BaseBall america™

2000 ALMANAC

A Comprehensive Review
of the 1999 Season, Featuring
Statistics and Commentary

BaseBall america™
2000 ALMANAC

PUBLISHED BY
Baseball America Inc.

EDITOR
Allan Simpson

ASSISTANT EDITORS
Mark Derewicz, John Royster

CONTRIBUTING EDITORS
James Bailey, Will Lingo, Lacy Lusk, John Manuel, Geoff Wilson

CONTRIBUTING WRITERS
John Perrotto, David Rawnsley, Alan Schwarz

PRODUCTION
Phillip Daquila, Brandon Donnell, Alex Ladd

STATISTICAL PRODUCTION CONSULTANT
Howe Sportsdata
Boston, Mass.

BaseBall america™
PUBLISHER/Lee Folger
EDITOR/Allan Simpson
MANAGING EDITOR/Will Lingo
DESIGN & PRODUCTION DIRECTOR/Phillip Daquila

COVER PHOTOS/Pedro Martinez by John Williamson; Yankees by David Seelig;
Rick Ankiel by Cosimo Mellace; University of Miami by Rich Clarkson/NCAA Photos

EDITOR'S NOTE
  Major league statistics are based on final, unofficial 1999 averages. Minor league statistics are official.
  The organization statistics, which begin on Page 51, include all players who participated in at least one game during the 1999 season. Pitchers' batting statistics are not included, nor are the pitching statistics of field players who pitched on rare occasions. For players who played with more than one team in the same league, the player's cumulative statistics appear on the line immediately after the player's last-team statistics.
  Innings have been rounded off to the nearest full inning.

CONTENTS

MAJOR LEAGUES

1999 SEASON

Sequel was fun, but not quite as good as the original

BY JOHN PERROTTO

Sequels are rarely as good as the original, as anyone who ever watched "Major League II" will attest. And in many respects, the 1999 major league season was a sequel to 1998.

Once again, Cardinals first baseman Mark McGwire and Cubs right fielder Sammy Sosa hit home runs in huge numbers and drew national attention. Once again, the Yankees were the team people kept their eyes on.

McGwire, Sosa and the Yankees tried their best to recreate the magic they made in 1998. While they did a good job, somehow 1999 just didn't quite live up to its predecessor.

In 1998, McGwire shattered Roger Maris' single-season record of 61 home runs in 1961, as he finished with 70. Sosa was right behind with 66. The Yankees won an American League-record 114 games, then went 11-2 in the postseason, sweeping the Padres in the World Series.

In 1999, McGwire and Sosa both made a run at the record but fell short. McGwire caught Sosa with a late rush for the major league lead with 65 homers, and Sosa finished with 63.

The Yankees had another fine year in '99 but still had a 16-game dropoff from their 1998 total. In fact, no other AL team saw its victory total drop by more games than the Yankees, who still were plenty good enough to win the AL East.

While the Yankees may not have duplicated their amazing regular season success, they wound up doing even better in the postseason. They won an amazing 11 of 12 games in dispatching the Rangers in the AL Division Series and the Red Sox in the AL Championship Series before sweeping the Braves in the World Series.

"Everyone always wants to talk about last year," McGwire lamented one day in August. "How about this year? Some pretty amazing things are happening this year, too. Not every year can be like 1998, but

Ho hum
Sammy Sosa blasted 60-plus homers again

this has still been a pretty special year."

Indeed, it was. And it was also an interesting year.

It was a year in which runs were scored in record numbers. It was a year in which players hit major statistical milestones. It was a year in which the umpires gambled and lost while the league presidents lost their jobs entirely. It was a year in which the Orioles visited Cuba. It was a year in which the Hall of Fame inducted one of its strongest classes and lost four of its classiest members. It was a year in which baseball said farewell to four ballparks.

But McGwire and Sosa were again at the forefront of baseball in 1999. Both men validated everything they did in 1998, again entering 62-and-beyond terrain, where only they have made footprints. In the last two seasons, they have accounted for the four highest single-season homer totals in baseball history.

"I feel great to share that type of record with Mark," Sosa said on the final day of the season. "To be in that category makes me proud of myself."

McGwire and Sosa each have as many 60-homer seasons as everyone else in major league history combined. Until 1998, Babe Ruth had the second-highest season total with 60 in 1927. Now, thanks to McGwire and Sosa, Ruth's 60 are sixth on the all-time list.

"I'm very surprised I hit this many," McGwire said. "My goal was 50 and always will be 50. Hitting 65

HOME RUN LEADERS

SINGLE SEASON

Player, Team, Year	
1. Mark McGwire, Cardinals, 1998	70
2. Sammy Sosa, Cubs, 1998	66
3. Mark McGwire, Cardinals, 1999	**65**
4. Sammy Sosa, Cubs, 1999	**63**
5. Roger Maris, Yankees, 1961	61
6. Babe Ruth, Yankees, 1927	60
7. Babe Ruth, Yankees, 1921	59
8. Jimmie Foxx, Athletics, 1932	58
Hank Greenberg, Tigers, 1938	58
Mark McGwire, Athletics/Cardinals, 1997	58
11. Hack Wilson, Cubs, 1930	56
Ken Griffey, Mariners, 1997	56
Ken Griffey, Mariners, 1998	56

Player of the Year
Martinez masters foes with arm, brain

The American League's far-and-away leader in wins (23), strikeouts (313) and ERA (2.07), Pedro Martinez looks like a real pitcher left in the dryer too long. A mascot. A good-luck charm the Red Sox hang around their neck.

Yet when he stands atop the mound, baseball in hand, he doesn't just say, "You have no chance," which would suffice. He says, "I know more than you." And he proceeds to prove it.

He entered Game Five of the American League Division Series against the Indians in the fourth inning—he hadn't started and was still in pain because of a pulled muscle behind his shoulder blade. His mere presence spooked the Indians to the point where he gave up no hits in six shutout innings, winning the game 12-8 and the series for Boston.

"He brought normalcy to the game," Red Sox pitching coach Joe Kerrigan said afterward. "That's Pedro. That's the legend of Pedro."

With performances like those in October, Martinez has developed an eerie, Buddha-like presence in baseball, a cherubic runt equal parts pitcher and poet. The Yankees' Paul O'Neill didn't even refer to him by name during the postseason, instead calling him,

"that little Dominican fellow" out of an abundance of respect, not a lack of it. Martinez commands the same from the press, using his precise and measured English to both inform and scold, tickle and intimidate.

Before his Game Five heroics against the Indians, Martinez sat down in the dugout next to Boston's starter that day, Bret Saberhagen, and said, "These guys are gonna swing tonight. You don't have to throw them strikes." Saberhagen admitted later, "I didn't do that," got shelled and needed Martinez to bail the Red Sox out in the fourth, to show them the way.

When Martinez studies opposing hitters, he looks for the emotional as much as the physical. "I look for everything—attitudes, frustrations, weakness," he says. "I look for everything I can look for to learn, and that's gonna help my game.

"Sometimes you can see that with just one pitch you can frustrate the whole game—with one batter. There's some of them that will let one at-bat frustrate them

Season for the ages
Pedro Martinez was amazing

forever. All you have to do is get a pitch that's one inch away from the plate from some hitters and that will get them dragging all day and get them upset. It takes away their whole game.

"Sometimes I look in a batter's face for almost a minute before I go to pitch, just to see his attitude, his eyes, what they're gonna say."

Baseball America's 1999 Major League Player of the Year, that little Dominican fellow, isn't merely on the bus anymore. He's driving it.

—ALAN SCHWARZ

---

blows me away. What I did last year blows me away."

Overcoming cancer
Joe Torre

What the Yankees did in '98 also blew everybody away. Yet they came back to win back-to-back World Series titles in 1999—giving them a total of 25—with their impressive postseason run.

"Everyone would talk this year about how we didn't have the same numbers as last year," said Yankees closer Mariano Rivera, the World Series MVP with one win and two saves. "Of course not. It's impossible to repeat those kinds of numbers. Last year was tremendous. I think those years only happen once in 100 years."

The Yankees, though, ran their World Series winning streak to 12 and became just the third team to sweep consecutive World Series.

"I think this team ranks up there with any of the great Yankee teams of the past," owner George Steinbrenner said.

The ability to overcome turmoil and tragedy defined the 1999 Yankees. Manager Joe Torre found out he had prostate cancer on March 10 and did not return to the dugout until May 18. Darryl Strawberry, recovering from colon cancer, was suspended after being arrested in April for cocaine possession. The fathers of Scott Brosius, Luis Sojo and Paul O'Neill all died within weeks of each other in September and October.

"In a lot of ways, winning the World Series this time is more special than 1998," Torre said. "All season, people kept comparing us to the '98 club and saying we weren't as good. It would be almost impossible to win 114 games again, but we really felt we had to win it all again this year to validate what we did last season. That's why this is so sweet. We came back and did it again under trying circumstances.

"In many ways, this is more satisfying than last year."

Hello, Home Plate

McGwire and Sosa were at the forefront of a continued offensive explosion in baseball. Scoring continued to be high in 1999, as a record 5,528 home runs flew out of major league parks.

An average major league game featured 10.2 runs and 2.3 home runs in 1999. The combined major league batting average was .271–.275 in the AL and .268 in the National League. The ERA was 4.56 in the NL and 4.86 in the hitter-happy AL.

To show how common home runs have become, consider the Pittsburgh Pirates set a club record with 171, from a franchise with a tradition of excellent hitters. Where did those 171 homers rank the Pirates in the 16-team NL? Tenth.

"You sit back and think we've really accomplished something pretty special," Pirates manager Gene Lamont said. "Then, you look around baseball and see everyone else is hitting as many or more home runs than you.

"The game has changed. It used to be that hitting 30 homers or driving in 100 runs in a season was a big accomplishment. It's still an accomplishment, but it isn't like it used to be."

The height of the preposterous offense probably came May 19 at Coors Field in Denver, appropriately enough, when the Reds beat the Rockies 24-12.

"It was like a summer league softball game in high school or something," Reds first baseman Sean Casey

Fast to 500
Mark McGwire hit homers at a dizzying rate

said. "It was like a beer league game. We should have walked away with the keg."

The Indians, who became the first team since 1950 to score more than 1,000 runs, came back from an eight-run deficit to win—three different times.

While many factors have contributed to the offensive explosion, some general managers are hinting that they'd like to make changes that would swing the pendulum back toward the pitchers. Some would like to raise the mound from 10 inches to 12-13 inches.

"A higher mound would at least be a start," Pirates GM Cam Bonifay said. "Something has to be done to bring some balance back to the game."

"A higher mound helps pitchers in general," Padres GM Kevin Towers said. "It's tougher for hitters with the ball on a downward plane, and it's easier on pitchers' arms to throw more downhill."

Other GMs want to get rid of the designated hitter, pointing out that it would take a potent bat out of the lineup and replace it with a pitcher, as well as increasing the strategy and nuance of the game.

"We can't have the game become too much like softball and that atmosphere where everybody who comes up is swinging for the fences," Rangers GM Doug Melvin said. "Remember when Paul Westhead was coaching in the NBA? His teams just tried to outscore the other team. Everybody thought it was new and exciting for a while, but the fans started getting bored. They got bored because there wasn't any strategy. That's what we've got to be careful of now."

Hitting The High Points

With runs being scored at a dizzying pace, it was not a surprise that hitters provided most of baseball's memorable milestones. In fact, the biggest milestones of the year came within three days in early August.

On Aug. 5, McGwire launched his 500th home run, connecting against the Padres' Andy Ashby in St.

Offense in ridiculous proportions
Sean Casey's Reds beat the Rockies 24-12

Major Leagues

DAVID SEELIG

DAVID SEELIG

Another hot-hitting Indian
Roberto Alomar returned to form in Cleveland

Dominating Diamondback
Randy Johnson overpowered NL hitters

Selected by Baseball America

FIRST TEAM

Pos.	Player, Team	B-T	Ht.	Wt.	Age	AVG	AB	R	H	2B	3B	HR	RBI	SB
C	Ivan Rodriguez, Rangers	R-R	5-9	205	27	.332	600	116	199	29	1	35	113	25
1B	Jeff Bagwell, Astros	R-R	6-0	195	31	.304	562	143	171	35	0	42	126	30
2B	Roberto Alomar, Indians	B-R	6-0	185	31	.323	563	138	182	40	3	24	120	37
3B	Chipper Jones, Braves	B-R	6-4	210	27	.319	567	116	181	41	1	45	110	25
SS	Derek Jeter, Yankees	R-R	6-3	195	25	.349	627	134	219	37	9	24	102	19
OF	Manny Ramirez, Indians	R-R	6-0	205	27	.333	522	131	174	34	3	44	165	2
OF	Ken Griffey, Mariners	L-L	6-3	205	29	.285	606	123	173	26	3	48	134	24
OF	Sammy Sosa, Cubs	R-R	6-0	210	30	.288	625	114	180	24	2	63	141	7
DH	Rafael Palmeiro, Rangers	L-L	6-0	190	34	.324	565	96	183	30	1	47	148	2

Pos.	Player, Team	B-T	Ht.	Wt.	Age	W	L	ERA	G	SV	IP	H	BB	SO
SP	Pedro Martinez, Red Sox	R-R	5-11	170	28	23	4	2.07	31	0	213	160	37	313
	Kevin Millwood, Braves	R-R	6-4	220	24	18	7	2.68	33	0	228	168	59	205
	Randy Johnson, Diamondbacks	R-L	6-10	230	35	17	9	2.48	35	0	272	207	70	364
	Mike Hampton, Astros	R-L	5-10	180	26	22	4	2.90	34	0	239	206	101	177
RP	Mariano Rivera, Yankees	R-R	6-2	170	29	4	3	1.83	66	45	69	43	18	52

SECOND TEAM

Pos.	Player, Team	B-T	Ht.	Wt.	Age	AVG	AB	R	H	2B	3B	HR	RBI	SB
C	Mike Piazza, Mets	R-R	6-3	215	30	.303	534	100	162	25	0	40	124	2
1B	Mark McGwire, Cardinals	R-R	6-5	250	35	.278	521	118	145	21	1	65	147	0
2B	Edgardo Alfonzo, Mets	R-R	5-11	187	25	.304	628	123	191	41	1	27	108	9
3B	Matt Williams, Diamondbacks	R-R	6-2	214	33	.303	627	98	190	37	2	35	142	2
SS	Nomar Garciaparra, Red Sox	R-R	6-0	180	25	.357	532	103	190	42	4	27	104	14
OF	Shawn Green, Blue Jays	L-L	6-4	200	26	.309	614	134	190	45	0	42	123	20
OF	Vladimir Guerrero, Expos	R-R	6-3	205	23	.316	610	102	193	37	5	42	131	14
OF	Bernie Williams, Yankees	B-R	6-2	205	30	.342	591	116	202	28	6	25	115	9
DH	Larry Walker, Rockies	L-R	6-3	237	32	.379	438	108	166	26	4	37	115	11

Pos.	Player, Team	B-T	Ht.	Wt.	Age	W	L	ERA	G	SV	IP	H	BB	SO
SP	Kevin Brown, Dodgers	R-R	6-4	200	34	18	9	3.00	35	0	252	210	59	221
	Jose Lima, Astros	R-R	6-2	205	26	21	10	3.58	35	0	246	256	44	187
	Mike Mussina, Orioles	B-R	6-2	185	30	18	7	3.50	31	0	203	207	52	172
	Bartolo Colon, Indians	R-R	6-0	225	24	18	5	3.95	32	0	205	185	76	161
RP	Billy Wagner, Astros	L-L	5-11	180	27	4	1	1.57	66	39	75	35	23	124

Ages as of July 1, 1999.

Position Player of the Year: Chipper Jones, 3b, Braves. **Pitcher of the Year:** Pedro Martinez, rhp, Red Sox. **Rookie of the Year:** Carlos Beltran, of, Royals. **Manager of the Year:** Jimy Williams, Red Sox. **Executive of the Year:** Jim Bowden, Reds.

NEWEST MEMBERS OF 3,000 CLUB

DAVID SCHOFIELD

JOHN KLEIN

WADE BOGGS' ROAD TO 3,000

Hit No.	Date	Opponent	Pitcher
1	April 26, 1982	White Sox	Rich Dotson
500	Sept. 9, 1984	Yankees	Mike Armstrong
1000	April 30, 1987	Mariners	Scott Bankhead
1500	July 21, 1989	Yankees	Melido Perez
2000	May 17, 1992	Angels	Mark Langston
2500	August 23, 1995	Athletics	Don Wengert
3000	August 7, 1999	Indians	Chris Haney

TONY GWYNN'S ROAD TO 3,000

Hit No.	Date	Opponent	Pitcher
1	July 19, 1982	Phillies	Sid Monge
500	August 18, 1985	Braves	Craig McMurtry
1000	April 22, 1988	Astros	Nolan Ryan
1500	August 15, 1990	Expos	Steve Frey
2000	August 6, 1993	Rockies	Bruce Ruffin
2500	Sept. 14, 1996	Reds	Hector Carrasco
3000	August 6, 1999	Expos	Dan Smith

Louis. (He also hit No. 501 in the same game.) Incredibly, McGwire became the first player in history to hit his 400th homer in one season and 500th the next. He finished the season with 522, giving him an outside chance of breaking Hank Aaron's all-time record of 755.

"I don't know what to say, other than it's an honor," McGwire said. "It's like when I hit 70, what do you say? I'm proud of what I've done but I don't get caught up in it all. It's nice, but these are all just numbers right now while I'm playing. Once I retire, I'll sit back and contemplate the numbers and I'm sure it will mean a lot more to me then."

On Aug. 6, Padres right fielder Tony Gwynn got his 3,000th hit when he singled to right field off Expos rookie righthander Dan Smith in Montreal. It was an emotional moment for Gwynn, who walked up the runway at Olympic Stadium, sank to his knees and sobbed.

"I was able to hold it off until I got off the field," Gwynn said. "Then, it just hit me. I just broke down. I was thinking about Pops (Gwynn's late father Charles) and everything in my whole life.

"You get thoughts about so many things but especially Dad. I was thinking about the impact he and my mom had on my life. My dad would always tell me I could do certain things. You'd listen but not really believe it. And then to see how significant the advice was, and have everything come true, is just unbelievable to me."

On Aug. 7, Devil Rays third baseman Wade Boggs

capped off the trifecta by homering off the Indians' Chris Haney for his 3,000th hit in front of the home fans in St. Petersburg. It was Boggs' second homer of the season. Of the 22 players who have 3,000 hits, Boggs was the first to reach the milestone with a home run.

"I love to hit home runs," joked Boggs, who has only 118 in his career. "It's the greatest feeling in the world to trot around the bases. I was a home run hitter in high school but then something happened—the parks got bigger."

Boggs then turned serious. "I finally put my flag in the mountain," he said. "So many guys have tried and come up short."

Orioles third baseman Cal Ripken would have been the third player to reach 3,000 hits in 1999, but back problems that caused him to make three trips to the disabled list forced him onto the operating table in September with 2,991 hits. Ripken did hit his 400th career homer in 1999, as did Devil Rays DH Jose Canseco.

MEL BAILEY

Grand slammer
Fernando Tatis

Cardinals third baseman Fernando Tatis also made history April 23 when he became the first player to

3,000-HIT CLUB

No.	Player	Hits
1.	Pete Rose	4,256
2.	Ty Cobb	4,191
3.	Hank Aaron	3,771
4.	Stan Musial	3,630
5.	Tris Speaker	3,514
6.	Honus Wagner	3,430
7.	Carl Yastrzemski	3,419
8.	Paul Molitor	3,319
9.	Eddie Collins	3,313
10.	Willie Mays	3,283
11.	Eddie Murray	3,255
12.	Nap Lajoie	3,251
13.	George Brett	3,154
14.	Paul Waner	3,152
15.	Robin Yount	3,142
16.	Dave Winfield	3,110
17.	**Tony Gwynn**	**3,067**
18.	Rod Carew	3,053
19.	Lou Brock	3,023
20.	Cap Anson	3,022
21.	**Wade Boggs**	**3,010**
22.	Al Kaline	3,007
23.	Roberto Clemente	3,000

Bold indicates active player

Waiting in the Wings

No.	Player	Hits
24.	Cal Ripken	2,991
39.	Rickey Henderson	2,816
41.	Harold Baines	2,783

400-HOME RUN CLUB

No.	Player	Home Runs
1.	Hank Aaron	755
2.	Babe Ruth	715
3.	Willie Mays	660
4.	Frank Robinson	586
5.	Harmon Killebrew	573
6.	Reggie Jackson	563
7.	Mike Schmidt	548
8.	Mickey Mantle	536
9.	Jimmie Foxx	534
10.	**Mark McGwire**	**522**
11.	Ted Williams	521
	Willie McCovey	521
13.	Eddie Mathews	512
	Ernie Banks	512
15.	Mel Ott	511
16.	Eddie Murray	504
17.	Lou Gehrig	493
18.	Stan Musial	475
	Willie Stargell	475
20.	Dave Winfield	465
21.	Carl Yastrzemski	452
22.	**Barry Bonds**	**445**
23.	Dave Kingman	442
24.	Andre Dawson	438
25.	**Jose Canseco**	**431**
26.	Billy Williams	426
27.	Darrell Evans	414
28.	Duke Snider	407
29.	**Cal Ripken**	**402**

Bold indicates active player

Waiting in the Wings

No.	Player	Home Runs
t31.	Ken Griffey	398
t33.	Fred McGriff	390

hit two grand slams in one inning. He connected both times off the Los Angeles Dodgers' Chan Ho Park.

Mets third baseman Robin Ventura became the first player to hit a grand slam in both games of a double-header when he turned the trick against the Brewers on May 20.

Led by right fielder Manny Ramirez' 165 RBIs, the Indians scored 1,009 runs to become the seventh team in baseball history to score 1,000 in a season. Ramirez posted the most RBIs since Jimmie Foxx drove home 175 in 1938.

DH Harold Baines, who split the season between the Orioles and Indians, notched his 1,500th career RBI. Braves outfielder Otis Nixon stole his 600th career base. The Rangers' Ivan Rodriguez hit 35 homers, a record for AL catchers.

Pitchers didn't get completely left out, though. Red Sox righthander Pedro Martinez, Baseball America's Major League Player of the Year, had one of the greatest seasons in history. He won the AL pitching triple crown with 23 victories, a 2.07 ERA and 313 strikeouts. Martinez' ERA was nearly three runs a game better than the league.

The Yankees' David Cone became the 14th pitcher in major league history to pitch a perfect game, against the Expos on July 18. Cone needed just 88 pitches on a 95-degree Sunday afternoon. The perfect game came on Yogi Berra Day at Yankee Stadium. Don Larsen, who threw the only perfect game in World Series history in 1956, threw out the ceremonial first pitch that day.

"You probably have a better chance of winning the lottery than having this happen," Cone said. "It makes you stop and think about Yankee magic and the mystique of this ballpark. You can't help but get caught up in it now."

The Cardinals' Jose Jimenez and Minnesota Twins' Eric Milton had the majors' other no-hitters in 1999, and both jewels were rather hard to fathom.

LARRY GOREN

Unlikely no-hitter
Jose Jimenez

Jimenez entered his June 25 start against the Diamondbacks in Phoenix having given up 60 runs, more than anyone else in the NL. He was 4-7 with an 8.04 ERA. Yet he held the Diamondbacks hitless in a 1-0 victory, beating the NL's most dominant pitcher, Randy Johnson, who had 17 strikeouts in the defeat. Johnson had the fourth-highest single-season strikeout total in major league history with 364.

Jimenez' moment was fleeting, though. Within two months, he was demoted to the minor leagues.

Milton had to get up early on the morning of Sept. 11 to throw his no-hitter against the visiting Anaheim Angels. The Twins were forced to play an 11 a.m. Saturday game as the University of Minnesota football team had a home game that evening in the Metrodome.

Despite taking a 6-11 record into the game, Milton

held the Angeles hitless, though Anaheim played a lineup filled with September callups and reserves. Third baseman Troy Glaus was the only regular to play.

Jesse Orosco, the Orioles' venerable lefthanded reliever, made history at age 42. Orosco surpassed Dennis Eckersley's all-time lead in games pitched when he made appearance No. 1,072 on Aug. 17 against the Twins in Baltimore.

Plodding Pennant Races

Just as there was no doubt about the outcome of the World Series, there was little suspense in the AL regular season races.

The Indians rolled to a 21½-game victory over the second-place White Sox for their fifth straight Central title. The Rangers won the West for the third time in four years, coasting to an eight-game edge over the Athletics. The Yankees won the East by four games over the Red Sox, who won the wild card by a four-game margin over the surprising Athletics. Oakland, Baseball America's Organization of the Year, stayed in the race until the season's last week despite having a payroll of $22 million.

The NL races were tighter, except in the West. The Diamondbacks, in just their second year of existence, became the fastest expansion team to get to the play-offs, winning the division by 14 games over the Giants.

The other NL races were filled with suspense. The Braves led the Mets by one game in the East with two weeks left. They pulled away by taking five of six from the Mets in that span, including a three-game sweep at Turner Field.

The Astros took the Central by one game over the Reds and their $33 million payroll. The Mets wound up with the wild card, winning 5-0 in a one-game tiebreaker at Cincinnati in the 163rd game of the season, as Al Leiter threw a two-hit shutout.

While the Athletics and Reds contended, the eight playoff teams were among the 12 with the highest payrolls. The disparity between the haves and have-nots of the game was evident.

The most intriguing Division Series came in the AL, as the Red Sox came from 2-0 down to beat the Indians 3-2 in the best-of-five series. The Red Sox scored 44 runs and became the first team to come from 2-0 down and win the fifth game on the road.

The Red Sox won 23-7 in Game Four, setting postseason records for runs and hits (24). The Red Sox then won 12-8 in the decisive fifth game behind a gutsy performance from Martinez. He had left Game

MORRIS FOSTOFF

Bailing out the Braves
Eddie Perez came through as NLCS MVP

One after four innings with a strained muscle behind his throwing shoulder. He came back in Game Five to pitch six hitless relief innings.

The Yankees swept the Rangers in the other AL Division Series. Both NL Division Series went four games, with the Braves downing the Astros and the Mets beating the Diamondbacks.

Hopes of a Subway Series between the Yankees and Mets were dashed in the League Championship Series, though.

The Yankees kept up their end of the bargain by beating the Red Sox in five games in the AL. The Mets, though, fell in six games to the Braves in the NL. Atlanta catcher Eddie Perez, who took over as the starter in July when Javy Lopez went down with a knee injury, was the surprise MVP as he went 10-for-20 with two homers and five RBIs.

The Braves, though, proved to be no match for the Yankees' juggernaut.

"You'd have to say the better team won because the Yankees were outstanding," Atlanta righthander John Smoltz said. "They played an absolutely perfect World Series. I can't think of one mistake they made. You have to tip your hat to them."

Twenty-Two Men Out

Off the field, umpires stirred the most controversy. An ill-fated plan by the umpires' union led to the resignations of 22 umpires, accepted by the commissioner's office Sept. 2. The two leagues hired 25 minor league umps as full-time staff members to replace them.

The umpires and union chief Richie Phillips announced July 15, two days after a glorious All-Star Game in Boston, that all umpires would resign their posts Sept. 2. The move was made in an effort to get

No.	Player, Team	Year	Strikeouts
1.	Nolan Ryan, Angels	1973	383
2.	Sandy Koufax, Dodgers	1965	382
3.	Nolan Ryan, Angels	1974	367
4.	**Randy Johnson, D'backs**	**1999**	**364**
5.	Rube Waddell, Phillies	1904	349
6.	Bob Feller, Indians	1948	348
7.	Nolan Ryan, Angels	1977	341
8.	Nolan Ryan, Angels	1972	329
	Randy Johnson, Mar./Astros	1998	329
10.	Nolan Ryan, Angels	1976	327

TOP STRIKEOUT SEASONS

BASEBALL'S ALL-CENTURY TEAM

The debate over the greatest baseball players has raged for years and will continue well into the next millennium. Major League Baseball let the fans speak in 1999, naming an all-century team composed of 25 players voted on by the fans and five named by a special committee to correct voting oversights.

The top vote-getters, perhaps predictably, came from the Yankee dynasties of the '20s and '30s. The surprise was that it was Lou Gehrig and not Babe Ruth who finished first. Gehrig garnered just more than 1.2 million votes to get the starting nod at first base. Ruth edged fellow outfielder Hank Aaron for second place.

Three great outfielders who brought baseball through World War II and/or into the modern age were the fourth-, fifth- and sixth-highest vote-getters—Ted Williams, Willie Mays and Joe DiMaggio. Catcher Johnny Bench was the only other player to receive more than a million votes.

Four active players were named to the team: single-season home run king Mark McGwire, iron man Cal Ripken, five-time Cy Young winner Roger Clemens and the youngest player elected to the team, Ken Griffey.

Nolan Ryan got the most votes of any pitcher, spurred by his record 5,714 strikeouts and seven no-hitters. All-time hits leader Pete Rose squeaked into the last outfield spot, allowing him to make an appearance at Turner Field in Atlanta when the team was introduced before Game Two of the World Series. For more on the controversy involving Rose and NBC's Jim Gray, see Page 24.

The players who were added to the team by the special committee were Pirates shortstop Honus Wagner, Cardinals outfielder Stan Musial and a trio of pitching giants: Lefty Grove, Christy Mathewson and Warren Spahn.

With any team like this, some omissions drew attention. Notable among them were Josh Gibson, the slugging catcher considered the Babe Ruth of the Negro Leagues, and Roberto Clemente, whose omission drew the ire of the Hispanic community. No Hispanic players or Negro League players made the team.

Other notable absences included: second base-

Yankees lead the way
Lou Gehrig beat out Babe Ruth as top vote-getter

man Joe Morgan; third baseman Eddie Mathews; shortstop Ozzie Smith; outfielder Frank Robinson; and pitchers Bob Feller, Tom Seaver and Greg Maddux, who missed out on the sixth pitching spot by less than 60,000 votes.

FAN SELECTIONS

Pos.	Player	Votes	Years	Primary Team
C	Johnny Bench	1,010,403	1967-83	Reds
	Yogi Berra	704, 208	1946-65	Yankees
1B	Lou Gehrig	1,207,982	1923-39	Yankees
	Mark McGwire	517,992	1986-99	Athletics
2B	Jackie Robinson	788,116	1947-56	Dodgers
	Rogers Hornsby	630,761	1915-37	Cardinals
3B	Mike Schmidt	855,654	1972-89	Phillies
	Brooks Robinson	761,700	1955-77	Orioles
SS	Cal Ripken	669,033	1981-99	Orioles
	Ernie Banks	598,168	1953-71	Cubs
OF	Babe Ruth	1,158,044	1914-35	Yankees
	Hank Aaron	1,156,782	1954-76	Braves
	Ted Williams	1,125,583	1939-42, 46-60	Red Sox
	Willie Mays	1,115,896	1951-73	Giants
	Joe DiMaggio	1,054,423	1936-42, 46-51	Yankees
	Mickey Mantle	988,163	1951-68	Yankees
	Ty Cobb	777,056	1905-28	Tigers
	Ken Griffey	645,389	1989-99	Mariners
	Pete Rose	629,742	1963-86	Reds
P	Nolan Ryan	992,040	1966-93	Angels
	Sandy Koufax	970,434	1955-66	Dodgers
	Cy Young	867,523	1900-11	Red Sox
	Roger Clemens	601,244	1984-99	Red Sox
	Bob Gibson	582,031	1959-75	Cardinals
	Walter Johnson	479,279	1907-27	Senators

COMMITTEE SELECTIONS

Pos.	Player		Years	Primary Team
SS	Honus Wagner		1900-17	Pirates
OF	Stan Musial		1941-44, 46-63	Cardinals
P	Warren Spahn		1942, 46-65	Braves
	Christy Mathewson		1900-16	Giants
	Lefty Grove		1925-41	Athletics

Cubs, Dodgers heroes
Ernie Banks, Sandy Koufax

the owners to begin negotiations on a new contract; the current one was set to expire Dec. 31.

The umpires cited a variety of other issues. They objected to an outside review of their performance, the revision of the strike zone ordered by the commissioner's office during spring training, and a plan by Sandy Alderson to centralize umpire control under the commissioner's office, rather than having the two league presidents oversee them.

"There are a multitude of issues," AL umpire Jim Evans said on the day the umpires announced their intentions. "These issues have been on the table for quite a while. Some are financial but many others are principles."

Alderson, Major League Baseball's executive vice president for baseball operations, quickly went on the offensive, saying that MLB would be glad to accept the resignations. MLB had its own reasons to be unhappy with the umpires. Among them were the lack of conditioning of some umpires and the confrontational nature and arrogance of others. MLB looked at this as a chance to get rid of those umpires it felt were bad apples.

The union quickly showed cracks. A total of 27 umpires either never turned in their resignations or rescinded them, 24 in the AL and three in the NL. Many in that group, upset by Phillips' negotiating tactics, tried to form their own union as the season came to a close and hire agent Ron Shapiro as their lead negotiator.

The major league umpires also miscalculated about the support they would receive from minor league umpires. The minor league umps jumped at the opportunity to leave behind their days of low pay and driving themselves from park to park. And because the major league umpires resigned, minor leaguers could accept jobs without fear of crossing a picket line or being labeled as scabs.

"Nothing against the big leagues—we support those guys—but we're not making hundreds of thousands of dollars and bitching," said Mike Billings, an umpire in the International League. "We're making close to minimum wage and just want it a little better."

Billings, in fact, tried to organize the minor league umpires into a union. At first the minor league umpires used Phillips and his law firm to help them in their efforts, but they later chose someone else.

On Sept. 1, 22 major league umpires lost their jobs. Two days of nearly around-the-clock negotiations in federal court resulted in the union dropping all legal action against MLB in exchange for full pay and benefits for the resigning umps for the rest of the year.

The resigned umpires' only hope for reinstatement was through arbitration, which wasn't scheduled by the National Labor Relations Board until sometime in 2000. The union agreed not to strike or stage any disturbances.

"We live today to fight tomorrow," union attorney Susan Davis said, moments after Judge J. Curtis Joyner announced the agreement in Philadelphia.

Phillips said it was "absolutely shameful" for commissioner Bud Selig to let the umpires lose their jobs, a disingenuous statement at best. It all made for an emotional final day for many of the umpires whose resignations were accepted.

"My heart is broken, I can tell you that," NL umpire

DAVID SCHOFIELD

Broken-hearted
Bill Hohn was burned by his union's tactics

Bill Hohn said. "I can't explain to you how badly my heart has been broken by baseball. I can't sell my services anywhere. My college education was Class A ball, Double-A ball. What do you do at 44?

"Don't these baseball people have hearts? I mean, we have families. They're ruining families and that's what hurts. (The union strategy) was a mistake but, my God, we're good people. We're the integrity of the game."

Hohn fumed every time he thought about why the union's strategy of mass resignations failed.

"Those 24 American League umps who bailed out, every one of them lied to us," Hohn said. "They didn't do anything but stab us in the back and keep pushing the knife in."

Streamlined Command

When baseball owners held their quarterly meeting in Cooperstown in September, it was fitting because the meeting had great historical significance.

The owners voted unanimously to eliminate the positions of AL and NL president, and they centralized everything the leagues had done individually in the office of the commissioner.

"This is a move long overdue," Selig said. "I've been in baseball 30 years and I remember centralization of the leagues being actively discussed in 1970.

"We had to reevaluate how we operate our business off the field. Having separate leagues becomes an encumbrance that inhibits sound and timely decisions. We're getting ready for the 21st century."

The elimination of the presidencies left the NL's Len Coleman and AL's Gene Budig out of jobs.

Organization of the Year
Athletics get results faster than expected

Back in the fall of 1993, the Oakland Athletics had paid the price of success. The team that won four consecutive American League West titles had aged and broken up. The farm system had been pulled apart like a Thanksgiving turkey to acquire veterans for immediate help.

The A's had two choices: join the escalating free-agent bidding or build from within and suffer for a few years. For a team lacking huge assets, it was not a difficult choice. The building process began and the organization languished through six losing seasons.

"Draft and development are areas where you can compete without spending an arm and a leg," scouting director Grady Fuson said. "We've drafted well, and we've developed well. And we've done it for half the money others have. It's judgment, sim-ple judgment."

For that astute judgment, Baseball America selected the A's as its Organization of the Year for 1999. Not only did Oakland jump its record to 87-75 at the major league level, but Vancouver also won the Triple-A World Series and teams thrived throughout the organization.

The process has been long and agonizing at times. Former general manager Sandy Alderson, now with the commissioner's office, put together the pieces, and his hand-picked successor, Billy Beane, followed the diagram.

From the beginning, the idea was to build the organization around a specific plan emphasizing power and patience: find on-base percentage hitters with the ability to drive the ball out of the park. On the mound, Oakland focuses on drafting college pitchers who can move quickly to the majors.

Everyone in the organization agrees with the concept, which has made it work. Beane, Fuson, assistant general manager Paul DePodesta and farm director Keith Lieppman are all on the same page.

"We have a young but experienced, energetic group," Beane said. "Grady does a great job in making the selections, especially when you realize we have restrictions as to what we can spend—it's not just trying to find the right guy, it's finding the guy we can afford. I think there's a real good

interaction between myself, player development and scouting."

The project began coming to fruition in '99, when the A's arrived ahead of schedule in the AL playoff race. It was not unusual for the A's to field a team containing seven or eight players drafted and developed by the system.

The team is built around such players as 23-year-old left fielder Ben Grieve, the No. 2 pick in the '94 draft; third baseman Eric Chavez, 22, the 10th overall selection in '96; and Dominican shortstop Miguel Tejada, 23. Emerging team leader Jason Giambi, 28, came as a second-rounder in '92.

Perhaps most stunning was the sudden development of righthander Tim Hudson, a 1997 sixth-round pick out of Auburn. He started the year 7-0 between Double-A Midland and Triple-A Vancouver, was promoted to the majors June 7 and finished 11-2, 3.23 in 21 big league starts. Behind him in the farm system are lefthanders Eric DuBose, Mark Mulder and Barry Zito and righthanders Chris Enochs and Brett Laxton.

—CASEY TEFERTILLER

PREVIOUS WINNERS

1982—Oakland Athletics
1983—New York Mets
1984—New York Mets
1985—Milwaukee Brewers
1986—Milwaukee Brewers
1987—Milwaukee Brewers
1988—Montreal Expos
1989—Texas Rangers
1990—Montreal Expos
1991—Atlanta Braves
1992—Cleveland Indians
1993—Toronto Blue Jays
1994—Kansas City Royals
1995—New York Mets
1996—Atlanta Braves
1997—Detroit Tigers
1998—New York Yankees

Coleman agreed to stay on with MLB as a senior adviser to the commissioner and president of MLB charities. Budig will move into the role of senior vice president for educational and government affairs with MLB.

"Over the past year, it was becoming increasingly evident being a league president was like being chairman of Studebaker," said Coleman, who had planned to resign at the end of the season. "I did not want to serve in a ceremonial post or be a figurehead."

Alderson will oversee much of the consolidation.

"This is all about eliminating redundancy and being more efficient in the league office," Diamondbacks owner Jerry Colangelo said. "Baseball's unique with two leagues. I know there's tradition involved, but I don't think this takes any-

Last league presidents
Gene Budig, Len Coleman

DAVID SEELIG

thing away from it."

The meeting also saw the end of the Marge Schott era as owner of the Reds. Under suspension for a second time in her 15-year reign as owner for making derogatory ethnic remarks, and under pressure from MLB to sell her majority share, the flamboyant Schott finally left quietly.

Owners unanimously approved the $67 million sale of Schott's shares to a group of limited partners led by Cincinnati businessman Carl Lindner, who took over as controlling partner.

Two other potential sales remained in limbo because of questions about the viability of baseball in small markets. Bay Area sports executive Andy Dolich was heading a group that expected to buy the Athletics for $122 million, while lawyer Miles Prentice headed a group that planned to purchase the Royals for $75 million.

Baltimore At Havana

Selig has long been a big proponent of increased international play and the globalization of the game. Baseball took a step forward in that direction when the Orioles played a Cuban national team in a home-and-home series.

Orioles owner Peter Angelos lobbied hard for the better part of three years to play the Cubans, and the series finally became a reality in mid-March with the help of the White House and President Bill Clinton's relaxed policy toward communist Cuba.

"Peter was relentless about doing this," Orioles vice chairman Joe Foss said. "When he puts his mind to something, I don't think he ever considers it can't be done."

The Orioles won the first meeting on March 28 at Havana's Estadio Latinoamericano, 3-2 in 11 innings. Cuban leader Fidel Castro watched the game from the seats behind home plate, flanked by Selig and Angelos. It was the first visit by an American team to Cuba in four decades, and the crowd of 55,000 was hand-picked by the Cuban government.

PERFECT GAMES

A list of the 16 perfect games in major league history, including David Cone's 6-0 gem over the Expos on July 18, 1999.

Pitcher, Team	Opponent	Date	Score
John Richmond, Worcester	Cleveland	June 12, 1880	1-0
John Ward, Providence	Buffalo	June 17, 1880	5-0
Cy Young, Boston (AL)	Philadelphia	May 5, 1904	3-0
Addie Joss, Cleveland (AL)	Chicago	Oct. 2, 1908	1-0
Charles Robertson, Chicago (AL)	Detroit	April 30, 1922	2-0
Don Larsen, New York	Brooklyn	Oct. 8, 1956	2-0
Jim Bunning, Philadelphia	New York (NL)	June 21, 1964	6-0
Sandy Koufax, Los Angeles	Chicago (NL)	Sept. 9, 1965	1-0
Jim "Catfish" Hunter, Oakland	Minnesota	May 8, 1968	4-0
Len Barker, Cleveland	Toronto	May 15, 1981	3-0
Mike Witt, California	Texas	Sept. 30, 1984	1-0
Tom Browning, Cincinnati	Los Angeles	Sept. 16, 1988	1-0
Dennis Martinez, Montreal	Los Angeles	July 28, 1991	2-0
Kenny Rogers, Texas	California	July 28, 1994	4-0
David Wells, New York (AL)	Minnesota	May 17, 1998	4-0
David Cone, New York (AL)	**Montreal**	**July 18, 1999**	**6-0**

PERFECTION

JOHN WILLIAMSON

Yankees righthander David Cone beat Montreal 6-0 on July 18, 1999, to become the 16th major leaguer to record a perfect game and the second in two years to do it while wearing pinstripes. Cone struck out 10, getting shortstop Orlando Cabrera to pop out to third baseman Scott Brosius to end the game and sealing the first perfect game in three years of interleague play. David Wells threw a perfect game on May 17, 1998, against the Twins at Yankee Stadium.

MONTREAL	ab	r	h	bi	bb	so	NEW YORK	ab	r	h	bi	bb	so
W. Guerrero dh	3	0	0	0	0	1	Knoblauch 2b	2	1	1	0	1	1
Jones cf	2	0	0	0	0	1	Jeter ss	4	1	1	2	0	0
Mouton cf	1	0	0	0	0	1	O'Neill rf	4	1	1	0	0	0
White lf	3	0	0	0	0	1	Be. Williams cf	4	0	1	1	0	0
V. Guerrero rf	3	0	0	0	0	1	Martinez 1b	4	0	1	0	0	0
Vidro 2b	3	0	0	0	0	0	Davis dh	3	1	1	0	1	0
Fullmer 1b	3	0	0	0	0	1	Ledee lf	4	1	1	2	0	1
Widger c	3	0	0	0	0	2	Brosius 3b	2	1	0	0	0	1
Andrews 3b	2	0	0	0	0	1	Girardi c	3	0	1	1	0	0
McGuire ph	1	0	0	0	0	0							
Cabrera ss	3	0	0	0	0	1							
Totals	27	0	0	0	0	10	Totals	30	6	8	6	2	3

```
Montreal     000 000 000—0
New York     050 000 01x—6
```

DP—Montreal 1. LOB—New York 4. 2B—O'Neill, Girardi. HR—Jeter, Ledee.

Montreal	ip	h	r	er	bb	so	New York	ip	h	r	er	bb	so
Vazquez L	7	7	6	6	2	3	Cone W	9	0	0	0	0	10
Ayala	1	1	0	0	0	0							

Vazquez pitched to two batters in eighth.
HBP—Brosius (by Vazquez), Knoblauch (by Vazquez).
Umpires: HP—Barrett; **1B**—McCoy; **2B**—Evans; **3B**—Meriwether.
T—2:16 (plus 33-minute rain delay in the third). **A**—41,930.

Impressive performances
Cuba looked good in two games against the Orioles

Baseball took another step internationally by opening the regular season in Monterrey, Mexico, with an April 4 game between the Rockies and Padres.

Rockies third baseman Vinny Castilla, an icon in his native Mexico, delighted the crowd of 27,104 at Monterrey Stadium by hitting three singles and a double. Rockies left fielder Dante Bichette led the way with four hits, including a home run, and four RBIs as Colorado won 8-2.

The only other time a major league game was played outside the United States or Canada was 1996, when the Padres and Mets played a three-game series in Monterrey. MLB found this opener so successful that it scheduled the Cubs and Mets to open the 2000 season with a two-game series in Japan.

"This makes a statement for us that we believe in taking the game internationally," MLB chief operating officer Paul Beeston said. "Don Fehr (head of the players' union) and the players believe in the internationalization of the game.

"Major League Baseball International has taken games to the Dominican Republic, gone into Cuba, is thinking about Puerto Rico and thinking about Venezuela. The union represents many from those countries, so it's natural to think about playing. We both agree we should be doing this."

Classy Class

The Hall of Fame inducted one of its strongest classes during ceremonies on July 25 in Cooperstown. George Brett, Nolan Ryan and Robin Yount were voted in by the baseball writers, while the veterans committee selected Orlando Cepeda, Nestor Chylak, Frank Selee and Smoky Joe Williams.

Brett was a .305 career hitter over 21 seasons with the Royals. He had 3,154 hits, 317 homers and 1,595 RBIs.

Catcher Charles Johnson's two-run homer off Cuban starter Jose Ibar staked the Orioles to a 2-0 lead. Righthander Jose Contreras replaced Ibar after the second inning and pitched eight scoreless innings of relief. Meanwhile, the Cubans forced extra innings by scoring single runs in the seventh and eighth innings.

"I was a little anxious because for 40 years no American team had come here," said Contreras, who pitched Cuba to the gold medal at the Pan American Games in August by beating Team USA. "But as the game went on I felt more comfortable."

The Orioles burst the Cubans' hopes of a victory by pushing across a run in the 11th on Baines' RBI single. Orosco pitched a scoreless bottom of the 11th for the save, helped by two fine defensive plays by rookie second baseman Jesse Garcia.

"I'm not sure I see enough power in the Cubans," Orioles manager Ray Miller said. "But I certainly see enough pitching. I've seen Cuban pitching in the United States and now here, and they are good."

Cuba rolled to a 12-6 victory over the Orioles in the rematch May 3 in Baltimore. The Orioles were an uninterested lot, off to a bad start to a season that saw them underachieve and finish 78-84.

"Obviously, Cuba's desire was much more than ours," Miller said.

Contreras didn't make it out of the second inning this time for Cuba, but neither did Orioles starter Scott Kamieniecki.

While there were no incidents in the Havana game, several demonstrators ran on the field in Baltimore. Second-base umpire Cesar Valdes, a Cuban, slammed one to the turf.

Impressive Cooperstown inductees
George Brett and Nolan Ryan led a strong class

Rookie of the Year

Royals can build around center fielder Beltran

STEVE MOORE

Carlos Beltran

Royals general manager Herk Robinson's career dates to 1962, when he was a scout for the Reds. So he has seen his share of baseball players, but only a few Carlos Beltrans.

"In my baseball career, there have been three players who have all been pretty good players, who were second-round draft choices and their last names all began with the letter B," Robinson says. "Their names are Johnny Bench, George Brett and Carlos Beltran."

The first two are in the Hall of Fame, and the third one has played just one major league season. But Beltran, a 22-year-old center fielder from Puerto Rico,

is off to quite a start. He was selected Baseball America's 1999 Rookie of the Year after hitting .293 with 22 homers, 108 RBIs, 112 runs, 27 stolen bases and 16 outfield assists.

Beltran became just the eighth rookie in the 1900s and the second since 1950 to score 100 runs and drive in 100 runs. The only other rookie to do that in the last half-century was Fred Lynn, with 103 runs and 105 RBIs for the 1975 Red Sox.

Two notable Hall of Famers accomplished the 100/100 feat as rookies: Joe DiMaggio in 1936 and Ted Williams in 1939. The others were Dale Alexander, Walt Dropo, Al Rosen and Hal Trosky.

In addition to the 100/100 statistical rarity and the other numbers, Beltran had 194 hits, 54 multi-hit games, 301 total bases and 56 extra-base hits. He also spent all season as the Royals' center fielder.

"Some people you might compare him to are like Bernie Williams, veteran players," Royals lefthander Jose Rosado says. "He's incredible. He scores 100 runs, drives in 100 runs, has almost 200 hits; he plays every day. I've never seen a guy grow up that quick and have the talent he has."

Not that Beltran is perfect. The Royals want him to cut down on his strikeouts, a team-leading 123, and walk more than 46 times, which would increase his .337 on-base percentage.

"I've been very low-profile on this, but this time of year I'll put on my party hat and blow my whistle," Royals manager Tony Muser said in October. "He is the Rookie of the Year. I think he's the epitome of an everyday player, and as a rookie that's pretty darn good."

—ALAN ESKEW

Ryan holds 53 major league records, including 5,714 career strikeouts and seven career no-hitters. He was 324-292 in 27 seasons with the Mets, Angels, Astros and Rangers, compiling a 3.19 ERA.

Yount hit .285 in 20 seasons with the Brewers, compiling 3,142 hits, 251 homers and 1,405 RBIs. He was a two-time MVP.

Cepeda hit .297 in 17 seasons with the Giants, Cardinals, Braves, Athletics, Red Sox and Royals. He had 379 homers and 1,365 RBIs.

Chylak was an AL umpire for 25 seasons from 1954-78. He also worked five World Series and six All-Star Games.

Selee was a successful 19th-century manager. He led the Boston Beaneaters to five NL titles, then transformed the lowly Chicago Colts (later the Cubs) into a winner. He had a .598 lifetime winning percentage.

Williams pitched in the Negro Leagues from 1910-

32 and was known for his exploding fastball and pinpoint control.

The ceremony set records for fans (an estimated 50,000) and media (more than 900 credentials).

"I'm 61 years old," Cepeda said. "For the last 10 years, they called me a future Hall of Famer. I figured with my numbers, I'd be here sooner or later. I used to say, 'Who cares about the Hall of Fame? Who needs it?' Well, now that I'm here, I found out that I need it. It's the greatest honor you could ever hope to achieve. And to go in with so many other great players just makes it more special."

The Great DiMaggio

While seven inductees entered the Hall of Fame, four Hall of Famers passed away in 1999. The biggest name was Joe DiMaggio, who died March 8 from lung cancer in Hollywood, Fla.

The Yankee Clipper went into Memorial Regional

1999 MAJOR LEAGUE ALL-STAR GAME

Hometown hero Martinez sets tone in 4-1 AL victory

As if his stellar performance during the regular season wasn't enough, the Red Sox' Pedro Martinez dominated the rest of the major leagues in the All-Star Game, played on July 13 at Boston's Fenway Park. He struck out five of the six National League hitters he faced while winning MVP honors in the American League's 4-1 victory.

After the introduction of almost 40 players, among 100 nominated to baseball's all-century team, and an emotional first pitch from Red Sox great Ted Williams, Martinez struck out Barry Larkin, Larry Walker and Sammy Sosa in the first inning. He followed up in the second with strike-outs of Mark McGwire and Jeff Bagwell.

Jim Thome and Cal Ripken provided all the offense the AL would need with first-inning RBI singles.

TOP VOTE-GETTERS

AMERICAN LEAGUE

CATCHER: 1. Ivan Rodriguez, Rangers, 1,897,774; 2. Sandy Alomar, Indians, 1,629,674; 3. Jorge Posada, Yankees, 252,739.
FIRST BASE: 1. Jim Thome, Indians, 1,364,692; 2. Rafael Palmeiro, Rangers, 684, 891; 3. Tino Martinez, Yankees, 551,154.
SECOND BASE: 1. Roberto Alomar, Indians, 2,793,891; 2. Chuck Knoblauch, Yankees, 673,351; 3. Delino DeShields, Orioles, 221,595.
THIRD BASE: 1. Cal Ripken, Orioles, 1,285,728; 2. Travis Fryman, Indians, 1,130,651; 3. Tony Fernandez, Blue Jays, 639,622.
SHORTSTOP: 1. Nomar Garciaparra, Red Sox, 1,089,974; 2. Derek Jeter, Yankees, 1,069,528; 3. Omar Vizquel, Indians, 1,038,362.
OUTFIELD: 1. Ken Griffey, Mariners, 2,918,055; 2. Manny Ramirez, Indians, 1,898,430; 3. Kenny Lofton, Indians, 1,676,595; 4. David Justice, Indians, 1,336,304; 5. Juan Gonzalez, Rangers, 834,962; 6. Bernie Williams, Yankees, 825,703; 7. Paul O'Neill, Yankees, 582,421; 8. Albert Belle, Orioles, 455,497; 9. Shawn Green, Blue Jays, 398,893.

NATIONAL LEAGUE

CATCHER: 1. Mike Piazza, Mets, 1,645,304; 2. Jason Kendall, Pirates, 511,587; 3. Javy Lopez, Braves, 487,022.
FIRST BASE: 1. Mark McGwire, Cardinals, 1,669,066; 2. Jeff Bagwell, Astros, 837,117; 3. Sean Casey, Reds, 441,372.
SECOND BASE: 1. Jay Bell, Diamondbacks, 1,203,902; 2. Craig Biggio, Astros, 1,171,574; 3. Bret Boone, Braves, 337,220.
THIRD BASE: 1. Matt Williams, Diamondbacks, 1,310,799; 2. Chipper Jones, Braves, 653,197; 3. Frenando Tatis, Cardinals, 543,099.
SHORTSTOP: 1. Barry Larkin, Reds, 858,203; 2. Rey Ordonez, Mets, 799,858; 3. Walt Weiss, Braves, 414,227.
OUTFIELD: 1. Sammy Sosa, Cubs, 2,315,204; 2. Larry Walker, Rockies, 1,147,524; 3. Tony Gwynn, Padres, 1,054,785; 4. Barry Bonds, Giants, 732,765; 5. Raul Mondesi, Dodgers, 520,581; 6. Steve Finley, Diamondbacks, 425,655; 7. Brian Giles, Pirates, 407,891; 8. Brian Jordan, Braves, 390,795; 9. Andruw Jones, Braves, 383,085.

ROSTERS

AMERICAN LEAGUE

MANAGER: Joe Torre, Yankees.
PITCHERS: David Cone, Yankees; Roberto Hernandez, Devil Rays; **Pedro Martinez, Red Sox**; Mike Mussina, Orioles; Charles Nagy, Indians; Troy Percival, Angels; Jose Rosado, Royals; John Wetteland, Rangers; Jeff Zimmerman, Rangers.
CATCHERS: Brad Ausmus, Tigers; **Ivan Rodriguez, Rangers.**

INFIELDERS: Roberto Alomar, Indians (2b); Ron Coomer, Twins; Tony Fernandez, Blue Jays; **Nomar Garciaparra, Red Sox (ss)**; John Jaha, Athletics; Derek Jeter, Yankees; Jose Offerman, Red Sox; y-**Rafael Palmeiro, Rangers (dh)**; **Cal Ripken, Orioles (3b)**; **Jim Thome, Indians (1b)**; Omar Vizquel, Indians.
OUTFIELDERS: Harold Baines, Orioles; x-Jose Canseco, Devil Rays; Shawn Green, Blue Jays; **Ken Griffey, Mariners (cf)**; **Kenny Lofton, Indians (lf)**; Magglio Ordonez, White Sox; **Manny Ramirez, Indians (rf)**; B.J. Surhoff, Orioles; Bernie Williams, Yankees.

NATIONAL LEAGUE

MANAGER: Bruce Bochy, Padres.
PITCHERS: Andy Ashby, Padres; Kent Bottenfield, Cardinals; Paul Byrd, Phillies; Mike Hampton, Astros; Trevor Hoffman, Padres; Randy Johnson, Diamondbacks; Jose Lima, Astros; Kevin Millwood, Braves; x-Robb Nen, Giants; **Curt Schilling, Phillies**; Billy Wagner, Astros; Scott Williamson, Reds.
CATCHERS: Mike Lieberthal, Phillies; Dave Nilsson, Brewers; **Mike Piazza, Mets.**
INFIELDERS: **Jeff Bagwell, Astros (dh)**; **Jay Bell, Diamondbacks (2b)**; Sean Casey, Reds; Alex Gonzalez, Marlins; Jeff Kent, Giants; **Barry Larkin, Reds (ss)**; **Mark McGwire, Cardinals (1b)**; Ed Sprague, Pirates; **Matt Williams, Diamondbacks (3b)**.
OUTFIELDERS: y-Jeromy Burnitz, Brewers (lf); Luis Gonzalez, Diamondbacks; Vladimir Guerrero, Expos; x-Tony Gwynn, Padres; Brian Jordan, Braves; Gary Sheffield, Dodgers; **Sammy Sosa, Cubs (cf)**; Larry Walker, Rockies (rf).

Starters in **boldface**.
x-injured, did not play; y-injury replacement.

July 13 in Boston
American League 4, National League 1

NATIONAL	ab	r	h	bi	AMERICAN	ab	r	h	bi
Larkin ss	3	0	1	1	Lofton lf-cf	3	1	1	0
A. Gonzalez ph-ss	1	0	0	0	B. Williams cf	1	0	0	0
Walker rf	2	0	0	0	Garciaparra ss	2	0	0	0
L. Gonzalez lf	2	0	1	0	Jeter ss	1	0	0	0
Sosa cf	3	0	0	0	Vizquel ss	1	0	0	0
Guerrero rf	1	0	0	0	Griffey cf	2	0	0	0
McGwire 1b	2	0	0	0	Surhoff lf	2	0	0	0
Casey 1b	1	0	0	0	Ramirez rf	1	1	0	0
M. Williams 3b	3	0	1	0	Green rf	1	0	1	0
Sprague 3b	1	0	0	0	Ordonez rf	1	0	0	0
Bagwell dh	3	0	1	0	Thome 1b	2	1	1	1
Sheffield dh	1	0	0	0	Coomer 1b	1	0	0	0
Piazza c	2	0	1	0	Ripken 3b	1	1	1	1
Lieberthal c	1	0	0	0	Fernandez 3b	2	0	0	0
Nilsson c	1	0	0	0	Palmeiro dh	2	0	1	1
Burnitz lf-rf	2	1	1	0	Baines dh	1	0	0	0
Jordan cf	1	0	1	0	Jaha dh	1	0	0	0
Bell 2b	1	0	0	0	Rodriguez c	2	0	0	0
Kent 2b	1	0	0	0	Ausmus c	1	0	0	0
					Alomar 2b	2	0	0	1
					Offerman ph-2b	1	0	0	0
Totals	32	1	7	1	**Totals**	31	4	6	4

National	001 000 000—1
American	200 200 00x—4

E—M. Williams, Alomar, Offerman. DP—American 3. LOB—National 8, American 6. 2B—Burnitz, L. Gonzalez. SB—Lofton. CS—M. Williams, Jordan.

National	ip	h	r	er	bb	so	American	ip	h	r	er	bb	so
Schilling L	2	3	2	2	1	3	Martinez W	2	0	0	0	0	5
Johnson	1	0	0	0	0	1	Cone	2	4	1	1	1	3
Bottenfield	1	1	2	2	1	2	Mussina	1	1	0	0	1	2
Lima	1	1	0	0	0	0	Rosado	1	1	0	0	0	1
Millwood	1	1	0	0	0	1	Zimmerman	1	0	0	0	2	0
Ashby	⅓	0	0	0	0	0	Hernandez	1	0	0	0	0	0
Hampton	⅔	0	0	0	0	0	Wetteland S	1	1	0	0	0	1
Hoffman	⅓	0	0	0	0	1							
Wagner	⅔	0	0	0	0	2							

HBP—Ripken (by Bottenfield).
Umpires: HP—Jim Evans; 1B—Terry Tata; 2B—Dale Ford; 3B—Angel Hernandez; LF—Mark Johnson; RF—Larry Vanover. T—2:53. A—34,187.

American icon
Joe DiMaggio transcended baseball

"Where have you gone, Joe DiMaggio, a nation turns its lonely eyes to you."

"Like his many fans across America, and indeed around the world, the Yankees are deeply saddened by the passing of Joe DiMaggio, one of our own and one of the greatest of all time," Steinbrenner said. "It was the class and dignity with which he led his life that made him part of all of us. I will forever treasure the close friendship we shared over the years."

DiMaggio was one of two Yankees Hall of Famers who died. Pitcher Jim "Catfish" Hunter succumbed to amyotrophic lateral sclerosis on Sept. 9 at his home in Hertford, N.C., less than a year after finding out he had Lou Gehrig's disease. Hunter pitched in the major leagues for 15 season with the Athletics (1965-74) and Yankees (1975-79). He went 224-166 with a 3.26 ERA.

Hunter was a pioneer who brought about the advent of free agency. After four straight 20-win seasons in Oakland, Hunter was declared a free agent on a contract technicality after the 1974 season in which he won the AL Cy Young Award.

Starting baseball's first free-agent bidding war, Hunter wound up signing a five-year, $3.75 million contract with the Yankees. He became the highest-paid player in the game and paved the way for full-scale free agency.

In New York, Hunter reached the 20-win mark again in 1975 and played for his fourth and fifth World Series champions in 1977 and '78.

"Catfish Hunter was the cornerstone of the Yankees' success over the last quarter century," Steinbrenner said. "We were not winning before Catfish arrived, and since his arrival in 1975 the Yankees have the best record in baseball. He exemplified class and dignity. He taught us how to win."

Longtime Dodgers captain and shortstop Pee Wee Reese died in his Louisville home Aug. 14 at 81. He had lung cancer.

In 15 seasons with the Brooklyn/Los Angeles Dodgers (1940-42, 1946-58), Reese hit .269 with 126 homers and 885 RBIs. He was known as much for his quiet leadership and his humanitarian side as his brilliant defensive play. Reese is credited with playing a major role in smoothing the way for Jackie Robinson to break baseball's color barrier in 1947.

"Pee Wee didn't ask for credit," Dodgers pitcher Carl Erskine said. "I never heard him say one word that he was able to help Jackie. He helped all of us by his leadership, his consistent play and just by being a good human being."

Early Wynn, a 300-game winner, died April 4 at 79 in Venice, Fla. He had a stroke and heart attack in recent years. Wynn pitched 23 years for the Washington Senators (1939, 1941-48), Indians (1948-57, 1963) and White Sox (1958-62), compiling a 300-244 record with a 3.54 ERA. Wynn was also a good hitter, belting 17 home runs in his career.

The Corner Bows Out

As baseball headed toward a new millennium and a new age of ballparks, it waved goodbye to four ballparks—the Kingdome in Seattle, Tiger Stadium in Detroit, 3Com (formerly Candlestick) Park in San Francisco and the Astrodome in Houston.

County Stadium in Milwaukee was also supposed to

Hospital on Oct. 12, 1998, and at one point was given last rites. He made a miraculous recovery and went home Jan. 19. The 84-year-old DiMaggio eventually took a turn for the worse, though, was hospitalized again and eventually lost his fight for life.

"Today, America lost one of the century's most beloved heroes, Joe DiMaggio," Clinton said. "This son of Italian immigrants gave every American something to believe in. He became the very symbol of American grace, power and skill.

"I have no doubt that when future generations look back at the best of America in the 20th century, they will think of the Yankee Clipper and all that he achieved."

Despite missing three years during World War II, DiMaggio finished his 13-year career (1936-42, 1946-51) with a .325 batting average, 361 home runs, 1,537 RBIs and 2,214 hits for the Yankees. He made 11 all-star teams and won three AL MVP awards. Of course, his greatest accomplishment was a record 56-game hitting streak in 1941. No one has come closer than 44 since.

However, the reclusive DiMaggio, once married to pop icon Marilyn Monroe, was remembered for more than his playing ability. DiMaggio maintained a mystique that no other ballplayer ever had.

DiMaggio transcended the playing field and became a part of American culture, and for more than just his short-lived marriage to Monroe. In the novel "The Old Man and the Sea," Ernest Hemingway's fictional character Santiago dreams of taking "the great DiMaggio fishing." Bandleader Les Brown and singer Betty Bonney recorded a 1941 song saluting the hitting streak. A generation later, Simon and Garfunkel looked back wistfully to lost innocence, asking,

MAJOR LEAGUE DEBUTS, 1999

AMERICAN LEAGUE

Anaheim Angels

Juan Alvarez, lhp	Sept. 1
Mike Colangelo, of	June 13
Brian Cooper, rhp	Sept. 7
Jeff DaVanon, of	Sept. 7
Trent Durrington, 2b	Aug. 6
Bret Hemphill, c	June 28
Ramon Ortiz, rhp	Aug. 19
Lou Pote, rhp	Aug. 11
Scott Schoeneweis, lhp	April 7

Baltimore Orioles

Tommy Davis, c	May 14
Brian Falkenborg, rhp	Oct. 1
Jesse Garcia, 2b	April 5
Gabe Molina, rhp	May 1
Matt Riley, lhp	Sept. 9

Boston Red Sox

Creighton Gubanich, c	April 16
Steve Lomasney, c	Oct. 3
Tomokazu Ohka, rhp	July 19
Juan Pena, rhp	May 8
Wilton Veras, 3b	July 1

Chicago White Sox

McKay Christensen, of	April 6
Pat Daneker, rhp	July 2
Joe Davenport, rhp	July 20
Jason Dellaero, ss	Sept. 7
Carlos Lee, of	May 7
Jeff Liefer, 1b	April 7
David Lundquist, rhp	April 6
Aaron Myette, rhp	Sept. 7
Josh Paul, c	Sept. 7
Jesus Pena, lhp	Aug. 7
Liu Rodriguez, 2b	June 9
Chris Singleton, of	April 10
Kip Wells, rhp	Aug. 2

Cleveland Indians

Jim Brower, rhp	Sept. 5
Sean DePaula, rhp	Aug. 31
John McDonald, ss	July 4
David Riske, rhp	Aug. 14
David Roberts, of	Aug. 7

Detroit Tigers

Dave Borkowski, rhp	July 17
Francisco Cordero, rhp	Aug. 2
Luis Garcia, ss	April 5
Beiker Graterol, rhp	April 9
Erik Hiljus, rhp	Sept. 10
Masao Kida, rhp	April 5
Jose Macias, 2b	May 12
Willis Roberts, rhp	July 2
Jeff Weaver, rhp	April 14

Kansas City Royals

Lance Carter, rhp	Sept. 15
Chad Durbin, rhp	Sept. 26
Mark Quinn, of	Sept. 14
Orber Moreno, rhp	May 25
Ken Ray, rhp	July 10
Dan Reichert, rhp	July 16

Minnesota Twins

Chad Allen, of	April 6
Cleatus Davidson, 2b	May 30
Cristian Guzman, ss	April 6
Jacque Jones, of	June 9
Mike Lincoln, rhp	April 7
Joe Mays, rhp	April 7
Dan Perkins, rhp	April 7
Rob Radlosky, rhp	May 25
Mark Redman, lhp	July 24
J.C. Romero, lhp	Sept. 15
Jason Ryan, rhp	Aug. 24

New York Yankees

Clay Bellinger, 2b-3b	April 9
D'Angelo Jimenez, ss	Sept. 15
Alfonso Soriano, ss	Sept. 14
Ed Yarnall, lhp	July 15

Oakland Athletics

Chad Harville, rhp	June 23
Ramon Hernandez, c	June 29
Tim Hudson, rhp	June 8
Brett Laxton, rhp	June 21
Frank Menechino, 2b	Sept. 6
Luis Vizcaino, rhp	July 23

Seattle Mariners

Ryan Franklin, rhp	May 15
Freddy Garcia, rhp	April 7
Brett Hinchliffe, rhp	April 5
Damaso Marte, lhp	June 30
Gil Meche, rhp	July 6
Rob Ramsay, lhp	Aug. 27
Aaron Scheffer, rhp	June 13
Sean Spencer, lhp	May 6
Denny Stark, rhp	Sept. 15
Jordan Zimmerman, lhp	May 17

Tampa Bay Devil Rays

Mickey Callaway, rhp	June 12
Steve Cox, 1b	Sept. 19
David Lamb, ss	April 12
Jim Morris, lhp	Sept. 18
Alan Newman, lhp	May 14
Ryan Rupe, rhp	May 5
Jeff Sparks, rhp	Sept. 12
Dan Wheeler, rhp	Sept. 1

Texas Rangers

Doug Davis, lhp	Aug. 9
Kelly Dransfeldt, ss	May 1
Ryan Glynn, rhp	May 16
Danny Kolb, rhp	June 4
Corey Lee, lhp	Aug. 24
Ruben Mateo, of	June 12
Mike Venafro, lhp	April 24
Jeff Zimmerman, rhp	April 13

Toronto Blue Jays

John Bale, lhp	Sept. 30
Casey Blake, 3b	Aug. 14
Tom Davey, rhp	April 6
Gary Glover, rhp	Sept. 30
Billy Koch, rhp	May 5
Peter Munro, rhp	April 6
Mike Romano, rhp	Sept. 5
Anthony Sanders, of	April 26
Vernon Wells, of	Aug. 30
Chris Woodward, ss	June 7

NATIONAL LEAGUE

Arizona Diamondbacks

Rod Barajas, c	Sept. 25
Jason Boyd, rhp	Sept. 10
Erubiel Durazo, 1b	July 26
Byung-Hyun Kim, rhp	May 29
Vicente Padilla, rhp	June 29
Rob Ryan, of	Aug. 20
Erik Sabel, rhp	July 9

Atlanta Braves

Micah Bowie, lhp	July 24
David Cortes, rhp	Aug. 30
Derrin Ebert, lhp	April 6
Pascual Matos, c	May 11
Kevin McGlinchy, rhp	April 5
Joe Winkelsas, rhp	April 10

Chicago Cubs

Richie Barker, rhp	April 25
Roosevelt Brown, of	May 18
Kyle Farnsworth, rhp	April 29
Ray King, lhp	May 21
Cole Liniak, 3b	Sept. 3
Brian McNichol, rhp	Sept. 7
Chad Meyers, 2b	Aug. 6
Jose Molina, c	Sept. 6
Bo Porter, of	May 9
Steve Rain, rhp	July 17

Cincinnati Reds

Travis Dawkins, ss	Sept. 3
Jason LaRue, c	June 15
B.J. Ryan, lhp	July 28
Scott Williamson, rhp	April 5

Colorado Rockies

Luther Hackman, rhp	Sept. 1
David Lee, rhp	May 22
Chris Petersen, ss	May 25
Ben Petrick, c	Sept. 1
Mike Porzio, lhp	July 9
Chris Sexton, ss	May 3
Juan Sosa, ss	Sept. 10

Florida Marlins

Armando Almanza, lhp	July 29
Hector Almonte, rhp	July 26
Brent Billingsley, lhp	May 20
A.J. Burnett, rhp	Aug. 17
Ramon Castro, c	Aug. 27
Chris Clapinski, of	July 17
Amaury Garcia, 2b	July 5
Julio Ramirez, of	Sept. 10
Michael Tejera, lhp	Sept. 8

Houston Astros

Glen Barker, of	April 7
Lance Berkman, of	July 16
Carlos Hernandez, 2b	May 26
Wade Miller, rhp	July 7

Los Angeles Dodgers

Jamie Arnold, rhp	April 20
Eric Gagne, rhp	Sept. 7
Matt Herges, rhp	Aug. 3
Onan Masaoka, lhp	April 5
Jeff Williams, lhp	Sept. 12

Milwaukee Brewers

Kevin Barker, 1b	Aug. 19
Robinson Cancel, c	Sept. 3
Carl Dale, rhp	Sept. 7
Horacio Estrada, lhp	May 4
Rick Greene, rhp	June 19
Kyle Peterson, rhp	July 19
Hector Ramirez, rhp	Aug. 28

Montreal Expos

Tony Armas, rhp	Aug. 16
Peter Bergeron, of	Sept. 7
Geoff Blum, ss	Aug. 9
Trace Coquillette, 2b-3b	Sept. 7
Darron Cox, c	April 6
Jose Fernandez, 3b	July 3
Ted Lilly, lhp	May 14
Guillermo Mota, rhp	May 2
J.D. Smart, rhp	April 6
Dan Smith, rhp	June 8
Chris Stowers, of	July 10
Scott Strickland, rhp	Aug. 14

New York Mets

Octavio Dotel, rhp	June 26
Terrence Long, of	April 14
Melvin Mora, of	May 30
Dan Murray, rhp	Aug. 9
Jorge Toca, of	Sept. 12
Vance Wilson, c	April 24

Philadelphia Phillies

Steve Schrenk, rhp	July 3
Anthony Shumaker, lhp	July 23
Randy Wolf, lhp	June 11

Pittsburgh Pirates

Jimmy Anderson, lhp	July 4
Kris Benson, rhp	April 9
Mike Garcia, rhp	Sept. 10
Yamid Haad, c	July 5
Chad Hermansen, of	Sept. 7
Warren Morris, 2b	April 5
Jason Phlips, rhp	April 5
Scott Sauerbeck, rhp	April 5

St. Louis Cardinals

Rick Ankiel, lhp	Aug. 23
Rick Heiserman, rhp	May 23
Adam Kennedy, 2b	Aug. 21

San Diego Padres

Buddy Carlyle, rhp	Aug. 29
Mike Darr, of	May 23
Wiki Gonzalez, c	Aug. 14
Domingo Guzman, rhp	Sept. 9
Gary Matthews Jr., of	June 4
David Newhan, 2b	June 4

San Francisco Giants

Miguel Del Toro, rhp	April 6
Edwards Guzman, 3b	April 6
Calvin Murray, of	June 22
Joe Nathan, rhp	April 21

close on the final day of the 1999 season. That farewell was delayed, however, because of a tragic construction accident at Miller Park that killed three ironworkers. Miller Park will now open in 2001.

Construction halted after a 567-foot crane collapsed July 14, dropping a 400-ton piece of the ballpark's retractable roof into the right-field stands. Damage was estimated at $75 million.

The Kingdome was the first stadium to go, closing its doors to baseball June 27 with the Mariners beating the Rangers 5-2. To the surprise of no one, Mariners center fielder Ken Griffey was the star, as he hit a three-run homer and reached over the fence to rob Juan Gonzalez of a homer.

The Kingdome opened in 1977 when the Mariners joined the AL as an expansion franchise. It was regarded almost since that time as one of the worst places to play in the major leagues. Seattle went back to the future 22 years later as it opened Safeco Field, an open-air park with a retractable roof. Safeco Field was hailed as one of the game's best new parks, as well it should be. It is the most expensive ballpark in baseball history, with a final price tag of $517 million. The Mariners opened Safeco on a losing note, dropping a 3-2 decision to the Padres.

Tiger Stadium, which opened in the same week the Titanic sank in 1912, closed its doors Sept. 27 with a grand ceremony. The Tigers won the game 8-2 behind rookie Rob Fick's grand slam.

They had been playing baseball at the corner of Michigan and Trumbull since 1892, when Bennett Field opened. Navin Field was built on the same site in 1912, with the name changing to Briggs Stadium in

Goodbye
Tiger Stadium closed its doors after almost a century of baseball

1938 and Tiger Stadium in 1961. The Tigers move into Comerica Park, a mile away, in 2000.

"This is the history of baseball in Detroit going down right here," said former Tigers star Kirk Gibson, a Michigan native. "My childhood. My dreams. This is where my dream came true."

San Francisco's 3Com Park was more like a nightmare, with its wind and cold on Candlestick Point. The park's final game on Sept. 30 arrived with more anticipation than sadness after a 39-year run, and the crowd seemed almost disappointed that the last game came on a warm, sunny day. The Giants move into Pacific Bell Park in downtown San Francisco in 2000.

"We leave this park with memories, but we're eagerly anticipating moving into Pacific Bell Ballpark," Giants CEO Larry Baer said. "We know this move is best for all concerned."

The Giants left Candlestick Point on a losing note, dropping a 9-4 decision to the Dodgers.

The Astros feel the same sense of anticipation about leaving the Astrodome, the world's first indoor stadium when it opened in 1965, for Enron Park, another retractable-roof facility. The Astros bowed out on a bitter note, losing 7-5 to the Braves on Oct. 9 in the fourth game of the NL Division Series.

"The Astrodome has a lot of fond memories for everyone involved with the Astros," said manager Larry Dierker, whose association with the club started in 1964 when he broke in as a pitcher. "But its time had come. It's time to move. Like everything in baseball, things change. Nothing ever stays the same. Now, it's time to turn the page and move on."

Good riddance
Few will be sorry to see 3Com/Candlestick Park go

Yankees leave no doubt about team of decade—or century

BY JOHN PERROTTO

The conventional wisdom going into the 1999 World Series: It would determine the team of the 1990s.

The Atlanta Braves, who prematurely had granted themselves that title after beating the Cleveland Indians in 1995, had won eight straight division titles and were making their fifth Fall Classic appearance of the decade.

The New York Yankees had won two of the previous three World Series and were looking for their third crown of the decade.

By the time the World Series was over, there was little doubt who the team of the '90s was. The Yankees blew past the Braves in four games for their second straight World Series sweep, after dusting the San Diego Padres in 1998.

The scoreboard at Yankee Stadium put the much broader perspective on the whole matter moments after the Yankees completed the sweep and sent all those broom-toting fans into delirium in the Bronx. It flashed this message: "New York Yankees. 25 World Championships. Team of the Century."

That pretty much said it all.

"We've won three World Series in four years, so I think you would have to say we're a dynasty, and we deserve our place alongside some of the other Yankee dynasties," Yankees shortstop Derek Jeter said after the celebration began to wind down. "To win three World Series in four years is quite an accomplishment. Not many teams have ever done that.

"But think about the big picture for a minute. The Yankees have won 25 World Series in this century. That's more than one-quarter of all the World Series ever played. That's something to be proud of. That's a dynasty if I ever heard of one."

And perhaps no Yankees team has ever been as special as this one. They won their 12th straight World Series game, tying a record. The Yankees set the record in 1927, 1928 and 1932. They also swept back-to-back World Series, only the third time that has happened. The Yankees also did it in 1927-28 and 1938-39.

The Yankees finished the World Series with 18 wins in their last 19 postseason games. They went 11-1 in 1999, sweeping the Texas Rangers in three games in the American League Division Series, eliminating the Boston Red Sox in five games in the AL Championship Series, then sweeping Atlanta.

"I think this team ranks up there with any of the great Yankee teams of the past," Yankees owner George Steinbrenner said. "Maybe this team isn't as talented as some of the other great clubs, but I don't think any team has ever had the heart of this year's club. These guys have been through a lot.

Familiar routine
Yankees celebrate World Series title No. 25

"In fact, I'd probably have to rank it at the top. Three tiers of playoffs (a system instituted in 1995) doesn't make it twice as hard or three times as hard, it makes it five times as hard. And what our guys had to overcome this season makes it 10 times as hard."

Thwarting Tragedy

Indeed, the ability to overcome turmoil and tragedy is what defined the 1999 Yankees and may separate them from other great teams of the past.

Yankees heroes Joe DiMaggio and Catfish Hunter died in '99. Doctors diagnosed prostate cancer in manager Joe Torre on March 10, and he didn't return to the dugout until May 18. Outfielder/designated hitter Darryl Strawberry, recovering from colon cancer, was arrested and suspended in April. Police charged him with cocaine possession after they said he solicited a female Tampa police officer posing as a prostitute.

Third baseman Scott Brosius lost his father in September, and infielder Luis Sojo missed the first two games of the World Series to attend his father's funeral. Right fielder Paul O'Neill's father died the day the Yankees finished their sweep of Atlanta.

WORLD SERIES YEAR-BY-YEAR

Year	Winner	Manager	Loser	Manager	Result	MVP
1903	Boston (AL)	Jimmy Collins	Pittsburgh (NL)	Fred Clarke	5-3	None Selected
1904	NO SERIES					
1905	New York (NL)	John McGraw	Philadelphia (AL)	Connie Mack	4-1	None Selected
1906	Chicago (AL)	Fielder Jones	Chicago (NL)	Frank Chance	4-2	None Selected
1907	Chicago (NL)	Frank Chance	Detroit (AL)	Hugh Jennings	4-0	None Selected
1908	Chicago (NL)	Frank Chance	Detroit (AL)	Hugh Jennings	4-1	None Selected
1909	Pittsburgh (NL)	Fred Clarke	Detroit (AL)	Hugh Jennings	4-3	None Selected
1910	Philadelphia (AL)	Connie Mack	Chicago (NL)	Frank Chance	4-1	None Selected
1911	Philadelphia (AL)	Connie Mack	New York (NL)	John McGraw	4-2	None Selected
1912	Boston (AL)	Jake Stahl	New York (NL)	John McGraw	4-3-1	None Selected
1913	Philadelphia (AL)	Connie Mack	New York (NL)	John McGraw	4-1	None Selected
1914	Boston (NL)	George Stallings	Philadelphia (AL)	Connie Mack	4-0	None Selected
1915	Boston (AL)	Bill Carrigan	Philadelphia (AL)	Pat Moran	4-1	None Selected
1916	Boston (AL)	Bill Carrigan	Brooklyn (NL)	Wilbert Robinson	4-1	None Selected
1917	Chicago (AL)	Pants Rowland	New York (NL)	John McGraw	4-2	None Selected
1918	Boston (AL)	Ed Barrow	Chicago (NL)	Fred Mitchell	4-2	None Selected
1919	Cincinnati (NL)	Pat Moran	Chicago (AL)	Kid Gleason	5-3	None Selected
1920	Cleveland (AL)	Tris Speaker	Brooklyn (NL)	Wilbert Robinson	5-2	None Selected
1921	New York (NL)	John McGraw	New York (AL)	Miller Huggins	5-3	None Selected
1922	New York (NL)	John McGraw	New York (AL)	Miller Huggins	4-0	None Selected
1923	New York (AL)	Miller Huggins	New York (NL)	John McGraw	4-2	None Selected
1924	Washington (AL)	Bucky Harris	New York (NL)	John McGraw	4-3	None Selected
1925	Pittsburgh (NL)	Bill McKechnie	Washington (AL)	Bucky Harris	4-3	None Selected
1926	St. Louis (NL)	Rogers Hornsby	New York (AL)	Miller Huggins	4-3	None Selected
1927	New York (AL)	Miller Huggins	Pittsburgh (NL)	Donie Bush	4-0	None Selected
1928	New York (AL)	Miller Huggins	St. Louis (NL)	Bill McKechnie	4-0	None Selected
1929	Philadelphia (AL)	Connie Mack	Chicago (NL)	Joe McCarthy	4-1	None Selected
1930	Philadelphia (AL)	Connie Mack	St. Louis (NL)	Gabby Street	4-2	None Selected
1931	St. Louis (NL)	Gabby Street	Philadelphia (AL)	Connie Mack	4-3	None Selected
1932	New York (AL)	Joe McCarthy	Chicago (NL)	Charlie Grimm	4-0	None Selected
1933	New York (NL)	Bill Terry	Washington (AL)	Joe Cronin	4-1	None Selected
1934	St. Louis (NL)	Frankie Frisch	Detroit (AL)	Mickey Cochrane	4-3	None Selected
1935	Detroit (AL)	Mickey Cochrane	Chicago (NL)	Charlie Grimm	4-2	None Selected
1936	New York (AL)	Joe McCarthy	New York (NL)	Bill Terry	4-2	None Selected
1937	New York (AL)	Joe McCarthy	New York (NL)	Bill Terry	4-1	None Selected
1938	New York (AL)	Joe McCarthy	Chicago (NL)	Gabby Hartnett	4-0	None Selected
1939	New York (AL)	Joe McCarthy	Cincinnati (NL)	Bill McKechnie	4-0	None Selected
1940	Cincinnati (NL)	Bill McKechnie	Detroit (AL)	Del Baker	4-3	None Selected
1941	New York (AL)	Joe McCarthy	Brooklyn (NL)	Leo Durocher	4-1	None Selected
1942	St. Louis (NL)	Billy Southworth	New York (AL)	Joe McCarthy	4-1	None Selected
1943	New York (AL)	Joe McCarthy	St. Louis (NL)	Billy Southworth	4-1	None Selected
1944	St. Louis (NL)	Billy Southworth	St. Louis (AL)	Luke Sewell	4-2	None Selected
1945	Detroit (AL)	Steve O'Neill	Chicago (NL)	Charlie Grimm	4-3	None Selected
1946	St. Louis (NL)	Eddie Dyer	Boston (AL)	Joe Cronin	4-3	None Selected
1947	New York (AL)	Bucky Harris	Brooklyn (NL)	Burt Shotton	4-3	None Selected
1948	Cleveland (AL)	Lou Boudreau	Boston (NL)	Billy Southworth	4-2	None Selected
1949	New York (AL)	Casey Stengel	Brooklyn (NL)	Burt Shotton	4-1	None Selected
1950	New York (AL)	Casey Stengel	Philadelphia (NL)	Eddie Sawyer	4-0	None Selected
1951	New York (AL)	Casey Stengel	New York (NL)	Leo Durocher	4-2	None Selected
1952	New York (AL)	Casey Stengel	Brooklyn (NL)	Chuck Dressen	4-3	None Selected
1953	New York (AL)	Casey Stengel	Brooklyn (NL)	Chuck Dressen	4-2	None Selected
1954	New York (NL)	Leo Durocher	Cleveland (AL)	Al Lopez	4-0	None Selected
1955	Brooklyn (NL)	Walter Alston	New York (AL)	Casey Stengel	4-3	Johnny Podres, p, Brooklyn
1956	New York (AL)	Casey Stengel	Brooklyn (NL)	Walter Alston	4-3	Don Larsen, p, New York
1957	Milwaukee (NL)	Fred Haney	New York (AL)	Casey Stengel	4-3	Lew Burdette, p, Milwaukee
1958	New York (AL)	Casey Stengel	Milwaukee (NL)	Fred Haney	4-3	Bob Turley, p, New York
1959	Los Angeles (NL)	Walter Alston	Chicago (AL)	Al Lopez	4-2	Larry Sherry, p, Los Angeles
1960	Pittsburgh (NL)	Danny Murtaugh	New York (AL)	Casey Stengel	4-3	Bobby Richardson, 2b, New York
1961	New York (AL)	Ralph Houk	Cincinnati (NL)	Fred Hutchinson	4-1	Whitey Ford, p, New York
1962	New York (AL)	Ralph Houk	San Francisco (NL)	Alvin Dark	4-3	Ralph Terry, p, New York
1963	Los Angeles (NL)	Walter Alston	New York (AL)	Ralph Houk	4-0	Sandy Koufax, p, Los Angeles
1964	St. Louis (NL)	Johnny Keane	New York (AL)	Yogi Berra	4-3	Bob Gibson, p, St. Louis
1965	Los Angeles (NL)	Walter Alston	Minnesota (AL)	Sam Mele	4-3	Sandy Koufax, p, Los Angeles
1966	Baltimore (AL)	Hank Bauer	Los Angeles (NL)	Walter Alston	4-0	Frank Robinson, of, Baltimore
1967	St. Louis (NL)	Red Schoendienst	Boston (AL)	Dick Williams	4-3	Bob Gibson, p, St. Louis
1968	Detroit (AL)	Mayo Smith	St. Louis (NL)	Red Schoendienst	4-3	Mickey Lolich, p, Detroit
1969	New York (NL)	Gil Hodges	Baltimore (AL)	Earl Weaver	4-1	Donn Clendenon, 1b, New York
1970	Baltimore (AL)	Earl Weaver	Cincinnati (NL)	Sparky Anderson	4-1	Brooks Robinson, 3b, Baltimore
1971	Pittsburgh (NL)	Danny Murtaugh	Baltimore (AL)	Earl Weaver	4-3	Roberto Clemente, of, Pittsburgh
1972	Oakland (AL)	Dick Williams	Cincinnati (NL)	Sparky Anderson	4-3	Gene Tenace, c, Oakland
1973	Oakland (AL)	Dick Williams	New York (NL)	Yogi Berra	4-3	Reggie Jackson, of, Oakland
1974	Oakland (AL)	Alvin Dark	Los Angeles (NL)	Walter Alston	4-1	Rollie Fingers, p, Oakland
1975	Cincinnati (NL)	Sparky Anderson	Boston (AL)	Darrell Johnson	4-3	Pete Rose, 3b, Cincinnati
1976	Cincinnati (NL)	Sparky Anderson	New York (AL)	Billy Martin	4-0	Johnny Bench, c, Cincinnati
1977	New York (AL)	Billy Martin	Los Angeles (NL)	Tom Lasorda	4-2	Reggie Jackson, of, New York
1978	New York (AL)	Bob Lemon	Los Angeles (NL)	Tom Lasorda	4-2	Bucky Dent, ss, New York
1979	Pittsburgh (NL)	Chuck Tanner	Baltimore (AL)	Earl Weaver	4-3	Willie Stargell, 1b, Pittsburgh
1980	Philadelphia (NL)	Dallas Green	Kansas City (AL)	Jim Frey	4-2	Mike Schmidt, 3b, Philadelphia
1981	Los Angeles (NL)	Tom Lasorda	New York (AL)	Bob Lemon	4-2	Cey/Guerrero/Yeager, L.A.
1982	St. Louis (NL)	Whitey Herzog	Milwaukee (AL)	Harvey Kuenn	4-3	Darrell Porter, c, St. Louis
1983	Baltimore (AL)	Joe Altobelli	Philadelphia (NL)	Paul Owens	4-1	Rick Dempsey, c, Baltimore
1984	Detroit (AL)	Sparky Anderson	San Diego (NL)	Dick Williams	4-1	Alan Trammell, ss, Detroit
1985	Kansas City (AL)	Dick Howser	St. Louis (NL)	Whitey Herzog	4-3	Bret Saberhagen, p, Kansas City
1986	New York (NL)	Dave Johnson	Boston (AL)	John McNamara	4-3	Ray Knight, 3b, New York
1987	Minnesota (AL)	Tom Kelly	St. Louis (NL)	Whitey Herzog	4-3	Frank Viola, p, Minnesota
1988	Los Angeles (NL)	Tom Lasorda	Oakland (AL)	Tony La Russa	4-1	Orel Hershiser, p, Los Angeles
1989	Oakland (AL)	Tony La Russa	San Francisco (NL)	Roger Craig	4-0	Dave Stewart, p, Oakland
1990	Cincinnati (NL)	Lou Piniella	Oakland (AL)	Tony La Russa	4-0	Jose Rijo, p, Cincinnati
1991	Minnesota (AL)	Tom Kelly	Atlanta (NL)	Bobby Cox	4-3	Jack Morris, p, Minnesota
1992	Toronto (AL)	Cito Gaston	Atlanta (NL)	Bobby Cox	4-2	Pat Borders, c, Toronto
1993	Toronto (AL)	Cito Gaston	Philadelphia (NL)	Jim Fregosi	4-2	Paul Molitor, dh, Toronto
1994	NO SERIES					
1995	Atlanta (NL)	Bobby Cox	Cleveland (AL)	Mike Hargrove	4-2	Tom Glavine, p, Atlanta
1996	New York (AL)	Joe Torre	Atlanta (NL)	Bobby Cox	4-2	John Wetteland, p, New York
1997	Florida (NL)	Jim Leyland	Cleveland (AL)	Mike Hargrove	4-3	Livan Hernandez, p, Florida
1998	New York (AL)	Joe Torre	San Diego (NL)	Bruce Bochy	4-0	Scott Brosius, 3b, New York
1999	New York (AL)	Joe Torre	Atlanta (NL)	Bobby Cox	4-0	Mariano Rivera, p, New York

"We've played with heavy hearts a lot this season," said righthander Roger Clemens, who came over in a trade with the Blue Jays in the spring. He did not prove to be the dominant ace the Yankees were looking for, but he was outstanding in getting the win in Game Four. "I don't know if I could have gone out there like Paul O'Neill did on the same day his father died. But that's the character of this ballclub. It's just amazing."

"I think we got in the pretty good habit of dealing with whatever lowlights there were and tragedies and hardships, and go out there and do the job we're capable of doing," Torre said. "Let's see how good we are in spite of the odds against us. Tragedy is a part of life. Just because you're an athlete doesn't mean you're exempt."

The Yankees also had the standard of the 1998 team to live up to. The '98 club won 125 games, an AL-record 114 in the regular season and 11 more in the postseason.

"Everyone would talk this year about how we didn't have the same numbers as last year," said closer Mariano Rivera, the World Series MVP after a win and two saves. "Of course not. It's impossible to repeat those numbers. Last year was tremendous. I think those years only happen once in 100 years."

Bridesmaids Again

Across the field, the Braves could only wonder again what might have been as they fell short in another World Series. The only other team to lose four World Series in a decade was the New York Giants

Earning his pinstripes
Roger Clemens came through in the clincher

from 1910-19.

"You can't play the season one way and turn on another way when you get to the World Series," Braves righthander John Smoltz said. "We've always relied on pitching and power hitting. But when you don't execute the little things, it sticks out like a thorn."

In the other World Series losses, the Braves had at least stretched them to six or seven games and played in some classic, close contests. This one was over in a hurry.

"It's not very much fun losing four in a row," Braves manager Bobby Cox said. "I thought we played a little

Gray's confrontation with Rose grabs center stage at Series

The most controversial–and perhaps memorable–figure from the 1999 World Series wasn't a member of the Yankees or Braves.

No, that honor went to NBC-TV sideline reporter Jim Gray, who created the Fall Classic's biggest stir with his interview of all-time hits leader Pete Rose before Game Two.

Baseball honored its all-century team at Atlanta's Turner Field before the game. Rose, who had been banned from baseball for gambling activities since 1989, was elected to the team by fans and was allowed to be part of the ceremonies.

After the ceremony, during which Rose received a 55-second cheer that was the loudest given any player, Gray interviewed Rose on the field. He grilled him about the gambling accusations live on the air for an excruciating and riveting two

Back in the limelight
Pete Rose

minutes and 20 seconds.

After opening with a question about why Rose wasn't taking the opportunity to come clean about betting on baseball, Gray refused to accept Rose's denials and continued to press him on the topic.

"I'm surprised you're bombarding me with this; I'm here to do an interview with you,"

Rose said during the segment. "You're bringing up something that happened 10 years ago."

Gray would not change the subject and said the commissioner's office had strong evidence that Rose bet on baseball. Rose tried to get Gray off the subject, saying: "I'm sure everyone's tired of hearing about that. It's too festive a night to worry about it. I'm just a small part of a big deal tonight."

Gray initially did not back down when asked about the interview, but two days later he apologized on the air to fans during the Game Three pregame show.

The controversy wasn't quite over, though. Yankees left fielder Chad Curtis snubbed Gray on the air after his game-winning home run in Game Three, and the Yankees reportedly considered a total media boycott after the game.

—JOHN PERROTTO

better than that. We would have liked to have made it a better contest, that's for sure. You don't want to get into these things and get swept. You want to at least take it to six or seven."

Rivera's near invincibility was a primary reason the Yankees swept again. He pitched 4⅔ scoreless innings in saving Games One and Four and winning Game Three.

In eight postseason appearances in '99, Rivera had two wins and six saves. He had not allowed a run in his last 25⅔ innings of postseason play, notching two wins and 12 saves.

Rivera's postseason ERA of 0.36–two earned runs in 47⅓ innings–is the lowest for any pitcher with at least 30 innings in postseason history. The Game Four save extended his streak to 12⅓ consecutive scoreless innings over eight games in three World Series.

Rivera was just as good in the regular season, as he ended '99 with a scoreless streak of 30⅔ innings over 28 games and converted his last 22 save opportunities. Rivera did not allow a run after July 21.

"He's the best," Yankees catcher Joe Girardi said of Rivera. "He's the best closer I've ever seen."

"I love the challenge of being a closer, especially in the World Series," Rivera said. "I love to be in that situation. I guess that's my motivation. Once you're there, you have butterflies in your stomach. You know you're there for real. You just want to do it."

No Doubt About It

The Yankees did it from start to finish in this World Series.

They rallied for four runs in the eighth inning to win 4-1 in Game One at Atlanta's Turner Field. Winner Orlando "El Duque" Hernandez allowed one run in seven innings, then watched his teammates score four runs in the eighth after being shut out by Greg Maddux through seven.

David Cone duplicated Hernandez' one-hit, seven-inning performance in Game Two, a 7-2 Yankee victory. Atlanta's Kevin Millwood, the best starter in the Braves rotation in '99, failed to make it past the third inning as the Yankees jumped to a 7-0 lead.

The killer for the Braves came in Game Three, when they failed to hold a 5-1 lead. Chad Curtis started the comeback with a solo homer in the fifth that made it 5-2, then capped it by leading off the 10th with another homer, this one a long drive to left field off Mike Remlinger. Homers by Tino Martinez and Chuck Knoblauch off starter Tom Glavine had tied it.

Clemens, the five-time Cy Young Award winner acquired at the beginning of spring training, finished off the sweep as he allowed only one run in 7⅔ innings in Game Four. It was the first title for Clemens.

"I finally know what it feels like to be a Yankee," a champagne-soaked Clemens said with a broad grin.

Being a Yankee in 1999 meant dominating a second straight World Series.

"You've got to tip your hat to the Yankees," Cox said. "Their pitching was excellent. We shook the hitting down as best we could. They're strong. They've got a great bunch of players."

"It's a ballclub that deserves to be world champions again."

WORLD SERIES
BOX SCORES

GAME ONE: October 23
Yankees 4, Braves 1

New York	ab	r	h	bi	bb	so	Atlanta	ab	r	h	bi	bb	so
Knoblauch 2b	4	1	0	0	0	0	G. Williams lf	4	0	0	0	0	2
Jeter ss	4	1	2	1	1	1	Boone 2b	4	0	1	0	0	2
O'Neill rf	4	0	1	2	0	1	C. Jones 3b	2	1	1	1	2	1
B. Williams cf	2	0	0	0	2	1	Jordan rf	4	0	0	0	0	1
Martinez 1b	3	0	0	0	1	2	Klesko 1b	3	0	0	0	0	0
Posada c	4	0	0	0	0	1	Hunter 1b	0	0	0	0	0	0
Ledee lf	3	0	0	0	0	1	Myers ph	1	0	0	0	0	0
Leyritz ph	0	0	0	1	1	0	A. Jones cf	2	0	0	0	1	1
Nelson p	0	0	0	0	0	0	Perez c	2	0	0	0	1	2
Stanton p	0	0	0	0	0	0	Weiss ss	2	0	0	0	0	1
Rivera p	0	0	0	0	0	0	Guillen ph	0	0	0	0	0	0
Brosius 3b	4	1	3	0	0	1	J. Hernandez ss	1	0	0	0	0	1
O. Hernandez p	1	0	0	0	0	0	Maddux p	2	0	0	0	0	2
Strawberry ph	0	0	0	0	1	0	Rocker p	0	0	0	0	0	0
Curtis pr-lf	1	1	0	0	0	0	Battle ph	0	0	0	0	0	0
							Lockhart ph	1	0	0	0	0	0
							Remlinger p	0	0	0	0	0	0
Totals	30	4	6	4	6	8	**Totals**	28	1	2	1	4	13

New York		000 000 040—4
Atlanta		000 100 000—1

E—Hunter 2 (2). DP—Atlanta 1. LOB—Atlanta 4, New York 7. HR—C. Jones (1). SB—Jeter (1), B. Williams (1). S—O. Hernandez, Knoblauch. CS—Jeter (1), C. Jones (1).

New York	ip	h	r	er	bb	so	Atlanta	ip	h	r	er	bb	so
O. Hernandez W	7	1	1	1	2	10	Maddux L	7	5	4	2	3	5
Nelson	⅓	0	0	0	1	1	Rocker	1	1	0	0	2	3
Stanton	⅓	0	0	0	0	1	Remlinger	1	0	0	0	1	0
Rivera S	1⅓	1	0	0	1	1							

IBB—B. Williams (by Rocker).
Umpires: HP—Marsh; 1B—Roe; 2B—Rippley; 3B—Cousins; LF—Davis; RF—Joyce.
T—2:57. A—51,342.

GAME TWO: October 24
Yankees 7, Braves 2

New York	ab	r	h	bi	bb	so	Atlanta	ab	r	h	bi	bb	so
Knoblauch 2b	4	1	2	1	1	1	G. Williams lf	4	0	0	0	0	1
Jeter ss	5	2	2	0	0	0	Guillen ss	4	0	0	0	0	0
O'Neill rf	4	0	1	1	1	0	C. Jones 3b	3	1	1	0	1	0
B. Williams cf	4	1	3	0	1	0	Jordan rf	3	0	0	0	1	0
Martinez 1b	5	2	2	2	0	1	Klesko 1b	4	0	0	0	0	1
Ledee lf	4	0	2	1	1	2	Lockhart 2b	2	1	0	0	2	0
Brosius 3b	5	1	2	1	0	2	Myers c	3	0	2	1	1	0
Girardi c	4	0	0	0	0	1	A. Jones cf	3	0	0	0	0	1
Cone p	4	0	0	0	0	0	McGlinchy p	0	0	0	0	0	0
Mendoza p	1	0	0	0	0	0	Boone ph	1	0	1	1	0	0
Nelson p	0	0	0	0	0	0	Millwood p	0	0	0	0	0	0
							Mulholland p	0	0	0	0	1	0
							Fabregas ph	1	0	0	0	0	1
							Springer p	0	0	0	0	0	0
							Nixon cf	2	0	1	0	0	0
Totals	40	7	14	6	4	8	**Totals**	30	2	5	2	6	4

New York		302 110 000—7
Atlanta		000 000 002—2

E—Cone (1), Guillen (1). DP—New York 3, Atlanta 1. LOB—New York 11, Atlanta 4. 2B—Ledee (1), Jeter (1), Brosius (1), Boone (1). S—Girardi. SB—Knoblauch (1).

New York	ip	h	r	er	bb	so	Atlanta	ip	h	r	er	bb	so
Cone W	7	1	0	0	5	4	Millwood L	2	8	5	4	2	2
Mendoza	1⅔	3	2	2	1	0	Mulholland	3	3	2	2	1	3
Nelson	⅓	1	0	0	0	0	Springer	2	1	0	0	0	1
							McGlinchy	2	2	0	0	1	2

IBB—B. Williams (by Mulholland).
Umpires: HP—Roe; 1B—Rippley; 2B—Cousins; 3B—Davis; LF—Joyce; RF—Marsh.
T—3:14. A—51,226.

GAME THREE: October 26
Yankees 6, Braves 5

Atlanta	ab	r	h	bi	bb	so	New York	ab	r	h	bi	bb	so
G. Williams lf	5	2	2	0	0	0	Knoblauch 2b	4	2	2	2	0	0
Boone 2b	5	1	4	1	0	0	Jeter ss	4	0	1	0	0	1
Nixon pr	0	0	0	0	0	0	O'Neill rf	4	0	1	1	0	0
Lockhart 2b	0	0	0	0	0	0	B. Williams cf	4	0	0	0	0	0
C. Jones 3b	4	0	1	1	1	1	Davis dh	4	0	0	0	0	2

Atlanta	ab	r	h	bi	bb	so	New York	ab	r	h	bi	bb	so
Jordan rf	3	1	1	1	2	0	Martinez 1b	4	1	1	1	0	0
A. Jones cf	5	1	1	0	0	0	Brosius 3b	4	0	0	0	0	1
J. Hernandez dh	4	0	1	2	0	1	Curtis lf	4	2	2	2	0	0
Guillen dh	1	0	0	0	0	1	Girardi c	3	1	2	0	0	0
Perez c	4	0	1	0	0	1							
Klesko ph-1b	1	0	1	0	0	0							
Hunter 1b	4	0	1	0	0	1							
Myers ph-c	1	0	0	0	0	0							
Weiss ss	4	0	1	0	0	0							
Totals	**41**	**5**	**14**	**5**	**3**	**5**	**Totals**	**35**	**6**	**9**	**6**	**0**	**4**

Atlanta	**103 100 000 0—5**
New York	**100 010 120 1—6**

E—Jordan (1). **DP**—New York 1, Atlanta 2. **LOB**—New York 2, Atlanta 9. **2B**—Boone 3 (4), J. Hernandez (1), Knoblauch (1). **3B**—G. Williams (1). **HR**—Curtis 2 (2), Martinez (1), Knoblauch (1). **SB**—J. Hernandez (1). **CS**—Boone (1), Nixon (1).

Atlanta	ip	h	r	er	bb	so	New York	ip	h	r	er	bb	so
Glavine	7	7	5	4	0	3	Pettitte	3⅔	10	5	5	1	1
Rocker	2	1	0	0	0	1	Grimsley	2⅓	2	0	0	2	0
Remlinger L	0	1	1	1	0	0	Nelson	2	0	0	0	0	2
							Rivera W	2	2	0	0	0	2

WP—Pettitte.

Umpires: HP—Rippley; **1B**—Cousins; **2B**—Davis; **3B**—Joyce; **LF**—Marsh; **RF**—Roe.

T—3:16. **A**—56,794.

GAME FOUR: October 27
Yankees 4, Braves 1

Atlanta	ab	r	h	bi	bb	so	New York	ab	r	h	bi	bb	so
G. Williams lf	4	0	1	0	0	1	Knoblauch 2b	4	1	1	0	0	2
Boone 2b	3	0	1	1	1	1	Sojo 2b	0	0	0	0	0	0
C. Jones 3b	4	0	0	0	0	0	Jeter ss	4	1	1	0	0	0
Jordan rf	3	0	0	0	1	1	O'Neill rf	3	0	0	0	1	1
Klesko 1b	4	0	1	0	0	0	B. Williams cf	3	1	0	0	1	1
Lockhart dh	4	0	1	0	0	0	Martinez 1b	3	0	1	2	1	1
Perez c	2	0	0	0	0	0	Strawberry dh	3	0	1	0	0	2
Myers ph-c	1	0	0	0	0	0	Leyritz ph-dh	1	1	1	1	0	0
A. Jones cf	3	0	0	0	0	1	Posada c	4	0	2	1	0	2
Weiss ss	3	1	1	0	0	0	Ledee lf	3	0	0	0	0	1
							Curtis ph-lf	1	0	0	0	0	0
							Brosius 3b	3	0	1	0	0	1
Totals	**31**	**1**	**5**	**1**	**2**	**4**	**Totals**	**32**	**4**	**8**	**4**	**3**	**11**

Atlanta	**000 000 010—1**
New York	**003 000 01x—4**

DP—New York 1. **LOB**—Atlanta 5, New York 7. **2B**—Posada (1). **HR**—Leyritz (1). **SB**—Jeter 2 (3).

Atlanta	ip	h	r	er	bb	so	New York	ip	h	r	er	bb	so
Smoltz L	7	6	3	3	3	11	Clemens W	7⅔	4	1	1	2	4
Mulholland	⅔	2	1	1	0	0	Nelson	0	1	0	0	0	0
Springer	⅓	0	0	0	0	0	Rivera S	1⅓	0	0	0	0	0

Umpires: HP—Cousins; **1B**—Davis; **2B**—Joyce; **3B**—Marsh; **LF**—Roe; **RF**—Rippley.

T—2:58. **A**—56,752.

COMPOSITE BOX

NEW YORK

Player, Pos.	AVG	G	AB	R	H	2B	3B	HR	RBI	BB	SO	SB
Jim Leyritz, ph/dh	1.000	2	1	1	1	0	0	1	2	1	0	0
Scott Brosius, 3b	.375	4	16	2	6	1	0	0	1	0	5	0
Derek Jeter, ss	.353	4	17	4	6	1	0	0	1	1	3	3
Chad Curtis, pr/lf	.333	3	6	3	2	0	0	2	2	0	0	0
D. Strawberry, ph/dh	.333	2	3	0	1	0	0	0	0	1	2	0
Chuck Knoblauch, 2b	.313	4	16	5	5	1	0	1	3	1	3	1
Joe Girardi, c	.286	2	7	1	2	0	0	0	0	0	1	0
Tino Martinez, 1b	.267	4	15	3	4	0	0	1	5	2	4	0
Jorge Posada, c	.250	2	8	0	2	1	0	0	1	0	3	0
Bernie Williams, cf	.231	4	13	2	3	0	0	0	0	4	2	1
Paul O'Neill, rf	.200	4	15	0	3	0	0	0	4	2	2	0
Ricky Ledee, lf	.200	3	10	0	2	1	0	0	1	1	4	0
David Cone, p	.000	1	4	0	0	0	0	0	0	0	0	0
Chili Davis, dh	.000	1	4	0	0	0	0	0	0	0	2	0
Orlando Hernandez, p	.000	1	1	0	0	0	0	0	0	0	0	0
Ramiro Mendoza, p	.000	1	1	0	0	0	0	0	0	0	0	0
Luis Sojo, 2b	000	1	0	0	0	0	0	0	0	0	0	0
Totals	**.270**	**4**	**137**	**21**	**37**	**5**	**0**	**5**	**20**	**13**	**31**	**5**

Pitching	W	L	ERA	G	GS	SV	IP	H	R	ER	BB	SO
David Cone	1	0	0.00	1	1	0	7	1	0	0	5	4
Mariano Rivera	1	0	0.00	3	0	2	5	3	0	0	1	3
Jeff Nelson	0	0	0.00	4	0	0	3	2	0	0	1	3
Jason Grimsley	0	0	0.00	1	0	0	2	2	0	0	2	0
Mike Stanton	0	0	0.00	1	0	0	0	0	0	0	0	1
Roger Clemens	1	0	1.17	1	1	0	8	4	1	1	2	4
Orlando Hernandez	1	0	1.29	1	1	0	7	1	1	1	2	10
Ramiro Mendoza	0	0	10.80	1	0	0	2	3	2	2	1	0
Andy Pettitte	0	0	12.27	1	1	0	4	10	5	5	1	1
Totals	**4**	**0**	**2.19**	**4**	**4**	**2**	**37**	**26**	**9**	**9**	**15**	**26**

DAVID SEELIG

Backbreaking blow
Chad Curtis' second homer in Game Three put the series away for the Yankees

ATLANTA

Player, Pos.	AVG	G	AB	R	H	2B	3B	HR	RBI	BB	SO	SB
Bret Boone, 2b/ph	.538	4	13	1	7	4	0	0	3	1	3	0
Otis Nixon, cf/pr	.500	2	2	0	1	0	0	0	0	0	0	0
Greg Myers, ph/c	.333	4	6	0	2	0	0	0	1	1	0	0
Brian Hunter, 1b	.250	2	4	0	1	0	0	0	0	0	1	0
Chipper Jones, 3b	.231	4	13	2	3	0	0	1	2	4	2	0
Walt Weiss, ss	.222	3	9	1	2	0	0	0	0	0	1	0
Jose Hernandez, ss/dh	.200	2	5	0	1	1	0	0	2	0	2	1
Gerald Williams, lf	.176	4	17	2	3	0	1	0	0	0	4	0
Ryan Klesko, 1b	.167	4	12	0	2	0	0	0	0	0	1	0
Keith Lockhart, 2b/dh	.143	4	7	1	1	0	0	0	0	2	0	0
Eddie Perez, c	.125	3	8	0	1	0	0	0	0	1	3	0
Andruw Jones, cf	.077	4	13	1	1	0	0	0	0	1	3	0
Brian Jordan, rf	.077	4	13	1	1	0	0	0	1	4	2	0
Ozzie Guillen, ss/dh	.000	3	5	0	0	0	0	0	0	0	1	0
Greg Maddux, p	.000	1	2	0	0	0	0	0	0	0	2	0
Jorge Fabregas, ph	.000	1	1	0	0	0	0	0	0	0	1	0
Howard Battle, ph	.000	1	0	0	0	0	0	0	0	0	0	0
Terry Mulholland, p	.000	2	0	0	0	0	0	0	0	1	0	0
Totals	**.200**	**4**	**130**	**9**	**26**	**5**	**1**	**1**	**9**	**15**	**26**	**1**

Pitcher	W	L	ERA	G	GS	SV	IP	H	R	ER	BB	SO
John Rocker	0	0	0.00	2	0	0	3	2	0	0	2	4
Russ Springer	0	0	0.00	2	0	0	2	1	0	0	0	1
Kevin McGlinchy	0	0	0.00	1	0	0	2	2	0	0	1	2
Greg Maddux	0	1	2.57	1	1	0	7	5	4	2	3	5
John Smoltz	0	1	3.86	1	1	0	7	6	3	3	3	11
Tom Glavine	0	0	5.14	1	1	0	7	7	5	4	0	3
Terry Mulholland	0	0	7.36	2	0	0	4	5	3	3	1	3
Mike Remlinger	0	1	9.00	2	0	0	1	1	1	1	1	0
Kevin Millwood	0	1	18.00	1	1	0	2	8	5	4	2	2
Totals	**0**	**4**	**4.37**	**4**	**4**	**0**	**35**	**37**	**21**	**17**	**13**	**31**

SCORE BY INNINGS

New York	**405 120 170 1—21**
Atlanta	**103 200 012 0— 9**

E—Cone, Hunter 2, Jordan, Guillen. **DP**—New York 5, Atlanta 4. **LOB**—New York 27, Atlanta 25. **CS**—Jeter, C. Jones, Boone, Nixon. **S**—Girardi, Knoblauch, O. Hernandez. **IBB**—B. Williams 3 (by Rocker, Mulholland, Smoltz).

Umpires—Randy Marsh, Rocky Roe, Steve Rippley, Derryl Cousins, Gerry Davis, Jim Joyce.

AMERICAN LEAGUE

Results same, but 1999 proved challenging for Yankees

BY LACY LUSK

The same four teams that had been in the American League playoffs in 1998 reached the playoffs in 1999. The same team—the Yankees—won the pennant. But the season wasn't routine by any means.

It was a season in which Don Larsen watched a Yankee throw a perfect game, and a group of early risers watched a Twin no-hit a lineup that could've been mistaken for that of the St. Paul Saints.

Red Sox fans didn't get their World Series title, but their team reached the AL Championship Series the season after first baseman Mo Vaughn signed with the Angels. And the Sox got there even after trailing the Division Series 2-0 to an Indians team that scored more than 1,000 runs in the regular season.

Boston won just one game as the AL's greatest rivals met in the ALCS, but even that one triumph was about as glorious as any Fenway faithful could imagine. Longtime Sox ace Roger Clemens was knocked out early, while Pedro Martinez capped one of the sport's best pitching performances ever with one last win.

After sweeping the Rangers in the Division Series for the second straight year, the Yankees rallied from a pair of one-run, seventh-inning deficits to win the first two games of the LCS. They saw Martinez only once and went on to their third pennant in four years.

The Yankees didn't dominate as they did in '98, but that was to be expected because no other AL team has ever won 114 games. The 1999 team's 98-64 season—after a 21-15 start while manager Joe Torre was away from the team because of prostate cancer—was no small feat, however.

"Everyone said how bad a season we had because we didn't win 114 games," said Yankees shortstop Derek Jeter, who hit .349 as he becomes the latest cornerstone of baseball's most storied franchise. "But we had the best record in the American League and now we've won the American League championship."

They followed that with the franchise's 25th World Series championship. After going 11-1 in the postseason, Torre joked that his team had really been undefeated—Martinez had been so inhuman that losing to him shouldn't count.

The Red Sox, though, failed to give Martinez a second start in the ALCS. Had he gone in Game Seven, Boston might have suddenly become the favorite. Instead, the Yankees rode timely hit-

Just win, baby
Derek Jeter led the Yankees to another title

LARRY GOREN

ting and strong pitching to the pennant.

Righthander Orlando Hernandez, in his first full season as a Yankee but his second postseason, cruised to a 6-1 victory in the clinching Game Five. The Cuban defector went 2-0 with a 1.17 ERA in three AL playoff starts.

In taking a 3-1 series lead, New York took advantage of a bad call at second base for the second time in the series.

In Game Four, Boston was within 3-2 in the eighth inning when Jose Offerman was ruled out on a phantom tag to start a double play. Had Tim Tschida not called Offerman out, batting champion Nomar Garciaparra would have come up with one out and the tying run on second. But Boston failed to score and New York pounced with a six-run ninth, highlighted by outfielder Ricky Ledee's grand slam.

Knoblauch said he wasn't sure whether he'd tagged Offerman, but the Red Sox second baseman said, "When somebody hits you with the glove, I think you feel it." Tschida even admitted later that he made the wrong call, much as fellow umpire Rick Reed confessed after a Red Sox rally was snuffed out when Knoblauch was credited with catching a ball for a force at second that he didn't really catch.

"All we want is a fair shake," Red Sox outfielder Darren Lewis said. "We're playing hard, busting our butts. We're professionals, just like they are. Give us a little benefit of the doubt, too, like you give those guys because they're world champions."

LARRY GOREN
Postseason ace
Orlando Hernandez

AMERICAN LEAGUE CHAMPIONS, 1901-1999

Year	Pennant	Pct.	GA	Year	Pennant	Pct.	GA	MVP
1901	Chicago	.610	4	1931	Philadelphia	.704	13½	Lefty Grove, lhp, Philadelphia
1902	Philadelphia	.610	5	1932	New York	.695	13	Jimmie Foxx, 1b, Philadelphia
1903	Boston	.659	14½	1933	Washington	.651	7	Jimmie Foxx, 1b, Philadelphia
1904	Boston	.617	1½	1934	Detroit	.656	7	Mickey Cochrane, c, Detroit
1905	Philadelphia	.622	2	1935	Detroit	.616	3	Hank Greenberg, 1b, Detroit
1906	Chicago	.616	3	1936	New York	.667	19½	Lou Gehrig, 1b, New York
1907	Detroit	.613	1½	1937	New York	.662	13	Charlie Gehringer, 2b, Detroit
1908	Detroit	.588	½	1938	New York	.651	9½	Jimmie Foxx, 1b, Boston
1909	Detroit	.645	3½	1939	New York	.702	17	Joe DiMaggio, of, New York
1910	Philadelphia	.680	14½	1940	Detroit	.584	1	Hank Greenberg, 1b, Detroit
1911	Philadelphia	.669	13½	1941	New York	.656	17	Joe DiMaggio, of, New York
1912	Boston	.691	14	1942	New York	.669	9	Joe Gordon, 2b, New York
1913	Philadelphia	.627	6½	1943	New York	.636	13½	Spud Chandler, rhp, New York
1914	Philadelphia	.651	8½	1944	St. Louis	.578	1	Hal Newhouser, lhp, Detroit
1915	Boston	.669	2½	1945	Detroit	.575	1½	Hal Newhouser, lhp, Detroit
1916	Boston	.591	2	1946	Boston	.675	12	Ted Williams, of, Boston
1917	Chicago	.649	9	1947	New York	.630	12	Joe DiMaggio, of, New York
1918	Boston	.595	2½	1948	Cleveland	.626	1	Lou Boudreau, ss, Cleveland
1919	Chicago	.629	3½	1949	New York	.630	1	Ted Williams, of, Boston
1920	Cleveland	.636	2	1950	New York	.636	3	Phil Rizzuto, ss, New York
1921	New York	.641	4½	1951	New York	.636	5	Yogi Berra, c, New York
1922	New York	.610	1	1952	New York	.617	2	Bobby Shantz, lhp, Philadelphia
1923	New York	.645	16	1953	New York	.656	8½	Al Rosen, 3b, Cleveland
1924	Washington	.597	2	1954	Cleveland	.721	8	Yogi Berra, c, New York
1925	Washington	.636	8½	1955	New York	.623	3	Yogi Berra, c, New York
1926	New York	.591	3	1956	New York	.630	9	Mickey Mantle, of, New York
1927	New York	.714	19	1957	New York	.636	8	Mickey Mantle, of, New York
1928	New York	.656	2½	1958	New York	.597	10	Jackie Jensen, of, Boston
1929	Philadelphia	.693	18	1959	Chicago	.610	5	Nellie Fox, 2b, Chicago
1930	Philadelphia	.662	8	1960	New York	.630	8	Roger Maris, of, New York
				1961	New York	.673	8	Roger Maris, of, New York
				1962	New York	.593	5	Mickey Mantle, of, New York
				1963	New York	.646	10½	Elston Howard, c, New York
				1964	New York	.611	1	Brooks Robinson, 3b, Baltimore
				1965	Minnesota	.630	7	Zoilo Versalles, ss, Minnesota
				1966	Baltimore	.606	9	Frank Robinson, of, Baltimore
				1967	Boston	.568	1	Carl Yastrzemski, of, Boston
				1968	Detroit	.636	12	Denny McLain, rhp, Detroit

Year	East. Div.	PCT	GA	West. Div.	PCT	GA	Pennant		MVP
1969	Baltimore	.673	19	Minnesota	.599	9	Baltimore	3-0	Harmon Killebrew, 1b-3b, Minnesota
1970	Baltimore	.667	15	Minnesota	.605	9	Baltimore	3-0	Boog Powell, 1b, Baltimore
1971	Baltimore	.639	12	Oakland	.627	16	Baltimore	3-0	Vida Blue, lhp, Oakland
1972	Detroit	.551	½	Oakland	.600	5½	Oakland	3-2	Dick Allen, 1b, Chicago
1973	Baltimore	.599	8	Oakland	.580	6	Oakland	3-2	Reggie Jackson, of, Oakland
1974	Baltimore	.562	2	Oakland	.556	5	Oakland	3-1	Jeff Burroughs, of, Texas
1975	Boston	.594	4½	Oakland	.605	7	Boston	3-0	Fred Lynn, of, Boston
1976	New York	.610	10½	Kansas City	.556	2½	New York	3-2	Thurman Munson, c, New York
1977	New York	.617	2½	Kansas City	.630	8	New York	3-2	Rod Carew, 1b, Minnesota
1978	New York	.613	1	Kansas City	.568	5	New York	3-1	Jim Rice, of, Boston
1979	Baltimore	.642	8	California	.543	3	Baltimore	3-1	Don Baylor, dh, California
1980	New York	.636	3	Kansas City	.599	14	Kansas City	3-0	George Brett, 3b, Kansas City
1981	New York*	.607	2	Oakland**	.587	—	New York	3-0	Rollie Fingers, rhp, Milwaukee
	Milwaukee	.585	1½	Kansas City	.566	1			
1982	Milwaukee	.586	1	California	.574	3	Milwaukee	3-2	Robin Yount, ss, Milwaukee
1983	Baltimore	.605	6	Chicago	.611	20	Baltimore	3-1	Cal Ripken, ss, Baltimore
1984	Detroit	.642	15	Kansas City	.519	3	Detroit	3-0	Willie Hernandez, lhp, Detroit
1985	Toronto	.615	2	Kansas City	.562	1	Kansas City	4-3	Don Mattingly, 1b, New York
1986	Boston	.590	5½	California	.568	5	Boston	4-3	Roger Clemens, rhp, Boston
1987	Detroit	.605	2	Minnesota	.525	2	Minnesota	4-1	George Bell, of, Toronto
1988	Boston	.549	1	Oakland	.642	13	Oakland	4-0	Jose Canseco, of, Oakland
1989	Toronto	.549	2	Oakland	.611	7	Oakland	4-1	Robin Yount, of, Milwaukee
1990	Boston	.543	2	Oakland	.636	9	Oakland	4-0	Rickey Henderson, of, Oakland
1991	Toronto	.562	7	Minnesota	.586	8	Minnesota	4-1	Cal Ripken, ss, Baltimore
1992	Toronto	.593	4	Oakland	.593	6	Toronto	4-2	Dennis Eckersley, rhp, Oakland
1993	Toronto	.586	7	Chicago	.580	8	Toronto	4-2	Frank Thomas, 1b, Chicago

Year	East Div.	PCT	GA	Central Div.	PCT	GA	West Div.	PCT	GA	MVP
1994	New York	.619	6½	Chicago	.593	1	Texas	.456	1	Frank Thomas, 1b, Chicago
1995	Boston	.597	7	Cleveland#	.694	30	Seattle	.545	1	Mo Vaughn, 1b, Boston
1996	New York@	.568	4	Cleveland	.615	14½	Texas	.556	4	Juan Gonzalez, of, Texas
1997	Baltimore	.605	2	Cleveland%	.534	6	Seattle	.556	6	Ken Griffey, of, Seattle
1998	New York&	.704	22	Cleveland	.549	9	Texas	.543	3	Juan Gonzalez, of, Texas
1999	New York^	.605	4	Cleveland	.599	21½	Texas	.586	8	Ivan Rodriquez, c, Texas

* Won first half; defeated Milwaukee 3-2 in best-of-5 playoff.   ** Won first half, defeated Kansas City 3-0 in best-of-5 playoff.
# Won AL pennant, defeating Seattle 4-2.   @ Won AL pennant, defeating Baltimore 4-1.   % Won AL pennant, defeating Baltimore 4-2.
& Won AL pennant, defeating Cleveland 4-2.   ^ Won AL pennant, defeating Boston 4-1.

Page	EAST	W	L	PCT	GB	Manager	General Manager	Attend./Dates	Last Penn.
174	New York Yankees	98	64	.605	—	Joe Torre	Brian Cashman	3,293,259 (81)	1999
81	Boston Red Sox*	94	68	.580	4	Jimy Williams	Dan Duquette	2,446,277 (81)	1986
248	Toronto Blue Jays	84	78	.519	14	Jim Fregosi	Gord Ash	2,163,486 (81)	1993
74	Baltimore Orioles	78	84	.481	20	Ray Miller	Frank Wren	3,432,099 (80)	1983
234	Tampa Bay Devil Rays	69	93	.426	29	Larry Rothschild	Chuck LaMar	1,749,557 (81)	None
Page	CENTRAL	W	L	PCT	GB	Manager	General Manager	Attend./Dates	Last Penn.
109	Cleveland Indians	97	65	.599	—	Mike Hargrove	John Hart	3,468,436 (81)	1997
88	Chicago White Sox	75	86	.466	21½	Jerry Manuel	Ron Schueler	1,338,851 (76)	1959
122	Detroit Tigers	69	92	.429	27½	Larry Parrish	Randy Smith	2,026,491 (81)	1984
141	Kansas City Royals	64	97	.398	32½	Tony Muser	Herk Robinson	1,501,292 (78)	1985
161	Minnesota Twins	63	97	.394	33	Tom Kelly	Terry Ryan	1,202,829 (81)	1991
Page	WEST	W	L	PCT	GB	Manager(s)	General Manager	Attend./Dates	Last Penn.
241	Texas Rangers	95	67	.586	—	Johnny Oates	Doug Melvin	2,774,501 (80)	None
189	Oakland Athletics	87	75	.537	8	Art Howe	Billy Beane	1,434,632 (81)	1990
227	Seattle Mariners	79	83	.488	16	Lou Piniella	Woody Woodward	2,915,828 (81)	None
53	Anaheim Angels	70	92	.432	25	T. Collins/J. Maddon	Bill Bavasi	2,253,040 (81)	None

*Won wild-card playoff berth

NOTE: Team's individual batting, pitching and fielding statistics can be found on page indicated in lefthand column.

But the Red Sox couldn't blame their finish on the umpiring or the Curse of the Bambino. No, selling Babe Ruth eight decades ago didn't prevent Boston from winning its first World Series since 1918.

The Sox made it back to the playoffs after team leader Vaughn left for the West Coast, and Martinez and Garciaparra battled injuries in the postseason.

"We definitely were good enough to win, but we didn't play well enough to win," Garciaparra said.

At least any more than one game—which was more than the Rangers or Braves could say.

Pedro's World

In a hitter-friendly era, Martinez had as dominant a year as any pitcher ever had. On his way to winning his second career Cy Young Award, he went 23-4, with a 2.07 ERA and 313 strikeouts in 213 innings.

After two years of Clemens winning the AL pitching triple crown with the Blue Jays, Martinez accomplished the feat in his second year in Boston. No other AL pitcher had led in wins, ERA and strikeouts in the same season since the Tigers' Hal Newhouser in 1945.

Martinez dazzled fans as much with his approach to pitching as his hard throwing. "I look for everything—attitudes, frustrations, weakness," he said. "I look for everything I can look for to learn, and that's gonna help my game.

"Sometimes you can see that with just one pitch you can frustrate the whole game—with one batter. There's some of them that will let one at-bat frustrate them forever. All you have to do is get a pitch that's one inch away from the plate from some hitters and that will get them dragging all day and get them upset. It takes away their whole game."

LARRY GOREN

Not quite enough
Nomar Garciaparra's Red Sox couldn't overcome the Yankees

Martinez backed up his regular season with a stellar postseason. In the decisive Game Five of the Division Series, he pitched six no-hit innings of relief as the Red Sox turned an 8-8 tie into a 12-8 triumph. The Sox had lost two Division Series to the Indians since 1995, but Martinez gave them an ace in the hole this time around.

His only start of the series had been in Game One, when he cruised through four shutout innings before leaving with a pulled muscle behind his shoulder blade. The Indians rallied to win that game after he left, but they couldn't duck Martinez entirely.

"There was a certain aura to (that) game when Pedro came in," Red Sox general manager Dan Duquette said. "There was a certain respect from Cleveland fans and players for this pitcher. When they saw he was throwing like Pedro Martinez, it got quiet. It got very quiet. I knew we were going to win the game. Pedro Martinez is what makes us better than

JOHN WILLIAMSON

Simply amazing
Pedro Martinez

AMERICAN LEAGUE YEAR-BY-YEAR BATTING LEADERS

Year	Batting Average	Home Runs	RBIs
1901	Nap Lajoie, Philadelphia .422	Nap Lajoie, Philadelphia 14	Nap Lajoie, Philadelphia 125
1902	Ed Delahanty, Wash. .376	Socks Seybold, Philadelphia 16	Buck Freeman, Boston 121
1903	Nap Lajoie, Cleveland .355	Buck Freeman, Boston 13	Buck Freeman, Boston 104
1904	Nap Lajoie, Cleveland .381	Harry Davis, Philadelphia 10	Nap Lajoie, Cleveland 102
1905	Elmer Flick, Cleveland .306	Harry Davis, Philadelphia 8	Harry Davis, Philadelphia 83
1906	George Stone, St. Louis .358	Harry Davis, Philadelphia 12	Harry Davis, Philadelphia 96
1907	Ty Cobb, Detroit .350	Harry Davis, Philadelphia 8	Ty Cobb, Detroit 116
1908	Ty Cobb, Detroit .324	Sam Crawford, Detroit 7	Ty Cobb, Detroit 101
1909	Ty Cobb, Detroit .377	Ty Cobb, Detroit 9	Ty Cobb, Detroit 115
1910	Ty Cobb, Detroit .385	Jake Stahl, Boston 10	Sam Crawford, Detroit 115
1911	Ty Cobb, Detroit .420	Frank Baker, Philadelphia 11	Ty Cobb, Detroit 144
1912	Ty Cobb, Detroit .410	2 tied at 10	Frank Baker, Philadelphia 133
1913	Ty Cobb, Detroit .390	Frank Baker, Philadelphia 12	Frank Baker, Philadelphia 126
1914	Ty Cobb, Detroit .368	Frank Baker, Philadelphia 9	Sam Crawford, Detroit 112
1915	Ty Cobb, Detroit .370	Braggo Roth, Cleveland 7	Sam Crawford, Detroit 116
1916	Tris Speaker, Cleveland .386	Wally Pipp, New York 12	Wally Pipp, New York 99
1917	Ty Cobb, Detroit .383	Wally Pipp, New York 9	Bob Veach, Detroit 115
1918	Ty Cobb, Detroit .382	2 tied at 11	2 tied at 74
1919	Ty Cobb, Detroit .384	Babe Ruth, Boston 29	Babe Ruth, Boston 112
1920	George Sisler, St. Louis .407	Babe Ruth, New York 54	Babe Ruth, New York 137
1921	Harry Heilmann, Detroit .394	Babe Ruth, New York 59	Babe Ruth, New York 171
1922	George Sisler, St. Louis .420	Kenny Williams, St. Louis 39	Kenny Williams, St. Louis 155
1923	Harry Heilmann, Detroit .403	Babe Ruth, New York 41	Babe Ruth, New York 131
1924	Babe Ruth, New York .378	Babe Ruth, New York 46	Goose Goslin, Wash. 129
1925	Harry Heilmann, Detroit .393	Bob Meusel, New York 33	Bob Meusel, New York 138
1926	Heinie Manush, Detroit .377	Babe Ruth, New York 47	Babe Ruth, New York 145
1927	Harry Heilmann, Detroit .398	Babe Ruth, New York 60	Lou Gehrig, New York 175
1928	Goose Goslin, Wash. .379	Babe Ruth, New York 54	2 tied at 142
1929	Lew Fonseca, Cleveland .369	Babe Ruth, New York 46	Al Simmons, Philadelphia 157
1930	Al Simmons, Philadelphia .381	Babe Ruth, New York 49	Lou Gehrig, New York 174
1931	Al Simmons, Philadelphia .390	2 tied at 46	Lou Gehrig, New York 184
1932	Dale Alexander, Det.-Bos. .367	Jimmie Foxx, Philadelphia 58	Jimmie Foxx, Philadelphia 169
1933	Jimmie Foxx, Philadelphia .356	Jimmie Foxx, Philadelphia 48	Jimmie Foxx, Philadelphia 163
1934	Lou Gehrig, New York .363	Lou Gehrig, New York 49	Lou Gehrig, New York 165
1935	Buddy Myer, Washington .349	2 tied at 36	Hank Greenberg, Detroit 170
1936	Luke Appling, Chicago .388	Lou Gehrig, New York 49	Hal Trosky, Cleveland 162
1937	Charlie Gehringer, Detroit .371	Joe DiMaggio, New York 46	Hank Greenberg, Detroit 183
1938	Jimmie Foxx, Boston .349	Hank Greenberg, Detroit 58	Jimmie Foxx, Boston 175
1939	Joe DiMaggio, New York .381	Jimmie Foxx, Boston 35	Ted Williams, Boston 145
1940	Joe DiMaggio, New York .352	Hank Greenberg, Detroit 41	Hank Greenberg, Detroit 150
1941	Ted Williams, Boston .406	Ted Williams, Boston 37	Joe DiMaggio, New York 125
1942	Ted Williams, Boston .356	Ted Williams, Boston 36	Ted Williams, Boston 137
1943	Luke Appling, Chicago .328	Rudy York, Detroit 34	Rudy York, Detroit 118
1944	Lou Boudreau, Cleve. .327	Nick Etten, New York 22	Vern Stephens, St. Louis 109
1945	Snuffy Stirnweiss, N.Y. .309	Vern Stephens, St. Louis 24	Nick Etten, New York 111
1946	Mickey Vernon, Wash. .353	Hank Greenberg, Detroit 44	Hank Greenberg, Detroit 127
1947	Ted Williams, Boston .343	Ted Williams, Boston 32	Ted Williams, Boston 114
1948	Ted Williams, Boston .369	Joe DiMaggio, New York 39	Joe DiMaggio, New York 155
1949	George Kell, Detroit .343	Ted Williams, Boston 43	Ted Williams, Boston 159
1950	Billy Goodman, Boston .354	Al Rosen, Cleveland 37	2 tied at 144
1951	Ferris Fain, Philadelphia .344	Gus Zernial, Chi.-Phil. 33	Gus Zernial, Chi.-Phil. 129
1952	Ferris Fain, Philadelphia .327	Larry Doby, Cleveland 32	Al Rosen, Cleveland 105
1953	Mickey Vernon, Wash. .337	Al Rosen, Cleveland 43	Al Rosen, Cleveland 145
1954	Bobby Avila, Cleveland .341	Larry Doby, Cleveland 32	Larry Doby, Cleveland 126
1955	Al Kaline, Detroit .340	Mickey Mantle, New York 37	2 tied at 116
1956	Mickey Mantle, New York .353	Mickey Mantle, New York 52	Mickey Mantle, New York 130
1957	Ted Williams, Boston .388	Roy Sievers, Washington 42	Roy Sievers, Washington 114
1958	Ted Williams, Boston .328	Mickey Mantle, New York 42	Jackie Jensen, Boston 122
1959	Harvey Kuenn, Detroit .353	2 tied at 42	Jackie Jensen, Boston 112
1960	Pete Runnels, Boston .320	Mickey Mantle, New York 40	Roger Maris, New York 112
1961	Norm Cash, Detroit .361	Roger Maris, New York 61	Roger Maris, New York 142
1962	Pete Runnels, Boston .326	Harmon Killebrew, Minn. 48	Harmon Killebrew, Minn. 126
1963	Carl Yastrzemski, Boston .321	Harmon Killebrew, Minn. 45	Dick Stuart, Boston 118
1964	Tony Oliva, Minnesota .323	Harmon Killebrew, Minn. 49	Brooks Robinson, Baltimore 118
1965	Tony Oliva, Minnesota .321	Tony Conigliaro, Boston 32	Rocky Colavito, Cleveland 108
1966	Frank Robinson, Balt. .316	Frank Robinson, Baltimore 49	Frank Robinson, Baltimore 122
1967	Carl Yastrzemski, Boston .326	2 tied at 44	Carl Yastrzemski, Boston 121
1968	Carl Yastrzemski, Boston .301	Frank Howard, Washington 44	Ken Harrelson, Boston 109
1969	Rod Carew, Minnesota .332	Harmon Killebrew, Minn. 49	Harmon Killebrew, Minn. 140
1970	Alex Johnson, California .329	Frank Howard, Washington 44	Frank Howard, Washington 126
1971	Tony Oliva, Minnesota .337	Bill Melton, Chicago 33	Harmon Killebrew, Minn. 119
1972	Rod Carew, Minnesota .318	Dick Allen, Chicago 37	Dick Allen, Chicago 113
1973	Rod Carew, Minnesota .350	Reggie Jackson, Oakland 32	Reggie Jackson, Oakland 117
1974	Rod Carew, Minnesota .364	Dick Allen, Chicago 32	Jeff Burroughs, Texas 118
1975	Rod Carew, Minnesota .359	2 tied at 36	George Scott, Milwaukee 109
1976	George Brett, Kansas City .333	Graig Nettles, New York 32	Lee May, Baltimore 109
1977	Rod Carew, Minnesota .388	Jim Rice, Boston 39	Larry Hisle, Minnesota 119
1978	Rod Carew, Minnesota .333	Jim Rice, Boston 46	Jim Rice, Boston 139
1979	Fred Lynn, Boston .333	Gorman Thomas, Mil. 45	Don Baylor, California 139
1980	George Brett, Kansas City .390	2 tied at 41	Cecil Cooper, Milwaukee 122
1981	Carney Lansford, Boston .336	4 tied at 22	Eddie Murray, Baltimore 78
1982	Willie Wilson, Kansas City .332	2 tied at 39	Hal McRae, Kansas City 133
1983	Wade Boggs, Boston .361	Jim Rice, Boston 39	2 tied at 126
1984	Don Mattingly, New York .343	Tony Armas, Boston 43	Tony Armas, Boston 123
1985	Wade Boggs, Boston .368	Darrell Evans, Detroit 40	Don Mattingly, New York 145
1986	Wade Boggs, Boston .357	Jesse Barfield, Toronto 40	Joe Carter, Cleveland 121
1987	Wade Boggs, Boston .363	Mark McGwire, Oakland 49	George Bell, Toronto 134
1988	Wade Boggs, Boston .366	Jose Canseco, Oakland 42	Jose Canseco, Oakland 124
1989	Kirby Puckett, Minn. .339	Fred McGriff, Toronto 36	Ruben Sierra, Texas 119
1990	George Brett, Kansas City .329	Cecil Fielder, Detroit 51	Cecil Fielder, Detroit 132
1991	Julio Franco, Texas .341	2 tied at 44	Cecil Fielder, Detroit 133
1992	Edgar Martinez, Seattle .343	Juan Gonzalez, Texas 43	Cecil Fielder, Detroit 124
1993	John Olerud, Toronto .363	Juan Gonzalez, Texas 46	Albert Belle, Cleveland 129
1994	Paul O'Neill, New York .359	Ken Griffey, Seattle 40	Kirby Puckett, Minnesota 112
1995	Edgar Martinez, Seattle .356	Albert Belle, Cleveland 50	2 tied at 126
1996	Alex Rodriguez, Seattle .358	Mark McGwire Oakland 52	Albert Belle, Cleveland 148
1997	Frank Thomas, Chicago .347	Ken Griffey, Seattle 56	Ken Griffey, Seattle 147
1998	Bernie Williams, New York .339	Ken Griffey, New York 56	Juan Gonzalez, Texas 157
1999	Nomar Garciaparra, Boston .357	Ken Griffey, Seattle 48	Manny Ramirez, Cleveland 165

AMERICAN LEAGUE YEAR-BY-YEAR PITCHING LEADERS

Year	Wins	ERA	Strikeouts
1901	Cy Young, Boston...33	Cy Young, Boston...1.63	Cy Young, Boston...158
1902	Cy Young, Boston...32	Ed Siever, Detroit...1.91	Rube Waddell, Philadelphia...210
1903	Cy Young, Boston...28	Earl Moore, Cleveland...1.77	Rube Waddell, Philadelphia...302
1904	Jack Chesbro, New York...41	Addie Joss, Cleveland...1.59	Rube Waddell, Philadelphia...349
1905	Rube Waddell, Phil....26	Rube Waddell, Philadelphia...1.48	Rube Waddell, Philadelphia...287
1906	Al Orth, New York...27	Doc White, Chicago...1.52	Rube Waddell, Philadelphia...196
1907	2 tied at...27	Addie Joss, Chicago...1.60	Rube Waddell, Philadelphia...232
1908	Ed Walsh, Chicago...40	Addie Joss, Cleveland...1.16	Ed Walsh, Chicago...269
1909	George Mullin, Detroit...29	Harry Krause, Philadelphia...1.39	Frank Smith, Chicago...177
1910	Jack Coombs, Phil....31	Ed Walsh, Chicago...1.27	Walter Johnson, Wash....313
1911	Jack Coombs, Phil....28	Vean Gregg, Cleveland...1.81	Ed Walsh, Chicago...255
1912	Joe Wood, Boston...34	Walter Johnson, Wash....1.39	Walter Johnson, Wash....303
1913	Walter Johnson, Wash....36	Walter Johnson, Wash....1.14	Walter Johnson, Wash....243
1914	Walter Johnson, Wash....28	Dutch Leonard, Bos....1.00	Walter Johnson, Wash....225
1915	Walter Johnson, Wash....27	Joe Wood, Boston...1.49	Walter Johnson, Wash....203
1916	Walter Johnson, Wash....25	Babe Ruth, Boston...1.75	Walter Johnson, Wash....228
1917	Ed Cicotte, Chicago...28	Ed Cicotte, Chicago...1.53	Walter Johnson, Wash....188
1918	Walter Johnson, Wash....23	Walter Johnson, Wash....1.27	Walter Johnson, Wash....162
1919	Ed Cicotte, Chicago...29	Walter Johnson, Wash....1.49	Walter Johnson, Wash....147
1920	Jim Bagby, Cleveland...31	Bob Shawkey, New York...2.45	Stan Coveleski, Cleveland...133
1921	2 tied at...27	Red Faber, Chicago...2.48	Walter Johnson, Wash....143
1922	Eddie Rommel, Phil....27	Red Faber, Chicago...2.80	Urban Shocker, St. Louis...149
1923	George Uhle, Cleveland...26	Stan Coveleski, Cleveland...2.76	Walter Johnson, Wash....130
1924	Walter Johnson, Wash....23	Walter Johnson, Wash....2.72	Walter Johnson, Wash....158
1925	2 tied at...21	Stan Coveleski, Wash....2.84	Walter Johnson, Wash....116
1926	George Uhle, Claveland...27	Lefty Grove, Philadelphia...2.51	Lefty Grove, Philadelphia...194
1927	2 tied at...22	Wilcy Moore, New York...2.28	Lefty Grove, Philadelphia...174
1928	2 tied at...24	Garland Braxton, Wash....2.52	Lefty Grove, Philadelphia...183
1929	George Earnshaw, Phil....24	Lefty Grove, Philadelphia...2.82	Lefty Grove, Philadelphia...170
1930	Lefty Grove, Philadelphia...28	Lefty Grove, Philadelphia...2.54	Lefty Grove, Philadelphia...209
1931	Lefty Grove, Philadelphia...31	Lefty Grove, Philadelphia...2.05	Lefty Grove, Philadelphia...175
1932	General Crowder, Wash....26	Lefty Grove, Philadelphia...2.84	Red Ruffing, New York...190
1933	2 tied at...24	Monte Pearson, Cleveland...2.33	Lefty Gomez, New York...163
1934	Lefty Gomez, New York...26	Lefty Gomez, New York...2.33	Lefty Gomez, New York...158
1935	Wes Ferrell, Boston...25	Lefty Grove, Boston...2.70	Tommy Bridges, Detroit...163
1936	Tommy Bridges, Detroit...23	Lefty Grove, Boston...2.81	Tommy Bridges, Detroit...175
1937	Lefty Gomez, New York...21	Lefty Gomez, New York...2.33	Lefty Gomez, New York...194
1938	Red Ruffing, New York...21	Lefty Grove, Philadelphia...3.07	Bob Feller, Cleveland...240
1939	Bob Feller, Cleveland...24	Lefty Grove, Philadelphia...2.54	Bob Feller, Cleveland...246
1940	Bob Feller, Cleveland...27	Bob Feller, Cleveland...2.62	Bob Feller, Cleveland...261
1941	Bob Feller, Cleveland...25	Thornton Lee, Chicago...2.37	Bob Feller, Cleveland...260
1942	Tex Hughson, Boston...22	Ted Lyons, Chicago...2.10	2 tied at...113
1943	2 tied at...20	Spud Chandler, New York...1.64	Allie Reynolds, Cleveland...151
1944	Hal Newhouser, Detroit...29	Dizzy Trout, Detroit...2.12	Hal Newhouser, Detroit...187
1945	Hal Newhouser, Detroit...25	Hal Newhouser, Detroit...1.81	Hal Newhouser, Detroit...212
1946	2 tied at...26	Hal Newhouser, Detroit...1.94	Bob Feller, Cleveland...348
1947	Bob Feller, Cleveland...20	Spud Chandler, New York...2.46	Bob Feller, Cleveland...196
1948	Hal Newhouser, Detroit...21	Gene Bearden, Cleveland...2.43	Bob Feller, Cleveland...164
1949	Mel Parnell, Boston...25	Mel Parnell, Boston...2.78	Virgil Trucks, Detroit...153
1950	Bob Lemon, Cleveland...23	Early Wynn, Cleveland...3.20	Bob Lemon, Cleveland...170
1951	Bob Feller, Cleveland...22	Saul Rogovin, Det.-Chi....2.78	Vic Raschi, New York...164
1952	Bobby Shantz, Philadelphia...24	Allie Reynolds, New York...2.07	Allie Reynolds, New York...160
1953	Bob Porterfield, Wash....22	Eddie Lopat, New York...2.43	Billy Pierce, Chicago...186
1954	2 tied at...23	Mike Garcia, Cleveland...2.64	Bob Turley, Baltimore...185
1955	3 tied at...18	Billy Pierce, Chicago...1.97	Herb Score, Cleveland...245
1956	Frank Lary, Detroit...21	Whitey Ford, New York...2.47	Herb Score, Cleveland...263
1957	2 tied at...20	Bobby Shantz, New York...2.45	Early Wynn, Cleveland...184
1958	Bob Turley, New York...21	Whitey Ford, New York...2.01	Early Wynn, Chicago...179
1959	Early Wynn, Chicago...22	Hoyt Wilhelm, Balt....2.19	Jim Bunning, Detroit...201
1960	2 tied at...18	Frank Baumann, Chicago...2.68	Jim Bunning, Detroit...201
1961	Whitey Ford, New York...25	Dick Donovan, Washington...2.40	Camilo Pascual, Minnesota...221
1962	Ralph Terry, New York...23	Hank Aguirre, Detroit...2.21	Camilo Pascual, Minnesota...206
1963	Whitey Ford, New York...24	Gary Peters, Chicago...2.33	Camilo Pascual, Minnesota...202
1964	2 tied at...20	Dean Chance, L.A....1.65	Al Downing, New York...217
1965	Mudcat Grant, Minnesota...21	Sam McDowell, Cleveland...2.18	Sam McDowell, Cleveland...325
1966	Jim Kaat, Minnesota...25	Gary Peters, Chicago...1.98	Sam McDowell, Cleveland...225
1967	2 tied at...22	Joel Horlen, Chicago...2.06	Jim Lonborg, Boston...246
1968	Denny McLain, Detroit...31	Luis Tiant, Cleveland...1.60	Sam McDowell, Cleveland...283
1969	Denny McLain, Detroit...24	Dick Bosman, Washington...2.19	Sam McDowell, Cleveland...279
1970	3 tied at...24	Diego Segui, Oakland...2.56	Sam McDowell, Cleveland...304
1971	Mickey Lolich, Detroit...25	Vida Blue, Oakland...1.82	Mickey Lolich, Detroit...308
1972	2 tied at...24	Luis Tiant, Boston...1.91	Nolan Ryan, California...329
1973	Wilbur Wood, Chicago...24	Jim Palmer, Baltimore...2.40	Nolan Ryan, California...383
1974	2 tied at...25	Catfish Hunter, Oakland...2.49	Nolan Ryan, California...367
1975	2 tied at...23	Jim Palmer, Baltimore...2.09	Frank Tanana, California...269
1976	Jim Palmer, Baltimore...22	Mark Fidrych, Detroit...2.34	Nolan Ryan, California...327
1977	3 tied at...20	Frank Tanana, California...2.54	Nolan Ryan, California...341
1978	Ron Guidry, New York...25	Ron Guidry, New York...1.74	Nolan Ryan, California...260
1979	Mike Flanagan, Baltimore...23	Ron Guidry, New York...2.78	Nolan Ryan, California...223
1980	Steve Stone, Baltimore...25	Rudy May, New York...2.47	Len Barker, Cleveland...187
1981	Steve McCatty, Oakland...14	Steve McCatty, Oak....2.32	Len Barker, Cleveland...127
1982	LaMarr Hoyt, Chicago...19	Rick Sutcliffe, Cleveland...2.96	Floyd Bannister, Seattle...209
1983	LaMarr Hoyt, Chicago...24	Rick Honeycutt, Texas...2.42	Jack Morris, Detroit...232
1984	Mike Boddicker, Balt....20	Mike Boddicker, Balt....2.79	Mark Langston, Seattle...204
1985	Ron Guidry, New York...22	Dave Stieb, Toronto...2.48	Bert Blyleven, Cleve.-Minn....206
1986	Roger Clemens, Boston...24	Roger Clemens, Boston...2.48	Mark Langston, Seattle...245
1987	2 tied at...20	Jimmy Key, Toronto...2.76	Mark Langston, Seattle...262
1988	Frank Viola, Minnesota...24	Allan Anderson, Minnesota...2.45	Roger Clemens, Boston...291
1989	Bret Saberhagen, K.C....23	Bret Saberhagen, K.C....2.16	Nolan Ryan, Texas...301
1990	Bob Welch, Oakland...27	Roger Clemens, Boston...1.93	Nolan Ryan, Texas...232
1991	2 tied at...20	Roger Clemens, Boston...2.62	Roger Clemens, Boston...241
1992	2 tied at...21	Roger Clemens, Boston...2.41	Randy Johnson, Seattle...241
1993	Jack McDowell, Chicago...22	Kevin Appier, Kansas City...2.56	Randy Johnson, Seattle...308
1994	Jimmy Key, New York...17	Steve Ontiveros, Oakland...2.65	Randy Johnson, Seattle...204
1995	Mike Mussina, Baltimore...19	Randy Johnson, Seattle...2.48	Randy Johnson, Seattle...294
1996	Andy Pettitte, New York...21	Juan Guzman, Toronto...2.93	Roger Clemens, Boston...257
1997	Roger Clemens, Toronto...21	Roger Clemens, Toronto...2.05	Roger Clemens, Toronto...292
1998	3 tied at...20	Roger Clemens, Toronto...2.65	Roger Clemens, Toronto...271
1999	Pedro Martinez, Boston...23	Pedro Martinez, Boston...2.07	Pedro Martinez, Boston...313

Not good enough
Cleveland came up short, and Mike Hargrove got fired

the Cleveland Indians."

In the other Division Series, the Yankees dispatched the Rangers in three games, just as they did in 1998. And the Rangers scored only one run in those three games, just as they did in 1998.

"It's mind-boggling," Rangers manager Johnny Oates said. "Just through pure luck, we should do more offensively."

Grover's Gone

Mike Hargrove was the Indians' manager for their first five postseason appearances since 1954, and he was within seven wins of becoming the franchise's winningest manager. After the first-round loss to the Red Sox, though, the Indians decided to make a change.

GM John Hart never warmed to Hargrove's easy-rider style. And Hargrove, who reached the World Series twice, was never comfortable with Hart's hovering, picking apart every aspect of every game.

"The nature of this business is change," Hart said. "We felt it was necessary to create a different environment and atmosphere."

The Indians, looking for a goal in the soft AL Central, had T-shirts made before the 1999 season with the slogan "100-plus." They won 97 games in the regular season, but their bullpen never came together, and it showed in Games Four and Five of the Division Series as the Red Sox won 23-7 and 12-8. Starters Bartolo Colon and Charles Nagy also were roughed up on three days rest.

Colon was brilliant after the all-star break, sharing league-high honors with 11 wins, but most of this team's success was at the plate. Its 1,009 runs were the most by any team since the 1950 Red Sox.

Manny Ramirez' 165 RBIs were an Indians record.

He scored 131 runs, while second baseman Roberto Alomar scored 138. First baseman Jim Thome led the AL in walks (127) and strikeouts (171).

In their last three games of '99, the Indians watched as Boston's offense provided hit after hit and run after run. After Colon and Nagy did their part in the first two games with just three innings of relief help between them, the Tribe staff unraveled.

Dave Burba had a 1-0 lead in Game Three, but left after four innings because of a forearm injury. Boston rallied off Jaret Wright and Ricardo Rincon to win that game 9-3.

The next time out, the Red Sox broke postseason records with 23 runs and 24 hits in a game. Cleveland's pitching didn't fare much better in the 12-8 loss in Game Five. Martinez' six hitless innings of relief, on a night when the Red Sox weren't even sure he could pitch, brought order to what had been a hitters' game. Boston outfielder Troy O'Leary was the main offensive star with a grand slam and three-run homer—both after intentional walks to Garciaparra.

All told, Boston hit .318 and slugged .597 against the Indians. Garciaparra hit .417 with two homers, first baseman Mike Stanley had 10 hits in 20 at-bats and third baseman John Valentin hit .318 with three homers and 12 RBIs.

Kiss It Goodbye

Of Wade Boggs' first 2,999 hits, just 117 were home runs. Then he became the first player to join the 3,000-hit club with a homer.

Boggs, the Devil Rays' third baseman, seemed as surprised as anyone when he connected off Indians

Major run producer
Manny Ramirez paced a potent Indians attack

lefthander Chris Haney on Aug. 7, to become the 23rd member of the elite group.

"Now I guess I'm going to be called a home run hitter," Boggs said. "When it left the bat, I said, 'Oh my God. That's a home run and I'll never get the ball back.'"

He was able to trade a jersey and bat for the ball, so all ended well for Boggs. On his way to 3,000, he did much of his damage from 1983-89, when he had at least 200 hits a season for the Red Sox.

While Boggs passed the 3,000-hit barrier, another rookie from the Class of 1982 will have to wait until next year. Orioles iron-man third baseman Cal Ripken had the first injury-riddled season of his career and finished with 2,991 career hits. With 113 hits for the year, Ripken hit .340.

Ripken, who holds the major league record for homers from the shortstop position, did manage the 400th home run of his career. And his teammate Jesse Orosco became baseball's all-time leader in games pitched at 1,090. They were temporary bright spots in another forgettable year for the Orioles.

Pitcher Perfect

For the second straight year, a Yankee pitched a perfect game. In '98 it was David Wells, a connoisseur of Babe Ruth history. In 1999, New York had a historical perspective again as Larsen, author of the only perfect game in World Series history, was on hand for a July 18 Yankees-Expos game.

It wound up being the perfect game to see, as Cone pitched the 16th perfect game in major league history. Second baseman Chuck Knoblauch, who had problems defensively all year just two seasons removed

from winning a Gold Glove, made the play of the game. He robbed Montreal's Jose Vidro of a hit on a ground ball in the eighth inning.

"When Knoblauch made the great play, I decided maybe there was some sort of Yankee aura," Cone said of the 6-0 win. "Maybe this was my day. Maybe there is something to this magic."

While 41,930 were at Yankee Stadium for Cone's gem, lefthander Eric Milton pitched his no-hitter on a smaller stage against an even less experienced lineup than the Expos used. But it was a major league no-hitter and those don't come easily.

Just 11,222 showed up for an 11 a.m. game at the Metrodome on Sept. 11 to watch Milton no-hit the Angels. Anaheim's lineup did not include Vaughn or its regular catcher, second baseman, shortstop and outfield.

Milton's no-hitter was the first by the Twins since righthander Scott Erickson threw one in April 1994. Milton struck out a career-high 13 batters. He walked

Early bird gets the no-hitter
Eric Milton shackled a toothless Angels lineup

AL: BEST TOOLS

A Baseball America survey of American League managers, conducted at midseason 1999, ranked AL players with the best tools:

BEST HITTER	BEST PICKOFF MOVE
1. Derek Jeter, Yankees	1. Andy Pettitte, Yankees
2. Nomar Garciaparra, Red Sox	2. Kenny Rogers, Athletics
3. Ken Griffey, Mariners	3. Jamie Moyer, Mariners
BEST POWER HITTER	**BEST RELIEVER**
1. Ken Griffey, Mariners	1. Mariano Rivera, Yankees
2. Juan Gonzalez, Rangers	2. John Wetteland, Rangers
3. Jose Canseco, Devil Rays	3. Troy Percival, Angels
BEST BUNTER	**BEST DEFENSIVE C**
1. Omar Vizquel, Indians	1. Ivan Rodriguez, Rangers
2. Kenny Lofton, Indians	2. Charles Johnson, Orioles
3. Roberto Alomar, Indians	3. Brad Ausmus, Tigers
BEST HIT-AND-RUN BATTER	**BEST DEFENSIVE 1B**
1. Joe Girardi, Yankees	1. David Segui, Mariners
2. Omar Vizquel, Indians	2. Will Clark, Orioles
3. Derek Jeter, Yankees	3. Rafael Palmeiro, Rangers
BEST BASERUNNER	**BEST DEFENSIVE 2B**
1. Roberto Alomar, Indians	1. Roberto Alomar, Indians
2. Derek Jeter, Yankees	2. Damion Easley, Tigers
3. Kenny Lofton, Indians	3. Carlos Febles, Royals
FASTEST BASERUNNER	**BEST DEFENSIVE 3B**
1. Tom Goodwin, Rangers	1. Travis Fryman, Indians
2. Brian Hunter, Mariners	2. Scott Brosius, Yankees
3. Kenny Lofton, Indians	3. Troy Glaus, Angels
BEST PITCHER	**BEST DEFENSIVE SS**
1. Pedro Martinez, Red Sox	1. Omar Vizquel, Indians
2. David Cone, Yankees	2. Derek Jeter, Yankees
3. Mike Mussina, Orioles	3. Alex Rodriguez, Mariners
BEST FASTBALL	**BEST INFIELD ARM**
1. Pedro Martinez, Red Sox	1. Alex Rodriguez, Mariners
2. Mariano Rivera, Yankees	2. Derek Jeter, Yankees
3. Billy Koch, Blue Jays	3. Nomar Garciaparra, Red Sox
BEST CURVEBALL	**BEST DEFENSIVE OF**
1. Mike Mussina, Orioles	1. Ken Griffey, Mariners
2. Tom Gordon, Red Sox	2. Kenny Lofton, Indians
3. Aaron Sele, Rangers	3. Bernie Williams, Yankees
BEST SLIDER	**BEST OUTFIELD ARM**
1. David Cone, Yankees	1. Ken Griffey, Mariners
2. Rolando Arrojo, Devil Rays	2. Paul O'Neill, Yankees
3. Orlando Hernandez, Yankees	3. Shawn Green, Blue Jays
BEST CHANGEUP	**MOST EXCITING PLAYER**
1. Pedro Martinez, Red Sox	1. Ken Griffey, Mariners
2. Jamie Moyer, Mariners	2. Nomar Garciaparra, Red Sox
3. Brad Radke, Twins	3. Derek Jeter, Yankees
BEST CONTROL	**BEST MANAGER**
1. Pedro Martinez, Red Sox	1. Joe Torre, Yankees
2. Brad Radke, Twins	2. Jimy Williams, Red Sox
3. Mike Mussina, Orioles	3. Johnny Oates, Rangers

JOHN WILLIAMSON

AMERICAN LEAGUE
DEPARTMENT LEADERS

BATTING

GAMES
B.J. Surhoff, Orioles 162
Albert Belle, Orioles 161
Mike Bordick, Orioles 160
Ken Griffey, Mariners 160
Roberto Alomar, Indians 159
Tino Martinez, Yankees 159
Miguel Tejada, Athletics 159

AT-BATS
B.J. Surhoff, Orioles 673
Carlos Beltran, Royals 663
Mike Bordick, Orioles 631
Randy Velarde, Angels/Athletics 631
Joe Randa, Royals 628

RUNS
Roberto Alomar, Indians 138
Shawn Green, Blue Jays 134
Derek Jeter, Yankees 134
Manny Ramirez, Indians 131
Ken Griffey, Mariners 123

HITS
Derek Jeter, Yankees 210
B.J. Surhoff, Orioles 207
Bernie Williams, Yankees 202
Randy Velarde, Angels/Athletics 200
Ivan Rodriguez, Rangers 199

TOTAL BASES
Shawn Green, Blue Jays 361
Rafael Palmeiro, Rangers 356
Ken Griffey, Mariners 349
Derek Jeter, Yankees 346
Manny Ramirez, Indians 346

EXTRA-BASE HITS
Shawn Green, Blue Jays 87
Carlos Delgado, Blue Jays 83
Manny Ramirez, Indians 81
Jermaine Dye, Royals 79
Rafael Palmeiro, Rangers 78

SINGLES
Randy Velarde, Angels/Athletics 152
Derek Jeter, Yankees 149
Omar Vizquel, Indians 146
Shannon Stewart, Blue Jays 144
Bernie Williams, Yankees 143

DOUBLES
Shawn Green, Blue Jays 45
Jermaine Dye, Royals 44
Mike Sweeney, Royals 44
Nomar Garciaparra, Red Sox 42

Breakout season
Shawn Green

Tony Fernandez, Blue Jays 41
Rusty Greer, Rangers 41
Todd Zeile, Rangers 41

TRIPLES
Jose Offerman, Red Sox.................... 11
Johnny Damon, Royals 9
Carlos Febles, Royals 9
Derek Jeter, Yankees 9
Ray Durham, White Sox 8
Jermaine Dye, Royals.......................... 8
Luis Polonia, Tigers 8
Joe Randa, Royals...............................8

HOME RUNS
Ken Griffey, Mariners 48
Rafael Palmeiro, Rangers................... 47
Carlos Delgado, Blue Jays 44
Manny Ramirez, Indians 44
Shawn Green, Blue Jays 42
Alex Rodriguez, Mariners 42

HOME RUN RATIO
(At-Bats per Home Run)
Manny Ramirez, Indians 11.9
Alex Rodriguez, Mariners................... 12.0
Rafael Palmeiro, Rangers 12.0
Ken Griffey, Mariners 12.6
Jose Canseco, Devil Rays 12.6

RUNS BATTED IN
Manny Ramirez, Indians 165
Rafael Palmeiro, Rangers................... 148
Carlos Delgado, Blue Jays 134
Ken Griffey, Mariners 134
Juan Gonzalez, Rangers 128

SACRIFICE BUNTS
Omar Vizquel, Indians........................ 17
Deivi Cruz, Tigers 14
Darren Lewis, Red Sox 14
Roberto Alomar, Indians 12
Carlos Febles, Royals......................... 12

SACRIFICE FLIES
Roberto Alomar, Indians 13
Juan Gonzalez, Rangers 12
Paul O'Neill, Yankees 10
Carlos Beltran, Royals 10
Mike Bordick, Orioles 10
John Flaherty, Devil Rays................... 10

HIT BY PITCH
Brady Anderson, Orioles..................... 24
Chuck Knoblauch, Yankees 21
Damion Easley, Tigers 19
Olmedo Saenz, Athletics 15
Carlos Delgado, Blue Jays 15

WALKS
Jim Thome, Indians............................ 127
Jason Giambi, Athletics 105
Albert Belle, Orioles 101
John Jaha, Athletics 101
Bernie Williams, Yankees 100

INTENTIONAL WALKS
Bernie Williams, Yankees 17
Ken Griffey, Mariners 17
Albert Belle, Orioles 15
Rafael Palmeiro, Rangers................... 14
Frank Thomas, White Sox 13
Jim Thome, Indians............................ 13

STRIKEOUTS
Jim Thome, Indians............................ 171
Dean Palmer, Tigers 153
Troy Glaus, Angels 143
Carlos Delgado, Blue Jays 141
Jose Canseco, Devil Rays 135

TOUGHEST TO STRIKE OUT
(Plate Appearances per SO)
Mike Caruso, White Sox 15.7
Nomar Garciaparra, Red Sox 15.3
Mike Sweeney, Royals...................... 13.4

Leader in strikeouts
Jim Thome

Omar Vizquel, Indians.......................13.3
Johnny Damon, Royals.....................13.2

STOLEN BASES
Brian Hunter, Tigers/Mariners............. 44
Omar Vizquel, Indians 42
Tom Goodwin, Rangers 39
Roberto Alomar, Indians 37
Shannon Stewart, Blue Jays............... 37

CAUGHT STEALING
Mike Caruso, White Sox 14
Shannon Stewart, Blue Jays............... 14
Jose Offerman, Red Sox..................... 12
Juan Encarnacion, Tigers 12
Ivan Rodriguez, Rangers 12

GIDP
Ivan Rodriguez, Rangers 32
Mike Bordick, Orioles 25
Paul O'Neill, Yankees 24
Magglio Ordonez, White Sox 24
Marty Cordova, Twins 22

HITTING STREAKS
Shawn Green, Blue Jays 28
Shannon Stewart, Blue Jays............... 26

MULTIPLE-HIT GAMES
Derek Jeter, Yankees 67
Omar Vizquel, Indians........................ 62
B.J. Surhoff, Orioles 62
Bernie Williams, Yankees 58
Shannon Stewart, Blue Jays............... 58

SLUGGING PERCENTAGE
Manny Ramirez, Indians .... .663
Rafael Palmeiro, Rangers .... .630
Nomar Garciaparra, Red Sox .... .603
Juan Gonzalez, Rangers .... .601
Shawn Green, Blue Jays .... .588

ON-BASE PERCENTAGE
Edgar Martinez, Mariners................. .447
Manny Ramirez, Indians .... .442
Derek Jeter, Yankees .... .438
Bernie Williams, Yankees .... .435
Tony Fernandez, Blue Jays .... .427

PITCHING

WINS
Pedro Martinez, Red Sox 23
Bartolo Colon, Indians........................ 18
Mike Mussina, Orioles 18
Aaron Sele, Rangers........................... 18
Freddy Garcia, Mariners 17
Orlando Hernandez, Yankees............. 17
David Wells, Blue Jays 17
Charles Nagy, Indians........................ 17

LOSSES
Brian Moehler, Tigers 16
Jim Parque, White Sox 15
Bobby Witt, Devil Rays 15
Kevin Appier, Royals/Athletics 14
Jose Rosado, Royals 14
LaTroy Hawkins, Twins........................ 14
Brad Radke, Twins 14

WINNING PERCENTAGE
Pedro Martinez, Red Sox................. .852
Bartolo Colon, Indians .... .783
Mike Mussina, Orioles .... .720
Freddy Garcia, Mariners .... .680
Aaron Sele, Rangers .... .667

GAMES
Buddy Groom, Athletics 76
Bob Wells, Twins 76
Mike Trombley, Twins........................ 75
Graeme Lloyd, Blue Jays 74
Derek Lowe, Red Sox......................... 74

GAMES STARTED
Rick Helling, Rangers 35
Pat Hentgen, Blue Jays 34
David Wells, Blue Jays 34
Scott Erickson, Orioles 34
Kevin Appier, Royals/Athletics 34
Dave Burba, Indians 34
Eric Milton, Twins 34

COMPLETE GAMES
David Wells, Blue Jays 7
Sidney Ponson, Orioles 6
Scott Erickson, Orioles 6
Eric Milton, Twins 5
Jose Rosado, Royals 5
Pedro Martinez, Red Sox 5

SHUTOUTS
Scott Erickson, Orioles 3
Eric Milton, Twins 2
Aaron Sele, Rangers 2
Bobby Witt, Devil Rays 2
Brian Moehler, Tigers 2

GAMES FINISHED
Roberto Hernandez, Devil Rays 66
Mike Jackson, Indians 65
Mariano Rivera, Yankees 63
Todd Jones, Tigers.............................. 62
Jose Mesa, Mariners 60

SAVES
Mariano Rivera, Yankees 45
Roberto Hernandez, Devil Rays 43
John Wetteland, Rangers 43
Mike Jackson, Indians 39
Jose Mesa, Mariners 33

Lots of goose eggs
Scott Erickson

Super closer
Mariano Rivera

INNINGS
David Wells, Blue Jays 232
Scott Erickson, Orioles 230
Jamie Moyer, Mariners 228
Dave Burba, Indians 220
Rick Helling, Rangers 219
Brad Radke, Twins 219

HITS ALLOWED
David Wells, Blue Jays 246
Scott Erickson, Orioles 244
Aaron Sele, Rangers......................... 244
Brad Radke, Twins 239
Charles Nagy, Indians........................ 238
LaTroy Hawkins, Twins...................... 238

RUNS ALLOWED
LaTroy Hawkins, Twins...................... 136
Jeff Fassero, Mariners/Rangers 135
David Wells, Blue Jays 132
Kevin Appier, Royals/Athletics 131
Bobby Witt, Devil Rays 130

HOME RUNS ALLOWED
Rick Helling, Rangers 41
Sidney Ponson, Orioles 35
Jeff Fassero, Mariners/Rangers 35
James Baldwin, White Sox 34
Pat Hentgen, Blue Jays 32
David Wells, Blue Jays 32

WALKS
Scott Erickson, Orioles 99
Bobby Witt, Devil Rays 96
Dave Burba, Indians 96
Chuck Finley, Angels 94
Freddy Garcia, Mariners 90
Roger Clemens, Yankees 90
David Cone, Yankees 90

FEWEST WALKS PER 9 INNINGS
Gil Heredia, Athletics 1.5
Pedro Martinez, Red Sox.................... 1.6
Brad Radke, Twins.............................. 1.8
Jamie Moyer, Mariners 1.9
Mike Mussina, Orioles 2.3

HIT BATSMEN
Jeff Weaver, Tigers 17
Rolando Arrojo, Devil Rays................. 14
Dave Mlicki, Tigers 12
Aaron Sele, Rangers........................... 12
Ryan Rupe, Devil Rays........................ 12

STRIKEOUTS
Pedro Martinez, Red Sox 313
Chuck Finley, Angels 200
Aaron Sele, Rangers......................... 186
David Cone, Yankees 177
Dave Burba, Indians 174

STRIKEOUTS PER 9 INNINGS
Pedro Martinez, Red Sox.................. 13.2
Chuck Finley, Angels 8.4

David Cone, Yankees 8.2
Aaron Sele, Rangers 8.2
Roger Clemens, Yankees 7.8

PICKOFFS
Sean Lowe, White Sox 6
Pat Hentgen, Blue Jays 5
Kenny Rogers, Athletics 5
Andy Pettitte, Yankees 5
John Halama, Mariners 5
Omar Olivares, Angels/Athletics 5

WILD PITCHES
Chuck Finley, Angels 15
Dave Burba, Indians 13
Tom Candiotti, Indians 13
Freddy Garcia, Mariners 12
Mac Suzuki, Mariners/Royals 11
James Baldwin, White Sox 11
John Snyder, White Sox 11

BALKS
C.J. Nitkowski, Tigers 3
Freddy Garcia, Mariners 3

OPPONENTS BATTING AVERAGE
Pedro Martinez, Red Sox.................. .205
David Cone, Yankees .... .229
Orlando Hernandez, Yankees .... .233
Bartolo Colon, Indians .... .242
Eric Milton, Twins............................. .243

FIELDING

PITCHER
PCT	Several tied at	1.000
PO	Scott Erickson, Orioles..............	24
A	Jamie Moyer, Mariners	47
E	Jimmy Haynes, Athletics	5
TC	Jamie Moyer, Mariners..............	64
DP	Jamie Moyer, Mariners...............	9

CATCHER
PCT	Brad Ausmus, Tigers..............	.998
PO	Jason Varitek, Red Sox	972
A	John Flaherty, Devil Rays	86
E	Jason Varitek, Red Sox	11
TC	Jason Varitek, Red Sox	1049
DP	Charles Johnson, Orioles.......	14
PB	Jason Varitek, Red Sox	25

FIRST BASE
PCT	Doug Mientkiewicz, Twins......	.997
PO	Carlos Delgado, Blue Jays	1306
A	Tino Martinez, Yankees	105
E	Carlos Delgado, Blue Jays	14
TC	Tino Martinez, Yankees	1409
DP	Carlos Delgado, Blue Jays......	134

SECOND BASE
PCT	Roberto Alomar, Indians	.992
PO	David Bell, Mariners	313
A	Randy Velarde, Angels/A's.....	492
E	Chuck Knoblauch, Yankees	26
TC	Randy Velarde, Angels/A's......	805
DP	David Bell, Mariners	117

THIRD BASE
PCT	Scott Brosius, Yankees	.962
PO	Joe Randa, Royals	119
A	Joe Randa, Royals	314
E	Two tied at................................	25
TC	Joe Randa, Royals	455
DP	Joe Randa, Royals	29

SHORTSTOP
PCT	Mike Bordick, Orioles	.989
PO	Miguel Tejada, Athletics	291
A	Mike Bordick, Orioles	513
E	Royce Clayton, Rangers	25
TC	Mike Bordick, Orioles	799
DP	Mike Bordick, Orioles	132

OUTFIELD
PCT	B.J. Surhoff, Orioles	1.000
PO	Carlos Beltran, Royals	395
A	Two tied at	17
E	Carlos Beltran, Royals	12
TC	Carlos Beltran, Royals	421
DP	Jermaine Dye, Royals	6

1999 American League Statistics

CLUB BATTING

	AVG	G	AB	R	H	2B	3B	HR	BB	SO	SB
Texas	.293	162	5651	945	1653	304	29	230	611	937	111
Cleveland	.289	162	5634	1009	1629	309	32	209	743	1099	147
New York	.282	162	5568	900	1568	302	36	193	718	978	104
Kansas City	.282	161	5624	856	1584	294	52	151	535	932	127
Toronto	.280	162	5642	883	1580	337	14	212	578	1077	119
Baltimore	.279	162	5637	851	1572	299	21	203	615	890	107
Boston	.278	162	5579	836	1551	334	42	176	597	929	67
Chicago	.277	162	5644	777	1563	298	37	162	499	810	110
Tampa Bay	.274	162	5586	772	1531	272	28	145	544	1042	73
Seattle	.269	162	5572	859	1499	263	21	244	610	1095	130
Minnesota	.264	161	5495	686	1450	285	30	105	500	978	118
Detroit	.261	161	5481	747	1433	289	34	212	458	1049	108
Oakland	.259	162	5519	893	1430	287	20	235	770	1129	70
Anaheim	.256	162	5494	711	1404	248	22	158	511	1022	71

CLUB PITCHING

	ERA	G	CG	SHO	SV	IP	H	R	ER	BB	SO
Boston	4.00	162	6	12	50	1437	1396	718	638	469	1131
New York	4.13	162	6	10	50	1440	1402	731	661	581	1111
Oakland	4.69	162	6	5	48	1438	1537	846	750	569	967
Baltimore	4.77	162	17	11	33	1435	1468	815	760	647	983
Anaheim	4.79	162	4	7	37	1431	1472	825	762	624	877
Cleveland	4.89	162	3	6	46	1450	1503	860	788	634	1120
Chicago	4.92	162	6	3	39	1438	1608	870	786	596	968
Toronto	4.92	162	14	9	39	1439	1582	862	787	575	1009
Minnesota	5.00	161	13	8	34	1423	1591	845	791	487	927
Tampa Bay	5.06	162	6	5	45	1433	1606	913	805	695	1055
Texas	5.07	162	6	9	47	1436	1626	859	809	509	979
Detroit	5.17	161	4	6	33	1421	1528	882	817	583	976
Seattle	5.24	162	7	6	40	1434	1613	905	834	684	980
Kansas City	5.35	161	11	3	29	1421	1607	921	844	643	831

CLUB FIELDING

	PCT	PO	A	E	DP		PCT	PO	A	E	DP
Baltimore	.986	4305	1781	89	191	Texas	.981	4309	1729	119	169
Minnesota	.985	4270	1613	92	150	Seattle	.981	4301	1689	113	182
Cleveland	.983	4351	1739	106	154	Oakland	.980	4315	1700	122	166
Anaheim	.983	4294	1723	106	156	Kansas City	.980	4262	1727	125	188
Toronto	.983	4317	1664	106	165	Boston	.979	4310	1548	127	132
New York	.982	4319	1577	111	132	Tampa Bay	.978	4299	1776	135	198
Detroit	.982	4263	1623	106	156	Chicago	.977	4315	1563	136	149

INDIVIDUAL BATTING LEADERS
(Minimum 502 Plate Appearances)

	AVG	G	AB	R	H	2B	3B	HR	RBI	BB	SO	SB
Garciaparra, Nomar, Boston	.357	135	532	103	190	42	4	27	104	51	39	14
Jeter, Derek, New York	.349	158	627	134	219	37	9	24	102	91	116	19
Williams, Bernie, New York	.342	158	591	116	202	28	6	25	115	100	95	9
Martinez, Edgar, Seattle	.337	142	502	86	169	35	1	24	86	97	99	7
Ramirez, Manny, Cleveland	.333	147	522	131	174	34	3	44	165	96	131	2
Vizquel, Omar, Cleveland	.333	144	574	112	191	36	4	5	66	65	50	42
Rodriguez, Ivan, Texas	.332	144	600	116	199	29	1	35	113	24	64	25
Fernandez, Tony, Toronto	.328	142	485	73	159	41	0	6	75	77	62	6
Gonzalez, Juan, Texas	.326	144	562	114	183	36	1	39	128	51	105	3
Palmeiro, Rafael, Texas	.324	158	565	96	183	30	1	47	148	97	69	2

INDIVIDUAL PITCHING LEADERS
(Minimum 162 Innings)

	W	L	ERA	G	GS	CG	SV	IP	H	R	ER	BB	SO
Martinez, Pedro, Boston	23	4	2.07	31	29	5	0	213	160	56	49	37	313
Cone, David, New York	12	9	3.45	31	31	1	0	193	164	84	74	90	177
Mussina, Mike, Baltimore	18	7	3.50	31	31	4	0	203	207	88	79	52	172
Radke, Brad, Minnesota	12	14	3.76	33	33	4	0	218	239	97	91	44	121
Rosado, Jose, Kansas City	10	14	3.85	33	33	5	0	208	197	103	89	72	141
Moyer, Jamie, Seattle	14	8	3.87	32	32	4	0	228	235	108	98	48	137
Colon, Bartolo, Cleveland	18	5	3.95	32	32	1	0	205	185	97	90	76	161
Sirotka, Mike, Chicago	11	13	4.00	32	32	3	0	209	236	108	93	57	125
Garcia, Freddy, Seattle	17	8	4.07	33	33	2	0	201	205	96	91	90	170
Hernandez, Orlando, N.Y.	17	9	4.12	33	33	2	0	214	187	108	98	87	157

AWARD WINNERS

Selected by Baseball Writers Association of America

MVP

Player, Team	1st	2nd	3rd	Total
Ivan Rodriguez, Tex.	7	6	7	252
Pedro Martinez, Bos.	8	6	4	239
Roberto Alomar, Cleve.	4	7	6	226
Manny Ramirez, Cleve.	4	4	5	226
Rafael Palmeiro, Tex.	4	1	2	193
Derek Jeter, New York	1	2	2	177
Nomar Garciaparra, Bos.	0	2	2	137
Jason Giambi, Oak.	0	0	0	49
Shawn Green, Toronto	0	0	0	44
Ken Griffey, Seattle	0	0	0	42
Bernie Williams, N.Y.	0	0	0	21
Carlos Delgado, Tor.	0	0	0	16
Juan Gonzalez, Texas	0	0	0	10
Mariano Rivera, N.Y.	0	0	0	9
Alex Rodriguez, Seattle	0	0	0	4
Omar Vizquel, Cleve.	0	0	0	3
Matt Stairs, Oakland	0	0	0	2
John Jaha, Oakland	0	0	0	1
B.J. Surhoff, Baltimore	0	0	0	1

CY YOUNG AWARD

Player, Team	1st	2nd	3rd	Total
Pedro Martinez, Bos.	28	0	0	140
Mike Mussina, Balt.	0	16	6	54
Mariano Rivera, N.Y.	0	6	9	27
Bartolo Colon, Cleve.	0	3	5	14
Aaron Sele, Texas	0	0	4	4
David Cone, New York	0	1	0	3
Jamie Moyer, Seattle	0	1	0	3
John Wetteland, Texas	0	1	0	3
Freddy Garcia, Seattle	0	0	2	2
Keith Foulke, Chicago	0	0	1	1
Roberto Hernandez, T.B.	0	0	1	1

ROOKIE OF THE YEAR

Player, Team	1st	2nd	3rd	Total
Carlos Beltran, K.C.	26	1	0	133
Freddy Garcia, Sea.	1	12	4	45
Jeff Zimmerman, Tex.	0	6	9	27
Brian Daubach, Bos.	1	3	2	16
Tim Hudson, Oakland	0	3	4	13
Chris Singleton, Chi.	0	2	3	9
Carlos Lee, Chicago	0	1	1	4
Billy Koch, Toronto	0	0	4	4
Trot Nixon, Boston	0	0	1	1

MANAGER OF THE YEAR

Manager, Team	1st	2nd	3rd	Total
Jimy Williams, Bos.	20	5	0	115
Art Howe, Oakland	5	19	3	85
Joe Torre, New York	0	4	9	21
Johnny Oates, Texas	1	0	13	18
Mike Hargrove, Cleve.	2	0	3	13

NOTE: MVP balloting based on 14 points for first-place vote, nine for second, eight for third, etc.; Cy Young Award, Rookie of the Year and Manager of the Year balloting based on five points for first-place vote, three for second and one for third.

GOLD GLOVE AWARDS

Selected by AL managers

C—Ivan Rodriguez, Texas. 1B—Rafael Palmeiro, Texas. 2B—Roberto Alomar, Cleveland. 3B—Scott Brosius, New York. SS—Omar Vizquel, Cleveland. OF—Shawn Green, Toronto; Ken Griffey, Seattle; Bernie Williams, New York. P—Mike Mussina, Baltimore.

two and faced only one more than the minimum in a 7-0 victory.

Odds And Ends

■ The Blue Jays began the year by deposing manager Tim Johnson in spring training and ended it by hiring former World Series-winning manager Cito Gaston as hitting coach.

They lost steam in a wild-card race eventually won by the Red Sox, but two of their young talents were among the best players in the league. Right fielder Shawn Green hit .309 with 42 homers and 123 RBIs, and first baseman/DH Carlos Delgado blossomed with 44 homers and 134 RBIs.

Meanwhile, 37-year-old third baseman Tony Fernandez had an average above .400 until close to the all-star break. He finished the year at .328.

■ With a payroll of a little more than $20 million, the Athletics stayed in the wild-card chase into September. Rookie righthander Tim Hudson (11-2, 3.23 ERA) gave the rotation a boost and outfielder Jason Giambi hit .315 with 33 homers and 123 RBIs.

The A's were the most trade-happy team in the league at the July 31 deadline. They dealt lefthander Kenny Rogers to the Mets in return for youth (including eventual Triple-A World Series MVP Terrence Long), but also tried to strengthen the big league club at the same time by dealing for righthanders Kevin Appier and Omar Olivares and second baseman Randy Velarde.

■ The Rangers nearly became the second team in major league history to have five players drive in at least 100 runs in the same season. Had third baseman Todd Zeile had two more, they would have joined the 1936 Yankees. Instead, they had to settle for first baseman/DH Rafael Palmeiro's 148 RBIs, outfielder Juan Gonzalez' 128, catcher Ivan Rodriguez' 113 and outfielder Rusty Greer's 101.

■ Royals center fielder Carlos Beltran became the first rookie to score 100 runs and drive in 100 runs in the same season since Fred Lynn in 1975. Beltran spent almost half the year in the leadoff spot before moving to the No. 3 hole.

■ Despite having one of baseball's richest payrolls, the Orioles reeled to a sub-.500 season and fired GM Frank Wren and manager Ray Miller after the season. Baltimore owner Peter Angelos drew criticism for an unusually toned release by the club after Wren's firing. The release castigated Wren for allowing a team charter to head for Anaheim without Cal Ripken aboard, despite a call from Ripken that he would soon be at the airport. The release stated that "the Orioles management cannot and will not abide having a general manager operate in such an unreasonable, authoritarian manner and treat anyone in this way, especially someone such as Cal who has done so much for the Orioles and for baseball."

■ The only in-season managerial change was in Anaheim, where Terry Collins had been given a contract extension during the season despite public criticism from his players. Along with Miller and Hargrove, Tigers manager Larry Parrish was fired after the season ended.

■ Though he was dealt from the Tigers to the Mariners during the season and hit just .232 with a .280 on-base percentage, outfielder Brian Hunter led the AL with 44 stolen bases.

LARRY GOREN

Unlikely contenders
Jason Giambi and the Athletics stunned the league

AMERICAN LEAGUE

DIVISION SERIES

NEW YORK vs. TEXAS

COMPOSITE BOX

NEW YORK

Player, Pos.	AVG	G	AB	R	H	2B	3B	HR	RBI	BB	SO	SB
Derek Jeter, ss	.455	3	11	3	5	1	1	0	0	2	3	0
Bernie Williams, cf	.364	3	11	2	4	1	0	1	6	1	2	0
Chili Davis, dh	.333	1	3	0	1	0	0	0	2	0	0	0
Darryl Strawberry, dh	.333	2	6	2	2	0	0	1	3	1	0	0
Ricky Ledee, lf	.273	3	11	3	3	2	0	0	2	1	5	0
Paul O'Neill, rf	.250	2	8	2	2	0	0	0	0	1	1	0
Jorge Posada, c	.250	1	4	0	1	1	0	0	0	0	0	0
Tino Martinez, 1b	.182	3	11	2	2	0	0	0	0	2	2	0
Chuck Knoblauch, 2b	.167	3	12	1	2	0	0	0	1	0	3	0
Scott Brosius, 3b	.100	3	10	0	1	1	0	0	1	0	0	0
Chad Curtis, ph	.000	3	3	1	0	0	0	0	0	0	0	0
Joe Girardi, c	.000	2	6	0	0	0	0	0	0	0	1	0
Jim Leyritz, ph	.000	2	2	0	0	0	0	0	1	1	0	0
Clay Bellinger, pr	.000	1	0	0	0	0	0	0	0	0	0	0
Totals	.237	3	98	14	23	6	1	2	13	10	19	0

Pitcher	W	L	ERA	G	GS	SV	IP	H	R	ER	BB	SO
Roger Clemens	1	0	0.00	1	1	0	7	3	0	0	2	2
Orlando Hernandez	1	0	0.00	1	1	0	8	2	0	0	6	4
Jeff Nelson	0	0	0.00	3	0	0	2	1	0	0	1	3
Mariano Rivera	0	0	0.00	2	0	2	3	1	0	0	0	3
Andy Pettitte	1	0	1.23	1	1	0	7	7	1	1	0	5
Totals	3	0	0.33	3	3	2	27	14	1	1	9	17

TEXAS

Player, Pos.	AVG	G	AB	R	H	2B	3B	HR	RBI	BB	SO	SB
Roberto Kelly, cf	.333	1	3	0	1	0	0	0	0	0	2	0
Rafael Palmeiro, 1b-dh	.273	3	11	0	3	0	0	0	0	1	1	0
Ivan Rodriguez, c	.250	3	12	0	3	1	0	0	0	0	2	1
Juan Gonzalez, rf	.182	3	11	1	2	0	0	1	1	1	3	0
Tom Goodwin, cf	.143	3	7	0	1	0	0	0	0	0	1	0
Rusty Greer, lf	.111	3	9	0	1	0	0	0	0	3	1	0
Lee Stevens, dh-1b	.111	3	9	0	1	1	0	0	0	1	2	0
Mark McLemore, 2b	.100	3	10	0	1	0	0	0	0	1	3	0
Todd Zeile, 3b	.100	3	10	0	1	0	0	0	0	2	1	0
Royce Clayton, ss	.000	3	10	0	0	0	0	0	0	0	1	0
Totals	.152	3	92	1	14	2	0	1	1	9	17	0

Pitcher	W	L	ERA	G	GS	SV	IP	H	R	ER	BB	SO
Danny Patterson	0	0	0.00	1	0	0	1	1	0	0	0	0
Mike Venafro	0	0	0.00	2	0	0	1	2	2	0	1	0
John Wetteland	0	0	0.00	1	0	0	1	0	0	0	0	1
Jeff Zimmerman	0	0	0.00	1	0	0	1	1	0	0	0	1
Rick Helling	0	1	2.84	1	1	0	6	5	2	2	1	8
Esteban Loaiza	0	1	3.86	1	1	0	7	5	3	3	1	4
Tim Crabtree	0	0	5.40	2	0	0	2	1	2	1	1	1
Aaron Sele	0	1	5.40	1	1	0	5	6	4	3	5	3
Jeff Fassero	0	0	9.00	1	0	0	1	2	1	1	1	1
Totals	0	3	3.60	3	3	0	25	23	14	10	10	19

SCORE BY INNINGS

New York	310 034 120	—14
Texas	000 100 000	— 1

E—Knoblauch, Zeile 2, Martinez. DP—New York 5, Texas 1. LOB—New York 21, Texas 19. S—Brosius. HBP—Williams (by Venafro). PB—Rodriguez.

CLEVELAND vs. BOSTON
COMPOSITE BOX

BOSTON

Player, Pos.	AVG	G	AB	R	H	2B	3B	HR	RBI	BB	SO	SB
Scott Hatteberg, c	1.000	1	1	1	1	0	0	0	1	0	0	0
Donnie Sadler, 2b	.500	2	2	1	1	1	0	0	0	0	1	0
Mike Stanley, 1b	.500	5	20	4	10	2	1	0	2	2	3	0
Nomar Garciaparra, ss	.417	4	12	6	5	2	0	2	4	3	3	0
Jose Offerman, 2b	.389	5	18	4	7	1	0	1	6	7	0	0
Darren Lewis, cf	.375	4	16	5	6	1	0	0	2	0	2	1
Lou Merloni, ss	.333	3	6	1	2	0	0	0	1	1	1	0
John Valentin, 3b	.318	5	22	6	7	2	0	3	12	0	4	0
Brian Daubach, dh	.250	4	16	3	4	2	0	1	3	0	7	0
Jason Varitek, c	.238	5	21	7	5	3	0	1	3	0	4	0
Trot Nixon, rf	.214	5	14	5	3	3	0	0	6	4	5	0
Butch Huskey, dh-ph	.200	2	5	0	1	0	0	0	0	0	1	0
Troy O'Leary, lf	.200	5	20	4	4	0	0	2	7	2	3	0
Damon Buford, cf	.000	1	3	0	0	0	0	0	0	1	0	0
Totals	.318	5	176	47	56	17	1	10	47	19	35	1

Pitcher	W	L	ERA	G	GS	SV	IP	H	R	ER	BB	SO
Rod Beck	0	0	0.00	2	0	0	2	2	0	0	0	2
Rheal Cormier	0	0	0.00	2	0	0	4	2	0	0	1	4
Pedro Martinez	1	0	0.00	2	1	0	10	3	0	0	4	11
Ramon Martinez	0	0	3.18	1	1	0	6	5	2	2	3	6
Rich Garces	1	0	3.86	2	0	0	2	2	1	1	3	2
Derek Lowe	1	1	4.32	3	0	0	8	6	7	4	1	7
Tom Gordon	0	0	4.50	2	0	0	2	1	1	1	1	3
Kent Mercker	0	0	10.80	1	1	0	3	2	3	2	3	1
Tim Wakefield	2	0	13.50	2	0	0	2	3	3	3	4	4
Bret Saberhagen	2	1	27.00	2	2	0	4	9	11	11	4	2
John Wasdin	0	0	27.00	1	0	0	2	2	5	5	4	1
Totals	3	2	6.02	5	5	0	43	38	32	29	28	43

CLEVELAND

Player, Pos.	AVG	G	AB	R	H	2B	3B	HR	RBI	BB	SO	SB
Wil Cordero, lf	.556	3	9	3	5	0	0	1	2	1	2	0
Roberto Alomar, 2b	.368	5	19	4	7	4	0	0	3	2	3	2
Harold Baines, dh	.357	4	14	1	5	0	0	1	4	2	1	0
Jim Thome, 1b	.353	5	17	7	6	0	0	4	10	4	5	0
Travis Fryman, 3b	.267	5	15	2	4	0	0	1	4	3	2	1
Omar Vizquel, ss	.238	5	21	3	5	1	1	0	3	2	3	0
Richie Sexson, dh-ph	.167	3	6	1	1	0	0	0	1	1	3	0
Sandy Alomar, c	.143	5	14	1	2	0	0	0	1	2	6	0
Kenny Lofton, cf	.125	5	16	5	2	1	0	0	1	5	6	2
Manny Ramirez, rf	.056	5	18	5	1	1	0	0	1	4	8	0
Einar Diaz, c-ph	.000	2	1	0	0	0	0	0	0	0	0	0
David Justice, dh	.000	3	8	0	0	0	0	0	1	2	2	0
Dave Roberts, cf	.000	2	3	0	0	0	0	0	0	0	2	0
Enrique Wilson, 3b	.000	3	2	0	0	0	0	0	0	0	0	0
Totals	.233	5	163	32	38	7	1	7	31	28	43	5

Pitcher	W	L	ERA	G	GS	SV	IP	H	R	ER	BB	SO
Dave Burba	0	0	0.00	1	1	0	4	1	0	0	1	0
Sean DePaula	0	0	1.80	3	0	0	5	2	1	1	3	5
Mike Jackson	0	0	4.50	2	0	0	2	2	1	1	1	1
Charles Nagy	1	0	7.20	2	2	0	10	11	9	8	2	6
Bartolo Colon	0	1	9.00	2	2	0	9	11	9	9	4	12
Steve Karsay	0	0	9.00	2	0	0	3	5	3	3	1	3
Paul Shuey	1	1	11.25	3	0	0	4	4	5	5	4	5
Jaret Wright	0	1	22.50	1	1	0	2	4	5	5	1	1
Paul Assenmacher	0	0	27.00	1	0	0	1	5	3	3	0	0
Steve Reed	0	0	30.86	2	0	0	2	9	8	8	1	1
Ricardo Rincon	0	0	40.50	1	0	0	1	2	3	3	1	1
Totals	2	3	9.63	5	5	0	43	56	47	46	19	35

SCORE BY INNINGS

Boston	469 751 (12)21	—47
Cleveland	439 643 102	—32

E—R. Alomar, S. Alomar, Lofton, Merloni, Valentin 2. DP—Boston 3, Cleveland 3. LOB—Boston 25, Cleveland 35. CS—Offerman. SF—Nixon 2, Valentin, Fryman, S. Alomar, R. Alomar, Justice. S—Vizquel. PB—Varitek 2. HBP—Garciaparra (by Reed), Lewis (by Reed), Varitek (by Wright), Fryman (by Gordon), Ramirez (by Lowe).

CHAMPIONSHIP SERIES
NEW YORK vs. BOSTON
COMPSITE BOX

NEW YORK

Player, Pos.	AVG	G	AB	R	H	2B	3B	HR	RBI	BB	SO	SB
Derek Jeter, ss	.350	5	20	3	7	1	0	1	3	2	3	0
Chuck Knoblauch, 2b	.333	5	18	3	6	1	0	0	1	3	0	1
Darryl Strawberry, dh-ph	.333	3	6	1	2	0	0	1	1	1	2	0
Paul O'Neill, rf	.286	5	21	2	6	0	0	0	1	1	5	0
Tino Martinez, 1b	.263	5	19	3	5	1	0	1	3	2	4	0
Bernie Williams, cf	.250	5	20	3	5	1	0	1	2	2	5	1
Joe Girardi, c	.250	3	8	0	2	0	0	0	0	2	0	0
Ricky Ledee, lf	.250	3	8	2	2	0	0	1	4	1	4	0
Scott Brosius, 3b	.222	5	18	3	4	0	1	2	3	1	4	0
Shane Spencer, lf-ph	.111	4	9	1	1	0	0	0	1	6	0	0
Jorge Posada, c	.100	4	10	1	1	0	0	1	2	1	2	0
Chili Davis, dh-ph	.091	5	11	0	1	0	0	0	1	3	4	0
Chad Curtis, lf-ph	.000	3	6	1	0	0	0	0	0	0	2	1
Clay Bellinger, ph-ss	.000	3	1	0	0	0	0	0	0	0	1	0
Luis Sojo, 2b-ph	.000	2	1	0	0	0	0	0	0	0	0	0
Totals	.239	5	176	23	42	4	1	8	21	18	44	3

Pitcher	W	L	ERA	G	GS	SV	IP	H	R	ER	BB	SO
Mariano Rivera	1	0	0.00	3	0	2	5	5	0	0	0	3
Ramiro Mendoza	0	0	0.00	2	0	1	2	0	0	0	0	2
Allen Watson	0	0	0.00	3	0	1	2	0	0	0	2	1
Jeff Nelson	0	0	0.00	3	0	0	1	0	0	0	1	0
Mike Stanton	0	0	0.00	3	0	0	1	1	0	0	1	0
Orlando Hernandez	1	0	1.80	2	2	0	15	12	4	3	6	13
Andy Pettitte	1	0	2.45	1	1	0	7	8	2	2	1	5
David Cone	1	0	2.57	1	1	0	7	7	2	2	3	9
Hideki Irabu	0	0	13.50	1	0	0	5	13	8	7	0	3
Roger Clemens	0	1	22.50	1	1	0	2	6	5	5	2	2
Totals	4	1	3.80	5	5	3	45	54	21	19	15	38

BOSTON

Player, Pos.	AVG	G	AB	R	H	2B	3B	HR	RBI	BB	SO	SB
Jose Offerman, 2b	.458	5	24	4	11	0	1	0	2	1	3	1
Nomar Garciaparra, ss	.400	5	20	2	8	2	0	2	5	2	2	1
Damon Buford, pr-cf	.400	4	5	1	2	0	0	0	0	0	2	1
Troy O'Leary, lf	.350	5	20	2	7	3	0	0	1	2	5	0
John Valentin, 3b	.348	5	23	3	8	2	0	1	5	2	4	0
Trot Nixon, rf	.286	4	14	2	4	2	0	0	1	5	0	0
Mike Stanley, 1b	.222	5	18	1	4	0	0	0	1	2	4	0
Jason Varitek, c	.200	5	20	1	4	1	1	1	1	1	4	0
Butch Huskey, ph-dh	.200	4	5	1	1	0	0	0	0	1	1	0
Brian Daubach, dh-1b	.176	5	17	2	3	1	0	1	3	1	4	0
Darren Lewis, cf-rf	.118	5	17	2	2	1	0	0	1	1	3	1
Scott Hatteberg, c-ph	.000	3	1	0	0	0	0	0	0	0	1	0
Lou Merloni, ph	.000	1	1	0	0	0	0	0	0	0	1	0
Donnie Sadler, 2b	.000	2	2	0	0	0	0	0	0	0	0	0
Totals	.293	5	184	21	54	13	2	5	19	15	38	4

Pitcher	W	L	ERA	G	GS	SV	IP	H	R	ER	BB	SO
Pedro Martinez	1	0	0.00	1	1	0	7	2	0	0	2	12
Rheal Cormier	0	0	0.00	4	0	0	4	3	0	0	3	4
Pat Rapp	0	0	0.00	1	0	0	1	0	0	0	1	0
Derek Lowe	0	0	1.42	3	0	0	6	6	3	1	2	7
Bret Saberhagen	0	1	1.50	1	1	0	6	5	3	1	1	5
Ramon Martinez	0	1	4.05	1	1	0	7	6	3	3	3	5
Kent Mercker	0	1	4.70	2	0	0	8	12	4	4	4	5
Rich Garces	0	0	12.00	2	0	0	3	3	5	4	1	2
Tom Gordon	0	0	13.50	3	0	0	2	3	3	3	1	3
Rod Beck	0	1	27.00	2	0	0	1	2	2	2	0	1
Totals	1	4	3.68	5	5	0	44	42	23	18	18	44

SCORE BY INNINGS

New York	230 300 518 1	—23
Boston	443 041 410 0	—21

E—Garciaparra 4, Offerman 2, Lewis, Saberhagen, Varitek, Stanley, Jeter 2, Knoblauch, Ledee, Posada. DP—New York 7. LOB—Boston 45, New York 42. CS—Lewis, Ledee. S—Varitek, Brosius, Knoblauch. HBP—Stanley (by Nelson), T. Martinez (by Mercker). PB—Girardi.

NATIONAL LEAGUE

Braves continue decade of dominance, at least in NL

BY JOHN MANUEL

In 1995, the Atlanta Braves won their first World Series since moving from Milwaukee in 1966. Their championship rings celebrated not only the World Series but also the franchise's sustained excellence in the decade, with the phrase "Team of the '90s" engraved on the side of the ring.

While that may be debatable for the game as a whole, in the National League there's no doubt about it. The Braves backed it up in 1999, again winning the pennant. It was Atlanta's first pennant since 1996 but the fifth of the decade, after its eighth trip to the NL Championship Series. This all started after Atlanta opened the 1990s with a seventh straight losing season, going 65-97.

"If you had told me (at the start of the decade) that we'd win eight straight division titles, I would have told you to check into drug rehab," said lefthander Tom Glavine, who along with righthander John Smoltz has been in Atlanta for the entire run.

In seven of those eight trips to the LCS, the Braves faced a different opponent—the Pirates in 1991 and '92 being the only repeat challenger. The new challenger in 1999 was the Mets, and again the Braves didn't flinch.

Of course, they did make it interesting, as is their custom. After losing Game One of the Division Series to the Astros, they won three straight with a spark from righthander Kevin Millwood, the newest member of the vaunted Braves rotation and its best member in 1999.

Millwood threw a one-hitter in Game Two and came out of the bullpen to save Game Three, a 12-inning classic that also featured closer John Rocker getting the team out of a bases-loaded, no-out jam in the 10th. The Braves closed out the series and the Astrodome in Game Four.

That moved the Braves into an Eastern Division showdown with the Mets, who had dispatched the Diamondbacks in four games in their Division Series. The two clubs already had a healthy rivalry. The Braves swept the Mets in '98 to deny them a wild-card spot, then won nine of 12 meetings in 1999, including five of six in September, to win the East.

Third baseman Chipper Jones sealed his MVP bid with four homers in a three-game sweep in Atlanta. The No. 1 pick in the 1990 draft, Jones established

Enjoying the ride
Tom Glavine can hardly believe what the Braves have built

JOHN WILLIAMSON

his place as one of the game's top players by producing his best season when the Braves needed it most.

With Andres Galarraga missing the season, catcher Javy Lopez missing the second half and Brian Jordan battling an injured hand that limited his power, Jones became the Braves' offense. He hit .319 with 45 home runs, 110 RBIs, 41 doubles, 25 stolen bases (in 28 attempts) and 126 walks.

Jones then started a war of words when he said Mets fans should "go home and put their Yankees stuff on." Rocker regaled reporters with his distaste for New York fans.

Atlanta backed up a talk by winning three close games to open the LCS, 4-2, 4-3 and 1-0 behind excellent pitching and the surprise bat of series MVP Eddie Perez. They then looked to Glavine to close out the series in New York. But the Mets won Game Four 3-2, setting the stage for two of the best playoff games ever.

In Game Five, the two teams used 46 players, 15 of them pitchers. The Braves left 19 runners on base, unable to put the feisty Mets away. New York erased a 2-0 deficit with a two-run homer by John Olerud off Greg Maddux in the fourth inning, and the game remained tied for the next 10 innings as the teams played through a steady rain.

Finally, the Braves broke through in the 15th on an RBI triple by reserve second baseman Keith Lockhart. But the Mets still wouldn't die. The game-winning rally off rookie reliever Kevin McGlinchy started when veteran Shawon Dunston, who had misplayed Lockhart's drive in the outfield in the top half of the

NATIONAL LEAGUE CHAMPIONS, 1901-1999

	Pennant	Pct.	GA
1901	Pittsburgh	.647	1½
1902	Pittsburgh	.741	27½
1903	Pittsburgh	.650	6½
1904	New York	.693	13
1905	New York	.686	9
1906	Chicago	.763	20
1907	Chicago	.704	17
1908	Chicago	.643	1
1909	Pittsburgh	.724	6½
1910	Chicago	.675	13
1911	New York	.647	7½
1912	New York	.682	10
1913	New York	.664	12½
1914	Boston	.614	10½
1915	Philadelphia	.592	7
1916	Brooklyn	.610	2½
1917	New York	.636	10
1918	Chicago	.651	10½
1919	Cincinnati	.686	9
1920	Brooklyn	.604	7
1921	New York	.614	4
1922	New York	.604	7
1923	New York	.621	4½
1924	New York	.608	1½
1925	Pittsburgh	.621	8½
1926	St. Louis	.578	2
1927	Pittsburgh	.610	1½
1928	St. Louis	.617	2
1929	Chicago	.645	10½
1930	St. Louis	.597	2

	Pennant	Pct.	GA	MVP
1931	St. Louis	.656	13	Frankie Frisch, 2b, St.Louis
1932	Chicago	.584	4	Chuck Klein, of, Philadelphia
1933	New York	.599	5	Carl Hubbell, lhp, New York
1934	St. Louis	.621	2	Dizzy Dean, rhp, St.Louis
1935	Chicago	.649	4	Gabby Hartnett, c, Chicago
1936	New York	.597	5	Carl Hubbell, lhp, New York
1937	New York	.625	3	Joe Medwick, of, St. Louis
1938	Chicago	.586	2	Ernie Lombardi, c, Cincinnati
1939	Cincinnati	.630	4½	Bucky Walters, rhp, Cincinnati
1940	Cincinnati	.654	12	Frank McCormick, 1b, Cincinnati
1941	Brooklyn	.649	2½	Dolf Camilli, 1b, Brooklyn
1942	St. Louis	.688	2	Mort Cooper, rhp, St. Louis
1943	St. Louis	.682	18	Stan Musial, of, St. Louis
1944	St. Louis	.682	14½	Marty Marion, ss, St. Louis
1945	Chicago	.636	3	Phil Cavarretta, 1b, Chicago
1946	St. Louis	.628	2	Stan Musial, 1b, St. Louis
1947	Brooklyn	.610	5	Bob Elliott, 3b, Boston
1948	Boston	.595	6½	Stan Musial, of, St. Louis
1949	Brooklyn	.630	1	Jackie Robinson, 2b, Brooklyn
1950	Philadelphia	.591	2	Jim Konstanty, rhp, Philadelphia
1951	New York	.624	1	Roy Campanella, c, Brooklyn
1952	Brooklyn	.627	4½	Hank Sauer, of, Chicago
1953	Brooklyn	.682	13	Roy Campanella, c, Brooklyn
1954	New York	.630	5	Willie Mays, of, New York
1955	Brooklyn	.641	13½	Roy Campanella, c, Brooklyn
1956	Brooklyn	.604	1	Don Newcombe, rhp, Brooklyn
1957	Milwaukee	.617	8	Hank Aaron, of, Milwaukee
1958	Milwaukee	.597	8	Ernie Banks, ss, Chicago
1959	Los Angeles	.564	2	Ernie Banks, ss, Chicago
1960	Pittsburgh	.617	7	Dick Groat, ss, Pittsburgh
1961	Cincinnati	.604	4	Frank Robinson, of, Cincinnati
1962	San Francisco	.624	1	Maury Wills, ss, Los Angeles
1963	Los Angeles	.611	6	Sandy Koufax, lhp, Los Angeles
1964	St. Louis	.574	1	Ken Boyer, 3b, St. Louis
1965	Los Angeles	.599	2	Willie Mays, of, San Francisco
1966	Los Angeles	.586	1½	Roberto Clemente, of, Pittsburgh
1967	St. Louis	.627	10½	Orlando Cepeda, 1b, St. Louis
1968	St. Louis	.599	9	Bob Gibson, rhp, St. Louis

	East. Div.	PCT	GA	West. Div.	PCT	GA	Pennant		MVP
1969	New York	.617	8	Atlanta	.574	3	New York	3-0	Willie McCovey, 1b, San Francisco
1970	Pittsburgh	.549	5	Cincinnati	.630	14½	Cincinnati	3-0	Johnny Bench, c, Cincinnati
1971	Pittsburgh	.599	7	San Francisco	.556	1	Pittsburgh	3-1	Joe Torre, 3b, St. Louis
1972	Pittsburgh	.619	11	Cincinnati	.617	10½	Cincinnati	3-2	Johnny Bench, c, Cincinnati
1973	New York	.509	1½	Cincinnati	.611	3½	New York	3-2	Pete Rose, of, Cincinnati
1974	Pittsburgh	.543	1½	Los Angeles	.630	4	Los Angeles	3-1	Steve Garvey, 1b, Los Angeles
1975	Pittsburgh	.571	6½	Cincinnati	.667	20	Cincinnati	3-0	Joe Morgan, 2b, Cincinnati
1976	Philadelphia	.623	9	Cincinnati	.630	10	Cincinnati	3-0	Joe Morgan, 2b, Cincinnati
1977	Philadelphia	.623	5	Los Angeles	.605	10	Los Angeles	3-1	George Foster, of, Cincinnati
1978	Philadelphia	.556	1½	Los Angeles	.586	2½	Los Angeles	3-1	Dave Parker, of, Pittsburgh
1979	Pittsburgh	.605	2	Cincinnati	.559	1½	Pittsburgh	3-0	Hernandez, St. Louis; Stargell, Pittsburgh
1980	Philadelphia	.562	1	Houston	.571	1	Philadelphia	3-2	Mike Schmidt, 3b, Philadelphia
1981	Montreal*	.566	½	Los Angeles**	.632	½	Los Angeles	3-2	Mike Schmidt, 3b, Philadelphia
	Philadelphia	.618	1½	Houston	.623	1			
1982	St. Louis	.568	3	Atlanta	.549	1	St. Louis	3-0	Dale Murphy, of, Atlanta
1983	Philadelphia	.556	6	Los Angeles	.562	3	Philadelphia	3-1	Dale Murphy, of, Atlanta
1984	Chicago	.596	6½	San Diego	.568	12	San Diego	3-2	Ryne Sandberg, 2b, Chicago
1985	St. Louis	.623	3	Los Angeles	.586	5½	St. Louis	4-2	Willie McGee, of, St. Louis
1986	New York	.667	21½	Houston	.593	10	New York	4-2	Mike Schmidt, 3b, Philadelphia
1987	St. Louis	.586	3	San Francisco	.556	6	St. Louis	4-3	Andre Dawson, of, Chicago
1988	New York	.625	15	Los Angeles	.584	7	Los Angeles	4-3	Kirk Gibson, of, Los Angeles
1989	Chicago	.571	6	San Francisco	.568	3	San Francisco	4-1	Kevin Mitchell, of, San Francisco
1990	Pittsburgh	.586	4	Cincinnati	.562	5	Cincinnati	4-2	Barry Bonds, of, Pittsburgh
1991	Pittsburgh	.605	14	Atlanta	.580	1	Atlanta	4-3	Terry Pendleton, 3b, Atlanta
1992	Pittsburgh	.593	9	Atlanta	.605	8	Atlanta	4-3	Barry Bonds, of, Pittsburgh
1993	Philadelphia	.599	3	Atlanta	.642	1	Philadelphia	4-2	Barry Bonds, of, San Francisco

	East Div.	PCT	GA	Central Div.	PCT	GA	West Div.	PCT	GA	MVP
1994	Montreal	.649	6	Cincinnati	.593	½	Los Angeles	.509	3½	Jeff Bagwell, 1b, Houston
1995	Atlanta#	.625	21	Cincinnati	.590	9	Los Angeles	.542	1	Barry Larkin, ss, Cincinnati
1996	Atlanta@	.593	8	St. Louis	.543	6	San Diego	.562	1	Ken Caminiti, 3b, San Diego
1997	Atlanta%	.623	9	Houston	.519	5	San Francisco	.556	2	Larry Walker, of, Colorado
1998	Atlanta	.654	18	Houston	.630	12½	San Diego &	.605	9½	Sammy Sosa, of, Chicago
1999	Atlanta^	.636	6½	Houston	.599	1½	Arizona	.617	14	Chipper Jones, 3b, Atlanta

* Won second half; defeated Philadelphia 3-2 in best-of-5 playoff.
** Won first half; defeated Houston 3-2 in best-of-5 playoff.
# Won NL pennant, defeating Cincinnati 4-2.
@ Won NL pennant, defeating St. Louis 4-3.
% Florida (wild card) won NL pennant, defeating Atlanta 4-2.
& Won NL pennant, defeating Atlanta 4-2.
^ Won NL pennant, defeating New York (wild card) 4-2.

STANDINGS

Page	EAST	W	L	PCT	GB	Manager	General Manager	Attend./Dates	Last Penn.
67	Atlanta Braves	103	59	.636	—	Bobby Cox	John Schuerholz	3,361,350 (81)	1999
181	New York Mets*	97	66	.595	6½	Bobby Valentine	Steve Phillips	2,287,942 (77)	1986
195	Philadelphia Phillies	77	85	.475	26	Terry Francona	Ed Wade	1,715,702 (79)	1993
167	Montreal Expos	68	94	.420	35	Felipe Alou	Jim Beattie	914,717 (81)	None
128	Florida Marlins	64	98	.395	39	John Boles	Dave Dombrowski	1,750,395 (79)	1997
Page	**CENTRAL**	**W**	**L**	**PCT**	**GB**	**Manager(s)**	**General Manager**	**Attend./Dates**	**Last Penn.**
135	Houston Astros	97	65	.599	—	Larry Dierker	Gerry Hunsicker	2,450,451 (80)	None
102	Cincinnati Reds	96	67	.589	1½	Jack McKeon	Jim Bowden	1,793,679 (81)	1990
202	Pittsburgh Pirates	78	83	.484	18½	Gene Lamont	Cam Bonifay	1,560,950 (80)	1979
209	St. Louis Cardinals	75	86	.466	21½	Tony La Russa	Walt Jocketty	3,195,021 (80)	1987
154	Milwaukee Brewers	74	87	.460	22½	P. Garner/J. Lefebvre	Sal Bando/Dean Taylor	1,811,548 (79)	None
95	Chicago Cubs	67	95	.414	30	Jim Riggleman	Ed Lynch	2,623,000 (80)	1945
Page	**WEST**	**W**	**L**	**PCT**	**GB**	**Manager**	**General Manager**	**Attend./Dates**	**Last Penn.**
60	Arizona Diamondbacks	100	62	.617	—	Buck Showalter	Joe Garagiola Jr.	3,602,856 (81)	None
221	San Francisco Giants	86	76	.531	14	Dusty Baker	Brian Sabean	1,925,634 (80)	1989
148	Los Angeles Dodgers	77	85	.475	23	Davey Johnson	Kevin Malone	3,089,222 (81)	1988
215	San Diego Padres	74	88	.457	26	Bruce Bochy	Kevin Towers	2,555,901 (79)	1998
116	Colorado Rockies	72	90	.444	28	Jim Leyland	Bob Gebhard	3,789,347 (81)	None

*Defeated Cincinnati in one-game playoff to win wild-card playoff berth
NOTE: Team's individual batting, pitching and fielding statistics can be found on page indicated in lefthand column.

inning, fouled off pitch after pitch before lacing a single to center.

Three walks (one intentional) and a sacrifice bunt left the game tied and the bases loaded for Robin Ventura, the third baseman signed by the Mets after the White Sox let him go as a free agent. Ventura drilled a 1-1 pitch over the fence in right field to win the game. It appeared to be a grand slam, but he was

Mets killer
Chipper Jones carried Atlanta's offense

mobbed by his teammates before he could circle the bases and was credited with a single in an improbable 4-3 Mets win.

"Baseball is a crazy game," McGlinchy said. "This was a crazy game."

Game Six, back in Atlanta, was no less crazy. New York went to veteran lefthander Al Leiter, who has a strong postseason resume but was pitching on three days' rest for the second time in his career. Leiter gave up five runs in the first inning without recording an out, hitting two batters, walking one and giving up two hits.

Again the Mets rallied, this time against Millwood. Millwood led all NL starters in opponents' batting average, but the Mets chased him with three runs in the sixth. Again Atlanta answered, this time with a two-run, pinch-hit single by Jose Hernandez.

The Braves turned again to a starter to do the job out of the bullpen. Smoltz, who had picked up a save in his first big league relief appearance in Game Two, got the call, but this time he didn't have it. He gave up four hits and four runs, capped by a game-tying two-run homer by Mike Piazza. New York took the lead in the eighth on rookie Melvin Mora's RBI single, then the Braves tied it again in the bottom of the eighth on a run-scoring single by Brian Hunter.

Both teams turned to their closers, and both Armando Benitez and Rocker gave up runs. Finally, the Braves broke through in the 11th against veteran lefthander Kenny Rogers, who took the loss in Game Two. Gerald Williams led off with a double and moved up on a sacrifice bunt. Two intentional walks loaded the bases for Andruw Jones with one out.

Rogers fell behind 3-1 before throwing a strike to run the count full. Finally, with the season on the line, Rogers missed by a mile, walking Jones and forcing home the winning run. Television cameras showed Mets manager Bobby Valentine slamming the top railing of the dugout and shouting, "No!" as the electrifying series came to an anticlimactic end in the Braves' 10-9 win.

"I told them they played like champions," Valentine

Major Leagues

BILL SETLIFF

NATIONAL LEAGUE YEAR-BY-YEAR BATTING LEADERS

Year	Batting Average	Home Runs	RBIs
1901	Jesse Burkett, St. Louis .382	Sam Crawford, Cincinnati 16	Honus Wagner, Pittsburgh 126
1902	Ginger Beaumont, Pitt. .357	Tom Leach, Pittsburgh 6	Honus Wagner, Pittsburgh 91
1903	Honus Wagner, Pitt. .355	Jim Sheckard, Brooklyn 9	Sam Mertes, New York 104
1904	Honus Wagner, Pitt. .349	Harry Lumley, Brooklyn 9	Bill Dahlen, New York 80
1905	Cy Seymour, Cincinnati .377	Fred Odwell, Cincinnati 9	Cy Seymour, Cincinnati 121
1906	Honus Wagner, Pitt. .339	Tim Jordan, Brooklyn 12	2 tied at 83
1907	Honus Wagner, Pitt. .350	Dave Brain, Boston 10	Sherry Magee, Philadelphia 85
1908	Honus Wagner, Pitt. .354	Tim Jordan, Brooklyn 12	Honus Wagner, Pittsburgh 109
1909	Honus Wagner, Pitt. .339	Red Murray, New York 7	Honus Wagner, Pittsburgh 100
1910	Sherry Magee, Phil. .331	2 tied at 10	Sherry Magee, Philadelphia 123
1911	Honus Wagner, Pitt. .334	Wildfire Schulte, Chicago 21	Wildfire Schulte, Chicago 121
1912	Heinie Zimmerman, Chi. .372	Heinie Zimmerman, Chi. 14	Heinie Zimmerman, Chi. 103
1913	Jake Daubert, Brooklyn .350	Gavvy Cravath, Phil. 19	Gavvy Cravath, Phil. 128
1914	Jake Daubert, Brooklyn .329	Gavvy Cravath, Phil. 19	Sherry Magee, Phil. 103
1915	Larry Doyle, New York .320	Gavvy Cravath, Phil. 24	Gavvy Cravath, Phil. 115
1916	Hal Chase, Cincinnati .339	2 tied at 12	Heinie Zimmerman, Chi.-N.Y. 126
1917	Edd Roush, Cincinnati .341	2 tied at 12	Heinie Zimmerman, N.Y. 102
1918	Zack Wheat, Brooklyn .335	Gavvy Cravath, Phil. 8	Sherry Magee, Cincinnati 76
1919	Edd Roush, Cincinnati .321	Gavvy Cravath, Phil. 12	Hy Myers, Brooklyn 73
1920	Rogers Hornsby, St.L. .370	Cy Williams, Philadelphia 15	2 tied at 94
1921	Rogers Hornsby, St.L. .397	George Kelly, New York 23	Rogers Hornsby, St. Louis 126
1922	Rogers Hornsby, St.L. .401	Rogers Hornsby, St. Louis 42	Rogers Hornsby, St. Louis 152
1923	Rogers Hornsby, St.L. .384	Cy Williams, Philadelphia 41	Emil Meusel, New York 125
1924	Rogers Hornsby, St.L. .424	Jack Fournier, Brooklyn 27	George Kelly, New York 136
1925	Rogers Hornsby, St.L. .403	Rogers Hornsby, St. Louis 39	Rogers Hornsby, St. Louis 143
1926	Bubbles Hargrave, Cinc. .353	Hack Wilson, Chicago 21	Jim Bottomley, St. Louis 120
1927	Paul Waner, Pittsburgh .380	2 tied at 30	Paul Waner, Pittsburgh 131
1928	Rogers Hornsby, St.L. .387	Jim Bottomley, St. Louis 31	Jim Bottomley, St. Louis 136
1929	Lefty O'Doul, Philadelphia .398	Chuck Klein, Philadelphia 43	Hack Wilson, Chicago 159
1930	Bill Terry, New York .401	Hack Wilson, Chicago 56	Hack Wilson, Chicago 190
1931	Chick Hafey, St. Louis .349	Chuck Klein, Philadelphia 31	Chuck Klein, Philadelphia 121
1932	Lefty O'Doul, Brooklyn .368	2 tied at 38	Frank Hurst, Philadelphia 143
1933	Chuck Klein, Philadelphia .368	Chuck Klein, Philadelphia 28	Chuck Klein, Philadelphia 120
1934	Paul Waner, Pittsburgh .362	2 tied at 35	Mel Ott, New York 135
1935	Arky Vaughan, Pittsburgh .385	Wally Berger, Boston 34	Wally Berger, Boston 130
1936	Paul Waner, Pittsburgh .373	Mel Ott, New York 33	Joe Medwick, St. Louis 138
1937	Joe Medwick, St. Louis .374	2 tied at 31	Joe Medwick, St. Louis 154
1938	Ernie Lombardi, Cinc. .342	Mel Ott, New York 36	Joe Medwick, St. Louis 122
1939	Johnny Mize, St. Louis .349	Johnny Mize, St. Louis 28	Frank McCormick, Cinc. 128
1940	Debs Garms, Pittsburgh .355	Johnny Mize, St. Louis 43	Johnny Mize, St. Louis 137
1941	Pete Reiser, Brooklyn .343	Dolf Camilli, Brooklyn 34	Dolf Camilli, Brooklyn 120
1942	Ernie Lombardi, Boston .330	Mel Ott, New York 30	Johnny Mize, New York 110
1943	Stan Musial, St. Louis .357	Bill Nicholson, Chicago 29	Bill Nicholson, Chicago 128
1944	Dixie Walker, Brooklyn .357	Bill Nicholson, Chicago 33	Bill Nicholson, Chicago 122
1945	Phil Cavarretta, Chicago .355	Tommy Holmes, Boston 28	Dixie Walker, Brooklyn 124
1946	Stan Musial, St. Louis .365	Ralph Kiner, Pittsburgh 23	Enos Slaughter, St. Louis 130
1947	Harry Walker, St.L-Phil. .363	2 tied at 51	Johnny Mize, New York 138
1948	Stan Musial, St. Louis .376	2 tied at 40	Stan Musial, St. Louis 131
1949	Jackie Robinson, Brooklyn .342	Ralph Kiner, Pittsburgh 54	Ralph Kiner, Pittsburgh 127
1950	Stan Musial, St. Louis .346	Ralph Kiner, Pittsburgh 47	Del Ennis, Philadelphia 126
1951	Stan Musial, St. Louis .355	Ralph Kiner, Pittsburgh 42	Monte Irvin, New York 121
1952	Stan Musial, St. Louis .336	2 tied at 37	Hank Sauer, Chicago 121
1953	Carl Furillo, Brooklyn .344	Eddie Mathews, Milwaukee 47	Roy Campanella, Brooklyn 142
1954	Willie Mays, New York .345	Ted Kluszewski, Cincinnati 49	Ted Kluszewski, Cincinnati 141
1955	Richie Ashburn, Phil. .338	Willie Mays, New York 51	Duke Snider, Brooklyn 136
1956	Hank Aaron, Milwaukee .328	Duke Snider, Brooklyn 43	Stan Musial, St. Louis 109
1957	Stan Musial, St. Louis .351	Hank Aaron, Milwaukee 44	Hank Aaron, Milwaukee 132
1958	Richie Ashburn, Phil. .350	Ernie Banks, Chicago 47	Ernie Banks, Chicago 129
1959	Hank Aaron, Milwaukee .355	Eddie Mathews, Milwaukee 46	Ernie Banks, Chicago 143
1960	Dick Groat, Pittsburgh .325	Ernie Banks, Chicago 41	Hank Aaron, Milwaukee 126
1961	Roberto Clemente, Pitt. .351	Orlando Cepeda, San Fran. 46	Orlando Cepeda, San Fran. 142
1962	Tommy Davis, L.A. .346	Willie Mays, San Francisco 49	Tommy Davis, Los Angeles 153
1963	Tommy Davis, L.A. .326	Hank Aaron, Milwaukee 44	Hank Aaron, Milwaukee 130
1964	Roberto Clemente, Pitt. .339	Willie Mays, San Francisco 47	Ken Boyer, St. Louis 119
1965	Roberto Clemente, Pitt. .329	Willie Mays, San Francisco 52	Deron Johnson, Cincinnati 130
1966	Matty Alou, Pittsburgh .342	Hank Aaron, Atlanta 44	Hank Aaron, Atlanta 127
1967	Roberto Clemente, Pitt. .357	Hank Aaron, Atlanta 39	Orlando Cepeda, San Fran. 111
1968	Pete Rose, Cincinnati .335	Willie McCovey, San Fran. 36	Willie McCovey, San Fran. 105
1969	Pete Rose, Cincinnati .348	Willie McCovey, San Fran. 45	Willie McCovey, San Fran. 126
1970	Rico Carty, Atlanta .366	Johnny Bench, Cincinnati 45	Johnny Bench, Cincinnati 148
1971	Joe Torre, St. Louis .363	Willie Stargell, Pittsburgh 48	Joe Torre, St. Louis 137
1972	Billy Williams, Chicago .333	Johnny Bench, Cincinnati 40	Johnny Bench, Cincinnati 125
1973	Pete Rose, Cincinnati .338	Willie Stargell, Pittsburgh 44	Willie Stargell, Pittsburgh 119
1974	Ralph Garr, Atlanta .353	Mike Schmidt, Philadelphia 36	Johnny Bench, Cincinnati 129
1975	Bill Madlock, Chicago .354	Mike Schmidt, Philadelphia 38	Greg Luzinski, Philadelphia 120
1976	Bill Madlock, Chicago .339	Mike Schmidt, Philadelphia 38	George Foster, Cincinnati 121
1977	Dave Parker, Pittsburgh .338	George Foster, Cincinnati 52	George Foster, Cincinnati 149
1978	Dave Parker, Pittsburgh .334	George Foster, Cincinnati 40	George Foster, Cincinnati 120
1979	Keith Hernandez, St.L. .344	Dave Kingman, Chicago 48	Dave Winfield, San Diego 118
1980	Bill Buckner, Chicago .324	Mike Schmidt, Philadelphia 48	Mike Schmidt, Philadelphia 121
1981	Bill Madlock, Pittsburgh .341	Mike Schmidt, Philadelphia 31	Mike Schmidt, Philadelphia 91
1982	Al Oliver, Montreal .331	Dave Kingman, New York 37	Dale Murphy, Atlanta 109
1983	Bill Madlock, Pittsburgh .323	Mike Schmidt, Philadelphia 40	Dale Murphy, Atlanta 121
1984	Tony Gwynn, San Diego .351	Dale Murphy, Atlanta 36	2 tied at 106
1985	Willie McGee, St. Louis .353	Dale Murphy, Atlanta 37	Dave Parker, Cincinnati 125
1986	Tim Raines, Montreal .334	Mike Schmidt, Philadelphia 37	Mike Schmidt, Philadelphia 119
1987	Tony Gwynn, San Diego .370	Andre Dawson, Chicago 49	Andre Dawson, Chicago 137
1988	Tony Gwynn, San Diego .313	Darryl Strawberry, N.Y. 39	Will Clark, San Francisco 109
1989	Tony Gwynn, San Diego .336	Kevin Mitchell, S.F. 47	Kevin Mitchell, S.F. 125
1990	Willie McGee, St. Louis .335	Ryne Sandberg, Chicago 40	Matt Williams, S.F. 122
1991	Terry Pendleton, Atlanta .319	Howard Johnson, New York 38	Howard Johnson, New York 117
1992	Gary Sheffield, S.D. .330	Fred McGriff, San Diego 35	Darren Daulton, Phil. 109
1993	Andres Galarraga, Colo. .370	Barry Bonds, San Francisco 46	Barry Bonds, S.F. 123
1994	Tony Gwynn, San Diego .394	Matt Williams, S.F. 43	Jeff Bagwell, Houston 116
1995	Tony Gwynn, San Diego .368	Dante Bichette, Colorado 40	Dante Bichette, Colorado 128
1996	Tony Gwynn, San Diego .353	Andres Galarraga, Colorado 47	Andres Galarraga, Colorado 150
1997	Tony Gwynn, San Diego .372	Larry Walker, Colorado 49	Andres Galarraga, Colorado 140
1998	Larry Walker, Colorado .363	Mark McGwire, St. Louis 70	Sammy Sosa, Chicago 158
1999	Larry Walker, Colorado .379	Mark McGwire, St. Louis 65	Mark McGwire, St. Louis 147

NATIONAL LEAGUE YEAR-BY-YEAR PITCHING LEADERS

Year	Wins	ERA	Strikeouts
1901	Bill Donovan, Brooklyn 25	Jesse Tannehill, Pittsburgh 2.18	Noodles Hahn, Cin. 233
1902	Jack Chesbro, Pittsburgh 28	Jack Taylor, Chicago 1.33	Vic Willis, Boston 226
1903	Joe McGinnity, New York 31	Sam Leever, Pittsburgh 2.06	Christy Mathewson, N.Y. 267
1904	Joe McGinnity, New York 35	Joe McGinnity, New York 1.61	Christy Mathewson, N.Y. 212
1905	Christy Mathewson, N.Y. 32	Christy Mathewson, N.Y. 1.27	Christy Mathewson, N.Y. 206
1906	Joe McGinnity, New York 27	Mordecai Brown, Chicago 1.04	Fred Beebe, Chi.-St.L. 171
1907	Christy Mathewson, N.Y. 24	Jack Pfiester, Chicago 1.15	Christy Mathewson, N.Y. 178
1908	Christy Mathewson, N.Y. 37	Christy Mathewson, N.Y. 1.43	Christy Mathewson, N.Y. 259
1909	Mordecai Brown, Chicago 27	Christy Mathewson, N.Y. 1.14	Orval Overall, Chicago 205
1910	Christy Mathewson, N.Y. 27	George McQuillan, Phil. 1.60	Christy Mathewson, N.Y. 190
1911	Grover Alexander, Phil. 28	Christy Mathewson, N.Y. 1.99	Rube Marquard, New York 237
1912	2 tied at 26	Jeff Tesreau, New York 1.96	Grover Alexander, Phil. 195
1913	Tom Seaton, Philadelphia 27	Christy Mathewson, N.Y. 2.06	Tom Seaton, Philadelphia 168
1914	2 tied at 27	Bill Doak, St. Louis 1.72	Grover Alexander, Phil. 214
1915	Grover Alexander, Phil. 31	Grover Alexander, Phil. 1.22	Grover Alexander, Phil. 241
1916	Grover Alexander, Phil. 33	Grover Alexander, Phil. 1.55	Grover Alexander, Phil. 167
1917	Grover Alexander, Phil. 30	Grover Alexander, Phil. 1.85	Grover Alexander, Phil. 200
1918	Hippo Vaughn, Chicago 22	Hippo Vaughn, Chicago 1.74	Hippo Vaughn, Chicago 148
1919	Jesse Barnes, New York 25	Grover Alexander, Chicago 1.72	Hippo Vaughn, Chicago 141
1920	Grover Alexander, Chicago 27	Grover Alexander, Chicago 1.91	Grover Alexander, Chicago 173
1921	2 tied at 22	Bill Doak, St. Louis 2.58	Burleigh Grimes, Brooklyn 136
1922	Eppa Rixey, Cincinnati 25	Rosy Ryan, New York 3.00	Dazzy Vance, Brooklyn 134
1923	2 tied at 27	Dolf Luque, Cincinnati 1.93	Dazzy Vance, Brooklyn 197
1924	Dazzy Vance, Brooklyn 28	Dazzy Vance, Brooklyn 2.16	Dazzy Vance, Brooklyn 262
1925	Dazzy Vance, Brooklyn 22	Dolf Luque, Cincinnati 2.63	Dazzy Vance, Brooklyn 221
1926	4 tied at 20	Ray Kremer, Pittsburgh 2.61	Dazzy Vance, Brooklyn 140
1927	Charlie Root, Chicago 26	Ray Kremer, Pittsburgh 2.47	Dazzy Vance, Brooklyn 184
1928	2 tied at 25	Dazzy Vance, Brooklyn 2.09	Dazzy Vance, Brooklyn 200
1929	Pat Malone, Chicago 22	Bill Walker, New York 3.08	Pat Malone, Chicago 166
1930	2 tied at 20	Dazzy Vance, Brooklyn 2.61	Bill Hallahan, St. Louis 177
1931	3 tied at 19	Bill Walker, New York 2.26	Bill Hallahan, St. Louis 159
1932	Lon Warneke, Chicago 22	Lon Warneke, Chicago 2.37	Dizzy Dean, St. Louis 191
1933	Carl Hubbell, New York 23	Carl Hubbell, New York 1.66	Dizzy Dean, St. Louis 199
1934	Dizzy Dean, St. Louis 30	Carl Hubbell, New York 2.30	Dizzy Dean, St. Louis 195
1935	Dizzy Dean, St. Louis 28	Cy Blanton, Pittsburgh 2.59	Dizzy Dean, St. Louis 182
1936	Carl Hubbell, New York 26	Carl Hubbell, New York 2.31	Van Lingle Mungo, Brooklyn 238
1937	Carl Hubbell, New York 22	Jim Turner, Boston 2.38	Carl Hubbell, New York 159
1938	Bill Lee, Chicago 22	Bill Lee, Chicago 2.66	Clay Bryant, Chicago 135
1939	Bucky Walters, Cincinnati 27	Bucky Walters, Cincinnati 2.29	2 tied at 137
1940	Bucky Walters, Cincinnati 22	Bucky Walters, Cincinnati 2.48	Kirby Higbe, Philadelphia 137
1941	2 tied at 22	Elmer Riddle, Cincinnati 2.24	Johnny Vander Meer, Cin. 202
1942	Mort Cooper, St. Louis 22	Mort Cooper, St. Louis 1.77	Johnny Vander Meer, Cin. 186
1943	3 tied at 21	Howie Pollet, St. Louis 1.75	Johnny Vander Meer, Cin. 174
1944	Bucky Walters, Cincinnati 23	Ed Heusser, Cincinnati 2.38	Bill Voiselle, New York 161
1945	Red Barrett, Bos.-St.L. 23	Hank Borowy, Chicago 2.14	Preacher Roe, Pittsburgh 148
1946	Howie Pollet, St. Louis 21	Howie Pollet, St. Louis 2.10	Johnny Schmitz, Chicago 135
1947	Ewell Blackwell, Cincinnati 22	Warren Spahn, Boston 2.33	Ewell Blackwell, Cincinnati 193
1948	Johnny Sain, Boston 24	Harry Brecheen, St. Louis 2.24	Harry Brecheen, St. Louis 149
1949	Warren Spahn, Boston 21	Dave Koslo, New York 2.50	Warren Spahn, Boston 151
1950	Warren Spahn, Boston 21	Jim Hearn, StL.-New York 2.49	Warren Spahn, Boston 191
1951	2 tied at 23	Chet Nichols, Boston 2.88	2 tied at 164
1952	Robin Roberts, Philadelphia 28	Hoyt Wilhelm, New York 2.43	Warren Spahn, Boston 183
1953	2 tied at 23	Warren Spahn, Milwaukee 2.10	Robin Roberts, Philadelphia 198
1954	Robin Roberts, Philadelphia 23	John Antonelli, New York 2.29	Robin Roberts, Philadelphia 185
1955	Robin Roberts, Philadelphia 23	Bob Friend, Pittsburgh 2.84	Sam Jones, Chicago 198
1956	Don Newcombe, Brooklyn 27	Lew Burdette, Milwaukee 2.71	Sam Jones, Chicago 176
1957	Warren Spahn, Milwaukee 21	Johnny Podres, Brooklyn 2.66	Jack Sanford, Philadelphia 188
1958	2 tied 22	Stu Miller, San Francisco 2.47	Sam Jones, St. Louis 225
1959	3 tied at 21	Sam Jones, S.F. 2.82	Don Drysdale, L.A. 242
1960	2 tied at 21	Mike McCormick, S.F. 2.70	Don Drysdale, L.A. 246
1961	2 tied at 21	Warren Spahn, Milwaukee 3.01	Sandy Koufax, L.A. 269
1962	Don Drysdale, Los Angeles 25	Sandy Koufax, L.A. 2.54	Don Drysdale, L.A. 232
1963	2 tied at 25	Sandy Koufax, L.A. 1.88	Sandy Koufax, L.A. 306
1964	Larry Jackson, Chicago 24	Sandy Koufax, L.A. 1.74	Bob Veale, Pittsburgh 250
1965	Sandy Koufax, Los Angeles 26	Sandy Koufax, L.A. 2.04	Sandy Koufax, L.A. 382
1966	Sandy Koufax, Los Angeles 27	Sandy Koufax, L.A. 1.73	Sandy Koufax, L.A. 317
1967	Mike McCormick, San Fran. 22	Phil Niekro, Atlanta 1.87	Jim Bunning, Philadelphia 253
1968	Juan Marichal, San Fran. 26	Bob Gibson, St. Louis 1.12	Bob Gibson, St. Louis 268
1969	Tom Seaver, New York 25	Juan Marichal, San Fran. 2.10	Ferguson Jenkins, Chicago 273
1970	2 tied at 23	Tom Seaver, New York 2.81	Tom Seaver, New York 283
1971	Ferguson Jenkins, Chicago 24	Tom Seaver, New York 1.76	Tom Seaver, New York 289
1972	Steve Carlton, Philadelphia 27	Steve Carlton, Philadelphia 1.98	Steve Carlton, Philadelphia 310
1973	Ron Bryant, San Francisco 24	Tom Seaver, New York 2.08	Tom Seaver, New York 251
1974	2 tied at 20	Buzz Capra, Atlanta 2.28	Steve Carlton, Philadelphia 240
1975	Tom Seaver, New York 22	Randy Jones, San Diego 2.24	Tom Seaver, New York 243
1976	Randy Jones, San Diego 22	John Denny, St. Louis 2.52	Tom Seaver, New York 235
1977	Steve Carlton, Philadelphia 23	John Candelaria, Pittsburgh 2.34	Phil Niekro, Atlanta 262
1978	Gaylord Perry, San Diego 21	Craig Swan, New York 2.43	J.R. Richard, Houston 303
1979	2 tied at 21	J.R. Richard, Houston 2.71	J.R. Richard, Houston 313
1980	Steve Carlton, Philadelphia 24	Don Sutton, Los Angeles 2.21	Steve Carlton, Philadelphia 286
1981	Tom Seaver, Cincinnati 14	Nolan Ryan, Houston 1.69	Fernando Valenzuela, L.A. 180
1982	Steve Carlton, Philadelphia 23	Steve Rogers, Montreal 2.40	Steve Carlton, Philadelphia 286
1983	John Denny, Philadelphia 19	Atlee Hammaker, San Fran. 2.25	Steve Carlton, Philadelphia 275
1984	Joaquin Andujar, St. Louis 20	Alejandro Pena, L.A. 2.48	Dwight Gooden, New York 276
1985	Dwight Gooden, New York 24	Dwight Gooden, New York 1.53	Dwight Gooden, New York 268
1986	Fernando Valenzuela, L.A. 21	Mike Scott, Houston 2.22	Mike Scott, Houston 306
1987	Rick Sutcliffe, Chicago 18	Nolan Ryan, Houston 2.76	Nolan Ryan, Houston 270
1988	2 tied at 23	Joe Magrane, St. Louis 2.18	Nolan Ryan, Houston 228
1989	Mike Scott, Houston 20	Scott Garrelts, San Fran. 2.28	Jose DeLeon, St. Louis 201
1990	Doug Drabek, Pittsburgh 22	Danny Darwin, Houston 2.21	David Cone, New York 233
1991	2 tied at 20	Dennis Martinez, Mon. 2.39	David Cone, New York 241
1992	2 tied at 20	Bill Swift, San Francisco 2.08	John Smoltz, Atlanta 215
1993	2 tied at 22	Greg Maddux, Atlanta 2.36	Jose Rijo, Cincinnati 227
1994	2 tied at 16	Greg Maddux, Atlanta 1.56	Andy Benes, San Diego 189
1995	Greg Maddux, Atlanta 19	Greg Maddux, Atlanta 1.63	Hideo Nomo, Los Angeles 236
1996	John Smoltz, Atlanta 24	Kevin Brown, Florida 1.89	John Smoltz, Atlanta 276
1997	Denny Neagle, Atlanta 20	Pedro Martinez, Montreal 1.90	Curt Schilling, Philadelphia 319
1998	Tom Glavine, Atlanta 20	Greg Maddux, Atlanta 2.22	Curt Schilling, Philadelphia 300
1999	Mike Hampton, Houston 22	Randy Johnson, Arizona 2.48	Randy Johnson, Arizona 364

Two-way threat
Edgardo Alfonzo's glove and bat paced the Mets

said. "We don't have a trophy, but they did everything they had to."

Wild Ride

That the Mets were in position to win a championship, with Valentine at the helm, came as a surprise after a roller-coaster season.

They stumbled out of the gate, losing seven straight in May, and at one point were just 27-28, prompting general manager Steve Phillips to fire pitching coach Bob Apodaca. Valentine stirred up controversy by claiming that if the Mets didn't turn their season around in the next 55 games, he would be gone, too.

The Mets did turn it around behind an airtight infield defense, a slugging lineup and a versatile, deep bullpen. The Mets caught the Braves for the division lead before falling a game behind heading into their pivotal series in Atlanta in September, when Jones virtually clinched the division with his four-homer performance.

The sweep sent the Mets into a seven-game spiral, not only dropping them out of contention in the East but also behind the Astros and Reds in the wild-card race. Heading into the season's final weekend, New York trailed Cincinnati by two games for the wild card, while Houston led the Reds by a game in the NL Central.

At the end of the skid, Valentine said he should be fired if the Mets missed the playoffs. Valentine certainly didn't have the tightest grip on his team. Rickey Henderson and Bobby Bonilla missed the latter stages of the Mets' thriller in Game Six of the LCS playing cards in the clubhouse. Henderson's lack of hustle earlier in the series had prompted reliever Turk Wendell to label him a quitter.

The turmoil that bubbled over in the postseason almost kept the Mets from getting there, but the veteran club proved resilient. It battled the Pirates at Shea Stadium, winning all three games, including the finale on a wild pitch.

The Astros, ravaged by injuries to Moises Alou, Ken Caminiti and rookie catcher Mitch Meluskey, rode Jeff Bagwell and Craig Biggio to another Central Division title, beating the Dodgers on the final weekend. Lefthander Mike Hampton (22-4, 2.90 ERA), who led the NL in wins, pitched on three days rest in the clincher after righthander Jose Lima (21-10) won the day before.

The Reds lost their first two games in Milwaukee, then had to wait out a rain delay that lasted almost six hours. Finally, with about 400 fans left at County Stadium, Pete Harnisch pitched the Reds past the Brewers.

That set up a one-game playoff for the wild card, the second straight year it was decided in Game 163. Leiter took command for New York and Edgardo Alfonzo hit a two-run homer in the first inning as the Mets cruised to a 5-0 victory. The win moved New York into the playoffs for the first time since 1988.

The loss spoiled a surprise season by the Reds, whose $33 million payroll was the lowest among NL playoff contenders. Manager Jack McKeon used a potent bullpen, led by NL rookie of the year Scott Williamson (12-7, 2.41 ERA, 19 saves) to supplement a patchwork rotation anchored by Harnisch (16-10).

McKeon coaxed plenty of offense from a blend of young talents such as first baseman Sean Casey (.332 with 25 home runs) and second baseman Pokey Reese (38 stolen bases) and veterans like Greg Vaughn (45 homers, 118 RBIs).

No Sophomore Slump

Once they got into the playoffs, the Mets dispatched the surprising Diamondbacks, who won the NL West. The division was tabbed as the NL's strongest in the preseason, but Arizona won 100 games and dominated. The Giants contended for much of the summer but couldn't overcome injuries that claimed, at various times, Barry Bonds, Ellis Burks, Jeff Kent and Robb Nen.

The Rockies struggled under manager Jim Leyland, who announced his retirement late in the season. The defending league champion Padres, who lost Kevin Brown to free agency and traded Vaughn in the offseason, played inconsistently. They had a 14-game winning streak, the NL's longest, but generally had trouble scoring runs and fell out of contention in August. And the Dodgers disintegrated into a team of malcontents, one that never seriously contended.

That left Arizona, buoyed by free-agent acquisitions such as lefthander Randy Johnson, righthanders Armando Reynoso and Todd

In and out
Jim Leyland

Stottlemyre and outfielder Steve Finley. Johnson got little support during the season—he once struck out 17 Cardinals and still lost 1-0 on the league's only no-hitter, thrown by rookie righthander Jose Jimenez.

But Johnson was the league's most dominant pitcher. He finished 17-9, with a 2.48 ERA and 364 strikeouts in 272 innings. Only Sandy Koufax, with 382 in

1965, had more strikeouts in a season in NL history. When Johnson wasn't pitching, the Diamondbacks displayed plenty of offense, led by the career years of second baseman Jay Bell (38 home runs and 112 RBIs) and outfielder Luis Gonzalez (.336 with 111 RBIs).

The Giants narrowed the gap on Arizona in mid-July and traded for righthander Livan Hernandez, so the Diamondbacks answered. They too went to the Marlins for help, acquiring closer Matt Mantei to solidify their bullpen. Mantei posted a 2.79 ERA for Arizona with 22 saves in 30 games to help the Diamondbacks reach the playoffs quicker than any expansion team in baseball history.

"This business is all about winning," team owner Jerry Colangelo said. "When I got into it, I wanted to win. People took their shots, but we operated by the rules. We wanted to compete. We did set out to make the playoffs in the second year. Obviously, you feel good about reaching goals. There is some satisfaction there."

McGwire-Sosa Part II

While the top of the league dealt with pennant races, many fans seemed more interested in the individual heroes of 1998 reprising their performances. Cardinals first baseman Mark McGwire and Cubs outfielder Sammy Sosa did have another home run race in 1999, albeit with less fanfare.

While both sluggers started slowly in comparison to '98, they picked up the pace as the weather heated up. McGwire hit 20 home runs in a 35-game span in July and August, while Sosa slugged 17 in 30 games. Sosa stayed hot in early September and kept a slim lead, but in the end Big Mac had a bigger finishing kick. McGwire's final tally, 65, included his 500th homer on Aug. 5 off San Diego's Andy Ashby and put him at 522 for his career, past Willie McCovey and Ted Williams and into 10th place all-time.

First to 60
Sammy Sosa

Sosa, who finished with 63, has now hit 129 homers the last two seasons and has yet to win a home run title. He did beat McGwire to 60 in 1999, becoming the first player to put together back-to-back 60-homer seasons.

"The whole thing is just crazy," Padres outfielder Tony Gwynn said in August. "Think about the transformation. Once, 61 looked like it couldn't be touched. Then these two guys just went right by it. Now 70 is the number, and they're right back doing it again."

Last Roundup

■ Gwynn clinched his spot in the Hall of Fame by becoming the 22nd player to reach 3,000 hits, doing it Aug. 6 at Montreal's Olympic Stadium against the Expos' Dan Smith. Gwynn got the hit on his mother's 64th birthday, six years to the day after collecting hit No. 2,000.

"The relief you feel is the first thing you think

about," Gwynn said. "Then I started to feel emotional. When I got back to the dugout, I couldn't sit down."

■ McGwire wasn't the Cardinals' only notable slugger. Third baseman Fernando Tatis became the first player in history to hit two grand slams in one inning, doing it in May at Dodger Stadium against Chan Ho Park.

"You have a better chance of winning the lottery," McGwire said. The Cardinals had not hit two grand slams in a game since 1929. Tatis went on to hit 34 home runs with 107 RBIs in his third season.

■ In a disappointing season for the team, outfielder Larry Walker provided the Rockies' biggest bright spot. Walker won his second consecutive batting championship, hitting .379, adding 37 homers and 115 RBIs. Walker also led the league in on-base (.458) and slugging percentage (.710). The last player to lead the NL in those three categories was the Cardinals' Stan Musial in 1943, while George Brett turned the

NL: BEST TOOLS

A Baseball America survey of National League managers, conducted at midseason 1999, ranked NL players with the best tools:

BEST HITTER
1. Tony Gwynn, Padres
2. Larry Walker, Rockies
3. Mike Piazza, Mets

BEST POWER HITTER
1. Mark McGwire, Cardinals
2. Sammy Sosa, Cubs
3. Jeff Bagwell, Astros

BEST BUNTER
1. Craig Biggio, Astros
2. Roger Cedeno, Mets
3. Tony Womack, D'backs

BEST HIT-AND-RUN BATTER
1. Tony Gwynn, Padres
2. Mark Loretta, Brewers
3. Jay Bell, Diamondbacks

BEST BASERUNNER
1. Larry Walker, Rockies
2. Barry Larkin, Reds
3. Craig Biggio, Astros

FASTEST BASERUNNER
1. Tony Womack, D'backs
2. Roger Cedeno, Mets
3. Eric Young, Dodgers

BEST PITCHER
1. Randy Johnson, D'backs
2. Curt Schilling, Phillies
3. Kevin Brown, Dodgers

BEST FASTBALL
1. Randy Johnson, D'backs
2. Billy Wagner, Astros
3. Curt Schilling, Phillies

BEST CURVEBALL
1. Darryl Kile, Rockies
2. Russ Ortiz, Giants
3. Mike Hampton, Astros

BEST SLIDER
1. John Smoltz, Braves
2. Randy Johnson, D'backs
3. Robb Nen, Giants

BEST CHANGEUP
1. Greg Maddux, Braves
2. Trevor Hoffman, Padres
3. Tom Glavine, Braves

BEST CONTROL
1. Greg Maddux, Braves
2. Shane Reynolds, Astros
3. Kevin Brown, Dodgers

BEST PICKOFF MOVE
1. Armando Reynoso, D'backs
2. Terry Mulholland, Cubs
3. Jesus Sanchez, Marlins

BEST RELIEVER
1. Billy Wagner, Astros
2. Robb Nen, Giants
3. Trevor Hoffman, Padres

BEST DEFENSIVE C
1. Jason Kendall, Pirates
2. Mike Lieberthal, Phillies
3. Javy Lopez, Braves

BEST DEFENSIVE 1B
1. J.T. Snow, Giants
2. Mark Grace, Cubs
3. Jeff Bagwell, Astros

BEST DEFENSIVE 2B
1. Bret Boone, Reds
2. Craig Biggio, Astros
3. Pokey Reese, Reds

BEST DEFENSIVE 3B
1. Scott Rolen, Phillies
2. Matt Williams, D'backs
3. Robin Ventura, Mets

BEST DEFENSIVE SS
1. Rey Ordonez, Mets
2. Barry Larkin, Reds
3. Alex Gonzalez, Marlins

BEST INFIELD ARM
1. Scott Rolen, Phillies
2. Adrian Beltre, Dodgers
3. Ken Caminiti, Padres

BEST DEFENSIVE OF
1. Andruw Jones, Braves
2. Larry Walker, Rockies
3. Barry Bonds, Giants

BEST OUTFIELD ARM
1. Vladimir Guerrero, Expos
2. Raul Mondesi, Dodgers
3. Larry Walker, Rockies

MOST EXCITING PLAYER
1. Sammy Sosa, Cubs
2. Mark McGwire, Cardinals
3. Larry Walker, Rockies

BEST MANAGER
1. Dusty Baker, Giants
2. Bruce Bochy, Padres
3. Bobby Cox, Braves

NATIONAL LEAGUE
DEPARTMENT LEADERS

BATTING

GAMES
Jeff Bagwell, Astros 162
Andruw Jones, Braves 162
John Olerud, Mets 162
Sammy Sosa, Cubs 162
Mark Grace, Cubs 161
Barry Larkin, Reds 161
J.T. Snow, Giants 161
Robin Ventura, Mets 161

AT-BATS
Neifi Perez, Rockies 690
Craig Biggio, Astros 639
Edgardo Alfonzo, Mets 628
Doug Glanville, Phillies 628
Matt Williams, Diamondbacks 627

RUNS
Jeff Bagwell, Astros 143
Jay Bell, Diamondbacks 132
Edgrado Alfonzo, Mets 123
Craig Biggio, Astros 123
Bobby Abreu, Phillies....................... 118
Mark McGwire, Cardinals 118

HITS
Luis Gonzalez, Diamondbacks 206
Doug Glanville, Phillies 204
Jeff Cirillo, Brewers 198
Sean Casey, Reds............................. 197
Vladimir Guerrero, Expos 193
Neifi Perez, Rockies 193

TOTAL BASES
Sammy Sosa, Cubs 397
Vladimir Guerrero, Expos 366
Mark McGwire, Cardinals 363
Chipper Jones, Braves 359
Todd Helton, Rockies 359

EXTRA-BASE HITS
Sammy Sosa, Cubs 89
Mark McGwire, Cardinals 87
Chipper Jones, Braves 87
Vladimir Guerrero, Expos 84
Todd Helton, Rockies 79

SINGLES
Doug Glanville, Phillies 149
Jeff Cirillo, Brewers 147
Neifi Perez, Rockies 143
Tony Womack, Diamondbacks 131
Luis Gonzalez, Diamondbacks 131

DOUBLES
Craig Biggio, Astros 56

Batting champion
Larry Walker

Career year
Luis Gonzalez

Luis Gonzalez, Diamondbacks 45
Jose Vidro, Expos 45
Mark Grace, Cubs 44
Geoff Jenkins, Brewers 43

TRIPLES
Bobby Abreu, Phillies 11
Neifi Perez, Rockies........................... 11
Steve Finley, Diamondbacks 10
Tony Womack, Diamondbacks 10
Mike Cameron, Reds 9
Mark Kotsay, Marlins 9

HOME RUNS
Mark McGwire, Cardinals 65
Sammy Sosa, Cubs 63
Chipper Jones, Braves 45
Greg Vaughn, Reds 45
Jeff Bagwell, Astros 42
Vladimir Guerrero, Expos 42

HOME RUN RATIO
(At-Bats per Home Run)
Mark McGwire, Cardinals 8.0
Sammy Sosa, Cubs 9.9
Larry Walker, Rockies...................... 11.8
Greg Vaughn, Reds 12.2
Chipper Jones, Braves 12.6

RUNS BATTED IN
Mark McGwire, Cardinals................. 147
Matt Williams, Diamondbacks 142
Sammy Sosa, Cubs 141
Dante Bichette, Rockies................... 133
Vladimir Guerrero, Expos................. 131

SACRIFICE BUNTS
Shane Reynolds, Astros 17
Greg Maddux, Braves 13
Jose Lima, Astros 13
Abraham Nunez, Pirates 13
Kevin Brown, Dodgers 13

SACRIFICE FLIES
Mark Grace, Cubs 10
Dante Bichette, Rockies..................... 10
Gary Sheffield, Dodgers.....................9
Jay Bell, Diamondbacks........................ 9
Edgardo Alfonzo, Mets 9
Brian Jordan, Braves 9
Mark Kotsay, Marlins 9

HIT BY PITCH
Ed Sprague, Pirates........................... 17
Jeromy Burnitz, Brewers 16
Fernando Tatis, Cardinals 16
Kevin Young, Pirates 12
Jason Kendall, Pirates 12

Larry Walker, Rockies 12
Alex Gonzalez, Marlins 12

WALKS
Jeff Bagwell, Astros 149
Mark McGwire, Cardinals.................. 133
Chpper Jones, Braves 126
John Olerud, Mets 125
Bobby Abreu, Phillies........................ 109

INTENTIONAL WALKS
Mark McGwire, Cardinals.................. 21
Chipper Jones, Braves 18
Jeff Bagwell, Astros 16
Vladimir Guerrero, Expos.................. 14
Sean Casey, Reds 13

STRIKEOUTS
Sammy Sosa, Cubs 171
Preston Wilson, Marlins 156
Jose Hernandez, Cubs/Braves 145
Mike Cameron, Reds 145
Ruben Rivera, Padres 143

TOUGHEST TO STRIKE OUT
(Plate Appearances per SO)
Eric Young, Dodgers........................ 20.5
Mark Grace, Cubs............................. 15.6
Darryl Hamilton, Rockies/Mets 14.6
Neifi Perez, Rockies 13.6
Barry Larkin, Reds 12.1

STOLEN BASES
Tony Womack, Diamondbacks 72
Roger Cedeno, Mets 66
Eric Young, Dodgers 51
Luis Castillo, Marlins 50
Mike Cameron, Reds 38
Pokey Reese, Reds 38

CAUGHT STEALING
Eric Young, Dodgers 22
Luis Castillo, Marlins 17
Roger Cedeno, Mets 17
Quilvio Veras, Padres 17
Marvin Benard, Giants 14
Craig Biggio, Astros 14
Rickey Henderson, Mets 14

GIDP
Mike Piazza, Mets 27
John Olerud, Mets 22
Chipper Jones, Braves 20
Derek Bell, Astros 20
Jeff Bagwell, Astros 18
Rico Brogna, Phillies 18
Michael Barrett, Expos 18
Vladimir Guerrero, Expos.................. 18
Eric Karros, Dodgers 18

HITTING STREAKS
Vladimir Guerrero, Expos.................. 31
Luis Gonzalez, Diamondbacks 30
Joe McEwing, Cardinals 25
Mike Piazza, Mets 24
Luis Castillo, Marlins 22

MULTIPLE-HIT GAMES
Sean Casey, Reds 66
Jeff Cirillo, Brewers 64
Doug Glanville, Phillies 62
Luis Gonzalez, Diamondbacks 61
Neifi Perez, Rockies........................... 60

SLUGGING PERCENTAGE
Larry Walker, Rockies .... .710
Mark McGwire, Cardinals .... .697
Sammy Sosa, Cubs .... .635
Chipper Jones, Braves .... .633
Brian Giles, Pirates .... .614

ON-BASE PERCENTAGE
Larry Walker, Rockies...................... .458
Mark McGwire, Cardinals .... .454
Bobby Abreu, Phillies .... .446
Chipper Jones, Braves .... .441

John Olerud, Mets............................ .427

PITCHING

WINS
Mike Hampton, Astros 22
Jose Lima, Astros 21
Greg Maddux, Braves 19
Kent Bottenfield, Cardinals 18
Kevin Millwood, Braves 18
Kevin Brown, Dodgers 18
Russ Ortiz, Giants 18

LOSSES
Steve Trachsel, Cubs 18
Dennis Springer, Marlins 16
Brian Meadows, Marlins....................... 15
Several tied at 14

WINNING PERCENTAGE
Mike Hampton, Astros....................... .846
Steve Parris, Reds .... .733
Kent Bottenfield, Cardinals .... .720
Kevin Millwood, Braves.................... .720
Curt Schilling, Phillies .... .714

GAMES
Steve Kline, Expos............................. 82
Turk Wendell, Mets 80
Scott Sullivan, Reds 79
Anthony Telford, Expos 79
Armando Benitez, Mets 77

GAMES STARTED
Jose Lima, Astros 35
Shane Reynolds, Astros 35
Kevin Brown, Dodgers 35
Randy Johnson, Diamondbacks 35
Tom Glavine, Braves 35

COMPLETE GAMES
Randy Johnson, Diamondbacks 12
Curt Schilling, Phillies 8
Pedro Astacio, Rockies 7
Kevin Brown, Dodgers 5
Steve Trachsel, Cubs 4
Greg Maddux, Braves 4
Shane Reynolds, Astros 4
Andy Ashby, Padres 4

SHUTOUTS
Andy Ashby, Padres 3
Several tied at 2

GAMES FINISHED
Robb Nen, Giants 64
Dave Veres, Rockies 63
Bob Wickman, Brewers 63
Ugueth Urbina, Expos 62
John Rocker, Braves 61

SAVES
Ugueth Urbina, Expos 41
Trevor Hoffman, Padres...................... 40
Billy Wagner, Astros 39
John Rocker, Braves 38
Robb Nen, Giants 37
Bob Wickman, Brewers 37

INNINGS
Randy Johnson, Diamondbacks 272
Kevin Brown, Dodgers 252
Jose Lima, Astros 246
Mike Hampton, Astros 239
Tom Glavine, Braves 234

HITS ALLOWED
Tom Glavine, Braves 259
Greg Maddux, Braves 258
Pedro Astacio, Rockies 258
Jose Lima, Astros 256
Shane Reynolds, Astros 250

RUNS ALLOWED
Darryl Kile, Rockies 150
Brain Bohanon, Rockies 146
Pedro Astacio, Rockies 140
Steve Trachsel, Cubs 133
Dennis Springer, Marlins 121
Scott Karl, Brewers 121
Shawn Estes, Giants 121

HOME RUNS ALLOWED
Pedro Astacio, Rockies 38
Chad Ogea, Phillies 36
Paul Byrd, Phillies 34
Andy Benes, Diamondbacks 34
Woody Williams, Padres 33
Darryl Kile, Rockies 33

WALKS
Russ Ortiz, Giants 125
Shawn Estes, Giants 112
Darryle Kile, Rockies 109
Mike Hampton, Astros 101
Chan Ho Park, Dodgers.................... 100

FEWEST WALKS PER 9 INNINGS
Shane Reynolds, Astros 1.4
Greg Maddux, Braves 1.5
Jose Lima, Astros 1.6
Steve Woodard, Brewers 1.8
John Smoltz, Braves 1.9

HIT BATSMEN
Paul Byrd, Phillies 17
Brian Bohanon, Rockies 14
Chan Ho Park, Dodgers..................... 14
Darren Oliver, Cardinals 11
Orel Hershiser, Mets 11
Jose Jimenez, Cardinals 11
Pedro Astacio, Rockies 11

STRIKEOUTS
Randy Johnson, Diamondbacks 364
Kevin Brown, Dodgers 221
Pedro Astacio, Rockies 210
Kevin Millwood, Braves 205
Shane Reynolds, Astros 197

STRIKEOUTS PER 9 INNINGS
Randy Johnson, Diamondbacks 12.1
Sterling Hitchcock, Padres 8.5
Jon Lieber, Cubs............................... 8.2
Hideo Nomo, Brewers....................... 8.2
Pedro Astacio, Rockies..................... 8.2

PICKOFFS
Todd Ritchie, Pirates 6
Ron Villone, Reds 5
Several tied at 4

WILD PITCHES
Shawn Estes, Giants 15
Sterling Hitchcock, Padres................. 15
Russ Ortiz, Giants 13
Scott Williamson, Reds 13
Darryl Kile, Rockies 13

BALKS
Darren Dreifort, Dodgers 4
Jason Schmidt, Pirates 4

OPPONENTS BATTING AVERAGE
Kevin Millwood, Braves..................... .202

Singles guy
Doug Glanville

Randy Johnson, Diamondbacks ...... .208
Kevin Brown, Dodgers .... .222
Omar Daal, Diamondbacks............... .236
Curt Schilling, Phillies .... .237

FIELDING

PITCHER
PCT Shane Reynolds, Astros 1.000
PO   Kevin Brown, Dodgers 41
A   Tom Glavine, Braves 59
E   Three tied at.............................. 6
TC   Kevin Brown, Dodgers 93
DP   Three ties at.............................. 6

CATCHER
PCT Mike Lieberthal, Phillies .... .997
PO   Mike Piazza, Mets 953
A   Mike Lieberthal, Phillies 61
E   Todd Hundley, Dodgers........... 16
TC   Mike Piazza, Mets 1011
DP   Four tied at.............................. 12
PB   Two tied at.............................. 11

FIRST BASE
PCT Travis Lee, Diamondbacks .... .997
PO   Kevin Young, Pirates 1413
A   Eric Karros, Dodgers 126
E   Kevin Young, Pirates 23
TC   Kevin Young, Pirates 1533
DP   Todd Helton, Rockies 152

SECOND BASE
PCT Edgardo Alfonzo, Mets .... .993
PO   Craig Biggio, Astros 359
A   Craig Biggio, Astros 430
E   Jay Bell, Diamondbacks 22
TC   Craig Biggio, Astros 804
DP   Craig Biggio, Astros 117

THIRD BASE
PCT Robin Ventura, Mets .... .980
PO   Jeff Cirillo, Brewers 125
A   Robin Ventura, Mets 320
E   Two tied at.............................. 29
TC   Robin Ventura, Mets 451
DP   Jeff Cirillo, Brewers 34

SHORTSTOP
PCT Rey Ordonez, Mets............... .994
PO   Neifi Perez, Rockies 260
A   Neifi Perez, Rockies 480
E   Rich Aurilia, Giants 28
TC   Neifi Perez, Rockies 755
DP   Neifi Perez, Rockies 124

OUTFIELD
PCT Darryl Hamilton, Rockies/Mets .. .997
PO   Andruw Jones, Braves............ 492
A   Mark Kotsay, Marlins 19
E   Vladimir Guerrero, Expos 19
TC   Andruw Jones, Braves............ 516
DP   J.D. Drew, Cardinals 6

Big winner
Mike Hampton

1999 National League Statistics

CLUB BATTING

	AVG	G	AB	R	H	2B	3B	HR	BB	SO	SB
Colorado	.289	162	5716	906	1644	305	39	223	508	863	70
New York	.279	163	5572	853	1553	297	14	181	717	994	150
Arizona	.277	162	5658	908	1566	289	46	216	588	1045	137
Philadelphia	.275	162	5598	841	1539	302	44	161	631	1081	125
Milwaukee	.273	161	5582	815	1524	299	30	165	658	1065	81
Cincinnati	.272	163	5649	865	1536	312	37	209	569	1125	164
San Francisco	.271	162	5563	872	1507	307	18	188	696	1028	109
Houston	.267	162	5485	823	1463	293	23	168	728	1138	166
Atlanta	.266	162	5569	840	1481	309	23	197	608	962	148
Los Angeles	.266	162	5567	793	1480	253	23	187	594	1030	167
Montreal	.265	162	5559	718	1473	320	47	163	438	939	70
Florida	.263	162	5578	691	1465	266	44	128	479	1145	92
St. Louis	.262	161	5570	809	1461	274	27	194	613	1202	134
Pittsburgh	.259	161	5468	775	1417	282	40	171	573	1197	112
Chicago	.257	162	5482	747	1411	255	35	189	571	1170	60
San Diego	.252	162	5394	710	1360	256	22	153	631	1169	174

CLUB PITCHING

	ERA	G	CG	SHO	SV	IP	H	R	ER	BB	SO
Atlanta	3.65	162	9	1	45	1471	1398	661	596	507	1197
Arizona	3.77	162	16	4	42	1467	1387	676	615	543	1198
Houston	3.84	162	12	5	48	1459	1485	675	622	478	1204
Cincinnati	3.99	163	6	3	55	1462	1309	711	648	636	1081
New York	4.27	163	5	3	49	1457	1372	711	691	617	1172
Pittsburgh	4.35	161	8	0	34	1433	1444	782	692	633	1083
Los Angeles	4.45	162	8	3	37	1453	1438	787	718	594	1077
San Diego	4.47	162	5	3	43	1420	1454	781	705	529	1078
Montreal	4.69	162	6	3	44	1434	1505	853	748	572	1043
San Francisco	4.71	162	6	1	42	1456	1486	831	762	655	1076
St. Louis	4.76	161	5	3	38	1445	1519	838	764	667	1025
Florida	4.90	162	6	2	33	1436	1560	852	781	655	943
Philadelphia	4.93	162	11	2	32	1438	1494	846	788	627	1030
Milwaukee	5.06	161	2	0	40	1442	1618	886	815	616	987
Chicago	5.27	162	11	3	32	1431	1619	920	837	529	980
Colorado	6.03	162	12	1	33	1429	1700	1028	957	737	1032

CLUB FIELDING

	PCT	PO	A	E	DP		PCT	PO	A	E	DP
New York	.989	4370	1607	68	147	Florida	.979	4307	1682	127	150
Arizona	.983	4402	1580	104	132	Milwaukee	.979	4328	1657	127	146
Cincinnati	.983	4386	1547	105	139	San Diego	.979	4261	1635	129	151
Houston	.983	4376	1729	106	175	Los Angeles	.978	4359	1719	137	137
Philadelphia	.983	4315	1593	100	144	St. Louis	.978	4336	1626	132	163
San Francisco	.983	4369	1627	105	155	Chicago	.977	4292	1598	139	135
Atlanta	.982	4413	1651	111	127	Pittsburgh	.976	4300	1740	147	179
Colorado	.981	4287	1736	118	189	Montreal	.974	4303	1622	160	125

INDIVIDUAL BATTING LEADERS
(Minimum 502 Plate Appearances)

	AVG	G	AB	R	H	2B	3B	HR	RBI	BB	SO	SB
Walker, Larry, Colorado	.379	127	438	108	166	26	4	37	115	57	52	11
Gonzalez, Luis, Arizona	.336	153	614	112	206	45	4	26	111	66	63	9
Abreu, Bob, Philadelphia	.335	152	546	118	183	35	11	20	93	109	113	27
Casey, Sean, Cincinnati	.332	151	594	103	197	42	3	25	99	61	88	0
Cirillo, Jeff, Milwaukee	.326	157	607	98	198	35	1	15	88	75	83	7
Grudzielanek, Mark, L.A.	.326	123	488	72	159	23	5	7	46	31	65	6
Everett, Carl, Houston	.325	123	464	86	151	33	3	25	108	50	94	27
Glanville, Doug, Phil.	.325	150	628	101	204	38	6	11	73	48	82	34
Helton, Todd, Colorado	.320	159	578	114	185	39	5	35	113	68	77	7
Jones, Chipper, Atlanta	.319	157	567	116	181	41	1	45	110	126	94	25

INDIVIDUAL PITCHING LEADERS
(Minimum 162 Innings)

	W	L	ERA	G	GS	CG	SV	IP	H	R	ER	BB	SO
Johnson, Randy, Arizona	17	8	2.48	35	35	12	0	272	207	86	75	70	364
Millwood, Kevin, Atlanta	18	7	2.68	33	33	2	0	228	168	80	68	59	205
Hampton, Mike, Houston	22	4	2.90	34	34	3	0	239	206	86	77	101	177
Brown, Kevin, Los Angeles	18	9	3.00	35	35	5	0	252	210	99	84	59	221
Smoltz, John, Atlanta	11	8	3.19	29	29	1	0	186	168	70	66	40	156
Ritchie, Todd, Pittsburgh	15	9	3.49	28	26	2	0	173	169	79	67	54	107
Schilling, Curt, Phil.	15	6	3.54	24	24	8	0	180	159	74	71	44	152
Maddux, Greg, Atlanta	19	9	3.57	33	33	4	0	219	258	103	87	37	136
Lima, Jose, Houston	21	10	3.58	35	35	3	0	246	256	108	98	44	187
Daal, Omar, Arizona	16	9	3.65	32	32	2	0	215	188	92	87	79	148

AWARD WINNERS

Selected by Baseball Writers Association of America

MVP

Player, Team	1st	2nd	3rd	Total
Chipper Jones, Atl.	29	2	1	432
Jeff Bagwell, Houston	1	20	6	276
Matt Williams, Arizona	2	7	21	269
Greg Vaughn, Cin.	0	1	2	121
Mark McGwire, St.L.	0	1	1	115
Robin Ventura, N.Y.	0	1	0	113
Mike Piazza, N.Y.	0	0	0	109
Edgardo Alfonzo, N.Y.	0	0	1	88
Sammy Sosa, Chicago	0	0	0	87
Larry Walker, Col.	0	0	0	35
Vladimir Guerrero, Mon.	0	0	0	34
Craig Biggio, Hou.	0	0	0	32
Jay Bell, Arizona	0	0	0	31
Sean Casey, Cin.	0	0	0	23
Randy Johnson, Ariz.	0	0	0	21
Billy Wagner, Hou.	0	0	0	19
Carl Everett, Hou.	0	0	0	15
Luis Gonzalez, Ariz.	0	0	0	12
Brian Jordan, Atlanta	0	0	0	11
Brian Giles, Pitt.	0	0	0	11
Mike Hampton, Hou.	0	0	0	10
Barry Larkin, Cin.	0	0	0	7
Bob Abreu, Phil.	0	0	0	6
Barry Bonds, S.F.	0	0	0	3
Matt Mantei, Arizona	0	0	0	3
Jeff Kent, S.F.	0	0	0	2
Kevin Millwood, Atl.	0	0	0	2
Trevor Hoffman, S.D.	0	0	0	1

CY YOUNG AWARD

Player, Team	1st	2nd	3rd	Total
Randy Johnson, Ariz.	20	11	1	134
Mike Hampton, Hou.	11	17	4	110
Kevin Millwood, Atl.	1	4	19	36
Jose Lima, Houston	0	0	3	3
Billy Wagner, Houston	0	0	3	3
Kevin Brown, L.A.	0	0	1	1
Trevor Hoffman, S.D.	0	0	1	1

ROOKIE OF THE YEAR

Player, Team	1st	2nd	3rd	Total
Scott Williamson, Cin.	17	9	6	118
Preston Wilson, Fla.	9	11	10	88
Warren Morris, Pitt.	6	10	9	69
Kris Benson, Pitt.	0	1	2	5
Alex Gonzalez, Fla.	0	1	1	4
Joe McEwing, St.L.	0	0	3	3
Kevin McGlinchy, Atl.	0	0	1	1

MANAGER OF THE YEAR

Manager, Team	1st	2nd	3rd	Total
Jack McKeon, Cin.	17	9	3	115
Bobby Cox, Atlanta	10	14	6	98
Larry Dierker, Hou.	4	6	10	48
Buck Showalter, Ariz.	1	1	9	17
Bobby Valentine, N.Y.	0	2	4	10

NOTE: MVP balloting based on 14 points for first place vote, nine for second, eight for third, etc.; Cy Young Award, Rookie of the Year and Manager of the Year balloting based on five points for first-place vote, three for second and one for third.

GOLD GLOVE AWARDS

Selected by NL managers

C—Mike Lieberthal, Philadelphia. **1B**—J.T. Snow, San Francisco. **2B**—Pokey Reese, Cincinnati. **3B**—Robin Ventura, New York. **SS**—Rey Ordonez, New York. **OF**—Steve Finley, Arizona; Andruw Jones, Atlanta; Larry Walker, Colorado. **P**—Greg Maddux, Atlanta.

Player, Pos.	AVG	G	AB	R	H	2B	3B	HR	RBI	BB	SO	SB
Brett Boone, 2b	.474	4	19	3	9	1	0	0	1	0	4	1
Brian Jordan, rf	.471	4	17	2	8	1	0	1	7	1	2	0
Gerald Williams, lf	.389	4	18	2	7	1	0	0	3	0	3	1
Ryan Klesko, 1b	.333	4	12	3	4	0	0	0	1	1	4	0
Kevin Millwood, p	.250	2	4	0	1	0	0	0	0	0	3	0
Eddie Perez, c	.250	4	16	1	4	0	0	0	3	0	3	0
Chipper Jones, 3b	.231	4	13	2	3	0	0	0	1	5	2	0
Andruw Jones, cf	.222	4	18	1	4	1	0	0	2	1	3	0
Walt Weiss, ss	.167	3	6	1	1	0	0	0	0	0	2	0
Jose Hernandez, ss	.091	4	11	1	1	0	0	0	0	1	3	1
Howard Battle, ph	.000	1	1	0	0	0	0	0	0	0	0	0
Tom Glavine, p	.000	1	2	0	0	0	0	0	0	0	1	0
Ozzie Guillen, ss	.000	1	1	0	0	0	0	0	0	0	0	0
Brian Hunter, 1b	.000	3	4	0	0	0	0	0	0	1	3	0
Keith Lockhart, ph-pr	.000	3	1	0	0	0	0	0	0	0	1	0
Greg Maddux, p	.000	2	1	0	0	0	0	0	0	0	1	0
John Rocker, p	.000	2	0	0	0	0	0	0	0	1	0	0
Totals	**.304**	**4**	**148**	**18**	**45**	**5**	**0**	**1**	**18**	**11**	**31**	**4**

Pitcher	W	L	ERA	G	GS	SV	IP	H	R	ER	BB	SO
Kevin McGlinchy	0	0	0.00	1	0	0	1	0	0	0	0	0
John Rocker	1	0	0.00	2	0	1	3	0	0	0	2	5
Russ Springer	0	0	0.00	1	0	0	1	2	0	0	1	1
Kevin Millwood	1	0	0.90	2	1	0	10	1	1	1	0	9
Greg Maddux	0	1	2.57	2	1	0	7	10	2	2	5	5
Tom Glavine	0	0	3.00	1	1	0	6	5	2	2	3	6
John Smoltz	1	0	5.14	1	1	0	7	6	4	4	3	3
Mike Remlinger	0	0	9.82	2	0	0	4	4	4	4	3	4
Terry Mulholland	0	0	27.00	2	0	0	1	3	2	2	0	0
Totals	**3**	**1**	**3.46**	**4**	**4**	**2**	**39**	**31**	**15**	**15**	**17**	**33**

HOUSTON

Player, Pos.	AVG	G	AB	R	H	2B	3B	HR	RBI	BB	SO	SB
Russ Johnson, ph	1.000	2	1	0	1	1	0	0	0	1	0	0
Tim Bogar, ss	.750	2	4	0	3	1	0	0	1	1	0	0
Ken Caminiti, 3b	.471	4	17	3	8	0	0	3	8	2	1	0
Derek Bell, rf	.333	2	3	0	1	0	0	0	0	0	0	0
Stan Javier, rf	.273	4	11	1	3	0	0	0	0	1	1	0
Bill Spiers, lf	.273	4	11	0	3	0	0	0	1	0	1	1
Tony Eusebio, c	.267	4	15	2	4	0	0	1	3	1	2	0
Shane Reynolds, p	.250	2	4	0	1	0	0	0	0	0	0	0
Jeff Bagwell, 1b	.154	4	13	3	2	0	0	0	0	5	4	0
Daryle Ward, rf-lf	.143	3	7	1	1	0	0	1	1	0	2	0
Carl Everett, cf	.133	4	15	2	2	0	0	0	1	2	8	1
Craig Biggio, 2b	.105	4	19	1	2	0	0	0	1	5	0	0
Glen Barker, pr-of	.000	2	3	1	0	0	0	0	0	0	2	1
Ricky Gutierrez, ss	.000	3	10	0	0	0	0	0	0	2	5	0
Mike Hampton, p	.000	1	2	0	0	0	0	0	0	0	1	0
Jose Lima, p	.000	1	2	0	0	0	0	0	0	0	1	0
Matt Mieske, rf	.000	2	4	1	0	0	0	0	0	1	0	0
Totals	**.220**	**4**	**141**	**15**	**31**	**2**	**0**	**5**	**15**	**17**	**33**	**3**

Pitcher	W	L	ERA	G	GS	SV	IP	H	R	ER	BB	SO
Jose Cabrera	0	0	0.00	1	0	0	2	2	0	0	0	6
Doug Henry	0	0	0.00	2	0	0	4	1	0	0	3	2
Trever Miller	0	0	0.00	2	0	0	1	1	0	0	0	2
Billy Wagner	0	0	0.00	1	0	0	1	0	0	0	0	1
Scott Elarton	0	0	3.86	2	0	0	2	4	1	1	1	3
Mike Hampton	0	0	3.86	1	1	0	7	6	3	3	1	9
Shane Reynolds	1	1	4.09	2	2	0	11	16	5	5	3	5
Jose Lima	0	1	5.40	1	1	0	7	9	4	4	2	4
Jay Powell	0	1	6.00	3	0	0	3	3	2	2	1	3
Chris Holt	0	0	---	1	0	0	0	3	3	3	0	0
Totals	**1**	**3**	**4.26**	**4**	**4**	**0**	**38**	**45**	**18**	**18**	**11**	**35**

SCORE BY INNINGS

Atlanta	201 019 300 002—18
Houston	220 001 244 000—15

E—Ward, Gutierrez, Eusebio, Spiers, C. Jones, Hernandez. **DP**—Atlanta 4, Houston 4. **LOB**—Atlanta 59, Houston 62. **CS**—Caminiti, Jordan. **S**—Barker, Reynolds, Maddux. **SF**—Everett, Perez, Jordan, C. Jones. **HBP**—Bagwell (by Glavine), Everett (by Smoltz).

LARRY GOREN

Speedy recovery
Larry Dierker came back from a frightening seizure to lead Houston to another division title

feat with the Royals in 1980.

■ Several of 1998's top stars never got on the field in '99. Cubs righthander Kerry Wood, Baseball America's 1998 Rookie of the Year, missed the season after having Tommy John surgery in spring training. The Braves played without first baseman Andres Galarraga, who had cancer in his back. And the Astros lost Alou to a knee injury in spring training.

■ Perhaps the strangest occurrence of spring training came when the Padres let country singer Garth Brooks suit up as a nonroster invitee to big league camp. Brooks, 37, didn't get a hit and gave up his quest at the end of the spring, though not before the Padres' minor league affiliates clamored for him to be assigned to them for the regular season. Brooks did it mostly to raise money for his foundation, which helps children's charities. The Padres donated $100,000 to the foundation instead of paying Brooks' salary.

■ The Astros played part of the season without manager Larry Dierker, who collapsed in the dugout July 13 in the eighth inning of a game against the Padres. Doctors said Dierker had a seizure caused when a collection of blood vessels dislodged in his brain. Dierker was hospitalized for 10 days but returned to the dugout to lead the Astros to their third straight division title.

NATIONAL LEAGUE
DIVISION SERIES

ATLANTA vs. HOUSTON
COMPOSITE BOX

ATLANTA

Player, Pos.	AVG	G	AB	R	H	2B	3B	HR	RBI	BB	SO	SB
Otis Nixon, ph	1.000	1	1	1	1	0	0	0	0	0	0	1
John Smoltz, p	.667	1	3	1	2	1	0	0	0	0	1	0

ARIZONA vs. NEW YORK
COMPOSITE BOX

ARIZONA

Player, Pos.	AVG	G	AB	R	H	2B	3B	HR	RBI	BB	SO	SB
Turner Ward, ph	.500	3	2	2	1	0	0	1	3	1	0	0
Greg Colbrunn, 1b	.400	2	5	1	2	1	0	1	2	2	2	0
Steve Finley, cf	.385	4	13	0	5	1	0	0	5	3	1	0
Matt Williams, 3b	.375	4	16	3	6	1	0	0	0	1	0	0
Randy Johnson, p	.333	1	3	0	1	0	0	0	0	0	1	0
Jay Bell, 2b	.286	4	14	3	4	1	0	0	3	1	0	0
Luis Gonzalez, lf	.200	4	10	3	2	1	0	1	2	5	1	0

Major Leagues

Player, Pos.	AVG	G	AB	R	H	2B	3B	HR	RBI	BB	SO	SB
Erubiel Durazo, 1b	.143	2	7	1	1	0	0	1	1	1	0	0
Kelly Stinnett, c	.143	4	14	1	2	1	0	0	0	1	4	0
Tony Womack, rf-ss	.111	4	18	2	2	0	1	0	0	6	0	0
Brian Anderson, p	.000	1	2	0	0	0	0	0	0	0	0	0
Omar Daal, p	.000	1	1	0	0	0	0	0	0	0	1	0
Andy Fox, ss	.000	1	3	0	0	0	0	0	0	0	1	0
Hanley Frias, ss-ph	.000	4	7	0	0	0	0	0	0	0	3	0
Bernard Gilkey, rf	.000	2	6	0	0	0	0	0	0	0	0	0
Lenny Harris, 3b-ph	.000	2	2	0	0	0	0	0	0	0	1	0
Todd Stottlemyre, p	.000	1	3	0	0	0	0	0	0	0	1	0
Totals	.206	4	126	16	26	7	1	4	16	14	22	0

Pitcher	W	L	ERA	G	GS	SV	IP	H	R	ER	BB	SO
Gregg Olson	0	0	0.00	2	0	0	1	0	1	0	1	0
Greg Swindell	0	0	0.00	3	0	0	3	1	0	0	3	1
Todd Stottlemyre	1	0	1.35	1	1	0	7	4	1	1	5	6
Brian Anderson	0	0	2.57	1	1	0	7	7	2	2	0	4
Bobby Chouinard	0	0	4.50	2	0	0	2	3	1	1	0	1
Matt Mantei	0	1	4.50	1	0	0	2	1	1	1	3	1
Omar Daal	0	1	6.75	1	1	0	4	6	3	3	3	4
Randy Johnson	0	1	7.56	1	1	0	8	8	7	7	3	11
Darren Holmes	0	0	27.00	1	0	0	1	1	4	4	3	0
Dan Plesac	0	0	54.00	1	0	0	1	3	2	2	0	0
Totals	1	3	5.35	4	4	0	35	34	22	21	21	28

NEW YORK

Player, Pos.	AVG	G	AB	R	H	2B	3B	HR	RBI	BB	SO	SB
John Olerud, 1b	.438	4	16	3	7	0	0	1	6	3	2	0
Rickey Henderson, lf	.400	4	15	5	6	0	0	0	1	3	1	6
Benny Agbayani, rf	.300	4	10	1	3	1	0	0	1	0	3	0
Roger Cedeno, rf	.286	4	7	1	2	0	0	0	2	1	1	1
Rey Ordonez, ss	.286	4	14	1	4	1	0	0	2	0	5	1
Edgardo Alfonzo, 2b	.250	4	16	6	4	1	0	3	6	3	2	0
Mike Piazza, c	.222	2	9	0	2	0	0	0	0	0	4	0
Robin Ventura, 3b	.214	4	14	1	3	2	0	0	1	4	2	0
Shawon Dunston, cf-rf	.167	4	6	0	1	0	0	0	0	0	1	0
Darryl Hamilton, cf	.125	4	8	0	1	0	0	0	2	2	0	0
Todd Pratt, c	.125	3	8	2	1	0	0	1	1	2	1	0
Bobby Bonilla, ph	.000	2	1	0	0	0	0	0	0	1	0	0
Melvin Mora, ph-lf	.000	3	1	1	0	0	0	0	0	1	0	0
Rick Reed, p	.000	1	1	0	0	0	0	0	0	0	1	0
Kenny Rogers, p	.000	1	2	0	0	0	0	0	0	0	2	0
Turk Wendell, p	.000	2	1	0	0	0	0	0	0	0	1	0
Masato Yoshii, p	.000	1	2	0	0	0	0	0	0	0	1	0
Matt Franco, ph	.000	1	0	0	0	0	0	0	0	0	1	0
Totals	.254	4	133	22	34	5	0	5	22	21	28	8

Pitcher	W	L	ERA	G	GS	SV	IP	H	R	ER	BB	SO
Armando Benitez	0	0	0.00	2	0	0	2	2	0	0	1	2
Dennis Cook	0	0	0.00	1	0	0	2	1	0	1	1	1
John Franco	1	0	0.00	3	0	0	4	1	0	0	0	2
Orel Hershiser	0	0	0.00	1	0	0	1	0	0	0	0	1
Turk Wendell	1	0	0.00	2	0	0	2	0	0	0	2	0
Rick Reed	1	0	3.00	1	1	0	6	4	2	2	3	2
Al Leiter	0	0	3.52	1	1	0	8	3	3	3	4	4
Pat Mahomes	0	0	5.40	1	0	0	2	3	1	1	0	1
Masato Yoshii	0	0	6.75	1	1	0	5	6	4	4	0	3
Kenny Rogers	0	1	8.31	1	1	0	4	5	4	4	2	6
Octavio Dotel	0	0	54.00	1	0	0	1	1	2	2	2	0
Totals	3	1	4.00	4	4	0	36	26	16	16	14	22

SCORE BY INNINGS

New York	115 207 014 1—22
Arizona	004 152 220 0—16

E—Womack 2, Bell, Daal, Fox. DP—New York 5, Arizona 2. LOB—Arizona 20, New York 32. CS—Bell. S—Ordonez 2, Reed, Mora. SF—Bell, Cedeno. HBP—Bell (by Leiter), Gonzalez (by Rogers), Colbrunn (by Dotel).

CHAMPIONSHIP SERIES

ATLANTA vs. NEW YORK

COMPOSITE BOX

ATLANTA

Player, Pos.	AVG	G	AB	R	H	2B	3B	HR	RBI	BB	SO	SB
Eddie Perez, c	.500	6	20	2	10	2	0	2	5	1	5	0
Jose Hernandez, ph	.500	2	2	0	1	0	0	0	0	2	1	0
Keith Lockhart, ph-2b	.400	3	5	0	2	0	1	0	1	0	2	0
Ozzie Guillen, ss-ph	.333	3	3	0	1	0	0	0	0	1	0	0

Player, Pos.	AVG	G	AB	R	H	2B	3B	HR	RBI	BB	SO	SB
Walt Weiss, ss	.286	6	21	2	6	2	0	0	1	2	4	2
Chipper Jones, 3b	.263	6	19	3	5	2	0	0	1	9	7	3
Andruw Jones, cf	.217	6	23	5	5	0	0	0	1	4	3	0
Brian Jordan, rf	.200	6	25	3	5	0	0	2	5	3	5	0
Bret Boone, 2b	.182	6	22	2	4	1	0	0	1	1	7	2
Gerald Williams, lf	.179	6	28	4	5	2	0	0	1	2	2	3
Ryan Klesko, 1b	.125	4	8	1	1	0	0	1	1	2	1	0
Brian Hunter, 1b-ph	.100	6	10	1	1	0	0	0	2	5	2	1
Greg Maddux, p	.000	2	5	0	0	0	0	0	0	0	4	0
Kevin Millwood, p	.000	2	4	0	0	0	0	0	0	1	0	0
Howard Battle, ph-1b	.000	3	2	0	0	0	0	0	0	0	2	1
John Smoltz, p	.000	3	2	0	0	0	0	0	0	0	0	0
Jorge Fabregas, ph	.000	2	2	0	0	0	0	0	0	0	1	0
Greg Myers, c	.000	2	2	0	0	0	0	0	0	1	1	0
Tom Glavine, p	.000	1	2	0	0	0	0	0	0	0	1	0
Kevin McGlinchy, p	.000	1	1	0	0	0	0	0	0	1	0	0
Otis Nixon, pr	.000	2	0	0	0	0	0	0	0	0	0	2
Totals	.223	6	206	24	46	9	1	5	22	31	47	14

Pitching	W	L	ERA	G	GS	SV	IP	H	R	ER	BB	SO
Tom Glavine	1	0	0.00	1	1	0	7	7	0	0	1	8
John Rocker	0	0	0.00	6	0	1	7	3	2	0	2	9
Terry Mulholland	0	0	0.00	2	0	0	3	1	0	0	1	2
Russ Springer	1	0	0.00	2	0	0	2	0	0	0	1	1
Greg Maddux	0	1	1.93	2	2	0	14	12	3	3	1	7
Mike Remlinger	0	1	3.18	5	0	0	6	3	2	2	3	4
Kevin Millwood	1	0	3.55	2	2	0	13	13	6	5	1	9
John Smoltz	0	0	6.23	3	1	1	9	8	6	6	0	8
Kevin McGlinchy	0	1	18.00	1	0	0	1	2	2	2	4	1
Totals	4	2	2.69	6	6	2	60	49	21	18	14	49

NEW YORK

Player, Pos.	AVG	G	AB	R	H	2B	3B	HR	RBI	BB	SO	SB
Roger Cedeno, rf-pr	.500	5	12	2	6	1	0	0	1	1	1	2
Matt Franco, ph	.500	5	2	1	1	0	0	0	1	0	0	0
Todd Pratt, ph-c	.500	4	2	0	1	0	0	0	3	1	1	0
Melvin Mora, lf-cf	.429	6	14	3	6	0	0	1	2	3	2	2
Darryl Hamilton, cf	.353	5	17	0	6	1	0	0	2	0	4	0
Bobby Bonilla, ph	.333	3	3	0	1	0	0	0	0	1	0	0
John Olerud, 1b	.296	6	27	4	8	0	0	2	6	2	3	0
Edgardo Alfonzo, 2b	.222	2	27	2	6	4	0	0	1	2	9	0
Rickey Henderson, lf	.174	6	23	2	4	1	0	0	1	0	5	1
Mike Piazza, c	.167	6	24	1	4	0	0	1	4	0	6	0
Shawon Dunston, ph-cf	.143	5	7	2	1	0	0	0	0	0	2	1
Robin Ventura, 3b	.120	6	25	2	3	1	0	0	1	1	5	0
Benny Agbayani, ph-of	.143	4	7	2	1	0	0	0	0	4	2	1
Rey Ordonez, ss	.042	6	24	0	1	0	0	0	0	0	2	0
Masato Yoshii, p	.000	2	3	0	0	0	0	0	0	1	0	0
Al Leiter, p	.000	2	2	0	0	0	0	0	0	0	1	0
Pat Mahomes, p	.000	3	2	0	0	0	0	0	0	2	0	0
Rick Reed, p	.000	1	2	0	0	0	0	0	0	0	2	0
Kenny Rogers, p	.000	3	1	0	0	0	0	0	0	0	1	0
Orel Hershiser, p	.000	2	1	0	0	0	0	0	0	0	0	0
Totals	.218	6	225	21	49	9	0	4	21	15	49	7

Pitching	W	L	ERA	G	GS	SV	IP	H	R	ER	BB	SO
Orel Hershiser	0	0	0.00	2	0	0	4	1	0	0	3	5
Dennis Cook	0	0	0.00	3	0	0	1	1	0	0	2	1
Armando Benitez	0	0	1.35	5	0	1	7	3	1	1	2	9
Pat Mahomes	0	0	1.42	3	0	0	6	4	1	1	3	3
Rick Reed	0	0	2.57	1	1	0	7	3	2	2	0	5
Octavio Dotel	1	0	3.00	1	0	0	3	4	1	1	2	5
John Franco	0	0	3.38	3	0	0	3	3	1	1	1	3
Masato Yoshii	0	1	4.70	2	2	0	8	9	4	4	3	4
Turk Wendell	1	0	4.76	5	0	0	6	2	3	3	4	5
Kenny Rogers	0	2	5.87	3	1	0	8	11	5	5	7	2
Al Leiter	0	1	6.43	2	2	0	7	5	6	5	4	5
Totals	2	4	3.49	6	6	1	59	46	24	23	31	47

SCORE BY INNINGS

Atlanta	700 217 040 110 001—24
New York	210 114 441 100 002—21

E—Piazza 3, Olerud 2, Leiter, Alfonzo, Henderson, C. Jones 2, Klesko 2, Hunter, Williams, Weiss. DP—New York 9, Atlanta 4. LOB—New York 42, Atlanta 47. CS—Agbayani, Dunston, Cedeno, Williams, A. Jones, Boone. SF—Pratt, Piazza, Hunter. S—Perez 2, Ordonez, Alfonzo, Rogers, Boone, Weiss, A. Jones, Maddux, Glavine. IBB—Jordan 3 (by Cook 2, Rogers), C. Jones 4 (by Rogers, Hershiser, Dotel, Yoshii), Hunter (by Wendell), Williams (by Mahomes), Perez (by Hershiser) Olerud (by McGlinchy), Piazza (by Rocker). HBP—Boone (by Hershiser), Jordan (by Wendell), C. Jones (by Leiter), Williams (by Leiter). PB—Perez.

ORGANIZATION STATISTICS

ANAHEIM ANGELS

Clubhouse implodes during strife-filled season for Angels

BY BILL SHAIKIN

The owner wanted out. The manager and general manager got out before they were booted out. One of the players who got out (Randy Velarde) compared his trade to the Athletics to fleeing the Titanic.

Nice 1999 season.

So much went so wrong for the Angels. When Disney spent $80 million to sign Mo Vaughn, the reviews were glowing. General manager Bill Bavasi had assembled a core of young stars and signed them to long-term contracts at bargain prices. Manager Terry Collins had never finished below second place. And with Vaughn, fellow free agent Tim Belcher and returning players like Velarde, Gary DiSarcina, Darin Erstad and Troy Percival, this was a clubhouse full of gamers.

Chemistry? Well, yes, but it was toxic. Players objected to a contract extension for Collins. Bavasi gave him one anyway, but not before the players turned on each other. Erstad called the Angels "soft." Vaughn preferred "lackadaisical." DiSarcina branded his teammates "unprofessional." Belcher pronounced the situation "embarrassing" and Angels president Tony Tavares described the clubhouse as "a day-care center."

When Vaughn, the vaunted leader, didn't charge onto the field after Percival incited a brawl by hitting an Indians batter–recklessly, Vaughn thought–Percival called Vaughn on it. Teammates backed Percival, demanding Collins yank Vaughn from the lineup the next day. Collins quit two days later. Bavasi quit two days before season's end.

Off the field, Disney negotiated for four months to sell the Angels–and the NHL's Mighty Ducks–to a group led by Orange County high-tech billionaire Henry T. Nicholas III. On the day Bavasi quit, Nicholas did too, saying he would pursue only a minority investment.

The Angels had other problems. They finished last in the American League West, and their 92 losses were within three of the franchise record. They finished last in the league in runs, hits, batting average and on-base percentage. They talked a lot about injuries, but the Braves and Indians survived worse and advanced to the playoffs.

If there was good news, Troy Glaus played outstanding defense and hit .240 with 29 homers and 79 RBIs, anchoring himself at third base. The Angels promoted several other youngsters, with pitchers Brian Cooper, Ramon Ortiz and Jarrod Washburn showing enough to contend for a rotation spot in spring training.

The Angels' minor league teams fared little better than the parent club, albeit without the public displays of affliction. Of the six teams, two finished with winning records, and only Double-A Erie advanced to the playoffs.

The Angels stacked Erie with an all-prospect rotation under the tutelage of pitching guru Howie Gershberg. They steered the SeaWolves into the Eastern League playoffs but were gone by playoff time–Cooper and Ortiz to Anaheim, Seth Etherton to Triple-A Edmonton and Mark Harriger and Matt Wise to the operating room. Erie fell to Harrisburg in the first round.

Doug Bridges won 18 games, tops in the minors, between Class A stops at Cedar Rapids and Lake Elsinore. Steve Fish (11-11, 4.90) led the minors with 197 innings at Lake Elsinore and led the California League with 180 strikeouts. Erie first baseman Larry Barnes drove in 100 runs (.286-20-100) and short-season Boise third baseman Robb Quinlan, the Northwest League MVP, hit .322-9-77 in 73 games.

Mo Vaughn

Ramon Ortiz

Players of the Year

MAJOR LEAGUE: Mo Vaughn, 1b

Vaughn led the Angels with 33 home runs and 108 RBIs in his first year with the team.

MINOR LEAGUE: Ramon Ortiz, rhp

Anaheim's top prospect proved he was recovered from his elbow injury, going 14-7 with a 3.25 ERA at Edmonton and Erie.

ORGANIZATION LEADERS

BATTING		
*AVG	Del Lindsey, Butte	.341
R	Darren Blakely, Lake Elsinore	88
H	Shawn Wooten, Erie	151
TB	Larry Barnes, Erie	245
2B	Darren Blakely, Lake Elsinore	38
3B	Elpidio Guzman, Cedar Rapids	13
HR	Larry Barnes, Erie	20
RBI	Larry Barnes, Erie	100
BB	Justin Ross, Lake Elsinore/Cedar Rapids	69
SO	Darren Blakely, Lake Elsinore	159
SB	Trent Durrington, Erie	59
PITCHING		
W	Doug Bridges, Lake Elsinore/Cedar Rapids	18
L	Brandon Emanuel, Lake Elsinore/Cedar Rapids	14
#ERA	Scot Shields, Erie/Lake Elsinore	2.67
G	Scott Brow, Edmonton	64
CG	Two tied at	6
SV	Steve Mintz, Edmonton/Erie	18
IP	Steve Fish, Lake Elsinore	197
BB	Paul Morse, Edmonton/Erie	88
SO	Scot Shields, Erie/Lake Elsinore	194

*Minimum 250 At-Bats #Minimum 75 Innings

Anaheim ANGELS

Manager: Terry Collins/Joe Maddon

1999 Record: 70-92, .432 (4th, AL West)

BATTING	AVG	G	AB	R	H	2B	3B	HR	RBI	BB	SO	SB	CS	B	T	HT	WT	DOB	1st Yr	Resides
Anderson, Garret	.303	157	620	88	188	36	2	21	80	34	81	3	4	L	L	6-3	215	6-30-72	1990	Valencia, Calif.
Colangelo, Mike	.500	1	2	0	1	0	0	0	0	1	0	0	0	R	R	6-1	185	10-22-76	1997	Dumfries, Va.
DaVanon, Jeff	.200	7	20	4	4	0	1	1	4	2	7	0	1	S	R	6-0	185	12-8-73	1995	Del Mar, Calif.
Decker, Steve	.238	28	63	5	15	6	0	0	5	13	9	0	0	R	R	6-3	220	10-25-65	1988	Keizer, Ore.
DiSarcina, Gary	.229	81	271	32	62	7	1	1	29	15	32	2	2	R	R	6-2	205	11-19-67	1988	East Sandwich, Mass.
Durrington, Trent	.180	43	122	14	22	2	0	0	2	9	28	4	3	R	R	5-10	172	8-27-75	1994	Broadbeach Waters, Aus.
Edmonds, Jim	.250	55	204	34	51	17	2	5	23	28	45	5	4	L	L	6-1	218	6-27-70	1988	Yorba Linda, Calif.
Erstad, Darin	.253	142	585	84	148	22	5	13	53	47	101	13	7	L	L	6-2	210	6-4-74	1995	Fargo, N.D.
Glaus, Troy	.240	154	551	85	132	29	0	29	79	71	143	5	1	R	R	6-5	225	8-3-76	1997	Newport Beach, Calif.
Greene, Todd	.243	97	321	36	78	20	0	14	42	12	63	1	4	R	R	5-10	208	5-8-71	1993	Evans, Ga.
Hemphill, Bret	.143	12	21	3	3	0	0	0	2	4	4	0	0	S	R	6-2	196	4-29-75	1994	Lakewood, Calif.
Huson, Jeff	.262	97	225	21	59	7	1	0	18	16	27	10	1	L	R	6-3	180	8-15-64	1986	Parker, Colo.
Luke, Matt	.300	18	30	4	9	0	0	3	6	2	10	0	0	L	L	6-5	220	2-26-71	1992	Huntington Beach, Calif.
Molina, Ben	.257	31	101	8	26	5	0	1	10	6	6	0	1	R	R	5-11	200	7-20-74	1993	Vega Alta, P.R.
O'Brien, Charlie	.097	27	62	3	6	0	0	1	4	1	12	0	0	R	R	6-2	205	5-1-61	1982	Tulsa, Okla.
Palmeiro, Orlando	.278	109	317	46	88	12	1	1	23	39	30	5	5	L	R	5-11	155	1-19-69	1991	Miami, Fla.
Pritchett, Chris	.156	20	45	3	7	1	0	1	2	2	9	1	1	L	R	6-4	212	1-31-70	1991	Modesto, Calif.
Salmon, Tim	.266	98	353	60	94	24	2	17	69	63	82	4	1	R	R	6-3	241	8-24-68	1989	Scottsdale, Ariz.
Sheets, Andy	.197	87	244	22	48	10	0	3	29	14	59	1	2	R	R	6-2	180	11-19-71	1992	Lafayette, La.
Silvestri, Dave	.091	3	11	0	1	1	0	0	1	0	1	0	0	R	R	6-0	180	9-29-67	1989	St. Louis, Mo.
Unroe, Tim	.241	27	54	5	13	2	0	1	6	4	16	0	0	R	R	6-3	200	10-7-70	1992	Antioch, Ill.
Vaughn, Mo	.281	139	524	63	147	20	0	33	108	54	127	0	0	L	R	6-1	245	12-15-67	1989	Easton, Mass.
Velarde, Randy	.306	95	376	57	115	15	4	9	48	43	56	13	4	R	R	6-0	200	11-24-62	1985	Midland, Texas
Walbeck, Matt	.240	107	288	26	69	8	1	3	22	26	46	2	3	S	R	5-11	206	10-2-69	1987	Sacramento, Calif.
Williams, Reggie	.222	30	63	8	14	1	2	1	6	5	21	2	1	S	R	6-1	180	5-5-66	1988	Laurens, S.C.

PITCHING	W	L	ERA	G	GS	CG	SV	IP	H	R	ER	BB	SO	B	T	HT	WT	DOB	1st Yr	Resides
Alvarez, Juan	0	1	3.00	8	0	0	0	3	1	1	1	4	4	L	L	6-1	175	8-9-73	1995	Miami, Fla.
Belcher, Tim	6	8	6.73	24	24	0	0	132	168	104	99	46	52	R	R	6-3	225	10-19-61	1984	Mount Gilead, Ohio
Cooper, Brian	1	1	4.88	5	5	0	0	28	23	15	15	18	15	R	R	6-5	185	8-19-74	1995	Glendora, Calif.
Finley, Chuck	12	11	4.43	33	33	1	0	213	197	117	105	94	200	L	L	6-6	226	11-26-62	1985	Newport Beach, Calif.
Fyhrie, Mike	0	4	5.05	16	7	0	0	52	61	32	29	21	26	R	R	6-2	190	12-9-69	1991	Mission Viejo, Calif.
Hasegawa, Shigetoshi	4	2	4.91	64	1	0	2	77	80	45	42	34	44	R	R	5-11	171	8-1-68	1997	Newport Beach, Calif.
Hill, Ken	4	11	4.77	26	22	0	0	128	129	72	68	76	76	R	R	6-2	214	12-14-65	1985	Southlake, Texas
Holtz, Mike	2	3	8.06	28	0	0	0	22	26	20	20	15	17	L	L	5-9	180	10-10-72	1994	Hollidaysburg, Pa.
Levine, Alan	1	1	3.39	50	1	0	0	85	76	40	32	29	37	L	R	6-3	180	5-22-68	1991	Belleville, Ill.
Magnante, Mike	5	2	3.38	53	0	0	0	69	68	30	26	29	44	L	L	6-1	185	6-17-65	1988	Burbank, Calif.
McDowell, Jack	0	4	8.05	4	4	0	0	19	31	17	17	5	12	R	R	6-5	190	1-16-66	1987	Rancho Sante Fe, Calif.
Mintz, Steve	0	0	3.60	3	0	0	0	5	8	2	2	2	2	L	R	5-11	190	11-24-68	1990	Vero Beach, Fla.
Olivares, Omar	8	9	4.05	20	20	3	0	131	135	62	59	49	49	R	R	6-1	205	7-6-67	1987	San German, P.R.
Ortiz, Ramon	2	3	6.52	9	9	0	0	48	50	35	35	25	44	R	R	6-0	165	3-23-76	1995	Cotui, D.R.
Percival, Troy	4	6	3.79	60	0	0	31	57	38	24	24	22	58	R	R	6-3	230	8-9-69	1990	Riverside, Calif.
Petkovsek, Mark	10	4	3.47	64	0	0	1	83	85	37	32	21	43	R	R	6-0	195	11-18-65	1987	Beaumont, Texas
Pote, Lou	1	1	2.15	20	0	0	3	29	23	9	7	12	20	R	R	6-3	190	8-27-71	1991	Chicago, Ill.
Schoeneweis, Scott	1	1	5.49	31	0	0	0	39	47	27	24	14	22	L	L	6-0	186	10-2-73	1996	Mount Laurel, N.J.
Sparks, Steve	5	11	5.42	28	26	0	0	148	165	101	89	82	73	R	R	6-0	180	7-2-65	1987	Sugar Land, Texas
Washburn, Jarrod	4	5	5.25	16	10	0	0	62	61	36	36	26	39	L	L	6-1	200	8-13-74	1995	Webster, Wis.

FIELDING

Catcher	PCT	G	PO	A	E	DP	PB
Decker	.987	17	73	4	1	0	5
Greene	.984	12	55	7	1	0	5
Hemphill	.955	12	36	6	2	1	1
Molina	.991	30	192	19	2	2	3
O'Brien	.993	27	140	11	1	2	0
Walbeck	.989	97	407	46	5	9	6

First Base	PCT	G	PO	A	E	DP
Decker	1.000	6	30	4	0	2
Edmonds	1.000	2	19	1	0	2
Erstad	.999	78	669	41	1	59
Huson	1.000	1	8	0	0	0
Luke	1.000	4	20	4	0	5
Pritchett	.990	15	96	8	1	8
Vaughn	.995	72	584	35	3	62

Second Base	PCT	G	PO	A	E	DP
Durrington	.966	41	73	98	6	19
Huson	.993	41	53	92	1	20
Sheets	.929	7	6	7	1	0
Silvestri	1.000	1	0	3	0	0
Unroe	.000	1	0	0	0	0
Velarde	.986	95	191	307	7	61

Third Base	PCT	G	PO	A	E	DP
Glaus	.954	153	114	277	19	25
Huson	.971	9	11	22	1	4
Sheets	.500	1	0	1	1	0
Unroe	1.000	1	3	1	2	0

Shortstop	PCT	G	PO	A	E	DP
DiSarcina	.963	81	138	249	15	62
Huson	.939	22	14	32	3	7
Sheets	.966	76	107	174	10	37

	PCT	G	PO	A	E	DP
Silvestri	.833	1	2	3	1	0

Outfield	PCT	G	PO	A	E	DP
Anderson	.993	153	406	7	3	1
Colangelo	1.000	1	1	1	0	1
DaVanon	1.000	5	5	0	0	0
Edmonds	.992	42	119	4	1	1
Erstad	1.000	69	185	7	0	1
Greene	.974	30	36	1	1	0
Huson	1.000	2	1	0	0	0
Luke	1.000	6	8	0	0	0
Palmeiro	.994	92	154	6	1	0
Salmon	.981	89	204	7	4	1
Silvestri	1.000	1	1	0	0	0
Unroe	1.000	12	13	1	0	0
Williams	.974	24	34	3	1	3

Director of Player Development: Jeff Parker

Class	Farm Team	League	W	L	Pct.	Finish*	Manager	First Yr
AAA	Edmonton (Alberta) Trappers	Pacific Coast	65	74	.468	t-11th (16)	Carney Lansford	1999
AA	Erie (Pa.) SeaWolves	Eastern	81	61	.570	2nd (12)	Garry Templeton	1999
A#	Lake Elsinore (Calif.) Storm	California	63	77	.450	8th (10)	Mario Mendoza	1994
A	Cedar Rapids (Iowa) Kernels	Midwest	61	77	.442	12th (14)	Mitch Seoane	1993
A	Boise (Idaho) Hawks	Northwest	43	33	.566	2nd (8)	Tom Kotchman	1989
Rookie#	Butte (Mont.) Copper Kings	Pioneer	32	43	.427	6th (8)	Joe Urso	1997

*Finish in overall standings (No. of teams in league)   #Advanced level

PACIFIC COAST LEAGUE

BATTING	AVG	G	AB	R	H	2B	3B	HR	RBI	BB	SO	SB	CS	B	T	HT	WT	DOB	1st Yr	Resides
Betten, Randy	.379	12	29	5	11	1	0	0	3	0	5	0	0	R	R	5-11	170	7-28-71	1995	Highland, Calif.
Burke, Jamie	.336	46	149	29	50	9	0	3	16	23	18	0	1	R	R	6-0	195	9-24-71	1993	Roseburg, Ore.
Carvajal, Jovino	.245	108	367	38	90	15	3	5	40	20	63	17	13	S	R	6-2	200	9-2-68	1987	La Romana, D.R.
Christian, Eddie	.236	44	148	24	35	5	1	5	15	12	31	4	3	S	L	5-11	180	8-26-71	1992	Richmond, Calif.
Colangelo, Mike	.362	26	105	13	38	7	1	0	9	13	18	2	1	R	R	6-1	185	10-22-76	1997	Dumfries, Va.
DaVanon, Jeff	.326	34	132	35	43	8	3	6	19	20	27	11	4	S	R	6-0	185	12-8-73	1995	Del Mar, Calif.
Decker, Steve	.284	64	225	51	64	19	2	15	51	44	38	0	0	R	R	6-3	220	10-25-65	1988	Keizer, Ore.
Foster, Jim	.295	24	88	13	26	10	0	2	15	4	13	1	0	R	R	6-3	220	8-18-71	1993	Warwick, R.I.
2-team (11 Tucson)	.289	35	114	17	33	11	0	2	18	8	15	1	0							
Graves, Bryan	.400	2	5	2	2	1	0	0	1	1	2	0	0	R	R	5-11	210	10-8-74	1995	Bogalusa, La.
Greene, Todd	.243	19	74	10	18	6	0	5	14	0	12	0	0	R	R	5-10	208	5-8-71	1993	Evans, Ga.
Hemphill, Bret	.313	74	246	29	77	16	1	7	31	31	58	1	0	S	R	6-2	196	4-29-75	1994	Lakewood, Calif.
Herrick, Jason	.208	25	72	6	15	3	0	1	7	1	27	0	2	L	L	6-0	175	7-29-73	1991	Franklin, Wis.
Hutchins, Norm	.250	126	521	80	130	27	6	7	51	40	127	25	17	S	L	5-11	198	11-20-75	1994	Greenburgh, N.Y.
Johns, Keith	.208	81	236	32	49	9	2	3	26	26	38	2	0	R	R	6-1	175	7-19-71	1992	St. Louis, Mo.
Kieschnick, Brooks	.314	77	296	54	93	20	3	23	73	19	60	0	1	L	R	6-4	228	6-6-72	1993	Caldwell, Texas
Luke, Matt	.429	6	21	7	9	2	1	5	15	6	4	0	0	L	L	6-5	220	2-26-71	1992	Huntington Beach, Calif.
Luuloa, Keith	.285	115	396	54	113	23	1	4	46	44	53	7	7	R	R	6-0	185	12-24-74	1994	Canyon Lake, Calif.
Molina, Ben	.286	65	241	28	69	16	0	7	41	15	17	1	2	R	R	5-11	200	7-20-74	1993	Vega Alta, P.R.
Pennyfeather, Will	.212	34	99	16	21	5	1	2	10	5	21	3	0	R	R	6-2	215	5-25-68	1988	Perth Amboy, N.J.
Perez, Tomas	.260	83	296	31	77	17	1	4	40	19	43	2	2	S	R	5-11	177	12-29-73	1991	Barquisimeto, Venez.
Pritchett, Chris	.279	96	348	60	97	15	1	12	45	47	70	1	1	L	R	6-4	212	1-31-70	1991	Modesto, Calif.
Sheets, Andy	.289	12	45	6	13	1	1	0	4	2	11	0	1	R	R	6-2	180	11-19-71	1992	Lafayette, La.
Silvestri, Dave	.318	79	318	55	101	18	0	6	42	22	43	4	3	R	R	6-0	180	9-29-67	1989	St. Louis, Mo.
Stoner, Mike	.346	22	81	12	28	5	1	3	12	4	11	0	1	R	R	6-0	200	5-23-73	1996	Simpsonville, Ky.
2-team (14 Tucson)	.363	36	102	14	37	6	1	3	18	6	14	0	1							
Tejero, Fausto	.294	5	17	3	5	0	0	1	2	3	3	0	0	R	R	6-2	205	10-26-68	1990	Miami Lakes, Fla.
t'Hoen, E.J.	.138	9	29	2	4	0	0	0	2	7	0	0	0	R	R	6-2	185	11-8-75	1996	Alphen Aan Denryn, Netherlands
Unroe, Tim	.386	10	44	10	17	5	1	5	18	5	9	0	0	R	R	6-3	200	10-7-70	1992	Antioch, Ill.
Williams, Reggie	.314	35	137	25	43	9	1	6	31	16	29	3	2	S	R	6-1	180	5-5-66	1988	Laurens, S.C.

PITCHING	W	L	ERA	G	GS	CG	SV	IP	H	R	ER	BB	SO	B	T	HT	WT	DOB	1st Yr	Resides
Alvarez, Juan	0	3	3.49	27	0	0	0	28	30	13	11	8	25	L	L	6-1	175	8-9-73	1995	Miami, Fla.
Borland, Toby	2	1	7.00	21	0	0	0	27	31	24	21	23	34	R	R	6-6	204	5-29-69	1989	Quitman, La.
Brow, Scott	1	6	5.70	64	0	0	15	79	94	53	50	31	48	R	R	6-3	215	3-17-69	1990	Hillsboro, Ore.
Cooper, Brian	2	1	3.77	5	5	0	0	31	30	17	13	10	32	R	R	6-1	185	8-19-74	1995	Glendora, Calif.
Edsell, Geoff	1	4	5.01	30	0	0	0	47	46	27	26	25	37	R	R	6-2	194	12-10-71	1993	Muncy, Pa.
Etherton, Seth	0	2	5.48	4	4	0	0	21	25	13	13	6	19	R	R	6-1	200	10-17-76	1998	Las Vegas, Nev.
Fyhrie, Mike	9	5	3.47	19	18	0	0	114	90	47	44	40	113	R	R	6-2	190	12-9-69	1991	Mission Viejo, Calif.
Hawblitzel, Ryan	4	4	5.34	24	7	0	0	64	81	47	38	24	37	R	R	6-2	170	4-30-71	1990	Lake Worth, Fla.
Holtz, Mike	2	1	2.30	20	0	0	1	27	20	7	7	11	39	L	L	5-9	180	10-10-72	1994	Hollidaysburg, Pa.
Jacobsen, Joe	0	1	7.20	12	0	0	0	15	24	13	12	5	6	R	R	6-3	225	12-26-71	1992	Clovis, Calif.
James, Mike	1	2	8.64	8	1	0	0	8	16	14	8	2	3	R	R	6-3	190	8-15-67	1988	Mary Esther, Fla.
Lomon, Kevin	7	8	5.75	23	17	0	0	124	170	86	79	35	91	R	R	6-1	195	11-20-71	1991	Cameron, Okla.
Lubozynski, Matt	0	0	0.00	1	0	0	0	2	1	0	0	1	1	R	L	6-4	190	11-9-76	1998	San Antonio, Texas
McDowell, Jack	1	0	5.73	2	2	0	0	11	12	7	7	3	2	R	R	6-5	190	1-16-66	1987	Rancho Sante Fe, Calif.
Menhart, Paul	3	3	6.80	9	9	0	0	42	58	34	32	14	21	R	R	6-2	190	3-25-69	1990	Covington, Ga.
Michalak, Chris	1	0	5.72	24	0	0	0	28	28	20	18	14	25	L	L	6-2	195	1-4-71	1993	Lemont, Ill.
Mintz, Steve	4	3	2.35	31	0	0	9	31	31	11	8	6	17	L	R	5-11	190	11-24-68	1990	Vero Beach, Fla.
Montoya, Norm	4	1	5.61	38	3	0	0	67	92	49	42	17	30	L	L	6-2	215	9-24-70	1990	Fremont, Calif.
Morse, Paul	1	5	7.11	10	9	0	0	49	64	44	39	34	30	R	R	6-2	185	2-27-73	1995	Danville, Ky.
Ortiz, Ramon	5	3	4.05	9	9	0	0	53	46	26	24	19	64	R	R	6-0	165	3-23-76	1995	Cotui, D.R.
Pote, Lou	7	9	4.50	24	23	3	0	150	171	80	75	41	118	R	R	6-3	190	8-27-71	1991	Chicago, Ill.
Schoeneweis, Scott	2	4	7.64	9	7	0	0	35	58	35	30	12	29	L	L	6-0	186	10-2-73	1996	Mount Laurel, N.J.
Troutman, Keith	1	0	3.54	6	3	0	0	20	23	12	8	2	22	R	R	6-1	200	5-29-73	1992	Candler, N.C.
Washburn, Jarrod	1	5	4.73	11	11	1	0	59	50	31	31	17	55	L	L	6-1	200	8-13-74	1995	Webster, Wis.
Williams, Shad	5	3	3.72	16	11	1	0	75	73	36	31	19	35	R	R	6-0	198	3-10-71	1991	Fresno, Calif.

FIELDING

Catcher	PCT	G	PO	A	E	DP	PB
Burke	.909	5	8	2	1	0	0
Decker	1.000	4	28	0	0	0	0
Foster	.987	18	138	16	2	1	2
Graves	1.000	2	13	3	0	0	1
Hemphill	.995	56	348	44	2	4	7

	PCT	G	PO	A	E	DP
Molina	.993	54	351	47	3	5	3
Tejero	.978	5	39	5	1	0	1

First Base	PCT	G	PO	A	E	DP
Burke	1.000	3	25	0	0	1
Decker	.993	14	126	8	1	12

	PCT	G	PO	A	E	DP
Foster	1.000	3	7	0	0	2
Hemphill	.975	6	36	3	1	4
Kieschnick	.981	31	238	24	5	29
Luuloa	1.000	5	25	1	0	2
Pennyfeather	1.000	2	10	1	0	2

Organization Statistics

	PCT	G	PO	A	E	DP
Pritchett	.989	86	714	63	9	74
R. Williams	1.000	2	9	1	0	1

Second Base	PCT	G	PO	A	E	DP
Betten	1.000	3	10	8	0	2
Burke	1.000	1	2	2	0	0
Johns	.976	21	31	51	2	15
Luuloa	.971	62	118	186	9	39
Perez	1.000	11	26	34	0	11
Sheets	1.000	2	3	2	0	1
Silvestri	.975	42	65	94	4	23
t'Hoen	1.000	6	10	24	0	5
R. Williams	1.000	1	1	0	0	0

Third Base	PCT	G	PO	A	E	DP
Betten	.933	4	3	11	1	1
Burke	.949	33	19	56	4	6

	PCT	G	PO	A	E	DP
Decker	.929	38	15	64	6	3
Johns	1.000	7	4	10	0	2
Kieschnick	1.000	1	0	2	0	0
Luuloa	.925	37	26	72	8	4
Silvestri	.968	21	9	21	1	1
Unroe	.900	2	5	4	1	1
t'Hoen	1.000	3	1	10	0	1
R. Williams	.667	1	1	1	1	0

Shortstop	PCT	G	PO	A	E	DP
Johns	.954	48	81	145	11	37
Perez	.968	73	123	209	11	53
Sheets	.977	10	10	32	1	9
Silvestri	.965	15	25	30	2	9

Outfield	PCT	G	PO	A	E	DP
Betten	1.000	3	2	0	0	0

	PCT	G	PO	A	E	DP
Burke	1.000	1	2	1	0	0
Carvajal	.968	101	172	9	6	0
Christian	.964	33	52	1	2	0
Colangelo	.941	26	29	3	2	0
DaVanon	1.000	33	74	6	0	1
Greene	1.000	12	23	0	0	0
Herrick	.947	19	34	2	2	1
Hutchins	.983	125	294	2	5	0
Kieschnick	1.000	7	8	0	0	0
Luke	1.000	3	6	0	0	0
Luuloa	.952	13	20	0	1	0
Pennyfeather	.942	29	46	3	3	0
Pritchett	1.000	1	3	1	0	0
Stoner	.917	10	21	1	2	0
Unroe	1.000	8	12	0	0	0
R. Williams	.979	23	44	3	1	0

ERIE — Class AA

EASTERN LEAGUE

BATTING

	AVG	G	AB	R	H	2B	3B	HR	RBI	BB	SO	SB	CS	B	T	HT	WT	DOB	1st Yr	Resides
Abbott, Chuck	.239	125	444	70	106	13	1	6	46	47	138	9	10	R	R	6-1	180	1-26-75	1996	Schaumburg, Ill.
Barnes, Larry	.286	130	497	73	142	25	9	20	100	49	99	14	3	L	L	6-1	195	7-23-74	1995	Bakersfield, Calif.
Betten, Randy	.150	7	20	3	3	0	1	0	1	0	7	3	0	R	R	5-11	170	7-28-71	1995	Highland, Calif.
Christian, Eddie	.283	53	205	29	58	11	1	3	27	20	34	14	3	S	L	5-11	180	8-26-71	1992	Richmond, Calif.
Colangelo, Mike	.339	28	109	24	37	10	3	1	13	14	22	3	3	R	R	6-1	185	10-22-76	1997	Dumfries, Va.
Dewey, Jason	.223	40	139	17	31	7	0	4	14	17	50	0	1	R	R	6-1	200	4-18-77	1997	Tampa, Fla.
DiSarcina, Gary	.300	5	20	1	6	0	0	0	2	0	4	0	2	R	R	6-2	205	11-19-67	1988	East Sandwich, Mass.
Durrington, Trent	.288	107	396	84	114	26	1	3	34	52	66	59	17	R	R	5-10	172	8-27-75	1994	Broadbeach Waters, Aus .
Foster, Jim	.250	4	16	2	4	1	0	1	3	2	0	0	0	R	R	6-3	220	8-18-71	1993	Warwick, R.I.
Graves, Bryan	.194	37	103	22	20	2	1	1	8	32	32	1	0	R	R	5-11	210	10-8-74	1995	Bogalusa, La.
Guiel, Jeff	.263	57	175	34	46	10	3	6	24	33	33	3	3	L	R	5-11	195	1-12-74	1997	Langley, B.C.
Haynes, Nathan	.158	5	19	3	3	1	0	0	0	5	5	0	0	L	L	5-9	170	9-7-79	1997	Hercules, Calif.
Herrick, Jason	.167	25	78	9	13	5	1	2	6	8	28	1	0	L	L	6-0	175	7-29-73	1991	Franklin, Wis.
Leggett, Adam	.167	24	72	8	12	0	0	1	6	21	14	2	3	S	R	6-0	190	4-3-76	1997	Carthage, Texas
Murphy, Nate	.267	104	359	48	96	17	8	14	56	54	85	6	5	L	L	6-1	210	4-15-75	1996	Montague, Mass.
Pennyfeather, Will	.205	11	39	4	8	1	0	0	4	5	13	1	2	R	R	6-2	215	5-25-68	1988	Perth Amboy, N.J.
Rapp, Travis	.250	3	8	1	2	1	0	0	0	2	4	0	0	R	R	6-2	205	1-28-75	1997	Sebring, Fla.
Simonton, Benji	.242	62	182	13	44	10	1	1	19	28	55	4	4	R	R	6-1	236	5-12-72	1992	Pittsburg, Calif.
Stoner, Mike	.339	14	62	10	21	4	0	3	15	2	8	0	1	R	R	6-0	205	5-23-73	1996	Simpsonville, Ky.
Tejero, Fausto	.213	62	211	19	45	9	0	3	18	13	38	0	2	R	R	6-2	205	10-26-68	1990	Miami Lakes, Fla.
t'Hoen, E.J.	.203	56	187	18	38	12	1	2	21	13	52	6	2	R	R	6-2	185	11-8-75	1996	Alphen Aan Denryn, Netherlands
Tolentino, Juan	.252	136	489	61	123	19	5	9	61	47	116	47	14	R	R	6-0	165	3-12-76	1995	San Pedro de Marcois, D.R.
Walther, Chris	.355	9	31	5	11	2	1		6	4	4	0	0	R	R	6-2	200	8-28-76	1995	Tampa, Fla.
Wolff, Mike	.248	91	307	43	76	21	3	10	40	63	85	4	6	R	R	6-1	195	12-19-70	1992	Wilmington, N.C.
Wooten, Shawn	.292	137	518	70	151	27	1	19	88	50	102	3	1	R	R	5-10	205	7-24-72	1993	La Verne, Calif.

PITCHING

	W	L	ERA	G	GS	CG	SV	IP	H	R	ER	BB	SO	B	T	HT	WT	DOB	1st Yr	Resides
Alvarez, Juan	1	2	2.05	23	0	0	4	31	20	14	7	6	22	L	L	6-1	175	8-9-73	1995	Miami, Fla.
Anderson, Bill	1	1	5.40	5	5	0	0	18	20	12	11	8	12	R	R	6-0	190	9-23-71	1994	Alta Loma, Calif.
Beaumont, Matt	5	6	4.73	32	12	0	1	107	97	64	56	59	76	L	L	6-3	210	4-22-73	1994	Rittman, Ohio
Bovee, Mike	1	1	1.32	26	0	0	12	34	26	6	5	5	33	R	R	5-11	219	8-21-73	1991	Poway, Calif.
Brown, Alvin	0	1	6.75	4	0	0	2	7	9	6	5	7	6	R	R	6-1	200	9-2-70	1989	Los Angeles, Calif.
2-team (7 Altoona)	..4	2	6.55	13	6	0	2	33	38	28	24	24	21							
Callier, Jeremy	0	0	18.00	1	0	0	1	2	2	2	2	2	2	R	R	6-0	195	11-18-75	1998	Ballwin, Mo.
Cooper, Brian	10	5	3.30	22	22	6	0	158	146	61	58	29	143	R	R	6-1	185	8-19-74	1995	Glendora, Calif.
Cummings, Ryan	1	1	5.09	3	3	0	0	18	18	12	10	10	7	R	R	6-2	210	6-3-76	1997	Marietta, Ga.
Edsell, Geoff	2	3	3.46	26	2	0	2	39	45	20	15	13	28	R	R	6-2	194	12-10-71	1993	Muncy, Pa.
Etherton, Seth	10	10	3.27	24	24	4	0	168	153	72	61	43	153	R	R	6-1	200	10-17-76	1998	Las Vegas, Nev.
Green, Steve	3	1	3.32	6	6	1	0	41	34	25	15	19	32	R	R	6-2	195	1-26-78	1997	Longueuil, Quebec
Hancock, Ryan	0	1	5.27	8	0	0	1	14	23	8	8	2	6	R	R	6-2	220	11-11-71	1993	Draper, Utah
Harriger, Mark	2	1	4.70	6	6	0	0	31	31	16	16	15	13	R	R	6-2	196	4-29-75	1996	Lakewood, Calif.
Hill, Jason	1	2	9.96	23	0	0	0	28	37	37	31	24	14	R	L	5-11	180	4-14-72	1994	Redding, Calif.
Johnson, Greg	0	0	12.00	2	0	0	0	3	8	4	4	1	4	L	L	6-0	185	4-28-74	1996	Frostburg, Md.
Mintz, Steve	1	1	2.23	26	0	0	9	32	26	12	8	3	33	L	R	5-11	190	11-24-68	1990	Vero Beach, Fla.
Morse, Paul	8	6	3.33	15	14	2	0	97	83	44	36	54	52	R	R	6-2	195	2-27-73	1995	Danville, Ky.
Nina, Elvin	3	0	4.07	4	4	0	0	24	20	12	11	15	19	R	R	6-0	185	11-25-75	1997	East Orange, N.J.
Ortiz, Ramon	9	4	2.82	15	15	2	0	102	88	32	32	40	86	R	R	6-0	165	3-23-76	1995	Cotui, D.R.
Petroff, Dan	0	0	9.45	8	0	0	0	13	21	17	14	4	8	R	R	6-4	220	4-5-74	1994	Punxsutawney, Pa.
Salter, Cody	3	2	4.10	27	3	0	0	53	65	29	24	14	16	R	R	6-4	200	10-8-75	1998	Plainfield, Ill.
Shields, Scot	4	4	2.89	10	10	1	0	75	57	26	24	26	81	R	R	6-1	175	7-22-75	1997	Fort Lauderdale, Fla.
Troutman, Keith	5	4	4.12	38	0	0	6	59	66	32	27	19	49	R	R	6-1	200	5-29-73	1992	Candler, N.C.
Wise, Matt	8	5	3.77	16	16	3	0	98	102	48	41	24	72	R	R	6-4	190	11-18-75	1997	La Verne, Calif.

FIELDING

Catcher	PCT	G	PO	A	E	DP	PB
Dewey	.981	40	277	28	6	3	2
Foster	1.000	4	30	1	0	1	0
Graves	.978	37	245	23	6	3	3
Rapp	1.000	3	16	4	0	0	0
Tejero	.987	62	399	41	6	5	4
Wooten	1.000	2	9	2	0	1	1

First Base	PCT	G	PO	A	E	DP
Barnes	.992	123	1047	87	9	87

	PCT	G	PO	A	E	DP	PB
Simonton	.909	1	10	0	1		1
Tejero	.833	1	4	1	1		1
Walther	1.000	1	9	0	0		3
Wolff	.994	17	161	15	1		19
Wooten	1.000	1	1	1	0	0	

Second Base	PCT	G	PO	A	E	DP
Betten	1.000	1	1	4	0	3

	PCT	G	PO	A	E	DP	PB
Durrington	.974	107	212	312	14	54	
Leggett	1.000	21	42	67	0	17	
t'Hoen	.933	19	26	44	5	12	
Wolff	1.000	1	0	2	0	0	

Third Base	PCT	G	PO	A	E	DP
Betten	1.000	2	0	3	0	0
Leggett	.800	3	0	4	1	0

Organization Statistics

	PCT	G	PO	A	E	DP	PB
t'Hoen	.884	22	11	27	5		3
Walther	1.000	3	0	5	0		1
Wooten	.938	124	91	243	22		24
Shortstop	**PCT**	**G**	**PO**	**A**	**E**	**DP**	
Abbott	.945	125	185	309	29	72	
Betten	1.000	3	2	4	0	0	
DiSarcina	1.000	5	5	12	0	1	

	PCT	G	PO	A	E	DP	PB
t'Hoen	.887	15	21	42	8		8
Outfield	**PCT**	**G**	**PO**	**A**	**E**	**DP**	
Betten	1.000	2	5	5	0	0	
Christian	.978	46	85	6	2	1	
Colangelo	.950	27	35	3	2	0	
Guiel	.977	46	78	6	2	2	
Haynes	1.000	5	5	1	0	0	

	PCT	G	PO	A	E	DP	PB
Herrick	.961	23	44	5	2	1	
Murphy	.977	101	207	5	5	1	
Pennyfeather	.952	9	19	1	1	1	
Simonton	.987	41	74	2	1	0	
Stoner	.909	6	10	0	1	0	
Tolentino	.968	134	293	7	10	1	
Wolff	1.000	1	2	0	0	0	

LAKE ELSINORE — Class A

CALIFORNIA LEAGUE

BATTING	AVG	G	AB	R	H	2B	3B	HR	RBI	BB	SO	SB	CS	B	T	HT	WT	DOB	1st Yr	Resides
Betten, Randy	.327	15	52	11	17	2	0	1	7	3	10	3	0	R	R	5-11	170	7-28-71	1995	Highland, Calif.
Blakely, Darren	.251	124	510	88	128	38	10	12	63	36	159	23	13	S	R	6-0	195	3-14-77	1998	Pensacola, Fla.
Castro, Nelson	.250	125	444	68	111	16	12	1	50	36	75	53	19	R	R	5-10	190	6-4-76	1994	Villa Vasquez, D.R.
Curtis, Matt	.261	126	460	72	120	26	2	17	76	68	84	2	2	S	R	6-0	195	8-14-74	1996	Visalia, Calif.
Dewey, Jason	.322	66	242	48	78	23	0	10	31	30	62	0	0	R	R	6-1	200	4-18-77	1997	Tampa, Fla.
DiSarcina, Gary	.083	4	12	0	1	0	0	0	0	1	0	0	0	R	R	6-2	205	11-19-67	1988	East Sandwich, Mass.
Dougherty, Jeb	.260	115	381	66	99	13	4	7	45	54	68	35	13	R	R	5-11	190	7-16-75	1997	Yucca Valley, Calif.
Edmonds, Jim	.421	5	19	4	8	2	0	0	3	4	2	0	0	L	L	6-1	218	6-27-70	1988	Yorba Linda, Calif.
Freitas, Joe	.111	3	9	1	1	1	0	0	1	1	3	0	0	R	R	6-3	215	8-2-73	1995	Hanford, Calif.
Graves, Bryan	.237	15	38	3	9	2	0	0	6	7	13	0	0	R	R	5-11	210	10-8-74	1995	Bogalusa, La.
Guiel, Jeff	.328	15	58	12	19	4	2	3	12	11	18	2	1	L	R	5-11	195	1-12-74	1997	Langley, B.C.
Hagins, Steve	.262	40	141	21	37	14	1	4	22	5	39	2	1	R	R	6-1	205	3-7-75	1997	Aliso Viejo, Calif.
Haynes, Nathan	.327	26	110	19	36	5	5	1	15	12	19	10	5	L	L	5-9	170	9-7-79	1997	Hercules, Calif.
2-team (35 Visalia)	.318	61	255	47	81	12	6	2	29	29	46	22	15							
Hood, Jay	.235	102	374	48	88	14	5	3	43	24	81	8	9	R	R	6-0	185	3-8-77	1998	Germantown, Tenn.
Huisman, Jason	.275	91	346	50	95	17	3	3	43	24	64	10	5	R	R	6-3	195	4-16-76	1998	Thornton, Ill.
Johnson, Patrick	.205	26	78	7	16	0	0	1	6	10	26	0	0	R	R	6-3	200	4-18-75	1996	Taylorsville, Utah
Kennedy, Gus	.204	29	93	13	19	5	0	3	13	15	25	4	2	R	R	5-10	205	12-26-73	1994	Seligman, Ariz.
Leggett, Adam	.243	57	185	19	45	14	0	3	25	20	30	6	3	S	R	6-0	190	4-3-76	1997	Carthage, Texas
Lopez, Norberto	.000	2	4	0	0	0	0	0	0	0	2	0	0	R	R	5-8	180	12-9-76	1999	Hialeah, Fla.
Luke, Matt	.340	13	53	10	18	5	3	0	7	7	14	2	0	L	L	6-5	220	2-26-71	1992	Huntington Beach, Calif.
Mott, Bill	.318	25	88	16	28	5	1	1	12	10	18	6	3	L	R	6-1	180	1-2-76	1998	San Luis Obispo, Calif.
Murphy, Nate	.355	28	107	21	38	8	1	5	20	11	27	9	4	L	L	6-1	210	4-15-75	1996	Montague, Mass.
Rapp, Travis	.176	12	34	2	6	2	0	0	1	2	14	0	0	R	R	6-2	205	1-28-75	1997	Sebring, Fla.
Rodriguez, Juan	.302	86	315	54	95	12	6	6	50	32	70	7	5	S	L	5-10	180	12-16-74	1994	Arecibo, P.R.
Ross, Justin	.258	22	66	10	17	3	1	0	5	16	16	2	1	L	L	6-2	193	12-24-76	1998	Wexford, Pa.
Salmon, Tim	.600	1	5	0	3	2	0	0	2	0	1	0	0	R	R	6-3	241	8-24-68	1989	Scottsdale, Ariz.
Simonton, Benji	.370	49	184	39	68	14	2	8	48	29	52	0	0	R	R	6-1	236	5-12-72	1992	Pittsburg, Calif.
Stuart, Rich	.186	11	43	3	8	1	1	0	3	1	11	1	2	R	R	5-11	170	7-31-76	1994	Arecibo, P.R.
Walther, Chris	.295	100	380	48	112	26	2	3	60	27	31	3	11	R	R	6-2	200	8-28-76	1995	Tampa, Fla.

GAMES BY POSITION: C—Curtis 11, Dewey 62, Graves 13, Hagins 31, P. Johnson 25, Lopez 2, Rapp 11. **1B**—Betten 1, Curtis 48, Hagins 1, Rodriguez 44, Simonton 3, Walther 52. **2B**—Betten 8, Hood 82, Huisman 17, Leggett 42, Rodriguez 1. **3B**—Betten 6, Curtis 18, Hood 1, Huisman 70, Leggett 5, Walther 47. **SS**—Castro 123, DiSarcina 3, Hood 21. **OF**—Blakely 121, Curtis 4, Dougherty 112, Guiel 15, Haynes 26, Kennedy 20, Luke 9, Murphy 30, Simonton 37, Stuart 11.

PITCHING	W	L	ERA	G	GS	CG	SV	IP	H	R	ER	BB	SO	B	T	HT	WT	DOB	1st Yr	Resides
Bridges, Doug	3	2	4.33	5	2	0	0	35	42	19	17	11	34	L	L	6-2	185	7-20-76	1998	Columbia, S.C.
Brooks, Jacob	3	3	7.12	27	0	0	4	37	38	33	29	29	43	R	R	6-1	175	3-23-78	1998	Largo, Fla.
Callier, Jeremy	5	3	3.86	34	7	0	2	96	107	48	41	33	69	R	R	6-0	195	11-18-75	1998	Ballwin, Mo.
Cowsill, Brendon	4	10	5.37	27	20	4	1	126	155	87	75	36	62	R	R	6-3	190	1-7-75	1994	Burbank, Calif.
Cummings, Ryan	3	1	3.28	7	1	0	0	47	43	19	17	15	41	R	R	6-2	210	6-3-76	1997	Marietta, Ga.
Duarte, Renney	0	1	6.43	3	3	0	0	14	22	13	10	8	6	R	R	6-0	200	11-7-78	1996	Maracaibo, Venez.
Emanuel, Brandon	0	2	5.14	2	2	0	0	14	15	11	8	7	12	R	R	6-3	215	4-9-76	1998	Panama City, Fla.
Fish, Steve	11	11	4.90	32	29	5	0	197	220	125	107	72	180	R	R	6-1	190	10-25-74	1997	Bend, Ore.
Gangemi, Joe	3	11	7.16	21	15	1	0	82	118	81	65	41	55	R	L	6-3	195	5-3-76	1997	Denville, N.J.
Green, Steve	7	6	3.95	19	19	4	0	121	130	70	53	37	91	R	R	6-2	195	1-26-78	1997	Longueuil, Quebec
Hill, Jason	2	13.06	10	0	0	2	10	16	19	15	12	12	R	L	5-11	175	4-14-72	1994	Redding, Calif.
James, Mike	0	0	5.79	3	3	0	0	9	12	6	6	0	8	R	R	6-3	195	8-15-67	1988	Mary Esther, Fla.
Johnson, Greg	4	4	3.21	39	5	1	1	81	83	36	29	15	63	L	L	6-0	185	4-28-74	1996	Frostburg, Md.
Lubozynski, Matt	1	1	2.31	30	0	0	3	39	35	12	10	17	18	R	L	6-4	190	11-9-76	1998	San Antonio, Texas
McDowell, Jack	0	1	7.36	1	1	0	0	7	11	7	6	1	7	R	R	6-5	200	1-16-66	1987	Rancho Sante Fe, Calif.
Morrison, Cody	4	8	5.32	45	0	0	3	68	65	57	40	50	64	R	R	6-2	200	9-26-74	1998	Kelso, Wash.
Perozo, Felix	0	5	5.70	32	0	0	2	36	44	26	23	18	23	R	R	6-5	193	3-24-74	1991	San Pedro de Macoris, D.R.
Pipes, Joey	1	0	1.69	2	2	1	0	16	16	3	3	4	19	R	R	6-4	200	11-9-73	1998	Pacific, Mo.
Salter, Cody	1	0	4.91	7	2	0	0	22	27	12	12	8	9	R	R	6-4	200	10-8-75	1998	Plainfield, Ill.
Shepherd, Alvie	0	0	15.88	5	0	0	0	6	11	11	11	3	1	R	R	6-7	225	5-12-74	1996	Bellwood, Ill.
Shields, Scot	10	3	2.52	24	9	2	1	107	91	37	30	39	113	R	R	6-1	195	7-22-75	1997	Fort Lauderdale, Fla.
Stephens, Jason	3	3	4.19	15	11	1	0	69	84	39	32	24	66	R	R	6-0	180	9-10-75	1996	Springhill, La.

CEDAR RAPIDS — Class A

MIDWEST LEAGUE

BATTING	AVG	G	AB	R	H	2B	3B	HR	RBI	BB	SO	SB	CS	B	T	HT	WT	DOB	1st Yr	Resides
Ahlers, Steve	.265	74	260	27	69	5	1	1	29	30	44	15	9	R	R	6-0	175	11-18-78	1997	Livermore, Calif.
Christensen, Mike	.282	127	504	68	142	36	2	18	71	42	102	1	2	R	R	6-2	190	5-24-76	1998	Fort Myers, Fla.
Condon, Mike	.122	13	41	2	5	0	0	0	1	3	7	0	0	R	R	5-10	180	2-13-74	1997	Brielle, N.J.
Croud, Will	.231	87	281	39	65	11	5	2	31	46	44	5	5	S	R	5-11	170	12-29-75	1998	Miramar, Fla.
Delgado, Ariel	.259	102	359	52	93	27	1	3	47	29	63	14	1	L	L	6-2	190	9-11-76	1994	Carolina, P.R.
Diaz, Angel	.242	81	281	43	68	11	1	10	42	34	65	3	0	R	R	6-0	190	7-27-76	1998	Lakeland, Fla.
Diaz, Michael	.181	25	72	12	13	1	0	0	6	14	22	3	1	L	L	5-10	160	8-5-76	1998	Tampa, Fla.
Downing, Brad	.234	13	47	7	11	3	0	2	7	3	10	0	0	L	R	6-0	200	5-10-76	1998	Celina, Texas
Encarnacion, Bien	.262	57	206	28	54	3	2	1	23	11	33	4	2	R	R	5-11	155	2-24-78	1995	Bani, D.R.

BATTING

BATTING	AVG	G	AB	R	H	2B	3B	HR	RBI	BB	SO	SB	CS	B	T	HT	WT	DOB	1st Yr	Resides
Gastelum, Carlos	.227	19	66	8	15	1	0	0	8	6	5	2	2	R	R	5-8	158	10-29-81	1999	Huatabampo, Mexico
Gay, Dennis	.191	16	47	4	9	3	0	0	8	4	14	0	0	R	R	6-2	180	7-12-76	1999	Macclenny, Fla.
Guzman, Elpidio	.274	130	526	74	144	26	13	4	48	41	84	52	17	L	L	6-2	165	2-24-79	1996	Santo Domingo, D.R.
Hill, Jason	.287	111	390	59	112	22	0	9	52	36	59	3	2	R	R	6-3	210	3-17-77	1998	Danville, Calif.
Knight, Marcus	.216	132	462	69	100	20	7	9	52	61	97	21	8	S	R	6-0	180	9-10-78	1996	Pembroke Pines, Fla.
Lopez, Norberto	.167	2	6	0	1	0	0	0	1	1	2	0	0	R	R	5-8	180	12-9-76	1999	Hialeah, Fla.
Medosch, Keith	.125	20	40	4	5	0	0	0	9	15	0	1	0	R	R	5-11	175	1-31-75	1997	St. Petersburg, Fla.
Oliver, Bill	.082	21	61	6	5	1	0	1	1	6	28	0	0	R	R	6-2	205	5-27-75	1998	San Jose, Calif.
Oliver, Brian	.274	66	252	43	69	16	1	6	29	26	30	12	1	R	R	5-10	170	11-7-76	1998	Antioch, Calif.
Pond, Ryan	.246	44	167	18	41	12	0	4	21	11	34	2	1	R	R	6-0	185	10-10-74	1999	Logan, Utah
Rapp, Travis	.189	14	37	6	7	3	0	1	8	2	16	0	0	R	R	6-2	205	1-28-75	1997	Sebring, Fla.
Ross, Justin	.288	51	184	43	53	14	0	3	23	53	30	10	3	L	L	6-2	193	12-24-76	1998	Wexford, Pa.
Stuart, Rich	.288	67	250	46	72	16	2	15	55	30	53	8	4	R	R	5-11	170	7-31-76	1994	Arecibo, P.R.
Ticen, Kevin	.284	27	88	8	25	4	0	1	10	8	24	0	1	R	R	5-11	195	4-9-76	1999	Bellevue, Wash.

GAMES BY POSITION: C—Christensen 1, A. Diaz 32, Hill 96, Lopez 2, Rapp 8, Ticen 6. **1B**—Delgado 97, A. Diaz 18, Bi. Oliver 15, Ross 5, Ticen 10. **2B**—Ahlers 24, Condon 13, Encarnacion 20, Gastelum 11, Gay 9, Medosch 8, Br. Oliver 20, Pond 38. **3B**—Ahlers 5, Christensen 125, Gastelum 3, Gay 5, Medosch 3, Ticen 4. **SS**—Ahlers 47, Encarnacion 37, Gastelum 5, Gay 2, Medosch 5, Bi. Oliver 1, Br. Oliver 47. **OF**—Croud 76, M. Diaz 21, Downing 11, Guzman 130, Knight 130, Ross 32, Stuart 21.

PITCHING

PITCHING	W	L	ERA	G	GS	CG	SV	IP	H	R	ER	BB	SO	B	T	HT	WT	DOB	1st Yr	Resides
Bridges, Doug	15	5	3.59	22	22	3	0	150	136	67	60	45	128	L	L	6-2	185	7-20-76	1998	Columbia, S.C.
Cummings, Ryan	5	8	4.39	19	19	3	0	121	104	69	59	35	97	R	R	6-2	210	6-3-76	1997	Marietta, Ga.
Demouy, Chris	2	1	2.40	46	0	0	16	49	39	18	13	28	51	R	L	6-1	205	11-3-75	1998	Baton Rouge, La.
Dobson, Dwayne	1	7	8.51	22	6	0	0	61	94	75	58	43	31	R	R	6-5	205	2-23-76	1997	Clearwater, Fla.
Duarte, Renney	6	11	4.75	31	18	3	1	133	145	81	70	33	102	R	R	6-0	220	11-7-76	1996	Maracaibo, Venez.
Emanuel, Brandon	7	12	4.47	23	23	5	0	153	173	92	76	50	88	R	R	6-3	215	4-9-76	1998	Panama City, Fla.
Ferrier, Shayne	0	0	5.06	7	0	0	0	11	11	10	6	8	8	R	R	6-0	200	4-13-76	1999	Springfield, Mo.
Freehill, Mike	0	0	11.57	2	0	0	0	2	2	3	3	4	2	R	R	6-2	175	6-2-71	1994	Phoenix, Ariz.
Gangemi, Joe	1	2	3.58	5	5	0	0	28	37	17	11	13	23	R	L	6-3	195	5-3-76	1997	Denville, N.J.
Gilich, Denny	3	7	4.22	51	0	0	2	64	62	36	30	31	79	R	R	6-7	210	8-21-75	1998	Gig Harbor, Wash.
Harwas, Oliver	3	4	5.61	37	0	0	2	51	50	40	32	29	37	R	R	6-7	210	8-7-75	1998	Okeechobee, Fla.
Hundley, Jeff	9	9	4.04	25	25	6	0	158	163	99	71	62	140	L	L	6-2	205	2-19-77	1998	Warren, Ohio
Jacobs, Greg	2	5	4.44	36	10	0	1	105	108	62	52	37	106	L	L	5-10	180	10-9-76	1998	Anaheim Hills, Calif.
Jones, Greg	2	4	3.83	34	0	0	13	40	37	18	17	13	41	R	R	6-2	190	11-15-76	1997	Seminole, Fla.
Parker, Allan	0	0	54.00	1	0	0	0	1	7	6	6	0	0	R	R	5-11	165	5-27-72	1994	Odessa, Fla.
Pipes, Joey	4	1	2.95	7	6	1	0	43	45	24	14	11	23	R	R	6-4	220	11-9-73	1998	Pacific, Mo.
Shepherd, Alvie	0	0	4.70	6	0	0	0	8	4	5	4	3	8	R	R	6-7	220	5-12-74	1996	Bellwood, Ill.
Suarez, Luis	1	1	7.00	4	4	0	0	18	25	19	14	9	15	R	R	6-2	180	3-12-76	1998	Sunrise, Fla.

BOISE Short-Season Class A

NORTHWEST LEAGUE

BATTING

BATTING	AVG	G	AB	R	H	2B	3B	HR	RBI	BB	SO	SB	CS	B	T	HT	WT	DOB	1st Yr	Resides
Amezaga, Alfredo	.322	48	205	52	66	6	4	2	29	23	29	14	3	R	R	5-10	165	1-16-78	1999	Ciudad Obregon, Mexico
Barski, Chris	.348	53	184	39	64	14	0	6	39	30	44	1	0	L	R	6-2	210	1-14-78	1999	Langley, B.C.
Bikowski, Scott	.297	65	246	59	73	22	0	2	45	46	42	11	4	L	L	6-0	185	2-12-77	1999	Suffield, Conn.
Boeth, Tim	.296	51	169	36	50	11	2	2	22	24	21	9	6	R	R	6-0	185	11-3-76	1999	Tallahassee, Fla.
Doudt, Anthony	.242	23	62	9	15	4	0	2	12	6	17	0	0	R	R	6-4	205	5-22-77	1999	Muncie, Ind.
Gay, Dennis	.242	10	33	5	8	2	0	0	5	3	6	0	0	R	R	6-2	180	7-12-76	1999	Macclenny, Fla.
Gregorio, Thomas	.296	52	186	29	55	10	1	5	36	11	33	0	1	R	R	6-2	200	5-5-77	1999	Staten Island, N.Y.
Hart, Dickie	.000	4	2	0	0	0	0	0	0	0	2	0	0	R	R	5-9	165	12-15-76	1999	Palm Harbor, Fla.
Johnson, Gary	.314	71	264	56	83	17	1	2	48	34	44	6	2	L	L	6-3	210	10-29-75	1999	Atherton, Calif.
Kelleher, Pat	.176	9	17	4	3	2	0	0	2	8	4	3	0	L	R	6-1	185	10-27-76	1997	Paradise Valley, Ariz.
Kelley, Casey	.307	61	205	45	63	12	4	7	37	32	60	2	1	L	R	6-2	220	11-4-76	1998	Ellensburg, Wash.
Lombardi, Dominick	.292	6	24	1	7	2	0	0	5	2	3	0	0	R	R	5-10	205	3-10-76	1998	Mission Viejo, Calif.
Lopez, Norberto	.231	5	13	1	3	1	0	0	0	2	5	0	0	R	R	5-8	180	12-9-76	1999	Hialeah, Fla.
O'Keefe, Mike	.326	72	264	52	86	13	1	9	70	54	41	4	1	L	L	5-10	205	6-28-78	1999	Hamden, Conn.
Palmieri, Jon	.325	48	151	34	49	10	2	2	31	17	10	4	4	R	R	6-1	205	6-19-77	1999	Melville, N.Y.
Quinlan, Robb	.322	73	295	51	95	20	1	9	77	35	52	5	3	R	R	6-1	195	3-17-77	1999	Maplewood, Minn.
Santos, Jose	.000	1	1	0	0	0	0	0	0	0	0	0	0	R	R	6-0	205	5-12-77	1995	San Pedro de Macoris, D.R.
Seever, Brian	.320	36	103	32	33	5	1	0	7	21	27	14	3	R	R	6-0	196	8-18-76	1998	Fairfield, Calif.
Shaffer, Josh	.209	66	225	46	47	11	0	1	21	30	65	3	4	L	R	6-1	175	6-26-80	1999	Las Vegas, Nev.
Ticen, Kevin	.292	14	48	5	14	5	0	0	9	3	10	1	0	R	R	5-11	195	4-9-76	1999	Bellevue, Wash.

GAMES BY POSITION: C—Barski 6, Doudt 17, Gregorio 51, Lombardi 6, Lopez 5. **1B**—Kelley 53, Palmieri 31, Quinlan 2. **2B**—Amezaga 40, Boeth 29, Gay 6, Hart 3, Quinlan 6. **3B**—Boeth 3, Quinlan 64, Santos 1, Ticen 11. **SS**—Amezaga 10, Gay 4, Shaffer 66. **OF**—Bikowski 61, Boeth 4, Johnson 69, Kelleher 6, O'Keefe 72, Seever 7.

PITCHING

PITCHING	W	L	ERA	G	GS	CG	SV	IP	H	R	ER	BB	SO	B	T	HT	WT	DOB	1st Yr	Resides
Bergman, Dusty	5	5	6.54	15	15	0	0	74	102	58	54	18	46	L	L	6-4	200	2-1-78	1999	Carson City, Nev.
Berryman, Chad	1	1	2.35	24	0	1	0	46	34	16	12	13	42	R	R	6-3	190	8-2-76	1998	Kannapolis, N.C.
Brummett, Sean	1	2	6.68	17	3	0	0	32	41	25	24	12	26	L	L	6-0	200	1-10-78	1999	Brookston, Ind.
Crawford, Wesley	5	1	2.21	11	9	2	0	61	52	23	15	17	54	S	L	6-3	220	12-14-77	1999	Panama City Beach, Fla.
Diaz, Zach	1	2	2.43	17	0	0	2	30	36	11	8	7	24	L	L	6-0	600	6-5-76	1999	Lakeland, Fla.
Ebanks, Palmer	6	3	3.94	27	0	0	3	48	44	23	21	22	53	R	R	6-1	170	1-14-77	1999	Tampa, Fla.
Ferrier, Shayne	0	0	27.00	4	0	0	0	3	9	10	10	4	2	R	R	6-0	200	4-13-76	1999	Springfield, Mo.
Glysch, Craig	3	4	3.62	22	0	0	2	32	30	15	13	7	28	L	R	6-3	215	11-15-76	1999	Green Bay, Wis.
Grezlovski, Ben	0	1	2.16	14	0	0	7	17	11	5	4	3	20	R	R	5-11	180	11-22-76	1999	Miami, Fla.
Haworth, Brent	0	0	5.40	14	0	0	0	20	30	26	15	14	14	R	R	6-6	205	2-26-77	1999	Orlando, Fla.
Hurtado, Ed	0	0	18.00	4	0	0	0	4	8	9	8	3	3	R	R	6-1	200	9-29-76	1998	Riverside, Calif.
Lackey, John	6	2	4.98	15	15	1	0	81	81	59	45	50	77	R	R	6-6	205	10-23-78	1999	Abilene, Texas
LaCorte, Vince	2	6	5.40	11	9	0	0	50	64	38	30	13	38	R	R	6-3	190	9-10-76	1998	Gilroy, Calif.
Mendoza, Mario	8	2	5.49	15	15	0	0	79	93	58	48	29	47	R	R	6-3	200	1-19-79	1999	Navojoa, Mexico
Moore, Greg	2	2	5.02	10	4	0	0	29	39	22	16	6	24	R	R	6-6	215	5-23-79	1999	San Ramon, Calif.
Padilla, Charly	1	0	7.23	10	0	0	0	19	21	16	15	13	14	R	R	6-4	180	9-11-76	1996	San Felipe, Venez.

PITCHING	W	L	ERA	G	GS	CG	SV	IP	H	R	ER	BB	SO	B	T	HT	WT	DOB	1st Yr	Resides
Rodriguez, Francisco ..	1	0	5.40	1	1	0	0	5	3	4	3	1	6	R	R	6-0	165	1-7-82	1999	Caracas, Venez.
Schreyer, Brett	0	0	1.08	9	0	0	2	8	6	5	1	7	8	R	R	6-2	215	10-15-76	1999	Waterford, N.J.
Suarez, Felipe	1	2	6.07	5	5	0	0	30	32	26	20	11	33	R	R	6-2	185	3-12-76	1998	Sunrise, Fla.
Sullivan, Luke	0	0	13.50	2	0	0	0	1	2	2	2	2	1	L	L	5-11	170	7-10-76	1999	Johnstown, Colo.

BUTTE   Rookie

PIONEER LEAGUE

BATTING	AVG	G	AB	R	H	2B	3B	HR	RBI	BB	SO	SB	CS	B	T	HT	WT	DOB	1st Yr	Resides
Amezaga, Alfredo	.294	8	34	11	10	2	0	0	5	5	5	6	2	R	R	5-10	165	1-16-78	1999	Ciudad Obregon, Mexico
Curtis, Bill	.319	66	238	40	76	18	1	6	46	35	58	0	2	S	R	6-2	195	11-11-77	1999	Middleville, Mich.
Diaz, Michael	.327	14	49	22	16	1	0	0	2	15	7	11	2	L	L	5-10	160	8-5-76	1998	Tampa, Fla.
Duran, Francisco	.249	53	209	39	52	6	1	2	43	26	40	8	4	R	R	5-11	160	6-3-79	1996	La Vega, D.R.
Duverge, Alcides	.213	26	89	12	19	3	2	1	7	5	28	1	1	R	R	6-2	195	10-5-79	1999	South Ozone Park, N.Y.
Gastelum, Carlos	.261	58	211	37	55	12	2	0	28	22	28	11	5	R	R	5-8	158	10-29-81	1999	Huatabampo, Mexico
Gosewisch, Chip	.246	55	207	29	51	10	2	1	30	12	43	0	2	R	R	5-8	170	2-28-77	1999	Scottsdale, Ariz.
Hills, Chris	.217	31	92	15	20	3	0	0	13	8	30	2	1	R	R	6-0	180	8-31-77	1999	Luling, La.
Jackson, Brandon	.279	22	68	16	19	2	1	3	13	10	28	3	1	R	L	6-4	195	1-1-77	1999	Savannah, Ga.
Lindsey, Del	.341	63	255	72	87	23	7	10	58	23	46	13	5	R	R	6-1	190	3-8-78	1999	Houston, Texas
Lopez, Norberto	.118	8	17	1	2	0	0	0	0	0	8	0	0	R	R	5-8	180	12-9-76	1999	Hialeah, Fla.
Martin, Brandon	.246	45	142	22	35	4	4	1	21	23	40	11	4	L	R	5-11	170	10-9-79	1999	Fontana, Calif.
Orgill, Peter	.323	58	217	43	70	8	1	5	36	26	38	0	0	L	R	6-3	225	3-16-77	1999	Yakima, Wash.
Ortiz, Miguel	.387	31	124	24	48	8	3	6	29	2	19	3	3	L	R	6-1	175	2-19-79	1996	Villa de Cura, Venez.
Pichardo, Gilberto	.234	41	137	32	32	6	2	4	16	9	39	2	0	R	R	6-1	195	1-8-79	1997	Brooklyn, N.Y.
Sharp, Preston	.327	26	98	25	32	3	4	1	12	11	15	9	2	S	R	6-0	185	4-22-77	1999	Chico, Calif.
Templeton, Garry	.204	33	93	16	19	0	0	0	11	8	28	4	1	R	R	5-9	175	8-24-78	1999	Poway, Calif.
Wagner, Jeff	.382	8	34	7	13	4	0	2	10	0	5	0	0	R	R	6-3	240	1-5-77	1999	Louisville, Ky.
Welch, Ed	.344	31	122	29	42	4	2	0	19	18	30	24	6	L	R	6-0	190	2-22-80	1998	Vancouver, B.C.
White, Greg	.327	55	205	37	67	15	2	9	47	26	50	1	2	R	R	6-5	210	2-17-76	1999	Waynesboro, Pa.

GAMES BY POSITION: C—Duverge 23, Gosewisch 37, Lopez 8, Orgill 15. **1B**—Gosewisch 3, Martin 2, Orgill 43, Ortiz 4, Sharp 1, White 32. **2B**—Amezaga 6, Duran 35, Gosewisch 6, Ortiz 9, Sharp 10, Templeton 20. **3B**—Duran 8, Lindsey 57, Ortiz 10, White 5. **SS**—Amezaga 2, Duran 18, Gastelum 58, Lindsey 4. **OF**—Curtis 38, Diaz 14, Duverge 1, Hills 29, Jackson 22, Martin 41, Pichardo 39, Sharp 15, Templeton 13, Welch 31, White 6.

PITCHING	W	L	ERA	G	GS	CG	SV	IP	H	R	ER	BB	SO	B	T	HT	WT	DOB	1st Yr	Resides
Bowen, Patrick	2	2	7.64	20	7	0	0	55	81	59	47	35	48	R	R	6-3	220	2-28-77	1999	Millersville, Md.
Brunet, Michael	1	0	1.69	9	0	0	3	11	8	2	2	4	12	R	R	6-2	175	3-5-77	1997	Land O' Lakes, Fla.
Bukowski, Stan	1	2	3.21	10	5	0	0	28	26	13	10	16	29	R	R	6-4	210	9-16-81	1999	Clearwater, Fla.
Easton, Eric	0	1	12.00	16	0	0	0	18	29	37	24	20	18	R	R	6-7	220	3-6-79	1998	Tarpon Springs, Fla.
Flading, Cameron	1	0	7.24	20	0	0	0	27	39	26	22	17	19	L	R	6-2	200	8-25-78	1999	Anaheim, Calif.
Franke, Aaron	4	5	4.35	15	15	0	0	79	76	52	38	32	69	R	R	6-3	220	8-13-79	1999	Oregon, Ohio
Gomez, Odalis	2	7	10.22	22	5	0	0	37	44	58	42	50	42	R	R	5-8	170	11-30-78	1998	San Diego, Calif.
Harris, J.T.	3	4	4.35	23	0	0	0	39	43	25	19	13	34	R	R	5-11	165	6-29-76	1998	San Jose, Calif.
Harris, Julian	2	9	8.38	17	16	0	0	82	132	95	76	36	67	L	L	6-3	175	9-26-77	1998	San Jose, Calif.
Haworth, Brent	0	0	10.38	5	0	0	1	4	4	6	5	4	3	R	R	6-6	205	2-26-77	1999	Orlando, Fla.
Matias, Adalberto	3	2	7.85	17	7	0	0	47	68	47	41	23	27	R	R	6-1	165	6-20-79	1998	Cotui, D.R.
McClain, Kevin	4	5	8.95	18	11	0	0	58	85	67	58	28	51	R	R	6-4	180	2-22-78	1998	Palm Bay, Fla.
Nebel, Jeff	3	2	4.06	29	0	0	5	31	34	15	14	12	26	R	R	6-1	215	7-7-76	1999	Lawrenceville, Ga.
Rodriguez, Francisco ..	1	1	3.31	12	9	1	0	52	33	21	19	21	69	R	R	6-0	165	1-7-82	1999	Caracas, Venez.
Sanchez, Sinuhe	3	3	5.94	27	0	0	2	36	52	36	24	11	33	L	L	6-1	160	7-21-77	1997	Mexicali, Mexico
Schreyer, Brett	0	0	2.53	10	0	0	0	11	9	3	3	9	6	R	R	6-2	215	10-15-76	1999	Waterford, N.J.
Wakefield, Doug	0	0	4.15	3	0	0	0	4	5	2	2	1	3	R	L	6-7	240	8-17-76	1998	Apple Valley, Calif.
Warren, Josh	2	0	10.93	14	0	0	1	28	44	38	34	16	16	R	R	6-5	220	2-4-79	1999	Kirkland, Wash.

ARIZONA DIAMONDBACKS

Diamondbacks set new standard for expansion franchises

BY JACK MAGRUDER

Meet the new model of the expansion experience. The 1999 Diamondbacks made all the others obsolete in their second year, when their lavish offseason spending brought them a division title and a long list of firsts.

The Diamondbacks were the quickest of the 14 expansion franchises since 1961 to reach the franchise .500 mark, to win a division title, to make it to the postseason and to win 100 games.

"This business is all about winning," team owner Jerry Colangelo said. "When I got into it, I wanted to win. People took their shots, but we operated by the rules. We wanted to compete. We did set out to make the playoffs in the second year. Obviously, you feel good about reaching goals. There is some satisfaction there."

The Diamondbacks, who lost 97 games in their inaugural season in 1998, committed $118.9 million on reinforcements–free agents Randy Johnson ($52.4 million), Todd Stottlemyre ($32 million), Steve Finley ($21.5 million), Armando Reynoso, Greg Colbrunn and Greg Swindell.

Those new faces, combined with the addition of Luis Gonzalez, Tony Womack and Matt Mantei through trades, helped the Diamondbacks to a 35-game turnaround, the biggest in major league history.

With Womack adding speed at the top of the order, the Diamondbacks lineup gelled. Nos. 2-3-4 hitters Jay Bell, Gonzalez and Matt Williams had career years. Bell, playing second base full-time for the first time in his career, hit 38 home runs, almost double his previous career high of 21. Gonzalez, acquired from the Tigers for outfielder Karim Garcia, led the National League with a career-high 206 hits and had five hitting streaks

Randy Johnson | **Jack Cust**

Players of the Year

MAJOR LEAGUE: Randy Johnson, lhp
Johnson led the NL with a 2.48 ERA and his 364 strikeouts were the most in the league since Sandy Koufax had 382 in 1965.

MINOR LEAGUE: Jack Cust, of
Cust hit .334 and led Diamondbacks minor leaguers with 32 home runs and 112 RBIs at High Desert.

of at least 10 games, including a 30-gamer in April and May. Williams set career highs in RBIs (142) and hits (190) while making a run at the MVP award. Finley had a career-high 34 homers and 103 RBIs.

And while the hitters hit, the pitchers had the second-best ERA in the league behind stopper Johnson. He made a run at Nolan Ryan's season strikeout record of 383, finishing with 364. Johnson went 17-9 and led the NL with a 2.48 ERA. A string of tough losses in the middle of the season cost him a 20-win season. Closer Mantei had 22 of his 32 saves after arriving in a July 9 trade with the Marlins, adding the final piece.

Rookie first baseman Erubiel Durazo and Korean righthander Byung-Hyun Kim were examples of the Diamondbacks' system-wide aggressiveness. Durazo, signed out of the Mexican League, hit .329 in 52 games after hitting .404 in two minor league stops.

The Diamondbacks were able to make the Mantei trade by sending prospects Vladimir Nunez and Brad Penny, among their best minor league talent, to the Marlins. But the system remained strong. Righthander John Patterson was the first-game starter for Team USA in the Pan American Games, while outfielders Jack Cust and Abraham Nunez were among the Class A California League's top prospects. Cust had one of the best offensive seasons in the minors, hitting .334 with 32 homers and 112 RBIs for High Desert.

Rookie-level Missoula won the Pioneer League title, led by third baseman Jeff Brooks, who homered in both games of the final series. Shortstop Corey Myers, the No. 4 overall pick in the draft, made his pro debut at Missoula.

ORGANIZATION LEADERS

BATTING

*AVG	Erubiel Durazo, Tucson/El Paso	.404
R	Jarrod Patterson, Tucson/El Paso	109
H	Jarrod Patterson, Tucson/El Paso	187
TB	Jarrod Patterson, Tucson/El Paso	308
2B	Jarrod Patterson, Tucson/El Paso	52
3B	Jamie Sykes, South Bend	10
HR	Jack Cust, High Desert	32
RBI	Jack Cust, High Desert	112
BB	J.D. Closser, South Bend/Missoula	105
SO	Jack Cust, High Desert	145
SB	Abraham Nunez, High Desert	40

PITCHING

W	Ben Norris, El Paso/High Desert	12
L	Hatuey Mendoza, S. Bend/Missoula/AZL	16
#ERA	Chris Cervantes, High Desert/South Bend	3.59
G	Two tied at	45
CG	Eric Knott, El Paso	3
SV	Chris Bloomer, South Bend	21
IP	Eric Knott, El Paso	161
BB	Hatuey Mendoza, South Bend/Missoula/AZL	78
SO	Two tied at	146

*Minimum 250 At-Bats #Minimum 75 Innings

Arizona
DIAMONDBACKS

Manager: Buck Showalter

1999 Record: 100-62, .617 (1st, NL West)

BATTING	AVG	G	AB	R	H	2B	3B	HR	RBI	BB	SO	SB	CS	B	T	HT	WT	DOB	1st Yr	Resides
Barajas, Rod	.250	5	16	3	4	1	0	1	3	1	1	0	0	R	R	6-2	220	9-5-75	1996	Norwalk, Calif.
Batista, Tony	.257	44	144	16	37	5	0	5	21	16	17	2	0	R	R	6-0	195	12-9-73	1992	Mao Valverde, D.R.
Bell, Jay	.289	151	589	132	170	32	6	38	112	82	132	7	4	R	R	6-0	182	12-11-65	1984	Valrico, Fla.
Colbrunn, Greg	.326	67	135	20	44	5	3	5	24	12	23	1	1	R	R	6-0	200	7-26-69	1988	Weston, Fla.
Dellucci, David	.394	63	109	27	43	7	1	1	15	11	24	2	0	L	L	5-10	180	10-31-73	1995	Baton Rouge, La.
Diaz, Edwin	.400	4	5	2	2	2	0	0	1	3	1	0	0	R	R	5-11	170	1-15-75	1993	Vega Alta, P.R.
Durazo, Erubiel	.329	52	155	31	51	4	2	11	30	26	43	1	1	L	L	6-3	225	1-23-74	1997	Hermosillo, Mexico
Finley, Steve	.264	156	590	100	156	32	10	34	103	63	94	8	4	L	L	6-2	180	3-12-65	1987	Del Mar, Calif.
Fox, Andy	.255	99	274	34	70	12	2	6	33	33	61	4	1	L	R	6-4	185	1-12-71	1989	Sacramento, Calif.
Frias, Hanley	.273	69	150	27	41	3	2	1	16	29	18	4	3	S	R	6-0	165	12-5-73	1991	Villa Ariagracia, D.R.
Gilkey, Bernard	.294	94	204	28	60	16	1	8	39	29	42	2	2	R	R	6-0	200	9-24-66	1985	St. Louis, Mo.
Gonzalez, Luis	.336	153	614	112	206	45	4	26	111	66	63	9	5	L	R	6-2	190	9-2-67	1988	Sugar Land, Texas
Harris, Lenny	.379	19	29	2	11	1	0	1	7	0	1	1	0	L	R	5-10	210	10-28-64	1983	Miami, Fla.
2-team (91 Colo.)	.310	110	187	17	58	13	0	1	20	6	7	2	1							
Klassen, Danny	1.000	1	1	0	1	0	0	0	0	0	0	0	0	R	R	6-0	175	9-22-75	1993	Stuart, Fla.
Lee, Travis	.237	120	375	57	89	16	2	9	50	58	50	17	3	L	L	6-3	210	5-26-75	1997	Olympia, Wash.
Miller, Damian	.270	86	296	35	80	19	0	11	47	19	78	0	0	R	R	6-2	190	10-13-69	1990	La Crosse, Wis.
Powell, Dante	.160	22	25	4	4	3	0	0	1	2	6	2	1	R	R	6-2	185	8-25-73	1994	Long Beach, Calif.
Ryan, Rob	.241	20	29	4	7	1	0	2	5	1	8	0	0	L	L	5-11	190	6-24-73	1996	Spokane, Wash.
Stinnett, Kelly	.232	88	284	36	66	13	0	14	38	24	83	2	1	R	R	5-11	195	2-4-70	1990	Lawton, Okla.
Ward, Turner	.348	10	23	6	8	1	0	2	7	2	6	0	0	S	R	6-2	190	4-11-65	1986	Saraland, Ala.
2-team (49 Pitt.)	.237	59	114	8	27	3	0	2	15	15	15	2	2							
Williams, Matt	.303	154	627	98	190	37	2	35	142	41	93	2	0	R	R	6-2	210	11-28-65	1986	Scottsdale, Ariz.
Womack, Tony	.277	144	614	111	170	25	10	4	41	52	68	72	13	L	R	5-9	155	9-25-69	1991	Greensboro, N.C.
Young, Ernie	.182	6	11	1	2	0	0	0	0	3	2	0	0	R	R	6-1	234	7-8-69	1990	Mesa, Ariz.

PITCHING	W	L	ERA	G	GS	CG	SV	IP	H	R	ER	BB	SO	B	T	HT	WT	DOB	1st Yr	Resides
Anderson, Brian	8	2	4.57	31	19	2	1	130	144	69	66	28	75	S	L	6-1	190	4-26-72	1993	North Olmstead, Ohio
Benes, Andy	13	12	4.81	33	32	0	0	198	216	117	106	82	141	R	R	6-6	245	8-20-67	1989	Phoenix, Ariz.
Carlson, Dan	0	0	9.00	2	0	0	0	4	5	4	4	0	3	R	R	6-1	185	1-26-70	1990	Portland, Ore.
Chouinard, Bobby	5	2	2.68	32	0	0	1	40	31	16	12	12	23	R	R	6-1	188	5-1-72	1990	Forest Grove, Ore.
Daal, Omar	16	9	3.65	32	32	2	0	215	188	92	87	79	148	L	L	6-3	185	3-1-72	1990	Maracaibo, Venez.
Frascatore, John	1	4	4.09	26	0	0	3	33	31	16	15	12	15	R	R	6-1	200	2-4-70	1991	Oceanside, N.Y.
Holmes, Darren	4	3	3.70	44	0	0	0	49	50	21	20	25	35	R	R	6-0	202	4-25-66	1984	Fletcher, N.C.
Johnson, Randy	17	9	2.48	35	35	12	0	272	207	86	75	70	364	R	L	6-10	230	9-10-63	1985	Glendale, Ariz.
Kim, Byung-Hyun	1	2	4.61	25	0	0	1	27	20	15	14	20	31	R	R	5-11	176	1-21-79	1999	Kwangsan-Ku, Korea
Kubenka, Jeff	0	1	11.74	6	0	0	0	8	13	12	10	4	2	R	L	6-1	191	8-24-74	1996	Schulenburg, Texas
Mantei, Matt	0	1	2.79	30	0	0	22	29	20	10	9	19	49	R	R	6-1	190	7-7-73	1991	Pembroke Pines, Fla.
2-team (35 Florida)	1	3	2.76	65	0	0	32	65	44	21	20	44	99							
Nunez, Vladimir	3	2	2.91	27	0	0	1	34	29	15	11	20	28	R	R	6-4	235	3-15-75	1996	Santo Domingo, D.R.
Olson, Gregg	9	4	3.71	61	0	0	14	61	54	28	25	25	45	R	R	6-4	210	10-11-66	1988	Reisterstown, Md.
Padilla, Vicente	0	1	16.88	5	0	0	0	3	7	5	5	3	0	R	R	6-2	200	9-27-77	1998	Managua, Nicaragua
Plesac, Dan	2	1	3.32	34	0	0	1	22	22	9	8	8	27	L	L	6-5	217	2-4-62	1983	Valparaiso, Ind.
Reynoso, Armando	10	6	4.37	31	27	0	0	167	178	90	81	67	79	R	R	6-0	196	5-1-66	1989	Lagos de Moreno, Mex.
Sabel, Erik	0	0	6.52	7	0	0	0	10	12	7	7	6	6	R	R	6-3	193	10-14-74	1996	West Lafayette, Ind.
Stottlemyre, Todd	6	3	4.09	17	17	0	0	101	106	51	46	40	74	L	R	6-3	195	5-20-65	1986	Yakima, Wash.
Swindell, Greg	4	0	2.51	63	0	0	1	65	54	19	18	21	51	R	L	6-3	230	1-2-65	1986	Houston, Texas
Telemaco, Amaury	1	0	7.50	5	0	0	0	6	7	5	5	6	2	R	R	6-3	210	1-19-74	1991	La Romana, D.R.
Vosberg, Ed	1	1	3.38	4	0	0	0	3	6	1	1	0	2	L	L	6-1	210	9-28-61	1983	Tucson, Ariz.
2-team (15 S.D.)	0	1	8.18	19	0	0	0	11	22	12	10	3	8							

FIELDING

Catcher	PCT	G	PO	A	E	DP	PB
Barajas	1.000	5	30	1	0	0	1
Miller	.991	86	622	61	6	9	11
Stinnett	.990	86	549	37	6	7	5

First Base	PCT	G	PO	A	E	DP
Colbrunn	.996	39	203	19	1	21
Durazo	1.000	44	324	20	0	25
Lee	.997	114	802	62	3	65

Second Base	PCT	G	PO	A	E	DP
Bell	.968	148	320	339	22	86
Diaz	1.000	2	0	3	0	0
Frias	1.000	8	4	6	0	2
Harris	.924	24	46	51	8	19
Womack	.971	19	30	36	2	6

Third Base	PCT	G	PO	A	E	DP
Colbrunn	.000	1	0	0	0	0
Fox	.909	12	5	15	2	2
Harris	1.000	5	3	5	0	2
Williams	.977	153	123	299	10	30

Shortstop	PCT	G	PO	A	E	DP
Batista	.979	43	60	130	4	27
Bell	.000	1	0	0	0	0
Diaz	1.000	2	4	2	0	0
Fox	.958	82	95	181	12	33
Frias	.965	53	42	95	5	16
Womack	.982	19	16	40	1	5

Outfield	PCT	G	PO	A	E	DP
Dellucci	1.000	31	37	1	0	0
Finley	.995	155	397	5	2	0
Gilkey	.969	53	90	3	3	0
Gonzalez	.983	148	271	10	5	1
Harris	1.000	2	3	0	0	0
Lee	1.000	2	3	0	0	0
Powell	.929	15	13	0	1	0
Ryan	1.000	5	7	0	0	0
Ward	1.000	5	11	0	0	0
Womack	.992	123	247	9	2	2
Young	1.000	4	10	1	0	1

Matt Williams

MEL BAILEY

Director, Minor League Operations: Tommy Jones

Class	Farm Team	League	W	L	Pct.	Finish*	Manager	First Yr
AAA	Tucson (Ariz.) Sidewinders	Pacific Coast	66	76	.465	13th (16)	Chris Speier	1998
AA	El Paso (Texas) Diablos	Texas	64	76	.457	7th (8)	Don Wakamatsu	1999
A#	High Desert (Calif.) Mavericks	California	68	72	.486	6th (10)	Derek Bryant	1997
A	South Bend (Ind.) Silver Hawks	Midwest	68	71	.489	9th (14)	Mike Brumley	1997
Rookie#	Missoula (Mont.) Osprey	Pioneer	45	31	.592	+3rd (8)	Joe Almaraz	1999
Rookie	Tucson (Ariz.) Diamondbacks	Arizona	24	32	.429	6th (8)	Roly de Armas	1996

*Finish in overall standings (No. of teams in league) #Advanced level +Won league championship

TUCSON — Class AAA

PACIFIC COAST LEAGUE

BATTING	AVG	G	AB	R	H	2B	3B	HR	RBI	BB	SO	SB	CS	B	T	HT	WT	DOB	1st Yr	Resides
Belliard, Francisco	.143	3	7	0	1	0	0	0	2	1	3	0	0	S	R	5-11	165	11-27-79	1997	Santiago, D.R.
Conti, Jason	.290	133	520	100	151	23	8	9	57	55	89	22	8	L	R	5-11	180	1-27-75	1996	Cranberry Township, Pa.
Coolbaugh, Scott	.255	74	212	28	54	14	1	7	31	32	49	1	1	R	R	5-11	195	6-13-66	1987	Seguin, Texas
Diaz, Edwin	.311	107	415	72	129	24	1	11	50	17	77	6	7	R	R	5-11	170	1-15-75	1993	Vega Alta, P.R.
Durazo, Erubiel	.407	30	118	27	48	7	0	10	28	14	18	1	0	L	L	6-3	225	1-23-74	1997	Hermosillo, Mexico
Foster, Jim	.269	11	26	4	7	1	0	0	3	4	2	0	0	R	R	6-3	208	8-18-71	1993	Warwick, R.I.
Frias, Hanley	.300	23	80	15	24	3	0	0	6	7	15	3	1	S	R	6-0	165	12-5-73	1991	Villa Ariagracia, D.R.
Hanel, Marcus	.067	6	15	1	1	0	0	0	4	2	0	0	0	R	R	6-4	205	10-19-71	1989	Racine, Wis.
Huckaby, Ken	.301	107	355	44	107	20	1	2	42	13	33	0	0	R	R	6-1	205	1-27-71	1991	Philadelphia, Pa.
Incaviglia, Pete	.156	8	32	3	5	4	0	0	7	1	11	1	0	R	R	6-1	230	4-2-64	1986	Colleyville, Texas
Johnson, Keith	.287	107	356	61	102	19	0	12	46	30	71	2	4	R	R	5-11	200	4-17-71	1992	Stockton, Calif.
Klassen, Danny	.269	64	245	38	66	16	3	6	33	20	51	5	3	R	R	6-0	175	9-22-75	1993	Stuart, Fla.
Koeyers, Ramsey	.128	15	39	6	5	1	0	0	1	4	7	0	0	R	R	6-1	187	8-7-74	1991	Willemstad, Neth. Antilles
Pachot, John	.265	35	102	10	27	4	0	1	11	3	10	1	0	R	R	6-2	168	11-11-74	1993	Ponce, P.R.
Patterson, Jarrod	.336	75	274	46	92	25	3	11	47	36	37	4	1	L	R	6-1	195	9-7-73	1993	Clanton, Ala.
Powell, Dante	.332	51	187	29	62	14	2	7	30	14	38	22	6	R	R	6-2	185	8-25-73	1994	Long Beach, Calif.
Rios, Eduardo	.375	3	8	1	3	1	0	1	2	0	3	0	0	R	R	5-11	178	10-13-72	1991	Charallave, Venez.
Ryan, Rob	.290	117	414	72	120	30	5	19	88	56	70	4	3	L	L	5-11	190	6-24-73	1996	Spokane, Wash.
Sell, Chip	.357	30	84	12	30	5	2	1	18	3	14	4	3	L	R	6-2	205	6-19-71	1994	Otis, Ore.
Stoner, Mike	.429	14	21	2	9	1	0	0	6	2	3	0	0	R	R	6-0	200	5-23-73	1996	Simpsonville, Ky.
Sveum, Dale	.209	20	67	3	14	1	0	1	4	3	23	0	1	S	R	6-2	212	11-23-63	1982	Scottsdale, Ariz.
Ward, Turner	.375	12	40	9	15	2	0	2	8	7	4	4	1	S	R	6-2	204	4-11-65	1986	Saraland, Ala.
2-team (35 Nashville)	.318	47	129	24	41	5	1	4	25	23	18	7	2							
White, Walt	.203	54	153	18	31	8	1	3	13	14	39	0	0	R	R	6-0	195	12-12-71	1994	Torrance, Calif.
Wilson, Desi	.323	130	452	65	146	27	7	6	62	34	76	2	3	L	L	6-7	230	5-9-69	1991	Glen Cove, N.Y.
Womack, Tony	.250	4	16	1	4	1	0	0	3	2	3	0	1	L	R	5-9	155	9-25-69	1991	Greensboro, N.C.
Young, Ernie	.294	126	453	78	133	25	1	30	95	57	129	4	1	R	R	6-1	234	7-8-69	1990	Mesa, Ariz.

PITCHING	W	L	ERA	G	GS	CG	SV	IP	H	R	ER	BB	SO	B	T	HT	WT	DOB	1st Yr	Resides
Anderson, Brian	0	1	5.40	2	2	0	0	7	9	5	4	1	8	S	L	6-1	190	4-26-72	1993	North Olmstead, Ohio
Batchelor, Rich	0	4	4.50	30	0	0	12	28	29	19	14	12	23	R	R	6-1	195	4-8-67	1990	Hartsville, S.C.
Bierbrodt, Nick	1	4	7.27	11	11	0	0	43	57	42	35	30	43	L	L	6-5	190	5-16-78	1996	Long Beach, Calif.
Boyd, Jason	6	5	4.52	44	0	0	5	76	76	42	38	27	60	R	R	6-3	170	2-23-73	1994	Edwardsville, Ill.
Brohawn, Troy	1	0	3.29	3	2	0	0	14	22	8	5	3	12	L	L	6-1	190	1-14-73	1994	Woolford, Md.
Bross, Terry	0	0	11.57	2	0	0	0	2	6	3	3	1	0	R	R	6-9	230	3-30-66	1987	Commack, N.Y.
Carlson, Dan	4	9	5.43	32	18	0	0	118	130	82	71	52	118	R	R	6-1	185	1-26-70	1990	Portland, Ore.
Chouinard, Bobby	4	1	4.06	12	9	0	0	62	70	33	28	13	63	R	R	6-1	188	5-1-72	1990	Forest Grove, Ore.
Clemons, Chris	6	4	5.93	45	3	0	1	68	77	53	45	44	75	R	R	6-4	225	10-31-72	1994	Waco, Texas
Cummings, John	1	1	8.31	11	1	0	0	22	33	24	20	9	18	L	L	6-3	200	5-10-69	1990	Laguna Niguel, Calif.
Eischen, Joey	3	9	9.07	27	1	0	1	42	63	47	42	26	36	L	L	6-1	190	5-25-70	1989	West Covina, Calif.
Figueroa, Nelson	11	6	3.94	24	21	1	0	128	128	59	56	41	106	S	R	6-1	155	5-18-74	1995	Brooklyn, N.Y.
Hernandez, Fernando	0	2	8.44	5	1	0	0	16	22	16	15	4	14	R	R	6-2	185	6-16-71	1990	Santiago, D.R.
Holmes, Darren	0	0	0.00	1	1	0	0	1	0	0	0	1	0	R	R	6-0	202	4-25-66	1984	Fletcher, N.C.
Jensen, Jason	0	1	3.86	1	1	0	0	5	6	6	2	4	3	L	L	6-2	175	11-4-75	1997	Portland, Maine
Kim, Byung-Hyun	4	0	2.40	11	3	0	1	30	21	9	8	16	50	R	R	5-11	176	1-21-79	1999	Kwangsan-Ku, Korea
Michalak, Chris	5	0	3.66	21	6	0	3	64	64	30	26	26	41	L	L	6-2	195	1-4-71	1993	Lemont, Ill.
2-team (24 Edmonton)	6	0	4.29	45	6	0	3	92	92	50	44	40	66							
Nunez, Vladimir	1	0	6.75	3	0	0	0	3	5	2	2	0	3	R	R	6-4	235	3-15-75	1996	Santo Domingo, D.R.
Padilla, Vicente	7	4	3.75	18	14	0	0	94	107	47	39	24	58	R	R	6-2	200	9-27-77	1998	Managua, Nicaragua
Patterson, John	1	5	7.04	7	6	0	0	31	43	26	24	18	29	R	R	6-6	197	1-30-78	1996	Orange, Texas
Peters, Don	0	1	3.86	3	0	0	0	5	1	2	2	2	2	R	R	6-0	190	10-7-69	1990	Crestwood, Ill.
Randolph, Stephen	0	7	6.91	11	10	1	0	42	47	37	32	32	26	L	L	6-3	185	5-1-74	1995	Austin, Texas
Rooney, Mike	0	0	0.00	1	0	0	0	2	3	1	0	2	0	R	R	6-1	175	10-6-75	1997	Stony Point, N.Y.
Ruebel, Matt	1	3	7.00	6	2	0	0	27	32	26	21	10	19	L	L	6-2	180	10-16-69	1991	Oklahoma City, Okla.
Sabel, Erik	5	2	3.34	22	9	0	2	73	79	36	27	24	38	R	R	6-3	193	10-14-74	1996	West Lafayette, Ind.
Shouse, Brian	3	4	6.25	30	0	0	0	45	63	35	31	18	32	L	L	5-11	180	9-26-68	1990	Peoria, Ill.
Swartzbaugh, Dave	0	0	6.23	13	0	0	0	22	27	16	15	14	20	R	R	6-2	205	2-11-68	1989	Glenshaw, Pa.
Telemaco, Amaury	3	3	5.09	13	12	0	0	18	21	11	10	6	17	R	R	6-3	210	1-19-74	1991	La Romana, D.R.
Tuttle, Dave	2	5	6.51	35	9	0	0	84	100	62	61	48	55	R	R	6-3	190	9-29-69	1992	Los Gatos, Calif.
Verplancke, Joe	0	0	0.00	2	0	0	0	2	1	0	0	1	4	R	R	6-2	200	5-11-75	1996	Ontario, Calif.
Vosberg, Ed	0	1	0.78	26	0	0	7	35	26	5	3	8	30	L	L	6-1	210	9-28-61	1983	Tucson, Ariz.
2-team (8 Las Vegas)	1	1	0.84	34	0	0	8	43	29	6	4	12	42							
Ward, Jeremy	0	0	0.00	1	0	0	0	2	2	0	0	2	1	R	R	6-3	220	2-24-78	1999	Rocky Mount, N.C.
Weber, Neil	1	1	10.66	9	0	0	0	13	23	16	15	4	16	L	L	6-5	215	12-6-72	1993	Harrisburg, Pa.

Organization Statistics

Catcher	PCT	G	PO	A	E	DP	PB
Foster	.968	10	56	5	2	0	1
Hanel	1.000	6	46	3	0	1	1
Huckaby	.988	101	695	52	9	3	8
Koeyers	.990	13	95	7	1	0	0
Pachot	.974	31	159	27	5	6	2
Ja. Patterson	1.000	1	6	0	0	0	0

First Base	PCT	G	PO	A	E	DP
Coolbaugh	.990	16	93	8	1	9
Durazo	.996	29	241	20	1	31
Huckaby	1.000	1	10	1	0	1
Johnson	1.000	3	17	3	0	1
Sveum	.970	4	30	2	1	5
Wilson	.976	99	757	55	20	79

Second Base	PCT	G	PO	A	E	DP
Belliard	1.000	2	4	6	0	1
Diaz	.982	58	111	165	5	44

	PCT	G	PO	A	E	DP
Frias	1.000	5	12	9	0	3
Johnson	.986	43	94	110	3	37
Klassen	.000	1	0	0	0	0
Rios	1.000	2	4	6	0	2
White	.980	40	88	105	4	24

Third Base	PCT	G	PO	A	E	DP
Coolbaugh	.920	40	29	75	9	6
Frias	.917	14	9	24	3	0
Huckaby	.750	7	1	2	1	0
Johnson	.800	8	4	4	2	1
Ja. Patterson	.916	73	41	101	13	12
Sveum	.879	8	7	22	4	2
White	.000	1	0	0	0	0

Shortstop	PCT	G	PO	A	E	DP
Diaz	.926	44	70	117	15	30

	PCT	G	PO	A	E	DP
Frias	.909	4	2	8	1	1
Johnson	.964	33	49	113	6	24
Klassen	.969	59	87	193	9	42
White	1.000	6	6	15	0	3

Outfield	PCT	G	PO	A	E	DP
Conti	.974	126	278	17	8	3
Incaviglia	1.000	7	6	0	0	0
Johnson	1.000	6	8	0	0	0
Powell	.952	45	94	5	5	0
Ryan	.969	104	182	8	6	1
Sell	1.000	22	27	1	0	0
Stoner	1.000	4	5	0	0	0
T. Ward	.905	11	18	1	2	1
Wilson	1.000	12	18	0	0	0
Womack	1.000	4	8	1	0	0
Young	.987	107	142	11	2	0

EL PASO — Class AA

Organization Statistics

TEXAS LEAGUE

BATTING

	AVG	G	AB	R	H	2B	3B	HR	RBI	BB	SO	SB	CS	B	T	HT	WT	DOB	1st Yr	Resides
Barajas, Rod	.318	127	510	77	162	41	2	14	95	24	73	2	0	R	R	6-2	220	9-5-75	1996	Norwalk, Calif.
Bautista, Juan	.000	2	3	0	0	0	0	0	0	0	2	0	0	R	R	6-1	165	7-20-78	1996	San Francisco de Macoris, D.R.
Brock, J.J.	.191	43	136	13	26	4	2	0	8	4	26	0	1	R	R	5-11	175	12-4-74	1998	South Bend, Ind.
Calloway, Ron	.219	11	32	4	7	0	0	0	1	7	7	1	2	L	L	6-0	195	9-6-76	1997	Los Banos, Calif.
Clark, Kevin	.298	106	373	44	111	24	3	8	64	21	75	0	2	R	R	6-1	200	4-30-73	1993	Henderson, Nev.
Coolbaugh, Scott	.279	18	61	12	17	3	0	3	17	13	9	1	0	R	R	5-11	195	6-13-66	1987	Seguin, Texas
Durazo, Erubiel	.403	64	226	53	91	18	3	14	55	44	37	2	1	L	L	6-3	225	1-23-74	1997	Hermosillo, Mexico
Gann, Jamie	.262	109	443	69	116	24	6	9	56	32	141	7	11	R	R	6-1	197	5-1-75	1996	Norman, Okla.
Hartman, Ron	.195	24	82	6	16	3	1	0	7	5	8	0	0	R	R	6-1	200	12-12-74	1996	Baltimore, Md.
Herrick, Jason	.301	49	173	23	52	18	1	6	20	14	45	2	5	L	L	6-0	175	7-29-73	1991	Franklin, Wis.
Johnson, Keith	.300	17	70	17	21	10	1	3	15	4	17	0	1	R	R	5-11	200	4-17-71	1992	Stockton, Calif.
Koeyers, Ramsey	.208	26	77	6	16	9	0	1	10	4	20	0	0	R	R	6-1	187	8-7-74	1993	Willemstad, Neth. Antilles
Maddox, Garry	.295	127	492	80	145	35	9	15	75	31	106	22	5	R	R	6-3	180	10-24-74	1996	Philadelphia, Pa.
Martin, Jared	.258	19	62	9	16	4	0	1	5	4	13	0	0	S	R	5-10	180	3-3-75	1997	Tallahassee, Fla.
Matos, Julius	.280	120	425	54	119	17	5	5	41	13	37	5	2	R	R	5-11	175	12-12-74	1996	Racine, Wis.
McKinnon, Sandy	.250	3	12	1	3	0	0	0	2	0	2	0	0	R	R	5-8	175	9-20-72	1993	Nicholls, Ga.
Neubart, Adam	.209	13	43	7	9	3	0	1	4	5	14	0	1	R	R	5-11	165	7-23-77	1998	Livingston, N.J.
Owens, Ryan	.319	31	113	11	36	5	1	1	18	8	36	1	2	R	R	6-2	200	3-18-78	1999	Anaheim Hills, Calif.
Patterson, Jarrod	.382	67	249	63	95	27	3	8	51	51	45	3	2	L	R	6-1	195	9-7-73	1993	Clanton, Ala.
Rexrode, Jackie	.319	37	144	30	46	7	2	2	11	29	16	7	3	L	R	5-11	175	9-16-78	1996	Laurel, Md.
Rios, Eduardo	.283	16	60	8	17	3	0	0	10	4	8	0	0	R	R	5-10	178	10-13-72	1991	Charallave, Venez.
Sandoval, Jhensy	.222	34	126	10	28	6	1	1	23	7	42	1	1	R	R	6-0	200	9-14-78	1996	Santo Domingo, D.R.
Sell, Chip	.307	92	329	50	101	16	1	8	35	20	66	19	6	L	R	6-2	205	6-19-71	1994	Otis, Ore.
Spivey, Junior	.293	44	164	40	48	10	4	3	19	36	27	14	10	R	R	6-0	185	1-28-75	1996	Oklahoma City, Okla.
Stoner, Mike	.000	1	0	1	0	0	0	0	0	1	0	0	0	R	R	6-0	200	5-23-73	1996	Simpsonville, Ky.
Van Rossum, Chris	.280	26	75	11	21	5	0	3	9	8	21	1	0	L	L	6-2	180	2-15-74	1996	Turlock, Calif.
White, Walt	.120	13	50	4	6	3	0	1	2	13	0	0		R	R	6-0	195	12-12-71	1994	Torrance, Calif.
Wolff, Mike	.226	52	155	14	35	8	1	1	17	11	23	0	0	L	L	6-3	205	2-17-73	1996	Granger, Ind.

PITCHING

	W	L	ERA	G	GS	CG	SV	IP	H	R	ER	BB	SO	B	T	HT	WT	DOB	1st Yr	Resides
Andrews, Jeff	3	8	5.30	35	8	0	7	73	87	47	43	24	40	R	R	6-3	190	9-1-74	1997	Beverly, Mass.
Bierbrodt, Nick	5	6	4.62	14	14	2	0	76	78	45	39	37	55	L	L	6-5	190	5-16-78	1996	Long Beach, Calif.
Burgus, Travis	1	1	4.33	17	0	0	2	27	26	14	13	13	32	L	L	6-2	190	11-6-72	1995	Mission Viejo, Calif.
Crews, Jason	3	4	5.66	35	2	0	0	56	73	47	35	23	30	R	R	6-2	205	8-28-73	1996	Plantation, Fla.
Dace, Derek	2	2	5.19	40	0	0	0	52	58	33	30	23	34	L	L	6-7	200	4-11-75	1994	Rolla, Mo.
Jacob, Russell	0	0	6.75	3	0	0	0	3	5	4	2	2	3	R	R	6-6	240	1-2-75	1994	Winter Haven, Fla.
Jensen, Jason	0	1	8.49	4	2	0	0	12	20	11	11	9	8	L	L	6-2	175	11-4-75	1997	Portland, Maine
Kermode, Al	4	4	3.01	12	11	1	0	72	68	31	24	12	56	R	R	6-4	185	12-10-70	1992	Chandler, Ariz.
Kim, Byung-Hyun	2	0	2.11	10	0	0	0	21	6	5	5	9	32	R	R	5-11	176	1-21-79	1999	Kwangsan-Ku, Korea
Knott, Eric	7	11	4.57	27	27	3	0	161	198	95	82	42	83	L	L	6-0	188	9-23-74	1997	Sebring, Fla.
Mayo, Blake	1	1	5.40	15	1	0	1	25	41	16	15	13	18	R	R	6-2	210	12-18-72	1996	Gadsden, Ala.
2-team (41 San Antonio)	3	3	5.68	56	1	0	4	76	104	56	48	33	49							
McCutcheon, Mike	1	1	6.23	3	1	0	0	9	7	8	6	9	8	L	L	5-11	158	7-5-77	1996	Mauna Loa, Hawaii
Miadich, Bart	2	2	8.10	12	0	0	1	20	37	22	18	7	16	R	R	6-4	205	2-3-76	1997	Lake Oswego, Ore.
Norris, Ben	10	6	4.16	20	20	0	0	119	132	61	55	53	87	L	L	6-3	185	12-6-77	1996	Austin, Texas
Patterson, John	8	6	4.77	18	18	2	0	100	98	61	53	42	117	R	R	6-6	197	1-30-78	1996	Orange, Texas
Penny, Brad	2	7	4.80	17	17	0	0	90	109	54	48	25	100	R	R	6-4	200	5-24-78	1996	Broken Arrow, Okla.
Peters, Don	3	3	5.71	32	0	0	4	41	57	36	26	16	29	R	R	6-0	190	10-7-69	1990	Crestwood, Ill.
Randolph, Stephen	2	2	2.64	8	8	0	0	44	39	14	13	23	38	L	L	6-3	185	5-14-74	1995	Austin, Texas
Sabel, Erik	0	1	6.30	8	1	0	1	10	16	9	7	4	7	R	R	6-3	193	10-14-74	1996	West Lafayette, Ind.
Sanchez, Martin	4	4	3.90	42	9	0	6	97	95	57	42	41	73	R	R	6-2	180	1-19-77	1994	Santo Domingo, D.R.
Schroeffel, Scott	4	4	6.72	41	1	0	2	64	75	55	48	34	52	S	R	6-0	190	12-30-73	1996	Wexford, Pa.
Verplancke, Joe	0	1	135.00	1	0	0	0	5	5	5	0	0	2	R	R	6-2	200	5-11-75	1996	Ontario, Calif.
Ward, Jeremy	1	1	2.45	19	0	0	7	26	18	7	7	9	26	R	R	6-3	220	2-24-78	1999	Rocky Mount, N.C.

FIELDING

Catcher	PCT	G	PO	A	E	DP	PB
Barajas	.984	110	787	95	14	3	10
Clark	.983	21	107	12	2	2	4
Koeyers	.952	14	73	6	4	0	0

First Base	PCT	G	PO	A	E	DP
Barajas	1.000	4	40	2	0	4

	PCT	G	PO	A	E	DP
Clark	.985	35	239	25	4	17
Durazo	.982	63	523	36	10	53
Ja. Patterson	1.000	3	24	2	0	0
Wolff	.995	45	325	38	2	30

Second Base	PCT	G	PO	A	E	DP
Bautista	.667	1	1	1	1	0
Brock	.938	28	45	75	8	18
Coolbaugh	1.000	1	5	3	0	1
Johnson	1.000	6	10	12	0	2
Martin	.949	17	40	35	4	6

	PCT	G	PO	A	E	DP	PB
Matos	.957	6	4	18	1	2	
Rexrode	.949	37	73	93	9	13	
Rios	.981	15	18	35	1	5	
Spivey	.960	35	96	95	8	25	
White	.962	4	15	10	1	3	

Third Base	PCT	G	PO	A	E	DP
Brock	1.000	3	0	4	0	0
Clark	1.000	1	1	2	0	0
Coolbaugh	.904	17	15	32	5	2
Hartman	.906	23	20	38	6	4
Johnson	.923	4	4	8	1	0
Martin	1.000	1	0	1	0	0

	PCT	G	PO	A	E	DP	PB
Owens	.888	31	17	54	9	6	
Ja. Patterson	.929	63	34	124	12	8	
White	1.000	2	0	4	0	1	

Shortstop	PCT	G	PO	A	E	DP
Brock	.912	11	12	19	3	3
Johnson	.955	6	7	14	1	3
Matos	.953	114	197	336	26	65
Spivey	.977	10	19	24	1	3
White	.906	7	13	16	3	3

Outfield	PCT	G	PO	A	E	DP
Calloway	1.000	11	17	1	0	

	PCT	G	PO	A	E	DP	PB
Gann	.975	108	224	9	6	2	
Herrick	.963	43	71	6	3	1	
Johnson	.000	2	0	0	0	0	
Maddox	.975	112	187	9	5	2	
McKinnon	.750	3	3	0	1	0	
Neubart	.882	13	14	1	2	0	
Ja. Patterson	.000	2	0	0	0	0	
Sandoval	.949	33	71	3	4	1	
Sell	.985	85	124	9	2	2	
Van Rossum	.909	21	37	3	4	2	
White	.000	1	0	0	0	0	

HIGH DESERT — Class A

CALIFORNIA LEAGUE

BATTING	AVG	G	AB	R	H	2B	3B	HR	RBI	BB	SO	SB	CS	B	T	HT	WT	DOB	1st Yr	Resides
Belliard, Francisco	.255	16	47	4	12	1	1	0	1	4	16	1	1	S	R	5-11	165	11-27-79	1997	Santiago, D.R.
Calloway, Ron	.316	60	196	41	62	14	1	3	23	30	34	22	7	L	L	6-0	195	9-6-76	1997	Los Banos, Calif.
Cintron, Alex	.307	128	499	78	153	25	4	3	64	19	65	15	8	S	R	6-2	180	12-17-78	1997	Yabucoa, P.R.
Cruz, Hector	.220	14	41	8	9	1	0	0	3	2	11	0	1	S	R	6-0	175	9-22-78	1999	Arroyo, P.R.
Cuntz, Casey	.265	86	257	46	68	11	1	10	39	38	61	0	2	R	R	6-3	185	2-4-75	1997	Metairie, La.
Cust, Jack	.334	125	455	107	152	42	3	32	112	96	145	1	4	L	R	6-1	205	1-16-79	1997	Flemington, N.J.
Goldfield, Josh	.400	5	5	2	2	0	0	0	0	1	0	0	0	L	R	6-1	185	7-11-79	1999	Thousand Oaks, Calif.
Graham, Justin	.100	4	10	1	1	0	0	0	1	0	4	0	0	R	R	5-10	190	8-9-77	1999	Fairmont, W.Va.
Hammock, Robert	.332	114	379	80	126	20	7	9	72	47	63	3	6	R	R	5-11	190	5-3-76	1997	Marietta, Ga.
Hartman, Ron	.250	33	124	13	31	6	0	2	22	7	13	0	0	R	R	6-1	200	12-12-74	1996	Baltimore, Md.
Johnson, Patrick	.313	37	99	15	31	6	0	2	15	19	27	0	2	R	R	6-3	200	4-18-75	1996	Taylorsville, Utah
2-team (26 Lake Els.)	.266	63	177	22	47	6	0	3	21	29	53	0	2							
Koeyers, Ramsey	.235	5	17	3	4	0	0	1	2	1	3	0	0	R	R	6-1	187	8-7-74	1991	Willemstad, Neth. Antilles
Lopez, Miguel	.200	9	20	1	4	1	0	0	3	0	7	0	0	R	R	5-11	180	10-12-78	1996	Scottsdale, Ariz.
Martin, Jared	.240	89	283	38	68	12	2	2	30	29	46	2	4	S	R	5-10	180	3-3-75	1997	Tallahassee, Fla.
Martinez, Belvani	.333	109	477	84	159	23	9	8	55	18	69	35	30	R	R	5-11	164	12-14-78	1996	San Cristobal, D.R.
McKinnon, Sandy	.667	1	3	0	2	0	0	0	1	0	0	1	0	R	R	5-8	175	9-20-72	1993	Nicholls, Ga.
Meier, Dan	.268	129	418	85	112	25	4	24	89	70	138	0	0	L	L	6-0	202	8-13-77	1998	Aurora, Colo.
Neal, Steve	.250	6	20	3	5	0	0	2	2	1	7	0	0	L	L	6-2	260	2-14-77	1998	Pine Bluff, Ark.
Neubart, Adam	.321	55	212	47	68	9	6	8	38	20	52	10	10	R	R	5-11	165	7-23-77	1998	Livingston, N.J.
Nunez, Abraham	.273	130	488	106	133	29	6	22	93	86	122	40	13	S	R	6-2	165	2-5-80	1996	Haina, D.R.
Osborne, Mark	.248	113	335	52	83	15	3	11	69	40	88	1	3	L	R	6-4	220	2-1-78	1996	Sanford, N.C.
Owens, Ryan	.398	26	103	19	41	7	3	4	28	9	30	1	2	R	R	6-2	200	3-18-78	1999	Anaheim Hills, Calif.
Rinne, James	.280	104	268	45	75	10	0	11	39	27	66	5	5	R	R	6-3	215	7-29-76	1998	Bloomington, Ill.
Steelmon, Wyley	.220	32	91	13	20	6	0	1	10	9	19	1	1	L	L	6-3	225	8-29-75	1997	Enid, Okla.
Van Rossum, Chris	.311	28	90	13	28	5	1	4	16	9	27	2	1	L	L	6-2	180	2-15-74	1996	Turlock, Calif.

GAMES BY POSITION: C—Goldfield 3, Hammock 89, Johnson 30, Koeyers 5, Lopez 8, Osborne 37. **1B**—Cuntz 15, Hartman 7, Meier 113, Neal 5, Osborne 14, Steelmon 18. **2B**—Belliard 2, Cintron 5, Cruz 5, Cuntz 21, Martin 16, Martinez 106. **3B**—Belliard 7, Cruz 3, Cuntz 36, Hammock 1, Hartman 3, Martin 60, Martinez 1, Owens 2. **SS**—Belliard 4, Cintron 125, Cruz 7, Cuntz 9, Martin 9. **OF**—Belliard 1, Calloway 49, Cuntz 18, Cust 114, Graham 3, Hammock 2, McKinnon 3, Meier 1, Neubart 52, Nunez 130, Rinne 64, Van Rossum 28.

PITCHING	W	L	ERA	G	GS	CG	SV	IP	H	R	ER	BB	SO	B	T	HT	WT	DOB	1st Yr	Resides
Andrews, Jeff	0	3	6.37	6	6	0	0	30	41	27	21	13	25	R	R	6-3	190	9-1-74	1997	Beverly, Mass.
Bido, Jose	0	0	12.46	11	0	0	3	13	23	19	18	9	14	R	R	6-2	188	12-20-78	1996	San Francisco de Macoris, D.R.
Cepeda, Wellington	6	6	5.71	42	3	0	2	87	106	64	55	42	74	R	R	6-3	195	11-25-77	1998	Santo Domingo, D.R.
Cervantes, Chris	0	0	162.00	1	0	0	0	0	5	6	6	1	1	L	L	6-1	165	2-4-79	1998	Tucson, Ariz.
Davis, Clint	1	0	4.50	2	0	0	0	2	0	1	1	2	3	R	R	6-3	205	9-26-69	1991	Irving, Texas
De la Rosa, Jorge	0	0	0.00	2	0	0	0	3	1	0	0	2	3	L	L	6-1	192	4-5-81	1998	San Nicolas, Mexico
Fahrner, Evan	0	1	6.00	3	1	0	0	3	3	3	2	7	3	R	R	6-2	200	3-4-78	1999	Peoria, Ill.
Immel, Steve	4	1	5.53	19	0	0	0	41	61	36	25	12	35	R	R	5-10	175	2-27-77	1999	Escondido, Calif.
Jensen, Jason	2	2	4.47	9	9	0	0	44	43	24	22	22	24	L	L	6-2	175	11-4-75	1997	Portland, Maine
Kees, Justin	6	2	5.57	30	7	0	1	86	89	60	53	51	68	R	R	6-1	190	8-5-77	1998	Danville, Ill.
Kohl, Doug	9	5	7.38	30	11	0	0	89	114	79	73	40	74	R	R	6-4	210	7-9-79	1997	Henderson, Nev.
Manzueta, Roberto	2	2	3.51	40	0	0	2	67	63	29	26	31	59	L	R	6-1	197	12-28-78	1996	Cotui, D.R.
Martines, Jason	9	7	2.26	43	0	0	9	72	68	33	18	28	73	L	R	6-2	190	1-21-76	1997	Hanover, Mich.
Miadich, Bart	3	8	5.42	21	16	0	0	98	125	71	59	40	85	R	R	6-4	205	2-3-76	1997	Lake Oswego, Ore.
Norris, Ben	2	2	4.43	8	8	0	0	41	39	27	20	24	45	L	L	6-3	185	12-6-77	1996	Austin, Texas
O'Reilly, John	1	4	7.24	21	4	0	1	46	53	46	37	36	47	R	R	6-2	200	8-11-74	1996	Elmwood Park, N.J.
Oleksik, George	0	0	3.86	4	0	0	0	7	14	11	3	6	5	R	R	6-4	210	4-19-74	1996	McMinnville, Tenn.
Padilla, Vicente	4	1	3.73	9	9	0	0	51	50	27	21	17	55	R	R	6-2	200	9-27-77	1998	Managua, Nicaragua
Rubio, Miguel	2	5	6.14	27	11	0	1	78	96	61	53	33	53	R	R	5-10	168	1-10-80	1997	Monterrey, Mexico
Sanchez, Duaner	0	0	7.53	3	0	0	0	14	15	13	12	9	9	R	R	6-0	160	10-14-79	1996	Cotui, D.R.
Sanchez, Simon	3	5	5.27	40	1	0	7	72	79	45	42	31	53	R	R	6-1	195	3-24-78	1996	San Francisco de Macoris, D.R.
Sundbeck, Cody	4	5	7.08	14	14	0	0	67	81	59	53	35	68	R	R	6-1	205	2-22-78	1999	Plano, Texas
Trejo, Francisco	0	0	6.75	3	0	0	0	5	6	5	7	6	6	L	L	6-0	154	3-6-80	1997	Santo Domingo, D.R.
Verplancke, Joe	1	0	10.38	3	0	0	0	4	5	5	5	4	5	R	R	6-2	200	5-11-75	1996	Ontario, Calif.
Ward, Jeremy	0	0	2.08	4	0	0	0	9	5	2	2	3	12	R	R	6-3	220	2-24-78	1999	Rocky Mount, N.C.
White, Matt	2	8	5.79	31	17	0	0	92	101	70	59	49	78	R	R	6-2	200	9-15-77	1998	Portland, Ore.
Wilson, Jeff	7	4	4.31	32	17	0	1	111	106	66	53	67	122	R	L	6-2	180	5-30-76	1997	Greensboro, N.C.

SOUTH BEND — Class A

MIDWEST LEAGUE

BATTING	AVG	G	AB	R	H	2B	3B	HR	RBI	BB	SO	SB	CS	B	T	HT	WT	DOB	1st Yr	Resides
Adams, John	.288	74	285	38	82	19	1	10	38	11	66	10	5	R	R	6-5	225	8-10-76	1997	Olathe, Kan.
Belliard, Francisco	.249	70	265	28	66	11	1	0	15	20	64	3	2	S	R	5-11	165	11-27-79	1997	Santiago, D.R.
Bolling, Kirk	.184	16	49	6	9	5	0	1	6	6	18	1	0	R	R	6-2	185	4-14-77	1998	Torrance, Calif.

BATTING	AVG	G	AB	R	H	2B	3B	HR	RBI	BB	SO	SB	CS	B	T	HT	WT	DOB	1st Yr	Resides
Brock, J.J.	.221	48	172	19	38	8	3	1	13	12	27	2	2	R	R	5-11	175	12-4-74	1998	South Bend, Ind.
Burns, Kevan	.318	43	157	22	50	8	1	2	25	14	27	3	4	L	L	6-0	185	11-10-76	1999	Beloit, Wis.
Closser, J.D.	.241	52	174	29	42	8	0	3	27	34	37	0	1	S	R	5-10	195	1-15-80	1998	Alexandria, Ind.
Downing, Lance	.289	118	439	65	127	18	5	1	51	35	69	7	3	L	R	5-10	185	3-9-79	1997	Pine Bluff, Ark.
Gordon, Brian	.212	48	184	21	39	9	3	0	17	9	35	8	3	L	R	6-0	180	8-16-78	1997	Round Rock, Texas
Kasper, Todd	.188	34	101	7	19	1	0	0	9	12	37	1	1	L	R	6-3	205	1-25-77	1999	Aurora, Colo.
Kata, Matt	.261	78	318	40	83	14	5	3	33	28	46	5	6	S	R	6-1	185	3-14-78	1999	Willoughby Hills, Ohio
Lopez, Jose	.165	26	91	5	15	3	0	1	8	3	19	0	0	R	R	5-10	187	12-23-78	1996	San Francisco de Macoris, D.R.
McAffee, Josh	.246	68	232	32	57	16	0	5	24	35	76	0	1	R	R	6-0	209	11-4-77	1996	Rock Springs, Wyo.
Moye, Tutu	.254	72	244	33	62	13	1	3	30	19	75	4	2	R	R	5-11	201	9-8-78	1997	Greenville, N.C.
Neal, Steve	.281	69	249	41	70	14	2	7	53	40	72	6	2	L	L	6-2	260	2-14-77	1998	Pine Bluff, Ark.
Neubart, Adam	.231	27	91	14	21	3	1	1	9	6	20	4	4	R	R	5-11	165	7-23-77	1998	Livingston, N.J.
Noboa, Joel	.179	11	39	2	7	2	0	0	3	0	17	0	0	R	R	6-0	172	11-27-79	1997	Santo Domingo, D.R.
Singletary, Dan	.235	95	306	47	72	8	6	5	43	54	53	15	9	L	L	6-0	180	8-23-75	1998	Paterson, N.J.
Sykes, Jamie	.286	127	479	75	137	34	10	15	83	53	111	17	8	R	R	5-11	190	1-14-75	1997	Kankakee, Ill.
Urquiola, Carlos	.362	93	384	66	139	13	3	0	35	22	32	20	14	L	R	5-8	150	4-22-80	1997	Caracas, Venez.
Valera, Greg	.156	53	186	18	29	4	2	0	10	9	46	1	2	R	R	6-0	150	4-11-79	1996	Palenque, D.R.
Van Rossum, Chris	.167	2	6	2	1	0	0	0	1	3	1	0	0	L	L	6-2	180	2-15-74	1996	Turlock, Calif.
Williford, Dan	.083	8	24	1	2	0	0	0	0	2	10	0	0	L	L	6-0	195	3-15-77	1999	Spanish Fort, Ala.
Wolff, Mike	.291	66	237	31	69	18	1	5	45	20	28	1	4	L	L	6-3	205	2-17-73	1994	Granger, Ind.

GAMES BY POSITION: C—Closser 34, Kasper 32, Jo. Lopez 22, McAffee 59. **1B**—Bolling 1, Downing 1, Jo. Lopez 2, Neal 69, Williford 4, Wolff 66. **2B**—Belliard 55, Brock 41, Downing 8, Urquiola 38. **3B**—Belliard 10, Bolling 10, Brock 1, Downing 99, Moye 13, Noboa 9. **SS**—Belliard 5, Brock 9, Kata 75, Valera 53. **OF**—Adams 72, Burns 40, Downing 1, Gordon 46, Moye 33, Neubart 27, Singletary 49, Sykes 123, Urquiola 30, Van Rossum 2, Williford 3.

PITCHING	W	L	ERA	G	GS	CG	SV	IP	H	R	ER	BB	SO	B	T	HT	WT	DOB	1st Yr	Resides
Bloomer, Chris	1	2	3.99	43	0	0	21	50	44	28	22	16	54	R	R	6-4	215	5-6-75	1997	White Bear Lake, Minn.
Cardona, Steve	1	2	6.23	14	0	0	0	22	31	18	15	5	26	R	R	6-3	190	2-18-74	1996	Stockton, Calif.
Cervantes, Chris	8	5	3.13	38	10	0	3	115	109	49	40	34	89	L	L	6-1	165	2-4-79	1998	Tucson, Ariz.
Crews, Jason	0	2	2.08	9	0	0	1	13	11	6	3	2	14	R	R	6-2	205	8-28-73	1996	Plantation, Fla.
Fahrner, Evan	3	1	6.08	20	1	0	1	37	39	27	25	21	45	R	R	6-2	200	3-4-78	1999	Peoria, Ill.
Fuller, Jody	7	4	4.49	36	11	0	0	116	133	68	58	43	83	R	R	6-3	225	9-12-76	1998	Huntingdon, Tenn.
Good, Andrew	11	10	4.10	27	27	0	0	154	160	80	70	42	146	R	R	6-2	166	9-19-79	1998	Rochester Hills, Mich.
Jensen, Jason	2	3	2.64	18	2	0	2	44	26	19	13	21	22	L	L	6-2	175	11-4-75	1997	Portland, Maine
Jones, Charlie	2	3	2.70	7	6	0	0	30	27	13	9	19	25	L	R	5-11	188	2-6-76	1997	Vero Beach, Fla.
Koplove, Mike	5	2	2.04	45	0	0	7	84	70	23	19	29	98	R	R	6-0	160	8-30-76	1998	Philadelphia, Pa.
Lopez, Javier	4	6	6.00	20	20	0	0	99	122	74	66	43	70	L	L	6-4	208	7-11-77	1998	Fairfax, Va.
McCutcheon, Mike	6	2	4.00	28	8	0	0	88	87	48	39	36	74	L	L	5-11	158	7-5-77	1996	Mauna Loa, Hawaii
Mendoza, Hatuey	3	9	8.27	13	11	0	0	58	64	57	53	45	36	R	R	6-0	164	3-16-80	1997	Santo Domingo, D.R.
O'Reilly, John	0	1	8.74	4	2	0	0	11	17	11	11	5	15	R	R	6-2	200	8-11-74	1996	Elmwood Park, N.J.
Prinz, Bret	6	10	4.48	30	23	0	0	139	129	82	69	52	98	R	R	6-3	200	6-15-77	1998	Peoria, Ariz.
Royer, Jason	7	7	4.69	32	18	0	1	119	135	77	62	43	62	R	R	6-5	200	7-3-78	1997	Del City, Okla.
Valverde, Jose	0	0	0.00	2	0	0	0	3	2	0	0	2	3	R	R	6-4	220	7-24-79	1997	El Seibo, D.R.
Verplancke, Joe	2	2	4.81	18	0	0	0	34	16	22	18	24	43	R	R	6-2	200	5-11-75	1996	Ontario, Calif.

MISSOULA — Rookie

PIONEER LEAGUE

BATTING	AVG	G	AB	R	H	2B	3B	HR	RBI	BB	SO	SB	CS	B	T	HT	WT	DOB	1st Yr	Resides
Brooks, Jeff	.339	73	295	48	100	18	4	12	60	17	77	6	2	R	R	6-5	235	9-4-79	1997	Nottingham, Pa.
Burns, Kevan	.364	16	55	15	20	2	2	1	14	6	10	3	0	L	L	6-0	185	11-10-76	1999	Beloit, Wis.
Closser, J.D.	.324	76	275	73	89	22	0	10	54	71	57	9	3	S	R	5-10	195	1-15-80	1998	Alexandria, Ind.
Conyer, Darryl	.263	49	190	55	50	9	2	3	23	43	56	20	7	L	L	5-10	200	12-10-79	1998	San Diego, Calif.
Cruz, Hector	.184	15	49	10	9	1	0	0	4	8	13	2	2	S	R	6-0	175	9-22-78	1999	Arroyo, P.R.
DeVore, Doug	.235	32	115	22	27	4	4	3	22	14	36	2	0	L	L	6-4	200	12-14-77	1999	Dublin, Ohio
Freeman, T.J.	.238	16	42	3	10	1	2	0	6	7	15	1	1	L	L	6-3	210	7-18-77	1999	Bowling Green, Ky.
Goldfield, Josh	.254	35	122	15	31	4	0	0	23	13	31	2	0	L	R	6-1	185	7-11-79	1999	Thousand Oaks, Calif.
Graham, Justin	.226	23	62	12	14	2	1	1	5	10	19	0	0	R	R	5-10	190	8-9-77	1999	Fairmont, W.Va.
Hall, Victor	.279	34	147	27	41	4	0	0	11	15	30	18	7	L	L	6-0	170	9-16-80	1998	Arleta, Calif.
Kalczynski, Joe	.197	23	61	12	12	4	0	1	8	11	17	2	0	R	R	6-5	205	1-25-78	1999	Farmington Hills, Mich.
Lopez, Jose	.571	5	14	5	8	4	1	1	3	2	1	0	0	R	R	5-10	187	12-23-78	1996	San Francisco de Macoris, D.R.
Myers, Corey	.276	66	272	43	75	13	2	5	44	22	65	6	3	R	R	6-2	205	6-5-80	1999	Phoenix, Ariz.
Noboa, Joel	.111	5	18	1	2	0	0	0	2	1	9	1	0	R	R	6-0	172	11-27-79	1997	Santo Domingo, D.R.
Oglesby, Travis	.000	3	5	0	0	0	0	0	0	0	2	0	0	R	R	6-3	225	12-17-77	1999	Windsor, Calif.
Overbay, Lyle	.343	75	306	66	105	25	7	12	101	40	53	10	3	L	L	6-2	215	1-28-77	1999	Centralia, Wash.
Santora, Jack	.262	51	195	46	51	9	1	1	31	34	33	36	7	S	R	5-7	145	10-6-76	1999	Monterey, Calif.
Santos, Luis	.244	43	123	19	30	3	0	0	15	26	24	5	2	R	R	5-11	170	5-21-79	1999	Huntington Beach, Calif.
Terrero, Luis	.287	71	272	74	78	13	7	8	40	32	91	27	10	R	R	6-2	183	5-18-80	1997	Barahona, D.R.
Williford, Dan	.140	16	50	6	7	4	0	1	6	4	19	0	0	L	L	6-0	195	3-15-77	1999	Spanish Fort, Ala.

GAMES BY POSITION: C—Closser 65, Goldfield 6, Kalczynski 8, Lopez 2, Oglesby 3. **1B**—Freeman 2, Overbay 68, Williford 7. **2B**—Cruz 12, Santora 51, Santos 18. **3B**—Brooks 70, C. Myers 6, Noboa 1, Santos 2. **SS**—C. Myers 58, Santos 23. **OF**—Burns 7, Conyer 45, DeVore 31, Goldfield 16, Graham 15, Hall 34, Noboa 3, Overbay 5, Terrero 71, Williford 5.

PITCHING	W	L	ERA	G	GS	CG	SV	IP	H	R	ER	BB	SO	B	T	HT	WT	DOB	1st Yr	Resides
Bevis, P.J.	6	2	4.62	15	15	0	0	86	83	51	44	30	69	R	R	6-3	175	7-28-80	1998	Capalaba, Australia
De la Rosa, Jorge	0	1	7.98	13	0	0	2	15	22	17	13	9	14	L	L	6-1	192	4-5-81	1998	San Nicolas, Mexico
Eames, Todd	2	1	2.95	19	1	0	1	40	37	19	13	17	28	R	R	6-6	210	1-20-78	1999	Billings, Mont.
Forbes, Derek	3	1	5.64	13	12	0	0	59	77	45	37	20	63	R	R	6-2	185	9-11-78	1999	Scottsdale, Ariz.
Gentile, Mark	7	4	5.88	15	14	0	0	78	100	62	51	25	45	L	L	6-4	170	7-28-80	1998	Orland Park, Ill.
Harris, Toby	1	3	5.04	22	4	1	1	61	80	48	34	14	43	R	R	6-3	205	12-24-76	1999	Las Vegas, Nev.
Matzenbacher, Brian	3	3	3.12	24	0	0	11	26	22	13	9	13	28	R	R	6-3	190	3-23-77	1999	Marissa, Ill.
Mendoza, Hatuey	0	0	0.00	1	0	0	0	3	3	5	0	2	3	R	R	6-0	164	3-16-80	1997	Santo Domingo, D.R.
Myers, Todd	0	0	12.86	5	1	0	0	7	12	11	10	6	4	R	R	6-1	195	3-15-77	1999	Fairfield, Pa.
Ross, Lew	4	3	2.79	20	0	0	4	39	27	21	12	13	50	L	L	6-4	185	8-26-77	1999	Hancock, Md.
Sanchez, Duaner	5	3	3.13	13	11	0	0	63	54	34	22	23	51	R	R	6-0	160	10-14-79	1996	Cotui, D.R.

PITCHING	W	L	ERA	G	GS	CG	SV	IP	H	R	ER	BB	SO	B	T	HT	WT	DOB	1st Yr	Resides
Stanton, Tim	3	3	3.90	21	0	0	0	32	35	19	14	9	35	L	L	6-1	190	12-31-76	1999	Sandwich, Mass.
Williamson, Charlie	2	2	2.52	25	0	0	2	36	33	16	10	12	34	R	R	6-6	220	8-2-77	1999	Gilbert, Ariz.
Wollscheid, Jim	3	5	5.78	18	9	0	0	62	65	50	40	31	55	R	R	6-0	190	8-24-77	1999	Sachse, Texas
Wood, Brandon	6	0	3.88	19	9	0	0	72	69	46	31	31	71	R	R	6-0	200	2-20-79	1999	Nacogdoches, Texas

TUCSON   Rookie

ARIZONA LEAGUE

BATTING	AVG	G	AB	R	H	2B	3B	HR	RBI	BB	SO	SB	CS	B	T	HT	WT	DOB	1st Yr	Resides
Cruz, Hector	.176	24	85	9	15	1	1	0	8	11	23	2	0	S	R	6-0	175	9-22-78	1999	Arroyo, P.R.
Delgado, Jorge	.294	20	68	11	20	5	1	1	6	6	14	1	0	R	R	6-0	208	7-8-80	1997	Acarigua, Venez.
Egly, John	.254	51	197	25	50	8	1	1	20	12	54	1	1	S	R	6-3	200	12-23-79	1998	Mountain View, Mo.
Goldfield, Josh	.333	2	3	3	1	0	0	0	0	2	0	0	0	L	R	6-1	185	7-11-79	1999	Thousand Oaks, Calif.
Hall, Victor	.365	27	104	19	38	2	1	0	14	13	25	10	5	L	L	6-0	170	9-16-80	1998	Arleta, Calif.
Jorgenson, Chris	.000	3	3	1	0	0	0	0	0	2	2	0	0	L	R	6-2	190	3-9-81	1999	New Brigden, Alberta
Kail, Tom	.305	55	220	33	67	15	3	5	41	16	48	1	0	R	R	6-4	196	7-22-79	1998	Pittsburgh, Pa.
Klassen, Danny	.235	6	17	2	4	1	0	0	1	1	4	0	0	R	R	6-0	175	9-22-75	1993	Stuart, Fla.
Knorr, Mario	.233	50	193	16	45	5	2	0	21	6	32	2	0	L	R	5-11	175	12-4-79	1998	Lakeside, Calif.
Lagana, Shawn	.258	39	159	28	41	8	1	0	21	10	33	5	3	R	R	6-2	170	4-28-81	1999	Cypress, Calif.
McCarty, Brock	.319	53	191	28	61	5	2	1	18	7	41	5	3	R	R	6-1	205	10-1-79	1998	Monroe, La.
Noboa, Joel	.312	52	215	31	67	11	1	12	41	6	60	5	1	R	R	6-0	172	11-27-79	1997	Santo Domingo, D.R.
Oglesby, Travis	.220	35	109	20	24	8	0	4	13	19	40	0	0	R	R	6-3	225	12-17-77	1999	Windsor, Calif.
Tomshack, Steven	.333	44	144	21	48	9	1	3	22	19	24	0	0	R	R	6-1	210	5-25-77	1999	Glen Burnie, Md.
Van Rossum, Chris	.250	6	16	1	4	0	0	0	0	1	3	1	0	L	L	6-2	180	2-15-74	1996	Turlock, Calif.
Vizcaino, Maximo	.283	12	46	7	13	0	1	0	4	4	3	1	0	R	R	6-1	175	11-28-80	1997	Palenque, D.R.
Yakopich, Joe	.305	47	154	37	47	5	3	0	22	30	31	6	2	L	R	5-11	160	6-19-81	1999	Amherstburg, Ontario

GAMES BY POSITION: C—Delgado 18, Goldfield 1, Oglesby 18, Tomshack 21. **1B**—Egly 50, Noboa 2, Oglesby 5. **2B**—Cruz 11, Vizcaino 4, Yakopich 44. **3B**—Cruz 4, Noboa 51, Vizcaino 3. **SS**—Cruz 10, Klassen 6, Lagana 39, Vizcaino 6. **OF**—Hall 27, Jorgenson 1, Kail 47, Knorr 44, McCarty 44, Tomshack 8, Van Rossum 4, Yakopich 1.

PITCHING	W	L	ERA	G	GS	CG	SV	IP	H	R	ER	BB	SO	B	T	HT	WT	DOB	1st Yr	Resides
Arauz, Alexis	2	3	4.41	16	8	0	1	51	60	40	25	26	38	R	R	6-3	200	10-10-79	1997	Panama City, Panama
De la Rosa, Jorge	0	0	3.21	8	0	0	2	14	12	5	5	3	17	L	L	6-1	192	4-5-81	1998	San Nicolas, Mexico
Deveraux, Dale	3	2	10.41	16	0	0	0	28	42	38	32	20	17	R	R	6-3	220	9-28-79	1999	American Fork, Utah
Figueroa, Nelson	0	1	0.00	1	1	0	0	3	3	1	0	0	2	S	R	6-1	155	5-18-74	1995	Brooklyn, N.Y.
Holmes, Darren	0	0	0.00	2	2	0	0	3	1	0	0	0	4	R	R	6-0	202	4-25-66	1984	Fletcher, N.C.
Kim, Byung-Hyun	0	0	0.00	1	1	0	0	2	1	0	0	1	2	R	R	5-11	176	1-21-79	1999	Kwangsan-Ku, Korea
Mendoza, Hatuey	2	7	5.65	13	13	0	0	72	83	64	45	31	69	R	R	6-0	164	3-16-80	1997	Santo Domingo, D.R.
Montoya, Saul	2	1	4.03	17	0	0	1	29	33	14	13	11	39	R	R	6-2	210	12-17-80	1998	Los Mochis, Mexico
Morel, Francis	2	1	8.04	7	0	0	1	16	23	15	14	5	18	R	R	6-5	206	12-22-78	1996	Cabrera, D.R.
Moreno, Victor	1	2	9.90	7	0	0	2	10	17	13	11	6	7	R	R	6-1	193	6-10-80	1997	Puerto Cabello, Venez.
Myers, Todd	0	0	1.69	3	0	0	0	5	6	3	1	3	4	R	R	6-1	195	3-15-77	1999	Fairfield, Pa.
Ovalles, Juan	7	2	2.40	14	7	0	0	60	48	25	16	25	36	R	R	6-1	165	5-15-82	1999	Caracas, Venez.
Perkins, Greg	0	0	6.75	4	3	0	0	12	13	11	9	8	11	R	R	6-3	195	4-15-81	1999	Kingwood, Texas
Randolph, Stephen	0	0	4.50	2	2	0	0	6	5	3	3	2	7	L	L	6-3	185	5-1-74	1995	Austin, Texas
Rubio, Miguel	0	1	6.00	2	2	0	0	3	6	2	2	3	3	R	R	5-10	168	1-10-80	1997	Monterrey, Mexico
Stottlemyre, Todd	2	0	0.53	3	3	1	0	17	11	1	1	1	25	L	R	6-3	195	5-20-65	1986	Yakima, Wash.
Trejo, Francisco	0	2	3.18	17	0	0	1	28	28	18	10	19	30	L	L	6-0	170	3-6-80	1997	Santo Domingo, D.R.
Valera, Greg	1	2	3.79	13	2	0	0	19	17	11	8	13	20	R	R	6-0	150	4-11-79	1996	Palenque, D.R.
Valverde, Jose	1	2	4.08	20	0	0	8	29	34	21	13	10	47	R	R	6-4	220	7-24-79	1997	El Seibo, D.R.
Villarreal, Oscar	1	5	3.78	14	11	0	0	64	64	39	27	25	51	L	R	6-0	177	11-22-81	1999	San Nicolas, Mexixo

Organization Statistics

ATLANTABRAVES

Team of '90s ends decade with another near-miss

BY BILL BALLEW

Finally, it seemed, the Braves' run of luck had run out.

The bad news in 1999 began just prior to spring training when first baseman Andres Galarraga was diagnosed with lymphoma, sidelining him for the entire campaign. The Braves lost their closer in March after Kerry Ligtenberg had season-ending Tommy John surgery. Former closer Mark Wohlers proved once the regular season started that he was no longer capable of throwing the ball over the plate with consistency.

The final obstacles occurred within three days of one another in late July. Rookie lefthander Odalis Perez tore the medial collateral ligament in his left elbow, and all-star catcher Javy Lopez was lost for the remainder of the season with a partial tear of the anterior cruciate ligament. Add to that the lingering ailments to righthander John Smoltz' elbow, and it appeared the Braves had little chance of holding off the improved Mets in the National League East.

Atlanta, however, showed its resiliency by winning the division and extending its major league record by reaching the playoffs for the eighth straight year. The Braves also became just the fourth team in major league history to win at least 100 games in three straight seasons, joining the 1929-31 Philadelphia Athletics, 1942-44 Cardinals and 1969-71 Orioles.

"This year everybody thought it was going to be more of a struggle and maybe it was," said manager Bobby Cox. "We played awfully good baseball and pretty consistently all season long."

The Braves were at their best during the playoffs, eliminating Houston in four games during the Division

Chipper Jones   **Rafael Furcal**

Players of the Year

MAJOR LEAGUE: Chipper Jones, 3b

Jones led the Braves with 45 homers, 116 runs, a .319 average and a .441 on-base percentage while driving in 110 runs.

MINOR LEAGUE: Rafael Furcal, ss

Furcal made a run at becoming the only minor leaguer to steal 100 bases in the '90s, but finished with 96 while batting .322.

Series before outlasting the Mets in six games during the NL Championship Series. Yet, as well as Atlanta played during those two series, the team was shut down in the World Series by the Yankees, whose pitchers silenced the Braves' bats in three of the four games to sweep the Fall Classic.

While the major league club continued its winning ways, the farm system showed improvement and displayed strong talent in the lower reaches of the organization. Atlanta's seven minor league teams improved their winning percentage, going from .439 in 1998 (tied for last among the 30 organizations) to .496 (tied for 16th). Only the Braves' two full-season Class A teams reached the playoffs, with Myrtle Beach being named co-champion with Kinston in the Carolina League.

The Braves continued to produce talent for the major league club. Reliever Kevin McGlinchy made the team in spring training and was a solid addition to the bullpen. Perez was an adequate starter, while lefthander Bruce Chen was inconsistent while shuttling between Triple-A Richmond and Atlanta.

The greatest amount of talent in the organization was seen in Myrtle Beach and Macon. Second baseman Marcus Giles led the Carolina League in batting average, hits and doubles, and was named league MVP. Shortstop Rafael Furcal led the minors with 96 stolen bases while splitting his season between Macon and Myrtle Beach and hitting a combined .322.

At Macon, Furcal joined second baseman Travis Wilson and lefthander Jimmy Osting, who led the South Atlantic League with 14 wins, on the postseason all-star team.

ORGANIZATION LEADERS

BATTING

*AVG	Marcus Giles, Myrtle Beach	.326
R	Rafael Furcal, Myrtle Beach/Macon	105
H	Rafael Furcal, Myrtle Beach/Macon	167
TB	Marcus Giles, Myrtle Beach	255
2B	Marcus Giles, Myrtle Beach	40
3B	Jason Ross, Myrtle Beach	13
HR	Howard Battle, Richmond	24
RBI	Brad Tyler, Richmond	79
BB	Brad Tyler, Richmond	69
SO	A.J. Zapp, Macon	163
SB	Rafael Furcal, Myrtle Beach/Macon	96

PITCHING

W	Jimmy Osting, Macon	14
L	Richard Dishman, Greenville	13
ERA	Winston Abreu, Myrtle Beach/Macon	2.48
G	Joe Winkelsas, Greenville	55
CG	Two tied at	2
SV	David Cortes, Richmond	22
IP	Jon Ratliff, Richmond	158
BB	Jacob Shumate, Greenville/Myrtle Beach	94
SO	Winston Abreu, Myrtle Beach/Macon	171

*Minimum 250 At-Bats #Minimum 75 Innings

Atlanta
BRAVES

Manager: Bobby Cox   **1999 Record:** 103-59, .636 (1st, NL East)

BATTING	AVG	G	AB	R	H	2B	3B	HR	RBI	BB	SO	SB	CS	B	T	HT	WT	DOB	1st Yr	Resides
Battle, Howard	.353	15	17	2	6	0	0	1	5	2	3	0	0	R	R	6-0	197	3-25-72	1990	Ocean Springs, Miss.
Boone, Bret	.252	152	608	102	153	38	1	20	63	47	112	14	9	R	R	5-10	180	4-6-69	1990	Orlando, Fla.
DeRosa, Mark	.000	7	8	0	0	0	0	0	0	0	2	0	0	R	R	6-1	195	2-2-75	1996	Carlstadt, N.J.
Fabregas, Jorge	.000	6	8	0	0	0	0	0	0	0	0	0	0	L	R	6-3	215	3-13-70	1991	Miami Beach, Fla.
2-team (82 Florida)	.199	88	231	20	46	10	2	3	21	26	27	0	0.							
Garcia, Freddy	.500	2	2	1	1	0	0	1	1	1	0	0	0	R	R	6-2	224	8-1-72	1991	La Romana, D.R.
2-team (55 Pittsburgh)	.235	57	132	17	31	5	0	7	24	5	42	0	0							
Guillen, Ozzie	.241	92	232	21	56	16	0	1	20	15	17	4	2	L	R	5-11	165	1-20-64	1981	Caracas, Venez.
Hernandez, Jose	.253	48	166	22	42	8	0	4	19	12	44	4	1	R	R	6-1	180	7-14-69	1987	Dorado, P.R.
2-team (99 Chicago)	.266	147	508	79	135	20	2	19	62	52	145	11	3							
Hunter, Brian	.249	114	181	28	45	12	1	6	30	31	40	0	1	R	L	6-0	195	3-4-68	1987	Anaheim, Calif.
Jones, Andruw	.275	162	592	97	163	35	5	26	84	76	103	24	12	R	R	6-1	185	4-23-77	1994	Willemstad, Curacao
Jones, Chipper	.319	157	567	116	181	41	1	45	110	126	94	25	3	S	R	6-4	210	4-24-72	1990	Alpharetta, Ga.
Jordan, Brian	.283	153	576	100	163	28	4	23	115	51	81	13	8	R	R	6-1	205	3-29-67	1988	Alpharetta, Ga.
Klesko, Ryan	.297	133	404	55	120	28	2	21	80	53	69	5	2	L	L	6-3	220	6-12-71	1989	Boynton Beach, Fla.
Lockhart, Keith	.261	108	161	20	42	3	1	1	21	19	21	3	1	L	R	5-10	170	11-10-64	1986	Overland Park, Kan.
Lombard, George	.333	6	6	1	2	0	0	0	1	2	2	0	0	L	R	6-0	212	9-14-75	1994	Atlanta, Ga.
Lopez, Javy	.317	65	246	34	78	18	1	11	45	20	41	0	3	R	R	6-3	200	11-5-70	1988	Ponce, P.R.
Matos, Pascual	.125	6	8	0	1	0	0	0	2	0	1	0	0	R	R	6-2	160	12-23-74	1992	Barahona, D.R.
Myers, Greg	.222	34	72	10	16	2	0	2	9	13	16	0	0	L	R	6-2	208	4-14-66	1984	Riverside, Calif.
2-team (50 San Diego)	.265	84	200	19	53	6	0	5	24	26	30	0	0							
Nixon, Otis	.205	84	151	31	31	2	1	0	8	23	15	26	7	S	R	6-2	180	1-9-59	1979	Alpharetta, Ga.
Perez, Eddie	.249	104	309	30	77	17	0	7	30	17	40	0	1	R	R	6-1	185	5-4-68	1987	Maracaibo, Venez.
Simon, Randall	.317	90	218	26	69	16	0	5	25	17	25	2	2	L	L	6-0	180	5-26-75	1993	Willemstad, Curacao
Weiss, Walt	.226	110	279	38	63	13	4	2	29	35	48	7	3	S	R	6-0	188	11-28-63	1985	Aurora, Colo.
Williams, Gerald	.275	143	422	76	116	24	1	17	68	33	67	19	11	R	R	6-2	187	8-10-66	1987	La Place, La.

PITCHING	W	L	ERA	G	GS	CG	SV	IP	H	R	ER	BB	SO	B	T	HT	WT	DOB	1st Yr	Resides
Bergman, Sean	1	0	2.84	6	0	0	0	6	5	2	2	3	6	R	R	6-4	225	4-11-70	1991	Joliet, Ill.
2-team (19 Houston)	5	6	5.21	25	16	2	0	105	135	62	61	29	44.							
Bowie, Micah	0	1	13.50	3	0	0	0	4	8	6	6	4	2	L	L	6-4	185	11-10-74	1993	Humble, Texas
Cather, Mike	1	0	10.13	4	0	0	0	3	5	3	3	1	0	R	R	6-2	205	12-17-70	1993	Folsom, Calif.
Chen, Bruce	2	2	5.47	16	7	0	0	51	38	32	31	27	45	S	L	6-1	180	6-19-77	1994	Panama City, Panama
Cortes, David	0	0	4.91	4	0	0	0	4	3	3	2	4	2	R	R	5-11	195	10-15-73	1996	El Centro, Calif.
Ebert, Derrin	0	1	5.63	5	0	0	1	8	9	5	5	5	4	R	L	6-3	200	8-21-76	1994	Hesperia, Calif.
Glavine, Tom	14	11	4.12	35	35	2	0	234	259	115	107	83	138	L	L	6-0	185	3-25-66	1984	Alpharetta, Ga.
Hudek, John	0	1	6.48	15	0	0	0	17	21	14	12	11	18	S	R	6-2	210	8-8-66	1988	Sugar Land, Texas
2-team (2 Cincinnati)	0	2	7.64	17	0	0	0	18	25	17	15	14	18							
Maddux, Greg	19	9	3.57	33	33	4	0	219	258	103	87	37	136	R	R	6-0	185	4-14-66	1984	Las Vegas, Nev.
McGlinchy, Kevin	7	3	2.82	64	0	0	0	70	66	25	22	30	61	R	R	6-5	220	6-28-77	1996	Ocala, Fla.
Millwood, Kevin	18	7	2.68	33	33	2	0	228	168	80	68	59	205	R	R	6-4	220	12-24-74	1993	Bessemer City, N.C.
Mulholland, Terry	4	2	2.98	16	8	0	1	60	64	24	20	13	39	R	L	6-3	220	3-9-63	1984	Scottsdale, Ariz.
2-team (26 Chicago)	10	8	4.39	42	24	0	1	170	201	95	83	45	83							
Perez, Odalis	4	6	6.00	18	17	0	0	93	100	65	62	53	82	L	L	6-0	150	6-7-78	1994	Las Matas de Farfan, D.R.
Remlinger, Mike	10	1	2.37	73	0	0	1	84	66	24	22	35	81	L	L	6-1	210	3-23-66	1987	Scottsdale, Ariz.
Rocker, John	4	5	2.49	74	0	0	38	72	47	24	20	37	104	R	L	6-4	225	10-17-74	1994	Macon, Ga.
Seanez, Rudy	6	1	3.35	56	0	0	3	54	47	21	20	21	41	R	R	5-11	205	10-20-68	1986	El Centro, Calif.
Smoltz, John	11	8	3.19	29	29	1	0	186	168	70	66	40	156	R	R	6-3	220	5-15-67	1986	Duluth, Ga.
Speier, Justin	0	0	5.65	19	0	0	0	29	28	18	18	13	22	R	R	6-4	205	11-6-73	1995	Paradise Valley, Ariz.
Springer, Russ	2	1	3.42	49	0	0	1	47	31	20	18	22	49	R	R	6-4	205	11-7-68	1989	Pollack, La.
Stull, Everett	0	0	13.50	1	0	0	0	1	2	3	1	2	0	R	R	6-3	200	8-24-71	1992	Stone Mountain, Ga.
Winkelsas, Joe	0	0	54.00	1	0	0	0	4	4	2	2	1	0	R	R	6-3	188	9-14-73	1996	Buffalo, N.Y.
Wohlers, Mark	0	0	27.00	2	0	0	0	1	1	2	2	6	0	R	R	6-4	207	1-23-70	1988	Alpharetta, Ga.

FIELDING

Catcher	PCT	G	PO	A	E	DP	PB
Fabregas	1.000	4	21	0	0	0	0
Lopez	.991	60	413	29	4	3	6
Matos	1.000	5	13	1	0	0	0
Myers	.994	31	166	12	1	2	0
E. Perez	.993	98	616	48	5	7	4

First Base	PCT	G	PO	A	E	DP
Fabregas	1.000	1	0	1	0	0
Garcia	1.000	1	0	0	0	0
Hernandez	1.000	1	1	0	0	0
Hunter	.991	101	425	36	4	37
Klesko	.989	75	493	30	6	37
E. Perez	1.000	2	4	0	0	0
Simon	.994	70	462	27	3	38

Second Base	PCT	G	PO	A	E	DP
Boone	.982	151	270	424	13	78
Guillen	1.000	1	1	0	0	0
Lockhart	1.000	25	26	58	0	11

Third Base	PCT	G	PO	A	E	DP
Battle	1.000	6	2	4	0	0
Garcia	.938	9	1	14	1	1
Guillen	1.000	6	3	9	0	1
C. Jones	.950	156	88	237	17	10
Lockhart	.875	10	1	6	1	1

Shortstop	PCT	G	PO	A	E	DP
DeRosa	1.000	2	2	2	0	0
Guillen	.965	53	54	137	7	29

	PCT	G	PO	A	E	DP
Hernandez	.964	45	48	114	6	24
C. Jones	1.000	1	0	1	0	0
Weiss	.963	102	108	203	12	41

Outfield	PCT	G	PO	A	E	DP
Garcia	.000	1	0	0	0	0
Hernandez	1.000	1	5	0	0	0
Hunter	1.000	8	10	0	0	0
A. Jones	.981	162	492	13	10	1
Jordan	.990	150	295	9	3	3
Klesko	1.000	53	61	2	0	0
Lombard	1.000	4	4	0	0	0
Nixon	.981	52	52	0	1	0
Williams	.985	139	188	9	3	2

Kevin Millwood
Led Braves with 2.68 ERA

DAVID SEELIG

Marcus Giles
Hit .326 for Myrtle Beach

ROBERT GURGANUS

FARM SYSTEM

Director, Player Development: Deric Ladnier/Dick Balderson

Class	Farm Team	League	W	L	Pct.	Finish*	Manager	First Yr
AAA	Richmond (Va.) Braves	International	64	78	.451	10th (14)	Randy Ingle	1966
AA	Greenville (S.C.) Braves	Southern	58	80	.420	10th (10)	Paul Runge	1984
A#	Myrtle Beach (S.C.) Pelicans	Carolina	79	60	.568	@2nd (8)	Brian Snitker	1999
A	Macon (Ga.) Braves	South Atlantic	74	64	.536	4th (14)	Jeff Treadway	1991
A	Jamestown (N.Y.) Jammers	New York-Penn	38	38	.500	9th (14)	Jim Saul	1999
Rookie#	Danville (Va.) Braves	Appalachian	38	31	.551	5th (10)	J.J. Cannon	1993
Rookie	Orlando (Fla.) Braves	Gulf Coast	27	33	.450	10th (14)	Rick Albert	1976

*Finish in overall standings (No. of teams in league)   #Advanced level   @League co-champion

RICHMOND   Class AAA

INTERNATIONAL LEAGUE

BATTING	AVG	G	AB	R	H	2B	3B	HR	RBI	BB	SO	SB	CS	B	T	HT	WT	DOB	1st Yr	Resides
Bass, Jayson	.209	59	153	20	32	4	1	1	10	19	46	9	2	S	R	6-0	180	6-2-76	1994	Fayette, Ala.
Battle, Howard	.284	121	454	80	129	29	1	24	74	33	66	2	3	R	R	6-0	197	3-25-72	1990	Ocean Springs, Miss.
DeRosa, Mark	.272	105	364	41	99	16	2	1	40	21	49	7	6	R	R	6-1	195	2-2-75	1996	Carlstadt, N.J.
Johnson, Adam	.333	14	42	7	14	2	0	1	6	2	5	1	1	L	L	6-0	185	7-18-75	1996	Naples, Fla.
Lombard, George	.206	74	233	25	48	11	3	7	29	35	98	21	6	L	R	6-0	212	9-14-75	1994	Atlanta, Ga.
Mahoney, Mike	.228	55	145	10	33	7	0	2	20	6	25	0	1	R	R	6-1	200	12-5-72	1995	Des Moines, Iowa
Malloy, Marty	.292	114	407	58	119	23	1	7	36	53	52	19	15	L	R	5-10	165	7-6-72	1992	Trenton, Fla.
Martinez, Pablo	.194	63	186	18	36	7	3	1	18	25	42	13	3	S	R	5-10	155	6-29-69	1989	Sabana Grande, D.R.
Matos, Pascual	.210	66	224	17	47	7	0	3	21	6	47	3	1	R	R	6-2	160	12-23-74	1992	Barahona, D.R.
McNabb, Buck	.229	17	48	8	11	0	0	1	8	6	9	0	1	L	R	6-0	180	1-17-73	1991	Fort Walton Beach, Fla.
Roberts, Lonell	.262	19	442	66	116	19	5	3	41	33	95	17	9	S	R	6-0	172	6-7-71	1989	Bloomington, Calif.
Rumfield, Toby	.274	111	383	57	105	23	1	15	62	31	57	1	2	R	R	6-3	190	9-4-72	1991	Belton, Texas
Schall, Gene	.293	100	355	49	104	25	1	12	53	35	84	0	1	R	R	6-3	205	6-5-70	1991	Harleysville, Pa.
Simon, Randall	.271	15	59	7	16	4	0	1	8	3	10	0	1	L	L	6-0	180	5-26-75	1993	Willemstad, Curacao
Sisco, Steve	.311	128	495	80	154	36	2	18	76	38	74	13	7	R	R	5-10	190	12-2-69	1992	Thousand Oaks, Calif.
Tyler, Brad	.286	122	413	73	118	20	2	21	79	69	99	18	3	L	R	6-2	180	3-3-69	1990	Aurora, Ind.
Whatley, Gabe	.271	82	251	35	68	14	2	8	34	38	65	8	4	L	R	6-0	180	12-29-71	1993	Stone Mountain, Ga.

PITCHING	W	L	ERA	G	GS	CG	SV	IP	H	R	ER	BB	SO	B	T	HT	WT	DOB	1st Yr	Resides
Bowie, Micah	4	4	2.96	13	13	0	0	73	65	24	24	14	82	L	L	6-4	185	11-10-74	1993	Humble, Texas
Brooks, Antone	3	5	3.86	43	0	0	1	56	57	28	24	21	39	L	L	6-0	170	12-20-73	1995	Florence, S.C.
Butler, Adam	0	1	2.25	9	0	0	3	8	10	4	2	3	6	L	L	6-2	225	8-17-73	1995	Burke, Va.
Cather, Mike	2	7	6.78	45	0	0	1	68	71	57	51	34	60	R	R	6-2	205	12-17-70	1993	Folsom, Calif.
Chen, Bruce	6	3	3.81	14	14	0	0	78	73	36	33	26	90	S	L	6-1	180	6-19-77	1994	Panama City, Panama
Cortes, David	2	3	3.35	47	0	0	22	46	50	19	17	14	42	R	R	5-11	195	10-15-73	1996	El Centro, Calif.

PITCHING	W	L	ERA	G	GS	CG	SV	IP	H	R	ER	BB	SO	B	T	HT	WT	DOB	1st Yr	Resides
Dawley, Joey	0	3	5.18	7	7	1	0	40	43	26	23	12	31	R	R	6-4	205	9-19-71	1993	Moreno Valley, Calif.
Ebert, Derrin	8	7	4.30	25	24	2	0	151	173	79	72	44	82	R	L	6-3	200	8-21-76	1994	Hesperia, Calif.
Harrison, Tommy	0	0	8.10	4	0	0	0	10	17	9	9	6	6	R	R	6-2	185	9-30-71	1993	Miamisburg, Ohio
Hudek, John	0	0	6.35	12	0	0	0	11	14	8	8	5	17	S	R	6-2	210	8-8-66	1988	Sugar Land, Texas
Iglesias, Mike	0	2	15.75	3	0	0	0	4	6	7	7	4	7	R	R	6-5	223	11-9-72	1991	Castro Valley, Calif.
Nelson, Joe	2	3	4.54	12	3	0	1	34	33	18	17	15	31	R	R	6-2	185	10-25-74	1996	Alameda, Calif.
Pisciotta, Marc	3	2	6.06	23	0	0	0	36	34	25	24	17	27	R	R	6-5	225	8-7-70	1991	Marietta, Ga.
Quevedo, Ruben	6	5	5.37	21	21	0	0	106	112	65	63	34	98	R	R	6-1	180	1-5-79	1996	Valencia, Venez.
Ratliff, Jon	5	12	4.45	27	27	0	0	158	154	88	78	44	129	R	R	6-4	195	12-22-71	1993	Clay, N.Y.
Seelbach, Chris	6	1	5.15	13	8	1	0	58	51	34	33	34	48	R	R	6-4	180	12-18-72	1991	Lufkin, Texas
Speier, Justin	2	4	5.62	27	0	0	3	42	51	28	26	22	39	R	R	6-4	205	11-6-73	1995	Paradise Valley, Ariz.
Springer, Russ	1	0	1.17	11	0	0	2	15	9	2	2	1	13	R	R	6-4	205	11-7-68	1989	Pollack, La.
Stull, Everett	8	8	4.47	30	22	0	0	139	124	75	69	73	126	R	R	6-3	200	8-24-71	1992	Stone Mountain, Ga.
Villegas, Ismael	6	7	4.40	44	2	0	1	92	93	51	45	39	61	R	R	6-0	188	8-12-76	1995	Caguas, P.R.
Wengert, Don	0	0	4.50	1	1	0	0	6	7	3	3	0	3	R	R	6-3	205	11-6-69	1992	Des Moines, Iowa
2-team (6 Columbus)	0	1	6.75	7	3	0	0	21	32	16	16	3	8							
Willoughby, Justin	0	0	9.00	1	0	0	0	1	3	1	1	0	1	L	L	6-3	170	4-9-78	1996	Princeton, N.C.

FIELDING

Catcher	PCT	G	PO	A	E	DP	PB
Mahoney	.989	42	237	24	3	1	4
Matos	.990	66	456	43	5	2	6
Rumfield	.987	50	347	23	5	3	6
Sisco	1.000	2	1	1	0	0	0

First Base	PCT	G	PO	A	E	DP
Battle	.926	3	23	2	2	3
Rumfield	.992	49	345	18	3	43
Schall	.991	74	535	36	5	40
Simon	1.000	14	115	14	0	9
Tyler	1.000	14	106	5	0	13

Second Base	PCT	G	PO	A	E	DP
Battle	1.000	1	1	3	0	1
Malloy	.990	65	111	172	3	31

	PCT	G	PO	A	E	DP	PB
Martinez	.963	13	18	34	2	5	
Sisco	.983	70	131	151	5	46	
Tyler	1.000	3	5	5	0	0	

Third Base	PCT	G	PO	A	E	DP
Battle	.939	84	41	114	10	13
Malloy	.933	31	20	50	5	7
Martinez	1.000	1	0	3	0	0
Sisco	.966	31	22	62	3	3
Tyler	.000	1	0	0	0	0

Shortstop	PCT	G	PO	A	E	DP
DeRosa	.951	102	139	249	20	55
Malloy	.936	11	18	26	3	9
Martinez	.969	33	41	113	5	19

	PCT	G	PO	A	E	DP	PB
Sisco	.929	4	5	8	1	2	

Outfield	PCT	G	PO	A	E	DP
Bass	.969	52	92	3	3	0
Johnson	1.000	11	20	2	0	1
Lombard	.974	67	108	3	3	0
Malloy	.000	1	0	0	0	0
Martinez	1.000	8	8	0	0	0
McNabb	.950	15	37	1	2	0
Roberts	.983	117	278	5	5	0
Schall	1.000	22	28	1	0	0
Sisco	1.000	10	23	0	0	0
Tyler	.977	92	206	2	5	2
Whatley	.992	67	118	2	1	0

GREENVILLE   Class AA
SOUTHERN LEAGUE

BATTING	AVG	G	AB	R	H	2B	3B	HR	RBI	BB	SO	SB	CS	B	T	HT	WT	DOB	1st Yr	Resides
Cepeda, Jose	.276	58	196	19	54	8	2	1	17	13	15	2	3	R	R	6-0	185	8-1-74	1995	Fajardo, P.R.
Glavine, Mike	.269	107	305	47	82	24	0	17	52	49	65	0	3	L	L	6-3	210	1-24-73	1995	Billerica, Mass.
Goodell, Steve	.299	102	338	69	101	25	2	15	58	55	61	8	6	R	R	6-3	196	4-23-75	1995	Danville, Calif.
Helms, Wes	.301	30	113	15	34	6	0	8	26	7	34	1	0	R	R	6-4	230	5-12-76	1994	Gastonia, N.C.
Horn, Jeff	.229	66	166	19	38	6	0	2	27	16	28	0	1	R	R	6-1	213	8-23-70	1992	Las Vegas, Nev.
Johnson, Adam	.289	104	394	50	114	27	2	14	72	31	74	1	6	L	L	6-0	185	7-18-75	1996	Naples, Fla.
Lackey, Steve	.292	80	315	50	92	18	3	4	38	21	55	9	8	R	R	5-11	159	9-25-74	1992	Riverside, Calif.
Lunar, Fernando	.224	105	343	33	77	15	1	3	35	12	64	0	1	R	R	6-1	190	5-25-77	1994	Anaco Aneoa, Venez.
Martinez, Pablo	.237	57	228	28	54	9	3	1	19	20	41	6	8	S	R	5-10	155	6-29-69	1989	Sabana Grande, D.R.
McNabb, Buck	.323	25	93	9	30	4	0	0	5	5	18	2	2	L	R	6-0	180	1-17-73	1991	Fort Walton Beach, Fla.
Mortimer, Mark	.233	11	30	4	7	1	0	0	5	3	7	0	0	R	R	6-1	215	9-15-75	1997	Forest Park, Ga.
Norris, Dax	.278	120	403	59	112	27	0	15	66	41	59	2	1	R	R	5-10	190	1-14-73	1996	La Grange, Ga.
Pendergrass, Tyrone	.262	100	344	60	90	12	6	3	31	37	61	19	14	S	R	6-1	180	7-31-76	1995	Hartsville, S.C.
Pimentel, Jose	.214	106	364	55	78	18	1	8	45	24	80	20	10	R	R	6-0	160	12-3-74	1993	San Cristobal, D.R.
Smith, Demond	.305	132	416	70	127	20	7	9	59	55	72	31	13	S	R	5-11	170	11-6-72	1990	Rialto, Calif.
Trippy, Joe	.221	79	131	26	29	5	0	2	15	30	25	6	7	L	L	5-10	185	7-31-73	1995	Seattle, Wash.
Williams, Glenn	.225	57	204	19	46	11	0	4	15	7	58	1	4	R	R	6-2	170	7-18-77	1994	Chipping North, Australia

PITCHING	W	L	ERA	G	GS	CG	SV	IP	H	R	ER	BB	SO	B	T	HT	WT	DOB	1st Yr	Resides
Beasley, Ray	7	4	4.63	50	0	0	3	82	84	45	42	26	71	R	L	5-11	168	10-26-76	1996	Lake City, Fla.
Bullard, Jason	0	1	18.78	5	0	0	0	8	16	18	16	12	5	R	R	6-2	185	10-23-68	1991	College Station, Texas
Butler, Adam	1	3	7.65	27	0	0	1	42	71	44	36	12	29	L	L	6-2	225	8-17-73	1995	Burke, Va.
Carlyle, Ken	1	6	5.93	17	12	0	0	71	89	60	47	42	33	R	R	6-1	195	4-16-71	1992	Cordova, Tenn.
Cruz, Charlie	1	0	3.45	11	0	0	1	16	23	6	6	9	11	L	L	5-10	175	10-22-73	1995	Miami, Fla.
Dawley, Joey	5	3	4.03	26	11	0	0	92	76	54	41	37	89	R	R	6-4	205	9-19-71	1993	Moreno Valley, Calif.
Dishman, Richard	6	13	4.19	30	24	1	1	140	146	76	65	58	131	R	R	6-5	220	4-26-75	1997	Roosevelt Island, N.Y.
Flach, Jason	1	2	6.63	12	2	0	1	37	44	29	27	10	15	R	R	6-0	165	11-25-73	1996	Davenport, Iowa
Forney, Rick	3	3	2.99	12	12	0	0	72	67	27	24	19	70	R	R	6-4	230	10-24-71	1991	Frederick, Md.
Harrison, Tommy	3	7	7.39	16	12	0	0	63	75	59	52	43	42	R	R	6-2	185	9-30-71	1993	Miamisburg, Ohio
Iglesias, Mike	0	3	7.07	4	4	0	0	14	19	11	11	6	5	R	R	6-5	223	11-9-72	1991	Castro Valley, Calif.
Kent, Nathan	0	0	18.00	1	0	0	0	1	1	2	2	2	2	R	R	6-6	210	8-16-78	1999	Frankfort, Ky.
Manzano, Adrian	5	2	3.21	42	0	0	2	62	61	24	22	22	51	R	R	5-9	185	11-27-78	1995	Jalisco, Mexico
Marquis, Jason	3	4	4.58	12	12	1	0	55	52	33	28	29	35	L	R	6-1	185	8-21-78	1996	Coral Springs, Fla.
Milburn, Adam	1	0	4.74	14	0	0	0	19	23	10	10	7	10	R	L	6-1	195	4-27-74	1996	Springfield, Ky.
Moss, Damian	1	3	8.54	7	7	0	0	33	50	33	31	21	22	R	L	6-0	187	11-24-76	1994	Sadler, Australia
Nelson, Joe	1	1	2.37	25	0	0	8	30	19	15	8	14	33	R	R	6-2	185	10-25-74	1996	Alameda, Calif.
Salamon, John	2	4	8.29	28	1	0	1	42	42	41	39	42	41	R	R	6-3	220	3-30-72	1991	McKees Rocks, Pa.
Seelbach, Chris	3	2	3.89	8	6	1	0	39	31	18	17	19	47	R	R	6-4	180	12-18-72	1991	Lufkin, Texas
Shumate, Jacob	3	4	4.74	14	12	0	0	57	43	30	30	61	48	R	R	6-2	185	1-22-76	1994	Hartsville, S.C.
Smoltz, John	0	0	4.50	2	1	0	0	4	5	2	2	1	7	R	R	6-3	220	5-15-67	1986	Duluth, Ga.
Steenstra, Kennie	2	1	3.79	8	0	0	0	19	25	8	8	1	12	R	R	6-5	215	10-13-70	1992	Liberty, Mo.
Steinmetz, Earl	0	2	6.75	6	2	0	0	11	13	9	8	16	6	R	R	6-1	189	5-17-71	1989	San Antonio, Texas
Trippy, Joe	0	0	14.54	5	0	0	0	4	10	7	7	3	1	L	L	5-10	185	7-31-73	1995	Seattle, Wash.
Winkelsas, Joe	4	4	3.75	55	0	0	12	62	71	32	26	30	38	R	R	6-3	188	9-14-73	1996	Buffalo, N.Y.
Yankosky, L.J.	5	8	4.24	20	20	1	0	108	122	70	51	43	62	R	R	6-2	208	2-1-75	1998	Springfield, Va.

FIELDING

Catcher	PCT	G	PO	A	E	DP	PB
Horn	.988	28	153	18	2	1	2
Lunar	.986	96	611	88	10	12	9
Norris	.979	26	161	24	4	1	2

First Base	PCT	G	PO	A	E	DP
Cepeda	1.000	1	1	0	0	0
Glavine	.994	64	487	44	3	47
Goodell	.909	2	9	1	1	1
Helms	.984	30	226	18	4	23
Johnson	.990	15	91	10	1	10
Mortimer	1.000	1	3	0	0	0
Norris	.991	47	295	18	3	30

Second Base	PCT	G	PO	A	E	DP
Cepeda	.969	56	80	138	7	32
Goodell	1.000	5	8	4	0	1
Lackey	.975	11	15	24	1	1
Pimentel	.985	27	57	77	2	19
Williams	.976	52	112	134	6	33

Third Base	PCT	G	PO	A	E	DP
Goodell	.880	90	69	143	29	13
Horn	.795	20	13	18	8	2
Pimentel	.910	38	22	69	9	2
Williams	1.000	5	1	11	0	1

Shortstop	PCT	G	PO	A	E	DP
Goodell	1.000	11	19	30	0	6

	PCT	G	PO	A	E	DP
Lackey	.926	71	111	203	25	44
Martinez	.961	56	90	182	11	39
Pimentel	.941	5	3	13	1	3

Outfield	PCT	G	PO	A	E	DP
Glavine	.959	30	46	1	2	1
Johnson	.972	91	164	9	5	4
McNabb	.977	20	41	2	1	0
Mortimer	1.000	8	8	0	0	0
Pendergrass	.975	96	230	8	6	4
Pimentel	.949	40	72	2	4	0
Smith	.991	129	211	12	2	2
Trippy	.958	51	66	3	3	0

MYRTLE BEACH — Class A

CAROLINA LEAGUE

BATTING	AVG	G	AB	R	H	2B	3B	HR	RBI	BB	SO	SB	CS	B	T	HT	WT	DOB	1st Yr	Resides
Bass, Jayson	.220	44	164	20	36	7	3	2	19	15	45	8	3	S	R	6-0	180	6-2-76	1994	Fayette, Ala.
Brignac, Junior	.228	64	254	32	58	7	2	7	35	24	84	11	10	R	R	6-3	175	2-15-78	1996	Sun Valley, Calif.
Bronowicz, Scott	.143	21	56	9	8	1	1	0	4	6	12	0	0	L	R	5-11	195	4-14-76	1998	Pittsburgh, Pa.
Cepeda, Jose	.000	1	5	1	0	0	0	0	0	0	1	0	0	R	R	6-0	185	8-1-74	1995	Fajardo, P.R.
2-team (w Wilmington)	.306	60	232	36	71	7	2	0	25	22	20	5	8							
Furcal, Rafael	.293	43	184	32	54	9	3	0	12	14	42	23	8	S	R	5-10	150	8-24-80	1997	Loma de Cabrera, D.R.
Giles, Marcus	.326	126	497	80	162	40	7	13	73	54	89	9	6	R	R	5-8	180	5-18-78	1997	El Cajon, Calif.
Hessman, Mike	.247	103	365	62	90	25	0	23	54	47	135	0	3	R	R	6-5	215	3-5-78	1996	Westminster, Calif.
Lackey, Steve	.273	53	216	24	59	10	2	0	16	15	33	13	4	R	R	5-11	159	9-25-74	1992	Riverside, Calif.
Lehr, Ryan	.255	109	423	59	108	18	4	14	68	45	63	3	2	R	R	5-11	205	2-1-79	1997	La Mesa, Calif.
Martinez, Louis	.133	5	15	1	2	1	0	0	0	1	2	0	0	R	R	6-0	175	1-1-76	1999	Tampa, Fla.
Mortimer, Mark	.276	73	250	29	69	13	0	3	31	28	48	1	0	R	R	6-1	215	9-15-75	1997	Forest Park, Ga.
Pugh, Josh	.165	41	115	4	19	2	0	0	12	10	32	0	0	R	R	6-0	200	9-10-77	1996	Lexington, Ky.
Rodriguez, Jeff	.000	1	1	0	0	0	0	0	0	0	1	0	0	R	R	5-11	195	12-20-76	1999	Miami, Fla.
Ross, Jason	.268	133	482	80	129	23	13	12	64	43	136	31	5	R	R	6-4	215	6-10-76	1994	Augusta, Ga.
Scharrer, Jim	.260	119	466	52	121	18	0	7	54	30	120	0	1	R	R	6-4	220	11-5-76	1995	Erie, Pa.
Smothers, Stewart	.151	56	185	19	28	8	3	1	14	15	71	2	2	R	R	5-10	180	4-29-76	1997	Los Angeles, Calif.
Spencer, Jeff	.247	111	397	59	98	28	4	11	42	34	126	2	6	R	R	6-2	170	6-25-77	1995	Melbourne, Australia
Terhune, Mike	.224	92	312	24	70	10	3	1	26	27	51	3	2	S	R	6-1	185	10-14-75	1996	Pocono Manor, Pa.
Torrealba, Steve	.211	52	175	23	37	9	0	6	23	13	47	1	0	R	R	6-0	175	2-24-78	1996	Barquisimeto, Venez.
Wong, Jerrod	.224	58	201	27	45	11	4	5	31	6	52	1	2	L	L	6-3	200	5-29-74	1996	Boise, Idaho

GAMES BY POSITION: C—Bronowicz 18, Mortimer 45, Pugh 41, Rodriguez 1, Torrealba 50. **1B**—Lehr 59, Scharrer 74, Wong 7. **2B**—Giles 121, Lo. Martinez 2, Terhune 19. **3B**—Hessman 97, Lo. Martinez 3, Mortimer 7, Terhune 36. **SS**—Cepeda 1, Furcal 43, Hessman 6, Lackey 53, Terhune 38. **OF**—Bass 41, Brignac 64, Bronowicz 1, Mortimer 1, Ross 131, Scharrer 1, Smothers 56, Spencer 99, Wong 35.

PITCHING	W	L	ERA	G	GS	CG	SV	IP	H	R	ER	BB	SO	B	T	HT	WT	DOB	1st Yr	Resides
Abreu, Winston	3	2	3.28	13	12	0	0	69	53	26	25	41	76	R	R	6-2	155	4-5-77	1994	Cotui, D.R.
Corey, Michael	2	1	4.78	22	0	0	6	32	32	19	17	11	31	R	R	6-2	215	9-29-74	1998	Pendleton, Ore.
Embry, Byron	0	0	0.00	2	0	0	0	6	1	0	0	0	5	R	R	6-2	240	9-5-76	1997	Richmond, Ky.
Flach, Jason	9	4	3.07	24	14	0	0	108	101	50	37	37	63	R	R	6-0	165	11-25-73	1996	Davenport, Iowa
Fleck, Will	10	10	6.48	40	0	0	0	75	67	56	54	52	72	R	R	6-0	175	3-29-76	1997	Milford, N.J.
Frachiseur, Zach	7	3	2.76	37	5	0	2	98	75	34	30	31	93	R	R	6-0	190	9-30-76	1998	Conyers, Ga.
Greene, Ryan	3	5	3.40	44	0	0	16	82	65	32	31	29	85	R	R	6-4	215	8-6-74	1997	Menlo Park, Calif.
Lee, Garrett	1	1	5.09	3	0	0	0	18	21	12	10	3	12	R	R	6-5	210	8-17-76	1996	Montrose, Calif.
Lewis, Derrick	8	4	2.40	24	23	0	0	131	100	44	35	81	102	R	R	6-3	215	5-7-76	1997	Montgomery, Ala.
Marquis, Jason	3	0	0.28	6	6	0	0	32	22	2	1	17	41	L	R	6-1	185	8-21-78	1996	Coral Springs, Fla.
Martinez, Lionel	1	0	0.00	1	0	0	0	1	0	0	0	0	1	R	R	6-3	165	11-28-79	1996	San Felix, Venez.
Milburn, Adam	2	4	4.20	39	0	0	15	45	53	27	21	14	27	R	L	6-1	195	4-27-74	1996	Springfield, Fla.
Nation, Joey	5	4	4.39	19	17	0	0	96	88	51	47	37	87	L	L	6-2	175	9-28-78	1997	Oklahoma City, Okla.
Pacheco, Delvis	6	5	3.44	40	0	0	2	99	87	47	38	42	87	R	R	6-2	180	6-25-79	1995	Maracay, Venez.
Rivera, Luis	0	2	3.11	25	13	0	0	67	45	25	23	23	81	R	R	6-3	163	6-21-78	1995	Chihuahua, Mexico
Shiell, Jason	6	7	3.77	26	17	0	0	115	118	51	48	36	90	R	R	6-0	180	10-19-76	1995	Savannah, Ga.
Shumate, Jacob	3	3	7.15	20	0	0	0	23	15	19	18	33	31	R	R	6-2	190	1-22-76	1994	Hartsville, S.C.
Sobkowiak, Scott	9	4	2.84	27	26	0	0	139	100	50	44	63	161	R	R	6-5	230	10-26-77	1998	Loveland, Ohio
Voyles, Brad	1	1	2.25	5	0	0	0	12	7	3	3	9	13	R	R	6-1	195	12-30-76	1998	Green Bay, Wis.

MACON — Class A

SOUTH ATLANTIC LEAGUE

BATTING	AVG	G	AB	R	H	2B	3B	HR	RBI	BB	SO	SB	CS	B	T	HT	WT	DOB	1st Yr	Resides
Aldridge, Cory	.251	124	443	48	111	19	4	12	65	33	123	9	6	L	R	6-0	210	6-13-79	1997	Abilene, Texas
Boscan, Jean	.226	105	368	40	83	17	0	4	38	26	94	2	4	R	R	6-2	160	12-26-79	1996	Maracaibo, Venez.
Brignac, Junior	.299	69	268	35	80	18	3	7	38	11	68	17	5	R	R	6-3	175	2-15-78	1996	Sun Valley, Calif.
Cameron, Troy	.238	130	462	71	110	28	2	22	77	64	161	7	9	R	R	5-11	180	8-31-78	1997	Plantation, Fla.
Castro, Ramon	.260	105	350	32	91	12	4	3	33	24	55	13	5	S	R	6-0	195	10-23-79	1996	Valencia, Venez.
Dalton, David	.288	39	132	19	38	7	1	3	12	14	34	3	3	R	R	5-10	190	6-30-76	1998	Tampa, Fla.
Furcal, Rafael	.337	83	335	73	113	15	1	1	29	41	36	73	22	S	R	5-10	150	8-24-80	1997	Loma de Cabrera, D.R.
Green, Nick	.200	3	10	1	2	0	0	1	3	0	4	1	0	R	R	6-0	178	9-10-78	1999	Duluth, Ga.
James, Drue	.185	40	119	10	22	2	0	1	8	15	37	0	0	R	R	5-10	215	7-1-76	1998	Blanchard, Okla.
Langerhans, Ryan	.268	121	448	66	120	30	1	9	49	52	99	19	11	L	L	6-3	195	2-20-80	1998	Round Rock, Texas
Maluchnik, Gregg	.206	57	131	18	27	3	0	1	9	21	35	2	3	R	R	6-3	205	9-14-76	1998	Raleigh, N.C.
Manning, Pat	.259	43	170	25	44	11	2	4	19	14	42	3	1	R	R	6-1	185	1-27-80	1999	Anaheim Hills, Calif.
Smothers, Stewart	.283	63	219	32	62	12	0	7	39	16	61	2	3	R	R	5-10	180	4-29-76	1997	Los Angeles, Calif.
Stewart, Colin	.208	29	72	8	15	4	0	0	3	5	16	3	1	R	R	6-2	185	9-2-76	1998	San Jose, Calif.
Strickland, Greg	.261	86	314	58	82	13	8	7	34	26	74	27	12	L	L	5-10	175	11-8-75	1997	McKenzie, Tenn.

Organization Statistics

BATTING	AVG	G	AB	R	H	2B	3B	HR	RBI	BB	SO	SB	CS	B	T	HT	WT	DOB	1st Yr	Resides
Wilson, Travis	.309	90	363	65	112	20	4	11	63	9	66	14	8	R	R	6-2	185	7-10-77	1996	Christchurch, New Zealand
Zapp, A.J.	.229	119	428	60	98	24	1	22	65	40	163	4	1	L	R	6-3	190	4-24-78	1996	Greenwood, Ind.

GAMES BY POSITION: C—Boscan 95, James 31, Maluchnik 22. 1B—Maluchnik 21, Wilson 10, Zapp 115. 2B—Castro 39, Dalton 28, Green 2, Wilson 72. 3B—Cameron 118, Castro 16, Dalton 7, James 1, Maluchnik 3. SS—Cameron 1, Castro 29, Dalton 1, Furcal 74, Manning 38. OF—Aldridge 116, Brignac 69, Castro 3, Langerhans 112, Maluchnik 6, Smothers 62, Stewart 27, Strickland 42.

PITCHING	W	L	ERA	G	GS	CG	SV	IP	H	R	ER	BB	SO	B	T	HT	WT	DOB	1st Yr	Resides
Abreu, Winston	7	2	1.69	14	14	0	0	69	41	17	13	26	95	R	R	6-2	155	4-5-77	1994	Cotui, D.R.
Blanco, Roger	1	3	9.71	19	6	0	0	38	63	46	41	16	28	R	R	6-6	215	8-29-76	1993	La Sabana, Venez.
Blythe, Billy	0	0	9.00	1	0	0	0	1	2	1	1	0	1	R	R	6-2	195	1-25-76	1994	Lexington, Ky.
Bong, Jung	6	5	3.98	26	20	0	1	109	111	61	48	50	100	L	L	6-3	175	7-15-80	1997	Norcross, Ga.
Chavez, Chris	1	2	3.52	13	0	0	3	15	14	9	6	6	18	R	R	6-0	180	7-23-75	1998	Tallahassee, Fla.
Corey, Michael	1	1	0.53	21	0	0	7	34	18	4	2	7	39	R	R	6-2	215	9-29-74	1998	Pendleton, Ore.
Dansby, Justin	0	2	7.50	4	0	0	0	6	7	5	5	6	7	R	R	6-1	190	2-28-78	1998	Ada, Okla.
Dent, Doug	4	5	3.44	17	17	0	0	89	78	42	34	29	64	R	R	6-8	210	3-23-77	1998	Citrus Heights, Calif.
Embry, Byron	5	2	2.38	25	0	0	0	45	35	17	12	25	42	R	R	6-0	240	9-5-76	1997	Richmond, Ky.
Frachiseur, Zach	0	1	6.75	4	0	0	0	4	5	3	3	2	6	R	R	6-0	190	9-30-76	1998	Conyers, Ga.
Gray, Michael	5	4	3.65	46	1	0	8	81	88	45	33	12	57	L	L	6-1	170	12-6-76	1999	Paso Robles, Calif.
Herndon, Eric	5	4	4.00	27	2	0	1	72	72	42	32	27	75	L	R	6-1	190	10-4-76	1998	Upper Marlboro, Md.
Mikels, Jason	0	1	3.00	5	0	0	1	12	9	7	4	4	6	R	R	6-4	185	7-27-79	1999	Rio Linda, Calif.
Moss, Damian	0	3	4.32	12	12	0	0	42	33	20	20	15	49	R	L	6-0	187	11-24-76	1994	Sadler, Australia
Nation, Joey	1	1	2.96	6	6	0	0	27	27	10	9	9	31	L	L	6-2	175	9-28-78	1997	Oklahoma City, Okla.
Osting, Jimmy	14	4	2.88	27	22	0	2	147	130	52	47	30	131	R	L	6-5	190	4-7-77	1995	Louisville, Ky.
Parra, Christian	1	1	3.31	6	0	0	0	33	33	15	12	12	31	R	R	6-1	255	2-28-78	1999	Yuma, Ariz.
Pierce, Tony	0	0	1.80	8	0	0	0	15	11	3	3	7	23	R	R	6-0	205	6-21-76	1999	Midland, Ga.
Ramirez, Horacio	6	3	2.67	17	14	1	0	78	70	30	23	25	43	L	L	6-1	170	11-24-79	1997	Inglewood, Calif.
Simpson, Chris	3	5	6.04	14	9	0	0	51	37	37	34	44	40	R	R	6-5	215	2-1-78	1997	Kentwood, La.
Spooneybarger, Tim ...	0	1	3.60	7	0	0	0	10	7	4	4	10	17	R	R	6-3	190	10-21-79	1998	Pensacola, Fla.
Sylvester, Billy	5	4	3.12	44	1	0	2	84	78	37	29	37	75	R	R	6-5	218	10-1-76	1997	Florence, S.C.
Taylor, Aaron	6	7	4.88	27	8	0	1	79	86	56	43	27	78	R	R	6-5	205	8-20-77	1996	Hahira, Ga.
Voyles, Brad	3	3	2.98	38	0	0	14	51	27	21	17	39	65	R	R	6-1	195	12-30-76	1998	Green Bay, Wis.

JAMESTOWN — Short-Season Class A

NEW YORK-PENN LEAGUE

BATTING	AVG	G	AB	R	H	2B	3B	HR	RBI	BB	SO	SB	CS	B	T	HT	WT	DOB	1st Yr	Resides
Burke, Paul	.178	34	101	5	18	5	0	0	9	9	27	1	0	R	R	6-2	200	9-2-77	1998	Louisville, Ky.
Calais, Ian	.210	68	224	19	47	8	1	0	20	23	47	4	5	R	R	6-1	180	9-8-76	1999	Breaux Bridge, La.
Celli, Mick	.272	72	246	39	67	16	1	2	33	32	55	8	0	S	L	5-11	185	1-19-77	1999	Pembroke Pines, Fla.
Dalton, David	.317	27	104	23	33	1	4	1	15	9	20	14	3	R	R	5-10	190	6-30-76	1998	Tampa, Fla.
Ewan, Bry	.193	31	109	9	21	3	0	1	15	13	33	0	0	R	R	6-2	205	8-2-78	1997	Belton, Texas
Francisco, Joe	.199	42	146	17	29	10	0	2	10	9	37	9	1	R	R	5-10	185	11-26-77	1999	Middle Village, N.Y.
Geisbush, David	.232	26	69	11	16	2	1	3	12	5	25	2	0	R	R	5-11	185	12-19-76	1999	San Antonio, Texas
Green, Nick	.297	73	273	52	81	15	0	11	41	26	66	14	4	R	R	6-0	178	9-10-78	1999	Duluth, Ga.
Langlois, Jean	.245	59	220	24	54	7	2	3	20	25	54	10	2	R	R	6-0	200	7-20-78	1999	Ste-Foy, Quebec
Leal, Jaeme	.273	33	99	16	27	5	0	8	28	8	37	0	0	R	R	6-0	195	8-23-78	1999	Riverside, Calif.
Oropeza, Asdrubal	.293	74	266	56	78	12	1	14	46	32	60	10	2	R	R	6-2	170	7-3-80	1996	Barquisimeto, Venez.
Poulsen, Chris	.220	37	123	19	27	8	0	2	14	2	22	2	2	R	R	6-1	190	6-13-76	1998	Fresno, Calif.
Rodriguez, Jeff	.287	48	174	23	50	10	0	0	14	11	27	3	0	R	R	5-11	185	12-20-76	1999	Miami, Fla.
Simmons, Jerry	.216	62	232	37	50	9	5	4	27	20	46	19	6	R	R	6-0	195	6-4-76	1998	Charleston, S.C.
Villar, Jose	.248	39	133	14	33	6	1	4	17	11	43	5	3	R	R	6-0	195	5-1-79	1996	Santo Domingo, D.R.

GAMES BY POSITION: C—Burke 13, Poulsen 24, Rodriguez 40. 1B—Burke 17, Ewan 28, Geisbush 1, Leal 33, Poulsen 7. 2B—Dalton 2, Geisbush 6, Green 73. 3B—Dalton 1, Geisbush 1, Oropeza 74, Rodriguez 2. SS—Calais 68, Dalton 8, Geisbush 4. OF—Celli 61, Francisco 26, Geisbush 2, Langlois 54, Simmons 52, Villar 38.

PITCHING	W	L	ERA	G	GS	CG	SV	IP	H	R	ER	BB	SO	B	T	HT	WT	DOB	1st Yr	Resides
Colon, Roman	7	5	4.54	15	15	1	0	77	77	48	39	25	61	R	R	6-3	170	8-13-79	1996	Montecristi, D.R.
Cox, Brian	1	4	4.82	17	1	0	1	28	23	17	15	18	29	R	R	6-2	180	11-30-75	1998	Shelby, N.C.
Curtis, Daniel	5	6	4.58	15	15	1	0	75	74	41	38	24	61	R	R	6-3	215	11-3-79	1998	Chattanooga, Tenn.
Dansby, Justin	1	4	6.57	24	0	0	4	38	45	29	28	24	43	R	R	6-1	190	2-28-78	1998	Ada, Okla.
Gawer, Matt	2	1	3.30	21	0	0	6	30	24	12	11	18	44	L	L	6-4	235	4-15-78	1999	Sullivan, Mo.
Hutchinson, Brian	1	2	6.35	14	0	0	0	23	24	19	16	12	22	L	L	6-0	190	1-10-77	1999	Fairview, N.C.
Kent, Nathan	3	3	4.13	14	11	0	1	52	57	31	24	11	49	R	R	6-5	210	8-16-78	1999	Frankfort, Ky.
Lee, Garrett	4	3	4.07	13	13	1	0	77	79	39	35	16	47	R	R	6-5	210	8-17-76	1996	Montrose, Calif.
McClendon, Matt	1	1	3.91	7	7	0	0	23	18	11	10	11	24	R	R	6-6	220	10-13-77	1999	Orlando, Fla.
Parra, Christian	2	2	3.10	9	9	0	0	49	46	21	17	19	62	R	R	6-1	255	2-28-78	1999	Yuma, Ariz.
Pierce, Tony	0	1	2.70	17	0	0	8	27	14	9	8	12	44	R	R	6-0	205	6-21-76	1999	Midland, Ga.
Samadani, A.J.	3	1	5.36	22	0	0	1	40	41	28	24	17	37	R	R	6-2	205	12-27-75	1999	San Diego, Calif.
Satterfield, Jeremy	2	2	4.28	23	0	0	1	34	25	17	16	22	36	R	R	6-3	200	12-2-75	1998	Santa Barbara, Calif.
Truitt, Derrick	2	3	4.63	18	0	0	1	35	28	20	18	18	30	R	R	6-1	200	2-2-78	1998	Columbia, Tenn.
Willoughby, Justin	5	3	5.29	19	5	0	0	48	55	35	28	16	49	L	L	6-3	170	4-9-78	1996	Princeton, N.C.

DANVILLE — Rookie

APPALACHIAN LEAGUE

BATTING	AVG	G	AB	R	H	2B	3B	HR	RBI	BB	SO	SB	CS	B	T	HT	WT	DOB	1st Yr	Resides
Argento, Shaun	.233	16	43	5	10	3	0	0	8	2	10	0	0	R	R	6-1	205	12-24-75	1999	Oroville, Calif.
Betemit, Wilson	.320	67	259	39	83	18	2	5	53	27	63	6	3	S	R	6-2	155	7-28-80	1996	Santo Domingo, D.R.
Crocker, Nick	.256	63	242	52	62	15	3	3	32	31	56	5	4	L	L	6-3	195	8-8-77	1999	Carlyle, Ill.
Donato, Greg	.288	53	215	30	62	15	3	2	37	19	45	13	6	R	R	6-0	185	11-10-80	1998	Clovis, Calif.
Fiore, Curt	.333	53	198	35	66	13	0	3	24	22	39	0	5	R	R	6-2	195	7-28-77	1999	San Juan Capistrano, Calif.
Forbes, Michael	.280	58	207	47	58	11	4	1	34	53	47	1	4	L	R	6-1	195	5-27-80	1998	West Lakes, Australia
Green, Kevin	.174	44	149	24	26	8	0	5	16	13	68	4	2	R	R	6-0	180	9-10-79	1999	Duluth, Ga.
Hambrick, Marcus	.258	38	120	21	31	4	1	1	9	14	39	9	3	L	L	5-11	170	6-19-79	1999	Montgomery, Ala.

BATTING	AVG	G	AB	R	H	2B	3B	HR	RBI	BB	SO	SB	CS	B	T	HT	WT	DOB	1st Yr	Resides
Heffernan, Chris	.109	23	55	10	6	0	2	0	2	11	25	4	0	L	R	6-2	193	6-15-78	1997	London, Ontario
Jones, Damien	.296	68	284	56	84	6	5	1	29	37	58	27	11	L	L	6-2	200	7-10-79	1998	Mobile, Ala.
Lopez, Guillermo	.083	14	36	6	3	1	0	0	2	14	15	0	0	R	R	6-1	210	4-10-79	1998	Miami, Fla.
Milton, Prinz	.173	36	127	20	22	4	1	0	15	9	31	6	1	R	R	6-3	225	3-2-79	1997	Gardena, Calif.
Rivas, Justo	.312	60	215	35	67	11	6	2	42	21	44	10	5	R	R	6-1	175	1-9-80	1997	Masaya, Nicaragua
Terveen, Bryce	.242	50	157	21	38	9	0	5	27	25	44	0	1	L	R	6-1	205	3-1-78	1999	Modesto, Calif.
Thompson, Alva	.361	11	36	7	13	3	1	2	10	6	10	0	0	R	R	5-10	210	10-16-76	1999	Atlanta, Ga.

GAMES BY POSITION: C—Argento 15, Lopez 14, Terveen 39, Thompson 10. **1B**—Crocker 52, Fiore 16, Terveen 1. **2B**—Donato 30, Green 41. **3B**—Donato 5, Fiore 30, Forbes 37. **SS**—Betemit 67, Donato 1, Fiore 2. **OF**—Crocker 1, Hambrick 37, Heffernan 18, Jones 68, Milton 35, Rivas 60.

PITCHING	W	L	ERA	G	GS	CG	SV	IP	H	R	ER	BB	SO	B	T	HT	WT	DOB	1st Yr	Resides
Belisle, Matt	2	5	4.67	14	14	0	0	71	86	50	37	23	60	S	R	6-3	195	6-6-80	1998	McCallum, Texas
Chavez, Chris	1	1	3.75	11	0	0	4	12	9	5	5	5	15	R	R	6-0	180	7-23-75	1999	Tallahassee, Fla.
Clifton, Derek	4	4	6.60	13	13	0	0	60	81	52	44	16	46	R	R	6-3	185	1-7-80	1999	League City, Texas
Curtis, Tom	2	2	4.45	18	0	0	3	32	35	25	16	9	48	R	L	6-4	215	12-19-76	1999	Ardmore, Pa.
Dukeman, Greg	0	1	3.38	17	0	0	2	24	30	16	9	6	21	R	R	6-7	175	12-6-78	1998	Costa Mesa, Calif.
Ennis, John	4	3	5.07	13	13	0	0	66	71	46	37	21	60	R	R	6-5	220	10-17-79	1998	North Hills, Calif.
Foster, John	4	1	1.38	18	0	0	1	39	28	10	6	6	36	L	L	6-0	200	5-17-78	1999	Stockton, Calif.
Lelless, Alex	1	0	7.07	18	0	0	1	28	35	26	22	18	20	R	R	6-3	195	11-22-79	1998	Cambridge, Mass.
McGinnis, Johnny	6	5	5.01	14	14	0	0	70	70	48	39	23	70	R	R	6-3	208	9-23-79	1998	Stone Mountain, Ga.
Mendez, David	6	3	3.25	12	12	0	0	61	61	32	22	28	74	L	L	6-2	190	10-1-79	1996	Pubelo Nuevo, Panama
Mikels, Jason	1	2	2.65	16	3	0	1	37	32	20	11	16	42	R	R	6-4	185	7-27-79	1999	Rio Linda, Calif.
Perez, Elvis	2	1	9.82	21	0	0	0	29	37	42	32	22	28	R	R	6-3	160	7-4-79	1999	Santo Domingo, D.R.
Schmidt, Pat	0	1	4.76	13	0	0	0	17	9	11	9	37	16	L	L	6-3	185	4-3-79	1997	Bellefontaine, Ohio
Spooneybarger, Tim	3	0	2.22	12	0	0	0	24	15	11	6	14	36	R	R	6-3	190	10-21-79	1999	Pensacola, Fla.
Veronie, Shanin	2	2	0.70	18	0	0	3	26	12	4	2	4	42	R	R	6-1	190	8-18-76	1999	West Sacramento, Calif.

ORLANDO — Rookie

GULF COAST LEAGUE

BATTING	AVG	G	AB	R	H	2B	3B	HR	RBI	BB	SO	SB	CS	B	T	HT	WT	DOB	1st Yr	Resides
Castellanos, Jose	.229	23	70	11	16	3	1	1	11	8	18	1	1	R	R	6-1	180	8-23-80	1999	Santo Domingo, D.R.
Clark, Tommy	.170	38	112	18	19	8	0	4	13	30	46	5	3	R	R	6-2	205	12-21-79	1998	Brunswick, Ga.
Geisbush, David	.231	23	78	12	18	4	0	2	11	8	21	1	1	R	R	5-11	185	12-19-76	1999	San Antonio, Texas
Guilliams, Earl	.114	18	35	1	4	1	0	0	4	7	0	0	0	R	R	6-0	190	6-22-81	1999	Danville, Va.
Harper, Shaun	.246	51	191	20	47	8	0	2	16	9	61	6	1	R	R	6-1	175	3-30-80	1999	Atlanta, Ga.
Helms, Wes	.455	9	33	1	15	2	0	0	10	5	4	0	1	R	R	6-4	230	5-12-76	1994	Gastonia, N.C.
Jones, Garrett	.241	46	170	17	41	3	0	3	18	16	47	1	2	L	L	6-4	205	6-21-81	1999	Tinley Park, Ill.
King, Jason	.196	45	168	15	33	4	3	1	11	13	40	5	2	R	R	6-0	175	1-20-80	1999	Jacksonville, Fla.
Machado, Alejandro	.278	56	223	45	62	11	0	0	14	20	22	19	6	R	R	6-0	160	4-26-82	1998	Caracas, Venez.
Manning, Pat	.416	24	89	21	37	9	1	4	19	14	14	4	1	R	R	6-1	185	2-27-80	1999	Anaheim Hills, Calif.
Martinez, Louis	.309	26	97	10	30	5	1	0	16	12	14	0	2	R	R	6-0	175	11-1-76	1999	Tampa, Fla.
Rasmussen, Wes	.221	36	122	16	27	5	1	1	15	19	40	2	2	R	R	6-0	165	5-2-81	1999	Moorpark, Calif.
Romero, Gabe	.200	13	35	4	7	1	0	0	2	2	12	0	0	R	R	6-1	170	10-18-79	1999	Union City, N.J.
Salas, Jose	.271	42	140	19	38	7	1	1	16	14	27	2	1	S	R	6-3	210	2-16-82	1998	Caracas, Venez.
Serrano, Raymond	.258	38	97	14	25	6	0	5	21	13	15	1	0	R	R	5-9	180	1-19-81	1999	Ponce, P.R.
Smith, Toebius	.191	29	94	11	18	3	0	0	7	10	24	6	0	R	R	6-0	180	10-27-79	1998	Clarkton, N.C.
Thompson, Alva	.224	27	76	11	17	3	0	3	11	13	22	1	1	R	R	5-10	210	10-16-76	1999	Atlanta, Ga.
Zumwalt, Alec	.207	51	188	19	39	3	1	3	22	15	48	1	2	R	R	6-2	190	1-20-81	1999	Kernersville, N.C.

GAMES BY POSITION: C—Guilliams 17, Salas 26, Serrano 26, Thompson 15. **1B**—Castellanos 5, Geisbush 11, Helms 3, Jones 45, Thompson 3. **2B**—Machado 56, Lo. Martinez 4, Rasmussen 4. **3B**—Geisbush 10, King 35, Lo. Martinez 12, Rasmussen 2, Romero 2. **SS**—Geisbush 1, King 11, Manning 19, Lo. Martinez 7, Rasmussen 21, Romero 3. **OF**—Castellanos 16, Clark 36, Harper 50, Romero 6, Smith 29, Zumwalt 48.

PITCHING	W	L	ERA	G	GS	CG	SV	IP	H	R	ER	BB	SO	B	T	HT	WT	DOB	1st Yr	Resides
Albertus, Roberto	1	2	6.06	13	4	0	0	33	36	23	22	17	27	L	L	6-4	190	11-14-81	1998	San Nicholaas, Aruba
Brown, Andrew	1	1	2.34	11	11	0	0	42	40	15	11	16	57	R	R	6-6	230	2-17-81	1999	Deltona, Fla.
Bureau, Stephen	0	0	10.03	11	0	0	0	12	13	17	13	14	8	R	R	6-2	185	8-24-80	1998	Fort Pierce, Fla.
Butler, Matt	2	4	4.03	11	10	0	0	38	36	20	17	22	38	R	R	6-3	190	9-24-79	1998	Hattiesburg, Miss.
Cespedes, Rafael	1	5	3.45	14	0	0	0	29	19	16	11	11	24	R	R	6-2	150	7-10-80	1997	Azua, D.R.
Cetani, Bryan	1	3	4.57	13	9	0	0	41	48	27	21	15	17	L	L	6-4	200	10-9-81	1999	Ukiah, Calif.
Colton, Kyle	2	1	1.79	13	10	0	0	50	35	11	10	27	30	R	R	6-2	175	11-16-80	1999	Longwood, Fla.
Evert, Brett	5	3	2.03	13	10	0	0	49	37	17	11	9	39	L	R	6-6	200	10-23-80	1999	Salem, Ore.
Kozlowski, Ben	1	1	1.87	15	0	0	3	34	28	9	7	6	29	L	L	6-6	220	8-16-80	1999	Seminole, Fla.
Martinez, Lionel	2	1	3.42	12	0	0	0	26	28	16	10	8	16	R	R	6-3	165	11-28-79	1996	San Felix, Venez.
Mejia, Juan	0	3	5.90	16	0	0	0	29	40	23	19	8	24	R	R	6-2	165	12-11-79	1999	Azua, D.R.
Rodriguez, Jose	1	2	3.61	16	6	0	1	42	33	22	17	21	38	R	R	6-0	175	1-15-82	1998	Lara, Venez.
Sclafani, Anthony	3	2	2.57	17	0	0	0	28	21	9	8	9	22	R	R	6-1	175	7-28-81	1999	Staten Island, N.Y.
Trevino, Chris	1	3	5.95	11	0	0	1	20	28	17	13	5	17	L	L	6-3	195	11-14-80	1999	Andrews, Texas
Walker, Adrian	0	2	4.18	13	0	0	0	24	22	11	11	15	30	L	L	6-2	180	1-21-80	1999	San Diego, Calif.
Watkins, David	5	0	0.92	13	0	0	2	29	15	5	3	11	24	R	R	6-1	190	8-18-81	1999	Leitchfield, Ky.

BALTIMORE ORIOLES

Cloud of uncertainty hangs over O's after disastrous year

BY ROCH KUBATKO

What does $84 million buy these days? For the 1999 Orioles, one day over .500.

A 10-7 season-opening win against the Devil Rays marked the only time the Orioles had a winning record in 1999. April ended with their record at 6-16. The first half concluded with it at 36-51.

Right fielder Albert Belle, signed to a five-year, $65 million contract in the offseason, collected 27 of his 37 homers and 82 of his 117 RBIs after the Orioles had fallen 15 games under .500 on June 8. Will Clark, signed to replace Rafael Palmeiro at first base, provided only 10 homers and 29 RBIs in 77 games. Delino DeShields, who replaced Roberto Alomar at second base, also had a disappointing, injury-filled year.

The Orioles finished 78-84 in Ray Miller's second year as manager, one game worse than his first. A 13-game winning streak in September wasn't enough to save Miller's job.

And Miller wasn't the only employee fired after another dismal season. Frank Wren was dismissed after just one season as general manager, thickening the cloud of uncertainty that hangs over owner Peter Angelos' organization.

The 1999 season also will be remembered for Cal Ripken's two trips to the disabled list, the first of his career, and Sept. 23 surgery to relieve nerve irritation in his lower back. He played enough to hit his 400th career homer and creep within nine hits of 3,000.

Mike Mussina put together another strong year, going 18-7 with a 3.50 ERA. Mussina was denied his first 20-win season because of bullpen meltdowns,

B.J. Surhoff   **Matt Riley**

Players of the Year

MAJOR LEAGUE: B.J. Surhoff, of

Surhoff was the only Oriole to play in all 162 games and he led the team with a .308 average and 331 total bases.

MINOR LEAGUE: Matt Riley, lhp

In his second pro season, Riley posted a 3.05 ERA and 189 strikeouts in 177 innings of work at Frederick and Bowie.

shoddy run and defensive support, and a bruised shoulder that cost him four starts. In the bullpen, lefthander Jesse Orosco became baseball's all-time leader in games pitched.

Offensively, left fielder B.J. Surhoff enjoyed one of his best seasons, playing in the All-Star Game and batting .308 with career highs in hits (207), home runs (28) and RBIs (107). The Orioles set a club record for hits in a season, tied the record for doubles and belted 203 homers. They finished first in the AL in defense and fourth in hitting.

Triple-A Rochester was just as big a disappointment as the Orioles, going 61-85 to finish in fifth place in the International League's Northern Division. Double-A Bowie lost 14 of its last 18 to miss the Eastern League playoffs, but prized lefthander Matt Riley went 10-6 with a 3.22 ERA in 20 games. He was 3-2, 2.61 in eight starts at Class A Frederick to start the year.

Frederick landed in second place in the Northern Division of the Carolina League and placed three players on the league's postseason all-star team: shortstop Eddy Martinez, catcher Jayson Werth and outfielder Luis Matos.

With the Orioles out of contention, Wren did land several young prospects in stretch-drive deals. The Orioles picked up righthander Jacobo Sequea and lefthander B.J. Ryan from the Reds for righthander Juan Guzman. DH Harold Baines was sent to the Indians for righthander Juan Aracena and lefthander Jimmy Hamilton. The team also managed to sign all of its record seven first-round draft picks, though it cost them more than $8 million to do so.

ORGANIZATION LEADERS

BATTING

*AVG	Rick Short, Bowie	.314
R	Two tied at	81
H	Julio Vinas, Rochester	151
TB	Julio Vinas, Rochester	247
2B	Julio Vinas, Rochester	32
3B	Alex Gordon, Bluefield/GCL	10
HR	Ryan Minor, Rochester	21
RBI	Two tied at	83
BB	Richard Paz, Bowie/Frederick	98
SO	Franky Figueroa, Frederick	138
SB	Tim Raines Jr., Delmarva	49

PITCHING

W	Two tied at	13
L	Ricky Casteel, Delmarva	14
#ERA	Scott Eibey, Bowie/Frederick	3.02
G	David Evans, Rochester	60
CG	Josh Towers, Bowie	5
SV	Ryan Kohlmeier, Bowie	23
IP	Josh Towers, Bowie	189
BB	John Parrish, Bowie/Frederick/Delmarva	61
SO	John Stephens, Delmarva	217

*Minimum 250 At-Bats #Minimum 75 Innings

Baltimore
ORIOLES

Manager: Ray Miller   **1999 Record:** 78-84, .481 (4th, AL East)

BATTING	AVG	G	AB	R	H	2B	3B	HR	RBI	BB	SO	SB	CS	B	T	HT	WT	DOB	1st Yr	Resides
Amaral, Rich	.277	91	137	21	38	8	1	0	11	15	20	9	6	R	R	6-0	175	4-1-62	1983	Seattle, Wash.
Anderson, Brady	.282	150	564	109	159	28	5	24	81	96	105	36	7	L	L	6-1	202	1-18-64	1985	Lake Tahoe, Nev.
Baines, Harold	.322	107	345	57	111	16	1	24	81	43	38	1	2	L	L	6-2	195	3-15-59	1977	St. Michaels, Md.
Belle, Albert	.297	161	610	108	181	36	1	37	117	101	82	17	3	R	R	6-2	210	8-25-66	1987	Euclid, Ohio
Bordick, Mike	.277	160	631	93	175	35	7	10	77	54	102	14	4	R	R	5-11	175	7-21-65	1986	Ruxton, Md.
Clark, Will	.303	77	251	40	76	15	0	10	29	38	42	2	2	L	L	6-1	200	3-13-64	1985	Southlake, Texas
Conine, Jeff	.291	139	444	54	129	31	1	13	75	30	40	0	3	R	R	6-1	220	6-27-66	1988	Weston, Fla.
Davis, Tommy	.167	5	6	0	1	0	0	0	0	0	2	0	0	R	R	6-1	195	5-21-73	1994	Semmes, Ala.
DeShields, Delino	.264	96	330	46	87	11	2	6	34	37	52	11	8	L	R	6-1	175	1-15-69	1987	West Palm Beach, Fla.
Figga, Mike	.221	41	86	12	19	4	0	1	5	2	27	0	2	R	R	6-0	200	7-31-70	1990	Tampa, Fla.
Garcia, Jesse	.207	17	29	6	6	0	0	2	2	2	3	0	0	R	R	5-10	155	9-24-73	1993	Robstown, Texas
Hairston, Jerry	.269	50	175	26	47	12	1	4	17	11	24	9	4	R	R	5-10	172	5-29-76	1997	Naperville, Ill.
Johnson, Charles	.251	135	426	58	107	19	1	16	54	55	107	0	0	R	R	6-2	220	7-20-71	1992	Pembroke Pines, Fla.
Kingsale, Eugene	.247	28	85	9	21	2	0	0	7	5	13	1	3	S	R	6-3	190	8-20-76	1994	Oranjestad, Aruba
May, Derrick	.265	26	49	5	13	0	0	4	12	4	6	0	0	L	R	6-4	200	7-14-68	1986	Newark, Del.
Minor, Ryan	.194	46	124	13	24	7	0	3	10	8	43	1	0	R	R	6-7	225	1-5-74	1996	Edmond, Okla.
Otanez, Willis	.213	29	80	7	17	3	0	2	11	6	16	0	*0	R	R	6-1	200	4-19-73	1990	Contui, D.R.
Pickering, Calvin	.125	23	40	4	5	1	0	1	5	11	16	0	0	L	L	6-5	283	9-29-76	1995	Temple Terrace, Fla.
Rebonlet, Jeff	.162	99	154	25	25	4	0	0	4	33	29	1	0	R	R	6-0	175	4-30-64	1986	Kettering, Ohio
Ripken, Cal	.340	86	332	51	113	27	0	18	57	13	31	0	1	R	R	6-4	220	8-24-60	1978	Reisterstown, Md.
Surhoff, B.J.	.308	162	673	104	207	38	1	28	107	43	78	5	1	L	R	6-1	200	8-4-64	1985	Cockeysville, Md.
Webster, Lenny	.167	16	36	1	6	1	0	0	3	8	5	0	0	R	R	5-9	195	2-10-65	1987	Charlotte, N.C.

PITCHING	W	L	ERA	G	GS	CG	SV	IP	H	R	ER	BB	SO	B	T	HT	WT	DOB	1st Yr	Resides
Bones, Ricky	0	3	5.98	30	2	0	0	44	59	29	29	19	26	R	R	6-0	202	4-7-69	1986	Guayama, P.R.
Coppinger, Rocky	0	1	8.31	11	2	0	0	22	25	21	20	19	17	R	R	6-5	245	3-19-74	1994	El Paso, Texas
Corsi, Jim	0	1	2.70	13	0	0	0	13	15	4	4	1	8	R	R	6-1	220	9-9-61	1982	Natick, Mass.
2-team (23 Boston)	1	3	4.34	36	0	0	0	37	40	19	18	20	22							
Erickson, Scott	15	12	4.81	34	34	6	0	230	244	127	123	99	106	R	R	6-4	230	2-2-68	1989	Stateline, Nev.
Falkenborg, Brian	0	0	0.00	2	0	0	0	3	2	0	0	2	1	R	R	6-6	187	1-18-78	1996	Redmond, Wash.
Fetters, Mike	1	0	5.81	27	0	0	0	31	35	23	20	22	22	R	R	6-4	226	12-19-64	1986	Gilbert, Ariz.
Guzman, Juan	5	9	4.18	21	21	1	0	123	124	63	57	65	95	R	R	5-11	195	10-28-66	1985	Miami, Fla.
Johns, Doug	6	4	4.47	32	5	0	0	87	81	45	43	25	50	R	L	6-2	195	12-19-67	1990	Plantation, Fla.
Johnson, Jason	8	7	5.46	22	21	0	0	115	120	74	70	55	71	R	R	6-6	220	10-27-73	1992	Burlington, Ky.
Kamieniecki, Scott	2	4	4.95	43	3	0	2	56	52	32	31	29	39	R	R	6-0	200	4-19-64	1987	Flint, Mich.
Linton, Doug	1	4	5.95	14	8	0	0	59	69	41	39	25	32	R	R	6-1	190	9-2-65	1987	Overland Park, Kan.
Molina, Gabe	1	2	6.65	20	0	0	0	23	22	19	17	16	14	R	R	5-11	190	5-3-75	1996	Denver, Colo.
Mussina, Mike	18	7	3.50	31	31	4	0	203	207	89	79	52	172	S	R	6-2	185	12-8-68	1990	Montoursville, Pa.
Orosco, Jesse	0	2	5.34	65	0	0	1	32	28	21	19	20	35	R	L	6-2	205	4-21-57	1978	San Diego, Calif.
Ponson, Sidney	12	12	4.71	32	32	6	0	210	227	118	110	80	112	R	R	6-1	220	11-2-76	1994	Oranjestad, Aruba
Reyes, Al	2	3	4.85	27	0	0	0	30	23	16	16	16	28	R	R	6-0	165	4-10-71	1988	Santo Domingo, D.R.
Rhodes, Arthur	3	4	5.43	43	0	0	3	53	43	37	32	45	59	L	L	6-2	204	10-24-69	1988	Sarasota, Fla.
Riley, Matt	0	0	7.36	3	3	0	0	11	17	9	9	13	6	L	L	6-1	205	8-2-79	1998	Oakley, Calif.
Ryan, B.J.	1	0	2.95	13	0	0	0	18	9	6	6	12	28	L	L	6-6	230	12-28-75	1998	Benton, La.
Slocumb, Heathcliff	0	0	12.46	10	0	0	0	9	15	12	12	9	12	R	R	6-3	220	6-7-66	1984	Richmond Hills, N.Y.
Timlin, Mike	3	9	3.57	62	0	0	27	63	51	30	25	23	50	R	R	6-4	210	3-10-66	1987	Midland, Texas

FIELDING

Catcher	PCT	G	PO	A	E	DP	PB
Davis	.909	4	9	1	1	0	0
Figga	.973	43	169	12	5	1	2
C. Johnson	.994	135	770	66	5	14	3
Webster	.986	12	67	6	1	2	0

First Base	PCT	G	PO	A	E	DP
Amaral	1.000	2	4	2	0	1
Clark	.995	63	575	42	3	54
Conine	.993	99	831	52	6	108
Davis	1.000	1	2	0	0	0
Minor	.917	1	10	1	1	1
Otanez	1.000	5	6	0	0	0
Pickering	.960	8	46	2	2	8

Second Base	PCT	G	PO	A	E	DP
Amaral	.000	2	0	0	0	0
DeShields	.977	93	178	249	10	54
Garcia	1.000	6	7	8	0	3
Hairston	1.000	50	115	154	0	47
Rebonlet	.993	36	54	83	1	21

Third Base	PCT	G	PO	A	E	DP
Amaral	.000	1	0	0	0	0

	PCT	G	PO	A	E	DP
Conine	.000	4	0	0	1	0
Garcia	1.000	2	0	1	0	0
Minor	.963	45	25	79	4	8
Otanez	.917	22	16	28	4	2
Rebonlet	.987	56	19	56	1	4
Ripken	.932	85	36	142	13	11
Surhoff	1.000	2	1	5	0	0

Shortstop	PCT	G	PO	A	E	DP
Bordick	.989	159	277	511	9	132
Garcia	1.000	7	9	13	0	5
Rebonlet	1.000	10	6	13	0	0

Outfield	PCT	G	PO	A	E	DP
Amaral	1.000	50	66	0	0	0
Anderson	.997	136	308	3	1	1
Belle	.985	154	252	17	4	2
Conine	1.000	13	17	1	0	0
Kingsale	.980	24	48	1	1	0
May	1.000	5	7	1	0	1
Surhoff	1.000	148	282	16	0	5

Albert Belle

Director of Player Development: Tom Trebelhorn

Class	Farm Team	League	W	L	Pct.	Finish*	Manager(s)	First Yr
AAA	Rochester (N.Y.) Red Wings	International	61	83	.424	12th (14)	Dave Machemer	1961
AA	Bowie (Md.) Baysox	Eastern	70	71	.496	6th (12)	Joe Ferguson	1993
A#	Frederick (Md.) Keys	Carolina	67	71	.486	5th (8)	Andy Etchebarren	1989
A	Delmarva (Md.) Shorebirds	South Atlantic	58	80	.420	14th (14)	Butch Davis	1997
Rookie#	Bluefield (W.Va.) Orioles	Appalachian	25	43	.368	8th (10)	Duffy Dyer	1958
Rookie	Sarasota (Fla.) Orioles	Gulf Coast	31	28	.525	6th (14)	Jesus Alfaro	1991

*Finish in overall standings (No. of teams in league)   #Advanced level

ROCHESTER   Class AAA

INTERNATIONAL LEAGUE

BATTING	AVG	G	AB	R	H	2B	3B	HR	RBI	BB	SO	SB	CS	B	T	HT	WT	DOB	1st Yr	Resides
Beltre, Esteban	.264	92	314	45	83	19	3	1	23	23	64	5	3	R	R	5-10	180	12-26-67	1984	San Pedro de Macoris, D.R.
Clark, Howie	.294	79	279	33	82	19	4	6	28	34	24	1	2	L	R	5-10	179	2-13-74	1992	Huntington Beach, Calif.
Davis, Tommy	.257	110	413	49	106	18	0	11	56	24	65	1	4	R	R	6-1	195	5-21-73	1994	Semmes, Ala.
Dent, Darrell	.133	9	30	4	4	0	0	2	5	3	8	4	0	L	L	6-2	172	5-26-77	1995	Panorama City, Calif.
DeCinces, Tim	.264	16	53	7	14	5	0	2	8	0	12	0	0	L	R	6-2	195	4-26-74	1996	Newport Beach, Calif.
Dunn, Todd	.173	30	98	8	17	5	0	2	15	8	35	1	2	R	R	6-5	230	7-29-70	1993	Jacksonville, Fla.
2-team (40 Louisville)	.196	70	204	22	40	6	1	7	31	22	67	3	3							
Forbes, P.J.	.264	88	349	49	92	16	1	0	19	26	40	5	0	R	R	5-10	160	9-22-67	1990	Pittsburg, Kan.
Foster, Jim	.229	35	118	6	27	3	1	0	11	12	19	4	2	R	R	6-3	220	8-18-71	1993	Warwick, R.I.
Garcia, Jesse	.255	62	220	25	56	10	2	2	23	11	21	9	6	R	R	5-10	155	9-24-73	1993	Robstown, Texas
Hairston, Jerry	.291	107	413	65	120	24	5	7	48	30	50	19	10	R	R	5-10	172	5-29-76	1997	Naperville, Ill.
Herrera, Jose	.205	39	127	11	26	7	1	2	16	2	20	3	1	L	L	6-0	164	8-30-72	1991	Santo Domingo, D.R.
Isom, Johnny	.345	34	119	19	41	12	0	2	10	10	28	1	1	R	R	5-11	210	8-9-73	1995	Fort Worth, Texas
Kingsale, Eugene	.309	48	191	31	59	9	0	2	20	13	23	10	9	S	R	6-3	190	8-20-76	1994	Oranjestad, Aruba
Livingstone, Scott	.372	14	43	5	16	4	0	0	7	7	4	1	1	L	R	6-0	198	7-15-65	1988	Southlake, Texas
May, Derrick	.278	71	295	39	82	19	3	5	43	22	28	4	2	L	R	6-4	200	7-14-68	1986	Newark, Del.
Minor, Ryan	.256	101	383	56	98	24	1	21	67	37	119	3	1	R	R	6-7	225	1-5-74	1996	Edmond, Okla.
Mouton, Lyle	.222	44	162	25	36	9	1	4	17	13	31	3	1	R	R	6-4	240	5-13-69	1991	Lafayette, La.
Murphy, Mike	.226	70	217	35	49	6	3	1	21	34	63	7	3	R	R	6-2	185	1-23-72	1990	Albuquerque, N.M.
Ojeda, Augie	.000	1	1	1	0	0	0	0	0	0	0	0	0	S	R	5-9	165	12-20-74	1996	South Gate, Calif.
Otero, Ricky	.231	53	199	16	46	11	4	4	21	16	23	5	5	S	L	5-7	150	4-15-72	1991	Vega Baja, P.R.
Pickering, Calvin	.285	103	372	63	106	20	0	16	63	60	99	1	3	L	L	6-5	283	9-29-76	1995	Temple Terrace, Fla.
Rust, Brian	.000	1	3	0	0	0	0	0	1	0	0	0	0	R	R	6-2	205	8-1-74	1995	Portland, Ore.
Vinas, Julio	.312	126	484	67	151	32	2	20	83	25	73	4	3	R	R	6-1	205	2-14-73	1991	Hialeah, Fla.
Webster, Lenny	.302	13	43	8	13	5	0	3	9	4	8	0	0	R	R	5-9	195	2-10-65	1986	Charlotte, N.C.

PITCHING	W	L	ERA	G	GS	CG	SV	IP	H	R	ER	BB	SO	B	T	HT	WT	DOB	1st Yr	Resides
Blood, Darin	0	4	8.66	12	10	0	0	44	53	43	42	38	21	S	R	6-2	200	8-31-74	1995	Scottsdale, Ariz.
Burrows, Terry	1	6	3.97	17	17	0	0	93	74	49	41	39	75	L	L	6-1	190	11-28-68	1990	Lake Charles, La.
Coppinger, Rocky	2	2	3.66	5	5	0	0	32	28	13	13	12	37	R	R	6-5	245	3-19-74	1994	El Paso, Texas
Corsi, Jim	2	0	3.48	10	0	0	2	10	12	4	4	3	7	R	R	6-1	220	9-9-61	1982	Natick, Mass.
Delahoya, Javier	4	3	5.09	14	14	0	0	81	88	49	46	26	58	R	R	6-2	160	2-21-70	1989	North Hollywood, Calif.
Dykhoff, Radhames	2	0	3.94	47	0	0	1	82	69	42	36	31	57	L	L	6-0	160	9-27-74	1993	Oranjestad, Aruba
Evans, David	2	11	5.35	60	0	0	2	71	70	48	42	27	65	R	R	6-3	205	1-1-68	1990	Houston, Texas
Fetters, Mike	0	0	0.00	4	0	0	0	4	0	0	0	2	6	R	R	6-4	226	12-19-64	1986	Gilbert, Ariz.
Hamilton, Jimmy	0	0	13.50	3	0	0	0	2	1	3	3	4	2	L	L	6-3	190	8-1-75	1996	Weyers Cave, Va.
2-team (26 Buffalo)	1	2	5.81	29	0	0	0	26	25	25	17	31	27							
Hartmann, Pete	1	5	8.93	34	3	0	0	44	56	45	44	27	43	L	L	6-2	200	5-13-71	1993	Arvada, Colo.
Johns, Doug	1	1	4.85	6	6	1	0	30	34	20	16	6	18	R	L	6-2	195	12-19-67	1990	Plantation, Fla.
Johnson, Jason	4	2	3.65	8	8	0	0	44	35	19	18	27	47	R	R	6-6	220	10-27-73	1992	Burlington, Ky.
Kamieniecki, Scott	1	2	5.09	4	4	0	0	23	23	13	13	6	14	R	R	6-0	200	4-19-64	1987	Flint, Mich.
Linton, Doug	7	5	3.65	18	18	1	0	118	120	58	48	27	97	R	R	6-1	190	9-2-65	1987	Overland Park, Kan.
Maduro, Calvin	11	11	3.99	29	28	2	0	169	179	88	75	60	149	R	R	6-0	180	9-5-74	1992	Santa Cruz, Aruba
McCommon, Jason	7	10	4.98	29	18	1	0	125	143	73	69	50	68	R	R	6-0	190	8-9-71	1994	Memphis, Tenn.
Molina, Gabe	2	2	3.14	45	0	0	18	57	45	22	20	28	58	R	R	5-11	190	5-3-75	1996	Denver, Colo.
Pina, Rafael	8	10	4.37	48	10	0	5	111	113	60	54	48	88	R	R	6-1	170	8-16-71	1991	San Gabriel, Calif.
Plantenberg, Erik	2	1	5.64	17	0	0	0	22	25	16	14	13	21	S	L	6-1	180	10-30-68	1990	Bellevue, Wash.
2-team (23 Durham)	7	5	5.91	40	7	0	0	81	100	59	53	41	72							
Rogers, Jason	0	2	8.10	9	0	0	0	10	15	9	9	6	7	L	L	6-6	220	4-5-73	1994	Reno, Nev.
Ryan, B.J.	0	0	2.51	11	0	0	1	14	8	4	4	4	20	L	L	6-6	230	12-28-75	1998	Benton, La.
2-team (11 Indy)	1	0	3.09	22	0	0	1	23	17	8	8	7	32							
Snyder, Matt	6	6	5.21	48	3	0	1	85	95	60	49	30	59	R	R	5-11	190	7-7-74	1995	Newton, Pa.

FIELDING

Catcher	PCT	G	PO	A	E	DP	PB
Davis	.984	60	398	35	7	7	3
DeCinces	.988	12	78	7	1	0	0
Foster	.993	34	257	22	2	0	2
Vinas	.978	38	253	17	6	1	1
Webster	1.000	9	49	4	0	1	

First Base	PCT	G	PO	A	E	DP
Clark	1.000	2	9	1	0	0
Davis	.986	18	135	10	2	11
Livingstone	1.000	3	13	0	0	1

	PCT	G	PO	A	E	DP
Minor	.992	15	116	13	1	11
Pickering	.985	97	821	45	13	75
Vinas	1.000	17	138	12	0	18

Second Base	PCT	G	PO	A	E	DP
Clark	1.000	7	6	11	0	3
Forbes	.989	35	71	102	2	29
Garcia	.947	21	41	48	5	10
Hairston	.974	89	182	230	11	50

Third Base	PCT	G	PO	A	E	DP
Beltre	1.000	13	6	27	0	2

	PCT	G	PO	A	E	DP
Clark	1.000	4	3	6	0	0
Davis	.900	6	3	15	2	0
Forbes	.982	40	33	74	2	7
Livingstone	.833	2	2	3	1	0
Minor	.940	83	54	135	12	12
Rust	1.000	1	1	6	0	0
Vinas	.889	5	3	5	1	0

Shortstop	PCT	G	PO	A	E	DP
Beltre	.951	78	106	206	16	40
Forbes	.951	11	22	36	3	9

Organization Statistics

	PCT	G	PO	A	E	DP
Garcia	.942	41	54	108	10	23
Hairston	.934	18	24	47	5	9
Ojeda	.000	1	0	0	0	0
Outfield	PCT	G	PO	A	E	DP
Clark	.984	70	122	4	2	0
Dent	1.000	9	18	0	0	0

	PCT	G	PO	A	E	DP
Dunn	.946	24	35	0	2	0
Forbes	1.000	8	14	0	0	0
Herrera	.975	36	76	1	2	0
Isom	1.000	33	55	4	0	0
Kingsale	.975	47	118	1	3	0
Livingstone	1.000	1	2	0	0	0

	PCT	G	PO	A	E	DP
May	.969	68	116	7	4	0
Mouton	.941	34	63	1	4	1
Murphy	.976	69	158	5	4	2
Otero	.979	52	90	4	2	0
Pickering	1.000	2	1	0	0	0
Vinas	.000	1	0	0	0	0

BOWIE — Class AA

EASTERN LEAGUE

BATTING

	AVG	G	AB	R	H	2B	3B	HR	RBI	BB	SO	SB	CS	B	T	HT	WT	DOB	1st Yr	Resides
Alley, Chip	.111	5	9	4	1	1	0	0	0	1	3	0	0	S	R	6-3	190	12-20-76	1995	West Palm Beach, Fla.
Almonte, Wady	.293	124	482	68	141	27	4	17	83	31	72	10	10	R	R	6-0	195	4-20-75	1993	Higuey, D.R.
Casimiro, Carlos	.221	139	526	73	116	23	1	18	64	39	101	7	12	R	R	5-11	175	11-8-76	1994	San Pedro de Macoris, D.R.
Clark, Howie	.294	39	126	17	37	6	0	2	12	10	14	2	0	L	R	5-10	179	2-13-74	1992	Huntington Beach, Calif.
Coffie, Ivanon	.185	57	195	21	36	9	3	3	23	20	46	2	2	L	R	6-1	170	5-16-77	1995	Curacao, Neth. Antilles
Dent, Darrell	.212	108	250	41	53	9	2	0	17	37	58	24	5	L	L	6-2	172	5-26-77	1995	Panorama City, Calif.
Devarez, Cesar	.265	58	200	25	53	11	0	4	29	16	24	2	2	R	R	5-10	175	9-22-69	1988	San Francisco de Macoris, D.R.
DeCinces, Tim	.260	84	258	38	67	15	0	12	36	54	52	0	2	L	R	6-2	195	4-26-74	1996	Newport Beach, Calif.
DeShields, Delino	.267	4	15	2	4	1	0	0	0	3	2	0	0	L	R	6-1	175	1-15-69	1987	West Palm Beach, Fla.
Hage, Tom	.277	128	426	53	118	21	4	8	65	50	60	1	1	L	R	6-3	210	8-2-74	1996	Bronx, N.Y.
Isom, Johnny	.228	38	127	19	29	6	0	2	16	12	25	0	1	R	R	5-11	210	8-9-73	1995	Fort Worth, Texas
Kingsale, Eugene	.235	67	268	43	63	11	4	3	23	33	46	14	10	S	R	6-0	175	8-20-76	1994	Oranjestad, Aruba
Lopez-Cao, Mike	.255	16	47	5	12	1	0	2	7	2	8	0	0	L	R	5-6	180	8-14-75	1997	Miami, Fla.
Matos, Luis	.237	66	283	41	67	11	1	9	36	15	39	14	5	R	R	6-0	155	10-30-78	1996	Bayamon, P.R.
Ojeda, Augie	.267	134	460	73	123	18	4	10	60	57	47	6	2	S	R	5-9	175	12-20-74	1996	South Gate, Calif.
Paz, Richard	.286	79	273	39	78	12	2	2	20	51	35	11	3	R	R	5-8	130	7-30-77	1994	Los Teques, Venez.
Rivera, Roberto	.222	9	36	0	8	0	0	1	1	9	2	0	0	S	R	6-2	160	11-25-76	1994	La Romana, D.R.
Ronca, Joe	.242	46	153	12	37	12	1	5	25	13	43	1	3	R	R	6-2	200	7-3-71	1989	Cantonment, Fla.
Rust, Brian	.309	52	149	24	46	11	0	4	21	17	29	2	0	R	R	6-2	205	8-1-74	1995	Portland, Ore.
Short, Rick	.314	112	392	60	123	19	0	16	62	43	48	6	1	R	R	6-0	190	12-6-72	1994	Peoria, Ill.
Werth, Jayson	.273	35	121	18	33	5	1	1	11	17	26	7	1	R	R	6-6	191	5-20-79	1997	Chatham, Ill.

PITCHING

	W	L	ERA	G	GS	CG	SV	IP	H	R	ER	BB	SO	B	T	HT	WT	DOB	1st Yr	Resides
Bell, Mike	7	7	4.59	41	13	0	1	131	134	80	67	49	79	L	L	6-2	195	10-14-72	1995	Sarasota, Fla.
Blazier, Ron	1	1	7.39	19	0	0	0	32	40	27	26	12	28	R	R	6-5	249	7-30-71	1990	Bellwood, Pa.
Delahoya, Javier	9	1	3.36	12	12	1	0	78	64	29	29	18	68	R	R	6-2	160	2-21-70	1989	North Hollywood, Calif.
Eibey, Scott	2	0	2.63	27	4	0	0	51	49	17	15	25	29	L	L	6-4	210	1-19-74	1995	Waterloo, Iowa
Falkenborg, Brian	3	6	3.78	16	16	0	0	83	77	40	35	36	77	R	R	6-6	187	1-18-78	1996	Redmond, Wash.
Gentile, Scott	1	2	8.36	10	0	0	0	14	15	13	13	9	12	R	R	5-10	205	12-21-70	1992	Berlin, Conn.
Hartmann, Pete	1	1	1.72	11	0	0	0	16	11	4	3	8	12	L	L	6-2	200	5-13-71	1993	Arvada, Colo.
Heredia, Maximo	6	4	4.24	50	0	0	0	76	80	42	36	33	56	R	R	6-0	163	9-27-76	1994	San Pedro de Macoris, D.R.
Iglesias, Mario	4	4	7.52	14	2	0	0	26	28	23	22	16	27	S	R	6-3	195	6-2-74	1996	Castro Valley, Calif.
Kamieniecki, Scott	0	1	3.60	1	1	0	0	5	6	2	2	0	1	R	R	6-0	200	4-19-64	1987	Flint, Mich.
Kohlmeier, Ryan	3	7	3.16	55	0	0	23	63	44	23	22	29	78	R	R	6-2	195	6-25-77	1996	Cottonwood Falls, Kan.
Lynch, Ryan	1	0	6.89	9	0	0	1	16	23	15	12	16	11	L	L	6-4	220	8-10-74	1996	Solano Beach, Calif.
Maloney, Sean	0	0	3.38	4	0	0	0	11	10	4	4	3	17	R	R	6-7	210	5-25-71	1993	North Kingstown, R.I.
McDougal, Mike	5	7	4.26	48	0	0	8	61	70	34	29	31	47	L	R	6-4	210	3-22-75	1994	Las Vegas, Nev.
McNatt, Josh	1	0	5.14	2	1	0	0	7	8	5	4	6	1	S	L	6-4	200	7-23-77	1996	Jackson, Tenn.
Medina, Carlos	3	6	5.54	15	15	0	0	78	86	52	48	37	70	L	L	6-2	160	5-16-77	1994	La Vega, D.R.
Moreno, Julio	2	2	5.28	10	10	0	0	44	46	29	26	25	23	R	R	6-1	165	10-23-75	1994	Cayacoa, D.R.
Paronto, Chad	0	4	8.12	15	9	0	0	41	59	39	37	32	27	R	R	6-5	250	7-28-75	1996	Haverhill, N.H.
Parrish, John	0	2	4.04	12	10	0	0	56	49	28	25	43	42	L	L	5-11	165	11-26-77	1996	Lancaster, Pa.
Riley, Matt	10	6	3.22	20	20	3	0	126	113	53	45	42	131	L	L	6-1	205	8-2-79	1998	Oakley, Calif.
Rogers, Jason	0	1	1.54	7	0	0	0	12	11	5	2	9	9	L	L	6-6	220	4-5-73	1994	Reno, Nev.
Rosenkranz, Terry	3	1	3.98	26	0	0	0	43	36	20	19	26	36	L	L	6-4	205	11-5-70	1992	Greenville, Ky.
Towers, Josh	12	7	3.76	29	28	5	0	189	204	86	79	26	106	R	R	6-1	150	2-26-77	1996	Port Hueneme, Calif.

FIELDING

Catcher	PCT	G	PO	A	E	DP	PB
Alley	1.000	5	31	2	0	1	0
Clark	.000	1	0	0	0	0	0
Devarez	.994	58	322	18	2	3	4
DeCinces	.991	67	421	36	4	7	3
Lopez-Cao	.972	14	63	7	2	0	0
Werth	.996	29	203	22	1	2	1

First Base	PCT	G	PO	A	E	DP
Clark	1.000	3	24	1	0	6
Hage	.987	101	746	59	11	64
Rust	.990	29	186	17	2	15
Short	.988	34	221	16	3	24

Second Base	PCT	G	PO	A	E	DP
Casimiro	.970	136	281	331	19	87
Clark	1.000	4	4	9	0	1

	PCT	G	PO	A	E	DP
DeShields	1.000	3	5	5	0	1
Paz	1.000	1	2	7	0	2
Rust	1.000	1	0	2	0	0
Short	1.000	4	2	2	0	1

Third Base	PCT	G	PO	A	E	DP
Casimiro	.667	1	0	2	1	0
Coffie	.941	55	39	89	8	6
Ojeda	1.000	1	1	0	0	0
Paz	.934	70	51	118	12	8
Rust	.925	18	16	33	4	1
Short	.917	12	5	17	2	1

Shortstop	PCT	G	PO	A	E	DP
Coffie	1.000	2	0	1	0	0
Ojeda	.969	133	210	379	19	79

	PCT	G	PO	A	E	DP
Paz	.919	9	14	20	3	7
Outfield	PCT	G	PO	A	E	DP
Almonte	.959	109	195	13	9	5
Clark	1.000	3	3	0	0	0
Dent	.994	104	150	4	1	1
Devarez	.800	2	4	0	1	0
Isom	.981	27	49	2	1	0
Kingsale	.978	67	173	2	4	1
Matos	.982	66	152	8	3	1
Rivera	.938	9	15	0	1	0
Ronca	.938	21	29	1	2	0
Short	.984	60	119	2	2	1
Werth	1.000	1	1	0	0	0

FREDERICK — Class A

CAROLINA LEAGUE

BATTING

	AVG	G	AB	R	H	2B	3B	HR	RBI	BB	SO	SB	CS	B	T	HT	WT	DOB	1st Yr	Resides
Alley, Chip	.227	41	132	21	30	6	0	1	12	23	27	0	1	S	R	6-3	190	12-20-76	1995	West Palm Beach, Fla.
Benham, Jason	.148	16	27	3	4	0	0	0	2	2	2	0	0	L	R	6-1	190	10-13-75	1998	Garland, Texas
Coffie, Ivanon	.283	73	276	35	78	18	4	11	53	28	62	7	4	L	R	6-1	170	5-16-77	1995	Curacao, Neth. Antilles

BATTING	AVG	G	AB	R	H	2B	3B	HR	RBI	BB	SO	SB	CS	B	T	HT	WT	DOB	1st Yr	Resides
Daedelow, Craig	.100	16	50	6	5	1	0	0	2	4	7	0	0	R	R	5-11	165	4-3-76	1994	Huntington Beach, Calif.
DeShields, Delino	.125	2	8	1	1	0	0	1	2	0	1	0	0	L	R	6-1	175	1-15-69	1987	West Palm Beach, Fla.
Escalante, Jaime	.333	5	3	0	1	1	0	0	1	0	1	0	0	S	R	6-2	210	4-5-77	1997	Federalsburg, Md.
Evans, Pat	.333	1	3	2	1	1	0	0	1	1	0	0	0	S	R	5-10	175	12-5-72	1994	San Ramon, Calif.
Figueroa, Franky	.250	132	527	59	132	20	3	17	78	32	138	2	3	R	R	6-6	225	2-9-77	1996	Hialeah, Fla.
Garabito, Eddy	.256	132	539	76	138	24	4	6	77	52	68	38	18	S	R	5-8	170	12-2-78	1996	Manrreza, D.R.
Hammond, Joey	.290	79	245	41	71	14	1	3	37	57	66	3	3	R	R	6-0	180	10-27-77	1998	Frederick, Md.
Hughes, Brian	.246	90	272	38	67	14	3	2	26	45	67	5	4	R	R	5-9	180	8-5-75	1998	Metairie, La.
Leon, Alfredo	.214	6	14	3	3	0	0	0	1	1	3	1	0	R	R	6-0	170	3-14-80	1996	Puerto Ordaz, Venez.
Lopez-Cao, Mike	.239	29	88	12	21	4	0	2	11	9	16	1	0	L	R	5-6	180	8-14-75	1997	Miami, Fla.
Martinez, Eddy	.291	127	416	68	121	21	1	2	55	52	99	8	4	R	R	6-2	150	10-23-77	1995	San Pedro de Macoris, D.R.
Matos, Luis	.297	68	273	40	81	15	1	7	41	20	35	27	6	R	R	6-0	155	10-30-78	1996	Bayamon, P.R.
McDonald, Darnell	.266	130	507	81	135	23	5	6	73	61	92	26	9	R	R	5-11	190	11-17-78	1997	Glendale, Colo.
McGee, Tom	.200	7	30	2	6	1	0	0	3	1	6	0	0	R	R	5-11	190	1-29-75	1997	Rialto, Calif.
Ndungidi, Ntema	.266	60	192	40	51	10	3	0	18	39	43	4	2	L	R	6-2	165	3-15-79	1997	Montreal, Quebec
Paxton, Chris	.249	58	169	26	42	8	0	6	28	34	54	0	0	L	R	6-2	210	12-11-76	1995	Palmdale, Calif.
Paz, Richard	.252	54	163	27	41	9	0	0	18	47	27	15	6	R	R	5-8	130	7-30-77	1994	Los Teques, Venez.
Rivera, Roberto	.274	118	460	70	126	21	4	12	53	39	89	18	9	S	R	6-2	160	11-25-76	1994	La Romana, D.R.
Rust, Brian	.148	9	27	7	4	1	0	0	1	5	7	0	0	R	R	6-2	205	8-1-74	1995	Portland, Ore.
Salargo, Steve	.100	3	10	0	1	0	0	0	0	0	5	0	0	R	R	6-2	195	12-24-76	1999	Wilson, N.C.
Werth, Jayson	.305	66	236	41	72	10	1	3	30	37	37	16	3	R	R	6-6	191	5-20-79	1997	Chatham, Ill.

GAMES BY POSITION: C—Alley 41, Daedelow 1, Escalante 5, Leon 2, Lopez-Cao 22, McGee 7, Paxton 14, Werth 61. **1B**—Benham 3, Figueroa 132, Hammond 2, Paxton 7. **2B**—Benham 1, Daedelow 1, DeShields 2, Garabito 117, Hammond 26. **3B**—Benham 8, Coffie 54, Daedelow 1, Hammond 28, Leon 3, Paz 50, Rust 6. **SS**—Coffie 13, Daedelow 2, Hammond 1, Martinez 124, Paz 1. **OF**—Daedelow 7, Hammond 3, Hughes 76, Matos 66, McDonald 110, Ndungidi 54, Paz 1, Rivera 112, Salargo 2.

PITCHING	W	L	ERA	G	GS	CG	SV	IP	H	R	ER	BB	SO	B	T	HT	WT	DOB	1st Yr	Resides
Achilles, Matt	5	8	4.31	16	15	1	0	94	103	57	45	32	77	R	R	6-3	175	8-18-76	1996	Moline, Ill.
Aracena, Juan	0	0	0.00	2	0	0	0	2	2	1	0	0	0	R	R	6-0	150	12-17-76	1994	La Vega, D.R.
2-team (5 Kinston)	1	1	2.00	7	0	0	0	9	9	3	2	1	7							
Bauer, Rick	10	9	4.56	26	26	4	0	152	159	85	77	54	123	R	R	6-5	190	1-10-77	1997	Eagle, Idaho
Brown, Derek	6	5	4.03	43	0	0	14	51	49	31	23	20	36	R	R	6-1	180	7-23-76	1994	Clear Spring, Md.
Douglass, Sean	5	6	3.32	16	16	1	0	98	101	48	36	35	89	R	R	6-6	200	4-28-79	1997	Lancaster, Calif.
Eibey, Scott	0	2	3.72	15	0	0	0	29	26	14	12	10	27	L	L	6-4	210	1-19-74	1995	Waterloo, Iowa
Fischer, Sean	1	1	13.50	3	0	0	0	5	10	7	7	6	3	L	L	6-1	205	12-13-77	1998	Philadelphia, Pa.
Gentile, Scott	0	0	0.00	2	0	0	0	2	0	0	0	0	4	R	R	5-10	205	12-21-70	1992	Berlin, Conn.
Halpin, Jeremy	5	3	3.56	45	1	0	2	83	95	44	33	18	53	R	R	6-3	190	11-20-74	1997	Rome, N.Y.
Huntsman, Brandon	4	4	6.85	11	10	0	0	45	58	37	34	19	29	R	R	6-4	195	11-19-75	1994	Pleasant Grove, Utah
Kamieniecki, Scott	0	0	0.00	1	1	0	0	4	0	0	0	1	3	R	R	6-0	200	4-19-64	1987	Flint, Mich.
Lynch, Ryan	1	1	4.87	12	1	0	0	20	18	12	11	20	23	L	L	6-4	220	8-10-74	1996	Solano Beach, Calif.
Maloney, Sean	1	0	1.42	15	0	0	2	25	21	10	4	10	22	R	R	6-7	210	5-25-71	1993	North Kingston, R.I.
Mastrolonardo, David	0	0	7.88	8	0	0	1	8	6	7	7	6	5	R	R	6-4	200	8-23-74	1997	Satellite Beach, Fla.
McNatt, Josh	2	3	6.00	19	6	0	0	45	41	36	30	44	29	S	L	6-4	200	7-23-77	1996	Jackson, Tenn.
Medina, Carlos	4	0	1.72	5	5	0	0	31	22	6	6	13	30	L	L	6-2	160	5-16-77	1994	La Vega, D.R.
Murphy, Brian	1	2	4.22	26	0	0	3	53	51	36	25	10	39	L	R	6-6	200	1-20-76	1998	Northstreet, Mich.
Paronto, Chad	3	5	4.73	13	13	1	0	72	81	46	38	26	55	R	R	6-5	250	7-28-75	1996	Haverhill, N.H.
Parrish, John	2	2	4.17	6	6	0	0	37	34	17	17	12	44	L	L	5-11	165	11-26-77	1996	Lancaster, Pa.
Paxton, Chris	0	0	1.59	6	0	0	0	5	4	2	1	1	1	L	R	6-2	210	12-11-76	1995	Palmdale, Calif.
Perez, Randy	0	1	9.00	2	1	0	0	7	14	8	7	1	4	L	L	6-1	170	4-13-80	1998	Lakeside, Calif.
Richardson, Kasey	5	2	5.31	38	0	0	2	61	63	38	36	32	44	L	L	6-3	191	8-27-76	1994	Huntington, Md.
Riley, Matt	3	2	2.61	8	8	0	0	52	34	19	15	14	58	L	L	6-1	205	8-2-79	1998	Oakley, Calif.
Romero, Jordan	0	0	2.93	9	0	0	0	15	11	9	5	13	11	R	R	6-1	170	10-30-76	1997	San Jose, Calif.
Shepherd, Alvie	0	2	11.81	3	2	0	0	5	7	7	7	10	6	R	R	6-7	220	5-12-74	1996	Bellwood, Ill.
Sims, Ken	4	4	4.17	35	1	0	2	69	83	38	32	19	41	R	R	6-4	187	7-24-75	1996	Union, S.C.
Spurgeon, Jay	6	9	4.75	26	26	1	0	146	176	99	77	53	87	R	R	6-6	225	7-5-76	1997	Coarsegold, Calif.

DELMARVA   Class A

SOUTH ATLANTIC LEAGUE

BATTING	AVG	G	AB	R	H	2B	3B	HR	RBI	BB	SO	SB	CS	B	T	HT	WT	DOB	1st Yr	Resides
Benham, Jason	.095	7	21	1	2	2	0	0	3	3	6	0	0	L	R	6-1	190	10-13-75	1998	Garland, Texas
Bigbie, Larry	.279	43	165	18	46	7	3	2	27	29	42	3	1	L	L	6-4	190	11-4-77	1999	Hobart, Ind.
Bonilla, Juan	.273	6	11	1	3	0	0	0	0	1	4	0	0	R	R	6-1	200	5-6-78	1998	Crestview, Fla.
Calzado, Napolean	.278	6	18	2	5	1	0	0	1	0	4	0	0	R	R	6-3	165	2-9-80	1996	Santo Domingo, D.R.
Daedelow, Craig	.313	45	160	28	50	3	2	0	21	35	26	1	3	R	R	5-11	165	4-3-76	1994	Huntington Beach, Calif.
Davison, Ashanti	.159	53	170	20	27	5	0	1	13	31	45	8	6	R	R	5-10	170	10-31-78	1996	Stockton, Calif.
DeShields, Delino	.286	2	7	1	2	0	0	1	2	1	1	0	1	L	R	6-1	175	1-15-69	1987	West Palm Beach, Fla.
Diaz, Maikell	.276	91	322	45	89	8	3	2	34	42	68	31	15	R	R	5-10	158	9-29-78	1996	Miranda, Venez.
Elder, Rick	.083	11	36	7	3	0	0	2	4	10	15	0	0	L	L	6-6	230	2-24-80	1998	Marietta, Ga.
Escalante, Jaime	.191	45	141	15	27	4	0	2	14	20	45	0	0	S	R	6-2	210	4-5-77	1997	Federalsburg, Md.
Gutierrez, Derrick	.262	30	103	12	27	6	0	1	14	3	28	1	1	R	R	5-11	175	10-6-78	1998	Jacksonville, Fla.
Haman, Mack	.220	68	246	27	54	9	4	3	37	14	67	4	2	R	R	6-4	205	12-11-75	1997	Newark, Del.
Hammond, Joey	.271	21	81	10	21	1	2	1	7	13	22	0	0	R	R	6-0	180	10-27-77	1998	Frederick, Md.
Harris, Willie	.265	66	272	42	72	13	5	2	32	20	41	17	11	L	R	5-9	175	6-22-78	1999	Cairo, Ga.
Hoch, Corey	.209	36	115	7	24	2	0	0	12	23	27	0	2	R	R	6-0	190	9-10-75	1998	Salisbury, Md.
Hooper, Daren	.244	24	90	13	22	7	2	0	5	3	30	0	1	R	R	6-1	230	5-15-77	1996	Woodside, Calif.
Johnson, Eric	.234	11	47	5	11	5	0	0	7	6	15	1	2	R	R	6-0	190	11-16-74	1997	Vidalia, Ga.
Lopez-Cao, Mike	.167	2	6	2	1	0	0	1	3	1	0	0	0	L	R	5-6	180	8-14-75	1997	Miami, Fla.
McGee, Tom	.271	71	218	37	59	16	2	4	27	34	52	0	4	R	R	5-11	190	1-29-75	1997	Rialto, Calif.
Ndungidi, Ntema	.194	64	217	33	42	8	2	0	24	49	54	18	2	L	R	6-2	165	3-15-79	1997	Montreal, Quebec
Nolasco, Regino	.119	23	59	10	7	0	0	0	6	5	16	1	1	R	R	6-0	145	7-28-79	1996	San Pedro de Macoris, D.R.
Price, Corey	.244	22	82	8	20	4	0	0	9	8	24	0	0	S	R	6-0	165	9-18-76	1996	Mount Pleasant, Texas
Purkiss, Matt	.210	107	366	44	77	15	0	11	46	57	124	0	0	L	R	6-3	220	7-15-75	1997	Visalia, Calif.
Raines, Tim	.248	117	415	80	103	24	8	2	49	71	130	49	16	R	R	5-10	185	8-31-79	1998	Sanford, Fla.
Reed, Keith	.258	61	240	36	62	14	3	4	25	22	53	3	2	R	R	6-4	215	10-8-78	1999	Yarmouth Port, Mass.

BATTING

	AVG	G	AB	R	H	2B	3B	HR	RBI	BB	SO	SB	CS	B	T	HT	WT	DOB	1st Yr	Resides
Riordan, Matt	.289	54	204	22	59	12	4	3	38	24	46	6	5	R	R	6-1	190	6-24-78	1999	Thousand Oaks, Calif.
Roberts, Brian	.240	47	167	22	40	12	1	0	21	27	42	17	5	S	R	5-9	165	10-9-77	1999	Chapel Hill, N.C.
Rumfield, Brock	.228	119	421	60	96	13	1	4	56	47	101	3	0	R	R	6-1	185	11-20-75	1998	Belton, Texas
Rust, Brian	.260	21	77	11	20	9	1	1	16	6	27	0	0	R	R	6-2	205	8-1-74	1995	Portland, Ore.
Seestedt, Michael	.263	27	80	8	21	3	0	0	3	10	20	0	0	R	R	6-0	195	11-10-77	1999	Mount Pleasant, Mich.

GAMES BY POSITION: C—Bonilla 5, Daedelow 19, Escalante 39, Lopez-Cao 2, McGee 63, Seestedt 24. **1B**—Elder 11, Escalante 2, Hoch 9, McGee 1, Purkiss 84, Rumfield 31, Rust 10. **2B**—Benham 4, Daedelow 20, DeShields 2, Diaz 6, Gutierrez 4, Hammond 5, Harris 64, Hoch 8, Nolasco 18, Price 16, Rumfield 1. **3B**—Benham 2, Calzado 6, Diaz 28, Gutierrez 1, Hammond 13, Hoch 5, McGee 1, Rumfield 80, Rust 8. **SS**—Diaz 60, Gutierrez 26, Hoch 10, Nolasco 5, Roberts 46. **OF**—Bigbie 32, Davison 50, Haman 55, Hammond 1, Harris 3, Hooper 7, Johnson 9, Ndungidi 57, Price 4, Raines 115, Reed 58, Riordan 36.

PITCHING

	W	L	ERA	G	GS	CG	SV	IP	H	R	ER	BB	SO	B	T	HT	WT	DOB	1st Yr	Resides
Andrade, Jancy	2	5	5.52	26	8	0	0	75	73	61	46	44	63	R	R	6-2	165	6-29-78	1995	Cumana, Venez.
Babula, Shaun	0	2	3.29	16	0	0	2	14	17	7	5	5	16	R	L	5-11	185	5-21-77	1998	Burlington, N.J.
Bechler, Steve	8	12	3.54	26	26	1	0	152	137	69	60	58	139	R	R	6-2	195	11-18-79	1998	Medford, Ore.
Bello, Jilberto	6	4	3.97	38	0	0	4	66	68	36	29	29	46	R	R	6-3	150	2-26-77	1994	San Pedro de Macoris, D.R.
Blazier, Ron	1	0	3.60	2	0	0	1	5	4	2	2	0	7	R	R	6-5	249	7-30-71	1990	Bellwood, Pa.
Casteel, Ricky	3	14	5.01	29	21	2	0	135	152	92	75	53	100	R	R	6-2	195	10-29-77	1997	Texarkana, Texas
Fleming, Travis	2	1	4.70	14	1	0	1	38	36	24	20	14	33	R	R	6-3	185	9-26-76	1999	McKinleyville, Calif.
Garcia, Sonny	3	5	5.81	13	12	0	0	62	68	46	40	19	44	R	R	6-3	220	9-10-76	1998	Houston, Texas
Guzman, Juan	9	5	3.55	29	18	0	3	124	124	51	49	44	134	R	R	6-2	160	3-4-78	1995	Los Llanos, D.R.
Huntsman, Brandon	1	1	4.43	7	2	0	0	22	20	12	11	9	25	R	R	6-4	195	11-19-75	1994	Pleasant Grove, Utah
McDougal, Mike	1	0	0.00	1	0	0	0	2	3	0	0	0	3	L	R	6-4	210	3-22-75	1994	Las Vegas, Nev.
Ormond, Rodney	1	2	2.89	17	1	0	3	37	29	16	12	19	38	R	R	6-4	210	6-17-77	1999	Princeton, N.C.
Paradis, Mike	0	1	15.00	2	0	0	0	3	3	5	5	4	6	R	R	6-2	214	5-3-78	1999	Auburn, Mass.
Parrish, John	0	1	7.20	4	0	0	0	10	9	8	8	6	10	L	L	5-11	165	11-26-77	1996	Lancaster, Pa.
Perez, Norberto	0	4	6.15	25	2	0	1	41	43	31	28	17	39	R	R	6-4	195	10-10-77	1995	El Seibo, D.R.
Perez, Randy	0	2	7.11	21	0	0	2	25	28	22	20	15	9	L	L	6-1	170	4-13-80	1998	Lakeside, Calif.
Rakers, Aaron	4	1	1.42	18	0	0	8	25	9	6	4	13	38	R	R	6-3	205	1-22-77	1999	Trenton, Ill.
Romero, Jordan	3	7	4.74	24	9	0	2	76	87	55	40	38	61	R	R	6-1	170	10-8-76	1997	San Jose, Calif.
Schwager, Matt	0	1	5.48	10	0	0	0	21	32	15	13	6	20	R	R	6-5	215	10-10-77	1998	Rio Piedras, P.R.
Sequea, Jacobo	0	2	3.90	6	6	0	0	30	35	19	13	16	25	R	R	6-0	175	8-31-81	1997	Anaco, Venez.
Stephens, John	10	8	3.22	28	27	4	0	170	148	75	61	36	217	R	R	6-1	190	11-15-79	1996	Berala, Australia
Tapia, Rafael	3	0	2.35	7	2	0	0	23	18	7	6	6	16	R	R	6-2	160	4-28-78	1995	San Pedro de Macoris, D.R.
Theodile, Simeon	1	2	5.83	33	1	0	0	54	68	44	35	27	45	R	R	6-2	190	4-15-77	1997	Jeanerette, La.

BLUEFIELD · Rookie

APPALACHIAN LEAGUE

BATTING

	AVG	G	AB	R	H	2B	3B	HR	RBI	BB	SO	SB	CS	B	T	HT	WT	DOB	1st Yr	Resides
Berrien, Sam	.239	30	92	13	22	3	1	0	9	18	22	1	1	L	L	6-0	235	4-30-79	1998	Philadelphia, Pa.
Bigbie, Larry	.267	8	30	3	8	0	0	0	4	3	8	1	3	L	L	6-4	190	11-4-77	1999	Hobart, Ind.
Bonilla, Juan	.240	34	100	12	24	5	0	1	17	12	23	0	0	R	R	6-1	200	5-6-78	1998	Crestview, Fla.
Cabrera, Ray	.274	31	117	21	32	9	0	2	9	6	14	1	3	R	R	6-3	170	11-10-78	1996	Upata, Venez.
Calzado, Napolean	.291	52	199	46	58	11	2	6	31	20	32	9	1	R	R	6-0	165	2-9-80	1996	Santo Domingo, D.R.
Centeno, Edwin	.250	5	8	1	2	0	0	0	0	0	2	1	0	S	R	6-0	165	3-15-78	1996	Baruta, Venez.
Elder, Rick	.329	46	158	35	52	8	4	10	40	30	57	2	0	L	L	6-6	230	2-24-80	1998	Marietta, Ga.
Gordon, Alex	.333	27	105	26	35	4	0	9	32	13	35	4	1	L	L	6-4	215	3-13-80	1998	Seattle, Wash.
Griswold, Matt	.275	40	149	30	41	8	1	6	26	32	50	2	1	L	R	6-0	188	11-10-77	1999	Severna Park, Md.
Gutierrez, Derrick	.203	34	123	18	25	2	3	2	15	20	44	3	1	R	R	5-11	175	10-6-78	1998	Jacksonville, Fla.
Gutierrez, Fernando	.269	23	78	5	21	7	0	0	11	4	19	0	1	R	R	6-2	175	9-25-80	1997	Araure, Venez.
Harris, Willie	.273	5	22	3	6	1	0	0	3	4	2	1	0	L	R	5-9	175	6-22-78	1999	Cairo, Ga.
Ide, Antoine	.224	24	85	17	19	2	2	0	8	7	10	2	1	R	R	6-0	170	3-2-79	1997	Portland, Ore.
Kessick, Jon	.204	28	93	13	19	3	0	4	14	4	33	0	0	R	R	6-5	215	1-9-78	1998	Muncie, Ind.
Monzon, Francisco	.244	24	82	14	20	4	0	1	7	9	20	1	1	R	R	6-0	175	11-8-79	1998	Carolina, P.R.
Nelson, Tim	.226	33	115	19	26	3	2	3	16	6	35	0	0	R	R	6-3	210	5-10-78	1998	Calgary, Alberta
Nolasco, Regino	.202	58	198	35	40	5	3	1	26	19	49	5	1	R	R	6-0	145	7-28-79	1996	San Pedro de Macoris, D.R.
Reed, Keith	.188	4	16	2	3	0	0	0	0	1	3	0	1	R	R	6-4	215	10-8-78	1999	Yarmouth Port, Mass.
Riordan, Matt	.333	5	21	2	7	1	1	1	6	3	3	1	1	R	R	6-1	190	6-24-78	1999	Thousand Oaks, Calif.
Salargo, Steve	.306	50	170	46	52	12	1	5	45	37	28	8	2	R	R	6-2	195	12-24-76	1999	Wilson, N.C.
Sowers, Doug	.249	53	181	32	45	14	1	8	35	33	54	2	1	L	R	6-1	205	9-16-77	1999	Knoxville, Md.
Tucker, Mamon	.253	58	233	52	59	9	5	2	10	18	29	44	7	R	R	6-0	190	10-8-77	1999	Austin, Texas

GAMES BY POSITION: C—Bonilla 3, F. Gutierrez 23, Kessick 27, Monzon 23. **1B**—Berrien 23, Bonilla 24, Elder 23, Nelson 4, Tucker 1. **2B**—Bonilla 1, Centeno 1, Harris 5, Nolasco 50, Sowers 17. **3B**—Calzado 23, Nelson 26, Sowers 26. **SS**—Calzado 29, D. Gutierrez 34, Nolaso 7. **OF**—Bigbie 5, Cabrera 23, Centeno 2, Elder 1, Gordon 23, Griswold 32, Ide 21, Reed 3, Riordan 5, Salargo 47, Tucker 50.

PITCHING

	W	L	ERA	G	GS	CG	SV	IP	H	R	ER	BB	SO	B	T	HT	WT	DOB	1st Yr	Resides
Andrade, Jancy	1	0	2.87	3	3	0	0	16	17	8	5	5	10	R	R	6-2	165	6-29-78	1995	Cumana, Venez.
Babula, Shaun	1	0	1.13	4	0	0	0	8	4	2	1	5	10	R	L	5-11	185	5-21-77	1999	Burlington, N.J.
Brewer, Dustin	0	0	0.00	1	0	0	1	2	1	0	1	4		R	R	6-5	225	7-14-80	1998	Granite City, Ill.
Cenate, Josh	1	5	4.46	9	9	0	0	38	45	32	19	20	55	L	L	6-1	195	1-28-81	1999	Charleston, W.Va.
Fischer, Sean	1	2	6.89	17	1	0	0	33	38	37	25	24	32	L	L	6-1	205	12-13-77	1998	Philadelphia, Pa.
Houle, Marc	3	7	7.16	20	0	0	0	44	57	44	35	27	36	R	R	6-3	210	2-18-78	1998	Montreal, Quebec
Jones, Sean	1	3	6.12	13	11	0	0	60	82	54	41	33	52	R	R	6-7	180	4-12-78	1997	Hamilton, Ontario
Knapp, Ben	4	6	9.24	14	14	0	0	61	88	77	63	40	50	R	R	6-5	190	11-8-79	1998	Oviedo, Fla.
Mastrolonardo, David	0	0	0.00	1	0	0	0	2	0	0	0	2	4	R	R	6-4	220	8-23-74	1997	Satellite Beach, Fla.
Ormond, Rodney	1	0	0.00	2	0	0	0	9	2	4	0	3	11	R	R	6-4	210	6-17-77	1999	Princeton, N.C.
Perez, Randy	4	3	2.70	14	5	1	0	50	51	26	15	12	39	L	L	6-1	170	4-13-80	1998	Lakeside, Calif.
Plank, Terry	1	3	6.68	20	1	0	0	32	42	26	24	12	46	L	R	6-5	200	4-19-78	1999	Hampton, Va.
Pruitt, Jason	2	4	6.00	17	8	0	1	54	56	41	36	31	57	L	L	6-3	190	8-6-80	1998	Philadelphia, Pa.
Rakers, Aaron	0	0	2.57	3	0	0	0	7	5	2	2	3	12	R	R	6-3	205	1-22-77	1999	Trenton, Ill.
Ramirez, Enrique	0	1	3.07	13	0	0	1	15	18	9	5	9	14	R	R	6-2	180	8-15-79	1996	El Seibo, D.R.
Ryba, Jason	5	5	5.94	18	3	0	0	47	55	40	31	23	42	R	R	6-3	190	10-5-78	1997	Brooklyn Heights, Ohio
Schwager, Matt	3	1	3.60	22	0	0	7	30	31	19	12	5	29	R	R	6-5	215	10-10-77	1998	Rio Piedras, P.R.

PITCHING	W	L	ERA	G	GS	CG	SV	IP	H	R	ER	BB	SO	B	T	HT	WT	DOB	1st Yr	Resides
Shepherd, Alvie	1	1	4.00	2	2	0	0	9	11	8	4	4	7	R	R	6-7	220	5-12-74	1996	Bellwood, Ill.
Tomaszewski, Eliot	0	0	7.20	1	1	0	0	5	8	5	4	1	1	R	R	6-4	190	1-13-80	1998	Albuquerque, N.M.
Whitecotton, Billy	3	8	7.22	15	10	0	0	62	82	67	50	37	60	R	R	6-3	170	8-18-80	1998	Baltimore, Md.

SARASOTA   Rookie

GULF COAST LEAGUE

BATTING	AVG	G	AB	R	H	2B	3B	HR	RBI	BB	SO	SB	CS	B	T	HT	WT	DOB	1st Yr	Resides
Alley, Chip	.000	2	3	2	0	0	0	0	0	2	0	0	0	S	R	6-3	190	12-20-76	1995	West Palm Beach, Fla.
Cabrera, Ray	.310	16	58	8	18	3	2	0	12	1	6	4	0	R	R	6-3	170	11-10-78	1996	Upata, Venez.
Cates, Gary	.268	45	127	20	34	7	0	1	20	15	20	11	2	R	R	5-8	155	7-3-81	1999	Brandon, Fla.
Centeno, Edwin	.272	33	92	22	25	4	3	2	15	4	26	12	3	S	R	6-0	165	3-15-78	1996	Baruta, Venez.
Davison, Ashanti	.258	8	31	5	8	3	0	0	3	3	7	6	1	R	R	5-10	170	10-31-78	1996	Stockton, Calif.
Dees, Charlie	.215	56	186	21	40	12	1	9	32	20	41	5	6	R	R	6-0	215	7-19-77	1999	Montgomery, Ala.
Del Rosario, Emmanuel	.244	40	123	19	30	2	0	0	8	22	10	10	5	S	R	5-11	145	7-8-81	1997	Hato Mayor, D.R.
Elder, Rick	.600	3	10	2	6	2	0	2	4	2	1	0	0	L	L	6-6	230	2-24-80	1998	Marietta, Ga.
Garcia, Nick	.229	21	70	12	16	5	0	3	15	4	10	1	2	R	R	5-11	165	5-2-80	1999	Obregon, Mexico
Gordon, Alex	.360	36	125	25	45	7	6	6	34	14	37	12	2	L	L	6-4	215	3-13-80	1998	Seattle, Wash.
Green, Ricky	.000	2	1	0	0	0	0	0	0	0	1	0	0	R	R	6-2	185	12-6-78	1998	Tullahoma, Tenn.
Griswold, Matt	.346	10	26	4	9	3	0	0	4	6	4	0	1	L	R	6-0	188	11-10-77	1999	Severna Park, Md.
Hernandez, Argenis	.178	39	118	10	21	3	0	2	15	9	20	0	1	L	L	6-2	180	8-4-80	1997	Caracas, Venez.
Ide, Antoine	.280	15	50	12	14	2	0	1	5	5	12	8	2	R	R	6-0	170	3-2-79	1997	Portland, Ore.
Leon, Alfredo	.327	29	107	18	35	6	3	1	15	6	11	3	3	R	R	6-0	170	3-14-80	1996	Puerto Ordaz, Venez.
Mack, Antonio	.247	48	170	36	42	6	1	0	5	17	46	20	7	R	R	5-11	185	3-19-79	1998	Orlando, Fla.
Martin, Kyle	.268	29	82	11	22	4	1	0	8	9	20	3	2	R	R	5-11	215	6-12-80	1999	Yakima, Wash.
Martinez, Octavio	.237	36	114	11	27	8	1	0	15	4	11	8	1	R	R	6-0	195	7-30-79	1999	Bakersfield, Calif.
Pickering, Kelvin	.194	23	72	8	14	2	0	1	3	4	25	0	0	R	R	6-1	215	9-7-79	1999	Tampa, Fla.
Riordan, Matt	.250	8	24	4	6	1	0	0	3	2	2	2	1	R	R	6-1	190	6-24-78	1999	Thousand Oaks, Calif.
Rogers, Ed	.288	53	177	34	51	5	1	1	19	23	22	20	3	R	R	6-1	165	8-10-81	1997	San Pedro de Macoris, D.R.
Seestedt, Michael	.200	6	15	0	3	1	0	0	4	0	1	0	0	R	R	6-0	195	11-10-77	1999	Mount Pleasant, Mich.
Shier, Pete	.346	9	26	6	9	1	0	0	1	3	4	3	4	R	R	6-1	170	3-16-81	1999	Columbus, Ohio
Sowers, Doug	.286	4	14	0	4	0	0	0	1	0	1	1	1	L	R	6-1	205	9-16-77	1999	Knoxville, Md.
Storke, Jon	.155	25	71	13	11	3	1	0	5	12	28	4	1	R	R	6-2	205	6-23-78	1999	Gardnerville, Nev.
Wade, Mike	.000	2	4	0	0	0	0	0	0	0	2	0	0	R	R	6-5	200	10-31-75	1998	Moore, Okla.

GAMES BY POSITION: C—Alley 1, Green 2, Leon 1, Martin 27, Martinez 31, Pickering 8, Seestedt 6. **1B**—Dees 25, Hernandez 39, Ide 1, Leon 3, Mack 1, Storke 3, Wade 1. **2B**—Cates 19, Del Rosario 40, E. Rogers 4. **3B**—Cates 15, Centeno 1, Dees 3, Garcia 4, Leon 16, Martinez 1, E. Rogers 10, Sowers 3, Storke 15. **SS**—Cates 5, Garcia 17, Leon 1, E. Rogers 32, Shier 9, Storke 3. **OF**—Cabrera 13, Cates 6, Centeno 29, Davison 8, Dees 30, Elder 1, Gordon 28, Griswold 8, Ide 13, Leon 2, Mack 47, Riordan 7, Storke 4.

PITCHING	W	L	ERA	G	GS	CG	SV	IP	H	R	ER	BB	SO	B	T	HT	WT	DOB	1st Yr	Resides
Advincola, Jose	1	1	5.46	12	5	0	0	28	37	20	17	16	23	L	L	6-0	140	5-20-80	1998	San Cristobal, D.R.
Anez, Omar	1	6	8.33	14	6	0	0	31	38	38	29	29	23	R	R	6-3	170	2-1-81	1997	Valencia, Venez.
Bedard, Erik	2	1	1.86	8	6	0	0	29	20	7	6	13	41	L	L	6-1	180	3-5-79	1999	Navan, Ontario
Berube, Martin	0	0	0.53	11	0	0	2	17	8	5	1	10	11	L	R	6-1	190	9-12-81	1998	Montreal, Quebec
Brewer, Dustin	1	1	2.89	4	0	0	0	9	13	11	3	2	8	R	R	6-5	225	7-14-80	1998	Granite City, Ill.
Burrows, Terry	0	0	0.00	2	2	0	0	5	0	1	0	1	4	L	L	6-1	190	11-28-68	1990	Lake Charles, La.
De la Rosa, Cristian	1	3	6.52	15	0	0	0	19	30	19	14	16	13	R	R	6-1	150	2-5-79	1998	San Pedro de Macoris, D.R.
Falkenborg, Brian	1	0	2.00	3	2	0	0	9	6	2	2	3	11	R	R	6-6	187	1-18-78	1996	Redmond, Wash.
Farren, Dave	1	1	0.95	10	2	0	2	19	17	6	2	7	12	R	R	6-2	175	3-20-81	1999	Texarkana, Texas
Fleming, Travis	1	1	1.13	4	3	0	0	16	12	2	2	2	21	R	R	6-3	185	9-26-76	1999	McKinleyville, Calif.
Halisky, Scott	0	0	7.20	3	0	0	0	5	7	4	4	3	3	R	R	6-7	210	9-28-77	1998	Clearwater, Fla.
Maloney, Sean	0	0	0.00	1	0	0	0	2	1	0	0	1	3	R	R	6-7	210	5-25-71	1993	North Kingston, R.I.
Mastrolonardo, Dave	2	0	2.08	3	0	0	0	4	2	1	1	2	9	R	R	6-4	220	8-23-74	1997	Satellite Beach, Fla.
McNatt, Josh	1	0	0.00	1	0	0	0	2	1	0	0	0	2	S	L	6-4	200	7-23-77	1996	Jackson, Tenn.
Moreno, Julio	1	0	1.80	4	2	0	0	10	8	4	2	1	5	R	R	6-1	165	10-23-75	1994	Cayacoa, D.R.
Paz, Rolando	1	1	8.64	13	0	0	0	25	23	28	24	25	23	R	R	6-2	180	1-31-79	1997	Vacamonte, Panama
Phillips, James	1	1	3.90	15	0	0	2	28	25	16	12	17	16	R	R	6-2	180	10-24-80	1999	Zanesville, Ohio
Ramirez, Enrique	0	0	2.45	9	0	0	5	11	9	3	3	3	7	R	R	6-1	180	8-15-79	1996	El Seibo, D.R.
Rice, Scott	1	4	10.38	9	6	0	0	17	26	34	20	20	14	L	L	6-6	220	9-21-81	1999	Simi Valley, Calif.
Rogers, Brad	1	1	1.69	6	0	0	0	11	11	3	2	3	8	R	R	6-4	195	12-6-81	1999	Nanaimo, B.C.
Tate, Matt	2	2	3.59	11	11	0	0	58	40	26	23	26	44	R	R	6-3	185	9-21-80	1999	Bonifay, Fla.
Tavarez, David	9	0	2.14	12	9	0	0	67	60	22	16	12	55	R	R	6-3	190	1-13-82	1998	Santiago, D.R.
Tomaszewski, Eliot	3	1	1.85	10	6	0	2	44	35	22	9	19	36	R	R	6-4	190	1-13-80	1998	Albuquerque, N.M.
Trinidad, Fernando	0	4	5.09	15	0	0	1	35	40	23	20	9	19	R	R	6-2	180	11-1-79	1997	Hato Mayor, D.R.

Organization Statistics

BOSTON RED SOX

Pedro, Nomar and 23 overachievers lift Red Sox to ALCS

BY TONY MASSAROTTI

When the 1999 season finally came to an end, an exhausted Mike Stanley stood proudly before his Fenway Park locker, the very same space that had previously been home to Mo Vaughn.

"Nobody gave us an ounce of respect all year," Stanley said.

Now, maybe somebody will.

Despite entering the season without Vaughn, who signed with the Angels as a free agent after the '98 campaign, the Red Sox reached the American League Championship Series in 1999. The team went 94-68 in the regular season—two wins better than the previous year—then ousted the Indians in the AL division series before losing in five games to the rival Yankees.

Clearly, the highlight for this team was its come-from-behind, first-round series win in which Red Sox hitters torched the Indians for 44 runs in the final three games. The decisive Game Five 12-8 win featured a heroic performance by inimitable ace Pedro Martinez.

Lifted from Game One of the series because of a back strain, Martinez threw six innings of no-hit relief as the Sox advanced to the ALCS for the first time since 1990. He was a landslide winner for the Cy Young Award and was Baseball America's Major League Player of the Year.

Said pitching coach Joe Kerrigan: "That's the legend of Pedro. It just adds to it. It amazes everybody, even all the guys on the bench."

Martinez finished the season with a 23-4 record, 2.07 ERA and 313 strikeouts, a new club record. He had just 37 walks in 213 innings as he led the AL in the triple crown pitching categories.

Pedro Martinez   **Tomokazu Ohka**

Players of the Year

MAJOR LEAGUE: Pedro Martinez, rhp

Martinez enjoyed a truly dominant season, leading the majors with 23 wins and a 2.07 ERA while striking out 313 and walking just 37.

MINOR LEAGUE: Tomokazu Ohka, rhp

Ohka was unbeatable at Trenton and Pawtucket, going 15-0 overall with a 2.31 ERA in his first season in the United States.

As good as Martinez was, he had considerable help. Shortstop Nomar Garciaparra, hitting .357, added a batting title to his growing trophy case. DH Brian Daubach came out of nowhere to emerge as the No. 3 hitter for much of the year. And righthander Derek Lowe developed into one of the most dominant relievers in the league, helping to offset the loss of an injured Tom Gordon.

And lest anyone forget, the Sox did it all under the guidance of manager Jimy Williams, AL manager of the year.

Along the way, the Red Sox exorcised a truckload of demons. While overcoming the loss of Vaughn, they reached the playoffs in consecutive years for the first time since 1915-16. And they manhandled Roger Clemens in Game Three of the ALCS, riding the golden right arm of Martinez to a lopsided 13-1 victory at Fenway.

The only thing the Sox didn't do, it seemed, was win their first World Series title since 1918, though New Englanders had reason to believe that could change in coming years.

The Red Sox did win a championship in their minor league system, the first since 1983. Class A Augusta won the South Atlantic League title, with Gordon starting the clincher in a rehabilitation appearance.

Led by undefeated Japanese righthander Tomokazu Ohka and second baseman David Eckstein, Double-A Trenton earned BA's Minor League Team of the Year award after leading the Eastern League all season. Ohka went a combined 15-0, 2.31 between Trenton and Triple-A Pawtucket, which opened a rebuilt McCoy Stadium.

ORGANIZATION LEADERS

BATTING

*AVG	Raul Gonzalez, Trenton	.335
R	David Eckstein, Trenton	109
H	Raul Gonzalez, Trenton	169
TB	Morgan Burkhart, Trenton/Sarasota	283
2B	Two tied at	33
3B	Angel Mendoza, Augusta	8
HR	Morgan Burkhart, Trenton/Sarasota	35
RBI	Morgan Burkhart, Trenton/Sarasota	108
BB	David Eckstein, Trenton	89
SO	Michael Coleman, Pawtucket	128
SB	David Eckstein, Trenton	32

PITCHING

W	Two tied at	15
L	Two tied at	13
#ERA	Tomokazu Ohka, Pawtucket/Trenton	2.31
G	Terrance Hill, Augusta	53
CG	Jin Ho Cho, Pawtucket	4
SV	Mark Cisar, Augusta	27
IP	Jared Fernandez, Pawtucket/Trenton	182
BB	Jason Sekany, Pawtucket/Trenton	68
SO	Jason Norton, Augusta	150

*Minimum 250 At-Bats #Minimum 75 Innings

Boston RED SOX

Manager: Jimy Williams.

1999 Record: 94-68, .580 (2nd, AL East)

BATTING	AVG	G	AB	R	H	2B	3B	HR	RBI	BB	SO	SB	CS	B	T	HT	WT	DOB	1st Yr	Resides
Buford, Damon	.242	91	297	39	72	15	2	6	38	21	74	9	2	R	R	5-10	170	6-12-70	1990	Phoenix, Ariz.
Coleman, Michael	.200	2	5	1	1	0	0	0	0	1	0	0	0	R	R	5-11	207	8-16-75	1994	Nashville, Tenn.
Daubach, Brian	.294	110	381	61	112	33	3	21	73	36	92	0	1	L	R	6-1	201	2-11-72	1990	Belleville, Ill.
Fonville, Chad	.000	3	2	1	0	0	0	0	0	2	0	1	0	S	R	5-7	155	3-5-71	1992	Midway Park, N.C.
Frye, Jeff	.281	41	114	14	32	3	0	1	12	14	11	2	2	R	R	5-9	165	8-31-66	1988	Arlington, Texas
Garciaparra, Nomar	.357	135	532	103	190	42	4	27	104	51	39	14	3	R	R	6-0	175	7-23-73	1994	Las Vegas, Nev.
Gubanich, Creighton	.277	18	47	4	13	2	1	1	11	3	13	0	0	R	R	6-3	200	3-27-72	1991	Phoenixville, Pa.
Hatteberg, Scott	.275	30	80	12	22	5	0	1	11	18	14	0	0	L	R	6-1	195	12-14-69	1991	Tacoma, Wash.
Huskey, Butch	.266	45	124	18	33	6	0	7	28	7	20	0	0	R	R	6-3	244	11-10-71	1989	Lawton, Okla.
2-team (74 Seattle)	.282	119	386	62	109	15	0	22	77	34	65	3	1							
Jefferson, Reggie	.277	83	206	21	57	13	1	5	17	17	55	0	0	L	L	6-4	215	9-25-68	1986	Tallahassee, Fla.
Lewis, Darren	.240	135	470	63	113	14	6	2	40	45	52	16	10	R	R	6-0	189	8-28-67	1988	San Carlos, Calif.
Lomasney, Steve	.000	1	2	0	0	0	0	0	0	0	2	0	0	R	R	6-0	185	8-29-77	1995	Peabody, Mass.
Merloni, Lou	.254	43	126	18	32	7	0	1	13	8	16	0	0	R	R	5-10	194	4-6-71	1993	Framingham, Mass.
Nixon, Trot	.270	124	381	67	103	22	5	15	52	53	75	3	1	L	L	6-2	196	4-11-74	1993	Charlotte, N.C.
Nunnally, Jon	.286	10	14	4	4	1	0	0	1	0	6	0	0	L	R	5-10	190	11-9-71	1992	Keeling, Va.
O'Leary, Troy	.280	157	596	84	167	36	4	28	103	56	91	1	2	L	L	6-0	190	8-4-69	1987	Phoenix, Ariz.
Offerman, Jose	.294	149	586	107	172	37	11	8	69	96	79	18	12	S	R	6-0	190	11-8-68	1988	San Pedro de Macoris, D.R.
Sadler, Donnie	.280	49	107	18	30	5	1	0	4	5	20	2	1	R	R	5-6	165	6-17-75	1994	Valley Mills, Texas
Stanley, Mike	.281	136	427	59	120	22	0	19	72	70	94	0	0	R	R	6-0	190	6-25-63	1985	Maitland, Fla.
Valentin, John	.254	113	449	58	114	27	1	12	70	40	68	0	1	R	R	6-0	180	2-18-67	1988	Homdel, N.J.
Varitek, Jason	.269	144	483	70	130	39	2	20	76	46	85	1	2	S	R	6-2	210	4-11-72	1995	Longwood, Fla.
Veras, Wilton	.286	36	119	14	34	5	1	2	13	5	14	0	2	R	R	6-2	186	1-19-78	1995	Santo Domingo, D.R.
Webster, Lenny	.000	6	14	0	0	0	0	0	1	2	2	0	0	R	R	5-9	195	2-10-65	1986	Charlotte, N.C.
2-team (16 Balt.)	.120	22	50	1	6	1	0	0	4	10	7	0	0							

PITCHING	W	L	ERA	G	GS	CG	SV	IP	H	R	ER	BB	SO	B	T	HT	WT	DOB	1st Yr	Resides
Beck, Rod	0	1	1.93	12	0	0	3	14	9	3	3	5	12	R	R	6-1	235	8-3-68	1986	Scottsdale, Ariz.
Bullinger, Kirk	0	0	4.50	4	0	0	0	2	2	1	1	2	0	R	R	6-2	170	10-28-69	1992	Hammond, La.
Cho, Jin Ho	2	3	5.72	9	7	0	0	39	45	26	25	8	16	R	R	6-3	207	8-16-75	1998	Jun Ju City, Korea
Cormier, Rheal	2	0	3.69	60	0	0	0	63	61	34	26	18	39	L	L	5-10	185	4-23-67	1989	Saint John, New Brunswick
Corsi, Jim	1	2	5.25	23	0	0	0	24	25	15	14	19	14	R	R	6-1	220	9-9-61	1982	Natick, Mass.
Florie, Bryce	2	0	4.80	14	2	0	0	30	33	19	16	15	25	R	R	5-11	192	5-21-70	1988	Goose Creek, S.C.
2-team (27 Detroit)	4	1	4.65	41	5	0	0	81	94	50	42	35	65							
Garces, Rich	5	1	1.55	30	0	0	2	41	25	9	7	18	33	R	R	6-0	215	5-18-71	1988	Maracay, Venez.
Gordon, Tom	0	2	5.60	21	0	0	11	18	17	11	11	12	24	R	R	5-9	180	11-18-67	1986	Avon Park, Fla.
Gross, Kip	0	2	7.82	11	1	0	0	13	15	11	11	8	9	R	R	6-2	190	8-24-64	1987	Gering, Neb.
Guthrie, Mark	1	1	5.83	46	0	0	2	46	50	32	30	20	36	L	L	6-4	211	9-22-65	1987	Bradenton, Fla.
Harikkala, Tim	1	1	6.23	7	0	0	0	13	15	9	9	6	7	R	R	6-2	185	7-15-71	1992	Lake Worth, Fla.
Lowe, Derek	6	3	2.63	74	0	0	15	109	84	35	32	25	80	R	R	6-6	170	6-1-73	1991	Dearborn, Mich.
Martinez, Pedro	23	4	2.07	31	29	5	0	213	160	56	49	37	313	R	R	5-11	170	10-25-71	1988	Santo Domingo, D.R.
Martinez, Ramon	2	1	3.05	4	4	0	0	21	14	8	7	8	15	S	R	6-4	184	3-22-68	1985	Santo Domingo, D.R.
Mercker, Kent	2	0	3.51	5	5	0	0	26	23	12	10	13	17	L	L	6-2	195	2-1-68	1986	Dublin, Ohio
Ohka, Tomokazu	1	2	6.23	8	2	0	0	13	21	12	9	6	8	R	R	6-1	179	3-18-76	1999	Kyoto, Japan
Pena, Juan	2	0	0.69	2	2	0	0	13	9	1	1	3	15	R	R	6-5	211	6-27-77	1995	Miami, Fla.
Portugal, Mark	7	12	5.51	31	27	1	0	150	179	100	92	41	79	R	R	6-0	190	10-30-62	1981	Barrington, R.I.
Rapp, Pat	6	7	4.12	37	26	0	0	146	147	78	67	69	90	R	R	6-3	215	7-13-67	1989	Sulphur, La.
Rose, Brian	7	6	4.87	22	18	0	0	98	112	59	53	29	51	R	R	6-3	215	2-13-76	1995	Dartmouth, Mass.
Saberhagen, Bret	10	6	2.95	22	22	0	0	119	122	43	39	11	81	R	R	6-1	200	4-11-64	1983	Babylon, N.Y.
Santana, Julio	1	4	7.32	22	5	0	0	55	66	49	45	32	34	R	R	6-1	175	1-20-73	1992	Santo Domingo, D.R.
Santana, Marino	0	0	15.75	3	0	0	0	4	8	7	7	3	4	R	R	6-1	175	5-10-72	1990	Santo Domingo, D.R.
Wakefield, Tim	6	11	5.08	49	17	0	15	140	146	93	79	72	104	R	R	6-2	204	8-2-66	1988	Melbourne, Fla.
Wasdin, John	8	3	4.12	45	0	0	2	74	66	38	34	18	57	R	R	6-2	195	8-5-72	1993	Jacksonville, Fla.
Wolcott, Bob	0	0	8.10	4	0	0	0	7	8	6	6	3	2	R	R	6-0	190	9-8-73	1992	Kent, Wash.

FIELDING

Catcher	PCT	G	PO	A	E	DP	PB
Gubanich	.979	14	39	8	1	1	3
Hatteberg	.993	23	128	14	1	1	2
Lomasney	1.000	1	7	2	0	0	0
Varitek	.990	140	972	66	11	8	25
Webster	1.000	6	25	3	0	1	1

First Base	PCT	G	PO	A	E	DP
Daubach	.983	61	418	35	8	35
Huskey	.988	10	76	3	1	10
Jefferson	1.000	2	8	1	0	0
Merloni	.909	1	9	1	1	0
Offerman	1.000	8	48	3	0	7
Stanley	.988	111	830	60	11	71

Second Base	PCT	G	PO	A	E	DP
Fonville	.900	2	6	3	1	1

	PCT	G	PO	A	E	DP
Frye	.980	26	41	56	2	9
Merloni	.949	8	17	20	2	4
Offerman	.975	128	237	318	14	70
Sadler	.935	10	7	22	2	4

Third Base	PCT	G	PO	A	E	DP
Daubach	.000	1	0	0	0	0
Frye	.882	7	5	10	2	0
Gubanich	1.000	1	1	3	0	0
Huskey	1.000	3	1	3	0	0
Merloni	.885	9	6	17	3	1
Sadler	.813	9	7	6	3	0
Valentin	.954	111	84	208	14	16
Veras	.929	35	23	56	6	7

Shortstop	PCT	G	PO	A	E	DP
Frye	1.000	2	6	5	0	1

	PCT	G	PO	A	E	DP
Garciaparra	.972	134	232	357	17	72
Merloni	.956	24	36	50	4	12
Sadler	.930	14	18	22	3	5

Outfield	PCT	G	PO	A	E	DP
Buford	.985	84	189	6	3	2
Coleman	1.000	2	0	0	0	0
Daubach	1.000	2	2	0	0	0
Huskey	1.000	4	4	1	0	0
Lewis	.994	130	309	4	2	2
Merloni	.000	1	0	0	0	0
Nixon	.968	121	210	3	7	1
Nunnally	.000	2	0	0	0	0
O'Leary	.993	157	295	9	2	3
Sadler	.941	8	14	2	1	1

Nomar Garciaparra
Led AL with .357 average

Morgan Burkhart
Led organization with 35 homers and 108 RBIs

FARM SYSTEM

Director of Player Development: Kent Qualls

Class	Farm Team	League	W	L	Pct.	Finish*	Manager	First Yr
AAA	Pawtucket (R.I.) Red Sox	International	76	68	.528	6th (14)	Gary Jones	1973
AA	Trenton (N.J.) Thunder	Eastern	92	50	.648	1st (12)	DeMarlo Hale	1995
A#	Sarasota (Fla.) Red Sox	Florida State	67	72	.482	9th (14)	Butch Hobson	1994
A	Augusta (Ga.) Greenjackets	South Atlantic	69	70	.496	+8th (14)	Billy Gardner Jr.	1999
A	Lowell (Mass.) Spinners	New York-Penn	34	42	.447	t-10th (14)	Luis Aguayo	1996
Rookie	Fort Myers (Fla.) Red Sox	Gulf Coast	30	29	.508	7th (14)	John Sanders	1993

*Finish in overall standings (No. of teams in league)   #Advanced level   +Won league championship

PAWTUCKET   Class AAA

INTERNATIONAL LEAGUE

BATTING	AVG	G	AB	R	H	2B	3B	HR	RBI	BB	SO	SB	CS	B	T	HT	WT	DOB	1st Yr	Resides
Abad, Andy	.297	102	377	61	112	21	4	15	65	51	50	7	2	L	L	6-1	184	8-25-72	1993	Jupiter, Fla.
Alcantara, Israel	.272	24	81	13	22	3	0	9	23	9	29	0	0	R	R	6-2	165	5-6-73	1991	Santo Domingo, D.R.
Chamblee, Jim	.274	127	464	84	127	21	3	24	88	43	126	5	3	R	R	6-4	175	5-6-75	1995	Denton, Texas
Coleman, Michael	.268	115	467	95	125	29	2	30	74	51	128	14	6	R	R	5-11	207	8-16-75	1994	Nashville, Tenn.
Daubach, Brian	.290	9	31	4	9	2	0	1	6	6	8	0	0	L	R	6-1	201	2-11-72	1990	Belleville, Ill.
DePastino, Joe	.253	77	257	35	65	13	0	13	52	27	40	1	1	R	R	6-2	210	9-4-73	1992	Sarasota, Fla.
Fonville, Chad	.253	74	257	31	65	3	2	1	14	20	31	6	4	S	R	5-7	155	3-5-71	1992	Midway Park, N.C.
Frye, Jeff	.333	3	9	0	3	0	0	0	2	2	1	0	0	R	R	5-9	165	8-31-66	1988	Arlington, Texas
Gubanich, Creighton	.283	27	92	12	26	3	0	5	10	6	23	0	0	R	R	6-3	200	3-27-72	1991	Phoenixville, Pa.
Hatteberg, Scott	.176	10	34	3	6	2	0	0	4	4	6	0	0	L	R	6-1	195	12-14-69	1991	Tacoma, Wash.
Hyzdu, Adam	.229	12	35	4	8	0	0	1	6	4	13	0	0	R	R	6-2	210	12-6-71	1990	Mesa, Ariz.
Ingram, Garey	.247	85	296	49	73	15	3	9	39	17	52	11	2	R	R	5-11	195	7-25-70	1990	Columbus, Ga.
Jackson, Gavin	.164	49	140	17	23	3	0	0	5	27	32	2	0	R	R	5-10	170	7-19-73	1993	Sylvester, Ga.
Jefferson, Reggie	.000	3	10	1	0	0	0	0	0	2	3	0	0	L	L	6-4	215	9-25-68	1986	Tallahassee, Fla.
Liniak, Cole	.264	95	348	55	92	25	0	12	42	40	57	0	5	R	R	6-1	181	8-23-76	1995	Encinitas, Calif.
Merloni, Lou	.279	66	229	45	64	14	1	7	36	30	38	1	1	R	R	5-10	194	4-6-71	1993	Framingham, Mass.
Mitchell, Keith	.258	117	431	71	111	32	4	12	52	78	69	9	1	R	R	5-10	195	8-6-69	1987	San Diego, Calif.
Nunnally, Jon	.267	133	494	90	132	24	3	23	76	85	103	26	4	L	R	5-10	190	11-9-71	1992	Keeling, Va.
Rodriguez, Luis	.000	2	3	0	0	0	0	0	0	0	1	0	0	R	R	5-9	160	1-3-74	1991	Tampa, Fla.
Romero, Mandy	.217	46	143	8	31	7	0	3	22	13	26	0	0	S	R	5-11	196	10-19-67	1988	Miami, Fla.
Sadler, Donnie	.291	43	172	23	50	12	4	1	17	16	36	4	2	R	R	5-6	165	6-17-75	1994	Valley Mills, Texas
Snopek, Chris	.247	24	81	10	20	7	0	3	10	5	15	2	0	R	R	6-1	185	9-20-70	1992	Cynthiana, Ky.
Stenson, Dernell	.270	121	440	64	119	28	2	18	82	55	119	2	1	L	L	6-1	230	6-17-78	1996	La Grange, Ga.
Tebbs, Nathan	.600	4	5	1	3	1	0	0	1	2	1	0	1	S	R	5-10	170	12-14-72	1993	Riverton, Utah

PITCHING	W	L	ERA	G	GS	CG	SV	IP	H	R	ER	BB	SO	B	T	HT	WT	DOB	1st Yr	Resides
Adams, Willie	4	5	5.15	11	11	1	0	65	82	46	37	10	37	R	R	6-7	225	10-8-72	1993	Scottsdale, Ariz.
Adamson, Joel	2	4	6.02	25	3	0	2	43	60	35	29	8	14	L	L	6-4	185	7-2-71	1990	Phoenix, Ariz.
Baptist, Travis	4	2	5.31	17	3	0	0	42	49	27	25	19	30	L	L	6-0	185	12-30-71	1990	Aloha, Ore.
Barkley, Brian	0	1	5.14	3	3	0	0	14	11	9	8	7	5	L	L	6-2	180	12-8-75	1994	Waco, Texas
Bullinger, Kirk	0	2	2.39	35	0	0	15	38	37	14	10	13	27	R	R	6-2	170	10-28-69	1992	Hammond, La.
Cho, Jin Ho	9	3	3.45	17	17	4	0	110	99	46	42	29	80	R	R	6-3	207	8-16-75	1998	Jun Ju City, Korea
Cumberland, Chris	4	3	4.45	36	1	0	0	63	66	33	31	30	35	R	L	6-1	189	1-15-73	1993	Mandeville, La.

PITCHING	W	L	ERA	G	GS	CG	SV	IP	H	R	ER	BB	SO	B	T	HT	WT	DOB	1st Yr	Resides
Dixon, Tim	0	1	9.00	2	0	0	0	5	6	5	5	3	4	L	L	6-2	215	2-26-72	1995	San Jose, Calif.
2-team (2 Ottawa)	0	1	8.53	4	0	0	0	6	9	6	6	3	5							
Farrell, Jim	2	3	4.19	14	5	0	0	43	45	25	20	16	35	R	R	6-1	180	11-1-73	1995	Hartville, Ohio
Fernandez, Jared	12	9	4.24	27	20	3	0	163	172	88	77	39	76	R	R	6-2	230	2-2-72	1994	West Valley, Utah
Garces, Rich	1	0	3.25	21	0	0	7	28	24	11	10	10	24	R	R	6-0	215	5-18-71	1988	Maracay, Venez.
Gross, Kip	1	0	5.40	10	2	0	0	22	24	14	13	12	16	R	R	6-2	190	8-24-64	1987	Gering, Neb.
Guthrie, Mark	0	0	0.00	1	1	0	0	1	0	0	0	0	1	R	L	6-4	211	9-22-65	1987	Bradenton, Fla.
Harikkala, Tim	1	2	5.40	14	1	0	0	30	44	19	18	7	19	R	R	6-2	185	7-15-71	1992	Lake Worth, Fla.
Martinez, Ramon	1	0	9.00	2	2	0	0	9	10	9	9	6	7	S	R	6-4	184	3-22-68	1985	Santo Domingo, D.R.
Mix, Greg	4	4	3.69	46	4	0	1	85	89	45	35	40	79	R	R	6-4	225	8-21-71	1993	Albuquerque, N.M.
Ohka, Tomokazu	7	0	1.58	12	12	1	0	68	60	17	12	11	63	R	R	6-1	179	3-18-76	1999	Kyoto, Japan
Pena, Juan	4	2	4.13	10	10	0	0	48	44	28	22	13	61	R	R	6-5	211	6-27-77	1995	Miami, Fla.
Ramsay, Robert	6	6	5.35	20	20	0	0	114	114	81	68	36	79	L	L	6-5	230	12-3-73	1996	Washougal, Wash.
Rose, Brian	2	1	2.89	7	7	0	0	28	28	10	9	8	30	R	R	6-3	215	2-13-76	1995	Dartmouth, Mass.
Santana, Marino	2	3	2.95	25	0	0	1	40	28	15	13	17	45	R	R	6-1	175	5-10-72	1990	Santo Domingo, D.R.
Sekany, Jason	0	4	4.76	1	1	0	0	6	7	4	3	4	1	R	R	6-4	200	7-20-75	1996	Fort Myers, Fla.
Stanifer, Rob	3	1	2.04	31	0	0	3	40	34	21	9	15	29	R	R	6-3	205	3-10-72	1994	Easley, S.C.
Urso, Sal	1	0	3.52	4	0	0	0	8	10	4	3	5	6	R	L	5-11	195	1-19-72	1997	Tampa, Fla.
Wasdin, John	1	1	2.12	5	5	0	0	30	19	9	7	7	28	R	R	6-2	195	8-5-72	1993	Jacksonville, Fla.
Wolcott, Bob	6	13	3.59	26	16	2	2	125	131	67	50	28	69	R	R	6-0	190	9-8-73	1992	Kent, Wash.

FIELDING

Catcher	PCT	G	PO	A	E	DP	PB
DePastino	.991	75	423	43	4	3	4
Gubanich........	.974	24	135	14	4	3	3
Hatteberg	1.000	9	47	4	0	0	3
Rodriguez.......	.857	2	6	0	1	0	0
Romero	.994	46	316	20	2	3	6

First Base	PCT	G	PO	A	E	DP
Abad..............	.977	20	157	13	4	15
Alcantara.......	1.000	5	37	2	0	4
Chamblee.....	1.000	3	23	4	0	1
Daubach.........	.969	3	30	1	1	3
DePastino	1.000	1	1	0	0	0
Gubanich......	1.000	1	1	0	0	0
Jefferson	1.000	2	18	1	0	3
Merloni	1.000	3	9	0	0	0
Snopek.........	1.000	1	1	0	0	0
Stenson..........	.966	115	919	56	34	78

Second Base	PCT	G	PO	A	E	DP
Chamblee.......	.976	103	207	238	11	55
Fonville...........	.952	23	38	42	4	7
Frye...............	1.000	3	1	11	0	1
Ingram...........	1.000	22	30	57	0	11
Jackson........	1.000	5	3	11	0	1
Merloni	.833	2	3	2	1	2

Third Base	PCT	G	PO	A	E	DP
Chamblee.......	.860	28	15	28	7	0
Fonville...........	.824	6	4	10	3	1
Liniak.............	.941	94	66	156	14	17
Merloni	.951	26	24	53	4	4
Snopek.........	1.000	1	1	0	0	0

Shortstop	PCT	G	PO	A	E	DP
Fonville...........	.914	23	23	51	7	12
Jackson........	.966	45	70	129	7	26

	PCT	G	PO	A	E	DP
Merloni	.943	31	43	72	7	14
Sadler.............	.944	36	73	96	10	19
Snopek.........	.969	20	27	36	2	7
Tebbs	.750	3	2	1	1	0

Outfield	PCT	G	PO	A	E	DP
Abad..............	.985	68	127	3	2	1
Alcantara.......	1.000	14	25	0	0	0
Coleman........	.980	108	299	2	6	0
Daubach.......	1.000	2	1	1	0	0
Fonville...........	.950	19	37	1	2	0
Hyzdu............	1.000	8	10	0	0	0
Ingram...........	.969	35	58	4	2	0
Mitchell..........	.987	76	148	1	2	1
Nunnally........	.983	119	271	12	5	1
Tebbs	1.000	1	5	0	0	0

TRENTON — Class AA

EASTERN LEAGUE

BATTING	AVG	G	AB	R	H	2B	3B	HR	RBI	BB	SO	SB	CS	B	T	HT	WT	DOB	1st Yr	Resides
Alcantara, Israel	.294	77	293	48	86	26	0	20	60	27	78	4	2	R	R	6-2	165	5-6-73	1991	Santo Domingo, D.R.
Burkhart, Morgan	.230	66	239	40	55	14	1	12	41	31	43	3	0	S	L	5-11	225	1-29-72	1995	St. Louis, Mo.
Chevalier, Virgil	.293	131	509	81	149	29	4	13	76	50	73	9	9	R	R	6-2	240	10-31-73	1995	Burnt Hills, N.Y.
DePastino, Joe	.217	6	23	5	5	1	0	2	5	3	3	1	0	R	R	6-2	210	9-4-73	1992	Sarasota, Fla.
Eckstein, David	.313	131	483	109	151	22	5	6	52	89	48	32	13	R	R	5-8	168	1-20-75	1997	Sanford, Fla.
Epperson, Chad	.197	55	188	24	37	10	1	2	15	31	46	1	2	S	R	6-3	221	3-26-72	1992	Fort Myers, Fla.
Espinal, Juan	.185	17	65	11	12	1	0	2	7	5	19	0	1	R	R	5-11	165	4-15-75	1992	La Vega, D.R.
Everett, Adam	.263	98	338	56	89	11	0	10	44	41	64	21	5	R	R	6-1	167	2-6-77	1998	Kennesaw, Ga.
Faurot, Adam	.250	33	108	11	27	4	1	0	8	6	20	1	1	R	R	5-11	175	8-7-74	1996	Blountstown, Fla.
Gibralter, David	.299	124	448	76	134	22	1	24	97	32	68	5	5	R	R	6-3	215	6-19-75	1993	Duncanville, Texas
Gonzalez, Raul	.335	127	505	80	169	33	4	18	103	51	71	12	3	R	R	5-8	190	12-27-73	1991	Villa Carolina, P.R.
Hillenbrand, Shea	.259	69	282	41	73	15	0	7	36	14	27	6	5	R	R	6-1	175	7-27-75	1996	Mesa, Ariz.
Jackson, Gavin	.211	27	71	11	15	1	0	0	5	15	12	2	1	R	R	5-10	170	7-28-73	1995	Sylvester, Ga.
Lomasney, Steve	.245	47	151	24	37	6	0	12	31	31	44	7	5	R	R	6-0	185	8-29-77	1995	Peabody, Mass.
Mashore, Justin	.375	5	16	3	6	2	2	0	5	1	4	1	0	R	R	5-9	190	2-14-72	1991	Concord, Calif.
Newfield, Marc	.154	4	13	3	2	1	0	1	2	1	3	1	0	R	R	6-4	225	10-19-72	1990	Huntington Beach, Calif.
Rodriguez, Luis	.272	32	114	10	31	7	0	4	14	3	25	2	1	R	R	5-9	160	1-3-74	1991	Tampa, Fla.
Soriano, Jose	.253	61	166	38	42	9	1	2	20	12	31	15	6	R	R	6-0	165	4-20-74	1992	Bani, D.R.
Tebbs, Nathan	.271	107	365	49	99	14	1	8	35	29	67	21	10	S	R	5-10	170	12-14-73	1992	Riverton, Utah
Veras, Wilton	.281	116	474	65	133	23	2	11	75	23	55	7	6	R	R	6-2	186	1-19-78	1995	Santo Domingo, D.R.

PITCHING	W	L	ERA	G	GS	CG	SV	IP	H	R	ER	BB	SO	B	T	HT	WT	DOB	1st Yr	Resides
Adams, Willie	1	1	4.63	2	2	0	0	12	17	6	6	2	6	R	R	6-7	225	10-8-72	1993	Scottsdale, Ariz.
Barkley, Brian	5	0	2.55	7	7	0	0	35	32	10	10	6	18	L	L	6-2	180	12-8-75	1994	Waco, Texas
Beale, Chuck	2	5	5.95	29	1	0	1	59	71	45	39	36	41	R	R	6-0	210	3-19-74	1996	Dublin, Ga.
Belovsky, Josh	0	0	33.75	1	0	0	0	1	4	5	5	2	2	R	R	6-2	225	4-8-74	1998	Orange, Calif.
Betancourt, Rafael	6	2	3.62	39	0	0	13	55	50	24	22	10	57	R	R	6-2	176	4-29-75	1994	Cumana, Venez.
Bullinger, Kirk	1	1	0.53	17	0	0	10	17	6	2	1	5	16	R	R	6-2	170	10-28-69	1992	Hammond, La.
Crawford, Paxton	7	8	4.08	28	28	1	0	163	151	81	74	59	111	R	R	6-3	193	8-4-77	1995	Morrialton, Ark.
Cressend, Jack	1	0	7.20	3	3	0	0	15	19	12	12	7	11	R	R	6-1	185	5-13-75	1993	Covington, La.
Cumberland, Chris	2	0	0.43	14	0	0	1	21	12	1	1	13	18	R	L	6-1	189	1-15-73	1993	Mandeville, La.
Dixon, Tim	2	0	2.95	8	2	0	0	18	15	6	6	6	10	L	L	6-2	215	2-26-72	1995	San Jose, Calif.
2-team (2 Harrisburg) ..	2	1	3.52	10	2	0	0	23	19	10	9	8	14							
Dougherty, Tony	0	0	8.22	6	1	0	1	8	12	8	7	6	10	R	R	6-2	200	4-12-73	1994	Beaver Falls, Pa.
2-team (9 Altoona)	0	0	7.71	15	1	0	1	23	41	27	20	13	16							
Farrell, Jim	2	2	3.33	7	5	0	0	27	26	13	10	9	26	R	R	6-1	180	11-1-73	1995	Hartville, Ohio
Fernandez, Jared	3	0	3.38	7	0	0	1	19	18	9	7	8	10	R	R	6-2	230	2-2-72	1994	West Valley, Utah
Hazlett, Andy	9	9	4.16	27	26	2	1	164	155	84	76	41	123	L	L	6-3	195	8-27-75	1997	The Dalles, Ore.
Kim, Sun	9	8	4.89	26	26	1	0	149	160	86	81	44	130	R	R	6-2	180	9-4-77	1997	Seoul, Korea
Matthews, Mike	0	0	4.63	3	3	0	0	12	11	7	6	9	8	L	L	6-2	175	10-24-73	1992	Woodbridge, Va.

PITCHING	W	L	ERA	G	GS	CG	SV	IP	H	R	ER	BB	SO	B	T	HT	WT	DOB	1st Yr	Resides
2-team (6 Akron)	0	5	7.47	9	9	0	0	37	47	37	31	24	18							
McMullen, Jerry	1	0	6.00	3	0	0	0	3	4	2	2	2	2	L	L	6-2	190	10-13-73	1995	Redmond, Ore.
Ohka, Tomokazu	8	0	3.00	12	12	0	0	72	63	26	24	25	53	R	R	6-1	179	3-18-76	1999	Kyoto, Japan
Saberhagen, Bret	1	0	0.00	1	1	0	0	6	2	0	0	0	5	R	R	6-1	200	4-11-64	1983	Babylon, N.Y.
Sekany, Jason	14	4	3.35	27	22	3	0	161	143	65	60	64	116	R	R	6-4	200	7-20-75	1996	Fort Myers, Fla.
Smetana, Steve	5	4	3.99	39	3	0	1	86	90	39	38	26	61	L	L	6-0	205	4-14-73	1996	Chardon, Ohio
Stanifer, Rob	0	0	0.00	5	0	0	1	9	6	0	0	4	11	R	R	6-3	205	3-10-72	1994	Easley, S.C.
Taglienti, Jeff	0	0	2.79	10	0	0	2	19	9	6	6	5	17	R	R	6-0	208	11-13-75	1997	Walpole, Mass.
Thompson, Chris	0	0	9.00	1	0	0	0	1	2	1	1	1	1	R	R	6-2	202	9-29-72	1996	Elyria, Ohio
Tweedlie, Brad	6	0	3.65	44	0	0	3	57	59	28	23	21	31	R	R	6-2	210	12-9-71	1993	Agawam, Mass.
Urso, Sal	2	2	1.86	22	0	0	5	29	25	11	6	14	39	R	L	5-11	195	1-19-72	1990	Tampa, Fla.
Young, Tim	4	4	4.37	31	0	0	2	45	38	26	22	26	52	L	L	5-9	170	10-15-73	1996	Bristol, Fla.

FIELDING

Catcher	PCT	G	PO	A	E	DP	PB
Chevalier......	1.000	2	14	1	0	1	2
DePastino......	1.000	1	6	1	0	0	0
Epperson......	1.000	12	89	11	0	0	1
Hillenbrand.....	.987	55	337	41	5	7	12
Lomasney......	.970	46	355	33	12	1	5
Rodriguez.......	.995	30	192	25	1	4	2

First Base	PCT	G	PO	A	E	DP
Alcantara.....	1.000	15	82	6	0	10
Burkhart.......	.987	25	215	7	3	19
Chevalier........	.750	3	3	0	1	0
Epperson.......	.982	14	102	7	2	13
Gibralter.......	.991	100	868	59	8	76
Rodriguez.....	1.000	1	4	0	0	0

Second Base	PCT	G	PO	A	E	DP
Eckstein	.985	127	232	359	9	87
Faurot.........	.971	12	24	44	2	7
Jackson........	1.000	2	5	5	0	2
Tebbs	.900	3	3	6	1	3

Third Base	PCT	G	PO	A	E	DP
Espinal	.828	16	4	20	5	0
Faurot...........	.897	11	7	19	3	1
Tebbs	.750	2	0	3	1	0
Veras	.945	115	83	245	19	27

Shortstop	PCT	G	PO	A	E	DP
Everett........	.959	98	150	273	18	61
Faurot...........	.952	5	7	13	1	2
Jackson...........	.947	25	34	56	5	10

	PCT	G	PO	A	E	DP
Tebbs	.988	21	30	52	1	9

Outfield	PCT	G	PO	A	E	DP
Alcantara	.982	50	103	4	2	1
Chevalier.......	.973	129	239	12	7	1
Epperson........	.000	1	0	0	0	0
Faurot..............	.000	1	0	0	0	0
Gibralter	1.000	2	4	0	0	0
Gonzalez	.993	120	268	4	2	1
Mashore	1.000	5	8	1	0	0
Newfield	.889	4	8	0	1	0
Soriano...........	.983	59	109	4	2	1
Tebbs	.993	85	136	6	1	2

SARASOTA — Class A

FLORIDA STATE LEAGUE

BATTING	AVG	G	AB	R	H	2B	3B	HR	RBI	BB	SO	SB	CS	B	T	HT	WT	DOB	1st Yr	Resides
Alevras, Chad	.143	2	7	2	1	0	0	1	2	0	0	0	0	R	R	6-1	195	1-8-75	1997	Littleton, Colo.
Benham, David	.238	33	105	10	25	5	0	3	11	5	18	0	0	R	R	6-2	190	10-12-75	1998	Garland, Texas
Burkhart, Morgan	.363	68	245	56	89	18	0	23	67	37	33	5	2	S	L	5-11	225	1-29-72	1995	St. Louis, Mo.
Capista, Aaron	.264	130	518	64	137	18	3	5	47	45	60	25	10	S	R	6-2	185	5-31-79	1997	Shorewood, Ill.
Cheek, Shawn	.080	15	25	1	2	0	0	0	1	2	10	0	0	R	R	6-3	215	4-30-74	1997	Albany, Ga.
DeLeon, Jorge	.274	66	219	33	60	11	2	1	18	24	33	3	2	R	R	6-2	170	9-26-74	1997	Guayama, P.R.
Epperson, Chad	.242	26	99	9	24	1	1	3	14	3	18	2	1	S	R	6-3	221	3-26-72	1992	Fort Myers, Fla.
Espinal, Juan	.299	111	411	78	123	26	0	10	67	47	83	12	4	R	R	5-11	165	4-15-75	1992	La Vega, D.R.
Fischer, Mark	.253	106	359	42	91	14	3	5	40	28	85	11	6	R	R	6-1	185	4-15-76	1997	Atlanta, Ga.
Fuentes, Javier	.290	64	176	28	51	4	0	0	13	33	17	6	1	R	R	6-1	185	9-27-74	1996	Austin, Texas
Graham, Jess	.268	129	462	66	124	33	5	7	65	49	77	5	4	L	L	6-0	185	10-12-75	1997	Fairmont, W.Va.
Haas, Danny	.241	87	241	18	58	8	5	0	24	22	54	4	3	L	R	5-11	184	1-4-76	1997	Paducah, Ky.
Hatteberg, Scott	1.000	1	1	0	1	0	0	0	1	0	0	0	0	L	R	6-1	195	12-14-69	1991	Tacoma, Wash.
Jefferson, Reggie	.429	3	14	4	6	2	0	1	2	1	2	0	0	L	L	6-4	215	9-25-68	1986	Tallahassee, Fla.
Johnson, Rontrez	.300	132	494	97	148	30	4	8	59	74	63	18	15	R	R	5-10	165	12-8-76	1995	Marshall, Texas
Key, Jeff	.234	25	77	9	18	6	1	1	13	10	12	4	2	L	R	6-1	210	11-22-74	1993	Covington, Ga.
Leon, Carlos	.156	47	154	16	24	1	1	0	14	12	16	9	1	S	R	5-10	169	8-31-79	1997	Cabimas, Venez.
Lomasney, Steve	.270	55	189	35	51	10	0	8	28	26	57	5	2	R	R	6-0	185	8-29-77	1995	Peabody, Mass.
Malone, Nick	.156	15	32	3	5	2	0	0	2	4	5	0	0	R	R	6-0	174	3-9-73	1998	Cape Coral, Fla.
Marsh, Roy	.375	7	24	6	9	0	1	0	3	1	5	3	0	R	R	5-8	191	11-6-73	1994	Baltimore, Md.
Mashore, Justin	.163	17	49	6	8	3	0	2	4	5	13	1	0	R	R	5-9	190	2-14-72	1991	Concord, Calif.
McBride, Gator	.360	36	136	25	49	10	3	9	29	7	13	2	1	R	R	5-10	170	8-12-73	1993	Catlettsburg, Ky.
Olmeda, Jose	.269	53	160	20	43	12	1	3	20	6	39	1	3	S	R	6-1	155	7-7-77	1995	Fajardo, P.R.
Rodriguez, Luis	.289	31	114	19	33	8	0	3	14	8	17	5	1	R	R	5-9	160	1-3-74	1991	Tampa, Fla.
Rodriguez, Ronny	.250	4	12	4	3	1	0	0	0	2	0	0	0	R	R	6-0	172	1-7-81	1998	Maracaibo, Venez.
Sapp, Damian	.197	86	289	38	57	11	1	13	48	44	102	0	0	R	R	6-3	219	5-20-76	1994	Pleasant Grove, Utah
Uccello, Jeff	.281	10	32	4	9	4	0	0	2	3	6	0	0	R	R	6-0	205	6-16-74	1997	Newington, Conn.
Whitby, Cory	.200	3	5	0	1	0	0	0	2	1	0	0	0	L	R	5-8	180	1-27-76	1998	Richmond, Va.

GAMES BY POSITION: C—Alevras 1, Benham 16, S. Cheek 15, Epperson 10, Hatteberg 1, Lomasney 47, L. Rodriguez 27, R. Rodriguez 1, Sapp 29, Uccello 7, Whitby 3. **1B**—Benham 16, Burkhart 57, Epperson 9, Espinal 17, Jefferson 1, Key 10, Lomasney 2, L. Rodriguez 2, Sapp 30, Uccello 1. **2B**—DeLeon 53, Fuentes 15, Haas 1, Leon 47, Malone 4, Olmeda 24, R. Rodriguez 3. **3B**—DeLeon 4, Espinal 90, Fuentes 1, Olmeda 8. **SS**—Capista 128, DeLeon 4, Malone 5, Olmeda 1. **OF**—S. Cheek 1, Epperson 1, Fischer 92, Fuentes 1, Graham 120, Haas 46, Johnson 132, Key 14, Malone 1, Marsh 7, Mashore 12, McBride 17.

PITCHING	W	L	ERA	G	GS	CG	SV	IP	H	R	ER	BB	SO	B	T	HT	WT	DOB	1st Yr	Resides
Adams, Willie	1	1	1.98	2	2	0	0	14	14	5	3	1	6	R	R	6-7	225	10-8-72	1993	Scottsdale, Ariz.
Barkley, Brian	1	0	0.00	1	0	0	0	3	2	0	0	1	2	L	L	6-2	225	12-8-75	1994	Waco, Texas
Belovsky, Josh	6	2	2.36	48	0	0	20	53	42	15	14	23	53	R	R	6-2	225	4-8-74	1998	Orange, Calif.
Betancourt, Rafael	0	0	0.00	6	0	0	4	7	5	0	0	1	6	R	R	6-2	176	4-29-75	1994	Cumana, Venez.
Castro, Eleuterio	1	0	4.15	3	1	0	0	13	13	6	6	6	8	R	R	6-1	195	2-20-78	1998	El Seibo, D.R.
Cheek, Andrew	0	0	13.50	2	0	0	0	4	8	6	6	6	0	R	L	6-2	200	5-28-78	1999	West Jefferson, N.C.
Darrell, Tommy	4	10	4.99	30	12	1	3	101	118	75	56	30	67	R	R	6-6	220	7-21-76	1995	Dunbar, Pa.
Dougherty, Tony	0	1	3.00	4	0	0	3	3	1	1	1	2	7	R	R	6-2	200	4-12-73	1994	Beaver Falls, Pa.
Duchscherer, Justin	7	7	4.49	20	18	0	0	112	101	62	56	30	105	R	R	6-3	150	11-19-77	1996	Lubbock, Texas
Garrett, Josh	8	10	4.59	26	26	0	0	149	189	87	76	50	95	R	R	6-4	195	1-12-78	1997	Richland, Ind.
Lampley, Danny	10	8	4.55	25	25	2	0	140	152	85	71	54	108	L	L	6-2	205	11-1-75	1998	Rockingham, N.C.
Lyons, Jonathan	1	2	5.92	23	0	0	0	24	44	25	16	11	18	R	R	6-3	215	1-13-75	1997	Olive Branch, Miss.
Maroth, Mike	11	6	4.04	20	19	0	0	111	124	65	50	35	64	L	L	6-0	180	8-17-77	1998	Orlando, Fla.
Martinez, Jesus	1	0	5.23	16	2	0	0	33	36	20	19	17	20	L	L	6-2	190	3-13-74	1991	Santo Domingo, D.R.
Martinez, Ramon	1	0	3.00	3	0	0	0	12	11	7	4	7	9	S	R	6-4	184	3-22-68	1985	Santo Domingo, D.R.

PITCHING	W	L	ERA	G	GS	CG	SV	IP	H	R	ER	BB	SO	B	T	HT	WT	DOB	1st Yr	Resides
McLeary, Marty	1	0	12.08	8	0	0	0	13	29	20	17	7	11	R	R	6-5	220	10-26-74	1997	Mansfield, Ohio
McMullen, Jerry	1	3	2.85	41	0	0	2	47	47	21	15	19	56	L	L	6-2	190	10-13-73	1995	Redmond, Ore.
Partenheimer, Brian	1	0	1.80	17	0	0	2	30	26	8	6	3	28	R	L	6-5	230	4-13-75	1997	Birdseye, Ind.
Pena, Juan	0	1	7.11	2	2	0	0	6	12	6	5	0	5	R	R	6-5	211	6-27-77	1995	Miami, Fla.
Pineda, Isauro	2	1	5.23	11	8	0	0	52	56	32	30	24	32	R	R	6-0	168	11-10-78	1997	Mazatlan, Mexico
Reitsma, Chris	4	10	5.61	19	19	0	0	96	116	71	60	31	79	R	R	6-5	195	12-31-77	1996	Calgary, Alberta
Roller, Adam	0	0	16.88	1	0	0	0	3	5	5	5	2	2	R	R	6-2	205	6-27-78	1997	Lakeland, Fla.
Rose, Brian	1	0	6.14	5	0	0	1	7	10	5	5	5	9	R	R	6-1	190	10-7-72	1994	Potsdam, N.Y.
Spinelli, Mike	2	2	3.14	38	0	0	2	80	73	36	28	44	58	L	L	6-3	205	10-5-76	1996	Revere, Mass.
Taglienti, Jeff	1	1	3.00	14	0	0	3	30	26	12	10	12	27	R	R	6-0	208	11-13-75	1997	Walpole, Mass.
Thompson, Chris	2	5	5.61	28	2	0	1	43	48	33	27	22	41	R	R	6-2	202	9-29-72	1996	Elyria, Ohio

AUGUSTA — Class A

SOUTH ATLANTIC LEAGUE

BATTING	AVG	G	AB	R	H	2B	3B	HR	RBI	BB	SO	SB	CS	B	T	HT	WT	DOB	1st Yr	Resides
Ahumada, Alejandro ...	.259	125	455	72	118	24	4	10	57	41	107	9	7	R	R	6-1	171	1-20-79	1996	Culiacan, Mexico
Alevras, Chad	.294	5	17	2	5	1	0	0	3	2	6	0	0	R	R	6-1	195	1-8-75	1997	Littleton, Colo.
Benham, David	.000	3	9	0	0	0	0	0	0	0	7	0	0	R	R	6-2	190	10-12-75	1998	Garland, Texas
Brown, Tonayne	.261	135	541	82	141	24	7	4	45	46	89	25	22	R	L	5-11	190	8-24-77	1998	Tallahassee, Fla.
Cheek, Shawn	.375	5	16	3	6	2	0	0	2	0	1	0	0	R	R	6-3	215	4-30-74	1997	Albany, Ga.
DeRosso, Tony	.297	36	128	19	38	7	1	6	27	16	21	0	0	R	R	6-3	216	11-7-75	1994	Moultrie, Ga.
Fuentes, Javier	.254	39	130	16	33	4	1	1	13	22	13	6	1	R	R	6-1	185	9-27-74	1996	Austin, Texas
Hart, Keith	.262	86	336	29	88	14	2	5	50	12	72	2	0	R	R	6-0	220	2-4-76	1998	Baytown, Texas
James, Chris	.224	55	170	17	38	8	0	2	19	10	35	3	3	R	R	5-10	180	5-16-76	1998	Victorville, Calif.
Keaveney, Jeff	.205	23	78	10	16	3	0	4	18	10	31	0	0	R	R	6-5	240	10-7-75	1996	Framingham, Mass.
Kerrigan, Joe	.200	9	35	7	7	1	0	0	1	6	6	1	2	L	R	5-10	180	11-1-77	1999	Ardmore, Pa.
Key, Jeff	.212	78	255	32	54	9	3	4	27	29	61	11	1	L	R	6-1	210	11-22-74	1993	Covington, Ga.
Larned, Andrew	.258	34	93	8	24	4	0	1	13	12	18	1	1	R	R	6-0	195	11-13-75	1998	Mentor, Ohio
Leon, Carlos	.233	60	210	34	49	7	0	1	19	23	42	13	4	S	R	5-10	169	8-31-79	1997	Cabimas, Venez.
Mendoza, Angel	.263	119	429	58	113	7	8	7	46	34	97	19	8	R	R	6-2	165	11-30-78	1996	San Pedro de Macoris, D.R.
Oliver, Johnny	.208	33	120	9	25	4	0	0	7	10	36	1	0	R	R	6-2	180	5-14-78	1996	Dallas, Ba.
Pena, Jose	.226	49	168	23	38	8	1	5	24	10	50	1	2	R	R	6-1	175	2-10-80	1997	Bani, D.R.
Pena, Rodolfo	.238	99	320	35	76	15	1	3	37	16	79	1	1	R	R	6-0	180	3-7-79	1997	Montecristi, D.R.
Rodriguez, Carlos	.193	33	119	14	23	6	1	3	8	8	41	1	2	R	R	6-2	210	6-12-77	1998	Louisville, Ky.
Santos, Angel	.270	130	466	83	126	30	2	15	55	62	88	25	10	S	R	5-11	185	8-14-79	1997	Cayey, P.R.
Soriano, Jose	.345	38	148	28	51	7	5	5	28	10	37	12	5	R	R	6-0	165	4-20-74	1997	Bani, D.R.
Terni, Chaz	.179	36	123	10	22	3	4	1	10	9	36	1	1	R	R	5-10	175	10-1-78	1997	Uncasville, Conn.
Warren, Chris	.170	42	153	16	26	4	0	5	16	11	53	4	0	R	R	6-3	205	9-30-76	1998	Fayetteville, N.C.
Whitby, Cory	.214	35	70	12	15	4	0	1	5	18	20	2	1	L	R	5-8	180	1-27-76	1998	Richmond, Va.
Wiese, Brian	.118	23	68	7	8	2	0	0	2	10	18	1	0	R	R	5-11	511	8-15-76	1999	Grenwell Springs, La.

GAMES BY POSITION: C—Alevras 3, Benham 3, Cheek 5, Larned 32, R. Pena 96, Whitby 20. **1B**—Alevras 1, Benham 1, DeRosso 15, Hart 85, Keaveney 15, Key 27, R. Pena 2. **2B**—Fuentes 2, James 33, Kerrigan 4, Leon 59, Santos 48. **3B**—Ahumada 32, Fuentes 28, James 13, Kerrigan 1, Santos 34, Terni 36. **SS**—Ahumada 94, Fuentes 4, Santos 45. **OF**—Brown 126, Key 22, Mendoza 100, Oliver 22, J. Pena 40, Rodriguez 29, Soriano 37, Warren 31, Wiese 19.

PITCHING	W	L	ERA	G	GS	CG	SV	IP	H	R	ER	BB	SO	B	T	HT	WT	DOB	1st Yr	Resides
Cisar, Mark	3	6	2.24	52	0	0	27	68	57	22	17	22	64	R	R	5-11	185	5-22-75	1998	New Martinsville, W.Va.
Duchscherer, Justin	4	0	0.22	6	6	0	0	41	21	1	1	8	39	R	R	6-3	150	11-19-77	1998	Lubbock, Texas
Giese, Daniel	1	0	2.08	9	0	0	0	17	15	4	4	5	11	R	R	6-3	200	5-19-77	1999	San Clemente, Calif.
Glaser, Eric	1	0	0.00	1	1	0	0	5	2	0	0	1	7	R	R	6-2	208	1-23-78	1997	Fort Thomas, Ky.
Hancock, Josh	6	8	3.80	25	25	0	0	140	154	79	59	46	106	R	R	6-3	210	4-11-78	1998	Tupelo, Miss.
Hill, Terrance	3	6	2.73	53	0	0	1	92	77	30	28	25	95	L	L	5-10	170	10-17-75	1998	Thibodaux, La.
Lontayo, Alex	2	4	4.30	40	0	0	0	59	55	31	28	26	80	L	L	6-1	195	12-12-75	1999	Chula Vista, Calif.
Lyons, Jonathan	1	1	2.15	19	0	0	2	29	26	9	7	9	32	R	R	6-3	215	1-13-75	1997	Olive Branch, Miss.
Martinez, Anastacio	2	4	6.30	10	10	0	0	40	44	37	28	18	36	R	R	6-2	180	11-3-80	1998	Santo Domingo, D.R.
McLeary, Marty	5	6	3.12	35	9	0	3	81	73	34	28	25	90	R	R	6-5	220	10-26-74	1997	Mansfield, Ohio
Miller, Greg	10	6	3.10	25	25	1	0	137	109	54	47	56	146	L	L	6-5	215	9-30-79	1997	Aurora, Ill.
Mowel, Mike	5	13	4.90	21	21	0	0	101	131	68	55	40	76	R	R	6-0	190	7-16-79	1997	North Kingston, R.I.
Norton, Jason	9	6	2.32	30	17	2	0	136	106	50	35	28	150	R	R	6-3	205	4-9-76	1998	Mobile, Ala.
Phillips, Matt	2	5	4.76	39	1	0	1	74	85	55	39	23	69	R	R	6-1	210	5-22-75	1998	Seaford, Del.
Pineda, Isauro	2	1	3.38	8	8	0	0	43	51	24	16	15	36	R	R	6-0	168	11-10-78	1997	Mazatlan, Mexico
Solano, Alex	1	2	4.82	9	5	0	0	28	32	25	15	7	18	R	R	6-1	150	4-22-80	1997	La Romana, D.R.
Spencer, Corey	1	0	4.63	7	1	0	1	12	13	6	6	5	13	L	L	6-1	220	9-4-76	1998	Andover, Mass.
Surridge, Lance	9	5	3.05	37	10	0	0	106	102	52	36	38	88	L	R	6-4	200	7-17-76	1998	Burnsville, Minn.
Zallie, Chris	2	1	4.32	9	0	0	0	8	4	4	4	10	14	L	L	6-1	195	2-4-75	1998	Harleysville, Pa.

LOWELL — Short-Season Class A

NEW YORK-PENN LEAGUE

BATTING	AVG	G	AB	R	H	2B	3B	HR	RBI	BB	SO	SB	CS	B	T	HT	WT	DOB	1st Yr	Resides
Anderson, Jon	.266	35	124	20	33	5	0	0	11	13	10	7	4	S	R	5-9	150	10-17-76	1999	South Barrington, Ill.
Dwyer, Mike	.247	71	271	24	67	12	0	3	41	34	50	3	2	L	L	6-2	200	7-13-77	1999	Stony Point, N.Y.
Ford, Lew	.280	62	250	48	70	17	4	7	34	19	35	15	2	R	R	6-0	190	8-12-76	1999	Grand Prairie, Texas
Jarvais, Kregg	.193	36	109	13	21	6	1	0	6	8	31	3	0	R	R	6-2	215	12-25-76	1999	Skowhegan, Maine
Kerrigan, Joe	.314	63	242	38	76	6	3	0	19	43	52	5	6	L	R	5-10	180	11-1-77	1999	Ardmore, Pa.
Ledesma, Phil	.270	30	74	19	20	3	2	1	12	16	15	8	2	R	R	5-11	175	3-14-75	1998	Upland, Calif.
Malone, Nick	.250	6	16	3	4	2	0	0	1	1	5	1	0	R	R	6-0	174	3-9-73	1998	Cape Coral, Fla.
Miley, Perry	.245	46	147	19	36	6	1	2	19	18	29	9	3	R	R	6-3	195	8-31-75	1998	Mendenhall, Miss.
Minus, Steve	.249	66	237	32	59	13	2	5	26	39	67	6	1	R	R	6-2	210	12-30-76	1999	San Antonio, Texas
Riepe, Andrew	.310	31	100	16	31	12	0	1	15	6	14	0	0	R	R	6-1	200	3-26-77	1999	Danbury, Conn.
Rodriguez, Carlos	.250	60	228	37	57	13	5	12	46	13	66	17	3	R	R	6-2	210	6-12-77	1998	Louisville, Ky.
Saba, Cesar	.275	69	284	38	78	16	3	2	30	28	49	1	3	S	R	6-0	160	8-2-81	1998	San Cristobal, D.R.
Terni, Chaz	.202	38	119	10	24	6	1	0	7	10	35	1	2	R	R	5-10	175	10-1-78	1997	Uncasville, Conn.

BATTING	AVG	G	AB	R	H	2B	3B	HR	RBI	BB	SO	SB	CS	B	THT	WT	DOB	1st Yr	Resides
Waldron, Jeff	.176	39	125	17	22	3	1	1	13	14	22	0	1	L	R 6-1	205	10-4-76	1999	Lynn, Mass.
Warren, Chris	.223	56	215	29	48	13	3	5	25	12	69	3	2	R	R 6-3	205	9-30-76	1998	Fayetteville, N.C.
Wiese, Brian	.316	21	79	16	25	4	1	5	18	9	25	2	2	R	R 5-11	511	8-15-76	1999	Grenwell Springs, La.

GAMES BY POSITION: C—Jarvais 35, Riepe 30, Waldron 23. **1B**—Dwyer 68, Minus 12. **2B**—Anderson 26, Kerrigan 48, Terni 4. **3B**—Minus 50, Terni 29. **SS**—Anderson 2, Kerrigan 3, Malone 4, Saba 69. **OF**—Dwyer 2, Ford 55, Ledesma 23, Miley 40, Rodriguez 52, Waldron 1, Warren 46, Wiese 16.

PITCHING	W	L	ERA	G	GS	CG	SV	IP	H	R	ER	BB	SO	B	T	HT	WT	DOB	1st Yr	Resides
Bottenfield, Jason	1	2	5.70	23	0	0	0	36	36	29	23	17	24	R	R	6-1	195	6-4-77	1999	Flower Mound, Texas
Fossum, Casey	0	1	1.26	5	5	0	0	14	6	2	2	5	16	S	L	6-0	160	1-9-78	1999	Nashville, Tenn.
Gamble, Jerome	1	0	1.75	5	5	0	0	26	18	7	5	9	37	R	R	6-3	190	4-5-80	1998	Concord, Mass.
Garcia, Ramon	0	0	3.60	5	0	0	2	5	5	2	2	2	5	R	R	6-4	198	1-23-77	1997	Mazatlan, Mexico
Giese, Daniel	3	0	1.83	18	0	0	2	34	17	8	7	10	27	R	R	6-3	200	5-19-77	1999	San Clemente, Calif.
Glaser, Eric	4	5	3.43	14	14	0	0	79	65	37	30	26	82	R	R	6-6	208	1-23-78	1997	Fort Thomas, Ky.
Leach, Bryan	5	2	3.57	13	4	0	0	45	41	23	18	18	52	R	R	5-11	175	8-3-77	1999	Seminole, Fla.
Ledesma, Phil	0	0	8.10	3	0	0	0	3	6	3	3	3	5	R	R	5-11	175	3-14-75	1998	Upland, Calif.
Lee, Andy	2	1	3.51	26	1	0	0	49	52	22	19	16	58	L	L	6-0	200	8-25-74	1998	Bolton, Miss.
Martinez, Anastacio	0	3	3.68	11	11	0	0	51	61	36	21	18	43	R	R	6-2	180	11-3-80	1998	Santo Domingo, D.R.
Martinez, Ramon	0	0	0.00	1	1	0	0	2	0	0	0	3	1	S	R	6-4	184	3-22-68	1985	Santo Domingo, D.R.
McClain, Jeremy	3	6	5.40	16	7	0	0	52	59	41	31	17	53	R	R	6-3	190	5-27-76	1999	Houlka, Miss.
Norris, Shon	4	4	5.05	27	0	0	3	41	41	25	23	13	29	R	R	6-2	185	6-29-77	1998	Pittsburgh, Pa.
Riccobono, Rick	4	6	5.24	15	14	0	0	77	93	63	45	30	54	R	R	6-3	230	1-3-80	1998	Commack, N.Y.
Roller, Adam	4	5	2.54	23	0	0	2	39	30	16	11	29	41	R	R	6-3	205	6-27-78	1997	Lakeland, Fla.
Rupp, Mike	1	5	5.81	18	8	0	0	57	72	46	37	33	48	R	R	6-5	170	2-21-78	1997	Spring Valley, Calif.
Solano, Alex	1	2	5.61	6	6	0	0	34	40	23	21	7	26	R	R	6-1	150	4-22-80	1997	La Romana, D.R.
Spencer, Corey	1	0	2.48	19	0	0	1	29	33	12	8	7	38	L	L	6-1	220	9-4-76	1999	Andover, Mass.

FORT MYERS — Rookie

GULF COAST LEAGUE

BATTING	AVG	G	AB	R	H	2B	3B	HR	RBI	BB	SO	SB	CS	B	T	HT	WT	DOB	1st Yr	Resides
Anderson, Jon	.182	3	11	1	2	1	0	0	1	1	3	0	1	S	R	5-9	150	10-17-76	1999	South Barrington, Ill.
Barnowski, Bryan	.227	32	88	13	20	5	1	0	4	10	23	3	1	R	R	6-2	205	9-3-80	1999	Granville, Mass.
Borjas, Henry	.191	49	152	18	29	5	3	0	11	16	26	3	4	S	R	6-0	193	6-5-79	1997	Barquisimeto, Venez.
Caridi, Tony	.167	25	72	9	12	2	0	0	3	9	19	1	0	S	R	6-3	175	10-26-79	1998	Spring, Texas
De los Santos, Hector	.243	56	218	36	53	8	0	3	21	15	38	11	8	R	R	6-3	216	1-19-80	1997	San Pedro de Macoris, D.R.
DeRosso, Tony	.278	5	18	3	5	3	0	1	7	2	2	0	1	R	R	6-3	216	11-7-75	1994	Moultrie, Ga.
Frye, Jeff	.400	6	20	4	8	1	0	0	1	2	2	0	0	R	R	5-9	165	8-31-66	1988	Arlington, Texas
Guerrero, James	.196	22	46	3	9	1	0	0	4	7	20	0	1	R	R	6-3	170	1-6-82	1999	Santo Domingo, D.R.
Guerrero, Julio	.207	32	116	17	24	1	1	0	11	10	18	8	5	R	R	6-3	170	10-18-80	1998	Bani, D.R.
Hatteberg, Scott	.400	6	15	4	6	2	0	1	6	7	1	0	0	L	R	6-1	195	12-14-69	1991	Tacoma, Wash.
Hattig, John	.270	50	163	28	44	7	3	1	17	16	20	1	1	S	R	6-1	205	2-27-80	1999	Piti, Guam
Kanaya, Takeshi	.313	14	32	6	10	1	0	1	9	3	4	1	0	R	R	6-1	220	7-30-78	1999	Nagano, Japan
Kawabata, Kenichiro	.297	46	145	35	43	4	4	1	15	31	34	15	4	S	L	6-2	170	5-8-79	1997	Kadoma, Japan
Lopez, Youanny	.243	51	181	18	44	10	2	3	26	21	41	3	5	R	R	6-0	170	6-16-80	1997	Santiago, D.R.
Malone, Nick	.120	12	25	4	3	2	0	0	1	3	8	2	1	R	R	6-0	174	3-9-73	1998	Cape Coral, Fla.
Marbury, Ben	.170	20	53	5	9	3	0	1	6	4	20	1	1	R	R	6-0	180	5-31-79	1999	Rockford, Ala.
Martinez, Edgar	.239	33	113	12	27	3	0	1	20	9	13	1	2	R	R	6-0	160	10-23-81	1998	Guigue, Venez.
Pena, Jose	.375	12	32	9	12	1	0	1	7	2	7	2	1	R	R	6-1	175	2-10-80	1997	Bani, D.R.
Rodriguez, Ronny	.247	54	170	19	42	5	1	1	13	14	32	7	2	R	R	6-0	172	1-7-81	1998	Maracaibo, Venez.
Sadler, Donnie	.385	4	13	2	5	2	0	0	1	2	1	0	0	R	R	5-6	165	6-17-75	1994	Valley Mills, Texas
Santoro, Patrick	.174	8	23	2	4	1	0	1	3	2	6	0	1	R	R	6-0	175	11-9-78	1998	River Forest, Ill.
Seiber, Antron	.261	13	46	6	12	0	2	0	10	4	11	2	2	R	R	6-1	180	5-19-80	1999	Independence, La.
Stenson, Dernell	.217	6	23	2	5	0	0	2	7	3	5	0	0	L	L	6-1	230	6-17-78	1996	La Grange, Ga.
Tyson, Torre	.105	10	19	4	2	0	0	0	3	4	2	1	1	S	R	5-10	185	12-31-75	1998	St. Louis, Mo.
Williams, Brady	.256	39	121	19	31	4	2	5	25	29	45	3	3	R	R	6-1	180	10-18-79	1999	Dunedin, Fla.

GAMES BY POSITION: C—Barnowski 25, Caridi 10, Hatteberg 13, Kanaya 8, E. Martinez 26. **1B**—Borjas 33, Caridi 15, DeRosso 1, Ja. Guerrero 17, Ju. Guerrero 1, Stenson 2. **2B**—Anderson 3, Borjas 4, de los Santos 13, Frye 5, Malone 2, Rodriguez 31, Santoro 7, Tyson 7. **3B**—Borjas 2, DeRosso 4, Hattig 38, Malone 3, Rodriguez 1, Williams 22. **SS**—Borjas 15, de los Santos 24, Ja. Guerrero 1, Malone 4, Rodriguez 22, Sadler 4, Tyson 1, Williams 2. **OF**—Borjas 1, Caridi 2, de los Santos 25, Ja. Guerrero 1, Ju. Guerrero 30, Kawabata 46, Lopez 47, Marbury 19, Jo. Pena 10, Seiber 13, Williams 3.

PITCHING	W	L	ERA	G	GS	CG	SV	IP	H	R	ER	BB	SO	B	T	HT	WT	DOB	1st Yr	Resides
Baker, Brad	1	0	0.79	4	3	0	0	11	10	3	1	2	8	R	R	6-2	180	11-6-80	1999	Stuart, Fla.
Benitez, Fabricio	4	4	3.28	13	8	0	1	58	55	34	21	14	40	R	R	6-3	175	5-10-81	1997	Santo Domingo, D.R.
Castro, Eleuterio	0	1	3.60	6	0	0	0	15	15	7	6	4	8	R	R	6-1	195	2-20-78	1999	El Seibo, D.R.
Cheek, Andrew	2	1	3.41	18	0	0	2	29	27	16	11	17	20	R	L	6-2	200	5-28-78	1999	West Jefferson, N.C.
Curtice, John	0	5	7.36	8	6	0	0	15	16	22	12	12	19	L	L	6-2	210	11-1-79	1997	Chesapeake, Va.
Francisco, Franklin	2	4	4.56	12	7	0	0	53	58	39	27	35	48	R	R	6-2	179	6-11-80	1997	Santo Domingo, D.R.
Garcia, Ramon	2	0	2.96	21	0	0	5	24	24	10	8	15	26	R	R	6-4	198	1-23-79	1997	Mazatlan, Mexico
Leach, B.J.	0	0	0.00	1	0	0	0	2	2	1	0	1	1	R	R	5-11	175	8-3-77	1999	Seminole, Fla.
Ledezma, Wilfredo	5	1	3.30	13	6	0	1	57	51	28	21	20	52	L	L	6-3	152	1-21-81	1998	Maracay, Venez.
Linarelli, Tom	0	0	13.50	1	1	0	0	1	2	3	2	2	1	R	R	6-3	210	11-11-76	1998	Kirkland, Wash.
Martinez, Ramon	1	0	1.38	4	4	0	0	13	9	4	2	3	15	S	R	6-4	184	3-22-68	1985	Santo Domingo, D.R.
Miniel, Rene	1	2	4.06	21	0	0	1	38	40	28	17	16	37	R	R	6-2	175	4-26-81	1998	Santo Domingo, D.R.
Pena, Juan	0	0	0.00	1	1	0	0	2	0	0	0	0	4	R	R	6-5	211	6-27-77	1995	Miami, Fla.
Rundles, Richard	1	0	2.13	5	1	0	0	13	13	3	3	1	11	L	L	6-3	170	6-3-81	1999	New Market, Tenn.
Seo, Jung Min	3	2	2.81	13	0	0	1	32	29	14	10	10	26	R	R	6-3	218	6-8-74	1999	Pusan, Korea
Solano, Alex	1	3	2.39	5	5	0	0	26	30	12	7	7	15	R	R	6-1	150	4-22-80	1997	La Romana, D.R.
Song, Seung	5	5	2.30	13	9	0	0	55	47	29	14	20	61	R	R	6-1	192	6-29-80	1999	Pusan, Korea
Tankersley, Dennis	1	0	0.76	11	6	0	1	36	14	7	3	9	57	R	R	6-2	185	2-24-79	1999	St. Charles, Mo.
Thompson, Mat	0	0	1.20	5	2	0	0	15	7	3	2	4	12	R	R	6-2	210	8-28-81	1999	Boise, Idaho
Vail, Garet	1	1	3.21	7	0	0	0	14	15	10	5	6	13	R	R	6-1	180	9-28-76	1998	Big Flats, N.Y.
Wasdin, John	0	0	0.00	1	1	0	0	2	1	0	0	0	4	R	R	6-2	195	8-5-72	1993	Jacksonville, Fla.

CHICAGO WHITE SOX

Manuel's troops exceed expectations in rebuilding season

BY PHIL ROGERS

Jerry Manuel didn't believe things could get tougher than his first season on the job. Then he watched as White Sox owner Jerry Reinsdorf allowed both slugger Albert Belle and the team's only leader, Robin Ventura, to continue the exodus that began with the controversial White Flag trade in 1997.

Now Manuel knows adversity. It was a tribute both to the talent in the White Sox farm system and the quagmire that is the American League Central that Manuel was able to produce a fourth consecutive second-place season in 1999.

"When you consider everything we lost, we could have lost 100," general manager Ron Schueler said. "We did exceed my expectations, but we have to add players to get better."

The White Sox saw their victory total drop below 80 for the first time in a non-strike season since 1989. They were above .500 as late as July 9 before finishing 75-86.

"I'm not satisfied with 75 wins," Manuel said. "It's nothing to hang your hat on. But when you consider that we subtracted Robin and Albert and went much younger, you can say we did a good job."

Manuel opened the season with the league's youngest team and finished it with second baseman Ray Durham and catcher Brook Fordyce as the only three-year veterans in the lineup. The highlight was the continued development of right fielder Magglio Ordonez and the emergence of rookie outfielders Chris Singleton and Carlos Lee.

Frank Thomas was expected to provide direction for his younger teammates, but he couldn't deliver on his vow to return to his pre-1998 form. He finished the season as a full-fledged enigma, clashing with Manuel

Magglio Ordonez   **Kip Wells**

Players of the Year

MAJOR LEAGUE: Magglio Ordonez, of
Ordonez hit .301 and led the White Sox with 30 home runs and 117 RBIs in his second full major league season.

MINOR LEAGUE: Kip Wells, rhp
Wells struck out 139 and led all White Sox minor leaguers with a 3.29 ERA in his first professional season.

about his willingness to play injured before having season-ending surgery to remove a bone spur from his ankle in September. He hit .305 with 15 homers.

Ordonez became the team's most reliable run producer and was the lone White Sox all-star. Singleton, acquired from the Yankees in a minor league trade the previous winter, barely won a roster spot in spring training but became the regular center fielder and hit .300-17-72 with 20 stolen bases. Lee moved from third base to left field and stepped in as a regular when Jeff Abbott slumped in April. Lee finished the season hitting .293-16-84.

The young pitching staff continued to develop. Third-year righthander Keith Foulke dominated in middle relief, striking out 123 in 105 innings while walking just 21. Rookie righthanders Pat Daneker, Aaron Myette and 1998 first-round pick Kip Wells made cameo starts as the White Sox prepared for spirited competition in the spring of 2000.

Myette's September promotion was delayed by Charlotte's trip to the Triple-A World Series in Las Vegas. Manager Tom Spencer won the International League with a nucleus built around minor league veterans such as Chad Mottola and Luis Raven.

Righthander Jon Garland, a 19-year-old acquired from the Cubs in a 1998 trade for Matt Karchner, started the year at Class A Winston-Salem and ended it by turning in the best pitching performance in Las Vegas. But Charlotte lost the series to Vancouver in five games.

First baseman Eric Battersby led Class A Burlington to a Midwest League championship. Battersby hit four home runs in the deciding game of the semifinal series over Kane County.

ORGANIZATION LEADERS

BATTING

*AVG	Mario Valenzuela, Burlington	.323
R	Luis Raven, Charlotte	97
H	Chad Mottola, Charlotte	164
TB	Luis Raven, Charlotte	289
2B	Aaron Rowand, Winston-Salem	37
3B	Terrell Merriman, Burlington	9
HR	Luis Raven, Charlotte	33
RBI	Luis Raven, Charlotte	125
BB	Ryan Hankins, Burlington	91
SO	Jason Dellaero, Birmingham/Win.-Salem	135
SB	Chad Durham, Burlington/Bristol	59

PITCHING

W	Two tied at	13
L	Three tied at	12
#ERA	Kip Wells, Birmingham/Winston-Salem	3.29
G	Todd Rizzo, Charlotte	53
CG	Carlos Castillo, Charlotte	5
SV	Brannon Whatley, Burlington	20
IP	Juan Figueroa, Winston-Salem/Burlington	172
BB	Dwayne Jacobs, Winston-Salem	79
SO	Juan Figueroa, Winston-Salem/Burlington	189

*Minimum 250 At-Bats #Minimum 75 Innings

Chicago
WHITE SOX

Organization Statistics

Manager: Jerry Manuel   **1999 Record:** 75-86, .466 (2nd, AL Central)

BATTING	AVG	G	AB	R	H	2B	3B	HR	RBI	BB	SO	SB	CS	B	T	HT	WT	DOB	1st Yr	Resides
Abbott, Jeff	.158	17	57	5	9	0	0	2	6	5	12	1	1	R	L	6-2	200	8-17-72	1994	Dunwoody, Ga.
Caruso, Mike	.250	136	529	60	132	11	4	2	35	20	36	12	14	L	R	6-1	172	5-27-77	1996	Coral Springs, Fla.
Christensen, McKay	.226	28	53	10	12	1	0	1	6	4	7	2	1	L	L	5-11	180	8-14-75	1995	Clovis, Calif.
Dellaero, Jason	.091	11	33	1	3	0	0	0	2	1	13	0	0	S	R	6-2	195	12-17-76	1997	Brewster, N.Y.
Durham, Ray	.296	153	612	109	181	30	8	13	60	73	105	34	11	S	R	5-8	180	11-30-71	1990	Charlotte, N.C.
Fordyce, Brook	.297	105	333	36	99	25	1	9	49	21	48	2	0	R	R	6-1	185	5-7-70	1989	Jensen Beach, Fla.
Jackson, Darrin	.275	73	149	22	41	9	1	4	16	3	20	4	1	R	R	6-0	198	8-22-63	1981	Mesa, Ariz.
Johnson, Mark	.227	73	207	27	47	11	0	4	16	36	58	3	1	L	R	6-0	185	9-12-75	1994	Warner Robins, Ga.
Konerko, Paul	.294	142	513	71	151	31	4	24	81	45	68	1	0	R	R	6-3	211	3-5-76	1994	Scottsdale, Ariz.
Lee, Carlos	.293	127	492	66	144	32	2	16	84	13	72	4	2	R	R	6-2	202	6-20-76	1994	Aguadulce, Panama
Liefer, Jeff	.248	45	113	8	28	7	1	0	14	8	28	2	0	L	R	6-3	195	8-17-74	1996	Upland, Calif.
Norton, Greg	.255	132	436	62	111	26	0	16	50	69	93	4	4	S	R	6-1	205	7-6-72	1993	Norman, Okla.
Ordonez, Magglio	.301	157	624	100	188	34	3	30	117	47	64	13	6	R	R	6-0	200	1-28-74	1991	Coro Falcon, Venez.
Paul, Josh	.222	6	18	2	4	1	0	0	1	0	4	0	0	R	R	6-1	185	5-19-75	1996	Buffalo Grove, Ill.
Rodriguez, Liu	.237	39	93	8	22	2	2	1	12	12	11	0	0	S	R	5-9	170	11-5-76	1995	Caracas, Venez.
Simmons, Brian	.230	54	126	14	29	3	3	4	17	9	30	4	0	S	R	6-2	190	9-4-73	1995	McMurray, Pa.
Singleton, Chris	.300	133	496	72	149	31	6	17	72	22	45	20	5	L	L	6-2	195	8-15-72	1993	Mesa, Ariz.
Thomas, Frank	.305	135	486	74	148	36	0	15	77	87	66	3	3	R	R	6-5	270	5-27-68	1989	Oak Brook, Ill.
Wilson, Craig	.238	98	252	28	60	8	1	4	26	23	22	1	1	R	R	6-0	185	9-3-70	1992	Phoenix, Ariz.

PITCHING	W	L	ERA	G	GS	CG	SV	IP	H	R	ER	BB	SO	B	T	HT	WT	DOB	1st Yr	Resides
Baldwin, James	12	13	5.10	35	33	1	0	199	219	119	113	81	123	R	R	6-3	235	7-15-71	1990	Southern Pines, N.C.
Bradford, Chad	0	0	19.64	3	0	0	0	4	9	8	8	5	0	R	R	6-5	205	9-14-74	1996	Jackson, Miss.
Castillo, Carlos	2	2	5.71	18	2	0	0	41	45	26	26	14	23	R	R	6-2	250	4-21-75	1994	Miami, Fla.
Daneker, Pat	0	0	4.20	3	2	0	0	15	14	8	7	6	5	R	R	6-3	195	1-14-76	1997	Williamsport, Pa.
Davenport, Joe	0	0	0.00	3	0	0	0	2	1	0	0	2	0	R	R	6-5	225	3-24-76	1994	Santee, Calif.
Eyre, Scott	1	1	7.56	21	0	0	0	25	38	22	21	15	17	L	L	6-1	200	5-30-72	1991	West Valley, Utah
Foulke, Keith	3	3	2.22	67	0	0	9	105	72	28	26	21	123	R	R	6-0	200	10-19-72	1994	Huffman, Texas
Howry, Bobby	5	3	3.59	69	0	0	28	68	58	34	27	38	80	L	R	6-5	220	8-4-73	1994	Glendale, Ariz.
Lowe, Sean	4	1	3.67	64	0	0	0	96	90	39	39	46	62	R	R	6-2	205	3-29-71	1992	Mesquite, Texas
Lundquist, David	1	1	8.59	17	0	0	0	22	28	21	21	12	18	R	R	6-2	200	6-4-73	1993	Carson City, Nev.
Myette, Aaron	0	2	6.32	4	3	0	0	16	17	11	11	14	11	R	R	6-4	195	9-26-77	1997	Gig Harbor, Wash.
Navarro, Jaime	8	13	6.09	32	27	0	0	160	206	126	108	71	74	R	R	6-4	250	3-27-68	1986	Milwaukee, Wis.
Parque, Jim	9	15	5.13	31	30	1	0	174	210	111	99	79	111	L	L	5-11	165	2-8-75	1997	La Crescenta, Calif.
Pena, Jesus	0	0	5.31	26	0	0	0	20	21	15	12	23	20	L	L	6-0	170	3-8-75	1993	Santo Domingo, D.R.
Rizzo, Todd	0	2	6.75	3	0	0	0	4	2	1	3	2	2	R	L	6-2	220	5-24-71	1992	Conshohocken, Pa.
Simas, Bill	6	3	3.75	70	0	0	2	72	73	36	30	32	41	R	R	6-3	235	11-28-71	1992	Fresno, Calif.
Sirotka, Mike	11	13	4.00	32	32	3	0	209	236	108	93	57	125	L	L	6-1	200	5-13-71	1993	Houston, Texas
Snyder, John	9	12	6.68	25	25	1	0	129	167	103	96	49	57	R	R	6-3	200	8-16-74	1992	Joliet, Ill.
Sturtze, Tanyon	0	0	0.00	1	1	0	0	6	4	0	0	2	2	R	R	6-5	205	10-12-70	1990	Irving, Texas
Ward, Bryan	0	1	7.55	40	0	0	0	39	63	36	33	11	35	L	L	6-2	205	1-25-72	1993	Mount Holly, N.J.
Wells, Kip	4	1	4.04	7	7	0	0	36	33	17	16	15	29	R	R	6-3	196	4-21-77	1999	Missouri City, Texas

FIELDING

Catcher	PCT	G	PO	A	E	DP	PB
Fordyce	.987	103	561	30	8	5	4
Johnson	.993	72	413	33	3	6	10
Paul	1.000	6	40	2	0	0	0
Simmons	.000	1	0	0	0	0	0

First Base	PCT	G	PO	A	E	DP
Konerko	.995	92	740	58	4	72
Lee	.966	5	24	4	1	3
Liefer	1.000	15	96	11	0	11
Norton	.972	26	67	3	2	9
Thomas	.990	49	385	18	4	40
Wilson	1.000	1	4	0	0	0

Second Base	PCT	G	PO	A	E	DP
Durham	.974	148	305	412	19	100
Rodriguez	.985	22	25	41	1	6
Wilson	.938	7	6	9	1	1

Third Base	PCT	G	PO	A	E	DP
Konerko	.000	1	0	0	0	0

	PCT	G	PO	A	E	DP
Norton	.922	120	93	201	25	17
Rodriguez	.000	1	0	0	0	0
Wilson	.969	72	47	108	5	10

Shortstop	PCT	G	PO	A	E	DP
Caruso	.957	132	183	348	24	86
Dellaero	.917	11	16	28	4	5
Rodriguez	.958	14	20	26	2	6
Wilson	.985	22	29	38	1	8

Outfield	PCT	G	PO	A	E	DP
Abbott	.962	17	25	0	1	0
Christensen	.943	27	50	0	3	0
Jackson	.972	64	103	2	3	0
Lee	.981	105	201	3	4	0
Liefer	1.000	17	28	1	0	1
Ordonez	.991	153	332	12	3	4
Simmons	.976	46	79	2	2	1
Singleton	.990	127	375	9	4	3

MEL BAILEY

Bobby Howry

Paul Konerko
Hit .294-24-81 in first season in Chicago

Aaron Myette
Won 12 games for Birmingham

FRANK RAGSDALE

LARRY GOREN

FARM SYSTEM

Vice President, Player Development: Ken Williams

Class	Farm Team	League	W	L	Pct.	Finish*	Manager(s)	First Yr
AAA	Charlotte (N.C.) Knights	International	82	62	.569	+3rd (16)	Tom Spencer	1999
AA	Birmingham (Ala.) Barons	Southern	73	67	.521	4th (10)	Chris Cron	1986
A#	Winston-Salem (N.C.) Warthogs	Carolina	63	75	.457	7th (8)	Jerry Terrell	1997
A	Burlington (Iowa) Bees	Midwest	71	68	.511	+7th (14)	Nick Capra	1999
Rookie#	Bristol (Va.) Sox	Appalachian	45	24	.652	2nd (10)	Gary Pellant	1995
Rookie	Tucson (Ariz.) White Sox	Arizona	23	33	.411	7th (8)	Jerry Hairston	1998

*Finish in overall standings (No. of teams in league)   #Advanced level   +Won league championship

CHARLOTTE   Class AAA

INTERNATIONAL LEAGUE

BATTING	AVG	G	AB	R	H	2B	3B	HR	RBI	BB	SO	SB	CS	B	T	HT	WT	DOB	1st Yr	Resides
Abbott, Jeff	.318	67	277	42	88	24	1	9	37	16	27	2	3	R	L	6-2	200	8-17-72	1994	Dunwoody, Ga.
Beamon, Trey	.259	18	54	11	14	5	0	1	6	3	10	4	0	L	R	6-3	192	2-11-74	1992	Garland, Texas
Beltre, Esteban	.256	38	121	27	31	8	0	2	17	7	16	4	0	R	R	5-10	180	12-26-67	1984	San Pedro de Macoris, D.R.
2-team (92 Rochester)	.262	130	435	72	114	27	3	3	40	30	80	9	3							
Brito, Tilson	.318	111	406	60	129	30	5	11	58	34	66	6	4	R	R	6-0	180	5-28-72	1990	Santo Domingo, D.R.
Christensen, McKay	.250	1	4	0	1	0	0	0	0	0	0	1	0	L	L	5-11	180	8-14-75	1995	Clovis, Calif.
Christopherson, Eric	.314	63	188	36	59	17	0	3	27	30	39	4	0	R	R	6-1	190	4-25-69	1990	Westminster, Calif.
Eddie, Steve	.252	33	119	14	30	4	0	2	12	7	19	0	0	R	R	6-1	190	1-6-71	1993	Storm Lake, Iowa
2-team (10 Indy)	.273	43	143	17	39	6	0	2	15	8	20	0	0							
Gonzalez, Jose	.286	9	14	3	4	1	0	0	1	0	3	1	0	R	R	5-10	170	9-24-77	1996	Anzoategui, Venez.
Gonzalez, Manny	.310	48	129	14	40	6	1	1	25	5	20	1	4	S	R	6-2	190	5-5-76	1994	Santo Domingo, D.R.
Hollins, Dave	.317	63	199	49	63	18	0	8	33	33	37	5	1	S	R	6-1	232	5-25-66	1987	Orchard Park, N.Y.
2-team (4 Syracuse)	.308	67	214	51	66	19	0	8	34	34	42	5	1.							
Inglin, Jeff	.205	14	39	8	8	0	0	3	8	4	9	0	1	R	R	5-11	185	10-8-75	1996	Petaluma, Calif.
Lee, Carlos	.351	25	94	16	33	5	0	4	20	8	14	2	1	R	R	6-2	202	6-20-76	1994	Aguadulce, Panama
Liefer, Jeff	.339	46	171	36	58	17	1	9	34	21	26	2	1	L	R	6-3	195	8-17-74	1996	Upland, Calif.
Lydy, Scott	.212	19	66	11	14	2	0	2	13	8	15	1	0	R	R	6-5	195	10-28-68	1989	Chandler, Ariz.
Machado, Robert	.204	16	54	4	11	3	0	2	7	4	13	0	0	R	R	6-1	205	6-3-73	1989	Caracas, Venez.
Magdaleno, Ricky	.235	27	81	7	19	5	1	0	7	7	20	0	1	R	R	6-0	185	7-6-74	1993	Baldwin Park, Calif.
Martinez, Gabby	.286	16	49	8	14	1	0	4	5	6	3	3	3	R	R	6-2	170	1-7-74	1992	Santurce, P.R.
Moore, Brandon	.284	90	299	44	85	21	2	1	41	21	41	3	2	R	R	5-11	175	8-23-72	1994	Springville, Ala.
Mottola, Chad	.321	140	511	95	164	32	4	20	94	60	83	18	6	R	R	6-3	220	10-15-71	1992	Fort Lauderdale, Fla.
Ramirez, Dan	.143	6	14	2	2	1	0	0	2	1	3	1	0	R	R	6-0	180	2-22-74	1992	San Pedro de Macoris, D.R.
Raven, Luis	.282	139	532	97	150	32	4	33	125	50	127	5	0	R	R	6-4	230	11-19-68	1989	La Guaira, Venez.
Simmons, Brian	.270	78	285	53	77	14	0	10	44	37	60	8	2	S	R	6-2	190	9-4-73	1995	McMurray, Pa.
Simons, Mitch	.289	119	474	65	137	32	1	7	52	45	67	22	6	R	R	5-9	172	12-13-68	1991	Midwest City, Okla.
Toth, Dave	.245	79	261	36	64	14	0	6	33	24	38	1	2	R	R	6-2	208	12-8-69	1990	Macon, Ga.
Valdez, Mario	.274	121	402	78	110	17	2	26	76	76	91	1	0	L	R	6-2	190	11-19-74	1994	Hialeah, Fla.

PITCHING	W	L	ERA	G	GS	CG	SV	IP	H	R	ER	BB	SO	B	T	HT	WT	DOB	1st Yr	Resides
Andujar, Luis	4	5	3.00	52	0	0	16	60	62	21	20	13	59	R	R	6-2	215	11-22-72	1991	Sarasota, Fla.
Beirne, Kevin	5	5	5.42	20	20	0	0	113	134	75	68	36	63	L	R	6-4	210	1-1-74	1995	The Woodlands, Texas
Bradford, Chad	9	3	1.94	47	0	0	5	74	63	19	16	15	56	R	R	6-5	205	9-14-74	1996	Jackson, Miss.
Castillo, Carlos	9	6	5.15	20	20	0	0	136	150	88	78	30	105	R	R	6-2	250	4-21-75	1994	Miami, Fla.
Daneker, Pat	4	4	6.57	9	9	1	0	49	64	36	36	16	36	R	R	6-3	195	1-14-76	1997	Williamsport, Pa.
Davenport, Joe	0	0	8.00	6	0	0	0	9	13	8	8	1	6	R	R	6-5	225	3-24-76	1994	Santee, Calif.
Eyre, Scott	6	4	3.82	12	11	0	0	68	75	32	29	23	63	L	L	6-1	205	5-30-72	1991	West Valley, Utah
Fordham, Tom	4	7	7.31	29	21	0	0	112	144	101	91	66	101	L	L	6-2	205	2-20-74	1993	El Cajon, Calif.
Hasselhoff, Derek	6	6	4.82	49	0	0	4	71	83	46	38	25	65	R	R	6-2	185	10-10-73	1995	Pasadena, Md.
Heathcott, Mike	10	8	5.17	32	21	1	0	139	177	89	80	64	77	R	R	6-3	180	5-16-69	1991	Chicago, Ill.
Lundquist, David	0	0	0.00	3	0	0	0	4	3	0	0	1	4	R	R	6-2	200	6-4-73	1993	Carson City, Nev.
Olsen, Jason	2	4	7.11	22	10	0	0	62	84	59	49	29	49	R	R	6-4	210	3-16-75	1995	Fairfield, Calif.
Rizzo, Todd	4	5	4.06	53	0	0	8	71	68	37	32	31	46	R	L	6-0	195	5-24-71	1992	Conshohocken, Pa.
Secoda, Jason	2	5	5.28	7	7	3	0	44	54	35	26	10	33	R	R	6-1	195	9-2-74	1995	Fullerton, Calif.
Snyder, John	3	0	4.24	3	3	0	0	17	17	9	8	3	15	R	R	6-3	200	8-16-74	1992	Joliet, Ill.
Sturtze, Tanyon	9	4	4.05	33	14	2	3	104	83	53	47	41	107	R	R	6-5	205	10-12-70	1990	Irving, Texas
VanRyn, Ben	3	2	5.93	47	8	0	5	68	83	47	45	30	54	L	L	6-5	195	8-19-71	1990	San Antonio, Texas
Virchis, Adam	0	0	1.42	3	0	0	0	6	6	1	1	1	4	R	R	6-3	185	10-15-73	1995	Chula Vista, Calif.
Ward, Bryan	2	0	3.52	14	0	0	1	15	15	7	6	3	15	L	L	6-2	205	1-25-72	1993	Mount Holly, N.J.

FIELDING

Catcher	PCT	G	PO	A	E	DP	PB
Christopherson	.986	62	396	27	6	3	5
Machado	.976	16	111	12	3	1	0
Toth	.987	75	475	55	7	4	6

First Base	PCT	G	PO	A	E	DP
Eddie	1.000	3	25	0	0	4
Hollins	.985	9	62	3	1	7
Lee	1.000	4	33	2	0	4
Liefer	.991	29	207	20	2	15
Lydy	.938	3	12	3	1	1
Magdaleno	1.000	1	2	0	0	0
Raven	.980	14	93	5	2	8
Valdez	.991	99	732	54	7	65

Second Base	PCT	G	PO	A	E	DP
Brito	.965	95	183	255	16	53
J. Gonzalez	1.000	6	6	12	0	0
Magdaleno	1.000	1	0	0	0	0
Moore	1.000	3	6	6	0	2
Simons	.990	49	92	116	2	28

	PCT	G	PO	A	E	DP
Brito	1.000	5	3	9	0	1
Eddie	.942	29	20	45	4	4
J. Gonzalez	.000	3	0	0	0	0
M. Gonzalez	.000	1	0	0	0	0
Hollins	.904	49	30	55	9	2
Lee	.882	13	10	20	4	1

Third Base	PCT	G	PO	A	E	DP
Liefer	.000	1	0	0	0	0
Magdaleno	1.000	2	0	2	0	1
Moore	.973	21	10	26	1	1
Raven	.889	5	1	7	1	0
Simons	.960	46	27	68	4	2

Shortstop	PCT	G	PO	A	E	DP
Beltre	.963	38	45	113	6	19
Brito	1.000	1	1	3	0	0
Eddie	.750	4	3	6	3	3
Magdaleno	.943	23	32	50	5	14
Martinez	.946	16	18	35	3	5

	PCT	G	PO	A	E	DP
Moore	.946	67	87	191	16	44

Outfield	PCT	G	PO	A	E	DP
Simons	.824	8	5	9	3	0
Abbott	.979	67	136	4	3	1
Beamon	1.000	11	16	0	0	0
Brito	1.000	10	24	0	0	0
Christensen	1.000	1	2	0	0	0
M. Gonzalez	.987	41	71	6	1	0
Inglin	1.000	12	7	0	0	0
Lee	1.000	9	13	0	0	0
Liefer	.958	25	19	4	1	0
Lydy	1.000	17	31	1	0	0
Moore	1.000	4	6	0	0	0
Mottola	.981	138	288	17	6	4
Ramirez	1.000	6	15	0	0	0
Simmons	.973	78	171	6	5	1
Simons	.977	25	41	2	1	0
Toth	1.000	3	1	0	0	0
Valdez	1.000	22	30	0	0	0

BIRMINGHAM — Class AA

SOUTHERN LEAGUE

BATTING	AVG	G	AB	R	H	2B	3B	HR	RBI	BB	SO	SB	CS	B	T	HT	WT	DOB	1st Yr	Resides
Aude, Rich	.290	129	486	63	141	33	2	12	85	34	90	15	3	R	R	6-5	220	7-13-71	1989	Chatsworth, Calif.
Bravo, Danny	.281	76	270	49	76	12	1	2	38	41	39	6	5	S	R	5-11	175	5-27-77	1996	Maracaibo, Venez.
Christensen, McKay	.290	75	293	53	85	8	6	3	28	31	46	18	6	L	L	5-11	180	8-14-75	1995	Clovis, Calif.
Connacher, Kevin	.222	7	18	1	4	0	0	0	0	2	5	1	0	R	R	5-9	175	4-6-75	1997	West Palm Beach, Fla.
Crede, Joe	.251	74	291	37	73	14	1	4	42	22	47	2	6	R	R	6-3	195	4-26-78	1996	Westphalia, Mo.
Dellaero, Jason	.268	81	272	40	73	13	3	10	44	14	76	6	8	S	R	6-2	195	12-17-76	1997	Brewster, N.Y.
Eaglin, Mike	.227	27	75	7	17	2	0	0	8	4	17	1	2	R	R	5-10	170	4-25-73	1992	Vallejo, Calif.
Eddie, Steve	.199	46	136	13	27	8	0	1	10	12	27	0	3	R	R	6-1	190	1-6-71	1993	Storm Lake, Iowa
2-team (6 Chatt.)	.197	52	157	15	31	8	0	1	12	12	30	0	3							
Gomez, Ramon	.285	99	274	47	78	10	5	0	26	31	81	26	10	R	R	6-2	175	10-6-75	1994	San Pedro de Macoris, D.R.
Hyde, Brandon	.278	7	18	4	5	3	0	0	2	3	4	0	1	R	R	6-3	210	10-3-73	1997	Santa Rosa, Calif.
Inglin, Jeff	.292	117	432	63	126	26	4	15	63	58	62	20	2	R	R	5-11	185	10-8-75	1996	Petaluma, Calif.
Lydy, Scott	.265	111	400	74	106	25	1	20	65	67	61	18	3	R	R	6-5	195	10-28-68	1989	Chandler, Ariz.
Moore, Brandon	.193	36	119	11	23	3	2	0	13	17	20	4	2	R	R	5-11	195	8-23-72	1994	Springville, Calif.
Newstrom, Doug	.285	82	253	30	72	11	1	3	23	29	42	3	4	L	R	6-1	195	9-18-71	1993	Goodyear, Ariz.
Olson, Dan	.165	33	97	14	16	4	0	6	13	15	44	1	1	L	L	6-2	210	4-10-75	1996	Cape May, N.J.
Paul, Josh	.279	93	319	47	89	19	3	4	42	29	68	6	6	R	R	6-1	185	5-19-75	1996	Buffalo Grove, Ill.
Pemberton, Rudy	.277	85	307	49	85	14	3	18	60	27	55	8	3	R	R	6-1	185	12-17-69	1987	San Pedro de Macoris, D.R.
Ramirez, Jose	.197	32	127	16	25	5	0	0	10	3	31	6	4	R	R	6-0	180	2-22-74	1992	San Pedro de Macoris, D.R.
Rexrode, Jackie	.268	70	213	34	57	7	5	0	25	28	30	14	4	L	R	5-11	175	9-16-78	1996	Laurel, Md.
Rodriguez, Liu	.291	64	244	42	71	11	1	3	37	22	35	5	3	S	R	5-9	170	11-5-76	1995	Caracas, Venez.
Ryder, Derek	.148	12	27	4	4	1	0	0	2	2	3	0	0	R	R	6-1	190	3-30-73	1995	Wellingford, Pa.

PITCHING	W	L	ERA	G	GS	CG	SV	IP	H	R	ER	BB	SO	B	T	HT	WT	DOB	1st Yr	Resides
Barcelo, Lorenzo	0	1	3.60	4	4	0	0	20	14	8	8	6	14	R	R	6-4	220	8-10-77	1994	San Pedro de Macoris, D.R.
Chantres, Carlos	6	8	3.50	28	21	1	2	141	122	64	55	61	105	R	R	6-3	175	4-1-76	1994	Miami, Fla.
Daneker, Pat	6	8	3.22	16	16	3	0	109	106	46	39	30	71	R	R	6-3	195	1-14-76	1997	Williamsport, Pa.
Davenport, Joe	3	5	3.10	40	0	0	10	49	43	26	17	19	24	R	R	6-5	225	3-24-76	1994	Santee, Calif.
Fogg, Josh	3	2	5.89	10	10	0	0	55	60	37	36	18	40	R	R	6-0	205	12-13-76	1998	Margate, Fla.
Garland, Jon	3	1	4.38	7	7	0	0	39	39	22	19	18	22	R	R	6-6	205	9-27-79	1997	Granada Hills, Calif.
Iglesias, Mario	5	5	4.68	23	2	0	0	50	51	29	26	21	29	S	R	6-3	195	6-2-74	1996	Castro Valley, Calif.
Lakman, Jason	0	0	15.00	3	0	0	0	3	5	5	5	9	3	R	R	6-4	220	10-17-76	1995	Woodinville, Wash.
Myette, Aaron	12	7	3.66	28	28	0	0	165	138	76	67	77	135	R	R	6-4	195	9-26-77	1997	Gig Harbor, Wash.
Olsen, Jason	1	3	3.82	9	4	1	0	33	33	15	14	10	25	R	R	6-4	210	3-16-75	1995	Fairfield, Calif.
Pena, Jesus	3	2	2.36	40	0	0	5	46	31	12	12	18	49	L	L	6-0	170	3-8-75	1993	Santo Domingo, D.R.
Roberts, Mark	5	8	3.40	33	17	0	2	124	108	64	47	41	84	R	R	6-2	205	9-29-75	1996	Zephyrhills, Fla.
Schmack, Brian	4	4	3.43	43	0	0	6	63	60	31	24	18	56	R	R	6-2	195	12-7-73	1996	Barrington, Ill.

PITCHING	W	L	ERA	G	GS	CG	SV	IP	H	R	ER	BB	SO	B	T	HT	WT	DOB	1st Yr	Resides
Secoda, Jason	8	7	3.44	22	17	1	0	115	100	49	44	39	94	R	R	6-1	195	9-2-74	1995	Fullerton, Calif.
Tokarse, Brian	0	1	5.06	6	0	0	0	11	12	7	6	3	11	R	R	6-3	180	2-28-75	1997	Whittier, Calif.
Tucker, Julien	2	1	5.33	37	0	0	5	49	52	30	29	22	32	L	R	6-7	200	4-19-73	1993	Chateauguay, Quebec
Vining, Ken	0	2	9.26	3	3	0	0	12	20	16	12	9	8	L	L	6-0	180	12-5-74	1996	Hopkins, S.C.
Virchis, Adam	0	0	0.00	1	0	0	0	3	3	0	0	0	1	R	R	6-3	185	10-15-73	1995	Chula Vista, Calif.
Wells, Kip	8	2	2.94	11	11	0	0	70	49	24	23	31	44	R	R	6-3	196	4-21-77	1999	Missouri City, Texas
Whitley, Curtis	4	2	5.01	36	0	0	1	50	58	31	28	25	24	L	L	6-4	240	1-9-74	1997	Goldsboro, N.C.

FIELDING

Catcher	PCT	G	PO	A	E	DP	PB
Bravo..............	1.000	1	0	1	0	0	0
Hyde..............	.968	7	28	2	1	0	0
Newstrom.......	.988	51	281	37	4	4	4
Paul..............	.992	85	526	66	5	4	7
Ryder..............	.983	12	47	10	1	0	3

First Base	PCT	G	PO	A	E	DP
Aude..............	.995	107	884	46	5	85
Eddie............	1.000	20	106	7	0	11
Lydy..............	1.000	3	16	0	0	0
Moore..........	1.000	2	21	2	0	2
Newstrom.......	.981	19	145	10	3	7
Rodriguez......	1.000	5	7	1	0	0

Second Base	PCT	G	PO	A	E	DP
Bravo..............	.972	29	47	56	3	9

	PCT	G	PO	A	E	DP
Connacher	.963	7	13	13	1	1
Eaglin	.937	21	20	39	4	8
Eddie	1.000	1	1	2	0	0
Rexrode	.958	67	129	169	13	43
Rodriguez......	.981	39	86	72	3	18

Third Base	PCT	G	PO	A	E	DP
Bravo..............	.931	47	34	87	9	5
Crede	.910	72	68	133	20	10
Eddie	.922	28	17	54	6	4
Lydy..............	1.000	2	1	1	0	0
Moore..........	1.000	3	0	9	0	1
Newstrom	.333	1	0	1	2	0
Rodriguez......	1.000	1	2	3	0	1

Shortstop	PCT	G	PO	A	E	DP
Bravo..............	.966	12	10	46	2	8

	PCT	G	PO	A	E	DP
Dellaero..........	.948	80	138	227	20	39
Moore..........	.979	31	48	93	3	23
Rodriguez.......	.942	27	24	73	6	14

Outfield	PCT	G	PO	A	E	DP
Bravo..............	1.000	1	1	0	0	0
Christensen....	.990	74	190	2	2	0
Gomez	.973	92	177	6	5	2
Inglin	.978	105	166	9	4	1
Lydy..............	.991	108	216	9	2	1
Olson..........	.966	16	28	0	1	0
Pemberton	.960	13	23	1	1	0
Ramirez..........	.944	31	64	3	4	1
Rodriguez......	1.000	1	1	0	0	0

CAROLINA LEAGUE

BATTING	AVG	G	AB	R	H	2B	3B	HR	RBI	BB	SO	SB	CS	B	T	HT	WT	DOB	1st Yr	Resides
Albert, Rashad	.111	21	54	3	6	1	1	0	1	4	23	0	2	R	R	6-1	165	9-18-75	1994	Fernandina Beach, Fla.
Berger, Matt	.225	90	329	41	74	17	0	10	49	34	86	1	3	R	R	6-1	195	10-2-74	1997	Fort Mitchell, Ky.
Caradonna, Brett	.251	128	505	68	127	28	4	9	62	48	108	18	7	L	R	6-1	185	12-3-78	1997	San Diego, Calif.
Connacher, Kevin	.259	121	413	60	107	14	5	10	48	63	101	27	13	R	R	5-9	175	4-6-75	1997	West Palm Beach, Fla.
Dellaero, Jason	.223	54	184	22	41	13	0	2	19	18	59	9	4	S	R	6-2	195	12-17-76	1997	Brewster, N.Y.
Downs, Brian	.180	20	61	7	11	1	0	1	5	2	13	1	0	R	R	6-2	210	4-10-75	1995	Chino, Calif.
Heintz, Chris	.293	118	417	55	122	33	2	7	60	40	72	6	3	R	R	6-1	200	8-6-74	1996	Clearwater, Fla.
Klee, Chuck	.211	73	199	19	42	11	0	4	24	14	50	3	0	R	R	6-3	175	5-15-77	1995	Lighthouse Point, Fla.
Manning, Brian	.240	106	350	45	84	20	4	5	47	32	55	24	4	R	R	6-2	200	2-1-75	1996	Hazlet, N.J.
Olson, Dan	.319	64	216	36	69	16	0	9	41	39	80	1	1	L	L	6-2	210	4-10-75	1996	Cape May, N.J.
Ramirez, Luis	.267	85	360	56	96	4	3	1	19	29	58	44	17	R	R	6-0	180	2-22-74	1992	San Pedro de Macoris, D.R.
Rowand, Aaron	.279	133	512	96	143	37	3	24	88	33	94	15	10	R	R	6-1	190	8-29-77	1998	Glendora, Calif.
Ryder, Derek	.208	39	120	11	25	4	0	0	8	5	17	0	3	R	R	6-1	190	3-30-73	1995	Wellingford, Pa.
Sheppard, Greg	.201	79	224	22	45	5	0	7	27	21	74	6	2	R	R	6-0	190	3-1-75	1996	Palmdale, Calif.
Suarez, Luis	.203	74	241	20	49	7	2	2	26	22	66	3	2	R	R	6-1	175	9-5-78	1998	Hialeah, Fla.
Terrell, Jim	.271	119	436	74	118	31	5	3	47	52	79	16	6	L	R	6-1	175	9-8-77	1996	Blue Springs, Mo.

GAMES BY POSITION: C—Downs 12, Heintz 92, Olson 1, Ryder 39, Sheppard 3. **1B**—Berger 77, Downs 4, Heintz 10, Klee 9, Olson 30, Sheppard 18. **2B**—Connacher 121, Klee 22, Terrell 1. **3B**—Berger 17, Klee 17, Terrell 112. **SS**—Dellaero 54, Klee 23, Suarez 74, Terrell 1. **OF**—Albert 20, Caradonna 127, Manning 65, Olson 15, Ramirez 85, Rowand 99, Sheppard 18.

PITCHING	W	L	ERA	G	GS	CG	SV	IP	H	R	ER	BB	SO	B	T	HT	WT	DOB	1st Yr	Resides
Borne, Matt	1	2	7.02	10	1	0	0	17	21	14	13	12	8	R	R	6-3	190	9-12-76	1998	Lexington, Ky.
Cardona, Steve	1	0	6.23	17	0	0	1	26	29	20	18	17	24	R	R	6-3	190	2-18-74	1998	Stockton, Calif.
Currens, Tim	1	1	2.49	14	0	0	0	22	21	8	6	13	17	L	R	6-4	195	10-2-75	1997	Bowling Green, Ky.
Felix, Miguel	1	0	1.93	9	0	0	1	14	11	8	3	7	7	R	R	6-3	155	12-30-76	1995	La Romana, D.R.
Figueroa, Juan	2	5	5.27	10	10	1	0	56	67	47	33	19	50	R	R	6-3	150	6-24-79	1998	Santo Domingo, D.R.
Fogg, Josh	10	5	2.96	17	17	1	0	103	93	44	34	33	109	R	R	6-2	205	12-13-76	1998	Margate, Fla.
Freeman, Kai	2	6	4.91	32	8	0	1	95	100	58	52	32	64	R	R	6-2	182	3-11-77	1998	Shorewood, Ill.
Garland, Jon	5	7	3.33	19	19	2	0	119	109	57	44	39	84	R	R	6-6	205	9-27-79	1997	Granada Hills, Calif.
Guerrier, Matt	0	0	5.40	4	0	0	2	3	3	2	2	0	5	R	R	6-3	190	8-2-78	1999	Shaker Heights, Ohio
Izquierdo, Hansel	3	5	4.14	18	13	0	0	83	76	46	38	46	72	R	R	6-2	205	1-2-77	1995	Miami, Fla.
Jacobs, Dwayne	1	3	5.03	46	1	0	4	59	33	38	33	79	76	R	R	6-10	225	7-17-76	1994	Jacksonville, Fla.
Johnson, Solomon	1	2	3.33	17	0	0	0	24	25	11	9	15	22	L	L	6-1	215	8-27-78	1998	Mexia, Texas
Lakman, Jason	9	8	4.36	20	20	2	0	120	108	69	58	55	110	R	R	6-4	220	10-17-76	1995	Woodinville, Wash.
Lopez, Jose	0	1	4.73	19	0	0	1	27	38	22	14	14	10	S	R	6-2	175	4-16-76	1996	Ridgewood, N.Y.
Manning, Brian	0	0	3.00	2	0	0	0	3	4	1	1	2	0	R	R	6-2	200	2-1-75	1996	Hazlet, N.J.
Rauch, Jon	0	0	3.00	1	0	0	0	6	4	3	2	1	9	R	R	6-10	230	9-27-78	1999	Westport, Ill.
Scott, Brian	8	8	3.41	25	25	1	0	148	135	75	56	60	132	R	R	6-2	190	4-29-76	1997	Ramona, Calif.
Thompson, John	0	1	7.00	2	2	0	0	9	10	9	7	8	9	R	R	6-2	200	1-18-73	1992	Spokane, Wash.
Tokarse, Brian	4	2	2.31	40	0	0	14	47	37	15	12	22	55	R	R	6-3	180	2-28-75	1997	Whittier, Calif.
Virchis, Adam	3	5	4.73	33	7	0	1	78	82	50	41	33	59	R	R	6-3	185	10-15-73	1995	Chula Vista, Calif.
Wells, Kip	5	6	3.57	14	14	0	0	86	78	39	34	34	95	R	R	6-3	196	4-21-77	1999	Missouri City, Texas
Weymouth, Marty	5	6	4.71	41	0	0	2	57	62	35	30	21	42	R	R	6-2	180	8-6-77	1995	Romeo, Mich.
Whitley, Curtis	0	0	4.50	9	0	0	2	8	9	4	4	4	8	L	L	6-4	240	1-9-74	1997	Goldsboro, N.C.

MIDWEST LEAGUE

BATTING	AVG	G	AB	R	H	2B	3B	HR	RBI	BB	SO	SB	CS	B	T	HT	WT	DOB	1st Yr	Resides
Acevas, Jonathan	.188	65	202	28	38	9	2	4	23	35	52	3	2	R	R	6-2	187	3-7-78	1997	Sonora, Mexico
Battersby, Eric	.290	132	472	78	137	27	2	18	93	83	90	13	2	R	L	6-1	205	2-28-76	1998	San Antonio, Texas
Durham, Chad	.200	7	25	3	5	1	0	0	0	4	6	2	3	R	R	5-8	175	6-23-78	1997	Charlotte, N.C.
Fennell, Jason	.279	114	398	78	111	28	7	6	79	75	56	22	6	S	R	6-3	210	11-15-77	1996	Pittsburgh, Pa.

BATTING	AVG	G	AB	R	H	2B	3B	HR	RBI	BB	SO	SB	CS	B	T	HT	WT	DOB	1st Yr	Resides
Garcia, Tony	.235	73	230	35	54	10	0	2	20	22	76	3	4	R	R	6-1	213	3-12-78	1998	Miami, Fla.
Garza, Rolando	.209	40	148	13	31	4	0	1	8	12	30	4	3	R	R	6-3	180	12-14-79	1997	Coachella, Calif.
Gonzalez, Jose	.278	70	266	36	74	11	2	3	28	19	52	13	8	R	R	5-10	170	9-24-77	1996	Anzoategui, Venez.
Hankins, Ryan	.294	129	487	93	143	36	4	15	74	91	118	11	6	R	R	5-11	200	6-30-76	1997	Simi Valley, Calif.
Hyde, Brandon	.286	65	210	33	60	15	0	6	40	33	60	1	1	R	R	6-3	210	10-3-73	1997	Santa Rosa, Calif.
Jenkins, Corey	.195	32	113	8	22	5	0	3	12	16	51	1	0	R	R	6-2	200	8-25-76	1995	Columbia, S.C.
Merriman, Terrell	.306	109	382	77	117	18	9	15	85	70	84	27	4	L	L	6-0	180	7-30-77	1998	Cheraw, S.C.
Mounts, J.R.	.212	95	326	40	69	14	1	6	32	25	129	11	7	R	R	6-0	190	11-13-78	1997	Key West, Fla.
Parker, Clark	.156	32	77	13	12	1	1	0	4	16	24	6	2	L	R	5-8	165	9-26-75	1997	Beverly Hills, Calif.
Sandoval, Danny	.227	76	255	34	58	5	1	3	37	17	39	8	5	S	R	5-11	160	4-7-79	1997	Lara, Venez.
Santamarina, Juan	.179	29	95	12	17	2	0	1	10	14	15	5	0	L	R	6-1	180	10-3-79	1998	Miami, Fla.
Suarez, Luis	.243	51	173	24	42	10	0	4	25	19	32	5	4	R	R	6-1	175	9-5-78	1998	Hialeah, Fla.
Torres, Bernie	.257	65	268	40	69	12	4	2	21	15	32	7	2	R	R	5-9	168	9-26-79	1997	Lara, Venez.
Valenzuela, Mario	.323	122	477	89	154	31	6	17	74	60	77	13	6	R	R	6-3	190	3-10-77	1996	Isla San Marcos, Mexico

GAMES BY POSITION: C—Acevas 61, Fennell 1, Garcia 64, Hyde 19, **1B**—Battersby 93, Fennell 6, Garcia 4, Garza 34, Hankins 6, Hyde 2. **2B**—Gonzalez 55, Hankins 11, Parker 29, Santamarina 2, Torres 56. **3B**—Garcia 3, Garza 5, Gonzalez 3, Hankins 106, Santamarina 28, Torres 8. **SS**—Hankins 9, Sandoval 75, Suarez 51, Torres 10. **OF**—Battersby 41, Durham 6, Fennell 41, Garcia 2, Jenkins 27, Merriman 104, Mounts 90, Valenzuela 7.

PITCHING	W	L	ERA	G	GS	CG	SV	IP	H	R	ER	BB	SO	B	T	HT	WT	DOB	1st Yr	Resides
Almonte, Edwin	9	12	3.03	37	5	2	5	116	107	48	39	28	85	R	R	6-3	200	12-17-76	1998	New York, N.Y.
Barcelo, Lorenzo	1	0	3.60	1	1	0	0	5	3	2	2	0	6	R	R	6-4	220	8-10-77	1994	San Pedro de Macoris, D.R.
Borne, Matt	2	4	4.75	22	0	0	2	30	35	20	16	22	24	R	R	6-4	195	9-12-76	1998	Lexington, Ky.
Brown, Tighe	0	0	7.71	4	0	0	0	5	3	4	4	6	8	R	R	6-4	195	9-10-76	1995	Louisville, Ky.
Buehrle, Mark	7	4	4.10	20	14	1	3	99	105	49	45	16	91	L	L	6-2	195	3-23-79	1999	St. Charles, Mo.
Currens, Tim	1	3	6.68	22	0	0	0	34	50	31	25	14	26	L	R	6-4	195	10-2-75	1997	Bowling Green, Ky.
Fauske, Josh	0	0	5.14	5	0	0	0	7	6	6	4	7	6	R	R	6-4	230	3-16-74	1995	Mercer Island, Wash.
Felix, Miguel	0	2	7.86	30	0	0	0	45	60	52	39	39	29	R	R	6-1	155	12-30-76	1995	La Romana, D.R.
Figueroa, Juan	8	4	3.12	17	16	2	0	115	100	51	40	44	139	R	R	6-3	205	6-24-79	1996	Santo Domingo, D.R.
Fischer, Eric	10	11	5.19	25	25	2	0	137	160	89	79	50	78	S	L	6-7	205	2-19-80	1998	Cincinnati, Ohio
Ginter, Matt	4	2	4.05	9	9	0	0	40	38	20	18	19	39	R	R	6-2	220	12-24-77	1999	Jacksonville, Fla.
Jacobson, Andrew	1	1	6.05	13	1	0	0	19	28	19	13	12	10	R	R	6-8	210	1-25-76	1997	McRain, Mich.
Johnson, Solomon	3	2	4.92	19	8	0	0	53	70	38	29	17	39	L	L	6-1	215	8-27-78	1998	Mexia, Texas
Kane, Kyle	1	0	13.50	12	0	0	1	18	28	29	27	12	17	L	R	6-3	215	2-4-76	1997	Reno, Nev.
Majewski, Gary	0	0	37.80	2	0	0	0	3	11	14	14	4	1	R	R	6-2	190	2-26-80	1999	Houston, Texas
Mendoza, Geronimo	9	8	4.63	28	28	0	0	157	186	96	81	60	119	L	R	6-4	160	1-23-78	1995	Santo Domingo, D.R.
Purvis, Rob	0	0	2.38	6	0	0	1	11	10	5	3	4	8	R	R	6-2	200	8-11-77	1999	Tipton, Ind.
Rodgers, Marcus	0	0	33.75	4	0	0	0	3	10	10	10	3	5	R	R	6-3	225	11-1-76	1996	Saraland, Ala.
Stewart, Josh	2	0	7.28	16	0	0	1	30	32	25	24	21	35	L	L	6-3	210	12-5-78	1999	Ledbetter, Ky.
Stumm, Jason	3	3	5.32	10	10	0	0	44	47	31	26	27	33	R	R	6-2	210	4-13-81	1999	Centralia, Wash.
Whatley, Brannon	3	5	3.47	45	0	0	20	57	48	29	22	34	52	R	R	6-1	190	10-11-76	1998	Marietta, Ga.
Williams, Mike	6	7	4.45	37	16	2	2	127	119	78	63	65	83	R	R	6-3	190	8-9-78	1998	Cypress, Texas
Wright, Dan	0	0	6.00	2	0	0	0	6	5	4	4	3	3	R	R	6-5	215	12-14-77	1999	Batesville, Ark.
Wylie, Mitch	1	0	1.97	6	6	0	0	32	33	11	7	11	27	R	R	6-3	190	1-14-77	1998	Princeton, Iowa

BRISTOL — Rookie

APPALACHIAN LEAGUE

BATTING	AVG	G	AB	R	H	2B	3B	HR	RBI	BB	SO	SB	CS	B	T	HT	WT	DOB	1st Yr	Resides
Aguirregaviria, Frank	.239	17	46	3	11	2	0	1	3	3	16	0	1	R	R	6-1	180	2-11-78	1997	Miami, Fla.
Blankenship, Tony	.103	12	29	4	3	0	0	1	5	16	0	1	R	R	5-10	184	2-3-77	1999	Toledo, Ohio
Delgado, Chris	.300	61	217	36	65	10	1	14	54	33	64	1	0	R	R	6-3	215	10-8-77	1997	Pembroke Pines, Fla.
Durham, Chad	.324	68	278	66	90	12	2	0	36	33	44	57	13	R	R	5-8	175	6-23-78	1997	Charlotte, N.C.
Garcia, Yosnel	.253	29	83	9	21	2	1	0	11	9	12	4	1	R	R	6-2	175	2-21-79	1996	Palo Negro, Venez.
Garza, Rolando	.253	62	198	30	50	10	0	1	17	21	32	3	3	R	R	6-3	180	12-14-79	1997	Coachella, Calif.
Harrelson, Casey	.150	18	40	3	6	1	0	0	1	5	11	0	1	L	R	6-3	190	2-8-78	1999	Orlando, Fla.
Holt, Todd	.292	36	113	14	33	8	0	1	13	8	33	4	5	R	R	6-4	225	5-15-78	1999	Chesterfield, Va.
Manuel, Marcellous	.300	66	240	38	72	13	1	6	48	23	37	8	3	L	L	5-10	165	10-9-75	1998	Stone Mountain, Ga.
Quintero, Humberto	.277	48	155	30	43	5	2	0	15	9	19	11	1	R	R	5-10	180	8-2-79	1997	Zulia, Venez.
Roman, Junior	.260	44	131	21	34	8	0	0	12	16	22	15	2	S	R	5-11	160	8-30-80	1997	Santo Domingo, D.R.
Rummel, Jason	.267	56	191	39	51	10	1	8	36	48	32	11	2	R	R	5-10	180	7-21-76	1999	Walkersville, Md.
Santamarina, Juan	.254	60	213	36	54	1	1	5	22	16	41	5	5	L	R	6-1	180	10-3-79	1998	Miami, Fla.
Stanley, Derek	.230	39	135	20	31	5	3	1	9	17	31	6	6	R	R	6-2	170	2-27-80	1999	Hopewell, Va.
Teilon, Nilson	.296	68	240	43	71	12	2	9	51	29	68	6	4	R	R	6-0	168	6-10-81	1998	San Pedro de Macoris, D.R.

GAMES BY POSITION: C—Aguirregaviria 3, Garcia 28, Garza 1, Quintero 46. **1B**—Aguirregaviria 2, Delgado 58, Garza 8, Harrelson 8, Santamarina 1. **2B**—Blankenship 4, Garza 1, Rummel 25, Teilon 46. **3B**—Aguirregaviria 7, Blankenship 3, Garza 15, Rummel 7, Santamarina 42. **SS**—Blankenship 3, Garza 5, Roman 42, Rummel 8, Teilon 20. **OF**—Blankenship 1, Durham 67, Garza 31, Harrelson 1, Holt 36, Manuel 46, Stanley 38.

PITCHING	W	L	ERA	G	GS	CG	SV	IP	H	R	ER	BB	SO	B	T	HT	WT	DOB	1st Yr	Resides
Brown, Tighe	1	2	10.24	7	0	0	1	10	18	12	11	5	11	R	R	6-4	195	9-10-76	1995	Louisville, Ky.
Caraballo, Angel	8	2	4.00	13	13	1	0	81	88	40	36	27	88	R	R	6-0	160	1-20-80	1997	Guanta, Venez.
Curreri, Joe	1	0	2.92	16	0	0	5	25	17	10	8	9	24	R	R	6-1	190	6-29-77	1998	Valley Cottage, N.Y.
Guerrier, Matt	5	1	1.05	21	0	0	10	26	18	9	3	14	37	R	R	6-3	190	8-2-78	1999	Shaker Heights, Ohio
Kane, Kyle	2	0	2.57	5	5	0	0	28	19	8	8	11	23	L	R	6-3	215	2-4-76	1997	Reno, Nev.
Majewski, Gary	7	1	3.05	13	13	1	0	77	67	34	26	37	91	R	R	6-2	190	2-26-80	1999	Houston, Texas
Mazur, Graham	2	2	2.05	10	0	0	0	22	17	7	5	3	34	L	L	6-2	200	12-2-75	1999	Coto de Caza, Calif.
McWhirter, Kris	0	1	4.21	12	1	0	2	26	25	16	12	12	23	R	R	6-4	175	5-11-79	1999	Goodlettsville, Tenn.
Mozingo, Dan	4	7	6.04	13	13	1	0	67	79	59	45	30	70	L	L	6-2	210	6-3-80	1998	Ashtabula, Ohio
Rauch, Jon	4	4	4.45	14	9	0	2	57	65	44	28	16	66	R	R	6-10	230	9-27-78	1999	Westport, Ky.
Rohling, Stuart	0	2	4.41	16	1	0	1	33	34	19	16	17	44	R	R	6-4	185	6-29-78	1998	Leoma, Tenn.
Simpson, Andre	1	3	3.00	13	13	1	0	72	69	33	24	22	79	R	R	6-3	170	1-1-80	1998	Lemon Grove, Calif.
Stewart, Josh	1	0	1.50	5	0	0	1	18	13	5	3	5	25	L	L	6-3	210	12-5-78	1999	Ledbetter, Ky.
Valentine, Joe	0	0	7.02	11	0	0	0	17	27	17	13	9	14	R	R	6-2	195	12-24-79	1999	Pensacola, Fla.

PITCHING	W	L	ERA	G	GS	CG	SV	IP	H	R	ER	BB	SO	B	T	HT	WT	DOB	1st Yr	Resides
West, Brian	1	2	10.50	8	1	0	2	18	26	25	21	14	17	R	R	6-4	230	8-4-80	1999	West Monroe, La.
Wright, Dan	2	0	1.00	10	0	0	1	18	14	8	2	9	18	R	R	6-5	215	12-14-77	1999	Batesville, Ark.

TUCSON   Rookie

ARIZONA LEAGUE

BATTING	AVG	G	AB	R	H	2B	3B	HR	RBI	BB	SO	SB	CS	B	T	HT	WT	DOB	1st Yr	Resides
Blankenship, Tony	.348	9	23	7	8	0	2	0	4	4	4	1	1	R	R	5-10	184	2-3-77	1999	Toledo, Ohio
Cochrane, Mark	.220	29	82	13	18	5	1	0	2	10	19	0	0	R	R	6-0	185	5-31-80	1999	Coral Springs, Fla.
Flores, Ralph	.337	55	193	30	65	9	7	0	30	23	26	10	5	R	R	5-11	160	2-13-80	1997	Caracas, Venez.
Gauch, Barry	.230	26	61	7	14	3	0	0	11	11	7	1	0	R	R	6-0	205	11-28-76	1999	Woodbridge, Va.
Goolsby, Kevin	.252	45	155	28	39	5	1	2	17	22	35	7	1	R	R	5-10	180	9-30-74	1999	Oxford, Miss.
Kashirsky, Michael	.125	15	32	5	4	0	0	0	1	9	7	0	2	R	L	6-1	205	10-21-77	1999	Orland Park, Ill.
Lowe, Ernesto	.320	50	181	29	58	8	3	0	23	11	42	7	4	R	R	6-0	180	10-1-78	1998	Miami, Fla.
McCall, Gerard	.268	46	168	33	45	12	5	3	26	20	36	6	3	R	R	6-0	215	11-19-79	1998	Meridian, Miss.
Perez, Rafael	.207	51	179	26	37	7	5	3	22	20	64	11	5	L	R	6-3	175	10-15-79	1998	Santo Domingo, D.R.
Reyes, Guillermo	.250	54	200	27	50	5	3	0	15	20	25	18	10	S	R	5-9	160	12-29-81	1999	Santo Domingo, D.R.
Reyes, Julio	.307	33	127	23	39	8	3	2	20	7	16	1	2	L	R	6-2	195	6-30-80	1999	Sonora, Mexico
Roehler, Trent	.067	9	15	1	1	1	0	0	0	1	6	0	0	R	R	6-3	230	10-28-76	1999	Topeka, Kan.
Rogowski, Casey	.288	52	160	23	46	7	2	0	27	26	34	2	1	L	L	6-2	220	5-1-81	1999	Livonia, Mich.
Solorzano, Lenin	.267	51	180	21	48	6	5	1	30	13	45	5	5	R	R	6-0	160	2-14-80	1997	Caracas, Venez.
Tapia, Roman	.300	21	50	7	15	4	0	0	6	7	12	0	3	R	R	6-3	190	12-7-79	1999	Dominican Republic
Wheat, Trey	.293	16	58	7	17	1	0	0	4	5	9	7	0	R	R	6-1	195	3-27-76	1999	Petersburg, Va.

GAMES BY POSITION: C—Cochrane 22, Gauch 14, McCall 25, Roehler 4. **1B**—Blankenship 1, Gauch 1, Kashirsky 14, Lowe 1, Rogowski 46, Tapia 3, Wheat 1. **2B**—Blankenship 3, Flores 1, G. Reyes 52, Tapia 1. **3B**—Blankenship 1, Solorzano 48, Tapia 12. **SS**—Blankenship 1, Flores 53, Solorzano 4. **OF**—Goolsby 42, Lowe 38, McCall 1, Perez 50, J. Reyes 28, Rogowski 1, Wheat 14.

PITCHING	W	L	ERA	G	GS	CG	SV	IP	H	R	ER	BB	SO	B	T	HT	WT	DOB	1st Yr	Resides
Asencio, Domingo	1	0	10.97	11	0	0	0	11	24	13	13	4	5	R	R	6-3	160	8-20-81	1998	Bani, D.R.
Barcelo, Lorenzo	2	1	1.69	9	9	0	0	43	36	14	8	6	57	R	R	6-4	220	8-10-77	1994	San Pedro de Macoris, D.R.
Beltre, Sandy	5	4	4.12	13	10	0	0	68	85	38	31	21	58	R	R	6-1	160	4-20-82	1998	Bani, D.R.
Ferrand, Dario	2	5	4.46	13	13	1	0	73	80	46	36	25	44	R	R	6-1	160	9-19-81	1998	Santo Domingo, D.R.
Ginter, Matt	1	0	3.24	3	0	0	1	8	5	4	3	3	10	R	R	6-2	220	12-24-77	1999	Jacksonville, Fla.
Hollifield, Alec	1	0	6.87	16	0	0	0	18	29	19	14	11	14	R	R	6-3	170	7-18-80	1999	Fort Lauderdale, Fla.
Hughes, Rocky	3	3	3.33	13	6	0	1	46	53	23	17	20	47	L	L	6-0	155	4-29-79	1999	Owasso, Okla.
Lopez, Juan	2	2	7.33	14	2	0	2	27	32	27	22	16	27	L	L	6-1	170	3-19-80	1997	Cua, Venez.
Malone, Corwin	0	2	8.00	10	0	0	0	18	16	19	16	16	24	R	L	6-3	200	7-3-80	1999	Thomasville, Ala.
Martinez, Daniel	2	0	2.35	13	0	0	1	15	18	6	4	10	20	L	L	6-6	235	12-31-78	1999	National City, Calif.
Munoz, Arnaldo	0	2	5.25	14	0	0	1	12	13	10	7	8	12	L	L	5-9	170	6-21-82	1999	Santo Domingo, D.R.
Patten, Mike	0	4	4.19	15	5	0	0	39	27	22	18	30	27	R	R	6-3	210	11-26-80	1999	Tecumseh, Okla.
Purvis, Rob	0	1	4.00	4	0	0	2	9	12	10	4	6	7	R	R	6-2	200	8-11-77	1999	Tipton, Ind.
Sanders, David	1	0	1.10	7	1	0	1	16	12	3	2	6	26	L	L	6-0	200	8-29-79	1999	Derby, Kan.
Stumm, Jason	0	0	3.27	3	2	0	0	11	13	8	4	3	9	R	R	6-2	210	4-13-81	1999	Centralia, Wash.
Ulacia, Dennis	3	2	3.79	8	8	0	0	38	36	19	16	11	52	L	L	6-1	185	4-2-81	1999	Hialeah, Fla.
Valentine, Joe	0	0	0.00	3	0	0	0	4	2	0	0	1	2	R	R	6-2	195	12-24-79	1999	Pensacola, Fla.
West, Brian	0	1	13.50	2	0	0	0	5	10	7	7	2	3	R	R	6-4	230	8-4-80	1999	West Monroe, La.
Zorrilla, Reinaldo	0	1	7.07	14	0	0	1	14	16	13	11	5	17	R	R	6-0	170	5-31-82	1999	Santo Domingo, D.R.

Organization Statistics

CHICAGO CUBS

Bottom falls out for Cubs after quick start to '99 season

BY BRUCE MILES

The 1999 season was going to be a crossroads for the Cubs no matter what happened, but they reached the fork in the road more quickly and painfully than anyone thought possible.

The Cubs brought back the same group that won the National League wild card in 1998, and the club looked like it was in good shape on June 9, when it trailed Houston by one game in the NL Central with a 32-23 record.

Then the pitching, defense and timely hitting all took summer vacations, and the Cubs wound up 67-95 to finish last for the second time in three years.

The fallout from the organization's overall failure and misjudging of talent was that manager Jim Riggleman was fired after five years on the job. The team also fired pitching coach Marty DeMerritt, first-base coach Dan Radison and third-base coach Tom Gamboa.

DeMerritt was in his first year on the job, and the Cubs finished with a team ERA of 5.27, worst in team history. But the pitching coach could do little about a staff decimated by injuries. Most notably, 1998 rookie sensation Kerry Wood had Tommy John surgery in April and missed the entire season. Righthander Jeremi Gonzalez suffered a setback from 1998 elbow surgery and wound up having reconstructive surgery as well.

Starters Kevin Tapani and Jon Lieber both did time on the disabled list, as did relievers Terry Adams, Rick Aguilera and Rod Beck, who eventually was dealt to the Red Sox for third baseman Cole Liniak.

On the bright side, Sammy Sosa nearly duplicated his 1998 66-homer season, with 63. He became the first man in baseball history to hit 60 home runs in two seasons, but when the season ended he found

Sammy Sosa   **Corey Patterson**

Players of the Year

MAJOR LEAGUE: Sammy Sosa, of
Sosa followed up his amazing 1998 performance with 63 home runs and 141 RBIs, giving him 129 homers and 299 RBIs over the last two years.

MINOR LEAGUE: Corey Patterson, of
Patterson collected 62 extra-base hits in his pro debut at Lansing and ranked second in the organization with 33 steals.

himself behind Mark McGwire again, this time 65-63. First baseman Mark Grace earned the title of hits leader of the 1990s, finishing with 1,754 to beat out Rafael Palmeiro. But those accomplishments were overshadowed by the team's dismal performance.

With the team out of the race by midseason, the youth movement began with such players as second baseman Chad Meyers and shortstop Jose Nieves getting significant playing time. They performed well enough after their callups from Triple-A Iowa that they were penciled in as the starting middle infield for 2000.

Righthander Kyle Farnsworth had an up-and-down season after his first callup from Iowa in late April, but he showed enough promise to merit strong consideration for a rotation spot.

The minor league system sent two teams deep into postseason action. Double-A West Tenn, under manager Dave Trembley, advanced to the Southern League finals before losing to Orlando three games to one. Class A Lansing went to the second round of the Midwest League playoffs under manager Oscar Acosta before bowing out 2-0 to Wisconsin.

Several of the Cubs' top young prospects played at Lansing, including center fielder Corey Patterson, first baseman Hee Seop Choi and third baseman David Kelton. Patterson, the third overall pick in the 1998 draft, hit .320 with 35 doubles, 17 triples, 20 home runs and 33 stolen bases in his pro debut.

The Cubs' first-rounder in 1999, righthander Ben Christensen, came to the club amid controversy. He was suspended for the end of his season at Wichita State after an incident in which he hit an opposing batter with a pitch before the start of a game.

ORGANIZATION LEADERS

BATTING
*AVG	Roosevelt Brown, Iowa/West Tenn	.338
R	Corey Patterson, Lansing	94
H	Corey Patterson, Lansing	152
TB	Corey Patterson, Lansing	281
2B	Scott Vieira, West Tenn	44
3B	Corey Patterson, Lansing	17
HR	Bo Porter, Iowa	27
RBI	Julio Zuleta, West Tenn	97
BB	Tony Schrager, Lansing	103
SO	Tom Quinlan, Iowa	159
SB	Chad Meyers, Iowa/West Tenn	39

PITCHING
W	Mike Meyers, West Tenn/Daytona	14
L	Four tied at	12
#ERA	Mike Meyers, West Tenn/Daytona	1.73
G	Two tied at	58
CG	David Manning, Iowa/West Tenn	6
SV	Steve Rain, Iowa/West Tenn	26
IP	Phillip Norton, West Tenn/Daytona	166
BB	Matt Bruback, Lansing	87
SO	Mike Meyers, West Tenn/Daytona	173

*Minimum 250 At-Bats #Minimum 75 Innings

Chicago CUBS

Manager: Jim Riggleman   **1999 Record:** 67-95, .414 (6th, NL Central)

BATTING	AVG	G	AB	R	H	2B	3B	HR	RBI	BB	SO	SB	CS	B	T	HT	WT	DOB	1st Yr	Resides
Alexander, Manny	.271	90	177	17	48	11	2	0	15	10	38	4	0	R	R	5-10	180	3-20-71	1988	San Pedro de Macoris, D.R.
Andrews, Shane	.254	19	67	13	17	4	0	5	14	7	21	0	1	R	R	6-1	205	8-28-71	1990	Carlsbad, N.M.
2-team (98 Montreal)	.195	117	348	41	68	12	0	16	51	50	109	1	1							
Blauser, Jeff	.240	104	200	41	48	5	2	9	26	26	52	2	2	R	R	6-1	190	11-8-65	1984	Alpharetta, Ga.
Brown, Roosevelt	.219	33	64	6	14	6	1	1	10	2	14	1	0	L	R	5-11	195	8-3-75	1993	Vicksburg, Miss.
Gaetti, Gary	.204	113	280	22	57	9	1	9	46	21	51	0	1	R	R	6-0	205	8-19-58	1979	St. Louis, Mo.
Goodwin, Curtis	.242	89	157	15	38	6	1	0	9	13	38	2	4	L	L	5-11	180	9-30-72	1991	San Leandro, Calif.
Grace, Mark	.309	161	593	107	183	44	5	16	91	83	44	3	4	L	L	6-2	200	6-28-64	1986	Chicago, Ill.
Hernandez, Jose	.272	99	342	57	93	12	2	15	43	40	101	7	2	R	R	6-1	180	7-14-69	1987	Dorado, P.R.
Hill, Glenallen	.300	99	253	43	76	9	1	20	55	22	61	5	1	R	R	6-3	230	3-22-65	1983	Santa Cruz, Calif.
Houston, Tyler	.233	100	249	26	58	9	1	9	27	28	67	1	1	L	R	6-1	210	1-17-71	1989	Las Vegas, Nev.
Jennings, Robin	.200	5	5	0	1	0	0	0	0	0	2	0	0	L	L	6-2	210	4-11-72	1992	Scottsdale, Ariz.
Johnson, Lance	.260	95	335	46	87	11	6	1	21	37	20	13	3	L	L	5-11	165	7-6-63	1984	Mobile, Ala.
Liniak, Cole	.241	12	29	3	7	2	0	0	2	1	4	0	1	R	R	6-1	181	8-23-76	1995	Encinitas, Calif.
Martinez, Sandy	.167	17	30	1	5	0	0	1	1	0	11	0	0	L	R	6-2	215	10-3-72	1990	Santo Domingo, D.R.
Meyers, Chad	.232	43	142	17	33	9	0	0	4	9	27	4	2	R	R	6-0	190	8-8-75	1996	Omaha, Neb.
Molina, Jose	.263	10	19	3	5	1	0	0	1	2	4	0	0	R	R	6-1	195	6-3-75	1993	Vega Alta, P.R.
Morandini, Mickey	.241	144	456	60	110	18	5	4	37	48	61	6	6	L	R	5-11	180	4-22-66	1989	Chesterton, Ind.
Nieves, Jose	.249	54	181	16	45	9	1	2	18	8	25	0	2	R	R	6-1	185	6-16-75	1992	Guacara, Venez.
Porter, Bo	.192	24	26	2	5	1	0	0	0	2	13	0	0	R	R	6-2	195	7-5-72	1994	Newark, N.J.
Reed, Jeff	.260	57	150	18	39	11	2	1	17	28	34	1	1	L	R	6-2	190	11-12-62	1980	Elizabethton, Tenn.
2-team (46 Colo.)	.258	103	256	29	66	16	2	3	28	45	58	1	2							
Rodriguez, Henry	.304	130	447	72	136	29	0	26	87	56	113	2	4	L	L	6-2	220	11-8-67	1986	Santo Domingo, D.R.
Santiago, Benito	.249	109	350	28	87	18	3	7	36	32	71	1	1	R	R	6-1	195	3-9-65	1983	Lighthouse Point, Fla.
Sosa, Sammy	.288	162	625	114	180	24	2	63	141	78	171	7	8	R	R	6-0	210	11-12-68	1986	San Pedro de Macoris, D.R.

PITCHING	W	L	ERA	G	GS	CG	SV	IP	H	R	ER	BB	SO	B	T	HT	WT	DOB	1st Yr	Resides
Adams, Terry	6	3	4.02	52	0	0	13	65	60	33	29	28	57	R	R	6-3	205	3-6-73	1991	Semmes, Ala.
Aguilera, Rick	6	3	3.69	44	0	0	8	46	44	22	19	10	32	R	R	6-5	208	12-31-61	1983	Rancho Santa Fe, Calif.
Ayala, Bobby	0	1	2.81	13	0	0	0	16	11	7	5	5	15	R	R	6-3	210	7-8-69	1988	Avondale, Ariz.
2-team (53 Montreal)	1	7	3.51	66	0	0	0	82	71	43	32	39	79							
Barker, Richie	0	0	7.20	5	0	0	0	5	6	4	4	4	3	R	R	6-2	220	10-29-72	1994	Malden, Mass.
Beck, Rod	2	4	7.80	31	0	0	7	30	41	26	26	13	13	R	R	6-1	235	8-3-68	1986	Scottsdale, Ariz.
Bowie, Micah	2	6	9.96	11	11	0	0	47	73	54	52	30	39	L	L	6-4	185	11-10-74	1993	Humble, Texas
2-team (3 Atlanta)	2	7	10.24	14	11	0	0	51	81	60	58	34	41							
Creek, Doug	0	0	10.50	3	0	0	0	6	6	7	7	8	6	L	L	6-0	200	3-1-69	1991	Dallas, Texas
Farnsworth, Kyle	5	9	5.05	27	21	1	0	130	140	80	73	52	70	R	R	6-4	220	4-14-76	1995	Roswell, Ga.
Guthrie, Mark	0	2	3.65	11	0	0	0	12	7	6	5	4	9	R	L	6-4	211	9-22-65	1987	Bradenton, Fla.
Heredia, Felix	3	1	4.85	69	0	0	1	52	56	35	28	25	50	L	L	6-0	180	6-18-76	1993	Santo Domingo, D.R.
Karchner, Matt	1	0	2.50	16	0	0	0	18	16	5	5	9	9	R	R	6-4	215	6-28-67	1989	Manassas, Va.
King, Ray	0	0	5.91	10	0	0	0	11	11	8	7	10	5	L	L	6-1	225	1-15-74	1995	Chicago, Ill.
Lieber, Jon	10	11	4.07	31	31	3	0	203	226	107	92	46	186	L	R	6-3	225	4-2-70	1992	Mobile, Ala.
Lorraine, Andrew	2	5	5.55	11	11	2	0	62	71	42	38	22	40	L	L	6-3	205	8-11-72	1993	Scottsdale, Ariz.
McNichol, Brian	0	2	6.75	4	2	0	0	11	15	8	8	7	12	L	L	6-5	225	5-20-74	1995	Woodbridge, Va.
Miller, Kurt	0	0	18.00	4	0	0	0	3	6	6	6	3	1	R	R	6-5	225	8-24-72	1990	Bakersfield, Calif.
Mulholland, Terry	6	6	5.15	26	16	0	0	110	137	71	63	32	44	R	L	6-3	220	3-9-63	1984	Scottsdale, Ariz.
Myers, Rodney	3	1	4.38	46	0	0	0	64	71	34	31	25	41	R	R	6-1	205	6-26-69	1990	Chandler, Ariz.
Rain, Steve	0	1	9.20	16	0	0	0	15	28	17	15	7	12	R	R	6-6	250	6-2-75	1993	Walnut, Calif.
Sanders, Scott	4	7	5.52	67	6	0	2	104	112	69	64	53	89	R	R	6-4	220	3-25-69	1990	Poway, Calif.
Serafini, Dan	3	2	6.93	42	4	0	1	62	86	51	48	32	17	S	L	6-1	195	1-25-74	1992	San Bruno, Calif.
Tapani, Kevin	6	12	4.83	23	23	1	0	136	151	81	73	33	73	R	R	6-1	195	2-18-64	1986	Chicago, Ill.
Trachsel, Steve	8	18	5.56	34	34	4	0	206	226	133	127	64	149	R	R	6-3	205	10-31-70	1991	Mesa, Ariz.
Woodall, Brad	0	1	5.63	6	3	0	0	16	17	12	10	6	7	S	L	6-0	175	6-25-69	1991	Blythewood, S.C.

FIELDING

Catcher	PCT	G	PO	A	E	DP	PB
Houston	.952	18	73	6	4	1	1
Martinez	.959	12	45	2	2	0	0
Molina	1.000	10	44	5	0	1	1
Reed	.987	49	282	17	4	3	2
Santiago	.990	107	560	43	6	8	10

First Base	PCT	G	PO	A	E	DP
Andrews	.000	1	0	0	0	0
Gaetti	.957	8	39	6	2	6
Grace	.994	160	1335	93	8	115
Hernandez	1.000	1	2	0	0	0
Houston	1.000	2	1	0	0	0
Santiago	1.000	1	2	0	0	0

Second Base	PCT	G	PO	A	E	DP
Alexander	.927	17	21	17	3	4
Blauser	.961	25	41	32	3	9

	PCT	G	PO	A	E	DP
Meyers	.983	32	49	68	2	13
Morandini	.991	132	239	319	5	72

Third Base	PCT	G	PO	A	E	DP
Alexander	.893	22	8	17	3	0
Andrews	.956	19	8	35	2	6
Blauser	.897	18	7	19	3	0
Gaetti	.962	81	35	140	7	8
Houston	.901	63	35	83	13	7
Liniak	1.000	10	8	8	0	1
Reed	.000	1	0	0	0	0

Shortstop	PCT	G	PO	A	E	DP
Alexander	.988	30	27	54	1	9
Blauser	.985	22	21	43	1	7
Gaetti	1.000	1	0	1	0	0
Hernandez	.971	92	114	249	11	51

	PCT	G	PO	A	E	DP
Nieves	.935	52	67	162	16	29

Outfield	PCT	G	PO	A	E	DP
Alexander	.000	2	0	0	0	0
Blauser	1.000	1	1	0	0	0
Brown	.955	18	20	1	1	0
Goodwin	.983	76	115	3	2	2
Hernandez	1.000	20	24	0	0	0
Hill	.955	62	81	3	4	0
Houston	.000	1	0	0	0	0
Johnson	.988	91	235	6	3	2
Meyers	1.000	14	27	0	0	0
Porter	.941	21	16	0	1	0
Rodriguez	.974	122	222	7	6	1
Sosa	.978	162	399	8	9	3

Mark Grace
Collected 1,754 hits in the '90s

Julio Zuleta
Led system with 97 RBIs

FARM SYSTEM

Director, Player Development: Jim Hendry

Class	Farm Team	League	W	L	Pct.	Finish*	Manager	First Yr
AAA	Iowa Cubs	Pacific Coast	65	76	.461	14th (16)	Terry Kennedy	1981
AA	West Tenn Diamond Jaxx	Southern	83	57	.593	1st (10)	Dave Trembley	1998
A#	Daytona (Fla.) Cubs	Florida State	63	75	.457	11th (14)	Nate Oliver	1993
A	Lansing (Mich.) Lugnuts	Midwest	73	67	.511	6th (14)	Oscar Acosta	1999
A	Eugene (Ore.) Emeralds	Northwest	29	47	.382	8th (8)	Bob Ralston	1999
Rookie	Mesa (Ariz.) Cubs	Arizona	18	37	.327	8th (8)	Carmelo Martinez	1997

*Finish in overall standings (No. of teams in league)   #Advanced level

IOWA   Class AAA

PACIFIC COAST LEAGUE

BATTING	AVG	G	AB	R	H	2B	3B	HR	RBI	BB	SO	SB	CS	B	T	HT	WT	DOB	1st Yr	Resides
Almanzar, Richard	.215	33	93	13	20	2	3	1	4	6	7	6	1	R	R	5-10	165	4-3-76	1993	San Francisco de Macoris, D.R.
Battle, Allen	.245	35	110	16	27	7	0	3	14	14	30	2	1	R	R	6-1	180	11-29-68	1991	Mobile, Ala.
Bridges, Kary	.120	10	25	1	3	0	0	0	0	1	5	0	0	L	R	5-10	170	10-27-72	1993	Hattiesburg, Miss.
Brown, Roosevelt	.358	74	268	50	96	25	2	22	79	19	54	3	3	L	R	5-11	195	8-3-75	1993	Vicksburg, Miss.
Cline, Pat	.228	98	290	27	66	20	1	6	42	26	73	1	2	R	R	6-3	225	10-9-74	1993	Bradenton, Fla.
Gazarek, Marty	.320	40	128	13	41	12	0	5	16	5	13	0	1	R	R	6-2	205	6-1-73	1994	North Baltimore, Ohio
Hinske, Eric	.267	4	15	3	4	0	1	1	2	1	4	0	0	L	R	6-2	225	8-5-77	1998	Menasha, Wis.
Jennings, Robin	.309	67	259	47	80	20	5	9	43	25	34	6	4	L	L	6-2	210	4-11-72	1992	Scottsdale, Ariz.
King, Brett	.196	32	112	16	22	6	0	4	10	17	27	6	1	R	R	6-1	190	7-20-72	1993	Apopka, Fla.
Lisanti, Bob	.173	31	52	5	9	3	0	0	1	1	14	0	0	R	R	5-10	180	5-28-73	1996	Chicago, Ill.
Martinez, Sandy	.232	36	125	8	29	6	0	2	18	5	29	1	0	L	R	6-2	215	10-3-72	1990	Santo Domingo, D.R.
Meyers, Chad	.354	44	175	39	62	13	2	0	16	29	20	17	7	R	R	6-0	190	8-8-75	1996	Omaha, Neb.
Molina, Jose	.263	74	240	24	63	11	1	4	26	20	54	0	1	R	R	6-1	195	6-3-75	1993	Vega Alta, P.R.
Nieves, Jose	.268	104	392	55	105	25	3	11	59	24	65	11	8	R	R	6-1	185	6-16-75	1992	Guacara, Venez.
Porter, Bo	.292	111	414	86	121	24	2	27	64	65	121	15	17	R	R	6-2	195	7-5-72	1994	Newark, N.J.
Quinlan, Tom	.250	133	472	62	118	26	1	17	58	41	159	1	1	R	R	6-4	220	3-27-68	1987	Maplewood, Minn.
Rennhack, Mike	.226	49	146	8	33	7	1	2	11	20	40	2	1	S	R	6-3	200	8-25-74	1992	Holiday, Fla.
Stahoviak, Scott	.237	83	274	51	65	16	1	14	44	44	88	4	1	L	R	6-5	220	3-6-70	1991	Round Lake Beach, Ill.
White, Derrick	.262	132	503	75	132	31	0	13	77	47	94	10	8	R	R	6-1	225	10-12-69	1991	Marin City, Calif.
Wilson, Brandon	.278	123	472	82	131	28	6	12	49	34	76	31	5	R	R	6-1	190	2-26-69	1990	Scottsdale, Ariz.
Zinter, Alan	.255	14	51	7	13	2	0	3	8	5	13	0	0	S	R	6-2	200	5-19-68	1989	Tucson, Ariz.

Organization Statistics

PITCHING

PITCHING	W	L	ERA	G	GS	CG	SV	IP	H	R	ER	BB	SO	B	T	HT	WT	DOB	1st Yr	Resides
Barker, Richie	4	4	4.26	55	2	0	7	74	72	37	35	30	52	R	R	6-2	220	10-29-72	1994	Malden, Mass.
Beck, Rod	0	0	0.00	2	0	0	0	2	1	0	0	0	2	R	R	6-1	235	8-3-68	1986	Scottsdale, Ariz.
Cole, Victor	2	1	4.69	19	2	0	0	40	41	24	21	23	33	L	R	5-10	180	1-23-68	1988	Cordova, Tenn.
Creek, Doug	7	3	3.79	25	20	0	1	131	116	66	55	62	140	L	L	6-0	200	3-1-69	1991	Dallas, Texas
Farnsworth, Kyle	2	2	3.20	6	6	0	0	39	38	16	14	9	29	R	R	6-4	220	4-14-76	1995	Roswell, Ga.
Gajkowski, Steve	5	8	3.73	58	0	0	9	80	79	36	33	25	64	R	R	6-3	215	12-30-69	1990	Olympia, Wash.
Gonzalez, Jeremi	0	1	4.50	3	3	0	0	10	10	8	5	6	10	R	R06-2		210	1-8-75	1992	Maracaibo, Venez.
Juelsgaard, Jarod	4	7	5.59	23	12	2	0	84	92	57	52	26	54	R	R	6-3	205	6-27-68	1991	Ridgeway, Iowa
Karchner, Matt	0	0	6.35	5	1	0	0	6	6	4	4	1	6	R	R	6-4	210	6-28-67	1989	Manassas, Va.
King, Ray	4	4	1.88	37	0	0	2	43	31	11	9	22	41	L	L	6-1	225	1-15-74	1995	Chicago, Ill.
Lacy, Kerry	3	8	5.44	49	5	0	0	93	105	65	56	44	69	R	R	6-2	215	8-7-72	1991	Higdon, Ala.
Lorraine, Andrew	9	8	3.71	22	21	1	0	143	149	67	59	34	96	L	L	6-3	205	8-11-72	1993	Scottsdale, Ariz.
Manning, David	0	0	4.66	7	0	0	0	10	9	6	5	8	7	R	R	6-3	215	8-14-72	1992	Lantana, Fla.
McNichol, Brian	10	11	5.58	28	28	2	0	161	194	108	100	55	120	L	L	6-5	225	5-20-74	1995	Woodbridge, Va.
Miller, Kurt	1	2	5.09	8	2	0	1	18	17	10	10	8	23	R	R	6-5	205	8-24-72	1990	Bakersfield, Calif.
Myers, Rodney	2	4	4.06	20	1	0	2	31	29	18	14	11	24	R	R	6-1	205	6-26-69	1990	Chandler, Ariz.
Nomo, Hideo	1	1	3.71	3	3	0	0	17	12	7	7	12	18	R	R	6-2	210	8-31-68	1995	Kobe, Japan
Norton, Phillip	5	6	6.67	14	14	0	0	80	98	63	59	33	61	R	L	6-1	185	2-1-76	1996	Texarkana, Texas
Quevedo, Ruben	3	1	3.45	7	7	1	0	44	34	18	17	21	50	R	R	6-1	180	1-5-79	1996	Valencia, Venez.
Rain, Steve	0	0	2.00	8	0	0	2	9	7	2	2	4	9	R	R	6-6	250	6-2-75	1993	Walnut, Calif.
Serafini, Dan	0	0	2.77	2	2	0	0	13	12	6	4	5	11	S	L	6-1	195	1-25-74	1992	San Bruno, Calif.
Watkins, Scott	1	2	6.14	47	3	0	0	63	71	47	43	33	54	L	L	6-2	195	5-15-70	1992	Sand Springs, Okla.
Woodall, Brad	2	2	6.84	15	9	0	1	53	67	40	40	23	41	S	L	6-0	175	6-25-69	1991	Blythewood, S.C.

FIELDING

Catcher	PCT	G	PO	A	E	DP	PB
Cline	.966	30	187	11	7	1	10
Lisanti	.971	11	64	4	2	1	2
Martinez	.996	34	239	17	1	0	3
Molina	.987	71	488	44	7	5	9
Zinter	1.000	7	44	5	0	1	2

First Base	PCT	G	PO	A	E	DP
Hinske	.947	2	17	1	1	1
Jennings	1.000	1	3	0	0	0
Quinlan	.986	22	187	17	3	16
Stahoviak	.990	71	563	44	6	50
White	.991	48	388	33	4	25
Zinter	1.000	8	66	7	0	7

Second Base	PCT	G	PO	A	E	DP
Almanzar	.935	12	25	18	3	8

	PCT	G	PO	A	E	DP
Bridges	1.000	2	0	1	0	0
Meyers	.980	39	95	99	4	28
Nieves	1.000	1	1	6	0	0
Wilson	.975	93	187	239	11	44

Third Base	PCT	G	PO	A	E	DP
Almanzar	.906	12	6	23	3	2
Bridges	1.000	5	0	7	0	0
Hinske	1.000	1	0	2	0	0
Quinlan	.963	116	85	257	13	28
Wilson	.926	20	6	44	4	1

Shortstop	PCT	G	PO	A	E	DP
Almanzar	1.000	4	4	8	0	1
B. King	.934	32	51	105	11	23
Nieves	.958	101	121	309	19	54

	PCT	G	PO	A	E	DP
Wilson	.972	8	14	21	1	1

Outfield	PCT	G	PO	A	E	DP
Battle	.960	13	23	1	1	0
Brown	.959	67	107	11	5	1
Cline	.923	18	24	0	2	0
Gazarek	.989	38	84	5	1	1
Jennings	.977	61	123	7	3	1
Meyers	1.000	5	9	0	0	0
Porter	1.000	107	223	5	0	3
Rennhack	1.000	43	69	3	0	1
Stahoviak	.952	8	18	2	1	0
White	1.000	82	125	6	0	0

WEST TENN — Class AA

SOUTHERN LEAGUE

BATTING	AVG	G	AB	R	H	2B	3B	HR	RBI	BB	SO	SB	CS	B	T	HT	WT	DOB	1st Yr	Resides
Almanzar, Richard	.305	42	151	27	46	7	0	2	16	18	19	13	7	R	R	5-10	165	4-3-76	1993	San Francisco de Macoris, D.R.
Bowers, Brent	.160	35	100	10	16	4	0	2	9	11	16	4	0	L	R	6-4	215	5-2-71	1989	Bridgeview, Ill.
Brock, Tarrik	.217	54	189	29	41	10	4	1	9	33	60	9	4	L	L	6-3	170	12-25-73	1991	Hawthorne, Calif.
2-team (66 Carolina)	.233	120	407	69	95	20	5	8	32	72	127	16	8							
Brown, Roosevelt	.296	34	125	12	37	12	0	3	12	14	29	6	1	L	R	5-11	195	8-3-75	1993	Vicksburg, Miss.
Encarnacion, Angelo	.257	30	101	16	26	6	1	1	10	4	12	2	0	R	R	5-8	190	4-18-73	1990	Santo Domingo, D.R.
Font, Franklin	.344	25	96	14	33	2	1	1	17	8	14	4	4	R	R	5-10	190	11-4-77	1995	Caracas, Venez.
Gazarek, Marty	.297	35	128	16	38	9	1	6	27	4	7	2	5	R	R	6-2	205	6-1-73	1994	North Baltimore, Ohio
Jennings, Robin	.321	13	53	11	17	3	0	5	17	5	7	1	0	L	L	6-2	205	4-11-72	1992	Scottsdale, Ariz.
King, Brad	.228	92	232	29	53	10	0	0	25	38	34	2	1	R	R	6-2	205	12-3-74	1996	Boca Raton, Fla.
King, Brett	.218	54	142	27	31	6	0	3	13	39	49	7	6	R	R	6-1	190	7-20-72	1993	Apopka, Fla.
Manning, Nate	.222	13	27	0	6	2	0	0	5	2	8	1	0	R	R	6-2	215	12-20-73	1996	Keosauqua, Iowa
Meyers, Chad	.290	64	238	45	69	19	2	3	29	26	40	22	8	R	R	6-0	190	8-8-75	1996	Omaha, Neb.
Micucci, Mike	.169	52	124	7	21	1	0	0	7	7	32	1	0	L	R	5-11	190	12-15-72	1994	Emerson, N.J.
Molina, Jose	.171	14	35	2	6	3	0	0	5	2	14	0	0	R	R	6-1	195	6-3-75	1993	Vega Alta, P.R.
Nelson, Bry	.268	129	471	66	126	24	5	16	78	42	52	10	7	S	R	5-10	205	1-27-74	1994	Crossett, Ark.
Polanco, Enohel	.240	116	354	44	85	21	5	3	30	20	89	12	8	R	R	5-11	165	8-11-75	1992	Puerto Plata, D.R.
Rennhack, Mike	.254	66	189	29	48	11	0	5	21	34	46	4	0	S	R	6-3	205	8-25-74	1992	Holiday, Fla.
Rivers, Jonathan	.182	35	88	10	16	3	0	1	6	8	20	5	0	R	R	6-3	205	8-17-74	1992	Tallassee, Ala.
Speed, Dorian	.267	121	415	70	111	21	8	14	57	27	106	22	11	R	R	6-3	205	3-1-74	1995	Tempe, Ariz.
Vieira, Scott	.292	126	455	63	133	44	4	10	58	53	126	10	6	R	R	5-11	185	8-17-73	1995	Hermitage, Tenn.
Walker, Ron	.219	105	302	42	66	20	1	9	42	39	86	2	0	R	R	6-2	215	12-29-75	1997	Indian Mills, N.J.
Zuleta, Julio	.295	133	482	75	142	37	4	21	97	35	122	4	3	R	R	6-6	230	3-28-75	1993	Mesa, Ariz.

PITCHING	W	L	ERA	G	GS	CG	SV	IP	H	R	ER	BB	SO	B	T	HT	WT	DOB	1st Yr	Resides
Adams, Terry	0	0	16.88	2	1	0	0	3	9	6	6	4	4	R	R	6-3	205	3-6-73	1991	Semmes, Ala.
Cole, Victor	3	1	3.91	17	0	0	0	23	21	11	10	18	17	L	R	5-10	180	1-23-68	1988	Cordova, Tenn.
Downs, Scott	8	1	1.35	13	12	1	0	80	56	13	12	28	101	L	L	6-2	180	3-17-76	1997	Louisville, Ky.
Duncan, Courtney	1	7	7.13	11	8	0	0	42	44	42	33	42	42	L	R	6-0	185	10-9-74	1996	Daphne, Ala.
Fennell, Barry	0	0	0.00	1	0	0	0	1	2	0	0	1	0	R	L	6-4	225	9-30-76	1994	Pennsauken, N.J.
Gissell, Chris	3	8	5.99	20	18	0	0	98	121	76	65	62	57	R	R	6-5	205	1-4-78	1996	Vancouver, Wash.
Gonzalez, Jeremi	0	0	1.74	3	3	0	0	10	7	2	2	9	12	R	R	6-2	210	1-8-75	1992	Maracaibo, Venez.
Hernandez, Elvin	9	9	4.94	29	25	1	1	151	174	100	83	50	98	R	R	6-1	195	8-20-77	1994	Laguna Salada Monte, D.R.
Manning, David	8	5	3.94	23	18	6	0	123	113	59	54	51	78	R	R	6-3	215	8-14-72	1992	Lantana, Fla.
Meyers, Mike	4	0	1.09	5	5	0	0	33	21	5	4	10	51	R	R	6-2	210	10-18-77	1997	Tillsonburg, Ontario
Negrette, Richard	1	0	5.40	3	0	0	0	3	3	2	2	2	2	R	R	6-2	175	3-6-76	1994	Maracaibo, Venez.
Newman, Eric	5	3	3.20	58	0	0	8	84	61	37	30	49	90	R	R	6-4	220	8-27-72	1995	Fremont, Calif.
Norton, Phillip	7	4	2.39	14	13	0	0	87	72	32	23	42	81	R	L	6-1	185	2-1-76	1996	Texarkana, Texas

PITCHING	W	L	ERA	G	GS	CG	SV	IP	H	R	ER	BB	SO	B	T	HT	WT	DOB	1st Yr	Resides
Piersoll, Chris	0	0	0.63	8	1	0	1	14	12	1	1	3	14	R	R	6-4	195	9-25-77	1997	Carlsbad, Calif.
Rain, Steve	3	1	1.59	40	0	0	24	45	32	9	8	16	55	R	R	6-6	250	6-2-75	1993	Walnut, Calif.
Ricketts, Chad	6	4	3.09	57	0	0	8	67	55	25	23	21	80	R	R	6-5	225	2-12-75	1995	Thorold, Ontario
Ryan, Jason	5	0	1.41	8	7	0	0	45	29	12	7	15	53	S	R	6-3	185	1-23-76	1994	Charlotte, N.C.
Schutz, Carl	3	1	4.38	40	0	0	1	51	54	30	25	30	46	L	L	5-10	200	8-22-71	1993	Gonzales, La.
Smith, Dan	5	3	4.22	56	0	0	2	75	70	38	35	31	78	L	L	6-5	190	8-20-69	1990	Arlington, Texas
Yoder, Jeff	10	5	3.08	29	22	0	0	134	115	54	46	70	109	L	R	6-2	210	2-16-76	1996	Pottsville, Pa.
Young, Danny	3	5	3.28	27	8	0	0	60	48	25	22	38	67	L	R	6-4	210	11-3-71	1991	Woodbury, Tenn.

FIELDING

Catcher	PCT	G	PO	A	E	DP	PB
Encarnacion	.992	29	221	25	2	1	1
Bra. King	.989	85	571	49	7	6	9
Micucci	.993	49	267	24	2	2	8
Molina	.982	12	97	13	2	0	4

First Base	PCT	G	PO	A	E	DP
Vieira	.990	36	178	14	2	15
Walker	1.000	2	1	0	0	0
Zuleta	.991	120	897	63	9	89

Second Base	PCT	G	PO	A	E	DP
Almanzar	.984	41	77	104	3	29
Font	.971	20	33	34	2	10
Bre. King	.944	9	9	8	1	3
C. Meyers	.966	63	106	148	9	29

	PCT	G	PO	A	E	DP
Nelson	.989	23	43	45	1	13
Polanco	1.000	7	7	12	0	2

Third Base	PCT	G	PO	A	E	DP
Font	1.000	1	1	2	0	0
Bre. King	1.000	1	0	1	0	0
N. Manning	1.000	8	4	11	0	1
Nelson	.905	92	56	134	20	11
Walker	.888	62	32	87	15	10

Shortstop	PCT	G	PO	A	E	DP
Font	.913	8	8	13	2	2
Bre. King	.962	43	54	121	7	25
Nelson	.833	5	3	2	1	0
Polanco	.948	103	146	237	21	53

Outfield	PCT	G	PO	A	E	DP
Bowers	.988	34	80	3	1	0
Brock	.993	52	136	6	1	1
Brown	.983	33	52	5	1	0
Gazarek	.960	33	47	1	2	0
Jennings	1.000	13	18	1	0	0
Bra. King	1.000	6	4	0	0	0
Nelson	1.000	15	17	1	0	0
Rennhack	.965	46	81	1	3	1
Rivers	.923	29	33	3	3	0
Speed	.980	116	197	2	4	0
Vieira	.980	101	144	4	3	0

DAYTONA — Class A

FLORIDA STATE LEAGUE

BATTING	AVG	G	AB	R	H	2B	3B	HR	RBI	BB	SO	SB	CS	B	T	HT	WT	DOB	1st Yr	Resides
Abreu, Dennis	.257	105	374	44	96	10	2	2	30	13	69	29	9	R	R	6-0	180	4-22-78	1995	Tumero, Venez.
Amrhein, Mike	.278	127	449	55	125	27	1	10	58	31	67	1	1	R	R	6-2	215	6-14-75	1997	Oak Park, Ill.
Bly, Derrick	.235	41	149	22	35	13	0	4	15	16	34	1	1	R	R	6-0	190	9-19-74	1996	Tucson, Ariz.
Carter, Quincy	.000	1	3	0	0	0	0	0	0	0	1	0	0	R	R	6-3	215	10-13-77	1996	Ellenwood, Ga.
Clarke, Jason	.240	81	254	24	61	6	1	2	29	25	27	8	3	S	R	5-9	170	10-17-75	1998	Frederiksted, V.I.
Connally, Chris	.233	29	90	10	21	3	0	0	9	5	19	2	1	R	R	5-11	190	3-24-76	1998	Midland, Texas
Font, Franklin	.295	87	315	48	93	7	4	2	33	21	38	14	6	R	R	5-10	190	11-4-77	1995	Caracas, Venez.
Hall, Doug	.248	31	101	9	25	8	0	0	8	2	11	2	0	L	L	6-1	190	12-12-74	1996	Gallatin, Tenn.
Hargreaves, Brad	.168	39	101	6	17	3	0	0	6	4	27	1	0	R	R	6-0	175	10-30-77	1997	Cincinnati, Ohio
Hinske, Eric	.297	130	445	76	132	28	6	19	79	62	90	16	10	L	R	6-2	225	8-5-77	1998	Menasha, Wis.
Jimenez, Felipe	.196	18	51	5	10	0	0	0	7	4	13	2	1	R	R	6-3	200	12-22-76	1994	Camatagua, Venez.
Johnson, Gary	.229	108	323	46	74	16	1	7	38	39	53	4	6	R	R	6-3	200	9-6-76	1997	Baldwin Park, Calif.
Manning, Nate	.252	110	393	48	99	23	3	11	57	33	83	2	2	R	R	6-2	215	12-20-73	1996	Keosauqua, Iowa
Ramsey, Brad	.212	105	330	47	70	15	0	9	44	40	67	1	3	R	R	6-4	215	11-7-76	1997	West Monroe, La.
Randolph, Jaisen	.272	130	511	70	139	16	5	2	37	43	86	25	26	R	R	6-0	180	1-19-79	1997	Tampa, Fla.
Rico, Diego	.282	100	344	50	97	22	5	4	42	26	66	10	4	L	L	6-0	180	3-24-76	1997	Tucson, Ariz.
Smith, Jason	.261	39	142	22	37	5	2	5	26	12	29	9	3	L	R	6-3	190	7-24-77	1997	Coatopa, Ala.
Vessel, Andrew	.208	20	77	7	16	4	0	2	8	6	19	1	1	R	R	6-3	225	3-11-75	1993	Richmond, Calif.

GAMES BY POSITION: C—Amrhein 45, Hargreaves 38, Ramsey 65. **1B**—Amrhein 50, Bly 9, Hinske 57, Manning 27. **2B**—Abreu 103, Clarke 36, Font 10. **3B**—Bly 14, Clarke 8, Font 3, Hinske 60, Manning 61. **SS**—Clarke 29, Font 76, Smith 39. **OF**—Bly 18, Carter 1, Connally 11, Hall 12, Hinske 6, Jimenez 17, Johnson 105, Manning 19, Randolph 130, Rico 93, Vessel 17.

PITCHING	W	L	ERA	G	GS	CG	SV	IP	H	R	ER	BB	SO	B	T	HT	WT	DOB	1st Yr	Resides
Booker, Chris	2	5	3.95	42	0	0	6	73	72	45	32	37	68	R	R	6-3	220	12-9-76	1995	Monroeville, Ala.
Cannon, Jon	3	5	4.42	33	11	1	0	96	83	55	47	66	77	R	L	6-3	200	1-1-75	1996	Los Altos, Calif.
Christensen, Ben	1	3	6.35	4	4	0	0	23	25	16	16	11	18	R	R	6-4	205	2-7-78	1999	Port Orange, Fla.
Downs, Scott	5	0	1.88	7	7	1	0	48	41	12	10	11	41	L	L	6-2	180	3-17-76	1997	Louisville, Ky.
2-team (2 Ft. Myers)	5	1	1.56	9	9	1	0	58	48	15	10	17	50							
Duncan, Courtney	4	5	5.54	15	11	1	1	65	70	60	40	34	48	L	R	6-0	185	10-9-74	1996	Daphne, Ala.
Fennell, Barry	2	4	4.99	22	0	0	5	31	33	21	17	18	21	R	L	6-4	225	9-30-76	1994	Pennsauken, N.J.
Fisher, Louis	3	8	5.56	40	0	0	9	70	63	59	43	50	64	R	R	6-0	200	10-14-75	1995	Oakland, Calif.
Gonzalez, Jeremi	0	0	0.00	2	2	0	0	5	2	0	0	0	4	R	R	6-2	210	1-8-75	1992	Maracaibo, Venez.
Gulin, Lindsay	2	0	0.00	3	1	0	0	14	7	0	0	7	19	L	L	6-3	165	11-22-76	1995	Issaquah, Wash.
Hammons, Matt	2	4	4.98	15	11	0	1	60	54	36	33	32	53	L	L	6-3	205	4-9-77	1995	San Diego, Calif.
Johnston, Sean	2	5	5.00	26	3	0	0	68	91	54	38	39	28	L	L	6-4	190	6-28-76	1994	Highland Park, Ill.
Lohse, Kyle	5	3	2.89	9	9	1	0	53	48	21	17	16	41	R	R	6-2	190	10-4-78	1997	Glenn, Calif.
Meyers, Mike	10	3	1.93	19	17	2	0	107	68	30	23	40	122	R	R	6-2	210	10-18-77	1997	Tillsonburg, Ontario
Nation, Joey	2	0	1.38	2	2	0	0	13	8	2	2	2	11	L	L	6-2	175	9-28-78	1997	Oklahoma City, Okla.
Ohman, Will	4	7	3.46	31	15	2	5	107	102	59	41	41	97	L	L	6-2	195	8-13-77	1998	Parker, Colo.
Piersoll, Chris	7	3	3.72	33	0	0	5	68	68	30	28	24	74	R	R	6-4	195	9-25-77	1997	Carlsbad, Calif.
Sams, Aaron	2	5	4.75	10	10	1	0	55	53	31	29	26	41	L	L	6-1	195	4-30-76	1998	Bedford, Pa.
Sullivan, Shane	1	0	6.75	4	0	0	0	12	17	10	9	7	5	R	R	6-2	175	12-17-77	1997	Pinon Hills, Calif.
Teut, Nate	5	12	6.38	26	26	1	0	133	180	113	94	41	91	R	L	6-7	205	3-11-76	1997	Monroe, Iowa
Williams, Randy	3	4	4.75	14	9	0	1	53	55	36	28	30	47	L	L	6-3	195	9-18-75	1997	Dickinson, Texas
Yoder, Jeff	0	0	0.84	5	0	0	1	11	8	2	1	5	11	L	R	6-2	210	2-16-76	1996	Pottsville, Pa.

LANSING — Class A

MIDWEST LEAGUE

BATTING	AVG	G	AB	R	H	2B	3B	HR	RBI	BB	SO	SB	CS	B	T	HT	WT	DOB	1st Yr	Resides
Bly, Derrick	.295	63	220	36	65	14	4	4	29	9	48	1	1	R	R	6-0	190	9-19-74	1996	Tucson, Ariz.
Choi, Hee	.321	79	290	71	93	18	6	18	70	50	68	2	1	L	L	6-5	240	3-16-79	1999	Kwang Ju, Korea
De la Cruz, Henry	.215	71	209	26	45	14	0	6	31	29	75	7	4	R	R	6-0	180	8-25-76	1994	Santo Domingo, D.R.

BATTING	AVG	G	AB	R	H	2B	3B	HR	RBI	BB	SO	SB	CS	B	T	HT	WT	DOB	1st Yr	Resides
Dorsett, Chris	.231	57	130	20	30	8	0	2	19	37	24	2	2	R	R	6-2	215	4-5-75	1998	Cranford, N.J.
Frese, Nate	.265	107	373	68	99	27	4	4	49	58	67	10	4	R	R	6-3	190	7-10-77	1998	Norway, Iowa
Fukuhara, Pete	.311	60	235	39	73	19	2	11	40	24	31	7	5	R	R	5-10	175	10-21-75	1998	Palo Alto, Calif.
German, Franklin	.242	84	281	49	68	12	2	5	31	23	75	12	4	R	R	5-10	175	2-28-80	1997	Santo Domingo, D.R.
Goldbach, Jeff	.271	112	399	82	108	27	3	18	72	64	66	1	4	R	R	6-0	190	12-20-79	1998	Princeton, Ind.
Griffin, Matt	.182	5	11	0	2	1	0	0	1	1	4	0	0	R	R	6-1	175	12-24-75	1998	Toccoa, Ga.
Hall, Doug	.278	33	90	16	25	8	0	2	18	16	23	3	2	L	L	6-1	190	12-12-74	1996	Gallatin, Tenn.
Kelton, David	.269	124	509	75	137	17	4	13	68	39	121	22	9	R	R	6-2	190	12-17-79	1998	West Point, Ga.
Mauck, Matt	.221	107	298	37	66	9	4	8	59	45	100	2	1	L	R	6-3	215	2-12-79	1997	Jasper, Ind.
Meadows, Tydus	.301	126	449	80	135	32	6	17	74	66	85	18	10	R	R	6-2	215	9-5-77	1998	Evans, Ga.
Moreno, Mikel	.158	5	19	1	3	0	1	1	2	0	2	1	0	R	R	5-10	180	9-5-76	1998	Mesa, Ariz.
Navarro, Ibrahim	.199	55	156	19	31	7	1	1	18	15	39	2	0	R	R	5-10	180	10-8-79	1997	Caracas, Venez.
Patterson, Corey	.320	112	475	94	152	35	17	20	79	25	85	33	9	L	R	5-10	175	8-13-79	1999	Kennesaw, Ga.
Pinero, Juan	.293	27	82	19	24	5	0	1	8	13	14	1	2	S	R	5-10	175	1-25-78	1996	Valle de Pascua, Venez.
Schrager, Tony	.270	122	392	83	106	31	4	16	73	103	101	8	3	R	R	6-1	185	6-14-77	1998	Omaha, Neb.
Vessel, Andrew	.308	13	52	7	16	4	2	0	11	2	3	1	0	R	R	6-3	225	3-11-75	1993	Richmond, Calif.

GAMES BY POSITION: C—Dorsett 39, Goldbach 85, Mauck 36. **1B**—Bly 29, Choi 79, de la Cruz 2, Griffin 2, Mauck 37, Navarro 1. **2B**—German 15, Griffin 1, Navarro 12, Schrager 122. **3B**—Bly 6, German 7, Kelton 113, Mauck 11, Navarro 13. **SS**—Frese 104, German 21, Griffin 1, Kelton 1, Navarro 22. **OF**—Bly 11, de la Cruz 62, Fukuhara 58, German 28, Hall 38, Meadows 121, Moreno 5, Patterson 102, Pinero 22, Vessel 13.

PITCHING	W	L	ERA	G	GS	CG	SV	IP	H	R	ER	BB	SO	B	T	HT	WT	DOB	1st Yr	Resides
Bruback, Matt	9	8	5.40	25	25	0	0	135	151	92	81	87	118	R	R	6-6	205	1-12-79	1998	Sarasota, Fla.
Dant, Larry	3	1	4.97	43	0	0	12	54	54	35	30	19	52	R	R	6-4	230	9-2-76	1998	Walnut, Iowa
Delano, Mike	0	1	3.48	2	2	0	0	10	7	5	4	2	10	L	L	6-7	200	11-9-77	1997	Las Vegas, Nev.
Delatori, Keola	3	5	7.63	15	4	0	1	31	34	28	26	20	27	R	R	6-0	180	12-23-78	1998	Schaumburg, Ill.
Gomer, Jeramy	2	1	5.86	7	5	0	0	28	27	18	18	12	21	L	L	6-2	195	6-12-79	1998	Plant City, Fla.
Gunderson, Matt	0	0	9.61	13	0	0	0	20	28	23	21	11	11	S	R	6-1	175	4-29-77	1998	Salem, Ore.
Krug, Dustin	3	7	3.36	46	0	0	5	59	75	34	22	25	32	R	R	6-2	205	3-6-77	1998	Kodiak, Alaska
Mallory, Andrew	0	0	13.50	5	0	0	0	5	12	11	7	4	2	R	R	6-2	170	9-25-76	1996	St. Petersburg, Fla.
Murphy, Matt	3	1	3.50	25	2	0	2	46	50	22	18	16	39	L	L	6-2	175	10-31-78	1998	Delano, Tenn.
Palma, Ricardo	7	7	2.94	22	22	2	0	135	134	61	44	44	79	L	L	6-1	160	9-26-79	1996	Maracay, Venez.
Polanco, Elvis	0	4	6.45	25	0	0	4	38	54	34	27	16	29	R	R	6-2	195	3-10-78	1994	Puerto Cabello, Venez.
Sams, Aaron	6	4	4.67	17	17	0	0	96	99	57	50	52	83	L	L	6-1	195	4-30-76	1998	Bedford, Pa.
Smyth, Steve	5	3	6.93	10	10	0	0	51	68	40	39	30	46	S	L	6-0	195	6-3-78	1999	Temecula, Calif.
Sullivan, Shane	2	0	8.15	13	0	0	0	18	28	20	16	13	9	R	R	6-2	215	12-10-77	1997	Pinon Hills, Calif.
Torres, Leo	2	0	2.74	51	0	0	3	62	51	22	19	28	47	L	L	6-4	205	5-11-76	1998	Yuma, Ariz.
Waligora, Tom	2	6	4.28	50	1	0	5	82	78	44	39	38	56	R	R	6-8	235	8-7-76	1997	Richmond, Va.
Wuertz, Mike	11	12	4.80	28	28	1	0	161	191	104	86	44	127	R	R	6-3	180	12-15-78	1997	Austin, Minn.
Zamarripa, Tony	2	0	7.20	11	0	0	0	15	21	13	12	5	7	R	R	6-4	240	12-17-76	1998	Austin, Texas
Zambrano, Carlos	13	7	4.17	27	24	2	0	153	150	87	71	62	98	L	R	6-4	220	6-1-81	1998	Puerto Cabello, Venez.

EUGENE — Short-Season Class A

NORTHWEST LEAGUE

BATTING	AVG	G	AB	R	H	2B	3B	HR	RBI	BB	SO	SB	CS	B	T	HT	WT	DOB	1st Yr	Resides
Aldrup, Morey	.169	31	65	6	11	1	0	1	4	2	17	2	0	R	R	5-10	165	12-23-78	1997	Santa Ana, Calif.
Bass, Kevin	.191	59	188	23	36	8	2	8	30	25	79	4	4	S	R	6-2	205	6-22-79	1998	Fayette, Ala.
Cohens, Derrick	.212	43	118	14	25	5	0	0	11	15	29	3	5	R	R	6-0	205	4-25-79	1999	Interlachen, Fla.
Curry, Chris	.227	41	132	18	30	6	0	2	9	5	35	0	2	R	R	6-1	210	11-17-77	1999	Conway, Ark.
Deschaine, Jim	.298	73	272	49	81	12	0	10	48	29	59	7	7	R	R	6-0	190	9-18-77	1998	Bristol, Conn.
Dzurilla, Mike	.291	70	278	43	81	14	2	5	44	16	33	12	4	R	R	5-11	190	5-4-78	1999	Bayside, N.Y.
Gripp, Ryan	.308	73	266	40	82	18	1	12	48	27	65	2	1	R	R	6-1	205	4-20-78	1999	Indianola, Iowa
Gsell, Tony	.250	76	276	50	69	21	1	12	43	23	69	12	5	R	R	6-0	195	12-31-76	1998	Somerville, N.J.
Johnstone, Ben	.333	54	186	34	62	9	0	1	11	9	30	16	14	R	R	6-0	195	2-5-78	1999	Atlanta, Ga.
Koen, Nate	.185	23	27	1	5	3	0	0	3	4	6	0	0	R	R	6-0	190	7-17-76	1998	Chatham, Ill.
Kopitzke, Casey	.209	37	110	19	23	3	0	0	12	15	25	3	3	R	R	6-2	210	5-31-78	1999	Greenleaf, Wis.
Longmire, Marcel	.000	1	2	0	0	0	0	0	1	0	1	0	0	R	R	6-3	215	4-18-78	1996	Vallejo, Calif.
Marquez, Eduardo	.205	32	73	9	15	2	1	0	8	1	15	3	1	R	R	6-2	190	2-24-77	1999	Orange, Calif.
Medina, Luis	.337	56	202	30	68	6	0	3	31	11	21	2	1	R	R	6-2	195	5-14-79	1998	Valencia, Venez.
Pinero, Juan	.235	10	34	5	8	1	1	0	6	4	4	5	1	S	R	5-10	175	1-25-78	1996	Valle de Pascua, Venez.
Ryan, Jeff	.275	45	149	26	41	6	5	2	16	17	39	9	1	R	R	5-10	185	9-7-76	1999	Coppell, Texas
Shipp, Charles	.267	6	15	3	4	1	0	0	1	1	3	0	0	R	R	6-2	205	11-25-76	1998	Chicago, Ill.
Zoccolillo, Pete	.235	64	183	20	43	7	1	1	15	22	26	3	2	L	R	6-2	205	2-6-77	1999	White Plains, N.Y.

GAMES BY POSITION: C—Curry 38, Cohens 18, Kopitzke 37. **1B**—Aldrup 1, Curry 1, Cohens 3, Longmire 1, Medina 34, Zoccolillo 47. **2B**—Aldrup 3, Dzurilla 68, Gsell 7, Ryan 7. **3B**—Aldrup 1, Gripp 70, Medina 13. **SS**—Aldrup 3, Deschaine 15, Gsell 62. **OF**—Aldrup 20, Bass 39, Cohens 36, Deschaine 26, Johnstone 48, Marquez 30, Pinero 9, Ryan 40, Shipp 4, Zoccolillo 10.

PITCHING	W	L	ERA	G	GS	CG	SV	IP	H	R	ER	BB	SO	B	T	HT	WT	DOB	1st Yr	Resides
Acosta, Jhon	1	0	6.62	13	3	0	0	35	39	29	26	14	43	S	R	6-3	210	10-30-79	1998	Maracay, Venez.
Adams, Chris	1	1	5.30	17	0	0	4	19	24	14	11	14	17	R	R	6-5	175	6-3-78	1999	McGregor, Texas
Beltran, Francis	0	2	8.36	16	0	0	0	28	41	32	26	14	28	R	R	6-5	220	7-25-80	1997	Santo Domingo, D.R.
Christensen, Ben	0	2	5.91	5	5	0	0	21	21	14	14	14	21	R	R	6-4	205	2-7-78	1999	Port Orange, Fla.
Conroy, Ken	5	3	4.37	11	11	0	0	60	75	37	29	23	48	R	R	6-4	220	12-19-78	1998	Gastonia, N.C.
Cruz, Juan	5	6	5.94	15	15	0	0	80	97	59	53	33	65	R	R	6-2	155	10-15-80	1997	Bonao, D.R.
Cueto, Jose	0	2	4.50	4	4	0	0	24	26	13	12	5	21	R	R	6-2	170	9-13-78	1996	San Pedro de Macoris, D.R.
Eppeneder, James	3	1	2.87	20	0	0	1	31	21	10	10	22	42	L	L	6-3	210	11-17-78	1999	Antioch, Calif.
Gomer, Jeramy	2	11	7.32	16	15	0	0	82	106	70	67	28	52	L	L	6-2	195	6-12-79	1998	Plant City, Fla.
Gunderson, Matt	1	3	5.11	8	0	0	1	12	16	11	7	6	15	S	R	6-1	175	4-29-77	1998	Salem, Ore.
Jackson, Stosh	2	0	3.24	10	0	0	1	17	20	12	6	5	24	L	L	6-1	190	10-13-75	1999	Gresham, Ore.
Lavery, Tim	3	2	3.63	15	2	0	3	40	42	21	16	17	43	L	L	6-3	195	11-16-78	1999	Naperville, Ill.
Ohm, Joe	1	4	6.31	21	1	0	0	41	50	31	29	14	39	R	R	6-3	205	9-13-76	1998	Rochester, Minn.
Polanco, Elvis	0	0	8.22	10	0	0	0	15	22	16	14	9	13	R	R	6-2	195	3-10-78	1994	Puerto Cabello, Venez.
Shaffar, Ben	4	5	5.79	14	13	0	0	65	79	54	42	27	76	R	R	6-3	185	9-28-77	1999	Leitchfield, Ky.
Smyth, Steve	1	1	4.38	5	5	0	0	25	29	17	12	7	14	S	L	6-0	195	6-3-78	1999	Temecula, Calif.

PITCHING	W	L	ERA	G	GS	CG	SV	IP	H	R	ER	BB	SO	B	T	HT	WT	DOB	1st Yr	Resides
Stephenson, Brian	0	1	4.50	2	2	0	0	4	4	5	2	4	4	R	R	6-3	210	7-17-73	1994	Fullerton, Calif.
Vracar, Paul	1	0	10.69	20	0	0	0	32	46	45	38	26	26	R	R	6-5	200	12-5-79	1997	Stoney Creek, Ontario
Waldrum, Kevin	0	0	6.14	4	0	0	0	7	10	6	5	3	1	L	R	6-4	200	3-22-79	1997	Mineral Wells, Texas
Webb, John	1	0	0.00	2	0	0	1	4	1	0	0	1	3	R	R	6-3	190	5-23-79	1999	Pensacola, Fla.
Wiggins, Dan	1	0	6.00	3	0	0	0	6	4	5	4	3	8	R	R	6-3	220	10-4-76	1999	Waynesboro, Ga.

MESA — Rookie

ARIZONA LEAGUE

BATTING	AVG	G	AB	R	H	2B	3B	HR	RBI	BB	SO	SB	CS	B	T	HT	WT	DOB	1st Yr	Resides
Anderson, Syketo	.295	37	139	16	41	11	3	0	14	5	22	8	9	L	R	5-11	180	2-12-79	1999	Prattville, Ala.
Battle, Allen	.308	3	13	2	4	0	1	0	0	1	4	1	0	R	R	6-1	180	11-29-68	1991	Mobile, Ala.
Cash, Condor	.268	49	194	29	52	10	1	9	29	10	46	4	3	R	R	6-2	210	9-22-79	1999	Toccoa, Ga.
Hines, Derek	.236	36	123	14	29	4	5	0	9	11	39	6	1	R	R	6-2	205	3-31-77	1999	Arvada, Colo.
Johnstone, Ben	.429	2	7	1	3	0	0	0	1	0	2	0	0	R	R	6-0	195	2-5-78	1999	Atlanta, Ga.
Mallory, Mike	.242	42	149	20	36	6	0	4	15	12	48	2	2	R	R	6-4	205	12-8-80	1999	Dinwiddie, Va.
Martinez, Dionnar	.254	41	126	13	32	5	0	0	11	15	20	5	2	S	R	6-5	185	1-15-81	1998	Barcelona, Venez.
McClure, Trey	.268	47	164	30	44	9	2	7	25	21	25	3	0	R	R	6-0	195	11-20-75	1999	Baton Rouge, La.
Morrissey, Adam	.296	44	169	23	50	7	3	2	23	21	28	4	7	R	R	5-11	170	6-8-81	1999	Ourimbah, Australia
Paredes, Reny	.279	35	122	16	34	10	0	2	17	2	32	2	3	R	R	6-2	190	9-9-79	1997	Santo Domingo, D.R.
Paulino, Robert	.208	21	53	3	11	1	0	0	4	3	22	1	1	R	R	5-11	160	3-29-82	1998	San Cristobal, D.R.
Pimentel, Francisco	.289	29	83	13	24	4	3	1	8	10	27	3	0	R	R	5-11	177	10-9-80	1997	Pimentel, D.R.
Pina, Emmanuel	.216	18	51	3	11	1	0	0	3	4	11	2	2	R	R	6-2	190	4-28-80	1997	Santo Domingo, D.R.
Robinson, Coby	.188	30	80	12	15	1	2	2	9	11	25	0	1	R	R	6-5	225	12-30-78	1998	Jonesboro, Ga.
Rohena, Omar	.250	20	60	11	15	2	0	1	5	4	21	0	0	R	R	6-3	200	8-14-80	1998	Rio Grande, P.R.
Rowden, Monte	.189	15	37	4	7	0	1	1	7	2	8	0	0	R	R	6-4	195	6-9-77	1999	Dixon, Mo.
Sing, Brandon	.265	17	68	4	18	4	1	2	12	5	16	1	1	R	R	6-3	200	3-13-81	1999	Joliet, Ill.
Sprowl, Jon	.392	31	97	19	38	9	2	0	14	18	14	1	1	L	L	6-1	196	8-1-80	1999	Panama City, Fla.
Thornton-Murray, Jandin	.205	34	112	12	23	2	1	0	4	9	24	0	3	S	R	6-0	190	6-24-81	1999	Ewa Beach, Hawaii
Van Horn, Ryan	.150	18	40	4	6	2	0	0	4	0	8	1	0	R	R	5-11	195	9-6-77	1999	Modesto, Calif.

GAMES BY POSITION: C—Pina 18, Rowden 13, Sprowl 18, Van Horn 18. **1B**—McClure 42, Rohena 11, Sprowl 8. **2B**—Martinez 1, Morrissey 44, Pimentel 2, Thonton-Murray 13. **3B**—Paulino 3, Pimentel 23, Sing 16, Thornton-Murray 17. **SS**—Martinez 40, Paulino 17, Thornton-Murray 4. **OF**—Anderson 27, Cash 39, Hines 33, Johnstone 2, Mallory 33, McClure 1, Paredes 28, Robinson 15, Rohena 4.

PITCHING	W	L	ERA	G	GS	CG	SV	IP	H	R	ER	BB	SO	B	T	HT	WT	DOB	1st Yr	Resides
Acosta, Jhon	1	0	0.00	5	0	0	1	9	7	1	0	0	9	S	R	6-3	210	10-30-79	1996	Maracay, Venez.
Alvarez, Larry	2	0	3.18	8	0	0	0	17	17	7	6	8	10	R	R	6-1	200	9-24-79	1998	Walnut, Calif.
Bailey, David	0	0	9.45	4	0	0	1	7	8	7	7	2	10	R	R	6-1	200	2-2-77	1900	Chesapeake, Va.
Beltran, Francis	0	1	0.00	7	0	0	2	11	5	3	0	1	8	R	R	6-5	220	7-25-80	1997	Santo Domingo, D.R.
Benitez, Angel	0	3	7.76	16	0	0	0	27	37	24	23	11	15	R	R	6-2	190	1-28-81	1999	Caracas, Venez.
Chavez, Wilton	5	5	5.88	14	13	1	0	67	89	57	44	31	68	R	R	6-2	155	4-30-81	1998	Montecristi, D.R.
Christensen, Ben	0	1	3.00	3	3	0	0	9	8	3	3	5	10	R	R	6-4	205	2-7-78	1999	Port Orange, Fla.
Cordero, Frangil	2	6	4.02	14	13	0	0	69	68	48	31	31	78	S	L	5-10	170	12-8-80	1997	Bani, D.R.
Cueto, Jose	3	4	2.86	11	9	0	0	57	49	32	18	22	66	R	R	6-2	170	9-13-78	1996	San Pedro de Macoris, D.R.
Diaz, Eddy	0	6	8.39	17	2	0	2	34	47	44	32	23	30	R	R	6-3	200	2-5-81	1998	Azua, D.R.
Ericks, Dave	1	3	8.38	16	1	0	0	29	35	31	27	29	22	R	R	6-4	180	12-4-79	1998	St. John, Ind.
Hoff, Steve	0	1	4.50	3	3	0	0	6	6	4	3	5	9	L	L	6-4	220	7-1-77	1996	San Bruno, Calif.
Jackson, Stosh	0	1	1.69	6	0	0	0	11	8	5	2	4	23	L	L	6-1	190	10-13-75	1999	Gresham, Ore.
Pate, Dustin	1	5	9.62	12	11	0	0	49	70	53	52	21	42	R	R	6-5	185	3-14-81	1999	Clemson, S.C.
Reyes, Junior	0	1	19.41	7	0	0	0	11	24	24	23	13	5	L	L	6-3	160	7-16-81	1997	Santo Domingo, D.R.
Stephenson, Brian	0	0	0.00	1	0	0	0	2	1	0	0	0	2	R	R	6-3	210	7-17-73	1994	Fullerton, Calif.
Webb, John	0	0	3.58	18	0	0	3	33	33	20	13	8	39	R	R	6-3	190	5-23-79	1999	Pensacola, Fla.
Wiggins, Dan	3	0	2.88	17	0	0	2	34	29	16	11	11	47	R	R	6-3	220	10-4-76	1999	Waynesboro, Ga.

CINCINNATI REDS

Surprising season accelerates timetable for upstart Reds

BY MARK SCHMETZER

When the 1999 season opened, postseason play was in the Reds' future—the distant future. The projection was 2003, when their new ballpark is scheduled to open.

Even with the offseason acquisitions of lefthander Denny Neagle and left fielder Greg Vaughn, these Reds were supposed to be more entertaining than effective. In the end, they were both. They battled all season and found themselves in a one-game playoff with the Mets for the National League wild-card berth. They lost 5-0.

"It's a shame," manager Jack McKeon said. "You win 96 games and then go home. That's tough. But this has been a tremendous experience for these guys, and they're certainly going to be better because of it."

The 1999 Reds set club records for the number of players with double-figure homer seasons (10) and pounded out the second-highest number of homers in club history (209). Vaughn rebounded from a slow start to hit 14 home runs in September. He finished with 45, matching Johnny Bench for the fourth-highest total in franchise history.

Other than second-year first baseman Sean Casey, the Reds opened the season slowly. They were in last place as late as May 15. Casey led the league in hitting for much of the first half of the season, but the pitching rotation was hampered by the aches and pains of Neagle and Pete Harnisch and put too much pressure on a youthful bullpen.

Perhaps the biggest surprise was Pokey Reese, the former shortstop who batted .285 and played Gold Glove-caliber defense in his first full year at second base.

Sean Casey · **Travis Dawkins**

Players of the Year

MAJOR LEAGUE: Sean Casey, 1b
Casey keyed the Reds offense in 1999 with a .332 average, 25 home runs and 99 RBIs in his second major league season.

MINOR LEAGUE: Travis Dawkins, ss
Dawkins climbed from Rockford to Chattanooga to the big leagues and even took time off to play with Team USA in the Pan American Games.

"It was the simultaneous development of our young players, like Casey, Reese, Mike Cameron, Aaron Boone, Dmitri Young, Scott Williamson, Danny Graves and Dennis Reyes," general manager Jim Bowden said. "You don't see that many young players come together at the same time too often."

The news off the field was promising as well, as Marge Schott completed her sale of the controlling interest in the franchise to a group of her limited partners.

Even the farm system showed improvement, putting together a combined winning percentage of .521 (362-333), eighth-best in baseball. Reds farm teams turned in the fifth-worst cumulative record in 1998. Both Reds affiliates in the Class A Midwest League, Clinton and Rockford, qualified for the playoffs.

Double-A Chattanooga outfielder Brady Clark, who missed more than half of the 1998 season with a stress fracture in his leg, was named the Southern League MVP after leading the league in hitting. Righthander Rob Bell, the organization's top prospect, missed more than half the season nursing a sore elbow but finished 3-6 with a 3.13 ERA in 12 starts.

Lefthander Ty Howington, the club's first-round pick in June, held out until August before signing for $1.75 million. The real story of the draft, though, was outfielder Ben Broussard, a second-round pick out of McNeese State. He hit .407-14-48 in 145 at-bats at Rookie-level Billings, earning a promotion to Clinton and then to Chattanooga.

There will be one significant change in the Reds' minor league lineup in 2000, with Louisville replacing Indianapolis as the Triple-A affiliate.

ORGANIZATION LEADERS

BATTING

*AVG	Jason Williams, Indianapolis/Chattanooga	.339
R	Brady Clark, Chattanooga	103
H	Jason Williams, Indianapolis/Chattanooga	167
TB	D.T. Cromer, Indianapolis	301
2B	Jason Williams, Indianapolis/Chattanooga	45
3B	DeWayne Wise, Rockford	13
HR	D.T. Cromer, Indianapolis	30
RBI	D.T. Cromer, Indianapolis	107
BB	Brady Clark, Chattanooga	89
SO	Samone Peters, Clinton/Billings	188
SB	Travis Dawkins, Chattanooga/Rockford	53

PITCHING

W	Two tied at	14
L	Justin Atchley, Indianapolis/Chattanooga	10
#ERA	Bo Donaldson, Chattanooga/Rockford	2.32
G	Pat Flury, Indianapolis/Chattanooga	66
CG	James Manias, Chattanooga/Rockford	4
SV	Brandon Puffer, Clinton	34
IP	Denny Harriger, Indianapolis	172
BB	Jim Crowell, Chattanooga	85
SO	Dave Therneau, Indianapolis/Chatta./Rockford	139

*Minimum 250 At-Bats #Minimum 75 Innings

Cincinnati REDS

Manager: Jack McKeon

1999 Record: 96-67, .589 (2nd, NL Central)

BATTING	AVG	G	AB	R	H	2B	3B	HR	RBI	BB	SO	SB	CS	B	T	HT	WT	DOB	1st Yr	Resides
Boone, Aaron	.280	139	472	56	132	26	5	14	72	30	79	17	6	R	R	6-2	200	3-9-73	1994	Villa Park, Calif.
Cameron, Mike	.256	146	542	93	139	34	9	21	66	80	145	38	12	R	R	6-2	190	1-8-73	1991	La Grange, Ga.
Casey, Sean	.332	151	594	103	197	42	3	25	99	61	88	0	2	L	R	6-4	215	7-2-74	1995	Pittsburgh, Pa.
Dawkins, Travis	.143	7	7	1	1	0	0	0	0	0	4	0	0	R	R	6-1	180	5-12-79	1997	Chappells, S.C.
Garcia, Guillermo	.250	4	4	0	1	0	0	0	0	0	2	0	0	R	R	6-3	215	4-4-72	1990	Santiago, D.R.
Hammonds, Jeffrey	.279	123	262	43	73	13	0	17	41	27	64	3	6	R	R	6-0	195	3-5-71	1992	Scotch Plains, N.J.
Johnson, Brian	.231	45	117	12	27	7	0	5	18	9	31	0	0	R	R	6-2	210	1-8-68	1989	Chicago, Ill.
Larkin, Barry	.293	161	583	108	171	30	4	12	75	93	57	30	8	R	R	6-0	185	4-28-64	1985	Cincinnati, Ohio
LaRue, Jason	.211	36	90	12	19	7	0	3	10	11	32	4	1	R	R	5-11	200	3-19-74	1995	Spring Branch, Texas
Lewis, Mark	.254	88	173	18	44	16	0	6	28	7	24	0	0	R	R	6-1	185	11-30-69	1988	Hamilton, Ohio
Morris, Hal	.284	80	102	10	29	9	0	0	16	10	21	0	0	L	L	6-2	195	4-9-65	1986	Orlando, Fla.
Reese, Pokey	.285	149	585	85	167	37	5	10	52	35	81	38	7	R	R	5-11	180	6-10-73	1991	Columbia, S.C.
Robinson, Kerry	.000	9	1	0	0	0	0	0	0	0	1	0	1	L	L	6-0	175	10-3-73	1994	Spanish Lake, Mo.
Stynes, Chris	.239	73	113	18	27	1	0	2	14	12	13	5	2	R	R	5-10	185	1-19-73	1991	Boca Raton, Fla.
Sweeney, Mark	.355	37	31	6	11	3	0	2	7	4	9	0	0	L	L	6-1	195	10-26-69	1991	Scottsdale, Ariz.
Taubensee, Eddie	.311	126	424	58	132	22	2	21	87	30	67	0	2	L	R	6-4	225	10-31-68	1986	Windermere, Fla.
Tucker, Michael	.253	133	296	55	75	8	5	11	44	37	81	11	4	L	R	6-2	185	6-25-71	1992	Lehigh Acres, Fla.
Vaughn, Greg	.245	153	550	104	135	20	2	45	118	85	137	15	2	R	R	6-0	202	7-3-65	1986	Elk Grove, Calif.
Young, Dmitri	.300	127	373	63	112	30	2	14	56	30	71	3	1	S	R	6-2	235	10-11-73	1991	Huntington, Ind.

PITCHING	W	L	ERA	G	GS	CG	SV	IP	H	R	ER	BB	SO	B	T	HT	WT	DOB	1st Yr	Resides
Avery, Steve	6	7	5.16	19	19	0	0	96	75	62	55	78	51	L	L	6-4	205	4-14-70	1988	Taylor, Mich.
Belinda, Stan	3	1	5.27	29	0	0	2	43	42	26	25	18	40	R	R	6-3	215	8-6-66	1985	Alexandria, Pa.
Bere, Jason	3	0	6.85	12	10	0	0	43	56	37	33	40	28	R	R	6-3	215	5-26-71	1990	Wilmington, Mass.
Graves, Danny	8	7	3.08	75	0	0	27	111	90	42	38	49	69	R	R	5-11	200	8-7-73	1995	Loveland, Ohio
Greene, Rick	0	0	4.76	1	0	0	0	6	7	4	3	1	3	R	R	6-5	200	1-2-71	1992	Miami, Fla.
Guzman, Juan	6	3	3.03	12	12	1	0	77	70	33	26	21	60	R	R	5-11	195	10-28-66	1985	Miami, Fla.
Harnisch, Pete	16	10	3.68	33	33	2	0	198	190	86	81	57	120	R	R	6-0	228	9-23-66	1987	Lake Mary, Fla.
Hudek, John	0	1	27.00	2	0	0	0	1	4	3	3	3	0	S	R	6-2	210	8-8-66	1988	Sugar Land, Texas
Neagle, Denny	9	5	4.27	20	19	0	0	112	95	54	53	40	76	L	L	6-2	225	9-13-68	1989	Alpharetta, Ga.
Parris, Steve	11	4	3.50	22	21	2	0	129	124	59	50	52	86	R	R	6-0	195	12-17-67	1989	Plainfield, Ill.
Reyes, Dennis	2	2	3.79	65	1	0	2	62	53	30	26	39	72	R	L	6-3	246	4-19-77	1994	Zaragoza, Mexico
Ryan, B.J.	0	0	4.50	1	0	0	0	2	4	1	1	1	1	L	L	6-6	230	12-28-75	1998	Benton, La.
Sullivan, Scott	5	4	3.01	79	0	0	3	114	88	41	38	47	78	R	R	6-3	210	3-13-71	1993	Livingston, Ala.
Tomko, Brett	5	7	4.92	33	26	1	0	172	175	103	94	60	132	R	R	6-4	215	4-7-73	1995	San Diego, Calif.
Villone, Ron	9	7	4.23	29	22	0	2	143	114	70	67	73	97	L	L	6-3	237	1-16-70	1992	Westwood, N.J.
White, Gabe	1	2	4.43	50	0	0	0	61	68	31	30	14	61	L	L	6-2	200	11-20-71	1990	Sebring, Fla.
Williamson, Scott	12	7	2.41	62	0	0	19	93	54	29	25	43	107	R	R	6-0	185	2-17-76	1997	Friendswood, Texas

FIELDING

Catcher	PCT	G	PO	A	E	DP	PB
Garcia	1.000	3	5	0	0	0	0
Johnson	.995	39	201	11	1	2	4
LaRue	.990	35	179	15	2	0	2
Taubensee	.989	124	733	48	9	8	5

First Base	PCT	G	PO	A	E	DP
Casey	.995	148	1190	55	6	109
Morris	.991	25	107	6	1	10
Sweeney	1.000	1	2	0	0	1
Young	1.000	9	56	1	0	5

Second Base	PCT	G	PO	A	E	DP
Lewis	.500	2	0	1	1	0

	PCT	G	PO	A	E	DP
Reese	.991	146	325	409	7	91
Stynes	.956	43	48	61	5	11

Third Base	PCT	G	PO	A	E	DP
Boone	.958	136	86	253	15	17
Lewis	.938	52	21	54	5	7
Stynes	.929	8	2	11	1	0

Shortstop	PCT	G	PO	A	E	DP
Boone	1.000	6	1	5	0	2
Dawkins	1.000	7	2	4	0	1
Larkin	.978	161	220	401	14	77
Reese	1.000	16	15	16	0	4

Outfield	PCT	G	PO	A	E	DP
Cameron	.979	146	371	7	8	3
Hammonds	1.000	106	156	5	0	2
Morris	1.000	4	3	0	0	0
Robinson	.000	2	0	0	0	0
Stynes	.000	4	0	0	0	0
Sweeney	1.000	1	1	0	0	0
Tucker	.990	114	182	8	2	0
Vaughn	.986	144	264	8	4	2
Young	.976	91	161	4	4	0

FARM SYSTEM

Director of Player Development: Muzzy Jackson/Buddy Bell

Class	Farm Team	League	W	L	Pct.	Finish*	Manager	First Yr
AAA	Indianapolis (Ind.) Indians	International	75	69	.521	7th (14)	Dave Miley	1993
AA	Chattanooga (Tenn.) Lookouts	Southern	78	62	.557	2nd (10)	Phillip Wellman	1988
A	Clinton (Iowa) LumberKings	Midwest	68	69	.496	8th (14)	Freddie Benavides	1999
A	Rockford (Ill.) Reds	Midwest	76	63	.547	4th (14)	Mike Rojas	1999
#R	Billings (Mont.) Mustangs	Pioneer	42	33	.560	4th (8)	Russ Nixon	1974
R	Sarasota (Fla.) Reds	Gulf Coast	23	37	.383	14th (14)	Donnie Scott	1999

*Finish in overall standings (No. of teams in league)   #Advanced level

INTERNATIONAL LEAGUE

BATTING

BATTING	AVG	G	AB	R	H	2B	3B	HR	RBI	BB	SO	SB	CS	B	T	HT	WT	DOB	1st Yr	Resides
Baerga, Carlos	.290	52	221	32	64	10	0	3	27	10	18	2	1	S	R	5-11	215	11-4-68	1986	Bayamon, P.R.
Baez, Kevin	.300	20	40	4	12	3	0	0	7	11	4	1	0	R	R	6-0	170	1-10-67	1988	San Juan, P.R.
Boone, Aaron	.341	11	41	6	14	2	1	0	7	3	4	2	2	R	R	6-2	200	3-9-73	1994	Villa Park, Calif.
Branson, Jeff	.253	124	430	57	109	18	2	7	56	46	86	2	2	L	R	6-0	180	1-26-67	1989	Millry, Ala.
Cromer, D.T.	.310	136	535	83	166	37	4	30	107	44	98	4	2	L	L	6-2	190	3-19-71	1992	Lexington, S.C.
Davis, James	.288	16	52	7	15	4	1	0	10	3	6	0	0	R	R	6-4	215	4-14-73	1995	Franklin, Ky.
Eddie, Steve	.375	10	24	3	9	2	0	0	3	1	1	0	0	R	R	6-1	190	1-6-71	1993	Storm Lake, Iowa
Frank, Mike	.296	121	433	73	128	36	7	9	62	36	55	10	6	L	L	6-2	190	1-14-75	1997	Santa Clara, Calif.
Garcia, Guillermo	.288	65	233	30	67	9	0	10	28	22	44	1	1	R	R	6-3	215	4-4-72	1990	Santiago, D.R.
Hardtke, Jason	.329	101	416	74	137	37	2	12	61	35	43	7	4	S	R	5-10	175	9-15-71	1990	Port Washington, N.Y.
Hiatt, Phil	.238	78	311	46	74	11	0	18	54	30	103	0	0	R	R	6-3	200	5-1-69	1990	Pensacola, Fla.
Hollins, Damon	.262	106	328	58	86	19	0	9	43	31	44	11	2	R	L	5-11	180	6-12-74	1992	Vallejo, Calif.
Johnson, Brian	.211	6	19	2	4	3	0	0	4	1	3	0	0	R	R	6-2	210	1-8-68	1989	Chicago, Ill.
LaRue, Jason	.251	70	263	42	66	12	2	12	37	15	52	0	3	R	R	5-11	200	3-19-74	1995	Spring Branch, Texas
McCall, Rod	.259	47	139	21	36	7	0	6	28	32	49	1	0	L	R	6-7	235	11-4-71	1990	Stanton, Calif.
Melo, Juan	.333	3	9	2	3	0	0	1	3	0	2	1	0	S	R	6-1	180	11-5-76	1994	Bani, D.R.
2-team (41 Syracuse)	.240	44	150	23	36	9	1	4	16	10	33	9	4							
Owens, Jayhawk	.208	18	53	7	11	1	0	4	10	4	18	0	0	R	R	6-1	213	2-10-69	1990	Cincinnati, Ohio
Robinson, Kerry	.264	34	129	24	34	3	2	1	14	4	12	14	4	L	L	6-0	175	10-3-73	1994	Spanish Lake, Mo.
Salzano, Jerry	.091	7	11	0	1	0	0	0	2	0	6	0	0	R	R	6-0	175	10-27-74	1992	Trenton, N.J.
Snopek, Chris	.281	103	381	66	107	24	3	9	64	42	51	17	6	R	R	6-1	185	9-20-70	1992	Cynthiana, Ky.
2-team (24 Pawtucket)	.275	127	462	76	127	31	3	12	74	47	66	19	6							
Sweeney, Mark	.322	86	311	66	100	17	1	12	51	59	40	3	2	L	L	6-1	195	10-26-69	1991	Scottsdale, Ariz.
Tinsley, Lee	.211	30	76	5	16	2	1	1	6	5	14	1	4	S	R	5-10	180	3-4-69	1987	Shelbyville, Ky.
Whitmore, Darrell	.282	83	238	39	67	17	1	10	42	24	64	2	1	L	R	6-1	220	11-18-68	1990	Miramar, Fla.
Williams, Jason	.381	40	160	30	61	18	2	2	19	14	25	4	1	R	R	5-8	180	12-18-73	1996	Gonzales, La.

PITCHING

PITCHING	W	L	ERA	G	GS	CG	SV	IP	H	R	ER	BB	SO	B	T	HT	WT	DOB	1st Yr	Resides
Atchley, Justin	2	1	5.40	5	4	0	1	23	39	14	14	2	6	L	L	6-3	215	9-5-73	1995	Mount Vernon, Wash.
Barrios, Manny	2	7	5.28	49	8	0	0	90	94	60	53	35	73	R	R	6-0	185	9-21-74	1993	Rock Island, Ill.
Belinda, Stan	2	0	2.38	10	0	0	0	11	7	3	3	6	10	R	R	6-3	215	8-6-66	1985	Alexandria, Pa.
Bere, Jason	0	2	10.19	5	4	0	0	18	25	20	20	19	8	R	R	6-3	215	5-26-71	1990	Wilmington, Mass.
Carrara, Giovanni	12	7	3.47	39	21	2	0	158	144	68	61	58	114	R	R	6-2	210	3-4-68	1990	Anzoategui, Venez.
Etler, Todd	2	1	6.39	26	0	0	0	38	42	29	27	29	35	R	R	6-0	205	4-18-74	1992	Villa Hills, Ky.
Flury, Pat	1	1	7.04	23	0	0	6	23	27	18	18	20	20	R	R	6-1	220	3-14-73	1993	Sparks, Nev.
Glauber, Keith	3	3	5.82	12	12	1	0	68	84	49	44	20	51	R	R	6-2	190	1-18-72	1994	Morganville, N.J.
Greene, Rick	5	7	3.69	61	0	0	9	78	78	37	32	35	40	R	R	6-5	200	1-2-71	1992	Miami, Fla.
Harriger, Denny	14	6	4.08	27	27	1	0	172	183	82	78	36	110	R	R	5-11	185	7-21-69	1987	Ford City, Pa.
Janzen, Marty	1	1	4.86	9	1	0	0	17	16	9	9	8	8	R	R	6-3	197	5-31-73	1991	Gainesville, Fla.
Klingenbeck, Scott	4	4	4.82	14	12	0	1	75	89	44	40	26	53	R	R	6-2	205	2-3-71	1992	Cincinnati, Ohio
LeBlanc, Eric	1	2	7.11	14	3	0	1	44	57	43	35	19	26	L	R	6-0	195	7-6-73	1996	North Troy, Ver.
Meacham, Rusty	1	3	6.98	16	1	0	1	30	38	27	23	15	19	R	R	6-2	175	1-27-68	1988	Palm City, Fla.
Merrell, Phil	0	3	14.73	3	3	0	0	11	21	21	18	4	6	R	R	6-3	190	3-11-78	1996	Nampa, Idaho
Neagle, Denny	2	0	4.67	3	3	0	0	17	11	9	9	2	9	L	L	6-2	225	9-13-68	1989	Alpharetta, Ga.
Pall, Donn	1	0	8.44	4	0	0	0	5	9	7	5	1	1	R	R	6-1	180	1-11-62	1985	Bloomingdale, Ill.
Parris, Steve	2	4	4.04	6	6	0	0	36	39	16	16	9	31	R	R	6-0	195	12-17-67	1989	Plainfield, Ill.
Priest, Eddie	6	5	5.35	18	12	0	2	69	86	41	41	20	35	R	L	6-1	200	4-8-74	1994	Chattanooga, Tenn.
Riedling, John	1	0	1.54	24	0	0	1	35	19	9	6	18	26	R	R	5-11	190	8-29-75	1994	Pompano Beach, Fla.
Robertson, Rich	0	0	9.82	9	0	0	0	7	17	9	8	4	7	L	L	6-4	175	9-15-68	1990	Waller, Texas
Ryan, B.J.	1	0	4.00	11	0	0	0	9	9	4	4	3	12	L	L	6-6	230	12-28-75	1998	Benton, La.
Sager, A.J.	6	3	4.67	24	7	0	0	52	79	45	27	25	18	R	R	6-4	200	3-3-65	1988	Perrysburg, Ohio
Therneau, Dave	0	2	8.17	7	7	0	0	36	52	36	33	14	22	R	R	6-5	195	12-23-75	1998	Denton, Texas
Thompson, Mark	2	6	5.13	11	10	0	0	54	50	31	31	29	28	R	R	6-2	205	4-7-71	1992	Russellville, Ky.
Tolar, Kevin	1	0	2.08	8	1	0	0	13	8	4	3	7	18	R	L	6-3	225	1-28-71	1989	Brandon, Fla.
Tomko, Brett	2	0	4.97	2	2	0	0	13	15	7	7	1	9	R	R	6-4	215	4-7-73	1995	San Diego, Calif.
Villone, Ron	2	0	1.42	18	0	0	1	19	9	3	3	13	23	L	L	6-3	237	1-16-70	1992	Westwood, N.J.
Williams, Todd	1	3	5.10	38	0	0	24	42	38	24	24	13	35	R	R	6-4	190	2-13-71	1991	Syracuse, N.Y.
Wohlers, Mark	0	0	108.00	1	0	0	0	0	1	4	4	5	1	R	R	6-4	207	1-23-70	1988	Alpharetta, Ga.

FIELDING

Catcher	PCT	G	PO	A	E	DP	PB
Davis	.966	16	75	9	3	0	2
Garcia	.991	50	307	22	3	4	7
Johnson	1.000	5	22	2	0	0	1
LaRue	.984	67	384	45	7	6	8
Owens	.990	14	87	8	1	0	1

First Base	PCT	G	PO	A	E	DP
Baerga	1.000	7	51	0	0	8
Branson	1.000	1	8	0	0	2
Cromer	.989	50	422	35	5	48
Garcia	.986	13	138	6	2	10
Hiatt	.997	38	319	37	1	51
McCall	1.000	29	237	25	0	21
Snopek	1.000	1	12	2	0	1
Sweeney	1.000	17	151	7	2	17
Tinsley	1.000	1	2	0	0	1

Second Base	PCT	G	PO	A	E	DP
Baerga	.978	16	34	57	2	14

	PCT	G	PO	A	E	DP
Baez	1.000	10	20	11	0	3
Boone	1.000	1	3	2	0	2
Branson	.875	3	4	3	1	1
Eddie	.967	6	14	15	1	3
Hardtke	.982	51	106	160	5	42
Snopek	.976	26	45	76	3	18
J. Williams	.990	40	75	120	2	33

Third Base	PCT	G	PO	A	E	DP
Baerga	.957	31	21	69	4	5
Baez	1.000	2	0	2	0	0
Boone	.929	9	5	21	2	1
Branson	.970	10	10	22	1	4
Garcia	.857	2	3	3	1	1
Hardtke	.933	36	31	81	8	10
Hiatt	.975	16	9	30	1	3
Salzano	1.000	3	0	2	0	0
Snopek	.907	42	16	81	10	13

Shortstop	PCT	G	PO	A	E	DP
Baez	.917	4	3	8	1	1
Boone	.900	1	3	6	1	1
Branson	.974	106	160	335	13	81
Hardtke	1.000	10	16	29	0	7
Melo	1.000	2	5	7	0	0
Snopek	.984	31	31	94	2	21

Outfield	PCT	G	PO	A	E	DP
Cromer	.957	69	85	3	4	0
Frank	.996	113	220	10	1	1
Hiatt	1.000	16	33	1	0	0
Hollins	.983	101	219	14	4	4
Robinson	.977	33	83	3	2	0
Snopek	1.000	1	1	0	0	0
Sweeney	.973	53	106	2	3	1
Tinsley	1.000	22	27	0	0	0
Whitmore	.977	56	83	1	2	0

Organization Statistics

SOUTHERN LEAGUE

BATTING	AVG	G	AB	R	H	2B	3B	HR	RBI	BB	SO	SB	CS	B	T	HT	WT	DOB	1st Yr	Resides
Broussard, Ben	.213	35	127	26	27	5	0	8	21	11	41	1	0	L	L	6-2	220	9-24-76	1999	Sour Lake, Texas
Burress, Andy	.272	63	257	42	70	12	1	7	28	18	41	11	4	R	R	6-0	185	7-18-77	1995	McRae, Ga.
Clark, Brady	.326	138	506	103	165	37	4	17	75	89	58	25	17	R	R	6-2	195	4-18-73	1996	Beaverton, Ore.
Conner, Decomba	.179	45	123	17	22	3	2	5	19	17	31	1	2	R	R	5-10	185	7-17-73	1994	Mooresville, N.C.
Davis, James	.241	16	54	7	13	5	0	4	16	1	5	0	1	R	R	6-4	215	4-14-73	1995	Franklin, Ky.
Dawkins, Travis	.364	32	129	24	47	7	0	2	13	14	17	15	5	R	R	6-1	180	5-12-79	1997	Chappells, S.C.
Diaz, Alejandro	.264	55	220	27	58	9	8	7	35	8	31	6	2	R	R	5-9	509	7-9-78	1999	San Pedro de Macoris, D.R.
Eddie, Steve	.190	6	21	2	4	0	0	0	2	0	3	0	0	R	R	6-1	190	1-6-71	1993	Storm Lake, Iowa
Florez, Tim	.252	39	139	24	35	8	1	5	22	15	23	7	2	R	R	5-10	170	7-23-69	1991	Goleta, Calif.
Garcia, Guillermo	.310	10	42	11	13	3	3	1	7	2	6	0	0	R	R	6-3	215	4-4-72	1990	Santiago, D.R.
Ingram, Darron	.221	85	267	42	59	11	3	11	40	28	95	5	7	R	R	6-3	226	6-7-76	1994	Lexington, Ky.
Larkin, Stephen	.299	104	264	34	79	16	2	4	42	31	44	7	3	L	L	6-0	190	7-24-73	1994	Cincinnati, Ohio
Larson, Brandon	.285	43	172	28	49	10	0	12	42	10	51	4	5	R	R	6-0	205	5-24-76	1997	San Antonio, Texas
Lawrence, Tony	.125	4	8	0	1	0	0	0	1	1	4	0	0	R	R	6-1	205	3-7-75	1997	Monroe, La.
Luzinski, Ryan	.246	55	171	17	42	10	0	2	26	24	43	1	2	R	R	6-1	215	8-22-73	1992	Medford, N.J.
Miller, Corky	.221	33	104	20	23	10	0	4	16	11	30	0	0	R	R	6-1	215	3-18-76	1998	Calimesa, Calif.
Milliard, Ralph	.294	32	102	19	30	3	1	4	23	20	13	2	3	R	R	5-11	175	12-30-73	1993	Amsterdam, Netherlands
Monds, Wonderful	.260	75	311	48	81	14	2	11	32	17	49	14	8	R	R	6-3	190	1-11-73	1993	Fort Pierce, Fla.
Nevers, Tom	.295	111	380	61	112	23	2	17	65	15	74	3	5	R	R	6-1	175	9-13-71	1990	Edina, Minn.
Owens, Jayhawk	.222	47	153	24	34	6	1	6	21	31	45	3	0	R	R	6-1	213	2-10-69	1990	Cincinnati, Ohio
Presto, Nick	.268	73	224	34	60	8	0	2	28	38	34	5	7	R	R	5-10	175	7-8-74	1996	Jupiter, Fla.
Salzano, Jerry	.327	72	263	44	86	19	1	4	38	39	38	14	10	R	R	6-0	175	10-27-74	1992	Trenton, N.J.
Saunders, Chris	.315	58	216	31	68	13	1	7	35	34	42	0	1	R	R	6-1	203	7-19-70	1992	Clovis, Calif.
Snusz, Chris	.500	2	6	0	3	1	0	0	2	1	0	0	0	R	R	6-0	190	11-8-72	1995	Buffalo, N.Y.
Stegall, Randy	.207	13	29	0	6	0	0	0	1	2	5	0	0	R	R	6-3	190	2-16-75	1998	Longwood, Fla.
Williams, Jason	.319	87	332	65	106	27	2	7	45	46	40	3	4	R	R	5-8	180	12-18-73	1996	Gonzales, La.

PITCHING	W	L	ERA	G	GS	CG	SV	IP	H	R	ER	BB	SO	B	T	HT	WT	DOB	1st Yr	Resides
Atchley, Justin	4	9	3.42	17	17	0	0	97	114	48	37	22	70	L	L	6-3	215	9-5-73	1995	Mount Vernon, Wash.
Averette, Robert	2	1	5.20	6	6	1	0	36	42	22	21	19	15	R	R	6-2	185	9-30-76	1997	Sylacauga, Ala.
Bell, Rob	3	6	3.13	12	12	2	0	72	75	30	25	17	68	R	R	6-5	225	1-17-77	1995	Marlboro, N.Y.
Crowell, Jim	10	5	5.10	27	27	0	0	148	173	99	84	85	80	R	L	6-4	230	5-14-74	1995	Valparaiso, Ind.
Donaldson, Bo	5	3	2.98	38	0	0	6	51	30	18	17	16	67	R	R	6-0	200	10-10-74	1997	Philadelphia, Pa.
Etler, Todd	2	0	2.35	14	0	0	0	23	17	6	6	8	26	R	R	6-0	205	4-18-74	1992	Villa Hills, Ky.
Flury, Pat	1	1	2.87	43	0	0	15	53	36	20	17	31	69	R	R	6-1	220	3-14-73	1993	Sparks, Nev.
Glauber, Keith	5	0	1.98	7	7	0	0	50	42	12	11	8	26	R	R	6-2	190	1-18-72	1994	Morganville, N.J.
Haring, Brett	2	1	3.72	7	4	0	0	36	46	18	15	12	15	R	L	5-11	180	2-7-75	1997	Mount Pleasant, Mich.
Janzen, Marty	1	3	4.94	30	4	0	0	55	54	32	30	29	41	R	R	6-3	197	5-31-73	1991	Gainesville, Fla.
LeBlanc, Eric	3	3	3.84	15	9	0	0	66	63	33	28	20	37	L	R	6-0	195	7-6-73	1996	North Troy, Ver.
MacRae, Scott	8	7	4.42	39	17	0	0	128	139	76	63	49	81	R	R	6-3	205	8-13-74	1995	Marietta, Ga.
Mallard, Randi	4	5	6.78	14	14	0	0	72	92	61	54	45	45	R	R	6-1	180	8-11-75	1996	Tampa, Fla.
Manias, James	0	0	0.00	1	0	0	0	1	0	0	0	0	0	L	L	6-4	190	10-21-74	1996	Florham Park, N.J.
Merrell, Phil	2	2	6.62	7	7	0	0	35	47	32	26	14	15	R	R	6-3	190	3-11-78	1996	Nampa, Idaho
Meyer, Jake	2	2	5.96	20	0	0	0	23	24	17	15	14	16	R	R	6-1	195	1-7-75	1997	San Diego, Calif.
Pearsall, J.J.	3	1	5.90	32	0	0	0	40	40	31	26	28	36	L	L	6-2	202	9-9-73	1995	Burnt Hills, N.Y.
Priest, Eddie	4	3	3.97	12	12	0	0	77	99	42	34	14	60	R	L	6-1	200	4-8-74	1994	Chattanooga, Ala.
Riedling, John	9	5	3.43	40	0	0	5	42	41	23	16	20	38	R	R	5-11	190	8-29-75	1994	Pompano Beach, Fla.
Rose, Ted	2	0	4.24	13	0	0	2	17	17	8	8	9	23	L	R	6-2	185	8-23-73	1996	St. Clairsville, Ohio
Ryan, B.J.	2	1	2.59	35	0	0	6	42	33	13	12	17	46	L	L	6-6	230	12-28-75	1998	Benton, La.
Therneau, Dave	2	0	2.57	3	3	0	0	21	22	7	6	8	11	R	R	6-5	195	12-23-75	1998	Denton, Texas
Tolar, Kevin	4	4	4.97	47	1	0	1	54	61	32	30	45	60	R	L	6-3	225	1-28-71	1989	Brandon, Fla.
Wohlers, Mark	0	0	16.20	2	0	0	0	2	1	3	3	3	3	R	R	6-4	207	1-23-70	1988	Alpharetta, Ga.

FIELDING

Catcher	PCT	G	PO	A	E	DP	PB
Davis	.971	13	88	12	3	1	1
Garcia	1.000	5	29	5	0	1	0
Lawrence	.938	3	14	1	1	1	1
Luzinski	.985	47	300	30	5	6	10
Miller	.989	33	227	35	3	6	8
Owens	.985	44	311	26	5	3	5
Snusz	1.000	2	14	1	0	0	0

First Base	PCT	G	PO	A	E	DP
Broussard	1.000	13	113	9	0	12
Eddie	1.000	1	10	1	0	1
Garcia	1.000	1	6	1	0	2
Larkin	.993	53	428	23	3	48
Luzinski	1.000	2	5	2	0	2
Nevers	.991	14	94	13	1	13
Owens	1.000	1	2	0	0	0
Presto	.990	10	95	6	1	15
Saunders	.993	54	502	37	4	47

Second Base	PCT	G	PO	A	E	DP
Stegall	1.000	4	39	3	0	4
Eddie	1.000	2	3	3	0	1
Florez	.992	31	48	69	1	19
Nevers	.967	11	20	38	2	12
Presto	.925	14	29	45	6	11
Stegall	1.000	5	9	8	0	2
Williams	.988	82	159	246	5	73

Third Base	PCT	G	PO	A	E	DP
Clark	.000	1	0	0	1	0
Florez	1.000	1	0	1	0	0
Garcia	1.000	1	0	3	0	0
Larson	.885	42	22	93	15	8
Luzinski	.778	5	3	11	4	0
Nevers	.910	22	12	49	6	8
Presto	.750	3	0	6	2	1

	PCT	G	PO	A	E	DP
Salzano	.903	71	34	152	20	13
Stegall	.000	1	0	0	0	0

Shortstop	PCT	G	PO	A	E	DP
Dawkins	.979	32	52	89	3	22
Eddie	1.000	1	1	2	0	0
Milliard	.963	29	44	87	5	22
Nevers	.954	49	70	156	11	40
Presto	.929	37	61	97	12	24

Outfield	PCT	G	PO	A	E	DP
Broussard	.931	19	26	1	2	0
Burress	.957	52	85	5	4	0
Clark	.985	133	255	10	4	2
Conner	.967	33	55	3	2	0
Diaz	.987	55	144	5	2	2
Ingram	.989	55	83	4	1	0
Larkin	.905	14	18	1	2	0
Monds	.972	70	132	9	4	1

MIDWEST LEAGUE

BATTING	AVG	G	AB	R	H	2B	3B	HR	RBI	BB	SO	SB	CS	B	T	HT	WT	DOB	1st Yr	Resides
Baderdeen, Kevin	.252	113	405	47	102	22	4	9	49	35	128	9	6	R	R	6-3	175	1-12-77	1997	Goshen, Ind.
Beattie, Andrew	.230	108	335	58	77	11	3	6	41	60	75	18	4	S	R	5-10	170	2-28-78	1998	Clearwater, Fla.
Broussard, Ben	.550	5	20	8	11	4	1	2	6	3	4	0	0	L	L	6-2	220	9-24-76	1999	Sour Lake, Texas
Caceres, Wilmy	.261	117	476	77	124	18	5	1	30	30	65	52	22	S	R	6-0	170	10-2-78	1997	Santo Domingo, D.R.
Copley, Travis	.200	4	15	3	3	0	0	0	0	3	0	0	0	L	R	6-4	215	1-8-76	1998	Hixson, Tenn.

BATTING	AVG	G	AB	R	H	2B	3B	HR	RBI	BB	SO	SB	CS	B	T	HT	WT	DOB	1st Yr	Resides
Davis, James	.200	3	10	0	2	0	0	0	0	1	2	1	0	R	R	6-4	215	4-14-73	1995	Franklin, Ky.
Diaz, Alejandro	.285	55	221	39	63	14	3	6	41	12	35	28	11	R	R	5-9	190	7-9-78	1999	SanPedro de Macoris, D.R.
Goudie, Jaime	.321	84	340	56	109	20	4	3	50	21	46	16	6	R	R	5-10	170	3-8-79	1997	Columbus, Ga.
Howard, Jason	.162	25	68	5	11	3	0	0	6	3	17	0	0	R	R	6-3	210	9-26-76	1999	Greenville, N.C.
Ingram, Darron	.355	22	76	15	27	5	0	5	18	14	20	1	1	R	R	6-3	226	6-7-76	1994	Lexington, Ky.
Johnerson, Ryan	.208	40	120	17	25	5	1	2	16	9	37	3	3	R	R	6-2	195	11-23-76	1999	Bozeman, Mont.
Kison, Robbie	.236	20	55	7	13	2	1	1	5	8	12	0	1	R	R	5-11	155	5-11-77	1999	Bradenton, Fla.
2-team (7 Rockford)	.229	27	70	10	16	2	1	1	6	12	16	0	1							
Layton, Blane	.294	42	109	19	32	6	2	2	12	25	31	5	2	L	L	6-2	190	8-17-76	1998	Plant City, Fla.
Markray, Thad	.100	3	10	1	1	0	0	0	0	1	2	0	0	R	R	6-4	220	9-20-79	1997	Springhill, La.
Oliver, Johnny	.115	17	52	7	6	0	0	1	2	5	16	0	2	R	R	6-2	180	5-14-78	1996	Dallas, Pa.
Peters, Samone	.221	83	290	32	64	13	1	15	46	17	131	0	2	R	R	6-8	260	7-30-78	1998	Alameda, Calif.
Price, Jason	.167	37	96	8	16	1	0	0	5	9	30	4	2	R	R	6-0	190	9-5-75	1998	College Station, Texas
Rios, Fernando	.276	75	275	36	76	16	0	2	42	21	34	3	2	R	R	6-2	175	12-15-78	1997	Glendale, Calif.
2-team (24 Rockford)	.278	99	356	45	99	23	0	2	50	32	43	5	5							
Rivera, Francisco	.320	15	50	7	16	6	1	0	6	4	10	0	0	L	R	6-3	225	10-4-79	1996	Veracruz, Mexico
Rodriguez, Hernandez	.252	28	115	10	29	4	2	1	6	4	17	6	0	R	R	6-0	188	10-12-78	1997	Veracruz, Mexico
Ruiz, Randy	.625	2	8	3	5	2	0	0	2	1	0	0	0	R	R	6-3	225	10-19-77	1999	Bronx, N.Y.
Santonocito, Justin	.180	26	61	5	11	2	0	1	5	5	12	0	0	L	R	6-1	195	12-15-76	1998	West Seneca, N.Y.
Snusz, Chris	.190	4	21	2	4	1	1	0	3	1	8	0	0	R	R	6-0	190	11-8-72	1995	Buffalo, N.Y.
Stegall, Randy	.250	71	252	39	63	12	4	4	44	27	64	3	2	R	R	6-3	190	2-16-75	1998	Longwood, Fla.
Suarez, Marc	.158	33	95	8	15	2	0	2	10	16	31	0	3	R	R	6-4	230	1-18-76	1997	Miami, Fla.
Thorpe, A.D.	.333	6	12	2	4	2	0	0	1	0	2	1	2	S	R	5-11	160	6-19-77	1996	Rougemont, N.C.
Toomey, Chris	.261	100	307	51	80	19	1	6	41	41	87	5	3	R	R	6-2	195	8-5-77	1998	Dana Point, Calif.
Vaughn, Clint	.238	104	374	45	89	25	4	3	54	18	87	2	2	R	R	6-4	225	12-30-76	1998	Edmond, Okla.
Whitehead, Braxton	.298	82	272	41	81	19	0	3	38	30	42	0	0	R	R	6-2	215	10-20-75	1997	Newton, Miss.
Zeber, Ryan	.000	2	2	0	0	0	0	0	0	1	0	0	0	R	R	6-2	190	5-24-78	1996	Santa Ana, Calif.
2-team (180 Rockford)	.250	41	108	11	27	6	1	0	10	8	21	1	5							

GAMES BY POSITION: C—Davis 3, Howard 22, Rivera 15, Snusz 4, Suarez 33, Whitehead 71, Zeber 2. **1B**—Baderdeen 4, Broussard 3, Johnerson 8, Markray 1, Ruiz 2, Santonocito 2, Stegall 20, Vaughn 101, Whitehead 3. **2B**—Beattie 52, Goudie 58, Kison 15, Santonocito 10, Stegall 9, Thorpe 2. **3B**—Baderdeen 100, Beattie 4, Goudie 6, Howard 1, Johnserson 4, Kison 1, Markray 2, Santonocito 1, Stegall 25, Whitehead 1. **SS**—Baderdeen 1, Beattie 19, Caceres 110, Kison 1, Stegall 13. **OF**—Baderdeen 4, Beattie 14, Broussard 3, Diaz 55, Goudie 1, Howard 1, Ingram 14, Johnerson 25, Kison 1, Layton 32, Oliver 16, Peters 50, Price 37, Rios 72, Rodriguez 28, Stegall 1, Suarez 1, Thorpe 1, Toomey 88.

PITCHING	W	L	ERA	G	GS	CG	SV	IP	H	R	ER	BB	SO	B	T	HT	WT	DOB	1st Yr	Resides
Acevedo, Jose	8	6	3.77	24	24	1	0	134	119	65	56	43	136	R	R	6-0	185	12-18-77	1997	Santiago, D.R.
Altman, Gene	0	2	3.86	3	3	0	0	14	7	9	6	7	19	R	R	6-7	209	9-1-78	1996	Lynchburg, S.C.
Bailey, Ben	1	0	5.06	9	2	0	0	21	20	12	12	8	16	R	R	6-2	220	8-31-74	1995	Howe, Ind.
Birdsong, Tim	5	8	4.27	24	23	0	0	129	131	75	61	50	95	R	R	6-5	210	5-4-77	1998	Bokchito, Okla.
Brewer, Clint	8	2	4.15	24	9	0	0	74	61	41	34	28	39	R	R	6-4	185	11-22-78	1997	Dibble, Okla.
Brown, Zay	0	1	4.15	3	0	0	0	4	4	2	2	3	1	R	R	6-1	180	1-5-79	1997	Warrenville, S.C.
Chighisola, Lou	0	1	2.77	7	1	0	0	13	11	4	4	7	8	L	L	6-3	200	5-7-76	1999	Plympton, Mass.
Cooper, Eric	2	5	6.08	12	10	1	0	47	49	38	32	36	37	R	R	6-4	210	9-5-77	1998	Fremont, Calif.
2-team (4 Rockford)	3	6	6.93	16	14	1	0	61	70	53	47	47	43							
Darnell, Paul	2	3	3.06	6	6	0	0	35	35	19	12	13	23	R	L	6-5	190	6-4-76	1999	Hubbard, Texas
DeHart, Casey	2	0	3.38	24	0	0	0	21	16	10	8	16	17	L	L	6-2	180	11-1-77	1998	Burleson, Texas
Escamilla, Paco	1	6	5.24	12	9	0	0	55	56	36	32	20	52	R	R	6-2	205	12-16-76	1999	Cedar Park, Texas
Gooch, Arnold	1	1	4.50	2	2	0	0	8	8	5	4	3	5	R	R	6-2	210	11-12-76	1994	Doylestown, Pa.
Hart, Damien	2	5	5.45	26	0	0	0	35	34	25	21	18	20	L	L	6-4	215	6-24-75	1998	Indianapolis, Ind.
Hayden, Terry	8	6	2.38	33	14	1	0	110	98	51	29	39	72	L	L	6-6	215	6-26-75	1997	Taylor, Mich.
Levy, Tye	1	1	4.15	7	0	0	1	9	12	4	4	4	6	L	L	6-2	185	4-20-78	1997	Alexandria, Pa.
Mallard, Randi	0	1	6.89	6	1	0	0	16	18	12	12	3	21	R	R	6-1	180	8-11-75	1996	Tampa, Fla.
McEvoy, Casey	0	1	10.24	7	0	0	0	10	12	12	11	8	13	R	R	6-3	210	7-29-76	1998	Florence, Ky.
Merrell, Phil	8	3	2.20	16	16	3	0	102	75	32	25	31	87	R	R	6-3	190	3-11-78	1996	Nampa, Idaho
Minaya, Pedro	4	6	5.57	36	11	0	0	84	88	65	52	58	54	R	R	6-3	170	7-30-77	1994	Santo Domingo, D.R.
Puffer, Brandon	1	2	1.99	59	0	0	34	63	53	20	14	24	60	R	R	6-3	195	10-5-75	1994	Mission Viejo, Calif.
Robinson, Dustin	3	6	4.76	44	1	0	0	70	67	51	37	29	53	R	R	6-6	215	9-13-75	1997	Chandler, Okla.
Rose, Brian	7	0	0.55	24	1	0	0	33	27	2	2	11	24	R	R	6-1	190	10-7-72	1994	Potsdam, N.Y.
Schurman, Ryan	3	3	3.54	44	3	0	2	86	74	41	34	50	83	R	R	6-3	190	8-28-76	1995	Tualatin, Ore.
Valdez, Jose	0	1	15.88	3	1	0	0	6	16	10	10	4	3	R	R	6-1	164	6-11-79	1996	San Cristobal, D.R.

ROCKFORD — Class A

MIDWEST LEAGUE

BATTING	AVG	G	AB	R	H	2B	3B	HR	RBI	BB	SO	SB	CS	B	T	HT	WT	DOB	1st Yr	Resides
Burress, Andy	.304	72	270	45	82	24	2	4	32	17	45	17	6	R	R	6-0	185	7-18-77	1995	McRae, Ga.
Conley, Brian	.228	89	285	39	65	7	3	2	22	19	69	13	8	R	R	5-11	180	12-5-74	1995	Cincinnati, Ohio
Dawkins, Travis	.272	76	305	56	83	10	6	8	32	35	38	38	13	R	R	6-1	180	5-12-79	1997	Chappells, S.C.
Dunn, Adam	.307	93	313	62	96	16	2	11	44	46	64	21	10	L	R	6-5	240	11-9-79	1998	Porter, Texas
Elliott, Dawan	.133	19	30	3	4	0	0	1	6	4	10	0	1	L	L	6-3	200	7-30-76	1995	Long Branch, N.J.
Garrett, Scott	.200	8	20	4	4	1	0	0	1	3	7	0	0	R	R	6-5	205	3-8-74	1996	Denver, N.C.
Godfrey, Tim	.247	34	77	10	19	2	0	1	7	9	23	3	3	S	R	6-2	185	8-26-77	1999	Checotah, Okla.
Kearns, Austin	.258	124	426	72	110	36	5	13	48	50	120	21	8	R	R	6-4	210	5-20-80	1998	Lexington, Ky.
Kison, Robbie	.200	7	15	3	3	0	0	0	1	4	4	0	0	R	R	5-11	155	5-11-77	1999	Bradenton, Fla.
Larson, Brandon	.300	69	250	38	75	18	1	13	52	25	67	12	2	R	R	6-0	205	5-24-76	1997	San Antonio, Texas
Lawrence, Tony	.171	10	35	2	6	0	0	5	2	12	0	0	0	R	R	6-1	205	3-7-75	1997	Monroe, La.
2-team (46 Ft. Wayne)	.192	56	177	13	34	10	1	0	13	23	57	1	1							
Layton, Blane	.273	34	110	19	30	10	3	2	20	6	27	4	3	L	L	6-2	190	8-17-76	1998	Plant City, Fla.
2-team (3 Clinton)	.283	76	219	38	62	16	5	4	32	31	58	9	5							
Markray, Thad	.194	59	180	21	35	6	0	4	22	21	47	3	4	R	R	6-4	220	9-20-79	1997	Springhill, La.
2-team (3 Clinton)	.189	62	190	22	36	6	0	4	22	22	49	3	4							
Matan, James	.254	116	393	39	100	17	0	10	56	38	90	5	6	R	R	6-3	230	4-18-76	1998	Kensington, Md.
Miller, Corky	.287	66	195	43	56	10	1	10	40	33	42	3	6	R	R	6-1	215	3-18-76	1998	Calimesa, Calif.
Perez, Antonio	.288	119	385	69	111	20	3	7	41	43	80	35	24	R	R	5-11	175	7-26-81	1998	Bani, D.R.
Price, Corey	.000	6	9	0	0	0	0	0	1	0	2	0	0	S	R	6-2	165	12-15-78	1997	Mt. Pleasant, Texas
Rios, Fernando	.284	24	81	9	23	7	0	0	8	11	9	2	3	R	R	6-2	175	12-15-78	1997	Glendale, Calif.

BATTING	AVG	G	AB	R	H	2B	3B	HR	RBI	BB	SO	SB	CS	B	T	HT	WT	DOB	1st Yr	Resides
Sanchez, Marcos	.246	20	57	6	14	2	2	1	7	3	23	4	1	S	R	6-0	190	9-25-74	1992	Santo Domingo, D.R.
Santiago, Daniel	.000	1	2	0	0	0	0	0	0	0	2	0	0	S	R	5-10	190	6-17-79	1999	Cleveland, Ohio
Snusz, Chris	.170	19	53	6	9	1	0	1	2	3	13	1	0	R	R	6-0	190	11-8-72	1995	Buffalo, N.Y.
2-team (4 Clinton)	.176	23	74	8	13	2	1	1	5	4	21	1	0							
Stegall, Randy	.313	26	99	14	31	4	1	0	18	3	20	3	4	R	R	6-3	190	2-16-75	1998	Longwood, Fla.
2-team (71 Clinton)	.268	97	351	53	94	16	5	4	62	30	84	6	6							
Suarez, Marc	.462	4	13	4	6	1	0	1	1	3	2	2	0	R	R	6-4	230	1-18-76	1997	Miami, Fla.
2-team (3 Clinton)	.194	37	108	12	21	3	0	3	11	19	33	2	3							
Thorpe, A.D.	.250	7	8	3	2	0	0	0	0	1	0	1	1	S	R	5-11	160	6-19-77	1996	Rougemont, N.C.
2-team (6 Clinton)	.300	13	20	5	6	2	0	0	1	1	2	2	3							
Welsh, Eric	.280	101	368	52	103	23	0	16	64	23	57	3	2	L	L	6-3	210	9-17-76	1997	Lockport, Ill.
Wise, DeWayne	.253	131	502	70	127	20	13	11	81	42	81	35	13	L	L	6-1	172	2-24-78	1997	Chapin, S.C.
Zeber, Ryan	.255	39	106	11	27	6	1	0	10	7	21	1	5	R	R	6-2	190	5-24-78	1996	Santa Ana, Calif.

GAMES BY POSITION: C—Garrett 8, Lawrence 10, Miller 66, Sanchez 20, Santiago 1, Snusz 19, Zeber 38. **1B**—Markray 5, Matan 55, Stegall 3, Welsh 93. **2B**—Conley 70, Godfrey 21, Kison 3, Perez 58, Price 3, Stegall 3. **3B**—Conley 11, Godfrey 5, Larson 69, Markray 58, Matan 1, Price 2, Stegall 12. **SS**—Conley 7, Dawkins 75, Godfrey 2, Kison 1, Perez 59, Thorpe 2. **OF**—Burress 63, Dunn 70, Elliott 8, Kearns 121, Layton 22, Matan 4, Rios 6, Stegall 11, Wise 131.

PITCHING	W	L	ERA	G	GS	CG	SV	IP	H	R	ER	BB	SO	B	T	HT	WT	DOB	1st Yr	Resides
Altman, Gene	2	6	6.08	11	11	0	0	53	63	41	36	34	51	R	R	6-7	209	9-1-78	1996	Lynchburg, S.C.
2-team (3 Clinton)	2	8	5.61	14	14	0	0	67	70	50	42	41	70							
Averette, Robert	9	5	2.58	19	19	2	0	126	117	54	36	40	98	R	R	6-2	185	9-30-76	1997	Sylacauga, Ala.
Brewer, Clint	1	0	6.11	10	0	0	0	18	19	15	12	9	16	R	R	6-4	185	11-22-78	1997	Dibble, Okla.
2-team (4 Clinton)	9	2	4.53	34	9	0	0	91	80	56	46	37	55							
Cooper, Eric	1	1	9.88	4	4	0	0	14	21	15	15	11	6	R	R	6-4	210	9-5-77	1998	Fremont, Calif.
Davis, Lance	7	5	3.82	22	20	1	0	127	135	62	54	49	95	R	L	5-11	165	9-1-76	1995	Polk City, Fla.
Donaldson, Bo	2	1	1.20	19	0	0	1	30	17	7	4	6	12	R	R	6-0	200	10-10-74	1997	Philadelphia, Pa.
Gardner, Nathan	3	2	5.09	34	0	0	2	46	51	31	26	31	27	R	R	5-11	195	9-10-74	1997	Newton, N.C.
Giuliano, Joe	3	4	4.03	43	1	0	2	74	79	51	33	39	54	R	R	6-2	175	1-1-76	1994	Hamilton, Ohio
Haring, Brett	10	3	3.34	25	18	3	1	124	113	53	46	42	94	R	L	5-11	180	2-7-75	1997	Mount Pleasant, Mich.
Hayden, Terry	0	0	7.71	5	0	0	0	7	10	6	6	3	7	L	L	6-6	215	6-26-75	1997	Taylor, Mich.
2-team (33 Clinton)	8	6	2.70	38	14	1	0	117	108	57	35	42	79							
Key, Scott	0	0	27.00	1	0	0	0	1	0	2	2	2	0	R	R	5-10	150	10-4-76	1995	Cantonment, Fla.
Koziara, Matt	1	2	4.08	8	3	0	0	29	39	19	13	13	15	R	R	6-2	205	11-8-76	1999	Franklin, Pa.
LeBlanc, Eric	0	0	1.86	2	1	0	1	10	5	2	2	4	5	L	R	6-0	195	7-6-73	1996	North Troy, Ver.
Lovingood, Ray	1	0	4.85	16	1	0	0	30	27	16	16	16	24	L	L	6-6	200	4-8-78	1998	Riceville, Tenn.
Manias, James	9	7	3.67	30	10	4	0	91	84	46	37	36	103	L	L	6-4	190	10-21-74	1996	Florham Park, N.J.
McEvoy, Casey	1	2	7.77	6	5	1	0	24	32	26	21	10	21	R	R	6-3	210	7-29-76	1998	Florence, Ky.
2-team (7 Clinton)	1	3	8.47	13	5	1	0	34	44	38	32	18	34							
Meyer, Jake	3	2	2.54	33	0	0	16	46	40	16	13	18	51	R	R	6-1	195	1-7-75	1997	San Diego, Calif.
Neu, Michael	0	1	4.50	9	0	0	1	18	17	10	9	12	23	S	R	5-10	185	3-9-78	1999	Napa, Calif.
Oleksik, George	1	0	6.35	21	0	0	2	28	32	22	20	12	24	R	R	6-4	200	4-19-74	1996	McMinnville, Tenn.
Rose, Brian	4	2	5.19	24	0	0	6	35	38	22	20	12	40	R	R	6-1	190	10-7-72	1994	Potsdam, N.Y.
2-team (24 Clinton)	11	2	2.94	48	1	0	6	67	65	24	22	23	64							
Sequea, Jacobo	4	6	4.92	16	16	2	0	90	88	52	49	44	67	R	R	6-0	175	8-31-81	1997	Anaco, Venez.
Soriano, Gabriel	0	2	13.97	8	0	0	0	10	18	21	15	16	10	R	R	6-1	158	6-19-76	1995	Santo Domingo, D.R.
Therneau, Dave	12	3	3.41	16	16	2	0	100	95	41	38	33	106	R	R	6-5	195	12-23-75	1998	Denton, Texas
Torres, Manny	1	6	6.05	8	7	1	0	39	48	33	26	11	29	R	R	6-2	195	5-27-77	1999	Bridgeport, Conn.
Whitesides, Johnny	1	1	8.04	13	1	0	0	16	24	19	14	10	11	R	R	6-2	195	3-2-78	1997	Sarasota, Fla.
Winchester, Scott	1	1	2.79	6	6	0	0	19	19	7	6	3	11	R	R	6-2	210	4-20-73	1995	Midland, Mich.
Wohlers, Mark	0	0	4.50	2	0	0	0	2	1	1	1	2	4	R	R	6-4	207	1-23-70	1988	Alpharetta, Ga.

BILLINGS — Rookie

PIONEER LEAGUE

BATTING	AVG	G	AB	R	H	2B	3B	HR	RBI	BB	SO	SB	CS	B	T	HT	WT	DOB	1st Yr	Resides
Bookout, Casey	.363	50	204	49	74	14	1	13	63	26	37	0	1	L	R	6-5	225	9-5-76	1999	Norman, Okla.
Broussard, Ben	.407	38	145	39	59	11	2	14	48	34	30	1	0	L	L	6-2	220	9-24-76	1999	Sour Lake, Texas
Burnett, Mark	.326	60	224	56	73	13	2	4	29	46	32	12	9	L	R	5-11	185	2-16-77	1999	Benton, Ark.
Campana, Wandel	.268	45	157	27	42	10	2	1	20	7	22	6	4	R	R	6-0	185	6-13-80	1998	Santo Domingo, D.R.
Dehner, Matt	.307	61	225	34	69	11	1	3	25	23	73	7	2	R	R	6-0	190	4-23-77	1999	Bakersfield, Calif.
Haver, Lance	.343	11	35	5	12	4	0	0	4	0	15	0	1	R	R	6-1	220	12-17-76	1999	Molalla, Ore.
Howard, Jason	.190	6	21	2	4	1	0	0	3	1	7	0	0	R	R	6-3	210	9-26-76	1999	Greenville, N.C.
Hurtado, Omar	.260	60	223	33	58	18	4	4	35	19	56	3	1	R	R	6-0	187	10-24-78	1996	Aragua, Venez.
Huth, Jason	.279	59	251	52	70	12	9	1	29	25	53	3	3	S	R	5-11	180	2-16-77	1999	Englewood, Colo.
Kison, Robbie	.148	9	27	4	4	0	0	0	2	6	4	0	0	R	R	5-11	155	5-11-77	1999	Bradenton, Fla.
LeFlore, Alex	.000	2	6	0	0	0	0	0	0	1	0	0	0	R	R	6-1	198	8-14-80	1999	Pinellas Park, Fla.
Liriano, Ruddy	.352	17	54	10	19	2	0	1	8	6	12	1	0	R	R	6-0	175	6-3-81	1998	Haina, D.R.
Peters, Samone	.225	29	111	13	25	3	0	9	23	5	57	0	0	R	R	6-8	260	7-30-78	1998	Alameda, Calif.
Price, Duane	.207	10	29	6	6	0	0	0	7	6	5	2	1	R	R	6-0	190	9-5-75	1998	College Station, Texas
Rewers, Nate	.067	3	15	3	1	1	0	0	2	1	2	1	0	S	R	5-6	175	11-30-76	1999	Elma, N.Y.
Rivera, Francisco	.214	31	112	11	24	1	0	2	15	4	14	2	0	L	R	6-2	215	10-4-79	1996	Veracruz, Mexico
Rodriguez, Serafin	.293	33	150	30	44	13	1	0	13	2	23	2	0	R	R	6-0	188	10-12-78	1997	Veracruz, Mexico
Schnall, Kevin	.315	18	54	22	17	4	0	2	14	20	10	0	0	R	R	6-2	185	1-30-77	1999	Mercerville, N.J.
Spoerl, Josh	.287	66	258	43	74	15	1	8	45	24	64	1	0	R	R	6-2	230	9-30-78	1999	Mesquite, Texas
Wallis, Jacob	.234	26	94	10	22	6	0	0	12	8	31	0	0	R	R	6-2	200	2-1-80	1998	Joshua, Texas
Ward, Corey	.269	49	167	24	45	7	4	3	19	12	49	8	4	R	R	6-2	195	9-27-78	1999	Dallas, Texas
Weber, Jon	.238	22	80	16	19	6	5	1	7	16	15	1	1	S	R	5-11	185	1-20-78	1999	Lakewood, Calif.

GAMES BY POSITION: C—Haver 8, Howard 6, Rivera 24, Schnall 17, Wallis 26. **1B**—Bookout 41, Broussard 8, Dehner 1, Huth 6, Rivera 4, Spoerl 17. **2B**—Burnett 52, Huth 7, Kison 9, Liriano 6, Rewers 3. **3B**—Burnett 4, Dehner 33, Huth 33, Spoerl 6. **SS**—Burnett 1, Campana 44, Dehner 23, Huth 9. **OF**—Broussard 31, Hurtado 59, Huth 4, LeFlore 2, Liriano 10, Peters 16, Price 9, Rodriguez 30, Spoerl 2, Ward 48, Weber 22.

PITCHING	W	L	ERA	G	GS	CG	SV	IP	H	R	ER	BB	SO	B	T	HT	WT	DOB	1st Yr	Resides
Bradley, David	5	4	4.87	17	9	0	0	65	69	43	35	24	51	R	R	6-1	175	8-28-77	1999	Walker, Wyo.
Brown, Zay	3	3	3.70	18	7	1	0	56	60	30	23	21	36	R	R	6-1	180	1-5-79	1997	Warrenville, S.C.
Chighisola, Lou	0	2	5.14	16	0	0	0	21	25	23	12	12	19	L	L	6-3	220	5-7-76	1999	Plympton, Mass.
Cooper, Matt	1	1	9.00	2	2	0	0	8	11	8	8	3	6	R	R	6-4	210	9-5-77	1998	Fremont, Calif.

PITCHING	W	L	ERA	G	GS	CG	SV	IP	H	R	ER	BB	SO	B	T	HT	WT	DOB	1st Yr	Resides
Darnell, Paul	3	3	5.21	9	9	0	0	48	55	37	28	22	39	R	L	6-5	190	6-4-76	1999	Hubbard, Texas
Dunn, Scott	1	3	4.31	9	8	0	0	40	36	24	19	24	36	R	R	6-3	185	5-23-78	1999	San Antonio, Texas
Erazo, Rafael	2	1	8.18	9	2	0	1	22	32	23	20	6	16	R	R	6-4	210	9-16-78	1999	Parsons, Kan.
Escamilla, Paco	3	0	3.54	5	5	0	0	28	18	11	11	9	33	R	R	6-2	205	12-16-76	1999	Cedar Park, Texas
Horney, Michael	4	1	2.81	8	0	0	1	16	15	6	5	4	11	R	R	6-0	210	7-5-77	1999	Greensboro, N.C.
Koronka, John	2	3	5.58	7	7	0	0	40	41	26	25	17	34	L	L	6-1	180	6-11-80	1998	Clermont, Fla.
Landkamer, Michael	2	2	7.06	20	0	0	1	22	23	17	17	19	19	R	R	5-11	190	4-19-77	1999	Mankato, Minn.
Levy, Tye	0	0	5.79	9	0	0	0	9	11	8	6	3	10	L	L	6-2	185	4-20-78	1997	Alexandria, Pa.
Martin, Kelly	2	0	4.66	5	3	0	0	19	16	13	10	8	25	R	R	6-4	190	9-27-78	1900	Phoenix, Ariz.
McEvoy, Casey	4	0	2.18	5	5	0	0	33	28	10	8	7	35	R	R	6-3	210	7-29-76	1998	Florence, Ky.
Nanninga, Matt	1	3	7.81	14	0	0	0	28	40	30	24	10	19	R	R	6-2	195	11-4-76	1999	Le Mars, Iowa
Pike, Tom	2	2	3.00	26	0	0	12	27	31	18	9	12	28	R	R	6-1	195	1-1-77	1999	Garvin, Okla.
Salmon, Brad	2	2	7.48	16	6	0	1	49	67	46	41	19	43	R	R	6-4	210	1-3-80	1999	Pensacola, Fla.
Stanley, Cody	1	2	3.65	26	0	0	2	37	43	36	15	24	35	R	R	6-3	185	9-21-78	1998	San Antonio, Texas
Stewart, Cory	2	0	3.14	10	10	0	0	49	50	25	17	21	37	L	L	6-4	180	11-14-79	1999	Boerne, Texas
Thompson, Travis	1	0	0.00	8	0	0	0	21	14	1	0	3	27	R	R	6-5	210	7-3-77	1900	Matthews, N.C.
Torres, Manny	1	1	3.48	7	2	0	0	21	17	9	8	7	18	R	R	6-1	195	5-27-77	1999	Bridgeport, Conn.

GULF COAST LEAGUE

BATTING	AVG	G	AB	R	H	2B	3B	HR	RBI	BB	SO	SB	CS	B	T	HT	WT	DOB	1st Yr	Resides
Abreu, Cesar	.197	26	76	4	15	2	0	1	6	5	23	2	1	R	R	6-0	170	7-17-78	1997	Santo Domingo, D.R.
Barrow, Corey	.171	54	175	19	30	7	3	2	19	26	56	10	1	R	R	5-10	180	3-30-80	1999	Athens, Ga.
Caceres, Wilmy	.333	2	9	2	3	0	0	0	0	1	0	0	0	S	R	6-0	170	10-2-78	1997	Santo Domingo, D.R.
Camarero, Rafael	.210	31	81	4	17	2	0	1	10	9	17	1	2	R	L	6-2	175	8-22-81	1997	Veracruz, Mexico
Campana, Wandel	.239	17	71	12	17	5	1	1	10	1	12	1	1	R	R	6-0	175	6-13-80	1998	Santo Domingo, D.R.
Copley, Travis	.208	7	24	5	5	2	0	0	1	4	6	0	0	L	R	6-4	215	1-8-76	1998	Hixson, Tenn.
Damato, Gabriel	.200	5	10	0	2	0	0	0	0	1	0	0	1	R	R	6-0	210	1-30-77	1999	Melrose Park, Ill.
Dolton, Odis	.177	32	96	11	17	2	1	1	12	5	43	3	0	R	R	6-4	200	4-3-80	1998	Abilene, Texas
Foltynowicz, Roger	.250	22	68	1	17	5	0	0	7	4	11	2	0	R	R	6-2	195	1-13-77	1999	Manitowoc, Wis.
Garabito, Vianney	.284	35	141	11	40	4	0	3	16	1	9	7	2	R	R	6-1	185	12-12-79	1996	Santo Domingo, D.R.
Goudie, Jaime	.500	1	2	0	1	0	0	0	1	0	0	0	0	R	R	5-10	170	3-8-79	1997	Columbus, Ga.
Hawes, B.J.	.302	45	162	23	49	11	5	0	18	13	22	11	2	R	R	6-1	175	6-2-79	1999	Appling, Ga.
Jenkins, Robert	.059	6	17	1	1	0	0	0	1	1	11	0	0	R	R	6-6	225	3-11-76	1999	Glendale, Wis.
Johnseron, Ryan	.478	7	23	7	11	1	0	0	3	6	3	3	1	R	R	6-2	195	11-23-76	1999	Bozeman, Mont.
Kison, Robbie	.273	7	11	2	3	0	0	0	2	0	0	1	0	R	R	5-11	195	5-11-77	1999	Bradenton, Fla.
LeFlore, Alex	.175	19	63	5	11	1	1	0	2	8	24	5	2	R	R	6-0	175	6-3-81	1998	Haina, D.R.
Liriano, Ruddy	.203	22	69	10	14	2	1	0	9	4	9	4	0	R	R	6-1	185	3-5-80	1999	Oklahoma City, Okla.
Lundquist, Ryan	.667	1	3	1	2	0	0	0	2	1	0	1	0	R	R	6-1	200	11-26-76	1999	Oklahoma City, Okla.
Martinez, Orlando	.308	4	13	4	4	1	1	0	1	0	2	0	0	R	R	5-11	165	6-8-79	1997	Santo Domingo, D.R.
Moncrief, Kyle	.175	39	97	11	17	3	1	1	7	22	41	3	1	L	L	6-6	255	2-4-80	1999	West Monroe, La.
Olmedo, Ranier	.236	54	195	30	46	12	1	1	19	12	28	13	7	R	R	5-11	155	5-31-81	1999	Maracay, Venez.
Presto, Nick	.375	3	8	2	3	2	0	0	0	1	1	0	0	R	R	5-10	175	7-8-74	1996	Jupiter, Fla.
Ruiz, Randy	.284	33	102	12	29	8	0	3	9	12	33	5	2	R	R	6-3	225	10-19-77	1999	Bronx, N.Y.
Santiago, Daniel	.108	24	65	7	7	0	0	0	2	9	20	2	1	S	R	5-10	510	6-17-79	1999	Cleveland, Ohio
Santonocito, Justin	.100	3	10	1	1	0	0	0	0	0	1	0	0	L	R	6-1	195	12-15-76	1998	West Seneca, N.Y.
Schnall, Kevin	1.000	1	1	0	1	0	0	0	0	0	0	0	0	R	R	6-0	200	1-30-77	1999	Mercerville, N.J.
Senegal, Terence	.203	50	148	17	30	2	0	0	9	11	36	8	1	R	R	6-1	185	11-25-78	1998	Lafayette, La.
Smith, Tony	.246	21	65	12	16	2	2	0	11	6	10	3	0	L	R	6-0	205	9-6-80	1999	Appling, Ga.
Taylor, Lonnie	.667	1	3	2	2	0	0	0	1	2	0	0	0	R	R	6-0	185	10-2-74	1998	Monroe, La.
Wallis, Jacob	.128	15	47	3	6	1	0	0	2	7	8	0	3	R	R	6-2	200	2-1-80	1998	Joshua, Texas
Zeber, Ryan	.167	3	6	1	1	0	0	0	1	0	0	0	0	R	R	6-2	190	5-24-78	1996	Santa Ana, Calif.

GAMES BY POSITION: C—Damata 5, Foltynowicz 20, Santiago 24, Schnall 1, Wallis 15, Zeber 3. **1B**—Abreu 11, Camarero 11, Moncrief 35, Ruiz 14. **2B**—Caceres 1, Campana 15, Garabito 12, Goudie 1, Kison 3, Olmedo 27, Presto 2, Santonocito 2. **3B**—Abreu 8, Camarero 8, Foltynowicz 1, Garabito 23, Hawes 2, Kison 1, Liriano 21, Olmedo 2, Santonocito 1. **SS**—Caceres 1, Campana 2, Hawes 34, Olmedo 26. **OF**—Abreu 3, Barrow 54, Camarero 10, Dolton 32, Jenkins 6, Johnerson 7, LeFlore 19, Liriano 1, O. Martinez 4, Ruiz 3, Senegal 48, Taylor 1.

PITCHING	W	L	ERA	G	GS	CG	SV	IP	H	R	ER	BB	SO	B	T	HT	WT	DOB	1st Yr	Resides
Altman, Gene	1	0	1.80	3	3	0	0	10	6	2	2	4	10	R	R	6-7	209	9-1-78	1996	Lynchburg, S.C.
Bell, Rob	0	0	1.13	2	2	0	0	8	3	1	1	0	11	R	R	6-2	225	1-17-77	1995	Marlboro, N.Y.
Brown, Paul	0	3	4.31	14	4	1	1	48	53	30	23	13	20	L	L	6-1	185	10-11-78	1999	Madison, Miss.
Chighisola, Lou	1	2	3.86	7	0	0	3	9	9	4	4	4	11	L	L	6-3	220	5-7-76	1999	Plympton, Mass.
Coffey, Todd	1	3	3.38	5	2	0	0	16	9	12	6	14	14	R	R	6-5	245	9-9-80	1998	Caroleen, N.C.
Cooper, Eric	0	2	7.84	3	2	0	0	10	13	12	9	5	5	R	R	6-4	200	9-5-77	1998	Fremont, Calif.
DeHart, Casey	0	1	7.71	2	2	0	0	5	7	4	4	2	6	L	L	6-2	180	11-1-77	1998	Burleson, Texas
Gooch, Arnold	1	1	1.13	2	2	0	0	8	5	2	1	1	6	R	R	6-2	210	11-12-76	1994	Doylestown, Pa.
Guillen, Elvin	0	0	9.00	7	0	0	0	8	9	9	8	11	7	R	R	6-3	185	5-12-81	1998	Santo Domingo, D.R.
Harrell, Scott	0	0	6.75	2	0	0	0	4	6	4	3	1	2	R	R	6-2	170	11-25-74	1997	Savannah, Ga.
Hines, Carlos	0	0	8.10	5	0	0	0	10	15	12	9	8	7	R	R	6-4	190	9-26-80	1999	Smithfield, N.C.
Joseph, Glen	1	0	7.20	2	0	0	0	5	8	4	4	1	3	R	R	6-3	190	9-3-80	1998	Tampa, Fla.
Koronka, John	3	3	1.69	7	7	0	0	37	25	11	7	14	27	L	L	6-1	180	6-11-80	1998	Clermont, Fla.
Koziara, Matt	3	2	2.05	13	1	0	0	26	24	15	6	16	26	R	R	6-2	205	11-8-76	1999	Franklin, Pa.
Lopez, Jorge	1	1	6.12	10	0	0	0	25	31	19	17	9	17	L	R	6-0	185	8-28-81	1998	Maracay, Venez.
Loudon, Gary	1	2	6.44	15	5	0	1	36	34	27	26	33	45	R	R	6-5	195	5-19-76	1999	Cortland, N.Y.
Love, Brandon	0	4	7.66	7	6	0	0	25	30	21	21	9	21	R	R	6-1	195	4-5-80	1999	Viola, Ark.
Lutz, Ken	0	4	6.50	12	9	0	0	44	58	40	32	20	37	R	R	6-2	210	10-4-81	1999	Collinsville, Ill.
Martinez, Erineido	3	3	3.71	17	0	0	2	27	27	14	11	16	17	R	R	6-1	153	11-30-80	1998	Santo Domingo, D.R.
Minaya, Richard	2	2	4.61	16	0	0	0	27	25	19	14	16	19	R	R	6-3	185	10-10-81	1999	Nagua, D.R.
Nanninga, Matt	1	1	9.60	6	2	0	0	15	17	19	16	10	4	R	R	6-2	195	11-4-76	1999	Le Mars, Iowa
Rose, Ted	0	0	9.00	1	0	0	0	2	4	2	2	1	3	L	R	6-2	185	8-23-73	1996	St. Clairsville, Ohio
Roundtree, Monte	1	1	2.42	7	3	0	0	22	16	8	6	11	19	L	L	6-4	180	2-7-78	1997	Greenville, N.C.
Russo, Dennis	0	0	4.50	2	2	0	0	4	6	3	2	2	1	R	R	6-2	180	1-10-80	1998	Auburndale, Fla.
Sager, A.J.	0	1	4.50	1	1	0	0	2	4	1	1	0	1	R	R	6-4	220	3-3-65	1988	Perrysburg, Ohio
Sequea, Jacobo	0	0	4.50	1	1	0	0	2	2	1	1	0	3	R	R	6-0	185	8-31-81	1997	Anaco, Venez.
Valdez, Jose	3	3	1.96	12	6	0	2	41	20	12	9	25	36	R	R	6-1	164	6-11-79	1996	San Cristobal, D.R.
Washington, Porter	0	0	9.26	10	0	0	0	12	19	12	13	13	13	R	R	6-1	175	9-1-79	1999	Pensacola, Fla.

CLEVELAND INDIANS

Tribe's inability to win in October costs Hargrove his job

BY JIM INGRAHAM

The 1999 season was one of extremes for the Indians. They were extremely prolific offensively, but their pitching was extremely inconsistent. And the roster was unsettled due to an extreme number of injuries.

The Indians were successful in the regular season, but extremely disappointing in the postseason, leading to the team's most extreme decision of all: the firing of manager Mike Hargrove.

Less than a week after an embarrassing collapse in the American League Division Series against the Red Sox, the team dumped Hargrove and his entire coaching staff, with the exception of bullpen coach Luis Isaac and hitting coach Charlie Manuel, who became the new manager.

It was a stunning conclusion to what in many ways was a season of positives. The club won 97 games in the regular season—the fifth-highest total in franchise history—won its fifth consecutive AL Central title and was the first major league team in 49 years to score 1,000 runs in a season.

Then the season came crashing down around the Tribe. After taking a 2-0 lead on the Red Sox, the Indians lost the last three in a row. They were outscored 44-18 in the process, including a 23-7 loss in Game Four, the worst postseason loss in major league history.

Four days after a 12-8 loss in Game Five, general manager John Hart fired Hargrove, who had been the manager since July 1991 and was within eight victories of becoming the franchise's all-time winningest manager.

Hargrove's firing overshadowed spectacular team

Roberto Alomar　　**Tim Drew**

Players of the Year

MAJOR LEAGUE: Roberto Alomar, 2b
In his first season with the Tribe, Alomar hit .323 with 138 runs and 120 RBIs, and committed just six errors at second base.

MINOR LEAGUE: Tim Drew, rhp
Drew went 13-5 with a 3.73 ERA in 28 starts in his first full season as a pro at Kinston.

and individual accomplishments. The club finished with a record of 97-65, winning the Central Division by 21½ games over the White Sox.

The Indians scored 1,009 runs, the fifth-highest total in major league history. Manny Ramirez led the majors with a club-record 165 RBIs, the most by a major leaguer in 61 years. Ramirez also hit .333 with 44 home runs and finished in the top 10 in the league in eight offensive categories. Roberto Alomar had a spectacular all-around season, playing outstanding defense at second base and hitting .323 with 24 home runs, 120 RBIs, 138 runs and 37 stolen bases.

Bartolo Colon, at 18-5 the first Indian to win 18 games since Greg Swindell in 1988, joined Charles Nagy (17-11) and Dave Burba (15-9) to give the Indians three 15-game winners for the first time since 1956.

With 16 different players spending time on the disabled list, the Indians had to rely on the farm system to provide reinforcements. The system came through with contributors such as righthander Sean DePaula, catcher Einar Diaz, infielder Enrique Wilson and outfielders Jacob Cruz, Alex Ramirez, Dave Roberts and Richie Sexson.

The trickle-down effect meant the Indians' minor league teams had to scramble to keep their rosters in order, and the result was an overall record of .500 (354-354) by the club's six affiliates.

Most encouraging was the development of the club's first-round draft picks from 1998 and 1997, pitchers C.C. Sabathia and Tim Drew. Sabathia, a lefthander, pitched at three levels and was a combined 5-3 with a 3.29 ERA. The righthanded Drew was 13-5, 3.73 at Class A Kinston.

ORGANIZATION LEADERS

BATTING

*AVG	Nate Grindell, Mahoning Valley	.315
R	Scott Morgan, Buffalo/Akron	104
H	John McDonald, Buffalo/Akron	142
TB	Scott Morgan, Buffalo/Akron	282
2B	Scott Morgan, Buffalo/Akron	35
3B	Tyler Minges, Columbus	11
HR	Scott Morgan, Buffalo/Akron	34
RBI	Scott Morgan, Buffalo/Akron	100
BB	Mike Edwards, Kinston	93
SO	Russell Branyan, Buffalo	187
SB	Scott Pratt, Kinston	47

PITCHING

W	Mark Watson, Akron/Kinston	15
L	Two tied at	11
#ERA	Sean DePaula, Buff./Akron/Kinston	2.56
G	Jimmy Hamilton, Buffalo/Akron	51
CG	Two tied at	2
SV	Two tied at	19
IP	Willie Martinez, Buffalo/Akron	170
BB	Mike Spiegel, Kinston/Columbus	65
SO	Rob Pugmire, Kinston/Columbus	160

*Minimum 250 At-Bats　#Minimum 75 Innings

Cleveland INDIANS

Manager: Mike Hargrove

BATTING

	AVG	G	AB	R	H	2B	3B	HR	RBI	BB	SO	SB	CS	B	T	HT	WT	DOB	1st Yr	Resides
Alomar, Roberto	.323	159	563	138	182	40	3	24	120	99	96	37	6	S	R	6-0	185	2-5-68	1985	Salinas, P.R.
Alomar, Sandy	.307	37	137	19	42	13	0	6	25	4	23	0	1	R	R	6-5	220	6-18-66	1984	Westlake, Ohio
Baerga, Carlos	.228	22	57	4	13	0	0	1	5	4	10	1	1	S	R	5-11	215	11-4-68	1986	Bayamon, P.R.
Baines, Harold	.271	28	85	5	23	2	0	1	22	11	10	0	0	L	L	6-2	195	3-15-59	1977	St. Michaels, Md.
2-team (107 Balt.)	.312	135	430	62	134	18	1	25	103	54	48	1	2							
Borders, Pat	.300	6	20	2	6	0	1	0	3	0	3	0	1	R	R	6-2	200	5-14-63	1982	Lake Wales, Fla.
Branyan, Russell	.211	11	38	4	8	2	0	1	6	3	19	0	0	L	R	6-3	195	12-19-75	1994	Warner Robins, Ga.
Cabrera, Jolbert	.189	30	37	6	7	1	0	0	1	8	3	0		R	R	6-0	177	12-8-72	1991	Cartagena, Colombia
Cordero, Wil	.299	54	194	35	58	15	0	8	32	15	37	2	0	R	R	6-2	200	10-3-71	1988	Mayaguez, P.R.
Cruz, Jacob	.330	32	88	14	29	5	1	3	17	5	13	0	2	L	L	6-0	179	1-28-73	1994	Oxnard, Calif.
Diaz, Einar	.281	119	392	43	110	21	1	3	32	23	41	11	4	R	R	5-10	165	12-28-72	1991	Chesnee, S.C.
Fryman, Travis	.255	85	322	45	82	16	2	10	48	25	57	2	1	R	R	6-1	195	3-25-69	1987	Cantonment, Fla.
Houston, Tyler	.148	13	27	2	4	1	0	1	3	3	11	0	0	L	R	6-1	210	1-17-71	1989	Las Vegas, Nev.
Justice, Dave	.287	133	429	75	123	18	0	21	88	94	90	1	3	L	L	6-3	200	4-14-66	1985	Cincinnati, Ohio
Levis, Jesse	.154	10	26	0	4	0	0	0	3	1	6	0	0	L	R	5-9	200	4-14-68	1989	Elkins Park, Pa.
Lofton, Kenny	.301	120	465	110	140	28	6	7	39	79	84	25	6	L	L	6-0	190	5-31-67	1988	Tucson, Ariz.
Manto, Jeff	.200	12	25	5	5	0	0	2	11	1	11	0	0	R	R	6-3	210	8-23-64	1985	Langhorne, Pa.
McDonald, John	.333	18	21	2	7	0	0	0	0	0	3	0	1	R	R	5-11	175	9-24-74	1996	East Lyme, Conn.
Ramirez, Juan	.299	48	97	11	29	6	1	3	18	3	26	1	1	R	R	5-11	190	10-3-74	1991	Winter Haven, Fla.
Ramirez, Manny	.333	147	522	131	174	34	3	44	165	96	131	2	4	R	R	6-0	205	5-30-72	1991	New York, N.Y.
Roberts, David	.238	41	143	26	34	4	0	2	12	9	16	11	3	L	L	5-10	172	5-31-72	1994	Oceanside, Calif.
Sexson, Richie	.255	134	479	72	122	17	7	31	116	34	117	3	3	R	R	6-7	210	12-29-74	1993	Scottsdale, Ariz.
Thome, Jim	.277	146	494	101	137	27	2	33	108	127	171	0	0	L	R	6-4	225	8-27-70	1989	Aurora, Ohio
Turner, Chris	.190	12	21	3	4	0	0	0	0	1	8	1	0	R	R	6-1	190	3-23-69	1991	Bowling Green, Ky.
Vizquel, Omar	.333	144	574	112	191	36	4	5	66	65	50	42	9	S	R	5-9	170	4-24-67	1984	Issaquah, Wash.
Whiten, Mark	.160	8	25	2	4	1	0	1	4	3	4	0	0	S	R	6-3	235	11-25-66	1986	Clearwater, Fla.
Wilson, Enrique	.262	113	332	41	87	22	1	2	24	25	41	5	4	S	R	5-11	170	7-27-75	1992	Santo Domingo, D.R.

PITCHING

	W	L	ERA	G	GS	CG	SV	IP	H	R	ER	BB	SO	B	T	HT	WT	DOB	1st Yr	Resides
Assenmacher, Paul	2	1	8.18	55	0	0	0	33	50	32	30	17	29	L	L	6-3	210	12-10-60	1983	Duluth, Ga.
Brower, Jim	3	1	4.56	9	2	0	0	26	27	13	13	10	18	R	R	6-2	205	12-29-72	1994	Minnetonka, Minn.
Burba, Dave	15	9	4.25	34	34	1	0	220	211	113	104	96	174	R	R	6-4	240	7-7-66	1987	Gilbert, Ariz.
Candiotti, Tom	1	1	11.05	7	2	0	0	15	19	18	18	7	11	R	R	6-2	221	8-31-57	1979	Clayton, Calif.
2-team (11 Oakland)	4	6	7.32	18	13	0	0	71	86	64	58	30	41							
Colon, Bartolo	18	5	3.95	32	32	1	0	205	185	97	90	76	161	R	R	6-0	225	5-24-75	1994	Puerto Plata, D.R.
DeLucia, Rich	0	0	6.75	6	0	0	0	9	13	7	7	9	7	R	R	6-0	190	10-7-65	1986	Shillington, Pa.
DePaula, Sean	0	0	4.63	11	0	0	0	12	8	6	6	3	18	R	R	6-4	215	11-7-73	1996	Derry, N.H.
Gooden, Dwight	3	4	6.26	26	22	0	0	115	127	90	80	67	88	R	R	6-3	210	11-16-64	1982	St. Petersburg, Fla.
Haney, Chris	0	2	4.69	13	4	0	0	40	43	22	21	16	22	L	L	6-3	210	11-16-68	1990	Barboursville, Va.
Jackson, Mike	3	4	4.06	72	0	0	39	69	60	32	31	26	55	R	R	6-2	223	12-22-64	1984	Spring, Texas
Karsay, Steve	10	2	2.97	50	3	0	1	79	71	29	26	30	68	R	R	6-3	209	3-24-72	1990	Scottsdale, Ariz.
Langston, Mark	1	2	5.25	25	5	0	0	62	69	40	36	29	43	R	L	6-2	185	8-20-60	1981	Anaheim Hills, Calif.
Martin, Tom	0	1	8.68	6	0	0	0	9	13	9	9	3	8	L	L	6-1	200	5-21-70	1989	Panama City, Fla.
Nagy, Charles	17	11	4.95	33	32	1	0	202	238	120	111	59	126	L	R	6-3	200	5-5-67	1989	Westlake, Ohio
Poole, Jim	1	0	18.00	3	0	0	0	1	2	2	2	3	0	L	L	6-1	203	4-28-66	1988	Alpharetta, Ga.
Rakers, Jason	0	0	4.50	1	0	0	0	2	2	1	1	1	0	R	R	6-2	197	6-29-73	1995	Pittsburgh, Pa.
Reed, Steve	3	2	4.23	63	0	0	0	62	69	33	29	20	44	R	R	6-2	212	3-11-66	1988	Arvada, Colo.
Rincon, Ricardo	2	3	4.43	59	0	0	0	45	41	22	22	24	30	L	L	5-10	188	4-13-70	1997	Veracruz, Mexico
Riske, David	1	1	8.36	12	0	0	0	14	20	15	13	6	16	R	R	6-2	175	10-23-76	1997	Kent, Wash.
Shuey, Paul	8	5	3.53	72	0	0	6	82	68	37	32	40	103	R	R	6-3	215	9-16-70	1992	Wake Forest, N.C.
Spradlin, Jerry	0	0	18.00	4	0	0	0	3	6	6	6	3	2	R	R	6-7	246	6-14-67	1988	Anaheim, Calif.
Stevens, Dave	0	0	10.00	5	0	0	0	9	10	10	10	8	6	R	R	6-3	215	3-4-70	1990	Yorba Linda, Calif.
Tam, Jeff	0	0	81.00	1	0	0	0	2	3	3	1	0	0	R	R	6-1	202	8-19-70	1993	Melbourne, Fla.
Wagner, Paul	1	0	4.15	3	0	0	0	4	5	4	2	3	0	R	R	6-1	210	11-14-67	1989	Slinger, Wis.
Wright, Jaret	8	10	6.06	26	26	0	0	134	144	99	90	77	91	R	R	6-2	230	12-29-75	1994	Newport Beach, Calif.

FIELDING

Catcher	PCT	G	PO	A	E	DP	PB
S. Alomar	.974	35	257	10	7	2	1
Borders	.943	5	32	1	2	0	2
Diaz	.988	119	751	81	10	8	5
Houston	1.000	1	4	0	0	0	0
Levis	1.000	9	53	3	0	0	0
Turner	.964	12	50	3	2	0	0

First Base	PCT	G	PO	A	E	DP
Manto	1.000	1	5	0	0	0
Sexson	.988	61	517	51	7	48
Thome	.994	111	930	83	6	93

Second Base	PCT	G	PO	A	E	DP
R. Alomar	.992	156	270	466	6	102
Baerga	1.000	6	5	9	0	3

	PCT	G	PO	A	E	DP
Cabrera	1.000	6	4	4	0	1
McDonald	1.000	7	7	11	0	4
Wilson	1.000	21	16	19	0	2

Third Base	PCT	G	PO	A	E	DP
Baerga	.964	15	8	19	1	1
Branyan	.960	8	6	18	1	0
Fryman	.969	85	41	146	6	12
Houston	1.000	10	3	11	0	1
Manto	1.000	10	7	16	0	2
Wilson	.965	61	24	86	4	2

Shortstop	PCT	G	PO	A	E	DP
McDonald	.917	6	1	10	1	1
Vizquel	.976	143	221	396	15	88

	PCT	G	PO	A	E	DP
Wilson	.960	35	37	58	4	21

Outfield	PCT	G	PO	A	E	DP
Cabrera	.957	16	22	0	1	0
Cordero	.981	29	51	0	1	0
Cruz	1.000	24	48	0	0	0
Justice	.977	93	161	7	4	3
Lofton	.989	119	255	11	3	3
A. Ramirez	.920	29	22	1	2	0
M. Ramirez	.975	146	267	7	7	2
Roberts	1.000	39	87	0	0	0
Sexson	1.000	49	66	3	0	0
Vizquel	.000	1	0	0	0	0
Whiten	1.000	7	11	1	0	0

Organization Statistics

Director, Player Development: Neal Huntington

Class	Farm Team	League	W	L	Pct.	Finish*	Manager	First Yr
AAA	Buffalo (N.Y.) Bisons	International	72	72	.500	9th (14)	Jeff Datz	1995
AA	Akron (Ohio) Aeros	Eastern	69	71	.493	7th (12)	Joel Skinner	1997
A#	Kinston (N.C.) Indians	Carolina	79	58	.577	1st (8)	Eric Wedge	1987
A	Columbus (Ga.) RedStixx	South Atlantic	70	71	.496	7th (14)	Brad Komminsk	1991
A	Mahoning Valley (Ohio) Indians	New York-Penn	43	33	.566	1st (14)	Ted Kubiak	1999
Rookie#	Burlington (N.C.) Indians	Appalachian	21	49	.300	10th (10)	Jack Mull	1986

*Finish in overall standings (No. of teams in league)   #Advanced level

BUFFALO   Class AAA

INTERNATIONAL LEAGUE

BATTING	AVG	G	AB	R	H	2B	3B	HR	RBI	BB	SO	SB	CS	B	T	HT	WT	DOB	1st Yr	Resides
Alomar, Sandy	.273	10	33	9	9	2	1	2	10	6	3	0	0	R	R	6-5	220	6-18-66	1984	Westlake, Ohio
Borders, Pat	.237	55	198	17	47	7	0	5	23	12	31	0	1	R	R	6-2	200	5-14-63	1982	Lake Wales, Fla.
Branyan, Russell	.208	109	395	51	82	11	1	30	67	52	187	8	1	L	R	6-3	195	12-19-75	1994	Warner Robins, Ga.
Budzinski, Mark	.286	47	133	24	38	7	3	2	17	22	36	4	2	L	L	6-2	175	8-26-73	1995	Severna Park, Md.
Cabrera, Jolbert	.265	71	279	44	74	13	4	0	27	26	43	20	4	R	R	6-0	177	12-8-72	1991	Cartagena, Colombia
Cruz, Jacob	.272	54	202	29	55	7	2	7	31	21	39	4	2	L	L	6-0	179	1-28-73	1994	Oxnard, Calif.
Fryman, Travis	.182	3	11	1	2	0	0	1	2	0	3	0	0	R	R	6-1	195	3-25-69	1987	Cantonment, Fla.
Harriss, Robin	.000	2	3	0	0	0	0	0	0	1	1	0	0	R	R	6-1	205	8-7-71	1994	San Angelo, Texas
Manto, Jeff	.296	66	203	47	60	9	0	23	44	66	47	3	1	R	R	6-3	210	8-23-64	1985	Langhorne, Pa.
McDonald, John	.316	66	237	30	75	12	1	0	25	11	23	6	3	R	R	5-11	175	9-24-74	1996	East Lyme, Conn.
Miller, David	.240	101	325	37	78	21	3	2	37	33	57	12	5	L	L	6-4	200	12-9-73	1996	Wyndmoor, Pa.
Miller, Orlando	.258	68	233	27	60	17	0	7	33	12	52	5	0	R	R	6-3	205	1-13-69	1988	Changuinola, Panama
Morgan, Scott	.257	48	171	32	44	9	0	8	31	18	38	2	3	R	R	6-7	230	7-19-73	1995	Lompoc, Calif.
Ortiz, Nick	.255	22	51	7	13	4	0	0	1	3	10	0	0	R	R	6-0	160	7-9-73	1991	Cidra, P.R.
Perry, Chan	.282	79	273	44	77	17	0	10	59	19	34	5	1	R	R	6-2	200	9-13-72	1994	Mayo, Fla.
Ramirez, Alex	.305	75	305	50	93	20	2	12	50	17	52	5	5	R	R	5-11	190	10-3-74	1991	Winter Haven, Fla.
Roberts, David	.271	89	350	65	95	17	10	0	38	43	52	39	3	L	L	5-10	172	5-31-72	1994	Oceanside, Calif.
Scutaro, Marcos	.273	129	462	76	126	24	2	8	51	61	69	21	6	R	R	5-10	170	10-30-75	1995	Yaracuy, Venez.
Selby, Bill	.295	122	447	75	132	32	5	20	85	57	63	4	3	L	R	5-9	190	6-11-70	1992	Walls, Miss.
Soliz, Steve	.259	40	112	15	29	6	0	2	14	6	24	0	0	R	R	5-10	180	1-27-71	1993	Oxnard, Calif.
Turner, Chris	.273	69	231	36	63	9	0	9	33	34	45	2	2	R	R	6-1	190	3-23-69	1991	Bowling Green, Ky.
Whiten, Mark	.280	48	175	32	49	10	0	6	19	22	38	3	1	S	R	6-3	235	11-25-66	1986	Clearwater, Fla.

PITCHING	W	L	ERA	G	GS	CG	SV	IP	H	R	ER	BB	SO	B	T	HT	WT	DOB	1st Yr	Resides
Brower, Jim	11	11	4.73	27	27	0	0	160	164	101	84	59	76	R	R	6-2	205	12-29-72	1994	Minnetonka, Minn.
Brown, Jamie	1	0	5.40	1	0	0	0	5	8	4	3	1	2	R	R	6-2	205	3-31-77	1997	Meridian, Miss.
Cadaret, Greg	0	0	2.70	10	0	0	0	7	6	3	2	7	8	L	L	6-3	215	2-27-62	1983	Mesa, Ariz.
Cairncross, Cam	0	3	5.21	19	0	0	0	19	22	13	11	6	13	L	L	6-2	212	5-11-72	1991	Cairns, Australia
Camp, Jared	0	0	0.84	10	0	0	1	11	4	2	1	13	14	R	R	6-2	195	5-4-75	1995	Huntington, W.Va.
DePaula, Sean	0	0	0.00	5	0	0	2	5	0	0	0	3	7	R	R	6-4	215	11-7-73	1996	Derry, N.H.
Dedrick, Jim	2	2	4.08	30	0	0	0	46	49	23	21	27	26	S	R	6-0	190	4-4-68	1990	Everett, Wash.
DeLucia, Rich	2	3	4.18	44	0	0	19	47	39	24	22	29	46	R	R	6-0	190	10-7-65	1986	Shillington, Pa.
Dougherty, Tony	0	2	5.63	16	1	0	0	24	28	17	15	15	8	R	R	6-2	200	4-12-73	1994	Beaver Falls, Pa.
Driskill, Travis	9	8	4.83	31	18	0	0	132	146	78	71	32	90	R	R	6-0	185	8-1-71	1993	Austin, Texas
Gooden, Dwight	0	1	2.45	1	1	0	0	4	6	1	1	3	3	R	R	6-3	210	11-16-64	1982	St. Petersburg, Fla.
Hamilton, Jimmy	1	4	5.18	26	0	0	0	24	24	22	14	27	25	L	L	6-3	190	8-1-75	1996	Weyers Cave, Va.
Haney, Chris	2	5	3.22	13	10	0	0	59	50	25	21	22	37	L	L	6-3	215	11-16-68	1990	Barboursville, Va.
Langston, Mark	0	1	3.86	4	4	0	0	19	16	9	8	8	11	R	L	6-2	185	8-20-60	1981	Anaheim Hills, Calif.
Martin, Tom	1	0	3.00	5	0	0	0	6	5	2	2	1	6	L	L	6-1	200	5-21-70	1989	Panama City, Fla.
Martinez, Willie	2	2	6.85	4	4	0	0	22	28	17	17	7	12	R	R	6-2	195	1-4-78	1995	Barquisimeto, Venez.
Matthews, Mike	1	2	7.59	25	0	0	0	21	23	18	18	18	16	L	L	6-2	175	10-24-73	1992	Woodbridge, Va.
Menhart, Paul	2	1	4.85	7	0	0	0	13	18	7	7	4	10	R	R	6-2	190	3-25-69	1990	Covington, Ga.
Rakers, Jason	7	8	4.92	23	20	1	0	132	151	83	72	31	85	R	R	6-2	197	6-29-73	1995	Pittsburgh, Pa.
Rigdon, Paul	7	4	4.53	19	19	0	0	103	114	60	52	28	60	R	R	6-5	210	11-2-75	1996	Jacksonville, Fla.
Riske, David	0	1	0.65	23	0	0	6	28	14	3	2	7	22	R	R	6-2	175	10-23-76	1997	Kent, Wash.
Sanders, Frankie	0	1	9.00	1	1	0	0	5	6	5	5	4	3	R	R	5-11	165	8-27-75	1995	Sarasota, Fla.
Sexton, Jeff	0	1	6.52	23	1	0	0	29	47	24	21	14	22	R	R	6-2	190	10-4-71	1993	Kingston, Okla.
Shuey, Paul	0	0	0.00	1	0	0	1	1	0	0	0	1	1	R	R	6-3	215	9-16-70	1992	Wake Forest, N.C.
Stevens, Dave	1	0	1.52	20	0	0	12	24	12	4	4	14	28	R	R	6-3	215	3-4-70	1990	Yorba Linda, Calif.
Tam, Jeff	2	2	2.08	16	0	0	0	26	23	9	6	8	13	R	R	6-1	202	8-19-70	1993	Melbourne, Fla.
2-team (16 Norfolk)	..	2	3	2.53	32	0	0	3	46	47	16	13	11	23							
Telgheder, Dave	8	8	3.95	29	14	1	0	107	109	56	47	21	60	R	R	6-3	223	11-11-66	1989	West Town, N.Y.
Wagner, Paul	8	4	3.82	23	23	0	0	130	123	67	55	55	95	R	R	6-1	210	11-14-67	1989	Slinger, Wis.
Walker, Mike	2	1	5.60	29	0	0	2	35	43	29	22	26	15	R	R	6-1	205	10-4-66	1986	Brooksville, Fla.
Wright, Jaret	0	0	0.00	1	1	0	0	3	0	1	0	4	4	R	R	6-2	230	12-29-75	1994	Newport Beach, Calif.

FIELDING

Catcher	PCT	G	PO	A	E	DP	PB
Alomar	.921	8	35	0	3	0	2
Borders	.986	54	316	25	5	1	2
Harriss	1.000	2	10	2	0	1	1
Soliz	.980	39	180	19	4	0	7
Turner	.989	52	316	34	4	4	5

	PCT	G	PO	A	E	DP
D. Miller	.996	30	232	13	1	20
O. Miller	1.000	3	16	3	0	1
Ortiz	1.000	3	3	0	0	0
Perry	.986	53	405	32	6	32
Turner	.984	16	108	13	2	13

	PCT	G	PO	A	E	DP
McDonald	1.000	2	4	5	0	2
O. Miller	1.000	2	1	2	0	1
Scutaro	.974	123	230	331	15	67
Selby	1.000	13	25	29	0	5

First Base	PCT	G	PO	A	E	DP
Manto	.993	54	417	22	3	37

Second Base	PCT	G	PO	A	E	DP
Cabrera	.968	6	15	15	1	2

Third Base	PCT	G	PO	A	E	DP
Branyan	.921	108	63	205	23	11
Cabrera	.900	3	2	7	1	0

	PCT	G	PO	A	E	DP
Fryman	.750	2	0	3	1	0
McDonald	1.000	3	1	9	0	0
O. Miller	.960	8	5	19	1	1
Selby	.929	24	14	51	5	2
Shortstop	**PCT**	**G**	**PO**	**A**	**E**	**DP**
Cabrera	.956	23	29	57	4	9
McDonald	.953	61	82	180	13	36

	PCT	G	PO	A	E	DP
O. Miller	.964	43	60	129	7	20
Ortiz	.973	17	26	46	2	10
Scutaro	.966	6	9	19	1	4
Outfield	**PCT**	**G**	**PO**	**A**	**E**	**DP**
Budzinski	1.000	45	114	1	0	1
Cabrera	1.000	40	107	3	0	0
Cruz	.953	43	77	5	4	1

	PCT	G	PO	A	E	DP
D. Miller	.972	56	100	4	3	1
Morgan	.972	45	101	3	3	0
Perry	.967	21	28	1	1	1
Ramirez	.977	71	167	6	4	3
Roberts	.996	87	247	4	1	1
Selby	1.000	17	26	0	0	0
Whiten	.989	35	88	4	1	1

AKRON — Class AA

EASTERN LEAGUE

BATTING	AVG	G	AB	R	H	2B	3B	HR	RBI	BB	SO	SB	CS	B	T	HT	WT	DOB	1st Yr	Resides
Alomar, Sandy	.310	10	29	8	9	0	0	1	6	3	2	1	0	R	R	6-5	220	6-18-66	1984	Westlake, Ohio
Bady, Ed	.243	69	230	42	56	13	3	2	33	32	68	19	5	S	R	5-11	170	2-5-73	1994	Queens, N.Y.
Benefield, Brian	.193	44	145	14	28	3	2	3	14	16	32	3	3	R	R	6-0	181	8-12-76	1997	Carrollton, Texas
Betances, Junior	.294	89	306	41	90	14	5	2	28	31	53	9	6	R	R	5-11	165	5-26-73	1991	La Vega, D.R.
Betts, Todd	.280	104	375	60	105	24	1	19	67	61	65	2	1	L	R	6-0	185	6-24-73	1993	Scarborough, Ontario
Budzinski, Mark	.283	86	297	58	84	17	6	6	46	48	63	9	4	L	L	6-2	175	8-26-73	1995	Severna Park, Md.
Cordero, Wil	.364	3	11	2	4	2	0	0	0	0	3	0	0	R	R	6-2	200	10-3-71	1988	Mayaguez, P.R.
Dishington, Nate	.237	17	59	12	14	2	0	5	14	6	30	0	0	L	R	6-3	210	1-8-75	1993	Glendale, Calif.
Dorman, John	.143	3	7	0	1	0	0	0	0	0	1	0	0	R	R	5-9	170	8-29-73	1997	Weston, Conn.
Encarnacion, Angelo	.213	34	127	9	27	7	0	1	21	6	19	1	1	R	R	5-8	190	4-18-73	1990	Santo Domingo, D.R.
Fryman, Travis	.250	4	12	4	3	0	0	1	4	2	4	0	0	R	R	6-1	195	3-25-69	1987	Cantonment, Fla.
Harriss, Robin	.167	17	48	9	8	1	0	2	6	1	12	1	0	R	R	6-1	205	8-7-71	1994	San Angelo, Texas
Hayes, Heath	.266	119	418	51	111	15	2	16	68	41	111	2	1	R	R	6-3	195	2-29-72	1994	Citrus Heights, Calif.
Hernaiz, Juan	.190	7	21	3	4	0	0	1	1	0	7	0	0	R	R	5-10	192	2-15-75	1992	Carolina, P.R.
Huelsmann, Mike	.277	43	177	20	49	5	1	1	10	15	30	12	3	S	R	5-11	165	11-21-74	1996	St. Louis, Mo.
Kilburg, Joe	.271	42	144	20	39	8	0	1	14	23	28	1	2	L	R	5-11	180	12-20-75	1997	Bay Village, Ohio
McDonald, John	.296	55	226	31	67	12	0	1	26	19	26	7	3	R	R	5-11	175	9-24-74	1996	East Lyme, Conn.
McKinley, Dan	.257	111	463	70	119	20	6	3	37	24	87	3	5	L	R	6-0	180	5-15-76	1997	Chandler, Ariz.
Mohr, Dustan	.167	12	42	3	7	2	1	0	2	5	7	0	1	R	R	6-2	210	6-19-76	1997	Hattiesburg, Miss.
Morgan, Scott	.282	88	344	72	97	26	2	26	70	38	96	6	1	R	R	6-7	230	7-19-73	1995	Lompoc, Calif.
Ortiz, Nick	.267	55	195	24	52	15	2	2	13	17	40	1	2	R	R	6-0	160	7-9-73	1991	Cidra, P.R.
Peoples, Danny	.251	127	494	75	124	23	3	21	78	55	142	2	1	R	R	6-1	207	1-20-75	1996	Austin, Texas
Perry, Chan	.279	37	154	24	43	14	0	7	30	11	27	1	0	R	R	6-2	200	9-13-72	1994	Mayo, Fla.
Robinson, Adam	.277	66	238	37	66	12	4	5	30	20	49	4	1	R	R	6-0	185	6-28-75	1997	Long Valley, N.J.
Schwab, Chris	.000	2	6	0	0	0	0	0	1	3	0	0	0	R	L	6-3	215	7-25-74	1993	Eagan, Minn.
Soliz, Steve	.130	7	23	1	3	0	0	0	3	1	4	0	0	R	R	5-10	180	1-27-71	1993	Oxnard, Calif.
Taveras, Frank	.190	16	42	6	8	1	0	1	4	4	17	0	0	L	R	6-1	158	9-6-75	1993	Santiago, D.R.
Whitaker, Chad	.322	41	149	18	48	12	2	5	38	15	40	0	1	L	R	6-2	195	9-16-76	1995	Fort Lauderdale, Fla.

PITCHING	W	L	ERA	G	GS	CG	SV	IP	H	R	ER	BB	SO	B	T	HT	WT	DOB	1st Yr	Resides
Atkins, Ross	6	8	5.77	33	7	0	3	87	90	60	56	47	43	R	R	6-2	195	8-7-73	1995	Coral Gables, Fla.
Bacsik, Mike	11	11	4.64	26	26	1	0	149	164	84	77	47	84	L	L	6-3	190	11-11-77	1996	Duncanville, Texas
Brammer, J.D.	3	2	4.76	47	0	0	8	76	53	44	40	60	69	R	R	6-4	235	1-30-75	1996	West Logan, W.Va.
Brown, Jamie	5	9	4.57	23	23	1	0	138	140	72	70	39	98	R	R	6-2	205	3-31-77	1997	Meridian, Miss.
Camp, Jared	1	2	6.50	17	0	0	7	18	22	17	13	16	18	R	R	6-2	195	5-4-75	1995	Huntington, W.Va.
DePaula, Sean	1	0	3.54	14	0	0	1	28	20	11	11	17	31	R	R	6-4	215	11-7-73	1996	Derry, N.H.
Dedrick, Jim	1	0	9.00	2	0	0	0	3	4	3	3	0	0	S	R	6-0	195	4-4-68	1990	Everett, Wash.
Deschenes, Marc	4	3	3.31	43	0	0	3	65	57	28	24	31	64	R	R	6-0	175	1-6-73	1995	Dracut, Mass.
Escobar, Ruben	0	0	16.20	1	0	0	0	2	5	3	3	0	0	R	R	6-1	185	6-8-76	1998	Hesperia, Calif.
Garza, Albert	3	5	9.35	10	9	0	0	42	54	46	44	41	38	R	R	6-3	195	5-25-77	1996	Wapato, Wash.
Gooden, Dwight	0	0	3.00	1	1	0	0	3	3	2	1	1	2	R	R	6-3	210	11-16-64	1982	St. Petersburg, Fla.
Hamilton, Jimmy	0	2	3.73	25	0	0	2	31	19	14	13	24	27	L	L	6-3	190	8-1-75	1996	Weyers Cave, Va.
Martin, Tom	0	0	1.00	3	3	0	0	9	4	1	1	3	9	L	L	6-1	200	5-21-70	1989	Panama City, Fla.
Martinez, Willie	9	8	4.09	24	24	0	0	147	163	83	67	45	91	R	R	6-2	175	1-4-78	1995	Barquisimeto, Venez.
Matthews, Mike	0	5	8.77	6	6	0	0	26	36	30	25	15	10	L	L	6-2	175	10-24-73	1992	Woodbridge, Va.
Negrette, Richard	1	3	6.13	33	0	0	1	47	49	35	32	47	34	R	R	6-2	175	3-6-76	1994	Maracaibo, Venez.
Poole, Jim	0	0	0.00	2	0	0	0	3	0	0	0	0	5	L	L	6-1	203	4-28-66	1988	Alpharetta, Ga.
Rigdon, Paul	7	0	0.90	8	7	0	0	50	20	5	5	10	25	R	R	6-5	210	11-2-75	1996	Jacksonville, Fla.
Rincon, Ricardo	0	0	5.40	2	2	0	0	2	2	1	1	0	2	L	L	5-10	188	4-13-70	1997	Veracruz, Mexico
Riske, David	0	0	1.90	23	0	0	12	24	5	5	5	13	33	R	R	6-2	175	10-23-76	1997	Kent, Wash.
Sanders, Frankie	6	6	4.85	33	13	0	2	121	139	72	65	51	72	R	R	5-11	165	8-27-75	1995	Sarasota, Fla.
Sexton, Jeff	1	0	3.60	15	0	0	2	20	24	10	8	9	16	R	R	6-2	190	10-4-71	1993	Kingston, Okla.
St. Pierre, Bob	0	0	18.00	4	0	0	0	4	9	8	8	4	2	R	R	6-1	190	4-11-74	1995	Huntington, Md.
Turnbow, Mark	1	0	3.00	1	1	0	0	6	4	3	2	3	4	R	R	6-3	205	11-26-78	1997	Saltillo, Tenn.
Watson, Mark	9	8	4.34	19	17	0	0	110	143	64	53	38	57	R	L	6-4	215	1-23-74	1996	Atlanta, Ga.
Wright, Jaret	1	0	0.00	1	1	0	0	3	1	0	0	1	6	R	R	6-2	230	12-29-75	1994	Newport Beach, Calif.

FIELDING

Catcher	PCT	G	PO	A	E	DP	PB
Alomar	.929	5	12	1	1	0	0
Encarnacion	.978	34	203	24	5	3	4
Harriss	.981	17	98	8	2	2	3
Hayes	.982	87	484	69	10	7	10
Soliz	1.000	7	50	9	0	0	2

First Base	PCT	G	PO	A	E	DP
Betts	1.000	18	153	7	0	16
Dishington	1.000	2	12	0	0	2
Hayes	1.000	15	135	11	0	15
Kilburg	.980	6	46	3	1	3
Peoples	.984	91	775	81	14	71
Perry	.983	12	98	16	2	9

Second Base	PCT	G	PO	A	E	DP
Bady	1.000	3	1	1	0	0
Benefield	.951	38	64	112	9	16
Betances	.981	36	53	106	3	14
Dorman	1.000	3	4	6	0	1
Kilburg	.992	21	50	74	1	20
McDonald	1.000	1	0	1	0	0
Ortiz	1.000	3	3	6	0	2
Robinson	.968	40	67	115	6	29

Third Base	PCT	G	PO	A	E	DP
Benefield	.667	4	0	2	1	1
Betances	.889	21	20	28	6	2
Betts	.935	77	54	134	13	11
Fryman	1.000	1	0	2	0	0

	PCT	G	PO	A	E	DP
Hayes	.895	15	8	26	4	0
Ortiz	.934	22	19	52	5	2
Taveras	1.000	12	3	10	0	0
Shortstop	**PCT**	**G**	**PO**	**A**	**E**	**DP**
Betances	.946	31	45	112	9	23
McDonald	.969	55	102	152	8	42
Ortiz	.992	28	40	78	1	14
Robinson	.959	27	52	66	5	19
Taveras	.875	2	3	4	1	1
Outfield	**PCT**	**G**	**PO**	**A**	**E**	**DP**
Bady	.966	49	105	8	4	0
Budzinski	.989	81	175	3	2	0

Organization Statistics

	PCT	G	PO	A	E	DP		PCT	G	PO	A	E	DP		PCT	G	PO	A	E	DP
Cordero	.000	2	0	0	0	0	Kilburg	1.000	8	16	0	0	0	Perry	1.000	3	3	0	0	0
Dishington	.000	1	0	0	0	0	McKinley	.983	111	234	2	4	1	Schwab	.000	1	0	0	0	0
Hernaiz	1.000	1	2	0	0	0	Mohr	1.000	11	28	1	0	1	Taveras	1.000	1	1	0	0	0
Huelsmann	.990	43	93	3	1	0	Morgan	.967	80	170	6	6	0	Whitaker	.957	36	66	1	3	0

KINSTON — Class A

CAROLINA LEAGUE

BATTING	AVG	G	AB	R	H	2B	3B	HR	RBI	BB	SO	SB	CS	B	T	HT	WT	DOB	1st Yr	Resides
Allison, Cody	.215	43	121	15	26	4	0	1	11	17	32	1	0	L	R	6-1	200	8-8-74	1996	Odessa, Texas
Cruz, Edgar	.150	35	133	13	20	11	0	2	14	9	46	0	0	R	R	6-3	195	8-12-78	1997	Juncos, P.R.
DePippo, Jeff	.213	68	174	33	37	8	1	2	19	29	51	3	1	R	R	5-7	170	4-29-76	1998	Garden Grove, Calif.
Edwards, Mike	.289	133	456	76	132	25	4	16	89	93	117	8	3	R	R	6-1	185	11-24-76	1995	Mechanicsburg, Pa.
Fitzgerald, Jason	.239	82	310	26	74	17	3	4	39	22	77	15	7	L	L	6-1	200	9-16-75	1997	Belle Chasse, La.
Gonzalez, Luis	.000	1	1	0	0	0	0	0	0	0	0	0	0	R	R	5-11	170	6-26-79	1997	El Tigre, Venez.
Hamilton, Jon	.279	131	473	74	132	29	5	13	65	61	114	9	4	L	L	6-1	195	10-23-77	1997	San Ramon, Calif.
Huelsmann, Mike	.305	58	177	35	54	6	4	2	22	29	19	14	3	S	R	5-11	165	11-21-74	1996	St. Louis, Mo.
Kilburg, Joe	.299	42	137	34	41	8	1	3	17	29	19	3	3	L	R	5-11	180	12-20-75	1997	Bay Village, Ohio
Mohr, Dustan	.280	112	429	46	120	29	3	8	60	26	104	6	6	R	R	6-2	210	6-19-76	1997	Hattiesburg, Miss.
Munoz, Billy	.254	106	378	46	96	25	1	9	55	48	108	3	2	L	L	6-2	220	6-30-75	1998	Mesa, Ariz.
Pratt, Scott	.247	133	486	86	120	27	6	9	54	77	95	47	11	L	R	5-10	185	2-4-77	1998	Tooele, Utah
Santana, Osmany	.241	43	145	16	35	8	0	3	20	8	26	7	0	L	L	5-11	185	8-9-76	1998	Hialeah, Fla.
Smith, Casey	.163	39	129	15	21	6	0	2	15	14	48	0	1	R	R	6-3	200	5-7-77	1997	Carrollton, Texas
Sorensen, Zach	.238	130	508	79	121	16	7	7	59	62	126	24	12	S	R	6-0	190	1-3-77	1998	Mesquite, Nev.
Taveras, Frank	.234	31	107	11	25	7	1	1	11	6	27	0	0	L	R	6-1	158	9-6-75	1993	Santiago, D.R.
Taylor, Adam	.188	6	16	2	3	0	0	1	2	2	7	0	1	R	R	5-11	195	3-14-74	1996	Chelsea, Mich.
Whitaker, Chad	.239	76	280	34	67	14	0	9	36	21	62	2	3	L	R	6-2	190	9-16-76	1997	Fort Lauderdale, Fla.
Whitlock, Brian	.250	13	32	3	8	1	0	0	3	1	10	0	2	R	R	6-1	185	9-16-74	1996	San Francisco, Calif.

GAMES BY POSITION: C—Allison 3, Cruz 30, DePippo 68, Smith 39, Taylor 6. **1B**—Allison 30, Kilburg 3, Munoz 104, Taveras 5. **2B**—Kilburg 5, Pratt 130, Taveras 1, Whitlock 1. **3B**—Edwards 127, Kilburg 3, Taveras 11, Whitlock 2. **SS**—Sorensen 129, Taveras 8, Whitlock 2. **OF**—Fitzgerald 1, Hamilton 127, Huelsmann 49, Kilburg 19, Mohr 108, Santana 43, Taveras 9, Whitaker 60, Whitlock 7.

PITCHING	W	L	ERA	G	GS	CG	SV	IP	H	R	ER	BB	SO	B	T	HT	WT	DOB	1st Yr	Resides
Aracena, Juan	1	1	2.57	5	0	0	0	7	7	2	2	1	8	R	R	6-0	150	12-17-76	1994	La Vega, D.R.
Bautista, Martin	6	1	2.76	20	0	0	2	42	31	16	13	20	44	R	R	6-0	155	2-22-78	1996	San Pedro de Macoris, D.R.
Brewington, Jamie	1	10	3.87	36	5	0	4	81	74	42	35	37	81	R	R	6-4	175	9-28-71	1992	Phoenix, Ariz.
Cairncross, Cam	2	0	0.00	6	0	0	2	10	5	1	0	4	11	L	L	6-2	212	5-11-72	1991	Cairns, Australia
Camp, Jared	3	2	1.98	18	6	1	4	55	48	15	12	16	59	R	R	6-2	195	5-4-75	1995	Huntington, W.Va.
DePaula, Sean	4	2	2.28	23	0	0	7	51	36	17	13	17	75	R	R	6-4	215	11-7-73	1996	Derry, N.H.
Drese, Ryan	5	4	4.93	15	15	1	0	69	46	47	38	52	81	R	R	6-3	220	4-5-76	1998	Oakland, Calif.
Drew, Tim	13	5	3.73	28	28	2	0	169	154	79	70	60	125	R	R	6-1	195	8-31-78	1997	Hahira, Ga.
Garza, Alberto	2	3	3.62	6	6	0	0	27	25	13	11	17	27	R	R	6-3	195	5-25-77	1996	Wapato, Wash.
Gross, Rafael	1	0	3.12	4	0	0	0	9	9	3	3	1	5	R	R	5-10	155	8-8-74	1993	Port St. Lucie, Fla.
Guillory, Dan	1	3	5.12	25	0	0	5	32	36	20	18	16	32	R	R	6-3	205	5-12-76	1998	Baton Rouge, La.
Mays, Jarrod	5	5	2.09	45	1	0	19	73	48	23	17	18	75	R	R	6-4	190	10-8-74	1995	El Dorado Springs, Mo.
Padilla, Roy	0	0	4.15	8	0	0	1	13	9	6	6	10	7	L	L	6-5	227	8-4-75	1993	Panama City, Panama
Percell, Brody	0	0	4.30	5	0	0	0	23	25	12	11	11	22	L	L	6-2	200	8-29-75	1998	Portland, Ore.
Pirkl, Greg	0	1	7.11	6	0	0	2	6	11	6	5	3	5	R	R	6-5	225	8-7-70	1988	Surprise, Ariz.
Pugmire, Rob	7	1	3.66	16	16	0	0	96	85	44	39	25	89	R	R	6-3	205	9-5-78	1997	Snohomish, Wash.
Romero, Jordan	0	0	9.00	1	0	0	0	1	1	1	1	1	2	R	R	6-1	170	10-8-76	1997	San Jose, Calif.
2-team (9 Frederick)	0	0	3.31	10	0	0	0	16	12	10	6	14	13							
Sabathia, C.C.	3	3	5.34	7	7	0	0	32	30	22	19	19	29	L	L	6-7	235	7-21-80	1998	Vallejo, Calif.
Sido, Wilson	1	2	5.94	9	7	0	0	36	33	26	24	22	22	R	R	6-2	178	6-18-76	1998	Barahona, D.R.
Spenser, Kaipo	3	4	3.25	35	5	0	1	72	65	33	26	26	46	R	R	6-3	220	8-4-75	1998	Phoenix, Ariz.
Spiegel, Mike	5	3	3.09	18	18	0	0	96	69	46	33	51	103	L	L	6-5	200	11-24-75	1996	Carmichael, Calif.
Turnbow, Mark	5	4	6.41	12	12	0	0	60	76	48	43	25	42	R	R	6-3	205	11-26-78	1997	Saltillo, Tenn.
Wagner, Ken	1	1	6.75	14	0	0	0	27	31	25	20	12	21	R	R	6-4	218	8-3-74	1995	West Palm Beach, Fla.
Watson, Mark	6	0	1.04	11	4	0	0	43	28	7	5	10	40	R	L	6-4	215	1-23-74	1996	Atlanta, Ga.
Weidert, Chris	4	3	2.58	27	2	0	0	52	49	15	15	22	42	R	R	6-3	215	4-3-74	1994	Emporia, Kan.

COLUMBUS — Class A

SOUTH ATLANTIC LEAGUE

BATTING	AVG	G	AB	R	H	2B	3B	HR	RBI	BB	SO	SB	CS	B	T	HT	WT	DOB	1st Yr	Resides
Alvarez, Carlos	.257	96	319	56	82	18	2	14	49	33	70	9	7	R	R	6-0	170	4-28-76	1995	Bachayuero, Venez.
Bastardo, Angel	.245	19	53	6	13	0	2	3	9	5	13	0	0	R	R	6-0	170	4-2-79	1997	Miraflores, Venez.
Benefield, Brian	.274	81	303	60	83	14	1	15	50	43	67	18	12	R	R	6-0	181	8-12-76	1997	Carrollton, Texas
Cruz, Edgar	.216	62	232	22	50	10	0	4	23	20	54	0	0	R	R	6-3	195	8-12-78	1997	Juncos, P.R.
Dampeer, Kelly	.258	94	299	37	77	13	5	5	39	25	52	10	4	R	R	5-11	190	1-25-75	1997	Roanoke, Va.
Esquerra, Marques	.256	122	403	53	103	14	4	3	44	32	65	9	8	S	R	5-11	185	5-17-76	1998	Tucson, Ariz.
Ewing, Byron	.243	47	173	19	42	11	0	3	19	16	41	10	1	R	R	6-3	215	10-22-76	1999	Jacksonville, Fla.
Fowler, Ben	.258	28	97	12	25	4	0	3	11	5	23	2	2	S	R	6-4	185	1-21-77	1995	Alpharetta, Ga.
Garcia, Oscar	.241	8	29	3	7	2	0	1	4	1	11	1	1	R	R	5-9	160	11-3-80	1998	Colon, Panama
Gonzalez, Luis	.294	83	299	41	88	18	2	7	50	26	40	6	5	R	R	5-11	170	6-26-79	1997	El Tigre, Venez.
Gordnier, Aaron	.254	64	177	30	45	10	2	8	29	23	49	3	2	R	R	5-11	185	9-4-74	1998	Rocklin, Calif.
Hernandez, Jesus	.306	70	255	43	78	22	3	12	56	30	53	8	2	L	L	6-2	170	6-6-77	1995	Laguna Salada, D.R.
Isturiz, Maicer	.300	57	220	46	66	5	3	4	23	20	28	14	2	S	R	5-8	155	9-12-80	1998	Barquisimeto, Venez.
Malave, Dennis	.267	44	150	16	40	6	1	3	15	14	44	8	8	L	L	5-9	165	1-6-80	1997	Caracas, Venez.
Minges, Tyler	.242	127	492	64	119	25	11	10	62	19	113	23	7	R	R	6-0	185	11-15-79	1998	Hamilton, Ohio
Olmeda, Jose	.264	30	106	16	28	3	2	3	16	11	32	5	1	S	R	6-1	155	7-7-77	1995	Fajardo, P.R.
Powers, Jeff	.266	76	233	34	62	10	0	2	30	24	24	2	3	L	R	6-0	175	3-20-76	1998	Scottsdale, Ariz.
Pursell, Mike	.217	18	69	9	15	4	1	0	6	6	11	1	0	L	R	6-0	187	12-22-75	1998	Pensacola, Fla.
Santana, Osmany	.323	38	133	23	43	6	0	0	17	10	21	15	6	L	L	5-11	185	8-9-76	1998	Hialeah, Fla.

BATTING	AVG	G	AB	R	H	2B	3B	HR	RBI	BB	SO	SB	CS	B	T	HT	WT	DOB	1st Yr	Resides
Schwab, Chris	.288	54	177	25	51	10	1	9	26	26	54	13	6	R	L	6-3	215	7-25-74	1993	Eagan, Minn.
Smith, Casey	.235	47	153	21	36	6	0	1	13	28	48	0	2	R	R	6-3	200	5-7-77	1997	Carrollton, Texas
Taylor, Adam	.296	8	27	4	8	2	0	1	4	2	9	0	0	R	R	5-11	195	3-14-74	1996	Chelsea, Mich.
Thompson, Eric	.250	74	280	48	70	9	0	0	15	31	83	22	9	L	L	6-0	170	5-1-79	1997	Fayetteville, N.C.

GAMES BY POSITION: C—Bastardo 12, Cruz 50, Fowler 27, Powers 1, Smith 47, Taylor 8. **1B**—Alvarez 12, Dampeer 8, Esquerra 39, Ewing 46, Fowler 1, Gordnier 2, Hernandez 1, Pursell 18, Schwab 26. **2B**—Benefield 68, Dampeer 35, Garcia 6, Gonzalez 22, Gordnier 1, Powers 16. **3B**—Benefield 2, Dampeer 31, Esquerra 80, Garcia 1, Gonzalez 23, Powers 14. **SS**—Dampeer 11, Garcia 2, Gonzalez 35, Isturiz 45, Olmeda 29, Powers 34. **OF**—Alvarez 65, Bastardo 1, Dampeer 1, Esquerra 2, Gordnier 38, Hernandez 65, Malave 44, Minges 113, Santana 35, Schwab 10, Thompson 71.

PITCHING	W	L	ERA	G	GS	CG	SV	IP	H	R	ER	BB	SO	B	T	HT	WT	DOB	1st Yr	Resides
Aracena, Juan	2	0	3.28	32	0	0	18	36	32	13	13	3	30	R	R	6-0	150	12-17-76	1994	La Vega, D.R.
Bautista, Martin	6	3	4.95	15	12	0	0	67	80	46	37	20	51	R	R	6-0	155	2-22-78	1996	San Pedro de Macoris, D.R.
Dampeer, Kelly	0	0	0.00	2	0	0	0	2	0	0	0	1	2	R	R	5-11	190	1-25-75	1997	Roanoke, Va.
Drese, Ryan	0	2	4.50	2	2	0	0	12	9	6	6	4	15	R	R	6-3	220	4-5-76	1998	Oakland, Calif.
Everett, Matt	1	2	4.55	18	0	0	1	32	30	17	16	14	19	R	R	6-4	215	10-2-75	1998	Monroe, Ga.
Granadillo, Adel	0	1	15.00	2	0	0	0	3	3	5	5	3	1	R	R	6-0	165	8-29-78	1997	Maracaibo, Venez.
Gross, Rafael	6	1	2.60	42	0	0	7	62	51	19	18	14	62	R	R	5-10	155	8-8-74	1993	Port St. Lucie, Fla.
Guillory, Dan	1	1	1.93	15	0	0	0	33	21	9	7	10	43	R	R	6-3	205	5-12-76	1998	Baton Rouge, La.
Hughes, Mike	0	0	4.50	6	2	0	1	18	15	11	9	3	22	L	L	6-1	192	12-5-75	1997	East Meadow, N.Y.
Kearney, Ryan	0	1	5.65	6	0	0	0	14	17	10	9	5	6	R	R	6-1	190	1-9-76	1998	Salem, N.H.
Layne, Roger	1	0	1.50	1	1	0	0	6	4	1	1	0	7	R	R	6-3	185	6-27-77	1997	Whitwell, Tenn.
Macias, Jose	0	0	0.00	1	0	0	0	2	1	0	0	0	2	R	R	6-2	165	12-21-79	1997	Santo Domingo, D.R.
Madison, Scott	2	4	4.60	10	4	0	0	31	37	19	16	13	22	L	L	6-2	190	9-12-74	1996	Latham, N.Y.
Marietta, Ron	3	6	8.25	11	11	0	0	48	71	48	44	19	40	L	L	6-0	190	8-12-77	1998	Brooklyn, N.Y.
Matsko, Rick	7	5	4.55	42	0	0	0	85	70	49	43	43	93	R	R	6-2	210	4-26-77	1998	Johnstown, Pa.
Padilla, Roy	2	2	3.02	30	0	0	3	60	53	27	20	27	56	L	L	6-5	227	8-4-75	1993	Panama City, Panama
Percell, Brody	1	3	4.30	6	6	0	0	29	22	15	14	10	30	L	L	6-2	200	8-29-75	1997	Portland, Ore.
Pugmire, Rob	6	1	2.65	10	10	0	0	58	43	20	17	14	71	R	R	6-3	205	9-5-78	1997	Snohomish, Wash.
Reinike, Chris	3	4	4.31	11	11	0	0	48	55	28	23	21	41	R	R	6-0	195	11-16-76	1998	Gulfport, Miss.
Sabathia, C.C.	2	0	1.08	3	3	0	0	17	8	2	2	5	20	L	L	6-7	235	7-21-80	1998	Vallejo, Calif.
Sanchez, Willmen	1	1	6.45	13	0	0	1	22	29	23	16	10	19	L	L	5-11	170	2-19-79	1997	Charallaue, Venez.
Sido, Wilson	3	7	7.35	13	12	0	0	49	63	43	40	23	51	R	R	6-2	178	6-18-76	1998	Barahona, D.R.
Spiegel, Mike	2	0	2.83	7	7	0	0	35	27	13	11	14	38	L	L	6-5	200	11-24-75	1996	Carmichael, Calif.
Suttles, Donnie	4	6	4.56	16	16	1	0	77	86	55	39	29	66	R	R	6-2	185	1-8-77	1998	Marion, N.C.
Turnbow, Mark	3	4	3.72	13	13	1	0	73	78	38	30	13	75	R	R	6-3	205	11-26-78	1997	Saltillo, Tenn.
Vael, Rob	5	4	4.86	42	7	0	0	93	89	50	50	53	91	R	R	6-3	200	1-8-76	1997	Surrey, B.C.
Vargas, Jose	2	5	4.66	34	6	0	2	85	88	47	44	29	103	R	R	6-0	175	3-25-77	1998	Barahona, D.R.
White, Matt	3	10	5.29	19	18	1	0	95	99	67	56	31	75	R	L	6-1	180	8-19-77	1998	Windsor, Mass.
Zamarripa, Mark	4	0	3.45	15	0	0	1	29	26	13	11	12	31	R	R	6-0	175	7-28-74	1996	Los Angeles, Calif.

MAHONING VALLEY — Short-Season Class A

NEW YORK-PENN LEAGUE

BATTING	AVG	G	AB	R	H	2B	3B	HR	RBI	BB	SO	SB	CS	B	T	HT	WT	DOB	1st Yr	Resides
Bost, Tom	.186	23	70	11	13	0	1	5	13	11	35	0	0	L	R	6-2	220	10-5-75	1998	West Monroe, La.
Centile, Raul	.239	25	88	15	21	5	2	1	13	5	17	3	1	S	R	6-0	160	5-31-79	1996	San Pedro de Macoris, D.R.
Day, Paul	.219	9	32	4	7	1	1	0	5	5	6	0	0	R	R	6-1	200	12-20-76	1998	Mission Viejo, Calif.
Ewing, Byron	.273	15	44	7	12	2	0	1	6	9	9	1	0	S	R	6-3	215	10-22-76	1999	Jacksonville, Fla.
Fowler, Ben	.210	17	62	5	13	3	0	3	15	2	21	0	1	S	R	6-4	185	1-21-77	1995	Alpharetta, Ga.
Gallaher, T.T.	.316	6	19	7	6	1	1	1	5	5	0	2	0	R	R	5-10	185	11-5-77	1998	Middletown, Conn.
Gay, Curtis	.231	65	234	34	54	13	2	2	24	24	98	3	2	L	L	6-6	225	9-12-77	1999	Enid, Okla.
Griffin, Justin	.111	5	9	2	1	0	0	0	2	5	0	0	0	R	R	5-10	170	10-5-76	1998	Eatontown, N.J.
Grindell, Nate	.315	71	267	42	84	20	2	5	47	24	39	6	5	R	R	6-1	180	4-9-77	1998	Carrollton, Texas
Johnson, Eric	.257	28	105	23	27	4	1	1	10	18	17	12	1	R	R	6-1	210	8-14-77	1999	Shallotte, N.C.
LaFlair, Jay	.200	16	30	8	6	0	0	3	5	6	2	0	0	R	R	6-0	215	9-18-75	1999	Temple, Texas
Lotterhos, Chris	.210	41	124	21	26	7	2	1	9	23	33	5	6	R	R	5-10	165	4-26-77	1999	Germantown, Tenn.
Lowe, Steve	.232	33	95	19	22	3	0	2	11	12	26	4	3	R	R	6-0	195	9-3-76	1999	Victoria, B.C.
MacMillan, Chris	.167	7	24	2	4	1	0	0	4	4	5	0	0	R	R	6-2	195	2-19-76	1998	El Monte, Calif.
Malave, Dennis	.244	12	41	11	10	0	0	1	8	7	9	1	1	L	L	5-9	165	1-6-80	1997	Caracas, Venez.
Martinez, Victor	.277	64	235	37	65	9	0	4	36	27	31	0	1	S	R	6-2	160	12-23-78	1997	Ciudad Bolivar, Venez.
Moraga, Omar	.230	67	248	35	57	21	2	4	37	21	69	3	2	L	R	5-9	180	5-23-77	1998	Tucson, Ariz.
Moreno, Jorge	.257	69	230	38	59	10	2	9	38	31	61	15	7	R	R	5-10	180	10-26-80	1998	Ciudad Ojeda, Venez.
Pichardo, Henry	.400	2	5	0	2	1	0	0	1	0	1	0	0	R	R	5-10	145	1-15-79	1996	Tamboril, D.R.
Requena, Alex	.234	61	214	44	50	6	3	0	18	36	64	44	12	S	R	5-11	155	8-13-80	1998	Maracay, Venez.
Rickon, Jim	.200	8	25	3	5	0	0	1	4	2	7	0	0	R	R	6-4	225	6-1-76	1999	Maple Heights, Ohio
Sherrill, J.J.	.375	3	8	1	3	0	0	0	1	1	4	0	0	S	R	5-7	170	8-11-80	1999	Seaside, Calif.
Williams, Jewell	.273	62	220	37	60	9	0	8	42	31	60	14	7	R	R	6-2	185	6-25-77	1995	Las Vegas, Nev.

GAMES BY POSITION: C—Fowler 10, LaFlair 16, Martinez 51, Rickon 6. **1B**—Ewing 9, Gay 65, Grindell 2, Rickon 1. **2B**—Centile 2, Lotterhos 7, Moraga 66, Pichardo 2. **3B**—Centile 2, Griffin 1, Grindell 67, MacMillan 7. **SS**—Centile 17, Lotterhos 34, Lowe 28. **OF**—Bost 9, Gallaher 5, Griffin 2, Grindell 2, Johnson 25, Malave 12, Moreno 66, Requena 56, Sherrill 3, Williams 53.

PITCHING	W	L	ERA	G	GS	CG	SV	IP	H	R	ER	BB	SO	B	T	HT	WT	DOB	1st Yr	Resides
Bonner, Luke	4	3	4.74	19	1	0	0	38	46	20	20	8	37	R	R	6-1	200	12-20-79	1999	Taylor, Mich.
Brown, Craig	1	1	6.14	18	0	0	1	29	34	20	20	15	33	L	L	5-9	170	8-10-76	1998	Tampa, Fla.
Byrd, Mike	2	0	2.70	9	0	0	1	20	17	12	6	10	23	R	R	6-5	220	5-5-78	1999	Lake Wales, Fla.
Cowie, Stephen	2	5	4.67	12	10	0	0	62	66	38	32	7	83	R	R	6-2	190	11-9-76	1998	Belmont, N.C.
Denney, Kyle	1	0	1.80	1	1	0	0	5	5	1	1	0	5	R	R	6-2	195	7-27-77	1999	Prague, Okla.
Drese, Ryan	0	2	2.65	5	5	0	0	17	8	6	5	7	26	R	R	6-3	220	4-5-76	1998	Oakland, Calif.
Escobar, Ruben	2	0	3.67	17	0	0	1	42	47	20	17	5	22	R	R	6-1	185	6-8-76	1998	Hesperia, Calif.
Everett, Matt	0	0	4.50	3	0	0	0	4	4	2	2	1	5	R	R	6-4	215	10-2-75	1998	Monroe, Ga.
Jackson, Brian	6	3	4.44	14	13	0	0	71	75	38	35	27	30	R	R	6-4	190	8-12-77	1998	Tiburon, Calif.
Kearney, Ryan	0	1	1.44	11	2	0	0	25	23	4	4	5	26	R	R	6-1	190	1-9-76	1998	Salem, N.H.
Kelley, Chris	3	4	5.63	13	11	0	0	48	44	40	30	34	54	R	R	6-2	180	4-29-78	1999	Portsmouth, Va.

Organization Statistics

PITCHING	W	L	ERA	G	GS	CG	SV	IP	H	R	ER	BB	SO	B	T	HT	WT	DOB	1st Yr	Resides
Layne, Roger	0	0	5.40	4	0	0	0	7	8	4	4	7	9	R	R	6-3	185	6-27-77	1997	Whitwell, Tenn.
Macias, Jose	1	0	1.80	1	1	0	0	5	2	1	1	2	1	R	R	6-2	165	12-21-79	1997	Santo Domingo, D.R.
Maleski, Eric	4	1	4.82	22	0	0	8	37	42	21	20	6	32	R	R	6-2	195	7-25-76	1998	Des Plaines, Ill.
Manning, Mike	2	1	2.67	20	0	0	3	34	25	11	10	12	34	R	R	6-3	195	10-23-77	1999	Bradford, Pa.
Marini, Anthony	5	3	3.60	13	11	0	0	65	64	31	26	25	56	R	L	6-0	185	1-22-77	1999	Vero Beach, Fla.
Novits, Carey	2	4	5.45	12	3	0	1	35	46	30	21	19	33	L	L	6-1	185	9-5-75	1998	San Dimas, Calif.
Roberts, Phil	0	0	6.23	3	0	0	0	4	6	5	3	4	4	R	R	6-0	190	12-8-76	1999	Saginaw, Mich.
Rosengren, Phil	2	3	5.07	11	9	0	0	50	40	30	28	24	41	R	R	6-5	215	2-10-77	1999	Barrington, Ill.
Sabathia, C.C.	0	0	1.83	6	6	0	0	20	9	5	4	12	27	L	L	6-7	235	7-21-80	1998	Vallejo, Calif.
Sadler, Carl	0	1	31.50	1	1	0	0	2	8	7	7	3	3	L	L	6-2	180	10-11-76	1996	Perry, Fla.
Sirianni, Jay	2	0	2.70	3	2	1	0	13	15	6	4	4	16	L	L	5-10	185	7-17-75	1999	Indianola, Iowa
Sullivan, Ted	1	1	6.57	13	0	0	4	12	14	9	9	1	13	R	R	6-2	190	2-22-77	1999	Washington, D.C.
Sunderman, Nick	0	0	4.50	2	0	0	0	4	2	2	2	2	4	L	L	6-0	185	7-7-78	1999	Fort Worth, Texas

BURLINGTON — Rookie

APPALACHIAN LEAGUE

BATTING	AVG	G	AB	R	H	2B	3B	HR	RBI	BB	SO	SB	CS	B	T	HT	WT	DOB	1st Yr	Resides
Bastardo, Angel	.262	17	61	7	16	3	0	0	4	4	13	1	0	R	R	6-0	170	4-2-79	1997	Miraflores, Venez.
Batista, Carlos	.234	45	171	16	40	8	0	3	29	8	49	0	2	R	R	6-3	174	7-3-79	1997	San Pedro de Macoris, D.R.
Centile, Raul	.167	9	24	2	4	0	0	0	1	4	7	1	0	S	R	6-0	160	5-31-79	1998	San Pedro de Macoris, D.R.
Colmenter, Jesus	.243	36	140	15	34	6	0	0	12	6	39	4	2	S	R	5-10	155	12-1-81	1998	Cabudare, Venez.
Edge, Michael	.207	29	92	9	19	1	0	0	9	9	26	1	2	R	R	6-0	180	8-13-79	1997	Winnabow, N.C.
Finnerty, Francis	.237	37	131	12	31	2	0	1	15	12	34	0	2	S	R	6-3	200	3-19-81	1999	West Palm Beach, Fla.
Garcia, Oscar	.289	56	194	39	56	9	1	5	41	33	42	17	4	R	R	5-9	160	11-3-80	1998	Colon, Panama
Griffin, Justin	.179	14	39	7	7	2	0	0	1	1	13	0	1	R	R	5-10	170	10-5-76	1998	Eatontown, N.J.
Hartley, Will	.159	48	151	19	24	3	0	4	14	41	51	3	0	S	R	6-2	205	12-24-80	1999	Starke, Fla.
Jackson, Chris	.153	22	59	8	9	2	0	0	5	10	16	0	0	R	R	6-2	200	3-7-79	1997	Birmingham, Ala.
Johnson, Eric	.231	39	147	26	34	9	1	3	22	25	29	13	1	R	R	6-1	210	8-14-77	1999	Shallotte, N.C.
Lantigua, Denys	.133	14	45	7	6	1	0	0	2	4	8	1	0	R	R	5-10	160	3-17-80	1998	Montecristi, D.R.
Lugo, Carlos	.141	25	71	5	10	0	1	0	5	1	31	1	1	R	R	6-2	180	8-27-79	1997	Santiago, D.R.
Lynn, Brody	.140	37	121	17	17	0	0	2	9	19	56	2	4	S	R	6-2	200	9-24-80	1999	Wichita, Kan.
Morla, Gilberto	.111	5	9	0	1	0	0	0	0	1	6	0	1	R	R	5-11	185	10-10-79	1997	Santo Domingo, D.R.
Moyer, Kyle	.265	38	132	15	35	5	0	1	10	21	40	0	0	L	L	6-2	240	2-2-81	1999	Tiffin, Ohio
Pichardo, Henry	.262	62	233	44	61	12	3	4	32	14	30	8	5	R	R	5-10	145	1-15-79	1996	Tamboril, D.R.
Rickon, Jim	.302	31	96	16	29	5	0	4	17	19	25	2	1	R	R	6-4	225	6-1-76	1999	Maple Heights, Ohio
Santini, Travis	.284	44	169	17	48	6	2	4	29	10	45	0	1	R	R	5-11	175	11-23-80	1999	Naples, Fla.
Sherrill, J.J.	.206	64	233	55	48	11	6	3	24	29	64	28	9	S	R	5-7	170	8-11-80	1999	Seaside, Calif.

GAMES BY POSITION: C—Bastardo 17, Hartley 4, Jackson 11, Lantigua 14, Morla 5, Rickon 30. **1B**—Batista 44, Finnerty 2, Griffin 1, Moyer 28. **2B**—Centile 5, Colmenter 2, Garcia 7, Griffin 1, Pichardo 60. **3B**—Finnerty 34, Garcia 1, Lynn 37. **SS**—Centile 2, Colmenter 22, Garcia 47, Griffin 1. **OF**—Edge 29, Griffin 8, Jackson 10, Johnson 39, Lugo 22, Pichardo 3, Santini 44, Sherrill 64.

PITCHING	W	L	ERA	G	GS	CG	SV	IP	H	R	ER	BB	SO	B	T	HT	WT	DOB	1st Yr	Resides
Barr, Adam	0	4	7.50	9	7	0	0	18	21	22	15	28	21	L	L	6-0	175	4-30-81	1999	South Williamsport, Pa.
Button, Sammy	1	5	5.19	13	12	0	0	50	55	38	29	26	44	L	L	6-2	210	12-8-77	1999	Covington, Ga.
Christ, John	3	4	4.08	23	0	0	4	35	35	19	16	18	36	L	R	6-2	215	9-10-77	1999	East Amherst, N.Y.
Colon, Jose	2	0	3.24	13	0	0	0	25	19	14	9	6	29	R	R	6-0	175	7-24-77	1993	Puerto Plata, D.R.
Daboin, Jorge	1	1	3.73	15	0	0	1	31	29	16	13	9	26	R	R	6-4	180	7-17-79	1997	Trujillo, Venez.
Denney, Kyle	3	4	3.44	12	3	0	1	34	26	17	13	15	37	R	R	6-2	195	7-27-77	1999	Prague, Okla.
Koeth, Mark	3	4	5.32	20	2	0	1	47	54	40	28	19	51	R	R	6-3	215	4-11-78	1998	Carrollton, Texas
Layne, Roger	1	2	4.50	11	0	0	0	30	36	23	15	8	22	R	R	6-3	185	6-27-77	1997	Whitwell, Tenn.
Lugo, Carlos	0	1	0.00	3	0	0	0	3	2	1	0	2	1	R	R	6-2	180	8-27-79	1997	Santiago, D.R.
Macias, Jose	0	2	7.85	12	3	0	1	29	30	28	25	5	37	R	R	6-2	165	12-21-79	1997	Santo Domingo, D.R.
Manning, Mike	0	2	4.50	4	0	0	0	8	9	6	4	4	9	R	R	6-3	195	10-23-77	1999	Bradford, Pa.
Reynolds, Jacob	0	2	9.00	3	3	0	0	10	13	14	10	8	7	R	R	6-2	200	1-7-80	1998	Ardmore, Tenn.
Rivera, Leyson	0	1	7.71	17	0	0	0	23	29	30	20	19	25	R	R	5-10	185	6-23-81	1999	Carolina, P.R.
Rogers, Devin	0	2	7.52	8	6	0	0	20	26	23	17	15	21	R	R	6-6	606	8-4-78	1999	Harvey, La.
Sadler, Carl	1	0	3.13	5	5	0	0	23	18	10	8	10	22	L	L	6-2	180	10-11-76	1996	Perry, Fla.
Sanchez, Willmen	1	3	3.22	10	0	0	1	22	26	8	8	3	26	L	L	5-11	170	2-19-79	1997	Charallaue, Venez.
Sirianni, Jay	1	5	4.50	11	10	1	0	56	62	36	28	12	66	L	L	5-10	185	7-17-75	1999	Indianola, Iowa
Sunderman, Nick	0	0	3.60	16	0	0	0	30	30	17	12	15	42	L	L	6-0	185	7-7-78	1999	Fort Worth, Texas
Tommasi, Carlos	1	1	3.55	12	0	0	0	25	29	22	10	9	24	R	R	6-0	185	3-15-80	1997	El Tigre, Venez.
Wade, Matt	3	3	1.09	7	7	0	0	33	26	10	4	3	33	R	R	6-2	195	1-14-80	1998	Lilburn, Ga.
Wallace, Shane	1	5	5.25	12	12	0	0	48	58	35	28	15	38	L	L	6-2	200	12-29-80	1999	Carrollton, Texas

COLORADO ROCKIES

Leyland era in Coors Field ends after only one season

BY BARNEY HUTCHINSON

Instead of igniting a franchise looking for a spark, Jim Leyland's short, undistinguished era will end up as a mere footnote in Rockies history.

The 1999 season began with an 8-2 win against the Padres in Monterrey, Mexico, the first season opener held outside the United States and Canada. That day and two days in June when they were 33-32 and 34-33 were the only times the Rockies were above .500 under Leyland. They had a losing record at Coors Field (39-42) for the first time since moving there in 1995.

The team never responded to Leyland and went 72-90, the franchise's worst record since the 67-95 inaugural season. Leyland, signed to a three-year, $6 million contract that made him the highest-paid manager in baseball, decided to retire after his first season in Colorado.

The Rockies' poor play put Bob Gebhard, the only general manager in team history, on the hot seat. He resigned Aug. 20 under fire for not doing enough to improve a team that went 77-85 in 1998. His departure signaled an organization-wide housecleaning that will have a much different front office leading the organization into the 2000 season. The first step in that came when the team selected Dan O'Dowd, former assistant general manager of the Indians, as the new GM Sept. 20.

A ballclub with a payroll of almost $60 million limped to a last-place finish in the National League West for the first time in franchise history. Still, positive notes came out of 1999. Not surprisingly, most of them were on offense.

Outfielder Larry Walker won his second consecutive NL batting title, hitting .379. Walker, Todd Helton,

Larry Walker   **Ben Petrick**

Players of the Year

MAJOR LEAGUE: Larry Walker, of

Walker won his second consecutive NL batting title with a .379 average while hitting 37 homers and driving in 115 runs.

MINOR LEAGUE: Ben Petrick, c

Petrick blossomed as an offensive catcher with 23 homers and 86 RBIs in 350 at-bats at Colorado Springs and Carolina.

Dante Bichette and Vinny Castilla each finished with at least 30 home runs and 100 RBIs. The Rockies led the league in hitting (.279) for a record fifth consecutive season and broke 69-year-old NL records for total bases (2,696) and extra-base hits (567). Leyland's choice for closer, Dave Veres, set a club record with 31 saves. Pedro Astacio tied the club record for wins at 17 and finished fifth in the NL in strikeouts with 210.

Otherwise, pitching numbers were bleak. The Rockies gave up 1,700 hits, 1,028 runs—955 earned—and were last in the majors with a club-worst 6.01 ERA. Those numbers were the highest by a National League team since Philadelphia in 1930. The Rockies' 737 walks and 237 home runs allowed set league records.

Lack of success at the major league level trickled down through the organization. Short-season Portland (39-37) had the only winning record in the system, winning a division title in the Northwest League on the final day of the season. Spokane swept Portland in the best-of-three playoffs.

In one of the few organization bright spots, catcher Ben Petrick played to his potential and earned a big league callup. Petrick hit .311 with 23 homers between Double-A and Triple-A and will compete for the big league catching job in 2000.

Class A Salem lefthander Josh Kalinowski led the Carolina League with 176 strikeouts, cementing his place as one of the organization's top pitching prospects. And righthander Jason Jennings, Baseball America's 1999 College Player of the Year and the Rockies' first-round pick, pitched well for Portland and Class A Asheville in his professional debut.

ORGANIZATION LEADERS

BATTING

*AVG	Rene Reyes, Asheville/AZL Rockies	.354
R	Juan Pierre, Asheville	93
H	Juan Pierre, Asheville	187
TB	J.R. Phillips, Colorado Springs	294
2B	Dave Hajek, Colorado Springs	43
3B	Jody Gerut, Salem	11
HR	J.R. Phillips, Colorado Springs	41
RBI	J.R. Phillips, Colorado Springs	100
BB	Jody Gerut, Salem	61
SO	J.R. Phillips, Colorado Springs	143
SB	Juan Pierre, Asheville	66

PITCHING

W	Two tied at	13
L	Four tied at	12
#ERA	Ryan Kibler, Portland/AZL Rockies	3.30
G	Travis Thompson, Salem	56
CG	Two tied at	3
SV	Travis Thompson, Salem	27
IP	Ryan Price, Salem	172
BB	Two tied at	72
SO	Josh Kalinowski, Salem	176

*Minimum 250 At-Bats #Minimum 75 Innings

Organization Statistics

Colorado ROCKIES

Manager: Jim Leyland

1999 Record: 72-90, .444 (5th, NL West)

BATTING	AVG	G	AB	R	H	2B	3B	HR	RBI	BB	SO	SB	CS	B	T	HT	WT	DOB	1st Yr	Resides
Abbott, Kurt	.273	96	286	41	78	17	2	8	41	16	69	3	2	R	R	6-0	190	6-2-69	1989	Davie, Fla.
Barry, Jeff	.268	74	168	19	45	16	0	5	26	19	29	0	4	S	R	6-0	200	9-22-68	1990	San Diego, Calif.
Bichette, Dante	.298	151	593	104	177	38	2	34	133	54	84	6	6	R	R	6-3	235	11-18-63	1984	Palm Beach Gardens, Fla.
Blanco, Henry	.232	88	263	30	61	12	3	6	28	34	38	1	1	R	R	5-11	220	8-29-71	1990	Guarenas, Venez.
Cangelosi, John	.167	7	6	0	1	1	0	0	0	4	0	0	0	S	L	5-8	160	3-10-63	1982	Chicago, Ill.
Castilla, Vinny	.275	158	615	83	169	24	1	33	102	53	75	2	3	R	R	6-1	185	7-4-67	1990	Oaxaca, Mexico
Clemente, Edgard	.253	57	162	24	41	10	2	8	25	7	46	0	0	R	R	6-0	170	12-15-75	1993	Guaynabo, P.R.
Echevarria, Angel	.293	102	191	28	56	7	0	11	35	17	34	1	3	R	R	6-4	215	5-25-71	1992	Bridgeport, Conn.
Gibson, Derrick	.179	10	28	2	5	1	0	2	6	0	7	0	0	R	R	6-2	238	2-5-75	1993	Winter Haven, Fla.
Hamilton, Darryl	.303	91	337	63	102	11	3	4	24	38	21	4	5	L	R	6-0	180	12-3-64	1986	Sugar Land, Texas
Harris, Lenny	.297	91	158	15	47	12	0	0	13	6	6	1	1	L	R	5-10	210	10-28-64	1983	Miami, Fla.
Helton, Todd	.320	159	578	114	185	39	5	35	113	68	77	7	6	L	L	6-2	195	8-20-73	1995	Powell, Tenn.
Kelly, Mike	.500	2	2	0	1	0	0	0	1	0	0	0	0	R	R	6-4	195	6-2-70	1991	Los Alamitos, Calif.
Lansing, Mike	.310	35	145	24	45	9	0	4	15	7	22	2	0	R	R	6-0	175	4-3-68	1990	Casper, Wyo.
Manwaring, Kirt	.299	48	137	17	41	7	1	2	14	12	23	0	0	R	R	5-11	203	7-15-65	1986	Scottsdale, Ariz.
McRae, Brian	.261	7	23	1	6	2	0	1	2	7	2	0	0	S	R	6-0	195	8-27-67	1985	Leawood, Kan.
Perez, Neifi	.280	157	690	108	193	27	11	12	70	28	54	13	5	S	R	6-0	175	6-2-75	1993	Villa Mella, D.R.
Petersen, Chris	.154	7	13	1	2	0	0	0	2	2	3	0	0	R	R	5-11	180	11-6-70	1992	Orlando, Fla.
Petrick, Ben	.323	19	62	13	20	3	0	4	12	10	13	1	0	R	R	6-0	195	4-7-77	1996	Hillsboro, Ore.
Phillips, J.R.	.231	25	39	5	9	4	0	2	4	0	13	0	0	L	L	6-1	185	4-29-70	1988	Moreno Valley, Calif.
Reed, Jeff	.255	46	106	11	27	5	0	2	11	17	24	0	1	L	R	6-2	190	11-12-62	1980	Elizabethton, Tenn.
Sexton, Chris	.237	35	59	9	14	0	1	1	7	11	10	4	2	R	R	5-11	180	8-3-71	1993	Cincinnati, Ohio
Shumpert, Terry	.347	92	262	58	91	26	3	10	37	31	41	14	0	R	R	5-11	185	8-16-66	1987	Paducah, Ky.
Sosa, Juan	.222	11	9	3	2	0	0	0	0	2	2	0	0	R	R	6-1	175	8-19-75	1993	San Francisco de Macoris, D.R.
Walker, Larry	.379	127	438	108	166	26	4	37	115	57	52	11	4	L	R	6-2	185	12-1-66	1985	Maple Ridge, B.C.
Watkins, Pat	.053	16	19	2	1	0	0	0	0	2	5	0	0	R	R	6-2	195	9-2-72	1993	Garner, N.C.

PITCHING	W	L	ERA	G	GS	CG	SV	IP	H	R	ER	BB	SO	B	T	HT	WT	DOB	1st Yr	Resides
Astacio, Pedro	17	11	5.04	34	34	7	0	232	258	140	130	75	210	R	R	6-2	195	11-28-69	1988	Miami, Fla.
Beltran, Rigo	0	0	7.36	12	0	0	0	11	20	9	9	7	15	L	L	5-11	185	11-13-69	1991	San Diego, Calif.
2-team (21 New York)	1	1	4.50	33	0	0	0	42	50	24	21	19	50							
Bohanon, Brian	12	12	6.20	33	33	3	0	197	236	146	136	92	120	L	L	6-2	219	8-1-68	1987	Houston, Texas
Brownson, Mark	0	2	7.89	7	7	0	0	30	42	26	26	8	21	L	R	6-2	175	6-17-75	1994	Wellington, Fla.
DeJean, Mike	2	4	8.41	56	0	0	0	61	83	61	57	32	31	R	R	6-2	205	9-28-70	1992	Denham Springs, La.
DiPoto, Jerry	4	5	4.26	63	0	0	1	87	91	44	41	44	69	R	R	6-2	200	5-24-68	1989	North Olmsted, Ohio
Hackman, Luther	1	2	10.69	5	3	0	0	16	26	19	19	12	10	R	R	6-4	195	10-10-74	1994	Columbus, Miss.
Jones, Bobby	6	10	6.33	30	20	0	0	112	132	91	79	77	74	R	L	6-0	175	4-11-72	1992	Rutherford, N.J.
Kile, Darryl	8	13	6.61	32	32	1	0	191	225	150	140	109	116	R	R	6-5	185	12-2-68	1988	Corona, Calif.
Lee, David	3	2	3.67	36	0	0	0	49	43	21	20	29	38	R	R	6-2	200	3-12-73	1995	Pittsburgh, Pa.
Leskanic, Curt	6	2	5.08	63	0	0	0	85	87	54	48	49	77	R	R	6-0	180	4-2-68	1990	Pineville, La.
McElroy, Chuck	3	1	6.20	41	0	0	0	41	48	29	28	28	37	L	L	6-0	195	10-1-67	1986	Friendswood, Texas
Porzio, Mike	0	0	8.59	16	0	0	0	15	21	14	14	10	10	L	L	6-3	190	8-20-72	1993	Norwalk, Conn.
Ramirez, Roberto	1	5	8.26	32	4	0	1	40	68	42	37	22	32	R	L	5-11	170	8-17-72	1990	Veracruz, Mexico
Thomson, John	1	10	8.04	14	13	1	0	63	85	62	56	36	34	R	R	6-3	175	10-1-73	1993	Sulphur, La.
Veres, Dave	4	8	5.14	73	0	0	31	77	88	46	44	37	71	R	R	6-2	195	10-19-66	1986	Gresham, Ore.
Wainhouse, David	0	0	6.91	19	0	0	0	29	37	22	22	16	18	L	R	6-2	185	11-7-67	1989	Mercer Island, Wash.
Wright, Jamey	4	3	4.87	16	16	0	0	94	110	52	51	54	49	R	R	6-6	205	12-24-74	1993	Moore, Okla.

FIELDING

Catcher	PCT	G	PO	A	E	DP	PB
Blanco	.992	86	562	58	5	12	5
Manwaring	.981	44	243	21	5	4	1
Petrick	.982	19	100	7	2	1	3
Reed	.983	36	160	15	3	1	0

First Base	PCT	G	PO	A	E	DP
Abbott	1.000	8	57	3	0	6
Echevarria	1.000	10	58	4	0	6
Helton	.993	156	1243	103	9	152
Phillips	1.000	4	3	0	0	1

Second Base	PCT	G	PO	A	E	DP
Abbott	.989	66	124	145	3	34
Lansing	.990	35	91	98	2	40
Petersen	.955	6	9	12	1	5
Sexton	.949	10	19	18	2	3
Shumpert	.988	54	102	151	3	35

Third Base	PCT	G	PO	A	E	DP
Castilla	.954	157	96	299	19	32
Harris	1.000	2	2	0	0	0
Shumpert	.947	14	6	12	1	3

Shortstop	PCT	G	PO	A	E	DP
Abbott	.857	3	3	3	1	2
Perez	.981	157	260	480	14	124
Petersen	1.000	1	3	4	0	1
Sexton	1.000	6	3	7	0	1
Shumpert	1.000	2	1	2	0	1
Sosa	.875	2	4	3	1	1

Outfield	PCT	G	PO	A	E	DP
Abbott	1.000	4	4	0	0	0
Barry	1.000	56	90	4	0	0
Bichette	.951	144	238	17	13	3
Blanco	.000	1	0	0	0	0

	PCT	G	PO	A	E	DP
Cangelosi	1.000	1	1	0	0	0
Clemente	.972	49	101	2	3	1
Echevarria	.985	49	64	3	1	1
Gibson	.944	10	15	2	1	1
Hamilton	1.000	82	205	1	0	0
Harris	.933	14	12	2	1	1
Kelly	1.000	1	0	0	0	0
McRae	1.000	7	14	0	0	0
Phillips	.933	7	11	3	1	2
Sexton	1.000	13	12	1	0	0
Shumpert	.952	19	20	0	1	0
Sosa	1.000	6	2	0	0	0
Walker	.982	114	204	13	4	3
Watkins	1.000	10	10	0	0	0

Director of Player Development: Paul Egins

Class	Farm Team	League	W	L	Pct.	Finish*	Manager	First Yr
AAA	Colo. Springs (Colo.) Sky Sox	Pacific Coast	66	73	.475	9th (16)	Bill Hayes	1993
AA	Carolina (N.C.) Mudcats	Southern	60	80	.429	9th (10)	Jay Loviglio	1999
A#	Salem (Va.) Avalanche	Carolina	69	69	.500	4th (8)	Ron Gideon	1995
A	Asheville (N.C.) Tourists	South Atlantic	64	77	.454	11th (14)	Jim Eppard	1994
A	Portland (Ore.) Rockies	Northwest	39	37	.513	4th (8)	Alan Cockrell	1995
Rookie	Tucson (Ariz.) Rockies	Arizona	27	28	.491	5th (8)	P.J. Carey	1992

*Finish in overall standings (No. of teams in league)   #Advanced level

COLORADO SPRINGS   Class AAA

PACIFIC COAST LEAGUE

BATTING	AVG	G	AB	R	H	2B	3B	HR	RBI	BB	SO	SB	CS	B	T	HT	WT	DOB	1st Yr	Resides
Barry, Jeff	.341	64	185	36	63	15	0	10	27	19	31	6	3	S	R	6-0	200	9-22-68	1990	San Diego, Calif.
Blanco, Henry	.333	15	57	8	19	4	0	3	12	1	12	0	1	R	R	5-11	220	8-29-71	1990	Guarenas, Venez.
Cangelosi, John	.330	29	109	22	36	7	0	1	13	24	16	4	3	S	L	5-8	160	3-10-63	1982	Chicago, Ill.
Clemente, Edgard	.304	75	273	45	83	24	1	16	59	20	55	5	5	R	R	6-0	170	12-15-75	1993	Guaynabo, P.R.
Cotton, John	.315	70	235	50	74	18	1	15	48	14	64	4	2	L	R	6-0	190	10-30-70	1989	Houston, Texas
Gibson, Derrick	.275	110	385	68	106	19	6	17	67	30	82	12	6	R	R	6-2	238	2-5-75	1993	Winter Haven, Fla.
Hajek, Dave	.295	127	533	84	157	43	3	8	58	25	42	13	8	R	R	5-10	165	10-14-67	1990	Colorado Springs, Colo.
Hatcher, Chris	.344	98	334	63	115	24	2	21	69	23	89	12	4	R	R	6-3	220	1-7-69	1990	Carter Lake, Iowa
Kelly, Mike	.277	114	394	69	109	27	3	9	50	57	93	10	7	R	R	6-4	195	6-2-70	1991	Los Alamitos, Calif.
Manwaring, Kirt	.227	7	22	3	5	0	0	1	2	1	2	0	0	R	R	5-11	203	7-15-65	1986	Scottsdale, Ariz.
Pena, Elvis	.163	13	43	5	7	1	0	0	1	3	7	4	1	S	R	5-11	155	9-15-76	1994	Santo Domingo, D.R.
Petersen, Chris	.259	107	370	56	96	21	1	6	33	29	85	4	0	R	R	5-11	180	11-6-70	1992	Orlando, Fla.
Petrick, Ben	.312	84	282	56	88	16	5	19	64	44	58	9	6	R	R	6-0	195	4-7-77	1996	Hillsboro, Ore.
Phillips, J.R.	.311	124	479	87	149	22	0	41	100	54	143	4	3	L	L	6-1	185	4-29-70	1988	Moreno Valley, Calif.
Sexton, Chris	.339	60	171	23	58	9	0	0	17	28	22	5	1	R	R	5-11	180	8-3-71	1993	Cincinnati, Ohio
Shumpert, Terry	.380	29	79	15	30	8	1	6	17	4	9	3	1	R	R	5-11	185	8-16-66	1987	Paducah, Ky.
Sosa, Juan	.393	6	28	3	11	1	1	1	5	0	1	1	0	R	R	6-1	175	8-19-75	1993	San Francisco de Macoris, D.R.
Strittmatter, Mark	.215	71	195	16	42	10	1	4	31	20	45	0	0	R	R	6-1	200	4-4-69	1992	Ridgewood, N.J.
Tatum, Jim	.313	109	396	57	124	23	1	14	64	33	85	1	2	R	R	6-2	200	10-9-67	1985	San Diego, Calif.
Watkins, Pat	.333	12	30	4	10	1	0	2	2	6	0	0	R	R	6-2	195	9-2-72	1993	Garner, N.C.

PITCHING	W	L	ERA	G	GS	CG	SV	IP	H	R	ER	BB	SO	B	T	HT	WT	DOB	1st Yr	Resides
Bailey, Roger	0	0	7.06	4	4	0	0	22	31	19	17	14	15	R	R	6-1	180	10-3-70	1992	Tallahassee, Fla.
Beltran, Rigo	1	0	2.25	6	0	0	0	8	12	3	2	5	12	L	L	5-11	185	11-13-69	1991	San Diego, Calif.
Bost, Heath	5	4	5.53	38	0	0	6	86	120	59	53	12	67	R	R	6-4	200	10-13-74	1995	Taylorsville, N.C.
Briggs, Anthony	1	1	7.64	10	1	0	0	18	30	25	15	10	5	R	R	6-1	155	9-14-73	1994	Manning, S.C.
Brownson, Mark	6	6	6.20	17	16	2	0	103	120	75	71	24	81	L	R	6-2	175	6-17-75	1994	Wellington, Fla.
DeJean, Mike	0	0	0.00	1	0	0	0	1	1	0	0	0	0	R	R	6-2	205	9-28-70	1992	Denham Springs, La.
De la Rosa, Maximo	0	1	2.45	8	0	0	0	11	12	3	3	4	5	R	R	5-11	170	7-12-71	1990	Villa Mella, D.R.
2-team (15 Tacoma)	0	3	4.91	23	0	0	1	33	46	21	18	14	29							
Farmer, Mike	8	10	7.86	25	20	2	0	113	170	111	99	44	75	S	L	6-1	200	7-3-68	1990	Gary, Ind.
Gonzalez, Lariel	1	10	10.13	11	0	0	0	13	18	16	15	12	9	R	R	6-4	240	5-25-76	1994	San Cristobal, D.R.
Hackman, Luther	7	6	3.74	15	15	1	0	101	106	49	42	44	88	R	R	6-4	195	10-10-74	1994	Columbus, Miss.
Holzemer, Mark	3	2	5.69	41	1	0	1	55	77	39	35	24	49	L	L	6-0	165	8-20-69	1988	Littleton, Colo.
Jones, Bobby	2	1	5.40	3	3	0	0	17	17	13	10	15	14	R	L	6-0	175	4-11-72	1992	Rutherford, N.J.
Lee, David	0	0	0.00	6	0	0	3	6	0	0	0	1	7	R	R	6-2	200	3-12-73	1995	Pittsburgh, Pa.
Porzio, Mike	5	1	3.38	35	0	0	0	43	44	16	16	30	33	L	L	6-3	190	8-20-72	1993	Norwalk, Conn.
Ramirez, Roberto	3	2	3.50	10	10	0	0	62	64	26	24	17	55	R	L	5-11	170	8-17-72	1990	Veracruz, Mexico
Randall, Scott	1	4	7.93	9	9	0	0	42	62	41	37	22	25	R	R	6-3	178	10-29-75	1995	Goleta, Calif.
Rossiter, Mike	2	0	3.89	24	0	0	0	37	37	16	16	20	31	R	R	6-6	230	6-20-73	1991	Burbank, Calif.
Saipe, Mike	1	5	4.83	11	11	0	0	54	62	36	29	20	39	R	R	6-1	190	9-10-73	1994	San Diego, Calif.
Seifert, Ryan	0	0	4.50	1	1	0	0	4	4	2	2	2	2	R	R	6-5	215	8-14-75	1997	Chaska, Minn.
Shoemaker, Stephen	4	6	6.00	16	16	2	0	81	100	59	54	47	46	L	R	6-1	195	2-3-73	1994	Phoenixville, Pa.
Stoops, Jim	3	7	5.18	55	5	0	3	89	93	54	51	56	57	R	R	6-2	195	6-30-72	1995	Somerset, N.J.
Thomson, John	2	2	9.45	5	5	1	0	26	36	25	21	8	19	R	R	6-3	175	10-1-73	1993	Sulphur, La.
Wainhouse, David	1	3	3.19	38	0	0	22	42	42	19	15	7	42	L	R	6-2	195	11-7-67	1989	Mercer Island, Wash.
Walker, Pete	8	4	4.48	48	0	0	5	62	64	37	31	28	57	R	R	6-2	195	4-8-69	1990	East Lyme, Conn.
Wright, Jamey	5	7	6.46	17	16	2	0	100	133	87	72	38	73	R	R	6-6	205	12-24-74	1993	Moore, Okla.

FIELDING

Catcher	PCT	G	PO	A	E	DP	PB
Blanco	.990	14	87	12	1	2	2
Manwaring	1.000	4	32	0	0	0	0
Petrick	.980	66	411	32	9	4	14
Strittmatter	.995	60	379	40	2	6	0
Tatum	.972	5	33	2	1	0	0

First Base	PCT	G	PO	A	E	DP
Cotton	1.000	2	5	0	0	2
Hatcher	.957	13	82	7	4	12
Phillips	.990	122	993	114	11	131
Strittmatter	1.000	2	3	0	0	0
Tatum	1.000	4	41	6	0	6

Second Base	PCT	G	PO	A	E	DP
Cotton	1.000	13	19	40	0	11
Hajek	.979	117	262	341	13	88
Pena	.917	5	12	10	2	3

	PCT	G	PO	A	E	DP
Sexton	.933	4	14	14	2	5
Shumpert	.963	5	9	17	1	6
Watkins	1.000	1	1	0	0	0

Third Base	PCT	G	PO	A	E	DP
Barry	1.000	6	3	12	0	3
Cotton	.937	26	13	61	5	7
Hajek	1.000	4	5	3	0	0
Sexton	.923	18	7	17	2	1
Shumpert	.941	11	4	12	1	2
Tatum	.913	87	57	132	18	11

Shortstop	PCT	G	PO	A	E	DP
Hajek	.947	5	7	11	1	4
Pena	.872	8	11	23	5	6
Petersen	.961	106	196	340	22	94
Sexton	.989	20	29	59	1	16

	PCT	G	PO	A	E	DP
Shumpert	.842	5	9	7	3	2
Sosa	1.000	2	6	8	0	3

Outfield	PCT	G	PO	A	E	DP
Barry	1.000	44	87	3	0	0
Cangelosi	.980	26	47	2	1	0
Clemente	.992	63	114	8	1	1
Cotton	.917	18	21	1	2	0
Gibson	.957	101	171	5	8	0
Hatcher	.936	59	81	7	6	1
Kelly	.975	104	188	10	5	2
Petrick	.000	1	0	0	0	0
Phillips	.000	1	0	0	0	0
Sexton	1.000	14	32	0	0	0
Shumpert	1.000	3	1	0	0	0
Sosa	.900	4	9	0	1	0
Watkins	1.000	7	13	0	0	0

SOUTHERN LEAGUE

BATTING	AVG	G	AB	R	H	2B	3B	HR	RBI	BB	SO	SB	CS	B	T	HT	WT	DOB	1st Yr	Resides
Anthony, Brian	.222	64	171	20	38	9	1	7	20	11	39	1	2	L	R	6-2	218	10-22-73	1996	Walnut Creek, Calif.
Bair, Rod	.303	125	472	70	143	34	6	13	81	28	78	14	12	R	R	5-11	190	10-29-74	1996	Tempe, Ariz.
Barthol, Blake	.280	96	322	41	90	18	3	8	27	32	62	0	1	R	R	6-0	200	4-7-73	1995	Emmaus, Pa.
Berry, Mike	.242	90	306	36	74	15	2	9	38	26	61	0	2	R	R	5-10	185	8-12-70	1993	Rolling Hills, Calif.
Brock, Tarrik	.248	66	218	40	54	10	1	7	23	39	67	7	4	L	L	6-3	170	12-25-73	1991	Hawthorne, Calif.
Cotton, John	.282	42	163	27	46	9	0	10	21	10	48	0	1	L	R	6-0	190	10-30-70	1989	Houston, Texas
Feuerstein, Dave	.220	101	287	27	63	9	3	1	18	18	43	6	2	R	R	6-2	200	7-19-73	1995	Scarsdale, N.Y.
Keck, Brian	.200	5	15	0	3	0	1	0	2	4	3	2	1	R	R	6-3	185	1-15-74	1996	Dodge City, Kan.
Kirgan, Chris	.222	133	474	55	105	27	2	13	84	60	115	1	0	R	R	6-4	235	6-29-73	1994	Littleton, Colo.
Light, Tal	.185	80	259	26	48	18	0	9	30	16	121	0	3	R	R	6-3	205	11-28-73	1995	Lumberton, Texas
Livingston, Doug	.202	43	119	11	24	2	1	1	9	13	24	4	2	R	R	5-8	160	4-9-74	1996	Thonotosassa, Fla.
Malave, Jose	.274	44	146	21	40	10	1	10	26	16	28	0	1	R	R	6-2	195	5-31-71	1990	Cumana, Venez.
Pena, Elvis	.301	110	356	57	107	24	6	2	31	48	64	21	6	S	R	5-11	155	9-15-76	1994	Santo Domingo, D.R.
Petrick, Ben	.309	20	68	18	21	5	1	4	22	9	15	3	1	R	R	6-0	195	4-7-77	1996	Hillsboro, Ore.
Raleigh, Matt	.209	48	115	13	24	8	0	4	12	23	60	0	0	R	R	5-11	235	7-18-70	1992	Endicott, N.Y.
Sosa, Juan	.276	125	490	70	135	22	5	7	42	31	65	38	15	R	R	6-1	175	8-19-75	1993	San Francisco de Macoris, D.R.
Vidal, Gilbert	.240	45	129	10	31	8	0	2	12	8	30	0	0	R	R	5-10	188	4-21-75	1995	Virginia Gardens, Fla.
Watkins, Pat	.298	88	312	38	93	27	1	3	40	24	49	6	5	R	R	6-2	195	9-2-72	1993	Garner, N.C.

PITCHING	W	L	ERA	G	GS	CG	SV	IP	H	R	ER	BB	SO	B	T	HT	WT	DOB	1st Yr	Resides
Bailey, Roger	0	3	7.00	4	4	0	0	18	21	16	14	10	14	R	R	6-1	180	10-3-70	1992	Tallahassee, Fla.
Bevel, Bobby	3	7	4.43	48	0	0	7	67	70	37	33	27	58	L	L	5-10	180	10-10-73	1995	West Plains, Mo.
Brester, Jason	2	6	5.76	11	11	0	0	59	71	45	38	26	44	L	L	6-3	190	12-7-76	1995	Burlington, Wash.
Briggs, Anthony	0	1	11.25	4	0	0	0	4	7	5	5	4	4	R	R	6-1	155	9-14-73	1994	Manning, S.C.
Colmenares, Luis	0	0	8.10	8	0	0	0	16	16	9	9	8	10	R	R	5-11	189	11-25-76	1994	Valencia, Venez.
DeWitt, Scott	1	2	3.92	45	0	0	2	67	84	34	29	21	65	R	L	6-3	210	10-6-74	1995	Springfield, Ore.
Gonzalez, Lariel	2	1	5.29	30	0	0	14	34	39	27	20	22	41	R	R	6-4	240	5-25-76	1994	San Cristobal, D.R.
Hackman, Luther	4	3	4.04	11	10	0	0	62	53	33	28	28	50	R	R	6-4	195	10-10-74	1994	Columbus, Miss.
Hartvigson, Chad	0	5	6.28	30	0	0	1	43	48	35	30	11	32	L	L	6-1	170	12-15-70	1994	Kirkland, Wash.
Jacobs, Ryan	6	12	5.29	28	21	1	0	114	120	76	67	68	89	R	L	6-2	175	2-3-74	1992	Louisville, Ky.
Lee, David	0	0	1.04	16	0	0	10	17	8	3	2	3	16	R	R	6-2	200	3-12-73	1995	Pittsburgh, Pa.
Martin, Chandler	13	8	3.78	27	27	2	0	164	153	82	69	63	130	R	R	6-1	180	10-29-75	1995	Salem, Ore.
Randall, Scott	5	8	3.43	16	16	3	0	100	101	52	38	34	102	R	R	6-3	178	10-29-75	1995	Goleta, Calif.
Rawitzer, Kevin	3	2	3.60	33	4	0	1	70	73	33	28	26	54	L	L	5-9	180	2-28-71	1993	Danville, Calif.
Roberts, Chris	5	4	3.78	43	1	0	1	81	76	46	34	36	52	R	L	5-10	185	6-25-71	1992	Middleburg, Fla.
Robertson, Rich	3	2	3.21	11	7	0	0	48	48	20	17	16	42	L	L	6-4	175	9-15-68	1990	Waller, Texas
Rossiter, Mike	0	0	2.08	16	0	0	2	22	11	5	5	9	24	R	R	6-6	230	6-20-73	1991	Burbank, Calif.
Vavrek, Mike	1	5	7.38	10	9	0	0	46	71	42	38	19	41	L	L	6-2	185	4-23-74	1995	Glendale Heights, Ill.
Walls, Doug	10	9	3.65	26	26	2	0	150	159	74	61	44	140	L	R	6-3	200	3-21-74	1993	Union, Ohio
Zamarripa, Mark	2	1	4.43	5	4	0	0	20	20	11	10	14	12	R	R	6-0	175	7-28-74	1996	Los Angeles, Calif.

FIELDING

Catcher	PCT	G	PO	A	E	DP	PB
Barthol	.983	92	656	53	12	2	13
Petrick	.992	16	113	10	1	0	1
Vidal	.974	42	279	17	8	2	3

First Base	PCT	G	PO	A	E	DP
Anthony	.968	12	85	5	3	8
Kirgan	.989	121	1010	91	12	85
Raleigh	.964	8	52	2	2	4

Second Base	PCT	G	PO	A	E	DP
Berry	.987	23	34	41	1	10
Livingston	.981	35	69	84	3	15
Pena	.970	79	166	193	11	43

	PCT	G	PO	A	E	DP
Watkins	.964	17	24	29	2	4

Third Base	PCT	G	PO	A	E	DP
Anthony	.928	24	12	52	5	0
Berry	.883	63	28	116	19	9
Cotton	.854	36	22	54	13	4
Keck	1.000	3	2	7	0	0
Raleigh	.863	18	8	36	7	5

Shortstop	PCT	G	PO	A	E	DP
Keck	1.000	1	1	4	0	0
Livingston	1.000	2	1	0	0	0
Pena	.983	29	40	74	2	12

	PCT	G	PO	A	E	DP
Sosa	.958	114	191	361	24	62
Watkins	.750	2	2	4	2	0

Outfield	PCT	G	PO	A	E	DP
Bair	.977	121	209	7	5	1
Brock	1.000	61	138	2	0	0
Feuerstein	.973	84	134	11	4	0
Keck	1.000	1	2	0	0	0
Light	.955	60	78	7	4	0
Malave	1.000	39	50	2	0	0
Sosa	1.000	9	11	0	0	0
Watkins	.973	69	107	3	3	1

CAROLINA LEAGUE

BATTING	AVG	G	AB	R	H	2B	3B	HR	RBI	BB	SO	SB	CS	B	T	HT	WT	DOB	1st Yr	Resides
Alviso, Jerome	.251	128	491	48	123	16	3	2	43	28	67	5	6	S	R	6-1	180	9-4-75	1997	Livermore, Calif.
Anthony, Brian	.242	36	128	13	31	7	0	3	13	8	28	0	2	L	R	6-2	218	10-22-73	1996	Walnut Creek, Calif.
Arias, Rogelio	.259	76	263	28	68	11	2	0	24	15	33	3	0	R	R	6-0	165	6-9-76	1993	Santo Domingo, D.R.
Correa, Miguel	.255	100	373	48	95	19	6	11	79	25	72	11	12	S	R	6-2	165	9-10-71	1990	Arroyo, P.R.
Figgins, Chone	.239	123	444	65	106	12	3	2	41	86	27	13	9	S	R	5-8	155	1-22-78	1997	Brandon, Fla.
Gerut, Jody	.289	133	499	80	144	33	11	11	63	61	65	25	12	L	L	6-0	190	9-18-77	1998	Lombard, Ill.
Gonzales, Jose	.170	44	141	9	24	6	0	0	18	12	35	1	0	R	R	6-0	205	4-25-75	1997	Lubbock, Texas
Hamlin, Mark	.248	103	363	45	90	20	3	7	48	35	111	4	3	R	R	6-3	220	2-9-74	1996	Augusta, Ga.
Hemme, Justin	.192	22	78	8	15	4	0	2	4	7	22	0	1	L	L	6-3	215	12-15-75	1999	Tulsa, Okla.
Jackson, Jeremy	.246	36	122	12	30	7	1	0	5	5	36	4	1	L	R	6-2	195	5-9-76	1997	Moline, Ill.
Jones, Jay	.150	18	60	4	9	3	0	0	8	4	9	0	0	L	R	6-0	195	10-24-74	1996	Trussville, Ala.
Keck, Brian	.242	103	347	54	84	10	3	3	30	37	53	14	2	R	R	6-3	185	1-15-74	1996	Dodge City, Kan.
Lindsey, John	.208	75	260	32	54	15	1	4	35	20	69	2	1	R	R	6-3	215	1-30-77	1995	Hattiesburg, Miss.
Livingston, Doug	.258	64	233	33	60	13	2	0	24	30	39	10	2	R	R	5-8	160	4-9-74	1996	Thonotosassa, Fla.
Mitchell, Andres	.183	33	109	10	20	3	1	1	11	11	35	7	2	R	R	6-1	185	5-26-76	1996	Brentwood, Tenn.
Schwartzbauer, Whitey	.257	58	179	21	46	3	1	2	19	26	44	1	3	L	R	6-1	185	5-4-77	1996	White Bear Lake, Minn.
Sears, Todd	.281	109	385	58	108	21	0	14	59	58	99	11	2	L	R	6-6	205	10-23-75	1997	Ankeny, Iowa
Vidal, Gilbert	.196	13	46	6	9	3	0	1	6	7	12	1	0	R	R	5-10	188	4-21-75	1995	Virginia Gardens, Fla.

GAMES BY POSITION: C—Arias 76, Gonzales 44, Jones 17, Vidal 5. **1B**—Hemme 17, Keck 15, Lindsey 47, Schwartzbauer 17, Sears 47. **2B**—Alviso 117, Keck 7, Livingston 17. **3B**—Anthony 25, Keck 55, Livingston 12, Schwartzbauer 19, Sears 32. **SS**—Alviso 8, Figgins 122, Keck 10. **OF**—Correa 94, Gerut 128, Hamlin 97, Jackson 26, Keck 9, Livingston 32, Mitchell 33.

PITCHING	W	L	ERA	G	GS	CG	SV	IP	H	R	ER	BB	SO	B	T	HT	WT	DOB	1st Yr	Resides
Brueggemann, Dean	3	3	5.90	37	0	0	2	61	64	46	40	43	52	L	L	6-4	195	3-11-76	1996	Smithton, Ill.
Chacon, Shawn	5	5	4.13	12	12	0	0	72	69	44	33	34	66	R	R	6-3	195	12-23-77	1996	Greeley, Colo.
Christman, Tim	1	2	2.42	38	0	0	2	48	38	18	13	12	64	L	L	6-2	180	3-31-75	1996	Oneonta, N.Y.
Colmenares, Luis	5	3	4.64	26	7	0	0	76	80	43	39	34	65	R	R	5-11	189	11-25-74	1994	Valencia, Venez.
DiFelice, Mark	8	12	3.86	27	23	3	0	156	142	71	67	36	142	R	R	6-2	190	8-23-76	1998	Havertown, Pa.
Emiliano, Jamie	5	1	3.52	45	0	0	7	54	50	26	21	29	47	R	R	5-10	210	8-2-74	1995	Andrews, Texas
Johnson, D.J.	0	0	3.00	4	0	0	0	6	4	2	2	2	6	R	R	6-3	220	10-6-74	1997	Baxter Springs, Kan.
Kalinowski, Josh	11	6	2.11	27	27	1	0	162	119	47	38	71	176	L	L	6-2	190	12-12-76	1997	Casper, Wyo.
Kringen, Jake	0	1	6.62	8	0	0	0	18	30	14	13	9	17	L	L	6-2	215	6-25-76	1997	Elma, Wash.
Matcuk, Steve	8	11	5.07	26	26	1	0	153	157	100	86	64	103	R	R	6-2	185	4-8-76	1996	Pasadena, Md.
Miller, Justin	1	2	4.14	8	8	0	0	37	35	18	17	11	35	R	R	6-2	200	8-27-77	1997	Torrance, Calif.
Price, Justin	10	12	4.93	28	27	1	0	172	198	102	94	57	143	R	R	6-3	190	1-31-78	1997	Roswell, N.M.
Rosa, Cristy	1	1	2.91	8	2	0	0	22	27	13	7	7	12	R	R	6-1	165	10-5-77	1995	Guanica, P.R.
Seifert, Ryan	3	5	3.50	24	0	0	0	46	40	24	18	21	51	R	R	6-5	215	8-14-75	1997	Chaska, Minn.
Thompson, Travis	3	3	1.74	56	0	0	27	62	54	19	12	24	53	R	R	6-4	190	1-10-75	1996	Greenfield, Wis.
Thomson, John	0	1	9.00	1	1	0	0	2	4	2	2	0	2	R	R	6-3	175	10-1-73	1993	Sulphur, La.
Vavrek, Mike	3	1	1.85	10	5	0	0	49	32	10	10	13	38	L	L	6-2	185	4-23-74	1995	Glendale Heights, Ill.
Wrigley, Jase	2	0	0.96	8	0	0	0	9	9	1	1	0	6	R	R	6-4	220	11-6-75	1998	Atlanta, Ga.

ASHEVILLE — Class A

SOUTH ATLANTIC LEAGUE

BATTING	AVG	G	AB	R	H	2B	3B	HR	RBI	BB	SO	SB	CS	B	T	HT	WT	DOB	1st Yr	Resides
Colina, Javier	.302	124	516	70	156	37	3	6	81	26	101	12	11	R	R	6-1	180	2-15-79	1997	Cocorote, Venez.
Duck, Kevin	.225	105	338	37	76	15	0	8	36	42	98	0	2	L	L	6-3	210	7-7-77	1998	Irvine, Calif.
Freeman, Choo	.274	131	485	82	133	22	4	14	66	39	132	16	4	R	R	6-2	200	10-20-79	1998	Dallas, Texas
Holliday, Matt	.264	121	444	76	117	28	0	16	64	53	116	10	3	R	R	6-4	215	1-15-80	1998	Stillwater, Okla.
Jackson, Jeremy	.250	17	52	6	13	4	0	0	3	3	14	2	0	L	R	6-2	195	5-9-76	1997	Moline, Ill.
Johnson, Erik	.293	87	311	40	91	20	2	9	43	18	34	7	2	R	R	5-11	195	3-2-77	1998	Naples, Fla.
Johnson, Tom	.333	2	9	1	3	0	0	0	1	0	4	1	1	R	R	6-5	193	1-25-76	1996	Elizabeth, N.J.
Jones, Jay	.297	43	148	22	44	8	0	8	28	8	16	2	0	L	R	6-0	195	10-24-74	1996	Trussville, Ala.
Landaeta, Luis	.280	117	453	61	127	22	1	4	51	20	80	9	7	L	L	6-0	180	3-4-77	1996	Valencia, Venez.
Leon, Richy	.245	62	212	28	52	10	0	5	31	6	29	2	3	R	R	5-8	175	6-21-76	1998	Yuma, Ariz.
Pierre, Juan	.320	140	585	93	187	28	5	1	55	38	37	66	19	L	L	6-0	170	8-14-77	1998	Alexandria, La.
Reyes, Rene	.350	40	160	26	56	6	1	3	19	6	22	1	0	S	R	5-11	202	2-21-78	1996	Porlamar, Venez.
Smith, Sam	.272	87	316	42	86	16	0	8	39	12	79	7	2	R	R	6-1	180	3-21-79	1997	Jasper, Texas
Uribe, Juan	.267	125	430	57	115	28	3	9	46	20	79	11	7	R	R	5-11	173	7-22-79	1997	San Cristobal, D.R.
Whitehurst, Tom	.240	33	100	15	24	1	0	1	6	2	33	3	2	R	R	5-11	175	7-20-77	1998	Blakely, Ga.
Winchester, Jeff	.232	86	310	45	72	18	1	18	48	27	92	0	1	R	R	6-0	205	1-21-80	1998	Metairie, La.

GAMES BY POSITION: C—E. Johnson 44, Jones 33, Winchester 72. **1B**—Duck 105, Reyes 4, Smith 44. **2B**—Colina 118, Leon 25. **3B**—Colina 3, Holliday 108, Leon 11, Smith 21. **SS**—Colina 1, Leon 19, Uribe 125. **OF**—Freeman 130, Jackson 13, T. Johnson 2, Landaeta 112, Leon 8, Pierre 140, Whitehurst 29.

PITCHING	W	L	ERA	G	GS	CG	SV	IP	H	R	ER	BB	SO	B	T	HT	WT	DOB	1st Yr	Resides
Brantley, Brian	6	6	5.88	34	3	0	3	90	89	65	59	44	100	R	R	6-4	185	4-23-76	1998	Chesapeake, Va.
Cameron, Ryan	3	1	2.34	17	0	0	2	35	18	10	9	18	40	R	R	6-1	180	9-13-77	1998	Williamstown, Mass.
Carter, Justin	13	6	3.56	27	26	2	0	144	138	79	57	72	146	R	L	6-2	185	3-8-77	1998	Birmingham, Ala.
Cook, Aaron	4	12	6.44	25	25	2	0	122	157	99	87	62	73	R	R	6-3	175	2-8-79	1997	Loveland, Ohio
Evans, Mike	5	6	4.29	38	0	0	7	84	81	52	40	35	70	L	L	5-11	185	4-1-76	1996	West Palm Beach, Fla.
Gordon, Kevin	0	1	2.57	2	1	0	0	7	7	4	2	3	8	L	R	6-3	200	9-16-76	1998	Clearwater, Fla.
Houser, Kyle	0	1	8.18	4	3	0	0	11	14	12	10	3	19	R	R	6-0	150	1-21-75	1993	Dallas, Texas
Hudson, Luke	6	5	4.30	21	20	1	0	88	89	47	42	24	96	R	R	6-3	195	5-2-77	1998	Fountain Valley, Calif.
Jennings, Jason	2	2	3.70	12	12	0	0	58	55	27	24	8	69	L	R	6-2	230	7-17-78	1999	Mesquite, Texas
Kidd, Jake	2	1	1.48	9	1	0	2	24	16	7	4	3	21	R	R	6-6	190	2-11-78	1997	Hesperia, Calif.
Labitzke, Jesse	0	2	8.07	14	1	0	0	32	40	29	29	25	35	L	L	6-5	220	11-23-77	1996	Laramie, Wyo.
LaMattina, Ryan	3	4	3.50	38	0	0	9	80	68	36	31	29	78	R	L	6-2	210	1-14-76	1998	Fredonia, N.Y.
Lynch, Pat	1	1	3.00	2	2	0	0	12	8	4	4	2	14	R	R	6-3	195	6-27-78	1996	Milton, Ontario
Mundy, Mike	3	3	5.90	37	0	0	2	58	65	43	38	42	59	L	R	6-1	185	3-26-76	1998	Belleville, N.J.
Pacheco, Enemencio ..	3	9	5.29	15	15	1	0	85	98	60	50	29	59	R	R	6-0	160	3-30-79	1997	Santo Domingo, D.R.
Rosa, Cristy	0	2	6.45	7	4	0	1	22	26	21	16	9	11	R	R	6-1	165	10-5-77	1995	Guanica, P.R.
Thompson, Doug	3	3	4.34	25	0	0	3	56	56	29	27	18	72	R	R	6-1	195	7-22-76	1998	Biloxi, Miss.
Van Buren, Jermaine ..	7	10	4.91	28	28	0	0	143	143	87	78	70	133	R	R	6-2	200	7-2-80	1998	Hattiesburg, Miss.
Wrigley, Jase	3	2	3.09	28	0	0	6	58	63	32	20	16	58	R	R	6-4	220	11-6-75	1998	Atlanta, Ga.

PORTLAND — Short-Season Class A

NORTHWEST LEAGUE

BATTING	AVG	G	AB	R	H	2B	3B	HR	RBI	BB	SO	SB	CS	B	T	HT	WT	DOB	1st Yr	Resides
Burford, Kevin	.306	64	216	55	66	22	2	7	33	52	45	9	6	L	L	6-0	190	11-7-77	1997	Westminster, Calif.
Catalanotte, Greg	.282	68	245	38	69	8	2	14	47	30	75	4	2	S	R	6-3	210	6-18-77	1999	Glendale, Ariz.
Gasparino, Billy	.260	62	242	48	63	9	2	6	23	40	57	10	8	R	R	6-0	185	11-28-76	1999	Valrico, Fla.
Hemme, Justin	.276	71	275	48	76	16	1	14	59	29	56	2	1	L	L	6-3	215	12-15-75	1999	Tulsa, Okla.
Lincoln, Justin	.241	68	253	36	61	14	2	6	44	28	102	6	2	R	R	6-3	200	4-4-79	1999	Sarasota, Fla.
Mahoney, Ricardo	.252	63	226	31	57	13	2	4	28	17	33	4	2	R	R	6-3	180	10-13-78	1996	Panama City, Panama
McQueen, Eric	.255	46	153	14	39	8	1	1	14	10	52	0	1	R	R	6-3	220	6-10-77	1999	Winder, Ga.
Moore, Chris	.265	63	260	69	19	2	4	38	15	64	0	3	L	R	5-11	180	11-16-76	1999	Wilmington, N.C.
Ortega, Sixto	.250	1	4	1	1	0	0	0	0	0	1	0	R	R	5-10	180	12-24-79	1997	Santo Domingo, D.R.
Phillips, Dan	.286	71	280	38	80	19	4	10	53	14	72	8	4	R	R	6-3	190	8-23-78	1999	Northridge, Calif.
Rosario, Melvin	.243	50	185	29	45	5	3	0	8	15	46	12	2	L	L	6-2	175	9-22-78	1998	Carolina, P.R.
Sanchez, Agustin	.168	31	101	10	17	3	1	1	9	9	11	0	0	S	R	6-0	175	2-3-79	1997	Yauco, P.R.

Organization Statistics

BATTING	AVG	G	AB	R	H	2B	3B	HR	RBI	BB	SO	SB	CS	B	T	HT	WT	DOB	1st Yr	Resides
Sosa, Jorge	.204	35	113	15	23	3	0	2	8	13	57	2	3	S	R	6-2	190	4-28-78	1995	Santo Domingo, D.R.
Vilorio, Miguel	.338	21	77	14	26	3	0	1	5	7	14	13	4	R	R	5-10	152	7-22-79	1997	Santo Domingo, D.R.

GAMES BY POSITION: C—Mahoney 3, McQueen 46, Ortega 1, Sanchez 31. **1B**—Hemme 69, Mahoney 8. **2B**—Gasparino 11, Moore 48, Vilorio 20. **3B**—Gasparino 43, Lincoln 2, Mahoney 22, Moore 12. **SS**—Gasparino 10, Lincoln 66, Moore 3. **OF**—Burford 11, Catalanotte 67, Mahoney 16, Phillips 68, Rosario 48, Sosa 26.

PITCHING	W	L	ERA	G	GS	CG	SV	IP	H	R	ER	BB	SO	B	T	HT	WT	DOB	1st Yr	Resides
Cameron, Ryan	1	0	0.00	4	0	0	1	5	1	0	0	1	4	R	R	6-1	180	9-13-77	1998	Williamstown, Mass.
Cercy, Rick	1	2	5.34	13	1	0	0	29	29	19	17	17	25	R	R	6-1	195	10-10-76	1999	Ormond Beach, Fla.
Crowder, Chuck	2	1	4.33	6	6	0	0	27	24	14	13	16	39	L	L	6-2	200	9-30-76	1999	Mantua, Ohio
DePaula, Julio	6	6	6.01	16	16	0	0	85	97	67	57	43	77	R	R	6-1	160	7-27-79	1997	Santo Domingo, D.R.
Esslinger, Cam	6	3	3.83	14	14	0	0	80	76	37	34	35	68	R	R	6-0	180	12-28-76	1999	Hewitt, N.J.
Garner, Brandon	0	0	9.00	1	0	0	0	1	2	1	1	1	1	R	R	6-0	190	3-28-80	1998	Jackson, Tenn.
Gomez, Diogenes	3	2	2.30	24	0	0	7	27	25	12	7	13	17	R	R	5-11	165	3-27-79	1997	La Represa, Panama
Gordon, Kevin	0	1	9.31	8	0	0	0	10	14	18	10	7	11	L	R	6-3	200	9-16-76	1998	Clearwater, Fla.
Haase, Frank	0	1	6.62	14	0	0	0	18	18	20	13	14	10	R	L	6-3	175	7-21-79	1999	Atwater, Calif.
Hoffman, Matt	4	1	6.27	23	0	0	1	33	35	27	23	23	22	R	R	6-6	225	1-15-77	1999	Claremore, Okla.
House, Craig	2	1	2.08	26	0	0	11	35	28	14	8	14	58	R	R	6-2	210	7-8-77	1999	Bartlett, Tenn.
Jennings, Jason	1	0	1.00	2	2	0	0	9	5	1	1	2	11	L	R	6-2	230	7-17-78	1999	Mesquite, Texas
Kibler, Ryan	0	0	21.60	1	1	0	0	3	8	8	8	4	4	R	R	6-2	185	9-17-80	1999	Tampa, Fla.
Kidd, Jake	2	1	2.65	11	0	0	0	17	10	6	5	5	17	R	R	6-6	190	2-11-78	1997	Hesperia, Calif.
Labitzke, Jesse	1	1	3.67	18	0	0	3	27	24	15	11	17	30	L	L	6-5	220	11-23-77	1996	Laramie, Wyo.
Little, Rodney	0	1	13.00	6	0	0	0	9	12	15	13	17	4	R	R	6-1	182	8-14-78	1997	Combs, Ky.
Little, Roger	0	4	6.21	12	4	0	0	33	41	27	23	15	21	R	R	6-2	180	8-14-78	1997	Combs, Ky.
Monzon, Yoel	3	4	4.74	17	7	0	1	57	65	43	30	29	37	R	R	6-2	185	5-14-77	1999	San Jose, Costa Rica
Pacheco, Enemencio	4	3	3.95	12	12	1	0	73	73	43	32	21	44	R	R	6-0	160	3-30-79	1997	Santo Domingo, D.R.
Vargas, Derrick	1	0	3.98	18	0	0	0	32	26	17	14	32	33	L	L	6-4	204	5-13-77	1997	Newark, Calif.
Young, Colin	2	5	4.88	15	13	0	0	59	59	39	32	28	74	L	L	6-0	185	8-1-77	1999	West Newbury, Mass.

TUCSON — Rookie

ARIZONA LEAGUE

BATTING	AVG	G	AB	R	H	2B	3B	HR	RBI	BB	SO	SB	CS	B	T	HT	WT	DOB	1st Yr	Resides
Bernard, Dagoberto	.325	34	117	14	38	5	0	0	21	6	17	7	6	R	R	6-0	159	2-23-80	1997	San Pedro de Macoris, D.R.
Daly, Sean	.182	25	77	12	14	3	0	0	8	12	35	3	0	R	R	6-2	195	1-5-81	1999	Visalia, Calif.
Figueroa, Carlos	.221	49	181	29	40	10	2	0	28	23	30	10	5	R	R	5-10	165	5-25-81	1999	Carolina, P.R.
Gearlds, Aaron	.311	51	180	37	56	4	4	1	29	18	43	22	2	R	R	6-1	190	12-13-79	1999	Jackson, Miss.
Guzman, Javier	.367	13	49	11	18	4	2	2	11	1	12	5	0	S	R	6-2	175	11-9-79	1998	Rio Piedras, P.R.
Londono, Alex	.268	38	142	29	38	7	3	4	28	11	46	10	3	R	R	6-2	180	2-10-80	1997	Los Teques, Venez.
Morency, Vernand	.294	44	160	36	47	7	4	2	18	19	49	25	5	R	R	5-11	200	2-4-80	1998	Miami, Fla.
Mulqueen, Dave	.249	53	169	32	42	9	3	1	17	42	63	6	3	S	R	6-3	225	10-16-80	1999	Milwaukee, Wis.
Ortega, Sixto	.232	25	82	8	19	3	0	0	14	4	20	3	2	R	R	5-10	180	12-24-79	1997	Santo Domingo, D.R.
Reyes, Rene	.361	22	97	21	35	4	4	1	20	4	14	6	1	S	R	5-11	202	2-21-78	1996	Porlamar, Venez.
Samuel, Tomas	.288	42	170	30	49	18	1	2	35	11	48	6	1	R	R	5-11	175	7-2-79	1996	San Pedro de Macoris, D.R.
Testa, Chris	.292	47	168	22	49	10	1	1	22	24	27	11	6	L	L	6-2	175	5-23-81	1999	Palmdale, Calif.
Ventura, Juan	.399	46	193	35	77	9	4	0	23	12	24	25	9	R	R	6-1	160	12-10-80	1997	Puerto Plata, D.R.
Warren, Chris	.257	40	144	30	37	4	1	1	16	23	22	18	2	R	R	6-0	175	11-24-76	1999	Athens, Ga.

GAMES BY POSITION: C—Daly 6, Ortega 24, Samuel 29. **1B**—Daly 10, Londono 5, Mulqueen 27, Reyes 18. **2B**—Bernard 14, Ventura 45. **3B**—Mulqueen 19, Warren 40. **SS**—Bernard 21, Figueroa 39, Warren 1. **OF**—Gearlds 47, Guzman 12, Londono 24, Morency 42, Testa 47.

PITCHING	W	L	ERA	G	GS	CG	SV	IP	H	R	ER	BB	SO	B	T	HT	WT	DOB	1st Yr	Resides
Briggs, Anthony	0	0	2.45	3	3	0	0	7	11	3	2	1	5	R	R	6-1	155	9-14-73	1994	Manning, S.C.
Christensen, Deryck	2	1	3.55	18	0	0	0	25	33	14	10	18	20	R	R	5-11	180	5-1-81	1999	Issaquah, Wash.
Ferrand, Julian	0	1	8.27	13	0	0	1	21	25	22	19	15	14	R	R	6-2	165	11-22-79	1997	Santo Domingo, D.R.
Garner, Brandon	4	5	3.63	14	13	1	0	79	74	37	32	5	67	R	R	6-0	190	3-28-80	1998	Jackson, Tenn.
Gonzalez, Miguel	0	1	6.61	10	1	0	0	16	24	18	12	12	15	R	R	6-3	200	11-7-79	1999	Guasave, Mexico
Granados, Bernie	1	1	5.60	16	0	0	0	27	38	28	17	12	25	R	R	6-2	180	6-6-79	1999	San Jose, Costa Rica
Johnson, Roney	2	3	8.64	9	8	0	0	33	48	34	32	18	22	R	R	6-2	205	7-20-80	1999	Antelope, Calif.
Kibler, Ryan	6	2	2.55	14	14	2	0	81	77	35	23	14	56	R	R	6-2	185	9-17-80	1999	Tampa, Fla.
Kusiewicz, Mike	1	3	5.47	6	6	0	0	25	26	16	15	9	27	R	L	6-2	185	11-1-76	1995	Nepean, Ontario
Lorenzo, Javier	6	4	4.28	20	1	0	2	34	36	23	16	19	41	R	R	5-11	180	12-26-78	1999	Hialeah, Fla.
Matos, Jesus	2	1	5.50	18	3	0	0	36	48	28	22	12	31	R	R	6-0	165	3-21-79	1997	San Pedro de Macoris, D.R.
Moore, Joel	0	1	13.06	4	3	0	0	10	25	19	15	1	9	L	R	6-2	180	8-13-72	1993	Elgin, Ill.
Rossiter, Mike	0	0	0.00	1	0	0	0	2	0	0	0	0	5	R	R	6-6	230	6-20-73	1991	Burbank, Calif.
Serrano, Alex	3	2	1.20	18	0	0	5	30	21	10	4	14	23	R	R	6-1	180	2-18-81	1998	Barcelona, Venez.
Simpson, Joe	1	3	6.11	14	3	0	0	35	39	28	24	31	21	R	R	6-2	175	10-10-78	1999	Fairfield, Ohio
Trask, Cody	0	0	8.31	9	1	0	0	17	26	21	16	13	12	R	R	6-3	205	3-19-78	1998	Chino Hills, Calif.

DETROIT TIGERS

Tigers' high expectations give way to disappointment

BY PAT CAPUTO

Another season of high expectations. Another season of bitter disappointments.

The Tigers continued to spin their wheels in 1999, as the nucleus of young veterans they signed to multiyear contracts fizzled and the young prospects they brought up from their minor league system struggled.

The rebuilding program that was supposed to make the Tigers a contender as they move into Comerica Park in 2000 is in question. The club did close out Tiger Stadium in style when rookie Robert Fick hit a grand slam to beat the Royals in the ballpark's final game.

The Tigers haven't had a winning season since 1993 and had just two winning seasons during the 1990s. No one expected them to contend in 1999, but it would have been difficult to envision the 69-92 record the club produced.

Adding to the disappointment is that several players the Tigers traded away or released in the recent past—Kent Bottenfield, Luis Gonzalez, Jose Lima, Jamie Moyer and Joe Randa—had big seasons elsewhere. The hitters they counted on—first baseman Tony Clark, second baseman Damion Easley and outfielder Bobby Higginson—struggled.

For the second straight season, Clark started slowly as the whole team struggled. He hit .240 with eight home runs in the first half, though he did rebound to hit .317 with 23 homers in the second half. Easley hit .188 with runners in scoring position on his way to hitting .266 on the season. Higginson, in the second year of a four-year, $16 million contract, hit just .239.

The team's young players also struggled. The Tigers

Dean Palmer   **Francisco Cordero**

JOHN SPEAR

Players of the Year

MAJOR LEAGUE: Dean Palmer, 3b
Palmer led the Tigers with 38 home runs, 100 RBIs and 92 runs scored in his first season with the team.

MINOR LEAGUE: Francisco Cordero, rhp
After missing much of the '98 season, Cordero bounced back with 27 saves and a 1.38 ERA in 52 innings at Jacksonville.

traded center fielder Brian Hunter to the Mariners early in the season and handed the job to rookie Gabe Kapler. But Kapler, who had a Southern League-record 146 RBIs for Double-A Jacksonville in 1998, appeared overmatched, hitting .245.

The young pitchers also had troubles in 1999. From 1996-98, the first three years of general manager Randy Smith's regime, the Tigers used their first-round picks on college righthanders.

After winning five of his last seven starts in 1998, 1996 first-round choice Seth Greisinger missed all of 1999 after Tommy John surgery. Matt Anderson, the No. 1 pick in 1997, took a step back and had a long stint at Triple-A Toledo. Jeff Weaver, the first-rounder in 1998, won six of his first nine decisions. But a stretch of 14 starts in which his ERA was 8.92 brought him back to earth.

Despite Anderson's struggles, the bullpen was solid with veterans Doug Brocail and Todd Jones joined late by Francisco Cordero, who was brilliant at Double-A Jacksonville and impressed in a September callup.

It was a dismal season for the farm system as well. After three straight seasons over .500, Tigers affiliates finished 335-363 (.480), and none of them qualified for the playoffs. Worst of all was Triple-A Toledo, which finished 57-87.

Most of the organization's recent top prospects (Anderson, Cordero, Juan Encarnacion and Kapler) reached the major leagues. The Tigers hope 1999 first-rounder Eric Munson, the third overall pick, will soon be there as well. Munson, a catcher at Southern California, played mostly first base while leading Class A West Michigan in home runs in his debut.

ORGANIZATION LEADERS

BATTING

*AVG	Javier Cardona, Jacksonville	.309
R	Kurt Airoso, Jacksonville	95
H	Kurt Airoso, Jacksonville	146
TB	Dave McCarty, Toledo	248
2B	Rob Sasser, Jacksonville	38
3B	Richard Gomez, West Michigan	12
HR	Dave McCarty, Toledo	31
RBI	Javier Cardona, Jacksonville	92
BB	Andres Torres, West Michigan	92
SO	Rod Lindsey, Jacksonville/Lakeland	135
SB	Richard Gomez, West Michigan	66

PITCHING

W	David Darwin, Jacksonville	14
L	Matt Drews, Toledo	14
#ERA	Jason Frasor, West Michigan/Oneonta	1.96
G	Bill Snyder, Jacksonville/Lakeland	61
CG	Two tied at	4
SV	Francisco Cordero, Jacksonville	27
IP	David Darwin, Jacksonville	187
BB	Matt Drews, Toledo	91
SO	Victor Santos, Jacksonville	146

*Minimum 250 At-Bats #Minimum 75 Innings

Detroit TIGERS

Manager: Larry Parrish

1999 Record: 69-92, .429 (3rd, AL Central)

BATTING	AVG	G	AB	R	H	2B	3B	HR	RBI	BB	SO	SB	CS	B	T	HT	WT	DOB	1st Yr	Resides
Alvarez, Gabe	.208	22	53	5	11	3	0	2	4	3	9	0	0	R	R	6-1	205	3-6-74	1995	El Monte, Calif.
Ausmus, Brad	.275	127	458	62	126	25	6	9	54	51	71	12	9	R	R	5-11	195	4-14-69	1988	San Diego, Calif.
Bartee, Kimera	.195	41	77	11	15	1	3	0	3	9	20	3	3	S	R	6-0	200	7-21-72	1993	Glendale, Ariz.
Catalanotto, Frank	.276	100	286	41	79	19	0	11	35	15	49	3	4	L	R	6-0	195	4-27-74	1992	Smithtown, N.Y.
Clark, Tony	.280	143	536	74	150	29	0	31	99	64	133	2	1	S	R	6-7	245	6-15-72	1990	Glendale, Ariz.
Cruz, Deivi	.284	155	518	64	147	35	0	13	58	12	57	1	4	R	R	6-0	184	11-6-75	1993	Nizao, D.R.
Easley, Damion	.266	151	549	83	146	30	1	20	65	51	124	11	3	R	R	5-11	185	11-11-69	1989	Glendale, Ariz.
Encarnacion, Juan	.255	132	509	62	130	30	6	19	74	14	113	33	12	R	R	6-3	187	3-8-76	1993	Las Matas de Farfan, D.R.
Fick, Robert	.220	15	41	6	9	0	0	3	10	7	6	1	0	L	R	6-1	189	3-15-74	1996	Thousand Oaks, Calif.
Garcia, Karim	.240	96	288	38	69	10	3	14	32	20	67	2	4	L	L	6-0	172	10-29-75	1993	Obregon, Mexico
Garcia, Luis	.111	8	9	0	1	1	0	0	0	0	2	0	0	R	R	6-0	174	5-20-75	1993	San Francisco de Macoris, D.R.
Haselman, Bill	.273	48	143	13	39	8	0	4	14	10	26	2	0	R	R	6-3	223	5-25-66	1987	New Castle, Wash.
Higginson, Bob	.239	107	377	51	90	18	0	12	46	64	66	4	6	L	R	5-11	195	8-18-70	1992	Bloomfield Hills, Mich.
Hunter, Brian	.236	18	55	8	13	2	1	0	0	5	11	0	3	R	R	6-3	180	3-25-71	1989	Vancouver, Wash.
Jefferies, Gregg	.200	70	205	22	41	8	0	6	18	13	11	3	4	S	R	5-10	185	8-1-67	1985	Pleasanton, Calif.
Kapler, Gabe	.245	130	416	60	102	22	4	18	49	42	74	11	5	R	R	6-2	208	8-31-75	1995	Reseda, Calif.
Macias, Jose	.250	5	4	2	1	0	0	1	2	0	1	0	0	S	R	5-10	173	1-25-74	1994	Panama City, Panama
Palmer, Dean	.263	150	560	92	147	25	2	38	100	57	153	3	3	R	R	6-1	210	12-27-68	1986	Tallahassee, Fla.
Polonia, Luis	.324	87	333	46	108	21	8	10	32	16	32	17	9	L	L	5-8	150	10-27-64	1984	Santiago, D.R.
Wood, Jason	.159	27	44	5	7	1	0	1	8	2	13	0	0	R	R	6-1	190	12-16-69	1991	Fresno, Calif.

PITCHING	W	L	ERA	G	GS	CG	SV	IP	H	R	ER	BB	SO	B	T	HT	WT	DOB	1st Yr	Resides
Anderson, Matt	2	1	5.68	37	0	0	0	38	33	27	24	35	32	R	R	6-4	200	8-17-76	1998	Houston, Texas
Blair, Willie	3	11	6.85	39	16	0	0	134	169	107	102	44	82	R	R	6-1	185	12-18-65	1986	Lexington, Ky.
Borkowski, David	2	6	6.10	17	12	0	0	77	86	58	52	40	50	R	R	6-1	200	2-7-77	1995	Sterling Heights, Mich.
Brocail, Doug	4	4	2.52	70	0	0	2	82	60	23	23	25	78	L	R	6-5	235	5-16-67	1986	Missouri City, Texas
Brunson, Will	1	0	6.00	17	0	0	0	12	18	9	8	6	9	L	L	6-5	185	3-20-70	1992	Bulverde, Texas
Cordero, Francisco	2	2	3.32	20	0	0	0	19	19	7	7	18	19	R	R	6-2	200	8-11-77	1994	Santo Domingo, D.R.
Cruz, Nelson	2	5	5.67	29	6	0	0	67	74	44	42	23	46	R	R	6-1	185	9-13-72	1991	Washington, D.C.
Florie, Bryce	2	1	4.56	27	3	0	0	51	61	31	26	20	40	R	R	5-11	192	5-21-70	1988	Goose Creek, S.C.
Graterol, Beiker	0	1	15.75	1	1	0	0	4	4	7	7	4	2	R	R	6-2	165	11-9-74	1993	Barquisimeto, Venez.
Hiljus, Erik	0	0	5.19	6	0	0	0	9	7	5	5	5	1	R	R	6-5	230	12-25-72	1991	Northridge, Calif.
Jones, Todd	4	4	3.80	65	0	0	30	66	64	30	28	35	64	L	R	6-3	230	4-24-68	1989	Pell City, Ala.
Kida, Masao	1	0	6.26	49	0	0	1	65	73	48	45	30	50	R	R	6-2	209	9-12-68	1988	Tokyo, Japan
Lira, Felipe	0	0	10.80	2	0	0	0	3	7	5	4	2	3	R	R	6-1	205	4-26-72	1990	Miranda, Venez.
Mlicki, Dave	14	12	4.60	31	31	2	0	192	209	108	98	70	119	R	R	6-4	205	6-8-68	1990	Columbus, Ohio
Moehler, Brian	10	16	5.04	32	32	2	0	196	229	116	110	59	106	R	R	6-3	235	12-31-71	1993	Marietta, Ga.
Nitkowski, C.J.	4	5	4.30	68	7	0	0	82	63	44	39	45	66	L	L	6-3	205	3-9-73	1994	Sugar Land, Texas
Roberts, Willis	0	0	13.50	1	0	0	0	1	3	4	2	0	0	R	R	6-3	175	6-19-75	1992	San Cristobal, D.R.
Rojas, Mel	0	0	22.74	5	0	0	0	6	12	16	16	4	6	R	R	5-11	212	12-10-66	1986	Santo Domingo, D.R.
Runyan, Sean	0	1	3.38	12	0	0	0	11	9	4	4	3	6	L	L	6-3	210	6-21-74	1992	Urbandale, Iowa
Thompson, Justin	9	11	5.11	24	24	0	0	143	152	85	81	59	83	L	L	6-4	215	3-8-73	1991	Montgomery, Texas
Weaver, Jeff	9	12	5.55	30	29	0	0	164	176	104	101	56	114	R	R	6-5	200	8-22-76	1998	Simi Valley, Calif.

FIELDING

Catcher	PCT	G	PO	A	E	DP	PB
Ausmus	.998	127	754	56	2	5	7
Fick	1.000	4	24	1	0	0	1
Haselman	.996	39	231	13	1	0	4

First Base	PCT	G	PO	A	E	DP
Catalanotto	1.000	32	219	11	0	29
Clark	.992	132	1126	86	10	111
Jefferies	1.000	3	19	4	0	1
Wood	.972	5	35	0	1	3

Second Base	PCT	G	PO	A	E	DP
Catalanotto	.966	32	24	61	3	7
Easley	.989	147	302	421	8	111
L. Garcia	.000	1	0	0	0	0
Jefferies	1.000	2	0	1	0	0
Macias	1.000	1	1	6	0	0
Wood	1.000	1	0	1	0	0

Third Base	PCT	G	PO	A	E	DP
Alvarez	1.000	2	0	1	0	0
Catalanotto	.946	21	9	26	2	4
Palmer	.945	141	89	240	19	24
Wood	.909	9	5	5	1	0

Shortstop	PCT	G	PO	A	E	DP
D. Cruz	.983	155	230	453	12	106
Easley	1.000	19	16	24	0	5
L. Garcia	1.000	7	3	2	0	0
Wood	.818	9	2	7	2	1

Outfield	PCT	G	PO	A	E	DP
Alvarez	1.000	5	3	0	0	0
Bartee	.985	38	66	0	1	0
Encarnacion	.968	131	264	10	9	2
K. Garcia	.958	81	152	7	7	1
Higginson	.983	88	175	2	3	0
Hunter	1.000	18	49	1	0	0
Jefferies	1.000	2	2	0	0	0
Kapler	.981	128	303	4	6	2
Polonia	.986	40	68	4	1	0

DAVID SEELIG

Tony Clark

Assistant General Manager: Steve Lubratich

Class	Farm Team	League	W	L	Pct.	Finish*	Manager(s)	First Yr
AAA	Toledo (Ohio) Mud Hens	International	57	87	.396	14th (14)	Gene Roof	1987
AA	Jacksonville (Fla.) Suns	Southern	75	66	.532	3rd (10)	Dave Anderson	1995
A#	Lakeland (Fla.) Tigers	Florida State	65	73	.471	10th (14)	Mark Meleski	1960
A	West Michigan Whitecaps	Midwest	68	72	.486	10th (14)	Bruce Fields	1997
A	Oneonta (N.Y.) Tigers	New York-Penn	41	34	.547	5th (14)	Kevin Bradshaw	1999
Rookie	Lakeland (Fla.) Tigers	Gulf Coast	29	31	.483	t-8th (14)	Gary Green	1995

*Finish in overall standings (No. of teams in league)   #Advanced level

TOLEDO   Class AAA

INTERNATIONAL LEAGUE

BATTING

	AVG	G	AB	R	H	2B	3B	HR	RBI	BB	SO	SB	CS	B	T	HT	WT	DOB	1st Yr	Resides
Alvarez, Gabe	.285	110	410	70	117	24	0	21	67	57	80	1	3	R	R	6-1	205	3-6-74	1995	El Monte, Calif.
Ashley, Billy	.286	29	112	19	32	9	0	9	25	9	32	0	0	R	R	6-6	240	7-11-70	1988	Thousand Oaks, Calif.
Bartee, Kimera	.286	104	416	64	119	13	8	12	43	38	76	21	9	S	R	6-0	200	7-21-72	1993	Glendale, Ariz.
Bonnici, Jim	.224	22	58	10	13	3	0	2	4	6	25	0	0	R	R	6-4	230	1-21-72	1991	Ortonville, Mich.
Casanova, Raul	.206	44	160	21	33	9	0	6	23	7	28	0	0	S	R	6-0	195	8-23-72	1990	Ponce, P.R.
Clark, Tony	.000	1	3	0	0	0	0	0	0	1	1	0	0	S	R	6-7	245	6-15-72	1990	Glendale, Calif.
Cradle, Rickey	.239	110	348	57	83	27	2	10	52	42	82	11	6	R	R	6-2	180	6-20-73	1991	Cerritos, Calif.
Fick, Robert	.313	14	48	11	15	0	1	2	8	8	5	1	0	L	R	6-1	189	3-15-74	1996	Thousand Oaks, Calif.
Garcia, Luis	.266	89	308	30	82	19	1	3	34	5	41	3	3	R	R	6-0	174	5-20-75	1993	San Francisco de Macoris, D.R.
Hamelin, Bob	.221	46	149	20	33	9	0	5	20	24	29	4	1	L	L	6-0	235	11-29-67	1988	Leawood, Kan.
Jefferies, Gregg	.250	2	8	0	2	0	0	0	0	0	2	0	0	S	R	5-10	185	8-1-67	1985	Pleasanton, Calif.
Kapler, Gabe	.315	14	54	11	17	6	2	3	14	9	10	0	1	R	R	6-2	208	8-31-75	1995	Reseda, Calif.
Lennon, Pat	.264	74	280	49	74	16	1	21	50	33	66	1	2	R	R	6-2	200	4-27-68	1986	Whiteville, N.C.
2-team (37 Syracuse)	.287	111	414	75	119	21	1	30	83	55	106	4	5							
Macias, Jose	.244	112	438	44	107	18	8	2	36	36	60	10	5	S	R	5-10	173	1-25-74	1994	Panama City, Panama
Maxwell, Jason	.236	119	419	60	99	17	2	15	62	53	87	6	3	R	R	6-1	180	3-26-72	1993	Lewisburg, Tenn.
McCarty, Dave	.268	132	466	85	125	24	3	31	77	70	110	6	6	R	L	6-5	215	11-23-69	1991	Menlo Park, Calif.
McKeel, Walt	.242	67	215	21	52	9	1	7	37	26	32	2	2	R	R	6-2	200	1-17-72	1990	Stantonsburg, N.C.
Polonia, Luis	.323	42	161	20	52	7	1	3	22	10	28	13	3	L	L	5-8	150	10-27-64	1984	Santiago, D.R.
Siddall, Joe	.193	84	244	29	47	15	0	8	33	34	74	4	1	L	R	6-1	200	10-25-67	1988	Windsor, Ontario
Swann, Pedro	.259	103	332	51	86	14	2	10	37	36	67	3	1	L	R	6-0	195	10-27-70	1991	Townsend, Del.
Wood, Jason	.286	48	185	34	53	11	0	6	34	14	22	2	2	R	R	6-1	190	12-16-69	1991	Fresno, Calif.

PITCHING

	W	L	ERA	G	GS	CG	SV	IP	H	R	ER	BB	SO	B	T	HT	WT	DOB	1st Yr	Resides
Alberro, Jose	2	2	5.25	14	0	0	0	24	28	16	14	11	21	R	R	6-2	190	6-29-69	1991	Arecibo, P.R.
Anderson, Matt	0	4	6.39	24	4	0	5	38	32	27	27	31	35	R	R	6-4	200	8-17-76	1998	Houston, Texas
Borkowski, David	6	8	3.50	19	19	3	0	126	119	59	49	43	94	R	R	6-1	200	2-7-77	1995	Sterling Heights, Mich.
Brunson, Will	3	1	4.53	38	1	0	3	48	45	28	24	17	41	L	L	6-5	185	3-20-70	1992	Bulverde, Texas
Checo, Robinson	0	0	0.00	2	1	0	0	5	2	0	0	1	6	R	R	6-1	185	9-9-71	1989	Santiago, D.R.
Corey, Bryan	5	2	2.86	48	0	0	2	69	63	27	22	34	36	R	R	6-0	170	10-21-73	1993	Phoenix, Ariz.
Cruz, Nelson	7	1	2.73	10	10	4	0	63	47	20	19	21	41	R	R	6-1	185	9-13-72	1991	Washington, D.C.
Drews, Matt	2	14	8.27	28	22	0	0	136	171	136	125	91	70	R	R	6-8	230	8-29-74	1994	Sarasota, Fla.
Drumright, Mike	6	10	5.97	21	21	1	0	121	116	88	80	59	76	L	R	6-4	210	4-19-74	1995	Valley Center, Kan.
Goldsmith, Gary	0	3	6.95	6	5	0	0	22	29	21	17	9	14	R	R	6-2	205	7-4-71	1993	Alamogordo, N.M.
Graterol, Beiker	3	9	5.83	17	15	0	0	79	89	55	51	38	47	R	R	6-2	165	11-9-74	1993	Barquisimeto, Venez.
Greisinger, Seth	0	1	5.87	2	2	0	0	8	9	5	5	3	4	R	R	6-3	200	7-29-75	1996	Falls Church, Va.
Grzanich, Mike	1	0	9.28	14	0	0	1	21	21	24	22	25	17	R	R	6-1	180	8-24-72	1992	Champaign, Ill.
Hiljus, Erik	2	3	4.40	33	0	0	5	59	49	31	29	16	73	R	R	6-5	230	12-25-72	1991	Northridge, Calif.
Keagle, Greg	1	4	7.16	7	7	0	0	33	50	29	26	13	19	R	R	6-2	195	6-28-71	1993	Horseheads, N.Y.
Kida, Masao	0	0	3.18	3	0	0	0	6	6	2	2	1	4	R	R	6-2	209	9-12-68	1988	Tokyo, Japan
Lira, Felipe	2	11	6.71	30	17	0	1	114	163	97	85	35	70	R	R	6-1	205	4-26-72	1990	Miranda, Venez.
Looney, Brian	3	0	6.22	47	1	0	2	55	51	38	38	44	52	L	L	5-10	180	6-26-69	1991	Cheshire, Conn.
Martinez, Romulo	0	0	5.40	6	0	0	0	7	7	5	4	6	2	R	R	6-1	170	12-5-76	1994	Santiago, D.R.
Ramirez, Jose	0	0	1.80	1	1	0	0	5	3	1	1	4	3	L	L	6-1	170	9-1-75	1994	Santo Domingo, D.R.
Reed, Brandon	8	5	4.14	44	6	1	3	91	101	53	42	26	59	R	R	6-4	185	12-18-74	1994	Flint, Mich.
Roach, Petie	1	1	4.50	4	0	0	0	8	6	4	4	2	5	L	L	5-9	170	9-19-70	1992	Redding, Calif.
Roberts, Willis	5	8	6.26	31	12	2	0	92	112	68	64	59	52	R	R	6-3	175	6-19-75	1992	San Cristobal, D.R.
Runyan, Sean	0	0	3.48	10	0	0	0	10	7	4	4	1	7	L	L	6-3	210	6-21-74	1992	Urbandale, Iowa

FIELDING

Catcher	PCT	G	PO	A	E	DP	PB
Casanova	.985	31	173	21	3	3	5
Fick	.970	5	31	1	1	0	0
McKeel	.986	45	266	25	4	2	8
Siddall	.998	72	410	33	1	5	6
Wood	1.000	2	2	0	0	0	1

First Base	PCT	G	PO	A	E	DP
Bonnici	1.000	4	26	2	0	1
Clark	1.000	1	10	1	0	0
Fick	.963	7	46	6	2	3
Hamelin	.991	13	106	5	1	14
Maxwell	1.000	1	10	1	0	0
McCarty	.999	115	968	104	1	102
McKeel	.909	2	18	2	2	2
Wood	.987	8	67	7	1	13

Second Base	PCT	G	PO	A	E	DP
Macias	.971	107	204	339	16	74
Maxwell	.984	40	69	111	3	26
Wood	1.000	2	2	7	0	2

Third Base	PCT	G	PO	A	E	DP
Alvarez	.893	86	48	160	25	9
Fick	.333	1	0	1	2	0
Garcia	.972	16	14	21	1	2
Maxwell	.861	15	4	27	5	2
McKeel	1.000	1	0	1	0	0
Wood	.974	30	20	54	2	6

Shortstop	PCT	G	PO	A	E	DP
Alvarez	1.000	1	2	2	0	1
Garcia	.955	72	124	235	17	48
Macias	.895	3	6	11	2	1
Maxwell	.967	68	108	189	10	53

	PCT	G	PO	A	E	DP
Wood	.957	6	7	15	1	3

Outfield	PCT	G	PO	A	E	DP
Alvarez	.976	20	37	3	1	2
Ashley	1.000	13	25	0	0	0
Bartee	.996	104	239	5	1	1
Cradle	.981	107	206	6	4	0
Kapler	1.000	14	33	0	0	0
Lennon	.959	40	68	3	3	1
Macias	1.000	5	8	1	0	0
McCarty	.972	20	33	2	1	1
McKeel	.900	5	9	0	1	0
Polonia	.985	36	64	2	1	0
Siddall	1.000	3	1	0	0	0
Swann	.993	83	141	8	1	0
Wood	1.000	2	2	0	0	0

Organization Statistics

SOUTHERN LEAGUE

BATTING	AVG	G	AB	R	H	2B	3B	HR	RBI	BB	SO	SB	CS	B	T	HT	WT	DOB	1st Yr	Resides
Airoso, Kurt	.272	134	536	95	146	28	6	10	72	89	113	10	3	R	R	6-2	190	2-12-75	1996	Tulare, Calif.
Candelaria, Ben	.269	120	464	65	125	31	3	18	77	35	93	6	7	L	R	5-11	167	1-29-75	1992	Hatillo, P.R.
Cardona, Javier	.309	108	418	84	129	31	0	26	92	46	69	4	2	R	R	6-1	185	9-15-75	1994	Dorado, P.R.
Freire, Alejandro	.296	66	243	45	72	20	0	10	43	23	44	2	0	R	R	6-2	185	8-23-74	1992	Caracas, Venez.
Gillespie, Eric	.306	118	474	80	145	28	6	19	88	53	89	12	2	L	R	5-10	200	6-6-75	1996	Long Beach, Calif.
Ibarra, Jesse	.157	18	70	9	11	1	0	1	6	10	20	0	0	S	R	6-3	195	7-12-72	1994	El Monte, Calif.
Jones, Ryan	.253	125	487	66	123	21	3	19	73	50	115	1	1	R	R	6-3	225	11-5-74	1993	Irvine, Calif.
Lemonis, Chris	.283	75	265	35	75	16	1	5	38	19	45	1	2	L	R	5-11	185	8-21-73	1995	New York, N.Y.
Lindsey, Rod	.185	7	27	3	5	1	0	0	2	1	6	0	0	S	R	5-8	175	1-28-76	1994	Opelika, Ala.
Lindstrom, David	.271	66	214	30	58	17	1	7	35	24	35	1	3	R	R	5-10	185	8-6-74	1996	Brooklyn Park, Minn.
Mitchell, Derek	.242	124	422	56	102	17	1	7	49	53	117	4	2	R	R	6-2	170	3-9-75	1996	Gurnee, Ill.
Riley, Marquis	.255	54	161	30	41	4	0	0	16	30	29	16	3	S	R	5-10	170	12-27-70	1992	Ashdown, Ark.
Rivera, Mike	.174	7	23	3	4	1	0	2	6	2	5	0	0	R	R	6-0	190	9-8-76	1997	Bayamon, P.R.
Santana, Pedro	.279	120	512	89	143	35	6	5	49	34	98	34	9	R	R	5-11	180	9-21-76	1995	San Pedro de Macoris, D.R.
Sasser, Rob	.283	117	424	60	120	38	1	7	61	57	101	9	5	R	R	6-3	205	3-9-75	1993	Oakland, Calif.
Wakeland, Chris	.321	55	212	42	68	16	3	13	36	35	53	6	5	L	L	6-0	185	6-15-74	1996	St. Helens, Ore.

PITCHING	W	L	ERA	G	GS	CG	SV	IP	H	R	ER	BB	SO	B	T	HT	WT	DOB	1st Yr	Resides
Alberro, Jose	0	0	3.38	1	0	0	0	3	4	2	1	1	1	R	R	6-2	190	6-29-69	1991	Arecibo, P.R.
Blanco, Alberto	3	2	3.75	37	4	0	1	72	58	37	30	37	62	L	L	6-1	200	6-27-76	1993	Miranda, Venez.
Bruner, Clay	1	3	8.88	7	5	0	1	25	47	32	25	10	9	R	R	6-3	180	10-16-76	1995	Weatherford, Okla.
Cordero, Francisco	4	1	1.38	47	0	0	27	52	35	9	8	22	58	R	R	6-2	200	8-11-77	1994	Santo Domingo, D.R.
Darwin, David	14	12	3.56	28	28	3	0	187	194	95	74	58	100	L	L	6-0	185	12-19-73	1996	Cornelius, N.C.
Garcia, Apostol	0	0	0.00	3	0	0	0	4	0	0	0	1	0	R	R	6-0	155	8-3-76	1994	Las Matas de Farfan, D.R.
Goldsmith, Gary	3	4	3.87	33	5	0	2	79	84	35	34	24	30	R	R	6-2	205	7-4-71	1993	Alamogordo, N.M.
Hiljus, Erik	1	0	1.04	10	0	0	0	17	5	4	2	5	28	R	R	6-5	230	12-25-72	1991	Northridge, Calif.
Keagle, Greg	4	2	2.85	9	9	1	0	54	58	22	17	22	28	R	R	6-2	195	6-28-71	1993	Horseheads, N.Y.
Maroth, Mike	1	2	4.79	4	4	0	0	21	27	15	11	7	10	L	L	6-0	180	8-17-77	1998	Orlando, Fla.
Martinez, Romulo	3	7	4.98	52	0	0	1	72	85	48	40	21	46	R	R	6-1	170	12-5-74	1994	Santiago, D.R.
Miles, Chad	3	2	6.14	45	0	0	0	59	78	49	40	30	50	S	L	6-3	195	2-26-73	1994	Renton, Wash.
Miller, Matt	4	1	4.43	7	7	0	0	41	43	23	20	12	25	L	L	6-3	175	8-2-74	1996	Lubbock, Texas
Pettyjohn, Adam	9	5	4.69	20	20	0	0	127	134	76	66	35	92	R	L	6-3	190	6-11-77	1998	Exeter, Calif.
Romo, Greg	2	2	8.27	8	3	0	0	21	29	20	19	7	15	L	R	6-2	165	5-14-75	1995	Wasco, Calif.
Santos, Victor	12	6	3.49	28	28	2	0	173	150	86	67	58	146	R	R	6-3	175	10-2-76	1995	Garfield, N.J.
Smith, Keilan	1	2	6.61	19	0	0	0	31	35	25	23	23	24	R	R	6-4	175	12-20-73	1993	Memphis, Tenn.
Snyder, Bill	1	0	2.50	14	0	0	2	18	16	6	5	5	17	R	R	6-0	190	1-29-75	1997	Hannibal, N.Y.
Swartzbaugh, Dave	0	4	10.25	6	5	0	0	26	36	31	30	12	22	R	R	6-2	205	2-11-68	1989	Glenshaw, Pa.
Villafuerte, Brandon	0	2	1.88	15	0	0	5	24	17	6	5	12	20	R	R	5-11	165	12-17-75	1995	Morgan Hill, Calif.
Weaver, Jeff	0	0	3.00	1	1	0	0	6	5	2	2	0	6	R	R	6-5	200	8-22-76	1998	Simi Valley, Calif.
Webb, Alan	9	9	4.95	26	22	0	0	140	140	87	77	64	88	L	L	5-10	165	9-26-79	1997	Las Vegas, Nev.

FIELDING

Catcher	PCT	G	PO	A	E	DP	PB
Cardona	.983	88	565	58	11	7	13
Lindstrom	.988	52	306	30	4	5	4
Rivera	1.000	7	46	4	0	1	0

First Base	PCT	G	PO	A	E	DP
Freire	.980	33	259	28	6	18
Ibarra	.923	2	12	0	1	1
Jones	.991	106	963	58	9	93
Lemonis	1.000	2	29	0	0	2
Lindstrom	1.000	1	2	1	0	0

Second Base	PCT	G	PO	A	E	DP
Lemonis	.968	25	63	57	4	16
Santana	.969	119	277	338	20	85

Third Base	PCT	G	PO	A	E	DP
Gillespie	.902	31	18	65	9	6
Lemonis	1.000	3	0	10	0	0
Sasser	.911	109	82	276	35	27

Shortstop	PCT	G	PO	A	E	DP
Lemonis	.911	21	28	54	8	10
Mitchell	.936	123	155	361	35	67

Outfield	PCT	G	PO	A	E	DP
Airoso	.987	134	362	12	5	3
Candelaria	.964	118	180	10	7	1
Freire	1.000	4	9	0	0	0
Gillespie	.985	64	124	6	2	3
Lemonis	1.000	4	6	0	0	0
Lindsey	.929	7	12	1	1	0
Lindstrom	1.000	6	6	1	0	0
Riley	.963	43	78	0	3	0
Wakeland	.944	54	97	4	6	0

FLORIDA STATE LEAGUE

BATTING	AVG	G	AB	R	H	2B	3B	HR	RBI	BB	SO	SB	CS	B	T	HT	WT	DOB	1st Yr	Resides
Bautista, Rayner	.228	96	303	35	69	11	4	1	32	21	75	7	3	R	R	5-11	155	8-17-79	1996	Nizao, D.R.
Besco, Dave	.287	122	456	70	131	28	4	9	66	37	88	10	7	R	R	6-2	200	1-21-76	1998	Westland, Mich.
Bunkley, Antuan	.272	133	493	52	134	26	0	4	69	49	69	1	1	R	R	6-1	205	9-20-75	1994	West Palm Beach, Fla.
Capellan, Rene	.177	34	113	14	20	2	0	1	9	3	10	2	2	R	R	5-11	160	4-24-78	1995	Santo Domingo, D.R.
Casanova, Raul	.500	4	12	3	6	2	0	1	6	0	1	0	0	S	R	6-0	195	8-23-72	1990	Ponce, P.R.
Forbush, Nate	.288	84	250	38	72	14	0	5	28	43	62	1	3	S	R	6-2	220	11-7-75	1998	West Jordan, Utah
Freeman, Terrance	.278	101	381	64	106	19	2	0	47	43	59	37	12	S	R	5-10	180	1-24-75	1995	Brandon, Fla.
Freire, Alejandro	.220	13	41	6	9	3	0	1	5	10	7	0	0	R	R	6-2	185	8-23-74	1992	Caracas, Venez.
Grimmett, Ryan	.203	50	133	32	27	4	1	3	16	25	41	24	4	R	R	5-9	165	3-4-75	1997	Cincinnati, Ohio
Lauterhahn, Dan	.270	63	152	19	41	7	1	2	14	13	22	4	3	R	R	6-1	175	4-23-76	1997	Wallington, N.J.
Lindsey, Rodney	.266	120	485	81	129	20	8	7	51	25	129	61	20	S	R	5-8	175	1-28-76	1994	Opelika, Ala.
Lutz, Manuel	.288	46	177	19	51	15	0	3	23	9	45	0	2	L	R	6-2	230	6-14-76	1995	Spring Valley, Calif.
Moore, LaCarlo	.245	36	94	15	23	4	1	0	6	9	18	6	3	L	R	5-10	175	1-15-76	1998	Chicago, Ill.
Mora, Juan	.125	3	8	1	1	1	0	0	0	3	0	0	0	L	L	5-11	170	11-26-77	1998	Bayamon, P.R.
Munson, Eric	.333	2	6	0	2	0	0	0	1	1	1	0	0	L	R	6-3	220	10-3-77	1999	San Diego, Calif.
Nelson, Bryce	.286	3	7	0	2	0	0	0	0	0	1	0	0	R	R	5-10	165	3-30-79	1998	San Diego, Calif.
Ozarowski, Rich	.272	52	173	24	47	8	6	2	23	14	23	4	1	S	R	5-9	175	10-19-74	1997	Boca Raton, Fla.
Parker, Chris	.125	3	8	1	1	0	0	0	0	0	3	0	0	R	R	6-2	185	8-16-79	1997	Thousand Oaks, Calif.
Rios, Brian	.281	119	430	60	121	27	7	6	44	24	47	7	3	R	R	6-3	190	7-25-74	1996	Corona, Calif.
Rivera, Mike	.278	104	370	44	103	20	2	14	72	20	59	1	1	R	R	6-0	190	9-8-76	1997	Bayamon, P.R.
Steele, Alex	.212	16	52	3	11	3	0	0	3	6	17	0	0	R	R	6-3	225	12-9-75	1997	Harrington Park, N.J.
Vargas, Arias	.122	21	41	2	5	0	0	0	2	4	13	0	0	R	R	6-0	185	3-1-78	1996	Santo Domingo, D.R.
Wakeland, Chris	.412	4	17	3	7	1	0	0	7	0	0	1	0	L	L	6-0	185	6-15-74	1996	St. Helens, Ore.
Wood, Jason	.235	5	17	0	4	0	0	0	1	4	2	0	1	R	R	6-1	190	12-16-69	1991	Fresno, Calif.
Zapata, Alexis	.245	115	404	52	99	15	5	5	45	33	116	7	5	R	R	6-3	190	5-20-77	1996	Santo Domingo, D.R.

GAMES BY POSITION: C—Casanova 3, Forbush 34, Parker 3, Rivera 94, Vargas 18. 1B—Bunkley 102, Forbush 36, Freire 6, Lutz 3, Rios 1, Wood 1. 2B—Capellan 13, Freeman 100, Lauterhahn 7, Nelson 2, Ozarowski 23, Wood 1. 3B—Capellan 7, Lutz 7, Moore 1, Ozarowski 10, Rios 117. SS—Bautista 93, Lauterhahn 47, Ozarowski 6, Wood 3. OF—Besco 94, Capellan 3, Grimmett 45, Lindsey 117, Lutz 30, Moore 28, Mora 3, Wakeland 4.

PITCHING	W	L	ERA	G	GS	CG	SV	IP	H	R	ER	BB	SO	B	T	HT	WT	DOB	1st Yr	Resides
Baginski, Tom	0	0	6.43	6	0	0	0	7	10	5	5	7	5	L	L	5-11	185	1-3-77	1999	Pittsburgh, Pa.
Bauder, Mike	1	3	4.40	28	0	0	1	43	56	22	21	19	30	L	L	5-9	171	5-13-75	1996	Las Vegas, Nev.
Buller, Sean	0	0	9.00	1	0	0	0	3	4	3	3	2	2	L	L	6-5	235	11-28-75	1998	Signal Hill, Calif.
Castillo, Jose	2	1	2.63	8	0	0	0	14	7	4	4	5	11	R	R	6-2	170	6-12-77	1994	Santo Domingo, D.R.
Cepeda, Victor	0	6	7.07	11	3	0	0	28	41	27	22	15	23	R	R	6-0	160	4-3-78	1997	Loiza, P.R.
Davis, Keith	3	0	3.41	25	0	0	0	34	36	15	13	10	24	R	R	6-2	210	11-1-72	1991	Vacherie, La.
2-team (11 Tampa)	5	1	3.04	36	0	0	0	50	53	24	17	15	39							
Durkovic, Peter	1	1	4.71	17	0	0	3	21	19	12	11	5	11	L	L	6-4	215	7-9-73	1995	Flushing, N.Y.
Florie, Bryce	0	0	0.00	1	1	0	0	3	0	0	0	0	7	R	R	5-11	192	5-21-70	1988	Goose Creek, S.C.
Greisinger, Seth	0	0	3.86	1	1	0	0	5	2	2	2	1	2	R	R	6-3	200	7-29-75	1996	Falls Church, Va.
Hiljus, Erik	0	0	2.25	3	0	0	0	4	4	1	1	0	9	R	R	6-5	230	12-25-72	1991	Northridge, Calif.
Hostetler, Jim	0	0	8.49	31	0	0	0	41	51	44	39	31	27	R	R	6-7	230	7-19-76	1998	Yorba Linda, Calif.
Infante, Asdrubal	0	1	4.50	1	1	0	0	4	6	2	2	3	3	R	R	6-1	185	9-28-81	1999	Guanta, Venez.
Johnson, Craig	11	11	5.13	26	25	0	0	144	176	93	82	31	98	R	R	6-3	200	11-8-75	1997	Tuftonboro, N.H.
Keagle, Greg	1	3	4.50	6	6	0	0	36	35	19	18	13	26	R	R	6-2	195	6-28-71	1993	Horseheads, N.Y.
Kirsten, Rick	2	0	0.54	2	2	1	0	17	7	1	1	6	8	R	R	6-0	165	7-23-78	1996	Rolling Meadows, Ill.
Loux, Shane	6	5	4.05	17	17	0	0	91	92	48	41	47	52	R	R	6-2	205	8-13-79	1997	Gilbert, Ariz.
Maroth, Mike	2	1	3.24	3	3	0	0	17	18	7	6	7	11	L	L	6-0	180	8-17-77	1998	Orlando, Fla.
2-team (20 Sarasota)	13	7	3.94	23	22	0	0	128	142	72	56	42	75							
Miller, Matt	4	9	4.15	19	19	1	0	108	108	58	50	45	82	L	L	6-3	175	8-2-74	1996	Lubbock, Texas
Mobley, Kevin	7	4	3.82	46	5	0	2	97	107	48	41	26	73	R	R	6-7	245	1-26-75	1997	Vidalia, Ga.
Pettyjohn, Adam	3	4	3.77	9	9	2	0	60	62	35	25	11	51	R	L	6-3	190	6-11-77	1998	Exeter, Calif.
Pineda, Luis	0	1	1.04	8	0	0	0	9	6	2	1	7	8	R	R	6-1	160	6-10-78	1995	Santo Domingo, D.R.
Quintal, Craig	1	11	4.84	26	16	2	2	110	129	74	59	27	45	R	R	6-0	190	1-21-75	1996	New Orleans, La.
Ramirez, Jose	5	5	5.00	29	6	0	0	85	79	53	47	46	62	L	L	6-1	170	9-1-75	1994	Santo Domingo, D.R.
Rodney, Fernando	1	0	1.42	4	0	0	2	6	7	1	1	1	5	R	R	5-11	180	3-17-81	1997	Santo Domingo, D.R.
Romo, Greg	8	4	3.49	25	15	1	2	106	90	46	41	46	89	L	R	6-2	165	5-14-75	1995	Wasco, Calif.
Smith, Clint	3	2	5.06	7	7	0	0	37	42	29	21	18	32	R	R	6-4	185	9-4-76	1998	Claremore, Okla.
Snyder, Bill	4	1	1.92	47	0	0	16	52	34	13	11	18	39	R	R	6-0	190	1-29-75	1997	Hannibal, N.Y.
Spear, Russell	0	0	9.24	8	2	0	0	13	15	17	13	24	8	R	R	6-3	190	8-30-77	1995	Albanvale, Australia

WEST MICHIGAN — Class A

MIDWEST LEAGUE

BATTING	AVG	G	AB	R	H	2B	3B	HR	RBI	BB	SO	SB	CS	B	T	HT	WT	DOB	1st Yr	Resides
Boone, Matt	.242	116	421	46	102	24	1	9	56	29	119	8	7	R	R	6-2	175	7-18-79	1997	Villa Park, Calif.
Bush, Ron	.255	118	444	56	113	23	4	1	60	44	57	14	10	R	R	6-1	170	10-10-76	1998	Glen Allen, Va.
Cedeno, Jesus	.236	47	157	14	37	9	0	3	16	6	34	3	3	R	R	5-11	160	6-24-76	1994	Santo Domingo, D.R.
Da Luz, Craig	.264	87	314	36	83	14	5	3	49	20	46	3	1	R	R	6-3	195	2-4-75	1998	San Diego, Calif.
Daigle, Leo	.276	108	406	59	112	36	1	5	60	33	121	3	0	R	R	6-3	225	9-18-79	1998	Spring Valley, Calif.
Fick, Robert	.273	3	11	2	3	0	0	0	2	0	1	0	1	L	R	6-1	189	3-15-74	1996	Thousand Oaks, Calif.
Gomez, Richard	.303	130	479	89	145	26	12	8	81	54	122	66	10	R	R	5-11	185	8-19-77	1997	San Francisco de Macoris, D.R.
Inge, Brandon	.244	100	352	54	86	25	2	9	46	39	87	15	3	R	R	5-11	185	5-19-77	1998	Evington, Va.
Jimenez, Carlos	.228	87	272	57	62	12	2	3	24	49	78	14	5	R	R	5-11	160	5-26-80	1997	San Pedro de Macoris, D.R.
Meran, Jorge	.197	44	152	18	30	9	4	2	23	7	38	1	3	R	R	6-1	168	6-18-77	1994	Santo Domingo, D.R.
Moore, LaCarlo	.299	43	164	27	49	4	1	0	17	16	26	8	3	L	R	5-10	170	1-15-76	1998	Chicago, Ill.
Munson, Eric	.266	67	252	42	67	16	1	14	44	37	47	3	1	L	R	6-3	220	10-3-77	1999	San Diego, Calif.
Reyes, Deurys	.246	46	134	23	33	11	3	5	27	16	53	8	1	L	L	5-11	155	8-8-79	1996	Santo Domingo, D.R.
Rich, Billy	.251	108	394	64	99	20	1	9	50	47	87	6	4	R	R	6-2	205	7-26-76	1998	Meriden, Conn.
Runnells, T.J.	.229	88	288	35	66	10	1	0	32	29	42	5	4	R	R	5-10	160	2-15-78	1997	Greeley, Colo.
Sassanella, Jeremy	.073	14	41	2	3	1	0	0	6	1	18	0	0	S	R	6-1	225	10-21-78	1997	Auburn, Ind.
Torres, Andres	.236	117	407	72	96	20	5	2	34	92	116	39	18	S	R	5-10	175	1-26-78	1998	Aguada, P.R.

GAMES BY POSITION: C—Fick 1, Inge 95, Meran 40, Munson 5. 1B—da Luz 39, Daigle 72, Fick 1, Munson 33, Sassanella 1. 2B—Bush 64, Runnells 83. 3B—Boone 105, Bush 1, da Luz 39. SS—Bush 57, Jimenez 87. OF—Cedeno 34, da Luz 2, Gomez 115, Moore 30, Reyes 37, Rich 101, Torres 112.

PITCHING	W	L	ERA	G	GS	CG	SV	IP	H	R	ER	BB	SO	B	T	HT	WT	DOB	1st Yr	Resides
Bernero, Adam	8	4	2.54	15	15	2	0	96	75	36	27	23	80	R	R	6-4	205	11-28-76	1999	Elk Grove, Calif.
Bess, Stephen	1	1	0.93	12	0	0	3	19	12	2	2	7	23	R	R	6-4	225	9-1-76	1999	Nashville, Tenn.
Buller, Sean	10	10	4.94	31	17	0	0	120	133	78	66	55	72	L	L	6-5	235	11-28-75	1998	Signal Hill, Calif.
Cornejo, Nate	9	11	3.71	28	28	4	0	175	173	87	72	67	125	R	R	6-5	200	9-24-79	1998	Wellington, Kan.
Frasor, Jason	2	1	2.63	4	4	1	0	24	17	10	7	9	33	R	R	5-10	170	8-9-77	1999	Oak Forest, Ill.
Gutierrez, Laz	2	1	4.66	35	0	0	1	46	50	26	24	15	56	L	L	6-2	195	2-7-76	1998	Hialeah, Fla.
Heams, Shane	5	4	2.35	51	0	0	10	69	41	26	18	39	101	R	R	6-1	175	9-29-75	1995	Lambertville, Mich.
Kalita, Tim	4	1	4.18	9	9	0	0	47	46	26	22	27	35	R	L	6-2	220	11-21-78	1999	Oak Park, Ill.
Keller, Kris	5	3	2.92	49	0	0	8	77	63	28	25	31	78	R	R	6-2	225	3-1-78	1996	Atlantic Beach, Fla.
Koutrouba, Tom	3	2	5.40	31	11	0	0	85	110	56	51	24	46	L	L	6-0	190	10-9-77	1998	North Attleboro, Mass.
Loux, Shane	1	3	6.27	8	8	0	0	47	55	39	33	16	43	R	R	6-2	205	8-13-79	1997	Gilbert, Ariz.
Madson, Will	1	2	10.13	8	0	0	0	8	15	10	9	6	9	R	R	6-0	215	4-18-76	1998	Sheboygan, Wis.
McGowan, Brian	2	5	5.05	39	0	0	0	62	66	58	35	47	40	R	R	6-4	245	12-14-76	1998	Sunnyside, N.Y.
Pineda, Luis	0	2	3.57	34	0	3	0	40	30	18	16	26	55	R	R	6-1	160	6-10-78	1995	Santo Domingo, D.R.
Roberts, Rick	0	0	12.00	1	1	0	0	3	5	5	4	2	1	L	L	6-1	175	5-20-79	1997	Summer Hill, Pa.
Sismondo, Bobby	9	12	3.67	27	27	1	0	169	153	86	69	62	135	L	L	6-1	180	11-14-76	1998	Mingo Junction, Ohio
Smith, Clint	4	7	4.23	20	14	0	0	87	86	60	41	48	73	R	R	6-4	185	9-4-76	1998	Claremore, Okla.
Yount, Andy	2	2	5.61	24	3	0	1	43	38	31	27	36	28	R	R	6-2	185	2-14-77	1995	Kingwood, Texas

ONEONTA — Short-Season Class A

NEW YORK-PENN LEAGUE

BATTING	AVG	G	AB	R	H	2B	3B	HR	RBI	BB	SO	SB	CS	B	T	HT	WT	DOB	1st Yr	Resides
Beam, Dusty	.170	50	165	20	28	5	0	0	3	17	45	2	1	R	R	6-2	205	4-18-77	1999	Tipp City, Ohio

Organization Statistics

BATTING	AVG	G	AB	R	H	2B	3B	HR	RBI	BB	SO	SB	CS	B	T	HT	WT	DOB	1st Yr	Resides
Drobiak, Jayson	.225	31	102	10	23	8	1	0	14	4	23	2	3	L	R	6-2	190	3-3-79	1999	Jewett, Conn.
Gordon, Johnny	.155	44	110	13	17	4	3	0	5	14	30	4	1	L	L	6-2	205	2-7-77	1999	Naples, Fla.
Hlousek, Robert	.220	36	109	15	24	3	0	0	3	12	11	9	1	R	R	5-9	175	7-29-77	1999	Waukegan, Ill.
Jackson, Kevin	.216	38	125	11	27	5	0	3	20	11	48	2	0	R	R	6-0	205	9-28-77	1999	Lake City, Fla.
Lara, Balmes	.276	63	232	30	64	10	4	7	37	14	63	9	1	R	R	6-3	180	6-19-78	1996	Santo Domingo, D.R.
McKinney, Antonio	.249	68	229	36	57	9	1	2	20	18	60	26	4	R	R	5-10	175	1-2-78	1996	Portland, Ore.
Nelson, Reggie	.237	67	249	44	59	11	3	1	20	36	42	32	8	R	R	5-10	165	3-30-79	1998	San Diego, Calif.
Nunez, Hector	.284	33	102	6	29	9	2	0	15	6	13	0	0	R	R	5-10	170	8-7-77	1996	Santo Domingo, D.R.
Parker, Chris	.198	38	116	10	23	5	0	2	17	12	38	0	1	R	R	6-2	185	8-16-79	1997	Thousand Oaks, Calif.
Reyes, Deurys	.342	12	38	8	13	3	1	2	9	5	12	3	0	L	L	5-11	155	8-8-79	1996	Santo Domingo, D.R.
Richardson, Corey	.264	41	125	25	33	2	1	0	9	25	34	19	4	R	R	6-0	165	3-9-77	1999	Lone Star, Texas
Santiago, Ramon	.340	12	50	9	17	1	2	1	8	2	12	5	0	S	R	5-11	150	8-31-81	1998	Las Matas de Farfan, D.R.
Sassanella, Jeremy	.271	54	170	16	46	7	0	0	13	13	57	1	0	R	R	6-1	225	10-21-78	1997	Auburn, Ind.
Siegfried, Jason	.164	24	61	6	10	3	0	0	3	6	28	0	0	R	R	6-2	225	10-13-76	1999	Alliance, Ohio
St. Pierre, Maxim	.251	51	175	12	44	7	0	1	22	11	29	9	0	R	R	6-0	175	4-17-80	1997	Montreal, Quebec
Ust, Brant	.261	58	226	23	59	12	3	5	34	16	54	3	4	R	R	6-2	200	7-17-78	1999	Redmond, Wash.
Williamson, Casey	.245	48	139	19	34	8	0	1	15	14	38	5	1	L	L	6-2	200	10-10-76	1998	Dothan, Ala.

GAMES BY POSITION: C—Parker 36, Siegfried 8, St. Pierre 42. **1B**—Jackson 30, Sassanella 54. **2B**—Drobiak 4, Hlousek 33, Nelson 44. **3B**—Beam 4, Drobiak 14, Nunez 17, Ust 48. **SS**—Beam 45, Nelson 20, Santiago 12. **OF**—Gordon 31, Lara 57, McKinney 62, Reyes 9, Richardson 37, Williamson 45.

PITCHING	W	L	ERA	G	GS	CG	SV	IP	H	R	ER	BB	SO	B	T	HT	WT	DOB	1st Yr	Resides
Baginski, Tom	1	1	4.50	3	0	0	1	6	8	4	3	4	6	L	L	5-11	185	1-3-77	1999	Pittsburgh, Pa.
Barnett, Aaron	5	0	5.05	23	0	0	0	36	35	21	20	22	35	L	L	6-2	196	3-25-77	1999	Smyrna, Tenn.
Bess, Stephen	0	0	1.06	7	1	0	2	17	9	2	2	7	23	R	R	6-4	225	9-1-76	1999	Nashville, Tenn.
Burke, Erick	1	1	8.82	15	0	0	0	16	28	26	16	25	15	L	L	6-4	230	8-14-77	1999	Houston, Texas
Chipperfield, Calvin	4	4	3.28	15	15	0	0	80	55	32	29	33	83	R	R	6-1	170	3-7-78	1998	Adelaide, Australia
Frasor, Jason	3	3	1.69	12	11	0	0	59	36	16	11	22	69	R	R	5-10	170	8-9-77	1999	Oak Forest, Ill.
Johnston, Rikki	1	6	4.05	12	12	1	0	60	57	33	27	30	36	L	L	6-4	185	4-2-81	1998	Victoria, Australia
Kalita, Tim	0	0	0.00	3	3	0	0	12	3	1	0	5	15	R	L	6-2	220	11-21-78	1999	Oak Park, Ill.
Law, Keith	2	2	3.40	22	1	0	2	45	35	23	17	28	32	R	R	6-2	165	1-12-77	1998	Hiram, Ga.
Leek, Randy	6	3	1.56	21	3	1	1	63	58	16	11	9	66	L	L	6-0	175	4-18-77	1999	Levittown, N.Y.
Marx, Tommy	2	1	3.22	6	4	0	0	22	20	14	8	13	19	R	L	6-7	200	9-5-79	1998	West Bloomfield, Mich.
McDonald, Corey	3	3	4.67	19	0	0	0	35	34	18	18	23	30	L	L	6-3	200	10-2-76	1999	Greensboro, N.C.
Rivera, Homero	5	2	2.72	23	0	0	0	50	44	19	15	22	47	R	L	5-10	160	8-13-78	1995	Nizao, D.R.
Rowe, Casey	3	4	3.43	15	15	1	0	76	76	42	29	30	50	R	R	6-3	210	9-7-78	1999	Fresno, Calif.
VanHekken, Andrew	4	2	2.15	11	10	0	0	67	57	17	16	16	50	L	L	6-3	175	7-31-79	1998	Holland, Mich.
Watson, Greg	1	1	3.21	31	0	0	19	34	23	18	12	17	33	R	R	6-2	170	1-8-77	1999	Tampa, Fla.

LAKELAND — Rookie

GULF COAST LEAGUE

BATTING	AVG	G	AB	R	H	2B	3B	HR	RBI	BB	SO	SB	CS	B	T	HT	WT	DOB	1st Yr	Resides
Altagen, Matt	.250	3	8	0	2	0	0	0	2	1	4	2	0	R	L	6-2	180	9-5-79	1998	Malibu, Calif.
Anderson, Nat	.130	19	46	6	6	2	0	0	3	11	16	5	0	L	R	6-4	195	8-8-81	1999	South Australia, Australia
Campos, Juan	.218	43	147	23	32	6	0	0	12	17	29	12	7	S	R	5-8	155	3-12-80	1996	Caracas, Venez.
Casanova, Raul	.800	2	5	1	4	0	0	1	1	0	0	1	5	S	R	6-0	195	8-23-72	1990	Ponce, P.R.
Cleveland, Russell	.311	37	132	13	41	5	0	0	13	5	33	2	2	R	R	6-3	205	12-26-79	1998	Las Vegas, Nev.
Davis, Daniel	.184	45	147	14	27	6	0	1	11	23	59	2	2	L	L	6-2	195	6-11-81	1999	Kissimmee, Fla.
DeShetler, Chris	.298	33	114	17	34	5	2	2	21	15	15	1	1	L	R	5-10	180	12-25-76	1999	Allen Park, Mich.
Fick, Robert	.333	3	9	2	3	1	0	0	2	2	0	1	0	L	R	6-1	189	3-15-74	1996	Thousand Oaks, Calif.
Infante, Omar	.268	25	97	11	26	4	0	0	7	4	11	4	0	R	R	6-0	150	12-26-81	1999	Guanta, Venez.
Jenkins, Neil	.297	33	111	18	33	13	3	2	15	16	37	2	1	R	R	6-5	210	7-17-80	1999	Jupiter, Fla.
Leer, David	.271	32	107	12	29	3	2	0	12	7	26	11	4	R	R	6-1	175	2-2-77	1997	San Nicolas, Aruba
Leonardo, Santos	.258	32	116	16	31	6	1	0	13	14	31	12	7	R	R	5-11	170	8-8-81	1997	Guaymate, D.R.
Nunez, Hector	.308	10	26	4	8	4	0	0	6	4	3	4	1	R	R	5-10	170	8-7-77	1996	Santo Domingo, D.R.
Reynolds, Dustin	.241	19	54	5	13	2	1	0	5	10	6	1	2	S	R	5-10	170	3-24-77	1999	Littlestown, Pa.
Rodriguez, Steve	.275	50	178	18	49	14	0	4	29	11	50	2	2	R	R	6-4	210	1-28-78	1998	Arcadia, Calif.
Ross, Cody	.218	42	142	19	31	8	3	4	18	16	28	3	1	R	L	5-11	180	12-23-80	1999	Carlsbad, N.M.
Santiago, Ramon	.321	35	134	25	43	9	2	0	11	9	17	20	7	S	R	5-11	150	8-31-81	1998	Las Matas de Farfan, D.R.
Tolli, Barry	.241	43	137	19	33	7	1	2	17	15	39	12	3	R	R	6-2	195	8-17-79	1998	Newbury Park, Calif.
Vargas, Inakel	.400	5	10	2	4	0	0	1	2	1	1	0	0	R	R	6-0	185	3-1-78	1999	Santo Domingo, D.R.
Wakeland, Chris	.071	4	14	2	1	0	0	0	1	6	4	0	0	L	L	6-0	185	6-15-74	1996	St. Helens, Ore.
Ware, Anthony	.186	33	102	11	19	2	0	2	8	6	48	0	0	R	R	6-0	180	1-7-81	1999	Los Angeles, Calif.
Yingling, Joe	.091	5	11	2	1	1	0	0	0	3	6	0	0	R	R	6-1	185	9-25-80	1999	Camarillo, Calif.

GAMES BY POSITION: C—Casanova 2, Cleveland 36, Fick 1, Reynolds 19, Vargas 2, Yingling 5. **1B**—Anderson 13, Fick 1, Rodriguez 48, Vargas 2. **2B**—Campos 43, DeShetler 17, Nunez 1. **3B**—DeShetler 11, Jenkins 22, Nunez 9, Ware 19. **SS**—O. Infante 20, Santiago 35. **OF**—Altagen 1, Davis 37, Leer 23, Leonardo 36, Ross 41, Tolli 41, Wakeland 4.

PITCHING	W	L	ERA	G	GS	CG	SV	IP	H	R	ER	BB	SO	B	T	HT	WT	DOB	1st Yr	Resides
Arias, Pablo	3	2	3.02	12	12	1	0	66	57	31	22	22	60	R	R	6-2	160	1-9-79	1996	Bani, D.R.
Baginski, Tom	2	0	1.80	10	0	0	0	20	11	4	4	4	24	L	L	5-11	185	1-3-77	1999	Pittsburgh, Pa.
Diaz, Luis	1	2	1.99	22	0	0	2	32	24	9	7	20	36	R	R	6-1	180	12-3-78	1998	Aguas Buenas, P.R.
Earl, Ryan	3	2	4.58	7	7	0	0	37	34	20	19	18	20	L	L	6-6	175	8-24-80	1998	Thousand Oaks, Calif.
Fuell, Jerrod	0	3	8.05	6	6	0	0	19	29	19	17	13	8	R	R	6-4	210	10-3-80	1999	Tucson, Ariz.
Infante, Asdrubal	3	0	1.09	15	2	1	2	33	17	5	4	20	51	R	R	6-1	185	9-28-81	1999	Guanta, Venez.
Kirsten, Rick	1	1	5.26	11	4	0	0	26	18	15	15	17	27	R	R	6-0	165	7-23-78	1996	Rolling Meadows, Ill.
Lewis, Jeremy	4	5	2.70	10	10	0	0	40	34	16	12	28	31	R	L	6-4	180	9-12-80	1999	Concord, N.C.
Lima, Frank	1	5	4.28	20	3	0	0	48	48	28	23	14	53	R	R	6-2	190	5-20-79	1997	Santiago, D.R.
Marx, Tommy	3	2	3.43	8	8	0	0	42	35	24	16	32	39	R	L	6-7	200	9-5-79	1998	West Bloomfield, Mich.
Rivera, Samuel	1	0	2.35	7	1	0	1	15	9	6	4	11	19	R	R	6-0	170	4-7-80	1997	San Pedro de Macoris, D.R.
Rodney, Fernando	0	3	2.40	22	0	0	9	30	20	8	8	21	39	R	R	5-11	170	3-17-81	1997	Santo Domingo, D.R.
Serrano, Willy	0	3	6.39	6	5	0	0	25	30	19	18	13	14	R	R	6-1	160	3-13-81	1997	Santo Domingo, D.R.
Taylor, Jason	3	5	2.97	18	1	0	0	33	33	15	11	17	26	R	R	6-5	205	7-14-76	1999	Parkersburg, W.Va.
Torres, Alex	1	1	7.23	13	1	0	0	24	28	20	19	25	15	R	L	6-2	210	11-15-78	1999	Bronx, N.Y.

FLORIDA MARLINS

Marlins lose 98 games, but see progress in 1999

BY MIKE BERARDINO

Perhaps their standards and expectations had become ridiculously low, but the Marlins still believed they made progress in 1999.

There was a 10-game improvement over the six-month nightmare that was the 1998 season. Not only did they avoid a second straight 100-loss season, going 64-98, but they also edged the Twins by percentage points to escape the majors' worst record.

And the organization managed to move another season away from the embarrassing talent dispersal that followed the World Series title. That was at least as important as anything that happened on the field.

Even as the losses mounted, the new-look Marlins refused to sulk. They took their cue from new owner John Henry and new manager John Boles, whose upbeat stewardship stood in sharp contrast to the performance of their predecessors, Wayne Huizenga and Jim Leyland.

On-field highlights included the comebacks of ace righthander Alex Fernandez and third baseman Mike Lowell. Fernandez, 18 months removed from major shoulder surgery, won seven games and would have ranked among the National League ERA leaders had he pitched enough innings to qualify. Lowell, acquired from the Yankees over the winter, learned he had testicular cancer on the eve of spring training. Surgery and the resulting radiation treatments kept Lowell from regaining his strength and swing until August, but he finished with a flourish.

A year after using 27 rookies, the Marlins received strong contributions from a smaller group of first-year players. Center fielder Preston Wilson hit .280-26-71 to

Preston Wilson   **Julio Ramirez**

Players of the Year

MAJOR LEAGUE: Preston Wilson, of
Wilson hit .280 in his first full major league season and led all rookies with 26 home runs.

MINOR LEAGUE: Julio Ramirez, of
Ramirez tied for sixth-best in the minor leagues with 64 steals and pounded out 53 extra-base hits at Portland.

make a late push for Rookie of the Year honors. Alex Gonzalez became the first NL rookie shortstop chosen for the All-Star Game in 55 years.

The payroll edged up slightly to $18 million, with $7 million of that going to Fernandez. Left fielder Cliff Floyd signed a four-year, $19 million contract before the season, then played just 69 games because of injuries.

General manager Dave Dombrowski continued the roster overhaul originally mandated by Huizenga, with an eye on a return to contention by 2002. Two more World Series heroes were traded, with second baseman Craig Counsell going to the Dodgers in a minor deal and Livan Hernandez going to the Giants for righthanders Jason Grilli and Nate Bump. Young closer Matt Mantei also was dealt, going to the Diamondbacks for righthanders Vladimir Nunez and Brad Penny.

The Marlins waded back into high-stakes international waters for the first time since signing Hernandez in February 1996. They signed 16-year-old shortstop Miguel Cabrera for a Venezuela-record $1.8 million.

Then there was Texas high school righthander Josh Beckett, the No. 2 overall pick in the June draft. It took nearly three months, but the Marlins managed to sign Beckett to a four-year, $7 million major league contract, easily eclipsing the franchise record ($1.6 million to Josh Booty in 1994).

The minor league system managed to improve its winning percentage by 18 points over the previous year (.459 to .477), despite a last-place showing at Triple-A Calgary. Just two affiliates had winning records, with Class A Kane County and short-season Utica both making the playoffs.

ORGANIZATION LEADERS

BATTING

*AVG	Joe Funaro, Portland	.366
R	Amaury Garcia, Calgary	94
H	Quincy Foster, Brevard County	167
TB	John Roskos, Calgary	278
2B	John Roskos, Calgary	44
3B	Julio Ramirez, Portland	10
HR	Chris Norton, Portland	38
RBI	Jose Santos, Kane County	105
BB	Jose Santos, Kane County	83
SO	Julio Ramirez, Portland	150
SB	Julio Ramirez, Portland	64

PITCHING

W	Gary Knotts, Portland/Brevard County	15
L	Mark Richards, Brevard County	14
#ERA	Nate Robertson, Kane County/Utica	2.45
G	Gabe Gonzalez, Calgary/Portland	50
CG	Scott Comer, Brevard County	5
SV	Hector Almonte, Portland	23
IP	Gary Knotts, Portland/Brevard County	176
BB	A.J. Burnett, Portland	71
SO	Michael Tejera, Calgary/Portland	157

*Minimum 250 At-Bats #Minimum 75 Innings

Florida
MARLINS

Manager: John Boles   **1999 Record:** 64-98, .395 (5th, NL East)

BATTING

BATTING	AVG	G	AB	R	H	2B	3B	HR	RBI	BB	SO	SB	CS	B	T	HT	WT	DOB	1st Yr	Resides
Aven, Bruce	.289	137	381	57	110	19	2	12	70	44	82	3	0	R	R	5-9	180	3-4-72	1994	Orange, Texas
Bautista, Danny	.288	70	205	32	59	10	1	5	24	4	30	3	0	R	R	5-11	170	5-24-72	1989	Santo Domingo, D.R.
Berg, Dave	.286	109	304	42	87	18	1	3	25	27	59	2	2	R	R	5-11	185	9-3-70	1993	Roseville, Calif.
Castillo, Luis	.302	128	487	76	147	23	4	0	28	67	85	50	17	S	R	5-11	175	9-12-75	1993	San Pedro de Macoris, D.R.
Castro, Ramon	.179	24	67	4	12	4	0	2	4	10	14	0	0	R	R	6-3	225	3-1-76	1994	Vega Baja, P.R.
Clapinski, Chris	.232	36	56	6	13	1	2	0	2	9	12	1	0	S	R	6-0	175	8-20-71	1992	Cape Canaveral, Fla.
Counsell, Craig	.152	37	66	4	10	1	0	0	2	5	10	0	0	L	R	6-0	175	8-21-70	1992	Fort Lauderdale, Fla.
Dunwoody, Todd	.220	64	186	20	41	6	3	2	20	12	41	3	4	L	L	6-1	195	4-11-75	1993	West Lafayette, Ind.
Fabregas, Jorge	.206	82	223	20	46	10	2	3	21	26	27	0	0	L	R	6-3	215	3-13-70	1991	Miami Beach, Fla.
Floyd, Cliff	.303	69	251	37	76	19	1	11	49	30	47	5	6	L	R	6-4	235	12-5-72	1991	Weston, Ill.
Garcia, Amaury	.250	10	24	6	6	0	1	2	2	3	11	0	0	R	R	5-10	160	5-20-75	1993	Santo Domingo, D.R.
Gonzalez, Alex	.277	136	560	81	155	28	8	14	59	15	113	3	5	R	R	6-0	170	2-15-77	1994	Turmero, Venez.
Hyers, Tim	.222	58	81	8	18	4	1	2	12	14	11	0	0	L	L	6-1	195	10-3-71	1990	Covington, Ga.
Kotsay, Mark	.271	148	495	57	134	23	9	8	50	29	50	7	6	L	L	6-0	190	12-2-75	1996	Sante Fe Springs, Calif.
Lee, Derrek	.206	70	218	21	45	9	1	5	20	17	70	2	1	R	R	6-5	225	9-6-75	1993	Folsom, Calif.
Lowell, Mike	.253	97	308	32	78	15	0	12	47	26	69	0	0	R	R	6-4	205	2-24-74	1995	Coral Gables, Fla.
Millar, Kevin	.285	105	351	48	100	17	4	9	67	40	64	1	0	R	R	6-0	185	9-24-71	1993	Encino, Calif.
Orie, Kevin	.254	77	240	26	61	16	0	6	29	22	43	1	0	R	R	6-4	215	9-1-72	1993	Pittsburgh, Pa.
Ramirez, Julio	.143	15	21	3	3	1	0	0	2	1	6	0	1	R	R	5-11	170	8-10-77	1994	Santo Domingo, D.R.
Redmond, Mike	.302	84	242	22	73	9	0	1	27	26	34	0	0	R	R	6-1	185	5-5-71	1993	Spokane, Wash.
Roskos, John	.167	13	12	0	2	2	0	0	1	1	7	0	0	R	R	5-11	195	11-19-74	1993	Rio Rancho, N.M.
Wilson, Preston	.280	149	482	67	135	21	4	26	71	46	156	11	4	R	R	6-2	193	7-19-74	1993	Eastover, S.C.

PITCHING

PITCHING	W	L	ERA	G	GS	CG	SV	IP	H	R	ER	BB	SO	B	T	HT	WT	DOB	1st Yr	Resides
Alfonseca, Antonio	4	5	3.24	73	0	0	21	78	79	28	28	29	46	R	R	6-5	235	4-16-72	1990	La Romana, D.R.
Almanza, Armando	0	1	1.72	14	0	0	0	16	8	4	3	9	20	L	L	6-3	205	10-26-72	1993	El Paso, Texas
Almonte, Hector	0	2	4.20	15	0	0	0	15	20	7	7	6	8	R	R	6-2	190	10-17-75	1993	Santo Domingo, D.R.
Billingsley, Brent	0	0	16.43	8	0	0	0	8	11	14	14	10	3	L	L	6-2	200	4-19-75	1996	Chino Hills, Calif.
Burnett, A.J.	4	2	3.48	7	7	0	0	41	37	23	16	25	33	R	R	6-5	205	1-3-77	1995	North Little Rock, Ark.
Corbin, Archie	0	1	7.29	17	0	0	0	21	25	20	17	15	30	R	R	6-4	230	12-30-67	1986	Beaumont, Texas
Cornelius, Reid	1	0	3.26	5	2	0	0	19	16	7	7	5	12	R	R	6-0	210	6-2-70	1989	West Palm Beach, Fla.
Darensbourg, Vic	0	1	8.83	56	0	0	0	35	50	36	34	21	16	L	L	5-10	165	11-13-70	1992	Las Vegas, Nev.
Dempster, Ryan	7	8	4.71	25	25	0	0	147	146	77	77	93	126	R	R	6-1	201	5-3-77	1995	Gibsons, B.C.
Edmondson, Brian	5	8	5.84	68	0	0	1	94	106	65	61	44	58	R	R	6-2	175	1-29-73	1991	Riverside, Calif.
Fernandez, Alex	7	8	3.38	24	24	1	0	141	135	60	53	41	91	R	R	6-1	225	8-13-69	1990	Miami Lakes, Fla.
Hernandez, Livan	5	9	4.76	20	20	2	0	136	161	78	72	55	97	R	R	6-2	225	2-20-75	1996	Miami Beach, Fla.
Looper, Braden	3	3	3.80	72	0	0	0	83	96	43	35	31	50	R	R	6-5	225	10-28-74	1996	Palm Beach Gardens, Fla.
Mantei, Matt	1	2	2.72	35	0	0	10	36	24	11	11	25	50	R	R	6-1	190	7-7-73	1991	Pembroke Pines, Fla.
Meadows, Brian	11	15	5.60	31	31	0	0	178	214	117	111	57	72	R	R	6-4	200	11-21-75	1994	Troy, Ala.
Medina, Rafael	1	1	5.79	20	0	0	0	23	20	15	15	20	16	R	R	6-3	240	2-15-75	1993	Panama City, Panama
Nunez, Vladimir	4	8	4.58	17	12	0	0	75	66	48	38	34	58	R	R	6-4	235	3-15-75	1996	Santo Domingo, D.R.
2-team (27 Arizona)	7	10	4.06	44	12	0	1	109	95	63	49	54	86							
Ojala, Kirt	0	1	14.34	8	1	0	0	11	21	17	17	6	5	L	L	6-2	215	12-24-68	1990	Grand Rapids, Mich.
Sanchez, Jesus	5	7	6.01	59	10	0	0	76	84	53	51	60	62	L	L	5-10	155	10-11-74	1992	Bani, D.R.
Springer, Dennis	6	16	4.86	38	29	3	1	196	231	121	106	64	83	R	R	5-10	185	2-12-65	1987	Fresno, Calif.
Tejera, Michael	0	0	11.37	3	1	0	0	6	10	8	8	5	7	L	L	5-9	175	10-18-76	1995	Miami, Fla.

FIELDING

Catcher	PCT	G	PO	A	E	DP	PB
Castro	.992	24	105	17	1	1	3
Fabregas	.989	78	404	52	5	2	4
Redmond	.992	82	444	45	4	5	3
Roskos	1.000	1	5	0	0	0	0

First Base	PCT	G	PO	A	E	DP
Hyers	1.000	14	71	3	0	6
Kotsay	1.000	19	104	8	0	9
Lee	.994	66	463	47	3	44
Millar	.995	94	720	52	4	80
Orie	1.000	1	1	0	0	1

Second Base	PCT	G	PO	A	E	DP
Berg	1.000	29	51	80	0	16
Castillo	.976	126	257	343	15	75
Clapinski	1.000	2	0	2	0	0
Counsell	.980	12	20	29	1	4
Garcia	.932	8	15	26	3	5

Third Base	PCT	G	PO	A	E	DP
Berg	.911	19	13	28	4	3
Clapinski	.882	9	6	9	2	1

	PCT	G	PO	A	E	DP
Lowell	.981	83	59	143	4	12
Millar	1.000	1	0	2	0	0
Orie	.961	64	51	120	7	8

Shortstop	PCT	G	PO	A	E	DP
Berg	.969	37	39	87	4	12
Clapinski	.955	6	9	12	1	4
Gonzalez	.955	135	237	339	27	85

Outfield	PCT	G	PO	A	E	DP
Aven	.984	102	181	4	3	1
Bautista	.979	60	140	3	3	0
Berg	.000	3	0	0	0	0
Clapinski	1.000	3	2	0	0	0
Dunwoody	.981	55	102	3	2	0
Floyd	.952	62	115	4	6	0
Hyers	1.000	15	15	0	0	0
Kotsay	.981	129	245	19	5	5
Millar	1.000	1	1	0	0	0
Ramirez	.950	11	19	0	1	0
Wilson	.973	136	320	10	9	1

DAVID SEELIG

Alex Gonzalez

Luis Castillo
Hit .302 with 50 steals

Wes Anderson
Struck out 134 at Kane County

FARM SYSTEM

Assistant General Manager: Dave Littlefield

Class	Farm Team	League	W	L	Pct.	Finish*	Manager	First Yr
AAA	Calgary (Alberta) Cannons	Pacific Coast	57	82	.410	15th (16)	Lynn Jones	1999
AA	Portland (Maine) Sea Dogs	Eastern	65	77	.458	t-9th (12)	Frank Cacciatore	1994
A#	Brevard County (Fla.) Manatees	Florida State	61	74	.452	12th (14)	Dave Huppert	1994
A	Kane County (Ill.) Cougars	Midwest	78	59	.569	1st (14)	Rick Renteria	1993
A	Utica (N.Y.) Blue Sox	New York-Penn	42	33	.560	2nd (14)	Ken Joyce	1996
Rookie	Melbourne (Fla.) Marlins	Gulf Coast	25	35	.417	12th (14)	Jon Deeble	1992

*Finish in overall standings (No. of teams in league)   #Advanced level

CALGARY   Class AAA

PACIFIC COAST LEAGUE

BATTING	AVG	G	AB	R	H	2B	3B	HR	RBI	BB	SO	SB	CS	B	T	HT	WT	DOB	1st Yr	Resides
Bautista, Danny	.319	38	135	25	43	8	1	8	28	11	18	3	3	R	R	5-11	170	5-24-72	1989	Santo Domingo, D.R.
Castro, Ramon	.258	97	349	43	90	22	0	15	61	24	64	0	0	R	R	6-3	225	3-1-76	1994	Vega Baja, P.R.
Clapinski, Chris	.322	81	267	51	86	21	6	8	35	30	53	5	1	S	R	6-0	175	8-20-71	1992	Cape Canaveral, Fla.
Duncan, Mariano	.200	2	5	0	1	1	0	0	0	0	2	0	0	R	R	6-0	185	3-13-63	1982	Miami, Fla.
Dunwoody, Todd	.272	65	246	35	67	16	7	9	36	10	56	7	8	L	L	6-1	195	4-11-75	1993	West Lafayette, Ind.
Floyd, Cliff	.387	9	31	6	12	1	0	3	8	2	8	0	1	L	R	6-4	235	12-5-72	1991	Weston, Ill.
Franco, Raul	.273	16	55	7	15	0	0	0	4	2	4	0	0	R	R	5-11	170	1-14-76	1994	San Pedro de Macoris, D.R.
Garcia, Amaury	.317	119	479	94	152	37	9	17	53	44	79	17	11	R	R	5-10	160	5-20-75	1993	Santo Domingo, D.R.
Gil, Benji	.279	116	412	74	115	29	1	17	64	27	101	17	5	R	R	6-2	190	10-6-72	1991	San Diego, Calif.
Gulan, Mike	.276	84	286	41	79	23	2	13	51	10	82	2	1	R	R	6-1	190	12-18-70	1992	Steubenville, Ohio
Hastings, Lionel	.267	34	75	8	20	4	1	1	4	5	13	2	0	R	R	5-9	165	1-26-73	1994	Hermosa Beach, Calif.
Hyers, Tim	.268	51	179	25	48	12	0	4	20	14	22	1	1	L	L	6-1	195	10-3-71	1990	Covington, Ga.
Jones, Jaime	.246	41	138	12	34	6	0	0	7	10	30	1	3	L	L	6-3	190	8-2-76	1995	Poway, Calif.
Lee, Derrek	.283	89	339	60	96	20	1	19	73	30	90	3	4	R	R	6-5	225	9-6-75	1993	Folsom, Calif.
Lobaton, Jose	.189	36	90	9	17	6	0	0	4	6	26	2	2	R	R	5-11	154	3-29-74	1992	Acarigua, Venez.
Lowell, Mike	.313	24	83	11	26	3	0	2	9	8	19	0	0	R	R	6-4	205	2-24-74	1995	Coral Gables, Fla.
Millar, Kevin	.301	36	143	24	43	11	1	7	26	11	19	2	0	R	R	6-0	185	9-24-71	1993	Encino, Calif.
Morman, Russ	.327	21	52	10	17	1	0	3	12	7	6	1	0	R	R	6-4	215	4-28-62	1983	Blue Springs, Mo.
Orie, Kevin	.319	23	72	10	23	9	0	3	8	13	7	0	0	R	R	6-4	215	9-1-72	1993	Pittsburgh, Pa.
Reese, Nate	.250	9	20	4	5	1	0	0	2	1	5	0	0	R	R	5-11	215	10-17-74	1997	Shawnee Mission, Kan.
Reeves, Glenn	.216	91	236	33	51	8	1	2	21	37	42	3	6	R	R	6-0	195	1-19-74	1993	Glen Waverly, Australia
Robertson, Ryan	.302	59	169	16	51	10	0	1	19	26	29	0	2	L	R	6-4	210	9-30-72	1996	Port Neches, Texas
Roskos, John	.320	134	506	85	162	44	0	24	90	52	112	2	1	R	R	5-11	195	11-19-74	1993	Rio Rancho, N.M.
Stovall, DaRond	.189	37	106	10	20	3	3	3	13	11	44	0	0	S	L	6-1	185	1-3-73	1991	East St. Louis, Ill.
Walton, Jerome	.321	26	84	12	27	8	1	0	12	5	12	5	1	R	R	6-1	200	7-8-65	1986	Fairburn, Ga.

PITCHING	W	L	ERA	G	GS	CG	SV	IP	H	R	ER	BB	SO	B	T	HT	WT	DOB	1st Yr	Resides
Alberro, Jose	3	2	6.64	24	8	0	0	60	79	46	44	16	43	R	R	6-2	190	6-29-69	1991	Arecibo, P.R.
Almanza, Armando	2	2	10.90	15	0	0	0	17	29	27	21	18	20	L	L	6-3	205	10-26-72	1993	El Paso, Texas
Arroyo, Luis	2	1	6.48	22	0	0	0	33	42	33	24	17	26	L	L	6-0	174	9-29-73	1992	Bajadero, P.R.
Benz, Jake	1	0	0.00	2	0	0	0	4	3	1	0	3	4	L	L	5-9	162	2-27-72	1994	Pleasant Hill, Calif.
Billingsley, Brent	2	9	5.55	21	21	0	0	117	133	81	72	48	79	L	L	6-2	200	4-19-75	1996	Chino Hills, Calif.
Burgus, Travis	1	0	5.40	20	0	0	1	23	33	17	14	8	15	L	L	6-2	190	11-6-72	1995	Mission Viejo, Calif.
Corbin, Archie	0	1	6.75	12	0	0	0	13	13	11	10	10	16	R	R	6-4	230	12-30-67	1986	Beaumont, Texas
Cornelius, Reid	10	6	4.49	27	27	2	0	172	184	96	86	68	135	R	R	6-0	210	6-2-70	1989	West Palm Beach, Fla.
Darensbourg, Vic	0	0	4.63	9	0	0	1	12	13	6	6	0	12	L	L	5-10	165	11-13-70	1992	Las Vegas, Nev.
Dempster, Ryan	1	1	4.99	5	5	0	0	31	30	17	17	10	29	R	R	6-1	201	5-3-77	1995	Gibsons, B.C.
Drumright, Mike	0	2	13.71	12	0	0	0	21	39	33	32	13	15	L	R	6-4	210	4-19-74	1995	Valley Center, Kan.
Duncan, Geoff	1	0	4.00	5	0	0	1	9	4	4	4	10	5	R	R	6-2	185	4-1-75	1996	Roswell, Ga.
Fontenot, Joe	3	2	5.11	8	8	1	0	44	52	26	25	19	18	R	R	6-2	185	3-20-77	1995	Lafayette, La.
Gonzalez, Gabe	1	1	4.18	24	0	0	0	28	27	15	13	9	23	L	L	6-1	170	5-24-72	1995	Long Beach, Calif.
Grilli, Jason	1	5	7.68	8	8	0	0	41	56	48	35	23	27	R	R	6-4	185	11-11-76	1997	Baldwinsville, N.Y.
2-team (19 Fresno)	8	10	6.16	27	27	1	0	142	180	117	97	62	103							
Hanson, Erik	1	1	7.55	10	9	0	0	48	43	40	26	42	19	R	R	6-6	215	5-18-65	1986	Kirkland, Wash.
Ludwick, Eric	11	6	3.86	48	0	0	14	58	65	33	25	36	61	R	R	6-5	220	12-14-71	1993	Las Vegas, Nev.
Medina, Rafael	1	2	3.34	25	0	0	1	35	29	15	13	21	34	R	R	6-3	240	2-15-75	1993	Panama City, Panama
Menhart, Paul	2	2	4.89	8	8	0	0	39	48	26	21	23	30	R	R	6-2	190	3-25-69	1990	Covington, Ga.
2-team (9 Edmonton)	5	5	5.89	17	17	0	0	81	106	60	53	37	51							
Mercedes, Jose	1	2	3.12	4	4	0	0	26	30	13	9	3	13	R	R	6-1	210	3-5-71	1992	Las Palmillas, D.R.
2-team (15 Las Vegas)	3	8	4.03	19	18	0	0	114	140	70	51	23	70							
Ojala, Kirt	3	8	7.21	16	14	1	0	79	110	70	63	44	54	L	L	6-2	215	12-24-68	1990	Grand Rapids, Mich.
Perez, Dario	7	13	5.73	28	21	0	0	132	150	94	84	31	66	R	R	6-1	150	6-27-70	1988	Nagua, D.R.
Salkeld, Roger	1	1	4.63	27	2	0	1	35	37	21	18	20	32	R	R	6-5	215	3-6-71	1989	Gilbert, Ariz.
Sanchez, Jesus	0	0	5.79	4	1	0	1	9	8	6	6	5	14	L	L	5-10	155	10-11-74	1992	Bani, D.R.
Stanifer, Rob	1	2	12.38	16	0	0	0	16	32	23	22	6	15	R	R	6-3	205	3-10-72	1994	Easley, S.C.
Tejera, Michael	0	2	12.00	2	2	0	0	9	19	14	12	4	5	L	L	5-9	175	10-18-76	1995	Miami, Fla.
Villano, Mike	1	5	6.21	36	1	0	2	58	87	43	40	17	48	R	R	6-0	200	8-10-71	1994	Bay City, Mich.

FIELDING

Catcher	PCT	G	PO	A	E	DP	PB
Castro	.989	90	552	67	7	7	9
Hastings	1.000	11	66	6	0	0	2
Reese	1.000	4	17	1	0	0	1
Robertson	.975	35	220	14	6	5	4
Roskos	.951	7	53	5	3	1	3

First Base	PCT	G	PO	A	E	DP
Hyers	1.000	17	126	7	0	18
Lee	.983	88	718	68	14	86
Millar	1.000	5	21	0	0	2
Morman	1.000	8	32	5	0	8
Robertson	1.000	1	4	0	0	0
Roskos	1.000	31	218	14	0	28
Walton	1.000	1	4	2	0	0

Second Base	PCT	G	PO	A	E	DP
Clapinski	.978	11	24	21	1	11
Garcia	.971	119	227	308	16	90

Third Base	PCT	G	PO	A	E	DP
Clapinski	1.000	36	28	64	0	6
Gulan	.959	67	28	114	6	14
Hastings	1.000	4	0	3	0	0
Lowell	.939	21	11	51	4	6
Millar	.857	10	3	9	2	2
Orie	.875	21	12	30	6	7
Roskos	.750	2	1	2	1	0

Shortstop	PCT	G	PO	A	E	DP
Clapinski	.924	22	24	49	6	11
M. Duncan	1.000	2	0	4	0	1
Franco	.943	7	8	25	2	7
Gil	.943	110	173	304	29	75
Gulan	1.000	4	1	6	0	2
Lobaton	.868	17	19	27	7	8

Outfield	PCT	G	PO	A	E	DP
Bautista	.969	36	90	5	3	3
Clapinski	1.000	18	25	2	0	0
Dunwoody	.977	64	159	10	4	1
Floyd	1.000	9	8	0	0	0
Franco	1.000	3	2	0	0	0
Gil	1.000	5	10	0	0	0
Gulan	.895	9	16	1	2	0
Hastings	.000	7	0	0	0	0
Hyers	.985	33	65	2	1	1
Jones	.961	39	68	5	3	1
Millar	1.000	27	39	0	0	0
Morman	1.000	3	5	0	0	0
Reeves	.993	78	132	9	1	2
Roskos	.981	85	102	1	2	0
Stovall	.982	32	52	3	1	0
Walton	.959	22	46	1	2	0

PORTLAND — Class AA

EASTERN LEAGUE

BATTING	AVG	G	AB	R	H	2B	3B	HR	RBI	BB	SO	SB	CS	B	T	HT	WT	DOB	1st Yr	Resides
Bates, Fletcher	.253	139	537	72	136	28	9	9	55	39	109	18	6	S	R	6-1	193	3-24-74	1994	Rocky Point, N.C.
Erickson, Matt	.269	107	361	38	97	20	2	0	35	51	65	2	3	L	R	5-11	190	7-30-75	1997	Appleton, Wis.
Funaro, Joe	.366	74	268	42	98	19	3	3	31	22	6	6	5	R	R	5-9	180	3-20-73	1995	Hamden, Conn.
Hastings, Lionel	.228	61	197	26	45	5	1	3	14	32	45	2	2	R	R	5-9	165	1-26-73	1994	Hermosa Beach, Calif.
Heinrichs, Jon	.227	49	176	25	40	11	1	3	17	16	23	4	0	R	R	6-0	195	11-18-74	1997	La Mesa, Calif.
Jones, Jaime	.254	73	244	39	62	16	0	7	31	47	81	2	0	L	L	6-3	190	8-2-76	1995	Poway, Calif.
Kleinz, Larry	.261	94	276	30	72	21	1	5	43	39	50	2	3	R	R	6-1	205	3-3-74	1996	Hamilton Square, N.J.
Kuilan, Hector	.261	76	245	22	64	11	0	2	32	11	42	0	0	R	R	5-11	190	4-3-76	1994	Vega Alta, P.R.
Lobaton, Jose	.250	13	32	2	8	2	0	0	2	2	13	1	0	R	R	5-11	154	3-29-74	1992	Acarigua, Venez.
Niles, Drew	.230	46	135	12	31	3	0	0	9	21	34	0	2	S	R	6-1	175	3-17-77	1998	Irmo, S.C.
Norton, Chris	.291	120	406	74	118	25	0	38	97	71	124	1	2	R	R	6-2	215	9-21-70	1992	Longwood, Fla.
Ozuna, Pablo	.281	117	502	62	141	25	7	7	46	13	50	31	16	R	R	6-0	160	8-25-78	1996	Santo Domingo, D.R.
Ramirez, Julio	.261	138	568	87	148	30	10	13	64	39	150	64	15	R	R	5-11	170	8-10-77	1994	Santo Domingo, D.R.
Reese, Nate	.000	3	3	0	0	0	0	0	0	0	1	0	0	R	R	5-11	215	10-7-74	1997	Shawnee Mission, Kan.
Reeves, Glenn	.000	6	9	0	0	0	0	0	0	0	6	0	0	R	R	6-0	195	1-19-74	1993	Glen Waverly, Australia
Robertson, Ryan	.246	44	130	15	32	6	0	2	10	22	17	0	0	L	R	6-4	210	9-30-72	1996	Port Neches, Texas
Rodriguez, Victor	.206	38	97	13	20	3	1	1	12	10	9	0	1	R	R	5-11	190	10-25-76	1994	Guayama, P.R.
Rolison, Nate	.299	124	438	71	131	20	1	17	69	68	112	0	1	L	R	6-6	240	3-27-77	1995	Petal, Miss.
Schifano, Tony	.239	29	67	9	16	1	1	0	6	5	9	0	0	R	R	6-1	195	11-11-74	1997	Anaheim Hills, Calif.

PITCHING	W	L	ERA	G	GS	CG	SV	IP	H	R	ER	BB	SO	B	T	HT	WT	DOB	1st Yr	Resides
Almanza, Armando	1	0	3.97	10	0	0	3	11	5	5	5	4	20	L	L	6-3	205	10-26-72	1993	El Paso, Texas
Almonte, Hector	1	4	2.84	47	0	0	23	44	42	14	14	26	42	R	R	6-2	190	10-17-75	1994	Santo Domingo, D.R.
Arroyo, Luis	0	1	3.29	9	0	0	1	14	14	11	5	8	10	L	L	6-0	174	9-29-73	1992	Bajadero, P.R.
Benz, Jake	1	0	4.32	23	0	0	0	33	33	19	16	23	24	L	L	5-9	162	2-27-72	1994	Pleasant Hill, Calif.
Bump, Nate	2	6	6.07	8	8	0	0	43	57	38	29	12	33	R	R	6-2	185	7-24-76	1998	Monroeton, Pa.
Burgus, Travis	0	0	0.00	1	0	0	0	1	0	0	0	2	1	L	L	6-2	190	11-6-72	1995	Mission Viejo, Calif.
Burnett, A.J.	6	12	5.52	26	23	0	0	121	132	91	74	71	121	R	R	6-5	205	1-3-77	1995	North Little Rock, Ark.
Cames, Aaron	3	6	5.55	23	16	1	0	96	110	64	59	46	66	R	R	6-1	192	11-21-75	1996	Woodland, Calif.

PITCHING

PITCHING	W	L	ERA	G	GS	CG	SV	IP	H	R	ER	BB	SO	B	T	HT	WT	DOB	1st Yr	Resides
Clark, Chris	1	0	7.50	4	0	0	0	6	5	5	5	7	4	R	R	6-1	180	10-29-74	1994	Tucson, Ariz.
Duncan, Geoff	2	3	2.85	43	0	0	4	66	59	24	21	26	59	R	R	6-2	185	4-1-75	1996	Roswell, Ga.
Gonzalez, Gabe	2	4	3.55	26	0	0	0	38	38	19	15	8	34	L	L	6-1	170	5-24-72	1995	Long Beach, Calif.
Henderson, Scott	6	3	2.96	46	1	0	7	85	67	32	28	26	83	R	R	6-3	195	2-27-75	1997	Villa Park, Calif.
Knotts, Gary	6	3	3.75	12	12	1	0	82	79	39	34	33	63	R	R	6-4	200	2-12-77	1996	Decatur, Ala.
Larkin, Andy	1	1	7.11	7	1	0	0	13	16	10	10	4	7	R	R	6-4	205	6-27-74	1992	Sunrise, Fla.
Leese, Brandon	4	4	5.73	20	11	0	0	82	110	66	52	20	52	R	R	6-4	205	10-8-75	1996	Lincolnshire, Ill.
Pageler, Mick	4	2	4.76	31	1	0	1	51	70	33	27	13	44	R	R	6-2	205	4-30-76	1996	Mesa, Ariz.
Penny, Brad	1	0	3.90	6	6	0	0	32	28	15	14	14	35	R	R	6-4	200	5-24-78	1996	Broken Arrow, Okla.
Rector, Bobby	0	4	3.59	13	4	0	0	43	43	23	17	14	19	R	R	6-1	170	9-24-74	1994	Imperial Beach, Calif.
Rodgers, Bobby	5	10	5.43	26	22	0	0	123	147	85	74	70	109	R	R	6-3	225	7-22-74	1996	St. Charles, Mo.
Tejera, Michael	13	4	2.62	25	25	0	0	155	137	55	45	45	152	L	L	5-9	175	10-18-76	1995	Miami, Fla.
Vardijan, Dan	0	1	29.08	5	0	0	0	4	12	15	14	8	5	R	R	6-4	205	12-1-76	1995	Glenview, Ill.
Villafuerte, Brandon	6	8	3.50	22	12	0	0	100	97	45	39	40	85	R	R	5-11	165	12-17-75	1995	Morgan Hill, Calif.

FIELDING

Catcher	PCT	G	PO	A	E	DP	PB
Hastings	.988	41	293	34	4	4	18
Kuilan	.984	68	472	65	9	6	10
Robertson	.989	43	320	32	4	3	8

First Base	PCT	G	PO	A	E	DP
Niles	1.000	1	8	0	0	0
Norton	.992	30	231	17	2	21
Rodriguez	1.000	5	11	1	0	3
Rolison	.987	115	920	69	13	89
Schifano	1.000	1	1	0	0	1

Second Base	PCT	G	PO	A	E	DP
Erickson	.974	106	212	282	13	68
Funaro...........	.945	11	18	34	3	5
Hastings	1.000	1	4	3	0	2
Lobaton	1.000	3	5	4	0	1

	PCT	G	PO	A	E	DP
Niles	.953	22	47	55	5	7
Rodriguez.......	1.000	8	16	8	0	1
Schifano........	1.000	5	3	4	0	2

Third Base	PCT	G	PO	A	E	DP
Funaro............	.943	47	31	101	8	11
Hastings	1.000	9	1	13	0	0
Kleinz	.902	76	33	123	17	15
Lobaton	1.000	4	1	7	0	0
Niles	1.000	2	0	2	0	0
Rodriguez.......	.959	21	9	38	2	7
Schifano	1.000	8	8	5	0	2

Shortstop	PCT	G	PO	A	E	DP
Funaro...........	1.000	5	5	7	0	1
Lobaton	.909	4	2	8	1	0

	PCT	G	PO	A	E	DP
Niles	.933	20	28	42	5	9
Ozuna	.946	117	179	309	28	53
Rodriguez	1.000	3	1	2	0	0
Schifano........	.960	6	12	12	1	5

Outfield	PCT	G	PO	A	E	DP
Bates.............	.969	139	208	14	7	2
Funaro............	1.000	19	25	0	0	0
Hastings	.962	12	23	2	1	0
Heinrichs........	.948	48	68	5	4	1
Jones	.939	73	106	2	7	0
Niles	1.000	2	6	1	0	0
Norton	.875	6	7	0	1	0
Ramirez..........	.969	137	326	14	11	3
Reeves...........	1.000	4	2	0	0	0
Schifano.........	1.000	3	2	0	0	0

BREVARD COUNTY — Class A

FLORIDA STATE LEAGUE

BATTING

BATTING	AVG	G	AB	R	H	2B	3B	HR	RBI	BB	SO	SB	CS	B	T	HT	WT	DOB	1st Yr	Resides
Alvarez, Aaron	.667	1	3	1	2	0	0	1	1	0	0	0	0	R	R	6-3	210	11-5-79	1999	Duluth, Ga.
Crespo, Cesar	.286	115	427	63	122	17	2	6	40	62	86	22	8	S	R	5-11	170	5-23-79	1997	Caguas, P.R.
Feliz, Joselyn	.200	11	25	0	5	2	0	0	2	1	8	0	0	R	R	6-3	225	6-2-76	1994	Santo Domingo, D.R.
Foster, Quincy	.294	134	568	78	167	13	6	3	54	36	96	56	23	L	R	6-2	175	10-30-74	1996	Hendersonville, N.C.
Franco, Raul	.239	111	426	41	102	17	1	1	43	13	48	4	6	R	R	5-11	170	1-14-76	1994	San Pedro de Macoris, D.R.
Frick, Matt	.221	35	113	8	25	5	0	0	12	11	27	0	1	R	R	6-2	220	1-2-76	1998	Scottsdale, Ariz.
Gload, Ross	.298	133	490	80	146	26	3	10	74	53	76	3	1	L	L	6-2	210	4-5-76	1997	East Hampton, N.Y.
Green, Kevin	.167	11	24	1	4	0	0	0	2	1	10	0	1	R	R	6-1	190	8-9-75	1997	Rome, N.Y.
Harper, Brandon	.268	81	280	35	75	9	0	4	40	30	31	1	1	R	R	6-4	200	4-29-76	1997	Houston, Texas
Heinrichs, Jon	.250	67	252	40	63	12	0	6	44	22	34	7	2	R	R	6-0	195	11-18-74	1997	La Mesa, Calif.
Honeycutt, Heath	.285	103	376	58	107	18	8	5	50	25	78	6	1	R	R	6-4	210	7-30-76	1998	Alpharetta, Ga.
Kleinz, Larry	.227	11	44	8	10	3	0	0	6	4	8	0	0	R	R	6-1	205	3-3-74	1996	Hamilton Square, N.J.
Maduro, Remy	.231	29	91	14	21	5	0	2	8	8	17	1	0	L	R	5-11	185	9-18-76	1996	Hooffddorp, Netherlands
Melconian, Alex	.263	58	205	26	54	6	1	4	20	24	48	11	9	R	R	5-10	190	3-18-75	1997	Berwyn, Pa.
Niles, Drew	.171	40	117	12	20	1	1	1	12	15	30	0	0	S	R	6-1	175	3-17-77	1998	Irmo, S.C.
Reed, Brian	.214	19	56	3	12	2	0	0	1	3	20	2	1	R	R	5-8	190	3-3-78	1997	Henderson, Nev.
Reese, Nate	.266	70	237	25	63	12	0	7	38	18	44	0	0	R	R	5-11	215	10-17-74	1997	Shawnee Mission, Kan.
Rigsby, Randy	.262	106	362	41	95	16	6	2	37	34	76	6	3	L	L	6-0	190	8-7-76	1998	Goldsboro, N.C.
Schifano, Tony	.248	45	141	21	35	3	1	2	15	12	36	2	2	R	R	6-1	195	11-11-74	1997	Anaheim Hills, Calif.
Smalls, Terrence	.208	32	77	5	16	1	0	0	5	6	8	5	2	L	R	5-10	170	11-22-75	1998	Holly Hill, S.C.
Ugueto, Luis	.133	12	30	1	4	0	0	0	3	7	5	1	0	S	R	5-11	170	2-15-79	1996	Macaracuay, Venez.
Washington, Kelley	.269	57	197	30	53	6	4	4	30	11	56	5	1	R	R	6-2	200	8-21-79	1998	Stephens City, Va.

GAMES BY POSITION: C—Alvarez 1, Feliz 10, Frick 24, Harper 76, Melconian 1, Reese 34, Schifano 1. **1B**—Frick 2, Gload 134, Rigsby 4. **2B**—Crespo 97, Franco 38, Schifano 1, Smalls 4. **3B**—Franco 28, Honeycutt 98, Kleinz 1, Schifano 4, Smalls 13. **SS**—Franco 4, Niles 41, Schifano 31, Ugueto 12, Washington 57. **OF**—Foster 137, Franco 27, Green 10, Heinrichs 64, Maduro 26, Melconian 57, Reed 16, Rigsby 79, Schifano 11, Smalls 1.

PITCHING

PITCHING	W	L	ERA	G	GS	CG	SV	IP	H	R	ER	BB	SO	B	T	HT	WT	DOB	1st Yr	Resides
Akin, Aaron	5	8	5.13	27	15	1	0	109	149	79	62	34	55	R	R	6-2	190	6-13-77	1997	Manhattan, Kan.
Bowe, Brandon	2	0	3.15	9	0	0	1	20	18	7	7	10	21	R	R	6-3	215	3-13-76	1999	Stockton, Calif.
Cames, Aaron	2	0	0.77	4	4	0	0	23	17	3	2	5	23	R	R	6-1	192	11-21-75	1996	Woodland, Calif.
Campos, David	0	2	6.75	13	0	0	0	25	25	24	19	16	17	L	L	5-11	170	8-31-77	1998	Kerman, Calif.
Clark, Chris	3	8	5.55	28	12	0	1	86	93	60	53	48	48	R	R	6-1	180	10-29-74	1994	Tucson, Calif.
Comer, Scott	9	4	2.35	19	19	5	0	130	120	38	34	5	85	L	L	6-5	205	6-23-77	1996	Klamath Falls, Ore.
Cordova, Jorge	1	0	4.38	6	0	0	0	12	9	6	6	6	11	R	R	6-0	190	1-13-78	1998	La Asuncion, Venez.
Gagliano, Steve	2	5	4.62	15	7	0	0	49	59	38	25	14	29	R	R	6-3	200	8-4-77	1997	Rolling Meadows, Ill.
Garvin, Robert	0	0	0.00	1	0	0	0	3	2	0	0	2	3	R	R	6-0	180	3-14-79	1997	Charleston, S.C.
Hurtado, Victor	0	2	9.43	4	4	0	0	21	28	22	22	7	6	R	R	6-4	190	6-14-77	1994	Santo Domingo, D.R.
Knotts, Gary	9	6	4.60	16	16	3	0	94	101	52	48	29	65	R	R	6-4	200	2-12-77	1996	Decatur, Ala.
Larkin, Andy	0	1	2.40	4	4	0	0	15	16	5	4	2	5	R	R	6-4	205	6-27-74	1992	Sunrise, Fla.
Levan, Matt	2	3	4.07	35	2	0	2	66	52	39	30	39	84	L	L	6-3	205	6-24-75	1996	Coatesville, Pa.
Marriott, Mike	1	5	9.00	8	8	0	0	34	50	36	34	21	22	R	R	6-3	205	3-12-77	1995	Spring, Texas
McCurtain, Paul	3	2	3.43	40	0	0	12	58	59	32	22	25	49	R	R	6-1	190	2-5-76	1998	Mesa, Ariz.
Moore, Chris	0	0	5.40	13	0	0	0	28	20	20	17	20	16	R	R	6-1	190	8-3-78	1997	Hazel Crest, Ill.
Moskau, Ryan	4	3	2.69	9	9	2	0	64	50	22	19	21	40	R	L	6-3	210	8-22-77	1998	Tucson, Ariz.
2-team (17 Vero Beach) ..	9	8	3.60	26	26	2	0	168	149	76	67	61	108							
Olsen, Kevin	2	5	5.05	11	11	0	0	57	70	37	32	13	45	R	R	6-2	200	7-26-76	1998	Norco, Calif.

PITCHING	W	L	ERA	G	GS	CG	SV	IP	H	R	ER	BB	SO	B	T	HT	WT	DOB	1st Yr	Resides
Partenheimer, Brian	2	3	2.25	21	0	0	2	44	29	13	11	14	29	R	L	6-5	230	4-13-75	1997	Birdseye, Ind.
2-team (17 Sarasota)	3	3	3.07	38	0	0	4	74	55	21	17	17	57							
Richards, Mark	6	14	6.13	26	24	2	2	134	171	107	91	51	54	R	R	6-6	220	6-19-74	1997	Tipp City, Ohio
Seaman, John	5	2	4.45	25	0	0	0	55	47	32	27	27	47	R	R	6-4	190	2-14-77	1998	Wilmette, Ill.
Vardijan, Dan	3	1	2.60	34	0	0	7	45	43	14	13	20	33	R	R	6-4	205	12-1-76	1995	Glenview, Ill.

KANE COUNTY — Class A

MIDWEST LEAGUE

BATTING	AVG	G	AB	R	H	2B	3B	HR	RBI	BB	SO	SB	CS	B	T	HT	WT	DOB	1st Yr	Resides
Abreu, Miguel	.000	3	7	0	0	0	0	0	1	0	6	0	0	R	R	6-3	190	8-15-78	1995	San Pedro de Macoris, D.R.
Aguila, Chris	.244	122	430	74	105	21	7	15	78	40	127	14	4	R	R	5-11	180	2-23-79	1997	Reno, Nev.
Bailey, Jeff	.278	76	277	49	77	19	1	10	53	34	77	1	1	R	R	6-2	205	11-19-78	1997	Kelso, Wash.
Bautista, Jorge	.220	61	186	30	41	12	0	3	30	21	54	2	1	R	R	5-9	185	7-12-76	1995	San Cristobal, D.R.
Callahan, David	.245	124	457	65	112	22	4	2	53	51	105	2	1	L	L	5-11	200	12-7-79	1998	Palm Bay, Fla.
Ferrand, Francisco	.255	16	51	6	13	4	0	0	4	7	8	0	2	L	L	5-10	170	5-20-80	1997	Santo Domingo, D.R.
Frick, Matt	.275	21	80	14	22	5	0	3	10	9	27	0	1	R	R	6-2	220	1-2-76	1998	Scottsdale, Ariz.
Hill, Willy	.303	127	535	85	162	19	6	2	57	44	56	38	24	L	L	5-9	160	9-21-76	1998	Sapulpa, Okla.
Kelly, Heath	.249	69	189	34	47	8	2	1	31	36	69	7	3	R	R	6-1	185	2-16-76	1998	Pensacola, Fla.
Medrano, Jesus	.274	118	445	64	122	26	5	5	46	36	92	42	11	R	R	6-0	185	9-11-78	1997	La Puente, Calif.
Morales, Stephen	.271	28	96	12	26	5	0	2	11	4	16	0	0	S	R	5-10	195	5-4-78	1996	Mayaguez, P.R.
Padgett, Matt	.333	45	159	34	53	9	0	5	23	20	40	1	0	L	L	6-2	215	7-22-77	1998	Lexington, S.C.
Roneberg, Brett	.288	132	511	88	147	32	4	8	68	79	82	3	2	L	L	6-2	205	2-5-79	1996	Cairns, Australia
Santos, Jose	.270	128	459	93	124	30	5	19	105	83	130	18	4	R	R	5-10	165	3-18-79	1995	Santiago, D.R.
Smalls, Terrence	.227	8	22	2	5	0	1	0	2	1	2	1	0	L	R	5-10	170	11-22-75	1998	Holly Hill, S.C.
Treanor, Matt	.286	86	308	56	88	21	1	10	53	36	65	4	1	R	R	6-1	188	3-3-76	1994	Anaheim, Calif.
Wathan, Derek	.254	125	469	71	119	18	4	1	49	53	54	33	12	S	R	6-3	190	12-13-76	1998	Blue Springs, Mo.

GAMES BY POSITION: C—Bailey 21, Frick 16, Morales 23, Treanor 81. **1B**—Bautista 16, Callahan 123, Kelly 1, Roneberg 3. **2B**—Kelly 28, Medrano 116, Smalls 5. **3B**—Bautista 11, Kelly 3, Santos 125. **SS**—Kelly 25, Wathan 125. **OF**—Abreu 2, Aguila 121, Bautista 2, Ferrand 11, Hill 126, Kelly 13, Padgett 24, Roneberg 126.

PITCHING	W	L	ERA	G	GS	CG	SV	IP	H	R	ER	BB	SO	B	T	HT	WT	DOB	1st Yr	Resides
Anderson, Wes	9	5	3.21	23	23	2	0	137	111	55	49	51	134	R	R	6-4	175	9-10-79	1997	Pine Bluff, Ark.
Clackum, Scott	4	4	3.30	47	1	0	10	71	82	32	26	14	53	R	R	6-3	185	1-13-75	1998	North Augusta, S.C.
Cordova, Jorge	1	0	0.47	12	0	0	0	19	6	2	1	10	17	R	R	6-0	190	1-13-78	1998	La Asuncion, Venez.
Farizo, Brad	4	7	5.27	34	12	0	1	113	143	81	66	37	80	R	R	6-4	190	11-3-78	1996	Marrero, La.
Goetz, Geoff	5	3	4.26	16	12	0	0	51	52	28	24	24	43	L	L	5-11	163	4-3-79	1997	Lutz, Fla.
Harber, Ryan	3	5	3.57	24	14	0	0	98	110	50	39	33	77	L	L	6-4	210	9-25-76	1998	Fort Wayne, Ind.
Henriquez, Hector	2	5	7.59	14	10	0	0	53	65	47	45	40	31	L	L	6-3	190	8-27-78	1994	Santo Domingo, D.R.
Lara, Nelson	3	2	6.06	46	0	0	10	52	50	38	35	47	45	R	R	6-4	185	7-15-78	1995	Santo Domingo, D.R.
LaRoche, Jeff	1	4	4.65	17	0	0	0	31	32	18	16	20	15	L	L	6-3	185	3-17-78	1998	Fort Scott, Kan.
Lowery, Phill	1	0	1.80	1	1	0	0	5	5	1	1	0	3	L	L	6-1	205	4-7-77	1998	Petaluma, Calif.
Moore, Chris	3	0	2.15	25	0	0	2	46	41	12	11	23	52	R	R	6-1	190	8-3-78	1997	Hazel Crest, Ill.
Neal, Blaine	4	2	2.32	26	0	0	6	31	21	8	8	10	31	R	R	6-5	205	4-6-78	1996	Haddon Heights, N.J.
Noyce, David	7	3	3.30	16	16	2	0	101	82	43	37	29	86	L	L	6-5	195	3-2-77	1998	Marietta, Ga.
Olsen, Kevin	5	2	3.38	10	9	0	0	61	65	25	23	16	52	R	R	6-2	200	7-26-76	1998	Norco, Calif.
Pidgeon, Matt	7	6	4.95	40	7	0	0	100	126	59	55	36	64	R	R	6-4	200	6-25-77	1997	Eureka, Calif.
Robertson, Nathan	6	1	2.29	8	1	0	0	51	42	14	13	12	33	R	L	6-2	215	9-3-77	1999	Valley Center, Kan.
Seaman, John	1	2	5.57	13	0	0	0	21	27	15	13	4	12	R	R	6-4	190	2-14-77	1998	Wilmette, Ill.
Sergent, Joe	2	1	7.11	8	0	0	0	13	17	10	10	4	9	L	L	6-0	185	8-29-78	1999	Manteca, Calif.
Shields, Drew	1	0	5.48	14	0	0	0	23	30	14	14	9	20	R	R	6-4	205	9-9-78	1997	Tucson, Ariz.
Vargas, Claudio	5	5	3.88	19	19	1	0	100	97	47	43	41	88	R	R	6-3	210	5-19-79	1996	Santiago, D.R.
Ward, Matt	3	1	5.06	5	5	0	0	27	41	17	15	4	7	L	L	6-0	175	9-15-77	1999	Irvine, Calif.

UTICA — Short-Season Class A

NEW YORK-PENN LEAGUE

BATTING	AVG	G	AB	R	H	2B	3B	HR	RBI	BB	SO	SB	CS	B	T	HT	WT	DOB	1st Yr	Resides
Ambres, Chip	.267	28	105	24	28	3	6	5	15	21	25	11	4	R	R	6-1	190	12-19-79	1998	Beaumont, Texas
Anderson, Dennis	.188	30	96	10	18	1	1	1	8	7	28	2	0	R	R	6-0	200	2-1-78	1999	Tucson, Ariz.
Close, James	.181	59	188	23	34	7	1	3	26	16	60	6	7	R	R	5-10	165	10-18-77	1999	Issaquah, Wash.
Feliz, Joselyn	.230	25	87	7	20	4	1	2	18	2	19	1	0	R	R	6-3	225	6-2-76	1994	Santo Domingo, D.R.
Ferrand, Francisco	.293	63	229	26	67	16	0	2	27	15	38	3	1	L	L	5-10	170	5-20-80	1997	Santo Domingo, D.R.
Gomez, Jose	.173	25	75	6	13	3	1	0	6	5	27	2	0	R	R	5-10	185	12-27-78	1999	San Bruno, Calif.
Goodman, Scott	.262	68	221	38	58	15	1	7	29	43	43	4	7	L	L	6-1	210	8-15-77	1999	San Luis Obispo, Calif.
Hooper, Kevin	.280	73	289	52	81	18	6	0	22	39	35	14	8	R	R	5-10	160	12-7-76	1999	Lawrence, Kan.
Lucca, Tony	.321	67	240	35	77	20	1	7	47	36	47	7	2	L	L	6-0	245	1-26-75	1998	Daly City, Calif.
Niles, Drew	.227	18	66	4	15	3	0	0	7	9	15	0	3	S	R	6-1	175	3-17-77	1998	Irmo, S.C.
Pass, Patrick	.000	1	2	1	0	0	0	0	0	1	1	0	0	R	R	6-1	215	12-31-77	1996	Decatur, Ga.
Perkins, Kevin	.287	60	202	35	58	11	4	2	23	19	41	2	3	R	R	6-2	185	8-2-77	1999	Whittier, Calif.
Postell, Matt	.264	45	148	15	39	8	2	0	21	18	50	4	2	L	R	6-4	187	1-10-77	1999	Gastonia, N.C.
Reyes, Dadny	.256	30	78	20	20	3	2	0	3	6	17	2	1	S	R	5-10	180	8-22-78	1997	Bonao, D.R.
Schell, Barry	.179	33	95	13	17	2	1	2	10	7	37	2	0	L	L	6-2	215	11-19-77	1999	Poway, Calif.
Ugueto, Luis	.276	56	217	33	60	11	2	1	26	18	46	9	4	S	R	5-11	170	2-15-79	1996	Macaracuay, Venez.
Walker, Javon	.000	8	11	0	0	0	0	0	1	7	0	0	0	R	R	6-4	205	10-14-78	1997	Lafayette, La.
Woody, Dominic	.276	48	181	26	50	11	0	4	22	16	34	0	2	R	R	6-3	210	8-17-78	1999	Richland, Wash.

GAMES BY POSITION: C—Anderson 29, Feliz 19, Woody 30. **1B**—Lucca 61, Postell 15, Reyes 1. **2B**—Hooper 73, Reyes 4. **3B**—Gomez 20, Perkins 32, Postell 18, Reyes 18. **SS**—Niles 18, Perkins 2, Reyes 3, Ugueto 56. **OF**—Ambres 28, Close 54, Ferrand 62, Goodman 59, Pass 1, Perkins 24, Schell 14, Walker 3.

PITCHING	W	L	ERA	G	GS	CG	SV	IP	H	R	ER	BB	SO	B	T	HT	WT	DOB	1st Yr	Resides
Abreu, Miguel	1	0	6.45	15	0	0	0	22	23	16	16	17	12	R	R	6-3	190	8-15-78	1995	San Pedro de Macoris, D.R.
Bowe, Brandon	2	0	2.92	6	0	0	0	12	14	6	4	2	24	R	R	6-3	215	3-13-76	1999	Stockton, Calif.
Byron, Terence	1	0	1.24	6	6	1	0	29	17	7	4	7	31	R	R	6-0	200	3-28-79	1999	St. Croix, Virgin Islands

Organization Statistics

PITCHING	W	L	ERA	G	GS	CG	SV	IP	H	R	ER	BB	SO	B	T	HT	WT	DOB	1st Yr	Resides
Garvin, Robert	3	5	3.95	23	3	0	0	55	58	29	24	8	39	R	R	6-0	180	3-14-79	1997	Charleston, S.C.
Gordon, Kevin	1	0	6.75	1	0	0	0	1	3	1	1	1	1	L	R	6-3	200	9-16-76	1998	Clearwater, Fla.
Henriquez, Hector	1	1	6.19	12	1	0	0	16	16	12	11	13	12	L	L	6-3	190	8-27-78	1994	Santo Domingo, D.R.
Hickman, Ben	3	2	2.13	24	0	0	7	38	36	12	9	4	38	R	R	6-0	240	11-10-76	1999	Bryant, Ark.
LaRoche, Jeff	3	3	8.03	26	0	0	1	37	62	37	33	15	29	L	L	6-3	185	3-17-78	1998	Fort Scott, Kan.
Lopez, Gustavo	4	2	3.53	13	13	0	0	64	59	28	25	17	46	R	R	5-9	180	12-31-78	1996	Santiago, D.R.
Lowery, Phill	1	0	6.00	2	0	0	0	6	7	4	4	1	5	L	L	6-1	205	4-7-77	1998	Petaluma, Calif.
Moore, Bryan	2	1	1.54	26	0	0	9	35	29	13	6	5	36	R	R	6-8	215	9-6-76	1999	Garden Grove, Calif.
Morse, Bryan	3	5	3.45	14	14	0	0	78	73	41	30	19	74	L	L	5-11	165	9-12-77	1999	California, Md.
Moser, Todd	8	2	1.53	14	14	3	0	88	63	20	15	24	86	L	L	6-5	180	10-28-76	1999	Davie, Fla.
Robertson, Nate	2	0	2.77	5	5	0	0	26	22	9	8	8	26	R	L	6-2	215	9-3-77	1999	Valley Center, Kan.
Sergent, Joe	0	0	1.40	10	0	0	1	19	9	4	3	7	23	L	L	6-0	185	8-29-78	1999	Manteca, Calif.
Shields, Drew	2	3	8.51	13	2	0	0	24	30	28	23	17	33	R	R	6-4	205	9-9-78	1997	Tucson, Ariz.
Smuin, Shane	1	3	3.98	23	0	0	1	43	33	20	19	21	51	R	R	6-2	205	6-22-79	1999	Vernal, Utah
Thomas, Gaige	0	5	5.40	13	11	0	1	40	41	34	24	30	32	S	R	6-1	190	2-28-79	1997	Brenham, Texas
Ward, Matt	2	1	4.00	8	6	0	0	36	36	17	16	3	24	L	L	6-0	175	9-15-77	1999	Irvine, Calif.

MELBOURNE — Rookie

GULF COAST LEAGUE

BATTING	AVG	G	AB	R	H	2B	3B	HR	RBI	BB	SO	SB	CS	B	T	HT	WT	DOB	1st Yr	Resides
Alvarez, Aaron	.257	24	74	7	19	5	0	0	4	3	12	0	1	R	R	6-3	210	11-5-79	1999	Duluth, Ga.
Ambres, Chip	.353	37	139	29	49	13	3	1	15	25	19	22	3	R	R	6-1	190	12-19-79	1998	Beaumont, Texas
Davis, Quian	.191	26	47	1	9	1	1	0	4	2	13	1	0	R	R	6-2	210	7-28-80	1999	Minotola, N.J.
DeMarco, Matt	.218	46	156	12	34	8	1	0	10	11	19	1	3	L	R	5-10	160	1-24-80	1999	Clayton, N.J.
Encarnacion, Arismendy	.278	46	151	21	42	9	2	0	14	3	24	5	6	R	R	6-0	170	12-17-79	1996	Santo Domingo, D.R.
Fernandez, Medardo	.306	39	134	20	41	6	2	0	16	15	30	10	4	S	R	5-11	154	11-1-78	1996	Trujillo, Venez.
Frazier, Charlie	.288	35	125	12	36	6	0	0	9	13	31	5	1	R	R	6-3	185	7-6-80	1999	Toms River, N.J.
Herbert, Keith	.215	29	79	8	17	3	3	1	8	7	20	1	0	R	R	5-10	180	5-30-81	1999	Keedysville, Md.
Laidlaw, Jake	.264	56	201	24	53	9	4	3	32	22	49	3	4	R	R	6-2	190	10-5-81	1999	North Las Vegas, Nev.
Louwsma, Chris	.176	55	182	20	32	7	1	1	8	24	56	3	3	R	R	6-3	210	12-25-78	1998	Sanford, Fla.
Mendieta, Enrique	.163	30	49	2	8	3	0	0	6	9	14	1	1	R	R	6-0	175	8-22-79	1998	Newport News, Va.
Paulino, David	.199	46	141	21	28	0	0	0	4	18	24	22	7	R	L	5-7	135	11-20-79	1997	San Cristobal, D.R.
Soto, Jose	.229	49	175	17	40	8	0	4	20	14	56	10	8	S	R	6-0	160	6-20-80	1996	San Cristobal, D.R.
Ugueto, Luis	.000	1	3	0	0	0	0	0	2	1	0	0	0	S	R	5-11	170	2-15-79	1996	Macaracuay, Venez.
Venales, Luis	.090	28	67	6	6	2	0	0	5	18	27	1	2	R	R	6-3	176	5-26-80	1997	Caracas, Venez.
Washington, Kelley	.133	4	15	2	2	0	0	0	2	2	9	0	0	R	R	6-2	200	8-21-79	1997	Stephens City, Va.
Wilson, Josh	.266	53	203	29	54	9	4	0	27	24	36	14	2	R	R	6-1	165	3-26-81	1999	Pittsburgh, Pa.
Zapey, Winton	.216	29	74	8	16	6	0	1	10	7	17	1	0	R	R	6-1	190	3-21-80	1997	Santo Domingo, D.R.

GAMES BY POSITION: C—Alvarez 19, Venales 27, Zapey 26. **1B**—Alvarez 4, Davis 12, DeMarco 26, Laidlaw 3, Louwsma 29, Mendieta 2, Zapey 2. **2B**—DeMarco 5, Herbert 27, Paulino 40. **3B**—Laidlaw 36, Louwsma 23, Paulino 6. **SS**—DeMarco 16, Washington 3, Wilson 45. **OF**—Ambres 35, Davis 9, Encarnacion 43, Fernandez 30, Frazier 32, Mendieta 23, Soto 34.

PITCHING	W	L	ERA	G	GS	CG	SV	IP	H	R	ER	BB	SO	B	T	HT	WT	DOB	1st Yr	Resides
Alcantara, Over	0	0	0.90	4	0	0	0	10	7	1	1	3	4	R	R	6-1	178	9-11-80	1997	Azua, D.R.
Anderson, Antwoine	2	1	3.45	13	0	0	2	29	28	13	11	9	26	L	L	6-3	170	11-5-78	1998	Cincinnati, Ohio
Bell, Tom	1	0	4.01	13	0	0	3	25	21	11	11	7	9	R	R	6-0	185	1-5-81	1999	Vienna, Va.
Campos, David	3	1	4.19	8	0	0	0	19	20	9	9	6	20	L	L	5-11	170	8-31-77	1998	Kerman, Calif.
Castillo, Ramon	1	2	3.46	11	10	0	0	52	56	21	20	12	34	R	R	6-1	155	12-24-78	1996	La Vega, D.R.
Cordova, Jorge	1	0	1.29	7	0	0	1	14	8	3	2	2	18	R	R	6-0	190	1-13-78	1998	La Asuncion, Venez.
Haynes, Brad	1	4	4.08	11	11	0	0	46	45	31	21	30	40	R	R	6-5	187	9-29-81	1999	Glasgow, Ky.
Johnston, David	1	2	4.85	12	0	0	0	26	35	17	14	5	20	R	R	6-3	190	4-27-81	1999	Marshalltown, Iowa
Lajara, Eudy	1	2	2.08	8	2	0	0	22	13	6	5	14	23	L	L	5-10	160	8-20-79	1996	Santo Domingo, D.R.
Leahy, Bart	0	1	8.47	8	0	0	1	17	22	19	16	18	16	R	R	6-5	225	10-19-76	1998	Glenview, Ill.
Messenger, Randy	0	3	7.52	13	2	0	2	26	28	25	22	19	23	R	R	6-0	220	8-13-81	1999	Sparks, Nev.
Salazar, Luis	5	3	3.34	14	0	0	1	32	26	14	12	23	27	R	R	6-2	190	5-30-79	1996	Maracay, Venez.
Sauer, Marc	5	4	2.71	13	13	1	0	70	75	28	21	7	57	R	R	6-2	190	6-30-80	1999	Gloucester, N.J.
Targac, Matt	1	7	3.05	12	11	1	0	56	53	32	19	16	55	S	L	6-3	210	6-25-80	1998	Delano, Calif.
Villanueva, Bill	2	5	3.86	11	11	1	0	58	58	29	25	21	42	R	R	6-4	195	10-6-78	1996	Santo Domingo, D.R.
Wykoff, Jarred	1	0	3.63	11	0	0	1	22	20	11	9	8	12	R	R	6-5	190	9-29-80	1999	Kinder, La.

HOUSTONASTROS

Astrodome finale doesn't go according to plan for Astros

BY TOM HALLIBURTON

The Astrodome cost $31 million and played host to baseball in Houston for 35 seasons. But fittingly, perhaps, the last celebration in the dome was by a visiting playoff team.

After falling three games to one to the Braves in the 1999 National League Division Series, the Astros are still looking to win a playoff series for the first time in franchise history. That search will continue as they move downtown to Enron Field, a $300 million stadium with a retractable roof.

Despite the way the year ended, Houston had much to be proud of in 1999. An aggravating, unhealthy year for the manager and many of the players didn't prevent the Astros from winning a third straight NL Central title.

Mike Hampton won his 22nd game, a franchise record, on the final day of the regular season to end the Reds' bid to win the division. Hampton became the first Astros lefthander to win 20 games, fashioned the majors' longest winning streak—11 games—and led the big leagues with an .846 winning percentage.

Hampton was one of four Astros, including three pitchers, to represent Houston in the All-Star Game. The others were pitchers Jose Lima and Billy Wagner and first baseman Jeff Bagwell.

Lima (21-10) and Hampton (22-4) gave the Astros two 20-game winners for the first time, and Wagner set a major league record by averaging 14.9 strikeouts per nine innings and a club record with 39 saves.

Bagwell established franchise marks in five offensive categories, joining Barry Bonds as the only major leaguers to hit 40 home runs and steal 30 bases in two

Jeff Bagwell   **Aaron McNeal**

Players of the Year

MAJOR LEAGUE: Jeff Bagwell, 1b

Bagwell led the majors with 143 runs and 149 walks while hitting 42 home runs and collecting 126 RBIs.

MINOR LEAGUE: Aaron McNeal, 1b

McNeal exploded for a .310 average and 38 homers at Michigan in his fourth pro season. His 131 RBIs were second in the minors.

seasons.

Craig Biggio became the first player in 49 years, and the first National Leaguer in 62 years, to collect as many as 56 doubles. Biggio played in at least 160 games for a fourth consecutive year despite playing the second half with a shoulder injury.

By August, Bagwell and Biggio were the last position players from the Opening Day lineup who hadn't been on the disabled list. The Astros used the DL 16 times, beginning with Moises Alou, who tore the anterior cruciate ligament in his left knee falling off a treadmill before spring training.

Manager Larry Dierker missed 27 games due to brain surgery after a mid-June seizure. Hitting coach Tom McCraw took a three-month leave after discovering he had prostate cancer. First-base coach Jose Cruz missed 34 games while receiving treatment for an irregular heartbeat.

Houston's injuries greatly depleted Triple-A New Orleans. A year after winning the inaugural Triple-A World Series, the Zephyrs had the worst record in Triple-A. Outfielder Daryle Ward led New Orleans by hitting .353 with 28 home runs in just 61 games.

But two Astros affiliates did win league titles. Class A Kissimmee claimed the Florida State League, beating Dunedin in the finals. Cobras righthander Eric Ireland also threw the first perfect game in the organization's history. Rookie-level Martinsville also won its league, beating Pulaski in the Appalachian League finals.

Jackson completed its final season as Houston's Double-A affiliate with a 38-34 second half. The team is moving to Round Rock, Texas, for the 2000 season.

ORGANIZATION LEADERS

BATTING

*AVG	Randy Knorr, New Orleans	.352
R	Aaron McNeal, Michigan	95
H	Aaron McNeal, Michigan	166
TB	Aaron McNeal, Michigan	315
2B	Casey Candaele, New Orleans	34
3B	Colin Porter, Michigan	9
HR	Aaron McNeal, Michigan	38
RBI	Aaron McNeal, Michigan	131
BB	Mike Rose, Jackson/Kissimmee	72
SO	Eric Cole, Jackson/Kissimmee	131
SB	Modesto DeAza, Auburn	34

PITCHING

W	Two tied at	15
L	Derek Root, Jackson	16
#ERA	Eric Ireland, Jackson/Kissimmee	2.24
G	Wayne Franklin, Jackson/Kissimmee	58
CG	Eric Ireland, Jackson/Kissimmee	5
SV	Wayne Franklin, Jackson/Kissimmee	21
IP	Jeriome Robertson, Jackson	191
BB	Derek Root, Jackson	79
SO	Mike Nannini, Michigan/Auburn	154

*Minimum 250 At-Bats #Minimum 75 Innings

Houston ASTROS

Manager: Larry Dierker

1999 Record: 97-65, .599 (1st, NL Central)

BATTING	AVG	G	AB	R	H	2B	3B	HR	RBI	BB	SO	SB	CS	B	T	HT	WT	DOB	1st Yr	Resides
Bagwell, Jeff	.304	162	562	143	171	35	0	42	126	149	127	30	11	R	R	6-0	195	5-27-68	1989	Houston, Texas
Bako, Paul	.256	73	215	16	55	14	1	2	17	26	57	1	1	L	R	6-2	205	6-20-72	1993	Lafayette, La.
Barker, Glen	.288	81	73	23	21	2	0	1	11	11	19	17	6	S	R	5-10	180	5-10-71	1993	Albany, N.Y.
Bell, Derek	.236	128	509	61	120	22	0	12	66	50	129	18	6	R	R	6-2	215	12-11-68	1987	Tampa, Fla.
Berkman, Lance	.237	34	93	10	22	2	0	4	15	12	21	5	1	S	L	6-1	205	2-10-76	1997	New Braunfels, Texas
Biggio, Craig	.294	160	639	123	188	56	0	16	73	88	107	28	14	R	R	5-11	180	12-14-65	1987	Houston, Texas
Bogar, Tim	.239	107	309	44	74	16	2	4	31	38	52	3	5	R	R	6-2	198	10-28-66	1987	Normal, Ill.
Caminiti, Ken	.286	78	273	45	78	11	1	13	56	46	58	6	2	S	R	6-0	200	4-21-63	1985	Richmond, Texas
Diaz, Alex	.220	30	50	3	11	2	0	1	7	3	13	2	2	S	R	5-11	180	10-5-68	1987	San Sebastian, P.R.
Eusebio, Tony	.272	103	323	31	88	15	0	4	33	40	67	0	0	R	R	6-2	210	4-27-67	1985	Kissimmee, Fla.
Everett, Carl	.325	123	464	86	151	33	3	25	108	50	94	27	7	S	R	6-0	190	6-3-71	1990	Tampa, Fla.
Gutierrez, Ricky	.261	85	268	33	70	7	5	1	25	37	45	2	5	R	R	6-1	175	5-23-70	1988	Miami, Fla.
Hernandez, Carlos	.143	16	14	4	2	0	0	0	1	0	3	1	0	R	R	5-9	175	12-12-75	1993	Caracas, Venez.
Hidalgo, Richard	.227	108	383	49	87	25	2	15	56	56	73	8	5	R	R	6-3	190	7-2-75	1991	Guarenas, Venez.
Howell, Jack	.212	37	33	2	7	2	0	1	1	8	9	0	0	L	R	6-0	190	8-18-61	1983	Celina, Texas
Javier, Stan	.328	20	64	12	21	4	1	0	4	9	8	3	1	S	R	6-0	195	1-9-64	1981	Santo Domingo, D.R.
2-team (112 S.F.)	.285	132	397	61	113	19	2	3	34	38	63	16	7							
Johnson, Russ	.282	83	156	24	44	10	0	5	23	20	31	2	3	R	R	5-10	180	2-22-73	1994	Denham Springs, La.
Knorr, Randy	.167	13	30	2	5	1	0	0	1	8	0	0	0	R	R	6-2	215	11-12-68	1986	Covina, Calif.
Meluskey, Mitch	.212	10	33	4	7	1	0	1	3	5	6	1	0	S	R	6-0	185	9-18-73	1992	Yakima, Wash.
Mieske, Matt	.284	54	109	13	31	5	0	5	22	6	22	0	0	R	R	6-0	194	2-13-68	1990	Mesa, Ariz.
Spiers, Bill	.288	127	393	56	113	18	5	4	39	47	45	10	5	L	R	6-2	190	6-5-66	1987	Cameron, S.C.
Thompson, Ryan	.200	12	20	2	4	1	0	1	5	2	7	0	0	R	R	6-3	200	11-4-67	1987	Edesville, Md.
Ward, Daryle	.273	64	150	11	41	6	0	8	30	9	31	0	0	L	L	6-2	230	6-27-75	1994	Riverside, Calif.

PITCHING	W	L	ERA	G	GS	CG	SV	IP	H	R	ER	BB	SO	B	T	HT	WT	DOB	1st Yr	Resides
Bergman, Sean	4	6	5.36	19	16	2	0	99	130	60	59	26	38	R	R	6-4	225	4-11-70	1991	Joliet, Ill.
Cabrera, Jose	4	0	2.15	26	0	0	0	29	21	7	7	9	28	R	R	6-0	160	3-24-72	1991	Santiago, D.R.
Elarton, Scott	9	5	3.48	42	15	0	1	124	111	55	48	43	121	R	R	6-7	240	2-23-76	1994	Lamar, Colo.
Hampton, Mike	22	4	2.90	34	34	3	0	239	206	86	77	101	177	R	L	5-10	180	9-9-72	1990	Houston, Texas
Henry, Doug	2	3	4.65	35	0	0	2	41	45	24	21	24	36	R	R	6-4	205	12-10-63	1986	Chandler, Ariz.
Holt, Chris	5	13	4.66	32	26	0	1	164	193	92	85	57	115	R	R	6-4	205	9-18-71	1992	Dallas, Texas
Lima, Jose	21	10	3.58	35	35	3	0	246	256	108	98	44	187	R	R	6-2	205	9-30-72	1989	Plant City, Fla.
McCurry, Jeff	0	1	15.75	5	0	0	0	4	11	8	7	2	3	R	R	6-6	220	1-21-70	1991	Houston, Texas
Miller, Trever	3	2	5.07	47	0	0	1	50	58	29	28	29	37	R	L	6-4	195	5-29-73	1991	Mount Washington, Ky.
Miller, Wade	0	1	9.58	5	1	0	0	10	17	11	11	5	8	R	R	6-2	185	9-13-76	1996	Reading, Pa.
Powell, Jay	5	4	4.32	67	0	0	4	75	82	38	36	40	77	R	R	6-4	225	1-9-72	1993	Madison, Miss.
Reynolds, Shane	16	14	3.85	35	35	4	0	232	250	108	99	37	197	R	R	6-3	210	3-26-68	1989	Houston, Texas
Slusarski, Joe	0	0	0.00	3	0	0	0	4	1	0	0	3	3	R	R	6-4	195	12-19-66	1989	Springfield, Ill.
Wagner, Billy	4	1	1.57	66	0	0	39	75	35	14	13	23	124	L	L	5-11	180	7-25-71	1993	Pearland, Texas
Williams, Brian	2	1	4.41	50	0	0	0	67	69	35	33	35	53	R	R	6-2	195	2-15-69	1990	Cayce, S.C.

FIELDING

Catcher	PCT	G	PO	A	E	DP	PB
Bako	.988	71	461	35	6	10	4
Eusebio	.994	98	652	37	4	3	4
Knorr	1.000	11	54	3	0	0	1
Meluskey	1.000	10	62	6	0	1	0

First Base	PCT	G	PO	A	E	DP
Bagwell	.994	161	1337	106	8	141
Berkman	1.000	1	1	0	0	1
Howell	1.000	5	9	2	0	4
Spiers	1.000	1	3	0	0	0
Ward	1.000	10	36	2	0	6

Second Base	PCT	G	PO	A	E	DP
Biggio	.985	155	359	430	12	117
Bogar	1.000	1	1	2	0	1
Hernandez	1.000	7	5	11	0	3
Johnson	.960	15	16	32	2	6
Spiers	1.000	4	5	10	0	4

Third Base	PCT	G	PO	A	E	DP
Bogar	1.000	12	6	20	0	0
Caminiti	.931	75	52	138	14	17
Gutierrez	1.000	1	0	1	0	0
Howell	1.000	3	1	3	0	0

	PCT	G	PO	A	E	DP
Johnson	.944	36	16	52	4	8
Spiers	.958	71	40	143	8	11
Shortstop	PCT	G	PO	A	E	DP
Bogar	.977	90	123	255	9	65
Gutierrez	.971	80	102	203	9	37
Hernandez	.667	2	2	0	1	0
Johnson	.833	2	1	4	1	1
Spiers	1.000	13	22	23	0	7
Outfield	PCT	G	PO	A	E	DP
Barker	.981	57	50	2	1	1
Bell	.985	126	192	4	3	1
Berkman	.955	27	42	0	2	0
Biggio	1.000	6	6	1	0	0
Diaz	.900	8	8	1	1	0
Everett	.978	121	255	11	6	4
Hidalgo	.991	108	214	15	2	3
Javier	1.000	18	31	1	0	0
Mieske	1.000	37	54	0	0	0
Spiers	.976	31	40	0	1	0
Thompson	.800	10	3	1	1	1
Ward	.946	31	34	1	2	0

Mike Hampton

JOHN KLEIN

Organization Statistics

Director of Player Development: Tim Purpura

Class	Farm Team	League	W	L	Pct.	Finish*	Manager	First Yr
AAA	New Orleans (La.) Zephyrs	Pacific Coast	55	85	.393	16th (16)	Tony Pena	1997
AA	Jackson (Miss.) Generals	Texas	68	72	.486	5th (8)	Jim Pankovits	1991
A#	Kissimmee (Fla.) Cobras	Florida State	71	66	.518	+6th (14)	Manny Acta	1985
A	Michigan Battle Cats	Midwest	76	62	.551	3rd (14)	Al Pedrique	1999
A	Auburn (N.Y.) Doubledays	New York-Penn	39	37	.513	8th (14)	Lyle Yates	1982
Rookie	Martinsville (Va.) Astros	Appalachian	41	29	.586	+1st (14)	Brad Wellman	1999

*Finish in overall standings (No. of teams in league)   #Advanced level   +Won league championship

PACIFIC COAST LEAGUE

BATTING	AVG	G	AB	R	H	2B	3B	HR	RBI	BB	SO	SB	CS	B	T	HT	WT	DOB	1st Yr	Resides
Alexander, Chad	.240	28	96	7	23	5	0	2	8	6	22	0	1	R	R	6-1	190	5-22-74	1995	Lufkin, Texas
Bako, Paul	.191	12	47	2	9	3	1	1	4	1	11	0	0	L	R	6-2	205	6-20-72	1993	Lafayette, La.
Berkman, Lance	.323	64	226	42	73	20	0	8	49	39	47	7	1	S	L	6-1	205	2-10-76	1997	New Braunfels, Texas
Betzsold, James	.217	63	198	29	43	15	0	7	27	14	64	3	2	R	R	6-3	210	8-7-72	1994	Orange, Calif.
Caminiti, Ken	.350	6	20	6	7	4	0	0	3	2	1	0	0	S	R	6-0	200	4-21-63	1985	Richmond, Texas
Candaele, Casey	.266	126	467	56	124	34	3	7	42	47	54	3	9	S	R	5-9	165	1-12-61	1983	San Luis Obispo, Calif.
Gonzales, Rene	.253	27	79	9	20	4	0	0	11	11	11	1	0	R	R	6-3	200	9-3-61	1982	Hollywood Hills, Calif.
Gutierrez, Ricky	.214	4	14	0	3	0	0	0	1	2	3	0	0	R	R	6-1	175	5-23-70	1988	Miami, Fla.
Hernandez, Carlos	.293	94	355	56	104	14	0	0	43	27	65	22	13	R	R	5-9	175	12-12-75	1993	Caracas, Venez.
Incaviglia, Pete	.194	18	62	6	12	3	1	1	6	8	15	1	2	R	R	6-1	230	4-2-64	1986	Colleyville, Texas
2-team (8 Tucson)	.181	26	94	9	17	7	1	1	13	9	26	2	2							
Johnson, Russ	.351	22	77	17	27	6	0	1	12	16	13	1	3	R	R	5-10	180	2-22-73	1994	Denham Springs, La.
Knorr, Randy	.352	77	270	33	95	22	1	11	41	20	41	0	1	R	R	6-2	215	11-12-68	1986	Covina, Calif.
Lopez, Pedro	.267	19	60	11	16	4	0	2	11	7	8	0	0	R	R	6-1	200	3-29-69	1988	Toa, P.R.
Miller, Ryan	.276	64	174	19	48	8	0	1	25	5	29	0	2	R	R	6-0	175	10-22-72	1994	Tulare, Calif.
Neal, Mike	.202	94	243	33	49	10	1	6	28	27	61	3	0	R	R	6-1	180	11-5-71	1993	Hammond, La.
Ramirez, Omar	.253	110	379	56	96	15	2	6	51	30	49	8	3	R	R	5-9	170	11-2-70	1990	Santiago, D.R.
Russo, Paul	.263	48	133	19	35	6	0	4	18	21	28	1	0	R	R	5-11	215	8-26-69	1990	Tampa, Fla.
Saylor, Jamie	.224	113	330	38	74	14	5	4	36	34	83	8	10	L	R	5-11	185	9-11-74	1994	Garland, Texas
Thompson, Ryan	.309	112	404	60	125	23	2	16	58	37	78	4	9	R	R	6-3	200	11-4-67	1987	Edesville, Md.
Thurston, Jerrey	.220	21	59	7	13	0	0	4	4	15	0	1	R	R	6-4	200	4-17-72	1990	Longwood, Fla.
Villalobos, Carlos	.283	133	499	82	141	33	1	9	50	54	100	11	3	R	R	6-0	170	4-5-74	1994	Cartagena, Colombia
Ward, Daryle	.353	61	241	56	85	15	1	28	65	23	43	1	1	L	L	6-2	230	6-27-75	1994	Riverside, Calif.
Williams, George	.240	29	100	18	24	5	0	3	14	13	19	1	1	S	R	5-10	214	4-22-69	1991	West Salem, Wis.
2-team (74 Salt Lake)	.284	103	328	56	93	21	1	9	45	55	70	1	4							

PITCHING	W	L	ERA	G	GS	CG	SV	IP	H	R	ER	BB	SO	B	T	HT	WT	DOB	1st Yr	Resides
Bergman, Sean	0	1	9.95	3	1	0	0	6	9	8	7	2	2	R	R	6-4	225	4-11-70	1991	Joliet, Ill.
Cabrera, Jose	3	1	2.82	31	0	0	7	51	34	18	16	12	41	R	R	6-0	180	3-24-72	1991	Santiago, D.R.
Creek, Ryan	1	2	3.98	6	5	0	0	32	30	17	14	16	20	R	R	6-1	180	9-24-72	1993	Martinsburg, W.Va.
Crow, Dean	2	6	7.04	34	0	0	3	46	71	36	36	12	22	L	R	6-4	215	8-21-72	1993	Houston, Texas
Diorio, Mike	2	3	6.40	50	0	0	1	70	85	59	50	31	32	R	R	6-2	200	3-1-73	1993	Pueblo, Colo.
Ellis, Robert	7	12	5.43	27	27	1	0	156	176	106	94	51	105	R	R	6-5	220	12-15-70	1991	Baton Rouge, La.
Henry, Doug	0	0	4.50	3	3	0	0	4	4	2	2	3	3	R	R	6-4	205	12-10-63	1986	Chandler, Ariz.
Hodges, Kevin	1	3	7.24	5	5	0	0	27	34	23	22	11	16	R	R	6-4	200	6-24-73	1991	Spring, Texas
Huisman, Rick	3	1	3.61	35	0	0	3	52	42	23	21	16	67	R	R	6-3	210	5-17-69	1990	Holland, Mich.
Maxcy, Brian	0	0	12.38	4	1	0	0	8	12	11	11	2	6	R	R	6-1	170	5-4-71	1992	Amory, Miss.
McCurry, Jeff	0	7	4.15	40	0	0	14	43	48	23	20	14	26	R	R	6-6	220	1-21-70	1991	Houston, Texas
Meacham, Rusty	3	4	4.94	17	0	0	1	47	56	26	26	9	47	R	R	6-2	175	1-27-68	1988	Palm City, Fla.
Miller, Wade	11	9	4.38	26	26	2	0	162	156	85	79	64	135	R	R	6-2	185	9-13-76	1996	Reading, Pa.
Mounce, Tony	0	1	2.45	14	0	0	0	11	10	3	3	13	10	L	L	6-2	175	2-8-75	1994	Kennewick, Wash.
Powell, Brian	4	4	6.19	9	9	0	0	48	54	33	33	11	22	R	R	6-2	205	10-10-73	1995	Bainbridge, Ga.
Scanlan, Bob	8	15	5.61	28	28	2	0	164	208	116	102	55	78	R	R	6-7	215	8-9-66	1984	Beverly Hills, Calif.
Sikorski, Brian	7	10	4.95	28	27	2	0	158	169	92	87	58	122	R	R	6-1	190	7-27-74	1995	Roseville, Mich.
Slusarski, Joe	1	4	3.64	40	0	0	2	64	71	32	26	11	40	R	R	6-4	195	12-19-66	1989	Springfield, Ill.
Wallace, Kent	2	2	4.14	36	1	0	1	59	61	30	27	13	43	L	R	6-3	192	8-22-70	1992	Paducah, Ky.

FIELDING

Catcher	PCT	G	PO	A	E	DP	PB
Bako	.984	12	58	4	1	1	0
Candaele	1.000	1	1	0	0	0	0
Knorr	.991	67	396	35	4	4	1
Lopez	.993	19	126	15	1	3	3
Russo	.971	14	61	5	2	0	3
Thurston	1.000	21	118	10	0	1	2
Williams	.984	19	114	11	2	1	1

First Base	PCT	G	PO	A	E	DP
Berkman	1.000	4	29	1	0	1
Betzsold	.992	15	119	7	1	11
Candaele	1.000	1	1	0	0	0
Gonzales	.990	10	95	5	1	9
Knorr	.939	6	41	5	3	5
Neal	.991	14	98	11	1	4
Russo	.991	25	220	11	2	13
Saylor	1.000	8	55	4	0	3
Ward	.993	59	527	35	4	46
Williams	.991	9	69	6	2	4

Second Base	PCT	G	PO	A	E	DP
Candaele	.976	76	124	202	8	41
Gonzales	1.000	4	3	4	0	0
Hernandez	.987	14	22	53	1	13
Johnson	1.000	13	23	32	0	9
R. Miller	.915	17	29	36	6	9
Saylor	1.000	6	3	6	0	0
Villalobos	.901	26	37	45	9	3

Third Base	PCT	G	PO	A	E	DP
Caminiti	.700	6	2	5	3	0
Candaele	.917	9	4	7	1	0
Gonzales	.929	6	6	7	1	1
R. Miller	1.000	11	3	15	0	1
Neal	.897	13	9	26	4	2
Saylor	1.000	16	8	19	0	0
Villalobos	.927	100	59	244	24	18

Shortstop	PCT	G	PO	A	E	DP
Candaele	.980	27	30	70	2	8
Gutierrez	.875	4	10	11	3	3

	PCT	G	PO	A	E	DP
Hernandez	.963	82	123	239	14	39
Johnson	.925	9	9	28	3	8
R. Miller	.955	13	21	21	2	4
Saylor	.915	18	23	52	7	9

Outfield	PCT	G	PO	A	E	DP
Alexander	.985	28	64	2	1	1
Berkman	.965	56	106	5	4	1
Betzsold	.950	46	88	7	5	3
Candaele	1.000	16	32	1	0	0
Incaviglia	.905	14	19	0	2	0
Johnson	.000	1	0	0	0	0
Knorr	.000	1	0	0	0	0
Neal	.983	33	56	1	1	0
Ramirez	.995	103	188	6	1	3
Saylor	.965	55	101	8	4	1
Thompson	.965	104	209	12	8	3
Villalobos	.944	4	16	1	1	1
Ward	.500	3	1	0	1	0

TEXAS LEAGUE

BATTING	AVG	G	AB	R	H	2B	3B	HR	RBI	BB	SO	SB	CS	B	T	HT	WT	DOB	1st Yr	Resides
Alexander, Chad	.309	84	317	42	98	27	3	9	44	34	58	9	5	R	R	6-1	190	5-22-74	1995	Lufkin, Texas
Barr, Tucker	.252	41	107	8	27	0	0	5	15	12	20	0	0	R	R	6-1	205	5-26-75	1996	Atlanta, Ga.
Bearden, Doug	.181	25	83	7	15	3	0	0	3	2	24	0	0	R	R	6-2	180	9-11-75	1997	Lexington, S.C.
Betzsold, James	.238	38	126	30	30	6	1	6	17	22	35	4	3	R	R	6-3	210	8-7-72	1994	Orange, Calif.
Burns, Kevin	.281	113	352	55	99	21	2	12	58	42	74	6	3	L	L	6-5	220	9-9-75	1995	El Dorado, Ark.
Cole, Eric	.167	15	54	4	9	1	0	2	8	1	11	0	0	R	R	6-0	185	11-15-75	1995	Lancaster, Calif.
Dallimore, Brian	.267	70	251	38	67	13	1	5	19	16	44	13	3	R	R	6-1	185	11-15-73	1996	Las Vegas, Nev.
Duffy, Jim	.133	26	60	5	8	0	0	0	2	4	15	0	0	R	R	6-2	195	7-18-74	1997	Andover, N.J.
Ginter, Keith	.382	9	34	9	13	1	0	1	6	4	6	0	0	R	R	5-10	190	5-5-76	1998	Fullerton, Calif.
Gutierrez, Ricky	.333	4	12	4	4	1	0	0	1	4	3	0	1	R	R	6-1	175	5-23-70	1988	Miami, Fla.
Howell, Jack	.375	3	8	2	3	1	0	2	3	0	2	0	0	L	R	6-0	190	8-18-61	1983	Celina, Texas
Johnson, A.J.	.241	63	187	21	45	7	0	4	16	9	38	4	2	R	R	6-3	210	2-17-73	1995	Neptune, N.J.
Johnson, J.J.	.252	131	437	57	110	28	2	18	69	47	119	11	11	R	R	6-0	204	8-31-73	1991	Pine Plains, N.Y.
Johnson, Ric	.245	99	323	28	79	19	1	1	27	13	44	5	5	R	R	6-2	185	3-18-74	1995	Chicago, Ill.
Lopez, Pedro	.184	81	255	20	47	11	0	6	28	12	52	1	1	R	R	6-1	200	3-29-69	1988	Toa, P.R.
Lugo, Julio	.319	116	445	77	142	24	5	10	42	44	53	25	11	R	R	6-0	165	11-16-75	1995	Brooklyn, N.Y.
Miller, Ryan	.147	27	75	5	11	0	1	0	4	2	11	5	0	R	R	6-0	175	10-22-72	1994	Tulare, Calif.
Perez, Jhonny	.250	76	276	37	69	16	4	4	25	19	44	7	8	R	R	5-10	180	10-23-76	1994	Santo Domingo, D.R.
Rose, Mike	.244	15	45	8	11	0	0	3	8	13	10	0	2	S	R	6-1	185	8-25-76	1995	Sacramento, Calif.
Samboy, Nelson	.300	45	170	20	51	9	0	0	14	11	14	6	5	R	R	5-10	165	9-4-76	1994	Pedernales, D.R.
Sanchez, Victor	.251	125	407	61	102	18	0	17	68	40	93	11	9	R	R	5-10	180	9-20-71	1994	Stockton, Calif.
Truby, Chris	.282	124	465	78	131	21	3	28	87	36	88	20	8	R	R	6-2	190	12-9-73	1993	Mukilteo, Wash.

PITCHING	W	L	ERA	G	GS	CG	SV	IP	H	R	ER	BB	SO	B	T	HT	WT	DOB	1st Yr	Resides
Bennett, Erik	0	3	4.13	20	0	0	1	28	23	14	13	12	32	R	R	6-2	205	9-13-68	1989	Yreka, Calif.
Braswell, Bryan	9	10	4.52	28	28	1	0	171	180	104	86	54	131	L	L	6-1	200	6-30-75	1996	Springboro, Ohio
Creek, Ryan	4	3	4.57	8	7	0	0	43	47	25	22	16	32	R	R	6-1	180	9-24-72	1993	Martinsburg, W.Va.
Franklin, Wayne	3	1	1.61	46	0	0	20	50	31	11	9	16	40	L	L	6-2	195	3-9-74	1996	North East, Md.
Green, Jason	3	3	3.40	33	0	0	10	42	41	20	16	20	50	R	R	6-4	190	6-5-75	1994	Port Hope, Ontario
Henry, Doug	0	1	4.50	2	1	0	0	2	2	1	1	1	3	R	R	6-4	205	12-10-63	1986	Chandler, Ariz.
Hodges, Kevin	1	4	2.94	8	8	0	0	49	48	22	16	16	21	R	R	6-4	190	6-24-73	1991	Spring, Texas
Ireland, Eric	0	1	4.30	3	3	0	0	15	19	9	7	2	15	R	R	6-1	170	3-11-77	1996	Long Beach, Calif.
Kester, Tim	8	5	3.72	43	2	0	1	75	91	43	31	19	51	R	R	6-4	190	12-1-71	1993	Coral Springs, Fla.
McKnight, Tony	9	9	2.75	24	24	0	0	160	134	60	49	44	118	L	R	6-5	205	6-29-77	1995	Texarkana, Ark.
Mounce, Tony	5	2	3.69	31	6	0	0	68	64	33	28	30	80	L	L	6-2	175	2-8-75	1994	Kennewick, Wash.
Narcisse, Tyrone	0	2	7.30	10	0	0	0	12	14	12	10	1	9	R	R	6-6	220	2-4-72	1990	Port Arthur, Texas
O'Malley, Paul	1	3	5.60	36	7	0	0	71	75	53	44	48	65	R	R	6-2	190	12-20-72	1994	Skokie, Ill.
Persails, Mark	0	1	1.37	12	0	0	0	20	15	5	3	10	20	R	R	6-3	190	10-25-75	1995	Vassar, Mich.
Robertson, Jeriome	.. 15	7	3.06	28	28	1	0	191	184	81	65	45	133	L	L	6-1	190	3-30-77	1996	Exeter, Calif.
Root, Derek	7	16	4.65	28	26	0	0	157	167	103	81	79	129	L	L	6-5	215	5-26-75	1993	Lakewood, Ohio
Wallace, Kent	0	1	2.30	13	0	0	3	16	13	4	4	6	16	L	R	6-3	192	8-22-70	1992	Paducah, Ky.
Walter, Mike	2	1	4.81	34	0	0	4	49	35	32	26	31	44	R	R	6-1	190	10-23-74	1993	San Diego, Calif.

FIELDING

Catcher	PCT	G	PO	A	E	DP	PB
Barr	.954	36	191	17	10	1	4
Lopez	.986	79	507	51	8	1	8
Rose	.983	14	105	13	2	2	1
Sanchez	.980	30	171	24	4	0	8

First Base	PCT	G	PO	A	E	DP
Betzsold	.964	3	25	2	1	3
Burns	.984	97	763	53	13	74
Howell	1.000	3	20	2	0	2
Sanchez	.990	49	365	26	4	31

Second Base	PCT	G	PO	A	E	DP
Bearden	.980	10	24	24	1	6
Cole	1.000	3	5	6	0	1
Dallimore	.956	43	89	105	9	25
Ginter	.956	9	19	24	2	4

	PCT	G	PO	A	E	DP
Lugo	1.000	2	0	1	0	0
Miller	.966	6	12	16	1	5
Perez	.958	59	124	152	12	27
Samboy	.926	17	40	35	6	10

Third Base	PCT	G	PO	A	E	DP
Bearden	1.000	2	2	0	0	
Dallimore	.913	7	5	16	2	2
Miller	.818	6	2	7	2	0
Sanchez	.944	15	5	29	2	2
Truby	.950	120	93	270	19	35

Shortstop	PCT	G	PO	A	E	DP
Bearden	.881	12	9	28	5	6
Dallimore	.875	3	5	9	2	2
Gutierrez	1.000	3	2	5	0	0

	PCT	G	PO	A	E	DP
Lugo	.946	113	185	327	29	53
Miller	.857	6	12	18	5	5
Perez	.968	7	12	18	1	3
Truby	.875	4	2	5	1	1

Outfield	PCT	G	PO	A	E	DP
Alexander	.988	82	168	3	2	3
Betzsold	.962	34	72	3	3	1
Cole	.968	11	28	2	1	0
Dallimore	.900	15	18	0	2	0
Duffy	.978	24	45	0	1	0
A.J. Johnson	.951	54	73	4	4	0
J.J. Johnson	.980	119	185	9	4	2
R. Johnson	.978	85	179	3	4	1
Samboy	.939	20	30	1	2	1
Sanchez	.000	2	0	0	0	0

FLORIDA STATE LEAGUE

BATTING	AVG	G	AB	R	H	2B	3B	HR	RBI	BB	SO	SB	CS	B	T	HT	WT	DOB	1st Yr	Resides
Bearden, Doug	.268	45	149	19	40	7	1	2	16	8	35	1	4	R	R	6-2	180	9-11-75	1997	Lexington, S.C.
Buckley, Brandon	.199	51	146	13	29	5	0	1	11	11	29	1	3	R	R	6-1	200	1-25-77	1998	Danville, Calif.
Carter, Charley	.274	115	416	62	114	19	2	12	56	28	77	0	3	R	R	6-2	205	12-11-75	1998	Mount Pleasant, Texas
Chavera, Arnie	.277	62	213	29	59	13	0	14	43	26	59	1	0	L	R	5-10	195	9-24-73	1996	Arlington, Texas
Cole, Eric	.265	120	460	62	122	27	5	13	67	39	120	23	13	R	R	6-0	185	11-15-75	1995	Lancaster, Calif.
Craig, Benny	.077	4	13	0	1	0	0	0	0	0	6	0	0	S	R	6-4	205	1-15-75	1997	Santee, Calif.
Dallimore, Brian	.270	19	74	12	20	2	0	0	3	4	10	2	1	R	R	6-1	185	11-15-73	1996	Las Vegas, Nev.
Duffy, Jim	.248	60	149	26	37	8	2	3	25	17	48	5	5	R	R	6-2	195	7-18-74	1997	Andover, N.J.
Ensberg, Morgan	.239	123	427	72	102	25	2	15	69	68	90	17	6	R	R	6-2	210	8-26-75	1998	Redondo Beach, Calif.
Ginter, Keith	.263	103	376	66	99	15	4	13	46	61	90	9	10	R	R	5-10	190	5-5-76	1998	Fullerton, Calif.
Joyce, Jesse	.143	4	7	2	1	0	0	0	0	0	2	0	0	R	R	5-11	185	5-12-76	1998	Highland, Calif.
Logan, Kyle	.291	113	399	57	116	33	7	7	62	33	62	16	5	L	R	6-0	196	7-11-75	1997	Hattiesburg, Miss.
Matranga, David	.231	124	472	70	109	20	4	6	48	68	118	17	10	R	R	5-11	170	1-8-77	1998	Orange, Calif.
Rose, Mike	.277	95	303	61	84	16	2	11	32	59	64	12	6	S	R	6-1	185	8-25-76	1995	Sacramento, Calif.
Thomas, J.J.	.230	88	287	36	66	15	0	16	44	20	109	0	0	R	R	6-4	215	9-18-77	1997	Atlanta, Ga.
Vasquez, Alejandro	.236	79	275	31	65	6	4	4	29	14	40	3	5	L	L	5-11	190	7-5-77	1995	San Pedro de Macoris, D.R.

Organization Statistics

BATTING	AVG	G	AB	R	H	2B	3B	HR	RBI	BB	SO	SB	CS	B	T	HT	WT	DOB	1st Yr	Resides
Wesson, Barry	.216	115	352	32	76	15	1	4	34	26	84	8	7	R	R	6-2	195	4-6-77	1995	Brandon, Miss.
Yates, Chris	.250	16	36	2	9	1	0	0	4	4	8	3	4	R	L	6-0	165	8-24-75	1997	Eupora, Miss.

GAMES BY POSITION: C—Buckley 50, Chavera 8, Rose 88. **1B**—Bearden 1, Carter 107, Ensberg 1, J. Thomas 38. **2B**—Bearden 11, Cole 17, Dallimore 9, Ginter 102, Joyce 1. **3B**—Bearden 16, Carter 3, Dallimore 7, Ensberg 115. **SS**—Bearden 14, Ensberg 2, Matranga 122. **OF**—Cole 89, Craig 2, Dallimore 3, Duffy 47, Joyce 3, Logan 106, J. Thomas 13, Vasquez 60, Wesson 113, Yates 15.

PITCHING	W	L	ERA	G	GS	CG	SV	IP	H	R	ER	BB	SO	B	T	HT	WT	DOB	1st Yr	Resides
Creek, Ryan	2	4	4.08	7	7	0	0	35	36	19	16	12	23	R	R	6-1	180	9-24-72	1993	Martinsburg, W.Va.
Franklin, Wayne	3	0	1.53	12	0	0	1	18	11	4	3	6	22	L	L	6-2	195	3-9-74	1996	North East, Md.
Garcia, Gabe	0	1	13.50	1	0	0	0	2	5	3	3	1	0	R	R	6-2	215	3-15-77	1996	Union City, Calif.
Glick, David	0	3	4.70	32	0	0	0	44	47	29	23	22	41	L	L	6-1	190	4-2-76	1995	Palmdale, Calif.
Ireland, Eric	10	7	2.06	24	24	5	0	170	145	59	39	30	133	R	R	6-1	170	3-11-77	1996	Long Beach, Calif.
Lidge, Brad	0	2	3.38	6	6	0	0	21	13	8	8	11	19	R	R	6-3	200	12-23-76	1998	Englewood, Colo.
Love, Jeff	2	3	6.66	15	0	0	0	26	34	24	19	9	20	R	R	6-1	190	11-25-73	1996	Woodbridge, Conn.
Lynch, Jim	3	14	4.93	28	21	3	0	130	131	82	71	61	99	R	R	6-1	200	12-12-75	1994	Evansville, Ind.
Maldonado, Esteban	0	0	3.38	8	1	0	0	11	6	6	4	12	4	R	R	6-3	210	8-3-75	1996	Carolina, P.R.
Mercedes, Carlos	2	4	4.92	41	1	0	2	75	82	51	41	31	39	R	R	6-0	175	3-29-76	1994	El Seibo, D.R.
Messman, Joe	3	4	2.43	45	0	0	15	59	38	20	16	35	47	R	R	6-2	175	7-29-75	1997	Parkdale, Ore.
Narcisse, Tyrone	0	0	6.75	4	0	0	0	5	10	4	4	2	3	R	R	6-6	220	2-4-72	1990	Port Arthur, Texas
Navarro, Scott	8	3	2.88	37	11	1	0	113	108	39	36	17	86	L	L	6-0	180	11-13-74	1997	Chico, Calif.
Persails, Mark	1	1	2.21	10	0	0	0	20	26	9	5	4	15	R	R	6-3	190	10-25-75	1995	Vassar, Mich.
Rodriguez, Wilfredo	15	7	2.88	25	24	0	0	153	108	55	49	62	148	L	L	6-3	180	3-20-79	1996	San Felix, Venez.
Sessions, Doug	3	0	1.97	35	0	0	13	46	35	11	10	14	55	R	R	6-1	192	9-28-76	1998	Orange Park, Fla.
Shearn, Tom	10	6	3.90	24	24	0	0	145	144	75	63	53	107	R	R	6-4	200	8-28-77	1994	Columbus, Ohio
Thomas, Don	8	6	6.95	18	18	0	0	91	129	77	70	28	44	L	L	6-2	175	12-20-75	1997	Arlington, Texas
Wade, Travis	0	0	0.00	1	0	0	0	1	1	0	0	0	2	R	R	6-4	225	7-8-75	1997	Climax, Mich.
Whitesides, Johnny	1	1	4.26	14	0	0	0	25	34	20	12	6	11	R	R	6-4	195	3-2-78	1997	Sarasota, Fla.

MICHIGAN — Class A

MIDWEST LEAGUE

BATTING	AVG	G	AB	R	H	2B	3B	HR	RBI	BB	SO	SB	CS	B	T	HT	WT	DOB	1st Yr	Resides
Alfaro, Jason	.271	118	473	74	128	25	4	5	50	23	62	5	5	R	R	5-10	189	11-29-77	1997	Fort Worth, Texas
Alleyne, Roberto	.291	95	323	61	94	25	3	8	60	25	59	9	2	R	R	6-4	230	5-15-77	1994	Panama City, Panama
Buck, John	.100	4	10	1	1	1	0	0	0	2	3	0	0	R	R	6-3	200	7-7-80	1998	Salt Lake City, Utah
Chapman, Scott	.270	64	226	37	61	17	1	11	36	14	32	1	2	R	R	6-2	200	1-30-78	1995	Albany, Ohio
Cutshall, Pat	.238	8	21	3	5	0	0	0	2	2	3	0	1	R	R	5-9	175	10-29-74	1997	Beaver Falls, Pa.
Dimmick, Josh	.306	53	180	27	55	11	2	4	28	17	25	2	1	S	R	6-3	225	5-5-76	1998	Wharton, Texas
Escalona, Felix	.288	116	396	78	114	29	4	6	47	29	60	7	7	R	R	6-0	185	3-12-79	1996	Puerto Cabello, Venez.
Fatheree, Danny	.203	38	118	13	24	5	2	1	18	11	19	2	1	R	R	5-11	232	8-25-78	1997	Grand Prairie, Texas
Jordan, Kevin	.252	116	413	60	104	21	2	11	66	18	98	17	6	R	R	6-1	190	9-7-76	1998	Midland, Texas
Joyce, Jesse	.167	8	24	4	4	1	1	1	2	1	5	0	1	R	R	5-11	185	5-12-76	1998	Highland, Calif.
Lopez, Luis	.266	95	335	55	89	22	3	14	48	33	96	7	5	R	R	6-3	195	4-13-78	1995	San Felipe, Venez.
McNeal, Aaron	.310	133	536	95	166	29	3	38	131	40	121	7	1	R	R	6-3	230	4-28-76	1996	Castro Valley, Calif.
Miles, Aaron	.317	112	470	72	149	28	8	10	71	28	33	17	12	S	R	5-8	170	12-15-76	1995	Antioch, Calif.
Nicholson, Derek	.319	66	216	40	69	8	5	3	39	30	25	3	4	L	R	5-11	205	6-17-76	1998	Redondo Beach, Calif.
O'Connor, Brian	.156	21	64	8	10	2	0	0	5	9	29	0	1	R	R	6-2	225	6-21-77	1999	Arlington Heights, Ill.
Porter, Colin	.291	127	453	91	132	28	9	18	68	53	123	23	13	L	L	6-2	205	11-23-75	1998	Tucson, Ariz.
Rosamond, Michael	.100	4	10	0	1	0	0	0	2	2	3	0	1	R	R	6-5	225	4-18-78	1999	Nashville, Tenn.
Schaffer, Jason	.130	7	23	2	3	0	0	0	2	1	8	0	0	R	R	5-10	185	3-28-75	1997	Bloomington, Minn.
Turnquist, Tyler	.309	118	456	89	141	25	7	11	67	62	69	5	4	R	R	5-11	190	11-10-75	1998	Naperville, Ill.

GAMES BY POSITION: C—Buck 4, Chapman 54, Dimmick 42, Fatheree 28, O'Connor 20. **1B**—Fatheree 5, McNeal 129, Nicholson 6, Turnquist 3. **2B**—Escalona 63, Miles 73, Schaffer 2, Turnquist 2. **3B**—Alfaro 5, Cutshall 5, Escalona 22, Jordan 1, Joyce 1, Nicholson 3, Turnquist 105. **SS**—Alfaro 109, Escalona 31, Schaffer 3. **OF**—Alleyne 81, Jordan 103, Joyce 3, Lopez 91, Nicholson 22, Porter 122, Turnquist 4.

PITCHING	W	L	ERA	G	GS	CG	SV	IP	H	R	ER	BB	SO	B	T	HT	WT	DOB	1st Yr	Resides
Blackmore, John	3	4	7.48	37	0	0	7	49	64	44	41	29	43	R	R	6-3	200	11-5-77	1996	Plainville, Conn.
Borges, Reece	6	2	5.04	37	1	0	2	64	74	45	36	23	37	R	R	6-3	195	4-4-76	1997	Reno, Nev.
Ferguson, Tony	0	2	7.71	5	0	0	0	5	8	4	4	6	2	R	R	6-4	200	12-1-76	1999	Russellville, Ark.
Gallo, Mike	2	3	5.85	12	12	0	0	60	76	47	39	23	32	L	L	6-0	170	4-2-77	1999	Long Beach, Calif.
Garcia, Gabe	5	3	4.63	38	8	0	3	89	100	49	46	37	79	R	R	6-2	215	3-15-77	1996	Union City, Calif.
Glick, David	1	0	0.55	10	0	0	1	16	7	2	1	5	20	L	L	6-1	190	4-2-76	1995	Palmdale, Calif.
Hamulack, Tim	3	0	3.04	25	0	0	0	27	23	9	9	11	32	L	L	6-4	215	11-14-76	1996	Edgewood, Md.
Hecht, Brian	4	1	3.15	27	0	0	1	34	42	13	12	10	26	R	R	6-4	205	11-29-77	1997	Arlington Heights, Ill.
Nannini, Mike	4	10	4.43	15	15	0	0	87	107	56	43	31	68	R	R	5-11	175	8-9-80	1998	Henderson, Nev.
Oswalt, Roy	13	4	4.46	22	22	2	0	151	144	78	75	54	143	R	R	6-0	170	8-29-77	1997	Weir, Miss.
Peguero, Darwin	7	4	4.11	24	20	0	0	114	115	58	52	35	88	S	L	6-0	165	12-5-78	1996	Hato Mayor, D.R.
Pineda, Jairo	0	2	8.84	4	4	0	0	19	30	24	19	5	6	R	R	6-3	185	9-25-76	1997	Granada, Nicaragua
Redding, Tim	8	6	4.97	43	11	0	14	105	84	69	58	76	141	R	R	6-0	182	2-12-78	1998	Rochester, N.Y.
Santana, Johan	8	8	4.66	27	26	1	0	160	162	94	83	55	150	L	L	6-0	155	3-13-79	1996	Tovar, Venez.
Sessions, Doug	0	0	0.69	12	0	0	5	13	6	1	1	1	18	R	R	6-1	190	9-28-76	1998	Orange Park, Fla.
Smith, Brandon	1	2	6.66	18	0	0	0	24	25	19	18	20	19	R	R	6-1	210	4-10-76	1998	Tyler, Texas
Spykstra, Dave	0	0	6.75	5	0	0	0	5	2	4	4	6	3	R	R	6-2	190	8-26-73	1992	Denver, Colo.
Wade, Travis	0	0	9.64	10	0	0	0	2	14	22	18	15	11	9	R	R	6-4	225	7-8-75	1997	Climax, Mich.
Whitney, Jacob	9	8	4.61	33	19	2	1	137	152	81	70	29	121	L	L	6-1	195	5-23-76	1998	Edina, Minn.
Zyskowski, Garrett	2	0	7.71	14	0	0	1	16	21	14	14	12	12	L	L	6-1	185	9-3-75	1998	Utica, N.Y.

AUBURN — Short-Season Class A

NEW YORK-PENN LEAGUE

BATTING	AVG	G	AB	R	H	2B	3B	HR	RBI	BB	SO	SB	CS	B	T	HT	WT	DOB	1st Yr	Resides
Alfieri, Frank	.237	23	76	9	18	4	0	4	12	7	22	2	0	R	R	6-0	205	5-10-77	1999	Saugatauck, Mich.

BATTING	AVG	G	AB	R	H	2B	3B	HR	RBI	BB	SO	SB	CS	B	T	HT	WT	DOB	1st Yr	Resides
Armstrong, Chris	.325	22	77	17	25	4	1	0	11	4	9	7	1	R	R	6-2	205	1-30-77	1999	Glendale, Ariz.
Buck, John	.245	63	233	36	57	17	0	3	29	25	48	7	1	R	R	6-3	200	7-7-80	1998	Salt Lake City, Utah
De Aza, Modesto	.220	61	223	38	49	7	4	2	18	11	73	34	10	R	R	5-11	150	2-14-79	1996	La Romana, D.R.
Dominguez, Luis	.298	63	218	34	65	11	2	0	27	33	28	6	3	R	R	6-0	165	3-9-80	1996	Maracay, Venez.
Hill, Mike	.297	69	269	44	80	11	2	6	39	29	65	22	6	R	R	6-4	210	9-30-76	1999	Lawton, Okla.
Hoover, Steve	.202	32	94	4	19	2	2	1	5	8	18	2	2	R	R	6-2	205	8-11-77	1999	Discovery Bay, Calif.
Joyce, Jesse	.300	18	70	11	21	5	2	2	10	4	13	1	2	R	R	5-11	185	5-12-76	1998	Highland, Calif.
Lane, Jason	.279	74	283	46	79	18	5	13	59	38	46	6	4	R	L	6-2	220	12-22-76	1999	Sebastopol, Calif.
Maule, Jason	.221	35	86	12	19	3	0	0	11	21	20	10	1	L	R	5-11	170	7-1-77	1999	East Berlin, Conn.
Mendez, Donaldo	.209	25	86	9	18	1	1	0	10	2	23	10	5	R	R	6-1	155	6-7-78	1996	Barquisimeto, Venez.
Ochoa, Javier	.277	15	47	5	13	2	1	0	11	3	7	0	1	R	R	6-1	170	1-8-79	1996	Maracay, Venez.
Rosamond, Michael	.265	61	230	34	61	9	4	6	24	23	63	22	6	R	R	6-5	205	4-18-78	1999	Nashville, Tenn.
Ryden, Karl	.333	31	117	24	39	8	0	3	15	19	19	10	4	R	R	5-11	185	5-7-77	1997	League City, Texas
Sampson, Chris	.239	51	159	23	38	7	3	1	19	22	49	21	5	R	R	6-0	175	5-23-78	1999	Channelview, Texas
Topolski, Jon	.243	67	255	46	62	11	6	2	38	50	72	27	13	L	R	5-10	185	12-28-76	1999	Houston, Texas
Zapata, Juan	.227	16	44	7	10	0	0	1	5	0	10	4	0	R	R	5-11	160	5-30-78	1996	San Pedro de Macoris, D.R.

GAMES BY POSITION: C—Buck 63, Ochoa 15. 1B—Armstrong 5, Dominguez 1, Lane 72. 2B—De Aza 50, Maule 29, Mendez 1. 3B—Alfieri 20, Dominguez 57, Joyce 2, Sampson 1. SS—De Aza 9, Maule 1, Mendez 22, Sampson 48. OF—Hill 67, Hoover 23, Joyce 1, Rosamond 61, Ryden 9, Topolski 64, Zapata 13.

PITCHING	W	L	ERA	G	GS	CG	SV	IP	H	R	ER	BB	SO	B	T	HT	WT	DOB	1st Yr	Resides
Anderson, Travis	1	5	5.22	9	8	0	0	40	42	31	23	17	29	R	R	6-4	235	3-18-78	1999	Bellevue, Wash.
Barrett, Scott	0	0	3.18	5	2	0	0	11	8	5	4	6	13	L	L	5-10	175	11-18-78	1999	Houston, Texas
Blitstein, Jeff	4	5	4.31	17	5	0	1	54	58	33	26	9	29	R	R	6-2	190	10-21-75	1999	Aurora, Colo.
Brown, Steve	3	2	5.30	18	7	0	1	53	57	40	31	21	43	S	R	6-0	205	4-13-76	1999	Reseda, Calif.
Calvo, Jose	0	2	5.14	5	0	0	1	7	9	9	4	4	5	R	R	6-3	180	1-14-80	1996	Chame, Panama
Fereira, Ramon	2	4	5.33	21	3	0	1	49	42	41	29	28	49	R	R	6-1	165	2-24-79	1996	Valencia, Venez.
Ferguson, Tony	0	0	1.29	3	0	0	1	7	3	1	1	1	8	R	R	6-4	200	12-1-76	1999	Russellville, Ark.
Gallo, Mike	1	0	1.23	3	3	0	0	15	13	4	2	7	11	L	L	6-0	170	4-2-77	1999	Long Beach, Calif.
George, Chris	2	1	1.48	21	0	0	2	30	28	9	5	9	41	R	R	6-3	190	8-16-77	1999	St. Louis, Mo.
Jamison, Ryan	5	3	4.11	15	15	0	0	88	83	45	40	36	83	R	R	6-3	185	1-5-78	1999	El Cajon, Calif.
Nannini, Mike	5	3	1.90	11	11	2	0	76	55	19	16	17	86	R	R	5-11	175	8-9-80	1998	Henderson, Nev.
Ortiz, John	1	2	4.66	23	0	0	0	37	39	25	19	22	28	L	L	6-0	190	12-5-75	1999	Las Cruces, N.M.
Pineda, Jairo	9	2	2.88	15	15	1	0	84	70	35	27	31	67	R	R	6-3	185	9-25-76	1997	Granada, Nicaragua
Saladin, Miguel	1	4	7.13	8	0	0	0	18	23	19	14	7	10	R	R	5-11	165	5-22-78	1996	San Pedro de Macoris, D.R.
Wade, Travis	1	1	2.39	26	0	0	11	38	25	10	10	13	53	R	R	6-4	225	7-8-75	1997	Climax, Mich.
Whitesides, Johnny	1	0	2.51	6	0	0	0	14	13	12	4	8	13	R	R	6-4	195	3-2-78	1997	Sarasota, Fla.
Wilkerson, Byron	3	3	3.75	9	7	0	0	48	38	25	20	22	47	R	R	6-4	205	8-15-76	1998	Temple, Texas

Organization Statistics

MARTINSVILLE — Rookie

APPALACHIAN LEAGUE

BATTING	AVG	G	AB	R	H	2B	3B	HR	RBI	BB	SO	SB	CS	B	T	HT	WT	DOB	1st Yr	Resides
Andrianoff, Jon	.218	24	55	8	12	1	0	0	6	9	29	4	3	R	R	6-2	165	2-25-81	1999	Olean, N.Y.
Carrillo, Robert	.224	49	174	21	39	7	0	7	28	15	56	5	2	R	R	6-6	260	5-9-79	1998	San Diego, Calif.
Garcia, Kevys	.255	50	192	36	49	9	3	2	18	20	65	16	4	R	R	5-11	155	10-9-80	1997	Farriar, Venez.
Gentry, Garett	.239	33	117	16	28	4	2	2	14	9	26	4	0	L	R	5-10	210	6-27-81	1999	Victorville, Calif.
Helquist, Jon	.301	49	173	33	52	15	3	4	17	18	50	5	5	R	R	6-1	170	8-17-80	1999	Jacksonville, Fla.
Huffman, Royce	.296	53	196	39	58	16	7	2	36	31	29	18	2	R	R	6-0	195	1-11-77	1999	Missouri City, Texas
Kane, Pat	.204	35	98	15	20	5	0	1	8	16	33	4	3	R	R	5-10	190	1-9-77	1999	Springfield, Pa.
Ledesma, Luis	.183	26	93	10	17	3	0	0	7	5	26	1	2	R	R	5-11	175	11-9-79	1997	Santiago, D.R.
Lopez, Aristides	.220	41	132	13	29	4	1	0	8	5	31	9	6	R	R	6-0	170	1-30-79	1997	Caracas, Venez.
Maya, Johan	.239	42	138	22	33	7	1	1	12	7	15	9	5	S	R	6-1	150	2-16-80	1996	San Felipe, Venez.
O'Connor, Brian	.184	13	38	3	7	1	0	1	2	8	4	2	3	R	R	6-2	185	6-21-77	1999	Arlington Heights, Ill.
Perez, Jay	.273	42	139	25	38	9	0	2	36	24	47	17	4	S	R	6-2	210	2-24-80	1999	Seymour, Conn.
Ramirez, Anthony	.344	22	64	13	22	7	0	4	20	9	11	1	2	L	R	6-1	200	7-21-80	1998	Carson, Calif.
Rincon, Carlos	.239	55	180	29	43	12	2	3	21	16	59	24	6	R	R	6-2	170	2-2-80	1997	San Pedro de Macoris, D.R.
Salazar, Erick	.195	17	41	6	8	0	0	0	0	3	15	3	0	R	R	6-1	165	9-17-79	1997	Maiquetia, Venez.
Santillan, Manuel	.181	21	72	13	13	3	1	2	9	4	21	2	2	R	R	6-0	165	8-20-79	1996	La Romana, D.R.
Schmitt, Brian	.267	51	180	27	48	11	4	6	26	29	48	4	4	L	L	6-0	175	5-16-79	1999	Jayton, Texas
Wright, Gavin	.309	61	236	37	73	17	3	2	29	25	46	31	2	R	R	6-2	175	5-6-79	1999	Lufkin, Texas

GAMES BY POSITION: C—Gentry 18, O'Connor 12, Perez 22, Santillan 19. 1B—Carrillo 42, A. Ramirez 1, Schmitt 29. 2B—Andrianoff 1, Garcia 15, Huffman 3, Kane 34, Lopez 1, Maya 23. 3B—Garcia 18, Helquist 16, Huffman 3, Maya 5, A. Ramirez 8. SS—Andrianoff 18, Garcia 15, Helquist 25, Maya 19. OF—Huffman 17, Kane 1, Ledesma 26, Lopez 36, Rincon 54, Salazar 16, Schmitt 16, Wright 61.

PITCHING	W	L	ERA	G	GS	CG	SV	IP	H	R	ER	BB	SO	B	T	HT	WT	DOB	1st Yr	Resides
Barrett, Jimmy	0	1	4.42	6	3	0	0	18	15	9	9	10	12	R	R	6-2	190	6-7-81	1999	Cumberland, Md.
Ferguson, Tony	2	2	2.20	15	0	0	3	33	27	12	8	6	32	R	R	6-4	200	12-1-76	1999	Russellville, Ark.
Fitzgerald, Ryan	1	1	5.11	12	0	0	0	25	24	20	14	6	22	R	R	6-5	220	9-25-75	1999	Mont Belvieu, Texas
Hernandez, Carlos	5	1	1.79	13	9	0	0	55	36	21	11	23	82	L	L	5-10	145	4-22-80	1997	Yagua, Venez.
Johnson, Derrick	2	2	4.18	21	0	0	0	47	32	23	22	32	46	L	L	6-0	205	11-19-78	1999	Albany, Ga.
Kann, Kris	0	2	7.82	9	6	0	0	25	36	26	22	16	16	R	R	6-4	220	4-22-79	1999	Newville, Pa.
Latham, Jason	3	3	5.20	15	6	0	0	45	51	35	26	16	45	R	R	5-11	180	2-22-77	1999	Ludlow, Miss.
Parker, Daniel	6	4	3.91	14	13	1	0	74	73	47	32	30	71	R	R	6-1	190	8-19-79	1998	Alamo, Calif.
Ramirez, Santiago	2	1	1.45	25	0	0	17	31	26	9	5	14	35	R	R	5-11	160	8-15-80	1997	Bonao, D.R.
Roberts, Nick	4	2	1.90	10	7	1	1	47	43	11	10	6	42	R	R	6-2	185	11-6-76	1999	Annabella, Utah
Rosario, Rodrigo	5	5	4.69	14	14	0	0	79	78	46	41	32	86	R	R	6-2	165	12-14-79	1996	La Romana, D.R.
Saladin, Miguel	1	0	5.06	11	0	0	1	16	24	12	9	4	19	R	R	5-11	165	5-22-78	1996	San Pedro de Macoris, D.R.
Smith, Brandon	2	0	1.35	8	0	0	0	13	6	3	2	10	10	R	R	6-1	210	4-10-76	1998	Tyler, Texas
Stanford, Derek	4	3	2.87	11	9	0	0	60	39	28	19	25	75	R	R	6-2	190	9-6-78	1998	Temple, Texas
Vasquez, Luis	6	1	2.79	13	3	0	1	42	46	21	13	12	39	L	L	5-11	150	8-23-79	1997	Barquisimeto, Venez.

GAMES BY POSITION: (none shown)

KANSASCITYROYALS

Bright future outshines franchise-worst finish for Royals

BY ALAN ESKEW

After several youngsters stepped forward with booming bats in 1999, the Royals feel bullish about their future despite finishing with the worst record (64-97) in franchise history.

K C. Rookie center fielder Carlos Beltran, who had spent just a half season with Double-A Wichita in 1998 before making the leap to the majors, hit .293 with 22 home runs, 108 RBIs, 112 runs and 27 stolen bases. He was honored as Baseball America's Rookie of the Year.

Mike Sweeney, who had a .258 average with 19 home runs in 230 previous major league games, hit a team-leading .322 with 22 home runs, 102 RBIs and 101 runs. He tied an American League record in July by driving in a run in 13 consecutive games. Sweeney also went through a position change, moving from catcher to first base after Jeff King announced his retirement on May 23.

After spending considerable time on the disabled list since coming from the Braves in 1997, a healthy Jermaine Dye hit .294 and led the team with 27 home runs and 119 RBIs. He and Sweeney each collected 44 doubles, tying for second in the American League. Joe Randa returned to the Royals in a trade after hitting .254 in 1998 with the Tigers, and rebounded to hit .314. Johnny Damon, who had played in a club-record 305 consecutive games, had to sit after pulling a muscle in September, but he hit a career-high .307 and scored more than 100 runs for the second straight year.

The Royals hit .282 and scored a club-record 856 runs. So how could they lose 97 games? The pitching staff surrendered a franchise-record 921 runs, and the

Jermaine Dye   **Dee Brown**

Players of the Year

MAJOR LEAGUE: Jermaine Dye, of
Dye enjoyed a breakthrough season, leading the Royals with 27 home runs and 119 RBIs while batting .294.

MINOR LEAGUE: Dee Brown, of
Brown played even better at Wichita after a mid-season promotion from Wilmington to finish at .331 overall on the year.

5.35 ERA was the worst in the AL.

The Royals lost 35 games in which they led or were tied going into the seventh inning. The bullpen blew 30 saves while logging just 29. Closer Jeff Montgomery, who had led the Royals in saves in each of the previous 10 seasons, announced his retirement, leaving a big void.

None had a winning record in 1999, but the Royals like what they saw from four starters: lefthander Jose Rosado and righthanders Jeff Suppan, Jay Witasick and Blake Stein. Stein came over from the Athletics as part of the package for longtime ace Kevin Appier, who was finally dealt after several seasons of speculation.

On the farm, five Royals clubs qualified for their league playoffs and three won championships: Double-A Wichita in the Texas League, Class A Wilmington in the Carolina League and short-season Spokane in the Northwest League. Wilmington shared its championship with Myrtle Beach when the threat of Hurricane Floyd forced the cancellation of Game Five of their best-of-5 series.

John Mizerock, who directed Wichita to the TL crown, was named Baseball America's Minor League Manager of the Year. He was promoted to manage the Royals' Triple-A Omaha club for 2000.

Outfielder Mark Quinn led the Pacific Coast League with a .360 average, and on Sept. 14 became just the fourth player to hit two home runs in his major league debut.

Outfielder Dee Brown, a 1996 first-round pick, combined to hit 25 home runs with 102 RBIs for Wichita and Wilmington before getting a September callup.

ORGANIZATION LEADERS

BATTING

*AVG	Mark Quinn, Omaha	.360
R	Dee Brown, Wichita/Wilmington	107
H	Mark Quinn, Omaha	154
TB	Kit Pellow, Omaha	277
2B	Joe Vitiello, Omaha	33
3B	Vic Radcliff, Wilmington	8
HR	Sean McNally, Wichita	36
RBI	Sean McNally, Wichita	109
BB	Sean McNally, Wichita	93
SO	Sean McNally, Wichita	132
SB	Mike Curry, Wilmington/Charleston	85

PITCHING

W	Three tied at	13
L	Matt Burch, Charleston/GCL	13
#ERA	Junior Guerrero, Wilmington/Charleston	2.31
G	Jake Chapman, Wichita	52
CG	Edwin Gonzalez, Wilmington/Charleston	3
SV	Ken Ray, Omaha/Wichita	15
IP	Scott Mullen, Omaha/Wichita	169
BB	Jeremy Affeldt, Charleston	80
SO	Junior Guerrero, Wilmington/Charleston	181

*Minimum 250 At-Bats #Minimum 75 Innings

Kansas City ROYALS

Manager: Tony Muser

1999 Record: 64-97, .398 (4th, AL Central)

Organization Statistics

BATTING	AVG	G	AB	R	H	2B	3B	HR	RBI	BB	SO	SB	CS	B	T	HT	WT	DOB	1st Yr	Resides
Beltran, Carlos	.293	156	663	112	194	27	7	22	108	46	123	27	8	S	R	6-0	175	4-24-77	1995	Manati, P.R.
Brown, Dee	.080	12	25	1	2	0	0	0	2	7	0	0	0	L	R	6-0	215	3-27-78	1996	Orlando, Fla.
Damon, Johnny	.307	145	583	101	179	39	9	14	77	67	50	36	6	L	L	6-2	190	11-5-73	1992	Overland Park, Kan.
Dye, Jermaine	.294	158	608	96	179	44	8	27	119	58	119	2	3	R	R	6-4	220	1-28-74	1993	Overland Park, Kan.
Fasano, Sal	.233	23	60	11	14	2	0	5	16	7	17	0	1	R	R	6-2	230	8-10-71	1993	Overland Park, Kan.
Febles, Carlos	.256	123	453	71	116	22	9	10	53	47	91	20	4	R	R	5-11	170	5-24-76	1994	La Romana, D.R.
Giambi, Jeremy	.285	90	288	34	82	13	1	3	34	40	67	0	0	L	L	6-0	205	9-30-74	1996	Covina, Calif.
Hansen, Jed	.203	49	79	16	16	1	0	3	5	10	32	0	1	R	R	6-1	195	8-19-72	1994	Olympia, Wash.
Holbert, Ray	.280	34	100	14	28	3	0	0	5	8	20	7	4	R	R	6-0	185	9-25-70	1988	Glendale, Ariz.
King, Jeff	.236	21	72	14	17	2	0	3	11	15	10	2	0	R	R	6-1	190	12-26-64	1986	Hamilton, Mont.
Kreuter, Chad	.225	107	324	31	73	15	0	5	35	34	65	0	0	S	R	6-2	200	8-26-64	1985	La Quinta, Calif.
Leius, Scott	.203	37	74	8	15	1	0	1	10	4	8	1	0	R	R	6-3	200	9-24-65	1986	Eden Prairie, Minn.
Lopez, Mendy	.400	7	20	2	8	0	1	0	3	0	5	0	0	R	R	6-2	190	10-15-74	1992	Santo Domingo, D.R.
Martinez, Felix	.143	6	7	1	1	0	0	0	0	0	0	0	0	S	R	6-0	180	5-18-74	1993	Nagua, D.R.
Pose, Scott	.285	86	137	27	39	3	0	0	12	21	22	6	2	L	R	5-11	190	2-11-67	1989	Raleigh, N.C.
Quinn, Mark	.333	17	60	11	20	4	1	6	18	4	11	1	0	R	R	6-1	175	5-21-74	1995	West Covina, Calif.
Randa, Joe	.314	156	628	92	197	36	8	16	84	50	80	5	4	R	R	5-11	190	12-18-69	1991	Overland Park, Kan.
Sanchez, Rey	.294	134	479	66	141	18	6	2	56	22	48	11	5	R	R	5-9	170	10-5-67	1986	San Juan, P.R.
Scarsone, Steve	.206	46	68	2	14	5	0	0	6	9	24	1	0	R	R	6-2	195	4-11-66	1986	Scottsdale, Ariz.
Spehr, Tim	.206	60	155	26	32	7	0	9	26	22	47	1	0	R	R	6-2	200	7-2-66	1988	Dallas, Texas
Sutton, Larry	.225	43	102	14	23	6	0	2	15	13	17	1	0	L	L	6-0	185	5-14-70	1992	Temecula, Calif.
Sweeney, Mike	.322	150	575	101	185	44	2	22	102	54	48	6	1	R	R	6-2	215	7-22-73	1991	Overland Park, Kan.
Vitiello, Joe	.146	13	41	4	6	1	0	1	4	2	9	0	0	R	R	6-3	230	4-11-70	1991	Stoneham, Mass.

PITCHING	W	L	ERA	G	GS	CG	SV	IP	H	R	ER	BB	SO	B	T	HT	WT	DOB	1st Yr	Resides
Appier, Kevin	9	9	4.87	22	22	1	0	140	153	81	76	51	78	R	R	6-2	200	12-6-67	1987	Paola, Kan.
Barber, Brian	1	3	9.64	8	3	0	1	19	31	20	20	10	7	R	R	6-1	190	3-4-73	1991	Ocoee, Fla.
Byrdak, Tim	0	3	7.66	33	0	0	1	25	32	24	21	20	17	L	L	5-11	160	10-31-73	1994	Oak Forest, Ill.
Carter, Lance	0	1	5.06	6	0	0	0	5	3	3	3	3	3	R	R	6-1	190	12-18-74	1994	Bradenton, Fla.
Durbin, Chad	0	0	0.00	1	0	0	0	2	1	0	0	1	3	R	R	6-1	175	12-3-77	1996	Baton Rouge, La.
Fussell, Chris	0	5	7.39	17	8	0	2	56	72	51	46	36	37	R	R	6-2	200	5-19-76	1994	Oregon, Ohio
Mathews, Terry	2	1	4.38	24	1	0	1	39	44	21	19	17	19	L	R	6-2	225	10-5-64	1987	Alexandria, La.
Montgomery, Jeff	1	4	6.84	49	0	0	12	51	72	40	39	21	27	R	R	5-11	175	1-7-62	1983	Leawood, Kan.
Moreno, Orber	0	0	5.63	7	0	0	0	8	4	5	5	6	7	R	R	6-2	190	4-27-77	1994	Los Autos, Venez.
Morman, Alvin	2	4	4.05	49	0	0	1	53	66	27	24	23	31	R	L	6-3	210	1-6-69	1991	Fuquay-Varina, N.C.
Murray, Dan	0	0	6.48	4	0	0	0	8	9	8	6	4	8	R	R	6-1	193	11-21-73	1995	Garden Grove, Calif.
Pisciotta, Marc	0	2	8.64	8	0	0	0	8	9	8	8	10	3	R	R	6-5	225	8-7-70	1991	Marietta, Ga.
Pittsley, Jim	1	2	6.94	5	5	0	0	23	32	18	18	15	7	R	R	6-7	230	4-3-74	1992	Dubois, Pa.
Ray, Ken	1	0	8.74	13	0	0	0	11	23	12	11	6	0	R	R	6-2	200	11-27-74	1993	Dawsonville, Ga.
Reichert, Dan	2	2	9.08	8	8	0	0	37	48	38	37	32	20	R	R	6-3	175	7-12-76	1997	Turlock, Calif.
Rigby, Brad	1	2	7.17	20	0	0	0	21	33	20	17	5	10	R	R	6-6	213	5-14-73	1994	Altamonte Springs, Fla.
2-team (29 Oakland)	4	6	5.06	49	0	0	0	84	102	51	47	31	36							
Rosado, Jose	10	14	3.85	33	33	5	0	208	197	103	89	72	141	L	L	6-0	185	11-4-74	1994	Dorado, P.R.
Rusch, Glendon	0	1	15.75	3	0	0	0	4	7	7	7	3	4	L	L	6-1	200	11-7-74	1993	Seattle, Wash.
Santiago, Jose	3	4	3.42	34	0	0	2	47	46	23	18	14	15	R	R	6-3	215	11-5-74	1994	Loiza, P.R.
Service, Scott	5	5	6.09	68	0	0	8	75	87	51	51	42	68	R	R	6-6	240	2-26-67	1986	Cincinnati, Ohio
Stein, Blake	1	2	4.09	12	11	0	0	70	59	33	32	41	43	R	R	6-7	210	8-3-73	1994	Folsom, La.
2-team (1 Oakland)	1	2	4.56	13	12	0	0	73	65	38	37	47	47							
Suppan, Jeff	10	12	4.53	32	32	4	0	209	222	113	105	62	103	R	R	6-2	210	1-2-75	1993	West Hills, Calif.
Suzuki, Mac	2	3	5.16	22	9	0	0	68	77	45	39	30	36	R	R	6-3	195	5-31-75	1992	Kobe, Japan
2-team (16 Seattle)	2	5	6.79	38	13	0	0	110	124	92	83	64	68							
Wallace, Derek	0	1	3.24	8	0	0	0	8	7	4	3	5	5	R	R	6-3	215	9-1-71	1992	Oxnard, Calif.
Wengert, Don	0	1	9.25	11	1	0	0	24	41	26	25	5	10	R	R	6-3	205	11-6-69	1992	Des Moines, Iowa
Whisenant, Matt	4	4	6.35	48	0	0	1	40	40	28	28	26	27	R	L	6-3	215	6-8-71	1990	Overland Park, Kan.
Witasick, Jay	9	12	5.57	32	28	1	0	158	191	108	98	83	102	R	R	6-4	210	8-28-72	1993	Bel Air, Md.

FIELDING

Catcher	PCT	G	PO	A	E	DP	PB
Fasano	1.000	23	143	8	0	0	1
Hansen	.000	1	0	0	0	0	0
Kreuter	.994	101	460	44	3	8	6
Spehr	.990	59	274	11	3	4	3
Sweeney	1.000	4	4	2	0	0	0

First Base	PCT	G	PO	A	E	DP
Giambi	.991	26	208	8	2	22
Hansen	.000	1	0	0	0	0
King	.990	20	188	15	2	21
Leius	.971	13	61	6	2	13
Scarsone	1.000	12	69	9	0	8
Sutton	.987	30	215	14	3	19
Sweeney	.981	74	584	41	12	76
Vitiello	1.000	10	65	7	0	11

Second Base	PCT	G	PO	A	E	DP
Febles	.979	122	272	375	14	101

	PCT	G	PO	A	E	DP
Hansen	.989	21	44	44	1	18
Holbert	.978	11	14	30	1	4
Leius	1.000	1	0	0	0	0
Lopez	1.000	6	11	16	0	5
Martinez	1.000	1	1	2	0	1
Scarsone	.938	9	17	13	2	3

Third Base	PCT	G	PO	A	E	DP
Hansen	1.000	4	2	1	0	0
Holbert	1.000	1	0	0	0	0
Leius	1.000	10	7	14	0	3
Randa	.952	156	119	314	22	28
Scarsone	.000	3	0	0	0	0

Shortstop	PCT	G	PO	A	E	DP
Hansen	1.000	10	11	22	0	3
Holbert	.987	22	31	46	1	16

	PCT	G	PO	A	E	DP
Leius	.000	2	0	0	0	0
Lopez	.000	1	0	0	0	0
Martinez	.000	2	0	0	0	0
Sanchez	.982	134	242	452	13	111
Scarsone	.977	16	15	27	1	7

Outfield	PCT	G	PO	A	E	DP
Beltran	.972	154	395	16	12	2
Brown	.929	3	12	1	1	0
Damon	.987	140	301	8	4	0
Dye	.984	157	362	17	6	6
Giambi	1.000	5	5	0	0	0
Hansen	.000	2	0	0	0	0
Pose	.970	25	29	3	1	1
Quinn	.964	15	25	2	1	0
Sutton	.000	1	0	0	0	0

GEORGE GOJKOVICH

Carlos Beltran
Honored as Rookie of the Year

DAVID SCHOFIELD

Mark Quinn
Hit .360-25-84 at Omaha

FARM SYSTEM

Director, Minor League Operations: Bob Hegman

Class	Farm Team	League	W	L	Pct.	Finish*	Manager(s)	First Yr
AAA	Omaha (Neb.) Royals	Pacific Coast	81	60	.574	3rd (16)	Ron Johnson	1969
AA	Wichita (Kan.) Wranglers	Texas	83	57	.593	1st (8)	John Mizerock	1995
A#	Wilmington (Del.) Blue Rocks	Carolina	77	61	.558	@3rd (8)	Jeff Garber	1993
A	Charleston (W.Va.) Alley Cats	South Atlantic	61	80	.433	13th (14)	Tom Poquette	1999
A	Spokane (Wash.) Indians	Northwest	44	32	.579	+1st (8)	Kevin Long	1995
Rookie	Baseball City (Fla.) Royals	Gulf Coast	33	27	.550	4th (14)	Andre David	1993

*Finish in overall standings (No. of teams in league)　#Advanced level　+Won league championship @League co-champion

OMAHA · Class AAA

PACIFIC COAST LEAGUE

BATTING	AVG	G	AB	R	H	2B	3B	HR	RBI	BB	SO	SB	CS	B	T	HT	WT	DOB	1st Yr	Resides
Brito, Juan	.286	2	7	1	2	2	0	0	0	0	2	0	0	R	R	5-11	185	11-7-79	1996	Santiago Rodriguez, D.R.
Byington, Jimmie	.206	89	228	28	47	10	1	2	23	20	46	3	7	R	R	5-11	175	8-22-73	1993	Tulsa, Okla.
Carr, Jeremy	.262	73	275	47	72	12	1	4	25	42	58	15	8	R	R	5-9	180	3-30-71	1993	Boise, Idaho
Fasano, Sal	.275	88	280	63	77	15	0	21	49	42	69	4	2	R	R	6-2	230	8-10-71	1993	Overland Park, Kan.
Giambi, Jeremy	.346	35	127	31	44	5	1	12	28	31	30	1	1	L	L	6-0	205	9-30-74	1996	Covina, Calif.
Gibralter, Steve	.266	110	417	77	111	21	1	28	78	27	97	6	3	R	R	6-0	195	10-9-72	1990	Duncanville, Texas
Hansen, Jed	.274	54	175	35	48	8	5	7	22	32	72	8	3	R	R	6-1	195	8-19-72	1994	Olympia, Wash.
Holbert, Ray	.297	33	128	26	38	4	0	4	12	12	35	13	4	R	R	6-0	185	9-25-70	1988	Glendale, Ariz.
Lopez, Mendy	.311	61	222	41	69	8	0	12	40	18	41	2	2	R	R	6-2	190	10-15-74	1992	Santo Domingo, D.R.
Martinez, Felix	.304	8	23	2	7	5	0	0	2	2	6	0	1	S	R	6-0	180	5-18-74	1993	Nagua, D.R.
Medrano, Anthony	.313	33	112	14	35	6	1	2	23	10	15	0	1	R	R	5-10	175	12-8-74	1993	Long Beach, Calif.
Mendez, Carlos	.280	84	293	38	82	25	0	10	37	6	32	4	3	R	R	6-0	210	6-18-74	1991	Caracas, Venez.
Mercedes, Henry	.244	69	193	27	47	8	0	6	32	27	63	4	1	R	R	6-2	210	7-23-69	1988	Santo Domingo, D.R.
Norman, Les	.273	89	333	53	91	20	2	13	40	14	45	7	3	R	R	6-1	185	2-25-69	1991	Leawood, Kan.
Pellow, Kit	.286	131	475	88	136	28	4	35	99	20	117	6	5	R	R	6-1	205	8-28-73	1996	Olathe, Kan.
Quinn, Mark	.360	107	428	67	154	27	0	25	84	28	69	7	9	R	R	6-1	175	5-21-74	1995	West Covina, Calif.
Roberge, J.P.	.314	116	437	77	137	31	3	13	66	26	59	16	5	R	R	6-0	177	9-12-72	1994	Arcadia, Calif.
Scarsone, Steve	.172	18	58	9	10	1	0	5	7	7	21	1	0	R	R	6-2	195	4-11-66	1986	Scottsdale, Ariz.
Sutton, Larry	.277	39	148	28	41	8	1	3	12	27	24	4	1	L	L	6-0	185	5-14-70	1992	Temecula, Calif.
Unroe, Tim	.227	5	22	4	5	0	0	1	2	0	5	0	0	R	R	6-3	200	10-7-70	1992	Antioch, Ill.
2-team (10 Edmonton)	.333	15	66	14	22	5	1	6	20	5	14	0	0							
Vitiello, Joe	.318	122	447	70	142	33	0	28	98	66	84	3	4	R	R	6-3	230	4-11-70	1991	Stoneham, Mass.

PITCHING	W	L	ERA	G	GS	CG	SV	IP	H	R	ER	BB	SO	B	T	HT	WT	DOB	1st Yr	Resides
Barber, Brian	9	5	4.56	19	19	2	0	120	128	68	61	29	75	R	R	6-1	190	3-4-73	1991	Ocoee, Fla.
Bluma, Jaime	0	0	3.22	17	0	0	2	22	21	10	8	4	19	R	R	5-11	195	5-18-72	1994	Overland Park, Kan.

PITCHING	W	L	ERA	G	GS	CG	SV	IP	H	R	ER	BB	SO	B	T	HT	WT	DOB	1st Yr	Resides
Byrdak, Tim	3	1	1.81	33	0	0	4	50	39	19	10	28	51	L	L	5-11	160	10-31-73	1994	Oak Forest, Ill.
D'Amico, Jeff	1	3	4.34	12	0	0	2	19	29	13	9	3	12	R	R	6-3	195	11-9-74	1993	Seattle, Wash.
2-team (14 Vancouver)	3	5	3.53	26	0	0	5	36	45	19	14	13	22							
Evans, Bart	4	5	8.10	30	0	0	2	33	33	34	30	36	34	R	R	6-2	210	12-30-70	1992	Lee's Summit, Mo.
Fussell, Chris	10	3	3.54	14	13	1	0	81	66	35	32	27	80	R	R	6-2	200	5-19-76	1994	Oregon, Ohio
Gooding, Jason	0	1	6.00	1	1	0	0	6	8	4	4	1	2	R	L	5-11	190	7-29-74	1997	Cambridge, Ontario
Hanson, Erik	4	3	4.60	14	10	0	0	61	58	32	31	22	43	R	R	6-6	215	5-18-65	1986	Kirkland, Wash.
2-team (10 Calgary)	5	9	5.90	24	19	0	0	108	126	75	71	48	85							
Krivda, Rick	6	8	5.70	21	18	0	0	115	154	94	73	41	70	R	L	6-1	185	1-19-70	1991	McKeesport, Pa.
Lineweaver, Aaron	0	1	6.00	1	1	0	0	6	6	4	4	3	3	R	R	6-0	210	7-26-73	1996	Denton, Texas
Mathews, Terry	1	0	1.65	7	0	0	0	16	11	4	3	5	11	L	R	6-2	225	10-5-64	1987	Alexandria, La.
Montgomery, Jeff	0	0	0.00	4	0	0	1	5	1	0	0	1	3	R	R	5-11	175	1-7-62	1983	Leawood, Kan.
Moreno, Orber	3	1	2.10	16	0	0	4	26	17	6	6	4	30	R	R	6-2	190	4-27-77	1994	Los Autos, Venez.
Morman, Alvin	0	0	3.14	8	1	0	1	14	8	5	5	1	15	L	R	6-3	210	1-6-69	1991	Fuquay-Varina, N.C.
Mullen, Scott	6	7	6.26	20	20	0	0	119	150	91	83	53	87	R	L	6-2	190	1-17-75	1996	Beaufort, S.C.
Pisciotta, Marc	0	1	11.20	10	0	0	0	14	18	18	17	11	8	R	R	6-5	225	8-7-70	1991	Marietta, Ga.
Ray, Ken	1	0	5.19	27	0	0	8	43	41	27	25	12	36	R	R	6-2	200	11-24-74	1993	Dawsonville, Ga.
Reichert, Dan	9	2	3.71	17	17	1	0	112	92	51	46	50	123	R	R	6-3	175	7-12-76	1997	Turlock, Calif.
Rios, Dan	10	4	6.07	47	5	0	4	89	111	64	60	39	44	R	R	6-2	195	11-11-72	1993	Hialeah, Fla.
Ruffcorn, Scott	1	0	5.02	8	0	0	0	14	14	10	8	10	8	R	R	6-5	230	12-29-69	1991	Cedar Park, Texas
Rusch, Glendon	4	7	4.42	20	20	1	0	114	143	68	56	33	102	L	L	6-1	200	11-7-74	1993	Seattle, Wash.
Saier, Matt	4	4	5.09	9	9	1	0	58	69	37	33	8	44	R	R	6-2	190	1-29-73	1995	Gulf Breeze, Fla.
Santiago, Jose	0	0	0.00	1	0	0	0	2	3	0	0	0	0	R	R	6-3	215	11-5-74	1994	Loiza, P.R.
Veras, Dario	1	2	4.35	12	0	0	0	21	19	10	10	3	17	R	R	6-1	155	3-13-73	1991	Villa Vazquez, D.R.
Walker, Jamie	0	1	4.67	4	4	0	0	17	22	12	9	4	11	L	L	6-2	190	7-1-71	1992	Overland Park, Kan.
Wengert, Don	4	0	4.17	16	2	0	1	41	41	20	19	9	24	R	R	6-3	205	11-6-69	1992	Des Moines, Iowa
Wilson, Kris	0	1	8.44	1	1	0	0	5	8	5	5	0	3	R	R	6-4	225	8-6-76	1997	Palm Harbor, Fla.

FIELDING

Catcher	PCT	G	PO	A	E	DP	PB
Brito	1.000	2	16	1	0	0	0
Fasano	.981	82	576	50	12	3	8
Gibralter	.500	1	1	0	1	0	0
Mendez	1.000	4	12	2	0	0	0
Mercedes	.998	66	382	43	1	5	8
Norman	1.000	1	1	0	0	0	0

First Base	PCT	G	PO	A	E	DP
Byington	.000	1	0	0	0	0
Fasano	1.000	1	6	1	0	0
Giambi	.983	15	111	8	2	10
Gibralter	.965	9	49	6	2	8
Mendez	.991	44	319	12	3	32
Pellow	1.000	2	15	1	0	1
Roberge	.980	45	34	3	1	6
Sutton	.985	34	235	21	4	25
Vitiello	.981	43	289	21	6	34

Second Base	PCT	G	PO	A	E	DP
Byington	.950	14	16	22	2	4

	PCT	G	PO	A	E	DP
Carr	.875	7	5	9	2	2
Hansen	1.000	35	76	72	0	24
Holbert	.923	8	15	9	2	0
Lopez	.880	6	10	12	3	3
Medrano	.991	24	46	66	1	19
Roberge	.985	60	115	149	4	38
Scarsone	1.000	4	8	5	0	0

Third Base	PCT	G	PO	A	E	DP
Byington	1.000	3	1	7	0	2
Lopez	1.000	3	3	6	0	0
Pellow	.901	127	78	223	33	18
Roberge	.893	13	6	19	3	2

Shortstop	PCT	G	PO	A	E	DP
Byington	.883	22	34	57	12	15
Hansen	.927	22	39	63	8	16
Holbert	.980	24	36	63	2	17
Lopez	.979	53	85	153	5	27
Martinez	.963	7	8	18	1	4

	PCT	G	PO	A	E	DP
Medrano	1.000	8	26	19	0	7
Roberge	1.000	4	6	6	0	1
Scarsone	1.000	12	22	27	0	7

Outfield	PCT	G	PO	A	E	DP
Byington	.988	41	80	1	1	1
Carr	.958	66	110	5	5	1
Giambi	1.000	20	45	1	0	0
Gibralter	.962	86	167	12	7	3
Hansen	1.000	1	1	0	0	0
Medrano	.000	1	0	0	0	0
Mendez	1.000	14	23	0	0	0
Mercedes	.000	2	0	0	0	0
Norman	.996	87	215	8	1	1
Quinn	.983	101	216	13	4	2
Roberge	.941	28	45	3	3	0
Scarsone	1.000	1	3	0	0	0
Sutton	1.000	7	12	0	0	0
Unroe	1.000	2	3	0	0	0

WICHITA — Class AA

TEXAS LEAGUE

BATTING	AVG	G	AB	R	H	2B	3B	HR	RBI	BB	SO	SB	CS	B	T	HT	WT	DOB	1st Yr	Resides
Amado, Jose	.290	121	459	71	133	29	2	13	93	54	37	5	3	R	R	6-1	180	2-7-75	1994	San Cristobal, Venez.
Brito, Juan	.091	4	11	0	1	0	0	0	0	2	3	0	0	R	R	5-11	185	11-7-79	1996	Santiago Rodriguez, D.R.
Brown, Dee	.353	65	235	58	83	14	3	12	56	35	41	10	8	L	R	6-0	215	3-27-78	1996	Orlando, Fla.
Brown, Ray	.318	13	44	8	14	4	0	1	11	8	5	0	0	L	R	6-2	205	7-30-72	1994	Redding, Calif.
Dodson, Jeremy	.257	133	452	63	116	20	1	21	56	51	95	9	5	L	R	6-2	200	5-3-77	1998	Sherman, Texas
Escamilla, Roman	.244	60	201	21	49	13	0	1	28	13	46	3	0	R	R	5-10	200	1-21-74	1996	Corpus Christi, Texas
Escandon, Emiliano	.259	120	340	59	88	18	5	7	57	73	46	5	7	L	R	5-10	180	11-6-74	1995	Ontario, Calif.
Goodwin, David	.300	3	10	3	3	0	0	0	0	1	3	0	0	R	R	6-1	205	3-26-75	1998	Overland Park, Kan.
Hallmark, Pat	.285	75	242	35	69	7	2	5	24	21	62	14	7	R	R	6-0	170	12-31-73	1995	Houston, Texas
Layne, Jason	.217	30	92	13	20	4	0	2	12	15	24	1	2	L	R	6-2	215	5-17-73	1996	Tyler, Texas
Martinez, Felix	.269	87	327	57	88	22	2	4	37	37	43	19	12	S	R	6-0	180	5-18-74	1993	Nagua, D.R.
McNally, Sean	.282	129	440	97	124	24	2	36	109	93	132	7	3	R	R	6-4	210	12-14-72	1994	Rye, N.Y.
Medrano, Anthony	.339	73	257	45	87	15	1	5	32	21	23	4	2	R	R	5-10	175	12-8-74	1993	Long Beach, Calif.
Metzler, Rod	.500	3	10	5	5	2	0	2	4	0	3	0	0	S	R	5-11	185	11-19-74	1997	Zionsville, Ind.
Moore, Kenderick	.251	80	243	36	61	11	0	0	27	20	55	19	10	R	R	5-11	175	5-17-73	1996	Ardmore, Okla.
Phillips, Paul	.267	108	393	58	105	20	2	3	56	26	38	8	9	R	R	5-11	175	4-15-77	1998	Bailey, Miss.
Prieto, Alejandro	.294	114	360	56	106	23	4	6	45	35	47	12	6	R	R	5-11	175	6-9-76	1995	Caracas, Venez.
Tomlinson, Goef	.280	128	479	100	134	31	4	4	46	72	82	24	19	L	L	6-1	190	8-19-76	1997	Fort Worth, Texas

PITCHING	W	L	ERA	G	GS	CG	SV	IP	H	R	ER	BB	SO	B	T	HT	WT	DOB	1st Yr	Resides
Austin, Jeff	3	1	4.46	6	6	0	0	34	40	19	17	11	21	R	R	6-0	185	10-19-76	1999	Kingwood, Texas
Bluma, Jeff	2	6	5.40	30	0	0	6	38	40	25	23	16	21	R	R	5-11	195	11-8-72	1994	Overland Park, Kan.
Brewer, Ryan	5	2	5.54	42	1	0	3	67	85	45	41	17	34	L	R	6-2	185	10-31-73	1996	Denton, Texas
Calero, Kiko	9	3	4.11	26	23	1	1	129	143	67	59	57	92	R	R	6-1	170	1-9-75	1996	Rio Piedras, P.R.
Carter, Lance	5	2	0.78	44	0	0	13	70	69	11	6	1	46	R	R	6-1	190	12-18-74	1994	Bradenton, Fla.
Chapman, Jake	3	0	4.39	52	0	0	3	70	87	38	34	29	53	R	L	6-1	175	1-11-74	1996	Rensselaer, Ind.
Durbin, Chad	8	10	4.64	28	27	1	0	157	154	88	81	49	122	R	R	6-1	175	12-3-77	1996	Baton Rouge, La.
Gooding, Jason	13	7	4.73	23	23	0	0	139	176	80	73	39	63	R	L	5-11	190	7-29-74	1997	Cambridge, Ontario
Lineweaver, Aaron	4	3	5.28	9	7	0	1	44	49	32	26	15	20	R	R	6-0	210	7-26-73	1996	Denton, Texas

PITCHING	W	L	ERA	G	GS	CG	SV	IP	H	R	ER	BB	SO	B	T	HT	WT	DOB	1st Yr	Resides
Mathews, Terry	0	0	4.50	1	0	0	0	2	2	1	1	0	2	L	R	6-2	225	10-5-64	1987	Alexandria, La.
Montgomery, Jeff	0	0	9.00	1	0	0	1	2	1	1	1	1	1	R	R	5-11	175	1-7-62	1983	Leawood, Kan.
Morrison, Robbie	2	0	2.01	15	0	0	5	22	26	7	5	7	21	R	R	6-0	215	12-7-76	1998	Loxahatchee, Fla.
Mullen, Scott	4	3	4.01	9	9	0	0	49	47	28	22	18	30	R	L	6-2	190	1-17-75	1996	Beaufort, S.C.
Prihoda, Steve	6	3	4.00	49	0	0	2	79	91	43	35	15	51	R	L	6-6	215	12-7-72	1995	Weimer, Texas
Ray, Ken	0	0	5.06	14	0	0	7	21	23	12	12	10	18	R	R	6-2	200	11-27-74	1993	Dawsonville, Ga.
Saier, Matt	9	7	5.01	19	19	0	0	110	137	64	61	34	61	R	R	6-2	190	1-29-73	1995	Gulf Breeze, Fla.
Santiago, Jose	0	1	2.00	4	2	0	0	9	8	2	2	0	6	R	R	6-3	215	11-5-74	1994	Loiza, P.R.
Smith, Toby	5	2	2.94	22	13	0	1	80	86	30	26	18	40	R	R	6-6	225	11-16-71	1993	Guthrie, Okla.
Wilson, Kris	5	7	5.45	23	10	0	0	74	91	51	45	14	45	R	R	6-4	225	8-6-76	1997	Palm Harbor, Fla.

FIELDING

Catcher	PCT	G	PO	A	E	DP	PB
Brito	1.000	4	23	2	0	0	0
Escamilla	.984	44	212	29	4	4	3
Hallmark	1.000	1	5	1	0	0	0
Medrano	.000	1	0	0	0	0	0
Phillips	.984	99	549	79	10	10	16

First Base	PCT	G	PO	A	E	DP
Amado	.990	102	868	57	9	85
R. Brown	.989	8	82	6	1	5
Goodwin	.889	2	8	0	1	1
Layne	.980	24	231	15	5	24
McNally	.957	12	79	9	4	9

Second Base	PCT	G	PO	A	E	DP
Escandon	.971	43	69	101	5	28
Martinez	1.000	5	13	10	0	3

	PCT	G	PO	A	E	DP
Medrano	.969	59	142	167	10	40
Metzler	1.000	1	2	0	0	0
Moore	.903	8	15	13	3	6
Prieto	.967	40	72	73	5	19

Third Base	PCT	G	PO	A	E	DP
Amado	.857	1	0	6	1	0
Escandon	.913	10	7	14	2	1
Martinez	.786	3	3	8	3	2
McNally	.932	119	75	266	25	26
Medrano	1.000	1	2	2	0	1
Phillips	1.000	1	0	1	0	0
Prieto	.944	16	8	26	2	1

Shortstop	PCT	G	PO	A	E	DP
Amado	1.000	1	1	0	0	0

	PCT	G	PO	A	E	DP
Escandon	.917	4	6	5	1	3
Martinez	.950	80	125	256	20	49
Medrano	1.000	5	8	18	0	7
Prieto	.944	62	97	188	17	36

Outfield	PCT	G	PO	A	E	DP
D. Brown	.958	65	110	4	5	1
Dodson	.966	129	179	20	7	6
Hallmark	.933	54	81	3	6	1
Medrano	1.000	7	9	0	0	0
Metzler	1.000	2	7	0	0	0
Moore	1.000	54	101	4	0	0
Phillips	1.000	3	3	1	0	0
Prieto	.750	3	3	0	1	0
Tomlinson	.984	127	313	2	5	0

WILMINGTON — Class A

CAROLINA LEAGUE

BATTING	AVG	G	AB	R	H	2B	3B	HR	RBI	BB	SO	SB	CS	B	T	HT	WT	DOB	1st Yr	Resides
Berger, Brandon	.293	119	450	73	132	27	4	16	73	45	93	29	7	R	R	5-11	200	2-21-75	1996	Fort Mitchell, Ky.
Brito, Juan	.283	14	46	3	13	1	0	0	1	1	11	0	0	R	R	5-11	185	11-7-79	1996	Santiago Rodriguez, D.R.
Brown, Dee	.308	61	221	49	68	10	2	13	46	44	56	20	8	L	R	6-0	215	3-27-78	1996	Orlando, Fla.
Campbell, Wylie	.241	45	137	22	33	4	0	1	17	25	29	6	5	S	R	5-11	180	3-27-75	1996	Fort Worth, Texas
Caruso, Joe	.235	102	361	60	85	13	6	5	37	34	68	6	4	R	R	5-9	190	12-30-74	1997	Lock Haven, Pa.
Cepeda, Jose	.313	59	227	35	71	7	2	0	25	22	19	5	8	R	R	6-0	185	8-1-74	1995	Fajardo, P.R.
Conner, Decomba	.304	48	171	27	52	7	2	1	17	21	26	9	1	R	R	5-10	185	7-17-73	1994	Mooresville, N.C.
Curry, Mike	.230	54	200	31	46	2	1	16	34	39	24	9	1	L	R	5-10	190	2-15-77	1998	Jacksonville, Fla.
Dillon, Joe	.264	134	503	73	133	31	2	16	90	59	124	9	6	R	R	6-2	205	8-2-75	1997	Santa Rosa, Calif.
Hill, Jeremy	.234	92	304	37	71	12	1	4	27	38	75	2	0	R	R	5-10	185	8-8-77	1996	Dallas, Texas
Medrano, Steve	.251	98	362	41	91	4	3	0	24	30	66	12	10	S	R	6-0	150	10-8-77	1996	La Puente, Calif.
Montas, Ricardo	.246	98	349	46	86	15	0	2	31	47	60	4	2	R	R	6-1	170	3-9-77	1994	Santo Domingo, D.R.
Moore, Griffin	.059	6	17	1	1	1	0	0	4	1	7	0	0	R	R	6-2	195	4-29-76	1998	Columbia, Mo.
Pagan, Carlos	.000	4	8	0	0	0	0	0	0	0	3	0	0	R	R	5-9	195	11-2-75	1997	Vega Baja, P.R.
Radcliff, Vic	.265	114	393	62	104	22	8	7	56	28	69	13	3	R	R	5-9	180	9-23-76	1995	Belvedere, S.C.
Torres, Rafael	.242	76	252	15	61	7	0	1	20	15	51	0	4	R	R	6-0	185	10-7-78	1996	Santo Domingo, D.R.
Ullery, Dave	.231	60	199	20	46	18	0	2	27	18	70	0	0	L	R	6-3	225	12-16-74	1997	Brazil, Ind.
Willis, Dave	.261	116	441	58	115	26	1	16	72	20	84	4	4	L	R	6-5	240	7-18-74	1997	Arcadia, Calif.

GAMES BY POSITION: C—Brito 14, Hill 92, Pagan 4, Ullery 37. **1B**—Dillon 13, Montas 16, Ullery 1, Willis 113. **2B**—Campbell 22, Caruso 64, Cepeda 35, Montas 25, Moore 1. **3B**—Cepeda 9, Dillon 111, Montas 21, Moore 1. **SS**—Campbell 21, Cepeda 14, Medrano 98, Montas 11. **OF**—Berger 76, Brown 57, Caruso 38, Conner 44, Curry 54, Moore 1, Radcliff 110, Torres 56.

PITCHING	W	L	ERA	G	GS	CG	SV	IP	H	R	ER	BB	SO	B	T	HT	WT	DOB	1st Yr	Resides
Austin, Jeff	7	2	3.77	18	18	0	0	112	108	52	47	39	97	R	R	6-0	185	10-19-76	1999	Kingwood, Texas
Delaney, Donnie	0	3	5.40	23	0	0	3	25	25	17	15	28	26	R	R	5-10	200	3-24-74	1994	Bossier City, La.
Delgado, Joseph	0	1	4.70	2	1	0	0	8	6	4	4	2	5	R	R	6-2	185	5-10-80	1997	La Guaira, Venez.
George, Chris	9	7	3.60	27	27	0	0	145	142	65	58	53	142	L	L	6-1	165	9-16-79	1998	Spring, Texas
Gonzalez, Edwin	1	1	6.55	5	0	0	0	11	14	12	8	4	8	R	R	5-10	175	8-13-77	1995	Santo Domingo, D.R.
Guerrero, Junior	4	2	1.40	9	9	0	0	51	30	10	8	26	68	R	R	6-2	175	8-21-79	1996	Santo Domingo, D.R.
Lamber, Justin	5	3	3.67	39	2	0	6	69	68	29	28	33	67	R	L	6-0	210	5-22-76	1997	Hackensack, N.J.
Lineweaver, Aaron	8	6	3.55	17	16	0	0	101	96	45	40	36	75	R	R	6-0	210	7-26-73	1996	Denton, Texas
Morrison, Robbie	2	5	2.27	28	0	0	6	44	31	13	11	13	47	R	R	6-0	215	12-7-76	1998	Loxahatchee, Fla.
Paredes, Carlos	6	0	4.09	36	0	0	3	55	47	31	25	48	49	R	R	6-0	170	5-10-76	1995	Sabana de la Mar, D.R.
Pederson, Justin	4	4	4.54	34	4	0	2	77	67	46	39	40	61	R	R	6-1	190	9-5-74	1997	Chippewa Falls, Wis.
Roberts, Mike	0	0	1.74	9	0	0	1	10	10	2	2	1	6	R	R	6-4	220	8-28-75	1997	Wilbraham, Mass.
Sedlacek, Shawn	4	6	5.28	17	17	1	0	92	111	61	54	26	69	R	R	6-4	200	6-29-77	1998	Cedar Rapids, Iowa
Sonnier, Shawn	1	2	2.88	44	0	0	13	59	46	20	19	19	73	R	R	6-5	210	7-5-76	1998	Carencro, La.
Thompson, John	2	1	2.57	20	0	0	4	35	29	12	10	12	25	R	R	6-2	200	1-18-73	1992	Spokane, Wash.
2-team (2 Winston-Salem)	2	2	3.48	22	2	0	4	44	39	21	17	20	34							
Thorn, Todd	8	5	5.61	34	13	0	2	117	143	85	73	42	54	L	L	6-2	175	11-4-76	1995	Stratford, Ontario
Thurman, Corey	8	11	4.88	27	27	0	0	149	160	89	81	64	131	R	R	6-1	215	11-5-78	1996	Wake Village, Texas
Wilson, Kris	8	1	1.13	14	4	0	0	48	25	7	6	11	45	R	R	6-4	225	8-6-76	1997	Palm Harbor, Fla.
Yen, Buddy	0	1	45.00	2	0	0	0	1	3	5	5	4	0	R	R	6-3	212	9-11-76	1999	Spring, Texas

CHARLESTON, W.VA. — Class A

SOUTH ATLANTIC LEAGUE

BATTING	AVG	G	AB	R	H	2B	3B	HR	RBI	BB	SO	SB	CS	B	T	HT	WT	DOB	1st Yr	Resides
Alou, Felipe	.195	57	185	18	36	8	1	0	13	13	50	11	4	R	R	5-11	165	11-29-78	1998	Santo Domingo, D.R.
Ayres, Yancy	.169	25	65	4	11	0	0	0	2	7	17	0	0	R	R	6-0	185	5-10-76	1998	Smith Center, Kan.
Brito, Juan	.240	61	208	14	50	6	0	0	19	11	37	1	2	R	R	5-11	185	11-7-79	1996	Santiago Rodriguez, D.R.

BATTING	AVG	G	AB	R	H	2B	3B	HR	RBI	BB	SO	SB	CS	B	T	HT	WT	DOB	1st Yr	Resides
Calderon, Henry	.227	130	459	49	104	29	1	7	56	21	106	33	14	R	R	6-1	170	8-3-77	1996	Santo Domingo, D.R.
Curry, Mike	.311	85	318	70	99	13	3	0	25	48	58	61	13	L	R	5-10	190	2-15-77	1998	Jacksonville, Fla.
DiPace, Danny	.224	65	192	23	43	11	0	2	19	34	67	8	3	L	R	6-2	215	4-24-75	1998	Jensen Beach, Fla.
Felix, Hersy	.288	23	80	6	23	7	0	1	4	3	17	2	0	R	R	6-3	160	4-11-78	1996	Puerto Plata, D.R.
Freitas, Jeremy	.247	85	300	38	74	20	2	13	52	37	80	3	0	L	R	6-3	215	2-4-75	1998	Hanford, Calif.
Gettis, Byron	.295	43	149	19	44	7	2	3	13	10	36	10	3	R	R	6-2	220	3-13-80	1998	Centreville, Ill.
Goodwin, David	.286	128	490	68	140	29	6	9	73	45	123	10	5	R	R	6-1	205	3-26-75	1998	Overland Park, Kan.
Hart, Corey	.190	92	295	43	56	16	3	0	39	58	62	13	7	S	R	6-0	180	9-5-75	1998	Oklahoma City, Okla.
Hopper, Norris	.500	5	22	3	11	0	2	0	2	0	1	1	0	R	R	5-10	170	3-24-79	1998	Shelby, N.C.
Ligons, Merrell	.203	87	232	37	47	10	2	4	18	45	82	17	6	S	R	5-8	165	6-22-77	1996	Compton, Calif.
Melo, Ramon	.273	3	11	0	3	0	0	0	1	4	0	0	0	R	R	5-11	160	12-7-79	1996	Bani, D.R.
Metzler, Rod	.264	130	462	64	122	23	7	7	60	48	98	29	14	S	R	5-11	185	11-19-74	1997	Zionsville, Ind.
Moore, Griffin	.217	40	106	10	23	3	1	0	6	8	13	2	2	R	R	6-2	195	4-29-76	1998	Columbia, Mo.
Pagan, Carlos	.227	50	154	19	35	9	0	6	21	13	40	2	2	R	R	5-9	195	11-2-75	1997	Vega Baja, P.R.
Ramirez, Charlie	.200	28	70	5	14	0	0	0	4	7	16	1	2	R	R	6-1	175	6-1-79	1996	San Pedro de Macoris, D.R.
Rojas, Mo	.091	18	33	4	3	1	0	0	3	3	12	1	2	R	R	5-11	180	11-25-76	1995	Hialeah, Fla.
Ross, Donovan	.176	6	17	1	3	1	0	0	0	4	6	0	0	L	R	6-1	215	8-1-77	1999	Mount Juliet, Tenn.
Ruiz, Willy	.304	57	191	31	58	6	1	0	19	34	44	24	14	R	R	5-11	160	10-15-78	1996	Nagua, D.R.
Shackelford, Brian	.200	73	260	25	52	14	2	10	30	26	80	1	1	L	L	6-1	190	8-30-76	1998	McAlester, Okla.
Taveras, Jose	.245	91	335	41	82	14	2	4	29	19	78	38	10	R	R	5-11	170	12-17-76	1998	Nagua, D.R.
Vann, Eric	.074	14	27	1	2	0	0	0	1	4	11	2	1	S	R	5-8	210	1-8-76	1998	Lawrence, Kan.

GAMES BY POSITION: C—Ayres 25, Brito 59, Felix 23, Pagan 48. 1B—Brito 1, DiPace 4, Freitas 19, Gettis 1, Goodwin 119, Moore 1. 2B—Hart 3, Hopper 5, Ligons 9, Metzler 113, Ruiz 21. 3B—Calderon 8, Hart 84, Ligons 27, Moore 25, Ramirez 1, Ruiz 18. SS—Calderon 121, Hart 1, Ligons 10, Melo 3, Ruiz 13. OF—Alou 57, Curry 85, DiPace 26, Freitas 13, Gettis 43, Ligons 41, Metzler 12, Ramirez 27, Rojas 17, Ruiz 3, Shackelford 7, Taveras 89, Vann 11.

PITCHING	W	L	ERA	G	GS	CG	SV	IP	H	R	ER	BB	SO	B	T	HT	WT	DOB	1st Yr	Resides
Affeldt, Jeremy	7	7	3.83	27	24	2	0	143	140	78	61	80	111	L	L	6-4	185	6-6-79	1997	Medical Lake, Wash.
Ammons, Cary	8	5	2.98	16	16	0	0	91	80	41	30	34	92	L	L	6-1	165	10-14-76	1998	Durant, Okla.
Bautista, Francisco	0	1	4.35	7	0	0	0	10	11	7	5	12	5	R	R	6-0	170	4-22-76	1994	El Seibo, D.R.
Burch, Matt	3	11	6.35	21	15	0	1	74	95	62	52	41	43	R	R	6-4	195	12-21-76	1998	Horseheads, N.Y.
Delgado, Joseph	3	4	4.60	11	11	0	0	45	53	29	23	21	31	R	R	6-2	170	5-10-80	1997	La Guaira, Venez.
Douglass, Ryan	3	4	4.71	10	9	0	0	42	55	28	22	13	22	R	R	6-3	200	12-3-78	1997	Pittsburgh, Pa.
Gilfillan, Jason	0	1	14.66	8	0	0	0	12	22	11	19	6	9	R	R	6-6	215	8-31-76	1997	Blacksburg, S.C.
Gonzalez, Edwin	7	6	2.24	27	13	3	2	120	101	37	30	28	136	R	R	5-10	175	8-13-77	1995	Santo Domingo, D.R.
Guerrero, Junior	7	3	2.76	19	19	0	0	104	90	39	32	45	113	R	R	6-2	175	8-21-79	1996	Santo Domingo, D.R.
Jackson, Jeremy	4	5	4.41	19	13	0	0	82	82	52	40	30	65	L	L	6-4	205	6-4-76	1998	Meridian, Miss.
Lee, Wayne	7	2	3.96	48	0	0	6	89	82	45	39	26	77	R	R	6-0	210	10-15-76	1998	Lakewood, Wash.
Maas, Steve	0	4	5.20	21	0	0	2	28	28	17	16	12	33	R	R	6-6	225	7-31-73	1996	Houston, Texas
Mancha, Tony	4	3	5.23	40	3	0	2	83	89	50	48	38	76	S	R	6-2	205	10-9-78	1997	Las Cruces, N.M.
Pamus, Javier	3	3	2.79	44	0	0	4	90	87	37	28	34	81	R	R	6-1	195	2-11-75	1998	Santee, Calif.
Pichardo, Carlos	2	3	2.57	10	8	0	0	42	44	19	12	22	24	R	R	5-10	145	3-5-78	1996	Esperanza, Venez.
Russo, Mike	0	2	13.94	10	0	0	0	10	18	18	16	10	10	R	R	6-4	230	8-9-77	1998	Hewlett, N.Y.
Smith, Toby	0	1	2.08	2	1	0	0	4	1	4	1	3	4	R	R	6-6	225	11-16-71	1993	Guthrie, Okla.
Solano, Francisco	1	6	5.52	32	6	1	4	90	100	63	55	37	52	R	R	5-11	180	7-14-79	1996	Santo Domingo, D.R.
Ward, Monty	2	9	2.88	42	3	0	7	84	74	42	27	40	93	R	R	6-1	180	10-11-76	1998	Lubbock, Texas

SPOKANE — Short-Season Class A

NORTHWEST LEAGUE

BATTING	AVG	G	AB	R	H	2B	3B	HR	RBI	BB	SO	SB	CS	B	T	HT	WT	DOB	1st Yr	Resides
Alou, Felipe	.238	17	42	4	10	1	1	0	4	5	12	2	0	R	R	5-11	165	11-29-78	1998	Santo Domingo, D.R.
Baker, Jacob	.282	65	234	34	66	15	2	3	39	32	46	9	4	R	R	6-3	220	6-18-76	1999	Houston, Texas
Clay, Michael	.151	31	86	9	13	4	0	1	4	4	15	1	0	R	R	6-0	200	10-3-76	1999	Rattan, Okla.
Cordova, Ben	.250	4	16	4	4	0	1	2	7	3	5	0	0	L	L	6-0	205	12-3-79	1998	Chula Vista, Calif.
Dunn, Casey	.294	58	218	34	64	7	1	11	49	19	28	0	1	R	R	5-10	190	10-3-76	1999	Vestavia Hills, Ala.
Ellis, Mark	.327	71	281	67	92	14	0	7	47	47	40	21	7	R	R	5-11	180	6-6-77	1999	Rapid City, S.D.
Gonzalez, Julian	.250	16	52	5	13	2	1	1	6	9	17	1	3	R	R	6-2	220	2-10-77	1999	Greenbelt, Md.
Harvey, Ken	.397	56	204	49	81	17	0	8	41	23	30	7	3	R	R	6-2	240	3-1-78	1999	Cerritos, Calif.
Healy, Liam	.240	17	50	8	12	2	0	3	12	6	12	0	1	R	R	6-1	215	12-21-76	1999	Baltimore, Md.
Johnson, Brian	.248	41	137	18	34	7	0	1	22	12	20	4	3	R	R	6-1	190	4-20-77	1999	Derby, Kan.
Lucas, Kevin	.256	38	121	28	31	3	1	0	11	4	12	5	1	R	R	5-11	180	7-13-77	1999	Festus, Mo.
McAuley, James	.143	12	35	7	5	1	0	1	6	9	10	2	0	R	R	6-0	185	12-17-77	1999	Dunwoody, Ga.
Nelson, Eric	.277	69	285	51	79	18	4	8	52	33	65	12	2	S	R	5-11	180	5-2-77	1999	Missouri City, Texas
Ramirez, Charlie	.263	54	179	34	47	7	3	2	15	14	30	8	3	R	R	6-1	175	6-1-79	1996	San Pedro de Macoris, D.R.
Raymundo, Gregg	.323	67	254	44	82	16	1	11	44	32	37	1	1	R	R	6-1	188	3-3-77	1999	Clovis, Calif.
Ruiz, Willy	.273	6	11	3	3	1	0	0	0	1	3	2	1	R	R	5-11	160	10-15-78	1996	Nagua, D.R.
Shanks, James	.258	69	260	41	67	9	0	0	29	19	52	19	5	R	R	6-0	180	1-26-79	1998	Appling, Ga.
Shearin, Jarrett	.251	51	183	37	46	14	1	3	20	31	42	16	5	R	R	6-1	195	8-10-76	1999	Wake Forest, N.C.

GAMES BY POSITION: C—Dunn 33, Johnson 39, McAuley 8. 1B—Baker 34, Clay 6, Harvey 37, Healy 6. 2B—Lucas 8, Nelson 66, Ruiz 3. 3B—Baker 3, Clay 20, Lucas 10, Raymundo 52, Ruiz 2. SS—Clay 1, Ellis 71, Lucas 8. OF—Alou 15, Baker 16, Cordova 4, Dunn 1, Gonzalez 16, Healy 7, Lucas 12, Ramirez 53, Shanks 67, Shearin 51.

PITCHING	W	L	ERA	G	GS	CG	SV	IP	H	R	ER	BB	SO	B	T	HT	WT	DOB	1st Yr	Resides
Baerlocher, Ryan	7	2	4.70	15	15	0	0	75	78	43	39	32	68	R	R	6-5	220	8-6-77	1999	Lewiston, Idaho
Cogan, Tony	1	3	1.36	27	0	0	4	40	26	10	6	14	37	L	L	6-2	195	12-21-76	1999	Highland Park, Ill.
Douglass, Ryan	0	0	4.43	4	4	0	0	20	24	13	10	6	14	R	R	6-3	200	12-3-78	1997	Pittsburgh, Pa.
Franco, Edwin	0	0	2.08	3	1	0	0	4	5	1	1	2	6	L	L	5-11	160	5-18-77	1999	Santo Domingo, D.R.
Garcia, Raul	9	2	2.39	32	0	0	1	53	47	18	14	21	64	R	R	5-9	170	12-23-76	1999	Miami, Fla.
Gehrke, Jay	5	5	5.59	32	0	0	13	29	34	21	18	21	33	R	R	6-6	225	11-1-77	1999	Scottsdale, Ariz.
Gilfillan, Jason	4	1	5.71	25	0	0	1	35	31	23	22	22	37	R	R	6-6	215	8-31-76	1997	Blacksburg, S.C.
Herrera, Pedro	1	0	6.30	16	0	0	0	20	27	18	14	14	14	R	R	6-2	180	5-24-78	1999	Santo Domingo, D.R.
Jackson, Jonathan	0	2	5.60	19	0	0	0	35	49	27	22	18	32	R	R	6-4	200	8-3-77	1999	Laurinburg, N.C.
Jones, Craig	1	1	6.23	2	2	0	0	9	11	8	6	1	4	R	R	6-2	190	5-18-77	1999	Westminster, Calif.

PITCHING	W	L	ERA	G	GS	CG	SV	IP	H	R	ER	BB	SO	B	T	HT	WT	DOB	1st Yr	Resides
King, James	7	2	3.88	17	7	0	0	72	60	38	31	29	63	S	L	5-11	195	7-21-77	1999	Pensacola, Fla.
Kurtz-Nicholl, Jesse	5	2	3.08	24	0	0	0	38	39	19	13	14	38	L	L	6-0	185	6-7-77	1999	Malibu, Calif.
MacDougal, Mike	2	2	4.47	11	11	0	0	46	43	25	23	17	57	S	R	6-5	190	3-5-77	1999	Marco Island, Fla.
Medrano, Juan	3	5	4.85	15	15	0	0	69	77	46	37	25	30	R	R	6-3	185	12-30-78	1996	Montecristy, D.R.
Pichardo, Carlos	1	2	3.77	4	4	0	0	14	14	15	6	10	10	R	R	5-10	145	3-5-78	1996	Esperanza, Venez.
Russo, Mike	1	2	3.46	21	1	0	0	42	39	19	16	23	29	R	R	6-4	230	8-9-77	1998	Hewlett, N.Y.
Sanches, Brian	1	1	4.76	9	9	0	0	34	32	19	18	12	51	R	R	6-1	175	8-8-78	1999	Nederland, Texas
Snyder, Kyle	1	0	4.13	7	7	0	0	24	20	13	11	7	25	S	R	6-8	215	9-9-77	1999	Sarasota, Fla.
Turner, Kyle	0	1	4.40	8	0	0	0	14	13	7	7	10	12	L	L	6-2	215	10-14-78	1998	Antioch, Calif.

BASEBALL CITY — Rookie

GULF COAST LEAGUE

BATTING	AVG	G	AB	R	H	2B	3B	HR	RBI	BB	SO	SB	CS	B	T	HT	WT	DOB	1st Yr	Resides
Alvarez, Henry	.183	29	104	10	19	8	2	0	11	1	37	2	0	R	R	5-11	175	10-20-79	1997	San Juan de la Magana, D.R.
Cordova, Ben	.286	52	168	36	48	9	2	5	26	51	50	12	3	L	L	6-0	205	12-3-79	1998	Chula Vista, Calif.
Essian, James	.197	30	71	13	14	4	1	0	8	24	26	3	1	S	R	6-3	215	11-8-79	1998	Troy, Mich.
Gettis, Byron	.316	28	95	20	30	6	2	5	21	17	21	3	2	R	R	6-2	220	3-13-80	1998	Centreville, Ill.
Gomez, Alexis	.276	56	214	44	59	12	1	5	31	32	48	13	5	L	L	6-2	160	8-6-80	1997	Loma de Cabrera, D.R.
Guzman, Jonathan	.241	43	141	23	34	4	1	2	14	21	46	11	2	R	R	6-1	170	8-8-80	1998	Santiago, D.R.
Guzman, Juan	.167	30	96	11	16	4	0	0	7	10	36	7	0	S	R	5-10	150	5-27-80	1997	Santiago, D.R.
Holbert, Ray	.188	5	16	5	3	2	0	0	1	1	4	1	0	R	R	6-0	185	9-25-70	1988	Glendale, Ariz.
Hopper, Norris	.257	46	179	33	46	3	2	0	13	19	20	22	6	R	R	5-10	170	3-24-79	1998	Shelby, N.C.
Lopez, Mendy	.200	3	5	0	1	0	0	0	2	3	1	0	0	R	R	6-2	190	10-15-74	1992	Santo Domingo, D.R.
Lora, Thomas	.274	47	175	31	48	3	4	1	17	31	37	20	2	S	R	5-10	165	10-14-78	1997	Montecristi, D.R.
Mercado, Wilkins	.266	41	128	17	34	5	1	3	15	17	23	1	0	R	R	6-2	185	10-5-78	1996	Esperanza, D.R.
Perea, Carlos	.000	4	8	1	0	0	0	0	0	1	1	0	0	R	R	6-0	150	8-16-79	1997	Ceiba, P.R.
Rodgers, Mackeel	.200	31	105	10	21	3	0	1	14	4	30	3	2	S	R	6-1	175	4-30-81	1999	Miami, Fla.
Ross, Donavon	.253	34	91	12	23	10	0	0	19	25	34	1	1	L	R	6-1	215	8-1-77	1999	Mount Juliet, Tenn.
Santana, Emmanuel	.157	26	83	8	13	3	0	0	14	19	18	1	1	L	R	6-0	185	8-4-80	1998	Vega Alta, P.R.
Santos, Chad	.271	48	177	20	48	9	0	4	35	12	54	1	0	L	L	6-1	215	4-28-81	1999	Kaneohe, Hawaii
Smiley, Jermaine	.067	5	15	0	1	0	0	0	1	0	6	0	0	L	L	6-2	190	3-5-80	1999	Seattle, Wash.
Sutton, Larry	.258	9	31	7	8	2	0	1	6	7	6	0	0	L	L	6-0	185	5-14-70	1992	Temecula, Calif.
Walker, Keronn	.324	18	37	4	12	1	0	1	4	9	9	0	0	S	R	6-2	215	8-29-78	1999	Chicago, Ill.

GAMES BY POSITION: C—Alvarez 28, Essian 2, Santana 24, K. Walker 14. **1B**—Essian 11, Ross 1, Santos 47, Sutton 6. **2B**—Ju. Guzman 1, Hopper 27, Lora 32, Perea 1. **3B**—Gettis 2, Mercado 41, Ross 23. **SS**—Ju. Guzman 25, Holbert 3, Lopez 2, Lora 2, Perea 2, Rodgers 30. **OF**—Cordova 51, Essian 8, Gettis 19, Gomez 56, Jo. Guzman 43, Ju. Guzman 3, Ross 1, Smiley 5, Sutton 1.

PITCHING	W	L	ERA	G	GS	CG	SV	IP	H	R	ER	BB	SO	B	T	HT	WT	DOB	1st Yr	Resides
Baranowski, Brannon ..	1	2	2.83	24	0	0	1	35	27	14	11	19	53	R	R	6-4	200	12-19-76	1999	Cypress, Texas
Burch, Matt	0	2	4.50	5	4	0	0	14	17	10	7	10	9	R	R	6-4	195	12-21-76	1998	Horseheads, N.Y.
Cabaj, Chris	6	0	2.66	11	2	0	0	44	42	15	13	6	38	R	R	6-10	245	11-12-77	1999	Western Springs, Ill.
Coa, Jesus	1	1	5.74	7	2	0	0	27	36	22	17	13	11	R	R	6-0	170	1-25-80	1997	Bolivar, Venez.
Delgado, Joseph	1	0	0.00	1	1	0	0	6	2	0	0	1	4	R	R	6-2	170	5-10-80	1997	La Guaira, Venez.
Franco, Edwin	0	0	0.00	2	0	0	0	3	1	0	0	0	4	L	L	5-11	160	5-18-77	1999	Santo Domingo, D.R.
Gamboa, Javier	0	0	3.60	3	3	0	0	5	6	2	2	2	4	R	R	6-1	195	3-17-74	1994	Fort Myers, Fla.
Garcia, Abel	0	0	4.20	3	2	0	0	15	17	9	7	2	13	L	L	6-0	195	6-21-78	1999	San Antonio, Texas
Garcia, Rafael	4	2	4.61	9	5	0	0	41	44	24	21	13	44	R	R	6-0	150	6-11-78	1996	Caracas, Venez.
Gobble, Jimmy	0	0	2.70	4	1	0	0	7	6	3	2	5	8	L	L	6-3	175	7-19-81	1999	Bristol, Va.
Herrera, Pedro	0	0	0.00	3	0	0	3	6	1	0	0	3	5	R	R	6-2	185	5-24-78	1996	Santo Domingo, D.R.
Hill, Ryan	0	0	81.00	1	0	0	0	0	3	3	3	3	1	R	R	6-3	210	8-27-78	1998	Washington, Ind.
Martinez, Carlos	4	3	3.04	11	7	1	0	50	40	20	17	7	36	L	L	5-11	155	7-29-78	1996	Santo Domingo, D.R.
Mathews, Terry	0	0	0.00	1	1	0	0	2	0	0	0	0	2	L	R	6-2	225	10-5-64	1987	Alexandria, La.
Moreno, Orber	0	0	0.00	1	1	0	0	1	0	0	0	0	1	R	R	6-2	190	4-27-77	1994	Los Autos, Venez.
Myers, Taylor	0	2	18.00	3	0	0	0	4	10	8	8	2	3	R	R	6-0	180	11-8-77	1996	Henderson, Nev.
Obermueller, Wes	2	1	2.58	11	7	0	0	38	33	16	11	12	39	R	R	6-2	195	12-22-76	1999	Vinton, Iowa
Ortega, Jose	2	1	3.62	17	0	0	3	37	41	17	15	18	32	L	L	5-11	145	8-2-78	1996	San Francisco de Macoris, D.R.
Ortega, Oscar	1	5	5.91	12	9	0	0	53	67	48	35	30	27	R	R	5-11	170	9-20-79	1997	La Vega, D.R.
Rasmussen, Brent	2	1	2.25	17	0	0	0	32	28	8	8	11	16	R	R	6-1	190	4-22-77	1998	Omaha, Neb.
Rusch, Glendon	0	0	1.50	2	2	0	0	6	3	1	1	3	9	L	L	6-1	200	11-7-74	1993	Seattle, Wash.
Santiago, Jose	0	0	1.80	3	3	0	0	5	1	1	1	0	4	R	R	6-3	215	11-5-74	1994	Loiza, P.R.
Sopkin, Josh	3	1	5.70	16	1	0	0	30	37	22	19	23	19	R	R	6-2	190	12-14-79	1998	Blue Island, Ill.
Stiles, Brad	0	1	1.80	4	0	0	1	5	3	3	1	3	5	L	L	6-6	215	2-9-81	1999	Lamar, Colo.
Turner, Kyle	1	0	0.00	2	1	0	0	4	2	0	0	0	3	L	L	6-2	215	10-14-78	1998	Antioch, Calif.
Veras, Dario	0	0	0.00	3	2	0	0	4	3	0	0	3	3	R	R	6-1	155	3-13-73	1991	Villa Vazquez, D.R.
Walker, Jamie	1	0	3.38	2	2	0	0	8	10	3	3	0	9	L	L	6-2	190	7-1-71	1992	Overland Park, Kan.
Yen, Buddy	3	2	2.40	25	0	0	10	30	18	11	8	6	34	R	R	6-3	212	9-11-76	1999	Spring, Texas

Organization Statistics

LOSANGELESDODGERS

Offseason acquisitions don't add up to in-season success

BY GEOFF SMITH

No team made more noise than the Dodgers during the 1998-99 offseason. The record signing of free agent Kevin Brown to a seven-year, $105 million contract put huge expectations on a team that hadn't won a postseason game since the 1988 World Series.

Add to that the signing of Devon White and the acquisition of catcher Todd Hundley, and the 1999 Dodgers were feeling pretty good about themselves. So good, in fact, that general manager Kevin Malone spouted off about facing the Yankees in the World Series.

It didn't take long before Malone was eating his words. The Dodgers struggled all season, finishing 77-85 and placing third in the National League West, 23 games behind the second-year Diamondbacks.

Hundley missed most of spring training recuperating from 1997 elbow surgery. The switch-hitter was expected to provide lefthanded power in the lineup to break up righthanders Gary Sheffield, Raul Mondesi and Eric Karros. Instead, Hundley struggled at the plate and behind it, briefly lost his job to rookie Angel Pena and didn't show promise until the second half.

Lefthander Carlos Perez, expected to be a staple of the rotation, was 2-10 with a 7.43 ERA before being sent to Triple-A Albuquerque. Chan Ho Park and Darren Dreifort didn't blossom into the frontline starters the Dodgers had envisioned.

Karros, Sheffield and Mondesi all finished with impressive individual statistics, but those numbers didn't tell the story. Mondesi started strong, including a game-winning homer against Arizona on Opening Day, but suffered the worst slump of his career and

Kevin Brown **Chin-Feng Chen**

Players of the Year

MAJOR LEAGUE: Kevin Brown, rhp
Brown went 18-9 with a 3.00 ERA and 221 strikeouts in his first season with the Dodgers after signing a $105 million contract.

MINOR LEAGUE: Chin-Feng Chen, of
Chen earned MVP honors in the California League after becoming the first 30-30 man in league history.

later demanded to be traded. Karros and Sheffield did most of their damage in the second half, long after the team fell out of contention.

Young third baseman Adrian Beltre was inconsistent. Shortstop Mark Grudzielanek played well, but not until coming off the disabled list for a hand injury sustained when he punched a wall in frustration. Second baseman Eric Young didn't provide the spark at the top of the lineup that first-year manager Davey Johnson was looking for.

Pitching coach Charlie Hough was the first casualty, fired at the end of May and replaced by Claude Osteen. Later in the season, Albuquerque manager and Dodgers favorite Mike Scioscia announced he was leaving the organization. Team president Bob Graziano—Peter O'Malley's hand-picked successor—was fired during the final week of the season.

If there was some good news, it came from a farm system thought to be devoid of talent. Class A San Bernardino won the California League title, led by pitchers Randey Dorame and Adrian Burnside.

Taiwanese outfielder Chin-Feng Chen hit .316 with 31 home runs, 123 RBIs and 31 stolen bases for San Bernardino. He was the first 30-30 player in the history of the Cal League and was named MVP of the league, as well as its top prospect. Chen's teammate Marcos Castillo pitched a perfect game against Lake Elsinore.

Righthander Eric Gagne emerged as a contender for a spot in the rotation in 2000, going 12-4 with a 2.63 ERA at Double-A San Antonio. During a late-season stint with the Dodgers, Gagne was 1-1 with a 2.10 ERA in five starts.

ORGANIZATION LEADERS

BATTING

*AVG	Tony Mota, San Antonio	.325
R	Eric Riggs, San Bernardino	105
H	Robb Gorr, San Bernardino	174
TB	Chin-Feng Chen, San Bernardino	296
2B	Shawn Gilbert, Albuquerque	35
3B	Luke Allen, San Antonio	12
HR	Chin-Feng Chen, San Bernardino	31
RBI	Chin-Feng Chen, San Bernardino	123
BB	Chin-Feng Chen, San Bernardino	75
SO	Glenn Davis, San Antonio	130
SB	Mike Metcalfe, San Antonio	57

PITCHING

W	Two tied at	14
L	Craig Taczy, Vero Beach	14
#ERA	Victor Alvarez, San Antonio/Vero Beach	2.71
G	Bill Everly, San Bernardino	60
CG	Six tied at	2
SV	Bill Everly, San Bernardino	34
IP	Two tied at	168
BB	Lance Caraccioli, San Bernardino	126
SO	Eric Gagne, San Antonio	185

*Minimum 250 At-Bats #Minimum 75 Innings

Los Angeles DODGERS

Manager: Davey Johnson　　　　　　　　　　　**1999 Record:** 77-85, .475 (3rd, NL West)

BATTING	AVG	G	AB	R	H	2B	3B	HR	RBI	BB	SO	SB	CS	B	T	HT	WT	DOB	1st Yr	Resides
Beltre, Adrian	.275	152	538	84	148	27	5	15	67	61	105	18	7	R	R	5-11	165	4-7-78	1995	Santo Domingo, D.R.
Brumfield, Jacob	.294	18	17	4	5	0	1	0	1	0	5	0	0	R	R	6-0	190	5-27-65	1983	Atlanta, Ga.
Castro, Juan	.000	2	1	0	0	0	0	0	0	0	1	0	0	R	R	5-10	187	6-20-72	1991	Los Mochis, Mexico
Cookson, Brent	.200	3	5	0	1	0	0	0	0	0	1	0	0	R	R	5-11	200	9-7-69	1991	Santa Paula, Calif.
Cora, Alex	.167	11	30	2	5	1	0	0	3	0	4	0	0	L	R	6-0	180	10-18-75	1996	Caguas, P.R.
Counsell, Craig	.259	50	108	20	28	6	0	0	9	9	14	1	0	L	R	6-0	175	8-21-70	1992	Fort Lauderdale, Fla.
2-team (37 Florida)	.218	87	174	24	38	7	0	0	11	14	24	1	0							
Cromer, Tripp	.192	33	52	5	10	0	0	2	8	5	10	0	0	R	R	6-2	160	11-21-67	1989	Lexington, S.C.
Grudzielanek, Mark	.326	123	488	72	159	23	5	7	46	31	65	6	6	R	R	6-1	170	6-30-70	1991	El Paso, Texas
Hansen, Dave	.252	100	107	14	27	8	1	2	17	26	20	0	0	L	R	6-0	195	11-24-68	1986	Laguna Hills, Calif.
Hollandsworth, Todd	.284	92	261	39	74	12	2	9	32	24	61	5	2	L	L	6-2	215	4-20-73	1991	San Ramon, Calif.
Hubbard, Trenidad	.314	82	105	23	33	5	0	1	13	13	24	4	3	R	R	5-9	185	5-11-66	1986	Houston, Texas
Hundley, Todd	.207	115	376	49	78	14	0	24	55	44	113	3	0	S	R	5-11	199	5-27-69	1987	Port St. Lucie, Fla.
Karros, Eric	.304	153	578	74	176	40	0	34	112	53	119	8	5	R	R	6-4	226	11-4-67	1988	Manhattan Beach, Calif.
LoDuca, Paul	.232	36	95	11	22	1	0	3	11	10	9	1	2	R	R	5-10	185	4-12-72	1993	Phoenix, Ariz.
Mondesi, Raul	.253	159	601	98	152	29	5	33	99	71	134	36	9	R	R	5-11	215	3-12-71	1988	San Cristobal, D.R.
Pena, Angel	.208	43	120	14	25	6	0	4	21	12	24	0	1	R	R	5-10	228	2-16-75	1993	San Pedro de Macoris, D.R.
Sanford, Chance	.250	5	8	1	2	0	0	0	2	0	1	0	0	L	R	5-10	175	6-2-72	1992	Houston, Texas
Sheffield, Gary	.301	152	549	103	165	20	0	34	101	101	64	11	5	R	R	5-11	205	11-18-68	1986	St. Petersburg, Fla.
Vizcaino, Jose	.252	94	266	27	67	9	0	1	29	20	23	2	1	S	R	6-1	180	3-26-68	1987	El Cajon, Calif.
White, Devon	.268	134	474	60	127	20	2	14	68	39	88	19	5	S	R	6-2	190	12-29-62	1981	Paradise Valley, Ariz.
Wilkins, Rick	.000	3	4	0	0	0	0	0	0	0	2	0	0	L	R	6-2	215	6-4-67	1987	Jacksonville, Fla.
Young, Eric	.281	119	456	73	128	24	2	2	41	63	26	51	22	R	R	5-9	180	5-18-67	1989	Chattanooga, Tenn.

PITCHING	W	L	ERA	G	GS	CG	SV	IP	H	R	ER	BB	SO	B	T	HT	WT	DOB	1st Yr	Resides
Arnold, Jamie	2	4	5.48	36	3	0	1	69	81	50	42	34	26	R	R	6-2	188	3-24-74	1992	Kissimmee, Fla.
Bochtler, Doug	0	0	5.54	12	0	0	0	13	11	8	8	6	7	R	R	6-3	200	7-5-70	1989	West Palm Beach, Fla.
Borbon, Pedro	4	3	4.09	70	0	0	1	51	39	23	23	29	33	L	L	6-1	205	11-15-67	1988	Houston, Texas
Brown, Kevin	18	9	3.00	35	35	5	0	252	210	99	84	59	221	R	R	6-4	200	3-14-65	1986	Macon, Ga.
Checo, Robinson	2	2	10.34	9	2	0	0	16	24	20	18	13	11	R	R	6-1	185	9-9-71	1989	Santiago, D.R.
Dreifort, Darren	13	13	4.79	30	29	1	0	179	177	105	95	76	140	R	R	6-2	211	5-3-72	1994	Wichita, Kan.
Gagne, Eric	1	1	2.10	5	5	0	0	30	18	8	7	15	30	R	R	6-2	195	1-7-76	1996	Mascouche, Quebec
Herges, Matt	0	2	4.07	17	0	0	0	24	24	13	11	8	18	L	R	6-0	200	4-1-70	1992	Champaign, Ill.
Judd, Mike	3	1	5.46	7	4	0	0	28	30	17	17	12	22	R	R	6-1	217	6-30-75	1995	La Mesa, Calif.
Maddux, Mike	1	1	3.29	49	0	0	0	55	54	21	20	19	41	L	R	6-2	188	8-27-61	1982	Las Vegas, Nev.
2-team (4 Montreal)	1	1	3.77	53	0	0	0	60	63	26	25	22	45							
Masaoka, Onan	2	4	4.32	54	0	0	1	67	55	33	32	47	61	R	L	6-0	188	10-27-77	1995	Hilo, Hawaii
Mills, Alan	3	4	3.73	68	0	0	0	72	70	33	30	43	49	S	R	6-1	195	10-18-66	1986	Lakeland, Fla.
Mlicki, Dave	0	0	4.91	2	0	0	0	7	10	4	4	2	1	R	R	6-4	205	6-8-68	1990	Columbus, Ohio
Osuna, Antonio	0	0	7.71	5	0	0	0	5	4	5	4	3	5	R	R	5-11	160	4-12-73	1991	Juan Jose Rios, Mexico
Park, Chan Ho	13	11	5.23	33	33	0	0	194	208	120	113	100	174	R	R	6-2	204	6-30-73	1994	Los Angeles, Calif.
Perez, Carlos	2	10	7.43	17	16	0	0	90	116	77	74	39	40	L	L	6-3	200	4-14-71	1990	San Cristobal, D.R.
Rojas, Mel	0	0	12.60	5	0	0	0	5	5	7	7	3	3	R	R	5-11	212	12-10-66	1986	Santo Domingo, D.R.
Shaw, Jeff	2	4	2.78	64	0	0	34	68	64	25	21	15	43	R	R	6-2	200	7-7-66	1986	Washington Courthouse, Ohio
Valdes, Ismael	9	14	3.98	32	32	2	0	203	213	97	90	58	143	R	R	6-3	215	8-21-73	1991	Victoria, Mexico
Williams, Jeff	2	0	4.08	3	0	0	0	18	12	10	8	7	9	R	L	6-0	185	6-6-72	1997	Page, Australia

FIELDING

Catcher	PCT	G	PO	A	E	DP	PB
Hubbard	1.000	1	1	0	0	0	0
Hundley	.979	108	681	51	16	5	7
LoDuca	.990	36	178	21	2	3	0
Pena	.989	43	233	26	3	5	6
Wilkins	1.000	1	1	0	0	0	0

First Base	PCT	G	PO	A	E	DP
Cromer	1.000	1	1	0	0	0
Hansen	.982	20	52	4	1	6
Hollandsworth	.990	13	91	9	1	12
Karros	.991	151	1291	126	13	108

Second Base	PCT	G	PO	A	E	DP
Castro	1.000	1	1	4	0	1
Cora	.857	3	3	9	2	2
Counsell	.993	38	54	85	1	13

	PCT	G	PO	A	E	DP
Cromer	1.000	9	7	18	0	5
Hubbard	.000	1	0	0	0	0
Sanford	1.000	2	1	1	0	0
Vizcaino	.991	30	36	70	1	9
Young	.984	116	216	321	9	62

Third Base	PCT	G	PO	A	E	DP
Beltre	.932	152	121	274	29	24
Cromer	1.000	2	2	1	0	0
Hansen	.900	13	5	13	2	0
Vizcaino	1.000	9	2	13	0	2

Shortstop	PCT	G	PO	A	E	DP
Castro	.000	1	0	0	0	0
Cora	1.000	8	10	11	0	2
Counsell	1.000	2	0	1	0	0

	PCT	G	PO	A	E	DP
Cromer	1.000	9	10	17	0	4
Grudzielanek	.973	119	171	306	13	66
Vizcaino	.966	44	60	109	6	20

Outfield	PCT	G	PO	A	E	DP
Brumfield	1.000	11	11	0	0	0
Cookson	1.000	3	4	0	0	0
Cromer	1.000	2	1	0	0	0
Hansen	1.000	2	1	0	0	0
Hollandsworth	.984	67	120	2	2	0
Hubbard	.980	51	49	1	1	0
Mondesi	.982	158	315	7	6	5
Sheffield	.972	145	235	7	7	1
Vizcaino	.000	1	0	0	0	0
White	.986	128	273	3	4	1

FARM SYSTEM

Assistant to General Manager, Minor Leagues: Bill Geivett

Class	Farm Team	League	W	L	Pct.	Finish*	Manager(s)	First Yr
AAA	Albuquerque (N.M.) Dukes	Pacific Coast	65	74	.468	t-11th (16)	Mike Scioscia	1963
AA	San Antonio (Texas) Missions	Texas	67	73	.479	6th (8)	Jim Johnson	1977
A#	San Bernardino (Calif.) Stampede	California	79	61	.564	+2nd (10)	Rick Burleson	1995
A#	Vero Beach (Fla.) Dodgers	Florida State	48	85	.361	14th (14)	Alvaro Espinoza	1980
A	Yakima (Wash.) Bears	Northwest	33	43	.434	7th (8)	Dino Ebel	1988
Rookie#	Great Falls (Mont.) Dodgers	Pioneer	29	47	.382	7th (8)	Tony Harris	1984

*Finish in overall standings (No. of teams in league)   #Advanced level   +Won league championship

ALBUQUERQUE   Class AAA

PACIFIC COAST LEAGUE

BATTING	AVG	G	AB	R	H	2B	3B	HR	RBI	BB	SO	SB	CS	B	T	HT	WT	DOB	1st Yr	Resides
Anthony, Eric	.300	7	20	4	6	2	0	1	3	3	5	0	0	L	L	6-2	210	11-8-67	1986	Houston, Texas
Castro, Juan	.274	116	423	52	116	25	4	7	51	34	70	2	3	R	R	5-10	187	6-20-72	1991	Los Mochis, Mexico
Chamberlain, Wes	.307	111	375	53	115	19	3	18	78	24	66	3	7	R	R	6-2	219	4-13-66	1987	Chicago, Ill.
Clark, Dave	.324	37	108	19	35	7	1	3	17	26	26	2	0	L	R	6-2	210	9-3-62	1983	Germantown, Tenn.
Cookson, Brent	.321	85	277	57	89	18	1	28	70	38	56	7	1	R	R	5-11	200	9-7-69	1991	Santa Paula, Calif.
Cora, Alex	.308	80	302	51	93	11	7	4	37	12	37	9	5	L	R	6-0	180	10-18-75	1996	Caguas, P.R.
Cromer, Tripp	.267	5	15	1	4	2	0	0	1	1	3	0	1	R	R	6-2	160	11-21-67	1989	Lexington, S.C.
Gibbs, Kevin	.286	11	21	4	6	3	0	0	1	4	6	2	2	S	R	6-2	182	4-3-74	1995	Davidsonville, Md.
Gilbert, Shawn	.304	114	421	88	128	35	3	10	52	62	84	25	8	R	R	5-9	185	3-12-65	1987	Glendale, Ariz.
Grijak, Kevin	.317	119	401	58	127	28	1	18	80	19	50	2	6	L	R	6-2	215	8-6-70	1991	Sterling Heights, Mich.
Hubbard, Trenidad	.333	32	123	24	41	8	2	5	24	16	27	16	4	R	R	5-9	185	5-11-66	1986	Houston, Texas
Livingstone, Scott	.205	28	78	11	16	1	0	1	4	9	12	2	1	L	R	6-0	198	7-15-65	1988	Southlake, Texas
LoDuca, Paul	.368	26	76	17	28	9	0	1	8	10	1	1	1	R	R	5-10	185	4-12-72	1993	Phoenix, Ariz.
Mejia, Roberto	.146	16	41	6	6	0	0	1	5	1	8	0	1	R	R	5-11	160	4-14-72	1989	Hato Mayor, D.R.
Newson, Warren	.260	95	285	42	74	22	0	8	38	44	70	2	4	L	L	5-7	200	7-3-64	1986	Southlake, Texas
Ortiz, Hector	.305	55	164	21	50	9	0	6	20	7	27	2	3	R	R	6-0	205	10-14-69	1988	Canovanas, P.R.
Pena, Angel	.291	34	127	15	37	10	1	1	24	10	24	3	2	R	R	5-10	228	2-16-75	1993	San Pedro de Macoris, D.R.
Riggs, Adam	.292	133	513	87	150	29	7	13	81	54	114	25	17	R	R	6-0	190	10-4-72	1994	Andover, N.J.
Sanford, Chance	.247	77	227	37	56	14	1	8	29	31	55	6	3	L	R	5-10	175	6-2-72	1992	Houston, Texas
Steed, Dave	.210	30	62	8	13	4	0	0	5	7	17	0	1	R	R	6-1	205	2-25-73	1993	Starkville, Miss.
Stovall, DaRond	.219	46	160	30	35	12	0	7	21	22	65	8	4	S	L	6-1	185	1-3-73	1991	East St. Louis, Ill.
2-team (37 Calgary)	.207	83	266	40	55	15	3	10	34	33	109	8	4							
Wilkins, Rick	.253	92	300	39	76	8	1	8	33	29	87	1	8	L	R	6-2	215	6-4-67	1987	Jacksonville, Fla.

PITCHING	W	L	ERA	G	GS	CG	SV	IP	H	R	ER	BB	SO	B	T	HT	WT	DOB	1st Yr	Resides
Alston, Garvin	1	2	5.06	5	0	0	0	11	12	6	6	4	5	R	R	6-2	188	12-8-71	1992	Mount Vernon, N.Y.
Arnold, Jamie	0	2	5.59	7	2	0	0	19	28	14	12	7	13	R	R	6-2	188	3-24-74	1992	Kissimmee, Fla.
Beckett, Robbie	1	3	7.57	15	5	0	0	44	48	39	37	37	54	R	L	6-5	235	7-16-72	1990	Austin, Texas
Bochtler, Doug	3	4	3.18	18	0	0	3	23	16	9	8	11	25	R	R	6-3	200	7-5-70	1989	West Palm Beach, Fla.
Boskie, Shawn	1	4	5.84	15	15	0	0	86	111	66	56	37	62	R	R	6-3	205	3-28-67	1986	Reno, Nev.
Checo, Robinson	3	6	4.33	16	15	0	0	79	68	40	38	39	98	R	R	6-1	185	9-9-71	1989	Santiago, D.R.
Croghan, Andy	2	1	2.81	35	0	0	2	42	43	16	13	14	31	R	R	6-5	220	10-26-69	1991	Yorba Linda, Calif.
Garrett, Hal	0	1	15.43	1	0	0	0	2	3	4	4	1	1	R	R	6-2	175	4-27-75	1993	Mount Juliet, Tenn.
Herges, Matt	8	3	4.73	21	21	2	0	131	135	82	69	47	88	L	R	6-0	200	4-1-70	1992	Champaign, Ill.
Jordan, Ricardo	4	1	7.20	37	0	0	2	30	33	26	24	21	35	L	L	6-0	190	6-27-70	1990	Palm Harbor, Fla.
Judd, Mike	8	7	6.67	21	21	1	0	111	132	90	82	47	122	R	R	6-3	217	6-30-75	1995	La Mesa, Calif.
Kubenka, Jeff	4	4	3.22	51	0	0	11	67	62	33	24	23	63	R	L	6-1	191	8-24-74	1996	Schulenburg, Texas
Mitchell, Dean	2	1	7.36	31	0	0	0	48	61	41	39	28	42	R	R	5-11	175	3-19-74	1996	Waco, Texas
Osteen, Gavin	6	8	5.12	34	12	0	2	104	127	64	59	33	65	R	L	6-0	195	11-27-69	1989	Bethany Beach, Del.
Perez, Carlos	3	3	5.92	6	6	2	0	38	46	28	25	10	14	L	L	6-3	200	4-14-71	1990	San Cristobal, D.R.
Ruffin, Johnny	1	1	3.17	46	0	0	10	54	41	21	19	26	66	R	R	6-3	170	7-29-71	1988	Butler, Ala.
Stone, Ricky	6	10	5.50	27	27	2	0	167	205	123	102	71	132	R	R	6-1	168	2-28-75	1994	Hamilton, Ohio
Weber, Neil	0	1	10.26	9	0	0	0	17	30	19	19	9	14	L	L	6-5	215	12-6-72	1993	Harrisburg, Pa.
2-team (9 Tucson)	1	2	10.43	18	0	0	0	29	53	35	34	13	30							
West, David	0	1	6.43	2	1	0	0	7	9	5	5	0	7	L	L	6-6	247	9-1-64	1983	Palm City, Fla.
Williams, Jeff	9	7	5.01	42	14	1	4	126	151	77	70	47	86	R	L	6-0	185	6-6-72	1997	Page, Australia

FIELDING

Catcher	PCT	G	PO	A	E	DP	PB
LoDuca	.975	17	147	11	4	1	0
Ortiz	.971	33	213	23	7	2	0
Pena	.987	30	200	28	3	2	3
Steed	1.000	8	51	7	0	1	0
Wilkins	.992	59	428	39	4	4	6

First Base	PCT	G	PO	A	E	DP
Anthony	1.000	1	2	0	0	0
Chamberlain	.989	66	431	36	5	52
Clark	.976	7	41	0	1	5
Cromer	1.000	1	8	1	0	1
Grijak	.991	28	208	13	2	25
Livingstone	.987	16	136	11	2	22
LoDuca	1.000	2	15	4	0	3
Ortiz	.973	18	99	9	3	11
Steed	1.000	10	68	4	0	5
Wilkins	.962	19	118	10	5	9

Second Base	PCT	G	PO	A	E	DP
Castro	.986	16	28	40	1	8
Cora	1.000	1	1	1	0	0
Cromer	1.000	2	8	7	0	3
Gilbert	1.000	3	8	7	0	2
Riggs	.964	112	259	299	21	86
Sanford	.980	12	22	28	1	7

Third Base	PCT	G	PO	A	E	DP
Castro	.943	42	24	76	6	11
Gilbert	.973	33	14	58	2	6
Livingstone	1.000	1	0	1	0	0
Mejia	.905	10	6	13	2	1
Riggs	.946	17	5	30	2	3
Sanford	.921	51	27	90	10	10
Steed	1.000	4	5	4	0	2

Shortstop	PCT	G	PO	A	E	DP
Castro	.953	59	74	170	12	42

	PCT	G	PO	A	E	DP
Cora	.968	76	133	233	12	58
Cromer	1.000	1	1	3	0	0
Gilbert	.945	13	14	38	3	6

Outfield	PCT	G	PO	A	E	DP
Anthony	1.000	5	6	0	0	0
Chamberlain	.900	24	18	0	2	0
Clark	.970	25	31	1	1	0
Cookson	.989	81	169	4	2	1
Gibbs	1.000	4	11	0	0	0
Gilbert	.984	71	111	10	2	3
Grijak	.993	90	137	7	1	1
Hubbard	.974	31	72	2	2	0
Livingstone	1.000	1	1	0	0	0
Mejia	1.000	3	1	0	0	0
Newson	.980	77	91	5	2	0
Sanford	1.000	13	8	0	0	0
Stovall	.981	44	99	2	2	0

Organization Statistics

TEXAS LEAGUE

BATTING

	AVG	G	AB	R	H	2B	3B	HR	RBI	BB	SO	SB	CS	B	T	HT	WT	DOB	1st Yr	Resides
Allen, Luke	.281	137	533	90	150	16	12	14	82	44	102	14	8	L	R	6-2	208	8-4-78	1997	Covington, Ga.
Bocachica, Hiram	.291	123	477	84	139	22	10	11	60	60	71	30	15	R	R	5-11	165	3-4-76	1994	Bayamon, P.R.
Collins, Michael	.333	7	12	1	4	0	0	0	0	5	2	0	1	R	R	5-9	166	1-29-77	1998	Phoenix, Ariz.
Cuevas, Trent	.500	2	2	0	1	0	0	0	0	0	0	0	0	R	R	5-11	170	12-25-76	1995	Placentia, Calif.
Davis, Glenn	.260	134	492	72	128	33	4	10	63	69	130	6	7	S	L	6-1	200	11-25-75	1997	Aston, Pa.
Diaz, Juan	.303	66	254	42	77	21	1	9	52	26	77	0	0	R	R	6-2	228	2-19-76	1996	Santo Domingo, D.R.
Dubose, Brian	.264	42	121	15	32	9	3	3	22	11	25	0	1	L	R	6-3	208	5-17-71	1990	Detroit, Mich.
Gil, Geronimo	.283	106	343	47	97	26	1	15	59	49	58	2	0	R	R	6-2	195	8-7-75	1996	Oaxaca, Mexico
Metcalfe, Mike	.293	123	461	78	135	25	3	3	57	65	47	57	21	S	R	5-10	175	1-2-73	1994	Orlando, Fla.
Moreta, Ramon	.305	117	397	56	121	13	3	2	42	18	66	26	16	R	R	5-11	185	9-5-75	1994	La Romana, D.R.
Mota, Tony	.325	98	345	65	112	31	2	15	75	41	56	13	5	S	R	6-1	170	10-31-77	1996	Miami, Fla.
Myers, Rod	.252	46	147	21	37	11	0	2	16	18	35	2	2	L	L	6-1	190	1-14-73	1991	Conroe, Texas
Ortiz, Hector	.240	40	121	10	29	4	0	0	13	10	17	0	1	R	R	6-0	205	10-14-69	1988	Canovanas, P.R.
Ortiz, Nick	.175	14	40	4	7	1	0	0	2	3	7	0	0	R	R	6-0	160	7-9-73	1991	Cidra, P.R.
Phoenix, Wynter	.249	60	169	22	42	6	1	5	22	21	41	1	2	L	L	6-2	208	12-7-74	1996	El Cajon, Calif.
Saitta, Rich	.291	91	254	25	74	11	4	2	34	8	43	7	4	R	R	5-10	170	7-28-75	1996	Marlboro, N.J.
Skeels, Andy	1.000	1	1	0	1	0	0	0	0	0	0	0	0	L	R	5-11	185	7-25-65	1987	Thousand Oaks, Calif.
Snow, Casey	.253	61	170	21	43	8	2	4	16	13	45	0	0	S	R	5-10	185	12-8-74	1996	Canoga Park, Calif.
Stovall, DaRond	.367	12	49	9	18	3	0	4	11	7	10	1	1	S	L	6-1	185	1-3-73	1991	East St. Louis, Ill.
Warner, Mike	.330	62	191	35	63	16	5	3	25	34	29	12	6	L	L	5-10	170	5-9-71	1992	Palm Beach Gardens, Fla.

PITCHING

	W	L	ERA	G	GS	CG	SV	IP	H	R	ER	BB	SO	B	T	HT	WT	DOB	1st Yr	Resides
Alvarez, Victor	4	3	3.67	9	9	0	0	56	58	27	23	10	43	L	L	5-10	150	11-8-76	1997	Culiacan, Mexico
Beckett, Robbie	7	7	5.18	18	16	1	1	97	82	63	56	68	92	R	L	6-5	235	7-16-72	1990	Austin, Texas
Davis, Allen	7	10	4.22	29	20	1	0	130	140	83	61	46	87	L	L	6-4	195	10-1-75	1998	Ovilla, Texas
Foster, Kris	0	2	3.59	33	0	0	4	53	43	24	21	26	53	R	R	6-1	200	8-30-74	1993	Lehigh Acres, Fla.
Gagne, Eric	12	4	2.63	26	26	0	0	168	122	55	49	64	185	R	R	6-2	195	1-7-76	1996	Mascouche, Quebec
Garcia, Apostol	7	5	3.36	32	11	0	1	102	110	57	38	45	50	R	R	6-0	155	8-3-76	1994	Las Matas de Farfan, D.R.
Garrett, Hal	5	9	3.61	42	4	0	2	95	70	47	38	55	76	R	R	6-2	175	4-27-75	1993	Mount Juliet, Tenn.
Jarvis, Matt	0	1	27.00	3	0	0	0	3	10	10	9	3	1	R	L	6-4	185	2-22-72	1991	Albuquerque, N.M.
Mayo, Blake	2	2	5.82	41	0	0	3	51	63	40	33	20	31	R	R	6-2	210	12-18-72	1996	Gadsden, Ala.
Mitchell, Dean	1	2	3.13	10	7	0	0	32	36	20	11	14	28	R	R	5-11	175	3-19-74	1996	Waco, Texas
Montgomery, Matt	5	6	2.60	58	0	0	26	55	65	35	16	17	39	R	R	6-4	210	5-13-76	1997	Anaheim, Calif.
Newton, Geronimo	0	1	3.21	11	0	0	0	14	17	6	5	10	14	L	L	6-0	165	12-31-73	1992	Christiansted, Virgin Islands
Niebla, Ruben	2	1	3.77	12	0	0	0	14	19	7	6	5	12	L	L	5-10	175	12-19-71	1995	Calexico, Calif.
Pearsall, J.J.	0	0	4.50	10	0	0	0	16	14	11	8	8	13	L	L	6-2	202	9-9-73	1995	Burnt Hills, N.Y.
Prokopec, Luke	8	12	5.42	27	27	0	0	158	172	113	95	46	124	L	R	5-11	166	2-23-78	1997	Renmark, Australia
Weber, Neil	4	5	5.24	12	11	0	0	55	62	39	32	24	31	L	L	6-5	215	12-6-72	1993	Harrisburg, Pa.
Workman, Widd	1	5	6.97	9	9	0	0	50	73	48	39	27	27	R	R	6-1	195	5-23-74	1996	Gilbert, Ariz.
Zamora, Pete	2	1	6.08	35	0	0	3	64	79	48	43	30	41	L	L	6-3	185	8-13-75	1997	Mission Viejo, Calif.

FIELDING

Catcher	PCT	G	PO	A	E	DP	PB
Gil	.988	74	529	54	7	4	10
H. Ortiz	.978	38	238	26	6	2	2
Snow	.984	43	246	5	4	2	0

First Base	PCT	G	PO	A	E	DP
G. Davis	.992	64	468	45	4	49
Diaz	.984	61	511	28	9	40
Dubose	.989	26	175	12	2	19
Gil	1.000	1	1	0	0	0
N. Ortiz	.000	1	0	0	0	0

Second Base	PCT	G	PO	A	E	DP
Bocachica	.946	122	227	313	31	77
Collins	.962	5	9	16	1	1

	PCT	G	PO	A	E	DP
Metcalfe	1.000	1	0	2	0	0
N. Ortiz	1.000	4	4	4	0	0
Saitta	.980	14	23	26	1	5
Snow	1.000	1	2	0	0	0

Third Base	PCT	G	PO	A	E	DP
Allen	.851	134	80	222	53	16
Cuevas	.000	1	0	0	0	0
Gil	.000	1	0	0	1	0
N. Ortiz	.000	1	0	0	0	0
Saitta	.833	7	6	9	3	1

Shortstop	PCT	G	PO	A	E	DP
Metcalfe	.945	114	160	335	29	58

	PCT	G	PO	A	E	DP
N. Ortiz	.952	8	15	25	2	7
Saitta	.982	27	39	72	2	16

Outfield	PCT	G	PO	A	E	DP
G. Davis	.946	75	114	9	7	0
Gil	.976	26	38	2	1	0
Metcalfe	1.000	7	9	0	0	0
Moreta	.974	114	251	9	7	2
Mota	.975	60	111	8	3	0
Myers	.985	43	66	0	1	0
Phoenix	.958	56	108	6	5	1
Saitta	.935	24	27	2	2	0
Stovall	.962	11	25	0	1	0
Warner	.988	46	80	5	1	1

CALIFORNIA LEAGUE

BATTING

	AVG	G	AB	R	H	2B	3B	HR	RBI	BB	SO	SB	CS	B	T	HT	WT	DOB	1st Yr	Resides
Blair, James	.256	25	78	13	20	2	1	2	7	16	15	3	2	R	R	6-0	190	5-18-77	1998	San Antonio, Texas
Bledsoe, Hunter	.265	45	166	17	44	10	1	2	13	9	27	3	0	R	R	6-4	215	1-24-76	1999	Nashville, Tenn.
Brown, Jason	.218	68	234	28	51	11	2	6	28	23	64	1	2	R	R	6-2	205	5-22-74	1997	Rolling Hills Estates, Calif.
Chatman, Karl	.267	79	300	40	80	13	2	4	37	29	87	13	9	R	R	6-1	190	1-17-75	1996	Chatman, Miss.
Chen, Chin-Feng	.316	131	510	98	161	22	10	31	123	75	129	31	7	R	R	6-1	189	10-28-77	1999	Tainan City, Taiwan
Cromer, Tripp	.500	4	18	3	9	1	0	0	3	0	3	0	0	R	R	6-2	160	11-21-67	1989	Lexington, S.C.
Crosby, Bubba	.296	96	371	53	110	21	3	1	37	42	71	19	8	L	L	5-11	185	8-11-76	1998	Bellaire, Texas
Gallo, Ismael	.314	104	338	66	106	15	3	2	42	40	30	3	1	L	R	5-11	165	1-14-77	1997	Ontario, Calif.
Gonzalez, Jimmy	.316	111	471	58	149	28	6	5	53	20	55	5	9	R	R	5-9	155	8-13-78	1996	Juigalpa, Nicaragua
Gorr, Robb	.319	132	546	67	174	22	6	11	106	30	59	5	2	R	R	6-0	195	9-14-76	1998	Vista, Calif.
Grudzielanek, Mark	.250	4	16	2	4	0	0	0	0	0	1	0	2	R	R	6-1	170	6-30-70	1991	El Paso, Texas
Hernandez, John	.261	61	199	31	52	17	0	7	25	21	44	0	1	R	R	6-2	190	9-1-79	1997	La Puente, Calif.
Hollandsworth, Todd	.385	4	13	3	5	2	0	0	3	2	4	0	1	L	L	6-2	215	4-20-73	1991	San Ramon, Calif.
Illig, Brett	.236	75	276	33	65	11	2	2	25	23	74	7	3	R	R	6-3	208	9-4-77	1995	Phoenixville, Pa.
Matthews, Lamont	.267	4	15	2	4	1	0	1	3	2	7	0	1	L	L	6-2	210	6-15-78	1997	Petersburg, Va.
McCrotty, Will	.254	93	319	43	81	12	3	4	43	27	49	0	2	R	R	6-2	195	6-22-79	1997	Russellville, Ark.
Newton, Kimani	.245	40	143	19	35	3	4	0	16	13	39	9	3	R	R	6-1	195	6-16-79	1996	Christiansted, Virgin Islands
Piedra, Jorge	.300	8	30	6	9	2	0	0	3	3	3	1	0	L	L	6-0	195	4-17-79	1997	Van Nuys, Calif.
Riggs, Eric	.275	130	526	103	144	18	10	16	69	70	92	27	11	S	R	6-2	190	8-19-76	1998	Brownsburg, Ind.

BATTING	AVG	G	AB	R	H	2B	3B	HR	RBI	BB	SO	SB	CS	B	T	HT	WT	DOB	1st Yr	Resides
Theodorou, Nick	.310	104	355	57	110	11	4	0	44	72	62	14	14	S	R	5-11	182	6-7-75	1998	Rialto, Calif.
Thurston, Joe	.000	2	3	0	0	0	0	0	0	0	1	0	0	L	R	5-11	175	9-29-79	1999	Vallejo, Calif.
Young, Eric	.250	3	12	0	3	0	0	0	0	0	2	0	0	R	R	5-9	180	5-18-67	1989	Chattanooga, Tenn.

GAMES BY POSITION: C—Brown 5, Hernandez 55, Illig 1, McCrotty 90. 1B—Bledsoe 10, Brown 7, Cromer 1, Gorr 126. 2B—Cromer 1, Gallo 40, Gonzalez 43, Illig 27, McCrotty 1, Riggs 30, Theodorou 6, Young 3. 3B—Blair 21, Bledsoe 1, Cromer 1, Gallo 2, Gonzalez 58, Illig 46, Theodorou 17. SS—Cromer 1, Gallo 41, Grudzielanek 4, Riggs 101, Thurston 1. OF—Bledsoe 2, Brown 22, Chatman 69, Chen 117, Crosby 90, Gonzalez 4, Hollandsworth 4, Matthews 1, Newton 40, Piedra 8, Theodorou 77.

PITCHING	W	L	ERA	G	GS	CG	SV	IP	H	R	ER	BB	SO	B	T	HT	WT	DOB	1st Yr	Resides
Bell, Scott	2	5	6.04	28	0	0	3	51	66	40	34	22	37	R	R	6-4	210	1-19-76	1998	New Orleans, La.
Burnside, Adrian	10	9	4.17	26	22	0	0	132	124	69	61	55	129	R	L	6-4	190	3-15-77	1996	Alice Springs, Australia
Caraccioli, Lance	6	7	5.01	28	26	0	0	140	124	90	78	126	98	L	L	6-4	190	12-14-77	1998	Walker, La.
Castillo, Marcos	14	9	4.10	27	27	1	0	167	182	76	76	48	130	R	R	6-2	172	2-15-79	1998	Bolivar, Venez.
Cervantes, Peter	4	3	4.18	40	1	0	2	80	92	38	37	21	89	L	R	6-2	185	10-13-74	1995	Los Angeles, Calif.
Checo, Robinson	0	0	10.80	2	2	0	0	5	5	6	6	3	6	R	R	6-1	185	9-9-71	1989	Santiago, D.R.
Chung, Rocky	1	0	1.71	9	0	0	0	21	13	5	4	3	23	R	R	6-2	176	7-1-73	1998	Seoul, Korea
Colyer, Steve	7	9	4.70	27	25	1	0	146	145	82	76	86	131	L	L	6-4	205	2-22-79	1998	St. Peters, Mo.
Correa, Elvis	2	2	4.98	40	0	0	1	69	87	42	38	17	40	R	R	6-2	200	11-10-78	1996	Milwaukee, Wis.
Dorame, Randey	14	3	2.51	24	24	1	0	154	130	52	43	37	159	L	L	6-2	205	1-23-79	1997	Huatabampo, Mexico
Everly, Bill	7	4	3.41	60	0	0	34	63	66	26	24	21	51	R	R	6-1	175	6-15-75	1997	Atglen, Pa.
Fischer, Mike	1	0	4.91	3	3	0	0	11	13	6	6	4	7	R	R	6-4	200	12-10-76	1998	Crestline, Ohio
Flores, Pedro	2	3	7.61	32	0	0	1	47	68	47	40	30	35	L	L	6-0	210	3-30-77	1996	Baldwin Park, Calif.
Harrell, Tim	5	2	4.82	44	0	0	2	75	78	44	40	36	78	R	R	6-4	205	10-31-75	1998	Weaverville, N.C.
Hebert, Cedric	2	2	5.89	16	5	0	1	44	57	34	29	19	37	R	R	6-1	175	9-19-77	1998	Kaplan, La.
Maddux, Mike	0	0	3.00	5	0	0	2	9	8	4	3	2	10	L	R	6-2	188	8-27-61	1982	Las Vegas, Nev.
Madero, Francisco	3	2	2.70	12	2	0	0	27	28	10	8	9	33	R	R	5-10	175	1-6-79	1997	Mazatlan, Mexico
Niebla, Ruben	0	1	4.76	3	0	0	0	6	9	3	3	1	6	L	L	5-10	175	12-19-71	1995	Calexico, Calif.
Osuna, Antonio	0	0	2.33	13	4	0	0	19	19	6	5	5	27	R	R	5-11	160	4-12-73	1991	Juan Jose Rios, Mexico

VERO BEACH — Class A

FLORIDA STATE LEAGUE

BATTING	AVG	G	AB	R	H	2B	3B	HR	RBI	BB	SO	SB	CS	B	T	HT	WT	DOB	1st Yr	Resides
Auterson, Jeff	.206	104	349	39	72	19	2	2	27	34	118	5	18	R	R	6-2	190	2-22-78	1996	Riverside, Calif.
Bell, Ricky	.234	100	376	37	88	26	1	5	46	27	81	1	3	R	R	6-2	180	4-5-79	1997	Cincinnati, Ohio
Castellano, John	.444	6	18	3	8	0	0	0	2	0	0	0	0	R	R	5-11	185	9-8-77	1998	North Babylon, N.Y.
Collins, Michael	.267	101	356	37	95	10	2	3	31	34	68	8	12	R	R	5-9	166	1-29-77	1998	Phoenix, Ariz.
Feliciano, Jesus	.254	98	370	44	94	13	0	0	21	29	38	20	10	L	L	5-11	150	6-6-79	1998	Bayamon, P.R.
Feramisco, Derek	.208	18	53	7	11	3	0	1	4	11	12	0	2	R	R	6-5	195	11-7-74	1997	Clovis, Calif.
Hill, Nakia	.180	19	50	6	9	3	0	4	4	12	12	0	1	R	R	6-0	175	2-24-76	1998	San Diego, Calif.
Jaramillo, Milko	.203	99	320	26	65	4	1	1	31	14	67	15	5	S	R	5-11	165	1-21-80	1996	Caracas, Venez.
Kellner, Ryan	.207	54	179	21	37	1	1	2	14	10	51	1	1	R	R	6-2	205	12-9-77	1998	Morganton, N.C.
Leach, Nick	.283	128	449	58	127	21	0	20	74	62	73	10	5	L	R	6-1	190	12-7-77	1996	Madera, Calif.
Mejia, Max	.218	28	87	14	19	4	0	1	20	8	25	4	2	R	R	6-0	150	7-17-77	1996	Azua, D.R.
Moore, Kevin	.500	2	6	0	3	0	0	0	0	2	1	0	1	S	R	6-2	210	6-20-75	1999	Beverly Hills, Calif.
Newton, Kimani	.265	62	211	29	56	7	2	0	18	29	67	7	5	R	R	6-1	195	6-16-79	1996	Christiansted, Virgin Islands
Perez, Josue	.279	62	201	24	56	14	1	2	22	21	29	14	11	S	R	6-0	180	8-12-77	1998	Santo Domingo, D.R.
Phoenix, Wynter	.347	62	202	43	70	10	2	5	31	42	30	6	5	L	L	6-2	208	12-7-74	1996	El Cajon, Calif.
Piedra, Jorge	.288	15	59	13	17	3	1	1	6	7	2	2	2	L	L	6-0	195	4-17-79	1997	Van Nuys, Calif.
Rolls, Damian	.297	127	474	68	141	26	2	9	54	36	66	24	13	R	R	6-2	205	9-15-77	1996	Kansas City, Kan.
Ross, David	.227	114	375	47	85	19	1	7	39	46	111	5	10	R	R	6-2	205	3-19-77	1998	Tallahassee, Fla.
Stodgel, Jeff	.211	44	123	14	26	1	2	0	8	10	24	3	4	S	R	5-9	155	4-5-76	1999	Anaheim, Calif.

GAMES BY POSITION: C—Castellano 6, Kellner 35, Ross 96, Stodgel 4. 1B—Auterson 1, Collins 1, Feliciano 1, Feramisco 1, Kellner 2, Leach 123, Phoenix 5, Ross 5, Stodgel 1. 2B—Bell 67, Collins 45, Hill 13, Jaramillo 1, Rolls 1, Stodgel 20. 3B—Bell 17, Collins 6, Leach 1, Rolls 113, Stodgel 1. SS—Collins 36, Hill 1, Jaramillo 98, Kellner 1, Stodgel 2. OF—Auterson 74, Collins 7, Feliciano 95, Feramisco 17, Mejia 27, Moore 2, Newton 52, Perez 62, Phoenix 47, Piedra 15, Ross 1, Stodgel 21.

PITCHING	W	L	ERA	G	GS	CG	SV	IP	H	R	ER	BB	SO	B	T	HT	WT	DOB	1st Yr	Resides
Alvarez, Victor	4	4	1.97	12	12	1	0	73	56	21	16	16	57	L	L	5-10	150	11-8-76	1997	Culiacan, Mexico
Avery, Paul	2	7	4.83	32	7	0	0	78	82	51	42	66	57	R	L	6-1	180	1-29-77	1998	Clovis, Calif.
Barnsby, Scott	0	0	8.22	4	0	0	0	8	12	10	7	2	7	R	R	6-1	185	11-20-75	1998	Torrington, Conn.
Bullinger, Jim	0	2	7.58	6	6	0	0	19	23	17	16	10	18	R	R	6-2	190	8-21-65	1986	Sarasota, Fla.
Dorame, Randey	0	2	5.73	3	2	0	0	11	15	9	7	1	5	L	L	6-2	205	1-23-79	1997	Huatabampo, Mexico
Dotel, Melido	6	5	4.46	31	6	0	1	73	56	45	36	73	57	R	R	6-3	163	4-20-77	1994	San Cristobal, D.R.
Foster, Kris	1	1	1.76	8	0	0	0	15	10	5	3	2	15	R	R	6-1	200	8-30-74	1993	Lehigh Acres, Fla.
Gomes, Tony	4	5	6.28	37	0	0	2	62	67	45	43	32	70	R	R	6-0	190	9-10-77	1998	Delano, Calif.
Hebert, Cedric	1	0	3.12	7	0	0	0	9	8	3	3	7	6	R	R	6-1	175	9-19-77	1998	Kaplan, La.
Husted, Brent	2	4	4.17	47	0	0	27	54	42	30	25	17	41	R	R	6-3	198	3-31-76	1997	Reno, Nev.
Lanzetta, Tobin	0	1	3.38	4	0	0	0	5	3	2	2	3	2	R	R	6-2	185	7-31-75	1997	Tucson, Ariz.
Madero, Francisco	2	6	5.09	12	10	1	0	69	75	43	39	25	45	R	R	5-10	175	1-6-79	1997	Mazatlan, Mexico
Montgomery, Steve	0	4	2.43	9	6	0	0	37	28	12	10	10	33	R	R	6-7	230	2-21-74	1994	Warren, Ohio
Moskau, Ryan	5	5	4.15	17	17	0	0	104	99	54	48	40	68	R	L	6-3	210	8-22-77	1998	Tucson, Ariz.
Niebla, Ruben	0	0	0.00	1	0	0	0	2	1	0	0	4	0	L	L	5-10	175	12-19-71	1995	Calexico, Calif.
Regalado, Maximo	2	12	5.80	20	19	1	0	90	110	65	58	49	58	R	R	6-2	165	11-18-76	1994	Montecristi, D.R.
Roberts, Rick	1	4	6.04	11	10	0	0	45	54	35	30	25	29	L	L	6-1	180	5-20-79	1997	Summer Hill, Pa.
Simon, Ben	7	4	3.45	38	5	0	2	89	79	44	34	29	89	R	R	6-1	175	11-12-74	1996	Berlin Heights, Ohio
Taczy, Craig	5	14	4.66	28	25	2	0	160	172	93	83	50	83	L	L	6-7	215	4-15-77	1995	Crestwood, Ill.
Urdaneta, Lino	5	4	4.84	27	5	0	0	67	74	42	36	20	43	R	R	6-1	168	11-20-79	1997	Guarenas, Venez.
Workman, Widd	1	1	7.35	25	3	0	0	56	79	53	46	25	32	R	R	6-1	195	5-23-74	1996	Gilbert, Ariz.

YAKIMA — Short-Season Class A

NORTHWEST LEAGUE

BATTING	AVG	G	AB	R	H	2B	3B	HR	RBI	BB	SO	SB	CS	B	T	HT	WT	DOB	1st Yr	Resides
Allen, Shane	.243	33	111	15	27	10	0	0	11	6	25	4	2	R	R	6-0	185	4-25-79	1997	Glenns Ferry, Idaho

BATTING	AVG	G	AB	R	H	2B	3B	HR	RBI	BB	SO	SB	CS	B	T	HT	WT	DOB	1st Yr	Resides
Covington, Kevin	.302	43	169	24	51	13	1	2	23	7	37	3	4	R	R	6-1	190	4-18-78	1997	Centre, Ala.
Dalton, Josh	.251	59	203	33	51	12	0	1	28	42	45	11	5	S	R	6-1	170	3-13-77	1999	Fort Dodge, Iowa
Duplissea, William	.152	13	33	5	5	2	0	1	4	5	7	2	1	R	R	6-0	200	9-27-77	1999	San Carlos, Calif.
Glassey, Josh	.228	28	92	13	21	4	0	2	14	19	24	0	1	L	R	6-1	190	5-6-77	1996	Longview, Texas
Goelz, Jim	.282	42	142	19	40	3	1	1	17	12	22	2	5	R	R	5-10	170	2-13-76	1998	St. James, N.Y.
Jaroncyk, Ryan	.355	8	31	6	11	4	0	0	4	5	10	2	1	S	R	6-1	175	3-26-77	1995	Valley Center, Calif.
Kluver, Hayden	.203	25	79	9	16	2	0	1	9	6	26	0	1	L	L	6-2	190	3-18-80	1998	Brisbane, Australia
Matthews, Lamont	.225	66	249	46	56	11	2	17	52	34	87	4	4	L	L	6-2	210	6-15-78	1999	Petersburg, Va.
Moreno, Omar	.195	44	133	30	26	1	0	0	8	33	28	11	8	S	R	6-0	155	3-14-80	1997	Panama City, Panama
Proctor, Jerry	.194	10	36	4	7	2	0	0	3	5	15	0	0	S	R	6-6	220	3-5-78	1996	Pasadena, Calif.
Rozich, John	.231	40	134	20	31	5	2	2	16	23	41	1	3	R	R	6-2	210	3-23-77	1999	Oxford, Pa.
Ruiz, Ray	.293	46	167	34	49	10	1	8	32	24	33	6	2	R	R	5-11	200	10-24-75	1997	Montebello, Calif.
Thurston, Joe	.285	71	277	48	79	10	3	0	32	27	34	27	18	L	R	5-11	175	9-29-79	1999	Vallejo, Calif.
Valdez, Eladio	.243	39	136	20	33	5	0	4	21	4	18	1	2	R	R	5-10	194	5-6-77	1996	Nizao, D.R.
Vasquez, Sandy	.262	75	271	46	71	11	1	6	44	44	91	18	8	R	R	6-3	210	9-7-76	1997	San Pedro de Macoris, D.R.
Wren, Cliff	.315	46	224	46	80	21	0	10	44	18	39	11	5	R	R	6-1	225	4-13-77	1999	Hattiesburg, Miss.

GAMES BY POSITION: C—Duplissea 12, Glassey 28, Rozich 40. **1B**—Vasquez 23, Wren 55. **2B**—Dalton 46, Goelz 30, Ruiz 1, Thurston 1. **3B**—Goelz 11, Ruiz 35, Valdez 32. **SS**—Dalton 9, Goelz 1, Thurston 68. **OF**—Allen 25, Covington 35, Jaroncyk 8, Kluver 15, Matthews 66, Moreno 36, Vasquez 51.

PITCHING	W	L	ERA	G	GS	CG	SV	IP	H	R	ER	BB	SO	B	T	HT	WT	DOB	1st Yr	Resides
Berry, Jonathan	1	6	8.69	16	10	0	0	58	81	68	56	46	31	R	R	6-1	195	11-17-77	1999	Branchville, S.C.
Burgos, Ricardo	1	2	4.32	18	0	0	4	42	50	31	20	9	24	R	R	6-2	215	5-15-79	1998	Cayey, P.R.
Castillo, Wilson	1	0	8.10	8	0	0	0	20	26	25	18	22	11	R	R	6-3	195	12-9-78	1996	Higuey, D.R.
Devey, Phil	5	4	3.91	13	13	1	0	78	70	43	34	27	56	L	L	6-0	170	5-31-77	1999	Lachute, Quebec
Hadden, Randy	6	5	4.78	16	11	0	1	87	94	51	46	25	53	R	R	6-2	191	11-1-77	1999	Jacksonville, Fla.
Junge, Eric	5	7	5.82	15	15	0	0	82	98	60	53	31	55	R	R	6-5	215	1-5-77	1999	Rye, N.Y.
Parker, Beau	1	0	0.00	3	1	0	0	7	6	0	0	1	4	R	R	6-4	185	6-7-79	1997	Vancouver, Wash.
Parrish, Wade	4	3	4.05	17	8	0	2	60	57	30	27	24	48	L	L	6-1	205	11-13-77	1999	Othello, Wash.
Proctor, Scott	4	2	7.20	16	6	0	0	50	57	45	40	26	41	R	R	6-1	210	1-2-77	1998	Jensen Beach, Fla.
Rijo, Fernando	1	2	7.69	18	4	0	2	57	63	57	49	31	39	R	R	5-11	155	11-14-77	1999	La Romana, D.R.
Roberts, Rick	1	3	7.27	11	6	0	0	35	52	34	28	23	26	L	L	6-1	180	5-20-79	1997	Summer Hill, Pa.
Springston, Adam	0	0	4.00	6	0	0	0	9	8	6	4	7	4	R	R	6-6	230	9-7-77	1999	Oxnard, Calif.
Ugas, Juan	3	5	4.62	20	2	0	3	51	55	32	26	26	45	R	R	6-0	190	3-21-80	1997	Caracas, Venez.
Wallace, Jeff	0	1	3.28	11	0	0	2	25	20	12	9	14	26	R	R	6-1	175	9-10-76	1999	Sacramento, Calif.
Walters, Jason	0	1	8.22	8	0	0	3	8	9	10	7	7	13	R	R	6-3	235	8-5-77	1997	Petal, Miss.

GREAT FALLS — Rookie
PIONEER LEAGUE

BATTING	AVG	G	AB	R	H	2B	3B	HR	RBI	BB	SO	SB	CS	B	T	HT	WT	DOB	1st Yr	Resides
Castellano, John	.246	37	134	13	33	6	1	1	25	9	8	3	2	R	R	5-11	185	9-8-77	1998	North Babylon, N.Y.
Curry, Zane	.244	27	90	10	22	3	0	0	8	15	16	1	3	R	R	6-2	210	11-8-76	1999	Houston, Texas
Detienne, Dave	.216	47	153	22	33	3	0	1	16	11	34	9	5	R	R	6-3	190	8-16-79	1998	Dartmouth, Nova Scotia
Escalera, Jose	.254	32	114	14	29	4	0	2	10	6	20	1	2	R	R	6-3	200	10-21-80	1999	Loiza, P.R.
Godbolt, Keith	.267	43	150	26	40	7	1	1	18	12	24	2	3	R	R	6-1	190	11-6-80	1999	Tampa, Fla.
King, Brennan	.291	61	247	37	72	13	1	2	30	24	45	9	6	R	R	6-3	185	1-20-81	1999	Murfreesboro, Tenn.
Martinez, Candido	.234	69	265	43	62	8	3	4	42	22	87	11	2	R	R	6-3	210	10-26-80	1997	Santo Domingo, D.R.
Ramirez, Frankelis	.292	74	281	39	82	9	3	3	42	22	34	7	4	L	L	6-0	160	12-27-78	1996	Cutupu, D.R.
Repko, Jason	.304	49	207	51	63	9	9	8	32	21	43	12	5	R	R	5-11	175	12-27-80	1999	West Richland, Wash.
Sampson, Jake	.265	37	102	17	27	6	1	2	17	12	24	7	3	R	R	5-11	170	9-9-78	1998	Tacoma, Wash.
Snow, Chris	.275	12	40	9	11	0	1	0	2	1	4	2	1	R	R	6-1	175	12-19-80	1999	Phoenix, Ariz.
Story-Harden, Thomari	.200	13	45	7	9	2	0	2	6	5	17	2	0	R	R	6-5	220	4-6-80	1998	Richmond, Calif.
Thomas, Charles	.253	54	194	32	49	11	4	3	23	22	48	10	2	R	R	6-0	200	6-10-80	1998	Fresno, Calif.
Tomaszewski, Dane	.298	34	131	22	39	9	1	5	24	5	25	3	2	R	R	6-3	230	8-14-79	1997	Sydney, Australia
Van Buizen, Rodney	.286	69	259	43	74	9	0	4	33	17	38	9	4	R	R	6-0	190	9-25-80	1998	New South Wales, Australia
Victorino, Shane	.280	55	225	53	63	7	6	2	25	20	31	20	5	R	R	5-9	160	11-30-80	1999	Wailuku, Hawaii

GAMES BY POSITION: C—Castellano 35, Curry 24, Tomaszewski 17. **1B**—Ramirez 71, Story-Harden 1, Tomaszewski 6. **2B**—Detienne 5, Sampson 8, Van Buizen 67. **3B**—Detienne 9, King 53, Thomas 12, Van Buizen 3. **SS**—Detienne 30, Repko 49, Sampson 1. **OF**—Castellano 2, Escalera 26, Godbolt 29, Martinez 66, Ramirez 3, Sampson 26, Snow 9, Story-Harden 1, Thomas 27, Victorino 55.

PITCHING	W	L	ERA	G	GS	CG	SV	IP	H	R	ER	BB	SO	B	T	HT	WT	DOB	1st Yr	Resides
Arellan, Felix	1	2	8.42	15	3	0	0	31	32	31	29	32	38	L	L	6-2	145	2-23-81	1997	Maracay, Venez.
Bridenbaugh, Christian	0	6	7.29	17	12	0	0	79	114	77	64	25	54	L	L	6-1	185	9-26-79	1998	Martinsburg, Pa.
Castillo, Wilson	1	3	4.50	5	0	0	0	10	11	6	5	3	8	R	R	6-3	195	12-9-78	1996	Higuey, D.R.
Cordero, Jesus	0	5	10.43	11	6	0	0	29	51	43	34	24	20	R	R	6-2	185	5-14-79	1998	San Pedro de Macoris, D.R.
Davis, Billy	0	0	46.29	5	0	0	0	2	4	12	12	14	0	R	R	6-1	175	11-6-76	1999	Perry, Fla.
Gomera, Rafael	2	5	11.05	19	2	0	3	37	64	54	45	24	23	R	R	6-1	205	9-28-77	1995	San Cristobal, D.R.
Hosford, Clinton	1	0	6.11	10	0	0	1	18	18	13	12	11	16	R	R	6-2	185	8-8-80	1999	North Vancouver, B.C.
Martin, Scott	4	4	3.86	16	15	2	0	103	115	55	44	23	69	R	R	6-4	230	12-2-77	1999	Plainville, Conn.
Nall, T.J.	3	8	4.95	15	14	2	0	93	115	60	51	13	70	R	R	6-1	175	11-4-80	1999	Schaumburg, Ill.
Neal, Brian	0	2	5.79	15	4	0	1	33	32	23	21	29	23	R	L	6-3	173	6-10-80	1999	Creekside, Pa.
Ortega, Carlos	3	3	2.30	17	6	0	2	55	45	25	14	23	52	L	L	6-1	170	9-20-78	1996	Tucacas, Venez.
Pearson, Dale	1	1	4.50	7	0	0	0	16	16	10	8	8	11	L	L	6-0	210	9-27-76	1999	Stillwater, Okla.
Piedra, Alex	3	2	5.64	18	0	0	0	30	22	21	19	36	25	S	R	6-2	210	2-1-80	1998	Miami, Fla.
Springston, Adam	1	1	2.08	4	0	0	0	9	4	4	2	3	12	R	R	6-6	230	9-7-77	1999	Oxnard, Calif.
Toropov, Alexander	0	0	6.75	2	0	0	0	2	1	1	1	2	1	S	R	6-7	245	2-1-80	1998	Moscow, Russia
Wallace, Jeff	0	0	3.86	4	0	0	0	5	5	2	2	5	5	R	R	6-1	175	9-10-76	1999	Sacramento, Calif.
Williams, Adam	7	2	4.36	15	14	0	0	89	70	45	43	35	95	R	L	6-3	236	11-29-78	1997	Montgomery, Ala.
Williams, Joel	2	3	8.34	13	0	0	1	23	30	26	21	16	15	R	R	6-2	200	11-26-79	1998	Yoncalla, Ore.

MILWAUKEE BREWERS

Brewers clean house after seventh straight losing season

BY TOM HAUDRICOURT

Whatever could go wrong, did, on and off the field for the Brewers in 1999. It would be difficult to imagine a more discouraging summer, in terms of the organization's present and immediate future.

Not only did the team suffer through its seventh straight losing season, but a tragic construction accident at the site of Miller Park also pushed back its opening from 2000 to 2001. The extra money from the new ballpark was supposed to help the Brewers become competitive, but now they must scramble for another year.

When the club bottomed out in August, it cost manager Phil Garner and general manager Sal Bando their jobs. Before the season was done, the Brewers hired Braves assistant general manager Dean Taylor to run their baseball operation.

A bad season spiraled out of control the day after the All-Star Game in Boston. A crane collapsed at Miller Park as a beam was being raised for the roof, killing three workers and badly damaging the structure.

A couple of days later, right fielder Jeromy Burnitz broke his right hand when he was hit by a pitch from the Royals' Jose Rosado. Burnitz was out for five weeks, and the offense went stone cold. Then righthander Steve Woodard, the club's most reliable starter, broke his hand and was lost for a month. Already thin, the Brewers could not absorb the key losses.

And the hits just kept coming. In early August, catcher David Nilsson broke his thumb and was lost for the rest of the season.

The starting pitching was a mess from the start,

Jeff Cirillo   Kevin Barker

Players of the Year

MAJOR LEAGUE: Jeff Cirillo, 3b
Cirillo ranked fifth in the NL with a .326 average and led the Brewers with 98 runs and 198 hits.

MINOR LEAGUE: Kevin Barker, 1b
Barker earned a ticket to Milwaukee after hitting .278 with 23 home runs and 87 RBIs in Triple-A at Louisville.

with lefthanders Rafael Roque (1-6, 6.36) and Jim Abbott (2-8, 6.84) falling by the wayside. Cal Eldred, the long-ago ace of the staff, continued his descent by going 2-8 with a 7.79 ERA.

If not for the good fortune of signing Hideo Nomo, the pitching would have been an absolute nightmare. Nomo, released by the Mets and Cubs, stabilized the rotation somewhat with a 12-8 record.

In addition to Nomo, there was other good news. Veterans Jeff Cirillo and Marquis Grissom rallied for strong finishes. Left fielder Geoff Jenkins, playing on a regular basis for the first time, proved he could be counted on by batting .313 with 21 home runs and 82 RBIs.

Closer Bob Wickman set a club record with 37 saves, though the bullpen wore down by season's end through overuse.

Down on the farm, the news wasn't much better. The six minor league clubs finished 83 games below .500 (316-399), with only Rookie-level Helena posting a winning record.

First baseman Kevin Barker hit 23 homers and drove in 87 runs at Triple-A Louisville, earning a late-season promotion. And third baseman Scott Kirby had a big year with 27 homers and 83 RBIs for the Class A clubs in Beloit and Stockton.

Righthander Kyle Peterson, a 1997 first-round pick, worked his way to the big leagues, but another top pitching prospect, Jose Garcia, missed the year with an elbow injury. The biggest splash was made by 1998 second-round pick Nick Neugebauer, who led all minor league starters with 13.78 strikeouts per nine innings at Beloit.

ORGANIZATION LEADERS

BATTING

*AVG	Ryan Knox, Helena	.349
R	Mickey Lopez, Louisville/Huntsville	101
H	Jeff Pickler, Huntsville/Stockton	156
TB	Scott Kirby, Stockton/Beloit	251
2B	Lyle Mouton, Louisville	34
3B	Scott Sollmann, Huntsville/Stockton	10
HR	Scott Kirby, Stockton/Beloit	27
RBI	Scott Krause, Louisville	89
BB	Scott Sollmann, Huntsville/Stockton	86
SO	Scott Sollmann, Huntsville/Stockton	150
SB	Greg Martinez, Louisville/Huntsville	56

PITCHING

W	Al Hawkins, Huntsville/Stockton	11
L	Rickey Lewis, Beloit/Ogden	13
#ERA	Kevin Grater, Beloit/Helena	3.07
G	Two tied at	58
CG	Paul Stewart, Stockton	5
SV	Reggie Harris, Louisville	16
IP	Paul Stewart, Stockton	170
BB	Rickey Lewis, Beloit/Ogden	99
SO	James Johnson, Stockton	135

*Minimum 250 At-Bats #Minimum 75 Innings

Milwaukee
BREWERS

Manager: Phil Garner/Jim Lefebvre

1999 Record: 74-87, .460 (5th, NL Central)

BATTING	AVG	G	AB	R	H	2B	3B	HR	RBI	BB	SO	SB	CS	B	T	HT	WT	DOB	1st Yr	Resides
Banks, Brian	.242	105	219	34	53	7	1	5	22	25	59	6	1	S	R	6-3	200	9-28-70	1993	Mesa, Ariz.
Barker, Kevin	.282	38	117	13	33	3	0	3	23	9	19	1	0	L	L	6-3	205	7-26-75	1996	Mendota, Va.
Becker, Rich	.252	89	139	15	35	5	2	5	16	33	38	5	0	L	L	5-10	193	2-1-72	1990	Cape Coral, Fla.
Belliard, Ron	.295	124	457	60	135	29	4	8	58	64	59	4	5	R	R	5-9	176	4-7-75	1994	Miami, Fla.
Berry, Sean	.228	106	259	26	59	11	1	2	23	17	50	0	0	R	R	5-11	200	3-22-66	1986	Paso Robles, Calif.
Burnitz, Jeromy	.270	130	467	87	126	33	2	33	103	91	124	7	3	L	R	6-0	205	4-14-69	1990	Tavernier, Fla.
Cancel, Robinson	.182	15	44	5	8	2	0	0	5	2	12	0	0	R	R	6-0	195	5-4-76	1994	Lajas, P.R.
Cirillo, Jeff	.326	157	607	98	198	35	1	15	88	75	83	7	4	R	R	6-2	193	9-23-69	1991	Seattle, Wash.
Collier, Lou	.259	74	135	18	35	9	0	2	21	14	32	3	2	R	R	5-10	183	8-21-73	1993	Chicago, Ill.
Greene, Charlie	.190	32	42	4	8	1	0	0	1	5	11	0	0	R	R	6-2	190	1-23-71	1991	Miami, Fla.
Grissom, Marquis	.267	154	603	92	161	27	1	20	83	49	109	24	6	R	R	5-11	192	4-17-67	1988	Fairburn, Ga.
Hughes, Bobby	.257	48	101	10	26	2	0	3	8	5	28	0	0	R	R	6-4	240	3-10-71	1992	North Hollywood, Calif.
Jenkins, Geoff	.313	135	447	70	140	43	3	21	82	35	87	5	1	L	R	6-1	205	7-21-74	1996	Stateline, Nev.
Loretta, Mark	.290	153	587	93	170	34	5	5	67	52	59	4	1	R	R	6-0	180	8-14-71	1993	Laguna Niguel, Calif.
Mouton, Lyle	.176	14	17	2	3	1	0	1	3	2	3	0	0	R	R	6-4	240	5-13-69	1991	Lafayette, La.
Nilsson, Dave	.309	115	343	56	106	19	1	21	62	53	64	1	2	L	R	6-3	230	12-14-69	1987	Samford, Australia
Ochoa, Alex	.300	119	277	47	83	16	3	8	40	45	43	6	4	R	R	6-0	195	3-29-72	1991	Pembroke Pines, Fla.
Valentin, Jose	.227	89	256	45	58	9	5	10	38	48	52	3	2	L	R	5-10	175	10-12-69	1987	Manati, P.R.
Vina, Fernando	.266	37	154	17	41	7	0	1	16	14	6	6	5	L	R	5-9	170	4-16-69	1991	Elk Grove, Calif.
Zosky, Eddie	.143	8	7	1	1	0	0	0	0	1	2	0	0	R	R	6-0	180	2-10-68	1989	Fresno, Calif.

PITCHING	W	L	ERA	G	GS	CG	SV	IP	H	R	ER	BB	SO	B	T	HT	WT	DOB	1st Yr	Resides
Abbott, Jim	2	8	6.91	20	15	0	0	82	110	71	63	42	37	L	L	6-3	210	9-19-67	1989	Newport Beach, Calif.
Bere, Jason	2	0	4.63	5	4	0	0	23	23	15	12	10	19	R	R	6-3	215	5-26-71	1990	Wilmington, Mass.
2-team (12 Cincinnati)	..5	5	6.08	17	14	0	0	67	79	52	45	50	47							
Coppinger, Rocky	5	3	3.68	29	0	0	0	37	35	16	15	23	39	R	R	6-5	245	3-19-74	1994	El Paso, Texas
D'Amico, Jeff	0	0	0.00	1	0	0	0	1	1	0	0	0	1	R	R	6-7	250	12-27-75	1993	Pinellas Park, Fla.
Dale, Carl	0	1	20.25	4	0	0	0	4	8	9	9	6	4	R	R	6-2	215	12-7-72	1994	Cookeville, Tenn.
De los Santos, Valerio	0	1	6.48	7	0	0	0	8	12	6	6	7	5	L	L	6-4	185	10-6-75	1993	Santo Domingo, D.R.
Eldred, Cal	2	8	7.79	20	15	0	0	82	101	75	71	46	60	R	R	6-4	235	11-24-67	1989	Chandler, Ariz.
Estrada, Horacio	0	0	7.36	4	0	0	0	7	10	6	6	4	5	L	L	6-1	185	10-19-75	1992	San Joaquin, Venez.
Falteisek, Steve	0	0	7.50	10	0	0	0	12	18	10	10	3	5	R	R	6-2	200	1-28-72	1992	Floral Park, N.Y.
Fox, Chad	0	0	10.80	6	0	0	0	7	11	8	8	4	12	R	R	6-3	190	9-3-70	1992	Houston, Texas
Harris, Reggie	0	0	3.00	8	0	0	0	12	8	4	4	7	11	R	R	6-2	217	8-12-68	1987	Waynesboro, Va.
Karl, Scott	11	11	4.78	33	33	0	0	198	246	121	105	69	74	L	L	6-2	205	8-9-71	1992	Solana Beach, Calif.
Myers, Mike	2	1	5.23	71	0	0	0	41	46	24	24	13	35	L	L	6-4	205	6-26-69	1990	Charlotte, N.C.
Nomo, Hideo	12	8	4.54	28	28	0	0	176	173	96	89	78	161	R	R	6-2	210	8-31-68	1995	Kobe, Japan
Peterson, Kyle	4	7	4.56	17	12	0	0	77	87	46	39	25	34	L	R	6-3	215	4-9-76	1997	Henderson, Nev.
Pittsley, Jim	0	1	4.82	15	0	0	0	19	20	12	10	10	13	R	R	6-7	230	4-3-74	1992	Dubois, Pa.
Plunk, Eric	4	4	5.02	68	0	0	0	75	71	44	42	43	63	R	R	6-6	220	9-3-63	1981	Riverside, Calif.
Pulsipher, Bill	5	6	5.98	19	16	0	0	87	100	65	58	36	42	L	L	6-3	200	10-9-73	1992	Port St. Lucie, Calif.
Ramirez, Hector	1	2	3.43	15	0	0	0	21	19	8	8	11	9	R	R	6-3	218	12-15-71	1988	El Seibo, D.R.
Reyes, Al	2	0	4.25	26	0	0	0	36	27	17	17	25	39	R	R	6-0	165	4-10-71	1988	Santo Domingo, D.R.
Roque, Rafael	1	6	5.34	43	9	0	1	84	96	52	50	42	66	L	L	6-4	186	1-1-72	1991	Santo Domingo, D.R.
Weathers, David	7	4	4.65	63	0	0	2	93	102	49	48	38	74	R	R	6-3	220	9-25-69	1988	Loretto, Tenn.
Wickman, Bob	3	8	3.39	71	0	0	37	74	75	31	28	38	60	R	R	6-1	220	2-6-69	1990	Abrams, Wis.
Woodard, Steve	11	8	4.52	31	29	2	0	185	219	101	93	36	119	L	R	6-4	235	5-15-75	1994	Hartselle, Ala.

FIELDING

Catcher	PCT	G	PO	A	E	DP	PB
Banks	.982	40	148	14	3	3	5
Cancel	.980	15	84	12	2	2	0
Greene	.991	31	104	8	1	0	1
Hughes	.988	44	149	15	2	2	5
Nilsson	.991	101	531	44	5	3	2

First Base	PCT	G	PO	A	E	DP
Banks	.992	44	221	20	2	18
Barker	.996	31	254	17	1	19
Berry	.989	64	438	27	5	50
Loretta	.994	66	474	31	3	44

Second Base	PCT	G	PO	A	E	DP
Belliard	.978	119	247	331	13	75
Collier	1.000	4	7	0	0	0
Loretta	.956	17	28	37	3	8
Vina	.995	37	84	104	1	31
Zosky	1.000	2	1	3	0	0

Third Base	PCT	G	PO	A	E	DP
Belliard	1.000	1	1	0	0	0

	PCT	G	PO	A	E	DP
Cirillo	.967	155	124	312	15	35
Collier	.800	7	0	4	1	0
Loretta	.900	14	11	16	3	2
Zosky	1.000	4	0	1	0	0

Shortstop	PCT	G	PO	A	E	DP
Belliard	1.000	1	2	3	0	0
Collier	.948	31	21	52	4	7
Loretta	.986	74	112	176	4	40
Valentin	.937	85	113	214	22	38

Outfield	PCT	G	PO	A	E	DP
Banks	1.000	5	1	0	0	0
Becker	.970	50	62	3	2	1
Burnitz	.982	127	262	8	5	2
Collier	1.000	10	14	0	0	0
Grissom	.987	149	374	1	5	2
Jenkins	.974	128	250	14	7	4
Mouton	1.000	3	1	0	0	0
Ochoa	.979	85	133	5	3	0

MEL BAILEY

Jeromy Burnitz

Geoff Jenkins
Hit .313 in first full season

Kyle Peterson
Won 11 games between Milwaukee and Louisville

FARM SYSTEM

Director of Player Development: Cecil Cooper

Class	Farm Team	League	W	L	Pct.	Finish*	Manager(s)	First Yr
AAA	Louisville (Ky.) Redbirds	International	63	81	.438	11th (14)	Gary Allenson	1998
AA	Huntsville (Ala.) Stars	Southern	64	76	.457	8th (10)	Darrell Evans	1999
A#	Stockton (Calif.) Ports	California	57	83	.407	9th (10)	Bernie Moncallo/Carlos Ponce	1979
A	Beloit (Wis.) Snappers	Midwest	59	80	.424	14th (14)	Don Money	1982
Rookie#	Helena (Mont.) Brewers	Pioneer	47	28	.627	2nd (8)	Carlos Lezcano	1985
Rookie#	Ogden (Utah) Raptors	Pioneer	26	50	.342	8th (8)	Jon Pont/Ed Sedar	1996

*Finish in overall standings (No. of teams in league)   #Advanced level

LOUISVILLE   Class AAA

INTERNATIONAL LEAGUE

BATTING	AVG	G	AB	R	H	2B	3B	HR	RBI	BB	SO	SB	CS	B	T	HT	WT	DOB	1st Yr	Resides
Andreopoulos, Alex	.264	71	201	19	53	8	0	5	31	25	21	1	0	L	R	5-10	190	8-19-72	1995	Toronto, Ontario
Banks, Brian	.208	6	24	3	5	2	1	1	6	2	5	0	0	S	R	6-3	200	9-28-70	1993	Mesa, Ariz.
Barker, Kevin	.278	121	442	89	123	27	5	23	87	59	94	2	2	L	L	6-3	205	7-26-75	1996	Mendota, Va.
Belliard, Ronnie	.241	29	108	14	26	4	0	1	8	14	13	12	3	R	R	5-9	176	4-7-75	1994	Miami, Fla.
Benitez, Yamil	.214	99	341	47	73	24	2	12	49	29	103	13	4	R	R	6-2	195	10-5-72	1990	Rio Piedras, P.R.
Brito, Jorge	.056	4	18	0	1	0	0	0	0	0	9	0	0	R	R	6-1	188	6-22-66	1986	Athens, Ala.
Cancel, Robinson	.368	39	117	22	43	8	0	5	28	14	28	6	2	R	R	6-0	195	5-4-76	1994	Lajas, P.R.
Collier, Lou	.385	27	91	25	35	10	0	4	11	15	14	6	3	R	R	5-10	183	8-21-73	1993	Chicago, Ill.
Cromer, Brandon	.215	115	330	46	71	12	1	24	61	40	103	6	0	L	R	6-2	175	1-25-74	1992	Lexington, S.C.
Dunn, Todd	.217	40	106	14	23	1	1	5	16	14	32	2	1	R	R	6-5	230	7-29-70	1993	Jacksonville, Fla.
Greene, Charlie	.211	56	161	16	34	8	0	4	15	7	26	0	0	R	R	6-0	190	1-23-71	1991	Miami, Fla.
Hughes, Bobby	.188	10	32	5	6	2	0	1	2	2	7	0	0	R	R	6-4	240	3-10-71	1992	North Hollywood, Calif.
Iapoce, Anthony	.169	26	83	6	14	2	0	0	0	7	30	6	3	S	L	5-10	178	8-23-73	1994	Ridgewood, N.Y.
Krause, Scott	.277	133	499	57	138	26	7	15	89	33	104	10	6	R	R	6-1	195	8-16-73	1994	Willowick, Ohio
Lopez, Mickey	.320	49	181	43	58	17	2	5	31	37	25	11	7	S	R	5-10	165	11-17-73	1995	Miami, Fla.
Martinez, Greg	.265	107	419	79	111	13	4	4	29	53	50	48	7	S	R	5-10	168	1-27-72	1993	Las Vegas, Nev.
Mouton, Lyle	.357	83	305	64	109	34	2	19	77	27	67	19	0	R	R	6-4	240	5-13-69	1991	Lafayette, La.
2-team (44 Rochester)	.310	127	467	89	145	43	3	23	94	40	98	22	1							
Ortiz, Luis	.263	96	304	36	80	11	0	11	33	23	41	0	2	R	R	6-0	195	5-25-70	1991	Santo Domingo, D.R.
Perez, Santiago	.263	108	407	57	107	23	8	7	38	31	94	21	4	S	R	6-2	150	12-30-75	1993	Santo Domingo, D.R.
Valentin, Jose	.250	6	20	6	5	0	0	3	3	4	3	0	1	L	R	5-10	175	10-12-69	1987	Manati, P.R.
Williamson, Antone	.239	68	184	21	44	7	0	5	20	30	29	0	1	L	R	6-1	195	7-18-73	1994	Tempe, Ariz.
Zosky, Eddie	.294	116	415	60	122	22	3	12	47	23	68	5	1	R	R	6-0	180	2-10-68	1989	Fresno, Calif.

PITCHING	W	L	ERA	G	GS	CG	SV	IP	H	R	ER	BB	SO	B	T	HT	WT	DOB	1st Yr	Resides
Beck, Greg	0	0	81.00	1	0	0	0	0	3	3	3	0	0	R	R	6-3	215	10-21-72	1994	Fort Myers, Fla.
Bere, Jason	2	1	2.08	5	5	0	0	26	21	8	6	8	27	R	R	6-3	215	5-26-71	1990	Wilmington, Mass.
2-team (5 Indianapolis)	2	3	5.36	10	9	0	0	44	46	28	26	27	35							
Borowski, Joe	6	2	5.46	58	0	0	4	89	94	59	54	44	70	R	R	6-2	225	5-4-71	1989	Bayonne, N.J.
Converse, Jim	4	3	5.81	30	4	0	0	62	76	43	40	34	40	L	R	5-9	180	8-17-71	1990	Citrus Heights, Calif.
D'Amico, Jeff	0	0	13.50	1	1	0	0	3	6	5	5	2	1	R	R	6-7	250	12-27-75	1993	Pinellas Park, Fla.
Dale, Carl	0	1	4.63	7	0	0	1	12	8	6	6	5	8	R	R	6-2	215	12-7-72	1994	Cookeville, Tenn.
Eldred, Cal	0	1	5.30	4	4	0	0	19	19	12	11	10	21	R	R	6-4	235	11-24-67	1989	Chandler, Ariz.
Estrada, Horacio	6	6	5.67	25	24	1	0	132	128	87	83	65	112	L	L	6-1	185	10-19-75	1992	San Joaquin, Venez.
Falteisek, Steve	5	11	6.84	42	4	0	0	76	98	65	58	41	34	R	R	6-2	200	1-28-72	1992	Floral Park, N.Y.
Granger, Jeff	1	6	4.73	56	1	0	3	59	72	40	31	25	50	R	L	6-4	200	12-16-71	1993	College Station, Texas
Harris, Reggie	3	4	4.73	41	0	0	16	40	43	21	21	20	45	R	R	6-2	217	8-12-68	1987	Waynesboro, Va.
Henderson, Rod	7	11	6.34	28	22	0	0	121	119	109	85	64	76	R	R	6-4	195	3-11-71	1992	Glasgow, Ky.
Henderson, Ryan	1	0	6.37	21	0	0	0	35	35	32	25	25	34	R	R	6-1	190	9-30-69	1992	Dana Point, Calif.
Levrault, Allen	1	3	8.65	9	5	0	0	34	48	37	33	16	33	R	R	6-3	238	8-15-77	1996	Westport, Mass.
Minor, Blas	4	4	4.58	21	17	0	0	108	118	59	55	32	77	R	R	6-3	200	3-20-66	1988	Gilbert, Ariz.
Ontiveros, Steve	5	1	4.44	8	8	0	0	49	47	26	24	12	33	R	R	6-0	180	3-5-61	1982	Stafford, Texas
Passini, Brian	2	3	7.48	6	6	0	0	28	34	23	23	17	14	L	L	6-3	195	1-24-75	1996	Hennepin, Ill.
Peterson, Kyle	7	6	3.55	18	18	1	0	109	90	52	43	42	95	L	R	6-3	215	4-9-76	1997	Henderson, Nev.
Pittsley, Jim	2	4	8.77	8	8	0	0	39	55	42	38	16	26	R	R	6-7	230	4-3-74	1992	Dubois, Pa.
Pulsipher, Bill	0	2	4.28	6	6	0	0	27	22	14	13	19	21	L	L	6-3	200	10-9-73	1992	Port St. Lucie, Fla.
Ramirez, Hector	3	3	3.80	58	0	0	0	95	91	45	40	33	55	R	R	6-3	218	12-15-71	1988	El Seibo, D.R.
Reyes, Al	2	2	8.38	6	0	0	0	10	12	9	9	7	8	R	R	6-0	165	4-10-71	1988	Santo Domingo, D.R.
Roque, Rafael	1	0	0.00	2	2	0	0	10	4	0	0	3	3	L	L	6-4	186	1-1-72	1991	Santo Domingo, D.R.
Small, Aaron	1	1	9.43	11	0	0	0	21	38	23	22	15	11	R	R	6-5	226	11-23-71	1989	Loudon, Tenn.
VanEgmond, Tim	0	5	5.06	8	7	0	0	27	28	25	15	17	15	R	R	6-2	185	5-31-69	1992	Shreveport, La.
Wunsch, Kelly	2	1	4.75	16	2	0	0	42	52	23	22	14	20	L	L	6-5	192	7-12-72	1993	Houston, Texas

FIELDING

Catcher	PCT	G	PO	A	E	DP	PB
Andreopoulos	.992	63	360	35	3	8	4
Banks	1.000	1	6	0	0	0	0
Brito	1.000	4	26	1	0	1	0
Cancel	.992	36	210	25	2	1	3
Greene	.994	49	306	27	2	9	3
Hughes	1.000	8	41	2	0	0	0

First Base	PCT	G	PO	A	E	DP
Banks	.944	3	16	1	1	0
Barker	.991	120	1036	88	10	100
Mouton	.875	1	6	1	1	0
Ortiz	1.000	23	185	14	0	19
Williamson	1.000	3	12	1	0	2

Second Base	PCT	G	PO	A	E	DP
Belliard	.975	29	51	66	3	12

	PCT	G	PO	A	E	DP
Cromer	.985	45	92	111	3	29
Lopez	.976	47	104	141	6	42
Perez	.941	5	8	8	1	2
Zosky	.963	26	51	53	4	16

Third Base	PCT	G	PO	A	E	DP
Andreopoulos	.000	1	0	0	0	0
Collier	.951	20	10	48	3	4
Cromer	.968	39	22	68	3	7
Krause	1.000	1	1	0	0	0
Ortiz	.871	27	19	55	11	5
Williamson	.864	20	5	33	6	1
Zosky	.914	59	30	108	13	12

Shortstop	PCT	G	PO	A	E	DP
Collier	1.000	3	4	11	0	2

	PCT	G	PO	A	E	DP
Cromer	.875	6	9	12	3	1
Perez	.935	102	142	273	29	51
Valentin	1.000	6	7	17	0	2
Zosky	.989	37	60	117	2	35

Outfield	PCT	G	PO	A	E	DP
Banks	1.000	2	7	0	0	0
Barker	.000	1	0	0	0	0
Benitez	.963	85	175	8	7	2
Collier	1.000	2	3	0	0	0
Cromer	1.000	4	7	0	0	0
Dunn	.961	32	46	3	2	0
Iapoce	.984	25	57	3	1	0
Krause	.972	123	201	8	6	3
Martinez	.996	103	233	7	1	3
Mouton	.995	75	175	6	1	0

HUNTSVILLE   Class AA

SOUTHERN LEAGUE

BATTING	AVG	G	AB	R	H	2B	3B	HR	RBI	BB	SO	SB	CS	B	T	HT	WT	DOB	1st Yr	Resides
Alfano, Jeff	.247	83	247	20	61	15	0	5	31	35	65	4	1	R	R	6-3	210	8-16-76	1996	Visalia, Calif.
Azuaje, Jesus	.281	119	391	63	110	21	0	10	60	70	26	34	8	R	R	5-10	170	1-16-73	1992	Bolivar, Venez.
Brito, Jorge	.299	26	67	11	20	2	1	3	7	4	15	0	0	R	R	6-1	188	6-22-66	1986	Athens, Ala.
Cancel, Robinson	.251	66	223	35	56	10	1	5	32	23	38	8	5	R	R	6-0	195	11-4-76	1994	Lajas, P.R.
DiPace, Dan	.115	11	26	2	3	1	0	0	2	3	9	0	0	L	R	6-2	215	4-24-75	1996	Jensen Beach, Fla.
Elliott, Dave	.233	123	404	69	94	23	0	12	55	59	111	11	6	R	R	6-2	205	8-10-73	1995	Gladstone, Mich.
Faurot, Adam	.260	22	50	5	13	2	0	0	7	1	7	1	0	R	R	5-11	175	8-7-74	1996	Blountstown, Fla.
Green, Chad	.246	116	422	56	104	23	3	10	46	46	109	28	13	S	R	5-10	180	6-28-75	1996	Mentor, Ohio
Iapoce, Anthony	.263	50	133	17	35	7	0	0	5	12	25	2	2	S	L	5-10	178	8-23-73	1994	Ridgewood, N.Y.
Jacobsen, Bucky	.193	47	150	20	29	6	1	3	19	20	32	4	1	R	R	6-4	220	8-30-75	1997	Hermiston, Ore.
Klimek, Josh	.239	123	431	46	103	28	0	14	71	33	78	3	2	L	R	6-1	175	2-2-74	1996	St. Louis, Mo.
Kominek, Toby	.232	128	456	56	106	20	3	12	59	52	118	7	10	R	R	6-1	200	6-13-73	1995	Erie, Mich.
Lobaton, Jose	.281	45	128	23	36	6	0	2	18	13	34	2	0	R	R	5-11	154	3-29-74	1996	Acarigua, Venez.
Lopez, Mickey	.298	83	315	58	94	16	5	5	40	46	46	31	4	S	R	5-10	165	11-17-73	1995	Miami, Fla.
Macalutas, Jon	.265	93	306	50	81	20	1	5	45	38	32	4	3	R	R	6-0	200	1-3-74	1996	Stockton, Calif.
Marrero, Oreste	.216	15	37	2	8	3	0	1	7	1	8	0	0	L	L	6-0	205	10-31-69	1987	Bayamon, P.R.
Martinez, Greg	.276	25	98	18	27	3	2	0	6	12	13	8	2	S	R	5-10	168	1-27-72	1993	Las Vegas, Nev.
Mathis, Jared	.225	74	218	23	49	5	1	2	24	8	32	2	3	R	R	5-10	175	8-8-75	1997	Port Orange, Fla.
Pickler, Jeff	.279	51	183	20	51	8	1	1	23	15	25	9	4	L	R	5-10	185	1-6-76	1998	Santa Ana, Calif.
Sollmann, Scott	.314	55	191	34	60	4	5	1	9	34	31	17	8	L	L	5-10	167	5-2-75	1996	Cincinnati, Ohio
Williamson, Antone	.342	12	38	5	13	3	0	0	6	7	6	3	0	L	R	6-1	195	7-18-73	1994	Tempe, Ariz.

PITCHING	W	L	ERA	G	GS	CG	SV	IP	H	R	ER	BB	SO	B	T	HT	WT	DOB	1st Yr	Resides
Akin, Jay	2	5	4.18	46	1	0	0	84	93	51	39	31	62	L	L	6-2	200	7-9-74	1997	Memphis, Tenn.
Beck, Greg	10	9	4.45	26	25	0	0	152	157	79	75	48	93	R	R	6-3	215	10-21-72	1994	Fort Myers, Fla.
Chavez, Carlos	0	3	10.64	13	3	0	0	22	37	27	26	13	12	R	R	6-1	210	8-25-72	1997	El Paso, Texas
Converse, Jim	1	1	2.86	16	0	0	5	22	14	8	7	7	25	L	R	5-9	180	8-17-71	1990	Citrus Heights, Calif.
D'Amico, Jeff	0	1	36.00	1	1	0	0	2	6	8	8	2	2	R	R	6-7	250	12-27-75	1993	Pinellas Park, Fla.
Dawsey, Jason	1	0	9.00	4	0	0	0	18	22	18	18	10	8	L	L	5-8	165	5-27-74	1995	Lexington, S.C.
Dixon, Tim	0	0	2.75	24	1	0	6	39	33	16	12	19	43	L	L	6-2	215	2-26-72	1995	San Jose, Calif.
Eldred, Cal	0	1	7.50	2	2	1	0	12	13	10	10	3	10	R	R	6-4	235	11-24-67	1989	Chandler, Ariz.
Gordon, Mike	1	0	0.00	7	0	0	0	6	8	0	0	7	5	L	R	6-2	210	11-30-72	1992	Havana, Fla.
Hawkins, Al	8	9	5.33	19	19	0	0	100	126	71	59	29	56	R	R	6-3	210	1-1-78	1998	Elizabeth, N.J.
Helmer, Chad	1	0	8.38	7	0	0	0	10	15	12	9	9	7	R	R	6-4	210	9-12-75	1997	Ruskin, Fla.

PITCHING

PITCHING	W	L	ERA	G	GS	CG	SV	IP	H	R	ER	BB	SO	B	T	HT	WT	DOB	1st Yr	Resides
Henderson, Ryan	2	0	0.63	12	0	0	6	14	12	2	1	6	13	R	R	6-1	190	9-30-69	1992	Dana Point, Calif.
Huntsman, Scott	1	4	3.63	47	0	0	5	69	72	33	28	25	31	R	R	6-2	235	10-28-72	1994	Zanesville, Ohio
Johnston, Doug	7	11	5.01	21	21	1	0	119	128	72	66	43	80	R	R	6-5	180	3-16-78	1996	Omaha, Neb.
Kelley, Rich	1	3	5.72	25	0	0	3	28	30	19	18	8	26	L	L	6-3	210	5-27-70	1991	Scituate, Mass.
Lee, Derek	8	8	3.86	26	21	4	0	140	143	70	60	51	77	L	L	6-4	185	8-20-74	1997	Fort Worth, Texas
Levrault, Allen	9	2	3.43	16	16	2	0	100	77	44	38	33	82	R	R	6-5	238	8-15-77	1996	Westport, Mass.
Minor, Blas	0	1	9.39	2	2	0	0	8	11	12	8	5	6	R	R	6-3	200	3-20-66	1988	Gilbert, Ariz.
Nomo, Hideo	1	0	0.00	1	1	0	0	7	5	0	0	1	7	R	R	6-2	210	8-31-68	1995	Kobe, Japan
Paredes, Roberto	2	3	3.96	28	0	0	1	52	48	26	23	29	35	R	R	6-3	170	10-16-73	1993	Santo Domingo, D.R.
Passini, Brian	0	4	3.62	8	8	0	0	37	33	19	15	19	22	L	L	6-3	195	1-24-75	1996	Hennepin, Ill.
Priebe, Kevin	0	0	2.57	3	0	0	0	7	7	2	2	2	4	R	L	6-2	225	1-1-75	1997	North Fond du Lac, Wis.
Smith, Travis	3	5	5.87	7	7	0	0	38	40	27	25	18	23	R	R	5-10	170	11-7-72	1995	Bend, Ore.
Theodile, Robert	3	7	5.75	47	3	0	0	92	118	71	59	56	60	R	R	6-3	190	9-16-72	1992	Jeanerette, La.
VanEgmond, Tim	0	1	3.27	3	3	0	0	11	11	6	4	6	9	R	R	6-2	185	5-31-69	1992	Shreveport, La.
Wunsch, Kelly	4	1	1.95	22	3	0	1	51	40	13	11	23	35	L	L	6-5	192	7-12-72	1993	Houston, Texas

FIELDING

Catcher	PCT	G	PO	A	E	DP	PB
Alfano	.985	73	416	49	7	2	23
Brito	.976	17	73	9	2	0	2
Cancel	.977	51	292	48	8	5	5
Mathis	.967	15	55	3	2	1	0

First Base	PCT	G	PO	A	E	DP
Jacobsen	.961	13	112	11	5	10
Kominek	.991	48	427	24	4	49
Macalutas	.991	75	617	57	6	55
Marrero	.985	8	62	5	1	3
Williamson	.960	7	45	3	2	3

Second Base	PCT	G	PO	A	E	DP
Azuaje	1.000	4	11	7	0	2
Faurot	.909	2	3	7	1	1
Lopez	.973	82	208	225	12	49
Mathis	.962	12	27	23	2	7

	PCT	G	PO	A	E	DP
Pickler	.972	51	117	124	7	43
Third Base	PCT	G	PO	A	E	DP
Azuaje	.930	31	15	38	4	3
Cancel	1.000	4	5	4	0	0
Elliott	.923	7	0	12	1	2
Faurot	1.000	6	1	6	0	0
Klimek	.924	100	81	197	23	15
Lobaton	.000	1	0	0	0	0
Mathis	.950	9	8	11	1	2
Williamson	1.000	4	5	10	0	0

Shortstop	PCT	G	PO	A	E	DP
Azuaje	.974	85	133	273	11	61
Faurot	.938	5	7	8	1	2
Klimek	1.000	1	1	8	0	1
Lobaton	.910	35	37	85	12	8

	PCT	G	PO	A	E	DP
Lopez	1.000	1	0	2	0	0
Mathis	.962	29	42	83	5	15
Outfield	PCT	G	PO	A	E	DP
Cancel	.667	1	2	0	1	0
DiPace	1.000	7	9	0	0	0
Elliott	.980	111	196	5	4	1
Faurot	1.000	2	3	0	0	0
Green	.984	112	240	6	4	1
Iapoce	.980	27	50	0	1	0
Jacobsen	.881	28	37	0	5	0
Kominek	.987	83	147	10	2	2
Lobaton	.000	2	0	0	0	0
Macalutas	1.000	6	7	0	0	0
Martinez	1.000	22	49	0	0	0
Mathis	.857	8	5	1	1	1
Sollmann	.982	50	106	1	2	1

STOCKTON — Class A

CALIFORNIA LEAGUE

BATTING

BATTING	AVG	G	AB	R	H	2B	3B	HR	RBI	BB	SO	SB	CS	B	T	HT	WT	DOB	1st Yr	Resides
Beatriz, Ramy	.242	41	149	21	36	7	2	1	10	7	24	3	5	L	L	5-11	180	1-15-79	1997	San Pedro de Macoris, D.R.
Caiazzo, Nick	.300	114	430	51	129	21	4	8	56	25	85	2	3	R	R	6-4	215	5-17-75	1997	Portland, Maine
Colon, Jose	.258	97	264	49	68	9	2	3	28	23	62	15	6	R	R	6-2	205	1-25-76	1995	Globe, Ariz.
Cridland, Mark	.261	124	437	51	114	26	5	13	87	33	64	14	7	L	R	6-3	185	5-15-75	1998	Galveston, Texas
Deardorff, Jeff	.266	126	436	59	116	22	2	10	47	40	150	2	7	R	R	6-3	205	8-14-78	1997	Clermont, Fla.
Fox, Jason	.234	70	248	34	58	8	3	1	18	14	63	15	4	S	R	6-2	185	3-30-77	1998	York, Pa.
Jacobsen, Bucky	.250	46	156	22	39	8	0	5	22	21	40	3	3	R	R	6-4	220	8-30-75	1997	Hermiston, Ore.
Jaramillo, Lee	.229	23	48	4	11	2	1	1	10	5	13	1	2	R	R	5-11	185	12-14-76	1998	Franksville, Wis.
Kirby, Scott	.287	60	202	35	58	15	3	10	36	25	59	3	3	R	R	6-2	190	7-18-77	1996	Destin, Fla.
Kraus, Jake	.236	25	72	4	17	4	1	0	11	6	11	0	1	R	R	6-4	225	10-13-73	1997	Malone, Wis.
Light, Tal	.118	4	17	1	2	0	0	0	2	0	13	0	0	R	R	6-3	205	11-28-73	1995	Lumberton, Texas
Macalutas, Jon	.281	32	121	12	34	7	0	2	20	15	16	2	2	R	R	6-0	200	1-3-74	1996	Stockton, Calif.
Mathis, Jared	.230	23	61	7	14	1	0	0	10	2	3	1	3	R	R	5-10	175	8-8-75	1997	Port Orange, Fla.
Montenegro, Jose	.164	21	55	1	9	0	0	1	5	2	8	0	1	R	R	6-0	185	4-26-76	1998	South Gate, Calif.
Moon, Brian	.265	116	385	52	102	14	2	2	30	37	40	6	6	S	R	6-0	190	7-15-77	1997	Mansfield, Ga.
Osilka, Garret	.255	100	278	43	71	11	4	4	28	24	60	7	9	R	R	6-1	195	9-14-77	1996	Jacksonville, Fla.
Pickler, Jeff	.338	80	311	40	105	14	3	1	42	23	29	7	6	L	R	5-10	185	1-6-76	1998	Santa Ana, Calif.
Rogue, Francisco	.333	8	15	2	5	1	0	0	1	0	1	0	1	R	R	6-1	170	11-22-75	1993	Janesville, Wis.
Rowan, Chris	.237	121	431	53	102	25	4	11	55	30	142	9	5	R	R	6-1	190	3-18-79	1997	Mount Vernon, N.Y.
Schaub, Greg	.251	119	422	51	106	18	5	5	43	21	71	4	7	R	R	6-1	200	3-30-77	1995	Kirkwood, Pa.
Sollmann, Scott	.349	67	249	61	87	10	5	0	33	52	38	32	14	L	L	5-10	167	5-2-75	1996	Cincinnati, Ohio

GAMES BY POSITION: C—Caiazzo 21, Jaramillo 10, Mathis 1, Montenegro 5, Moon 115, Rogue 6. **1B**—Caiazzo 55, Cridland 5, Deardorff 2, Jacobsen 2, Jaramillo 2, Kirby 39, Kraus 16, Light 2, Macalutas 28. **2B**—Mathis 11, Montenegro 12, Osilka 53, Pickler 76. **3B**—Deardorff 122, Jaramillo 1, Kirby 13, Montenegro 5, Osilka 14. **SS**—Mathis 5, Osilka 20, Rowan 121. **OF**—Beatriz 39, Caiazzo 1, Colon 87, Cridland 80, Fox 63, Jacobsen 14, Kirby 1, Light 2, Macalutas 1, Schaub 117, Sollmann 55.

PITCHING

PITCHING	W	L	ERA	G	GS	CG	SV	IP	H	R	ER	BB	SO	B	T	HT	WT	DOB	1st Yr	Resides
Barton, Chris	1	1	10.31	7	2	0	0	18	23	23	21	15	8	R	R	6-5	214	7-30-76	1998	Carlisle, Mass.
Childers, Jason	2	8	3.56	12	12	1	0	73	78	39	29	11	73	R	R	6-0	165	1-13-75	1997	Douglas, Ga.
Hawkins, Al	3	0	3.60	4	4	0	0	25	26	12	10	6	11	R	R	6-3	210	1-1-78	1996	Elizabeth, N.J.
Helmer, Chad	1	4	2.86	20	4	0	6	35	35	18	11	18	33	R	R	6-4	210	9-12-75	1997	Ruskin, Fla.
Johnson, James	5	6	4.73	29	23	1	0	129	146	83	68	47	135	S	L	6-1	195	8-7-76	1998	San Diego, Calif.
Kendall, Phil	0	10	5.68	18	18	1	0	103	113	71	65	63	60	R	R	6-4	220	8-22-77	1996	Jasper, Ind.
Kirst, Mark	3	7	6.45	32	4	0	2	60	67	55	43	31	58	R	R	6-4	200	5-23-75	1997	Green Bay, Wis.
Krawczyk, Jack	5	4	4.68	41	1	0	2	77	87	48	40	19	74	R	R	6-4	205	8-12-75	1998	Scottsdale, Ariz.
Mallette, Brian	2	0	1.50	28	0	0	4	36	38	16	6	16	34	R	R	6-0	185	1-19-75	1997	Glenwood, Ga.
Miller, Jim	8	9	4.42	28	17	1	1	124	137	91	61	44	101	S	R	6-6	195	8-1-75	1997	Des Plaines, Ill.
Myers, Aaron	3	4	4.55	22	10	0	1	83	88	52	42	25	81	R	R	6-2	215	5-14-76	1994	Santa Maria, Calif.
Paredes, Roberto	1	3	7.41	12	6	0	0	34	31	28	28	27	30	R	R	6-3	170	10-16-73	1993	Santo Domingo, D.R.
Pasqualicchio, Mike	0	1	5.27	4	4	0	0	14	15	9	8	4	12	R	L	6-1	205	8-17-74	1995	Astoria, N.Y.
Priebe, Kevin	3	2	2.76	34	0	0	6	42	40	20	13	22	46	R	L	6-2	225	1-1-75	1997	North Fond du Lac, Wis.
Schubmehl, Brian	6	6	4.07	43	1	0	9	77	81	52	35	47	71	R	R	6-1	185	11-3-74	1997	Wayland, N.Y.
Sheets, Ben	1	0	3.58	5	5	0	0	28	23	11	11	14	28	R	R	6-1	195	7-18-78	1999	St. Amant, La.
Simonson, Chris	2	1	3.16	15	1	0	2	31	31	13	11	12	31	R	R	6-4	210	4-8-77	1999	Plover, Wis.
Smith, Travis	0	2	6.14	3	3	0	0	7	9	6	5	3	8	R	R	5-10	170	11-7-72	1995	Bend, Ore.
Stewart, Paul	10	11	3.96	27	25	5	0	170	171	90	75	61	117	R	R	6-5	225	10-21-78	1996	Raleigh, N.C.
Zapata, Juan	1	4	6.67	30	0	0	1	54	65	52	40	33	30	R	R	6-2	205	9-3-75	1993	Bani, D.R.

MIDWEST LEAGUE

BATTING	AVG	G	AB	R	H	2B	3B	HR	RBI	BB	SO	SB	CS	B	T	HT	WT	DOB	1st Yr	Resides
Beatriz, Ramy	.296	70	243	43	72	14	2	3	26	29	39	5	3	L	L	5-11	180	1-15-79	1997	San Pedro de Macoris, D.R.
Bordenick, Ryan	.270	73	248	40	67	19	1	6	36	25	60	2	0	R	R	6-1	205	12-7-75	1998	Greenville, S.C.
Brito, Obispo	.234	101	364	44	85	24	1	7	48	13	76	7	0	R	R	5-11	186	3-17-78	1996	Monte Plata, D.R.
Candela, Frank	.299	30	107	15	32	4	0	0	5	9	12	14	6	R	R	5-9	180	7-26-78	1997	Peabody, Mass.
Darula, Bobby	.304	120	438	63	133	24	8	4	75	62	57	19	5	L	R	5-10	175	10-29-74	1996	Elkhorn, Neb.
De la Cruz, Erickson	.215	95	260	19	56	8	0	0	13	19	35	1	4	R	R	5-10	160	12-6-78	1997	Santo Domingo, D.R.
Figueroa, Eduardo	.253	70	233	38	59	19	0	7	43	29	72	0	0	L	L	6-2	205	9-9-76	1998	San Juan, P.R.
Fox, Jason	.221	41	163	18	36	3	1	1	6	11	34	8	3	S	R	6-2	185	3-30-77	1998	York, Pa.
Guillen, Jose	.268	76	228	45	61	7	4	1	20	48	65	12	4	S	R	6-0	156	8-10-79	1996	Santo Domingo, D.R.
Hammond, Derry	.229	107	380	65	87	17	2	17	50	43	141	1	1	R	R	6-2	205	10-19-79	1998	West Point, Miss.
Jaramillo, Frank	.307	65	244	48	75	12	2	12	40	24	41	6	2	R	R	5-11	170	11-28-74	1996	Franksville, Wis.
Kirby, Scott	.304	68	247	54	75	14	1	17	47	47	59	3	1	R	R	6-2	190	7-18-77	1996	Destin, Fla.
Mackiewitz, Richard	.262	102	355	44	93	19	1	8	57	28	57	1	0	L	L	6-2	217	6-6-76	1998	Brandon, Fla.
Montenegro, Jose	.333	2	6	1	2	1	0	1	2	1	0	0	0	R	R	6-0	185	4-26-76	1998	South Gate, Calif.
Morrow, Alvin	.233	82	296	29	69	11	0	3	44	47	121	0	0	R	R	6-5	240	4-28-77	1997	St. Louis, Mo.
Patten, Chris	.285	124	478	69	136	16	7	7	65	30	100	6	5	R	R	6-1	180	12-8-78	1997	Tempe, Ariz.
Sanchez, Wellington	.261	71	261	35	68	14	3	0	23	25	58	9	3	R	R	6-0	162	5-27-77	1995	Nagua, D.R.
Tucent, Francisco	.186	38	102	9	19	4	0	1	10	0	26	0	1	S	R	6-2	165	6-16-77	1997	Villa Mella, D.R.
Vina, Fernando	.200	2	10	1	2	1	0	0	0	0	2	0	1	L	R	5-9	170	4-16-69	1991	Elk Grove, Calif.

GAMES BY POSITION: C—Bordenick 44, Brito 100, Darula 2. **1B**—Bordenick 17, Figueroa 38, Kirby 1, Mackiewitz 89. **2B**—Guillen 16, Patten 118, Tucent 11, Vina 1. **3B**—Bordenick 1, Jaramillo 49, Kirby 67, Montenegro 2, Patten 6, Tucent 22. **SS**—Guillen 57, Jaramillo 21, Sanchez 69, Tucent 2. **OF**—Beatriz 68, Bordenick 2, Candela 13, Darula 64, de la Cruz 94, Fox 25, Guillen 1, Hammond 105, Mackiewitz 1, Morrow 78, Tucent 2.

PITCHING	W	L	ERA	G	GS	CG	SV	IP	H	R	ER	BB	SO	B	T	HT	WT	DOB	1st Yr	Resides
Barton, Chris	0	1	5.46	16	0	0	2	28	31	27	17	16	18	R	R	6-5	214	7-30-76	1998	Carlisle, Mass.
Childers, Matt	3	10	5.94	20	19	0	0	100	129	72	66	30	52	R	R	6-5	195	12-3-78	1997	Augusta, Ga.
D'Amico, Jeff	1	0	0.00	2	2	0	0	8	7	0	0	1	6	R	R	6-7	250	12-27-75	1993	Pinellas Park, Fla.
Gagliano, Steve	5	3	4.10	15	9	1	1	75	71	40	34	23	45	R	R	6-3	200	8-4-77	1997	Rolling Meadows, Ill.
Geitz, Scott	1	3	5.19	52	0	0	3	69	75	44	40	31	56	R	R	6-4	190	4-6-76	1998	St. Louis, Mo.
Gold, J.M.	6	10	5.40	21	21	2	0	112	120	82	67	54	93	R	R	6-5	225	4-10-80	1998	Toms River, N.J.
Grater, Kevin	5	3	2.39	9	8	1	0	60	47	17	16	17	65	R	R	6-1	195	9-30-77	1999	Fond du Lac, Wis.
Greeny, Burdette	0	0	5.79	19	0	0	3	28	38	20	18	7	22	R	R	6-5	215	4-23-75	1998	Port Angeles, Wash.
Incantalupo, Todd	4	4	6.04	40	7	0	1	95	115	71	64	40	62	L	L	6-2	185	5-18-76	1997	Norwalk, Conn.
Jones, Fontella	4	3	4.34	36	5	0	4	77	84	44	37	35	76	R	R	6-2	210	5-25-75	1998	Pass Christian, Miss.
Krawczyk, Jack	0	0	0.00	6	0	0	3	6	5	0	0	1	11	R	R	6-4	195	8-12-75	1998	Scottsdale, Ariz.
Lewis, Rickey	5	6	6.02	16	14	0	0	64	70	59	43	55	42	R	R	6-2	220	4-3-77	1998	Biloxi, Miss.
Mathews, Dan	3	4	8.69	19	3	0	3	29	41	34	28	25	26	R	R	6-0	175	12-22-75	1998	South Bend, Ind.
Miller, Jim	0	1	3.77	6	1	0	0	14	13	6	6	5	9	S	R	6-6	195	8-1-75	1997	Des Plaines, Ill.
Miniel, Roberto	0	0	9.37	10	0	0	0	16	23	19	17	16	11	R	R	6-4	160	12-5-80	1996	Santo Domingo, D.R.
Neugebauer, Nick	7	5	3.90	18	18	0	0	81	50	41	35	80	125	R	R	6-3	225	7-15-80	1999	Riverside, Calif.
Penney, Mike	9	12	4.24	27	27	4	0	170	171	94	80	70	109	R	R	6-0	185	3-29-77	1998	Laguna Niguel, Calif.
Pine, Chris	0	1	3.14	7	0	0	0	14	13	7	5	10	17	R	R	6-2	205	9-25-76	1998	Tigard, Ore.
Poe, Ryan	6	10	3.56	49	5	0	9	96	94	46	38	16	108	R	R	6-2	220	9-3-77	1998	Mission Viejo, Calif.
Rosado, Juan	0	0	9.90	8	0	0	0	10	11	12	11	14	4	L	L	5-11	180	6-16-79	1994	Camuy, P.R.
Wooten, Shane	0	2	3.09	33	0	0	1	35	29	16	12	25	35	S	L	6-0	170	3-14-75	1998	Goodlettsville, Tenn.
Zapata, Juan	0	2	8.03	7	0	0	0	12	22	16	11	9	9	R	R	6-2	205	9-3-75	1993	Bani, D.R.

PIONEER LEAGUE

BATTING	AVG	G	AB	R	H	2B	3B	HR	RBI	BB	SO	SB	CS	B	T	HT	WT	DOB	1st Yr	Resides
Brazoban, Jose	.234	45	158	28	37	5	1	1	18	18	43	18	5	R	R	5-11	183	7-28-77	1997	Santo Domingo, D.R.
Buccheri, Joe	.200	21	65	6	13	2	0	0	13	3	15	4	4	R	R	5-11	180	10-31-78	1999	Dunnellon, Fla.
Ceriani, Matt	.302	57	162	22	49	11	0	1	25	15	23	4	0	R	R	6-2	210	10-9-76	1998	Vacaville, Calif.
Doucet, Brandon	.239	48	134	20	32	7	0	0	11	15	31	4	0	R	R	6-1	215	3-24-76	1998	Abbeville, La.
Foster, Brian	.152	20	46	4	7	0	0	0	2	5	16	0	0	R	R	6-2	190	8-21-81	1999	Burlington, N.C.
Garcia, Hector	.307	68	264	48	81	10	2	16	62	12	46	8	1	R	R	6-3	165	12-19-79	1997	Haina, D.R.
Geraldo, Anulfo	.261	45	161	28	42	8	0	2	22	20	26	2	3	R	R	6-0	165	12-1-79	1998	Santo Domingo, D.R.
Kenney, Jeff	.261	48	153	40	40	8	2	4	29	37	33	8	4	R	R	5-11	185	9-14-77	1999	Pitman, N.J.
Knox, Ryan	.349	72	275	58	96	17	1	2	25	25	27	44	11	R	R	6-0	185	6-28-77	1999	Peoria, Ill.
Martinez, Alejandro	.289	38	128	14	37	7	0	2	16	18	20	1	0	S	R	6-1	210	5-22-77	1997	Santo Domingo, D.R.
Mayo, Terry	.163	36	104	5	17	3	0	1	12	6	47	0	3	R	R	6-4	180	7-1-81	1999	Greensboro, N.C.
Reyes, Eduardo	.291	66	223	51	65	12	3	6	33	19	38	13	4	R	R	5-11	160	8-28-79	1997	Santo Domingo, D.R.
Rojas, Eliser	.278	43	151	26	42	4	1	3	20	14	21	7	1	R	R	5-10	170	1-14-79	1997	Santo Domingo, D.R.
Scarborough, Steve	.327	32	113	29	37	11	0	5	18	19	16	6	2	R	R	6-0	160	3-10-78	1999	Duncanville, Texas
2-team (16 Ogden)	.303	48	152	36	46	14	1	5	24	23	26	9	4							
Stryhas, Paul	.285	37	123	18	35	8	0	2	14	13	24	1	1	R	R	5-10	180	12-20-76	1999	Sarasota, Fla.
Tindell, Matt	.280	29	100	20	28	6	0	2	11	7	24	4	1	R	R	6-0	180	4-22-80	1999	Augusta, Ga.
Truitt, Steve	.308	54	185	51	57	10	1	11	50	37	40	19	5	R	R	5-9	185	12-2-77	1999	Missouri City, Texas

GAMES BY POSITION: C—Ceriani 56, Foster 12, Tindell 23. **1B**—Ceriani 2, Garcia 67, Kenney 2, Martinez 10. **2B**—Buccheri 5, Geraldo 40, Kenney 6, Rojas 29. **3B**—Geraldo 6, Kenney 8, Reyes 43, Rojas 7, Stryhas 20. **SS**—Buccheri 5, Kenney 20, Reyes 22, Scarborough 32. **OF**—Brazoban 44, Buccheri 3, Doucet 41, Knox 69, Mayo 36, Reyes 1, Rojas 1, Truitt 52.

PITCHING	W	L	ERA	G	GS	CG	SV	IP	H	R	ER	BB	SO	B	T	HT	WT	DOB	1st Yr	Resides
Aponte, Carlos	3	3	5.75	21	1	0	1	36	36	24	23	17	28	R	R	6-2	175	5-17-79	1997	San Pedro de Macoris, D.R.
Arieta, Corey	6	3	3.86	15	15	1	0	89	83	51	38	27	60	L	L	6-6	180	10-8-76	1999	St. Francisville, La.
Briceno, Pablo	1	4	4.46	12	6	0	0	42	36	26	21	21	23	R	R	6-2	165	1-3-78	1997	Lara, Venez.
Burkhart, B.J.	1	1	3.38	8	0	0	0	8	13	4	3	1	4	L	L	6-0	190	2-13-77	1999	La Salle, Ill.
2-team (10 Ogden)	2	1	4.55	18	0	0	0	30	40	25	15	6	17							

PITCHING	W	L	ERA	G	GS	CG	SV	IP	H	R	ER	BB	SO	B	T	HT	WT	DOB	1st Yr	Resides
Cordero, Victor	5	3	6.92	22	0	0	1	40	45	39	31	22	41	R	R	6-2	183	9-7-79	1997	Santo Domingo, D.R.
Gordon, Justin	1	2	6.03	15	4	0	0	31	31	31	21	29	36	L	L	6-5	215	5-26-79	1999	Taunton, Mass.
Grater, Kevin	1	1	4.40	6	5	0	0	31	34	16	15	7	30	R	R	6-1	195	9-30-77	1999	Fond du Lac, Wis.
Horne, Travis	1	0	7.94	3	2	0	0	6	5	5	5	9	2	L	L	6-4	245	4-16-81	1999	Jacksonville, Fla.
Krismer, Jeremy	4	3	4.86	12	9	0	0	46	49	26	25	17	27	R	R	6-6	230	8-5-76	1999	Tulsa, Okla.
Mieses, Jose	10	2	2.67	15	15	3	0	108	79	36	32	28	87	R	R	6-0	178	10-14-79	1998	Santo Domingo, D.R.
Mosher, Andy	1	1	5.61	24	0	0	12	26	25	17	16	15	30	R	R	6-3	175	10-24-75	1999	Flagstaff, Ariz.
Olean, Chris	6	1	2.76	14	8	2	4	59	56	30	18	12	27	R	R	6-0	185	5-29-77	1999	Minneapolis, Minn.
2-team (2 Ogden)	6	1	3.50	16	8	2	4	62	60	36	24	15	30							
Poturnicki, Adam	3	0	4.79	16	2	0	0	36	37	27	19	16	32	R	R	6-5	230	8-15-76	1999	Middlefield, Conn.
Robinson, Jeff	0	0	1.29	1	1	0	0	7	4	4	1	3	14	R	R	6-4	215	6-2-77	1999	Lake Charles, La.
2-team (9 Ogden)	5	2	2.77	10	9	2	0	62	49	29	19	19	65							
Simonson, Chris	3	0	1.95	6	6	0	0	37	34	21	8	8	29	R	R	6-4	210	4-8-77	1999	Plover, Wis.
Smith, Jesse	2	3	4.35	19	1	0	3	31	37	23	15	16	29	R	R	6-2	195	5-15-76	1997	Pikeville, Ky.
Wagner, Frank	0	1	12.71	11	0	0	1	11	18	19	16	16	6	L	L	6-2	602	9-25-77	1999	Colstrip, Mont.
Walker, Josh	0	0	5.40	3	0	0	0	7	10	4	4	0	3	R	R	6-2	190	5-19-76	1999	Gardnerville, Nev.

OGDEN — Rookie

PIONEER LEAGUE

BATTING	AVG	G	AB	R	H	2B	3B	HR	RBI	BB	SO	SB	CS	B	T	HT	WT	DOB	1st Yr	Resides
Ayala, Elio	.267	66	240	41	64	14	0	1	19	20	27	8	3	R	R	5-8	160	11-7-78	1998	Bronx, N.Y.
Buccheri, Joe	.190	10	21	3	4	0	0	0	1	6	5	0	1	R	R	5-11	180	10-31-78	1999	Dunnellon, Fla.
2-team (21 Helena)	.198	31	86	9	17	2	0	0	14	9	20	4	5							
Correa, Nelson	.288	50	156	25	45	9	2	9	34	17	30	2	2	L	L	6-3	205	8-27-77	1999	Rio Grande, P.R.
De los Santos, Nelson	.252	48	131	27	33	4	2	4	23	16	39	9	3	S	R	5-10	180	10-19-78	1997	San Juan de la Maguan, D.R.
Ernster, Mark	.227	5	22	3	5	1	1	0	2	1	1	1	0	R	R	6-0	190	12-10-77	1999	Glendale, Ariz.
Ford, Will	.341	53	179	38	61	14	4	5	46	22	27	5	5	L	L	6-0	190	10-6-76	1999	Houston, Texas
Forelli, Anthony	.294	64	228	22	67	17	0	3	37	18	51	3	3	R	R	6-4	220	4-16-77	1999	Ridgewood, N.Y.
Frank, Nick	.300	59	203	35	61	13	0	4	40	25	44	13	5	R	R	5-11	195	6-9-76	1999	Tucson, Ariz.
Guerrero, Cristian	.310	65	226	51	70	7	3	5	28	23	59	26	2	R	R	6-4	198	4-12-81	1997	Bani, D.R.
Hall, Bill	.289	69	280	41	81	15	2	6	31	15	61	19	8	R	R	6-0	175	12-28-79	1998	Nettleton, Miss.
Jaramillo, Lee	.308	43	143	20	44	11	2	3	18	21	27	2	3	R	R	5-11	185	12-14-76	1998	Franksville, Wis.
Montenegro, Jose	.247	18	54	8	14	3	0	0	4	2	8	0	0	R	R	6-0	185	4-26-76	1998	South Gate, Calif.
Palomares, Luis	.247	66	223	40	55	4	1	9	34	18	59	10	5	R	R	6-2	190	1-30-79	1997	Bachaquero, Venez.
Paterson, Joe	.245	35	94	11	23	4	0	2	20	9	26	0	2	R	R	6-0	195	12-22-78	1997	Ontario, Calif.
Pregnalato, Bob	.331	42	130	34	43	7	1	3	14	18	19	14	4	R	R	6-0	173	7-5-77	1999	Burlington, Ontario
Scarborough, Steve	.231	16	39	7	9	3	1	0	6	4	10	3	2	R	R	6-0	160	3-10-78	1999	Duncanville, Texas
Schilling, Chris	.303	16	33	3	10	1	0	0	2	3	8	0	1	R	R	5-11	192	1-14-81	1999	Central, S.C.
Trout, Casey	.246	49	142	14	35	5	0	1	11	14	26	2	3	R	R	6-2	185	4-9-77	1999	Gambrills, Md.
Warren, Tom	.149	35	87	14	13	5	0	0	3	13	34	5	2	S	R	6-4	180	11-1-79	1997	Inglewood, Calif.

GAMES BY POSITION: C—de los Santos 36, Jaramillo 28, Montenegro 15, Schilling 60. **1B**—Correa 36, Forelli 42, Frank 4, Trout 2. **2B**—Ayala 61, Buccheri 7, Ernster 5, Montenegro 1, Trout 9. **3B**—Ayala 3, Frank 37, Jaramillo 14, Montenegro 4, Scarborough 8, Trout 22. **SS**—Hall 65, Scarborough 8, Trout 10. **OF**—de los Santos 2, Forelli 44, Frank 2, Guerrero 61, Palomares 65, Paterson 23, Pregnolato 35, Trout 4, Warren 28.

PITCHING	W	L	ERA	G	GS	CG	SV	IP	H	R	ER	BB	SO	B	T	HT	WT	DOB	1st Yr	Resides
Burkhart, B.J.	1	0	4.98	10	0	0	0	22	27	21	12	5	13	L	L	6-0	190	2-13-77	1998	La Salle, Ill.
Charles, Juan	0	1	11.88	6	0	0	0	8	18	11	11	4	8	R	R	5-11	175	7-24-78	1997	Villa Altagracia, D.R.
Childers, Jason	0	0	1.38	3	3	0	0	13	10	4	2	3	14	R	R	6-0	165	1-13-75	1997	Douglas, Ga.
Durkee, Jeremy	2	3	4.06	16	1	0	2	31	31	19	14	13	32	L	L	6-1	205	11-30-80	1999	Cuyahoga Falls, Ohio
Greeny, Burdette	0	3	9.00	5	0	0	0	12	20	13	12	6	7	R	R	6-6	215	4-23-75	1998	Port Angeles, Wash.
House, Jeff	1	3	8.18	17	0	0	0	33	47	41	30	19	31	R	R	6-2	200	2-24-77	1999	Goose Creek, S.C.
Kelley, Jason	2	3	6.00	15	3	0	1	45	70	37	30	12	34	R	R	5-11	175	11-8-76	1999	Dayton, Ohio
Lewis, Rickey	1	7	7.24	11	11	0	0	60	75	53	48	44	35	R	R	6-2	220	4-3-77	1998	Biloxi, Miss.
Lugo, Ruddy	1	2	7.88	6	6	0	0	24	35	23	21	12	26	R	R	5-11	175	5-22-80	1999	Brooklyn, N.Y.
Martinez, Luis	0	7	6.97	15	7	0	1	50	66	65	39	34	43	L	L	6-7	195	1-20-80	1997	Santo Domingo, D.R.
McConnell, Gary	1	2	5.24	17	0	0	0	34	38	24	20	28	34	R	R	6-3	190	5-6-78	1998	Donalsonville, Ga.
McGee, Chris	3	1	3.00	17	0	0	7	24	18	8	8	7	28	R	R	6-3	215	7-28-77	1999	Laceyville, Pa.
Miniel, Roberto	5	4	4.41	15	14	1	0	86	98	58	42	34	77	R	R	6-4	160	5-12-80	1998	Santo Domingo, D.R.
Montero, Oscar	2	7	5.31	13	8	0	0	61	67	47	36	42	63	R	R	6-4	195	5-9-78	1997	Bolivar, Venez.
Olean, Chris	0	0	18.00	2	0	0	0	3	4	6	6	3	3	R	R	6-0	185	5-29-77	1999	Minneapolis, Minn.
Robinson, Jeff	5	2	2.96	9	8	2	0	55	45	25	18	16	51	R	R	6-4	215	6-2-77	1999	Lake Charles, La.
Sheets, Ben	0	1	5.63	2	2	0	0	8	8	5	5	2	12	R	R	6-1	195	7-18-78	1999	St. Amant, La.
Smith, Travis	0	0	0.00	1	1	0	0	1	0	1	0	0	3	R	R	5-10	170	11-7-72	1995	Bend, Ore.
Stewart, Steve	2	3	3.95	13	10	0	0	71	73	47	31	27	50	L	L	6-0	183	8-9-76	1999	Jacksonville, Fla.
Wallace, Ben	0	1	9.78	16	2	0	0	23	37	33	25	25	13	L	L	6-2	190	2-18-81	1999	Burton, Ohio

MINNESOTA TWINS

Twins field 17 rookies during another cost-cutting season

BY SCOTT MILLER

It was another year of clipping coupons, cutting costs and wondering about the future for the Twins, as they spent the 1999 season running in place while continuing to seek an agreement on a new ballpark.

The Twins started the season knowing they wouldn't have much of a chance. In December 1998, owner Carl Pohlad announced his decision to cut costs. Worse than the decision was the timing. Pohlad dropped the news on general manager Terry Ryan at such late notice—just a few days before the Winter Meetings—that Ryan couldn't tender a contract to shortstop Pat Meares, who was arbitration-eligible.

Word of the Twins' plan got out before Ryan could get any kind of decent offer in return for Meares, who eventually signed as a free agent with the Pirates. The Twins, after playing with a payroll of a little more than $20 million in 1998, were forced to scale back to $16 million in 1999. And by that edict, Meares wasn't the only player who was unavailable to the Twins: On May 21, they had to deal closer Rick Aguilera and his $3 million contract to the Cubs.

Consequently, manager Tom Kelly at times looked like a Cub Scout leader. The Twins used 17 rookies during the season, frequently starting six: first baseman Doug Mientkiewicz, third baseman Corey Koskie, shortstop Cristian Guzman, left fielder Chad Allen, either Torii Hunter or Jacque Jones in center field, and one of several options on the mound.

The Twins were competitive through the first four months of the season, even spending time in third place in the American League Central ahead of the Tigers and Royals. But by the end of the year, the kids appeared

Brad Radke   **Matthew LeCroy**

Players of the Year

MAJOR LEAGUE: Brad Radke, rhp

Radke quietly put up another solid season as the ace of the Twins rotation, going 12-14 with a 3.75 ERA in 33 starts.

MINOR LEAGUE: Matthew LeCroy, c

LeCroy hit .303 in Triple-A after jumping from Class A, where he hit .279 with 20 home runs and 69 RBIs in 333 at-bats.

drained and the Twins had their worst September ever on the way to a 63-97 finish, last in the division.

From all the rookies, though, several bright spots emerged. Guzman handled himself well for a 21-year-old who had never played above Double-A. He developed into a superb bunter but hit just .226.

Allen was steady in left field, finishing at .277. While Hunter didn't progress in center as much as the club hoped, Jones showed potential.

The highlight among rookies came during a stretch from mid-July to mid-August, when righthander Joe Mays pitched 20 consecutive scoreless innings. He spent time among the league's ERA leaders before finishing 6-11 with a 4.37 ERA.

But the Twins' story of the year came from a second-year big leaguer, when lefthander Eric Milton no-hit the Angels in a Sept. 11 breakfast matinee. In a game that began at 11 a.m. because the University of Minnesota had a home football game that evening, Milton produced the club's first no-hitter since Scott Erickson threw one against the Brewers in April 1994.

The stadium question still hangs over the club. Within a couple of weeks of the end of the season, Kelly and other club officials walked the streets of St. Paul in a lobbying effort to gain people's support for a stadium referendum. Pohlad announced he would sell the team to a local group if a new ballpark is built in St. Paul.

With so many young players in the big leagues, Minnesota's minor league teams combined to go 342-347 (.496). Only Triple-A Salt Lake made its postseason, and the Buzz lost in the first round of the Pacific Coast League playoffs.

ORGANIZATION LEADERS

BATTING

*AVG	Ruben Salazar, Elizabethton	.401
R	Jon Schaeffer, Quad City	97
H	Michael Restovich, Quad City	154
TB	David Ortiz, Salt Lake	281
2B	Two tied at	36
3B	Cleatus Davidson, New Britain	10
HR	Two tied at	30
RBI	David Ortiz, Salt Lake	110
BB	Jon Schaeffer, Quad City	92
SO	Allen Butler, Fort Myers	121
SB	Cleatus Davidson, New Britain	40

PITCHING

W	Juan Rincon, Quad City	14
L	Jose Espinal, New Britain	12
#ERA	Juan Rincon, Quad City	2.92
G	Two tied at	60
CG	Two tied at	3
SV	Saul Rivera, Quad City	23
IP	Juan Rincon, Quad City	163
BB	Ryan Mills, Fort Myers	87
SO	Juan Rincon, Quad City	153

*Minimum 250 At-Bats #Minimum 75 Innings

Organization Statistics

Minnesota TWINS

Manager: Tom Kelly

BATTING	AVG	G	AB	R	H	2B	3B	HR	RBI	BB	SO	SB	CS	B	T	HT	WT	DOB	1st Yr	Resides
Allen, Chad	.277	137	481	69	133	21	3	10	46	37	89	14	7	R	R	6-1	195	2-6-75	1996	DeSoto, Texas
Coomer, Ron	.263	127	467	53	123	25	1	16	65	30	69	2	1	R	R	5-11	206	11-18-66	1987	Minneapolis, Minn.
Cordova, Marty	.285	124	425	62	121	28	3	14	70	48	96	13	4	R	R	6-0	206	7-10-69	1989	Las Vegas, Nev.
Cummings, Midre	.263	16	38	1	10	0	0	1	9	3	7	2	0	L	R	6-0	190	10-14-71	1990	Clearwater, Fla.
Davidson, Cleatus	.136	12	22	3	3	0	0	0	3	0	4	2	0	S	R	5-10	170	11-1-76	1994	Haines City, Fla.
Gates, Brent	.255	110	306	40	78	13	2	3	38	34	56	1	3	S	R	6-1	190	3-14-70	1991	Grandville, Mich.
Guzman, Cristian	.226	131	420	47	95	12	3	1	26	22	90	9	7	S	R	6-0	188	3-21-78	1995	Santo Domingo, D.R.
Hocking, Denny	.267	136	386	47	103	18	2	7	41	22	54	11	7	S	R	5-10	183	4-2-70	1990	Anaheim, Calif.
Hunter, Torii	.255	135	384	52	98	17	2	9	35	26	72	10	6	R	R	6-2	205	7-18-75	1993	Pine Bluff, Ark.
Jones, Jacque	.289	95	322	54	93	24	2	9	44	17	63	3	4	L	L	5-10	196	4-25-75	1996	San Diego, Calif.
Koskie, Corey	.310	117	342	42	106	21	0	11	58	40	72	4	4	L	R	6-3	217	6-28-73	1994	White Rock, B.C.
Latham, Chris	.091	14	22	1	2	0	0	0	3	0	13	0	0	S	R	6-0	198	5-26-73	1991	Las Vegas, Nev.
Lawton, Matt	.259	118	406	58	105	18	0	7	54	57	42	26	4	L	R	5-10	186	11-3-71	1991	Saucier, Miss.
Mientkiewicz, Doug	.229	118	327	34	75	21	3	2	32	43	51	1	1	L	R	6-2	193	6-19-74	1995	Fort Myers, Fla.
Ortiz, David	.000	10	20	1	0	0	0	0	0	5	12	0	0	L	L	6-4	230	11-18-75	1993	Haina, D.R.
Pierzynski, A.J.	.273	9	22	3	6	2	0	0	3	1	4	0	0	L	R	6-3	220	12-30-76	1994	Jacksonville, Fla.
Steinbach, Terry	.284	101	338	35	96	16	4	4	42	38	54	2	2	R	R	6-1	211	3-2-62	1983	Corcoran, Minn.
Valentin, Javier	.248	78	218	22	54	12	1	5	28	22	39	0	0	S	R	5-10	192	9-19-75	1993	Manati, P.R.
Walker, Todd	.279	143	531	62	148	37	4	6	46	52	83	18	10	L	R	6-0	181	5-25-73	1994	Bossier City, La.

PITCHING	W	L	ERA	G	GS	CG	SV	IP	H	R	ER	BB	SO	B	T	HT	WT	DOB	1st Yr	Resides
Aguilera, Rick	3	1	1.27	17	0	0	6	21	10	3	3	2	13	R	R	6-5	208	12-31-61	1983	Rancho Santa Fe, Calif.
Carrasco, Hector	2	3	4.96	39	0	0	1	49	48	29	27	18	35	R	R	6-2	220	10-22-69	1988	San Pedro de Macoris, D.R.
Guardado, Eddie	2	5	4.50	63	0	0	2	48	37	24	24	25	50	R	L	6-0	194	10-2-70	1991	Stockton, Calif.
Hawkins, LaTroy	10	14	6.66	33	33	1	0	174	238	136	129	60	103	R	R	6-5	204	12-21-72	1991	Merrillville, Ind.
Lincoln, Mike	3	10	6.84	18	15	0	0	76	102	59	58	26	27	R	R	6-2	211	4-10-75	1996	Citrus Heights, Calif.
Mays, Joe	6	11	4.37	49	20	2	0	171	179	92	83	67	115	S	R	6-1	185	12-10-75	1995	Bradenton, Fla.
Miller, Travis	2	2	2.72	52	0	0	0	50	55	19	15	16	40	R	L	6-3	209	11-2-72	1994	Eaton, Ohio
Milton, Eric	7	11	4.49	34	34	5	0	206	190	111	103	63	163	L	L	6-3	220	8-4-75	1996	Fort Myers, Fla.
Perkins, Dan	1	7	6.54	29	12	0	0	87	117	69	63	43	44	R	R	6-2	193	3-15-75	1993	South Miami, Fla.
Radke, Brad	12	14	3.75	33	33	4	0	219	239	97	91	44	121	R	R	6-2	188	10-27-72	1991	Largo, Fla.
Radlosky, Rob	0	1	12.46	7	0	0	0	9	15	12	12	4	3	R	R	6-2	204	1-7-74	1994	Lantana, Fla.
Rath, Gary	0	1	11.57	5	1	0	0	5	6	6	6	5	1	L	L	6-2	186	1-10-73	1994	Long Beach, Miss.
Redman, Mark	1	0	8.53	5	1	0	0	13	17	13	12	7	11	L	L	6-5	220	1-5-74	1995	Tulsa, Okla.
Romero, J.C.	0	0	3.72	5	0	0	0	10	13	4	4	0	4	S	L	5-11	193	6-4-76	1997	San Juan, P.R.
Ryan, Jason	1	4	4.87	8	8	1	0	41	46	23	22	17	15	R	R	6-3	185	1-23-76	1994	Charlotte, N.C.
Sampson, Benj	3	2	8.11	30	4	0	0	71	107	65	64	34	56	R	L	6-2	210	4-27-75	1993	Ankeny, Iowa
Trombley, Mike	2	8	4.33	75	0	0	24	87	93	42	42	28	82	R	R	6-2	204	4-14-67	1989	Fort Myers, Fla.
Wells, Bob	8	3	3.81	76	0	0	1	87	79	41	37	28	44	R	R	6-0	200	11-1-66	1989	Cowiche, Wash.

FIELDING

Catcher	PCT	G	PO	A	E	DP	PB
Pierzynski	1.000	9	35	2	0	1	1
Steinbach	.991	96	539	30	5	5	5
Valentin	.998	76	387	27	1	4	6

First Base	PCT	G	PO	A	E	DP
Coomer	.996	71	518	47	2	57
Gates	1.000	5	27	0	0	2
Hocking	1.000	2	7	0	0	0
Mientkiewicz	.997	110	882	50	3	75
Ortiz	1.000	1	7	0	0	1

Second Base	PCT	G	PO	A	E	DP
Davidson	.973	6	13	23	1	7
Gates	1.000	47	44	95	0	19
Hocking	.994	56	77	85	1	22
Walker	.984	103	168	270	7	54

Third Base	PCT	G	PO	A	E	DP
Coomer	.969	57	24	101	4	9
Gates	.972	61	27	79	3	10
Hocking	1.000	6	1	5	0	1

	PCT	G	PO	A	E	DP
Koskie	.962	79	33	143	7	8

Shortstop	PCT	G	PO	A	E	DP
Davidson	1.000	4	5	5	0	1
Gates	.000	1	0	0	0	0
Guzman	.959	131	196	363	24	82
Hocking	.987	61	62	95	2	22

Outfield	PCT	G	PO	A	E	DP
Allen	.975	133	267	9	7	3
Coomer	.000	1	0	0	0	0
Cordova	.927	29	38	0	3	0
Cummings	1.000	6	5	0	0	0
Hocking	1.000	38	46	5	0	0
Hunter	.997	130	284	7	1	3
Jones	.980	93	231	9	5	2
Koskie	.962	25	25	0	1	0
Latham	1.000	14	13	0	0	0
Lawton	.982	109	213	3	4	0
Ortiz	.000	1	0	0	0	0

Ron Coomer

LARRY GOREN

Organization Statistics

Director, Minor Leagues: Jim Rantz

Class	Farm Team	League	W	L	Pct.	Finish*	Manager	First Yr
AAA	Salt Lake (Utah) Buzz	Pacific Coast	73	68	.518	6th (16)	Phil Roof	1994
AA	New Britain (Conn.) Rock Cats	Eastern	59	82	.418	11th (12)	John Russell	1995
A#	Fort Myers (Fla.) Miracle	Florida State	60	79	.432	13th (14)	Mike Boulanger	1993
A	Quad City (Iowa) River Bandits	Midwest	77	62	.554	2nd (14)	Jose Marzan	1999
Rookie#	Elizabethton (Tenn.) Twins	Appalachian	40	30	.571	4th (10)	Jon Mathews	1974
Rookie	Fort Myers (Fla.) Twins	Gulf Coast	33	26	.559	3rd (14)	Al Newman	1989

*Finish in overall standings (No. of teams in league)   #Advanced level

SALR LAKE   Class AAA

PACIFIC COAST LEAGUE

BATTING	AVG	G	AB	R	H	2B	3B	HR	RBI	BB	SO	SB	CS	B	T	HT	WT	DOB	1st Yr	Resides
Alvarez, Rafael	.375	6	16	3	6	1	0	0	2	0	1	0	0	S	L	5-11	192	1-22-77	1994	Valencia, Venez.
Buchanan, Brian	.297	107	391	67	116	24	1	10	60	28	85	11	2	R	R	6-4	230	7-21-73	1994	Clifton, Va.
Cey, Dan	.295	117	403	63	119	18	3	11	56	32	66	10	2	R	R	5-11	168	11-8-75	1996	Woodland Hills, Calif.
Cummings, Midre	.322	69	261	50	84	19	4	13	68	23	43	4	4	L	R	6-0	190	10-14-71	1990	Clearwater, Fla.
Ferguson, Jeff	.265	95	298	44	79	16	2	4	48	28	39	7	5	R	R	5-10	184	6-18-73	1994	Whittier, Calif.
Hacker, Steve	.150	8	20	2	3	0	0	2	3	5	7	0	1	R	R	6-5	230	9-6-74	1995	St. Louis, Mo.
Huls, Steve	.233	17	30	6	7	0	0	2	3	7	0	1	0	R	R	6-0	178	10-11-74	1996	Cold Spring, Minn.
Jones, Jacque	.298	52	198	32	59	13	2	4	26	9	36	9	2	L	L	5-10	176	4-25-75	1996	San Diego, Calif.
Latham, Chris	.322	94	382	93	123	24	8	15	51	54	95	18	13	S	R	6-0	198	5-26-73	1991	Las Vegas, Nev.
LeCroy, Matthew	.303	29	119	23	36	4	1	10	30	5	22	0	1	R	R	6-2	225	12-13-75	1997	Belton, S.C.
Marsters, Brandon	.200	11	25	4	5	1	0	1	8	2	6	0	0	R	R	5-11	190	3-14-75	1996	Sarasota, Fla.
Moriarty, Mike	.258	128	380	63	98	21	7	4	51	56	62	6	4	R	R	6-0	190	3-8-74	1995	Mount Laurel, N.J.
Nicholas, Darrell	.293	106	348	55	102	19	2	5	44	33	76	14	7	R	R	5-11	180	5-26-72	1994	Garyville, La.
Ortiz, David	.315	130	476	85	150	35	3	30	110	79	105	2	2	L	L	6-4	230	11-18-75	1993	Haina, D.R.
Pierzynski, A.J.	.259	67	228	29	59	10	0	1	25	16	29	0	0	L	R	6-3	220	12-30-76	1994	Jacksonville, Fla.
Richardson, Brian	.277	130	451	77	125	23	4	18	73	54	104	0	0	R	R	6-2	215	8-31-75	1992	Diamond Bar, Calif.
Rupp, Chad	.193	37	119	18	23	3	0	7	18	17	48	3	0	R	R	6-2	225	9-30-71	1993	Tampa, Fla.
Smith, Jeff	.389	5	18	5	7	3	0	1	3	0	1	0	0	L	R	6-3	216	6-17-74	1996	Naples, Fla.
Williams, Eddie	.316	97	345	56	109	24	0	17	57	35	68	0	1	R	R	6-0	215	11-1-64	1983	La Mesa, Calif.
Williams, George	.303	74	228	38	69	16	1	6	31	42	51	0	3	S	R	5-10	214	4-22-69	1991	West Salem, Wis.

PITCHING	W	L	ERA	G	GS	CG	SV	IP	H	R	ER	BB	SO	B	T	HT	WT	DOB	1st Yr	Resides
Baptist, Travis	1	3	5.35	17	6	0	1	39	46	24	23	17	23	L	L	6-0	195	12-30-71	1990	Aloha, Ore.
Bell, Jason	5	5	6.37	18	15	0	0	76	96	58	54	35	72	R	R	6-3	214	9-30-74	1995	Orlando, Fla.
Bowers, Shane	7	4	5.68	31	18	0	0	122	149	86	77	54	103	R	R	6-5	220	7-27-71	1993	Covina, Calif.
Carrasco, Hector	1	0	0.00	3	0	0	1	4	3	0	0	1	3	R	R	6-2	220	10-22-69	1988	San Pedro de Macoris, D.R.
Carroll, Dave	0	1	6.55	36	0	0	2	34	34	25	25	19	26	R	L	6-3	205	7-23-72	1993	Fairfax, Va.
Fiore, Tony	2	1	3.47	40	0	0	19	47	45	21	18	26	38	R	R	6-4	210	10-12-71	1992	Oak Park, Ill.
Gandarillas, Gus	2	2	4.55	42	0	0	2	61	73	37	31	20	47	R	R	6-1	183	7-9-71	1993	Hialeah, Fla.
Harris, Jeff	4	3	6.90	36	0	0	0	46	61	38	35	26	20	R	R	6-0	195	7-4-74	1995	San Pablo, Calif.
Lincoln, Mike	5	2	7.78	9	9	0	0	59	82	52	51	21	39	R	R	6-2	211	4-10-75	1996	Citrus Heights, Calif.
Mahaffey, Alan	1	2	5.48	7	5	0	0	21	28	17	13	15	11	L	L	6-1	199	2-2-74	1995	Downers Grove, Ill.
Miller, Travis	1	2	2.50	16	0	0	1	18	16	7	5	6	19	R	L	6-3	209	11-2-72	1994	Eaton, Ohio
Ohme, Kevin	5	3	3.83	51	3	0	2	82	94	44	35	31	48	L	L	6-1	185	4-13-71	1993	Brandon, Fla.
Perkins, Dan	0	0	4.26	3	2	0	0	13	11	6	6	4	7	R	R	6-2	193	3-15-75	1993	South Miami, Fla.
Radlosky, Rob	8	4	3.91	22	20	1	0	101	98	49	44	38	68	R	R	6-2	204	1-7-74	1994	Lantana, Fla.
Rath, Fred	7	5	3.92	56	0	0	3	83	88	41	36	24	36	R	R	6-3	220	1-5-73	1995	Tampa, Fla.
Rath, Gary	3	8	5.62	20	18	1	0	99	129	76	62	27	67	L	L	6-2	186	1-10-73	1994	Long Beach, Miss.
Redman, Mark	9	9	5.05	24	24	1	0	134	141	87	75	51	114	L	L	6-5	220	1-5-74	1995	Tulsa, Okla.
Rodriguez, Frank	3	4	6.70	9	9	1	0	43	40	34	32	14	33	R	R	6-0	210	12-11-72	1991	New York, N.Y.
Romero, J.C.	4	1	3.20	15	0	0	1	20	18	11	7	14	20	S	L	5-11	193	6-4-76	1997	San Juan, P.R.
Ryan, Jason	4	4	5.13	9	9	0	0	54	57	36	31	24	34	S	R	6-3	185	1-23-76	1994	Charlotte, N.C.
Sampson, Benj	1	1	8.04	3	3	0	0	16	25	16	14	1	7	R	L	6-2	210	4-27-75	1993	Ankeny, Iowa
Stentz, Brent	0	3	11.22	23	0	0	0	26	43	34	33	21	23	R	R	6-5	225	7-24-75	1995	Brooksville, Fla.

FIELDING

Catcher	PCT	G	PO	A	E	DP	PB
LeCroy	1.000	19	100	6	0	0	4
Marsters	1.000	10	42	4	0	2	0
Pierzynski	.984	63	376	45	7	1	3
Smith	.969	4	31	0	1	0	1
G. Williams	.988	53	325	15	4	0	1

First Base	PCT	G	PO	A	E	DP
Ortiz	.980	111	896	77	20	98
Richardson	.971	8	30	3	1	3
Rupp	.987	19	127	20	2	13
E. Williams	1.000	16	116	10	0	9

Second Base	PCT	G	PO	A	E	DP
Cey	.967	115	235	319	19	76

	PCT	G	PO	A	E	DP
Ferguson	.969	35	66	88	5	20
Huls	.889	2	4	4	1	0
Richardson	.000	2	0	0	0	0

Third Base	PCT	G	PO	A	E	DP
Ferguson	.898	37	13	66	9	3
Huls	1.000	5	1	4	0	0
Moriarty	1.000	1	0	1	0	0
Richardson	.928	110	53	203	20	21
Rupp	.000	1	0	0	0	0
E. Williams	1.000	3	1	3	0	1

Shortstop	PCT	G	PO	A	E	DP
Ferguson	.986	24	21	47	1	8
Huls	.833	1	2	3	1	1

	PCT	G	PO	A	E	DP
Moriarty	.953	127	176	426	30	85

Outfield	PCT	G	PO	A	E	DP
Alvarez	1.000	6	3	0	0	0
Buchanan	.980	101	184	9	4	0
Cummings	.954	64	101	3	5	1
Ferguson	1.000	4	5	0	0	0
Huls	1.000	6	8	0	0	0
Jones	.987	52	150	2	2	1
Latham	.978	94	262	9	6	0
Nicholas	.952	98	149	10	8	0
Richardson	.912	15	30	1	3	1
Rupp	1.000	6	4	0	0	0
G. Williams	1.000	5	7	1	0	0

NEW BRITAIN   Class AA

EASTERN LEAGUE

BATTING	AVG	G	AB	R	H	2B	3B	HR	RBI	BB	SO	SB	CS	B	T	HT	WT	DOB	1st Yr	Resides
Barnes, John	.263	129	452	62	119	21	1	13	58	49	40	10	2	R	R	6-2	205	4-24-76	1996	El Cajon, Calif.

BATTING	AVG	G	AB	R	H	2B	3B	HR	RBI	BB	SO	SB	CS	B	T	HT	WT	DOB	1st Yr	Resides
Cranford, Joey	.208	57	159	19	33	4	1	5	14	10	38	0	3	R	R	6-0	192	2-10-75	1996	Macon, Ga.
Cummings, Midre	.376	24	93	28	35	7	0	2	15	17	14	3	1	L	R	6-0	190	10-14-71	1990	Clearwater, Fla.
Davidson, Cleatus	.244	127	491	88	120	16	10	2	40	53	110	40	14	S	R	5-10	170	11-1-76	1994	Haines City, Fla.
Felston, Anthony	.207	36	135	17	28	3	2	0	12	13	15	12	2	L	L	5-9	180	11-26-74	1996	Leland, Miss.
Gunderson, Shane	.253	46	154	15	39	11	1	3	16	7	37	1	1	R	R	6-0	216	10-16-73	1995	Faribault, Minn.
Hacker, Steve	.302	118	461	71	139	36	0	27	97	39	103	0	2	R	R	6-5	230	9-6-74	1995	St. Louis, Mo.
Huls, Steve	.217	56	152	13	33	1	0	0	10	23	32	4	3	R	R	6-0	178	10-11-74	1996	Cold Spring, Minn.
Lane, Ryan	.286	17	49	6	14	0	1	3	6	7	10	2	2	R	R	6-1	185	7-6-74	1993	Bellefontaine, Ohio
Lewis, Marc	.260	101	384	38	100	27	0	9	52	38	79	6	4	R	R	6-2	185	5-20-75	1994	Decatur, Ala.
Moeller, Chad	.248	89	250	29	62	11	3	4	24	21	44	0	0	R	R	6-3	207	2-18-75	1996	Upland, Calif.
Moss, Rick	.270	90	252	28	68	13	0	4	29	24	37	0	5	L	R	6-2	197	9-18-75	1996	Lockport, Ill.
Mucker, Kelcey	.272	109	368	26	100	16	0	1	25	32	57	0	3	L	R	6-4	250	2-17-75	1993	Lawrenceburg, Ind.
Peterman, Tommy	.262	140	538	68	141	28	0	20	84	61	84	1	2	L	L	6-0	228	5-5-75	1996	Marietta, Ga.
Rivas, Luis	.254	132	527	78	134	30	7	7	49	41	92	31	14	R	R	5-10	175	8-30-79	1996	Caracas, Venez.
Smith, Jeff	.253	79	265	25	67	13	0	6	31	23	40	1	0	L	R	6-3	216	6-17-74	1996	Naples, Fla.

PITCHING	W	L	ERA	G	GS	CG	SV	IP	H	R	ER	BB	SO	B	T	HT	WT	DOB	1st Yr	Resides
Babineaux, Darrin	0	0	6.52	5	0	0	0	10	14	10	7	4	7	R	R	6-4	210	7-10-74	1995	Rayne, La.
Bell, Jason	3	3	3.42	7	7	0	0	47	46	21	18	11	34	R	R	6-3	214	9-30-74	1995	Orlando, Fla.
Cressend, Jack	7	10	4.34	25	24	2	0	145	152	79	70	50	125	R	R	6-1	185	5-13-75	1996	Covington, La.
2-team (3 Trenton) ..	8	10	4.61	28	27	2	0	160	171	91	82	57	136							
Downs, Scott	0	0	8.69	6	3	0	0	20	33	21	19	10	22	L	L	6-2	180	3-17-76	1997	Louisville, Ky.
Espinal, Jose	3	12	5.54	29	20	2	0	132	160	100	81	41	90	R	R	6-3	195	8-31-76	1994	Pedernales, D.R.
Gandarillas, Gus	1	3	8.63	18	0	0	1	32	38	32	31	21	26	R	R	6-1	183	7-19-71	1992	Hialeah, Fla.
Garza, Chris	1	0	2.08	31	0	0	0	30	14	10	7	19	40	L	L	5-11	187	7-23-75	1996	Los Angeles, Calif.
Guardado, Eddie	0	0	1.93	3	0	0	0	5	3	1	1	0	5	R	L	6-0	190	10-2-70	1991	Stockton, Calif.
Haigler, Phil	1	4	6.32	19	6	0	0	53	74	53	37	20	18	R	R	6-3	217	6-13-74	1996	Pascagoula, Miss.
Harris, Jeff	3	1	1.48	20	0	0	0	24	21	5	4	14	12	R	R	6-0	195	7-4-74	1995	San Pablo, Calif.
Hooten, David	6	6	3.56	52	5	0	1	104	94	55	41	49	89	R	R	6-0	182	5-8-75	1996	Shreveport, La.
Kinney, Matt	4	7	7.12	14	13	0	0	61	69	54	48	36	50	R	R	6-4	200	12-16-76	1995	Bangor, Maine
Lohse, Kyle	3	4	5.89	11	11	1	0	70	87	49	46	23	41	R	R	6-2	190	10-4-78	1997	Glenn, Calif.
Mahaffey, Alan	8	6	4.12	33	12	1	1	98	109	47	45	34	89	L	L	6-1	199	2-2-74	1995	Downers Grove, Ill.
Mota, Danny	0	1	3.55	6	0	0	0	13	11	5	5	5	12	R	R	6-0	180	10-9-75	1994	La Romana, D.R.
Niedermaier, Brad	2	2	4.35	41	0	0	9	50	50	29	24	27	47	R	R	6-2	209	2-9-73	1995	Niles, Ill.
Padilla, Juan	1	1	6.63	11	0	0	2	19	31	15	14	7	12	R	R	6-0	188	2-17-77	1998	Levittown, P.R.
Romero, J.C.	4	4	3.40	36	1	0	7	53	51	25	20	34	53	S	L	5-11	193	6-4-76	1997	San Juan, P.R.
Ryan, Juan	2	4	4.80	8	8	0	0	51	48	29	27	24	42	S	R	6-3	185	1-23-76	1994	Charlotte, N.C.
Spiers, Corey	5	2	3.47	8	8	1	0	47	50	21	18	12	21	L	L	6-0	204	6-19-75	1996	Houston, Texas
Stentz, Brent	0	1	3.73	32	0	0	9	31	23	13	13	12	44	R	R	6-5	225	7-24-75	1995	Brooksville, Fla.
Yeskie, Nate	5	11	5.28	25	23	0	0	130	157	83	76	47	102	R	R	6-3	201	8-13-74	1996	Henderson, Nev.

FIELDING

Catcher	PCT	G	PO	A	E	DP	PB
Moeller	.984	84	548	59	10	4	8
Smith	.980	69	437	49	10	4	8

First Base	PCT	G	PO	A	E	DP
Cranford	1.000	1	9	1	0	1
Hacker	.978	5	42	2	1	5
Mucker	1.000	1	6	0	0	0
Peterman	.986	134	1129	110	17	121
Smith	1.000	1	6	0	0	0

Second Base	PCT	G	PO	A	E	DP
Cranford	.906	7	12	17	3	1
Davidson	.982	110	264	323	11	78

	PCT	G	PO	A	E	DP
Huls	.966	19	34	52	3	11
Lane	1.000	2	4	5	0	2
Rivas	.951	9	14	25	2	9

Third Base	PCT	G	PO	A	E	DP
Cranford	.915	29	14	61	7	5
Gunderson	.000	1	0	0	0	0
Huls	.932	39	15	67	6	9
Lane	.886	14	5	34	5	1
Moss	.904	78	40	110	16	11

Shortstop	PCT	G	PO	A	E	DP
Cranford	1.000	1	4	2	0	1

	PCT	G	PO	A	E	DP
Davidson	.943	18	31	51	5	14
Rivas	.933	123	150	367	37	78

Outfield	PCT	G	PO	A	E	DP
Barnes	.985	127	247	12	4	2
Cranford	1.000	15	27	0	0	0
Cummings	1.000	24	50	2	0	0
Felston	.924	35	60	1	5	1
Gunderson	.907	31	34	5	4	1
Lewis	.982	101	211	10	4	3
Mucker	.978	104	174	4	4	1
Peterman	1.000	1	4	0	0	0

FORT MYERS — Class A

FLORIDA STATE LEAGUE

BATTING	AVG	G	AB	R	H	2B	3B	HR	RBI	BB	SO	SB	CS	B	T	HT	WT	DOB	1st Yr	Resides
Alvarez, Rafael	.293	83	304	47	89	22	4	10	58	38	48	8	4	S	L	5-9	192	1-22-77	1994	Valencia, Venez.
Bolivar, Papo	.305	114	433	54	132	21	3	3	37	27	56	8	9	R	R	5-9	195	10-18-78	1996	Catia La Mar, Venez.
Borrego, Ramon	.221	27	86	9	19	3	0	0	6	7	15	4	0	S	R	5-6	163	6-7-78	1996	Valencia, Venez.
Butler, Allen	.253	137	491	73	124	36	2	14	73	65	121	3	3	L	R	6-3	190	1-22-75	1996	Clinchport, Va.
Cranford, Joey	.242	38	124	18	30	4	1	3	14	17	22	3	2	R	R	6-0	192	2-10-75	1996	Macon, Ga.
Cuddyer, Michael	.298	130	466	87	139	24	4	16	82	76	91	14	4	R	R	6-2	202	3-27-79	1997	Chesapeake, Va.
Felston, Anthony	.296	81	311	66	92	11	3	3	47	52	41	21	10	L	L	5-9	180	11-26-74	1996	Leland, Miss.
Harrison, Jamal	.189	30	95	6	18	1	0	2	11	16	24	0	2	R	R	6-4	216	7-15-77	1995	Palo Alto, Calif.
Lawton, Matt	.571	4	14	3	8	1	0	2	3	1	3	1	0	L	R	5-10	186	11-3-71	1991	Saucier, Miss.
LeCroy, Matthew	.279	89	333	54	93	20	1	20	69	42	51	0	1	R	R	6-2	225	12-13-75	1997	Belton, S.C.
Lopez, Manny	.244	86	291	44	71	7	2	2	26	30	58	7	5	R	R	5-9	188	3-20-78	1996	El Portal, D.R.
Lorenzo, Juan	.257	119	421	51	108	11	1	3	48	9	68	8	3	S	R	6-0	190	6-10-78	1995	Cambito Garabitos, D.R.
Lough, Aaron	.143	5	14	0	2	0	0	0	0	0	3	0	0	R	R	6-3	194	6-3-77	1998	Dayton, Va.
Marsters, Brandon	.237	54	173	18	41	11	0	2	28	19	33	1	0	R	R	5-11	190	3-14-75	1996	Sarasota, Fla.
McConnell, Jason	.238	48	151	23	36	6	0	0	13	20	24	5	0	S	R	5-9	169	5-21-76	1997	Magnolia, Ark.
Pagan, Felix	.083	7	24	2	2	0	0	0	1	4	10	1	0	R	R	5-11	185	6-12-75	1997	Bayamon, P.R.
Ryan, Mike	.274	131	507	85	139	26	5	8	71	63	60	3	4	L	R	5-10	175	7-6-77	1996	Indiana, Pa.
Smith, Nestor	.283	96	329	39	93	14	6	4	34	16	67	8	7	S	R	5-11	188	1-21-78	1995	Maturin, Venez.
Torres, Gabby	.221	22	68	7	15	3	0	1	6	3	8	0	0	R	R	5-10	189	3-20-78	1996	Acarigua, Venez.

GAMES BY POSITION: C—Alvarez 1, LeCroy 65, Lough 5, Marsters 53, Torres 21. **1B**—Butler 137, Harrison 1, Torres 1. **2B**—Borrego 6, McConnell 9, Ryan 126. **3B**—Cuddyer 128, McConnell 12. **SS**—Borrego 2, Lorenzo 119, McConnell 26. **OF**—Alvarez 77, Bolivar 70, Borrego 15, Cranford 29, Felston 79, Lawton 4, LeCroy 1, Lopez 88, Pagan 4, Smith 86.

PITCHING	W	L	ERA	G	GS	CG	SV	IP	H	R	ER	BB	SO	B	T	HT	WT	DOB	1st Yr	Resides
Carnes, Matt	4	4	3.67	52	1	0	4	81	74	48	33	26	67	R	R	6-3	201	8-18-75	1997	Miami, Okla.
Carrasco, Hector	0	0	4.50	1	1	0	0	2	2	1	1	1	1	R	R	6-2	220	10-22-69	1988	San Pedro de Macoris, D.R.

PITCHING	W	L	ERA	G	GS	CG	SV	IP	H	R	ER	BB	SO	B	T	HT	WT	DOB	1st Yr	Resides
Cosgrove, Mike	0	1	3.38	7	0	0	1	11	12	8	4	6	9	R	R	6-1	190	2-14-76	1997	Downey, Calif.
Davies, Bob	10	10	4.59	25	23	1	0	137	156	82	70	38	105	R	R	6-1	194	4-2-76	1997	Warren, Ohio
Downs, Scott	0	1	0.00	2	2	0	0	10	7	3	0	6	9	L	L	6-0	180	3-17-76	1997	Louisville, Ky.
Fisher, Pete	5	10	3.74	25	24	0	0	147	171	74	61	38	91	R	R	6-3	219	7-7-77	1998	Stoneham, Mass.
Gandy, Josh	4	3	3.67	47	1	0	3	74	75	33	30	36	64	R	L	6-1	203	10-12-75	1997	Ringgold, Ga.
Garza, Chris	1	2	3.12	21	1	0	2	40	36	16	14	18	30	L	L	5-11	187	7-23-75	1996	Los Angeles, Calif.
Haigler, Phil	6	3	4.25	11	9	1	0	53	68	27	25	10	24	R	R	6-3	217	6-13-74	1996	Pascagoula, Miss.
Hill, Kendall	2	5	6.41	39	4	0	2	80	99	68	57	42	55	R	R	6-3	192	7-18-74	1994	Monroeville, Ala.
Howard, Tom	1	2	5.06	22	0	0	0	43	43	28	24	25	22	R	L	6-5	230	7-29-75	1993	Cocoa Beach, Fla.
Lohse, Kyle	2	3	5.18	7	7	0	0	42	47	28	24	9	33	R	R	6-2	190	10-4-78	1997	Glenn, Calif.
2-team (9 Daytona)	7	6	3.90	16	16	1	0	95	95	49	41	25	74							
Malko, Bryan	7	9	4.49	30	18	2	1	110	120	60	55	48	102	R	R	6-3	215	1-23-77	1995	Piscataway, N.J.
Marshall, Lee	2	2	1.47	28	0	0	5	37	32	10	6	5	25	R	R	6-5	204	9-25-76	1995	Ariton, Ala.
Mills, Ryan	3	10	8.87	27	21	0	0	95	121	107	94	87	70	R	L	6-5	205	7-21-77	1998	Scottsdale, Ariz.
Mota, Danny	1	1	2.41	11	0	0	0	19	19	5	5	5	22	R	R	6-0	180	10-9-75	1994	La Romana, D.R.
Nakamura, Mike	2	0	1.83	14	0	0	2	20	9	5	4	5	18	R	R	6-0	171	9-6-76	1998	Melbourne, Australia
Padilla, Juan	2	2	3.48	22	0	0	0	34	32	14	13	17	28	R	R	6-0	188	2-17-77	1998	Levittown, P.R.
Thomas, Brad	8	11	4.78	27	27	1	0	153	182	99	81	46	108	L	L	6-3	204	10-22-77	1996	Seven Hills, Australia

QUAD CITY — Class A

MIDWEST LEAGUE

BATTING	AVG	G	AB	R	H	2B	3B	HR	RBI	BB	SO	SB	CS	B	T	HT	WT	DOB	1st Yr	Resides
Almonte, Claudio	.213	46	150	19	32	4	2	0	12	19	41	4	3	R	R	6-0	185	8-2-78	1996	Los Prados, D.R.
Alvarez, Jimmy	.253	121	435	69	110	20	1	6	48	81	112	15	10	S	R	5-11	168	10-4-79	1997	Santo Domingo, D.R.
Dimmick, Josh	.262	24	84	9	22	5	1	2	12	10	12	0	0	S	R	6-3	225	5-5-76	1998	Wharton, Texas
2-team (53 Michigan)	.292	77	264	36	77	16	3	6	40	27	37	2	1							
Hawthorne, Kyle	.238	84	315	44	75	14	2	2	31	27	61	14	5	R	R	6-2	185	3-13-78	1998	Baton Rouge, La.
Hodge, Kevin	.240	125	425	65	102	30	3	13	73	78	85	6	6	R	R	6-0	185	10-28-76	1998	Bryan, Texas
Jordan, Yustin	.200	47	150	28	30	11	0	7	30	26	42	0	1	R	R	6-3	214	8-15-78	1996	Monticello, Ark.
Kielty, Bobby	.294	69	245	52	72	13	1	13	43	43	56	12	3	S	R	6-1	215	8-5-76	1999	Moreno Valley, Calif.
Leatherman, Dan	.259	74	255	41	66	12	0	2	31	35	28	2	5	L	L	5-11	170	5-29-76	1999	Orland Hills, Ill.
Lough, Aaron	.250	3	12	1	3	0	0	0	1	1	4	0	0	R	R	6-3	194	6-3-77	1998	Dayton, Va.
Marciniak, Dave	.261	47	165	20	43	7	0	3	19	20	19	2	1	R	R	6-2	200	2-3-77	1998	Arenel, N.J.
McConnell, Jason	.212	27	99	12	21	1	1	0	3	7	24	3	3	S	R	5-9	169	5-21-76	1997	Magnolia, Ark.
McMillin, Brian	.266	116	414	69	110	21	3	19	74	53	75	19	4	R	R	5-10	205	5-24-77	1998	Franklin, Ind.
Restovich, Michael	.312	131	493	91	154	30	6	19	107	74	100	7	9	R	R	6-4	233	1-3-79	1997	Rochester, Minn.
Rodriguez, Luis	.270	119	434	63	117	20	0	3	50	53	49	8	4	S	R	5-9	170	6-27-80	1997	Tinaco, Venez.
Scanlon, Matt	.189	16	53	8	10	2	1	1	5	2	8	0	0	L	R	5-11	187	6-19-78	1999	Richfield, Minn.
Schaeffer, Jon	.290	116	390	47	113	33	4	17	65	92	69	2	3	R	R	6-1	197	1-20-76	1997	Tarzana, Calif.
Selander, Craig	.226	100	345	41	78	17	3	2	32	21	56	2	1	L	R	6-2	180	8-31-76	1998	West St. Paul, Minn.
Shrum, Allen	.236	68	191	14	45	12	0	1	22	16	52	0	0	R	R	6-3	215	5-13-76	1998	Hermitage, Tenn.

GAMES BY POSITION: C—Dimmick 18, Lough 1, Schaeffer 73, Shrum 65. **1B**—Hawthorne 11, Jordan 25, Leatherman 64, Marciniak 14, Schaeffer 42, Selander 1. **2B**—Alvarez 14, Hawthorne 11, Hodge 9, Marciniak 10, McConnell 11, Rodriguez 93, Scanlon 1. **3B**—Hawthorne 13, Hodge 104, Jordan 1, Marciniak 1, McConnell 6, Restovich 1, Rodriguez 12, Scanlon 12. **SS**—Alvarez 100, Hawthorne 39, McConnell 7. **OF**—Almonte 40, Hawthorne 1, Hodge 7, Jordan 16, Kielty 56, Leatherman 4, McConnell 1, McMillin 103, Restovich 124, Selander 82.

PITCHING	W	L	ERA	G	GS	CG	SV	IP	H	R	ER	BB	SO	B	T	HT	WT	DOB	1st Yr	Resides
Balfour, Grant	8	5	3.53	19	14	0	1	92	66	39	36	37	95	R	R	6-2	170	12-30-77	1997	Sydney, Australia
Cento, Anthony	1	0	1.08	11	0	0	8	6	2	1	3	11	L	L	5-11	165	8-16-77	1999	Edgewood, Ky.
Cosgrove, Mike	7	7	4.74	42	0	0	1	63	71	37	33	24	46	R	R	6-1	190	2-14-76	1997	Downey, Calif.
Dobis, Jason	5	1	5.05	23	4	0	1	57	67	36	32	17	36	R	R	6-2	200	1-17-76	1998	Orange, Calif.
Eyre, Willie	1	0	4.26	2	2	0	0	13	8	6	6	6	10	R	R	6-0	185	7-21-78	1999	West Valley City, Utah
Fitts, Brian	6	4	5.58	37	12	0	1	100	109	73	62	32	71	R	R	6-2	187	7-25-76	1998	Gallatin, Tenn.
Foote, Joe	7	5	3.93	44	18	1	2	135	131	72	59	44	111	R	R	6-2	190	8-30-79	1997	Sterling, Va.
Frazier, Brad	1	3	5.40	33	0	0	0	48	52	37	29	39	26	R	R	5-11	180	12-16-76	1998	Semmes, Ala.
Hoard, Brent	12	7	3.43	28	28	1	0	150	143	68	57	64	139	R	L	6-4	210	11-3-76	1998	Los Gatos, Calif.
Howard, Tom	2	1	1.53	15	1	0	0	29	26	6	5	4	22	R	L	6-5	230	7-29-75	1993	Cocoa Beach, Fla.
Jacobs, Jake	0	3	4.79	48	0	0	0	71	63	52	38	55	70	R	R	6-6	233	3-28-78	1996	Pensacola, Fla.
Miller, Aaron	6	6	4.32	25	18	0	1	83	55	53	40	73	87	R	L	6-3	235	7-31-76	1997	Middletown, Del.
Padilla, Juan	0	2	2.40	12	0	0	0	15	18	8	4	6	16	R	R	6-0	188	2-17-77	1998	Levittown, P.R.
Rincon, Juan	14	8	2.92	28	28	0	0	163	146	67	53	66	153	R	R	5-11	187	1-23-79	1996	Maracaibo, Venez.
Rivera, Saul	4	1	1.42	60	0	0	23	70	42	12	11	36	102	R	R	5-11	155	9-27-77	1998	San Juan, P.R.
Schoening, Brent	0	1	2.45	6	1	0	1	11	7	3	3	5	11	R	R	6-2	205	4-7-78	1999	Columbus, Ga.
Sturdy, Tim	2	7	6.27	13	13	0	0	60	85	48	42	16	39	R	R	6-2	179	10-8-78	1997	Albuquerque, N.M.
Victoria, Lester	1	1	4.03	41	0	0	0	51	41	30	23	42	58	R	L	5-11	175	6-14-76	1998	Curacao, Neth. Antilles

ELIZABETHTON — Rookie

APPALACHIAN LEAGUE

BATTING	AVG	G	AB	R	H	2B	3B	HR	RBI	BB	SO	SB	CS	B	T	HT	WT	DOB	1st Yr	Resides
Almonte, Claudio	.314	45	172	32	54	15	2	2	23	21	41	4	6	R	R	6-0	185	8-2-78	1996	Los Prados, D.R.
Collura, Todd	.313	23	67	13	21	4	0	2	18	7	20	0	0	R	R	6-3	200	12-7-78	1998	Boca Raton, Fla.
Dillard, Thomas	.264	34	110	17	29	6	1	1	17	4	28	4	2	R	R	5-10	170	12-20-76	1999	Bristol, Tenn.
Garbe, B.J.	.316	41	171	33	54	8	0	3	32	20	34	4	1	R	R	6-2	195	2-3-81	1999	Moses Lake, Wash.
Jordan, Yustin	.371	11	35	7	13	5	0	3	8	5	7	0	0	R	R	6-3	214	8-15-78	1996	Monticello, Ark.
Lough, Aaron	.220	32	100	14	22	3	2	2	9	12	33	0	0	R	R	6-3	194	6-3-77	1998	Dayton, Va.
Nanita, Manny	.230	38	135	20	31	6	1	2	19	9	40	5	6	R	R	5-11	197	12-25-79	1997	Santo Domingo, D.R.
Salazar, Ruben	.401	64	262	66	105	24	2	14	65	48	43	11	4	R	R	5-9	162	1-16-78	1997	San Felix, Venez.
Sandberg, Eric	.306	67	255	60	78	16	2	15	62	45	51	3	2	L	L	6-1	215	8-15-79	1998	Spokane, Wash.
Scanlon, Matt	.354	57	240	54	85	16	5	6	48	36	45	8	0	L	R	5-11	180	6-19-78	1999	Richfield, Minn.
Southward, DeShawn	.249	50	173	34	43	10	2	1	25	28	30	16	4	R	R	5-11	187	5-16-78	1997	Dade City, Fla.
Torres, Franklin	.251	52	187	44	47	7	3	7	30	32	60	12	3	R	R	5-9	180	9-10-79	1996	Santiago, D.R.

BATTING	AVG	G	AB	R	H	2B	3B	HR	RBI	BB	SO	SB	CS	B	T	HT	WT	DOB	1st Yr	Resides
Torres, Gabby	.250	7	24	5	6	1	0	1	3	4	1	1	1	R	R	5-10	189	3-20-78	1996	Acarigua, Venez.
Wandall, Chad	.247	65	271	56	67	12	1	2	27	46	71	6	4	R	R	5-11	190	8-26-76	1999	Sarasota, Fla.
West, Kevin	.314	63	229	43	72	12	6	12	55	22	68	4	2	R	R	6-2	195	1-1-80	1999	Redwood Valley, Calif.
Williamson, Bryan	.254	24	67	6	17	3	1	0	6	7	11	0	1	R	R	6-6	210	10-29-76	1999	Kennewick, Wash.

GAMES BY POSITION: C—Collura 19, Dillard 34, Lough 26, Nanita 1, G. Torres 6. **1B**—Jordan 2, Lough 6, Nanita 2, Sandberg 66. **2B**—Nanita 27, F. Torres 40. **3B**—Jordan 1, Lough 1, Salazar 16, Scanlon 53, F. Torres 1. **SS**—F. Torres 7, Wandall 63. **OF**—Almonte 34, Garbe 40, Jordan 6, Nanita 14, Southward 50, West 63, Williamson 18.

PITCHING	W	L	ERA	G	GS	CG	SV	IP	H	R	ER	BB	SO	B	T	HT	WT	DOB	1st Yr	Resides
Cento, Tony	1	2	1.86	18	0	0	5	19	22	6	4	6	35	L	L	5-11	165	8-16-77	1999	Edgewood, Ky.
Cooke, Andrew	1	4	5.27	16	9	0	0	55	65	44	32	9	58	L	L	6-3	197	2-17-81	1997	New South Wales, Australia
Eyre, Willie	6	3	4.53	16	10	1	0	58	60	38	29	34	59	R	R	6-0	185	7-21-78	1999	West Valley City, Utah
Flock, Rick	2	3	4.55	22	0	0	3	28	30	19	14	7	37	R	R	6-3	205	6-19-78	1997	Fort Myers, Fla.
Lockridge, Sherwin	0	1	6.11	16	0	0	0	17	18	17	12	16	21	R	R	5-11	190	6-16-77	1999	Welaka, Fla.
Melson, Nate	3	1	2.48	22	0	0	2	36	40	22	10	10	23	R	R	6-6	203	10-28-78	1997	Rogers, Ark.
Nowakowski, Brian	1	0	3.05	16	0	0	0	21	17	12	7	11	26	R	R	6-1	189	11-27-79	1997	Chicago, Ill.
Poplin, Paul	6	3	4.38	21	0	0	3	37	50	25	18	11	37	R	R	6-0	165	10-5-77	1999	Norwood, N.C.
Pridie, Jon	5	6	4.48	14	14	0	0	76	93	44	38	33	64	R	R	6-4	205	12-7-79	1998	Prescott, Ariz.
Riviere, Rhett	1	0	2.25	7	0	0	0	8	7	3	2	4	6	R	R	6-4	205	12-17-79	1999	Austin, Texas
Sents, Marcus	5	1	6.14	13	0	0	0	63	56	48	43	48	60	R	R	6-2	210	8-12-80	1998	Cookeville, Tenn.
Sheets, Matt	3	3	4.79	12	12	0	0	62	69	40	33	20	55	R	R	6-2	205	9-16-77	1996	Grand Rapids, Mich.
Sturdy, Tim	6	1	3.31	12	12	0	0	73	71	33	27	17	64	R	R	6-2	179	10-8-78	1997	Albuquerque, N.M.
Underhill, Ray	0	1	7.20	17	0	0	0	25	36	24	20	15	18	R	R	6-4	195	1-26-79	1997	De Land, Fla.
Weis, John	0	1	2.16	26	0	0	3	33	24	15	8	17	39	L	L	6-1	190	11-29-77	1999	Winter Park, Fla.

FORT MYERS — Rookie

GULF COAST LEAGUE

BATTING	AVG	G	AB	R	H	2B	3B	HR	RBI	BB	SO	SB	CS	B	T	HT	WT	DOB	1st Yr	Resides
Boitel, Rafael	.286	45	161	23	46	6	2	0	14	18	39	6	4	S	R	6-3	165	1-21-81	1998	Santo Domingo, D.R.
Bowen, Rob	.260	29	77	10	20	4	0	0	11	20	15	2	2	S	R	6-3	205	2-24-81	1997	Fort Wayne, Ind.
Edwards, John	.230	33	100	17	23	2	0	2	16	9	20	3	1	R	R	6-1	180	6-27-78	1998	Melton, Australia
Gonzalez, Reggie	.301	44	143	17	43	6	3	1	14	7	20	3	3	R	R	5-11	160	10-14-79	1998	Santo Domingo, D.R.
Johnson, Kareem	.266	40	128	20	34	2	2	0	15	13	39	5	1	R	R	6-1	185	8-15-80	1998	Trail, B.C.
Jones, A.J.	.151	33	73	11	11	0	0	0	4	5	18	4	1	R	R	6-1	185	2-24-78	1999	Dade, Fla.
Lawton, Matt	.250	1	4	0	1	0	0	0	1	0	2	0	0	L	R	5-10	186	11-3-71	1991	Saucier, Miss.
Manning, Ricky	.196	19	51	12	10	0	0	0	7	14	13	5	1	L	L	5-10	170	11-18-80	1999	Fresno, Calif.
Maza, Luis	.262	25	61	11	16	4	0	0	10	10	15	1	1	R	R	5-9	145	6-22-80	1997	Cumana, Venez.
Morneau, Justin	.302	17	53	3	16	5	0	0	9	2	6	0	1	L	R	6-4	195	5-15-81	1999	New Westminster, B.C.
Nunez, Edward	.233	29	43	9	10	1	1	0	5	10	9	3	2	L	R	5-6	152	1-13-80	1997	Caracas, Venez.
Quickstad, Barry	.240	32	96	20	23	4	2	1	9	21	29	11	0	L	R	6-1	198	7-20-80	1999	Waseca, Minn.
Reed, Matthew	.185	27	65	8	12	1	0	0	7	4	10	1	1	R	R	5-11	155	10-13-80	1999	Haines City, Fla.
Sandoval, Michael	.320	55	194	30	62	13	3	0	34	15	21	5	7	R	R	5-9	160	7-8-81	1997	Puerto Cabello, Venez.
Santana, Gamalier	.341	20	44	7	15	1	1	0	6	8	4	3	0	L	R	5-9	170	11-24-80	1999	Vega Alta, P.R.
Tamburrino, Brett	.209	14	43	9	9	0	0	0	5	7	10	1	0	S	R	5-11	165	11-10-81	1998	Sunbury, Australia
Tope, Stephen	.200	18	55	14	11	3	0	0	10	9	10	2	1	R	R	5-11	176	1-12-82	1999	Ballajura, Australia
Torres, Digno	.277	53	166	20	46	7	1	1	26	26	36	10	2	L	L	6-5	175	8-27-79	1999	Morouis, P.R.
Watkins, Tommy	.263	49	152	30	40	10	0	1	12	28	21	4	4	R	R	5-10	180	6-18-80	1998	Fort Myers, Fla.
Wrenn, Michael	.256	42	129	24	33	8	1	4	21	15	19	6	0	R	R	6-0	185	9-8-77	1999	Land O' Lakes, Fla.

GAMES BY POSITION: C—Bowen 24, Edwards 30, Wrenn 15. **1B**—Johnson 1, Quickstad 3, Sandoval 1, Tamburrino 12, Torres 24, Wrenn 26. **2B**—Gonzalez 17, Reed 1, Santana 15, Watkins 36. **3B**—Sandoval 48, Tope 3, Watkins 13, Wrenn 1. **SS**—Gonzalez 28, Maza 18, Reed 24, Santana 1, Tamburrino 1, Watkins 2. **OF**—Boitel 44, Edwards 1, Johnson 38, Jones 27, Lawton 1, Manning 18, Nunez 24, Quickstad 21, Torres 33.

PITCHING	W	L	ERA	G	GS	CG	SV	IP	H	R	ER	BB	SO	B	T	HT	WT	DOB	1st Yr	Resides
Barreto, Joel	4	3	2.56	11	9	3	0	56	45	18	16	17	41	R	R	5-11	152	10-14-80	1997	La Guaira, Venez.
Bowyer, Travis	1	0	0.00	1	0	0	0	1	0	0	0	0	1	R	R	6-4	195	8-3-81	1999	Big Island, Va.
Boyanich, Vince	2	5	7.56	15	0	0	2	33	45	33	28	11	38	R	R	5-11	200	1-25-77	1999	Vallejo, Calif.
Espinal, Jose	4	3	6.90	10	4	0	0	30	35	29	23	13	23	R	R	6-1	172	12-3-79	1998	Canovanas, P.R.
Flanagan, Ryan	1	2	3.92	8	4	0	0	21	10	11	9	16	14	R	R	6-2	190	8-20-78	1998	Pittsburgh, Pa.
Frederick, Kevin	0	0	15.43	2	0	0	0	2	6	5	4	1	3	L	R	6-2	203	11-4-76	1998	Lincolnshire, Ill.
Kinney, Matt	0	1	4.76	3	3	0	0	6	6	4	3	8	8	R	R	6-4	200	12-16-76	1995	Bangor, Maine
LaRosa, Dancy	5	2	3.66	11	11	2	0	59	66	30	24	20	42	R	R	6-0	155	1-21-79	1997	Carupano, Venez.
Lesner, Ken	0	2	4.70	13	0	0	1	23	32	16	12	9	13	R	R	6-2	219	9-26-76	1999	Sylvania, Ohio
Morel, Jason	0	1	4.55	14	0	0	1	32	34	26	16	15	31	R	R	6-2	170	7-15-80	1998	Nagua, D.R.
Odom, Lance	2	2	5.79	20	0	0	5	23	33	18	15	7	13	R	R	6-1	210	1-2-79	1999	Altamonte Springs, Fla.
Palki, Jeromy	0	0	0.00	3	1	0	0	5	0	0	0	1	3	R	R	6-0	215	4-14-76	1995	Oakland, Ore.
Richardson, Jason	1	2	2.37	12	10	0	0	49	46	21	13	23	54	R	R	6-2	210	6-10-80	1998	Lakeland, Fla.
Romero, Josmir	5	3	3.22	11	11	3	0	67	61	33	24	7	40	R	R	6-2	193	11-18-80	1997	Guarenas, Venez.
Turner, Jess	6	0	4.11	17	2	0	0	35	38	18	16	13	39	L	R	6-2	195	10-27-78	1999	Kelso, Wash.
Wolfe, Brian	4	0	2.84	9	5	2	0	38	33	14	12	9	40	R	R	6-3	210	11-29-80	1999	Irvine, Calif.

Organization Statistics

MONTREALEXPOS

Attendance lags as Expos endure another building season

BY MICHAEL LEVESQUE

The Expos ended the 1999 season as they have most recent years, with a young but promising team struggling to win and their future in Montreal still up in the air.

Ground hadn't been broken for a new downtown ballpark, but potential new owner Jeffrey Loria was confident enough about becoming general partner that he met informally with Expos players late in the season in Philadelphia.

Loria believes he can get a new park and turn around the fortunes of the team in Montreal. The stadium was sorely needed, as the team drew just 773,267 fans–9,546 fans a game–to Olympic Stadium during a 68-94 season. The Expos were the only major league team that didn't draw at least one million fans.

On the field, Vladimir Guerrero continued his rise to superstardom with another monster season. The 23-year-old Dominican earned his first all-star appearance and finished the year with a .316 average, 42 home runs and 131 RBIs. He threw in a 31-game hitting streak that was the longest of the decade and became the first Expo to put together back-to-back 30-homer, 100-RBI seasons. He also broke team records for consecutive games played (277), home runs and RBIs.

Center fielder Rondell White enjoyed a productive season after moving up to the leadoff spot. He finished with a .312 average and 22 home runs. After a strong winter, second baseman Jose Vidro had a breakout year. He led the club with 45 doubles and had a .304 average.

Michael Barrett had a solid rookie season, splitting his time between third base and catcher. The Expos said they will decide his permanent position before

Vladimir Guerrero   **Andy Tracy**

Players of the Year

MAJOR LEAGUE: Vladimir Guerrero, of
Guerrero led the Expos with a .316 average and ranked fifth in the NL with 42 home runs, 131 RBIs and 193 hits.

MINOR LEAGUE: Andy Tracy, 3b
Tracy led Expos minor leagues with 37 home runs, 128 RBIs and 96 runs in his second taste of Double-A.

2000 and will stop moving him back and forth.

Ugueth Urbina continued his dominance as the closer. The 25-year-old led the league with 41 saves. Righthander Dustin Hermanson had a strong finish to an otherwise disappointing season, while Javier Vazquez pitched well after returning from a stint at Triple-A Ottawa. Rookie reliever Guillermo Mota and righthander Mike Thurman had promising seasons.

On the farm, Double-A Harrisburg had another banner season, winning its fourth straight Eastern League title and fifth since becoming an Expos affiliate in 1993. Outfielder Milton Bradley won the championship series over Norwich with a grand slam with two out in the bottom of the ninth of the deciding game. It was a nice way to end the season for Bradley, who had been suspended for seven games earlier in the season for spitting gum on an umpire.

Both Class A affiliates Jupiter and Cape Fear reached postseason play, with Cape Fear falling in the South Atlantic League championship series.

Speedy outfielder Peter Bergeron began the season with Harrisburg and ended it with Montreal. Between he played for Team USA at the Pan American Games. He should find a home in Montreal in 2000.

Top pitching prospects Tony Armas, T.J. Tucker and Jake Westbrook all had impressive campaigns. Armas pitched in the Futures Game and finished the season 9-7 with a 2.89 ERA. Tucker blasted out of the gate, going 5-1 with a 1.23 ERA with Jupiter before being promoted to Harrisburg, where a tired arm slowed him late in the season. Westbrook started slowly but finished the season dominating Eastern League hitters.

ORGANIZATION LEADERS

BATTING

*AVG	Matt Watson, Vermont	.380
R	Andy Tracy, Harrisburg	96
H	Talmadge Nunnari, Harrisburg/Jupiter	172
TB	Andy Tracy, Harrisburg	276
2B	Al Benjamin, Cape Fear	38
3B	Tootie Myers, Cape Fear	8
HR	Andy Tracy, Harrisburg	37
RBI	Andy Tracy, Harrisburg	128
BB	Albenis Machado, Cape Fear	102
SO	Tootie Myers, Cape Fear	147
SB	Kenny James, Harrisburg/Jupiter	44

PITCHING

W	Matt Blank, Harrisburg/Jupiter	15
L	Keith Evans, Ottawa/Harrisburg	15
#ERA	Bryan Hebson, Jupiter/Cape Fear	2.17
G	Scott Forster, Ottawa/Harrisburg	55
CG	Matt Blank, Harrisburg/Jupiter	3
SV	Ryan Saylor, Harrisburg/Jupiter	17
IP	Matt Blank, Harrisburg/Jupiter	175
BB	Roberto Duran, Ottawa/Harrisburg/Jupiter	73
SO	Cristobal Rodriguez, Cape Fear	128

*Minimum 250 At-Bats #Minimum 75 Innings

Montreal EXPOS

Manager: Felipe Alou

1999 Record: 68-94, .420 (4th, NL East)

BATTING	AVG	G	AB	R	H	2B	3B	HR	RBI	BB	SO	SB	CS	B	T	HT	WT	DOB	1st Yr	Resides
Andrews, Shane	.181	98	281	28	51	8	0	11	37	43	88	1	0	R	R	6-1	205	8-28-71	1990	Carlsbad, N.M.
Barrett, Michael	.293	126	433	53	127	32	3	8	52	32	39	0	2	R	R	6-3	185	10-22-76	1995	West Palm Beach, Fla.
Bergeron, Peter	.244	16	45	12	11	2	0	0	1	9	5	0	0	L	R	6-2	185	11-9-77	1996	Greenfield, Mass.
Blum, Geoff	.241	45	133	21	32	7	2	8	18	17	25	1	0	S	R	6-3	193	4-26-73	1994	Chino, Calif.
Cabrera, Orlando	.254	104	382	48	97	23	5	8	39	18	38	2	2	R	R	5-11	165	3-2-74	1994	Cartagena, Colombia
Coquillette, Trace	.265	17	49	2	13	3	0	0	4	4	7	1	0	R	R	5-11	165	6-4-74	1993	Orangevale, Calif.
Cox, Darron	.240	15	25	2	6	1	0	1	2	0	5	0	0	R	R	6-1	205	11-21-67	1989	Norman, Okla.
Fernandez, Jose	.208	8	24	0	5	2	0	0	1	1	7	0	0	R	R	6-2	190	11-2-74	1993	Santiago, D.R.
Fullmer, Brad	.277	100	347	38	96	34	2	9	47	22	35	2	3	L	R	6-1	185	1-17-75	1994	Chatsworth, Calif.
Guerrero, Vladimir	.316	160	610	102	193	37	5	42	131	55	62	14	7	R	R	6-2	195	2-9-76	1993	Nizao, D.R.
Guerrero, Wilton	.292	132	315	42	92	15	7	2	31	13	38	7	6	R	R	5-11	175	10-24-74	1992	Nizao, D.R.
Jones, Terry	.270	17	63	4	17	1	1	0	3	3	14	1	2	R	R	5-10	160	2-15-71	1993	Pinson, Ala.
Machado, Robert	.182	17	22	3	4	1	0	0	0	2	6	0	0	R	R	6-1	205	6-3-73	1989	Caracas, Venez.
Martinez, Manny	.245	137	331	48	81	12	7	2	26	17	51	19	6	R	R	6-2	169	10-3-70	1988	San Pedro de Macoris, D.R.
McGuire, Ryan	.221	88	140	17	31	7	2	2	18	27	33	1	1	L	L	6-1	195	11-23-71	1993	Woodland Hills, Calif.
Merced, Orlando	.268	93	194	25	52	12	1	8	26	26	27	2	1	L	R	6-1	195	11-2-66	1985	Orlando, Fla.
Mordecai, Mike	.235	109	226	29	53	10	2	5	25	20	31	2	5	R	R	5-11	175	12-13-67	1989	Pinson, Ala.
Mouton, James	.262	95	122	18	32	5	1	2	13	18	31	6	2	R	R	5-9	175	12-29-68	1991	Missouri City, Texas
Seguignol, Fernando	.257	35	105	14	27	9	0	5	10	5	33	0	0	S	R	6-5	179	1-19-75	1993	Panama City, Panama
Stowers, Chris	.000	4	2	0	0	0	0	0	0	0	0	0	0	L	L	6-3	195	8-18-74	1996	Marietta, Ga.
Vidro, Jose	.304	140	494	67	150	45	2	12	59	29	51	0	4	S	R	5-11	175	8-27-74	1992	Sabana Grande, P.R.
White, Rondell	.312	138	539	83	168	26	6	22	64	32	85	10	6	R	R	6-1	193	2-23-72	1990	Gray, Ga.
Widger, Chris	.264	124	383	42	101	24	1	14	56	28	86	1	4	R	R	6-3	195	5-21-71	1992	Pennsville, N.J.

PITCHING	W	L	ERA	G	GS	CG	SV	IP	H	R	ER	BB	SO	B	T	HT	WT	DOB	1st Yr	Resides
Armas, Tony	0	1	1.50	1	1	0	0	6	8	4	1	2	2	R	R	6-4	175	4-29-78	1994	Puerto Piritu, Venez.
Ayala, Bobby	1	6	3.68	53	0	0	0	66	60	36	27	34	64	R	R	6-3	210	7-8-69	1988	Avondale, Ariz.
Batista, Miguel	8	7	4.88	39	17	2	1	135	146	88	73	58	95	R	R	6-0	160	2-19-71	1988	San Pedro de Macoris, D.R.
Bennett, Shayne	0	1	14.29	5	1	0	0	11	24	18	18	3	4	R	R	6-5	200	4-10-72	1993	Worongary, Australia
DeHart, Rick	0	0	21.60	3	0	0	0	2	6	4	4	3	1	R	L	6-1	180	3-21-70	1992	Topeka, Kan.
Hermanson, Dustin	9	14	4.20	34	34	0	0	216	225	110	101	69	145	R	R	6-3	195	12-21-72	1994	Springfield, Ohio
Johnson, Mike	0	0	8.64	3	1	0	0	8	12	8	8	7	6	L	R	6-2	175	10-3-75	1993	Edmonton, Alberta
Kline, Steve	7	4	3.75	82	0	0	0	70	56	32	29	33	69	S	L	6-2	200	8-22-72	1993	Winfield, Pa.
Lilly, Ted	0	1	7.61	9	3	0	0	24	30	20	20	9	28	L	L	6-1	177	1-4-76	1996	Fresno, Calif.
Maddux, Mike	0	0	9.00	4	0	0	0	5	9	5	5	3	4	L	R	6-2	188	8-27-61	1982	Las Vegas, Nev.
Mota, Guillermo	2	4	2.93	51	0	0	0	55	54	24	18	25	27	R	R	6-5	185	7-25-73	1991	San Pedro de Macoris, D.R.
Pavano, Carl	6	8	5.63	19	18	1	0	104	117	66	65	35	70	R	R	6-5	230	1-8-76	1994	Southington, Conn.
Powell, Jeremy	4	8	4.73	17	17	0	0	97	113	60	51	44	44	R	R	6-5	230	6-18-76	1994	Sacramento, Calif.
Rojas, Mel	0	0	16.88	3	0	0	0	3	5	5	5	2	4	R	R	5-11	212	12-10-66	1986	Santo Domingo, D.R.
2-team (5 L.A.)	0	0	14.09	8	0	0	0	8	10	12	12	5	4							
Smart, J.D.	0	1	5.02	29	0	0	0	52	56	30	29	17	21	R	R	6-2	185	11-12-73	1995	Austin, Texas
Smith, Dan	4	9	6.02	20	17	0	0	90	104	64	60	39	72	R	R	6-3	210	9-15-75	1993	Girard, Kan.
Strickland, Scott	0	1	4.50	17	0	0	0	18	15	10	9	11	23	R	R	5-11	180	4-26-76	1997	Spring, Texas
Telford, Anthony	5	4	3.94	79	0	0	2	96	112	52	42	38	69	R	R	6-0	175	3-6-66	1987	Pinellas Park, Fla.
Thurman, Mike	7	11	4.05	29	27	0	0	147	140	84	66	52	85	R	R	6-5	190	7-22-73	1994	Philomath, Ore.
Urbina, Ugueth	6	6	3.69	71	0	0	41	76	59	35	31	36	100	R	R	6-2	170	2-15-74	1991	Caracas, Venez.
Vazquez, Javier	9	8	5.00	26	26	3	0	155	154	98	86	52	113	R	R	6-2	175	6-25-76	1994	Ponce, P.R.

FIELDING

Catcher	PCT	G	PO	A	E	DP	PB
Barrett	.986	59	329	25	5	2	7
Cox	.963	14	48	4	2	1	0
Machado	1.000	17	33	3	0	0	1
Widger	.992	117	662	54	6	6	8

First Base	PCT	G	PO	A	E	DP
Andrews	.985	18	122	7	2	12
Fullmer	.991	94	700	41	7	48
McGuire	.997	58	267	37	1	19
Merced	.917	7	21	1	2	2
Mordecai	1.000	1	2	0	0	0
Seguignol	.989	23	172	11	2	20
Vidro	.970	14	59	5	2	7

Second Base	PCT	G	PO	A	E	DP
Blum	1.000	2	0	2	0	0
Coquillette	1.000	6	10	14	0	4
W. Guerrero	.931	54	65	98	12	17
Mordecai	.962	38	17	33	2	11
Vidro	.982	121	208	291	9	61

Third Base	PCT	G	PO	A	E	DP
Andrews	.932	82	37	127	12	9
Barrett	.943	66	45	104	9	4

	PCT	G	PO	A	E	DP
Coquillette	.944	11	3	14	1	1
Fernandez	.889	6	7	9	2	0
Mordecai	.984	32	15	47	1	4
Vidro	1.000	2	1	0	0	0

Shortstop	PCT	G	PO	A	E	DP
Barrett	1.000	2	0	1	0	0
Blum	.929	42	47	83	10	11
Cabrera	.979	102	186	289	10	61
Mordecai	.966	38	38	75	4	20

Outfield	PCT	G	PO	A	E	DP
Bergeron	.967	13	27	2	1	1
V. Guerrero	.948	160	332	15	19	3
W. Guerrero	1.000	22	21	0	0	0
Jones	1.000	17	47	2	0	0
Martinez	.968	126	234	10	8	1
McGuire	.960	23	23	1	1	0
Merced	.963	44	74	3	3	0
Mouton	.981	56	50	2	1	1
Seguignol	1.000	8	11	0	0	0
Stowers	1.000	2	1	0	0	0
Vidro	1.000	4	2	0	0	0
White	.964	135	286	7	11	2

MORRIS FOSTOFF

Ugueth Urbina

Organization Statistics

Rondell White
Hit .312-22-64 for Montreal

Tony Armas
Allowed just 123 hits in 150 innings at Harrisburg

FARM SYSTEM

Director of Player Development: Don Reynolds

Class	Farm Team	League	W	L	Pct.	Finish*	Manager	First Yr
AAA	Ottawa (Ontario) Lynx	International	59	85	.410	13th (14)	Jeff Cox	1993
AA	Harrisburg (Pa.) Senators	Eastern	76	66	.535	+4th (12)	Rick Sweet/Doug Sisson	1991
A#	Jupiter (Fla.) Hammerheads	Florida State	73	65	.529	5th (14)	Luis Dorante	1998
A	Cape Fear (N.C.) Crocs	South Atlantic	75	65	.536	5th (14)	Frank Kremblas	1997
A	Vermont Expos	New York-Penn	33	43	.434	12th (14)	Tony Barbone	1994
Rookie	Jupiter (Fla.) Expos	Gulf Coast	29	31	.483	t-8th (14)	Billy Masse	1998

*Finish in overall standings (No. of teams in league)   #Advanced level   +Won league championship

OTTAWA — Class AAA

INTERNATIONAL LEAGUE

BATTING	AVG	G	AB	R	H	2B	3B	HR	RBI	BB	SO	SB	CS	B	T	HT	WT	DOB	1st Yr	Resides
Adolfo, Carlos	.189	16	53	5	10	2	1	2	9	3	11	0	0	R	R	5-11	160	4-20-76	1994	Santo Domingo, D.R.
Andrews, Shane	.250	2	8	1	2	0	0	1	4	0	2	0	0	R	R	6-1	205	8-28-71	1990	Carlsbad, N.M.
Barrett, Michael	.429	2	7	1	3	0	0	0	2	1	0	0	1	R	R	6-3	185	10-22-76	1995	West Palm Beach, Fla.
Bergeron, Peter	.314	58	194	36	61	12	3	3	20	23	40	14	8	L	R	6-2	185	11-9-77	1996	Greenfield, Mass.
Blum, Geoff	.265	77	268	43	71	14	1	10	37	37	39	6	1	S	R	6-3	193	4-26-73	1994	Chino, Calif.
Bradshaw, Terry	.197	56	127	13	25	5	3	0	10	16	31	4	2	L	R	6-0	195	2-3-69	1990	Zuni, Va.
Burkhart, Lance	.125	2	8	1	1	0	0	0	0	0	5	0	0	R	R	5-9	190	12-16-74	1997	Florissant, Mo.
Camilli, Jason	.265	35	102	12	27	6	0	0	8	11	19	4	1	R	R	6-0	178	10-18-75	1994	Phoenix, Ariz.
Carvajal, Jhonny	.231	106	355	28	82	20	4	0	34	21	67	7	3	R	R	5-10	165	7-24-74	1993	Barcelona, Venez.
Coquillette, Trace	.326	98	334	56	109	32	3	14	55	44	68	10	4	R	R	5-11	165	6-4-74	1993	Orangevale, Calif.
Cox, Darron	.000	3	9	0	0	0	0	0	0	1	2	0	0	R	R	6-1	205	11-21-67	1989	Norman, Okla.
Fernandez, Jose	.271	124	465	73	126	30	2	14	68	31	136	14	7	R	R	6-2	190	11-2-74	1993	Santiago, D.R.
Fullmer, Brad	.317	39	142	31	45	9	0	11	32	12	16	2	2	L	R	6-1	185	1-17-75	1994	Chatsworth, Calif.
Hosey, Dwayne	.181	33	94	16	17	3	1	1	10	15	26	6	4	S	R	5-10	170	3-11-67	1987	Altadena, Calif.
Hunter, Scott	.225	78	280	22	63	13	0	8	41	21	64	2	5	R	R	6-1	210	12-17-75	1994	Philadelphia, Pa.
2-team (50 Norfolk)	.226	128	460	42	104	17	0	16	64	29	106	8	11							
Jones, Terry	.262	88	332	49	87	17	2	0	23	24	66	30	10	R	R	5-10	160	2-15-71	1993	Pinson, Ala.
Machado, Robert	.227	21	75	6	17	5	0	0	3	0	13	0	1	R	R	6-1	205	6-3-73	1989	Caracas, Venez.
2-team (16 Charlotte)	.217	37	129	10	28	8	0	2	10	4	26	0	1							
Malave, Jaime	.250	3	8	2	2	0	0	0	0	1	4	0	0	R	R	6-0	196	3-22-75	1995	Fort Lauderdale, Fla.
McGuire, Ryan	.251	53	183	23	46	6	1	4	27	35	37	1	3	L	L	6-1	195	11-23-71	1993	Woodland Hills, Calif.
Morales, Francisco	.229	99	345	43	79	11	1	10	44	31	93	1	1	R	R	6-3	180	1-31-73	1991	San Pedro de Macoris, D.R.
Pachot, John	.214	17	56	7	12	4	0	0	6	6	9	0	0	R	R	6-2	168	11-11-74	1993	Ponce, P.R.
Post, Dave	.259	108	375	49	97	17	2	10	36	34	56	12	8	R	R	5-11	170	9-3-73	1992	Kingston, N.Y.
Seguignol, Fernando	.285	87	312	54	89	17	3	23	74	40	96	3	8	S	R	6-5	179	1-19-75	1993	Panama City, Panama
Snusz, Chris	.286	21	63	6	18	3	0	3	9	1	18	0	0	R	R	6-0	190	11-8-72	1995	Buffalo, N.Y.
Staton, T.J.	.190	14	42	5	8	3	1	0	5	10	11	2	0	L	L	6-3	210	2-17-75	1993	Elyria, Ohio
Stowers, Chris	.237	118	431	60	102	17	4	5	37	39	92	28	9	L	L	6-3	195	8-18-74	1996	Marietta, Ga.

PITCHING

PITCHING	W	L	ERA	G	GS	CG	SV	IP	H	R	ER	BB	SO	B	T	HT	WT	DOB	1st Yr	Resides
Baker, Jason	1	0	8.53	11	0	0	0	13	18	12	12	14	9	R	R	6-4	195	11-21-74	1993	Midland, Texas
Batista, Miguel	0	1	2.25	3	3	0	0	8	3	2	2	4	7	R	R	6-0	160	2-19-71	1988	San Pedro de Macoris, D.R.
Bautista, Jose	0	1	5.72	16	0	0	4	28	33	19	18	5	24	R	R	6-2	207	7-25-64	1981	Cooper City, Fla.
Bennett, Shayne	3	9	5.04	38	8	0	8	89	96	53	50	37	70	R	R	6-5	200	4-10-72	1993	Worongary, Australia
Benz, Jake	2	3	5.93	18	0	0	1	30	42	27	20	20	34	L	L	5-9	162	2-27-72	1994	Pleasant Hill, Calif.
DeHart, Rick	2	4	4.78	15	2	0	0	26	33	19	14	11	22	R	L	6-1	180	3-21-70	1992	Topeka, Kan.
DeSilva, John	4	1	2.89	22	15	0	0	90	73	35	29	41	75	R	R	6-0	193	9-30-67	1989	Fort Bragg, Calif.
Dixon, Tim	0	0	6.75	2	0	0	0	1	3	1	1	0	1	L	L	6-2	215	2-26-72	1995	San Jose, Calif.
Duran, Roberto	1	1	5.25	5	2	0	0	12	10	8	7	13	10	L	L	6-0	205	3-6-73	1990	Moca, D.R.
Durocher, Jayson	1	3	1.51	17	0	0	4	36	17	12	6	20	22	R	R	6-3	195	8-18-74	1993	Scottsdale, Ariz.
Evans, Keith	2	13	4.80	24	18	2	0	122	143	79	65	22	74	R	R	6-5	200	11-2-75	1996	Woodland Hills, Calif.
Field, Nathan	0	0	3.00	2	0	0	0	3	4	1	1	4	4	R	R	6-2	185	12-11-75	1998	Littleton, Colo.
Forster, Scott	0	4	5.16	53	0	0	2	52	49	32	30	47	32	R	L	6-1	194	10-27-71	1994	Flourtown, Pa.
Johnson, Mike	6	12	5.38	28	27	0	0	147	174	105	88	63	120	L	R	6-2	175	10-3-75	1993	Edmonton, Alberta
Lilly, Ted	8	5	3.84	16	16	0	0	89	81	40	38	23	78	L	L	6-1		1-4-76	1996	Fresno, Calif.
Marquez, Robert	1	1	4.88	18	0	0	1	28	33	19	15	14	16	R	R	6-0	180	4-21-73	1995	Houston, Texas
Mitchell, Scott	4	4	5.63	18	9	0	0	62	78	43	39	25	28	R	R	5-11	170	3-19-73	1995	Citrus Heights, Calif.
Moraga, David	1	2	6.19	4	3	0	0	16	24	14	11	5	10	L	L	6-0	184	7-8-75	1994	Suisun City, Calif.
Mota, Guillermo	2	0	1.89	14	0	0	5	19	16	6	4	5	17	R	R	6-5	185	7-25-73	1991	San Pedro de Macoris, D.R.
Parker, Christian	0	1	7.59	7	0	0	0	11	10	9	9	7	5	R	R	6-1	200	7-3-75	1996	Albuquerque, N.M.
Pavano, Carl	0	1	9.00	2	2	0	0	5	7	5	5	0	3	R	R	6-5	230	1-8-76	1994	Southington, Conn.
Powell, Jeremy	3	5	2.97	16	16	0	0	91	85	37	30	37	72	R	R	6-5	230	6-18-76	1994	Sacramento, Calif.
Rojas, Mel	0	0	5.14	12	0	0	2	21	25	13	12	12	16	R	R	5-11	212	12-10-66	1986	Santo Domingo, D.R.
Salyers, Jeremy	0	0	1.50	1	1	0	0	6	6	2	1	2	2	R	R	6-3	205	1-31-76	1996	Pound, Va.
Small, Mark	4	5	5.54	42	0	0	2	67	85	50	41	32	43	R	R	6-3	205	11-12-67	1989	Seattle, Wash.
Smart, J.D.	0	0	2.61	6	4	0	0	21	22	7	6	5	8	R	R	6-2	185	11-12-73	1995	Austin, Texas
Smith, Dan	5	4	3.68	11	11	0	0	71	61	31	29	27	59	R	R	6-3	210	9-15-75	1993	Girard, Kan.
Stevenson, Rod	2	1	3.93	17	0	0	2	18	15	9	8	7	12	R	R	6-2	210	3-21-74	1996	Columbus, Ga.
Strickland, Scott	3	0	1.63	19	0	0	5	28	23	5	5	11	34	R	R	5-11	180	4-26-76	1997	Spring, Texas
Vazquez, Javier	4	2	4.85	7	7	0	0	43	45	24	23	16	46	R	R	6-2	175	6-25-76	1994	Ponce, P.R.

FIELDING

Catcher	PCT	G	PO	A	E	DP	PB
Cox	1.000	3	17	2	0	0	
Machado	.981	20	141	12	3	3	2
Morales	.990	97	661	64	7	9	16
Pachot	.982	16	100	11	2	2	3
Snusz	.989	13	84	7	1	0	2

	PCT	G	PO	A	E	DP
Camilli	.969	11	9	22	1	3
Carvajal	.969	18	28	35	2	5
Coquillette	.966	85	150	196	12	46
Fernandez	1.000	1	3	2	0	1
Post	.977	34	47	82	3	21

	PCT	G	PO	A	E	DP
Carvajal	.973	72	123	206	9	53
Post	.985	20	19	47	1	10

First Base	PCT	G	PO	A	E	DP
Blum	1.000	6	59	3	0	6
Camilli	.988	9	76	9	1	5
Coquillette	1.000	1	6	0	0	0
Fernandez	1.000	10	88	4	0	6
Fullmer	.990	25	187	13	2	20
McGuire	.996	34	247	14	1	25
Morales	1.000	1	2	0	0	1
Post	1.000	10	92	7	0	13
Seguignol	.977	50	388	39	10	41
Snusz	1.000	6	34	0	0	2

Second Base	PCT	G	PO	A	E	DP
Blum	.971	6	14	20	1	6

Third Base	PCT	G	PO	A	E	DP
Andrews	1.000	2	1	2	0	0
Barrett	.800	2	0	4	1	0
Blum	.900	3	3	6	1	2
Camilli	.929	4	4	9	1	1
Carvajal	1.000	2	3	2	0	1
Coquillette	.826	9	3	16	4	2
Fernandez	.911	113	94	223	31	20
Pachot	.800	2	2	2	1	0
Post	.909	16	11	29	4	0

Shortstop	PCT	G	PO	A	E	DP
Blum	.958	59	78	150	10	30
Camilli	.000	1	0	0	0	0

Outfield	PCT	G	PO	A	E	DP
Adolfo	.952	16	39	1	2	1
Bergeron	.973	39	64	8	2	0
Bradshaw	1.000	30	50	0	0	0
Burkhart	1.000	1	1	0	0	0
Camilli	.000	4	0	0	0	0
Carvajal	1.000	5	3	0	0	0
Hosey	.980	26	47	1	1	0
Hunter	.968	78	148	3	5	1
Jones	.984	80	172	9	3	2
McGuire	1.000	17	28	1	0	0
Post	.956	23	40	3	2	1
Seguignol	1.000	6	9	1	0	0
Staton	1.000	11	20	0	0	0
Stowers	.993	114	284	11	2	2

HARRISBURG

Class AA

EASTERN LEAGUE

BATTING	AVG	G	AB	R	H	2B	3B	HR	RBI	BB	SO	SB	CS	B	T	HT	WT	DOB	1st Yr	Resides
Adolfo, Carlos	.271	76	221	37	60	16	0	10	41	25	51	3	2	R	R	6-2	160	4-20-76	1994	Santo Domingo, D.R.
Bergeron, Peter	.327	42	162	29	53	14	2	4	18	24	29	9	7	L	R	6-2	185	11-9-77	1996	Greenfield, Mass.
Bradley, Milton	.329	87	346	62	114	22	5	12	50	33	61	14	11	S	R	6-0	170	4-15-78	1996	Long Beach, Calif.
Bravo, Danny	.143	12	28	0	4	1	0	0	2	1	6	0	0	S	R	5-11	175	5-27-77	1996	Maracaibo, Venez.
Camilli, Jason	.214	63	154	26	33	7	0	4	16	23	31	0	2	R	R	6-0	178	10-18-75	1994	Phoenix, Ariz.
Carroll, Jamey	.292	141	561	78	164	34	5	5	63	48	58	21	10	R	R	5-11	165	2-18-75	1996	Newburgh, Ind.
Cossins, Tim	.172	41	93	8	16	2	0	4	14	4	21	0	0	R	R	6-1	192	3-31-70	1993	Windsor, Calif.
De la Rosa, Tomas	.261	135	467	70	122	22	3	6	43	42	64	28	15	R	R	5-10	155	1-28-78	1996	La Victoria, D.R.
James, Kenny	.255	29	102	8	26	4	2	0	6	1	19	7	3	S	R	6-0	198	10-9-76	1995	Sebring, Fla.
Johannes, Todd	.250	1	4	1	0	0	0	0	0	2	0	0	0	R	R	6-3	185	10-25-76	1993	Sunnyvale, Calif.
Malave, Jaime	.222	12	18	4	4	0	0	3	4	2	4	0	0	R	R	6-0	196	3-22-75	1995	Fort Lauderdale, Fla.
Nunnari, Talmadge	.331	63	239	45	79	17	1	6	29	39	46	7	2	L	L	6-1	205	4-9-75	1997	Pensacola, Fla.
Post, Dave	.381	5	21	5	8	1	0	1	3	1	2	0	0	R	R	5-11	170	9-3-73	1992	Kingston, N.Y.
Preston, Brian	.067	6	15	1	1	0	0	0	2	1	4	0	0	R	R	5-10	190	12-11-76	1999	Augusta, Kan.
Schneider, Brian	.264	121	421	48	111	19	1	17	66	32	56	2	2	L	R	6-1	180	11-26-76	1995	Cherryville, Pa.
Snusz, Chris	.308	5	13	4	4	1	0	0	3	1	3	0	0	R	R	6-0	190	11-8-72	1995	Buffalo, N.Y.
Tracy, Andy	.274	134	493	96	135	26	2	37	128	70	139	6	1	L	R	6-3	220	12-11-73	1996	Bowling Green, Ohio
Tucker, Jon	.257	112	362	53	93	21	2	13	55	50	85	4	4	L	L	6-4	200	12-17-76	1995	Northridge, Calif.
Ware, Jeremy	.262	111	381	57	100	23	2	9	56	41	79	12	5	R	R	6-1	190	10-23-75	1995	Guelph, Ontario
Wilkerson, Brad	.235	138	422	66	99	21	3	8	49	88	100	3	5	L	L	6-0	190	6-1-77	1999	Owensboro, Ky.
Zech, Scott	.278	22	72	8	20	4	1	1	10	4	13	3	2	R	R	5-11	175	6-6-74	1997	Boca Raton, Fla.

PITCHING	W	L	ERA	G	GS	CG	SV	IP	H	R	ER	BB	SO	B	T	HT	WT	DOB	1st Yr	Resides
Agamennone, Brandon	5	2	3.10	22	4	0	0	52	44	19	18	14	41	R	R	6-2	190	11-6-75	1998	Crofton, Md.
Armas, Tony	9	7	2.89	24	24	2	0	150	123	62	48	55	106	R	R	6-4	175	4-29-78	1994	Puerto Piritu, Venez.
Baker, Jason	1	3	6.03	23	1	0	2	31	29	22	21	28	24	R	R	6-4	195	11-21-74	1993	Midland, Texas
Blank, Matt	6	3	3.92	15	14	0	0	85	94	41	37	26	42	L	L	6-2	200	4-5-76	1997	Arlington, Texas
Dixon, Tim	0	1	5.79	2	0	0	0	5	4	4	3	2	4	L	L	6-2	215	2-26-72	1995	San Jose, Calif.

PITCHING	W	L	ERA	G	GS	CG	SV	IP	H	R	ER	BB	SO	B	T	HT	WT	DOB	1st Yr	Resides
Duran, Roberto	2	2	8.31	19	1	0	1	22	15	20	20	31	20	L	L	6-0	205	3-6-73	1990	Moca, D.R.
Durocher, Jayson	1	3	3.48	29	1	0	4	52	44	29	20	25	36	R	R	6-3	195	8-18-74	1993	Scottsdale, Ariz.
Evans, Keith	0	2	3.67	5	5	0	0	27	29	14	11	5	21	R	R	6-5	200	11-2-75	1996	Woodland Hills, Calif.
Forster, Scott	0	0	0.00	2	0	0	0	5	3	0	0	0	1	R	L	6-1	194	10-27-71	1994	Flourtown, Pa.
Lara, Yovanny	0	0	7.90	9	0	0	0	14	19	12	12	8	10	R	R	6-4	180	9-20-75	1993	San Cristobal, D.R.
Marquez, Robert	2	2	4.56	18	0	0	1	26	31	15	13	8	22	R	R	6-0	180	4-21-73	1995	Houston, Texas
Mattes, Troy	5	8	5.36	20	19	0	0	97	114	67	58	38	58	R	R	6-7	185	8-26-75	1994	Sarasota, Fla.
Mitchell, Scott	2	0	4.26	3	3	1	0	19	16	9	9	3	10	R	R	5-11	170	3-19-73	1995	Citrus Heights, Calif.
Moraga, David	1	0	0.00	1	0	0	0	3	1	0	0	0	1	L	L	6-0	184	7-8-75	1994	Suisun City, Calif.
Niebla, Ruben	2	0	5.58	29	0	0	1	31	31	22	19	22	23	L	L	5-10	175	12-19-71	1995	Calexico, Calif.
Parker, Christian	8	5	3.65	36	6	0	3	89	86	39	36	37	45	R	R	6-1	200	7-3-75	1996	Albuquerque, N.M.
Phelps, Tommy	3	6	5.71	13	13	1	0	65	76	53	41	26	36	L	L	6-3	192	3-4-74	1993	Tampa, Fla.
Quezada, Edward	0	0	1.80	3	0	0	0	5	2	1	1	1	4	R	R	6-2	150	1-15-75	1993	Nizao, D.R.
Salyers, Jeremy	1	0	2.81	12	1	0	0	26	20	9	8	11	9	R	R	6-3	205	1-31-76	1996	Pound, Va.
Saylor, Ryan	6	1	3.62	28	3	0	7	60	50	28	24	24	55	L	R	5-10	175	5-20-75	1997	Greenville, Ohio
Stevenson, Rod	2	9	4.38	37	0	0	4	51	54	32	25	21	34	R	R	6-2	210	3-21-74	1996	Columbus, Ga.
Strickland, Scott	1	1	2.48	14	1	0	3	29	25	8	8	10	36	R	R	5-11	180	4-26-76	1997	Spring, Texas
Tucker, T.J.	8	5	4.10	19	19	1	0	116	110	55	53	38	85	R	R	6-3	245	10-20-78	1997	New Port Richey, Fla.
Westbrook, Jake	11	5	3.92	27	27	2	0	175	180	88	76	63	90	R	R	6-3	180	9-29-77	1996	Danielsville, Ga.

FIELDING

Catcher	PCT	G	PO	A	E	DP	PB
Cossins	.989	31	163	10	2	1	2
Johannes	1.000	1	4	0	0	0	0
Malave	1.000	7	18	2	0	0	1
Preston	1.000	6	26	1	0	0	1
Schneider	.992	112	613	91	6	7	6
Snusz	.917	3	16	6	2	1	0

First Base	PCT	G	PO	A	E	DP
Cossins	1.000	4	17	0	0	2
Nunnari	.992	40	334	21	3	35
Schneider	1.000	1	9	1	0	1
Snusz	1.000	1	5	1	0	0
Tracy	.994	18	138	18	1	8
J. Tucker	.992	91	744	48	6	79
Wilkerson	1.000	1	1	0	0	0

Second Base	PCT	G	PO	A	E	DP
Bravo	.941	4	6	10	1	0
Camilli	.987	20	33	41	1	6
Carroll	.982	120	220	379	11	86
Post	1.000	1	4	1	0	1
Zech	.944	7	19	15	2	3

Third Base	PCT	G	PO	A	E	DP
Bravo	.900	5	2	7	1	1
Camilli	.875	25	15	27	6	4
Tracy	.918	110	88	182	24	18
Zech	.943	12	7	26	2	0

Shortstop	PCT	G	PO	A	E	DP
Camilli	1.000	1	2	3	0	0
Carroll	.952	18	24	36	3	9
De la Rosa	.946	129	219	381	34	83

Outfield	PCT	G	PO	A	E	DP
Adolfo	.968	51	87	5	3	0
Bergeron	.986	40	72	1	1	1
Bradley	.971	77	166	3	5	3
Camilli	1.000	8	6	1	0	0
James	1.000	25	65	0	0	0
Nunnari	.974	22	38	0	1	0
Post	1.000	3	6	1	0	0
Tracy	1.000	1	1	0	0	0
J. Tucker	.917	6	11	0	1	0
Ware	.977	96	201	7	5	1
Wilkerson	.972	123	233	11	7	4
Zech	.000	1	0	0	0	0

JUPITER — Class A

FLORIDA STATE LEAGUE

BATTING	AVG	G	AB	R	H	2B	3B	HR	RBI	BB	SO	SB	CS	B	T	HT	WT	DOB	1st Yr	Resides
Albert, Rashad	.224	76	245	25	55	3	5	1	21	34	74	14	16	R	R	6-0	165	9-18-75	1994	Fernandina Beach, Fla.
Bravo, Danny	.300	7	20	5	6	3	0	1	3	1	5	0	0	S	R	5-11	175	5-27-77	1996	Maracaibo, Venez.
Burkhart, Lance	.214	45	131	19	28	8	0	5	21	13	35	1	1	R	R	5-9	190	12-16-74	1997	Florissant, Mo.
Calloway, Ron	.270	54	211	30	57	8	4	3	25	15	45	5	6	L	L	6-0	195	9-6-76	1997	Los Banos, Calif.
Carreno, Jose	.000	2	6	0	0	0	0	0	0	0	2	0	0	R	R	5-11	160	4-23-78	1996	El Tigre, Venez.
Diaz, Miguel	.000	2	4	0	0	0	0	0	0	0	2	0	0	R	R	5-11	160	9-29-77	1995	San Pedro de Macoris, D.R.
Dito, Robert	.000	1	2	0	0	0	0	0	0	0	0	0	0	R	R	6-1	195	7-31-77	1998	Queens Village, N.Y.
Hall, Noah	.236	119	398	57	94	10	3	8	49	49	60	32	11	R	R	5-11	180	6-9-77	1998	Aptos, Calif.
Hook, Kevin	.239	34	88	16	21	5	0	1	6	16	21	3	1	R	R	6-0	180	9-14-76	1998	Clovis, Calif.
James, Kenny	.237	99	372	68	88	9	1	2	32	31	57	37	7	S	R	6-0	198	10-9-76	1995	Sebring, Fla.
Lentz, Ryan	.207	114	362	39	75	16	1	6	35	50	84	1	3	L	R	6-2	210	5-29-77	1998	Woodinville, Wash.
Malave, Jaime	.400	3	10	2	4	2	0	0	2	2	1	0	0	R	R	6-0	196	3-22-75	1995	Fort Lauderdale, Fla.
Mateo, Henry	.260	118	447	69	116	27	7	4	58	44	112	32	16	S	R	5-11	170	10-14-76	1995	Santurce, P.R.
Moore, Ryan	.200	5	10	2	2	0	0	1	1	1	5	0	0	L	R	5-11	180	7-28-76	1999	Pomona, Calif.
Nunnari, Talmadge	.356	71	261	41	93	17	1	5	44	27	36	10	0	L	L	6-1	205	4-9-75	1997	Pensacola, Fla.
Pond, Simon	.256	127	434	47	111	25	1	10	77	48	83	4	8	L	R	6-1	175	10-27-76	1996	North Vancouver, B.C.
Quero, Pedro	.239	114	419	36	100	16	2	4	52	16	83	13	12	R	R	6-4	180	11-17-75	1995	Caracas, Venez.
Reding, Josh	.263	121	415	54	109	10	2	2	31	22	73	30	9	R	R	6-2	165	3-7-77	1997	Anaheim, Calif.
Sandusky, Scott	.254	108	354	31	90	9	1	1	22	20	72	4	5	R	R	6-0	180	3-6-76	1998	Arvada, Colo.
Tucker, Jon	.400	3	10	0	4	0	0	0	1	1	0	2	0	L	L	6-4	200	12-17-76	1995	Northridge, Calif.
Urquhart, Derick	.182	23	44	5	8	1	0	0	5	7	7	2	0	L	L	5-8	175	12-20-75	1998	Florence, S.C.
Ware, Jeremy	.320	7	25	5	8	2	0	2	11	2	5	3	0	R	R	6-1	190	10-23-75	1995	Guelph, Ontario
Zech, Scott	.281	68	203	28	57	13	0	1	18	29	30	15	5	R	R	5-11	175	6-6-74	1997	Boca Raton, Fla.

GAMES BY POSITION: C—Burkhart 35, Carreno 2, Lentz 1, Malave 2, Sandusky 107, Zech 1. **1B**—Carreno 1, Lentz 1, Nunnari 43, Pond 49, Quero 49, J. Tucker 2, Zech 1. **2B**—Bravo 2, Hook 9, Mateo 100, Moore 2, Pond 2, Zech 31. **3B**—James 1, Lentz 87, Moore 3, Pond 22, Zech 34. **SS**—Bravo 4, Hook 22, Reding 118, Zech 3. **OF**—Albert 75, Calloway 51, Hall 113, James 96, Nunnari 7, Quero 67, Urquhart 22, Ware 6, Zech 1.

PITCHING	W	L	ERA	G	GS	CG	SV	IP	H	R	ER	BB	SO	B	T	HT	WT	DOB	1st Yr	Resides
Agamennone, Brandon	4	2	3.15	19	9	0	0	66	51	31	23	15	41	R	R	6-2	190	11-6-75	1998	Crofton, Md.
Albin, Scott	0	1	4.50	2	0	0		1	2	4	1	1	3	R	R	6-0	180	9-27-75	1999	Redondo Beach, Calif.
Blank, Matt	9	5	2.40	14	14	3	0	90	64	26	24	19	66	L	L	6-2	200	4-5-76	1997	Arlington, Texas
Bridges, Donnie	4	8	4.09	18	18	1	0	99	116	53	45	36	63	R	R	6-4	195	12-10-78	1997	Purvis, Miss.
Chiavacci, Ron	4	4	2.23	8	8	0	0	48	36	15	12	17	32	R	R	6-3	203	9-5-77	1998	Scranton, Pa.
Duran, Roberto	0	2	4.13	7	6	0	0	24	13	15	11	29	24	L	L	6-0	205	3-6-73	1990	Moca, D.R.
Hebson, Bryan	7	6	2.00	17	16	0	0	103	86	33	23	16	67	R	R	6-6	210	3-12-76	1997	Phenix City, Ala.
Hughes, Mike	1	2	4.70	17	2	0	0	31	41	17	16	16	22	L	L	6-1	190	12-5-75	1997	East Meadow, N.Y.
Julio, Jorge	4	8	3.92	23	22	0	0	115	116	62	50	34	80	R	R	6-1	190	3-3-79	1996	Caracas, Venez.
Lara, Giovanny	3	1	2.76	33	0	0	0	65	59	24	20	18	42	R	R	6-4	180	9-20-75	1993	San Cristobal, D.R.
Marquez, Robert	3	0	0.00	13	0	0	3	16	5	2	0	6	15	R	R	6-0	180	4-21-73	1995	Houston, Texas
Marrero, Darwin	0	0	13.50	2	0	0	0	1	1	2	2	2	4	R	R	6-1	192	2-9-81	1997	Valencia, Venez.
Mattes, Troy	3	0	3.70	5	5	0	0	24	27	11	10	7	12	R	R	6-7	185	8-26-75	1994	Sarasota, Fla.
Matz, Brian	5	2	2.36	41	1	0	7	91	77	30	24	31	46	L	L	6-1	195	9-23-74	1996	Towson, Md.

PITCHING	W	L	ERA	G	GS	CG	SV	IP	H	R	ER	BB	SO	B	T	HT	WT	DOB	1st Yr	Resides
Moraga, David	8	6	3.66	23	23	2	0	138	124	63	56	44	91	L	L	6-0	184	7-8-75	1994	Suisun City, Calif.
Mori, Kazuma	0	1	7.36	3	0	0	0	4	3	4	3	2	2	R	R	6-0	185	12-12-75	1999	Hiroshima, Japan
Nicholson, John	0	4	21.60	4	4	0	0	8	9	21	20	19	3	S	R	6-4	205	12-6-77	1996	Houston, Texas
Quezada, Edward	2	6	4.38	34	1	0	0	64	64	34	31	17	25	R	R	6-2	150	1-15-75	1993	Nizao, D.R.
Saylor, Ryan	1	0	0.40	21	0	0	10	22	15	1	1	6	21	L	R	5-10	175	5-20-75	1997	Greenville, Ohio
Serrano, Jim	8	5	2.13	44	1	0	8	93	59	25	22	27	118	R	R	5-8	165	5-9-76	1998	Grand Junction, Colo.
Sheldon, Kyle	1	1	3.34	20	0	0	1	30	37	13	11	7	22	R	R	6-2	180	12-8-76	1998	Winter Haven, Fla.
Strickland, Scott	1	1	3.51	12	1	0	2	26	21	11	10	4	33	R	R	5-11	180	4-26-76	1997	Spring, Texas
Tucker, T.J.	5	1	1.23	7	7	0	0	44	24	7	6	16	35	R	R	6-3	245	8-20-78	1997	New Port Richey, Fla.
Van Gilder, Ryan	0	1	7.50	5	0	0	0	6	5	5	5	3	6	R	R	6-0	175	12-1-75	1997	Watertown, S.D.

CAPE FEAR — Class A

SOUTH ATLANTIC LEAGUE

BATTING	AVG	G	AB	R	H	2B	3B	HR	RBI	BB	SO	SB	CS	B	T	HT	WT	DOB	1st Yr	Resides
Ackerman, Scott	.268	67	224	30	60	14	0	6	31	16	58	5	2	R	R	6-2	195	4-23-79	1997	Oregon City, Ore.
Benjamin, Al	.322	128	488	66	157	38	2	10	77	27	110	14	17	R	R	6-1	200	9-9-77	1996	Houston, Texas
Burkhart, Lance	.167	2	6	2	1	1	0	0	0	2	4	0	0	R	R	5-9	190	12-16-74	1997	Florissant, Mo.
Carreno, Jose	.221	41	140	11	31	2	0	0	10	5	16	4	3	R	R	5-11	180	4-23-78	1996	El Tigre, Venez.
Castro, Martires	.290	9	31	1	9	2	1	0	3	0	7	1	0	R	R	6-0	170	12-6-76	1995	Caracas, Venez.
Diaz, Miguel	.000	1	2	0	0	0	0	0	0	1	2	0	0	R	R	5-11	185	9-4-80	1999	Cayey, P.R.
Hendricks, Jason	.263	82	270	42	71	13	2	11	38	26	84	8	4	R	R	6-1	200	5-20-76	1998	Phoenix, Ariz.
Hodges, Scott	.258	127	449	62	116	31	2	8	59	45	105	8	15	L	R	6-0	185	12-26-78	1997	Lexington, Ky.
Hook, Kevin	.063	5	16	1	1	0	0	0	0	2	4	0	0	R	R	6-0	180	9-14-76	1998	Clovis, Calif.
Machado, Albenis	.247	124	434	84	107	16	5	2	34	102	77	19	28	S	R	6-0	175	3-20-79	1996	Caracas, Venez.
McKinley, Josh	.262	48	168	18	44	12	0	0	17	16	38	9	6	S	R	6-2	190	9-14-79	1998	York, Pa.
Meadows, Randy	.227	50	141	18	32	5	1	0	9	7	35	2	5	R	R	6-0	185	8-15-76	1998	Nesbit, Miss.
Myers, Tootie	.223	137	515	61	115	19	8	11	52	35	147	30	16	R	R	5-11	165	9-8-78	1997	Petal, Miss.
Na, Jim	.217	67	221	24	48	10	4	1	18	17	45	7	5	L	R	6-0	205	10-5-75	1998	Randle, Wash.
Ortiz, Juan	.159	16	44	7	7	1	0	0	2	7	21	1	1	R	R	5-10	205	2-26-79	1998	Brooklyn, N.Y.
Piercy, Brad	.232	90	323	40	75	12	2	6	23	17	111	17	11	L	R	6-4	200	12-23-76	1998	Shelby, N.C.
Pittman, Thomas	.283	131	505	74	143	26	3	22	97	25	146	12	17	R	R	6-4	270	1-2-79	1997	Garyville, La.
Ruan, Wilken	.224	112	397	43	89	16	4	1	47	18	79	29	17	R	R	6-0	160	11-18-79	1996	Guaymate, D.R.
Urquhart, Derick	.308	54	169	31	52	4	4	3	18	26	19	6	8	L	L	5-8	175	12-20-75	1998	Florence, S.C.
Zech, Scott	.300	3	10	1	3	0	0	0	1	3	1	0	0	R	R	5-11	175	6-6-74	1997	Boca Raton, Fla.

GAMES BY POSITION: C—Ackerman 61, Burkhart 2, Carreno 41, Diaz 1, Piercy 40. 1B—Meadows 11, Na 14, Pittman 119. 2B—Machado 2, Meadows 4, Myers 136. 3B—Hodges 123, Meadows 21, Na 2, Zech 1. SS—Hook 2, Machado 108, McKinley 22, Meadows 11. OF—Benjamin 89, Castro 8, Hendricks 70, Hook 1, Na 36, Ortiz 16, Piercy 48, Ruan 112, Urquhart 52.

PITCHING	W	L	ERA	G	GS	CG	SV	IP	H	R	ER	BB	SO	B	T	HT	WT	DOB	1st Yr	Resides
Arthurs, Shane	7	8	4.16	25	21	2	0	136	144	77	63	52	87	R	R	6-5	185	8-30-79	1997	Oklahoma City, Okla.
Becks, Ryan	10	6	3.84	34	6	0	1	94	96	52	40	32	62	L	L	6-3	185	4-7-76	1997	San Jose, Calif.
Bridges, Donnie	6	1	2.28	8	8	1	0	47	37	12	12	17	44	R	R	6-4	195	12-10-78	1997	Purvis, Miss.
Castelli, Robert	2	2	3.71	29	0	0	3	44	39	30	18	16	46	R	R	6-1	190	3-14-77	1998	Ottawa, Ill.
Chiavacci, Ron	5	3	3.59	20	8	0	1	63	60	39	25	34	67	R	R	6-3	230	9-5-77	1998	Scranton, Pa.
Crumpton, Chuck	2	1	0.47	13	0	0	7	19	15	3	1	3	15	R	R	6-4	220	12-30-76	1999	Mesquite, Texas
Field, Nathan	4	8	5.40	42	0	0	2	65	75	49	39	22	55	R	R	6-2	185	12-11-75	1998	Littleton, Colo.
Hebson, Bryan	0	1	2.67	6	6	0	0	34	22	13	10	17	34	R	R	6-6	210	3-12-76	1997	Phenix City, Ala.
Kanovich, Jason	4	2	3.19	36	0	0	2	62	52	28	22	28	46	L	L	6-2	200	2-18-77	1998	Harrisburg, Pa.
Mangum, Mark	10	11	3.50	26	26	1	0	159	156	85	62	54	107	R	R	6-2	165	8-24-78	1997	Kingwood, Texas
Martinez, Obispo	0	0	10.13	7	0	0	0	8	12	10	9	3	4	R	R	6-0	176	4-2-78	1996	San Cristobal, D.R.
Rodriguez, Cristobal	5	8	4.17	26	25	0	0	121	100	68	56	65	128	R	R	6-2	190	1-27-79	1996	Chichiriviche, Venez.
Salyers, Jeremy	2	3	3.29	22	7	0	1	63	62	22	16	18	37	R	R	6-3	185	1-31-76	1996	Pound, Va.
Seale, Dustin	1	0	1.80	3	0	0	0	5	3	1	1	4	1	L	L	6-1	170	12-2-77	1997	Safford, Ariz.
Sheldon, Kyle	5	1	2.05	26	0	0	9	44	39	13	10	10	30	R	R	6-2	180	12-8-76	1998	Winter Haven, Fla.
Tetz, Kris	3	3	4.35	10	9	0	0	50	54	25	24	12	36	R	R	6-5	200	9-3-78	1997	Lodi, Calif.
Toriz, Steve	0	1	6.75	1	1	0	0	4	2	3	3	2	1	R	R	6-1	200	11-30-78	1998	Lynwood, Calif.
Van Gilder, Ryan	0	0	54.00	1	0	0	0	1	2	4	4	2	0	R	R	6-0	175	12-1-75	1997	Watertown, S.D.
Waldron, Brad	3	2	3.38	25	9	0	5	93	104	40	35	20	72	R	R	6-3	200	4-17-77	1998	Ottawa, Ill.
Wamback, Trevor	6	3	2.84	24	14	1	1	105	98	39	33	14	77	L	R	6-2	183	12-22-76	1998	Halifax, Nova Scotia

VERMONT — Short-Season Class A

NEW YORK-PENN LEAGUE

BATTING	AVG	G	AB	R	H	2B	3B	HR	RBI	BB	SO	SB	CS	B	T	HT	WT	DOB	1st Yr	Resides
Caracciolo, Anthony	.200	7	15	2	3	1	0	0	3	6	5	1	0	R	R	6-1	180	7-12-79	1997	Henderson, Nev.
Cepicky, Matt	.307	74	323	50	99	15	5	12	53	20	49	10	9	L	R	6-2	215	11-10-77	1999	Sun City Center, Fla.
Espinoza, Andres	.211	29	71	9	15	3	0	0	2	4	15	1	1	R	R	6-2	180	11-12-78	1996	Caracas, Venez.
Johannes, Todd	.298	24	84	5	25	2	0	0	11	10	15	1	0	R	R	6-3	185	10-25-76	1999	Sunnyvale, Calif.
Lugo, Felix	.206	46	170	19	35	6	3	5	25	12	67	3	2	S	R	6-2	173	8-1-80	1996	Catalina, D.R.
McKinley, Josh	.251	69	283	47	71	12	3	4	32	33	52	9	5	S	R	6-2	190	9-14-79	1998	York, Pa.
Meadows, Randy	.200	9	30	4	6	0	0	0	3	2	7	1	2	R	R	6-0	185	8-15-76	1998	Nesbit, Miss.
Melucci, Lou	.195	33	123	13	24	3	1	0	7	10	34	6	1	R	R	5-9	175	9-20-77	1999	Clarks Summit, Pa.
Moore, Ryan	.262	26	103	16	27	4	1	2	12	13	21	1	3	L	R	5-11	185	7-28-76	1999	Pomona, Calif.
Ortiz, Juan	.235	32	115	16	27	0	1	1	9	6	29	6	1	R	R	5-10	205	2-26-79	1998	Brooklyn, N.Y.
Pascucci, Valentino	.351	72	259	62	91	26	1	7	48	53	46	17	2	R	R	6-6	225	11-17-78	1999	Cerritos, Calif.
Preston, Brian	.214	28	103	14	22	8	0	2	16	13	25	2	0	R	R	6-0	190	12-11-76	1999	Augusta, Kan.
Rivera, Luis	.227	31	97	14	22	6	1	1	12	14	28	0	2	R	R	6-3	185	12-21-77	1996	Bayamon, P.R.
Thomas, Mark	.316	44	152	23	48	5	3	1	23	27	28	10	3	L	L	6-1	195	1-20-76	1999	Concord Township, Ohio
Valdez, Wilson	.246	36	130	19	32	7	0	1	10	7	21	4	3	R	R	5-11	150	5-20-80	1997	Nizao, D.R.
Van Pareren, Tim	.207	30	82	9	17	2	0	0	3	12	23	4	1	S	R	6-0	180	1-2-80	1997	Amsterdam, Netherlands
Watson, Matt	.380	70	284	55	108	13	3	7	47	30	27	17	7	L	R	5-11	190	9-5-78	1999	Lancaster, Pa.
Williams, Clyde	.234	63	256	23	60	14	2	2	37	16	85	1	4	L	L	6-2	180	7-7-79	1998	Sanford, Fla.

GAMES BY POSITION: C—Johannes 23, Preston 28, Rivera 29. 1B—Rivera 2, Thomas 31, Williams 47. 2B—Caracciolo 1, McKinley 16, Melucci 32, Moore 2, Valdez 6, Van Pareren 24. 3B—Caracciolo 2, Lugo 46, McKinley 3, Meadows 8, Moore 16, Van Pareren 4. SS—Caracciolo 4, McKinley 46, Valdez 30. OF—Cepicky 53, Espinoza 25, Ortiz 31, Pascucci 63, Watson 63, Williams 2.

PITCHING	W	L	ERA	G	GS	CG	SV	IP	H	R	ER	BB	SO	B	T	HT	WT	DOB	1st Yr	Resides
Albin, Scott	4	2	2.62	26	0	0	6	55	50	22	16	11	57	R	R	6-0	180	9-27-75	1999	Redondo Beach, Calif.
Andujar, Jesse	0	0	18.69	5	0	0	0	4	2	11	9	10	2	R	R	6-1	175	7-23-79	1996	San Pedro de Macoris, D.R.
Baldassano, J.R.	0	1	6.75	6	0	0	0	8	9	7	6	9	11	R	R	5-11	170	11-15-79	1998	Riverside, Calif.
Chisnall, Wes	2	5	8.64	9	9	0	0	42	57	57	40	20	26	R	R	6-4	180	7-18-80	1998	Alta Loma, Calif.
Collins, Pat	2	4	3.48	12	11	0	0	54	57	35	21	21	39	R	R	6-5	230	3-3-78	1999	Union, N.J.
Crumpton, Chuck	1	1	1.93	19	0	0	5	23	24	11	5	6	24	R	R	6-4	220	12-30-76	1999	Mesquite, Texas
Dorn, Grant	3	3	3.15	23	1	0	3	54	55	23	19	19	54	R	R	6-4	195	2-26-78	1999	New Alexandria, Pa.
Finnegan, Mike	1	1	5.74	14	0	0	0	27	38	18	17	18	17	R	R	6-6	235	6-15-77	1999	West St. Paul, Minn.
Fraser, Joe	0	1	24.75	4	0	0	0	4	9	14	11	7	2	R	R	6-1	195	10-23-77	1996	Anaheim, Calif.
Good, Eric	5	5	5.79	15	15	0	0	70	77	49	45	30	59	R	L	6-3	170	4-10-80	1998	Niles, Mich.
Harris, Silas	0	5	7.20	23	1	0	0	30	32	24	24	30	32	L	L	6-3	210	3-15-77	1999	Edmond, Okla.
Humrich, Chris	1	1	3.97	22	0	0	0	45	45	29	20	20	52	R	R	5-11	188	12-28-77	1999	Bethune, Calif.
Klepacki, Ed	5	4	4.73	14	14	1	0	78	92	54	41	18	40	R	R	6-5	180	4-26-78	1998	Midwest City, Okla.
Marrero, Darwin	3	3	5.28	14	14	0	0	77	86	53	45	27	74	R	R	6-1	192	2-9-81	1997	Valencia, Venez.
Roque, Darryl	2	2	4.63	12	7	0	0	45	44	22	12	12	37	S	R	6-4	210	4-20-77	1998	Nashville, Tenn.
Seale, Dustin	2	1	0.44	14	0	0	2	20	13	1	1	13	16	L	L	6-1	170	12-2-77	1997	Safford, Ariz.
2-team (3 St. Cath.)	2	2	0.76	17	0	0	2	24	15	2	2	15	20							
Toriz, Steve	2	2	4.58	21	4	0	3	39	34	25	20	31	31	R	R	6-1	200	11-30-76	1998	Lynwood, Calif.

JUPITER — Rookie

GULF COAST LEAGUE

BATTING	AVG	G	AB	R	H	2B	3B	HR	RBI	BB	SO	SB	CS	B	T	HT	WT	DOB	1st Yr	Resides
Ambrosini, Dom	.161	19	62	5	10	1	0	0	0	8	19	1	0	L	L	5-10	185	2-21-81	1999	Ronkonkoma, N.Y.
Boyer, Bret	.172	32	93	6	16	1	0	0	8	6	20	6	1	R	R	6-0	170	8-8-80	1999	Indian Rocks Beach, Fla.
Brown, Nick	.162	31	99	11	16	1	0	3	8	11	38	3	0	R	R	6-1	185	9-23-80	1999	Randleman, N.C.
Castro, Martires	.237	11	38	5	9	2	1	1	7	1	9	1	0	R	R	6-0	170	12-6-76	1995	Caracas, Venez.
Diaz, Miguel	.179	20	56	7	10	2	1	0	5	6	12	2	0	R	R	5-11	185	9-4-80	1999	Cayey, P.R.
Dito, Robert	.229	18	48	5	11	0	0	1	9	5	13	0	0	R	R	6-1	195	7-31-77	1998	Queens Village, N.Y.
Gonzalez, Felix	.209	44	115	11	24	4	1	0	12	14	13	5	3	R	R	5-11	150	9-18-79	1998	San Lorenzo, P.R.
Harris, Karl	.202	28	89	4	18	4	0	0	6	4	19	0	1	R	R	6-2	200	2-5-81	1999	Luddenham, Australia
Henley, Bob	.250	2	4	0	1	0	0	0	1	1	1	0	0	R	R	6-2	190	1-30-73	1993	Grand Bay, Ala.
Hernandez, Nicolas	.143	4	7	0	1	0	0	0	1	1	0	0	0	S	R	6-2	180	6-4-80	1997	Maracay, Venez.
Infante, Juan	.254	26	67	5	17	0	0	0	3	10	11	2	3	S	R	5-11	170	10-8-81	1998	Caracas, Venez.
Lane, Richard	.222	41	144	16	32	5	0	1	14	10	30	4	2	L	L	6-3	195	1-4-80	1999	Santana, Calif.
Lugo, Felix	.368	6	19	6	7	2	1	1	4	3	4	2	0	S	R	6-2	173	8-1-80	1996	Catalina, D.R.
Lutz, David	.318	44	154	21	49	8	1	0	15	14	14	4	1	L	R	6-3	195	9-25-81	1999	Spring Valley, Calif.
McMillan, Drew	.210	31	100	11	21	4	0	0	2	8	19	2	1	R	R	6-2	195	10-25-80	1999	Placentia, Calif.
Phillips, Brandon	.290	47	169	23	49	11	3	1	21	15	35	12	3	R	R	5-10	170	6-28-81	1999	Stone Mountain, Ga.
Rombley, Danny	.246	45	134	20	33	4	1	0	15	12	29	8	4	R	R	6-1	170	11-26-79	1999	Amersfoort, Netherlands
Rooi, Vince	.189	36	111	17	21	4	0	0	10	22	24	3	2	R	R	6-0	185	12-13-81	1999	Amsterdam, Netherlands
Rosado, Omar	.236	41	140	12	33	7	0	0	22	9	10	4	1	R	R	6-1	170	11-12-80	1999	Toa Baja, P.R.
Valdez, Darlin	.271	14	48	3	13	2	1	0	4	4	10	0	0	R	R	6-1	180	2-21-80	1997	Nizao, D.R.
Valdez, Wilson	.293	22	82	12	24	2	0	0	7	5	7	10	0	R	R	5-11	150	5-20-80	1997	Nizao, D.R.
Watson, Brandon	.303	33	119	12	36	2	0	0	10	9	14	11	0	L	L	6-0	170	9-30-81	1999	Inglewood, Calif.

GAMES BY POSITION: C—Diaz 17, Dito 17, Henley 1, McMillan 28, D. Valdez 6. 1B—Ambrosini 3, Gonzalez 1, Harris 24, Lugo 1, Lutz 18, Rosado 19. 2B—Boyer 29, Infante 10, Rosado 18, W. Valdez 9. 3B—Brown 17, Infante 5, Lugo 4, Lutz 18, Rooi 30. SS—Infante 10, Phillips 40, W. Valdez 13. OF—Ambrosini 14, Brown 8, Castro 10, Gonzalez 40, Hernandez 4, Lane 34, Lutz 12, Rombley 42, Watson 31.

PITCHING	W	L	ERA	G	GS	CG	SV	IP	H	R	ER	BB	SO	B	T	HT	WT	DOB	1st Yr	Resides
Baldassano, J.R.	1	2	9.15	12	0	0	4	20	27	22	20	13	20	R	R	5-11	170	11-15-79	1998	Riverside, Calif.
Barker, Billy	2	2	3.14	10	0	0	3	14	13	6	5	8	10	L	L	6-0	175	10-5-76	1999	Yakima, Wash.
Casadiego, Gerardo	1	1	2.79	9	4	0	0	19	19	10	6	8	8	R	R	6-1	168	12-19-80	1998	Barquisimeto, Venez.
Charron, Eric	0	2	5.86	9	8	0	0	43	44	32	28	19	25	R	R	5-11	170	4-3-79	1999	Montreal, Quebec
Chisnall, Wes	0	2	7.36	4	4	0	0	15	20	13	12	6	8	R	R	6-4	180	7-18-80	1998	Alta Loma, Calif.
Crowther, John	2	2	3.12	13	0	0	1	35	30	14	12	11	26	R	R	6-4	195	9-14-76	1999	Riverside, Calif.
Dubuc, Charles	1	2	2.70	16	5	0	2	47	39	21	14	27	34	L	L	6-1	185	8-19-80	1999	Iberville, Quebec
Finnegan, Mike	1	0	0.00	1	0	0	0	2	5	0	0	0	1	R	R	6-6	235	6-15-77	1999	West St. Paul, Minn.
Fraser, Joe	0	0	0.00	4	0	0	0	6	1	0	0	9	4	R	R	6-1	195	10-23-77	1996	Anaheim, Calif.
Garris, Antonio	3	2	4.02	15	1	0	1	40	32	19	18	19	33	L	R	6-0	180	3-23-78	1999	Wadesboro, N.C.
Girdley, Josh	0	2	3.32	12	11	0	0	43	41	19	16	16	49	L	L	6-3	185	8-29-80	1999	Jasper, Texas
Grantham, Ryan	2	2	3.42	8	5	0	0	26	24	10	10	18	30	R	R	6-4	190	6-1-80	1998	Hamilton, Ontario
Hughes, Mike	0	0	0.00	2	2	0	0	8	4	1	0	0	9	L	L	6-1	170	12-5-75	1997	East Meadow, N.Y.
Lockwood, Luke	1	2	4.57	11	7	0	0	41	46	21	21	13	32	L	L	6-2	165	7-21-81	1999	Victorville, Calif.
Merrill, Darren	2	0	3.09	6	0	0	0	12	13	4	4	2	5	R	R	6-0	175	7-6-76	1999	Hacienda Heights, Calif.
Morel, Ramon	0	1	27.00	2	0	0	0	2	7	8	6	4	1	R	R	6-2	200	8-15-74	1991	Villa Gonzalez, D.R.
Nicholson, John	0	0	0.00	2	0	0	0	3	0	0	0	2	4	S	R	6-4	205	12-6-77	1996	Houston, Texas
Rijo, Hector	1	3	3.42	15	0	0	3	26	25	11	10	12	16	L	L	6-1	160	4-26-81	1998	La Romana, D.R.
Roque, Darryl	1	0	0.00	1	0	0	0	1	1	0	0	0	6	S	R	6-4	210	4-20-77	1998	Nashville, Tenn.
Tetz, Kris	0	0	2.25	1	0	0	0	4	1	1	1	1	4	R	R	6-5	220	9-3-78	1997	Lodi, Calif.
Torres, Luis	5	2	2.85	12	9	1	0	60	55	28	19	28	36	R	R	6-5	180	3-12-81	1999	Caracas, Venez.
Urbina, Ulmer	3	2	6.39	14	0	0	2	25	22	19	18	24	20	R	R	6-1	180	4-20-80	1998	Miranda, Venez.
Wamback, Trevor	1	0	2.92	2	2	0	0	12	5	4	4	1	12	R	R	6-2	183	12-22-76	1998	Halifax, Nova Scotia

NEW YORK YANKEES

Third title in four years makes Yankees a true dynasty

BY GEORGE KING

What can a team possibly do for an encore after setting the American League record for wins in a season with 114 and annexing the franchise's 24th World Series championship with 125 victories overall in 1998?

Try winning the 25th World Series crown, going 11-1 in the postseason and recording a second consecutive World Series sweep.

When the 1999 World Series against the Braves opened, the winner was supposed to be the "Team of the Decade." When it ended, nobody argued with those calling the Yankees the "Team of the Century."

When the Yankees started spring training, they knew they couldn't live up to 1998 from a wins-and-losses standpoint.

"That was a once-in-a-lifetime year. It never happened before and it may never happen again," manager Joe Torre said in February.

Torre, of course, was right. The Yankees won their second straight AL East title, winning 98 games while overcoming several obstacles. Torre missed three weeks of spring training and the first six weeks of the season due to prostate cancer.

Roger Clemens wasn't David Wells, the pitcher he was traded for on the first day of spring training. Third baseman Scott Brosius' dream season of 1998 was replaced with a productive, if not spectacular, year, and he and outfielder Paul O'Neill dealt with ailing fathers.

All of that, however, didn't do a thing to the Yankees' postseason excellence. For the second straight October, they started their march toward the World Series by sweeping the Rangers in three straight

Derek Jeter   Nick Johnson

Players of the Year

MAJOR LEAGUE: Derek Jeter, ss

Jeter finished second in the AL with a .349 average and tied for second with 134 runs while hitting 24 homers.

MINOR LEAGUE: Nick Johnson, 1b

Johnson hit .345 and scored 114 runs at Norwich, while leading the minors with 123 walks and 37 hit-by-pitches.

in the Division Series.

The only blip on the postseason screen surfaced in Game Three of the American League Championship Series against the Red Sox, when Pedro Martinez and the Red Sox blasted Clemens at Fenway Park. From there, the Yankees won six straight, including four in a row against the Braves in the World Series.

Outside of shortstop Derek Jeter and closer Mariano Rivera, no Yankee had what could be called a career year. Jeter's .349 batting average left him second in the AL hitting race. He also led the majors with 219 hits. Rivera led all big leaguers with 45 saves and didn't allow a run from July 21 until the final out of the World Series.

The organization that was named Baseball America's Organization of the Year in 1998 continued to thrive on the minor league level as well.

Triple-A Columbus, Double-A Norwich and Class A Greensboro made it to the postseason, with Norwich coming within an out of winning the Eastern League championship.

Columbus lefty Ed Yarnall went 13-4 with a 3.47 ERA and should get a good shot at making the Yankees rotation in 2000. Clippers shortstop D'Angelo Jimenez received a September callup after hitting .327 with 15 homers and 88 RBIs.

Yet Norwich trotted out the jewels of the farm system in first baseman Nick Johnson and shortstop Alfonso Soriano. Johnson hit .345-14-87 while sporting an unlikely .525 on-base percentage. Soriano batted .305-15-68 and hit two homers in the inaugural Futures Game during the all-star break.

ORGANIZATION LEADERS

BATTING

*AVG	Nick Johnson, Norwich	.345
R	Nick Johnson, Norwich	114
H	D'Angelo Jimenez, Columbus	172
TB	Scott Seabol, Greensboro	283
2B	Scott Seabol, Greensboro	55
3B	Jackson Melian, Tampa	13
HR	Alonzo Powell, Columbus	24
RBI	Donny Leon, Norwich	100
BB	Nick Johnson, Norwich	123
SO	Andy Brown, Greensboro/Staten Island	146
SB	Donzell McDonald, Norwich	54

PITCHING

W	Jason Beverlin, Norwich	15
L	Jake Robbins, Norwich/Tampa	15
#ERA	Denny Lail, Norwich/Tampa	1.94
G	Joe Lisio, Norwich	59
CG	Jeff Juden, Columbus	4
SV	Jason Ellison, Tampa	35
IP	Jeff Juden, Columbus	176
BB	Jason Beverlin, Norwich	81
SO	Geraldo Padua, Greensboro	155

*Minimum 250 At-Bats #Minimum 75 Innings

New York
YANKEES

Manager: Joe Torre

1999 Record: 98-64, .605 (1st, AL East)

BATTING	AVG	G	AB	R	H	2B	3B	HR	RBI	BB	SO	SB	CS	B	T	HT	WT	DOB	1st Yr	Resides
Bellinger, Clay	.200	32	45	12	9	2	0	1	2	1	10	1	0	R	R	6-3	195	11-18-68	1989	Oneonta, N.Y.
Brosius, Scott	.247	133	473	64	117	26	1	17	71	39	74	9	3	R	R	6-1	202	8-15-66	1987	McMinnville, Ore.
Curtis, Chad	.262	96	195	37	51	6	0	5	24	43	35	8	4	R	R	5-10	185	11-6-68	1989	Middleville, Mich.
Davis, Chili	.269	146	476	59	128	25	1	19	78	73	100	4	1	S	R	6-3	240	1-17-60	1978	Scottsdale, Ariz.
Figga, Mike	.000	2	0	0	0	0	0	0	0	0	0	0	0	R	R	6-0	200	7-31-70	1990	Tampa, Fla.
Girardi, Joe	.239	65	209	23	50	16	1	2	27	10	26	3	1	R	R	5-11	200	10-14-64	1986	Tampa, Fla.
Jeter, Derek	.349	158	627	134	219	37	9	24	102	91	116	19	8	R	R	6-3	195	6-26-74	1992	Tampa, Fla.
Jimenez, D'Angelo	.400	7	20	3	8	2	0	0	4	3	4	0	0	S	R	6-0	160	12-21-77	1995	Santo Domingo, D.R.
Knoblauch, Chuck	.292	150	603	120	176	36	4	18	68	83	57	28	9	R	R	5-9	170	7-7-68	1989	Houston, Texas
Ledee, Ricky	.276	88	250	45	69	13	5	9	40	28	73	4	3	L	L	06-1	160	11-22-73	1990	Salinas, P.R.
Leyritz, Jim	.227	31	66	8	15	4	1	0	5	13	17	0	0	R	R	6-0	195	12-27-63	1986	Cooper City, Fla.
Manto, Jeff	.125	6	8	0	1	0	0	0	0	2	4	0	0	R	R	6-3	210	8-23-64	1985	Langhorne, Pa.
2-team (12 Cleve.)	.182	18	33	5	6	0	0	1	2	13	15	0	0							
Martinez, Tino	.263	159	589	95	155	27	2	28	105	69	86	3	4	L	R	6-2	210	12-7-67	1989	Tampa, Fla.
O'Neill, Paul	.285	153	597	70	170	39	4	19	110	66	89	11	9	L	L	6-4	215	2-25-63	1981	Cincinnati, Ohio
Posada, Jorge	.245	112	379	50	93	19	2	12	57	53	91	1	0	S	R	6-2	205	8-17-71	1991	Rio Piedras, P.R.
Sojo, Luis	.252	49	127	20	32	6	0	2	16	4	17	1	0	R	R	5-11	175	1-3-66	1987	Barquisimeto, Venez.
Soriano, Alfonso	.125	9	8	2	1	0	0	1	1	0	3	0	1	R	R	6-1	160	1-7-78	1999	Los Angeles, Calif.
Spencer, Shane	.234	71	205	25	48	8	0	8	20	18	51	0	4	R	R	5-11	210	2-20-72	1990	El Cajon, Calif.
Strawberry, Darryl	.327	24	49	10	16	5	0	3	6	17	16	2	0	L	L	6-6	215	3-12-62	1980	Rancho Mirage, Calif.
Tarasco, Tony	.161	14	31	5	5	2	0	0	3	3	5	1	0	L	R	6-0	205	12-9-70	1988	Santa Monica, Calif.
Williams, Bernie	.342	158	591	116	202	28	6	25	115	100	95	9	10	S	R	6-2	205	9-13-68	1986	Armonk, N.Y.

PITCHING	W	L	ERA	G	GS	CG	SV	IP	H	R	ER	BB	SO	B	T	HT	WT	DOB	1st Yr	Resides
Buddie, Mike	0	0	4.50	2	0	0	0	2	3	1	1	0	1	R	R	6-3	210	12-12-70	1992	Advance, N.C.
Clemens, Roger	14	10	4.60	30	30	1	0	188	185	101	96	90	163	R	R	6-4	230	8-4-62	1983	Houston, Texas
Cone, David	12	9	3.44	31	31	1	0	193	164	84	74	90	177	L	R	6-1	190	1-2-63	1981	Greenwich, Conn.
Erdos, Todd	0	0	3.86	4	0	0	0	7	5	4	3	4	4	R	R	6-1	190	11-21-73	1992	Meadville, Pa.
Fossas, Tony	0	0	36.00	5	0	0	0	1	6	4	4	1	0	L	L	6-0	198	9-23-57	1979	Fort Lauderdale, Fla.
Grimsley, Jason	7	2	3.60	55	0	0	1	75	66	39	30	40	49	R	R	6-3	180	8-7-67	1985	Lafayette, La.
Hernandez, Orlando	17	9	4.12	33	33	2	0	214	187	108	98	87	157	R	R	6-2	210	10-11-69	1998	Miami, Fla.
Irabu, Hideki	11	7	4.84	32	27	2	0	169	180	98	91	46	133	R	R	6-4	240	5-5-69	1997	Chiba, Japan
Juden, Jeff	0	1	1.59	2	1	0	0	6	5	9	1	3	9	R	R	6-8	265	1-19-71	1989	Salem, Mass.
Mendoza, Ramiro	9	9	4.29	53	6	0	3	124	141	68	59	27	80	R	R	6-2	170	6-15-72	1992	Los Santos, Panama
Naulty, Dan	1	0	4.38	33	0	0	0	49	40	24	24	22	25	R	R	6-6	224	1-6-70	1992	Tustin, Calif.
Nelson, Jeff	2	1	4.15	39	0	0	1	30	27	14	14	22	35	R	R	6-8	235	11-17-66	1984	Issaquah, Wash.
Pettitte, Andy	14	11	4.70	31	31	0	0	192	216	105	100	89	121	L	L	6-5	225	6-15-72	1991	Deer Park, Texas
Rivera, Mariano	4	3	1.83	66	0	0	45	69	43	15	14	18	52	R	R	6-4	170	11-29-69	1990	La Chorrera, Panama
Stanton, Mike	2	2	4.33	73	1	0	0	62	71	30	30	18	59	L	L	6-1	215	6-2-67	1987	Houston, Texas
Tessmer, Jay	0	0	14.85	6	0	0	0	7	16	11	11	4	3	R	R	6-3	190	12-26-71	1995	Port St. Lucie, Fla.
Watson, Allen	4	0	2.10	21	0	0	0	34	30	8	8	10	30	L	L	6-3	195	11-18-70	1991	Middle Village, N.Y.
2-team (3 Seattle)	4	1	2.89	24	0	0	0	37	36	17	12	13	32							
Yarnall, Ed	1	0	3.71	5	2	0	0	17	17	8	7	10	13	L	L	6-3	234	12-4-75	1997	Coral Springs, Fla.

FIELDING

Catcher	PCT	G	PO	A	E	DP	PB
Figga	1.000	2	3	0	0	0	
Girardi	.984	65	452	34	8	5	1
Leyritz	.000	1	0	0	0	0	0
Posada	.993	109	705	46	5	7	17

First Base	PCT	G	PO	A	E	DP
Bellinger	1.000	8	7	1	0	1
Leyritz	.985	9	59	8	1	5
Manto	1.000	3	14	1	0	1
Martinez	.995	158	1300	106	7	110
Posada	1.000	1	4	1	0	1
Sojo	1.000	4	8	0	0	0

Second Base	PCT	G	PO	A	E	DP
Bellinger	.000	1	0	0	0	0
Jimenez	1.000	1	1	1	0	0
Knoblauch	.963	150	254	425	26	67
Sojo	.986	16	30	40	1	12

Third Base	PCT	G	PO	A	E	DP
Bellinger	1.000	16	12	16	0	1

	PCT	G	PO	A	E	DP
Brosius	.962	132	87	239	13	20
Jimenez	1.000	6	2	8	0	2
Leyritz	.800	1	2	2	1	0
Manto	.000	1	0	0	0	0
Sojo	.974	20	15	23	1	3

Shortstop	PCT	G	PO	A	E	DP
Bellinger	1.000	1	2	1	0	0
Jeter	.978	158	230	391	14	88
Sojo	1.000	6	12	9	0	2
Soriano	.500	1	0	1	1	1

Outfield	PCT	G	PO	A	E	DP
Bellinger	1.000	2	2	0	0	0
Curtis	.990	81	99	2	1	0
Ledee	.942	77	143	3	9	0
O'Neill	.974	151	292	10	8	3
Spencer	1.000	64	107	5	0	3
Tarasco	1.000	12	11	0	0	0
Williams	.987	155	380	9	5	3

DAVID SEELIG

Bernie Williams

FARM SYSTEM

Vice President, Player Development: Mark Newman

Class	Farm Team	League	W	L	Pct.	Finish*	Manager	First Yr
AAA	Columbus (Ohio) Clippers	International	83	58	.589	1st (14)	Trey Hillman	1979
AA	Norwich (Conn.) Navigators	Eastern	78	64	.549	3rd (12)	Lee Mazzilli	1995
A#	Tampa (Fla.) Yankees	Florida State	78	58	.574	2nd (14)	Tom Nieto	1994
A	Greensboro (N.C.) Bats	South Atlantic	77	64	.546	3rd (14)	Stan Hough	1990
A	Staten Island (N.Y.) Yankees	New York-Penn	39	35	.527	7th (14)	Joe Arnold	1999
Rookie	Tampa (Fla.) Yankees	Gulf Coast	32	28	.533	5th (14)	Ken Dominguez	1980

*Finish in overall standings (No. of teams in league)   #Advanced level

COLUMBUS — Class AAA

INTERNATIONAL LEAGUE

BATTING	AVG	G	AB	R	H	2B	3B	HR	RBI	BB	SO	SB	CS	B	T	HT	WT	DOB	1st Yr	Resides
Ashby, Chris	.267	70	206	46	55	13	1	9	32	21	39	6	3	R	R	6-3	196	12-15-74	1993	Boca Raton, Fla.
Bellinger, Clay	.234	40	141	19	33	10	1	2	14	13	32	6	0	R	R	6-3	195	11-18-68	1989	Oneonta, N.Y.
Bierek, Kurt	.280	135	532	84	149	42	4	23	95	48	99	5	3	L	R	6-4	220	9-13-72	1993	Hillsboro, Ore.
Carpenter, Bubba	.283	101	325	78	92	20	2	22	81	75	68	7	3	L	L	6-1	195	7-23-68	1991	Springdale, Ark.
Cedeno, Andujar	.293	62	215	27	63	14	3	6	38	11	31	1	1	R	R	6-1	168	8-21-69	1987	La Romana, D.R.
Coolbaugh, Mike	.276	114	391	65	108	31	2	15	66	38	112	5	7	R	R	6-1	185	6-5-72	1990	San Antonio, Texas
Glass, Chip	.277	53	159	32	44	7	3	2	30	22	32	5	4	L	L	5-11	180	6-24-71	1994	Golden, Colo.
Jimenez, D'Angelo	.327	126	526	97	172	32	5	15	88	59	75	26	14	S	R	6-0	160	12-21-77	1995	Santo Domingo, D.R.
Ledee, Ricky	.252	30	115	18	29	7	1	4	15	17	29	4	2	L	L	6-1	160	11-22-73	1990	Salinas, P.R.
Molina, Izzy	.246	97	338	44	83	16	1	4	51	18	47	4	2	R	R	5-11	224	6-3-71	1990	Miami, Fla.
Powell, Alonzo	.315	130	470	97	148	23	4	24	90	82	110	1	3	R	R	6-2	190	12-12-64	1983	Indianapolis, Ind.
Raabe, Brian	.327	130	493	93	161	35	5	11	77	48	19	5	7	R	R	5-9	176	11-5-67	1990	North Branch, Minn.
Soriano, Alfonso	.183	20	82	8	15	5	1	2	11	5	18	1	1	R	R	6-1	160	1-7-78	1999	Los Angeles, Calif.
Spencer, Shane	.360	14	50	17	18	2	0	2	10	9	8	0	0	R	R	5-11	210	2-20-72	1990	El Cajon, Calif.
Stankiewicz, Andy	.276	50	163	34	45	8	3	1	20	23	27	6	1	R	R	5-9	165	8-10-64	1986	Gilbert, Ariz.
Strawberry, Darryl	.288	21	73	12	21	5	1	4	15	11	13	1	2	L	L	6-6	215	3-12-62	1980	Rancho Mirage, Calif.
Tarasco, Tony	.295	95	346	72	102	23	0	19	61	49	39	9	5	L	R	6-0	205	12-9-70	1988	Santa Monica, Calif.
Waszgis, B.J.	.277	63	191	36	53	12	0	6	31	27	55	4	2	R	R	6-2	215	8-24-70	1991	Camilla, Ga.

PITCHING	W	L	ERA	G	GS	CG	SV	IP	H	R	ER	BB	SO	B	T	HT	WT	DOB	1st Yr	Resides
Bradley, Ryan	5	12	6.21	29	24	1	0	145	163	112	100	73	118	R	R	6-4	226	10-26-75	1997	Chino Hills, Calif.
Buddie, Mike	9	2	2.86	49	2	0	0	79	80	30	25	22	68	R	R	6-3	210	12-12-70	1992	Advance, N.C.
Carroll, Dave	0	0	9.00	1	0	0	0	1	1	2	1	0	1	R	L	6-3	205	7-23-72	1993	Fairfax, Va.
De los Santos, Luis	6	3	4.77	12	12	0	0	66	81	42	35	24	45	R	R	6-2	187	11-1-77	1995	San Pedro de Macoris, D.R.
Erdos, Todd	2	2	6.56	27	8	0	0	59	70	47	43	25	53	R	R	6-1	190	11-21-73	1992	Meadville, Pa.
Ford, Ben	6	3	4.73	53	0	0	3	70	69	42	37	39	40	R	R	6-7	200	8-15-75	1994	Cedar Rapids, Iowa
Fossas, Tony	1	0	4.05	26	0	0	0	20	17	10	9	6	15	L	L	6-0	188	9-23-57	1979	Fort Lauderdale, Fla.
Juden, Jeff	11	12	5.56	27	26	4	0	176	164	124	109	76	151	R	R	6-8	265	1-19-71	1989	Salem, Mass.
McCarthy, Greg	2	1	3.86	29	0	0	1	35	24	19	15	19	21	L	L	6-2	215	10-30-68	1987	Shelton, Conn.
Naulty, Dan	2	1	4.35	7	0	0	0	10	14	6	5	4	5	R	R	6-6	224	1-6-70	1992	Tustin, Calif.
Nichting, Chris	8	5	5.29	25	21	2	0	128	135	80	75	47	110	R	R	6-1	205	5-13-66	1988	Cincinnati, Ohio
Pavlas, Dave	4	2	4.04	38	2	0	1	62	69	32	28	9	49	S	R	6-2	205	8-12-62	1985	Shiner, Texas
Spence, Cam	0	1	5.14	1	1	0	0	7	8	4	4	2	5	R	R	6-3	195	10-11-74	1996	Lithonia, Ga.
Tessmer, Jay	3	3	3.34	51	0	0	28	57	52	22	21	12	42	R	R	6-3	190	12-26-71	1995	Port St. Lucie, Fla.
Watson, Allen	0	0	6.14	2	2	0	0	7	7	5	5	2	5	L	L	6-3	195	11-18-70	1991	Middle Village, N.Y.
Wengert, Don	0	1	7.63	6	2	0	0	15	25	13	13	5	5	R	R	6-3	205	11-6-69	1992	Des Moines, Iowa
Williams, Matt	0	2	3.86	13	1	0	0	21	15	9	9	11	22	S	L	6-0	175	4-12-71	1992	Virginia Beach, Va.
Wilson, Trevor	3	2	3.56	19	4	0	1	48	47	25	19	12	41	L	L	6-0	204	6-7-66	1985	Scottsdale, Ariz.
Yarnall, Ed	13	4	3.47	23	23	1	0	145	136	61	56	57	146	L	L	6-3	234	12-4-75	1997	Coral Springs, Fla.
Zancanaro, Dave	7	2	4.17	13	11	3	0	78	85	40	36	28	45	L	L	6-1	185	1-8-69	1990	Carmichael, Calif.

FIELDING

Catcher	PCT	G	PO	A	E	DP	PB
Molina	.985	95	618	52	10	2	10
Waszgis	.986	55	388	26	6	4	10

First Base	PCT	G	PO	A	E	DP
Bellinger	1.000	3	21	4	0	0
Bierek	.994	128	1082	73	7	106
Coolbaugh	.976	10	76	6	2	7
Waszgis	.882	5	29	1	4	6

Second Base	PCT	G	PO	A	E	DP
Bellinger	1.000	4	6	14	0	3
Cedeno	.667	5	1	3	2	1
Jimenez	1.000	4	9	11	0	0
Raabe	.981	94	165	249	8	67
Soriano	1.000	1	1	2	0	1

	PCT	G	PO	A	E	DP
Stankiewicz	.983	43	69	108	3	21
Third Base	PCT	G	PO	A	E	DP
Bellinger	.966	24	16	40	2	3
Cedeno	.936	37	16	57	5	5
Coolbaugh	.903	64	44	105	16	11
Jimenez	.952	6	5	15	1	1
Raabe	.979	22	8	38	1	5
Soriano	.929	5	3	10	1	0
Shortstop	PCT	G	PO	A	E	DP
Bellinger	1.000	11	17	31	0	7
Cedeno	.900	3	2	7	1	1
Jimenez	.955	116	188	346	25	73
Soriano	.959	14	15	32	2	6

	PCT	G	PO	A	E	DP
Stankiewicz	1.000	1	0	2	0	0
Outfield	PCT	G	PO	A	E	DP
Ashby	.981	65	99	7	2	1
Bellinger	1.000	5	8	0	0	0
Bierek	1.000	8	10	0	0	0
Carpenter	.981	101	197	7	4	2
Coolbaugh	.958	44	68	3	3	0
Glass	.988	52	79	4	1	0
Ledee	.953	30	59	2	3	0
Powell	.973	41	70	2	2	0
Spencer	.958	13	23	0	1	0
Strawberry	1.000	8	14	0	0	0
Tarasco	.990	94	204	1	2	0

NORWICH — Class AA

EASTERN LEAGUE

BATTING	AVG	G	AB	R	H	2B	3B	HR	RBI	BB	SO	SB	CS	B	T	HT	WT	DOB	1st Yr	Resides
Ashby, Chris	.250	29	108	11	27	5	1	3	16	11	20	3	4	R	R	6-3	196	12-15-74	1993	Boca Raton, Fla.
Brown, Richard	.261	104	383	46	100	18	8	6	54	34	81	5	8	L	L	6-1	196	4-28-77	1996	Plantation, Fla.
Brown, Vick	.251	132	482	86	121	19	1	5	48	83	101	50	14	R	R	6-1	170	11-14-72	1993	Cypress, Fla.

BATTING

BATTING	AVG	G	AB	R	H	2B	3B	HR	RBI	BB	SO	SB	CS	B	T	HT	WT	DOB	1st Yr	Resides
Dennis, Les	.250	53	176	27	44	10	0	0	12	27	50	0	3	R	R	6-0	175	6-3-73	1995	West Linn, Ore.
Emmons, Scott	.235	37	102	13	24	1	0	3	16	6	25	0	0	R	R	6-4	205	12-25-73	1995	Norco, Calif.
Glass, Chip	.251	65	239	36	60	9	3	6	34	31	49	5	5	L	L	5-11	180	6-24-71	1994	Golden, Colo.
Johnson, Nick	.345	132	420	114	145	33	5	14	87	123	88	8	6	L	L	6-3	195	9-19-78	1996	Sacramento, Calif.
Leon, Donny	.302	118	457	69	138	34	2	21	100	34	102	0	0	S	R	6-2	185	5-7-76	1995	Ponce, P.R.
McDonald, Donzell	.272	137	533	95	145	19	10	4	33	90	110	54	20	S	R	5-11	165	2-20-75	1995	Glendale, Colo.
McLamb, Brian	.159	48	126	11	20	5	0	2	14	4	46	1	1	S	R	6-3	185	12-13-72	1993	Jacksonville, Fla.
Mirizzi, Marc	.106	15	47	6	5	0	0	1	6	5	13	0	0	S	R	6-1	190	6-17-75	1997	Los Gatos, Calif.
Morris, Jeremy	.247	111	392	50	97	16	1	9	52	31	91	8	2	R	R	6-3	225	10-7-74	1997	Quincy, Fla.
Ottavinia, Paul	.288	59	191	26	55	11	3	7	31	14	40	5	3	L	L	6-1	190	4-22-73	1994	Drakestown, N.J.
Shumpert, Derek	.217	54	166	25	36	8	0	7	15	13	63	3	2	S	R	6-2	185	9-30-75	1993	St. Louis, Mo.
Smith, Rod	.600	1	5	1	3	0	0	0	1	0	1	2	0	S	R	6-0	185	9-2-75	1994	Lexington, Ky.
Soriano, Alfonso	.305	89	361	57	110	20	3	15	68	32	67	24	16	R	R	6-1	160	1-7-78	1999	Los Angeles, Calif.
Thames, Marcus	.225	51	182	25	41	6	2	4	26	22	40	0	1	R	R	6-2	185	3-6-77	1997	Louisville, Miss.
Valencia, Victor	.222	119	396	57	88	18	0	22	72	45	142	0	0	R	R	6-2	185	5-13-77	1994	Maracay, Venez.

PITCHING

PITCHING	W	L	ERA	G	GS	CG	SV	IP	H	R	ER	BB	SO	B	T	HT	WT	DOB	1st Yr	Resides
Beverlin, Jason	15	9	3.69	28	27	1	0	173	153	91	71	81	147	L	R	6-5	220	11-27-73	1994	Royal Oak, Mich.
Carroll, Dave	0	0	0.00	3	0	0	1	6	5	3	0	2	4	R	L	6-3	175	7-23-72	1993	Fairfax, Va.
De la Cruz, Francisco	6	5	4.59	29	19	1	0	133	141	89	68	73	91	R	R	6-2	175	7-9-73	1991	La Romana, D.R.
Dingman, Craig	8	6	1.57	55	0	0	9	74	56	16	13	12	90	R	R	6-4	195	3-12-74	1994	Wichita, Kan.
Einertson, Darrell	2	2	4.97	21	0	0	0	29	39	23	16	10	16	R	R	6-2	190	9-4-72	1995	Urbandale, Iowa
Flores, Randy	0	1	6.48	4	4	0	0	25	32	20	18	11	19	L	L	6-0	180	7-31-75	1997	Pico Rivera, Calif.
Johnson, Mark	9	9	3.68	16	15	0	0	88	88	51	36	39	52	R	R	6-3	205	5-2-75	1996	Leesburg, Fla.
Kaufman, Brad	3	2	4.12	40	5	0	1	83	76	45	38	38	81	R	R	6-2	210	4-26-72	1993	Traer, Iowa
Keisler, Randy	3	4	4.57	8	8	0	0	43	45	24	22	17	33	L	L	6-3	190	2-24-76	1998	Richards, Texas
Lail, Denny	5	0	1.74	6	6	0	0	41	24	12	8	11	29	R	R	6-1	172	9-10-74	1995	Taylorsville, N.C.
Lisio, Joe	2	6	4.13	59	0	0	33	57	58	27	26	27	49	R	R	6-2	205	8-5-73	1994	West Hempstead, N.Y.
Maeda, Kats	3	2	4.34	25	7	1	1	77	82	41	37	40	48	R	R	6-2	215	6-23-71	1996	Tokyo, Japan
Mairena, Oswaldo	4	3	2.67	49	0	0	2	57	48	24	17	27	47	L	L	5-11	165	7-30-75	1996	Chinandega, Nicaragua
Resz, Greg	3	2	4.36	20	5	0	0	43	40	25	21	20	45	L	R	6-5	215	12-25-71	1993	Springfield, Mo.
Robbins, Jake	3	12	5.43	20	19	2	0	111	118	80	67	60	63	R	R	6-5	190	5-23-76	1994	Charlotte, N.C.
Spence, Cam	5	5	5.79	19	16	0	0	92	118	75	59	32	62	R	R	6-3	195	10-11-74	1996	Lithonia, Ga.
Williams, Matt	1	1	2.40	22	0	0	0	30	22	9	8	18	44	S	L	6-0	175	4-12-71	1992	Virginia Beach, Va.
Zancanaro, Dave	6	1	2.28	15	11	1	0	79	64	25	20	32	61	L	L	6-1	185	1-8-69	1990	Carmichael, Calif.

FIELDING

Catcher	PCT	G	PO	A	E	DP	PB
Emmons	.984	32	164	22	3	2	3
Valencia	.983	115	822	80	16	4	14

First Base	PCT	G	PO	A	E	DP
Emmons	1.000	2	9	1	0	2
N. Johnson	.983	132	1070	85	20	103
Morris	.944	5	34	0	2	2
Ottavinia	.973	10	63	8	2	3

Second Base	PCT	G	PO	A	E	DP
V. Brown	.958	131	239	334	25	68
Dennis	1.000	3	0	7	0	1

Third Base	PCT	G	PO	A	E	DP
Dennis	.000	1	0	0	0	0
Emmons	.000	3	0	0	0	0
Leon	.882	115	87	175	35	12
McLamb	.840	18	12	30	8	3
Mirizzi	.920	11	4	19	2	3
Morris	.786	5	3	8	3	1

Shortstop	PCT	G	PO	A	E	DP
Dennis	.925	48	69	116	15	29
McLamb	1.000	9	19	14	0	5

	PCT	G	PO	A	E	DP
Mirizzi	.833	1	2	3	1	0
Soriano	.937	87	160	243	27	53

Outfield	PCT	G	PO	A	E	DP
Ashby	1.000	16	35	3	0	0
R. Brown	.955	94	166	4	8	1
Glass	.985	65	128	7	2	4
McDonald	.973	134	314	8	9	4
Morris	.882	20	26	4	4	0
Ottavinia	1.000	34	63	2	0	0
Shumpert	.983	30	55	2	1	0
Thames	.929	49	84	8	7	1

TAMPA — Class A

FLORIDA STATE LEAGUE

BATTING	AVG	G	AB	R	H	2B	3B	HR	RBI	BB	SO	SB	CS	B	T	HT	WT	DOB	1st Yr	Resides
Almonte, Erick	.257	61	230	36	59	8	2	5	25	18	49	3	1	R	R	6-2	180	2-1-78	1996	Santo Domingo, D.R.
August, Brian	.270	92	318	40	86	21	1	5	42	41	72	1	0	R	R	6-2	180	3-7-76	1997	Newark, Del.
Barr, Clint	.154	7	13	1	2	0	0	0	2	6	0	0	0	R	R	6-2	190	9-27-76	1999	Greeley, Colo.
Brosius, Scott	.333	1	3	0	1	0	0	0	0	0	0	0	0	R	R	6-1	202	8-15-66	1987	McMinnville, Ore.
Chambliss, Russ	.000	5	6	0	0	0	0	0	0	2	0	0	0	L	R	6-3	190	6-12-75	1997	Briarcliff Manor, N.Y.
Dennis, Les	.303	23	89	20	27	3	1	0	7	15	20	0	1	R	R	6-0	175	6-3-73	1995	West Linn, Ore.
Fuentes, Omar	.246	19	57	4	14	0	0	0	8	3	7	0	0	R	R	6-1	175	4-6-80	1996	Maracay, Venez.
Harrell, Ken	1.000	1	1	1	1	0	0	0	1	0	0	0	0	R	R	6-0	193	1-29-75	1997	Las Cruces, N.M.
Henson, Drew	.280	69	254	37	71	12	0	13	37	26	71	3	1	R	R	6-5	220	2-13-80	1998	Brighton, Mich.
Hernandez, Michel	.246	82	281	26	69	10	1	2	23	18	49	2	2	R	R	6-0	211	8-12-78	1998	Caracas, Venez.
Jones, Aaron	.278	132	454	50	126	25	11	4	57	76	92	6	5	L	L	6-4	210	9-7-75	1997	Newport, Mich.
Kofler, Eric	.358	15	53	7	19	6	2	0	14	5	10	1	0	L	L	6-1	170	2-11-76	1994	Palm Harbor, Fla.
Maxwell, Vernon	.085	23	47	4	4	0	0	1	3	14	0	0	R	R	6-3	205	10-22-76	1996	Midwest City, Okla.
Melian, Jackson	.283	128	467	65	132	17	13	6	61	49	98	11	8	R	R	6-2	190	1-7-80	1996	Barcelona, Venez.
Mirizzi, Marc	.239	90	330	40	79	16	3	6	30	37	87	1	0	S	R	6-1	190	6-17-75	1997	Los Gatos, Calif.
Montilla, Miguel	.121	12	33	2	4	0	0	0	8	10	0	0	S	R	6-1	175	12-18-73	1993	Miami, Fla.
Pinto, Rene	.229	22	70	9	16	5	2	1	6	3	19	0	0	R	R	6-0	185	7-17-77	1994	Palo Negro, Venez.
Rivera, Juan	.263	109	426	50	112	20	2	14	77	26	67	5	4	R	R	6-0	170	7-3-78	1996	Guarenas, Venez.
Rodriguez, John	.305	71	269	37	82	14	3	8	43	41	52	2	5	L	L	5-10	185	1-20-78	1997	New York, N.Y.
Smith, Rod	.264	126	507	92	134	33	8	6	45	69	102	38	16	S	R	6-0	185	9-2-75	1994	Lexington, Ky.
Soules, Ryan	.254	22	71	12	18	5	1	2	12	14	22	0	0	L	R	6-2	185	2-27-76	1997	Seattle, Wash.
Thames, Marcus	.244	69	266	47	65	12	4	11	38	33	58	3	0	R	R	6-2	205	3-6-77	1997	Louisville, Miss.
Torres, Jaime	.273	9	33	1	9	1	0	0	3	4	1	0	R	R	6-0	185	3-12-71	1992	Aragua, Venez.
Twombley, Dennis	.243	15	37	3	9	1	0	0	3	6	11	0	0	R	R	6-2	218	6-8-75	1996	San Diego, Calif.
Vento, Mike	.259	70	255	37	66	10	1	7	28	17	69	2	3	R	R	6-0	195	5-25-78	1998	Albuquerque, N.M.
Winrow, Gary	.429	3	7	1	3	0	0	0	0	0	0	0	L	L	6-2	185	7-12-80	1999	Fort Myers, Fla.

GAMES BY POSITION: C—Barr 6, Fuentes 18, Hernandez 81, Pinto 19, Torres 9, Twombley 14. **1B**—August 5, Jones 128, Mirizzi 2, Pinto 1, Soules 4, Vento 1. **2B**—Mirizzi 9, Montilla 3, Smith 126. **3B**—August 54, Brosius 1, Fuentes 1, Henson 51, Mirizzi 33. **SS**—Almonte 61, August 4, Dennis 23, Mirizzi 42, Montilla 8. **OF**—Chambliss 3, Kofler 1, Maxwell 16, Melian 126, Mirizzi 1, Montilla 1, Rivera 93, Rodriguez 69, Soules 1, Thames 48, Vento 57, Winrow 2.

Orlando Hernandez
Led Yankees with 17 wins

Alfonso Soriano
Hit .282-17-79 in first season in U.S.

PITCHING	W	L	ERA	G	GS	CG	SV	IP	H	R	ER	BB	SO	B	T	HT	WT	DOB	1st Yr	Resides
Blevins, Jeremy	0	0	0.00	1	0	0	0	2	4	3	0	1	0	R	R	6-3	190	10-5-77	1995	Bristol, Tenn.
Carroll, Dave	0	0	2.08	2	1	0	0	4	6	1	1	2	5	R	L	6-3	205	7-23-72	1993	Fairfax, Va.
Choate, Randy	2	2	4.50	47	0	0	1	50	51	25	25	24	62	L	L	6-3	180	9-5-75	1997	Tallahassee, Fla.
Cubillan, Darwin	7	4	2.51	55	0	0	3	75	57	27	21	32	76	R	R	6-2	170	11-15-74	1994	Bobure, Venez.
Davis, Keith	2	1	2.25	11	0	0	0	16	17	9	4	5	15	R	R	6-2	210	11-1-72	1994	Vacherie, La.
De la Cruz, Luis	2	0	2.08	5	0	0	0	9	9	2	2	5	1	R	R	6-3	190	3-15-81	1999	La Romana, D.R.
Einertson, Darrell	0	0	1.93	2	1	0	0	5	1	1	1	1	3	R	R	6-2	190	9-4-72	1995	Urbandale, Iowa
Ellison, Jason	0	2	2.15	49	0	0	35	54	42	15	13	19	56	R	R	6-4	180	7-24-75	1996	Buffalo, Texas
Flores, Randy	11	4	2.87	21	20	1	0	135	118	56	43	38	99	L	L	6-0	180	7-31-75	1997	Pico Rivera, Calif.
Grace, Bryan	2	0	2.04	9	0	0	0	18	17	7	4	18	10	R	R	6-1	190	4-1-76	1999	Baton Rouge, La.
Johnson, Mark	1	0	1.50	1	1	0	0	6	4	1	1	1	6	R	R	6-3	226	5-2-75	1996	Leesburg, Fla.
Keisler, Randy	10	3	3.30	15	15	1	0	90	67	43	33	40	77	L	L	6-3	190	2-24-76	1998	Richards, Texas
Lail, Denny	1	3	2.08	22	4	0	2	61	45	17	14	16	53	R	R	6-1	172	9-10-74	1995	Taylorsville, N.C.
Lewis, Craig	0	1	5.27	5	1	0	0	14	18	9	8	3	12	R	R	6-5	210	12-30-76	1997	Sydney, Australia
Nelson, Jeff	0	0	0.00	3	3	0	0	3	1	0	0	2	5	R	R	6-8	235	11-17-66	1984	Issaquah, Wash.
Noel, Todd	3	7	4.34	17	17	0	0	93	101	56	45	33	80	R	R	6-4	185	9-28-78	1996	Maurice, La.
Pettitte, Andy	1	0	0.00	1	1	0	0	5	4	0	0	2	8	L	L	6-5	225	6-15-72	1991	Deer Park, Texas
Rangel, Julio	3	3	2.93	12	9	0	1	55	48	23	18	17	36	R	R	6-3	160	9-28-75	1994	Panama City, Panama
Reith, Brian	9	9	4.70	26	23	0	0	140	174	87	73	35	101	R	R	6-5	190	2-28-78	1996	Fort Wayne, Ind.
Robbins, Jake	3	3	4.75	7	7	0	0	42	44	30	22	19	31	R	R	6-5	190	5-23-76	1994	Charlotte, N.C.
Rogers, Brian	8	10	3.83	25	23	1	0	134	141	62	57	43	129	R	R	6-6	200	2-13-77	1998	Carthage, N.C.
Salamon, John	0	0	0.00	2	0	0	0	2	3	2	0	2	2	R	R	6-1	220	3-30-72	1991	McKees Rocks, Pa.
Spence, Cam	3	0	1.93	7	7	1	0	47	32	13	10	11	36	R	R	6-3	195	10-11-74	1996	Lithonia, Ga.
Swiatkiewicz, Chris	0	0	0.00	2	0	0	0	2	1	0	0	1	1	R	R	6-1	190	5-24-76	1999	Spring Lake Park, Minn.
Tovar, Angel	1	1	10.80	3	0	0	0	2	5	2	2	1	1	R	R	6-4	195	4-25-78	1996	San Joaquin, Venez.
Wallace, Chris	3	4	5.06	30	0	0	0	37	46	24	21	15	21	R	R	6-2	210	4-5-76	1997	Marion, Ohio
Willis, Jason	2	0	2.03	3	3	0	0	13	9	3	3	7	10	R	R	6-4	210	1-3-79	1999	Philadelphia, Miss.
Wood, Stanton	4	1	3.75	50	0	0	0	82	89	43	34	23	66	R	R	6-2	185	12-5-76	1997	Torrance, Calif.

GREENSBORO | Class A

SOUTH ATLANTIC LEAGUE

BATTING	AVG	G	AB	R	H	2B	3B	HR	RBI	BB	SO	SB	CS	B	T	HT	WT	DOB	1st Yr	Resides
Brown, Andy	.176	29	108	14	19	5	1	5	15	10	49	0	1	L	L	6-6	190	4-14-80	1998	Richmond, Ind.
Brown, Billy	.294	134	520	102	153	28	6	19	62	71	144	21	10	R	R	6-0	195	3-9-76	1997	Plantation, Fla.
Castri, Andrea	.239	78	264	35	63	14	1	6	33	25	91	2	3	R	R	6-4	210	6-26-74	1998	Lecce, Italy
Darjean, John	.249	113	398	47	99	18	4	2	43	19	80	20	11	R	R	6-1	175	4-3-76	1997	Baton Rouge, La.
Elwood, Brad	.232	81	259	35	60	11	2	3	30	24	72	3	2	R	R	6-1	195	10-22-75	1998	Clear Spring, Md.
Greene, Alan	.247	115	437	74	108	16	5	16	68	26	118	7	2	S	R	6-1	190	4-10-77	1998	Renton, Wash.
Gregg, Neal	.208	11	24	1	5	0	0	0	2	0	7	0	0	L	R	6-4	220	2-9-76	1998	Hattiesburg, Miss.
Heine, Kyle	.254	19	59	5	15	5	0	0	7	5	14	0	1	R	R	6-1	190	1-25-76	1998	Arlington, Texas
Kidd, Scott	.274	115	463	74	127	31	4	15	84	25	103	4	2	R	R	5-10	180	1-15-74	1997	Cupertino, Calif.
Massucco, Scott	.000	3	4	0	0	0	0	0	0	0	2	0	0	R	R	6-1	190	8-20-79	1998	Tamarac, Fla.
Mirizzi, Marc	.265	9	34	5	9	0	1	1	3	5	9	0	0	S	R	6-1	190	6-17-75	1997	Los Gatos, Calif.
Olivares, Teuris	.279	110	451	78	126	18	6	11	52	26	78	14	7	R	R	6-0	164	12-15-78	1996	San Pedro de Macoris, D.R.
Pinto, Rene	.259	19	58	9	15	1	1	2	6	5	13	0	1	R	R	6-0	185	7-17-77	1994	Palo Negro, Venez.

BATTING

BATTING	AVG	G	AB	R	H	2B	3B	HR	RBI	BB	SO	SB	CS	B	T	HT	WT	DOB	1st Yr	Resides
Rodriguez, Junior	.188	69	191	28	36	3	3	5	25	37	75	1	2	R	R	6-0	175	9-9-77	1998	Brea, Calif.
Seabol, Scott	.315	138	543	86	171	55	6	15	89	45	91	6	5	R	R	6-4	200	5-17-75	1996	McKeesport, Pa.
Taylor, Seth	.300	4	10	1	3	1	0	0	1	1	0	1	0	R	R	6-1	185	8-23-77	1999	Cantonment, Fla.
Twombley, Dennis	.239	44	142	19	34	6	0	7	22	17	44	0	0	R	R	6-2	218	6-8-75	1996	San Diego, Calif.
Valdez, Angel	.272	35	125	11	34	4	0	1	14	2	32	2	3	R	R	6-2	178	5-22-78	1996	Santo Domingo, D.R.
Vento, Mike	.250	40	148	20	37	11	1	3	16	14	46	3	1	R	R	6-0	195	5-25-78	1998	Albuquerque, N.M.
Washington, Dion	.218	84	284	46	62	14	2	7	34	30	107	15	6	R	R	6-4	235	12-21-76	1997	Las Vegas, Nev.

GAMES BY POSITION: C—Elwood 76, Heine 19, Massucco 3, Pinto 15, Twombley 38. **1B**—Castri 55, Greene 22, Gregg 3, Washington 67. **2B**—Kidd 115, Mirizzi 3, Olivares 1, Rodriguez 20, Taylor 3. **3B**—Castri 1, Rodriguez 6, Seabol 138. **SS**—Kidd 1, Mirizzi 6, Olivares 109, Rodriguez 28, Taylor 1. **OF**—A. Brown 29, B. Brown 110, Darjean 107, Elwood 2, Greene 58, Rhodes 62, Rodriguez 6, Valdez 34, Vento 23, Washington 2.

PITCHING

PITCHING	W	L	ERA	G	GS	CG	SV	IP	H	R	ER	BB	SO	B	T	HT	WT	DOB	1st Yr	Resides
Aramboles, Ricardo	1	2	2.34	6	6	1	0	35	25	9	9	12	34	R	R	6-2	170	12-4-81	1996	Santo Domingo, D.R.
Blevins, Jeremy	10	5	4.05	19	19	0	0	107	105	56	48	30	81	R	R	6-3	190	10-5-77	1995	Bristol, Tenn.
Buchanan, Brian	4	3	3.00	48	0	0	1	51	41	21	17	40	58	L	L	6-3	190	4-23-77	1995	Oviedo, Fla.
Carpenter, Justin	3	2	4.06	40	0	0	0	58	57	39	26	29	45	R	R	6-4	215	1-18-77	1997	Prague, Okla.
Claussen, Brandon	0	1	10.50	1	1	1	0	6	8	7	7	2	5	L	L	6-2	175	5-1-79	1999	Roswell, N.M.
Day, Zach	0	1	2.25	2	2	0	0	8	14	11	2	1	4	R	R	6-4	185	6-15-78	1996	West Harrison, Ind.
De la Cruz, Andres	0	0	10.13	3	0	0	0	3	5	3	3	2	2	R	R	6-4	190	5-12-79	1996	Santo Domingo, D.R.
Dunn, Keith	9	9	3.13	35	18	1	5	135	134	61	47	16	109	R	R	6-3	195	4-18-78	1998	Tunica, Miss.
Eavenson, Clay	0	0	1.38	5	1	0	0	11	12	7	4	3	6	R	R	6-3	185	3-6-78	1997	Loganville, Ga.
Garcia, Rosman	2	3	6.38	9	9	0	0	42	60	33	30	20	31	R	R	6-2	165	1-3-79	1996	San Joaquin, Venez.
Jodie, Brett	9	6	3.81	25	20	2	1	120	125	59	51	18	106	R	R	6-4	208	3-25-77	1998	Lexington, S.C.
Keisler, Randy	1	1	2.38	4	4	0	0	23	12	6	6	10	42	L	L	6-3	190	2-24-76	1998	Richards, Texas
Knowles, Mike	1	1	8.23	11	2	0	0	27	45	27	25	10	27	R	R	6-5	215	7-15-79	1997	Daytona Beach, Fla.
Lewis, Craig	4	0	2.66	9	5	0	1	47	42	17	14	7	51	R	R	6-5	210	12-30-76	1997	Sydney, Australia
Oliver, Scott	1	1	3.71	7	7	1	0	44	42	22	18	8	37	R	R	6-2	195	6-30-77	1999	Mount Pleasant, S.C.
Padua, Geraldo	9	4	2.84	21	21	1	0	140	120	53	44	35	155	R	R	6-2	165	2-9-77	1995	Santo Domingo, D.R.
Ridenour, Ryan	0	2	9.58	17	1	0	0	31	33	35	33	31	32	L	L	6-6	215	4-6-77	1998	Southlake, Texas
Spurling, Chris	4	6	3.66	49	0	0	4	76	78	34	31	23	68	R	R	6-6	240	6-28-77	1998	Englewood, Ohio
Vogtli, Robb	3	2	5.17	25	0	0	1	38	39	25	22	18	38	R	R	6-0	190	4-11-75	1998	Olean, N.Y.
Weber, Brett	8	4	1.97	52	0	0	23	73	56	24	16	17	83	R	R	6-2	185	8-21-76	1998	Highland Park, Ill.
Whiteley, Shad	1	9	7.64	15	8	0	0	55	67	52	47	42	62	R	R	6-6	220	3-19-75	1998	Fort Worth, Texas
Wiggins, Scott	7	1	3.95	17	17	0	0	93	84	45	41	32	110	L	L	6-3	205	3-24-76	1997	Newport, Ky.

STATEN ISLAND — Short-Season Class A

NEW YORK-PENN LEAGUE

BATTING	AVG	G	AB	R	H	2B	3B	HR	RBI	BB	SO	SB	CS	B	T	HT	WT	DOB	1st Yr	Resides
Brazeal, Spencer	.100	8	10	3	1	0	0	0	1	1	4	0	0	R	R	6-0	190	3-9-77	1999	Oklahoma City, Okla.
Brown, Andy	.214	67	215	38	46	8	5	7	22	27	97	5	2	L	L	6-6	190	4-14-80	1998	Richmond, Ind.
Correa, Dominic	.208	56	144	17	30	8	0	4	22	14	36	1	2	R	R	5-11	185	6-12-77	1999	Sacramento, Calif.
DeGroote, Casey	.095	7	21	3	2	1	0	0	0	2	12	0	0	L	R	6-3	190	7-13-79	1998	Harte, Ind.
Fuentes, Omar	.279	50	129	15	36	7	1	3	21	19	18	0	1	R	R	6-1	175	4-6-80	1996	Maracay, Venez.
Green, Jason	.200	25	25	6	5	1	0	0	1	7	3	0	0	R	R	6-0	190	10-20-76	1999	San Diego, Calif.
Gregg, Neal	.212	17	33	4	7	3	0	1	8	5	14	0	0	L	R	6-4	220	3-29-78	1998	Hattiesburg, Miss.
Jaworowski, Aaron	.200	11	30	2	6	2	0	0	4	3	8	0	0	L	R	6-3	216	8-7-75	1997	Ellisville, Mo.
Leaumont, Jeff	.241	67	212	35	51	12	1	0	20	21	61	7	4	L	L	6-4	205	3-22-77	1999	Alexandria, La.
Mitchell, Todd	.270	65	248	34	67	13	1	1	23	21	39	11	2	R	R	6-2	178	8-12-78	1999	Bloomington, Ill.
Perini, Mike	.186	43	97	11	18	4	1	2	13	6	40	1	0	L	R	6-2	210	4-27-78	1996	Carlsbad, N.M.
Phillips, Andy	.322	64	233	35	75	11	7	7	48	37	40	3	3	R	R	6-0	205	4-6-77	1999	Demopolis, Ala.
Rhodes, Dusty	.249	45	169	28	42	11	0	1	13	33	42	3	5	L	R	6-1	190	2-6-76	1998	Madison, N.J.
Rodriguez, Felix	.000	1	2	0	0	0	0	0	0	0	1	0	0	R	R	6-2	180	3-19-78	1998	Ponce, P.R.
Santana, Pedro	.321	67	237	35	76	18	1	9	41	9	57	5	4	R	R	6-1	190	5-19-76	1996	Santo Domingo, D.R.
Sutter, Chad	.130	36	77	8	10	1	0	2	7	11	18	1	0	R	R	6-2	224	7-1-77	1998	Kennesaw, Ga.
Taylor, Seth	.293	74	283	57	83	11	1	5	36	35	40	23	6	R	R	6-1	185	8-23-77	1999	Cantonment, Fla.
Ticehurst, Brad	.253	63	221	29	56	12	5	8	39	22	51	4	3	L	R	6-2	195	5-24-77	1999	Los Alamitos, Calif.
Valdez, Angel	.211	34	71	11	15	3	0	1	13	5	16	3	2	R	R	6-2	178	5-22-78	1996	Santo Domingo, D.R.

GAMES BY POSITION: C—Brazeal 8, Fuentes 48, Green 25, F. Rodriguez 1, Sutter 34. **1B**—Fuentes 4, Gregg 8, Jaworowski 6, Leaumont 65, Valdez 4. **2B**—Correa 18, Mitchell 61, Taylor 1. **3B**—Correa 4, DeGroote 1, Mitchell 3, Phillips 63. **SS**—Mitchell 4, Taylor 73. **OF**—Brown 59, Perini 6, Rhodes 44, Santana 55, Ticehurst 58, Valdez 25.

PITCHING	W	L	ERA	G	GS	CG	SV	IP	H	R	ER	BB	SO	B	T	HT	WT	DOB	1st Yr	Resides
Carlson, Jeff	0	0	2.70	6	0	0	0	7	2	2	2	3	8	R	R	6-5	220	11-3-75	1998	Niantic, Conn.
Claussen, Brandon	6	4	3.38	12	12	1	0	72	70	30	27	12	89	L	L	6-2	175	5-1-79	1999	Roswell, N.M.
De la Cruz, Andres	0	2	13.50	5	0	0	2	4	7	6	6	2	3	R	R	6-4	190	5-12-79	1996	Santo Domingo, D.R.
Eavenson, Clay	0	0	6.75	1	0	0	0	1	2	1	1	0	0	R	R	6-3	185	3-6-78	1997	Loganville, Ga.
Faigin, Jason	1	1	3.18	18	0	0	1	23	22	9	8	5	27	R	R	6-2	190	9-20-78	1998	Marlboro, N.J.
Franco, Jose	3	3	2.83	30	0	0	5	41	29	14	13	14	58	R	R	6-2	190	8-29-81	1999	Santo Domingo, D.R.
Garcia, Rosman	2	6	4.26	18	10	0	1	70	86	40	33	14	40	R	R	6-2	165	1-3-79	1996	San Joaquin, Venez.
Grace, Bryan	0	4	5.68	8	1	0	0	13	13	14	8	9	11	R	R	6-1	190	4-1-76	1999	Baton Rouge, La.
Graman, Alex	6	3	2.99	14	14	0	0	81	74	30	27	16	85	L	L	6-4	195	11-17-77	1999	Huntingburg, Ind.
Klein, Cody	0	0	3.57	16	0	0	0	23	17	9	9	6	23	L	L	6-2	205	2-4-79	1997	Andrews, Texas
Knowles, Mike	0	0	14.21	3	2	0	0	6	15	12	10	4	5	R	R	6-5	215	7-15-79	1997	Daytona Beach, Fla.
Kremer, John	3	0	2.84	23	0	0	0	38	31	14	12	17	59	R	R	6-1	220	11-19-76	1999	Indianapolis, Ind.
Langston, David	0	0	20.25	2	0	0	0	1	3	3	3	3	0	R	R	6-5	215	12-11-78	1997	Ringgold, Ga.
Oliver, Scott	1	0	9.95	2	2	0	0	6	9	9	7	4	4	R	R	6-2	195	6-30-77	1999	Mount Pleasant, S.C.
Ridenour, Ryan	0	0	4.50	2	0	0	0	2	2	1	1	0	4	L	L	6-6	215	4-6-77	1998	Southlake, Texas
Rodriguez, Anthony	1	0	6.87	13	0	0	0	18	24	15	14	13	19	R	R	6-2	180	11-8-78	1997	New York, N.Y.
Swiatkiewicz, Chris	0	0	6.23	6	0	0	2	9	13	8	6	3	6	R	R	6-1	190	5-24-76	1998	Spring Lake Park, Minn.
Wallace, Chris	0	1	4.02	14	0	0	8	16	9	7	7	13	12	R	R	6-2	210	4-5-76	1997	Marion, Ohio
Walling, Dave	8	2	3.14	14	14	0	0	80	76	31	28	18	82	R	R	6-5	210	11-12-78	1999	Las Vegas, Nev.
Whiteley, Shad	3	4	4.96	12	12	0	0	62	69	39	34	26	71	R	R	6-6	220	3-19-75	1998	Fort Worth, Texas

PITCHING	W	L	ERA	G	GS	CG	SV	IP	H	R	ER	BB	SO	B	T	HT	WT	DOB	1st Yr	Resides
Whiteley, Jason	3	4	4.96	12	12	0	0	62	69	39	34	26	71	R	R	6-6	220	1-3-75	1998	Fort Worth, Texas
Willis, Jason	1	2	4.09	7	7	0	0	33	45	18	15	12	27	R	R	6-4	210	1-3-79	1999	Philadelphia, Miss.
Witte, Lou	5	2	3.05	25	0	0	1	41	42	21	14	12	39	R	R	5-11	175	10-30-76	1999	Richmond, Ind.

TAMPA — Rookie

GULF COAST LEAGUE

BATTING	AVG	G	AB	R	H	2B	3B	HR	RBI	BB	SO	SB	CS	B	T	HT	WT	DOB	1st Yr	Resides
Almonte, Erick	.300	9	30	5	9	2	0	2	9	3	10	1	0	R	R	6-2	180	2-1-78	1996	Santo Domingo, D.R.
Baker, Casey	.192	35	104	12	20	3	0	0	9	18	20	4	2	R	R	5-9	165	8-7-80	1999	Wysox, Pa.
Barr, Clint	.136	11	22	2	3	1	0	0	2	2	8	0	0	R	R	6-2	190	9-27-76	1999	Greeley, Colo.
Brazeal, Spencer	.206	26	68	13	14	3	0	0	5	17	19	1	1	R	R	6-0	190	3-9-77	1999	Oklahoma City, Okla.
Brazoban, Yhency	.320	56	200	33	64	14	5	1	26	12	47	7	3	R	R	6-1	170	6-11-80	1997	Santo Domingo, D.R.
Castillo, Victor	.314	42	153	24	48	8	1	0	16	22	38	9	8	R	R	6-0	160	2-15-81	1998	Aragua, Venez.
Corporan, Elvis	.278	56	212	29	59	13	3	4	30	19	41	3	1	S	R	6-2	205	6-9-80	1999	Catano, P.R.
Dennis, Les	.250	3	8	2	2	0	0	0	1	0	1	0	0	R	R	6-0	175	6-3-73	1995	West Linn, Ore.
DeGroote, Casey	.150	7	20	1	3	0	0	0	2	3	6	1	0	L	R	6-3	190	7-13-79	1998	Harte, Ind.
Evans, Mitch	.182	24	44	11	8	0	0	0	4	16	10	1	1	R	R	6-1	180	4-11-81	1999	Sydney, Australia
Fernandez, Alejandro ..	.214	12	28	2	6	3	0	0	3	6	8	0	0	R	R	6-2	175	12-19-80	1997	Maracaibo, Venez.
Fowler, David	.251	57	187	28	47	9	2	4	25	27	63	6	5	R	R	6-3	190	10-17-79	1998	St. Louis, Mo.
Harrell, Ken	.600	1	5	0	3	1	0	0	0	0	0	0	0	R	R	6-0	193	1-29-75	1997	Las Cruces, N.M.
Kofler, Eric	.667	1	3	1	2	1	0	1	4	1	0	0	0	L	L	6-1	170	2-11-76	1994	Palm Harbor, Fla.
Llamas, Juan	.500	4	4	1	2	0	0	0	0	2	1	0	0	R	R	6-1	165	6-24-80	1997	Cartagena, Colombia
Massucco, Scott	.154	6	13	1	2	0	0	0	1	2	0	0	1	R	R	6-0	190	8-20-79	1998	Tamarac, Fla.
Maxwell, Vernon	.500	1	4	0	2	0	0	0	0	0	1	0	0	R	R	6-3	205	10-22-76	1996	Midwest City, Okla.
Morris, Jeremy	.400	5	15	7	6	0	0	2	7	6	5	0	0	R	R	6-3	225	10-7-74	1997	Quincy, Fla.
Nettles, Jeff	.275	44	142	24	39	8	1	6	31	15	27	1	2	R	R	6-2	200	8-20-78	1998	Encinitas, Calif.
Pena, Wily	.247	45	166	21	41	10	1	7	26	12	54	3	2	R	R	6-3	190	1-23-82	1998	Laguna Salada, D.R.
Reyes, Ivan	.131	45	122	15	16	5	1	0	12	25	55	1	4	R	R	6-2	175	6-6-81	1999	Toa Baja, P.R.
Rivera, Juan	.333	5	18	7	6	0	0	1	4	4	1	0	0	R	R	6-2	170	7-3-78	1996	Guarenas, Venez.
Rodriguez, John	.286	3	7	1	2	0	1	0	1	3	0	0	0	L	L	6-0	185	1-20-78	1997	New York, N.Y.
Sein, Javier	.211	37	114	9	24	4	0	2	15	15	39	0	1	L	R	6-4	210	10-16-78	1998	Aguadilla, P.R.
Sheffield, Jeff	.000	3	4	0	0	0	0	0	0	0	1	0	0	S	R	6-2	195	6-1-79	1998	Spokane, Wash.
Soriano, Alfonso	.263	5	19	7	5	2	0	1	5	1	3	0	0	R	R	6-1	160	1-7-78	1999	Los Angeles, Calif.
Torres, Jaime	.333	11	30	5	10	2	0	1	3	2	1	0	1	R	R	6-0	176	3-12-71	1992	Aragua, Venez.
Winrow, Gary	.317	46	180	31	57	9	3	0	28	21	28	5	1	L	L	6-2	185	7-12-80	1999	Fort Myers, Fla.

GAMES BY POSITION: C—Barr 11, Brazeal 24, Evans 24, Fernandez 4, Harrell 1, Massucco 5, Torres 9. 1B—Dennis 1, Nettles 29, Sein 35. 2B—Baker 33, Castillo 31, Dennis 3. 3B—Corporan 53, DeGroote 4, Llamas 2, Nettles 2. SS—Almonte 7, Castillo 9, Nettles 1, Reyes 44, Soriano 4. OF—Brazoban 50, Fowler 55, Maxwell 1, Nettles 6, Pena 24, Rivera 5, Rodriguez 3, Sheffield 3, Winrow 42.

PITCHING	W	L	ERA	G	GS	CG	SV	IP	H	R	ER	BB	SO	B	T	HT	WT	DOB	1st Yr	Resides
Aldridge, Mike	2	0	8.59	7	0	0	0	7	6	7	7	5	12	R	R	6-5	215	3-17-77	1999	Franklin, Ohio
Aramboles, Ricardo	2	3	3.89	9	7	0	0	35	35	18	15	14	42	R	R	6-2	170	12-4-81	1996	Santo Domingo, D.R.
Chacon, Ernesto	4	0	3.09	18	1	0	1	35	30	14	12	21	55	R	R	6-3	180	10-21-79	1997	Maracaibo, Venez.
Claussen, Brandon	0	1	3.18	2	2	0	0	11	7	4	4	2	16	L	L	6-2	175	5-1-79	1999	Roswell, N.M.
Day, Zach	1	1	3.78	5	4	0	0	17	20	10	7	4	17	R	R	6-4	185	6-15-78	1996	West Harrison, Ind.
De los Santos, Luis	0	0	0.00	2	2	0	0	8	5	0	0	0	7	R	R	6-2	187	11-1-77	1995	San Pedro de Macoris, D.R.
De la Cruz, Luis	0	0	0.00	3	0	0	1	3	2	0	0	2	2	R	R	6-3	190	3-15-81	1999	La Romana, D.R.
Einertson, Darrell	0	1	0.00	1	0	0	0	2	3	3	0	1	4	R	R	6-2	190	9-4-72	1995	Urbandale, Iowa
Gardea, Mario	1	3	2.84	14	0	0	0	19	11	10	6	13	34	R	R	6-2	220	2-26-80	1999	Odessa, Texas
Igualada, Eric	1	3	3.80	11	0	0	0	24	16	10	10	12	30	R	R	6-2	175	4-1-79	1998	Los Santos, Panama
Jelovcic, Rich	1	1	3.12	14	0	0	0	17	12	6	6	15	10	R	R	6-3	215	12-4-77	1999	Whitestone, N.Y.
Johnson, Mark	0	0	8.18	3	2	0	0	11	15	11	10	5	10	R	R	6-2	226	5-2-75	1996	Leesburg, Fla.
Lankford, Frank	0	0	4.50	1	1	0	0	2	2	1	1	1	2	R	R	6-2	190	3-26-71	1993	Atlanta, Ga.
LaPlante, Reggie	1	2	5.21	8	7	0	0	38	40	25	22	15	40	L	R	6-3	185	12-22-79	1999	Beauport, Quebec
Lyons, Curt	0	0	0.00	1	0	0	0	2	1	0	0	2	3	R	R	6-5	225	10-17-74	1992	Richmond, Ky.
Martinez, David	5	3	2.97	12	11	2	0	67	52	29	22	22	67	L	L	6-1	165	6-7-80	1997	Venezuela
Martinez, Oscar	2	1	1.85	23	0	0	9	24	23	8	5	8	29	R	R	6-2	185	10-7-78	1999	Araure, Venez.
McCloud, Josh	0	0	27.00	3	0	0	0	3	9	8	8	3	4	R	R	6-3	205	10-4-80	1999	Holland, Ohio
Nelson, Jeff	0	0	0.00	2	2	0	0	2	1	0	0	1	3	R	R	6-8	235	11-17-66	1984	Issaquah, Wash.
Obando, Omar	1	0	0.00	2	0	0	0	4	5	4	0	3	3	R	R	6-2	180	3-23-77	1996	Chimandega, Nicaragua
Ochsner, Alan	1	1	5.79	4	0	0	0	5	4	4	3	4	6	R	R	6-4	205	12-10-75	1999	Brenham, Texas
Oliver, Scott	4	1	1.65	6	5	0	0	33	28	7	6	8	31	R	R	6-2	195	6-30-77	1999	Mount Pleasant, S.C.
Ortiz, Javier	3	2	5.68	12	10	1	0	51	63	40	32	35	46	R	R	6-0	155	11-28-79	1996	Cartagena, Colombia
Peeples, Jim	0	0	4.96	16	0	0	0	16	21	13	9	16	21	L	L	6-0	195	7-5-80	1998	Jacksonville, Fla.
Reisinger, Justin	1	0	11.05	8	0	0	0	7	11	12	9	6	7	R	R	6-3	185	3-22-80	1998	Clarksburg, Ohio
Ridenour, Ryan	0	2	2.08	7	0	0	0	9	5	5	2	5	13	L	L	6-6	215	4-6-77	1998	Southlake, Texas
Spears, Ricky	0	0	0.84	7	1	0	0	11	5	1	1	7	8	R	R	6-3	185	7-27-80	1999	Gore, Okla.
Swiatkiewicz, Chris	1	0	0.82	9	0	0	5	11	5	1	1	2	13	R	R	6-1	190	5-24-76	1999	Spring Lake Park, Minn.
Tovar, Angel	0	1	8.22	8	0	0	0	8	12	8	7	5	7	R	R	6-4	195	4-25-78	1996	San Joaquin, Venez.
Willis, Jason	1	1	2.20	4	4	0	0	16	13	4	4	6	17	R	R	6-4	210	1-3-79	1999	Philadelphia, Miss.
Zgoda, Derek	0	0	3.60	2	0	0	0	5	5	2	2	0	5	R	R	6-0	205	4-20-73	1999	Amherst, N.Y.

NEWYORKMETS

Mets fight to the finish but fall just shy of World Series

BY MARTY NOBLE

Perhaps the best thing the Mets did in their most rewarding season in 11 years was lose the first three games of their National League Championship Series against the Braves. The compelling comeback they executed in the subsequent two games and their 11-inning, albeit futile, effort in the sixth game gripped the New York market and energized the organization.

Nothing captures the imagination like gallantry in underdog circumstances.

The Mets took their nemesis of the last two years to the brink of a decisive seventh game and, in the process, demonstrated remarkable resilience and an ability they didn't know they had: They could beat the Braves. Beat them in successive games, in fact, and scare the devil out of the team they couldn't catch in the regular season.

Only four teams in the history of the Mets franchise (1969, 1985, 1986 and 1988) won more games than the 1999 edition. New York needed a 163rd game—a one-game playoff in Cincinnati against the Reds for the NL wild-card berth—but it reached the playoffs for the first time since 1988. Lefthander Al Leiter pitched the Mets into the postseason with a complete-game, 5-1 win.

No Mets team had ever scored more runs (853), hit more doubles (297), produced a higher batting average (.279), committed fewer errors (68, a major league record) and allowed fewer unearned runs (20, also a major league record).

But with all the offense, it was the defense of the infield that made the Mets special.

John Olerud at first, Edgardo Alfonzo at second, Rey

Edgardo Alfonzo   **Dicky Gonzalez**

Players of the Year

MAJOR LEAGUE: Edgardo Alfonzo, 2b
Alfonzo hit .304 with 27 home runs and 108 RBIs while committing just five errors after moving to second base from third.

MINOR LEAGUE: Dicky Gonzalez, rhp
Gonzalez led the organization with 14 wins and a 2.82 ERA while walking just 31 hitters and striking out 146.

Ordonez at shortstop and Robin Ventura at third provided the best defense in the league as the Mets set a record for fewest infield errors (33). Ordonez completed the regular season with 100 consecutive error-less games, a record for shortstops.

The Mets succeeded while changing closers on the fly from injured John Franco to intimidating Armando Benitez; despite losing streaks of seven and eight games, the former in September; without a pitcher with more than 13 wins; and with half the coaching staff departing at midseason.

At the same time, the Mets had unexpected contributions from outfielders Roger Cedeno (90 runs, 66 stolen bases) and Benny Agbayani (.286-14-42 in 276 at-bats); righthanders Octavio Dotel (8-3) and Pat Mahomes (8-0, 3.68); and, in the postseason, outfielder Melvin Mora.

While the farm system provided Dotel, Abgayani and Mora, the development of its top prospect, center fielder Alex Escobar, was undermined by injuries (back and left shoulder) that cost him the season.

The club was encouraged by the development at Double-A Binghamton of center fielder Jason Tyner (.313, 49 SB), its first-round selection in the 1998 draft, and delighted by the progress of another center fielder, Brian Cole (.316-18-71, 50 SB at Class A Capital City). The club considers Cole the fastest and most exciting player in the organization.

The Mets' minor league teams produced a .515 composite record with the team in the Rookie-level Gulf Coast League winning the championship for the second time in three years. The organization will not operate a team in the GCL beginning in 2000.

ORGANIZATION LEADERS

BATTING

*AVG	Jorge Toca, Norfolk/Binghamton	.319
R	Brian Cole, Capital City	97
H	Jason Tyner, Norfolk/Binghamton	162
TB	Brian Cole, Capital City	261
2B	Brian Cole, Capital City	41
3B	Three tied at	7
HR	Earl Snyder, Capital City	28
RBI	Earl Snyder, Capital City	97
BB	Todd Haney, Norfolk	73
SO	Bryon Gainey, Binghamton	184
SB	Brian Cole, Capital City	50

PITCHING

W	Dicky Gonzalez, Norfolk/St. Lucie	14
L	Two tied at	13
#ERA	Dicky Gonzalez, Norfolk/St. Lucie	2.82
G	Mark Guerra, Norfolk	63
CG	Three tied at	3
SV	Heath Bell, Capital City	25
IP	Dicky Gonzalez, Norfolk/St. Lucie	175
BB	Todd Cutchins, St. Lucie	82
SO	Rene Vega, Capital City	148

*Minimum 250 At-Bats #Minimum 75 Innings

New York METS

Manager: Bobby Valentine   **1999 Record:** 97-66, .595 (2nd, NL East)

BATTING	AVG	G	AB	R	H	2B	3B	HR	RBI	BB	SO	SB	CS	B	T	HT	WT	DOB	1st Yr	Resides
Agbayani, Benny	.286	101	276	42	79	18	3	14	42	32	60	6	4	R	R	6-0	225	12-28-71	1993	Aiea, Hawaii
Alfonzo, Edgardo	.304	158	628	123	191	41	1	27	108	85	85	9	2	R	R	5-11	187	11-8-73	1991	Caracas, Venez.
Allensworth, Jermaine	.219	40	73	14	16	2	0	3	9	9	23	2	1	R	R	6-0	190	1-11-72	1993	Anderson, Ind.
Bonilla, Bobby	.160	60	119	12	19	5	0	4	18	19	16	0	1	S	R	6-4	240	2-23-63	1981	Greenwich, Conn.
Cedeno, Roger	.313	155	453	90	142	23	4	4	36	60	100	66	17	S	R	6-1	205	8-16-74	1992	Valencia, Venez.
Dunston, Shawon	.344	42	93	12	32	6	1	0	16	0	16	4	1	R	R	6-1	175	3-21-63	1982	Corona, N.Y.
2-team (62 St. Louis)	.321	104	243	35	78	11	3	5	41	2	39	10	4							
Franco, Matt	.235	122	132	18	31	5	0	4	21	28	21	0	0	L	R	6-1	210	8-19-69	1987	Thousand Oaks, Calif.
Hamilton, Darryl	.339	55	168	19	57	8	1	5	21	19	18	2	3	L	R	6-1	180	12-3-64	1986	Sugar Land, Texas
2-team (91 Colorado)	.315	146	505	82	159	19	4	9	45	57	39	6	8							
Henderson, Rickey	.315	121	438	89	138	30	0	12	42	82	82	37	14	R	L	5-10	190	12-25-58	1976	Hillsborough, Calif.
Kinkade, Mike	.196	28	46	3	9	2	1	2	6	3	9	1	0	R	R	6-1	210	5-6-73	1995	Tigard, Ore.
Long, Terrence	.000	3	3	0	0	0	0	0	0	0	2	0	0	L	L	6-1	190	2-29-76	1994	Millbrook, Ala.
Lopez, Luis	.212	68	104	11	22	4	0	2	13	12	33	1	1	S	R	5-11	166	9-4-70	1988	Cidra, P.R.
McRae, Brian	.221	96	298	36	66	12	1	8	36	39	57	2	6	S	R	6-0	195	8-27-67	1985	Leawood, Kan.
Mora, Melvin	.161	66	31	6	5	0	0	0	1	4	7	2	1	R	R	5-10	160	2-2-72	1991	Naquanqua, Venez.
Olerud, John	.298	162	581	107	173	39	0	19	96	125	66	3	0	L	L	6-5	220	8-5-68	1989	Phoenix, Ariz.
Ordonez, Rey	.258	154	520	49	134	24	2	1	60	49	59	8	4	R	R	5-9	159	11-11-72	1993	Miami, Fla.
Payton, Jay	.250	13	8	1	2	1	0	0	1	0	2	1	2	R	R	5-10	185	11-22-72	1994	Zanesville, Ohio
Piazza, Mike	.303	141	534	100	162	25	0	40	124	51	70	2	2	R	R	6-3	223	9-4-68	1989	Valley Forge, Pa.
Pratt, Todd	.293	71	140	18	41	4	0	3	21	15	32	2	0	R	R	6-3	230	2-9-67	1985	Sunrise, Fla.
Toca, Jorge	.333	4	3	0	1	0	0	0	0	0	2	0	0	R	R	6-3	220	1-7-75	1999	Los Angeles, Calif.
Ventura, Robin	.301	161	588	88	177	38	0	32	120	74	109	1	1	L	R	6-1	198	7-14-67	1989	Santa Maria, Calif.

PITCHING	W	L	ERA	G	GS	CG	SV	IP	H	R	ER	BB	SO	B	T	HT	WT	DOB	1st Yr	Resides
Beltran, Rigo	1	1	3.48	21	0	0	0	31	30	15	12	12	35	L	L	5-11	185	11-13-69	1991	San Diego, Calif.
Benitez, Armando	4	3	1.85	77	0	0	22	78	40	17	16	41	128	R	R	6-4	225	11-3-72	1990	San Pedro de Macoris, D.R.
Cook, Dennis	10	5	3.86	71	0	0	3	63	50	27	27	27	68	L	L	6-3	190	10-4-62	1985	Austin, Texas
Dotel, Octavio	8	3	5.38	19	14	0	0	85	69	52	51	49	85	R	R	6-0	160	11-25-75	1993	Santo Domingo, D.R.
Franco, John	0	2	2.88	46	0	0	19	41	40	14	13	19	41	L	L	5-10	185	9-17-60	1981	Staten Island, N.Y.
Hershiser, Orel	13	12	4.58	32	32	0	0	179	175	92	91	77	89	R	R	6-3	195	9-16-58	1979	Windermere, Fla.
Isringhausen, Jason	1	3	6.41	13	5	0	1	39	43	29	28	22	31	R	R	6-3	210	9-7-72	1992	Brighton, Ill.
Jones, Bobby	3	3	5.61	12	9	0	0	59	69	37	37	11	31	R	R	6-4	216	2-10-70	1991	Fresno, Calif.
Leiter, Al	13	12	4.23	32	32	1	0	213	209	107	100	93	162	L	L	6-3	220	10-23-65	1984	Plantation, Fla.
Mahomes, Pat	8	0	3.68	39	0	0	0	64	44	26	26	37	51	R	R	6-4	210	8-9-70	1988	Lindale, Texas
Manzanillo, Josias	0	0	5.79	12	0	0	0	19	19	12	12	4	25	R	R	6-0	190	10-16-67	1983	Hyde Park, Mass.
McElroy, Chuck	0	0	3.38	15	0	0	0	13	12	5	5	8	7	L	L	6-0	195	10-1-67	1986	Friendswood, Texas
2-team (41 Colo.)	3	1	5.50	56	0	0	0	54	60	34	33	36	44							
McMichael, Greg	1	1	4.82	19	0	0	0	19	20	10	10	8	18	R	R	6-3	222	12-1-66	1988	Alpharetta, Ga.
Murray, Dan	0	0	13.50	1	0	0	0	2	4	3	3	2	1	R	R	6-1	193	11-21-73	1995	Garden Grove, Calif.
Reed, Rick	11	5	4.58	26	26	1	0	149	163	77	76	47	104	R	R	6-1	195	8-16-65	1986	Huntington, W.Va.
Rogers, Kenny	5	1	4.03	12	12	2	0	76	71	35	34	28	58	L	L	6-1	205	11-10-64	1982	Tampa, Fla.
Rusch, Glendon	0	0	0.00	1	0	0	0	1	1	0	0	0	0	L	L	6-1	200	11-7-74	1993	Seattle, Wash.
Tam, Jeff	0	0	3.18	9	0	0	0	11	6	4	4	3	8	R	R	6-1	202	8-19-70	1993	Melbourne, Fla.
Taylor, Billy	0	1	8.10	18	0	0	0	13	20	12	12	9	14	R	R	6-8	230	10-16-61	1980	Thomasville, Ga.
Watson, Allen	2	2	4.08	14	4	0	1	40	36	18	18	22	32	L	L	6-3	195	11-18-70	1991	Middle Village, N.Y.
Wendell, Turk	5	4	3.05	80	0	0	3	86	80	31	29	37	77	L	R	6-2	205	5-19-67	1988	Denver, Colo.
Yoshii, Masato	12	8	4.40	31	29	1	0	174	168	86	85	58	105	R	R	6-2	210	4-20-65	1998	Tokyo, Japan

FIELDING

Catcher	PCT	G	PO	A	E	DP	PB
Kinkade	1.000	1	3	0	0	0	0
Piazza	.989	137	953	47	11	5	7
Pratt	.996	52	262	13	1	1	3

First Base	PCT	G	PO	A	E	DP
Bonilla	.962	4	23	2	1	2
Dunston	1.000	8	37	2	0	3
M. Franco	1.000	19	41	5	0	8
Kinkade	.000	1	0	0	0	0
Olerud	.994	160	1344	105	9	127
Pratt	.000	1	0	0	0	0
Toca	1.000	2	0	0	0	0
Ventura	1.000	1	1	0	0	0

Second Base	PCT	G	PO	A	E	DP
Alfonzo	.993	158	298	409	5	98

	PCT	G	PO	A	E	DP
Cedeno	.000	1	0	0	0	0
Lopez	.966	16	8	20	1	5
Mora	1.000	4	1	1	0	1

Third Base	PCT	G	PO	A	E	DP
Dunston	1.000	1	1	1	0	0
M. Franco	.950	12	1	18	1	1
Kinkade	1.000	3	1	1	0	0
Lopez	.857	9	3	3	1	1
Mora	1.000	3	2	5	0	1
Ventura	.980	160	123	320	9	33

Shortstop	PCT	G	PO	A	E	DP
Dunston	.929	7	1	12	1	3
Lopez	.971	33	23	45	2	8
Mora	1.000	1	0	1	0	0

	PCT	G	PO	A	E	DP
Ordonez	.994	154	220	416	4	91

Outfield	PCT	G	PO	A	E	DP
Agbayani	.984	80	121	2	2	0
Allensworth	1.000	33	47	1	0	1
Bonilla	.974	25	36	2	1	0
Cedeno	.989	149	256	9	3	2
Dunston	.978	27	43	1	1	0
M. Franco	1.000	19	13	0	0	0
Hamilton	1.000	52	100	2	0	0
Henderson	.988	116	168	0	2	0
Kinkade	1.000	17	14	1	0	0
McRae	.994	87	152	1	1	0
Mora	1.000	45	18	0	0	0
Payton	1.000	6	3	0	0	0
Pratt	1.000	1	1	0	0	0

JOHN WILLIAMSON

Mike Piazza
Led Mets with 40 homers and 124 RBIs

MORRIS FOSTOFF

Jason Tyner
Stole 49 bases for Binghamton

FARM SYSTEM

Assistant General Manager, Player Personnel: Jim Duquette

Class	Farm Team	League	W	L	Pct.	Finish*	Manager	First Yr
AAA	Norfolk (Va.) Tides	International	77	63	.550	4th (14)	John Gibbons	1969
AA	Binghamton (N.Y.) Mets	Eastern	54	88	.380	12th (12)	Doug Davis	1992
A#	St. Lucie (Fla.) Mets	Florida State	68	70	.493	8th (14)	Howie Freiling	1988
A	Capital City (S.C.) Bombers	South Atlantic	83	58	.589	2nd (14)	Dave Engle	1983
A	Pittsfield (N.Y.) Mets	New York-Penn	41	35	.539	6th (14)	Tony Tijerina	1989
Rookie#	Kingsport (Tenn.) Mets	Appalachian	34	36	.486	6th (10)	Guy Conti	1980
Rookie	Port St. Lucie (Fla.) Mets	Gulf Coast	39	21	.650	+1st (14)	John Stephenson	1988

*Finish in overall standings (No. of teams in league)   #Advanced level   +Won league championship

NORFOLK   Class AAA

INTERNATIONAL LEAGUE

BATTING	AVG	G	AB	R	H	2B	3B	HR	RBI	BB	SO	SB	CS	B	T	HT	WT	DOB	1st Yr	Resides
Agbayani, Benny	.356	28	101	21	36	8	1	8	32	16	19	5	3	R	R	6-0	225	12-28-71	1993	Aiea, Hawaii
Allensworth, Jermaine ..	.264	81	273	44	72	20	5	5	20	36	39	10	5	R	R	6-0	190	1-11-72	1993	Anderson, Ind.
Baez, Kevin	.263	60	175	15	46	5	0	1	26	17	21	2	0	R	R	6-0	170	1-10-67	1988	San Juan, P.R.
2-team (20 Indianapolis)	.270	80	215	19	58	8	0	1	33	28	25	3	0							
Bell, Mike	.274	39	135	11	37	11	1	1	25	9	23	4	2	R	R	6-2	195	12-7-74	1993	Cincinnati, Ohio
Bonilla, Bobby	.231	3	13	1	3	0	0	1	0	1	0	0	0	S	R	6-4	240	2-23-63	1981	Greenwich, Conn.
Brooks, Jerry	.237	79	241	32	57	13	1	9	27	34	50	0	2	R	R	6-0	195	3-23-67	1988	Syracuse, N.Y.
Buccheri, Jim	.228	32	92	9	21	3	0	0	5	4	15	4	1	R	R	5-11	165	11-12-68	1988	Fountain Valley, Calif.
2-team (6 Durham)	.220	38	100	11	22	4	0	0	7	6	15	6	1							
Darden, Tony	.121	18	33	4	4	1	0	0	3	7	4	2	2	R	R	6-0	180	5-29-74	1994	Gilmer, Texas
Grifol, Pedro	.260	59	177	11	46	5	0	4	27	12	33	1	1	R	R	6-1	197	11-28-69	1991	Miami, Fla.
Halter, Shane	.274	127	474	77	130	22	3	6	35	60	90	19	18	R	R	6-0	180	11-8-69	1991	Overland Park, Kan.
Haltiwanger, Garrick	.000	6	13	2	0	0	0	0	0	0	8	0	0	R	L	6-2	190	3-3-75	1996	Irmo, S.C.
Haney, Todd	.311	122	447	82	139	25	6	5	48	73	43	7	9	R	R	5-9	165	7-30-65	1987	San Antonio, Texas
Hunter, Scott	.228	50	180	20	41	4	0	8	23	8	42	6	6	R	R	6-1	210	12-17-75	1994	Philadelphia, Pa.
Kinkade, Mike	.308	84	312	53	96	20	2	7	49	21	31	7	1	R	R	6-1	210	5-6-73	1995	Tigard, Ore.
Livingstone, Scott	.298	36	114	10	34	7	0	1	20	7	9	2	0	L	R	6-0	198	7-15-65	1988	Southlake, Texas
2-team (14 Rochester) ...	.318	50	157	15	50	11	0	1	27	14	13	3	0							
Long, Terrence	.326	78	304	41	99	20	4	7	47	23	41	14	6	L	L	6-1	190	2-29-76	1994	Millbrook, Ala.
Mora, Melvin	.303	82	304	55	92	17	2	8	36	41	54	18	8	R	R	5-10	160	2-2-72	1991	Naquanqua, Venez.
Neubart, Garrett	.158	13	38	6	6	0	0	0	2	6	7	5	1	R	R	5-10	160	11-7-73	1995	Livingston, N.J.
Paquette, Craig	.272	70	283	40	77	20	3	15	54	10	47	3	0	R	R	6-0	190	3-28-69	1989	Tempe, Ariz.
Payton, Jay	.389	38	144	27	56	13	2	8	35	12	13	2	2	R	R	5-10	185	11-22-72	1994	Zanesville, Ohio
Rodriguez, Sammy	.222	5	9	2	2	0	0	2	4	3	2	0	0	R	R	5-9	185	8-20-75	1995	New York, N.Y.
Romero, Mandy	.258	28	97	7	25	6	0	1	9	9	18	0	0	S	R	5-11	196	10-19-67	1988	Miami, Fla.
2-team (46 Pawtucket) ...	.233	74	240	15	56	13	0	4	31	22	44	0	0							

BATTING	AVG	G	AB	R	H	2B	3B	HR	RBI	BB	SO	SB	CS	B	T	HT	WT	DOB	1st Yr	Resides
Toca, Jorge	.335	49	176	25	59	12	1	5	29	6	23	0	3	R	R	6-3	220	1-7-75	1999	Los Angeles, Calif.
Tomberlin, Andy	.310	97	303	60	94	21	1	16	61	40	74	2	1	L	L	5-11	185	11-7-66	1986	Monroe, N.C.
Tyner, Jason	.000	3	8	0	0	0	0	0	0	0	5	0	0	L	L	6-1	170	4-23-77	1998	Beaumont, Texas
Valera, Yohanny	.154	23	65	3	10	2	0	1	6	4	16	0	0	R	R	6-1	196	8-17-76	1993	San Cristobal, D.R.
Wilson, Vance	.264	15	53	10	14	3	0	3	5	4	8	1	0	R	R	5-11	190	3-17-73	1994	Mesa, Ariz.

PITCHING	W	L	ERA	G	GS	CG	SV	IP	H	R	ER	BB	SO	B	T	HT	WT	DOB	1st Yr	Resides
Bautista, Jose	7	4	5.33	20	12	0	0	83	111	53	49	21	41	R	R	6-2	207	7-25-64	1981	Cooper City, Fla.
2-team (16 Ottawa)	7	5	5.43	36	12	0	4	111	144	72	67	26	65							
Beltran, Rigo	2	1	1.61	21	0	0	0	22	16	5	4	12	27	L	L	5-11	185	11-13-69	1991	San Diego, Calif.
Cammack, Eric	0	0	3.12	9	0	0	4	9	7	3	3	1	17	R	R	6-1	175	8-14-75	1997	Port Neches, Texas
Dotel, Octavio	5	2	3.84	13	13	1	0	70	52	33	30	34	90	R	R	6-0	160	11-25-75	1993	Santo Domingo, D.R.
Fleetham, Ben	1	2	14.85	6	0	0	0	7	11	15	11	10	9	R	R	6-1	205	8-3-72	1994	Minneapolis, Minn.
Gonzalez, Dicky	0	1	2.70	1	1	0	0	7	5	2	2	1	3	R	R	5-11	170	10-21-78	1996	Bayamon, P.R.
Guerra, Mark	8	3	2.93	63	2	0	0	89	90	45	29	39	70	R	R	6-2	200	11-4-71	1994	Pensacola Beach, Fla.
Henderson, Ryan	0	2	8.10	7	2	0	0	13	14	13	12	9	12	R	R	6-1	190	9-30-69	1992	Dana Point, Calif.
2-team (21 Louisville)	0	1	6.84	28	2	0	0	49	49	45	37	34	46							
Henriquez, Oscar	3	4	4.00	53	0	0	23	54	54	31	24	38	65	R	R	6-6	220	1-28-74	1991	La Guaira, Venez.
Isringhausen, Jason	3	1	2.29	12	8	0	0	51	33	18	13	20	51	R	R	6-3	210	9-7-72	1992	Brighton, Ill.
Jones, Bobby	2	0	2.45	2	2	0	0	11	11	3	3	3	8	R	R	6-4	216	2-10-70	1991	Fresno, Calif.
Lewis, Richie	7	8	5.06	20	20	3	0	123	128	82	69	49	101	R	R	5-10	175	1-25-66	1987	Fort Lauderdale, Fla.
Lopez, Jose	3	5	4.15	33	8	0	1	102	98	49	47	44	84	R	R	6-2	200	4-4-75	1992	Yaracuy, Venez.
Lyons, Mike	0	0	21.00	2	0	0	0	3	7	7	7	3	5	R	R	6-3	195	5-20-75	1996	Altamonte Springs, Fla.
Mahomes, Pat	4	1	3.49	6	6	0	0	39	38	17	15	12	24	R	R	6-4	210	8-9-70	1988	Lindale, Texas
McMichael, Greg	0	0	2.70	3	1	0	0	3	4	1	1	3	4	R	R	6-3	222	12-1-66	1988	Alpharetta, Ga.
Mercado, Hector	0	0	1.50	2	2	0	0	6	3	1	1	1	2	L	L	6-3	205	4-29-74	1992	Dorado, P.R.
Mercedes, Jose	2	1	2.53	6	0	0	0	32	36	15	9	11	19	R	R	6-1	210	3-5-71	1992	Las Palmillas, D.R.
Murray, Dan	12	10	4.97	29	27	3	0	145	149	91	80	70	96	R	R	6-1	193	11-21-73	1995	Garden Grove, Calif.
Myers, Jimmy	0	0	17.18	3	0	0	0	4	11	8	7	2	2	R	R	6-1	185	4-28-69	1987	Crowder, Okla.
Palacios, Vicente	2	1	1.86	7	0	0	1	10	9	2	2	4	9	R	R	6-2	180	7-19-63	1983	Veracruz, Mexico
Pontes, Dan	0	0	9.39	14	0	0	0	23	36	25	24	11	14	R	R	6-3	200	4-27-71	1993	Geneva, N.Y.
Reed, Rick	1	0	27.00	1	1	0	0	3	10	9	9	2	2	R	R	6-1	195	8-16-65	1986	Huntington, W.Va.
Roberts, Grant	2	1	4.50	5	5	0	0	28	32	15	14	11	30	R	R	6-3	205	9-13-77	1995	El Cajon, Calif.
Ruebel, Matt	3	0	4.50	7	7	0	0	40	40	20	20	17	23	L	L	6-2	180	10-16-69	1991	Oklahoma City, Okla.
Stewart, Scott	6	4	4.42	35	14	0	0	100	109	55	49	36	85	R	L	6-2	205	8-14-75	1994	Stanley, N.C.
Tam, Jeff	0	1	3.10	16	0	0	3	20	24	7	7	3	10	R	R	6-1	202	8-19-70	1993	Melbourne, Fla.
Treadwell, Jody	1	2	9.93	11	3	0	0	23	27	25	25	18	19	R	R	6-0	190	12-14-68	1990	Jacksonville, Fla.
Turrentine, Rich	0	1	6.75	2	0	0	0	3	6	2	2	1	3	R	R	6-0	185	5-21-71	1989	Texarkana, Ark.
Villano, Mike	0	0	4.50	2	0	0	0	2	3	1	1	2	1	R	R	6-0	200	8-10-71	1994	Bay City, Mich.
Wallace, Derek	2	5	3.60	36	0	0	7	55	53	24	22	25	38	R	R	6-3	215	9-1-71	1992	Oxnard, Calif.
Welch, Mike	2	2	3.58	24	0	0	0	33	33	17	13	13	17	L	R	6-2	210	8-25-72	1993	Nashua, N.H.
2-team (13 Scranton)	3	4	5.81	37	5	0	0	67	78	47	43	26	28							

FIELDING

Catcher	PCT	G	PO	A	E	DP	PB
Brooks	.993	23	125	8	1	0	4
Grifol	.993	53	382	29	3	5	5
Halter	1.000	1	1	0	0	0	0
Kinkade	.990	16	89	9	1	0	6
Rodriguez	1.000	5	16	0	0	0	2
Romero	.983	23	162	10	3	3	3
Valera	.974	22	138	14	4	4	5
Wilson	.991	14	95	11	1	2	0

First Base	PCT	G	PO	A	E	DP
Agbayani	.987	8	71	6	1	6
Bell	1.000	17	90	6	0	9
Brooks	.985	38	252	17	4	23
Grifol	1.000	1	4	0	0	1
Kinkade	.989	12	81	10	1	3
Livingstone	1.000	13	82	15	0	6
Paquette	.991	16	98	8	1	9
Toca	.987	44	351	41	5	46
Tomberlin	.988	12	80	0	1	4

Second Base	PCT	G	PO	A	E	DP
Baez	.974	26	47	65	3	19

	PCT	G	PO	A	E	DP
Bell	.936	22	47	41	6	12
Darden	.000	1	0	0	0	0
Halter	1.000	17	23	38	0	10
Haney	.967	88	172	205	13	43
Mora	1.000	1	1	2	0	0

Third Base	PCT	G	PO	A	E	DP
Baez	1.000	2	1	1	0	0
Brooks	.000	1	0	0	0	0
Darden	.950	11	5	14	1	2
Halter	.895	14	15	19	4	1
Haney	.868	32	24	55	12	7
Kinkade	.926	42	20	67	7	7
Livingstone	.889	14	12	20	4	2
Mora	.000	1	0	0	1	0
Paquette	.941	39	26	69	6	5

Shortstop	PCT	G	PO	A	E	DP
Baez	.972	28	28	75	3	16
Halter	.955	69	92	181	13	40
Haney	1.000	1	1	1	0	0
Mora	.928	49	63	130	15	23

	PCT	G	PO	A	E	DP
Paquette	1.000	1	1	2	0	0

Outfield	PCT	G	PO	A	E	DP
Agbayani	.977	18	42	0	1	0
Allensworth	.975	74	155	3	4	2
Bucceri	1.000	25	31	0	0	0
Darden	1.000	1	3	0	0	0
Halter	.950	32	56	1	3	0
Haltiwanger	1.000	6	7	0	0	0
Haney	.000	1	0	0	0	0
Hunter	1.000	48	84	3	0	0
Kinkade	.955	11	19	2	1	0
Long	.980	75	192	8	4	1
Mora	1.000	30	62	2	0	0
Neubart	1.000	11	18	1	0	0
Paquette	.979	19	43	3	1	0
Payton	.984	34	59	3	1	1
Toca	1.000	1	0	1	0	0
Tomberlin	.991	53	102	6	1	3
Tyner	1.000	2	4	0	0	0

BINGHAMTON — Class AA

EASTERN LEAGUE

BATTING	AVG	G	AB	R	H	2B	3B	HR	RBI	BB	SO	SB	CS	B	T	HT	WT	DOB	1st Yr	Resides
Beamon, Trey	.240	71	246	32	59	13	0	2	20	29	41	13	10	L	R	6-3	192	2-11-74	1992	Garland, Texas
Bennett, Ryan	.000	1	4	1	0	0	0	0	0	0	2	0	0	R	R	6-0	195	7-26-74	1996	Waukegan, Ill.
Bruce, Mo	.270	133	500	80	135	25	4	9	76	61	134	33	11	R	R	5-10	190	5-1-75	1996	Kansas City, Mo.
Bucceri, Jim	.294	4	17	1	5	1	1	0	1	0	4	0	0	R	R	5-11	165	11-12-68	1988	Fountain Valley, Calif.
Darden, Tony	.354	49	164	25	58	8	1	5	23	19	30	5	4	R	R	6-0	180	5-29-74	1996	Gilmer, Texas
Dina, Allen	.229	49	192	25	44	10	3	0	15	9	46	9	3	R	R	5-10	180	9-28-73	1998	Stratford, Conn.
Dubose, Brian	.174	30	69	8	12	3	0	0	4	14	19	5	1	L	R	6-3	208	5-17-71	1990	Detroit, Mich.
Gainey, Bryon	.237	137	502	68	119	28	6	25	78	40	184	1	2	L	R	6-5	215	1-23-76	1994	Mobile, Ala.
Haltiwanger, Garrick	.273	4	11	1	3	0	0	1	2	1	1	0	0	R	L	6-2	190	3-3-75	1996	Irmo, S.C.
Huff, B.J.	.249	57	205	26	51	9	1	7	32	19	46	9	2	R	R	6-1	195	8-1-75	1996	Chandler, Ind.
Lopez, Jose	.145	20	55	2	8	2	0	0	6	2	24	2	1	R	R	6-1	175	8-4-75	1994	Haverstraw, N.Y.
Mashore, Justin	.214	13	42	4	9	2	0	1	3	0	13	1	0	R	R	5-9	190	2-14-72	1991	Concord, Calif.
2-team (5 Trenton)	.259	18	58	7	15	4	2	1	8	1	17	2	0							

Organization Statistics

BATTING

	AVG	G	AB	R	H	2B	3B	HR	RBI	BB	SO	SB	CS	B	T	HT	WT	DOB	1st Yr	Resides
Meggers, Mike	.161	18	56	6	9	4	0	1	6	7	29	0	0	R	R	6-2	200	7-6-70	1992	Sacramento, Calif.
Neubart, Garrett	.288	83	260	36	75	14	4	3	21	22	40	17	5	R	R	5-10	160	11-7-73	1995	Livingston, N.J.
Phillips, Jason	.227	39	141	13	32	5	0	7	23	13	20	0	0	R	R	6-1	171	9-27-76	1997	El Cajon, Calif.
Rodriguez, Sammy	.227	69	203	15	46	10	0	3	24	21	49	2	3	R	R	5-9	185	8-20-75	1995	New York, N.Y.
Sanchez, Yuri	.231	116	381	43	88	10	1	5	30	37	135	6	5	L	R	6-1	165	11-11-73	1992	Lynn, Mass.
Stoffels, Alex	.000	3	8	0	0	0	0	0	0	2	4	0	0	R	R	5-10	190	6-12-77	1998	San Bernardino, Calif.
Tamargo, John	.215	112	363	27	78	13	3	4	37	40	55	7	5	S	R	5-9	172	5-3-75	1996	Tampa, Fla.
Toca, Jorge	.308	75	279	60	86	15	1	20	67	32	43	5	5	R	R	6-3	220	1-7-75	1999	Los Angeles, Calif.
Tyner, Jason	.313	129	518	91	162	19	5	0	33	62	46	49	16	L	L	6-1	170	4-23-77	1998	Beaumont, Texas
Valera, Yohanny	.289	57	204	33	59	14	3	9	39	17	57	2	1	R	R	6-1	196	8-17-76	1993	San Cristobal, D.R.
Zamora, Junior	.239	67	255	28	61	17	0	10	33	12	62	2	1	R	R	6-2	195	5-3-76	1994	San Pedro de Macoris, D.R.

PITCHING

	W	L	ERA	G	GS	CG	SV	IP	H	R	ER	BB	SO	B	T	HT	WT	DOB	1st Yr	Resides
Arteaga, J.D.	3	1	5.72	11	3	0	0	28	32	21	18	14	24	L	L	6-3	220	8-2-74	1997	Miami, Fla.
Bohannon, Gary	0	0	49.50	2	0	0	0	2	12	13	11	3	0	R	R	6-4	175	2-19-76	1998	Harrison, Tenn.
Brittan, Corey	2	4	2.78	54	0	0	7	91	84	36	28	23	60	R	R	6-6	195	2-23-75	1996	Scott City, Kan.
Cammack, Eric	4	2	2.38	45	0	0	15	57	28	17	15	38	83	R	R	6-1	175	8-14-75	1997	Port Neches, Texas
Corey, Mark	7	13	5.40	29	27	0	0	155	175	108	93	64	111	R	R	6-2	220	11-16-74	1995	Austin, Pa.
Della Ratta, Pete	1	4	2.18	41	3	0	0	83	75	22	20	13	68	R	R	6-4	200	2-14-74	1996	Gulf Breeze, Fla.
Franco, John	0	0	0.00	1	1	0	0	1	0	0	0	0	1	L	L	5-10	185	9-17-60	1981	Staten Island, N.Y.
Hafer, Jeff	0	2	3.14	7	0	0	0	14	12	5	5	0	9	R	R	6-1	185	10-27-74	1996	Springfield, Va.
Henderson, Ryan	0	2	7.04	5	2	0	0	8	9	6	6	6	8	R	R	6-1	190	9-30-69	1992	Dana Point, Calif.
Herbison, Brett	5	13	5.85	27	26	1	0	149	161	115	97	81	60	R	R	6-5	180	6-13-77	1995	Elgin, Ill.
Jones, Bobby	1	2	3.86	3	3	0	0	12	11	5	5	5	12	R	R	6-4	216	2-10-70	1991	Fresno, Calif.
Lopez, Johan	0	0	13.50	2	0	0	0	2	3	3	3	3	1	R	R	6-2	200	4-4-75	1992	Yaracuy, Venez.
Lyons, Mike	4	7	3.40	53	0	0	5	79	76	41	30	37	70	R	R	6-3	195	5-20-75	1996	Altamonte Springs, Fla.
McCrary, Scott	1	5	4.86	17	6	0	0	54	72	34	29	21	29	R	R	6-4	204	1-8-74	1997	Vacaville, Calif.
McEntire, Ethan	0	2	13.17	4	3	0	0	14	26	23	20	8	7	L	L	6-1	194	7-19-75	1993	Clarkesville, Ga.
McMichael, Greg	0	0	0.00	2	2	0	0	3	2	1	0	1	5	R	R	6-3	222	12-1-66	1988	Alpharetta, Ga.
Pontes, Dan	3	1	5.01	19	0	0	1	32	29	18	18	15	37	R	R	6-3	200	4-27-71	1993	Geneva, N.Y.
Pumphrey, Ken	6	9	4.80	25	23	0	0	131	146	95	70	71	84	R	R	6-6	208	9-10-76	1994	Glen Burnie, Md.
Reed, Rick	0	0	1.80	1	1	0	0	5	1	1	1	1	5	R	R	6-1	195	8-16-65	1986	Huntington, W.Va.
Roberts, Grant	7	6	4.87	23	23	0	0	131	135	81	71	49	94	R	R	6-3	205	9-13-77	1995	El Cajon, Calif.
Ruebel, Matt	2	0	2.73	6	5	0	0	26	24	13	8	8	25	L	L	6-2	180	10-16-69	1991	Oklahoma City, Okla.
Short, Barry	0	7	3.48	24	0	0	0	41	43	29	16	16	22	R	R	6-3	182	12-15-73	1994	Mansfield, Mo.
Stewart, Scott	1	0	0.00	1	1	0	0	5	3	0	0	5	2	R	L	6-2	224	8-14-75	1994	Stanley, N.C.
Turrentine, Rich	0	2	4.66	17	0	0	0	19	20	13	10	20	16	R	R	6-0	220	5-21-71	1989	Texarkana, Ark.
Vasquez, Leo	1	2	3.83	27	0	0	1	42	39	18	18	23	45	L	L	6-4	196	7-1-73	1996	La Romana, D.R.
Walker, Tyler	6	4	6.22	13	13	0	0	68	78	49	47	32	59	R	R	6-3	250	5-15-76	1997	Ross, Calif.

FIELDING

Catcher	PCT	G	PO	A	E	DP	PB
Bennett	.800	1	4	0	1	0	0
Phillips	.984	38	271	28	5	1	0
Rodriguez	.992	59	325	34	3	5	2
Stoffels	.923	1	12	0	1	0	0
Valera	.967	55	363	46	14	3	5

First Base	PCT	G	PO	A	E	DP
Dubose	1.000	5	41	2	0	5
Gainey	.986	120	1004	90	16	86
Meggers	.935	3	27	2	2	2
Toca	.994	22	158	13	1	19
Valera	1.000	1	4	1	0	0

Second Base	PCT	G	PO	A	E	DP
Bruce	.963	112	255	343	23	74

	PCT	G	PO	A	E	DP
Mashore	.000	1	0	0	1	0
Tamargo	.953	34	62	101	8	20

Third Base	PCT	G	PO	A	E	DP
Bruce	.979	17	17	30	1	4
Darden	.939	18	10	36	3	4
Jos. Lopez	.684	7	1	12	6	1
Tamargo	.883	43	25	81	14	7
Toca	1.000	2	2	1	0	0
Zamora	.926	62	47	127	14	9

Shortstop	PCT	G	PO	A	E	DP
Sanchez	.937	114	150	284	29	56
Tamargo	.932	33	45	79	9	19
Zamora	.900	5	12	15	3	6

Outfield	PCT	G	PO	A	E	DP
Beamon	.947	55	106	1	6	0
Bruce	1.000	3	3	0	0	0
Buccheri	1.000	3	8	0	0	0
Darden	1.000	3	7	0	0	0
Dina	.981	48	103	3	2	1
Dubose	1.000	4	5	0	0	0
Haltiwanger	.923	4	12	0	1	0
Huff	.969	55	89	5	3	1
Jos. Lopez	.889	9	8	0	1	0
Mashore	1.000	12	25	3	0	1
Meggers	.917	7	10	1	1	0
Neubart	1.000	65	114	11	0	2
Toca	.961	49	91	8	4	0
Tyner	.993	127	255	11	2	2

ST. LUCIE — Class A

FLORIDA STATE LEAGUE

BATTING

	AVG	G	AB	R	H	2B	3B	HR	RBI	BB	SO	SB	CS	B	T	HT	WT	DOB	1st Yr	Resides
Bennett, Ryan	.224	56	165	19	37	4	0	0	12	9	32	2	1	R	R	6-0	195	7-26-74	1996	Waukegan, Ill.
Burns, Pat	.238	133	488	54	116	26	2	6	54	50	122	6	3	S	L	6-1	185	9-16-77	1996	Denton, Texas
Chavez, Endy	.311	45	183	33	57	8	3	2	18	22	22	9	3	L	L	6-0	170	2-7-78	1996	Valencia, Venez.
Copeland, Brandon	.128	16	39	3	5	1	0	1	4	4	18	2	0	R	R	6-0	205	3-31-77	1996	Topeka, Kan.
Dina, Allen	.344	85	343	65	118	16	4	12	47	25	54	34	10	R	R	5-10	180	9-28-73	1996	Stratford, Conn.
Escobar, Alex	.667	1	3	1	2	0	0	1	3	1	1	1	1	R	R	6-1	185	9-6-78	1996	Valencia, Venez.
Haltiwanger, Garrick	.265	111	423	67	112	18	6	10	71	31	77	20	12	R	L	6-2	190	3-3-76	1996	Irmo, S.C.
Johnson, Tom	.256	56	199	25	51	12	0	1	10	21	57	12	5	R	R	6-5	193	1-25-76	1996	Elizabeth, N.J.
Mashore, Justin	.212	28	104	13	22	4	2	1	10	7	25	1	4	R	R	5-9	190	2-14-72	1991	Concord, Calif.
2-team (17 Sarasota)	.196	45	153	19	30	7	2	3	14	12	38	2	4							
McGrath, Sean	.222	35	72	7	16	1	0	0	6	3	17	0	0	R	R	6-0	202	4-4-76	1997	North Adams, Mass.
Mento, Alfredo	.000	1	1	0	0	0	0	0	0	0	1	0	0	R	R	6-1	175	2-21-78	1995	La Romana, D.R.
Miller, Kenny	.237	93	304	32	72	13	1	3	24	18	50	3	5	R	R	5-11	170	6-25-76	1997	Joliet, Ill.
Moreno, Juan	.300	120	424	64	127	18	5	4	47	51	70	28	11	R	R	6-2	175	3-19-76	1993	Monte Plata, D.R.
Patton, Cory	.077	9	13	3	1	0	0	0	0	3	8	0	0	R	R	6-2	189	10-18-75	1996	Harrisburg, Ill.
Payton, Jay	.346	7	26	3	9	1	1	0	3	4	5	0	1	R	R	5-10	185	11-22-72	1994	Zanesville, Ohio
Perez, Jersen	.256	128	468	60	120	15	7	7	45	27	117	7	5	R	R	5-8	178	1-20-76	1996	Lynn, Mass.
Phillips, Jason	.258	81	283	36	73	12	1	9	48	23	28	0	0	R	R	6-1	171	9-27-76	1997	El Cajon, Calif.
Ramos, Kelly	.188	24	80	6	15	3	1	2	11	8	16	0	0	S	R	6-0	168	10-15-76	1994	San Pedro de Macoris, D.R.
Roach, Jason	.215	115	409	51	88	21	0	15	62	30	122	6	0	R	R	6-4	188	4-20-76	1997	Kinston, N.C.
Stanton, Tom	.171	37	82	10	14	6	1	2	5	12	38	1	1	L	R	6-0	208	2-3-76	1996	Middleburg, Fla.
Tomberlin, Andy	.379	9	29	4	11	0	1	4	4	8	2	0	1	L	L	5-11	185	11-7-66	1986	Monroe, N.C.
Wigginton, Ty	.292	123	456	69	133	23	5	21	73	56	82	9	12	R	R	6-0	190	10-11-77	1998	Chula Vista, Calif.

GAMES BY POSITION: C—Bennett 46, Phillips 68, Ramos 24, Stanton 8. 1B—Burns 125, McGrath 1, Roach 13, Tomberlin 3. 2B—McGrath

15, Perez 13, Wigginton 118. **3B**—McGrath 6, Miller 45, Roach 94. **SS**—McGrath 12, Miller 33, Perez 106. **OF**—Chavez 39, Copeland 12, Dina 84, Escobar 1, Haltiwanger 90, Johnson 51, Mashore 27, Moreno 98, Patton 7, Payton 7, Roach 6, Tomberlin 5.

PITCHING	W	L	ERA	G	GS	CG	SV	IP	H	R	ER	BB	SO	B	T	HT	WT	DOB	1st Yr	Resides
Arteaga, J.D.	0	1	3.60	1	1	0	0	5	3	2	2	2	0	L	L	6-3	220	8-2-74	1997	Miami, Fla.
Barry, Shawn	3	4	6.99	46	0	0	0	37	35	33	29	46	40	L	L	6-3	205	7-15-74	1997	Colchester, Conn.
Berger, Craig	1	3	4.89	36	0	0	9	39	49	22	21	25	21	R	R	6-4	210	10-20-75	1997	Orefield, Pa.
Bohannon, Gary	6	6	4.42	32	12	1	2	108	131	66	53	30	58	R	R	6-4	175	2-19-76	1998	Harrison, Tenn.
Brea, Lesli	1	7	3.73	32	18	0	3	121	95	64	50	48	136	R	R	5-11	170	10-12-78	1996	Santo Domingo, D.R.
Cerros, Juan	2	0	0.00	5	0	0	0	8	5	1	0	4	6	R	R	6-1	203	9-25-76	1999	Nuevo Leon, Mexico
Cutchins, Todd	6	7	3.96	25	25	1	0	130	127	68	57	82	106	R	L	6-0	190	7-14-75	1996	Westlake, La.
Gaskill, Derek	2	0	8.04	22	0	0	0	28	34	30	25	24	28	R	R	6-6	191	5-6-74	1992	Chesapeake, Va.
German, Yon	1	7	5.40	10	9	0	0	55	67	41	33	21	40	L	L	5-11	155	2-28-78	1995	Bani, D.R.
Gonzalez, Dicky	14	9	2.83	25	25	3	0	169	156	66	53	30	143	R	R	5-11	170	10-21-78	1996	Bayamon, P.R.
Hafer, Jeff	4	2	3.22	36	2	0	5	67	74	43	24	16	51	R	R	6-1	185	10-27-74	1996	Springfield, N.J.
Kessel, Kyle	1	2	4.63	8	8	0	0	35	35	22	18	16	24	R	L	6-0	160	6-2-76	1994	Mundelein, Ill.
Lohrman, Dave	4	0	3.08	43	1	0	0	76	64	33	26	46	75	R	R	6-6	205	9-16-75	1997	East Amherst, N.Y.
McEntire, Ethan	8	10	3.84	22	21	0	0	129	130	68	55	62	63	L	L	6-1	194	7-19-75	1993	Clarkesville, Ga.
Pontes, Dan	0	0	2.70	4	0	0	0	7	7	2	2	7	2	R	R	6-3	200	4-27-71	1993	Geneva, N.Y.
Riggan, Jerrod	5	5	3.33	44	0	0	12	73	69	33	27	24	66	R	R	6-4	185	5-16-74	1996	Brewster, Wash.
Seo, Jae	2	0	1.84	3	3	0	0	15	8	3	3	2	14	R	R	6-1	215	5-24-77	1997	La Canada, Calif.
Short, Barry	2	2	4.32	10	0	0	0	17	19	8	8	4	9	R	R	6-3	182	12-15-73	1994	Mansfield, Mo.
Tam, Jeff	0	0	3.38	2	0	0	0	3	4	1	1	0	3	R	R	6-1	202	8-19-70	1993	Melbourne, Fla.
Walker, Tyler	6	5	2.94	13	13	2	0	80	64	31	26	29	64	R	R	6-3	250	5-15-76	1997	Ross, Calif.

CAPITAL CITY — Class A

SOUTH ATLANTIC LEAGUE

BATTING	AVG	G	AB	R	H	2B	3B	HR	RBI	BB	SO	SB	CS	B	T	HT	WT	DOB	1st Yr	Resides
Brett, Jason	.242	32	95	11	23	3	0	0	1	12	25	4	2	R	R	6-0	167	4-28-77	1997	Perry, Ga.
Chavez, Endy	.253	73	253	40	64	8	1	0	15	34	36	20	12	L	L	6-0	170	2-7-78	1996	Valencia, Venez.
Cole, Brian	.316	125	500	97	158	41	4	18	71	37	77	50	16	R	R	5-9	168	3-28-78	1998	Meridian, Miss.
Copeland, Brandon	.198	33	101	14	20	4	0	5	17	15	39	5	1	R	R	6-0	205	3-31-77	1996	Topeka, Kan.
Erickson, Corey	.236	129	424	64	100	21	1	23	57	46	120	9	3	R	R	5-11	190	1-10-77	1995	Springfield, Ill.
Hill, Bobby	.245	86	278	31	68	12	3	3	14	16	57	12	3	L	R	5-9	160	6-25-79	1997	Waldo, Fla.
Jenkins, Brian	.290	107	400	69	116	15	7	20	79	30	69	19	7	R	R	5-11	195	10-11-78	1997	Port St. Joe, Fla.
Lebron, Francisco	.222	10	36	4	8	0	0	2	2	6	9	0	0	R	R	6-6	220	5-10-75	1999	Bayamon, P.R.
Malinowski, Scott	.208	100	313	30	65	2	2	1	20	15	51	3	3	L	R	6-2	170	9-23-76	1998	Joliet, Ill.
Martin, Billy	.236	64	220	38	52	19	1	8	30	24	82	1	1	R	R	6-2	205	6-10-76	1998	Abilene, Texas
McGrath, Sean	.179	30	95	13	17	6	1	0	13	1	31	0	0	R	R	6-0	202	4-4-76	1997	North Adams, Mass.
Mento, Alfredo	.333	3	12	5	4	1	0	0	2	0	2	2	0	R	R	6-1	175	2-21-78	1995	La Romana, D.R.
Mulvehill, Chase	.286	116	427	65	122	23	6	9	58	29	97	29	13	R	R	6-2	185	2-24-78	1996	Pell City, Ala.
Ramos, Kelly	.256	82	262	31	67	14	0	10	34	9	52	4	2	S	R	6-0	168	10-15-76	1994	San Pedro de Macoris, D.R.
Ribaudo, Mike	.246	58	199	22	49	12	0	7	33	4	53	0	1	R	R	6-2	170	7-19-75	1995	Sarasota, Fla.
Smith, Ryan	.000	1	3	0	0	0	0	0	0	0	1	0	0	R	R	5-10	180	6-20-79	1998	Mobile, Ala.
Snyder, Earl	.267	136	486	73	130	25	4	28	97	55	117	2	2	R	R	6-0	195	5-6-76	1998	Plainville, Conn.
Stratton, Robert	.274	95	318	58	87	17	3	21	60	48	112	7	1	R	R	6-2	220	10-7-77	1996	Santa Barbara, Calif.
Thompson, Andrew	.227	61	185	14	42	11	0	0	17	22	45	0	0	L	R	6-1	225	1-26-74	1999	Cleveland, Tenn.
Velazquez, Gil	.227	21	75	9	17	4	1	0	6	3	14	0	0	R	R	6-2	170	10-17-79	1998	South Gate, Calif.

GAMES BY POSITION: C—Ramos 75, Ribaudo 39, Smith 1, Thompson 37. **1B**—Jenkins 6, Lebron 9, Martin 3, McGrath 6, Snyder 126. **2B**—Brett 8, Erickson 126, Malinowski 6, McGrath 8. **3B**—Brett 2, Erickson 2, Hill 9, Malinowski 68, Martin 56, McGrath 11, Snyder 9. **SS**—Brett 20, Hill 76, Malinowski 27, McGrath 4, Velazquez 21. **OF**—Chavez 72, Cole 118, Copeland 21, Jenkins 70, Malinowski 1, Martin 1, Mento 3, Mulvehill 108, Ribaudo 1, Stratton 52.

PITCHING	W	L	ERA	G	GS	CG	SV	IP	H	R	ER	BB	SO	B	T	HT	WT	DOB	1st Yr	Resides
Behn, Brendan	0	0	36.00	1	0	0	0	1	4	4	4	1	1	L	L	6-1	212	10-10-75	1997	Merced, Calif.
Bell, Heath	1	7	2.60	55	0	0	25	62	47	23	18	17	68	R	R	6-2	225	9-29-77	1998	Tustin, Calif.
Bellhorn, Todd	4	4	4.30	38	0	0	0	59	55	38	28	32	46	R	L	6-0	210	10-13-76	1998	Oviedo, Fla.
Carr, Tim	6	4	1.58	45	0	0	0	68	58	18	12	20	64	R	R	6-5	195	2-26-77	1998	Danville, Va.
Cook, Andy	12	7	2.83	27	26	0	1	150	150	66	47	42	124	R	R	6-5	195	2-26-77	1998	Danville, Va.
Corcoran, Tim	0	3	4.44	40	3	0	3	75	62	43	37	41	89	R	R	6-2	195	4-15-78	1997	Slaughter, La.
Gaskill, Derek	2	1	3.10	12	0	0	0	20	13	7	7	9	23	R	R	6-6	191	5-6-74	1992	Chesapeake, Va.
German, Yon	8	2	2.26	14	14	0	0	88	82	33	22	15	68	L	L	5-11	155	2-28-78	1995	Bani, D.R.
Gorman, Pat	1	1	11.78	15	0	0	0	18	28	27	24	19	19	R	R	6-2	222	8-16-77	1997	Valley Cottage, N.Y.
Heffernan, Greg	0	0	5.14	5	0	0	0	7	7	8	4	5	5	R	R	6-2	180	9-18-74	1996	Guelph, Ontario
Jackson, Jeremy	1	0	1.61	5	4	0	0	28	22	5	5	3	26	L	L	6-4	205	6-4-76	1998	Meridian, Miss.
2-team (19 Char., W.Va.)	5	5	3.69	24	17	0	0	110	104	57	45	33	91							
Lowe, Matt	0	0	9.00	1	0	0	0	2	3	2	2	0	2	R	R	6-4	220	4-3-79	1997	Walhalla, S.C.
Maness, Nick	5	6	4.95	23	22	0	0	107	92	74	59	57	99	R	R	6-4	195	10-17-78	1997	Robbins, N.C.
Mattson, John	0	0	9.00	1	0	0	0	3	6	3	3	2	2	R	R	6-4	205	10-1-76	1997	Port Orchard, Wash.
Ochoa, Pablo	0	0	0.00	3	0	0	1	6	2	0	0	1	4	R	R	6-0	185	10-21-75	1996	Nuevo Leon, Mexico
Prokop, Michael	5	2	3.83	37	0	0	4	40	51	21	17	17	28	R	R	6-1	190	1-28-78	1998	Kennesaw, Ga.
Saenz, Jason	10	8	5.44	27	27	0	0	134	147	89	81	68	125	L	L	6-2	185	2-13-77	1998	Santa Ana, Calif.
Santana, Humberto	3	1	3.24	10	2	0	1	25	19	12	9	4	19	L	L	5-11	175	3-25-77	1995	Espaillat Province, D.R.
Strange, Pat	12	5	2.63	28	21	2	1	154	138	57	45	29	113	R	R	6-5	240	8-23-80	1998	Springfield, Mass.
Vega, Rene	11	7	3.14	29	22	1	1	146	101	57	51	50	148	L	L	5-11	185	8-4-76	1998	Mobile, Ala.
Viole, Paul	0	0	0.00	2	0	0	0	2	1	1	0	2	1	R	R	5-10	510	11-12-77	1999	Demarest, N.J.
Weslowski, Robert	1	0	6.45	9	0	0	0	22	22	18	16	13	21	R	R	6-2	165	9-23-78	1997	Marcellus, N.Y.

PITTSFIELD — Short-Season Class A

NEW YORK-PENN LEAGUE

BATTING	AVG	G	AB	R	H	2B	3B	HR	RBI	BB	SO	SB	CS	B	T	HT	WT	DOB	1st Yr	Resides
Acuna, Ronald	.225	22	71	7	16	3	0	0	6	8	26	8	6	R	R	5-11	175	6-30-79	1996	Gustiro, Venez.

Organization Statistics

BATTING	AVG	G	AB	R	H	2B	3B	HR	RBI	BB	SO	SB	CS	B	T	HT	WT	DOB	1st Yr	Resides
Brett, Jason	.211	42	109	20	23	3	0	0	7	10	20	12	2	R	R	6-0	167	4-28-77	1997	Perry, Ga.
Deschenes, Pat	.313	5	16	7	5	0	0	1	3	4	2	0	0	L	R	6-0	200	4-26-78	1999	Quebec City, Quebec
Dyer, Matt	.500	2	4	0	2	0	0	0	2	0	1	0	0	R	R	6-2	200	1-6-77	1999	North Manchester, Ind.
Elzy, Steve	.244	40	131	16	32	10	1	0	18	9	15	2	0	R	R	6-0	185	1-6-78	1999	Douglas, Ariz.
Johnson, Tony	.202	63	178	31	36	8	4	5	28	39	59	14	2	S	R	5-10	189	10-11-77	1996	Oakland, Calif.
Lebron, Francisco	.289	75	266	46	77	17	0	9	43	46	53	6	1	R	R	6-6	220	5-10-75	1999	Bayamon, P.R.
Lopez, Sam	.429	2	7	0	3	0	0	0	0	0	3	0	0	R	R	6-0	180	12-11-77	1999	Dinuba, Calif.
Ludvigsen, Marc	.220	30	100	11	22	5	1	2	13	5	43	0	1	L	L	6-4	215	5-2-77	1998	Statesville, N.C.
Meadows, Mike	.261	48	134	23	35	10	0	5	24	21	57	3	0	R	R	6-1	185	10-19-78	1996	Sanford, Fla.
Mento, Alfredo	.251	72	275	42	69	12	3	2	23	24	55	24	11	R	R	6-1	175	2-21-78	1995	La Romana, D.R.
Mize, Matt	.263	69	281	32	74	15	2	3	27	22	78	22	7	S	R	5-10	190	5-11-77	1999	Austin, Texas
Nye, Rodney	.306	70	255	45	78	30	2	7	48	32	36	10	4	R	R	6-4	212	12-2-76	1999	Cameron, Okla.
Shipp, Brian	.238	65	240	25	57	10	4	1	19	18	56	8	6	R	R	6-2	195	8-15-78	1999	Zachary, La.
Smith, Ryan	.143	12	35	1	5	0	0	1	5	0	5	0	0	R	R	5-10	180	6-20-79	1998	Mobile, Ala.
Stockam, Travis	.219	41	128	19	28	4	1	4	19	8	32	1	3	R	R	6-3	205	5-11-76	1998	Joplin, Mo.
Stoffels, Alex	.114	26	70	5	8	1	0	0	9	6	19	6	2	R	R	5-10	190	6-12-77	1998	San Bernardino, Calif.
Wright, Brad	.258	63	236	38	61	9	3	1	23	18	31	9	4	L	L	6-1	205	9-11-75	1999	San Marcos, Calif.

GAMES BY POSITION: C—Dyer 2, Elzy 38, Smith 12, Stockam 12, Stoffels 26. 1B—Lebron 60, Ludvigsen 1, Meadows 5, Wright 14. 2B—Brett 20, Lopez 2, Mize 58. 3B—Meadows 13, Nye 65, Shipp 2. SS—Brett 17, Shipp 64. OF—Acuna 22, Johnson 57, Lebron 5, Ludvigsen 23, Meadows 12, Mento 70, Mize 9, Wright 47.

PITCHING	W	L	ERA	G	GS	CG	SV	IP	H	R	ER	BB	SO	B	T	HT	WT	DOB	1st Yr	Resides
Behn, Brendan	2	2	3.15	15	1	0	1	40	39	18	14	11	39	L	L	6-1	212	10-10-75	1997	Merced, Calif.
Encarnacion, Orlando	3	6	4.81	15	15	0	0	86	102	51	46	13	61	R	R	6-0	202	3-1-79	1997	Bronx, N.Y.
Gorman, Pat	3	2	3.21	19	0	0	1	34	30	17	12	20	40	R	R	6-2	185	8-16-77	1997	Valley Cottage, N.Y.
Hawkins, Barry	1	2	3.86	16	0	0	0	37	39	20	16	12	24	R	R	6-5	230	5-16-77	1998	Laguna Niguel, Calif.
Hendricks, John	5	4	3.04	15	14	0	0	80	78	38	27	19	64	L	L	6-1	200	8-6-77	1999	Winston-Salem, N.C.
Joseph, Jake	3	2	2.91	11	6	0	1	43	35	19	14	27	26	R	R	6-1	205	1-24-78	1999	Sacramento, Calif.
Lowe, Matt	3	5	4.57	16	11	0	2	69	67	42	35	37	33	R	R	6-4	220	4-3-79	1997	Walhalla, S.C.
Mattson, John	1	3	9.00	11	0	0	0	18	32	20	18	10	20	R	R	6-4	205	10-1-76	1997	Port Orchard, Wash.
McCarter, Jason	4	0	3.34	21	0	0	2	35	33	17	13	25	36	R	R	6-3	210	9-26-76	1996	Seaside, Calif.
Queen, Mike	3	3	3.26	15	15	0	0	77	68	33	28	24	69	L	L	6-4	220	12-5-77	1996	Gravette, Ark.
Santana, Humberto	1	0	0.00	4	0	0	0	9	7	2	0	2	12	L	L	5-11	175	3-25-77	1995	Provincia Espaillat, D.R.
Terry, Mike	2	1	5.34	18	0	0	1	32	33	19	19	14	24	L	L	6-4	210	1-5-76	1999	Tulsa, Okla.
Viole, Paul	3	0	0.00	18	0	0	11	23	7	0	0	7	28	R	R	5-11	190	11-12-77	1999	Demarest, N.J.
Weslowski, Robert	4	4	3.33	14	14	0	0	84	79	35	31	22	62	R	R	6-2	165	9-23-78	1997	Marcellus, N.Y.
Williamson, Brian	1	1	4.91	6	0	0	1	7	6	5	4	4	2	R	R	6-2	185	1-6-77	1999	San Luis Obispo, Calif.

KINGSPORT — Rookie

APPALACHIAN LEAGUE

BATTING	AVG	G	AB	R	H	2B	3B	HR	RBI	BB	SO	SB	CS	B	T	HT	WT	DOB	1st Yr	Resides
Abreu, David	.438	5	16	5	7	0	0	0	1	8	2	3	1	S	R	6-0	160	6-28-79	1996	San Pedro de Macoris, D.R.
Acuna, Ronald, Nell	.285	38	123	26	35	8	0	1	24	14	32	15	5	R	R	5-11	175	6-30-79	1996	Gustiro, Venez.
Alvarez, Nell	.270	53	159	32	43	5	2	7	27	17	43	9	7	R	R	6-0	175	9-27-78	1997	Orangeburg, N.Y.
Brazell, Craig	.385	59	221	27	85	16	1	6	39	7	34	6	5	L	R	6-3	185	5-10-80	1998	Montgomery, Ala.
Ciarrachi, Kevin	.000	2	1	0	0	0	0	0	0	0	1	0	0	R	R	6-1	195	3-27-78	1999	Lombard, Ill.
De la Cruz, Ruddi	.225	54	160	30	36	6	2	2	12	25	47	10	5	R	R	6-0	165	11-2-79	1997	San Pedro de Macoris, D.R.
Deschenes, Pat	.377	40	151	30	57	8	3	3	30	25	18	6	2	L	R	6-0	200	4-26-78	1999	Quebec City, Quebec
Dyer, Matt	.200	22	40	2	8	2	0	0	3	3	10	0	0	R	R	6-2	200	1-6-77	1999	North Manchester, Ind.
Fafard, Mathias	.353	9	17	4	6	1	0	1	6	1	3	0	0	R	R	6-1	190	12-21-76	1997	Cocoa, Fla.
Guyton, Eric	.263	59	186	17	49	11	1	2	28	11	39	6	1	R	R	6-3	210	1-7-77	1999	Hagerstown, Md.
Hernandez, Carlos	.000	5	4	1	0	0	0	0	0	1	2	0	0	R	R	6-1	170	3-2-79	1998	Juarez, Mexico
Hunter, David	.250	19	32	5	8	1	0	2	4	2	10	0	0	L	L	6-5	210	5-26-80	1998	Delano, Calif.
Lugo, Roberto	.179	25	39	5	7	1	0	1	4	2	8	0	0	L	L	6-3	200	3-7-80	1998	San Sebastian, P.R.
O'Sullivan, Sean	.267	51	161	22	43	8	0	4	23	10	42	4	2	R	R	6-3	220	3-22-77	1999	Rockford, Ill.
Redman, Prentice	.295	58	200	40	59	14	1	6	29	24	42	16	11	R	R	6-3	185	8-23-79	1999	Duncanville, Ala.
Seale, Marvin	.233	63	210	46	49	7	3	2	20	24	75	22	4	S	R	6-0	190	6-16-79	1998	Durango, Colo.
Smith, Ryan	.186	31	86	8	16	2	1	0	9	7	20	1	1	R	R	5-10	180	6-20-79	1998	Mobile, Ala.
Velazquez, Gil	.262	62	225	24	59	8	0	1	19	19	43	4	1	R	R	6-2	170	10-17-79	1998	South Gate, Calif.
Yancy, Michael	.284	65	215	36	61	6	3	2	29	15	50	24	7	R	R	5-11	180	3-26-79	1997	San Diego, Calif.
Zaragoza, Anthony	.155	36	84	8	13	2	1	0	3	15	27	4	2	R	R	5-10	185	4-18-73	1996	Boise, Idaho
Zardis, Alex	.116	33	43	10	5	4	0	0	3	7	18	0	3	R	R	6-3	190	2-17-78	1998	Seattle, Wash.

GAMES BY POSITION: C—Alvarez 42, Dyer 21, R. Smith 27. 1B—Alvarez 3, Brazell 30, Deschenes 25, Guyton 6, Hunter 18, Lugo 20, O'Sullivan 1, Redman 1. 2B—Abreu 5, de la Cruz 48, Fafard 2, Guyton 1, Hernandez 1, Velazquez 3, Zaragoza 26, Zardis 5. 3B—Deschenes 14, Fafard 6, Guyton 51, Hernandez 3, Velazquez 1, Zaragoza 1, Zardis 17. SS—de la Cruz 7, Velazquez 59, Zaragoza 9. OF—Acuna 35, Deschenes 5, Fafard 1, O'Sullivan 16, Redman 48, Seale 57, Yancy 59.

PITCHING	W	L	ERA	G	GS	CG	SV	IP	H	R	ER	BB	SO	B	T	HT	WT	DOB	1st Yr	Resides
Brown, Graeme	4	3	3.50	18	3	0	1	46	47	24	18	19	46	R	R	6-4	216	12-30-77	1999	Avon, Conn.
Chenard, Ken	6	3	3.07	14	13	1	0	76	64	32	26	25	80	R	R	6-3	175	8-30-78	1995	Victorville, Calif.
Chivers, Jason	3	1	4.26	20	1	0	0	25	29	18	12	29	30	L	L	6-6	235	12-19-78	1997	Lancaster, Calif.
Gomez, Rafael	3	3	4.66	25	0	0	4	37	35	21	19	20	23	R	R	6-1	180	9-18-77	1995	Cabral, D.R.
Graham, Frank	3	3	3.71	14	14	0	0	80	69	42	33	33	79	R	R	6-2	180	8-7-78	1998	Johnstown, Ohio
Griffiths, Jeremy	3	5	3.30	14	14	1	0	76	68	40	28	36	74	R	R	6-7	233	3-22-78	1999	Avon Lakes, Ohio
Hee, Aaron	0	4	7.58	12	12	0	0	49	64	48	41	37	38	L	L	6-0	175	3-4-79	1998	Las Vegas, Nev.
James, Nick	0	0	0.00	2	0	0	0	1	1	0	0	1	2	S	R	6-2	185	4-21-78	1999	South Portland, Maine
Mikkola, Shaun	0	0	10.64	8	0	0	0	11	17	13	13	12	10	R	R	6-1	190	8-3-79	1997	Largo, Fla.
Nunez, Jose	3	4	3.75	13	13	0	0	70	75	36	29	15	63	L	L	6-2	165	3-14-79	1996	Montecristi, D.R.
Polk, Scott	4	5	3.19	23	0	0	4	48	32	24	17	30	70	R	R	6-2	220	8-25-76	1998	Ridgeland, Miss.
Rogers, Lionel	3	1	1.84	14	0	0	2	29	17	7	6	17	34	R	R	5-11	177	10-29-77	1999	Chowchilla, Calif.
Smith, Matt	1	1	10.88	18	0	0	0	24	33	35	29	20	28	R	R	6-5	230	8-14-78	1999	Godfrey, Ill.
Sweeney, Mike	3	1	5.64	19	0	0	1	30	34	20	19	11	20	R	R	6-3	205	4-24-77	1999	Keene, N.H.
Wheeler, David	0	0	4.00	7	0	0	0	9	10	9	4	6	8	R	R	6-2	185	2-11-76	1998	Spokane, Wash.

GULF COAST LEAGUE

BATTING	AVG	G	AB	R	H	2B	3B	HR	RBI	BB	SO	SB	CS	B	T	HT	WT	DOB	1st Yr	Resides
Abreu, David	.327	32	98	25	32	3	1	0	9	20	10	13	2	S	R	6-0	160	6-28-79	1996	San Pedro de Macoris, D.R.
Acuna, Ronald	.250	5	20	1	5	1	0	0	3	1	4	2	0	R	R	5-11	175	6-30-79	1996	Gustiro, Venez.
Arias, Leandro	.301	47	173	38	52	14	6	5	33	23	30	10	9	S	R	5-10	160	5-4-81	1998	Santo Domingo, D.R.
Bell, Josh	.222	31	90	14	20	0	0	0	7	11	27	4	3	R	R	5-10	175	12-15-79	1998	Loysville, Pa.
Brito, Justo	.219	43	128	18	28	4	0	3	20	15	26	0	1	R	R	5-11	180	1-26-79	1996	Santo Domingo, D.R.
Cruz, Enrique	.306	54	183	34	56	14	2	4	24	28	41	0	0	R	R	6-1	175	11-21-81	1998	Santo Domingo, D.R.
Deschenes, Pat	.380	24	79	16	30	3	0	1	12	15	8	4	2	L	R	6-0	200	4-26-78	1999	Quebec City, Quebec
Devanez, Noel	.286	44	147	31	42	8	1	4	26	15	41	2	2	R	R	6-0	175	12-24-81	1998	San Francisco de Macoris, D.R.
Dyer, Matt	.000	2	1	0	0	0	0	0	0	1	0	0	0	R	R	6-2	200	1-6-77	1999	North Manchester, Ind.
Escobar, Alex	.375	2	8	1	3	2	0	0	1	1	2	0	0	R	R	6-1	185	9-6-78	1996	Valencia, Venez.
Fafard, Mathias	.182	5	11	4	2	0	0	1	2	1	0	0	0	R	R	6-1	190	12-21-76	1997	Cocoa, Fla.
Garcia, Kenji	.083	32	72	9	6	2	0	1	6	17	46	0	0	R	R	6-4	215	7-29-80	1998	Caracas, Venez.
Hamn, Larnell	.117	32	60	6	7	2	0	0	4	3	22	0	2	R	R	6-0	180	11-21-79	1998	Triangle, Va.
Harris, Corey	.259	49	185	26	48	11	6	1	28	18	27	6	0	R	R	5-10	180	12-7-79	1999	Davenport, Iowa
Hunter, David	.220	25	82	12	18	2	1	0	8	5	26	1	1	L	L	6-5	210	5-26-80	1998	Delano, Calif.
Jacobs, Mike	.333	44	147	18	49	12	0	4	30	14	30	2	0	L	R	6-2	200	10-30-80	1999	Chula Vista, Calif.
Lawson, Forrest	.250	37	116	15	29	3	1	0	11	17	36	1	1	R	R	6-3	195	11-9-80	1999	Puyallup, Wash.
Lugo, Roberto	.286	14	21	1	6	2	0	0	2	1	3	0	1	L	L	6-3	200	3-7-80	1998	San Sebastian, P.R.
Lydon, Wayne	.183	37	60	13	11	3	0	0	5	7	13	0	1	R	R	6-3	190	4-17-81	1999	Jessup, Pa.
McIntyre, Robert	.304	32	102	18	31	2	0	0	15	15	19	7	2	R	R	5-10	170	12-8-80	1999	Tampa, Fla.
Osborn, Jason	.667	1	3	0	2	1	0	0	2	0	0	0	0	R	R	6-2	190	5-28-80	1998	Bellingham, Wash.
Perich, Josh	.272	47	158	24	43	5	1	0	22	20	37	6	2	R	R	6-4	210	11-15-79	1998	Allentown, Pa.
Reyes, Manuel	.182	11	22	3	4	0	0	0	3	1	5	0	0	R	R	5-11	180	10-25-79	1998	Cora, Venez.
Rosario, Vicente	.200	3	5	0	1	0	0	0	0	0	2	0	0	R	R	5-9	178	2-2-78	1997	New York, N.Y.

GAMES BY POSITION: C—Brito 41, Deschenes 1, Dyer 1, Jacobs 22, Lydon 1, Reyes 8. **1B**—Deschenes 6, Garcia 31, Hunter 25, Jacobs 4, Lugo 14, Reyes 1. **2B**—Abreu 10, Arias 45, Bell 9, Harris 1. **3B**—Abreu 13, Arias 1, Bell 20, Cruz 21, Deschenes 15, Fafard 3. **SS**—Abreu 2, Arias 1, Bell 2, Cruz 36, McIntyre 26. **OF**—Acuna 5, Devanez 39, Dyer 1, Escobar 1, Hamn 28, Harris 46, Lawson 34, Lydon 28, Osborn 1, Perich 37, Rosario 3.

PITCHING	W	L	ERA	G	GS	CG	SV	IP	H	R	ER	BB	SO	B	T	HT	WT	DOB	1st Yr	Resides
Arteaga, J.D.	0	0	6.75	2	1	0	0	4	4	3	3	0	3	L	L	6-3	220	8-2-74	1997	Miami, Fla.
Cabrera, Yunior	2	3	3.81	13	11	0	0	54	58	35	23	26	59	L	L	6-0	160	7-25-80	1996	San Pedro de Macoris, D.R.
Cole, Joey	5	1	4.41	13	8	0	0	51	52	30	25	23	55	L	R	6-7	235	9-15-77	1999	Nacogdoches, Texas
Gauger, Michael	2	0	3.30	18	0	0	3	30	27	17	11	8	30	L	L	6-2	215	12-24-76	1999	St. Marks, Fla.
Guerrero, Neftali	1	2	1.66	15	0	0	5	22	16	6	4	5	17	R	R	6-0	175	4-20-80	1997	Monte Plata, D.R.
Halvorson, Greg	1	2	3.86	5	3	0	0	21	22	14	9	9	20	R	R	6-4	225	1-17-77	1998	Tucson, Ariz.
Hopper, Josh	3	1	1.62	16	2	0	2	44	42	13	8	19	50	L	L	6-2	175	8-16-77	1999	Silver Creek, Ga.
Kessel, Kyle	0	1	3.38	3	3	0	0	8	5	4	3	2	11	R	L	6-0	160	6-2-76	1994	Mundelein, Ill.
Lopez, Jose	0	2	8.53	2	2	0	0	6	12	8	6	8	4	S	R	6-2	165	7-13-79	1998	Santo Domingo, D.R.
Lopez, Rafael	7	1	2.17	12	8	0	0	58	43	20	14	29	42	R	R	6-4	180	10-24-80	1997	Hato Mayor, D.R.
Mikkola, Shaun	1	0	4.13	5	4	0	0	24	28	14	11	15	9	R	R	6-1	190	8-3-79	1997	Largo, Fla.
Musser, Neal	2	1	2.01	8	7	0	0	31	26	13	7	18	22	L	L	6-2	185	8-25-80	1999	Otterbein, Ind.
Nichols, Brian	3	1	4.95	9	0	0	0	20	22	12	11	8	11	R	R	6-3	185	4-23-78	1999	Burbank, Calif.
Pepen, Robert	3	1	1.47	19	0	0	2	31	20	7	5	7	34	R	R	6-1	180	12-17-78	1996	Bani, D.R.
Pidgeon, Chip	0	0	10.38	4	0	0	0	4	5	6	5	6	4	R	L	6-5	250	12-26-78	1997	Shoreham, N.Y.
Roman, Orlando	6	0	2.36	12	11	1	0	61	41	20	16	21	64	R	R	6-2	185	11-28-78	1999	Vega Baja, P.R.
Santana, Humberto	1	0	0.00	2	0	0	0	3	0	0	0	0	2	L	L	5-11	175	3-25-77	1995	Espaillat Province, D.R.
Sawvell, Matt	0	0	6.30	8	0	0	0	10	14	7	7	4	13	R	L	5-10	175	11-21-76	1998	Wilton, Iowa
Sollenberger, Matt	1	5	3.58	18	0	0	2	28	30	16	11	6	27	R	L	6-2	185	1-26-77	1999	Kendallville, Ind.
Sweeney, Mike	1	0	0.00	1	0	0	0	2	1	0	0	0	2	R	R	6-3	205	4-24-77	1999	Keene, N.H.
Terry, Mike	0	0	0.00	2	0	0	1	2	1	0	0	0	0	L	L	6-4	210	1-5-76	1999	Tulsa, Okla.
Turrentine, Rich	0	0	1.13	5	0	0	0	8	4	2	1	2	7	R	R	6-0	220	5-21-71	1989	Texarkana, Ark.

OAKLAND ATHLETICS

BA's Organization of the Year enjoys glimpse of future

BY CASEY TEFERTILLER

It wasn't quite worst to first—more like worst to respectability. But a franchise that had been virtually given up for dead showed it is very much alive and threatening to become a force soon.

The Athletics made a 13-game improvement, going from 74-88 in 1998 to 87-75 in '99, and stayed in the wild-card race until the final week of the season. The legacy of 1999 should not be just an anomaly after six losing seasons. Instead, the A's are poised to become a winner again and an example that medium-market teams can thrive in an age of free spending.

And what happened in the majors was only part of the story. Baseball America named the Athletics as its Organization of the Year, and affiliate Vancouver prevailed in the Triple-A World Series.

After years of building through scouting and development, the A's saw a payoff. Manager Art Howe's team staged a second-half run to respectability, mildly threatened the Rangers for the American League West title and seriously battled the Red Sox for the wild card. Oakland took off after midseason trades for righthanders Kevin Appier and Omar Olivares and second baseman Randy Velarde.

The improvement came so suddenly that it almost surprised the organization. For years, the emphasis has been on the future, then the future suddenly showed up. But several young players arrived ahead of schedule.

Foremost was righthander Tim Hudson, a sixth-round pick in 1997 who tore through the minor leagues to become the new ace. He used his sinking fastball and nasty slider to become the A's best pitcher at 11-2.

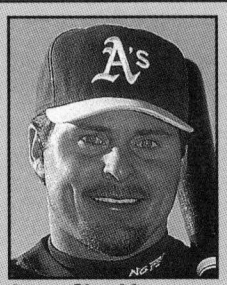 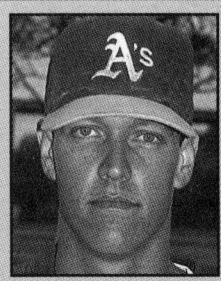

Jason Giambi   **Adam Piatt**

Players of the Year

MAJOR LEAGUE: Jason Giambi, 1b
Giambi was one of the keys to Oakland's revived offense with a .315 average, 33 homers and 123 RBIs.

MINOR LEAGUE: Adam Piatt, 3b
Piatt hit .345 with 39 homers and 135 RBIs at Midland to become the Texas League's first triple crown winner since 1927.

The most heralded of the rookie crop, 1998 Minor League Player of the Year Eric Chavez, struggled early before a strong finish to hit .247 with 13 homers.

Several veterans also came through, including surprising DH John Jaha. His career had been ravaged by shoulder injuries, but he recovered for an outstanding season in the middle of the order with first baseman Jason Giambi and outfielder Matt Stairs.

Reigning AL rookie of the year Ben Grieve moved from right field to left at the end of spring training, struggled mightily through May, then joined the offensive onslaught. The A's expect the continued development of Grieve, Chavez and shortstop Miguel Tejada (.251-21-84) to provide a deep and balanced lineup for the future.

The farm system has more talent to come as well. In BA's postseason ratings of the top prospects in each minor league, 13 A's players appeared, more than any other organization.

Vancouver's rise to the Triple-A World Series championship was built around pitching prospects such as righthander Brett Laxton and lefthanders Mark Mulder and Barry Zito, the club's last two first-round picks.

Third baseman Adam Piatt won the Texas League triple crown and emerged as a legitimate power prospect. Both California League affiliates, Modesto and Visalia, reached the playoffs, and the A's finished first in the Rookie-level Arizona League.

The A's also took a step to assure their future comes to fruition by signing general manager Billy Beane to a three-year contract extension.

ORGANIZATION LEADERS

BATTING

*AVG	Mike Lockwood, Southern Oregon	.361
R	Adam Piatt, Vancouver/Midland	129
H	Two tied at	168
TB	Adam Piatt, Vancouver/Midland	340
2B	Adam Piatt, Vancouver/Midland	49
3B	Oscar Salazar, Modesto	18
HR	Adam Piatt, Vancouver/Midland	39
RBI	Adam Piatt, Vancouver/Midland	138
BB	Esteban German, Modesto	102
SO	Caonabo Cosme, Modesto	148
SB	Carlos Rosario, Visalia/Southern Oregon	42

PITCHING

W	Brett Laxton, Vancouver	13
L	Kevin Gregg, Vancouver/Midland/Visalia	11
#ERA	Elvin Nina, Midland/Modesto	2.88
G	Ray Noriega, Visalia	60
CG	Two tied at	3
SV	Jim Brink, Midland/Modesto	29
IP	Brett Laxton, Vancouver	161
BB	Tom Bennett, Visalia	94
SO	Jesus Colome, Modesto	127

*Minimum 250 At-Bats #Minimum 75 Innings

Oakland ATHLETICS

Manager: Art Howe

1999 Record: 87-75, .537 (2nd, AL West)

BATTING	AVG	G	AB	R	H	2B	3B	HR	RBI	BB	SO	SB	CS	B	T	HT	WT	DOB	1st Yr	Resides
Becker, Rich	.264	40	125	21	33	3	0	1	10	25	43	3	2	L	L	5-10	193	2-1-72	1990	Cape Coral, Fla.
Chavez, Eric	.247	115	356	47	88	21	2	13	50	46	56	1	1	L	R	6-1	195	12-7-77	1996	San Diego, Calif.
Christenson, Ryan	.209	106	268	41	56	12	1	4	24	38	58	7	5	R	R	5-11	175	3-28-74	1995	Apple Valley, Calif.
Giambi, Jason	.315	158	575	115	181	36	1	33	123	105	106	1	1	L	R	6-3	235	1-8-71	1992	Palm Desert, Calif.
Grieve, Ben	.265	148	486	80	129	21	0	28	86	63	108	4	0	L	R	6-4	226	5-4-76	1994	Arlington, Texas
Hernandez, Ramon	.279	40	136	13	38	7	0	3	21	18	11	1	0	R	R	6-0	203	5-20-76	1994	Caracas, Venez.
Hinch, A.J.	.215	76	205	26	44	4	1	7	24	11	41	6	2	R	R	6-1	205	5-15-74	1996	Midwest City, Okla.
Jaha, John	.276	142	457	93	126	23	0	35	111	101	129	2	0	R	R	6-1	225	5-25-66	1985	Camas, Wash.
Macfarlane, Mike	.243	81	226	24	55	17	0	4	31	13	52	0	0	R	R	6-1	210	4-12-64	1985	Overland Park, Kan.
McDonald, Jason	.209	100	187	26	39	2	1	3	8	25	48	6	3	S	R	5-7	182	3-20-72	1993	Sacramento, Calif.
Menechino, Frank	.222	9	9	0	2	0	0	0	0	0	4	0	0	R	R	5-9	175	1-7-71	1993	Staten Island, N.Y.
Phillips, Tony	.244	106	406	76	99	24	4	15	49	71	94	11	3	S	R	5-10	175	4-25-59	1978	Scottsdale, Ariz.
Raines, Tim	.215	58	135	20	29	5	0	4	17	26	17	4	1	S	R	5-8	185	9-16-59	1977	Heathrow, Fla.
Saenz, Olmedo	.275	97	255	41	70	18	0	11	41	22	47	1	1	R	R	6-0	185	10-8-70	1990	Chitre Herrera, Panama
Spiezio, Scott	.243	89	247	31	60	24	0	8	33	29	36	0	0	S	R	6-2	222	9-21-72	1993	Morris, Ill.
Stairs, Matt	.258	146	531	94	137	26	3	38	102	89	124	2	7	L	R	5-9	206	2-27-69	1989	Stanley, New Brunswick
Tejada, Miguel	.251	159	593	93	149	33	4	21	84	57	94	8	7	R	R	5-9	192	5-25-76	1994	Bani, D.R.
Velandia, Jorge	.188	63	48	4	9	1	0	0	2	2	13	2	0	R	R	5-9	160	1-12-75	1992	Caracas, Venez.
Velarde, Randy	.333	61	255	48	85	10	3	7	28	27	42	11	4	R	R	6-0	200	11-24-62	1985	Midland, Texas
2-team (95 Anaheim)	.317	156	631	105	200	25	7	16	76	70	98	24	8							

PITCHING	W	L	ERA	G	GS	CG	SV	IP	H	R	ER	BB	SO	B	T	HT	WT	DOB	1st Yr	Resides
Appier, Kevin	7	5	5.77	12	12	0	0	69	77	50	44	33	53	R	R	6-2	200	12-6-67	1987	Paola, Kan.
2-team (22 K.C.)	16	14	5.17	34	34	1	0	209	230	131	120	84	131							
Candiotti, Tom	3	5	6.35	11	11	0	0	57	67	46	40	23	30	R	R	6-2	221	8-31-57	1979	Clayton, Calif.
Groom, Buddy	3	2	5.09	76	0	0	0	46	48	29	26	18	32	L	L	6-2	208	7-10-65	1987	Waxahachie, Texas
Harville, Chad	0	2	6.91	15	0	0	0	14	18	11	11	10	15	R	R	5-9	180	9-16-76	1997	Savannah, Tenn.
Haynes, Jimmy	7	12	6.34	30	25	0	0	142	158	112	100	80	93	R	R	6-3	180	9-5-72	1991	La Grange, Ga.
Heredia, Gil	13	8	4.81	33	33	1	0	200	228	119	107	34	117	R	R	6-1	195	10-26-65	1987	Tucson, Ariz.
Hudson, Tim	11	2	3.23	21	21	1	0	136	121	56	49	62	132	R	R	6-0	160	7-14-75	1997	Salem, Ala.
Isringhausen, Jason	0	1	2.13	20	0	0	8	25	21	6	6	12	20	R	R	6-3	210	9-7-72	1992	Brighton, Ill.
Jarvis, Kevin	0	1	11.57	4	1	0	0	14	28	19	18	6	11	S	R	6-2	200	8-1-69	1991	Lexington, Ky.
Jones, Doug	5	5	3.55	70	0	0	10	104	106	43	41	24	63	R	R	6-2	225	6-24-57	1978	Tucson, Ariz.
Kubinski, Tim	0	0	5.84	14	0	0	0	12	14	8	8	5	7	L	L	6-4	205	1-20-72	1993	San Luis Obispo, Calif.
Laxton, Brett	0	1	7.45	3	2	0	0	10	12	12	8	7	9	L	R	6-2	205	10-5-73	1996	Audubon, N.J.
Mahay, Ron	2	0	1.86	6	1	0	1	19	8	4	4	3	15	L	L	6-2	185	6-28-71	1991	Crestwood, Ill.
Mathews, T.J.	9	5	3.81	50	0	0	3	59	46	28	25	20	42	R	R	6-2	200	1-19-70	1992	Columbia, Ill.
McMichael, Greg	0	0	5.40	17	0	0	0	15	15	9	9	12	3	R	R	6-3	222	12-1-66	1988	Alpharetta, Ga.
Olivares, Omar	7	2	4.34	12	12	1	0	75	82	43	36	32	36	R	R	6-1	205	7-6-67	1987	San German, P.R.
2-team (20 Anaheim)	15	11	4.16	32	32	4	0	206	217	105	95	81	85							
Oquist, Mike	9	10	5.37	28	24	0	0	141	158	86	84	64	89	R	R	6-2	189	5-30-68	1989	La Junta, Colo.
Rigby, Brad	3	4	4.33	29	0	0	0	62	69	31	30	26	26	R	R	6-6	213	5-14-73	1994	Altamonte Springs, Fla.
Rogers, Kenny	5	3	4.30	19	19	3	0	119	135	66	57	41	68	L	L	6-1	205	11-10-64	1982	Tampa, Fla.
Stein, Blake	0	0	16.88	1	1	0	0	3	6	5	5	6	4	R	R	6-7	210	8-3-73	1994	Folsom, La.
Taylor, Billy	1	5	3.98	43	0	0	26	43	48	23	19	14	38	R	R	6-8	230	10-16-61	1980	Thomasville, Ga.
Vizcaino, Luis	0	0	5.40	1	0	0	0	3	3	2	2	3	2	R	R	6-1	170	6-10-77	1995	Bani, D.R.
Worrell, Tim	2	2	4.15	53	0	0	0	69	69	38	32	34	62	R	R	6-4	215	7-5-67	1990	Glendale, Ariz.

FIELDING

Catcher	PCT	G	PO	A	E	DP	PB
Hernandez	.980	40	274	19	6	5	2
Hinch	.987	73	368	26	5	4	10
Macfarlane	.997	79	351	43	1	8	6

First Base	PCT	G	PO	A	E	DP
Giambi	.995	142	1251	45	7	128
Jaha	1.000	8	42	4	0	3
Saenz	.994	28	153	12	1	11
Spiezio	1.000	10	51	1	0	6
Stairs	1.000	1	2	0	0	0

Second Base	PCT	G	PO	A	E	DP
McDonald	1.000	1	1	0	0	0
Phillips	.974	66	96	164	7	41
Spiezio	.984	42	57	127	3	25
Velandia	.989	52	36	57	1	13
Velarde	.977	61	107	186	7	43

Third Base	PCT	G	PO	A	E	DP
Chavez	.961	105	69	155	9	13
Giambi	.000	1	0	0	0	0

	PCT	G	PO	A	E	DP
Menechino	1.000	1	1	1	0	0
Phillips	.000	2	0	0	0	0
Saenz	.938	56	27	79	7	12
Spiezio	.927	31	16	35	4	1
Velandia	1.000	2	1	1	0	0

Shortstop	PCT	G	PO	A	E	DP
Chavez	.000	2	0	0	0	0
Menechino	1.000	5	3	6	0	2
Phillips	.000	1	0	0	0	0
Tejada	.973	159	291	471	21	110
Velandia	.938	8	9	21	2	4

Outfield	PCT	G	PO	A	E	DP
Becker	.986	39	67	4	1	1
Christenson	.969	104	213	3	7	1
Grieve	.988	137	232	6	3	2
McDonald	.993	89	149	3	1	1
Phillips	.937	62	85	4	6	1
Raines	1.000	38	61	0	0	0
Stairs	.981	139	245	13	5	1

STEVE MOORE

Tim Hudson

Organization Statistics

Director of Player Development: Keith Lieppman

Class	Farm Team	League	W	L	Pct.	Finish*	Manager	First Yr
AAA	Vancouver (B.C.) Canadians	Pacific Coast	84	58	.592	+1st (16)	Mike Quade	1999
AA	Midland (Texas) RockHounds	Texas	74	66	.529	t-2nd (10)	Tony DeFrancesco	1999
A#	Modesto (Calif.) A's	California	88	52	.629	1st (10)	Bob Geren	1975
A#	Visalia (Calif.) Oaks	California	75	65	.536	5th (10)	Juan Navarrete	1997
A	Southern Oregon Timberjacks	Northwest	38	38	.500	5th (8)	Greg Sparks	1979
Rookie	Phoenix (Ariz.) Athletics	Arizona	39	17	.696	+1st (8)	John Kuehl	1988

*Finish in overall standings (No. of teams in league)   #Advanced level   +Won league championship

VANCOUVER   Class AAA

PACIFIC COAST LEAGUE

BATTING	AVG	G	AB	R	H	2B	3B	HR	RBI	BB	SO	SB	CS	B	T	HT	WT	DOB	1st Yr	Resides
Ardoin, Danny	.253	109	336	53	85	13	2	8	46	50	78	3	3	R	R	6-0	205	7-8-74	1995	Ville Platte, La.
Ball, Jeff	.309	96	346	50	107	22	2	8	51	37	57	7	2	R	R	5-10	185	4-17-69	1990	Merced, Calif.
Christenson, Ryan	.344	33	128	30	44	8	1	1	16	22	21	7	2	R	R	5-11	175	3-28-74	1995	Apple Valley, Calif.
Encarnacion, Mario	.241	39	145	18	35	5	0	3	17	6	44	5	4	R	R	6-2	187	9-24-77	1994	Bani, D.R.
Espada, Joe	.308	6	26	2	8	1	0	0	3	4	1	2	0	R	R	5-10	175	8-30-75	1996	Carolina, P.R.
Freeman, Ricky	.223	61	202	27	45	14	0	4	24	20	39	0	0	R	R	6-4	210	2-3-72	1994	Houston, Texas
Hernandez, Ramon	.261	77	291	38	76	11	3	13	55	23	37	1	2	R	R	6-0	203	5-20-76	1994	Caracas, Venez.
Hinch, A.J.	.377	15	61	9	23	3	0	2	7	3	12	1	1	R	R	6-1	205	5-15-74	1996	Midwest City, Okla.
Lesher, Brian	.292	103	387	66	113	29	2	14	64	41	71	8	2	R	L	6-5	216	3-5-71	1992	Scottsdale, Ariz.
Long, Terrence	.247	40	154	16	38	6	2	2	21	10	29	7	5	L	L	6-1	190	2-29-76	1994	Millbrook, Ala.
Luderer, Brian	.321	10	28	6	9	1	0	0	4	4	2	0	0	R	R	5-11	195	8-19-78	1996	Tarzana, Calif.
Martins, Eric	.239	97	301	39	72	15	5	3	33	31	47	2	1	R	R	5-9	170	11-19-72	1994	Rowland Heights, Calif.
McDonald, Jason	.326	32	129	27	42	9	1	4	18	19	33	8	5	S	R	5-7	182	3-20-72	1993	Sacramento, Calif.
Menechino, Frank	.309	130	501	103	155	31	9	15	88	73	97	4	5	R	R	5-9	175	1-7-71	1993	Staten Island, N.Y.
Morales, Willie	.143	5	14	2	2	1	0	0	2	1	4	0	0	R	R	5-10	182	9-7-72	1993	Tucson, Ariz.
Neill, Mike	.296	96	365	61	108	23	2	10	61	57	97	10	5	L	L	6-2	190	4-27-70	1991	Seaford, Del.
Newfield, Marc	.143	7	28	1	4	0	0	0	1	1	2	0	0	R	R	6-4	225	10-19-72	1990	Huntington Beach, Calif.
Ortiz, Jose	.284	107	377	66	107	29	2	9	45	29	50	13	4	R	R	5-9	160	6-13-77	1995	Santo Domingo, D.R.
Piatt, Adam	.222	6	18	1	4	1	0	0	3	6	2	0	0	R	R	6-2	195	2-8-76	1997	Fort Myers, Fla.
Saenz, Olmedo	.600	2	5	1	3	1	0	0	2	0	0	0	0	R	R	6-0	185	10-8-70	1993	Chitre Herrera, Panama
Sheff, Chris	.287	118	421	62	121	24	1	15	70	45	87	9	6	R	R	6-3	215	2-4-71	1992	Laguna Hills, Calif.
Spiezio, Scott	.390	28	105	27	41	9	1	7	25	15	16	0	0	S	R	6-2	222	9-21-72	1993	Morris, Ill.
Vaz, Roberto	.264	109	367	54	97	18	4	7	38	51	72	7	5	L	L	5-9	195	3-15-75	1997	Tuscaloosa, Ala.

PITCHING	W	L	ERA	G	GS	CG	SV	IP	H	R	ER	BB	SO	B	T	HT	WT	DOB	1st Yr	Resides
Baez, Benito	0	2	3.50	11	0	0	1	18	18	7	7	7	19	L	L	6-0	160	5-6-77	1994	Bonao, D.R.
Chavez, Anthony	4	6	3.91	54	0	0	14	69	67	42	30	37	72	R	R	5-11	180	10-22-70	1992	Merced, Calif.
Clark, Terry	3	4	4.79	14	7	0	0	41	47	25	22	14	17	R	R	6-2	195	10-10-60	1979	Fontana, Calif.
D'Amico, Jeff	2	2	2.65	14	0	0	3	17	16	6	5	10	10	R	R	6-3	195	11-9-74	1993	Seattle, Wash.
Dale, Carl	4	3	3.48	29	0	0	4	44	41	19	17	18	27	R	R	6-2	195	12-7-72	1994	Cookeville, Tenn.
Delamaza, Roland	0	0	12.00	4	0	0	0	3	5	4	4	4	4	R	R	6-2	195	11-9-71	1993	Arleta, Calif.
Gregg, Kevin	1	0	3.60	1	1	0	0	5	6	2	2	2	4	R	R	6-6	200	6-20-78	1996	Corvallis, Ore.
Harville, Chad	1	0	1.75	22	0	0	11	26	24	5	5	11	36	R	R	5-9	180	9-16-76	1997	Savannah, Tenn.
Hudson, Tim	4	0	2.20	8	8	0	0	49	38	16	12	21	61	R	R	6-0	160	7-14-75	1997	Salem, Ala.
Jarvis, Kevin	10	2	3.41	17	16	2	0	103	110	47	39	26	64	S	R	6-2	200	8-1-69	1991	Lexington, Ky.
Jones, Marcus	2	1	2.40	3	3	0	0	15	23	11	4	5	5	R	R	6-5	215	3-29-75	1997	Yorba Linda, Calif.
King, Bill	9	6	3.49	45	7	0	4	98	105	52	38	22	60	R	R	6-5	215	2-18-73	1994	Chipley, Fla.
Kubinski, Tim	5	3	3.44	46	1	0	6	73	70	30	28	27	56	L	L	6-4	205	1-20-72	1993	San Luis Obispo, Calif.
Lawrence, Sean	2	2	4.81	25	2	0	0	39	51	25	21	21	37	L	L	6-1	215	9-2-70	1992	Hillside, Ill.
Laxton, Brett	13	8	3.46	25	25	3	0	161	158	68	62	49	112	L	R	6-2	205	10-5-73	1996	Audubon, N.J.
Mahay, Ron	7	2	4.29	32	15	0	0	107	116	57	51	43	73	L	L	6-2	185	6-28-71	1991	Crestwood, Ill.
Manwiller, Tim	4	2	6.46	11	11	0	0	54	72	42	39	14	30	R	R	6-2	205	9-5-74	1997	Annville, Pa.
Mathews, T.J.	0	0	9.00	1	1	0	0	1	1	1	1	1	1	R	R	6-2	200	1-19-70	1992	Columbia, Ill.
Mulder, Mark	6	7	4.06	22	22	1	0	129	152	69	58	31	81	L	L	6-6	200	8-5-77	1999	South Holland, Ill.
Oquist, Mike	1	0	0.00	1	1	0	0	6	2	0	0	1	2	R	R	6-2	189	5-30-68	1989	La Junta, Colo.
Perez, Juan	0	4	6.96	20	1	0	0	32	42	25	25	15	22	L	L	6-0	155	3-28-73	1992	La Romana, D.R.
Rigby, Brad	0	1	1.93	1	1	0	0	5	6	3	1	2	6	R	R	6-6	213	5-14-73	1994	Altamonte Springs, Fla.
Snow, Bert	1	0	3.86	2	0	0	0	2	3	1	1	1	3	R	R	6-1	190	3-23-77	1998	Brooksville, Fla.
Stein, Blake	4	2	4.10	19	19	0	0	110	94	54	50	43	111	R	R	6-7	210	8-3-73	1994	Folsom, La.
Vasquez, Leo	0	0	5.40	1	0	0	0	2	2	1	1	2	0	L	L	6-4	196	7-1-73	1996	La Romana, D.R.
Vizcaino, Luis	0	1	1.38	7	0	0	0	13	13	4	2	6	7	R	R	6-1	170	6-10-77	1995	Bani, D.R.
Zito, Barry	1	0	1.50	1	1	0	0	6	5	1	1	2	6	L	L	6-4	205	5-13-78	1999	Las Vegas, Nev.

FIELDING

Catcher	PCT	G	PO	A	E	DP	PB
Ardoin	.989	83	498	59	6	9	6
Hernandez	.997	44	302	27	1	6	3
Hinch	.989	12	83	3	1	1	1
Luderer	.984	10	60	1	1	0	0

First Base	PCT	G	PO	A	E	DP
Ardoin	.975	6	35	4	1	8
Ball	.989	24	172	12	2	20
Freeman	.981	49	394	20	8	42
Hernandez	1.000	4	26	0	0	3
Lesher	.993	63	543	35	4	64
Morales	.971	4	33	0	1	7

Second Base	PCT	G	PO	A	E	DP
Espada	.968	6	13	17	1	4
Martins	.971	82	137	197	10	54
McDonald	1.000	1	2	3	0	1
Menechino	1.000	40	57	106	0	23
Ortiz	1.000	4	11	12	0	5
Spiezio	.967	24	48	70	4	19

Third Base	PCT	G	PO	A	E	DP
Ardoin	.857	10	5	13	3	2
Ball	.914	56	30	98	12	12
Hernandez	.857	11	11	13	4	0
Martins	.952	9	4	16	1	0

	PCT	G	PO	A	E	DP
Menechino	.964	57	34	99	5	12
Morales	.000	2	0	0	0	0
Piatt	.875	5	3	11	2	1
Saenz	1.000	2	1	0	0	0
Spiezio	1.000	3	2	3	0	1

Shortstop	PCT	G	PO	A	E	DP
Martins	.926	4	8	17	2	5
Menechino	.975	42	61	136	5	33
Ortiz	.942	103	168	283	28	71
Piatt	1.000	1	3	5	0	2

Outfield	PCT	G	PO	A	E	DP
Ball	.000	1	0	0	0	0
Christenson	.978	33	88	1	2	0
Encarnacion	.960	37	91	6	4	2
Freeman	1.000	8	10	0	0	0

	PCT	G	PO	A	E	DP
Lesher	1.000	37	56	2	0	0
Long	.961	38	95	3	4	1
McDonald	.988	32	77	3	1	2
Neill	.967	80	136	9	5	2

	PCT	G	PO	A	E	DP
Newfield	1.000	4	10	0	0	0
Sheff	.991	102	213	9	2	3
Vaz	.957	66	103	8	5	2

MIDLAND — Class AA

TEXAS LEAGUE

BATTING	AVG	G	AB	R	H	2B	3B	HR	RBI	BB	SO	SB	CS	B	T	HT	WT	DOB	1st Yr	Resides
Bellhorn, Mark	.298	17	57	12	17	3	0	2	8	11	13	1	0	S	R	6-1	190	8-23-74	1995	Oviedo, Fla.
Berroa, Angel	.059	4	17	3	1	1	0	0	0	0	2	0	0	R	R	6-0	175	1-27-80	1997	Santo Domingo, D.R.
Bowles, Justin	.286	131	489	73	140	27	8	20	73	44	122	10	7	L	L	6-0	185	8-20-73	1996	Lake Jackson, Texas
Byrnes, Eric	.238	43	164	25	39	14	0	1	22	17	32	6	3	R	R	6-2	200	2-16-76	1998	Woodside, Calif.
Castro, Jose	.261	119	368	69	96	17	3	7	42	38	90	21	7	S	R	5-10	160	10-15-74	1994	Villa Vasquez, D.R.
Cesar, Dionys	.190	35	105	15	20	4	3	3	15	18	28	1	4	S	R	5-10	170	9-27-76	1994	Santo Domingo, D.R.
Chirinos, Germain	.214	4	14	1	3	1	0	0	0	3	3	1	0	R	R	6-0	170	8-29-78	1996	Yaracuy, Venez.
DaVanon, Jeff	.342	100	374	87	128	29	11	11	60	53	68	18	10	S	R	6-0	185	12-8-73	1995	Del Mar, Calif.
Encarnacion, Mario	.309	94	353	69	109	21	4	18	71	47	86	9	9	R	R	6-2	187	9-24-77	1994	Bani, D.R.
Espada, Joe	.338	113	435	85	147	15	2	6	51	62	51	22	16	R	R	5-10	175	8-30-75	1996	Carolina, P.R.
Garland, Tim	.289	119	463	84	134	23	10	6	55	29	59	28	13	R	R	6-0	185	7-15-68	1989	Danville, Va.
Garrison, Webster	.274	43	124	17	34	9	0	4	21	16	15	1	1	R	R	5-11	170	8-24-65	1984	Marrero, La.
Marcinczyk, T.R.	.279	127	477	87	133	39	1	23	111	62	109	2	0	R	R	6-2	195	10-11-73	1996	Plainville, Conn.
McKay, Cody	.294	94	333	59	98	21	1	6	43	38	40	1	2	L	R	6-0	190	1-11-74	1996	Scottsdale, Ariz.
Morales, Willie	.280	102	343	43	96	27	0	16	71	24	54	2	0	R	R	5-11	182	9-7-72	1993	Tucson, Ariz.
Piatt, Adam	.345	129	476	128	164	48	3	39	135	93	101	7	3	R	R	6-2	195	2-8-76	1997	Fort Myers, Fla.
Skeels, David	.273	23	66	6	18	5	0	1	12	6	15	2	0	R-R		6-2	195	6-23-73	1996	Thousand Oaks, Calif.
Stuckenschneider, Eric	.163	29	92	17	15	4	2	0	16	17	22	6	1	R	R	6-0	200	8-24-71	1994	Freeburg, Mo.
Vaz, Roberto	.406	10	32	4	13	3	0	1	12	8	5	0	1	L	L	5-9	175	3-15-75	1997	Tuscaloosa, Ala.

PITCHING	W	L	ERA	G	GS	CG	SV	IP	H	R	ER	BB	SO	B	T	HT	WT	DOB	1st Yr	Resides
Anderson, Jason	4	9	6.89	23	23	0	0	111	148	103	85	47	74	L	L	6-2	195	4-6-76	1997	Salem, Va.
Baez, Benito	5	1	5.47	37	0	0	3	54	68	35	33	15	51	L	L	6-0	160	5-6-77	1994	Bonao, D.R.
Bertotti, Mike	2	3	8.42	20	0	0	1	26	30	26	24	37	25	L	L	6-1	185	1-18-70	1991	Highland Mills, N.Y.
Brink, Jim	1	1	7.88	5	0	0	0	8	10	7	7	1	4	R	R	6-0	185	9-11-76	1998	Stockton, Calif.
D'Amico, Jeff	1	2	4.96	32	0	0	3	45	53	31	25	16	38	R	R	6-3	195	11-9-74	1993	Seattle, Wash.
DuBose, Eric	4	2	5.49	21	14	0	1	77	89	57	47	44	68	L	L	6-3	215	5-15-76	1997	Nashville, Tenn.
Enochs, Chris	3	5	10.00	13	11	0	0	45	69	57	50	34	33	R	R	6-3	225	10-11-75	1997	Newell, W.Va.
Gorrell, Chris	2	0	7.83	30	0	0	1	56	92	63	49	23	41	R	R	6-2	188	1-27-76	1996	Las Vegas, Nev.
Gregg, Kevin	4	7	3.74	16	16	2	0	91	75	45	38	31	66	R	R	6-6	200	6-20-78	1996	Corvallis, Ore.
Harville, Chad	2	0	2.01	17	0	0	7	22	13	6	5	9	35	R	R	5-9	180	9-16-76	1997	Savannah, Tenn.
Hudson, Tim	3	0	0.50	3	3	0	0	18	9	1	1	3	18	R	R	6-0	160	7-14-75	1997	Salem, Ala.
Kimball, Andy	9	5	5.44	47	0	0	2	89	112	64	54	40	87	R	R	6-0	190	8-23-75	1997	Oshkosh, Wis.
Leyva, Julian	3	4	6.03	12	11	1	0	63	86	46	42	12	39	L	R	6-0	200	2-11-78	1996	Riverside, Calif.
Manwiller, Tim	6	2	3.51	17	13	0	0	85	95	43	33	24	58	R	R	6-2	195	9-5-74	1997	Annville, Pa.
Nelson, Chris	1	1	7.92	19	0	0	0	31	45	30	27	22	24	S	R	6-2	180	1-26-73	1995	San Diego, Calif.
Niles, Randy	4	6	5.73	23	14	0	0	88	126	78	56	47	46	R	R	6-2	200	8-28-75	1997	Key West, Fla.
Nina, Elvin	3	2	4.80	7	4	0	0	30	36	21	16	18	16	R	R	6-0	185	11-25-75	1997	East Orange, N.J.
O'Dell, Jake	0	2	11.31	9	3	0	0	25	36	31	31	15	16	R	R	6-1	205	9-22-73	1996	Round Rock, Texas
Perez, Juan	2	2	6.94	23	0	0	3	35	47	29	27	18	30	L	L	5-11	155	3-28-77	1992	La Romana, D.R.
Snow, Bert	1	1	1.71	21	0	0	13	21	14	4	4	9	32	R	R	6-1	190	3-23-77	1998	Brooksville, Fla.
Vasquez, Leo	3	1	3.09	13	0	0	1	23	18	11	8	13	24	L	L	6-4	196	7-1-73	1996	La Romana, D.R.
Vizcaino, Luis	8	7	5.85	25	19	0	0	105	120	74	68	48	88	R	R	6-1	170	6-10-77	1995	Bani, D.R.
Wagner, Denny	1	2	4.23	5	5	0	0	28	28	22	13	14	12	R	R	6-0	205	11-8-76	1997	Castlewood, Va.
Zito, Barry	2	1	4.91	4	4	0	0	22	22	15	12	11	29	L	L	6-4	205	5-13-78	1999	Las Vegas, Nev.

FIELDING

Catcher	PCT	G	PO	A	E	DP	PB
McKay	.982	56	384	48	8	3	16
Morales	.996	81	469	54	2	5	8
Skeels	.962	22	108	19	5	1	3

First Base	PCT	G	PO	A	E	DP
Bowles	1.000	1	2	0	0	0
Garrison	.993	16	126	12	1	8
Marcinczyk	.986	125	1051	93	16	101
McKay	.962	6	46	4	2	4
Morales	1.000	1	1	0	0	0

Second-Base	PCT	G	PO	A	E	DP
Bellhorn	.973	15	30	41	2	10
Castro	.961	65	114	181	12	39
Cesar	.943	32	55	94	9	16
Espada	.965	25	49	60	4	13
Garrison	.930	14	14	39	4	10

Third Base	PCT	G	PO	A	E	DP
Castro	.889	6	3	5	1	0
Garrison	.000	1	0	0	0	0
McKay	.937	24	16	43	4	6
Piatt	.910	115	73	220	29	17

Shortstop	PCT	G	PO	A	E	DP
Berroa	.889	4	10	6	2	2
Castro	.923	48	72	143	18	25
Espada	.918	85	127	222	31	45
Piatt	.962	10	18	33	2	10

Outfield	PCT	G	PO	A	E	DP
Bowles	.952	98	150	8	8	2
Byrnes	.923	41	59	1	5	0
Chirinos	.917	4	10	1	1	1
DaVanon	.960	86	162	8	7	1
Encarnacion	.936	74	126	6	9	1
Garland	.985	104	191	5	3	0
Garrison	1.000	1	2	0	0	0
Marcinczyk	1.000	1	0	0	0	0
Stuckenschneider	.939	18	29	2	2	0
Vaz	1.000	5	11	0	0	0

MODESTO — Class A

CALIFORNIA LEAGUE

BATTING	AVG	G	AB	R	H	2B	3B	HR	RBI	BB	SO	SB	CS	B	T	HT	WT	DOB	1st Yr	Resides
Basabe, Jesus	.235	95	310	45	73	21	1	15	51	36	97	12	5	R	R	6-2	195	5-14-77	1995	Bobures, Venez.
Byrnes, Eric	.337	96	365	86	123	28	1	6	66	58	37	28	8	R	R	6-2	200	2-16-76	1998	Woodside, Calif.
Cosbey, Chris	.200	39	90	16	18	4	0	0	7	3	23	9	4	L	L	5-9	165	11-14-74	1998	Arcadia, Calif.
Cosme, Caonabo	.214	122	444	55	95	21	2	12	47	45	148	14	7	R	R	6-3	200	3-18-79	1996	La Vega, D.R.
German, Esteban	.311	128	501	107	156	16	12	4	52	102	128	40	16	R	R	5-10	180	12-26-78	1996	Santo Domingo, D.R.
Hart, Jason	.305	135	550	96	168	48	2	19	123	56	105	2	5	R	R	6-4	240	9-5-77	1998	Springfield, Mo.
Landry, Jacques	.311	133	508	92	158	46	6	27	111	47	128	18	4	R	R	6-3	205	8-15-73	1996	LaMarque, Texas
Luderer, Brian	.286	55	182	22	52	13	2	1	22	16	25	3	3	R	R	5-11	195	8-19-78	1996	Tarzana, Calif.
Ludwick, Ryan	.275	43	171	28	47	11	3	4	34	19	45	2	1	R	L	6-3	603	7-13-78	1999	Las Vegas, Nev.
Olivo, Miguel	.305	73	243	46	74	13	6	9	42	21	60	4	5	R	R	6-1	212	7-15-78	1996	Villa Vasquez, D.R.

BATTING	AVG	G	AB	R	H	2B	3B	HR	RBI	BB	SO	SB	CS	B	T	HT	WT	DOB	1st Yr	Resides
Pujols, Rafael	.236	71	233	28	55	16	0	3	32	24	34	5	6	S	R	6-1	208	1-20-78	1995	Bani, D.R.
Rosario, Omar	.298	116	419	82	125	23	6	5	57	70	94	19	12	L	L	6-1	185	1-14-78	1996	Santo Domingo, D.R.
Salazar, Oscar	.295	130	525	100	155	26	18	18	105	39	106	14	6	R	R	6-0	155	6-27-78	1994	Maracay, Venez.
Thomas, Gary	.323	99	344	69	111	14	4	7	38	33	45	23	6	R	R	5-6	175	9-6-79	1997	Houma, La.

GAMES BY POSITION: C—Luderer 48, Olivo 71, Pujols 40. **1B**—Hart 127, Landry 1, Pujols 15, Salazar 1. **2B**—German 110, Landry 2, Salazar 33. **3B**—Landry 111, Pujols 7, Salazar 28. **SS**—Cosme 122, Salazar 20. **OF**—Basabe 84, Byrnes 96, Cosbey 32, Ludwick 40, Rosario 98, Salazar 1, Thomas 97.

PITCHING	W	L	ERA	G	GS	CG	SV	IP	H	R	ER	BB	SO	B	T	HT	WT	DOB	1st Yr	Resides
Adkins, Jon	9	5	4.76	26	15	0	1	102	113	65	54	30	93	R	R	6-1	200	8-30-77	1998	Wayne, W.Va.
Brink, Jim	3	0	4.57	47	0	0	29	45	53	19	23	18	38	R	R	6-0	185	9-11-76	1998	Stockton, Calif.
Calandriello, Donato	4	1	3.56	38	0	0	1	48	36	22	19	31	44	L	L	6-2	210	7-1-75	1998	Caracas, Venez.
Colome, Jesus	8	4	3.36	31	22	0	1	129	125	63	48	60	127	R	R	6-2	190	3-23-79	1996	San Pedro de Macoris, D.R.
Holmes, Mike	9	6	4.88	34	18	0	6	146	184	100	79	15	84	R	R	6-2	200	10-11-75	1997	Greensboro, N.C.
Jarvis, Kevin	0	0	1.29	2	2	0	0	7	4	1	1	1	10	S	R	6-2	200	8-1-69	1991	Lexington, Ky.
Jones, Marcus	2	1	2.81	7	5	0	0	32	29	18	10	14	36	R	R	6-5	235	3-29-75	1997	Yorba Linda, Calif.
2-team (18 Visalia)	8	5	4.02	25	20	0	0	123	132	74	55	46	118							
Kenny, Seth	0	3	3.52	18	0	0	0	23	26	13	9	13	18	R	R	6-2	195	7-21-76	1998	Novato, Calif.
Maurer, Mike	1	0	2.65	15	0	0	1	17	23	8	5	5	15	R	R	6-2	185	7-4-72	1994	Burnsville, Minn.
McCall, Travis	3	3	4.54	43	0	0	3	71	79	46	36	31	67	L	L	5-11	185	12-20-77	1996	Chino Hills, Calif.
Moore, Brad	3	2	5.11	34	0	0	0	37	37	24	21	31	42	R	R	6-0	185	2-25-76	1998	Waterloo, Iowa
Moore, Darin	1	1	11.76	12	0	0	0	21	21	27	27	26	21	R	R	6-0	195	12-19-76	1999	Acampo, Calif.
Niles, Randy	3	0	3.15	8	4	0	2	34	39	13	12	8	35	R	R	6-2	200	8-28-75	1997	Key West, Fla.
Nina, Elvin	5	2	2.09	17	12	0	0	73	59	31	17	41	74	R	R	6-0	185	11-25-75	1997	East Orange, N.J.
Nix, Wayne	9	6	4.22	34	18	0	2	119	109	76	56	69	105	R	R	6-5	230	9-16-76	1995	North Hills, Calif.
O'Dell, Jake	1	0	2.57	3	0	0	0	7	7	2	2	3	10	R	R	6-1	205	9-22-73	1996	Round Rock, Texas
Schultz, Jeff	2	9	5.44	23	11	0	3	83	90	58	50	49	63	R	R	6-1	200	5-22-76	1998	Long Beach, Calif.
Seaver, Mark	12	4	4.30	34	17	0	2	134	158	85	64	57	112	R	R	6-8	250	4-6-75	1996	Hickory, Pa.
Wagner, Denny	7	4	3.56	27	15	0	3	114	116	57	45	42	99	R	R	6-0	205	11-8-76	1997	Castlewood, Va.
Worrell, Tim	0	0	0.00	1	1	0	0	2	0	0	0	0	5	R	R	6-4	215	7-5-67	1990	Glendale, Ariz.

VISALIA — Class A

CALIFORNIA LEAGUE

BATTING	AVG	G	AB	R	H	2B	3B	HR	RBI	BB	SO	SB	CS	B	T	HT	WT	DOB	1st Yr	Resides
Camilo, Juan	.284	82	285	58	81	17	2	17	52	34	89	7	6	R	R	6-0	205	6-24-78	1996	Santo Domingo, D.R.
Cesar, Dionys	.322	77	320	59	103	21	5	7	62	41	51	21	11	S	R	5-10	170	9-27-76	1994	Santo Domingo, D.R.
Clifton, Rodney	.261	110	371	67	97	30	4	9	56	63	81	12	5	R	R	6-2	195	11-7-76	1996	Elgin, Ill.
De la Cruz, Jose	.209	43	115	17	24	5	1	4	17	12	32	3	1	R	R	6-1	200	1-27-78	1995	Santo Domingo, D.R.
Flores, Javier	.296	103	362	48	107	22	1	5	63	27	59	6	3	R	R	6-0	200	12-20-75	1997	Broken Arrow, Okla.
Haynes, Nathan	.310	35	145	28	45	7	1	1	14	17	27	12	10	L	L	5-9	170	9-7-79	1997	Hercules, Calif.
Howe, Matt	.200	42	120	14	24	3	1	1	11	18	27	3	4	R	R	6-0	205	9-16-76	1998	Houston, Texas
Jones, Tim	.205	72	185	31	38	8	2	5	31	40	76	9	1	L	R	6-0	208	9-13-77	1995	Buena Park, Calif.
Keith, Rusty	.313	124	448	87	140	28	3	10	62	82	59	10	8	R	R	6-0	209	9-18-77	1998	Brookings, Ore.
Lara, Eddie	.299	105	358	67	107	20	6	9	56	44	45	25	16	R	R	5-10	180	10-30-75	1993	Bani, D.R.
Martinez, Hipolito	.267	113	431	93	115	24	3	21	77	59	119	8	4	R	R	6-1	210	1-30-77	1995	Bani, D.R.
Mensik, Todd	.291	134	505	93	147	29	4	29	123	79	114	5	1	L	L	6-2	215	2-27-75	1996	Orland Park, Ill.
Nieckula, Aaron	.277	25	65	13	18	4	0	0	10	8	17	2	0	R	R	5-11	200	9-7-76	1998	Stickney, Ill.
Pecci, Jay	.252	119	377	60	95	14	2	1	43	42	56	12	7	S	R	5-11	185	9-26-76	1998	Novato, Calif.
Pimentel, Franklin	.500	3	2	0	1	0	0	0	1	0	0	1	0	S	R	6-0	197	1-20-79	1996	Bani, D.R.
Rosario, Carlos	.236	37	123	27	29	5	1	0	16	21	29	11	6	S	R	5-9	160	2-22-80	1997	Bani, D.R.
Schneidmiller, Gary	.276	85	239	56	66	8	2	0	22	49	57	4	2	R	R	6-1	185	1-26-80	1998	Chino, Calif.
Sosa, Nick	.218	100	339	53	74	14	1	13	67	65	106	4	2	R	R	6-2	220	7-18-77	1996	Longwood, Fla.

GAMES BY POSITION: C—de la Cruz 41, Flores 97, Nieckula 25. **1B**—de la Cruz 2, Howe 1, T. Jones 1, Keith 1, Mensik 78, Sosa 66. **2B**—Cesar 76, Howe 3, Lara 28, Pecci 8, Pimentel 2, Rosario 35. **3B**—Flores 9, Howe 35, Lara 32, Schneidmiller 76. **SS**—Lara 45, Pecci 111. **OF**—Camilo 60, Clifton 105, Haynes 35, T. Jones 31, Keith 114, Martinez 102.

PITCHING	W	L	ERA	G	GS	CG	SV	IP	H	R	ER	BB	SO	B	T	HT	WT	DOB	1st Yr	Resides
Anderson, Jason	2	1	2.52	4	4	0	0	25	32	9	7	7	17	L	L	6-2	195	4-6-76	1997	Salem, Va.
Bazzell, Shane	2	4	5.13	8	8	0	0	40	50	27	23	19	29	L	R	6-2	190	3-7-77	1998	Columbus, Miss.
Bennett, Tom	1	9	8.01	36	8	0	0	88	113	91	78	94	87	R	R	6-4	190	5-13-76	1995	Alameda, Calif.
Calzada, Jancor	2	0	6.63	8	0	0	0	19	24	17	14	4	15	R	R	6-2	195	2-28-79	1996	Bani, D.R.
Enochs, Chris	0	0	4.91	4	4	0	0	18	24	10	10	10	19	R	R	6-3	225	10-11-75	1997	Newell, W.Va.
Gorrell, Chris	4	3	5.09	16	0	0	4	23	33	14	13	7	31	R	R	6-2	188	1-27-76	1998	Las Vegas, Nev.
Gregg, Kevin	4	4	3.80	13	11	1	1	64	60	34	27	23	48	R	R	6-6	200	6-20-78	1996	Corvallis, Ore.
Jensen, Jared	9	7	4.20	32	22	0	0	141	154	82	66	41	110	R	R	6-1	190	3-6-74	1997	Blackfoot, Idaho
Jones, Marcus	6	4	4.45	18	15	0	0	91	103	56	45	32	82	R	R	6-5	235	3-29-75	1997	Yorba Linda, Calif.
Klein, Matt	1	1	5.55	11	2	0	0	24	35	24	15	20	18	R	R	6-1	190	5-15-75	1998	Solvang, Calif.
Leyva, Julian	7	3	4.25	15	14	0	1	83	87	50	39	25	67	L	R	6-0	200	2-11-78	1996	Riverside, Calif.
Nogowski, Brandon	5	4	4.02	33	2	0	3	65	71	40	29	19	60	L	L	6-0	187	5-13-76	1995	Phoenix, Ariz.
Noriega, Ray	3	4	4.02	60	0	0	11	69	67	36	31	32	62	R	R	5-10	170	3-28-74	1996	Tucson, Ariz.
Pena, Juan	9	5	5.76	33	18	0	1	131	168	106	84	61	107	L	L	6-3	195	6-4-79	1996	Santo Domingo, D.R.
Snow, Bert	3	2	5.15	31	0	0	5	65	55	43	37	40	90	R	R	6-1	190	3-23-77	1998	Brooksville, Fla.
Thompson, Eric	9	6	5.61	31	20	0	1	127	150	91	79	56	110	R	R	6-2	195	9-7-77	1998	Fairborn, Ohio
Waites, David	1	4	5.87	32	0	0	7	38	30	25	25	29	28	R	R	6-3	220	2-2-76	1997	Albuquerque, N.M.
Yates, Tyler	2	5	5.47	47	1	0	4	82	98	64	50	35	74	R	R	6-4	225	8-7-77	1998	Koloa, Hawaii
Zito, Barry	3	0	2.45	8	8	0	0	40	21	13	11	22	62	L	L	6-4	205	5-13-78	1999	Las Vegas, Nev.

SOUTHERN OREGON — Short-Season Class A

NORTHWEST LEAGUE

BATTING	AVG	G	AB	R	H	2B	3B	HR	RBI	BB	SO	SB	CS	B	T	HT	WT	DOB	1st Yr	Resides
Asche, Kirk	.288	66	260	53	75	14	3	17	67	34	56	10	0	R	R	6-2	195	7-10-77	1999	Brandon, Fla.
Clements, Jason	.181	36	105	20	19	2	0	1	8	13	32	0	3	S	R	5-11	170	3-1-78	1999	Temecula, Calif.

BATTING

BATTING	AVG	G	AB	R	H	2B	3B	HR	RBI	BB	SO	SB	CS	B	T	HT	WT	DOB	1st Yr	Resides
De la Cruz, Jose	.157	18	51	7	8	4	0	1	8	9	16	0	0	R	R	6-1	200	1-27-78	1995	Santo Domingo, D.R.
Declet, Miguel	.380	14	50	13	19	7	0	2	6	3	16	1	0	R	R	6-3	185	9-9-79	1997	Caguas, P.R.
Forbes, Matt	.279	63	258	50	72	17	6	4	34	34	77	13	6	R	R	5-10	165	2-17-78	1998	Davenport, Iowa
Hall, Justin	.300	5	20	2	6	3	0	0	2	1	4	1	0	R	R	5-10	180	9-23-76	1998	Mesa, Ariz.
Henderson, Brad	.269	57	197	30	53	9	1	5	36	27	33	3	1	R	R	6-1	185	10-15-76	1999	Tupelo, Miss.
Hochgesang, Josh	.155	21	71	10	11	2	0	1	8	14	23	0	1	R	R	6-3	210	4-16-77	1999	Fullerton, Calif.
Howe, Matt	.301	64	229	44	69	12	2	14	45	48	49	9	2	R	R	6-0	205	9-16-76	1998	Houston, Texas
Keller, G.W.	.242	28	95	10	23	5	0	0	13	17	10	5	1	R	R	5-10	180	6-4-77	1998	Bakersfield, Calif.
Laird, Gerald	.285	60	228	45	65	7	2	2	39	28	43	10	5	R	R	6-2	195	11-13-79	1999	Garden Grove, Calif.
Lockwood, Mike	.361	69	255	48	92	18	5	7	51	39	49	6	5	L	L	6-1	195	12-27-76	1999	Powell, Ore.
Nieckula, Aaron	.260	15	50	11	13	4	0	1	9	9	12	2	1	R	R	5-11	200	9-7-76	1998	Stickney, III.
Porter, Jamie	.240	44	129	30	31	5	1	2	16	11	32	9	4	R	R	6-1	195	5-16-76	1997	Bellevue, Wash.
Rosario, Carlos	.227	63	260	51	59	9	5	2	27	44	56	31	13	S	R	5-9	160	2-22-80	1997	Bani, D.R.
Schied, Jeremy	.254	60	213	28	54	9	1	3	35	32	60	0	0	L	L	6-0	190	3-24-76	1998	Grand Junction, Colo.
Soto, Jorge	.244	45	160	37	39	9	0	11	30	38	63	1	2	R	R	6-0	210	4-14-78	1999	Patillas, P.R.

GAMES BY POSITION: C—de la Cruz 15, Laird 51, Nieckula 14. 1B—de la Cruz 4, Schied 53, Soto 24. 2B—Henderson 40, Keller 7, Rosario 35, Soto 1. 3B—Henderson 5, Hochgesang 9, Howe 53, Keller 10, Nieckula 1. SS—Clements 33, Declet 13, Hall 5, Rosario 31. OF—Asche 63, Forbes 61, Keller 10, Lockwood 65, Porter 38.

PITCHING

PITCHING	W	L	ERA	G	GS	CG	SV	IP	H	R	ER	BB	SO	B	T	HT	WT	DOB	1st Yr	Resides
Bazzell, Shane	3	1	1.86	5	5	0	0	29	27	15	6	9	18	L	R	6-2	190	3-22-79	1998	Columbus, Miss.
Chiasson, Scott	2	2	5.22	15	13	0	0	69	80	52	40	39	51	R	R	6-5	185	8-14-77	1998	Norwich, Conn.
Crawford, Jay	2	1	3.96	19	0	0	2	39	40	20	17	14	24	L	L	6-0	185	12-27-78	1997	Chatham, Ill.
Gage, Matt	8	7	5.68	18	5	0	0	65	78	49	41	16	39	R	R	6-5	205	3-23-78	1999	Westmont, Ill.
German, Franklyn	3	5	5.99	15	15	0	0	74	89	52	49	45	58	R	R	6-5	210	1-20-80	1996	San Cristobal, D.R.
Hilton, Nate	2	4	6.82	16	14	0	0	67	80	63	51	28	50	R	R	6-6	230	4-21-78	1999	Boone, Iowa
Lehr, Justin	2	6	5.95	14	4	0	0	42	62	36	28	17	40	R	R	6-1	200	8-3-77	1999	West Covina, Calif.
Mazur, Bryan	5	2	3.35	23	0	0	8	40	36	20	15	17	29	L	L	6-0	175	7-26-77	1999	Elizabethtown, N.C.
Meeks, Eric	0	0	9.00	6	3	0	0	19	21	22	19	11	10	R	R	6-4	225	4-12-79	1997	Orlando, Fla.
Miller, Corey	1	1	2.25	5	0	0	0	12	5	4	3	2	10	R	R	5-11	175	7-31-76	1999	Oakhurst, Calif.
Moore, Darin	1	0	1.42	5	2	0	0	13	9	4	2	6	14	R	R	6-0	195	12-19-76	1999	Acampo, Calif.
Negron, Alex	0	4	5.61	13	1	0	1	26	16	21	16	23	25	R	R	6-6	200	5-2-78	1998	Dorado, P.R.
Oyler, Scott	0	0	15.43	4	0	0	0	7	11	14	12	6	4	R	R	6-4	200	12-16-75	1998	Portland, Ore.
Pomar, Jason	2	0	3.81	16	1	0	0	50	55	31	21	9	52	R	R	6-3	215	3-8-77	1999	Vero Beach, Fla.
Sanchez, Cade	0	1	3.80	9	0	0	0	21	20	15	9	21	15	L	R	6-0	205	3-7-77	1998	Salina, Kan.
Surkont, Keith	5	3	4.48	17	13	0	1	74	85	45	37	35	39	R	R	6-2	205	4-4-77	1999	Pawtucket, R.I.
Tauscher, Ryan	2	1	6.84	12	0	0	0	25	27	22	19	19	16	S	L	6-2	200	10-4-76	1998	Glendale, Ariz.

PHOENIX

Rookie

ARIZONA LEAGUE

BATTING

BATTING	AVG	G	AB	R	H	2B	3B	HR	RBI	BB	SO	SB	CS	B	T	HT	WT	DOB	1st Yr	Resides
Bellhorn, Mark	.233	12	43	11	10	3	0	0	5	11	9	0	0	S	R	6-1	190	8-23-74	1995	Oviedo, Fla.
Berroa, Angel	.290	46	169	42	49	11	4	2	24	16	26	11	4	R	R	6-0	175	1-27-80	1997	Santo Domingo, D.R.
Betts, DeWayne	.129	34	70	13	9	3	0	0	6	8	25	0	0	R	R	6-0	175	6-14-80	1998	Lakewood, Calif.
Castillo, Carlos	.205	31	88	9	18	4	1	1	13	3	23	0	0	R	R	6-0	190	5-6-81	1998	Santo Domingo, D.R.
Chirinos, German	.271	54	199	34	54	9	5	6	56	28	47	13	4	R	R	6-0	170	8-29-78	1996	Yaracuy, Venez.
Ellis, Alvyn	.216	34	102	13	22	5	2	0	12	8	45	0	0	R	R	6-3	195	6-6-80	1999	Beaverton, Ore.
Gregg, Mitch	.237	37	118	21	28	9	1	1	16	32	40	4	2	L	R	6-6	230	7-7-76	1999	Issaquah, Wash.
Halgren, Chris	.182	10	22	4	4	0	0	0	3	11	11	0	0	R	R	6-3	200	4-11-79	1999	Beaverton, Ore.
Hall, Justin	.350	7	20	5	7	1	0	0	4	5	5	0	1	R	R	5-10	180	9-23-76	1998	Mesa, Ariz.
Ortiz, Jorge	.192	22	52	6	10	1	0	0	5	13	29	1	1	R	R	6-4	210	9-24-80	1999	Cayey, P.R.
Pellerano, Cristi	.275	48	178	34	49	11	1	3	29	11	45	1	1	R	R	6-2	185	8-25-78	1996	Santo Domingo, D.R.
Pena, Wilton	.240	41	129	18	31	14	1	5	21	14	39	0	0	R	R	6-1	210	12-16-78	1996	Bani, D.R.
Pimentel, Franklin	.276	54	174	40	48	6	2	8	40	38	36	6	4	S	R	6-0	197	1-20-79	1996	Bani, D.R.
Reyes, Christian	.283	49	187	39	53	11	8	1	39	26	54	3	1	S	R	6-0	175	6-22-78	1995	Santo Domingo, D.R.
Rosa, Ivan	.194	32	72	18	14	4	0	2	11	11	30	0	2	L	L	6-0	170	6-12-79	1996	Santo Domingo, D.R.
Schmidt, J.P.	.278	34	90	20	25	2	2	0	14	28	21	2	5	L	R	6-1	180	1-4-80	1998	Palmdale, Calif.
Wenner, Michael	.386	49	207	56	80	12	7	2	28	17	31	36	12	R	R	5-10	180	12-9-78	1999	Allentown, Pa.

GAMES BY POSITION: C—Castillo 31, Halgren 7, Pena 33. 1B—Ellis 31, Gregg 25, Pena 5, Reyes 6. 2B—Bellhorn 7, Berroa 10, Hall 1, Pimentel 44, Schmidt 1. 3B—Berroa 9, Ortiz 13, Pimentel 6, Reyes 41. SS—Berroa 31, Hall 3, Schmidt 33. OF—Berroa 2, Betts 33, Chirinos 50, Pellerano 45, Rosa 21, Wenner 48.

PITCHING

PITCHING	W	L	ERA	G	GS	CG	SV	IP	H	R	ER	BB	SO	B	T	HT	WT	DOB	1st Yr	Resides
Beckman, Jacob	4	1	3.81	12	0	0	1	28	31	16	12	10	19	R	R	6-2	180	4-4-79	1999	Niles, Mich.
Blumenstock, Brad	0	0	5.40	3	2	0	0	5	10	4	3	6	4	R	R	6-6	225	2-19-75	1996	Marion, Ill.
Calzada, Javier	5	1	2.54	10	8	0	0	46	32	19	13	11	30	R	R	6-2	195	2-28-79	1996	Bani, D.R.
Diaz, Alex	2	1	3.19	22	0	0	5	42	54	21	15	10	26	R	R	6-3	175	7-15-79	1996	Santo Domingo, D.R.
Dunphy, Micah	2	1	3.19	16	1	0	1	31	35	18	11	17	34	L	L	6-1	180	11-7-79	1999	Dixon, Ill.
Galva, Claudio	6	2	2.38	14	11	0	0	68	64	23	18	16	59	L	L	6-2	200	11-28-79	1996	Santo Domingo, D.R.
Jacobs, Frankey	1	2	5.48	12	0	0	0	21	20	14	13	11	15	R	R	6-6	190	1-15-78	1997	Durham, N.C.
Maurer, Mike	0	0	1.23	7	0	0	2	7	4	1	1	1	8	R	R	6-2	185	7-4-72	1994	Burnsville, Minn.
Miller, Corey	2	0	0.78	18	0	0	11	23	15	3	2	9	28	R	R	5-11	175	7-31-76	1999	Oakhurst, Calif.
Minaya, Edwin	5	3	6.18	14	11	0	0	60	76	49	41	24	41	R	R	6-3	180	6-20-80	1997	Montecristi, D.R.
Nantkes, Kurt	5	4	2.19	15	11	0	0	70	55	25	17	18	64	R	R	6-4	195	11-12-79	1998	Aurora, Colo.
Sobchuk, Justin	3	1	5.77	15	6	0	1	48	51	34	31	28	47	L	R	6-2	195	11-19-80	1999	Bellingham, Wash.
Velazquez, Elih	4	1	3.70	16	4	0	0	41	44	18	17	11	38	L	L	6-2	190	6-2-80	1999	San Lorenzo, P.R.
Weinberg, Todd	0	0	4.15	6	0	0	0	4	5	2	0	3	1	R	L	6-3	235	6-13-72	1994	Somerset, Mass.

PHILADELPHIA PHILLIES

Offensive nucleus brings optimism despite soft finish

BY PAUL HAGEN

To borrow a line from an old television game show, will the real Phillies please stand up? Were they the team that was 13 games over .500 as late as Aug. 6? Or were they the team that lost 34 of its next 44 after that to plunge out of contention?

The Phillies, of course, claim it's the former. But it's hard to ignore the record. The Phillies finished 77-85 in 1999, just a two-game improvement from 1998.

"Our record is what it is," manager Terry Francona said. "And we're disappointed to finish where we finished because of the way we played the first four months. But I really believe we're in a better position to improve than we were before."

That optimism is based on several outstanding individual performances, as well as the fact that general manager Ed Wade has a significant payroll increase, from $30 million to about $45 million, to work with.

"I think knowledgeable people around baseball think we have the nucleus to be a legitimate contender if we do one or two things," Wade said.

Here's what the nucleus accomplished:

■ Center fielder Doug Glanville became the first Phillies player since Pete Rose in 1979 to have 200 hits in a season.

■ Catcher Mike Lieberthal had a breakthrough season, making the all-star team and batting .300 with 31 homers.

■ Right fielder Bob Abreu finished third in the batting race. His .335 average was the highest for the Phillies since Tony Gonzalez hit .339 in 1967.

■ Third baseman Scott Rolen appeared on his way to his best season yet before spraining his lower back

Bob Abreu   **Pat Burrell**

Players of the Year

MAJOR LEAGUE: Bob Abreu, of
Abreu ranked third in the NL with a .335 average and a .446 on-base percentage and led the Phillies with 118 runs.

MINOR LEAGUE: Pat Burrell, 1b/of
Burrell led Phillies farmhands with a .320 average and 29 homers while learning to play left field.

sliding into third base in Milwaukee on July 21. At the time, he had hit five homers in five games. He hit only two more the rest of the year and didn't play at all the final month of the season.

Suspect pitching, however, offset those offensive milestones. Righthander Chad Ogea, who opened the season as the No. 2 starter, finished it deep in the bullpen and was released when the season ended. Lefthander Paul Spoljaric, the fifth starter in April, went 0-3 with a 15.09 ERA in five games and was traded to the Blue Jays for righthander Robert Person.

When the season ended, 20 pitchers had won at least one game and the Phillies had allowed 212 home runs.

Righthanders Curt Schilling and Paul Byrd each made the all-star team, with Schilling getting the honor of starting for the National League at Fenway Park. But Schilling succumbed in the second half to shoulder tendinitis, pitching just 31 innings after the break. Byrd slumped, winning just four more games.

Help could be on the way from the farm system, which produced lefthander Randy Wolf for '99. Wolf started strong before a second-half fade. Pat Burrell, drafted No. 1 overall in 1998, tore up the Eastern League and finished the season with Triple-A Scranton/Wilkes-Barre in the International League playoffs. The Phillies moved him to left field late in the season.

Righthander Adam Eaton, a 1996 first-round pick, pitched a no-hitter in his first start for Reading, though he got the loss. The organization had more pitching emerge with Class A Piedmont. The Boll Weevils had the lowest team ERA in the minors, led by righthander Brad Baisley and lefthander Greg Kubes.

ORGANIZATION LEADERS

BATTING

*AVG	Pat Burrell, Scranton/Reading	.320
R	Billy McMillon, Scranton	97
H	Wendell Magee, Scranton	160
TB	Pat Burrell, Scranton/Reading	271
2B	Billy McMillon, Scranton	38
3B	Reggie Taylor, Reading	10
HR	Pat Burrell, Scranton/Reading	29
RBI	Two tied at	106
BB	Jon Zuber, Scranton	86
SO	Shomari Beverly, Piedmont/Batavia	137
SB	Alejandro Fajardo, Piedmont	44

PITCHING

W	Robert Dodd, Scranton/Reading	14
L	Greg Kubes, Piedmont	12
#ERA	Robert Dodd, Scranton/Reading	3.04
G	Doug Nickle, Clearwater	60
CG	Three tied at	4
SV	Doug Nickle, Clearwater	28
IP	Adam Eaton, Reading	167
BB	Rob Burger, Reading/Clearwater/GCL	84
SO	Derrick Turnbow, Piedmont	149

*Minimum 250 At-Bats #Minimum 75 Innings

Philadelphia
PHILLIES

Manager: Terry Francona

Organization Statistics

BATTING	AVG	G	AB	R	H	2B	3B	HR	RBI	BB	SO	SB	CS	B	T	HT	WT	DOB	1st Yr	Resides
Abreu, Bob	.335	152	546	118	183	35	11	20	93	109	113	27	9	L	R	6-0	185	3-11-74	1991	Tumero, Venez.
Anderson, Marlon	.252	129	452	48	114	26	4	5	54	24	61	13	2	L	R	5-11	190	1-6-74	1995	Prattville, Ala.
Arias, Alex	.303	118	347	43	105	20	1	4	48	36	31	2	2	R	R	6-3	185	11-20-67	1987	Plantation, Fla.
Bennett, Gary	.273	36	88	7	24	4	0	1	21	4	11	0	0	R	R	6-0	190	4-17-72	1990	Waukegan, Ill.
Brogna, Rico	.278	157	619	90	172	29	4	24	102	54	132	8	5	L	L	6-2	200	4-18-70	1988	Watertown, Conn.
Cedeno, Domingo	.152	32	66	5	10	4	0	1	5	5	22	0	1	S	R	6-0	170	11-4-68	1989	La Romana, D.R.
Doster, Dave	.196	99	97	9	19	2	0	3	10	12	23	1	0	R	R	5-11	185	10-8-70	1993	Fort Wayne, Ind.
Ducey, Rob	.261	104	188	29	49	10	2	8	33	38	57	2	1	L	R	6-2	180	5-24-65	1984	Palm Harbor, Fla.
Estalella, Bobby	.167	9	18	2	3	0	0	0	1	4	7	0	1	R	R	6-1	200	8-23-74	1993	Pembroke Pines, Fla.
Gant, Ron	.260	138	516	107	134	27	5	17	77	85	112	13	3	R	R	6-0	200	3-2-65	1983	Smyrna, Ga.
Glanville, Doug	.325	150	628	101	204	38	6	11	73	48	82	34	2	R	R	6-2	175	8-25-70	1991	Teaneck, N.J.
Jordan, Kevin	.285	120	347	36	99	17	3	4	51	24	34	0	0	R	R	6-1	185	10-9-69	1990	Birkdale, Australia
Lieberthal, Mike	.300	145	510	84	153	33	1	31	96	44	86	0	0	R	R	6-0	186	1-18-72	1990	Westlake Village, Calif.
Lovullo, Torey	.211	17	38	3	8	0	0	2	5	3	11	0	0	S	R	6-0	185	7-25-65	1987	Northridge, Calif.
Magee, Wendell	.357	12	14	4	5	1	0	2	5	1	4	0	0	R	R	6-0	220	8-3-72	1994	Birmingham, Ala.
Prince, Tom	.167	4	6	1	1	0	0	0	1	1	0	0	0	R	R	5-11	206	8-13-64	1984	Bradenton, Fla.
Relaford, Desi	.242	65	211	31	51	11	2	1	26	19	34	4	3	S	R	5-8	170	9-16-73	1991	Palm Harbor, Fla.
Rolen, Scott	.268	112	421	74	113	28	1	26	77	67	114	12	2	R	R	6-4	223	4-4-75	1993	Jasper, Ind.
Sefcik, Kevin	.278	111	209	28	58	15	3	1	11	29	24	9	4	R	R	5-10	181	2-10-71	1993	Lockport, Ill.

PITCHING	W	L	ERA	G	GS	CG	SV	IP	H	R	ER	BB	SO	B	T	HT	WT	DOB	1st Yr	Resides
Aldred, Scott	1	1	3.90	29	0	0	1	32	33	15	14	15	19	L	L	6-4	195	6-12-68	1987	Lakeland, Fla.
Bennett, Joel	2	1	9.00	5	3	0	0	17	26	17	17	7	13	R	R	6-1	161	1-31-70	1991	Sydney, N.Y.
Brantley, Jeff	1	2	5.19	10	0	0	5	9	5	6	5	8	11	R	R	5-10	189	9-5-63	1985	Clinton, Miss.
Brewer, Billy	1	1	7.01	25	0	0	2	26	30	20	20	14	28	L	L	6-1	175	4-15-68	1990	Waco, Texas
Byrd, Paul	15	11	4.60	32	32	1	0	200	205	119	102	70	106	R	R	6-1	185	12-3-70	1991	Louisville, Ky.
Gomes, Wayne	5	5	4.26	73	0	0	19	74	70	38	35	56	58	R	R	6-2	226	1-15-73	1993	Cherry Hill, N.J.
Grace, Mike	1	4	7.69	27	5	0	0	55	80	48	47	30	28	R	R	6-4	210	6-20-70	1991	Clearwater, Fla.
Grahe, Joe	1	4	3.86	13	5	0	0	33	40	16	14	17	16	R	R	6-0	200	8-14-67	1989	Palm Beach Gardens, Fla.
Loewer, Carlton	2	6	5.12	20	13	2	0	90	100	54	51	26	48	S	R	6-6	220	9-24-73	1995	Eunice, La.
Montgomery, Steve	1	5	3.34	53	0	0	3	65	54	25	24	31	55	R	R	6-4	200	12-25-70	1992	Corona Del Mar, Calif.
Ogea, Chad	6	12	5.63	36	28	0	0	168	192	110	105	61	77	R	R	6-2	200	11-9-70	1991	Lake Charles, La.
Perez, Yorkis	3	1	3.94	35	0	0	0	32	29	15	14	15	26	S	L	6-0	180	9-30-67	1983	Bajos de Haina, D.R.
Person, Robert	10	5	4.27	31	22	0	0	137	130	72	65	70	127	R	R	6-0	195	1-8-69	1989	St. Louis, Mo.
Politte, Cliff	1	0	7.13	13	0	0	0	18	19	14	14	15	15	R	R	5-11	185	2-27-74	1995	St. Louis, Mo.
Poole, Jim	1	1	4.33	51	0	0	1	35	48	20	17	15	22	L	L	6-1	203	4-28-66	1988	Alpharetta, Ga.
Ryan, Ken	1	2	6.32	15	0	0	0	16	16	11	11	11	9	R	R	6-3	230	10-24-68	1986	Attleboro, Mass.
Schilling, Curt	15	6	3.54	24	24	8	0	180	159	74	71	44	152	R	R	6-4	228	11-14-66	1986	Philadelphia, Pa.
Schrenk, Steve	1	3	4.29	32	2	0	1	50	41	24	24	14	36	R	R	6-3	185	11-20-68	1987	Aurora, Ore.
Shumaker, Anthony	0	3	5.96	8	4	0	0	23	23	17	15	14	17	L	L	6-5	223	5-14-73	1995	Kokomo, Ind.
Spoljaric, Paul	0	3	15.09	5	3	0	0	11	23	24	19	7	10	L	L	6-3	210	9-24-70	1990	Kelowna, B.C.
Telemaco, Amaury	3	0	5.55	44	0	0	0	47	45	29	29	20	41	R	R	6-3	210	1-19-74	1991	La Romana, D.R.
2-team (5 Arizona)	4	0	5.77	49	0	0	0	53	52	34	34	26	43							
Wolf, Randy	6	9	5.55	22	21	0	0	122	126	78	75	67	116	L	L	6-0	190	8-22-76	1997	Canoga Park, Calif.

FIELDING

Catcher	PCT	G	PO	A	E	DP	PB
G. Bennett	.971	32	129	6	4	0	2
Estalella	.976	7	38	2	1	0	0
Lieberthal	.997	143	881	62	3	12	11
Prince	1.000	4	13	1	0	0	0

First Base	PCT	G	PO	A	E	DP
Brogna	.995	157	1240	123	7	119
Jordan	1.000	13	55	4	0	6
Lovullo	1.000	6	22	5	0	3

Second Base	PCT	G	PO	A	E	DP
Anderson	.979	121	234	284	11	59
Arias	.000	1	0	0	0	0
Cedeno	1.000	1	1	2	0	0
Doster	.993	77	69	72	1	21
Jordan	.984	33	56	67	2	22
Lovullo	1.000	6	14	8	0	0
Sefcik	.977	15	25	17	1	4

Third Base	PCT	G	PO	A	E	DP
Arias	1.000	2	1	1	0	0
Doster	1.000	6	3	7	0	1
Jordan	.943	62	40	93	8	10
Rolen	.960	112	111	227	14	21

Shortstop	PCT	G	PO	A	E	DP
Arias	.988	95	119	207	4	43
Cedeno	.982	19	19	35	1	6
Doster	1.000	5	6	9	0	3
Relaford	.952	63	97	182	14	43

Outfield	PCT	G	PO	A	E	DP
Abreu	.989	146	260	8	3	0
Ducey	1.000	58	89	1	0	0
Gant	.993	133	260	7	2	2
Glanville	.980	148	385	13	8	3
Magee	1.000	4	5	0	0	0
Sefcik	.986	64	68	1	1	0

DIAMOND IMAGES

Curt Schilling

Mike Lieberthal
Enjoyed breakthrough year with 31 home runs

Adam Eaton
Threw a no-hitter and lost

FARM SYSTEM

Director, Minor League Operations: Steve Noworyta

Class	Farm Team	League	W	L	Pct.	Finish*	Manager	First Yr
AAA	Scranton/W-B (Pa.) Red Barons	International	78	66	.542	5th (14)	Marc Bombard	1989
AA	Reading (Pa.) Phillies	Eastern	73	69	.514	5th (12)	Gary Varsho	1967
A#	Clearwater (Fla.) Phillies	Florida State	77	59	.566	3rd (14)	Bill Dancy	1985
A	Piedmont (N.C.) Boll Weevils	South Atlantic	69	71	.493	9th (14)	Ken Oberkfell	1995
A	Batavia (N.Y.) Muckdogs	New York-Penn	42	34	.553	t-3rd (14)	Greg Legg	1988
Rookie#	Clearwater (Fla.) Phillies	Gulf Coast	26	34	.433	11th (14)	Ramon Aviles	1999

*Finish in overall standings (No. of teams in league) #Advanced level

SCRANTON/WILKES-BARRE | Class AAA

INTERNATIONAL LEAGUE

BATTING	AVG	G	AB	R	H	2B	3B	HR	RBI	BB	SO	SB	CS	B	T	HT	WT	DOB	1st Yr	Resides
Alvarez, Clemente	.250	9	28	4	7	4	0	0	6	3	9	0	0	R	R	5-11	180	5-18-68	1987	Anzoategui, Venez.
Burrell, Pat	.152	10	33	4	5	0	0	1	4	4	8	0	1	R	R	6-4	230	10-10-76	1998	Miami, Fla.
Burton, Darren	.262	118	409	61	107	30	3	13	63	44	96	7	2	S	R	6-1	185	9-16-72	1990	Somerset, Ky.
Carter, Michael	.161	9	31	2	5	1	1	1	4	0	8	0	1	R	R	5-9	170	5-5-69	1990	Vicksburg, Miss.
Carver, Steve	.236	98	288	33	68	18	1	11	38	34	101	2	0	L	R	6-3	215	9-27-72	1995	Jacksonville, Fla.
Estalella, Bobby	.231	110	386	58	89	23	2	15	62	55	100	4	1	R	R	6-1	200	8-23-74	1993	Pembroke Pines, Fla.
Finn, John	.218	42	124	18	27	1	0	4	10	15	12	2	0	R	R	5-8	168	10-18-67	1989	Oakland, Calif.
Flores, Jose	.246	64	228	35	56	6	2	0	18	37	43	13	3	R	R	5-11	180	6-28-73	1994	New York, N.Y.
Frazier, Lou	.247	89	308	54	76	16	7	6	32	44	79	21	3	S	R	6-2	175	1-26-65	1986	Chandler, Ariz.
Guiliano, Matt	.190	71	216	20	41	15	0	2	24	17	61	3	2	R	R	5-9	180	10-7-72	1994	Ronkonkoma, N.Y.
Huff, Larry	.235	9	17	4	4	2	0	0	1	5	2	0	0	R	R	6-0	175	1-24-72	1994	Palm Harbor, Fla.
Lovullo, Torey	.279	139	519	90	145	36	3	21	106	78	89	3	4	S	R	6-0	185	7-25-65	1987	Northridge, Calif.
Lucca, Lou	.268	136	533	61	143	33	2	12	70	22	94	4	6	R	R	5-11	210	10-13-70	1992	South San Francisco, Calif.
Magee, Wendell	.283	142	566	95	160	34	2	20	79	55	124	10	8	R	R	6-0	220	8-3-72	1994	Birmingham, Ala.
McMillon, Billy	.304	132	464	97	141	38	4	16	85	65	79	11	2	L	L	5-11	179	11-17-71	1993	Sumter, S.C.
Millan, Adan	.000	1	2	0	0	0	0	0	0	1	2	0	0	R	R	6-0	195	3-26-72	1994	Montebello, Calif.
Prince, Tom	.091	7	22	2	2	0	0	1	1	3	5	1	0	R	R	5-11	206	8-13-64	1984	Bradenton, Fla.
Rollins, Jimmy	.077	4	13	0	1	1	0	0	0	1	1	1	0	S	R	5-8	160	11-27-78	1996	Alameda, Calif.
Ronan, Marc	.165	38	115	14	19	5	0	2	10	8	28	1	2	L	R	6-2	190	9-19-69	1990	Tallahassee, Fla.
Zuber, Jon	.295	111	387	69	114	24	2	6	54	86	48	7	1	L	L	6-0	190	12-10-69	1992	Moraga, Calif.

PITCHING

PITCHING	W	L	ERA	G	GS	CG	SV	IP	H	R	ER	BB	SO	B	T	HT	WT	DOB	1st Yr	Resides
Bennett, Joel	10	4	4.61	20	20	1	0	127	134	71	65	47	125	R	R	6-1	161	1-31-70	1991	Sydney, N.Y.
Bolton, Rod	11	10	3.82	24	24	4	0	153	161	76	65	52	85	R	R	6-2	190	9-23-68	1990	Chattanooga, Tenn.
Brewer, Billy	6	1	3.78	33	5	0	2	69	59	32	29	28	57	L	L	6-1	175	4-15-68	1990	Waco, Texas
Dodd, Robert	4	0	0.91	6	4	1	0	30	19	5	3	6	23	L	L	6-3	188	3-14-73	1994	Plano, Texas
Eaton, Adam	1	1	3.00	3	3	0	0	21	17	10	7	6	10	R	R	6-2	190	11-23-77	1996	Snohomish, Wash.
Fesh, Sean	4	3	4.39	45	0	0	1	53	50	29	26	31	38	L	L	6-2	165	11-3-72	1991	Bethel, Conn.
Fiore, Tony	0	0	6.64	13	0	0	0	20	28	19	15	15	13	R	R	6-4	210	10-12-71	1992	Oak Park, Ill.
Grace, Mike	2	2	4.44	10	9	0	0	47	52	25	23	17	27	R	R	6-4	210	6-20-70	1991	Clearwater, Fla.
Grahe, Joe	3	1	3.00	23	4	0	10	36	38	15	12	15	25	R	R	6-0	200	8-14-67	1989	Palm Beach Gardens, Fla.
Green, Tyler	4	6	7.69	19	7	1	0	50	78	47	43	24	31	R	R	6-5	208	2-18-70	1991	Englewood, Colo.
Jacquez, Tom	0	1	2.45	3	0	0	0	4	4	1	1	0	4	L	L	6-2	195	12-29-75	1997	Stockton, Calif.
Johnson, Barry	6	10	5.02	31	18	1	0	136	157	83	76	49	88	R	R	6-4	200	8-21-69	1991	Joliet, Ill.
Looney, Brian	1	0	3.94	3	3	0	0	16	19	9	7	6	12	L	L	5-10	180	6-26-69	1991	Cheshire, Conn.
2-team (47 Toledo)...	4	0	5.70	50	4	0	2	71	70	47	45	50	64							
Montgomery, Steve	0	0	6.23	14	0	0	7	13	17	9	9	11	13	R	R	6-4	200	12-25-70	1992	Corona Del Mar, Calif.
Myers, Jimmy	1	0	3.77	11	0	0	1	14	15	6	6	3	6	R	R	6-1	185	4-28-69	1987	Crowder, Okla.
2-team (3 Norfolk) ...	1	1	6.50	14	0	0	1	18	26	14	13	5	8							
Nye, Ryan	5	4	5.10	14	10	0	0	65	69	41	37	20	63	R	R	6-2	195	6-24-73	1994	Cameron, Okla.
Ryan, Ken	2	2	5.66	31	0	0	6	41	54	30	26	19	33	R	R	6-3	230	10-24-68	1986	Attleboro, Mass.
Schrenk, Steve	3	1	2.93	32	0	0	2	43	38	17	14	31	34	R	R	6-3	185	11-20-68	1987	Aurora, Ore.
Scott, Darryl	7	6	4.09	57	4	0	10	106	100	53	48	47	91	R	R	6-1	185	8-6-68	1990	Prior Lake, Minn.
Shumaker, Anthony	3	5	5.72	14	14	1	0	90	119	60	57	32	49	L	L	6-5	223	5-14-73	1995	Kokomo, Ind.
Welch, Mike	1	2	7.94	13	5	0	0	34	45	30	30	13	11	L	R	6-2	210	8-25-72	1993	Nashua, N.H.
Williams, Shad	0	2	19.80	2	2	0	0	5	17	11	11	3	2	R	R	6-0	198	3-10-71	1991	Fresno, Calif.
Wolf, Randy	4	5	3.61	12	12	0	0	77	73	36	31	29	72	L	L	6-0	190	8-22-76	1997	Canoga Park, Calif.

FIELDING

Catcher	PCT	G	PO	A	E	DP	PB
Alvarez	1.000	9	59	6	0	0	1
Estalella	.993	101	652	43	5	10	3
Millan	1.000	1	8	0	0	0	0
Prince	1.000	6	31	2	0	0	0
Ronan	.981	32	185	19	4	2	3

First Base	PCT	G	PO	A	E	DP
Burrell	1.000	6	58	1	0	8
Carver	.990	67	572	33	6	64
Lovullo	.929	5	24	2	2	2
Ronan	1.000	1	1	0	0	0
Zuber	.997	73	588	74	2	65

Second Base	PCT	G	PO	A	E	DP
Finn	.973	10	19	17	1	6
Guiliano	.917	5	6	5	1	1
Huff	1.000	3	4	3	0	3
Lovullo	.982	132	262	390	12	99

Third Base	PCT	G	PO	A	E	DP
Finn	1.000	1	1	0	0	0
Guiliano	.933	8	3	11	1	1
Huff	1.000	3	0	7	0	2
Lovullo	1.000	2	2	6	0	0
Lucca	.960	136	76	310	16	27

Shortstop	PCT	G	PO	A	E	DP
Finn	.944	28	33	85	7	19
Flores	.960	63	90	175	11	38
Guiliano	.921	57	70	174	21	44
Huff	.000	1	0	0	0	0
Rollins	.960	4	9	15	1	4

Outfield	PCT	G	PO	A	E	DP
Burrell	1.000	4	4	0	0	0
Burton	.975	98	191	8	5	4
Carter	1.000	6	7	0	0	0
Carver	.000	1	0	0	0	0
Frazier	.969	56	155	2	5	0
Magee	.975	140	310	7	8	1
McMillon	.979	129	219	11	5	2
Zuber	1.000	13	20	1	0	0

READING   Class AA

EASTERN LEAGUE

BATTING

BATTING	AVG	G	AB	R	H	2B	3B	HR	RBI	BB	SO	SB	CS	B	T	HT	WT	DOB	1st Yr	Resides
Alvarez, Clemente	.176	48	142	12	25	5	1	2	12	11	38	1	1	R	R	5-11	180	5-18-68	1987	Anzoategui, Venez.
Antczak, Chuck	.000	8	19	0	0	0	0	0	0	0	4	0	0	R	R	6-0	185	10-8-73	1995	Sarasota, Fla.
Burnham, Gary	.249	116	354	47	88	20	0	12	49	41	49	11	3	L	L	5-11	200	10-13-74	1997	South Windsor, Conn.
Burrell, Pat	.333	117	417	84	139	28	6	28	90	79	103	3	3	R	R	6-4	230	10-10-76	1998	Miami, Fla.
Finn, John	.209	40	115	15	24	8	1	0	9	20	16	7	1	R	R	5-8	168	10-18-67	1989	Oakland, Calif.
Francia, David	.271	107	339	41	92	22	5	4	43	21	57	13	4	L	L	6-0	167	4-16-75	1996	Mobile, Ala.
Harris, Reggie	.221	119	380	42	84	13	3	5	41	46	58	9	5	S	R	5-10	180	4-28-75	1997	Carmel, Ind.
Horne, Tyrone	.267	80	262	37	70	13	2	5	37	43	64	13	9	L	R	5-10	185	11-2-70	1989	Troy, N.C.
Huff, Larry	.260	121	427	72	111	28	3	3	54	60	69	28	6	R	R	6-0	175	1-24-72	1994	Palm Harbor, Fla.
McNamara, Rusty	.249	50	177	26	44	9	1	5	20	17	22	0	4	R	R	5-9	185	1-23-75	1997	Riverside, Calif.
Pierce, Kirk	.259	83	255	37	66	10	0	9	40	42	56	4	4	R	R	6-3	200	5-26-73	1995	Murrieta, Calif.
Raynor, Mark	.209	14	43	4	9	0	1	0	3	6	4	0	1	R	R	6-0	180	4-1-73	1995	Williamston, N.C.
Rollins, Jimmy	.273	133	532	81	145	21	8	11	56	51	47	24	13	S	R	5-8	168	11-27-78	1996	Alameda, Calif.
Royster, Aaron	.291	91	309	53	90	17	2	8	48	48	90	11	5	R	R	6-1	220	11-30-72	1994	Chicago, Ill.
Stewart, Andy	.300	54	190	23	57	19	0	7	40	16	18	0	3	R	R	5-11	205	12-5-70	1990	Wilmington, Del.
Taylor, Reggie	.266	127	526	75	140	17	10	15	61	18	79	38	22	L	R	6-1	175	1-12-77	1995	Newberry, S.C.
Tinoco, Luis	.271	39	96	18	26	4	0	1	10	22	23	2	2	R	R	6-2	215	7-24-74	1992	Maracaibo, Venez.

PITCHING

PITCHING	W	L	ERA	G	GS	CG	SV	IP	H	R	ER	BB	SO	B	T	HT	WT	DOB	1st Yr	Resides
Bailie, Matt	1	0	0.00	1	1	0	0	6	3	0	0	1	6	R	R	5-10	195	10-1-75	1998	Aloha, Ore.
Barnett, Marty	2	3	2.53	35	0	0	7	53	43	19	15	24	33	R	R	6-3	210	3-10-74	1995	Harlan, Iowa
Brannan, Ryan	0	0	16.62	5	0	0	0	4	9	8	8	4	1	R	R	6-3	225	4-27-75	1996	Huntington Beach, Calif.
Brester, Jason	7	5	3.76	16	16	3	0	105	105	48	44	26	87	L	L	6-3	190	12-7-76	1995	Burlington, Wash.
Burger, Rob	0	6	13.50	9	9	0	0	27	29	43	41	45	23	R	R	6-1	175	3-25-76	1994	Willow Street, Pa.
Cedeno, Blas	2	2	4.26	19	0	0	0	32	30	16	15	12	18	R	R	6-0	165	11-15-72	1991	Campo Carabobo, Venez.
Censale, Silvio	1	6	11.77	16	11	0	0	52	74	76	68	48	36	L	L	6-2	195	11-21-71	1993	Lodi, N.J.
Coggin, Dave	5	7	7.50	9	9	0	0	42	55	37	35	20	21	R	R	6-4	195	10-30-76	1995	Upland, Calif.
Dodd, Robert	10	2	3.83	42	0	0	5	80	78	38	34	23	79	L	L	6-3	188	3-14-73	1994	Plano, Texas
Eason, Clay	0	2	10.38	10	1	0	1	13	14	15	15	14	13	R	R	5-11	175	11-18-75	1997	Dunn, N.C.
Eaton, Adam	5	4	2.92	12	12	2	0	77	60	30	25	28	67	R	R	6-2	190	11-23-77	1996	Snohomish, Wash.
Grahe, Joe	0	0	0.90	7	0	0	4	10	7	3	1	2	12	R	R	6-0	200	8-14-67	1989	Palm Beach Gardens, Fla.
Herbert, Russ	3	5	4.75	26	9	0	3	83	90	53	44	32	55	R	R	6-3	195	4-21-72	1994	Mentor, Ohio
Hubbs, Dan	0	0	5.63	3	1	0	0	8	10	5	5	5	8	R	R	6-2	200	1-23-71	1993	Renton, Wash.
Jacquez, Tom	6	5	5.28	38	14	0	1	123	149	84	72	32	68	L	L	6-2	195	12-29-75	1997	Stockton, Calif.
Kawabata, Kyle	0	0	6.00	8	0	0	0	12	20	9	8	2	7	R	R	6-0	195	1-2-74	1995	Kailua, Hawaii
Kershner, Jason	4	4	5.73	57	2	0	8	93	99	67	59	40	86	L	L	6-2	165	12-19-76	1995	Scottsdale, Ariz.

PITCHING	W	L	ERA	G	GS	CG	SV	IP	H	R	ER	BB	SO	B	T	HT	WT	DOB	1st Yr	Resides
Politte, Cliff	9	8	3.63	37	13	1	5	109	112	45	44	33	97	R	R	5-11	185	2-27-74	1995	St. Louis, Mo.
Pyc, David	5	2	4.33	17	13	1	0	81	95	44	39	15	51	L	L	6-3	235	2-11-71	1992	Depew, N.Y.
Rutherford, Mark	1	0	0.98	4	4	0	0	18	11	3	2	9	10	R	R	6-2	211	11-9-74	1997	Livonia, Mich.
Shumaker, Anthony	4	3	1.78	10	10	1	0	61	48	17	12	17	60	L	L	6-5	223	5-14-73	1995	Kokomo, Ind.
Thomas, Evan	9	5	3.25	36	15	1	3	127	123	53	46	50	127	R	R	5-10	171	6-14-74	1996	Pembroke Pines, Fla.
Williams, Shad	2	2	3.13	16	2	0	2	32	30	17	11	10	19	R	R	6-0	198	3-10-71	1991	Fresno, Calif.

FIELDING

Catcher	PCT	G	PO	A	E	DP	PB
Alvarez	.992	48	326	24	3	2	4
Antczak	.980	8	46	4	1	0	2
Pierce	.990	70	468	48	5	3	9
Stewart	1.000	29	172	24	0	1	1

First Base	PCT	G	PO	A	E	DP
Burnham	.985	52	368	31	6	33
Burrell	.985	85	665	55	11	49
Huff	1.000	1	4	0	0	0
McNamara	1.000	3	22	2	0	1
Stewart	.992	15	113	10	1	11

Second Base	PCT	G	PO	A	E	DP
Finn	.979	14	16	31	1	3
Harris	.973	113	210	298	14	58

	PCT	G	PO	A	E	DP
Huff	.923	16	19	41	5	6
McNamara	1.000	3	6	10	0	3
Raynor	.953	9	18	23	2	7

Third Base	PCT	G	PO	A	E	DP
Finn	.906	21	19	39	6	4
Huff	.934	96	67	189	18	9
McNamara	.918	31	25	42	6	2
Raynor	.875	3	0	7	1	0
Stewart	1.000	4	2	7	0	2

Shortstop	PCT	G	PO	A	E	DP
Finn	.923	3	4	8	1	2
Harris	1.000	5	10	11	0	2

	PCT	G	PO	A	E	DP
Huff	1.000	2	5	5	0	1
Raynor	1.000	2	1	2	0	0
Rollins	.965	133	211	392	22	72

Outfield	PCT	G	PO	A	E	DP
Burnham	.973	40	70	2	2	0
Burrell	.981	27	50	1	1	0
Francia	.973	99	207	9	6	2
Horne	.962	51	73	2	3	0
Huff	1.000	7	7	4	0	0
McNamara	1.000	9	20	1	0	0
Royster	1.000	71	114	4	0	1
Taylor	.971	122	295	9	9	1
Tinoco	.895	24	32	2	4	0

CLEARWATER — Class A

FLORIDA STATE LEAGUE

BATTING	AVG	G	AB	R	H	2B	3B	HR	RBI	BB	SO	SB	CS	B	T	HT	WT	DOB	1st Yr	Resides
Acevedo, Carlos	.286	12	42	4	12	2	1	0	6	3	7	2	1	R	R	6-0	167	1-31-81	1997	Santo Domingo, D.R.
Antczak, Chuck	.258	15	31	3	8	2	0	0	4	2	6	0	0	R	R	6-0	185	10-8-73	1995	Sarasota, Fla.
Casillas, Uriel	.283	32	113	23	32	5	0	0	24	17	10	4	2	R	R	5-11	185	8-22-75	1997	Downey, Calif.
Collier, Lamonte	.264	104	318	50	84	11	3	0	28	49	60	4	3	R	R	5-9	185	4-1-75	1997	St. Louis, Mo.
Connell, Jerry	.289	25	90	11	26	4	1	2	18	8	27	2	0	R	R	6-2	200	7-17-77	1995	Avenel, N.J.
Dominique, Andy	.255	130	487	77	124	29	5	14	92	69	84	3	3	R	R	6-0	210	10-30-75	1997	Reno, Nev.
Estalella, Bobby	.423	8	26	3	11	3	0	1	8	3	3	0	0	R	R	6-1	200	8-23-74	1993	Pembroke Pines, Fla.
Estrada, Johnny	.277	98	346	35	96	15	0	9	52	14	26	1	0	S	R	5-11	209	6-27-76	1997	Fresno, Calif.
Kiil, Skip	.298	86	305	74	91	15	8	14	55	70	101	24	5	R	R	6-0	172	4-10-74	1996	Salinas, Calif.
Knupfer, Jason	.289	15	45	13	13	2	0	0	3	12	5	1	0	R	R	6-0	185	9-21-74	1996	Redwood City, Calif.
Machado, Anderson	.000	1	2	0	0	0	0	0	0	0	1	0	0	S	R	5-11	165	1-25-81	1998	Caracas, Venez.
McNamara, Rusty	.321	69	274	40	88	12	2	3	43	29	22	5	3	R	R	5-9	185	1-23-75	1997	Riverside, Calif.
Michaels, Jason	.306	122	451	91	138	31	6	14	65	68	103	10	7	R	R	6-0	205	5-4-76	1998	Tampa, Fla.
Perez, Josue	.247	23	93	15	23	2	0	0	6	7	17	6	1	S	R	6-0	180	8-12-77	1998	Santo Domingo, D.R.
2-team (62 Vero Beach)	.269	85	294	39	79	16	1	2	28	28	46	20	12							
Polidor, Wil	.238	52	151	18	36	9	0	0	14	11	18	1	0	S	R	6-1	158	9-23-73	1991	Caracas, Venez.
Prince, Tom	.364	9	33	5	12	0	0	2	9	3	3	1	0	R	R	5-11	206	8-13-64	1984	Bradenton, Fla.
Punto, Nick	.305	106	400	65	122	18	6	1	48	67	53	16	7	S	R	5-10	170	11-8-77	1998	Mission Viejo, Calif.
Relaford, Desi	.286	2	7	1	2	0	0	0	1	1	1	0	0	S	R	5-8	170	9-16-73	1991	Palm Harbor, Fla.
Royster, Aaron	.317	11	41	6	13	2	2	0	5	3	10	1	0	R	R	6-1	220	11-30-72	1994	Chicago, Ill.
Salazar, Jeremy	.300	2	10	1	3	1	0	0	1	0	2	0	0	R	R	5-11	185	3-18-76	1998	Springfield, Ill.
Terrell, Jeff	.283	109	385	63	109	18	4	2	45	42	44	13	8	L	R	6-1	175	10-22-74	1997	Blue Springs, Mo.
Thompson, Nick	.111	9	27	4	3	1	0	0	1	4	12	0	1	R	R	6-0	190	8-23-74	1996	Dunwoody, Ga.
Tinoco, Luis	.182	32	110	15	20	3	0	0	6	8	23	1	0	R	R	6-2	215	7-24-74	1992	Maracaibo, Venez.
Valent, Eric	.288	134	520	91	150	31	9	20	106	58	110	5	3	L	L	6-0	191	4-4-77	1998	Anaheim, Calif.
Van Iten, Bob	.264	98	345	48	91	16	1	5	51	31	63	3	4	L	R	6-1	170	7-1-77	1996	Independence, Mo.

GAMES BY POSITION: C—Antczak 8, Dominique 46, Estalella 6, Estrada 75, Prince 9, Salazar 2, Thompson 1. **1B**—Dominique 34, McNamara 28, Polidor 1, Van Iten 78. **2B**—Casillas 6, Knupfer 15, Polidor 31, Terrell 100. **3B**—Casillas 17, Collier 84, McNamara 31, Polidor 13, Terrell 4, Van Iten 6. **SS**—Casillas 11, Collier 18, Machado 1, Polidor 3, Punto 106, Relaford 2. **OF**—Acevedo 12, Antczak 2, Collier 6, Connell 21, Kiil 83, McNamara 11, Michaels 90, Perez 23, Royster 6, Thompson 3, Tinoco 28, Valent 129, Van Iten 7.

PITCHING	W	L	ERA	G	GS	CG	SV	IP	H	R	ER	BB	SO	B	T	HT	WT	DOB	1st Yr	Resides
Adair, Derek	1	0	3.21	9	0	0	3	14	16	5	5	1	9	R	R	6-4	188	8-25-75	1997	Albertson, N.Y.
Bailie, Matt	0	0	3.00	2	0	0	0	3	2	1	1	3	5	R	R	5-10	195	10-1-75	1998	Aloha, Ore.
Beech, Matt	0	0	7.71	2	2	0	0	5	7	5	4	2	1	L	L	6-2	194	1-20-72	1994	Voorhees, N.J.
Black, Brett	3	3	5.16	34	0	0	3	45	55	30	26	6	27	R	R	6-0	218	10-3-74	1997	Apopka, Fla.
Brannan, Ryan	4	4	4.89	28	13	0	0	77	86	63	42	40	39	R	R	6-3	225	4-27-75	1996	Huntington Beach, Calif.
Burger, Rob	1	2	3.00	6	5	0	0	24	15	10	8	24	23	R	R	6-1	175	3-25-76	1994	Willow Street, Pa.
Cedeno, Blas	4	4	4.21	34	0	0	1	58	63	33	27	17	42	R	R	6-0	165	11-15-72	1991	Campo Carabobo, Venez.
Cotton, Joe	3	3	1.95	38	3	0	1	69	41	17	15	15	43	R	R	6-2	185	3-25-75	1996	Uniontown, Ohio
Duckworth, Brandon	11	5	4.84	27	17	0	1	132	164	84	71	40	101	S	R	6-2	185	1-23-76	1997	Kearns, Utah
Eason, Clay	1	1	4.00	18	0	0	0	27	26	18	12	17	31	R	R	5-11	175	11-18-75	1997	Dunn, N.C.
Eaton, Adam	5	5	3.91	13	13	0	0	69	81	39	30	24	50	R	R	6-2	190	11-23-77	1996	Snohomish, Wash.
Geary, Geoff	10	5	3.95	24	19	2	0	139	175	77	61	31	77	R	R	6-0	175	8-26-76	1998	El Cajon, Calif.
Kawabata, Kyle	3	1	1.15	33	0	0	7	47	36	11	6	10	37	R	R	6-0	195	1-2-74	1995	Kailua, Hawaii
Loewer, Carlton	0	0	7.71	3	3	0	0	7	10	6	6	1	5	R	R	6-6	220	9-24-73	1995	Eunice, La.
Nickle, Doug	2	4	2.29	60	0	0	28	71	60	25	18	23	70	R	R	6-4	210	10-2-74	1997	Sonoma, Calif.
Pyc, David	3	0	0.00	7	0	0	0	10	7	0	0	1	9	L	L	6-3	235	2-11-71	1992	Depew, N.Y.
Rose, Johnathan	0	1	6.75	8	0	0	0	9	12	7	7	6	7	L	L	6-4	225	8-18-76	1997	Haw River, N.C.
Rutherford, Mark	0	4	9.20	9	9	0	0	46	64	57	47	25	23	R	R	6-2	211	11-9-74	1997	Livonia, Mich.
Shipp, Kevin	7	4	5.51	32	7	0	0	83	108	56	51	22	54	R	R	5-11	190	2-8-75	1997	Baton Rouge, La.
Walker, Adam	9	7	3.93	26	25	3	0	149	156	80	65	52	100	L	L	6-7	210	5-28-76	1997	Albuquerque, N.M.
Wedel, Jeremy	0	0	1.69	4	0	0	0	5	4	1	1	3	2	R	R	6-0	195	11-27-76	1998	Wasco, Calif.
Westmoreland, Ken	8	4	4.20	20	20	0	0	111	130	59	52	40	40	R	R	6-1	205	2-26-75	1998	Decatur, Ala.

SOUTH ATLANTIC LEAGUE

BATTING	AVG	G	AB	R	H	2B	3B	HR	RBI	BB	SO	SB	CS	B	T	HT	WT	DOB	1st Yr	Resides
Acevedo, Carlos	.282	56	188	22	53	10	0	1	19	11	30	7	2	R	R	6-0	167	1-31-81	1997	Santo Domingo, D.R.
Avila, Rob	.222	3	9	1	2	1	0	0	0	0	4	0	0	R	R	5-10	175	9-4-78	1999	Fresno, Calif.
Beverly, Shomari	.197	50	173	18	34	7	0	6	12	11	62	4	2	R	R	6-0	165	2-16-78	1997	Alameda, Calif.
Bush, Brian	.233	38	129	12	30	3	0	0	7	7	32	4	5	R	R	6-1	180	1-3-77	1999	Warren, Ohio
Carnes, Shayne	.268	106	396	45	106	28	0	10	55	26	78	1	1	L	L	6-2	200	9-16-76	1998	Nogales, Ariz.
Casillas, Uriel	.227	73	225	30	51	11	2	0	20	48	33	4	5	R	R	5-11	185	8-22-75	1997	Downey, Calif.
Cody, Ryan	.333	1	3	1	1	0	0	0	0	1	0	0	0	R	R	6-1	190	6-13-78	1997	Vancouver, Wash.
Connell, Jerry	.239	31	109	9	26	9	1	3	15	10	46	1	1	R	R	6-2	200	7-17-77	1995	Avenel, N.J.
Duncan, Carlos	.217	73	276	41	60	15	3	11	40	19	88	15	4	R	R	6-1	155	6-30-77	1995	San Pedro de Macoris, D.R.
Espy, Nate	.254	83	295	37	75	18	2	11	38	48	56	3	1	R	R	6-3	215	4-24-78	1998	Pensacola, Fla.
Fajardo, Alejandro	.243	118	444	66	108	16	6	6	43	52	91	44	10	R	R	6-0	180	2-6-76	1995	Moca, D.R.
Giron, Alejandro	.287	99	387	43	111	15	6	8	59	15	75	12	6	R	R	6-2	180	4-26-79	1996	Santo Domingo, D.R.
Guzman, Carlos	.163	16	49	5	8	2	0	0	5	3	17	2	0	L	L	5-9	160	6-28-78	1995	Santiago, D.R.
Hannahan, Buzz	.123	22	65	5	8	0	0	0	3	6	12	3	1	R	R	6-2	180	6-29-76	1998	Torrance, Calif.
Ishida, Takehito	.242	10	33	2	8	1	1	0	0	1	7	0	1	R	R	6-2	165	7-30-78	1998	Hokkaido, Japan
Johnson, Jason	.264	111	447	51	118	21	5	1	31	22	61	27	11	R	R	6-1	170	8-21-77	1996	Collinsville, Va.
Machado, Anderson	.233	20	60	7	14	4	2	0	7	7	20	2	1	S	R	5-11	165	1-25-81	1998	Caracas, Venez.
Padilla, Jorge	.208	44	168	13	35	10	1	3	17	5	44	0	0	R	R	6-2	210	8-11-79	1998	Carolina, P.R.
Polidor, Wil	.221	26	95	7	21	3	1	0	7	2	15	0	1	S	R	6-1	158	9-23-73	1991	Caracas, Venez.
Reyes, Ambiorix	.245	78	257	30	63	7	3	0	15	11	23	14	5	R	R	5-11	166	2-6-79	1996	Rancho Viejo, D.R.
Richardson, Juan	.167	4	12	0	2	1	0	0	2	1	5	0	0	R	R	6-1	175	1-10-81	1998	Bani, D.R.
Salazar, Jeremy	.252	98	345	37	87	17	0	10	36	27	90	1	0	R	R	5-11	185	3-18-76	1998	Springfield, Ill.
Schreimann, Eric	.241	78	257	35	62	10	5	12	37	16	77	1	1	R	R	6-1	205	4-22-75	1994	Jefferson City, Mo.
Valdez, Jerry	.222	39	126	11	28	5	0	2	13	11	26	0	1	R	R	5-11	195	6-6-74	1997	El Paso, Texas

GAMES BY POSITION: C—Avila 2, Cody 1, Salazar 92, Schreimann 27, Valdez 20. **1B**—Carnes 57, Espy 74, Hannahan 1, Schreimann 9. **2B**—Casillas 6, Fajardo 116, Hannahan 3, Ishida 6, Reyes 10. **3B**—Casillas 37, Duncan 43, Hannahan 17, Ishida 4, Polidor 23, Reyes 8, Richardson 4, Schreimann 6. **SS**—Casillas 30, Duncan 30, Hannahan 1, Machado 20, Reyes 60. **OF**—Acevedo 53, Beverly 49, Bush 38, Carnes 13, Connell 13, Fajardo 2, Giron 90, Guzman 15, Johnson 111, Padilla 42.

PITCHING	W	L	ERA	G	GS	CG	SV	IP	H	R	ER	BB	SO	B	T	HT	WT	DOB	1st Yr	Resides
Adair, Derek	2	4	4.70	8	6	0	0	38	44	28	20	6	15	R	R	6-4	188	8-25-75	1997	Albertson, N.Y.
Bailie, Matt	0	0	1.47	6	1	0	1	18	13	5	3	7	24	R	R	5-10	195	10-1-75	1998	Aloha, Ore.
Baisley, Brad	10	7	2.26	23	23	3	0	148	116	56	37	55	110	R	R	6-9	200	8-24-79	1998	Tampa, Fla.
Eason, Clay	0	1	2.18	10	0	0	2	21	13	5	5	11	33	R	R	5-11	175	11-18-75	1997	Dunn, N.C.
Espina, Rendy	0	2	4.63	15	0	0	3	35	35	20	18	10	31	L	L	6-0	180	5-11-78	1995	Cabimas, Venez.
Fenus, Justin	2	0	2.43	10	4	0	0	37	29	16	10	10	27	R	R	6-2	195	5-19-75	1996	Mountain View, Wyo.
Hiles, Cary	3	2	2.21	44	0	0	26	61	52	20	15	12	84	R	R	5-10	175	11-29-75	1998	Memphis, Tenn.
Keelin, Chris	1	0	3.00	4	0	0	0	6	9	6	2	3	2	R	R	6-2	190	3-30-77	1999	Sussex, N.J.
Kubes, Greg	11	12	2.62	27	27	4	0	165	162	65	48	47	147	L	L	6-6	205	11-10-76	1998	East Bernard, Texas
Montero, Francisco	4	3	3.05	25	9	0	2	86	84	48	29	20	70	R	R	6-2	185	1-6-76	1994	Barahona, D.R.
Nunez, Franklin	4	8	3.39	13	13	1	0	77	69	39	29	25	88	R	R	6-0	165	1-18-77	1995	Nagua, D.R.
Pilato, Chris	1	2	4.50	4	4	0	0	22	20	12	11	8	15	R	R	6-3	180	9-8-77	1998	Rochester, N.Y.
Ramos, Fernando	3	6	2.88	38	0	0	4	69	61	31	22	19	73	R	R	6-1	169	5-3-76	1994	Moca, D.R.
Rose, Johnathan	0	5	6.30	21	1	0	1	30	40	24	21	17	34	L	L	6-4	225	8-18-76	1997	Haw River, N.C.
Silva, Carlos	11	8	3.12	26	26	3	0	164	176	79	57	41	99	R	R	6-4	198	4-23-79	1996	Calle las Mangas, Venez.
Turnbow, Derrick	12	8	3.35	26	26	4	0	161	130	67	60	53	149	R	R	6-3	180	1-25-78	1997	Franklin, Tenn.
Wedel, Jeremy	5	3	2.16	23	0	0	3	50	46	19	12	8	40	R	R	6-2	195	11-27-76	1998	Wasco, Calif.

NEW YORK-PENN LEAGUE

BATTING	AVG	G	AB	R	H	2B	3B	HR	RBI	BB	SO	SB	CS	B	T	HT	WT	DOB	1st Yr	Resides
Avila, Rob	.148	10	27	3	4	3	0	0	2	6	6	0	0	R	R	5-10	175	9-4-78	1999	Fresno, Calif.
Batson, Tom	.298	65	245	52	73	10	4	8	33	35	36	11	5	R	R	5-11	180	2-9-77	1999	Alvin, Texas
Beverly, Shomari	.243	65	267	35	65	13	3	5	34	16	75	19	4	R	R	6-0	165	2-16-78	1997	Alameda, Calif.
Byrd, Marlon	.296	65	243	40	72	7	6	13	50	28	70	8	2	R	R	5-11	225	8-30-77	1999	Marietta, Ga.
Cody, Ryan	.111	3	9	1	1	1	0	0	0	1	4	0	0	R	R	6-1	190	6-13-78	1997	Vancouver, Wash.
Collazo, Julio	.250	5	16	0	4	0	0	0	2	2	6	1	0	R	R	5-11	155	12-24-80	1999	Ponce, P.R.
Deitrick, Jeremy	.265	26	83	16	22	10	0	2	13	5	21	0	0	R	R	6-0	210	9-14-76	1998	Williamsport, Pa.
Duarte, Justin	.250	45	140	15	35	8	0	1	20	8	36	0	0	R	R	6-2	210	9-14-76	1999	Glendora, Calif.
Eberly, Rod	.205	50	171	17	35	5	0	2	18	15	26	0	0	L	R	6-2	205	10-30-76	1999	Clarinda, Iowa
Hitchcox, Brian	.223	54	166	22	37	5	1	2	18	19	14	7	1	L	R	5-11	175	7-21-78	1999	Dayton, Tenn.
McArthur, Kennon	.194	31	103	13	20	10	0	2	4	5	31	0	0	R	R	6-2	205	10-23-79	1998	Sylacauga, Ala.
Merhoff, Aaron	.137	16	51	3	7	2	1	0	6	6	16	0	0	R	R	6-2	220	11-20-75	1999	Klamath Falls, Ore.
Muthig, Dean	.262	31	107	16	28	7	2	1	18	4	28	1	0	R	R	5-11	205	8-24-77	1999	Embarrass, Wis.
Norrell, Troy	.250	28	100	16	25	7	2	6	21	8	45	1	0	R	R	6-0	185	10-25-76	1997	Lake Jackson, Texas
O'Neill, Dan	.189	34	106	11	20	2	0	1	8	14	27	7	2	R	L	6-1	180	12-1-76	1999	Champaign, Ill.
Padilla, Jorge	.252	65	238	28	60	10	1	3	30	22	79	2	1	R	R	6-2	210	8-11-79	1998	Carolina, P.R.
Reyes, Ambiorix	.234	25	77	4	18	1	0	0	5	3	7	6	2	R	R	5-11	166	2-6-79	1996	Rancho Viejo, D.R.
Richardson, Juan	.125	7	24	1	3	1	0	1	2	2	8	0	1	R	R	6-1	175	1-10-81	1998	Bani, D.R.
Rojas, Alex	.284	45	176	38	50	6	3	0	16	15	37	39	7	R	R	5-9	145	3-2-78	1996	La Vega, D.R.
Schley, Joe	.197	36	71	15	14	3	1	1	7	16	24	8	3	R	R	5-9	165	7-5-76	1999	Shorewood, Ill.
Sitzman, Jay	.296	49	169	33	50	5	5	2	22	9	37	15	5	L	L	6-3	195	3-13-78	1999	Scottsdale, Ariz.

GAMES BY POSITION: C—Cody 3, Deitrick 26, McArthur 28, Norrell 24. **1B**—Avila 2, Duarte 40, Eberly 30, Muthig 18, O'Neill 1. **2B**—Batson 33, Hitchcox 1, Rojas 45, Schley 9. **3B**—Avila 5, Batson 31, Eberly 20, Hitchcox 10, Muthig 16, Richardson 7. **SS**—Batson 9, Collazo 5, Hitchcox 46, Reyes 25. **OF**—Beverly 57, Byrd 44, Merhoff 7, O'Neill 21, Padilla 56, Schley 16, Sitzman 38.

PITCHING	W	L	ERA	G	GS	CG	SV	IP	H	R	ER	BB	SO	B	T	HT	WT	DOB	1st Yr	Resides
Alston, Travis	1	1	4.22	15	3	0	0	32	35	19	15	17	29	R	R	6-2	195	7-24-76	1999	Birmingham, Ala.
Bailie, Matt	2	2	4.15	10	0	0	3	17	15	8	8	4	23	R	R	5-10	195	10-1-75	1998	Aloha, Ore.
Brookman, Ryan	1	0	0.46	14	0	0	1	20	17	5	1	7	13	R	R	6-0	190	2-24-77	1999	Tomah, Wis.

PITCHING	W	L	ERA	G	GS	CG	SV	IP	H	R	ER	BB	SO	B	T	HT	WT	DOB	1st Yr	Resides
Brooks, Frank	7	3	2.91	16	12	1	0	77	64	26	25	33	58	L	L	6-2	200	9-6-78	1999	Brooklyn, N.Y.
Dagley, Corey	5	5	4.27	15	12	0	0	65	77	35	31	19	44	R	R	6-2	180	4-15-77	1998	Centralia, Ill.
Espina, Rendy	0	1	36.00	1	0	0	0	1	5	4	4	1	1	L	L	6-0	180	5-11-78	1995	Cabimas, Venez.
Fry, Justin	4	0	1.35	25	0	0	6	33	18	5	5	10	59	R	R	6-3	195	8-20-76	1999	Munhall, Pa.
Keelin, Chris	1	0	5.06	14	0	0	0	21	19	18	12	16	27	R	R	6-2	190	3-30-77	1999	Sussex, N.J.
Lawson, Jarrod	0	4	8.31	4	4	0	0	17	27	19	16	12	11	R	R	6-4	200	4-2-79	1998	Potosi, Mo.
Madson, Ryan	5	5	4.72	15	15	0	0	88	80	51	46	43	75	R	R	6-5	175	8-28-80	1998	Moreno Valley, Calif.
Outlaw, Mark	1	1	1.62	23	0	0	4	33	26	10	6	9	45	L	L	5-11	180	1-2-77	1999	Waco, Texas
Pautz, Brad	8	4	4.06	13	13	2	0	78	77	37	35	30	58	R	R	6-3	190	1-3-77	1999	Reedsville, Wis.
Pilato, Chris	0	0	4.50	11	0	0	0	14	15	8	7	9	18	R	R	6-3	180	9-8-77	1998	Rochester, N.Y.
Serrano, Elio	0	4	4.12	19	3	0	1	39	38	22	18	20	29	R	R	6-3	180	12-4-78	1996	Valencia, Venez.
Smith, Chad	0	0	10.80	3	0	0	0	5	9	8	6	1	8	R	R	5-9	200	8-11-77	1999	Gas City, Ind.
Tucker, Brad	0	1	3.81	17	1	0	0	26	24	15	11	11	15	R	R	6-2	200	11-11-76	1999	Fresno, Calif.
Wilson, Mike	5	3	3.64	13	13	1	0	84	66	42	34	29	73	R	R	6-6	222	6-12-80	1998	El Cajon, Calif.
Zipser, Mike	2	1	2.76	9	0	0	0	16	17	9	5	6	16	R	R	6-0	215	9-14-76	1998	Las Vegas, Nev.

CLEARWATER — Rookie

GULF COAST LEAGUE

BATTING	AVG	G	AB	R	H	2B	3B	HR	RBI	BB	SO	SB	CS	B	T	HT	WT	DOB	1st Yr	Resides
Avila, Rob	.328	16	58	6	19	3	0	2	5	4	10	2	0	R	R	5-10	175	9-4-78	1999	Fresno, Calif.
Bishop, Bennie	.232	28	82	9	19	4	1	0	9	7	23	4	1	R	R	5-11	170	1-2-79	1997	Inglewood, Calif.
Bradley, Wade	.000	2	5	0	0	0	0	0	0	0	3	0	0	L	L	6-0	190	8-7-78	1999	Lexington, S.C.
Collazo, Julio	.256	52	176	34	45	3	0	0	7	33	36	25	1	R	R	5-11	155	12-24-80	1999	Ponce, P.R.
Deitrick, Jeremy	.353	5	17	3	6	2	1	0	3	0	2	0	1	R	R	6-0	210	9-14-76	1998	Williamsport, Pa.
Delgado, Dario	.324	19	71	12	23	3	1	2	17	5	16	1	2	R	R	6-1	186	3-30-80	1997	Santo Domingo, D.R.
Driggers, Richard	.229	17	48	6	11	2	0	0	3	1	11	1	0	R	R	6-2	185	8-30-81	1999	Goose Creek, S.C.
Eagle, Todd	.128	14	39	1	5	1	0	0	3	1	5	1	0	R	R	6-2	190	8-2-80	1999	Albany, Calif.
Eberly, Rod	.192	7	26	4	5	1	0	0	3	4	5	1	0	L	R	6-2	205	10-30-76	1999	Clarinda, Iowa
Ishida, Takehito	.318	27	85	8	27	11	0	1	14	9	11	1	1	R	R	6-2	165	7-30-78	1998	Hokkaido, Japan
Jewson, Ben	.238	31	101	5	24	3	0	0	11	9	32	1	0	R	R	6-3	205	6-29-79	1998	Waukesha, Wis.
Machado, Anderson	.259	43	143	26	37	6	3	2	12	15	38	6	3	S	R	5-11	165	1-25-81	1998	Caracas, Venez.
Merhoff, Aaron	.321	22	78	10	25	6	2	1	12	10	15	2	1	R	R	6-2	220	11-20-75	1999	Klamath Falls, Ore.
O'Neill, Dan	.333	10	27	6	9	3	1	0	4	10	7	2	0	R	L	6-1	180	12-1-76	1999	Champaign, Ill.
Prince, Tom	.238	7	21	3	5	3	0	0	3	4	0	0	0	R	R	5-11	206	8-13-64	1984	Bradenton, Fla.
Rauls, Ian	.303	51	175	31	53	8	0	0	17	34	32	27	8	L	L	6-2	170	10-27-98	1998	Trenton, N.J.
Richardson, Juan	.226	46	164	27	37	14	0	5	23	11	46	7	6	R	R	6-1	175	1-10-81	1999	Bani, D.R.
Rivera, Erick	.150	31	100	8	15	4	0	2	10	4	32	0	2	R	R	6-2	185	5-22-81	1999	Utuado, P.R.
Rodeheaver, Roger	.236	40	123	14	29	7	1	1	14	16	36	4	1	R	R	6-2	215	10-16-76	1998	Carmel, Ind.
Serrano, Elio	.200	2	5	2	1	0	0	0	1	3	1	0	0	R	R	6-3	180	12-4-78	1996	Valencia, Venez.
Serrano, Hector	.115	10	26	0	3	0	0	0	1	4	14	0	0	S	R	6-0	180	12-7-79	1999	Arecibo, P.R.
Tosca, Dan	.236	50	157	19	37	8	0	4	22	22	38	3	1	L	R	6-0	180	11-1-80	1999	Seffner, Fla.
Van Vark, Wade	.208	34	106	6	22	1	0	0	6	12	26	4	2	S	R	6-4	185	3-25-77	1999	Pella, Iowa
Wigand, Tom	.148	15	27	8	4	0	0	0	2	10	11	2	3	R	R	6-0	175	10-3-77	1999	Plainview, N.Y.

GAMES BY POSITION: C—Avila 9, Deitrick 5, Eagle 7, Prince 5, E. Serrano 2, H. Serrano 9, Tosca 31. **1B**—Delgado 16, Eberly 6, Jewson 8, Rodeheaver 31. **2B**—Collazo 3, Ishida 15, Machado 35, Wigand 14. **3B**—Jewson 19, Machado 1, Richardson 43. **SS**—Collazo 49, Ishida 1, Machado 9, Richardson 1, Wigand 1. **OF**—Bishop 28, Bradley 2, Driggers 14, Jewson 1, Merhoff 22, O'Neill 10, Rauls 47, Rivera 30, Van Vark 34.

PITCHING	W	L	ERA	G	GS	CG	SV	IP	H	R	ER	BB	SO	B	T	HT	WT	DOB	1st Yr	Resides
Ascencio, Miguel	1	4	5.97	9	5	0	0	29	35	24	19	16	14	R	R	6-2	160	9-29-80	1993	Santo Domingo, D.R.
Brito, Eude	0	1	5.02	12	3	0	0	29	39	22	16	19	23	L	L	6-0	160	9-18-81	1998	Sabana de la Mar, D.R.
Burger, Rob	1	1	2.78	9	2	0	0	23	19	8	7	15	31	R	R	6-1	175	3-25-76	1994	Willow Street, Pa.
Carey, Ben	2	2	3.66	17	4	0	0	39	40	20	16	15	35	L	L	6-1	175	1-1-79	1999	San Luis Obispo, Calif.
Espina, Rendy	1	0	0.00	2	0	0	1	1	1	0	0	0	1	L	L	6-0	180	5-11-78	1995	Cabimas, Venez.
Herrera, Carlos	0	3	4.37	12	5	0	0	45	46	30	22	25	40	R	R	6-0	145	5-3-81	1997	Santo Domingo, D.R.
Jimenez, Ronal	6	2	3.51	20	0	0	4	33	29	13	13	16	30	R	R	5-11	155	10-11-80	1997	Carabobo, Venez.
Legette, Richard	2	1	7.26	12	6	0	0	31	34	26	25	23	23	L	R	6-2	210	2-6-81	1999	Summerville, S.C.
Loewer, Carlton	0	0	0.00	1	1	0	0	2	2	0	0	0	2	R	R	6-6	220	9-24-73	1995	Eunice, La.
McGinnis, Ron	0	0	22.50	4	0	0	0	4	9	10	10	8	2	R	R	6-3	215	8-17-76	1998	Las Vegas, Nev.
Myers, Brett	2	1	2.33	7	5	0	0	27	17	8	7	7	30	R	R	6-4	215	8-17-80	1999	Jacksonville, Fla.
Perez, Franklin	3	4	6.31	12	7	0	0	41	44	36	29	27	35	R	R	6-2	175	6-10-81	1998	Bani, D.R.
Rodriguez, Alejandro	1	1	2.63	5	0	0	0	24	24	9	7	8	22	S	R	5-11	155	10-13-80	1997	Barcelona, Venez.
Rose, Johnathan	2	1	2.50	5	2	0	0	18	15	5	5	7	17	L	L	6-4	225	8-18-76	1997	Haw River, N.C.
Silverio, Carlos	1	0	5.59	5	1	0	0	10	12	6	6	5	8	R	R	6-0	157	4-1-79	1997	Puerto Plata, D.R.
Smith, Chad	3	5	2.88	22	2	0	8	34	29	19	11	9	31	R	R	5-9	200	8-11-77	1999	Gas City, Ind.
Staples, Dave	0	3	7.12	15	2	0	0	37	45	31	29	13	38	L	L	6-4	197	4-6-78	1999	Moscow, Mo.
Tejeda, Robinson	1	3	4.27	12	9	0	0	46	47	27	22	27	39	R	R	6-3	188	3-24-82	1999	Santo Domingo, D.R.
Thrasher, Jesse	0	1	15.12	5	1	0	0	8	15	16	14	15	6	R	R	6-3	225	12-20-80	1999	St. Joseph, Mo.
Zipser, Mike	0	1	4.00	6	0	0	0	9	11	5	4	5	11	R	R	6-0	215	9-14-76	1998	Las Vegas, Nev.

PITTSBURGH PIRATES

Strong finish has Bucs feeling like contenders for 2000

BY JOHN PERROTTO

The Pirates used their last homestand of 1999 as a measuring stick. They played the Astros and Reds, the two best teams in the National League Central, and went 4-2 against teams that won 97 and 96 games, taking two of three in each series.

That gave the third-place Pirates a good feeling.

"We're not Houston and we're not Cincinnati, but we're not that far away," manager Gene Lamont said. "We're getting better and I like to think that next year we'll have a contending team. A lot of people are talking about 2001 and our new ballpark opening that year, but I don't want to hear talk about 2001 right now. I want to hear about 2000. I think we can win in 2000."

The Pirates will have to make up 18½ games. That's how far they finished behind Houston in 1999. Pittsburgh had a 78-83 record.

"It seems like we're far away but we're not," first baseman Kevin Young said. "There's definitely a gap there between the contenders and ourselves, but it's not a huge gap. It's a gap that can be closed in the not-too-distant future."

Indeed, the Pirates won nine more games than 1998, when they lost 25 of their last 30. If not for injuries, the Pirates might have had their first winning season since 1992. The injuries hit early and often, as the Pirates had 21 players go on the disabled list, missing 1,313 games.

The most serious injury occurred July 4, when catcher Jason Kendall dislocated his right ankle while trying to beat out a bunt, and missed the rest of the season. Shortstop Pat Meares, signed as a free agent in

Brian Giles   **Chad Hermansen**

Players of the Year

MAJOR LEAGUE: Brian Giles, of
Giles led the Pirates in nearly every offensive category after coming over from the Indians in a trade for reliever Ricardo Rincon.

MINOR LEAGUE: Chad Hermansen, of
Nashville's Hermansen led all Pirates minor leaguers with 32 home runs and tied for tops with 97 RBIs.

February, was limited to 21 games because of surgery to repair damaged tendons in his left hand. Third baseman Ed Sprague (hand) and center fielder Brian Giles (finger) missed a significant portion of the season's final month with broken bones. They led an offense that set a club record with 171 home runs.

Rich Loiselle, who had a combined 48 saves in 1997-98, had reconstructive elbow surgery in July. Many other relievers also missed time, including closer Mike Williams, Jason Christiansen, Jeff Wallace, Chris Peters and Jose Silva.

"I think when you take everything into consideration, we had a pretty good year," said Giles, nabbed from the Indians in a trade for lefthanded reliever Ricardo Rincon. "You never like to use injuries as an excuse, but we had more than our fair share. If we could have kept everyone healthy, I'm not saying we would have contended to the last day of the season, but we would have made things more interesting."

The Pirates' six minor league affiliates combined for a 337-355 record. Triple-A Nashville was the only club with a winning record, going 80-60. Class A Hickory sneaked into the South Atlantic League playoffs with a 70-70 record and won a first-round series before bowing in the semifinals.

Center fielder Chad Hermansen and third baseman Aramis Ramirez, two of the Pirates' most highly touted prospects of the decade, led the way at Nashville. But the top individual minor league honor went to short-season Williamsport third baseman Antonio Alvarez, who was the New York-Penn League MVP after hitting .321 with seven homers in 58 games.

ORGANIZATION LEADERS

BATTING

*AVG	Ray Montgomery, Nashville	.331
R	Rico Washington, Lynchburg/Hickory	101
H	Rico Washington, Lynchburg/Hickory	160
TB	Chad Hermansen, Nashville	263
2B	Two tied at	35
3B	Tike Redman, Altoona	12
HR	Chad Hermansen, Nashville	32
RBI	Two tied at	97
BB	Eddy Furniss, Lynchburg	94
SO	Corey Pointer, Lynchburg	147
SB	Kory DeHaan, Altoona/Lynchburg	46

PITCHING

W	Bronson Arroyo, Nashville/Altoona	15
L	Andy Bausher, Lynchburg	15
#ERA	Luis Torres, Hickory/GCL	2.43
G	Matt Dunbar, Nashville/Altoona	60
CG	Sam McConnell, Altoona/Lynchburg	5
SV	Tony Pavlovich, Hickory	20
IP	Bronson Arroyo, Nashville/Altoona	166
BB	Brian O'Connor, Altoona	92
SO	John Grabow, Hickory	164

*Minimum 250 At-Bats #Minimum 75 Innings

Pittsburgh PIRATES

Manager: Gene Lamont **1999 Record:** 78-83, .484 (3rd, NL Central)

BATTING	AVG	G	AB	R	H	2B	3B	HR	RBI	BB	SO	SB	CS	B	T	HT	WT	DOB	1st Yr	Resides
Benjamin, Mike	.247	110	368	42	91	26	7	1	37	20	90	10	1	R	R	6-0	169	11-22-65	1987	Chandler, Ariz.
Brown, Adrian	.270	116	226	34	61	5	2	4	17	33	39	5	3	S	R	6-0	185	2-7-74	1992	Summit, Miss.
Brown, Brant	.232	130	341	49	79	20	3	16	58	22	114	3	4	L	L	6-3	205	6-22-71	1992	Fresno, Calif.
Brown, Emil	.143	6	14	0	2	1	0	0	0	0	3	0	0	R	R	6-2	192	12-29-74	1994	Chicago, Ill.
Cruz, Ivan	.400	5	10	3	4	0	0	1	2	0	2	0	0	L	L	6-2	225	5-3-68	1989	Jacksonville, Fla.
Garcia, Freddy	.231	55	130	16	30	5	0	6	23	4	41	0	0	R	R	6-2	224	8-1-72	1991	La Romana, D.R.
Giles, Brian	.315	141	521	109	164	33	3	39	115	95	80	6	2	L	L	5-10	200	1-20-71	1989	Las Vegas, Nev.
Guillen, Jose	.267	40	120	18	32	6	0	1	18	10	21	1	0	R	R	5-11	195	5-17-76	1993	San Cristobal, D.R.
Haad, Yamid	.000	1	1	0	0	0	0	0	0	0	0	0	0	R	R	6-2	204	9-2-77	1995	Cartagena, Colombia
Hermansen, Chad	.233	19	60	5	14	3	0	1	1	7	19	2	2	R	R	6-2	185	9-10-77	1995	Henderson, Nev.
Kendall, Jason	.332	78	280	61	93	20	3	8	41	38	32	22	3	R	R	6-0	193	6-26-74	1992	Manhattan Beach, Calif.
Laker, Tim	.333	6	9	0	3	0	0	0	0	0	2	0	0	R	R	6-2	175	11-27-69	1988	Simi Valley, Calif.
Martin, Al	.277	143	541	97	150	36	8	24	63	49	119	20	3	L	L	6-2	214	11-24-67	1985	Scottsdale, Ariz.
Meares, Pat	.308	21	91	15	28	4	0	0	7	9	20	0	0	R	R	6-0	187	9-6-68	1990	Wichita, Kan.
Morris, Warren	.288	147	511	65	147	20	3	15	73	59	88	3	7	L	R	5-11	185	1-11-74	1997	Alexandria, La.
Nunez, Abraham	.220	90	259	25	57	8	0	0	17	28	54	9	1	S	R	5-11	175	3-16-76	1994	Santo Domingo, D.R.
Oliver, Joe	.201	45	134	10	27	8	0	1	13	10	33	2	0	R	R	6-3	220	7-24-65	1983	Orlando, Fla.
Osik, Keith	.186	66	167	12	31	3	1	2	13	11	30	0	0	R	R	6-0	198	10-22-68	1990	Shoreham, N.Y.
Ramirez, Aramis	.179	18	56	2	10	2	1	0	7	6	9	0	0	R	R	6-1	215	6-25-78	1995	Santo Domingo, D.R.
Sprague, Ed	.267	137	490	71	131	27	2	22	81	50	93	3	6	R	R	6-2	215	7-25-67	1989	Stockton, Calif.
Sveum, Dale	.211	49	71	7	15	5	1	3	13	7	28	0	0	S	R	6-2	212	11-23-63	1982	Scottsdale, Ariz.
Tremie, Chris	.071	9	14	1	1	0	0	1	2	4	0	0	0	R	R	6-0	215	10-19-69	1992	New Waverly, Texas
Ward, Turner	.209	49	91	2	19	2	0	1	8	13	9	2	2	S	R	6-2	204	4-11-65	1986	Saraland, Ala.
Wehner, John	.185	39	65	6	12	2	0	1	4	7	12	1	0	R	R	6-3	205	6-29-67	1988	Pittsburgh, Pa.
Young, Kevin	.298	156	584	103	174	41	6	26	106	75	124	22	10	R	R	6-3	240	6-16-69	1990	Phoenix, Ariz.

PITCHING	W	L	ERA	G	GS	CG	SV	IP	H	R	ER	BB	SO	B	T	HT	WT	DOB	1st Yr	Resides
Anderson, Jimmy	2	1	3.99	13	4	0	0	29	25	15	13	16	13	L	L	6-1	190	1-22-76	1994	Chesapeake, Va.
Benson, Kris	11	14	4.07	31	31	2	0	197	184	105	89	83	139	R	R	6-4	190	11-7-74	1996	Marietta, Ga.
Boyd, Jason	0	0	3.38	4	0	0	0	5	5	2	2	4	4	R	R	6-3	170	2-23-73	1994	Edwardsville, Ill.
Christiansen, Jason	2	3	4.06	39	0	0	3	38	26	17	17	22	35	R	L	6-5	242	9-21-69	1991	Omaha, Neb.
Clontz, Brad	1	3	2.74	56	0	0	2	49	49	21	15	24	40	R	R	6-1	195	4-25-71	1992	Alpharetta, Ga.
Cordova, Francisco	8	10	4.43	27	27	2	0	161	166	83	79	59	98	R	R	6-1	191	4-26-72	1996	Veracruz, Mexico
Dougherty, Jim	0	0	9.00	2	0	0	0	2	3	3	2	3	1	R	R	6-1	225	3-8-68	1991	Kitty Hawk, N.C.
Garcia, Mike	1	0	1.29	7	0	0	0	7	2	1	1	3	9	R	R	6-2	220	5-11-68	1989	Moreno Valley, Calif.
Hansell, Greg	1	3	3.89	33	0	0	0	39	42	20	17	11	34	R	R	6-5	245	3-12-71	1989	La Palma, Calif.
Loiselle, Rich	3	2	5.28	13	0	0	0	15	16	9	9	9	14	R	R	6-5	245	1-12-72	1991	Phoenix, Ariz.
Peters, Chris	5	4	6.59	19	11	0	0	71	98	59	52	27	46	L	L	6-1	165	1-28-72	1993	Bethel Park, Pa.
Phillips, Jason	0	0	11.57	6	0	0	0	7	11	9	9	6	7	R	R	6-6	225	3-22-74	1992	Hughesville, Pa.
Ritchie, Todd	15	9	3.49	28	26	2	0	173	169	79	67	54	107	R	R	6-3	215	11-7-71	1990	Kerens, Texas
Sauerbeck, Scott	4	1	2.00	65	0	0	2	68	53	19	15	38	55	R	L	6-3	190	11-9-71	1994	Cincinnati, Ohio
Schmidt, Jason	13	11	4.19	33	33	2	0	213	219	110	99	85	148	R	R	6-5	211	1-29-73	1991	Longview, Wash.
Schourek, Pete	4	7	5.34	30	17	0	0	113	128	75	67	49	94	L	L	6-5	205	5-10-69	1987	Clifton, Va.
Silva, Jose	2	8	5.73	34	12	0	4	97	108	70	62	39	77	R	R	6-5	227	12-19-73	1991	San Diego, Calif.
Wallace, Jeff	1	0	3.69	41	0	0	0	39	26	17	16	38	41	L	L	6-2	228	4-12-76	1995	Louisville, Ohio
Wilkins, Marc	2	3	4.24	46	0	0	0	51	49	28	24	26	44	R	R	5-11	221	10-21-70	1992	Pittsburgh, Pa.
Williams, Mike	3	4	5.09	58	0	0	23	58	63	36	33	37	76	R	R	6-2	209	7-29-68	1990	Newport, Va.

FIELDING

Catcher	PCT	G	PO	A	E	DP	PB
Kendall	.988	75	505	48	7	13	6
Laker	1.000	2	9	0	0	0	1
Oliver	.993	44	285	12	2	4	1
Osik	.997	50	289	22	1	4	1
Tremie	1.000	8	29	2	0	1	1

First Base	PCT	G	PO	A	E	DP
B. Brown	1.000	7	37	3	0	2
Cruz	1.000	1	13	1	0	3
Sveum	1.000	4	23	2	0	5
Young	.985	155	1413	97	23	148

Second Base	PCT	G	PO	A	E	DP
Benjamin	1.000	12	21	31	0	5
Morris	.979	144	263	403	14	102
Nunez	.985	14	24	42	1	13
Sveum	1.000	2	1	2	0	1
Wehner	1.000	1	4	2	0	2

Third Base	PCT	G	PO	A	E	DP
Benjamin	1.000	6	1	5	0	0
Ramirez	.930	17	11	29	3	2
Sprague	.920	134	79	254	29	22

	PCT	G	PO	A	E	DP
Sveum	.941	12	2	14	1	0
Wehner	1.000	2	1	1	0	0
Shortstop	**PCT**	**G**	**PO**	**A**	**E**	**DP**
Benjamin	.982	93	140	298	8	77
Meares	.939	21	26	67	6	13
Nunez	.953	65	89	172	13	37
Sveum	1.000	4	1	5	0	1
Wehner	1.000	2	0	1	0	0
Outfield	**PCT**	**G**	**PO**	**A**	**E**	**DP**
A. Brown	.966	96	111	3	4	2
B. Brown	.981	82	150	4	3	0
E. Brown	1.000	6	8	0	0	0
Cruz	.000	1	0	0	0	0
F. Garcia	.977	24	43	0	1	0
Giles	.990	138	294	8	3	2
Guillen	.952	37	58	1	3	1
Hermansen	1.000	18	29	0	0	0
Martin	.952	134	196	3	10	0
Sveum	1.000	1	2	0	0	0
Ward	.955	34	41	1	2	0
Wehner	.958	17	23	0	1	0

GEORGE GOJKOVICH

Warren Morris

FARM SYSTEM

Director of Player Development: Paul Tinnell

Class	Farm Team	League	W	L	Pct.	Finish*	Manager	First Yr
AAA	Nashville (Tenn.) Sounds	Pacific Coast	80	60	.571	4th (16)	Trent Jewett	1998
AA	Altoona (Pa.) Curve	Eastern	67	73	.479	8th (12)	Marty Brown	1999
A#	Lynchburg (Va.) Hillcats	Carolina	64	73	.467	6th (8)	Scott Little	1995
A	Hickory (N.C.) Crawdads	South Atlantic	70	70	.500	6th (14)	Tracy Woodson	1999
A	Williamsport (Pa.) Crosscutters	New York-Penn	32	44	.421	13th (14)	Curtis Wilkerson	1999
Rookie	Bradenton (Fla.) Pirates	Gulf Coast	24	35	.407	13th (14)	Woody Huyke	1967

*Finish in overall standings (No. of teams in league)   #Advanced level

NASHVILLE — Class AAA

PACIFIC COAST LEAGUE

BATTING	AVG	G	AB	R	H	2B	3B	HR	RBI	BB	SO	SB	CS	B	T	HT	WT	DOB	1st Yr	Resides
Bieser, Steve	.231	6	13	3	3	1	0	0	3	2	4	0	0	L	R	5-10	180	8-4-67	1989	St. Genevieve, Mo.
Brinkley, Darryl	.323	111	372	68	120	35	2	14	75	31	58	5	5	R	R	5-11	205	12-23-68	1994	Stamford, Conn.
Brown, Adrian	.321	17	56	10	18	3	1	0	4	11	8	6	1	S	R	6-0	185	2-7-74	1992	Summit, Miss.
Brown, Emil	.307	110	430	97	132	20	5	18	60	35	80	16	5	R	R	6-2	192	12-29-74	1994	Chicago, Ill.
Cruz, Ivan	.326	75	273	57	89	20	1	25	81	21	56	0	2	L	L	6-2	225	5-3-68	1989	Jacksonville, Fla.
Garcia, Freddy	.000	4	9	0	0	0	0	0	0	1	3	0	0	R	R	6-2	224	8-1-72	1991	La Romana, D.R.
Guillen, Jose	.333	35	132	28	44	10	0	5	22	8	21	0	1	R	R	5-11	195	5-17-76	1993	San Cristobal, D.R.
Hermansen, Chad	.270	125	496	89	134	27	3	32	97	35	119	19	10	R	R	6-2	185	9-10-77	1995	Henderson, Nev.
Howard, Matt	.293	114	399	41	117	17	2	2	44	25	24	13	10	R	R	5-10	170	9-22-67	1989	San Diego, Calif.
Hyzdu, Adam	.250	14	44	6	11	1	0	5	13	4	11	0	0	R	R	6-2	210	12-6-71	1990	Mesa, Ariz.
Laker, Tim	.269	112	405	48	109	29	3	12	65	29	68	3	0	R	R	6-2	175	11-27-69	1988	Simi Valley, Calif.
Meares, Pat	.167	5	18	3	3	0	0	0	1	3	1	0	R	R	6-0	187	9-6-68	1990	Wichita, Kan.
Montgomery, Ray	.331	90	272	57	90	23	2	16	52	24	49	5	3	R	R	6-2	225	8-8-70	1990	Pearland, Texas
Nunez, Abraham	.310	15	58	12	18	0	0	0	3	5	8	1	0	S	R	5-11	175	3-16-76	1994	Santo Domingo, D.R.
Osik, Keith	.091	4	11	0	1	0	0	0	0	0	1	0	0	R	R	6-0	198	10-22-68	1990	Shoreham, N.Y.
Patzke, Jeff	.220	59	173	20	38	5	1	2	14	32	29	2	3	S	R	6-0	190	11-19-73	1992	Klamath Falls, Ore.
Polcovich, Kevin	.240	80	233	37	56	10	1	3	25	20	52	6	4	R	R	5-9	185	6-28-70	1992	Auburn, N.Y.
Ramirez, Aramis	.328	131	460	92	151	35	1	21	74	73	56	5	3	R	R	6-1	215	6-25-78	1995	Santo Domingo, D.R.
Robertson, Mike	.309	74	220	34	68	16	1	9	31	10	32	2	1	L	L	6-0	189	10-9-70	1991	Las Vegas, Nev.
Secrist, Reed	.265	46	102	12	27	8	1	2	15	8	22	1	1	L	R	6-1	210	5-7-70	1992	Santa Clara, Utah
Strange, Doug	.077	5	13	2	1	1	0	0	0	2	0	0	0	S	R	6-1	188	4-13-64	1985	Greenville, S.C.
Sveum, Dale	.344	42	125	25	43	14	1	3	25	18	30	1	0	S	R	6-2	212	11-23-63	1982	Scottsdale, Ariz.
2-team (20 Tucson)	.297	62	192	28	57	15	1	4	29	21	53	1	1							
Tremie, Chris	.248	47	121	20	30	7	0	3	16	14	29	4	0	R	R	6-0	215	10-17-69	1992	New Waverly, Texas
Ward, Turner	.292	35	89	15	26	3	1	2	17	16	14	3	1	S	R	6-2	204	4-11-65	1986	Saraland, Ala.
Wehner, John	.431	17	58	14	25	3	0	8	15	3	6	0	0	R	R	6-3	205	6-29-67	1988	Pittsburgh, Pa.

PITCHING	W	L	ERA	G	GS	CG	SV	IP	H	R	ER	BB	SO	B	T	HT	WT	DOB	1st Yr	Resides
Ah Yat, Paul	4	3	5.71	13	11	1	0	65	75	45	41	24	41	R	L	6-1	186	10-13-74	1996	Honolulu, Hawaii
Anderson, Jimmy	11	2	3.84	21	21	1	0	134	153	67	57	41	93	L	L	6-1	190	1-22-76	1994	Chesapeake, Va.
Arroyo, Bronson	0	2	10.38	3	3	0	0	13	22	15	15	10	11	R	R	6-5	185	2-24-77	1995	Brooksville, Fla.
Boyd, Jason	0	0	0.00	5	0	0	0	5	2	0	0	0	2	R	R	6-3	170	2-23-73	1994	Edwardsville, Ill.
2-team (44 Tucson)	6	5	4.26	49	0	0	5	80	78	42	38	27	62							
Castillo, Frank	7	5	4.68	19	19	0	0	119	139	72	62	32	90	R	R	6-1	200	4-1-69	1987	Cave Creek, Ariz.
Christiansen, Jason	0	0	0.00	2	0	0	0	2	0	0	0	0	1	R	L	6-5	242	9-21-69	1991	Omaha, Neb.
Clontz, Brad	0	2	3.50	12	0	0	7	18	12	8	7	6	23	R	R	6-1	195	4-25-71	1992	Alpharetta, Ga.
Cordova, Francisco	2	2	0.75	2	2	0	0	12	10	2	1	1	7	R	R	6-1	191	4-26-72	1996	Veracruz, Mexico
Davis, Kane	3	2	6.75	12	9	0	0	49	65	38	37	17	31	R	R	6-4	194	6-25-75	1993	Reedy, W.Va.
Dougherty, Jim	3	3	5.43	53	0	0	10	60	69	38	36	27	55	R	R	6-1	225	3-8-68	1991	Kitty Hawk, N.C.
Dunbar, Matt	1	0	4.35	11	0	0	0	10	13	6	5	4	9	L	L	6-0	175	10-15-68	1990	Tallahassee, Fla.
Garcia, Mike	0	2	3.95	23	0	0	2	27	24	12	12	10	35	R	R	6-2	220	5-11-68	1989	Moreno Valley, Calif.
Giard, Ken	0	0	4.32	14	0	0	0	17	16	10	8	11	21	R	R	6-3	219	4-2-73	1991	Warwick, R.I.
Hansell, Greg	3	3	2.00	22	0	0	2	27	18	8	6	9	36	R	R	6-5	223	3-12-71	1989	La Palma, Calif.
Long, Joey	2	1	4.50	35	0	0	0	36	39	25	18	22	37	R	L	6-2	215	7-15-70	1991	Rosewood, Ohio
Milacki, Bob	6	8	4.86	22	20	0	0	111	130	82	60	43	79	R	R	6-4	230	7-28-64	1984	Lake Havasu, Ariz.
Peters, Chris	3	1	2.19	11	9	0	1	49	54	18	12	15	34	L	L	6-1	165	1-28-72	1993	Bethel Park, Pa.
Phillips, Jason	0	0	15.00	1	1	0	0	3	6	6	5	5	5	R	R	6-6	223	3-22-74	1992	Hughesville, Pa.
Ritchie, Todd	0	0	1.80	1	1	0	0	5	6	1	1	1	2	R	R	6-3	215	11-7-71	1990	Kerens, Texas
Robertson, Jeriome	3	7	7.98	7	6	0	0	29	39	27	26	20	29	L	L	6-4	175	9-15-68	1990	Waller, Texas
2-team (3 Oklahoma)	2	4	7.94	10	6	0	0	34	46	32	30	23	33							
Ryan, Ken	1	1	3.86	6	0	0	0	7	7	3	3	8	9	R	R	6-3	230	10-24-68	1986	Attleboro, Mass.
Ryan, Matt	6	5	4.42	48	6	0	8	79	87	48	39	35	52	R	R	6-5	190	3-20-72	1993	Oxford, Miss.
Sauveur, Rich	5	2	1.95	53	0	0	7	65	62	21	14	16	61	L	L	6-4	195	11-23-63	1983	Bradenton, Fla.
Scott, Tim	1	3	5.09	19	0	0	0	23	29	14	13	7	21	R	R	6-2	220	11-16-66	1984	Hanford, Calif.
Silva, Jose	2	0	1.50	2	2	0	0	12	14	4	2	4	10	R	R	6-5	227	12-19-73	1991	San Diego, Calif.
Sparks, Jeff	5	3	3.83	34	0	0	0	49	37	25	21	23	69	R	R	6-2	220	4-4-72	1995	Houston, Texas
Van Poppel, Todd	10	6	4.95	27	27	2	0	164	173	95	90	62	157	R	R	6-5	241	12-9-71	1990	Southlake, Texas
Wallace, Jeff	2	2	8.79	15	0	0	3	14	18	15	14	8	14	L	L	6-2	228	4-12-76	1995	Louisville, Ohio
Wilkins, Marc	0	0	0.79	8	0	0	3	11	9	3	1	3	8	R	R	5-11	221	10-21-70	1992	Pittsburgh, Pa.

FIELDING

Catcher	PCT	G	PO	A	E	DP	PB
Bieser	.000	2	0	0	0	0	1
Laker	.984	95	660	64	12	2	7
Osik	1.000	4	24	3	0	0	0
Secrist	1.000	20	83	6	0	0	4

	PCT	G	PO	A	E	DP	PB
Tremie	.988	42	292	29	4	2	0

First Base	PCT	G	PO	A	E	DP
Cruz	.993	65	571	37	4	51

	PCT	G	PO	A	E	DP
Laker	.972	15	65	5	2	5
Montgomery	.982	14	100	7	2	7
M. Robertson	.993	55	384	28	3	40
Secrist	.921	7	34	1	3	6

Organization Statistics

	PCT	G	PO	A	E	DP
Sveum	.944	8	32	2	2	8
Second Base	PCT	G	PO	A	E	DP
Bieser	1.000	3	7	7	0	1
Howard	.982	100	189	259	8	68
Patzke	.981	35	75	83	3	15
Polcovich	1.000	4	3	9	0	1
Strange	.846	2	7	4	2	1
Sveum	.963	9	15	11	1	2
Wehner	1.000	1	2	5	0	1
Third Base	PCT	G	PO	A	E	DP
Bieser	1.000	1	0	1	0	0
F. Garcia	1.000	2	1	2	0	0
Howard	.923	7	4	8	1	1
Laker	.500	2	1	0	1	0

	PCT	G	PO	A	E	DP
Polcovich	.000	1	0	0	0	0
Ramirez	.884	124	70	250	42	19
Secrist	.875	8	3	11	2	1
Strange	.000	1	0	0	0	0
Sveum	.929	6	3	10	1	0
Tremie	1.000	1	0	2	0	0
Shortstop	PCT	G	PO	A	E	DP
Howard	.864	4	3	16	3	0
Meares	.800	5	2	6	2	1
Nunez	.971	15	23	43	2	10
Patzke	.949	25	30	63	5	16
Polcovich	.969	71	85	229	10	42
Sveum	.949	16	11	63	4	14
Wehner	.943	14	19	31	3	11

Outfield	PCT	G	PO	A	E	DP
Brinkley	.969	81	118	7	4	2
A. Brown	.969	17	31	0	1	0
E. Brown	.948	107	173	10	10	1
Guillen	.939	30	57	5	4	1
Hermansen	.989	117	258	9	3	3
Howard	.000	1	0	0	0	0
Hyzdu	1.000	12	26	1	0	0
Montgomery	.953	65	80	2	4	0
Osik	1.000	1	0	0	0	0
Patzke	.000	1	0	0	0	0
Polcovich	.000	1	0	0	0	0
M. Robertson	1.000	5	4	0	0	0
Secrist	1.000	2	4	0	0	0
Ward	.900	14	17	1	2	0
Wehner	1.000	2	1	1	0	0

ALTOONA | Class AA

EASTERN LEAGUE

BATTING

	AVG	G	AB	R	H	2B	3B	HR	RBI	BB	SO	SB	CS	B	T	HT	WT	DOB	1st Yr	Resides
Asche, Mike	.412	7	17	3	7	2	0	0	3	1	3	1	1	R	R	6-2	189	2-13-72	1994	Kearney, Neb.
Bieser, Steve	.209	40	148	24	31	5	2	4	23	21	32	3	4	L	R	5-10	180	8-4-67	1989	St. Genevieve, Mo.
Bryant, Matt	.250	12	24	1	6	0	0	0	1	2	7	0	0	R	R	6-0	180	4-28-75	1997	Denver, Colo.
Cruz, Ivan	.154		13	1	2	1	0	0	3	1	8	0	0	L	L	6-2	225	5-3-68	1989	Jacksonville, Fla.
DeHaan, Kory	.268	47	190	26	51	13	2	3	24	11	46	14	6	L	R	6-2	187	7-16-76	1997	Pella, Iowa
Dunn, Todd	.167	8	30	0	5	2	0	0	2	2	10	0	1	R	R	6-5	230	7-29-70	1993	Jacksonville, Fla.
Figueroa, Luis	.263	131	418	61	110	15	5	3	50	52	44	9	9	S	R	5-9	146	2-16-74	1997	Vega Alta, P.R.
Haad, Yamid	.182	43	137	20	25	3	0	6	10	19	32	7	3	R	R	6-2	204	9-2-77	1995	Cartagena, Colombia
Haverbusch, Kevin	.286	93	332	57	95	22	2	14	61	12	60	6	4	R	R	6-3	197	6-16-76	1997	Massapequa, N.Y.
Hernandez, Alex	.257	126	475	76	122	26	3	15	63	54	110	11	8	L	L	6-4	186	5-28-77	1995	Levittown, P.R.
Hyzdu, Adam	.316	91	345	64	109	26	2	24	78	40	62	8	4	R	R	6-2	210	12-6-71	1990	Mesa, Ariz.
Iglesias, Luis	.281	31	89	13	25	6	0	6	16	14	26	0	1	R	R	6-3	210	2-3-67	1984	Panama City, Panama
Jorgensen, Tim	.130	7	23	1	3	1	0	0	2	0	6	0	0	L	R	6-3	200	11-30-72	1995	Luxemburg, Wis.
Long, Garrett	.245	109	355	61	87	12	4	18	56	63	100	6	6	R	R	6-3	205	10-5-76	1995	Houston, Texas
Lorenzana, Luis	.216	34	74	9	16	2	1	2	8	14	17	0	0	R	R	6-0	180	11-9-78	1996	San Diego, Calif.
Mackowiak, Rob	.262	53	195	21	51	15	3	3	27	8	34	0	2	L	R	5-10	165	6-20-76	1996	Schererville, Ind.
Patzke, Jeff	.298	53	198	31	59	12	1	2	25	33	45	4	2	S	R	6-0	190	11-19-73	1992	Klamath Falls, Ore.
Redman, Tike	.269	136	532	84	143	20	12	3	60	52	52	29	16	L	L	5-11	166	3-10-77	1996	Duncanville, Ala.
Robertson, Mike	.280	46	175	31	49	12	0	9	28	24	26	0	3	L	L	6-0	189	10-9-70	1991	Las Vegas, Nev.
Rosario, Mel	.241	26	87	11	21	9	0	1	11	6	15	0	0	S	R	6-0	200	5-25-73	1992	Miami, Fla.
Secrist, Reed	.168	36	95	9	16	5	0	0	10	13	23	0	0	L	R	6-1	210	5-7-70	1992	Santa Clara, Utah
Sweet, Jonathan	.257	37	105	15	27	5	1	2	13	11	15	0	1	L	R	6-0	182	11-10-71	1994	Cincinnati, Ohio
Ward, Turner	.000	1	3	1	0	0	0	0	0	2	2	0	0	S	R	6-2	204	4-11-65	1986	Saraland, Ala.
Wehner, John	.167	4	12	2	2	0	0	0	2	0	0	1	1	R	R	6-3	205	6-29-67	1988	Pittsburgh, Pa.
Wilson, Craig	.268	111	362	57	97	21	3	20	69	40	104	1	3	R	R	6-2	220	11-30-76	1995	Huntington Beach, Calif.
Wimmer, Chris	.252	27	107	9	27	5	2	1	6	8	12	5	2	R	R	5-11	175	9-25-70	1992	Oklahoma City, Okla.
Wright, Ron	.213	24	80	2	17	6	0	4	9		27	0	0	R	R	6-1	230	1-21-76	1994	St. George, Utah

PITCHING

	W	L	ERA	G	GS	CG	SV	IP	H	R	ER	BB	SO	B	T	HT	WT	DOB	1st Yr	Resides
Ah Yat, Paul	8	4	3.02	16	15	0	0	95	86	41	32	30	90	R	L	6-1	186	10-13-74	1996	Honolulu, Hawaii
Arroyo, Bronson	15	4	3.65	25	25	2	0	153	167	73	62	58	100	R	R	6-5	180	2-24-77	1995	Brooksville, Fla.
Ayers, Mike	0	0	1.59	11	0	0	0	17	10	4	3	11	16	L	L	5-10	188	12-23-73	1996	Cincinnati, Ohio
Baron, Jim	9	9	3.97	29	20	0	0	145	141	73	64	44	75	L	L	6-3	210	2-22-74	1992	Humble, Texas
Beltran, Alonso	0	2	9.00	13	0	0	1	18	27	18	18	9	18	R	R	6-3	180	3-4-72	1991	El Paso, Texas
Brown, Alvin	4	1	6.49	7	6	0	0	26	29	22	19	17	15	R	R	6-3	200	9-2-70	1995	Los Angeles, Calif.
Burgos, Enrique	2	1	2.25	5	0	0	0	4	1	1	1	3	2	L	L	6-5	230	10-7-65	1983	Panama City, Panama
Christiansen, Jason	0	0	0.00	2	1	0	0	3	1	0	0	1	2	R	L	6-5	242	9-21-69	1991	Omaha, Neb.
Cordova, Francisco	1	1	4.66	2	2	0	0	10	13	8	5	4	12	R	R	6-1	191	4-26-72	1991	Veracruz, Mexico
Daniels, David	2	2	2.67	55	0	0	8	67	55	21	20	19	63	R	R	6-2	184	7-25-73	1996	Nashville, Tenn.
Davis, Kane	4	6	3.78	16	16	0	0	95	97	51	40	41	53	R	R	6-3	194	6-25-75	1993	Reedy, W.Va.
Donnelly, Brendan	0	0	7.71	2	0	0	1	2	4	2	2	2	0	R	R	6-2	205	7-4-71	1992	Albuquerque, N.M.
Dougherty, Tony	0	0	7.47	9	0	0	0	16	29	19	13	7	6	R	R	6-2	200	4-12-73	1994	Beaver Falls, Pa.
Duff, Matt	2	4	2.81	44	0	0	12	58	43	19	18	35	59	R	R	6-1	192	10-6-74	1997	Alligator, Miss.
Dunbar, Matt	3	5	3.42	49	0	0	2	47	35	19	18	23	35	L	L	6-0	175	10-15-68	1990	Tallahassee, Fla.
France, Aaron	4	5	3.67	33	11	0	0	96	79	50	39	48	70	L	R	6-3	186	4-17-74	1994	Anaheim, Calif.
Garcia, Al	0	0	4.50	2	0	0	0	4	6	4	2	3	1	S	R	6-4	225	6-11-74	1993	Buena Park, Calif.
Giard, Ken	2	2	1.71	38	0	0	6	42	34	12	8	25	48	R	R	6-3	219	4-2-73	1991	Warwick, R.I.
Gonzalez, Mike	2	3	8.10	7	5	0	0	27	34	25	24	19	31	R	L	6-2	218	5-23-78	1997	Pasadena, Texas
Long, Joey	0	0	5.91	8	0	0	0	11	16	8	7	4	5	R	L	6-2	215	7-15-70	1991	Rosewood, Ohio
Martinez, Javier	0	0	6.10	10	0	0	0	10	11	8	7	14	16	R	R	6-2	235	2-5-77	1994	Toa Alta, P.R.
Mathews, Del	1	1	6.00	9	0	0	0	12	21	15	8	6	8	L	L	6-4	224	10-31-74	1993	Fernandina Beach, Fla.
McConnell, Sam	1	7	6.64	13	12	1	0	62	82	52	46	33	40	L	L	6-5	212	12-31-75	1997	Fairfield, Ohio
O'Connor, Brian	7	11	3.28	28	27	1	0	153	152	98	80	92	106	L	L	6-2	190	1-1-74	1995	Cincinnati, Ohio
Pena, Alex	0	3	3.86	9	0	0	0	21	22	12	9	9	20	R	R	6-2	175	9-9-77	1995	Santo Domingo, D.R.
Runion, Tony	1	4	3.59	31	0	0	2	43	52	23	17	9	39	R	R	6-3	229	12-6-71	1993	Florence, Ky.
Wilkins, Marc	0	1	1.50	4	0	0	0	6	3	1	1	2	8	R	R	5-11	221	10-21-70	1992	Pittsburgh, Pa.

FIELDING

Catcher	PCT	G	PO	A	E	DP	PB
Asche	1.000	1	2	0	0	0	0
Bieser	.988	12	65	15	1	3	2
Haad	.969	41	272	37	10	2	8
Rosario	.978	23	161	19	4	0	4
Secrist	.985	19	115	16	2	1	2
Sweet	1.000	21	117	15	0	2	2

	PCT	G	PO	A	E	DP	PB
Wilson	.988	34	220	33	3	3	7

First Base	PCT	G	PO	A	E	DP
Asche	.889	1	7	1	1	0
Hernandez	1.000	6	60	4	0	7
Hyzdu	.974	18	176	11	5	16
Iglesias	.980	6	44	4	1	4

	PCT	G	PO	A	E	DP
G. Long	.994	47	419	40	3	38
Robertson	.983	35	328	22	6	37
Secrist	.981	5	46	6	1	2
Sweet	.889	1	8	0	1	2
Wilson	.962	13	118	7	5	9
Wright	.991	11	94	12	1	5

Second Base	PCT	G	PO	A	E	DP
Bieser	.962	11	26	24	2	6
Bryant	1.000	3	4	4	0	1
Figueroa	1.000	1	0	5	0	1
Lorenzana	.967	8	10	19	1	6
Mackowiak	.971	52	112	158	8	39
Patzke	.974	46	98	129	6	32
Wimmer	.965	26	42	67	4	6

Third Base	PCT	G	PO	A	E	DP
Bieser	.854	13	4	31	6	3
Bryant	.000	2	0	0	0	0
Haverbusch	.861	79	45	159	33	12
Hyzdu	.800	10	3	13	4	2
Iglesias	.875	13	9	26	5	0
Jorgensen	.944	5	4	13	1	1

	PCT	G	PO	A	E	DP
Lorenzana	.931	20	6	21	2	3
Secrist	.500	4	1	3	4	0
Sweet	.913	9	3	18	2	0
Wehner	.857	3	1	5	1	1

Shortstop	PCT	G	PO	A	E	DP
Bryant	.944	6	9	8	1	1
Figueroa	.956	129	222	391	28	78
Haverbusch	1.000	4	0	6	0	0
Lorenzana	.941	6	3	13	1	4
Patzke	.919	7	14	20	3	5

Outfield	PCT	G	PO	A	E	DP
Asche	.875	5	6	1	1	0
Bieser	1.000	4	1	1	0	0

	PCT	G	PO	A	E	DP
DeHaan	.989	46	88	1	1	0
Dunn	.857	7	6	0	1	0
Hernandez	.976	103	189	11	5	1
Hyzdu	.980	60	96	3	2	0
Iglesias	.800	5	3	1	1	0
G. Long	.964	48	75	6	3	0
Mackowiak	1.000	1	2	0	0	0
Redman	.972	133	301	12	9	2
Robertson	.750	3	3	0	1	0
Secrist	1.000	3	2	0	0	0
Sweet	.000	1	0	0	0	0
Wehner	1.000	1	1	0	0	0
Wilson	.929	14	12	1	1	0

LYNCHBURG — Class A

CAROLINA LEAGUE

BATTING	AVG	G	AB	R	H	2B	3B	HR	RBI	BB	SO	SB	CS	B	T	HT	WT	DOB	1st Yr	Resides
Anderson, Frank	.171	12	35	4	6	0	0	0	3	3	12	0	1	R	R	6-1	200	9-1-75	1995	Lake City, Ga.
Bone, Billy	.250	38	104	17	26	5	0	1	13	22	35	3	1	R	R	6-1	179	1-5-76	1998	Jacksonville, Fla.
Bryant, Matt	.284	26	102	9	29	4	0	0	11	11	12	4	1	R	R	6-0	180	4-28-75	1997	Denver, Colo.
Bultmann, Kurt	.195	30	87	7	17	3	1	0	3	17	15	0	0	R	R	5-9	165	2-10-77	1999	Seminole, Fla.
Cortez, Santos	.224	48	161	19	36	6	0	1	10	8	34	1	3	R	R	6-0	210	1-18-75	1998	Long Beach, Calif.
DeHaan, Kory	.325	78	295	55	96	19	5	7	42	36	63	32	10	L	R	6-2	187	7-16-76	1997	Pella, Iowa
Evans, Lee	.225	117	413	44	93	18	2	11	58	37	129	3	6	S	R	6-1	177	7-20-77	1996	Northport, Ala.
Furniss, Eddy	.261	128	444	96	116	33	1	23	87	94	113	5	4	L	L	6-4	217	9-18-75	1998	Nacogdoches, Texas
Gutierrez, Victor	.234	114	428	55	100	11	8	1	33	37	68	23	9	R	R	5-11	164	12-23-77	1995	Santo Domingo, D.R.
Haad, Yamid	.254	59	209	31	53	11	1	5	33	33	42	5	2	R	R	6-2	204	9-2-77	1995	Cartagena, Colombia
Jorgensen, Tim	.278	64	230	32	64	21	3	4	34	26	47	0	1	L	R	6-3	200	11-30-72	1995	Luxemburg, Wis.
Lankford, Derrick	.292	123	456	80	133	28	8	20	88	52	124	4	0	L	R	6-4	220	9-21-74	1997	Harrison, Tenn.
Lorenzana, Luis	.256	49	156	15	40	7	0	2	14	11	37	2	3	R	R	6-0	180	11-9-74	1996	San Diego, Calif.
Mackowiak, Rob	.304	74	263	51	80	7	4	7	30	18	57	9	4	L	R	5-10	165	6-20-76	1996	Schererville, Ind.
Maxwell, Keith	.250	35	132	10	33	6	1	3	16	6	29	0	2	R	R	6-1	203	4-18-75	1997	Bristol, Fla.
May, Freddy	.295	126	441	61	130	20	4	8	56	85	105	17	11	L	L	6-2	205	1-24-76	1995	Seattle, Wash.
Pointer, Corey	.180	108	327	55	59	18	1	15	44	44	147	13	12	R	R	6-2	208	9-2-75	1994	Waxahachie, Texas
Reyes, Jose	.154	30	65	7	10	4	0	1	4	11	28	1	0	R	R	6-1	188	5-1-73	1993	Villa Vazquez, D.R.
Washington, Rico	.283	57	205	31	58	7	0	7	32	30	45	4	1	L	R	5-10	179	5-30-78	1997	Gray, Ga.

GAMES BY POSITION: C—Anderson 11, Evans 79, Haad 31, Reyes 10, Washington 14. 1B—Bone 1, Bryant 3, Furniss 87, Haad 5, Jorgensen 3, Lankford 34, Maxwell 19. 2B—Bone 14, Bryant 5, Bultmann 30, Jorgensen 1, Lorenzana 25, Mackowiak 62, Washington 11. 3B—Bone 23, Bryant 5, Haad 1, Jorgensen 63, Lankford 9, Lorenzana 19, Maxwell 3, Washington 33. SS—Bone 2, Bryant 15, Gutierrez 114, Lorenzana 11. OF—Cortez 38, DeHaan 78, Evans 1, Haad 2, Lankford 79, Mackowiak 11, Maxwell 12, May 122, Pointer 104.

PITCHING	W	L	ERA	G	GS	CG	SV	IP	H	R	ER	BB	SO	B	T	HT	WT	DOB	1st Yr	Resides
Alvarado, Carlos	4	6	4.57	20	18	0	0	91	89	52	46	46	75	R	R	6-4	218	1-24-75	1995	Arecibo, P.R.
Ayers, Mike	1	2	2.70	27	0	0	2	37	34	13	11	16	28	L	L	5-10	188	12-23-73	1996	Cincinnati, Ohio
Bausher, Andy	6	15	4.83	25	24	1	0	143	165	98	77	52	89	R	L	6-3	190	8-17-76	1997	Bechtelsville, Pa.
Breitenstein, Keith	1	2	2.65	33	8	0	0	85	85	37	25	25	62	R	L	6-1	155	1-12-72	1994	Dayton, Ohio
Carrasco, Danny	0	1	6.35	2	0	0	0	6	9	8	4	3	4	R	R	6-3	200	4-12-77	1997	Safford, Ariz.
Combs, Chris	5	3	6.52	32	13	0	0	90	112	73	65	40	69	L	R	6-8	232	5-19-75	1997	Raleigh, N.C.
Duff, Matt	2	3	5.08	7	7	0	0	39	41	22	22	13	40	R	R	6-1	190	10-6-74	1997	Alligator, Miss.
Gonzalez, Mike	10	4	4.02	20	20	0	0	112	98	55	50	63	119	R	L	6-2	218	5-23-78	1997	Pasadena, Texas
Guy, Brad	6	4	4.11	49	0	0	10	72	77	35	33	17	60	R	R	6-2	179	10-25-75	1997	Eureka, Calif.
Guzman, Wilson	1	2	3.44	35	0	0	2	65	70	35	25	12	78	L	L	5-11	199	7-14-77	1995	Palo Verde, D.R.
Halla, Ryan	2	7	5.13	46	0	0	7	54	60	34	31	20	56	S	R	6-4	243	10-3-73	1997	Birmingham, Ala.
Lambert, Kris	1	3	2.60	13	5	0	0	45	43	16	13	13	37	L	L	6-0	178	11-25-75	1997	Houston, Texas
Martin, Jeff	2	1	5.58	10	3	0	0	31	34	27	19	13	27	R	R	6-1	185	1-25-74	1995	Las Vegas, Nev.
McConnell, Sam	7	3	3.19	15	15	4	0	102	84	41	36	27	70	L	L	6-5	212	12-31-75	1997	Fairfield, Ohio
Minter, Matt	3	2	5.03	41	0	0	3	63	67	40	35	16	55	L	L	6-0	185	2-22-73	1996	Bellaire, Texas
Prempas, Lyle	2	3	5.68	6	6	0	0	25	27	19	16	7	25	L	L	6-7	205	12-3-74	1993	Westchester, Ill.
Sparks, Steve	2	3	6.23	5	5	1	0	26	36	20	18	15	20	R	R	6-5	204	3-28-75	1998	Mobile, Ala.
Williams, Larry	4	4	3.55	34	3	0	0	63	58	36	25	21	51	R	R	6-0	200	11-15-75	1996	Spring City, Pa.
Wimberly, Larry	5	5	5.04	11	10	0	0	55	77	40	31	13	41	L	L	6-1	185	8-22-75	1994	Zellwood, Fla.

HICKORY — Class A

SOUTH ATLANTIC LEAGUE

BATTING	AVG	G	AB	R	H	2B	3B	HR	RBI	BB	SO	SB	CS	B	T	HT	WT	DOB	1st Yr	Resides
Anderson, Frank	.194	38	129	15	25	4	0	4	11	8	52	0	2	R	R	6-1	200	9-1-75	1995	Lake City, Ga.
Barns, B.J.	.230	52	174	16	40	8	4	6	25	25	47	5	3	L	R	6-4	205	7-21-77	1999	Loysville, Pa.
Bone, Billy	.200	7	20	7	4	2	0	1	3	7	6	0	0	R	R	6-1	179	1-5-76	1998	Jacksonville, Fla.
Bultmann, Kurt	.356	13	45	4	16	2	0	0	9	6	4	1	1	R	R	5-9	165	2-10-77	1999	Seminole, Fla.
Caballero, Antonio	.079	13	38	3	3	0	0	0	2	3	13	0	1	L	L	6-0	155	6-13-79	1997	Valencia, Venez.
Cleto, Ambioris	.106	24	66	6	7	1	0	0	6	17	23	0	2	R	R	6-0	157	1-5-80	1996	Santo Domingo, D.R.
Cota, Humberto	.271	37	133	28	36	11	2	0	20	21	20	3	1	R	R	6-0	175	2-7-79	1996	San Luis Rio Colorado, Mexico
2-team (85 Char, S.C.)	.277	122	469	70	130	32	3	11	81	41	71	4	2							
Davis, J.J.	.265	86	317	58	84	26	1	19	65	44	99	2	5	R	R	6-6	231	10-25-78	1997	Pomona, Calif.
Diaz, Diogenes	.205	13	39	1	8	2	0	0	1	1	12	0	0	R	R	6-0	206	10-10-78	1998	Villa Mella, D.R.
Harts, Jeremy	.132	22	68	8	9	1	0	0	1	10	24	1	0	S	L	6-2	186	6-6-80	1998	Decatur, Ga.
Hobbs, Jay	.252	124	409	60	103	22	1	21	73	75	116	5	5	L	L	6-2	190	5-12-75	1999	Falkville, Ala.
House, J.R.	.273	4	11	3	3	0	0	0	0	3	3	0	0	R	R	6-2	215	11-11-79	1999	Ormond Beach, Fla.
Martin, Justin	.294	23	85	14	25	1	0	2	5	17	19	12	2	S	R	5-8	160	2-19-76	1999	Reno, Nev.
Maxwell, Keith	.262	62	206	26	54	11	1	8	39	19	49	2	2	R	R	6-1	203	4-18-75	1997	Bristol, Fla.
Perez, Deivi	.205	25	83	13	17	4	0	2	9	14	26	2	0	R	R	6-1	190	4-8-80	1997	Bani, D.R.

BATTING

BATTING	AVG	G	AB	R	H	2B	3B	HR	RBI	BB	SO	SB	CS	B	T	HT	WT	DOB	1st Yr	Resides
Piercy, Mike	.167	8	18	7	3	0	0	0	0	3	2	1	1	L	L	6-0	200	6-24-76	1999	Hillside, N.J.
Prieto, Jonathan	.303	61	244	42	74	9	1	1	21	22	55	10	7	L	R	5-11	176	6-24-80	1997	San Bernardino, Venez.
Ralph, Brian	.167	16	48	7	8	3	0	0	2	6	8	3	2	L	L	5-11	185	6-25-76	1998	Laguna Niguel, Calif.
Reyes, Jose	.275	23	80	11	22	4	1	5	15	4	18	3	1	R	R	6-1	188	5-1-73	1993	Villa Vazquez, D.R.
Risinger, Ben	.249	124	449	56	112	20	3	4	44	39	80	2	4	R	R	6-1	170	11-25-77	1999	Perth, Australia
Rivera, Carlos	.322	119	457	63	147	30	4	13	86	15	45	2	1	L	L	6-1	221	6-10-78	1996	Rio Grande, P.R.
Segura, Rolando	.303	40	142	23	43	8	0	6	21	12	30	0	3	R	R	6-2	203	12-21-78	1996	San Pedro de Macoris, D.R.
Shelley, Jason	.259	20	54	8	14	2	0	1	6	1	14	0	1	R	R	6-2	195	3-19-77	1999	Plainfield, Ill.
Skrehot, Shaun	.234	115	461	53	108	17	5	1	37	16	72	12	8	R	R	5-11	166	12-5-75	1998	Spring, Texas
Sosa, Jovanny	.209	108	402	61	84	16	1	22	53	37	145	2	2	R	R	6-2	207	4-10-80	1997	Santo Domingo, D.R.
Washington, Rico	.355	76	287	70	102	15	1	13	50	48	45	5	5	L	R	5-10	179	5-30-78	1997	Gray, Ga.
Weichard, Paul	.225	89	316	44	71	7	3	5	37	28	92	23	7	S	L	5-11	185	11-7-79	1997	Melbourne, Australia

GAMES BY POSITION: C—Anderson 38, Cota 30, Diaz 11, Reyes 14, Washington 54. 1B—Hobbs 19, Maxwell 16, Risinger 9, Rivera 114. 2B—Bone 5, Bultmann 13, Martin 15, Perez 1, Prieto 61, Risinger 24, Skrehot 29. 3B—House 1, Maxwell 1, Risinger 83, Segura 39, Shelley 1, Skrehot 9, Washington 5. SS—Cleto 24, Perez 25, Risinger 22, Shelley 1, Skrehot 82. OF—Barns 50, Caballero 11, Davis 51, Harts 22, Hobbs 81, House 1, Martin 7, Maxwell 13, Piercy 7, Ralph 14, Sosa 89, Weichard 88.

PITCHING

PITCHING	W	L	ERA	G	GS	CG	SV	IP	H	R	ER	BB	SO	B	T	HT	WT	DOB	1st Yr	Resides
Beimel, Joe	5	11	4.43	29	22	0	0	130	146	81	64	43	102	L	L	6-4	203	4-19-77	1998	Kersey, Pa.
Bennett, Jeff	2	2	5.91	8	6	0	0	35	48	25	23	9	16	R	R	6-3	186	6-10-80	1998	Brush Creek, Tenn.
Bravo, Franklin	7	1	3.22	34	8	0	0	95	82	47	34	42	81	R	R	6-2	200	12-24-78	1996	Santo Domingo, D.R.
Buirley, Matt	8	4	3.76	46	0	0	11	55	44	34	23	32	63	R	R	6-3	207	7-21-75	1996	Gambier, Ohio
Crawford, Danny	6	4	4.07	16	9	0	0	60	66	35	27	21	38	R	R	6-6	232	2-25-75	1997	Houston, Texas
Glaser, Scott	1	1	4.43	17	0	0	0	20	23	12	10	3	10	R	L	5-10	160	5-13-76	1999	Seminole, Fla.
Grabow, John	9	10	3.80	26	26	0	0	156	152	82	66	32	164	L	L	6-2	189	11-4-78	1997	San Gabriel, Calif.
Johnston, Clint	5	6	4.73	34	10	0	0	93	92	63	49	49	94	L	L	6-2	207	7-2-77	1998	Vero Beach, Fla.
Martin, Jeff	0	2	1.88	13	0	0	0	24	19	6	5	8	23	R	R	6-1	205	1-25-74	1995	Las Vegas, Nev.
Martinez, Javier	0	0	3.52	6	0	0	0	8	6	6	3	6	13	R	R	6-2	235	2-5-77	1994	Toa Alta, P.R.
Montilla, Felix	0	0	5.40	2	0	0	0	3	6	2	2	0	1	R	R	6-1	192	3-7-80	1997	Santo Domingo, D.R.
Pavlovich, Tony	5	1	2.33	56	0	0	20	73	55	29	19	16	78	R	R	6-0	180	8-23-74	1994	Pavo, Ga.
Pena, Alex	0	4	6.60	22	7	0	0	46	68	42	34	31	37	R	R	6-2	175	9-9-77	1995	Santo Domingo, D.R.
Prater, Andy	2	3	5.80	15	12	0	0	64	71	46	41	18	52	R	R	6-4	170	9-27-77	1996	Florissant, Mo.
Siciliano, Jess	0	2	9.53	6	0	0	0	6	11	8	6	4	4	R	R	6-2	193	8-31-76	1996	East White Plains, N.Y.
Simontacchi, Jason	4	6	4.02	23	7	0	1	69	71	34	31	19	66	R	R	6-2	185	11-13-73	1996	Santa Clara, Calif.
Sparks, Steve	4	4	4.47	25	12	1	0	89	97	60	44	51	72	R	R	6-5	204	3-28-75	1998	Mobile, Ala.
Stabile, Paul	3	3	4.00	46	0	0	1	74	70	42	33	42	87	L	L	6-0	175	1-16-76	1997	Staten Island, N.Y.
Torres, Luis	3	2	3.26	7	7	0	0	39	40	17	14	20	26	R	R	5-11	175	6-6-80	1998	Falcon, Venez.
Williams, David	3	1	3.20	9	9	1	0	59	42	22	21	11	46	L	L	6-2	208	3-12-79	1998	Camden, Del.
Wimberly, Larry	1	1	1.51	17	5	0	0	48	32	8	8	11	57	L	L	6-1	185	8-22-75	1994	Zellwood, Fla.

WILLIAMSPORT   Short-Season Class A

NEW YORK-PENN LEAGUE

BATTING	AVG	G	AB	R	H	2B	3B	HR	RBI	BB	SO	SB	CS	B	T	HT	WT	DOB	1st Yr	Resides
Alvarez, Antonio	.321	58	196	44	63	14	1	7	45	21	36	38	9	R	R	6-1	202	5-10-79	1996	Los Teques, Venez.
Barns, B.J.	.400	14	50	10	20	4	0	1	11	12	11	0	2	L	R	6-4	205	7-21-77	1999	Loysville, Pa.
Batcheller, Chris	.148	23	81	2	12	1	0	1	9	1	31	1	0	R	R	6-3	215	2-17-78	1999	Stuart, Va.
Bonifay, Josh	.260	52	200	42	52	10	2	4	17	25	55	2	2	R	R	6-0	185	7-30-78	1999	Gibsonia, Pa.
Cotten, Jeremy	.200	50	175	16	35	13	1	1	24	18	67	0	0	R	R	6-3	226	9-24-80	1998	Fuquay-Varina, N.C.
Daggett, Jesse	.222	5	18	1	4	3	0	0	1	4	3	0	0	R	R	6-4	227	7-3-78	1998	La Crescenta, Calif.
Diaz, Diogenes	.300	9	30	3	9	3	0	1	3	4	7	1	2	R	R	6-0	206	10-10-78	1996	Villa Mella, D.R.
Hernandez, Jose	.237	35	118	5	28	4	0	0	9	3	20	1	1	R	R	6-1	186	11-3-80	1998	Valencia, Venez.
House, J.R.	.300	26	100	11	30	6	0	1	13	9	21	0	1	R	R	6-2	215	11-11-79	1999	Ormond Beach, Fla.
Hudson, Danny	.214	37	117	14	25	6	2	0	9	22	41	5	3	R	R	6-2	185	10-24-77	1999	Lucedale, Miss.
Landreth, Jason	.314	62	210	35	66	14	1	6	37	34	35	5	5	R	R	6-2	205	10-18-75	1998	Lubbock, Texas
Langston, Jay	.275	54	200	15	55	8	1	1	20	6	40	2	1	S	R	6-3	205	3-23-78	1999	Lawrenceville, Ga.
Martin, Justin	.248	31	109	26	27	2	0	0	8	21	26	16	1	S	R	5-8	160	2-19-76	1999	Reno, Nev.
Nicolas, Jose	.202	29	99	8	20	6	1	1	11	7	32	2	2	R	R	6-3	205	1-1-79	1997	Miami, Fla.
Pelfrey, Brice	.120	14	50	1	6	0	1	0	2	1	12	1	0	R	R	6-2	147	5-16-80	1998	Cantonment, Fla.
Perez, Deivi	.189	48	148	20	28	7	0	3	9	18	35	2	0	R	R	6-1	190	4-8-80	1997	Bani, D.R.
Piercy, Mike	.192	8	26	3	5	0	0	1	5	6	7	0	3	L	L	6-0	200	6-24-76	1999	Hillside, N.J.
Ravelo, Manuel	.214	55	201	27	43	2	1	1	10	17	43	23	7	R	R	5-10	152	8-8-81	1997	Santo Domingo, D.R.
Sarabia, Eliot	.200	34	100	12	20	1	1	0	10	14	12	7	1	R	R	5-11	165	2-25-76	1998	Las Vegas, Nev.
Schneider, Matt	.197	24	76	10	15	4	1	2	11	9	27	1	0	L	R	6-6	235	5-19-78	1999	Jacksonville, Fla.
Segura, Rolando	.333	29	108	26	36	10	0	4	24	12	26	1	1	R	R	6-2	203	12-21-78	1996	San Pedro de Macoris, D.R.
Sickles, Jeremy	.160	27	94	4	15	2	0	1	1	4	19	0	1	R	R	6-3	205	1-16-78	1999	Long Beach, Calif.
Washington, Mo	.125	5	16	0	2	0	0	0	0	2	11	0	0	R	R	6-1	201	5-22-79	1997	North Las Vegas, Nev.

GAMES BY POSITION: C—Alvarez 1, Daggett 3, Diaz 9, Hernandez 35, House 14, Sickles 19. 1B—Alvarez 1, Cotton 45, House 8, Landreth 24. 2B—Alvarez 7, Bonifay 31, Martin 19, Pelfrey 14. 3B—Alvarez 33, Bonifay 6, Langston 17, Segura 24. SS—Alvarez 1, Perez 48, Sarabia 33. OF—Alvarez 5, Barns 14, Batcheller 22, Bonifay 1, Hudson 37, Landreth 25, Langston 37, Martin 7, Nicolas 21, Piercy 8, Ravelo 49, Schneider 13, Washington 4.

PITCHING	W	L	ERA	G	GS	CG	SV	IP	H	R	ER	BB	SO	B	T	HT	WT	DOB	1st Yr	Resides
Alcala, Jason	0	0	4.38	6	0	0	0	12	11	7	6	6	11	R	R	6-2	175	9-18-80	1997	Cumana, Venez.
Bazan, Juan	4	3	3.02	8	8	1	0	48	37	17	16	16	33	R	R	6-0	192	4-7-78	1996	Chitre, Panama
Biddlestone, Jason	0	1	9.00	1	1	0	0	5	7	6	5	3	2	R	R	6-4	205	8-12-78	1999	Westerville, Ohio
Carrasco, Danny	4	2	2.96	18	4	0	0	52	43	20	17	23	49	R	R	6-3	200	4-12-77	1997	Safford, Ariz.
Classen, Ender	0	0	3.12	3	1	0	0	9	9	3	3	2	5	S	R	6-3	192	4-1-78	1996	Arecibo, P.R.
Glaser, Scott	0	1	4.50	3	0	0	0	4	5	2	2	1	6	R	L	5-10	160	5-13-76	1999	Seminole, Fla.
Hancock, Rodney	1	2	1.69	8	4	0	0	32	27	13	6	13	35	L	L	6-0	205	7-19-78	1998	Goose Creek, S.C.
Johnston, Michael	3	2	4.25	14	2	0	2	42	46	26	20	18	30	L	L	6-3	192	3-30-79	1998	Colwyn, Pa.
Montilla, Felix	1	2	3.99	23	0	0	10	29	29	14	13	11	29	R	R	6-1	192	3-7-80	1997	Santo Domingo, D.R.
Prater, Andy	2	2	6.10	10	10	1	0	38	45	36	26	18	21	R	R	6-4	170	9-27-77	1996	Florissant, Mo.
Reid, Justin	2	6	4.62	16	11	0	1	62	71	41	32	23	68	R	R	6-6	205	6-30-77	1999	Folsom, Calif.

PITCHING	W	L	ERA	G	GS	CG	SV	IP	H	R	ER	BB	SO	B	T	HT	WT	DOB	1st Yr	Resides
Rojas, Chris	5	7	4.87	15	15	1	0	81	72	57	44	43	85	R	R	6-2	180	3-30-77	1998	Glendale, N.Y.
Sabens, Mike	1	1	10.80	5	0	0	0	7	8	8	9	6	9	R	R	6-1	195	1-21-77	1999	Hiram, Ga.
Satterfield, Troy	2	1	1.70	17	0	0	0	37	33	11	7	11	28	R	L	6-6	200	10-27-76	1999	McDonough, Ga.
Vinton, Drew	1	4	4.16	17	7	1	0	63	58	43	29	33	49	R	R	6-2	195	5-1-76	1999	Jenison, Mich.
Wallace, Justin	0	0	5.40	19	0	0	2	32	35	22	19	16	23	L	L	6-5	220	10-1-76	1998	Fairlawn, Ohio
Williams, David	4	2	2.56	7	7	1	0	46	33	17	13	11	47	L	L	6-2	208	3-12-79	1998	Camden, Del.
Wright, Shane	2	6	2.81	17	6	2	1	58	53	29	18	19	38	R	R	6-3	215	10-28-76	1999	Overland Park, Kan.

BRADENTON · Rookie

GULF COAST LEAGUE

BATTING	AVG	G	AB	R	H	2B	3B	HR	RBI	BB	SO	SB	CS	B	T	HT	WT	DOB	1st Yr	Resides
Araujo, Victor	.286	51	199	30	57	8	0	4	32	8	29	13	5	R	R	6-0	173	1-16-80	1997	San Pedro de Macoris, D.R.
Batcheller, Chris	.261	6	23	3	6	1	0	0	3	2	4	1	0	R	R	6-3	215	2-17-78	1999	Stuart, Va.
Bone, Billy	.125	7	24	3	1	0	0	0	3	2	3	0	0	R	R	6-1	179	1-5-76	1998	Jacksonville, Fla.
Cabrera, Yoelmis	.282	27	78	17	22	7	0	0	6	10	15	8	0	R	R	5-11	155	10-40-81	1997	Santo Domingo, D.R.
Cardona, Raynier	.216	14	37	2	8	3	0	0	7	9	9	1	0	S	R	5-11	195	8-26-80	1998	San Sebastian, P.R.
Castillo, Jose	.266	47	173	27	46	9	0	4	30	11	23	8	0	R	R	6-0	180	3-19-81	1997	Las Mercedes, Venez.
Castro, Vicente	.280	43	161	21	45	9	0	3	21	6	30	3	0	R	R	6-0	180	5-19-80	1997	San Pedro de Macoris, D.R.
Cortes, Jorge	.301	32	93	14	28	4	1	0	14	14	19	2	1	L	L	6-0	169	10-17-80	1998	Barranquilla, Colombia
Diaz, David	.184	17	38	4	7	2	0	0	1	1	10	0	0	R	R	6-4	202	7-3-80	1998	Hialeah, Fla.
Dorsey, Ryan	.175	14	40	4	7	1	1	0	2	6	18	0	0	R	R	6-2	175	8-29-81	1999	Wheaton, Md.
Douglas, Mo	.161	26	87	6	14	2	1	1	7	8	33	1	0	L	L	6-2	238	6-6-77	1999	O'Fallon, Mo.
Doumit, Ryan	.282	29	85	17	24	5	0	1	7	15	14	4	2	S	R	6-0	180	4-3-81	1999	Moses Lake, Wash.
Harts, Jeremy	.295	28	122	20	36	3	2	2	15	8	21	8	3	S	L	6-2	186	6-6-80	1998	Decatur, Ga.
Herrera, Elvis	.111	7	18	5	2	0	0	0	1	4	6	0	0	R	R	6-2	178	1-18-81	1998	Santo Domingo, D.R.
House, J.R.	.327	33	113	13	37	9	3	5	23	11	23	1	0	R	R	6-2	215	11-11-79	1999	Ormond Beach, Fla.
Hudnall, Josh	.195	25	82	6	16	3	0	0	6	4	28	1	2	R	R	6-2	185	2-22-80	1999	Monroe, La.
Hudson, Danny	.211	7	19	5	4	1	1	0	3	3	3	4	1	R	R	6-2	185	10-24-77	1999	Lucedale, Miss.
Miller, Josh	.091	6	22	0	2	2	0	0	0	0	6	0	0	L	R	6-1	214	12-1-78	1998	Aiken, S.C.
Paulino, Ronny	.253	29	83	6	21	2	4	1	13	8	19	1	2	R	R	6-3	190	4-21-81	1998	Santo Domingo, D.R.
Pelfrey, Brice	.241	31	108	19	26	1	0	0	7	8	15	6	3	R	R	6-2	147	5-16-80	1998	Cantonment, Fla.
Piercy, Mike	.314	10	35	6	11	1	0	0	3	7	7	3	1	L	L	6-0	200	6-24-76	1999	Hillside, N.J.
Riek, Clifford	.226	24	84	10	19	2	0	1	6	6	22	1	0	R	R	6-2	195	4-15-81	1999	Cary, N.C.
Shelley, Jason	.000	8	17	0	0	0	0	0	1	2	4	0	0	R	R	6-2	195	3-19-77	1999	Plainfield, Ill.
Weston, Aron	.218	33	119	26	26	1	2	1	5	20	36	14	5	L	L	6-5	173	11-5-80	1999	Solon, Ohio
Young, Walter	.231	37	130	9	30	6	2	0	15	4	34	2	2	L	R	6-5	280	2-18-80	1999	Purvis, Miss.

GAMES BY POSITION: C—Cardona 11, Diaz 16, Doumit 13, Paulino 26. **1B**—Douglas 1, House 16, Riek 11, Young 35. **2B**—Araujo 3, Bone 3, Castillo 23, Herrera 5, Hudnall 1, Pelfrey 28. **3B**—Araujo 39, Bone 4, Herrera 2, House 3, Hudnall 1, Riek 9, Shelley 6. **SS**—Castillo 24, Dorsey 14, Hudnall 23, Pelfrey 2. **OF**—Araujo 1, Batcheller 4, Cabrera 22, Castro 38, Cortez 25, Douglas 20, Harts 28, Hudson 5, Miller 3, Piercy 9, Weston 32.

PITCHING	W	L	ERA	G	GS	CG	SV	IP	H	R	ER	BB	SO	B	T	HT	WT	DOB	1st Yr	Resides
Alcala, Jason	0	1	1.23	10	0	0	2	15	12	7	2	0	9	R	R	6-2	175	9-18-80	1997	Cumana, Venez.
Bennett, Jeff	3	4	4.23	8	8	0	0	45	53	27	21	9	28	R	R	6-3	186	6-10-80	1998	Brush Creek, Tenn.
Biddlestone, Jason	4	1	2.91	12	4	0	0	46	39	19	15	16	45	R	R	6-4	205	8-12-78	1999	Westerville, Ohio
Bradley, Bobby	1	0	2.90	6	6	0	0	31	31	13	10	4	31	R	R	6-1	170	12-15-80	1999	Wellington, Fla.
Bumatay, Mike	2	1	2.90	11	3	0	2	40	35	16	13	8	39	L	L	6-0	165	10-9-79	1998	Clovis, Calif.
Burruezo, Joe	0	1	4.82	7	0	0	0	9	6	6	5	9	8	R	R	6-3	180	9-10-80	1999	Tampa, Fla.
Classen, Ender	3	1	1.82	6	6	0	0	35	21	13	7	9	28	S	R	6-3	192	4-1-78	1996	Arecibo, P.R.
Hlodan, George	0	0	3.60	4	0	0	1	10	11	4	4	3	3	R	R	6-1	176	6-25-76	1996	Elizabeth, Pa.
Josephson, Jared	1	0	1.80	8	0	0	1	10	8	2	2	2	8	R	R	6-4	220	12-30-76	1999	Concord, Calif.
Levesque, Ben	2	7	7.53	11	11	1	0	43	38	44	36	40	20	R	R	6-3	186	10-9-79	1998	Longwood, Fla.
Lewter, John	2	1	5.63	13	0	0	1	24	28	20	15	8	14	L	R	6-1	180	4-12-77	1999	Frostproof, Fla.
Mendible, Franklin	0	1	1.59	4	0	0	0	6	4	1	1	4	3	R	R	6-3	160	8-4-79	1996	Valencia, Venez.
Messer, Brian	0	1	4.50	3	2	0	0	6	7	3	3	1	5	R	R	6-5	210	4-6-77	1999	Shawnee, Kan.
Parkerson, Michael	0	1	3.27	14	0	0	1	33	25	14	12	21	31	R	L	6-2	185	4-26-79	1997	Columbus, Ga.
Rhea, Thad	0	1	3.38	2	0	0	0	3	2	1	1	3	1	S	R	6-1	195	1-27-77	1997	College Station, Texas
Sabens, Mike	0	1	3.38	7	0	0	0	8	6	4	3	9	9	R	R	6-1	195	1-21-77	1999	Hiram, Ga.
Searles, Jon	1	0	4.15	8	0	0	0	13	14	10	6	9	9	R	R	6-3	185	1-18-81	1999	Huntington, N.Y.
Story, Aaron	2	2	3.58	12	1	0	0	28	26	14	11	13	27	L	L	6-1	185	10-2-80	1999	Lawrenceburg, Tenn.
Torres, Luis	1	2	1.69	8	8	0	0	43	24	9	8	7	33	R	R	5-11	175	6-6-80	1998	Falcon, Venez.
Vogt, Robert	0	0	12.00	3	0	0	0	3	5	4	4	2	3	L	L	6-6	190	10-19-78	1996	Brandon, Fla.
White, James	2	8	4.86	13	11	0	0	63	70	44	34	24	35	R	R	6-2	192	11-6-79	1998	Chico, Calif.

ST.LOUISCARDINALS

McGwire's feats again tempered by team's poor showing

BY MIKE EISENBATH

A year after Mark McGwire set the sports world afire with his 70 home runs, he put together one of the best seasons in history for an encore, batting .278 with 65 home runs and 147 RBIs. But his efforts didn't garner nearly as much attention as in 1998.

Again, a disappointing season for the Cardinals accompanied McGwire's feat. The Cardinals' pitching woes, injuries to key players and poor fundamentals doomed St. Louis to finish 11 games under .500.

McGwire's power display, phenomenal as it was, almost was expected. That's why the Cardinals set a franchise attendance record at Busch Stadium and were baseball's best attraction on the road. McGwire trailed Sammy Sosa for the home run lead for most of the season, but his typical late-season surge allowed him to win the race once more.

The Cardinals did have several pleasant surprises. Third baseman Fernando Tatis became the first infielder in club history to hit at least 20 homers and steal 20 bases, and he set a franchise record for third basemen with 34 homers. He also became the first hitter in major league history to hit two grand slams in an inning, doing it against Dodgers righthander Chan Ho Park.

Journeyman righthander Kent Bottenfield emerged as a surprise ace. Pitching for his sixth organization, he pitched in the All-Star Game and won 18 games, double his career total. Minor league veteran Joe McEwing captivated fans with his hot first-half bat, constant hustle and versatility. Starter Garrett Stephenson had a promising final two months, during which he won six games.

But the disappointments were plentiful. Ray

Mark McGwire   **Rick Ankiel**

Players of the Year

MAJOR LEAGUE: Mark McGwire, 1b
McGwire made another run at history, finishing with 65 home runs and 147 RBIs to lead the NL in both categories.

MINOR LEAGUE: Rick Ankiel, lhp
Ankiel won Minor League Player of the Year honors after going 13-3 with a 2.35 ERA and 194 strikeouts at Memphis and Arkansas.

Lankford, moved to left field because of achy knees, slumped to 15 homers after belting 31 each of the two previous seasons. Right fielder Eric Davis spent the second half on the disabled list, and center fielder J.D. Drew never realized predictions that he would be the league's best rookie. Catcher Eli Marrero never found his swing and spent considerable time on the bench.

The pitching staff took its biggest hit in spring training, when Matt Morris had Tommy John surgery. A shaky rotation resulted in an overworked bullpen, which lacked a defined closer in the first place. Bottenfield was the only Cardinal to reach double digits in wins.

Rookie righthander Jose Jimenez epitomized the pitching. He beat the Diamondbacks with a 1-0 no-hitter, beating Randy Johnson in late June, but he was in the minor leagues less than two months later and finished 5-14 with a 5.85 ERA.

Cardinals minor league affiliates struggled just as much, producing a cumulative winning percentage of .442. Only Triple-A Memphis, at 74-64, had a winning record.

The Redbirds featured lefthander Rick Ankiel, the 1999 Minor League Player of the Year. Ankiel went 6-0 with a 0.91 ERA at Double-A Arkansas, then 7-3 with a 3.16 ERA for the Redbirds. He had 194 strikeouts in 137 innings before a September callup.

Second baseman Adam Kennedy started with Ankiel in the inaugural Futures Game during the all-star break. Kennedy was one of two players who played in a classification all-star game, the Futures Game and the Pan American Games. He finished his season in the big leagues.

ORGANIZATION LEADERS

BATTING

*AVG	Adam Kennedy, Memphis	.327
R	Andy Bevins, Potomac	92
H	Jack Wilson, Potomac/Peoria	162
TB	Chris Richard, Memphis/Arkansas	261
2B	Bill Ortega, Arkansas/Potomac	36
3B	Four tied at	8
HR	Chris Richard, Memphis/Arkansas	30
RBI	Chris Richard, Memphis/Arkansas	98
BB	Esix Snead, Potomac/Peoria	67
SO	Chris Haas, Memphis	155
SB	Esix Snead, Potomac/Peoria	64

PITCHING

W	Two tied at	13
L	Two tied at	13
#ERA	Rick Ankiel, Memphis/Arkansas	2.35
G	Two tied at	59
CG	Four tied at	2
SV	Jason Marr, Potomac	21
IP	Jason Karnuth, Arkansas	160
BB	Chad Hutchinson, Memphis/Arkansas	93
SO	Rick Ankiel, Memphis/Arkansas	194

*Minimum 250 At-Bats #Minimum 75 Innings

St. Louis
CARDINALS

Manager: Tony La Russa   **1999 Record:** 75-86, .466 (4th, NL Central)

BATTING	AVG	G	AB	R	H	2B	3B	HR	RBI	BB	SO	SB	CS	B	T	HT	WT	DOB	1st Yr	Resides
Bragg, Darren	.260	93	273	38	71	12	1	6	26	44	67	3	0	L	R	5-9	180	9-7-69	1991	Roswell, Ga.
Castillo, Alberto	.263	93	255	21	67	8	0	4	31	24	48	0	0	R	R	6-0	185	2-10-70	1987	Port St. Lucie, Fla.
Davis, Eric	.257	58	191	27	49	9	2	5	30	30	49	5	4	R	R	6-3	200	5-29-62	1980	Woodland Hills, Calif.
Drew, J.D.	.242	104	368	72	89	16	6	13	39	50	77	19	3	L	R	6-1	195	11-20-75	1997	Hahira, Ga.
Dunston, Shawon	.307	62	150	23	46	5	2	5	25	2	23	6	3	R	R	6-1	175	3-21-63	1982	Corona, N.Y.
Howard, David	.207	52	82	3	17	4	0	1	6	7	27	0	2	S	R	6-0	175	2-26-67	1987	Sarasota, Fla.
Howard, Thomas	.292	98	195	16	57	10	0	6	28	17	26	1	1	S	R	6-2	205	12-11-64	1986	Elk Grove, Calif.
Jensen, Marcus	.235	16	34	5	8	5	0	1	6	12	0	0	1	S	R	6-4	204	12-14-72	1990	Scottsdale, Ariz.
Kennedy, Adam	.255	33	102	12	26	10	1	1	16	3	8	0	1	L	R	6-1	180	1-10-76	1997	Riverside, Calif.
Lankford, Ray	.306	122	422	77	129	32	1	15	63	49	110	14	4	L	L	5-11	180	6-5-67	1987	Modesto, Calif.
Marrero, Eli	.192	114	317	32	61	13	1	6	34	18	56	11	2	R	R	6-1	180	11-17-73	1993	Miami, Fla.
McEwing, Joe	.275	152	513	65	141	28	4	9	44	41	87	7	4	R	R	5-10	170	10-19-72	1992	Bristol, Pa.
McGee, Willie	.251	132	271	25	68	7	0	0	20	17	60	7	4	S	R	6-1	185	11-2-58	1977	Hercules, Calif.
McGwire, Mark	.278	153	521	118	145	21	1	65	147	133	141	0	0	R	R	6-5	225	10-1-63	1984	Claremont, Calif.
Oliver, Darren	.274	35	73	7	20	4	0	0	6	3	23	0	0	R	L	6-2	210	10-6-70	1988	Arlington, Texas
Ordaz, Luis	.111	10	9	3	1	0	0	0	2	1	2	1	0	R	R	5-11	170	8-12-75	1993	Maracaibo, Venez.
Paquette, Craig	.287	48	157	21	45	6	0	10	37	6	38	1	0	R	R	6-0	190	3-28-69	1989	Tempe, Ariz.
Perez, Eduardo	.344	21	32	6	11	2	0	1	9	7	6	0	0	R	R	6-4	225	9-11-69	1991	Calabasas, Calif.
Polanco, Placido	.277	88	220	24	61	9	3	1	19	5	15	24	1	R	R	5-10	168	10-10-75	1994	Miami, Fla.
Renteria, Edgar	.275	154	585	92	161	36	2	11	63	53	82	37	8	R	R	6-1	180	8-7-75	1992	Barranquilla, Colombia
Tatis, Fernando	.298	149	537	104	160	31	2	34	107	82	128	21	9	R	R	5-10	170	1-1-75	1993	San Pedro de Macoris, D.R.

PITCHING	W	L	ERA	G	GS	CG	SV	IP	H	R	ER	BB	SO	B	T	HT	WT	DOB	1st Yr	Resides
Acevedo, Juan	6	8	5.89	50	12	0	4	102	115	71	67	48	52	R	R	6-2	228	5-5-70	1992	Carpentersville, Ill.
Ankiel, Rick	0	1	3.27	9	5	0	1	33	26	12	12	14	39	L	L	6-1	210	7-19-79	1997	Fort Pierce, Fla.
Aybar, Manny	4	5	5.47	65	1	0	3	97	104	67	59	36	74	R	R	6-1	177	10-5-74	1991	Bani, D.R.
Benes, Adam	0	0	0.00	2	0	0	0	2	2	0	0	0	2	L	R	6-2	195	3-12-73	1995	Lake Forest, Ill.
Bottalico, Ricky	3	7	4.91	68	0	0	20	73	83	45	40	49	66	L	R	6-1	217	8-26-69	1991	Rocky Hill, Conn.
Bottenfield, Kent	18	7	3.97	31	31	0	0	190	197	91	84	89	124	R	R	6-3	240	11-14-68	1986	Brownsburg, Ind.
Busby, Mike	0	1	7.13	15	0	0	0	18	21	15	14	14	7	R	R	6-4	225	12-27-72	1991	Glendale, Ariz.
Croushore, Rich	3	7	4.14	59	0	0	3	72	68	42	33	43	88	R	R	6-4	210	8-7-70	1993	Houston, Texas
Heiserman, Rick	0	0	8.31	3	0	0	0	4	8	4	4	4	4	R	R	6-7	220	2-22-73	1994	Omaha, Neb.
Jimenez, Jose	5	14	5.85	29	28	2	0	163	173	114	106	71	113	R	R	6-3	170	7-7-73	1992	San Pedro de Macoris, D.R.
King, Curtis	0	0	18.00	2	0	0	0	1	3	2	2	0	1	R	R	6-5	205	10-25-70	1994	Conshohocken, Pa.
Luebbers, Larry	3	3	5.12	8	8	1	0	46	46	27	26	16	16	R	R	6-6	190	10-11-69	1990	Florence, Ky.
Mercker, Kent	6	5	5.12	25	18	0	0	104	125	73	59	51	64	L	L	6-2	195	2-1-68	1986	Dublin, Ohio
Mohler, Mike	1	1	4.38	48	0	0	1	49	47	26	24	23	31	R	L	6-2	208	7-26-68	1990	Gonzales, La.
Oliver, Darren	9	9	4.26	30	30	2	0	196	197	96	93	74	119	R	L	6-2	210	10-6-70	1988	Arlington, Texas
Osborne, Donovan	1	3	5.52	6	6	0	0	29	34	18	18	10	21	L	L	6-2	195	6-21-69	1990	Carson City, Nev.
Painter, Lance	4	5	4.83	56	4	0	1	63	63	37	34	25	56	L	L	6-1	195	7-21-67	1990	Milwaukee, Wis.
Radinsky, Scott	2	1	4.88	43	0	0	3	28	27	16	15	18	17	L	L	6-3	221	3-3-68	1986	Simi Valley, Calif.
Slocumb, Heathcliff	3	2	2.36	40	0	0	2	53	49	16	14	30	48	R	R	6-3	220	6-7-66	1984	Richmond Hills, N.Y.
Sodowsky, Clint	0	1	15.63	3	1	0	0	6	15	11	11	6	2	L	R	6-4	200	7-13-72	1991	Lamont, Okla.
Stephenson, Garrett	6	3	4.22	18	12	0	0	85	90	43	40	29	59	R	R	6-5	208	1-2-72	1992	Kimberly, Idaho
Thompson, Mark	1	3	2.76	5	0	0	0	29	26	12	9	17	22	R	R	6-2	205	4-7-71	1992	Russellville, Ky.

FIELDING

Catcher	PCT	G	PO	A	E	DP	PB
Castillo	.991	91	514	38	5	10	5
Jensen	.988	14	72	9	1	1	1
Marrero	.987	96	490	42	7	12	2

First Base	PCT	G	PO	A	E	DP
D. Howard	1.000	9	33	1	0	4
Marrero	1.000	20	47	5	0	2
McEwing	1.000	2	5	0	0	0
McGee	1.000	3	9	0	0	0
McGwire	.990	151	1181	80	13	119
Paquette	1.000	6	19	3	0	1
Perez	.952	5	18	2	1	2

Second Base	PCT	G	PO	A	E	DP
D. Howard	1.000	9	10	16	0	4
Kennedy	.971	29	68	64	4	14
McEwing	.980	96	202	238	9	51
Ordaz	1.000	1	0	1	0	0
Paquette	.962	7	10	15	1	4
Polanco	.980	66	116	123	5	32

Third Base	PCT	G	PO	A	E	DP
Dunston	.909	5	2	8	1	2
D. Howard	1.000	4	3	6	0	1
McEwing	.875	6	2	5	1	2

	PCT	G	PO	A	E	DP
Ordaz	.000	1	0	0	0	0
Paquette	1.000	10	4	24	0	0
Polanco	.889	9	0	8	1	0
Tatis	.958	147	100	267	16	30

Shortstop	PCT	G	PO	A	E	DP
D. Howard	.966	13	10	18	1	2
McEwing	.000	1	0	0	0	0
Ordaz	.786	8	4	7	3	4
Polanco	.931	9	7	20	2	5
Renteria	.959	151	219	393	26	88

Outfield	PCT	G	PO	A	E	DP
Bragg	.982	88	155	7	3	1
Davis	1.000	51	93	4	0	0
Drew	.972	98	235	9	7	6
Dunston	1.000	23	38	1	0	0
D. Howard	1.000	5	3	0	0	0
T. Howard	.987	48	77	0	1	0
Lankford	.987	106	214	6	3	0
McEwing	.991	66	111	3	1	1
McGee	.972	89	103	2	3	1
Paquette	.955	27	42	0	2	0
Perez	1.000	6	10	1	0	1

Kent Bottenfield

LARRY GOREN

Director of Player Development: Mike Jorgensen

Class	Farm Team	League	W	L	Pct.	Finish*	Manager	First Yr
AAA	Memphis (Tenn.) Redbirds	Pacific Coast	74	64	.536	5th (16)	Gaylen Pitts	1998
AA	Arkansas Travelers	Texas	59	81	.421	8th (8)	Chris Maloney	1966
A#	Potomac (Va.) Cannons	Carolina	54	85	.388	8th (8)	Joe Cunningham	1997
A	Peoria (Ill.) Chiefs	Midwest	63	76	.453	11th (14)	Brian Rupp	1995
A	New Jersey Cardinals	New York-Penn	30	46	.395	14th (14)	Jeff Shireman	1994
Rookie#	Johnson City (Tenn.) Cardinals	Appalachian	30	39	.435	7th (10)	Steve Turco	1975

*Finish in overall standings (No. of teams in league)   #Advanced level

Organization Statistics

MEMPHIS   Class AAA

PACIFIC COAST LEAGUE

BATTING	AVG	G	AB	R	H	2B	3B	HR	RBI	BB	SO	SB	CS	B	T	HT	WT	DOB	1st Yr	Resides
Ametler, Jesus	.250	2	4	0	1	0	0	0	0	0	0	0	0	L	R	5-8	175	7-25-74	1997	Hialeah, Fla.
Belk, Tim	.200	21	55	10	11	4	0	3	8	9	9	1	0	R	R	6-3	200	4-6-70	1992	Houston, Texas
Bieser, Steve	.311	58	180	25	56	13	2	4	16	16	30	8	0	L	R	5-10	180	8-4-67	1989	St. Genevieve, Mo.
2-team (6 Nashville)	.306	64	193	28	59	14	2	4	19	18	34	8	0							
Clapp, Stubby	.260	110	393	72	102	26	2	14	62	53	96	7	7	L	R	5-8	175	2-24-73	1996	Windsor, Ontario
Dishington, Nate	.209	72	196	34	41	11	1	8	32	25	96	1	4	L	R	6-3	210	1-8-75	1993	Glendale, Calif.
Drew, J.D.	.299	25	87	11	26	5	1	2	15	8	20	6	1	L	R	6-1	195	11-20-75	1997	Hahira, Ga.
Haas, Chris	.229	114	397	63	91	19	2	18	73	66	155	4	4	L	R	6-2	210	10-15-76	1995	Paducah, Ky.
Howard, David	.263	8	19	3	5	0	0	0	2	1	6	2	0	S	R	6-0	175	2-26-67	1987	Sarasota, Fla.
Howard, Thomas	.361	35	119	24	43	10	2	2	21	13	21	1	2	S	R	6-2	205	12-11-64	1986	Elk Grove, Calif.
Hulse, David	.335	74	200	37	67	13	2	4	31	9	39	4	2	L	L	5-11	170	2-25-68	1990	San Angelo, Texas
Jensen, Marcus	.291	72	237	38	69	19	4	8	44	30	59	0	0	S	R	6-4	204	12-14-72	1990	Scottsdale, Ariz.
Kennedy, Adam	.327	91	367	69	120	22	4	10	63	29	36	20	6	L	R	6-1	180	1-10-76	1997	Riverside, Calif.
Lariviere, Jason	.286	133	497	90	142	35	3	9	47	47	64	18	4	R	R	5-10	180	9-30-73	1995	Biddeford, Maine
Little, Mark	.296	51	196	40	58	11	5	3	22	10	48	12	5	R	R	6-0	195	7-11-72	1994	Edwardsville, Ill.
McDonald, Keith	.301	39	113	20	34	7	0	5	27	20	25	1	0	R	R	6-2	215	2-8-73	1994	Yorba Linda, Calif.
Ordaz, Luis	.285	107	362	31	103	25	4	1	45	24	40	3	4	R	R	5-11	170	8-12-75	1993	Maracaibo, Venez.
Pemberton, Rudy	.260	25	73	13	19	7	0	2	11	6	13	1	0	R	R	5-11	185	12-17-69	1987	San Pedro de Macoris, D.R.
Perez, Eduardo	.320	119	416	67	133	31	0	18	82	45	92	7	8	R	R	6-4	225	9-11-69	1991	Calabasas, Calif.
Polanco, Placido	.275	29	120	18	33	4	1	0	10	3	11	2	0	R	R	5-10	168	10-10-75	1994	Miami, Fla.
Richard, Chris	.412	4	17	3	7	2	0	1	4	1	2	0	0	L	L	6-2	185	6-7-74	1995	San Diego, Calif.
Stefanski, Mike	.299	64	201	27	60	12	0	4	22	17	28	3	0	R	R	6-2	190	9-12-69	1991	Redford, Mich.
Warner, Ron	.290	90	245	35	71	14	4	2	32	32	70	4	3	R	R	6-3	185	12-2-68	1991	Redlands, Calif.

PITCHING	W	L	ERA	G	GS	CG	SV	IP	H	R	ER	BB	SO	B	T	HT	WT	DOB	1st Yr	Resides
Ankiel, Rick	7	3	3.16	16	16	0	0	88	73	37	31	46	119	L	L	6-1	210	7-19-79	1997	Fort Pierce, Fla.
Barnes, Brian	4	3	5.50	36	10	0	0	90	104	55	55	33	88	L	L	5-9	170	3-25-67	1989	Dacula, Ga.
Benes, Alan	0	1	3.18	3	3	0	0	6	8	3	2	3	1	R	R	6-5	235	1-21-72	1993	Cedar Hill, Mo.
Busby, Mike	3	4	7.43	29	10	0	0	73	112	69	60	36	50	R	R	6-4	225	12-27-72	1991	Glendale, Ariz.
Crafton, Kevin	0	1	22.85	4	0	0	0	4	12	12	11	0	2	R	R	6-1	185	5-10-74	1996	Russellville, Ark.
Croushore, Rich	1	0	6.75	7	0	0	4	7	8	5	5	6	1	R	R	6-4	210	8-7-70	1993	Houston, Texas
Detmers, Kris	6	8	5.10	23	22	0	0	125	135	74	71	44	90	S	L	6-5	185	6-22-74	1994	Nokomis, Ill.
Eversgerd, Bryan	6	6	2.86	59	0	0	2	66	56	26	21	15	46	R	L	6-1	185	2-11-69	1989	Centralia, Ill.
Heiserman, Rick	2	3	5.11	52	0	0	20	62	67	37	35	21	57	R	R	6-7	220	2-22-73	1994	Omaha, Neb.
Hutchinson, Chad	2	0	2.19	2	2	0	0	12	4	3	3	8	16	R	R	6-3	220	2-21-77	1998	San Diego, Calif.
Jimenez, Jose	2	2	3.04	4	4	0	0	27	30	10	9	9	18	R	R	6-3	170	7-7-73	1992	San Pedro de Macoris, D.R.
King, Curtis	2	2	2.61	27	3	0	7	31	21	13	9	10	25	R	R	6-3	205	10-25-70	1994	Conshohocken, Pa.
Lovingier, Kevin	3	4	4.85	51	0	0	0	78	66	44	42	40	66	L	L	6-1	185	8-29-71	1994	Mission Viejo, Calif.
Luebbers, Larry	13	4	4.03	21	19	1	0	130	134	61	58	33	84	R	R	6-6	190	10-11-69	1990	Florence, Ky.
Mlicki, Doug	3	1	5.78	38	0	0	0	67	78	48	43	26	26	R	R	6-3	175	4-12-71	1992	Galloway, Ohio
Mohler, Mike	2	1	3.07	10	0	0	1	15	16	5	5	5	17	R	L	6-2	185	7-26-68	1990	Gonzales, La.
Nussbeck, Mark	6	10	8.23	36	16	0	0	102	145	100	93	37	82	L	R	6-4	180	5-25-74	1996	Kansas City, Mo.
Opipari, Mario	0	0	10.13	3	0	0	0	3	2	3	3	3	0	S	R	6-2	185	1-24-75	1996	Henderson, Nev.
Slocumb, Heathcliff	0	0	4.50	2	0	0	0	2	3	1	1	0	2	R	R	6-3	220	6-7-66	1984	Richmond Hills, N.Y.
Smith, Pete	2	3	6.87	8	8	0	0	38	53	35	29	16	35	R	R	6-2	210	2-27-66	1984	Smyrna, Ga.
Sodowsky, Clint	4	5	4.82	19	13	2	3	80	85	55	43	32	52	L	R	6-4	200	7-13-72	1991	Lamont, Okla.
Stechschulte, Gene	0	0	7.71	2	0	0	0	2	2	2	2	5	2	R	R	6-5	210	8-12-73	1996	Kalida, Ohio
Stephenson, Garrett	1	1	3.16	4	4	0	0	26	22	9	9	7	19	R	R	6-5	208	1-2-72	1992	Kimberly, Idaho
Thompson, Mark	4	2	2.94	9	8	0	0	52	50	22	17	20	27	R	R	6-2	205	4-7-71	1992	Russellville, Ky.
Weibl, Clint	1	0	5.40	5	0	0	0	8	10	9	5	2	8	R	R	6-3	180	3-17-75	1996	Dawson, Pa.

FIELDING

Catcher	PCT	G	PO	A	E	DP	PB
Bieser	1.000	2	4	1	0	0	0
Jensen	.995	59	380	32	2	1	2
McDonald	1.000	25	162	7	0	2	0
Stefanski	.980	58	411	26	9	4	5

First Base	PCT	G	PO	A	E	DP
Belk	.986	10	71	2	1	7
Dishington	1.000	11	73	4	0	7
Haas	.996	31	256	15	1	30
McDonald	1.000	1	12	0	0	0
Perez	.991	90	708	64	7	78
Richard	1.000	4	34	5	0	4

	PCT	G	PO	A	E	DP
Stefanski	1.000	1	1	0	0	0
Warner	.964	9	48	6	2	8

Second Base	PCT	G	PO	A	E	DP
Ametler	1.000	1	1	1	0	1
Bieser	1.000	2	1	2	0	1
Clapp	.972	68	119	157	8	42
D. Howard	1.000	4	8	8	0	3
Kennedy	.972	52	117	123	7	37
Polanco	.990	22	34	65	1	24
Warner	1.000	9	11	24	0	6

Third Base	PCT	G	PO	A	E	DP
Bieser	.938	9	9	21	2	2
Clapp	1.000	12	3	16	0	4
Haas	.953	81	56	165	11	25
Kennedy	.870	7	8	12	3	0
Lariviere	.000	1	0	0	0	0
Perez	.950	16	7	31	2	1
Polanco	1.000	3	5	9	0	1
Warner	.923	21	17	43	5	3

Shortstop	PCT	G	PO	A	E	DP
Clapp	.000	1	0	0	0	0
D. Howard	1.000	2	3	3	0	0

	PCT	G	PO	A	E	DP
Kennedy	.918	25	19	71	8	11
Ordaz	.956	103	150	346	23	72
Polanco	.933	4	4	10	1	1
Warner	.933	16	15	41	4	8

Outfield	PCT	G	PO	A	E	DP
Belk	1.000	2	2	0	0	0

	PCT	G	PO	A	E	DP
Bieser	.973	38	69	2	2	1
Clapp	1.000	39	50	4	0	0
Dishington	1.000	34	43	3	0	0
Drew	1.000	25	44	2	0	1
Eversgerd	.000	1	0	0	0	0
D. Howard	1.000	1	1	0	0	0
T. Howard	.982	34	54	2	1	0

	PCT	G	PO	A	E	DP
Hulse	.946	55	66	4	4	1
Kennedy	1.000	10	16	0	0	0
Lariviere	.993	131	247	18	2	4
Little	.960	51	114	6	5	2
Pemberton	1.000	20	22	2	0	0
Warner	.971	24	32	2	1	0

ARKANSAS   Class AA

TEXAS LEAGUE

BATTING	AVG	G	AB	R	H	2B	3B	HR	RBI	BB	SO	SB	CS	B	T	HT	WT	DOB	1st Yr	Resides
Ametller, Jesus	.307	116	397	53	122	26	2	10	53	5	21	2	1	L	R	5-8	175	7-25-74	1994	Hialeah, Fla.
Butler, Brent	.269	139	528	68	142	21	1	13	54	26	47	0	4	R	R	6-0	180	2-11-78	1996	Laurinburg, N.C.
Deck, Billy	.061	18	33	1	2	1	0	0	1	0	16	0	0	L	L	6-0	180	9-16-76	1995	Summerville, S.C.
Eckelman, Alex	.241	41	116	5	28	4	3	1	13	5	20	0	0	R	R	5-11	187	7-16-74	1997	St. Louis, Mo.
Farley, Cordell	.259	122	421	43	109	16	8	8	41	19	97	24	16	R	R	6-0	185	3-29-73	1996	Blackstone, Va.
Feramisco, Derek	.182	57	121	10	22	5	0	2	9	19	27	1	2	R	R	6-5	195	11-7-74	1997	Clovis, Calif.
Garcia, Ossie	.125	5	8	0	1	0	0	0	1	1	2	0	0	R	R	6-1	180	10-14-73	1993	Hialeah, Fla.
Hardge, Mike	.227	54	141	15	32	3	1	5	11	25	43	3	3	R	R	5-11	183	1-27-72	1990	Killeen, Texas
Hogan, Todd	.200	91	280	36	56	7	6	4	21	21	68	8	7	R	R	6-2	180	9-18-75	1996	Dublin, Ga.
Kleiner, Stacy	.221	85	235	23	52	8	2	2	16	24	60	2	1	R	R	6-0	185	1-12-75	1996	Las Vegas, Nev.
Leon, Jose	.233	112	335	37	78	17	0	18	54	25	114	3	3	R	R	6-0	160	12-8-76	1994	Cayey, P.R.
Martine, Chris	.150	18	40	3	6	1	0	0	1	2	12	0	0	R	R	6-2	190	7-10-75	1997	Cherry Hill, N.J.
McDonald, Keith	.307	49	163	21	50	10	0	2	14	15	35	1	0	R	R	6-2	215	2-8-73	1994	Yorba Linda, Calif.
Munoz, Juan	.667	2	3	1	2	0	0	0	0	0	0	0	0	L	L	5-9	170	3-27-75	1995	Miami, Fla.
Ortega, Bill	.377	20	69	10	26	9	0	2	10	10	9	0	0	R	R	6-4	205	7-24-75	1997	San Jose, Costa Rica
Richard, Chris	.294	133	442	78	130	26	3	29	94	43	75	7	1	L	L	6-2	185	6-7-74	1995	San Diego, Calif.
Saturria, Luis	.244	139	484	66	118	30	4	16	61	35	134	16	8	R	R	6-2	185	7-21-76	1994	Boca Chica, D.R.
Schmidt, Dave	.221	48	113	6	25	4	0	3	15	11	34	1	1	L	R	6-1	195	10-11-73	1996	Spokane, Wash.
Woolf, Jason	.272	86	320	46	87	18	4	8	15	28	86	11	3	S	R	6-1	170	6-6-77	1995	Miami, Fla.

PITCHING	W	L	ERA	G	GS	CG	SV	IP	H	R	ER	BB	SO	B	T	HT	WT	DOB	1st Yr	Resides
Ambrose, John	4	12	4.73	34	16	0	9	107	108	65	56	68	78	R	R	6-5	180	11-1-74	1994	Evansville, Ind.
Ankiel, Rick	6	0	0.91	8	8	1	0	49	25	6	5	16	75	L	L	6-1	210	7-19-79	1997	Fort Pierce, Fla.
Avrard, Corey	1	1	3.12	25	0	0	6	26	15	12	9	14	31	R	R	6-0	190	12-6-76	1994	Metairie, La.
Benes, Adam	1	1	5.36	28	0	0	0	40	51	30	24	15	19	L	R	6-2	185	3-12-73	1995	Lake Forest, Ill.
Benes, Alan	0	0	6.23	2	2	0	0	4	6	3	3	1	0	R	R	6-5	235	1-21-72	1993	Cedar Hill, Mo.
Brunette, Justin	1	2	1.96	18	0	0	0	18	21	12	4	7	23	L	L	6-1	200	10-7-75	1997	Huntington Beach, Calif.
Crafton, Kevin	7	7	7.58	42	0	0	2	46	57	41	39	16	41	R	R	6-1	185	5-10-74	1996	Russellville, Ark.
DeWitt, Matt	9	8	4.43	26	26	0	0	148	153	87	73	59	107	R	R	6-4	220	9-4-77	1995	Las Vegas, Nev.
Geis, John	2	5	6.83	45	0	0	5	55	65	44	42	29	29	L	L	6-2	191	12-21-73	1996	Central Square, N.Y.
Hutchinson, Chad	7	11	4.72	25	25	0	0	141	127	79	74	85	150	R	R	6-5	230	2-21-77	1998	San Diego, Calif.
Karnuth, Jason	7	11	5.22	26	26	2	0	160	175	105	93	55	71	R	R	6-2	190	5-15-76	1997	Glen Ellyn, Ill.
Matthews, Mike	2	0	0.00	2	1	0	0	12	3	0	0	1	10	L	L	6-2	175	10-24-73	1992	Woodbridge, Va.
Nussbeck, Mark	0	1	6.17	2	2	0	0	12	12	8	8	9	11	L	R	6-4	185	5-25-74	1996	Kansas City, Mo.
Opipari, Mario	1	0	3.51	20	0	0	0	26	30	11	10	11	16	S	R	6-2	185	1-24-75	1996	Henderson, Nev.
Painter, Lance	0	0	0.00	1	1	0	0	2	1	0	0	0	4	L	L	6-1	195	7-21-67	1990	Milwaukee, Wis.
Reed, Steve	4	5	5.42	36	9	0	0	81	87	59	49	28	45	R	R	6-2	205	9-24-75	1994	Juno Beach, Fla.
Rodriguez, Jose	1	2	3.25	30	0	0	0	36	38	16	13	25	30	L	L	6-1	205	12-18-74	1997	Cayey, P.R.
Stechschulte, Gene	2	6	3.40	39	0	0	19	42	41	26	16	20	41	R	R	6-5	210	8-12-73	1996	Kalida, Ohio
Stephenson, Garrett	0	0	3.38	1	1	0	0	5	8	3	2	1	2	R	R	6-2	208	1-2-72	1992	Kimberly, Idaho
Weibl, Clint	4	9	4.66	28	17	1	0	110	121	59	57	49	75	R	R	6-3	180	3-17-75	1996	Dawson, Pa.
Woodward, Finley	0	2	4.94	5	3	0	0	27	36	19	15	10	15	R	R	5-11	200	8-15-75	1997	Molino, Fla.

FIELDING

Catcher	PCT	G	PO	A	E	DP	PB
Kleiner	.993	62	402	50	3	5	4
Martine	1.000	13	72	11	0	1	3
McDonald	.977	40	236	22	6	4	2
Schmidt	.979	32	167	21	4	1	2

First Base	PCT	G	PO	A	E	DP
Deck	.979	7	46	1	1	4
Hardge	.987	10	74	2	1	5
Kleiner	1.000	1	2	0	0	0
Richard	.989	128	1071	67	13	119
Schmidt	1.000	2	17	1	0	1

Second Base	PCT	G	PO	A	E	DP
Ametller	.966	91	167	255	15	64
Butler	.975	38	71	83	4	22

	PCT	G	PO	A	E	DP
Eckelman	.950	3	5	14	1	1
Hardge	.986	15	23	45	1	17

Third Base	PCT	G	PO	A	E	DP
Ametller	.786	4	5	6	3	0
Butler	.983	46	30	86	2	13
Eckelman	1.000	14	5	32	0	2
Hardge	.500	2	1	0	1	0
Kleiner	1.000	7	3	11	0	1
Leon	.903	75	34	153	20	12

Shortstop	PCT	G	PO	A	E	DP
Butler	.957	60	82	164	11	44
Eckelman	.961	11	16	33	2	7
Woolf	.943	74	122	209	20	48

Outfield	PCT	G	PO	A	E	DP
Deck	1.000	2	2	0	0	0
Eckelman	1.000	6	12	0	0	0
Farley	.949	114	177	8	10	1
Feramisco	.933	37	53	3	4	1
Garcia	1.000	2	2	0	0	0
Hardge	1.000	17	26	1	0	1
Hogan	.962	81	143	7	6	1
Leon	.846	10	11	0	2	0
Munoz	.000	1	0	0	0	0
Ortega	1.000	20	43	0	0	0
Richard	1.000	6	8	1	0	0
Saturria	.968	138	255	13	9	1
Woolf	1.000	10	16	0	0	0

POTOMAC   Class A

CAROLINA LEAGUE

BATTING	AVG	G	AB	R	H	2B	3B	HR	RBI	BB	SO	SB	CS	B	T	HT	WT	DOB	1st Yr	Resides
Benham, David	.154	9	26	2	4	1	0	0	1	1	7	0	0	R	R	6-2	190	10-12-75	1998	Garland, Texas
Bevins, Andy	.277	138	513	92	142	30	2	25	97	44	128	6	2	R	R	6-3	215	10-10-75	1997	Port Coquitlam, B.C.
Britt, Bryan	.192	11	26	1	5	0	0	1	3	1	11	0	0	R	R	6-2	215	4-16-75	1998	Wilmington, N.C.
Deck, Billy	.260	71	235	35	61	12	4	3	32	31	54	4	2	L	L	6-0	180	9-16-76	1995	Summerville, S.C.
Eckelman, Alex	.193	52	161	20	31	5	2	4	14	13	39	3	3	R	R	5-11	187	7-16-74	1997	St. Louis, Mo.
Freeman, Brad	.234	109	342	36	80	17	2	2	37	45	75	9	13	R	R	6-2	210	9-13-75	1998	Oxford, Miss.
Garrick, Matt	.167	70	216	17	36	10	1	3	17	32	57	1	5	R	R	6-0	185	8-19-75	1997	Duncanville, Texas
Gentry, Aaron	.159	66	138	13	22	4	1	1	8	13	54	4	3	R	R	6-2	185	5-22-75	1997	Tulsa, Okla.

BATTING	AVG	G	AB	R	H	2B	3B	HR	RBI	BB	SO	SB	CS	B	T	HT	WT	DOB	1st Yr	Resides
Kim, David	.259	123	440	68	114	23	1	19	72	42	107	7	6	R	R	6-0	200	4-2-76	1997	Cherry Hill, N.J.
Lee, Jason	.212	44	113	15	24	4	0	1	9	18	35	11	0	L	R	6-1	185	4-22-77	1995	Burlington, Iowa
Maier, T.J.	.263	102	353	53	93	15	0	2	38	55	61	12	7	R	R	6-0	180	2-24-75	1997	Santa Clara, Calif.
Martine, Chris	.206	42	136	11	28	7	2	1	14	16	42	1	2	R	R	6-2	190	7-10-75	1997	Cherry Hill, N.J.
Macrory, Rob	.233	114	434	52	101	15	2	2	29	24	70	27	10	R	R	6-1	165	2-18-75	1997	Montgomery, Ala.
Ortega, Bill	.306	110	421	66	129	27	4	9	74	38	69	7	7	R	R	6-4	205	7-24-75	1997	San Jose, Costa Rica
Quaccia, Luke	.247	125	429	46	106	26	2	13	80	42	112	4	5	L	R	6-6	220	2-27-75	1997	Oakdale, Calif.
Rupert, Bryan	.190	40	121	13	23	7	1	2	16	9	42	0	0	R	R	5-10	200	2-18-75	1997	Green Cove Spring, Fla.
Snead, Esix	.181	67	249	37	45	8	5	0	14	32	57	35	12	S	R	5-10	175	6-7-76	1998	Williston, Fla.
Wilson, Jack	.296	64	257	44	76	10	1	2	18	19	31	7	4	R	R	6-0	170	12-29-77	1998	Thousand Oaks, Calif.

GAMES BY POSITION: C—Garrick 70, Martine 42, Rupert 37. **1B**—Britt 3, Deck 36, Gentry 2, Quaccia 110, Rupert 1. **2B**—Eckelman 17, Maier 22, Macrory 113. **3B**—Eckelman 20, Freeman 34, Gentry 40, Maier 61. **SS**—Eckelman 9, Freeman 66, Gentry 5, Wilson 64. **OF**—Bevins 56, Britt 3, Deck 41, Eckelman 1, Freeman 3, Gentry 4, Kim 115, Lee 44, Maier 2, Ortega 109, Snead 67.

PITCHING	W	L	ERA	G	GS	CG	SV	IP	H	R	ER	BB	SO	B	T	HT	WT	DOB	1st Yr	Resides
Avrard, Corey	2	2	4.41	28	0	0	0	33	32	19	16	26	40	R	R	6-4	190	12-6-76	1994	Metairie, La.
Benes, Alan	0	0	1.80	2	2	0	0	5	1	1	1	4	2	R	R	6-5	235	1-21-72	1993	Cedar Hill, Mo.
Coogan, Patrick	4	7	5.79	19	19	2	0	101	112	73	65	43	67	R	R	6-3	195	9-12-75	1997	Baton Rouge, La.
DeLeon, Jose	5	6	5.48	19	0	0	5	71	68	48	43	42	47	R	R	6-3	152	10-2-76	1994	Azua, D.R.
Franks, Lance	5	1	2.63	54	0	0	0	79	63	25	23	17	61	R	R	5-11	180	8-20-75	1997	Russellville, Ark.
Gonzales, Rick	3	4	6.13	47	3	0	0	72	88	58	49	38	39	R	R	6-1	205	10-25-74	1998	Albuquerque, N.M.
Held, Travis	2	10	5.40	24	21	0	0	112	140	76	67	25	85	R	R	6-3	215	3-19-77	1998	Jupiter, Fla.
Huffaker, Mike	1	5	3.86	54	0	0	0	68	59	33	29	51	79	R	R	6-2	215	10-8-75	1997	Florence, Ala.
Jerue, Tristan	0	1	7.36	4	3	0	0	15	18	12	12	8	9	R	R	6-1	185	12-12-75	1997	Westfield, Mass.
Lanfranco, Otoniel	4	8	4.29	21	21	0	0	115	105	59	55	35	83	R	R	6-0	160	7-17-76	1996	Cotui, D.R.
Marr, Jason	1	6	5.26	50	0	0	21	53	57	36	31	21	40	R	R	6-1	195	9-9-75	1998	Downey, Calif.
Navarro, Jason	5	13	6.06	39	14	0	0	111	134	82	75	49	66	L	L	6-4	225	7-5-75	1997	Lilburn, Ga.
Opipari, Mario	0	1	3.12	7	0	0	0	9	12	7	3	3	9	S	R	6-2	185	1-24-75	1996	Henderson, Nev.
Reames, Britt	3	2	3.19	10	8	0	0	37	34	21	13	21	22	R	R	5-11	170	8-19-73	1995	Seneca, S.C.
Sheredy, Kevin	5	5	3.98	41	12	0	0	104	100	58	46	53	69	R	R	6-4	210	1-3-75	1996	Antioch, Calif.
Smith, Robert	4	9	2.96	18	18	0	0	103	91	47	34	32	93	L	L	6-0	170	10-23-79	1998	Lakewood, Calif.
Woodward, Finley	6	7	4.10	24	18	1	0	121	126	61	55	28	82	R	R	5-11	200	8-15-75	1997	Molino, Fla.

PEORIA — Class A

MIDWEST LEAGUE

BATTING	AVG	G	AB	R	H	2B	3B	HR	RBI	BB	SO	SB	CS	B	T	HT	WT	DOB	1st Yr	Resides
Araujo, Danilo	.277	105	361	53	100	10	2	1	36	43	75	21	16	R	R	5-10	160	1-17-77	1995	Bani, D.R.
Bowers, Jason	.263	112	414	53	109	14	8	2	49	32	78	10	9	R	R	6-2	175	1-27-78	1998	Uniontown, Pa.
Clark, Greg	.214	68	229	26	49	11	0	3	23	29	76	0	4	R	R	6-2	175	1-5-77	1998	Phoenix, Ariz.
Diaz, Miguel	.254	105	343	44	87	18	6	3	34	8	59	10	6	R	R	5-11	160	9-29-77	1995	San Pedro de Macoris, D.R.
Dyt, Darren	.237	81	253	30	60	15	1	1	24	24	55	4	2	L	R	6-5	195	12-15-75	1998	Tulare, Calif.
Escobar, Gustavo	.319	24	94	11	30	2	3	0	18	6	14	2	2	R	R	5-10	170	1-30-80	1997	Anzoategui, Venez.
Farnsworth, Troy	.250	134	500	76	125	33	3	19	78	55	124	3	2	R	R	6-2	200	2-4-76	1998	Salt Lake City, Utah
Folkers, Brandon	.249	86	257	35	64	15	2	7	36	45	96	6	3	L	L	6-2	180	8-25-77	1998	St. Petersburg, Fla.
Kelly, Chris	.169	18	59	5	10	1	0	0	7	7	18	0	0	R	R	6-3	210	5-29-77	1998	Trumbull, Conn.
Kidwell, Tommy	.257	50	167	23	43	6	2	0	15	5	27	2	1	R	R	5-9	175	11-19-76	1998	St. Petersburg, Fla.
Lee, Jason	.232	66	224	31	52	14	0	2	26	24	58	5	3	L	R	6-1	185	4-22-77	1995	Burlington, Iowa
McNaughton, Troy	.273	125	484	57	132	25	6	14	84	37	123	5	4	L	L	6-0	195	1-27-75	1998	Tacoma, Wash.
Nykoluk, Kevin	.260	55	177	24	46	13	1	2	19	14	25	0	1	R	R	6-0	210	4-2-75	1997	Simi Valley, Calif.
Secoda, Joe	.253	116	400	61	101	14	2	2	30	62	97	15	9	R	R	6-1	190	11-19-77	1997	Fullerton, Calif.
Snead, Esix	.193	59	181	35	35	7	1	2	18	35	42	29	9	S	R	5-10	175	6-7-76	1998	Williston, Fla.
William, Jovany	.204	67	240	30	49	8	0	8	27	14	59	2	3	R	R	6-2	165	1-29-77	1994	San Pedro de Macoris, D.R.
Wilson, Jack	.343	64	251	47	86	22	4	3	28	15	23	11	5	R	R	6-0	170	12-29-77	1998	Thousand Oaks, Calif.

GAMES BY POSITION: C—Clark 66, Nykoluk 20, William 55. **1B**—Dyt 12, Farnsworth 42, Folkers 81, Kelly 9, Nykoluk 10, William 4. **2B**—Araujo 101, Bowers 18, Escobar 7, Kidwell 24, Secoda 1. **3B**—Bowers 26, Escobar 13, Farnsworth 89, Kidwell 18. **SS**—Bowers 71, Escobar 4, Kidwell 6, Wilson 64. **OF**—Diaz 100, Dyt 25, Folkers 1, Lee 63, McNaughton 71, Nykoluk 3, Secoda 1, Snead 59.

PITCHING	W	L	ERA	G	GS	CG	SV	IP	H	R	ER	BB	SO	B	T	HT	WT	DOB	1st Yr	Resides
Book, Jeremy	6	5	5.33	27	16	0	0	103	110	70	61	32	67	R	R	6-4	205	8-3-77	1998	Trenton, Ill.
Brunette, Justin	3	1	1.81	38	0	0	2	45	34	9	9	16	44	L	L	6-2	200	10-7-75	1997	Huntington Beach, Calif.
Christenson, Ryan	4	4	5.32	29	8	0	0	90	101	63	53	42	84	R	R	6-5	205	8-10-76	1998	New Hope, Minn.
Correa, Cristobal	0	2	10.35	5	5	0	0	20	26	24	23	14	15	R	R	6-1	175	12-27-79	1998	Guarico, Venez.
Fahs, Paul	1	0	0.00	2	0	0	0	2	3	0	0	0	2	R	R	6-3	195	3-17-78	1999	Carmel, N.Y.
Folkers, Brandon	0	0	4.50	5	0	0	0	6	6	3	3	3	5	L	L	6-2	180	8-29-75	1998	St. Petersburg, Fla.
Gooden, Derek	3	2	4.82	38	0	0	12	37	41	20	20	12	21	R	R	6-0	175	6-26-75	1997	Adel, Ga.
Griffin, Kirk	3	4	3.60	57	0	0	11	65	42	28	26	22	53	R	R	6-1	185	6-4-75	1998	Sacramento, Calif.
Hand, Jon	3	3	3.64	58	0	0	1	82	90	43	33	22	55	R	R	6-2	200	12-14-75	1998	Mount Pleasant, Texas
Held, Travis	1	0	2.53	2	2	0	0	11	14	3	3	4	7	R	R	6-3	215	3-19-77	1998	Jupiter, Fla.
Lambert, Jeremy	2	1	8.91	11	0	0	0	34	48	36	34	27	27	R	R	6-1	192	1-10-79	1997	Kearns, Utah
Prather, Scott	9	10	3.85	27	27	0	0	147	134	81	63	77	132	L	L	6-4	205	10-8-76	1998	Atlanta, Ga.
Rodriguez, Jose	2	3	3.31	15	0	0	0	16	14	7	6	8	15	L	L	6-1	205	12-18-74	1997	Cayey, P.R.
Shibilo, Andy	4	13	5.11	27	24	2	0	136	157	105	77	41	89	R	R	6-7	220	9-16-76	1998	Belleville, N.J.
Smith, Robert	4	1	2.83	9	9	0	0	54	53	20	17	16	59	L	L	6-0	170	10-23-79	1998	Lakewood, Calif.
Stemle, Steve	7	10	5.47	28	28	0	0	148	177	104	90	67	113	R	R	6-4	200	5-20-77	1998	Louisville, Ky.
Viles, Jeff	3	5	5.93	49	0	0	0	71	59	47	42	34	79	R	R	6-2	220	4-1-76	1998	Kansas City, Mo.
Walrond, Les	7	10	5.70	21	20	0	0	109	115	77	69	59	78	L	L	6-0	195	11-7-76	1998	Tulsa, Okla.
Yates, Chad	1	2	2.59	22	0	0	0	24	16	8	7	14	26	R	R	6-1	185	12-16-76	1999	Ruston, La.

NEW JERSEY — Short-Season Class A

NEW YORK-PENN LEAGUE

BATTING	AVG	G	AB	R	H	2B	3B	HR	RBI	BB	SO	SB	CS	B	T	HT	WT	DOB	1st Yr	Resides
Alfonzo, Eliezer	.326	46	178	14	58	12	2	3	28	3	39	3	4	R	R	6-0	170	2-7-79	1996	Puerto la Cruz, Venez.

BATTING	AVG	G	AB	R	H	2B	3B	HR	RBI	BB	SO	SB	CS	B	T	HT	WT	DOB	1st Yr	Resides
Bailey, Travis	.228	66	241	37	55	9	8	8	31	17	81	6	2	R	R	6-2	198	1-26-77	1999	Loxahatchee, Fla.
Carvajal, Ramon	.250	65	240	35	60	9	8	6	30	13	59	12	7	S	R	5-10	155	3-4-81	1997	Bani, D.R.
Escobar, Gustavo	.271	31	96	17	26	2	3	0	12	7	22	5	2	R	R	5-10	170	1-30-80	1997	Anzoategui, Venez.
Espino, Jose	.199	42	136	12	27	4	2	0	10	9	44	5	4	R	R	6-0	164	11-6-79	1997	Cotui, D.R.
Ewing, Chris	.130	26	54	5	7	1	1	0	0	9	25	1	1	R	R	5-11	180	1-26-76	1999	Lemoore, Calif.
Floyd, Mike	.219	38	137	17	30	8	0	1	16	4	40	4	1	R	R	6-1	210	9-1-77	1999	Brandon, Fla.
Hart, Bo	.184	50	163	23	30	3	3	3	15	10	38	4	2	R	R	5-11	175	9-27-76	1999	Capitola, Calif.
Hernandez, Johnny	.394	10	33	4	13	1	0	0	2	10	9	1	4	S	L	6-1	185	9-11-79	1999	Brooklyn, N.Y.
Johnson, Gabe	.194	35	124	12	24	5	2	5	14	9	49	1	1	R	R	6-1	190	9-21-79	1998	Delray Beach, Fla.
Lee, Monte	.223	38	121	20	27	4	0	0	10	18	25	14	6	R	L	6-0	195	2-9-77	1999	Mount Pleasant, S.C.
Lemon, Tim	.198	72	242	25	48	5	3	4	29	22	62	16	16	R	R	6-1	180	9-23-80	1998	La Mirada, Calif.
Nunez, Jose	.306	45	157	29	48	11	1	1	13	20	18	6	3	R	R	5-10	175	12-8-78	1997	Cotui, D.R.
Ortega, Jose	.190	30	100	12	19	1	0	0	8	1	32	4	0	R	R	6-3	180	1-7-78	1996	El Tigre, Venez.
Pemberthy, Aaron	.250	15	48	6	12	4	1	0	6	3	17	0	0	R	R	6-1	210	7-13-76	1999	Fresno, Calif.
Schumacher, Shawn	.227	47	154	14	35	6	0	3	23	11	8	2	3	L	R	6-1	200	8-18-76	1999	Carthage, Texas
Thames, Damon	.228	47	180	22	41	5	1	0	16	7	42	10	5	R	R	6-1	175	11-15-76	1999	Humble, Texas
Williams, Charles	.244	28	90	16	22	4	4	2	8	19	25	3	5	S	L	6-0	185	2-9-78	1999	Humble, Texas

GAMES BY POSITION: C—Alfonzo 23, Johnson 20, Pemberthy 9, Schumacher 31. 1B—Bailey 49, Ortega 30. 2B—Carvajal 56, Hart 19, Nunez 2. 3B—Bailey 18, Carvajal 1, Escobar 15, Hart 8, Nunez 38. SS—Escobar 15, Hart 20, Thames 46. OF—Espino 39, Ewing 20, Floyd 35, Hernandez 10, Lee 35, Lemon 70, Williams 28.

PITCHING	W	L	ERA	G	GS	CG	SV	IP	H	R	ER	BB	SO	B	T	HT	WT	DOB	1st Yr	Resides
Butler, Mark	2	0	7.32	18	0	0	0	20	22	18	16	22	8	R	R	6-4	235	1-3-77	1999	Beaver Lake, Neb.
Caple, Chance	0	4	4.38	7	7	0	0	37	35	24	18	18	36	R	R	6-6	215	8-9-78	1999	Southlake, Texas
Cook, B.R.	5	1	2.84	9	8	0	0	44	42	19	14	16	42	R	R	6-4	200	3-2-78	1999	Salem, Ore.
Correa, Cristobal	3	3	2.94	9	9	0	0	52	41	20	17	26	59	R	R	6-1	175	12-27-79	1998	Guarico, Venez.
Cummings, Jeremy	6	6	3.60	14	14	1	0	85	88	42	34	7	62	R	R	6-2	215	11-7-76	1999	Hurricane, W.Va.
Dinkel, Aaron	0	0	9.58	13	0	0	0	10	16	13	11	15	6	R	R	6-1	200	10-8-77	1999	Magna, Conn.
Fahs, Paul	1	2	3.38	10	0	0	7	35	25	17	13	19	21	R	R	6-3	195	3-17-78	1999	Carmel, N.Y.
Gargano, Mike	1	4	5.69	21	7	0	0	49	57	34	31	27	20	R	R	6-1	200	7-28-78	1998	Salt Lake City, Utah
Janke, Cheyenne	2	5	3.67	15	14	0	0	83	85	40	34	20	63	R	R	6-5	235	2-16-77	1999	Elk Mound, Wis.
Langen, Brian	1	3	4.60	26	0	0	0	29	26	20	15	21	24	L	L	6-7	210	2-13-78	1998	Litchfield, Ill.
Layfield, Scotty	2	2	3.15	23	3	0	0	34	27	16	12	21	26	R	R	6-2	205	9-13-76	1999	Montezuma, Ga.
Matew, Francisco	1	1	3.58	19	0	0	0	33	34	17	13	8	28	R	R	5-11	165	4-12-79	1997	San Pedro de Macoris, D.R.
Pearce, Josh	3	7	4.98	14	14	1	0	78	78	45	43	20	78	R	R	6-3	215	8-20-77	1999	Yakima, Wash.
Peck, Brandon	1	1	4.04	31	0	0	0	36	37	17	16	11	29	L	L	5-10	170	8-5-76	1999	Bethany, Okla.
Sansom, Trevor	1	3	7.71	20	0	0	0	23	34	28	20	16	18	R	R	6-4	190	5-6-76	1999	Winfield, W.Va.
Yates, Chad	1	1	3.71	12	0	0	1	17	9	7	7	10	20	R	R	6-1	185	12-18-76	1999	Ruston, La.

JOHNSON CITY — Rookie

APPALACHIAN LEAGUE

BATTING	AVG	G	AB	R	H	2B	3B	HR	RBI	BB	SO	SB	CS	B	T	HT	WT	DOB	1st Yr	Resides
Acosta, Emilio	.243	36	107	11	26	6	2	1	16	8	16	2	0	R	R	6-1	172	1-14-80	1998	San Joaquin, Venez.
Albertson, Justin	.234	41	128	17	30	1	1	5	16	17	60	11	2	R	R	6-3	210	10-10-79	1999	Los Angeles, Calif.
Banez, Marco	.200	2	5	1	1	0	0	0	1	0	0	1	0	L	L	6-1	175	9-24-79	1997	Maracay, Venez.
Buckley, Chris	.251	47	171	19	43	8	2	3	23	13	68	10	4	R	R	5-11	180	1-18-77	1999	Pine Bluff, Ark.
Crisp, Covelli	.258	65	229	55	59	5	4	3	22	44	41	27	6	S	R	6-0	185	11-1-79	1999	Desert Hot Springs, Calif.
De los Santos, Santo	.214	55	159	22	34	2	2	1	10	16	58	3	5	R	R	6-1	160	12-29-80	1998	Bani, D.R.
Diaz, Aneuris	.229	56	205	30	47	9	2	4	27	10	55	6	2	R	R	6-2	165	1-20-81	1998	Azua, D.R.
Diaz, Johnny	.111	3	9	0	1	0	0	0	0	0	0	0	0	R	R	6-1	162	10-11-80	1999	Guarico, Venez.
Duncan, Chris	.214	55	201	23	43	8	1	6	34	25	62	3	1	L	R	6-5	210	5-5-81	1999	Tucson, Ariz.
Franco, Pascual	.310	18	58	12	18	2	0	2	14	3	22	1	0	R	R	6-1	160	3-9-79	1996	Boca Chica, D.R.
Hernandez, Johnny	.262	60	225	45	59	12	3	1	32	38	45	23	7	S	L	6-1	185	9-11-79	1999	Brooklyn, N.Y.
Johnson, Ben	.330	57	203	38	67	9	1	10	51	29	57	14	6	R	R	6-1	180	6-18-81	1999	Memphis, Tenn.
Mejias, Aureliano	.227	33	75	9	17	3	1	0	5	10	29	2	2	S	R	6-2	170	7-7-80	1998	Caracas, Venez.
Pemberthy, Aaron	.000	1	2	0	0	0	0	0	0	0	4	0	0	R	R	6-1	210	7-13-76	1999	Fresno, Calif.
Perez, Juan	.234	46	171	31	40	11	1	1	11	18	41	13	7	R	R	6-2	165	12-10-80	1998	San Francisco de Macoris, D.R.
Pimentel, Hector	.300	3	10	0	3	1	0	0	2	0	0	0	0	R	R	6-1	180	2-23-79	1996	Bani, D.R.
Spooner, Brent	.214	42	126	17	27	9	0	1	10	16	24	0	3	R	R	5-11	180	9-1-77	1999	Tallahassee, Fla.
Torres, Reynaldo	.152	36	105	8	16	6	0	1	10	6	52	1	0	R	R	6-5	235	3-14-79	1997	Guanica, P.R.
Vasquez, Geraldo	.228	49	167	28	38	6	0	5	25	13	43	7	5	R	R	5-11	145	11-5-79	1997	San Pedro de Macoris, D.R.

GAMES BY POSITION: C—Acosta 29, Franco 9, Pemberthy 1, Spooner 42. 1B—Acosta 1, Albertson 1, Banez 2, A. Diaz 1, Duncan 53, Torres 18. 2B—Crisp 64, Torres 1, Vasquez 11. 3B—Acosta 2, A. Diaz 54, J. Diaz 2, Pimentel 3, Torres 1, Vasquez 16. SS—de los Santos 55, Franco 1, Mejias 1, Vasquez 28. OF—Albertson 26, Buckley 19, Hernandez 57, Johnson 54, Mejias 24, Perez 41.

PITCHING	W	L	ERA	G	GS	CG	SV	IP	H	R	ER	BB	SO	B	T	HT	WT	DOB	1st Yr	Resides
Crudale, Mike	0	1	3.27	24	0	0	1	33	29	15	12	14	36	R	R	6-0	205	1-3-77	1999	Danville, Calif.
Fiora, Chris	0	3	8.69	18	0	0	2	20	27	21	19	14	31	R	R	6-3	200	12-3-78	1999	Riva, Md.
Graves, Donovan	3	1	3.71	19	5	0	1	44	40	24	18	17	51	R	R	6-4	205	1-3-81	1999	Boonville, Mo.
Grippo, Mike	1	1	8.35	14	0	0	1	18	21	18	17	12	18	L	L	5-11	511	5-6-76	1999	Staten Island, N.Y.
Olivo, Carlos	2	1	4.22	6	6	0	0	32	35	19	15	13	31	R	R	6-2	161	10-19-79	1998	Montecristi, D.R.
Parker, Matt	1	1	2.59	23	0	0	2	31	22	13	9	11	43	R	R	6-3	210	12-13-78	1999	Hartsfield, Ga.
Perkins, Mike	6	1	4.09	15	11	0	0	62	71	34	28	19	50	R	R	6-1	195	5-29-79	1999	Punta Gorda, Fla.
Polo, Bienvenido	0	5	12.96	20	0	0	0	25	47	47	36	19	11	R	R	6-2	162	1-4-79	1997	El Seibo, D.R.
Rayborn, Kris	1	7	5.79	13	13	0	0	65	79	54	42	33	34	L	L	6-4	170	8-10-79	1998	Purvis, Miss.
Riveles, Mike	0	0	4.91	4	0	0	0	7	12	10	4	4	4	R	R	6-1	180	8-10-77	1999	Hopewell Junction, N.Y.
Rizo, Miguel	2	3	3.16	20	0	0	0	31	26	12	11	14	22	R	R	6-2	175	6-23-80	1997	Maracay, Venez.
Samora, Santo	2	0	2.48	18	2	0	1	33	26	12	9	11	17	R	R	6-2	165	12-10-79	1997	San Pedro de Macoris, D.R.
Sprague, Kevin	5	3	3.23	11	11	0	0	64	47	27	23	27	73	L	L	6-4	215	3-10-77	1999	Kansas City, Kan.
Teekel, Josh	1	0	5.35	8	0	0	0	34	41	26	20	8	42	R	R	6-5	185	9-18-80	1999	Greenwell Springs, La.
Tejeda, Franklin	2	1	3.08	14	2	0	1	26	24	15	9	7	28	R	R	6-0	165	4-7-80	1998	Bani, D.R.
Vincent, Matt	1	2	3.81	24	0	0	2	28	24	14	12	18	36	L	L	6-1	190	5-10-77	1999	Floyds Knobs, Ind.
Zazueta, Peter	3	6	5.72	11	11	0	0	57	62	43	36	26	56	R	R	6-2	180	12-9-79	1999	Tucson, Ariz.

Organization Statistics

SANDIEGOPADRES

Padres build for 2002 with nucleus of young players

BY JOHN MAFFEI

Don't say "fire sale" around Padres general manager Kevin Towers unless you're looking for trouble.

The team's purge of players like Kevin Brown, Ken Caminiti, Steve Finley and Greg Vaughn from the 1998 National League champions was based on reasonable financial thinking. Towers made good offers to free agents Finley, Caminiti and Brown but was blown away by better offers.

Vaughn, who hit 50 home runs in '98, was traded to the Reds in February for outfielder Reggie Sanders and shortstop Damian Jackson. While Vaughn was a huge help to the Reds, the Padres got two good players who could be around for a while in return.

The Padres are building toward the 2002 season, when they move into their new waterfront stadium. In the meantime, the team is trying to get younger and build from within.

The strategy looked surprisingly successful for a time, when the Padres ran off 14 straight wins to move within 4½ games of first place in the NL West on July 2. They couldn't sustain the pace, though, and slipped to a 74-88 finish, 26 games behind the Diamondbacks.

Right fielder Tony Gwynn supplied yet another special moment when he collected his 3,000th hit on Aug. 6 against the Expos. He finished the season with 3,067, 18th on the all-time list. His .338 average gave him 17 straight .300 seasons.

Four Padres stole 30 bases or more, with Sanders leading the way at 36. The others were Jackson, utilityman Eric Owens and second baseman Quilvio Veras. Third baseman Phil Nevin provided an unexpected boost, breaking through with 24 home runs and a

Trevor Hoffman   **Sean Burroughs**

Players of the Year

MAJOR LEAGUE: Trevor Hoffman, rhp

Hoffman again was one of the top relievers in baseball, allowing opponents just a .194 average and finishing with 40 saves.

MINOR LEAGUE: Sean Burroughs, 3b

Burroughs finished 1999 by reaching base in 54 consecutive games while ranking second in the minors with a .363 average.

team-leading 85 RBIs.

The team saw not one, but two impressive young catchers earn playing time as the season concluded, with both Ben Davis and Wiki Gonzalez getting long looks. Davis came up at midseason and started off hot, but he tailed off both offensively and defensively as the season progressed.

The club's pitching was solid, with closer Trevor Hoffman again ranking as one of the top relievers in the game. Hoffman finished with 40 saves and a 2.14 ERA. The front four members of the rotation all pitched well, with rookie Matt Clement showing improvement after struggling early.

There is little pitching help at Triple-A Las Vegas, though after that there is promise. But the star of the farm system was third baseman Sean Burroughs, who played the season as an 18-year-old. He had a spectacular year at Class A Fort Wayne and briefly at Class A Rancho Cucamonga. He finished the season with an incredible run, reaching base via hit or walk in his last 54 games, including California League playoff contests.

With six first-round picks, the Padres brought in a new wave of prospects in the draft. Outfielder Vince Faison enjoyed an outstanding debut in the Rookie-level Arizona League. Several pitchers contributed to the success of Idaho Falls, which finished first in the Rookie-level Pioneer League but fell in the first round of the playoffs.

To lead the next generation of Padres, the organization brought in former Pirates GM Ted Simmons late in the season to run the farm system. He replaced Jim Skaalen, who was fired.

ORGANIZATION LEADERS

BATTING

*AVG	Sean Burroughs, Rancho Cuca./Fort Wayne	.363
R	Jeremy Owens, Rancho Cuca./Fort Wayne	113
H	Sean Burroughs, Rancho Cuca./Fort Wayne	163
TB	Brandon Pernell, Rancho Cucamonga	255
2B	Kevin Nicholson, Mobile	38
3B	Jeremy Owens, Rancho Cuca./Fort Wayne	12
HR	John Curl, Mobile	22
RBI	Dusty Allen, Las Vegas	89
BB	Dusty Allen, Las Vegas	79
SO	Jeremy Owens, Rancho Cuca./Fort Wayne	166
SB	Jeremy Owens, Rancho Cuca./Fort Wayne	67

PITCHING

W	Rick Guttormson, Rancho Cucamonga	14
L	Two tied at	12
#ERA	Jacob Peavy, Idaho Falls/AZL	1.17
G	Kevin Hite, Mobile/Rancho Cucamonga	58
CG	Brian Lawrence, Rancho Cucamonga	4
SV	Clay Condrey, Rancho Cuca./Fort Wayne	20
IP	Bryan Wolff, Las Vegas	178
BB	Ben Howard, Fort Wayne	110
SO	Brian Lawrence, Rancho Cucamonga	166

*Minimum 250 At-Bats #Minimum 75 Innings

San Diego
PADRES

Manager: Bruce Bochy **1999 Record:** 74-88, .457 (4th, NL West)

BATTING	AVG	G	AB	R	H	2B	3B	HR	RBI	BB	SO	SB	CS	B	T	HT	WT	DOB	1st Yr	Resides
Arias, George	.244	55	164	20	40	8	0	7	20	6	54	0	0	R	R	5-11	190	3-12-72	1993	Tucson, Ariz.
Baerga, Carlos	.250	33	80	6	20	1	0	2	5	6	14	1	0	S	R	5-11	215	11-4-68	1986	Bayamon, P.R.
Darr, Mike	.271	25	48	6	13	1	0	2	3	5	18	2	1	L	R	6-3	205	3-21-76	1994	Corona, Calif.
Davis, Ben	.244	76	266	29	65	14	1	5	30	25	70	2	1	S	R	6-4	205	3-10-77	1995	Aston, Pa.
Garcia, Carlos	.182	6	11	1	2	0	0	0	0	1	3	0	0	R	R	6-1	193	10-15-67	1987	Lancaster, N.Y.
Giovanola, Ed	.190	56	58	10	11	0	1	0	3	9	8	2	0	L	R	5-10	170	3-4-69	1990	San Jose, Calif.
Gomez, Chris	.252	76	234	20	59	8	1	1	15	27	49	1	2	R	R	6-1	195	6-16-71	1992	Carlsbad, Calif.
Gonzalez, Wiki	.253	30	83	7	21	2	1	3	12	1	8	0	0	R	R	5-11	175	5-17-74	1992	Palo Negro, Venez.
Gwynn, Tony	.338	111	411	59	139	27	0	10	62	29	14	7	2	L	L	5-11	220	5-9-60	1981	Poway, Calif.
Jackson, Damian	.224	133	388	56	87	20	2	9	39	53	105	34	10	R	R	5-10	160	8-16-73	1992	Concord, Calif.
Joyner, Wally	.248	110	323	44	80	14	2	5	43	58	54	0	1	L	L	6-2	200	6-16-62	1983	Rancho Santa Fe, Calif.
Leyritz, Jim	.239	50	134	17	32	5	0	8	21	15	37	0	0	R	R	6-0	195	12-27-63	1986	Cooper City, Fla.
Magadan, Dave	.274	116	248	20	68	12	1	2	30	45	36	1	3	L	R	6-4	215	9-30-62	1983	Tampa, Fla.
Matthews, Gary	.222	23	36	4	8	0	0	0	7	9	9	2	0	S	R	6-3	200	8-25-74	1994	Canoga Park, Calif.
Myers, Greg	.289	50	128	9	37	4	0	3	15	13	14	0	0	L	R	6-2	208	4-14-66	1984	Riverside, Calif.
Nevin, Phil	.269	128	383	52	103	27	0	24	85	51	82	1	0	R	R	6-2	231	1-19-71	1992	Anaheim Hills, Calif.
Newhan, David	.140	32	43	7	6	1	0	2	6	1	11	2	1	L	R	5-10	180	9-7-73	1995	Yorba Linda, Calif.
Owens, Eric	.266	149	440	55	117	22	3	9	61	38	50	33	7	R	R	6-1	184	2-3-71	1992	Rocky Mount, Va.
Rivera, Ruben	.195	147	411	65	80	16	1	23	48	55	143	18	7	R	R	6-3	200	11-14-73	1992	La Chorrera, Panama
Sanders, Reggie	.285	133	478	92	136	24	7	26	72	65	108	36	13	R	R	6-1	185	12-1-67	1988	Tampa, Fla.
Vander Wal, John	.272	132	246	26	67	18	0	6	41	37	59	2	1	L	L	6-1	180	4-29-66	1987	Hudsonville, Mich.
Veras, Quilvio	.280	132	475	95	133	25	2	6	41	65	88	30	17	S	R	5-8	168	4-3-71	1990	Santo Domingo, D.R.

PITCHING	W	L	ERA	G	GS	CG	SV	IP	H	R	ER	BB	SO	B	T	HT	WT	DOB	1st Yr	Resides
Almanzar, Carlos	0	0	7.47	28	0	0	0	37	48	32	31	15	30	R	R	6-2	200	11-6-73	1991	Santo Domingo, D.R.
Ashby, Andy	14	10	3.80	31	31	4	0	206	204	95	87	54	132	R	R	6-5	190	7-11-67	1986	Pittston, Pa.
Boehringer, Brian	6	5	3.24	33	11	0	0	94	97	38	34	35	64	S	R	6-2	190	1-8-69	1991	Fenton, Mo.
Carlyle, Buddy	1	3	5.97	7	7	0	0	38	36	28	25	17	29	L	R	6-3	175	12-21-77	1996	Bellevue, Neb.
Clement, Matt	10	12	4.48	31	31	0	0	181	190	106	90	86	135	R	R	6-3	190	8-12-74	1994	Butler, Pa.
Cunnane, Will	2	1	5.23	24	0	0	0	31	34	19	18	12	22	R	R	6-2	175	4-24-74	1993	Congers, N.Y.
Guzman, Domingo	0	1	21.60	7	0	0	0	5	13	12	12	3	4	R	R	6-3	195	4-5-75	1994	San Cristobal, D.R.
Hitchcock, Sterling	12	14	4.11	33	33	1	0	206	202	99	94	76	194	L	L	6-1	192	4-29-71	1989	Brandon, Fla.
Hoffman, Trevor	2	3	2.14	64	0	0	40	67	48	23	16	15	73	R	R	6-0	205	10-13-67	1989	Southlake, Texas
Miceli, Danny	4	5	4.46	66	0	0	2	69	67	39	34	36	59	R	R	6-0	216	9-9-70	1990	Winter Springs, Fla.
Murray, Heath	0	4	5.76	22	0	0	0	50	60	33	32	26	25	L	L	6-4	205	4-19-73	1994	Troy, Ohio
Reyes, Carlos	2	4	3.72	65	0	0	1	77	76	38	32	24	57	S	R	6-1	190	4-19-69	1991	Tampa, Fla.
Rivera, Roberto	1	2	3.86	12	0	0	0	7	6	4	3	3	3	L	L	6-0	200	1-1-69	1988	Bayamon, P.R.
Spencer, Stan	0	7	9.16	9	8	0	0	38	56	44	39	11	36	R	R	6-4	205	8-7-69	1991	Battleground, Wash.
Vosberg, Ed	0	0	9.72	15	0	0	0	8	16	11	9	3	6	L	L	6-1	210	9-28-61	1983	Tucson, Ariz.
Wall, Donne	7	4	3.07	55	0	0	0	70	58	31	24	23	53	R	R	6-1	180	7-11-67	1989	Houston, Texas
Whisenant, Matt	0	1	3.68	19	0	0	0	15	10	6	6	10	10	L	L	6-3	215	6-8-71	1990	Overland Park, Kan.
Whiteside, Matt	1	0	13.91	10	0	0	0	11	19	17	17	5	9	R	R	6-0	205	8-8-67	1990	Arlington, Texas
Williams, Woody	12	12	4.41	33	33	0	0	208	213	106	102	73	137	R	R	6-0	190	8-19-66	1988	Alvin, Texas

FIELDING

Catcher	PCT	G	PO	A	E	DP	PB
Davis	.986	74	471	29	7	7	4
Gonzalez	.992	17	109	15	1	2	1
Leyritz	.994	24	150	16	1	0	6
Myers	.986	41	199	14	3	0	0
Nevin	.994	31	155	14	1	0	4

First Base	PCT	G	PO	A	E	DP
Baerga	.000	2	0	0	0	0
Garcia	1.000	1	2	0	0	0
Joyner	.995	105	731	66	4	83
Leyritz	.984	19	116	7	2	10
Magadan	.985	42	186	15	3	19
Nevin	.988	11	74	9	1	5
Newhan	.000	1	0	0	0	0
Owens	1.000	12	77	4	0	7
Vander Wal	.994	28	156	8	1	14

Second Base	PCT	G	PO	A	E	DP
Baerga	1.000	13	16	20	0	7
Giovanola	.982	19	26	28	1	9
Jackson	.988	21	37	44	1	13
Newhan	.970	19	28	36	2	10
Owens	1.000	1	1	0	0	0
Veras	.981	118	271	334	12	78

Third Base	PCT	G	PO	A	E	DP
Arias	.941	50	35	93	8	4
Baerga	.882	13	5	10	2	2
Garcia	.778	4	4	3	2	0
Giovanola	.938	25	4	11	1	0
Leyritz	.000	1	0	0	0	0
Magadan	.969	52	23	70	3	5
Nevin	.982	67	36	131	3	12
Newhan	.000	1	0	0	0	0
Owens	.714	4	1	4	2	0

Shortstop	PCT	G	PO	A	E	DP
Giovanola	1.000	7	6	8	0	2
Gomez	.961	75	101	195	12	48
Jackson	.940	100	136	258	25	57

Outfield	PCT	G	PO	A	E	DP
Darr	1.000	22	28	0	0	0
Gwynn	.993	104	147	4	1	0
Jackson	1.000	3	1	1	0	0
Matthews	1.000	17	22	0	0	0
Nevin	1.000	13	11	0	0	0
Owens	.990	116	199	4	2	1
Ru. Rivera	.976	143	312	8	8	2
Sanders	.975	129	233	4	6	0
Vander Wal	1.000	48	71	2	0	1

Reggie Sanders

Director of Player Development: Jim Skaalen

Class	Farm Team	League	W	L	Pct.	Finish*	Manager	First Yr
AAA	Las Vegas (Nev.) Stars	Pacific Coast	67	75	.472	10th (16)	Mike Ramsey	1983
AA	Mobile (Ala.) BayBears	Southern	66	73	.475	7th (10)	Mike Basso	1997
A#	Rancho Cucamonga (Calif.) Quakes	California	76	64	.543	3rd (10)	Tom LeVasseur	1993
A	Fort Wayne (Ind.) Wizards	Midwest	61	79	.436	13th (14)	Dan Simonds	1999
Rookie#	Idaho Falls (Idaho) Braves	Pioneer	48	27	.640	1st (8)	Don Werner	1995
Rookie	Peoria (Ariz.) Padres	Arizona	31	24	.564	3rd (8)	Randy Whisler	1988

*Finish in overall standings (No. of teams in league)   #Advanced level

LAS VEGAS — Class AAA

PACIFIC COAST LEAGUE

BATTING	AVG	G	AB	R	H	2B	3B	HR	RBI	BB	SO	SB	CS	B	T	HT	WT	DOB	1st Yr	Resides
Allen, Dusty	.273	128	454	68	124	30	3	18	89	79	143	3	5	R	R	6-4	215	8-9-72	1995	Oklahoma City, Okla.
Arias, George	.284	26	95	30	27	7	2	10	30	17	28	1	0	R	R	5-11	190	3-12-72	1993	Tucson, Ariz.
Baerga, Carlos	.286	21	91	15	26	7	0	2	9	9	5	0	0	S	R	5-11	215	11-4-68	1986	Bayamon, P.R.
Charles, Frank	.246	80	272	25	67	19	2	2	28	10	61	0	1	R	R	6-4	210	2-23-69	1991	Anaheim, Calif.
Darr, Mike	.298	100	383	57	114	34	0	10	62	50	103	10	3	L	R	6-3	205	3-21-76	1994	Corona, Calif.
Davis, Ben	.308	58	201	27	62	18	1	7	44	24	41	4	1	S	R	6-4	205	3-10-77	1995	Aston, Pa.
Garcia, Carlos	.281	78	274	36	77	19	0	3	28	17	61	5	0	R	R	6-1	193	10-15-67	1987	Lancaster, N.Y.
Giovanola, Ed	.283	36	106	23	30	6	1	2	10	16	23	2	0	L	R	5-10	170	3-4-69	1990	San Jose, Calif.
Gomez, Chris	.333	10	27	3	9	1	0	0	4	2	6	0	0	R	R	6-1	195	6-16-71	1992	Carlsbad, Calif.
Gonzalez, Jimmy	.295	40	112	10	33	9	1	3	19	14	29	0	0	R	R	6-3	235	3-8-73	1991	Hartford, Conn.
Gonzalez, Wiki	.272	24	92	13	25	6	0	6	12	5	10	0	0	R	R	5-11	175	5-17-74	1992	Palo Negro, Venez.
Guiel, Aaron	.245	84	257	46	63	25	2	12	39	44	86	5	4	L	R	5-10	190	10-5-72	1993	Langley, B.C.
Hamel, Jon	.000	1	2	0	0	0	0	0	0	1	1	0	0	R	R	5-11	195	1-11-77	1999	Phoenix, Ariz.
Joyner, Wally	.235	6	17	4	4	0	0	0	2	3	2	0	0	L	L	6-2	200	6-16-62	1983	Rancho Santa Fe, Calif.
Kirby, Wayne	.300	66	160	29	48	7	3	10	31	28	36	2	4	L	R	5-10	185	1-22-64	1983	Yorktown, Va.
LaRocca, Greg	.275	14	51	3	14	2	0	0	2	2	10	2	2	R	R	5-11	185	11-10-72	1994	Bedford, N.H.
Leyritz, Jim	.000	2	8	0	0	0	0	0	0	0	5	0	0	R	R	6-0	195	12-27-63	1986	Cooper City, Fla.
Lidle, Kevin	.276	10	29	5	8	3	0	2	5	3	8	0	0	R	R	5-11	170	3-22-72	1992	West Covina, Calif.
Matthews, Gary	.256	121	422	57	108	22	3	6	52	58	104	17	6	S	R	6-3	200	8-25-74	1994	Canoga Park, Calif.
Melo, Juan	.201	45	169	17	34	3	2	2	13	7	34	1	1	S	R	6-4	180	11-5-76	1994	Bani, D.R.
Mitchell, Mike	.241	27	87	7	21	5	0	1	11	12	20	0	0	L	R	6-3	205	4-5-73	1994	Camarillo, Calif.
Nevin, Phil	.200	3	10	2	2	0	0	2	2	0	2	0	0	R	R	6-2	231	1-19-71	1992	Anaheim Hills, Calif.
Newhan, David	.286	98	374	49	107	25	1	14	49	30	84	22	4	L	R	5-10	180	9-7-73	1995	Yorba Linda, Calif.
Pelaez, Alex	.308	5	13	1	4	0	0	0	2	0	2	0	0	R	R	5-9	190	4-6-76	1998	Chula Vista, Calif.
Prieto, Chris	.241	108	348	66	84	14	6	6	29	46	51	21	6	L	L	5-11	180	8-24-72	1993	Carmel, Calif.
Rossy, Rico	.255	93	259	42	66	12	0	10	29	41	27	4	1	R	R	5-10	175	2-16-64	1985	Bayamon, P.R.
Snellgrove, Clay	.667	1	3	1	2	2	0	0	0	0	0	0	0	R	R	6-0	180	11-22-74	1997	Lafayette, Ind.
Thrower, Jake	.288	72	267	40	77	17	4	4	30	27	56	4	4	S	R	5-11	180	11-19-75	1997	Yuma, Ariz.

PITCHING	W	L	ERA	G	GS	CG	SV	IP	H	R	ER	BB	SO	B	T	HT	WT	DOB	1st Yr	Resides
Almanzar, Carlos	1	3	9.53	11	3	0	0	23	32	25	24	8	18	R	R	6-2	200	11-6-73	1991	Santo Domingo, D.R.
Carlyle, Buddy	11	8	4.89	25	25	0	0	160	180	99	87	42	138	L	R	6-3	175	12-21-77	1996	Bellevue, Neb.
Cooke, Steve	0	0	30.00	5	0	0	0	3	6	10	10	12	0	R	L	6-6	240	1-14-70	1990	Aloha, Ore.
Cunnane, Will	2	1	0.98	28	0	0	11	37	30	5	4	16	54	R	R	6-2	175	4-24-74	1993	Congers, N.Y.
Darwin, Jeff	1	1	13.50	8	0	0	0	10	19	17	15	5	9	R	R	6-3	180	7-6-69	1989	Gainesville, Texas
Dennis, Shane	3	10	5.59	34	18	0	0	116	140	83	72	60	104	R	L	6-3	200	7-3-71	1994	Uniontown, Kan.
Drumheller, Al	6	4	4.90	20	7	0	0	61	72	36	33	22	46	R	L	6-0	185	7-31-71	1993	Shenandoah, Pa.
Kolb, Brandon	2	1	3.94	42	0	0	4	62	72	36	27	29	63	R	R	6-1	190	11-20-73	1995	Danville, Calif.
Mercedes, Jose	2	6	4.30	15	14	0	0	88	110	57	42	20	57	R	R	6-1	210	3-5-71	1992	Las Palmillas, D.R.
Murray, Heath	5	4	4.26	15	15	1	0	82	99	45	39	32	65	L	L	6-4	205	4-19-73	1994	Troy, Ohio
Rivera, Roberto	1	2	10.16	20	3	0	0	34	61	39	38	14	25	L	L	6-0	200	1-1-69	1988	Bayamon, P.R.
Sak, Jim	2	2	3.58	23	0	0	6	28	22	11	11	17	32	R	R	6-1	195	8-18-73	1995	Chicago, Ill.
Skrmetta, Matt	2	1	3.45	20	0	0	1	29	20	13	11	11	25	S	R	6-3	200	11-6-72	1993	Satellite Beach, Fla.
Smith, Pete	4	5	3.64	13	12	2	0	72	77	40	29	13	47	R	R	6-2	210	2-27-66	1984	Smyrna, Ga.
2-team (8 Memphis)	6	8	4.76	21	20	2	0	110	130	75	58	29	82							
Spencer, Stan	2	4	5.47	12	10	0	0	54	69	35	33	15	50	R	R	6-4	205	8-7-69	1991	Battleground, Wash.
Sullivan, Brendan	2	4	7.60	45	0	0	0	66	88	60	56	38	50	R	R	6-3	190	12-15-74	1996	Washington, D.C.
Tollberg, Brian	1	2	4.85	15	0	0	0	30	34	17	16	6	23	R	R	6-3	195	9-16-72	1994	Bradenton, Fla.
Vosberg, Ed	0	0	1.08	8	0	0	1	8	3	1	1	4	12	L	L	6-1	200	9-28-61	1983	Tucson, Ariz.
Whiteside, Matt	9	5	5.12	47	3	1	7	90	99	59	51	29	88	R	R	6-0	205	8-8-67	1990	Arlington, Texas
Wolff, Bryan	8	12	4.66	28	27	2	0	178	199	99	92	57	151	R	R	6-1	195	3-16-72	1993	St. Louis, Mo.

FIELDING

Catcher	PCT	G	PO	A	E	DP	PB
Charles	.990	27	195	12	2	1	0
Davis	.992	58	454	32	4	5	5
J. Gonzalez	.991	28	200	21	2	4	2
W. Gonzalez	.984	23	175	10	3	3	1
Hamel	1.000	1	4	0	0	0	0
Lidle	1.000	10	55	7	0	1	1
Nevin	1.000	2	10	2	0	1	0

First Base	PCT	G	PO	A	E	DP
Allen	.985	69	507	35	8	58
Charles	.988	22	153	12	2	15
Garcia	.983	38	256	26	5	27

	PCT	G	PO	A	E	DP
J. Gonzalez	.667	1	2	0	1	0
Joyner	1.000	6	38	2	0	3
Leyritz	1.000	2	17	1	0	2
Mitchell	.978	23	165	11	4	15
Nevin	1.000	1	1	1	0	0

Second Base	PCT	G	PO	A	E	DP
Baerga	.944	2	5	12	1	4
Garcia	1.000	7	19	14	0	5
Giovanola	1.000	3	8	5	0	1
LaRocca	.875	1	5	2	1	1
Newhan	.952	95	162	233	20	58

	PCT	G	PO	A	E	DP
Pelaez	1.000	1	1	1	0	0
Rossy	.978	10	23	21	1	4
Snellgrove	1.000	1	0	4	0	0
Thrower	.984	29	44	83	2	21

Third Base	PCT	G	PO	A	E	DP
Arias	.950	25	20	37	3	4
Baerga	.909	19	11	29	4	5
Charles	.829	21	11	18	6	2
Garcia	.965	24	13	42	2	4
Giovanola	.940	23	9	38	3	7
LaRocca	.957	7	5	17	1	4

Organization Statistics

	PCT	G	PO	A	E	DP
Melo	.000	2	0	0	0	0
Nevin	1.000	1	1	1	0	0
Pelaez	.833	4	0	5	1	0
Rossy	.750	4	3	6	3	1
Thrower	.933	28	13	57	5	8
Shortstop	**PCT**	**G**	**PO**	**A**	**E**	**DP**
Garcia	.889	2	2	6	1	1

	PCT	G	PO	A	E	DP
Giovanola	.967	11	10	19	1	4
Gomez	.933	9	8	20	2	5
LaRocca	.944	6	5	12	1	3
Melo	.957	44	70	108	8	24
Newhan	1.000	1	2	2	0	1
Rossy	.978	72	85	186	6	41
Thrower	.963	16	28	49	3	10

Outfield	PCT	G	PO	A	E	DP
Allen	.966	57	79	6	3	1
Charles	1.000	1	1	0	0	0
Darr	.989	97	172	11	2	1
Guiel	.944	49	81	4	5	0
Kirby	.969	32	63	0	2	0
Matthews	.976	120	273	7	7	1
Prieto	.994	94	154	6	1	1

MOBILE — Class AA

SOUTHERN LEAGUE

BATTING	AVG	G	AB	R	H	2B	3B	HR	RBI	BB	SO	SB	CS	B	T	HT	WT	DOB	1st Yr	Resides
Ahrendt, Jay	.200	8	15	2	3	1	0	0	2	4	8	0	0	L	R	6-2	210	1-23-74	1996	Homewood, Ill.
Balfe, Ryan	.280	111	400	69	112	31	3	11	70	50	95	0	1	S	R	6-1	180	11-11-75	1994	Cornwall, N.Y.
Curl, John	.285	133	474	79	135	30	3	22	76	77	137	9	5	L	R	6-3	205	11-10-72	1995	Logansport, Ind.
Eberwein, Kevin	.171	10	35	5	6	1	0	1	2	3	16	0	0	R	R	6-4	200	3-30-77	1998	Las Vegas, Nev.
Faggett, Ethan	.243	128	527	82	128	18	11	6	43	53	126	63	14	L	L	6-0	190	8-21-74	1992	Burleson, Texas
Gonzalez, Jimmy	.265	21	68	15	18	3	0	2	8	7	16	0	0	R	R	6-3	235	3-8-73	1991	Hartford, Conn.
Gonzalez, Wiki	.338	61	225	38	76	16	2	10	49	29	28	0	0	R	R	5-11	175	5-17-74	1992	Palo Negro, Venez.
Johnson, A.J.	.243	44	136	12	33	7	0	4	18	6	35	1	3	R	R	6-3	210	2-17-73	1995	Neptune, N.J.
Jorgensen, Randy	.321	72	252	41	81	15	0	7	54	36	46	2	2	L	L	6-2	195	4-3-72	1993	Glendale, Ariz.
Kent, Robbie	.271	109	336	48	91	17	3	8	56	44	71	2	0	R	R	5-10	185	1-8-74	1996	Evansville, Ind.
Lidle, Kevin	.222	63	180	23	40	8	0	6	26	30	40	1	3	R	R	5-11	170	3-22-72	1992	West Covina, Calif.
Luzinski, Ryan	.371	22	62	11	23	10	0	4	13	15	0	0	0	R	R	6-1	215	8-22-73	1992	Medford, N.J.
2-team (55 Chatt.)	.279	77	233	28	65	20	0	2	30	37	58	1	2							
McClure, Brian	.207	51	169	17	35	10	3	1	27	17	34	0	0	L	R	6-0	170	1-15-74	1996	Chatham, Ill.
Morenz, Shea	.263	21	57	6	15	5	0	0	7	4	27	1	1	L	R	6-2	205	1-22-74	1995	San Antonio, Texas
Nicholson, Kevin	.288	127	489	84	141	38	3	13	81	46	92	16	5	S	R	5-10	190	3-29-76	1997	Surrey, B.C.
Paciorek, Pete	.221	83	226	38	50	9	2	4	17	38	60	2	3	L	L	6-3	195	5-19-76	1995	San Gabriel, Calif.
Prieto, Rick	.287	118	359	61	103	14	4	6	43	57	55	28	5	S	R	5-10	175	8-24-72	1993	Carmel, Calif.
Schmidt, Bryan	.188	17	32	7	6	1	0	0	3	5	8	0	0	R	R	6-2	180	6-28-75	1998	Stockton, Calif.
Thrower, Jake	.242	40	149	15	36	9	2	3	26	21	26	3	3	S	R	5-11	180	11-19-75	1997	Yuma, Ariz.
Tucci, Pete	.250	83	312	45	78	15	0	11	35	26	83	11	6	R	R	6-2	205	10-8-75	1996	Norwalk, Conn.

PITCHING	W	L	ERA	G	GS	CG	SV	IP	H	R	ER	BB	SO	B	T	HT	WT	DOB	1st Yr	Resides
Agosto, Stevenson	3	3	5.89	40	1	0	0	81	81	61	53	59	59	L	L	5-10	175	9-2-75	1994	Rio Grande, P.R.
Anderson, Bill	0	0	7.00	4	4	0	0	18	20	14	14	13	19	R	R	6-0	190	9-23-71	1994	Alta Loma, Calif.
Doughty, Brian	8	10	4.77	36	15	0	1	138	161	85	73	29	69	R	R	6-5	235	9-21-74	1992	Bothell, Wash.
Drumheller, Al	5	2	4.33	12	12	0	0	69	78	40	33	29	55	R	L	6-0	185	7-31-71	1993	Shenandoah, Pa.
Estes, Eric	0	1	10.90	8	2	0	0	17	33	22	21	9	4	R	R	6-4	185	9-4-72	1997	Vancouver, Wash.
Giron, Isabel	4	7	6.32	11	11	0	0	63	71	49	44	15	45	R	R	6-2	190	11-17-77	1995	Villa Mella, D.R.
2-team (17 Knoxville)	11	12	5.46	28	27	0	0	158	168	108	96	54	126							
Guzman, Domingo	1	2	5.47	41	0	0	6	51	60	33	31	25	38	R	R	6-3	195	4-5-75	1994	San Cristobal, D.R.
Hart, Len	0	0	3.38	2	0	0	0	3	4	1	1	2	4	L	L	5-11	190	10-8-73	1996	Oliver Springs, Tenn.
Herndon, Junior	10	9	4.69	26	26	2	0	163	172	96	85	52	87	R	R	6-1	190	9-11-78	1997	Craig, Colo.
Hite, Henry	2	4	4.32	51	0	0	15	58	71	30	28	17	52	R	R	6-1	155	7-23-74	1996	Hermitage, Tenn.
Kolb, Brandon	0	2	0.79	7	0	0	2	11	8	4	1	4	14	R	R	6-1	180	11-20-73	1995	Danville, Calif.
Lopez, Rodrigo	10	8	4.41	28	28	2	0	169	187	91	83	58	138	R	R	6-1	180	12-14-75	1995	Mexico City, Mexico
Maurer, Dave	4	4	3.63	54	0	0	3	72	59	30	29	15	73	R	L	6-2	195	2-23-75	1997	Burnsville, Minn.
Middlebrook, Jason	4	6	8.06	13	13	0	0	64	78	59	57	30	38	R	R	6-3	215	6-26-75	1996	Grass Lake, Mich.
Ricken, Ray	7	7	5.37	20	19	3	0	111	122	73	66	55	67	R	R	6-5	225	8-11-73	1994	Warren, Mich.
Sak, Jim	4	1	1.69	18	0	0	2	27	15	11	5	15	37	R	R	6-1	195	8-18-73	1995	Chicago, Ill.
Serrano, Wascar	2	3	5.53	7	7	0	0	42	48	27	26	17	29	R	R	6-2	178	7-2-78	1995	Bani, D.R.
Skrmetta, Matt	1	3	6.27	25	1	0	1	37	42	28	26	24	45	S	R	6-3	220	11-6-72	1993	Satellite Beach, Fla.
Szymborski, Tom	1	0	5.40	6	0	0	0	7	10	9	4	5	3	R	R	6-3	210	3-7-75	1996	Chicago, Ill.
Walters, Brett	0	1	5.40	9	0	0	0	13	13	8	8	9	12	R	R	6-0	185	9-30-74	1994	Bateman, Australia

FIELDING

Catcher	PCT	G	PO	A	E	DP	PB
Ahrendt	.974	8	34	3	1	0	0
J. Gonzalez	.968	16	81	9	3	1	2
W. Gonzalez	.982	52	329	43	7	3	5
Lidle	.981	53	310	48	7	3	3
Luzinski	.994	22	143	12	1	2	2

First Base	PCT	G	PO	A	E	DP
Curl	.985	22	187	13	3	15
Jorgensen	.991	58	498	34	5	50
Paciorek	.989	62	499	32	6	44
Tucci	.875	1	7	0	1	1

Second Base	PCT	G	PO	A	E	DP
Kent	.957	63	124	144	12	37

	PCT	G	PO	A	E	DP
McClure	.982	45	100	113	4	31
Prieto	1.000	1	1	0	0	0
Schmidt	1.000	8	9	8	0	3
Thrower	.941	37	59	85	9	13

Third Base	PCT	G	PO	A	E	DP
Balfe	.922	108	70	213	24	18
Eberwein	.957	10	3	19	1	1
J. Gonzalez	.500	1	1	1	2	2
Kent	.887	32	24	39	8	6

Shortstop	PCT	G	PO	A	E	DP
Kent	.940	13	20	27	3	5
McClure	.000	1	0	0	0	0

	PCT	G	PO	A	E	DP
Nicholson	.948	126	187	402	32	75
Schmidt	1.000	1	0	4	0	0
Thrower	.867	4	8	5	2	1

Outfield	PCT	G	PO	A	E	DP
Curl	.955	102	190	3	9	1
Faggett	.971	125	293	11	9	2
Johnson	.981	28	51	2	1	0
Morenz	1.000	6	9	0	0	0
Prieto	.979	97	182	3	4	1
Tucci	.975	78	156	2	4	0

RANCHO CUCAMONGA — Class A

CALIFORNIA LEAGUE

BATTING	AVG	G	AB	R	H	2B	3B	HR	RBI	BB	SO	SB	CS	B	T	HT	WT	DOB	1st Yr	Resides
Ahrendt, Jay	.256	40	121	14	31	5	1	1	14	16	44	0	1	L	R	6-2	210	1-23-74	1996	Homewood, Ill.
Arias, George	.190	7	21	1	4	2	0	1	4	2	9	0	0	R	R	5-11	190	3-12-72	1993	Tucson, Ariz.
Briones, Chris	.184	27	76	3	14	3	0	1	6	3	23	0	0	R	R	5-11	205	6-5-73	1995	Brea, Calif.
Burroughs, Sean	.435	6	23	3	10	3	0	1	5	3	3	0	1	L	R	6-1	195	9-12-80	1999	Long Beach, Calif.
Bush, Darren	.282	77	238	35	67	9	1	8	36	36	51	7	4	L	R	6-0	200	1-18-74	1996	Dunedin, Fla.
Eberwein, Kevin	.259	110	417	69	108	30	4	18	69	42	139	7	5	R	R	6-4	200	3-30-77	1998	Las Vegas, Nev.
French, Ron	.150	7	20	2	3	0	1	0	3	1	5	0	0	R	R	5-10	200	5-24-78	1998	Concord, Calif.
Halloran, Matt	.217	95	309	39	67	11	2	0	22	17	75	15	9	R	R	6-2	185	3-3-78	1996	Niceville, Fla.
Hunter, Johnny	.217	25	106	11	23	4	0	0	9	8	32	1	2	R	R	6-1	190	6-14-75	1997	Mansfield, Texas

Organization Statistics

BATTING	AVG	G	AB	R	H	2B	3B	HR	RBI	BB	SO	SB	CS	B	T	HT	WT	DOB	1st Yr	Resides
Koonce, Graham	.285	132	474	76	135	16	1	19	79	76	110	4	1	L	L	6-4	225	5-15-75	1994	Julian, Calif.
Leyritz, Jim	.000	1	4	0	0	0	0	0	0	0	1	0	0	R	R	6-0	195	12-27-63	1986	Cooper City, Fla.
McClure, Brian	.224	36	116	26	26	5	1	2	15	26	22	4	1	L	R	6-0	170	1-15-74	1996	Chatham, Ill.
Myers, Greg	.000	3	3	0	0	0	0	0	0	1	1	0	0	L	R	6-2	208	4-14-66	1984	Riverside, Calif.
Nieves, Wilbert	.328	120	427	58	140	26	2	7	61	40	54	2	7	R	R	5-11	190	9-25-77	1996	Santurce, P.R.
Owens, Jeremy	.158	9	38	2	6	1	0	0	1	1	13	2	1	R	R	6-1	200	12-9-76	1998	Johnson City, Tenn.
Pelaez, Alex	.298	117	443	62	132	21	4	4	54	35	53	7	3	R	R	5-9	190	4-6-76	1998	Chula Vista, Calif.
Pernell, Brandon	.280	133	529	96	148	30	7	21	84	50	156	33	14	R	R	6-2	195	4-11-77	1995	Torrance, Calif.
Seal, Scott	.248	123	439	67	109	23	2	13	70	45	96	7	3	L	L	6-1	205	8-16-75	1997	Irvine, Calif.
Snellgrove, Clay	.293	116	426	62	125	20	2	3	43	19	42	8	7	R	R	6-0	180	11-22-74	1997	Lafayette, Ind.
Wickersham, Jack	.282	56	174	28	49	10	0	0	14	15	37	13	5	R	R	5-11	175	10-19-75	1998	La Canada, Calif.
Wilson, Andy	.293	105	351	60	103	18	5	1	39	48	50	26	14	R	R	5-6	160	8-12-75	1998	Thousand Oaks, Calif.

GAMES BY POSITION: C—Ahrendt 16, Briones 16, Bush 1, French 2, Myers 2, Nieves 117. **1B**—Eberwein 3, Koonce 126, Pelaez 14. **2B**—McClure 32, Pelaez 17, Snellgrove 49, Wickersham 45, Wilson 1. **3B**—Arias 4, Burroughs 2, Eberwein 91, McClure 1, Pelaez 41, Snellgrove 10, Wickersham 1. **SS**—Eberwein 1, Halloran 91, Snellgrove 49, Wickersham 3. **OF**—Bush 61, Hunter 25, Owens 9, Pernell 132, Seal 118, Snellgrove 3, Wilson 85.

PITCHING	W	L	ERA	G	GS	CG	SV	IP	H	R	ER	BB	SO	B	T	HT	WT	DOB	1st Yr	Resides
Aragon, Angel	2	7	3.54	53	0	0	19	69	55	33	27	28	76	R	R	6-1	215	12-19-73	1998	Oxnard, Calif.
Bynum, Mike	3	1	3.29	7	7	0	0	38	35	17	14	8	44	L	L	6-4	200	3-20-78	1999	Middleburg, Fla.
Camp, Shawn	1	5	3.95	53	0	0	6	66	68	37	29	25	78	R	R	6-1	200	11-18-75	1997	Fairfax, Va.
Condrey, Clay	0	0	3.68	6	0	0	0	7	4	3	3	3	9	R	R	6-3	195	11-19-75	1998	Navasota, Texas
Diaz, Antonio	0	0	5.11	9	0	0	0	12	7	7	7	7	7	R	R	5-11	170	1-28-79	1997	Juncos, P.R.
Fikac, Jeremy	8	3	5.08	40	6	0	0	85	94	50	48	43	75	R	R	6-2	185	4-8-75	1998	Shiner, Texas
Foran, John	9	5	4.80	25	20	0	0	105	113	70	56	53	89	R	R	6-1	185	10-22-73	1995	Alford, Fla.
Guttormson, Rick	14	8	3.72	28	28	1	0	174	165	83	72	36	125	R	R	6-2	185	1-11-77	1997	Anacortes, Wash.
Hart, Len	2	1	0.83	33	0	0	3	43	19	5	4	18	54	L	L	5-11	190	Oliver Springs, Tenn.		
Hite, Kevin	0	1	4.05	7	0	0	4	7	6	3	3	1	8	R	R	6-1	155	7-23-74	1996	Hermitage, Tenn.
Kramer, Aaron	9	9	3.63	23	23	0	0	139	154	73	56	31	98	S	R	6-1	210	6-25-75	1998	Glendale, Ariz.
Lawrence, Brian	12	8	3.39	27	27	4	0	175	178	72	66	30	166	R	R	6-0	195	5-14-76	1998	Queen City, Texas
Luque, Roger	0	0	10.80	3	0	0	0	2	3	2	2	2	2	L	L	6-1	170	1-8-80	1997	Charallave, Venez.
Padua, Geraldo	3	3	4.65	7	7	0	0	41	43	21	21	18	41	R	R	6-2	165	2-9-77	1995	Santo Domingo, D.R.
Serrano, Wascar	9	8	3.33	21	21	1	0	132	110	58	49	43	129	R	R	6-2	178	7-2-78	1995	Bani, D.R.
Szymborski, Tom	1	2	4.78	28	0	0	0	43	48	26	23	23	33	R	R	6-3	200	3-7-75	1996	Chicago, Ill.
Volkman, Keith	2	2	5.40	49	0	0	2	53	59	38	32	37	41	L	L	6-2	225	1-13-76	1994	Pasadena, Md.
Walker, Kevin	1	1	3.46	27	1	0	4	39	35	19	15	19	35	L	L	6-4	190	9-20-76	1995	Glen Rose, Texas

FORT WAYNE — Class A

MIDWEST LEAGUE

BATTING	AVG	G	AB	R	H	2B	3B	HR	RBI	BB	SO	SB	CS	B	T	HT	WT	DOB	1st Yr	Resides
Berroa, Cristian	.240	119	442	49	106	12	3	4	40	14	71	25	11	S	R	5-11	150	4-27-79	1996	Haina, D.R.
Burroughs, Sean	.359	122	426	65	153	30	3	5	80	74	59	17	15	L	R	6-1	195	9-12-80	1998	Long Beach, Calif.
Campbell, Sean	.265	102	343	48	91	17	4	7	54	27	71	10	4	L	R	6-3	180	4-15-77	1998	Fresno, Calif.
Cook, Jon	.213	107	315	60	67	12	1	2	32	54	94	39	11	R	R	6-1	195	4-26-77	1998	San Jose, Calif.
Cosentino, Tony	.244	37	127	11	31	5	0	0	11	22	33	1	1	R	R	6-0	195	12-7-78	1997	Torrance, Calif.
Dunaway, Jason	.216	85	255	34	55	10	2	1	17	27	58	12	6	R	R	6-1	177	1-12-77	1997	Durango, Colo.
Dusan, Joe	.293	53	184	29	54	10	2	5	37	29	50	1	3	L	L	6-1	190	7-30-77	1998	Bend, Ore.
Faison, Vince	.208	11	48	10	10	2	0	0	1	6	18	7	1	L	R	6-0	180	1-22-81	1999	Lyons, Ga.
French, Ron	.269	65	219	24	59	11	0	4	31	23	58	0	3	R	R	5-10	200	5-24-78	1998	Concord, Calif.
Garcia, Alex	.299	71	201	27	42	9	1	2	26	25	62	5	2	R	R	5-11	165	4-14-79	1996	Haina, D.R.
Hazen, Mike	.203	72	222	23	45	8	0	3	24	37	62	6	5	R	L	6-1	195	1-7-76	1998	Abington, Mass.
Hemmings, Scot	.111	12	36	3	4	1	0	0	4	5	18	1	0	R	R	6-4	197	5-6-77	1997	Columbus, Ga.
Lawrence, Tony	.197	46	142	11	28	8	1	0	8	21	45	1	1	R	R	6-1	205	3-7-75	1997	Monroe, La.
Loggins, Josh	.297	136	522	75	155	29	7	14	85	60	119	24	12	R	R	6-1	190	11-29-76	1998	West Lafayette, Ind.
Owens, Jeremy	.281	129	513	111	144	26	12	9	66	63	153	65	14	R	R	6-1	200	12-9-76	1998	Johnson City, Tenn.
Scheschuk, John	.252	66	242	35	61	14	0	3	36	43	34	3	1	L	L	6-2	208	2-2-77	1999	Houston, Texas
Schmidt, Bryan	.238	67	227	23	54	7	1	0	13	20	49	2	4	R	R	6-2	180	6-28-75	1998	Stockton, Calif.
Vandemore, Anthony	.278	5	18	0	5	2	0	0	1	5	0	0	1	L	R	6-3	200	6-10-77	1998	Geneseo, Ill.
Wagner, Mike	.261	13	46	10	12	1	0	2	8	8	15	0	0	R	R	6-0	185	9-11-77	1999	Loveland, Ohio
Wickersham, Jack	.236	39	140	24	33	7	1	0	20	12	28	6	6	R	R	5-11	175	10-19-75	1998	La Canada, Calif.

GAMES BY POSITION: C—Campbell 79, Cosentino 27, French 21, Lawrence 28. **1B**—Dusan 51, Lawrence 7, Loggins 7, Scheschuk 66, Schmidt 7, Wickersham 1. **2B**—Dunaway 49, French 1, Garcia 54, Schmidt 21, Wickersham 26. **3B**—Burroughs 120, Garcia 21, Schmidt 19. **SS**—Berroa 118, Dunaway 16, Schmidt 17. **OF**—Cook 94, Dunaway 2, Faison 11, Hazen 46, Hemmings 7, Loggins 128, Owens 128, Schmidt 1, Vandemore 4, Wagner 11.

PITCHING	W	L	ERA	G	GS	CG	SV	IP	H	R	ER	BB	SO	B	T	HT	WT	DOB	1st Yr	Resides
Bartosh, Cliff	5	12	4.44	35	20	1	0	130	136	76	64	49	100	L	L	6-2	175	9-5-79	1998	Duncanville, Texas
Bauer, Ryan	4	9	4.89	36	15	1	5	110	111	75	60	55	86	R	R	6-3	225	7-11-76	1998	Smithboro, Ill.
Bell, Casey	0	0	6.75	2	0	0	0	7	8	5	5	3	3	R	R	6-2	186	7-14-78	1998	Elkins, Ark.
Berryman, Brian	4	2	4.05	9	9	0	0	47	43	25	21	24	19	R	R	6-4	200	7-13-77	1998	Canton, Mich.
Condrey, Clay	2	3	3.78	42	0	0	20	48	40	24	20	19	47	R	R	6-3	195	11-19-75	1998	Navasota, Texas
Darr, Jay	1	1	5.87	7	4	0	0	23	27	19	15	12	12	R	R	6-3	190	2-26-79	1997	Benton, Ark.
Dent, Doug	4	1	3.51	8	8	0	0	49	43	23	19	17	32	R	R	6-8	210	3-23-77	1998	Citrus Heights, Calif.
Diaz, Antonio	6	3	4.18	27	9	0	0	75	77	41	35	28	54	R	R	5-11	170	1-28-79	1997	Juncos, P.R.
Dobson, Mark	2	0	6.50	41	0	0	0	80	92	65	58	48	83	R	R	6-3	212	9-23-75	1998	Littleton, Colo.
Forbes, Keith	3	4	6.18	42	2	0	0	67	60	52	46	65	70	R	R	6-1	195	1-28-77	1998	Malden, Mass.
Harris, Josh	5	7	7.43	17	7	0	0	53	67	39	33	40	76	R	R	6-3	220	10-23-77	1996	Canyon Lake, Texas
Howard, Ben	6	10	4.73	28	28	0	0	145	123	100	76	110	131	R	R	6-2	195	1-15-79	1997	Jackson, Tenn.
Jones, Travis	8	2	3.15	41	7	0	0	91	90	42	32	57	72	L	L	6-3	190	12-3-77	1996	Konawa, Okla.
Luque, Roger	3	5	3.84	46	3	0	2	77	67	39	33	40	79	L	L	6-1	170	1-8-80	1997	Charallave, Venez.
Ortiz, Omar	1	2	6.75	4	4	0	0	19	17	16	14	20	9	S	R	6-1	195	9-11-77	1999	Brownsville, Texas
Perry, Tim	2	5	5.08	10	10	0	0	51	50	39	29	34	46	R	R	6-0	190	8-17-75	1996	Carlsbad, N.M.
Pesqueira, Omar	x	x	5.08	47	2	0	2	78	84	49	44	54	66	R	R			8-8-79	1999	Nogales, Mexico
Van De Weg, Ryan	3	4	6.71	13	8	0	1	54	71	46	40	28	41	R	R	6-0	180	2-24-74	1995	West Olive, Mich.
Viator, Dustin	0	1	17.18	5	0	0	0	4	7	7	7	1	2	R	R	6-3	192	7-12-75	1997	New Iberia, La.
Watkins, Steve	0	3	8.47	4	4	0	0	17	24	17	16	9	21	R	R	6-4	190	7-19-78	1998	Lubbock, Texas

PIONEER LEAGUE

BATTING

BATTING	AVG	G	AB	R	H	2B	3B	HR	RBI	BB	SO	SB	CS	B	T	HT	WT	DOB	1st Yr	Resides
Boykin, Paul	.248	45	149	30	37	6	1	1	10	14	44	24	9	L	R	5-11	190	10-3-77	1998	Littleton, Colo.
Bystrowski, Robby	.297	44	155	37	46	8	3	3	19	27	44	19	5	R	R	6-1	195	9-27-76	1997	Fair Oaks, Calif.
Cosentino, Tony	.375	20	88	14	33	5	2	2	30	6	11	0	0	R	R	6-0	195	12-7-78	1997	Torrance, Calif.
Curry, Jesse	.264	47	159	28	42	12	5	7	35	22	53	5	0	L	L	6-4	205	10-25-78	1997	Gresham, Ore.
Donovan, Todd	.298	53	198	57	59	11	3	1	22	25	39	40	5	R	R	6-1	175	8-12-78	1999	East Lyme, Conn.
Garrett, Shawn	.307	53	192	46	59	14	1	7	33	21	46	5	3	S	R	6-3	190	11-2-78	1998	Kinmundy, Ill.
Gutierrez, Said	.310	26	87	10	27	5	0	1	11	3	14	0	1	R	R	5-10	196	3-26-80	1998	Merida, Mexico
Huff, Jake	.315	30	108	25	34	7	0	4	29	17	25	0	0	R	R	6-3	210	7-8-77	1999	Springville, Utah
Ienni, Greg	.228	53	193	34	44	13	0	6	29	12	58	10	6	R	R	6-1	188	8-8-77	1999	Ontario, Calif.
Moore, Jason	.270	64	252	54	68	16	3	6	43	43	54	16	1	S	R	6-0	180	1-4-78	1999	Miami, Fla.
Motley, Brittan	.235	41	153	23	36	6	0	1	20	16	40	11	1	S	R	6-2	180	10-18-78	1997	Kansas City, Mo.
Rizzo, Jeff	.206	29	97	19	20	3	2	1	19	21	28	3	0	L	R	6-0	190	1-17-78	1999	San Diego, Calif.
Scales, Bobby	.290	44	169	47	49	14	6	1	30	29	31	7	2	S	R	6-0	175	10-4-77	1999	Roswell, Ga.
Schader, Troy	.336	68	268	61	90	16	7	19	69	35	75	2	2	R	R	6-1	200	3-5-77	1999	La Centre, Wash.
Stone, Jonathon	.204	28	98	11	20	6	0	0	8	11	38	5	1	R	R	5-11	185	12-23-78	1999	Lodi, Calif.
Ward, Brian	.317	68	287	50	91	23	2	7	60	32	46	6	3	R	R	5-8	188	7-7-77	1999	Orlando, Fla.

GAMES BY POSITION: C—Cosentino 10, Gutierrez 26, Huff 19, Stone 26. **1B**—Curry 47, Garrett 32, Huff 2, Rizzo 1. **2B**—Rizzo 3, Scales 38, Ward 38. **3B**—Garrett 9, Rizzo 12, Schader 35, Ward 23. **SS**—Moore 58, Rizzo 1, Schader 19. **OF**—Boykin 41, Bystrowski 38, Donovan 48, Garrett 8, Ienni 52, Motley 41, Rizzo 1, Stone 1.

PITCHING

PITCHING	W	L	ERA	G	GS	CG	SV	IP	H	R	ER	BB	SO	B	T	HT	WT	DOB	1st Yr	Resides
Barbarossa, Josh	1	0	2.89	3	3	0	0	9	8	4	3	4	7	L	L	6-3	215	1-4-80	1999	Valparaiso, Ind.
Baxter, Gerik	2	0	4.81	5	5	0	0	24	21	15	13	17	29	R	R	6-2	185	3-11-80	1999	Edmonds, Wash.
Bell, Casey	3	6	4.71	15	13	0	0	78	85	57	41	39	37	R	R	6-2	186	7-14-78	1998	Elkins, Ark.
Burns, Casey	1	2	3.63	12	9	0	0	40	44	24	16	22	48	R	R	6-1	185	7-24-77	1999	Pennington, N.J.
Bynum, Mike	1	0	0.00	5	3	0	0	17	7	0	0	4	21	L	L	6-4	200	3-20-78	1999	Middleburg, Fla.
Carmona, Cesarin	4	1	4.92	25	0	0	0	53	58	33	29	24	47	R	R	5-10	180	12-20-76	1994	Bani, D.R.
Cyr, Eric	1	0	1.80	1	1	0	0	5	5	1	1	1	3	R	L	6-4	200	2-11-79	1999	Ada, Okla.
Darr, Jay	2	1	6.79	19	8	0	0	57	80	48	43	20	62	R	R	6-3	190	2-26-79	1997	Benton, Ark.
DeHart, Blair	3	1	3.20	10	10	0	0	56	50	28	20	17	43	R	R	6-1	190	5-4-78	1999	Herndon, Va.
Devine, Travis	1	2	4.26	8	4	0	0	25	32	17	12	9	13	R	R	6-3	190	12-3-79	1998	Lawrenceville, Ga.
Hunter, Johnny	3	4	5.51	29	0	0	3	49	55	41	30	34	54	R	R	6-1	190	6-14-75	1997	Mansfield, Texas
Meyer, John	0	1	14.40	2	1	0	0	5	13	13	8	3	1	R	R	6-5	230	6-19-79	1998	Fort Worth, Texas
Ortiz, Omar	2	1	3.41	6	5	0	0	29	25	18	11	13	24	S	R	6-1	210	9-11-77	1999	Brownsville, Texas
Peavy, Jacob	2	0	0.00	2	2	0	0	11	5	0	0	1	13	R	R	6-1	180	5-31-81	1999	Semmes, Ala.
Rosario, Hipolito	0	0	4.50	2	0	0	0	4	3	2	2	2	2	R	R	6-0	165	2-10-80	1997	San Cristobal, D.R.
Shiyuk, Todd	5	0	5.67	23	0	0	4	40	46	30	25	17	49	L	L	6-0	190	1-31-77	1999	Delta, B.C.
Silverio, Marcelino	7	3	6.80	23	0	0	0	46	47	38	35	20	41	R	R	6-3	180	3-7-79	1996	Haina, D.R.
Verdugo, Oswaldo	5	1	2.35	33	0	0	13	38	34	13	10	9	54	R	R	5-11	163	4-4-81	1998	Los Mochis, Mexico
Watkins, Steve	5	2	4.40	12	11	0	0	61	60	39	30	25	75	R	R	6-4	190	7-19-78	1998	Lubbock, Texas
Webster, Jeremy	0	2	6.63	12	0	0	0	19	22	19	14	18	11	L	L	6-0	195	3-20-79	1999	Sandy, Utah

ARIZONA LEAGUE

BATTING

BATTING	AVG	G	AB	R	H	2B	3B	HR	RBI	BB	SO	SB	CS	B	T	HT	WT	DOB	1st Yr	Resides
Duenas, Manuel	.192	45	156	28	30	8	2	1	20	15	60	4	0	R	R	6-1	181	12-17-79	1999	Obregon, Mexico
Encarnacion, Santos	.283	52	187	31	53	2	4	0	23	21	40	22	2	R	R	6-2	155	9-21-79	1996	Haina, D.R.
Faison, Vince	.309	44	178	40	55	6	6	4	28	18	45	30	4	L	R	6-0	180	1-22-81	1999	Lyons, Ga.
Gould, Elliott	.196	21	56	7	11	1	0	0	4	5	19	6	3	R	R	6-0	185	10-17-77	1999	Missouri City, Texas
Gutierrez, Said	.316	7	19	2	6	0	0	1	6	2	0	0	0	R	R	5-10	196	3-26-80	1998	Merida, Mexico
Hamel, Jon	.175	27	80	9	14	2	0	0	7	18	23	2	2	R	R	5-11	195	1-11-77	1999	Phoenix, Ariz.
Klatt, Jason	.293	47	174	34	51	7	3	4	38	25	19	12	9	R	R	6-2	175	12-29-75	1999	Arvada, Colo.
Morenz, Shea	.417	4	12	5	5	2	1	0	3	3	2	0	0	L	R	6-2	205	1-22-74	1995	San Antonio, Texas
Pagan, Andres	.187	27	91	15	17	3	0	1	6	9	25	3	0	R	R	6-3	170	3-18-81	1999	Yauco, P.R.
Puccinelli, John	.266	50	177	34	47	12	0	1	20	22	35	3	2	R	R	6-4	180	3-5-81	1999	Sherman Oaks, Calif.
Romero, Nicholas	.293	45	181	31	53	4	3	3	23	16	59	16	4	R	R	5-10	150	1-12-80	1997	Haina, D.R.
Sobet, Renato	.225	39	129	11	29	4	1	2	13	13	28	3	1	R	R	6-2	185	12-30-79	1996	Haina, D.R.
Trzesniak, Nick	.241	29	108	17	26	3	1	0	16	14	39	7	1	R	R	6-0	600	11-19-80	1999	Tinley Park, Ill.
Vandemore, Anthony	.276	50	185	32	51	7	3	3	39	23	51	2	6	L	R	6-3	200	6-10-77	1999	Geneseo, Ill.
Wagner, Mike	.313	34	128	27	40	9	4	5	27	21	37	13	4	R	R	6-0	185	9-11-77	1999	Loveland, Ohio

GAMES BY POSITION: C—Gutierrez 7, Hamel 21, Pagan 19, Trzesniak 13. **1B**—Encarnacion 47, Klatt 10, Pagan 5. **2B**—Duenas 38, Klatt 21. **3B**—Duenas 6, Encarnacion 4, Klatt 3, Puccinelli 48. **SS**—Klatt 13, Puccinelli 1, Romero 43. **OF**—Encarnacion 6, Faison 42, Gould 15, Morenz 3, Sobet 34, Vandemore 46, Wagner 8.

PITCHING

PITCHING	W	L	ERA	G	GS	CG	SV	IP	H	R	ER	BB	SO	B	T	HT	WT	DOB	1st Yr	Resides
Baxter, Gerik	3	0	1.50	8	7	0	0	36	27	7	6	15	45	R	R	6-2	185	3-11-80	1999	Edmonds, Wash.
Cyr, Eric	2	1	3.26	11	5	0	0	39	34	19	14	15	39	R	L	6-4	200	2-11-79	1999	Ada, Okla.
Dowell, Brian	0	0	45.00	2	0	0	0	1	2	8	5	6	0	R	R	6-3	210	12-31-77	1998	Houston, Texas
Jones, Geoff	4	2	4.15	14	0	0	2	39	38	25	18	18	32	L	L	6-5	220	8-10-79	1999	Dolores, Colo.
Meyer, John	1	3	6.06	21	0	0	6	33	34	29	22	30	31	R	R	6-5	230	6-19-79	1998	Fort Worth, Texas
Middlebrook, Jason	1	0	7.20	1	1	0	0	5	9	5	4	1	3	R	R	6-3	215	6-26-75	1996	Grass Lake, Mich.
Peavy, Jacob	7	1	1.34	13	11	1	0	74	52	16	11	23	90	R	R	6-1	180	5-31-81	1999	Semmes, Ala.
Perez, Oliver	1	2	5.08	15	2	0	3	28	28	20	16	16	37	L	L			8-15-81	1999	Culiacan, Mexico
Rosario, Hipolito	0	1	9.82	16	0	0	1	26	47	34	28	13	16	R	R	6-0	165	2-10-80	1997	San Cristobal, D.R.
Soto, Darwin	2	2	3.69	15	4	0	1	39	39	22	16	16	32	R	R	6-1	160	1-15-82	1998	Bani, D.R.
Thompson, Mike	1	7	6.09	13	13	0	0	65	78	52	44	27	62	R	R	6-4	185	11-6-80	1999	Lamar, Colo.
Tollberg, Brian	0	0	4.50	2	2	0	0	4	4	2	2	0	6	R	R	6-3	195	9-16-72	1994	Bradenton, Fla.
Velazquez, Ernesto	2	3	3.71	18	0	0	2	34	44	19	14	3	15	R	R			7-31-81	1999	Culiacan, Mexico
Vitek, Josh	6	2	3.99	12	10	0	0	47	43	22	21	24	48	R	R	6-3	200	6-18-80	1999	Fayetteville, Texas
Webster, Jeremy	1	0	4.26	7	0	0	0	13	13	11	6	13	16	L	L	6-0	195	3-20-79	1999	Sandy, Utah

Organization Statistics

SANFRANCISCOGIANTS

Injuries prove costly during final season at Candlestick

BY MARK GONZALES

The Giants left Candlestick (3Com) Park for the final time in a manner like their brave fans who attended the cold, wind swept stadium for the past 40 years—aching.

A productive 1999 season was marred by injuries that cost the team a shot at seriously competing for the National League West title. The Giants were knocked out of first place on July 24 and slowly faded, thanks largely to injuries. Eleven players spent time on the disabled list.

In their final season at the Stick, the Giants went 49-32 at home and finished with a 1,776-1,398 record in 40 seasons.

Barry Bonds, who had served only one stint on the disabled list in his 13 previous seasons, missed 7½ weeks because of surgery to repair a torn tendon and remove bone chips in his left elbow. Bonds still recovered to hit a team-high 34 home runs, including 14 during a 16-game stretch in August. But he had to miss the final three games because of arthroscopic surgery on his right knee. He hit .262, his lowest average in 10 years.

Perhaps the boldest performance came from right fielder Ellis Burks, who played 120 games despite painful knees that required surgery less than a week after the season ended. Burks managed to hit 31 homers and drive in 96 runs in 390 at-bats. The Giants were left playing "what if," as the foursome of Bonds, Burks, Jeff Kent (who missed 2½ weeks because of an injured toe on his left foot) and J.T. Snow played only 48 games together.

The farm system, under scrutiny during the 1990s for its perceived lack of development and its will-

Jeff Kent   **Calvin Murray**

Players of the Year

MAJOR LEAGUE: Jeff Kent, 2b
Kent hit .290 with 23 home runs and led the Giants with 101 RBIs despite missing 24 games due to injury.

MINOR LEAGUE: Calvin Murray, of
Murray broke through in his seventh pro season for a .334 average, 24 home runs, 122 runs and 42 stolen bases at Fresno.

ingness to trade top prospects, produced two pitchers for the rotation. Righthander Russ Ortiz, a closer during his first two professional seasons, emerged as an ace in his first full major league season, winning 18 games and leading the staff in innings and strikeouts.

Righthander Joe Nathan, who was drafted in 1995 as a shortstop and sat out 1996 to contemplate his career, won seven games, the most by a Giants rookie in five years. Nathan surfaced as one of the staff's top pitchers once he was called up to stay on Aug. 16.

The Giants move into Pacific Bell Park in 2000 and expect more help from their farm system. Speedy center fielder Calvin Murray, a 1992 first-round pick who had never lived up to expectations, was the Pacific Coast League player of the year and could provide speed and defense in the spacious outfield at Pac Bell. Murray hit .334, scored 122 runs and stole 42 bases.

The Giants decided they had enough pitching depth to trade two first-round picks, righthanders Nate Bump and Jason Grilli, to the Marlins for righthander Livan Hernandez. Righthander Jake Esteves earned a midseason promotion after going 6-1 with a 2.01 ERA for Class A San Jose, then went 8-2 with a 3.63 ERA with Double-A Shreveport.

First-round pick Kurt Ainsworth lived up to his billing, striking out 61 in 45 innings while posting a 1.61 ERA for short-season Salem-Keizer. Ainsworth, who signed for a $1.3 million bonus, then went 2-0 with a 0.44 ERA in three starts in the California League playoffs for San Jose.

ORGANIZATION LEADERS

BATTING
*AVG	Sean McGowan, San Jose/Salem-Keizer	.336
R	Calvin Murray, Fresno	122
H	Calvin Murray, Fresno	183
TB	Calvin Murray, Fresno	297
2B	Three tied at	33
3B	Arturo McDowell, Bakersfield	10
HR	Mike Glendenning, Shreveport/San Jose	28
RBI	Mike Glendenning, Shreveport/San Jose	99
BB	Mike Glendenning, Shreveport/San Jose	83
SO	Tim Flaherty, San Jose	168
SB	Calvin Murray, Fresno	42

PITCHING
W	Two tied at	14
L	Manny Bermudez, Bakersfield	14
#ERA	Jake Esteves, Shreveport/San Jose	2.92
G	Robbie Crabtree, Fresno/Shreveport	58
CG	15 tied at	1
SV	Todd Ozias, Bakersfield	26
IP	Tony Coscia, Bakersfield	172
BB	Chris Jones, San Jose	87
SO	Aaron Fultz, Fresno	151

*Minimum 250 At-Bats #Minimum 75 Innings

San Francisco GIANTS

Manager: Dusty Baker

Organization Statistics

1999 Record: 86-76, .531 (2nd, NL West)

BATTING	AVG	G	AB	R	H	2B	3B	HR	RBI	BB	SO	SB	CS	B	T	HT	WT	DOB	1st Yr	Resides
Aurilia, Rich	.281	152	558	68	157	23	1	22	80	43	71	2	3	R	R	6-0	170	9-2-71	1992	Hazlet, N.J.
Benard, Marvin	.290	149	562	100	163	36	5	16	64	55	97	27	14	L	L	5-10	180	1-20-71	1992	Scottsdale, Ariz.
Bonds, Barry	.262	102	355	91	93	20	2	34	83	73	62	15	2	L	L	6-1	206	7-24-64	1985	Redwood Shores, Calif.
Burks, Ellis	.282	120	390	73	110	19	0	31	96	69	86	7	5	R	R	6-2	205	9-11-64	1983	Denver, Colo.
Canizaro, Jay	.444	12	18	5	8	2	0	1	9	1	2	1	0	R	R	5-10	175	7-4-73	1993	Orange, Texas
Delgado, Wilson	.254	35	71	7	18	2	1	0	3	5	9	1	0	S	R	5-11	165	7-15-75	1993	San Cristobal, D.R.
Guzman, Edwards	.000	14	15	0	0	0	0	0	0	0	4	0	0	L	R	5-11	205	9-11-76	1996	Naranjito, P.R.
Hayes, Charlie	.205	95	264	33	54	9	1	6	48	33	41	3	1	R	R	6-0	215	5-29-65	1983	Tomball, Texas
Javier, Stan	.276	112	333	49	92	15	1	3	30	29	55	13	6	S	R	6-0	195	1-9-64	1981	Santo Domingo, D.R.
Kent, Jeff	.290	138	511	86	148	40	2	23	101	61	112	13	6	R	R	6-1	185	3-7-68	1989	Spicewood, Texas
Martinez, Ramon	.264	61	144	21	38	6	0	5	19	14	17	1	2	R	R	6-1	170	10-10-72	1993	Toa Alta, P.R.
Mayne, Brent	.301	117	322	39	97	32	0	2	39	43	65	2	2	L	R	6-1	190	4-19-68	1989	Corona Del Mar, Calif.
Mirabelli, Doug	.253	33	87	10	22	6	0	1	10	9	25	0	0	R	R	6-1	215	10-18-70	1992	Wichita, Kan.
Mueller, Bill	.290	116	414	61	120	24	0	2	36	65	52	4	2	S	R	5-11	173	3-17-71	1993	Maryland Heights, Mo.
Murray, Calvin	.263	15	19	1	5	2	0	0	5	2	4	1	0	R	R	5-11	185	7-30-71	1993	Houston, Texas
Rios, Armando	.327	72	150	32	49	9	0	7	29	24	35	7	4	L	L	5-9	178	9-13-71	1994	Supply, N.C.
Santangelo, F.P.	.260	113	254	49	66	17	3	3	26	53	54	12	4	S	R	5-10	165	10-24-67	1989	El Dorado Hills, Calif.
Servais, Scott	.273	69	198	21	54	10	0	5	21	13	31	0	0	R	R	6-2	210	6-4-67	1989	Castle Rock, Colo.
Snow, J.T.	.274	161	570	93	156	25	2	24	98	86	121	0	4	S	L	6-2	202	2-26-68	1989	Corona Del Mar, Calif.

PITCHING	W	L	ERA	G	GS	CG	SV	IP	H	R	ER	BB	SO	B	T	HT	WT	DOB	1st Yr	Resides
Brock, Chris	6	8	5.48	19	19	0	0	107	124	69	65	41	76	R	R	6-0	175	2-5-70	1992	Altamonte Springs, Fla.
Del Toro, Miguel	0	0	4.18	14	0	0	0	24	24	11	11	11	20	R	R	6-1	170	6-22-72	1992	Sonora, Mexico
Embree, Alan	3	2	3.38	68	0	0	0	59	42	22	22	26	53	L	L	6-2	190	1-23-70	1990	Vancouver, Wash.
Estes, Shawn	11	11	4.92	32	32	1	0	203	209	121	111	112	159	R	L	6-2	200	2-18-73	1991	San Francisco, Calif.
Gardner, Mark	5	11	6.47	29	21	1	0	139	142	103	100	57	86	R	R	6-1	215	3-1-62	1985	Fresno, Calif.
Hernandez, Livan	3	3	4.38	10	10	0	0	64	66	32	31	21	47	R	R	6-2	225	2-20-75	1996	Miami Beach, Fla.
2-team (20 Florida)	8	12	4.64	30	30	2	0	200	227	110	103	76	144							
Johnstone, John	4	6	2.60	62	0	0	3	66	48	24	19	20	56	R	R	6-3	195	11-25-68	1987	Scottsdale, Ariz.
Nathan, Joe	7	4	4.18	19	14	0	1	90	84	45	42	46	54	R	R	6-4	195	11-22-74	1995	Circleville, N.Y.
Nen, Robb	3	8	3.98	72	0	0	37	72	79	36	32	27	77	R	R	6-5	210	11-28-69	1987	Weston, Fla.
Ortiz, Russ	18	9	3.81	33	33	3	0	208	189	109	88	125	164	R	R	6-1	190	6-5-74	1995	Norman, Okla.
Patrick, Bronswell	1	0	10.13	6	0	0	1	5	9	7	6	3	6	R	R	6-1	220	9-16-70	1988	Winterville, N.C.
Rodriguez, Felix	2	3	3.80	47	0	0	0	66	67	32	28	29	55	R	R	6-1	180	12-5-72	1990	Montecristi, D.R.
Rodriguez, Rich	3	0	5.24	62	0	0	0	57	60	33	33	28	44	L	L	6-0	200	3-1-63	1984	Duluth, Ga.
Rueter, Kirk	15	10	5.41	33	33	1	0	185	219	118	111	55	94	L	L	6-2	210	12-1-70	1991	Nashville, Ill.
Spradlin, Jerry	3	1	4.19	59	0	0	0	58	59	31	27	29	52	S	R	6-7	246	6-14-67	1988	Anaheim, Calif.
Tavarez, Julian	2	0	5.93	47	0	0	0	55	65	38	36	25	33	L	R	6-2	190	5-22-73	1990	Broadway Heights, Ohio

FIELDING

Catcher	PCT	G	PO	A	E	DP	PB
Guzman	1.000	1	1	0	0	0	0
Mayne	.995	105	597	47	3	9	2
Mirabelli	1.000	30	156	11	0	2	0
Servais	.992	62	362	23	3	5	6

First Base	PCT	G	PO	A	E	DP
Hayes	1.000	20	103	8	0	9
Kent	1.000	1	7	2	0	2
Servais	1.000	1	1	0	0	0
Snow	.996	160	1221	122	6	123

Second Base	PCT	G	PO	A	E	DP
Canizaro	1.000	4	2	5	0	1
Delgado	.963	15	17	9	1	2
Kent	.984	133	279	325	10	90
Martinez	.992	27	50	68	1	15
Mueller	1.000	3	2	0	0	0
Santangelo	1.000	11	13	21	0	1

Third Base	PCT	G	PO	A	E	DP
Guzman	1.000	5	2	7	0	0

	PCT	G	PO	A	E	DP
Hayes	.940	55	27	83	7	3
Martinez	1.000	11	5	9	0	0
Mueller	.958	108	81	195	12	17
Santangelo	1.000	3	1	0	0	0

Shortstop	PCT	G	PO	A	E	DP
Aurilia	.957	150	218	411	28	97
Delgado	.932	20	22	33	4	10
Martinez	.878	12	11	25	5	4
Santangelo	.000	1	0	0	0	0

Outfield	PCT	G	PO	A	E	DP
Benard	.988	142	323	5	4	1
Bonds	.984	96	177	4	3	2
Burks	.991	107	210	3	2	2
Hayes	.000	1	0	0	0	0
Javier	.976	94	158	4	4	3
Murray	1.000	9	6	0	0	0
Rios	.978	53	84	5	2	1
Santangelo	.993	81	130	4	1	1

DAVID SEELIG

Russ Ortiz

Barry Bonds
Hit 34 homers in limited playing time

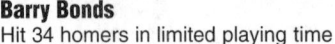

Mike Glendenning
Led system with 28 homers and 99 RBIs

FARM SYSTEM

Director of Player Personnel: Dick Tidrow

Class	Farm Team	League	W	L	Pct.	Finish*	Manager	First Yr
AAA	Fresno (Calif.) Grizzlies	Pacific Coast	73	69	.514	7th (16)	Ron Roenicke	1998
AA	Shreveport (La.) Captains	Texas	71	69	.507	4th (8)	Shane Turner	1979
A#	Bakersfield (Calif.) Blaze	California	64	76	.457	7th (10)	Keith Comstock	1997
A#	San Jose (Calif.) Giants	California	75	65	.536	t-4th (10)	Lenn Sakata	1988
A	Salem-Keizer (Ore.) Volcanoes	Northwest	37	39	.487	6th (8)	Frank Reberger	1997

*Finish in overall standings (No. of teams in league)   #Advanced level

FRESNO — Class AAA

PACIFIC COAST LEAGUE

BATTING	AVG	G	AB	R	H	2B	3B	HR	RBI	BB	SO	SB	CS	B	T	HT	WT	DOB	1st Yr	Resides
Byas, Michael	.364	5	22	4	8	2	0	0	2	5	4	2	1	S	R	6-0	170	4-21-76	1997	Chesterfield, Mo.
Campusano, Carlos	.283	16	46	2	13	2	0	0	3	2	9	0	0	R	R	5-11	160	9-2-75	1994	Palave, D.R.
Canizaro, Jay	.280	106	364	77	102	20	2	26	78	49	79	16	5	R	R	5-10	175	7-4-73	1993	Orange, Texas
Crespo, Felipe	.332	112	385	98	128	27	5	24	84	78	73	17	8	S	R	5-11	200	3-5-73	1991	Caguas, P.R.
Delgado, Wilson	.300	57	213	28	64	10	3	1	33	18	35	4	2	S	R	5-11	165	7-15-75	1993	San Cristobal, D.R.
Faircloth, Chad	.000	1	1	0	0	0	0	0	0	0	0	0	0	L	R	6-0	180	4-25-75	1997	Winston-Salem, N.C.
Guzman, Edwards	.274	90	358	48	98	13	0	7	48	17	50	6	5	L	R	5-11	205	9-11-76	1996	Naranjito, P.R.
Leach, Jalal	.294	116	371	58	109	19	5	15	75	27	67	8	7	L	L	6-2	200	3-14-69	1990	Novato, Calif.
Martinez, Ramon	.325	29	114	13	37	7	1	2	17	10	17	2	0	R	R	6-1	170	10-10-72	1993	Toa Alta, P.R.
Marval, Raul	.300	97	280	41	84	15	1	7	46	16	48	2	3	R	R	6-0	170	12-13-75	1993	Cabodare, Venez.
Mashore, Damon	.262	110	347	62	91	20	1	20	69	38	98	7	3	R	R	5-11	195	10-31-69	1991	Concord, Calif.
Mayes, Craig	.260	62	169	19	44	12	0	3	16	8	26	1	1	L	R	5-10	195	5-8-70	1992	Washington, Mich.
Mirabelli, Doug	.313	86	320	63	100	24	1	14	51	48	56	8	2	R	R	6-1	215	10-18-70	1992	Wichita, Kan.
Mueller, Bill	.417	3	12	3	5	0	1	0	6	0	0	0	0	S	R	5-11	173	3-17-71	1993	Maryland Heights, Mo.
Murray, Calvin	.334	130	548	122	183	31	7	23	73	49	88	42	14	R	R	5-11	185	7-30-71	1993	Houston, Texas
Rios, Armando	.275	31	109	24	30	3	0	4	21	11	22	3	1	L	L	5-9	178	9-13-71	1994	Supply, N.C.
Servais, Scott	.273	3	11	3	3	1	1	0	2	0	1	0	0	R	R	6-2	210	6-4-67	1989	Castle Rock, Colo.
Tavarez, Jesus	.167	2	6	0	1	0	0	0	0	0	0	0	0	S	R	6-0	170	3-26-71	1990	Santo Domingo, D.R.
Torrealba, Yorvit	.254	17	63	9	16	2	0	2	10	4	11	0	1	R	R	5-11	180	7-19-78	1995	Guarenas, Venez.
Voigt, Jack	.194	23	67	12	13	4	1	1	5	17	21	1	0	R	R	6-1	178	5-17-66	1987	Venice, Fla.
Williams, Keith	.282	89	294	46	83	23	3	11	50	34	50	4	2	R	R	6-0	190	4-21-72	1993	Bedford, Pa.
Woods, Ken	.324	124	469	77	152	23	4	6	73	33	45	19	4	R	R	5-10	175	8-2-70	1992	Los Angeles, Calif.
Young, Travis	.250	26	92	15	23	1	1	2	11	9	23	3	2	R	R	6-1	185	9-8-74	1997	Albuquerque, N.M.

PITCHING	W	L	ERA	G	GS	CG	SV	IP	H	R	ER	BB	SO	B	T	HT	WT	DOB	1st Yr	Resides
Bailey, Cory	2	1	3.30	43	0	0	18	46	47	24	17	17	52	R	R	6-1	202	1-24-71	1991	Marion, Ill.
Connelly, Steve	6	4	5.25	54	0	0	2	72	93	58	42	32	47	R	R	6-4	210	4-27-74	1995	Long Beach, Calif.
Corps, Edwin	0	0	3.86	4	0	0	0	7	9	7	3	3	11	R	R	5-11	190	11-3-72	1994	Carolina, P.R.

PITCHING	W	L	ERA	G	GS	CG	SV	IP	H	R	ER	BB	SO	B	T	HT	WT	DOB	1st Yr	Resides
Crabtree, Robbie	1	4	5.24	22	1	0	1	34	37	23	20	10	40	R	R	6-1	175	11-25-72	1996	Anaheim, Calif.
Del Toro, Miguel	4	2	4.42	40	0	0	0	71	76	41	35	29	71	R	R	6-1	170	6-22-72	1992	Sonora, Mexico
Estrella, Luis	0	1	12.34	8	0	0	0	12	23	16	16	7	5	R	R	6-2	220	10-7-74	1996	Santa Ana, Calif.
Fultz, Aaron	9	8	4.98	37	20	1	0	137	141	87	76	51	151	L	L	6-0	196	9-4-73	1992	Northport, Ala.
Grilli, Jason	7	5	5.54	19	19	1	0	101	124	69	62	39	76	R	R	6-4	185	11-11-76	1997	Baldwinsville, N.Y.
Jensen, Ryan	11	10	5.12	27	27	0	0	156	160	96	89	68	150	R	R	6-0	205	9-17-75	1996	West Valley, Utah
McMullen, Mike	2	2	4.36	41	0	0	0	66	52	36	32	41	56	R	R	6-2	185	10-13-73	1993	St. Louis, Mo.
Nathan, Joe	6	4	4.46	13	13	1	0	75	68	44	37	36	82	R	R	6-4	195	11-22-74	1995	Circleville, N.Y.
Oropesa, Eddie	6	5	4.85	21	18	1	0	102	113	69	55	49	61	L	L	6-3	215	11-23-71	1993	Conoga Park, Calif.
Patrick, Bronswell	14	11	4.88	28	28	1	0	164	194	116	89	42	142	R	R	6-1	220	9-16-70	1988	Winterville, N.C.
Soderstrom, Steve	2	8	6.78	22	13	0	0	72	90	64	54	35	58	R	R	6-3	215	4-3-72	1993	Turlock, Calif.
Tavarez, Julian	0	0	2.25	4	1	0	0	8	3	2	2	3	9	L	R	6-2	190	5-22-73	1990	Broadway Heights, Ohio
Verdugo, Jason	1	0	4.87	9	2	0	0	20	19	14	11	9	29	R	R	6-2	195	3-28-75	1997	Tempe, Ariz.
Weber, Ben	2	4	3.34	51	0	0	8	86	78	34	32	28	67	R	R	6-4	180	11-17-69	1991	Groves, Texas

FIELDING

Catcher	PCT	G	PO	A	E	DP	PB
Guzman	.957	31	229	13	11	1	7
Mayes	.992	39	239	15	2	0	3
Mirabelli	.993	66	473	58	4	2	2
Servais	1.000	3	23	1	0	0	1
Torrealba	.988	17	155	12	2	1	6

First Base	PCT	G	PO	A	E	DP
Crespo	.993	70	560	47	4	61
Guzman	.935	4	27	2	2	3
Mayes	1.000	2	11	2	0	3
Mirabelli	.994	19	146	15	1	12
Je. Tavarez	1.000	1	14	1	0	0
Voigt	.994	16	148	6	1	13
Williams	.964	11	74	6	3	2
Woods	.984	31	225	15	4	20

Second Base	PCT	G	PO	A	E	DP
Campusano	1.000	2	2	2	0	0
Canizaro	.969	99	181	263	14	59
Crespo	.886	9	14	17	4	2
Delgado	1.000	1	1	0	0	0
Marval	1.000	6	10	10	0	4
Woods	.789	5	6	9	4	1
Young	.992	26	46	76	1	22

Third Base	PCT	G	PO	A	E	DP
Campusano	.885	11	6	17	3	1
Canizaro	.667	1	0	2	1	0
Crespo	.813	5	6	7	3	0
Guzman	.915	58	26	114	13	11
Martinez	1.000	1	2	1	0	0
Marval	.857	12	5	19	4	1
Mueller	.800	3	2	10	3	0
Voigt	1.000	5	1	10	0	0
Woods	.877	54	29	92	17	12

Shortstop	PCT	G	PO	A	E	DP
Canizaro	1.000	2	3	3	0	2
Crespo	1.000	2	4	4	0	0
Delgado	.944	56	85	166	15	34
Martinez	.950	26	24	71	5	10
Marval	.940	59	72	146	14	32
Woods	.909	6	5	15	2	3

Outfield	PCT	G	PO	A	E	DP
Byas	1.000	5	10	1	0	0
Crespo	.950	24	36	2	2	0
Leach	.975	90	153	5	4	0
Mashore	.993	92	133	5	1	0
Murray	.980	129	284	8	6	0
Rios	1.000	20	28	1	0	0
Williams	1.000	59	85	7	0	1
Woods	1.000	24	34	3	0	1

SHREVEPORT — Class AA

TEXAS LEAGUE

BATTING	AVG	G	AB	R	H	2B	3B	HR	RBI	BB	SO	SB	CS	B	T	HT	WT	DOB	1st Yr	Resides
Byas, Michael	.271	129	487	76	132	9	1	0	41	68	79	31	15	S	R	6-0	170	4-21-76	1997	Chesterfield, Mo.
Campusano, Carlos	.154	15	39	5	6	0	2	1	6	3	10	1	0	R	R	5-11	160	9-2-75	1994	Palave, D.R.
Chiaramonte, Giuseppe	.245	114	400	54	98	20	2	19	74	40	88	4	2	R	R	6-0	200	2-19-76	1997	Santa Cruz, Calif.
Clark, Doug	.220	15	50	6	11	3	0	1	6	4	9	0	0	L	R	6-2	205	3-5-76	1998	Springfield, Mass.
Dilone, Juan	.253	112	340	52	86	19	6	5	44	46	87	11	7	S	R	6-1	188	5-10-73	1991	Higuey, D.R.
Faircloth, Chad	.216	23	37	4	8	2	0	0	3	2	14	0	0	L	R	6-0	180	4-25-75	1997	Winston-Salem, N.C.
Feliz, Pedro	.253	131	491	52	124	24	6	13	77	19	90	4	2	R	R	6-1	180	4-27-77	1994	Azua, D.R.
Glendenning, Mike	.264	32	106	14	28	6	0	5	19	12	30	1	1	R	R	6-0	225	8-26-76	1996	West Hills, Calif.
Gulseth, Mark	.228	62	145	13	33	6	0	1	17	18	26	1	0	L	R	6-4	215	11-12-71	1993	Callaway, Minn.
Magruder, Chris	.256	133	476	78	122	21	4	6	60	69	85	17	12	S	R	5-11	200	4-26-77	1998	Yakima, Wash.
Marval, Raul	.250	2	4	0	1	0	0	0	0	0	1	0	1	R	R	6-0	170	12-13-75	1993	Cabodare, Venez.
Mendoza, Carlos	.202	111	332	35	67	16	4	3	34	36	65	1	4	S	R	6-0	175	11-27-79	1996	Barquisimeto, Venez.
Minor, Damon	.273	136	473	76	129	33	4	20	82	80	115	1	0	L	L	6-7	230	1-5-74	1996	Edmond, Okla.
Priess, Matt	.167	5	12	1	2	0	0	1	1	1	3	0	0	R	R	6-2	200	11-24-74	1997	Brea, Calif.
Ransom, Cody	.122	14	41	6	5	0	0	2	4	4	22	0	0	R	R	6-2	190	2-17-76	1998	Chandler, Ariz.
Torrealba, Yorvit	.244	65	217	25	53	10	1	4	19	9	34	0	2	R	R	5-11	180	7-19-78	1995	Guarenas, Venez.
Tyler, Josh	.263	105	331	41	87	17	0	3	39	30	53	14	5	R	R	6-1	185	9-6-73	1994	Green Lane, Pa.
Young, Travis	.264	108	416	68	110	28	2	5	38	33	75	16	11	R	R	6-1	185	9-8-74	1997	Albuquerque, N.M.

PITCHING	W	L	ERA	G	GS	CG	SV	IP	H	R	ER	BB	SO	B	T	HT	WT	DOB	1st Yr	Resides
Bump, Nate	4	10	3.31	17	17	1	0	92	85	40	34	32	59	R	R	6-2	185	7-24-76	1998	Monroeton, Pa.
Chavarria, David	0	1	7.47	10	1	0	0	16	24	22	13	9	16	L	R	6-7	235	5-19-73	1991	Lake Suzy, Fla.
Corps, Edwin	4	4	4.59	24	12	0	0	84	98	54	43	29	34	R	R	5-11	190	11-3-72	1994	Carolina, P.R.
Crabtree, Robbie	4	2	2.56	36	0	0	2	63	50	21	18	18	65	R	R	6-1	175	11-25-72	1996	Anaheim, Calif.
Davis, Jason	5	1	1.27	52	0	0	21	64	42	9	9	22	54	L	L	6-3	195	8-15-74	1996	Winters, Calif.
Esteves, Jake	8	2	3.63	15	14	0	0	92	76	40	37	23	53	R	R	6-1	200	7-31-75	1998	Auburn, Calif.
Estrella, Luis	6	4	3.02	40	5	0	4	92	77	33	31	33	75	R	R	6-2	220	10-7-74	1996	Santa Ana, Calif.
Heckman, Andy	10	6	4.08	23	23	1	0	132	142	67	60	43	70	R	L	6-3	185	10-17-71	1992	Pine Bush, N.Y.
Joseph, Kevin	0	2	1.42	7	0	0	0	13	8	4	2	5	16	R	R	6-4	200	8-1-76	1997	Dallas, Texas
Knoll, Brian	9	7	3.51	33	17	1	1	128	117	54	50	34	91	R	R	6-3	200	8-4-73	1995	Corona, Calif.
Linebrink, Scott	1	8	6.44	10	10	0	0	43	48	31	31	14	33	R	R	6-3	185	8-4-76	1997	Austin, Texas
Malloy, Bill	2	0	6.26	17	0	0	1	27	31	20	19	15	16	R	R	6-2	225	5-22-75	1996	Piscataway, N.J.
Nathan, Joe	0	1	3.12	2	2	0	0	9	5	4	3	7	7	R	R	6-4	195	11-22-74	1995	Circleville, N.Y.
Ricabal, Dan	2	0	4.91	8	0	0	0	11	15	6	6	5	4	R	R	6-1	185	7-8-72	1994	Temple City, Calif.
Riley, Michael	8	3	2.11	30	13	1	1	111	80	35	26	53	107	L	L	6-2	165	1-2-75	1996	Seaford, Del.
Tucker, Ben	3	3	4.18	18	0	0	1	28	37	19	13	12	12	R	R	6-4	220	11-6-73	1995	Fresno, Calif.
Urban, Jeff	2	7	5.81	14	14	0	0	70	100	54	45	19	54	R	L	6-8	215	1-25-77	1998	Alexandria, Ind.
Verdugo, Jason	2	3	3.02	40	0	0	8	63	58	34	21	12	46	R	R	6-2	195	3-28-75	1997	Tempe, Ariz.
Vogelsong, Ryan	0	2	7.31	6	6	0	0	28	40	25	23	15	23	R	R	6-3	195	7-22-77	1998	North Grafton, Mass.
Zerbe, Chad	1	3	1.96	7	6	0	0	41	32	13	9	10	16	L	L	6-0	190	4-27-72	1991	Tampa, Fla.

FIELDING

Catcher	PCT	G	PO	A	E	DP	PB
Chiaramonte	.987	88	550	40	8	3	9
Priess	.963	5	24	2	1	0	0
Torrealba	.994	49	299	43	2	0	3
Tyler	1.000	1	1	0	0	0	0

First Base	PCT	G	PO	A	E	DP
Dilone	1.000	5	20	0	0	1
Gulseth	.976	12	76	4	2	12
Minor	.993	130	1160	104	9	95
Tyler	1.000	2	5	0	0	1

Second Base	PCT	G	PO	A	E	DP
Campusano	.750	2	3	0	1	0

FIELDING

	PCT	G	PO	A	E	DP
Mendoza	1.000	1	0	1	0	0
Tyler	.942	33	63	67	8	8
Young	.974	108	242	319	15	77

Third Base	PCT	G	PO	A	E	DP
Campusano..	1.000	1	0	1	0	0
Feliz	.934	129	76	304	27	23
Tyler	.875	12	11	17	4	1

Shortstop	PCT	G	PO	A	E	DP
Campusano....	.940	10	11	36	3	6
Marval	1.000	2	1	3	0	1
Mendoza	.951	110	137	329	24	52
Ransom.........	.953	14	13	48	3	7
Tyler	.909	19	25	35	6	11

Outfield	PCT	G	PO	A	E	DP
Byas	.985	127	306	14	5	3

	PCT	G	PO	A	E	DP
Clark............	1.000	13	19	1	0	0
Dilone............	.974	90	141	7	4	2
Faircloth	.900	10	9	0	1	0
Glendenning...	.979	26	44	2	1	0
Gulseth..........	.917	13	11	0	1	0
Magruder........	.988	128	241	5	3	1
Tyler	.945	39	48	4	3	0

BAKERSFIELD — Class A

CALIFORNIA LEAGUE

BATTING	AVG	G	AB	R	H	2B	3B	HR	RBI	BB	SO	SB	CS	B	T	HT	WT	DOB	1st Yr	Resides
Allen, Jeff	.265	130	480	80	127	32	3	10	65	47	130	24	5	R	R	6-1	190	6-8-76	1998	Oak Brook, Ill.
Bertrand, Ben	.190	12	21	3	4	1	0	0	0	3	7	0	0	R	R	6-0	195	8-5-75	1998	Hillsboro, Ore.
Burns, Xavier	.218	80	229	28	50	9	3	3	29	19	70	10	9	R	R	5-11	190	5-8-75	1996	Chicago, Ill.
Campusano, Carlos	.353	14	51	7	18	2	0	1	4	1	13	2	2	R	R	5-11	160	9-2-75	1994	Palave, D.R.
2-team (27 San Jose) ..	.326	41	135	20	44	4	1	2	11	7	28	6	3							
Clark, Doug	.326	118	420	67	137	17	2	11	58	59	89	17	11	L	R	6-2	205	3-5-76	1998	Springfield, Mass.
Faircloth, Chad	.262	51	145	14	38	12	1	0	16	14	35	5	4	L	R	6-0	180	4-25-75	1997	Winston-Salem, N.C.
Fuentes, Joel	.198	64	162	20	32	5	0	0	16	19	38	5	1	S	R	6-0	178	5-27-76	1997	Juncos, P.R.
Greene, Clay	.257	46	148	19	38	2	0	0	17	18	44	16	4	R	R	6-0	185	11-10-74	1997	Cleveland, Tenn.
Hill, Steve	.266	135	522	78	139	16	6	0	60	40	99	39	13	S	R	5-10	180	12-10-75	1998	Enid, Okla.
Luster, Jeremy	.201	52	184	26	37	4	3	0	19	22	54	9	4	S	R	6-3	212	6-10-77	1999	Kennesaw, Ga.
Mapes, Jake	.176	11	17	3	3	2	0	0	3	1	7	0	0	R	R	6-4	210	3-1-79	1999	Hemet, Calif.
McDowell, Arturo	.222	121	441	66	98	16	10	2	37	49	140	28	23	L	L	6-1	175	9-7-79	1998	Jackson, Miss.
Messner, Jake	.291	55	172	33	50	11	6	7	35	16	45	2	2	L	L	6-1	205	5-18-77	1995	Sacramento, Calif.
Niemet, Jake	.263	27	57	7	15	4	0	0	7	13	9	3	1	R	R	6-2	204	8-23-76	1999	Columbus, Ohio
Ransom, Cody	.275	99	356	69	98	12	6	11	47	54	108	15	8	R	R	6-2	190	2-17-76	1998	Chandler, Ariz.
Rodriguez, Guillermo ..	.290	41	93	10	27	5	0	1	11	3	18	4	0	R	R	5-11	190	5-15-78	1996	Barquisimeto, Venez.
Serrano, Sammy	.276	125	463	55	128	30	1	9	80	30	78	4	6	R	R	6-2	205	12-3-76	1998	Woodbridge, Va.
Summers, John	.295	114	403	50	119	19	2	7	51	40	65	2	5	S	R	6-0	195	11-16-76	1998	Butte, Mont.
Torcato, Tony	.291	110	422	50	123	25	0	4	58	30	67	2	1	L	R	6-1	195	10-25-79	1998	Woodland, Calif.

GAMES BY POSITION: C—Bertrand 10, Mapes 7, Rodriguez 36, Serrano 114. **1B**—Luster 48, Messner 3, Niemet 14, Rodriguez 3, Summers 86. **2B**—Fuentes 49, Hill 107. **3B**—Burns 61, Fuentes 9, Hill 2, Niemet 1, Summers 4, Torcato 82. **SS**—Campusano 14, Fuentes 3, Hill 32, Ransom 99. **OF**—Allen 123, Clark 109, Faircloth 39, Greene 31, McDowell 116, Messner 30.

PITCHING	W	L	ERA	G	GS	CG	SV	IP	H	R	ER	BB	SO	B	T	HT	WT	DOB	1st Yr	Resides
Bermudez, Manny	5	14	5.99	32	22	1	0	146	183	121	97	66	65	R	R	6-1	195	12-15-76	1995	Antioch, Calif.
Connolly, Keith	7	8	4.34	54	0	0	3	83	61	41	40	47	95	R	R	6-3	205	12-9-74	1998	Washingtonville, N.Y.
Coscia, Tony	10	11	4.51	28	28	1	0	172	186	100	86	38	133	R	R	6-1	170	4-6-74	1995	Mill Valley, Calif.
Cox, Ryan	1	4	4.86	7	7	0	0	33	46	22	18	3	30	R	R	6-3	195	12-25-76	1999	Stewardson, Ill.
Featherstone, Deron ...	0	0	7.59	6	0	0	0	11	13	17	9	17	13	R	R	6-2	175	6-20-77	1998	Hendersonville, N.C.
Fields, Brian	2	0	5.80	20	0	0	1	36	43	25	23	12	22	R	L	6-1	175	8-21-74	1998	Greenville, N.C.
Flores, Benito	2	1	3.67	34	6	0	0	81	81	42	33	34	63	L	L	6-1	185	1-24-76	1998	Placentia, Calif.
Horgan, Joe	6	10	5.22	25	19	1	0	117	129	76	68	43	101	L	L	6-1	200	6-7-77	1996	Rancho Cordova, Calif.
Huller, Mike	0	0	18.00	1	0	0	0	1	2	2	2	2	0	R	L	6-1	190	8-25-77	1998	Bel Air, Md.
Johnson, Eric	1	0	5.82	17	0	0	0	22	22	14	14	21	14	R	R	6-4	195	9-12-77	1997	Newberg, Ore.
Oropesa, Eddie	2	0	3.60	2	1	0	0	10	13	5	4	1	10	L	L	6-3	215	11-23-71	1993	Conoga Park, Calif.
Ozias, Todd	5	5	2.56	52	0	0	26	56	47	21	16	25	67	R	R	6-1	185	8-19-76	1998	Coral Springs, Fla.
Prata, Danny	9	9	3.91	27	27	0	0	143	143	80	62	54	87	L	L	6-0	190	9-13-78	1999	Repentigny, Quebec
Rajotte, Jason	1	1	5.23	47	0	0	2	53	63	35	31	26	43	L	L	6-0	180	12-15-72	1993	West Warwick, R.I.
Rice, Nathan	0	0	22.85	3	0	0	0	4	11	14	11	10	3	L	L	6-5	215	4-19-74	1997	Visalia, Calif.
Travis, Jesse	2	5	8.74	14	9	0	0	45	71	47	44	20	27	R	R	6-1	195	11-4-74	1997	Seattle, Wash.
Valenti, Jon	4	1	5.12	46	0	0	1	84	85	55	48	39	69	R	R	6-1	195	11-26-73	1994	Bakersfield, Calif.
Wells, Zach	0	0	3.00	4	0	0	0	6	6	4	2	1	3	R	R	6-4	205	2-23-77	1997	Clayton, Calif.
Zerbe, Chad	7	7	3.64	21	21	0	0	126	124	66	51	33	81	L	L	6-0	190	4-27-72	1991	Tampa, Fla.

SAN JOSE — Class A

CALIFORNIA LEAGUE

BATTING	AVG	G	AB	R	H	2B	3B	HR	RBI	BB	SO	SB	CS	B	T	HT	WT	DOB	1st Yr	Resides
Bazzani, Matt	.237	34	93	18	22	4	1	7	12	8	29	0	0	R	R	6-0	205	9-17-73	1994	Foster City, Calif.
Campusano, Carlos	.310	27	84	13	26	2	1	1	7	6	15	4	1	R	R	5-11	160	9-2-75	1994	Palave, D.R.
Casper, Brett	.266	121	436	71	116	22	2	16	77	56	135	20	10	R	R	6-3	215	11-24-75	1997	Omaha, Neb.
Cepeda, Ali	.077	9	13	0	1	0	0	0	0	0	4	0	0	R	R	6-0	200	9-27-76	1999	Orlando, Fla.
Daeley, Scott	.222	9	9	1	2	0	0	0	0	2	1	0	0	R	R	5-10	178	2-25-77	1999	Orange, Calif.
Dean, Mike	.284	23	81	16	23	4	2	1	12	11	15	13	3	R	R	5-11	190	8-2-77	1998	Okmulgee, Okla.
Flaherty, Tim	.267	132	490	82	131	33	3	25	88	69	168	11	3	R	R	6-4	220	7-11-76	1997	Williamstown, Mass.
Glendenning, Mike	.245	104	368	71	90	26	1	23	80	71	112	7	4	R	R	6-0	225	8-26-76	1996	West Hills, Calif.
McGowan, Sean	.375	2	8	1	3	1	0	0	1	0	3	0	1	R	R	6-6	240	5-15-77	1999	Burlington, Mass.
McKinley, Dan	.226	15	53	7	12	2	1	1	3	7	13	2	0	L	R	6-0	180	5-15-76	1997	Chandler, Ariz.
Melendez, Angel	.222	101	370	32	82	17	1	5	41	24	100	10	8	R	R	6-0	192	10-21-75	1996	Caguas, P.R.
Mota, Pedro	.269	50	171	26	46	3	4	3	19	12	38	3	7	L	L	6-1	195	2-28-78	1995	San Pedro de Macoris, D.R.
Otero, William	.333	96	402	81	134	28	3	10	56	37	67	20	4	R	R	5-11	175	9-30-76	1997	Bayamon, P.R.
Pernalete, Marco	.238	99	370	50	88	19	0	3	32	30	105	10	3	S	R	6-1	165	10-12-78	1996	Barquisimeto, Venez.
Priess, Matt	.229	86	293	35	67	11	2	1	28	38	38	1	2	R	R	6-2	200	11-24-74	1997	Brea, Calif.
Reynoso, Ismael	.249	79	253	26	63	12	1	3	26	12	48	12	3	R	R	5-10	170	6-17-78	1995	La Romana, D.R.
Tommasino, Kevin	.254	108	382	52	97	17	2	6	34	48	86	3	3	R	R	6-1	205	1-18-75	1998	Winston, Ore.
Torrealba, Yorvit	.315	19	73	10	23	3	0	2	14	6	15	0	0	R	R	5-11	180	7-19-78	1995	Guarenas, Venez.
Tsoukalas, John	.322	64	208	36	67	15	1	9	41	25	42	0	1	R	L	6-1	190	8-24-70	1991	Everett, Wash.
Valderrama, Carlos	.256	26	90	12	23	2	0	0	12	4	19	4	0	R	R	5-11	175	11-30-77	1995	Maracaibo, Venez.
Zuniga, Tony	.270	136	533	82	144	33	3	10	66	65	89	9	4	R	R	6-0	185	1-13-75	1996	Santa Ana, Calif.

GAMES BY POSITION: C—Bazzani 29, Dean 17, Flaherty 1, Priess 86, Tommasini 1, Torrealba 19. **1B**—Flaherty 127, Tsoukalas 17. **2B**—Otero 92, Pernalete 50. **3B**—Tsoukalas 7, Zuniga 135. **SS**—Campusano 26, Otero 2, Pernalete 43, Reynoso 76. **OF**—Casper 121, Cepeda 3, Daeley 2, Dean 6, Glendenning 55, McKinley 15, Melendez 100, Mota 46, Tommasini 67, Valderrama 21.

PITCHING	W	L	ERA	G	GS	CG	SV	IP	H	R	ER	BB	SO	B	T	HT	WT	DOB	1st Yr	Resides
Andra, Jeff	4	2	4.50	13	7	0	0	50	54	28	25	19	54	L	L	6-5	210	9-9-75	1997	Lenexa, Kan.
Chavarria, David	0	2	7.58	21	0	0	0	30	43	25	25	16	26	L	R	6-7	235	5-19-73	1991	Lake Suzy, Fla.
Esteves, Jake	6	1	2.01	12	11	1	1	72	59	21	16	17	56	R	R	6-1	200	7-31-75	1998	Auburn, Calif.
Fernandez, Ozzie	0	1	6.00	4	4	0	0	9	6	6	6	2	5	R	R	6-2	190	11-4-68	1996	Miami, Fla.
Gardner, Mark	1	0	4.50	2	0	0	0	10	10	5	5	3	13	R	R	6-1	215	3-1-62	1985	Fresno, Calif.
Goodrich, Randy	8	8	4.81	38	18	0	1	137	174	95	73	34	82	R	R	6-4	210	11-8-76	1998	Arcadia, Calif.
Jones, Chris	8	12	4.61	28	27	0	0	131	121	85	67	87	118	R	L	6-4	200	8-29-79	1998	Charlotte, N.C.
Joseph, Kevin	1	2	2.35	20	0	0	2	31	17	9	8	13	30	R	R	6-4	200	8-1-76	1997	Dallas, Texas
Kiyono, Masashi	2	1	7.46	32	3	0	0	57	87	62	47	29	31	R	R	6-2	190	3-16-75	1997	Kanagawa, Japan
Malerich, Will	5	4	4.46	45	0	0	1	73	95	43	36	38	59	L	L	5-11	180	10-25-75	1997	Alexandria, Va.
Malloy, Bill	5	4	4.18	17	13	0	0	80	87	45	37	37	66	R	R	6-2	225	5-22-75	1996	Piscataway, N.J.
Messman, Joe	0	0	27.00	2	0	0	0	2	6	5	5	3	0	R	R	6-2	175	7-29-75	1997	Parkdale, Ore.
Miller, Benji	3	2	3.02	47	0	0	20	60	53	26	20	17	61	R	R	6-2	180	5-2-76	1998	Charleston, Calif.
Pourron, Joe	2	0	6.17	14	0	0	0	23	17	18	16	32	23	R	R	6-7	222	3-12-77	1997	Jonesboro, Ga.
Ramirez, Erasmo	2	0	2.67	31	0	0	5	57	42	18	17	8	52	L	L	6-0	180	4-29-76	1998	Santa Ana, Calif.
Ricabal, Dan	1	0	4.91	7	0	0	1	7	13	7	4	5	1	R	R	6-4	185	7-8-72	1994	Temple City, Calif.
Santos, Josh	3	6	4.32	13	13	1	0	67	75	47	32	29	47	L	L	6-0	195	2-3-77	1998	East Haven, Conn.
Tavarez, Julian	0	0	0.00	1	1	0	0	4	1	0	0	1	3	R	R	6-2	190	5-22-73	1990	Broadway Heights, Ohio
Tucker, Ben	4	6	4.57	16	15	0	0	83	106	46	42	26	65	R	R	6-4	220	11-6-73	1995	Fresno, Calif.
Urban, Jeff	8	5	3.76	15	13	0	0	81	78	41	34	18	89	R	L	6-8	215	1-25-77	1998	Alexandria, Ind.
Vogelsong, Ryan	4	4	2.45	13	13	0	0	70	37	26	19	27	86	R	R	6-3	195	7-22-77	1998	North Grafton, Mass.
Wells, Matt	8	5	3.67	57	0	0	7	91	73	41	37	65	100	R	R	6-2	210	5-25-75	1996	Rocklin, Calif.

SALEM-KEIZER   Short-Season Class A

NORTHWEST LEAGUE

BATTING	AVG	G	AB	R	H	2B	3B	HR	RBI	BB	SO	SB	CS	B	T	HT	WT	DOB	1st Yr	Resides
Cepeda, Ali	.250	24	44	9	11	2	0	0	5	11	15	4	2	R	R	6-0	200	9-27-76	1999	Orlando, Fla.
Cook, Josh	.241	35	112	16	27	9	0	1	16	11	24	5	6	R	R	6-2	195	6-1-78	1999	Yuba City, Calif.
Cordido, Julio	.264	70	242	36	64	10	2	1	28	29	44	8	4	R	R	6-1	192	7-30-80	1997	Caracas, Venez.
Daeley, Scott	.246	69	268	42	66	12	1	0	22	43	29	29	9	R	R	5-10	178	2-25-77	1999	Orange, Calif.
Grochol, Bryan	.241	28	79	9	19	1	0	1	10	7	15	2	3	L	L	6-1	205	10-4-77	1999	Pacifica, Calif.
Holst, Micah	.289	57	204	37	59	8	2	4	28	6	32	20	5	R	R	6-2	205	3-5-77	1999	Independence, Mo.
Jester, Jon	.300	72	263	67	79	19	1	8	40	50	57	13	6	R	R	5-11	180	7-17-78	1999	Ashdown, Ark.
Luster, Jeremy	.219	39	146	22	32	7	1	1	14	16	48	7	1	S	R	6-3	212	6-10-77	1999	Kennesaw, Ga.
Luther, Ryan	.300	61	220	34	66	12	1	4	38	18	35	12	4	R	R	6-0	185	1-21-77	1999	North Bend, Wash.
Mapes, Ryan	.172	12	29	2	5	2	0	0	4	2	11	0	2	R	R	6-4	210	3-1-79	1999	Hemet, Calif.
Mattern, Erik	.220	17	41	11	9	1	1	1	6	16	9	1	1	R	R	5-11	185	3-23-76	1998	Fountain Valley, Calif.
McGowan, Sean	.335	63	257	40	86	12	1	15	62	20	56	3	1	R	R	6-6	240	5-15-77	1999	Burlington, Mass.
Messner, Jake	.263	9	19	4	5	0	0	1	5	5	4	0	0	L	L	6-1	205	5-18-77	1995	Sacramento, Calif.
Niemet, Bob	.214	18	56	8	12	1	0	0	4	6	5	1	2	R	R	6-2	204	8-23-76	1999	Columbus, Ohio
Pene, Ryan	.192	40	125	18	24	5	0	2	21	19	40	1	0	L	L	6-3	205	2-11-77	1999	Salina, Utah
Ransom, Troy	.140	26	50	6	7	1	2	0	6	5	19	1	2	R	R	6-2	180	7-9-78	1999	Chandler, Ariz.
Rodriguez, Guillermo	.254	33	114	16	29	5	0	6	34	9	28	1	3	R	R	5-11	190	5-15-78	1996	Barquisimeto, Venez.
Turco, Paul	.181	44	116	8	21	3	0	0	5	10	27	3	1	L	R	5-10	162	10-17-76	1999	Sarasota, Fla.
Valderrama, Carlos	.291	40	134	27	39	3	1	2	18	12	34	17	2	R	R	5-11	175	11-30-77	1999	Maracaibo, Venez.
Wright, Michael	.270	24	63	14	17	4	0	1	7	17	12	0	0	R	R	6-2	210	3-13-76	1999	San Jose, Calif.

GAMES BY POSITION: C—Luther 22, Mapes 11, Rodriguez 31, Wright 22. **1B**—Luster 35, McGowan 32, Niemet 10, Pene 5, Wright 1. **2B**—Cook 23, Jester 26, Luther 15, Mattern 13, Ransom 1, Turco 15. **3B**—Cook 6, Cordido 70, Luther 3, Mattern 1. **SS**—Cook 7, Jester 48, Luther 1, Turco 25. **OF**—Cepeda 15, Daeley 69, Grochol 6, Holst 53, Jester 1, Niemet 6, Pene 30, Ransom 21, Turco 1, Valderrama 36.

PITCHING	W	L	ERA	G	GS	CG	SV	IP	H	R	ER	BB	SO	B	T	HT	WT	DOB	1st Yr	Resides
Ainsworth, Kurt	3	3	1.61	10	10	1	0	45	34	18	8	18	64	R	R	6-3	185	9-9-78	1999	Kingwood, Texas
Cox, Ryan	2	1	3.15	8	8	0	0	34	39	13	12	10	20	R	R	6-3	195	12-25-76	1999	Stewardson, Ill.
Cozier, Vance	5	4	4.57	15	10	0	0	61	61	34	31	24	46	R	R	6-6	245	9-26-77	1999	Ajax, Ontario
Cunningham, Jeremy	0	2	4.70	7	5	0	1	15	25	11	8	6	13	R	R	6-5	190	8-4-78	1999	Cupertino, Calif.
Featherstone, Hal	0	1	46.29	4	0	0	0	2	7	12	12	6	0	R	R	6-2	175	6-20-77	1999	Hendersonville, N.C.
Fields, Brian	2	3	3.12	24	0	0	8	35	30	14	12	14	38	R	L	6-1	175	8-21-74	1998	Greenville, N.C.
Hills, Mark	0	2	6.71	16	7	0	0	52	70	49	39	27	41	L	L	6-1	202	8-12-78	1999	Salem, Ore.
Huller, Mike	0	0	12.00	3	0	0	0	3	6	5	4	3	4	R	L	6-1	190	8-25-77	1998	Bel Air, Md.
Jimenez, Reinaldo	2	5	5.54	24	0	0	0	37	44	29	23	27	23	R	R	6-1	175	1-4-78	1997	Cabudare, Venez.
Johnson, Eric	1	1	7.71	15	1	0	0	16	18	15	14	17	18	R	R	6-4	195	9-12-77	1999	Newberg, Ore.
Lee, Fletcher	2	1	3.11	26	0	0	5	38	33	15	13	20	34	R	R	6-1	190	1-29-76	1999	Honolulu, Hawaii
Meagher, Brian	2	4	4.88	17	6	0	0	52	56	32	28	28	41	L	L	6-2	185	5-11-77	1999	Lowell, Mass.
Ojeda, Joseph	2	3	6.55	16	0	0	0	33	39	27	24	17	20	R	R	6-4	190	9-27-76	1998	Brooklyn, N.Y.
Pourron, Joe	0	0	11.57	8	0	0	0	7	13	10	9	6	8	R	R	6-7	222	3-12-77	1997	Jonesboro, Ga.
Sabino, Miguel	2	6	6.44	10	6	0	0	43	48	35	31	18	29	R	R	5-11	185	8-29-76	1996	San Pedro de Macoris, D.R.
Taschner, Jack	3	2	2.51	7	6	0	0	29	26	12	8	10	36	L	L	6-3	190	4-21-78	1999	Racine, Wis.
Vent, Kevin	2	3	5.03	17	6	0	3	39	44	25	22	18	31	R	R	6-0	185	6-1-77	1999	Maumelle, Ark.
Wells, Zach	4	1	3.48	15	0	0	1	21	17	13	8	13	13	R	R	6-4	205	2-23-77	1997	Clayton, Calif.
Williams, Jerome	1	1	2.19	7	7	1	0	37	29	13	9	11	34	R	R	6-3	190	12-4-81	1999	Las Vegas, Nev.
Yacco, Anthony	0	1	13.15	9	4	0	1	13	16	19	19	14	12	R	R	6-3	200	12-2-80	1999	Mahopac, N.Y.
Zirelli, Mike	1	4	4.41	25	0	0	2	51	50	31	25	17	47	R	R	6-4	210	1-21-77	1999	San Carlos, Calif.

SEATTLE MARINERS

Future of Griffey, A-Rod casts shadow over Mariners

BY SUSAN WADE

Instead of celebrating the achievements of Ken Griffey and Alex Rodriguez and enjoying their move out of the Kingdome in 1999, the Mariners ended another disappointing season worrying that the club couldn't afford to keep them.

It was typical in a year of oscillation for Seattle fans. They oohed at the opening of retro-chic Safeco Field as it ushered in the open-air era of baseball in Seattle. They gave Randy Johnson, whose spat with management set a bad tone at the start of the 1998 season, a standing ovation when he reappeared as a starter for the Diamondbacks. They embraced rookie starters Freddy Garcia and John Halama and speculated how splendid Carlos Guillen will be at second base when he returns in 2000 from a torn anterior cruciate ligament. They also endured a team that was 79-83 and never seriously in contention. Then they bid an apathetic adieu to retiring general manager Woody Woodward. Former Blue Jays GM Pat Gillick was selected to replace Woodward.

New team president Howard Lincoln, a former Nintendo executive, and Gillick were left to deal with Griffey and Rodriguez. After the season the duo was offered the richest contracts in the history of baseball. Lincoln also announced the Mariners would increase their payroll from $53 million to as much as $70 million in 2000.

Griffey, though, asked to be traded. He finished the season with a .285 average, a league-leading 48 home runs, 134 RBIs and 24 stolen bases. After the final season of his 20s, he has 1,742 career hits and 398 home runs. He became just the third player in major league

Ken Griffey   **Bo Robinson**

Players of the Year

MAJOR LEAGUE: Ken Griffey, of
Griffey led the AL with 48 home runs and was tops on the Mariners with 123 runs and 134 RBIs.

MINOR LEAGUE: Bo Robinson, 3b
Robinson led Mariners minor leaguers with a .329 average, 50 doubles and 108 walks, and drove in 102 runs for Wisconsin.

history to hit 200 homers in a four-season span, and just the seventh to hit 40 in four consecutive seasons. He fell six RBIs short of Babe Ruth's feat of 140 or more in six straight seasons.

If 1999 was Rodriguez' last in Seattle, it was memorable. He hit .285 with 42 home runs, 111 RBIs and stole 21 bases, despite missing 31 games early in the year with a torn meniscus in his left knee.

Edgar Martinez showed he had more hits left in him. He got his 1,500th career hit Aug. 14 and ended with a .337 mark, his sixth season at .320 or better with at least 15 home runs. He hit 24 homers and drove in 86 runs.

Pitching remains the key for the Mariners. The boost from their young starters—Garcia, Halama and Gil Meche—was encouraging, but collectively, the staff set franchise records it would rather forget, allowing 902 runs, 833 earned runs, 1,602 hits and 679 walks. It also hit the most batters (70) on the way to the highest ERA (5.26).

The organization enjoyed success at the lower levels of the minor leagues, with Class A Wisconsin reaching the Midwest League finals and short-season Everett and Rookie-level Peoria finishing second in their leagues.

Lefthander Ryan Anderson, the team's top prospect, led the Double-A Eastern League with 162 strikeouts. Meche, who began the season alongside Anderson in the New Haven rotation, landed in Seattle at midseason and posted respectable numbers as a rookie.

Righthander Cha Seung Baek, the club's Korean bonus baby, enjoyed a strong pro debut in the Arizona League. Two other newcomers, catcher Ryan Christianson and righthander Jeff Heaverlo, played well after signing as first-round picks.

ORGANIZATION LEADERS

BATTING

*AVG	Bo Robinson, Wisconsin	.329
R	Jermaine Clark, Lancaster	112
H	Bo Robinson, Wisconsin	164
TB	Two tied at	259
2B	Bo Robinson, Wisconsin	50
3B	Kerry Robinson, Tacoma	9
HR	Peanut Williams, Lancaster/Wisconsin	28
RBI	Juan Silvestre, Wisconsin	107
BB	Bo Robinson, Wisconsin	108
SO	Jayson Bass, New Haven	160
SB	Ramon Valera, Lancaster/Wisconsin	46

PITCHING

W	Two tied at	13
L	Joel Pineiro, New Haven	15
#ERA	Pat Ahearne, New Haven	2.61
G	Justin Kaye, Lancaster	53
CG	Two tied at	4
SV	Justin Kaye, Lancaster	14
IP	Melqui Torres, Wisconsin	172
BB	Ryan Anderson, New Haven	86
SO	Ryan Anderson, New Haven	162

*Minimum 250 At-Bats #Minimum 75 Innings

Seattle MARINERS

Manager: Lou Piniella **1999 Record:** 79-83, .488 (3rd, AL West)

BATTING	AVG	G	AB	R	H	2B	3B	HR	RBI	BB	SO	SB	CS	B	T	HT	WT	DOB	1st Yr	Resides
Bell, David	.268	157	597	92	160	31	2	21	78	58	90	7	4	R	R	5-10	175	9-14-72	1990	Seattle, Wash.
Blowers, Mike	.239	19	46	2	11	1	0	2	7	4	12	0	0	R	R	6-2	210	4-24-65	1986	Tacoma, Wash.
Bournigal, Rafael	.274	55	95	16	26	5	0	2	14	7	6	0	0	R	R	5-11	175	5-12-66	1987	Lakeland, Fla.
Buhner, Jay	.222	87	266	37	59	11	0	14	38	69	100	0	0	R	R	6-3	210	8-13-64	1984	Issaquah, Wash.
Cedeno, Domingo	.214	21	42	4	9	2	0	2	8	5	9	1	1	S	R	6-0	170	11-4-68	1989	La Romana, D.R.
Davis, Russ	.245	124	432	55	106	17	1	21	59	32	111	3	3	R	R	6-0	195	9-13-69	1988	Birmingham, Ala.
Gipson, Charles	.225	55	80	16	18	5	2	0	9	6	13	3	4	R	R	6-2	180	12-16-72	1992	Orange, Calif.
Griffey, Ken	.285	160	606	123	173	26	3	48	134	91	108	24	7	L	L	6-3	205	11-21-69	1987	Issaquah, Wash.
Guevara, Giomar	.250	10	12	2	3	2	0	0	2	0	2	0	0	S	R	5-8	150	10-23-72	1991	Guarenas, Venez.
Guillen, Carlos	.158	5	19	2	3	0	0	1	3	1	6	0	0	S	R	6-1	180	9-30-75	1993	Aragua, Venez.
Hunter, Brian	.231	121	484	71	112	11	5	4	34	32	80	44	5	R	R	6-3	180	3-25-71	1989	Vancouver, Wash.
2-team (18 Detroit)	.232	139	539	79	125	13	6	4	34	37	91	44	8							
Huskey, Butch	.290	74	262	44	76	9	0	15	49	27	45	3	1	R	R	6-3	244	11-10-71	1989	Lawton, Okla.
Ibanez, Raul	.258	87	209	23	54	7	0	9	27	17	32	5	1	L	R	6-2	200	6-2-72	1992	Miami, Fla.
Jackson, Ryan	.235	32	68	4	16	3	0	0	10	6	19	3	3	L	L	6-3	185	11-15-71	1994	Sarasota, Fla.
Lampkin, Tom	.291	76	206	29	60	11	2	9	34	13	32	1	3	L	R	5-11	195	3-4-64	1986	Vancouver, Wash.
Mabry, John	.244	87	262	34	64	14	0	9	33	20	60	2	1	L	R	6-4	210	10-17-70	1991	St. Louis, Mo.
Martinez, Edgar	.337	142	502	86	169	35	1	24	86	97	99	7	2	R	R	5-11	200	1-2-63	1983	Kirkland, Wash.
Mieske, Matt	.366	24	41	11	15	0	0	4	7	2	9	0	0	R	R	6-0	194	2-13-68	1990	Mesa, Ariz.
Monahan, Shane	.133	16	15	3	2	0	0	0	0	0	6	0	0	L	R	6-0	195	8-12-74	1995	Phoenix, Ariz.
Rodriguez, Alex	.285	129	502	110	143	25	0	42	111	56	109	21	7	R	R	6-3	195	7-27-75	1994	Miami, Fla.
Segui, David	.293	90	345	43	101	22	3	9	39	32	43	1	2	S	L	6-1	202	7-19-66	1988	Kansas City, Kan.
Timmons, Ozzie	.114	26	44	4	5	2	0	1	3	4	12	0	1	R	R	6-2	220	9-18-70	1991	Tampa, Fla.
Wilson, Dan	.266	123	414	46	110	23	2	7	38	29	83	5	0	R	R	6-3	190	3-25-69	1990	Seattle, Wash.

PITCHING	W	L	ERA	G	GS	CG	SV	IP	H	R	ER	BB	SO	B	T	HT	WT	DOB	1st Yr	Resides
Abbott, Paul	6	2	3.10	25	7	0	0	73	50	31	25	32	68	R	R	6-3	195	9-15-67	1985	Fullerton, Calif.
Bunch, Mel	0	0	11.70	5	1	0	0	10	20	13	13	7	4	R	R	6-1	170	11-4-71	1992	Texarkana, Texas
Carmona, Rafael	1	0	7.94	9	0	0	0	11	18	11	10	9	6	L	R	6-2	185	10-2-72	1993	Comerio, P.R.
Cloude, Ken	4	4	7.96	31	6	0	1	72	106	67	64	46	35	R	R	6-3	205	1-9-75	1994	Baltimore, Md.
Davey, Tom	1	0	4.71	16	0	0	0	21	22	13	11	14	17	R	R	6-7	230	9-11-73	1994	Canton, Mich.
2-team (31 Toronto)	2	1	4.71	45	0	0	1	65	62	41	34	40	59							
Fassero, Jeff	4	14	7.38	30	24	0	0	139	188	123	114	73	101	L	L	6-1	195	1-5-63	1984	Mercer Island, Wash.
Franklin, Ryan	0	0	4.76	6	0	0	0	11	10	6	6	8	6	R	R	6-3	165	3-5-73	1993	Spiro, Okla.
Garcia, Freddy	17	8	4.07	33	33	2	0	201	205	96	91	90	170	R	R	6-4	210	10-6-76	1994	Baruta, Venez.
Halama, John	11	10	4.22	38	24	1	0	179	193	88	84	56	105	L	L	6-5	200	2-22-72	1994	Brooklyn, N.Y.
Henry, Butch	2	0	5.04	7	4	0	0	25	30	15	14	10	15	L	L	6-1	205	10-7-68	1987	El Paso, Texas
Hinchliffe, Brett	0	4	8.80	11	4	0	0	31	41	31	30	21	14	R	R	6-5	190	7-21-74	1992	Detroit, Mich.
Leiter, Mark	0	0	6.75	2	0	0	0	1	2	1	1	0	1	R	R	6-3	220	4-13-63	1983	Lanoka Harbor, N.J.
Marte, Damaso	0	1	9.35	5	0	0	0	9	16	9	9	6	3	L	L	6-0	170	2-14-75	1993	San Carlos, D.R.
Meche, Gil	8	4	4.73	16	15	0	0	86	73	48	45	57	47	R	R	6-3	180	9-8-78	1996	Scott, La.
Mesa, Jose	3	6	4.98	68	0	0	33	69	84	42	38	40	42	R	R	6-3	225	5-22-66	1982	Westlake, Ohio
Moyer, Jamie	14	8	3.87	32	32	4	0	228	235	108	98	48	137	L	L	6-0	170	11-18-62	1984	Granger, Ill.
Paniagua, Jose	6	11	4.06	59	0	0	3	78	75	37	35	52	74	R	R	6-2	185	8-20-73	1991	Santo Domingo, D.R.
Ramsay, Robert	0	2	6.38	6	3	0	0	18	23	13	13	9	11	L	L	6-5	230	12-3-73	1996	Washougal, Wash.
Rodriguez, Frank	2	4	5.65	28	5	0	3	73	94	47	46	30	47	R	R	6-0	210	12-11-72	1991	New York, N.Y.
Scheffer, Aaron	0	0	1.93	4	0	0	0	5	6	5	1	3	4	L	R	6-2	165	10-15-75	1994	Westland, Mich.
Sinclair, Steve	0	1	3.95	18	0	0	0	14	15	8	6	10	15	L	L	6-2	190	8-2-71	1991	Victoria, B.C.
2-team (3 Toronto)	0	1	6.52	21	0	0	0	19	22	16	14	14	18							
Spencer, Sean	0	0	21.60	2	0	0	0	5	4	4	3	2	1	L	L	5-11	185	5-29-75	1996	Port Orchard, Wash.
Stark, Denny	0	0	9.95	5	0	0	0	6	10	8	7	4	4	R	R	6-2	210	10-27-74	1996	Edgerton, Ohio
Suzuki, Mac	0	2	9.43	16	4	0	0	42	47	47	44	34	32	R	R	6-3	195	5-31-75	1992	Kobe, Japan
Watson, Allen	0	1	12.00	3	0	0	0	6	9	4	3	2	1	L	L	6-3	195	11-18-70	1991	Middle Village, N.Y.
Weaver, Eric	0	1	10.61	8	0	0	0	9	14	12	11	8	14	R	R	6-5	230	8-4-73	1991	Springfield, Ill.
Williams, Todd	0	0	4.66	13	0	0	0	10	11	5	5	7	7	R	R	6-4	190	2-13-71	1991	Syracuse, N.Y.
Zimmerman, Jordan	0	0	7.88	12	0	0	0	8	14	8	7	4	3	R	L	6-0	200	4-28-75	1995	Brenham, Texas

FIELDING

Catcher	PCT	G	PO	A	E	DP	PB
Ibanez	1.000	1	4	0	0	0	0
Lampkin	.985	56	292	27	5	5	5
Wilson	.995	121	743	46	4	7	3

First Base	PCT	G	PO	A	E	DP
Bell	1.000	4	15	1	0	2
Blowers	1.000	14	72	6	0	14
Buhner	1.000	1	9	0	0	1
Ibanez	.987	21	147	7	2	18
Jackson	.989	29	167	11	2	19
Mabry	.992	20	120	10	1	11
Martinez	1.000	5	29	2	0	2
Segui	.996	90	700	61	3	86
Timmons	1.000	1	1	0	0	0

	PCT	G	PO	A	E	DP
Wilson	1.000	5	10	2	0	1
Second Base	**PCT**	**G**	**PO**	**A**	**E**	**DP**
Bell	.978	154	313	426	17	118
Bournigal	.983	17	26	33	1	10
Cedeno	1.000	1	1	2	0	0
Gipson	1.000	3	1	1	0	1
Guillen	1.000	2	6	6	0	5
Third Base	**PCT**	**G**	**PO**	**A**	**E**	**DP**
Blowers	.875	4	2	5	1	1
Bournigal	.900	8	5	4	1	0
Cedeno	.000	1	0	0	0	0
Davis	.958	124	71	206	12	17

	PCT	G	PO	A	E	DP
Huskey	.000	1	0	0	0	0
Mabry	.873	24	21	34	8	1
Shortstop	**PCT**	**G**	**PO**	**A**	**E**	**DP**
Bell	1.000	1	1	0	0	0
Bournigal	.987	28	28	47	1	13
Cedeno	.941	20	17	47	4	11
Davis	.000	2	0	0	0	0
Gipson	.750	3	2	1	1	0
Guevara	.870	9	6	14	3	2
Guillen	.938	3	6	9	1	1
A. Rodriguez	.977	129	213	382	14	103

Outfield	PCT	G	PO	A	E	DP
Bournigal	.000	1	0	0	0	0
Buhner	.993	85	127	7	1	2
Gipson	.960	28	19	5	1	0
Griffey	.978	158	387	10	9	5

	PCT	G	PO	A	E	DP
Hunter	.985	121	252	14	4	3
Huskey	1.000	53	101	1	0	0
Ibanez	.988	57	83	1	1	0
Jackson	.000	1	0	0	0	0
Lampkin	.000	2	0	0	0	0

	PCT	G	PO	A	E	DP
Mabry	.989	43	80	6	1	1
Mieske	1.000	20	25	1	0	0
Monahan	1.000	9	7	0	0	0
Timmons	1.000	17	12	0	0	0

Alex Rodriguez
Hit .285-42-111 for Seattle

Ryan Anderson
Led farm system with 162 strikeouts

FARM SYSTEM

Farm Director: Benny Looper

Class	Farm Team	League	W	L	Pct.	Finish*	Manager	First Yr
AAA	Tacoma (Wash.) Rainiers	Pacific Coast	69	70	.496	7th (16)	Dave Myers	1995
AA	New Haven (Conn.) Ravens	Eastern	65	77	.458	t-9th (12)	Dan Rohn	1997
A#	Lancaster (Calif.) JetHawks	California	55	85	.393	10th (10)	Darrin Garner	1996
A	Wisconsin Timber Rattlers	Midwest	72	66	.522	t-5th (14)	Steve Roadcap	1993
A	Everett (Wash.) Aquasox	Northwest	41	35	.539	3rd (8)	Terry Pollreisz	1995
Rookie	Peoria (Ariz.) Mariners	Arizona	32	24	.571	2nd (8)	Gary Thurman	1988

*Finish in overall standings (No. of teams in league)   #Advanced level

TACOMA   Class AAA

PACIFIC COAST LEAGUE

BATTING	AVG	G	AB	R	H	2B	3B	HR	RBI	BB	SO	SB	CS	B	T	HT	WT	DOB	1st Yr	Resides
Akers, Chad	.313	48	192	31	60	9	3	1	14	18	25	7	3	R	R	5-8	160	5-30-72	1993	Lake, W.Va.
Alcala, Juan	.000	1	1	0	0	0	0	0	0	0	0	0	0	R	R	6-2	185	4-15-78	1995	San Pedro de Macoris, D.R.
Blowers, Mike	.231	3	13	1	3	1	0	0	2	0	4	0	0	R	R	6-2	210	4-24-65	1986	Tacoma, Wash.
Brown, Randy	.256	44	156	15	40	7	1	6	27	9	48	4	2	R	R	5-11	160	5-1-70	1989	Houston, Texas
Buhner, Shawn	.240	43	146	17	35	8	0	1	12	10	43	0	1	R	R	6-2	200	8-29-72	1994	League City, Texas
Carroll, Mark	.000	1	1	0	0	0	0	0	0	0	1	0	0	R	R	6-0	195	10-19-78	1996	Athens, N.Y.
Cedeno, Domingo	.268	33	112	17	30	8	1	1	13	7	36	1	3	S	R	6-0	170	11-4-68	1989	La Romana, D.R.
Chavez, Raul	.268	102	354	39	95	20	1	3	40	28	63	1	3	R	R	5-11	210	3-18-74	1990	Valencia, Venez.
Durango, Ariel	.000	1	4	0	0	0	0	0	0	0	0	0	0	S	R	5-10	170	4-5-79	1996	Panama City, Panama
Flores, Jose	.308	42	143	33	44	6	1	3	15	37	23	4	3	R	R	5-11	180	6-28-73	1994	New York, N.Y.
Gipson, Charles	.299	47	174	26	52	6	3	0	21	14	24	18	4	R	R	6-2	180	12-16-72	1992	Orange, Calif.
Guevara, Giomar	.293	32	116	15	34	13	0	3	15	12	22	0	1	S	R	5-8	150	10-23-72	1991	Guarenas, Venez.
Hills, Rich	.000	1	4	0	0	0	0	0	0	0	0	0	0	R	R	6-0	195	7-28-73	1995	Springdale, Ark.
Ibanez, Raul	.355	8	31	6	11	1	0	3	5	1	7	1	0	L	R	6-2	200	6-2-72	1992	Miami, Fla.
Jackson, Ryan	.308	105	409	57	126	25	2	8	62	36	64	12	3	L	L	6-3	185	11-15-71	1994	Sarasota, Fla.
Johnson, Earl	.236	17	55	6	13	2	0	0	4	8	6	5	1	S	R	5-10	165	10-3-71	1991	Detroit, Mich.
Mathis, Joe	.250	26	84	8	23	5	1	0	7	6	25	3	0	L	R	5-11	180	8-10-74	1993	Johnston, S.C.
Matos, Francisco	.310	100	393	43	122	24	3	3	33	18	41	4	6	R	R	6-1	160	7-23-69	1988	Azua, D.R.
Monahan, Shane	.256	108	399	51	102	21	2	7	32	19	81	9	3	L	R	6-0	195	8-12-74	1995	Phoenix, Ariz.

BATTING

BATTING	AVG	G	AB	R	H	2B	3B	HR	RBI	BB	SO	SB	CS	B	T	HT	WT	DOB	1st Yr	Resides
Murphy, Mike	.295	38	129	22	38	7	3	2	22	13	36	10	4	R	R	6-2	185	1-23-72	1990	Albuquerque, N.M.
Pledger, Kinnis	.275	43	153	20	42	8	1	8	30	19	37	0	2	L	R	6-4	220	7-17-68	1987	Benton, Ark.
Radmanovich, Ryan	.286	109	420	69	120	24	3	17	80	53	83	10	4	L	R	6-2	200	8-9-71	1993	Calgary, Alberta
Robinson, Kerry	.322	79	335	53	108	16	9	0	34	14	44	30	7	L	L	6-0	175	10-3-73	1994	Spanish Lake, Mo.
Sachse, Matt	.200	11	35	2	7	1	0	0	0	4	13	1	0	L	L	6-4	205	6-29-76	1995	Spokane, Wash.
Sealy, Scot	.184	67	201	22	37	4	0	6	24	20	56	0	0	R	R	6-2	225	2-10-71	1992	Saraland, Ala.
Seitzer, Brad	.287	130	474	80	136	34	1	9	66	89	86	1	2	R	R	6-2	195	2-2-70	1991	Lincoln, Ill.
Timmons, Ozzie	.273	82	297	56	81	22	0	21	66	53	81	0	2	R	R	6-2	220	9-18-70	1991	Tampa, Fla.

PITCHING

PITCHING	W	L	ERA	G	GS	CG	SV	IP	H	R	ER	BB	SO	B	T	HT	WT	DOB	1st Yr	Resides
Abbott, Paul	1	1	6.43	2	2	0	0	14	21	11	10	4	10	R	R	6-3	195	9-15-67	1985	Fullerton, Calif.
Adamson, Joel	2	2	5.15	14	6	0	0	37	48	25	21	15	15	L	L	6-4	185	7-2-71	1990	Phoenix, Ariz.
Bertotti, Mike	0	2	10.29	3	3	0	0	7	6	8	8	17	6	L	L	6-1	185	1-18-70	1991	Highland Mills, N.Y.
Bunch, Mel	10	2	3.10	21	19	1	0	125	112	53	43	40	117	R	R	6-1	170	11-4-71	1992	Texarkana, Texas
Carmona, Rafael	1	3	3.53	27	0	0	2	43	39	18	17	20	38	L	R	6-2	185	10-2-72	1993	Comerio, P.R.
Cloude, Ken	5	1	2.33	6	6	2	0	39	19	11	10	15	33	R	R	6-1	205	1-9-75	1994	Baltimore, Md.
De la Rosa, Maximo	0	0	6.14	15	0	0	1	22	34	18	15	10	24	R	R	5-11	170	7-12-71	1990	Villa Mella, D.R.
Delgado, Danny	0	1	6.00	2	0	0	0	3	4	2	2	2	2	R	R	6-2	180	2-10-78	1997	Miami Lakes, Fla.
Fleetham, Ben	1	2	3.38	14	0	0	1	19	19	9	7	12	16	R	R	6-1	205	8-3-72	1994	Minneapolis, Minn.
Flener, Huck	4	4	5.45	22	5	0	1	66	72	41	40	26	48	S	L	5-11	180	2-25-69	1990	Fairfield, Calif.
Franklin, Ryan	6	9	4.71	29	19	2	2	136	142	81	71	33	94	R	R	6-3	165	3-5-73	1993	Spiro, Okla.
Henry, Butch	2	0	0.00	4	0	0	0	5	4	0	0	1	3	L	L	6-1	205	10-7-68	1987	El Paso, Texas
Hinchliffe, Brett	9	7	5.15	21	21	3	0	131	141	78	75	44	107	R	R	6-5	190	7-21-74	1992	Detroit, Mich.
Hodges, Kevin	3	3	3.25	14	12	0	1	83	88	31	30	27	42	R	R	6-4	200	6-24-73	1991	Spring, Texas
2-team (5 New Orleans)	4	6	4.22	19	17	0	1	110	122	54	52	38	58							
Holdridge, David	5	6	4.34	41	0	0	10	66	67	38	32	23	68	R	R	6-3	215	2-5-69	1988	Huntington Beach, Calif.
Kroon, Marc	3	2	6.11	13	5	0	0	35	31	24	24	21	38	R	R	6-2	195	4-2-73	1991	Phoenix, Ariz.
Leiter, Mark	0	0	4.50	1	1	0	0	2	2	1	1	0	3	R	R	6-3	220	4-13-63	1983	Lanoka Harbor, N.J.
Luce, Rob	0	0	8.44	3	0	0	0	16	22	15	15	7	6	S	R	6-0	168	7-19-74	1996	Rescue, Calif.
Marte, Damaso	3	3	5.13	31	11	0	0	74	79	43	42	40	59	L	L	6-0	170	2-14-75	1993	San Carlos, D.R.
McCarthy, Greg	0	1	2.05	18	0	0	0	22	18	6	5	13	14	L	L	6-2	215	10-30-68	1987	Shelton, Conn.
Meche, Gil	2	2	3.19	6	6	0	0	31	31	12	11	13	24	R	R	6-3	180	9-8-78	1996	Scott, La.
Ramsay, Robert	4	1	1.08	5	5	0	0	33	20	6	4	14	37	L	L	6-5	230	12-3-73	1996	Washougal, Wash.
Scheffer, Aaron	2	3	2.87	35	1	0	9	60	47	25	19	23	62	L	R	6-2	165	10-15-75	1994	Westland, Mich.
Sinclair, Steve	1	0	4.50	2	0	0	0	2	2	1	1	1	1	L	L	6-2	190	8-2-71	1991	Victoria, B.C.
Spencer, Sean	2	1	3.47	44	0	0	7	49	41	21	19	23	53	L	L	5-11	185	5-29-75	1996	Port Orchard, Wash.
Steenstra, Kennie	1	4	5.57	13	10	0	0	52	60	40	32	15	24	R	R	6-5	215	10-13-70	1992	Liberty, Mo.
Stevens, Dave	1	1	12.60	7	0	0	0	10	14	14	14	6	8	R	R	6-2	215	3-4-70	1990	Yorba Linda, Calif.
Sweeney, Brian	0	2	6.75	5	1	0	0	16	26	17	12	2	10	R	R	6-2	185	6-13-74	1996	Yonkers, N.Y.
Weaver, Eric	1	2	3.86	16	3	0	1	26	22	11	11	7	22	R	R	6-5	230	8-4-73	1991	Springfield, Ill.
Williams, Todd	0	0	0.00	1	0	0	1	2	1	0	0	0	0	R	R	6-2	190	2-13-71	1991	Syracuse, N.Y.
Zimmerman, Jordan	0	0	5.14	9	0	0	1	7	13	4	4	4	4	R	L	6-0	200	4-28-75	1995	Brenham, Texas

FIELDING

Catcher	PCT	G	PO	A	E	DP	PB
Chavez	.988	95	664	74	9	5	9
Sealy	.985	53	361	38	6	7	2

First Base	PCT	G	PO	A	E	DP
Blowers	1.000	3	21	0	0	3
Buhner	.994	20	143	13	1	16
Chavez	.000	1	0	0	0	0
Ibanez	1.000	1	1	0	0	0
Jackson	.990	91	704	55	8	76
Pledger	.987	19	142	10	2	17
Sealy	1.000	3	10	1	0	1
Seitzer	.986	6	65	4	1	3

Second Base	PCT	G	PO	A	E	DP
Akers	.972	6	14	21	1	5
Brown	.961	28	64	59	5	20
Cedeno	1.000	5	14	9	0	3
Chavez	.800	1	2	2	1	0
Durango	1.000	1	0	1	0	0
Gipson	1.000	4	7	9	0	1
Guevara	1.000	8	15	18	0	5

	PCT	G	PO	A	E	DP
Matos	.980	89	177	208	8	53
Monahan	1.000	1	0	2	0	1
Sealy	1.000	2	0	1	0	0

Third Base	PCT	G	PO	A	E	DP
Akers	.912	14	4	27	3	2
Buhner	.905	6	7	12	2	1
Chavez	1.000	1	1	2	0	0
Flores	1.000	1	0	4	0	0
Gipson	1.000	5	1	4	0	1
Hills	1.000	1	0	3	0	0
Matos	1.000	3	1	3	1	1
Radmanovich	.800	5	1	3	1	0
Seitzer	.928	108	79	204	22	23

Shortstop	PCT	G	PO	A	E	DP
Akers	.976	15	29	52	2	12
Brown	.955	17	19	45	3	7
Cedeno	.939	26	31	62	6	13
Chavez	1.000	1	2	4	0	0
Flores	.946	41	66	126	11	22

	PCT	G	PO	A	E	DP
Gipson	.903	24	34	50	9	17
Guevara	.965	24	41	69	4	13
Matos	1.000	1	0	2	0	0
Seitzer	1.000	1	0	1	0	0

Outfield	PCT	G	PO	A	E	DP
Akers	1.000	11	23	2	0	0
Gipson	1.000	14	34	2	0	2
Ibanez	1.000	6	12	0	0	0
Jackson	.917	5	10	1	1	0
Johnson	1.000	17	49	1	0	1
Mathis	1.000	25	39	1	0	0
Monahan	.995	88	205	7	1	2
Murphy	1.000	35	87	0	0	0
Pledger	.667	1	2	0	1	0
Radmanovich	.985	92	184	12	3	3
Robinson	.974	70	141	6	4	2
Sachse	1.000	11	18	1	0	0
Timmons	.973	53	106	3	3	1

NEW HAVEN — Class AA

EASTERN LEAGUE

BATTING	AVG	G	AB	R	H	2B	3B	HR	RBI	BB	SO	SB	CS	B	T	HT	WT	DOB	1st Yr	Resides
Akers, Chad	.000	1	0	1	0	0	0	0	0	0	0	0	0	R	R	5-8	160	5-30-72	1993	Lake, W.Va.
Bass, Jayson	.265	123	431	79	114	23	5	21	67	72	160	34	14	L	L	6-3	205	6-22-74	1993	Seattle, Wash.
Brown, Randy	.257	46	167	30	43	7	5	6	22	19	37	0	4	R	R	5-11	160	5-1-70	1989	Houston, Texas
Cruz, Cirilo	.158	18	57	5	9	3	0	0	9	10	13	0	0	R	R	6-0	185	5-29-75	1995	Arroyo, P.R.
Estrada, Marco	.150	8	20	3	3	1	0	0	1	3	8	0	0	S	R	6-2	187	12-11-76	1999	El Segundo, Calif.
Gipson, Charles	.000	5	18	2	0	0	0	0	0	3	2	1	0	R	R	6-2	180	12-16-72	1992	Orange, Calif.
Harrison, Adonis	.272	120	449	54	122	16	0	2	45	38	75	22	18	L	R	5-9	165	9-28-76	1995	Pasadena, Calif.
Hills, Rich	.262	83	282	30	74	15	0	4	29	40	47	1	3	R	R	6-0	195	7-28-73	1995	Springdale, Ark.
Horner, Jim	.270	76	278	29	75	17	0	6	50	17	51	1	1	R	R	6-0	210	11-11-73	1996	Twin Falls, Idaho
Johnson, Earl	.245	37	139	18	34	3	0	0	10	8	31	11	4	S	R	5-10	165	10-3-71	1991	Detroit, Mich.
Kingman, Brendan	.279	130	509	58	142	20	0	10	56	26	71	0	0	R	R	6-1	235	5-22-73	1992	Sydney, Australia
Lopez, Pee Wee	.188	8	32	1	6	1	0	0	1	0	5	0	0	R	R	6-0	195	10-22-76	1996	Miami, Fla.
Magdaleno, Ricky	.271	68	258	30	70	13	1	1	24	21	45	1	3	R	R	6-0	185	7-6-74	1993	Baldwin Park, Calif.
Maness, Dwight	.241	27	87	11	21	2	1	5	12	11	18	9	5	R	R	6-3	188	4-3-74	1992	New Castle, Del.

BATTING	AVG	G	AB	R	H	2B	3B	HR	RBI	BB	SO	SB	CS	B	T	HT	WT	DOB	1st Yr	Resides
Marn, Kevin	.286	2	7	0	2	0	0	0	1	1	3	1	0	R	R	6-4	205	3-23-74	1996	Broadview Heights, Ohio
Martinez, Victor	.000	2	4	0	0	0	0	0	0	1	3	0	0	R	R	5-11	180	3-12-78	1996	New York, N.Y.
Mathis, Joe	.271	67	240	29	65	13	5	2	30	15	45	9	5	L	R	5-11	180	8-10-74	1993	Johnston, S.C.
Regan, Jason	.213	45	150	12	32	9	1	3	13	17	46	2	1	R	R	5-9	175	6-30-76	1996	Belton, Texas
Sachse, Matt	.113	27	97	12	11	1	0	1	4	10	36	1	2	L	L	6-4	205	6-29-76	1995	Spokane, Wash.
Thomas, Juan	.243	71	267	47	65	13	0	16	51	14	92	0	0	R	R	6-5	270	4-17-72	1991	New Boston, Ohio
Vazquez, Ramon	.258	127	438	58	113	27	3	5	45	62	77	8	1	L	R	5-11	170	8-21-76	1995	Cayey, P.R.
Wathan, Dusty	.279	96	333	37	93	16	2	4	37	24	60	4	1	R	R	6-4	215	8-22-73	1994	Blue Springs, Mo.
Weber, Jake	.256	136	489	64	125	22	2	11	59	66	73	5	7	L	R	5-11	188	4-22-76	1998	Wappingers Falls, N.Y.

PITCHING	W	L	ERA	G	GS	CG	SV	IP	H	R	ER	BB	SO	B	T	HT	WT	DOB	1st Yr	Resides
Ahearne, Pat	8	3	2.61	17	17	4	0	124	114	41	36	27	80	R	R	6-3	195	12-10-69	1992	Atascadero, Calif.
Anderson, Ryan	9	13	4.50	24	24	0	0	134	131	77	67	86	162	L	L	6-10	215	7-12-79	1997	Westland, Mich.
Brosnan, Jason	3	0	2.34	28	1	0	6	50	32	14	13	15	44	L	L	6-1	190	1-26-68	1989	San Leandro, Calif.
De la Rosa, Maximo	0	1	2.53	10	0	0	4	11	9	4	3	3	7	R	R	5-11	170	7-12-71	1990	Villa Mella, D.R.
Dunham, Pat	0	1	2.57	3	0	0	0	7	1	2	2	16	5	R	R	6-5	200	3-16-76	1997	Portage, Mich.
Fitzgerald, Brian	2	2	3.83	29	1	0	3	54	58	24	23	18	37	L	L	5-11	175	12-26-74	1996	Lake Ridge, Va.
Fuentes, Brian	3	3	4.95	15	14	0	0	60	53	36	33	46	66	L	L	6-4	220	8-9-75	1996	Merced, Calif.
Gryboski, Kevin	2	5	2.89	47	0	0	10	62	67	27	20	20	41	R	R	6-5	220	11-15-73	1995	Plains, Pa.
Kirkreit, Daron	2	2	2.63	5	4	0	0	24	33	8	7	7	15	R	R	6-6	225	8-7-72	1993	Norco, Calif.
Luce, Rob	0	0	8.59	2	0	0	0	7	11	10	7	3	3	S	R	6-0	168	7-19-74	1996	Rescue, Calif.
McClaskey, Tim	0	0	2.25	4	0	0	0	8	4	2	2	1	7	R	R	6-1	180	1-11-76	1996	Melbourne, Fla.
Meche, Gil	3	4	3.05	10	10	0	0	59	51	24	20	26	56	R	R	6-3	180	9-8-78	1996	Scott, La.
Montane, Ivan	4	2	2.47	41	0	0	10	55	38	16	15	22	70	R	R	6-2	195	6-3-73	1992	Miami, Fla.
Newton, Geronimo	2	1	3.97	31	2	0	0	59	60	32	26	26	48	L	L	6-0	165	12-31-73	1992	Christiansted, V.I.
Pineiro, Joel	10	15	4.72	28	25	4	0	166	190	105	87	52	116	R	R	6-1	180	9-25-78	1997	Orlando, Fla.
Scheffer, Aaron	2	0	3.71	10	0	0	0	17	19	9	7	8	24	L	L	6-2	165	10-15-75	1994	Westland, Mich.
Smith, Cam	1	4	5.07	41	0	0	0	55	42	39	31	61	59	R	R	6-3	190	9-20-73	1993	Selkirk, N.Y.
Stark, Denny	9	11	4.40	26	26	2	0	147	151	82	72	62	103	R	R	6-2	210	10-27-74	1996	Edgerton, Ohio
Sweeney, Brian	4	6	4.69	23	18	0	1	111	125	65	58	31	83	R	R	6-2	185	6-13-74	1996	Yonkers, N.Y.
Zimmerman, Jordan	1	4	1.08	22	0	0	2	33	26	8	4	19	33	R	L	6-0	200	4-28-75	1995	Brenham, Texas

FIELDING

Catcher	PCT	G	PO	A	E	DP	PB
Horner	.998	68	522	49	1	3	15
Wathan	.989	78	562	64	7	5	4

First Base	PCT	G	PO	A	E	DP
Cruz	1.000	6	41	2	0	4
Kingman	.993	115	943	84	7	103
Thomas	.992	14	125	5	1	16
Wathan	.989	12	85	7	1	11

Second Base	PCT	G	PO	A	E	DP
Brown	1.000	1	2	4	0	2
Gipson	1.000	2	8	6	0	2
Harrison	.958	117	248	319	25	77
Hills	.944	10	11	23	2	5
Vazquez	.953	16	34	47	4	15

Third Base	PCT	G	PO	A	E	DP
Brown	.897	24	18	43	7	5
Gipson	.667	1	1	1	1	0
Hills	.909	53	26	94	12	9
Kingman	.857	5	3	15	3	1
Regan	.906	22	14	44	6	1
Vazquez	.922	44	25	82	9	9

Shortstop	PCT	G	PO	A	E	DP
Brown	.957	12	19	25	2	3
Gipson	.000	1	0	0	0	0
Magdaleno	.971	66	97	202	9	49
Vazquez	.945	67	98	214	18	43

Outfield	PCT	G	PO	A	E	DP
Bass	.954	110	220	8	11	2

	PCT	G	PO	A	E	DP
Brown	.500	2	1	0	1	0
Gipson	1.000	1	1	0	0	0
Hills	1.000	23	23	1	0	0
Johnson	.986	37	64	4	1	2
Kingman	1.000	9	13	0	0	0
Lopez	1.000	8	9	1	0	0
Magdaleno	1.000	3	4	0	0	0
Maness	.955	27	41	1	2	0
Marn	1.000	2	4	0	0	0
Mathis	.978	62	125	6	3	0
Sachse	.957	24	43	1	2	0
Wathan	1.000	1	1	0	0	0
Weber	.988	133	226	15	3	2

LANCASTER — Class A

CALIFORNIA LEAGUE

BATTING	AVG	G	AB	R	H	2B	3B	HR	RBI	BB	SO	SB	CS	B	T	HT	WT	DOB	1st Yr	Resides
Alcala, Juan	.071	8	14	0	1	1	0	0	2	1	7	0	0	R	R	6-2	185	4-15-78	1995	San Pedro de Macoris, D.R.
Amador, Jerry	.270	19	74	12	20	3	1	1	9	3	24	2	1	R	R	6-0	185	1-13-80	1999	Hatillo, P.R.
Clark, Jermaine	.315	126	502	112	158	27	8	6	61	58	80	33	15	L	R	5-10	175	9-29-76	1997	Vacaville, Calif.
Connors, Greg	.268	117	448	72	120	20	7	16	84	40	91	10	7	R	R	6-2	185	8-22-74	1996	Smithtown, N.Y.
Cruz, Cirilo	.249	94	342	51	85	12	1	12	44	28	73	1	1	R	R	6-0	185	5-29-75	1995	Arroyo, P.R.
Eady, Gerald	.245	52	151	20	37	4	3	1	18	27	57	7	12	R	R	6-2	200	10-25-75	1996	Jacksonville, Fla.
Estrada, Marco	.200	13	35	3	7	2	0	0	3	2	8	1	0	S	R	6-0	187	12-11-76	1999	El Segundo, Calif.
Fernandez, Alex	.282	118	426	63	120	29	2	14	62	21	83	21	11	L	L	6-1	205	5-15-81	1998	Cotui, D.R.
Figueroa, Luis	.356	39	146	21	52	8	1	4	20	18	8	2	2	R	R	6-0	175	3-2-77	1995	Carolina, P.R.
Hargrove, Harvey	.294	130	510	83	150	20	2	11	80	51	116	17	16	R	R	5-11	175	10-9-75	1997	Upper Marlboro, Md.
Kuzmic, Craig	.204	32	108	19	22	4	0	5	15	20	43	3	1	S	R	6-1	195	5-27-78	1998	Fountain Valley, Calif.
Lopez, Pee Wee	.287	72	247	37	71	10	3	5	28	15	36	5	4	R	R	6-0	195	10-22-76	1996	Miami, Fla.
Magdaleno, Ricky	.348	23	89	12	31	4	2	1	14	11	12	2	1	R	R	6-0	185	7-6-74	1993	Baldwin Park, Calif.
Marchiano, Mike	.313	47	182	25	57	11	1	3	29	16	28	4	1	R	R	6-0	215	2-3-75	1997	Oak Ridge, N.J.
Maynard, Scott	.259	8	27	6	7	4	0	1	3	4	8	0	0	R	R	6-2	215	8-28-77	1995	Laguna Niguel, Calif.
McCorkle, Shawn	.275	83	302	45	83	22	1	9	52	35	97	1	1	L	R	6-5	230	7-14-77	1998	Newton, N.J.
Moreno, Jose	.162	23	68	9	11	2	0	0	4	7	12	4	1	R	R	5-11	176	8-9-77	1995	San Pedro de Macoris, D.R.
Quintana, Wilfredo	.297	10	37	7	11	1	1	3	8	2	14	1	0	R	R	5-11	181	6-29-77	1998	Loiza, P.R.
Ramirez, Joel	.239	106	376	55	90	17	7	2	42	29	64	10	8	R	R	5-10	155	8-17-73	1994	Miami, Fla.
Regan, Jason	.255	64	231	50	59	17	1	15	45	33	77	4	1	R	R	5-9	175	6-30-76	1996	Belton, Texas
Sachse, Matt	.305	69	236	40	72	18	2	7	41	33	67	5	4	L	L	6-4	205	6-29-76	1995	Spokane, Wash.
Southall, Rick	.000	1	2	0	0	0	0	0	0	0	2	0	0	L	R	6-3	225	2-9-77	1998	Beaverton, Ore.
Taylor, Josh	.077	6	13	0	1	0	0	0	2	1	6	0	0	R	R	5-9	155	7-5-77	1997	Shawnee, Okla.
Valera, Ramon	.185	17	54	10	10	1	0	0	1	10	10	4	4	S	R	5-11	160	8-21-75	1994	Santo Domingo, D.R.
Williams, Peanut	.324	68	272	60	88	12	0	26	59	35	89	0	0	R	R	6-3	235	10-3-77	1995	Nacogdoches, Texas

GAMES BY POSITION: C—Alcala 7, Connors 55, Kuzmic 14, Lopez 63, Maynard 8, Williams 4. **1B**—Connors 11, Cruz 26, Kuzmic 2, McCorkle 59, Williams 51. **2B**—Clark 122, Hargrove 1, Moreno 6, Ramirez 11, Regan 4, Taylor 4, Valera 5. **3B**—Connors 6, Cruz 30, Figueroa 32, Hargrove 1, Kuzmic 10, Magdaleno 3, Moreno 2, Ramirez 2, Regan 62, Taylor 2. **SS**—Estrada 13, Hargrove 6, Magdaleno 19, Moreno 5, Ramirez 95, Valera 12. **OF**—Amador 17, Connors 6, Cruz 33, Eady 46, Fernandez 114, Hargrove 123, Marchiano 33, Moreno 1, Quintana 3, Sachse 6, Williams 2.

PITCHING	W	L	ERA	G	GS	CG	SV	IP	H	R	ER	BB	SO	B	T	HT	WT	DOB	1st Yr	Resides
Bello, Emerson	0	0	6.75	9	0	0	0	13	15	12	10	9	13	R	R	6-0	180	10-4-77	1995	Maracaibo, Venez.
Bieniasz, Derek	1	8	7.91	15	9	0	0	52	75	48	46	20	29	R	R	6-4	175	4-19-74	1993	Toronto, Ontario

PITCHING	W	L	ERA	G	GS	CG	SV	IP	H	R	ER	BB	SO	B	T	HT	WT	DOB	1st Yr	Resides
Carmody, Brian	3	3	3.66	16	2	0	0	39	43	22	16	18	45	L	L	6-3	195	7-1-75	1996	San Jose, Calif.
Dunham, Pat	1	4	7.78	9	8	0	0	39	49	40	34	28	33	R	R	6-5	200	3-16-76	1997	Portage, Mich.
Farnsworth, Jeff	3	6	6.50	26	9	0	3	72	91	61	52	43	43	R	R	6-2	190	10-6-75	1996	Pensacola, Fla.
Fitzgerald, Brian	1	3	7.15	6	6	0	0	34	50	35	27	4	23	L	L	5-11	200	12-26-74	1996	Lake Ridge, Va.
Hoerman, Jared	0	0	7.04	4	0	0	0	8	8	6	6	7	6	R	R	6-4	215	4-25-77	1999	Ardmore, Okla.
Kaye, Justin	3	5	5.75	53	0	0	14	61	68	42	39	40	66	R	R	6-4	195	6-9-76	1995	Las Vegas, Nev.
Kirkreit, Daron	4	4	5.36	9	9	0	0	47	65	34	28	17	35	R	R	6-6	225	8-7-72	1993	Norco, Calif.
Klepaski, Jose	0	0	0.00	1	0	0	0	2	0	0	0	1	0	R	R	6-2	194	4-9-78	1999	Key West, Fla.
Koehler, Russ	0	3	8.03	7	7	0	0	25	33	28	22	18	19	R	R	6-5	215	10-5-74	1995	Medford, Ore.
Longo, Neil	6	7	5.71	23	19	0	0	128	163	87	81	46	76	R	R	6-5	200	9-5-77	1998	Miller Place, N.Y.
McClaskey, Tim	3	3	6.36	30	0	0	0	58	83	51	41	11	54	R	R	6-1	180	1-11-76	1996	Melbourne, Fla.
Mears, Chris	3	6	7.08	10	10	0	0	55	71	44	43	18	45	R	R	6-4	190	1-20-78	1996	Victoria, B.C.
Parker, Brandon	9	7	5.09	27	27	0	0	140	164	95	79	67	147	R	R	6-1	200	12-9-75	1997	Long Beach, Miss.
Ramos, Juan	1	4	6.28	42	0	0	1	62	82	58	43	36	41	R	R	6-0	185	2-1-76	1995	Santo Domingo, D.R.
Schmidt, Donnie	1	2	3.50	21	0	0	0	36	46	20	14	25	21	R	R	6-1	175	2-18-75	1996	Sherwood, Ore.
Simpson, Allan	0	0	6.33	9	0	0	0	21	17	16	15	14	25	R	R	6-4	185	8-26-77	1997	Las Vegas, Nev.
Stark, Zac	1	2	3.99	49	0	0	2	79	75	44	35	29	72	R	L	6-6	225	8-7-74	1994	Leawood, Kan.
Sweeney, Brian	0	0	6.75	5	0	0	0	9	14	7	7	3	14	R	R	6-2	185	6-13-74	1996	Yonkers, N.Y.
Turman, Jason	4	10	5.20	31	12	1	1	97	116	66	56	35	78	R	R	6-10	210	11-10-75	1996	Gordo, Ala.
Victery, Joe	1	4	8.51	10	5	0	0	31	51	35	29	13	15	R	R	6-2	205	4-26-75	1996	Ninnekah, Okla.
Wooten, Greg	10	4	4.33	17	17	3	0	114	123	62	55	30	72	R	R	6-7	210	3-30-74	1996	Vancouver, Wash.

WISCONSIN — Class A

MIDWEST LEAGUE

BATTING	AVG	G	AB	R	H	2B	3B	HR	RBI	BB	SO	SB	CS	B	T	HT	WT	DOB	1st Yr	Resides
Castillo, Ruben	.205	20	44	7	9	0	0	0	4	5	9	1	1	R	R	6-2	155	8-16-80	1996	San Pedro de Macoris, D.R.
Espino, Fernando	.293	130	481	71	141	29	0	11	69	38	91	5	8	R	R	6-0	165	11-26-76	1994	La Vega, D.R.
Freeman, Corey	.190	18	63	6	12	6	0	0	9	1	18	0	0	R	R	5-11	180	10-13-79	1998	Tampa, Fla.
Haynes, Larry	.261	67	176	36	46	5	5	6	23	18	58	9	3	R	R	5-11	180	8-31-77	1997	West Covina, Calif.
Hernandez, Orlando	.231	15	26	3	6	1	0	0	1	8	0	0	0	R	R	6-2	190	3-26-79	1996	Charallave, Venez.
Kuzmic, Craig	.238	91	323	48	77	18	1	10	55	61	84	7	4	S	R	6-1	195	5-2-77	1998	Fountain Valley, Calif.
Maldonado, Carlos	.308	92	302	35	93	13	0	0	33	43	32	4	6	R	R	6-2	185	1-3-79	1996	Maracaibo, Venez.
Martinez, Victor	.224	69	254	41	57	10	3	3	28	21	37	3	2	R	R	5-11	180	3-12-78	1996	New York, Venez.
Maynard, Scott	.200	50	135	16	27	4	0	2	15	10	29	1	3	R	R	6-2	215	8-28-77	1995	Laguna Niguel, Calif.
Moreno, Jose	.000	3	4	0	0	0	0	0	0	0	0	0	1	R	R	5-11	176	8-9-77	1995	San Pedro de Macoris, D.R.
Nelson, Brian	.205	58	171	17	35	10	0	3	21	22	54	2	1	R	R	6-1	185	5-11-76	1996	Sarasota, Fla.
Robinson, Bo	.329	138	499	101	164	50	3	13	102	108	75	4	1	R	R	6-2	195	8-21-75	1998	Charlotte, N.C.
Schill, Vaughn	.354	25	79	13	28	4	0	0	7	13	16	7	1	R	R	6-2	175	9-10-77	1999	Audubon, N.J.
Silvestre, Juan	.288	137	534	89	154	34	4	21	107	47	124	5	4	R	R	5-11	180	1-10-78	1996	San Pedro de Macoris, D.R.
Southall, Rick	.246	102	337	47	83	19	1	10	51	42	101	4	1	L	R	6-3	225	2-9-77	1998	Beaverton, Ore.
Valera, Ramon	.270	99	382	72	103	14	4	2	33	75	92	42	19	S	R	5-11	160	8-21-75	1994	Santo Domingo, D.R.
Williams, P.J.	.299	115	371	65	111	14	5	2	46	48	63	22	7	R	R	6-2	165	5-7-77	1997	Rockdale, Texas
Williams, Peanut	.250	9	32	6	8	1	0	2	7	4	12	0	0	R	R	6-3	235	10-3-77	1996	Nacogdoches, Texas
Woodward, Matt	.213	58	150	15	32	1	0	0	9	24	45	0	3	R	R	6-2	192	12-1-75	1998	Kirkland, Wash.
Zambrano, Alan	.202	90	282	33	57	14	0	5	30	29	79	6	7	S	S	5-11	170	1-7-79	1996	Maracaibo, Venez.

GAMES BY POSITION: C—Kuzmic 6, Maldonado 88, Maynard 45, Nelson 18. **1B**—Kuzmic 1, Nelson 4, Robinson 19, Southall 69, Pe. Williams 4, Woodward 56. **2B**—Kuzmic 1, Martinez 31, Valera 36, Zambrano 83. **3B**—Kuzmic 58, Martinez 5, Maynard 4, Moreno 1, Robinson 83. **SS**—Castillo 19, Freeman 18, Kuzmic 1, Martinez 22, Moreno 2, Schill 24, Valera 63. **OF**—Espino 123, Freeman 2, Haynes 66, Hernandez 15, Kuzmic 36, Martinez 10, Maynard 1, Nelson 2, Robinson 1, Silvestre 99, Southall 1, P.J. Williams 111, Zambrano 2.

PITCHING	W	L	ERA	G	GS	CG	SV	IP	H	R	ER	BB	SO	B	T	HT	WT	DOB	1st Yr	Resides
Atchison, Scott	4	5	3.42	15	13	0	0	82	67	34	31	25	85	R	R	6-2	180	3-29-76	1999	Grainbury, Texas
Balbuena, Caleb	1	3	5.32	8	8	0	0	44	48	33	26	18	31	R	R	6-7	240	3-23-77	1998	Tuolumne, Calif.
Berroa, Oliver	1	0	1.84	21	0	0	1	29	22	8	6	17	28	R	R	6-1	204	3-24-78	1996	San Pedro de Macoris, D.R.
Chrysler, Clint	5	7	2.06	51	0	0	8	57	47	22	13	22	59	L	L	6-0	191	11-4-75	1997	St. Petersburg, Fla.
Dunham, Pat	0	1	7.53	12	0	0	1	14	23	15	12	7	13	R	R	6-5	200	3-16-76	1997	Portage, Mich.
Dunning, Justin	4	4	5.61	25	8	0	2	69	79	50	43	36	76	R	R	6-3	210	2-16-77	1998	Tustin, Calif.
Heaverlo, Jeff	1	0	2.55	3	3	1	0	18	15	6	5	7	24	R	R	6-1	185	1-13-78	1999	Ephrata, Wash.
Longo, Neil	2	2	0.96	5	5	3	0	38	24	9	4	8	35	R	R	6-5	200	9-5-77	1998	Miller Place, N.Y.
Looper, Aaron	9	6	4.10	38	7	0	3	90	89	47	41	26	73	R	R	6-2	185	9-7-76	1998	Ada, Okla.
Mateo, Julio	1	3	4.34	20	0	0	4	29	31	18	14	8	27	R	R	6-0	177	8-22-79	1996	Bani, D.R.
Matos, Gonzalo	9	9	4.63	25	22	2	0	138	143	78	71	44	110	R	R	6-4	190	3-15-78	1997	Cabo Rojo, P.R.
Mears, Chris	10	1	2.43	13	13	2	0	89	76	33	24	16	78	R	R	6-4	190	1-20-78	1996	Victoria, B.C.
Montane, Ivan	0	0	0.71	10	0	0	3	13	5	1	1	5	18	R	R	6-2	195	6-3-73	1992	Miami, Fla.
Schmidt, Donnie	0	1	4.50	5	0	0	0	8	5	6	4	9	8	R	R	6-1	175	2-18-75	1996	Sherwood, Ore.
Simpson, Allan	2	9	4.38	24	13	1	0	90	83	56	44	48	88	R	R	6-4	185	8-26-77	1997	Las Vegas, Nev.
Smith, Justin	1	1	4.82	7	7	0	0	37	41	22	20	10	29	L	L	5-11	185	1-13-77	1999	Elk City, Okla.
Thornton, Matt	0	0	4.91	25	1	0	1	29	39	19	16	25	34	L	L	6-6	220	9-15-76	1998	Allendale, Mich.
Torres, Melqui	13	9	4.51	27	27	3	0	172	185	99	86	45	129	R	R	6-1	165	5-27-77	1996	San Pedro de Macoris, D.R.
Ulloa, Enmanuel	7	3	4.60	35	10	0	5	88	90	50	45	36	98	R	R	6-2	170	11-26-78	1997	New York, N.Y.
Willis, Craig	2	2	5.90	39	1	0	0	61	81	47	40	26	49	R	R	6-3	195	7-8-76	1998	Ferndale, Wash.

EVERETT — Short-Season Class A

NORTHWEST LEAGUE

BATTING	AVG	G	AB	R	H	2B	3B	HR	RBI	BB	SO	SB	CS	B	T	HT	WT	DOB	1st Yr	Resides
Abate, Mike	.254	57	185	34	47	15	0	5	23	17	57	1	2	R	R	6-3	205	7-16-78	1999	Norwalk, Conn.
Alcala, Juan	.207	17	58	4	12	4	0	1	8	0	17	1	0	R	R	6-2	185	4-15-78	1995	San Pedro de Macoris, D.R.
Amador, Jerry	.293	14	58	10	17	3	0	2	12	6	12	3	1	R	R	6-0	185	1-13-80	1999	Hatillo, P.R.
Barnett, Nathan	.225	18	40	4	9	4	0	0	5	3	12	0	0	L	L	6-2	205	9-26-76	1999	Arlington, Wash.
Bloomquist, Willie	.287	42	178	35	51	10	3	2	27	22	25	17	5	R	R	5-11	180	11-27-77	1999	Port Orchard, Wash.
Carroll, Mark	.228	45	127	22	29	6	0	1	14	29	39	0	0	R	R	6-0	195	10-29-76	1996	Athens, N.Y.
Castillo, Ruben	.288	62	226	38	65	10	2	2	27	19	48	11	2	R	R	6-2	155	8-16-80	1996	San Pedro de Macoris, D.R.

BATTING	AVG	G	AB	R	H	2B	3B	HR	RBI	BB	SO	SB	CS	B	T	HT	WT	DOB	1st Yr	Resides
Christianson, Ryan	.280	30	107	19	30	7	0	8	17	14	31	3	1	R	R	6-2	202	4-21-81	1999	Riverside, Calif.
Durango, Ariel	.269	25	93	19	25	5	1	2	9	9	25	11	5	S	R	5-10	170	4-5-79	1996	Panama City, Panama
Estrella, Gorky	.250	28	84	15	21	4	1	1	11	31	22	2	2	R	R	6-2	205	6-11-77	1996	New York, N.Y.
Gipson, Charles	.500	1	2	0	1	0	1	0	1	2	0	1	0	R	R	6-2	180	12-16-72	1992	Orange, Calif.
Gundrum, Kris	.297	29	91	13	27	4	0	2	15	10	27	5	0	L	L	6-0	190	4-18-77	1999	Dublin, Ga.
Hertel, Brian	.357	5	14	5	5	1	0	0	0	3	3	0	0	R	R	6-5	200	4-28-78	1999	Fresno, Calif.
Leone, Justin	.263	62	205	34	54	14	2	6	35	32	49	5	3	R	R	6-1	190	3-9-77	1999	Las Vegas, Nev.
Martinez, Victor	.212	28	113	9	24	2	1	1	15	4	24	1	3	R	R	5-11	180	3-12-78	1996	New York, N.Y.
Parnell, Sean	.244	36	131	25	32	8	0	0	18	12	24	5	3	R	R	6-3	225	11-8-77	1999	Deer Park, Wis.
Quintana, Wilfredo	.161	19	62	6	10	3	0	1	5	0	21	0	1	R	R	5-11	181	6-22-78	1998	Loiza, P.R.
Ramirez, Oscar	.308	6	13	4	4	3	0	0	5	4	3	0	0	R	R	5-11	180	9-14-78	1999	Mexico City, Mexico
Robles, Kevin	.262	62	214	27	56	12	0	5	32	16	44	0	0	R	R	6-1	210	2-11-78	1999	Dorado, P.R.
Sledge, Terrmel	.318	62	233	43	74	8	3	5	32	27	35	9	8	L	L	6-0	190	3-18-77	1999	Granada Hills, Calif.
Snelling, Chris	.306	69	265	46	81	15	3	10	50	33	24	8	9	L	L	5-10	165	12-3-81	1999	Gorokan, Australia
Taylor, Josh	.211	42	90	11	19	1	0	1	8	17	21	0	1	R	R	5-9	155	5-1-77	1997	Shawnee, Okla.

GAMES BY POSITION: C—Alcala 15, Carroll 44, Christianson 13, Robles 13. **1B**—Abate 1, Barnett 16, Estrella 10, Gundrum 20, Hertel 5, Martinez 10, Robles 34. **2B**—Bloomquist 37, Durango 22, Martinez 3, Taylor 20. **3B**—Durango 1, Estrella 19, Leone 40, Martinez 14, Ramirez 5, Robles 1, Taylor 9. **SS**—Castillo 62, Durango 2, Gipson 1, Leone 18, Taylor 1. **OF**—Abate 44, Amador 14, Booomquist 1, Gundrum 9, Martinez 4, Parnell 29, Quintana 14, Sledge 62, Snelling 69.

PITCHING	W	L	ERA	G	GS	CG	SV	IP	H	R	ER	BB	SO	B	T	HT	WT	DOB	1st Yr	Resides
Anderson, Craig	10	2	3.20	15	15	2	0	90	81	42	32	13	82	L	L	6-2	182	10-30-80	1999	Ourimbah, Australia
Barnes, Pat	3	3	5.66	15	10	1	0	49	59	40	31	26	39	R	L	6-3	196	9-25-79	1999	Jacksonville, Fla.
Burton, Tim	2	3	3.72	26	0	0	1	39	40	25	16	21	28	R	R	6-3	225	12-16-76	1999	Stuart, Fla.
Carreras, Marino	1	4	7.18	22	0	0	2	31	37	29	25	24	30	L	L	6-1	170	1-25-80	1996	Monte Plata, D.R.
Delgado, Danny	2	3	3.05	17	1	0	3	38	35	18	13	12	35	R	R	6-2	180	2-10-78	1997	Miami Lakes, Fla.
Duprey, Pete	3	1	1.00	22	0	0	3	36	26	7	4	12	32	R	L	6-4	225	11-26-78	1997	Ocala, Fla.
Grunwald, Erik	0	0	2.25	4	0	0	1	4	5	1	1	4	4	R	R	6-4	220	4-25-77	1999	Ontario, Calif.
Heaverlo, Jeff	1	0	2.08	3	0	0	0	9	5	5	2	2	9	R	R	6-1	185	1-13-78	1999	Ephrata, Wash.
Kent, Steven	3	2	5.35	21	0	0	4	37	31	24	22	26	43	L	L	5-11	170	10-3-78	1999	Killeen, Texas
Klepaski, Jose	0	0	6.75	3	0	0	0	5	6	4	4	5	5	R	R	6-2	194	4-9-78	1999	Key West, Fla.
Lopez, Aquilino	7	6	3.80	15	15	1	0	88	76	44	37	30	93	R	R	6-3	165	4-21-80	1997	Villa Altagracia, D.R.
Olore, Kevin	0	0	4.88	22	0	0	2	31	31	21	17	21	31	L	R	6-2	200	9-21-99	1999	Southington, Conn.
Putz, J.J.	0	0	4.84	10	0	0	2	22	23	13	12	11	17	R	R	6-5	220	2-22-77	1999	Trenton, Mich.
Smith, Justin	1	0	3.18	2	0	0	0	6	3	3	2	1	8	L	L	5-11	511	1-13-77	1999	Elk City, Okla.
Soriano, Rafael	5	4	3.11	14	14	0	0	75	56	34	26	49	83	R	R	6-1	175	12-19-79	1996	Boca Chica, D.R.
Walton, Sam	3	3	4.94	14	14	0	0	62	55	39	34	36	59	L	L	6-4	215	12-1-78	1997	Dallas, Texas
Wayne, Hawkeye	0	2	8.29	15	7	0	0	34	47	39	31	32	34	R	R	6-1	205	11-24-77	1999	Honolulu, Hawaii
Wells, Roy	0	2	19.29	3	0	0	0	2	5	5	5	4	3	S	R	6-3	195	11-17-78	1999	Hazard, Ky.
Zimmerman, Jordan	0	0	27.00	1	0	0	0	1	3	2	2	0	1	R	L	6-0	200	4-28-75	1995	Brenham, Texas

PEORIA   Rookie

ARIZONA LEAGUE

BATTING	AVG	G	AB	R	H	2B	3B	HR	RBI	BB	SO	SB	CS	B	T	HT	WT	DOB	1st Yr	Resides
Christianson, Ryan	.263	11	38	3	10	8	0	0	7	2	12	2	0	R	R	6-2	202	4-21-81	1999	Riverside, Calif.
Clark, Jamie	.344	26	96	26	33	3	3	3	17	17	29	5	2	L	L	6-1	190	6-1-79	1998	Valrico, Fla.
Cruz, Israel	.286	13	28	4	8	1	0	0	4	2	6	1	0	R	R	6-0	170	9-23-79	1998	Carolina, P.R.
Diaz, Jose	.182	23	66	7	12	2	0	0	7	5	16	0	2	R	R	6-1	175	6-27-80	1997	Cabimas, Venez.
Doakes, Schuyler	.254	34	138	21	35	7	3	0	11	13	30	9	1	S	R	5-7	160	8-23-76	1998	Detroit, Mich.
Durango, Ariel	.312	20	24	5	1	2	12	8	7	6	2	6	2	S	R	5-10	170	4-5-79	1996	Panama City, Panama
Figueroa, Luis	.500	3	10	2	5	1	0	0	1	0	0	0	0	R	R	6-0	175	3-2-77	1995	Carolina, P.R.
Freeman, Corey	.272	28	103	20	28	9	0	0	13	8	25	8	2	R	R	5-11	165	10-13-79	1998	Tampa, Fla.
Fulse, Sheldon	.247	31	97	15	24	11	0	0	9	22	34	12	8	S	R	6-1	170	11-10-81	1999	Bartow, Fla.
Hernandez, Orlando	.245	27	106	17	26	7	1	1	19	5	17	1	2	R	R	6-2	180	3-26-79	1996	Charallave, Venez.
Hertel, Brian	.280	33	125	22	35	5	1	3	19	6	20	1	0	R	R	6-5	200	4-28-78	1999	Fresno, Calif.
Kent, Mat	.227	34	119	18	27	3	3	3	15	5	28	1	0	L	R	6-3	185	7-2-80	1998	Melbourne, Australia
Lara, Franklin	.288	30	104	13	30	4	1	0	6	9	13	1	2	R	R	5-11	175	10-14-79	1996	Ciudad Bolivar, Venez.
Lopez, Orlando	.254	42	138	18	35	6	2	0	10	16	27	11	7	R	R	6-0	180	9-26-80	1997	Lecherias, Venez.
Marchiano, Mike	.444	3	9	2	4	0	0	1	5	2	0	1	1	R	R	6-0	215	3-2-75	1997	Oak Ridge, N.J.
Martinez, Guillermo	.306	42	160	24	49	7	0	1	19	4	33	3	6	S	R	6-0	158	6-24-80	1997	Maracay, Venez.
Pena, Pelagio	.364	21	77	11	28	5	1	0	14	4	13	3	1	R	R	6-0	210	6-27-80	1997	Santo Domingo, D.R.
Pines, Greg	.299	31	97	14	29	7	2	3	17	8	15	0	0	R	R	6-0	180	8-3-78	1999	Garden Grove, Calif.
Quintana, Wilfredo	.379	16	58	10	22	8	0	2	18	2	11	2	2	R	R	5-11	181	6-22-78	1998	Loiza, P.R.
Ramirez, Oscar	.327	47	159	32	52	15	2	1	26	28	28	9	4	R	R	5-11	180	9-14-78	1999	Mexico City, Mexico
Richardson, Miguel	.273	37	128	26	35	3	4	7	26	13	49	1	1	R	R	6-5	200	8-5-80	1997	San Pedro de Macoris, D.R.

GAMES BY POSITION: C—Christianson 6, Diaz 15, Kent 22, Pena 18, Pines 6. **1B**—Hertel 32, Kent 10, Pines 18. **2B**—Doakes 29, Durango 12, Martinez 12, Ramirez 6. **3B**—Durango 2, Figueroa 1, Lara 26, Pines 1, Ramirez 30. **SS**—Durango 5, Freeman 27, Martinez 29. **OF**—J. Clark 24, K. Clark 2, Fulse 26, Hernandez 27, Lopez 41, Marchiano 1, Pines 4, Quintana 16, Ramirez 1, Richardson 35.

PITCHING	W	L	ERA	G	GS	CG	SV	IP	H	R	ER	BB	SO	B	T	HT	WT	DOB	1st Yr	Resides
Baek, Cha	3	0	3.67	8	4	0	0	27	30	13	11	6	25	R	R	6-4	190	5-29-80	1999	Pusan, Korea
Clark, Kevin	2	0	5.72	16	0	0	0	28	34	22	18	20	22	R	R	6-5	250	3-3-78	1999	Lake Worth, Fla.
Drain, Brad	6	5	4.27	13	11	0	0	65	63	38	31	13	71	R	R	6-5	200	1-16-80	1998	Wonona, Australia
Dunham, Pat	0	2	9.58	7	0	0	3	10	13	11	11	7	11	R	R	6-5	200	3-16-76	1997	Portage, Mich.
Earle, Scott	1	1	1.46	7	0	0	0	12	14	4	2	2	13	R	R	6-2	175	8-6-76	1999	Puyallup, Wash.
Encarnacion, Luis	0	0	10.88	15	0	0	1	22	26	30	27	24	25	R	R	6-0	195	3-27-80	1996	Santo Domingo, D.R.
Espinal, Juan	3	3	7.12	15	5	0	0	43	56	38	34	20	31	R	R	6-1	190	8-1-80	1997	Santiago, D.R.
Garcia, Joaquin	3	4	4.61	12	7	0	0	53	64	33	27	13	51	R	R	6-3	190	6-21-78	1997	San Cristobal, D.R.
Grunwald, Erik	3	2	2.63	18	0	0	3	24	22	10	7	9	23	R	R	6-4	220	4-25-77	1999	Ontario, Calif.
Herrera, Jose	3	5	5.83	12	11	0	0	54	56	46	35	29	48	R	R	6-6	170	11-11-79	1996	Santo Domingo, D.R.
Hoerman, Jared	1	0	1.41	11	1	0	2	32	24	6	5	6	46	R	R	6-4	215	4-25-77	1999	Ardmore, Okla.
Kesten, Mike	2	0	6.55	13	0	0	0	22	17	18	16	20	17	L	L	6-2	185	9-22-81	1999	Bellflower, Calif.
Koehler, Russ	1	2	0.96	4	4	0	0	19	16	5	2	5	21	R	R	6-5	215	10-5-74	1995	Medford, Ore.
Kroon, Marc	0	0	3.86	4	4	0	0	7	5	3	3	0	9	R	R	6-2	195	4-23-73	1991	Phoenix, Ariz.
Montenegro, Chris	0	1	3.00	19	0	0	7	27	19	11	9	15	35	R	R	6-1	205	1-26-77	1999	Howell, N.J.
Wells, Roy	3	0	2.70	10	9	0	0	47	39	22	14	22	52	S	R	6-3	195	11-17-78	1999	Hazard, Ky.

TAMPA BAY DEVIL RAYS

"Good, bad and ugly" season shows Rays where they stand

BY MARC TOPKIN

The Devil Rays learned a lot during the 1999 season. They discovered that some young players weren't ready. They found out that some veterans weren't done. They saw how much injuries can hurt.

And they realized just how much work they have ahead. The Devil Rays finished 69-93, six games better than their inaugural season but a long way from where they want to be.

"Good, bad and ugly," closer Roberto Hernandez said. "That about covers everything."

The worst was the stream of injuries that came to define the season. The Rays were 22-20 in mid-May, but a brutal two-week stretch of injuries launched a 2-16 skid that wrecked their record and their season.

Three players went down with season-ending injuries—righthander Jim Mecir, fractured elbow; outfielder Quinton McCracken, torn anterior cruciate ligament; and lefthander Tony Saunders, broken arm. Two more would join them later in the summer, when shortstop Kevin Stocker and third baseman Wade Boggs both went down for knee surgery.

One veteran who came through was Boggs, who reached the 3,000-hit plateau on Aug. 7. First baseman Fred McGriff, Hernandez and lefthander Wilson Alvarez were among the other veterans who proved they can still produce.

The injuries were not the only disappointment. The Rays also found out that some of the young players who starred in 1998, such as third baseman Bobby Smith and center fielder Randy Winn, were not ready for full-time duty.

Not all was lost, however. The injuries allowed the

Fred McGriff   **Steve Cox**

Players of the Year

MAJOR LEAGUE: Fred McGriff, 1b
McGriff rebounded from a disappointing '98 season with a .310 average, 32 home runs and 104 RBIs.

MINOR LEAGUE: Steve Cox, 1b
Cox was named MVP of the International League after hitting .341 with 25 home runs and 127 RBIs.

club to take long looks at a number of other players, which will help their decision-making as they move into year three. Further, they got some immediate help from the farm system, finding two righthanders ready to perform—Ryan Rupe, who was consistently good for much of the season after an early-May promotion, and Dan Wheeler, who was impressive in September.

"I think all in all when you win 69 games and you withstand some devastating injuries, you've got to feel you're moving in the right direction," catcher John Flaherty said. "I think things look bright for this organization going into spring training next year, especially in the pitching department."

Stability was another theme. General manager Chuck LaMar and manager Larry Rothschild both received contract extensions, as did McGriff and Flaherty. And the Rays decided to bring back Jose Canseco, who was on a record home run pace until his July back surgery.

"I'm not satisfied with what we've done this year, but I'm satisfied knowing what we have to do to get to the level we need to play at," Rothschild said.

The biggest infusion of talent came in the draft, where the organization held the No. 1 overall pick. The Rays selected high school outfielder Josh Hamilton, who signed almost immediately for a $3.96 million bonus and proceeded to tear up the Rookie-level Appalachian League. After a promotion to short-season Hudson Valley, he helped lead the Renegades to the New York-Penn League championship.

Double-A Orlando also won a championship, in the Southern League. Triple-A Durham, powered by league MVP Steve Cox, reached the International League finals for the second straight season.

ORGANIZATION LEADERS

BATTING

*AVG	Steve Cox, Durham	.341
R	Steve Cox, Durham	107
H	Steve Cox, Durham	182
TB	Steve Cox, Durham	314
2B	Steve Cox, Durham	49
3B	Two tied at	8
HR	Luke Wilcox, Durham/Orlando	29
RBI	Steve Cox, Durham	127
BB	Scott McClain, Durham	73
SO	Brian Martin, Charleston/Hudson Valley	177
SB	Alex Sanchez, Durham/Orlando	48

PITCHING

W	Jason Standridge, St. Petersburg/Charleston	13
L	Pablo Ortega, Durham/Orlando/St. Pete	13
#ERA	Jason Standridge, St. Petersburg/Charleston	2.57
G	Trevor Enders, Orlando	60
CG	Jason Standridge, St. Petersburg/Charleston	3
SV	Eddy Reyes, Orlando/St. Petersburg	27
IP	Delvin James, St. Petersburg/Charleston	175
BB	Terrell Wade, Durham	80
SO	Travis Harper, Orlando/St. Petersburg	147

*Minimum 250 At-Bats #Minimum 75 Innings

Tampa Bay
DEVIL RAYS

Manager: Larry Rothschild   **1999 Record:** 69-93, .426 (5th, AL East)

BATTING	AVG	G	AB	R	H	2B	3B	HR	RBI	BB	SO	SB	CS	B	T	HT	WT	DOB	1st Yr	Resides
Boggs, Wade	.301	90	292	40	88	14	1	2	29	38	23	1	0	L	R	6-2	197	6-15-58	1976	Tampa, Fla.
Butler, Rich	.150	7	20	2	3	1	0	0	0	2	4	0	0	L	R	6-1	180	5-1-73	1991	East York, Ontario
Cairo, Miguel	.295	120	465	61	137	15	5	3	36	24	46	22	7	R	R	6-1	190	5-4-74	1991	Anaco, Venez.
Canseco, Jose	.279	113	430	75	120	18	1	34	95	58	135	3	0	R	R	6-4	240	7-2-64	1982	Fort Lauderdale, Fla.
Clyburn, Danny	.198	28	81	8	16	4	0	3	5	7	21	0	0	R	R	6-4	220	4-6-74	1992	Lancaster, S.C.
Cox, Steve	.211	6	19	0	4	1	0	0	0	0	2	0	0	L	L	6-4	225	10-31-74	1992	Strathmore, Calif.
Difelice, Mike	.307	51	179	21	55	11	0	6	27	8	23	0	0	R	R	6-2	205	5-28-69	1991	Knoxville, Tenn.
Flaherty, John	.278	117	446	53	124	19	0	14	71	19	64	0	2	R	R	6-1	202	10-21-67	1988	West Nyack, N.Y.
Franco, Julio	.000	1	1	0	0	0	0	0	0	0	1	0	0	R	R	6-1	188	8-23-61	1978	San Pedro de Macoris, D.R.
Graffanino, Tony	.315	39	130	20	41	9	4	2	19	9	22	3	2	R	R	6-1	195	6-6-72	1990	Marietta, Ga.
Guillen, Jose	.244	47	168	24	41	10	0	2	13	10	36	0	0	R	R	5-11	195	5-17-76	1993	San Cristobal, D.R.
Lamb, David	.226	55	124	18	28	5	1	1	13	10	18	0	1	S	R	6-2	165	6-6-75	1993	Newbury Park, Calif.
Ledesma, Aaron	.265	93	294	32	78	15	0	0	30	14	35	1	1	R	R	6-2	200	6-3-71	1990	Union City, Calif.
Lowery, Terrell	.259	66	185	25	48	15	1	2	17	19	53	0	2	R	R	6-3	195	10-25-70	1991	Vallejo, Calif.
Martinez, Dave	.284	143	514	79	146	25	5	6	66	60	76	13	6	L	L	5-10	175	9-26-64	1983	Safety Harbor, Fla.
McCracken, Quinton	.250	40	148	20	37	6	1	1	18	14	23	6	5	S	R	5-8	170	3-16-70	1992	Southport, N.C.
McGriff, Fred	.310	144	529	75	164	30	1	32	104	86	107	1	0	L	L	6-3	215	10-31-63	1981	Tampa, Fla.
Perry, Herbert	.254	66	209	29	53	10	1	6	32	16	42	0	0	R	R	6-2	210	9-15-69	1991	Mayo, Fla.
Smith, Bobby	.181	68	199	18	36	4	1	3	19	16	64	4	4	R	R	6-3	190	4-10-74	1992	Oakland, Calif.
Sorrento, Paul	.235	99	294	40	69	14	1	11	42	49	101	1	1	L	R	6-2	220	11-17-65	1986	Peabody, Mass.
Stocker, Kevin	.299	79	254	39	76	11	2	1	27	24	41	9	7	S	R	6-1	175	2-13-70	1991	Spokane, Wash.
Trammell, Bubba	.290	82	283	49	82	19	0	14	39	43	37	0	2	R	R	6-2	205	11-6-71	1994	Knoxville, Tenn.
Winn, Randy	.267	79	303	44	81	16	4	2	24	17	63	9	9	S	R	6-2	175	6-9-74	1995	Danville, Calif.

PITCHING	W	L	ERA	G	GS	CG	SV	IP	H	R	ER	BB	SO	B	T	HT	WT	DOB	1st Yr	Resides
Aldred, Scott	3	2	5.18	37	0	0	0	24	26	15	14	14	22	L	L	6-4	195	6-12-68	1987	Lakeland, Fla.
Alvarez, Wilson	9	9	4.22	28	28	1	0	160	159	92	75	79	128	L	L	6-1	235	3-24-70	1987	Maracaibo, Venez.
Arrojo, Rolando	7	12	5.18	24	24	2	0	141	162	84	81	60	107	R	R	6-4	210	7-18-68	1997	San Jose, Costa Rica
Callaway, Mickey	1	2	7.45	5	4	0	0	19	30	20	16	14	11	R	R	6-2	190	5-13-75	1996	Germantown, Tenn.
Charlton, Norm	2	3	4.44	42	0	0	0	51	49	29	25	36	45	S	L	6-3	205	1-6-63	1984	Tilden, Texas
Duvall, Mike	1	1	4.05	40	0	0	0	40	46	21	18	27	18	R	L	6-0	185	10-11-74	1995	Morgantown, W.Va.
Eiland, Dave	4	8	5.60	21	15	0	0	80	98	59	50	27	53	R	R	6-3	205	7-5-66	1987	Dade City, Fla.
Gaillard, Eddie	1	0	2.08	8	0	0	0	9	12	9	2	4	7	R	R	6-1	200	8-13-70	1993	Denver, Colo.
Hernandez, Roberto	2	3	3.07	72	0	0	43	73	68	27	25	33	69	R	R	6-4	235	11-11-64	1986	Cobo Rojo, P.R.
Lidle, Cory	1	0	7.20	5	1	0	0	5	8	4	4	2	4	R	R	5-11	180	3-22-72	1991	West Covina, Calif.
Lopez, Albie	3	2	4.64	51	0	0	1	64	66	40	33	24	37	R	R	6-2	205	8-18-71	1991	Mesa, Ariz.
Mecir, Jim	0	1	2.61	17	0	0	0	21	15	7	6	14	15	R	R	6-1	195	5-16-70	1991	St. James, N.Y.
Morris, Jim	0	0	5.79	5	0	0	0	5	3	3	3	2	3	L	L	6-2	215	1-19-64	1984	San Angelo, Texas
Newman, Alan	2	2	6.89	18	0	0	0	16	22	12	12	9	20	L	L	6-6	240	10-2-69	1988	Pineville, La.
Rekar, Bryan	6	6	5.80	27	12	0	0	95	121	68	61	41	55	R	R	6-3	205	6-3-72	1993	Orland Park, Ill.
Rupe, Ryan	8	9	4.55	24	24	0	0	142	136	81	72	57	97	R	R	6-6	240	3-31-75	1998	Houston, Texas
Saunders, Tony	3	3	6.43	9	9	0	0	42	53	39	30	29	30	L	L	6-1	189	4-29-74	1992	Ellicott City, Md.
Sparks, Jeff	0	0	5.40	8	0	0	1	10	6	6	6	12	17	R	R	6-3	220	4-4-72	1995	Houston, Texas
Wheeler, Dan	0	4	5.87	6	6	0	0	31	35	20	20	13	32	R	R	6-3	215	12-10-77	1997	Warwick, R.I.
White, Rick	5	3	4.08	63	1	0	0	108	132	56	49	38	81	R	R	6-4	215	12-23-68	1990	Springfield, Ohio
Witt, Bobby	7	15	5.84	32	32	3	0	180	213	130	117	96	123	R	R	6-2	205	5-11-64	1985	Colleyville, Texas
Yan, Esteban	3	4	5.90	50	1	0	0	61	77	41	40	32	46	R	R	6-4	180	6-22-74	1991	La Higuera, D.R.

FIELDING

Catcher	PCT	G	PO	A	E	DP	PB
Difelice	.987	51	344	28	5	5	8
Flaherty	.993	115	726	87	6	12	4

First Base	PCT	G	PO	A	E	DP
Boggs	1.000	4	32	0	0	3
Cox	1.000	4	19	1	0	5
Franco	1.000	1	2	0	0	0
Ledesma	1.000	4	27	6	0	4
McGriff	.989	125	1038	87	13	132
Perry	1.000	14	77	4	0	13
Sorrento	.995	27	203	9	1	19

Second Base	PCT	G	PO	A	E	DP
Cairo	.986	117	250	379	9	102
Graffanino	.990	17	38	65	1	14
Lamb	.949	15	12	25	2	6
Ledesma	.990	17	43	56	1	18
Smith	.964	13	22	32	2	7

Third Base	PCT	G	PO	A	E	DP
Boggs	.942	74	45	100	9	14
Graffanino	.000	1	0	0	0	0
Ledesma	.907	26	11	28	4	1

	PCT	G	PO	A	E	DP
Perry	.955	42	32	75	5	11
Smith	.933	59	26	100	9	13

Shortstop	PCT	G	PO	A	E	DP
Graffanino	.951	17	28	49	4	14
Lamb	.945	35	46	75	7	28
Ledesma	.977	50	83	134	5	37
Stocker	.957	76	137	216	16	55

Outfield	PCT	G	PO	A	E	DP
Butler	1.000	6	8	0	0	0
Canseco	1.000	6	7	1	0	0
Clyburn	1.000	24	39	3	0	1
Cox	1.000	2	1	0	0	0
Guillen	.966	47	80	5	3	0
Lowery	.971	60	97	4	3	1
Martinez	.985	140	253	8	4	1
McCracken	.988	40	80	1	1	0
Perry	1.000	6	4	0	0	0
Sorrento	.957	57	87	2	4	1
Trammell	.993	74	142	2	1	1
Winn	.995	77	180	4	1	0

Roberto Hernandez

Jose Canseco
Led Tampa Bay with 34 home runs

Alex Sanchez
Led organization with 48 stolen bases

FARM SYSTEM

Director, Minor League Operations: Tom Foley

Class	Farm Team	League	W	L	Pct.	Finish*	Manager	First Yr
AAA	Durham (N.C.) Bulls	International	83	60	.580	2nd (14)	Bill Evers	1998
AA	Orlando (Fla.) Rays	Southern	70	68	.507	+5th (10)	Bill Russell	1999
A#	St. Petersburg (Fla.) Devil Rays	Florida State	74	63	.540	4th (14)	Roy Silver	1997
A	Charleston (S.C.) RiverDogs	South Atlantic	65	77	.458	10th (14)	Charlie Montoyo	1997
A	Hudson Valley (N.Y.) Renegades	New York-Penn	42	34	.553	+t-3rd (14)	Edwin Rodriguez	1996
Rookie#	Princeton (W.Va.) Devil Rays	Appalachian	25	45	.357	9th (10)	Bobby Ramos	1997

*Finish in overall standings (No. of teams in league)   #Advanced level   +Won league championship

DURHAM   Class AAA

INTERNATIONAL LEAGUE

BATTING	AVG	G	AB	R	H	2B	3B	HR	RBI	BB	SO	SB	CS	B	T	HT	WT	DOB	1st Yr	Resides
Buccheri, Jim	.125	6	8	2	1	1	0	0	2	2	0	2	0	R	R	5-11	165	11-12-68	1988	Fountain Valley, Calif.
Butler, Rich	.289	90	332	52	96	28	2	10	63	41	70	2	5	L	R	6-1	180	5-1-73	1991	East York, Ontario
Clyburn, Danny	.234	82	303	38	71	11	1	9	33	19	74	2	0	R	R	6-4	220	4-6-74	1992	Lancaster, S.C.
Cox, Steve	.341	134	534	107	182	49	4	25	127	67	74	3	3	L	L	6-4	225	10-31-74	1992	Strathmore, Calif.
Fraraccio, Dan	.267	15	30	5	8	3	0	1	4	4	4	2	0	R	R	5-11	175	9-18-70	1992	Bradenton, Fla.
Garcia, Neil	.091	12	33	1	3	1	0	1	2	2	8	1	0	S	R	6-0	185	4-6-73	1994	Tustin, Calif.
Graffanino, Tony	.313	87	345	66	108	25	6	9	58	37	46	16	9	R	R	6-1	195	6-6-72	1990	Marietta, Ga.
Guillen, Jose	.382	9	34	8	13	1	0	3	12	7	7	0	1	R	R	5-11	195	5-17-76	1993	San Cristobal, D.R.
Holbert, Aaron	.311	100	347	77	108	18	4	12	56	25	56	14	5	R	R	6-0	160	1-9-73	1990	Torrance, Calif.
Kieschnick, Brooks	.200	23	75	6	15	5	0	1	5	5	14	0	0	L	R	6-4	228	6-6-72	1993	Caldwell, Texas
Lamb, David	.233	7	30	7	7	3	0	0	7	2	4	0	1	S	R	6-2	165	6-6-75	1993	Newbury Park, Calif.
Ledesma, Aaron	.100	2	10	0	1	0	0	0	0	0	0	0	0	R	R	6-2	200	6-6-71	1990	Union City, Calif.
Levis, Jesse	.330	27	94	20	31	5	0	1	8	15	9	0	0	L	R	5-9	200	4-14-68	1989	Elkins Park, Pa.
Lowery, Terrell	.335	71	275	69	92	20	5	15	57	43	62	10	5	R	R	6-3	195	10-25-70	1991	Vallejo, Calif.
Martin, Chris	.273	120	399	64	109	20	1	9	53	48	61	14	2	R	R	6-1	170	1-25-68	1990	Los Angeles, Calif.
McClain, Scott	.251	137	533	106	134	33	1	28	104	73	156	4	2	R	R	6-3	209	5-19-72	1990	Glendale, Ariz.
Mendoza, Carlos	.293	75	266	57	78	8	3	1	25	32	38	9	8	L	L	5-11	160	11-4-74	1994	Bolivar, Venez.
Oliver, Joe	.301	57	219	27	66	18	1	7	43	7	50	1	0	R	R	6-3	220	7-24-65	1983	Orlando, Fla.
Perry, Herbert	.311	27	103	21	32	8	0	5	20	6	21	0	0	R	R	6-2	210	9-15-69	1991	Mayo, Fla.
Sanchez, Alex	.200	3	10	2	2	1	0	0	0	1	0	0	0	L	L	5-10	179	8-26-76	1996	Miami, Fla.
Silvestri, Dave	.000	1	3	0	0	0	0	0	0	0	0	0	0	R	R	6-0	180	9-29-67	1989	St. Louis, Mo.
Smith, Bobby	.333	57	225	52	75	15	3	14	47	27	61	13	4	R	R	6-3	190	4-10-74	1992	Oakland, Calif.
Trammell, Bubba	.269	47	186	25	50	12	0	7	31	15	36	0	0	R	R	6-2	205	11-6-71	1994	Knoxville, Tenn.
Wilcox, Luke	.328	39	134	32	44	12	5	9	34	22	18	1	3	L	R	6-4	190	11-15-73	1995	St. Johns, Mich.
Wilson, Tom	.279	67	215	41	60	19	0	16	44	49	59	0	2	R	R	6-3	210	12-19-70	1991	Fullerton, Calif.
Winn, Randy	.353	46	207	38	73	20	3	3	30	16	27	9	6	S	R	6-2	175	6-9-74	1995	Danville, Calif.

PITCHING

PITCHING	W	L	ERA	G	GS	CG	SV	IP	H	R	ER	BB	SO	B	T	HT	WT	DOB	1st Yr	Resides
Bailey, Roger	1	0	5.67	7	4	0	0	27	28	21	17	13	17	R	R	6-1	180	10-3-70	1992	Tallahassee, Fla.
Barnett, Marty	1	0	5.46	16	0	0	0	28	30	17	17	14	19	R	R	6-3	210	3-10-74	1995	Harlan, Iowa
Callaway, Mickey	7	1	4.20	15	15	0	0	81	86	45	38	28	56	R	R	6-2	190	5-13-75	1996	Germantown, Tenn.
Charlton, Norm	3	2	3.69	18	0	0	1	32	27	13	13	10	29	S	L	6-3	205	1-6-63	1984	Tilden, Texas
Daniels, John	2	0	4.89	21	0	0	0	35	37	19	19	9	25	S	R	6-3	185	2-7-74	1993	Little Chute, Wis.
Davis, Tim	0	0	9.00	3	0	0	0	2	2	2	2	1	1	L	L	5-11	165	7-14-70	1992	Bristol, Fla.
Donnelly, Brendan	5	5	3.05	37	1	0	2	62	53	23	21	18	61	R	R	6-3	205	7-4-71	1992	Albuquerque, N.M.
Duvall, Mike	2	2	5.40	19	1	0	2	30	32	20	18	12	27	R	L	6-0	185	10-11-74	1995	Morgantown, W.Va.
Eiland, Dave	5	3	3.36	10	10	0	0	59	60	26	22	9	46	R	R	6-3	205	7-5-66	1987	Dade City, Fla.
Gaillard, Eddie	3	6	2.89	59	0	0	26	62	67	30	20	23	67	R	R	6-1	200	8-13-70	1993	Denver, Colo.
Hernandez, Santos	0	2	10.80	6	4	0	0	18	34	25	22	11	12	R	R	6-1	172	11-3-72	1994	Chiriqui, Panama
Lidle, Cory	0	0	4.76	3	2	0	0	6	9	3	3	1	6	R	R	5-11	180	3-22-72	1991	West Covina, Calif.
Morris, Jim	3	1	5.48	18	0	0	0	23	21	14	14	19	16	L	L	6-2	215	1-19-64	1984	San Angelo, Texas
Munoz, Bobby	3	3	4.39	39	3	0	5	55	55	35	27	31	50	R	R	6-7	210	3-3-68	1989	Hialeah, Fla.
Newman, Alan	10	0	2.24	50	0	0	0	80	59	24	20	20	76	L	L	6-6	240	10-2-69	1988	Pineville, La.
Nunez, Maximo	1	0	5.40	21	0	0	2	32	25	20	19	28	31	R	R	6-5	165	1-15-73	1991	Villa Mella, D.R.
Ortega, Pablo	0	1	34.71	1	1	0	0	2	10	9	9	0	2	S	R	6-2	170	1-7-76	1994	Nuevo Laredo, Mexico
Plantenberg, Erik	5	4	6.02	23	7	0	0	58	75	43	39	28	51	S	L	6-1	180	10-30-68	1990	Bellevue, Wash.
Rekar, Bryan	4	1	3.86	6	5	0	0	35	29	15	15	8	26	R	R	6-3	205	6-3-72	1993	Orland Park, Ill.
Saunders, Tony	0	0	2.57	1	1	0	0	7	8	3	2	2	7	L	L	6-1	189	4-29-74	1992	Ellicott City, Md.
Small, Aaron	4	6	6.34	21	18	0	0	99	118	81	70	32	52	R	R	6-5	226	11-23-71	1989	Loudon, Tenn.
2-team (11 Louisville)	5	7	6.88	32	18	0	0	120	156	104	92	47	63							
Sparks, Jeff	3	0	3.38	18	0	0	0	24	16	11	9	14	31	R	R	6-3	220	4-4-72	1995	Houston, Texas
Strong, Joe	0	1	7.98	6	1	0	1	15	20	13	13	8	12	S	R	6-0	200	9-9-62	1984	Seattle, Wash.
Tatis, Ramon	12	8	5.50	28	28	0	0	155	178	100	95	74	97	L	L	6-2	180	1-5-73	1991	Guayubin, D.R.
Valdes, Marc	1	2	5.18	9	9	0	0	40	39	25	23	12	23	R	R	6-0	170	12-20-71	1993	Tampa, Fla.
Wade, Terrell	1	7	9.49	34	19	0	0	99	140	112	104	80	61	L	L	6-3	204	1-25-73	1991	Rembert, S.C.
Wheeler, Dan	7	5	4.92	14	14	2	0	82	103	59	45	25	58	R	R	6-3	215	12-10-77	1997	Warwick, R.I.

FIELDING

Catcher	PCT	G	PO	A	E	DP	PB
Garcia	.981	12	46	7	1	2	1
Levis	1.000	24	142	9	0	1	6
McClain	1.000	1	1	0	0	0	
Oliver	.984	55	399	27	7	2	11
Wilson	.986	60	391	41	6	8	6

First Base	PCT	G	PO	A	E	DP
Cox	.996	123	1125	73	5	121
Fraraccio	1.000	2	13	0	0	1
McClain	.973	13	104	3	3	11
Perry	.967	7	53	6	2	2
Wilson	1.000	2	1	1	0	0

Second Base	PCT	G	PO	A	E	DP
Fraraccio	1.000	6	8	14	0	4
Graffanino	.998	84	182	231	1	73
Holbert	.977	53	100	154	6	38
Lamb	1.000	3	5	5	0	1
Ledesma	1.000	1	2	4	0	1

	PCT	G	PO	A	E	DP
Martin	.000	1	0	0	0	0
Silvestri	1.000	1	3	0	0	0

Third Base	PCT	G	PO	A	E	DP
Fraraccio	.857	1	3	3	1	1
Graffanino	1.000	1	0	2	0	0
Holbert	.889	4	1	7	1	0
McClain	.938	83	64	162	15	19
Oliver	.000	1	0	0	0	0
Perry	1.000	4	3	6	0	1
Smith	.944	54	44	126	10	15
Trammell	1.000	1	0	2	0	0

Shortstop	PCT	G	PO	A	E	DP
Fraraccio	1.000	2	3	8	0	1
Holbert	.958	22	32	60	4	15
Lamb	.897	5	8	18	3	1
Ledesma	.917	1	5	6	1	3
Martin	.952	116	159	380	27	75

	PCT	G	PO	A	E	DP
Smith	1.000	2	2	0	0	0

Outfield	PCT	G	PO	A	E	DP
Buccheri	1.000	3	3	0	0	0
Butler	.981	79	148	3	3	1
Clyburn	.976	69	116	4	3	0
Fraraccio	.000	1	0	0	0	0
Guillen	1.000	9	19	1	0	0
Holbert	1.000	7	11	0	0	0
Kieschnick	1.000	8	15	0	0	0
Lowery	.992	69	129	3	1	0
Mendoza	.983	71	107	8	2	0
Sanchez	1.000	3	8	0	0	0
Trammell	.959	44	65	6	3	1
Wilcox	.959	28	46	1	2	1
Wilson	1.000	6	8	4	0	0
Winn	.966	46	113	2	4	0

ORLANDO — Class AA

SOUTHERN LEAGUE

BATTING	AVG	G	AB	R	H	2B	3B	HR	RBI	BB	SO	SB	CS	B	T	HT	WT	DOB	1st Yr	Resides
Badeaux, Brooks	.500	3	2	1	1	0	0	1	1	0	0	0	0	S	R	5-10	175	10-20-76	1998	Scott, La.
Becker, Brian	.252	129	480	67	121	24	1	18	74	42	89	0	0	R	R	6-7	220	5-26-75	1996	Tempe, Ariz.
Buccheri, Jim	.311	45	161	18	50	8	1	1	16	15	24	5	4	R	R	5-11	165	11-12-68	1988	Fountain Valley, Calif.
Cairo, Miguel	.385	3	13	1	5	2	0	0	1	0	1	0	1	R	R	6-1	190	5-4-74	1991	Anaco, Venez.
Carr, Dustin	.302	125	461	76	139	22	3	6	63	70	62	7	2	R	R	6-0	190	6-7-75	1997	Mount Vernon, Texas
Colina, Roberto	.273	99	315	45	86	20	1	6	53	37	47	0	1	L	L	6-0	200	1-29-71	1997	San Jose, Costa Rica
Cruz, Luis	.281	13	32	2	9	2	0	0	1	1	6	0	0	R	R	6-0	180	1-21-77	1997	Santo Domingo, D.R.
De los Santos, Eddy	.275	128	448	53	123	24	4	3	49	29	69	3	2	R	R	6-2	165	2-24-78	1996	Santo Domingo, D.R.
Fraraccio, Dan	.287	82	254	48	73	19	3	7	28	25	43	1	4	R	R	5-11	185	9-18-70	1992	Bradenton, Fla.
Garcia, Neil	.284	31	95	13	27	6	0	1	11	10	16	0	1	S	R	6-0	180	4-6-73	1994	Tustin, Calif.
Hall, Toby	.254	46	173	20	44	7	0	9	34	4	10	1	1	R	R	6-3	205	10-21-75	1997	Placerville, Calif.
Hawkins, Kraig	.301	94	296	41	89	10	1	0	27	38	45	19	10	R	R	6-2	170	12-4-71	1992	Lake Charles, La.
Huff, Aubrey	.301	133	491	85	148	40	3	22	78	64	77	2	3	L	R	6-4	220	12-20-76	1998	Fort Worth, Texas
Levis, Jesse	.396	13	48	6	19	7	0	1	11	6	4	0	0	L	R	5-9	200	4-14-68	1989	Elkins Park, Pa.
Long, Ryan	.233	8	30	2	7	1	0	0	4	1	3	0	0	R	R	6-2	215	2-3-73	1991	Pearland, Texas
Mosquera, Julio	.305	80	259	36	79	13	1	4	37	15	40	1	0	R	R	6-0	190	1-29-72	1991	Dunedin, Fla.
Pigott, Anthony	.250	4	8	0	2	1	0	0	0	0	2	0	0	R	R	6-1	195	6-13-76	1997	Wilmington, N.C.
Pomierski, Joe	.261	62	188	31	49	10	3	9	33	22	44	1	1	L	R	6-2	192	4-15-74	1992	Biloxi, Miss.
Quatraro, Matt	.250	1	4	1	1	0	0	1	2	0	2	0	0	R	R	6-2	205	11-14-73	1996	East Selkirk, N.Y.
Sanchez, Alex	.254	121	500	68	127	12	4	2	29	26	88	48	27	L	L	5-10	179	8-26-76	1996	Miami, Fla.
Wilcox, Luke	.270	90	315	60	90	24	1	20	64	35	54	3	2	L	R	6-4	190	11-15-73	1995	St. Johns, Mich.
Wilson, Tom	.288	30	104	12	30	2	0	7	23	18	34	0	0	R	R	6-3	210	12-19-70	1991	Fullerton, Calif.

PITCHING	W	L	ERA	G	GS	CG	SV	IP	H	R	ER	BB	SO	B	T	HT	WT	DOB	1st Yr	Resides
Aquino, Julio	0	0	18.47	5	0	0	0	6	18	15	13	4	4	R	R	6-1	173	12-12-72	1991	Estorga, D.R.
Belitz, Todd	9	9	5.77	28	28	0	0	161	169	114	103	65	118	L	L	6-1	218	10-23-75	1997	Huntington Beach, Calif.
Bowers, Cedrick	6	9	5.98	27	27	1	0	125	125	94	83	76	138	R	L	6-2	190	2-10-78	1996	Chiefland, Fla.
Brown, Elliot	0	2	7.71	10	1	0	0	19	25	18	16	12	12	S	R	6-3	185	6-7-75	1996	Metairie, La.
Callaway, Mickey	1	1	4.50	2	2	0	0	10	15	6	5	2	7	R	R	6-2	190	5-13-75	1996	Germantown, Tenn.
Daniels, John	3	2	1.90	38	0	0	14	52	33	14	11	15	40	S	R	6-3	185	2-7-74	1993	Little Chute, Wis.

PITCHING	W	L	ERA	G	GS	CG	SV	IP	H	R	ER	BB	SO	B	T	HT	WT	DOB	1st Yr	Resides
Enders, Trevor	8	2	3.30	60	0	0	1	95	86	37	35	33	63	R	L	6-1	205	12-22-74	1996	Houston, Texas
Gardner, Lee	0	0	9.00	1	0	0	0	2	3	2	2	1	1	R	R	6-0	200	1-16-75	1998	Hartland, Mich.
Harper, Travis	6	3	5.38	14	14	1	0	72	73	45	43	26	68	R	R	6-4	200	5-21-76	1997	Riverton, W.Va.
Hernandez, Santos	5	4	3.70	35	4	0	5	56	43	31	23	15	47	R	R	6-1	172	11-3-72	1994	Chiriqui, Panama
Kaufman, John	1	3	8.83	21	2	0	0	36	54	39	35	14	22	L	L	5-10	170	10-23-74	1996	Tampa, Fla.
LeRoy, John	0	0	4.50	4	0	0	0	6	7	3	3	5	5	R	R	6-3	175	4-19-75	1993	Bellevue, Wash.
Manon, Julio	3	3	5.10	30	5	0	0	67	80	43	38	23	53	R	R	6-1	183	7-10-73	1992	Boca Chica, D.R.
Morris, Jim	0	1	1.80	3	0	0	1	5	6	1	1	1	6	L	L	6-2	215	1-19-64	1984	San Angelo, Texas
Nunez, Maximo	0	2	3.46	26	0	0	9	26	23	11	10	17	19	R	R	6-5	165	1-15-73	1991	Villa Mella, D.R.
Ortega, Pablo	8	10	3.87	22	22	1	0	130	147	77	56	47	74	S	R	6-2	170	11-7-76	1995	Nuevo Laredo, Mexico
Pujals, Denis	5	3	3.86	42	0	0	0	72	82	35	31	19	39	R	R	6-4	215	2-5-73	1996	Miami, Fla.
Reyes, Eddy	1	3	4.08	18	0	0	2	29	31	16	13	11	25	R	R	6-4	200	4-24-76	1997	Miami, Fla.
Rupe, Ryan	2	2	2.73	5	5	0	0	26	18	13	8	6	22	R	R	6-6	240	3-31-75	1998	Houston, Texas
Seay, Bobby	1	2	7.94	6	6	0	0	17	22	15	15	15	16	L	L	6-2	190	6-20-78	1996	Sarasota, Fla.
Strong, Joe	1	4	5.68	11	7	2	0	38	40	24	24	18	34	S	R	6-0	200	9-9-62	1984	Seattle, Wash.
Valdes, Marc	0	1	5.87	2	2	0	0	8	7	5	5	2	5	R	R	6-0	170	12-20-71	1993	Tampa, Fla.
Wheeler, Dan	3	0	3.26	9	9	0	0	58	56	27	21	8	53	R	R	6-3	215	12-10-77	1997	Warwick, R.I.
Zambrano, Victor	7	2	4.59	40	4	0	1	82	92	55	42	38	81	R	R	6-1	170	8-6-74	1994	Los Teques, Venez.

FIELDING

Catcher	PCT	G	PO	A	E	DP	PB
Garcia	.990	23	181	26	2	1	5
Hall	.986	37	261	27	4	5	5
Levis	.982	7	52	4	1	0	0
Mosquera	.988	57	374	36	5	0	8
Quatraro	1.000	1	9	3	0	0	0
Wilson	.971	20	121	15	4	0	1

First Base	PCT	G	PO	A	E	DP
Becker	.992	127	1006	57	9	110
Colina	.961	18	115	8	5	10

Second Base	PCT	G	PO	A	E	DP
Badeaux	.000	1	0	0	0	0

	PCT	G	PO	A	E	DP
Cairo	1.000	3	2	7	0	2
Carr	.977	123	273	332	14	98
Cruz	1.000	7	7	6	0	0
Fraraccio	.977	13	19	23	1	4

Third Base	PCT	G	PO	A	E	DP
Fraraccio	1.000	9	5	11	0	1
Huff	.927	133	93	273	29	23

Shortstop	PCT	G	PO	A	E	DP
Badeaux	1.000	1	2	0	0	0
Cruz	1.000	1	0	2	0	0
De los Santos	.928	128	155	344	39	75
Fraraccio	.907	15	21	28	5	10

Outfield	PCT	G	PO	A	E	DP
Buccheri	.975	38	77	2	2	1
Carr	.000	1	0	0	0	0
Colina	.947	18	18	0	1	0
Cruz	1.000	1	1	0	0	0
Fraraccio	.957	45	67	0	3	0
Hawkins	.978	91	129	6	3	0
Long	.833	7	14	1	3	0
Mosquera	1.000	2	2	0	0	0
Pigott	1.000	3	3	0	0	0
Pomierski	.972	56	99	7	3	1
Sanchez	.958	121	314	8	14	2
Wilcox	.972	71	132	5	4	1

ST. PETERSBURG — Class A

FLORIDA STATE LEAGUE

BATTING	AVG	G	AB	R	H	2B	3B	HR	RBI	BB	SO	SB	CS	B	T	HT	WT	DOB	1st Yr	Resides
Alamo, Efrain	.138	8	29	1	4	1	0	0	0	0	9	0	0	R	R	6-2	190	10-5-76	1994	Canovanas, P.R.
Backe, Brandon	.197	41	132	21	26	6	1	1	11	21	34	0	3	R	R	6-0	190	4-5-78	1998	Webster, Texas
Badeaux, Brooks	.284	96	342	68	97	6	1	0	19	57	44	2	7	S	R	5-10	175	10-20-76	1998	Scott, La.
Batista, Angel	.250	6	16	4	4	0	0	0	0	1	0	0	1	L	L	6-3	190	1-14-80	1996	Santo Domingo, D.R.
Belliard, Fernando	.167	6	12	1	2	0	0	0	0	0	6	0	0	R	R	6-1	175	1-15-81	1998	Santo Domingo, D.R.
Berns, Robert	.209	14	43	4	9	3	0	0	7	3	2	0	1	R	L	6-1	200	10-18-74	1997	San Jose, Calif.
Butler, Garrett	.249	94	329	36	82	14	3	2	31	17	61	16	6	S	R	6-2	170	5-20-76	1994	Miami, Fla.
Cairo, Miguel	.385	3	13	2	5	0	0	0	0	1	2	1	1	R	R	6-1	190	5-4-74	1991	Anaco, Venez.
Cruz, Luis	.220	58	218	25	48	5	0	2	17	10	38	1	2	R	R	6-0	180	1-21-77	1998	Santo Domingo, D.R.
Hall, Toby	.297	56	212	24	63	13	1	4	36	17	9	0	2	R	R	6-3	205	10-21-75	1997	Placerville, Calif.
Hoover, Paul	.272	118	408	66	111	13	6	8	54	54	81	23	7	R	R	6-0	200	4-14-76	1997	Steubenville, Ohio
Jorgensen, Randy	.219	26	96	6	21	6	0	1	5	5	11	0	0	L	L	6-2	195	4-3-72	1993	Glendale, Ariz.
Kelly, Kenny	.277	51	206	39	57	10	4	3	21	18	46	14	5	R	R	6-3	180	1-26-79	1997	Plant City, Fla.
Ledesma, Aaron	.143	2	7	0	1	0	0	0	1	0	0	0	0	R	R	6-2	200	6-3-71	1990	Union City, Calif.
Mahoney, Sean	.152	35	112	8	17	6	0	1	8	13	32	2	0	R	R	6-4	220	12-23-75	1998	Miami, Fla.
Neuberger, Scott	.260	127	442	55	115	14	3	10	63	24	104	1	2	R	R	6-3	210	8-14-77	1997	Millersville, Md.
Perez, Nestor	.264	111	364	33	96	8	1	0	23	10	53	4	5	R	R	5-10	160	11-24-76	1997	Tenerife, Canary Islands
Pigott, Anthony	.268	105	339	41	91	9	4	2	33	11	84	16	8	R	R	6-5	195	6-13-76	1997	Wilmington, N.C.
Quatraro, Matt	.261	73	218	20	57	14	2	3	23	14	47	3	1	R	R	6-2	205	11-14-73	1996	East Selkirk, N.Y.
Rhodes, Nick	.500	1	2	2	1	0	0	1	1	1	0	0	0	R	R	6-4	200	8-9-78	1998	Danbury, Conn.
Salinas, Trey	.250	10	32	5	8	6	0	0	2	0	6	0	0	R	R	6-1	190	6-29-75	1996	Corpus Christi, Texas
Sandberg, Jared	.276	136	504	73	139	24	1	22	96	51	133	8	2	R	R	6-3	185	3-2-78	1996	Olympia, Wash.
Stocker, Kevin	.091	3	11	2	1	0	0	0	0	0	2	0	0	S	R	6-1	175	2-13-70	1991	Spokane, Wash.
Velazquez, Jose	.260	112	404	43	105	15	2	3	69	37	46	2	5	L	L	6-3	190	8-24-75	1994	Guayama, P.R.

GAMES BY POSITION: C—Hall 30, Hoover 87, Quatraro 25, Rhodes 1. 1B—Alamo 1, Backe 1, Berns 10, Hoover 4, Jorgensen 25, Quatraro 11, Velazquez 92. 2B—Backe 2, Badeaux 80, Cairo 3, Cruz 55. 3B—Hoover 3, Ledesma 1, Quatraro 1, Salinas 1, Sandberg 134. SS—Backe 11, Badeaux 15, Ledesma 1, Perez 111, Stocker 3. OF—Alamo 5, Backe 30, Badeaux 1, Batista 6, Butler 85, Kelly 51, Mahoney 33, Neuberger 122, Pigott 84, Quatraro 14.

PITCHING	W	L	ERA	G	GS	CG	SV	IP	H	R	ER	BB	SO	B	T	HT	WT	DOB	1st Yr	Resides
Arrojo, Rolando	0	1	4.50	2	2	0	0	10	11	6	5	1	10	R	R	6-4	210	7-18-68	1997	San Jose, Costa Rica
Box, John	2	2	5.05	42	0	0	0	57	71	34	32	15	31	R	L	6-3	180	4-30-75	1996	Houston, Texas
Brown, Elliot	5	3	2.67	38	0	0	3	57	44	20	17	14	42	S	R	6-3	185	6-7-75	1996	Metairie, La.
Davis, Tim	0	0	27.00	1	0	0	0	1	3	2	2	1	1	L	L	5-11	165	7-14-70	1992	Bristol, Fla.
Flohr, Adam	6	6	3.80	31	18	0	0	135	164	78	57	30	64	L	L	6-2	185	3-29-77	1998	Longview, Wash.
Gardner, Lee	2	0	1.96	20	0	0	7	23	20	7	5	9	22	R	R	6-0	200	1-16-75	1998	Hartland, Mich.
Garibaldi, Cecilio	6	4	4.36	21	15	0	0	99	109	56	48	28	52	R	R	6-2	190	1-5-78	1998	Guasave, Mexico
Haines, Talley	0	0	0.00	2	0	0	0	4	1	0	0	4	2	R	R	6-5	200	11-16-76	1998	Cape Girardeau, Mo.
Harper, Travis	5	4	3.43	14	14	0	0	81	82	36	31	23	79	R	R	6-4	200	5-21-76	1997	Riverton, W.Va.
James, Delvin	3	0	3.18	3	2	0	0	17	18	6	6	4	6	R	R	6-3	215	1-3-78	1996	Nacogdoches, Texas
Jimenez, Jason	4	4	2.38	41	1	0	5	57	46	23	15	21	47	R	L	6-2	210	1-10-76	1997	Elk Grove, Calif.
Kaufman, John	1	2	3.57	16	0	0	0	23	29	10	9	6	22	L	L	5-10	170	10-23-74	1996	Tampa, Fla.
Lidle, Cory	0	0	0.00	2	2	0	0	5	2	0	0	2	5	R	R	5-11	180	3-22-72	1991	West Covina, Calif.
Lira, James	4	1	3.05	36	0	0	0	44	45	18	15	17	25	R	R	6-1	160	5-19-77	1998	Fountain Valley, Calif.
Lopez, Albie	0	0	5.40	2	1	0	0	3	7	5	2	0	3	R	R	6-1	190	8-18-71	1991	Mesa, Ariz.

PITCHING	W	L	ERA	G	GS	CG	SV	IP	H	R	ER	BB	SO	B	T	HT	WT	DOB	1st Yr	Resides
McDonald, Jon	1	0	6.00	10	0	0	0	15	19	12	10	6	10	L	L	6-0	190	12-1-76	1998	Humble, Texas
Ortega, Pablo	1	2	1.93	4	1	0	0	9	9	6	2	1	5	S	R	6-2	170	11-7-76	1995	Nuevo Laredo, Mexico
Phelps, Travis	10	8	4.24	24	23	1	0	134	148	70	63	39	101	R	R	6-2	170	7-25-77	1997	Rocky Comfort, Mo.
Reyes, Eddy	0	2	1.88	37	0	0	25	38	31	13	8	23	30	R	R	6-4	200	4-24-76	1997	Miami, Fla.
Rosario, Juan	5	3	2.67	15	15	0	0	94	80	34	28	25	37	R	R	6-4	195	11-3-75	1993	Perth Amboy, N.J.
Ruhl, Nathan	2	0	2.57	4	0	0	0	7	9	2	2	3	5	R	R	6-4	200	7-16-76	1996	Lee's Summit, Mo.
Schuldt, Matt	2	0	4.83	19	2	0	0	32	36	19	17	16	23	R	R	6-2	205	9-17-75	1998	Sioux Falls, S.D.
Seay, Bobby	2	6	3.00	12	11	0	0	57	56	25	19	23	45	L	L	6-2	190	6-20-78	1996	Sarasota, Fla.
Standridge, Jason	4	4	3.91	8	8	0	0	48	49	21	21	20	26	R	R	6-4	205	11-9-78	1997	Birmingham, Ala.
White, Matt	9	7	5.18	21	20	2	0	113	125	75	65	33	92	R	R	6-5	215	8-13-78	1996	South Pasadena, Fla.
Yan, Esteban	0	0	0.00	2	2	0	0	4	3	1	0	1	0	R	R	6-4	180	6-22-74	1991	La Higuera, D.R.
Zambrano, Victor	0	2	4.00	7	0	0	0	9	10	6	4	5	15	R	R	6-1	170	8-6-74	1994	Los Teques, Venez.

CHARLESTON, S.C. — Class A

SOUTH ATLANTIC LEAGUE

BATTING	AVG	G	AB	R	H	2B	3B	HR	RBI	BB	SO	SB	CS	B	T	HT	WT	DOB	1st Yr	Resides
Alamo, Efrain	.246	97	346	46	85	14	8	10	53	16	96	4	6	R	R	6-2	190	10-5-76	1994	Canovanas, P.R.
Arias, Jeison	.148	30	81	9	12	2	2	0	6	7	34	1	0	R	R	6-1	195	9-27-78	1996	San Jose de Ocoa, D.R.
Backe, Brandon	.232	84	272	43	63	11	2	9	40	35	81	3	5	R	R	6-0	190	4-5-78	1998	Webster, Texas
Chwan, Brian	.221	49	136	16	30	8	0	3	9	10	29	0	0	L	R	6-2	195	8-30-76	1998	Anaheim, Calif.
Cota, Humberto	.280	85	336	42	94	21	1	9	61	20	51	1	1	R	R	6-0	175	2-7-79	1996	San Luis Rio Colorado, Mexico
Grummitt, Dan	.133	8	30	6	4	1	0	1	4	1	12	0	0	R	R	6-5	230	6-16-76	1998	Twinsburg, Ohio
Joffrion, Jack	.209	83	292	32	61	15	1	5	28	9	89	7	3	R	R	5-11	170	9-19-75	1997	Seabrook, Texas
Katz, Glenn	.246	55	179	18	44	7	0	0	17	6	24	6	7	R	R	5-10	185	1-30-77	1999	Norwalk, Conn.
LaForest, Pete	.256	125	445	64	114	21	3	13	53	55	97	9	3	L	R	6-1	190	1-27-78	1995	Gatineau, Quebec
Lebron, Hector	.229	57	188	26	43	3	2	1	21	8	42	7	2	L	R	6-3	225	7-22-77	1997	Catano, P.R.
Llanos, Alex	.000	5	13	1	0	0	0	0	0	2	4	1	0	L	R	6-1	185	9-20-76	1995	Carolina, P.R.
Mann, Derek	.283	124	449	86	127	20	1	5	45	71	88	22	10	L	R	6-0	165	3-8-78	1996	Midland, Ga.
Martin, Brian	.172	40	145	9	25	1	2	3	13	9	70	1	2	R	R	6-2	220	6-14-80	1998	El Centro, Calif.
Pressley, Josh	.243	118	437	50	106	22	0	9	64	49	80	1	4	L	R	6-6	220	4-2-80	1998	Fort Lauderdale, Fla.
Rhodes, Nick	.239	19	46	6	11	0	2	0	5	5	11	0	0	R	R	6-4	200	8-9-78	1998	Danbury, Conn.
Ryan, Kelvin	.236	128	478	63	113	20	3	12	66	30	107	12	4	R	R	6-1	185	8-10-78	1997	La Romana, D.R.
Scioneaux, Damian	.111	5	18	1	2	0	0	0	0	2	3	2	0	L	R	5-8	165	6-4-75	1997	Kenner, La.
Soler, Ramon	.237	108	389	74	92	17	2	1	28	56	93	46	14	S	R	6-0	147	7-6-81	1997	Las Caobas, D.R.
Suriel, Miguel	.226	80	257	24	58	18	0	3	22	31	35	2	1	R	R	6-0	165	11-15-76	1994	Palmirito, D.R.
Wilder, Paul	.173	44	150	15	26	4	0	4	13	21	61	7	1	L	R	6-4	230	1-9-78	1996	Raleigh, N.C.
Winter, Jon	.250	13	32	3	8	2	0	0	3	7	10	0	1	R	R	5-11	170	4-11-77	1999	Wausau, Wis.

GAMES BY POSITION: C—Chwan 40, Cota 61, Rhodes 15, Suriel 38. **1B**—Backe 5, Cota 2, Grummitt 4, Lebron 37, Pressley 100, Suriel 4. **2B**—Backe 8, Joffrion 17, LaForest 1, Llanos 2, Mann 117, Winter 7. **3B**—Backe 1, Chwan 1, Joffrion 1, LaForest 118, Llanos 1, Suriel 24. **SS**—Backe 3, Joffrion 48, Mann 1, Soler 91, Winter 6. **OF**—Alamo 92, Arias 26, Backe 63, Katz 52, Lebron 10, Martin 31, Ryan 125, Scioneaux 5, Suriel 13, Wilder 31.

PITCHING	W	L	ERA	G	GS	CG	SV	IP	H	R	ER	BB	SO	B	T	HT	WT	DOB	1st Yr	Resides
Box, John	1	0	0.00	2	0	0	0	2	2	0	0	0	1	R	L	6-3	180	4-30-75	1996	Houston, Texas
Carter, Roger	0	3	8.76	12	1	0	1	12	11	15	12	17	14	R	R	6-2	200	8-17-78	1997	Fort Gibson, Okla.
Cornejo, Jesse	5	4	3.50	51	0	0	2	72	66	35	28	33	75	L	L	6-3	190	10-26-76	1998	Wellington, Kan.
Haines, Talley	3	2	3.25	47	0	0	18	61	51	33	22	12	68	R	R	6-5	200	11-16-76	1998	Cape Girardeau, Mo.
Hertzel, Patrick	7	7	3.98	35	16	0	0	127	142	66	56	46	96	R	R	6-5	210	7-9-76	1998	Manhattan, Kan.
James, Delvin	8	8	3.64	25	25	1	0	158	142	76	64	33	106	R	R	6-3	215	1-3-78	1996	Nacogdoches, Texas
Kofler, Ed	9	11	4.00	27	27	2	0	157	153	85	70	37	136	R	R	6-2	165	12-23-77	1996	Palm Harbor, Fla.
McDonald, Jon	0	0	6.97	14	0	0	0	21	26	19	16	5	19	L	L	6-0	190	12-1-76	1998	Humble, Texas
Peguero, Radhame	0	4	4.15	11	11	0	0	56	61	31	26	25	29	R	R	6-0	160	4-15-78	1996	San Pedro de Macoris, D.R.
Robinson, Jeremy	5	8	4.41	29	16	0	0	116	144	59	57	29	67	L	L	6-1	205	10-13-77	1998	Gonzales, La.
Rodriguez, Jose	0	1	6.57	7	0	0	1	12	20	15	9	7	11	R	R	6-2	160	2-27-76	1996	Cotui, D.R.
Ruhl, Nathan	4	4	2.93	36	0	0	2	55	31	20	18	34	82	R	R	6-4	200	7-16-76	1996	Lee's Summit, Mo.
Schuldt, Matt	1	4	4.91	26	1	0	1	33	31	24	18	15	20	R	R	6-2	205	9-17-75	1998	Sioux Falls, S.D.
Seberino, Ronni	6	2	2.65	50	0	0	0	75	57	29	22	38	73	L	L	6-1	177	5-27-76	1996	San Pedro de Macoris, D.R.
Standridge, Jason	9	1	2.02	18	18	3	0	116	80	35	26	31	84	R	R	6-4	205	11-9-78	1997	Birmingham, Ala.
Wright, Barrett	2	6	5.37	13	13	0	0	64	67	55	38	41	34	R	R	6-3	200	1-5-79	1997	Charlotte, N.C.
Wright, Chris	5	12	4.02	38	14	0	8	105	108	54	47	22	89	R	R	6-2	195	6-6-77	1997	Dale, Okla.

HUDSON VALLEY — Short-Season Class A

NEW YORK-PENN LEAGUE

BATTING	AVG	G	AB	R	H	2B	3B	HR	RBI	BB	SO	SB	CS	B	T	HT	WT	DOB	1st Yr	Resides
Arias, Jeison	.143	17	49	5	7	1	0	0	2	3	20	0	1	R	R	6-1	195	9-27-78	1996	San Jose de Ocoa, D.R.
Batista, Angel	.183	53	164	19	30	5	0	0	12	22	46	8	4	L	L	6-3	190	1-14-80	1996	Santo Domingo, D.R.
Beinbrink, Andrew	.339	76	292	46	99	24	2	11	51	39	49	13	4	R	R	6-3	205	9-24-76	1999	San Diego, Calif.
Cantu, Jorge	.260	72	281	33	73	17	2	1	33	20	59	3	4	R	R	6-1	185	1-30-82	1998	Reynosa, Mexico
Diaz, Matt	.245	54	208	22	51	15	2	1	20	6	43	6	2	R	R	6-1	215	3-3-78	1999	Lakeland, Fla.
Goodeill, Harold	.174	8	23	3	4	1	1	0	2	2	6	0	0	R	R	6-4	210	10-6-77	1999	Salida, Calif.
Grummitt, Dan	.254	73	287	44	73	13	1	22	58	30	78	3	1	R	R	6-5	230	6-16-76	1998	Twinsburg, Ohio
Hamilton, Josh	.194	16	72	7	14	3	0	0	7	1	14	1	1	L	L	6-4	205	5-21-81	1999	Raleigh, N.C.
Isenia, Chairon	.263	33	118	17	31	9	0	3	16	4	22	0	1	R	R	5-11	190	1-23-79	1996	Curacao, Neth. Antilles
Lebron, Hector	.250	17	56	3	14	3	0	1	6	3	13	0	0	L	R	6-3	225	7-22-77	1997	Catano, P.R.
Martin, Brian	.195	70	262	34	51	7	6	5	27	40	107	12	5	R	R	6-2	220	6-14-80	1998	El Centro, Calif.
Moore, Frank	.304	74	319	53	97	12	5	2	20	21	68	24	9	L	R	6-2	200	7-2-78	1998	Douglas, Ga.
Murch, Jeremy	.214	39	131	18	28	7	2	5	18	12	36	1	2	L	L	6-1	180	9-22-78	1998	Sarasota, Fla.
Ramirez, Edgar	.192	34	120	14	23	6	1	2	6	10	46	2	1	R	R	6-2	165	8-7-79	1996	San Pedro de Macoris, D.R.
Suriel, Miguel	.231	33	121	15	28	8	0	0	7	8	15	1	1	R	R	6-0	165	11-15-76	1994	Palmirito, D.R.
Valdez, Castulo	.231	12	26	4	6	0	0	0	0	5	4	0	0	R	R	5-11	180	9-20-77	1999	Houston, Texas
Vazquez, Carlos	.198	29	91	3	18	1	0	0	7	7	18	0	0	R	R	6-3	190	1-10-79	1997	Ponce, P.R.

GAMES BY POSITION: C—Isenia 33, Suriel 32, Valdez 12, Vazquez 6. **1B**—Grummitt 68, Lebron 7, Suriel 1, Vazquez 2. **2B**—Moore 74, Ramirez 4. **3B**—Beinbrink 75, Ramirez 1. **SS**—Cantu 72, Ramirez 4. **OF**—Arias 15, Batista 52, Diaz 54, Goodeill 3, Hamilton 16, Lebron 1, Martin 69, Murch 9, Ramirez 18.

PITCHING	W	L	ERA	G	GS	CG	SV	IP	H	R	ER	BB	SO	B	T	HT	WT	DOB	1st Yr	Resides
Andersen, Derek	2	3	2.60	20	5	0	0	55	46	19	16	14	56	L	L	6-3	190	10-6-77	1999	West Lynnwood, Wash.
Crawford, Chris	0	0	0.00	1	0	0	0	1	0	0	0	1	2	R	R	6-3	205	10-14-77	1999	Marietta, Ga.
Dailey, Matt	0	1	7.08	14	0	0	0	20	27	19	16	12	17	L	L	6-4	205	6-5-78	1999	Castro Valley, Calif.
Frendling, Neal	3	1	3.10	9	9	0	0	49	39	21	17	10	50	R	R	6-3	195	10-7-79	1999	Dyer, Ind.
Getz, Cody	5	1	2.85	11	11	0	0	60	56	22	19	17	69	L	L	6-8	200	9-19-78	1998	Walnut Creek, Calif.
Kennedy, Joe	6	5	2.65	16	16	1	0	95	78	33	28	26	101	R	L	6-4	220	5-24-79	1998	El Cajon, Calif.
Ledden, Ryan	3	1	6.53	20	0	0	0	30	33	23	22	27	16	R	R	6-4	195	10-19-77	1997	Lilburn, Ga.
Marin, Willy	2	3	3.34	23	1	0	2	57	43	23	21	13	47	R	R	6-1	165	7-28-78	1998	Miami, Fla.
McCormick, Terry	3	1	3.94	9	6	0	0	30	22	15	13	15	23	L	L	6-1	170	10-14-78	1997	Tampa, Fla.
McKoin, Heath	2	7	6.28	15	14	0	0	57	67	52	40	33	51	R	L	6-2	185	8-25-79	1997	Pine Bluff, Ark.
Minix, Travis	2	2	1.44	27	0	0	7	56	36	11	9	12	68	R	R	6-1	190	8-8-77	1999	Hamlet, Ind.
Oase, Ryan	0	0	6.75	1	0	0	0	1	3	1	1	1	1	S	R	6-2	220	4-9-78	1998	Everett, Wash.
Ortiz, Jose	4	3	1.74	29	0	0	9	47	31	14	9	14	35	R	R	6-3	175	12-12-77	1995	Guayubin, D.R.
Peguero, Radhame	2	1	2.42	4	4	0	0	26	13	8	7	11	24	R	R	6-0	160	4-15-78	1996	San Pedro de Macoris, D.R.
Pruett, Jason	4	2	1.99	25	0	0	1	41	32	13	9	8	29	L	L	6-3	160	1-21-79	1999	Princeton, Texas
Valera, Nelson	0	1	16.88	2	1	0	0	3	4	5	5	2	3	R	R	6-3	165	9-1-78	1996	Bani, D.R.
Wright, Barrett	4	2	3.70	10	9	0	1	58	55	29	24	24	40	R	R	6-3	200	1-5-79	1997	Charlotte, N.C.

APPALACHIAN LEAGUE

BATTING	AVG	G	AB	R	H	2B	3B	HR	RBI	BB	SO	SB	CS	B	T	HT	WT	DOB	1st Yr	Resides
Aaron, Oginga	.000	2	4	0	0	0	0	0	0	0	2	0	0	R	R	6-0	165	9-21-79	1999	Tustin, Calif.
Batista, Angel	.138	7	29	4	4	1	0	0	1	1	8	0	0	L	L	6-3	190	1-14-80	1996	Santo Domingo, D.R.
Candelario, Luis	.130	13	54	3	7	1	0	1	8	1	18	1	0	R	R	6-2	200	8-9-81	1999	San Pedro de Macoris, D.R.
Crawford, Carl	.319	60	260	62	83	14	4	0	25	13	47	17	4	L	L	6-2	195	8-5-81	1999	Houston, Texas
DeCaster, Yurendell	.257	48	183	37	47	12	0	11	36	20	65	4	2	R	R	6-1	175	9-26-79	1996	Curacao, Neth. Antilles
Hamilton, Josh	.347	56	236	49	82	20	4	10	48	13	43	17	3	L	L	6-4	200	5-21-81	1999	Raleigh, N.C.
Helena, Roberto	.274	61	223	31	61	7	0	1	14	10	44	4	6	R	R	6-2	175	8-23-81	1998	Santo Domingo, D.R.
Isenia, Chairon	.275	30	102	19	28	7	2	2	12	8	16	5	2	R	R	5-11	190	1-23-79	1996	Curacao, Neth. Antilles
Jacobs, John	.257	65	241	39	62	19	1	4	36	29	72	15	6	R	R	6-1	185	11-7-79	1998	Rohnert Park, Calif.
Lama, Jesus	.262	20	65	16	17	5	1	4	13	12	26	4	1	R	R	6-1	160	5-30-80	1997	Santo Domingo, D.R.
Maduro, Jorge	.241	24	83	5	20	4	0	0	6	4	20	1	2	R	R	6-2	200	3-11-81	1999	Miami, Fla.
Mansfield, Doug	.145	22	69	9	10	2	0	0	8	5	30	0	0	L	R	6-5	190	8-13-79	1997	Sherwood, Ark.
Ortiz, Daniel	.156	43	141	15	22	4	1	1	11	16	74	0	3	R	R	6-5	205	12-19-80	1999	Nuevo, Calif.
Osorio, Isrrael	.278	60	205	36	57	15	2	12	50	37	79	8	4	R	R	6-2	185	2-4-81	1997	Maracay, Venez.
Salas, Juan	.259	53	193	19	50	9	0	2	15	13	50	1	7	R	R	6-2	170	12-6-81	1998	Santo Domingo, D.R.
Schuda, Justin	.315	33	111	17	35	9	0	4	19	14	44	0	0	L	R	6-3	185	2-24-81	1999	Murrieta, Calif.
Serrano, Yalian	.000	7	10	0	0	0	0	0	0	0	8	0	0	R	R	5-10	170	8-15-80	1997	San Jose, Costa Rica
Volquez, Bolivar	.272	58	202	23	55	8	1	1	20	13	57	9	4	R	R	6-3	175	7-3-81	1998	Santo Domingo, D.R.

GAMES BY POSITION: C—Isenia 26, Maduro 24, Osorio 3, Schuda 21, Serrano 6. **1B**—Ortiz 21, Osorio 51, Salas 1, Schuda 2. **2B**—Aaron 1, DeCaster 48, Isenia 1, Salas 22. **3B**—Jacobs 60, Salas 9, Volquez 2. **SS**—Salas 18, Volquez 53. **OF**—Batista 7, Candelario 7, Crawford 58, Hamilton 55, Helena 59, Jacobs 4, Lama 7, Mansfield 16, Ortiz 3.

PITCHING	W	L	ERA	G	GS	CG	SV	IP	H	R	ER	BB	SO	B	T	HT	WT	DOB	1st Yr	Resides
Armstrong, Charles	0	0	13.50	3	0	0	0	3	7	5	4	3	2	L	L	6-4	210	9-28-76	1998	Oakland, Calif.
Campbell, Jarrett	4	2	5.05	11	9	0	0	46	51	35	26	15	29	R	R	6-2	185	9-8-79	1998	Corpus Christi, Texas
Cromer, Jason	1	5	7.46	11	8	0	0	41	69	45	34	14	26	R	L	6-4	220	12-11-80	1999	Des Moines, Iowa
Cromer, Nathan	0	4	11.44	13	7	0	0	39	72	69	50	33	28	L	L	6-4	220	12-11-80	1999	Des Moines, Iowa
Dailey, Matt	0	0	1.29	4	0	0	0	7	5	1	1	3	6	L	L	6-4	205	6-5-78	1999	Castro Valley, Calif.
Dittmer, Greg	1	3	3.27	28	0	0	1	44	48	28	16	16	32	L	L	6-7	220	1-24-79	1999	Davenport, Iowa
Frendling, Neal	2	1	2.50	4	3	0	0	18	16	8	5	5	18	R	R	6-3	195	10-7-79	1999	Dyer, Ind.
Frias, Juan	2	2	5.84	30	0	0	2	37	40	28	24	18	38	R	R	6-0	160	6-27-79	1996	San Pedro de Macoris, D.R.
Kolb, Jason	0	0	10.13	2	0	0	0	3	4	3	3	1	1	L	L	6-4	195	9-2-77	1999	Corona, Calif.
McClung, Seth	2	4	7.69	13	10	0	0	46	53	47	39	48	46	R	R	6-6	235	2-7-81	1999	Lewisburg, W.Va.
McKey, Dustin	1	1	8.73	26	0	0	0	44	62	49	43	18	31	R	R	6-4	195	5-1-78	1999	Cumming, Ga.
Price, Kevin	0	0	9.00	4	0	0	0	5	9	14	5	5	6	R	R	6-9	180	3-7-79	1997	Riverton, Utah
Silverthorn, Will	0	0	1.86	7	0	0	0	10	16	10	2	7	9	L	L	6-1	190	4-9-79	1998	Richardson, Texas
Stokes, Brian	2	3	3.89	13	0	0	9	37	33	20	16	21	39	R	R	6-1	190	9-7-79	1999	Chino, Calif.
Valera, Nelson	5	2	2.91	23	1	0	1	59	55	26	19	15	52	R	R	6-3	165	9-1-78	1996	Bani, D.R.
Vandermeer, Scott	2	8	6.63	14	11	0	0	58	58	54	43	36	32	R	R	6-4	185	2-16-81	1999	New Orleans, La.
Veras, Enger	3	5	7.12	14	14	0	0	61	74	57	48	50	48	R	R	6-5	197	6-5-81	1998	Santo Domingo, D.R.
Waechter, Doug	0	5	9.77	11	7	0	0	35	46	45	38	35	38	R	R	6-4	210	1-28-81	1999	St. Petersburg, Fla.

TEXASRANGERS

October failures take shine off strong 1999 showing

BY EVAN GRANT

Judged by all the numbers, 1999 was a runaway success for the Rangers. They took over first place during the second week of the season and held onto it the rest of the way to win their third American League West title in four years. They set a franchise record for wins with 95.

Catcher Ivan Rodriguez had his best offensive season, and first baseman/DH Rafael Palmeiro was a smash success in his return. After slow starts, righthanders Rick Helling and Aaron Sele again emerged as horses at the front of the rotation.

The farm system had the fourth-best record among all organizations, and the minor leagues produced major league contributors such as righthanders Dan Kolb and Jeff Zimmerman, lefthander Mike Venafro and outfielder Ruben Mateo.

So how come October was even more glum than usual around the Rangers offices?

Because in the one true measure of success in the American League—beating the Yankees—the Rangers failed again. A disastrous Division Series in which the Rangers scored one run in three games ended the promising season just like 1998.

That aside, 1999 was perhaps the brightest season in Rangers history. A look at some of the highlights:

■ In April, needing an extra arm for the bullpen, the Rangers purchased the contract of Zimmerman, a non-drafted refugee of the independent Northern League. All he did was win his first nine decisions and post an ERA of 0.86 in the first half to help the Rangers take control of the AL West. Along the way, Zimmerman earned an invitation to the All-Star Game and started a

Rafael Palmeiro   **Jason Romano**

Players of the Year

MAJOR LEAGUE: Rafael Palmeiro, 1b
  Palmeiro finished second in the AL with 47 home runs and 148 RBIs in his first season back in Texas.

MINOR LEAGUE: Jason Romano, 2b
  Romano hit .312 with 34 stolen bases and 54 extra-base hits at Charlotte, including an organization-best 14 triples.

stream of callups.

■ The callups indicated a return to productivity for the farm system. The Rangers called up nine players before September, and many of them could be back in 2000. Among them are infielder Kelly Dransfeldt, who could take over at second base for Mark McLemore, and lefthanders Doug Davis and Corey Lee, who will battle with September callup Matt Perisho for a spot in the rotation.

■ The Rangers set an organization record by placing four minor league teams—Triple-A Oklahoma, Double-A Tulsa, Rookie-level Pulaski and the Rookie-level Gulf Coast League team—in the postseason.

Though no teams won league titles, it marked the second straight year the Rangers sent at least three affiliates to the playoffs.

Oklahoma set an organization record for wins by a Triple-A affiliate with 83. Tulsa, which won the Texas League in 1998, qualified for the playoffs by winning three of five in a season-ending series with Jackson. Pulaski had the best record in the Appalachian League. And the GCL Rangers went to the playoffs for the fourth consecutive season.

■ Perhaps most promising, the Rangers' minor league teams went 373-317 (.541), with the 373 wins matching the most in Rangers history. The last time the minor league system did that was 1989, when, among others, Juan Gonzalez, Rodriguez and Dean Palmer were in the system.

Gonzalez was traded for salary reasons after the season. The organization is fortunate the minor league system has shown promise, because the Rangers intend to rely on it more and more.

ORGANIZATION LEADERS

BATTING

*AVG	Kevin Mench, Savannah/Pulaski	.357
R	Mike Lamb, Oklahoma/Tulsa	98
H	Mike Lamb, Oklahoma/Tulsa	177
TB	Mike Lamb, Oklahoma/Tulsa	301
2B	Mike Lamb, Oklahoma/Tulsa	51
3B	Jason Romano, Charlotte	14
HR	Two tied at	28
RBI	Travis Hafner, Savannah	111
BB	Two tied at	74
SO	Travis Hafner, Savannah	151
SB	Craig Monroe, Oklahoma/Charlotte	40

PITCHING

W	Matt Perisho, Oklahoma	15
L	Two tied at	14
#ERA	Doug Davis, Oklahoma/Tulsa	2.72
G	Matt Miller, Tulsa/Charlotte	56
CG	Brandon Knight, Oklahoma	5
SV	Allen McDill, Oklahoma	18
IP	Brady Raggio, Oklahoma	168
BB	Matt Perisho, Oklahoma	78
SO	Doug Davis, Oklahoma/Tulsa	153

*Minimum 250 At-Bats #Minimum 75 Innings

Texas RANGERS

Manager: Johnny Oates

1999 Record: 95-67, .586 (1st, AL West)

Organization Statistics

BATTING	AVG	G	AB	R	H	2B	3B	HR	RBI	BB	SO	SB	CS	B	T	HT	WT	DOB	1st Yr	Resides
Alicea, Luis	.201	68	164	33	33	10	0	3	17	28	32	2	1	S	R	5-9	176	7-29-65	1988	Loxahatchie, Fla.
Clayton, Royce	.288	133	465	69	134	21	5	14	52	39	100	8	6	R	R	6-0	183	1-2-70	1988	Inglewood, Calif.
Dransfeldt, Kelly	.189	16	53	3	10	1	0	1	5	3	12	0	0	R	R	6-2	195	4-16-75	1996	Morris, Ill.
Gonzalez, Juan	.326	144	562	114	183	36	1	39	128	51	105	3	3	R	R	6-3	220	10-16-69	1986	Levittown, P.R.
Goodwin, Tom	.259	109	405	63	105	12	6	3	33	40	61	39	11	L	R	6-1	175	7-27-68	1989	Fresno, Calif.
Green, Scarborough	.308	18	13	4	4	0	0	0	0	1	2	0	1	S	R	5-10	170	6-9-74	1993	Florissant, Mo.
Greer, Rusty	.300	147	556	107	167	41	3	20	101	96	67	2	2	L	L	6-0	195	1-21-69	1990	Colleyville, Texas
Kelly, Roberto	.300	87	290	41	87	17	1	8	37	21	57	6	1	R	R	6-2	202	10-1-64	1982	Panama City, Panama
Mateo, Ruben	.238	32	122	16	29	9	1	5	18	4	28	3	0	R	R	6-0	170	2-10-78	1995	San Cristobal, D.R.
McLemore, Mark	.274	144	566	105	155	20	7	6	45	83	79	16	8	S	R	5-11	207	10-4-64	1982	Grapevine, Texas
Palmeiro, Rafael	.324	158	565	96	183	30	1	47	148	97	69	2	4	L	L	6-0	190	9-24-64	1985	Colleyville, Texas
Rodriguez, Ivan	.332	144	600	116	199	29	1	35	113	24	64	25	12	R	R	5-9	205	11-30-71	1989	Vega Baja, P.R.
Shave, Jon	.288	43	73	10	21	4	0	0	9	5	17	1	0	R	R	6-0	185	11-4-67	1990	Fernandina Beach, Fla.
Sheldon, Scott	.000	2	2	0	0	0	0	0	0	0	0	0	0	R	R	6-3	185	11-20-68	1991	Houston, Texas
Simms, Mike	.500	4	2	0	1	0	0	0	0	0	1	0	0	R	R	6-4	230	1-12-67	1985	Arlington, Texas
Stevens, Lee	.282	146	517	76	146	31	1	24	81	52	132	2	3	L	L	6-4	235	7-10-67	1986	Grapevine, Texas
Zaun, Greg	.247	43	93	12	23	2	1	1	12	10	7	1	0	S	R	5-10	180	4-14-71	1989	Glendale, Calif.
Zeile, Todd	.293	156	587	80	172	41	1	24	98	56	94	1	2	R	R	6-1	204	9-9-65	1986	Westlake Village, Calif.

PITCHING	W	L	ERA	G	GS	CG	SV	IP	H	R	ER	BB	SO	B	T	HT	WT	DOB	1st Yr	Resides
Burkett, John	9	8	5.62	30	25	0	0	147	184	95	92	46	96	R	R	6-3	215	11-28-64	1983	Southlake, Texas
Clark, Mark	3	7	8.60	15	15	0	0	74	103	73	71	34	44	R	R	6-5	235	5-12-68	1988	Bath, Ill.
Crabtree, Tim	5	1	3.46	68	0	0	0	65	71	26	25	18	54	R	R	6-4	205	10-13-69	1992	Jackson, Mich.
Davis, Doug	0	0	33.75	2	0	0	0	3	12	10	10	0	3	R	L	6-3	185	9-21-75	1996	Sparks, Nev.
Fassero, Jeff	1	0	5.71	7	3	0	0	17	20	12	11	10	13	L	L	6-1	195	1-5-63	1984	Mercer Island, Wash.
2-team (30 Seattle)	5	14	7.20	37	27	0	0	156	208	135	125	83	114							
Glynn, Ryan	2	4	7.24	13	10	0	0	55	71	46	44	35	39	R	R	6-3	195	11-1-74	1995	Portsmouth, Va.
Gunderson, Eric	0	0	7.20	11	0	0	0	10	20	8	8	2	6	R	L	6-0	190	3-29-66	1987	Portland, Ore.
Helling, Rick	13	11	4.84	35	35	3	0	219	228	127	118	85	131	R	R	6-3	220	12-15-70	1992	West Fargo, N.D.
Johnson, Jonathan	0	0	15.00	1	0	0	0	3	9	5	5	2	3	R	R	6-0	180	7-16-74	1995	West Columbia, S.C.
Kolb, Dan	2	1	4.65	16	0	0	0	31	33	18	16	15	15	R	R	6-4	185	3-29-75	1995	Sterling, Ill.
Lee, Corey	0	1	27.00	1	0	0	0	1	2	3	3	1	0	S	L	6-2	180	12-26-74	1996	Clayton, N.C.
Loaiza, Esteban	9	5	4.56	30	15	0	0	120	128	65	61	40	77	R	R	6-3	205	12-31-71	1991	Imperial Beach, Calif.
Morgan, Mike	13	10	6.24	34	25	1	0	140	184	108	97	48	61	R	R	6-2	220	10-8-59	1978	Park City, Utah
Munoz, Mike	2	1	3.93	56	0	0	1	53	52	24	23	18	27	L	L	6-2	190	7-12-65	1986	West Covina, Calif.
Patterson, Danny	2	0	5.67	53	0	0	0	60	77	38	38	19	43	R	R	6-0	180	2-17-71	1990	Arlington, Texas
Perisho, Matt	0	0	2.61	4	1	0	0	10	8	3	3	2	17	L	L	6-0	190	6-8-75	1993	Phoenix, Ariz.
Sele, Aaron	18	9	4.79	33	33	2	0	205	244	115	109	70	186	R	R	6-5	215	6-25-70	1991	Kirkland, Wash.
Venafro, Mike	3	2	3.29	65	0	0	0	68	63	29	25	22	37	L	L	5-10	170	8-2-73	1995	Chantilly, Va.
Wetteland, John	4	4	3.68	62	0	0	43	66	67	30	27	19	60	R	R	6-2	215	8-21-66	1985	Cedar Crest, N.M.
Zimmerman, Jeff	9	3	2.36	65	0	0	3	88	50	24	23	23	67	R	R	6-1	200	8-9-72	1997	Fairmont, W.Va.

FIELDING

Catcher	PCT	G	PO	A	E	DP	PB
Rodriguez	.993	141	850	83	7	13	1
Zaun	.984	37	165	15	3	0	1

First Base	PCT	G	PO	A	E	DP
Palmeiro	.996	28	261	13	1	23
Shave	1.000	9	43	1	0	7
Simms	1.000	1	1	0	0	0
Stevens	.994	133	1228	60	8	128
Zeile	1.000	1	1	0	0	0

Second Base	PCT	G	PO	A	E	DP
Alicea	.980	37	60	87	3	19
McLemore	.983	135	261	433	12	93
Shave	1.000	1	1	1	0	1

Third Base	PCT	G	PO	A	E	DP
Alicea	.905	10	6	13	2	3
Shave	.889	6	2	6	1	1

	PCT	G	PO	A	E	DP
Sheldon	1.000	2	2	3	0	0
Zeile	.941	155	104	294	25	23

Shortstop	PCT	G	PO	A	E	DP
Clayton	.961	133	204	406	25	91
Dransfeldt	.966	16	31	54	3	13
Shave	.953	24	26	55	4	14

Outfield	PCT	G	PO	A	E	DP
Alicea	.000	1	0	0	0	0
Gonzalez	.983	131	223	7	4	3
Goodwin	.989	107	258	4	3	0
Green	1.000	9	6	0	0	0
Greer	.983	145	286	3	5	1
Kelly	.981	85	155	4	3	2
Mateo	1.000	31	62	3	0	0
McLemore	1.000	11	15	0	0	0
Simms	.000	1	0	0	0	0

MEL BAILEY

Ivan Rodriguez

DAVID SEELIG

Aaron Sele
Led Rangers with 18 wins

MORRIS FOSTOFF

Matt Perisho
Won 15 games for Oklahoma

FARM SYSTEM

Director of Player Development: Reid Nichols

Class	Farm Team	League	W	L	Pct.	Finish*	Manager	First Yr
AAA	Oklahoma RedHawks	Pacific Coast	83	59	.585	2nd (16)	Greg Biagini	1983
AA	Tulsa (Okla.) Drillers	Texas	74	66	.529	t-2nd (8)	Bobby Jones	1977
A#	Charlotte (Fla.) Rangers	Florida State	69	70	.496	7th (14)	James Byrd	1987
A	Savannah (Ga.) Sand Gnats	South Atlantic	62	78	.443	12th (14)	Paul Carey	1998
Rookie#	Pulaski (Va.) Rangers	Appalachian	48	21	.696	1st (10)	Bruce Crabbe	1997
Rookie	Port Charlotte (Fla.) Rangers	Gulf Coast	37	23	.617	2nd (14)	Darryl Kennedy	1973

*Finish in overall standings (No. of teams in league)   #Advanced level

OKLAHOMA   Class AAA

PACIFIC COAST LEAGUE

BATTING	AVG	G	AB	R	H	2B	3B	HR	RBI	BB	SO	SB	CS	B	T	HT	WT	DOB	1st Yr	Resides
Barkett, Andy	.307	132	486	70	149	32	5	10	76	44	71	7	7	L	L	6-1	205	9-5-74	1995	Raleigh, N.C.
Bournigal, Rafael	.375	17	56	16	21	6	0	3	14	12	5	1	1	R	R	5-11	175	5-12-66	1987	Lakeland, Fla.
Bridges, Kary	.343	75	239	38	82	14	0	7	39	21	14	6	3	L	R	5-10	170	10-27-72	1993	Hattiesburg, Miss.
2-team (10 Iowa)	.322	85	264	39	85	14	0	7	39	22	19	6	3							
Brumbaugh, Cliff	.250	4	12	1	3	0	0	0	1	0	2	0	0	R	R	6-2	205	4-21-74	1995	New Castle, Del.
Clayton, Royce	.143	2	7	1	1	0	0	0	1	3	3	0	0	R	R	6-0	183	1-2-70	1988	Inglewood, Calif.
Cuyler, Milt	.173	20	52	3	9	4	0	0	6	2	12	1	1	S	R	5-10	185	10-7-68	1986	Lakeland, Fla.
Demetral, Chris	.262	65	183	29	48	7	1	4	18	28	35	1	2	L	R	5-11	175	12-8-69	1991	Sterling Heights, Mich.
Dransfeldt, Kelly	.237	102	359	55	85	21	2	10	44	24	108	6	3	R	R	6-2	195	4-16-75	1996	Morris, Ill.
Evans, Tom	.280	128	439	84	123	35	3	12	68	66	100	5	4	R	R	6-1	200	7-9-74	1992	Issaquah, Wash.
Forbes, P.J.	.104	22	67	4	7	1	0	0	2	5	12	0	0	R	R	5-10	160	9-22-67	1990	Pittsburg, Kan.
Green, Scarborough	.248	104	359	68	89	16	6	3	29	34	86	26	12	S	R	5-10	170	6-9-74	1993	Florissant, Mo.
Hubbard, Mike	.283	110	392	48	111	19	0	9	49	25	70	4	1	R	R	6-1	205	2-16-71	1992	Madison Heights, Va.
Lamb, Mike	.500	2	2	0	1	0	0	0	0	1	0	0	1	L	R	6-1	185	8-9-75	1997	Valinda, Calif.
Marzano, John	.244	44	160	15	39	10	0	2	16	8	19	0	1	R	R	5-11	195	2-14-63	1985	Westboro, Mass.
Mateo, Ruben	.336	63	253	53	85	12	0	18	62	14	36	6	3	R	R	6-0	170	2-10-78	1995	San Cristobal, D.R.
Monroe, Craig	.250	6	16	2	4	1	0	0	1	1	4	0	0	R	R	6-1	195	2-27-77	1995	Texarkana, Texas
Reeder, Cory	.190	8	21	3	4	2	0	0	1	0	6	0	0	R	R	6-2	220	3-17-71	1994	Columbus, Neb.
Rosario, Mel	.192	7	26	2	5	1	0	0	3	0	8	1	0	S	R	6-0	200	5-25-73	1992	Miami, Fla.
Sagmoen, Marc	.272	83	268	42	73	11	3	13	43	24	58	3	2	L	L	5-11	185	4-16-71	1993	Seattle, Wash.
Sheldon, Scott	.311	122	453	94	141	35	3	28	97	56	112	12	2	R	R	6-3	185	11-20-68	1991	Houston, Texas
Simms, Mike	.274	22	73	7	20	1	0	2	16	16	25	0	0	R	R	6-4	230	1-12-67	1985	Arlington, Texas
Solano, Danny	.000	3	6	0	0	0	0	0	0	1	0	4	0	0	R R	5-9	155	12-3-78	1997	Santo Domingo, D.R.
Valdes, Pedro	.327	110	394	72	129	27	1	21	72	52	60	1	2	L	L	6-1	190	6-29-73	1991	Loiza, P.R.
Zywica, Mike	.265	135	495	80	131	31	3	9	79	33	119	4	1	R	R	6-4	190	9-14-74	1996	Richton Park, Ill.

PITCHING	W	L	ERA	G	GS	CG	SV	IP	H	R	ER	BB	SO	B	T	HT	WT	DOB	1st Yr	Resides
Davis, Doug	7	0	3.00	13	11	0	0	78	77	27	26	31	74	R	L	6-3	185	9-21-75	1996	Sparks, Nev.
Dickey, R.A.	2	2	4.37	6	2	0	0	23	23	12	11	7	17	R	R	6-2	205	10-29-74	1997	Nashville, Tenn.
Frey, Steve	1	2	4.47	30	0	0	9	44	51	25	22	15	38	L	L	5-9	170	7-29-63	1983	Newtown, Pa.
Glynn, Ryan	6	2	3.39	16	16	2	0	90	81	46	34	36	55	R	R	6-3	195	11-1-74	1995	Portsmouth, Va.
Gunderson, Eric	0	1	8.10	5	0	0	1	7	11	6	6	1	3	R	L	6-0	190	3-29-66	1987	Portland, Ore.
Hudson, Joe	1	1	5.00	5	0	0	0	9	15	6	5	4	4	R	R	6-1	180	9-29-70	1992	Medford, N.J.
Johnson, Jonathan	8	4	6.25	21	8	0	2	68	91	53	47	23	38	R	R	6-0	180	7-16-74	1995	West Columbia, S.C.
Karp, Ryan	2	2	7.49	8	6	1	0	40	62	34	33	14	28	L	L	6-4	205	4-5-70	1992	Coral Gables, Fla.
Knight, Brandon	9	8	4.91	27	26	5	0	163	173	96	89	47	97	L	R	6-0	170	10-1-75	1995	Oxnard, Calif.
Kolb, Dan	5	3	5.10	11	8	0	0	60	74	35	34	27	21	R	R	6-4	185	3-29-75	1995	Sterling, Ill.
Lee, Corey	3	0	2.03	4	4	0	0	27	21	6	6	8	25	S	L	6-2	180	12-26-74	1996	Clayton, N.C.
Loaiza, Esteban	0	0	0.00	2	2	0	0	4	3	0	0	3	6	R	R	6-3	205	12-31-71	1991	Imperial Beach, Calif.
McDill, Allen	1	3	3.72	42	0	0	18	48	45	22	20	17	46	L	L	6-1	155	8-23-71	1992	Hot Springs, Ark.
Moody, Eric	7	4	3.42	39	1	0	4	74	78	33	28	13	31	R	R	6-6	185	1-6-71	1993	Williamston, S.C.
Patterson, Danny	1	0	0.00	2	0	0	0	3	1	0	0	1	4	R	R	6-0	180	2-17-71	1990	Arlington, Texas
Perisho, Matt	15	7	4.61	27	27	2	0	156	160	86	80	78	150	L	L	6-0	190	6-8-75	1993	Phoenix, Ariz.
Pickett, Ricky	3	4	8.13	29	3	0	2	55	77	53	50	43	55	L	L	6-1	200	1-19-70	1992	Greenville, Fla.
Raggio, Brady	6	11	5.14	30	24	4	1	168	193	100	96	49	114	R	R	6-4	210	9-17-72	1992	Danville, Calif.
Robertson, Rich	0	1	7.71	3	0	0	0	5	7	5	4	3	4	L	L	6-4	175	9-15-68	1990	Waller, Texas
Sievert, Mark	0	0	10.32	7	0	0	0	11	17	13	13	8	5	L	R	6-4	195	2-16-73	1991	Janesville, Wis.
Smith, Chuck	5	4	2.96	32	4	2	4	85	73	31	28	28	76	R	R	6-1	175	10-21-69	1991	Cleveland, Ohio
Venafro, Mike	0	0	5.40	6	0	0	1	12	16	7	7	0	7	L	L	5-10	170	8-2-73	1995	Chantilly, Va.
Zimmerman, Jeff	1	0	0.00	2	0	0	1	4	0	0	0	0	2	R	R	6-1	200	8-9-72	1997	Fairmont, W.Va.

FIELDING

Catcher	PCT	G	PO	A	E	DP	PB
Hubbard	.994	105	675	47	4	5	9
Marzano	.978	32	170	11	4	6	1
Reeder	1.000	8	33	2	0	0	1
Rosario	.976	7	39	1	1	0	0
Sheldon	.955	4	19	2	1	0	0

First Base	PCT	G	PO	A	E	DP
Barkett	.995	122	1003	87	6	125
Brumbaugh	1.000	1	3	2	0	0
Evans	1.000	1	1	0	0	0
Hubbard	1.000	1	7	0	0	2
Marzano	.000	1	0	0	0	0
Sheldon	.978	12	82	7	2	11
Simms	.969	5	29	2	1	2
Valdes	1.000	11	107	6	0	8

Second Base	PCT	G	PO	A	E	DP
Bournigal	1.000	7	14	30	0	5
Bridges	.991	32	44	63	1	20
Demetral	.994	41	74	86	1	26

	PCT	G	PO	A	E	DP
Dransfeldt	1.000	8	11	18	0	6
Forbes	.976	18	30	53	2	14
Marzano	.000	1	0	0	0	0
Sheldon	.997	60	99	195	1	49

Third Base	PCT	G	PO	A	E	DP
Bournigal	.800	2	2	2	1	1
Bridges	.909	16	5	25	3	3
Evans	.951	126	81	266	18	24
Forbes	1.000	1	1	0	0	0
Lamb	.000	2	0	0	0	0
Marzano	.000	1	0	0	0	0
Sheldon	.889	6	6	18	3	2

Shortstop	PCT	G	PO	A	E	DP
Bournigal	.950	6	6	13	1	4
Clayton	1.000	2	4	7	0	2
Demetral	.977	13	16	27	1	6
Dransfeldt	.958	96	151	279	19	72
Forbes	1.000	2	2	3	0	1

	PCT	G	PO	A	E	DP
Marzano	.000	1	0	0	0	0
Sheldon	.987	33	48	103	2	23
Solano	.714	3	3	7	4	4

Outfield	PCT	G	PO	A	E	DP
Barkett	.000	1	0	0	0	0
Bridges	.944	17	17	0	1	0
Brumbaugh	.000	3	0	0	0	0
Cuyler	.966	19	28	0	1	0
Demetral	1.000	15	11	0	0	0
Green	.975	103	219	13	6	1
Hubbard	.000	1	0	0	0	0
Marzano	1.000	1	1	0	0	0
Mateo	.963	59	128	3	5	1
Monroe	1.000	6	17	0	0	0
Sagmoen	.986	81	133	4	2	1
Sheldon	.000	1	0	0	0	0
Simms	1.000	7	6	0	0	0
Valdes	.981	29	51	2	1	0
Zywica	.970	134	247	12	8	6

TULSA — Class AA

TEXAS LEAGUE

BATTING	AVG	G	AB	R	H	2B	3B	HR	RBI	BB	SO	SB	CS	B	T	HT	WT	DOB	1st Yr	Resides
Bautista, Juan	.246	127	471	60	116	14	3	8	45	25	114	18	9	R	R	6-0	170	6-24-75	1992	San Pedro de Macoris, D.R.
Brumbaugh, Cliff	.281	135	513	94	144	35	3	25	89	71	88	18	4	R	R	6-2	205	4-21-74	1995	New Castle, Del.
Cuyler, Milt	.326	36	138	30	45	4	4	0	13	18	29	7	6	S	R	5-10	185	10-7-68	1986	Lakeland, Fla.
Diaz, Freddie	.096	16	52	5	5	3	0	0	9	6	15	1	0	S	R	5-11	190	9-10-72	1992	El Monte, Calif.
Gallagher, Shawn	.283	112	452	61	128	30	3	18	78	26	84	1	0	R	R	6-0	180	11-8-76	1995	Lakeland, Fla.
Goodwin, Joe	.235	30	98	15	23	7	0	0	8	7	16	0	1	R	R	5-10	180	4-19-76	1995	New Windsor, Md.
Grabowski, Jason	.167	2	6	1	1	0	0	0	0	2	2	0	0	L	R	6-3	200	5-24-76	1997	Clinton, Conn.
Ibarra, Jesse	.222	90	325	32	72	10	1	11	49	41	88	0	0	S	R	6-3	195	7-12-72	1994	El Monte, Calif.
King, Cesar	.227	95	321	41	73	19	2	11	45	32	70	2	1	R	R	6-0	175	2-28-78	1995	La Romana, D.R.
Lamb, Mike	.324	137	544	98	176	51	5	21	100	53	65	4	3	L	R	6-1	185	8-9-75	1997	Valinda, Calif.
Lane, Ryan	.273	77	264	38	72	23	5	9	48	26	47	5	2	R	R	6-0	175	7-6-74	1993	Bellefontaine, Ohio
Morris, Bobby	.333	6	21	0	7	2	0	0	2	4	1	0	0	L	R	6-0	175	11-22-72	1993	Munster, Ind.
Myers, Adrian	.235	99	357	60	84	12	4	1	28	44	63	33	7	R	R	5-10	175	5-10-75	1996	Bassfield, Miss.
Piniella, Juan	.264	124	458	69	121	23	2	9	46	61	120	15	6	R	R	5-10	160	3-13-78	1996	Stafford, Va.
Podsednik, Scott	.155	37	116	10	18	4	0	0	1	5	13	6	2	L	L	6-0	170	3-18-76	1994	West, Texas
Rosario, Mel	.208	28	96	12	20	3	0	0	8	19	3	28	1	0	S	R	6-0	200	5-25-73	1992	Miami, Fla.
Sasser, Rob	.263	5	19	3	5	2	0	0	0	1	2	0	0	R	R	6-3	205	3-9-75	1993	Oakland, Calif.
Sergio, Tom	.291	128	512	88	149	38	6	10	72	58	59	19	5	L	R	5-9	175	6-27-75	1997	Norristown, Pa.
Valdes, Pedro	.353	11	34	3	12	4	0	1	4	8	6	0	0	L	L	6-1	190	6-29-73	1991	Loiza, P.R.

PITCHING	W	L	ERA	G	GS	CG	SV	IP	H	R	ER	BB	SO	B	T	HT	WT	DOB	1st Yr	Resides
Buckles, Bucky	10	4	3.73	36	5	0	1	72	71	40	30	34	39	R	R	6-1	190	6-19-73	1994	Victorville, Calif.
Burkett, John	0	1	2.70	2	1	0	0	7	7	5	2	3	3	R	R	6-3	215	11-28-64	1983	Southlake, Texas
Cobb, Trevor	4	5	5.26	35	3	0	1	75	79	52	44	33	44	L	L	6-2	190	7-13-73	1992	Marysville, Wash.
Cook, Derrick	7	6	5.67	21	21	2	0	114	137	81	72	45	71	R	R	6-3	195	8-6-76	1996	Staunton, Va.
Davis, Doug	4	4	2.42	12	12	1	0	74	65	26	20	25	79	R	L	6-3	185	9-21-75	1996	Sparks, Nev.
Dickey, R.A.	6	7	4.55	35	11	0	10	95	105	60	48	40	59	R	R	6-2	205	10-29-74	1997	Nashville, Tenn.
Elder, David	1	0	8.10	3	0	0	0	7	8	7	6	6	7	R	R	6-0	185	9-23-75	1997	Pensacola, Fla.
Johnson, Jonathan	0	0	9.53	1	1	0	0	6	12	6	6	0	4	R	R	6-0	180	7-16-74	1995	West Columbia, S.C.
Karp, Ryan	2	2	2.78	11	9	1	0	65	50	21	20	21	49	L	L	6-4	205	4-5-70	1992	Coral Gables, Fla.
Kolb, Dan	1	2	2.79	7	7	1	0	39	38	16	12	18	32	R	R	6-4	185	3-29-75	1995	Sterling, Ill.
Lee, Corey	8	5	4.44	22	22	0	0	128	132	76	63	44	121	S	L	6-2	180	12-26-74	1996	Clayton, N.C.
Martinez, Jose	4	4	5.42	33	9	0	3	98	112	69	59	36	70	R	R	6-0	165	2-4-75	1995	Santiago, D.R.
Miller, Matt	6	4	3.38	34	0	0	7	56	42	24	21	28	83	R	R	6-2	215	11-23-71	1997	Greenville, Miss.

PITCHING	W	L	ERA	G	GS	CG	SV	IP	H	R	ER	BB	SO	B	T	HT	WT	DOB	1st Yr	Resides
Moreno, Juan	4	3	2.30	42	0	0	3	63	33	20	16	32	83	L	L	6-1	190	2-28-75	1994	Cagua, Venez.
Poland, Trey	5	8	4.93	21	21	2	0	119	139	74	65	56	80	L	L	6-1	190	4-3-75	1997	Shreveport, La.
Quarnstrom, Rob	1	0	1.98	10	0	0	0	14	12	3	3	4	7	R	L	5-11	200	10-30-76	1998	Cabot, Ark.
Silva, Ted	6	3	4.00	13	11	0	0	72	64	34	32	14	48	R	R	6-0	170	8-4-74	1995	Redondo Beach, Calif.
Sollecito, Gabe	5	4	2.43	53	0	0	11	96	85	28	26	29	80	S	R	6-1	190	3-3-72	1993	Monterey, Calif.
Woodman, Hank	0	4	5.46	6	6	0	0	30	27	24	18	19	25	S	R	6-1	185	11-16-72	1993	Fort Myers, Fla.

FIELDING

Catcher	PCT	G	PO	A	E	DP	PB
Goodwin	.985	26	184	10	3	1	2
King	.983	94	614	75	12	6	17
Lamb	1.000	1	2	0	0	0	
Rosario	.987	26	208	24	3	1	4

First Base	PCT	G	PO	A	E	DP
Brumbaugh	.994	21	154	12	1	18
Gallagher	.985	107	922	46	15	77
Goodwin	1.000	1	1	1	0	0
Ibarra	1.000	8	78	8	0	6
Lane	.000	1	0	0	0	0
Valdes	.971	4	34	0	1	1

Second Base	PCT	G	PO	A	E	DP
Brumbaugh ..	1.000	1	4	1	0	1
Diaz	1.000	1	4	1	0	0
Lane	.963	17	18	34	2	4
Morris	1.000	1	1	3	0	0
Sergio	.962	123	289	346	25	73

Third Base	PCT	G	PO	A	E	DP
Brumbaugh	.000	1	0	0	0	0
Lamb	.930	137	88	284	28	25
Lane	.900	5	3	6	1	1

Shortstop	PCT	G	PO	A	E	DP
Bautista	.929	126	161	378	41	63

	PCT	G	PO	A	E	DP
Lane	.900	15	16	47	7	6

Outfield	PCT	G	PO	A	E	DP
Brumbaugh	.975	114	188	8	5	1
Cuyler	.986	35	68	1	1	1
Diaz	1.000	2	4	0	0	0
Ibarra	.882	10	13	2	2	0
Lane	.958	10	20	3	1	1
Myers	.975	94	190	6	5	0
Piniella	.986	124	276	13	4	5
Podsednik	.987	35	72	3	1	1
Sasser	1.000	4	7	0	0	0
Valdes	1.000	1	2	0	0	0

CHARLOTTE — Class A

FLORIDA STATE LEAGUE

BATTING	AVG	G	AB	R	H	2B	3B	HR	RBI	BB	SO	SB	CS	B	T	HT	WT	DOB	1st Yr	Resides
Acevedo, Inocencio	.000	1	3	1	0	0	0	0	0	0	0	1	0	R	R	5-10	155	6-15-79	1997	Santo Domingo, D.R.
Baker, Derek	.260	119	419	69	109	16	2	7	55	58	83	3	2	L	R	6-2	220	10-5-75	1996	Tustin, Calif.
Boughton, Mike	.179	14	39	5	7	0	0	0	4	3	9	2	1	S	R	6-3	180	11-8-74	1996	Flower Mound, Texas
Ellis, John	.270	48	152	15	41	7	1	0	17	11	21	0	1	R	R	6-1	195	8-4-75	1996	Niantic, Conn.
Garcia, Douglas	.298	112	386	57	115	14	5	0	34	26	69	14	8	L	L	6-1	165	4-25-79	1997	Barquisimeto, Venez.
Goodwin, Tom	.364	3	11	2	4	1	0	0	1	4	0	0	1	L	R	6-1	175	7-27-68	1989	Fresno, Calif.
Grabowski, Jason	.313	123	434	68	136	31	6	12	87	65	66	13	10	L	R	6-3	200	5-24-76	1997	Clinton, Conn.
Jaramillo, Frank	.216	12	37	1	8	0	0	0	4	1	9	1	1	R	R	5-11	170	11-28-74	1996	Franksville, Wis.
Jones, Jeremy	.194	11	31	4	6	1	0	1	4	4	10	1	0	R	R	6-3	195	8-12-77	1998	Raymore, Mo
Marzano, John	.000	1	4	0	0	0	0	0	0	0	0	0	0	R	R	5-11	195	2-14-63	1985	Westboro, Mass.
Mejias, Erick	.500	1	4	0	2	0	0	0	1	0	1	0	0	S	R	6-1	172	12-13-80	1998	Barcelona, Venez.
Monroe, Craig	.260	130	480	77	125	21	1	17	81	42	102	40	16	R	R	6-1	195	2-27-77	1995	Texarkana, Texas
Nina, Amuarys	.265	112	430	113	15	5	2	29	45	101	24	12	R	R	5-11	155	8-10-77	1995	San Cristobal, D.R.
Pena, Carlos	.255	136	501	85	128	31	8	18	103	74	135	2	5	L	L	6-2	210	5-17-78	1998	Haverhill, Mass.
Pena, Jose	.230	64	187	39	43	9	3	2	24	17	32	8	7	R	R	6-2	175	10-13-76	1995	Santiago, D.R.
Quinones, Marcus	.261	7	23	2	6	1	0	0	3	1	5	0	1	S	R	6-1	190	2-26-76	1998	Houston, Texas
Richards, Rowan	.265	9	34	5	9	1	0	1	5	0	8	0	1	R	R	6-0	195	5-17-74	1996	Bloomfield, N.J.
Romano, Jason	.312	120	459	84	143	27	14	13	71	39	72	34	16	R	R	6-0	185	6-24-79	1997	Tampa, Fla.
Simms, Mike	.220	12	41	7	9	1	0	2	9	8	3	0	0	R	R	6-4	230	1-12-67	1985	Arlington, Texas
Solano, Danny	.271	116	421	64	114	18	4	7	44	74	74	21	13	R	R	5-9	155	12-3-78	1997	Santo Domingo, D.R.
Taveras, Luis	.263	95	308	36	81	18	4	6	46	30	69	10	4	R	R	5-10	165	8-1-77	1995	Santiago, D.R.
Ware, Ryan	.182	67	181	16	33	7	1	5	22	15	22	4	0	R	R	5-11	180	2-6-76	1997	Houston, Texas

GAMES BY POSITION: C—Ellis 47, Jones 9, Taveras 95. **1B**—Boughton 1, Grabowski 3, C. Pena 135. **2B**—Acevedo 1, Mejias 1, Quinones 6, Romano 112, Ware 24. **3B**—Ellis 2, Grabowski 117, Jaramillo 3, Richards 1, Taveras 1, Ware 20. **SS**—Boughton 8, Jaramillo 7, Quinones 1, Solano 116, Ware 14. **OF**—Boughton 3, Garcia 107, Goodwin 3, Jaramillo 1, Jones 2, Monroe 130, Nina 112, J. Pena 59, Richards 9, Ware 3.

PITCHING	W	L	ERA	G	GS	CG	SV	IP	H	R	ER	BB	SO	B	T	HT	WT	DOB	1st Yr	Resides
Belcher, B.J.	2	2	4.62	15	4	0	0	37	48	22	19	19	15	R	R	6-2	225	7-2-77	1998	Milford, Va.
Benoit, Joaquin	7	4	5.31	22	22	0	0	105	117	67	62	50	83	R	R	6-3	160	7-26-79	1996	Santiago, D.R.
Bond, Aaron	6	4	6.45	8	7	0	0	38	54	34	27	23	18	R	R	6-2	230	12-2-76	1997	Las Vegas, Nev.
Cedeno, Jovanny	1	0	5.40	1	1	0	0	5	7	3	3	1	2	R	R	6-0	160	10-25-79	1997	La Romana, D.R.
Clark, Mark	0	0	1.29	2	2	0	0	7	5	1	1	1	2	R	R	6-5	235	5-12-68	1988	Bath, Ill.
Duncan, Sean	7	6	3.15	45	0	0	8	80	71	38	28	52	65	L	L	6-2	195	6-9-73	1994	Arlington, Texas
Elder, David	4	2	2.84	24	1	0	4	44	33	15	14	25	42	R	R	6-2	210	10-14-76	1996	Pensacola, Fla.
Fleming, Emar	9	9	4.30	24	22	1	0	142	138	81	68	62	100	R	R	6-3	210	10-14-76	1996	Baltimore, Md.
Freehill, Mike	2	2	3.57	17	0	0	8	18	15	11	7	9	18	R	R	6-2	175	6-2-71	1994	Phoenix, Ariz.
Frey, Chris	0	1	6.75	2	0	0	0	4	10	3	3	2	3	R	R	6-3	210	4-15-74	1998	Etters, Pa.
Guzman, Delby	5	6	5.88	19	18	0	0	93	114	67	61	40	45	R	R	6-5	160	9-27-76	1994	Hato Del Media Abajo, D.R.
LaMarsh, Robert	0	0	2.70	1	1	0	0	3	9	1	1	0	0	R	L	6-4	245	7-14-76	1998	Alton, Ill.
Lundberg, Dave	14	7	2.83	30	21	4	0	156	162	63	49	44	81	S	R	6-1	185	5-4-77	1997	San Diego, Calif.
Marsonek, Sam	3	9	5.54	15	15	2	0	91	111	69	56	27	61	R	R	6-6	225	7-10-78	1997	Tampa, Fla.
Miller, Matt	1	2	3.03	22	0	0	8	30	27	12	10	13	39	R	R	6-1	215	11-23-71	1997	Greenville, Miss.
Mlodik, Kevin	0	4	4.07	25	0	0	0	49	52	29	22	30	33	R	R	6-1	205	8-21-74	1995	Rosholt, Wis.
Moody, Eric	0	0	9.00	1	1	0	0	2	2	2	2	0	1	R	R	6-6	185	1-6-71	1993	Williamston, S.C.
Poeck, Chad	0	0	1.20	9	0	0	1	15	10	3	2	6	12	R	R	6-2	190	10-18-72	1996	Houston, Texas
Poland, Trey	2	2	0.84	5	5	1	0	32	16	4	3	9	28	L	L	6-1	190	4-3-75	1997	Shreveport, La.
Quarnstrom, Rob	2	2	3.51	30	0	0	4	59	68	30	23	16	38	R	L	5-11	200	10-30-76	1998	Cabot, Ark.
Schultz, Eric	2	5	5.36	19	1	0	1	45	56	30	27	9	44	R	R	6-5	220	12-4-74	1997	St. John, Ind.
Silva, Doug	4	3	3.90	24	12	0	0	95	103	58	41	25	55	R	R	6-3	190	7-8-79	1997	Miranda, Venez.
Vigeland, Ole	0	0	7.27	5	0	0	0	9	14	7	7	4	9	R	R	6-1	185	10-26-76	1998	Redmond, Wash.
Woodman, Hank	2	2	4.11	6	6	2	0	31	35	17	14	14	19	S	R	6-1	185	11-16-72	1993	Fort Myers, Fla.

SAVANNAH — Class A

SOUTH ATLANTIC LEAGUE

BATTING	AVG	G	AB	R	H	2B	3B	HR	RBI	BB	SO	SB	CS	B	T	HT	WT	DOB	1st Yr	Resides
Acevedo, Luis	.000	6	15	1	0	0	0	0	0	3	5	0	0	R	R	5-11	180	11-19-77	1996	Isabela, P.R.
Baez, Ernies	.000	1	3	0	0	0	0	0	0	1	2	0	0	S	R	6-0	180	1-2-78	1998	Dorado, P.R.

BATTING	AVG	G	AB	R	H	2B	3B	HR	RBI	BB	SO	SB	CS	B	T	HT	WT	DOB	1st Yr	Resides
Blalock, Hank	.240	7	25	3	6	1	0	1	2	1	3	0	0	L	R	6-1	192	11-21-80	1999	San Diego, Calif.
Boughton, Mike	.267	26	90	7	24	4	0	0	3	12	22	1	2	S	R	6-3	180	11-8-74	1996	Flower Mound, Texas
Castaneda, Cesar	.202	103	331	33	67	13	2	12	47	29	105	2	4	R	R	6-3	210	11-30-76	1998	Los Angeles, Calif.
Castillo, Geramel	.301	114	405	42	122	21	4	3	40	19	94	4	4	S	R	6-1	160	10-3-77	1995	La Romana, D.R.
Cordero, Willy	.246	101	366	51	90	20	4	6	37	27	70	11	6	R	R	6-1	155	8-20-78	1995	San Cristobal, D.R.
Cruz, Rafael	.065	23	62	0	4	1	0	0	3	7	30	1	1	R	R	6-2	180	5-19-79	1996	Santiago, D.R.
Guerrero, Pedro	.183	42	131	20	24	2	3	3	12	11	39	11	0	R	R	5-10	165	8-21-79	1996	Santo Domingo, D.R.
Hafner, Travis	.292	134	480	94	140	30	4	28	111	67	151	5	4	L	R	6-3	215	6-3-77	1997	Sykeston, N.D.
Harris, Kevin	.161	59	180	15	29	5	2	3	11	3	72	8	6	R	R	6-2	220	3-27-78	1997	Tampa, Fla.
Hazelton, Justin	.154	4	13	0	2	1	0	0	1	1	8	0	0	R	R	6-2	175	8-9-78	1996	Philipsburg, Pa.
Jones, Jeremy	.241	43	133	18	32	6	2	0	16	15	27	0	1	R	R	6-3	195	8-12-77	1998	Raymore, Mo
Marciante, Frank	.290	84	286	36	83	12	1	5	37	16	50	1	2	S	R	6-3	185	8-16-78	1998	Sunrise, Fla.
Meliah, David	.296	93	358	53	106	21	3	8	49	16	80	3	6	L	R	6-3	185	3-11-77	1998	Walla Walla, Wash.
Mench, Kevin	.304	6	23	4	7	1	1	2	8	2	4	0	0	R	R	6-0	215	1-7-78	1999	Newark, Del.
Novak, John	.251	66	215	38	54	13	1	8	36	28	65	3	2	R	R	6-1	215	1-15-77	1999	Tarzana, Calif.
Nowlin, Cody	.181	56	204	25	37	6	1	4	26	19	58	1	2	L	R	6-3	190	11-27-79	1998	Fresno, Calif.
Ottevaere, Derek	.273	97	337	45	92	11	5	7	43	27	70	3	1	R	R	6-2	215	12-24-75	1998	Houston, Texas
Quinones, Marcus	.203	37	123	17	25	9	0	0	9	14	28	2	1	S	R	6-1	180	2-26-76	1998	Houston, Texas
Rollins, Antwon	.242	8	33	7	8	0	0	0	1	4	14	3	0	R	R	6-0	190	3-18-80	1998	Alameda, Calif.
Romano, Jimmie	.201	44	134	13	27	2	0	2	14	5	26	1	0	R	R	5-10	185	3-31-77	1998	Tampa, Fla.
Sienko, Ryan	.151	37	86	7	13	3	0	1	6	8	25	0	0	R	R	6-4	220	9-16-75	1997	Elgin, Ill.
Torres, Jason	.167	43	126	6	21	3	2	0	8	10	31	2	1	L	R	5-10	170	12-11-78	1997	Vero Beach, Fla.
Warriax, Brandon	.153	43	144	10	22	3	1	1	13	15	43	7	1	R	R	6-0	165	6-23-79	1997	Maxton, N.C.
Wright, Corey	.263	95	316	61	83	15	5	1	23	64	73	13	13	L	L	5-11	185	11-26-79	1997	La Puente, Calif.

GAMES BY POSITION: C—Cruz 23, Jones 42, Romano 38, Sienko 21, Torres 37. **1B**—Castaneda 2, Hafner 108, Marciante 29, Ottevaere 9, Romano 1, Sienko 6. **2B**—Acevedo 2, Boughton 13, Castaneda 1, Cordero 21, Guerrero 42, Meliah 66, Quinones 6, Romano 2. **3B**—Acevedo 3, Blalock 7, Castaneda 100, Cordero 19, Hafner 5, Meliah 22, Quinones 1, Romano 2, Sienko 1. **SS**—Acevedo 1, Boughton 11, Cordero 61, Quinones 30, Romano 1, Warriax 40. **OF**—Baez 2, Castillo 99, Harris 54, Hazelton 4, Meliah 7, Mench 6, Novak 64, Nowlin 34, Ottevaere 71, Rollins 8, Romano 4, Sienko 1, Torres 3, Wright 94.

PITCHING	W	L	ERA	G	GS	CG	SV	IP	H	R	ER	BB	SO	B	T	HT	WT	DOB	1st Yr	Resides
Beitey, Jason	1	3	5.36	21	1	0	2	49	54	38	29	28	38	R	R	6-1	170	11-18-77	1997	Vancouver, Wash.
Boublis, Dan	7	3	6.32	30	9	2	0	84	116	66	59	35	59	R	R	6-0	215	3-7-77	1998	Cedar Rapids, Iowa
Brazoban, Melvin	1	2	7.09	29	5	0	2	66	72	63	52	60	75	R	R	6-3	165	1-20-77	1994	Santo Domingo, D.R.
Clark, Mark	0	0	0.00	1	1	0	0	4	2	0	0	1	1	R	R	6-5	235	5-12-68	1988	Bath, Ill.
Figueroa, Carlos	0	0	5.85	10	0	0	1	20	19	14	13	16	30	L	L	6-1	190	10-5-78	1997	Carolina, P.R.
Frey, Chris	2	0	2.44	31	0	0	5	59	53	27	16	15	55	R	R	6-3	210	4-15-74	1998	Etters, Pa.
Guzman, Ambiorix	3	7	4.40	29	1	0	6	72	71	37	35	16	73	R	R	6-2	160	5-20-78	1995	Santiago, D.R.
Hughes, Travis	11	7	2.81	30	23	1	2	157	127	60	49	54	150	R	R	6-5	215	5-25-78	1998	Elwood, Neb.
Kosderka, Matt	12	9	3.81	31	20	1	4	135	133	69	57	50	114	R	R	6-2	215	4-13-76	1998	Roseburg, Ore.
McGill, Frankie	8	14	5.22	26	26	0	0	141	163	92	82	56	128	R	R	5-11	210	9-10-79	1998	Cantonment, Fla.
Mlodik, Kevin	2	2	0.90	14	0	0	5	20	12	5	2	8	32	R	R	6-1	205	8-21-74	1995	Rosholt, Wis.
Moore, Eric	1	1	2.86	23	0	0	1	35	38	16	11	7	28	R	R	6-3	203	5-26-76	1998	Houston, Texas
Pratt, Andy	4	4	2.89	13	13	1	0	72	66	30	23	16	100	L	L	5-11	180	8-27-79	1998	Mesa, Ariz.
Rosado, Juan	0	1	4.86	20	0	0	4	33	35	29	18	23	35	L	L	5-11	180	8-6-74	1994	Camuy, P.R.
Silva, Doug	0	1	2.04	7	0	0	1	18	15	5	4	3	18	R	R	6-3	190	7-8-79	1997	Miranda, Venez.
Stewart, John	6	14	5.04	30	20	1	0	130	144	99	73	24	79	R	L	6-4	180	7-9-77	1998	Streamwood, Ill.
Tynan, Chris	4	10	6.99	21	21	0	0	112	140	96	87	38	97	R	R	6-2	170	11-15-78	1997	Vancouver, Wash.

PULASKI — Rookie

APPALACHIAN LEAGUE

BATTING	AVG	G	AB	R	H	2B	3B	HR	RBI	BB	SO	SB	CS	B	T	HT	WT	DOB	1st Yr	Resides
Acevedo, Luis	.087	9	23	4	2	0	0	0	1	9	9	4	0	R	R	5-11	180	11-19-77	1996	Isabela, P.R.
Baez, Ernies	.192	8	26	3	5	0	0	2	5	4	6	1	0	S	R	6-0	180	1-2-78	1998	Dorado, P.R.
Cadiente, Brett	.354	68	274	69	97	16	7	7	48	38	51	18	3	L	L	5-11	180	6-17-77	1999	Mesa, Ariz.
Cruz, Rafael	.222	15	54	7	12	3	0	0	8	4	14	0	0	R	R	6-2	180	5-19-79	1996	Santiago, D.R.
Cubillan, Jose	.100	5	10	4	1	0	0	0	1	2	8	0	0	S	R	6-4	180	12-27-78	1996	Zulia, Venez.
Guerrero, Pedro	.216	63	218	57	47	7	2	5	22	49	59	19	7	R	R	5-10	165	8-21-79	1996	Santo Domingo, D.R.
Jaramillo, Tony	.185	25	81	10	15	4	0	0	11	11	25	0	0	L	R	5-10	175	8-16-78	1998	Dallas, Texas
Jimenez, Jonathan	.239	61	213	25	51	11	1	3	27	17	65	3	2	R	R	6-0	160	1-30-79	1997	Santo Domingo, D.R.
Jones, Jason	.355	69	262	65	93	24	1	11	58	33	55	1	2	S	R	6-3	210	10-17-76	1999	Marietta, Ga.
Mench, Kevin	.362	65	260	63	94	22	1	16	60	28	48	12	2	R	R	6-0	215	1-7-78	1999	Newark, Del.
Nowlin, Cody	.278	58	227	45	63	10	1	8	49	21	34	5	0	L	R	6-3	190	11-27-79	1998	Fresno, Calif.
Poe, Adam	.298	49	171	26	51	12	0	2	31	16	30	11	3	R	R	6-0	177	4-28-78	1999	Kennesaw, Ga.
Torres, Frederick	.304	60	240	35	73	19	0	8	45	7	53	1	0	R	R	6-2	165	3-16-80	1997	Santiago, D.R.
Torres, Jason	.277	25	65	18	18	4	1	4	8	12	16	0	0	L	R	5-10	170	12-11-78	1997	Vero Beach, Fla.
Warriax, Brandon	.254	65	232	44	59	9	2	9	35	18	68	11	1	R	R	6-0	165	6-23-79	1997	Maxton, N.C.

GAMES BY POSITION: C—Cruz 7, F. Torres 50, J. Torres 17. **1B**—Jones 67, J. Torres 3. **2B**—Acevedo 1, Guerrero 60, Jaramillo 12. **3B**—Acevedo 7, Jaramillo 5, Jimenez 60. **SS**—Acevedo 2, Guerrero 3, Jimenez 1, Warriax 64. **OF**—Baez 8, Cadiente 66, Jones 3, Mench 51, Nowlin 48, Poe 36.

PITCHING	W	L	ERA	G	GS	CG	SV	IP	H	R	ER	BB	SO	B	T	HT	WT	DOB	1st Yr	Resides
Backsmeyer, Justin	3	1	6.75	12	7	0	0	43	55	41	32	30	31	R	R	6-4	205	1-24-80	1998	Ballwin, Mo.
Bullock, Jeremiah	2	3	5.72	13	13	0	0	68	78	60	43	31	39	L	L	6-1	180	12-27-79	1998	Cedar Rapids, Iowa
Cullen, Ryan	1	2	3.54	19	0	0	6	41	33	20	16	17	47	L	L	6-2	170	1-20-80	1999	Satellite Beach, Fla.
Dittfurth, Ryan	7	2	2.60	14	14	1	0	83	66	35	24	42	85	R	R	6-6	175	10-18-79	1998	Plano, Texas
Harang, Aaron	9	2	2.30	16	10	1	1	78	64	22	20	17	87	R	R	6-7	240	5-9-78	1999	San Diego, Calif.
Hollingsworth, Scott	0	1	5.49	12	0	0	0	20	24	18	12	14	20	R	R	6-3	180	10-5-75	1999	Brooklyn, Minn.
Lewis, Colby	7	3	1.95	14	11	1	0	65	46	24	14	27	84	R	R	6-4	215	8-2-79	1999	Bakersfield, Calif.
Regilio, Nick	4	2	1.63	11	8	1	0	50	30	12	9	16	58	R	R	6-2	185	9-4-78	1999	Deltona, Fla.
Rochez, Angel	2	1	8.24	18	3	0	3	39	54	40	36	20	29	R	R	5-9	155	3-5-79	1996	La Romana, D.R.
Rodriguez, Alfredo	0	1	9.72	6	0	0	0	8	13	10	9	5	5	R	R	6-3	185	11-1-77	1995	Zalaya, D.R.
Rodriguez, Luis	0	0	0.00	1	0	0	0	1	2	0	0	1	1	R	R	6-2	185	7-24-81	1998	Caracas, Venez.
Scuglik, Mike	2	2	3.10	18	0	0	3	29	36	15	10	10	36	L	L	6-2	190	5-24-77	1999	Kenosha, Wis.

PITCHING	W	L	ERA	G	GS	CG	SV	IP	H	R	ER	BB	SO	B	T	HT	WT	DOB	1st Yr	Resides
Valdez, Domingo	0	0	6.75	3	3	0	0	16	20	14	12	7	14	R	R	6-3	220	6-27-80	1998	Corpus Christi, Texas
Weaver, Joe	6	0	6.43	18	0	0	0	21	30	17	15	15	17	L	R	6-4	220	9-6-77	1998	Centerville, Miss.
Wessel, Travis	5	1	4.03	21	0	0	7	29	28	15	13	11	36	L	L	6-2	205	5-21-76	1999	Denison, Iowa

PORT CHARLOTTE — Rookie

GULF COAST LEAGUE

BATTING	AVG	G	AB	R	H	2B	3B	HR	RBI	BB	SO	SB	CS	B	T	HT	WT	DOB	1st Yr	Resides
Acevedo, Inocencio	.217	27	115	23	25	4	3	0	9	8	18	16	1	R	R	5-10	155	6-15-79	1997	Santo Domingo, D.R.
Angell, Ricky	.251	60	203	35	51	12	2	2	32	20	30	14	3	R	R	5-9	175	11-24-76	1999	Rhinelander, Wis.
Baez, Ernies	.286	12	42	4	12	1	0	1	8	3	15	2	1	S	R	6-0	180	1-2-78	1998	Dorado, P.R.
Baez, Fleming	.000	4	9	0	0	0	0	0	0	0	5	0	0	R	R	6-0	172	6-10-81	1900	Santo Domingo, D.R.
Blalock, Hank	.361	51	191	34	69	17	6	3	38	25	23	3	2	L	R	6-1	192	11-21-80	1999	San Diego, Calif.
Bryan, Jason	.350	6	20	3	7	2	0	0	1	3	9	1	1	R	R	6-2	195	11-18-81	1999	Brooklyn, N.Y.
Cruz, Orlando	.184	46	136	12	25	5	2	0	11	15	44	0	2	R	R	6-0	170	10-5-81	1999	Juncos, P.R.
Gajewski, Matt	.210	52	162	31	34	7	1	4	26	34	41	1	0	S	R	6-2	205	10-8-77	1999	Ashley, Ill.
Jaile, Chris	.173	39	139	16	24	5	0	2	14	22	32	0	0	R	R	6-3	195	2-20-81	1999	Miami, Fla.
Jones, Jason	.206	11	34	1	7	2	0	0	3	2	12	1	0	L	R	6-0	170	9-20-77	1999	Martinez, Ga.
Leed, Adam	.273	12	44	5	12	2	0	2	8	3	12	1	1	R	R	6-2	210	12-29-76	1999	Lancaster, Pa.
Matos, Angel	.279	36	122	21	34	12	2	2	22	18	36	2	1	R	R	5-10	160	1-2-80	1997	Santiago, D.R.
Mejias, Erick	.258	56	194	35	50	7	1	1	23	22	36	11	3	S	R	6-1	172	12-13-80	1998	Barcelona, Venez.
Morban, Jose	.283	54	205	45	58	10	5	4	18	31	70	19	14	R	R	6-1	160	12-2-79	1997	Santo Domingo, D.R.
Podsednik, Scott	.412	5	17	6	7	2	0	0	5	2	3	1	0	L	L	6-0	170	3-18-76	1994	West, Texas
Ramos, Eddy	.200	55	180	20	36	0	2	0	16	21	54	12	1	S	R	6-1	170	9-28-78	1996	Santiago, D.R.
Richards, Rowan	.267	10	30	4	8	1	0	1	8	2	8	0	0	R	R	6-0	195	5-17-74	1996	Bloomfield, N.J.
Rollins, Antwon	.250	1	4	1	1	0	0	0	2	0	0	0	0	R	R	6-0	190	3-18-80	1998	Alameda, Calif.
Valdez, Toribio	.037	10	27	0	1	0	0	0	1	2	5	0	0	S	R	6-0	170	3-23-80	1998	Nizao, D.R.
Villegas, Ernest	.286	11	35	6	10	1	2	0	5	5	7	1	1	R	R	6-1	200	11-29-78	1999	Irving, Texas

GAMES BY POSITION: C—F. Baez 2, Gajewski 9, Jaile 30, Matos 20. **1B**—Angell 4, E. Baez 1, Gajewski 43, Matos 2, Mejias 1, Villegas 11. **2B**—Acevedo 11, Angell 2, Mejias 47. **3B**—Angell 2, Blalock 48, Gajewski 1, Matos 1, Mejias 5, T. Valdez 7. **SS**—Acevedo 15, Mejias 1, Morban 44, T. Valdez 1. **OF**—Angell 50, E. Baez 6, Bryan 6, Cruz 44, Jones 7, Leed 9, Matos 4, Mejias 2, Podsednik 3, Ramos 53, Richards 7, Rollins 1, T. Valdez 2.

PITCHING	W	L	ERA	G	GS	CG	SV	IP	H	R	ER	BB	SO	B	T	HT	WT	DOB	1st Yr	Resides
Buckles, Bucky	0	1	4.50	1	1	0	0	2	4	2	1	0	1	R	R	6-1	190	6-19-73	1994	Victorville, Calif.
Cavazos, Andy	2	0	3.72	10	7	0	0	36	35	16	15	12	15	R	R	6-3	185	1-5-81	1999	Clute, Texas
Cedeno, Jovanny	3	0	0.33	6	6	1	0	27	13	3	1	4	32	R	R	6-0	160	10-25-79	1997	La Romana, D.R.
Echols, Justin	2	2	2.60	14	4	0	0	35	27	14	10	21	32	R	R	6-3	185	10-6-80	1999	Roby, Mo.
Figueroa, Carlos	4	0	0.84	6	0	0	0	11	5	1	1	3	17	L	L	6-1	170	10-5-78	1997	Carolina, P.R.
Garcia, Reynaldo	4	4	3.23	12	11	0	0	64	55	30	23	26	42	R	R	6-3	170	4-15-78	1997	Santo Domingo, D.R.
Guzman, Leiby	0	0	0.00	1	1	0	0	3	2	0	0	0	1	R	R	6-5	160	9-27-76	1994	Hato Del Media Abajo, D.R.
Hill, Jamie	2	0	2.35	21	1	0	2	46	32	12	12	20	38	L	L	6-1	205	2-22-77	1999	Panama City, Fla.
Johnson, Jonathan	0	0	1.80	1	1	0	0	5	3	1	1	0	5	R	R	6-0	180	7-16-74	1995	West Columbia, S.C.
LaMarsh, Robert	2	0	2.00	3	0	0	0	9	7	2	2	1	6	R	L	6-4	245	7-14-76	1998	Alton, Ill.
Lopez, Ignacio	7	2	2.70	12	9	0	1	57	60	22	17	5	31	R	R	6-2	185	5-5-80	1997	Santiago, D.R.
Mead, David	1	3	5.00	11	7	0	0	36	40	23	20	11	34	R	R	6-5	180	3-21-81	1999	Sale Creek, Tenn.
Rahrer, Josh	4	4	4.36	15	0	0	3	33	29	18	16	12	16	R	R	6-3	195	12-11-80	1999	Emmett, Idaho
Rodriguez, Alfredo	0	1	2.19	9	0	0	3	12	14	6	3	1	8	R	R	6-2	185	11-1-77	1995	Zalaya, D.R.
Rodriguez, Luis	4	2	3.47	17	5	1	1	49	46	24	19	18	26	R	R	6-2	185	7-24-81	1998	Caracas, Venez.
Stamm, Steven	1	2	1.74	20	0	0	8	31	15	11	6	15	30	S	L	5-11	180	4-28-77	1999	Joliet, Ill.
Valdez, Domingo	0	1	4.91	8	7	0	0	29	29	22	16	18	34	R	R	6-3	220	6-27-80	1998	Corpus Christi, Texas
Villamil, William	0	1	4.94	14	0	0	1	24	24	14	13	12	17	L	L	6-1	165	8-20-80	1998	Villa Carolina, P.R.

Organization Statistics

TORONTO BLUE JAYS

Jays fall short of wild card in roller-coaster '99 season

BY LARRY MILLSON

It was a good season for individual efforts in 1999, but the Blue Jays again fell short of their team goal of making the postseason for the first time since 1993.

Jim Fregosi took over as manager from Tim Johnson on March 17, after Johnson was forced out. Johnson admitted over the winter that he had never served in Vietnam, as he had told some people. He had served only in the Marine reserves.

That move came after an eventful offseason in which the Blue Jays traded five-time Cy Young Award winner Roger Clemens to the Yankees for lefthanders Graeme Lloyd and David Wells and second baseman Homer Bush.

Toronto rode a roller coaster all season. After a 12-4 start, the Blue Jays dropped to nine games below .500 on June 12. But they rode a 19-7 July to a season-high 14 games above .500 on Aug. 11, the next-to-last day in which they occupied the wild-card lead. After an August and September slide, they finished 84-78, four games worse than 1998.

First baseman Carlos Delgado and right fielder Shawn Green had career years. Delgado hit 44 home runs and had 134 RBIs, which tied George Bell's 1987 club record, before his season ended Sept. 22. He broke his tibia when he fouled a ball off his leg. Green batted .308 with 42 home runs, 123 RBIs and a club-record 134 runs. He also had a club-record 28-game hitting streak.

Righthander Billy Koch set a league record for saves by a rookie with 31. Shortstop Alex Gonzalez' season ended in mid-May because of a torn labrum, but Tony Batista filled the vacancy. The Blue Jays' July run started when they acquired Batista and reliever John Frascatore from the Diamondbacks for lefthander Dan

Shawn Green

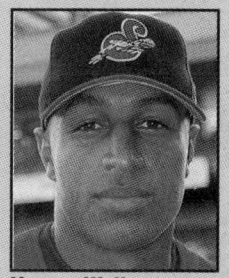

Vernon Wells

Players of the Year

MAJOR LEAGUE: Shawn Green, of
Green blossomed into a star, leading the Blue Jays with 134 runs while hitting .309 with 42 home runs and 123 RBIs.

MINOR LEAGUE: Vernon Wells, of
Wells was named top prospect in three different leagues in a season in which he climbed from Class A to the majors.

Plesac. Batista hit .285 with 26 home runs and 79 RBIs.

Injuries also hit the starting pitching. Joey Hamilton had late-season shoulder surgery and Chris Carpenter had elbow surgery to remove bone chips. Both righthanders missed substantial stretches of the season.

After the season, five coaches Fregosi inherited were fired: Jim Lett, Gary Matthews, Lloyd Moseby, Marty Pevey and Mel Queen.

Outfielder Vernon Wells provided the organization's best story. Wells, the club's first-round pick in 1997, made a rapid rise through the minors to play the final month in the majors. He was MVP of the Florida State League and tore through Double-A Knoxville and Triple-A Syracuse. He was named the No. 1 prospect in all three leagues in Baseball America's postseason ratings, the first player ever to accomplish that feat.

With Wells in the lineup, the major league team fielded six first-round picks: Carpenter, righthander Roy Halladay, Green, Koch, outfielder Shannon Stewart and Wells.

Three teams in the organization made their league playoffs. Class A Dunedin lost in the FSL championship series, while Knoxville and Class A Hagerstown both lost in the first round of the playoffs.

Among the minor league stars, first baseman Tim Giles set a Knoxville record with 114 RBIs; Dunedin's Cesar Izturis showed surprising hitting to go with a sterling glove, and was the FSL's all-star shortstop; and righthander Pasqual Coco had a brilliant start with Hagerstown, going 11-1 with a 2.21 ERA. He cooled to 4-6 with a 5.64 ERA at Dunedin.

ORGANIZATION LEADERS

BATTING

*AVG	Rob Butler, Knoxville	.337
R	Jorge Nunez, Hagerstown	116
H	Luis Lopez, Syracuse	171
TB	Jay Gibbons, Dunedin/Hagerstown	268
2B	Brent Abernathy, Knoxville	42
3B	Cesar Izturis, Dunedin	12
HR	Andy Thompson, Syracuse/Knoxville	31
RBI	Tim Giles, Knoxville	114
BB	Adam Melhuse, Syracuse/Knoxville	118
SO	Felipe Lopez, Hagerstown	157
SB	Jorge Nunez, Hagerstown	51

PITCHING

W	Pasqual Coco, Dunedin/Hagerstown	15
L	Joe Casey, Hagerstown	14
#ERA	David Bleazard, Knoxville/Dunedin	2.74
G	Two tied at	58
CG	Four tied at	2
SV	Jarrod Kingrey, Hagerstown	27
IP	David Bleazard, Knoxville/Dunedin	177
BB	Mike Romano, Syracuse	84
SO	Scott Cassidy, Hagerstown	178

*Minimum 250 At-Bats #Minimum 75 Innings

Toronto
BLUE JAYS

Organization Statistics

Manager: Jim Fregosi **1999 Record:** 84-78, .519 (3rd, AL East)

BATTING	AVG	G	AB	R	H	2B	3B	HR	RBI	BB	SO	SB	CS	B	T	HT	WT	DOB	1st Yr	Resides
Batista, Tony	.285	98	375	61	107	25	1	26	79	22	79	2	0	R	R	6-0	195	12-9-73	1992	Mao Valverde, D.R.
Berroa, Geronimo	.194	22	62	11	12	3	0	1	6	9	15	0	0	R	R	6-0	210	3-18-65	1984	New York, N.Y.
Blake, Casey	.256	14	39	6	10	2	0	1	1	2	7	0	0	R	R	6-2	195	8-23-73	1996	Indianola, Iowa
Borders, Pat	.214	6	14	1	3	0	0	1	3	1	2	0	0	R	R	6-2	200	5-14-63	1982	Lake Wales, Fla.
2-team (6 Cleve.)	.265	12	34	3	9	0	1	1	6	1	5	0	1							
Brown, Kevin	.444	2	9	1	4	2	0	0	1	0	3	0	0	R	R	6-2	215	4-21-73	1994	Mount Vernon, Ind.
Brumfield, Jacob	.235	62	170	25	40	8	3	2	19	19	39	1	2	R	R	6-0	190	5-27-65	1983	Atlanta, Ga.
Bush, Homer	.320	128	485	69	155	26	4	5	55	21	82	32	8	R	R	5-10	175	11-11-72	1991	East St. Louis, Ill.
Butler, Rob	.143	8	7	1	1	0	0	0	1	0	0	0	0	L	L	5-11	185	4-10-70	1991	Toronto, Ontario
Cruz, Jose	.241	106	349	63	84	19	3	14	45	64	91	14	4	S	R	6-0	195	4-19-74	1995	Houston, Texas
Dalesandro, Mark	.185	16	27	3	5	0	0	0	1	0	2	1	0	R	R	6-0	195	5-14-68	1990	Chicago, Ill.
Delgado, Carlos	.272	152	573	113	156	39	0	44	134	86	141	1	1	L	R	6-3	225	6-25-72	1989	Aguadilla, P.R.
Fernandez, Tony	.328	142	485	73	159	41	0	6	75	77	62	6	7	S	R	6-2	195	6-30-62	1980	Boca Raton, Fla.
Fletcher, Darrin	.291	115	412	48	120	26	0	18	80	26	47	0	0	L	R	6-2	200	10-3-66	1987	Oakwood, Ill.
Gonzalez, Alex	.292	38	154	22	45	13	0	2	12	16	23	4	2	R	R	6-0	200	4-8-73	1991	Miami, Fla.
Goodwin, Curtis	.000	2	8	0	0	0	0	0	0	0	3	0	0	L	L	5-11	180	9-30-72	1991	San Leandro, Calif.
Grebeck, Craig	.363	34	113	18	41	7	0	0	10	15	13	0	0	R	R	5-7	155	12-29-64	1987	Laguna Niguel, Calif.
Green, Shawn	.309	153	614	134	190	45	0	42	123	66	117	20	7	L	L	6-4	200	11-10-72	1992	Newport Beach, Calif.
Greene, Willie	.204	81	226	22	46	7	0	12	41	20	56	0	0	L	R	5-11	192	9-23-71	1989	Haddock, Ga.
Hollins, Dave	.222	27	99	12	22	5	0	2	6	5	22	0	0	S	R	6-0	182	5-25-66	1987	Orchard Park, N.Y.
Kelly, Pat	.267	37	116	17	31	7	0	6	20	10	23	0	1	R	R	6-0	182	10-14-67	1988	Clearwater Beach, Fla.
Lennon, Pat	.207	9	29	3	6	2	0	1	6	2	12	0	0	R	R	6-2	200	4-27-68	1986	Whiteville, N.C.
Martin, Norberto	.222	9	27	3	6	2	0	0	0	4	4	0	0	R	R	5-10	164	12-10-66	1984	Hato Rey, P.R.
Matheny, Mike	.215	57	163	16	35	6	0	3	17	12	37	0	0	R	R	6-3	205	9-22-70	1991	Chesterfield, Mo.
McRae, Brian	.195	31	82	11	16	3	1	3	11	16	22	0	1	S	R	6-0	195	8-27-67	1985	Leawood, Kan.
Otanez, Willis	.252	42	127	21	32	8	0	5	13	9	30	0	0	R	R	6-1	200	4-19-73	1990	Cotui, D.R.
2-team (29 Baltimore)	.237	71	207	28	49	11	0	7	24	15	46	0	0							
Sanders, Anthony	.286	3	7	1	2	1	0	0	2	0	2	0	0	R	R	6-2	200	3-2-74	1993	Tucson, Ariz.
Segui, David	.316	31	95	14	30	5	0	5	13	8	17	0	0	S	L	6-1	202	7-19-66	1988	Kansas City, Kan.
2-team (90 Seattle)	.298	121	440	57	131	27	3	14	52	40	60	1	2							
Stewart, Shannon	.304	145	608	102	185	28	2	11	67	59	83	37	14	R	R	6-1	205	2-25-74	1992	Miami, Fla.
Wells, Vernon	.261	25	88	8	23	5	0	1	8	4	18	1	1	R	R	6-1	210	12-8-78	1997	Arlington, Texas
Witt, Kevin	.206	15	34	3	7	1	0	1	5	2	9	0	0	L	R	6-4	200	1-5-76	1994	Jacksonville, Fla.
Woodward, Chris	.231	14	26	1	6	1	0	0	2	2	6	0	0	R	R	6-0	160	6-27-76	1995	Duarte, Calif.

PITCHING	W	L	ERA	G	GS	CG	SV	IP	H	R	ER	BB	SO	B	T	HT	WT	DOB	1st Yr	Resides
Bale, John	0	0	13.50	1	0	0	0	2	2	3	3	2	4	L	L	6-4	195	5-22-74	1996	Crestview, Fla.
Carpenter, Chris	9	8	4.38	24	24	4	0	150	177	81	73	48	106	R	R	6-6	215	4-27-75	1994	Raymond, N.H.
Davey, Tom	1	1	4.70	29	0	0	1	44	40	28	23	26	42	R	R	6-7	230	9-11-73	1994	Canton, Mich.
Escobar, Kelvim	14	11	5.69	33	30	1	0	174	203	118	110	81	129	R	R	6-1	195	4-11-76	1992	Caracas, Venez.
Frascatore, John	7	1	3.41	33	0	0	1	37	42	16	14	9	22	R	R	6-1	200	2-4-70	1991	Oceanside, N.Y.
Glover, Gary	0	0	0.00	1	0	0	0	1	0	0	0	1	0	R	R	6-5	205	12-3-76	1994	DeLand, Fla.
Halladay, Roy	8	7	3.92	36	18	1	1	149	156	76	65	79	82	R	R	6-5	205	5-14-77	1995	Arvada, Colo.
Hamilton, Joey	7	8	6.52	22	18	0	0	98	118	73	71	39	56	R	R	6-4	230	9-9-70	1991	Atlanta, Ga.
Hentgen, Pat	11	12	4.79	34	34	1	0	199	225	115	106	65	118	R	R	6-2	195	11-13-68	1986	Palm Harbor, Fla.
Hudek, John	0	0	12.27	3	0	0	0	4	8	5	5	1	2	S	R	6-2	210	8-8-66	1988	Sugar Land, Texas
Koch, Billy	0	5	3.39	56	0	0	31	64	55	26	24	30	57	R	R	6-3	218	12-14-74	1996	Clearwater, Fla.
Lloyd, Graeme	5	3	3.63	74	0	0	3	72	68	36	29	23	47	L	L	6-7	234	4-9-67	1988	Gnarwarre, Australia
Ludwick, Eric	0	0	27.00	1	0	0	0	1	3	3	3	2	0	R	R	6-5	220	12-14-71	1993	Las Vegas, Nev.
Munro, Peter	0	2	6.02	31	2	0	0	55	70	38	37	23	38	R	R	6-2	200	6-14-75	1994	Little Neck, N.Y.
Person, Robert	0	2	9.82	11	0	0	2	11	9	12	12	15	12	R	R	6-0	195	1-8-69	1989	St. Louis, Mo.
Plesac, Dan	0	3	8.34	30	0	0	0	23	28	21	21	9	26	L	L	6-5	217	2-4-62	1983	Valparaiso, Ind.
Quantrill, Paul	3	2	3.33	41	0	0	0	49	53	19	18	17	28	L	R	6-1	180	11-3-68	1989	Tarpon Springs, Fla.
Rodriguez, Nerio	0	1	13.50	2	0	0	0	2	3	3	3	2	2	R	R	6-1	195	3-22-73	1991	San Pedro de Macoris, D.R.
Romano, Mike	0	0	11.81	3	0	0	0	5	8	8	7	5	3	R	R	6-2	195	3-3-72	1993	Chalmette, La.
Sinclair, Steve	0	0	12.71	3	0	0	0	6	7	8	8	4	3	L	L	6-2	190	8-2-71	1991	Victoria, B.C.
Spoljaric, Paul	2	2	4.65	37	2	0	0	62	62	41	32	32	63	L	L	6-3	210	9-24-70	1990	Kelowna, B.C.
Wells, David	17	10	4.82	34	34	7	0	232	246	132	124	62	169	L	L	6-4	225	5-20-63	1982	Palm Harbor, Fla.

FIELDING

Catcher	PCT	G	PO	A	E	DP	PB
Borders	1.000	3	7	2	0	0	0
Brown	1.000	2	10	1	0	0	0
Dalesandro	1.000	8	22	2	0	2	1
Fletcher	.997	113	638	42	2	4	10
Matheny	.995	57	346	33	2	8	2

First Base	PCT	G	PO	A	E	DP
Delgado	.990	147	1306	84	14	134
Otanez	1.000	3	89	7	0	11
Segui	.955	4	19	2	1	3

Second Base	PCT	G	PO	A	E	DP
Bush	.984	109	220	350	9	81

	PCT	G	PO	A	E	DP
Fernandez	1.000	1	0	2	0	0
Grebeck	.959	17	32	39	3	7
Kelly	.962	35	60	92	6	17
Martin	.974	8	9	29	1	8

Third Base	PCT	G	PO	A	E	DP
Blake	1.000	14	12	23	0	4
Borders	.000	1	0	0	0	0
Dalesandro	1.000	2	0	1	0	0
Fernandez	.939	132	65	211	18	21
Grebeck	1.000	2	1	0	0	0
Greene	.917	7	4	7	1	0

	PCT	G	PO	A	E	DP
Otanez	.953	24	16	25	2	6
Woodward	1.000	2	0	3	0	0

Shortstop	PCT	G	PO	A	E	DP
Batista	.975	98	165	309	12	72
Bush	.920	18	26	54	7	5
Gonzalez	.980	37	69	132	4	34
Grebeck	.882	4	9	6	2	3
Martin	.000	1	0	0	0	0
Woodward	.939	10	8	23	2	2

Outfield	PCT	G	PO	A	E	DP
Berroa	1.000	2	4	0	0	0

248 • BASEBALL AMERICA 2000 ALMANAC

	PCT	G	PO	A	E	DP
Brumfield	.978	53	126	5	3	0
Butler	1.000	2	1	0	0	0
Cruz	.990	106	277	8	3	2
Goodwin	1.000	2	7	1	0	0

	PCT	G	PO	A	E	DP
Green	.997	152	340	5	1	1
Greene	1.000	3	3	0	0	0
Lennon	1.000	8	23	1	0	1
McRae	1.000	13	28	1	0	1

	PCT	G	PO	A	E	DP
Sanders	1.000	1	1	0	0	0
Stewart	.981	142	256	4	5	1
V. Wells	1.000	24	51	4	0	1

Carlos Delgado
Led Toronto with 44 homers and 134 RBIs

Jay Gibbons
Drove in 108 runs at two Class A stops

FARM SYSTEM

Director of Player Development: Jim Hoff

Class	Farm Team	League	W	L	Pct.	Finish*	Manager	First Yr
AAA	Syracuse (N.Y.) SkyChiefs	International	73	71	.507	8th (14)	Terry Bevington	1978
AA	Knoxville (Tenn.) Smokies	Southern	71	69	.507	6th (10)	Omar Malave	1980
A#	Dunedin (Fla.) Blue Jays	Florida State	86	51	.628	1st (14)	Rocket Wheeler	1987
A	Hagerstown (Md.) Suns	South Atlantic	84	56	.600	1st (14)	Rolando Pino	1993
A	St. Catharines (Ontario) Stompers	New York-Penn	34	42	.447	t-10th (14)	Eddie Rodriguez	1986
Rookie#	Medicine Hat (Alberta) Blue Jays	Pioneer	33	43	.434	5th (8)	Paul Elliott	1978

*Finish in overall standings (No. of teams in league)   #Advanced level

SYRACUSE
Class AAA

INTERNATIONAL LEAGUE

BATTING	AVG	G	AB	R	H	2B	3B	HR	RBI	BB	SO	SB	CS	B	T	HT	WT	DOB	1st Yr	Resides
Berroa, Geronimo	.273	10	33	7	9	0	0	3	8	8	5	0	0	R	R	6-0	210	3-18-65	1984	New York, N.Y.
Blake, Casey	.245	110	387	69	95	16	2	22	75	61	82	9	5	R	R	6-2	195	8-23-73	1996	Indianola, Iowa
Brown, Kevin	.258	88	295	39	76	18	2	13	51	21	79	0	1	R	R	6-2	215	4-21-73	1994	Mount Vernon, Ind.
Carter, Shannon	.111	2	9	0	1	0	0	0	0	0	2	0	0	L	L	6-0	170	3-23-79	1997	El Reno, Okla.
Cruz, Jose	.184	31	103	17	19	3	1	3	14	28	20	5	0	S	R	6-0	195	4-19-74	1995	Houston, Texas
Dalesandro, Mark	.225	20	71	3	16	2	0	0	5	1	7	1	0	R	R	6-0	195	5-14-68	1990	Chicago, Ill.
Delgado, Alex	.206	37	107	11	22	7	0	2	12	14	14	0	0	R	R	6-0	160	1-11-71	1988	Palmarejo, Venez.
Fletcher, Darrin	.267	4	15	0	4	0	0	0	0	1	1	0	0	L	R	6-2	200	10-3-66	1987	Oakwood, Ill.
Freel, Ryan	.299	20	77	15	23	3	2	1	11	8	13	10	3	R	R	5-10	175	3-8-76	1995	Jacksonville, Fla.
Grebeck, Craig	.250	4	16	3	4	1	0	1	2	1	1	0	0	R	R	5-7	155	12-29-64	1987	Laguna Niguel, Calif.
Greene, Willie	.327	14	52	12	17	1	0	5	11	6	14	0	0	L	R	5-11	192	9-23-71	1989	Haddock, Ga.
Hollins, Dave	.200	4	15	2	3	1	0	0	1	1	5	0	0	S	R	6-1	232	5-25-66	1987	Orchard Park, N.Y.
Hurst, Jimmy	.282	29	103	18	29	3	0	3	10	15	32	4	3	R	R	6-6	225	3-1-72	1991	Tuscaloosa, Ala.
Jones, Chris	.237	81	279	45	66	12	3	8	40	19	74	11	3	R	R	6-2	210	11-16-65	1984	Utica, N.Y.
Lennon, Pat	.336	37	134	26	45	5	0	9	33	22	40	3	3	R	R	6-2	200	4-27-68	1986	Whiteville, N.C.
Lopez, Luis	.322	136	531	76	171	35	2	4	69	40	58	1	0	R	R	6-0	200	10-5-73	1996	Spring Hill, Fla.
Martin, Norberto	.295	81	319	45	94	11	2	5	34	12	33	14	1	R	R	5-10	164	12-10-66	1984	Hato Rey, P.R.
Melhuse, Adam	.282	21	71	15	20	5	0	2	16	10	20	1	1	S	R	6-2	185	3-27-72	1993	Stockton, Calif.
Melo, Juan	.234	41	141	21	33	9	1	3	13	10	31	8	4	S	R	6-1	180	11-5-76	1994	Bani, D.R.
Mummau, Rob	.242	123	433	52	105	29	3	5	58	28	61	2	1	R	R	5-11	185	8-21-71	1993	Clearwater, Fla.
Pohle, Ike	.200	2	5	0	1	0	0	0	0	0	2	0	0	R	R	6-3	210	6-3-77	1999	Minnetonka, Minn.

BATTING

BATTING	AVG	G	AB	R	H	2B	3B	HR	RBI	BB	SO	SB	CS	B	T	HT	WT	DOB	1st Yr	Resides
Probst, Alan	.220	23	59	6	13	2	0	1	5	4	18	0	0	R	R	6-4	215	10-24-70	1992	Avis, Pa.
Sanders, Anthony	.244	124	496	71	121	22	5	18	59	46	111	18	10	R	R	6-2	200	3-2-74	1993	Tucson, Ariz.
Solano, Fausto	.214	9	28	4	6	0	0	1	3	1	2	0	1	R	R	5-9	144	6-19-74	1992	Santo Domingo, D.R.
Soriano, Fred	.389	5	18	3	7	0	0	0	2	0	4	0	0	R	R	5-9	160	8-5-74	1992	Bani, D.R.
Strange, Mike	.156	15	32	4	5	3	0	0	2	8	13	1	0	R	R	6-0	172	4-21-74	1994	Melbourne, Fla.
Thompson, Andy	.293	62	229	42	67	17	2	16	42	21	45	5	0	R	R	6-3	210	10-8-75	1995	Sun Prairie, Wis.
Wells, Vernon	.310	33	129	20	40	8	1	4	21	10	22	5	1	R	R	6-1	210	12-8-78	1997	Arlington, Texas
Witt, Kevin	.278	114	421	72	117	24	3	24	71	64	109	0	0	L	R	6-4	200	1-5-76	1994	Jacksonville, Fla.
Woodward, Chris	.292	75	281	46	82	20	3	1	20	38	49	4	1	R	R	6-0	160	6-27-76	1995	Duarte, Calif.

PITCHING

PITCHING	W	L	ERA	G	GS	CG	SV	IP	H	R	ER	BB	SO	B	T	HT	WT	DOB	1st Yr	Resides
Andrews, Clayton	0	1	7.80	3	3	0	0	15	10	14	13	13	9	R	L	6-0	175	5-15-78	1996	Largo, Fla.
Arroyo, Luis	0	1	8.53	9	0	0	0	13	18	13	12	9	10	L	L	6-0	174	9-29-73	1992	Bajadero, P.R.
Bale, John	0	3	3.97	6	4	0	0	23	16	14	10	10	10	L	L	6-4	195	5-22-74	1996	Crestview, Fla.
Bochtler, Doug	4	0	2.63	14	0	0	0	27	18	9	8	10	28	R	R	6-3	200	7-5-70	1989	West Palm Beach, Fla.
Bogott, Kurt	8	6	4.62	46	4	0	1	86	80	52	44	44	76	L	L	6-4	195	9-30-72	1993	Sterling, Ill.
Bovee, Mike	0	2	7.32	19	3	0	1	36	49	29	29	20	32	R	R	5-11	219	8-21-73	1991	Poway, Calif.
Bradford, Josh	0	1	18.00	1	1	0	0	4	9	8	8	3	2	R	R	6-5	185	4-19-74	1996	Sterling, Kan.
Croghan, Andy	0	0	0.00	2	0	0	2	3	0	0	0	2	4	R	R	6-5	220	10-26-69	1991	Yorba Linda, Calif.
Davey, Tom	1	2	3.48	6	6	0	0	34	30	15	13	19	20	R	R	6-7	230	9-11-73	1994	Canton, Mich.
Delgado, Ernie	0	4	9.43	14	4	0	0	28	38	29	29	19	15	R	R	6-2	190	7-21-75	1993	Tucson, Ariz.
Dimma, Doug	0	0	9.00	1	0	0	0	1	2	1	1	0	1	R	L	5-11	180	7-3-73	1999	Richmond Hill, Ontario
Donnelly, Brendan	0	1	2.89	5	0	0	0	9	8	4	3	4	9	R	R	6-3	205	7-4-71	1992	Albuquerque, N.M.
2-team (37 Durham)	5	6	3.03	42	1	0	2	71	61	27	24	22	70							
Glover, Gary	4	6	5.19	14	14	0	0	76	93	50	44	35	57	R	R	6-5	205	12-3-76	1994	De Land, Fla.
Hamilton, Joey	0	1	5.11	3	3	0	0	12	15	8	7	5	9	R	R	6-4	230	9-9-70	1991	Atlanta, Ga.
Harris, D.J.	0	0	7.71	7	0	0	0	14	20	15	12	10	6	R	R	5-10	190	4-11-71	1993	Las Vegas, Nev.
Hudek, John	0	2	5.50	12	0	0	1	18	17	12	11	8	15	S	R	6-2	210	8-8-66	1988	Sugar Land, Texas
2-team (12 Richmond)	0	2	5.83	24	0	0	1	29	31	20	19	13	32							
Koch, Billy	3	0	3.86	5	5	0	0	26	27	11	11	10	22	R	R	6-3	218	12-14-74	1996	Clearwater, Fla.
Lukasiewicz, Mark	4	4	5.34	37	9	1	3	98	109	59	58	40	77	L	L	6-3	230	3-8-73	1994	Secaucus, N.J.
Mann, Jim	6	5	4.64	47	0	0	5	66	53	35	34	39	72	R	R	6-3	225	11-17-74	1994	Holbrook, Mass.
McClellan, Sean	0	0	3.86	8	0	0	2	7	6	4	3	4	5	R	R	6-2	215	4-26-73	1996	Seminole, Fla.
Moore, Marcus	0	1	11.25	7	0	0	0	12	14	15	15	13	12	S	R	6-5	204	11-2-70	1989	Tampa, Fla.
Munro, Peter	6	1	3.10	18	11	0	0	70	70	29	24	33	68	R	R	6-2	200	6-14-75	1994	Little Neck, N.Y.
Pennington, Brad	3	0	4.24	27	0	0	1	34	30	20	16	30	34	L	L	6-6	215	4-14-69	1989	Salem, Ind.
Quantrill, Paul	0	0	0.00	2	0	0	0	2	1	0	0	0	1	L	R	6-1	180	11-3-68	1989	Tarpon Springs, Fla.
Reece, Dana	0	0	0.00	1	0	0	0	2	1	0	0	2	1	L	L	6-0	170	6-12-77	1999	Columbus, Ga.
Rodriguez, Nerio	10	8	4.54	27	27	1	0	163	161	84	82	53	137	R	R	6-1	195	3-22-73	1991	San Pedro de Macoris, D.R.
Romano, Mike	12	8	4.13	29	28	2	0	174	160	90	80	84	104	R	R	6-2	195	3-3-72	1993	Chalmette, La.
Sinclair, Steve	2	2	2.06	34	0	0	18	39	24	11	9	12	31	L	L	6-2	190	8-2-71	1991	Victoria, B.C.
Smith, Brian	7	4	3.50	29	0	0	7	46	45	22	18	24	46	R	R	5-11	185	7-19-72	1994	Salisbury, N.C.
Stevenson, Jason	1	2	6.05	7	7	0	0	39	52	30	26	21	15	R	R	6-3	180	8-11-74	1994	Phenix City, Ala.
Yennaco, Jay	2	6	6.86	15	15	0	0	80	107	68	61	34	50	R	R	6-4	238	11-17-75	1996	Windham, N.H.

FIELDING

Catcher	PCT	G	PO	A	E	DP	PB
Brown	.979	82	575	42	13	7	6
Dalesandro	1.000	2	7	0	0	0	0
A. Delgado	.977	34	201	12	5	2	1
Fletcher	1.000	3	18	5	0	0	1
Melhuse	1.000	18	121	8	0	0	0
Mummau	1.000	2	12	2	0	0	2
Pohle	1.000	1	6	1	0	0	0
Probst	1.000	16	74	6	0	0	0

First Base	PCT	G	PO	A	E	DP
Lopez	.994	82	641	55	4	62
Probst	1.000	3	6	0	0	0
Witt	.995	66	500	51	3	32

Second Base	PCT	G	PO	A	E	DP
Grebeck	.882	3	8	7	2	2
Martin	.982	36	64	99	3	14
Melo	1.000	3	4	7	0	2
Mummau	.980	80	155	187	7	44

	PCT	G	PO	A	E	DP
Solano	1.000	1	1	4	0	0
Strange	.977	12	18	24	1	4
Woodward	.949	16	30	45	4	8

Third Base	PCT	G	PO	A	E	DP
Blake	.967	109	94	168	9	13
Dalesandro	1.000	2	0	4	0	1
Lopez	.969	30	17	45	2	2
Mummau	.889	6	3	5	1	0

Shortstop	PCT	G	PO	A	E	DP
Blake	.500	1	0	1	1	0
Freel	.800	3	1	7	2	0
Grebeck	1.000	1	1	3	0	0
Martin	.955	37	48	102	7	11
Melo	.966	38	68	103	6	23
Mummau	.000	1	0	0	0	0
Solano	.962	8	8	17	1	3
Soriano	.960	5	9	15	1	7
Woodward	.972	59	84	155	7	40

Outfield	PCT	G	PO	A	E	DP
Berroa	.941	5	15	1	1	0
Carter	1.000	1	2	0	0	0
Cruz	1.000	29	75	2	0	1
Dalesandro	1.000	15	25	1	0	1
A. Delgado	1.000	2	4	0	0	0
Freel	.976	16	39	2	1	0
Greene	1.000	14	24	2	0	0
Hurst	.938	20	44	1	3	0
Jones	.983	25	57	2	1	1
Lennon	1.000	21	39	2	0	1
Martin	1.000	8	12	0	0	0
Mummau	.971	36	64	2	2	2
Probst	1.000	2	1	0	0	0
Sanders	.980	123	279	17	6	3
Thompson	1.000	45	89	4	0	0
Wells	.976	33	79	2	2	0
Witt	.988	50	79	4	1	0

KNOXVILLE   Class AA

SOUTHERN LEAGUE

BATTING	AVG	G	AB	R	H	2B	3B	HR	RBI	BB	SO	SB	CS	B	T	HT	WT	DOB	1st Yr	Resides
Abernathy, Brent	.291	136	577	108	168	42	1	13	62	55	47	34	15	R	R	6-1	185	9-23-77	1996	Marietta, Ga.
Butler, Rob	.337	64	258	48	87	13	6	2	36	19	21	4	5	L	L	5-11	185	4-10-70	1991	Toronto, Ontario
Chiaffredo, Paul	.077	11	39	3	3	1	0	1	3	0	10	0	0	R	R	6-2	195	5-30-76	1997	San Jose, Calif.
Cripps, Bobby	.172	25	87	13	15	6	0	2	9	6	37	0	0	L	R	6-2	200	5-9-77	1996	Powell River, B.C.
Freel, Ryan	.283	11	46	9	13	5	1	1	9	8	4	4	2	R	R	5-10	175	3-8-76	1995	Jacksonville, Fla.
Giles, Tim	.311	133	505	76	157	24	2	18	114	56	93	0	2	L	R	6-3	215	9-12-75	1996	Gambrills, Md.
Gomez, Rudy	.281	122	427	74	120	26	3	17	92	75	63	10	4	R	R	5-11	180	5-14-75	1995	Miami, Fla.
Hayes, Chris	.287	36	129	25	37	11	1	2	16	18	29	4	4	R	R	6-2	190	12-23-73	1995	Jacksonville, Fla.
Langaigne, Selwyn	.244	40	123	18	30	4	1	0	10	10	25	3	4	L	L	6-0	185	3-22-76	1994	Las Acaias, Venez.
Lawrence, Joe	.264	70	250	52	66	16	2	7	24	56	48	7	6	R	R	6-2	190	2-13-77	1996	Lake Charles, La.
Loyd, Brian	.280	104	364	53	102	18	1	11	65	46	57	9	2	R	R	6-2	210	12-3-73	1996	Yorba Linda, Calif.
Melhuse, Adam	.294	107	374	79	110	25	0	19	69	108	76	5	6	S	R	6-2	185	3-27-72	1993	Stockton, Calif.
Probst, Alan	.212	21	66	5	14	3	0	1	7	5	23	0	0	R	R	6-4	215	10-24-70	1992	Avis, Pa.

BATTING	AVG	G	AB	R	H	2B	3B	HR	RBI	BB	SO	SB	CS	B	T	HT	WT	DOB	1st Yr	Resides
Rupp, Chad	.257	67	241	49	62	19	2	16	44	44	73	7	2	R	R	6-2	225	9-30-71	1993	Tampa, Fla.
Schifano, Tony	.272	27	92	12	25	4	1	0	15	3	15	5	3	R	R	6-1	195	11-11-74	1997	Anaheim Hills, Calif.
Solano, Fausto	.305	104	348	62	106	18	0	14	61	57	54	11	15	R	R	5-9	144	6-19-74	1992	Santo Domingo, D.R.
Strange, Mike	.093	29	54	10	5	0	0	0	4	26	24	1	0	R	R	6-0	172	4-21-74	1994	Melbourne, Fla.
Stromsborg, Ryan	.249	99	377	54	94	17	3	9	45	28	91	5	4	R	R	6-3	185	12-19-74	1996	Encino, Calif.
Thompson, Andy	.244	67	254	56	62	16	3	15	53	34	55	7	3	R	R	6-3	210	10-8-75	1995	Sun Prairie, Wis.
Wells, Vernon	.340	26	106	18	36	6	2	3	17	12	15	6	2	R	R	6-1	210	12-8-78	1997	Arlington, Texas

PITCHING	W	L	ERA	G	GS	CG	SV	IP	H	R	ER	BB	SO	B	T	HT	WT	DOB	1st Yr	Resides
Andrews, Clayton	10	8	3.93	25	25	0	0	133	143	85	58	69	93	R	L	6-0	175	5-15-78	1996	Largo, Fla.
Arroyo, Luis	0	0	1.35	5	0	0	1	7	2	1	1	0	7	L	L	6-0	174	9-29-73	1992	Bajadero, P.R.
Bale, John	2	2	3.75	33	4	0	1	62	64	32	26	16	91	L	L	6-4	195	5-22-74	1996	Crestview, Fla.
Bleazard, David	5	3	3.22	15	15	1	0	87	81	36	31	34	49	R	R	6-0	175	3-7-74	1996	Tooele, Utah
Bradford, Josh	5	4	5.31	34	12	0	2	105	109	66	62	53	83	R	R	6-5	185	4-19-74	1996	Sterling, Kan.
Delgado, Ernie	4	1	3.51	31	0	0	0	51	49	27	20	23	33	R	R	6-2	190	7-21-75	1993	Tucson, Ariz.
Giron, Isabel	7	5	4.89	17	16	0	0	96	97	59	52	39	81	R	R	6-2	170	11-17-77	1995	Villa Mella, D.R.
Glover, Gary	8	2	3.56	13	13	1	0	86	70	39	34	27	77	R	R	6-5	205	12-3-76	1994	DeLand, Fla.
Harris, D.J.	2	4	7.05	25	4	0	0	60	73	50	47	31	36	R	R	5-10	190	4-11-73	1993	Las Vegas, Nev.
Hartshorn, Ty	4	1	4.79	10	7	0	0	47	60	32	25	15	24	R	R	6-5	190	8-3-74	1993	Lamar, Colo.
Hendrickson, Mark	2	7	6.63	12	11	0	0	56	73	46	41	21	39	L	L	6-9	230	6-23-74	1998	Syracuse, N.Y.
Hibbard, Billy	0	0	8.10	3	0	0	0	3	7	3	3	1	0	R	R	6-3	198	6-24-76	1994	Orlando, Fla.
Lowe, Benny	4	6	5.14	58	0	0	3	68	68	44	39	40	70	L	L	5-10	185	6-13-74	1994	Key West, Fla.
Mann, Jim	1	2	0.93	6	0	0	0	10	6	2	1	1	12	R	R	6-3	225	11-17-74	1994	Holbrook, Mass.
McClellan, Sean	1	0	3.48	14	0	0	1	21	18	8	8	11	24	R	R	6-2	215	4-26-73	1996	Seminole, Fla.
Rivette, Scott	4	7	3.81	56	0	0	10	78	85	40	33	29	74	S	R	6-2	200	2-8-74	1995	Upland, Calif.
Schaffer, Trevor	1	3	5.67	38	0	0	1	54	69	43	34	38	23	R	R	6-3	210	1-13-74	1996	Menlo Park, Calif.
Smith, Brian	1	2	5.14	29	0	0	13	35	42	25	20	6	27	R	R	5-11	185	7-19-72	1994	Salisbury, N.C.
Sneed, John	3	1	5.08	6	6	0	0	28	33	17	16	21	28	L	R	6-6	235	6-30-76	1997	Houston, Texas
Stevenson, Jason	4	7	6.24	21	19	1	0	92	99	69	64	57	73	R	R	6-3	180	8-11-74	1994	Phenix City, Ala.
Yennaco, Jay	3	4	6.60	8	1	0	0	44	52	34	32	17	30	R	R	6-4	238	11-17-75	1996	Windham, N.H.

FIELDING

Catcher	PCT	G	PO	A	E	DP	PB
Chiaffredo	.980	11	88	8	2	0	0
Cripps	.974	6	35	3	1	0	3
Loyd	.980	102	740	80	17	3	5
Melhuse	1.000	7	35	1	0	0	2
Probst	.985	16	112	16	2	1	0

First Base	PCT	G	PO	A	E	DP
Cripps..........	1.000	4	36	2	0	5
Giles	.992	102	831	75	7	91
Hayes	.882	2	13	2	2	1
Langaigne	1.000	2	3	2	0	0
Melhuse	.991	27	203	15	2	21
Rupp	.943	5	32	1	2	3
Strange	.973	5	31	5	1	2

Second Base	PCT	G	PO	A	E	DP
Abernathy.......	.976	132	292	361	16	89

	PCT	G	PO	A	E	DP
Gomez	.933	6	13	15	2	1
Strange	.929	3	8	5	1	1

Third Base	PCT	G	PO	A	E	DP
Gomez	.968	43	20	71	3	11
Hayes	.895	17	7	27	4	3
Lawrence	.910	67	29	112	14	14
Melhuse	.913	6	6	15	2	2
Solano	.909	7	3	7	1	0
Strange	.917	5	3	8	1	0
Stromsborg ...	.500	2	1	1	2	0

Shortstop	PCT	G	PO	A	E	DP
Gomez	.924	44	68	102	14	22
Lawrence	1.000	1	2	0	0	0
Schifano	1.000	8	12	15	0	5

	PCT	G	PO	A	E	DP
Solano............	.948	93	157	265	23	58

Outfield	PCT	G	PO	A	E	DP
Butler.............	.975	62	111	7	3	1
Cripps............	.667	1	2	0	1	0
Freel..............	1.000	1	23	1	0	0
Giles	1.000	1	2	0	0	0
Gomez	1.000	8	11	0	0	0
Hayes	1.000	17	37	3	0	0
Langaigne	.989	38	86	3	1	1
Melhuse	.973	44	66	5	2	1
Rupp	.986	42	71	2	1	0
Schifano	1.000	20	32	2	0	0
Stromsborg	.976	97	194	7	5	0
Thompson.......	.965	66	108	3	4	1
Wells	1.000	26	56	4	0	3

DUNEDIN — Class A

FLORIDA STATE LEAGUE

BATTING	AVG	G	AB	R	H	2B	3B	HR	RBI	BB	SO	SB	CS	B	T	HT	WT	DOB	1st Yr	Resides
Bagley, Lorenzo	.280	90	275	46	77	11	2	12	44	35	70	9	7	R	R	5-9	225	12-30-75	1996	Citra, Fla.
Berroa, Geronimo	.200	4	5	1	1	0	0	2	2	1	0	0	0	R	R	6-0	210	3-18-65	1984	New York, N.Y.
Bush, Homer	.357	4	14	3	5	2	0	0	0	1	1	0	0	R	R	5-10	175	11-17-72	1991	East St. Louis, Ill.
Chiaffredo, Paul	.253	88	261	39	66	22	2	3	21	17	44	1	4	R	R	6-2	195	5-30-76	1997	San Jose, Calif.
Cripps, Bobby	.063	5	16	1	1	0	0	0	1	1	7	0	0	L	R	6-2	200	5-9-77	1996	Powell River, B.C.
Delgado, Alex	.170	13	47	6	8	0	0	2	4	1	6	0	0	R	R	6-0	160	1-11-71	1988	Palmarejo, Venez.
Fleming, Ryan	.228	51	123	17	28	7	1	0	9	10	19	4	3	L	L	5-11	180	2-11-76	1998	Grove City, Ohio
Gibbons, Jay	.311	60	212	34	66	14	0	9	39	25	38	2	1	L	L	6-0	200	3-2-77	1998	Lakewood, Calif.
Hayes, Chris	.305	60	190	42	58	15	2	6	41	26	37	12	4	R	R	6-2	190	12-23-73	1995	Jacksonville, Fla.
Izturis, Cesar	.308	131	536	77	165	28	12	3	77	22	58	32	16	S	R	5-9	155	2-10-80	1996	Lara, Venez.
Langaigne, Selwyn	.294	62	201	35	59	9	1	2	25	16	29	5	5	L	L	6-0	185	3-22-76	1994	Las Acaias, Venez.
Morillo, Luis	.000	4	3	1	0	0	0	0	0	0	1	0	0	L	L	5-11	155	1-13-76	1996	Santo Domingo, D.R.
Morrison, Greg	.265	81	260	31	69	17	1	2	34	15	32	2	1	L	L	6-1	205	2-23-76	1995	Medicine Hat, Alberta
Peeples, Mike	.288	132	541	100	156	34	6	20	68	49	80	20	11	R	R	6-0	175	9-3-76	1994	Green Cove Springs, Fla.
Peters, Tony	.244	116	316	58	77	12	2	14	50	44	97	15	4	R	R	6-0	210	10-28-74	1995	Mesa, Ariz.
Phelps, Josh	.328	110	406	72	133	27	4	20	88	28	104	6	3	R	R	6-3	215	5-12-78	1996	Rathdrum, Idaho
Rodriguez, Mike	.281	80	260	36	73	17	1	4	30	17	40	3	2	R	R	5-11	185	4-1-75	1996	Stephenville, Texas
Rupp, Chad	.308	4	13	4	4	2	0	1	7	5	4	0	0	R	R	6-2	225	9-30-71	1993	Tampa, Fla.
Soriano, Fred	.213	46	136	21	29	5	0	4	17	9	35	3	4	R	R	5-9	160	8-5-74	1992	Bani, D.R.
Strange, Mike	.375	3	8	2	3	0	0	1	3	1	3	0	0	R	R	6-0	172	4-21-74	1994	Melbourne, Fla.
Stromsborg, Ryan	.224	20	76	5	17	10	0	1	9	3	17	1	1	R	R	6-3	185	12-19-74	1996	Encino, Calif.
Wells, Vernon	.343	70	265	43	91	16	2	11	43	26	34	13	2	R	R	6-1	210	12-8-78	1997	Arlington, Texas
Young, Mike	.313	129	495	86	155	36	3	5	83	61	78	30	6	R	R	6-0	175	10-19-76	1997	Covina, Calif.

GAMES BY POSITION: C—Chiaffredo 88, Cripps 2, Delgado 10, Peters 8, Phelps 27, Rodriguez 25. **1B**—Gibbons 57, Hayes 13, Morrison 46, Peters 24, Rodriguez 23, Rupp 4, Strange 1. **2B**—Bush 3, Izturis 45, Peeples 7, Soriano 17, Young 74. **3B**—Hayes 28, Izturis 2, Peeples 49, Peters 6, Rodriguez 37, Soriano 25, Strange 2. **SS**—Izturis 84, Soriano 3, Young 53. **OF**—Bagley 69, Berroa 2, Fleming 47, Hayes 5, Langaigne 61, Morillo 3, Morrison 26, Peeples 78, Peters 85, Rodriguez 1, Rupp 1, Stromsborg 20, Wells 69.

PITCHING	W	L	ERA	G	GS	CG	SV	IP	H	R	ER	BB	SO	B	T	HT	WT	DOB	1st Yr	Resides
Bleazard, David	6	6	2.28	14	13	1	0	91	73	36	23	30	58	R	R	6-0	175	3-7-74	1996	Tooele, Utah
Brackeen, Colin	2	1	3.88	40	0	0	3	53	60	29	23	28	33	L	L	6-0	200	3-8-75	1997	Arden Hills, Minn.

PITCHING	W	L	ERA	G	GS	CG	SV	IP	H	R	ER	BB	SO	B	T	HT	WT	DOB	1st Yr	Resides
Coco, Pasqual	4	6	5.64	13	13	2	0	75	81	50	47	36	59	R	R	6-1	160	9-24-77	1995	Santo Domingo, D.R.
Estrella, Leo	14	7	3.21	27	24	2	0	168	166	74	60	47	116	R	R	6-1	176	2-20-75	1994	Port St. Lucie, Fla.
File, Bob	4	1	1.70	47	0	0	26	53	30	13	10	14	48	R	R	6-4	215	1-28-77	1998	Philadelphia, Pa.
Hartshorn, Ty	3	1	6.68	7	7	0	0	31	43	25	23	16	30	R	R	6-5	190	8-3-74	1993	Lamar, Colo.
Heath, Woody	6	4	5.00	22	14	0	1	103	109	67	57	47	89	R	R	6-0	170	8-19-76	1997	Issaquah, Wash.
Hibbard, Billy	3	2	4.72	31	1	0	0	55	54	29	29	18	34	R	R	6-3	198	6-24-76	1994	Orlando, Fla.
Huggins, David	2	3	3.09	42	3	0	1	70	72	29	24	52	57	R	R	6-5	190	12-19-75	1997	Chester, Texas
LaChapelle, Yan	2	3	5.24	15	7	0	1	45	46	28	26	22	36	R	R	5-10	190	10-26-75	1996	Gatineau, Quebec
Lawrence, Clint	1	2	7.61	15	3	0	1	24	29	23	20	20	16	L	L	6-4	200	10-19-76	1995	Oakville, Ontario
McClellan, Matt	13	5	3.79	26	25	1	0	147	114	69	62	61	146	R	R	6-7	205	8-13-76	1997	Toledo, Ohio
McClellan, Sean	0	0	6.00	3	0	0	0	3	1	2	2	1	5	R	R	6-2	215	4-26-73	1996	Seminole, Fla.
Person, Robert	0	0	3.00	1	1	0	0	3	4	1	1	1	3	R	R	6-0	195	1-8-69	1989	St. Louis, Mo.
Quantrill, Paul	0	1	4.50	5	4	0	0	6	5	3	3	1	2	L	R	6-1	180	11-3-68	1989	Tarpon Springs, Fla.
Schaffer, Trevor	3	1	1.98	8	0	0	0	14	8	3	3	6	10	R	R	6-3	210	1-13-74	1996	Menlo Park, Calif.
Seabury, Jaron	4	3	5.37	35	0	0	3	54	59	33	32	19	34	R	R	6-4	215	1-31-76	1995	Mount Vernon, Wash.
Sneed, John	11	5	3.45	21	20	0	0	125	107	53	48	36	143	L	R	6-6	235	6-30-76	1997	Houston, Texas
Weimer, Matt	6	3	2.89	46	0	0	6	65	60	23	21	20	37	R	R	6-2	190	11-21-74	1997	Annapolis, Md.
Yennaco, Jay	2	0	0.82	3	2	0	0	11	10	2	1	0	11	R	R	6-4	238	11-17-75	1996	Windham, N.H.

HAGERSTOWN — Class A

SOUTH ATLANTIC LEAGUE

BATTING	AVG	G	AB	R	H	2B	3B	HR	RBI	BB	SO	SB	CS	B	T	HT	WT	DOB	1st Yr	Resides
Bundy, Ryan	.222	46	153	19	34	5	1	5	17	18	62	5	3	R	R	6-1	210	8-5-77	1998	Everett, Wash.
Davies, Justin	.197	127	396	69	78	6	1	0	23	86	55	36	15	L	R	6-0	170	11-10-76	1998	West Babylon, N.Y.
Dusan, Joe	.239	69	243	26	58	14	0	8	37	28	82	3	1	L	L	6-1	190	7-30-77	1998	Bend, Ore.
Fleming, Ryan	.335	61	227	34	76	9	2	4	35	23	26	7	6	L	L	5-11	180	2-11-76	1998	Grove City, Ohio
Gibbons, Jay	.305	71	292	53	89	20	2	16	69	32	56	3	0	L	L	6-0	200	3-2-77	1998	Lakewood, Calif.
Hudson, Orlando	.267	132	513	66	137	36	6	7	74	42	85	8	6	S	R	6-0	175	12-12-77	1998	Darlington, S.C.
Kremblas, Mike	.206	58	165	22	34	7	0	0	7	15	28	2	0	R	R	6-0	180	10-1-75	1998	Carroll, Ohio
Logan, Matt	.243	119	453	55	110	21	1	9	57	32	130	3	2	L	R	6-3	200	7-22-79	1997	Brampton, Ontario
Lopez, Felipe	.277	134	537	87	149	27	4	14	80	61	157	21	14	S	R	6-0	175	5-12-80	1998	Apopka, Fla.
Maloney, Jeff	.233	88	305	36	71	17	1	7	37	26	70	8	4	S	R	6-4	190	11-27-76	1995	Basking Ridge, N.J.
Nieves, Juan	.146	47	130	14	19	3	1	1	12	14	28	7	1	R	R	6-3	175	2-19-76	1996	Carabobo, Venez.
Nunez, Jorge	.268	133	564	116	151	28	11	14	61	40	103	51	8	R	R	5-10	158	3-3-78	1995	Villa Mella, D.R.
Thompson, Tyler	.261	130	440	84	115	28	3	17	81	79	122	20	3	R	R	6-0	205	8-28-75	1998	Bloomington, Ind.
Umbria, Jose	.290	62	186	24	54	5	0	3	26	26	36	2	2	R	R	6-2	205	1-20-78	1996	Barquisimeto, Venez.
Zepeda, Jesse	.225	89	222	26	50	8	1	5	34	42	36	3	0	S	R	5-10	165	5-4-74	1998	Santa Maria, Calif.

GAMES BY POSITION: C—Bundy 43, Kremblas 54, Umbria 55. **1B**—Dusan 40, Gibbons 22, Logan 80, Umbria 4. **2B**—Hudson 2, Nunez 122, Zepeda 27. **3B**—Hudson 103, Kremblas 1, Nunez 2, Umbria 1, Zepeda 63. **SS**—Lopez 133, Nunez 17. **OF**—Davies 123, Fleming 58, Gibbons 11, Hudson 22, Maloney 69, Nieves 46, Thompson 124.

PITCHING	W	L	ERA	G	GS	CG	SV	IP	H	R	ER	BB	SO	B	T	HT	WT	DOB	1st Yr	Resides
Bowles, Brian	6	2	3.97	48	1	0	3	79	73	41	35	39	80	R	R	6-5	205	8-18-76	1995	Manhattan Beach, Calif.
Casey, Joe	7	14	4.69	28	28	0	0	142	150	99	74	64	79	R	R	6-0	185	1-25-79	1997	Honeybrook, Pa.
Cassidy, Scott	13	7	3.27	27	27	1	0	171	151	78	62	30	178	R	R	6-3	175	10-3-75	1998	Clay, N.Y.
Coco, Pasqual	11	4	2.21	14	14	0	0	98	67	29	24	25	83	R	R	6-1	160	9-24-77	1995	Santo Domingo, D.R.
Dreier, Thom	0	0	6.75	8	0	0	0	9	12	11	7	8	10	R	R	6-4	235	10-17-76	1999	Union, Mo.
Gourlay, Matt	0	1	13.50	7	0	0	0	7	10	10	10	13	5	R	R	6-5	200	6-26-79	1996	Cheltenham, Australia
Kingrey, Jarrod	3	2	3.10	56	0	0	27	61	49	24	21	26	69	R	R	6-1	205	8-23-76	1998	Fortson, Ga.
LaRosa, Tom	0	0	4.76	12	0	0	1	11	9	8	6	16	18	R	R	5-10	188	6-28-75	1996	Henderson, Nev.
Lewis, Peyton	0	0	0.00	2	0	0	0	2	0	0	0	1	5	L	R	6-1	205	10-18-75	1999	Yutan, Neb.
Lynch, Pat	10	5	3.52	24	18	0	1	128	133	55	50	22	106	R	R	6-3	195	6-27-78	1996	Milton, Ontario
2-team (2 Asheville)	11	6	3.48	26	20	0	1	140	141	59	54	24	120							
Place, Eric	6	4	3.13	40	0	0	7	72	55	34	25	38	56	R	R	6-1	160	12-29-80	1997	Carabobo, Venez.
Sandoval, Marcos	4	3	4.55	27	10	0	4	83	89	47	42	32	53	R	R	6-3	195	12-15-78	1997	Henderson, Nev.
Smith, Taylor	7	10	3.78	28	28	1	0	171	158	87	72	51	119	L	L	6-3	180	11-11-76	1999	Cincinnati, Ohio
Spille, Ryan	1	1	2.20	14	11	0	0	70	49	20	17	15	49	L	L	6-3	180	8-24-78	1998	Canton, Mich.
Stafford, Mike	3	2	2.70	39	0	0	5	50	37	15	15	10	40	S	L	6-3	180	5-7-77	1999	Pottersville, Mo.
Stine, Justin	0	0	3.86	17	0	0	0	28	30	13	12	7	20	R	L	6-1	195	1-2-78	1997	Sacramento, Calif.
Woodards, Orlando	7	4	4.15	44	3	0	2	80	66	45	37	43	79	R	R	6-3	205				

ST. CATHARINES — Short-Season Class A

NEW YORK-PENN LEAGUE

BATTING	AVG	G	AB	R	H	2B	3B	HR	RBI	BB	SO	SB	CS	B	T	HT	WT	DOB	1st Yr	Resides
Bernhardt, Jossephang .	.243	70	267	20	65	10	1	5	35	8	67	2	1	R	R	6-1	165	9-22-80	1996	San Pedro de Macoris, D.R.
Blake, Casey	.667	1	3	0	2	0	0	0	0	1	0	0	0	R	R	6-2	195	8-23-73	1996	Indianola, Iowa
Carter, Shannon	.279	61	215	38	60	5	4	1	16	11	54	15	6	L	L	6-0	170	3-23-77	1998	El Reno, Okla.
Cripps, Bobby	.290	10	31	3	9	0	0	2	7	2	9	0	0	L	R	6-2	200	5-9-77	1996	Powell River, B.C.
Davis, Jermaine	.158	33	101	7	16	5	1	2	11	2	36	1	2	R	R	6-4	230	9-9-78	1997	Chesnee, S.C.
Estevez, Domingo	.255	61	212	31	54	21	2	3	28	21	32	12	9	S	R	6-2	165	7-1-77	1995	Santiago Rodriguez, D.R.
Gonzalez, Santos	.233	42	150	14	35	3	1	3	14	13	41	9	2	S	R	5-11	170	6-25-77	1994	Bani, D.R.
Holliday, Josh	.255	71	216	50	55	13	1	10	37	63	57	1	2	S	R	5-11	195	9-14-76	1999	Stillwater, Okla.
Jackson, Brandon	.332	62	214	37	71	13	1	2	25	28	45	3	8	R	R	6-1	180	10-28-75	1998	Chicago, Ill.
Johnson, Reed	.241	60	191	24	46	8	2	2	23	24	31	5	5	R	R	5-10	185	12-8-76	1999	Temecula, Calif.
Lebron, Jesus	.239	65	218	37	52	11	1	6	29	27	90	15	4	R	R	5-11	185	7-25-77	1998	Orlando, Fla.
Morales, Victor	.220	43	141	23	29	4	0	0	16	11	24	7	0	S	R	6-1	158	1-24-78	1996	Betania, Panama
Pohle, Ike	.239	46	142	19	34	10	0	4	20	21	47	0	1	R	R	6-3	210	6-3-77	1999	Minnetonka, Minn.
Riggins, Auntwan	.238	44	105	16	25	3	1	0	11	12	34	12	2	S	R	6-1	170	6-17-76	1998	Houston, Texas
Santos, Juan	.172	43	128	16	22	6	0	1	8	20	38	1	1	S	R	6-3	186	3-14-78	1997	Bayamon, P.R.
Smith, Fred	.223	40	130	16	29	3	1	1	12	22	50	13	3	R	R	6-2	172	5-27-78	1998	Lexington, Ky.

GAMES BY POSITION: C—Cripps 1, Holliday 18, Pohle 38, Santos 29. **1B**—Bernhardt 6, Holliday 19, Morales 23, Riggins 25, Santos 15. **2B**—Estevez 58, Jackson 10, Morales 10, Riggins 2. **3B**—Bernhardt 63, Blake 1, Gonzalez 2, Holliday 4, Jackson 1, Morales 10, Riggins 1. **SS**—Gonzalez 40, Jackson 41, Morales 1. **OF**—Carter 49, Davis 29, Johnson 57, Lebron 60, Riggins 7, Smith 39.

PITCHING	W	L	ERA	G	GS	CG	SV	IP	H	R	ER	BB	SO	B	T	HT	WT	DOB	1st Yr	Resides
Baker, Chris	2	4	6.20	12	10	0	0	49	61	37	34	14	55	R	R	6-1	185	8-24-77	1999	Valencia, Calif.
Bluma, Marc	3	4	5.92	24	0	0	13	24	22	16	16	7	32	R	R	5-11	215	12-22-76	1999	Owasso, Okla.
Bost, Ronald	0	0	7.36	4	0	0	0	4	2	3	3	3	2	L	L	6-2	175	7-24-79	1997	Harrisburg, N.C.
Carpenter, Chris	0	0	4.50	1	1	0	0	4	5	2	2	1	6	R	R	6-6	215	4-27-75	1994	Raymond, N.H.
Dean, Aaron	4	0	2.34	17	8	0	1	62	50	18	16	13	68	L	L	6-2	200	11-21-76	1997	Newhall, Calif.
Detwiler, Jim	2	4	3.27	14	6	0	0	44	45	23	16	25	45	L	L	6-1	190	6-11-76	1999	Pottstown, Pa.
Dimma, Doug	3	1	3.78	17	2	0	1	48	48	29	20	28	42	R	L	5-11	180	7-3-78	1999	Richmond Hill, Ontario
Dreier, Thom	1	0	2.53	4	0	0	0	11	6	3	3	9	15	R	R	6-4	235	10-17-76	1999	Union, Mo.
Gourlay, Matt	1	1	5.21	14	0	0	0	19	14	17	11	18	24	R	R	6-5	200	6-26-79	1996	Cheltenham, Australia
Gracesqui, Franklyn	2	3	5.05	15	10	0	1	46	44	30	26	41	45	S	L	6-5	200	8-20-79	1998	New York, N.Y.
Hubbel, Travis	0	0	1.80	5	3	0	1	20	16	5	4	7	19	R	R	6-1	185	6-27-79	1997	Edmonton, Alberta
Lewis, Peyton	2	1	1.31	15	1	0	2	41	26	8	6	15	54	L	R	6-1	205	10-18-75	1999	Yutan, Neb.
Markwell, Diegomar	3	4	7.58	14	13	0	0	59	72	55	50	38	54	L	L	6-2	165	8-8-80	1996	Curacao, Neth. Antilles
Murray, Steve	1	4	5.68	12	8	0	1	57	68	46	36	16	46	L	L	6-1	185	6-29-80	1998	Ennismore, Ontario
Needle, Chad	1	2	5.85	15	0	0	0	20	18	13	13	5	20	R	R	6-5	225	5-17-79	1996	Perth, Australia
Nunley, Robert	0	0	3.12	7	0	0	0	9	8	3	3	2	10	R	R	6-1	185	9-13-80	1999	Jacksonville, Fla.
Orloski, Joe	3	9	4.59	17	7	0	1	65	80	48	33	22	57	R	R	6-3	175	5-17-79	1998	Las Vegas, Nev.
Reece, Dana	1	0	2.70	5	0	0	0	7	4	2	2	3	7	L	L	6-0	170	6-12-77	1999	Columbus, Ga.
Renwick, Tyler	2	4	5.31	16	5	0	0	39	35	28	23	33	32	R	R	6-3	195	8-12-78	1998	Langley, B.C.
Seale, Dustin	0	1	2.70	3	0	0	0	3	2	1	1	2	4	L	L	6-1	170	12-2-77	1997	Safford, Ariz.
Southard, Lee	0	0	10.38	5	0	0	0	4	2	5	5	14	6	R	R	6-4	180	5-2-78	1999	Oklahoma City, Okla.
Spille, Ryan	1	0	0.00	1	1	0	0	5	2	0	0	0	5	L	L	6-3	180	11-11-76	1999	Cincinnati, Ohio
Stine, Justin	2	0	1.08	2	1	0	0	8	5	1	1	1	4	R	L	5-7	175	5-7-99	1999	Pottersville, Mo.

MEDICINE HAT — Rookie

PIONEER LEAGUE

BATTING	AVG	G	AB	R	H	2B	3B	HR	RBI	BB	SO	SB	CS	B	T	HT	WT	DOB	1st Yr	Resides
Clark, Chivas	.270	70	267	56	72	18	3	6	29	38	78	12	5	L	L	6-2	185	11-25-78	1997	Macon, Ga.
Cornett, Robert	.289	49	166	26	48	9	3	3	36	25	31	1	1	R	R	6-2	208	9-1-76	1999	Gainesville, Ga.
Cosby, Robert	.270	46	178	22	48	9	1	3	25	12	29	10	3	S	R	6-2	195	4-2-81	1999	Rio Piedras, P.R.
Fera, Aaron	.221	61	213	26	47	10	1	6	29	18	58	3	2	R	R	6-2	215	11-13-77	1999	Sault Ste. Marie, Ontario
Fierro, Robert	.237	22	59	10	14	2	0	0	10	16	9	0	0	R	R	5-11	183	7-6-77	1999	Levittown, N.Y.
Gutierrez, Roberto	.150	7	20	1	3	0	1	0	1	2	2	0	0	R	R	5-11	186	3-3-81	1998	Nata, Panama
Guzman, Alexis	.215	47	149	28	32	8	1	0	10	18	39	3	1	S	R	6-0	170	4-23-80	1997	Barcelona, Venez.
Juarez, Jonny	.255	29	102	11	26	1	0	1	10	8	14	8	2	L	L	6-0	165	6-22-78	1996	Caracas, Venez.
Mitchell, Brian	.226	30	84	13	19	4	1	2	11	12	20	1	3	R	R	5-10	180	4-28-79	1999	Iowa City, Iowa
Quiroz, Guillermo	.221	63	208	25	46	7	0	9	28	18	55	0	2	R	R	6-1	195	11-29-81	1999	Maracaibo, Venez.
Rios, Alexis	.269	67	234	35	63	7	3	0	13	17	31	8	4	R	R	6-5	178	2-18-81	1999	Guaynabo, P.R.
Roper, Doug	.248	45	137	20	34	7	2	0	10	20	25	8	2	S	R	5-9	155	7-20-77	1999	Vidalia, Ga.
Sherlock, Brian	.291	73	265	43	77	16	0	6	50	46	49	17	5	R	R	5-10	188	6-29-76	1999	Medford, N.J.
Snyder, Mike	.209	62	196	30	41	7	0	3	19	31	47	3	4	L	R	6-5	220	2-11-81	1999	Chino Hills, Calif.
Weekly, Chris	.300	71	257	43	77	14	2	6	42	29	43	12	2	L	L	6-1	171	12-4-76	1999	Mesa, Ariz.

GAMES BY POSITION: C—Cornett 2, Fierro 20, Quiroz 61. **1B**—Cornett 21, Juarez 1, Sherlock 57. **2B**—Mitchell 15, Weekly 66. **3B**—Cosby 32, Gutierrez 4, Guzman 1, Mitchell 1, Roper 7, Snyder 38. **SS**—Guzman 44, Roper 38, Snyder 1. **OF**—Clark 69, Fera 52, Gutierrez 2, Juarez 28, Mitchell 12, Rios 67, Snyder 8.

PITCHING	W	L	ERA	G	GS	CG	SV	IP	H	R	ER	BB	SO	B	T	HT	WT	DOB	1st Yr	Resides
Baker, Chris	0	1	3.12	3	1	0	0	9	8	4	3	2	9	R	R	6-1	185	8-24-77	1999	Valencia, Calif.
Cardwell, Brian	2	1	5.16	10	4	0	0	30	34	22	17	8	26	R	R	6-10	210	12-30-80	1999	Kiefer, Okla.
Chacin, Gustavo	4	3	3.09	15	9	0	1	64	68	33	22	23	50	L	L	5-11	170	12-4-80	1998	Maracaibo, Venez.
Curtis, Mark	1	3	6.89	10	5	0	0	31	47	29	24	15	36	R	L	6-5	200	12-1-77	1997	St. Albert, Alberta
Detwiler, Jim	0	0	4.91	3	2	0	0	11	10	6	6	6	14	L	L	6-1	190	6-11-76	1999	Pottstown, Pa.
Ford, Matt	4	0	2.05	13	7	0	0	48	31	11	11	23	68	S	L	6-2	165	4-8-81	1999	Tamarac, Fla.
Gaud, Perfecto	0	1	8.27	14	2	0	0	21	23	22	19	16	26	L	L	6-4	210	12-4-78	1998	Yauco, P.R.
Hamann, Robert	2	8	3.93	15	13	0	0	76	95	54	33	17	45	R	R	6-7	215	12-15-76	1999	Franklin Park, Ill.
Hanson, David	1	2	5.32	14	7	0	0	46	64	33	27	21	35	R	R	5-11	180	8-7-80	1999	Richland, Wash.
Houston, Ryan	3	4	6.70	14	7	0	1	46	61	41	34	19	30	R	R	6-4	180	9-22-79	1999	Pensacola, Fla.
McCullem, Ryan	2	1	6.08	9	5	0	0	24	34	17	16	11	19	L	L	6-4	195	10-8-80	1999	Columbia, Mo.
Mowday, Chris	2	6	5.97	16	1	0	1	29	34	25	19	12	28	R	R	6-1	191	8-24-81	1997	Strathpine, Australia
Newman, Tim	1	0	4.73	23	0	0	2	27	26	21	14	13	29	R	R	6-2	190	8-15-78	1999	Yakima, Wash.
Perez, George	2	2	5.79	15	8	0	1	56	65	46	36	26	41	R	R	6-4	207	3-20-79	1997	San Pedro de Macoris, D.R.
Porter, Scott	1	3	5.49	18	0	0	8	20	23	16	12	10	29	R	R	6-1	195	3-18-77	1999	Doctors Inlet, Fla.
Reece, Dana	2	1	7.71	13	0	0	0	12	19	11	10	8	14	L	L	6-0	170	6-12-77	1999	Columbus, Ga.
Reimers, Cam	1	5	3.25	13	5	0	0	44	39	21	16	12	29	R	R	6-5	190	9-15-78	1999	Missoula, Mont.
St. Amand, Reuben	0	1	6.11	15	0	0	0	28	31	23	19	17	24	R	R	6-4	215	8-4-79	1998	Olympia, Wash.
Stevens, Josh	5	1	2.45	23	0	0	4	29	27	14	8	5	34	R	R	6-4	200	6-6-79	1998	Riverside, Calif.

MINOR LEAGUES

Futures Game, Pan American Games give minor leaguers more opportunities to shine

BY LACY LUSK

For many of the minor leagues' most elite players, the most memorable part of 1999 didn't even take place in official minor league games.

History was made as professional players were showcased in two ways they never had been. In July, the inaugural Futures Game showcased tomorrow's stars in a major league setting and the Pan American Games, a qualifying event for the 2000 Olympics, introduced professionals on an international stage.

The Futures Game took place on July 11 at Boston's Fenway Park as part of the major league All-Star Game festivities. A team of American-born prospects took on a team of foreign-born players. Yankees prospect Alfonso Soriano, a shortstop for Double-A Norwich, stole the show with a two-homer, five-RBI game to lead the World to a 7-0 thumping of the United States.

Going out as winners
The Vancouver Canadians won the Triple-A title in their last year

But the 21-year-old Dominican, playing in his first season in the United States, wasn't the only player who enjoyed the game and the concept. Twins Class A prospect Michael Cuddyer, who had played in the Midwest League all-star game the previous year, said, "You can't even compare them. Everything about this is just amazing."

Even major league all-star Mike Piazza of the New York Mets was impressed with the event, which will return as part of the 2000 All-Star Game in Atlanta.

"I played in the Triple-A all-star game, and it wasn't really an all-star game because a lot of older players were there," Piazza said. "And anytime you get to play in a nice stadium and eat in first-class restaurants, who wouldn't want to do that?"

Two weeks later, a mix of older players and young prospects assured the United States of a spot in the 2000 Olympics by finishing second at the Pan Am Games in Winnipeg, Manitoba.

With the door now open to the use of professional players in international competition, USA Baseball, the governing body of amateur baseball in the U.S., sought the aid of Major League Baseball in its efforts to field the best team possible as it set out to secure one of two Olympic berths allocated for the Americas.

MLB not only allowed Team USA the use of minor leaguers not on 40-man rosters, but freed up players from other nations as well. In all, about 70 minor leaguers took about two weeks off to participate in the Pan Am Games.

Yet Cuba, an international dynasty whose government forbids its players to play professionally, still won the tournament. The Cubans beat the U.S. 5-1 in the gold-medal game.

"This was the greatest international tournament ever," proclaimed Baseball Canada general manager Kevin Briand, whose team narrowly missed an Olympic bid. Canada, a team composed almost entirely of minor leaguers, lost to Cuba 3-2 in the semifinals—its only loss of the tournament.

All five of Team USA's victories came from pitchers on the way up in their current organizations—Ryan

TRIPLE-A WORLD SERIES

Las Vegas
Sept. 20-25, 1999

STANDINGS	W	L	RF	RA
Vancouver (Pacific Coast)	3	2	37	23
Charlotte (International)	2	3	23	37

SEMIFINALS: International League—Charlotte defeated Durham 3-1 in best-of-5 series. **Pacific Coast League**—Vancouver defeated Oklahoma 3-2 in best-of-5 series.

INDIVIDUAL BATTING LEADERS
(Minimum 13 Plate Appearances)

	AVG	AB	R	H	2B	3B	HR	RBI	SB
Beltre, Esteban, Char	.429	14	4	6	0	1	0	1	0
Encarnacion, Mario, Van	.429	14	3	6	2	0	0	3	0
Long, Terrence, Van	.429	21	1	9	1	2	0	10	0
Mottola, Chad, Char	.400	20	4	8	1	0	1	1	0
Brito, Tilson, Charlotte	.333	21	2	7	0	0	2	3	1
Espada, Joe, Van	.333	18	8	6	0	0	0	1	1
Ortiz, Jose, Vancouver	.318	22	3	7	1	0	1	6	0

INDIVIDUAL PITCHING LEADERS
(Minimum 5 Innings)

	W	L	ERA	G	SV	IP	H	BB	SO
Garland, Jon, Charlotte	1	0	0.00	1	0	8	5	0	8
Bradford, Chad, Char	0	0	0.00	4	1	4	4	1	5
Heathcott, Mike, Char	0	0	1.80	2	0	5	2	3	4
Mulder, Mark, Vancouver	1	0	2.87	2	0	16	16	3	5

Most Valuable Player: Terrence Long, of, Vancouver.

Minor Leagues

MINOR LEAGUE ALL-STARS
Selected by Baseball America

Pos. Player, Team (League)	AVG	AB	R	H	2B	3B	HR	RBI	BB	SO	SB
C Ben Petrick, Carolina (SL)/Colo. Springs (PCL)	.311	350	74	109	21	6	23	86	53	73	12
1B Steve Cox, Durham (International)	.341	534	107	182	49	4	25	127	67	74	3
2B Adam Kennedy, Memphis (Pacific Coast)	.327	367	69	120	22	4	10	63	29	36	20
3B Adam Piatt, Midland (TL)/Vancouver (PCL)	.340	494	129	168	49	3	39	138	99	103	7
SS Rafael Furcal, Macon (SAL)/Myrtle Beach (CL)	.322	519	105	167	24	4	1	41	55	78	96
OF Chin-Feng Chen, San Bernardino (California)	.316	510	98	161	22	10	31	123	75	129	31
Corey Patterson, Lansing (Midwest)	.320	475	94	152	35	17	20	79	25	85	33
Vernon Wells, Dunedin (FSL)/Knox. (SL)/Syr. (IL)	.334	500	81	167	30	5	18	81	48	71	24
DH Jack Cust, High Desert (California)	.334	455	107	152	42	3	32	112	96	145	1

	W	L	ERA	G	GS	CG	SV	IP	H	BB	SO
SP Rick Ankiel, Arkansas (TL)/Memphis (PCL)	13	3	2.35	24	24	1	0	138	98	62	194
Eric Gagne, San Antonio (Texas)	12	4	2.63	26	26	0	0	168	122	64	185
Tomokazu Ohka, Trenton (EL)/Pawtucket (IL)	15	0	2.31	24	24	1	0	140	123	36	116
Matt Riley, Frederick (CL)/Bowie (EL)	13	8	3.05	28	28	3	0	177	147	56	189
RP Francisco Cordero, Jacksonville (Southern)	4	1	1.38	47	0	0	27	52	35	22	58

Player of the Year: Rick Ankiel, Arkansas/Memphis. **Manager of the Year:** John Mizerock, Wichita.

Anderson (Mariners), Mark Mulder (Athletics), John Patterson (Diamondbacks), J.C. Romero (Twins) and Dan Wheeler (Devil Rays). Most of the club's offense was provided by two Cardinals farmhands, second base prospect Adam Kennedy (.367-0-5) and veteran catcher Marcus Jensen (.300-3-9).

"There's nothing in the minor leagues that compares to this," said Phillies veteran minor leaguer Jon Zuber, a first baseman/DH for Team USA. "We played every game with such intensity, every single game meant something, and you just don't get that in the minor leagues. If I'm not in the big leagues, I could definitely do something like this again."

It was undetermined which players would compete for the U.S. in the Olympics, but with the event scheduled for Septemebr of 2000, it was assumed minor leaguers would comprise the roster.

Going Out In Style

Unlike the Pan Am competition, minor league games generally don't have a lot at stake. But the Vancouver Canadians and Harrisburg Senators placed a little extra importance on games in September in 1999.

Vancouver, in its last season in the Pacific Coast League before moving to Sacramento and a new ball-park in 2000, rallied from a two-games-to-one deficit to take the second Triple-A World Series in five games. The competition matching champions from the International and Pacific Coast leagues was played before sparse crowds in Las Vegas.

In the clinching game against the IL's Charlotte Knights, Mulder went the distance and had 20 hits of support in a 16-2 blowout. Series MVP Terrence Long had four of his series-high 10 RBIs in the last game.

Mark Mulder

"It's a hell of a way to go out—or start," said Art Savage, a northern California businessman who bought the Canadians in 1998 for $7.5 million (U.S.).

In the second year of a three-year deal between Minor League Baseball and the Las Vegas Convention and Visitors Bureau, the series drew an announced 4,002 fans a game. That represented a small increase from the 3,368 a game who watched New Orleans win the inaugural event at Cashman Field, but the series has hardly developed into a national spectacle.

The first four games all started after 8 p.m. Pacific time—and were shown on national cable in the east at 11 p.m.

"I think we've got a lot of work to do to make this

ORGANIZATION STANDINGS

Cumulative farm club standings for the 30 major league farm systems:

TEAM	1999 W	1999 L	1999 Pct.	1998 Pct.	1997 Pct.	1996 Pct.
Oakland (6)	398	296	.573	.524	.534	.536
New York-AL (6)	387	307	.558	.516	.556	.525
Kansas City (6)	379	317	.545	.558	.484	.521
Texas (6)	373	317	.541	.526	.486	.501
Toronto (6)	381	332	.534	.558	.445	.487
Boston (6)	368	331	.526	.521	.512	.503
Philadelphia (6)	365	333	.523	.503	.504	.493
Cincinnati (6)	362	333	.521	.454	.541	.485
Chicago-AL (6)	357	329	.520	.493	.501	.430
New York-NL (7)	396	371	.516	.535	.516	.574
Tampa Bay (6)	359	347	.508	.533	.497	.466
San Diego (6)	349	342	.505	.533	.486	.530
San Francisco (5)	320	318	.502	.490	.512	.527
Cleveland (6)	354	354	.500	.513	.507	.542
Houston (6)	350	351	.499	.506	.468	.493
Atlanta (7)	378	384	.496	.439	.483	.465
Minnesota (6)	342	347	.496	.548	.520	.520
Montreal (6)	345	355	.493	.528	.483	.539
Pittsburgh (6)	337	355	.487	.449	.499	.486
Anaheim (6)	345	365	.486	.457	.484	.483
Arizona (6)	335	359	.483	.446	.501	.547
Seattle (6)	334	357	.483	.520	.509	.487
Chicago-NL (6)	332	359	.480	.515	.487	.499
Detroit (6)	335	363	.480	.501	.531	.501
Florida (6)	328	360	.477	.459	.512	.464
Colorado (6)	325	364	.472	.463	.479	.478
Los Angeles (6)	322	383	.457	.439	.485	.494
Baltimore (6)	312	376	.453	.499	.535	.503
Milwaukee (6)	316	399	.442	.469	.490	.524
St. Louis (6)	310	391	.442	.506	.459	.501

Number of farm teams in parentheses

Minor Leagues

CLASSIFICATION ALL-STAR TEAMS
Selected by Baseball America

TRIPLE-A

Pos.	Player, Team (League)	AVG	AB	R	H	2B	3B	HR	RBI	BB	SO	SB
C	Ben Petrick, Colorado Springs (Pacific Coast)	.312	282	56	88	16	5	19	64	44	58	9
1B	Steve Cox, Durham (International)	.341	534	107	182	49	4	25	127	67	74	3
2B	Adam Kennedy, Memphis (Pacific Coast)	.327	367	69	120	22	4	10	63	29	36	20
3B	Aramis Ramirez, Nashville (Pacific Coast)	.328	460	92	151	35	1	21	74	73	56	5
SS	Scott Sheldon, Oklahoma (Pacific Coast)	.311	453	94	141	35	3	28	97	56	112	12
OF	Ruben Mateo, Oklahoma (Pacific Coast)	.336	253	53	85	12	0	18	62	14	36	6
	Calvin Murray, Fresno (Pacific Coast)	.334	548	122	183	31	7	23	73	49	88	42
	Mark Quinn, Omaha (Pacific Coast)	.360	428	67	154	27	0	25	84	28	69	7
DH	David Ortiz, Salt Lake (Pacific Coast)	.315	476	85	150	35	3	30	110	79	105	2

Pos.	Player, Team (League)	W	L	ERA	G	GS	CG	SV	IP	H	BB	SO
SP	Brett Laxton, Vancouver (Pacific Coast)	13	8	3.46	25	25	3	0	161	158	49	112
	Matt Perisho, Oklahoma (Pacific Coast)	15	7	4.61	27	27	2	0	156	160	78	150
	Dan Reichert, Omaha (Pacific Coast)	9	2	3.71	17	17	1	0	112	92	50	123
	Ed Yarnall, Columbus (International)	13	4	3.47	23	23	1	0	145	136	57	146
RP	Jay Tessmer, Columbus (International)	3	3	3.34	51	0	0	28	57	52	12	42

Player of the Year: Steve Cox, 1b, Durham. **Manager of the Year:** Greg Biagini, Oklahoma (Pacific Coast).

DOUBLE-A

Pos.	Player, Team (League)	AVG	AB	R	H	2B	3B	HR	RBI	BB	SO	SB
C	Javier Cardona, Jacksonville (Southern)	.309	418	84	129	31	0	26	92	46	69	4
1B	Nick Johnson, Norwich (Eastern)	.345	420	114	145	33	5	14	87	123	88	8
2B	Brent Abernathy, Knoxville (Southern)	.291	577	108	168	42	1	13	62	55	47	34
3B	Adam Piatt, Midland (Texas)	.345	476	128	164	48	3	39	135	93	101	7
SS	Alfonso Soriano, Norwich (Eastern)	.305	361	57	110	20	3	15	68	32	67	24
OF	Pat Burrell, Reading (Eastern)	.333	417	84	139	28	6	28	90	79	103	3
	Brady Clark, Chattanooga (Southern)	.326	506	103	165	30	3	22	76	77	137	9
	Raul Gonzalez, Trenton (Eastern)	.335	505	80	169	33	4	18	103	51	71	12
DH	Mike Lamb, Tulsa (Texas)	.324	544	98	176	51	5	21	100	53	65	4

Pos.	Player, Team (League)	W	L	ERA	G	GS	CG	SV	IP	H	BB	SO
SP	Rick Ankiel, Arkansas (Texas)	6	0	0.91	8	8	1	0	49	25	16	75
	Eric Gagne, San Antonio (Texas)	12	4	2.63	26	26	0	0	168	122	64	185
	Matt Riley, Bowie (Eastern)	10	6	3.22	20	20	3	0	126	113	42	131
	Michael Tejera, Portland (Eastern)	13	4	2.62	25	25	0	0	155	137	45	152
RP	Francisco Cordero, Jacksonville (Southern)	4	1	1.38	47	0	0	27	52	35	22	58

Player of the Year: Adam Piatt, 3b, Midland. **Manager of the Year:** John Mizerock, Wichita (Texas).

CLASS A

Pos.	Player, Team (League)	AVG	AB	R	H	2B	3B	HR	RBI	BB	SO	SB
C	Matthew LeCroy, Fort Myers (Florida State)	.279	333	54	93	20	1	20	69	42	51	0
1B	Aaron McNeal, Michigan (Midwest)	.310	536	95	166	29	3	38	131	40	121	7
2B	Marcus Giles, Myrtle Beach (Carolina)	.326	497	80	162	40	7	13	73	54	89	9
3B	Sean Burroughs, Fort Wayne (MWL)/Rancho Cuca. (CAL)	.363	449	68	163	33	3	6	85	77	62	17
SS	Rafael Furcal, Macon (SAL)/Myrtle Beach (Carolina)	.322	519	105	167	24	4	1	41	55	78	96
OF	Chin-Feng Chen, San Bernardino (California)	.316	510	98	161	22	10	31	123	75	129	31
	Jack Cust, High Desert (California)	.334	455	107	152	43	2	32	112	96	145	1
	Corey Patterson, Lansing (Midwest)	.320	475	94	152	35	17	20	79	25	85	33
DH	Jacques Landry, Modesto (California)	.311	508	92	158	46	6	27	111	47	128	18

Pos.	Player, Team (League)	W	L	ERA	G	GS	CG	SV	IP	H	BB	SO
SP	Randey Dorame, San Bernardino (California)	14	3	2.51	24	24	1	0	154	130	37	159
	Josh Kalinowski, Salem (Carolina)	11	6	2.11	27	27	1	0	162	119	71	176
	Wilfredo Rodriguez, Kissimmee (Florida State)	15	7	2.88	25	24	0	0	153	108	62	148
	Jason Standridge, Charleston, S.C. (SAL)/St. Pete (FSL)	13	5	2.58	26	26	3	0	164	129	51	110
RP	Jason Ellison, Tampa (Florida State)	0	2	2.15	49	0	0	35	54	42	19	58

Player of the Year: Chin Feng-Chen, of, San Bernardino. **Manager of the Year:** Bob Geren, Modesto (California).

SHORT-SEASON

Pos.	Player, Team (League)	AVG	AB	R	H	2B	3B	HR	RBI	BB	SO	SB
C	J.D. Closser, Missoula (Pioneer)	.324	275	73	89	22	0	10	54	71	57	9
1B	Lyle Overbay, Missoula (Pioneer)	.343	306	66	105	25	7	12	101	40	53	10
2B	Ruben Salazar, Elizabethton (Appalachian)	.401	262	66	105	24	2	14	65	48	43	11
3B	Andrew Beinbrink, Hudson Valley (New York-Penn)	.339	292	46	99	24	2	11	51	39	49	13
SS	Mark Ellis, Spokane (Northwest)	.327	281	67	92	14	0	7	47	47	40	21
OF	Ben Broussard, Billings (Pioneer)	.407	145	35	59	11	2	14	48	34	30	1
	Josh Hamilton, Princeton (Appy)/Hudson Valley (NYP)	.312	308	56	96	23	4	10	55	14	57	19
	Kevin Mench, Pulaski (Appalachian)	.362	260	63	94	22	1	16	60	28	48	12
DH	Robb Quinlan, Boise (Northwest)	.322	295	51	95	20	1	9	77	35	52	5

Pos.	Player, Team (League)	W	L	ERA	G	GS	CG	SV	IP	H	BB	SO
SP	Craig Anderson, Everett (Northwest)	10	2	3.20	15	15	2	0	90	81	13	82
	Aaron Harang, Pulaski (Appalachian)	9	2	2.30	16	10	1	1	78	64	17	87
	Todd Moser, Utica (New York-Penn)	8	2	1.53	14	14	3	0	88	63	24	86
	David Walling, Staten Island (New York-Penn)	8	2	3.14	14	14	0	0	80	76	18	82
RP	Craig House, Portland (Northwest)	2	1	2.08	26	0	0	11	35	28	14	58

Player of the Year: Lyle Overbay, 1b, Missoula. **Manager of the Year:** Kevin Long, Spokane (Northwest).

Minor Leagues

Player of the Year
St. Louis prospect lives up to the hype

STAN DENNY

Rick Ankiel

For months before Rick Ankiel finally pulled on a Cardinals uniform and climbed the Busch Stadium pitcher's mound, his name was a hot topic in local baseball circles.

On St. Louis radio stations throughout the spring and summer of 1999, hardly a sports talk show would pass without his name being invoked as a possible answer to all that was frustrating about the Cardinals beleaguered pitching staff. The local newspaper regularly updated fans about Ankiel's latest minor league feat. During Cardinals games broadcast on television, Ankiel regularly was mentioned as a key part to the team's future.

Manager Tony La Russa frequently fielded questions about Ankiel. Even Cardinals players closely followed the progress Ankiel was making during the 1999 season, first as an almost unhittable ace at Double-A Arkansas and then as a successful (if slightly wild) farmhand at Triple-A Memphis. Eventually, those big leaguers thought that if the Cardinals wanted to win soon, they might as well get Ankiel to the majors right away and find out how good he might be.

Ankiel, who celebrated his 20th birthday in July, was a big-time celebrity in baseball before ever getting to the big leagues. Yet he had no idea.

"I'm just me," he said shortly after joining the Cardinals in late August. "I'd rather be seen than heard. I don't pay attention to all that other stuff, what people write about me or say about me."

He ought to pay more attention, because most of what people said and wrote about him in 1999 was positive.

At the end of the minor league season,

his recognition grew as Ankiel was selected as Baseball America's 1999 Minor League Player of the Year. He is the first Cardinals farmhand to ever win the award, and the first pitcher to win it since Tom Gordon in 1988.

On his way to the majors, Ankiel was voted the No. 1 prospect in both the Texas and Pacific Coast leagues in polls of managers. He went 6-0 with a 0.91 ERA in eight starts at Arkansas and was 7-3 with a 3.16 ERA in 16 starts at Memphis. In 137 minor league innings, he struck out 194 and walked 62. He lost his only major league decision after he was recalled by St. Louis late in August. He made nine appearances, including five starts, and posted a 3.27 ERA while striking out 39 in 33 innings.

Though his bonus demands got Ankiel's name in the limelight when he was drafted 72nd overall by the Cardinals in 1997, all the news since he signed has come from his ability.

"He is a unique talent," Memphis manager Gaylen Pitts said. "I've had a lot of fun seeing all the other managers in the league, the way their eyes light up when they see him throw. Some of them have told me that even if their team is losing to him, it's fun to watch him pitch."

After Ankiel signed for a then-record $2.5 million bonus on Aug. 28, 1997, he had to wait until 1998 to make his professional debut. But he led the minor leagues with 222 strikeouts between Class A Peoria and Class A Prince William. In 299 career innings in the minor leagues, Ankiel allowed 204 hits and 112 walks while striking out 416.

"When I see his minor league numbers," said John Messina, "they look like high school numbers."

Messina ought to know. He coached Ankiel at Port St. Lucie (Fla.) High, where he went 11-1 with a 0.47 ERA and 162 strikeouts in 74 innings his senior year. He was projected to be one of the top picks in that year's draft, but set such a price tag on his services that all clubs passed on him and he slid to the second round.

Ankiel is a 6-foot-1, 210-pound lefthander with a 95-mph fastball and three other quality pitches.

"I haven't changed at all," he said. "I still have the same friends I always had. A lot of them are gone to college when I'm home in the winter, so that's different. They go to college most of the year and do what they do. I play ball most of the year; this is what I do."

—MIKE EISENBATH

PREVIOUS WINNERS
1981—Mike Marshall, 1b, Albuquerque (Dodgers)
1982—Ron Kittle, of, Edmonton (White Sox)
1983—Dwight Gooden, rhp, Lynchburg (Mets)
1984—Mike Bielecki, rhp, Hawaii (Pirates)
1985—Jose Canseco, of, Huntsville/Tacoma (Athletics)
1986—Gregg Jefferies, ss, Columbia/Lynch./Jackson (Mets)
1987—Gregg Jefferies, ss, Jackson/Tidewater
1988—Tom Gordon, rhp, Apple./Memphis/Omaha (Royals)
1989—Sandy Alomar, c, Las Vegas (Padres)
1990—Frank Thomas, 1b, Birmingham (White Sox)
1991—Derek Bell, of, Syracuse (Blue Jays)
1992—Tim Salmon, of, Edmonton (Angels)
1993—Manny Ramirez, of, Canton/Charlotte (Indians)
1994—Derek Jeter, ss, Tampa/Albany/Columbus (Yankees)
1995—Andruw Jones, of, Macon (Braves)
1996—Andruw Jones, of, Durham/Green./Rich. (Braves)
1997—Paul Konerko, 1b, Albuquerque (Dodgers)
1998—Eric Chavez, 3b, Huntsville/Edmonton (Athletics)

Team of the Year
Trenton goes wire-to-wire, loses in playoffs

The season ended in disappointment in the first round of the Eastern League playoffs. But there was little argument that the combination of prospects and veteran minor leaguers the parent Boston Red Sox sent to Double-A Trenton for 1999 made the Thunder the nation's most dominant minor league team.

The Thunder went wire-to-wire in first place in the EL's Southern Division, reeling off nine consecutive victories to open the season, adding a 12-game winning streak to push its record to 35-11, and cresting at 90-43 on the way to a final 92-50 record.

Trenton finished 14 games ahead of second-place Norwich in the division, only to lose three games to two to the Navigators in the EL playoffs' first round.

Despite that loss, the Thunder's consistent play all season earned it recognition as

Baseball America's 1999 Minor League Team of the Year.

"After this, I couldn't imagine being on a team that would be 50-92," said lefthander Andy Hazlett, who finished 9-9 after a 2-5 start. "I showed up here early every day to see what was going on because it was so much fun."

The fun started with an offense ignited by former University of Florida walk-on David Eckstein, the second baseman. He batted .313 with six homers and 52 RBIs, stole 32 bases and was hit by pitches 25 times. In his leadoff role, Eckstein finished second in the league in runs (109) and on-base percentage (.440), third in walks (89) and fifth in hits (151).

The lineup that followed him was powerful, led by outfielders Virgil Chevalier (.293-13-76) and Raul Gonzalez (.335-18-103); first baseman/DH David Gibralter (.299-24-97); and when he wasn't playing at Fenway Park, 21-year-old third baseman Wilton Veras (.281-11-75).

Along the way, that lineup also included veteran outfielder Israel Alcantara (.294-20-60) for 77 games, independent league graduate Morgan Burkhart (.230-12-41) and Red Sox catching prospect Steve Lomasney (.245-12-31).

The Thunder's .279 team batting average was 11 points better than the next-best team (Norwich), and its 150 home runs were 10 more than the next-highest total (Harrisburg).

And Trenton wasn't just a smashmouth team. The Thunder finished second in the league with a 3.85 ERA and gave up the fewest runs in the league.

Japanese righthander Tomokazu Ohka, making his professional debut, went 8-0 with a 3.00 ERA before his promotion to Triple-A Pawtucket and eventually Boston. Righthander Jason Sekany emerged as the ace upon Ohka's departure and went 14-4, 3.35, including a 6-0 run in August.

—LARRY O'ROURKE

PREVIOUS WINNERS

1993—Harrisburg/Eastern (Expos)
1994—Wilmington/Carolina (Royals)
1995—Norfolk/International (Mets)
1996—Edmonton/Pacific Coast (Athletics)
1997—West Michigan/Midwest (Tigers)
1998—Mobile/Southern (Padres)

Minor Leagues

event better," Savage said. "It's obviously just the second year, so we're building on it. But Triple-A baseball has good players and good teams. It's a shame more people weren't here to see it."

While Vancouver's dominance quickly took all of the excitement out of the deciding game of the Triple-A series, the Double-A Eastern League playoffs had a fairy-tale ending.

Harrisburg won its fourth straight league title in dramatic fashion, getting a two-out, full-count grand slam from outfielder Milton Bradley to win the deciding game 12-11. Entering the bottom of the ninth,

MINOR ADJUSTMENTS

With Minor League Baseball requesting that all teams get in line to make their renewals with big league parent clubs in even-numbered years, the annual affiliation shuffle involved just one switch. The Reds moved into Triple-A Louisville with a five-year deal, leaving Indianapolis behind after seven seasons. The Brewers, displaced in Louisville, stepped into the void in Indianapolis. Twenty-eight minor league teams gained new affiliations after the 1998 season.

Triple-A	League	'99 affiliate	'00 affiliate
Indianapolis	International	Reds	Brewers
Louisville	International	Brewers	Reds

Norwich held an 11-7 lead but the Senators closed within three before Bradley's blast made them the first team in EL history to win four consecutive league crowns.

Bradley, one of the Expos' top prospects and a member of Team USA at the Pan Am Games, had been suspened early in the season after a run-in with an umpire. With his home run, he took home what had to have been the minor league honor for Best Drama.

"I couldn't believe it," Expos farm director Don Reynolds said. "It's not even a storybook finish because nobody would believe it. It would sound too hokey.

"The only thing that could have added to it was if Bradley hit it off the scoreboard and the scoreboard blew up."

Changing Identity

The minor leagues, known formally as the National Association of Professional Baseball Leagues since 1901, decided to change their name in 1999. At the Triple-A World Series, organization president Mike Moore announced that the NA will be known as Minor League Baseball.

As a practical matter, the change won't mean much, though it might make things easier for the average fan to figure out. Of more significance, it acknowledges that the stigma attached to the term "minor league" has at least decreased, if it hasn't disappeared altogether.

Minor league baseball has taken such a foothold in the American sporting conscience in the 1980s and

'90s that "minor league," which normally indicates something that is second-rate, no longer is thought of as a negative term.

"We will retain (NA) as our corporate name, but to do business in the public, it is now Minor League Baseball," Moore said. "I was comfortable with the term 10 years ago, but there are a number of people who thought the press and other people gave it a negative connotation because it was called 'minor league.' "

An overriding but unspoken reason for the name change might have been an attempt on the part of Minor League Baseball to distance itself from independent leagues. Independent leagues have sprung up in the '90s and in some cases, particularly in the crowded Northeast Corridor, have encroached on territories of traditional minor league teams. Independent team operators often have portrayed their clubs as minor league, creating confusion in the market.

Moore said the move was not an effort to squeeze out the independents.

"First of all, the more baseball that is being played, the better," Moore said. "Our only concern is when they're taking teams so close to other teams in the same market.

"(The name change) has been talked about for a number of years. I remember our first heavy-duty conversations about it were 10 years ago."

Moore said he just wants to make a distinction between Minor League Baseball and independent minor leagues. He said whenever he sees a reference to independent leagues, they are referred to as "independent minor leagues."

"We are concerned that the investments by many communities and clubs in new stadiums over the past few years be taken into consideration, in terms of the potential for oversaturating a market," he said.

Stt-rrr-ike?

One of the biggest scares the National Association had in 1999 came from its 228 minor league umpires. In a choice umpires say was unrelated to the controversial resignations of 22 major league umpires, the minor leaguers considered walking out in July in search of better pay and better conditions. But the threat never came to pass.

When association spokesman Mike Billings and his fellow umpires voted on a July 30 walkout, more than 80 percent opted instead to go to the National Labor Relations Board and request to become a union. The NLRB vote had not been decided late in the year.

"We'd like to negotiate a contract with Minor League Baseball (if the union is approved)," said Billings, an International League umpire. "If they give us a deal we can accept, we're not going to walk out. I haven't missed a game yet, and I don't plan to start now."

ALL-STAR FUTURES GAME

Yankees shortstop prospect Alfonso Soriano hit two home runs and had five RBIs in three at-bats to lead the World team to a 7-0 victory over the U.S. team at Boston's Fenway Park in the first Futures Game, featuring many of the game's top prospects.

The World team, made up of prospects who were born outside the United States, scored its runs on three home runs—two by Soriano and one by Mets prospect Jorge Toca. Eight pitchers did the rest, limiting the U.S. team to three hits in the seven-inning game.

The game was played in conjunction with the major league All-Star Game, with rosters selected by Baseball America.

UNITED STATES ROSTER

Pitchers: Ryan Anderson, Mariners; Rick Ankiel, Cardinals; A.J. Burnett, Marlins; Jason Grilli, Giants; Mark Mulder, Athletics; Brad Penny, Marlins; Kyle Peterson, Brewers; Matt Riley, Orioles; B.J. Ryan, Reds; Kip Wells, White Sox; Matt White, Devil Rays.

Catchers: Giuseppe Chiaramonte, Giants; Ben Petrick, Rockies.

Infielders: Russell Branyan, Indians; Pat Burrell, Phillies; Michael Cuddyer, Twins; Kelly Dransfeldt, Rangers; Nick Johnson, Yankees; Adam Kennedy, Cardinals; Joe Lawrence, Blue Jays.

Outfielders: Peter Bergeron, Expos; Lance Berkman, Astros; Dee Brown, Royals; Corey Patterson, Cubs; Vernon Wells, Blue Jays.

WORLD ROSTER

Pitchers: Tony Armas, Expos; Francisco Cordero, Tigers; Sun-Woo Kim, Red Sox; Chris Mears, Mariners; Aaron Myette, White Sox; Tomokazu Ohka, Red Sox; Ramon Ortiz, Angels; Luke Prokopec, Dodgers; J.C. Romero, Twins; Wascar Serrano, Padres.

Catchers: Javier Cardona, Tigers; Yamid Haad, Pirates; Cesar King, Rangers.

Infielders: Erubiel Durazo, Diamondbacks; Rafael Furcal, Braves; Pablo Ozuna, Marlins; Calvin Pickering, Orioles; Aramis Ramirez, Pirates; Alfonso Soriano, Yankees; E.J. t'Hoen, Angels.

Outfielders: Chin-Feng Chen, Dodgers; Alex Sanchez, Devil Rays; Jorge Toca, Mets; Goefrey Tomlinson, Royals.

World 7, USA 0

WORLD	ab	r	h	bi	USA	ab	r	h	bi
Furcal 2b	3	1	2	0	Patterson cf	2	0	0	0
Ozuna 2b	1	0	0	0	VWells cf	1	0	0	0
Soriano ss	3	2	2	5	Kennedy 2b	3	0	1	0
Durazo 1b	2	1	1	0	Berkman rf	3	0	0	0
Pickering 1b	1	0	0	0	Burrell dh/1b	3	0	0	0
Toca lf	4	1	2	2	Johnson 1b/dh	3	0	1	0
Ramirez 3b	3	0	0	0	Branyan 3b	2	0	0	0
t'Hoen 3b	1	0	0	0	Cuddyer 3b	1	0	0	0
Cardona dh	3	0	0	0	Brown lf	2	0	0	0
Chen rf	3	0	1	0	Bergeron lf	0	0	0	0
King c	2	1	1	0	Petrick c	1	0	0	0
Haad c	1	0	1	0	Chiaramonte c	1	0	0	0
Sanchez cf	2	1	1	0	Dransfeldt ss	2	0	1	0
Tomlinson cf	1	0	0	0					
Totals	32	7	11	7	Totals	24	0	3	0
World						005	200	0—7	
USA						000	000	0—0	

E—Dransfeldt. DP—USA 1. LOB—World 4, USA 5. 2B—Durazo, Kennedy. HR—Soriano 2, Toca. CS—Furcal.

WORLD	ip	h	r	er	bb	so	USA	ip	h	r	er	bb	so
Ohka	1	1	0	0	0	1	Ankiel	1	1	0	0	1	1
Kim W	1	0	0	0	0	0	Grilli	⅔	0	0	0	0	0
Armas	1	1	0	0	0	1	Mulder L	⅔	5	5	5	0	0
Mears	1	0	0	0	0	0	White	⅔	0	0	0	0	0
Serrano	1	0	0	0	1	0	Anderson	⅔	2	1	1	0	0
Prokopec	½	0	0	0	0	0	Peterson	⅓	1	1	1	0	0
Romero	⅔	0	0	0	0	0	KWells	⅔	0	0	0	0	0
Cordero	1	0	0	0	1	3	Penny	1	2	0	0	0	0
							Burnett	⅓	0	0	0	0	1
							Ryan	½	0	0	0	1	1
							Riley	⅔	0	0	0	0	1

Manager of the Year
Former first rounder on fast track again

John Mizerock's big league career was brief and unfulfilling.

After being selected by the Astros with the eighth overall pick in the 1979 June draft, he played 103 games in the majors and hit .186 in 231 at-bats. He said like every other first-round pick, he thought he would be in the majors in two to three years.

"I was off and on for a few years in the majors, and when I did play I didn't play very well," Mizerock said. "I was good in Punxsutawney (the Pennsylvania city best known for Groundhog Day that also happens to be his

hometown), but it didn't take me but a few days to realize there were a lot of good players from around the country."

Mizerock was a lefthanded-hitting catcher with a significant problem. "I couldn't hit," he said. And two arm operations helped to squelch his catch-and-throw abilities.

"I didn't have enough physical tools and talent to be a good major league player," Mizerock said. "I hit that head-on early."

But his path to the majors has taken a different turn. Mizerock, 38, has developed into one of the minor leagues' top managers since join-

JIM VASALDUA

John Mizerock

ing the Royals organization in 1992.

In 1999, he directed Double-A Wichita to an 83-57 record, winning both halves of the Western Division and sweeping Tulsa in the Texas League championship series. For his accomplishments, Baseball America chose Mizerock as its Minor League Manager of the Year.

Mizerock actually left the game after his playing career ended.

"I wasn't looking to manage," he said. But after one year out of baseball, which he said "got boring," the Royals offered him a coaching job.

He served as a coach for the Royals' Class A Eugene club in 1992, and for the next seven years has managed in the Royals system. In that time he has had only one losing season.

He rose to Wichita in 1998, taking the Wranglers to a 75-65 overall record and a division title in the second half. In 1999 the Wranglers had no peer in the league.

—ALAN ESKEW

PREVIOUS WINNERS

1981—Ed Nottle, Tacoma (Athletics)
1982—Eddie Haas, Richmond (Braves)
1983—Bill Dancy, Reading (Phillies)
1984—Sam Perlozzo, Jackson (Mets)
1985—Jim Lefebvre, Phoenix (Giants)
1986—Brad Fischer, Huntsville (Athletics)
1987—Dave Trembley, Harrisburg (Pirates)
1988—Joe Sparks, Indianapolis (Expos)
1989—Buck Showalter, Albany (Yankees)
1990—Kevin Kennedy, Albuquerque (Dodgers)
1991—Butch Hobson, Pawtucket (Red Sox)
1992—Grady Little, Greenville (Braves)
1993—Terry Francona, Birmingham (White Sox)
1994—Tim Ireland, El Paso (Brewers)
1995—Marc Bombard, Indianapolis (Reds)
1996—Carlos Tosca, Portland (Marlins)
1997—Gary Jones, Edmonton (Athletics)
1998—Terry Kennedy, Iowa (Cubs)

Pat O'Conner, chief operating officer of Minor League Baseball and the vice president in charge of administration for the Professional Baseball Umpire Corporation, wasn't expecting the union to be approved.

"We have a good-faith doubt that leadership has the support it claims to have," O'Conner said. "We suggested that they file a petition and ask the NLRB to conduct a secret-ballot election."

In 1999, minor league umpire salaries ranged between $4,500 (for 2½ months in short-season leagues) and about $17,000 for the most experienced Triple-A umpires. Per diem allocations ranged between $15 and $20.

Piatt's All That

While prized Cardinals lefthander Rick Ankiel was selected Baseball America's 1999 Minor League Player of the Year, the most impressive offensive numbers came from Adam Piatt, a power-hitting third baseman in the Athletics organization.

Piatt, the A's eighth-round draft pick in 1997 from Mississippi State, became just the second player to ever win the Texas League triple crown. Before a late-

season callup to join eventual Triple-A champion Vancouver, he hit .345 with 39 homers and 135 RBIs for the Midland RockHounds. The only other Texas Leaguer to lead in all three categories was Del Pratt in 1927.

"Honestly, the magnitude of the whole deal hasn't hit me yet," said Piatt, 23. "It hadn't been done in a long time. And it was the last thing I expected this year."

Piatt played his home games at Christensen Stadium, which is notorious for wind-blown longballs. Of Piatt's 39 home runs, 22 came at home.

Adam Piatt

"I'll be the first to admit Midland is a home run hitter's park," Piatt said. "But I'm proudest of hitting a lot of homers on the road."

Piatt wasn't the only minor league position player to shine in 1999.

Blue Jays outfield prospect Vernon Wells became the first player ever selected the No. 1 prospect in

Minor Leagues

DEPARTMENT LEADERS
Minor Leagues

TEAM

WINS
Trenton (Eastern) 92
Modesto (California) 88
Dunedin (Florida State) 86
Hagerstown (South Atlantic) 84
Vancouver (Pacific Coast) 84
West Tenn (Southern) 84

LONGEST WINNING STREAK
High Desert (California) 15
Nashville (Pacific Coast) 15
Greensboro (South Atlantic) 14
Pulaski (Appalachian) 12
Trenton (Eastern) 12
West Michigan (Midwest) 12
Mariners (Arizona) 12

LOSSES
Binghamton (Eastern) 88
Toledo (International) 87
Lancaster (California) 85
New Orleans (Pacific Coast) 85
Ottawa (International) 85
Potomac (Carolina) 85
Vero Beach (Florida State) 85

LONGEST LOSING STREAK
Hickory (South Atlantic) 16
Peoria (Midwest) 13
Lancaster (California) 12
Stockton (California) 12
Clearwater (Florida State) 11
New Orleans (Pacific Coast) 11
Toledo (International) 11

BATTING AVERAGE*
Colorado Springs (Pacific Coast) .... .297
Durham (International) .... .295
Fresno (Pacific Coast) .... .294
Midland (Texas) .... .294
High Desert (California) .... .293

RUNS
Durham (International) 923
High Desert (California) 902
Midland (Texas) 884
Columbus (International) 879
Modesto (California) 872

HOME RUNS
Omaha (Pacific Coast) 231
Colorado Springs (Pacific Coast) 194
Pawtucket (International) 187

Diamondbacks' Erubiel Durazo
.404 average topped minors

GEORGE GOJKOVICH

Durham (International) 186
Nashville (Pacific Coast) 183

STOLEN BASES
Charleston, W.Va. (South Atlantic) .. 270
Rockford (Midwest) 227
Fort Wayne (Midwest) 225
Jupiter (Florida State) 206
Macon (South Atlantic) 199

EARNED RUN AVERAGE*
Piedmont (South Atlantic) 3.02
Jupiter (Florida State) 3.17
Augusta (South Atlantic) 3.35
Tampa (Florida State) 3.43
Myrtle Beach (Carolina) 3.50

STRIKEOUTS
Greensboro (South Atlantic) 1186
Columbus (South Atlantic) 1182
Augusta (South Atlantic) 1170
Asheville (South Atlantic) 1163
Myrtle Beach (Carolina) 1159

FIELDING AVERAGE*
Indianapolis (International) .... .981
Richmond (International) .... .979
Durham (International) .... .978
Oklahoma (Pacific Coast) .... .978
Syracuse (International) .... .978

INDIVIDUAL BATTING

BATTING AVERAGE
(Minimum 383 Plate Appearances)
Erubiel Durazo, El Paso/Tucson ..... .404
Sean Burroughs, Fort Wayne/R. Cuca. .. .363
Carlos Urquiola, South Bend .... .362
Mark Quinn, Omaha .... .360
Jarrod Patterson, El Paso/Tucson .. .358
Nick Johnson, Norwich .... .345
Talmadge Nunnari, Jupiter/Harrisburg .344
Steve Cox, Durham .... .341
Adam Piatt, Midland/Vancouver ...... .340
Jason Williams, Chatt./Indianapolis .339

RUNS
Adam Piatt, Midland/Vancouver 129
Jeff DaVanon, Midland/Edmonton ... 122
Calvin Murray, Fresno 122
Jorge Nunez, Hagerstown 116
Nick Johnson, Norwich 114

HITS
Jarrod Patterson, El Paso/Tucson 187
Juan Pierre, Asheville 187
Calvin Murray, Fresno 183
Steve Cox, Durham 182
Mike Lamb, Tulsa/Oklahoma 177

TOP HITTING STREAKS
Scott Seabol, Greensboro 35
Rob Butler, Knoxville 28
Aubrey Huff, Orlando 28
Chad Akers, Tacoma 26
Roosevelt Brown, Iowa 26

MOST HITS, ONE GAME
Michael Coleman, Pawtucket 7
Hiram Bocachica, San Antonio 6
Franklin German, Lansing 6
Jason Jones, Pulaski 6
Les Norman, Omaha 6
Robb Quinlan, Boise 6
Nate Tebbs, Trenton 6
Tyler Thompson, Hagerstown 6

TOTAL BASES
Adam Piatt, Midland/Vancouver 340
Aaron McNeal, Michigan 315
Steve Cox, Durham 314
Jarrod Patterson, El Paso/Tucson 308
D.T. Cromer, Indianapolis 301

Colorado Springs' J.R. Phillips
Led minors with 41 homers

COSIMO MELLACE

Mike Lamb, Tulsa/Oklahoma 301

EXTRA-BASE HITS
Adam Piatt, Midland/Vancouver 91
Jacques Landry, Modesto 79
Steve Cox, Durham 78
Mike Lamb, Tulsa/Oklahoma 77
Jarrod Patterson, El Paso/Tucson 77
Jack Cust, High Desert 77

DOUBLES
Scott Seabol, Greensboro 55
Jarrod Patterson, El Paso/Tucson 52
Mike Lamb, Tulsa/Oklahoma 51
Bo Robinson, Wisconsin 50
Steve Cox, Durham 49
Adam Piatt, Midland/Vancouver 49

TRIPLES
Oscar Salazar, Modesto 18
Corey Patterson, Lansing 17
Jeff DaVanon, Midland/Edmonton ... 14
Jason Romano, Charlotte (FSL) 14

HOME RUNS
J.R. Phillips, Colorado Springs 41
Adam Piatt, Midland/Vancouver 39
Chris Norton, Portland (EL) 38
Aaron McNeal, Michigan 38
Andy Tracy, Harrisburg 37

RUNS BATTED IN
Adam Piatt, Midland/Vancouver 138
Aaron McNeal, Michigan 131
Andy Tracy, Harrisburg 128
Steve Cox, Durham 127
Luis Raven, Charlotte (IL) 125

MOST RBIs, ONE GAME
Ben Broussard, Billings 11
Andy Phillips, Staten Island 9
Several tied with 8

STOLEN BASES
Rafael Furcal, Macon/Myrtle Beach 96
Mike Curry, Char., W.Va./Wilmington .. 85
Jeremy Owens, Fort Wayne/R. Cuca. .. 67
Richard Gomez, West Michigan 66
Juan Pierre, Asheville 66

CAUGHT STEALING
Rafael Furcal, Macon/Myrtle Beach ... 30
Belvani Martinez, High Desert 30
Albenis Machado, Cape Fear 28
Alex Sanchez, Orlando/Durham 27
Jaisen Randolph, Daytona 26

Minor Leagues

HIT BY PITCHES

Nick Johnson, Norwich 37
Corky Miller, Rockford/Chattanooga .. 31
Sal Fasano, Omaha 26
David Eckstein, Trenton 25
Trace Coquillette, Ottawa 24

WALKS

Nick Johnson, Norwich 123
Adam Melhuse, Knoxville/Syracuse .. 118
Bo Robinson, Wisconsin 108
Tony Schrager, Lansing 103
Esteban German, Modesto 102
Albenis Machado, Cape Fear 102

STRIKEOUTS

Russell Branyan, Buffalo 187
Bryon Gainey, Binghamton 184
Tim Flaherty, San Jose 168
Jeremy Owens, Fort Wayne/R. Cuca. .. 166
A.J. Zapp, Macon 163

SACRIFICE FLIES

Larry Barnes, Erie 16
Mark Cridland, Stockton 16
DeWayne Wise, Rockford 14
Jacques Landry, Modesto 12
Chris Truby, Jackson 12

SACRIFICE BUNTS

Augie Ojeda, Bowie/Rochester 25
Shane Halter, Norfolk 17
Cesar Izturis, Dunedin 17
Henry Mateo, Jupiter 17
Alex Cintron, High Desert 17

SLUGGING PERCENTAGE

Erubiel Durazo, El Paso/Tucson ...... .703
Adam Piatt, Midland/Vancouver ...... .688
Jack Cust, High Desert .... .651
Roosevelt Brown, West Tenn/Iowa .. .634
Chris Norton, Portland (EL) .... .633

ON-BASE PERCENTAGE

Nick Johnson, Norwich .... .525
Erubiel Durazo, El Paso/Tucson .... .489
Sean Burroughs, Fort Wayne/R. Cuca. .. .467
Adam Piatt, Midland/Vancouver .... .450
Jack Cust, High Desert .... .450

BATTING AVERAGE*
By Position
(Minimum 400 Plate Appearances)

CATCHERS

Robert Hammock, High Desert .... .332
Wilbert Nieves, Rancho Cucamonga .328
Rod Barajas, El Paso .... .318
Ben Petrick, Carolina/Colo. Springs .311
Javier Cardona, Jacksonville .... .309

FIRST BASEMEN

Erubiel Durazo, El Paso/Tucson ...... .404
Nick Johnson, Norwich .... .345
Talmadge Nunnari, Jupiter/Harris. .. .344
Steve Cox, Durham .... .341
Felipe Crespo, Fresno .... .332

SECOND BASEMEN

Carlos Urquiola, South Bend .... .362
Jason Williams, Chatt./Indianapolis .339
Joe Espada, Midland/Vancouver ..... .336
William Otero, San Jose .... .333
Belvani Martinez, High Desert .... .333

THIRD BASEMEN

Jarrod Patterson, El Paso/Tucson .. .358
Adam Piatt, Midland/Vancouver ...... .340
Bo Robinson, Wisconsin .... .329
Aramis Ramirez, Nashville .... .328
Rico Washington, Hickory/Lynch. .... .325

SHORTSTOPS

D'Angelo Jimenez, Columbus .... .327
Rafael Furcal, Macon/Myrtle Beach .322
Julio Lugo, Jackson .... .319
Jack Wilson, Peoria/Potomac .... .319
Ismael Gallo, San Bernardino .... .314

OUTFIELDERS

Mark Quinn, Omaha .... .360
Jeff DaVanon, Midland/Edmonton .. .338

Cubs' Mike Meyers
Minors' ERA leader

Roosevelt Brown, West Tenn/Iowa .. .338
Midre Cummings, New Britain/S.L. .. .336
Raul Gonzalez, Trenton .... .335

INDIVIDUAL PITCHING
EARNED RUN AVERAGE
(Minimum 112 Innings)

Mike Meyers, Daytona/West Tenn .. 1.73
Josh Kalinowski, Salem 2.11
Bryan Hebson, Cape Fear/Jupiter .. 2.17
Eric Ireland, Kissimmee/Jackson 2.24
Brad Baisley, Piedmont 2.26
Tomokazu Ohka, Trenton/Paw. 2.31
Junior Guerrero, Char., W.Va./Wilm. .. 2.31
Jason Norton, Augusta 2.32
Scott Downs, N.B./Daytona/W.T. 2.35
Scott Comer, Brevard County 2.35
Rick Ankiel, Arkansas/Memphis 2.35

WINS

Doug Bridges, Cedar Rapids/L.E. 18
Jared Fernandez, Trenton/Pawtucket .. 15
Tomokazu Ohka, Trenton/Pawtucket .. 15
Matt Perisho, Oklahoma 15
Mark Watson, Kinston/Akron 15
Jason Beverlin, Norwich 15
Pasqual Coco, Hagerstown/Dunedin .. 15
Jeriome Roberston, Jackson 15
Wilfredo Rodriguez, Kissimmee 15
Matt Blank, Jupiter/Harrisburg 15
Bronson Arroyo, Altoona/Nashville 15
Gary Knotts, Brevard/Portland (EL) 15

LOSSES

Nate Bump, Shreveport/Portland (EL) .. 16
Derek Root, Jackson 16
Andy Bausher, Lynchburg 15
Keith Evans, Harrisburg/Ottawa 15
Joel Pineiro, New Haven 15
Jake Robbins, Tampa/Norwich 15
Bob Scanlan, New Orleans................. 15

GAMES

Pat Flury, Chatt./Indianapolis 66
Scott Brow, Edmonton 64
John Riedling, Chatt./Indianapolis 64
Mark Guerra, Norfolk 63
Rick Greene, Indianapolis 61
Bill Snyder, Lakeland/Jacksonville 61

COMPLETE GAMES

Brian Cooper, Erie/Edmonton 6
Jeff Hundley, Cedar Rapids 6
David Manning, West Tenn/Iowa 6
Several tied with 5

SAVES

Jason Ellison, Tampa 35
Brandon Puffer, Clinton 34
Bill Everly, San Bernardino 34
Joe Lisio, Norwich 33
Jim Brink, Modesto/Midland 29

INNINGS

Steve Fish, Lake Elsinore 197
Jeriome Robertson, Jackson 191
Josh Towers, Bowie 189
Brian Cooper, Erie/Edmonton 189
Seth Etherton, Erie/Edmonton 189

WALKS

Lance Caraccioli, San Bernardino 126
Ben Howard, Fort Wayne 110
Robbie Beckett, S.A./Albuquerque .. 106
Tom Bennett, Visalia 94
Jacob Shumate, M.B./Greenville 94

STRIKEOUTS

John Stephens, Delmarva 217
Geraldo Padua, Greensboro/R. Cuca. .. 196
Scot Shields, Lake Elsinore/Erie 194
Rick Ankiel, Arkansas/Memphis 194
Matt Riley, Frederick/Bowie 189
Juan Figueroa, Burl. (MWL)/W-S....... 189

STRIKEOUTS/9 INNINGS*
(Starters)

Nick Neugebauer, Beloit 13.95
Rick Ankiel, Arkansas/Memphis 12.68
John Stephens, Delmarva 11.47
Winston Abreu, Macon/M.B. 11.15
Robinson Checo, Toledo/S.B./Alb. .. 11.12

STRIKEOUTS/9 INNINGS*
(Relievers)

Eric Cammack, Bing./Norfolk 13.78
Chad Harville, Midland/Vancouver .. 13.31
Saul Rivera, Quad City 13.18
Shane Heams, West Michigan 13.17
Bo Donaldson, Rockford/Chatt. 12.95

BATTING AVERAGE AGAINST*
(Starters)

Nick Neugebauer, Beloit .... .178
Mike Meyers, Daytona/West Tenn ... .179
Rene Vega, Capital City .... .188
Winston Abreu, Macon/M.B. .... .195
Rick Ankiel, Arkansas/Memphis ...... .196

BATTING AVERAGE AGAINST*
(Relievers)

David Riske, Akron/Buffalo .... .113
Juan Moreno, Tulsa .... .153
Brad Voyles, Macon/Myrtle Beach ... .155
Eric Cammack, Binghamton/Norfolk .160
Bob File, Dunedin .... .164

MOST STRIKEOUTS IN ONE GAME

Carlos Hernandez, Martinsville 18
Octavio Dotel, Norfolk 17
John Stephens, Delmarva 17

INDIVIDUAL FIELDING
MOST ERRORS

Luke Allen, 3b, San Antonio 53
Luis Suarez, ss, Burlington (MWL)/W-S. .. 52
Alejandro Fajardo, 2b, Piedmont 47
Chris Rowan, ss, Stockton 45
Chone Figgins, ss, Salem 45

Delmarva's John Stephens
Strikeout king at 217

MINOR LEAGUES BEST TOOLS

	International League (AAA)	Pacific Coast League (AAA)	Eastern League (AA)	Southern League (AA)	Texas League (AA)	California League (A)	Carolina League (A)	Florida State League (A)	Midwest League (A)	South Atlantic League (A)
Best Batting Prospect	Dernell Stenson, Pawtucket	Ruben Mateo, Oklahoma	Pat Burrell, Reading	Chris Wakeland, Jacksonville	Erubiel Durazo, El Paso	Chin-Feng Chen, San Bernardino	Aaron Rowand, Winston-Salem	Vernon Wells, Dunedin	Tydus Meadows, Lansing	Rafael Furcal, Macon
Best Power Prospect	Russell Branyan, Buffalo	Daryle Ward, New Orleans	Scott Morgan, Akron	Andy Thompson, Knoxville	Adam Piatt, Midland	Chin-Feng Chen, San Bernardino	Dee Brown, Wilmington	Matt LeCroy, Fort Myers	Aaron McNeal, Michigan	Jovanny Sosa, Hickory
Best Base Runner	Dave Roberts, Buffalo	Kerry Robinson, Tacoma	Trent Durrington, Erie	Alex Sanchez, Orlando	Mike Metcalfe, San Antonio	Scott Sollmann, Stockton	Kory DeHaan, Lynchburg	Rod Lindsey, Lakeland	Travis Dawkins, Rockford	Mike Curry, Charleston, W.Va.
Fastest Runner	Terry Jones, Ottawa	Kerry Robinson, Tacoma	Julio Ramirez, Portland	Ethan Faggett, West Tenn	Jason Woolf, Arkansas	Scott Sollmann, Stockton	Esix Snead, Potomac	Quincy Foster, Brevard County	Travis Dawkins, Rockford	Rafael Furcal, Macon
Best Pitching Prospect	Bruce Chen, Richmond	Rick Ankiel, Memphis	Tony Armas, Harrisburg	Phillip Norton, West Tenn	Rick Ankiel, Arkansas	Randey Dorame, San Bernardino	Jason Marquis, Myrtle Beach	John Sneed, Dunedin	Chris Mears, Wisconsin	Jason Standridge, Charleston, S.C.
Best Fastball	Octavio Dotel, Norfolk	Chad Harville, Vancouver	Ramon Ortiz, Erie	Francisco Cordero, Jacksonville	Chad Harville, Midland	Jesus Colome, Modesto	Luis Rivera, Myrtle Beach	Todd Noel, Tampa	Nick Neugebauer, Beloit	Franklin Nunez, Piedmont
Best Breaking Pitch	Ted Lilly, Ottawa	Rick Ankiel, Memphis	Ryan Anderson, New Haven	Phillip Norton, West Tenn	John Patterson, El Paso	Elvin Nina, Modesto	Kip Wells, Winston-Salem	Eric Ireland, Kissimmee	Shane Heams, West Michigan	Brad Baisley, Piedmont
Best Control	Jin Ho Cho, Pawtucket	Mike Fyhrie, Edmonton	Brian Cooper, Erie	Pat Daneker, Birmingham	Tony McKnight, Jackson	Randey Dorame, San Bernardino	Josh Fogg, Winston-Salem	Eric Ireland, Kissimmee	Chris Mears, Wisconsin	Geraldo Padua, Greensboro
Best Reliever	Todd Williams, Indianapolis	Cory Bailey, Fresno	Ryan Kohlmeier, Bowie	Francisco Cordero, Jacksonville	Chad Harville, Midland	Jim Brink, Modesto	Robbie Morrison, Wilmington	Eddy Reyes, St. Petersburg	Brandon Puffer, Clinton	Juan Aracena, Columbus
Best Defensive Catcher	Jason LaRue, Indianapolis	Sal Fasano, Omaha	Victor Valencia, Norwich	Wiki Gonzalez, Mobile	Rod Barajas, El Paso	Brian Moon, Stockton	Jayson Werth, Frederick	Luis Taveras, Charlotte	Corky Miller, Rockford	Jean Boscan, Macon
Best Defensive First Baseman	Steve Cox, Durham	Ryan Jackson, Tacoma	Nick Johnson, Norwich	Julio Zuleta, West Tenn	Chris Richard, Arkansas	Todd Mensik, Visalia	Billy Munoz, Kinston	Carlos Pena, Charlotte	Dan Leatherman, Quad City	Carlos Rivera, Hickory
Best Defensive Second Baseman	Jerry Hairston, Rochester	Adam Kennedy, Memphis	David Eckstein, Trenton	Jason Williams, Chattanooga	Hiram Bocachica, San Antonio	William Otero, San Jose	Ron Mackowiak, Lynchburg	Cesar Izturis, Dunedin	Jesus Medrano, Kane County	Javier Colina, Asheville
Best Defensive Third Baseman	Casey Blake, Syracuse	Aramis Ramirez, Nashville	Wilton Veras, Trenton	Joe Crede, Birmingham	Mike Lamb, Tulsa	Tony Zuniga, San Jose	Mike Edwards, Kinston	Michael Cuddyer, Fort Myers	Mike Christensen, Cedar Rapids	Troy Cameron, Macon
Best Defensive Shortstop	D'Angelo Jimenez, Columbus	Kelly Dransfeldt, Oklahoma	John McDonald, Akron	Kevin Nicholson, Mobile	Julio Lugo, Jackson	Nelson Castro, Lake Elsinore	Jason Dellaero, Winston-Salem	Mike Young, Dunedin	Travis Dawkins, Rockford	Rafael Furcal, Macon
Best Infield Arm	Ryan Minor, Rochester	Jose Nieves, Iowa	Wilton Veras, Trenton	Jason Dellaero, Birmingham	Luke Allen, San Antonio	Nelson Castro, Lake Elsinore	Jason Dellaero, Winston-Salem	Jason Grabowski, Charlotte	Sean Burroughs, Fort Wayne	Rafael Furcal, Macon
Best Defensive Outfielder	Anthony Sanders, Syracuse	Mark Quinn, Omaha	Reggie Taylor, Reading	Dorian Speed, West Tenn	Michael Byas, Shreveport	Gary Thomas, Modesto	Kory DeHaan, Lynchburg	Vernon Wells, Dunedin	Corey Patterson, Lansing	Ryan Langherans, Macon
Best Outfield Arm	Terrence Long, Norfolk	Ruben Mateo, Oklahoma	Julio Ramirez, Portland	Brady Clark, Chattanooga	Jeremy Dodson, Wichita	Abraham Nunez, High Desert	Luis Matos, Frederick	Scott Neuberger, St. Petersburg	Miguel Diaz, Peoria	Ryan Langherans, Macon
Most Exciting Player	George Lombard, Richmond	Ruben Mateo, Oklahoma	Alfonso Soriano, Norwich	McKay Christensen, Birmingham	Julio Lugo, Jackson	Abraham Nunez, High Desert	Dee Brown, Wilmington	Vernon Wells, Dunedin	Corey Patterson, Lansing	Rafael Furcal, Macon
Best Managerial Prospect	Trey Hillman, Columbus	Trent Jewett, Nashville	Garry Templeton, Erie	Chris Cron, Birmingham	John Mizerock, Wichita	Bob Geren, Modesto	Jeff Garber, Wilmington	Luis Dorante, Jupiter	Rick Renteria, Kane County	Dave Engle, Capital City

Selected at midseason, 1999 by minor league managers in consultation with Baseball America

Minor Leagues

three different leagues in Baseball America's annual survey of league managers. Wells, 20, began the season at Class A Dunedin, moved to Double-A Knoxville and Triple-A Syracuse, and ended it in Toronto.

On The Move

Vancouver's exodus to Sacramento for the 2000 season paralleled a trend that has seen National Hockey League teams leave Canada for greener pastures in the U.S. in recent years. Vancouver had a Triple-A team continuously since 1978.

In addition to Vancouver, two other Canadian teams were sold to U.S. interests.

The short-season Class A St. Catharines Stompers played their last game, with the team scheduled to move to Brooklyn, in 2000. Calgary Cannons owner Russ Parker also sold his Triple-A team to a group from Portland led by Oregon businessman Marshall Glickman, who planned to relocate the team to Portland after the 2000 season.

"It is simply time to give up the fight," Parker said. "The constant battles with Calgary's unpredictable weather conditions, together with the challenge of playing in an outdated city baseball facility, are insurmountable obstacles for the franchise."

When Triple-A returns to Portland in 2001, the city's short-season Rockies will have to find a new home. Rockies owners Jack and Mary Cain were forced to clear the way for the move.

"We've pretty much revived baseball in Portland, and we get kicked in the shins by the city," Jack Cain said. "People think money is the root of all happiness, but it isn't. People congratulate me. Don't congratulate me. This has been our baby for 19 years. You get emotionally attached to your business. I'd rather be doing what I'm doing right now for the next 20 years."

The St. Catharines sale and pending move to Brooklyn completes the Mets' and Yankees' plans to move their short-season New York-Penn League teams to New York City.

The Yankees brought their NY-P affiliate to Staten Island for the 1999 season, and as part of the arrangement that allowed that team into the New York territory, the Mets arranged to bring a team to Coney Island in Brooklyn.

Brooklyn Baseball Co., a Mets subsidiary, bought the team and was set to move it right away, though the new Coney Island ballpark won't be ready until 2001.

"This is not a particularly happy day for the Stompers ownership group," St. Catharines presi-

Freitas Awards
Louisville rolls with changes in nickname, league, affiliation, stadium

After a year in which all four of the Freitas Award winners won the honor in their first year of eligibility, the 1999 group has a club born before 1990. And it has two Portlands.

The Freitas Awards annually recognize long-term success by minor league franchises at the Triple-A, Double-A, Class A and short-season levels. They are named for Bob Freitas, a longtime minor league operator, promoter and ambassador who died in 1989. Franchises are eligible for the honor in their fifth year of operation.

Triple-A honoree Louisville has been in the minors' highest classification since 1982. The city had International League baseball from 1968-72 and an American Association team from 1982 until the AA disbanded before the 1998 season. After Triple-A realignment, Louisville fans took to the return to the IL in style.

Despite playing out the string at Cardinal Stadium, the club drew more than 360,000 fans in each of its two years as a Brewers affiliate. Louisville will move into 13,000-seat Slugger Field and

start an affiliation with the nearby Reds in 2000.

The Portland SeaDogs, winners in Double-A in their second year of eligibility, have brought Maine a team it can be proud of. They topped the 400,000 mark in '99 in attendance.

The other Portland winner in 1999 was the short-season Portland Rockies. The five-year-

old team owned by Jack and Mary Cain outgrew itself, as its popularity helped seal a deal to bring a Triple-A club from Calgary to Portland.

The Wilmington Blue Rocks seized the Class A honor after a seventh solid year as a Carolina League franchise. They led the CL with more than 320,000 in attendance in 1999.

PREVIOUS WINNERS

Triple-A	Class A
1989—Columbus (International)	1989—Durham (Carolina)
1990—Pawtucket (International)	1990—San Jose (California)
1991—Buffalo (American Association)	1991—Asheville (South Atlantic)
1992—Iowa (American Association)	1992—Springfield (Midwest)
1993—Richmond (International)	1993—South Bend (Midwest)
1994—Norfolk (International)	1994—Kinston (Carolina)
1995—Albuquerque (Pacific Coast)	1995—Kane County (Midwest)
1996—Indianapolis (American Association)	1996—Wisconsin (Midwest)
1997—Rochester (International)	1997—Rancho Cucamonga (California)
1998—Salt Lake (Pacific Coast)	1998—West Michigan (Midwest)
Double-A	**Short-Season**
1989—El Paso (Texas)	1989—Eugene (Northwest)
1990—Arkansas (Texas)	1990—Salt Lake City (Pioneer)
1991—Reading (Eastern)	1991—Spokane (Northwest)
1992—Tulsa (Texas)	1992—Boise (Northwest)
1993—Harrisburg (Eastern)	1993—Billings (Pioneer)
1994—San Antonio (Texas)	1994—Everett (Northwest)
1995—Midland (Texas)	1995—Great Falls (Pioneer)
1996—Carolina (Southern)	1996—Bluefield (Appalachian)
1997—Bowie (Eastern)	1997—Oneonta (New York-Penn)
1998—Trenton (Eastern)	1998—Hudson Valley (New York-Penn)

Minor Leagues

TOP 100 PROSPECTS

Through consultation with scouts and player-development people, Baseball America selects its annual list of the game's top 100 minor league prospects. The list emphasizes long-range major league potential and considers only players in professional baseball who had not exhausted their major league rookie status entering the 1999 season.
The highest level each player reached in 1999 is noted in parentheses.

1. J.D. Drew, of, Cardinals (Majors)
2. Rick Ankiel, lhp, Cardinals (Majors)
3. Eric Chavez, 3b, Athletics (Majors)
4. Bruce Chen, lhp, Braves (Majors)
5. Brad Penny, rhp, Marlins (AA)
6. Michael Barrett, 3b-c, Expos (Majors)
7. Ryan Anderson, lhp, Mariners (AA)
8. Pablo Ozuna, ss, Marlins (AA)
9. Ruben Mateo, of, Rangers (Majors)
10. Matt Clement, rhp, Padres (Majors)
11. Alex Escobar, of, Mets (A)
12. Roy Halladay, rhp, Blue Jays (Majors)
13. Lance Berkman, of, Astros (Majors)
14. Carlos Beltran, of, Royals (Majors)
15. John Patterson, rhp, D'backs (AAA)
16. Corey Patterson, of, Cubs (A)
17. Alex Gonzalez, ss, Marlins (Majors)
18. Nick Johnson, 1b, Yankees (AA)
19. Pat Burrell, 1b, Phillies (AAA)
20. Matt Riley, lhp, Orioles (Majors)
21. A.J. Burnett, rhp, Marlins (Majors)
22. Dernell Stenson, 1b, Red Sox (AAA)
23. Braden Looper, rhp, Marlins (Majors)
24. Ben Davis, c, Padres (Majors)
25. Ryan Bradley, rhp, Yankees (AAA)
26. George Lombard, of, Braves (Majors)
27. Mark Mulder, lhp, Athletics (AAA)
28. Carlos Lee, 3b-of, White Sox (Majors)
29. Russell Branyan, 3b, Indians (Majors)
30. Carlos Febles, 2b, Royals (Majors)
31. Odalis Perez, lhp, Braves (Majors)
32. Matt White, rhp, Devil Rays (A)
33. Billy Koch, rhp, Blue Jays (Majors)
34. Gabe Kapler, of, Tigers (Majors)
35. Rob Bell, rhp, Reds (AA)
36. Michael Cuddyer, ss-3b, Twins (A)
37. Chad Hermansen, of, Pirates (Majors)
38. Calvin Pickering, 1b, Orioles (Majors)
39. Alfonso Soriano, ss, Yankees (Majors)
40. Peter Bergeron, of, Expos (Majors)
41. Angel Pena, c, Dodgers (Majors)
42. Chad Hutchinson, rhp, Cardinals (Majors)

J.D. Drew

DAVID SEELIG

43. Mitch Meluskey, c, Astros (Majors)
44. Jason Grilli, rhp, Marlins (AAA)
45. Octavio Dotel, rhp, Mets (Majors)
46. Joe Crede, 3b, White Sox (AA)
47. Kevin McGlinchy, rhp, Braves (Majors)
48. Julio Ramirez, of, Marlins (Majors)
49. Ron Belliard, 2b, Brewers (Majors)
50. Michael Restovich, of, Twins (A)
51. Jeff Weaver, rhp, Tigers (Majors)
52. Jayson Werth, c, Orioles (AA)
53. Eric DuBose, lhp, Athletics (AA)
54. Brent Butler, ss, Cardinals (AA)
55. Jeff Austin, rhp, Royals (AA)
56. John Curtice, lhp, Red Sox (Rookie)
57. Orber Moreno, rhp, Royals (AAA)
58. Mike Lowell, 3b, Marlins (Majors)

59. Kris Benson, rhp, Pirates (Majors)
60. Rafael Furcal, ss, Braves (A)
61. Freddy Garcia, rhp, Mariners (Majors)
62. Junior Herndon, rhp, Padres (AA)
63. Luis Rivas, ss, Twins (AA)
64. Jeremy Giambi, of, Royals (Majors)
65. Kelly Dransfeldt, 2b-ss, Rangers (Majors)
66. Ted Lilly, lhp, Expos (Majors)
67. Felipe Lopez, ss, Blue Jays (A)
68. Cristian Guzman, ss, Twins (Majors)
69. Vernon Wells, of, Blue Jays (Majors)
70. Ricky Ledee, of, Yankees (Majors)
71. Luis Rivera, rhp, Braves (A)
72. Jackson Melian, of, Yankees (A)
73. Gary Matthews Jr., of, Padres (Majors)
74. Darnell McDonald, of, Orioles (A)
75. Choo Freeman, of, Rockies (A)
76. Austin Kearns, of, Reds (A)
77. Aaron Myette, rhp, White Sox (Majors)
78. Gil Meche, rhp, Mariners (Majors)
79. Grant Roberts, rhp, Mets (AAA)
80. Wade Miller, rhp, Astros (AAA)
81. Derrick Gibson, of, Rockies (Majors)
82. Sean Burroughs, 3b, Padres (A)
83. Marlon Anderson, 2b, Phillies (Majors)
84. Warren Morris, 2b, Pirates (Majors)
85. Ben Petrick, c, Rockies (Majors)
86. Milton Bradley, of, Expos (AA)
87. Carlos Guillen, 2b, Mariners (Majors)
88. Guillermo Mota, rhp, Expos (Majors)
89. Jason Marquis, rhp, Braves (AA)
90. Tony Armas, rhp, Expos (Majors)
91. Wes Anderson, rhp, Marlins (A)
92. Dee Brown, of, Royals (Majors)
93. Carlos Pena, 1b, Rangers (A)
94. Mike Darr, of, Padres (Majors)
95. Chad Harville, rhp, Athletics (Majors)
96. Randy Wolf, lhp, Phillies (Majors)
97. Scott Williamson, rhp, Reds (Majors)
98. Adam Kennedy, 2b, Cardinals (Majors)
99. Trot Nixon, of, Red Sox (Majors)
100. Drew Henson, 3b, Yankees (A)

dent Greg Sorbara said. "We bought this franchise five years ago because we love the game and wanted to keep a part of baseball's future in southern Ontario."

The Stompers became a prime target to be sold because St. Catharines' Community Park fell short of ballpark standards as enforced by Minor League Baseball. The ownership group could not raise the money to fix or replace it.

"Our park has always had a real hometown atmosphere, and we are very proud of what we've done over the past five years," said Terry O'Malley, one of the Stompers' owners. "But the reality of the more demanding standards left us with no option but to sell."

The franchise will remain a Blue Jays affiliate in 2000, but the Mets will take it over in 2001 after their affiliation with the Pittsfield Mets expires.

Around The Minors

■ In addition to the loss of Canadian teams, Fayetteville, N.C. , was set to lose its team. The Cape Fear Crocs (South Atlantic) were sold to a group that plans to move them to Lakewood, N.J., for the 2001 season—extending the northern boundary of the league. The Fayetteville team consistently ranked at or near the bottom of the league in attendance.

"That's what we've dealt with the last 13 years," Crocs owner Greg Padgett said. "Shoot, I'm 26 and this thing has been part of my life for half of my life. I feel like I'm giving up a puppy or something."

While the Lakewood team won't begin play until 2001, three full-season teams already planned fresh starts for 2000: Sacramento (formerly Vancouver), the Round Rock Express (formerly the Jackson Generals) and the Dayton Dragons (formerly the Rockford Reds).

Those three teams will have brand-new ballparks, as will the Louisville RiverBats (International) and Memphis Redbirds (Pacific Coast).

■ The first-year Mahoning Valley Scrappers set a New York-Penn League attendance record with 203,073 fans, while the minor leagues as a whole remained steady at the gate.

With two Double-A expansion teams in the Eastern League, minor league attendance was slightly higher in 1999 (32.3 million) than in 1998. That meant more fans watched National Association games in 1999 than in any year since the post-World War II boom, when more than 400 teams played in more than 50 leagues.

The average minor league crowd in '99 was 3,419 fans—down 29 fans a game from 1998.

INTERNATIONALLEAGUE

As White Sox' team, Charlotte travels Marlins' route

BY MATT MICHAEL

The Charlotte Knights are no longer affiliated with the Marlins, but they borrowed a page from Florida's book anyway.

In 1997, the Marlins chased the Braves all season and finished second to Atlanta in the National League East. But Florida, the NL's wild-card team, defeated the Braves in the NL Championship Series, then downed the Cleveland Indians to win the World Series.

The Knights, Florida's Triple-A affiliate from 1995-98, spent the 1999 season battling the Durham Bulls for the International League's Southern Division crown. Now the White Sox' top farm club, Charlotte earned the IL's wild-card spot by finishing 82-62, 1½ games behind the Bulls.

Charlotte, which joined the IL the same year the Marlins joined the NL (1993), beat Scranton/Wilkes-Barre in the first round of the IL playoffs, then overtook Durham when it counted most: in the Governors' Cup championship series.

The Knights' copycat season ran out of luck in the Triple-A World Series in Las Vegas, though, as the Vancouver Canadians took Games Four and Five to spoil Charlotte's bid for a Triple-A title.

"We feel like this is the toughest division in the International League," Charlotte manager Tom Spencer said after the Knights clinched a playoff spot. "There's a lot of satisfaction to have the opportunity to go to the playoffs."

Satisfaction didn't stop there as the Knights rallied to win both of their IL playoff series. In the first round, Charlotte fell behind two games to one, but won the final two games of the five-game series at Scranton/Wilkes-Barre to advance to the Governors' Cup series.

Charlotte dropped the first game against Durham,

MORRIS FOSTOFF

IL MVP Steve Cox
Durham's first baseman hit .341-25-127

but captured the next three to win its second IL championship and its first since 1993, when the Knights were affiliated with Cleveland.

In the title-clinching game against the Bulls at Knights Stadium, Jason Secoda and relievers Bryan Ward and Luis Andujar combined on a three-hitter.

The championship was the third in nine years as a minor league manager for Spencer, who was named the IL's manager of the year.

"We keep taking players from him, and he keeps winning," White Sox skipper manager Jerry Manuel said. "He'll be a manager in the big leagues soon."

Led by IL MVP Steve Cox, Durham posted the

Minor Leagues

STANDINGS

Page	EAST	W	L	PCT	GB	Manager	Attendance/Dates	Last Penn.
196	Scranton/W-B Red Barons (Phillies)	78	66	.542	—	Marc Bombard	439,171 (68)	None
82	Pawtucket Red Sox (Red Sox)	76	68	.528	2	Gary Jones	596,624 (72)	1984
249	Syracuse SkyChiefs (Blue Jays)	73	71	.507	5	Pat Kelly	446,025 (69)	1976
110	Buffalo Bisons (Indians)	72	72	.500	6	Jeff Datz	684,051 (68)	1998
75	Rochester Red Wings (Orioles)	61	83	.424	17	Dave Machemer	481,039 (68)	1997
168	Ottawa Lynx (Expos)	59	85	.410	19	Jeff Cox	195,979 (72)	1995
Page	**WEST**	**W**	**L**	**PCT**	**GB**	**Manager**	**Attendance/Dates**	**Last Penn.**
175	Columbus Clippers (Yankees)	83	58	.589	—	Trey Hillman	460,923 (64)	1996
103	Indianapolis Indians (Reds)	75	69	.521	9½	Dave Miley	658,250 (71)	1963
155	Louisville RiverBats (Brewers)	63	81	.438	21½	Gary Allenson	361,419 (72)	None
123	Toledo Mud Hens (Tigers)	57	87	.396	27½	Gene Roof	295,173 (68)	1967
Page	**SOUTH**	**W**	**L**	**PCT**	**GB**	**Manager**	**Attendance/Dates**	**Last Penn.**
235	Durham Bulls (Devil Rays)	83	60	.580	—	Bill Evers	464,001 (70)	None
89	Charlotte Knights (White Sox)	82	62	.569	1½	Tom Spencer	344,199 (70)	1999
182	Norfolk Tides (Mets)	77	63	.550	4½	John Gibbons	486,727 (72)	1985
68	Richmond Braves (Braves)	64	78	.451	18½	Randy Ingle	523,670 (70)	1994

GOVERNORS' CUP PLAYOFFS—Semifinals: Durham defeated Columbus 3-0 and Charlotte defeated Scranton/Wilkes-Barre 3-2 in best-of-5 series. **Finals:** Charlotte defeated Durham 3-1 in best-of-5 series.

NOTE: Team's individual batting and pitching statistics can be found on page indicated in lefthand column.

league's second-best record (83-60). Cox, a lefthanded-hitting first baseman, led the IL in batting average (.341), hits (182), extra-base hits (78), doubles (49), runs (107), RBIs (127) and slugging percentage (.588).

Durham swept IL Western Division winner

Columbus 3-0 in a first-round playoff series. The Clippers had the league's best record (83-58) and featured IL most valuable pitcher Ed Yarnall, who ranked second in the league in wins (13) and ERA (3.47), and third in strikeouts (146).

Scranton/Wilkes-Barre (78-66) used an eight-game winning streak late in the season to pull away from Pawtucket and Syracuse in the IL's Northern Division.

Ed Yarnall

The Red Barons made just their second playoff appearance since joining the IL in 1989.

Unlikely No-Hitter

It took two Ottawa pitchers to throw the IL's only no-hitter in 1999. On July 19 at Syracuse's P&C Stadium, starter Shayne Bennett (five perfect innings) and reliever Jayson Durocher (one walk in four innings) combined to no-hit the SkyChiefs 10-0. Bennett, who's normally a reliever, was an emergency starter, while Durocher was making his Triple-A debut. "It's one of those lucky things," Bennett said. "It doesn't happen very often."

The no-hitter was the IL's first since Pawtucket's Juan Pena no-hit Durham on July 22, 1998. And it was just the third combined nine-inning no-hitter in the IL's 116-year history.

On June 4 at Pawtucket's McCoy Stadium, the Red Sox' Michael Coleman went 7-for-7 with two singles, a double, a triple and three home runs in Pawtucket's 25-2 rout of Norfolk. Lee Tinsley, in 1993 with Calgary (Pacific Coast), was the last minor leaguer to collect seven hits in a nine-inning game.

Coleman is believed to be the first professional player to hit for the cycle and go 7-for-7 in the same game. Coleman had seven RBIs and 19 total bases.

Japanese pitcher Tomo Ohka went 7-0 with a 1.58 ERA at Pawtucket, finishing a perfect 15-0 year in the minor leagues. He was 8-0, 3.00 at Double-A Trenton.

Outfielder Vernon Wells played in just 33 games at Syracuse, but that was enough for IL managers to select him as the IL's top prospect. Wells batted a combined .334 with 18 homers and 81 RBIs at Class A Dunedin (70 games), Double-A Knoxville (24 games) and Syracuse, and he was named the top prospect in the Florida State, Southern and International leagues.

"He's one hell of a prospect," Blue Jays manager Jim Fregosi said. "I think he has a chance to be an all-star center fielder in the major leagues."

A short stint with the Indians probably saved third baseman Russell Branyan from setting an IL record for most strikeouts in a season. Branyan had 187 strikeouts, 12 shy of the record set by Richmond's Dave

LEAGUE CHAMPIONS

Last 30 Years

Year	Regular Season*	Pct.	Playoff
1970	Syracuse (Yankees)	.600	Syracuse (Yankees)
1971	Rochester (Orioles)	.614	Rochester (Orioles)
1972	Louisville (Red Sox)	.563	Tidewater (Mets)
1973	Charleston (Pirates)	.586	Pawtucket (Red Sox)
1974	Memphis (Expos)	.613	Rochester (Orioles)
1975	Tidewater (Mets)	.607	Tidewater (Mets)
1976	Rochester (Orioles)	.638	Syracuse (Yankees)
1977	Pawtucket (Red Sox)	.571	Charleston (Astros)
1978	Charleston (Astros)	.607	Richmond (Braves)
1979	Columbus (Yankees)	.612	Columbus (Yankees)
1980	Columbus (Yankees)	.593	Columbus (Yankees)
1981	Columbus (Yankees)	.633	Columbus (Yankees)
1982	Richmond (Braves)	.590	Tidewater (Mets)
1983	Columbus (Yankees)	.593	Tidewater (Mets)
1984	Columbus (Yankees)	.590	Pawtucket (Red Sox)
1985	Syracuse (Blue Jays)	.564	Tidewater (Mets)
1986	Richmond (Braves)	.571	Richmond (Braves)
1987	Tidewater (Mets)	.579	Columbus (Yankees)
1988	Tidewater (Mets)	.546	Rochester (Orioles)
	Rochester (Orioles)	.546	
1989	Syracuse (Blue Jays)	.572	Richmond (Braves)
1990	Rochester (Orioles)	.614	Rochester (Orioles)
1991	Columbus (Yankees)	.590	Columbus (Yankees)
1992	Columbus (Yankees)	.660	Columbus (Yankees)
1993	Charlotte (Indians)	.610	Charlotte (Indians)
1994	Richmond (Braves)	.567	Richmond (Braves)
1995	Norfolk (Mets)	.606	Ottawa (Expos)
1996	Columbus (Yankees)	.599	Columbus (Yankees)
1997	Rochester (Orioles)	.589	Rochester (Orioles)
1998	Buffalo (Indians)	.566	Buffalo (Indians)
1999	Columbus (Yankees)	.589	Charlotte (White Sox)

*Best overall record

Nicholson in 1968. The power-hitting Branyan also hit three home runs in a game twice—on April 17 against Ottawa and July 22 against Indianapolis.

The name of Buffalo's ballpark keeps changing (from Pilot Field to North AmeriCare Park to Dunn Tire Park), but the fans keep coming. The Bisons, who attracted 648,051 fans in 1999, have led the minors in attendance in each of the 12 years they have played at the 20,000-seat stadium. Indianapolis finished second in the minor league attendance race, with Pawtucket at refurbished McCoy Stadium going from 16th to third.

After the Bisons' next-to-last game of the year, which was at Dunn Tire Park, Buffalo slugger Jeff Manto announced he would retire from the minors after the season. Manto, 35, who left open the possibility of playing in the majors in 2000, had been the minors' active home run leader with 230.

In early September, the IL announced its only affiliation switch (and the minors' only one) for 2000.

Michael Coleman

The Reds moved their Triple-A team from Indianapolis to Louisville, forcing the Brewers to shift from Louisville to Indianapolis.

Indianapolis fans weren't thrilled with the change, because while the Reds were affiliated with Indianapolis from 1993-99, the Indians had the best record in Triple-A at 554-451 (.551). Louisville will move into 13,000-seat Slugger Field in 2000.

Minor Leagues

1999 International League Statistics

CLUB BATTING

	AVG	G	AB	R	H	2B	3B	HR	BB	SO	SB
Durham	.295	143	4951	923	1460	336	39	186	565	956	103
Charlotte	.290	144	4843	836	1405	309	22	164	506	850	95
Columbus	.289	141	4816	879	1391	305	34	171	576	853	96
Indianapolis	.284	144	4977	788	1411	296	30	156	479	878	83
Norfolk	.280	140	4688	675	1313	258	32	121	468	782	115
Buffalo	.269	144	4829	748	1301	254	34	154	542	947	143
Rochester	.269	144	4931	668	1325	277	31	114	414	858	91
Syracuse	.268	144	4891	744	1311	257	32	154	498	968	102
Louisville	.265	144	4893	731	1299	265	36	166	492	1003	168
Richmond	.265	142	4774	661	1263	249	24	126	455	956	132
Pawtucket	.263	144	4897	776	1286	265	28	187	593	1008	90
Toledo	.258	144	4814	706	1241	250	32	176	526	978	86
Ottawa	.255	144	4770	647	1216	246	32	120	460	1057	146
Scranton/W-B	.254	144	4799	728	1220	290	29	132	583	1035	90

CLUB PITCHING

	ERA	G	CG	SHO	SV	IP	H	R	ER	BB	SO
Pawtucket	4.01	144	11	9	31	1267	1283	682	565	393	900
Buffalo	4.34	144	2	5	42	1247	1278	706	601	491	818
Ottawa	4.48	144	2	6	36	1255	1321	725	624	531	954
Norfolk	4.58	140	7	7	39	1220	1283	712	620	532	984
Scranton/W-B	4.60	144	9	11	40	1253	1363	715	641	494	912
Richmond	4.65	142	4	8	34	1232	1256	693	637	466	1040
Rochester	4.67	144	5	8	30	1274	1290	740	662	511	1017
Columbus	4.70	141	9	5	34	1230	1262	725	643	470	986
Syracuse	4.88	144	4	4	41	1258	1284	752	682	618	974
Indianapolis	4.95	144	4	6	47	1265	1386	773	696	496	854
Charlotte	4.97	144	12	4	42	1225	1378	763	677	440	952
Durham	5.20	143	2	2	39	1253	1370	817	724	533	961
Louisville	5.41	144	2	7	33	1271	1361	868	765	586	929
Toledo	5.46	144	11	2	22	1241	1327	839	753	596	848

CLUB FIELDING

	PCT	PO	A	E	DP		PCT	PO	A	E	DP
Indianapolis	.981	3794	1639	106	171	Buffalo	.974	3740	1418	135	110
Richmond	.979	3696	1322	106	116	Louisville	.974	3815	1518	140	144
Durham	.978	3759	1537	117	154	Charlotte	.974	3675	1419	135	116
Syracuse	.978	3774	1376	116	113	Rochester	.974	3823	1429	142	128
Toledo	.977	3723	1564	127	147	Ottawa	.974	3764	1481	142	132
Scranton/W-B	.976	3759	1583	132	158	Norfolk	.971	3659	1372	151	122
Columbus	.975	3690	1437	130	129	Pawtucket	.970	3800	1395	162	114

INDIVIDUAL BATTING LEADERS
(Minimum 389 Plate Appearances)

	AVG	G	AB	R	H	2B	3B	HR	RBI	BB	SO	SB
Cox, Steve, Durham	.341	134	534	107	182	49	4	25	127	67	143	
Hardtke, Jason, Indy	.329	101	416	74	137	37	2	12	61	35	43	7
Jimenez, D'Angelo, Col.	.327	126	526	97	172	32	5	15	88	59	75	26
Raabe, Brian, Columbus	.327	130	493	93	161	35	5	11	77	48	19	5
Coquillette, Trace, Ottawa	.326	98	334	56	109	32	3	14	55	44	68	10
Lopez, Luis, Syracuse	.322	136	531	76	171	35	2	4	69	40	58	1
Mottola, Chad, Charlotte	.321	140	511	95	164	32	4	20	94	60	83	18
Brito, Tilson, Charlotte	.318	111	406	60	129	30	5	11	58	34	66	6
Powell, Alonzo, Columbus	.315	130	470	97	148	23	1	24	90	82	110	1
Graffanino, Tony, Durham	.313	87	345	66	108	25	6	9	58	37	46	16

INDIVIDUAL PITCHING LEADERS
(Minimum 115 Innings)

	W	L	ERA	G	GS	CG	SV	IP	H	R	ER	BB	SO
Yarnall, Ed, Columbus	13	4	3.47	23	23	1	0	145	136	61	56	57	146
Carrara, Giovanni, Indy	12	7	3.47	39	21	2	0	158	144	68	61	58	114
Borkowski, David, Toledo	6	8	3.50	19	19	3	0	126	119	59	49	43	94
Wolcott, Bob, Pawtucket	6	13	3.59	26	16	2	2	125	131	67	50	28	69
Linton, Doug, Rochester	7	5	3.65	18	18	1	0	118	120	58	48	27	97
Wagner, Paul, Buffalo	8	4	3.82	23	23	0	0	130	123	67	55	35	95
Bolton, Rod, Scranton	11	10	3.82	24	24	4	0	153	161	76	65	52	85
Maduro, Calvin, Rochester	11	11	3.99	29	28	2	0	169	179	88	75	60	149
Harriger, Denny, Indy	14	6	4.08	27	27	1	0	172	183	82	78	36	110
Romano, Mike, Syracuse	12	8	4.13	29	28	2	0	174	160	90	80	84	104

ALL-STAR TEAM

C—Jason LaRue, Indianapolis. **1B**—Steve Cox, Durham. **2B**—Brian Raabe, Columbus. **3B**—Scott McClain, Durham. **SS**—D'Angelo Jimenez, Columbus. **OF**—Michael Coleman, Pawtucket; D.T. Cromer, Indianapolis; Chad Mottola, Charlotte. **DH**—Luis Raven, Charlotte. **Util**—Jason Hardtke, Indianapolis. **SP**—Ed Yarnall, Columbus. **RP**—Jay Tessmer, Columbus.

Most Valuable Player: Steve Cox, Durham. **Most Valuable Pitcher:** Ed Yarnall, Columbus. **Rookie of the Year:** Kurt Bierek, Columbus. **Manager of the Year:** Tom Spencer, Charlotte.

TOP 10 PROSPECTS

1. Vernon Wells, of, Syracuse; **2.** Dernell Stenson, 1b, Pawtucket; **3.** Russell Branyan, 3b, Buffalo; **4.** Octavio Dotel, rhp, Norfolk; **5.** Bruce Chen, lhp, Richmond; **6.** Randy Wolf, lhp, Scranton/Wilkes-Barre; **7.** Terrence Long, of, Norfolk; **8.** D'Angelo Jimenez, ss, Columbus; **9.** Jerry Hairston, 2b, Rochester; **10.** Ed Yarnall, lhp, Columbus.

DEPT. LEADERS

BATTING
G	Wendell Magee, Scranton	142
AB	Wendell Magee, Scranton	566
R	Steve Cox, Durham	107
H	Steve Cox, Durham	182
TB	Steve Cox, Durham	314
XBH	Steve Cox, Durham	78
2B	Steve Cox, Durham	49
3B	Dave Roberts, Buffalo	10
HR	Luis Raven, Charlotte	33
RBI	Steve Cox, Durham	127
SH	Shane Halter, Norfolk	17
SF	Billy McMillon, Scranton	10
BB	Jon Zuber, Scranton	86
IBB	Steve Cox, Durham	11
HBP	Trace Coquillette, Ottawa	24
SO	Russell Branyan, Buffalo	187
SB	Greg Martinez, Louisville	48
CS	Shane Halter, Norfolk	17
GIDP	Luis Lopez, Syracuse	22
OB%	Trace Coquillette, Ottawa	.434
SL%	Steve Cox, Durham	.588

PITCHING
G	Mark Guerra, Norfolk	63
GS	Three tied at	28
CG	Carlos Castillo, Charlotte	5
ShO	Rod Bolton, Scranton	2
	Nelson Cruz, Toledo	2
GF	Eddie Gaillard, Durham	52
SV	Jay Tessmer, Columbus	28
W	Denny Harriger, Indianapolis	14
L	Matt Drews, Toledo	14
IP	Jeff Juden, Columbus	176
H	Denny Harriger, Indianapolis	183
R	Matt Drews, Toledo	136
ER	Matt Drews, Toledo	125
HR	Ryan Bradley, Columbus	28
	Carlos Castillo, Charlotte	28
HB	Jeff Juden, Columbus	17
BB	Matt Drews, Toledo	91
SO	Jeff Juden, Columbus	151
WP	Ryan Bradley, Columbus	23
BK	Ramon Tatis, Durham	9

FIELDING
C	AVG	Joe Siddall, Toledo	.998
	PO	Francisco Morales, Ottawa	661
	A	Francisco Morales, Ottawa	64
	E	Kevin Brown, Syracuse	13
	DP	Bobby Estalella, Scranton	10
	PB	Francisco Morales, Ottawa	16
1B	AVG	David McCarty, Toledo	.999
	PO	Steve Cox, Durham	1125
	A	David McCarty, Toledo	104
	E	Dernell Stenson, Pawtucket	34
	DP	Steve Cox, Durham	121
2B	AVG	Torey Lovullo, Scranton	.982
	PO	Torey Lovullo, Scranton	262
	A	Torey Lovullo, Scranton	390
	E	Tilson Brito, Charlotte	16
		Jose Macias, Toledo	16
	DP	Torey Lovullo, Scranton	99
3B	AVG	Casey Blake, Syracuse	.967
	PO	Casey Blake, Syracuse	94
		Jose Fernandez, Ottawa	94
	A	Lou Lucca, Scranton	310
	E	Jose Fernandez, Ottawa	31
	DP	Lou Lucca, Scranton	27
SS	AVG	Jeff Branson, Indianapolis	.974
	PO	D'Angelo Jimenez, Columbus	188
	A	Chris Martin, Durham	380
	E	Santiago Perez, Louisville	29
	DP	Jeff Branson, Indianapolis	81
OF	AVG	Kimera Bartee, Toledo	.996
	PO	Wendell Magee, Scranton	310
	A	Chad Mottola, Charlotte	17
		Anthony Sanders, Syracuse	17
	E	Wendell Magee, Scranton	8
	DP	Three tied at	4

PACIFICCOASTLEAGUE

Canadians take parting gifts on their way to Sacramento

BY PETER BARROUQUERE

The Vancouver Canadians exited the Pacific Coast League in style, taking the Triple-A World Series title on their way to Sacramento.

The Canadians, who had been in the PCL continuously since 1978 but were sold to Northern California businessman Art Savage for $7.5 million in 1998, blew out the Charlotte Knights 16-2 in the deciding Game Five. PCL teams have won both Triple-A World Series. The New Orleans Zephyrs beat the Buffalo Bisons in four games in the inaugural series in 1998.

In the clinching game in the '99 series in Las Vegas, lefthander Mark Mulder pitched a complete-game seven-hitter and allowed one earned run.

"You've got to give the hitters credit," Mulder said. "They made my job real easy. I was laying fastballs in there and letting the infielders and outfielders do their jobs. It was easy because of them."

Outfielder Terrence Long, whom the Canadians received in July when the parent Oakland Athletics shipped lefthander Kenny Rogers to the New York Mets, was named the series MVP. He had 10 RBIs in the series, including four in a 3-for-6 Game Five.

Terrence Long

"We had some guys struggling in the playoffs," Long said. "I myself struggled early in this series. But this is what you play for."

The Knights took two of the first three games, but Vancouver won Game Four, 9-7, after a two-run bottom of the eighth. Second baseman Josue Espada singled home the go-ahead run and Long added another RBI single.

The next night, Vancouver set franchise playoff records with 20 hits and the 16 runs.

The Canadians, the PCL's Western Division champion, also needed to win two straight games to take the best-of-5 PCL championship series from Oklahoma, the Eastern Division champion. Omaha won the Central and Salt Lake the South.

The best race was in the Southern Division, where the Buzz beat out Fresno on the last day of the season to win by half a game. The disparity in games was created by a Salt Lake rainout against New Orleans that was not made up.

Individual Achievements

For the second straight season, Omaha produced the league batting champion. PCL rookie of the year Mark Quinn hit .364 to win going away. His nearest pursuer was Fresno's Calvin Murray (.334), who led in runs (122), hits (183), total bases (297) and stolen bases (42).

The 28-year-old Murray was chosen the league's MVP. A two-time first-round pick, his career had stalled as he spent part of six straight seasons at

STANDINGS

AMERICAN CONFERENCE

Page	EAST	W	L	PCT	GB	Manager	Attendance/Dates	Last Penn.
242	Oklahoma RedHawks (Rangers)	83	59	.585	—	Greg Biagini	471,722 (67)	None
203	Nashville Sounds (Pirates)	80	60	.571	2	Trent Jewett	335,901 (69)	None
210	Memphis Redbirds (Cardinals)	74	64	.536	7	Gaylen Pitts	397,339 (70)	1965
136	New Orleans Zephyrs (Astros)	55	85	.393	27	Tony Pena	472,665 (70)	1998

Page	CENTRAL	W	L	PCT	GB	Manager	Attendance/Dates	Last Penn.
142	Omaha GoldenSpikes (Royals)	81	60	.574	—	Ron Johnson	411,233 (64)	None
117	Colorado Springs Sky Sox (Rockies)	66	73	.475	14	Bill Hayes	202,724 (62)	1995
149	Albuquerque Dukes (Dodgers)	65	74	.468	15	Mike Scioscia	319,339 (67)	1994
96	Iowa Cubs (Cubs)	65	76	.461	16	Terry Kennedy	416,804 (65)	None

PACIFIC CONFERENCE

Page	SOUTH	W	L	PCT	GB	Manager	Attendance/Dates	Last Penn.
162	Salt Lake Buzz (Twins)	73	68	.518	—	Phil Roof	505,547 (63)	1979
222	Fresno Grizzlies (Giants)	73	69	.514	½	Ron Roenicke	311,804 (69)	None
216	Las Vegas Stars (Padres)	67	75	.472	6½	Mike Ramsey	339,702 (71)	1988
61	Tucson Sidewinders (Diamondbacks)	66	76	.465	7½	Chris Speier	254,817 (68)	1993

Page	WEST	W	L	PCT	GB	Manager	Attendance/Dates	Last Penn.
190	Vancouver Canadians (Athletics)	84	58	.592	—	Mike Quade	241,461 (63)	1999
228	Tacoma Rainiers (Mariners)	69	70	.496	13½	Dave Myers	271,026 (69)	1978
54	Edmonton Trappers (Angels)	65	74	.468	17½	Carney Lansford	385,913 (65)	1997
129	Calgary Cannons (Marlins)	57	82	.410	25½	Lynn Jones	269,002 (61)	None

PLAYOFFS—Semifinals: Oklahoma defeated Omaha 3-1 and Vancouver defeated Salt Lake 3-2 in best-of-5 series. **Finals:** Vancouver defeated Oklahoma 3-1 in best-of-5 series.

NOTE: Team's individual batting and pitching statistics can be found on page indicated in lefthand column.

Minor Leagues

Double-A Shreveport. That changed in '99 as he made his major league debut after starring for the Grizzlies.

"Most of it is maturity and learning," Murray said of his big season. "I always felt, especially the last two years, I've been going in the right direction."

The most significant single-game accomplishments of 1999 included two no-hitters: The Canadians, who gave their fans the ultimate going-away gift in September, were on the road when Terry Clark, Bill King and Anthony Chavez combined to no-hit New Orleans on April 13.

Clark, who had just two days' rest after giving up seven runs and two homers against Oklahoma, pitched four perfect innings. He was starting in place of Mike Oquist, who was called up by Oakland.

King, the winner, went the next four and lost the perfect game when Carlos Villalobos reached on an error in the sixth. Chavez walked Villalobos to lead off the ninth.

Salt Lake's Frank Rodriguez—yet another high profile draft pick now in his mid- to late 20s—later pitched a seven-inning no-hitter, beating Iowa 2-1 on May 8. Rodriguez lost the shutout in the first inning when Allen Battle reached on an error and ultimately scored.

Less than three weeks later, the Twins organization released Rodriguez and the Mariners picked him up.

A Little Less Buzz

Attendance was down from 5,959,104 fans to 5,233,932 in the second year of a 16-team PCL.

The Salt Lake Buzz (505,547) and New Orleans Zephyrs (472,865) finished 1-2 for the second straight season. The Zephyrs attendance dropped just 46,919, even as the team went from Triple-A's champions to

LARRY GOREN

Late-blooming Calvin Murray
Two-time first-round pick had his best pro season

the team with Triple-A's worst record (55-85).

Entering 2000, the PCL was preparing for one new city and two new stadiums. Sacramento will rejoin the PCL after a 23-year absence. On Aug. 30, stadium bond financing was approved for 10,000-seat Raley Field in West Sacramento.

The Memphis Redbirds will move from Tim McCarver Stadium to AutoZone Park, a project that cost an estimated $71 million and includes a new minor league museum. The ballpark will seat 14,000.

After the 2000 season, the exodus of Canadian teams will continue as the Calgary Cannons move to Portland, Ore.

"It is simply time to give up the fight," Calgary owner Russ Parker. "The constant battles with Calgary's unpredictable weather conditions, together with the challenges of playing in an outdated city baseball facility, are insurmountable obstacles for the franchise."

Portland's Civic Stadium, which currently houses a short-season Northwest League team, will undergo major renovations.

"We're well on our way to our ultimate goal—renovation of Civic Stadium and bringing affordable family entertainment to Portland," said Mike Higgins, general manager of Portland Family Entertainment—the group bringing Triple-A baseball back to Oregon after a five-year absence. "These are important milestones for the stadium, for the city and our entire community."

The Edmonton Trappers avoided the same fate as Calgary and Vancouver, as they were sold to a local group, the same people who own the Canadian Football League's Edmonton Eskimos.

If anyone else was in jeopardy, it was the Fresno Grizzlies. The club hadn't dug up a spade of dirt toward constructing a new stadium, and the parent Giants said they would pull the team out of Fresno after the 2000 season if a new stadium isn't under construction.

LEAGUE CHAMPIONS

Last 30 Years

Year	Regular Season*	Pct.	Playoff
1970	Hawaii (Angels)	.671	Spokane (Dodgers)
1971	Tacoma (Cubs)	.545	Salt Lake City (Angels)
1972	Albuquerque (Dodgers)	.622	Albuquerque (Dodgers)
1973	Tucson (Athletics)	.583	Spokane (Rangers)
1974	Spokane (Rangers)	.549	Spokane (Rangers)
1975	Hawaii (Padres)	.611	Hawaii (Padres)
1976	Salt Lake City (Angels)	.625	Hawaii (Padres)
1977	Phoenix (Giants)	.579	Phoenix (Giants)
1978	Tacoma (Yankees)	.584	Tacoma (Yankees)#
			Albuquerque (Dodgers)#
1979	Albuquerque (Dodgers)	.581	Salt Lake City (Angels)
1980	Tucson (Astros)	.595	Albuquerque (Dodgers)
1981	Albuquerque (Dodgers)	.712	Albuquerque (Dodgers)
1982	Albuquerque (Dodgers)	.594	Albuquerque (Dodgers)
1983	Albuquerque (Dodgers)	.594	Portland (Phillies)
1984	Hawaii (Pirates)	.621	Edmonton (Angels)
1985	Hawaii (Pirates)	.587	Vancouver (Brewers)
1986	Vancouver (Brewers)	.616	Las Vegas (Padres)
1987	Calgary (Mariners)	.596	Albuquerque (Dodgers)
1988	Albuquerque (Dodgers)	.605	Las Vegas (Padres)
1989	Albuquerque (Dodgers)	.563	Vancouver (White Sox)
1990	Albuquerque (Dodgers)	.641	Albuquerque (Dodgers)
1991	Albuquerque (Dodgers)	.580	Tucson (Astros)
1992	Colo. Springs (Indians)	.596	Colo. Springs (Indians)
1993	Portland (Twins)	.608	Tucson (Astros)
1994	Albuquerque (Dodgers)	.597	Albuquerque (Dodgers)
1995	Tucson (Astros)	.608	Colo. Springs (Rockies)
1996	Edmonton (Athletics)	.592	Edmonton (Athletics)
1997	Phoenix (Giants)	.615	Edmonton (Athletics)
1998	Iowa (Cubs)	.590	New Orleans (Astros)
1999	Vancouver (Athletics)	.592	Vancouver (Athletics)

*Best overall record   #Co-champions

1999 Pacific Coast League Statistics

CLUB BATTING

	AVG	G	AB	R	H	2B	3B	HR	BB	SO	SB
Colorado Springs	.297	139	4793	793	1422	303	28	194	437	1012	100
Fresno	.294	142	4857	849	1430	262	37	170	483	883	145
Tucson	.292	142	4885	766	1427	282	36	141	449	941	86
Salt Lake	.291	141	4736	814	1379	274	38	159	521	951	84
Omaha	.289	141	4828	826	1395	277	20	231	457	990	104
Nashville	.289	140	4757	806	1373	292	26	183	440	855	93
Albuquerque	.284	139	4703	742	1338	288	32	148	472	979	119
Memphis	.284	138	4666	743	1323	300	34	127	472	1017	110
Vancouver	.282	142	4740	759	1339	272	37	124	547	902	93
Oklahoma	.282	142	4819	787	1360	286	27	151	469	970	84
Calgary	.282	139	4703	716	1327	315	34	159	403	995	73
Tacoma	.281	139	4841	689	1359	272	35	102	488	949	121
Edmonton	.281	139	4767	730	1338	272	31	137	444	860	84
New Orleans	.270	140	4711	674	1270	266	19	118	454	914	75
Las Vegas	.264	142	4771	692	1261	297	31	135	560	1106	105
Iowa	.263	141	4800	699	1261	287	29	156	461	1093	116

CLUB PITCHING

	ERA	G	CG	SHO	SV	IP	H	R	ER	BB	SO
Vancouver	3.84	142	6	11	43	1229	1287	617	525	436	925
Tacoma	4.35	139	8	6	36	1232	1245	664	595	476	998
Nashville	4.48	140	4	1	43	1216	1328	708	606	464	1042
Oklahoma	4.65	142	16	5	43	1234	1349	696	638	456	900
Iowa	4.66	141	6	4	25	1242	1290	716	644	495	1014
Omaha	4.77	141	6	5	29	1226	1313	744	650	438	957
Fresno	4.91	142	5	2	29	1230	1327	800	672	499	1107
Edmonton	4.94	139	5	4	25	1213	1365	746	666	421	936
Memphis	4.98	138	3	6	37	1195	1298	738	662	459	945
New Orleans	5.03	140	7	6	31	1210	1332	750	676	416	851
Las Vegas	5.08	142	6	6	30	1231	1437	791	695	451	1057
Tucson	5.15	142	2	6	32	1222	1400	807	700	523	1013
Albuquerque	5.30	139	8	5	34	1206	1363	805	711	514	1023
Salt Lake	5.32	141	4	2	35	1204	1387	807	711	494	858
Colorado Springs	5.50	139	10	2	34	1193	1457	830	730	504	909
Calgary	5.84	139	4	2	22	1171	1424	866	760	511	882

CLUB FIELDING

TEAM	PCT	PO	A	E	DP		PCT	PO	A	E	DP
Oklahoma	.978	3701	1549	119	169	Calgary	.972	3513	1452	144	155
Memphis	.976	3586	1501	126	142	Colo. Spr.	.972	3580	1504	148	166
Edmonton	.976	3640	1471	127	139	N. Orleans	.971	3629	1503	151	109
Iowa	.976	3727	1540	131	118	Omaha	.971	3678	1331	148	132
Tacoma	.974	3695	1384	134	131	Salt Lake	.971	3611	1548	156	129
Vancouver	.974	3687	1434	137	164	Tucson	.970	3667	1493	157	142
Las Vegas	.974	3692	1396	138	136	Nashville	.970	3648	1498	160	128
Albuquerque	.973	3618	1469	141	148	Fresno	.969	3690	1443	163	118

INDIVIDUAL BATTING LEADERS
(Minimum 383 Plate Appearances)

	AVG	G	AB	R	H	2B	3B	HR	RBI	BB	SO	SB
Quinn, Mark, Omaha	.360	107	428	67	154	27	0	25	84	28	69	7
Murray, Calvin, Fresno	.334	130	548	122	183	31	7	23	73	49	88	42
Crespo, Felipe, Fresno	.332	112	385	98	128	27	5	24	84	78	73	17
Ramirez, Aramis, Nashville	.328	131	460	92	151	35	1	21	76	73	56	5
Valdes, Pedro, Oklahoma	.327	110	394	72	129	27	1	21	72	52	60	1
Kennedy, Adam, Memphis	.327	91	367	69	120	22	4	10	63	29	36	20
Woods, Ken, Fresno	.324	124	469	77	152	23	4	6	73	33	45	19
Wilson, Desi, Tucson	.323	130	452	65	146	27	7	6	62	34	76	2

INDIVIDUAL PITCHING LEADERS
(Minimum 114 Innings)

	W	L	ERA	G	GS	CG	SV	IP	H	R	ER	BB	SO
Bunch, Mel, Tacoma	10	2	3.10	21	19	1	0	125	112	53	43	40	117
Laxton, Brett, Vancouver	13	8	3.46	25	25	3	0	161	158	68	62	49	112
Fyhrie, Mike, Edmonton	9	5	3.47	19	18	0	0	114	90	47	44	40	113
Lorraine, Andrew, Iowa	9	8	3.71	22	21	1	0	143	149	67	59	34	96
Creek, Doug, Iowa	7	3	3.79	25	20	0	1	131	116	66	55	62	140
Anderson, Jimmy, Nashville	11	2	3.84	21	21	1	0	134	153	67	57	41	93
Figueroa, Nelson, Tucson	11	6	3.94	24	21	1	0	128	128	59	56	41	106
Luebbers, Larry, Memphis	13	4	4.03	21	19	1	0	130	134	61	58	33	84

ALL-STAR TEAM

C—Sal Fasano, Omaha. **1B**—J.R. Phillips, Colorado Springs. **2B**—Adam Kennedy, Memphis. **3B**—Kit Pellow, Omaha. **SS**—Scott Sheldon, Oklahoma. **OF**—Chad Hermansen, Nashville; Calvin Murray, Fresno; Mark Quinn, Omaha. **DH**—David Ortiz, Salt Lake. **Util**—Frank Menechino, Vancouver. **RHP**—Brett Laxton, Vancouver. **LHP**—Matt Perisho, Oklahoma. **RP**—David Wainhouse, Colorado Springs.

Most Valuable Player: Calvin Murray, Fresno. **Rookie of the Year:** Mark Quinn, Omaha. **Manager of the Year:** Greg Biagini, Oklahoma.

TOP 10 PROSPECTS

1. Rick Ankiel, lhp, Memphis; **2.** Ruben Mateo, of, Oklahoma; **3.** Aramis Ramirez, 3b, Nashville; **4.** Chad Hermansen, of, Nashville; **5.** Ben Davis, c, Las Vegas; **6.** Ben Petrick, c, Colorado Springs; **7.** Tim Hudson, rhp, Vancouver; **8.** Mark Mulder, lhp, Vancouver; **9.** Ramon Ortiz, rhp, Edmonton; **10.** Daryle Ward, 1b, New Orleans.

DEPT. LEADERS

BATTING
G	Mike Zywica, Oklahoma	135
AB	Calvin Murray, Fresno	548
R	Calvin Murray, Fresno	122
H	Calvin Murray, Fresno	183
TB	Calvin Murray, Fresno	297
XBH	David Ortiz, Salt Lake	68
	John Roskos, Calgary	68
2B	John Roskos, Calgary	44
3B	Three tied at	9
HR	J.R. Phillips, Colo. Springs	41
RBI	David Ortiz, Salt Lake	110
SH	Mike Moriarty, Salt Lake	11
SF	Four tied at	9
BB	Brad Seitzer, Tacoma	89
IBB	Frank Menechino, Van.	7
HBP	Sal Fasano, Omaha	26
SO	Tom Quinlan, Iowa	159
SB	Calvin Murray, Fresno	42
CS	Bo Porter, Iowa	17
GIDP	Jeff Ball, Vancouver	19
OB%	Felipe Crespo, Fresno	.447
SL%	Felipe Crespo, Fresno	.616

PITCHING
G	Scott Brow, Edmonton	64
GS	Three tied at	28
CG	Brandon Knight, Oklahoma	5
ShO	Brady Raggio, Oklahoma	2
GF	Eric Ludwick, Calgary	44
SV	David Wainhouse, Colo. Spr.	22
W	Matt Perisho, Oklahoma	15
L	Bob Scanlan, New Orleans	15
IP	Bryan Wolff, Las Vegas	178
H	Bob Scanlan, New Orleans	208
R	Ricky Stone, Albuquerque	123
ER	Bob Scanlan, New Orleans	102
	Ricky Stone, Albuquerque	102
HR	Bronswell Patrick, Fresno	33
HB	Doug Creek, Iowa	12
	Bob Scanlan, New Orleans	12
BB	Matt Perisho, Oklahoma	78
SO	Todd Van Poppel, Nashville	157
WP	Steve Connelly, Fresno	14
BK	Robinson Checo, Albuquerque	4
	Eddie Oropesa, Fresno	4

FIELDING
C	AVG	Mike Hubbard, Oklahoma	.994
	PO	Ken Huckaby, Tucson	695
	A	Raul Chavez, Tacoma	74
	E	Sal Fasano, Omaha	12
		Tim Laker, Nashville	12
	DP	Danny Ardoin, Vancouver	9
	PB	Ben Petrick, Colo. Spr.	14
1B	AVG	Andy Barkett, Oklahoma	.995
	PO	Andy Barkett, Oklahoma	1003
	A	J.R. Phillips, Colorado Spr.	114
	E	David Ortiz, Salt Lake	20
		Desi Wilson, Tucson	20
	DP	J.R. Phillips, Colo. Spr.	131
2B	AVG	Matt Howard, Nashville	.982
	PO	Dave Hajek, Colo. Spr.	262
	A	Dave Hajek, Colo. Spr.	341
	E	Adam Riggs, Albuquerque	21
	DP	Amaury Garcia, Calgary	90
3B	AVG	Tom Quinlan, Iowa	.963
	PO	Tom Quinlan, Iowa	85
	A	Tom Evans, Oklahoma	266
	E	Aramis Ramirez, Nash.	42
	DP	Tom Quinlan, Iowa	28
SS	AVG	Chris Petersen, Colo. Spr.	.961
	PO	Chris Petersen, Colo. Spr.	196
	A	Mike Moriarty, Salt Lake	426
	E	Mike Moriarty, Salt Lake	30
	DP	Chris Petersen, Colo. Spr.	94
OF	AVG	Bo Porter, Iowa	1.000
	PO	Norm Hutchins, Edmonton	294
	A	Jason Lariviere, Memphis	18
	E	Emil Brown, Nashville	10
	DP	Mike Zywica, Oklahoma	6

Minor Leagues

EASTERNLEAGUE

Good to last drop, Harrisburg claims fourth title in row

BY ANDREW LINKER

Been away for awhile? Trying to catch up? Well, if you last remembered the Harrisburg Senators as the Eastern League champions, you have not missed much.

The Senators, in the most turbulent of their 13 storied seasons in the EL, turned a losing team for most of the season into a playoff team just in time to win an unprecedented fourth straight title in 1999.

Along the way, the Senators became the league's first team in 25 years to forfeit a game, when they used an ineligible player in a June 21 game at Portland.

"It was definitely an original season," catcher Brian Schneider said.

It definitely ended with the most dramatic postseason in the league's history as each of the Senators' nine playoff games was decided by one run, with three of those games ending in the bottom of the ninth.

None was more dramatic than the deciding Game Five of the finals, where the Senators began the bottom of the ninth trailing 11-7 only to finish with a five-run rally that was capped by Milton Bradley's two-out, two-strike grand slam off EL saves leader Joe Lisio.

Bradley's slam gave the Senators their fourth straight title, their fifth in the last seven seasons and their sixth since professional baseball returned to Harrisburg in 1987.

"I've been through a lot of stuff this year," said Bradley, who missed 55 combined games between a suspension for spitting at an umpire, numerous injuries and his participation with Team USA in the Pan American Games. "But it's turned out pretty good."

The Senators reached the playoffs after winning 32 of their final 51 games following Doug Sisson's return as manager, a position he briefly abdicated after accepting a job as an assistant coach at the University of Georgia only to return a week later.

The Senators didn't move into playoff position until 26 days remained in the season. No player was hotter for Harrisburg than third baseman Andy Tracy, who after the all-star break collected 18 of his franchise-record 37 home runs and 53 of his league-leading 128 RBIs.

Norwich won 32 of its final 51 games before eliminating Trenton in the first round of the Northern Division playoffs. From July 2 to the end of the regular season, the Navigators had been down at least 10 games to 1999 Minor League Team of the Year Trenton, which finished 92-50 and won the most games in the EL since Harrisburg took 94 in 1993.

The league's regular season included a no-hitter by Reading Phillies righthander Adam Eaton in a 1-0 Norwich victory on June 22. The no-hitter was first in the EL by a losing pitcher since 1969.

Akron, in just its third season since relocating from Canton, again led the EL in attendance by nearly 75,000. A year after becoming the first team in Double-A history to reach the 500,000 plateau in attendance, the Aeros topped their 1998 gate by 1,300 to finish with 522,459.

As for the league's newcomers in a year in which the EL expanded from 10 to 12 teams, Erie averaged 3,496 fans and Altoona 4,695. Erie, which had been in the New York-Penn League prior to Double-A expansion, averaged 4,941 fans a game before going up from short-season ball.

Milton Bradley
Dream homer

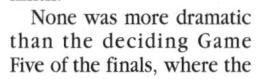

STANDINGS

Page	NORTH	W	L	PCT	GB	Manager	Attendance/Dates	Last Penn.
83	Trenton Thunder (Red Sox)	92	50	.648	—	DeMarlo Hale	440,033 (71)	None
175	Norwich Navigators (Yankees)	78	64	.549	14	Lee Mazzilli	244,442 (69)	None
130	Portland Sea Dogs (Marlins)	65	77	.458	27	Frank Cacciatore	402,582 (71)	None
229	New Haven Ravens (Mariners)	65	77	.458	27	Dan Rohn	197,163 (68)	None
162	New Britain Rock Cats (Twins)	59	82	.418	32 ½	John Russell	177,026 (66)	1983
183	Binghamton Mets (Mets)	54	88	.380	38	Doug Davis	203,674 (70)	1994
Page	SOUTH	W	L	PCT	GB	Manager(s)	Attendance/Dates	Last Penn.
55	Erie Seawolves (Angels)	81	61	.570	—	Garry Templeton	234,257 (67)	None
169	Harrisburg Senators (Expos)	76	66	.535	5	Doug Sisson/Rick Sweet	253,399 (66)	1999
197	Reading Phillies (Phillies)	73	69	.514	8	Gary Varsho	448,367 (70)	1995
76	Bowie BaySox (Orioles)	70	71	.496	10 ½	Joe Ferguson	421,398 (69)	None
111	Akron Aeros (Indians)	69	71	.493	11	Joel Skinner	522,459 (69)	None
204	Altoona Curve (Pirates)	67	73	.479	13	Marty Brown	323,932 (69)	None

PLAYOFFS—Semifinals: Norwich defeated defeated Trenton 3-2 and Harrisburg defeated Erie 3-1 in best-of-5 series. **Finals:** Harrisburg defeated Norwich 3-2 in best-of-5 series.

NOTE: Team's individual batting and pitching statistics can be found on page indicated in lefthand column.

1999 Eastern League Statistics

CLUB BATTING

	AVG	G	AB	R	H	2B	3B	HR	BB	SO	SB
Trenton	.279	142	4851	785	1352	251	23	150	495	801	151
Harrisburg	.268	142	4723	714	1265	256	29	140	543	910	119
Portland	.267	142	4774	646	1277	249	35	110	521	990	133
Akron	.265	140	4782	714	1266	248	40	132	495	1066	84
Norwich	.264	142	4766	755	1259	232	39	129	605	1129	168
Reading	.263	142	4710	680	1237	236	43	116	549	839	164
New Britain	.260	141	4730	611	1232	237	26	106	458	832	111
Bowie	.259	141	4798	676	1245	229	27	118	522	786	111
Erie	.258	142	4686	671	1210	234	41	110	581	1094	180
Altoona	.258	140	4723	695	1218	249	43	138	519	964	105
New Haven	.256	142	4754	610	1219	222	25	97	478	1000	110
Binghamton	.254	142	4789	635	1218	224	33	113	470	1130	168

CLUB PITCHING

	ERA	G	CG	SHO	SV	IP	H	R	ER	BB	SO
Erie	3.74	142	19	7	37	1249	1197	617	520	451	967
Trenton	3.85	142	7	17	42	1265	1200	603	541	453	986
New Haven	3.85	142	10	7	36	1244	1215	625	533	549	1059
Norwich	3.93	142	6	6	47	1242	1209	680	543	550	981
Altoona	4.07	140	4	5	32	1245	1252	680	563	570	935
Harrisburg	4.09	142	7	10	31	1233	1200	649	560	496	812
Bowie	4.28	141	9	7	33	1261	1264	670	600	534	989
Portland	4.29	142	2	5	39	1242	1301	708	593	520	1068
Binghamton	4.58	142	1	8	29	1256	1297	767	639	557	939
Akron	4.64	140	2	6	41	1216	1232	702	627	562	839
Reading	4.65	142	9	4	39	1250	1295	732	645	494	984
New Britain	4.78	141	7	9	30	1224	1336	759	651	500	982

CLUB FIELDING

	PCT	PO	A	E	DP		PCT	PO	A	E	DP
Trenton	.977	3796	1508	123	130	Erie	.971	3748	1485	154	128
Harrisburg	.974	3698	1517	140	138	Portland	.969	3726	1462	164	122
Bowie	.974	3782	1427	140	127	New Britain	.969	3673	1566	169	139
Reading	.972	3749	1515	151	103	Binghamton	.966	3767	1563	190	128
Akron	.972	3647	1501	148	126	Altoona	.965	3734	1606	194	126
New Haven	.972	3732	1538	152	147	Norwich	.960	3727	1381	212	121

INDIVIDUAL BATTING LEADERS
(Minimum 383 Plate Appearances)

	AVG	G	AB	R	H	2B	3B	HR	RBI	BB	SO	SB
Johnson, Nick, Norwich	.345	132	420	114	145	33	5	14	87	123	88	8
Gonzalez, Raul, Trenton	.335	127	505	80	169	33	4	18	103	51	71	12
Burrell, Pat, Reading	.333	117	417	84	139	28	6	28	90	79	103	3
Bradley, Milton, Harrisburg	.329	87	346	62	114	22	5	12	50	33	61	14
Hyzdu, Adam, Altoona	.316	91	345	64	109	26	2	24	78	40	62	8
Short, Rick, Bowie	.314	112	392	60	123	19	0	16	62	43	48	6
Tyner, Jason, Binghamton	.313	129	518	91	162	19	5	0	33	62	46	49
Eckstein, David, Trenton	.313	131	483	109	151	22	5	6	52	89	48	32
Soriano, Alfonso, Norwich	.305	89	361	57	110	20	3	15	68	32	67	24
Leon, Donny, Norwich	.302	118	457	69	138	34	2	21	100	34	102	0

INDIVIDUAL PITCHING LEADERS
(Minimum 114 Innings)

	W	L	ERA	G	GS	CG	SV	IP	H	R	ER	BB	SO
Ahearne, Pat, New Haven	8	3	2.61	17	17	4	0	124	114	41	36	27	80
Tejera, Michael, Portland	13	4	2.62	25	25	0	0	155	137	55	45	45	152
Armas, Tony, Harrisburg	9	7	2.89	24	24	2	0	150	123	62	48	55	106
Riley, Matt, Bowie	10	6	3.22	20	20	3	0	126	113	53	45	42	131
Thomas, Evan, Reading	9	5	3.25	36	15	1	3	127	123	53	46	50	103
Etherton, Seth, Erie	10	10	3.27	24	24	4	0	168	153	72	61	43	153
Cooper, Brian, Erie	10	5	3.30	22	22	6	0	158	146	61	58	29	143
Sekany, Jason, Trenton	14	4	3.35	27	22	3	0	161	143	65	50	64	116
Arroyo, Bronson, Altoona	15	4	3.65	25	25	2	0	153	167	73	62	58	100
Beverlin, Jason, Norwich	15	9	3.69	28	27	1	0	173	153	91	71	81	147

ALL-STAR TEAM

C—Brian Schneider, Harrisburg. **1B**—Nick Johnson, Norwich. **2B**—David Eckstein, Trenton. **3B**—Andy Tracy, Harrisburg. **SS**—Alfonso Soriano, Norwich. **OF**—Pat Burrell, Reading; Raul Gonzalez, Trenton; Scott Morgan, Akron; Julio Ramirez, Portland. **DH**—Chris Norton, Portland. **Util**—Larry Barnes, Erie. **RHP**—Tony Armas, Harrisburg; Brian Cooper, Erie. **LHP**—Matt Riley, Bowie; Michael Tejera, Portland. **RP**—Eric Cammack, Binghamton.

TOP 10 PROSPECTS

1. Pat Burrell, 1b-of, Reading; **2.** Alfonso Soriano, ss, Norwich; **3.** Nick Johnson, 1b, Norwich; **4.** Tony Armas, rhp, Harrisburg; **5.** Matt Riley, lhp, Bowie; **6.** Milton Bradley, of, Harrisburg; **7.** Julio Ramirez, of, Portland; **8.** Ramon Ortiz, rhp, Erie; **9.** Ryan Anderson, lhp, New Haven; **10.** Reggie Taylor, of, Reading.

DEPT. LEADERS

BATTING
G	Jamey Carroll, Harrisburg	141
AB	Julio Ramirez, Portland	568
R	Nick Johnson, Norwich	114
H	Raul Gonzalez, Trenton	169
TB	Andy Tracy, Harrisburg	276
XBH	Andy Tracy, Harrisburg	65
2B	Steve Hacker, New Britain	36
3B	Tike Redman, Altoona	12
HR	Chris Norton, Portland	38
RBI	Andy Tracy, Harrisburg	128
SH	Augie Ojeda, Bowie	25
SF	Larry Barnes, Erie	16
BB	Nick Johnson, Norwich	123
IBB	Larry Barnes, Erie	7
HBP	Nick Johnson, Norwich	37
SO	Bryon Gainey, Binghamton	184
SB	Julio Ramirez, Portland	64
CS	Donzell McDonald, Norwich	20
	Reggie Taylor, Reading	20
GIDP	Wilton Veras, Trenton	23
OB%	Nick Johnson, Norwich	.525
SL%	Chris Norton, Portland	.633

PITCHING
G	Joe Lisio, Norwich	59
GS	Paxton Crawford, Trenton	28
	Josh Towers, Bowie	28
CG	Brian Cooper, Erie	6
ShO	Several tied at	2
GF	Joe Lisio, Norwich	56
SV	Joe Lisio, Norwich	33
W	Bronson Arroyo, Altoona	15
	Jason Beverlin, Norwich	15
L	Joel Pineiro, New Haven	15
IP	Josh Towers, Bowie	189
H	Josh Towers, Bowie	204
R	Brett Herbison, Binghamton	115
ER	Brett Herbison, Binghamton	97
HR	Josh Towers, Bowie	26
HB	Christian Parker, Harrisburg	15
	Ken Pumphrey, Binghamton	15
BB	Brian OiConnor, Altoona	92
SO	Ryan Anderson, New Haven	162
WP	Brian OiConnor, Altoona	21
BK	Jim Baron, Altoona	5

FIELDING
C AVG	Brian Schneider, Harris.	.992
PO	Victor Valencia, Norwich	822
A	Brian Schneider, Harris.	91
E	Victor Valencia, Norwich	16
DP	Four tied at	7
PB	Lionel Hastings, Portland	18
1B AVG	Brendan Kingman, NH	.993
PO	Tommy Peterman, NB	1129
A	Tommy Peterman, NB	110
E	Nick Johnson, Norwich	20
DP	Tommy Peterman, NB	121
2B AVG	David Eckstein, Trenton	.985
PO	Carlos Casimiro, Bowie	281
A	Jamey Carroll, Harrisburg	379
E	Vick Brown, Norwich	25
	Adonis Harrison, NH	25
DP	Carlos Casimiro, Bowie	87
	David Eckstein, Trenton	87
3B AVG	Wilton Veras, Trenton	.945
PO	Shawn Wooten, Erie	91
A	Wilton Veras, Trenton	245
E	Donny Leon, Norwich	35
DP	Wilton Veras, Trenton	27
SS AVG	Augie Ojeda, Bowie	.969
PO	Luis Figueroa, Altoona	222
A	Jimmy Rollins, Reading	392
E	Luis Rivas, New Britain	37
DP	Tomas De la rosa, Harris.	83
OF AVG	Darrell Dent, Bowie	.994
PO	Julio Ramirez, Portland	326
A	Jake Weber, New Haven	15
E	Jayson Bass, New Haven	11
	Julio Ramirez, Portland	11
DP	Wady Almonte, Bowie	5

SOUTHERN LEAGUE

Rays win championship as sun sets on three stadiums

BY DAVID JENKINS

The 1999 Southern League season, when all is said and done, was one last, sometimes loving look at its past. Three of the SL's most storied stadiums—in Chattanooga, Knoxville and Orlando—enjoyed their last hurrahs with varied degrees of celebration.

In 2000, Chattanooga expects to have a new downtown stadium, Knoxville a new suburban, hillside home and Orlando a place in the Disney complex. Only Jacksonville's Wolfson Park will be more than 20 years old.

Not coincidentally, the three cities getting new ballparks ranked at the bottom of the league in attendance in '99. The most unwanted of those lame-duck fields, Orlando's Tinker Field, was the scene of a pennant celebration as

Brady Clark
SL batting champion

manager Bill Russell's Rays ran a gauntlet of travel and weather to claim the club's first SL pennant since 1991.

Russell had been cast out as Dodgers manager late in the 1998 season and was looking for a club to manage pretty much anywhere. He found a good one, as Orlando peaked at exactly the right moment. The Rays tied Jacksonville on the final day of the season, then beat the Suns in a one-game playoff to claim the second-half Eastern Division title.

Dodging two hurricanes along the way, the Toby Hall-led Rays defeated Knoxville in the first round and West Tenn in the finals, each series going three games to one. Hall, a catcher, punished the favored Diamond Jaxx (who won both halves of the West) by hitting .536 with 15 hits and seven RBIs in the championship series.

While Orlando claimed the league's top team award, Chattanooga outfielder Brady Clark doubled up on the league's top individual honors.

Clark, whose 1998 season was more than cut in half because of a stress fracture in his leg, was the second straight Lookouts player to win the SL batting championship. Additionally, he became the first Lookout to be named league MVP.

Following a 1998 season that saw the SL talent pool teeming with prospects, veteran observers rated 1999 as one of the least talented years for the league. So slim were the pickings that the consensus top prospect was Knoxville outfielder Vernon Wells, who spent all of 29 games in a Smokies uniform before moving up to Triple-A and eventually the Blue Jays.

Jacksonville closer Francisco Cordero, who likewise was in the big leagues before the season ended, earned the league's pitcher of the year award. Before going to the Tigers on Aug. 2, Cordero logged 27 saves while going 4-1 with a 1.38 ERA.

West Tenn's David Manning spun the league's only no-hitter, against Jacksonville on July 22 in a 1-0 win. His previous start July 17 against Huntsville, he came within one strike of another no-hitter.

Birmingham's Jeff Inglin earned the MVP award in the Southern League all-star game, which was held at West Tenn in June. At the Double-A all-star game at Mobile in July, BayBears outfielder John Curl gave the home team an MVP winner as his home run paved the way for a 3-0 win for the National League affiliates.

Minor Leagues

STANDINGS: SPLIT SEASON

FIRST HALF					SECOND HALF				
EAST	W	L	PCT	GB	EAST	W	L	PCT	GB
Knoxville	38	32	.543	—	Orlando	40	31	.563	—
Jacksonville	36	34	.514	2	Jacksonville	39	32	.549	1
Greenville	31	37	.456	6	Knoxville	33	37	.471	6½
Orlando	30	37	.448	6½	Carolina	29	41	.414	10½
Carolina	31	39	.443	7	Greenville	27	43	.386	12½
WEST	**W**	**L**	**PCT**	**GB**	**WEST**	**W**	**L**	**PCT**	**GB**
West Tenn	39	32	.549	—	West Tenn	45	25	.643	—
Huntsville	38	33	.535	1	Chattanooga	41	29	.586	4
Chattanooga	37	33	.529	1½	Birmingham	39	31	.557	6
Mobile	34	35	.493	4	Mobile	32	38	.457	13
Birmingham	34	36	.486	4½	Huntsville	26	44	.371	19

PLAYOFFS—Semifinals: West Tenn defeated Chattanooga 3-1 and Orlando defeated Knoxville 3-1 in best-of-5 series. **Finals:** Orlando defeated West Tenn 3-1 in best-of-5 series.

STANDINGS: OVERALL

Page		W	L	PCT	GB	Manager	Attendance/Dates	Last Penn.
97	West Tenn Diamond Jaxx (Cubs)	84	57	.596	—	Dave Trembley	302,203 (70)	None
104	Chattanooga Lookouts (Reds)	78	62	.557	5½	Phillip Wellman	218,946 (69)	1988
124	Jacksonville Suns (Tigers)	75	66	.532	9	Dave Anderson	233,630 (70)	1996
90	Birmingham Barons (White Sox)	73	67	.521	10½	Chris Cron	314,010 (70)	1993
236	Orlando Rays (Devil Rays)	70	68	.507	12½	Bill Russell	81,032 (62)	1999
250	Knoxville Smokies (Blue Jays)	71	69	.507	12½	Omar Malave	119,571 (67)	1978
217	Mobile BayBears (Padres)	66	73	.475	17	Mike Basso	293,147 (69)	1998
156	Huntsville Stars (Brewers)	64	77	.454	20	Darrell Evans	275,000 (68)	1994
118	Carolina Mudcats (Rockies)	60	80	.429	23½	Jay Loviglio	238,002 (66)	1995
69	Greenville Braves (Braves)	58	80	.420	24½	Paul Runge	257,171 (67)	1997

NOTE: Team's individual batting and pitching statistics can be found on page indicated in lefthand column.

1999 Southern League Statistics

CLUB BATTING

	AVG	G	AB	R	H	2B	3B	HR	BB	SO	SB
Orlando	.281	138	4695	686	1319	254	26	118	458	760	91
Knoxville	.278	140	4717	824	1312	274	29	151	666	860	122
Chattanooga	.277	140	4789	765	1327	270	35	147	530	919	130
Jacksonville	.276	141	4952	792	1367	305	31	149	561	1032	106
Birmingham	.268	140	4671	699	1253	229	38	101	491	883	160
Mobile	.264	139	4686	711	1235	265	36	116	570	1094	139
Greenville	.260	138	4558	640	1186	241	24	109	432	884	108
Carolina	.255	140	4587	597	1169	260	34	110	423	1017	103
West Tenn	.254	141	4648	646	1181	275	36	106	482	1044	144
Huntsville	.252	141	4698	646	1182	229	24	92	542	915	178

CLUB PITCHING

	ERA	G	CG	SHO	SV	IP	H	R	ER	BB	SO
West Tenn	3.58	141	8	9	45	1231	1115	579	489	590	1133
Birmingham	3.81	140	6	8	31	1207	1108	592	511	475	876
Chattanooga	4.23	140	3	8	35	1241	1308	682	583	533	948
Jacksonville	4.27	141	6	8	39	1252	1280	710	595	466	877
Carolina	4.32	140	8	7	38	1197	1249	685	575	489	1020
Huntsville	4.49	141	8	7	27	1241	1299	724	619	503	833
Knoxville	4.76	140	4	9	32	1222	1300	757	646	549	974
Orlando	4.78	138	5	11	33	1200	1259	742	638	469	953
Greenville	4.98	138	4	6	30	1186	1279	763	656	588	920
Mobile	5.09	139	7	6	30	1215	1334	772	687	493	874

CLUB FIELDING

	PCT	PO	A	E	DP		PCT	PO	A	E	DP
West Tenn	.974	3692	1330	135	119	Carolina	.969	3591	1426	159	102
Birmingham	.973	3622	1424	142	119	Mobile	.968	3644	1449	167	126
Huntsville	.972	3722	1525	150	133	Orlando	.968	3601	1341	163	127
Chattanooga	.972	3724	1583	155	160	Greenville	.968	3557	1445	168	130
Knoxville	.971	3667	1412	149	127	Jacksonville	.966	3757	1553	185	129

INDIVIDUAL BATTING LEADERS
(Minimum 378 Plate Appearances)

	AVG	G	AB	R	H	2B	3B	HR	RBI	BB	SO	SB
Clark, Brady, Chattanooga	.326	138	506	103	165	37	4	17	75	89	58	25
Williams, Jason, Chattanooga	.319	87	332	65	106	27	2	7	45	46	40	3
Giles, Tim, Knoxville	.311	133	505	76	157	24	2	18	114	56	93	0
Cardona, Javier, Jacksonville	.309	108	418	84	129	31	0	26	92	46	69	4
Gillespie, Eric, Jacksonville	.306	118	474	80	145	28	6	19	88	53	89	12
Smith, Demond, Greenville	.305	132	416	70	127	20	7	9	59	55	72	31
Solano, Fausto, Knoxville	.305	104	348	62	106	18	0	14	61	57	54	11
Bair, Rod, Carolina	.303	125	472	70	143	34	6	13	81	28	78	14
Carr, Dustin, Orlando	.302	125	461	76	139	22	3	6	63	70	62	7
Huff, Aubrey, Orlando	.301	133	491	85	148	40	3	22	78	64	77	2

INDIVIDUAL PITCHING LEADERS
(Minimum 112 Innings)

	W	L	ERA	G	GS	CG	SV	IP	H	R	ER	BB	SO
Yoder, Jeff, West Tenn	10	5	3.08	29	22	0	0	134	115	54	46	70	109
Roberts, Mark, Birmingham	5	8	3.40	33	17	0	2	124	108	64	47	41	84
Secoda, Jason, Birmingham	8	7	3.44	22	17	1	0	115	100	49	44	39	94
Santos, Victor, Jacksonville	12	6	3.49	28	28	2	0	173	150	86	67	58	146
Chantres, Carlos, Birm.	6	8	3.50	28	21	1	2	141	122	64	55	61	105
Darwin, David, Jacksonville	14	12	3.56	28	28	3	0	187	194	95	74	58	100
Walls, Doug, Carolina	10	9	3.65	26	26	2	0	150	159	74	61	44	140
Myette, Aaron, Birmingham	12	7	3.66	28	28	0	0	165	138	76	67	77	135
Martin, Chandler, Carolina	13	8	3.78	27	27	2	0	164	153	82	69	63	130
Lee, Derek, Huntsville	8	8	3.86	26	21	4	0	140	143	70	60	51	77

ALL-STAR TEAM

C—Javier Cardona, Jacksonville. **1B**—Julio Zuleta, West Tenn. **2B**—Dustin Carr, Orlando. **3B**—Aubrey Huff, Orlando. **SS**—Kevin Nicholson, Mobile. **OF**—Rod Bair, Carolina; Brady Clark, Chattanooga; John Curl, Mobile; Eric Gillespie, Jacksonville. **DH**—Tim Giles, Knoxville. **Util**—Adam Melhuse, Knoxville. **RHP**—Jeff Yoder, West Tenn. **LHP**—David Darwin, Jacksonville. **RP**—Francisco Cordero, Jacksonville.

Most Valuable Player: Brady Clark, Chattanooga. **Most Outstanding Pitcher:** Francisco Cordero, Jacksonville. **Manager of the Year:** Dave Trembley, West Tenn.

TOP 10 PROSPECTS

1. Vernon Wells, of, Knoxville; **2.** Francisco Cordero, rhp, Jacksonville; **3.** Kip Wells, rhp, Birmingham; **4.** Rob Bell, rhp, Chattanooga; **5.** Javier Cardona, c, Jacksonville; **6.** Wiki Gonzalez, c, Mobile; **7.** Alejandro Diaz, of, Chattanooga; **8.** Aaron Myette, rhp, Birmingham; **9.** Kevin Nicholson, ss, Mobile; **10.** Julio Zuleta, 1b, West Tenn.

DEPT. LEADERS

BATTING
G Brady Clark, Chattanooga 138
AB Brent Abernathy, Knoxville 577
R Brent Abernathy, Knoxville 108
H Brent Abernathy, Knoxville 168
TB Brady Clark, Chattanooga 261
XBH Aubrey Huff, Orlando 65
2B Scott Vieira, West Tenn 44
3B Ethan Faggett, Mobile 11
HR Javier Cardona, Jacksonville 26
RBI Tim Giles, Knoxville 114
SH Alex Sanchez, Orlando 10
SF Tim Giles, Knoxville 10
BB Adam Melhuse, Knoxville 108
IBB Adam Melhuse, Knoxville 7
HBP Julio Zuleta, West Tenn 20
SO John Curl, Mobile 137
SB Ethan Faggett, Mobile 63
CS Alex Sanchez, Orlando 26
GIDP Ryan Balfe, Mobile 18
OB% Adam Melhuse, Knoxville 454
SL% Javier Cardona, Jacksonville ...569

PITCHING
G Trevor Enders, Orlando 60
GS Five tied at 28
CG David Manning, West Tenn 6
ShO Three tied at 2
GF Francisco Cordero, Jacksonville . 43
SV Francisco Cordero, Jacksonville . 27
W David Darwin, Jacksonville 14
L Richard Dishman, Greenville 13
IP David Darwin, Jacksonville 187
H David Darwin, Jacksonville 194
R Todd Belitz, Orlando 108
ER Todd Belitz, Orlando 103
HR Isabel Giron, Mobile 29
HB Aaron Myette, Birmingham 15
BB Jim Crowell, Chattanooga 85
SO Victor Santos, Jacksonville 146
WP Randi Mallard, Chattanooga 15
BK Chandler Martin, Carolina 6

FIELDING
C **AVG** Josh Paul, Birmingham ..... .992
PO Brian Loyd, Knoxville 740
A Fernando Lunar, Green. 88
E Brian Loyd, Knoxville 17
DP Fernando Lunar, Green. 12
PB Jeff Alfano, Huntsville 23
1B **AVG** Rich Aude, Birmingham .... .995
PO Chris Kirgan, Carolina 1010
A Chris Kirgan, Carolina 91
E Chris Kirgan, Carolina 12
DP Brian Becker, Orlando 110
2B **AVG** Dustin Carr, Orlando .... .977
PO Brent Abernathy, Knox. 292
A Brent Abernathy, Knox. 361
E Pedro Santana, Jack. 20
DP Dustin Carr, Orlando 98
3B **AVG** Aubrey Huff, Orlando .... .927
PO Aubrey Huff, Orlando 93
A Rob Sasser, Jacksonville ... 276
E Rob Sasser, Jacksonville 35
DP Rob Sasser, Jacksonville 27
SS **AVG** Juan Sosa, Carolina .... .958
PO Juan Sosa, Carolina 191
A Kevin Nicholson, Mobile 402
E Eddy De los Santos, Orl. 39
DP Eddy De los Santos, Orl. 75
Kevin Nicholson, Mobile 75
OF **AVG** Demond Smith, Greenville .991
PO Kurt Airoso, Jacksonville 362
A Kurt Airoso, Jacksonville 12
Demond Smith, Greenville ... 12
E Alex Sanchez, Orlando 14
DP Adam Johnson, Greenville 4
Tyrone Pendergrass, Green. . 4

TEXASLEAGUE

Piatt's numbers, Wichita's wins baffle league opponents

BY GEORGE SCHROEDER

The statistics didn't tell the story. And even Minor League Manager of the Year John Mizerock struggled to explain his Wichita team's dominance in 1999.

The Wranglers swept both halves of the Texas League's Western Division, going 87-57, then swept through the playoffs to win the league title. They did it without many stars, and with mediocre statistics—Wichita's batting average (.280) and team ERA (4.27) each ranked fourth in the eight-team league.

"It's just something nobody can put a finger on," Mizerock said after the final victory. "People will come up to me and ask me why we're so good and I honestly answer, 'I don't know.' . . . It was something intangible. I guess you call it chemistry."

Call it anything, but it was clear Wichita was far and away the league's best team in 1999.

There were plenty of other success stories—the most notable being Midland third baseman Adam Piatt, who won only the second triple crown in league history. Piatt hit .345 with 39 homers and 135 RBIs.

Adam Piatt
Historic season

"I don't know how often triple crowns are won anywhere," league president Tom Kayser said. "It's part of his name now: Adam Piatt, who won the first triple crown in 72 years in the Texas League. And I think that's a wonderful thing."

Not everything was wonderful. While the Wranglers were celebrating their first title since 1992, members of the Jackson Generals front office were packing and preparing to vacate Smith-Wills Stadium. After 25 years in the league, the Generals will move to Round Rock, Texas, a suburb of Austin, in 2000.

Jackson's fate was sealed by years of low attendance. The franchise was sold to a group headed by baseball Hall of Famer Nolan Ryan and his son Reid during the 1998 season. Despite fielding a competitive team that was in the Eastern Division's pennant race until the final day, Jackson finished its final season with a league-low 99,240 attendance—56,176 fewer fans than seventh-place Shreveport.

Beginning in 2000, Wichita moves to the Eastern Division and Round Rock joins the Western Division. Also, the league has adopted a more balanced schedule in which teams will face every other team in each half.

The 1999 season featured plenty of prospects, led by everyone's favorite phenom, Minor League Player of the Year Rick Ankiel. The lefthander went 6-0 with a 0.91 ERA in eight starts as a 19-year-old at Arkansas.

Wichita didn't have a player among the league's top 10 batters, and its only pitcher in the top 10 in ERA was righthander Kiko Calero (8-3, 3.98). But third baseman Sean McNally hit 36 home runs and had 109 RBIs. Outfielder Dee Brown provided a significant second-half boost on his way to ranking second in a manager's poll of the league's Top 10 Prospects. Brown, reliever Lance Carter and shortstop Felix Martinez were promoted to the Royals.

Piatt was the overwhelming choice as the TL player of the year. San Antonio righthander Eric Gagne, who finished the season with the Dodgers, was the pitcher of the year; his season included a 10-1 roll during a 13-start stretch. Overall, Gagne went 12-4 with a league-leading 2.63 ERA.

STANDINGS: SPLIT SEASON

FIRST HALF					SECOND HALF				
EAST	W	L	PCT	GB	**EAST**	W	L	PCT	GB
Shreveport	39	29	.574	—	Tulsa	40	32	.556	—
Tulsa	34	34	.500	5	Jackson	38	34	.528	2
Arkansas	31	37	.456	8	Shreveport	32	40	.444	8
Jackson	30	38	.441	9	Arkansas	28	44	.389	12
WEST	W	L	PCT	GB	**WEST**	W	L	PCT	GB
Wichita	38	30	.559	—	Wichita	45	27	.625	—
Midland	36	32	.529	2	Midland	38	34	.528	7
El Paso	34	34	.500	4	San Antonio	37	35	.514	8
San Antonio	30	38	.441	8	El Paso	30	42	.417	15

PLAYOFFS—Semifinals: Tulsa defeated Shreveport 3-1 in best-of-5 series. **Finals:** Wichita defeated Tulsa 4-0 in best-of-7 series.

STANDINGS: OVERALL

Page		W	L	PCT	GB	Manager	Attendance/Dates	Last Penn.
143	Wichita Wranglers (Royals)	83	57	.593	—	John Mizerock	181,403 (66)	1999
243	Tulsa Drillers (Rangers)	74	66	.529	9	Bobby Jones	351,929 (66)	1998
191	Midland Rockhounds (Athletics)	74	66	.529	9	Tony DeFrancesco	176,369 (67)	1975
223	Shreveport Captains (Giants)	71	69	.507	12	Shane Turner	155,416 (67)	1995
137	Jackson Generals (Astros)	68	72	.486	15	Jim Pankovits	99,240 (70)	1996
150	San Antonio Missions (Dodgers)	67	73	.479	16	Jimmy Johnson	318,590 (68)	1997
62	El Paso Diablos (Diamondbacks)	64	76	.457	19	Don Wakamatsu	313,622 (65)	1994
211	Arkansas Travelers (Cardinals)	59	81	.421	24	Chris Maloney	191,346 (57)	1989

NOTE: Team's individual batting and pitching statistics can be found on page indicated in lefthand column.

1999 Texas League Statistics

CLUB BATTING

	AVG	G	AB	R	H	2B	3B	HR	BB	SO	SB
Midland	.294	140	4786	884	1406	311	48	164	586	916	138
El Paso	.284	140	4835	726	1375	303	46	107	416	986	88
San Antonio	.282	140	4733	710	1337	265	52	102	516	915	171
Wichita	.280	140	4596	785	1286	257	28	122	577	785	140
Tulsa	.265	140	4798	720	1272	284	38	132	491	910	130
Jackson	.257	140	4670	628	1199	233	23	133	402	918	127
Arkansas	.253	140	4405	527	1113	207	34	125	328	950	79
Shreveport	.249	140	4581	613	1140	222	32	89	484	944	103

CLUB PITCHING

	ERA	G	CG	SHO	SV	IP	H	R	ER	BB	SO
Shreveport	3.67	140	4	13	39	1208	1165	585	493	410	851
Jackson	3.76	140	2	10	39	1220	1183	632	510	465	988
Tulsa	4.12	140	7	10	36	1228	1218	666	563	487	984
Wichita	4.27	140	2	8	42	1197	1339	643	568	377	722
San Antonio	4.33	140	2	8	40	1212	1235	733	583	518	951
Arkansas	4.65	140	5	7	36	1153	1188	690	596	521	876
El Paso	4.69	140	8	7	31	1199	1352	741	625	470	944
Midland	5.66	140	3	2	35	1201	1448	903	756	552	958

CLUB FIELDING

	PCT	PO	A	E	DP		PCT	PO	A	E	DP
Shreveport	.973	3625	1551	142	121	Jackson	.965	3659	1482	185	121
Arkansas	.970	3459	1467	153	143	El Paso	.965	3596	1509	184	115
Wichita	.969	3590	1543	162	146	Midland	.962	3603	1517	204	124
Tulsa	.967	3685	1499	175	114	San Antonio	.961	3637	1398	202	117

INDIVIDUAL BATTING LEADERS
(Minimum 378 Plate Appearances)

	AVG	G	AB	R	H	2B	3B	HR	RBI	BB	SO	SB
Piatt, Adam, Midland	.345	129	476	128	164	48	3	39	135	93	101	7
DaVanon, Jeff, Midland	.342	100	374	87	128	29	11	11	60	53	68	18
Espada, Josue, Midland	.338	113	435	85	147	15	2	6	51	62	51	22
Mota, Tony, San Antonio	.325	98	345	65	112	31	2	15	75	41	56	13
Lamb, Mike, Tulsa	.324	137	544	98	176	51	5	21	100	53	65	4
Lugo, Julio, Jackson	.319	116	445	77	142	24	5	10	42	44	53	25
Barajas, Rod, El Paso	.318	127	510	77	162	41	2	14	95	24	73	2
Encarnacion, Mario, Midland	.309	94	353	69	109	21	4	18	71	47	86	9
Ametller, Jesus, Arkansas	.307	116	397	53	122	26	2	10	53	5	21	2
Moreta, Ramon, San Antonio	.305	127	397	56	121	13	3	2	42	18	66	26

INDIVIDUAL PITCHING LEADERS
(Minimum 112 Innings)

	W	L	ERA	G	GS	CG	SV	IP	H	R	ER	BB	SO
Gagne, Eric, San Antonio	12	4	2.63	26	26	0	0	168	122	55	49	64	185
McKnight, Tony, Jackson	9	9	2.75	24	24	0	0	160	134	60	49	44	118
Robertson, Jeriome, Jackson	15	9	3.06	28	28	1	0	191	184	81	65	45	133
Knoll, Brian, Shreveport	9	7	3.51	33	17	1	1	128	117	54	50	34	91
Heckman, Andy, Shreveport	10	6	4.08	23	23	1	0	132	142	67	60	43	70
Calero, Kiko, Wichita	9	3	4.11	26	23	1	1	129	143	67	59	57	92
Norris, Ben, El Paso	10	6	4.16	20	20	0	0	119	132	61	55	53	87
Davis, Allen, San Antonio	7	10	4.22	29	20	1	0	130	140	83	61	46	87
Dewitt, Matt, Arkansas	9	8	4.43	26	26	0	0	148	153	87	73	59	107
Lee, Corey, Tulsa	8	5	4.44	22	22	0	0	128	132	76	63	44	121

ALL-STAR TEAM

C—Rod Barajas, El Paso. **1B**—T.R. Marcinczyk, Midland; Chris Richard, Arkansas. **2B**—Tom Sergio, Tulsa. **3B**—Adam Piatt, Midland. **SS**—Julio Lugo, Jackson. **OF**—Jeff DaVanon, Midland; Mario Encarnacion, Midland; Tony Mota, San Antonio. **DH**—Sean McNally, Wichita. **Util**—Josue Espada, Midland; Mike Lamb, Tulsa. **RHP**—Eric Gagne, San Antonio; Tony McKnight, Jackson. **LHP**—Rick Ankiel, Arkansas; Jason Davis, Shreveport; Corey Lee, Tulsa.

Most Valuable Player: Adam Piatt, Midland. **Pitcher of the Year:** Eric Gagne, San Antonio. **Manager of the Year:** John Mizerock, Wichita.

TOP 10 PROSPECTS

1. Rick Ankiel, lhp, Arkansas; **2.** Dee Brown, of, Wichita; **3.** Erubiel Durazo, 1b, El Paso; **4.** John Patterson, rhp, El Paso; **5.** Brad Penny, rhp, El Paso; **6.** Eric Gagne, rhp, San Antonio; **7.** Chad Harville, rhp, Midland; **8.** Tony McKnight, rhp, Jackson; **9.** Adam Piatt, 3b, Midland; **10.** Chad Hutchinson, rhp, Arkansas.

DEPT. LEADERS

BATTING
G	Brent Butler, Arkansas	139
	Luis Saturria, Arkansas	139
AB	Mike Lamb, Tulsa	544
R	Adam Piatt, Midland	128
H	Mike Lamb, Tulsa	176
TB	Adam Piatt, Midland	335
XBH	Adam Piatt, Midland	90
2B	Mike Lamb, Tulsa	51
3B	Luke Allen, San Antonio	12
HR	Adam Piatt, Midland	39
RBI	Adam Piatt, Midland	135
SH	Alejandro Prieto, Wichita	13
SF	Chris Truby, Jackson	12
BB	Sean McNally, Wichita	93
	Adam Piatt, Midland	93
IBB	Adam Piatt, Midland	10
HBP	Hiram Bocachica, San Antonio	13
SO	Jamie Gann, El Paso	141
SB	Mike Metcalfe, San Antonio	57
CS	Mike Metcalfe, San Antonio	21
GIDP	Pedro Feliz, Shreveport	18
OB%	Adam Piatt, Midland	.451
SL%	Adam Piatt, Midland	.704

PITCHING
G	Matt Montgomery, SA	58
GS	Bryan Braswell, Jackson	28
	Jeriome Robertson, Jackson	28
CG	Eric Knott, El Paso	3
ShO	Several tied at	1
GF	Matt Montgomery, SA	56
SV	Matt Montgomery, SA	26
W	Jeriome Robertson, Jackson	15
L	Derek Root, Jackson	16
IP	Jeriome Robertson, Jackson	191
H	Eric Knott, El Paso	198
R	Luke Prokopec, San Antonio	113
ER	Luke Prokopec, San Antonio	95
HR	Bryan Braswell, Jackson	27
HB	Robbie Beckett, San Antonio	13
	Mike Walter, Jackson	13
BB	Chad Hutchinson, Arkansas	85
SO	Eric Gagne, San Antonio	185
WP	Chad Hutchinson, Arkansas	20
BK	Jeriome Robertson, Jackson	7

FIELDING
C	AVG	Willie Morales, Midland	.996
	PO	Rod Barajas, El Paso	787
	A	Rod Barajas, El Paso	95
	E	Rod Barajas, El Paso	14
	DP	Paul Phillips, Wichita	10
	PB	Cesar King, Tulsa	17
1B	AVG	Damon Minor, Shreveport	.993
	PO	Damon Minor, Shreveport	1160
	A	Damon Minor, Shreveport	104
	E	T.R. Marcinczyk, Midland	16
	DP	Chris Richard, Arkansas	119
2B	AVG	Travis Young, Shreveport	.974
	PO	Tom Sergio, Tulsa	288
	A	Tom Sergio, Tulsa	346
	E	Hiram Bocachica, SA	31
	DP	Hiram Bocachica, SA	77
		Travis Young, Shreveport	77
3B	AVG	Chris Truby, Jackson	.950
	PO	Chris Truby, Jackson	93
	A	Pedro Feliz, Shreveport	304
	E	Luke Allen, San Antonio	53
	DP	Chris Truby, Jackson	35
SS	AVG	Julius Matos, El Paso	.953
	PO	Julius Matos, El Paso	197
	A	Juan Bautista, Tulsa	378
	E	Juan Bautista, Tulsa	64
	DP	Julius Matos, El Paso	65
OF	AVG	Chris Magruder, Shreve.	.988
	PO	Goefrey Tomlinson, Wich.	313
	A	Jeremy Dodson, Wichita	20
	E	Cordell Farley, Arkansas	10
	DP	Jeremy Dodson, Wichita	6

Minor Leagues

CALIFORNIA LEAGUE

Chen leads Stampede to playoffs; teammates finish job

BY LANCE PUGMIRE

Surviving a three-series postseason without its best player, San Bernardino won its second California League championship in three years in 1999.

In Game Five of the final series against defending champion San Jose, Stampede second baseman and leadoff hitter Eric Riggs, who hit .435 in postseason play, contributed the deciding RBI double in the eighth inning of a 2-1 win. San Bernardino closer Bill Everly stranded a San Jose runner at second in the ninth for his fourth playoff save after tallying a league record-tying 34 during the regular season.

The Stampede won the playoffs without left fielder Chin-Feng Chen, a 22-year-old who became the first Taiwanese player in nearly a quarter-century to play in a major league organization. He became the first Cal League player with 30 home runs and 30 stolen bases in a season just in time: With two games left in the regular year, he had to leave for the Asian qualifying tournament for the 2000 Sydney Olympics.

Chin-Feng Chen
First 30-30 player

Taiwan didn't quite make the Olympics, but the Dodgers were happy to let the league's No. 1 prospect play for his country. The move didn't even wind up hurting the Stampede, who became the league's first repeat winner since Reno in 1975-76.

In addition to stealing 31 bases and hitting 31 homers, Chen batted .316 with 123 RBIs, tying Modesto first baseman Jason Hart and Visalia first baseman Todd Mensik for the RBI title.

San Bernardino was one strike away from bowing out in the Southern Division championship series against first-half champion Rancho Cucamonga, which reeled off a club-record 11-game winning streak during a 23-3 June.

Quakes closer Angel Aragon, however, couldn't record that final strike, walking a man to load the bases in Game Four and then permitting a two-out, two-run single by Stampede catcher Will McCrotty to end a 4-3 game. McCrotty also homered to win and end Game One of the series.

The league experienced a return to its power-hitting reputation in 1999. Modesto swatted a league-record eight home runs in a regular season game at San Jose and Rancho Cucamonga and Lancaster each hit seven in a game.

Individually, High Desert outfielder Jack Cust, a 1997 first-round pick, led the league in home runs, slugging percentage and on-base percentage while finishing second in batting and fourth in RBIs. The Mavericks won a league-best 15 consecutive games, tying Nashville's string for best in the minors in 1999.

San Bernardino's Marcos Castillo fired the only no-hitter in a 4-0 win over Lake Elsinore on June 14.

Stockton manager Bernie Moncallo was fired during the season as then-Brewers farm director Cecil Cooper witnessed a loss influenced by the manager's incorrect handling of a lineup card.

STANDINGS: SPLIT SEASON

FIRST HALF					SECOND HALF				
NORTH	**W**	**L**	**PCT**	**GB**	**NORTH**	**W**	**L**	**PCT**	**GB**
Modesto	44	26	.629	—	Modesto	44	26	.629	—
San Jose	38	32	.543	6	Visalia	43	27	.614	1
Bakersfield	36	34	.514	8	San Jose	37	33	.529	7
Stockton	34	36	.486	10	Bakersfield	28	42	.400	16
Visalia	32	38	.457	12	Stockton	23	47	.329	21
SOUTH	**W**	**L**	**PCT**	**GB**	**SOUTH**	**W**	**L**	**PCT**	**GB**
R.Cucamonga	42	28	.600	—	San Bern.	39	32	.549	—
San Bern.	41	29	.586	1	High Desert	38	33	.535	1
Lake Elsinore	30	40	.429	12	R.Cucamonga	34	36	.486	4½
High Desert	30	40	.429	12	Lake Elsinore	33	37	.471	5½
Lancaster	23	47	.329	19	Lancaster	32	38	.457	6½

PLAYOFFS—First Round: San Bernardino defeated High Desert and San Jose defeated Visalia 2-1 in best-of-3 series. **Semifinals:** San Bernardino defeated Rancho Cucamonga 3-2 and San Jose defeated Modesto 3-2 in best-of-5 series. **Finals:** San Bernardino defeated San Jose 3-2 in best-of-5 series.

STANDINGS: OVERALL

Page		W	L	PCT	GB	Manager(s)	Attendance/Dates	Last Penn.
191	Modesto A's (Athletics)	88	52	.629	—	Bob Geren	133,757 (68)	1984
150	San Bernardino Stampede (Dodgers)	80	61	.567	8½	Rick Burleson	167,437 (69)	1999
217	Rancho Cucamonga Quakes (Padres)	76	64	.543	12	Tom LeVasseur	321,682 (69)	1994
192	Visalia Oaks (Athletics)	75	65	.536	13	Juan Navarrete	65,538 (67)	1978
224	San Jose Giants (Giants)	75	65	.536	13	Lenn Sakata	157,598 (70)	1998
63	High Desert Mavericks (Diamondbacks)	68	73	.482	20½	Derek Bryant	146,772 (70)	1997
224	Bakersfield Blaze (Giants)	64	76	.457	24	Keith Comstock	107,747 (70)	1989
56	Lake Elsinore Storm (Angels)	63	77	.450	25	Mario Mendoza	282,533 (70)	1996
157	Stockton Ports (Brewers)	57	83	.407	31	B. Moncallo/C. Ponce	73,702 (68)	1992
230	Lancaster JetHawks (Mariners)	55	85	.393	33	Darrin Garner	218,479 (69)	None

NOTE: Team's individual batting and pitching statistics can be found on page indicated in lefthand column.

Minor Leagues

1999 California League Statistics

CLUB BATTING

	AVG	G	AB	R	H	2B	3B	HR	BB	SO	SB
High Desert	.293	141	4941	903	1449	268	51	159	583	1116	140
Modesto	.289	140	4885	872	1410	300	63	120	575	1075	193
San Bernardino	.287	141	4936	764	1416	224	57	95	517	918	145
Lancaster	.279	140	4892	812	1363	249	43	142	500	1112	137
Visalia	.274	140	4791	871	1312	259	39	132	701	1044	154
R. Cucamonga	.273	140	4755	715	1300	237	33	100	484	1016	136
Lake Elsinore	.273	140	4831	753	1320	274	61	92	496	1034	190
Stockton	.268	140	4787	654	1283	223	43	78	406	991	126
Bakersfield	.268	140	4786	685	1281	224	43	66	478	1116	187
San Jose	.264	140	4780	722	1260	254	28	126	529	1143	134

CLUB PITCHING

	ERA	G	CG	SHO	SV	IP	H	R	ER	BB	SO
R. Cucamonga	3.85	140	6	11	38	1233	1198	619	527	425	1110
Modesto	4.18	140	0	7	54	1246	1310	734	579	544	1099
San Jose	4.22	140	2	4	38	1227	1264	704	575	526	1068
San Bernardino	4.34	141	3	8	46	1266	1321	697	611	546	1126
Stockton	4.59	140	9	8	34	1228	1316	802	627	523	1048
Lake Elsinore	4.62	140	21	9	19	1239	1385	771	637	481	999
Bakersfield	4.81	140	3	2	33	1230	1329	787	658	493	926
Visalia	4.95	140	1	3	38	1235	1376	832	680	577	1118
High Desert	5.44	141	0	0	28	1231	1391	890	744	621	1099
Lancaster	5.74	140	4	4	21	1223	1504	915	780	533	972

CLUB FIELDING

	PCT	PO	A	E	DP		PCT	PO	A	E	DP
San Bern.	.972	3798	1440	151	112	Visalia	.963	3706	1507	199	106
R. Cuca.	.970	3698	1510	163	122	Stockton	.962	3684	1392	202	113
San Jose	.967	3681	1584	182	122	Modesto	.960	3738	1540	219	111
Lancaster	.967	3669	1440	177	138	Bakersfield	.959	3691	1514	225	123
Lake Elsinore	.964	3717	1613	197	137	High Desert	.958	3693	1427	225	125

INDIVIDUAL BATTING LEADERS

(Minimum 378 Plate Appearances)

	AVG	G	AB	R	H	2B	3B	HR	RBI	BB	SO	SB
Byrnes, Eric, Modesto	.337	96	365	86	123	28	1	6	66	58	37	28
Cust, Jack, High Desert	.334	125	455	107	152	42	3	32	112	96	145	1
Martinez, Belvani, HD	.333	109	477	84	159	23	9	8	55	18	69	35
Otero, William, San Jose	.333	96	402	81	134	28	3	10	56	37	67	20
Hammock, Robert, HD	.332	114	379	80	126	20	7	9	72	47	63	3
Nieves, Wilbert, R. Cuca.	.328	120	427	58	140	26	2	7	61	40	54	2
Clark, Doug, Bakersfield	.326	118	420	67	137	17	2	11	58	59	89	17
Thomas, Gary, Modesto	.323	99	344	69	111	14	4	7	38	33	45	23
Gorr, Robb, San Bernardino	.319	132	546	67	174	22	6	11	106	30	59	5
Gonzalez, Jimmy, SB	.316	111	471	78	149	28	6	5	53	20	55	9

INDIVIDUAL PITCHING LEADERS

(Minimum 112 Innings)

	W	L	ERA	G	GS	CG	SV	IP	H	R	ER	BB	SO
Dorame, Randey, San Bern.	14	3	2.51	24	24	1	0	154	130	52	43	37	159
Serrano, Wascar, R. Cuca.	9	8	3.33	21	21	1	0	132	110	58	49	43	129
Colome, Jesus, Modesto	8	4	3.36	31	22	0	1	129	125	63	48	60	127
Lawrence, Brian, R. Cuca.	12	8	3.39	27	27	4	0	175	178	72	66	30	166
Wagner, Denny, Modesto	7	4	3.56	27	15	0	3	114	116	57	45	42	99
Kramer, Aaron, R. Cuca.	9	9	3.63	23	23	0	0	139	154	73	56	31	98
Zerbe, Chad, Bakersfield	7	7	3.64	21	21	0	0	126	124	66	51	33	81
Guttormson, Rick, R. Cuca.	14	9	3.72	28	28	1	0	174	165	83	72	36	125
Prata, Danny, Bakersfield	9	9	3.91	27	27	0	0	143	143	80	62	54	87
Green, Steve, Lake Elsinore	7	6	3.95	19	19	4	0	121	130	70	53	37	91

ALL-STAR TEAM

C—Wilbert Nieves, Rancho Cucamonga. **1B**—Robb Gorr, San Bernardino. **2B**—Belvani Martinez, High Desert. **3B**—Jacques Landry, Modesto. **SS**—Nelson Castro, Lake Elsinore; Alex Cintron, High Desert. **OF**—Eric Byrnes, Modesto; Chin-Feng Chen, San Bernardino; Jack Cust, High Desert. **DH**—Todd Mensik, Visalia. **P**—Randey Dorame, San Bernardino; Bill Everly, San Bernardino; Rick Guttormson, Rancho Cucamonga; Scot Shields, Lake Elsinore.

Most Valuable Player: Chin-Feng Chen, San Bernardino. **Pitcher of the Year:** Randey Dorame, San Bernardino. **Rookie of the Year:** Chin-Feng Chen, San Bernardino. **Manager of the Year:** Bob Geren, Modesto.

TOP 10 PROSPECTS

1. Chin-Feng Chen, of, San Bernardino; **2.** Abraham Nunez, of, High Desert; **3.** Jack Cust, of, High Desert; **4.** Barry Zito, lhp, Visalia; **5.** Wascar Serrano, rhp, Rancho Cucamonga; **6.** Jesus Colome, rhp, Modesto; **7.** Miguel Olivo, c, Modesto; **8.** Jake Esteves, rhp, San Jose; **9.** Scot Shields, rhp, Lake Elsinore; **10.** Eric Byrnes, of, Modesto.

DEPT. LEADERS

BATTING

G	Tony Zuniga, San Jose	136
AB	Jason Hart, Modesto	550
R	Jermaine Clark, Lancaster	112
H	Robb Gorr, San Bernardino	174
TB	Jacques Landry, Modesto	297
XBH	Jacques Landry, Modesto	79
2B	Jason Hart, Modesto	48
3B	Oscar Salazar, Modesto	18
HR	Jack Cust, High Desert	32
RBI	Three tied at	123
SH	Alex Cintron, High Desert	17
SF	Mark Cridland, Stockton	16
BB	Esteban German, Modesto	102
IBB	Todd Mensik, Visalia	11
HBP	Darren Blakely, Lake Elsinore	20
SO	Tim Flaherty, San Jose	168
SB	Nelson Castro, Lake Elsinore	53
CS	Belvani Martinez, High Desert	30
GIDP	Alex Pelaez, Rancho Cuca.	24
OB%	Jack Cust, High Desert	.450
SL%	Jack Cust, High Desert	.651

PITCHING

G	Bill Everly, San Bernardino	60
	Ray Noriega, Visalia	60
GS	Steve Fish, Lake Elsinore	29
CG	Paul Stewart, Stockton	5
	Steve Fish, Lake Elsinore	5
ShO	Steve Green, Lake Elsinore	4
GF	Bill Everly, San Bernardino	57
SV	Bill Everly, San Bernardino	34
W	Three tied at	14
L	Manny Bermudez, Bakersfield	14
IP	Steve Fish, Lake Elsinore	197
H	Steve Fish, Lake Elsinore	220
R	Steve Fish, Lake Elsinore	125
ER	Steve Fish, Lake Elsinore	107
HR	Tony Coscia, Bakersfield	25
HB	Manny Bermudez, Bakersfield	18
BB	Lance Caraccioli, San Bern.	126
SO	Steve Fish, Lake Elsinore	180
WP	Tom Bennett, Visalia	39
BK	Three tied at	5

FIELDING

C	AVG	Wilbert Nieves, RC	.995
	PO	Wilbert Nieves, RC	902
	A	Brian Moon, Stockton	129
	E	Robert Hammock, HD	18
	DP	Robert Hammock, HD	11
		Brian Moon, Stockton	11
	PB	Javier Flores, Visalia	23
1B	AVG	Robb Gorr, San Bern.	.994
	PO	Jason Hart, Modesto	1147
	A	Robb Gorr, San Bern.	114
	E	Tim Flaherty, San Jose	18
	DP	Tim Flaherty, San Jose	103
2B	AVG	Jermaine Clark, Lancaster	.983
	PO	Jermaine Clark, Lancaster	243
	A	Jermaine Clark, Lancaster	346
	E	Esteban German, Modesto	38
	DP	Jermaine Clark, Lancaster	92
3B	AVG	Tony Zuniga, San Jose	.929
	PO	Jeff Deardorff, Stockton	91
	A	Tony Zuniga, San Jose	312
	E	Jeff Deardorff, Stockton	36
	DP	Tony Zuniga, San Jose	33
SS	AVG	Nelson Castro, LE	.962
	PO	Alex Cintron, High Desert	223
	A	Nelson Castro, LE	370
	E	Chris Rowan, Stockton	45
	DP	Nelson Castro, LE	74
OF	AVG	Rusty Keith, Visalia	.995
	PO	Harvey Hargrove, Lan.	273
		Brandon Pernell, RC	273
	A	Abraham Nunez, HD	20
	E	Abraham Nunez, HD	14
	DP	Five tied at	3

CAROLINA LEAGUE

Wilmington, Myrtle Beach swim to co-championship

BY DAVE UTNIK

The Carolina League finished its 1999 season without an undisputed champion for the first time in its 54-year history. The threat of Hurricane Floyd forced the largest peacetime evacuation in U.S. history along the southern Atlantic coast and prompted the league to cancel the deciding game of its championship series in Myrtle Beach.

"It was gut-wrenching for me to walk away from the very game you've spent all season trying to get to," Carolina League president John Hopkins said. "Everybody wanted to play, but with one of history's biggest hurricanes bearing down on us, we decided to err on the side of the safety of the players."

Pelicans' Marcus Giles
CL MVP

The championship series between Myrtle Beach and Wilmington was tied at two games apiece with the fifth and final game scheduled to be played at Myrtle Beach's Coastal Federal Field on Sept. 14. But after approximately 2.6 million people were urged to evacuate along the coastlines of Florida, Georgia and South Carolina in anticipation of the ferocious storm, Hopkins officially declared the Pelicans and Blue Rocks co-champions.

The first shared championship in the Carolina League allowed Wilmington to claim its fourth title in seven years. Myrtle Beach became the third team in league history, and the first since Hagerstown in 1981, to win a title in its first season. The Pelicans, who relocated to Myrtle Beach after spending 1998 in Danville, Va., were also the first Braves affiliate in 22 seasons to capture a Carolina League championship. They had won 11 of their last 13 regular-season games to take the Southern Division's second-half crown.

Led by league batting champion and MVP Marcus

Giles, Myrtle Beach went on to defeat first-half champion Kinston in the divisional playoffs before challenging Wilmington in the Mills Cup series.

The Blue Rocks continued to dominate the league by drawing a league-high 321,143 fans to Frawley Stadium and winning both halves in the Northern Division for the second straight season. Returning to the finals was a remarkable feat considering that their best players—outfielder Dee Brown and righthander Jeff Austin, among others—were promoted to Double-A at midseason.

In mid-July, the Blue Rocks dropped 11 consecutive games on the road and were mired in last place.

"We finished the first half on a downer and we didn't start well in the second half," Wilmington manager Jeff Garber said. "We were kind of losing our chemistry. Some of the guys had to take on new roles and we had to find a different way to win."

While the Blue Rocks and Pelicans were making team history, Potomac's Andy Bevins and Salem's Josh Kalinowski flirted with triple crown seasons.

Bevins, who hit three grand slams during the season, captured the league home run (25) and RBI titles (97), but an August hitting slump prevented him from challenging Giles for the batting crown. Kalinowski was named the league's pitcher of the year after posting a 2.11 ERA and 176 strikeouts. Only Tim Drew's 13-win season for Kinston kept Kalinowski from leading all three categories.

STANDINGS: SPLIT SEASON

FIRST HALF

NORTH	W	L	PCT	GB
Wilmington	39	30	.565	—
Frederick	37	33	.529	2½
Lynchburg	35	34	.507	4
Potomac	24	45	.348	15

SOUTH	W	L	PCT	GB
Kinston	37	32	.536	—
Winston-Salem	36	33	.522	1
Myrtle Beach	35	34	.507	2
Salem	34	36	.486	3½

SECOND HALF

NORTH	W	L	PCT	GB
Wilmington	38	31	.551	—
Frederick	30	38	.441	7½
Potomac	30	40	.429	8½
Lynchburg	29	39	.426	8½

SOUTH	W	L	PCT	GB
Myrtle Beach	44	26	.629	—
Kinston	42	26	.618	1
Salem	35	33	.515	8
Winston-Salem	27	42	.391	16½

PLAYOFFS—Semifinals: Myrtle Beach defeated Kinston 2-1 in best-of-3 series. **Final:** Final game of best-of-5 championship series cancelled due to Hurricane Floyd; Wilmington and Myrtle Beach declared co-champions.

STANDINGS: OVERALL

Page		W	L	PCT	GB	Manager	Attendance/Dates	Last Penn.
112	Kinston Indians (Indians)	78	58	.577	—	Eric Wedge	124,010 (66)	1995
70	Myrtle Beach Pelicans (Braves)	79	60	.568	1	Brian Snitker	232,619 (66)	1999
144	Wilmington Blue Rocks (Royals)	77	61	.558	2½	Jeff Garber	321,143 (70)	1999
118	Salem Avalanche (Rockies)	69	69	.500	10½	Ron Gideon	206,012 (67)	1987
76	Frederick Keys (Orioles)	67	71	.486	12½	Andy Etchebarren	313,603 (66)	1990
205	Lynchburg Hillcats (Pirates)	64	73	.467	15	Scott Little	110,937 (65)	1997
91	Winston-Salem Warthogs (White Sox)	63	75	.457	16½	Jerry Terrell	134,764 (64)	1993
211	Potomac Cannons (Cardinals)	54	85	.388	26	Joe Cunningham	209,168 (68)	1989

NOTE: Team's individual batting and pitching statistics can be found on page indicated in lefthand column.

Minor Leagues

1999 Carolina League Statistics

CLUB BATTING

	AVG	G	AB	R	H	2B	3B	HR	BB	SO	SB
Frederick	.264	138	4667	699	1232	222	30	79	589	952	171
Wilmington	.260	138	4641	653	1208	209	33	85	482	950	143
Lynchburg	.259	137	4568	680	1182	228	40	116	582	1146	126
Kinston	.252	137	4492	644	1132	241	36	92	554	1088	142
Winston-Salem	.251	138	4623	635	1159	242	29	94	458	1037	174
Myrtle Beach	.250	139	4763	637	1193	240	49	105	427	1190	108
Salem	.247	138	4521	574	1116	206	37	61	430	915	126
Potomac	.243	139	4610	619	1120	221	30	90	475	1051	138

CLUB PITCHING

	ERA	G	CG	SHO	SV	IP	H	R	ER	BB	SO
Myrtle Beach	3.50	139	0	10	41	1249	1056	552	486	559	1159
Kinston	3.63	137	4	11	47	1184	1031	569	478	492	1092
Salem	3.83	138	6	8	38	1205	1152	600	513	468	1078
Wilmington	3.99	138	1	9	40	1221	1165	607	541	503	1090
Winston-Salem	4.05	138	7	10	29	1209	1155	675	544	568	1065
Frederick	4.32	138	8	8	26	1219	1269	714	585	479	943
Lynchburg	4.38	137	6	7	24	1206	1271	706	587	431	1008
Potomac	4.59	139	3	8	26	1209	1243	718	617	497	894

CLUB FIELDING

	PCT	PO	A	E	DP		PCT	PO	A	E	DP
Wilmington	.975	3663	1450	132	123	Lynchburg	.969	3618	1477	165	113
Myrtle Beach	.973	3746	1346	143	95	Salem	.969	3616	1489	166	125
Kinston	.970	3552	1462	156	92	Frederick	.964	3657	1530	193	129
Potomac	.969	3627	1420	162	122	Winston-Salem	.960	3628	1469	211	132

INDIVIDUAL BATTING LEADERS
(Minimum 378 Plate Appearances)

	AVG	G	AB	R	H	2B	3B	HR	RBI	BB	SO	SB
Giles, Marcus, MB	.326	126	497	80	162	40	7	13	73	54	89	9
Ortega, Bill, Potomac	.306	110	421	66	129	27	4	9	74	38	69	7
May, Freddy, Lynchburg	.295	126	441	61	130	20	4	8	56	85	105	17
Berger, Brandon, Wilm.	.293	119	450	73	132	27	4	16	73	45	93	29
Heintz, Chris, Win.-Salem	.293	118	417	55	122	33	2	7	60	40	72	6
Lankford, Derrick, Lynch.	.292	123	456	80	133	28	8	20	88	52	124	4
Martinez, Eddy, Frederick	.291	127	416	68	121	21	1	2	55	52	99	8
Edwards, Mike, Kinston	.289	133	456	76	132	25	4	16	89	93	117	8
Gerut, Jody, Salem	.289	133	499	80	144	33	11	11	63	61	65	25
Sears, Todd, Salem	.281	109	385	58	108	21	0	14	59	58	99	11

INDIVIDUAL PITCHING LEADERS
(Minimum 112 Innings)

	W	L	ERA	G	GS	CG	SV	IP	H	R	ER	BB	SO
Kalinowski, Josh, Salem	11	6	2.11	27	27	1	0	162	119	47	38	71	176
Lewis, Derrick, Myrtle Beach	8	4	2.40	24	23	0	0	131	100	44	35	81	102
Sobkowiak, Scott, MB	9	4	2.84	27	26	0	0	139	100	50	44	63	161
Garland, Jon, Winston-Salem	5	7	3.33	19	19	2	0	119	109	57	44	39	84
Scott, Brian, Winston-Salem	8	8	3.41	25	25	1	0	148	135	75	56	60	132
George, Chris, Wilmington	9	9	3.60	27	27	0	0	145	142	65	58	53	142
Drew, Tim, Kinston	13	5	3.73	28	28	2	0	169	154	79	70	60	125
Austin, Jeffrey, Wilmington	7	2	3.77	18	18	0	0	112	108	52	47	39	97
Shiell, Jason, Myrtle Beach	8	7	3.77	26	17	0	0	115	118	51	48	36	90
Difelice, Mark, Salem	8	12	3.86	27	23	3	0	156	142	71	67	36	142

ALL-STAR TEAM

C—Chris Heintz, Winston-Salem. **1B**—Eddy Furniss, Lynchburg. **2B**—Marcus Giles, Myrtle Beach. **3B**—Mike Edwards, Kinston. **SS**—Eddy Martinez, Frederick. **OF**—Jody Gerut, Salem; Derrick Lankford, Lynchburg; Aaron Rowand, Winston-Salem. **DH**—Andy Bevins, Potomac. **Util**—Brandon Berger, Wilmington; Joe Dillon, Wilmington. **SP**—Josh Kalinowski, Salem. **RP**—Travis Thompson, Salem.

Most Valuable Player: Marcus Giles, Myrtle Beach. **Pitcher of the Year:** Josh Kalinowski, Salem. **Manager of the Year:** Eric Wedge, Kinston.

TOP 10 PROSPECTS

1. Kip Wells, rhp, Winston-Salem; **2.** Dee Brown, of, Wilmington; **3.** Rafael Furcal, ss, Myrtle Beach; **4.** Matt Riley, lhp, Frederick; **5.** Jeff Austin, rhp, Wilmington; **6.** Jon Garland, rhp, Winston-Salem; **7.** Tim Drew, rhp, Kinston; **8.** Luis Matos, of, Frederick; **9.** Aaron Rowand, of, Winston-Salem; **10.** Josh Kalinowski, lhp, Salem.

DEPT. LEADERS

BATTING
G	Andy Bevins, Potomac	138
AB	Eddy Garabito, Frederick	539
R	Eddy Furniss, Lynchburg	96
	Aaron Rowand, Winston-Salem	96
H	Marcus Giles, Myrtle Beach	162
TB	Aaron Rowand, Winston-Salem	258
XBH	Aaron Rowand, Winston-Salem	64
2B	Marcus Giles, Myrtle Beach	40
3B	Jason Ross, Myrtle Beach	13
HR	Andy Bevins, Potomac	25
RBI	Andy Bevins, Potomac	97
SH	Chone Figgins, Salem	14
	Brian Keck, Salem	14
SF	Eddy Garabito, Frederick	10
BB	Eddy Furniss, Lynchburg	94
IBB	Dee Brown, Wilmington	6
	Mike Edwards, Kinston	6
HBP	Vic Radcliff, Wilmington	18
SO	Corey Pointer, Lynchburg	147
SB	Scott Pratt, Kinston	47
CS	Eddy Garabito, Frederick	17
GIDP	Franky Figueroa, Frederick	21
OB%	Mike Edwards, Kinston	.413
SL%	Derrick Lankford, Lynchburg	.520

PITCHING
G	Jose DeLeon, Potomac	59
GS	Tim Drew, Kinston	28
CG	Rick Bauer, Frederick	4
	Sam McConnell, Lynchburg	4
ShO	Sam McConnell, Lynchburg	2
GF	Travis Thompson, Salem	52
SV	Travis Thompson, Salem	27
W	Tim Drew, Kinston	13
L	Andy Bausher, Lynchburg	15
IP	Ryan Price, Salem	172
H	Ryan Price, Salem	198
R	Ryan Price, Salem	102
ER	Ryan Price, Salem	94
HR	Mark Difelice, Salem	20
HB	Steve Matcuk, Salem	20
BB	Derrick Lewis, Myrtle Beach	81
SO	Josh Kalinowski, Salem	176
WP	Dwayne Jacobs, Winston-Salem	28
BK	Carlos Alvarado, Lynchburg	4

FIELDING
C	AVG	Jeremy Hill, Wilmington	.991
	PO	Chris Heintz, Win.-Salem	716
	A	Jeremy Hill, Wilmington	87
	E	Chris Heintz, Win.-Salem	15
	DP	Rogelio Arias, Salem	6
		Matt Garrick, Potomac	6
	PB	Chris Heintz, Win.-Salem	19
1B	AVG	Luke Quaccia, Potomac	.995
	PO	Franky Figueroa, Frederick	1144
	A	Franky Figueroa, Frederick	98
	E	Billy Munoz, Kinston	12
	DP	Franky Figueroa, Frederick	107
2B	AVG	Marcus Giles, Myrtle Beach	.985
	PO	Jerome Alviso, Salem	261
	A	Kevin Connacher, W-S	356
	E	Eddy Garabito, Frederick	23
		Scott Pratt, Kinston	23
	DP	Jerome Alviso, Frederick	84
3B	AVG	Mike Hessman, MB	.941
	PO	Joe Dillon, Wilmington	94
	A	Mike Edwards, Kinston	226
	E	Jim Terrell, Win.-Salem	31
	DP	Joe Dillon, Wilmington	20
SS	AVG	Victor Gutierrez, Lynch.	.966
	PO	Eddy Martinez, Frederick	189
	A	Zach Sorensen, Kinston	399
	E	Chone Figgins, Salem	45
	DP	Eddy Martinez, Frederick	80
OF	AVG	William Ortega, Potomac	.989
	PO	William Ortega, Potomac	252
	A	Dan Ramirez, W-S	15
	E	Corey Pointer, Lynchburg	12
	DP	Darnell McDonald, Fred.	4
		Dustan Mohr, Kinston	4

FLORIDA STATE LEAGUE

Wells leaps through Dunedin; Kissimmee takes crown

BY SEAN KERNAN

By the time Vernon Wells was officially named MVP of the Florida State League, the outfielder already had left Dunedin for points beyond—Knoxville, Syracuse and Toronto.

Wells, who reached the big leagues before his 21st birthday, easily convinced FSL managers he was the top prospect in the league in 1999. The 6-foot-1, 195-pound center fielder batted .343 with 11 home runs and 43 RBIs in 265 at-bats before embarking on quick visits to the Southern League, International League and eventually the American League.

Jays' Vernon Wells
Short but sweet

"This guy can hurt you with a home run, double, bunt, a great play in the outfield, his arm," Jupiter Hammerheads manager Luis Dorante said. "You don't see many guys like him with all those plus tools. He'll hurt you if you leave the breaking ball up."

Long after Wells was gone, some of his old teammates at Dunedin lost the FSL's championship series to Kissimmee, three games to one. Dunedin had posted the league's best overall record and won both halves of the Western Division split-season schedule.

Kissimmee, which has been in the league as an Astros affiliate since 1985, had posted only the league's sixth best record overall, at 71-66. It won its first league title.

In decisive Game Four against Dunedin, the Cobras scored twice in the top of the 10th inning for a 5-3 victory. Cobras righthander Eric Ireland started that game, and worked into the eighth inning. Ireland also worked the other most significant game the Cobras played in 1999. On June 23, he threw the first perfect game in the history of the Astros organization.

In addition to Wells, another short-timer in the FSL was 19-year-old Tampa third baseman Drew Henson, who hit .275 with 13 homers before returning to college. Henson, a two-sport standout, also is a highly rated quarterback for Michigan.

"If he can put the numbers up he did in Tampa playing part time, I'd say his baseball potential is really, really high," Lakeland manager Mark Meleski said. "He's got a very high ceiling."

For just the second time in the 38-year history of the league's all-star games, the game was ruled a tie. Wells went 4-for-6 with a home run to win the MVP award in a 9-9, 10-inning deadlock.

The league wasn't planning on having any franchise shifts heading into the 2000 season, especially after the Dodgers agreed to return to Vero Beach for another year of spring training.

STANDINGS: SPLIT SEASON

FIRST HALF

EAST	W	L	PCT	GB
Jupiter	39	29	.574	—
St. Lucie	31	37	.456	8
Kissimmee	30	37	.448	8½
Daytona	30	38	.441	9
Brevard	27	40	.403	11½
Vero Beach	26	42	.382	13

WEST	W	L	PCT	GB
Clearwater	46	23	.667	—
Dunedin	45	24	.652	1
Tampa	39	29	.574	6½
St. Petersburg	39	29	.574	6½
Sarasota	39	30	.565	7
Lakeland	33	36	.478	13
Charlotte	29	40	.420	17
Fort Myers	25	44	.362	21

SECOND HALF

EAST	W	L	PCT	GB
Kissimmee	41	29	.586	—
St. Lucie	37	33	.529	4
Brevard	34	34	.500	6
Jupiter	34	36	.486	7
Daytona	33	37	.471	8
Vero Beach	22	43	.338	16½

WEST	W	L	PCT	GB
Dunedin	41	27	.603	—
Tampa	39	29	.574	2
Charlotte	40	30	.571	2
St. Petersburg	35	24	.507	6½
Fort Myers	35	35	.500	7
Lakeland	32	37	.464	9½
Clearwater	31	36	.463	9½
Sarasota	28	42	.400	14

PLAYOFFS—Semifinals: Dunedin defeated Clearwater 2-1 and Kissimmee defeated Jupiter 2-1 in best-of-3 series. **Finals:** Kissimmee defeated Dunedin 3-1 in best-of-5 series.

STANDINGS: OVERALL

Page		W	L	PCT	GB	Manager	Attendance/Dates	Last Penn.
251	Dunedin Blue Jays (Blue Jays)	86	51	.628	—	Rocket Wheeler	51,819 (65)	None
176	Tampa Yankees (Yankees)	78	58	.574	7½	Tom Nieto	91,603 (63)	1994
198	Clearwater Phillies (Phillies)	77	59	.566	8½	Bill Dancy	70,147 (67)	1993
237	St. Petersburg Devil Rays (Devil Rays)	74	63	.540	12	Roy Silver	82,631 (64)	1997
170	Jupiter Hammerheads (Expos)	73	65	.529	13½	Luis Dorante	105,037 (69)	1991
137	Kissimmee Cobras (Astros)	71	66	.518	15	Manny Acta	33,789 (63)	1999
244	Charlotte Rangers (Rangers)	69	70	.496	18	James Byrd	42,119 (66)	1989
184	St. Lucie Mets (Mets)	68	70	.493	18½	Howie Freiling	40,928 (65)	1998
84	Sarasota Red Sox (Red Sox)	67	72	.482	20	Butch Hobson	51,148 (64)	1963
124	Lakeland Tigers (Tigers)	65	73	.471	21½	Mark Meleski	36,092 (64)	1992
98	Daytona Cubs (Cubs)	63	75	.457	23½	Nate Oliver	62,491 (64)	1995
131	Brevard County Manatees (Marlins)	61	74	.452	24	Dave Huppert	115,145 (65)	None
163	Fort Myers Miracle (Twins)	60	79	.432	27	Mike Boulanger	108,074 (61)	1985
151	Vero Beach Dodgers (Dodgers)	48	85	.361	36	Alvaro Espinoza	50,838 (59)	1990

NOTE: Team's individual batting and pitching statistics can be found on page indicated in lefthand column.

Minor Leagues

1999 Florida State League Statistics

CLUB BATTING

	AVG	G	AB	R	H	2B	3B	HR	BB	SO	SB
Dunedin	.288	137	4659	760	1341	285	39	120	414	835	159
Clearwater	.281	136	4653	756	1307	232	48	87	579	811	103
Fort Myers	.270	139	4635	686	1251	221	32	91	507	801	95
Sarasota	.269	139	4649	693	1250	238	31	106	498	841	121
Charlotte	.269	139	4583	702	1232	215	53	89	521	914	180
Brevard County	.264	135	4541	591	1201	174	33	58	396	842	140
Lakeland	.264	138	4623	638	1221	231	41	64	393	911	173
Tampa	.264	136	4577	622	1208	219	55	90	511	991	79
St. Lucie	.261	138	4595	625	1199	203	39	98	419	971	143
St. Petersburg	.258	137	4491	579	1160	174	29	63	367	851	93
Daytona	.258	138	4452	589	1147	206	30	79	378	795	128
Vero Beach	.253	133	4262	531	1079	181	21	59	428	884	125
Kissimmee	.252	137	4554	652	1149	227	34	121	486	1051	118
Jupiter	.252	138	4471	579	1126	184	28	57	428	895	206

CLUB PITCHING

	ERA	G	CG	SHO	SV	IP	H	R	ER	BB	SO
Jupiter	3.17	138	6	13	32	1210	1056	509	426	402	885
Tampa	3.43	136	4	9	48	1195	1154	561	455	415	1002
St. Petersburg	3.69	137	3	12	40	1177	1227	585	483	362	805
Kissimmee	3.72	137	9	8	31	1191	1143	595	492	416	918
St. Lucie	3.83	138	7	7	31	1201	1177	637	511	533	957
Dunedin	3.88	137	6	9	42	1196	1131	592	515	475	967
Charlotte	4.16	139	10	8	34	1190	1275	669	550	481	816
Clearwater	4.18	136	5	11	44	1205	1323	690	559	406	798
Daytona	4.25	138	10	9	34	1165	1151	694	550	540	981
Lakeland	4.38	138	7	3	28	1193	1243	681	581	471	843
Sarasota	4.43	139	3	7	38	1189	1311	709	586	443	929
Brevard County	4.44	135	13	7	27	1171	1228	686	578	430	789
Fort Myers	4.55	139	5	9	20	1188	1307	716	601	469	884
Vero Beach	4.67	133	5	5	32	1126	1145	679	584	482	819

CLUB FIELDING

	PCT	PO	A	E	DP		PCT	PO	A	E	DP
Jupiter	.973	3629	1489	140	91	Kissimmee	.967	3572	1483	175	123
St. Petersburg	.973	3532	1499	141	116	Sarasota	.966	3567	1488	179	103
Dunedin	.972	3587	1612	152	150	Charlotte	.965	3569	1397	179	131
Lakeland	.969	3578	1550	162	132	Vero Beach	.965	3378	1407	173	104
Brevard	.967	3514	1494	169	104	Daytona	.964	3494	1338	183	110
Fort Myers	.967	3563	1583	174	134	St. Lucie	.963	3603	1571	199	118
Tampa	.967	3584	1429	173	93	Clearwater	.962	3614	1557	204	119

INDIVIDUAL BATTING LEADERS

(Minimum 378 Plate Appearances)

	AVG	G	AB	R	H	2B	3B	HR	RBI	BB	SO	SB
Dina, Allen, St. Lucie	.344	85	343	65	118	16	4	12	47	25	54	34
Phelps, Josh, Dunedin	.328	110	406	72	133	27	4	20	88	28	104	6
Grabowski, Jason, Char.	.313	123	434	68	136	31	6	12	87	65	66	13
Young, Mike, Dunedin	.313	129	495	86	155	36	3	5	61	61	78	30
Romano, Jason, Charlotte	.312	120	459	84	143	27	14	13	71	39	72	34
Izturis, Cesar, Dunedin	.308	131	536	77	165	28	12	3	77	22	58	32
Michaels, Jason, Clear.	.306	122	451	91	138	31	6	14	65	68	103	10
Punto, Nick, Clearwater	.305	106	400	65	122	18	6	1	48	67	53	16
Bolivar, Papo, Ft. Myers	.305	114	433	54	132	21	3	3	37	27	56	8
Johnson, Rontrez, Sarasota	.300	132	494	97	148	30	4	8	59	74	63	18

INDIVIDUAL PITCHING LEADERS

(Minimum 112 Innings)

	W	L	ERA	G	GS	CG	SV	IP	H	R	ER	BB	SO
Ireland, Eric, Kissimmee	10	7	2.06	24	24	5	0	170	145	59	39	30	133
Comer, Scott, Brevard	9	4	2.35	19	19	5	0	130	120	38	34	5	85
Lundberg, Dave, Charlotte	14	7	2.83	30	21	4	0	156	162	63	49	44	81
Gonzalez, Dicky, St. Lucie	14	9	2.83	25	25	3	0	169	156	66	53	30	143
Flores, Randy, Tampa	11	4	2.87	21	20	1	0	135	118	56	43	38	99
Navarro, Scott, Kissimmee	8	3	2.88	37	11	1	0	113	108	39	36	17	86
Rodriguez, Wilfredo, Kiss.	15	7	2.88	25	24	0	0	153	108	55	49	62	148
Estrella, Leo, Dunedin	14	7	3.21	27	24	2	0	168	166	74	60	47	116

ALL-STAR TEAM

C—Matthew LeCroy, Fort Myers; Michael Rivera, Lakeland. **1B**—Eric Hinske, Daytona. **2B**—Jason Romano, Charlotte. **3B**—Jason Grabowski, Charlotte. **SS**—Cesar Izturis, Dunedin. **OF**—Quincy Foster, Brevard County; Eric Valent, Clearwater; Vernon Wells, Dunedin. **DH**—Josh Phelps, Dunedin. **Util**—Allen Dina, St. Lucie; Mike Young, Dunedin. **SP**—Eric Ireland, Kissimmee; Mike Meyers, Daytona; Wilfredo Rodriguez, Kissimmee; John Sneed, Dunedin. **RP**—Jason Ellison, Tampa; Bob File, Dunedin. **Most Valuable Player:** Vernon Wells, Dunedin. **Manager of the Year:** Rocket Wheeler.

TOP 10 PROSPECTS

1. Vernon Wells, of, Dunedin; **2.** Drew Henson, 3b, Tampa; **3.** Michael Cuddyer, 3b, Fort Myers; **4.** Wilfredo Rodriguez, lhp, Kissimmee; **5.** Cesar Izturis, ss, Dunedin; **6.** Jared Sandberg, 3b, St. Petersburg; **7.** Jason Grabowski, 3b, Charlotte; **8.** Matthew LeCroy, c, Fort Myers; **9.** Matt White, rhp, St. Petersburg; **10.** Jason Romano, 2b, Charlotte.

DEPT. LEADERS

BATTING

G	Allen Butler, Fort Myers	137
AB	Quincy Foster, Brevard	568
R	Mike Peeples, Dunedin	100
H	Quincy Foster, Brevard	167
TB	Mike Peeples, Dunedin	262
XBH	Mike Peeples, Dunedin	60
	Eric Valent, Clearwater	60
2B	Allen Butler, Fort Myers	36
	Mike Young, Dunedin	36
3B	Jason Romano, Charlotte	14
HR	Morgan Burkhart, Sarasota	23
RBI	Eric Valent, Clearwater	106
SH	Cesar Izturis, Dunedin	17
	Henry Mateo, Jupiter	17
SF	Simon Pond, Jupiter	11
BB	Michael Cuddyer, Fort Myers	76
	Aaron Jones, Tampa	76
IBB	Three tied at	7
HBP	Jess Graham, Sarasota	19
SO	Carlos Pena, Charlotte	133
	Jared Sandberg, St. Petersburg	133
SB	Rod Lindsey, Lakeland	61
CS	Jaisen Randolph, Daytona	24
GIDP	Michael Cuddyer, Fort Myers	20
OB%	Skip Kiil, Clearwater	.436
SL%	Josh Phelps, Dunedin	.562

PITCHING

G	Doug Nickle, Clearwater	60
GS	Brad Thomas, Fort Myers	27
CG	Scott Comer, Brevard	5
	Eric Ireland, Kissimmee	5
ShO	Several tied at	2
GF	Doug Nickle, Clearwater	50
SV	Jason Ellison, Tampa	35
W	Wilfredo Rodriguez, Kissimmee	15
L	Three tied at	14
IP	Eric Ireland, Kissimmee	170
H	Josh Garrett, Sarasota	189
R	Nate Teut, Daytona	113
ER	Nate Teut, Daytona	94
	Ryan Mills, Fort Myers	94
HR	Craig Johnson, Lakeland	20
HB	Danny Lampley, Sarasota	18
BB	Ryan Mills, Fort Myers	87
SO	Wilfredo Rodriguez, Kissimmee	148
WP	Ryan Mills, Fort Myers	20

FIELDING

C	AVG	Paul Chiaffredo, Dunedin	.992
	PO	Scott Sandusky, Jupiter	671
	A	Mike Rivera, Lakeland	104
	E	Luis Tavares, Charlotte	22
	DP	Brandon Marsters, Ft. Myers	9
	PB	Luis Tavares, Charlotte	26
1B	AVG	Allen Butler, Ft. Myers	.995
	PO	Allen Butler, Ft. Myers	1260
	A	Allen Butler, Ft. Myers	108
	E	Pat Burns, St. Lucie	22
	DP	Carlos Pena, Charlotte	119
2B	AVG	Ty Wigginton, St. Lucie	.973
	PO	Rod Smith, Tampa	270
	A	Mike Ryan, Ft. Myers	395
	E	Mike Ryan, Ft. Myers	35
	DP	Mike Ryan, Ft. Myers	81
3B	AVG	Brian Rios, Lakeland	.947
	PO	Jared Sandberg, St. Pete.	96
	A	Jared Sandberg, St. Pete.	278
	E	Jared Sandberg, St. Pete.	37
	DP	Michael Cuddyer, Ft. Myers	25
SS	AVG	Danny Solano, Charlotte	.972
	PO	Danny Solano, Charlotte	218
	A	David Matranga, Kissimmee	427
	E	Jersen Perez, St. Lucie	32
	DP	Danny Solano, Charlotte	95
OF	AVG	Diego Rico, Daytona	.993
	PO	Craig Monroe, Charlotte	326
	A	Jess Graham, Sarasota	19
	E	Quincy Foster, Brevard	15
	DP	Scott Neuberger, St. Pete.	5
		Tony Peters, Dunedin	5

MIDWEST LEAGUE

Bees finish on top with offense as season's buzzword

BY BRANSON WRIGHT

Don't tell pitchers in the Midwest League that the baseball wasn't juiced in 1999. Highlighted by a four-homer game by a player in a postseason game, it was a good year to be a hitter.

Baseballs were splattered all across and out of many league stadiums. Several offensive records were set.

The Lansing Lugnuts and the Michigan Battle Cats put up the top two total-base figures in MWL history. Wisconsin's Bo Robinson tied the league record for doubles. Michigan slugger Aaron McNeal made a strong run for the league record in RBIs and homers but fell short late in the season.

Then there was league champion Burlington. In their first year as a White Sox affiliate, the Bees finished the first half of the season seven games under .500. They slipped into the playoffs by winning the second half of the Western Division by one game.

Eric Battersby
Four-homer game

But the postseason belonged to Bees first baseman/outfielder Eric Battersby, who hit .290 with 18 homers in the regular season. In the postseason he hit .387 with five homers and an .871 slugging percentage. Four of the homers came in one game, tying a league record and lifting Burlington to victory in the decisive Game Three over Kane County to send the Bees to the finals.

"I was kind of excited after hitting the second one," Battersby said. "When I hit the third and fourth, it was just unbelievable. The last home run, I was pretty much floating around the bases."

Battersby's heroics against Kane County gave the Bees a jump-start against Wisconsin in the finals. The Bees won the first two games of the best-of-5 series. Wisconsin tied the series with two straight wins but the Bees, remaining true to the offensive theme of the '99 season, exploded to a 13-4 victory in the final.

The league's Top 10 Prospects, as chosen by the MWL managers, were all age 21 or younger, led by Lansing outfielder Corey Patterson. The Cubs' first-round pick in 1998, Patterson hit .320 with 35 doubles, 17 triples, 20 homers and 33 stolen bases.

The league's plans for 2000 include a switch from three to two divisions. The Reds affiliate in Rockford will move to Dayton, Ohio, and be known as the Dragons.

STANDINGS: SPLIT SEASON

FIRST HALF

EAST	W	L	PCT	GB
Lansing	38	32	.543	—
Michigan	35	34	.507	2½
South Bend	32	37	.464	5½
West Michigan	29	41	.414	9
Fort Wayne	29	41	.414	9
CENTRAL	W	L	PCT	GB
Rockford	45	24	.652	—
Kane County	40	27	.597	4
Peoria	37	32	.536	8
Wisconsin	32	36	.471	12½
Beloit	25	44	.362	20
WEST	W	L	PCT	GB
Clinton	41	27	.603	—
Quad City	38	31	.551	3½
Burlington	31	38	.449	10½
Cedar Rapids	30	38	.441	11

SECOND HALF

EAST	W	L	PCT	GB
Michigan	41	28	.594	—
West Michigan	39	31	.557	2½
South Bend	36	34	.514	5½
Lansing	35	35	.500	6½
Fort Wayne	32	38	.457	9½
CENTRAL	W	L	PCT	GB
Wisconsin	40	30	.571	—
Kane County	38	32	.543	2
Beloit	34	36	.486	6
Rockford	31	39	.443	9
Peoria	26	44	.371	14
WEST	W	L	PCT	GB
Burlington	40	30	.571	—
Quad City	39	31	.557	1
Cedar Rapids	31	39	.443	9
Clinton	27	42	.391	12½

PLAYOFFS—Quarterfinals: Kane County defeated Quad City 2-1, Burlington defeated Clinton 2-1, Lansing defeated Michigan 2-0 and Wisconsin defeated Rockford in best-of-3 series. **Semifinals:** Wisconsin defeated Lansing 2-0 and Burlington defeated Kane County 2-1 in best-of-3 series. **Finals:** Burlington defeated Wisconsin 3-2 in best-of-5 series.

STANDINGS: OVERALL

Page		W	L	PCT	GB	Manager	Attendance/Dates	Last Penn.
132	Kane County Cougars (Marlins)	78	59	.569	—	Rick Renteria	451,145 (64)	None
164	Quad City River Bandits (Twins)	77	62	.554	2	Jose Marzan	145,734 (66)	1990
138	Michigan Battle Cats (Astros)	76	62	.551	2½	Al Pedrique	108,033 (65)	None
105	Rockford Reds (Reds)	76	63	.547	3	Mike Rojas	63,705 (65)	None
231	Wisconsin Timber Rattlers (Mariners)	72	66	.522	6½	Steve Roadcap	223,814 (66)	1984
98	Lansing Lugnuts (Cubs)	73	67	.521	6½	Oscar Acosta	462,515 (67)	1997
91	Burlington Bees (White Sox)	71	68	.511	8	Nick Capra	66,178 (64)	1999
104	Clinton LumberKings (Reds)	68	69	.496	10	Freddie Benavides	61,485 (61)	1991
63	South Bend Silver Hawks (Diamondbacks)	68	71	.489	11	Mike Brumley	200,518 (64)	1993
125	West Michigan Whitecaps (Tigers)	68	72	.486	11½	Bruce Fields	457,350 (69)	1998
212	Peoria Chiefs (Cardinals)	63	76	.453	16	Brian Rupp	150,254 (65)	None
56	Cedar Rapids Kernels (Angels)	61	77	.442	17½	Mitch Seoane	127,612 (69)	1994
218	Fort Wayne Wizards (Padres)	61	79	.436	18½	Dan Simonds	201,395 (68)	None
158	Beloit Snappers (Brewers)	59	80	.424	20	Don Money	54,689 (67)	1995

NOTE: Team's individual batting and pitching statistics can be found on page indicated in lefthand column.

1999 Midwest League Statistics

CLUB BATTING

	AVG	G	AB	R	H	2B	3B	HR	BB	SO	SB
Michigan	.284	138	4747	810	1350	277	54	141	401	873	105
Lansing	.274	140	4670	822	1278	288	60	147	619	1031	133
Kane County	.270	137	4681	777	1263	251	40	86	554	1010	166
Wisconsin	.268	138	4645	721	1243	247	26	90	609	1027	122
Rockford	.266	139	4587	700	1221	243	43	116	451	975	227
Burlington	.263	139	4604	734	1213	239	39	99	610	1023	155
Beloit	.263	139	4664	680	1227	231	34	94	491	1056	94
South Bend	.262	139	4712	642	1236	229	45	63	447	986	108
Fort Wayne	.259	140	4668	672	1209	221	38	61	571	1102	225
Quad City	.258	139	4655	743	1203	252	28	110	658	893	96
Clinton	.255	137	4542	648	1159	234	38	75	425	1045	157
Cedar Rapids	.255	138	4627	636	1178	235	35	90	506	901	152
Peoria	.254	139	4634	641	1178	228	41	69	455	1049	125
West Michigan	.253	140	4688	696	1186	260	43	73	521	1091	197

CLUB PITCHING

	ERA	G	CG	SHO	SV	IP	H	R	ER	BB	SO
Clinton	3.91	137	6	5	37	1181	1093	643	513	516	964
Quad City	3.94	139	2	10	31	1221	1139	649	534	569	1103
West Michigan	4.04	140	10	9	30	1220	1170	682	548	570	1033
Kane County	4.06	137	6	11	29	1206	1247	617	545	466	955
Wisconsin	4.09	138	12	10	29	1198	1194	653	544	434	1110
Rockford	4.23	139	16	18	32	1204	1232	690	566	524	1046
South Bend	4.38	139	0	6	36	1214	1222	702	591	482	1003
Cedar Rapids	4.49	138	21	7	35	1196	1242	741	596	459	976
Lansing	4.73	140	5	4	32	1199	1312	750	630	528	893
Peoria	4.74	139	2	4	26	1201	1240	748	633	511	978
Burlington	4.78	139	9	4	35	1194	1291	763	635	519	953
Michigan	4.82	138	5	5	37	1192	1264	732	639	483	1055
Beloit	4.85	139	8	9	30	1202	1261	770	648	582	1002
Fort Wayne	4.98	140	2	5	33	1224	1237	812	678	675	991

CLUB FIELDING

	PCT	PO	A	E	DP		PCT	PO	A	E	DP
Kane County	.971	3618	1514	155	147	South Bend	.962	3643	1639	208	109
Michigan	.970	3576	1376	153	124	West Mich.	.962	3659	1626	209	115
Quad City	.966	3662	1517	185	133	Fort Wayne	.961	3673	1384	203	124
Peoria	.965	3603	1484	183	117	Rockford	.961	3613	1536	208	113
Beloit	.965	3605	1407	184	106	Burlington	.958	3582	1538	222	116
Wisconsin	.964	3593	1401	184	91	Clinton	.958	3542	1476	220	127
Lansing	.964	3596	1503	193	145	C. Rapids	.958	3587	1585	229	137

INDIVIDUAL BATTING LEADERS
(Minimum 378 Plate Appearances)

	AVG	G	AB	R	H	2B	3B	HR	RBI	BB	SO	SB
Urquiola, Carlos, SB	.362	93	384	66	139	13	3	0	35	22	32	20
Burroughs, Sean, Ft. Wayne	.359	122	426	65	153	30	3	5	80	74	59	17
Robinson, Bo, Wisconsin	.329	138	499	101	164	50	3	13	102	108	75	4
Valenzuela, Mario, Bur.	.323	122	477	89	154	31	6	10	70	44	77	13
Patterson, Corey, Lansing	.320	112	475	94	152	35	17	20	79	25	85	33
Miles, Aaron, Michigan	.317	112	470	72	149	28	8	10	71	28	33	17
Restovich, Michael, QC	.312	131	493	91	154	30	6	19	107	74	100	7
McNeal, Aaron, Michigan	.310	133	536	95	166	29	3	38	131	40	121	7
Turnquist, Tyler, Michigan	.309	118	456	89	141	25	7	11	67	62	69	5
Merriman, Terrell, Burlington	.306	109	382	77	117	18	9	15	85	70	84	27

INDIVIDUAL PITCHING LEADERS
(Minimum 112 Innings)

	W	L	ERA	G	GS	CG	SV	IP	H	R	ER	BB	SO
Averette, Robert, Rockford	9	5	2.58	19	19	2	0	126	117	54	36	40	98
Hayden, Terry, Rock./Clin.	8	6	2.70	38	14	1	0	117	108	57	35	42	79
Rincon, Juan, Quad City	14	8	2.92	28	28	0	0	163	146	67	53	66	153
Palma, Ricardo, Lansing	7	7	2.94	22	22	2	0	135	134	61	44	44	79
Almonte, Edwin, Burlington	9	12	3.03	37	5	2	5	116	107	48	39	28	85
Figueroa, Juan, Burlington	8	4	3.12	17	16	2	0	115	100	51	40	44	139
Cervantes, Chris, SB	8	5	3.13	38	10	0	3	115	109	49	40	34	89
Anderson, Wes, Kane Co.	9	5	3.21	23	23	2	0	137	111	55	49	51	134

ALL-STAR TEAM

C—Jeff Goldbach, Lansing. **1B**—Aaron McNeal, Michigan. **2B**—Aaron Miles, Michigan. **3B**—Sean Burroughs, Fort Wayne. **SS**—Travis Dawkins, Rockford. **OF**—Corey Patterson, Lansing; Michael Restovich, Quad City; Juan Silvestre, Wisconsin. **DH**—Eric Munson, West Michigan. **RHP**—Juan Rincon, Quad City. **LHP**—David Noyce, Kane County. **RH Reliever**—Brandon Puffer, Clinton. **LH Reliever**—Clint Chrysler, Wisconsin.

Most Valuable Player: Aaron McNeal, Michigan. **Prospect of the Year:** Corey Patterson, Lansing. **Manager of the Year:** Rick Renteria, Kane County.

TOP 10 PROSPECTS

1. Corey Patterson, of, Lansing; **2.** Travis Dawkins, ss, Rockford; **3.** Sean Burroughs, 3b, Fort Wayne; **4.** Michael Restovich, of, Quad City; **5.** Eric Munson, c-1b, West Michigan; **6.** Nick Neugebauer, rhp, Beloit; **7.** Aaron McNeal, 1b, Michigan; **8.** David Kelton, 3b, Lansing; **9.** Juan Rincon, rhp, Quad City; **10.** Hee Seop Choi, 1b, Lansing.

DEPT. LEADERS

BATTING
G	Bo Robinson, Wisconsin	138
AB	Aaron McNeal, Michigan	536
R	Jeremy Owens, Fort Wayne	111
H	Aaron McNeal, Michigan	166
TB	Aaron McNeal, Michigan	315
XBH	Corey Patterson, Lansing	72
2B	Bo Robinson, Wisconsin	50
3B	Corey Patterson, Lansing	17
HR	Aaron McNeal, Michigan	38
RBI	Aaron McNeal, Michigan	131
SH	Luis Rodriguez, Quad City	13
SF	DeWayne Wise, Rockford	14
BB	Bo Robinson, Wisconsin	108
IBB	Sean Burroughs, Fort Wayne	7
HBP	Corky Miller, Rockford	20
	Jon Schaeffer, Quad City	20
SO	Jeremy Owens, Fort Wayne	153
SB	Richard Gomez, West Mich.	66
CS	Willy Hill, Kane County	24
	Antonio Perez, Rockford	24
GIDP	Brian McMillin, Quad City	18
	Bo Robinson, Wisconsin	18
OB%	Sean Burroughs, Fort Wayne	.464
SL%	Corey Patterson, Lansing	.592

PITCHING
G	Saul Rivera, Quad City	60
GS	Several tied at	28
CG	Jeff Hundley, Cedar Rapids	6
ShO	Brett Haring, Rockford	3
	Phil Merrell, Clinton	3
GF	Brandon Puffer, Clinton	55
SV	Brandon Puffer, Clinton	34
W	Doug Bridges, Cedar Rapids	15
L	Andy Shibilo, Peoria	13
IP	Nate Cornejo, West Michigan	175
H	Mike Wuertz, Lansing	191
R	Andy Shibilo, Peoria	105
ER	Steve Stemle, Peoria	90
HR	Renney Duarte, Cedar Rapids	19
	Josue Matos, Wisconsin	19
HB	Jake Jacobs, Quad City	15
BB	Ben Howard, Fort Wayne	110
SO	Juan Rincon, Quad City	153
WP	Hatuey Mendoza, South Bend	20
BK	Several tied at	6

FIELDING
C	AVG	Sean Campbell, Ft. Wayne	.995
	PO	Obispo Brito, Beloit	722
	A	Brandon Inge, West Mich.	114
	E	Corky Miller, Rockford	14
	DP	Corky Miller, Rockford	6
		Matt Treanor, KC	6
	PB	Jeff Goldbach, Lansing	23
1B	AVG	Eric Battersby, Burlington	.987
	PO	David Callahan, KC	1050
	A	Aaron McNeal, Michigan	111
	E	Clint Vaughn, Clinton	21
	DP	David Callahan, KC	116
2B	AVG	Luis Rodriguez, Quad City	.984
	PO	Chris Patten, Beloit	259
	A	Tony Schrager, Lansing	325
	E	Danilo Araujo, Peoria	18
	DP	Tony Schrager, Lansing	81
3B	AVG	Ryan Hankins, Burlington	.925
	PO	Jose Santos, Kane County	104
	A	Mike Christensen, CR	306
	E	Jose Santos, Kane County	40
	DP	Mike Christensen, CR	39
SS	AVG	Derek Wathan, KC	.963
	PO	Derek Wathan, KC	185
	A	Derek Wathan, KC	394
	E	Wilmy Caceres, Clinton	42
	DP	Derek Wathan, KC	90
OF	AVG	Brian McMillin, Quad City	1.000
	PO	Jeremy Owens, Ft. Wayne	309
	A	Chris Aguila, Kane County	19
	E	Jeremy Owens, Ft. Wayne	17
	DP	Mario Valenzuela, Bur.	6

GreenJackets put losing season behind them in flash

BY GENE SAPAKOFF

For a more bizarre South Atlantic League championship series script, wait for the Steven Spielberg version.

The Cape Fear Crocs pulled even in the best-of-3 series just as Hurricane Floyd was taking aim at North Carolina's Cape Fear region. Red Sox closer Tom Gordon, on a rehabilitation assignment, started for Augusta and worked the first three innings as the GreenJackets won 1-0.

The title-winning home run came from native Georgian Tony DeRosso, who homered off Trevor Wamback in the eighth inning.

It was a remarkable postseason run for manager Billy Gardner's team, which finished the regular season with a sub-.500 record (69-70) but took advantage of the SAL's split-season and wild-card playoff format.

Bats' Scott Seabol
35-game streak

"This is a special bunch," Gardner said. "They busted their tails for six months and didn't pack it in when things were going bad."

Augusta's championship was the first for a Red Sox farm club since 1984, when Pawtucket won the Triple-A International League title. Augusta also won SAL championships in 1989 and 1995 as Pittsburgh Pirates farm clubs.

The story of the year came from Greensboro third baseman Scott Seabol, whose 35-game hitting streak shattered the record of 29 set by Charles Truesdell of Statesville in 1962 and established the third-longest minor league hitting streak since Howe Sportsdata began keeping track in 1987. Seabol, 24 and in his

third full season in the SAL, was named the league's most valuable player.

Macon shortstop Rafael Furcal was selected the SAL's top prospect in a poll of managers. Furcal, who turned 19 in August, won the batting title and led the league in stolen bases despite playing in just 83 games before a promotion to Class A Myrtle Beach.

Righthander Jason Standridge of the Charleston RiverDogs was named the SAL's most valuable pitcher. Standridge, once Auburn's top quarterback prospect, spent most of the second half in the Florida State League but hung around long enough to throw a seven-inning no-hitter against Hickory. Another righthander named Jason dominated after the draft. Jason Jennings, the College Player of the Year on his way from Baylor to Asheville, overmatched hitters with fastballs and sliders despite short pitch limits.

STANDINGS: SPLIT SEASON

FIRST HALF

NORTH	W	L	PCT	GB
Hagerstown	48	23	.676	—
Cape Fear	38	33	.535	10
Charleston, W.Va.	30	42	.417	18½
Delmarva	26	44	.371	21½

CENTRAL	W	L	PCT	GB
Capital City	44	27	.620	—
Greensboro	37	35	.514	7½
Piedmont	36	35	.507	8
Hickory	35	35	.500	8½
Charleston, S.C.	32	40	.444	12½
Asheville	29	42	.408	15

SOUTH	W	L	PCT	GB
Columbus	44	27	.620	—
Macon	40	30	.571	3½
Augusta	29	40	.420	14
Savannah	28	43	.394	16

SECOND HALF

NORTH	W	L	PCT	GB
Cape Fear	37	32	.536	—
Hagerstown	36	33	.522	1
Delmarva	32	36	.471	4½
Charleston, W.Va.	31	38	.449	6

CENTRAL	W	L	PCT	GB
Greensboro	40	29	.580	—
Capital City	39	31	.557	1½
Hickory	35	35	.500	5½
Asheville	35	35	.500	5½
Piedmont	33	36	.478	7
Charleston, S.C.	33	37	.471	7½

SOUTH	W	L	PCT	GB
Augusta	40	30	.571	—
Macon	34	34	.500	5
Savannah	34	35	.493	5½
Columbus	26	44	.371	14

PLAYOFFS—Quarterfinals: Augusta defeated Columbus 2-0, Hickory defeated Macon 2-0, Capital City defeated Greensboro 2-1 and Cape Fear defeated Hagerstown 2-0 in best-of-3 series. **Semifinals:** Augusta defeated Hickory 2-1 and Cape Fear defeated Capital City 2-0 in best-of-3 series. **Finals:** Augusta defeated Cape Fear 2-1 in best-of-3 series.

STANDINGS: OVERALL

Page		W	L	PCT	GB	Manager	Attendance/Dates	Last Penn.
252	Hagerstown Suns (Blue Jays)	84	56	.600	—	Rolando Pino	105,380 (69)	None
185	Capital City Bombers (Mets)	83	58	.589	1½	Dave Engle	133,273 (64)	1998
177	Greensboro Bats (Yankees)	77	64	.546	7½	Stan Hough	156,270 (67)	1982
70	Macon Braves (Braves)	74	64	.536	9	Jeff Treadway	115,897 (61)	None
171	Cape Fear Crocs (Expos)	75	65	.536	9	Frank Kremblas	72,856 (63)	None
205	Hickory Crawdads (Pirates)	70	70	.500	14	Tracy Woodson	188,531 (68)	None
112	Columbus Redstixx (Indians)	70	71	.496	14½	Brad Komminsk	104,153 (64)	None
85	Augusta GreenJackets (Red Sox)	69	70	.496	14½	Billy Gardner Jr.	156,685 (65)	1999
199	Piedmont Boll Weevils (Phillies)	69	71	.493	15	Ken Oberkfell	119,637 (64)	None
238	Charleston, S.C., RiverDogs (Devil Rays)	65	77	.458	20	Charlie Montoyo	238,184 (69)	None
119	Asheville Tourists (Rockies)	64	77	.454	20½	Jim Eppard	137,836 (64)	1984
244	Savannah Sand Gnats (Rangers)	62	78	.443	22	Paul Carey	132,017 (66)	1996
144	Charleston, W.Va., Alley Cats (Royals)	61	80	.433	23½	Tom Poquette	92,738 (66)	1990
77	Delmarva Shorebirds (Orioles)	58	80	.420	25	Butch Davis	296,004 (69)	1997

NOTE: Team's individual batting and pitching statistics can be found on page indicated in lefthand column.

1999 South Atlantic League Statistics

CLUB BATTING

	AVG	G	AB	R	H	2B	3B	HR	BB	SO	SB
Asheville	.278	141	4869	701	1352	263	20	106	320	956	149
Columbus	.263	141	4679	688	1231	222	40	110	453	1005	179
Greensboro	.262	141	4756	733	1245	251	46	122	430	1232	106
Macon	.261	138	4633	661	1210	235	31	115	415	1169	199
Capital City	.258	141	4682	688	1209	238	34	155	406	1089	167
Hickory	.256	140	4781	705	1222	226	25	134	498	1119	96
Cape Fear	.255	140	4553	616	1161	222	38	81	397	1109	173
Hagerstown	.254	140	4826	731	1225	234	34	110	562	1076	179
Augusta	.245	139	4657	626	1140	198	40	83	427	1064	139
Piedmont	.244	141	4548	528	1111	214	38	84	360	993	145
Charleston, W.Va.	.244	141	4661	593	1135	227	35	65	499	1138	270
Savannah	.242	140	4621	607	1118	203	41	95	424	1197	82
Delmarva	.240	138	4557	627	1092	203	41	47	615	1175	163
Charleston, S.C.	.237	142	4719	634	1118	207	29	88	450	1117	132

CLUB PITCHING

	ERA	G	CG	SHO	SV	IP	H	R	ER	BB	SO
Piedmont	3.02	140	16	12	42	1187	1099	540	399	352	1041
Augusta	3.35	139	3	14	35	1217	1157	585	453	407	1170
Cape Fear	3.57	140	5	4	32	1216	1172	613	483	441	952
Macon	3.59	138	1	5	40	1193	1083	585	476	466	1128
Hagerstown	3.63	140	2	11	43	1262	1138	616	509	440	1049
Capital City	3.64	141	3	11	37	1221	1115	611	494	448	1103
Charleston, S.C.	3.83	142	6	9	33	1243	1192	651	529	430	1010
Greensboro	3.98	141	7	6	36	1223	1204	646	541	406	1186
Hickory	3.99	140	2	9	33	1247	1243	702	553	470	1130
Charleston, W.Va.	4.02	141	6	10	28	1245	1252	689	556	532	1078
Delmarva	4.32	138	7	7	27	1213	1214	705	583	479	1134
Columbus	4.38	141	3	7	34	1220	1207	703	594	443	1182
Savannah	4.53	140	6	12	34	1207	1262	749	608	450	1113
Asheville	4.66	141	6	4	35	1211	1231	743	627	492	1163

CLUB FIELDING

	PCT	PO	A	E	DP		PCT	PO	A	E	DP
Hagerstown	.969	3786	1593	174	124	Delmarva	.962	3639	1386	196	88
Char., W.Va.	.964	3735	1607	197	122	Char., S.C.	.962	3730	1569	211	133
Hickory	.964	3742	1443	194	107	Asheville	.961	3633	1524	211	113
Cape Fear	.964	3648	1477	192	111	Capital City	.960	3662	1584	219	123
Augusta	.964	3650	1423	192	105	Savannah	.959	3620	1407	216	110
Macon	.963	3579	1293	186	95	Columbus	.958	3661	1454	227	107
Greensboro	.963	3670	1486	199	98	Piedmont	.955	3562	1474	235	102

INDIVIDUAL BATTING LEADERS
(Minimum 383 Plate Appearances)

	AVG	G	AB	R	H	2B	3B	HR	RBI	BB	SO	SB
Furcal, Rafael, Macon	.337	83	335	73	113	15	1	1	29	41	36	73
Benjamin, Al, Cape Fear	.322	128	488	66	157	38	2	10	77	27	110	14
Rivera, Carlos, Hickory	.322	119	457	63	147	30	1	13	86	15	45	2
Pierre, Juan, Asheville	.320	140	585	93	187	28	5	1	55	38	37	66
Cole, Brian, Columbus	.316	125	500	97	158	41	4	18	71	37	77	50
Seabol, Scott, Greensboro	.315	138	543	86	171	55	6	15	89	45	91	6
Curry, Mike, Char., W.Va.	.311	85	318	70	99	13	3	0	25	48	58	61
Wilson, Travis, Macon	.309	90	363	65	112	20	4	11	63	9	66	14
Colina, Javier, Asheville	.302	124	516	70	156	37	3	6	81	26	101	12
Castillo, Geramel, Savannah	.301	114	405	42	122	21	4	3	40	19	94	4

INDIVIDUAL PITCHING LEADERS
(Minimum 114 Innings)

	W	L	ERA	G	GS	CG	SV	IP	H	R	ER	BB	SO
Standridge, Jason, Char., S.C.	9	1	2.02	18	18	3	0	116	80	35	26	31	84
Gonzalez, Edwin, Char., W.Va.	7	6	2.24	27	13	3	2	120	101	37	30	28	136
Baisley, Brad, Piedmont	10	7	2.26	23	23	3	0	148	116	56	37	55	110
Norton, Jason, Augusta	9	6	2.32	30	17	2	0	136	106	50	35	28	150
Kubes, Greg, Piedmont	11	12	2.62	27	27	4	0	165	162	65	48	47	147
Strange, Patrick, Columbus	12	5	2.63	28	21	2	1	154	138	57	45	29	113
Hughes, Travis, Savannah	11	7	2.81	30	23	1	2	157	127	60	49	54	150
Cook, Andy, Columbus	12	7	2.83	27	26	0	1	150	150	66	47	42	124

ALL-STAR TEAM

C—Rico Washington, Hickory. **1B**—Travis Hafner, Savannah. **2B**—Javier Colina, Asheville. **3B**—Scott Seabol, Greensboro. **SS**—Rafael Furcal, Macon. **OF**—Al Benjamin, Cape Fear; Brian Cole, Capital City; Juan Pierre, Asheville. **DH**—Jay Gibbons, Hagerstown. **Util**—Mike Curry, Charleston (W.Va.); Travis Wilson, Macon. **RHP**—Jason Standridge, Charleston (S.C.). **LHP**—Jimmy Osting, Macon.

Most Valuable Player: Scott Seabol, Greensboro. **Most Valuable Pitcher:** Jason Standridge, Charleston (S.C.). **Most Outstanding Prospect:** Rafael Furcal, Macon. **Manager of the Year:** Rolando Pino, Hagerstown.

TOP 10 PROSPECTS

1. Rafael Furcal, ss, Macon; **2.** Jason Standridge, rhp, Charleston, S.C.; **3.** Jason Jennings, rhp, Asheville; **4.** Felipe Lopez, ss, Hagerstown; **5.** Brad Baisley, rhp, Piedmont; **6.** Rico Washington, c, Hickory; **7.** J.J. Davis, rhp, Hickory; **8.** Jorge Nunez, 2b, Hagerstown; **9.** Choo Freeman, of, Asheville; **10.** Humberto Cota, c, Charleston, S.C./Hickory.

BATTING

G	Juan Pierre, Asheville	140
AB	Juan Pierre, Asheville	585
R	Jorge Nunez, Hagerstown	116
H	Juan Pierre, Asheville	187
TB	Scott Seabol, Greensboro	283
XBH	Scott Seabol, Greensboro	76
2B	Scott Seabol, Greensboro	55
3B	Tyler Minges, Columbus	11
	Jorge Nunez, Hagerstown	11
HR	Travis Hafner, Savannah	28
	Earl Snyder, Capital City	28
RBI	Travis Hafner, Savannah	111
SH	Derek Mann, Charleston, S.C.	12
SF	Scott Seabol, Greensboro	11
BB	Albenis Machado, Cape Fear	102
IBB	Rico Washington, Hickory	7
HBP	Eric Schreimann, Piedmont	19
SO	A.J. Zapp, Macon	163
SB	Rafael Furcal, Macon	73
CS	Albenis Machado, Cape Fear	27
GIDP	Shayne Carnes, Piedmont	18
OB%	Rafael Furcal, Macon	.417
SL%	Travis Hafner, Savannah	.546

PITCHING

G	Jarrod Kingrey, Hagerstown	56
	Tony Pavlovich, Hickory	56
GS	Three tied at	28
CG	Three tied at	4
ShO	Jason Standridge, Charleston, S.C.	3
GF	Jarrod Kingrey, Hagerstown	48
	Heath Bell, Capital City	48
SV	Mark Cisar, Augusta	27
	Jarrod Kingrey, Hagerstown	27
W	Jimmy Osting, Macon	14
L	Four tied at	14
IP	Scott Cassidy, Hagerstown	171
	Taylor Smith, Hagerstown	171
H	Carlos Silva, Piedmont	176
R	Three tied at	99
ER	Aaron Cook, Asheville	87
HR	John Stewart, Savannah	19
	Chris Tynan, Savannah	19
HB	Scott Cassidy, Hagerstown	21
BB	Jeremy Affeldt, Char., W.Va.	80
SO	John Stephens, Delmarva	217
WP	Joe Casey, Hagerstown	25

FIELDING

C	AVG	Rodolfo Pena, Augusta	.993
	PO	Jean Boscan, Macon	798
	A	Rodolfo Pena, Augusta	125
	E	Casey Smith, Columbus	16
	DP	Several tied at	5
	PB	Brad Elwood, Greensboro	33
1B	AVG	Earl Snyder, Capital City	.993
	PO	Earl Snyder, Capital City	1106
	A	David Goodwin, Char., W.Va.	86
	E	A.J. Zapp, Macon	18
	DP	Earl Snyder, Capital City	96
2B	AVG	Derek Mann, Charleston, S.C.	.977
	PO	Tootie Myers, Cape Fear	263
	A	Derek Mann, Charleston, S.C.	375
	E	Alejandro Fajardo, Piedmont	47
	DP	Derek Mann, Charleston, S.C.	74
3B	AVG	Orlando Hudson, Hagerstown	.940
	PO	Scott Hodges, Cape Fear	105
	A	Scott Seabol, Greensboro	273
	E	Matt Holliday, Asheville	37
		Pete LaForest, Charleston, S.C.	37
	DP	Scott Hodges, Cape Fear	26
SS	AVG	Albenis Machado, Cape Fear	.964
	PO	Henry Calderon, Char., W.Va.	193
	A	Juan Uribe, Asheville	390
	E	Ramon Soler, Charleston, S.C.	40
	DP	Juan Uribe, Asheville	72
OF	AVG	Tyler Thompson, Hagerstown	.989
	PO	Tonayne Brown, Augusta	270
	A	Wilken Ruan, Cape Fear	18
	E	Geramel Castillo, Savannah	12
	DP	Juan Pierre, Asheville	4

Minor Leagues

NEW YORK PENN LEAGUE

Hudson Valley finishes atop mountain in fan-filled year

BY HOWARD HERMAN

The 1999 New York-Penn League featured bigger crowds and a first-time champion.

The Hudson Valley Renegades, with No. 1 overall draft pick Josh Hamilton in their outfield down the stretch, ousted the wildly popular Mahoning Valley Scrappers in the league's best-of-3 final, winning 11-3 in the deciding game. Hamilton, who spent most of his first season in the Rookie-level Appalachian League, went 6-for-13 with four RBIs in the series.

Dan Grummitt
Socked 22 homers

In the league's first year with a revised schedule, Hudson Valley and Mahoning Valley hadn't seen each other all year as interdivisional play was eliminated after the 1998 season. The Renegades won the McNamara Division and the Scrappers the Pinckney Division.

Even in a season in which the league started its invasion into New York City, two batting records fell and a no-hitter was thrown in a losing effort, Hudson Valley warranted much of the attention.

"We had the division wrapped up and we blew it," said Hudson Valley first baseman Dan Grummitt, referring to a critical three-game losing streak in the final four days of the season.

But the Renegades beat Utica 7-1 on the final night of the regular season to eliminate Pittsfield from post-season contention and claim the wild-card berth from the McNamara Division. The Renegades beat Utica in the first round of the playoffs, then took on Mahoning Valley, which had moved from Erie, Pa., after Double-A expansion stripped the NY-P of that market. The Scrappers, located in Niles, Ohio, took advantage of their Indians affiliation to draw a league-record 203,073 fans.

"We wanted this from the beginning," Grummitt said. "With the score as it was, it felt good to just go out there and appreciate the title."

Grummitt and Vermont outfielder Matt Watson came up just short in their efforts to get into the league's record books.

Watson, who led the league with a .380 batting average, missed out in his bid to become the first .400 hitter in the league since Jack Maloof did it for Auburn in 1971. He did, however, set a league record with 108 hits, beating by one the mark set by Rob Katzaroff of Jamestown in 1990.

Grummitt, meanwhile, hit 22 home runs, which was one shy of the league mark of 23 set by John Hennell of Utica in 1982.

Pittsfield's Rodney Nye shattered the league record for doubles, hitting 30. The record of 26 had been set by Demetrius Dowler of Geneva in 1993.

Staten Island, a Yankees farm team in its first season, drew 117,765 to their temporary stadium in 1999. The Lil' Yankees were one of six NY-P teams to draw at least 100,000 fans.

When Staten Island came into the league, it necessitated the change to a two-division setup. In 2000, they'll have company on the eastern side of the league because the New York Mets purchased the St. Catharines franchise and planned to relocate the team in Brooklyn. That team will be affiliated with the Blue Jays for one season as Pittsfield still had one year remaining as a Mets affiliation.

STANDINGS

Page	McNAMARA	W	L	PCT	GB	Manager	Attendance/Dates	Last Penn.
113	Mahoning Valley Scrappers (Indians)	43	33	.566	—	Ted Kubiak	203,073 (36)	none
199	Batavia Muckdogs (Phillies)	42	34	.553	1	Greg Legg	39,357 (37)	1963
138	Auburn Doubledays (Astros)	39	37	.513	4	Lyle Yates	57,933 (36)	1998
71	Jamestown Jammers (Braves)	38	38	.500	5	Jim Saul	62,428 (37)	1991
252	St. Catharines Stompers (Blue Jays)	34	42	.447	9	Eddie Rodriguez	46,905 (34)	1986
206	Williamsport Crosscutters (Pirates)	32	44	.421	11	Curtis Wilkerson	57,548 (35)	None

Page	STEDLER	W	L	PCT	GB	Manager	Attendance/Dates	Last Penn.
132	Utica Blue Sox (Marlins)	42	33	.560	—	Ken Joyce	64,468 (35)	1983
238	Hudson Valley Renegades (Devil Rays)	42	34	.553	½	Edwin Rodriguez	161,678 (38)	1999
125	Oneonta Tigers (Tigers)	41	34	.547	1	Kevin Bradshaw	51,047 (31)	1998
185	Pittsfield Mets (Mets)	41	35	.539	1½	Tony Tijerina	80,131 (38)	1997
178	Staten Island Yankees (Yankees)	39	35	.527	2½	Joe Arnold	117,765 (37)	None
85	Lowell Spinners (Red Sox)	34	42	.447	8½	Luis Aguayo	180,077 (37)	None
171	Vermont Expos (Expos)	33	43	.434	9½	Tony Barbone	112,842 (37)	1996
212	New Jersey Cardinals (Cardinals)	30	46	.395	12½	Jeff Shireman	135,802 (38)	1994

PLAYOFFS—Semifinals: Mahoning Valley defeated Batavia 2-0 and Hudson Valley defeated Utica 2-1 in best-of-3 series. **Final:** Hudson Valley defeated Mahoning Valley 2-1 in best-of-3 series.

NOTE: Team's individual batting and pitching statistics can be found on page indicated in lefthand column.

1999 New York-Penn League Statistics

CLUB BATTING

	AVG	G	AB	R	H	2B	3B	HR	BB	SO	SB
Vermont	.273	76	2680	400	732	126	24	45	289	577	94
Auburn	.262	76	2567	399	673	120	33	44	299	585	191
Utica	.259	75	2530	357	655	136	29	36	279	570	69
Lowell	.256	76	2620	379	671	137	27	44	283	574	81
Staten Island	.255	74	2457	372	626	126	23	51	278	597	67
Jamestown	.251	76	2520	365	632	117	16	55	235	599	101
Mahoning Valley	.250	76	2429	406	607	119	19	49	305	623	115
Pittsfield	.249	76	2536	368	631	137	21	41	270	591	125
Batavia	.248	76	2589	379	643	115	33	48	239	633	125
Hudson Valley	.247	76	2620	340	647	132	22	53	233	644	74
St. Catharines	.246	76	2455	332	604	115	16	42	286	655	96
Williamsport	.244	76	2522	329	616	120	13	36	270	617	108
Oneonta	.241	75	2523	313	607	112	21	25	236	637	131
New Jersey	.233	76	2494	320	582	94	39	36	192	635	97

CLUB PITCHING

	ERA	G	CG	SHO	SV	IP	H	R	ER	BB	SO
Oneonta	3.13	75	3	5	25	661	565	302	230	306	609
Hudson Valley	3.35	76	1	8	20	687	585	308	256	240	632
Pittsfield	3.69	76	0	6	20	675	655	336	277	247	540
Auburn	3.69	76	3	5	18	670	607	364	275	258	616
Utica	3.69	75	4	6	20	670	631	338	275	219	622
Batavia	3.84	76	4	6	15	668	629	341	285	277	602
Williamsport	3.89	76	7	4	16	656	622	372	284	276	565
Staten Island	3.95	74	1	3	20	647	660	333	284	207	670
Lowell	4.06	76	0	0	10	674	675	395	304	262	639
Mahoning Valley	4.19	76	1	2	19	648	650	363	302	243	638
New Jersey	4.25	76	2	2	16	665	656	377	314	277	540
Jamestown	4.48	76	3	4	23	656	630	377	327	263	638
St. Catharines	4.49	76	0	6	21	649	637	393	324	317	653
Vermont	4.81	76	1	1	19	676	724	460	362	302	573

CLUB FIELDING

	PCT	PO	A	E	DP		PCT	PO	A	E	DP
Hudson Valley	.967	2061	857	101	66	Batavia	.960	2004	769	117	63
Staten Island	.965	1942	740	96	45	St. Cath.	.959	1948	699	112	61
Utica	.965	2011	824	102	74	Mahoning	.957	1944	757	120	58
Jamestown	.964	1969	753	101	46	Williamsport	.955	1969	815	132	69
Pittsfield	.963	2025	856	112	75	Lowell	.954	2022	736	134	53
Oneonta	.961	1982	751	110	56	Vermont	.953	2028	771	138	39
New Jersey	.961	1996	855	116	65	Auburn	.946	2010	775	160	49

INDIVIDUAL BATTING LEADERS
(Minimum 205 Plate Appearances)

	AVG	G	AB	R	H	2B	3B	HR	RBI	BB	SO	SB
Watson, Matt, Vermont	.380	70	284	55	108	12	3	7	47	30	27	17
Pascucci, Valentino, Vermont	.351	72	259	62	91	26	1	7	48	53	46	17
Beinbrink, Andrew, HV	.339	76	292	46	99	24	2	11	51	39	49	13
Jackson, Brandon, St. Cath.	.332	62	214	37	71	13	1	2	25	28	45	3
Phillips, Andy, Staten Island	.322	64	233	35	75	11	7	7	48	37	40	3
Alvarez, Antonio, Williamsport	.321	58	196	44	63	14	1	7	45	21	36	38
Lucca, Tony, Utica	.321	67	240	35	77	20	1	7	47	36	47	7
Santana, Pedro, SI	.321	67	237	35	76	18	1	9	41	9	57	5
Grindell, Nate, MV	.315	71	267	42	84	20	2	5	47	24	39	6
Landreth, Jason, Williamsport	.314	62	210	35	66	14	1	6	37	34	35	5

INDIVIDUAL PITCHING LEADERS
(Minimum 61 Innings)

	W	L	ERA	G	GS	CG	SV	IP	H	R	ER	BB	SO
Moser, Todd, Utica	8	2	1.53	14	14	3	0	88	63	20	15	24	86
Leek, Randy, Oneonta	6	3	1.56	21	3	1	1	63	58	16	11	9	68
Nannini, Mike, Auburn	5	3	1.90	11	11	2	0	76	55	19	16	17	86
Dean, Aaron, St. Catharines	4	0	2.34	17	8	0	1	62	50	18	16	13	68
Kennedy, Joe, Hudson Valley	6	5	2.65	16	16	1	0	95	78	33	28	26	101
Pineda, Jairo, Auburn	9	2	2.88	15	15	1	0	84	70	35	27	31	67
Brooks, Frank, Batavia	7	3	2.91	16	12	1	0	77	64	26	25	33	58
Graman, Alex, Staten Island	3	2	2.99	14	14	0	0	81	74	30	27	16	85
Hendricks, John, Pittsfield	5	4	3.04	15	14	0	0	80	78	38	27	19	64
Walling, Dave, Staten Island	8	2	3.14	14	14	0	0	80	76	31	28	18	82

ALL-STAR TEAM

C—Victor Martinez, Mahoning Valley. **1B**—Jason Lane, Auburn. **2B**—Nick Green, Jamestown. **3B**—Andrew Beinbrink, Hudson Valley. **SS**—Seth Taylor, Staten Island. **Res. Inf.**—Antonio Alvarez, Williamsport. **OF**—Matt Cepicky, Vermont; Valentino Pascucci, Vermont; Matt Watson, Vermont. **DH**—Marlon Byrd, Batavia. **RHP**—Mike Nannini, Auburn; David Walling, Staten Island. **LHP**—Joe Kennedy, Hudson Valley; Todd Moser, Utica.

Most Valuable Players: Andrew Beinbrink, Hudson Valley (McNamara Division); Antonio Alvarez, Williamsport (Stedler Division).

TOP 10 PROSPECTS

1. Alex Graman, lhp, Staten Island; **2.** Terry Byron, rhp, Utica; **3.** Tony Alvarez, 3b, Williamsport; **4.** Chip Ambres, of, Utica; **5.** Mike Nannini, rhp, Auburn; **6.** David Walling, rhp, Staten Island; **7.** J.R. House, c-1b, Williamsport; **8.** Nick Green, 2b, Jamestown; **9.** Asdrubal Oropeza, 3b, Jamestown; **10.** Matt McClendon, rhp, Jamestown.

DEPT. LEADERS

BATTING
G	Andrew Beinbrink, HV	76
AB	Matt Cepicky, Vermont	323
R	Valentino Pascucci, Vermont	62
H	Matt Watson, Vermont	108
TB	Andrew Beinbrink, HV	160
	Matt Cepicky, Vermont	160
XBH	Rodney Nye, Pittsfield	39
2B	Rodney Nye, Pittsfield	30
3B	Travis Bailey, New Jersey	8
	Ramon Carvajal, New Jersey	8
HR	Dan Grummitt, Hudson Valley	22
RBI	Jason Lane, Auburn	59
SH	Three tied at	5
SF	Jossephang Bernhardt, St.C.	7
	Jorge Moreno, Mahoning Valley	7
BB	Josh Holliday, St. Catharines	63
IBB	Three tied at	3
HBP	Antonio Alvarez, Williamsport	16
SO	Brian Martin, Hudson Valley	107
SB	Alex Requena, Mahoning Valley	44
CS	Tim Lemon, New Jersey	16
GIDP	Scott Goodman, Utica	10
OB%	Valentino Pascucci, Vermont	.482
SL%	Andrew Beinbrink, HV	.548

PITCHING
G	Brandon Peck, New Jersey	31
	Greg Watson, Oneonta	31
GS	Joe Kennedy, Hudson Valley	16
CG	Todd Moser, Utica	3
ShO	Brad Pautz, Batavia	2
GF	Jose Ortiz, Hudson Valley	27
	Greg Watson, Oneonta	27
SV	Greg Watson, Oneonta	19
W	Jairo Pineda, Auburn	9
L	Joe Orloski, St. Catharines	9
IP	Joe Kennedy, Hudson Valley	95
H	Orlando Encarnacion, Pittsfield	102
R	Rick Riccobono, Lowell	63
ER	Diegomar Markwell, St.C.	50
HR	Four tied at	10
HB	Rick Riccobono, Lowell	11
	Chris Rojas, Williamsport	11
BB	Ryan Madson, Batavia	43
	Chris Rojas, Williamsport	43
SO	Joe Kennedy, Hudson Valley	101
WP	Gaige Thomas, Utica	16

FIELDING
C	AVG	Steve Elzy, Pittsfield	.989
	PO	John Buck, Auburn	549
	A	Victor Martinez, MV	56
	E	John Buck, Auburn	16
	DP	John Buck, Auburn	5
		Maxim St. Pierre, Oneonta	5
	PB	Dominic Woody, Utica	18
1B	AVG	Francisco Lebron, Pitt.	.998
	PO	Dan Grummitt, HV	620
	A	Jeff Leaumont, SI	59
	E	Dan Grummitt, HV	11
	DP	Tony Lucca, Utica	61
2B	AVG	Kevin Hooper, Utica	.989
	PO	Frank Moore, HV	148
	A	Kevin Hooper, Utica	215
	E	Frank Moore, HV	16
	DP	Kevin Hooper, Utica	50
3B	AVG	Andrew Beinbrink, HV	.952
	PO	Andrew Beinbrink, HV	52
	A	Andrew Beinbrink, HV	185
	E	Nate Grindell, MV	22
	DP	Andrew Beinbrink, HV	15
SS	AVG	Ian Calais, Jamestown	.946
	PO	Jorge Cantu, HV	111
	A	Brian Shipp, Pittsfield	217
	E	Cesar Saba, Lowell	35
	DP	Brian Shipp, Pittsfield	46
OF	AVG	Jesus Lebron, St. Cath.	.993
	PO	Alfredo Mento, Pittsfield	162
	A	Matt Diaz, Hudson Valley	12
	E	Shomari Beverly, Batavia	8
	DP	Five tied at	3

Minor Leagues

NORTHWESTLEAGUE

Spokane pops corks, while Portland waits to celebrate

BY SUSAN WADE

In Portland, partying was such sweet sorrow.

The Portland Rockies, expected to move as the city brings back Triple-A baseball for the 2001 season, showed that short-season baseball was electrifying in its own right. The Rockies won the Southern Division title and, armed with one of the Northwest League's better pitching staffs, they were poised to present the city with a triumphant—and maybe defiant—gift of a second championship in three years.

But the champagne went flat for owners Jack and Mary Cain, who had signed an agreement to sell the team to Portland Family Entertainment and allow for the Calgary Cannons' move to Oregon after the 2000 season.

The Spokane Indians swept Portland in the best-of-5 championship series to take their first pennant since 1990, when they completed a streak of four consecutive titles. Spokane's 5-1, 14-3 and 7-3 victories ended the Southern Division's dominance. The South's entry had won the league championship in five of the previous six seasons.

Spokane manager Kevin Long, who helped coach Wilmington to the 1998 Class A Carolina League championship, said after the clinching Game Three, "We played so free and easy, as relaxed as I've seen us play all year."

Boise's Robb Quinlan
League MVP

Neither Spokane nor Portland took an easy path to the final series.

The Indians' staff, which included NWL No. 1 prospect Kyle Snyder, led the league with a 4.19 ERA. Snyder, the Royals' first-round pick in 1999 out of the University of North Carolina, threw in the mid- to high 90s as he went 1-0 with a 4.13 ERA.

Spokane also had batting champion Ken Harvey, but the Indians topped Boise by just one game.

Harvey's .397 average fell just six points short of the NWL record set by Boise's Ron McNeely in 1976. Harvey, a fifth-round pick out of the University of Nebraska, also had the best on-base percentage (.477) and slugging percentage (.598).

Spokane had a franchise-record 12-game winning streak from July 17-28 to build a 5½-game lead, but needed to win at Yakima on the last day of the season because Boise had the tiebreaker advantage.

The Hawks couldn't quite catch Spokane, but they had league MVP and RBI champion Robb Quinlan.

FRANK RAGSDALE

Spokane's Kyle Snyder
Strict pitch count

Everett, with outstanding pitching, challenged, as well. The AquaSox boasted the second-best team ERA (4.29), behind the 10 wins of Australian lefthander Craig Anderson. Everett's Aquilino Lopez, Rafael Soriano and Anderson were 1-2-3 in the NWL in strikeouts.

The Rockies also earned their division crown on the final day. They were 5½ games out of first as late as Aug. 7.

Southern Oregon, which had held onto first place for 74 of the season's 76 days, lost 18 of its final 30 games. And Portland was 18-11 down the stretch.

The championship series pitted two teams that split 10 games in the regular season. However, Harvey immediately hammered away any notion that the series would be balanced. He hit a grand slam in the bottom of the eighth inning in the series opener. And that, Long said, was the pivotal point of the playoffs.

"If they (had won) that game, everything's different," he said.

With Portland out of the league after the 2000 season and Southern Oregon considering a move even sooner, Vancouver, Wash., and Vancouver, B.C., were among the cities seeking a relocated NWL team.

Minor Leagues

STANDINGS

Page	NORTH	W	L	PCT	GB	Manager	Attendance/Dates	Last Penn.
145	Spokane Indians (Royals)	44	32	.579	—	Kevin Long	187,315 (38)	1999
57	Boise Hawks (Angels)	43	33	.566	1	Tom Kotchman	132,885 (38)	1995
231	Everett AquaSox (Mariners)	41	35	.539	3	Terry Pollreisz	103,455 (35)	1985
151	Yakima Bears (Dodgers)	33	43	.434	11	Dino Ebel	74,977 (38)	1996

Page	SOUTH	W	L	PCT	GB	Manager	Attendance/Dates	Last Penn.
119	Portland Rockies (Rockies)	39	37	.513	—	Alan Cockrell	206,136 (38)	1997
192	Southern Oregon Timberjacks (Athletics)	38	38	.500	1	Greg Sparks	69,495 (38)	1983
225	Salem-Keizer Volcanoes (Giants)	37	39	.487	2	Frank Reberger	124,627 (37)	1998
99	Eugene Emeralds (Cubs)	29	47	.382	10	Bob Ralston	122,500 (36)	1980

PLAYOFFS—Spokane defeated Portland 3-0 in best-of-5 series.
NOTE: Team's individual batting and pitching statistics can be found on page indicated in lefthand column.

1999 Northwest League Statistics

CLUB BATTING

	AVG	G	AB	R	H	2B	3B	HR	BB	SO	SB
Boise	.302	76	2697	556	814	167	17	49	381	515	77
Spokane	.283	76	2648	477	749	138	16	62	303	476	110
Southern Oregon	.269	76	2631	489	708	136	26	73	401	631	101
Everett	.268	76	2589	423	693	139	17	55	310	563	83
Eugene	.266	76	2576	390	684	123	14	57	226	556	83
Portland	.263	76	2630	416	692	142	22	70	279	684	71
Salem-Keizer	.262	76	2582	426	677	117	13	48	312	544	128
Yakima	.260	76	2517	418	654	126	11	55	314	582	103

CLUB PITCHING

	ERA	G	CG	SHO	SV	IP	H	R	ER	BB	SO
Spokane	4.17	76	0	1	19	673	669	383	312	298	624
Everett	4.29	76	4	4	18	663	626	395	316	355	640
Portland	4.74	76	1	1	24	669	672	443	352	354	607
Salem-Keizer	4.87	76	2	1	21	664	705	432	359	319	570
Boise	4.89	76	3	2	17	669	738	451	364	254	554
Southern Oregon	5.16	76	0	1	12	672	742	486	386	333	484
Yakima	5.62	76	1	1	17	667	746	504	417	319	476
Eugene	5.85	76	0	4	12	650	773	501	423	294	596

CLUB FIELDING

	PCT	PO	A	E	DP		PCT	PO	A	E	DP
Spokane	.961	2019	858	118	59	Yakima	.957	2002	890	129	74
Salem-Keizer	.959	1991	808	119	70	So. Oregon	.955	2017	901	139	55
Boise	.958	2008	879	126	65	Everett	.952	1988	788	139	71
Eugene	.958	1951	727	117	67	Portland	.949	2006	782	150	51

INDIVIDUAL BATTING LEADERS
(Minimum 205 Plate Appearances)

	AVG	G	AB	R	H	2B	3B	HR	RBI	BB	SO	SB
Harvey, Ken, Spokane	.397	56	204	49	81	17	0	8	41	23	30	7
Lockwood, Mike, So. Oregon	.361	69	255	48	92	18	5	7	51	39	49	6
Barski, Chris, Boise	.348	53	184	39	64	14	0	6	39	30	44	1
Medina, Luis, Eugene	.337	56	202	30	68	6	0	3	31	11	21	2
McGowan, Sean, Salem-Keizer	.335	63	257	40	86	12	1	15	62	20	56	3
Johnstone, Benjamin, Eugene	.333	54	186	34	62	9	0	1	11	9	30	16
Ellis, Mark, Spokane	.327	71	281	67	92	14	0	7	47	47	40	21
O'Keefe, Michael, Boise	.326	72	264	52	86	13	1	9	70	54	41	4
Raymundo, Gregg, Spokane	.323	67	254	44	82	16	1	11	44	32	37	1
Quinlan, Robb, Boise	.322	73	295	51	95	20	1	9	77	44	18	5

INDIVIDUAL PITCHING LEADERS
(Minimum 61 Innings)

	W	L	ERA	G	GS	CG	SV	IP	H	R	ER	BB	SO
Crawford, Wesley, Boise	5	1	2.21	11	9	2	0	61	52	23	15	17	54
Soriano, Rafael, Everett	5	4	3.11	14	14	0	0	75	56	34	26	49	83
Anderson, Craig, Everett	10	2	3.20	15	15	2	0	90	81	42	32	13	82
Lopez, Aquilino, Everett	7	6	3.80	15	15	1	0	88	76	44	37	30	93
Esslinger, Cam, Portland	6	3	3.83	14	14	0	0	80	76	37	34	35	68
King, James, Spokane	7	2	3.88	17	7	0	0	72	60	38	31	29	63
Devey, Phil, Yakima	5	4	3.91	13	13	1	0	78	70	43	34	27	56
Pacheco, Enemencio, Portland	4	3	3.95	12	12	1	0	73	73	43	32	21	44
Surkont, Keith, So. Orgeon	5	3	4.48	17	13	0	1	74	85	45	37	35	39
Cozier, Vance, Salem-Keizer	5	4	4.57	15	10	0	0	61	61	34	31	24	46

ALL-STAR TEAM

C—Gerald Laird, Southern Oregon. **1B**—Sean McGowan, Salem-Keizer. **2B**—Alfredo Amezaga, Boise. **3B**—G.J. Raymundo, Spokane. **SS**—Mark Ellis, Spokane. **OF**—Kirk Asche, Southern Oregon; Michael O'Keefe, Boise; Chris Snelling, Everett. **DH**—Ken Harvey, Spokane. **RHP**—Cam Esslinger, Portland. **LHP**—Craig Anderson, Everett. **RH Reliever**—Jay Gehrke, Spokane. **LH Reliever**—Tony Cogan, Spokane; Bryan Mazur, Southern Oregon.

Most Valuable Player: Robb Quinlan, Boise. **Co-Managers of the Year:** Kevin Long, Spokane; Greg Sparks, Southern Oregon.

TOP 10 PROSPECTS

1. Kyle Snyder, rhp, Spokane; **2.** Ryan Christianson, c, Everett; **3.** Kurt Ainsworth, rhp, Salem-Keizer; **4.** Mike MacDougal, rhp, Spokane; **5.** Chris Snelling, of, Everett; **6.** Brian Sanches, rhp, Spokane; **7.** Gerald Laird, c, Southern Oregon; **8.** Willie Bloomquist, 2b, Everett; **9.** Ruben Castillo, ss, Everett; **10.** Craig House, rhp, Portland.

DEPT. LEADERS

BATTING

G	Tony Gsell, Eugene	76
AB	Robb Quinlan, Boise	295
R	Mark Ellis, Spokane	67
	Joe Jester, Salem-Keizer	67
H	Robb Quinlan, Boise	95
TB	Kirk Asche, Southern Oregon	146
XBH	Kirk Asche, Southern Oregon	34
	Tony Gsell, Eugene	34
2B	Kevin Burford, Portland	22
	Scott Bikowski, Boise	22
3B	Matt Forbes, So. Oregon	6
HR	Kirk Asche, Southern Oregon	17
	Lamont Matthews, Yakima	17
RBI	Robb Quinlan, Boise	77
SH	James Shanks, Spokane	11
SF	Brad Henderson, So. Oregon	7
BB	Michael OiKeefe, Boise	54
IBB	Three tied at	4
HBP	Joe Thurston, Yakima	21
SO	Justin Lincoln, Portland	102
SB	Carlos Rosario, So. Oregon	31
CS	Joe Thurston, Yakima	17
GIDP	Jacob Baker, Spokane	14
OB%	Ken Harvey, Spokane	.477
SL%	Ken Harvey, Spokane	.598

PITCHING

G	Raul Garcia, Spokane	32
	Jay Gehrke, Spokane	32
GS	Julio De Paula, Portland	16
CG	Craig Anderson, Everett	2
	Wesley Crawford, Boise	2
ShO	Three tied at	1
GF	Jay Gehrke, Spokane	32
SV	Jay Gehrke, Spokane	13
W	Craig Anderson, Everett	10
L	Jeramy Gomer, Eugene	11
IP	Craig Anderson, Everett	90
H	Jeramy Gomer, Eugene	106
R	Jeramy Gomer, Eugene	70
ER	Jeramy Gomer, Eugene	67
HR	Fernando Rijo, Yakima	14
HB	Paul Vracar, Eugene	13
BB	Sam Walton, Everett	60
SO	Aquilino Lopez, Everett	93
WP	Sam Walton, Everett	16
BK	Fletcher Lee, Salem-Keizer	6

FIELDING

C	AVG	Chris Curry, Eugene	.991
	PO	Eric McQueen, Portland	347
	A	Gerald Laird, So. Oregon	70
	E	Gerald Laird, So. Oregon	11
	DP	Eric McQueen, Portland	7
	PB	Gerald Laird, So. Oregon	19
1B	AVG	Casey Kelley, Boise	.994
	PO	Justin Hemme, Portland	579
	A	Jeremy Schied, So. Oregon	43
	E	Justin Hemme, Portland	15
	DP	Cliff Wren, Yakima	52
2B	AVG	Mike Dzurilla, Eugene	.966
	PO	Mike Dzurilla, Eugene	138
	A	Eric Nelson, Spokane	189
	E	Eric Nelson, Spokane	22
	DP	Mike Dzurilla, Eugene	35
3B	AVG	Ryan Gripp, Eugene	.938
	PO	Julio Cordido, S-K	60
	A	Robb Quinlan, Boise	147
	E	Robb Quinlan, Boise	23
	DP	Ryan Gripp, Eugene	21
SS	AVG	Mark Ellis, Spokane	.958
	PO	Mark Ellis, Spokane	137
	A	Joe Thurston, Yakima	246
	E	Joe Thurston, Yakima	29
	DP	Joe Thurston, Yakima	43
OF	AVG	Chris Snelling, Everett	.993
	PO	Lamont Matthews, Yakima	160
	A	Greg Catalanotte, Portland	12
	E	Kevin Bass, Eugene	8
		James Shanks, Spokane	8
	DP	Three tied at	3

APPALACHIAN LEAGUE

In win-starved Martinsville, Astros have Midas touch

BY JAMES BAILEY

The 1999 season might best be remembered by some as the year Josh Hamilton toured the Appalachian League. Others will recall Elizabethton infielder Ruben Salazar's .400 season and run at the triple crown. But fans in Martinsville will cherish it as the year they finally got to learn what a pennant race felt like.

After 11 seasons—and not a winning one among them—as a Phillies affiliate, Martinsville became an Astros farm club for the '99 season. The team battled hard in the Eastern Division all year, finally clinching first place on the next-to-last day of the season.

Martinsville lefthander Carlos Hernandez, who led the league with a 1.46 ERA, struck out 18 and allowed only one hit in seven innings against Elizabethton—the league's top-hitting team—in Martinsville's division-clinching win.

The Astros then went on to upset the favored Pulaski Rangers in the playoffs to win the league championship.

Pulaski's lineup featured many of the top hitters in the league, including left fielder Kevin Mench, who led the league with 16 home runs. But the key to the Rangers' charge through the regular season was their pitching staff.

Righthander Aaron Harang was named the Appy League's pitcher of the year after winning a league-best nine games and finishing third in both ERA and strikeouts. He was backed up by righthanders Ryan Dittfurth, Colby Lewis and Nick Regilio—all of whom could have been the ace of just about any rotation in the league. Lewis and Regilio were both among the first 100 players drafted in 1999.

Despite their outstanding rotation, the Rangers didn't clinch the Western Division title until the season's final day. Throughout the season they took turns in first place with the Bristol Sox, the reigning league champs.

In the postseason, the Astros took the first game of the series at Pulaski by a 6-5 margin and returned home for the first Appy League playoff game in Martinsville history. Third baseman Jonathan Helquist was the offensive star, hitting a three-run homer to start the scoring for the Astros, and they held on for another 6-5 win and the championship.

Hamilton's tour of the league came to an early end when he was promoted to short-season Hudson Valley in mid-August and helped that team win the New York-Penn League championship. But he certainly lived up to every expectation in his two-month stint. The No. 1 pick in the 1999 draft, Hamilton was a landslide selection as the top prospect in the league. He homered in his first and last games and had plenty of other hits in between, finishing at .347 with 10 homers and 48 RBIs.

He was upstaged only by Salazar's run at the triple crown. The Elizabethton infielder, who hit just .248 in the Gulf Coast League in 1998, made a run at the league batting record before settling at .401. A 4-for-4 game on the final day of the season would have put Salazar at .410 and slightly ahead of the record set by Wytheville's Tony Oliva in 1961. But Salazar, who was nursing a sore arm much of the season, was held out of the contest. He finished first in both batting and RBIs, and missed the triple crown by just two home runs.

Bristol center fielder Chad Durham stole 57 bases, falling just short of the 60 stolen the year before by Danville's Rafael Furcal.

In addition to Hamilton, the other 1999 first-round pick to play in the league was Elizabethton center fielder B.J. Garbe. Outfielders Larry Bigbie and Keith Reed also made brief appearances with Bluefield before moving on to the South Atlantic League.

Ruben Salazar
Hit .401

STANDINGS

Page	EAST	W	L	PCT	GB	Manager	Attendance/Dates	Last Penn.
139	Martinsville Astros (Astros)	41	29	.586	—	Brad Wellman	43,309 (34)	1999
71	Danville Braves (Braves)	38	31	.551	2 ½	J.J. Cannon	57,044 (32)	None
78	Bluefield Orioles (Orioles)	25	43	.368	15	Duffy Dyer	32,392 (32)	1997
239	Princeton Devil Rays (Devil Rays)	25	45	.357	16	Bobby Ramos	33,017 (34)	1994
114	Burlington Indians (Indians)	21	49	.300	20	Jack Mull	43,718 (33)	1993
Page	WEST	W	L	PCT	GB	Manager	Attendance/Dates	Last Penn.
245	Pulaski Rangers (Rangers)	48	21	.696	—	Bruce Crabbe	16,370 (31)	None
92	Bristol Sox (White Sox)	45	24	.652	3	Gary Pellant	22,194 (31)	1998
164	Elizabethton Twins (Twins)	40	30	.571	8 ½	Jon Mathews	11,823 (33)	1990
186	Kingsport Mets (Mets)	34	36	.486	14 ½	Guy Conti	55,457 (31)	1995
213	Johnson City Cardinals (Cardinals)	30	39	.435	18	Steve Turco	15,193 (35)	1976

PLAYOFFS—Martinsville defeated Pulaski 2-0 in best-of-3 series.
NOTE: Team's individual batting and pitching statistics can be found on page indicated in lefthand column.

1999 Appalachian League Statistics

CLUB BATTING

	AVG	G	AB	R	H	2B	3B	HR	BB	SO	SB
Elizabethton	.297	70	2515	505	748	148	28	73	346	589	74
Pulaski	.289	69	2356	475	681	141	16	75	269	545	86
Bristol	.275	69	2309	392	635	108	14	46	275	478	131
Kingsport	.272	70	2373	378	646	110	18	40	237	566	130
Danville	.269	69	2343	408	631	121	28	30	304	594	85
Princeton	.265	70	2411	384	640	137	16	53	209	703	86
Bluefield	.259	68	2375	445	616	111	30	59	310	587	51
Martinsville	.254	70	2318	366	589	131	24	37	253	611	159
Johnson City	.241	69	2357	366	569	98	20	44	266	674	123
Burlington	.228	70	2318	336	529	85	14	34	271	624	82

CLUB PITCHING

	ERA	G	CG	SHO	SV	IP	H	R	ER	BB	SO
Bristol	3.89	69	4	4	25	592	596	346	256	242	662
Pulaski	4.01	69	4	8	20	590	579	343	263	262	589
Kingston	4.32	70	2	2	12	612	595	369	294	314	603
Elizabethton	4.35	70	1	3	16	612	658	390	296	258	602
Danville	4.47	69	0	2	15	597	611	398	297	248	614
Burlington	4.66	70	1	1	9	602	634	429	312	269	617
Johnson City	4.77	69	1	5	12	611	637	408	324	268	584
Bluefield	5.76	68	1	0	9	585	696	505	374	291	571
Princeton	6.30	70	0	0	13	594	722	544	416	343	483

CLUB FIELDING

	PCT	PO	A	E	DP		PCT	PO	A	E	DP
Kingsport	.957	1836	744	117	55	Elizabethton	.947	1836	805	148	42
Martinsville	.956	1831	754	118	59	Danville	.944	1791	725	150	49
Pulaski	.956	1770	684	113	50	Princeton	.937	1783	774	173	52
Bristol	.951	1777	692	128	48	Bluefield	.933	1754	708	178	58
Johnson City	.949	1834	782	141	48	Burlington	.931	1807	687	185	44

INDIVIDUAL BATTING LEADERS
(Minimum 184 Plate Appearances)

	AVG	G	AB	R	H	2B	3B	HR	RBI	BB	SO	SB
Salazar, Ruben, Elizabethton	.401	64	262	66	105	24	2	14	65	48	43	11
Brazell, Craig, Kingsport	.385	59	221	27	85	16	1	6	39	7	34	6
Mench, Kevin, Pulaski	.362	65	260	63	94	22	1	16	60	28	48	12
Jones, Jason, Pulaski	.355	69	262	65	93	24	1	11	58	33	55	1
Scanlon, Matt, Elizabethton	.354	57	240	54	85	16	5	6	48	36	45	8
Cadiente, Brett, Pulaski	.354	68	274	69	97	16	7	7	48	28	51	18
Hamilton, Josh, Princeton	.347	56	236	49	82	20	4	10	48	13	43	17
Fiore, Curt, Danville	.333	53	198	35	66	13	0	3	24	22	39	0
Johnson, Ben, Johnson City	.330	57	203	38	67	9	1	10	51	29	57	14
Elder, Rick, Bluefield	.329	46	158	35	52	8	4	10	40	30	57	2

INDIVIDUAL PITCHING LEADERS
(Minimum 54 Innings)

	W	L	ERA	G	GS	CG	SV	IP	H	R	ER	BB	SO
Lewis, Colby, Pulaski	7	3	1.95	14	11	1	0	65	46	24	14	27	84
Harang, Aaron, Pulaski	9	2	2.30	16	10	1	1	78	64	22	20	17	87
Dittfurth, Ryan, Pulaski	7	2	2.60	14	14	1	0	83	66	35	24	42	85
Stanford, Derek, Martinsville	4	4	2.87	11	9	0	0	60	39	28	19	25	75
Valera, Nelson, Princeton	5	2	2.91	23	1	0	1	59	55	26	19	15	52
Simpson, Andre, Bristol	7	1	3.00	13	13	1	0	72	69	33	24	22	79
Majewski, Gary, Bristol	7	1	3.05	13	13	1	0	77	67	34	26	37	91
Chenard, Kenneth, Kingsport	5	6	3.07	14	13	1	0	76	64	32	26	25	80
Sprague, Kevin, Johnson City	5	3	3.23	11	11	0	0	64	47	27	23	27	73
Mendez, David, Danville	6	3	3.25	12	12	0	0	61	61	32	22	28	74

ALL-STAR TEAM

C—Frederick Torres, Pulaski. 1B—Chris Delgado, Bristol. 2B—Ruben Salazar, Elizabethton. 3B—Matt Scanlon, Pulaski. SS—Wilson Betemit, Danville. OF—Chad Durham, Bristol; Josh Hamilton, Princeton; Kevin Mench, Pulaski. DH—Rick Elder, Bluefield. Util—Eric Sandberg, Elizabethton; Gavin Wright, Martinsville. RHP—Aaron Harang, Pulaski. LHP—Randy Perez, Bluefield. RP—Santiago Ramirez, Martinsville.

Player of the Year: Ruben Salazar, Elizabethton. Pitcher of the Year: Aaron Harang, Pulaski. Manager of the Year: Bruce Crabbe, Pulaski.

TOP 10 PROSPECTS

1. Josh Hamilton, of, Princeton; 2. Wilson Betemit, ss, Danville; 3. B.J. Garbe, of, Elizabethton; 4. Colby Lewis, rhp, Pulaski; 5. Rick Elder, 1b-of, Bluefield; 6. Ryan Dittfurth, rhp, Pulaski; 7. Carl Crawford, of, Princeton; 8. Cody Nowlin, of, Pulaski; 9. Juan Salas, ss, Princeton; 10. Angel Caraballo, rhp, Bristol.

DEPT. LEADERS

BATTING

G	Five tied at	68
AB	Damien Jones, Danville	284
R	Brett Cadiente, Pulaski	69
H	Ruben Salazar, Elizabethton	105
TB	Ruben Salazar, Elizabethton	175
XBH	Ruben Salazar, Elizabethton	40
2B	Jason Jones, Pulaski	24
	Ruben Salazar, Elizabethton	24
3B	Brett Cadiente, Pulaski	7
	Royce Huffman, Martinsville	7
HR	Kevin Mench, Pulaski	16
RBI	Ruben Salazar, Elizabethton	65
SH	Covelli Crisp, Johnson City	8
SF	Oscar Garcia, Burlington	6
BB	Michael Forbes, Danville	53
IBB	Craig Brazell, Kingsport	4
HBP	J.J. Sherrill, Burlington	26
SO	Isrrael Osorio, Princeton	79
SB	Chad Durham, Bristol	57
CS	Chad Durham, Bristol	13
GIDP	Johnny Hernandez, Johnson City	9
	Eric Sandberg, Elizabethton	9
OB%	Ruben Salazar, Elizabethton	.498
SL%	Ruben Salazar, Elizabethton	.668

PITCHING

G	Brian Stokes, Princeton	33
GS	Several tied at	14
CG	Several tied at	1
ShO	Several tied at	1
GF	Brian Stokes, Princeton	27
SV	Santiago Ramirez, Martinsville	17
W	Aaron Harang, Pulaski	9
L	Scott Vandermeer, Princeton	8
	Billy Whitecotton, Bluefield	8
IP	Ryan Dittfurth, Pulaski	83
H	Jon Pridie, Elizabethton	93
R	Ben Knapp, Bluefield	77
ER	Ben Knapp, Bluefield	60
HR	Ben Knapp, Bluefield	12
HB	Ryan Dittfurth, Pulaski	15
BB	Enger Veras, Princeton	50
SO	Gary Majewski, Bristol	91
WP	Doug Waechter, Princeton	21
BK	Angel Caraballo, Bristol	5
	Kris McWhirter, Bristol	5

FIELDING

C	AVG	Humberto Quintero, Bristol	.987
	PO	Frederick Torres, Pulaski	410
	A	Nell Alvarez, Kingsport	66
	E	Fernando Gutierrez, Blue.	10
	DP	Brent Spooner, Johnson City	3
	PB	Frederick Torres, Pulaski	20
1B	AVG	Nickolas Crocker, Danville	.992
	PO	Eric Sandberg, Eliz.	586
	A	Isrrael Osorio, Princeton	39
		Eric Sandberg, Elizabethton	39
	E	Isrrael Osorio, Princeton	16
	DP	Jason Jones, Pulaski	40
2B	AVG	Regino Nolasco, Bluefield	.957
	PO	Yurendel De Caster, Prin.	131
	A	Covelli Crisp, Johnson City	149
	E	Covelli Crisp, Johnson City	24
	DP	Yurendel De Caster, Prin.	26
3B	AVG	Eric Guyton, Kingsport	.924
	PO	John Jacobs, Princeton	44
	A	John Jacobs, Princeton	126
	E	John Jacobs, Princeton	26
	DP	John Jacobs, Princeton	10
SS	AVG	Gil Velazquez, Kingsport	.950
	PO	Wilson Betemit, Danville	92
	A	Chad Wandall, Elizabethton	204
	E	Chad Wandall, Elizabethton	35
	DP	Gil Velazquez, Kingsport	38
OF	AVG	Kevin Mench, Pulaski	.989
	PO	J.J. Sherrill, Bristol	139
	A	Justo Rivas, Danville	14
	E	Damien Jones, Danville	13
	DP	Ben Johnson, Johnson City	2
		Aristides Lopez, Martinsville	2

PIONEER LEAGUE

Osprey fly sky-high in inaugural season in Missoula

BY JAMES BAILEY

Maybe it was beginner's luck. Or perhaps a change of scenery was enough to put them over the hump. Whatever the explanation, the Missoula Osprey went home with the Pioneer League crown in their first year of existence.

Missoula was led in the postseason by third baseman Jeff Brooks, who homered in each game of the championship series as his club swept the Billings Mustangs, 2-0. And it was a Brooks single that plated the winning run in the bottom of the ninth inning in Game Two, to give Missoula a 6-5 win and the league title.

For Brooks and a few other Diamondbacks farmhands, the victory washed away the disappointment of losing in the 1998 finals as members of the Lethbridge Black Diamonds, the club that moved to Missoula during the offseason.

Billings' Broussard
Memorable night

Brooks, who hit .339 with 12 homers and 60 RBIs during the season, was overshadowed on his own club by first baseman Lyle Overbay, who broke the league record with 101 RBIs. The next best total in the league was 69 by Idaho Falls third baseman Troy Schader.

Overbay, who batted .343 with 12 homers, was an easy choice as MVP. In addition to RBIs, he led the league in hits, total bases, doubles and extra-base hits.

Overbay was upstaged, at least for a day, by Billings outfielder Ben Broussard on July 12. Broussard, the Reds' second-round pick, exploded for three homers and two doubles in a 5-for-5 showing against Great Falls that day. His performance set league records for total bases (16) and RBIs (11) in a game. Broussard,

who also had five hits in a game six days earlier, soon earned a ticket out of Billings and finished the season in Double-A. He hit .407 in a 38-game stint for the Mustangs.

Butte righthander Francisco Rodriguez, 17, was named the league's top prospect. He struck out 69 hitters in 52 innings for the Copper Kings while posting a 3.31 ERA.

Eight first-rounders from the 1999 draft made their marks in the league, including Missoula shortstop Corey Myers, Medicine Hat outfielder Alex Rios, Great Falls shortstop Jason Repko and Ogden righthander Ben Sheets. Sheets made just a two-start tuneup with the Raptors before moving on to Class A Stockton.

The other four were all on Idaho Falls' pitching staff: righthanders Gerik Baxter, Casey Burns and Omar Ortiz and lefthander Mike Bynum. Bynum didn't yield an earned run in 17 innings of work, earning a promotion to Class A Rancho Cucamonga. With that stock of pitching on hand it was no wonder that Idaho Falls finished with the best overall record in the league.

But the Braves, like Helena which finished with second-best record, made an early exit in the postseason. Idaho Falls was swept by Missoula in the first round of the playoffs and Helena was swept by Billings.

STANDINGS: SPLIT SEASON

FIRST HALF

NORTH	W	L	PCT	GB
Missoula	28	10	.737	—
Helena	21	17	.553	7
Medicine Hat	16	22	.421	12
Great Falls	14	24	.368	14

SOUTH	W	L	PCT	GB
Idaho Falls	24	14	.632	—
Billings	22	16	.579	2
Butte	17	21	.447	7
Ogden	10	28	.263	14

SECOND HALF

NORTH	W	L	PCT	GB
Helena	26	11	.703	—
Missoula	17	21	.447	9½
Medicine Hat	17	21	.447	9½
Great Falls	15	23	.395	11½

SOUTH	W	L	PCT	GB
Idaho Falls	24	13	.649	—
Billings	20	17	.541	4
Ogden	16	22	.421	8½
Butte	15	22	.405	9

PLAYOFFS—Semifinals: Billings defeated Idaho Falls 2-0 and Missoula defeated Helena 2-0 in best-of-3 series. **Final:** Missoula defeated Billings 2-0 in best-of-3 series.

STANDINGS: OVERALL

Page		W	L	PCT	GB	Manager(s)	Attendance/Dates	Last Penn.
219	Idaho Falls Braves (Padres)	48	27	.640	—	Don Werner	64,134 (37)	1998
158	Helena Brewers (Brewers)	47	28	.627	1	Carlos Lezcano	25,979 (36)	1984
64	Missoula Osprey (Diamondbacks)	45	31	.592	3½	Joe Almaraz	56,099 (38)	1999
106	Billings Mustangs (Reds)	42	33	.560	6	Russ Nixon	92,147 (37)	1997
253	Medicine Hat Blue Jays (Blue Jays)	33	43	.434	15½	Paul Elliott	26,852 (36)	1982
58	Butte Copper Kings (Angels)	32	43	.427	16	Joe Urso	20,119 (37)	1981
152	Great Falls Dodgers (Dodgers)	29	47	.382	19½	Tony Harris	87,687 (38)	1990
159	Ogden Raptors (Brewers)	26	50	.342	22½	Jon Pont/Ed Sedar	81,345 (36)	None

NOTE: Team's individual batting and pitching statistics can be found on the page indicated in lefthand column.

1999 Pioneer League Statistics

CLUB BATTING

	AVG	G	AB	R	H	2B	3B	HR	BB	SO	SB
Butte	.290	75	2641	529	765	132	34	51	284	585	109
Billings	.288	75	2645	489	761	152	27	70	292	613	50
Idaho Falls	.285	75	2653	546	755	165	35	68	334	646	153
Missoula	.284	76	2668	552	759	142	33	59	376	658	150
Helena	.281	75	2545	468	715	129	11	58	283	490	143
Ogden	.280	76	2631	437	737	137	19	55	265	561	122
Great Falls	.268	76	2637	438	708	106	31	40	224	498	108
Medicine Hat	.255	76	2536	389	647	123	18	45	310	530	86

CLUB PITCHING

	ERA	G	CG	SHO	SV	IP	H	R	ER	BB	SO
Helena	4.31	75	6	3	22	651	633	404	312	264	509
Missoula	4.48	76	1	4	21	678	719	457	338	255	593
Idaho Falls	4.62	75	0	1	20	668	700	440	343	299	634
Billings	4.66	75	1	2	18	658	702	444	341	275	577
Medicine Hat	4.76	76	0	2	21	649	739	449	343	264	586
Ogden	5.56	76	3	1	11	663	787	541	410	336	577
Great Falls	5.83	76	4	1	9	663	755	511	430	327	533
Butte	6.66	75	1	0	12	648	812	602	479	348	572

CLUB FIELDING

	PCT	PO	A	E	DP		PCT	PO	A	E	DP
Great Falls	.953	1989	860	139	74	Med. Hat	.951	1946	810	142	57
Helena	.953	1954	819	136	57	Butte	.947	1943	721	150	53
Idaho Falls	.953	2004	829	139	75	Missoula	.942	2034	896	179	54
Billings	.952	1975	797	139	73	Ogden	.938	1990	799	185	90

INDIVIDUAL BATTING LEADERS

(Minimum 205 Plate Appearances)

	AVG	G	AB	R	H	2B	3B	HR	RBI	BB	SO	SB
Bookout, Casey, Billings	.363	50	204	49	74	14	1	13	63	26	37	0
Knox, Ryan, Helena	.349	72	275	58	96	17	1	2	25	25	27	44
Overbay, Lyle, Missoula	.343	75	306	66	105	25	7	12	101	40	53	10
Lindsey, Del, Butte	.341	63	255	72	87	23	7	10	58	23	46	13
Ford, Will, Ogden	.341	53	179	38	61	14	4	5	46	22	27	5
Brooks, Jeff, Missoula	.339	73	295	48	100	18	4	12	60	17	77	6
Schader, Troy, Idaho Falls	.336	68	268	61	90	16	7	19	69	35	75	2
White, Greg, Butte	.327	55	205	37	67	15	2	9	47	26	50	1
Burnett, Mark, Billings	.326	60	224	56	73	13	2	4	29	46	32	12
Closser, J.D., Missoula	.324	76	275	73	89	22	0	10	54	71	57	9

INDIVIDUAL PITCHING LEADERS

(Minimum 61 Innings)

	W	L	ERA	G	GS	CG	SV	IP	H	R	ER	BB	SO
Mieses, Jose, Helena	10	2	2.67	15	15	3	0	108	79	36	32	28	87
Robinson, Jeff, Ogd./Hel.	5	2	2.77	10	9	2	0	62	49	29	19	19	65
Chacin, Gustavo, Med. Hat	4	3	3.09	15	9	0	1	64	68	33	22	23	50
Sanchez, Duaner, Missoula	5	3	3.13	13	11	0	0	63	54	34	22	23	51
Olean, Chris, Ogden/Helena	6	1	3.50	16	8	2	4	62	60	36	24	15	30
Martin, Scott, Great Falls	4	4	3.86	16	15	2	0	103	115	55	44	23	69
Arieta, Corey, Helena	6	3	3.86	15	15	1	0	89	83	51	38	27	60
Wood, Brandon, Missoula	6	0	3.88	19	9	0	0	72	69	46	31	31	71
Hamann, Robert, Med. Hat	2	8	3.93	15	13	0	0	76	95	54	33	17	45
Stewart, Steve, Ogden	2	3	3.95	13	10	0	0	71	73	47	31	27	50

ALL-STAR TEAM

C—J.D. Closser, Missoula. **1B**—Lyle Overbay, Missoula. **2B**—Brian Ward, Idaho Falls. **3B**—Del Lindsey, Butte. **SS**—Jason Repko, Great Falls. **OF**—Ben Broussard, Billings; Cristian Guerrero, Ogden; Ryan Knox, Helena. **DH**—Casey Bookout, Billings. **RHP**—Jose Mieses, Helena. **LHP**—Gustavo Chacin, Medicine Hat. **RP**—Brian Matzenbacher, Missoula.

Most Valuable Player: Lyle Overbay, Missoula. **Manager of the Year:** Russ Nixon, Billings.

TOP 10 PROSPECTS

1. Francisco Rodriguez, rhp, Butte; **2.** Mike Bynum, lhp, Idaho Falls; **3.** Ben Broussard, of, Billings; **4.** Gerik Baxter, rhp, Idaho Falls; **5.** Cristian Guerrero, of, Ogden; **6.** Guillermo Quiroz, c, Medicine Hat; **7.** Jason Repko, ss, Great Falls; **8.** Luis Terrero, of, Missoula; **9.** Alexis Rios, of, Medicine Hat; **10.** Matt Ford, lhp, Medicine Hat.

DEPT. LEADERS

BATTING

G	J.D. Closser, Missoula	76
AB	Lyle Overbay, Missoula	306
R	Luis Terrero, Missoula	74
H	Lyle Overbay, Missoula	105
TB	Lyle Overbay, Missoula	180
XBH	Lyle Overbay, Missoula	44
2B	Lyle Overbay, Missoula	25
3B	Jason Repko, Great Falls	9
	Jason Huth, Billings	9
HR	Troy Schader, Idaho Falls	19
RBI	Lyle Overbay, Missoula	101
SH	Jonny Juarez, Medicine Hat	7
SF	Jeff Rizzo, Idaho Falls	7
BB	J.D. Closser, Missoula	71
IBB	Bill Curtis, Butte	4
HBP	Peter Orgill, Butte	12
SO	Luis Terrero, Missoula	91
SB	Ryan Knox, Helena	44
CS	Ryan Knox, Helena	11
GIDP	Lyle Overbay, Missoula	14
OB%	J.D. Closser, Missoula	.458
SL%	Troy Schader, Idaho Falls	.660

PITCHING

G	Oswaldo Verdugo, Idaho Falls	33
GS	Julian Harris, Butte	16
CG	Jose Mieses, Helena	3
ShO	Jose Mieses, Helena	1
	Jeff Robinson, Helena	1
GF	Oswaldo Verdugo, Idaho Falls	32
SV	Oswaldo Verdugo, Idaho Falls	13
W	Jose Mieses, Helena	10
L	Julian Harris, Butte	9
IP	Jose Mieses, Helena	108
H	Julian Harris, Butte	132
R	Julian Harris, Butte	95
ER	Julian Harris, Butte	76
HR	Kevin McClain, Butte	13
	T.J. Nall, Great Falls	13
HB	Justin Gordan, Helena	12
BB	Odalis Gomez, Butte	50
SO	Adam Williams, Great Falls	95
WP	Patrick Bowen, Butte	15
	Julian Harris, Butte	15

FIELDING

C	AVG	Matt Ceriani, Helena	.984
	PO	J.D. Closser, Missoula	492
	A	J.D. Closser, Missoula	74
	E	J.D. Closser, Missoula	21
	DP	Three tied at	4
	PB	J.D. Closser, Missoula	16
1B	AVG	Lyle Overbay, Missoula	.986
	PO	Lyle Overbay, Missoula	641
	A	Frank Ramirez, Great Falls	59
	E	Hector Garcia, Helena	13
		Frank Ramirez, Great Falls	13
	DP	Frank Ramirez, Great Falls	64
2B	AVG	Rodney Van Buizen, GF	.991
	PO	Rodney Van Buizen, GF	139
		Chris Weekly, Med. Hat	139
	A	Rodney Van Buizen, GF	197
	E	Jack Santora, Missoula	20
		Chris Weekly, Medicine Hat	20
	DP	Rodney Van Buizen, GF	47
3B	AVG	Del Lindsey, Butte	.910
	PO	Jeff Brooks, Missoula	51
	A	Jeff Brooks, Missoula	141
	E	Jeff Brooks, Missoula	40
	DP	Jason Huth, Billings	10
SS	AVG	Corey Myers, Missoula	.919
	PO	William Hall, Ogden	115
	A	William Hall, Ogden	204
	E	William Hall, Ogden	38
		Jason Repko, Great Falls	38
	DP	William Hall, Ogden	40
OF	AVG	Shane Victorino, Great Falls	.986
	PO	Luis Terrero, Missoula	129
	A	Shane Victorino, Great Falls	14
	E	Luis Terrero, Missoula	11

ARIZONALEAGUE

Wenner-led Athletics wind up as league's big winners

BY JAMES BAILEY

The Athletics coasted to an easy title in the Arizona League, finishing seven games ahead of the pack to claim their first crown since 1995. The complex-based league, in its 12th year of operation, has no playoffs.

The A's were led by Arizona League MVP Michael Wenner, who ranked second in the league with a .386 average and topped the league with 56 runs, 80 hits and 36 stolen bases.

Michael Wenner
Won MVP award

Wenner, an 11th-round pick in June out of Rider College, was one of the few Americans to shine for the A's, who got strong performances from several products of their rich Dominican program.

Outfielder German Chirinos led the league with 56 RBIs, while lefthander Claudio Galva, who ranked second in the Dominican Summer League with a 1.00 ERA in 1998, went 6-2 with a 2.38 ERA, and righthander Javier Calzada went 5-1, 2.54. Calzada was 9-0, 1.80 in the DSL in '98.

Calzada and Galva gave the A's three pitchers who were ranked in the top five in the league in ERA. Righthander Kurt Nantkes, who signed late after being taken in the 32nd round of the '98 draft, was 5-4, 2.19 in his pro debut. His ERA was second best in the league.

But the top pitcher in the league was Padres righthander Jacob Peavy, who won the pitching triple crown. Peavy, a 15th-round pick in the 1999 draft, finished at 7-1, 1.34 with 90 strikeouts in 74 innings. He tied for the league lead in wins and led outright in the other two categories.

In a managers survey of the league's top prospects, Peavy ranked seventh but another Padre earned top billing. Outfielder Vince Faison, the first of six San Diego first-round picks in '99, was No. 1. He showed a little bit of everything, batting .309 with four homers and 28 RBIs while stealing 30 bases. Padres righthander Gerik Baxter, another first-rounder, ranked third on the list. Baxter was 3-0, 1.50 in eight games before earning a promotion to the Pioneer League.

Heralded Mariners righthander Cha Seung Baek was named the No. 2 prospect. The 19-year-old Korean was 3-0, 3.67 in his pro debut.

Rockies second baseman Juan Ventura made a strong push for .400, but finished just a hair shy at .399. He became the second consecutive Rockies player to win the batting title. Rene Reyes won it with a .429 mark in 1998.

For the second year a team from the Mexican League academy played in the league, giving the league eight teams—four in Phoenix, four in Tucson. The Mexican team saw significantly more success than 1998's entry, finishing a game over .500 at 28-27—compared to 23-33 a year earlier. Two Mexican Leaguers made the league's postseason all-star team: catcher Ventura Cisneros and outfielder Luis Garcia. Cisneros ranked third in the league in batting while Garcia led with 13 homers and a .649 slugging percentage.

Young players weren't the only ones to make their mark on the league in 1999. Rehabbing Diamondbacks righthander Todd Stottlemyre earned pitcher of the week honors in early August. In three Arizona League starts he went 2-0, 0.53 with 25 strikeouts and one walk in 17 innings.

STANDINGS

Page	Club	Complex Site	W	L	PCT	GB	Manager	Last Penn.
193	Athletics	Phoenix	39	17	.696	—	John Kuehl	1999
232	Mariners	Peoria	32	24	.571	7	Gary Thurman	None
219	Padres	Peoria	31	24	.564	7½	Randy Whisler	1996
120	Rockies	Tucson	28	28	.500	11	P.J. Carey	1998
	Mexican All-Stars	Tucson	28	28	.500	11	————————	None
65	Diamondbacks	Tucson	24	32	.429	15	Roly de Armas	None
93	White Sox	Tucson	23	33	.411	16	Jerry Hairston	None
100	Cubs	Mesa	18	37	.327	20½	Carmelo Martinez	1997

PLAYOFFS—None.

NOTE: Team's individual batting and pitching statistics can be found on page indicated in lefthand column.

1999 Arizona League Statistics

CLUB BATTING

	AVG	G	AB	R	H	2B	3B	HR	BB	SO	SB
Rockies	.290	56	1929	346	559	97	29	15	210	450	157
Mariners	.285	56	1940	342	553	118	24	27	182	414	78
Diamondbacks	.283	56	1924	292	545	83	18	27	165	437	40
White Sox	.270	56	1864	287	504	81	37	11	209	387	76
Athletics	.266	56	1920	384	511	106	34	31	272	516	77
Padres	.262	55	1861	323	488	70	28	25	225	482	123
Cubs	.261	55	1887	249	493	88	25	31	164	442	44
Mexico	.260	56	1845	263	480	58	31	25	189	455	41

CLUB PITCHING

	ERA	G	CG	SHO	SV	IP	H	R	ER	BB	SO
Athletics	3.54	56	0	2	21	497	497	300	196	172	416
Padres	4.23	55	1	3	15	482	492	291	227	220	472
White Sox	4.42	56	1	0	10	475	519	301	233	204	461
Diamondbacks	4.49	56	1	3	16	474	513	330	237	216	449
Mariners	4.60	56	0	2	16	493	498	310	252	211	503
Mexico	4.65	56	5	4	11	470	522	289	243	177	397
Rockies	4.85	56	3	2	8	480	551	336	259	191	392
Cubs	5.52	55	1	1	11	481	541	379	295	225	493

CLUB FIELDING

	PCT	PO	A	E	DP		PCT	PO	A	E	DP
Mexico	.960	1411	532	81	48	Padres	.946	1446	505	111	46
Mariners	.957	1478	497	89	42	Cubs	.946	1442	485	110	22
Athletics	.953	1491	619	105	69	D'backs	.942	1423	599	125	39
White Sox	.947	1424	584	112	44	Rockies	.940	1441	606	130	51

INDIVIDUAL BATTING LEADERS
(Minimum 151 Plate Appearances)

	AVG	G	AB	R	H	2B	3B	HR	RBI	BB	SO	SB
Ventura, Juan, Rockies	.399	46	193	35	77	9	4	0	23	12	24	25
Wenner, Michael, Athletics	.386	49	207	56	80	12	7	2	28	17	31	36
Cisneros, Ventura, Mexico	.349	46	172	24	60	9	6	2	27	12	26	3
Flores, Ralph, White Sox	.337	55	193	30	65	9	7	0	30	23	26	10
Tomshack, Steven, D'backs	.333	44	144	21	48	9	1	3	22	19	24	0
Garcia, Luis, Mexico	.330	50	188	35	62	9	6	13	40	22	31	1
Ramirez, Oscar, Marlins	.327	47	159	44	52	15	2	1	26	28	28	9
Presichi, Cristian, Mexico	.321	52	190	29	61	8	6	4	23	16	37	4
Lowe, Ernesto, White Sox	.320	50	181	29	58	8	3	0	23	11	42	7
McCarty, Brock, D'backs	.319	53	191	28	61	5	2	1	18	7	41	5

INDIVIDUAL PITCHING LEADERS
(Minimum 45 Innings)

	W	L	ERA	G	GS	CG	SV	IP	H	R	ER	BB	SO
Peavy, Jacob, Padres	7	1	1.34	13	11	1	0	74	52	16	11	23	90
Nantkes, Kurt, Athletics	5	4	2.19	15	11	0	0	70	55	25	17	18	64
Galva, Claudio, Athletics	6	2	2.38	14	11	0	0	68	64	23	18	16	59
Ovalles, Juan, D'backs	7	2	2.40	14	7	0	0	60	48	25	16	25	36
Calzada, Javier, Athletics	5	1	2.54	10	8	0	0	46	32	19	13	11	30
Kibler, Ryan, Rockies	6	2	2.55	14	14	2	0	81	77	35	23	14	55
Wells, Roy, Mariners	3	0	2.70	10	9	0	0	47	39	22	14	22	52
Cueto, Jose, Cubs	3	4	2.86	11	9	0	0	57	49	32	18	22	66
Martinez, Juan, Mexico	5	5	3.27	15	13	3	1	85	76	36	31	27	86
Hughes, Rocky, White Sox	3	3	3.33	13	6	0	1	46	53	23	17	20	47

ALL-STAR TEAM

C—Ventura Cisneros, Mexican League Academy. **1B**—Casey Rogowski, White Sox. **2B**—Juan Ventura, Rockies. **3B**—Joel Noboa, Diamondbacks. **SS**—Angel Berroa, Athletics. **OF**—Vince Faison, Padres; Luis Garcia, Mexican League Academy; Michael Wenner, Athletics. **DH**—Luis Garcia, Mexican League Academy; Oscar Ramirez, Mariners. **RHP**—Ryan Kibler, Rockies; Jacob Peavy, Padres. **LHP**—Claudio Galva, Athletics. **RH Reliever**—Corey Miller, Athletics. **LH Reliever**—Geoff Jones, Padres.

Most Valuable Player: Michael Wenner, Athletics. **Co-Managers of the Year:** Gary Thurman, Mariners; Randy Whisler, Padres.

TOP 10 PROSPECTS

1. Vince Faison, of, Padres; **2.** Cha Sueng Baek, rhp, Mariners; **3.** Gerik Baxter, rhp, Padres; **4.** Jose Valverde, rhp, Diamondbacks; **5.** Angel Berroa, ss, Athletics; **6.** Germain Chirinos, of, Athletics; **7.** Jacob Peavy, rhp, Padres; **8.** Ryan Kibler, rhp, Rockies; **9.** Michael Wenner, of, Athletics; **10.** Joel Noboa, 3b, Diamondbacks.

DEPT. LEADERS

BATTING

G	Tom Kail, Diamondbacks	55
	Ralph Flores, White Sox	55
AB	Tom Kail, Diamondbacks	220
R	Michael Wenner, Athletics	56
H	Michael Wenner, Athletics	80
TB	Luis Garcia, Mexico	122
XBH	Luis Garcia, Mexico	28
2B	Tomas Samuel, Rockies	18
3B	Christian Reyes, Athletics	8
HR	Luis Garcia, Mexico	13
RBI	German Chirinos, Athletics	56
SH	Five tied at	4
SF	Jason Klatt, Padres	5
	Aaron Geralds, Rockies	5
BB	Dave Mulqueen, Rockies	42
IBB	Three tied at	2
HBP	Alex Londono, Rockies	10
	Juan Zavola, Mexico	10
SO	Rafael Perez, White Sox	64
	Osvaldo Felix, Mexico	64
SB	Michael Wenner, Athletics	36
CS	Michael Wenner, Athletics	12
GIDP	Tom Kail, Diamondbacks	8
	Lenin Solorzano, White Sox	8
OB%	Michael Wenner, Athletics	.442
SL%	Luis Garcia, Mexico	.649

PITCHING

G	Alex Diaz, Athletics	22
GS	Ryan Kibler, Rockies	14
CG	Juan Martinez, Mexico	3
ShO	Wilton Chavez, Cubs	1
	Juan Martinez, Mexico	1
GF	Edgar Moreno, Mexico	18
SV	Corey Miller, Athletics	11
W	Juan Ovalles, Diamondbacks	7
	Jacob Peavy, Padres	7
L	Michael Thompson, Padres	7
	Hatuey Mendoza, Diamondbacks	7
IP	Juan Martinez, Mexico	85
H	Wilton Chavez, Cubs	89
R	Hatuey Mendoza, Diamondbacks	64
ER	Dustin Pate, Cubs	52
HR	Michael Thompson, Padres	8
HB	Michael Patton, White Sox	11
BB	Four tied at	31
SO	Jacob Peavy, Padres	90
WP	Hatuey Mendoza, Diamondbacks	14

FIELDING

C	AVG	Wilton Pena, Athletics	.980
	PO	Wilton Pena, Athletics	207
	A	Wilton Pena, Athletics	33
	E	Steven Tomshack, Dibacks	11
	DP	Carlos Castillo, Athletics	4
	PB	Wilton Pena, Athletics	15
1B	AVG	Santos Encarnacion, Padres	.986
	PO	John Egly, Diamondbacks	.456
	A	Santos Encarnacion, Padres	31
	E	Casey Rogowski, White Sox	9
	DP	Santos Encarnacion, Padres	37
2B	AVG	Guillermo Reyes, White Sox	.964
	PO	Guillermo Reyes, White Sox	108
	A	Guillermo Reyes, White Sox	130
	E	Adam Morrissey, Cubs	14
	DP	Franklin Pimentel, D'backs	35
3B	AVG	Cristian Presichi, Mexico	.920
	PO	Cristian Presichi, Mexico	47
	A	Lenin Solorzano, White Sox	107
	E	John Puccinelli, Padres	16
	DP	Cristian Presichi, Mexico	14
SS	AVG	Jose Sanchez, Mexico	.945
	PO	Ralph Flores, White Sox	74
	A	Ralph Flores, White Sox	137
	E	Carlos Figueroa, Rockies	23
		Nicholas Romero, Padres	23
	DP	Angel Berroa, Athletics	28
OF	AVG	Anthony Vandemore, Padres	.977
	PO	Osvaldo Felix, Mexico	105
	A	Osvaldo Felix, Mexico	9
	E	Rafael Perez, White Sox	14

GULFCOASTLEAGUE

After year without trophy, Mets return it to St. Lucie

BY JAMES BAILEY

The Port St. Lucie Mets won the 1999 Gulf Coast League title, sweeping the Fort Myers Twins in two games in the championship series. The victory gave the Mets their second crown in three years. They beat the Rangers to win it in 1997.

Shortstop Enrique Cruz was the offensive star, homering in both games for the Mets. His home run in Game One was the only tally as the Mets won 1-0. He drove in two runs in Game Two with another homer as the Mets prevailed 4-3. The 17-year-old Dominican was named the shortstop on the league's all-star team, but he played third base in the playoffs. He batted .306 with four homers on the season for the Mets.

Chip Ambres
GCL's top prospect

In the first round of the playoffs, the Mets defeated the Royals 4-3 and the Twins beat the Rangers 7-0. With the three-division setup in the GCL, the top two finishers from the Western Division both make the playoffs. The league plays no interdivision games during its regular season schedule.

The Mets, who went 39-21 in the regular season, led the league in runs with 324 and batting with a .266 mark, and ranked second with a 3.10 ERA. Cruz, catcher Mike Jacobs (.333-4-30) and second baseman Leandro Arias (.301-5-33) all made the league's post-season all-star team, as did manager John Stephenson.

Rangers third baseman Hank Blalock had the best year of any player in the league. Blalock, a third-round pick of the Rangers in the 1999 draft, won the batting title with a .361 mark and ranked first in numerous other categories, including RBIs. The league doesn't name an MVP, but Blalock would have been a worthy choice.

Marlins outfielder Chip Ambres, not Blalock, was the choice of managers as the top prospect in the league. Ambres, a first-round pick in 1998, made an impressive professional debut, hitting .353 with 13 doubles and 22 stolen bases before moving on to short-season Utica.

Tigers shortstop Ramon Santiago, the league's No. 2 prospect, also finished the season in the New York-Penn League. The switch-hitting Santiago hit .321 and stole 20 bases in 35 GCL games.

The GCL featured seven first-round and supplemental first-round picks from the 1999 draft: Expos lefthander Josh Girdley, Pirates righthander Bobby Bradley, Phillies righthander Brett Myers, Red Sox righthander Brad Baker, Royals lefthander Jimmy Gobble, Orioles lefthander Scott Rice and Rangers righthander David Mead.

Braves shortstop Pat Manning, a third-round pick in the draft, upstaged them all by hitting .416 with four homers in 24 games before jumping to Class A Macon. Manning was named the GCL's player of the week in each of the first two weeks of the season.

Yankees outfielder Wily Mo Pena and Braves catcher Jose Salas made other noteworthy debuts. Pena signed with the Yankees in April for $3.7 million after having had contracts with the Marlins and Mets voided on technicalities, and Salas signed with Atlanta out of Venezuela for a $1.2 million bonus.

Minor Leagues

STANDINGS

Page	EAST	Complex Site	W	L	PCT	GB	Manager	Last Penn.
187	Mets	Port St. Lucie	39	21	.650	—	John Stephenson	1999
172	Expos	Jupiter	29	31	.483	10	Bill Masse	1991
72	Braves	Orlando	27	33	.450	12	Rick Albert	1964
133	Marlins	Melbourne	25	35	.417	14	Jon Deeble	None
Page	NORTH	Complex Site	W	L	PCT	GB	Manager	Last Penn.
146	Royals	Baseball City	33	27	.550	—	Andre David	1992
179	Yankees	Tampa	32	28	.533	1	Ken Dominguez	1996
126	Tigers	Lakeland	29	31	.483	4	Gary Green	None
200	Phillies	Clearwater	26	34	.433	7	Ramon Aviles	None
Page	WEST	Complex Site	W	L	PCT	GB	Manager	Last Penn.
246	Rangers	Port Charlotte	37	23	.617	—	Darryl Kennedy	1998
165	Twins	Fort Myers	33	26	.559	3 ½	Al Newman	None
79	Orioles	Sarasota	31	28	.525	5 ½	Jesus Alfaro	None
86	Red Sox	Fort Myers	30	29	.508	6 ½	John Sanders	None
207	Pirates	Bradenton	24	35	.407	12 ½	Woody Huyke	None
107	Reds	Sarasota	23	37	.383	14	Donnie Scott	None

PLAYOFFS—Semifinals: Twins defeated Rangers and Mets defeated Royals in one-game playoffs. **Final:** Mets defeated Twins 2-0 in best-of-3 series.

NOTE: Team's individual batting and pitching statistics can be found on page indicated in lefthand column.

1999 Gulf Coast League Statistics

CLUB BATTING

	AVG	G	AB	R	H	2B	3B	HR	BB	SO	SB
Mets	.266	60	1971	324	525	94	19	24	249	455	58
Twins	.262	60	1838	295	481	77	16	10	241	356	75
Yankees	.260	60	1922	292	500	98	18	32	255	486	44
Orioles	.258	60	1896	303	490	90	20	29	187	368	141
Tigers	.254	60	1851	240	470	98	15	19	190	463	96
Pirates	.250	60	1990	274	497	84	16	22	177	431	82
Phillies	.248	60	1860	248	461	93	10	20	228	450	94
Rangers	.247	60	1909	302	471	91	26	22	238	460	85
Royals	.247	60	1939	305	479	89	16	28	304	507	101
Braves	.244	60	2018	265	493	86	9	30	225	482	55
Marlins	.241	60	2015	239	486	95	20	11	218	456	100
Red Sox	.241	60	1915	279	461	72	19	23	226	401	65
Expos	.238	60	1898	215	451	66	10	8	180	348	73
Reds	.225	60	1861	220	418	75	17	14	172	427	87

CLUB PITCHING

	ERA	G	CG	SHO	SV	IP	H	R	ER	BB	SO
Red Sox	3.03	60	0	3	12	511	465	273	172	198	472
Mets	3.10	60	1	2	15	523	473	247	180	216	486
Rangers	3.10	60	2	4	16	510	441	221	176	179	385
Braves	3.49	60	0	4	7	526	479	258	204	214	440
Tigers	3.65	60	2	3	14	490	427	239	199	275	462
Royals	3.67	60	1	5	18	519	498	263	212	197	441
Pirates	3.72	60	1	1	8	514	467	275	213	196	383
Yankees	3.78	60	3	5	16	503	468	265	211	243	565
Marlins	3.78	60	3	5	11	529	522	274	222	201	428
Orioles	3.82	60	0	2	14	504	472	300	214	242	413
Expos	3.99	60	1	3	17	504	481	264	224	241	387
Twins	4.03	60	10	6	9	481	490	276	215	165	403
Reds	4.72	60	1	2	8	491	483	328	258	261	387
Phillies	4.85	60	0	4	13	492	516	318	265	262	438

CLUB FIELDING

	PCT	PO	A	E	DP		PCT	PO	A	E	DP
Tigers	.969	1471	553	65	47	Phillies	.956	1475	573	95	53
Rangers	.966	1531	648	76	41	Pirates	.953	1542	693	109	48
Royals	.965	1557	586	78	55	Twins	.949	1442	600	109	53
Marlins	.961	1586	654	91	52	Reds	.948	1473	666	117	52
Yankees	.961	1508	602	86	41	Mets	.948	1568	639	121	46
Expos	.960	1514	670	90	41	Red Sox	.945	1533	629	125	50
Braves	.958	1577	660	97	51	Orioles	.944	1512	675	129	58

INDIVIDUAL BATTING LEADERS
(Minimum 162 Plate Appearances)

	AVG	G	AB	R	H	2B	3B	HR	RBI	BB	SO	SB
Blalock, Hank, Rangers	.361	51	191	34	69	17	6	3	38	25	23	3
Ambres, Chip, Marlins	.353	37	139	29	49	13	3	1	15	25	19	22
Jacobs, Michael, Mets	.333	44	147	18	49	12	0	4	30	14	30	2
Brazoban, Yhency, Yankees	.320	56	200	33	64	14	5	1	26	12	47	7
Sandoval, Michael, Twins	.320	55	194	30	62	13	3	0	34	15	21	5
Lutz, David, Expos	.318	44	154	21	49	8	1	0	15	14	14	4
Winrow, Tommy, Yankees	.317	46	180	31	57	9	3	0	28	21	28	5
Castillo, Victor, Yankees	.314	42	153	24	48	8	1	0	16	22	38	9
Cruz, Enrique, Mets	.306	54	183	34	56	14	2	4	24	28	41	0
Rauls, Ian, Phillies	.303	51	175	31	53	8	0	0	17	34	32	27

INDIVIDUAL PITCHING LEADERS
(Minimum 48 Innings)

	W	L	ERA	G	GS	CG	SV	IP	H	R	ER	BB	SO
Colton, Kyle, Braves	2	1	1.79	13	10	0	0	50	35	11	10	27	30
Evert, Brett, Braves	5	3	2.03	13	10	0	0	49	37	11	11	9	39
Tavarez, David, Orioles	9	0	2.14	12	9	0	0	67	60	22	16	12	55
Lopez, Rafael, Mets	7	1	2.17	12	8	0	0	58	43	20	14	29	42
Song, Seung, Red Sox	5	5	2.30	13	9	0	0	55	47	29	14	20	61
Roman, Orlando, Mets	6	0	2.36	12	11	1	0	61	41	20	16	21	64
Richardson, Jason, Twins	1	2	2.37	12	10	0	0	49	46	21	13	23	54
Barreto, Joel, Twins	4	3	2.56	11	9	3	0	56	45	18	16	17	41
Lopez, Ignacio, Rangers	7	2	2.70	12	9	0	1	57	60	22	17	5	31
Sauer, Marc, Marlins	5	4	2.71	13	13	1	0	70	75	28	21	7	57

ALL-STAR TEAM

C—Mike Jacobs, Mets. **1B**—Steve Rodriguez, Tigers. **2B**—Leandro Arias, Mets. **3B**—Hank Blalock, Rangers. **SS**—Enrique Cruz, Mets. **OF**—Chip Ambres, Marlins; Yhency Brazoban, Yankees; Tommy Winrow. **SP**—David Tavarez, Orioles. **RP**—Buddy Yen, Royals.

Manager of the Year: John Stephenson, Mets.

TOP 10 PROSPECTS

1. Chip Ambres, of, Marlins; **2.** Ramon Santiago, ss, Tigers; **3.** Jose Morban, ss, Rangers; **4.** Alexis Gomez, of, Royals; **5.** Fernando Rodney, rhp, Tigers; **6.** Luis Torres, rhp, Pirates; **7.** Enrique Cruz, ss, Mets; **8.** Wily Mo Pena, of, Yankees; **9.** Hank Blalock, 3b, Rangers; **10.** Pat Manning, ss, Braves.

DEPT. LEADERS

BATTING
G	Ricky Angell, Rangers	60
AB	Alejandro Machado, Braves	223
R	Alejandro Machado, Braves	45
	Jose Morban, Rangers	45
H	Hank Blalock, Rangers	69
TB	Hank Blalock, Rangers	107
XBH	Hank Blalock, Rangers	26
2B	Hank Blalock, Rangers	17
3B	Four tied at	6
HR	Charlie Dees, Orioles	9
RBI	Hank Blalock, Rangers	38
SH	Anderson Machado, Phillies	7
SF	Three tied at	5
BB	Ben Cordova, Royals	51
IBB	Hank Blalock, Rangers	4
HBP	David Fowler, Yankees	10
SO	Jose Morban, Rangers	70
SB	Ian Rauls, Phillies	27
CS	Jose Morban, Rangers	14
GIDP	John Hattig, Red Sox	8
OB%	Chip Ambres, Marlins	.452
	Ben Cordova, Royals	.452
SL%	Hank Blalock, Rangers	.560

PITCHING
G	Buddy Yen, Royals	25
GS	Marc Sauer, Marlins	13
CG	Joel Barreto, Twins	3
	Josmir Romero, Twins	3
ShO	Several tied at	1
GF	Buddy Yen, Royals	21
SV	Buddy Yen, Royals	10
W	David Tavarez, Orioles	9
L	James White, Pirates	8
IP	Marc Sauer, Marlins	70
H	Marc Sauer, Marlins	75
R	Oscar Ortega, Royals	48
ER	Ben Levesque, Pirates	36
HR	Five tied at	5
HB	James White, Pirates	12
BB	Ben Levesque, Pirates	40
SO	David Martinez, Yankees	67
WP	Omar Anez, Orioles	13
BK	Jesus Morel, Twins	6

FIELDING
C	AVG	Russell Cleveland, Tigers	.987
	PO	Justo Brito, Mets	285
	A	Octavio Martinez, Orioles	42
	E	Edgar Martinez, Red Sox	12
	DP	Three tied at	4
	PB	Jose Salas, Braves	27
1B	AVG	Steve Rodriguez, Tigers	.989
	PO	Matt Gajewski, Rangers	420
	A	Steve Rodriguez, Tigers	31
	E	Kenji Garcia, Mets	13
	DP	Chad Santos, Royals	37
2B	AVG	Erick Mejias, Royals	.990
	PO	Alejandro Machado, Braves	117
	A	Alejandro Machado, Braves	176
	E	Emmanuel Del Rosario, Orioles	14
	DP	Alejandro Machado, Braves	36
3B	AVG	Juan Richardson, Phillies	.914
	PO	Juan Richardson, Phillies	37
	A	Hank Blalock, Rangers	103
	E	Michael Sandoval, Twins	19
	DP	Chris Louwsma, Marlins	10
SS	AVG	Julio Collazo, Phillies	.956
	PO	Jose Morban, Rangers	81
	A	Jose Morban, Rangers	144
	E	B.J. Hawes, Reds	20
	DP	Julio Collazo, Phillies	28
OF	AVG	Corey Harris, Mets	1.000
	PO	Alexis Gomez, Royals	131
	A	Antonio Mack, Orioles	10
	E	Terence Senegal, Reds	9
	DP	Rafael Boitel, Twins	3
		Terence Senegal, Reds	3

LATINAMERICA

Traditional afterthought Phillies pull out first DSL crown

DOMINICAN SUMMER LEAGUE

The Phillies, who had never come close to winning even a division title in their previous six years in the league, were the surprise champions of the Dominican Summer League in 1999.

Despite the poorest record among the league's four division winners, the Phillies turned back the Devil Rays in the semifinals and the Mets in the finals. Both series went the limit.

First baseman Dario Delgado was the only Phillies player selected to the league all-star team, but he was little factor in eight playoff games as he went just 3-for-31 with three RBIs. Catcher Carlos Rios (.429) and outfielder Claudio Soto (.419), who led the league with 37 stolen bases, picked up the slack by driving in 15 runs between them. Each hit two homers in the final series against the Mets.

The defending champion Athletics West had the second-best overall record in the league but failed to reach postseason play because they finished second in the Santo Domingo West Division to the Devil Rays.

The 15-year-old league had the full participation of every major league club for a second straight year—though the Twins, who have a greater presence in Venezuela, did not field a full team. The Athletics, Dodgers and Mets again fielded two teams, giving the league a record 33 teams—one more than in 1998.

Second basemen Lizandro Royer of the Mets and Amaury Pena of the White Sox shared league player of the year honors. Royer led the league with a .410 average while Pena was tops with 19 homers and second with 67 RBIs.

INDIVIDUAL BATTING LEADERS
(Minimum 170 Plate Appearances)

	AVG	AB	R	H	2B	3B	HR	RBI	SB
Royer, Lizandro, Mets	.410	178	43	73	12	6	2	35	37
Madera, Sandy, Athletics West	.374	187	32	70	14	4	5	45	6
Liriano, Pedro, Mariners	.367	199	63	73	10	3	13	47	25
Santana, Isidro, Tigers	.362	265	63	96	9	3	3	43	29
Docen, Jose, Expos	.361	244	63	88	9	1	2	23	49
Chourio, Jorjanys, Pirates ...	.361	155	49	56	5	1	6	21	31
%Santana, Roberto, Mets ..	.359	198	36	71	18	3	8	53	9
Martinez, Ramon, Rangers ..	.359	195	43	70	19	2	7	44	7
Castro, Juan, Cubs	.357	255	55	91	18	3	14	69	6
Taveras, Willy, Indians	.354	277	57	98	19	6	3	44	26
Montilla, Samuel, D'Backs ..	.348	184	23	64	10	2	2	28	7
Franco, Sterling, Astros	.347	251	70	87	17	3	4	35	11
Delgado, Dario, Phillies	.347	167	31	58	12	7	3	44	4
Francisco, Ruben, Orioles ..	.338	198	46	67	10	5	5	27	13
Rosario, Harold, Devil Rays	.336	274	56	92	16	4	11	64	13
Pena, Amaury, White Sox ..	.335	218	70	73	19	0	19	67	27
Agramonte, Antonio, Rangers	.332	262	44	87	19	9	2	46	7
Ramirez, Wagner, Cubs	.330	218	48	72	10	5	1	25	28
Garcia, Isaac, Athletics West	.330	276	61	91	14	5	3	44	13
Figueroa, Eduardo, Mariners	.327	214	48	70	13	2	6	37	18
Perez, Carlos, Dodgers II...	.324	222	43	72	4	5	2	33	23
Johnson, Luis, Indians	.324	139	22	45	5	2	0	19	2
Sosa, Francisco, Mets	.321	224	35	72	10	1	0	25	18
De la Paz, Camilo, Brewers	.321	262	46	84	22	6	6	50	5
Fermin, Jose, Phillies..........	.321	237	44	76	13	1	1	33	14
Candelaria, Luis, Devil Rays	.318	233	55	74	15	1	12	58	2
Santos, Sneider, D'backs.....	.314	242	39	76	19	3	3	40	3
Disla, Jose, Tigers	.314	223	48	70	12	3	0	40	20
Estevez, Jose, Mets...........	.313	192	50	60	10	0	4	47	18
Marrero, Domingo, Mariners..	.313	160	36	50	8	1	4	25	14
Soto, Claudio, Phillies	.313	240	59	75	16	4	4	36	37
Heredia, Yensy, Tigers........	.312	269	60	84	20	4	6	51	19
Hilario, Anderson, White Sox	.312	215	29	67	14	0	10	47	5
Guerrero, Jorge, Marlins	.312	279	60	87	14	2	7	52	11
Cespedes, Alex, Indians	.312	186	40	58	7	8	5	32	16
Mercedes, Ramon, Devil Rays	.310	242	39	75	15	3	0	34	7
*Boll, Javier, Twins	.310	229	47	71	14	4	4	27	34
Virgen, Constancio, Dodgers I	.311	171	27	53	9	0	4	39	4
Cabrera, Leonel, Giants......	.309	246	34	76	10	1	0	37	18
%Perez, Ismael, Mets	.309	204	39	63	17	4	1	32	5
Aracena, Sandy, Dodgers II	.307	202	36	62	10	1	3	34	5
Guzman, Kelvin, Giants......	.307	244	49	75	7	9	0	27	21

STANDINGS

SANTO DOMINGO EAST	W	L	PCT	GB
Mets I	53	20	.726	—
Tigers	52	21	.712	1
Brewers	45	26	.634	7
Mariners	41	30	.577	11
Diamondbacks	41	30	.577	11
Dodgers I	31	38	.449	20
Expos	29	42	.408	23
Marlins	27	44	.380	25
Cardinals	25	47	.347	27½
Athletics East	12	58	.171	39½

SANTO DOMINGO WEST	W	L	PCT	GB
Devil Rays	55	17	.764	—
Athletics West	53	18	.746	1½
Yankees	41	28	.594	12½
Pirates	34	36	.486	20
Reds	32	40	.444	23
Cubs	32	40	.444	23
Twins/Co-op	29	43	.403	26
Mets II/Co-op	28	43	.394	26½
Padres	27	45	.375	28
Rangers	24	45	.348	29½

SAN PEDRO de MACORIS	W	L	PCT	GB
Dodgers II	52	18	.743	—
Astros	47	23	.671	5
Angels	44	25	.638	7½
Orioles	38	31	.551	13½
Red Sox	30	40	.429	22
Blue Jays	26	43	.377	25½
Braves	21	49	.300	31
Giants	19	48	.284	31½

CIBAO	W	L	PCT	GB
Phillies	47	20	.701	—
Indians	40	28	.588	7½
White Sox	32	34	.485	14½
Royals	26	42	.382	21½
Rockies	23	44	.343	24

PLAYOFFS: Semifinals—Phillies defeated Devil Rays 2-1 and Mets I defeated Dodgers II 2-0 in best-of-3 series. **Finals**—Phillies defeated Mets I 3-2 in best-of-5 series.

ALL-STAR TEAM: C—Sandy Madera, Athletics West. **1B**—Dario Delgado, Phillies. **2B**—Lizandro Royer, Mets; Amaury Pena, White Sox. **3B**—Sterling Franco, Astros. **SS**—Jhonny Peralta, Indians. **OF**—Juan Castro, Cubs; Harold Rosario, Devil Rays; Willy Taveras, Indians. **DH**— Felipe Perez, Orioles. **RHP**—Gustavo Martinez, Mariners. **LHP**—Amaury Pena, White Sox.

Players of the Year: Lizandro Royer, Mets; Amaury Pena, White Sox. **Pitcher of the Year:** Gustavo Martinez, Mariners. **Manager of the Year:** Alex Taveras, Phillies.

Soriano, Carlos, Brewers	.306	242	63	74	13	1	12	44	40
Peguero, Miguel, Tigers	.305	239	52	73	15	4	3	39	8
Ruiz, Carlos, Phillies	.305	226	39	69	15	5	4	35	3
Rodriguez, Wilson, Indians	.305	259	48	79	14	3	10	64	5
Jimenez, Francisco, Braves	.304	181	39	55	10	2	4	24	11
De la Cruz, Miguel, Pirates	.303	231	46	70	9	0	11	56	11
DeLeon, Virgilio, Tigers	.303	231	63	70	11	2	13	51	23
Peralta, Jhonny, Indians......	.303	208	48	63	14	6	6	43	14
Solano, Francisco, Reds	.303	155	41	47	11	4	5	28	33
Romero, Flavio, Dodgers II	.303	188	56	57	7	4	0	24	14
Adames, Jonathan, Red Sox...	.302	245	39	74	11	1	3	26	14
Mendez, Charlie, Athletics West	.302	225	43	68	12	2	2	41	9
Starling, Ivan, Cubs	.302	189	43	57	7	2	13	43	6
Baez, Manuel, Rangers	.301	183	49	55	8	2	4	23	14
#German, Ramon, Astros ..	.289	249	48	72	**23**	1	9	47	19
#Quero, Luis, D'backs	.283	244	58	69	11	**9**	0	23	32

*Property of Diamondbacks   %Property of Indians

INDIVIDUAL PITCHING LEADERS
(Minimum 50 Innings)

	W	L	ERA	G	SV	IP	H	BB	SO
Valles, Rolando, Astros	7	2	0.35	36	**21**	51	29	23	48
Martinez, Gustavo, Mariners	5	0	**0.74**	29	8	73	29	38	122
Garcia, Jose, Mets	9	0	1.09	30	5	66	46	9	72
Pillier, Santo, Athletics West..	6	2	1.27	27	7	57	33	19	82
Martinez, Ramon, Dodgers II	4	4	1.38	24	10	59	31	31	71
Rincones, Rafael, Royals	7	4	1.39	17	0	84	68	30	94
Martinez, Renan, Angels	6	0	1.39	13	1	65	41	30	60
Chavez, Severino, Brewers	**10**	2	1.48	12	0	67	34	48	87
Williams, Ruddy, Astros	9	2	1.52	14	0	83	64	28	76
Tejeda, Santiago, Padres......	7	4	1.53	15	0	106	78	27	133
Rosario, Melvin, Dodgers II ..	6	0	1.58	17	0	51	32	37	60
Gonzalez, Cesar, D'backs	7	3	1.64	12	0	71	41	24	82
Castillo, Geraldo, Brewers	0	3	1.70	25	14	53	48	23	49
Lopez, Mariano, Dodgers II ..	5	2	1.71	12	0	67	56	18	73
Valdez, Marcelino, Angels	6	1	1.82	15	1	84	53	29	70
Liriano, Pedro, Angels	7	2	1.83	17	0	79	46	23	61
Perez, Franklin, Tigers	4	1	1.87	14	0	101	75	30	111
Gonzalez, Cristian, Athletics West	8	2	1.90	14	1	90	56	25	89
Perez, Luis, Red Sox	6	6	1.94	13	0	70	38	30	107
Ramirez, Joslin, D'backs	1	2	2.08	15	0	74	67	35	67
Leon, Brigmer, Athletics West	8	4	2.10	15	0	90	64	21	69
Lizarraga, Edgar, Dodgers II	2	2	2.10	21	2	64	52	16	74
Montano, Wilson, Devil Rays	8	2	2.12	12	0	81	41	40	94
Alcantara, Over, Marlins	5	1	2.13	10	0	72	63	19	59
Amancio, Jose, Athletics West	6	3	2.13	21	1	80	61	28	65
Armengo, Yorki, Mets............	5	2	2.15	24	6	67	65	29	58
Diaz, Franklin, Athletics West	9	1	2.17	15	0	95	61	31	89
De la Cruz, Pedro, Brewers ..	8	4	2.18	14	0	91	77	18	94
Alvarez, Javier, Mets	9	5	2.21	23	1	94	71	30	112
Valdez, Fernando, Dodgers II	6	3	2.23	13	0	69	56	17	101
Beltre, Frank, Brewers	4	1	2.34	13	1	50	44	32	23
Barrada, Roberto, Dodgers II	5	2	2.41	12	1	67	61	13	55
Espinal, Maximo, Tigers	8	2	2.42	14	0	78	62	17	84
Santana, Eddy, Yankees	3	4	2.45	11	0	51	42	25	42
Coscorrosa, Hermes, D'backs	5	4	2.49	15	0	72	62	32	93
Batista, Antonio, Red Sox......	2	4	2.51	14	0	61	51	25	35
Severino, Jose, Tigers	7	2	2.53	24	2	75	75	32	60
#Mejia, Andres, Mariners	**10**	1	3.21	23	3	81	74	30	64
#Paredes, Robert, Mariners ..	9	4	3.63	17	0	104	78	45	**146**

Statistics in **boldface** indicate league leader
League leader but nonqualifier

VENEZUELAN SUMMER LEAGUE

The Venezuelan Summer League expanded for the second consecutive year, growing from eight teams to 10 in its third season of operation. For the first time the league was broken into two divisions, with the four teams located in Barquisimeto making one division and the remaining six teams making up the other. There were no playoffs.

The league is open to players from all Latin American Spanish-speaking countries except the Dominican Republic and Puerto Rico, provided players have no more than three years of professional service. A vast majority were from Venezuela, but Colombia, Costa Rica, Curacao, Mexico, Nicaragua and Panama were represented.

Chino Canonico, a club in the Barquisimeto

Division, led the league with a .672 winning percentage. Not surprisingly, the team fielded players from the Blue Jays, Braves and Indians, three teams with a history of a strong presence in Venezuela. Most teams were supplied with players from three different major league organizations. All teams except Arizona, Oakland, San Diego and the Chicago White Sox provided talent.

STANDINGS

	W	L	PCT	T	GB
Cagua	32	24	.569	2	—
La Victoria	33	26	.558	1	½
Ciudad Alianza	29	26	.526	3	2½
La Pradera	28	30	.483	1	5
San Joaquin	27	32	.458	1	6½
Universidad of Carabobo	24	35	.407	0	9½
BARQUISIMETO	**W**	**L**	**PCT**	**T**	**GB**
Chino Canonico	39	19	.672	2	—
San Felipe	32	25	.561	3	6½
Chivacoa	26	31	.456	3	12½
Cabudare	19	41	.317	0	21

AFFLIATIONS: Cabudare (Orioles, Rangers); Cagua (Cubs, Reds, Red Sox); Chino Canonico (Blue Jays, Braves, Indians); Chivacoa (Devil Rays, Pirates); Ciudad Alianza (Astros, Marlins, Twins); La Pradera (Angels, Astros, Yankees); La Victoria (Brewers, Giants, Phillies); San Felipe (Indians, Mariners, Tigers); San Joaquin (Cardinals, Dodgers, Expos); Universidad of Carabobo (Mets, Rockies, Royals).

INDIVIDUAL BATTING LEADERS
(Minimum 115 At-Bats)

	AVG	AB	R	H	2B	3B	HR	RBI	SB
Cordova, Ricardo, Dodgers	**.368**	144	22	53	11	1	2	26	5
Bocaranda, Nestor, Tigers ..	.346	156	27	54	12	1	2	35	4
Chavez, Angel, Giants	.344	186	**40**	64	12	1	**14**	**49**	11
Domero, William, Tigers......	.344	131	20	45	6	2	3	18	3
Moncada, Rafael, Indians ...	.338	148	30	50	12	1	2	17	8
Asprilla, Avelino, Pirates	.337	196	35	66	10	**5**	1	25	30
Sanchez, Jean, Rangers	.332	199	25	66	11	4	1	33	1
Camacho, Juan, Yankees	.328	193	33	64	13	2	8	38	7
Aliendo, Humberto, Pirates	.328	189	37	62	**15**	2	6	37	12
Hidalgo, Reinaldo, Rangers	.325	160	35	52	3	0	3	12	4
Quinonez, Luis, Dodgers	.323	198	36	64	11	1	3	20	18
Salinas, Yilbert, Rockies	.319	138	21	44	5	0	7	21	3
Malpica, Martin, Blue Jays ..	.317	142	24	45	10	0	4	33	0
Gomez, Jose, Cardinals......	.310	126	14	39	7	1	0	19	10
Burguillos, Jose, Cubs	.308	172	22	53	8	4	2	31	2
Laya, Rayner, Braves..........	.308	172	35	53	6	2	0	23	11
Herrera, Harold, Mets..........	.305	128	19	39	1	1	0	13	5
Medina, Rodney, Blue Jays ..	.299	154	21	46	10	1	0	22	10
Hernandez, Javier, Indians	.298	188	46	56	8	0	8	39	15
Leal, Silverio, Brewers........	.298	205	34	61	10	0	6	33	3
Pastrano, Carlos, Blue Jays	.297	155	28	46	8	0	6	35	1
Linares, Jesus, Mets	.295	139	24	41	10	2	1	18	5
Mora, Juan, Pirates	.295	176	30	52	4	1	1	21	**32**
Centeno, Irwin, Devil Rays...	.294	170	36	50	7	1	0	22	14

INDIVIDUAL PITCHING LEADERS
(Minimum 40 Innings)

	W	L	ERA	G	SV	IP	H	BB	SO
Perez, Keino, Indians	4	1	0.58	14	2	47	32	8	44
Raudez Pavon, Julio, Giants	7	2	**0.74**	11	0	73	40	6	64
Moris, Carlos, Expos	**9**	1	0.98	15	1	73	46	16	81
Herrera, Alexander, Indians ..	3	2	1.28	16	5	56	42	20	74
Abache, Andrius, Phillies	5	2	1.61	14	0	61	49	23	61
Mendieta, Manuel, Cubs	4	4	1.69	21	0	48	37	15	31
Lara, Mauricio, Red Sox	7	0	1.71	10	0	58	44	17	63
Gonzalez, Kimi, Devil Rays ...	3	2	1.72	12	1	63	53	12	49
Lazo, Rafael, Mets	2	2	1.86	12	0	58	46	14	74
Medina, Frewing, Blue Jays ..	5	2	1.88	17	4	53	39	16	43
Romero, Luis, Indians...........	3	3	2.11	15	0	73	53	29	68
Rojas, Ivan, Braves	5	0	2.17	13	0	71	54	17	70
Reina, Dimas, Dodgers	3	4	2.19	15	0	66	52	23	53
Mieres, Alberto, Yankees	5	2	2.21	14	0	61	38	22	52
Lisardi, Gustavo, Twins	6	3	2.23	16	1	65	47	25	59
Figuera, Alejandro, Orioles....	5	6	2.29	30	7	59	59	39	35
#Nunez, Renny, Reds	1	2	2.50	25	**14**	36	24	15	33
#Esquivia, Manuel, Marlins...	5	4	3.00	13	0	69	47	37	**94**

INDEPENDENT LEAGUES

Independent leagues come of age in 1999; new leagues and old teams flourish

BY MARK DEREWICZ

After six seasons of fly-by-night franchises and leagues with shorter lifespans than fruit flies, independent baseball finally achieved stability in 1999.

Some of the attendance figures were still on the low side but that's nothing new in minor league baseball, independent or affiliated. As a matter of fact, most fans of independent league clubs don't seem to care that their town has nothing to do with the National Association of Professional Baseball Leagues—or Minor League Baseball, as it will now be known.

Bridgeport, Conn., for example, has become a haven for baseball fans who wanted to see quality baseball in a state-of-the-art facility, regardless of the team's affiliation. There were rumors that Bridgeport might one day be the Double-A affiliate of the nearby Boston Red Sox but until that day comes, the Bluefish front office will gladly take the 342,857 Atlantic League fans that came to Harbor Park in 1999.

The Northern League's St. Paul Saints averaged 6,329, capacity at Midway Stadium, for the third consecutive year and were followed closely by Winnipeg, Schaumburg and Fargo-Moorhead. Even Sioux Falls, the Northern League version of the Chicago Cubs, drew 118,333 fans. Sioux Falls Stadium was scheduled to get a $4 million overhaul, which should boost attendance.

The success of those teams and many others has helped independent baseball shed its reputation, not to imply that the bad rap wasn't earned.

In the previous six seasons, many club operators figured all they had to do was bring a team to town and the fans would flock to the ballyard in droves.

It didn't work that way, and as a result nine leagues and several franchises folded. But the leagues that survived have given independent baseball a more respectable image, which was anything but tarnished by the end of 1999.

The Northern League, which started this mad independent rush with the Frontier League in 1993, is still recognized as the premier independent circuit. But the gap has tightened.

The Northern League merged with the Northeast League after the 1998 season—a marriage that was somewhat puzzling considering the Northern League's stature. But the former Northeast League, now the Eastern Division of the Northern League, came out on top when Albany-Colonie defeated Winnipeg 3-1 in a best-of-5 series for the championship.

Quality product

Whether or not anyone wants to admit it, independent leaguers can play the game. None have the star potential of former Northern Leaguer J.D. Drew, now with the St. Louis Cardinals, but players like Jeff Zimmerman, Kerry Ligtenberg, Morgan Burkhart, Darryl Brinkley, Graham Koonce and Kevin Millar, just to name a few, are proving that independent leagues play a high level of baseball.

The Frontier League, which has improved by leaps and bounds since its first year in 1993, again was home to some rising stars in independent baseball. Outfielder Gator McBride, who spent five years in the Atlanta Braves chain, hit .456 with 15 homers and 48 RBIs for Chillicothe before the Boston Red Sox signed him at midseason. McBride, who went on to hit .360 at Class A Sarasota, was the second former Frontier Leaguer to perform well in the Red Sox system. Burkhart led the Florida State League in 1999 with 23 home runs while hitting .297 with 35 homers and 108 RBIs overall for Sarasota and Double-A Trenton.

In the Northern League, Ila Borders received standing ovations as a woman pitching professionally, though she was in her third season. Borders

Still the one to beat
St. Paul's Midway Stadium sells out every night

Gator McBride

Player of the Year
Cappuccio Completes Comeback

Whether it's done in the major leagues or independent leagues, a 39-game hitting streak is nothing to sneeze at. Outfielder Carmine Cappuccio, a sweet-swinging lefty for the Northern League's New Jersey Jackals, accomplished that feat to close out the 1999 season, helping him earn Baseball America's Independent Player of the Year award.

The old independent league record was 36 games, set by Greenville's Popeye Cole in the Texas-Louisiana League in 1998.

Carmine Cappuccio

During his run Cappuccio hit .402 with 10 homers and 48 RBIs. On the season, he hit .349 with 17 homers and 75 RBIs and was a major reason the Jackals landed in the Northern League Eastern Division championship series.

Cappuccio's professional career began in 1992 when the Chicago White Sox drafted him in the ninth round out of Rollins (Fla.) College. He spent six seasons in the White Sox chain hitting a combined .277 with 40 homers before he injured his back in 1997. He rehabbed for two months but was in too much pain when he returned to Triple-A Nashville. Once he hit just .220 with four homers in 55 games that year, he was released in the offseason.

The Red Sox, who have 1998 Independent Player of the Year Morgan Burkhart in their system, invited him to camp in 1998 but he still was hurting and they released him before the season started. Cappuccio decided not to play for a season in order to recuperate fully. He had a respectable spring training with the Indians in 1999, but Cleveland also couldn't find a place for him. Cappuccio hooked up with the Jackals, who already had two former White Sox farmhands in Essex Burton and Pete Rose II.

Healthy for the first time in two years, Cappuccio proved in 1999 he can still hit. His .349 average was seventh in the league and his 75 RBIs led the league.

Baseball America's 1999 independent league all-star team:

C—Chris Coste, Fargo-Moorhead (Northern). **1B**—John O'Brien, Alexandria (Texas-Louisiana). **2B**—Jeff Berblinger, Somerset (Atlantic). **3B**—Derek Henderson, Amarillo (Texas-Louisiana). **SS**—Angel Espada, Bridgeport (Atlantic). **OF**—Carmine Cappuccio, New Jersey (Northern); Mark Charbonnet, Zion (Western); Chris Vasquez, Madison (Northern). **DH**—Scott Pinoni, Chillicothe (Frontier).

SP—Michel Laplante, Quebec (Northern); Greg Salvevold, Fargo-Moorhead (Northern); Alan Sontag, Bridgeport (Atlantic); Chris White, Chico (Western). **RP**—Dave Adam, Bridgeport (Atlantic).

pitched two innings for the Duluth-Superior Dukes before getting traded to the Madison Black Wolf and going 1-0, 1.67 in 32 innings. Black Wolf manager Al Gallagher used Borders as a starter on occasion but usually relieved her after three innings despite her success.

Two major independent league records fell during the 1999 season. Texas-Louisiana League first baseman John O'Brien hit a record 39 home runs for the Alexandria Aces, and the Northern League's Carmine Cappuccio had a 39-game hitting streak which earned him Baseball America's Independent Player of the Year honor.

NORTHERN LEAGUE

The Northern League took an ambitious step toward moving independent baseball under one governing body when it merged with the eight-team Northeast League after the 1998 season. The merger gave the Northern League 16 teams.

The move was surprising for several reasons, not the least of which was the supposed gap in talent between the leagues. That, however, proved to be a non-issue when the underdog Albany-Colonie Diamond Dogs defeated the Winnipeg Goldeyes three games to one in the first championship series under the new alignment.

The Goldeyes came into the title series as hot as any team in independent baseball. They swept Sioux City and Fargo-Moorhead in a pair of best-of-5 series before traveling east.

Albany-Colonie's road wasn't so easy. The Diamond Dogs downed Adirondack three games to two with an exciting 2-1 win in Game Five. They then beat New Jersey three games to one to earn a spot in the championship series, where they defeated the Goldeyes 7-6 in each of their three wins, including a 10-inning victory in Game Four.

Only two franchises in the more established Central Division drew less than 115,000 fans, with the St. Paul Saints leading the way for the seventh consecutive year. The Saints sold out every home game from 1997 through 1999.

The Schaumburg Flyers, who averaged 5,499 fans while playing in the shadow of Chicago's Wrigley Field, made the playoffs in their first season after relocating from Thunder Bay, Ontario.

In the Eastern Division, Quebec City drew 110,559 fans in the city's first year back in professional ball since it was home to a Double-A Eastern League franchise in 1977.

The Eastern Division also assembled a talented cast of players including New Jersey's Carmine Cappuccio, who hit safely in 39 consecutive games to earn Baseball America's 1999 Independent Player of the Year award.

In the past, the Northern League has provided an alternative to players selected in the draft who choose not to sign with the team that drafted them. Celebrated holdout J.D. Drew decided not to play for Philadelphia in 1997 when he was drafted by the Phillies. He played for St. Paul that season.

The Saints also became home to Boston's ninth-round pick Hank Thoms in 1999 after he spurned the Red Sox' $3,500 bonus offer.

Independent Leagues

CENTRAL DIVISION

STANDINGS

FIRST HALF

EAST	W	L	PCT	GB
Schaumburg Flyers	19	24	.442	—
Duluth-Superior Dukes	18	24	.429	½
St. Paul Saints	18	25	.419	1
Madison Black Wolf	17	25	.405	1½
WEST	**W**	**L**	**PCT**	**GB**
Winnipeg Goldeyes	28	15	.651	—
Fargo-Moorhead RedHawks	27	16	.628	1
Sioux City Explorers	23	19	.548	4½
Sioux Falls Canaries	20	22	.476	7½

SECOND HALF

EAST	W	L	PCT	GB
Schaumburg Flyers	25	18	.581	—
St. Paul Saints	20	22	.476	4½
Madison Black Wolf	20	22	.476	4½
Duluth-Superior Dukes	17	25	.405	7½
WEST	**W**	**L**	**PCT**	**GB**
Sioux City Explorers	28	15	.651	—
Fargo-Moorhead RedHawks	23	19	.548	4½
Winnipeg Goldeyes	20	23	.465	8
Sioux Falls Canaries	17	26	.395	11

PLAYOFFS: First Round—Winnipeg defeated Sioux City 3-0 and Fargo-Moorhead defeated Schaumburg 3-0 in best-of-5 series. **Semifinals**—Winnipeg defeated Fargo-Moorhead 3-0 in best-of-5 series. **Finals**—Albany-Colonie defeated Winnipeg 3-1 in best-of-5 series.

MANAGERS: Duluth-Superior—Larry See. Fargo-Moorhead—Doug Simunic. Madison—Al Gallagher. St. Paul—Marty Scott. Schaumburg—Ron Kittle. Sioux City—Ed Nottle. Sioux Falls—Mike Burton. Winnipeg—Hal Lanier.

ATTENDANCE: St. Paul, 265,818, Winnipeg, 248,488; Schaumburg, 236,476; Fargo-Moorhead, 179,919; Sioux Falls, 118,765; Sioux City, 118,333; Duluth-Superior, 67,098; Madison, 64,259.

ALL-STAR TEAM: C—Chris Coste, Fargo-Moorhead. **1B**—Darin Everson, Winnipeg. **2B**—Steve Hine, Fargo-Moorhead. **3B**—Mike Busch, Fargo-Moorhead. **SS**—Chad Thornhill, Winnipeg. **OF**—Brian Ralph, Schaumburg; Chris Vasquez, Madison; Bryan Warner, Duluth-Superior. **DH**—Jamie Lopiccolo, Schaumburg. **RHP**—Rick Forney, Winnipeg. **LHP**—Lindsay Gulin, St. Paul. **RP**—Derek Fahs, Sioux City.

Player of the Year: Chris Vasquez, Madison. **Rookie of the Year:** Brian Ralph, Schaumburg. **Rookie Pitcher of the Year:** Greg Salvevold, Fargo-Moorhead. **Manager of the Year:** Ed Nottle, Sioux City.

INDIVIDUAL BATTING LEADERS
(Minimum 232 Plate Appearances)

	AVG	AB	R	H	2B	3B	HR	RBI	SB
Patton, Josh, Sioux City	.350	303	59	106	18	3	7	66	6
Vasquez, Chris, Madison	.346	344	58	119	26	1	16	70	0
Warner, Bryan, Duluth	.340	338	59	115	33	1	10	64	12
Coste, Chris, Fargo	.335	352	67	118	18	2	16	60	4
Hine, Steve, Fargo	.333	252	45	84	18	4	4	28	8
Lopiccolo, Jamie, Schaum.	.332	358	49	119	28	1	15	78	0
Hosey, Dwayne, Winnipeg	.330	206	47	68	18	2	6	46	6
Fortin, Troy, Winnipeg	.323	201	44	65	21	1	6	39	1
Ralph, Brian, Schaumburg	.322	345	73	111	20	7	1	34	42
Schwab, Chris, Fargo	.320	197	36	63	13	0	11	40	9

INDIVIDUAL PITCHING LEADERS
(Minimum 69 Innings)

	W	L	ERA	G	SV	IP	H	BB	SO
Forney, Rick, Winnipeg	9	3	2.13	13	0	84	93	13	62
Hyde, Rich, Sioux Falls	8	2	2.73	19	0	115	123	27	77
Salvevold, Greg, Fargo	10	1	3.06	16	0	97	84	29	50
Gulin, Lindsay, St. Paul	8	2	3.18	16	0	102	83	46	83
Marchesano, Mike, Sioux City	8	4	3.30	27	2	79	73	44	56
Bell, Richard, St. Paul	4	6	3.52	39	3	69	55	21	76
Thoms, Hank, St. Paul	5	2	3.55	13	0	71	68	25	46
Hill, Chris, Sioux City	6	5	3.81	28	0	76	76	37	50
Meyer, Dave, Fargo	5	2	4.05	21	0	93	105	31	64
Bittiger, Jeff, Fargo	5	4	4.26	15	0	74	83	25	68

DULUTH-SUPERIOR

BATTING	AVG	AB	R	H	2B	3B	HR	RBI	SB
Cardona, Ruben, 2b	.243	74	8	18	0	1	0	8	4
2-team (36 Madison)	.234	209	27	49	4	1	0	21	13
Corps, Erick, 2b-ss	.291	296	45	86	10	0	2	38	5
Cronin, Shane, 1b-3b	.318	305	45	97	13	0	10	50	3
Evans, Brandon, of	.292	343	73	100	18	1	9	32	37
Howell, Pat, of	.186	43	3	8	1	0	0	5	4
Jorgensen, Randy, 1b	.288	59	9	17	4	0	1	8	0
Krey, Kenny, ss	.219	270	33	59	12	3	2	30	14
Lewis, Anthony, dh-1b	.296	328	57	97	23	0	19	64	6
Mulligan, Sean, c	.250	200	23	50	10	0	5	25	1
Pagan, Felix, 3b	.271	277	41	75	16	0	17	52	3
Plambeck, Ricky, c	.333	6	1	2	0	0	1	2	0
Rojo, David, c	.223	121	10	27	2	0	1	10	0
Schmitz, Chris, of-dh	.317	139	31	44	10	0	2	10	9
See, Larry, 1b	.100	10	0	1	1	0	0	0	0
Smith, Ira, of	.325	194	36	63	10	4	7	44	6
Warner, Bryan, of	.340	338	59	115	33	1	10	64	12

PITCHING	W	L	ERA	G	SV	IP	H	BB	SO
Benesh, Ed	3	3	5.60	36	2	55	63	25	32
Borders, Ila	0	0	30.86	3	0	2	10	4	1
Brand, Cliff	3	8	6.72	16	0	86	109	31	47
Cannon, Kevan	4	2	4.35	35	7	41	42	30	31
2-team (5 Fargo)	4	2	4.15	40	7	48	46	32	36
Culp, Wes	0	0	8.22	5	0	8	7	8	3
Doyle, Tom	1	3	4.32	10	0	33	26	11	32
Fieldbinder, Mick	1	5	7.07	12	0	64	94	21	24
Giron, Roberto	0	1	8.76	4	0	12	18	6	7
Harrell, Scott	0	0	12.91	10	0	15	26	20	6
Hernandez, Ariel	1	6	6.56	11	0	23	35	10	15
Key, Scott	1	1	7.32	10	0	20	23	17	9
Montgomery, Joe	7	3	4.56	29	1	49	63	23	27
2-team (5 Winnipeg)	7	3	4.39	34	1	53	67	26	28
Nelson, Erick	1	1	8.22	18	1	23	23	18	10
Smith, Matt	1	1	6.43	9	1	14	17	9	11
2-team (30 Fargo)	3	3	4.48	39	5	60	68	28	32
Stockstill, Jason	6	8	6.14	21	0	110	142	55	84
Swiatkiewicz, Chris	0	2	3.38	10	3	21	19	8	22
Wagner, Rick	4	6	5.35	19	0	113	143	37	56
Williams, Juan	3	4	4.83	10	0	54	57	49	32
2-team (2 Winnipeg)	4	4	4.28	12	0	67	69	53	43

FARGO-MOORHEAD

BATTING	AVG	AB	R	H	2B	3B	HR	RBI	SB
Amundson, Aron, 3b-1b	.160	25	1	4	1	0	1	4	0
Brown, Bobby, of	.304	358	48	109	23	0	8	51	3
Busch, Mike, 1b-3b	.273	308	64	84	18	0	21	57	0
Butt, Gerald, c	.083	12	3	1	1	0	0	2	0
Coste, Chris, c	.335	352	67	118	18	2	16	60	4
Faulken, Matt, dh	.233	60	7	14	1	0	1	6	0
Fink, Marc, dh-1b	.345	177	24	61	12	1	8	40	0
Gutfeld, Marc, ss	.265	272	41	72	11	2	3	35	1
Hamilton, Joe, of	.274	175	25	48	10	2	3	23	3
Hine, Steve, of	.333	252	45	84	18	4	4	28	8
Knott, Johnny, 3b-2b	.284	271	57	77	14	1	17	58	14
Motley, Darryl, dh	.236	55	6	13	2	0	4	11	0
Prodanov, Peter, of-ss	.250	108	21	27	7	1	1	11	5
Richards, Tony, dh	.220	41	4	9	0	1	0	4	0
Schwab, Chris, of-1b	.320	197	36	63	13	0	11	40	9
Smith, Cory, of-2b	.256	254	61	65	13	4	3	28	16
Sumner, Sam, of	.250	52	8	13	3	0	1	8	4
Wambach, James, 1b	.189	37	1	7	1	0	0	4	0
Wilson, Mike, of	.083	12	1	1	0	0	0	0	0

PITCHING	W	L	ERA	G	SV	IP	H	BB	SO
Bittiger, Jeff	5	4	4.26	15	0	74	83	25	68
Bou, Edward	0	2	5.51	22	0	47	49	21	32
2-team (9 Madison)	0	4	5.58	31	0	60	66	27	43
Cannon, Kevan	0	0	2.84	5	0	6	4	2	5
Clark, Mark	0	0	27.00	2	0	1	1	3	2
DeWitt, Chris	3	1	5.59	8	0	37	46	15	16
Duffy, John	2	0	0.00	14	0	13	8	4	4
Fleetham, Ben	1	0	5.17	10	0	16	18	5	17
Fletschock, Justin	7	5	5.58	17	0	98	128	35	67
Isom, Jeff	1	1	4.80	15	0	30	32	19	23
Jersild, Aaron	4	6	4.58	16	0	96	97	42	69
Kunka, Tony	0	0	13.50	2	0	3	4	2	0
Mattson, Craig	3	4	3.00	23	0	36	33	16	16
Meyer, Dave	5	2	4.05	21	0	93	105	31	64
Salvevold, Greg	10	1	3.06	16	0	97	84	29	50
Schmidt, George	3	5	3.47	39	11	49	40	30	53

PITCHING	W	L	ERA	G	SV	IP	H	BB	SO
Smith, Matt	2	2	3.88	30	4	46	51	19	21
Vandemark, John	1	2	3.63	11	0	17	10	11	13

MADISON

BATTING	AVG	AB	R	H	2B	3B	HR	RBI	SB
Aylor, Brian, of	.074	54	6	4	1	0	0	1	5
Campos, Jesus, of	.292	353	56	103	14	2	2	37	25
Cardona, Ruben, 2b	.230	135	19	31	4	0	0	13	3
Copeland, Jason, 2b-3b	.288	212	30	61	13	0	4	24	1
Doskocil, Darren, 2b	.250	24	8	6	1	0	2	4	0
Estrada, Marco, ss	.171	41	7	7	0	0	1	1	0
Grice, Dan, ss-3b	.248	290	46	72	8	0	2	33	2
Harris, Donnie, of	.258	330	58	85	15	1	12	53	17
Imrisek, Jason, c	.251	187	25	47	8	0	4	22	6
Lewis, Danny, dh	.287	164	27	47	12	0	4	31	3
2-team (27 Sioux Falls)	.256	262	32	67	15	0	4	44	3
Marrero, Oreste, 1b-of	.239	92	14	22	7	0	2	12	3
McMaster, Eric, 2b	.208	53	13	11	1	1	0	1	6
Roper, Chad, 3b-of	.289	308	46	89	20	0	11	53	3
Slaughter, Caleb, c	.000	2	0	0	0	0	0	0	0
Swinton, Jermaine, 1b	.284	183	38	52	8	1	13	42	4
Vasquez, Chris, of-1b	.346	344	58	119	26	1	16	70	0
Wagner, Brian, c	.242	153	19	37	12	0	6	26	5
Wilson, Mike, of	.077	13	4	1	0	0	0	1	2
2-team (5 Fargo)	.080	25	5	2	0	0	0	2	2

PITCHING	W	L	ERA	G	SV	IP	H	BB	SO
Borders, Ila	1	0	1.67	15	0	32	33	10	8
2-team (3 Duluth)	1	0	3.63	18	0	35	43	14	9
Bou, Edward	0	2	5.84	9	0	12	17	6	11
Deremer, Brent	2	2	5.76	21	0	59	89	16	25
Deremer, Scott	7	6	4.58	21	0	141	163	36	84
Folkers, Ken	2	1	7.62	12	0	26	36	11	19
Garcia, Ariel	0	2	15.26	5	0	8	9	7	3
Heflin, Bronson	3	4	3.34	25	8	30	31	13	21
Isom, Jeff	0	0	10.38	5	0	4	10	1	2
Meyer, David	5	10	5.67	20	0	132	163	44	64
Moore, P.J.	0	2	7.99	17	1	24	34	20	21
Nall, John	0	0	8.31	7	0	4	6	5	0
Roup, Clay	1	3	9.95	16	0	25	42	22	17
Santori, Jeremy	0	0	18.00	3	0	3	7	1	2
Smith, Hut	3	1	5.32	7	0	44	58	8	19
Steppke, Terry	1	1	11.02	8	1	16	31	4	19
Stutz, Joe	4	6	4.08	35	4	46	47	27	43
Taylor, Donnie	7	7	4.88	18	0	120	130	47	87
Uceta, Victor	1	0	0.00	3	0	2	0	3	2
Zwirchitz, Andy	0	0	6.52	2	0	10	14	8	8
2-team (12 St. Paul)	0	4	5.82	14	0	60	82	31	44

ST. PAUL

BATTING	AVG	AB	R	H	2B	3B	HR	RBI	SB
Ashley, Billy, of-dh	.340	194	40	66	14	0	14	41	1
Bellinato, Tony, of	.190	42	13	8	3	0	0	4	0
Bustos, Saul, ss	.312	343	58	107	16	0	17	62	7
Chance, Tony, of	.347	49	8	17	2	0	0	5	1
Curtis, Brandon, 3b-of	.279	183	27	51	12	0	3	20	1
Gerald, Eddie, of	.321	56	11	18	6	0	1	10	0
2-team (65 Sioux Falls)	.236	305	43	72	13	6	9	41	13
Gonzalez, Manuel, of	.289	83	13	24	4	1	2	12	5
Habig, Keith, 3b-2b	.297	337	68	100	28	4	12	52	2
Hamilton, Joe, of	.173	81	15	14	2	0	1	10	1
2-team (46 Fargo)	.242	256	40	62	12	2	4	33	4
Hickey, Mike, 2b	.345	116	20	40	3	0	3	11	6
Kennedy, David, 1b-of	.268	314	60	84	21	0	12	44	6
Mirza, Erik, of	.197	137	17	27	4	2	0	7	2
Mota, Carlos, c	.277	213	25	59	13	0	6	34	2
Nelson, Charlie, of	.105	19	1	2	0	0	1	2	1
Nokes, Matt, dh-1b	.275	306	44	84	18	1	18	66	0
Ruiz, Ryan, of	.382	68	13	26	1	0	0	11	2
Senjem, Guye, c	.227	75	18	17	3	0	2	7	2
Tarpley, Andy, of-3b	.300	290	34	87	19	0	4	44	6
Torres, Bernie, 2b	.250	64	4	16	1	0	0	4	1

PITCHING	W	L	ERA	G	SV	IP	H	BB	SO
Bell, Richard	4	6	3.52	39	3	69	55	21	76
Dickinson, Rodney	3	3	6.59	31	2	55	59	38	44
Fieldbinder, Mick	0	0	3.97	2	0	11	14	5	6
2-team (12 Duluth)	1	5	6.60	14	0	75	108	26	30
Frazier, Harold	0	0	8.74	10	0	11	18	8	7
Gomez, Dennys	0	1	16.20	4	0	7	16	3	3
Gulin, Lindsay	8	2	3.18	16	0	102	83	46	83
Manon, Julio	1	1	2.21	4	0	20	18	7	21
Mota, Henry	3	8	5.55	20	0	96	116	38	38
O'Reilly, John	0	5	10.27	8	0	31	46	27	22
Ramirez, Marco	0	1	12.12	9	0	16	29	6	11
Ruffcorn, Scott	2	5	4.80	10	0	60	62	26	40
Secrist, Jon	0	1	9.35	2	0	9	16	5	2
Smith, Roy	4	2	3.21	8	0	42	38	23	43
Swinburnson, Tyler	5	4	3.79	39	0	55	61	28	29
Thoms, Hank	5	2	3.55	13	0	71	68	25	46
Tzelepis, Alex	1	0	8.10	4	0	7	6	6	7
Wright, Scott	2	2	3.12	36	18	35	25	13	42
Zwirchitz, Andy	0	4	5.68	12	0	51	68	23	36

SCHAUMBURG

BATTING	AVG	AB	R	H	2B	3B	HR	RBI	SB
Berrios, Harry, of	.309	359	65	111	15	1	11	59	26
Beyna, Terry, 3b	.248	149	20	37	3	0	4	17	2
Buckley, Reagan, c	.274	274	37	75	14	2	3	30	3
Burns, Xavier, 3b	.235	81	7	19	2	1	1	9	3
Cacini, Ron, ss	.000	10	0	0	0	0	0	0	0
Donohue, Gregg, c	.467	15	3	7	0	0	0	3	0
Franzese, Nick, c	.163	43	7	7	2	0	0	2	0
Hartsburg, Steve, 3b-ss	.256	82	9	21	7	0	0	12	0
Jaramillo, Frank, ss	.095	21	0	2	0	0	0	2	0
Lopiccolo, Jamie, dh-1b	.332	358	49	119	28	1	15	78	0
Mansavage, Jay, 2b	.273	77	11	21	2	0	1	9	3
Marshall, Mike, 1b	.307	137	17	42	8	1	2	21	1
Nunez, Sergio, 2b	.295	210	37	62	8	1	2	20	7
Ralph, Brian, of	.322	345	73	111	20	7	1	34	42
Rushford, Jim, of-1b	.289	166	26	48	12	2	2	28	7
Shultz, Brian, of	.301	269	40	81	18	1	6	36	1
Trahan, Mike, ss	.288	260	48	75	21	2	10	41	3
2-team (12 Winnipeg)	.286	294	50	84	23	2	10	47	3
Voigt, Jack, 1b-3b	.304	138	33	42	10	1	7	27	0
Wright, Bryan, ss	.176	34	5	6	1	0	0	4	4

PITCHING	W	L	ERA	G	SV	IP	H	BB	SO
Apana, Matt	2	1	6.89	7	0	31	38	19	17
Boynewicz, Jim	0	2	8.27	5	0	21	38	8	10
Calvert, Klae	6	4	4.29	17	0	94	106	18	56
Caruso, Gino	3	1	2.41	5	0	37	28	10	35
Castillo, Alberto	7	5	4.27	17	0	97	97	47	70
DeWitt, Chris	1	1	11.74	5	0	8	20	6	5
2-team (8 Fargo)	4	2	6.65	13	0	45	66	21	21
Durkovic, Peter	1	0	3.86	5	2	9	7	4	8
Franzese, Nick	0	0	4.50	2	0	4	4	1	1
Garcia, Ariel	0	0	2.70	4	0	3	4	2	2
Genke, Todd	6	6	4.34	16	0	93	97	19	52
Gomez, Javier	0	0	15.00	5	0	6	9	5	8
Keppen, Jeff	0	1	12.60	2	0	5	5	9	4
Lopez, Joe	0	0	0.79	8	3	11	3	11	12
Martinez, Johnny	0	1	6.14	4	0	7	6	4	1
Mattson, Craig	0	0	4.32	5	0	8	8	1	8
2-team (23 Fargo)	3	4	3.25	28	0	44	41	17	24
Miller, Shawn	3	3	5.17	12	0	54	52	21	30
Poeck, Chad	3	4	2.84	20	3	32	21	11	34
Prempas, Lyle	0	1	3.25	16	1	28	19	13	29
Rainford, Kevin	0	1	8.10	3	0	7	7	8	4
Rushing, Will	3	1	2.85	24	0	41	36	17	41
Santiago, Derek	0	0	9.64	4	0	5	10	3	5
Toronto, Brian	0	1	7.82	5	0	13	19	4	8
Tribe, Byron	4	7	6.18	31	6	67	88	42	62
Vandemark, John	0	1	6.35	3	0	6	6	2	4
Wise, Andy	3	1	3.52	11	1	38	46	11	26
2-team (4 Winnipeg)	3	4	5.03	15	1	59	78	14	34
Wright, Bryan	0	0	0.00	1	0	3	4	1	0
Zamarripa, Mark	2	0	1.83	5	0	39	26	26	25

SIOUX CITY

BATTING	AVG	AB	R	H	2B	3B	HR	RBI	SB
Amundson, Aron, 3b-1b	.200	10	4	2	1	0	0	2	0
2-team (9 Fargo)	.171	35	5	6	2	0	1	6	0
Baeza, Art, 3b	.319	144	22	46	10	1	3	27	0
2-team (42 Winnipeg)	.308	295	50	91	18	2	7	45	2
Caston, Bernard, of	.274	351	64	96	18	2	2	32	24
Hardtke, Brad, 3b	.273	11	5	3	0	0	0	0	0
Kirkpatrick, Jay, 1b	.434	145	34	63	7	1	8	43	0
Kopacz, Derek, of	.266	282	47	75	19	5	5	42	32
Mack, Bryan, c-1b	.247	93	22	23	4	0	5	20	0
Mackay, Tripp, ss	.281	146	24	41	9	0	0	17	3
2-team (46 Winnipeg)	.264	280	46	74	14	2	0	42	4
Miranda, Jose, dh-of	.276	163	34	45	17	0	3	22	2
Neff, Marty, 1b-of	.281	224	28	63	17	0	9	46	3
Patton, Josh, dh-3b	.350	303	59	106	18	3	7	66	6
Ramirez, J.D., 3b	.280	125	18	35	3	0	2	16	0
Sawyer, Chris, of	.275	276	44	76	14	5	7	52	11
Thornhill, Chad, ss	.338	157	31	53	8	1	1	28	3

Independent Leagues

BATTING	AVG	AB	R	H	2B	3B	HR	RBI	SB
Toven, John, 2b	.301	322	61	97	25	0	3	44	32
Unrat, Chris, c	.280	239	41	67	15	1	4	37	1

PITCHING	W	L	ERA	G	SV	IP	H	BB	SO
Bedinger, Doug	5	5	4.72	20	0	124	142	48	98
Cushman, Dwayne	0	1	10.38	7	0	13	27	4	8
Dixon, Gordon	0	0	54.00	1	0	1	1	2	1
Fahs, Derek	4	4	4.07	44	19	49	54	14	45
Green, Otis	2	1	4.66	4	0	29	26	8	22
Grife, Rich	0	0	6.08	5	0	13	15	5	3
Hill, Chris	6	5	3.81	28	0	76	76	37	50
Kammerer, James	4	1	5.08	35	3	34	30	19	27
Kosek, Kory	3	2	11.84	10	0	19	34	12	20
Marchesano, Mike	8	4	3.30	27	2	79	73	44	56
Marowski, Ray	0	0	4.50	3	0	6	4	7	1
Patino, Leonardo	8	2	5.77	28	0	106	121	41	87
Paull, Kalam	0	0	6.75	3	0	3	5	1	0
2-team (16 Winnipeg)	1	2	4.78	19	1	32	38	11	14
Ponte, Ed	4	1	3.25	9	0	55	60	8	39
Post, Bobby	3	3	5.96	10	0	54	65	22	37
Press, Gregg	3	4	6.85	10	0	47	75	16	26
Rodriguez, Carlos	0	0	12.00	8	0	15	18	17	8
Tilmon, Pat	1	1	4.25	6	0	36	49	9	17

SIOUX FALLS

BATTING	AVG	AB	R	H	2B	3B	HR	RBI	SB
Alvarez, Luis, 1b-of	.143	21	2	3	0	0	0	0	0
Antigua, Nilson, c	.239	88	16	21	8	2	1	12	2
Briller, Chris, 1b-3b	.313	316	44	99	21	2	4	37	12
Carter, Michael, of	.246	65	10	16	1	1	0	4	1
Cruz, Paul, of	.310	29	2	9	0	0	1	3	1
Dour, Craig, 1b	.276	87	21	24	4	1	2	14	6
Droptini, Bryan, of	.235	115	22	27	7	0	0	8	9
Fauske, Josh, c-1b	.396	53	12	21	4	1	2	16	2
Fisher, Eric, 3b-ss	.277	177	22	49	4	0	1	15	4
Gerald, Eddie, of	.217	249	32	54	7	6	8	31	13
Hannah, Josh, of-2b	.269	268	29	72	8	1	4	31	5
Jones, Ron, dh	.319	160	25	51	8	0	5	26	3
Lewis, Danny, dh	.204	98	5	20	3	0	3	10	6
Peterson, Charles, of	.289	318	48	92	17	1	10	53	23
Ramirez, Angel, of	.339	177	37	60	17	3	4	23	7
Rodrigues, Rich, c	.245	196	25	48	7	0	9	25	3
Tovar, Edgar, ss-2b	.314	318	51	100	13	2	10	51	9
Vopata, Nate, 2b-ss	.239	305	43	73	17	4	9	40	7

PITCHING	W	L	ERA	G	SV	IP	H	BB	SO
Arner, Mike	0	3	6.31	9	0	46	64	12	38
Blanc, Rick	3	2	2.93	32	5	43	37	18	27
Briller, Chris	0	1	4.91	2	0	4	5	3	4
Buckman, Tom	0	0	6.30	5	0	10	16	5	6
Callahan, Damon	0	1	5.23	2	0	10	14	4	6
Fauske, Josh	0	0	4.50	8	0	8	6	3	5
Garcia, Ariel	3	0	3.60	4	0	30	34	7	14
3-team (5 Mad., 4 Sch.)	3	2	5.71	13	0	41	47	16	19
Grant, Brian	2	1	6.75	9	2	11	13	4	2
Hahn, Steve	2	8	5.06	26	0	84	94	37	41
Hogan, Dennis	9	7	6.05	20	0	106	124	44	62
Hyde, Rich	8	2	2.73	19	0	115	123	27	77
Keppen, Dusty	1	2	5.16	17	1	30	42	10	22
Mercedes, Ruben	2	6	4.99	17	0	58	64	24	39
Moeller, Dennis	0	2	16.71	2	0	7	14	2	6
Palazzolo, Tony	0	2	11.17	3	0	10	16	4	2
Pearson, Jason	2	3	2.98	27	0	63	57	28	48
Roberts, Mike	4	1	0.88	18	5	31	21	4	22
Taulman, Jason	0	0	2.25	4	0	8	11	1	2
Veniard, Jay	1	6	4.58	14	0	90	85	49	77

WINNIPEG

BATTING	AVG	AB	R	H	2B	3B	HR	RBI	SB
Baeza, Art, 3b	.298	151	28	45	8	1	4	18	2
Chandler, Russell, dh-of	.167	18	1	3	0	0	0	1	0
Danton, Jeff, c-of	.182	11	4	2	1	0	0	1	0
Duva, Brian, 2b	.288	316	60	91	11	7	1	39	23
Everson, Darin, 1b	.306	333	60	102	20	1	12	69	1
Fortin, Troy, c	.323	201	44	65	21	1	6	39	1
French, Ned, of	.083	24	2	2	0	0	0	1	0
Hearn, Sean, of	.249	237	36	59	14	0	10	41	5
Hosey, Dwayne, of	.330	206	47	68	18	2	6	46	6
Kokinda, Chris, of	.285	337	66	96	18	1	3	39	9
Lane, Nolan, dh-of	.260	265	41	69	14	2	12	46	4
MacKay, Tripp, ss	.246	134	22	33	5	2	0	25	1
Matthews, Eric, of	.226	115	9	26	3	0	0	9	0
Myrow, Brian, 2b-3b	.284	67	11	19	7	0	1	15	0
Neff, Marty, 1b-of	.278	79	15	22	6	0	7	21	0

BATTING	AVG	AB	R	H	2B	3B	HR	RBI	SB
2-team (57 Sioux City)	.281	303	47	85	23	0	16	67	3
Neiles, Scott, of	.333	3	2	1	0	0	0	0	0
Sachs, Brent, 3b-of	.279	290	56	81	10	9	6	44	21
Thornhill, Chad, ss	.293	150	28	44	3	4	0	18	3
2-team (45 Sioux City)	.316	307	59	97	11	5	1	46	6
Trahan, Mike, 2b	.265	34	2	9	2	0	0	6	0

PITCHING	W	L	ERA	G	SV	IP	H	BB	SO
Anderson, Eric	9	6	4.81	18	0	110	121	36	66
Arnold, John	0	1	14.54	4	0	4	9	5	5
Bates, Shawn	0	0	5.40	3	0	3	6	1	1
Bettens, Jamie	0	0	6.35	3	0	6	8	5	2
Bowman, Noah	3	1	7.09	21	0	46	71	19	22
Cushman, Dwayne	0	1	9.43	14	0	21	35	7	14
2-team (7 Sioux City)	0	0	7.88	7	0	8	8	3	6
Forney, Rick	9	3	2.13	13	0	84	93	13	62
Fortin, Blaine	0	0	5.06	3	0	5	6	3	2
Gooden, Derek	1	0	2.61	11	4	10	8	6	14
Guehne, Dan	4	3	3.27	35	9	41	41	17	28
Hurtado, Victor	0	2	8.90	7	0	31	52	7	16
Keppen, Jeff	7	4	4.59	16	0	96	97	51	81
2-team (2 Schaumburg.)	7	5	4.99	18	0	101	102	60	85
Montgomery, Joe	0	0	2.25	5	0	4	4	3	1
Ochsner, Alan	2	0	0.96	17	5	28	24	10	32
Onley, Shawn	5	9	5.19	18	0	127	133	49	103
Osborn, Josh	1	1	7.25	6	0	22	30	8	15
Paull, Kalam	1	2	4.60	16	1	29	33	10	14
Spykstra, David	0	0	12.15	4	0	7	12	7	8
Steinmetz, Earl	2	1	4.40	5	0	31	35	11	29
Viano, Jacob	1	2	5.48	5	0	23	27	14	16
Williams, Juan	1	0	2.03	2	0	13	12	4	11
Wise, Andy	0	3	7.84	4	0	21	32	3	8
Ybarra, Jamie	0	0	2.51	10	6	14	10	14	15

EASTERN DIVISION

STANDINGS

FIRST HALF

NORTH	W	L	PCT	GB
Adirondack Lumberjacks	22	21	.512	—
Quebec Les Capitales	21	22	.488	1
Massachusetts Mad Dogs	21	22	.488	1
Albany-Colonie Diamond Dogs	21	22	.488	1
SOUTH	**W**	**L**	**PCT**	**GB**
New Jersey Jackals	23	19	.548	—
Waterbury Spirit	22	21	.512	1½
Elmira Pioneers	21	22	.500	2
Allentown Ambassadors	20	23	.465	3½

SECOND HALF

NORTH	W	L	PCT	GB
Albany-Colonie Diamond Dogs	24	19	.558	—
Quebec Les Capitales	22	21	.512	2
Adirondack Lumberjacks	21	22	.488	3
Massachusetts Mad Dogs	20	23	.465	4
SOUTH	**W**	**L**	**PCT**	**GB**
Allentown Ambassadors	27	16	.628	—
New Jersey Jackals	22	21	.512	5
Elmira Pioneers	22	21	.512	5
Waterbury Spirit	14	29	.326	13

PLAYOFFS: First Round—New Jersey defeated Allentown 3-0 and Albany-Colonie defeated Adirondack 3-2 in best-of-5 series. **Semifinals**—Albany-Colonie defeated New Jersey 3-1 in best-of-5 series. **Finals**—Albany-Colonie defeated Winnipeg 3-1 in best-of-5 series.

MANAGERS: Adirondack—Les Lancaster. Albany—Charlie Sullivan. Allentown—Ed Ott. Elmira—Dan Shwam. Massachusetts—George Scott. New Jersey—Kash Beauchamp. Quebec—Jay Ward. Waterbury—George Tsamis.

ATTENDANCE: New Jersey, 129,179; Allentown, 116,402; Quebec, 110,559; Albany-Colonie, 99,313; Elmira, 83,276; Adirondack, 54,903; Waterbury, 44,697; Massachusetts, 38,528.

ALL-STAR TEAM: C—D.C. Olsen, New Jersey. **1B**—Morgan Walker, Albany-Colonie. **2B**—Mike Pagan, Massachusetts. **3B**—Ruben Santana, Adirondack. **SS**—Chris Miyake, Adirondack. **OF**—Carmine Cappuccio, New Jersey; Brandon Naples, Allentown; Steve Walker, Allentown. **DH**—Jay Gainer, Allentown. **RHP**—Michel Laplante, Quebec. **LHP**—Chad Ward, Elmira. **RP**—Matt

Wagner, Adirondack.

Player of the Year: Carmine Cappuccio, New Jersey. **Pitcher of the Year**: Michel Laplante, Quebec. **Rookie of the Year**: Kasuaki Miyasaki, Adirondack. **Rookie Pitcher of the Year**: Jason Foulks, Albany-Colonie. **Manager of the Year**: Ed Ott, Allentown.

INDIVIDUAL BATTING LEADERS
(Minimum 232 Plate Appearances)

	AVG	AB	R	H	2B	3B	HR	RBI	SB
Naples, Brandon, Allentown .	.378	275	50	104	12	4	2	30	17
French, Anton, Queb.-Mass.	.377	228	39	86	18	3	4	42	27
Mitchell, Tony, Mass.	.375	224	56	84	11	1	27	70	0
Gainer, Jay, Allentown	.360	222	53	80	13	2	22	71	3
Pagana, Mike, Mass.	.355	349	67	124	14	5	1	57	14
Marsh, Roy, Mass.	.350	294	67	103	13	6	2	30	21
Cappuccio, Carmine, NJ	.349	301	59	105	28	1	17	75	0
Dean, Chris, Allentown	.346	211	52	73	15	2	5	28	12
Walker, Morgan, Adir.	.325	311	54	101	22	3	14	63	1
Santana, Ruben, Adir.	.322	307	63	99	19	5	12	65	15

INDIVIDUAL PITCHING LEADERS
(Minimum 69 Innings)

	W	L	ERA	G	SV	IP	H	BB	SO
Laplante, Michel, Quebec	11	2	2.06	20	0	131	108	23	143
Lancaster, Les, Adir.	3	3	2.20	11	0	70	75	14	41
Kelly, John, Waterbury	7	4	3.05	12	0	89	88	26	85
Sanford, Mo, Mass.	8	4	3.05	19	0	133	122	29	91
Pincavitch, Kevin, NJ	10	5	3.33	17	0	114	115	27	97
Grundy, Phil, Elmira	8	9	3.33	20	0	143	157	22	126
Newman, Damon, Adir.	9	3	3.53	19	0	117	124	36	62
Bauer, Chuck, Albany	6	2	3.56	17	0	94	92	9	64
Ward, Chad, Elmira	7	8	3.69	19	0	120	128	27	87
Arteaga, Ivan, Elmira	10	5	3.71	17	0	112	111	40	82

ADIRONDACK

BATTING	AVG	AB	R	H	2B	3B	HR	RBI	SB
Abrego, Keith, of	.143	7	0	1	0	0	0	0	0
Ahearne, Paul, 2b-ss	.132	38	5	5	1	0	0	3	1
Britt, Bryan, 1b	.264	333	58	88	26	0	20	63	4
Cano, Matt, 3b	.288	226	20	65	6	0	0	18	7
Church, Mike, c	.220	164	16	36	8	0	0	10	1
Ham, Kevin, of	.262	252	34	66	15	0	8	40	4
Hamilton, Joe, of	.273	44	7	12	2	0	0	3	2
Ikeda, Go, of	.313	16	3	5	0	0	0	0	0
Johnson, Andre, of	.243	37	6	9	0	0	4	8	2
2-team (29 Albany)	.240	146	24	35	1	1	8	18	14
Kimbler, Doug, 2b	.197	61	5	12	2	0	0	8	1
Kingston, Kelly, of	.291	275	62	80	16	2	12	41	15
2-team (1 Waterbury)	.000	2	1	0	0	0	0	1	0
Miyake, Chris, ss	.264	318	55	84	15	2	2	36	18
Miyasaki, Kasuaki, 2b	.322	273	62	88	18	6	0	29	37
Neikirk, Derick, c	.263	118	15	31	3	1	2	13	3
Porter, Kedric, of	.318	321	41	102	17	1	1	43	27
Santana, Ruben, dh-3b	.322	307	63	99	19	5	12	65	15
Strangfeld, Aaron, c	.000	4	0	0	0	0	0	0	0
Yelding, Eric, dh-2b	.202	94	10	19	4	1	0	2	11

PITCHING	W	L	ERA	G	SV	IP	H	BB	SO
Campbell, Chad	0	1	6.17	8	0	12	14	5	9
Coronado, Osvaldo	2	2	3.77	7	0	14	12	6	6
Eischen, Joey	4	2	3.75	7	0	48	52	11	49
Fry, Jeff	0	1	4.67	6	0	17	19	16	5
Grant, Brian	0	4	5.80	20	0	36	45	12	23
Gray, Jason	7	1	2.85	42	5	47	45	11	42
Holland, Wes	1	1	4.42	13	0	18	22	9	9
Kimihiko, Inoui	0	0	13.50	2	0	1	2	3	1
Kosek, Kory	2	5	6.99	10	0	55	55	14	49
Lancaster, Les	3	3	2.20	11	0	70	75	14	41
Larson, Toby	1	2	7.28	10	0	38	53	17	29
Newman, Damon	9	3	3.53	19	0	117	124	36	62
Ramirez, Marco	0	1	2.08	5	0	13	10	6	8
Santiago, Derek	7	4	3.71	16	0	97	100	40	62
Wagner, Matt	1	6	4.27	43	20	46	44	17	48
Wilkerson, Steven	0	1	14.73	3	0	7	17	5	5
Yoshimune, Wakita	6	6	5.25	23	0	82	83	34	53
Zambelli, Mike	0	0	3.75	7	0	12	8	11	10

ALBANY-COLONIE

BATTING	AVG	AB	R	H	2B	3B	HR	RBI	SB
Belliard, Rafael, ss	.310	168	28	52	5	0	1	18	2
Craddox, Kenny, of	.235	51	11	12	2	1	0	6	2
Davila, Vic, 3b-of	.270	248	39	67	16	1	6	33	5
Dockery, Tim, c	.260	50	11	13	2	0	5	15	1
2-team (14 Quebec)	.216	97	15	21	4	0	5	21	1

Durick, Chad, of	.254	59	3	15	3	0	0	6	0
2-team (5 Waterbury)	.247	77	7	19	3	0	1	8	1
Figueroa, Shaun, 2b	.167	18	0	3	0	0	0	1	0
Gabriel, Denio, ss	.200	35	5	7	0	0	0	4	2
2-team (13 Mass.)	.185	81	11	15	2	1	0	6	6
Heller, Brad, c	.271	59	9	16	2	0	0	12	3
Johnson, Andre, of	.239	109	18	26	1	1	4	10	12
Kopriva, Dan, dh-1b	.275	160	29	44	9	0	5	25	16
Lockett, Ron, of	.257	101	15	26	7	1	1	11	3
McKee, Scott, c-3b	.295	237	34	70	14	0	3	33	0
McWhite, Moe, 1b-of	.000	13	0	0	0	0	0	1	0
Mejia, Ramon, ss-of	.318	129	23	41	7	2	0	14	20
Mueller, Jon, dh	.290	214	37	62	11	0	13	43	1
Paxton, Chris, c	.275	51	10	14	5	0	1	2	0
Robertson, Matt, of-2b	.129	31	4	4	0	1	0	3	3
Roche, Marlon, of	.313	300	48	94	15	3	3	40	6
Thobe, Steve, 3b	.167	30	4	5	2	0	1	3	0
Valdez, Trovin, of	.188	128	14	24	5	0	1	6	9
Vasquez, Danny, of	.200	30	4	6	0	1	1	6	0
Walker, Morgan, 1b-of	.325	311	54	101	22	3	14	63	1
Zorrilla, Julio, 2b	.270	363	54	98	13	8	1	38	31

PITCHING	W	L	ERA	G	SV	IP	H	BB	SO
Bauer, Chuck	6	2	3.56	17	0	94	92	9	64
Brassington, Phil	10	2	3.87	17	0	105	117	35	99
Brito, Juan	0	1	6.52	12	0	19	24	14	15
Cruz, Fermin	1	7	8.14	12	0	49	69	12	38
Debrino, Rob	2	4	4.75	15	5	36	26	29	29
DeJesus, Jose	0	1	7.50	7	0	24	36	11	22
Durick, Chad	3	3	2.88	18	0	41	33	12	26
Foulks, Jason	1	0	1.08	8	3	8	9	7	9
2-team (25 Mass.)	5	3	1.70	33	8	48	36	28	53
Hasler, Jerry	7	6	4.67	18	0	106	121	33	77
Hooper, Jimmy	1	0	2.33	16	4	19	14	3	27
2-team (15 Elmira)	3	0	3.73	31	5	41	38	14	46
House, Sean	2	1	4.78	9	0	32	44	5	29
Johnson, Dane	0	0	2.38	9	3	11	8	4	12
Kosoc, Nate	0	0	8.31	3	0	4	9	0	2
Lawton, Bill	8	8	4.17	25	0	91	99	33	70
Metoyer, Tony	0	0	4.50	2	2	1	2	4	4
Newill, Max	1	0	7.03	22	1	24	20	13	24
Parantala, Mark	2	4	4.91	24	0	29	30	10	21
Santana, Cesar	0	0	6.08	7	0	13	20	6	11
Seely, Jason	2	4	3.29	24	0	27	28	13	14
Strahowski, Chris	0	0	0.90	11	0	10	2	4	6

ALLENTOWN

BATTING	AVG	AB	R	H	2B	3B	HR	RBI	SB
Anderson, Milt, of	.279	240	39	67	13	1	2	31	16
Bullett, Scott, of	.361	83	17	30	8	1	3	28	7
Dean, Chris, 2b	.346	211	52	73	15	2	5	28	12
Flanders, Shawnn, of-2b	.217	60	11	13	0	1	0	5	1
Gainer, Jay, dh	.360	222	53	80	13	2	22	71	3
Gilligan, Dan, c	.152	33	1	5	1	0	0	3	0
Johns, Mike, ss	.226	159	27	36	9	1	3	22	2
Kelley, Erskine, of	.283	46	5	13	1	0	2	6	6
Magallanes, Bobby, 3b	.296	125	17	37	16	0	1	24	0
Martinez, Rafael, 1b	.313	323	61	101	30	1	5	57	4
Matsushita, Makoto, 3b-ss	.351	97	19	34	5	0	0	18	7
Naples, Brandon, of	.378	275	50	104	12	4	2	30	17
Pell, Rich, 2b	.247	77	16	19	3	1	0	5	2
Sadlowski, Jared, c	.267	273	48	73	23	2	6	48	5
Sanchez, Manny, 3b-2b	.353	150	28	53	8	3	1	12	6
Schappacher, Scott, ss	.189	143	16	27	7	0	2	14	0
Walker, Steve, of	.299	324	72	97	31	4	17	68	25
Williams, Juan, dh-of	.155	58	7	9	2	0	2	10	1
Williams, Ryan, c	.276	87	5	24	6	0	0	10	0

PITCHING	W	L	ERA	G	SV	IP	H	BB	SO
Bair, Denny	1	3	6.94	5	0	23	32	5	9
Chambers, Scott	1	1	3.42	31	1	47	51	15	47
Davis, Jim	3	1	4.27	28	0	53	42	34	64
Flanders, Shawnn	0	1	6.75	6	0	12	14	9	12
Gaal, Bryan	0	0	2.67	19	2	30	25	7	37
Getz, Rod	0	1	11.57	2	0	2	3	5	3
Gonzalez, Juan	7	2	3.36	32	8	62	58	12	47
2-team (8 Mass.)	1	5	7.28	10	0	51	69	29	26
Hunter, Rich	10	8	4.70	19	0	119	143	39	82
Macey, Fausto	9	6	3.79	18	0	128	156	18	64
McNally, Andrew	3	0	1.91	17	0	28	23	10	25
Mitchell, Courtney	0	0	10.50	4	0	6	9	4	5
Petique, Marino	7	3	3.93	18	0	108	118	46	80
Phillips, Jon	2	1	4.85	11	2	13	15	4	9

Independent Leagues

	W	L	ERA	G	SV	IP	H	BB	SO
Ponte, Ed	2	5	2.84	9	0	57	63	10	29
Saneaux, Francisco	0	2	5.74	7	0	16	19	7	12
Smith, Hut	2	1	4.71	5	0	29	38	11	21
Sordo, Fernado	0	2	18.00	3	0	7	18	6	6

ELMIRA

BATTING	AVG	AB	R	H	2B	3B	HR	RBI	SB
Abreu, Nelson, of-3b	.277	332	53	92	13	6	3	38	39
Bell, Juan, 2b	.412	34	6	14	2	2	2	8	0
Bethea, Larry, 1b	.138	29	3	4	0	0	1	2	1
Dorrmann, Brian, 3b-2b	.298	121	15	36	11	1	0	15	3
Downs, Brian, 1b-c	.279	258	27	72	18	0	7	29	0
Edelstein, Chris, of	.291	86	12	25	3	1	1	11	4
2-team (22 New Jersey)	.277	137	19	38	4	2	1	19	6
Garcia, Ossie, of	.302	139	19	42	11	1	0	19	7
Groppuso, Mike, 3b-of	.265	313	48	83	20	0	13	64	3
Guerrero, Juan, 2b	.203	158	18	32	6	1	1	13	1
Kennedy, Gus, of	.264	125	21	33	8	0	3	14	8
Kopriva, Dan, dh	.351	57	9	20	4	0	2	9	5
2-team (46 Albany)	.295	217	38	64	13	0	7	34	14
McCladdie, Tony, ss	.143	7	1	1	1	0	0	1	1
2-team (10 Mass.)	.281	32	7	9	3	0	0	3	5
McNeal, Pepe, c	.261	226	38	59	17	3	5	36	8
Owen, Andy, of	.294	85	15	25	5	2	4	13	2
Reyes, Kiko, ss	.251	299	39	75	15	0	4	36	6
Riccio, John, 1b	.247	81	6	20	5	0	0	3	1
Rojas, Christian, of	.213	122	17	26	7	1	6	23	2
Stewart, Paxton, 1b	.000	3	0	0	0	0	0	0	0
Stockmann, Matt, c	.227	22	0	5	3	0	0	1	0
Taylor, Tom, of	.264	53	7	14	0	0	0	4	0
Tidwell, Dave, of-dh	.266	252	46	67	10	0	2	25	34

PITCHING	W	L	ERA	G	SV	IP	H	BB	SO
Arteaga, Ivan	10	5	3.71	17	0	112	111	40	82
Brown, Chris	0	1	2.33	14	1	19	18	4	22
Forsythe, Neil	5	1	2.77	29	0	39	42	10	21
Grundy, Phil	8	9	3.33	20	0	143	157	22	126
Hooper, Jimmy	2	0	4.98	15	1	22	24	11	19
Madison, Scott	0	0	0.00	1	0	1	1	0	1
McKeon, Shane	0	1	9.39	10	0	15	23	15	8
Nichols, Jamie	6	6	4.54	18	0	119	122	48	76
Parantala, Mark	1	0	4.85	10	0	13	16	5	11
2-team (24 Albany)	3	4	4.89	34	0	42	46	15	32
Steph, Rod	0	5	2.96	27	20	27	29	10	27
Totten, Kris	1	1	6.53	21	0	40	53	17	34
Turnier, Aaron	3	5	4.59	22	0	67	81	35	53
Ward, Chad	7	8	3.69	19	0	120	128	27	87

MASSACHUSETTS

BATTING	AVG	AB	R	H	2B	3B	HR	RBI	SB
Cameron, Dorian, dh-of	.143	7	1	1	1	0	0	0	0
Carrasco, Ricardo, of-1b	.265	102	19	27	4	2	5	14	1
Carver, Jerrell, dh	.266	64	6	17	4	0	1	10	1
French, Anton, of	.393	135	22	53	13	3	3	29	17
Gabriel, Denio, of	.174	46	6	8	2	1	0	2	4
Gandolfo, Robert, ss	.169	59	9	10	1	1	0	5	4
Garramore, Joe, dh-c	.238	21	3	5	0	0	0	2	2
Hasty, Chris, of	.103	39	6	4	2	0	2	8	0
Holmes, Tammy, of	.000	7	1	0	0	0	0	0	0
Kane, Ryan, 3b-1b	.294	306	50	90	17	4	7	65	10
Marsh, Roy, of	.350	294	67	103	13	6	2	30	21
McCain, Marcus, of	.182	22	5	4	0	0	0	1	6
McCladdie, Tony, ss	.320	25	6	8	2	0	0	2	4
Mitchell, Tony, of	.375	224	56	84	11	1	27	70	0
Murphy, Dan, c	.000	7	0	0	0	0	0	0	0
Oropeza, Willie, of	.236	144	20	34	9	0	3	21	1
2-team (18 New Jersey)	.223	197	25	44	11	0	3	25	1
Pagana, Mike, 2b	.355	349	67	124	14	5	1	57	14
Polanco, Juan, of	.266	214	36	57	11	5	6	39	5
Reinisch, Paul, 1b	.267	258	38	69	12	0	4	36	1
Rhodes, Danny, of	.310	84	20	26	5	1	1	13	4
Roa, Hector, 3b	.203	123	23	25	5	0	2	21	4
Rodriguez, Miguel, c	.286	14	2	4	0	0	0	4	1
Smetek, Peter, of	.174	23	2	4	0	0	0	2	0
Suero, Ignacio, c	.244	176	11	43	7	0	0	23	0
Thorpe, A.D., ss	.254	189	30	48	8	0	1	13	7
Williams, Tray, 3b-ss	.000	11	1	0	0	0	0	0	0

PITCHING	W	L	ERA	G	SV	IP	H	BB	SO
Bauldree, Joe	2	2	1.58	25	4	46	33	19	43
Cordova, Luis	0	0	54.00	2	0	1	5	4	0
Dunphy, Chris	0	0	0.00	2	0	1	0	2	0
Foulks, Jason	4	3	1.83	25	5	39	27	21	44
Giard, Jeremy	1	3	5.15	20	2	37	47	14	24
Gomez, Gus	2	3	7.01	13	2	44	49	26	40

	W	L	ERA	G	SV	IP	H	BB	SO
Guerrero, Jose	1	4	6.55	8	0	45	56	26	24
Hueston, Steve	7	9	5.26	21	0	115	133	68	70
Lima, Cory	5	3	4.77	16	0	66	77	37	42
Love, Farley	1	1	13.50	2	0	1	1	5	1
Macone, Mike	0	0	0.00	3	0	2	1	1	5
Mangieri, John	1	0	5.82	6	0	23	28	10	11
Manzanillo, Ravelo	2	0	1.29	3	0	21	16	4	25
Mercado, Manuel	0	0	6.23	2	0	4	6	4	4
2-team (2 New Jersey)	0	0	10.13	4	0	8	11	4	6
Reyes, Pablo	2	1	3.46	3	0	26	20	5	16
Romero, Elvis	0	2	7.94	6	0	6	6	3	3
Sanford, Mo	8	4	3.05	19	0	133	122	29	91
Smetek, Peter	0	0	9.00	2	0	3	8	2	2
Switala, Stan	0	2	7.94	6	0	17	20	13	5
Taylor, Tommy	0	4	10.87	6	0	27	40	17	28
2-team (8 Quebec)	4	5	6.28	14	0	67	77	26	54
Thoesen, Ian	0	2	11.15	5	0	15	25	5	10
Tillmon, Darrell	1	0	4.98	17	1	34	47	9	25
Walsh, Steve	4	2	4.83	17	1	41	45	14	23

NEW JERSEY

BATTING	AVG	AB	R	H	2B	3B	HR	RBI	SB
Anderson, Jeff, ss-2b	.262	202	41	53	9	2	2	27	2
Brinkley, Josh, 3b-ss	.282	291	50	82	16	1	10	43	16
Burke, Mark, 1b-dh	.291	237	35	69	15	1	5	39	7
Burton, Essex, 2b-of	.308	354	65	109	17	2	4	43	34
Campbell, Wylie, ss	.217	46	5	10	0	0	0	5	3
Cappuccio, Carmine, of	.349	301	59	105	28	1	17	75	0
Davis, Brian, of	.276	268	36	74	15	3	4	38	13
Deck, Ronnie, c	.125	8	0	1	0	0	0	1	0
Edelstein, Chris, of-dh	.255	51	7	13	1	1	0	8	2
Handy, Russell, dh-of	.276	58	12	16	1	0	2	10	5
Lewis, Joe, ss	.083	12	0	1	0	0	0	1	0
Martinez, Tony, 3b-2b	.279	262	45	73	20	2	5	37	2
Olsen, D.C., c-1b	.279	323	54	90	14	2	13	52	2
Oropeza, Willie, c-3b	.189	53	5	10	2	0	0	4	0
Peltz, Mike, c	.271	85	12	23	5	0	0	14	2
Rose, Pete, of	.300	303	70	91	27	1	15	53	7
Valdez, Trovin, of	.234	47	8	11	4	3	0	9	6
2-team (38 Albany)	.200	175	22	35	9	3	1	15	15
Wydner, Dan, of	.261	23	5	6	0	0	0	3	0

PITCHING	W	L	ERA	G	SV	IP	H	BB	SO
Bane, Jaymie	4	4	5.67	15	0	67	58	40	43
Brewer, Nevin	0	1	8.44	7	0	11	15	6	5
Carroll, Don	0	0	0.00	1	0	1	0	2	0
Cuchetti, Tony	0	0	6.35	13	0	23	31	9	21
DelPriore, Rob	0	0	10.13	6	0	11	11	7	8
Diono, Marty	0	0	9.00	1	0	1	0	2	0
Hartung, Michael	1	2	6.98	39	12	39	56	17	32
High, Andy	4	3	4.25	36	0	49	54	19	51
Lemke, Mark	5	1	6.68	11	0	34	33	30	19
Magrini, Paul	6	7	4.74	18	0	106	125	34	71
Mercado, Manuel	0	0	16.20	2	0	3	5	0	2
Nielsen, Tom	1	4	6.90	14	0	46	63	36	31
Pincavitch, Kevin	10	5	3.33	17	0	114	115	27	97
Reichow, Bob	6	7	5.26	30	1	92	121	33	50
Rohrbach, Mike	5	2	4.03	29	0	74	87	22	48
Terrana, Pete	0	1	5.23	3	1	10	5	8	6
Woodring, Jason	3	3	2.90	36	5	50	37	20	32

QUEBEC

BATTING	AVG	AB	R	H	2B	3B	HR	RBI	SB
Autry, Brian, 1b	.306	111	22	34	9	0	3	18	0
Baird, Matt, of	.223	148	16	33	8	0	2	9	1
Bellinato, Tony, of	.154	26	4	4	1	0	0	2	0
Campeau, Dominic, c	.269	67	6	18	3	0	0	10	1
Chimelis, Joel, 1b-2b	.271	59	9	16	3	0	1	6	0
Davis, Eddie, of	.111	45	5	5	0	0	1	4	1
Dionne, Stephane, dh	.316	19	2	6	0	0	0	0	0
DiMaggio, Frank, 3b-2b	.220	50	3	11	1	0	1	3	0
DiPrima, Giancarlo, 2b-ss	.241	266	31	64	3	1	0	19	11
Dockery, Tim, c	.170	47	4	8	2	0	0	6	0
Dumas, Mike, of-2b	.267	281	64	75	8	0	0	27	36
French, Anton, of	.355	93	17	33	5	0	1	13	10
2-team (32 Mass.)	.377	228	39	86	18	3	4	42	27
Hernandez, JoJo, 1b	.149	121	11	18	7	0	0	12	0
Hill, Jason, c	.303	198	30	60	12	0	8	39	1
Jackson, Jeremy, of	.042	24	1	1	0	0	0	1	2
Lantigua, Eddie, of-3b	.276	315	44	87	17	3	9	51	1
Lepine, Julien, 3b-ss	.302	139	17	42	3	0	1	11	3
Lepine, Olivier, of	.224	67	5	15	3	0	0	5	0
Lyden, Mitch, dh	.290	272	32	79	13	0	14	55	0
McDonald, Ashanti, ss	.307	228	33	70	9	2	6	33	18

Independent Leagues

	AVG	AB	R	H	2B	3B	HR	RBI	SB
Mora, Mike, of	.222	171	27	38	8	1	0	20	6
Rios, Eduardo, 3b	.333	9	1	3	1	0	0	2	0
Russin, Tom, of-1b	.250	44	8	11	4	0	3	9	0
Wayne, Tyrone, of	.184	49	5	9	1	1	1	4	3

PITCHING	W	L	ERA	G	SV	IP	H	BB	SO
Boynewicz, Jim	4	7	5.04	12	0	70	78	27	42
Carl, Todd	2	8	5.38	16	0	85	93	36	54
Lavenia, Mark	6	8	4.55	20	0	115	128	37	90
Lavigne, Martin	0	2	4.50	3	0	10	14	4	8
Laplante, Michel	11	2	2.06	20	0	131	108	23	143
Martineau, Yves	5	3	1.70	40	18	58	46	23	51
Ramos, Luis	1	3	5.07	38	0	82	83	39	78
Rizzo, Nick	1	3	6.83	7	0	29	43	11	26
Sanchez, Mike	5	3	5.34	43	5	61	62	29	54
Taylor, Tommy	4	1	3.15	8	0	40	37	9	26
Tinnish, Andrew	3	1	6.93	22	0	38	44	29	18
Warren, DeShawn	1	0	4.42	9	0	18	16	17	15
Westover, Richard	0	1	18.29	8	0	10	27	9	5
Ziobro, Jeff	0	1	4.50	2	0	2	2	0	0

WATERBURY

BATTING	AVG	AB	R	H	2B	3B	HR	RBI	SB
Asencio, Alex, of	.285	323	58	92	12	4	4	31	20
Belcher, Tim, 1b-of	.281	160	26	45	7	1	6	27	3
Benes, Richie, 2b-ss	.229	144	14	33	4	3	0	9	8
Bryant, Pat, of	.296	142	21	42	5	2	3	21	7
Cooney, Kyle, dh-c	.295	305	50	90	19	1	12	57	5
Durick, Chad, 1b	.222	18	4	4	0	0	1	2	1
Garbowski, Joe, c	.243	111	11	27	4	1	0	8	1
Guerrero, Rafael, of	.370	165	25	61	11	2	6	37	2
Hall, Joe, of	.391	46	9	18	3	1	3	10	0
Keaveney, Jeff, 1b	.293	188	35	55	16	1	10	39	0
Kingston, Kelly, of	.000	2	1	0	0	0	0	0	1
Lewis, Joe, ss	.167	72	8	12	1	0	0	9	2
2-team (3 New Jersey)	.155	84	8	13	1	0	0	10	2
Malave, Jaime, dh-c	.264	72	12	19	2	0	3	9	0
Melendez, Luis, c-2b	.205	88	9	18	3	0	0	9	0
Nunez, Sergio, 2b	.194	62	9	12	2	0	0	4	7
Penalver, Juan, 3b	.257	292	63	75	10	5	1	26	21
Reintjes, Steve, of	.288	205	30	59	8	0	3	35	0
Ricard, Toby, 2b-of	.279	330	43	92	16	3	5	50	8
Tanner, Paul, ss	.276	196	23	54	10	0	2	34	2

PITCHING	W	L	ERA	G	SV	IP	H	BB	SO
Barnsby, Scott	0	0	13.50	5	0	5	4	8	5
Bertotti, Mike	0	1	6.06	7	0	36	39	17	40
Debrino, Rob	0	0	13.50	2	0	2	4	0	1
2-team (15 Albany)	1	2	5.21	17	5	38	30	29	30
Frazier, Ron	5	4	4.63	19	0	107	119	26	54
Guerrero, Rafael	0	0	4.32	7	0	8	9	8	10
Holland, Wes	0	1	8.44	14	0	21	28	13	9
2-team (13 Adirondack)	1	2	6.58	27	0	40	50	22	18
Jimenez, John	2	6	3.35	29	0	48	47	17	32
Kelly, Chris	1	2	4.19	19	0	43	40	20	20
Kelly, Jeff	2	4	7.33	15	0	50	64	37	26
Kelly, John	7	4	3.05	12	0	89	88	26	85
Meady, Todd	5	5	3.34	35	3	65	65	17	41
Munoz, J.J.	3	6	2.88	29	13	34	37	12	35
Santana, Cesar	0	0	15.75	4	0	4	11	0	1
2-team (7 Albany)	0	0	8.31	11	0	17	31	6	12
Seely, Jason	1	2	27.00	4	0	8	24	5	2
2-team (24 Albany)	3	6	8.49	28	0	35	52	18	16
Shourds, Tony	2	4	6.60	8	0	30	36	23	7
Smith, Pete	2	6	7.24	17	0	60	82	22	32
Swanson, David	6	5	4.49	19	0	112	130	34	63
Thoesen, Ian	0	0	14.63	5	0	8	16	3	5
2-team (5 Mass.)	0	2	12.34	10	0	23	41	8	15

ATLANTIC LEAGUE

The Bridgeport Bluefish earned headlines in 1998 for helping revive an old industrial town with a new stadium and a winning ballclub. In 1999, the Bluefish did nothing to tarnish their image while drawing record numbers at the gate and winning another championship in the league's second season.

The Bluefish drew 342,857 fans, more than any other independent team and more than most affiliated minor league franchises.

Bridgeport wasn't the only story, though. The Som-erset Patriots drew 335,056 in their first year at Som-erset County Ballpark. They also proved to be a wor-thy opponent on the field by coming on strong down the stretch to win the second-half title. The victory, however, was short-lived. The Bluefish swept the Patriots three games to none in the title series.

Two costly throwing errors by Patriots' pitchers allowed the Bluefish to score several unearned runs late in two of the games. Bluefish righthander Al Sontag set the tone in the opener by allowing two earned runs on four hits in a 6-2 complete-game win. The Bluefish closed out the series with an 8-3 win behind another strong pitching performance by Steve Renko.

The Atlantic League, which began operating in 1998, is trying to establish itself as the premier inde-pendent league by attracting former major leaguers and playing a full-season schedule.

Former big leaguers like Ruben Sierra, Alex Cole, Gerald Young, Jose Lind, Jerome Walton and Kim Batiste have added instant credibility to a league try-ing to survive in the crowded Northeast corridor. So far, so good. The New Haven Ravens, the Seattle Mariners Double-A affiliate just down the road from Bridgeport, drew only 197,163 fans in 1999.

STANDINGS

FIRST HALF

	W	L	PCT	GB
Bridgeport Bluefish	43	17	.717	—
Atlantic City Surf	36	24	.600	7
Lehigh Valley Black Diamonds	26	33	.441	16½
Nashua Pride	26	34	.433	17
Newark Bears	24	35	.407	18½
Somerset Patriots	24	36	.400	19

SECOND HALF

	W	L	PCT	GB
Somerset Patriots	36	24	.600	—
Bridgeport Bluefish	35	25	.583	1
Newark Bears	31	29	.517	5
Nashua Pride	26	33	.441	9½
Lehigh Valley Black Diamonds	26	34	.433	10
Atlantic City Surf	25	34	.424	10½

PLAYOFFS: Bridgeport defeated Somerset 3-0 in best-of-5 series.

MANAGERS: Atlantic City—Doc Edwards. Bridgeport—Willie Upshaw. Lehigh Valley—Wayne Krenchicki. Nashua—Bobby Tolan. Newark—Tom O'Malley. Somerset—Sparky Lyle.

ATTENDANCE: Bridgeport 342,857; Somerset 335,056; Atlantic City 206,538; Newark 126,407; Nashua 106,139. Note: Lehigh Valley played season as a road team.

ALL-STAR TEAM: C—Mike Moyle, Bridgeport. 1B—Dan Held, Lehigh Valley. 2B—Jeff Berblinger, Somerset. 3B—Lipso Nava, Somerset. SS—Ken Arnold, Somerset. OF—Glenn Murray, Nashua; Danny Perez, Somerset; Ruben Sierra, Atlantic City. Util—Sharnol Adriana, Newark. DH—Mel Wearing, Bridgeport. RHP—Darrin Babineaux, Newark; Al Sontag, Bridgeport. LHP—Justin Jensen, Somerset. RP—Dave Adam, Bridgeport.

Player of the Year: Glenn Murray, Nashua. **Pitcher of the Year:** Justin Jensen, Somerset. **Manager of the Year:** Sparky Lyle, Somerset.

INDIVIDUAL BATTING LEADERS
(Minimum 270 Plate Appearances)

	AVG	AB	R	H	2B	3B	HR	RBI	SB
Espada, Angel, Bridgeport	.356	357	82	127	19	4	1	34	40
Adriana, Sharnol, Newark	.334	419	72	140	25	2	16	77	7
Lopez, Louis, Somerset	.329	255	41	84	14	0	15	60	5
Berblinger, Jeff, Somerset	.327	397	81	130	26	2	11	39	47
Cole, Alex, Bridgeport	.323	337	65	109	22	7	2	53	27
Soto, Emison, AC	.321	296	66	95	24	1	21	64	3
Wearing, Mel, Bridgeport	.313	364	87	114	24	1	20	84	5

Perez, Danny, LV	.310	432	69	134	27	7	10	49	20
Batiste, Kim, LV-AC	.305	302	50	92	19	1	17	58	4
Avila, Rolando, Newark	.302	374	81	113	21	4	6	37	29

INDIVIDUAL PITCHING LEADERS

(Minimum 80 Innings)

	W	L	ERA	G	SV	IP	H	BB	SO
Jensen, Justin, Somerset	12	5	2.76	24	0	156	120	77	111
Love, Jeff, Lehigh Valley	7	5	3.24	22	0	89	89	27	61
Babineaux, Darrin, Newark	10	5	3.59	35	1	125	118	48	104
St. Pierre, Bob, Newark	8	6	3.60	20	0	123	112	41	71
Davis, Ray, Somerset	7	2	3.68	20	3	86	69	38	97
Renko, Steve, Bridgeport	12	6	3.69	24	0	146	158	62	100
Sontag, Alan, Bridgeport	13	6	3.86	28	1	140	139	47	95
Montalvo, Rafael, AC	10	8	3.89	24	0	167	184	45	99
Cornett, Brad, LV	11	9	3.94	23	0	162	172	37	118
Adkins, Tim, Bridgeport	8	6	3.97	26	0	141	152	49	100

ATLANTIC CITY

BATTING	AVG	AB	R	H	2B	3B	HR	RBI	SB
Akers, Chad, ss-2b	.272	243	42	66	18	3	5	32	16
Antigua, Nilson, c-of	.286	63	11	18	3	1	1	10	0
Batiste, Kim, 3b-ss	.290	193	32	56	15	1	9	40	4
Brady, Doug, 2b	.271	273	39	74	16	6	2	24	17
Carr, Chuck, of	.263	190	32	50	7	1	8	21	14
Gordon, Keith, of	.306	216	32	66	17	1	8	29	19
2-team (27 Nashua)	.264	311	43	82	23	1	8	33	29
Henry, Santiago, 2b-ss	.332	208	34	69	5	4	12	43	2
Knott, Johnny, dh-3b	.204	93	23	19	4	0	2	10	5
McQuiniff, Jason, c	.091	11	0	1	0	1	0	0	0
Monell, Johnny, of-1b	.251	263	41	66	11	2	8	34	1
Pennyfeather, Will, of	.303	175	26	53	9	2	2	20	4
Pough, Chop, 3b	.270	115	19	31	9	1	4	14	3
Quinones, Luis, 3b-ss	.268	194	32	52	10	0	5	34	0
Quinones, Rey, ss	.235	132	21	31	6	0	4	11	0
Rocha, Juan, of	.275	331	59	91	18	3	15	55	9
Rodriguez, Joe, c	.191	115	17	22	2	1	7	24	0
Sierra, Ruben, dh-of	.294	422	76	124	22	2	28	82	3
Soto, Emison, c-of	.321	296	66	95	24	1	21	64	3
Thomas, Juan, 1b	.312	154	30	48	12	0	10	35	2
Velez, Jose, of	.213	61	4	13	3	0	0	5	0
2-team (72 Somerset)	.284	296	34	84	15	0	2	34	14
Villanueva, Hector, 1b-c	.323	186	43	60	7	0	16	45	2
Yan, Julian, 1b-of	.242	99	17	24	4	1	8	17	0

PITCHING	W	L	ERA	G	SV	IP	H	BB	SO
Abugherir, Amer	5	0	6.88	22	0	54	71	25	38
Davis, Clint	1	1	3.32	18	7	19	17	6	25
Eddy, Chris	2	5	5.34	33	17	29	30	10	23
Estes, Eric	1	0	11.25	3	0	4	6	5	3
Garcia, Apolinar	1	1	2.61	5	0	31	31	10	18
Hardwick, Bubba	0	4	3.12	12	1	17	18	7	20
2-team (25 LV)	3	11	4.30	37	1	107	123	35	85
Haught, Gary	3	1	1.57	23	6	34	24	10	30
Jacobsen, Joe	0	0	6.97	7	1	10	19	5	8
Keith, Jeff	1	0	10.80	3	0	5	5	9	3
Montalvo, Rafael	10	8	3.89	24	0	167	184	45	99
Moody, Jason	1	1	3.24	13	0	33	39	18	29
O'Brien, Mark	0	0	10.57	7	0	8	16	2	7
Ojeda, Erick	3	3	4.15	9	0	56	56	19	28
Olszewski, Eric	4	8	7.70	24	0	97	107	73	105
Rodriguez, Jorge	0	0	12.00	6	0	9	15	6	4
2-team (22 Somerset)	2	2	7.98	28	1	44	58	24	30
Siciliano, Jess	0	2	10.80	4	0	5	4	5	3
Smith, Michael	1	1	0.73	11	1	12	6	4	11
Sordo, Fernando	2	5	8.21	23	2	65	88	46	45
Soriano, Jose	1	0	6.14	14	0	22	29	13	16
Taylor, Kerry	4	2	4.79	13	0	68	72	23	49
Thompson, Frank	2	3	8.36	35	2	42	55	21	40
Valdez, Efrain	0	1	9.00	1	0	2	4	0	1
Ware, Jeff	4	7	8.43	15	0	74	96	42	57
Williams, Jimmy	13	4	4.55	26	0	156	162	56	124
Zappelli, Mark	2	1	3.78	3	0	17	16	8	17
2-team (23 Somerset)	7	8	5.13	26	0	105	118	49	92

BRIDGEPORT

BATTING	AVG	AB	R	H	2B	3B	HR	RBI	SB
Cole, Alex, of	.323	337	65	109	22	7	2	53	27
Duncan, Mariano, 2b-3b	.356	87	12	31	7	2	0	20	0
Edwards, Lamont, 3b	.256	277	38	71	13	2	3	37	5
Espada, Angel, ss	.356	357	82	127	19	4	1	34	40
Giudice, John, of	.309	149	28	46	6	0	4	28	1
Holifield, Rick, of	.224	125	23	28	4	4	4	23	27
Jenkins, Dee, 2b-ss	.280	214	37	60	12	1	7	37	12
2-team (9 Nashua)	.268	246	42	66	15	1	7	41	14
Landingham, James, of	.254	142	25	36	4	2	1	13	5
Lind, Jose, 2b	.262	172	23	45	9	0	4	26	2
McGriff, Terry, c	.313	217	32	68	20	0	4	40	0
Moyle, Mike, c-1b	.296	318	44	94	17	1	8	53	0
Mulligan, Sean, of-c	.177	62	7	11	3	0	1	6	0
Nunez, Jose, 2b-ss	.265	68	16	18	2	3	1	4	0
Ortiz, Asbel, 2b-3b	.209	196	25	41	10	1	8	41	6
Pledger, Kinnis, 1b	.298	225	46	67	15	2	16	63	6
Singleton, Duane, of	.255	306	57	78	12	2	6	36	17
Stark, Matt, dh	.348	66	6	23	3	0	0	14	0
Wearing, Mel, dh	.313	364	87	114	24	1	20	84	5
Wells, Forry, of-1b	.235	345	67	81	22	3	11	48	6

PITCHING	W	L	ERA	G	SV	IP	H	BB	SO
Adam, Dave	4	2	3.59	45	27	48	43	16	56
Adkins, Tim	8	6	3.97	26	0	141	152	49	100
Ahearne, Pat	6	0	2.53	7	0	46	35	14	43
Cintron, Jose	0	2	3.75	5	0	24	25	2	10
Conner, Scott	14	5	4.38	24	0	148	150	76	105
Gallaher, Kevin	4	2	7.49	33	0	52	45	72	44
Guilfoyle, Mike	4	2	3.98	48	2	52	56	29	50
Jean, Domingo	2	1	6.75	42	4	48	55	25	38
Jones, Kiki	4	4	4.50	14	0	58	52	24	51
Karp, Ryan	1	0	1.80	2	0	10	9	1	12
Klemyk, Jim	3	2	5.80	36	0	54	57	41	19
Nieves, Ernie	2	2	4.70	30	2	46	63	17	32
Pratt, Rich	0	2	8.24	12	0	20	30	8	22
Renko, Steve	12	6	3.69	24	0	146	158	62	100
Rosenkranz, Terry	1	0	1.40	14	0	19	14	10	22
Sontag, Alan	13	6	3.86	28	1	140	139	47	95

LEHIGH VALLEY

BATTING	AVG	AB	R	H	2B	3B	HR	RBI	SB
Batiste, Kim, 3b-ss	.330	109	18	36	4	0	8	18	0
2-team (50 AC)	.305	302	50	92	19	1	17	58	4
Connell, Lino, 2b	.277	480	59	133	25	12	11	79	34
Fowler, Maleke, of	.000	2	1	0	0	0	0	0	0
Garcia, Omar, of	.300	30	3	9	1	0	0	5	0
Held, Dan, 1b	.276	340	72	94	25	0	25	62	7
Hernandez, Victor, of	.224	156	22	35	4	1	3	22	8
Lawrence, Chip, ss	.233	347	41	81	13	3	4	31	12
Long, Ryan, of	.281	121	15	34	9	0	4	23	0
2-team (67 Newark)	.239	326	39	78	19	2	10	44	1
Martin, James, of	.214	126	25	27	8	1	4	15	8
Millan, Adan, c	.242	302	50	73	10	0	10	39	4
Pagan, Angel, ss	.145	69	5	10	2	3	0	5	1
Perez, Danny, of	.310	432	69	134	27	7	10	49	20
Raleigh, Matt, 1b-3b	.260	215	38	56	11	0	16	45	3
Rivero, Eddie, of	.261	429	59	112	36	3	20	72	1
Vecchioni, Jerry, 3b	.306	36	1	11	1	0	0	1	1
Viera, Jose, 3b-dh	.249	445	68	111	17	1	23	55	0
Viera, Rob, c	.244	160	19	39	10	0	2	20	0
Young, Gerald, of-dh	.247	304	49	75	13	0	6	36	7

PITCHING	W	L	ERA	G	SV	IP	H	BB	SO
Blais, Mike	2	6	2.40	45	23	56	56	13	41
Campbell, Mike	1	3	4.63	8	0	35	30	11	38
Cornett, Brad	11	9	3.94	23	0	162	172	37	118
Getz, Rod	0	0	6.65	14	0	22	26	17	9
Hardwick, Bubba	3	7	4.53	25	0	89	105	28	65
Hook, Chris	0	5	11.57	7	0	28	46	27	12
Hope, John	0	2	9.16	5	0	19	21	17	9
Kell, Rob	2	3	5.17	6	1	31	34	12	29
Love, Jeff	7	5	3.24	22	0	89	89	27	61
Maskivish, Joe	1	0	10.61	7	1	9	15	3	6
2-team (34 Newark)	3	2	6.31	41	2	51	69	21	30
Miranda, Angel	11	5	4.28	21	0	124	106	81	102
Murray, Matt	3	1	3.75	6	0	36	43	7	26
Neal, Billy	1	2	3.60	10	1	15	14	5	5
Nyari, Pete	1	6	5.85	32	0	60	75	35	48
Paul, Andy	4	6	4.89	27	0	103	104	63	95
Salamon, John	1	0	3.18	8	0	11	11	8	9
Sexton, Patrick	0	1	7.36	5	0	11	10	5	5
Stumpf, Brian	2	6	4.30	40	2	73	79	46	59
West, David	2	0	2.96	6	0	27	19	6	33
Yeager, Gary	0	0	27.00	1	0	2	9	3	0

NASHUA

BATTING	AVG	AB	R	H	2B	3B	HR	RBI	SB
Adorno, Wilson, c	.000	4	1	0	0	0	0	0	0
Beckhorn, Frank, 1b-2b	.261	161	20	42	3	1	4	26	0
Boston, D.J., 1b	.274	350	56	96	22	1	10	49	5
Diaz, Mario, 2b	.281	121	10	34	6	0	3	11	1
Eddie, Steve, 3b	.250	8	1	2	1	0	0	1	0
English, Chris, ph	.000	1	0	0	0	0	0	0	0

Independent Leagues

	AVG	AB	R	H	2B	3B	HR	RBI	SB
Florez, Tim, 3b	.267	180	25	48	8	1	1	12	5
2-team (9 Somerset)	.266	203	28	54	8	1	2	17	5
Forsberg, Dana, of-1b	.231	195	26	45	12	0	5	21	0
Garrett, Scott, c	.200	35	2	7	0	1	1	3	0
Gordon, Keith, of	.168	95	11	16	6	0	0	4	10
Green, Darrio, of	.143	7	0	1	0	0	0	0	0
Jenkins, Dee, 2b	.188	32	5	6	3	0	0	4	2
Laub, Jay, c	.250	36	4	9	2	0	0	7	1
2-team (37 Somerset)	.242	128	12	31	2	0	3	12	1
Malave, Jose, of	.304	207	30	63	19	1	6	34	5
McQuiniff, Jason, c	.268	56	9	15	3	0	1	10	1
2-team (4 AC)	.239	67	9	16	3	1	1	10	1
Medrano, Ryan, ss-3b	.291	309	58	90	21	4	11	47	1
Moore, Kevin, of	.256	332	45	85	18	2	5	42	12
Moore, Michael, of	.282	390	65	110	22	1	26	82	6
Murray, Glenn, of	.272	434	82	118	16	4	29	102	22
Pough, Chop, 3b	.208	48	9	10	1	1	3	7	1
2-team (30 AC)	.252	163	28	41	10	2	7	21	4
Pride, Curtis, dh	.063	32	0	2	0	0	0	2	0
Rodriguez, Carlos, ss-2b	.184	76	11	14	2	0	0	5	2
Rodriguez, Tony, ss	.320	153	30	49	9	3	6	25	11
Santana, Ruben, 3b	.356	45	5	16	5	0	0	3	0
Taylor, Matt, 2b-ss	.212	306	50	65	8	2	0	19	21
Walker, Joe, c	.252	326	58	82	22	0	16	54	3
Waller, Derric, of	.167	6	1	1	1	0	0	0	0
Yelding, Eric, 2b-of	.222	9	1	2	0	0	1	2	0

PITCHING	W	L	ERA	G	SV	IP	H	BB	SO
Ali, Sam	3	4	7.74	27	3	52	66	20	41
Anderson, Bill	5	1	2.08	10	1	39	32	7	32
Calderon, Jose	3	4	5.94	33	3	67	79	22	32
2-team (6 Somerset)	3	6	6.39	39	3	100	125	35	44
Crawford, Carlos	5	9	5.92	38	2	119	153	44	64
DeJesus, Javier	1	2	4.13	38	2	65	49	44	54
Donnelly, Brendan	0	0	3.00	3	0	3	1	3	4
Forsberg, Dana	0	0	2.45	6	0	7	4	6	5
Jacobsen, Joe	0	2	5.33	26	11	25	35	9	24
Juarbe, Ken	6	5	6.42	33	4	55	56	29	45
Kirkreit, Daron	1	2	5.90	7	0	40	53	18	24
Linares, Yonder	0	4	7.00	18	0	27	37	3	15
Marrero, Kenny	0	1	10.03	8	1	12	13	5	14
Mejia, Delfino	4	4	4.02	17	0	72	74	19	76
Ojeda, Erick	4	6	6.27	14	0	80	103	35	53
2-team (9 AC)	7	9	5.40	23	0	137	159	54	81
Ramos, Edgar	8	8	4.57	21	0	136	150	35	84
Riley, Ed	1	3	7.06	6	0	22	26	24	15
Roper, John	6	7	4.75	22	0	116	121	48	81
Silva, Luis	0	1	4.88	10	0	24	22	2	18
Woodson, Kerry	5	3	4.06	14	0	64	61	44	35
Yuscavage, Gerald	0	0	13.50	4	0	7	13	4	1

NEWARK

BATTING	AVG	AB	R	H	2B	3B	HR	RBI	SB
Adriana, Sharnol, 2b-3b	.334	419	72	140	25	2	16	77	7
Avila, Rolando, of	.302	374	81	113	21	4	6	37	29
Delgado, Reymundo, dh	.174	23	1	4	1	0	0	1	2
Garcia, Manny, ss	.100	10	2	1	1	0	0	1	0
Gorecki, Ryan, dh-2b	.268	164	22	44	8	0	0	14	0
Griffith, Tommy, dh-of	.111	18	1	2	0	0	0	1	2
Jennings, Doug, 1b	.263	293	46	77	16	0	17	51	1
Long, Ryan, of	.215	205	24	44	10	2	6	21	1
Longueira, Tony, ss-3b	.228	145	16	33	5	0	2	21	1
Martin, James, of	.222	90	18	20	5	2	4	15	3
3-team (9 Som, 48 LV)	.214	234	43	50	14	3	8	32	11
Meulens, Hensley, 3b-1b	.283	448	84	127	17	3	21	94	12
Morillo, Cesar, ss	.293	338	60	99	21	2	6	42	19
Pacheco, Juan, 2b-ss	.133	15	2	2	0	0	0	2	0
Ramirez, Peto, c	.238	265	38	63	16	0	12	40	1
Ratliff, Darryl, of	.159	44	2	7	0	0	0	0	2
Robertson, Greg, 1b-dh	.314	121	23	38	5	1	0	17	2
Smith, Brian, of-2b	.246	264	36	65	5	8	1	20	10
Stevenson, Chad, c-of	.233	150	15	35	2	0	6	16	0
Thomas, Keith, of-dh	.262	325	42	85	13	2	15	58	8
Worthington, Craig, 3b-dh	.282	234	37	66	10	0	16	43	0

PITCHING	W	L	ERA	G	SV	IP	H	BB	SO
Babineaux, Darrin	10	5	3.59	35	1	125	118	48	104
Beck, Matt	0	0	27.00	1	0	1	2	2	1
Cain, Tim	11	10	4.82	26	0	166	171	69	112
Cooke, Bill	1	0	2.13	2	0	13	12	0	6
Farley, Joe	1	6	5.78	23	0	73	81	38	44
Huber, Jeff	6	11	5.53	25	0	127	140	42	91
Logan, Marcus	3	4	5.30	13	0	56	57	30	41
Maskivish, Joe	2	2	5.36	34	1	42	54	18	24
Piddington, Brian	2	5	5.71	17	0	58	68	25	43

	W	L	ERA	G	SV	IP	H	BB	SO
Richards, Dave	3	3	1.77	54	10	66	49	30	62
Saneaux, Francisco	0	3	9.15	14	0	21	28	21	20
2-team (3 Somerset)	0	4	8.79	17	0	29	40	23	27
Smith, Matt	0	0	2.57	4	0	7	7	6	5
St. Pierre, Bob	8	6	3.60	20	0	123	112	41	71
Tajima, Tony	1	1	9.18	16	0	17	23	7	16
Thompson, Frank	3	1	3.50	17	2	18	11	8	12
2-team (35 AC)	5	4	6.90	52	4	60	66	29	52
Wagner, Hector	0	3	6.82	7	0	33	51	17	25
Whiteman, Mike	2	1	6.55	23	0	33	46	8	27
Zimmerman, Mike	2	3	4.80	30	9	30	27	27	38

SOMERSET

BATTING	AVG	AB	R	H	2B	3B	HR	RBI	SB
Alvarez, Jorge, of	.269	108	17	29	7	0	4	23	1
Arnold, Ken, ss	.279	365	54	102	9	7	7	46	10
Berblinger, Jeff, 2b	.327	397	81	130	26	2	11	39	47
Bonds, Bobby, of-dh	.289	228	49	66	10	2	12	30	15
Colon, Frank, c	.000	4	0	0	0	0	0	0	0
DiOrio, Andy, 3b-ss	.230	126	18	29	4	0	2	13	2
Dubose, Brian, 1b-of	.216	74	6	16	1	1	2	10	1
Florez, Tim, 2b-ss	.261	23	3	6	0	0	1	5	0
Garcia, Leo, of	.139	36	7	5	0	0	0	2	2
Keene, Andre, dh	.176	17	1	3	0	0	0	3	0
Laub, Jay, c	.239	92	8	22	0	0	3	5	0
Lopez, Louis, 1b-dh	.329	255	41	84	14	0	15	60	5
Lukachyk, Rob, of	.275	320	56	88	17	6	12	46	16
Lyle, Dane, 2b	.191	68	9	13	2	1	0	7	0
Maness, Dwight, of	.266	282	48	75	17	2	12	42	21
Martin, James, of	.167	18	0	3	1	0	0	2	0
Martinez, Gil, of-1b	.310	213	30	66	22	1	6	31	1
Morales, Jorge, of	.216	74	10	16	4	0	3	12	1
Nava, Lipso, 3b	.290	345	63	100	18	0	16	59	1
Reeder, Cory, c	.202	178	21	36	6	0	7	27	1
Reyes, Gilberto, c	.257	74	10	19	4	0	3	9	0
Rocha, Juan, of	.306	72	16	22	6	0	2	11	3
2-team (94 AC)	.280	403	75	113	24	3	17	66	12
Traxler, Brian, 1b	.251	387	34	97	23	1	12	61	1
Velez, Jose, of	.302	235	30	71	12	0	2	29	14
Walton, Jerome, of	.377	53	12	20	3	0	2	7	6

PITCHING	W	L	ERA	G	SV	IP	H	BB	SO
Briscoe, John	1	2	5.28	28	6	31	37	15	33
Bullard, Jason	3	3	3.96	46	6	50	55	23	43
Calderon, Jose	0	2	7.29	6	0	33	46	13	12
Davis, Ray	7	2	3.68	20	3	86	69	38	97
Duffy, John	0	1	4.91	6	0	7	8	10	4
Ettles, Mark	3	1	5.12	15	2	19	22	5	12
Gonzales, Frank	4	4	4.03	28	2	45	51	12	44
Henry, Dwayne	1	7	5.52	44	5	46	44	24	57
Heredia, Julian	1	0	3.72	6	1	19	19	7	25
Hook, Chris	1	1	8.31	2	0	9	11	7	9
2-team (7 LV)	1	6	10.80	9	0	37	57	34	21
Hoy, Wayne	2	4	5.20	13	0	54	50	17	34
Jacobsen, Joe	0	0	2.63	8	3	14	7	5	2
3-team (7 AC, 26 Nashua)	0	2	4.93	41	15	49	61	19	34
Jensen, Justin	12	5	2.76	24	0	156	120	77	111
Jordan, Ricardo	2	3	3.86	18	1	33	29	13	29
Olsen, Mario	0	0	7.02	14	0	17	17	13	15
Pulido, Carlos	9	4	4.42	22	0	149	137	36	105
Rodriguez, Jorge	2	2	6.94	22	1	35	43	18	26
Steed, Rick	2	3	3.25	8	0	36	27	25	24
Winston, Darrin	6	8	5.83	25	0	110	116	38	79
Zappelli, Mark	5	7	5.38	23	0	89	102	41	75

FRONTIER LEAGUE

The Frontier League plays in smaller towns but it has produced some of the best talent in independent baseball. In 1998, the Boston Red Sox finally gave perennial all-star Morgan Burkhart a shot in affiliated ball after the former Richmond Rooster won a triple crown.

In 1999, the Red Sox plucked Gator McBride from the Chillicothe Paints and several players were signed by major league organizations during the season. Dubois County closer John Oestreich was clocked in the mid-90s and was offered contracts by four teams. He declined each of them, opting to teach social studies and coach high school volleyball and baseball instead.

The Frontier League is like no other independent league because its rules encourage the use of younger players. Players older than 26 can't play, even if they've played only one season in the league or have become fan favorites. Burkhart aged out after the 1998 season.

The Frontier League had its share of franchise rumblings in 1999, including four new teams. The London Werewolves stole the show in their first season by winning the league title. The Werewolves, led by pitcher Brett Gray and slugger John Payne, won four consecutive playoff games to win the championship in easy fashion.

River City was the big winner at the gate. The Rascals drew 151,661 fans, more than any club in Frontier League history.

STANDINGS

EAST	W	L	PCT	GB
London Werewolves	54	30	.643	—
Chillicothe Paints	45	38	.542	8½
Johnstown Johnnies	43	41	.512	11
Richmond Roosters	40	43	.482	13½
Canton Crocodiles	33	51	.393	21

WEST	W	L	PCT	GB
Evansville Otters	43	41	.512	—
Dubois County Dragons	42	42	.500	1
Cook County Cheetahs	41	43	.488	2
Springfield Capitals	39	45	.464	4
River City Rascals	39	45	.464	4

PLAYOFFS: Semifinals—London defeated Johnstown 2-0 and Chillicothe defeated Evansville 2-1 in best-of-3 series. **Finals**—London defeated Chillicothe 2-0 in best-of-3 series.

MANAGERS: Canton—John Zizzo. Chillicothe—Roger Hanners. Cook County—Chico Walker. Dubois County—Joe Pass. Evansville—Greg Tagert. Johnstown—Mal Fichman. London—Andy McCauley. Richmond—John Cate. River City—Jack Clark. Springfield—Paul Fletcher.

ATTENDANCE: River City 151,661; Evansville 111,039; Cook County 86,248; Chillicothe 61,249; London 60,546; Johnstown 57,529; Springfield 53,503; Canton 50,295; Richmond 43,976; Dubois County 35,690.

ALL-STAR TEAM: C—Tony Girod, Johnstown. **1B**—Scott Pinoni, Chillicothe. **2B**—Joe Pass, Dubois County. **3B**—Chance Melvin, Chillicothe. **SS**—Dalphie Correa, London. **OF**—Rick Nadeau, London; Shane Hopper, Johnstown; Steve Barningham, Springfield. **DH**—Jason Kinchen, Richmond. **SP**—Tom Becker, Cook County. **RP**—John Oestreich, Dubois County.

Most Valuable Player: Scott Pinoni, Chillicothe. **Most Valuable Pitcher:** John Oestreich, Dubois County. **Manager of the Year:** Andy McCauley, London.

INDIVIDUAL BATTING LEADERS
(Minimum 216 Plate Appearances)

	AVG	AB	R	H	2B	3B	HR	RBI	SB
Pinoni, Scott, Chillicothe	.377	265	59	100	13	0	22	74	2
Hopper, Shane, Johnstown	.372	328	65	122	27	3	8	83	12
Goodwin, Keith, London	.369	187	37	69	17	3	4	45	18
Kinchen, Jason, Richmond	.357	280	65	100	19	0	27	78	2
Headley, Justin, Johnstown	.352	310	71	109	19	1	5	37	1
Barningham, Steve, Spring.	.351	319	76	112	21	11	5	60	44
Nadeau, Rick, London	.348	339	69	118	32	6	8	82	17
Villacres, Garry, Dubois	.345	264	50	91	16	6	0	33	24
Correa, Dalphie, London	.344	323	79	111	15	0	1	38	39
Pollard, Brandon, Cook Co.	.341	302	67	103	17	3	9	53	30

INDIVIDUAL PITCHING LEADERS
(Minimum 64 Innings)

	W	L	ERA	G	SV	IP	H	BB	SO
Becker, Tom, Cook County	9	4	2.54	24	4	96	88	30	107
Silcock, Matt, Evansville	10	3	2.70	14	0	90	81	26	52
Meurer, Josh, Canton	6	4	3.03	17	0	116	100	31	108
Pulizzano, Tim, Cook County	6	7	3.29	24	4	98	112	25	69
Kvasnicka, Jay, Cook County	6	4	3.37	17	0	115	94	46	82
Brown, Jeremy, Springfield	4	7	3.49	31	2	80	69	20	55

Loonam, Rick, Springfield	7	2	3.58	15	0	106	107	26	57
Byrd, Stephen, Chillicothe	9	4	3.60	18	0	110	107	49	92
Hessler, Landon, Johnstown	7	5	3.72	41	0	77	67	34	51
Scarcello, Brian, Chillicothe	5	2	3.80	15	0	73	71	34	57

CANTON

BATTING	AVG	AB	R	H	2B	3B	HR	RBI	SB
Alfieri, Frank, 3b	.233	43	5	10	0	2	1	10	0
Alguacil, Jose, ss	.200	30	6	6	1	0	0	0	2
Armstrong, Ryan, of	.242	33	4	8	1	0	0	3	8
Autry, Brian, 1b	.326	175	23	57	8	0	9	34	1
Chambliss, Russ, of	.296	186	32	55	7	3	1	16	9
Christy, Jack, of	.119	42	1	5	0	0	0	2	0
Clark, Nick, ss-2b	.206	34	6	7	0	0	1	6	0
Delgado, Jose, 2b-ss	.266	124	18	33	7	1	1	19	3
DeCastro, Raul, 1b	.268	41	7	11	0	1	0	6	0
Doskocil, Darren, of-2b	.100	30	3	3	1	0	0	2	0
Johnson, Jason, of	.288	160	33	46	6	1	0	14	23
Juarez, Jeff, of	.280	246	24	69	12	0	2	23	13
King, Willie, 1b	.203	74	7	15	2	1	1	6	1
Leoni, Raul, of	.143	35	5	5	1	0	0	1	2
Maysonet, Jose, ss	.284	74	15	21	1	1	0	8	5
Mongiardo, Chris, dh-c	.302	288	39	87	13	0	2	48	2
Moore, Jason, of-1b	.000	11	0	0	0	0	0	0	0
Pagan, Angel, ss	.258	163	31	42	9	2	2	21	8
Poss, John, 3b	.295	346	51	102	22	2	1	46	2
Pritchard, Jeff, of	.219	192	20	42	9	1	1	25	2
Santiago, Angel, 1b	.268	56	9	15	1	1	3	8	0
2-team (7 Johnstown)	.235	81	15	19	1	1	4	12	0
Sherrod, John, dh-1b	.250	48	6	12	1	1	1	7	1
Smith, Larry, c	.288	240	37	69	8	0	0	22	20
Urban, Trevor, of	.375	8	0	3	1	1	0	3	1
Wade, Jody, of	.222	27	4	6	0	0	0	2	2
Warga, Ron, 2b	.183	71	8	13	2	0	1	9	9
Zamilski, Cary, 2b	.229	118	16	27	5	0	1	14	9

PITCHING	W	L	ERA	G	SV	IP	H	BB	SO
Allen, Chris	3	9	5.71	19	0	99	110	40	67
Arnold, John	6	7	6.32	16	0	100	125	49	85
Baker, Ken	0	1	7.71	5	1	5	8	7	1
Bates, Chip	0	0	8.22	4	0	8	10	4	5
Behrens, Brett	1	1	5.28	9	0	15	25	1	16
Centeno, Ruben	1	2	4.58	9	0	18	18	9	9
Deubel, Ron	3	6	4.01	23	3	83	88	39	79
Donofrio, Andy	0	0	23.63	2	0	3	5	9	3
Galiher, Sean	1	0	15.43	3	0	2	6	6	3
Gibson, Scott	0	1	9.00	5	0	4	3	7	1
Key, Scott	0	1	9.00	2	0	1	2	2	1
Meurer, Josh	6	4	3.03	17	0	116	100	31	108
Moody, Jason	2	2	2.37	15	3	30	25	20	34
Moore, Jason	0	0	0.00	1	0	2	0	0	3
Mullikin, Robby	0	1	10.80	4	0	5	8	3	7
Rodriguez, Jorge	1	0	9.00	6	0	11	18	6	10
Ryan, Jason	0	2	4.12	20	0	39	39	19	47
Siciliano, Jess	3	4	4.62	24	1	64	63	39	42
Stenger, Pat	0	0	27.00	2	0	2	5	3	1
Sugar, Dylan	3	5	4.94	21	1	58	58	25	44
Thomas, Drew	3	4	4.50	24	0	66	64	29	46
Torres, Elvin	0	0	13.50	1	0	3	5	3	2
Viel, Chris	0	1	9.53	4	0	6	10	5	4

CHILLICOTHE

BATTING	AVG	AB	R	H	2B	3B	HR	RBI	SB
Black, Sam, dh-1b	.216	37	7	8	3	0	0	2	0
Boggs, Ronnie, c	.061	33	1	2	0	0	0	1	1
Cervenak, Mike, ss	.306	301	59	92	17	4	3	46	6
Choron, Joey, dh-of	.246	224	26	55	6	1	7	39	3
Colameco, Joe, of	.280	279	59	78	17	3	4	34	20
Hoffman, Jay, dh	.095	21	1	2	0	0	0	2	0
Horning, Mike, 2b	.272	327	63	89	18	3	2	37	28
Johnson, Jason, of	.287	101	17	29	4	1	2	15	7
2-team (43 Canton)	.287	261	50	75	10	2	2	29	30
Keefe, Jamie, ss	.239	88	20	21	5	0	1	8	9
Kerry, Bill, c	.167	36	2	6	0	0	0	2	0
McBride, Gator, of	.456	147	46	67	11	0	15	48	0
Melson, Bryant, c	.170	53	6	9	2	0	0	7	0
Melvin, Chance, 3b	.299	334	54	100	19	1	11	76	5
Middleton, Matt, 1b-3b	.165	91	8	15	2	0	0	4	0
Pinoni, Scott, 1b	.377	265	59	100	13	0	22	74	2
Robinson, Bryan, dh	.250	4	0	1	0	0	0	0	0
Roush, Ryan, of	.209	43	6	9	4	0	0	3	0
Streit, Josh, c	.206	160	19	33	3	0	3	16	0
Tucker, Jamie, of	.279	190	27	53	7	2	4	24	4
Woods, Eddie, of	.306	180	24	55	7	3	5	33	0

PITCHING	W	L	ERA	G	SV	IP	H	BB	SO
Blaesing, Jamie	1	1	5.23	31	0	41	37	24	55
Byrd, Stephen	9	4	3.60	18	0	110	107	49	92
Callahan, Todd	1	1	7.45	11	0	10	13	11	4
Chandler, Bobby	2	2	2.61	33	2	41	38	26	32
Fleming, Rip	1	1	3.95	15	0	14	10	14	15
Fullenkamp, Kurt	5	3	1.15	29	11	47	32	24	56
Golden, Jeff	1	1	7.23	6	0	19	25	15	8
Hughes, Chris	0	2	6.52	3	0	10	13	4	17
Koziara, Matt	1	0	6.43	2	0	7	7	4	7
Lee, Andy	6	5	3.88	14	0	93	94	37	84
Maness, Chris	2	1	3.19	34	8	37	28	20	34
McAninch, Joe	0	1	6.43	16	1	28	30	22	28
Middleton, Matt	1	0	4.76	3	0	6	6	4	2
Pittillo, Everett	0	1	18.00	2	0	2	1	6	2
Quick, Dave	3	1	4.39	11	1	41	45	21	28
Scarcello, Brian	5	2	3.80	15	0	73	71	34	57
Sieszputowski, Greg	1	1	11.57	2	0	7	11	7	5
Spears, Bob	2	6	5.64	11	0	61	79	28	55
Sundsmo, Aaron	0	1	5.87	5	0	8	8	6	6
White, Josh	4	2	6.14	14	0	63	68	34	64
Woods, Eddie	0	2	10.80	7	1	12	22	7	4

COOK COUNTY

BATTING	AVG	AB	R	H	2B	3B	HR	RBI	SB
Baker, Brett, c	.211	71	6	15	4	0	0	15	1
Bennett, Rick, ss	.263	179	31	47	5	1	0	18	28
Bradshaw, Neil, 2b	.247	73	3	18	2	0	0	6	3
Breyne, Corey, ss	.105	19	2	2	1	0	0	0	0
Davis, Mike, 2b-of	.271	214	40	58	8	2	2	24	25
Dye, Anthony, of	.167	18	1	3	0	0	0	0	1
Fefee, Theo, of	.240	121	13	29	5	1	3	20	8
Harer, Mac, of	.254	209	37	53	10	3	0	21	9
Hendrix, Thurman, 3b-2b	.268	239	33	64	6	0	1	27	9
Horton, Bill, c	.200	5	0	1	1	0	0	3	0
2-team (1 Canton)	.333	6	0	2	1	0	0	3	0
Koenig, Keith, 3b	.050	20	2	1	1	0	0	0	0
Les, Tom, 1b-of	.254	67	13	17	3	0	2	11	1
Mazurek, Brian, 1b	.300	253	36	76	14	1	6	40	0
Morey, Randy, ss-2b	.309	175	27	54	6	1	0	21	30
2-team (19 Evansville)	.280	236	36	66	7	2	2	34	35
Moutrey, Mike, 2b-3b	.268	56	11	15	4	0	0	4	3
Pierro, Justin, dh	.322	121	17	39	8	0	7	22	1
Pollard, Brandon, of	.341	302	67	103	17	3	9	53	30
Schmidt, Jim, 3b	.208	101	17	21	2	1	1	14	6
Serembiczky, Michael, c	.140	50	6	7	0	0	0	1	2
Shrewsbury, Aaron, dh-1b	.358	159	28	57	9	3	5	24	9
Utting, Andy, c-1b	.143	21	2	3	0	0	1	3	0
Voldness, Aaron, c	.240	171	25	41	9	2	4	28	4
White, Darren, of	.294	201	32	59	9	2	5	36	3
Zeedyk, Eric, c-1b	.154	13	2	2	0	0	1	2	0

PITCHING	W	L	ERA	G	SV	IP	H	BB	SO
Becker, Tom	9	4	2.54	24	4	96	88	30	107
Davis, Jason	5	5	4.38	19	0	86	79	43	88
Dunnett, Randy	3	5	4.90	26	1	75	85	28	68
Gillespie, Shawn	2	4	8.24	19	1	39	51	31	32
Justine, Brian	0	1	5.04	12	1	25	31	18	14
Kim, B.J.	2	2	7.20	9	2	25	32	14	29
Knollin, Chris	2	3	6.29	7	0	44	49	25	39
Kvasnicka, Jay	6	4	3.37	17	0	115	94	46	82
Lairsey, Eric	0	0	7.20	3	0	5	5	9	2
2-team (2 Springfield)	0	1	11.12	5	0	6	9	11	2
Leys, Michael	0	0	5.27	6	0	14	19	6	15
Mumma, Eric	1	4	6.62	20	0	34	43	23	29
Pulizzano, Tim	6	7	3.29	24	4	98	112	25	69
Sokol, Trad	5	4	4.48	24	1	74	71	26	49
Studeman, Matt	0	0	23.14	2	0	2	6	1	1

DUBOIS COUNTY

BATTING	AVG	AB	R	H	2B	3B	HR	RBI	SB
Bennett, Anthony, of	.083	12	1	1	0	0	0	1	1
Benson, Brad, dh	.150	20	0	3	0	0	0	2	0
Chiprez, Chris, of	.289	263	39	76	13	1	3	43	15
Dettman, Matt, 3b	.257	280	55	72	13	0	13	50	5
Feliciano, Edwin, c	.268	183	30	49	8	0	0	17	5
Forman, Brian, ss-of	.200	10	2	2	0	0	0	1	0
Freeman, Matt, c	.224	134	16	30	2	0	2	11	1
Heise, Eric, 1b-dh	.220	123	8	27	3	0	0	17	4
Knight, Nathan, 3b-2b	.250	108	18	27	4	1	1	20	6
Kuempel, Tom, of	.265	215	43	57	12	1	7	30	8
Marple, Scott, of	.303	238	47	72	16	0	7	49	11
Muro, Roy, dh	.266	94	10	25	3	0	1	16	1
Pass, Joe, 2b	.328	323	56	106	16	1	1	31	5

	AVG	AB	R	H	2B	3B	HR	RBI	SB
Riordan, Fran, 1b	.300	293	51	88	16	2	11	51	4
Tavares, John, ss	.296	304	55	90	14	1	6	50	20
Thimons, Nate, dh-of	.273	33	5	9	3	0	0	2	2
Villacres, Garry, of	.345	264	50	91	16	6	0	33	24

PITCHING	W	L	ERA	G	SV	IP	H	BB	SO
Allen, Rodney	2	2	5.25	9	0	60	67	13	47
2-team (6 Johnstown)	4	5	5.85	15	0	88	102	24	56
Anderson, Todd	4	0	2.27	24	2	32	30	10	28
Antonelli, Danny	4	1	5.62	9	0	42	39	28	26
Baggett, Nate	1	0	9.64	7	0	14	21	7	8
Bradley, Brian	5	9	6.82	18	0	96	126	39	59
Bryant, Keith	1	3	7.84	24	0	60	92	32	43
Dettman, Matt	0	0	2.45	4	2	4	2	3	6
Fry, Nolan	9	1	3.08	31	1	50	45	31	55
Hassell, John	5	2	5.90	13	0	61	65	45	35
Klomparens, Rob	3	5	6.83	14	0	55	81	24	37
Long, Lee	4	7	4.50	16	0	112	139	32	61
Oestreich, John	1	2	3.69	28	20	39	26	13	69
Possidento, Alec	0	1	10.57	6	0	15	27	11	6
Rainford, Kevin	0	0	15.88	2	0	6	11	8	2
2-team (4 Johnstown)	0	2	10.64	6	0	22	31	21	9
Stadelhofer, Mike	1	0	7.71	5	0	7	4	11	5
2-team (2 Richmond)	1	0	10.80	7	0	8	13	5	5
Tarnoff, Andy	1	6	6.44	18	1	57	79	24	23
Thimons, Nate	1	2	5.40	6	0	20	19	13	16
Warren, Peyton	0	1	7.20	2	0	5	3	11	4

EVANSVILLE

BATTING	AVG	AB	R	H	2B	3B	HR	RBI	SB
Anderson, John, 2b	.211	19	1	4	0	0	0	1	1
Arredondo, Rey, ss	.255	47	5	12	0	0	0	2	1
Bartolucci, Paul, ss-2b	.280	268	32	75	17	0	1	31	12
Becerra, Chris, of	.059	17	1	1	0	0	0	0	0
Brown, Todd, 3b-1b	.254	201	46	51	2	2	3	26	23
Bryan, Brooks, of	.285	263	53	75	9	4	11	47	23
Clark, Jason, of	.301	306	61	92	15	4	6	45	28
Cutchlow, Rohrk, c	.204	152	23	31	6	1	5	25	1
Ferres, David, 2b	.236	89	15	21	5	0	0	3	1
Foster, Brian, 1b	.325	289	52	94	15	2	18	73	4
Franzi, Rob, of	.133	15	1	2	1	0	0	1	0
Gilligan, Dan, dh-c	.154	13	0	2	0	0	0	2	0
Goff, Chad, 3b	.316	152	24	48	11	1	3	17	0
Joseph, Eric, of	.232	82	18	19	3	2	5	16	5
Levingston, Derrick, 1b	.229	48	5	11	0	0	3	8	0
McDaniel, Ryan, c	.182	11	0	2	0	0	0	1	0
McGraw, Josh, c	.262	65	12	17	2	0	0	5	0
Miranda, Migdoel, of-dh	.077	26	1	2	1	0	0	0	0
Mongello, Barry, c	.000	2	0	0	0	0	0	0	0
Morey, Randy, 2b-3b	.197	61	9	12	1	1	2	13	5
Rains, Adam, of-2b	.260	154	31	40	6	2	2	17	4
Rima, Todd, 2b	.111	27	1	3	1	0	0	5	2
Robinson, David, of-dh	.288	292	61	84	19	2	12	51	13
Tadlock, Jeremi, 1b	.286	7	0	2	0	0	0	0	0
Vaughn, Lateef, 2b-of	.310	84	15	26	5	1	0	11	7
Waugh, Michael, c	.222	27	0	6	0	0	0	3	0

PITCHING	W	L	ERA	G	SV	IP	H	BB	SO
Biggs, Adam	0	2	6.99	16	0	28	30	13	22
Connolly, Doug	1	0	11.91	4	0	11	22	3	7
Davis, Mark	0	2	6.75	10	0	12	17	3	9
Hayes, Chad	0	3	9.64	4	0	9	18	3	10
Kelley, Brent	5	5	4.37	16	0	101	102	34	79
Knollin, Chris	5	3	2.89	10	0	65	45	26	72
2-team (7 Cook County)	7	6	4.27	17	0	110	94	51	111
Kottmeyer, Matt	4	4	5.50	23	0	75	96	15	59
May, Kyle	2	1	3.35	29	16	38	37	25	54
Murphy, Rob	3	1	6.28	25	0	14	19	8	11
Perry, Josh	0	1	6.89	3	0	16	22	10	12
Rister, Nate	0	0	10.80	5	0	5	8	6	6
Rodgers, Jamie	1	1	9.25	16	0	24	40	19	17
Rushing, Donald	1	3	9.00	7	0	28	29	24	21
Sagara, Brendan	0	0	1.69	4	0	5	3	8	4
Sherrill, George	2	4	3.15	22	2	40	40	18	33
Silcock, Matt	10	3	2.70	14	0	90	81	26	52
Stafford, Dan	1	3	6.12	17	0	32	44	14	26
Tipton, Jeremiah	7	2	3.95	21	1	82	92	30	69
Wheeler, Matt	1	3	4.56	4	0	24	27	11	18

JOHNSTOWN

BATTING	AVG	AB	R	H	2B	3B	HR	RBI	SB
Aita, Colin, ss	.183	109	9	20	2	0	0	12	2
Becker, Jason, ss	.000	2	0	0	0	0	0	0	0
Beyna, Terry, 3b	.000	3	0	0	0	0	0	0	0

	AVG	AB	R	H	2B	3B	HR	RBI	SB
Clairmont, Kenton, c	.273	11	0	3	2	0	0	0	0
Close, Bart, dh-c	.262	42	9	11	1	0	2	9	0
Crowley, Ben, dh-of	.263	57	9	15	4	1	0	8	1
Cueto, Jim, of	.186	215	36	40	9	2	1	25	6
Edwards, Dytarious, ss	.091	11	3	1	0	0	0	1	3
Esposito, Paul, 2b	.283	325	54	92	15	0	2	35	2
Girod, Tony, c	.324	256	45	83	20	1	1	26	4
Haigler, Aaron, 3b	.200	15	4	3	1	0	0	0	0
Headley, Justin, 1b	.352	310	71	109	19	1	5	37	1
Hopper, Shane, of	.372	328	65	122	27	3	8	83	12
Karpell, Jeff, of	.000	4	0	0	0	0	0	0	0
Kubosh, Scott, ss	.250	12	3	3	1	0	0	2	0
Memmert, Gabe, dh	.332	205	34	68	15	0	5	43	2
Pilger, Mike, of-3b	.339	171	44	58	12	5	2	24	16
Santiago, Angel, 1b	.160	25	6	4	0	0	1	4	0
Serafin, Steven, ss-2b	.265	189	26	50	7	0	2	13	0
Smith, Chris, c	.244	41	2	10	3	0	0	4	1
Sorensen, Eric, c	.333	3	0	1	0	0	0	0	0
Taylor, Kirk, of	.294	320	59	94	29	1	11	73	14
West, George, 3b	.269	331	40	89	21	0	11	54	1

PITCHING	W	L	ERA	G	SV	IP	H	BB	SO
Allen, Rodney	2	3	7.16	6	0	28	35	11	9
Balazentis, Bob	1	1	6.23	4	0	17	27	6	11
Beller, Steve	1	0	3.86	2	0	5	4	6	2
Bruton, Wade	3	2	1.64	12	0	49	31	25	54
Cali, Joe	1	1	8.10	9	0	13	17	13	10
Cerbone, Marc	2	2	5.45	7	0	36	50	16	17
Donovan, Tom	7	4	4.90	18	0	75	100	29	49
Hessler, Landon	7	5	3.72	41	0	77	67	34	51
Hlodan, George	4	1	5.25	11	0	58	74	26	31
Jollife, Bryan	2	2	6.02	37	1	49	60	30	33
Kojack, Phill	1	1	5.04	5	0	25	25	9	22
Mathys, Jason	6	2	5.24	25	0	89	102	35	78
Mitchell, Courtney	2	1	5.81	30	0	26	34	9	25
Perry, Matthew	3	4	3.92	42	1	44	45	22	47
Petroff, Dan	0	1	7.07	3	0	14	21	6	10
Quick, Dave	0	2	8.31	6	0	26	38	11	24
2-team (11 Chillicothe)	3	3	5.91	17	1	67	83	32	52
Rainford, Kevin	0	2	8.82	4	0	16	20	13	7
Raino, Brian	0	4	6.11	8	0	35	51	11	30
Silver, Travis	0	0	3.68	2	0	7	8	6	4
Trujillo, J.J.	1	3	1.58	39	14	46	33	21	60

LONDON

BATTING	AVG	AB	R	H	2B	3B	HR	RBI	SB
Borghese, Jason, of	.254	264	56	67	18	2	10	37	19
Correa, Dalphie, ss	.344	323	79	111	15	0	1	38	39
DeGraffenreid, Todd, 3b	.340	200	44	68	9	1	8	43	11
Edwards, Willie, of-3b	.386	127	37	49	9	0	5	28	5
Galarraga, Simon, 1b	.182	11	1	2	2	0	0	0	0
Gavriel, Chris, dh-of	.299	271	49	81	15	0	15	64	1
Goodwin, Keith, of	.369	187	37	69	17	3	4	45	18
Kuseski, Matt, 2b-ss	.246	114	29	28	1	0	0	10	19
Matsumora, Kunihiro, ph	.000	1	0	0	0	0	0	0	0
Metzger, Erik, c	.301	173	33	52	10	0	3	34	13
Nadeau, Rick, of	.348	339	69	118	32	6	8	82	17
Neuman, Gregg, c-3b	.263	186	33	49	10	3	2	26	1
Payne, Joe, 2b	.316	237	51	75	10	2	3	32	6
Pettit, Ryan, 1b-of	.191	68	9	13	1	0	0	7	1
Pogue, Jamie, c-1b	.270	237	42	64	14	1	5	30	3
Swift, Dan, 1b	.261	88	13	23	6	0	7	31	0
Wilcox, Scot, of-1b	.247	198	30	49	5	1	8	42	2

PITCHING	W	L	ERA	G	SV	IP	H	BB	SO
Barendregt, Jake	1	0	5.91	8	0	21	26	17	29
Brungardt, Bobby	5	4	4.05	20	1	53	64	16	38
Clark, Mark	8	3	4.87	15	0	94	113	37	83
Conner, Scott	10	5	4.65	18	0	112	122	35	82
Fidge, Darren	4	5	5.21	18	0	114	140	42	103
Gray, Brett	9	5	4.18	19	0	125	141	29	129
Harvey, Ian	4	1	5.11	26	2	37	49	15	44
Jackson, Eric	0	0	21.60	1	0	2	6	1	2
Masse, Derek	0	0	9.00	2	0	4	10	0	4
Melehes, Meleti	6	2	6.63	27	3	38	44	21	36
Spottz, Jamie	0	0	7.71	8	0	12	16	10	9
Turberville, Kris	5	3	3.96	31	2	91	84	55	90
Waller, Jerry	2	2	1.88	29	14	43	35	21	51

RICHMOND

BATTING	AVG	AB	R	H	2B	3B	HR	RBI	SB
Bichelmeyer, Jason, of	.333	261	60	87	14	9	7	50	7
Crothers, K.C., 3b-ss	.328	305	60	100	19	1	5	59	6
Deck, Ronnie, of	.255	94	15	24	4	0	0	12	1

	AVG	AB	R	H	2B	3B	HR	RBI	SB
Dixon, Terrell, ph	.000	1	0	0	0	0	0	0	1
Flores, Freddy, ss-of	.262	172	34	45	4	1	3	21	13
Fout, Keith, c	.286	112	9	32	5	0	1	20	2
Harris, Steve, of	.140	43	5	6	2	0	0	3	0
Hennecke, Pete, dh-3b	.279	226	29	63	10	2	2	37	3
Kinchen, Jason, dh-1b	.357	280	65	100	19	0	27	78	2
Lopez, Mark, of	.194	93	11	18	3	0	1	8	2
Mathis, Chad, 2b	.167	12	5	2	0	0	0	1	1
Pemberton, Shawn, c	.143	7	0	1	0	0	0	2	0
Quire, Jeremy, c	.259	27	3	7	0	1	0	6	0
Robinson, Tony, 2b	.091	11	2	1	1	0	0	1	1
Schwade, Brian, ss-2b	.256	195	30	50	11	2	1	19	6
Sledd, Aaron, of	.303	261	66	79	24	2	8	44	2
Stiles, Shap, of	.271	166	35	45	7	0	0	25	18
Tarleton, Tory, c	.243	74	7	18	5	0	1	11	1
Voshell, Key, dh-ss	.317	259	50	82	15	1	2	42	6
Williams, Chris, of-3b	.266	64	11	17	1	0	0	9	2
Zerbe, Mike, 1b-dh	.285	214	52	61	15	0	14	41	1

PITCHING	W	L	ERA	G	SV	IP	H	BB	SO
Arnold, Jay	0	1	40.50	2	0	1	2	1	1
Baker, Ken	0	0	10.13	2	0	3	7	0	5
Cali, Joe	1	1	6.10	19	1	31	30	21	34
2-team (9 Johnstown)	2	2	6.70	28	1	44	47	34	44
Donohoo, Chris	1	0	8.44	4	0	5	5	3	3
Dyer, Rob	0	1	10.64	6	0	11	25	7	5
Finken, Brad	5	5	6.12	18	0	90	126	31	75
Fischer, Kenny	5	7	5.84	17	0	94	98	57	75
Flores, Freddy	0	0	4.05	6	0	7	8	3	7
Hartman, Kory	2	3	7.31	20	1	60	75	44	64
Hollowell, Todd	3	6	6.18	13	0	79	102	21	66
Klassen, Brett	3	2	4.54	21	0	42	45	23	42
Kojack, Phill	6	1	4.12	8	0	55	46	25	71
2-team (5 Johnstown)	7	2	4.41	13	0	80	71	34	93
Magill, Steve	6	0	4.76	13	1	57	60	29	62
Morgan, Robby	1	2	6.08	9	1	13	19	8	10
Parke, Brent	0	1	7.90	4	0	14	23	9	6
Silver, Travis	1	2	10.43	4	0	15	24	13	7
2-team (2 Johnstown)	1	2	8.18	6	0	22	32	19	11
Stadelhofer, Mike	0	0	27.00	2	0	1	4	2	0
Stephens, Jon	2	6	5.11	34	5	56	58	20	64
Tyo, Todd	0	1	6.33	19	0	27	31	10	32
Whitford, Chris	3	1	10.69	10	1	16	20	18	12
Woodman, Hank	1	3	1.64	5	0	38	34	18	37

RIVER CITY

BATTING	AVG	AB	R	H	2B	3B	HR	RBI	SB
Black, William, c	.311	183	26	57	14	0	3	29	2
Coggins, Justin, c	.207	82	7	17	4	0	1	9	1
2-team (10 Canton)	.114	35	4	4	1	0	0	2	1
Doskocil, Darren, 2b-ss	.200	5	1	1	0	0	0	0	1
Graham, Dan, of-c	.302	192	39	58	13	2	6	30	10
Jaworowski, Aaron, 3b-1b	.290	272	45	79	17	1	16	61	1
Nielson, Bret, of	.077	13	3	1	0	0	1	2	0
Olson, Cass, 1b	.278	309	54	86	15	2	10	51	4
Pitts, Kevin, of	.286	290	43	83	12	3	11	47	10
Rakers, Jason, ss-3b	.296	253	61	75	19	2	15	46	16
Robertson, Mike, of	.314	293	55	92	15	3	13	59	12
Rogelstad, Dustin, 3b-2b	.233	103	17	24	6	0	0	15	2
Salyers, Cody, of	.254	181	25	46	10	1	5	20	8
Schmidt, Jim, 3b-2b	.245	98	16	24	5	2	1	8	4
2-team (30 Cook County)	.226	199	33	45	7	3	2	22	10
Still, Tim, of	.249	253	51	63	8	3	13	42	11
Tripp, Terry, ss	.079	38	4	3	0	0	0	2	0
Tyson, Torre, 2b	.294	143	30	42	6	1	1	17	26
Weeks, Paul, 2b-ss	.252	151	22	38	6	0	2	16	6

PITCHING	W	L	ERA	G	SV	IP	H	BB	SO
Bailey, Chris	1	3	7.87	28	0	42	44	35	35
Berman, Ben	0	1	7.20	10	0	20	20	18	8
Blackwell, Corey	0	0	22.50	1	0	2	4	2	1
Bray, Chris	3	3	10.61	13	1	19	25	23	16
2-team (14 Springfield)	4	4	8.05	27	3	35	42	31	28
Cronk, Darryl	2	3	6.36	24	2	58	88	19	39
Eversgerd, Randy	5	7	6.22	19	0	116	148	24	108
Guerrero, Rich	5	1	5.59	24	2	47	60	23	35
Kearney, Bryan	0	0	20.25	4	0	1	1	6	1
Levey, Joshua	6	9	6.34	18	0	104	134	29	68
Miller, Tom	10	2	5.22	19	0	110	133	31	71
Moody, Brian	1	3	5.14	29	10	28	20	19	38
Pipes, Joey	4	6	4.46	11	1	69	71	19	54
Ridenour, Jeff	0	2	11.12	2	0	6	10	8	1
Rister, Nate	0	0	3.86	2	0	2	1	2	0
2-team (5 Evansville)	0	0	8.59	7	0	7	9	8	6
Squire, Mark	0	0	7.36	5	0	7	17	2	2

	W	L	ERA	G	SV	IP	H	BB	SO
Turnrose, Erik	1	1	4.15	33	1	30	29	26	29
Weeks, Paul	0	0	5.14	4	0	7	6	4	8
Whitford, Chris	1	3	5.79	13	0	51	63	29	43
2-team (10 Richmond)	4	4	6.95	23	1	67	83	47	55

SPRINGFIELD

BATTING	AVG	AB	R	H	2B	3B	HR	RBI	SB
Anarumo, Jason, 3b-2b	.266	177	27	47	10	4	2	28	1
Annicelli, Rob, 2b	.231	52	8	12	4	1	1	4	1
Barningham, Steve, of	.351	319	76	112	21	11	5	60	44
Brosseau, Matt, 2b	.286	14	1	4	0	0	0	2	1
Cook, Josh, c	.059	17	3	1	1	0	0	1	0
Fiermonte, Jeff, dh-of	.143	21	1	3	1	0	0	1	0
Forst, David, ss	.294	343	60	101	14	1	4	53	7
Gillis, Ed, 2b	.143	7	0	1	0	0	0	1	0
Jenkins, Brink, c	.209	129	21	27	8	1	2	15	0
Kidd, Bobby, c-dh	.295	224	38	66	12	0	8	41	0
Kirkpatrick, Mike, of-dh	.253	190	38	48	8	4	6	29	11
Lindekugel, Tyson, 3b-dh	.252	317	49	80	11	3	10	40	1
McDonald, Bobby, of	.319	310	46	99	24	0	11	67	0
Provines, Kip, 1b	.286	325	55	93	20	2	9	51	0
Sapp, Aaron, of	.273	44	6	12	4	0	0	3	0
Sundlie, Tod, 2b	.272	173	29	47	13	1	0	27	9
Tunali, Rauf, of	.275	193	43	53	14	4	1	22	8
Wiebe, Jay, of	.250	24	9	6	0	1	0	3	7

PITCHING	W	L	ERA	G	SV	IP	H	BB	SO
Arnold, Neal	6	5	5.27	17	0	101	120	37	70
Bray, Chris	1	1	5.06	14	2	16	17	8	12
Brown, Jeremy	4	7	3.49	31	2	80	69	20	55
Crozier, John	2	1	3.86	21	0	42	36	18	31
Danner, Andy	1	1	10.50	6	0	12	22	5	11
Denly, Greg	2	1	6.21	15	0	33	50	12	27
Dillahay, Art	3	4	4.11	26	7	31	33	15	32
Garmong, Aaron	1	6	5.33	20	0	73	91	50	47
Guess, Scott	0	0	8.68	5	0	9	13	6	6
Harden, Tony	4	8	5.49	17	0	98	115	38	86
Hegeman, Joel	0	0	2.84	6	0	6	4	6	2
Hubbard, Joel	0	0	7.56	8	0	8	11	4	6
Loonam, Rick	7	2	3.58	15	0	106	107	26	57
McDaniel, Lonnie	0	1	37.80	3	0	2	3	4	0
McDonald, Corey	0	0	8.31	2	0	4	4	1	1
Robertson, Doug	4	3	4.08	13	0	53	57	14	29
Tubb, Dustin	2	3	5.73	7	0	38	31	25	16
Zuk, David	1	1	4.15	11	0	13	10	5	9

TEXAS-LOUISIANA LEAGUE

The Texas-Louisiana League seems to have mirrored the major leagues in at least one respect. The same teams win year after year.

In 1999, the Amarillo Dillas and Alexandria Aces squared off in the league championship series for the third consecutive year. In the previous two, Alexandria pummeled Amarillo three games to none in 1998 and three games to one in 1997, and each time the celebration took place at Amarillo's Memorial Stadium. But 1999 proved to be a royal flush for the Dillas, who defeated the Aces 8-7 in 11 innings, 7-6 in 10 innings and 13-4 at home in front of 2,976 broom-waving fans.

The championship was a long time coming for the Amarillo faithful. They hadn't seen a winner since the Amarillo Gold Sox won the Double-A Texas League title in 1975.

The Dillas, who set a league record with a .750 winning percentage, were the second-best draw. They fell short of the Ozark Mountain Ducks, who drew 154,752 in their first season in the league. The Ducks finished 30 games behind the Dillas but the people of Springfield, Mo., finally got their professional baseball franchise. They had failed to get an affiliated minor league franchise in three attempts.

Pitching, as a whole, was not a selling point for the league. Only five qualifiers had ERAs lower than 4.00. But where there's no pitching, there's plenty of hit-

ting. Alexandria's John O'Brien hit an independent league record 39 home runs.

STANDINGS

	W	L	PCT	GB
Amarillo Dillas	63	21	.750	—
Alexandria Aces	48	36	.571	15
Abilene Prairie Dogs	46	38	.548	17
Rio Grande Valley Whitewings	45	38	.542	17½
Ozark Mountain Ducks	32	50	.390	30
Bayou Bullfrogs	32	51	.386	30½
Greenville Bluesmen	26	58	.310	37

PLAYOFFS: Semifinals—Amarillo defeated Rio Grande Valley 2-1 and Alexandria defeated Abilene 2-1 in best-of-3 series. **Finals**—Amarillo defeated Alexandria 3-0 in best-of-5 series.

MANAGERS: Abilene—Dan Madsen. **Alexandria**—Stan Cliburn. **Amarillo**—John Cook. **Bayou**—John Harris. **Greenville**—Bob Lacey. **Ozark**—Barry Jones. **Rio Grande Valley**—Eddie Dennis.

ATTENDANCE: Ozark, 154,752; Amarillo, 151,222; Rio Grande Valley, 77,866; Alexandria, 77,192; Bayou, 30,678; Greenville, 35,519; Abilene, 34,131.

ALL-STAR TEAM: C—Brent Bubela, Ozark; Eddie Fitzpatrick, Rio Grande Valley; Guy Guffre, Abilene. **1B**—John O'Brien, Alexandria. **2B**—Marvin Cole, Alexandria. **3B**—Derek Henderson, Amarillo. **SS**—Matt Hyers, Abilene. **OF**—Sergio Cairo, Rio Grande Valley/Ozark; Lonnie Maclin, Amarillo; Vince Moore, Amarillo; Ryan Rothe, Alexandria. **Util**—Jason Adams, Abilene; T.D. Taylor, Abilene. **DH**—Gabe Duross, Abilene. **P**—Mike Boebert, Amarillo; Josh Foshie, Amarillo; Steve Ortiz, Abilene; Keith Rockwell, Abilene; Mario Rodriguez, Rio Grande Valley; Russell Reeder, Alexandria; Mike Smith, Ozark; Darell White, Alexandria.

Most Valuable Player: John O'Brien, Alexandria. **Most Valuable Pitcher**: Darell White, Alexandria. **Rookie of the Year**: Sam Lee, Amarillo. **Co-Managers of the Year**: Daren Brown, Amarillo; Dan Madsen, Abilene.

INDIVIDUAL BATTING LEADERS
(Minimum 227 Plate Appearances)

	AVG	AB	R	H	2B	3B	HR	RBI	SB
Henderson, Derek, Amarillo	.398	319	87	127	31	3	15	89	5
Roland, William, Alex.	.365	318	48	116	17	1	7	56	7
Lee, Sam, Amarillo	.359	309	64	111	13	8	6	69	31
Adams, Jason, Abilene	.351	339	82	119	31	4	12	73	11
Duross, Gabe, Abilene	.350	374	68	131	27	3	10	110	5
Fingleson, Gavin, Bayou	.350	226	39	79	12	1	2	34	12
Cairo, Sergio, RGV-Ozark	.349	298	60	104	19	3	7	54	14
Maclin, Lonnie, Amarillo	.348	333	83	116	24	3	9	79	9
Moore, Vince, Amarillo	.348	319	74	111	26	2	13	84	19
Hyers, Matt, Abilene	.337	338	73	114	24	4	1	64	33

INDIVIDUAL PITCHING LEADERS
(Minimum 67 Innings)

	W	L	ERA	G	SV	IP	H	BB	SO
Rodriguez, Mario, RGV	6	1	3.13	11	0	69	58	28	50
Kermode, Al, Amarillo	6	2	3.35	11	0	75	69	15	61
Brown, Chris, Alexandria	4	3	3.88	33	6	70	71	45	47
Rockwell, Keith, Abilene	9	7	3.90	25	0	111	128	39	56
Smith, Mike, Ozark	10	7	3.94	21	0	162	177	59	104
McDermott, Toby, Abilene	8	4	4.00	17	0	115	103	66	101
Patrick, Jason, Amarillo	10	2	4.07	26	1	111	123	16	85
White, Darell, Alexandria	6	6	4.33	23	0	173	165	76	124
Kast, Nick, Amarillo	10	3	4.45	22	1	89	126	19	67
Hollins, Stacy, Bayou	5	7	4.48	14	0	92	80	31	85

ABILENE

BATTING	AVG	AB	R	H	2B	3B	HR	RBI	SB
Adams, Jason, 3b	.351	339	82	119	31	4	12	73	11
Billingsly, Kyle, dh-of	.400	180	38	72	12	0	2	19	2
Contreras, Efrain, dh-of	.183	82	12	15	4	0	0	9	0
Cooney, Jim, of	.100	10	0	1	0	0	0	1	0
DeCelle, Mike, of	.362	185	43	67	21	4	3	34	4
2-team (21 RGV)	.331	269	57	89	29	6	5	50	5
Donaldson, Rhodney, of	.290	269	69	78	13	2	1	41	22
Duross, Gabe, 1b	.350	374	68	131	27	3	10	110	5
Giuffre, Guy, c-dh	.304	273	52	83	20	2	16	66	0
Holder, Jody, of	.182	44	4	8	2	1	0	9	1
Hyers, Matt, ss	.337	338	73	114	24	4	1	64	33
McNabb, Brandon, 3b-of	.234	77	8	18	1	0	1	7	0
Melchione, Rafael, c	.125	8	0	1	0	0	0	2	0

Independent Leagues

BATTING	AVG	AB	R	H	2B	3B	HR	RBI	SB
Pettiford, Torrey, 2b	.255	165	32	42	7	2	3	20	8
Pitts, Rick, of	.314	328	65	103	15	1	3	56	32
Solis, Samuel, 2b	.333	9	3	3	0	0	0	0	1
Taylor, T.D., c-2b	.273	286	68	78	18	3	7	56	7

PITCHING	W	L	ERA	G	SV	IP	H	BB	SO
Arminio, Sam	0	0	0.00	1	0	1	1	0	0
Brown, Brandon	0	0	7.98	19	0	38	42	32	34
2-team (9 Ozark)	0	3	8.32	28	0	49	57	47	43
Gomez, Gus	0	0	13.50	2	0	2	4	2	4
2-team (4 Greenville)	1	1	4.88	6	0	31	35	15	28
MacKinlay, Gary	1	1	7.92	20	0	44	63	35	34
Maddock, Steve	1	2	7.01	6	0	26	34	15	15
McDaniel, Denny	0	2	4.10	36	9	42	47	21	39
McDermott, Toby	8	4	4.00	17	0	115	103	66	101
Naff, Todd	3	2	4.13	22	0	33	35	11	24
Ortiz, Steve	14	7	4.61	22	0	150	171	50	105
Perry, J.D.	0	2	9.00	6	0	25	40	12	24
Powell, Dax	0	0	12.00	2	0	3	4	4	2
Rockwell, Keith	9	7	3.90	25	0	111	128	39	56
Roque, Jorge	3	3	9.51	11	0	35	62	22	21
Thomas, Jeff	7	6	5.13	14	0	93	103	43	50
Wright, Jason	0	1	49.50	5	0	2	4	16	1

ALEXANDRIA

BATTING	AVG	AB	R	H	2B	3B	HR	RBI	SB
Cole, Marvin, 2b	.314	309	55	97	11	4	4	37	8
DeLeon, Ray, dh	.370	100	21	37	9	0	4	16	3
Diaz, Christian, c	.265	98	16	26	7	0	3	20	1
Hewes, Robert, 3b	.302	285	68	86	20	4	5	50	13
Matos, Malvin, of-dh	.314	334	69	105	19	0	26	78	8
Medlin, Eddie, c	.250	76	12	19	6	1	1	12	1
O'Brien, John, 1b	.324	296	80	96	16	1	39	104	0
Rengifo, Daliene, of	.236	55	12	13	1	1	0	5	4
2-team (4 Bayou)	.224	67	14	15	1	2	0	7	4
Roberts, Chris, dh-c	.250	20	3	5	1	0	2	4	0
Roland, William, ss	.365	318	48	116	17	1	7	56	7
Rothe, Ryan, of	.319	313	74	100	21	2	6	41	27
Sandoval, David, 2b-3b	.286	14	4	4	0	0	0	2	1
Shade, Kyle, of-1b	.359	181	48	65	10	5	6	44	1
Stroud, Cecil, c	.222	9	0	2	0	0	0	0	0
Trosclair, Brent, of	.309	333	54	103	19	9	2	41	17
Van Asselberg, Ricky, c	.216	171	21	37	3	0	2	24	3

PITCHING	W	L	ERA	G	SV	IP	H	BB	SO
Brown, Chris	4	3	3.88	33	6	70	71	45	47
Filson, Brian	3	6	8.43	15	0	58	91	42	34
Fleming, Rip	3	0	8.36	8	0	14	18	12	12
Hawkins, Brandon	0	1	6.48	9	0	17	19	18	8
Ishee, Gabe	8	8	5.28	18	0	123	127	48	91
Mack, Tony	0	2	8.62	9	0	31	37	20	13
McIntyre, Harvey	1	1	5.71	10	1	17	26	12	5
Moran, Eric	1	2	3.15	10	0	20	25	6	20
Perkins, Russ	1	0	10.43	6	0	15	23	16	14
Reeder, Russell	9	5	4.69	20	0	144	166	36	84
Viator, Dustin	3	2	6.02	6	0	40	48	16	32
2-team (11 Bayou)	8	6	4.70	17	0	105	121	45	62
White, Darell	15	6	4.33	23	0	173	165	76	124

AMARILLO

BATTING	AVG	AB	R	H	2B	3B	HR	RBI	SB
Anderson, Chris, c-3b	.246	207	45	51	9	2	6	26	5
Fowler, Maleke, of	.331	320	94	106	18	6	1	48	50
Hayes, Tim, of	.245	139	17	34	6	1	1	22	7
Hemond, Scott, dh	.091	33	3	3	0	0	0	5	0
Henderson, Derek, 3b	.398	319	87	127	31	3	15	89	5
Hook, Kenny, ss	.301	326	81	98	18	3	3	73	15
Hughes, Shawn, c	.257	206	39	53	15	0	6	42	2
Jones, Bryan, 2b	.276	134	36	37	8	2	6	20	14
Koerner, Pat, 1b-dh	.246	191	47	47	8	1	12	42	3
Lee, Sam, 2b-dh	.359	309	64	111	13	8	6	69	31
Maclin, Lonnie, of-dh	.348	333	83	116	24	3	9	79	9
McAlvain, Jared, 1b	.254	177	32	45	10	2	4	31	3
Moore, Vince, of	.348	319	74	111	26	2	13	84	19

PITCHING	W	L	ERA	G	SV	IP	H	BB	SO
Boebert, Mike	12	5	5.52	22	0	137	167	58	123
Brown, Daren	3	0	3.20	4	0	20	19	4	17
Duey, Kyle	3	1	4.47	18	6	52	55	17	41
Foshie, Josh	4	1	6.98	5	0	39	46	22	28
2-team (11 Bayou)	8	4	5.85	16	0	115	129	74	86
Frazier, Harold	1	1	4.45	15	0	28	31	15	23
Hayes, Tim	0	0	2.53	7	1	11	11	3	9
Kast, Nick	10	3	4.45	22	1	89	126	19	67
Kermode, Al	6	2	3.35	11	0	75	69	15	61
Leach, Mike	7	5	4.54	23	1	119	151	34	95
Neese, Josh	0	0	9.00	4	0	4	9	3	1
Patrick, Jason	10	2	4.07	26	1	111	123	16	85
Quinones, Rene	0	0	9.88	11	0	14	16	13	5
Whitson, Jason	7	1	2.23	35	10	44	31	19	30

BAYOU

BATTING	AVG	AB	R	H	2B	3B	HR	RBI	SB
Bardin, Brad, c	.289	242	27	70	15	0	3	30	0
Brooks, Anthony, of	.302	129	29	39	10	0	5	19	12
Chapman, Billy, c-of	.292	65	9	19	5	0	1	11	0
Cherry, Evan, of	.280	186	28	52	10	3	2	20	7
Craig, Benny, of-dh	.287	296	49	85	21	1	9	49	3
Davila, Leonard, 2b	.186	70	3	13	2	0	0	3	0
Dolias, Steven, 3b	.268	56	9	15	2	0	0	5	4
Doucet, Brandon, of	.222	27	3	6	0	0	0	0	1
Fingleson, Gavin, 2b	.350	226	39	79	12	1	2	34	12
Heinen, Shane, ss	.238	126	15	30	2	0	2	19	3
Hendricks, R.J., c-1b	.000	11	0	0	0	0	0	0	0
Horton, Bill, c	.091	33	3	3	0	0	0	2	1
Labruzzo, Joe, of	.318	22	2	7	1	1	0	0	1
Lorence, Tony, c	.083	12	1	1	1	0	0	1	0
Medina, Octavio, ss	.185	92	17	17	3	1	0	7	12
Missler, Ryan, 3b	.250	12	1	3	0	0	0	0	0
Niethammer, Marc, 1b	.206	141	14	29	3	1	4	22	0
O'Dwyer, George, 2b	.214	56	5	12	3	0	0	7	2
Perret, Kevin, 3b	.294	211	43	62	12	4	3	28	0
Powell, Chris, of	.339	56	19	19	2	2	1	11	14
Quinn, Eric, ss	.324	74	11	24	2	1	0	12	1
2-team (20 RGV)	.278	126	19	35	3	1	0	18	1
Rengifo, Daliene, of	.167	12	2	2	0	1	0	2	0
Schaub, Kent, of	.500	10	3	5	0	0	0	2	0
Taylor, Corey, of	.357	140	33	50	11	3	8	26	14
Van Allen, Larry, of	.217	115	11	25	6	2	1	11	6
Visser, Jon, of	.198	86	6	17	2	1	1	12	2
2-team (36 RGV)	.236	199	20	47	7	2	1	31	11
Waguespack, Macky, 1b-dh	.281	228	30	64	11	1	9	37	0

PITCHING	W	L	ERA	G	SV	IP	H	BB	SO
Aikens, Jeremy	0	1	8.31	9	0	13	10	22	9
Angerhofer, Chad	0	2	7.71	7	0	19	33	15	13
Brown, Alvin	0	0	3.00	1	0	6	3	1	5
Casey, Shaw	3	3	4.31	29	6	65	63	48	50
Chaney, Jason	0	1	9.82	6	0	7	18	4	9
Chapman, Billy	2	0	2.38	13	1	23	22	7	23
Foshie, Josh	4	3	5.28	11	0	77	83	52	58
Frisbie, James	0	0	4.50	1	0	2	3	2	0
Hardcastle, J.D.	5	9	5.33	18	0	105	132	63	49
Hollins, Stacy	5	7	4.48	14	0	92	80	31	85
Lanasa, Matt	0	0	1.50	2	0	6	3	1	4
Masters, Dayne	4	6	8.04	22	0	63	89	25	29
McNellie, Jackie	0	0	7.36	3	1	7	12	3	1
Nipper, Jarrod	0	1	21.94	3	0	5	14	6	5
Shoemaker, John	0	2	8.31	9	0	17	22	9	12
Viator, Dustin	5	4	3.88	11	0	65	73	29	30
Von Haefen, Jason	3	4	3.30	11	0	57	55	15	56
Warren, David	1	4	4.20	16	0	45	55	26	31
Wilkerson, Grey	0	1	36.00	2	0	1	6	2	1
Wilson, Michael	0	0	31.50	2	0	2	7	2	2
Winkle, Ken	0	2	7.16	15	5	16	15	13	26

GREENVILLE

BATTING	AVG	AB	R	H	2B	3B	HR	RBI	SB
Bryant, Chris, 3b-ss	.321	299	61	96	25	4	4	49	15
Capellan, Rene, ss-2b	.273	209	31	57	8	6	1	22	8
Case, Fred, c-3b	.276	239	35	66	10	1	3	32	1
Cassels, Chris, dh-of	.267	337	52	90	14	1	18	71	0
Cepeda, Malcom, 1b	.353	150	24	53	10	1	0	17	14
Cole, Popeye, of	.324	296	54	96	21	5	1	32	10
Garcia, Cip, c-1b	.304	230	32	70	19	0	5	48	3
Gower, Mack, 1b	.000	1	0	0	0	0	0	0	0
Hudson, Robert, of	.229	131	12	30	7	0	1	12	1
Jasco, Elinton, 2b	.353	34	8	12	2	0	0	2	4
Johnson, Alphonso, ss	.231	52	11	12	2	0	1	8	4
Jones, Andy, 2b	.167	42	4	7	0	0	0	2	0
Landrum, Tito, of	.333	294	57	98	21	5	6	50	22
Miller, Terry, ss	.400	10	2	4	1	0	0	1	0
Robinson, Manny, 2b	.264	125	18	33	6	0	0	12	5
Rushing, Shannon, of-1b	.254	291	42	74	13	7	1	44	8
Swindell, Mark, ss-2b	.252	107	17	27	4	0	0	12	0
2-team (23 RGV)	.240	175	32	42	4	1	0	20	0

PITCHING	W	L	ERA	G	SV	IP	H	BB	SO
Brack, A.J.	0	2	9.18	8	0	17	30	20	8
Calton, Eric	0	4	6.47	8	1	40	56	17	12

	W	L	ERA	G	SV	IP	H	BB	SO
Cravey, Brian	2	10	6.85	19	0	114	162	36	76
Frisbie, James	0	0	8.10	6	0	10	11	9	4
2-team (1 Bayou)	0	0	7.50	7	0	12	14	11	4
Haviland, Mike	0	0	11.81	5	0	5	7	9	4
Hobson, Craig	0	2	15.43	8	0	9	17	17	0
Holobinko, Mike	0	0	16.50	3	0	6	12	10	2
Gomez, Gus	1	1	4.30	4	0	29	31	13	24
Jessee, Jamie	5	12	7.22	29	2	125	169	91	87
Krahenbuhl, Ken	4	5	5.45	13	0	76	104	28	51
Lacey, Bob	0	0	2.57	4	0	7	4	6	6
Molina, Bryan	4	4	5.15	28	3	37	41	24	39
Moore, Ashley	0	7	7.26	27	1	57	89	31	34
Rayborn, Kenny	6	9	4.85	18	0	115	140	43	80
Roberts, Chris	0	0	9.88	10	0	14	21	17	9
Robinson, Lance	0	0	20.77	4	0	4	15	2	4
Rushing, Shannon	0	0	4.26	1	0	6	6	3	4
Smith, Mike	2	1	1.64	10	3	11	7	6	16
Swindell, Mark	1	1	4.50	5	0	22	23	5	9
2-team (3 RGV)	1	1	4.97	8	0	25	30	7	13
Warren, Peyton	0	0	40.50	2	0	2	4	8	0

OZARK

BATTING	AVG	AB	R	H	2B	3B	HR	RBI	SB
Benbow, Lou, ss-2b	.268	250	37	67	15	4	3	33	8
Bogan, Tre, of	.154	39	2	6	2	1	0	5	0
Brooks, Anthony, of	.000	4	1	0	0	0	0	0	0
3-team (36 Bayou, 19 RGV)	.265	196	41	52	13	0	7	25	20
Bubela, Brent, c-of	.315	314	56	98	25	7	6	53	3
Cairo, Sergio, of	.358	254	52	91	17	3	6	44	13
Cubillan, Tubalcain, dh-of	.190	42	3	8	0	1	1	7	2
Davis, Gerald, of	.250	44	4	11	4	0	0	5	1
Hall, Scott, of	.258	97	13	25	3	1	1	8	2
Harris, Kevin, of	.171	70	10	12	2	1	2	5	6
Holmberg, Brett, c	.229	35	2	8	0	0	0	2	2
Jones, Barry, dh-of	.338	207	29	70	9	1	4	45	5
Mason, Lamont, 2b-ss	.259	197	55	51	7	0	2	29	12
Medlin, Eddie, c	.286	42	5	12	2	0	0	4	0
2-team (21 Alexandria)	.292	65	8	19	3	1	0	9	0
Motes, Jeff, 3b-ss	.282	273	36	77	11	2	2	33	6
Nelson, Brian, of	.216	51	8	11	2	1	0	5	2
Nunez, Dimerson, c-1b	.152	33	3	5	1	0	0	4	4
Sheffield, Jeff, of	.188	32	5	6	1	1	0	1	3
Smithey, Russell, 2b-of	.264	182	22	48	10	0	1	26	4
Stevens, Brad, 3b-1b	.304	92	10	28	9	0	1	17	1
Thompson, Jason, of	.215	265	36	57	12	8	4	25	12
Underwood, Curtis, 1b	.290	255	32	74	14	1	8	36	1
Woodress, Bray, c	.158	57	6	9	2	0	0	4	1

PITCHING	W	L	ERA	G	SV	IP	H	BB	SO
Abbott, Jeff	1	1	10.69	9	0	16	26	10	14
Bethea, Bill	0	0	16.20	5	0	5	10	6	3
Brown, Brandon	0	3	9.58	9	0	10	15	15	9
Buchanan, Todd	1	5	6.03	14	0	72	91	35	55
Buschhorn, Bryan	1	1	0.71	5	0	13	5	8	9
Collazo, Rafael	0	0	0.00	1	1	3	1	0	3
2-team (3 RGV)	0	0	1.42	4	1	13	8	1	5
Deckard, Eddie	1	3	6.03	12	0	31	36	22	21
Derenches, Al	1	2	9.00	4	0	18	29	10	16
Giles, Denny	2	3	4.19	12	2	34	33	15	24
Hampton, Mark	4	3	4.96	28	7	69	63	62	54
Hovey, Charlie	1	1	5.77	16	1	34	33	17	19
Mozley, Brandon	1	7	5.54	8	0	52	73	11	37
2-team (20 RGV)	4	8	5.63	28	1	93	125	28	56
Peck, Jeff	1	1	5.40	11	0	15	16	7	7
Pierce, Byron	2	2	7.49	16	1	34	50	21	12
2-team (7 RGV)	2	2	7.29	23	1	42	64	27	19
Rhodes, Kendall	3	2	6.17	20	0	54	57	36	30
Santana, Alfredo	2	5	5.60	15	2	63	74	32	50
Shorter, Chris	1	1	9.16	11	0	19	25	29	14
Smith, Mike	10	7	3.94	21	0	162	177	59	140
Westcott, Christian	0	3	9.98	3	0	15	26	8	9

RIO GRANDE VALLEY

BATTING	AVG	AB	R	H	2B	3B	HR	RBI	SB
Brooks, Anthony	206	63	11	13	3	0	2	6	8
Cairo, Sergio, of	.295	44	8	13	2	0	1	10	1
2-team (65 Ozark)	.349	298	60	104	19	3	7	54	14
Chavez, Eric, dh-c	.264	277	48	73	19	0	20	63	0
Chavez, Steven, 3b	.250	288	36	72	13	4	12	49	4
DeCelle, Mike, of-1b	.262	84	14	22	8	2	2	16	1
Fitzpatrick, Eddie, c	.237	241	24	57	3	0	2	27	2
Hector, Ramon, 2b	.000	4	0	0	0	0	0	0	0
Johnson, Andre, dh-1b	.361	119	30	43	12	2	10	30	15
Keene, Andre, 1b	.339	59	10	20	3	0	3	16	4

Marquez, Ruben, ss-2b	.261	46	9	12	2	0	0	4	0
Martinez, Joey, of	.384	73	17	28	5	2	1	13	5
Medlin, Eddie, dh-c	.304	23	3	7	1	1	0	5	0
Mendoza, Alonso, of	.286	63	11	18	3	0	1	12	2
Michel, Domingo, 1b	.305	223	45	68	23	0	12	57	4
Pelfrey, Dennis, ss	.225	173	29	39	12	0	3	16	6
Quinn, Eric, ss	.212	52	8	11	1	0	0	6	0
Roa, Hector, 2b	.268	71	5	19	5	0	0	8	3
Rojas, Christian, of	.333	51	11	17	4	1	2	14	5
Samuels, Scott, of	.393	140	51	55	8	0	19	53	21
Swindell, Mark, ss-2b	.221	68	15	15	0	1	0	8	0
Vaughn, Derek, of	.278	302	64	84	16	3	3	30	48
Vela, Manuel, 2b-of	.294	310	82	91	20	0	5	26	11
Visser, Jon, of	.265	113	14	30	5	1	0	19	9

PITCHING	W	L	ERA	G	SV	IP	H	BB	SO
Abbott, Jeff	4	3	6.75	16	0	65	87	29	63
2-team (9 Ozark)	5	4	7.52	25	0	81	113	39	77
Buitron, Andy	1	0	6.82	21	0	32	40	26	20
Collazo, Rafael	0	0	1.80	3	0	10	7	1	2
Davis, Ray	2	1	6.00	4	0	30	35	15	26
Fields, Curtis	0	1	30.86	2	0	2	4	6	3
Giron, Roberto	5	2	4.58	24	6	35	31	22	38
Linares, Yfrain	3	3	6.48	17	1	33	46	15	41
Martinez, Johnny	3	9	8.05	18	1	79	119	40	60
Mozley, Brandon	3	1	5.75	20	1	41	52	17	19
Perez, Pablo	4	1	4.37	8	0	45	45	19	26
Pierce, Byron	0	0	6.48	7	0	8	14	6	7
Ramirez, Luis	2	0	2.25	14	4	24	20	7	25
Robell, Kevin	5	7	5.19	22	1	120	127	70	115
Rodriguez, Mario	6	1	3.13	11	0	69	58	28	50
Ruiz, Rafael	5	4	5.59	17	0	66	69	32	35
Santana, Alfredo	2	4	3.98	9	0	54	55	18	26
2-team (15 Ozark)	4	9	4.85	24	2	117	129	50	76
Swindell, Mark	0	0	8.10	3	0	3	7	2	4
Tellez, Eloy	0	1	5.59	7	0	19	18	10	13

WESTERN LEAGUE

The Chico Heat ran away with the regular season crown in the Western League in 1999, but as was the story a year earlier, the Heat ran out of gas in the playoffs.

Chico had a 63-27 record and had four pitchers in the top 10 in ERA for most of the season but still fell to the Tri-City Posse three games to one in the championship series. The Heat had the best record in 1998 but was swept out of the playoffs in the first round by Sonoma County.

The Posse won the championship for the first time after losses in the 1995 and 1996 title series, both times to the now-defunct Long Beach Riptide.

Former major leaguer Nelson Simmons hit .415 in the playoffs and .471 in the championship series to earn the league's postseason MVP award.

Righthander Ned Darley, who joined the Posse after returning to the United States from the Taiwan Major League, picked up four saves in the playoffs, including two in the title series.

The Western League underwent a major facelift before the season, with four teams folding and two others joining. The revamped six-team circuit made it through in fine fashion and plans for two new franchises were in the works.

The Sacramento Steelheads, one of the new franchises, didn't fare as well as projected. Sacramento was one of the best untapped minor league markets in the country before the Steelheads moved into a city-owned park. They drew 68,134 fans, second lowest in the Western League.

The arrival of a new Triple-A franchise in Sacramento has prompted the Steelheads to move to Vacaville, a smaller town about 35 miles northwest of Sacramento.

STANDINGS

	W	L	PCT	GB
Chico Heat	63	27	.700	—
Tri-City Posse	48	42	.533	15
Zion Pioneerzz	41	49	.456	22
Sonoma County Crushers	41	49	.456	22
Reno BlackJacks	41	49	.456	22
Sacramento Steelheads	36	54	.400	27

PLAYOFFS: Semifinals—Chico defeated Reno 3-2 and Tri-City defeated Sonoma County 3-0 in best-of-5 series. **Finals**—Tri-City defeated Chico 3-1 in best-of-5 series.

MANAGERS: Chico—Bill Plummer. Reno—Charlie Kerfeld. Sacramento—Bob Oliver. Sonoma County—Dick Dietz. Tri-City—Wally Backman. Zion—Bruce Hurst.

ATTENDANCE: Chico, 126,525; Tri-City, 90,964; Sonoma County, 85,362; Zion, 79,517; Sacramento, 68,134; Reno, 55,189.

ALL-STAR TEAM: **C**—Grant Fithian, Sonoma County. **1B**—Justin Drizos, Reno. **2B**—Sergio Guerrero, Reno. **3B**—Bo Durkac, Chico. **SS**—Tim Cooper, Chico. **OF**—Mark Charbonnet, Zion; Vernon Spearman, Sonoma County; Kevin Ellis, Tri-City. **DH**—Terrel Hansen, Chico. **Util**—Raul Rodarte, Tri-City. **SP**—Tom Bergan, Chico; Ryan Bowen, Sacramento; Randy Phillips, Reno; Marcus Moore, Zion; Kurt Takahashi, Sonoma County; Chris White, Chico. **RP**—Josh Montgomery, Chico.

Player of the Year: Justin Drizos, Reno. **Co-Pitchers of the Year**: Ryan Bowen, Sacramento; Chris White, Chico. **Manager of the Year**: Bill Plummer, Chico.

INDIVIDUAL BATTING LEADERS

(Minimum 243 Plate Appearances)

PLAYER, TEAM	AVG	AB	R	H	2B	3B	HR	RBI	SB
Ellis, Kevin, Tri-City	.366	331	72	121	27	3	12	71	7
Dowler, Dee, Reno	.365	241	59	88	7	6	1	36	17
McClendon, Travis, Zion	.362	276	59	100	17	4	3	36	23
Guerrero, Sergio, Reno	.354	367	73	130	26	5	5	54	7
Otero, Ricky, Zion	.353	323	81	114	25	6	8	47	31
Rodarte, Raul, Tri-City	.352	290	67	102	27	3	14	79	25
White, Eric, Sonoma	.352	327	68	115	25	0	7	59	12
Drizos, Justin, Reno	.351	296	78	104	22	1	24	85	2
Charbonnet, Mark, Zion	.350	371	77	130	24	4	28	103	7
Nadeau, Mike, Chico	.345	328	90	113	14	4	9	44	26

INDIVIDUAL PITCHING LEADERS

(Minimum 72 Innings)

	W	L	ERA	G	SV	IP	H	BB	SO
Bergan, Tom, Chico	9	4	2.93	19	0	117	103	56	71
White, Chris, Chico	10	1	3.21	15	0	98	86	29	72
Bowen, Ryan, Sacramento	9	4	3.56	17	0	109	108	49	89
Takahashi, Kurt, Sonoma	9	5	3.71	21	0	114	122	33	119
Moore, Marcus, Zion	8	3	3.87	17	0	100	95	64	114
Sobkoviak, Jeff, Chico	9	7	4.21	19	0	120	129	55	40
Phillips, Randy, Reno	8	3	4.56	19	0	118	116	56	104
Frierson, Andrew, Chico	7	2	4.73	28	3	86	91	52	43
Davidson, Tim, Sonoma	7	7	4.78	20	1	111	121	54	78
Flynt, Will, Tri-City	7	8	5.08	21	0	126	152	59	109

CHICO

BATTING	AVG	AB	R	H	2B	3B	HR	RBI	SB
Arntzen, Brian, c-1b	.269	308	39	83	13	0	7	48	3
Cooper, Tim, ss	.280	304	79	85	19	6	19	64	13
Durkac, Bo, 3b	.337	329	64	111	20	2	7	77	3
Fuller, Jon, c-1b	.305	272	59	83	16	0	11	54	0
Funderburk, Levi, dh-1b	.279	240	28	67	12	0	10	54	1
Gennaro, Brad, of	.291	364	63	106	25	0	10	72	2
Hansen, Terrel, 1b-of	.304	273	63	83	14	2	19	63	2
Kernan, Phil, of	.219	105	17	23	1	2	3	13	1
Lazerus, Erik, ss-2b	.221	68	12	15	6	0	0	6	1
Madden, Joey, of	.297	155	25	46	3	0	0	13	10
Moutrey, Mike, of-2b	.143	14	1	2	1	0	0	1	1
Nadeau, Mike, 2b	.345	328	90	113	14	4	9	44	26
Scott, Shawn, of	.293	294	54	86	12	2	6	45	19
2-team (16 Tri-City)	.284	366	61	104	18	2	7	49	22
Shamburg, Ken, dh-1b	.115	26	2	3	0	0	0	1	0
Stewart, Colin, of	.213	61	12	13	1	0	0	3	1
Wallace, Joe, c	.200	5	0	1	0	0	0	1	0

PITCHING	W	L	ERA	G	SV	IP	H	BB	SO
Arroyo, Joel	0	0	23.63	4	0	3	5	5	2
Bergan, Tom	9	4	2.93	19	0	117	103	56	71
Bryant, Adam	7	3	4.73	45	3	51	53	28	48
Frierson, Andrew	7	2	4.73	28	3	86	91	52	43
Johnson, D.J.	4	1	3.26	42	0	61	46	54	45
Kringen, Jake	0	1	5.21	4	0	19	16	17	13
Martineau, Brian	0	0	5.46	19	1	30	35	11	18
Mayer, Aaron	2	2	6.41	12	0	39	44	26	25
2-team (7 Reno)	3	7	6.37	19	0	76	93	42	44
Montgomery, Josh	4	2	1.93	40	19	42	32	15	51
Neier, Chris	1	1	6.94	5	0	23	29	9	21
Roach, Petie	4	2	6.06	18	0	65	82	28	50
Sobkoviak, Jeff	9	7	4.21	19	0	120	129	55	40
Sprinkle, Hank	0	0	0.00	2	0	3	1	0	3
Stoecklin, Tony	6	1	2.20	38	0	45	44	20	37
White, Chris	10	1	3.21	15	0	98	86	29	72

RENO

BATTING	AVG	AB	R	H	2B	3B	HR	RBI	SB
Cameron, Ken, of	.232	95	16	22	2	2	0	6	4
Cloud, Casey, c	.266	192	27	51	13	0	7	27	4
Cora, Manny, ss-2b	.297	249	42	74	11	4	2	33	3
Dowler, Dee, of	.365	241	59	88	7	6	1	36	17
Drizos, Justin, 1b-dh	.351	296	78	104	22	1	24	85	2
Garcia, Ismael, 3b	.299	87	13	26	3	1	1	13	1
Guerrero, Sergio, 2b-ss	.354	367	73	130	26	5	5	54	7
Johnson, Jack, c	.287	188	25	54	13	0	9	46	1
Kahl, Chris, of	.297	175	30	52	11	1	0	12	2
Kernan, Phil, of	.193	150	23	29	9	1	4	25	5
2-team (34 Chico)	.204	255	40	52	10	3	7	38	6
Kliner, Josh, 3b-2b	.307	296	56	91	16	10	7	54	3
Lawrence, Mike, 3b	.118	17	3	2	0	0	1	4	0
Mateo, Jose, ss	.200	15	0	3	0	0	0	3	1
Mattingly, Brandon, c	.300	30	6	9	1	0	1	4	1
Melendez, Dan, 1b	.340	194	44	66	14	0	9	47	0
Reed, Brian, of	.247	73	14	18	5	1	0	9	7
Sanchez, David, of	.321	349	74	112	24	2	14	77	10
Valdez, Trovin, of	.272	151	29	41	4	1	2	16	33

PITCHING	W	L	ERA	G	SV	IP	H	BB	SO
Alexander, Jordy	6	7	7.45	19	0	103	147	49	70
Bicknell, Greg	4	5	6.19	30	1	77	105	31	68
Brown, Duane	0	3	7.96	7	0	32	40	23	15
Gonzalez, Armando	0	1	7.65	14	0	20	30	10	17
Gould, Clint	3	1	8.18	36	1	55	75	26	33
Linares, Rich	6	7	6.64	48	9	60	89	19	67
Mahan, Dallas	5	2	5.35	30	1	67	75	36	56
Mayer, Aaron	1	5	6.32	7	0	37	49	16	19
McDermott, Toby	0	1	8.49	3	0	12	15	11	9
Niebla, Ruben	0	1	6.75	3	0	19	21	5	15
Oyler, Scott	0	1	5.87	6	0	8	8	8	9
Perez, Pablo	0	1	7.89	9	0	30	52	15	23
Phillips, Randy	8	3	4.56	19	0	119	116	56	104
Powalski, Rick	4	6	6.13	45	0	69	76	52	71
Walters, Brett	3	3	6.31	11	0	51	75	15	30
Warrecker, Teddy	0	0	4.15	4	0	4	3	6	3
Zuk, Dave	0	0	16.20	1	0	2	3	2	0
Zwemke, Bryan	1	2	6.92	6	0	26	36	11	13

SACRAMENTO

BATTING	AVG	AB	R	H	2B	3B	HR	RBI	SB
Bethea, Scott, ss-2b	.198	101	15	20	1	1	1	7	4
3-team (14 SC, 16 T-C)	.206	194	29	40	4	1	1	11	5
Blackwell, Juan, 2b-ss	.300	307	45	92	16	5	3	46	4
Bogle, Bryan, 3b	.143	42	2	6	1	0	0	6	1
Brown, Jeff, c	.210	124	17	26	5	0	2	12	0
Cheatle, David, of-2b	.260	246	36	64	16	2	0	24	10
Dodson, Bo, dh-1b	.328	271	62	89	28	0	13	59	2
Fraser, Joe, 2b-3b	.337	83	28	28	6	1	2	14	5
Fuller, Aaron, of	.261	211	48	55	8	5	2	31	17
Jenkins, Brett, of-dh	.365	85	18	31	7	1	4	26	2
McIntosh, Tim, c	.286	63	12	18	1	0	1	8	0
Miranda, Tony, of	.355	200	46	71	17	1	4	34	13
Musolino, Mike, c	.130	23	2	3	0	0	0	1	0
Phair, Kelly, ss	.246	130	25	32	11	1	0	14	2
Richardson, Scott, of	.289	360	71	104	22	2	7	73	24
Shipley, Matt, 2b	.208	72	7	15	1	0	0	2	5
Torres, Paul, 3b	.290	214	31	62	16	1	6	39	4
Underwood, Jake, c	.143	91	8	13	1	0	0	5	0
2-team (15 Tri-City)	.203	128	15	26	3	0	2	11	0
Vallarelli, Mike, c	.219	32	5	7	4	0	0	5	0
Washington, Kyle, of	.248	101	12	25	4	1	3	13	0
2-team (41 Zion)	.303	231	38	70	13	2	9	40	2
Weinheimer, Wayne, 1b-of	.319	326	62	104	26	0	6	65	4

PITCHING	W	L	ERA	G	SV	IP	H	BB	SO
Abeyta, Scott	3	3	7.32	33	0	59	90	41	37
Bowen, Ryan	9	4	3.56	17	0	109	108	49	89
Calmus, Lance	0	2	9.62	9	0	29	47	15	16

	W	L	ERA	G	SV	IP	H	BB	SO
Cheatle, David	0	0	6.08	5	1	13	21	5	3
Collazo, Rafael	0	0	30.00	1	0	3	11	2	2
Cruz, Charlie	0	1	11.05	2	0	7	12	9	7
Davis, Phil	0	0	8.53	4	0	6	8	6	5
Dawsey, Jason	3	3	5.44	20	0	50	57	38	43
Elias, Joseph	0	4	6.34	30	1	65	80	44	60
Grebe, Brett	0	0	0.00	5	2	6	4	0	5
2-team (27 Tri-City)	1	4	3.83	32	7	40	38	14	40
Grennan, Steve	1	2	12.71	3	0	11	20	10	8
2-team (4 Tri-City)	3	3	9.24	7	0	25	39	21	24
Hunt, Jared	1	1	5.84	4	0	12	15	6	8
Kawahara, Orin	0	4	11.28	10	0	22	38	19	17
2-team (9 Zion)	3	8	8.39	19	0	69	101	47	50
Lacey, Levi	3	4	6.58	11	0	66	80	60	55
2-team (15 Tri-City)	3	6	6.21	26	1	96	111	75	74
Lanzetta, Tobin	1	4	5.09	22	0	41	48	18	28
Leslie, Reggie	5	8	6.26	15	0	101	110	51	86
2-team (7 Tri-City)	6	12	6.99	22	0	139	159	71	123
Marifian, John	0	0	9.00	2	0	3	6	1	2
Mendes, Jaime	0	4	11.17	9	0	19	40	9	6
Ocasio, Mark	0	1	24.30	2	0	3	11	5	1
Palazzolo, Tony	0	1	11.05	3	0	7	16	7	3
Putnicki, Billy	5	2	4.01	35	6	43	46	27	28
Scott, Tim	1	1	1.59	17	6	17	11	3	23
Tyus, Wayne	0	0	16.20	5	0	5	10	2	3
Welch, Travis	0	0	4.91	8	0	7	11	9	4
Wilson, Gary	4	4	6.08	12	0	74	94	15	47

SONOMA COUNTY

BATTING	AVG	AB	R	H	2B	3B	HR	RBI	SB
Alguacil, Jose, ss	.285	253	37	72	15	2	1	33	12
Bethea, Scott, ss-3b	.170	47	5	8	1	0	0	2	0
Brown, Eric, of	.247	73	12	18	5	0	2	15	2
Fithian, Grant, c	.278	252	51	70	13	1	13	53	0
Fox, Brian, dh	.167	12	1	2	1	0	0	1	0
Hebert, Jeff, of	.276	105	14	29	10	0	6	23	0
Hopgood, Scott, ss-3b	.236	55	4	13	4	0	0	6	0
Horton, Conan, c	.214	14	4	3	0	0	0	0	0
Longmire, Marcel, c	.372	86	25	32	7	1	3	21	1
Marcano, Raul, of	.291	189	26	55	10	0	3	39	3
Mateo, Jose, ss	.294	17	3	5	0	0	0	1	2
2-team (5 Reno)	.250	32	3	8	0	0	0	4	3
McKeel, Walt, c	.444	9	1	4	0	1	0	1	0
Ozuna, Rafael, 2b	.254	319	46	81	16	3	6	51	12
Preston, Doyle, 3b	.230	135	13	31	3	0	0	17	1
2-team (12 Tri-City)	.245	159	14	39	3	0	0	19	1
Pridy, Todd, dh-1b	.292	325	62	95	22	2	12	76	1
Rendina, Mike, 1b	.287	307	58	88	22	1	11	53	1
Rico, Diego, of	.500	8	1	4	0	0	0	0	0
Sheppard, Don, of	.250	216	45	54	8	0	1	27	7
Spearman, Vernon, of	.285	376	89	107	19	5	2	36	55
White, Eric, 3b-of	.352	327	68	115	25	0	7	59	12
Wingate, Ervan, 2b	.000	3	0	0	0	0	0	0	0

PITCHING	W	L	ERA	G	SV	IP	H	BB	SO
Avila, David	2	4	4.54	22	6	38	48	22	38
Cooper, Chris	0	1	9.95	4	0	6	8	3	4
Davidson, Tim	7	7	4.78	20	1	111	121	54	78
Dishman, Glenn	0	1	9.20	5	0	15	27	6	9
Ewen, Jared	4	8	7.38	21	0	104	122	67	72
Harris, Ryan	3	2	5.24	32	0	55	54	30	33
Homan, John	3	7	6.75	27	2	77	114	41	47
Hopgood, Scott	0	0	9.35	6	0	9	16	7	4
Kishita, Kirt	1	4	4.54	26	7	38	36	19	29
Oyler, Scott	1	0	7.15	7	0	11	17	7	5
2-team (6 Reno)	1	1	6.63	13	0	19	25	15	14
Peck, John	0	0	27.00	1	0	1	2	2	0
Pool, Matt	4	6	5.27	21	3	96	112	48	55
Pourron, Joe	1	1	13.50	10	0	12	20	9	7
Takahashi, Kurt	9	5	3.71	21	0	114	122	33	119
Thobe, J.J.	0	0	6.75	1	0	4	8	0	4
Thobe, Tom	1	0	9.00	4	0	3	7	3	3
Warrecker, Teddy	0	0	81.00	2	0	1	3	0	0
2-team (4 Reno)	0	0	9.64	6	0	5	3	9	3
Wojciechowski, Steve	6	3	4.41	10	0	63	61	25	55
Woodrow, Jim	1	1	7.53	13	2	35	45	16	29

TRI-CITY

BATTING	AVG	AB	R	H	2B	3B	HR	RBI	SB
Baker, Jason, of	.210	100	13	21	8	0	1	10	0
Bethea, Scott, 2b-ss	.261	46	9	12	2	0	0	2	1
Ellis, Kevin, of	.366	331	72	121	27	3	12	71	7
Goodwin, Keith, of	.256	82	13	21	1	0	0	8	1
Johnson, Terry, of	.220	41	11	9	1	1	0	4	2

BATTING	AVG	AB	R	H	2B	3B	HR	RBI	SB
Kapano, Randy, of-1b	.242	99	24	24	7	0	3	18	2
Lofton, James, ss	.297	353	66	105	13	3	2	48	25
Longmire, Tony, of	.343	67	11	23	3	0	5	16	1
Madonna, Chris, c	.304	263	53	80	13	3	12	49	12
Michael, Jeff, ss-of	.200	5	1	0	0	0	0	0	0
Miranda, Tony, of	.300	80	19	24	9	0	4	22	4
2-team (49 Sac.)	.339	280	65	95	26	1	8	56	17
Mitchell, Greg, 1b-3b	.283	237	33	67	12	0	5	35	0
Moore, Kerwin, of	.202	129	36	26	4	1	0	11	19
Mowry, David, 1b	.309	97	15	30	2	0	6	17	0
Powell, Chris, of	.300	140	31	42	11	0	2	22	7
Preston, Doyle, 3b-2b	.333	24	1	8	0	0	0	2	0
Price, Dave, 2b-3b	.143	14	1	2	0	0	0	2	0
Rodarte, Raul, 3b	.352	290	67	102	27	3	14	79	25
Rutz, Ryan, 2b	.280	261	33	73	9	1	0	35	3
Sanders, Jeff, 2b	.125	8	0	1	0	0	0	1	0
Scherer, Jeff, c	.292	24	0	7	2	0	0	1	0
Scott, Shawn, of	.250	72	7	18	6	0	1	4	3
Simmons, Nelson, dh	.296	351	59	104	27	1	13	74	2
Underwood, Jake, c	.351	37	7	13	2	0	2	6	0

PITCHING	W	L	ERA	G	SV	IP	H	BB	SO
Bennett, Erik	2	1	0.49	22	2	37	16	11	40
Boyd, Chris	2	2	4.55	11	0	59	54	47	26
Campbell, Mike	0	1	12.00	1	0	3	6	3	1
Checketts, Andrew	4	4	6.11	13	0	74	74	34	59
Cowan, Bobby	8	5	3.91	46	5	71	72	46	58
Dopson, John	6	1	4.30	12	0	52	47	27	36
Flynt, Will	7	8	5.08	21	0	126	152	59	109
Grebe, Brett	1	4	4.50	27	5	34	34	14	35
Grennan, Steve	2	1	6.43	4	0	14	19	11	16
Kerley, Collin	4	5	6.55	18	0	99	115	46	72
Lacey, Levi	0	2	5.40	15	1	30	31	15	19
Leslie, Reggie	1	4	8.92	7	0	38	49	20	37
Raney, Zach	0	0	4.50	4	0	16	12	9	9
Salcedo, Jose	2	1	2.50	6	0	36	28	14	26
Sprinkle, Hank	2	0	5.97	31	1	32	36	24	25
2-team (2 Chico)	2	0	5.50	33	1	34	37	24	28
Thomas, Jeff	0	0	6.75	2	0	4	5	3	4
Thurmond, Travis	1	1	12.33	6	0	15	24	14	11
2-team (6 Zion)	2	2	8.72	12	0	43	53	33	31
Wheeler, David	0	0	1.93	3	0	5	4	5	2
Winkle, Ken	3	1	4.94	19	6	24	11	14	24
Wisler, Brian	2	2	3.94	24	0	32	36	16	20

ZION

BATTING	AVG	AB	R	H	2B	3B	HR	RBI	SB
Belk, Tim, 1b	.344	131	29	45	11	0	10	30	3
Charbonnet, Mark, of-dh	.350	371	77	130	24	4	28	103	7
Cowan, J.D., 3b-2b	.277	141	17	39	7	0	3	27	3
Diaz, Freddie, ss	.217	120	18	26	6	1	2	24	1
Edmondson, Tracy, 2b-ss	.241	145	21	35	7	1	1	17	3
Foulds, Kalin, of-2b	.280	268	58	75	9	4	3	38	30
Grebe, Brian, ss-2b	.259	220	52	57	10	0	12	41	6
Lewis, Dwight, of	.286	133	21	38	14	0	3	25	1
McCall, Rod, 1b	.262	145	34	38	5	1	13	42	0
McClendon, Travis, c	.362	276	59	100	17	4	3	36	23
Mealing, Al, of	.228	167	26	38	15	2	3	20	13
Mendoza, Alonso, 1b	.200	15	2	3	1	0	0	0	0
Mohler, Jacob, c	.226	93	13	21	4	0	0	11	0
Mosher, Willie, 1b	.239	46	8	11	2	0	2	9	1
Muro, Robert, 3b	.337	282	66	95	26	0	11	62	4
Otero, Ricky, of	.353	323	81	114	25	6	8	47	31
Rhein, Jeff, of	.276	116	20	32	8	0	2	20	8
Spencer, Glen, 3b-2b	.247	97	9	24	5	0	0	15	3
Washington, Kyle, dh-of	.346	130	26	45	9	1	6	27	2
West, Kyle, 1b-of	.087	23	4	2	0	0	0	1	2

PITCHING	W	L	ERA	G	SV	IP	H	BB	SO
Cooke, Steve	2	2	7.99	8	0	42	47	42	11
Corry, Delynn	1	4	7.97	20	6	20	28	15	17
Gledhill, Chance	3	5	6.47	18	0	81	109	32	34
Hancock, Ryan	2	2	8.28	13	0	29	45	15	18
Jimenez, Miguel	1	4	4.13	30	6	33	29	27	37
Kawahara, Orin	3	4	6.99	9	0	46	63	28	33
MacGillivray, Monte	0	2	14.85	8	0	7	11	12	8
Mazone, Brian	5	5	5.60	21	0	101	141	39	49
Mendoza, David	0	0	7.50	5	0	6	12	3	2
Moore, Marcus	8	3	3.87	17	0	100	95	64	114
Rand, Ian	2	5	6.92	38	1	68	92	42	34
Smith, Mike	8	7	5.96	20	0	128	149	36	94
Thurmond, Travis	1	1	6.75	6	0	28	29	19	20
Thomas, Jeremy	2	2	5.35	31	4	34	35	24	36
Tremblay, Max	3	2	4.75	41	1	55	58	35	51
Vanhof, Dave	0	1	2.35	14	0	15	12	15	16

Independent Leagues

FOREIGN LEAGUES

Embattled Johnson has success south of the border

BY JOHN ROYSTER

Toronto Blue Jays manager Tim Johnson was in the news seemingly every day for months early in 1999. Then after the Blue Jays fired him, he seemed to disappear.

But he didn't disappear. He went to the Mexican League and won a championship as manager of the Mexico City Red Devils.

The Blue Jays let Johnson go in spring training, after a winter of news that he had misrepresented his military record to his players, saying he had served in Vietnam when he had not. Jays general manager Gord Ash at first decided to keep Johnson on, then finally let him go as the pressure mounted.

Tim Johnson

In May, the Red Devils also came to a painful parting with their manager, Marco Antonio Vazquez, who had guided the team since 1993 and was the longest-tenured manager in the Mexican League. They hired Johnson, who had won two winter-ball championships as a manager in the Mexican Pacific League.

"I was raised in East Los Angeles speaking Spanish. I feel comfortable with Latinos and I have their trust," Johnson said. "Mexico is like my second home. I just wanted to get away, relax and have some fun, and Mexico was the perfect place."

The Reds won 22 of their first 28 games with Johnson as manager, and went on to beat the Mexico City Tigers in six games of the best-of-seven championship series. The 7-5 win in the final game was keyed by a three-run home run by third baseman Pedro Castellano, a former major league player with the Colorado Rockies.

The same two teams had met for the 1997 title, with the Tigers winning in five games. This time, Reds righthanded reliever Mike Garcia won one game and saved one to lead his team and win series MVP honors. Garcia finished the season in the major leagues with the Pittsburgh Pirates, who have a working agreement with the Red Devils.

The Reds' closest call in the playoffs came in the semifinals, when they were extended to 10 innings in Game Seven by the Saltillo Sarape Makers. Outfielder Tony Barron and third baseman Ray Martinez singled home the tying and winning runs in Saltillo's home park.

The league's other major 1999 news was the resignation of longtime league president Pedro Treto Cisneros. Treto, who had been president since 1983, left after the playoffs. An executive committee of team owners and presidents was to run the league until a new president was named.

Veracruz, a city that has had Mexican League franchises off and on for years, was back on again in '99. A 1998 expansion franchise in Chetumal lasted just one year in that city before moving to Veracruz, which had been without a team since 1995. The move didn't help much on the field: The team finished last in the South Zone in both halves of the season.

Luis Ayala, a 21-year-old sidearmer for Saltillo, broke the league saves record with 41. The old record of 39 was set by Miguel Alicea for Union Laguna in 1994.

Former Milwaukee Brewers lefthander Narciso Elvira pitched two no-hitters for the Campeche Pirates. The first came in April, in Elvira's first-ever start for the club. He beat the Cancun Lobstermen 5-0 in Cancun, striking out seven and walking three.

The second no-hitter was a 1-0, seven-inning win over the Two Laredos in June. That time Elvira struck out nine and walked two.

The league also announced the resumption in 2000 of its all-star series with the Texas League. Games were scheduled for San Antonio and Monterrey in 2000, and the agreement also calls for games in 2001 and 2002.

STANDINGS

NORTH ZONE	W	L	Pct.	GB
Saltillo Sarape Makers (15)	74	45	.622	—
Monclova Steelers (15)	71	46	.607	1
Monterrey Sultans (13)	64	54	.542	9½
Two Laredos Owls (11.5)	53	65	.449	20½
Union Laguna Cotton Pickers (11.5)	50	69	.420	24
Reynosa Broncos (10)	42	75	.359	31
CENTRAL ZONE	**W**	**L**	**Pct.**	**GB**
Mexico City Tigers (15)	75	38	.664	—
Mexico City Red Devils (15)	74	43	.632	3
Cordoba Coffeegrowers (13)	51	66	.436	26
Oaxaca Warriors (11.5)	49	70	.412	29
Aguascalientes Railroadmen (11.5)	47	74	.388	33
SOUTH ZONE	**W**	**L**	**Pct.**	**GB**
Cancun Lobstermen (14)	63	57	.525	—
Tabasco Cattlemen (13.5)	63	57	.525	—
Yucatan Lions (13.5)	60	56	.517	1
Campeche Pirates (14)	58	60	.492	4
Veracruz Eagle (11)	50	69	.420	12½

NOTE: League played a split-season schedule. Points were awarded on the basis of finish in each half (8 for first, 7 for second, 6.5 for third, 6 for fourth, 5.5 for fifth, 5 for sixth) to determine playoff pairings.

PLAYOFFS—Quarterfinals: Mexico City Red Devils defeated Monterrey 4-1, Mexico City Tigers defeated Tabasco 4-3, Monclova defeated Cancun 4-0 and Saltillo defeated Campeche 4-2 in best-of-7 series. **Semifinals:** Mexico City Red Devils defeated Saltillo 4-3 and Mexico City Tigers defeated Monclova 4-2 in best-of-7 series. **Finals:** Mexico City Red Devils defeated Mexico City Tigers 4-2 in best-of-7 series.

MANAGERS: Aguascalientes—Enrique Reyes, Porfirio Mendoza. Campeche—Marco Guzman, Eleno Cuen. Cancun—Francisco Estrada, Francisco Chavez. Cordoba—Ramon Arano, Jose Ruiz, Eduardo Diaz. Mexico City Red Devils—Marco Vazquez, Abelardo Vega, Tim Johnson. Mexico City Tigers—Dan Firova. Monclova—Aurelio Rodriguez. Monterrey—Juan Rodriguez. Oaxaca—Nelson Barrera. Reynosa—Leo Clayton, Jose Guerrero. Saltillo—Alfonso Jimenez. Tabasco—Alejandro Lizarraga, Mario Salazar, Juan Espino, Eddy Castro. Two Laredos—Andres Mora. Union Laguna—Pompeyo Davalillo, Alejandro Lizarraga. Veracruz—Raul Cano, Rolando Camarero. Yucatan—Carlos Paz.

REGULAR SEASON ATTENDANCE: Monterrey 457,328; Yucatan 428,296; Monclova 368,677; Cordoba 277,472; Saltillo 240,030; Veracruz 132,870; Mexico City Tigers 122,018; Tabasco 108,343; Mexico City Red Devils 106,420; Cancun 104,257;

Foreign Leagues

Oaxaca 103,232; Campeche 101,349; Reynosa 93,740; Two Laredos 85,785; Union Laguna 80,848; Aguascalientes 64,624.

INDIVIDUAL BATTING LEADERS

(Minimum 329 Plate Appearances)

	AVG	AB	R	H	2B	3B	HR	RBI	SB
Franco, Julio, Tigers	**.423**	326	90	138	22	6	14	77	9
Carrillo, Matias, Tigers	.416	421	107	**175**	27	2	20	98	3
Garcia, Cornelio, UL	.349	390	62	136	22	3	1	41	25
Rodriguez, Boi, Monclova	.342	459	99	157	33	5	26	**105**	**43**
Barron, Tony, Reds	.341	369	67	126	22	1	13	83	3
Gainey, Ty, Saltillo	.339	319	73	108	17	1	23	78	3
Gonzalez, Jesus, UL	.338	432	90	146	**36**	2	25	92	6
Gastelum, Sergio, Tigers	.337	415	92	140	16	3	6	61	12
Bullett, Scott, Campeche	.336	295	43	99	14	2	3	34	18
Castellano, Pedro, Reds	.336	455	92	153	28	2	22	99	4
Sherman, Darrell, Monclova	.336	396	93	133	23	3	4	41	20
Muñoz, Jose, Saltillo	.335	358	74	120	11	**11**	3	29	20
Vizcarra, Roberto, Agua./Tigers	.334	353	77	118	19	0	10	46	11
Romero, Wilfredo, Tigers/Sal.	.333	475	**110**	158	18	10	11	81	27
Garcia, Hector, Monterrey	.328	378	67	124	18	0	5	35	8
Arredondo, Luis, Yucatan	.327	462	71	151	15	7	2	50	20
Alvarez, Hector, Oaxaca	.324	404	65	131	17	2	3	41	6
Arano, Wilfredo, Laredo	.324	383	52	124	17	3	3	51	7
Guerrero, Epy, Campeche	.324	386	53	125	23	5	9	59	3
Espinosa, Ramon, Reynosa	.322	**509**	79	164	19	6	9	62	10
Fernandez, Daniel, Reds	.320	331	66	106	13	1	0	24	14
Chimelis, Joel, Laredo	.315	447	72	141	22	3	17	80	0
Esquer, Ramon, Oaxaca/Reds	.315	327	56	103	12	2	2	35	6
Rodriguez, Armando, Tigers	.315	327	50	103	16	3	5	66	6
Flores, Miguel, Monterrey	.314	420	71	132	20	4	3	54	13
Saenz, Ricardo, Monclova	.314	420	84	132	30	0	17	85	7
Liriano, Nelson, Reds	.313	323	78	101	10	5	10	54	24
Leyva, German, Veracruz	.312	391	53	122	19	0	8	49	4
Martinez, Ray, Reds	.312	359	68	112	19	0	19	75	3
Mendez, Roberto, Oaxaca	.311	273	51	85	11	1	9	40	17
Tellez, Alonso, Reynosa	.311	447	64	139	22	0	19	103	2
Arauz, Leobardo, Yucatan	.309	327	51	101	15	5	4	36	1
Sandoval, Jose, Reds	.309	418	67	129	29	2	12	77	1
Muñoz, Noe, Saltillo	.308	383	61	118	12	0	4	63	2
Bell, Juan, Cordoba	.307	420	67	129	23	7	5	63	20
Machiria, Pablo, Aguas.	.307	423	51	130	21	2	11	86	1
Martinez, Carlos, Saltillo	.307	449	58	138	22	2	1	42	8
Martinez, Enrique, Aguas.	.307	290	52	89	14	4	10	53	6
Alvarez, Jorge, Cordoba	.305	282	43	86	11	0	0	30	13
Gonzalez, Jose, Yuc./Aguas.	.301	392	86	118	22	5	16	65	19
Guizar, Hector, Monclova	.300	413	55	124	17	3	6	56	3
Zazueta, Mauricio, UL	.300	426	64	128	20	5	2	57	6
Brown, Ray, Tabasco	.299	355	58	106	21	1	6	54	4
Jimenez, Houston, Saltillo	.299	361	45	108	23	1	4	52	3
De Lima, Rafael, Aguas.	.298	322	62	96	16	6	2	36	13
Rodriguez, Fernando, Campeche	.298	410	50	122	23	2	6	49	3
Yan, Julian, Cordoba	.298	413	76	123	19	2	27	79	7
Canizalez, Juan, Monterrey	.296	392	43	116	22	1	3	50	5
Jimenez, Eduardo, Saltillo	.296	260	40	77	12	0	11	55	0
Saucedo, Roberto, Mont./Rey.	.296	277	37	82	9	3	15	50	0
#Meggers, Mike, Veracruz/UL	.263	365	62	96	15	0	**28**	61	2

(Other Select Players)

	AVG	AB	R	H	2B	3B	HR	RBI	SB
Magallanes, Ever, Monterrey	.399	228	59	91	15	0	5	32	7
Obando, Sherman, Oaxaca	.360	161	37	58	12	1	10	40	3
Poe, Charles, Tabasco/UL	.349	269	39	94	8	2	7	51	4
Bruno, Julio, Tabasco	.338	287	32	97	19	0	6	54	3
Kapano, Randy, Monterrey	.337	89	18	30	5	0	2	16	2
Lee, Derek, Yucatan/Reds	.333	156	27	52	6	0	4	32	1
Tavarez, Rafael, Veracruz	.331	254	25	84	11	2	1	20	7
Magallanes, Bobby, UL	.325	40	9	13	1	0	0	6	1
May, Derrick, Monterrey	.324	108	19	35	5	0	4	29	1
Incaviglia, Pete, Monterrey	.323	96	18	31	5	0	2	12	8
Stark, Matt, Reynosa/Mont.	.323	167	25	54	11	0	6	25	1
Carter, Michael, UL/Veracruz	.313	243	38	76	10	2	2	22	17
Tinsley, Lee, Monclova	.305	118	22	36	3	2	3	12	8
Martinez, Domingo, Reds	.302	215	34	65	8	0	8	50	0
Fink, Marc, Cordoba	.300	30	3	9	0	0	2	4	0
Canseco, Ozzie, Mont./Tab.	.297	158	20	47	7	1	7	38	2
Gonzales, Rene, Reynosa	.293	75	14	22	1	1	2	10	0
Stoner, Mike, Monterrey	.293	147	21	43	10	1	5	33	2
Gama, Ricardo, Tabasco	.288	358	46	103	17	4	0	28	5
Garcia, Leo, Oacaxa	.287	457	71	131	17	6	6	66	20
Bethea, Larry, Cordoba	.285	256	40	73	14	0	12	36	12
Trafton, Todd, Oaxaca	.272	173	27	47	12	0	6	30	0
Moore, Kerwin, Veracruz	.271	140	26	38	5	0	1	16	12
Mitchell, Tony, Veracruz	.268	164	15	44	6	0	7	25	2
Velazquez, Guillermo, Mont.	.264	197	24	52	10	0	3	36	0
Azocar, Oscar, Veracruz	.263	463	58	122	9	0	13	60	4
Jones, Tim, Aguascalientes	.260	77	18	20	1	1	4	11	3
Groppuso, Mike, Yucatan	.256	82	9	21	4	0	0	6	2
Chance, Tony, Mon./Tabasco	.249	406	60	101	14	3	20	81	4
Jones, Ron, Laredo	.246	57	11	14	4	0	1	6	0
Reyes, Gilberto, Veracruz	.243	115	6	28	4	0	2	13	1
Villanueva, Hector, Oaxaca	.225	71	12	16	3	0	3	13	1
Hall, Joe, Veracruz	.224	58	2	13	1	1	0	4	0
Berry, Mike, Veracruz	.222	27	1	6	2	0	0	6	0
Canale, George, Yucatan	.222	36	6	8	2	0	0	5	1
Mitchell, Kevin, Tabasco	.212	52	5	11	2	0	1	4	0
Nokes, Matt, Cordoba	.000	8	0	0	0	0	0	0	0

INDIVIDUAL PITCHING LEADERS

(Minimum 98 Innings)

	W	L	ERA	G	SV	IP	H	BB	SO
#Ayala, Luis, Saltilla	7	3	1.71	61	**41**	79	54	22	28
Alvarez, Juan, Tabasco	12	8	**2.20**	25	0	163	155	44	64
Elvira, Narciso, Campeche	10	6	2.25	20	0	144	97	57	**133**
Lopez, Gilberto, Cancun	7	6	2.29	48	18	102	79	46	35
Martinez, Miguel, Tabasco	**16**	5	2.33	25	0	166	153	37	77
Rivera, Oscar, Veracruz	7	4	2.54	21	0	120	93	61	83
Bourgeois, Steve, Saltillo	14	5	2.62	20	0	141	115	82	107
Palafox, Juan, Monclova	13	5	2.79	23	0	171	163	44	100
Quiñones, Enrique, Yucatan	10	9	2.87	25	0	151	169	47	71
Manzanillo, Ravelo, Mon./Yuc.	10	5	2.90	24	1	146	115	101	94
Meza, Leobardo, Veracruz	9	5	3.01	23	1	123	95	64	60
Acosta, Aaron, Laredo	5	4	3.10	21	0	116	101	62	84
Alvarez, Tavo, Reds	12	6	3.12	23	0	170	168	46	69
Turgeon, David, Reynosa	5	5	3.16	17	0	111	106	42	71
Valenzuela, Saul, Cancun	14	3	3.18	20	0	124	132	39	28
Loaiza, Sabino, Campeche	8	7	3.19	24	0	141	131	73	51
Alvarez, Antonio, Monclova	7	2	3.20	26	0	101	97	35	46
Ruiz, Cecilio, Tabasco	3	8	3.30	19	0	101	96	24	40
Grajales, Norberto, UL	8	6	3.32	27	1	117	121	29	49
Muñoz, Miguel, Cordoba	9	8	3.39	23	0	143	150	31	53
Fontes, Agustin, Cancun	7	5	3.42	21	0	116	134	35	34
Leyva, Edgar, Cordoba	7	4	3.54	24	1	109	101	60	73
Pimentel, Roberto, Tabasco	12	9	3.56	25	0	162	161	46	61
Jimenez, German, Laredo	4	6	3.59	20	0	105	110	66	34
Sanchez, Alejandro, Cancun	5	7	3.59	37	0	98	91	37	29
Navarro, Luis, Yucatan	**16**	4	3.62	42	2	134	145	53	44
Reyes, Pablo, Monterrey	12	7	3.65	28	1	170	169	70	79
Cota, Marino, Oaxaca	3	10	3.69	44	15	105	117	47	64
Campos, Francisco, Campeche	6	11	3.71	24	0	158	162	53	97
Lopez, Emigdio, Campeche	9	11	3.71	26	0	153	168	36	73
Hernandez, Martin, Can,/Sal.	7	4	3.76	18	0	117	112	54	43
Nuñez, Jose, Tigers	15	3	3.78	26	0	157	154	84	72
Lara, Hugo, Vera./Tabasco	5	8	3.83	24	0	106	118	28	38
Ochoa, Joel, Reynosa	8	11	3.86	24	0	142	136	78	128
Garcia, Carlos, Reds	12	4	4.05	25	0	153	170	78	58
Rios, Jesus, Monclova	6	5	4.12	17	0	109	117	33	60
CeceÒa, Jose, Monclova	9	6	4.17	24	0	117	109	38	69
Conde, Argenis, UL	9	6	4.18	53	0	140	163	71	75
Mora, Eleazar, Veracruz	7	10	4.19	22	0	127	138	41	50
Caruso, Gene, Laredo	6	9	4.30	22	0	132	135	76	83
Garcia, Alfredo, Reds	9	6	4.30	19	0	113	132	38	54

(Other Select Players)

	W	L	ERA	G	SV	IP	H	BB	SO
Garcia, Mike, Reds	0	0	0.75	12	8	12	5	3	20
Palacios, Vicente, Reynosa	5	2	0.95	43	10	66	47	20	68
Powell, Dennis, Campeche	5	4	1.10	45	20	65	51	25	45
Marquez, Isidro, Tigers	9	6	2.97	54	26	67	69	31	36
Metoyer, Tony, Can./Laredo	3	7	2.98	50	25	54	55	32	36
Higuera, Teddy, Monterrey	7	2	2.91	9	0	53	41	34	34
Heredia, Julian, Reynosa	3	9	3.09	15	0	90	91	41	82
Lewis, Richie, Reynosa	1	3	3.33	11	2	46	35	27	37
Green, Otis, Saltillo/UL	0	4	4.31	7	0	40	36	30	29
Boze, Marshall, Saltillo	10	6	4.36	25	0	149	152	90	85
Arocha, Rene, Yuc./Monterrey	1	7	4.55	12	0	57	67	14	47
Strong, Joe, Tigers	1	1	4.73	11	2	13	17	10	10
Garibay, Daniel, Tigers	2	5	5.06	16	0	89	91	56	59
Berumen, Andres, Monterrey	0	4	5.10	12	1	30	26	24	11
Haynes, Heath, Oaxaca	1	3	5.68	4	0	19	21	8	10
Ruffin, Johnny, Oaxaca	0	1	5.68	5	1	6	5	5	5
Fernandez, Osvaldo, Mont./Sal.	3	5	5.77	12	0	53	61	47	45
Salkeld, Roger, Tigers	2	1	6.14	6	0	29	38	16	13
Woodson, Kerry, Saltillo	0	1	6.30	3	0	10	11	12	9
Hollins, Stacy, UL	2	5	7.17	8	0	43	45	19	28
Mikkelsen, Linc, Saltillo	0	1	7.36	3	0	15	19	6	8
Heredia, Wilson, Tigers	1	1	11.42	5	0	17	18	23	20
Butcher, Mike, Aguas.	0	1	15.00	4	0	6	12	6	4

Statistics in **boldface** indicate league leader
# Indicates league leader but non-qualifier

Foreign Leagues

Home run king Oh leads Hawks to elusive title

JAPAN

BY WAYNE GRACZYK

The Fukuoka Daiei Hawks, consistent second-division finishers in the Pacific League over the past quarter-century, overcame scandal, a difficult economic situation and the death of their team president to win the 1999 Japan Series.

The Hawks won their first PL pennant since 1973, when the franchise was based in Osaka and known as the Nankai Hawks. The overall championship is the first for the city of Fukuoka since 1963, when the Nishitetsu (now Seibu) Lions were based in the southern Japanese city on Kyushu Island.

Daiei capped the season with a surprisingly easy four-games-to-one Japan Series victory over the Central League's Chunichi Dragons of Nagoya. The Hawks won three of the games by shutout.

Managed by former Yomiuri Giants slugger and manager Sadaharu Oh, the Hawks began the year as an unlikely contender, though a tie for third in 1998 in the six-team Pacific League was their best finish since a second-place showing in 1977.

The Hawks overcame a 1997 income-tax cheating scandal that led to the suspension of star player Hiroki Kokubo for 10 weeks in 1998, and a sign-stealing episode that cast a shadow over the team late in '98. They won the PL pennant by four games over the defending champion Lions.

Bobby Rose

The team was also handicapped by the poor financial condition of its parent company, one of Japan's top retailers with department stores and supermarkets throughout the nation. Daiei began the season with no foreign players because it couldn't afford them.

Eventually, enough cash was scraped together to hire reliever Rod Pedraza, a former Montreal Expos and Texas Rangers farmhand, and outfielder Melvin Nieves, who hit 24 home runs for the Detroit Tigers in 1996.

Both became key ingredients in the pennant drive. Pedraza went 3-1 with a 1.98 ERA and 27 saves in 48 appearances. Nieves, in half a season's worth of at-bats, hit .257 with 17 home runs and 43 RBIs.

The Daiei organization was shocked by the sudden death of team president Rikuo Nemoto, 74, on April 29.

A total of 57 foreign players saw action in Japan, and they were led—in terms of both longevity and performance—by Yokohama BayStars second baseman Bobby Rose. Playing his seventh year in Japan, the former California Angel won the CL batting title with a .369 average. His 153 RBIs were the second-highest total ever in Japan. He also had a league-record 192 hits and slammed 37 homers.

Yakult Swallows first baseman Roberto Petagine hit 44 homers to lead the Central League, while Kintetsu Buffaloes outfielder Tuffy Rhodes won the Pacific League homer (40) and RBI (101) titles.

Orix BlueWave outfielder Ichiro Suzuki won his sixth straight PL batting title, despite missing the final five weeks with a fractured wrist. He hit .343.

CENTRAL LEAGUE

STANDINGS

	W	L	PCT	GB
Chunichi Dragons	81	54	.600	—
Yomiuri Giants	75	60	.556	6
Yokohama BayStars	71	64	.511	10
Yakult Swallows	66	69	.474	15
Hiroshima Carp	57	78	.422	24
Hanshin Tigers	55	80	.412	26

INDIVIDUAL BATTING LEADERS
(Minimum 419 Plate Appearances)

	AVG	AB	R	H	2B	3B	HR	RBI	SB
Rose, Bobby, BayStars	.369	521	93	192	34	2	37	153	3
Sekikawa, Koichi, Dragons	.330	522	74	172	28	6	4	60	20
Suzuki, Takanori, BayStars	.328	542	110	178	31	6	17	92	7
Petagine, Roberto, Swallows	.325	452	97	147	23	3	44	112	10
Takahashi, Yoshinobu, Giants	.315	454	71	143	18	2	34	98	3
Manaka, Mitsuru, Swallows	.308	516	71	159	33	2	7	46	8
Ogata, Koichi, Carp	.305	495	111	151	23	3	36	69	18
Tsuboi, Tomochika, Tigers	.304	530	75	161	30	1	5	43	6
Matsui, Hideki, Giants	.304	471	100	143	24	2	42	95	0
Yano, Akihiro, Tigers	.304	369	39	112	13	2	3	27	5
Furuta, Atsuya, Swallows	.302	483	79	146	26	2	13	71	10
Maeda, Tomonori, Carp	.301	392	53	118	17	0	12	65	1
Nishi, Toshihisa, Giants	.298	510	79	152	28	4	9	42	18
Haru, Toshio, BayStars	.298	568	95	169	31	5	15	70	21
Gomez, Leo, Dragons	.297	474	84	141	19	1	36	109	4
#Ishii, Takuro, BayStars	.292	537	108	157	24	3	8	58	39
#Shinjo, Tsuyoshi, Tigers	.255	471	53	120	21	7	14	58	8

(Remaining U.S. and Latin Players)

	AVG	AB	R	H	2B	3B	HR	RBI	SB
Martinez, Domingo, Giants..	.324	262	31	85	14	0	16	56	1
Pozo, Arquimedez, BayStars	.297	229	31	68	9	0	9	30	0
Diaz, Eddy, Carp	.263	361	29	95	14	2	8	53	2
Smith, Mark, Swallows	.259	293	38	76	11	1	20	55	3
Johnson, Mark, Tigers	.253	376	52	95	23	1	20	66	1
Blowers, Mike, Tigers	.251	259	31	65	7	1	10	43	0
Perdomo, Felix, Carp	.200	45	3	9	3	0	1	4	0
Perez, Timoniel, Carp	.174	23	2	4	0	0	0	2	0
Liriano, Nelson, Dragons	.000	4	0	0	0	0	0	0	0

INDIVIDUAL PITCHING LEADERS
(Minimum 135 Innings)

	W	L	ERA	G	SV	IP	H	BB	SO
Uehara, Koji, Giants	20	4	2.38	25	0	198	153	24	179
Noguchi, Shigeki, Dragons..	19	7	2.65	29	0	204	202	67	145
Yamamoto, Masahiro, Dragons..	8	5	2.96	25	0	158	149	44	116
Kawamura, Takeo, BayStars	17	6	3.00	26	0	183	169	43	131
Sasaoka, Shinji, Carp	15	8	3.27	26	0	190	181	43	150
Takeda, Kazuhiro, Dragons ..	9	10	3.50	25	0	162	166	43	92
Galvez, Balvino, Giants	9	12	3.66	27	0	187	174	51	106
Takagi, Koji, Swallows	9	8	3.79	27	0	145	157	39	73
Kawasaki, Kenjiro, Swallows	7	11	3.85	24	0	166	188	41	79
Yabu, Keiichi, Tigers	6	16	3.95	28	0	173	175	57	95
Saito, Takashi, BayStars	14	3	3.95	26	0	185	178	31	125
Kuwata, Masumi, Giants	8	9	4.07	32	0	141	137	57	100

(Remaining U.S. and Latin Players)

	W	L	ERA	G	SV	IP	H	BB	SO
Rivera, Ben, Tigers	1	1	0.71	29	12	26	15	6	29
Dessens, Elmer, Giants	0	1	3.86	8	0	16	24	4	6
May, Darrell, Tigers	6	7	4.25	18	0	112	101	38	113
Jacome, Jason, Swallows ..	12	6	4.50	26	0	140	149	43	92

	W	L	ERA	G	SV	IP	H	BB	SO
Perdomo, Felix, Carp	1	2	4.56	17	0	26	24	10	25
Parra, Jose, Giants	2	3	5.32	12	0	47	43	23	25
Minchey, Nate, Carp	2	9	5.77	17	0	83	105	27	39
Miller, Kurt, Tigers	2	4	5.98	11	0	53	67	21	35
Batchelor, Rich, Swallows	0	0	7.94	7	0	6	7	1	2
DeHart, Rick, Carp	0	1	8.53	6	0	6	13	5	3
Pascual, Reinoso, Carp	0	2	9.00	0	0	13	13	13	4

PACIFIC LEAGUE

STANDINGS

	W	L	PCT	GB
Fukuoka Daiei Hawks	78	54	.591	—
Seibu Lions	75	59	.560	4
Orix BlueWave	68	65	.511	10½
Chiba Lotte Marines	63	70	.474	15½
Nippon Ham Fighters	60	73	.451	18½
Kintetsu Buffaloes	54	77	.412	23½

INDIVIDUAL BATTING LEADERS
(Minimum 419 Plate Appearances)

	AVG	AB	R	H	2B	3B	HR	RBI	SB
Suzuki, Ichiro, BlueWave	.343	411	80	141	27	2	21	68	12
Matsui, Kazuo, Lions	.330	539	87	178	29	4	15	67	32
Jojima, Kenji, Hawks	.306	493	65	151	33	1	17	77	6
Rhodes, Tuffy, Buffaloes	.301	491	94	148	38	1	40	101	3
Tani, Yoshitomo, BlueWave	.291	532	81	155	17	4	11	62	24
Clark, Phil, Buffaloes	.287	509	79	146	32	0	29	84	4
Ogasawara, Michihiro, Fighters	.285	547	90	156	34	4	25	83	3
Pulliam, Harvey, BlueWave	.280	446	59	125	21	0	20	85	0
Morozumi, Kenji, Marines	.280	432	56	121	19	5	2	33	10
Kosaka, Makoto, Marines	.280	482	64	135	18	10	3	40	31
Oshima, Koichi, BlueWave	.280	361	46	101	15	1	1	33	5
Yoshioka, Yuji, Buffaloes	.276	420	56	116	28	1	13	57	12
Yoshinaga, Koichiro, Hawks	.275	346	48	95	12	1	16	38	0
Kataoka, Atsushi, Fighters	.274	423	59	116	19	4	15	63	1
Kaneko, Makoto, Fighters	.274	416	56	114	17	3	3	29	4

(Remaining U.S. and Latin Players)

	AVG	AB	R	H	2B	3B	HR	RBI	SB
Obando, Sherman, Fighters	.306	346	49	106	23	0	20	62	0
Brede, Brent, Marines	.267	101	12	27	8	1	2	10	3
Neel, Troy, BlueWave	.262	252	37	66	8	0	17	52	1
Nieves, Melvin, Hawks	.257	245	37	63	16	1	17	43	0
Paul, Corey, Lions	.257	183	25	47	4	0	12	29	3
Perez, Robert, BlueWave	.253	166	16	42	10	2	2	23	0
Bolick, Frank, Marines	.250	348	50	87	17	1	26	61	1
Franklin, Micah, Fighters	.238	428	67	102	23	0	30	80	2
Zinter, Alan, Lions	.202	173	20	35	8	0	8	28	2
Blosser, Greg, Lions	.198	96	10	19	2	0	3	9	3
Gonzalez, Paul, BlueWave	.188	16	2	3	1	0	1	1	0
Cianfrocco, Archi, Lions	.163	43	3	7	0	0	2	5	2
Wilson, Nigel, Fighters	.136	22	1	3	0	0	0	0	0

INDIVIDUAL PITCHING LEADERS
(Minimum 135 Innings)

	W	L	ERA	G	SV	IP	H	BB	SO
Kudo, Kimiyasu, Hawks	11	7	2.38	26	0	196	143	34	196
Kuroki, Tomohiro, Marines	14	10	2.50	29	0	213	164	68	171
Matsuzaka, Daisuke, Lions	16	5	2.60	25	0	180	124	87	151
Kawagoe, Hidetaka, BlueWave	11	8	2.85	26	0	177	159	47	134
Nagai, Tomohiro, Hawks	10	5	3.06	27	0	141	124	70	98
Ishii, Takashi, Lions	13	8	3.07	26	0	179	177	43	108
Wakatabe, Kenichi, Hawks	10	6	3.29	26	0	159	153	42	114
Nishiguchi, Fumiya, Lions	14	10	3.41	29	0	179	141	55	141
Kaneda, Masahiko, BlueWave	11	10	3.49	30	0	188	165	76	116
Iwamoto, Tsutomu, Fighters	13	11	3.81	27	0	189	181	93	158

(Remaining U.S. and Latin Players)

	W	L	ERA	G	SV	IP	H	BB	SO
Manuel, Barry, Lions	0	0	0.00	1	0	1	0	1	0
Schullstrom, Erik, Fighters	2	1	1.69	14	7	16	15	2	21
Warren, Brian, Marines	1	2	1.82	49	30	54	38	7	25
Pedraza, Rod, Hakws	3	1	1.98	48	27	59	44	10	38
Hurtado, Edwin, BlueWave	4	2	2.29	34	4	63	53	39	44
Mimbs, Mark, BlueWave	3	6	3.42	42	1	76	77	27	43
Banks, Willie, BlueWave	3	3	3.94	13	1	30	27	21	26
De la Cruz, Fernando, Buffaloes	0	1	4.50	1	0	2	4	1	1
Mattson, Rob, Buffaloes	3	4	4.70	20	0	84	87	43	59
Valdez, Carlos, Buffaloes	3	4	4.84	48	8	58	51	32	35
Orellano, Rafael, Fighters	1	5	4.99	21	0	40	38	27	27
Leftwich, Phil, Buffaloes	4	6	5.25	15	0	70	73	32	52
Withem, Shannon, Fighters	6	7	5.76	17	0	86	116	36	31
Crawford, Joe, Marines	1	6	6.27	4	0	19	19	14	5
Hartgraves, Dean, Marines	0	2	7.45	3	0	10	11	10	4

TAIWAN

Taiwan professional baseball crowned two champions in 1999, but the real story was off the field.

The Mercury Tigers, one of the original four teams in the Chinese Professional Baseball League, announced they were folding after 10 years of operation.

Mercury officials said they hoped the elimination of the team will breathe new "health" into Taiwan baseball—a thinly veiled reference to underworld influence and game-fixing which has plagued the league for three seasons.

The Tigers are the second CPBL team to fold. The China Times Eagles officially dropped out after the 1998 season, a year after having all but one of their local players convicted on gambling-related charges.

The demise of the Tigers fueled speculation that other teams might fold, or that the entire league might suspend operations, as Taiwan's pro basketball league did in March.

On the field, the Weichuan Dragons won their third straight CPBL title, beating the regular season champion China Trust Whales four games to one in the championship series. It was Weichuan's fifth title in the 10 years of the league.

In the TML, the perennial doormat Taichung Robomen surprised the regular season champion Taipei Suns, 4-2, to take their first league championship.

Taichung championship series MVP Hsu Ming-chieh didn't stick around long. Three days after winning the title, the pitcher announced that he had signed with the Seibu Lions of Japan. Hsu is the first Taiwan player in six years to sign with a Japanese club.

In the CPBL, rookie pitcher Tsao Chun-yang was named league MVP.

—JEFFREY WILSON

CPBL

STANDINGS

	W	L	PCT	T	GB
China Trust Whales	60	29	.674	2	—
President Lions	56	37	.601	0	6
Weichuan Dragons	49	39	.557	4	10
Brother Elephants	39	52	.429	2	22
Mercury Tigers	37	53	.411	4	23
Sinon Bulls	30	61	.330	2	31

INDIVIDUAL BATTING LEADERS
(Minimum 282 Plate Appearances)

	AVG	AB	R	H	2B	3B	HR	RBI	SB
Hung Chi-feng, China Trust	.333	252	53	84	19	2	13	46	24
Chen Lien-hung, China Trust	.331	299	57	99	21	7	5	50	13
Cabrera, Alex, China Trust	.325	302	63	98	23	0	18	64	6
Wood, Ted, Brother	.322	329	51	106	18	2	19	68	12
Huang Kan-lin, President	.321	290	50	93	12	4	3	30	54
Chang Tai-shan, Weichuan	.321	327	60	105	12	3	17	70	18
Chen Kai-fa, Mercury	.316	310	51	98	13	7	9	35	8
Wang Kuang-hao, China Trust	.310	290	54	90	15	5	4	43	2
Cornelius, Brian, Mercury	.304	349	41	106	22	2	2	35	3
Parra, Juan, China Trust	.302	367	60	111	12	7	11	41	34

(Remaining U.S., Latin and Australian Players)

	AVG	AB	R	H	2B	3B	HR	RBI	SB
Olmeda, Jose, Mercury	.360	50	6	18	3	0	0	3	1
Mercedes, Rafaelito, China Trust	.333	12	6	4	1	0	0	3	2
Samuels, Scott, President	.333	111	30	37	7	1	6	23	12
Rodarte, Raul, President	.323	62	10	20	8	1	0	9	1
Martinez, Gabby, Mercury	.316	177	20	56	8	0	3	16	25
Bruno, Julio, Weichuan	.313	67	4	21	2	0	0	7	3
Kapano, Randy, President	.311	122	24	38	7	1	6	20	7
Batiste, Kim, China Trust	.308	13	2	4	1	0	0	2	0

Player	AVG	AB	R	H	2B	3B	HR	RBI	SB
Rodriguez, Luis, President..	.305	200	33	61	5	4	1	14	13
Hickey, Mike, Sinon	.304	92	8	28	4	1	4	13	1
Sievers, Carlos, Weichuan..	.295	78	12	23	4	1	2	14	1
Torres, Paul, Mercury	.288	66	6	19	5	0	1	8	0
Marrero, Oreste, Sinon	.287	167	29	48	6	0	8	25	5
Pegues, Steve, Mercury	.282	124	14	35	8	1	1	12	6
Mercedes, Guillermo, Brother	.278	331	41	92	12	1	2	30	13
De la Cruz, Lorenzo, President	.277	191	35	53	11	1	11	31	14
Maurer, Ron, Sinon	.264	163	22	43	9	0	6	31	1
Diaz, Remigio, President	.238	21	2	5	0	0	0	3	4
Kirkpatrick, Jay, Sinon	.234	145	16	34	5	0	3	14	0
Gonzalez, Jesus, China Trust	.231	26	3	6	1	0	1	3	0
Leyva, German, President	.227	22	3	5	0	0	0	0	0
Tatis, Bernie, Weichuan	.221	86	17	19	1	0	2	5	7
Ramirez, Robert, Weichuan	.154	13	1	2	0	0	0	0	0
Cruz, Fausto, China Trust	.143	35	2	5	0	0	0	0	0
Thomas, Keith, Mercury	.143	7	0	1	0	0	0	0	0
Lopez, Jose, Weichuan	.125	16	1	2	0	0	0	1	0
Held, Dan, President	.100	10	0	1	0	0	0	0	0
Pough, Pork Chop, Mercury	.000	5	0	0	0	0	0	0	0

INDIVIDUAL PITCHING LEADERS
(Minimum 91 Innings)

Player	W	L	ERA	G	SV	IP	H	BB	SO
Mirabel, Carlos, China Trust..	2	1	1.87	43	13	91	68	22	62
Lemon, Don, President	5	5	2.37	22	4	98	88	25	63
Hurst, Jonathan, Mercury	5	8	2.43	22	2	111	96	27	68
Kiefer, Mark, Sinon	6	10	2.45	30	2	198	153	72	155
Tsao Chun-yang, President	11	5	2.48	23	0	141	108	44	116
Henthorne, Kevin, China Trust..	15	5	2.48	26	1	181	165	47	121
Rivera, Lino, Mercury	8	10	2.66	26	0	152	142	40	116
Ozuna, Gab, Weichuan	10	5	2.69	26	0	167	159	39	127
Hsieh Chang-heng, President	10	5	2.86	20	1	104	103	24	52
Kuo Lee Chien-fu, China Trust	15	7	2.86	23	0	152	125	62	134

(Remaining U.S., Latin and Australian Players)

Player	W	L	ERA	G	SV	IP	H	BB	SO
Valdez, Armando, President..	5	0	1.26	10	1	35	25	10	27
Valdez, Efrain, China Trust...	2	0	1.52	11	0	23	21	3	14
Cruz, Javier, Weichuan	1	1	1.59	8	1	11	10	5	6
Turner, Matt, Weichuan	3	0	1.93	33	15	46	45	11	33
Drahman, Brian, President	4	3	1.98	36	22	59	50	12	68
Olivier, Rich, Brother	5	2	2.01	19	1	53	47	18	28
Jones, Calvin, China Trust	2	2	2.32	24	11	31	23	15	35
Garcia, Jose, Brother	2	3	2.34	45	15	65	60	15	32
Guzman, Geraldo, China Trust	0	0	2.48	9	1	13	15	3	6
Solano, Julio, Sinon	3	10	2.55	53	9	91	98	35	62
Richards, Dave, Mercury	0	0	2.70	6	2	6	3	1	6
Aguirre, Gaudencio, China Trust..	0	1	2.81	7	1	16	19	4	9
Valenzuela, Saul, Weichuan..	2	2	2.88	6	0	25	26	4	9
Jimenez, Miguel, President	1	1	3.00	8	0	15	12	12	16
Magee, Danny, President	8	4	3.00	25	0	111	82	60	95
Cano, Jose, Weichuan	7	5	3.12	18	0	106	93	42	74
Glinatsis, George, Sinon	0	2	3.12	5	0	17	18	12	14
Burgos, John, Mercury	5	9	3.15	30	4	125	128	34	85
Alston, Garvin, Weichuan	1	1	3.18	13	0	22	19	7	21
Darley, Ned, China Trust	1	1	3.21	28	2	42	36	28	38
Moreno, Angel, Weichuan	8	8	3.21	22	0	134	136	46	104
Matulevich, Jeff, Mercury	3	3	3.25	35	2	52	55	22	38
Alvarez, Juan, China Trust	3	1	3.27	5	0	22	25	7	10
Arriechi, Alejandro, Brother	0	0	3.38	4	0	13	10	7	5
Iglesias, Mike, Weichuan	1	3	3.39	16	1	58	66	25	27
Ramirez, Luis, President	0	2	3.42	15	5	26	23	10	9
Campos, Francisco, Brother..	0	3	3.57	3	0	22	20	3	12
Valera, Julio, President	8	4	3.59	28	0	105	115	32	69
Haught, Gary, Mercury	0	3	3.60	14	2	15	14	5	10
Martinez, Osvaldo, Sinon	8	15	3.83	30	1	178	181	54	135
Rivera, Oscar, Weichuan	2	2	3.83	8	0	40	55	23	16
Butler, Adam, Sinon	2	1	3.91	13	1	23	25	12	28
Revenig, Todd, Weichuan	7	5	3.92	23	3	64	69	14	33
Nieves, Ernie, President	1	0	3.94	10	0	16	28	5	13
Mimbs, Mike, Sinon	1	3	4.00	9	0	36	38	27	27
Kell, Rob, Sinon	2	5	4.13	18	1	69	71	37	60
Apana, Matt, Sinon	2	4	4.32	7	0	25	27	14	10
Rodriguez, Felix, Brother	2	4	4.40	8	0	47	41	24	27
Morillo, Santiago, Weichuan..	0	1	4.91	8	0	14	24	2	8
Abreu, Oscar, Brother	0	1	4.96	4	0	16	11	19	21
Mesa, Baltazar, Weichuan	0	0	5.23	8	0	10	14	8	8
Rosenkranz, Terry, Mercury..	1	1	5.25	3	0	12	20	8	9
Myers, Jimmy, Sinon	2	5	5.53	25	0	57	69	16	29
Gamez, Francisco, Weicihuan	2	4	5.63	11	0	32	45	22	21
Jones, Al, Brother	1	2	6.23	4	0	4	7	0	3
Perez, Julio, Brother	1	3	6.55	12	0	33	39	21	12
Burlingame, Ben, China Trust..	0	1	6.75	1	0	4	7	2	1
Woodson, Kerry, Brother	0	0	7.11	3	0	6	8	9	0
Marrero, Kenny, Mercury	0	2	7.52	15	0	32	41	10	20
Caruso, Gene, Brother	0	2	7.84	2	0	10	14	7	8
Rivera, Rafael, Weichuan	0	0	10.38	3	0	4	7	0	5

TAIWAN MAJOR LEAGUE

STANDINGS

	W	L	Pct.	T	GB
Taipei Suns	48	33	.593	3	—
Taichung Robomen	40	42	.488	2	8½
Chiayi Braves	40	42	.488	2	8½
Kaohsiung Thunder	36	47	.434	1	13

INDIVIDUAL BATTING LEADERS
(Minimum 260 Plate Appearances)

Player	AVG	AB	R	H	2B	3B	HR	RBI	SB
Strauss, Brad, Kao./Taichung	.387	248	61	96	16	5	11	57	10
Brewer, Rod, Chiayi	.364	283	62	103	23	4	19	71	2
Howard, Tim, Taichung	.349	335	67	117	18	6	15	48	26
Li Chu-ming, Kaohsiung	.338	281	33	95	12	3	3	34	5
Buckley, Matt, Chiayi	.336	226	44	76	22	2	2	33	12
Estrada, Manny, Taipei	.334	305	47	102	19	0	0	32	8
De los Santos, Luis, Kaohsiung	.317	306	54	97	25	3	11	58	2
Lin Kun-han, Taipei	.310	319	62	99	24	1	3	32	20
Powell, Corey, Kaohsiung ..	.307	336	70	103	20	0	25	66	7
Chiu Chang-jung, Taichung	.297	300	59	89	24	1	13	41	21

(Remaining U.S., Latin and Australian Players)

Player	AVG	AB	R	H	2B	3B	HR	RBI	SB
Hernandez, Alberto, Taichung	1.000	2	1	2	0	0	1	4	0
Paul, Corey, Taipei	.360	136	28	49	5	2	10	37	1
Byrne, Clayton, Taipei	.339	180	30	61	14	1	4	37	7
Lofton, James, Chiayi	.336	42	4	13	0	2	1	6	4
Campusano, Sil, Chiayi	.293	181	29	53	6	1	6	24	4
Rios, Eduardo, Taipei	.289	38	8	11	2	0	3	6	3
Charbonnet, Mark, Taipei....	.235	51	7	12	2	2	1	9	1
Cooper, Tim, Taichung	.226	31	7	7	2	0	1	4	3
Goldberg, Lonnie, Taichung	.224	154	29	36	7	0	1	12	24
Utting, Ben, Taichung	.220	82	13	18	3	2	1	6	2
Rhein, Jeff, Taipei	.182	44	8	8	2	0	1	5	3

INDIVIDUAL PITCHING LEADERS
(Minimum 84 Innings)

Player	W	L	ERA	G	SV	IP	H	BB	SO
Watanabe, Hisanobu, Chiayi	18	7	2.34	28	0	207	195	50	201
Tonkin, Shane, Taipei	7	7	2.73	33	4	171	139	52	105
Hsu Ming-chieh, Taichung ..	15	6	2.83	29	0	194	196	60	123
Curtis, Chris, Taipei	8	5	2.95	23	1	116	118	33	61
Liang Ju-hao, Taipei	14	7	3.09	34	2	169	160	66	135
Chen Hsien-hung, Taichung..	3	7	3.14	31	0	86	85	28	43
Chen Yi-hsin, Chiayi	11	14	3.38	28	0	200	231	41	136
Cederblad, Brett, Kaohsiung	7	6	3.55	17	0	106	97	29	67
Steed, Rick, Taichung	5	5	3.77	21	0	98	83	53	51
August, Don, Kaohsiung	5	13	3.82	25	0	162	198	52	89

(Remaining U.S., Latin, and Australian Players)

Player	W	L	ERA	G	SV	IP	H	BB	SO
Newman, Damon, Chiayi	1	0	1.50	3	0	6	3	3	3
Haynes, Heath, Taichung	0	0	2.21	19	8	29	27	6	29
Wisler, Brian, Taipei	2	1	2.21	8	1	20	18	5	14
Wishnevski, Rob, Taipei/Kao.	4	4	2.88	49	22	75	70	28	101
Bicknell, Greg, Chiayi	0	1	3.24	6	2	8	11	3	10
Knox, Kerry, Chiayi	3	7	3.87	34	13	74	84	32	67
Salcedo, Jose, Kaohsiung	2	4	4.08	12	2	35	39	12	25
Spears, Bob, Kaohsiung	1	3	4.53	15	4	51	56	30	41
Hemandez, Osvaldo, Kaohsiung ..	3	2	4.54	10	0	41	53	24	33
Kelly, John, Chia/Taichung..	8	6	4.80	21	1	90	102	33	64
Ettles, Mark, Taichung	0	2	5.19	14	3	17	26	3	16
Murray, Matt, Chiayi	2	4	5.64	9	0	52	71	34	16
White, Chris, Taichung	0	1	6.75	4	0	8	11	3	4
Narcisse, Tyrone, Taichung ..	0	1	7.24	8	0	13	14	10	10
Hampton, Mark, Taichung	0	2	9.95	5	1	12	15	14	13
Pinales, Aquiles, Kaohsiung..	0	0	13.50	4	0	5	7	4	7

KOREA

More important records were broken in 1999 than in any other season in Korea Baseball Organization history. But the year probably will be remembered for just one of the record-breakers: the one they call the Young Lion, Lee Seung-yeop of the Samsung Lions.

Lee, 24, became the most talked-about Asian player since Japan's Sadaharu Oh broke Hank Aaron's career home run record. He obliterated Korea's single-season record for homers, and nearly broke Oh's Asian record of 55.

Foreign Leagues

When Lee hit his 50th homer, he was on pace to break Oh's record by three. He then hit a 12-game homerless streak and finished the season one shy, at 54 in a 132-game season. Oh hit his 55 in a 140-game season.

In seven playoff games, Lee homered three more times to finish with 57 in 139 games. He set new league records for home runs, RBIs and walks, while finishing in the top 10 in batting.

The old league home run record was 42, set in 1998 by Tyrone Woods of the OB Bears. Lee finished with 38 that year after fading in the last two months.

Foreign players heavily influenced most of the league's teams. Former major league outfielder Felix Jose turned around the Lotte Giants, a club that brought up the rear of the league for many years. Jay Davis and Dan Rohrmeier had a similar effect on the Hanwha Eagles.

Those two teams met in the Korean Series, with Hanwha winning four games to one.

—THOMAS ST. JOHN

STANDINGS

DREAM LEAGUE	W	L	PCT	GB
Doosan Bears	76	51	.598	—
Lotte Giants	75	52	.591	1
Hyundai Unicorns	68	59	.535	8
Haitai Tigers	60	69	.465	17
MAGIC LEAGUE	W	L	PCT	GB
Samsung Lions	73	57	.562	—
Hanwha Unicorns	72	58	.554	1
LG Twins	61	70	.466	12½
Ssangbangwool Raiders	28	97	.224	42½

INDIVIDUAL BATTING LEADERS
(Minimum 400 At-Bats)

	AVG	AB	R	H	HR	RBI	SB
Ma Hae-yong, Lotte	.372	503	111	187	35	119	6
Lee Byung-kyu, LG	.349	550	117	192	30	99	31
Chang Sung-ho, Haitai	.342	485	110	166	24	62	5
Kim Han-su, Samsung	.340	497	87	169	18	89	7
Shim Jong-su, Doosan	.325	480	79	161	31	110	1
Lee Yong-woo, Hanwha	.334	425	83	142	13	49	16
Park Jong-tae, Lotte	.329	456	83	150	11	83	0
Davis, Jay, Hanwha	.328	525	93	172	30	106	35
Jose, Felix, Lotte	.327	462	93	151	36	122	12
Chong Su-kun, Doosan	.325	505	100	164	2	55	57

(Remaining North Americans)

	AVG	AB	R	H	HR	RBI	SB
Woods, Tyrone, Doosan	.297	454	90	135	34	101	5
Rohrmeier, Dan, Hanwha	.292	487	91	142	45	109	6
Bowers, Brent, Hyundai	.290	124	17	36	3	12	0
Pearson, Eddie, Hyundai	.287	502	67	145	31	108	0
Smith, Bubba, Samsung	.287	408	70	117	40	98	1
Briggs, Stoney, Haitai	.283	382	48	102	23	74	21
Dattola, Kevin, LG	.279	263	33	74	9	42	0
Felix, Junior, LG	.253	336	53	85	13	58	1
Caceres, Edgar, Doosan	.250	168	21	42	3	17	2
Sanders, Tracy, Haitai	.247	409	86	101	40	94	3
Hall, Billy, Samsung	.244	414	73	101	4	23	47
Canale, George, Hyundai	.184	38	2	7	1	3	0

INDIVIDUAL PITCHING LEADERS
(Minimum 120 Innings)

	W	L	ERA	G	SV	IP	H	BB	SO
Im Chang-yong, Samsung	13	4	2.14	71	38	139	91	29	141
Chong Min-tae, Hyundai	20	7	2.54	33	3	177	169	63	178
Lee Kyung-pil, Doosan	13	7	3.18	28	0	167	161	55	91
Moon Dong-hwan, Lotte	17	4	3.28	30	0	189	171	67	141
Park Seok-jin, Lotte	11	3	3.28	33	2	148	123	44	101
Chong Min-chul, Hanwha	18	8	3.58	32	1	202	179	57	151
Ju Hyung-kwang, Lotte	18	12	3.98	31	1	190	190	190	177
Song Jin-woo, Hanwha	15	5	4.00	35	6	187	180	61	132

(Remaining North Americans)

	W	L	ERA	G	SV	IP	H	BB	SO
Giron, Emiliano, Lotte	5	1	3.30	24	2	74	59	33	57
Viano, Jake, Ssang	3	3	7.06	29	0	73	88	55	37
Anderson, Mike, Ssang	2	9	6.75	19	0	69	94	41	31
Guilfoyle, Mike, Lotte	0	0	13.50	6	1	6	10	4	3

ITALY

Wood bats were re-introduced to Serie A/1, the Italian elite league, several weeks into the 1999 season, with predictable results. A power shortage ensued immediately and lasted for the rest of the summer. On average, only 0.78 home runs were hit per game during the regular season.

Bologna righthander Ercilio DeLeon (9-6, 3.11) threw a rain-shortened no-hitter against Collecchio early in the campaign. Former St. Louis Cardinals and Detroit Tigers lefthander Tom Urbani later pitched a perfect game for Rimini against San Marino.

The home team won all seven games in the national championship finals. Rimini prevailed to claim its first Italian title since 1992.

Parma won the European Cup, the continental club championship, with the help of ex-big league righthander Willie Fraser. In an all-Italian tournament final, Fraser threw a three-hitter as Parma defeated Nettuno 6-0.

STANDINGS

	W	L	PCT	GB
Rimini	40	8	.833	—
Nettuno	31	17	.646	9
Grosseto	29	19	.604	11
Parma	29	19	.604	11
Bologna	23	25	.479	17
Caserta	23	25	.479	17
Modena	19	29	.396	21
San Marino	14	34	.292	26
Collecchio	8	40	.167	32

HOLLAND

Former major league infielder Robert Eenhoorn made a triumphant return to his native land in 1999. The former New York Yankee and Anaheim Angel led Neptunus to the Dutch Major League pennant and a Holland Series victory over HCAW, the defending champion.

Neptunus Stadium in Rotterdam was officially opened for the biennial World Port Tournament, which saw the Dutch national team defeat a representative Cuban team for the first time in more than 30 attempts.

The Netherlands defeated Italy in the finals of the European Championships. Both countries qualified for the 2000 Olympics.

STANDINGS

	W	L	PCT	GB
Neptunus	38	7	.844	—
Kinheim	31	14	.689	7
HCAW	29	16	.644	9
Hoofddorp Pioniers	27	16	.622	10
Amsterdam Expos	27	18	.600	11
Sparta/Feyenoord	24	21	.533	14
ADO	21	24	.467	17
RCH	13	32	.289	25
Tilburg	7	36	.178	30
Twins	6	39	.133	32

WINTER BASEBALL

Dominicans squander one opportunity, but rally to win third straight Caribbean title

BY JOHN ROYSTER

Fans at the 1999 Caribbean World Series in San Juan, Puerto Rico, got an extra game to watch. And it was well worth seeing.

Licey of the Dominican Republic defeated Mayaguez of Puerto Rico 6-5 in 12 innings, after blowing a golden opportunity to close out the series the day before.

The Tigers carried a 5-0 lead over Mayaguez into the eighth inning of the final game of the double round-robin phase of the four-nation tournament.

Three errors and six runs later, Mayaguez had an improbable 6-5 win to force the extra game. Infielder Edwards Guzman (Giants) drove in outfielder Jose Cruz Jr. (Blue Jays) with the winning run, singling over the head of Licey shortstop Neifi Perez (Rockies). Licey committed six errors in the game.

Neifi Perez

For a while, the deciding game looked like a replay. Licey took a 4-1 lead after three innings, with two of the runs coming on a home run by first baseman David Ortiz (Twins).

Neither team scored again until the seventh, when the Indians tallied two runs to cut the deficit to 4-3. Mayaguez, which had mounted several comebacks during the regular season and the Puerto Rican League playoffs, completed its last one when left fielder Wil Cordero (Indians) homered to lead off the ninth against Cardinals righthander Manny Aybar, tying the score 4-4.

In the end, it was Licey that erased a deficit and won the championship, the third straight by a team from the Dominican Republic. Aguilas had won the previous two series and six of the past 10.

Mayaguez first baseman Boi Rodriguez hit his third home run in as many days to give the Indians a 5-4 lead in the top of the 12th.

But pinch-hitter Luis Castillo (Marlins) singled to lead off the bottom of the inning, and things began to unravel for Mayaguez. An out later, Castillo stole second and moved to third on a wild pitch by Mayaguez closer Miguel Alicea.

Alicea then walked second baseman Ron Belliard (Brewers), another good basestealer, and was replaced by lefthander Eddie Priest (Reds) for the purpose of holding Belliard at first base. Belliard stole second anyway, and after an intentional walk, Ortiz hit a liner that landed just inside the left-field foul line, driving home the tying and winning runs.

"We were aggressive on the basepaths all winter, and I figured that would be the key to our success in this tournament," said Licey manager Dave Jauss (Red Sox). "Mayaguez had done a good job of shutting us

1999 CARIBBEAN WORLD SERIES

San Juan, Puerto Rico
Feb. 2-8, 1999

ROUND-ROBIN STANDINGS

	W	L	PCT.	GB
Dominican Republic (Licey)	5	2	.714	—
Puerto Rico (Mayaguez)	4	3	.667	1
Venezuela (Lara)	2	4	.333	2½
Mexico (Mexicali)	2	4	.333	2½

INDIVIDUAL BATTING LEADERS
(Minimum 17 Plate Appearances)

	AVG	AB	R	H	2B	3B	HR	RBI	SB
Mendoza, Carlos, Venez.	.500	18	1	9	1	0	0	1	1
Garcia, Karim, Mexico	.500	14	3	7	2	0	2	6	0
Polonia, Luis, DR	.474	19	6	9	2	0	0	0	2
Perez, Neifi, DR	.400	30	6	12	1	0	1	6	2
Brinkley, Darryl, Mexico	.393	28	3	11	2	0	0	5	0
Chamberlain, W., Ven.	.389	18	7	7	2	0	3	6	0
Magallanes, Ever, Mex.	.381	21	5	8	2	0	2	7	0
Martinez, Ray, Mexico	.350	20	3	7	2	1	0	1	1
Belliard, Ron, DR	.308	26	6	8	3	0	0	1	6
Rodriguez, Boi, PR	.308	26	9	8	2	0	3	4	2
Beltre, Adrian, DR	.280	25	4	7	2	0	0	1	3
Castellano, Pedro, Ven.	.263	19	1	5	0	0	1	0	0

INDIVIDUAL PITCHING LEADERS
(Minimum 6 Innings)

	W	L	ERA	G	SV	IP	H	BB	SO
Batista, Miguel, DR	0	0	0.00	2	0	8	2	0	10
Vazquez, Javier, PR	1	0	0.00	1	0	6	4	0	7
Rosado, Jose, PR	1	0	0.77	2	0	12	7	3	13
Aybar, Manny, DR	1	0	1.35	2	0	7	4	2	3
Perez, Dario, DR	1	0	1.80	2	0	10	7	5	6
Chavez, Anthony, DR	2	0	2.84	5	0	6	5	0	9
Lopez, Johan, Venez	0	1	3.00	1	0	6	5	2	7
Dessens, Elmer, Mexico	0	0	3.00	1	0	6	5	0	3
Lopez, Emigdio, Mexico	1	1	3.68	3	0	15	12	7	5
De los Santos, Valerio, DR	1	0	3.68	2	0	7	6	4	4

ALL-TOURNAMENT TEAM: C—Ben Molina, Puerto Rico. **1B**—Boi Rodriguez, Puerto Rico. **2B**—Ever Magallanes, Mexico. **3B**—Adrian Beltre, Dominican Republic. **SS**—Neifi Perez, Dominican Republic. **OF**—Karim Garcia, Mexico; Carlos Mendoza, Venezuela; Luis Polonia, Dominican Republic. **DH**—Wes Chamberlain, Venezuela. **RHP**—Dario Perez, Dominican Republic. **LHP**—Jose Rosado, Puerto Rico. **RP**—Miguel Batista, Dominican Republic.

Most Valuable Player—Neifi Perez, Dominican Republic.

down in our second meeting, but we're a dangerous team when we get our leadoff man on."

Ortiz had gone just 4-for-21 in the Caribbean Series before his third-inning home run. Perez, who batted .400 with a homer in an earlier game, was named the series MVP for the second straight year.

Licey emerged from the playoffs in a Dominican League that was temporarily down to four teams. Hurricane Georges had ripped through the Dominican Republic in the fall of 1998, causing damage to ballparks that forced Azucareros and Estrellas to sit out the season.

The financially troubled Australian Baseball League was sold shortly after the winter to a group including Milwaukee Brewers catcher David Nilsson, an Australia native. The league played the 1998-99 season with six teams instead of the usual eight, but the new owners hoped to go back to eight.

1998-99 WINTER ALL-STAR TEAM

Selected by Baseball America

Player, Club (League)	Organization	AVG	AB	R	H	2B	3B	HR	RBI	SB
C Ramon Hernandez, Occidente (Venezuela)	Athletics	.294	265	22	78	13	0	6	34	1
1B Erubiel Durazo, Hermosillo (Mexico)	Diamondbacks	.334	272	58	91	23	1	14	59	2
2B Jose Vidro, Ponce (Puerto Rico)	Expos	.364	209	41	76	14	0	12	35	5
3B Adrian Beltre, Aguilas (Dom. Republic)	Dodgers	.288	267	44	77	11	0	11	41	20
SS Neifi Perez, Escogido (Dom. Republic)	Rockies	.304	207	36	63	7	1	4	34	10
OF Bob Abreu, Caracas (Venezuela)	Phillies	.390	213	43	83	15	3	4	46	17
Jacque Jones, Obregon (Mexico)	Twins	.343	251	40	86	18	1	8	30	12
Carlos Mendoza, Magallanes (Venezuela)	Devil Rays	.374	243	49	91	8	7	0	29	15
DH Luis Raven, Occidente/Caracas (Venez.)	White Sox	.307	349	53	107	17	0	25	72	1

		W	L	ERA	G	SV	IP	H	BB	SO
P Greg Beck, Caracas (Venezuela)	Brewers	11	2	3.05	19	0	118	122	21	49
Octavio Dotel, Escogido (Dom. Republic)	Mets	5	0	2.49	11	0	47	45	15	49
Eric Ludwick, Ponce (Puerto Rico)	Blue Jays	5	2	2.03	12	0	71	45	19	64
Mike Romano, Lara (Venezuela)	Blue Jays	12	3	2.78	20	0	107	85	39	61
RP Orber Moreno, Caracas (Venezuela)	Royals	3	0	1.32	36	15	41	29	15	38

PLAYER OF THE YEAR: Bob Abreu, Caracas (Venezuela).
Statistics include regular season, playoff and Caribbean World Series games.

DOMINICAN LEAGUE

It was anything but business as usual in the Dominican League in 1998-99, as Hurricane Georges rendered two stadiums unusable shortly before the season began.

Georges caused an estimated $2 billion in damage and killed more than 200 people when it made landfall in late September. The damage to both Francisco Micheli Stadium in La Romana and Tetelo Vargas Stadium in San Pedro de Macoris was extensive and, with other needs more pressing, no money was available to fix them.

The league cut down to four teams for the season, running a dispersal draft to temporarily distribute players from Azucareros and Estrellas to the other clubs.

On the field, Escogido won nine of its last 10 games to tie Aguilas, then beat Aguilas in a one-game playoff to claim the regular season title and the top seed in the playoffs.

But in the playoffs, third-place Licey claimed the league championship. Led by shortstop Ron Belliard (Brewers), the Tigers beat Aguilas three games to one and Escogido five games to four. Escogido took a 7-6 lead to the ninth inning of the decisive ninth game, but Licey erupted for four runs against ace closer Anthony Chavez (Athletics), who did not allow an earned run in 24 regular season appearances and led the league with 10 saves.

Belliard was named MVP of both the semifinals and finals. He hit a combined .426 in the two series with a homer and 12 RBIs.

Adrian Beltre

Aguilas third baseman Adrian Beltre (Dodgers) was named the league MVP after becoming only the third player in league history to reach double figures in home runs and stolen bases. Beltre hit .301 with 10 homers and stole 17 bases.

Escogido third baseman Freddy Garcia (Pirates) led the league with 14 homers, tying Dick Stuart's league record, and 41 RBIs.

The Nordeste Giants struggled all season, losing their final 30 games and all 20 games to Escogido. They had more rainouts (11) than wins (nine) and went through three managers.

STANDINGS

REGULAR SEASON	W	L	PCT	GB
Escogido Lions	40	21	.656	—
Aguilas	39	22	.639	1
Licey Tigers	33	27	.560	6 ½
Nordeste Giants	9	51	.150	30 ½

PLAYOFFS—Semifinals: Licey defeated Aguilas, 3-1, in best-of-5 series. Championship Series: Licey defeated Escogido, 5-4, in best-of-9 series.

Statistics in **boldface** indicate league leader.
#Indicates league leader but non-qualifier.

INDIVIDUAL BATTING LEADERS
(Minimum 135 Plate Appearances)

	AVG	AB	R	H	2B	3B	HR	RBI	SB
Polonia, Luis, Aguilas	.336	217	38	**73**	10	1	1	17	**19**
Castillo, Luis, Licey	.317	145	22	46	5	2	0	16	10
Perez, Neifi, Escogido	.314	140	27	44	6	1	3	25	6
Espinosa, Ramon, Escogido	.310	187	23	58	8	2	3	20	2
Beltre, Adrian, Aguilas	.301	226	39	68	9	0	10	37	17
Cruz, Fausto, Nordeste	.297	172	18	51	5	1	4	23	0
Herrera, Jesus, Escogido	.287	129	16	37	6	1	1	7	4
Ortiz, David, Escogido	.286	154	23	44	**12**	2	4	28	0
Ramirez, Omar, Aguilas	.282	142	21	40	8	1	1	18	6
McEwing, Joe, Aguilas	.278	126	10	35	**12**	0	1	14	2
Batista, Tony, Aguilas	.277	188	34	52	8	0	8	33	7
Perez, Santiago, Nordeste	.274	157	15	43	11	**3**	0	15	6
#Campos, Jesus, Nordeste	.273	121	13	33	2	**3**	0	6	2
Tejada, Miguel, Aguilas	.261	203	33	53	10	1	5	29	13
Castillo, Alberto, Aguilas	.260	131	19	34	5	0	5	21	3
Garcia, Freddy, Escogido	.259	232	**39**	60	10	2	**14**	**41**	0
Parra, Franklin, Nordeste	.250	148	12	37	6	1	0	9	0
Nunez, Abraham, Escogido	.247	170	26	32	6	0	1	17	6

INDIVIDUAL PITCHING LEADERS
(Minimum 40 Innings)

	W	L	ERA	G	SV	IP	H	BB	SO
#Chavez, Anthony, Escogido	3	0	0.00	24	**10**	27	11	8	33
Ramirez, Hector, Aguilas	2	1	**1.18**	18	0	46	37	12	29
Dotel, Octavio, Escogido	5	0	1.29	9	0	42	36	7	42
Cruz, Nelson, Escogido	6	1	1.74	10	0	52	44	9	47
#Batista, Miguel, Aguilas	6	3	2.04	16	1	35	26	7	31
Santana, Julio, Escogido	6	2	2.49	12	0	62	50	20	32
Hernandez, Fernando, Aguilas	6	3	2.71	14	0	70	46	30	**74**
Perez, Dario, Licey	5	2	2.74	12	0	62	57	7	29

Aybar, Manny, Licey	5	3	2.79	10	0	48	49	13	34
Dedrick, Jim, Licey	4	3	2.87	12	0	60	47	14	36
Magee, Bo, Aguilas	0	0	3.83	12	0	47	40	20	40
Rodriguez, Nerio, Nordeste	2	7	3.92	12	0	62	59	25	26

MEXICAN PACIFIC LEAGUE

The Mexicali Eagles, who finished in fourth place in the regular season, soared through the playoffs en route to the 1998-99 Mexican Pacific League championship.

Mexicali went 12-3 in its romp through the postseason. The Eagles split the first two games at home against Culiacan in the best-of-seven final, then wrapped up the series with three straight wins at Culiacan, earning their first trip to the Caribbean World Series in 10 years.

The turning point in the championship series came in Game Four with Mexicali trailing 2-0 entering the ninth inning. Eduardo Jimenez' two-run homer keyed a three-run uprising that resulted in a 3-2 win and a 3-1 series lead.

Third baseman George Arias (Padres) and closer Isidro Marquez led Mexicali in its postseason surge. Arias hit eight homers and drove in 19 runs in the three playoff series. He hit .450 with a homer and seven RBIs in the final. Marquez led the league with 13 saves during the regular season and added five more in postseason play. He went 2-0 and did not allow a run in 11 appearances.

Erubiel Durazo

JOHN SPEAR

Culiacan, which slumped badly in the second half, needed seven games to beat Hermosillo in the semifinals. Legendary Fernando Valenzuela, who went 3-0 with a 1.44 ERA in five regular season starts, started for Hermosillo in the deciding game but left in the third inning after giving up three runs and was charged with a 5-2 loss.

Hermosillo first baseman Erubiel Durazo challenged for a triple crown before falling short. He led the league with 48 RBIs and finished second with 12 home runs, two shy of league leader Bubba Smith. Durazo's .345 batting average was four points behind league leader Matt Stark. The young star was named the league's rookie of the year and signed with the Diamondbacks, for whom he became a sensation both in the minor and major leagues in 1999.

STANDINGS

REGULAR SEASON

	W	L	PCT	GB
Obregon Yaquis	38	29	.567	—
Hermosillo Orange Growers	38	29	.567	—
Los Mochis Sugarcane Growers	37	30	.552	1
Mexicali Eagles	35	32	.522	3
Guasave Cottoneers	35	32	.522	3
Culiacan Tomato Growers	32	35	.478	6
Mazatlan Deer	28	40	.412	10½
Navojoa Mayos	26	42	.382	12½

PLAYOFFS—Quarterfinals: Culiacan defeated Obregon, 4-1; Hermosillo defeated Guasave, 4-2; and Mexicali defeated Los Mochis, 4-2, in best-of-7 series. **Semifinals:** Culiacan defeated Hermosillo, 4-3; and Mexicali defeated Guasave, 4-0, in best-of-7 series. **Finals:** Mexicali defeated Culiacan, 4-1, in best-of-7 series.

INDIVIDUAL BATTING LEADERS
(Minimum 184 Plate Appearances)

	AVG	AB	R	H	2B	3B	HR	RBI	SB
Stark, Matt, Culiacan	.349	189	31	66	10	0	7	44	0
Williams, Eddie, Hermosillo	.346	217	58	75	13	0	12	44	2
Durazo, Erubiel, Hermosillo	.345	223	51	77	21	1	12	48	2
Jones, Jacque, Obregon	.343	251	40	86	18	1	8	30	12
White, Derrick, Mexicali	.322	233	45	75	15	0	6	31	8
Garcia, Luis, Hermosillo	.319	213	27	68	8	2	5	36	4
Leach, Jalal, Guasave	.314	245	39	77	20	1	4	37	13
Gil, Benji, Culiacan	.309	178	35	55	9	5	2	25	11
Martinez, Greg, Guasave	.306	209	36	64	4	2	2	19	12
Canizalez, Juan, Hermosillo	.304	204	39	62	15	3	4	40	3
Agbayani, Benny, LM	.303	218	31	66	9	1	5	39	4
Mendez, Roberto, Guasave	.294	160	28	47	10	0	5	23	8
Rodriguez, F., Mazatlan	.293	174	15	51	9	0	0	18	1
Ball, Jeff, Guasave	.291	213	36	62	10	1	3	18	9
Beamon, Trey, Los Mochis	.290	224	44	65	15	0	2	35	23
Garcia, Cornelio, Hermosillo	.288	170	29	49	4	2	1	6	9
Guizar, Hector, Guasave	.284	204	28	58	6	0	1	15	1
Seitzer, Brad, Guasave	.283	198	42	56	11	2	7	36	2
Jimenez, Eduardo, Mexicali	.282	195	32	54	15	0	11	46	0
Rojas, Homar, Obregon	.278	198	21	55	11	0	6	31	2
Guiel, Aaron, Mexicali	.277	195	32	54	8	0	10	32	3
Alvarez, Hector, Navojoa	.277	188	20	52	6	1	1	20	1
Smith, Bubba, Mazatlan	.277	188	34	52	8	0	14	39	3
Jimenez, Alfonso, Obregon	.276	217	25	60	17	0	1	20	5
Doster, David, Hermosillo	.276	225	38	61	11	0	4	37	7
Fernandez, Daniel, Mazatlan	.272	162	24	44	7	1	1	14	1
Roberts, Dave, Los Mochis	.272	151	33	41	5	0	2	18	20
Esquer, Ramon, Navojoa	.270	163	21	44	5	2	0	10	6
Sherman, Darrell, Culiacan	.267	221	38	59	10	1	1	21	26
#Salas, Heriberto, Guasave	.253	194	20	49	8	5	1	30	3

INDIVIDUAL PITCHING LEADERS
(Minimum 54 Innings)

	W	L	ERA	G	SV	IP	H	BB	SO
#Federico, Gustavo, Obregon	3	2	1.14	25	13	32	25	15	21
Hernandez, Jose, Culiacan	7	2	2.00	13	0	85	75	24	33
Garcia, Jose, Mazatlan	6	3	2.30	18	1	55	49	19	26
#Marquez, Isidro, Mexicali	4	1	2.35	28	13	31	28	13	24
Sinohui, David, Navojoa	1	1	2.37	24	0	68	53	37	40
Lomon, Kevin, Hermosillo	6	4	2.41	13	0	75	58	42	44
Garibay, Daniel, Mazatlan	6	5	2.73	14	0	96	79	36	77
Garcia, Alfredo, Obregon	6	3	2.74	14	0	85	86	33	32
Higuera, Ted, Los Mochis	5	1	2.77	13	0	65	49	43	42
Moreno, Leobardo, Obregon	5	2	2.81	14	0	74	66	36	54
Bailey, Cory, Culiacan	3	5	2.91	14	2	59	47	28	43
Rios, Jesus, Guasave	5	2	2.92	16	0	89	71	43	63
Rodriguez, Salvador, Obregon	8	4	2.93	13	0	92	91	29	50
Lopez, Rodrigo, Culiacan	2	5	2.93	13	0	77	51	30	52
Bernal, Manuel, Obregon	5	4	3.14	11	0	72	63	23	50
Ruiz, Cecilio, Obregon	6	3	3.30	11	1	57	59	18	24
Chavez, Carlos, Los Mochis	3	3	3.33	19	0	54	40	38	39
Esquer, Mercedes, Guasave	2	5	3.39	12	0	61	62	25	39
Gonzalez, Gilberto, Guasave	5	4	3.48	14	0	78	63	57	48
Gamez, Francisco, Her/Nav	4	1	3.49	24	0	59	51	43	36

PUERTO RICAN LEAGUE

The Mayaguez Indians, who barely finished above .500 in the regular season, lost just one of 10 playoff games and stormed away with the 1998-99 Puerto Rican League championship. They beat regular season champion Ponce decisively in the best-of-nine final, five games to one.

Ponce hit a meager .195 in the series and second baseman Jose Vidro (Expos), who won the batting title with a .417 average, slumped to .192 with one RBI. Mayaguez shortstop Jose Valentin (Brewers), who hit .320, scored nine runs and drove in seven, was selected MVP of the finals.

After splitting the first two games, the Indians ran off four straight wins, including a 2-1, 13-inning victory to clinch the series.

Vidro, a unanimous selection as the league's MVP despite missing 13 games because of an injury, won the batting title by more than 80 points. His .417 average was the highest in the league since Edgar Martinez hit .424 in 1990.

Jose Vidro

Vidro continued his hot hitting in the semifinals against Arecibo, as the Lions swept the Wolves in four straight games. Vidro hit .400 in the series. In the other semifinal, Mayaguez swept Santurce as second baseman Jose Munoz hit .333 with two homers and seven RBIs in the four-game sweep.

Ponce righthander Eric Ludwick (Blue Jays) was the pitching star of the league, going 4-1 with a league-best 1.33 ERA. Ludwick struck out 55 in 54 innings.

Hurricane Georges damaged many of the league's ballparks, but unlike in the Dominican Republic, all six teams were able to play the season.

STANDINGS

REGULAR SEASON	W	L	PCT	GB
Ponce Lions	29	18	.617	—
Santurce Crabbers	26	22	.542	3 ½
Mayaguez Indians	26	24	.520	4 ½
Arecibo Wolves	23	26	.469	7
San Juan Senators	21	28	.429	9
Caguas Criollos	21	28	.429	9

PLAYOFFS—Semifinals: Ponce defeated Arecibo, 4-0, and Mayaguez defeated Santurce, 4-0, in best-of-7 series. **Finals:** Mayaguez defeated Ponce, 5-1, in best-of-9 series.

INDIVIDUAL BATTING LEADERS
(Minimum 135 Plate Appearances)

	AVG	AB	R	H	2B	3B	HR	RBI	SB
Vidro, Jose, Ponce	.417	144	33	60	12	0	10	30	5
Villanueva, Hector, San Juan	.335	155	23	52	6	0	10	31	2
Diaz, Alex, Mayaguez	.333	177	37	59	20	0	6	26	21
Rodriguez, Boi, Mayaguez	.324	170	26	55	13	0	11	37	17
Cruz, Jose, Santurce	.319	166	34	53	9	1	6	29	5
Garcia, Omar, Arecibo	.316	177	19	56	8	2	4	29	0
Beltran, Carlos, Arecibo	.311	151	28	47	7	3	9	28	6
Gonzalez, Raul, San Juan	.310	174	21	54	7	1	4	22	0
Lucca, Lou, Mayaguez	.310	171	24	53	9	1	9	29	2
Crespo, Felipe, Caguas	.309	136	27	42	8	0	2	17	2
Vaz, Roberto, Arecibo	.302	169	21	51	12	2	4	15	6
Valentin, Jose, Mayaguez	.293	164	34	48	12	2	9	31	5
Martinez, Ramon, San Juan	.290	145	18	42	10	1	3	14	2
Otero, Ricky, Caguas	.289	135	8	39	11	0	1	8	2
Sierra, Ruben, Santurce	.285	172	29	49	14	1	7	31	2
Berg, Dave, Ponce	.281	146	23	41	6	1	2	19	4
Rodriguez, Victor, Arecibo	.273	161	25	44	8	0	1	14	1
Cora, Alex, Caguas	.269	130	15	35	7	3	2	15	5
Diaz, Edwin, Santurce	.259	158	18	41	8	0	2	20	7
Correa, Miguel, Ponce	.250	168	30	42	11	0	6	18	13
Guzman, Edwards, Mayaguez	.246	167	23	41	9	0	3	14	1
Lopez, Luis, Caguas	.239	184	24	44	6	0	3	19	3
LeBron, Juan, Caguas/SJ	.236	127	14	30	2	0	5	17	3
Ibanez, Raul, Santurce	.236	174	26	41	9	0	4	18	1
Latham, Chris, San Juan	.234	167	29	39	8	4	4	19	12
Young, Ernie, San Juan	.232	155	21	36	5	1	13	35	3
Vargas, Hector, Arecibo	.227	141	12	32	5	0	1	16	0

INDIVIDUAL PITCHING LEADERS
(Minimum 40 Innings)

	W	L	ERA	G	SV	IP	H	BB	SO
#Romero, J.C., Santurce	2	0	0.43	20	11	21	14	6	19
Ludwick, Eric, Ponce	4	1	1.33	9	0	54	31	14	55
Gonzalez, Dicky, San Juan	2	1	1.80	12	0	45	42	12	27
Priest, Eddie, Mayaguez	5	2	1.94	11	0	60	55	11	37
#Flury, Pat, Arecibo	6	2	2.67	24	4	34	22	18	27
DeSilva, John, Arecibo	3	4	3.08	11	0	61	51	28	52
Valera, Julio, Mayaguez	3	3	3.10	13	1	70	67	23	54
Pineiro, Joel, Ponce	2	0	3.20	12	0	51	43	18	39
Montalvo, Rafael, San Juan	3	3	3.23	16	1	47	44	14	25

Watkins, Scott, Santurce	3	2	3.32	10	0	57	46	19	39
Linton, Doug, Caguas	3	5	3.38	13	0	64	63	9	56
Krivda, Rick, Santurce	2	1	3.57	6	0	40	35	15	21
Weaver, Eric, Ponce	3	2	3.79	11	0	57	55	29	46
Pittsley, Jim, San Juan	1	2	4.07	9	0	42	51	14	34
Forster, Scott, Arecibo	2	4	5.23	11	0	43	44	26	22
Cepeda, Victor, Mayaguez	0	2	6.47	15	0	40	47	18	25

VENEZUELAN LEAGUE

For the second straight year, the Lara Cardinals rode stellar pitching to defeat the Caracas Lions and win the Venezuelan League championship. The Cardinals beat the Lions four games to two in the finals, after winning 4-3 a year earlier.

Righthander Mike Romano (Blue Jays) led Lara to the best overall record in the regular season by going 8-1 with a 2.49 ERA, and responded in the final, going 2-0, 1.42 in 19 innings.

Lara reached the finals thanks in large part to righthander Edwin Hurtado (Orix BlueWave, Japan). Hurtado went 4-0 with a 1.76 ERA in the five-team, 16-game round-robin segment of the playoffs.

But the best individual player in the league was Caracas outfielder Bob Abreu, Baseball America's Winter Player of the Year. Abreu (Phillies) hit .419 during the regular season, the highest average in league history. He batted .422 with 16 RBIs in the round-robin, but struggled against Lara's pitching in the finals, hitting .160.

Bob Abreu

Occidente outfielder Luis Raven (White Sox) led the league with 18 homers, double his closest pursuer. Raven was then added to the Caracas roster for the round-robin and added four more homers, while hitting .344 with 16 RBIs. But like Abreu, he was held in check by Lara in the finals, hitting just .190 with one homer.

Magallanes third baseman Edgardo Alfonzo (Mets) played only six games in the regular season but hit .375 in the round-robin while leading all players with four homers and 18 RBIs—foreshadowing his outstanding season in the majors in 1999. But the Navigators finished 7-9 after winning the regular season championship in the Eastern Division.

STANDINGS

EASTERN DIVISION	W	L	PCT	GB
Magallanes Navigators	35	27	.565	—
Caracas Lions	34	28	.548	1
La Guaira Sharks	30	33	.476	5 ½
Oriente Caribbeans	23	37	.393	10 ½

WESTERN DIVISION	W	L	PCT	GB
Lara Cardinals	35	26	.574	—
Aragua Tigers	34	28	.548	1 ½
Zulia Eagles	31	32	.492	5
Pastora	25	37	.403	10 ½

PLAYOFFS	W	L	PCT	GB
Caracas Lions	10	6	.625	—
Lara Cardinals	10	6	.625	—
Zulia Eagles	9	7	.563	1
Magallanes Navigators	7	9	.438	3
Aragua Tigers	4	12	.250	6

Championship Series: Lara defeated Caracas, 4-2, in best-of-7 series.

INDIVIDUAL BATTING LEADERS
(Minimum 162 Plate Appearances)

	AVG	AB	R	H	2B	3B	HR	RBI	SB
Abreu, Bob, Caracas	.419	124	24	52	12	1	3	26	13
Mendoza, Carlos, Magallanes	.348	164	34	57	2	4	0	17	10
Castellano, Pedro, Aragua	.328	198	34	65	15	0	2	31	0
Ordonez, Magglio, Oriente	.322	146	32	47	3	0	7	38	13
Raven, Luis, Pastora	.321	243	38	78	13	0	18	44	0
Sojo, Luis, Lara	.318	151	11	48	8	1	0	17	1
Zambrano, Roberto, Aragua	.316	171	36	54	17	0	4	40	3
Munoz, Orlando, Zulia	.315	216	34	68	8	0	1	17	4
Hernandez, Ramon, Pastora	.314	194	18	61	11	0	6	27	0
Roche, Marlon, Caracas	.301	196	27	59	10	2	3	18	3
Mendez, Carlos, Caracas	.297	172	12	51	9	0	1	16	0
Mora, Melvin, Magallanes	.297	175	27	52	9	5	0	18	7
Gonzalez, Jesus, Zulia	.293	205	40	60	11	0	9	47	2
Gonzalez, Alex, Caracas	.290	169	28	49	5	4	6	24	3
Velandia, Jorge, La Guaira	.287	171	27	49	6	0	0	16	1
Escobar, Alex, La Guaira	.285	186	33	53	10	3	3	29	7
Langaigne, Selwyn, Lara	.283	145	25	41	3	4	0	22	3
Machado, Robert, Magallanes	.280	186	24	52	12	1	1	28	5
Rivas, Luis, Magallanes	.280	186	33	52	6	5	0	12	6
Prieto, Alejandro, Zulia	.280	193	29	54	3	5	0	14	1
Cabrera, Jolbert, Zulia	.280	243	40	68	14	1	1	20	13
Owens, Eric, Caracas	.279	208	33	58	5	3	0	21	0
Clapinski, Chris, Pastora	.278	151	19	42	8	3	4	20	2
Abad, Andy, Magallanes	.278	194	25	54	11	1	3	33	1
Nava, Lipso, Zulia	.277	195	18	54	13	0	1	25	1
Borrego, Ramon, Oriente	.274	164	24	45	9	2	1	18	2
Hernandez, C., Magallanes	.268	231	26	62	6	3	0	20	9
Azocar, Oscar, Aragua	.265	189	15	50	7	1	2	27	2
Cedeno, Roger, Caracas	.263	152	29	40	7	3	1	14	13
#Long, Terrence, Magallanes	.255	161	24	41	5	8	1	23	4
#Garcia, Carlos, Aragua	.246	195	27	48	7	2	2	16	25

INDIVIDUAL PITCHING LEADERS
(Minimum 48 Innings)

	W	L	ERA	G	SV	IP	H	BB	SO
Ellis, Robert, Caracas	6	2	1.93	14	0	79	59	29	35
Guerra, Mark, Magallanes	4	3	2.41	14	0	75	70	24	41
Romano, Mike, Lara	8	1	2.49	12	0	65	59	26	37
Pote, Lou, La Guaira	5	6	2.55	17	1	109	91	31	66
Tapia, Jorge, La Guaira	4	2	2.61	18	0	52	43	21	30
Beck, Greg, Caracas	9	2	2.72	14	0	83	87	13	32
Franklin, Ryan, Aragua	7	3	2.74	13	0	85	85	13	34
Conde, Argenis, Oriente	2	5	2.90	25	1	59	53	19	46
Lira, Felipe, La Guaira	7	4	2.97	13	0	88	93	22	33
Armas, Tony, Oriente	2	3	3.19	9	0	48	49	19	46
Sauveur, Rich, Aragua	2	1	3.45	20	0	66	65	17	40
Silva, Luis, Lara	4	5	3.55	22	0	51	51	13	31
Bost, Heath, Pastora	3	2	3.58	13	0	55	53	14	34
Blanco, Alberto, Magallanes	7	4	3.63	13	0	67	54	24	39
#Hernandez, Santos, Pastora	0	4	4.66	28	16	29	25	11	29

ARIZONA FALL LEAGUE

The best record in the league was no help to the Grand Canyon Rafters when the 1998 Arizona Fall League playoffs rolled around. A depleted Rafters club fell in two straight games to a Sun Cities team that finished just .500 in the regular season.

Key players such as righthander Roy Halladay (Blue Jays), first baseman Steve Cox (Devil Rays), catcher Mike Figga (Yankees) and outfielder Luke Wilcox (Devil Rays) missed postseason play due to prior commitments, leaving the Rafters shorthanded when it counted.

Second baseman Marlon Anderson (Phillies) had seven hits and five runs in the two playoff games to key the Sun Cities attack. He had two doubles and a home run in Game One, a 7-4 Solar Sox win. Anderson added three hits in a 6-4 win in Game Two. Righthander Keith Evans (Expos) saved both games for Sun Cities.

Phoenix third baseman Carlos Lee (White Sox) set an AFL record with 19 doubles, and teammate Jason Rakers (Indians) had a record-low ERA of 0.97. Grand

Canyon righthander Jason Johnson (Devil Rays) tied a league record with seven wins.

Two brother combinations teamed up in AFL play. Catcher Ben Davis (Padres) and first baseman Glenn Davis (Dodgers) played for Scottsdale, while righthander Jeff Zimmerman (Rangers) and lefthander Jordan Zimmerman (Mariners) pitched for Peoria.

STANDINGS

NORTHERN DIVISION	W	L	PCT	GB
Sun Cities Solar Sox	22	22	.500	—
Scottsdale Scorpions	20	23	.465	1 ½
Maryvale Saguaros	19	25	.432	3
SOUTHERN DIVISION	**W**	**L**	**PCT**	**GB**
Grand Canyon Rafters	26	18	.591	—
Peoria Javelinas	23	21	.523	3
Phoenix Desert Dogs	21	22	.488	4 ½

PLAYOFFS—Finals: Sun Cities defeated Grand Canyon, 2-0, in best-of-3 series.

INDIVIDUAL BATTING LEADERS
(Minimum 122 Plate Appearances)

	AVG	AB	R	H	2B	3B	HR	RBI	SB
Zywica, Mike, Peoria	.330	115	30	38	11	1	2	15	1
Zuleta, Julio, Maryvale	.323	124	19	40	6	1	3	16	0
Anderson, Marlon, Sun Cities	.317	139	27	44	8	1	2	16	11
Lee, Carlos, Phoenix	.315	143	22	45	19	1	4	33	6
Singleton, Chris, GC	.313	112	21	35	7	3	1	14	10
Luuloa, Keith, Peoria	.310	113	21	35	8	0	4	20	0
Morris, Warren, Maryvale	.307	137	24	42	7	1	8	27	3
Stenson, Dernell, GC	.306	134	27	41	5	1	5	23	3
Jones, Jaime, Sun Cities	.306	108	11	33	7	1	2	25	1
DeRosa, Mark, Sun Cities	.302	149	23	45	7	1	1	22	5
Kapler, Gabe, Phoenix	.299	144	23	43	6	4	2	19	4
Hansen, Jed, Phoenix	.287	94	17	27	3	0	3	11	7
McDonald, John, Phoenix	.286	147	19	42	4	1	1	12	4
Brown, Roosevelt, Maryvale	.285	144	25	41	9	0	9	30	6
Mientkiewicz, Doug, Phoenix	.285	130	19	37	12	1	3	25	0
Mota, Tony, Scottsdale	.279	147	18	41	6	0	3	19	4
Barrett, Michael, Sun Cities	.275	160	29	44	9	0	2	24	4
Bergeron, Peter, Sun Cities	.274	135	25	37	3	1	1	10	11
Conti, Jason, Scottsdale	.274	146	20	40	13	1	1	6	12
Darr, Mike, Scottsdale	.272	125	19	34	9	0	3	21	3
Gibson, Derrick, Scottsdale	.269	145	21	39	10	0	6	25	5
Frank, Mike, Maryvale	.268	123	16	33	5	1	2	12	5
Dransfeldt, Kelly, Peoria	.264	121	20	32	9	1	3	29	5
Meyers, Chad, Maryvale	.264	110	16	29	6	1	2	16	14
Sasser, Rob, Peoria	.255	110	24	28	5	2	4	17	9

INDIVIDUAL PITCHING LEADERS
(Minimum 36 Innings)

	W	L	ERA	G	SV	IP	H	BB	SO
Rakers, Jason, Phoenix	1	2	0.97	9	0	37	31	7	29
#Rose, Ted, Maryvale	0	0	1.50	17	7	18	15	5	21
Wolff, Bryan, Scottsdale	3	0	2.33	9	0	46	32	16	56
Reichert, Dan, Phoenix	3	1	2.54	9	0	39	37	10	28
Harriger, Mark, Peoria	1	4	2.56	9	0	39	39	15	18
Randall, Scott, Scottsdale	3	2	2.88	9	0	41	29	17	27
Robertson, Jeriome, Maryvale	4	4	2.89	9	0	44	43	12	35
Weaver, Jeff, Phoenix	0	2	2.92	9	0	37	34	6	36
Lincoln, Mike, Phoenix	1	2	2.93	9	0	40	45	10	18
Yennaco, Jay, Grand Canyon	3	3	3.14	9	0	43	29	10	25
Anderson, Jimmy, Maryvale	2	2	3.15	9	0	40	38	12	35
Shumaker, Anthony, Sun Cities	1	0	3.32	9	0	38	33	13	35
Johnson, Jason, Grand Canyon	7	1	4.00	9	0	45	49	12	34
Johnson, Jonathan, Peoria	1	4	4.24	9	0	40	42	15	33
Fussell, Chris, Grand Canyon	2	2	4.50	8	0	36	35	15	29
Powell, Jeremy, Sun Cities	1	5	4.70	9	0	38	43	10	38
Bowie, Micah, Sun Cities	3	1	4.82	9	0	37	31	10	43
Arroyo, Bronson, Maryvale	2	4	6.51	9	0	37	49	13	26

MARYLAND FALL LEAGUE

In the inaugural—and only—season of the Maryland Fall League, the Frederick Regiment won the championship.

Led by player of the year Maurice Bruce (Mets) and pitcher of the year Brian Cooper (Angels), the Regiment won by 1½ games, topping Delmarva and Delaware. There were no playoffs.

The MFL replaced Hawaii Winter Baseball as a fall developmental league for Class A and Double-A prospects. Though it was run well and drew encouraging crowds, the MFL was replaced by a league that operated in Southern California in 1999. The decision was largely attributed to climate.

Outfielder Milton Bradley (Expos) led the MFL in batting with a .330 average. But his season came to an early end when he was suspended after a physical confrontation with umpire Matt Schaeffer over a strike call.

Bradley and Bruce, an infielder, were among the top prospects sent to the MFL. Others included Delaware righthander Adam Eaton (Phillies), Delaware righthander Matt Kinney (Twins), Frederick third baseman Mike Lamb (Rangers), Frederick righthander Grant Roberts (Mets), Delaware outfielder Luis Saturria (Cardinals), Delaware outfielder Eric Valent (Phillies) and Bowie catcher Jayson Werth (Orioles).

STANDINGS

STANDINGS	W	L	PCT	GB
Frederick Regiment	23	19	.548	—
Delmarva Rockfish	21	20	.512	1 ½
Delaware Stars	21	20	.512	1 ½
Bowie Nationals	18	24	.429	5

INDIVIDUAL BATTING LEADERS
(Minimum 113 Plate Appearances)

	AVG	AB	R	H	2B	3B	HR	RBI	SB
Bradley, Milton, Delmarva	.330	106	22	35	8	2	5	22	2
Lamb, Mike, Frederick...........	.321	109	18	35	8	1	5	26	3
Bruce, Maurice, Frederick.......	.307	114	23	35	5	1	5	15	12
Clark, Brady, Bowie	.305	128	24	39	11	0	2	25	13
Wakeland, Chris, Delaware	.295	122	18	36	6	2	2	10	5
Redman, Julian, Bowie..........	.293	133	19	39	4	1	0	15	9
Woodward, Chris, Frederick....	.267	101	24	27	3	1	1	6	2
Saturria, Luis, Delaware	.262	122	15	32	6	2	3	15	7
Valent, Eric, Delaware...........	.262	122	19	32	8	0	2	20	0
Garavito, Eddy, Bowie...........	.261	111	22	29	8	2	4	19	10
Pendergrass, T., Delmarva	.256	117	20	30	4	1	2	11	9
Mohr, Dustan, Delmarva	.254	114	18	29	6	1	8	18	0
Gallagher, Shawn, Frederick. ..	.252	123	15	31	5	0	5	22	0
Dillon, Joe, Delaware	.252	127	13	32	7	2	1	18	6
Alexander, Chad, Bowie........	.250	104	16	26	6	1	3	23	5
Smith, Rod, Bowie..............	.236	89	28	21	4	2	1	12	17
Davidson, Cleatus, Delaware ...	.234	124	19	29	5	4	0	12	15
Minor, Damon, Delmarva	.226	124	8	28	7	0	3	18	0

INDIVIDUAL PITCHING LEADERS
(Minimum 34 Innings)

	W	L	ERA	G	SV	IP	H	BB	SO
Kinney, Matt, Delaware	2	1	1.22	8	0	37	27	14	36
Cooper, Brian, Frederick	3	0	1.50	7	0	36	30	12	48
Lynch, Jim, Bowie	3	2	2.72	7	0	36	33	12	30
Averette, Robert, Bowie	2	1	3.34	8	0	35	34	13	18
Roberts, Grant, Frederick...........	1	1	3.38	7	0	35	33	13	42
#Blank, Matt, Delmarva..............	5	0	4.30	10	0	23	16	10	19
#Winkelas, Joe, Delmarva...........	1	1	4.50	16	6	22	28	11	17
McClaskey, Tim, Bowie..............	1	2	5.40	7	0	35	38	12	21
McKnight, Tony, Bowie..............	0	1	6.32	9	0	37	55	8	23

AUSTRALIAN LEAGUE

Two unlikely opponents met in the Australian League playoff final in 1999, with the Gold Coast Cougars coming out on top with a two-game sweep of the Sydney Storm.

Most of the drama was in Game One, which was won on a bottom-of-the-ninth home run by Gold Coast

third baseman Paul Gorman. His two-run blast came after a two-out single by Brandon Pollard, and turned a 7-6 deficit into an 8-7 win.

The second game was also close until the Cougars scored eight runs in the sixth inning. Only two of those runs were earned as the Storm committed eight errors in the game.

Gold Coast had charged from the second division to close the regular season in second place. Sydney finished below .500 in the regular season, then knocked off the first-place Adelaide Giants in two games in the playoff semifinals. Gold Coast also swept its semifinal series, beating the Melbourne Monarchs.

The league MVP came from a non-playoff team. Second baseman Adam Burton of the Melbourne Reds led the league in batting, home runs, slugging, runs and hits.

After the season, the league was sold to a group headed by Milwaukee Brewers catcher Dave Nilsson, an Australia native and a former player in the league. Nilsson's group planned to continue with six Australian teams for the 1999-2000 season, but intended to expand overseas after that. Toward that end, the league was renamed the International Baseball League Australia.

STANDINGS

REGULAR SEASON	W	L	PCT	GB
Adelaide Giants	28	17	.622	—
Gold Coast Cougars	24	20	.545	3 ½
Melbourne Monarchs	22	22	.500	5 ½
Sydney Storm	21	22	.488	6
Melbourne Reds	20	23	.465	7
Perth Heat	17	28	.378	11

PLAYOFFS—Semifinals: Gold Coast defeated Melbourne Monarchs, 2-0, and Sydney defeated Adelaide, 2-0, in best-of-3 series. **Finals:** Gold Coast defeated Sydney, 2-0, in best-of-3 series.

INDIVIDUAL BATTING LEADERS
(Minimum 120 Plate Appearances)

	AVG	AB	R	H	2B	3B	HR	RBI	SB
Burton, Adam, Reds	.372	148	39	55	10	0	14	40	6
White, Gary, Sydney	.366	145	20	53	12	0	6	27	4
Hogan, Shane, Reds.............	.359	131	24	47	14	0	8	31	2
Buckley, Matt, Sydney	.323	167	29	54	12	0	3	20	8
Sell, Chip, Adelaide	.320	128	21	41	10	0	2	13	11
Pollard, Brandon, Gold Coast..	.317	145	29	45	4	0	12	33	5
Dawes, Scott, Reds.............	.313	150	27	47	8	0	3	24	1
Gonzalez, Paul, Monarchs	.311	103	18	32	9	1	4	15	7
Robertson, Dean, Perth.........	.311	161	27	50	9	0	8	21	6
Scott, Andrew, Adelaide	.310	171	35	53	14	0	9	41	5
Phillips, Darren, Adelaide	.309	139	22	43	7	3	8	39	1
Johnson, Ron, Gold Coast	.307	101	15	31	4	0	5	19	1
White, Darren, Reds..............	.304	138	24	42	5	0	11	31	2
Utting, Ben, Reds	.299	144	20	43	4	2	3	15	1
Moyle, Mike, Perth...............	.293	116	21	34	4	0	6	20	1
#Macias, Jose, Gold Coast	.267	161	27	43	5	2	1	18	20
#Hewitt, Jason, Adelaide........	.244	176	32	43	7	4	3	24	6

INDIVIDUAL PITCHING LEADERS
(Minimum 40 Innings)

	W	L	ERA	G	SV	IP	H	BB	SO
Ahearne, Pat, Perth...................	7	3	2.17	14	0	87	58	25	72
Challinor, John, Giants.............	3	1	2.24	19	4	41	33	9	54
Cederblad, Brett, Gold Coast	4	1	2.35	7	0	42	33	11	39
Anderson, Craig, Sydney	5	4	2.38	16	0	69	57	26	45
Herges, Matt, Adelaide..............	7	3	2.52	15	0	83	67	21	81
Bennett, Shayne, Adelaide........	4	1	3.13	8	0	46	44	6	41
#Cassell, Grahame, Sydney.......	2	3	3.15	31	9	38	32	8	32
Glover, Gary, Sydney................	2	3	3.25	12	0	47	39	14	45
Brassington, Phil, Gold Coast ...	3	3	3.31	14	0	88	75	29	64
Mayo, Blake, Adelaide..............	3	4	3.83	19	3	54	42	17	45
White, David, Reds..................	7	4	4.43	20	3	82	82	18	57
Byrne, Earl, Monarchs..............	4	4	4.43	16	0	67	59	38	58
#Tonkin, Shane, Perth...............	1	7	5.33	24	9	58	79	15	33

COLLEGE BASEBALL

The monkey is off their backs
Miami's sixth consecutive trip to Omaha ended with a College World Series championship

Hurricanes banish ghost of Warren Morris, defeat Florida State for national championship

BY JOHN MANUEL

So much was new in college baseball in 1999, it seems fitting that an old standby like the University of Miami provided some continuity to the past.

The No. 1-seeded Hurricanes went undefeated in winning their third College World Series edging arch-rival and No. 2 seed Florida State 6-5 in the championship game.

But the overriding story of 1999 was an attempt by the NCAA to regulate aluminum bats, which contributed to record offensive numbers throughout college baseball a year earlier. An outcry for reform generated a groundswell of support after Southern California beat Arizona State 21-14 in the 1998 CWS. The controversy spilled into the 1999 season, even resulting in the first wood-bat games in college since 1974.

Victory, at last
Miami coach Jim Morris

The bats ultimately used were a little heavier, more narrow and a little less nuclear, and combined with excellent pitching, they helped keep offensive num-

bers in Omaha at reasonable levels after 1998's record output.

To get to Omaha and the traditional College World Series format in 1999, however, Division I teams had to get through a new, expanded 64-team regional field. The eight survivors had to win two sets of regionals—16 four-team, double-elimination tournaments followed by eight best-of-three series. The arrangement eliminated the old pitching-depleting, grinding six-team format, to the delight of pretty much everyone associated with college baseball.

While the national champion, Miami, was an old hand in Omaha, its 1999 lineup was relatively new. Gone were bashers such as Pat Burrell, Aubrey Huff and Jason Michaels who helped the Hurricanes smash a number of club offensive records on their way to a fifth-place finish in Omaha in 1998. The Hurricanes returned in '99 for the sixth consecutive time under coach Jim Morris with a team more dependent on pitching, speed and defense. They hung on to beat arch-rival Florida State in the championship game after beating the Seminoles five times in six previous meetings in 1999.

Relying on Little Ball

Morris and the 'Canes had come close in Omaha since last winning in 1985. They lost to Louisiana State on Warren Morris' historic two-run, bottom-of-the-ninth home run in 1996. And they came apart in 1998, when the 'Canes' minds seemed to be on the

COLLEGE WORLD SERIES

Omaha, Nebraska
June 11-19, 1999

STANDINGS

BRACKET ONE	W	L	RF	RA
Miami	4	0	27	12
Alabama	2	2	20	21
Rice	1	2	16	16
Oklahoma State	0	2	5	18

Bracket One Final: Miami 5, Alabama 2

BRACKET TWO	W	L	RF	RA
Florida State	4	2	47	38
Stanford	2	2	36	30
Cal State Fullerton	1	2	8	18
Texas A&M	0	2	5	11

Bracket Two Final: Florida State 14, Stanford 11 (13 innings)
CHAMPIONSHIP GAME: Miami 6, Florida State 5

INDIVIDUAL BATTING LEADERS
(Minimum 10 at-bats)

PLAYER, TEAM	AVG.	AB	R	H	2B	3B	HR	RBI	SB
Gall, John, Stanford	.611	18	5	11	1	0	2	6	2
Hill, Bobby, Miami	.571	14	5	8	0	0	1	2	2
Griffin, John-Ford, FSU	.500	14	6	7	3	0	0	4	0
Phillips, Andy, Alabama	.438	16	3	7	3	0	0	0	2
Keller, G.W., Alabama	.438	16	3	7	3	0	0	5	1
Bruntlett, Eric, Stanford	.429	14	3	6	0	0	0	2	0
Crespo, Manny, Miami	.400	10	3	4	1	0	0	2	0
Esquivel, Lale, Miami	.400	15	4	6	2	0	0	4	0
Barthelemy, Ryan, FSU	.391	23	6	9	0	1	2	3	0
Scott, Sam, FSU	.389	18	6	7	2	0	3	4	0

INDIVIDUAL PITCHING LEADERS
(Minimum 7 innings)

PLAYER, TEAM	W	L	ERA	G	SV	IP	H	BB	SO
Saarloos, Kirk, CSF	0	0	0.00	3	1	7	4	3	5
Sorensen, Matt, CSF	1	0	1.08	1	0	8	10	0	3
Neu, Michael, Miami	0	0	1.23	4	3	7	3	3	10
Chavez, Chris, FSU	2	0	1.26	3	0	14	9	4	13
Santos, Alex, Miami	2	0	1.54	2	0	12	8	9	10
Murphy, Scott, Alabama	1	0	2.16	3	1	8	6	3	9
Baugh, Kenny, Rice	1	0	2.35	1	0	8	9	4	5
Smith, Justin, Alabama	1	0	3.21	2	0	14	7	7	19

ALL-TOURNAMENT TEAM

C—Jeremiah Klosterman, Florida State. **1B**—John Gall, Stanford. **2B**—Marshall McDougall, Florida State. **3B**—Lale Esquivel, Miami. **SS**—Bobby Hill, Miami. **OF**—Manny Crespo, Miami; Matt Diaz, Florida State; G.W. Keller, Alabama. **DH**—Sam Scott, Florida State. **P**—Chris Chavez, Florida State; Michael Neu, Miami.

Most Outstanding Player—Marshall McDougall, Florida State.

CHAMPIONSHIP GAME
Hurricanes 6, Seminoles 5

FLORIDA ST.	ab	r	h	bi	MIAMI	ab	r	h	bi
Griffin lf	2	0	1	2	Hill ss	2	1	2	0
McDougall 2b	5	0	1	0	Seever cf	4	0	1	1
Diaz rf	4	1	2	0	Crespo rf	2	1	0	0
Scott dh	4	2	1	1	Esquivel 3b	3	1	1	0
Klosterman c	5	0	0	0	Brown 1b	4	1	2	4
Cash 3b	4	0	1	1	Rodriguez lf	3	0	0	0
Smith cf	4	0	0	0	Nettles dh	3	1	0	0
Groves ss	2	1	0	0	Lovelady c	4	0	0	0
Barthelemy 1b	4	1	1	0	Clute 2b	3	1	1	1
Totals	**34**	**5**	**7**	**4**	**Totals**	**28**	**6**	**8**	**6**

Florida State	011 000 210—5
Miami	010 050 00X—8

E—Whidden (1), Hill (16), Crespo (4). **DP**—Florida State 3. **LOB**—Florida State 10, Miami 5. **2B**—Brown (14). **3B**—Barthelemy (1). **HR**—Scott (12), Brown (22). **SB**—Hill (52). **SH**—Crespo (5), Griffin (2).

FLORIDA ST.	ip	h	r	er	bb	so	MIAMI	ip	h	r	er	bb	so
Varnes L	6	8	6	6	4	1	Santos W	5	4	2	1	5	4
Whidden	2	0	0	0	2	2	Vazquez	2	2	2	2	2	2
							Neu S	2	1	1	1	0	2

Varnes faced one batter in seventh
WP—Varnes (6), Vazquez (4). **T**—2:50. **A**—23,563.

major league draft more than on the task at hand.

That was not the case for the '99 Hurricanes, who asked their No. 3 hitter, Manny Crespo, to bunt in consecutive games. These Hurricanes stole a lot of bases, played great defense and used the home run as a fallback, not a major weapon. In fact, Morris explained the Miami philosophy as something almost foreign to the college game in the late '90s: fundamental baseball.

"I like to bunt and I like the running part of the game," Morris said. "That was part of the game before we got gorillas at the plate, with both aluminum and wood. We've gotta go with what's best for us and our team, and that's putting pressure on the other guys. When you do that, a lot of times they make mistakes. We've worked very hard on bunting this year, probably more than ever. I like this type of game; it's more fun to coach.

Four RBIs in final
CWS hero Kevin Brown

"We focus on getting a lead and getting the game to our bullpen. I believe in our setup guy and our closer. I feel like if we go into the seventh inning with a lead, we've got a great shot at getting a win."

Miami didn't deviate from that blueprint for victory all year, even at Rosenblatt Stadium, site of some of baseball's most offensive games in recent years. The 1998 championship game between USC and Arizona State was college baseball's ultimate offensive orgy, the cap on a prolific tournament that saw 56 offensive records broken or tied.

Against Florida State, Miami used some gorilla ball itself. Sophomore first baseman Kevin Brown was the offensive hero, driving in four runs with a mammoth solo home run and a three-run double in the Hurricanes' 6-5 victory.

The Seminoles rallied from a 6-2 deficit against Miami's normally stolid bullpen. Setup man Vince Vazquez gave up two runs in his two innings, and closer Michael Neu gave up one run as Florida State closed within a run. But Miami hung on to beat its cross-state rival for the national championship.

"That's the way we had to play," said junior shortstop Bobby Hill, who ignited Miami's lineup for three seasons. "We had to do the little things to win. Last year, we'd make mistakes and we still won. We just mashed our way through mistakes until we got to Omaha. This year, we couldn't afford to make mistakes, and we had to do all the little things like bunt, steal bases, hit the cutoff man, just to win games."

Miami reached the championship game by going undefeated in bracket play, beating Alabama 5-2 in the deciding game. Florida State's road to the final was a lot more difficult as it had to come through the losers' bracket and beat Stanford twice in a row, including a classic 14-11, 13-inning thriller in the deciding con-

Player of the Year
Bears' durable Jennings does it all

Jason Jennings is old-fashioned. Nobody's got a problem with that, least of all Jennings himself.

At 6-foot-2, 243 pounds, with a closely shaved head and thick build, he has the Texas country-boy look down pat. A junior righthander/DH, Jennings was an academic all-American at Baylor. He talks in a measured, almost deliberate tone, probably inherited from his grandfather James, a longtime public-address announcer for the Dallas Cowboys.

Doing things the old-fashioned way has always paid off for Jennings, like when he proposed to his high school sweetheart, Kelly Summers.

"I went over to her apartment here in Waco, and I gave her a rose with the ring on the stem. When I gave it to her, she thanked me, and I slid the ring off the rose," Jennings said. "I got down on one knee and said if the rose didn't make her happy, maybe the ring would. She just started bawling. I guess the tears were a good sign."

Jennings should have no trouble paying for the ring—he was drafted 16th overall by the Rockies in June and signed for a $1.675 million bonus.

In the span of a little more than a month, Jennings got engaged; led Baylor to a school-record win total; got drafted; was named the Big 12 Conference player of the year; led the Bears to within two innings of the College World Series; and, finally, he began his pro career in the Rockies organization.

To top all that, Jennings was named Baseball America's College Player of the Year.

Jennings was Baylor's closer as a freshman, going 3-5 with a 2.90 ERA and 10 saves, and he has all the school's save records. He moved into the rotation in 1998, going 11-4 with a 5.08 ERA and two saves while batting .327-18-58 and earning third-team All-America honors.

"I'm two players, in that sense," Jennings said. "I know it helps out the coaching staff and it helps us win games."

Jennings says he wished he played a position so he could have helped even more, but his special pitching talent and his lack of quickness persuaded Bears coach Steve Smith to keep him as a DH when he wasn't pitching.

"I wanted to work him at first base to give us more options," Smith said. "But my assistants reminded me he can't run out of sight by tomorrow, so we just kept him at DH."

Jennings had heard the knocks and the jokes about his size before, and he admits he's not fleet of foot. But in 1999, with his dominance on the mound (13-2, 2.58) and in the batter's box (.386-17-68), he turned the weight question into an answer.

Baylor two-way sensation Jason Jennings

"He's durable as hell," Rockies scouting director Pat Daugherty said after drafting Jennings. "He never missed a start and he's never been hurt."

That durability has its roots in Jennings' generous hips and thighs. He learned to use his frame to his advantage and never doubted himself, but he knew scouts found plenty of fault with his body before 1999.

"I've heard that my whole career," he said. "I've always had a big lower body. In high school, I didn't have a very strenuous weight-training program, but since I got to college I have, and that's helped me re-form the muscles and put things in different places.

"It used to bother me, but I've turned a shoulder to it."

He knows he's also going to have to turn away from hitting in pro ball. Jennings was excited to go to a National League team, so he'll at least still get to hit if he makes the majors. Smith also thinks it's a combination made for Coors Field—particularly at the plate.

"I'd pay to see his first at-bat," Smith says with a laugh. "That pitcher is going to be on the mound, and Jason's going to step in with his back foot dug in, six inches from the plate. He's going to open up in his big stance, and I'm just going to laugh when the pitcher steps off, wipes his brow and just kind of says, 'Whew.' He ain't gonna look like no pitcher."

What an old-fashioned notion: a pitcher who can hit.

—JOHN MANUEL

PREVIOUS WINNERS

1981—Mike Sodders, 3b, Arizona State
1982—Jeff Ledbetter, of-lhp, Florida State
1983—Dave Magadan, 1b, Alabama
1984—Oddibe McDowell, of, Arizona State
1985—Pete Incaviglia, of, Oklahoma State
1986—Casey Close, of, Michigan
1987—Robin Ventura, 3b, Oklahoma State
1988—John Olerud, 1b-lhp, Washington State
1989—Ben McDonald, rhp, Louisiana State
1990—Mike Kelly, of, Arizona State
1991—David McCarty, 1b, Stanford
1992—Phil Nevin, 3b, Cal State Fullerton
1993—Brooks Kieschnick, dh-rhp, Texas
1994—Jason Varitek, c, Georgia Tech
1995—Todd Helton, 1b-lhp, Tennessee
1996—Kris Benson, rhp, Clemson
1997—J.D. Drew, of, Florida State
1998—Jeff Austin, rhp, Stanford

test. Twice the Seminoles had to rally from two runs down in their final at-bat before winning on a three-run homer by Karl Jernigan.

Bats-Capades

A more well-rounded, lower-scoring game returned to the CWS as gorilla ball waned ever so slightly. That was exactly what the NCAA was hoping for in the off-season of 1998-99, when a spate of new bat regulations were debated, enacted, retracted and finally set.

The standards settled on for 1999 tempered the bats' power to a certain extent and offense was down marginally across the board in Division I, with batting averages, home runs, runs and ERA all down (see chart).

To get to that point, teams had to weather a bat crisis in the season's first month as conferences and bat companies struggled with liability questions. Trying to cover themselves from possible lawsuits stemming from batted-ball injuries resulting from aluminum bats, every conference had to work out an indemnification agreement with bat manufacturers.

The first game of the year, between Arizona State and Utah on Jan. 15, was played with wood bats, the first wood-bat college game since 1974. Officials with Louisville Slugger and the Pacific-10 Conference couldn't come to an insurance agreement on the new bats soon enough, leaving exasperated Sun Devils coach Pat Murphy to exclaim, "Whichever bat we're going to use, let's use it. We've got to get some leadership here."

The situation took a turn for the absurd when St. Mary's played Arizona a week later. The Gaels, again because of indemnification concerns, used wood

COLLEGE WORLD SERIES CHAMPIONS: 1947-99

Year	Champion	Coach	Record	Runner-Up	MVP
1947	California*	Clint Evans	31-10	Yale	None selected
1948	Southern California	Sam Barry	40-12	Yale	None selected
1949	Texas*	Bibb Falk	23-7	Wake Forest	Charles Teague, 2b, Wake Forest
1950	Texas	Bibb Falk	27-6	Washington State	Ray VanCleef, of, Rutgers
1951	Oklahoma*	Jack Baer	19-9	Tennessee	Sid Hatfield, 1b-p, Tennessee
1952	Holy Cross	Jack Berry	21-3	Missouri	Jim O'Neill, p, Holy Cross
1953	Michigan	Ray Fisher	21-9	Texas	J.L. Smith, p, Texas
1954	Missouri	Hi Simmons	22-4	Rollins	Tom Yewcic, c, Michigan State
1955	Wake Forest	Taylor Sanford	29-7	Western Michigan	Tom Borland, p, Oklahoma State
1956	Minnesota	Dick Siebert	33-9	Arizona	Jerry Thomas, p, Minnesota
1957	California*	George Wolfman	35-10	Penn State	Cal Emery, 1b-p, Penn State
1958	Southern California	Rod Dedeaux	35-7	Missouri	Bill Thom, p, Southern California
1959	Oklahoma State	Toby Greene	27-5	Arizona	Jim Dobson, 3b, Oklahoma State
1960	Minnesota	Dick Siebert	34-7	Southern California	John Erickson, 2b, Minnesota
1961	Southern California*	Rod Dedeaux	43-9	Oklahoma State	Littleton Fowler, p, Oklahoma State
1962	Michigan	Don Lund	31-13	Santa Clara	Bob Garibaldi, p, Santa Clara
1963	Southern California	Rod Dedeaux	37-16	Arizona	Bud Hollowell, c, Southern California
1964	Minnesota	Dick Siebert	31-12	Missouri	Joe Ferris, p, Maine
1965	Arizona State	Bobby Winkles	54-8	Ohio State	Sal Bando, 3b, Arizona State
1966	Ohio State	Marty Karow	27-6	Oklahoma State	Steve Arlin, p, Ohio State
1967	Arizona State	Bobby Winkles	53-12	Houston	Ron Davini, c, Arizona State
1968	Southern California*	Rod Dedeaux	45-14	Southern Illinois	Bill Seinsoth, 1b, Southern California
1969	Arizona State	Bobby Winkles	56-11	Tulsa	John Dolinsek, of, Arizona State
1970	Southern California	Rod Dedeaux	51-13	Florida State	Gene Ammann, p, Florida State
1971	Southern California	Rod Dedeaux	53-13	Southern Illinois	Jerry Tabb, 1b, Tulsa
1972	Southern California	Rod Dedeaux	50-13	Arizona State	Russ McQueen, p, Southern California
1973	Southern California*	Rod Dedeaux	51-11	Arizona State	Dave Winfield, of-p, Minnesota
1974	Southern California	Rod Dedeaux	50-20	Miami (Fla.)	George Milke, p, Southern California
1975	Texas	Cliff Gustafson	56-6	South Carolina	Mickey Reichenbach, 1b, Texas
1976	Arizona	Jerry Kindall	56-17	Eastern Michigan	Steve Powers, dh-p, Arizona
1977	Arizona State	Jim Brock	57-12	South Carolina	Bob Horner, 3b, Arizona State
1978	Southern California*	Rod Dedeaux	54-9	Arizona State	Rod Boxberger, p, Southern California
1979	Cal State Fullerton	Augie Garrido	60-14	Arkansas	Tony Hudson, p, Cal State Fullerton
1980	Arizona	Jerry Kindall	45-21	Hawaii	Terry Francona, of, Arizona
1981	Arizona State	Jim Brock	55-13	Oklahoma State	Stan Holmes, of, Arizona State
1982	Miami (Fla.)*	Ron Fraser	57-18	Wichita State	Dan Smith, p, Miami (Fla.)
1983	Texas*	Cliff Gustafson	66-14	Alabama	Calvin Schiraldi, p, Texas
1984	Cal State Fullerton	Augie Garrido	66-20	Texas	John Fishel, of, Cal State Fullerton
1985	Miami (Fla.)*	Ron Fraser	64-16	Texas	Greg Ellena, dh, Miami (Fla.)
1986	Arizona	Jerry Kindall	49-19	Florida State	Mike Senne, of, Arizona
1987	Stanford	Mark Marquess	53-17	Oklahoma State	Paul Carey, of, Stanford
1988	Stanford	Mark Marquess	46-23	Arizona State	Lee Plemel, p, Stanford
1989	Wichita State	Gene Stephenson	68-16	Texas	Greg Brummett, p, Wichita State
1990	Georgia	Steve Webber	52-19	Oklahoma State	Mike Rebhan, p, Georgia
1991	Louisiana State*	Skip Bertman	55-18	Wichita State	Gary Hymel, c, Louisiana State
1992	Pepperdine*	Andy Lopez	48-11	Cal State Fullerton	Phil Nevin, 3b, Cal State Fullerton
1993	Louisiana State	Skip Bertman	53-17	Wichita State	Todd Walker, 2b, Louisiana State
1994	Oklahoma*	Larry Cochell	50-17	Georgia Tech	Chip Glass, of, Oklahoma
1995	Cal State Fullerton*	Augie Garrido	57-9	Southern California	Mark Kotsay, of, CalState Fullerton
1996	Louisiana State*	Skip Bertman	52-15	Miami (Fla.)	Pat Burrell, 3b, Miami
1997	Louisiana State*	Skip Bertman	57-13	Alabama	Brandon Larson, ss, Louisiana State
1998	Southern California	Mike Gillespie	49-17	Arizona State	Wes Rachels, 2b, Southern California
1999	Miami*	Jim Morris	50-13	Florida State	Marshall McDougall, 2b, Florida State

*Undefeated

THE ROAD TO OMAHA

SUPER REGIONALS

June 4-6; 16 teams, 8 best-of-3 series (Winners advance to College World Series)

REGIONALS

May 28-31; 64 teams, 16 double-elimination tournaments (Winners advance to super regionals)
* Automatic qualifier

MIAMI

■ **Super Regional Site:** Coral Gables, Fla. (Miami).
Participants: Wake Forest (46-14) at Miami (44-13). (Miami wins 2-0).

❏ **Regional Site:** Coral Gables, Fla. (Miami).
Participants: No. 1 Miami (41-13), No. 2 Florida Atlantic (52-7), *No. 3 Florida International (43-17), *No. 4 Bethune-Cookman (27-29).
Champion: Miami (3-0). **Runner-Up:** Florida Atlantic (2-2).
Outstanding Player: Lale Esquivel, 3b, Miami.

❏ **Regional Site:** Winston-Salem, N.C. (Wake Forest).
Participants: *No. 1 Wake Forest (44-13), No. 2 Richmond (38-15), No. 3 Virginia Tech (41-15), No. 4 Siena (34-20).
Champion: Wake Forest (3-1). **Runner-Up:** Richmond (3-2).
Outstanding Player: Jon Palmieri, 1b, Wake Forest.
(Wake Forest advances to meet Miami in super regional).

FLORIDA STATE

■ **Super Regional Site:** Tallahassee, Fla. (Florida State).
Participants: Auburn (46-17) at Florida State (51-12). (Florida State wins 2-0).

❏ **Regional Site:** Tallahassee, Fla. (Florida State).
Participants: No. 1 Florida State (48-12), *No. 2 Providence (47-14), *No. 3 Jacksonville (40-21), *No. 4 The Citadel (41-18).
Champion: Florida State (3-0). **Runner-Up:** Providence (2-2).
Outstanding Player: Kevin Cash, 3b, Florida State.

❏ **Regional Site:** Auburn, Ala. (Auburn).
Participants: *No. 1 Tulane (45-15), No. 2 Auburn (43-16), No. 3 North Carolina State (37-23), *No. 4 Winthrop (39-21).
Champion: Auburn (3-1). **Runner-Up:** Tulane (3-2).
Outstanding Player: Mailon Kent, of, Auburn.
(Auburn advances to meet Florida State in super regional).

CAL STATE FULLERTON

■ **Super Regional Site:** Columbus, Ohio (Ohio State).
Participants: Cal State Fullerton (47-11) at Ohio State (49-12). (Cal State Fullerton wins 2-1).

❏ **Regional Site:** Columbus, Ohio (Ohio State).
Participants: No. 1 Ohio State (46-12), *No. 2 Nebraska (41-16), No. 3 Mississippi State (40-19), *No. 4 Bowling Green (36-22).
Champion: Ohio State (3-0). **Runner-Up:** Mississippi State (2-2).
Outstanding Players: E.J. Laratta, rhp, Ohio State; Matt Middleton, 3b, Ohio State.

❏ **Regional Site:** South Bend, Ind. (Notre Dame).
Participants: *No. 1 Cal State Fullerton (44-11), No. 2 Notre Dame (42-16), No. 3 Creighton (38-23), *No. 4 Michigan (32-28).
Champion: Cal State Fullerton (3-0). **Runner-Up:** Michigan (2-2).
Outstanding Player: Adam Johnson, rhp, Cal Sate Fullerton.
(Cal State Fullerton advances to meet Ohio State in super regional).

OKLAHOMA STATE

■ **Super Regional Site:** Waco, Texas (Baylor).
Participants: Oklahoma State (44-18) at Baylor (49-13). (Oklahoma State wins 2-1).

❏ **Regional Site:** Wichita (Wichita State).
Participants: *No. 1 Wichita (57-12), No. 2 Oklahoma State (40-17), No. 3 UCLA (30-29), *No. 4 Oral Roberts (46-13).
Champion: Oklahoma State (4-1). **Runner-Up:** Wichita State (2-2).
Outstanding Player: Lamont Matthews, of, Oklahoma State.

❏ **Regional Site:** Waco, Texas (Baylor).
Participants: No. 1 Baylor (46-13), No. 2 Minnesota (44-16), No. 3 Arizona (33-21), *No. 4 Eastern Illinois (32-21).
Champion: Baylor (3-0). **Runner-Up:** Minnesota (2-2).
Outstanding Player: Jason Jennings, rhp/dh, Baylor.
(Baylor advances to meet Oklahoma State in super regional).

ALABAMA

■ **Super Regional Site:** Tuscaloosa, Ala. (Alabama).
Participants: Louisiana State (41-22) at Alabama (49-14). (Alabama wins 2-0).

❏ **Regional Site:** Tuscaloosa, Ala. (Alabama).
Participants: *No. 1 Alabama (46-14), No. 2 South Alabama (38-18), No. 3 Southern Mississippi (38-21), *No. 4 Navy (27-20).
Champion: Alabama (3-0). **Runner-Up:** Southern Mississippi (2-2).
Outstanding Player: Andy Phillips, ss, Alabama.

❏ **Regional Site:** Baton Rouge (Louisiana State).
Participants: *No. 1 East Carolina (44-14), No. 2 Louisiana State (37-21), No. 3 Northeast Louisiana (36-20), *No. 4 Southern (28-14).
Champion: Louisiana State (4-1). **Runner-Up:** East Carolina (2-2).
Outstanding Player: Kurt Ainsworth, rhp, Louisiana State.
(Louisiana State advances to meet Alabama in super regional).

STANFORD

■ **Super Regional Site:** Stanford, Calif. (Stanford).
Participants: Southern California (36-24) at Stanford (46-13). (Stanford wins 2-0).

❏ **Regional Site:** Stanford, Calif. (Stanford).
Participants: *No. 1 Stanford (43-13), No. 2 Nevada (36-18), No. 3 North Carolina (40-16), *No. 4 Loyola Marymount (33-26).
Champion: Stanford (3-0). **Runner-Up:** Nevada (2-2).
Outstanding Player: Nick Day, of, Stanford.

❏ **Regional Site:** Los Angeles (Southern California).
Participants: No. 1 Pepperdine (43-14), No. 2 Southern California (33-23), No. 3 Virginia Commonwealth (40-18), *No. 4 Harvard (28-18).
Champion: Southern California (3-1). **Runner-Up:** Pepperdine (3-2).
Outstanding Player: Eric Munson, c, Southern California.
(Southern California advances to meet Stanford in super regional).

TEXAS A&M

■ **Super Regional Site:** College Station, Texas (Texas A&M).
Participants: Clemson (41-25) at Texas A&M (50-15) (Texas A&M wins 2-1)

❏ **Regional Site:** Fayetteville, Ark. (Arkansas).
Participants: No. 1 Arkansas (41-21), No. 2 Clemson (37-24), No. 3 Southwest Missouri State (36-17), *No. 4 Delaware (35-23).
Champion: Clemson (4-1). **Runner-Up:** Southwest Missouri State (2-2).
Outstanding Player: Matt Cepicky, of, Southwestern Missouri State

❏ **Regional Site:** College Station, Texas (Texas A&M).
Participants: No. 1 Texas A&M (46-14), No. 2 Long Beach State (33-23), No.3 Mississippi (33-26), *No. 4 Monmouth (26-22).
Champion: Texas A&M (4-1). **Runner-Up:** Long Beach State (2-2).
Outstanding Player: Steven Truitt, of, Texas A&M.
(Texas A&M advances to meet Clemson in super regional).

RICE

■ **Super Regional Site:** Houston (Rice).
Participants: Southwestern Louisiana (41-22) vs. Rice (56-12) at the Astrodome.
(Rice wins 2-1).

❏ **Regional Site:** Houston (Houston).
Participants: No. 1 Houston (38-22), No. 2 Southwestern Louisiana (38-22), No. 3 Texas (35-24), *No. 4 Southwest Texas State (27-30).
Champion: Southwestern Louisiana (3-0). **Runner-Up:** Houston (2-2).
Outstanding Player: Nathan Nelson, 3b, Southwestern Louisiana.

❏ **Regional Site:** Lubbock, Texas (Texas Tech).
Participants: *No. 1 Rice (56-12), No. 2 Texas Tech (40-15), No. 3 Rutgers (37-19), *No. 4 Wisconsin-Milwaukee (30-27).
Champion: Rice (4-1). **Runner-Up:** Texas Tech (2-2).
Outstanding Player: Will Ford, of, Rice.
(Rice advances to meet Southwestern Louisiana in super regional).

1999 COLLEGE ALL-AMERICA TEAM

Selected by Baseball America

Josh Bard **Willie Bloomquist** **Keith Reed** **Matt Cepicky** **Kurt Ainsworth**

FIRST TEAM

Pos., Player, School	Hometown	YR	AVG	AB	R	H	2B	3B	HR	RBI	SB	Drafted/Round
C Josh Bard, Texas Tech	Englewood, Colo.	Jr.	.353	238	49	84	28	2	13	92	1	Rockies (3)
1B Jon Palmieri, Wake Forest	Mellville, N.Y.	Sr.	.412	272	81	112	20	3	18	94	19	Angels (14)
2B Marshall McDougall, Florida St.	Valrico, Fla.	Jr.	.419	301	104	126	26	3	28	106	22	Red Sox (26)
3B Xavier Nady, California	Salinas, Calif.	So.	.374	227	56	85	17	1	23	62	5	Not eligible
SS Willie Bloomquist, Arizona St.	Port Orchard, Wash.	Jr.	.394	254	95	100	18	8	10	84	32	Mariners (3)
OF Matt Cepicky, SW Missouri St.	St. Louis	Jr.	.414	222	90	92	9	1	30	100	7	Expos (4)
OF Daylan Holt, Texas A&M	Mesquite, Texas	So.	.341	287	78	98	22	3	34	105	9	Not eligible
OF Keith Reed, Providence	Yarmouth Port, Mass.	Jr.	.398	274	73	109	22	2	17	79	15	Orioles (1)
DH Ken Harvey, Nebraska	Cerritos, Calif.	Jr.	.478	224	77	107	15	1	23	86	13	Royals (5)
UT Jason Jennings, Baylor	Mesquite, Texas	Jr.	.386	233	52	90	14	0	17	68	1	Rockies (1)

Pos., Player, School	Hometown	YR	W	L	ERA	G	SV	IP	H	BB	SO	
SP Kurt Ainsworth, Louisiana State	Baton Rouge	So.	13	6	3.45	22	1	130	114	48	157	Giants (1)
SP Mike MacDougal, Wake Forest	Mesa, Ariz.	Jr.	13	3	2.62	17	0	120	88	65	117	Royals (1)
SP Ben Sheets, NE Louisiana	St. Amant, La.	Jr.	14	1	3.11	18	2	116	100	31	156	Brewers (1)
SP Barry Zito, Southern California	El Cajon, Calif.	Jr.	12	3	3.28	17	0	113	93	58	154	Athletics (1)
RP Jay Gehrke, Pepperdine	Scottsdale, Ariz.	Jr.	1	1	0.86	31	18	31	19	12	40	Royals (1)
UT Jason Jennings, Baylor	Mesquite, Texas	Jr.	13	2	2.58	22	1	147	102	50	172	

SECOND TEAM

Pos., Player, School	Hometown	YR	AVG	AB	R	H	2B	3B	HR	RBI	SB	Drafted
C Casey Dunn, Auburn	Vestavia Hills, Ala.	Sr.	.379	269	70	102	19	1	16	86	1	Royals (15)
1B Ben Broussard, McNeese St.	Sour Lake, Texas	Sr.	.478	224	77	107	15	1	23	86	13	Reds (2)
2B James Jurries, Tulane	Lake Jackson, Texas	Fr.	.367	256	83	94	18	4	20	75	18	Not eligible
3B Ryan Gripp, Creighton	Indianola, Iowa	Jr.	.395	233	78	92	24	0	24	84	1	Cubs (3)
SS Brian Roberts, So. Carolina	Chapel Hill, N.C.	Jr.	.353	221	79	78	21	0	12	36	67	Orioles (1)
OF Larry Bigbie, Ball State	Hobart, Ind.	Jr.	.419	210	71	88	12	3	17	54	21	Dodgers (1)
OF Patrick Boyd, Clemson	Clearwater, Fla.	So.	.390	246	78	96	22	1	17	70	20	Not eligible
OF Bill Scott, UCLA	Granada Hills, Calif.	So.	.380	242	66	92	19	0	28	86	0	Not eligible
DH Taggert Bozied, San Fran.	Denver	So.	.412	204	71	84	13	2	30	82	7	Not eligible
UT Mike Dwyer, Richmond	Stony Point, N.Y.	Sr.	.412	228	77	94	20	4	21	78	3	Red Sox (13)

Pos., Player, School	Hometown	YR	W	L	ERA	G	SV	IP	H	BB	SO	
SP Mario Ramos, Rice	Pflugerville, Texas	Jr.	13	3	2.51	25	2	154	121	51	146	Athletics (6)
SP Brent Schoening, Auburn	Columbus, Ga.	Jr.	13	1	3.32	21	0	138	122	47	151	Twins (5)
SP Nick Stocks, Florida State	Tampa	So.	13	2	3.25	21	0	127	111	44	139	Cardinals (1)
SP Jason Young, Stanford	Berkeley, Calif.	So.	12	3	3.43	21	0	155	128	55	178	Not eligible
RP Jim Journell, Illinois	Springfield, Ohio	Jr.	7	2	1.78	26	8	35	24	15	53	Cardinals (4)
UT Mike Dwyer, Richmond	Stony Point, N.Y.	Sr.	10	5	3.56	17	0	94	85	29	82	

THIRD TEAM

Pos., Player, School	Hometown	YR	AVG	AB	R	H	2B	3B	HR	RBI	SB	Drafted
C Dane Sardinha, Pepperdine	Kahuku, Hawaii	So.	.365	260	51	95	26	2	15	63	5	Not eligible
1B Sean McGowan, Boston College	Burlington, Mass.	Sr.	.430	179	60	77	8	2	25	70	5	Giants (3)
2B Eric Nelson, Baylor	Missouri City, Texas	Sr.	.362	282	77	102	20	6	17	79	22	Royals (8)
3B Andrew Beinbrink, Arizona State	San Diego	Sr.	.402	234	78	94	22	2	14	85	16	Devil Rays (7)
SS Bobby Hill, Miami	San Jose	Jr.	.391	215	77	84	14	3	10	30	52	White Sox (2)
OF Lamont Matthews, Oklahoma St.	Petersburg, Va.	Jr.	.384	242	87	93	17	7	30	105	10	Dodgers (10)
OF Spencer Oborn, Cal St. Fullerton	Diamond Bar, Calif.	Jr.	.395	263	74	104	22	7	14	82	27	White Sox (14)
OF Steve Salargo, East Carolina	Wilson, N.C.	Jr.	.398	244	70	97	20	1	16	77	14	Orioles (20)
DH Andy Phillips, Alabama	Demopolis, Ala.	Sr.	.398	259	71	103	22	6	22	66	16	Yankees (7)
UT Peyton Lewis, Creighton	Yutan, Neb.	Sr.	.339	232	55	79	19	4	19	76	1	Blue Jays (18)

Pos., Player, School	Hometown	YR	W	L	ERA	G	SV	IP	H	BB	SO	
SP Casey Burns, Richmond	Pennington, N.J.	Jr.	9	3	3.21	14	0	95	72	37	124	Padres (1)
SP Phil Devey, SW Louisiana	Lachute, Quebec	Jr.	10	1	3.14	21	0	129	99	60	165	Dodgers (5)
SP Todd Moser, Florida Atlantic	Davie, Fla.	Sr.	15	1	2.34	19	0	104	96	31	130	Marlins (14)
SP David Walling, Arkansas	Lakeside, Calif.	Jr.	10	2	3.78	16	0	121	104	31	155	Yankees (1)
RP Chris Russ, Texas A&M	Kerrville, Texas	So.	12	2	3.27	28	3	83	77	28	51	Not eligible
UT Peyton Lewis, Creighton	Yutan, Neb.	Sr.	10	1	3.30	17	1	104	89	52	114	

bats, while Arizona used aluminum. The Wildcats swept the three-game series by a combined score of 35-8.

"That was ridiculous," Arizona freshman outfielder Shelley Duncan said after the series. "A lot of players are angry there's been a problem with that during the season, that it wasn't taken care of."

Over the course of the season, offense took a slight dip and coaches came to the conclusion that the players most affected by the new bats were players who didn't have a lot of power to begin with.

"The little guys, you notice a big difference with them because they don't hit as many out with the heavier bat," Louisiana State coach Skip Bertman said. "You see a lot more fly balls that go to the warning track, and we're all seeing that ball to the opposite field that used to go out gets caught now."

Still Swinging Big

Aluminum bats in use in 1999 were still aluminum and pretty potent, meaning there was plenty of offense.

The greatest single-game explosion in Division I history occurred when Florida State second baseman Marshall McDougall blasted an NCAA Division I record six home runs May 9 against Maryland in a 26-2 win.

"It's a great feeling because everyone was rooting for me," McDougall said after the game. "Seeing my teammates react and the fans react, it was great."

McDougall, a first-team All-American, also set D-I marks for RBIs (16) and total bases (25) while going 7-for-7, an Atlantic Coast Conference record. McDougall went on to hit .419 with 28 homers and 106 RBIs, and led the nation in hits (126), RBIs and runs (104). McDougall was also MVP of the CWS, but wasn't drafted until the 26th round by the Boston Red Sox. He did not sign and returned to Florida State for his senior year.

McDougall also put together one of the nation's longest hitting streaks, reaching 33 games before going hitless against Miami. Cal State Fullerton's Spencer Oborn had the longest streak of 1999, 37 games, while Alabama's Andy Phillips set a Southeastern Conference mark with a streak that reached 36 games before ending in Omaha. Kennesaw State (Ga.) senior outfielder Jason Jones set a new Division II hitting-streak record at 39 games.

Six home runs, one game
Florida State's Marshall McDougall

Three players hit four home runs in a game during the 1999 season: San Francisco's Taggert Bozied, Wichita State's Brian Preston and UCLA's Bill Scott.

Nebraska set NCAA records for runs and margin of victory in a 50-3 win against Chicago State. Senior first baseman Craig Moore had 10 RBIs in the game.

With all the big swings came a record number of strikeouts and some impressive strikeout feats. Northeast Louisiana righthander Ben Sheets, drafted No. 10 overall by the Milwaukee Brewers, had 20 strikeouts in a 6-2 win against Louisiana Tech. The Citadel lefthander Rodney Hancock had 20 as well in a 3-0 win against Furman during the Southern Conference tournament.

But possibly the most impressive pitching performance was turned in by Southern California lefthander Barry Zito, who was drafted ninth overall, just ahead of Sheets, by the Oakland Athletics. Zito recorded 16 strikeouts apiece in three consecutive starts in midseason. No Trojans pitcher had struck out 16 in a game since at least 1987, the last season for which USC had records available. Zito finished the 1999 season in Triple-A in the A's system.

Incident Costs Molina, Shockers

Aside from McDougall's six-home-run outburst, the college story that made the most national headlines in 1999 dealt one of the sport's top programs a black eye, as well as a major setback to its national championship hopes.

Wichita State lost righthander Ben Christensen for the rest of the season when he was suspended for a pregame beaning incident on April 23. Christensen, who was 9-1 and later was drafted in the first round by the Chicago Cubs, nailed Evansville leadoff hitter Anthony Molina in the face with a

Ben Christensen

pitch clocked at 91 mph during his warmups. Molina was several feet away from the plate when he was hit.

Christensen said he thought Molina was timing his pitches and Wichita State pitchers were instructed to throw a brushback pitch at those players. He said he didn't intend to hit Molina, who sustained a fractured cheekbone and a deep gash over his left eye that required more than 20 stitches. Months after the incident, Molina wasn't expected to ever regain 20/20 vision in his left eye.

In other news:

■ Pepperdine coach Frank Sanchez returned from his third bout with brain tumors in the last 15 years to lead the Waves to their best season since winning the national championship in 1992. But California coach Bob Milano's recovery from early season heart surgery didn't have as happy an ending. While Milano recovered, the Bears struggled and Milano retired at the end of the season. Pepperdine assistant Dave Esquer, a shortstop on Stanford's 1987-88 College World Series teams, replaced Milano.

Coach of the Year

Graham seizes first Division I opportunity by making Owls contenders

Wayne Graham freely admits he's a fan of daytime television. Soap operas such as ABC's "All My Children," are a Graham staple.

At 63, the Rice coach was in just his eighth year of coaching at the Division I level in 1999, after a life in baseball that took him to two brief major league stints as a player, years as a high school coach and a dominant stretch of junior-college coaching. He won plenty of awards in his varied career, but has just started to get national recognition for his work at Rice.

His wait for acclaim wasn't as long as that of "All My Children" star Susan Lucci, who won her first Emmy award in 1999 after being nominated 19 times for her portrayal of Erica Kane. Graham took home his own hardware in 1999 as Baseball America's Coach of the Year.

"I feel like Erica on 'All My Children.' It took (Lucci) 19 years to get an Emmy; it took me 20 years to get a Division I job,"

Wayne Graham

Graham said. "The thing is, they say what you survive makes you better. I feel like I survived 20 years of frustrated job aspirations."

Graham has taken Rice's program from an afterthought to a place among the nation's elite. The Owls made two College World Series trips in the last three years, the first two visits to Omaha in the program's history.

In fact, Rice has made all of its regional appearances under Graham (1995-1999) and produced four first-round picks since 1995: Jose Cruz Jr. (1995), Matt Anderson and Lance Berkman (1997), and Bubba Crosby (1998).

The Owls intend to be a force for a while, too. The school has razed Cameron Field, which Graham described as a glorified high school field. Reckling Park, a $6.4 million stadium that will seat 5,667 and enable

the Owls to stay at home for postseason play, will open in 2000.

"This stadium will help us sustain the program at the highest level," Graham said. "We've seen that more than 50 percent of the teams that make it to Omaha for the College World Series had hosted regionals, so this will help us stay at that level."

Few figured the Owls would ever compete at that level. Graham is managing to make the program work without compromising the school's reputation in the classroom. The 1999 team, which finished 59-15 after a 1-2 showing in Omaha, set a school record for wins and became the first Rice team to occupy the No. 1 spot in a poll in any sport.

Graham's track record indicated Rice would succeed under his leadership. He has coached his teams to 27 consecutive winning seasons and has a 908-267 record between Rice and San Jacinto (Texas) Junior College.

It was at San Jacinto that Graham's national reputation took root. His first team included freshman righthander Roger Clemens and went 43-7.

He was just getting started, though, as San Jac recorded seven consecutive 50-win seasons and won three straight national championships from 1985-87 and two more in 1989 and '90. The 1990 team included New York Yankees lefthander Andy Pettitte.

Graham needed a new challenge, and Rice was looking for new success in its program. It has become the perfect marriage.

PREVIOUS WINNERS

1981—Ron Fraser, Miami
1982—Gene Stephenson, Wichita State
1983—Barry Shollenberger, Alabama
1984—Augie Garrido, Cal State Fullerton
1985—Ron Polk, Mississippi State
1986—Skip Bertman, Louisiana State
          Dave Snow, Loyola Marymount
1987—Mark Marquess, Stanford
1988—Jim Brock, Arizona State
1989—Dave Snow, Long Beach State
1990—Steve Webber, Georgia
1991—Jim Hendry, Creighton
1992—Andy Lopez, Pepperdine
1993—Gene Stephenson, Wichita State
1994—Jim Morris, Miami
1995—Rod Delmonico, Tennessee
1996—Skip Bertman, Louisiana State
1997—Jim Wells, Alabama
1998—Pat Murphy, Arizona State

■ Florida Atlantic tied the Division I record for consecutive victories, winning 34 straight before a 2-1 loss to Jacksonville. That tied the record set by Texas' 1977 team.

■ Providence bowed out of Division I with the best season in school history. The Friars set a school record with 47 wins on the way to a Big East tournament championship. Providence fell two wins short of the CWS, losing to Florida State in the Tallahassee regional.

■ Baylor defeated Houston 8-2 in a 22-inning game, tying the Division I record set April 26, 1974, by Colorado and Nebraska.

■ UCLA's Gary Adams and Delaware's Bob Hannah pushed the number of college coaches with 1,000 career wins to 22. That fraternity lost one active member, however, when Georgia Southern's Jack Stallings, with 1,258 wins (fourth all-time), retired. Hannah announced he would retire at the end of the 2000 season, as did Auburn coach Hal Baird. But two veteran coaches returned: Ron Polk, who left Mississippi State in 1997, will coach Georgia in 2000, while Mike Roberts will coach UNC Asheville after leaving North Carolina after the 1998 season.

Freshman of the Year
Tulane's Jurries keeps award at second base

James Jurries didn't have a lot of experience at second base, but his coach is confident he'll be playing there for a long time.

"It doesn't take an astute baseball person to look at him and

know he's going to be a special player," Tulane coach Rick Jones said.

Jurries, 20, hit .374 with 20 home runs and 87 RBIs in 1999 and was the key player for 15th-ranked Tulane. Off that performance he edged out preseason favorite Mark Teixeira of Georgia Tech to become Baseball America's 1999 Freshman of the Year. He became the second straight second baseman honored, following California's Xavier Nady in 1998.

"I played a little bit better than I thought I would," said Jurries, who was the second baseman on BA's preseason All-Freshman team. "I figured I would come in and struggle at the beginning, which I did. But I made the adjustments."

Jurries had more adjustments to make than the typical freshman—both in the field and at the plate.

He began the season in the No. 2 hole before moving to the lead-off role when injuries created a need. Late in the season, when Jones decided he needed to put someone to protect senior catcher Chad Sutter in the lineup, he moved Jurries to the cleanup hole.

As his .440 on-base percentage and .698 slugging average indicate, he has the ability to get on base like a top-of-the-order hitter and the ability to hit with authority.

"It's just the way he swings," Jones said. "He stays back. He's got bat speed and bat control both. A lot of guys have one or the other. With that bat control he can make adjustments to reach pitches."

Jurries isn't just an offensive second baseman, though. He might be a little green in the field, but he's long on tools and he made great strides in 1999.

"I started figuring out second base," said Jurries, who started all 65 games there for the Green Wave. "I made a lot of dumb mistakes early."

But it didn't take long for him to learn when to hold the ball, where to position himself and how to execute the fundamentals of turning the double play.

"It's not a position you learn overnight," Jones said. "But his range and arm are outstanding."

James Jurries

A third baseman and shortstop at Brazoswood High in Lake Jackson, Texas, Jurries was told by scouts that his future would likely be at second base or in the outfield. His interest in changing positions made Tulane a perfect fit, as the Green Wave had lost second baseman Michael Pursell to graduation.

His commitment to the school was reinforced when he wasn't selected until the Indians took him in the 34th round in the 1998 draft.

"My mind was set to come to Tulane on draft day," he said. "It's probably the best move I've made in my life."

—JAMES BAILEY

FRESHMAN ALL-AMERICA TEAM

FIRST TEAM

Pos., Player, School	AVG	AB	R	H	2B	3B	HR	RBI	SB
C Beau Craig, Southern California	.319	204	46	65	17	3	4	50	2
1B Ryan Howard, Southwest Missouri State	.355	234	68	83	14	0	19	66	0
2B James Jurries, Tulane	.367	256	83	94	18	4	20	75	18
3B Mark Teixeira, Georgia Tech	.387	225	61	87	18	0	13	65	11
SS Jeff Keppinger, Georgia	.383	230	51	88	14	1	11	48	4
OF Shelley Duncan, Arizona	.294	211	47	62	13	0	20	68	3
OF Aaron Fausett, Vanderbilt	.356	216	34	77	12	1	8	41	11
OF Neal McCarthy, Providence	.376	218	65	82	22	2	17	69	7
DH Jeremy Brown, Alabama	.347	262	77	91	20	0	15	69	4
UT Ben Diggins, Arizona	.190	105	17	20	4	1	5	21	0

	W	L	ERA	G	SV	IP	H	BB	SO
P Lenny DiNardo, Stetson	9	6	3.78	19	0	95	99	38	98
P Charlie Isaacson, Arkansas	9	0	3.16	16	0	100	72	53	97
P Josh Karp, UCLA	8	3	4.26	16	0	87	84	44	79
P Brian Sager, Stanford	6	0	4.17	19	0	86	90	41	72
P Blair Varnes, Florida State	11	1	3.84	18	0	103	104	16	75
UT Ben Diggins, Arizona	8	5	6.86	19	2	85	86	57	86

SECOND TEAM

C—Chris Hamblen, Cincinnati (.299-11-62). **1B**—Brad Carlson, Iowa (.367-21-71). **2B**—Chris Burke, Tennessee (.372-2-41). **3B**—Greg Sain, San Diego (.339-12-66). **SS**—Lee Delfino, East Carolina (.317-12-50). **OF**—Tim Merritt, South Alabama (.330-11-44); Karl Nonemaker, Vanderbilt (.415-3-29); Mike Ross, Maine (.361-8-63). **DH**—Gabe Gross, Auburn (.363-7-65). **P**—Daniel Haren, Pepperdine (10-3, 3.08); Shane Komine, Nebraska (6-2, 3.58); E.J. Laratta, Ohio (10-3, 3.77); Preston Larrison, Evansville (8-5, 4.82); Justin Wechsler, Ball State (10-3, 3.39). **Util**—Mark Prior, Vanderbilt (.260-4-28; 4-8, 4.59).

College Baseball

NCAA DIVISION I LEADERS

TEAM BATTING

BATTING AVERAGE

	G	AVG
Arizona State	60	.356
Boston College	48	.354
Grambling	51	.352
Oral Roberts	61	.348
Southwest Missouri State	57	.345
New Mexico	60	.344
Rutgers	58	.343
Florida Atlantic	63	.341
Nevada-Las Vegas	61	.339
Nebraska	60	.338

RUNS SCORED

	G	R
Oklahoma State	67	696
Arizona State	60	679
Wichita State	73	657
Florida State	71	645
Alabama	69	617
Clemson	69	612
Southwest Missouri State	57	607
Providence	65	605
Rice	74	601
Nebraska	60	599

DOUBLES

	G	2B
Florida State	71	176
Rice	74	174
Wichita State	73	172
Minnesota	64	171
Clemson	69	169

TRIPLES

	G	3B
Rice	74	37
Nebraska	60	33
Bethune-Cookman	58	32
Oklahoma State	67	31
Alabama	69	31

HOME RUNS

	G	HR
Southwest Missouri State	57	144
Oklahoma State	67	132
Tulane	65	128
Texas A&M	70	128
Alabama	69	120
Troy State	59	118
Florida State	71	111
Florida Atlantic	63	109
Baylor	65	108
Louisiana State	66	104
Miami (Fla.)	63	104

STOLEN BASES

	G	SB	ATT
Oral Roberts	61	230	269
James Madison	44	182	231
Miami (Fla.)	63	164	222
UNC Greensboro	55	153	180
Bethune-Cookman	58	150	194
The Citadel	61	148	193
Baylor	65	146	172
Nebraska	60	144	170
Cal State Fullerton	64	144	202
South Carolina	58	143	176

TEAM PITCHING

W-L PERCENTAGE

	W	L	PCT
Florida Atlantic	54	9	.857
Wichita State	59	14	.808
Florida State	57	14	.803
Rice	59	15	.797
Miami (Fla.)	50	13	.794
Cal State Fullerton	50	14	.781
Ohio State	50	14	.781
Baylor	50	15	.769
Stanford	50	15	.769
Alabama	53	16	.768

EARNED RUN AVERAGE

	G	ERA
Florida International	63	3.07
Florida Atlantic	63	3.10
Florida State	71	3.18
Rice	74	3.34
Wichita State	73	3.59
Northeastern	49	3.67
Coastal Carolina	58	3.72
North Carolina	59	3.73
Pepperdine	62	3.80
Southwestern Louisiana	66	3.85

TEAM FIELDING

AVERAGE

	G	AVG
Mississippi State	63	.974
Pepperdine	62	.972
Texas Tech	59	.971
Oklahoma	59	.970
Wichita State	73	.969
Arizona	56	.969
Houston	64	.969
Georgia	56	.968
Towson	52	.968
Northwestern State	59	.967
Southwest Texas State	59	.967
Louisville	56	.967

INDIVIDUAL BATTING

BATTING AVERAGE
(Minimum 125 At-Bats)

	Yr.	AVG	G	AB	R	H	2B	3B	HR	RBI	BB	SO	SB
Ken Harvey, Nebraska	Jr.	.478	57	224	77	107	15	1	23	86	38	23	13
Hunter Bledsoe, Vandy	Sr.	.459	54	207	61	95	24	1	10	51	40	19	31
B.J. Barns, Duquesne	Jr.	.456	56	195	67	89	22	3	17	57	32	34	5
Joe Zeccardi, Long Island	Sr.	.444	43	153	58	68	15	2	13	58	39	26	3
Steve Tomshack, UMBC	Sr.	.439	35	132	33	58	16	2	5	32	16	14	1
Mark Ernster, Ariz. St.	Jr.	.439	44	155	49	68	13	2	5	45	19	25	11
John-Ford Griffin, Fla. St.	Fr.	.436	55	133	42	58	15	0	3	35	18	22	0
Joe Francisco, Wagner	Sr.	.436	42	163	32	52	8	1	5	19	20	20	30
Brian Thrash, UMBC	Sr.	.435	35	124	41	54	14	1	4	27	19	17	3
Sean McGowan, Bos. Coll.	Sr.	.430	47	179	60	77	8	2	25	70	28	32	5
Ben Johnstone, Yale	Sr.	.430	40	151	39	65	14	3	2	29	7	11	23
Gilbert Lanoix, Grambling	So.	.429	46	168	51	72	11	5	7	55	15	4	4
Kasey Weishaar, Kan. St.	So.	.429	53	191	53	82	9	4	7	31	30	30	4
Nick Danzuso, Duquesne	Jr.	.428	51	187	40	80	13	1	10	68	15	21	5
Ben Broussard, McNeese	Sr.	.427	56	211	74	90	14	4	27	91	53	40	10
Paul Esposito, Fair. Dick.	Sr.	.427	40	143	50	61	14	1	3	28	23	12	2
Darren Fenster, Rutgers	Jr.	.424	57	224	64	95	18	2	2	57	27	24	7
Mike Thiessen, Air Force	So.	.424	51	191	71	81	15	3	12	50	38	29	9
Ryan Neill, ORU	Jr.	.423	61	208	70	88	20	2	18	71	37	40	20
Royce Huffman, TCU	Jr.	.422	57	223	75	94	20	3	15	64	47	16	6
Mike Scott, Providence	So.	.420	64	286	87	120	21	13	5	64	27	13	7
Lyle Overbay, Nevada	Sr.	.420	58	243	76	102	24	3	15	88	35	47	4
Nathan Nelson, SW La.	Sr.	.420	41	162	30	68	17	3	4	42	12	13	6
Marshall McDougall, Fla. St.	Jr.	.419	71	301	104	126	26	3	28	106	39	46	22
Larry Bigbie, Ball State	Jr.	.419	60	210	71	88	12	3	17	54	38	28	21
Pete Zoccolillo, Rutgers	Jr.	.418	58	232	63	97	22	2	12	72	25	25	1
Jeff Stallings, ORU	Jr.	.417	61	228	81	95	19	3	7	42	38	23	49
Kelly Eddlemon, Sam Hous.	Jr.	.416	55	221	62	92	24	2	26	95	22	20	7
Chris Cottonham, Grambling	So.	.416	47	154	65	64	11	4	16	69	25	22	13
Aaron Runk, Iowa St.	Jr.	.415	36	142	48	59	15	3	6	28	23	26	22
Karl Nonemaker, Vandy	Fr.	.415	51	212	46	88	18	0	3	29	17	18	4
Matt Cepicky, SW Mo.	Sr.	.414	56	222	90	92	9	1	30	100	38	27	7
Robb Quinlan, Minn.	Sr.	.413	64	259	76	107	26	4	16	84	28	21	6
Nate Rewers, Richmond	Sr.	.413	58	225	71	93	14	0	14	54	37	20	16
Jon Palmieri, Wake Forest	Sr.	.412	63	272	81	112	20	3	18	94	26	13	19
Mike Dwyer, Richmond	Sr.	.412	58	228	77	94	20	4	21	78	36	40	3
Jake Anthony, Va. Comm.	Sr.	.412	58	204	48	84	14	0	8	53	29	37	4
Taggert Bozied, USF	So.	.412	56	204	71	84	13	2	30	82	40	25	7
Mike Grippo, Long Island	Sr.	.412	43	165	33	68	14	3	5	44	8	10	4
Jeremy Johnson, SE Mo	Jr.	.412	52	194	50	80	18	5	11	45	18	28	13
Mike Dzurilla, St. John's	Jr.	.410	56	223	51	94	24	2	16	65	21	22	17
Chris Beck, CS Fullerton	Jr.	.408	63	240	64	98	18	1	8	75	48	37	27
Michael Artman, So. Miss	Jr.	.408	63	260	74	106	15	3	6	43	31	33	19
Kevin Youkilis, Cincinnati	So.	.407	59	236	85	96	23	0	13	72	40	22	2
Mike McCarthy, Bucknell	Sr.	.407	53	199	54	81	15	8	6	58	16	33	13
Ryan Carville, Air Force	Sr.	.407	50	189	52	77	20	3	9	52	17	30	12
Charles Thomas, West. Car.	Jr.	.406	60	244	76	99	15	2	3	41	43	33	17
Jess Bechard, Kent	Jr.	.406	50	192	48	78	22	1	8	49	14	24	5
Mark Thomas, Young. St.	Jr.	.406	56	197	54	80	22	4	9	39	31	30	12
Tom Yost, Miami (Ohio)	So.	.406	46	128	25	52	3	1	5	27	12	31	6
Kevin Schnall, Co. Car.	Sr.	.405	55	185	46	75	13	0	7	48	35	19	1
Dino Dakuras, Beth.-Cook.	Sr.	.405	50	158	39	64	15	2	5	41	28	24	3
Blake Woods, Grand Canyon	So.	.404	53	225	55	91	20	0	1	37	27	21	0
Chris Clarke, Wm. & Mary	So.	.404	53	203	62	82	18	1	7	60	34	23	17
Travis Chapman, Miss. St.	Jr.	.404	63	245	66	99	18	0	6	49	38	28	2
Rob DeFabbia, Fair. Dick.	Sr.	.403	45	159	44	64	12	1	13	60	26	10	2
Kevin Hooper, Wich. St.	Sr.	.402	55	214	72	86	15	7	4	36	45	26	26
Buddy Dubois, Austin Peay	Jr.	.402	56	199	45	80	23	2	5	27	22	28	14
Andrew Beinbrink, Ariz. St.	Jr.	.402	60	234	78	94	22	2	14	85	48	26	16
Brian Leighton, Seton Hall	So.	.401	50	182	51	73	11	6	7	48	30	21	4
Ben Fjelland, Northern Iowa	Jr.	.400	53	220	49	88	20	1	7	44	16	24	4
Bob Niemet, Bowling Green	Sr.	.400	59	200	50	80	15	3	6	44	28	11	20
Al Candea, Ill.-Chicago	Sr.	.400	47	180	43	72	15	2	11	55	14	25	6
Brian Hitchcox, Samford	Jr.	.400	51	200	50	80	21	3	2	29	23	14	26

College Baseball

RUNS	Yr.	G	R
Marshall McDougall, Fla. St.	Jr.	71	104
Reed Johnson, CS Fullerton	.. Jr.	64	101
Billy Gasparino, Okla. St.	Sr.	66	96
Willie Bloomquist, Ariz. St.	Jr.	60	95
Matt Cepicky, SW Mo.	Jr.	56	90
James Jurries, Tulane	Fr.	65	90
Mike Scott, Providence	So.	64	87
Lamont Matthews, Okla. St.	Jr.	65	87
Blake Blasi, Wich. St.	So.	68	87
Joe Inglett, Nevada	Jr.	58	86
Damon Thames, Rice	Sr.	74	86
David DeJesus, Rutgers	So.	58	85
Kevin Youkilis, Cinc.	So.	59	85
G.W. Keller, Alabama	Sr.	63	85
Henri Stanley, Clemson	Jr.	69	85

HITS	Yr.	G	H
Marshall McDougall, Fla. St.	Jr.	71	126
Mike Scott, Providence	So.	64	120
Damon Thames, Rice	Sr.	74	118
Charles Williams, Rice	Jr.	74	116
Matt Diaz, Fla. State	So.	70	114
Jon Palmieri, Wake Forest	Sr.	63	112
Keith Reed, Providence	Jr.	65	109
Ken Harvey, Nebraska	Jr.	57	107
Robb Quinlan, Minn.	Sr.	64	107
G.W. Keller, Alabama	Sr.	69	107
Michael Artman, So. Miss	Jr.	63	106
Reed Johnson, CS Full	Jr.	64	106
Blake Blasi, Wich. St.	So.	68	106
Will Ford, Rice	Jr.	70	105
Spencer Oborn, CS Full	Jr.	64	104
James Jurries, Tulane	Fr.	65	104

SLUGGING PERCENTAGE

(Minimum 125 At-Bats)	Yr.	G	PCT
Taggert Bozied, USF	So.	56	.936
Sean McGowan, Bos. Coll	Sr.	47	.916
Ben Broussard, McNeese	Sr.	56	.915
Kelly Eddlemon, Sam Hous. ...	Jr.	55	.896
Lamont Matthews, Okla. St.	Jr.	67	.884
Matt Cepicky, SW Mo.	Jr.	56	.869
Ken Harvey, Nebraska	Jr.	57	.862
B.J. Barns, Duquesne	Jr.	56	.862
Chris Cottonham, Gram	So.	47	.851
Joe Zeccardi, Long Island	Sr.	43	.824

TOTAL BASES	Yr.	G	TB
Marshall McDougall, Fla. St.	Jr.	71	242
Daylan Holt, Texas A&M	So.	70	228
Lamont Matthews, Okla. St.	Jr.	65	214
Matt Diaz, Fla. State	So.	70	207
Andy Phillips, Alabama	Sr.	64	203
Kelly Eddlemon, Sam Hous.	Jr.	55	198
Bill Scott, UCLA	So.	61	195
James Jurries, Tulane	Fr.	65	194
Ben Broussard, McNeese	Sr.	56	193
Matt Cepicky, SW Mo.	Jr.	56	193

Texas A&M's Daylan Holt
Led nation with 34 homers

South Carolina's Brian Roberts
67 stolen bases led nation

Ken Harvey, Nebraska	Jr.	57	193
Jon Palmieri, Wake Forest	Sr.	63	192
Taggert Bozied, USF	So.	56	191
Robb Quinlan, Minn.	Sr.	64	189
Ryan Gripp, Creighton	Jr.	63	188

DOUBLES	Yr.	G	2B
Matt Scanlon, Minn.	Jr.	64	33
Casey Crume, Ark.-LR	Jr.	51	28
Josh Bard, Texas Tech	Jr.	58	28
Blake Blasi, Wich. St.	So.	68	28
Russell Harry, J'ville St.	Jr.	52	27
Matt Postell, N.C. State	Jr.	59	27
Scott Daeley, Wake Forest	Sr.	63	27
Sean Heaney, Texas A&M	Jr.	67	27
Dane Sardinha, Pepp.............	So.	62	26
Robb Quinlan, Minn.	Sr.	64	26
Marshall McDougall, Fla. St.	Jr.	71	26

TRIPLES	Yr.	G	3B
Mike Scott, Providence	So.	64	13
Charles Williams, Rice	Jr.	74	9
Jon Weber, Texas Tech	Jr.	50	8
Mike McCarthy, Bucknell	Jr.	53	8
Willie Bloomquist, Ariz. St.	Jr.	60	8
Jason Cox, Texas	Sr.	62	8
Jason Gray, Rice	Jr.	74	8

HOME RUNS	Yr.	G	HR
Daylan Holt, Texas A&M	So.	70	34
Matt Cepicky, SW Mo.	Jr.	56	30
Taggert Bozied, USF	So.	56	30
Lamont Matthews, Okla. St.	Jr.	67	30
Bill Scott, UCLA	So.	61	28
Marshall McDougall, Fla. St.	Jr.	71	28
Ben Broussard, McNeese	Sr.	56	27
Don Price, Nevada	Jr.	58	27
Kelly Eddlemon, Sam Hous.	Jr.	55	26
Steve Harris, W. Car.	Sr.	59	26
Jorge Soto, Troy State	Jr.	59	26
Sean McGowan, Bos. Coll.	Sr.	47	25
Jon Hale, SW Mo.	Sr.	56	25
Jaeme Leal, Long Beach St. ..	Jr.	59	24
Ryan Gripp, Creighton	Jr.	63	24
Billy Gasparino, Ok. St.	Sr.	66	24
Joe Beichert, Geo. Wash.	Sr.	56	23
Nick Kays, SW Mo.	So.	56	23
John Wilson, Ky.	So.	56	23
Ken Harvey, Nebraska	Jr.	57	23
Macky Waguespack, SE La. ..	Sr.	57	23
Xavier Nady, Cal	So.	58	23
Mike Hill, ORU	Jr.	59	23
Ryan Duncheon, Ill. St.	Jr.	59	23
Chad Sutter, Tulane	Sr.	63	23
Ryan Owens, CS Full	Jr.	64	23
Brian Preston, Wich. St.	Sr.	67	23
Ryan Pond, BYU	Sr.	55	23
Josh Pride, Mid Tenn	Jr.	59	22
Kevan Burns, Troy State	Jr.	59	22
Kevin Brown, Miami	So.	62	22

	Yr.	G	
Andy Phillips, Alabama	Sr.	63	22
Brad Carlson, Iowa	Fr.	54	21
Eric Storey, Butler	Jr.	55	21
Mike Dwyer, Richmond	Sr.	58	21
Chris Moore, West. Car.	Sr.	60	21
Matt Diaz, Fla. State	So.	70	21

RUNS BATTED IN	Yr.	G	RBI
Marshall McDougall, Fla. St. ...	Jr.	71	106
Lamont Matthews, Okla. St.	Jr.	67	105
Daylan Holt, Texas A&M	So.	70	105
Matt Cepicky, SW Mo.	Jr.	56	100
Kelly Eddlemon, Sam Houston	Jr.	55	95
Jon Palmieri, Wake Forest	Sr.	63	94
Matt Diaz, Fla. State	So.	70	94
Pat Magness, Wich. St.	Jr.	72	94
Josh Bard, Texas Tech	Jr.	58	92
Ben Broussard, McNeese	Sr.	56	91
Billy Gasparino, Ok. St.	Sr.	66	91
Don Price, Nevada	Jr.	58	89
Lyle Overbay, Nevada	Sr.	58	88
Mike Hill, Oral Roberts	Jr.	59	88
Chad Sutter, Tulane	Sr.	63	87
Ken Harvey, Nebraska	Jr.	57	86
Bill Scott, UCLA	So.	61	86
Casey Dunn, Auburn	Sr.	65	86
Andrew Beinbrink, Ariz. St.	Sr.	60	85
Ryan Owens, CS Fullerton	Jr.	64	85
Jon Weber, Texas Tech	Jr.	50	84
Chris Moore, West. Car.	Sr.	60	84
Willie Bloomquist, Ariz. St.	Jr.	60	84
Ryan Gripp, Creighton	Jr.	63	84
Robb Quinlan, Minn.	Sr.	64	84
Jody Pollock, Ga. South.	Jr.	58	83

WALKS	Yr.	G	BB
Bobby Hill, Miami	Jr.	63	73
Josh Holliday, Ok. St.	Sr.	67	71
Dan Moylan, No. Car.	So.	59	68
Pat Magness, Wich. St.	.Jr.	72	68
Jorge Soto, Troy State	Jr.	59	65

STRIKEOUTS	Yr.	G	SO
Phil Downing, So. Utah	Jr.	48	74
Darryl Clark, Char. So.	So.	58	73
Jaeme Leal, Long Beach St. ..	Jr.	59	73
Brian Kirby, Ark.	So.	65	73
Kevin Cash, Fla. St.	Jr.	68	72

TOUGHEST TO STRIKE OUT

(Minimum 125 At-Bats)	Yr.	AB	SO	Ratio
Gilbert Lanoix, Gram.	So.	168	4	42.0
Jeff Karpell, Fair. Dick. ...	Sr.	163	4	40.8
Glenn Katz, Conn.	Sr.	220	8	27.5
Vic Boccarossa, LeMoyne	Sr.	136	5	27.2
Shawn Schumacher, Tx A&M	Sr.	243	9	27.0

STOLEN BASES	Yr.	G	SB	ATT
Brian Roberts, So. Car. ..	Jr.	58	67	79
T Riley, James Madison	Jr.	51	54	60
Chris Morris, Citadel	So.	59	52	63
Bobby Hill, Miami	Jr.	63	52	67
Jeff Stallings, ORU	Jr.	61	49	55
Eric Johnson, W. Car.	Jr.	60	46	54
Billy Colome, Coll. Char. ..	Sr.	55	46	56
Tim Boeth, Cent. Fla.	Sr.	53	45	54
Shawn Pearson, ODU	Jr.	54	43	49
Mailon Kent, Auburn	Fr.	65	40	42
G.W. Keller, Alabama	Sr.	69	40	44
Tony Coleman, Gram.	Sr.	42	39	45
Brian Joyce, Davidson ..	Sr.	49	37	42
Marco Cunningham, Tx Tech	Jr.	59	37	45
Mike Harris, Citadel	So.	60	36	47
Ryan Ruiz, Texas Tech ..	Sr.	59	35	37
Joe Jester, Ark.	Jr.	65	35	37
Bryan Gann, ORU	Jr.	61	35	40
Rich Thompson, JMU	So.	44	35	42
Jason Clements, ORU	Jr.	49	35	42
Mark Dixon, More. St.	Sr.	53	35	43

HIT BY PITCH	Yr.	G	HBP
Luke Geddes, So. Utah	Jr.	46	24
Tony Hurtado, USF	So.	55	24
Billy Gasparino, Ok. St.	Sr.	66	24
Jaeme Leal, Long Beach St. ..	Jr.	59	23
Josh Holliday, Ok. St.	Sr.	71	22
Matt Maguire, Nevada	Fr.	57	22
Jake Anthony, Va. Comm.	Sr.	58	22
Joe Jester, Arkansas	Jr.	65	22

College Baseball

INDIVIDUAL PITCHING

EARNED RUN AVERAGE
(Minimum 60 Innings)

	Yr.	W	L	ERA	G	GS	CG	SV	IP	H	R	ER	BB	SO
Derrick DePriest, No. Car.	Jr.	7	6	1.71	36	1	0	7	74	73	35	14	22	72
Jeremy Sanders, E. Ill.	Sr.	10	1	1.76	34	1	0	5	72	53	26	14	14	48
Greg Montalbano, N'eastern	Jr.	8	2	2.09	11	10	8	0	65	44	18	15	24	71
Chris Chavez, Fla. State	Sr.	8	5	2.17	36	3	1	5	87	60	27	21	36	109
Mark Short, Pacific	Jr.	8	3	2.20	31	3	1	7	78	65	27	19	24	60
David Mittauer, FIU	So.	7	3	2.24	17	14	0	0	88	80	33	22	31	91
Kenny Baugh, Rice	So.	12	2	2.26	20	16	3	0	112	94	38	28	46	103
Adam Poturnicki, C. Conn.	Sr.	9	3	2.33	18	11	9	2	89	77	38	23	28	112
Todd Moser, Fla. Atl.	Sr.	15	1	2.34	19	16	3	0	104	96	42	27	31	130
Ben Christensen, Wich. St.	Jr.	9	1	2.40	11	11	3	0	71	46	21	19	17	77
Brandon Roberson, Tx Tech	Jr.	3	4	2.45	27	3	0	10	70	62	24	19	28	77
Brandon Belanger, Tulane	Jr.	3	5	2.45	41	0	0	16	66	66	27	18	15	68
Mike Gallo, Long Beach St.	Sr.	10	3	2.48	18	17	4	0	123	122	48	34	29	96
Scott Sturkie, Co. Car.	So.	10	4	2.49	20	16	4	0	116	107	45	32	39	106
Peter Moore, Temple	Sr.	5	6	2.50	24	10	10	8	94	76	33	26	33	103
Jeremy Griffiths, Toledo	Jr.	11	4	2.50	15	15	11	0	97	75	33	27	29	102
Mario Ramos, Rice	Jr.	13	3	2.51	25	20	6	2	154	121	56	43	51	146
Lucas Hocker, Coll. Char.	Jr.	9	4	2.52	16	14	2	0	96	100	43	27	25	87
Bryan Moore, Houston	Jr.	7	2	2.55	32	0	0	2	74	71	30	21	26	50
Jay Adams, Pepp.	So.	11	3	2.56	18	15	5	0	120	114	41	34	19	91
Randon Ho, Hawaii	Jr.	6	3	2.57	15	10	0	1	63	57	28	18	27	55
Jason Jennings, Baylor	Jr.	13	2	2.58	22	18	9	1	147	102	50	34	50	172
Scott Atchison, TCU	Jr.	10	4	2.58	15	14	4	0	101	101	44	29	26	115
Travis Minix, Ball State	Sr.	11	2	2.60	19	17	6	0	97	83	42	28	30	106
Jesse Kurtz-Nicholl, Rice	Sr.	7	1	2.61	38	0	0	8	76	68	31	22	25	100
Mike MacDougal, WF	Jr.	13	3	2.62	17	17	2	0	120	88	43	35	65	117
Andy Facey, Long Island	Jr.	6	3	2.64	12	9	6	0	72	73	36	21	7	51
Hank Thoms, Miss. St.	Sr.	7	6	2.66	18	16	2	1	118	127	47	35	37	121
Doug Connolly, Marist	Sr.	8	2	2.67	12	12	6	0	78	71	35	23	36	78
Ben Grezlovski, Fla.	Sr.	9	8	2.69	36	0	0	5	84	79	34	25	39	84
Alan Ochsner, SW La.	Sr.	6	0	2.72	26	3	0	6	76	59	35	23	30	93
Travis Thompson, E. Car.	Sr.	10	2	2.75	16	14	2	0	95	94	37	29	34	84
Bryan Mazur, UNC-W	Sr.	10	4	2.76	22	10	7	3	101	98	37	31	35	118
Kevin Barry, Rider	So.	5	2	2.76	12	10	4	0	65	54	28	20	26	57
Jody Harris, Missouri	Jr.	8	4	2.77	17	14	4	0	101	89	46	31	19	93
John Birtwell, Harvard	So.	4	5	2.83	11	9	4	0	64	53	24	20	10	69
Vince LaCorte, San Jose St.	Jr.	9	2	2.85	17	13	3	2	101	95	43	32	26	99

WINS

	Sr.	W	L
Todd Moser, Fla. Atl.	Sr.	15	1
Jeff Nichols, Rice	Jr.	15	4
Ben Sheets, NE La.	Jr.	14	1
Marc DesRoches, Prov.	Sr.	14	2
Brent Schoening, Auburn	Jr.	13	2
Ron Deubel, Co. Car.	Sr.	13	2
Jason Jennings, Baylor	Jr.	13	2
Nick Stocks, Fla. State	So.	13	2
Mike MacDougal, WF	Jr.	13	3
Alex Santos, Miami (Fla.)	Jr.	13	3
Mario Ramos, Rice	Jr.	13	3
Jared Berkowitz, Tulane	Jr.	13	3
Kurt Ainsworth, LSU	So.	13	6
Hayden Gliemmo, Auburn	So.	13	7
David Gil, Miami (Fla.)	Jr.	12	0
Matt Sorensen, CS Full	Sr.	12	0
Matt Koziara, Winthrop	Sr.	12	2
Chris Russ, So., Texas A&M	So.	12	2
Scott Siemon, Wake Forest	Sr.	12	2
Kenny Baugh, Rice	So.	12	2
Barry Zito, So. Cal	Jr.	12	3
Matt Baber, East Tenn.	Jr.	12	3
Jason Young, Stanford	So.	12	3
Jason Kelley, Bowl. Green	Sr.	12	4
Scott Glaser, So. Fla.	Sr.	12	5
Raul Garcia, FIU	Sr.	12	6
Casey Fossum, Texas A&M	Jr.	12	7

APPEARANCES

	Yr.	G
Michael Neu, Miami (Fla.)	Jr.	46
Brandon Belanger, Tulane	Jr.	41
Kirk Saarloos, CS Full	So.	39
Tyler Kee, Southern Miss	Sr.	39
Jesse Kurtz-Nicholl, Rice	Sr.	38
Hans Smith, Fresno State	Sr.	38

COMPLETE GAMES

	Yr.	GS	CG
Jason Kelley, Bowl. Green	Sr.	18	12
Matt Baber, East Tenn.	Jr.	13	11
Jeremy Griffiths, Toledo	Jr.	15	11
Peter Moore, Temple	Sr.	10	10
Martin Warfield, Ark.-PB	Jr.	13	10
Lou Witte, Xavier	Sr.	15	10

Stanford's Jason Young
178 strikeouts

Eugenio Melendez, Toledo	Jr.	15	10
Jason Young, Stanford	So.	21	10

SAVES

	Yr.	G	SV
Jay Gehrke, Pepp.	Jr.	31	18
Marc Bluma, Wich. St.	Sr.	28	17
Brandon Belanger, Tulane	Jr.	41	16
Michael Neu, Miami (Fla.)	Jr.	46	16
Mark Squire, Wright St.	Sr.	28	15
Dan Adams, Kent	Jr.	31	15
Steve Kent, FIU	Jr.	24	13
Kit Kadlec, Co. Car.	Jr.	36	13
Brian Gismonde, Monmouth	So.	26	12
Matt Hoffman, ORU	Jr.	28	11
Lance Cormier, Alabama	Fr.	29	11
Scott Yahraus, Creighton	Fr.	32	11
Aaron Sundsmo, Winthrop	Sr.	35	11

Pepperdine's Jay Gehrke
18 saves

Scott Porter, Jacksonville	Sr.	35	11

INNINGS PITCHED

	Yr.	G	IP
Jamie Bennett, Tenn.	Jr.	23	164
Jason Young, Stanford	So.	21	155
Mario Ramos, Rice	Jr.	25	154
Jason Jennings, Baylor	Jr.	22	147
Brent Schoening, Auburn	Jr.	21	138
Jeff Nichols, Rice	Jr.	25	138

WALKS

	Yr.	IP	BB
Joe Locklear, NC A&T	Fr.	64	76
Marlyn Tisdale, Tenn.	Jr.	86	67
Scott Dunn, Texas	Jr.	103	67
Mike MacDougal, Wake For	Jr.	120	65
Cade Sanchez, UT Arl.	Jr.	71	64

STRIKEOUTS

	Yr.	IP	SO
Jason Young, Stanford	So.	155	178
Jason Jennings, Baylor	Jr.	147	172
Phil Devey, SW La.	Jr.	129	165
Casey Fossum, Texas A&M	Jr.	134	162
Kurt Ainsworth, LSU	So.	130	157
Ben Sheets, NE La.	Jr.	116	156
David Walling, Ark.	Jr.	121	155
Barry Zito, USC	Jr.	113	154
Brent Schoening, Auburn	Jr.	138	151
Brian Wiley, Citadel	Sr.	93	150
Edwin Franco, FIU	Sr.	127	148
Mario Ramos, Rice	Jr.	154	146
Matt Smith, Okla. St.	So.	114	144
Alex Santos, Miami (Fla.)	Jr.	122	144
Jamie Bennett, Tenn.	Jr.	164	142
Nick Stocks, Fla. State	So.	127	139
Stephen Cowie, Duke	Sr.	116	137
Adam Johnson, CS Full	So.	117	136
Justin Wayne, Stanford	So.	118	135
Billy Traber, Loy. Mary.	So.	120	135
Omar Ortiz, Texas-PA	Jr.	102	132
Ron Deubel, Co. Car	Sr.	131	132
Jeff Heaverlo, Wash.	Jr.	108	131
Henry Bonilla, Tulane	Jr.	124	131
Todd Moser, Fla. Atl.	Sr.	104	130
Chuck Crowder, Ga. Tech	Sr.	117	130
Darin Moore, Pacific	Jr.	117	128
Dan Jackson, Fla. Atl.	Jr.	96	126

STRIKEOUTS/9 INNINGS
(Minimum 50 Innings)

	Yr.	IP	SO	AVG
Michael Neu, Miami (Fla.)	Jr.	67	110	14.7
Brian Wiley, Citadel	Sr.	93	150	14.5
Harold Eckert, FIU	Sr.	75	112	13.5
Rick Cercy, More. St.	Sr.	63	92	13.1
Barry Zito, USC	Jr.	113	154	12.3
Ben Sheets, NE La.	Jr.	116	158	12.3
Scott Martin, C. Conn.	Sr.	77	103	12.1
Dan Jackson, Fla. Atl.	Jr.	96	126	11.9
J. Kurtz-Nicholl, Rice	Sr.	76	100	11.8
Casey Burns, Richmond	Jr.	95	124	11.7

BASEBALL AMERICA'S
COLLEGE TOP 25

BATTERS: 10 or more at-bats.
PITCHERS: 5 or more innings.

Boldface indicates selected in 1999 draft.

1. MIAMI

Coach: Jim Morris   **Record:** 50-13

BATTING	YR	AVG	AB	R	H	2B	3B	HR	RBI	SB
Hill, Bobby, ss	Jr.	.391	215	77	84	14	3	10	30	52
Jacobson, Russ, c	Jr.	.380	150	42	57	13	1	14	41	1
Rodriguez, Mike, of	Fr.	.371	167	39	62	11	3	1	34	18
Crespo, Manny, of	So.	.364	173	49	63	11	0	12	54	12
Esquivel, Lale, 3b	So.	.354	229	52	81	16	1	13	58	6
Nettles, Marcus, of-dh	Jr.	.349	109	29	38	3	1	2	20	20
Rodriguez, Javier, 2b-3b	Fr.	.345	139	29	48	3	1	2	22	5
Brown, Kevin, 1b	So.	.319	216	63	69	14	0	22	66	4
Lovelady, Greg, c	So.	.318	129	24	41	9	1	4	36	0
Seever, Brian, of	So.	.304	138	36	42	7	2	2	23	18
Clute, Kris, 2b	So.	.301	163	32	49	10	0	3	38	8
Walker, Mark, of	Jr.	.292	168	46	49	5	2	9	43	14
Jimerson, Charlton, of	So.	.263	57	12	15	1	0	2	8	5
DiRosa, Mike, c	Fr.	.254	63	14	16	2	0	4	11	1
Grubbs, Waylon, dh	Jr.	.194	36	5	7	2	0	2	5	0
DeCastro, Raul, dh	Sr.	.150	20	7	3	0	0	2	4	0

PITCHING		W	L	ERA	G	SV	IP	H	BB	SO
Prendes, Alex, lhp	So.	0	0	2.30	17	0	16	11	8	15
Neu, Michael, rhp	Jr.	3	1	2.94	46	16	67	36	30	110
Santos, Alex, rhp	Jr.	13	3	2.95	20	0	122	106	46	144
Gil, David, rhp	Jr.	12	0	3.19	17	0	93	86	36	103
Farmer, Tom, rhp	So.	2	1	3.48	3	0	10	13	3	7
Roque, Darryl, rhp	Sr.	5	1	3.90	13	0	55	47	11	47
Sheffield, Chris, rhp	Fr.	1	1	3.93	8	0	18	20	20	24
Vazquez, Vince, rhp	So.	5	1	4.02	31	2	47	39	28	55
Howell, Greg, rhp	So.	1	0	4.22	9	0	11	10	5	15
Perez, Eduardo, lhp	Jr.	0	0	4.32	11	0	8	14	1	6
Roberson, Troy, rhp	Fr.	1	1	4.64	15	0	21	22	12	26
DeBold, Luke, rhp	Fr.	0	0	4.76	4	0	6	9	3	5
Spassoff, Darin, rhp	Sr.	2	1	6.46	6	0	15	18	6	11
Channell, Ryan, lhp	Jr.	1	0	6.57	7	0	12	16	6	13
Walker, Brian, lhp	Fr.	2	2	6.75	16	0	36	48	11	36
Kamalsky, Matt, rhp	So.	2	1	6.75	9	0	15	16	8	10
Smith, Dan, rhp	So.	0	0	7.20	4	0	5	6	5	4

2. FLORIDA STATE

Coach: Mike Martin   **Record:** 57-14

BATTING	YR	AVG	AB	R	H	2B	3B	HR	RBI	SB
Griffin, John-Ford, of-dh	Fr.	.436	133	42	58	15	0	3	35	0
McDougall, Marshall, 2b-3b	Jr.	.419	301	104	126	26	3	28	106	22
Diaz, Matt, of	So.	.379	301	80	114	24	3	21	94	10
Futrell, Michael, of	Jr.	.363	135	39	49	11	2	3	19	3
Barthelemy, Ryan, 1b-dh	Fr.	.343	99	23	34	6	1	5	24	0
Scott, Sam, 2b-dh	Jr.	.320	172	37	55	11	0	12	39	2
Cash, Kevin, 3b-1b	Jr.	.317	252	50	80	13	0	14	58	7
Klosterman, Jeremiah, c	Sr.	.298	248	38	74	18	0	5	55	0
Halliday, John, 1b-dh	Jr.	.298	205	44	61	16	0	10	50	2
Groves, Brett, ss	So.	.286	227	59	65	10	3	1	31	29
Smith, Chris, of-lhp	Fr.	.286	161	47	46	9	0	1	24	1
Hart, Chris, c-dh	Fr.	.241	79	15	19	7	0	2	19	0
Spano, Bobby, ss-2b	Jr.	.229	48	15	11	2	1	0	5	1
Jernigan, Karl, of	So.	.227	163	49	37	8	2	6	31	12
Hoguet, J.C., c	Jr.	.143	14	2	2	0	0	0	2	0

PITCHING		W	L	ERA	G	SV	IP	H	BB	SO
Ginn, Chris, lhp	So.	5	0	1.31	26	1	34	26	14	28
Diaz, Zach, lhp	Sr.	4	1	2.08	29	0	43	27	10	34
Chavez, Chris, rhp	Sr.	8	5	2.17	36	5	87	60	36	109
Whidden, Chris, rhp	Fr.	2	1	2.75	30	2	39	27	24	60

ROBERT GURGANUS

Automatic at the top of the order
Miami's Bobby Hill set the table for three years

Smalley, Mike, lhp	So.	4	0	2.93	15	0	31	27	25	31
Stocks, Nick, rhp	So.	13	2	3.25	21	0	127	111	44	139
McDonald, Jon, rhp	So.	9	3	3.57	20	0	116	112	51	123
Varnes, Blair, rhp	Fr.	11	2	4.13	19	0	109	112	20	76
DiBlasi, Mike, lhp	Jr.	0	0	4.33	28	9	27	22	20	46
Smith, Chris, lhp	Fr.	1	0	4.63	5	0	12	11	11	9

3. STANFORD

Coach: Mark Marquess   **Record:** 50-15

BATTING	YR	AVG	AB	R	H	2B	3B	HR	RBI	SB
Borchard, Joe, of	So.	.372	247	64	92	16	1	11	56	7
Gall, John, 1b	Jr.	.337	264	66	89	17	3	12	70	12
Salter, John, c-dh	Sr.	.333	30	6	10	1	0	2	6	0
Jacobson, Billy, of	So.	.321	131	32	42	3	2	2	18	9
Bruntlett, Eric, ss	Jr.	.316	187	38	59	10	0	1	28	11
Day, Nick, of-dh	Jr.	.312	202	34	63	15	4	4	41	1
Hochgesang, Josh, 3b	Sr.	.307	251	67	77	17	4	17	73	13
Muth, Edmund, of	Jr.	.305	187	39	57	13	4	6	30	8
Alvarado, Damien, c	Jr.	.299	231	39	69	15	2	5	51	2
Rizzo, Jeff, 2b	Jr.	.293	256	62	75	17	5	5	54	10
Thompson, Craig, of-dh	Jr.	.281	203	50	57	14	0	3	32	9
Savig, Joe, dh	Jr.	.234	47	8	11	4	0	1	15	0
Topham, Andy, ss-3b	Fr.	.192	26	5	5	0	0	0	1	0
VanMeetren, Jason, of	Fr.	.167	12	2	2	1	0	0	2	0
Dragicevich, Scott, ss	Fr.	.148	27	3	4	0	0	0	1	0
Chan, Stephen, dh	Fr.	.111	18	5	2	0	0	1	3	3

PITCHING	YR	W	L	ERA	G	SV	IP	H	BB	SO
Young, Jason, rhp	So.	12	3	3.43	21	0	155	128	55	178
Rich, Dan, lhp	Fr.	3	1	3.66	17	2	20	18	8	20
Cogan, Tony, lhp	Sr.	7	4	3.69	33	8	68	63	21	68
Sager, Brian, rhp	Fr.	6	0	4.17	19	0	86	90	41	72
Wayne, Justin, rhp	So.	10	1	4.94	21	0	118	117	43	135
Drew, Brad, lhp	So.	2	3	5.48	10	0	23	26	18	19
Wodnicki, Mike, rhp	Fr.	3	0	5.57	15	0	32	29	18	28
Coose, Austin, rhp	So.	3	0	5.68	16	0	25	30	16	25
Gosling, Mike, lhp	Fr.	1	2	5.73	17	0	38	49	26	40
Willcox, J.D., rhp	Fr.	2	1	6.46	14	1	24	23	9	16

4. ALABAMA

Coach: Jim Wells   **Record:** 53-16

BATTING	YR	AVG	AB	R	H	2B	3B	HR	RBI	SB
Phillips, Andy, ss	Sr.	.398	259	71	103	22	6	22	66	16

		YR	AVG	AB	R	H	2B	3B	HR	RBI	SB
Keller, G.W., of		Sr.	.396	270	85	107	15	4	15	72	40
Brown, Jeremy, 1b		Fr.	.347	262	77	91	20	0	15	69	4
Gulledge, Kelley, c		So.	.344	195	40	67	15	3	11	53	0
Wigginton, Derek, of-dh		So.	.328	180	44	59	6	6	5	32	6
Bostic, Antonio, of		Sr.	.357	70	18	25	4	4	2	20	7
McClanahan, Scott, of		Fr.	.321	84	21	27	5	1	1	10	8
Boyd, Brent, 3b		Sr.	.316	234	60	74	15	1	7	33	7
Bozanich, Sam, 2b		So.	.308	276	62	85	19	1	8	57	7
Wood, Darren, of		Jr.	.306	216	50	66	15	4	8	42	11
Smallwood, Erik, of		Jr.	.325	120	31	39	9	1	7	27	5
Mills, Rock, c		Fr.	.282	78	8	22	5	0	1	16	0
Cox, Jayson, dh		Jr.	.280	150	32	42	9	0	9	33	0
Chavers, Dan, ss		Jr.	.235	85	18	20	2	0	9	25	2

PITCHING		YR	W	L	ERA	G	SV	IP	H	BB	SO
Vaughn, Jeremy, rhp		Fr.	1	0	1.74	3	0	10	6	5	7
Moates, Jason, rhp		So.	3	2	3.82	17	0	61	67	32	58
Blankenship, Jon, lhp		So.	10	3	4.12	34	3	90	84	39	95
Marzion, Kevin, rhp		So.	4	0	4.60	8	0	29	34	8	29
Torres, Manny, rhp		Jr.	10	3	5.09	18	0	115	137	30	104
Murphy, Scott, rhp		Fr.	8	0	5.18	22	3	82	89	20	75
Smith, Justin, lhp		Jr.	6	4	5.44	16	0	81	86	28	100
Green, B.J., rhp		So.	5	1	5.59	20	1	58	74	23	40
Cormier, Lance, rhp		Fr.	6	3	6.24	29	11	66	70	42	62
Henderson, Shane, rhp		Jr.	0	0	6.32	12	1	16	19	8	17

5. RICE

Coach: Wayne Graham   **Record:** 59-15

BATTING		YR	AVG	AB	R	H	2B	3B	HR	RBI	SB
Ford, Will, of		Jr.	.398	264	65	105	24	3	12	74	4
Thames, Damon, ss		Sr.	.377	313	86	118	24	6	11	72	14
Williams, Charles, of		Jr.	.366	317	82	116	22	9	7	50	10
Michaelis, Derek, dh		So.	.364	11	1	4	1	0	0	3	0
Gray, Jason, of		Jr.	.327	294	74	96	12	8	20	72	19
Baker, Jacob, 1b		Sr.	.323	294	47	95	24	1	5	50	4
Berg, Justin, c		Jr.	.312	224	48	70	20	0	3	50	3
Fox, Matt, 3b		So.	.299	154	27	46	5	7	2	31	2
Smith, Brett, 2b		Jr.	.299	278	75	83	12	2	8	50	5
Ackal, Mitch, 3b-of		Jr.	.286	84	16	24	4	1	3	15	2
Curry, Zane, c		Sr.	.286	206	34	59	12	0	1	32	1
Lukin, John, c		Jr.	.279	61	14	17	5	0	3	12	0
Kurtz-Nicholl, J., dh-lhp		Sr.	.268	41	8	11	2	0	0	10	1
Arnold, Eric, 3b		Fr.	.238	105	16	25	7	0	3	18	5

PITCHING		YR	W	L	ERA	G	SV	IP	H	BB	SO
Baugh, Kenny, rhp		So.	12	2	2.26	20	0	112	94	46	103
Ramos, Mario, lhp		Jr.	13	3	2.51	25	2	154	121	51	146
Kurtz-Nicholl, Jesse, lhp		Sr.	7	1	2.61	38	8	76	68	25	100
Terrana, Peter, lhp		Sr.	1	0	2.86	11	0	22	19	10	15
Gwyn, Marc, rhp		Jr.	7	1	3.22	25	2	81	73	36	74
Skaggs, Jon, rhp		Fr.	1	1	4.41	12	1	33	28	24	21
Nichols, Jeff, rhp		Jr.	15	4	4.84	25	0	138	165	51	121
Bess, Stephen, rhp		Sr.	3	3	5.48	29	4	46	48	26	48

6. CAL STATE FULLERTON

Coach: George Horton   **Record:** 50-14

BATTING		YR	AVG	AB	R	H	2B	3B	HR	RBI	SB
Beck, Chris, dh		Jr.	.408	240	64	98	18	1	8	75	27
Johnson, Reed, of		Jr.	.396	268	101	106	22	3	13	59	18
Oborn, Spencer, of		Jr.	.395	263	74	104	22	7	14	82	27
Rifkin, Aaron, dh		So.	.378	185	47	70	18	1	6	47	4
Owens, Ryan, 3b		Jr.	.358	240	66	86	14	2	23	85	16
Bacani, David, 2b		So.	.332	226	74	75	16	3	7	33	17
Stringfellow, Chris, of		Jr.	.313	32	12	10	1	0	1	7	1
Guzman, Robert, of		Fr.	.291	175	38	51	5	3	2	26	11
Norris, Shawn, ss		Fr.	.286	154	22	44	9	1	6	34	6
Patterson, Craig, c		Jr.	.286	98	19	28	5	0	3	20	3
Gates, Jeff, c		Jr.	.281	135	21	38	3	1	2	25	1
Olszanski, Chad, ss-2b		So.	.267	86	18	23	7	0	1	10	7
Bischofberger, Sean, 3b-1b		Fr.	.224	58	8	13	1	0	2	13	2
Moore, Ryan, ss		Jr.	.222	36	7	8	2	0	1	5	1
Baum, Chad, dh		Sr.	.208	24	4	5	1	0	2	6	0
Kay, Brett, dh		Fr.	.133	15	3	2	0	0	0	2	0

PITCHING		YR	W	L	ERA	G	SV	IP	H	BB	SO
Smith, Jon, lhp		So.	7	1	3.16	15	1	68	53	20	60
Johnson, Adam, rhp		So.	10	4	3.55	17	1	117	104	47	136
Saarloos, Kirk, rhp		So.	7	3	3.63	39	7	74	66	20	68
Sorensen, Matt, rhp		So.	12	0	4.14	18	0	126	145	44	84
Hanlon, Marco, rhp		Sr.	6	1	4.37	22	0	60	65	26	42
Westemier, Jason, rhp		Jr.	1	1	5.40	6	0	7	11	5	5
Hawkins, Barry, rhp		Jr.	1	1	5.65	8	0	14	22	2	6
DeJong, Jordan, rhp		So.	4	1	5.75	18	1	56	71	33	47
Jurado, Ruben, rhp		So.	1	1	5.85	12	0	20	26	9	14

Steady line-drive hitter
Cal State Fullerton's Spencer Oborn

JEFF GOLDEN

		YR	W	L	ERA	G	SV	IP	H	BB	SO
Carralejo, George, lhp		So.	1	0	9.15	16	0	21	23	12	15
Garner, Mike, lhp		Jr.	0	1	18.56	7	1	5	16	3	5

7. TEXAS A&M

Coach: Mark Johnson   **Record:** 52-18

BATTING		YR	AVG	AB	R	H	2B	3B	HR	RBI	SB
Schumacher, Shawn, c		Sr.	.374	243	43	91	14	0	11	53	3
Scheschuk, John, 1b		Sr.	.363	248	62	90	20	0	10	54	2
Truitt, Steven, of		Jr.	.345	264	80	91	24	5	19	60	23
Sundstrom, Ken, 3b		Sr.	.344	32	4	11	3	0	0	7	2
Holt, Daylan, of		So.	.341	287	78	98	22	3	34	105	9
Heaney, Sean, 2b		Jr.	.333	282	70	94	27	5	11	48	9
Porter, Greg, dh		Fr.	.328	122	28	40	11	0	7	26	1
Scarborough, Steve, ss		Jr.	.326	264	64	86	10	1	6	41	8
Sobek, Erik, dh		Sr.	.314	105	21	33	5	0	7	29	1
Lindsey, Del, 3b		Jr.	.305	246	55	78	15	2	14	59	12
O'Jibway, Joe, c		Jr.	.283	60	15	17	2	0	1	12	4
Whealey, Blake, 3b		Fr.	.276	29	6	8	2	0	0	6	1
Hudson, Chad, of		Jr.	.265	132	23	35	6	3	4	29	6
Stephenson, Neal, 1b		Sr.	.240	50	19	12	2	2	2	5	4
Russ, Chris, rhp-if		So.	.214	14	1	3	0	0	0	2	1
Leonard, Steve, of		Sr.	.173	57	8	10	1	0	2	5	2
Clark, Tommy, of		Sr.	.132	38	6	5	2	0	0	5	2

PITCHING		YR	W	L	ERA	G	SV	IP	H	BB	SO
Fulbright, Chris, rhp		Jr.	0	0	0.00	3	1	5	2	2	4
Weller, Courtney, rhp		Jr.	1	0	3.10	17	1	29	23	24	21
Russ, Chris, rhp		So.	12	3	3.27	28	3	83	77	28	51
Fossum, Casey, lhp		Jr.	12	7	3.64	20	0	134	117	52	162
Ward, Matt, lhp		Sr.	8	1	3.66	15	0	91	109	9	63
King, Shane, lhp		So.	0	0	3.96	7	0	25	33	7	15
Caple, Chance, rhp		Jr.	8	5	4.26	17	0	114	107	45	125
Ballouli, Khalid, rhp		Fr.	7	2	5.45	18	0	66	96	19	42
Knight, Matt, lhp		Jr.	0	1	6.00	12	0	18	19	10	16
Holle, Kyle, rhp		Sr.	1	0	6.14	3	1	7	7	4	3
Scarcella, Chris, rhp		So.	2	0	8.49	14	0	35	51	15	30

8. BAYLOR

Coach: Steve Smith **Record:** 50-15

BATTING	YR	AVG	AB	R	H	2B	3B	HR	RBI	SB
Saccomanno, Mark, ss-2b	Fr.	.394	33	7	13	3	0	1	10	1
Jennings, Jason, dh-rhp	Jr.	.386	233	52	90	14	0	17	68	1
Dorneman, Steve, of	Fr.	.378	37	13	14	5	0	0	9	1
Nelson, Eric, 2b	Sr.	.362	282	77	102	20	6	17	79	22
Topolski, Jon, of	Sr.	.358	243	74	87	12	2	17	61	23
Hensley, Anthony, of	Jr.	.346	133	36	46	8	2	2	19	29
Zboril, Ron, 1b	Jr.	.342	38	8	13	4	0	3	13	0
Cogdill, Mark, of	Jr.	.330	224	56	74	12	4	5	37	16
Williams, Matt, 1b	So.	.318	239	59	76	14	1	19	67	9
Bubela, Jaime, of	So.	.312	192	44	60	8	4	3	28	21
Underdown, Preston, 3b	Jr.	.302	235	43	71	13	4	5	47	7
Brewer, Jace, ss	Fr.	.278	209	39	58	16	0	6	44	12
Loeb, Bryan, c	Jr.	.225	151	37	34	5	0	8	26	3
Shoppach, Kelly, c	Fr.	.222	72	12	16	5	0	4	13	1
Fredenburg, Denver, c	Sr.	.111	18	4	2	1	0	0	0	0

PITCHING	YR	W	L	ERA	G	SV	IP	H	BB	SO
Jennings, Jason, rhp	Jr.	13	2	2.58	22	1	147	102	50	172
Hawkins, Chad, lhp	Jr.	7	3	3.89	21	3	116	114	27	108
Evans, Kyle, rhp	So.	7	1	4.37	18	0	58	64	34	48
Scott, Josh, lhp	So.	10	2	4.87	21	0	105	104	29	110
Taylor, Justin, rhp	Fr.	5	4	5.06	22	1	48	53	22	41
Bartula, Daren, rhp	Jr.	0	0	5.46	11	1	28	38	17	21
Edens, Kyle, rhp	Fr.	3	0	5.49	11	1	20	26	8	23
Outlaw, Mark, lhp	Sr.	4	3	5.80	29	1	45	42	22	44
Ratliff, Joe, rhp	Jr.	1	0	6.19	12	0	16	19	6	19

9. OKLAHOMA STATE

Coach: Tom Holliday **Record:** 46-21

BATTING	YR	AVG	AB	R	H	2B	3B	HR	RBI	SB
Matthews, Lamont, of	Jr.	.384	242	87	93	17	7	30	105	10
Lorsbach, Mike, of	Fr.	.381	42	14	16	4	1	2	14	1
Smith, Lance, 2b-ss	Jr.	.372	43	16	16	8	0	3	16	1
Gasparino, Billy, ss	Sr.	.364	247	96	90	19	3	24	91	27
Gautreaux, Carlos, of-dh	Jr.	.361	147	35	53	11	3	3	32	7
Becerra, Chris, of	Jr.	.356	135	39	48	10	3	10	39	0
Myers, Michael, ss	Fr.	.350	20	8	7	1	0	0	6	1
Lucas, Kevin, 2b	Jr.	.342	269	74	92	12	4	7	46	24
Rhodes, Toby, of	Fr.	.329	76	26	25	4	1	7	22	6
Kitsch, Trent, c-1b	So.	.311	74	19	23	3	0	2	20	1
McAuliff, Jimbo, of	So.	.306	170	58	52	8	3	7	31	20
McCullough, Jay, 1b	So.	.306	206	49	63	12	2	13	57	2
Holliday, Josh, c-3b	Sr.	.290	221	77	64	12	1	15	65	2
Leu, Trevor, 1b-lhp	So.	.282	103	24	29	6	0	4	28	2
Budde, Ryan, c-3b	Fr.	.275	189	39	52	18	1	1	39	10
Mabrey, Matt, of	Jr.	.241	58	21	14	2	2	2	14	3
Haggard, Chris, c	Jr.	.182	55	11	10	5	0	1	9	0
Smith, Brad, 1b	So.	.176	17	2	3	0	0	1	3	0

PITCHING	YR	W	L	ERA	G	SV	IP	H	BB	SO
Rushing, Rusty, rhp	Jr.	4	1	2.77	22	4	39	27	13	47
Smith, Matt, lhp	So.	9	6	3.09	20	0	114	102	44	144
Leu, Trevor, lhp	So.	0	0	3.68	11	1	7	3	9	12
Dreier, Thom, rhp	Jr.	8	6	3.95	19	0	93	95	49	77
New, Denny, lhp	Jr.	2	2	4.19	11	0	39	46	14	39
Herrmann, Ryan, rhp	Fr.	4	3	5.04	25	0	50	54	31	38
Krismer, Jeremy, rhp	Jr.	6	0	5.27	20	0	55	58	24	60
Bergman, Grant, rhp	Jr.	1	0	5.56	9	0	23	26	4	26
Bludau, Frank, rhp	Jr.	3	0	5.73	13	0	33	42	20	25
Rollandini, David, rhp	Jr.	3	0	5.76	11	0	25	27	11	26
Pearson, Dale, lhp	So.	1	9	6.02	15	1	52	69	25	46
Hunt, Stu, lhp	So.	1	1	7.42	22	1	30	38	13	33
Kelly, Daniel, lhp	Jr.	0	1	7.71	4	1	5	11	2	6
Rosellini, Will, rhp	So.	2	0	8.38	5	0	10	11	8	4

10. SOUTHERN CALIFORNIA

Coach: Mike Gillespie **Record:** 36-26

BATTING	YR	AVG	AB	R	H	2B	3B	HR	RBI	SB
Lane, Jason, of-lhp	Jr.	.356	216	58	77	20	4	20	68	12
Munson, Eric, c	Jr.	.346	153	45	53	6	1	15	41	5
Davidson, Seth, ss	So.	.345	238	51	82	11	4	1	35	9
Correa, Dominic, 2b-rhp	Jr.	.330	233	56	77	12	2	12	51	1
Craig, Beau, 3b-c	Fr.	.319	204	46	65	17	3	4	50	2
Casillas, Carlos, 1b-dh	Jr.	.310	126	21	39	7	0	8	26	1
Persell, Josh, 1b-c	So.	.309	55	5	17	1	0	0	9	1
Hanoian, Greg, of	Jr.	.306	252	56	77	15	1	7	46	9
Gemoll, Justin, 3b-1b	Jr.	.300	203	39	61	11	1	4	26	6
Lehr, Justin, 1b-rhp	Sr.	.297	155	34	46	16	0	4	27	1
Ticehurst, Brad, of	Jr.	.267	195	48	52	10	0	10	39	16

11. WAKE FOREST

Coach: George Greer **Record:** 47-16

BATTING	YR	AVG	AB	R	H	2B	3B	HR	RBI	SB
Palmieri, Jon, 1b	Sr.	.412	272	81	112	20	3	18	94	19
Price, Matt, of	So.	.368	106	33	39	6	1	4	27	3
Borrell, Danny, 2b-lhp	So.	.365	222	57	81	14	3	20	73	1
Voshell, Chase, ss	So.	.353	224	49	79	15	4	9	37	16
Daeley, Scott, of	Sr.	.349	261	83	91	27	2	3	46	24
Riepe, Andrew, c	Jr.	.339	254	48	86	19	1	9	63	3
Danosky, Ben, of	Jr.	.318	170	36	54	14	0	7	37	1
Kubachka, John, of	Fr.	.307	88	14	27	8	0	2	19	0
Aquilante, Jason, 2b	So.	.286	220	67	63	12	1	5	36	5
Slavik, Corey, of	So.	.272	232	38	63	10	2	7	42	0
Brackley, Carlos, of	So.	.271	59	13	16	2	0	0	4	1
Turner, Chris, 2b	Jr.	.250	36	8	9	1	0	0	1	0
Mendez, Ricky, of	Jr.	.235	51	11	12	2	1	2	7	0
Sullivan, Stephen, of	Jr.	.220	59	9	13	3	0	3	12	0
Siemon, Scott, rhp-3b	So.	.158	19	3	3	2	0	0	2	0

PITCHING	YR	W	L	ERA	G	SV	IP	H	BB	SO
MacDougal, Mike, rhp	Jr.	13	3	2.63	17	0	120	88	65	117
Schmitt, Eric, rhp	Jr.	4	1	4.13	10	0	61	72	15	55
Briggs, Matt, rhp	Jr.	6	0	4.14	20	1	72	68	33	50
Siemon, Scott, rhp	So.	12	2	4.78	29	4	92	113	30	65
Hendricks, John, lhp	Sr.	10	6	5.44	20	1	131	150	52	88
Bush, David, rhp	Fr.	1	1	5.85	25	2	40	42	15	38
Borrell, Danny, lhp	So.	1	2	6.39	13	2	25	34	17	21
Paugh, Ricky, rhp	Jr.	0	0	10.38	5	0	9	13	8	2

12. OHIO STATE

Coach: Bob Todd **Record:** 50-14

BATTING	YR	AVG	AB	R	H	2B	3B	HR	RBI	SB
Check, Mike, ss	Jr.	.450	40	14	18	3	0	0	6	5
Palazzo, Joe, 3b	Fr.	.400	25	6	10	0	0	1	6	1
Garofalo, Marcello, dh-1b	Jr.	.378	37	7	14	5	0	3	14	0
Trott, Jason, 1b	Sr.	.367	221	70	81	20	0	7	52	11
Ehrnsberger, Chad, 2b	So.	.356	216	62	77	15	0	16	73	10
Durant, Tom, c	Sr.	.350	214	58	75	22	1	7	39	11
Lockwood, Mike, of	Sr.	.344	253	71	87	12	5	15	55	6
Middleton, Matt, 3b	So.	.330	221	42	73	17	2	9	55	5
Turner, Jason, of	Sr.	.310	226	57	70	10	4	7	59	3
Dendinger, Doug, dh	Fr.	.305	59	13	18	2	0	2	12	1
Wilkins, Joe, c	Fr.	.298	47	9	14	3	0	0	10	1
McIlvain, Trent, ss	So.	.297	192	45	57	13	1	4	24	3
Driscoll, Jason, of	Jr.	.286	224	39	64	8	4	5	47	5
Mayor, John, ss-dh	So.	.254	59	13	31	7	0	1	14	8
Alvord, Chris, c	So.	.200	60	7	12	0	0	0	8	0

PITCHING	YR	W	L	ERA	G	SV	IP	H	BB	SO
Fry, Justin, rhp	Sr.	11	2	3.70	17	0	114	117	27	104
Laratta, E.J., rhp	Fr.	10	3	3.77	15	0	86	86	18	59
Goodrum, Kevin, lhp	So.	4	0	4.35	29	3	52	47	37	38
Kalnins, Ted, rhp	Fr.	0	0	4.82	6	0	9	9	4	7
Lee, Andy, rhp	Sr.	9	2	5.63	19	1	96	123	26	76
Cox, Cory, rhp	So.	3	3	5.65	28	9	37	55	5	25
Smith, Nate, rhp	Fr.	5	3	5.98	19	0	59	73	19	56
Steen, Brandon, rhp	Fr.	4	0	6.26	9	0	23	24	13	11
Fullenkamp, Kurt, rhp	Jr.	4	1	6.62	24	1	50	59	9	40
Larrick, Greg, rhp	Fr.	0	0	11.85	7	0	14	21	16	9

13. AUBURN

Coach: Hal Baird **Record:** 46-19

BATTING	YR	AVG	AB	R	H	2B	3B	HR	RBI	SB
Kent, Mailon, of	So.	.379	269	79	102	18	2	45	40

	YR	W	L	ERA	G	SV	IP	H	BB	SO
Drumright, Greg, rhp	Sr.	3	0	2.85	20	4	47	41	13	50
Adair, Gary, lhp	Fr.	1	0	3.20	13	1	25	26	7	27
Bauer, Greg, rhp	Jr.	2	2	3.55	28	3	66	62	18	71
Sloan, Brandon, rhp ...	So.	10	3	3.66	17	0	93	92	40	86
Peterson, Adam, rhp	Fr.	2	0	3.72	7	0	19	15	8	9
Lee, Tymber, rhp	So.	6	0	3.93	20	2	37	33	12	29
Robertson, Nate, lhp ...	Jr.	8	0	4.13	14	0	81	88	29	77
Keiter, Ben, rhp	Fr.	7	0	4.22	13	2	63	71	17	53
Krafft, Jason, rhp	Sr.	7	2	4.62	14	0	64	66	26	57
Bryan, Erich, rhp	Jr.	2	3	5.59	5	0	19	28	4	14

15. TULANE

Coach: Rick Jones   **Record:** 48-17

BATTING	YR	AVG	AB	R	H	2B	3B	HR	RBI	SB
Sutter, Chad, c-dh	Sr.	.393	239	70	94	12	0	23	87	4
Jurries, James, 2b	Jr.	.374	278	90	104	22	4	20	79	18
Cannizaro, Andy, ss	So.	.370	219	66	81	14	1	1	38	31
Groff, Matt, of-3b	Jr.	.367	240	55	88	17	2	4	37	20
McKee, Mickey, 1b	Jr.	.326	224	52	73	15	1	4	32	7
Sparks, Jason, of	Sr.	.324	222	56	72	16	1	19	62	16
Shirley, Steve, of	So.	.311	135	31	42	5	0	8	27	0
Gautreau, Jake, 3b-dh ...	Jr.	.292	264	57	77	11	1	21	69	0
Herz, Nick, c	Jr.	.265	83	18	22	3	0	3	9	0
Burnham, Jake, of	Sr.	.261	245	46	64	15	0	20	60	3
Boudreaux, Paul, of	Jr.	.240	50	7	12	1	0	1	5	2
Belanger, Brandon, of-rhp	Jr.	.231	78	12	18	5	0	4	14	0
Heintz, Jay, of	So.	.200	25	6	5	0	0	0	1	1

PITCHING	YR	W	L	ERA	G	SV	IP	H	BB	SO
Belanger, Brandon, rhp ...	Jr.	3	5	2.45	41	16	66	66	15	68
Bonilla, Henry, rhp	Jr.	11	1	3.34	20	1	124	129	36	131
Berkowitz, Jared, lhp	Jr.	13	3	3.78	19	0	124	133	20	87
O'Gara, Dan, rhp	Jr.	8	2	4.59	22	0	86	106	40	61
Echeverz, Raul, lhp	Sr.	6	2	5.35	26	1	72	76	46	51
Robinson, Jared, lhp	Sr.	3	3	6.31	20	0	51	59	33	39
Hood, Jeremiah, rhp	So.	1	0	7.71	10	0	14	19	4	8
Melius, Barth, rhp	So.	2	1	8.84	10	0	19	27	4	17
Carroll, James, rhp	Fr.	0	0	10.03	9	0	12	17	13	12
Vogel, Bryan, rhp	Fr.	1	0	10.24	5	0	10	12	5	3

16. LOUISIANA STATE

Coach: Skip Bertman   **Record:** 41-24-1

BATTING	YR	AVG	AB	R	H	2B	3B	HR	RBI	SB
Leaumont, Jeff, 1b	Sr.	.342	257	63	88	15	3	18	82	5
Witten, Jeremy, of	So.	.330	209	64	69	18	3	8	46	15
Hawpe, Brad, of-dh	So.	.325	117	27	38	8	0	12	30	0
Theriot, Ryan, 2b	Fr.	.322	242	55	78	11	3	2	41	13
McClure, Trey, dh-c	Jr.	.319	229	61	73	13	1	18	55	1
Hendrickson, Eric, of	Jr.	.311	161	36	50	5	1	11	46	1
Cresse, Brad, c-dh	Jr.	.302	215	52	65	11	0	10	39	2
Dalton, Josh, ss	Jr.	.294	238	55	70	8	0	2	38	24
Barbier, Blair, 3b	Jr.	.293	263	66	77	14	2	13	51	2
Harris, Cedrick, of	So.	.245	208	42	51	8	0	6	45	10
Earnhart, Clint, dh-c	Sr.	.229	105	11	24	6	0	1	10	2
Lipari, Jeff, 1b	So.	.214	28	4	6	1	1	1	5	0
Simon, Antoine, of	Jr.	.150	20	8	3	2	0	0	5	2

PITCHING	YR	W	L	ERA	G	SV	IP	H	BB	SO
Brian, Billy, rhp	Fr.	0	0	0.96	5	0	9	5	9	12
Ainsworth, Kurt, rhp ...	So.	13	6	3.45	22	1	130	114	48	157
Youman, Shane, lhp	Fr.	0	0	3.52	4	0	8	7	8	4
Gomez, Hunter, rhp	Jr.	4	3	4.38	31	7	99	112	25	90
Saxon, Ben, rhp	Jr.	2	0	4.91	19	1	33	34	6	29
Tallet, Brian, lhp	So.	3	4	5.01	19	0	59	59	30	60
Nugent, Tim, lhp	So.	2	2	5.51	29	1	33	39	16	37
Bowe, Brandon, rhp	Sr.	9	4	6.38	19	0	96	120	20	88
Grace, Bryan, rhp	Sr.	5	2	6.79	15	2	54	76	26	43
Hodges, Trey, rhp	Jr.	3	2	7.08	13	0	34	50	8	38
Loftice, Jeremy, rhp	Jr.	0	1	7.43	12	0	13	17	10	18
Guidry, Weylin, rhp	Fr.	0	0	8.22	8	0	8	12	3	11

17. CLEMSON

Coach: Jack Leggett   **Record:** 42-27

BATTING	YR	AVG	AB	R	H	2B	3B	HR	RBI	SB
Boyd, Patrick, of	So.	.390	246	78	96	22	1	17	70	20
Greene, Khalil, 3b	Fr.	.358	274	58	98	20	1	8	69	9
Harris, Jason, 1b	Jr.	.339	248	68	84	17	0	10	66	17
Calitri, Mike, 1b	So.	.333	15	3	5	2	0	1	3	0
Bultmann, Kurt, 2b	Sr.	.327	272	73	89	23	2	12	72	6
Holstad, Brian, of	Jr.	.313	115	30	36	5	1	1	16	3
Borgert, Derek, c	Sr.	.306	121	27	37	10	0	4	36	1

Everything you could want in a Friday starter
Righthander Brent Schoening set the tone for Auburn

	YR	AVG	AB	R	H	2B	3B	HR	RBI	SB
Dunn, Casey, c	Sr.	.379	269	70	102	19	1	16	86	1
Gross, Gabe, of-3b	Fr.	.363	245	50	89	23	3	7	65	1
Gliemmo, Hayden, of-lhp	So.	.346	205	39	71	8	3	1	37	4
Kersh, Jamie, 3b-1b	Sr.	.341	255	57	87	23	0	11	59	4
Rich, Dominic, 2b-of	So.	.320	266	68	85	15	3	2	47	15
Slater, Andrew, c	So.	.312	16	2	5	1	0	0	0	0
Reif, Derek, of	Sr.	.308	117	20	36	11	2	1	23	3
Wandall, Chad, ss	Sr.	.303	244	58	74	17	2	2	49	3
Faulkner, Todd, 1b	So.	.281	249	53	70	20	2	6	50	3
Tyler, John, 2b-ss	Fr.	.279	122	31	34	1	0	1	23	6
Dearth, Tucker, of	Jr.	.217	23	6	5	2	0	0	4	0
Holder, Collin, c		.188	16	7	3	1	1	1	6	1
Zanthos, Joseph, of	So.	.188	16	2	3	0	0	0	0	0
Turco, Paul, ss	Sr.	.000	0	0	0	0	0	0	0	0

PITCHING	YR	W	L	ERA	G	SV	IP	H	BB	SO
Schoening, Brent, rhp ..	Jr.	13	1	3.32	21	0	138	122	47	151
Bean, Colter, rhp	Jr.	5	3	4.70	34	8	52	49	20	47
Gliemmo, Hayden, lhp ..	So.	13	7	4.96	21	0	123	132	37	105
Mayfield, Brandon, rhp ...	Jr.	0	0	5.54	14	0	13	23	2	13
Knorst, Kevin, rhp	Jr.	2	0	5.56	21	3	44	53	21	44
Bootcheck, Chris, rhp	So.	8	6	5.57	22	0	128	159	38	125
Renfro, Jon, rhp	So.	1	1	5.97	19	0	32	38	12	25
Weis, Brad, lhp	Jr.	4	1	6.69	23	0	35	45	22	36

14. WICHITA STATE

Coach: Gene Stephenson   **Record:** 59-14

BATTING	YR	AVG	AB	R	H	2B	3B	HR	RBI	SB
Hooper, Kevin, ss		.402	214	72	86	15	7	4	36	26
Blasi, Blake, 2b	So.	.396	268	87	106	28	5	4	54	22
Magness, Pat, 1b	Jr.	.364	250	60	91	15	0	18	94	2
Absher, Eric, of	Jr.	.351	57	14	20	4	0	2	21	3
Hill, Koyie, 3b	Jr.	.347	294	59	102	21	1	10	81	6
Welch, Tanner, 2b-ss.....	Fr.	.323	96	32	31	6	1	0	14	6
Schoenhofer, Brian, of	Jr.	.321	106	22	34	5	1	2	18	2
Wright, Bradley, of	Jr.	.321	156	35	50	14	2	1	28	4
Ryan, Jeff, of-ss	Jr.	.304	217	69	66	12	1	10	62	33
McCarty, Justin, of	Jr.	.302	189	57	57	14	2	0	26	18
Preston, Brian, c	Jr.	.299	244	55	73	7	0	23	59	1
Hayes, Tim, of	Jr.	.298	151	23	45	14	0	5	36	1
Schreiber, Andy, dh	Jr.	.281	89	19	25	3	1	8	29	1
Abram, Aaron, of	Jr.	.253	75	17	19	7	2	2	16	0
Walkup, Casey, 2b	Sr.	.250	12	4	3	0	0	0	2	0
Hawkins, Dustin, of	Jr.	.227	44	8	10	2	0	0	7	5
Akin, Jason, of	Fr.	.136	22	7	3	1	0	1	6	1
Bozarth, Dustin, c	Fr.	.125	32	11	4	0	0	0	2	0

PITCHING	YR	W	L	ERA	G	SV	IP	H	BB	SO
Bluma, Marc, rhp	Sr.	2	3	1.70	28	17	37	26	13	49
Christensen, Ben, rhp ..	Jr.	9	1	2.40	11	0	71	46	17	77

BATTING										
Stanley, Henri, of	Jr.	.296	257	85	76	20	2	8	60	27
LeCroy, Bradley, ss	So.	.286	220	42	63	14	1	3	44	13
Ellis, Brian, c	Jr.	.265	223	60	59	15	1	4	45	6
Frank, Kyle, of	Fr.	.255	94	19	24	6	1	0	16	2
Kane, Jeff, 3b	So.	.250	20	4	5	1	0	1	4	0
Stone, Casey, of	So.	.240	104	22	25	4	0	0	17	7
Singleton, Justin, of	So.	.237	156	32	37	10	0	3	23	7
Reames, Joe Don, c	Fr.	.200	15	2	3	0	0	0	0	0
Roper, Doug, ss-rhp	Jr.	.178	45	9	8	0	1	0	9	3

PITCHING	YR	W	L	ERA	G	SV	IP	H	BB	SO
Heck, Chris, lhp	Sr.	6	1	2.23	18	5	32	29	15	26
Paradis, Mike, rhp	Jr.	6	1	4.37	16	0	91	94	39	87
Roper, Doug, rhp	Jr.	1	0	5.04	13	1	25	24	8	20
Proto, Mike, lhp	So.	2	0	5.43	23	0	65	74	27	64
Adams, Brian, lhp	Jr.	5	5	5.85	23	1	80	98	42	62
Additon, Matt, rhp	Jr.	4	5	5.97	26	1	66	76	29	71
Mottl, Ryan, rhp	Jr.	4	8	6.14	19	0	100	120	53	84
Browning, Skip, rhp	Jr.	0	0	6.27	14	0	19	21	13	17
Boozer, Thomas, lhp	Fr.	6	3	6.98	15	1	49	67	26	34
Reba, Steve, rhp	Fr.	5	4	7.46	21	0	57	78	34	45
Cook, Brandt, lhp	Fr.	1	1	8.83	8	0	17	22	14	9
Lombardi, Justin, lhp	So.	0	0	11.57	10	0	9	13	12	17

18. PEPPERDINE

Coach: Frank Sanchez   **Record:** 46-16

BATTING	YR	AVG	AB	R	H	2B	3B	HR	RBI	SB
Raymundo, G.J., 3b	Sr.	.379	219	60	83	15	3	16	68	0
Sardinha, Dane, c	So.	.365	260	51	95	26	2	15	63	5
Evans, Austin, rf	So.	.362	149	41	54	9	2	0	16	20
Katz, Damon, 2b	Jr.	.343	216	29	74	11	2	5	48	4
Kramer, Michael, c-dh	Jr.	.333	45	12	15	3	0	2	6	1
Cliffords, Woody, cf	Fr.	.330	218	44	72	14	2	2	41	10
Pitney, Jared, 1b	So.	.314	242	47	76	16	2	4	51	2
Spieth, Chris, cf	Jr.	.313	99	14	31	6	0	1	14	1
Garcia, Tony, ss	Fr.	.308	201	43	62	15	0	10	35	3
White, Jeremy, dh	Jr.	.303	89	27	27	7	1	3	17	0
Garcia, Danny, of-2b	Fr.	.299	164	32	49	16	1	2	24	1
Haren, Daniel, rhp-dh	Fr.	.288	52	9	15	3	2	0	7	0
Coronado, Jeremy, cf	Jr.	.254	71	14	18	6	0	0	6	1
Ball, Dane, of	So.	.238	63	12	15	2	0	1	6	0
Bir, Dan, 1b	Sr.	.200	60	11	12	0	0	0	6	0
Merkle, Ryan, of	Sr.	.188	16	1	3	1	0	0	1	2

PITCHING	YR	W	L	ERA	G	SV	IP	H	BB	SO
Gehrke, Jay, rhp	Jr.	1	1	0.86	31	18	31	19	12	40
Adams, Jay, rhp	So.	11	3	2.56	18	0	120	114	19	91
Haren, Daniel, rhp	Fr.	10	3	3.08	19	0	108	105	27	77
Wersel, Matt, rhp	Fr.	0	0	3.38	7	0	16	16	3	3
Tucker, Brad, rhp	Sr.	9	3	4.09	20	0	112	105	48	68
Reed, Dave, lhp	Sr.	5	1	4.13	29	1	33	26	20	34
Sundstrom, Richard, rhp	Jr.	2	0	4.76	19	0	28	34	10	9
Askay, Michael, lhp	Fr.	2	1	4.86	13	0	17	13	11	10
Schenewerk, Steve, rhp	Jr.	6	3	5.78	22	0	76	88	33	46
Correa, Stephen, lhp	Fr.	0	1	18.47	9	1	6	15	11	3

19. EAST CAROLINA

Coach: Keith LeClair   **Record:** 46-16

BATTING	YR	AVG	AB	R	H	2B	3B	HR	RBI	SB
Brock, Chris, of	Fr.	.412	17	2	7	2	0	0	0	0
Salargo, Steve, of	Sr.	.398	244	70	97	20	1	16	77	14
Williamson, John, cf	So.	.369	241	63	89	19	1	15	65	3
Schnabel, Nick, 2b	Jr.	.357	224	56	80	20	1	3	35	7
Tracy, Chad, 1b	Jr.	.349	238	52	83	17	1	3	37	4
Howard, Jason, c	Jr.	.341	182	36	62	13	1	10	52	2
Bakich, Erik, 3b	Jr.	.324	244	43	79	16	0	7	54	9
Delfino, Lee, ss	Jr.	.317	218	61	69	9	3	12	50	4
Molinari, James, of	Jr.	.300	210	63	63	12	1	4	37	26
Simons, Brad, of	Jr.	.300	20	7	6	3	1	1	4	0
Hastings, Joe, dh	So.	.257	70	12	18	6	0	3	12	0
Godwin, Cliff, c-dh	Fr.	.246	122	23	30	7	0	4	20	0
Gentrup, Chris, 1b	So.	.200	35	8	7	1	1	1	4	0
Ward, Bryant, 2b-ss	Fr.	.188	32	6	6	2	0	0	4	0
Grieve, Kevin, dh	So.	.143	14	2	2	1	0	0	1	0
O'Sullivan, Kevin, 2b-ss	Fr.	.115	52	11	6	0	0	1	5	

PITCHING	YR	W	L	ERA	G	SV	IP	H	BB	SO
Scott, Cory, rhp	Jr.	2	0	2.53	14	1	32	28	15	29
Fulcher, Kevyn, rhp	Sr.	4	2	2.70	25	10	37	39	6	19
Thompson, Travis, rhp	Sr.	10	2	2.75	16	0	95	94	34	84
Outlaw, Bill, rhp	Sr.	2	2	3.69	10	0	39	49	6	25
Bucy, Josh, rhp	Sr.	4	0	3.79	16	1	38	31	15	41
Jernigan, Brooks, lhp	Sr.	9	4	4.03	19	0	105	99	50	79

BATTING										
Minton, Foye, lhp	So.	9	5	4.56	17	0	105	93	20	89
Mandryk, Jason, rhp	Fr.	2	1	5.20	11	0	28	32	17	18
Reikowski, Adam, rhp	Sr.	1	0	6.75	17	1	23	19	17	19
Schumacher, Jeremy, rhp	Jr.	3	0	7.28	12	1	30	37	15	23
Moncus, Curtis, rhp	Fr.	0	0	7.36	7	0	11	12	2	5

20. SOUTHWESTERN LOUISIANA

Coach: Tony Robichaux   **Record:** 42-24

BATTING	YR	AVG	AB	R	H	2B	3B	HR	RBI	SB
Nelson, Nathan, 3b-dh	Sr.	.420	162	30	68	17	3	4	42	6
Hawkins, Will, of	Jr.	.350	157	25	55	12	2	7	41	4
O'Dwyer, George, 2b	Sr.	.350	200	48	70	10	0	7	49	9
Bailey, Bret, c	So.	.333	12	0	4	0	0	0	0	1
Feehan, Steven, of	Jr.	.331	254	68	84	18	3	2	40	18
Massiatte, Danny, c	Jr.	.323	217	46	70	18	3	1	32	14
Calais, Ian, ss	Jr.	.318	157	38	50	8	1	0	27	2
Gill, Ryan, 3b-1b	Jr.	.312	215	50	67	12	2	3	23	19
Robinson, Jeff, 1b-rhp	Jr.	.303	185	36	56	9	1	5	41	12
Haydel, Rick, ss	Sr.	.277	83	20	23	5	0	3	13	5
Valdez, Castulo, dh-c	Sr.	.262	160	25	42	5	0	6	28	4
Poche, Jess, 1b-dh	Fr.	.250	72	10	18	4	0	1	9	1
Schaub, Kent, of	Sr.	.242	95	18	23	8	1	5	22	3
Arceneaux, Chad, of	Sr.	.218	101	11	22	1	0	2	10	2
Douglas, Mo, of	Sr.	.205	83	18	17	4	0	5	17	7
Gusman, Dan, dh	Jr.	.186	43	2	8	3	0	0	3	0
Judice, Adam, of	Sr.	.179	39	8	7	1	0	0	3	1
Simoneaux, Neil, ss-2b	Jr.	.091	22	9	2	2	0	0	0	2
Carboni, Scott, dh	Jr.	.083	12	2	1	0	0	0	0	1
Melancon, Ryker, of	Jr.	.000	11	0	0	0	0	0	1	0

PITCHING	YR	W	L	ERA	G	SV	IP	H	BB	SO
Baranowski, Br., rhp	Sr.	6	6	2.45	34	6	59	44	29	94
Ochsner, Alan, rhp	Sr.	6	0	2.72	26	6	76	59	30	93
Devey, Phil, lhp	Jr.	10	1	3.14	21	0	129	99	60	165
Bullinger, Trey, rhp	Jr.	2	2	3.67	11	0	34	32	19	33
O'Brien, Gordon, rhp	Fr.	0	0	3.81	12	0	26	28	7	40
Lally, Willis, rhp	Sr.	1	1	4.05	15	1	27	32	9	19
Templet, Eric, rhp	Sr.	7	5	4.58	20	0	88	108	27	81
Dohmann, Scott, rhp	So.	8	5	4.71	18	0	99	110	17	84
Robinson, Jeff, rhp	Jr.	2	1	4.82	10	1	19	19	8	26
Duplechain, Trent, rhp	Sr.	0	0	7.71	3	0	5	6	2	5
Yen, Buddy, rhp	Sr.	0	3	9.45	14	2	13	17	13	17

21. FLORIDA ATLANTIC

Coach: Kevin Cooney   **Record:** 54-9

BATTING	YR	AVG	AB	R	H	2B	3B	HR	RBI	SB
Conway, Clint, dh-1b	Jr.	.433	60	15	26	7	0	1	18	0
Withey, Ryan, of	Jr.	.385	179	61	69	15	2	5	28	24
Celli, Mick, of	Sr.	.374	214	70	80	10	1	15	64	10
Hart, Dickie, 2b	Jr.	.361	219	74	79	20	2	4	44	20
Roper, Zack, of	Jr.	.350	214	59	75	11	3	12	55	9
Biernbaum, L.J., 1b	Fr.	.333	24	8	8	0	1	0	5	0
Doudt, Anthony, c-dh	Jr.	.333	213	41	71	18	1	16	56	1
Stryhas, Paul, 3b	Jr.	.332	223	49	74	21	1	11	75	0
Murphy, Tommy, ss	So.	.330	209	57	69	18	2	11	37	13
Roig, George, 2b	Sr.	.326	46	19	15	1	2	0	13	2
Winsett, Chris, dh-c	Sr.	.321	159	37	51	10	0	15	50	1
Raffo, John-Edward, 1b	Jr.	.294	187	59	55	13	0	19	53	0
Somarriba, Gabe, of	Fr.	.281	57	13	16	1	0	0	8	3
Chirino, Mario, 2b-ss	Fr.	.265	34	6	9	1	1	0	5	1
Samaniego, Regan, of	So.	.250	16	1	4	1	0	0	3	0

PITCHING	YR	W	L	ERA	G	SV	IP	H	BB	SO
Piedra, Eddie, lhp	Jr.	0	0	0.63	13	0	14	12	9	17
Schreyer, Brett, rhp	Jr.	3	1	1.02	27	8	35	20	16	48
Burton, Tim, rhp	Sr.	3	0	1.80	17	4	35	26	15	34
Moser, Todd, lhp	Sr.	15	1	2.34	19	0	104	96	31	130
Cooney, Jim, lhp	Fr.	1	0	2.70	6	0	10	7	1	7
Gauger, Mike, lhp	Sr.	6	0	2.73	28	0	53	41	25	54
Cali, Carmen, lhp	So.	9	5	2.99	17	1	84	71	52	89
Mattoni, Nick, rhp	So.	6	0	3.40	17	0	53	54	27	54
Patterson, Steve, lhp	Fr.	1	0	3.60	3	0	5	7	1	6
Jackson, Dan, rhp	Jr.	10	2	4.61	17	0	96	88	55	126
Santom, Robert, rhp	Jr.	0	0	7.00	13	2	18	20	7	24
Eddinger, Dave, rhp	Fr.	0	0	8.10	6	0	7	10	3	2

22. PROVIDENCE

Coach: Charlie Hickey   **Record:** 49-16

BATTING	YR	AVG	AB	R	H	2B	3B	HR	RBI	SB
Scott, Mike, of	So.	.420	286	87	120	23	13	5	64	7
Reed, Keith, of	Jr.	.398	274	73	109	22	2	17	79	15

College Baseball

	YR	AVG	AB	R	H	2B	3B	HR	RBI	SB
McCarthy, Neal, of	Fr.	.376	218	65	82	22	2	17	69	7
O'Keefe, Mike, 1b	So.	.351	245	64	86	18	4	12	71	11
Athas, Jamie, ss	Fr.	.325	246	56	80	8	3	5	42	18
Ciminiello, Angelo, 3b	Sr.	.322	199	46	64	12	0	14	58	3
Conway, Dan, c-dh	So.	.312	221	59	69	11	0	10	50	5
Costello, Paul, 2b	Sr.	.312	250	67	78	13	1	2	43	9
O'Donnell, Coley, dh	Jr.	.275	109	21	30	7	2	2	22	0
Sweet, Jeremy, c	Jr.	.233	120	27	28	10	0	4	20	5
Hairston, Jason, of	Jr.	.231	91	21	21	5	3	0	10	8
Trainor, Brendan, 3b-2b	Fr.	.230	61	16	14	3	0	1	9	1

PITCHING	YR	W	L	ERA	G	SV	IP	H	BB	SO
Donovan, Brett, lhp	So.	1	0	1.98	8	0	14	12	4	11
DesRoches, Marc, rhp	Sr.	14	2	2.86	17	1	104	97	28	87
Swanjord, Scott, rhp	Sr.	0	0	3.38	10	1	13	20	6	6
Scott, Andrew, lhp	So.	7	2	3.70	17	4	73	74	34	43
Burnham, Josh, rhp	Sr.	10	3	5.30	17	1	114	139	36	75
Corraro, Rob, rhp	Sr.	8	3	5.54	15	0	104	127	36	43
Lewis, Ryan, lhp	Fr.	6	2	6.79	10	0	53	76	18	43
Stuart, Mike, lhp	Sr.	2	3	9.45	13	1	33	59	15	26
Murray, Todd, rhp	Sr.	0	1	9.78	15	2	19	34	15	13
Cox, Josh, rhp	Sr.	1	0	11.77	7	0	13	24	8	6

23. ARKANSAS

Coach: Norm DeBriyn   **Record: 42-23**

BATTING	YR	AVG	AB	R	H	2B	3B	HR	RBI	SB
Vorisek, John, of	Jr.	.400	10	3	4	0	0	0	4	0
Jester, Joe, 2b-ss	Jr.	.338	263	76	89	20	2	10	59	35
Crossett, Justin, of	So.	.335	182	30	61	8	1	4	33	9
Nye, Rodney, 3b-1b	Jr.	.327	269	69	88	19	0	20	78	17
McCrotty, Wes, 1b-lhp	So.	.325	120	21	39	8	0	0	24	1
Fletcher, Jeff, 2b	Fr.	.317	63	13	20	3	0	0	6	3
Pohle, Ike, c	Sr.	.306	186	42	57	14	0	6	36	7
Lundquist, Ryan, of	Sr.	.305	262	60	80	20	0	14	55	16
Burnett, Mark, ss-3b	Jr.	.297	182	47	54	11	0	5	29	21
Hagedorn, Brad, 3b-of	Jr.	.284	88	13	25	8	0	0	12	0
Kirby, Brian, of	So.	.272	217	39	59	14	0	10	42	3
Welsh, Jack, of	Jr.	.271	251	60	68	13	3	7	55	23
McMurry, John Paul, 1b	Jr.	.263	19	5	5	0	0	0	3	0
Blum, Greg, c	Jr.	.253	75	14	19	5	0	3	14	0
McDaniel, Travis, 3b	Jr.	.250	140	34	35	10	1	5	22	1
Bryant, Bo, of	Jr.	.100	10	2	1	0	0	0	0	0

PITCHING	YR	W	L	ERA	G	SV	IP	H	BB	SO
Nye, Rodney, rhp	Sr.	0	1	3.00	5	2	6	4	3	6
Isaacson, Charlie, rhp	Fr.	9	0	3.16	16	0	100	72	53	97
Manatt, Jared, lhp	Fr.	2	1	3.75	13	0	24	25	8	12
Walling, David, rhp	Jr.	10	2	3.78	18	0	121	104	31	155
Hurley, Scott, rhp	Sr.	1	1	5.14	18	0	21	24	16	11
Vent, Kevin, rhp	Sr.	3	3	5.28	31	4	58	57	39	61
Gilleland, Greg, lhp	Sr.	1	2	5.40	22	0	32	41	20	26
McCrotty, Wes, lhp	So.	5	2	5.75	21	1	83	100	39	74
Bohannan, Brad, rhp	Jr.	2	0	5.87	9	0	15	16	8	10
Wright, Dan, rhp	Jr.	1	8	6.27	25	4	47	49	29	53
Matheson, Derek, rhp	Jr.	0	0	6.39	9	0	13	15	6	7
Ens, Ryan, lhp	Fr.	2	0	7.94	6	0	11	12	7	4
Riethmaier, Matt, rhp	So.	5	2	9.19	15	0	31	38	31	24
Moriarity, Mike, lhp	Sr.	0	1	11.12	2	0	6	8	3	4
Tisher, Mitch, rhp	Jr.	0	0	19.06	6	0	6	11	2	6

24. HOUSTON

Coach: Rayner Noble   **Record: 40-24**

BATTING	YR	AVG	AB	R	H	2B	3B	HR	RBI	SB
Bitter, Jarrod, c	So.	.389	226	54	88	15	0	12	57	2
Woodward, J.P., 1b	So.	.381	218	55	83	17	3	18	66	8
Caraway, Brandon, 2b-of	Jr.	.363	267	72	97	18	4	6	37	27
Schweitzer, Tyson, of	Jr.	.343	213	46	73	24	0	6	48	9
Rios, Bruce, dh	Sr.	.298	114	23	34	5	0	4	24	4
Pekar, Jason, of	So.	.296	203	37	60	11	2	4	31	17
Lee, Eric, of	So.	.292	212	53	62	12	3	5	41	25
Melebeck, Aaron, ss	Jr.	.284	197	42	56	9	0	4	19	12
Wilken, Kris, 3b-c	So.	.277	256	34	71	14	2	7	47	2
Whatley, Keith, of-lhp	Fr.	.261	23	3	6	1	0	0	3	1
Allen, Sean, 2b	So.	.253	79	10	20	2	0	0	8	1
Sperring, Jayme, 1b-rhp	So.	.246	69	11	17	3	0	4	10	0
Medrano, Mike, of	Sr.	.242	132	18	32	5	0	2	17	4
Dieudonne, Robert, 3b-rhp	Jr.	.222	81	16	18	4	1	5	20	2
Nance, Shane, lhp-dh	Jr.	.200	10	2	2	0	0	0	2	0
Syfert, Justin, 2b	Sr.	.188	16	7	3	0	0	0	0	0

PITCHING	YR	W	L	ERA	G	SV	IP	H	BB	SO
Moore, Bryan, rhp	Sr.	7	2	2.55	32	2	74	71	26	50
Crowell, Kyle, rhp	So.	11	2	3.00	19	0	117	86	40	94

Dazzling tools that translated into results
Outfielder Keith Reed led Providence to Big East title

	YR	W	L	ERA	G	SV	IP	H	BB	SO
Sykes, Jerret, lhp	Jr.	5	3	4.26	18	0	76	90	19	52
Burke, Erick, lhp	Jr.	0	1	4.61	17	0	14	15	14	16
Torina, Nick, lhp	So.	1	0	4.72	16	0	27	26	17	23
Nance, Shane, lhp	Jr.	7	6	5.00	21	0	112	113	40	119
Dieudonne, Robert, rhp ..	Jr.	0	1	5.00	12	0	18	21	7	8
McAdoo, Duncan, rhp	Jr.	5	4	5.48	23	2	71	82	31	40
Jackson, Alex, lhp	Jr.	4	0	5.73	20	0	22	27	11	16
Hooper, Matt, rhp	Fr.	0	2	6.02	15	1	18	23	4	9
Mitchell, Nathan, rhp	Fr.	0	2	8.66	15	1	18	24	16	10
Sperring, Jayme, rhp	So.	0	1	9.00	13	0	14	14	10	13
Whatley, Keith, lhp	Fr.	0	0	14.29	5	0	6	9	4	3

25. NEBRASKA

Coach: Dave Van Horn   **Record: 42-18**

BATTING	YR	AVG	AB	R	H	2B	3B	HR	RBI	SB
Harvey, Ken, 1b	Jr.	.478	224	77	107	15	1	23	86	13
Cole, John, 2b-of	Fr.	.396	144	48	57	3	3	7	46	15
Shabala, Adam, of	Jr.	.373	177	48	66	8	3	0	37	28
Hedman, Jeff, dh-1b	Sr.	.371	167	42	62	8	2	13	48	0
Mumm, Erik, of	Sr.	.365	74	31	27	8	2	1	6	5
Bailey, Jim, dh-3b	Jr.	.349	63	21	22	1	1	4	29	0
Vlieger, Brandt, ss	Jr.	.348	207	48	72	10	3	4	41	16
Moore, Craig, dh-1b	So.	.346	26	11	9	2	0	1	14	1
Strong, Jamal, of	Jr.	.346	217	66	75	9	4	0	32	34
Cowan, Justin, of-c	So.	.312	221	52	69	21	1	9	60	7
Bolt, Will, 2b	So.	.278	227	48	63	16	7	4	43	8
Johnson, Brian, c	Jr.	.265	155	39	41	11	0	4	37	13
Kimura, Danny, 3b	So.	.259	193	40	50	8	4	4	45	2
Larsen, Scott, of	Jr.	.222	18	5	4	1	1	1	8	0
Stern, Adam, of	Fr.	.197	61	17	12	4	1	1	12	2

PITCHING	YR	W	L	ERA	G	SV	IP	H	BB	SO
Komine, Shane, rhp	Fr.	6	2	3.58	18	2	78	84	37	79
Wiles, Chad, rhp	Jr.	5	1	4.01	14	1	49	46	17	46
Bearinger, Jarod, rhp	Sr.	3	1	4.58	22	1	55	73	13	43
Hale, Steve, rhp	Jr.	3	2	4.80	9	1	30	34	10	34
Penas, Brandon, rhp	So.	4	0	5.20	16	1	38	28	10	28
Rodaway, Brian, lhp	So.	0	1	6.00	9	1	9	19	4	9
Schneider, Dave, rhp	Fr.	3	0	6.03	12	0	31	39	8	26
Spiehs, R.D., rhp	Fr.	5	1	6.27	23	1	56	68	23	43
Fries, Scott, lhp	Jr.	8	7	6.79	19	0	101	122	30	64
Sirianni, Jay, lhp	Sr.	6	3	6.87	18	1	75	103	30	58

CONFERENCE
Standings, Leaders

*Won conference tournament.
Boldface: NCAA regional participant/conference department leader.
#Conference department leader who is a non-qualifier.

AMERICA EAST CONFERENCE

	Conference W	L	Overall W	L
Towson	20	7	33	19
*Delaware	19	9	35	25
Northeastern	18	10	28	21
Maine	14	14	28	28
Hofstra	14	14	24	20
Vermont	10	18	21	26
Drexel	9	19	18	38
Hartford	7	20	12	34

ALL-CONFERENCE TEAM: C—Dusty Reynolds, Sr., Towson. **1B**—Vince Michello, Sr., Hofstra. **2B**—Jason Rummel, Sr., Towson. **3B**—Brian Poire, Sr., Maine. **SS**—Kevin Kim, Sr. Northeastern. **OF**—Nick Agoglia, Jr., Towson; James Caroleo, Sr., Hofstra; Kevin Mench, Jr., Delaware. **DH**—Dave Lohman, Sr., Hofstra. **P**—Greg Montalbano, Jr., Northeastern; Bryan Porcelli, Sr., Delaware.

Player of the Year: Kevin Mench, Delaware. **Pitcher of the Year:** Greg Montalbano, Northeastern. **Rookie of the Year:** Mike Ross, Maine. **Coach of the Year:** Mike Gottlieb, Towson.

INDIVIDUAL BATTING LEADERS
(Minimum 100 At-Bats)

	AVG	AB	R	H	2B	3B	HR	RBI	SB
Lohman, Dave, Hofstra	.442	113	27	50	15	0	7	31	2
Agoglia, Nick, Towson	**.392**	171	37	67	14	3	6	38	5
Avila, Ryan, Towson	.373	118	28	44	9	1	5	32	1
Mench, Kevin, Delaware	.373	204	48	**76**	17	1	**19**	**70**	11
Poire, Brian, Maine	.367	207	**55**	**76**	16	1	3	33	8
Tehonica, Josh, Vermont	.370	154	32	57	12	1	4	40	3
Acabbo, Bob, Vermont	.368	136	29	50	16	1	4	32	0
Boffalo, Matt, Hofstra	.368	117	33	43	10	2	6	29	9
Caroleo, James, Hofstra	.367	139	39	51	15	0	13	48	2
Keating, Matt, Northeastern	.363	168	38	61	13	1	7	40	8
Ross, Mike, Maine	.361	194	54	70	**20**	1	8	63	5
Michello, Vincent, Hofstra	.359	131	37	47	9	1	7	36	1
Lomuscio, Michael, North	.346	162	28	56	10	2	2	35	9
Marchetti, Lou, Drexel	.342	161	29	55	16	0	7	40	1
Denzine, Mark, Vermont	.339	124	14	42	10	0	3	24	0
Lewis, Jason, Northeastern	.338	160	42	54	11	3	1	15	13
Rummel, Jason, Towson	.337	163	42	55	11	0	9	44	12
Ciofrone, Paul, Hofstra	.333	111	35	37	8	2	6	29	20
Kim, Kevin, Northeastern	.329	164	37	54	14	3	4	37	4
Rikert, Wade, Vermont	.327	165	51	54	11	2	2	21	**27**
Quin, Peel, Maine	.322	180	28	58	2	0	4	39	2
Vukovich, Vince, Delaware	.322	152	22	49	6	2	3	23	4
Neiber, Matt, Drexel	.321	184	35	59	11	1	1	31	4
Russo, John, Hartford	.316	152	24	48	11	3	3	18	11
Salvo, Andrew, Delaware	.316	206	51	65	8	1	7	25	9
#Rikert, Kyle, Vermont	.301	156	47	47	3	**5**	1	22	20

INDIVIDUAL PITCHING LEADERS
(Minimum 40 Innings)

	W	L	ERA	G	SV	IP	H	BB	SO
Walsh, Chris, Northeastern	4	3	1.09	10	0	50	47	15	31
Montalbano, Greg, North.	8	2	**2.09**	11	0	65	44	24	71
Burns, John, Northeastern	4	4	2.63	8	0	55	41	24	33
Gillespie, Jason, Northeastern	5	2	2.86	9	0	63	59	23	53
Theberge, Casey, North.	5	3	3.00	16	1	48	36	14	40
Russ, Chris, Towson	6	3	3.11	12	0	55	53	23	61
Porcelli, Bryan, Delaware	**10**	3	3.24	17	1	103	102	39	**76**
Buck, Peter, Towson	6	0	3.43	12	0	79	81	19	54
McGuire, Rich, Delaware	7	4	3.58	17	0	73	89	14	40
Boehm, Bruce, Drexel	3	6	3.75	11	0	60	59	32	59

Setting the stage for draft 2000
Clemson outfielder Patrick Boyd hit .390-17-70

Mullin, Dave, Delaware	7	7	4.10	18	1	105	115	29	43
Wheeler, Todd, Hartford	2	6	4.25	16	0	59	63	24	40
Bailin, Jim, Maine	6	2	4.46	14	1	67	93	23	41
Steinberg, Howard, Hofstra	3	4	4.57	12	0	43	58	12	28
#Truman, Matt, Maine	2	3	4.71	17	**5**	21	20	10	18
Simmering, Bryan, Towson	2	3	4.81	10	0	49	48	15	33
Spaulding, Jason, Vermont	7	2	4.95	14	1	67	79	23	40
Lorito, Tim, Delaware	5	5	5.01	14	0	59	59	45	27

ATLANTIC COAST CONFERENCE

	Conference W	L	Overall W	L
Florida State	22	2	57	14
***Wake Forest**	16	7	47	16
Clemson	13	10	42	27
North Carolina	13	11	41	18
Georgia Tech	12	12	38	20
North Carolina State	11	13	37	25
Virginia	8	15	21	35
Maryland	6	17	23	33
Duke	4	18	24	31

ALL-CONFERENCE TEAM: C—Dan Moylan, So., North Carolina. **1B**—Jon Palmieri, Sr., Wake Forest. **2B**—Marshall McDougall, Jr., Florida State. **3B**—Mark Teixeira, Fr., Georgia Tech. **SS**—Vaughn Schill, Jr., Duke. **OF**—Matt Diaz, So., Florida State; Patrick Boyd, So., Clemson; Tyrell Godwin, So., North Carolina. **DH**—Danny Borrell, So., Wake Forest. **Util**—Matt Postell, Sr., North Carolina State. **P**—Chuck Crowder, Sr., Georgia Tech; Mike MacDougal, Jr., Wake Forest; Nick Stocks, So., Florida State. **RP**—Chris Chavez, Sr., Florida State.

Player of the Year: Marshall McDougall, Florida State. **Rookie of the Year:** Mark Teixeira, Georgia Tech. **Coach of the Year:** Mike Martin, Florida State.

INDIVIDUAL BATTING LEADERS
(Minimum 125 At-Bats)

	AVG	AB	R	H	2B	3B	HR	RBI	SB
Griffin, John-Ford, Fla. State	.436	133	42	58	15	0	3	35	0
McDougall, Marshall, FSU	.419	301	**104**	**126**	26	3	**28**	**106**	22
Palmieri, Jon, WF	.412	272	81	112	20	3	18	94	19
Boyd, Patrick, Clemson	.390	246	78	96	22	1	17	70	20
Teixeira, Mark, GT	.387	225	61	87	18	0	13	65	11
Schill, Vaughn, Duke	.386	220	67	85	24	2	5	30	5
Benick, Jon, Virginia	.384	229	38	88	16	1	10	54	4

College Baseball

ROBERT GURGANUS

Postell, Matt, NC State	.380	205	55	78	**27**	1	7	54	10
Diaz, Matt, Fla. State	.379	301	80	114	24	3	21	94	10
Godwin, Tyrell, UNC	.371	221	56	82	13	5	7	58	**29**
Ward, Brian, NC State	.367	237	65	87	18	3	16	73	9
Borrell, Danny, WF	.365	222	57	81	14	3	20	73	1
Wright, Brian, NC State	.363	190	47	69	14	1	6	35	12
Futrell, Michael, Fla. State	.363	135	39	49	11	2	3	19	3
Earey, Ryan, UNC	.362	207	50	75	13	2	15	63	9
Greene, Khalil, Clemson	.358	274	58	98	20	1	8	69	9
Voshell, Chase, WF	.353	224	49	79	15	4	9	37	16
Basil, Jason, GT	.349	209	43	73	18	0	8	56	5
Daeley, Scott, WF	.349	261	83	91	**27**	2	3	46	24
Riepe, Andrew, WF	.339	254	48	86	19	1	9	63	3
Harris, Jason, Clemson	.339	248	68	84	17	0	10	66	17
Moylan, Sean, UNC	.339	218	57	74	18	1	6	28	17
LaMarsh, Chris, UNC	.339	186	49	63	15	0	3	31	3
Lewis, Richard, GT	.338	148	26	50	3	0	1	14	7
Hooper, Clay, UNC	.336	244	56	82	14	1	11	37	6
Munroe, Craig, Maryland	.336	220	49	74	17	0	16	63	5
Acevedo, Adrean, NC State	.335	209	42	70	11	1	5	41	5
Donaghey, Stephen, GT	.333	153	28	51	9	0	12	53	2
Stockton, Brad, GT	.331	181	47	60	16	0	5	26	5
Bultmann, Kurt, Clemson	.327	272	73	89	23	2	12	72	6
Trout, Casey, Maryland	.323	198	49	64	15	2	5	35	8
Conrey, Ed, Duke	.321	209	41	67	11	**6**	8	47	1
Beer, Eric, Maryland	.321	221	48	71	12	1	6	30	18
Scott, Sam, Fla. State	.320	172	37	55	11	0	10	37	4
Stone, David, Virginia	.319	210	40	67	8	2	1	31	20
Goodner, Wes, Duke	.319	191	37	61	10	1	5	41	1
Danosky, Ben, WF	.318	170	36	54	14	0	7	37	1
Cash, Kevin, Fla. State	.317	252	50	80	13	0	14	58	7
Boggs, Matthew, GT	.316	206	56	65	5	0	0	16	14
McQueen, Eric, GT	.315	216	44	68	10	1	11	37	11
#Groves, Brett, Fla. State	.286	227	59	65	10	3	1	31	**29**

INDIVIDUAL PITCHING LEADERS
(Minimum 50 Innings)

	W	L	ERA	G	SV	IP	H	BB	SO
DePriest, Derrick, UNC	7	6	**1.71**	36	7	74	73	22	72
Chavez, Chris, Fla. State	8	5	2.17	36	5	87	60	36	109
MacDougal, Mike, WF	**13**	3	2.62	17	0	120	88	65	117
Snare, Ryan, UNC	6	5	2.94	17	0	80	73	46	82
Stocks, Nick, Fla. State	**13**	2	3.25	21	0	127	111	44	**139**
Metzger, Jon, Virginia	2	0	3.53	18	0	64	62	48	74
McDonald, Jon, Fla. State	9	3	3.57	20	0	116	112	51	123
Crowder, Chuck, GT	10	5	3.62	23	3	117	106	58	130
Snyder, Kyle, UNC	7	5	3.82	15	0	97	85	32	102
Kennedy, Casey, Virginia	4	6	3.86	12	0	70	80	15	38
Bynum, Mike, UNC	7	1	3.90	15	0	85	85	41	89
Young, Simon, GT	7	4	4.10	15	0	83	93	28	79
Varnes, Blair, Fla. State	11	2	4.13	19	0	109	112	20	76
Schmitt, Eric, WF	4	1	4.13	10	0	61	72	15	55
Briggs, Matt, WF	6	0	4.14	20	1	72	68	33	50
Ormond, Rodney, NC State	7	5	4.27	16	0	84	102	30	60
#DiBlasi, Mike, Fla. State	0	0	4.33	28	**9**	27	22	20	46
Paradis, Mike, Clemson	6	1	4.37	16	0	91	94	39	87
Vance, Cory, GT	9	3	4.43	18	1	104	118	50	103
Shrout, Kevin, Virginia	2	4	4.53	15	1	58	58	32	58
Creswell, Brandon, Virginia	6	7	4.59	17	0	100	116	37	86
Siemon, Scott, WF	12	4	4.78	29	4	92	113	33	65
D'Amato, Dan, NC State	7	2	5.11	23	2	88	102	26	52
Cowie, Stephen, Duke	8	9	5.18	18	0	116	129	28	137

ALL-CONFERENCE TEAM: C—Barry Gauch, Sr., Virginia Tech. **1B**—Joe Beichert, Sr., George Washington. **2B**—Mike Roberts, Sr., George Washington. **3B**—Nick Danzuso, Jr., Duquesne. **SS**—Joe Kerrigan, Sr., Temple. **OF**—B.J. Barns, Jr., Duquesne; Matt Griswold, Sr., Virginia Tech; Matt Watson, Jr., Xavier. **DH**—Colin Young, Jr., Fordham. **P**—Peter Moore, Sr., Temple; Lou Witte, Sr., Xavier.

Player of the Year: B.J. Barns, Duquesne. **Pitcher of the Year**: Peter Moore, Temple. **Rookie of the Year**: Jason Bush, Virginia Tech. **Coach of the Year**: Larry Conti, La Salle.

INDIVIDUAL BATTING LEADERS
(Minimum 125 At-Bats)

	AVG	AB	R	H	2B	3B	HR	RBI	SB
Barns, B.J., Duquesne	.456	195	**67**	89	22	3	17	57	5
Danzuso, Nick, Duquesne	.428	187	40	80	13	1	10	68	5
Bowles, Larry, Va. Tech	.390	210	49	82	17	3	14	58	1
Kerrigan, Joe, Temple	.387	204	43	79	14	1	2	44	10
Watson, Matt, Xavier	.386	189	52	73	**23**	2	14	51	5
Fuchs, Mike, La Salle	.378	217	48	82	23	1	9	57	0
Hemphill, Eric, St. Bona.	.377	159	34	60	3	0	7	36	2
Young, Colin, Fordham	.374	179	42	67	17	0	6	35	11
Gauch, Barry, Va. Tech	.374	227	51	85	17	3	10	61	4
Dacey, Ryan, Geo. Wash.	.371	224	53	83	22	1	5	46	8
La Barbera, Mike, RI	.367	196	43	72	14	1	1	23	20
Fisher, Toby, La Salle	.360	203	44	73	14	1	5	42	5
Rasey, Pat, Dayton	.356	202	31	72	17	0	4	33	5
Sprague, Bob, Fordham	.355	155	31	55	12	1	3	34	14
Bowman, Addison, Va. Tech	.352	227	50	80	18	0	8	36	7
Stein, Tom, Fordham	.351	131	26	46	9	0	3	26	5
Beichert, Joe, Geo. Wash	.349	215	54	75	17	0	**23**	**77**	0
Griswold, Matt, Va. Tech	.345	206	**67**	71	12	1	12	49	12
Scullin, Jon, RI	.344	195	50	67	6	4	3	31	20
Evers, Mark, St. Bona.	.343	143	34	49	13	0	1	22	14
Krusen, Chris, Temple	.341	135	23	46	8	3	0	23	6
Vega, Anthony, Fordham	.341	176	46	60	10	3	6	27	28
Braunstein, Aaron, Mass	.339	174	45	59	9	1	12	52	5
Shiflett, Eric, Va. Tech	.338	216	55	73	11	1	8	49	10
Berigen, Brent, Dayton	.338	213	60	72	14	6	13	52	13
#Wyatt, Eric, St. Joseph's	.335	188	38	63	5	**7**	5	31	26
#Mazzaferro, Bryan, Mass	.333	174	47	58	10	2	1	25	**32**

INDIVIDUAL PITCHING LEADERS
(Minimum 50 Innings)

	W	L	ERA	G	SV	IP	H	BB	SO
Moore, Peter, Temple	5	6	**2.50**	24	**8**	94	76	33	103
Veracka, Travis, Mass	6	4	3.08	12	0	76	85	19	63
Witte, Lou, Xavier	10	5	3.24	21	0	106	119	23	92
Young, Colin, Fordham	6	4	3.44	17	3	68	54	29	87
Fisher, Mike, Duquesne	4	0	3.55	11	0	66	80	18	26
Pinkman, Pat, Va. Tech	9	5	3.72	21	2	119	124	35	94
Wyatt, Eric, St. Joseph's	4	9	4.04	13	0	71	80	50	52
Szado, Craig, Mass	3	5	4.15	15	2	74	69	26	73
Cozier, Vance, St. Bona.	5	6	4.22	14	0	81	80	39	85
Bowles, Larry, Va. Tech	10	3	4.27	18	0	105	120	28	**106**
Antico, Matt, Fordham	4	6	4.30	14	0	73	79	24	56
Gaffney, Chris, RI	6	2	4.36	12	0	64	67	30	58
Siefker, James, Xavier	2	3	4.36	14	0	64	70	18	29
Scott, John, Dayton	6	1	4.39	25	0	55	63	20	30
Gray, Mike, St. Bona.	9	2	4.41	19	1	63	77	17	63
Carroll, Sean, RI	6	6	4.56	12	0	81	93	22	60
Bush, Jason, Va. Tech	**11**	2	4.59	16	0	84	81	26	56
Belicic, Adam, Geo. Wash.	6	6	4.76	12	0	74	79	32	63
Bouie, Aaron, St. Bona.	5	4	4.83	12	0	54	54	38	57
Wiggers, Greg, Xavier	6	5	4.92	20	0	79	73	36	74

ATLANTIC-10 CONFERENCE

EAST	Conference W	L	Overall W	L
Massachusetts	13	8	26	23
Temple	12	9	28	28
Rhode Island	10	11	22	28
Fordham	10	11	22	28
St. Bonaventure	10	11	24	22
St. Joseph's	5	16	21	33

WEST	W	L	W	L
*Virginia Tech	18	3	42	17
La Salle	10	11	27	29
Duquesne	10	11	24	32
George Washington	10	11	27	30
Xavier	10	11	24	31
Dayton	8	13	22	34

BIG EAST CONFERENCE

	Conference W	L	Overall W	L
Notre Dame	20	5	43	18
Rutgers	19	7	37	21
*Providence	18	8	49	16
Seton Hall	14	11	32	19
St. John's	13	11	32	22
West Virginia	12	13	29	28
Pittsburgh	11	15	27	27
Villanova	11	15	27	26
Boston College	10	15	26	21
Connecticut	10	16	27	24
Georgetown	2	24	18	34

ALL-CONFERENCE TEAM: C—Jeff Waldron, Sr., Boston College. **1B**—Sean McGowan, Sr., Boston College. **2B**—Matt Longo, So., Villanova. **3B**—Mike Dzurilla, Jr., St. John's. **SS**—Brant Ust, Jr., Notre Dame. **OF**—Keith Reed, Jr., Providence; Mike Scott, Sr., Providence; Pete Zoccolillo, Sr., Rutgers. **DH**—Jeff Wagner, Sr., Notre Dame; Eric Potts, So., St. John's. **Util**—Alfie Critelli, Jr., Seton Hall. **P**—Aaron Heilman, So., Notre Dame; Marc DesRoches, Sr., Providence; Cam Esslinger, Jr., Seton Hall.

Player of the Year: Keith Reed, Providence. **Pitcher of the Year**: Marc DesRoches, Providence. **Rookie of the Year**: Mike Scott, Providence. **Coach of the Year**: Charlie Hickey, Providence.

INDIVIDUAL BATTING LEADERS
(Minimum 125 At-Bats)

	AVG	AB	R	H	2B	3B	HR	RBI	SB
McGowan, Sean, BC	.430	179	60	77	8	2	25	70	5
Fenster, Darren, Rutgers	.424	224	64	95	18	2	2	57	7
Scott, Mike, Providence	.420	286	87	120	21	13	5	64	7
Zoccolillo, Pete, Rutgers	.418	232	63	97	22	2	12	72	1
Dzurilla, Mike, St. John's	.410	229	51	94	24	2	16	65	17
Leighton, Brian, Seton Hall	.401	182	51	73	11	6	7	48	4
Waldron, Jeff, BC	.399	168	46	67	15	1	7	33	1
Reed, Keith, Providence	.398	274	73	109	22	2	17	79	15
Critelli, Alfie, Seton Hall	.395	162	25	64	15	1	8	54	0
Williams, Lance, WV	.394	203	42	80	13	0	8	49	4
Bravetts, John, Seton Hall	.393	206	65	81	23	3	5	43	1
Kealty, Joe, BC	.393	178	29	70	15	2	0	44	7
McCarthy, Neal, Providence	.376	218	65	82	22	2	17	69	7
DeJesus, David, Rutgers	.373	233	85	87	20	6	8	45	20
Gonda, Mike, Pittsburgh	.367	180	33	66	8	3	9	34	13
Potts, Eric, St. John's	.367	196	45	72	9	1	9	48	9
Gambino, Mike, BC	.363	146	29	53	2	0	4	31	3
Longo, Matt, Villanova	.361	191	64	69	16	1	9	57	4
Cafiero, Rob, Villanova	.361	191	40	69	15	0	10	72	1
Pizzini, Dave, Villanova	.359	181	35	65	13	1	1	36	2
Ust, Brant, Notre Dame	.359	220	53	79	16	2	17	58	10
Caudill, Clarke, Conn	.354	198	50	70	20	2	8	46	10
O'Keefe, Mike, Providence	.351	245	64	86	18	4	12	71	11
Katz, Glenn, Conn	.350	220	44	77	15	3	4	40	24
McGee, Brian, Seton Hall	.349	172	40	60	9	1	2	26	17
Dickinson, Steve, Pittsburgh	.347	199	33	69	12	0	13	47	1
Daubert, Jake, Rutgers	.346	231	53	80	22	1	8	68	0
Fallon, Chris, St. John's	.346	159	37	55	14	0	11	33	6
Horowitz, Jeremy, George.	.345	142	26	49	10	0	1	13	5
Esposito, Brian, Conn	.343	181	30	62	10	2	6	36	5
Brock, Todd, WV	.340	191	32	65	17	1	8	53	2
#Graham, Pete, St. John's	.333	204	51	68	14	5	8	42	28
#Neumark, Tim, WV	.310	142	27	44	5	1	0	25	28

INDIVIDUAL PITCHING LEADERS
(Minimum 50 Innings)

	W	L	ERA	G	SV	IP	H	BB	SO
DesRoches, Marc, Prov.	14	2	2.86	17	1	104	97	28	87
Ponce de Leon, D., SH	7	1	3.08	14	0	50	56	9	38
Heilman, Aaron, ND	11	2	3.14	20	3	109	89	37	118
McKeown, Chris, ND	3	2	3.53	16	1	51	58	13	45
Schultz, John, Pitsburgh	4	7	3.65	14	0	79	94	24	70
Esslinger, Cam, SH	6	4	3.66	15	1	71	71	22	70
Cummings, Jeremy, WV	6	8	3.69	16	0	110	93	27	116
Cavey, Scott, Notre Dame	6	1	3.70	13	0	58	60	8	47
Scott, Andrew, Providence	7	2	3.70	17	4	73	74	34	43
Irvin, Matt, Pittsburgh	6	4	3.86	14	0	77	80	30	76
Wilson, James, Rutgers	8	3	4.04	18	1	93	97	36	70
McGerry, Kevin, St. John's	8	3	4.06	17	0	106	91	53	124
Wheeler, Tom, Rutgers	5	1	4.28	11	0	61	65	28	43
Brown, Eric, Rutgers	8	5	4.33	14	0	89	110	19	56
Langone, Steve, BC	8	4	4.43	15	2	85	112	20	78
#Corbin, John, Notre Dame	7	3	4.53	28	9	48	49	18	44
Probst, John, Seton Hall	3	3	4.53	19	1	54	54	20	42
Collins, Pat, St. John's	4	5	4.54	16	0	75	79	45	82
#Manning, Brian, Villanova	3	2	7.01	30	9	35	39	43	56

BIG SOUTH CONFERENCE

	Conference W	L	Overall W	L
Coastal Carolina	10	2	43	15
*Winthrop	9	6	40	23
Radford	7	7	22	30
Liberty	7	8	26	28
Charleston Southern	5	8	26	32
UNC Asheville	4	11	20	39

ALL-CONFERENCE TEAM: C—Kevin Schnall, Sr., Coastal Carolina. **1B**—Josh White, Sr., UNC Asheville. **2B**—Jordan Webb, So., Winthrop. **3B**—Jason Colson, So., Winthrop. **SS**—Jason Tarsuik, Sr., Winthrop. **OF**—Brooks Marzka, So., Coastal Carolina; Ryan Moffett, Fr., UNC Asheville; Anthony Pennix, Jr., Liberty. **DH**—Bill McCarthy, Fr., Radford. **P**—Ron Deubel, Sr., Coastal Carolina; Scott Sturkie, Sr., Coastal Carolina.

Most Valuable Player: Kevin Schnall, Coastal Carolina. **Rookie of the Year**: Ryan Moffett, UNC Asheville. **Coach of the Year**: Gary Gilmore, Coastal Carolina.

INDIVIDUAL BATTING LEADERS
(Minimum 100 At-Bats)

	AVG	AB	R	H	2B	3B	HR	RBI	SB
Schnall, Kevin, Coastal Car.	.405	185	46	75	13	0	7	48	1
Miller, Trey, Liberty	.374	107	32	40	5	1	5	22	11
Marzka, Brooks, Coast. Car.	.370	216	51	80	14	0	8	43	14
Moffett, Ryan, UNCA	.359	217	56	78	17	7	12	48	14
Pennix, Anthony, Liberty	.354	181	46	64	11	2	10	50	12
Owens, Justin, Coastal Car.	.353	102	26	36	5	1	1	21	4
Leathers, Todd, Winthrop	.349	175	27	61	8	2	8	35	2
Webb, Jordan, Winthrop	.345	238	60	82	11	1	3	29	20
Davis, Jason, Coastal Car.	.343	178	36	61	8	0	2	30	6
Tarasuik, Jason, Winthrop	.342	228	46	78	15	2	5	48	13
Woods, Eddie, UNCA	.338	228	34	77	9	1	6	37	5
McCarthy, Bill, Radford	.337	181	37	61	17	2	6	45	7
Walsh, Sean, Radford	.337	184	44	62	17	0	4	33	17
Ayala, Ricardo, Coastal Car.	.335	164	44	55	7	2	0	21	33
Busha, Brett, Winthrop	.333	222	47	74	13	0	6	59	8
Corrigale, Jay, Charlston So.	.332	214	37	71	13	1	4	36	18
Lombardi, Mike, Radford	.327	205	50	67	8	3	5	27	14
Potter, Mike, Radford	.327	101	27	33	7	0	1	8	6
Black, Travis, UNCA	.324	145	30	47	6	2	3	18	13
Colson, Jason, Winthrop	.321	240	55	77	18	1	15	57	4
Trees, Patrick, Coastal Car.	.318	107	23	34	5	0	3	17	0
Smith, Alan, Liberty	.317	104	13	33	4	1	0	13	5
Ury, Josh, Winthrop	.316	196	42	62	13	2	2	33	6
#Malikowski, Ted, Char. So.	.313	195	33	61	18	1	7	45	4

INDIVIDUAL PITCHING LEADERS
(Minimum 40 Innings)

	W	L	ERA	G	SV	IP	H	BB	SO
Sundsmo, Aaron, Winthrop	6	3	2.43	35	11	59	43	19	55
Sturkie, Scott, Coastal Car.	10	4	2.49	20	0	116	107	39	106
Kadlec, Kit, Coastal Car.	2	2	2.93	36	13	46	47	16	50
Koziara, Matt, Winthrop	12	2	3.18	17	0	125	110	48	103
Pennix, Anthony, Liberty	3	1	3.48	9	1	41	36	38	27
Tyree, Robert, Charleston So.	8	8	3.62	18	0	114	107	34	106
Thomas, Kevin, Coastal Car.	3	1	3.64	11	0	42	28	25	37
Johnson, Rett, Coastal Car.	9	3	3.69	19	0	83	84	37	85
Deubel, Ron, Coastal Car.	13	2	3.72	23	1	131	121	48	132
Viars, Andy, Charleston So.	2	3	4.09	16	0	51	46	30	40
Smith, Ryan, Charleston So.	6	2	4.42	15	0	73	86	10	49
Krosschell, Terry, Winthrop	10	5	4.48	17	0	98	84	62	98
Steffler, David, Winthrop	9	4	4.54	17	0	119	134	29	88
Adams, Darren, Liberty	6	2	4.75	12	0	55	65	20	32

BIG TEN CONFERENCE

	Conference W	L	Overall W	L
Ohio State	25	3	50	14
Minnesota	21	7	46	18
Illinois	15	12	34	22
*Michigan	15	13	34	30
Indiana	14	14	37	17
Penn State	12	15	32	23
Michigan State	10	17	28	25
Purdue	10	17	24	30
Northwestern	10	18	24	29
Iowa	6	22	22	34

ALL-CONFERENCE TEAM: C—Tom Durant, Sr., Ohio State. **1B**—Robb Quinlan, Sr., Minnesota. **2B**—Chad Ehrnsberger, So., Ohio State. **3B**—Mike Cervenak, Sr., Michigan. **SS**—Jeremy Kurella, So., Northwestern. **OF**—Mike Lockwood, Sr., Ohio State; Doug DeVore, Jr., Indiana; Michael Campo, Sr., Penn State. **DH**—Aron Amundson, Sr., Minnesota. **P**—Justin Fry, Sr., Ohio State; Jason Anderson, So., Illinois; Brad Pautz, Sr., Minnesota; E.J. Laratta, Fr., Ohio State. **RP**—Jim Journell, Jr., Illinois.

Player of the Year: Robb Quinlan, Minnesota. **Pitcher of the Year**: Justin Fry, Ohio State. **Freshman of the Year**: E.J. Laratta, Ohio State. **Coach of the Year**: Bob Todd, Ohio State.

All-conference Gopher
Brad Pautz helped Minnesota return to regionals

INDIVIDUAL BATTING LEADERS
(Minimum 125 At-Bats)

	AVG	AB	R	H	2B	3B	HR	RBI	SB
Quinlan, Robb, Minnesota	.413	259	76	107	26	4	16	84	6
Amundson, Aron, Minn.	.396	192	48	76	19	1	15	63	0
Basak, Chris, Illinois	.393	145	32	57	9	0	3	19	19
Simmons, Luke, Illinois	.386	127	33	49	8	0	7	38	0
Holthaus, Josh, Minnesota ...	.382	131	35	50	16	1	8	36	0
Scales, Bobby, Michigan	.371	248	75	92	20	4	9	50	4
Haegele, Dan, Indiana	.370	181	59	67	10	1	3	39	25
Marquie, Craig, Illinois	.368	193	56	71	10	2	14	55	2
Carlson, Brad, Iowa	.367	210	43	77	17	0	21	71	1
Scanlon, Matt, Minnesota	.367	264	70	97	33	3	10	78	5
Trott, Jason, Ohio State	.367	221	70	81	20	0	7	52	11
DeVore, Doug, Indiana	.360	200	48	72	15	3	19	65	7
Hannahan, Jim, Minn.	.360	139	28	50	9	0	4	30	2
Svihlik, D.J., Illinois	.359	198	59	71	10	2	15	52	5
Bush, Brian, Michigan	.357	263	55	94	14	5	7	43	13
Ehrnsberger, Chad, OSU	.356	216	62	77	15	0	16	73	10
Anderson, Jon, Illinois	.355	228	58	81	13	0	6	34	3
Frei, Eric, Purdue	.352	193	43	68	9	3	9	43	16
Humes, Toby, Iowa	.352	162	35	57	14	2	6	26	2
Burks, Brian, Iowa	.351	154	35	54	6	4	4	18	12
Campo, Michael, Penn State .	.351	211	63	74	9	4	6	34	27
Durant, Tom, Ohio State	.350	214	58	75	22	1	7	39	11
Rudden, Kevin, Illinois	.350	200	33	70	12	1	7	45	1
Kurella, Jeremy, NW	.348	210	53	73	6	0	5	29	18
Hallada, Daryl, Purdue	.346	228	39	79	20	2	5	39	8
St. Clair, Blake, Indiana	.346	133	40	46	6	5	8	40	14
Dainton, Robert, NW	.345	197	30	68	13	3	2	36	14
Fagan, Shawn, Penn State ..	.344	183	44	63	10	4	13	53	7
Hartley, Tom, Mich. State......	.344	180	42	62	12	0	7	37	2
Lockwood, Mike, OSU...........	.344	253	71	87	12	5	15	55	6
Hietpas, Joe, NW	.342	187	36	64	13	0	11	44	3
Cervenak, Mike, Michigan	.340	256	56	87	23	3	9	70	5
Howard, Scott, Minnesota	.335	203	46	68	11	2	1	29	13
Williams, Jason, Indiana	.335	161	38	54	14	1	3	31	7
Fernandez, Carlos, Mich. St.	.333	183	39	61	7	2	0	27	7
Walker, Chris, Purdue	.332	220	48	73	13	2	1	22	21
Dvorsky, Alex, Iowa	.331	178	35	59	12	1	9	37	4
Middleton, Matt, OSU	.330	221	42	73	17	2	9	55	5
Netwall, Chris, Penn State ...	.330	176	49	58	11	1	12	43	9
O'Connell, Frank, Indiana	.330	182	47	60	9	4	9	39	8
Richmond, John, Penn State .	.330	179	32	59	6	0	0	16	4
Sickler, Nate, Purdue	.330	194	51	64	16	1	11	43	9
McClure, Todd, Illinois	.328	198	48	65	17	1	6	41	6
Alcaraz, Jason, Michigan	.327	248	46	81	19	3	8	52	3
Pisani, Mike, Mich. State	.327	208	30	68	17	0	3	25	4
Williamson, J.P., NW	.326	193	35	63	4	0	4	29	9
Jansen, Andy, Iowa	.324	210	49	68	16	5	5	33	4

INDIVIDUAL PITCHING LEADERS
(Minimum 50 Innings)

	W	L	ERA	G	SV	IP	H	BB	SO
Torres, Jason, Indiana	4	2	3.41	14	1	74	57	48	86
Ralston, Bryce, Michigan	8	1	3.54	14	0	81	96	19	42
McCall, Dan, Penn State	5	3	3.69	13	0	68	60	39	69
Fry, Justin, Ohio State	11	2	3.70	17	0	114	117	27	104
Putz, J.J., Michigan	7	4	3.70	16	0	80	79	38	67
Laratta, E.J., Ohio State	10	3	3.77	15	0	86	86	18	59
Yodis, Peter, Penn State	6	5	4.02	15	0	63	55	30	56
Goodrum, Kevin, OSU	4	0	4.35	29	3	52	47	37	38
Magrane, James, Iowa	6	4	4.43	16	0	108	123	29	110
Bilke, Austin, Purdue	3	4	4.45	11	0	65	65	30	40
Werner, Kelly, Minnesota	6	2	4.54	14	0	75	87	25	46
Goebeler, Dan, Penn State	4	6	4.76	14	0	87	105	31	56
Horvath, Dan, Mich. State	4	5	4.85	16	0	52	76	11	25
Smith, Chad, Indiana	5	6	5.01	14	0	65	74	28	68
Pautz, Brad, Minnesota	9	3	5.04	16	0	100	126	33	65
Anderson, Jason, Illinois	9	2	5.12	20	0	97	124	32	61
Padgett, Dan, NW	4	4	5.18	18	1	57	52	36	56
Clarey, Chadd, Minnesota.........	7	3	5.26	16	0	79	87	31	53
#Cox, Cory, Ohio State	3	3	5.33	28	9	37	55	21	45
Brandell, Scott, Mich. State	5	4	5.37	15	0	69	86	21	41
Bonner, Luke, Michigan	5	7	5.40	16	1	70	83	30	56
Gassner, David, Purdue	4	5	5.47	16	1	79	85	31	64

BIG 12 CONFERENCE

	Conference W	L	Overall W	L
Texas A&M	23	6	52	18
Baylor	20	7	50	15
Texas Tech	18	8	42	17
Oklahoma State	18	9	46	21
***Nebraska**	16	9	42	18
Texas	17	13	36	26
Missouri	14	13	35	19
Oklahoma	12	18	30	29
Kansas State	11	18	26	29
Kansas	4	26	14	40
Iowa State	2	28	17	36

ALL-CONFERENCE TEAM: C—Josh Bard, Jr., Texas Tech. **1B**—Ken Harvey, Jr., Nebraska. **2B**—Eric Nelson, Sr., Baylor. **3B**—Josh Holliday, Sr., Oklahoma State. **SS**—Jason Moore, So., Texas. **OF**—Lamont Matthews, Jr., Oklahoma State; Daylan Holt, So., Texas A&M; Kasey Weishaar, So., Kansas State; Jon Topolski, Sr., Baylor. **DH**—Casey Bookout, Sr., Oklahoma. **Util**—Billy Gasparino, Sr., Oklahoma State. **P**—Casey Fossum, Jr., Texas A&M; Jason Jennings, Jr., Baylor; Matt Smith, So., Oklahoma State; Jody Harris, Jr., Missouri. **RP**—Brandon Roberson, Jr., Texas Tech; Chris Russ, Sr., Texas A&M.

Player of the Year: Jason Jennings, Baylor. **Newcomer of the Year**: Jody Harris, Missouri. **Freshman of the Year**: Shane Komine, Nebraska. **Coach of the Year**: Mark Johnson, Texas A&M.

INDIVIDUAL BATTING LEADERS
(Minimum 125 At-Bats)

	AVG	AB	R	H	2B	3B	HR	RBI	SB
Harvey, Ken, Nebraska	.478	224	77	107	15	1	23	86	13
Weishaar, Kasey, Kansas St.	.429	191	53	82	9	4	7	31	4
Runk, Aaron, Iowa State	.415	142	48	59	15	3	6	28	22
Cole, John, Nebraska	.396	144	48	57	3	3	7	46	15
Jennings, Jason, Baylor	.386	233	52	90	14	0	17	68	1
Matthews, Lamont, Okla. St.	.384	242	87	93	17	7	30	105	10
Schumacher, Shawn, A&M ...	.374	243	43	91	14	0	11	53	3
Shabala, Adam, Nebraska	.373	177	48	66	8	3	0	37	28
Wilson, Aaron, Missouri	.373	212	47	79	21	1	5	55	0
Hedman, Jeff, Nebraska	.371	167	42	62	8	2	13	48	0
Park, Richard, Oklahoma	.368	212	50	78	12	1	11	42	2
Bookout, Casey, Oklahoma ...	.367	215	48	79	16	2	16	60	0
Gasparino, Billy, Okla. State .	.364	247	96	90	19	3	24	91	27
Scheschuk, John, A&M	.363	248	62	90	14	0	10	54	2
Ruiz, Ryan, Texas Tech	.363	204	80	74	8	3	0	31	35
Nelson, Eric, Baylor	.362	282	77	102	20	6	17	79	22
Williams, Jon, Missouri	.362	188	39	68	17	1	4	40	3
Gautreaux, Carlos, Okla. St. .	.361	147	35	53	11	3	3	32	7
Topolski, Jon, Baylor	.358	243	74	87	12	2	17	61	23
Becerra, Chris, Okla. State ...	.356	135	39	48	10	3	10	39	0
Weber, Jon, Texas Tech	.356	194	64	69	18	8	13	84	6
Cunningham, Marco, TT	.355	234	72	83	16	4	3	34	37

	AVG	AB	R	H	2B	3B	HR	RBI	SB
Bard, Josh, Texas Tech	.353	238	49	84	**28**	2	13	92	1
Walters, Bobby, Oklahoma ...	.352	247	54	87	15	3	11	48	11
Paciorek, Mack, Iowa State ..	.349	215	30	75	21	1	3	37	3
Vlieger, Brandt, Nebraska	.348	207	48	72	10	3	4	41	16
Hensley, Anthony, Baylor	.346	133	36	46	8	2	2	19	29
Strong, Jamal, Nebraska	.346	217	66	75	9	4	0	32	34
Truitt, Steven, A&M	.345	264	80	91	24	5	19	60	23
Lucas, Kevin, Okla. State	.342	269	74	92	12	4	7	46	24
Holt, Daylan, A&M	.341	287	78	98	22	3	**34**	**105**	9
Silva, Andy, Kansas State	.340	150	23	51	12	1	4	31	1
Tabor, Chad, Kansas State ..	.335	221	53	74	8	2	4	24	19
Heaney, Sean, A&M	.333	282	70	94	27	5	11	48	9
Lekse, Zach, Oklahoma	.333	255	51	85	14	2	2	29	5
Warner, J.R., Missouri	.333	165	51	55	14	3	4	25	7
Cox, Jason, Texas	.332	259	56	86	15	**8**	2	43	16
Cogdill, Mark, Baylor	.330	224	56	74	12	4	5	37	16
Whiteman, Tommy, Okla.	.330	185	33	61	13	2	7	44	7

INDIVIDUAL PITCHING LEADERS
(Minimum 50 Innings)

	W	L	ERA	G	SV	IP	H	BB	SO
Roberson, Brandon, TT	3	4	2.45	27	**10**	70	62	28	77
Jennings, Jason, Baylor	**13**	2	2.58	22	1	147	102	50	**172**
George, Chris, Missouri	4	3	2.73	13	0	56	53	21	50
Harris, Jody, Missouri	8	4	2.77	17	0	101	89	19	93
Smith, Matt, Okla. State	9	6	3.09	20	0	114	102	44	144
Russ, Chris, Texas A&M	12	3	3.27	28	3	83	77	28	51
Hoerman, Jared, Oklahoma	7	6	3.40	19	0	127	111	58	114
Tracey, Kevin, Texas Tech	9	1	3.52	16	0	87	84	33	54
Romine, Shane, Nebraska	7	2	3.58	18	2	78	84	37	79
Fossum, Casey, A&M	12	7	3.64	20	0	134	117	52	162
Ward, Matt, A&M	8	1	3.66	15	0	91	109	9	63
Hawkins, Chad, Baylor	7	3	3.89	21	3	116	114	27	108
Wright, Shane, Texas Tech	10	4	3.93	19	1	126	140	23	100
Dreier, Thom, Okla. State	8	6	3.95	19	0	93	95	49	77
Caple, Chance, A&M	9	5	4.26	17	0	114	107	45	125
Ralston, Brad, Texas Tech	9	2	4.35	16	0	93	95	31	97
Evans, Kyle, Baylor	7	1	4.37	18	0	58	64	34	48
Stine, Justin, Missouri	9	4	4.34	18	0	116	124	43	107
Jones, D.J., Texas	10	7	4.73	24	3	122	137	34	77
Bearinger, Jarod, Nebraska	3	1	4.58	22	1	55	73	13	43
Scott, Josh, Baylor	10	2	4.87	21	0	105	104	29	110
Leone, Dax, Texas	7	6	5.13	21	0	114	132	34	75
Herrmann, Ryan, Okla. State ...	4	3	5.04	25	0	50	54	31	38
Krismer, Jeremy, Okla. State ...	6	0	5.27	20	0	55	58	24	60

BIG WEST CONFERENCE

	Conference		Overall	
	W	L	W	L
Cal State Fullerton	25	5	50	14
Nevada	21	9	38	20
Long Beach State	19	11	35	25
Pacific	17	13	32	24
UC Santa Barbara	14	16	27	26
Cal Poly San Luis Obispo	9	21	21	34
Sacramento State	8	22	18	39
New Mexico State	7	23	18	38

ALL-CONFERENCE TEAM: C—Matt Ortiz, Jr., Nevada. **1B**—Chris Beck, Jr., Cal State Fullerton; Don Price, Jr., Nevada. **2B**—David Bacani, So., Cal State Fullerton. **3B**—Ryan Owens, Jr., Cal State Fullerton. **SS**—Chris Weekly, Sr., New Mexico State. **OF**—Lyle Overbay, Sr., Nevada; Spencer Oborn, Jr., Cal State Fullerton; Reed Johnson, Jr., Cal State Fullerton. **DH**—Jaeme Leal, Jr., Long Beach State; Aaron Rifkin, So., Cal State Fullerton. **Util**—Brad Wright, Sr., UC Santa Barbara. **P**—Mike Gallo, Sr., Long Beach State; Darin Moore, Jr., Pacific; Matt Sorensen, So., Cal State Fullerton. **RP**—Mark Short, Jr., Pacific. **Player of the Year**: Spencer Oborn, Cal State Fullerton. **Pitcher of the Year**: Mike Gallo, Long Beach State. **Co-Coaches of the Year**: Gary Powers, Nevada; George Horton, Cal State Fullerton.

INDIVIDUAL BATTING LEADERS
(Minimum 125 At-Bats)

	AVG	AB	R	H	2B	3B	HR	RBI	SB
Overbay, Lyle, Nevada	**.420**	243	76	102	**24**	3	15	88	4
Beck, Chris, CS Full.	.408	240	64	98	18	1	8	75	**27**
Weekly, Chris, NM State	.397	242	69	96	14	5	13	62	4
Johnson, Reed, CS Full.	.396	268	**101**	**106**	22	3	13	59	18
Inglett, Joe, Nevada	.395	233	86	92	21	3	2	57	15
Oborn, Spencer, CS Full.	.395	263	74	104	22	**7**	14	82	**27**
Gant, Bryan, Cal Poly	.392	125	29	49	11	0	0	17	11

	AVG	AB	R	H	2B	3B	HR	RBI	SB
Rifkin, Aaron, CS Fullerton ...	.378	185	47	70	18	1	6	47	4
Wright, Brad, UCSB	.377	223	54	84	12	3	2	36	10
Barski, Chris, NM State	.376	213	61	80	17	1	19	72	2
Dobbs, Greg, Long Beach	.376	229	46	86	8	0	10	63	12
Ortiz, Matt, Nevada	.364	220	48	80	18	1	11	72	7
Molidor, Dave, UCSB	.361	191	34	69	12	1	8	44	1
Leal, Jaeme, Long Beach	.361	219	64	79	12	0	24	79	0
Price, Don, Nevada	.361	231	70	81	10	2	**27**	**89**	4
Owens, Ryan, CS Fullerton ..	.358	240	66	86	14	2	23	85	16
Martin, Justin, Nevada	.346	254	69	88	11	1	0	35	26
LaCour, Bryan, UCSB	.345	139	35	48	13	1	7	48	2
Roberson, Chris, NM State ..	.343	198	40	68	10	2	12	63	1
Marvel, Mike, NM State	.336	137	28	46	4	0	4	28	0
Sledge, Terrmel, LBS	.336	217	72	73	18	5	9	37	7
Duplisses, Bill, UCSB	.333	183	35	61	14	1	5	21	4
Bacani, David, CS Fullerton .	.332	226	74	75	16	3	7	33	17
Wright, Curtis, Long Beach ..	.332	199	45	66	12	6	2	37	3
Moya, Jay, NM State	.326	144	19	47	8	3	1	26	6
Marshall, Brandon, Sac.	.325	212	44	69	16	2	3	33	5
Reader, Presley, NM State ..	.325	206	54	67	10	1	1	31	15
Faltys, Jeremy, NM State	.323	186	45	60	9	0	4	28	13
Crosby, Bobby, Long Beach .	.316	190	31	60	6	0	2	25	13

INDIVIDUAL PITCHING LEADERS
(Minimum 50 Innings)

	W	L	ERA	G	SV	IP	H	BB	SO
Short, Mark, Pacific	8	3	**2.20**	31	7	78	65	24	60
Gallo, Mike, Long Beach	10	3	2.48	18	0	123	122	29	96
Albin, Scott, Nevada	4	4	2.77	26	6	55	49	17	74
Leuenberger, Jeff, Long Beach .	6	2	2.81	23	4	58	60	22	59
Moore, Darin, Pacific	9	3	3.09	16	0	116	83	59	128
Smith, Jon, CS Fullerton	7	1	3.16	15	1	68	53	20	60
Johnson, Adam, CS Full.	10	4	3.55	17	1	117	104	47	**136**
Saarloos, Kirk, CS Fullerton	7	3	3.63	39	7	74	66	20	68
Drakulich, Luke, Nevada	3	0	3.68	22	6	51	54	9	43
Fischer, Steve, Pacific	4	4	3.94	14	1	75	82	29	56
Olenberger, Kasey, LBS	6	2	4.02	21	0	63	57	32	40
Sorensen, Matt, CS Fullerton ..	**12**	0	4.14	18	0	126	145	44	84
Fleming, Travis, Pacific	4	4	4.17	15	1	78	81	33	65
Hanlon, Marco, CS Fullerton	6	1	4.37	22	0	60	65	26	42
Gates, Brian, Sac. State	3	8	4.54	14	0	85	101	34	39
Rainer, Matt, Nevada	11	3	4.76	17	0	96	103	59	68
Qualls, Chad, Nevada	11	3	4.79	16	0	103	118	41	56
Zirelli, Mike, Cal Poly	7	7	4.90	17	0	116	124	30	99
#Quiroz, Chris, UCSB	2	3	5.01	21	**10**	41	50	12	27
Sullivan, Luke, NM State	6	3	5.07	17	0	76	86	33	68
Edwards, Pat, Sac. State	4	7	5.27	16	0	94	102	45	56
Kinte, Troy, UCSB..............	4	3	5.48	16	0	66	63	43	55
Ward, Jeremy, Long Beach........	3	3	5.50	26	6	72	81	36	80

COLONIAL ATHLETIC ASSOCIATION

	Conference		Overall	
	W	L	W	L
Richmond	15	5	41	17
***East Carolina**	14	6	46	16
Virginia Commonwealth	14	6	42	20
George Mason	9	12	30	24
Old Dominion	7	11	38	17
UNC Wilmington	8	13	30	26
William & Mary	7	12	29	24
James Madison	6	15	22	35

ALL-CONFERENCE TEAM: C—Josh Lamberg, Jr., Richmond. **1B**—Mike Dwyer, Sr., Richmond. **2B**—Nate Rewers, Sr., Richmond. **3B**—Greg Miller, So., James Madison. **SS**—Tim Hummel, So., Old Dominion. **OF**—Chris Clarke, So., William & Mary; Eddie Jordan, So., George Mason; Steve Salargo, Sr., East Carolina. **DH**—Jason Dubois, So., Virginia Commonwealth. **LHP**—Bryan Mazur, Sr., UNC Wilmington. **RHP**—Casey Burns, Jr., Richmond. **RP**—Andy Lee, Sr., Old Dominion. **Player of the Year**: Mike Dwyer, Richmond. **Rookie of the Year**: Chad Tracy, East Carolina. **Co-Coaches of the Year**: Ronnie Atkins, Richmond; Keith LeClair, East Carolina.

INDIVIDUAL BATTING LEADERS
(Minimum 125 At-Bats)

	AVG	AB	R	H	2B	3B	HR	RBI	SB
Rewers, Nate, Richmond	**.413**	225	71	93	14	0	14	54	16
Anthony, Jake, VCU	.412	204	48	84	14	0	8	51	4
Dwyer, Mike, Richmond	.412	228	**77**	94	20	4	**21**	**78**	3
Clarke, Chris, Wm. & Mary ...	.404	203	62	82	18	1	7	60	17
Miller, Greg, James Madison	.398	221	61	88	16	2	6	59	21

College Baseball

Player	AVG	AB	R	H	2B	3B	HR	RBI	SB
Salargo, Steve, ECU	.398	244	70	97	20	1	16	77	14
Hairr, Kevin, UNCW	.386	202	53	78	19	1	9	44	18
Gsell, Tony, Old Dominion	.375	224	65	84	17	3	17	61	8
O'Kelly, Mike, Wm. & Mary	.369	176	38	65	18	0	11	64	1
Williamson, John, ECU	.369	241	63	89	19	1	15	65	3
Hummel, Tim, Old Dominion	.368	212	58	78	21	3	5	62	21
Johnson, Bryan, JMU	.368	220	42	81	10	2	4	42	17
Dubois, Jason, VCU	.364	242	56	88	16	3	9	54	5
Harris, Brendan, W&M	.362	210	54	76	20	6	9	49	9
Razler, Kevin, JMU	.357	182	52	65	19	2	6	44	17
Schnabel, Nick, ECU	.357	224	56	80	20	1	3	35	7
Forthofer, Brian, GMU	.356	188	47	67	14	3	16	44	9
Elrod, Kevin, VCU	.353	221	47	78	13	2	3	35	10
Lamberg, Josh, Richmond	.351	191	34	67	13	0	8	52	2
McIntosh, Benji, UNCW	.349	186	29	65	9	1	6	39	6
Tracy, Chad, East Carolina	.349	238	52	83	17	1	3	37	4
Schalick, G.R., Richmond	.343	204	43	70	13	1	11	47	0
Howard, Jason, ECU	.341	182	36	62	13	1	10	52	2
Jordan, Eddie, GMU	.341	205	65	70	14	2	11	47	28
Booker, Stephen, W&M	.338	216	66	73	15	6	0	30	19
Wilson, Charles, W&M	.337	166	39	56	8	0	1	19	13
Forelli, Anthony, ODU	.336	214	55	72	16	1	12	58	1
Gibbs, Mark, George Mason	.333	171	33	57	10	0	5	29	5
Rodio, Doug, George Mason	.333	132	23	44	6	1	5	35	1
Bakich, Erik, East Carolina	.324	244	43	79	16	0	7	54	9
Rogers, Brian, W&M	.324	176	60	57	10	2	11	53	11
#Anderson, Brian, GMU	.315	92	27	29	5	6	4	24	1
#Riley, T, James Madison	.288	205	49	59	9	0	2	28	54

INDIVIDUAL PITCHING LEADERS
(Minimum 50 Innings)

Player	W	L	ERA	G	SV	IP	H	BB	SO
#Lee, Andy, Old Dominion	3	1	1.91	25	10	33	29	11	40
#Fulcher, Kevyn, ECU	4	2	2.70	25	10	37	39	6	19
Thompson, Travis, ECU	10	2	2.75	16	0	95	94	34	84
Mazur, Bryan, UNCW	10	4	2.76	22	3	101	98	35	118
Dubois, Jason, VCU	10	3	3.03	16	0	119	97	33	102
Acors, Bo, VCU	5	1	3.09	20	1	67	61	28	61
Burns, Casey, Richmond	9	3	3.21	14	0	95	72	37	124
Davis, Marcus, George Mason	4	2	3.21	13	1	67	59	28	57
Smith, Mike, Richmond	11	2	3.47	17	0	114	112	46	87
Leek, Randy, William & Mary	5	5	3.49	19	0	111	106	24	97
Dwyer, Mike, Richmond	10	5	3.56	17	0	94	85	29	82
Detwiler, Jim, Old Dominion	8	3	3.66	15	0	93	79	48	73
Jernigan, Brooks, ECU	9	4	4.03	19	0	105	99	50	79
Bailey, David, Old Dominion	8	5	4.05	14	0	80	76	36	59
Martin, Davy, VCU	6	2	4.24	27	5	57	36	24	50
Coughlin, Chris, UNCW	5	1	4.27	19	0	59	51	24	51
Fisher, Marc, VCU	9	4	4.40	17	1	102	104	25	75
Trogdon, Bryan, UNCW	4	4	4.43	13	0	67	66	32	58
Minton, Foye, ECU	9	4	4.56	17	0	105	93	20	89
Weaver, Shawn, Old Dominion	9	4	4.65	15	0	81	80	27	62
Korn, John, VCU	8	5	4.92	18	1	108	112	32	84

CONFERENCE USA

	Conference		Overall	
	W	L	W	L
Houston	20	7	40	24
*Tulane	19	8	48	17
Southern Mississippi	18	9	40	23
Memphis	15	12	28	26
South Florida	15	12	31	27
Louisville	14	13	37	19
UNC Charlotte	13	14	26	25
Cincinnati	9	18	30	29
Alabama-Birmingham	7	20	22	31
Saint Louis	5	22	19	39

ALL-CONFERENCE TEAM: C—Chad Sutter, Sr., Tulane. **INF**—Michael Artman, Jr., Southern Miss.; Andy Cannizaro, So., Tulane; Brandon Caraway, Jr., Houston; James Jurries, Fr., Tulane; J.P. Woodward, Jr., Houston. **OF**—Jake Burnham, Sr., Tulane; Dusty Haley, So., Southern Mississippi; Matt Singer, So., Cincinnati; Jason Sparks, Sr., Tulane. **DH**—Craig House, Sr., Memphis. **P**—Jared Berkowitz, Jr., Tulane; Henry Bonilla, Jr., Tulane; Kyle Crowell, So., Houston; Craig House, Sr., Memphis. **RP**—Brandon Belanger, Jr., Tulane.

Player of the Year: Chad Sutter, Tulane. **Pitcher of the Year:** Kyle Crowell, Houston. **Freshman of the Year:** James Jurries, Tulane. **Coach of the Year:** Rayner Noble, Houston.

INDIVIDUAL BATTING LEADERS
(Minimum 125 At-Bats)

Player	AVG	AB	R	H	2B	3B	HR	RBI	SB
Artman, Michael, So. Miss	.408	260	74	106	15	3	6	43	19
Youkilis, Kevin, Cincinnati	.407	236	85	96	23	0	13	72	2
Sutter, Chad, Tulane	.393	239	70	94	12	0	23	87	4
Singer, Matt, Cincinnati	.391	238	70	93	20	1	17	79	16
Bitter, Jarrod, Houston	.389	226	54	88	15	0	12	57	2
Woodward, J.P., Houston	.381	218	55	83	17	3	18	66	8
McAuley, James, Louisville	.378	209	58	79	10	2	9	56	17
Jurries, James, Tulane	.374	278	90	104	22	4	20	79	18
Haley, Dusty, Southen Miss	.373	225	54	84	13	0	15	65	9
Cannizaro, Andy, Tulane	.370	219	66	81	14	1	1	38	31
Groff, Matt, Tulane	.367	240	55	88	17	2	4	37	20
Caraway, Brandon, Houston	.363	267	72	97	18	4	6	37	27
DeMent, Dan, UAB	.362	207	56	75	18	4	16	66	9
Wood, Jason, St. Louis	.362	221	64	80	14	6	3	32	25
Drawdy, Ben, South Florida	.359	217	40	78	14	3	3	50	5
Hill, Jason, UNCC	.359	195	40	70	20	3	4	39	2
Smith, Barrett, UAB	.355	197	53	70	13	4	0	15	19
Owen, David, UAB	.353	173	39	61	14	2	6	42	3
Steiner, Nick, St. Louis	.353	224	46	79	16	0	8	57	8
House, Craig, Memphis	.351	191	35	67	9	1	7	38	4
Tewes, Chad, Louisville	.345	206	61	71	13	1	15	65	0
Schweitzer, Tyson, Houston	.343	213	46	73	24	0	6	48	9
Crocker, Nick, St. Louis	.341	226	52	77	13	0	15	56	9
Lorenz, Doug, Louisville	.341	208	51	71	8	7	11	62	8
Smith, Brad, UNCC	.340	203	43	69	16	6	5	46	9
Raburn, Johnny, So. Florida	.338	210	59	71	6	1	0	22	21
Voshell, Key, Louisville	.335	221	48	74	23	2	1	44	5
Snowell, Anthony, Cincinnati	.327	217	73	71	17	6	10	37	6
McKee, Mickey, Tulane	.326	224	52	73	15	1	4	32	7
Cuccia, Chris, South Florida	.325	228	36	74	12	2	5	50	2
Reimers, Chris, UAB	.324	182	40	59	15	1	1	28	10
Sparks, Jason, Tulane	.324	222	56	72	18	1	19	62	16
#Pfister, Bubba, UNCC	.250	152	25	38	6	7	2	20	4

INDIVIDUAL PITCHING LEADERS
(Minimum 50 Innings)

Player	W	L	ERA	G	SV	IP	H	BB	SO
Belanger, Brandon, Tulane	3	5	2.45	41	16	66	66	15	68
Moore, Bryan, Houston	7	2	2.55	32	2	74	71	26	50
Crowell, Kyle, Houston	11	2	3.00	19	0	117	86	40	94
Bonilla, Henry, Tulane	11	3	3.34	20	1	124	129	36	131
Castellvi, Antonio, Louisville	4	2	3.34	20	0	57	55	28	45
Stewart, Josh, Memphis	7	4	3.70	18	0	90	79	41	84
Berkowitz, Jared, Tulane	13	3	3.78	19	0	124	133	20	87
Baker, Ryan, UNCC	3	3	3.91	15	1	53	51	15	65
House, Craig, Memphis	8	4	4.08	16	0	93	75	39	112
Williams, Denny, Louisville	4	1	4.09	18	1	55	41	28	31
Sykes, Jerret, Houston	5	3	4.26	18	0	76	90	19	52
Padgett, Josh, Memphis	1	2	4.30	17	1	52	60	26	42
Leicester, Jon, Memphis	3	6	4.32	19	0	75	80	36	68
Calcote, Colby, Southern Miss	2	4	4.46	17	0	67	75	18	58
Glaser, Scott, South Florida	12	5	4.47	21	1	111	127	41	101
Walker, Josh, Southern Miss	9	1	4.50	16	0	84	96	33	69
O'Gara, Dan, Tulane	4	2	4.59	22	0	86	106	40	61
Stanford, Jason, UNCC	8	6	4.71	17	0	92	102	34	97
McKay, John, UNCC	6	10	4.80	16	0	99	98	27	106
Cento, Tony, Cincinnati	4	4	4.90	18	1	94	102	40	103
McRae, Joe, UAB	5	8	4.98	17	1	90	117	31	65
Nance, Shane, Houston	7	6	5.00	21	0	112	113	40	114
Sementilli, Damon, Louisville	3	5	5.08	13	0	73	100	33	69
Poplin, Paul, UNCC	5	4	5.12	14	0	90	99	35	84
Green, Sean, Louisville	6	4	5.23	16	0	95	107	43	67
Stallings, Michael, UAB	5	7	5.23	19	0	103	126	44	62
Echeverz, Raul, Tulane	6	2	5.35	26	1	72	76	46	51

IVY LEAGUE

GEHRIG	Conference		Overall	
	W	L	W	L
Princeton	15	5	25	20
Cornell	7	13	12	28
Columbia	6	14	13	27
Pennsylvania	6	14	9	28
ROLFE	W	L	W	L
*Harvard	16	4	28	20
Brown	13	7	23	18
Dartmouth	9	11	17	24
Yale	6	14	16	29

ALL-CONFERENCE TEAM: C—Mike Levy, So., Dartmouth. **1B**—Pete DeYoung, Sr., Princeton. **2B**—Jeff Lawler, Jr., Brown. **3B**—Mike Conway, Jr., Dartmouth. **SS**—Dan Kantrovitz, So., Brown. **OF**—Andrew Huling, Sr., Harvard; Ben Johnstone, Jr., Yale; Todd Iarussi, So., Brown; James Little, Jr., Dartmouth. **DH**—Tony Coyne, Jr., Yale. **SP**—John Birtwell, So., Harvard; Chris Young, Fr., Princeton. **RP**—Jeff Golden, Sr., Princeton.

Player of the Year: Andrew Huling, Harvard. **Pitcher of the Year**: John Birtwell, Harvard. **Rookies of the Year**: Chris Young, Princeton; Ben Crockett, Harvard.

INDIVIDUAL BATTING LEADERS
(Minimum 100 At-Bats)

	AVG	AB	R	H	2B	3B	HR	RBI	SB
Johnstone, Ben, Yale	.430	151	39	65	14	3	2	29	23
Kantrovitz, Dan, Brown	.427	117	36	50	15	0	2	23	4
Coyne, Tony, Yale	.417	103	29	43	12	2	6	22	3
Lawler, Jeff, Brown	.388	134	35	52	12	2	5	41	25
Huling, Andrew, Harvard	.384	164	49	63	16	2	5	51	14
Woodfork, Peter, Harvard	.374	147	22	55	7	0	0	30	8
Levy, Michael, Dartmouth	.373	134	26	50	10	2	3	29	4
Teal, Ben, Yale	.372	113	14	42	10	0	3	24	1
Iarussi, Todd, Brown	.370	138	31	51	13	3	5	30	11
Holbert, Kevin, Columbia	.363	124	27	45	6	3	2	17	18
Luria, Andrew, Cornell	.363	113	24	41	6	0	3	21	9
Conway, Michael, Dartmouth	.359	156	35	56	11	1	1	23	8
Macrie, Michael, Cornell	.353	133	31	47	6	2	6	22	10
Evans, Matt, Princeton	.346	159	29	55	15	0	10	36	0
Meyer, Aaron, Dartmouth	.333	141	32	47	12	0	11	38	3
Carmack, Scott, Harvard	.328	116	33	38	7	1	1	16	2
Ambrosius, Glen, Penn	.331	130	28	43	11	1	3	22	
Gallagher, Shaun, Brown	.321	140	23	45	9	0	4	25	2
Rockers, Joe, Dartmouth	.321	131	26	42	10	2	1	20	2

INDIVIDUAL PITCHING LEADERS
(Minimum 40 Innings)

	W	L	ERA	G	SV	IP	H	BB	SO
Rowland, Tom, Princeton	4	2	2.45	10	1	51	57	18	23
Birtwell, John, Harvard	4	5	2.83	11	0	64	53	10	69
Vail, Garett, Harvard	2	3	3.18	15	3	57	56	17	58
Quintana, Jason, Princeton	5	4	3.52	11	0	64	66	14	53
#Golden, Jeff, Princeton	1	1	3.72	23	7	29	34	11	28
Horn, Howard, Princeton	3	2	4.00	9	0	45	49	21	28
Mattern, Mike, Penn	6	3	4.02	10	0	54	60	36	42
Bayer, Nick, Cornell	3	6	4.12	10	0	59	72	17	40
Johnson, Jim, Brown	6	0	4.12	8	0	44	48	12	32
Dutremble, Jeff, Dartmouth	4	2	4.24	8	0	47	37	27	32
Grillo, Jamie, Brown	5	3	4.24	12	0	51	49	24	33
Hepler, Matt, Penn	1	5	4.68	10	0	42	49	18	28
Gati, Dan, Columbia	4	3	4.72	11	0	55	71	18	21
Crockett, Ben, Harvard	5	1	4.88	12	0	52	55	6	47
McQuaid, Brendan, Cornell	4	2	5.17	8	0	47	52	11	27
#Finnegan, Mike, Yale	0	5	8.42	19	7	31	53	8	26

METRO ATLANTIC CONFERENCE

	Conference		Overall	
NORTH	**W**	**L**	**W**	**L**
*Siena	21	5	34	22
LeMoyne	17	9	21	16
Marist	14	12	27	23
Niagara	11	14	13	22
SOUTH	**W**	**L**	**W**	**L**
Iona	15	11	23	27
Rider	14	11	26	30
Fairfield	13	13	23	23
Manhattan	12	14	22	27
St. Peter's	4	22	10	36

MAAC North ALL-CONFERENCE TEAM: C—Ryan Mahoney, Sr., Canisius; Anthony Ambrosini, Jr., Marist. **1B**—Cam Pelton, Sr., LeMoyne. **2B**—Stephen O'Sullivan, Fr., Marist; Mike Mallozzi, Jr., Siena. **3B**—Geoff Hoover, Sr., Niagara; Trey Gethoefer, Sr., Siena. **SS**—Vic Boccarossa, Jr., LeMoyne. **OF**—Casey Saucke, Jr., LeMoyne; Anthony Cervini, Jr., Marist; Aaron Mindel, Sr., Niagara; Todd Donovan, Jr., Siena. **DH**—Kevin Wissner, So., Marist. **P**—Jaime Steward, So., LeMoyne; Doug Connolly, Marist.

Player of the Year: Todd Donovan, Siena. **Pitchers of the Year**: Jamie Steward, LeMoyne; Doug Connolly, Marist. **Rookie of the Year**: Ryan Finn, Siena. **Coach of the Year**: Tony Rossi, Siena.

MAAC South ALL-CONFERENCE TEAM: C—Mike Ryan, Jr., Rider. **1B**—Tom McDonough, Sr., Manhattan. **2B**—Cristian Jung, Sr., Fairfield; Kevin Rowett, Jr., Manhattan. **3B**—Mike Lorento, So., Manhattan. **SS**—Greg Toher, Sr., Iona. **OF**—Tom Lopusznick, Jr., Fairfield; Michael Wenner, Jr., Rider; Josh Loftin, Sr., Rider. **DH**—Mike Mornambe, Sr., Manhattan; Jason Healy, Sr., St. Peter's. **P**—Kevin Barry, So., Rider; Frank Brooks, Jr., St. Peter's.

Player of the Year: Josh Loftin, Rider. **Pitcher of the Year**: Kevin Barry, Rider. **Rookie of the Year**: Wendell Anderson, Manhattan. **Coach of the Year**: Sonny Pittaro, Rider.

INDIVIDUAL BATTING LEADERS
(Minimum 100 At-Bats)

	AVG	AB	R	H	2B	3B	HR	RBI	SB
Mindel, Aaron, Niagara	.390	118	35	46	10	1	2	12	18
Brady, Ryan, Marist	.377	162	38	61	9	1	1	34	9
Helbig, Kyle, Rider	.375	112	38	42	4	1	2	21	2
Bittner, Tim, Marist	.372	113	22	42	9	2	2	22	0
Donovan, Todd, Siena	.371	159	40	59	7	4	1	18	30
Loftin, Josh, Rider	.364	176	33	64	8	0	4	42	4
Cervini, Anthony, Marist	.362	199	50	72	14	3	4	24	8
Wenner, Mike, Rider	.361	133	37	48	9	2	5	15	31
Bocchino, Anthony, Marist	.357	185	38	66	13	4	3	39	3
Kalle, Jason, Iona	.351	174	36	61	16	1	9	49	8
Willis, Jimmy, Marist	.351	134	24	47	5	2	3	28	2
Finn, Ryan, Siena	.348	164	36	57	10	4	9	50	11
Pike, Cory, Niagara	.343	105	26	36	7	2	3	24	1
Miceli, Paul, Manhattan	.338	160	40	54	7	1	0	18	14
Lorento, Mike, Manhattan	.333	153	30	51	10	0	4	20	1
Lopusznick, Tom, Fairfield	.333	147	33	49	5	1	10	42	33
Pikolycky, Will, Iona	.333	171	44	57	16	4	5	26	21
Passerelle, Matt, Iona	.333	111	26	37	11	0	3	17	2
Jung, Cristian, Fairfield	.331	160	40	53	9	2	4	35	10
#Hoover, Geoff, Niagara	.325	114	31	37	7	2	10	32	1
#Spera, Nick, Siena	.323	167	54	54	11	1	1	33	27
#Gethoefer, Trey, Siena	.311	196	32	61	22	1	1	49	5
#Ramos-Romano, Angel, St.P	.275	142	26	39	8	5	1	25	11

INDIVIDUAL PITCHING LEADERS
(Minimum 40 Innings)

	W	L	ERA	G	SV	IP	H	BB	SO
Connolly, Doug, Marist	8	2	2.67	12	0	78	71	36	78
Barry, Kevin, Rider	5	2	2.76	12	0	65	54	26	57
Lenko, Jared, Rider	5	2	2.86	12	0	66	56	22	57
Dunford, Brendan, Canisius	3	4	2.88	10	0	50	46	17	40
Barone, John, Iona	6	5	3.00	13	1	66	56	31	69
Novinsky, John, Iona	2	3	3.54	9	0	56	40	45	52
West, Mark, Canisius	4	5	3.68	10	0	51	42	26	55
Olore, Kevin, Marist	5	2	3.75	11	0	70	65	26	71
Fugarino, Steve, Iona	3	6	3.77	12	0	57	63	20	43
Chudacik, Mike, LeMoyne	4	3	3.83	8	0	42	41	10	30
Adams, Steve, Manhattan	6	3	3.86	11	0	61	64	21	48
Perrucci, Kevin, Marist	3	6	3.88	12	0	65	54	19	53
Brooks, Frank, St. Peter's	5	6	3.89	14	0	74	75	47	81
Bechard, Steve, LeMoyne	5	3	4.01	9	0	61	65	8	48
Pahucki, Dave, Siena	9	1	4.03	13	0	76	76	25	46
Colcord, Steve, Fairfield	5	4	4.21	11	0	62	74	5	35
Brown, Kevin, Siena	8	2	4.50	15	0	80	94	23	51
#Widgren, Pat, Manhattan	1	3	5.79	16	8	23	29	7	8
#Smith, Mark, Siena	1	1	8.10	15	8	17	13	10	27

MID-AMERICAN CONFERENCE

	Conference		Overall	
EAST	**W**	**L**	**W**	**L**
*Bowling Green	22	10	36	24
Miami	20	12	34	27
Kent	19	12	33	25
Ohio	17	13	26	28
Akron	10	22	20	36
Marshall	4	27	12	44
WEST	**W**	**L**	**W**	**L**
Ball State	25	6	42	18
Toledo	23	9	39	20
Western Michigan	20	12	30	28
Central Michigan	15	15	24	32
Eastern Michigan	12	19	21	32
Northern Illinois	1	31	4	51

ALL-CONFERENCE TEAM: C—Alex Marconi, Jr., Kent. **1B**—Bob Niemet, Sr., Bowling Green. **2B**—Jeremy Ridley, Jr., Ball State. **3B**—Frank Alfieri, Sr., Western Michigan. **SS**—Shayne Rid-

College Baseball

ley, Jr., Ball State. **OF**—Larry Bigbie, Jr., Ball State; Jake Sanborn, Jr., Central Michigan; D.J. Eckhart, Sr., Miami; Chris Gundrum, Sr., Western Michigan. **DH**—Chuck Lombardy, So., Ohio. **Util**—Jess Bechard, Jr., Kent. **P**—Travis Minix, Sr., Ball State; Jason Kelley, Sr., Bowling Green; Jeremy Griffiths, Jr., Toledo; Eugenio Melendez, Jr., Toledo. **RP**—Dan Adams, Jr., Kent.

Player of the Year: Larry Bigbie, Ball State. **Pitcher of the Year**: Jeremy Griffiths, Toledo. **Freshman of the Year**: Justin Wechsler, Ball State. **Coach of the Year**: Joe Kruzel, Toledo.

INDIVIDUAL BATTING LEADERS
(Minimum 100 At-Bats)

	AVG	AB	R	H	2B	3B	HR	RBI	SB
Bigbie, Larry, Ball State	.419	210	71	88	12	3	17	54	21
Bechard, Jess, Kent	.406	192	48	78	22	1	8	49	5
Yost, Tom, Miami	.406	128	25	52	3	1	5	27	6
Neimet, Bob, Bowling Green	.400	200	50	80	15	3	6	44	20
Marcum, Matt, BG	.393	117	29	46	6	0	3	36	4
Malinowski, Scott, Ohio	.385	195	44	75	17	2	4	28	5
Ridley, Jeremy, Ball State	.383	222	59	85	17	1	12	68	20
Elias, Lee, Bowling Green	.381	160	49	61	19	0	7	42	2
Eckhart, D.J., Miami	.378	201	46	76	17	0	12	62	6
Carpenter, Ty, Kent	.377	175	31	66	12	1	3	41	0
Thewes, Mark, Miami	.376	197	38	74	6	1	0	14	13
Lombardy, Chuck, Ohio	.375	168	33	63	12	0	10	39	0
Mace, Clark, Miami	.371	224	52	83	13	2	3	32	18
Marconi, Alex, Kent	.371	210	43	78	14	1	11	55	1
Reinhart, Luke, Miami	.369	103	15	38	7	1	2	25	3
Williams, Aaron, Marshall	.369	187	42	69	11	2	2	20	33
Rook, Jeff, Ohio	.367	169	51	62	3	0	16	48	3
Hill, Jayson, Akron	.365	148	31	54	16	0	5	39	2
Lindsay, Derek, West. Mich.	.358	179	33	64	15	0	10	41	0
Doerbecker, Mike, Akron	.355	186	50	66	15	1	14	53	3
Wood, Matt, Ball State	.355	203	60	72	15	1	16	71	6
Sanborn, Jake, Central Mich.	.354	206	47	73	10	3	11	49	7
Morrison, Lee, BG	.347	121	21	42	8	1	3	26	2
Pinkerton, Eric, Marshall	.347	193	29	67	16	0	9	38	8
Alfieri, Frank, West. Mich.	.346	211	51	73	13	1	18	63	6
DeShetler, Chris, East. Mich.	.345	197	40	68	15	1	8	37	8
Ridley, Shayne, Ball State	.342	222	64	76	22	2	16	62	3
Arbinger, Jason, Ohio	.340	191	47	65	14	0	9	39	1
Gundrum, Kris, West. Mich.	.338	210	48	71	18	1	12	44	13
#Malaska, Mark, Akron	.318	198	52	62	22	2	6	41	9
#Roberts, Brian, Akron	.310	187	30	58	10	0	5	45	15

INDIVIDUAL PITCHING LEADERS
(Minimum 40 Innings)

	W	L	ERA	G	SV	IP	H	BB	SO
#Adams, Dan, Kent	3	1	1.99	31	15	32	21	6	29
Griffiths, Jeremy, Toledo	11	4	2.50	15	0	97	75	29	102
Minix, Travis, Ball State	11	2	2.60	19	0	97	83	30	106
Roberts, Phil, Central Mich.	4	3	2.66	19	0	44	43	13	46
Wilkinson, John, Akron	5	4	3.07	14	0	73	65	33	81
Melendez, Eugenio, Toledo	9	5	3.10	15	0	96	91	19	72
Fontana, Tony, Bowling Green	4	2	3.30	13	0	57	56	19	53
Bolthouse, Adam, Central Mich.	2	3	3.38	16	0	53	61	22	35
Wechsler, Justin, Ball State	10	3	3.39	20	0	88	79	30	67
Kelley, Jason, Bowling Green	12	4	3.42	18	0	116	95	34	93
Palazeti, Angelo, West. Mich.	10	6	3.92	19	1	101	98	33	86
Neal, Tyson, Miami	5	6	3.96	13	0	73	70	30	54
Jackson, Sage, Central Mich.	3	6	4.06	15	0	64	78	15	55
Fawcett, Mike, Central Mich.	5	6	4.24	13	0	76	83	23	59
Dyrlund, Jeff, Akron	2	7	4.32	17	2	73	100	26	45
Thomas, J.J., Marshall	3	6	4.39	19	2	41	44	20	26
Schell, Dan, Central Mich.	5	5	4.44	13	0	71	77	28	71
Perez, Keith, West. Mich.	3	8	4.57	16	0	85	76	35	74
Cheney, Joe, Bowling Green	5	6	4.64	15	0	66	75	28	42
Vaught, Chris, Bowling Green	5	6	4.67	17	0	89	99	48	62
Svala, Adam, Ohio	4	2	4.68	15	1	42	48	21	26
Bayer, Russ, Miami	8	3	4.71	13	0	63	70	30	39
Webb, Brad, Toledo	7	3	4.76	13	0	68	84	26	34
Tekavec, Nate, Miami	9	7	4.78	21	0	102	128	25	88
Reeder, Sean, Marshall	6	7	5.08	18	0	96	109	42	107

MID-CONTINTENT CONFERENCE

	Conference		Overall	
	W	L	W	L
*Oral Roberts	14	4	46	15
Valparaiso	12	8	30	27
Western Illinois	9	9	14	35
Chicago State	9	11	19	33
Youngstown State	8	10	20	36
Indiana-Purdue	4	14	7	43

ALL-CONFERENCE TEAM: **C**—Justin Wohlers, Sr., Western Illinois. **1B**—Ryan Neill, Jr., Oral Roberts. **2B**—Bryan Gann, Fr., Oral Roberts. **3B**—Justin Olson, Sr., Oral Roberts. **SS**—Jason Clements, Jr., Oral Roberts. **OF**—J.J. Swiatkowski, Jr., Valparaiso; Jeff Stallings, Jr., Oral Roberts; Mike Hill, Sr., Oral Roberts. **DH**—Mark Pedersen, So., Valparaiso. **Util**—Josh Shackelford, So., Oral Roberts. **SP**—Mike Rose, Sr., Oral Roberts; Dusty Barrett, Sr., Oral Roberts; Sean Galiher, Sr., Valparaiso. **RP**—Justin Craker, So., Valparaiso.

Player of the Year: Jeff Stallings, Oral Roberts. **Pitcher of the Year**: Mike Rose, Oral Roberts. **Newcomer of the Year**: Jason Lewin, Chicago State. **Coach of the Year**: Sunny Golloway, Oral Roberts.

INDIVIDUAL BATTING LEADERS
(Minimum 100 At-Bats)

	AVG	AB	R	H	2B	3B	HR	RBI	SB
Neill, Ryan, Oral Roberts	.423	208	70	88	20	2	18	71	20
Stallings, Jeff, Oral Roberts	.417	228	81	95	19	3	7	42	49
Thomas, Mark, Young. St.	.406	197	54	80	22	4	9	39	12
Hill, Mike, Oral Roberts	.398	226	74	90	19	3	23	88	25
Pedersen, Mark, Valparaiso	.395	157	43	62	14	3	10	34	6
Clements, Jason, ORU	.377	183	70	69	7	7	8	45	35
Olson, Justin, Western Ill.	.373	161	41	60	15	1	5	34	4
Moore, Chris, Valparaiso	.369	149	30	55	14	1	2	32	4
Keltner, David, Chicago St.	.368	174	57	64	13	1	11	31	26
Lewin, Jason, Chicago St.	.361	158	27	57	9	0	4	32	3
Langdon, Ryan, Western Ill.	.358	162	36	58	16	3	5	38	5
Vandeventer, Eric, ORU	.351	211	61	74	16	3	13	53	20
Santore, Todd, Young. St.	.350	157	23	55	9	2	0	30	3
O'Connor, Brian, Valparaiso	.349	166	24	58	14	1	2	38	3
Swiatkowski, J.J., Valparaiso	.340	191	44	65	18	2	14	44	7
Gann, Bryan, Oral Roberts	.339	224	60	76	18	3	3	53	35

INDIVIDUAL PITCHING LEADERS
(Minimum 40 Innings)

	W	L	ERA	G	SV	IP	H	BB	SO
#Hoffman, Matt, Oral Roberts	0	0	2.13	28	11	25	17	21	33
Mosley, Seth, Oral Roberts	4	2	2.98	17	1	45	33	21	27
Rose, Mike, Oral Roberts	11	5	4.07	19	0	104	96	47	83
McFarlan, Brian, Young. St.	6	6	4.14	16	0	76	95	25	55
Galiher, Sean, Valparaiso	7	4	4.28	11	0	67	66	32	62
Barrett, Dusty, Oral Roberts	9	2	4.47	19	0	95	86	57	68
Whitekiller, Jerel, Oral Roberts	4	1	4.67	10	0	44	53	12	23
Roy, Angus, Valparaiso	3	5	4.76	16	1	70	80	34	42
Pomeroy, Jim, Valparaiso	5	4	4.99	10	0	61	63	35	63
Chalek, Corey, Young. State	4	6	5.20	15	0	74	107	30	39
#Menges, Fred, Chicago State	5	10	6.39	20	0	113	150	38	94

MID-EASTERN CONFERENCE

	Conference		Overall	
NORTH	W	L	W	L
Delaware State	13	5	20	23
Howard	12	6	18	32
Maryland Eastern Shore	7	11	8	41
Coppin State	4	14	5	40
SOUTH	W	L	W	L
*Bethune-Cookman	13	5	27	31
Florida A&M	10	8	21	29
Norfolk State	9	9	23	29
North Carolina A&T	4	14	11	46

ALL-CONFERENCE TEAM: **C**—John Defere, Sr., Norfolk State. **INF**—Mark Circo, Sr., Delaware State; Dino Dakuras, Sr., Bethune-Cookman; Chris Warren, Sr., Howard; Eunique Johnson, Jr., Howard. **OF**—Jeante Nunez, Jr., Bethune-Cookman; Faheem Hammett, Sr., Maryland Eastern Shore; Shawn Bradley, Sr., Norfolk State. **DH**—Christian Morales, Jr., Bethune-Cookman. **P**—Mike Shirtcliffe, So., Bethune-Cookman.

Player of the Year: Mark Circo, Delaware State. **Rookie of the Year**: Steven McLeod, N.C. A&T. **Coach of the Year**: Joe Durant, Florida A&M.

INDIVIDUAL BATTING LEADERS
(Minimum 100 At-Bats)

	AVG	AB	R	H	2B	3B	HR	RBI	SB
Dakuras, Dino, Beth.-Cook.	.405	158	39	64	15	2	5	41	3
Nunez, Jeante, Beth.-Cook.	.381	181	38	69	17	4	9	49	16
Baez, Carlos, Beth.-Cook.	.361	155	33	56	4	3	3	30	19
Hammett, Faheem, UMES	.359	156	37	56	12	5	4	44	21
Mincey, Kevin, UMES	.348	161	39	56	15	3	0	26	14
Mercaldo, Mike, Del. St.	.343	137	36	47	9	1	2	33	3

Circo, Mark, Delaware St.	.338	154	42	52	6	0	**13**	43	10
Hernandez, Jose, B-C	.336	119	19	40	7	3	1	20	8
Bradley, Shawn, Norfolk St. ..	.333	180	45	60	15	**5**	4	37	12
Warren, Chris, Howard	.331	121	27	40	13	1	5	21	8
Jackson, Antonio, Nor. St.	.327	162	31	53	8	2	3	23	4
Ewing, Byron, Howard	.325	154	33	50	13	2	7	34	9
Griggs, Reggie, Florida A&M .321		137	16	44	6	0	2	31	0
Linares, Eddy, Delaware St. ..	.321	137	34	44	7	1	4	29	9
Morales, Christian, B-C	.321	168	35	54	12	2	1	24	8
Knox, Matthew, Beth.-Cook. ..	.316	193	42	61	10	4	1	30	**27**
#McInnis, Ed, Norfolk St.	.306	170	**49**	52	14	2	2	32	20
#Defere, John, Norfolk St.	.305	164	41	50	10	1	7	**50**	1

INDIVIDUAL PITCHING LEADERS
(Minimum 40 Innings)

	W	L	ERA	G	SV	IP	H	BB	SO
Jerue, Brook, Beth.-Cook.	5	1	3.49	24	5	57	67	20	59
Shirtcliffe, Mike, Beth.-Cook......	7	5	3.50	14	1	80	72	38	**99**
Gibson, Chris, Norfolk State	3	5	4.26	11	0	51	59	20	58
Featherstone, Ron, N.C. A&T	0	9	4.50	16	0	74	61	62	62
Baylor, Harry, Norfolk State	6	3	4.74	14	0	68	73	28	34
McLeod, Steve, N.C. A&T	3	6	5.05	14	1	73	87	44	24
#Johnson, Gorman, Del. State ..	4	2	5.08	20	**6**	39	42	13	16
Circo, Mark, Delaware State	**9**	2	5.52	12	0	73	73	48	58
Coker, Jason, Beth.-Cook.	2	5	5.53	17	0	54	64	18	45
Pallone, Adam, UMES	2	7	5.63	23	0	40	74	30	19
Beckford, Omar, Florida A&M ...	3	3	5.71	10	0	52	54	11	26

MIDWESTERN COLLEGIATE

	Conference		Overall	
	W	L	W	L
Butler	14	6	29	27
*Wisconsin-Milwaukee	11	7	31	29
Cleveland State	12	8	22	34
Wright State	8	10	26	28
Illinois-Chicago	6	12	18	30
Detroit	5	13	14	33

ALL-CONFERENCE TEAM: C—Todd Ludwig, Jr., Wisconsin-Milwaukee. **1B**—Chad Sadowski, Jr., Wisconsin-Milwaukee. **2B**—Eric Duke, Jr., Illinois-Chicago. **3B**—Jeff Haase, Jr., Cleveland State. **SS**—Dusty Beam, Jr., Wright State. **OF**—Al Candea, Sr., Illinois-Chicago; Luke Murphy, Jr., Butler; Jeremy Sinsabaugh, So., Butler. **DH**—Pete Lotus, Sr., Illinois-Chicago. **Util**—Paul Archambault, So., Wisconsin-Milwaukee. **P**—Chris Andrzejak, Jr., Detroit; Steve Magill, Sr., Butler.

Player of the Year: Jeff Haase, Cleveland State. **Pitcher of the Year**: Steve Magill, Butler. **Newcomer of the Year**: Steve Tylke, Wisconsin-Milwaukee. **Co-Coaches of the Year**: Steve Farley, Butler; Mike Dee, Illinois-Chicago.

INDIVIDUAL BATTING LEADERS
(Minimum 100 At-Bats)

	AVG	AB	R	H	2B	3B	HR	RBI	SB
Candea, Al, Ill.-Chicago	**.400**	180	43	72	15	2	11	55	6
Archambault, Paul, Wis.-Mil. ..	.397	121	23	48	10	1	2	21	2
Hart, Josh, Wright State	.390	177	26	69	8	0	1	25	1
Marshall, Scott, Wright State ..	.371	170	38	63	10	0	0	31	2
Duke, Eric, Illinois-Chicago ..	.368	193	36	71	16	1	0	38	9
Beam, Dusty, Wright State	.365	208	38	76	12	**4**	12	61	15
Dattilo, Franco, Butler	.365	170	33	62	12	0	5	30	4
Haase, Jeff, Cleveland State ..	.362	196	51	71	12	1	17	59	8
Gombos, Jason, Detroit	.361	180	37	65	16	0	2	29	2
Tylke, Steve, Wis.-Mil.	.361	219	47	**79**	**20**	1	5	43	2
Candea, Armand, Ill.-Chi.	.359	131	32	47	14	3	5	33	8
Sadowski, Chad, Wis.-Mil.	.358	215	55	77	**20**	1	17	68	7
Ludwig, Todd, Wis.-Mil.	.354	192	**61**	68	13	0	17	53	2
Karney, Chris, Detroit	.345	148	27	51	8	0	2	18	4
Bautsch, Brian, Wright St.	.333	201	25	67	10	1	2	34	1
#Haugom, Darin, Wis.-Mil.	.328	235	**61**	77	14	**4**	8	48	**24**
#Olszta, Eddie, Butler	.328	180	59	59	5	4	5	36	16
#Storey, Eric, Butler	.325	206	47	67	10	**4**	**21**	**74**	10

INDIVIDUAL PITCHING LEADERS
(Minimum 40 Innings)

	W	L	ERA	G	SV	IP	H	BB	SO
#Squire, Mark, Wright State	1	4	2.50	28	**15**	36	33	15	17
Hoane, Wes, Butler	4	7	**3.46**	17	0	81	87	25	67
Gilliam, Wes, Illinois-Chicago	5	3	3.50	13	1	56	56	31	52
Ritz, Mark, Cleveland State	4	2	3.63	30	2	54	67	17	41
Magill, Steve, Butler	**8**	6	4.10	19	0	87	95	27	80
McClarnon, Ryan, Cleve. St.	5	5	4.10	15	0	73	90	28	62
McFarland, Eric, Butler	4	3	4.17	16	0	55	77	20	36

Carlson, Steve, Illinois-Chicago	5	5	4.18	13	0	75	85	45	69
Bedford, Chris, Wright State	6	6	4.29	16	0	91	102	35	71
Stephens, Brian, Wright State ...	6	7	4.45	16	0	99	129	15	83
Krenzke, Jason, Wright State ...	3	4	4.50	12	0	47	44	41	36
Sadowski, Chad, Wis.-Mil.	7	5	4.53	16	0	95	104	37	**91**

MISSOURI VALLEY CONFERENCE

	Conference		Overall	
	W	L	W	L
*Wichita State	24	7	59	14
Southwest Missouri State	18	11	38	19
Creighton	18	13	38	25
Evansville	17	13	32	25
Illinois State	17	15	35	24
Bradley	15	17	26	31
Northern Iowa	13	17	28	26
Southern Illinois	9	22	25	29
Indiana State	8	24	21	34

ALL-CONFERENCE TEAM: C—Jon Hale, Sr., Southwest Missouri State. **1B**—Pat Magness, Jr., Wichita State. **2B**—Blake Blasi, So., Wichita State. **SS**—Ryan Gripp, Jr., Creighton. **SS**—Kevin Hooper, Sr., Wichita State. **OF**—Matt Cepicky, Jr., Southwest Missouri State; Joe Schley, Sr., Southern Illinois; Micah Holst, Sr., Southwest Missouri State. **DH**—Ryan Duncheon, Jr., Illinois State. **Util**—Ben Fjelland, Jr., Northern Iowa. **SP**—Peyton Lewis, Sr., Creighton; Evan Fahrner, Jr., Bradley; Eric Eckenstahler, Jr., Illinois State. **RP**—Marc Bluma, Sr., Wichita State; Matt Cobb, So., Northern Iowa.

Player of the Year: Matt Cepicky, SW Missouri State. **Pitcher of the Year**: Peyton Lewis, Creighton. **Newcomer of the Year**: Peyton Lewis, Creighton. **Freshman of the Year**: Ryan Howard, Southwest Missouri State. **Coach of the Year**: Jack Dahm, Creighton.

INDIVIDUAL BATTING LEADERS
(Minimum 125 At-Bats)

	AVG	AB	R	H	2B	3B	HR	RBI	SB
Cepicky, Matt, SW Mo.	**.414**	222	90	92	9	1	**30**	**100**	7
Hooper, Kevin, Wichita St. ..	.402	214	72	86	15	**7**	4	36	**26**
Fjelland, Ben, Northern Iowa	.400	220	49	88	20	1	7	44	4
Blasi, Blake, Wichita State ..	.396	268	87	**106**	**28**	5	4	54	22
Gripp, Ryan, Creighton	.395	233	78	92	24	0	24	84	1
Holst, Micah, SW Missouri ..	.392	240	75	94	16	4	11	62	15
Schley, Joe, Southern Illinois	.372	207	52	77	14	**7**	3	34	23
Gardner, Matt, SW Missouri .	.365	233	82	85	15	1	9	45	4
Correa, Nelson, Bradley	.365	208	51	76	17	2	15	47	2
Magness, Pat, Wichita St.	.364	250	60	91	15	0	18	94	2
Hale, Jon, SW Missouri	.363	204	64	74	10	0	25	68	5
Pietro, Vince, Creighton	.356	253	60	90	17	4	1	39	4
Howard, Ryan, SW Missouri .	.355	234	68	83	14	0	19	66	0
Duncheon, Ryan, Ill. State ...	.354	206	59	73	13	0	23	64	2
Worsley, Marty, So. Illinois ..	.353	204	31	72	16	2	7	44	4
Lawler, Dan, Creighton	.353	218	48	77	14	1	7	53	0
Smith, Jesse, Bradley	.353	218	47	77	18	3	8	50	5
Connors, Ryan, Evansville ...	.349	238	50	83	17	3	8	46	**26**
Hill, Koyie, Wichita State	.347	294	59	102	21	1	10	81	6
Ruggeri, Steve, So. Illinois ..	.347	225	47	78	18	1	4	22	15
Baker, J.C., Indiana State	.342	202	38	69	20	3	3	44	8
Perganson, Jacob, Illinois St.	.342	146	29	50	8	1	2	19	7
Busse, Jeff, Bradley	.341	214	49	73	16	2	15	58	3
Woodin, Greg, Northern Iowa	.340	200	40	68	11	1	5	29	5
Lewis, Peyton, Creighton	.339	233	55	79	18	4	19	76	2
Fuess, Brian, SW Missouri ...	.339	183	36	62	14	0	14	64	2
Smith, Brian, Creighton	.336	140	22	47	9	1	3	26	2
Welsch, Trav, Northern Iowa .	.336	134	31	45	4	0	4	20	4
Mitchell, Todd, Illinois St.	.335	233	45	78	15	0	13	45	14
Mojica, Ruben, Bradley	.333	231	50	77	13	6	4	34	10
Serafini, Vince, Evansville	.332	211	43	70	13	0	6	35	7
Von Behren, Seth, Illinois St.	.331	160	34	53	8	1	5	28	2
Brunner, Ryan, No. Iowa	.330	218	35	72	19	1	12	52	3
Tolzien, Ed, Illinois State	.330	194	35	64	9	3	3	41	10
Dufault, Jared, Illinois St.	.328	232	49	76	12	6	11	49	5
Witzenman, Ben, Indiana St.	.326	184	31	60	8	3	0	25	23
Schirmer, Scott, No. Iowa	.324	182	49	59	16	3	6	48	6

INDIVIDUAL PITCHING LEADERS
(Minimum 50 Innings)

	W	L	ERA	G	SV	IP	H	BB	SO
#Bluma, Marc, Wichita State	2	3	1.70	28	**17**	37	26	13	49
Christensen, Ben, Wichita State	9	1	**2.40**	11	0	71	46	17	77
Frasor, Jason, So. Illinois	5	5	3.27	16	0	96	80	35	110

College Baseball

College Baseball

	W	L	ERA	G	SV	IP	H	BB	SO
Lewis, Peyton, Creighton	10	1	3.30	17	1	104	89	52	114
Burkhart, B.J., Illinois St.	7	5	3.34	16	1	105	125	11	68
Yahraus, Scott, Creighton	5	5	3.42	32	11	55	48	19	42
Bauer, Greg, Wichita State	2	2	3.55	28	3	66	62	18	71
Sloan, Brandon, Wichita St.	10	3	3.66	17	0	93	92	40	86
Biggs, Adam, So. Illinois	5	8	3.86	19	0	89	93	22	67
Cobb, Matt, Northern Iowa	3	5	3.99	22	10	59	64	25	52
Purvis, Rob, Bradley	2	8	4.04	14	0	78	82	43	81
Keiter, Ben, Wichita State	7	0	4.12	13	2	63	71	17	53
Robertson, Nate, Wichita St.	8	4	4.13	14	0	81	88	29	77
Eckenstahler, Eric, Illinois St.	8	2	4.41	14	0	84	88	32	74
Graman, Alex, Indiana State	7	6	4.49	16	0	100	97	51	112
Krafft, Jason, Wichita St.	7	2	4.62	14	0	64	66	26	57
Fahrner, Evan, Bradley	6	3	4.77	15	0	83	91	54	102
Hearing, Brad, So. Illinois	4	4	4.81	13	0	64	75	36	51
Larrison, Preston, Evansville	8	5	4.82	15	0	93	91	57	91

	W	L	ERA	G	SV	IP	H	BB	SO
Martin, Scott, Central Conn	6	5	3.76	16	1	77	78	18	103
DeNicola, Anthony, St. Francis	3	2	3.88	16	0	49	47	31	44
Hinchcliff, George, FDU	8	2	4.46	14	0	73	78	39	74
Ustler, H.J., Wagner	4	3	4.65	9	0	41	55	16	20
Yanosy, David, Central Conn	4	4	4.87	12	1	57	74	9	25
Elliott, John, FDU	2	3	5.14	13	2	56	78	20	32
Severino, Dan, Monmouth	3	3	5.14	10	0	42	52	26	36
Lankford, Joe, St. Francis	6	5	5.18	12	0	66	77	36	62
Curreri, Joe, Long Island	5	4	5.26	12	0	65	84	25	82

NORTHEAST CONFERENCE

	Conference		Overall	
NORTH	W	L	W	L
Fairleigh Dickinson	12	8	22	24
Central Connecticut State	12	8	22	22
St. Francis (N.Y.)	11	9	18	30
Long Island	11	9	25	19
Quinnipiac	7	13	17	23
SOUTH	W	L	W	L
*Monmouth	12	7	26	24
Wagner	10	9	20	23
Maryland-Baltimore County	8	11	20	22
Mount St. Mary's	5	14	12	31

ALL-CONFERENCE TEAM: C—Rob DeFabbia, Sr., Fairleigh Dickinson. **1B**—Joe Zeccardi, Sr., Long Island. **2B**—Frank Castagna, Sr., St. Francis. **3B**—Joe Zangari, Jr., Quinnipiac. **SS**—Jason Maule, Sr., Central Connecticut State. **OF**—Michael Grippo, Sr., Long Island; Joe Francisco, Sr., Wagner; Will Vanjonack, Sr., Mount St. Mary's. **DH**—John Spinelli, Jr., Wagner. **P**—Scott Martin, Sr., Central Connecticut State; George Hinchcliff, Jr., Fairleigh Dickinson.

Player of the Year: Joe Zeccardi, Long Island. **Pitcher of the Year**: Adam Poturnicki, Central Connecticut State. **Newcomer of the Year**: Jason Law, Monmouth. **Coach of the Year**: Dennis Sasso, Fairleigh Dickinson.

INDIVIDUAL BATTING LEADERS
(Minimum 100 At-Bats)

	AVG	AB	R	H	2B	3B	HR	RBI	SB
Zeccardi, Joe, Long Island	.444		58	68	15	2	13	58	3
Tomshack, Steve, UMBC	.439	132	33	58	16	2	5	32	1
Francisco, Joe, Wagner	.436	163	46	71	8	1	5	19	30
Thrash, Brian, UMBC	.435	124	41	54	14	1	4	27	3
Esposito, Paul, FDU	.427	143	50	61	14	1	3	28	2
Grippo, Michael, Long Island	.412	165	33	68	14	3	5	44	4
DeFabbia, Robert, FDU	.403	159	44	64	12	1	13	60	2
Maule, Jason, Central Conn	.394	127	33	50	11	2	0	24	20
Karpell, Jeff, FDU	.393	163	38	64	11	3	4	59	8
Vanjonack, Will, MSM	.388	152	45	59	17	1	8	35	3
Moyer, Brian, Monmouth	.384	125	18	48	10	0	4	33	2
Crandell, Scott, UMBC	.383	154	44	59	14	2	8	36	9
Abbassi, Sami, Long Island	.382	157	45	60	13	3	10	44	3
Egan, Paul, St. Francis	.369	168	37	62	12	2	5	28	8
Burzynski, Nick, Long Island	.368	155	45	57	7	7	7	28	13
Cerminaro, Mike, Wagner	.366	142	32	52	13	3	7	37	6
Gildea, Sean, Mt. St. Mary's	.364	110	25	40	8	0	5	20	0
Santana, David, Monmouth	.363	168	37	61	10	2	3	34	7
Montenegro, Chris, Mon.	.360	169	41	61	12	1	4	42	13
Noyes, Nate, Quinnipiac	.361	155	37	56	9	1	14	45	1
Barkman, Gil, Wagner	.358	137	45	49	8	0	11	48	3
Koslowski, Kasey, St. Francis	.358	165	34	59	14	0	4	36	9
Castagna, Frank, St. Francis	.357	143	25	51	4	0	0	18	7
Zielinski, Mark, FDU	.357	157	43	56	13	2	3	29	7
Pagano, Andrew, FDU	.355	152	27	54	14	2	3	34	0
Zangari, Joe, Quinnipiac	.354	147	38	52	9	0	16	50	1

INDIVIDUAL PITCHING LEADERS
(Minimum 40 Innings)

	W	L	ERA	G	SV	IP	H	BB	SO
Gismonde, Brian, Monmouth	5	1	1.96	26	12	55	48	20	51
Poturnicki, Adam, Central Conn	9	3	2.33	18	2	89	77	28	112
Facey, Andy, Long Island	6	3	2.64	12	0	72	73	7	51
Sarrica, Santino, St. Francis	5	6	3.67	12	0	69	68	33	62

OHIO VALLEY CONFERENCE

	Conference		Overall	
	W	L	W	L
*Eastern Illinois	17	7	33	23
Southeast Missouri State	15	8	27	27
Eastern Kentucky	14	10	35	25
Middle Tennessee State	14	10	29	31
Austin Peay	13	10	29	27
Murray State	13	11	30	25
Morehead State	10	14	25	29
Tennessee Tech	7	17	17	36
Tennessee-Martin	4	20	15	40

ALL-CONFERENCE TEAM: C—Ryan Bridgewater, Sr., Eastern Illinois. **1B**—Lee Chapman, Jr., Eastern Kentucky. **2B**—Bryan Peck, Jr., Middle Tennessee State. **3B**—Josh Pride, Jr., Middle Tennessee State. **SS**—Sam Hoehner, Jr., Morehead State. **OF**—Jeremy Johnson, Jr., Southeast Missouri State; Buddy Dubois, Jr., Austin Peay; Sean Murray, Sr., Eastern Kentucky. **DH**—Joe Lancaster, Jr., Austin Peay. **Util**—Todd Fox, Sr., Murray State. **SP**—Ryan Spille, Sr., Southeast Missouri State; John Larson, Jr., Eastern Illinois. **RP**—Jeremy Sanders, Sr., Eastern Illinois.

Player of the Year: Josh Pride, Middle Tennessee State. **Pitcher of the Year**: John Larson, Eastern Illinois. **Coach of the Year**: Jim Schmitz, Eastern Illinois.

INDIVIDUAL BATTING LEADERS
(Minimum 100 At-Bats)

	AVG	AB	R	H	2B	3B	HR	RBI	SB
Johnson, Jeremy, SE Missouri	.412	194	50	80	18	5	11	45	13
Dubois, Buddy, Austin Peay	.402	199	45	80	23	2	5	27	14
Curley, Ty, Middle Tenn.	.384	190	39	73	12	1	12	50	3
Pride, Josh, Middle Tenn.	.382	225	73	86	11	1	22	53	10
Chapman, Lee, Eastern Ky.	.373	244	64	91	13	4	20	71	20
Lancaster, Joe, Austin Peay	.372	207	58	77	21	0	11	38	3
Sharp, Jason, Eastern Ky.	.371	197	39	73	17	0	9	35	10
O'Sullivan, Pat, Austin Peay	.369	205	41	76	19	1	17	69	4
Barker, Todd, More. State	.367	207	37	74	18	1	10	55	2
Zook, Gabe, Tenn. Tech	.364	195	43	71	19	2	6	31	5
Sayre, Jess, Austin Peay	.361	205	49	74	14	3	8	42	7
Hempel, Aaron, Austin Peay	.358	148	30	53	13	0	10	37	4
Murray, Sean, Eastern Ky.	.355	242	49	86	19	0	13	61	15
Adams, Neale, Tenn. Tech.	.354	113	27	40	10	0	5	26	5
Tomse, Mark, Eastern Illinois	.350	183	28	64	11	3	9	44	0
Reichert, Mike, More. State	.349	186	37	65	13	1	5	40	3
Fox, Todd, Murray State	.345	200	44	69	20	0	6	39	1
Basil, Adam, Eastern Ky.	.344	224	60	77	19	0	12	47	10
Bonilla, Clemente, SE Mo.	.341	173	38	59	14	0	4	29	5
Pack, Bryan, Middle Tenn	.339	218	50	74	23	1	17	56	7
#Dixon, Mark, Morehead St.	.317	189	45	60	10	5	5	34	35
#Lowe, Steve, SE Missouri	.316	152	38	48	15	5	4	30	7
#Leber, Aaron, Tenn. Tech	.282	156	27	44	10	5	3	14	5

INDIVIDUAL PITCHING LEADERS
(Minimum 40 Innings)

	W	L	ERA	G	SV	IP	H	BB	SO
#Fox, Todd, Murray State	2	2	1.09	12	6	25	21	9	22
Sanders, Jeremy, East. Illinois	10	1	1.76	34	5	72	53	14	48
Larson, John, Eastern Illinois	10	3	3.20	18	0	104	109	32	69
Huesgen, Dan, SE Missouri St.	8	5	3.39	19	0	96	111	20	73
Cercy, Rick, Morehead State	7	3	3.55	14	0	63	55	38	92
Spille, Ryan, SE Missouri St.	10	4	4.05	20	0	104	105	36	69
Bogenpohl, Chad, SE Mo. St.	5	2	4.07	17	1	55	49	15	55
Tarajack, Bill, Austin Peay	2	3	4.05	13	0	53	52	17	52
Albright, Chip, Eastern Ill.	5	4	4.12	17	0	98	95	36	64
Sherrill, George, Austin Peay	5	7	4.13	23	4	85	88	40	83
Martini, Mike, Eastern Ky.	6	1	4.22	24	5	53	45	29	40
Allen, T.J., Tenn.-Martin	5	4	4.30	13	0	44	51	16	28
Lammers, Kris, Middle Tenn	5	3	4.34	16	0	66	68	18	41
Glosser, Jason, Murray State	1	7	4.54	19	2	42	51	13	27
Harvey, Greg, Murray State	8	7	4.68	17	0	85	98	21	70
#Rauch, Jon, Morehead State	3	7	6.05	15	1	88	102	33	103

PACIFIC-10 CONFERENCE

	Conference		Overall	
	W	L	W	L
Stanford	19	5	50	15
Southern California	17	7	36	26
Arizona	13	11	33	23
UCLA	13	11	31	31
Arizona State	12	12	39	21
Washington	12	12	33	23
California	11	13	27	31
Oregon State	7	17	19	35
Washington State	4	20	24	31

ALL-CONFERENCE TEAM: C—Mike Tonis, So., California; Dominic Woody, Jr., Washington. **IF**—Garrett Atkins, So., UCLA; Andrew Beinbrink, Sr., Arizona State; Willie Bloomquist, Jr., Arizona State; Dominic Correa, Sr., Southern California; Seth Davidson, So., Southern California; Keoni DeRenne, So., Arizona; John Gall, Jr., Stanford; Joe Gerber, Jr., Oregon State; Ray Hattenburg, Jr., Washington State; Josh Hochgesang, Sr., Stanford; Xavier Nady, So., California. **OF**—Joe Borchard, So., Stanford; Greg Hanoian, Sr., Southern California; Jason Lane, Sr., Southern California; Bill Scott, So., UCLA, Chase Utley, So., UCLA. **P**—Jeff Heaverlo, Jr., Washington; Jason Young, So., Stanford; Barry Zito, Jr., Southern California.

Player of the Year: Will Bloomquist, Arizona State. **Pitcher of the Year**: Barry Zito, Southern California. **Coach of the Year**: Mark Marquess, Stanford.

INDIVIDUAL BATTING LEADERS
(Minimum 125 At-Bats)

	AVG	AB	R	H	2B	3B	HR	RBI	SB
Ernster, Mark, Arizona St.	.439	155	49	68	13	2	5	45	11
Beinbrink, Andrew, ASU	.402	234	78	94	**22**	2	14	85	16
Hattenburg, Ray, Wash. St.	.398	221	41	88	20	1	7	59	6
Bloomquist, Willie, ASU	.394	254	**95**	**100**	18	**8**	10	84	32
Grove, Jason, Wash. State	.393	173	54	68	10	1	18	61	2
Williamson, Bryan, Wash.	.392	194	56	76	15	1	10	46	2
Gerber, Joe, Oregon State	.387	191	45	74	15	0	13	57	1
Tonis, Mike, California	.384	211	55	81	17	1	17	60	8
Scott, Bill, UCLA	.380	242	66	92	19	0	**28**	**86**	0
Duncan, Jeff, Arizona State	.377	138	47	52	7	2	0	23	15
Atkins, Garrett, UCLA	.375	256	64	96	18	1	14	41	2
Woody, Dominic, Wash.	.375	208	58	78	22	0	19	73	5
Nady, Xavier, California	.374	227	56	85	17	1	23	62	5
Sitzman, Jay, Arizona State	.373	185	65	69	7	4	3	41	**33**
Borchard, Joe, Stanford	.372	247	64	92	16	1	11	56	7
DeRenne, Keoni, Arizona	.361	227	54	82	11	2	3	54	22
Rittenhouse, Marc, Wash.	.360	136	46	49	10	1	2	24	10
Lane, Jason, USC	.356	216	58	77	20	4	20	68	12
Anderson, Dennis, Arizona	.353	207	46	73	13	1	8	42	2
Gosewisch, Chip, ASU	.350	157	42	55	15	3	3	45	2
Munson, Eric, USC	.346	153	45	53	6	1	15	41	5
Davidson, Seth, USC	.345	238	51	82	11	4	1	35	9
Gall, John, Stanford	.337	264	66	89	17	3	12	70	12
Jones, Mitch, Arizona State	.333	156	46	52	13	1	11	39	2
Hedges, Drew, Oregon State	.332	184	32	61	12	0	4	31	1
Correa, Dominic, USC	.330	233	56	77	12	2	12	51	1
Gingrich, Troy, Arizona	.329	173	55	57	14	7	1	29	14
Myers, Casey, Arizona State	.329	170	39	56	11	0	6	51	1
Ticen, Kevin, Washington	.322	199	44	64	9	1	15	51	6
Willkie, Corrie, Oregon State	.322	205	46	66	14	0	1	25	3
Jacobson, Billy, Stanford	.321	131	32	42	3	2	2	18	9
Craig, Beau, USC	.319	204	46	65	17	3	4	50	2
Stevenson, Shawn, WSU	.318	245	61	78	18	3	1	42	14
Sharpe, Preston, California	.317	161	42	51	4	1	4	19	16
Utley, Chase, UCLA	.317	271	66	86	13	2	16	56	5
Bruntlett, Eric, Stanford	.316	187	38	59	10	0	1	28	11
Orgill, Pete, Washington	.315	146	34	46	7	0	9	31	0
Dryden, Tim, Oregon State	.314	153	23	48	8	0	2	31	0
Day, Nick, Stanford	.312	202	34	63	15	4	4	41	1
Casillas, Carlos, USC	.310	126	21	39	7	0	8	26	1
Scherer, Jeff, Wash. State	.310	171	27	53	14	0	9	30	0
Green, Jason, UCLA	.309	223	39	69	19	1	6	50	0
Reece, Eric, UCLA	.308	146	25	45	4	1	3	25	0
Hochgesang, Josh, Stanford	.307	251	67	77	17	4	17	73	13
Hanoian, Greg, USC	.306	252	56	77	15	1	7	46	9
Muth, Edmund, Stanford	.305	187	39	57	13	4	6	30	8
Gates, Bookie, Wash. State	.304	171	35	52	13	2	7	32	1
Jones, Rafell, Arizona	.303	142	23	43	9	0	2	23	2
Gemoll, Justin, USC	.300	203	39	61	11	1	4	26	6

BILL NICHOLS

Wildcat sparkplug
Shortstop Keoni DeRenne led Arizona in hitting

INDIVIDUAL PITCHING LEADERS
(Minimum 50 Innings)

	W	L	ERA	G	SV	IP	H	BB	SO
Zito, Barry, USC	**12**	3	3.28	17	0	113	93	58	154
Young, Jason, Stanford	**12**	3	3.43	21	0	155	128	55	**178**
Cogan, Tony, Stanford	7	4	3.69	33	**8**	68	63	21	68
Switzer, Jon, Arizona State	7	4	4.12	25	0	87	89	29	78
Waldrip, Will, Arizona State	10	3	4.16	21	0	115	100	59	103
Sager, Brian, Stanford	6	0	4.17	19	0	86	90	41	72
Brandt, Jon, UCLA	7	4	4.21	21	0	107	92	57	109
Karp, Josh, UCLA	8	3	4.26	16	0	87	84	44	79
Lehr, Justin, USC	7	3	4.29	22	3	113	114	42	109
Crumpton, Chuck, ASU	7	4	4.33	22	0	100	108	47	96
Roe, Bobby, UCLA	3	4	4.34	25	4	85	91	47	61
Shirley, Jon, California	6	5	4.40	15	0	94	86	42	88
Heaverlo, Jeff, Washington	10	4	4.72	19	1	109	112	45	131
Carlsen, Jeff, Washington	9	1	4.85	14	0	89	101	29	55
Wayne, Justin, Stanford	10	1	4.94	21	0	118	117	43	135
Atkinson, Ryan, California	5	7	5.23	18	1	84	87	43	52
Smyth, Steve, USC	6	8	5.27	29	3	84	91	42	81
Cook, B.R., Oregon State	6	9	5.44	16	1	101	97	48	92
Pearce, Josh, Arizona	7	6	5.48	17	0	107	135	47	100
Cislak, Chad, UCLA	5	3	5.91	25	6	53	60	42	57

PATRIOT LEAGUE

	Conference		Overall	
	W	L	W	L
Bucknell	15	5	26	28
*Navy	15	5	27	22
Holy Cross	9	11	14	26
Army	9	11	15	28
Lehigh	8	12	14	28
Lafayette	4	16	8	32

ALL-CONFERENCE TEAM: C—Frank Fresconi, Jr., Bucknell. **1B**—Mark Zematis, Jr., Navy. **2B**—Tyler Prout, Jr., Bucknell. **3B**—Bob Osipower, Jr., Lafayette. **SS**—Tony Mauro, Sr., Navy; Jeff Miller, Jr., Holy Cross. **OF**—Mike McCarthy, Sr., Bucknell; Shaun Salmon, Jr., Army; Brian Supko, Sr., Army. **DH**—Jim Sweeney, So., Holy Cross. **P**—Shane Groover, Jr., Navy; Kevin McDowell, So., Bucknell; Jim Sweeney, So., Holy Cross. **RP**—Chris Lackett, Fr., Bucknell.

Player of the Year: Jim Sweeney, Holy Cross. **Pitcher of the Year**: Shane Groover, Navy. **Coach of the Year**: Paul Pearl, Holy Cross.

INDIVIDUAL BATTING LEADERS
(Minimum 100 At-Bats)

	AVG	AB	R	H	2B	3B	HR	RBI	SB
Sweeney, Jim, Holy Cross ...	**.448**	116	20	52	6	3	2	31	2
McCarthy, Mike, Bucknell	.407	199	**54**	81	15	**8**	6	**58**	13
Miller, Jeff, Holy Cross	.399	143	35	57	15	0	4	28	8
Salmon, Shaun, Army	.398	118	18	47	11	0	0	29	8
Eiben, Kevin, Bucknell	.378	164	**54**	62	12	1	1	19	**24**
Clement, Eric, Lehigh	.375	104	14	39	3	1	1	11	7
D'Angelis, Vince, Lafayette ..	.364	107	25	39	8	1	1	17	10
Palos, Michael, Lafayette ...	.358	120	19	43	6	1	2	21	9
Mauro, Tony, Navy	.353	184	46	65	15	3	5	42	5
Gonser, Tye, Lafayette	.340	153	25	52	5	2	0	23	15
Osipower, Bob, Lafayette	.338	136	34	46	9	1	**12**	39	3
Zematis, Mark, Navy	.333	174	33	58	18	2	5	46	0
Fresconi, Frank, Bucknell	.320	197	28	63	20	0	5	37	3
Supko, Brian, Army	.312	154	43	48	8	0	2	11	16

INDIVIDUAL PITCHING LEADERS
(Minimum 40 Innings)

	W	L	ERA	G	SV	IP	H	BB	SO
Adams, Buck, Army	4	5	**3.11**	11	0	64	68	14	60
Deafenbaugh, Brad, Navy	7	2	3.33	15	1	73	68	20	43
Manfredi, Joseph, Holy Cross ...	3	3	3.41	13	0	63	70	23	35
Groover, Shane, Navy	**8**	3	3.51	15	1	85	84	27	73
Scott, Perry, Bucknell	2	2	3.52	20	1	46	52	18	22
Frey, Chris, Lehigh	3	3	3.72	10	1	58	58	14	35
Sweeney, Jim, Holy Cross	5	4	3.80	12	0	66	58	27	78
Cerminaro, Dave, Lehigh	1	4	4.13	10	0	48	53	19	31
Cini, Matt, Army	3	4	4.31	12	0	71	65	41	63
Kozink, Scott, Navy	7	4	4.55	14	0	97	99	40	**105**
Montano, Mike, Holy Cross	1	5	4.95	8	0	44	50	15	25
#Lackett, Chris, Bucknell	2	3	7.43	17	3	36	47	15	39

SOUTHEASTERN CONFERENCE

	Conference		Overall	
EAST	W	L	W	L
South Carolina	15	15	35	23
Kentucky	13	17	25	32
Florida	13	17	31	25
Tennessee	10	20	28	28
Georgia	8	20	25	30
Vanderbilt	8	22	22	33
WEST	W	L	W	L
Arkansas	22	8	42	23
*Alabama	21	9	53	16
Louisiana State	18	11	41	24
Auburn	18	12	46	19
Mississippi	17	13	34	28
Mississippi State	15	14	42	21

ALL-CONFERENCE TEAM: C—Casey Dunn, Sr., Auburn. **1B**—Cliff Wren, Sr., Mississippi State. **2B**—Brad Henderson, Sr., Mississippi. **3B**—Hunter Bledsoe, Sr., Vanderbilt. **SS**—Andy Phillips, Sr., Alabama. **OF**—G.W. Keller, Sr., Alabama; Brian Rainwater, Jr., Georgia; Brian Wiese, Jr., Mississippi State. **DH**—Tim Angiolini, Jr., South Carolina. **P**—Brent Schoening, Jr., Auburn; Charlie Isaacson, Fr., Arkansas. **RP**—Ben Grezlovski, Sr., Florida.

Player of the Year: Hunter Bledsoe, Vanderbilt. **Coach of the Year**: Norm DeBriyn, Arkansas.

INDIVIDUAL BATTING LEADERS
(Minimum 125 At-Bats)

	AVG	AB	R	H	2B	3B	HR	RBI	SB
Bledsoe, Hunter, Vanderbilt .	**.459**	207	61	95	24	1	10	51	31
Nonemaker, Karl, Vanderbilt .	.415	212	46	88	18	0	3	29	4
Chapman, Travis, Miss. St. ...	.404	245	66	99	18	0	6	49	2
Phillips, Andy, Alabama	.398	259	71	103	22	**6**	22	66	16
Keller, G.W., Alabama	.396	270	**85**	**107**	15	4	15	72	40
Henderson, Brad, Miss.	.388	260	60	101	24	2	11	48	5
Hudson, Josh, Georgia	.387	217	50	84	15	2	2	36	14
Keppinger, Jeff, Georgia	.383	230	51	88	14	1	11	48	4
Poe, Adam, South Carolina ..	.383	206	45	79	18	3	4	46	13
Dunn, Casey, Auburn	.379	269	70	102	19	1	16	**86**	1
Mailon, Kent, Auburn	.379	269	79	102	16	3	2	45	40
Burke, Chris, Tennessee	.372	234	50	87	**25**	2	2	41	19
Gross, Gabe, Auburn	.363	245	50	89	23	3	7	65	1
Wren, Cliff, Mississippi St.	.367	245	56	90	15	2	13	60	1
Rainwater, Brian, Georgia	.362	235	47	85	23	**6**	12	62	17
Wilson, John, Kentucky	.360	225	59	81	16	2	**23**	56	4
Fausett, Aaron, Vanderbilt ...	.356	216	34	77	12	1	8	41	11

Newton, Robert, Kentucky	.356	146	24	52	8	0	4	25	1
Roberts, Brian, South Caro. . .	.353	221	79	78	21	0	12	36	**67**
Brown, Jeremy, Alabama	.347	262	77	91	20	0	15	69	4
Daniel, Steve, Tennessee ...	.346	231	53	80	19	0	9	52	30
Gliemmo, Hayden, Auburn ...	.346	205	39	71	8	3	1	37	4
Lotterhos, Chris, Miss. State .	.346	256	64	85	16	4	1	41	4
Wiese, Brian, Mississippi St.	.345	252	74	87	16	2	19	66	8
Ellis, Mark, Florida	.344	244	56	84	18	3	10	42	20
Leaumont, Jeff, LSU	.342	257	63	88	15	3	18	82	5
Kersh, Jamie, Auburn	.341	255	57	87	23	0	11	59	4
Gulledge, Kelley, Alabama ...	.339	192	40	65	15	3	11	50	0
Wigginton, Derek, Alabama ..	.339	174	44	59	6	**6**	5	32	6
Jester, Joe, Arkansas	.338	263	76	89	20	2	10	59	35
Crossett, Scott, Arkansas	.335	182	30	61	8	1	4	33	9
Rock, Jamin, Mississippi St. .	.333	165	44	55	17	1	2	44	5
Witten, Jeremy, LSU	.330	209	64	69	18	3	8	46	15
Dyson, Trey, South Carolina .	.329	146	24	48	11	0	3	25	6
Catalanotte, Greg, Florida	.328	229	48	75	13	1	18	58	7
Dorminy, Josh, Georgia	.327	168	31	55	10	0	7	31	1
Luellwitz, Sean, Vanderbilt ...	.327	150	21	49	11	0	1	20	2
Nye, Rodney, Arkansas	.327	269	69	88	19	0	20	78	17
Christensen, Jeff, Tenn	.325	151	34	49	8	1	6	35	10
Janowicz, Nate, South Caro. .	.324	204	61	66	11	3	7	53	26
Kropf, Andy, Vanderbilt	.322	199	34	64	16	0	6	46	0
Theriot, Ryan, LSU	.322	242	55	78	11	3	2	41	13
Rich, Dominic, Auburn	.320	266	68	85	15	3	2	47	15
Boyd, Brent, Arkansas	.319	229	59	73	15	1	7	32	7
McClure, Trey, LSU	.319	229	61	73	13	1	18	55	1
Ross, Donnie, Tennessee ...	.316	196	51	62	19	1	15	59	5
Wright, Daron, Miss. St.	.316	155	35	49	16	1	0	29	5
Dill, Jason, Florida	.311	132	33	41	7	1	7	31	0
Hendrickson, Eric, LSU	.311	161	36	50	5	1	11	46	1
Rosamond, Michael, Miss	.310	232	55	72	13	**6**	18	41	6
Bozanich, Sam, Alabama	.309	275	62	85	19	1	8	57	7
Martin, Ty, Mississippi St.	.308	195	56	60	7	4	7	39	2
Angiolini, Tim, South Caro. ...	.307	199	26	61	13	0	9	62	0
McGlone, Aaron, Kentucky ...	.307	218	48	67	9	2	16	52	1
West, Josh, Mississippi St. ...	.307	140	34	43	12	1	6	27	0
Pohle, Ike, Arkansas	.306	186	42	57	14	0	6	36	7
Lundquist, Ryan, Arkansas ..	.305	162	60	80	20	0	14	55	16
Nelson, Shane, South Caro. .	.305	141	35	43	12	0	7	26	10
Price, Breck, Kentucky	.303	208	36	63	10	1	13	33	7
Wandall, Chad, Auburn	.303	244	58	74	17	2	2	49	3
Cresse, Brad, LSU	.302	215	52	65	11	0	10	39	2
Huisman, Justin, Miss	.302	215	35	65	10	1	7	45	2
Wood, Darren, Alabama	.302	215	47	65	15	4	8	42	11
Keene, Kurt, Florida	.300	223	48	67	12	1	7	37	20
Moore, Beau, Kentucky	.300	190	46	57	12	0	7	27	24

INDIVIDUAL PITCHING LEADERS
(Minimum 50 Innings)

	W	L	ERA	G	SV	IP	H	BB	SO
Thoms, Hank, Mississippi St.	7	6	**2.66**	18	1	118	127	37	121
Grezlovski, Ben, Florida	9	8	2.69	36	5	84	79	39	84
#Huisman, Justin, Mississippi ..	1	0	2.93	15	**10**	15	14	2	17
Isaacson, Charlie, Arkansas	9	0	3.16	16	0	100	72	53	97
Schoening, Brent, Auburn	**13**	1	3.32	21	0	138	122	47	151
Ainsworth, Kurt, LSU	**13**	6	3.45	22	1	130	114	48	**157**
Bryd, Mike, Vanderbilt	5	6	3.59	19	1	108	105	41	107
Walling, David, Arkansas	10	2	3.78	18	0	121	104	31	155
Bouknight, Kip, So. Carolina	7	4	3.86	18	1	119	111	49	124
Compton, Brian, Mississippi St.	6	1	3.86	27	2	70	68	31	77
Brice, Keith, Florida	7	3	3.99	25	1	68	71	34	55
Brand, Cliff, Georgia	4	7	4.03	16	0	103	101	27	93
McShea, Dan, Mississippi	7	3	4.05	22	1	87	88	29	55
Bennett, Jamie, Tennessee ..	11	5	4.12	23	0	164	159	61	142
Goodwin, Ronnie, Mississippi ..	2	4	4.26	18	1	57	58	13	32
Lyons, Nathan, Mississippi ...	4	5	4.34	23	1	64	73	35	50
Gomez, Hunter, LSU	4	3	4.38	31	7	99	112	25	90
Rodriguez, Sergio, Florida	2	0	4.58	23	1	57	70	21	34
Prior, Mark, Vanderbilt	4	8	4.59	13	0	82	107	23	71
McAvoy, Jeff, Mississippi	8	6	4.60	18	0	115	111	41	88
Bean, Colter, Auburn	5	3	4.70	34	8	52	49	20	47
Kent, Nathan, Kentucky	5	7	4.79	18	0	126	139	42	116
Ginter, Matt, Mississippi State ..	4	8	4.80	19	0	94	81	55	108
Fowler, Barry, Georgia	5	4	4.94	17	0	95	114	24	52
Gliemmo, Hayden, Auburn ...	**13**	7	4.96	21	0	123	132	37	105
Smith, Justin, Alabama	3	5	5.00	12	0	76	75	25	95
Tallet, Brian, LSU	3	4	5.01	19	0	59	59	30	60
McClendon, Matt, Florida	5	4	5.04	12	0	64	86	22	44
Torres, Manny, Alabama	9	3	5.04	17	0	114	136	30	104
Bauer, Peter, South Carolina .	5	3	5.09	17	1	69	72	27	54
Hadden, Randy, South Carolina	7	4	5.15	17	0	100	135	26	72
Vent, Kevin, Arkansas	3	5	5.28	31	4	58	57	39	61
Bootcheck, Chris, Auburn	8	6	5.57	22	0	128	159	38	125

College Baseball

	W	L	ERA	G	SV	IP	H	BB	SO
Polk, Scott, Mississippi State	5	3	5.71	19	2	65	56	33	65
Tisdale, Marlyn, Tennessee	4	9	5.73	17	0	86	90	67	89
Murphy, Scott, Alabama	5	0	5.74	10	0	53	62	12	52
McCrotty, Wes, Arkansas	5	2	5.75	21	1	83	100	39	74
Shaffer, Ben, Kentucky	5	5	5.87	17	1	87	78	55	108
Beal, Andy, Vanderbilt	3	3	5.91	22	0	81	104	32	84

SOUTHERN CONFERENCE

	Conference W	Conference L	Overall W	Overall L
*The Citadel	24	5	41	20
Charleston	19	10	31	24
Western Carolina	18	10	36	23
East Tennessee State	18	11	29	25
UNC Greensboro	16	12	29	26
Georgia Southern	13	15	29	29
Virginia Military	13	16	22	27
Furman	13	17	22	35
Appalachian State	10	20	14	38
Davidson	9	21	11	37
Wofford	7	23	14	36

ALL-CONFERENCE TEAM: C—Ronny Marmol, So., Charleston. **1B**—Philip Hartig, So., The Citadel. **2B**—Billy Colome, Sr., Charleston. **3B**—Eric Walker, Jr., Virginia Military. **SS**—Chris Moore, Sr., Western Carolina. **OF**—Charles Thomas, So., Western Carolina; Brandon Eierman, Sr., East Tennessee State; Eric Johnson, Jr., Western Carolina. **DH**—Scott Thompkins, Sr., Virginia Military. **P**—Brian Wiley, Sr., The Citadel; Lucas Hocker, Jr., Charleston. **RP**—Jay Morgan, Jr., The Citadel.

Player of the Year: Chris Moore, Western Carolina. **Pitcher of the Year:** Brian Wiley, The Citadel. **Freshman of the Year:** Brett Lewis, Georgia Southern. **Coach of the Year:** Fred Jordan, The Citadel.

INDIVIDUAL BATTING LEADERS
(Minimum 100 At-Bats)

	AVG	AB	R	H	2B	3B	HR	RBI	SB
Thomas, Charles, W. Car.	.406	244	76	99	15	2	3	41	17
Colome, Billy, Charleston	.393	206	63	81	14	7	5	39	46
Johnson, Eric, W. Carolina	.388	258	83	100	18	5	10	53	46
Moore, Chris, W. Carolina	.388	227	72	88	16	1	21	84	7
Pollack, Jody, Ga. Southern	.387	248	69	96	20	1	11	83	16
Marmol, Ronny, Charleston	.383	167	37	64	14	0	3	41	7
Deaton, Rad, Wofford	.378	193	38	73	12	1	6	39	8
Eierman, Brandon, ETSU	.376	189	59	71	14	3	15	54	5
Walker, Eric, VMI	.376	186	42	70	8	0	4	40	5
Blocker, Kevin, Wofford	.374	163	35	61	7	0	5	35	4
Howell, Travis, Charleston	.368	190	51	70	10	1	6	59	20
Sparks, Ed, East Tenn. St.	.368	155	34	57	14	0	9	41	2
Bradford, Ben, VMI	.367	139	40	51	12	0	3	36	5
Sigmon, Shane, App. State	.360	261	64	94	20	3	17	73	5
Blevins, Travis, ETSU	.354	223	66	79	16	1	2	31	7
Wade, Jody, Furman	.353	221	58	78	15	4	6	38	31
Catanzaro, Chris, VMI	.347	170	41	59	14	0	5	36	3
Cheek, Andy, App. State	.347	170	39	59	9	3	8	41	9
Henley, Scott, Ga. Southern	.347	239	44	83	18	0	9	55	12
Thompkins, Scott, VMI	.347	167	36	58	12	2	11	55	1
Brown, Ben, Davidson	.344	195	34	67	16	4	1	14	24
Yaniszewski, Scott, Wofford	.344	192	44	66	11	0	14	54	1
Frend, Tim, Davidson	.343	181	30	62	12	1	6	39	2
Behne, Chris, App. State	.342	199	36	68	13	2	8	52	8
Smith, Jeff, UNCG	.341	220	56	75	12	5	10	46	28
Huffstettler, Robbie, App. St.	.340	191	39	65	15	1	5	31	8
Foxhall, Joey, Charleston	.336	217	58	73	9	0	0	19	17
Swackhamer, Rusty, ETSU	.335	212	52	71	12	0	13	57	3
#Morris, Chris, The Citadel	.327	217	61	71	6	0	0	27	52
#Biggs, Tracy, W. Carolina	.325	166	48	54	8	7	0	12	19
#Sloan, Stewart, Davidson	.324	185	36	60	20	0	9	38	2
#Langley, Dustin, Ga. South.	.322	255	58	82	20	1	13	61	8
#Harris, Steve, W. Carolina	.304	224	57	68	10	3	26	73	11

INDIVIDUAL PITCHING LEADERS
(Minimum 40 Innings)

	W	L	ERA	G	SV	IP	H	BB	SO
Hocker, Lucas, Charleston	9	4	2.52	16	0	96	100	25	87
Hancock, Rodney, The Citadel	10	5	3.11	17	0	110	100	40	123
Oliver, Scott, Charleston	8	4	3.24	15	0	89	77	53	90
Wiley, Brian, The Citadel	9	3	3.47	19	1	93	73	56	150
#Davey, Brett, Charleston	4	2	3.80	24	7	24	32	9	15
Morgan, Jay, The Citadel	8	3	3.99	29	7	56	56	16	41
Bunn, Kyle, The Citadel	6	1	4.19	31	1	58	53	18	55
Overbay, Wesley, W. Carolina	5	4	4.25	11	1	89	102	29	46

	W	L	ERA	G	SV	IP	H	BB	SO
Pember, David, W. Carolina	8	5	4.36	19	1	120	153	42	76
Horne, Aaron, UNCG	2	1	4.37	16	1	58	52	27	37
David, Toby, Furman	3	8	4.68	17	0	85	98	42	62
McPherson, Dallas, The Citadel	3	4	4.70	18	0	88	89	41	74
Baber, Matt, ETSU	12	3	4.74	24	1	99	112	25	95
Bates, Chip, Furman	4	7	4.82	18	0	80	86	46	85
Gordon, Sean, UNCG	5	5	4.92	20	2	68	84	22	53
Klomparens, Robbie, Wofford	3	6	5.14	11	0	68	77	32	47
Lewis, Brett, Georgia Southern	9	5	5.20	22	0	119	132	47	121
#Ostlund, Ian, VMI	3	2	7.39	23	7	35	44	19	38

SOUTHLAND CONFERENCE

	Conference W	Conference L	Overall W	Overall L
Northeast Louisiana	19	7	36	22
Northwestern State	18	9	38	21
Texas-San Antonio	15	12	27	33
*Southwest Texas State	15	12	27	32
Texas-Arlington	14	13	26	35
Southeastern Louisiana	13	14	28	29
Lamar	12	14	34	21
McNeese State	12	15	31	25
Sam Houston State	8	19	22	33
Nicholls State	8	19	20	32

ALL-CONFERENCE TEAM: C—Chris Seaman, Jr., Southwest Texas State. **1B**—Ben Broussard, Sr., McNeese State. **2B**—Johnny Johnston, Sr., Texas-San Antonio. **3B**—Steve Minus, Sr., Texas-San Antonio. **SS**—Kelly Eddlemon, Jr., Sam Houston State. **OF**—Matt Mize, Sr, Texas-Arlington; Jason Wolfe, Sr, Northeast Louisiana; Jeff Juarez, Jr., Texas-San Antonio. **DH**—Macky Waguespack, Sr., Southeastern Louisiana. **P**—Adam Stout, Jr., Northwestern State; Ben Sheets, Jr., Northeast Louisiana; Cheyenne Janke, Sr., Nicholls State.

Player of the Year: Ben Sheets, Northeast Louisiana. **Hitter of the Year:** Ben Broussard, McNeese State. **Pitcher of the Year:** Ben Sheets, Northeast Louisiana. **Newcomer of the Year:** Adam Stout, Northwestern State. **Coach of the Year:** Smoke Laval, Northeast Louisiana.

INDIVIDUAL BATTING LEADERS
(Minimum 100 At-Bats)

	AVG	AB	R	H	2B	3B	HR	RBI	SB
Broussard, Ben, McNeese	.427	211	74	90	14	4	27	91	10
Eddlemon, Kelly, SHS	.416	221	62	92	24	2	26	95	7
Seaman, Chris, SW Texas	.399	183	35	73	6	0	3	37	9
Mize, Matt, Texas-Arlington	.374	238	59	89	19	4	16	48	27
Fingleson, Gavin, SE La.	.373	260	51	97	15	2	2	39	4
Dominguez, Anthony, SWT	.369	236	54	87	17	1	12	50	10
Juarez, Jeff, UTSA	.368	250	66	92	19	0	18	61	22
Johnston, Johnny, UTSA	.360	239	54	86	19	1	3	31	9
Janek, John David, SWT	.359	195	44	70	7	3	3	29	15
Bell, Steven, NW State	.352	193	58	68	14	0	10	58	4
Waguespack, Macky, SE La.	.351	231	44	81	15	2	23	82	1
Zander, Bryan, NE Louisiana	.351	211	51	74	12	0	4	42	7
Cooksey, Wes, Lamar	.349	129	34	45	15	1	7	40	2
Baez, Dariel, Nicholls State	.347	196	22	68	8	3	2	29	3
Prater, Nick, UTSA	.346	185	33	64	12	1	3	30	2
Wallis, Kent, UTSA	.344	227	50	78	22	5	10	67	16
Cliffe, Tommy, Sam Houston	.342	184	44	63	14	2	14	57	4
Tompkins, John, SW Texas	.341	229	39	78	12	7	9	64	5
Moore, Terrence, SW Texas	.340	200	54	68	12	7	4	26	7
Frank, Nick, NE Louisiana	.339	186	40	63	10	0	5	40	8
Cox, Chris, NW State	.338	142	31	48	11	6	6	36	1
Wolfe, Jason, NE Louisiana	.337	243	58	82	20	3	12	49	20
Jobert, Jacques, Nicholls St.	.336	214	35	72	11	2	8	39	6
Parker, Nolan, McNeese St.	.333	204	48	68	13	1	7	49	9
Perret, Kevin, Nicholls State	.333	186	45	62	15	2	4	40	7
Potramente, Darren, NE La	.333	174	30	58	8	1	5	40	2
Parrish, Brette, UTSA	.333	132	30	44	4	1	3	20	13
Smith, Ryan, UTSA	.333	174	42	58	11	2	9	29	9

INDIVIDUAL PITCHING LEADERS
(Minimum 40 Innings)

	W	L	ERA	G	SV	IP	H	BB	SO
Sanches, Brian, Lamar	4	1	1.82	12	1	49	38	14	45
Sheets, Ben, NE Louisiana	14	1	3.11	18	2	116	100	31	158
Janke, Cheyenne, Nicholls St.	5	4	3.26	13	0	97	106	13	91
McIntyre, Harvey, NW State	1	1	3.59	17	0	58	56	18	30
Sobczak, David, UTA	3	4	3.62	37	8	55	61	24	65
Stout, Adam, NW State	10	2	3.76	16	0	103	119	25	66
Fitzgerald, Ryan, Lamar	5	0	3.83	23	3	47	41	14	43

Player	W	L	ERA	G	SV	IP	H	BB	SO
Warren, Andy, Sam Houston	5	8	4.13	19	1	107	123	20	68
Ryan, Jason, McNeese State	6	1	4.31	14	0	63	80	30	58
Vanlandingham, Jeff, SHS	4	4	4.32	18	0	65	76	31	37
Castillo, Brian, Lamar	4	3	4.44	13	0	47	44	30	39
Bradley, Mike, Texas-Arlington	2	2	4.58	19	0	55	66	28	47
Sprague, Kevin, McNeese St.	5	2	4.70	16	1	90	103	48	76
Slanina, Jason, NW State	4	3	4.86	19	1	46	51	11	46
Sergent, Joe, Lamar	1	4	5.09	19	2	53	66	19	45
Balcer, David, NW State	7	5	5.16	19	1	106	136	36	84
Gonzales, Craig, SE Louisiana	5	2	5.23	16	0	72	91	33	51

SWAC

	Conference		Overall	
EAST	W	L	W	L
Jackson State	20	4	33	20
Alcorn State	11	8	22	22
Mississippi Valley State	5	12	11	20
Alabama State	4	16	13	32
WEST	W	L	W	L
*Southern	23	7	29	16
Grambling State	23	9	37	14
Texas Southern	17	15	24	23
Arkansas-Pine Bluff	11	21	15	33
Prairie View A&M	4	26	11	39

ALL-CONFERENCE TEAM: C—Alva Thompson, Sr., Southern. **1B**—Chris Atwell, Jr., Southern. **2B**—Dustin Ebanks, Jr., Grambling. **3B**—Delvon Matthews, Jr., Texas Southern. **SS**—Gilbert Lanoix, Grambling. **OF**—Stephen Cotton, Fr., Texas Southern; Chris Hills, Sr., Jackson State; Marvin Mister, Sr., Mississippi Valley. **DH**—Chris Cottonham, So., Grambling. **P**—Gabe Ashford, So., Southern; Torik Harrison, So., Southern; Demetrius Mitchell, Sr., Jackson State; Ricardo Salazar, So., Texas Southern.
Player of the Year: Gilbert Lanoix, Grambling. **Pitcher of the Year**: Ricardo Salazar, Texas Southern. **Hitter of the Year**: Chris Cottonham, Grambling. **Freshman of the Year**: Michael Woods, Southern. **Newcomer of the Year**: Gilbert Lanoix, Grambling. **Coach of the Year**: Roger Cador, Southern.

INDIVIDUAL BATTING LEADERS
(Minimum 100 At-Bats)

Player	AVG	AB	R	H	2B	3B	HR	RBI	SB
Lanoix, Gilbert, Grambling	.429	168	51	72	11	5	7	55	4
Cottonham, Chris, Gram.	.416	154	65	64	11	4	16	69	13
Alexander, Juan, Grambling	.400	110	37	44	9	0	4	35	19
May, Damion, Jackson St.	.396	106	29	42	11	1	5	24	3
Woods, Michael, Southern	.386	158	57	61	20	3	5	42	14
Navarro, Juan, Grambling	.385	109	32	42	5	1	8	38	1
Matthews, Delvon, Tex. So.	.382	144	48	55	9	1	5	33	9
Gould, Elliott, Texas So.	.379	103	36	39	7	1	5	40	19
Rosa, Dario, Alcorn State	.378	148	41	56	11	6	3	44	11
Parker, Jamar, Alabama St.	.377	114	28	43	6	1	2	20	21
Carter, Devontay, Alcorn St.	.367	147	48	54	11	2	3	34	18
Harrison, Jermaine, Ala. St.	.366	145	50	53	11	1	8	47	13
Atwell, Chris, Southern	.359	131	25	47	11	1	5	36	3
Beard, Lavon, Jackson St.	.358	109	32	39	12	0	3	38	13
Thompson, Alva, Southern	.358	109	29	39	9	1	8	34	2
Cowan, Bartowski, Ala. St.	.355	141	47	50	11	3	2	28	16
Cotton, Stephen, Texas So.	.355	124	33	44	7	3	0	24	20
Dotson, Arlo, Prairie View	.351	111	22	39	5	1	2	19	18
Phaure, Dwayne, Texas So.	.351	134	30	47	7	1	2	34	3
Sillman, Willie, Alabama St.	.349	149	37	52	6	4	6	43	5
#Hills, Chris, Jackson St.	.331	175	50	58	11	7	5	43	26
#Coleman, Tony, Grambling	.305	151	52	46	5	2	0	18	39

INDIVIDUAL PITCHING LEADERS
(Minimum 35 Innings)

Player	W	L	ERA	G	SV	IP	H	BB	SO
Salazar, Ricardo, Texas So.	5	4	3.48	11	0	54	61	19	49
Putman-Anderson, Jason, SU	6	3	3.65	10	0	62	60	20	41
Toliver, Melvin, Grambling	3	0	3.68	14	1	44	37	39	44
Harrison, Torik, Southern	7	4	3.69	12	0	71	76	32	78
Burel, Terry, Texas So.	2	3	3.76	13	0	41	35	38	43
Washington, Rasha, Grambling	5	1	4.01	12	1	52	55	31	27
Witt, Nathan, Ark.-PB	2	5	4.41	10	0	54	74	8	19
Foster, Roy, Grambling	8	1	4.48	13	0	62	70	10	35
Ashford, Gabe, Southern	5	4	4.50	12	0	62	52	34	46
Mitchell, Demetrius, Jack. St.	8	4	4.56	15	1	73	68	36	52
Winder, Marcus, Texas So.	5	1	5.14	11	0	56	61	34	42
Williams, Eric, Jackson St.	4	2	5.23	14	0	52	49	43	40
Moore, Trammel, Southern	6	0	5.28	13	0	60	53	32	45
#Clarke, Andre, Texas So.	0	2	6.23	10	4	22	20	16	21

SUN BELT CONFERENCE

	Conference		Overall	
TEAM	W	L	W	L
South Alabama	27	5	39	20
Southwestern Louisiana	24	9	42	24
Western Kentucky	21	12	38	24
*Florida International	17	16	44	19
New Orleans	15	18	25	34
Louisiana Tech	10	22	20	37
Arkansas-Little Rock	10	22	20	37
Arkansas State	6	26	18	38

ALL-CONFERENCE TEAM: C—Danny Massiatte, Jr., Southwestern Louisiana. **1B**—T.J. Freeman, Sr., Western Kentucky. **2B**—Brian Myrow, Sr., Louisiana Tech. **3B**—John Ballon, Jr., New Orleans. **SS**—Hiram Silfa, Sr., Florida International. **OF**—Eben Wells, Sr., South Alabama; Chris Yeo, Sr., Western Kentucky; Casey Crume, Jr., Arkansas-Little Rock. **DH**—Jabbar Wesley, Sr., Arkansas-Little Rock. **Util**—Jon Watson, Sr., New Orleans. **P**—Phil Devey, Jr., Southwestern Louisiana; Edwin Franco, Sr., Florida International; Daniel Head, Jr., South Alabama.
Player of the Year: T.J. Freeman, Western Kentucky. **Newcomer of the Year**: John Ballon, New Orleans. **Freshman of the Year**: Tim Merritt, South Alabama. **Coach of the Year**: Steve Kittrell, South Alabama.

INDIVIDUAL BATTING LEADERS
(Minimum 125 At-Bats)

Player	AVG	AB	R	H	2B	3B	HR	RBI	SB
Nelson, Nathan, SW La.	.420	162	30	68	17	3	4	42	6
Ballon, John, New Orleans	.386	220	60	85	23	1	12	54	3
Fernandez, Luis, FIU	.364	217	50	79	8	1	10	49	4
Taylor, Seth, South Alabama	.359	220	54	79	14	6	10	49	20
Gretz, Nick, South Alabama	.356	163	26	58	8	0	9	49	2
Wesley, Jabbar, Ark.-LR	.352	193	25	68	18	0	4	45	5
Hawkins, Will, SW La.	.350	157	25	55	12	2	7	41	4
O'Dwyer, George, SW La.	.350	200	48	70	10	0	7	49	9
Yeo, Chris, Western Ky.	.349	232	64	81	14	5	5	43	11
Paulk, Barry, Florida Int.	.348	132	35	46	6	2	2	17	27
Smitherman, Clay, Ark.-LR	.347	190	42	66	11	1	6	32	4
Bello, Joel, Florida Int.	.345	145	25	50	8	0	1	26	6
Hernandez, Vinnie, So. Ala.	.344	224	49	77	19	2	8	42	2
Wells, Eben, So. Alabama	.340	241	70	82	19	4	6	31	21
Myrow, Brian, La. Tech	.339	192	61	65	18	0	14	41	5
Soto, T.J., Louisiana Tech	.339	224	53	76	17	4	19	64	12
Freeman, T.J., West. Ky.	.336	214	57	72	19	1	18	59	9
Feehan, Steven, SW La.	.331	254	68	84	18	3	2	40	18
Merritt, Tim, So. Alabama	.330	206	46	68	4	1	11	44	15
Calahan, Scott, So. Alabama	.328	238	46	78	13	4	2	38	11
Crume, Casey, Ark.-LR	.326	190	50	62	28	2	3	38	3
Massiatte, Danny, SW La.	.323	217	46	70	18	3	1	32	14
Watson, Jon, New Orleans	.323	217	44	70	12	2	11	48	8
Calais, Ian, SW La.	.318	157	38	50	8	1	0	27	2
Gill, Ryan, SW La.	.312	215	50	67	12	2	3	23	19
Bredensteiner, Reed, Ark. St.	.311	177	29	55	12	0	13	48	4
Sapp, Aaron, New Orleans	.311	209	42	65	18	2	9	42	4
#Otero, George, Fla. Int.	.288	191	53	55	8	2	7	26	28

INDIVIDUAL PITCHING LEADERS
(Minimum 50 Innings)

Player	W	L	ERA	G	SV	IP	H	BB	SO
#Kent, Steve, Florida Int.	1	0	0.69	24	13	26	14	13	29
Mittauer, David, Fla. Int.	7	3	2.24	17	0	88	80	31	91
Baranowski, Brennan, SW La.	6	6	2.45	34	6	59	44	29	94
Ochsner, Alan, SW La.	6	2	2.72	26	6	76	59	30	93
Head, Daniel, So. Alabama	7	6	2.87	30	9	91	84	40	71
Janecek, Eric, So. Alabama	9	2	3.02	19	0	83	71	20	71
Franco, Edwin, Fla. Int.	11	3	3.11	18	0	127	105	41	148
Eckert, Harold, Fla. Int.	6	2	3.13	24	2	75	57	38	112
Devey, Phil, SW La.	10	1	3.14	21	0	129	99	60	165
Helpenstill, Clint, Ark. St.	2	3	3.34	29	5	62	60	16	34
Meyer, Layne, So. Alabama	8	3	3.48	17	0	106	89	33	108
Hutchison, Ryan, West. Ky.	10	4	3.51	17	0	105	96	36	74
Garcia, Raul, Florida Int.	12	6	3.66	21	0	103	96	44	110
Novotney, Josh, West. Ky.	8	4	3.86	18	0	121	132	25	102
Hickman, Ben, La. Tech	5	5	3.88	27	5	102	112	13	97
Houdek, Brian, West. Ky.	7	4	4.00	17	0	81	79	43	63
Isenberg, Nathan, West. Ky.	2	2	4.35	29	7	50	54	9	21
Templett, Eric, SW La.	3	4	4.58	20	0	88	108	27	81
Roach, Kyle, So. Alabama	7	3	4.69	19	1	71	69	18	66
Dohmann, Scott, SW La.	8	5	4.71	18	0	99	110	17	84
Rowland, Carl, Ark.-LR	6	10	5.12	19	0	97	132	35	67

TRANSAMERICA CONFERENCE

	Conference		Overall	
Florida Atlantic	26	4	54	9
*Jacksonville	22	8	41	23
Mercer	19	11	36	24
Central Florida	19	11	38	21
Troy State	15	15	31	28
Centenary	14	16	21	35
Georgia State	13	17	23	33
Jacksonville State	13	17	22	30
Stetson	11	19	23	31
Samford	8	22	20	33
Campbell	5	25	24	32

ALL-CONFERENCE TEAM: C—Bobby Kidd, Sr., Georgia State. **1B**—Dustin Brisson, Jr., Central Florida. **2B**—Dickie Hart, Sr., Florida Atlantic. **3B**—Paul Stryhas, Sr., Florida Atlantic. **SS**—Brian Hitchcox, Jr., Samford. **OF**—Matt Bowser, So., Central Florida; Mick Celli, Sr., Florida Atlantic; Jay Langston, Jr., Georgia State. **DH**—Brandon Blair, So., Mercer. **P**—Todd Moser, Sr., Florida Atlantic; Lenny DiNardo, Fr., Stetson. **RP**—Jason Arnold, So., Central Florida.

Player of the Year: Todd Moser, Florida Atlantic. **Coach of the Year**: Kevin Cooney, Florida Atlantic.

INDIVIDUAL BATTING LEADERS
(Minimum 125 At-Bats)

	AVG	AB	R	H	2B	3B	HR	RBI	SB
Hitchcox, Brian, Samford	.400	200	50	80	21	3	2	29	26
Kidd, Bobby, Ga. State	.398	166	33	66	17	0	8	42	0
Harry, Russell, Jack. St.	.396	192	35	76	27	1	6	48	1
Brisson, Dustin, Cent. Fla.	.388	206	50	80	19	2	17	76	1
Withey, Ryan, Fla. Atlantic	.385	179	61	69	15	2	5	28	24
Batia, Mark, Central Fla.	.378	135	55	51	7	3	0	18	12
Schmidt, Greg, Mercer	.377	235	67	90	10	1	8	49	19
Celli, Mick, Fla. Atlantic	.374	214	70	80	10	1	15	64	10
Bowser, Matt, Central Fla.	.371	178	49	66	21	0	13	62	3
Brooks, Wes, Jack. St.	.370	181	45	67	14	1	12	36	9
Barker, Ben, Campbell	.366	213	48	79	19	1	9	31	10
Asche, Kirk, Jacksonville	.361	216	59	78	20	1	14	56	16
Boeth, Tim, Central Fla.	.361	169	60	61	8	2	3	39	45
Hart, Dickie, Fla. Atlantic	.361	219	74	79	20	2	4	44	20
Kirkland, Derrel, Troy St.	.361	191	45	69	7	0	11	45	0
Grant, Sam, Jack. St.	.360	189	45	68	22	0	3	36	4
Wiley, Chris, Campbell	.354	127	22	45	6	0	2	17	0
Wicklund, Aaron, Centenary	.352	176	31	62	9	0	1	30	6
Burns, Kevan, Troy State	.350	226	71	79	11	1	22	62	5
Roper, Zack, Fla. Atlantic	.350	214	59	75	11	3	12	55	9
Vollstedt, John, Jacksonville	.349	218	70	76	12	1	8	41	33
McDonough, James, Mercer	.347	202	57	70	15	0	9	38	14
Langston, Jay, Ga. State	.343	216	45	74	20	0	16	70	7
French, Ned, Stetson	.341	208	51	71	15	0	4	33	25
Nebel, Jeff, Mercer	.339	218	55	74	19	2	10	63	5
Clayton, Chris, Mercer	.338	225	55	76	8	1	20	74	8
Doudt, Anthony, Fla. Atl.	.333	213	41	71	18	1	16	56	1
Hess, Merritt, Centenary	.333	150	36	50	8	0	0	20	9
Rinaldi, Vinnie, Stetson	.333	159	31	53	6	1	11	37	5
Rowe, Ricky, Troy State	.333	234	64	78	18	1	14	51	30
Youngbauer, Scott, Ga. St.	.333	213	34	71	16	1	4	42	10
Gregorio, Tom, Troy State	.332	211	47	70	12	0	15	48	2
Stryhas, Paul, Fla. Atlantic	.332	223	49	74	21	1	11	75	0
Hess, Merritt, Centenary	.331	151	36	40	8	0	0	20	9
Murphy, Tommy, Fla. Atl.	.330	209	57	69	18	2	11	37	13
Trujillo, Ivan, Cent. Fla.	.329	173	38	57	7	5	2	25	18
Crookes, Kyle, Centenary	.325	162	29	51	17	5	4	39	2
#Soto, Jorge, Troy State	.289	194	61	56	6	0	26	72	3

INDIVIDUAL PITCHING LEADERS
(Minimum 50 Innings)

	W	L	ERA	G	SV	IP	H	BB	SO
Moser, Todd, Fla. Atlantic	15	1	2.34	19	0	104	96	31	130
Arnold, Jason, Central Fla.	7	4	2.67	24	8	57	47	29	75
Gauger, Mike, Fla. Atlantic	6	0	2.73	28	0	53	41	25	54
Cali, Carmen, Fla. Atlantic	9	5	2.99	17	1	84	71	52	89
Mattioni, Nick, Fla. Atlantic	6	3	3.40	17	0	53	54	27	54
DiNardo, Lenny, Stetson	9	6	3.78	19	0	95	99	38	98
Ebanks, Palmer, Jacksonville	10	6	3.86	22	0	126	138	33	82
Rankin, David, Central Fla.	8	5	3.94	17	0	103	114	29	95
Williams, Bryan, Jacksonville	5	3	3.96	16	0	52	52	24	40
Alford, Ryan, Troy State	5	3	4.05	20	1	53	54	22	52
Porter, Scott, Jacksonville	4	5	4.22	35	11	53	47	26	78

WEST COAST CONFERENCE

WEST	Conference		Overall	
	W	L	W	L
*Loyola Marymount	18	12	33	28
Portland	16	14	23	28
Saint Mary's	14	16	22	32
Santa Clara	11	19	20	36
COAST	W	L	W	L
Pepperdine	21	9	46	16
Gonzaga	14	14	27	23
San Diego	13	16	28	27
San Francisco	11	18	21	34

ALL-CONFERENCE TEAM: C—Dane Sardinha, So., Pepperdine. **1B**—Travis Kermode, Sr., Saint Mary's. **2B**—Damon Katz, Jr., Pepperdine. **3B**—Taggert Bozied, So., San Francisco. **SS**—Bo Hart, Sr., Gonzaga. **OF**—Kevin Taylor, Sr., Gonzaga; Jason Bay, Jr., Gonzaga; Kevin Reese, Jr., San Diego. **Util**—Anthony Angel, Jr., Loyola Marymount; G.J. Raymundo, Jr., Pepperdine. **P**—Billy Traber, So., Loyola Marymount; Jay Adams, So., Pepperdine; Jay Gehrke, Jr., Pepperdine.

Player of the Year: Taggert Bozied, San Francisco. **Pitcher of the Year**: Jay Adams, Pepperdine. **Co-Freshmen of the Year**: Greg Sain, San Diego; Dan Haren, Pepperdine. **Coach of the Year**: Frank Sanchez, Pepperdine.

INDIVIDUAL BATTING LEADERS
(Minimum 125 At-Bats)

	AVG	AB	R	H	2B	3B	HR	RBI	SB
Bozied, Taggert, San Fran.	.412	204	71	84	13	2	30	82	7
Taylor, Kevin, Gonzaga	.384	216	64	83	13	5	3	47	7
Raymundo, G.J., Pepperdine	.379	219	60	83	15	3	16	68	0
Reese, Kevin, San Diego	.372	231	67	86	15	5	16	51	11
Fiore, Curt, LMU	.366	243	54	89	17	2	8	44	10
Sardinha, Dane, Pepperdine	.365	260	51	95	26	2	15	63	5
Evans, Austin, Pepperdine	.362	149	41	54	9	2	0	16	20
Bay, Jason, Gonzaga	.360	200	65	72	11	4	20	74	6
Stokey, Adam, Gonzaga	.353	204	50	72	20	0	15	67	2
Leuthard, Alan, San Diego	.345	142	21	49	9	0	3	28	1
Riordan, Matt, LMU	.344	262	53	90	21	2	6	42	21
Katz, Damon, Pepperdine	.343	216	29	74	11	2	5	48	4
Sain, Greg, San Diego	.339	233	45	79	21	1	12	66	11
Clements, Andrew, San Fran.	.338	160	31	54	12	0	3	24	12
Walter, Scott, LMU	.337	255	49	86	19	0	9	47	12
Queen, Matt, Santa Clara	.333	204	25	68	8	0	8	39	2
Cliffords, Woody, Pepperdine	.330	218	44	72	14	2	2	41	10
Liosi, Chris, San Diego	.330	203	54	67	7	1	4	21	14
Omori, Gregg, San Fran.	.326	218	49	71	14	1	8	46	4
Cohan, Olin, St. Mary's	.325	194	27	63	11	1	2	27	4
Angel, Anthony, LMU	.322	245	46	79	16	1	4	38	7
Pritchard, Jeff, San Fran.	.321	212	33	68	10	1	3	37	6
Walsh, Pat, San Fran.	.320	203	37	65	12	1	3	30	16
Sulentor, Joe, LMU	.315	241	39	76	15	0	5	33	6
Pitney, Jared, Pepperdine	.314	242	47	76	16	2	4	51	2
Powell, Ryan, Portland	.314	191	43	60	15	1	4	32	9
Maffei, David, LMU	.312	144	33	45	6	0	4	23	9
#Gavin Hare, Portland	.308	211	39	65	13	0	0	23	31

INDIVIDUAL PITCHING LEADERS
(Minimum 50 Innings)

	W	L	ERA	G	SV	IP	H	BB	SO
#Gehrke, Jay, Pepperdine	1	1	0.86	31	18	31	19	12	40
Adams, Jay, Pepperdine	11	3	2.56	18	0	120	114	19	91
Bennett, Steve, Gonzaga	6	1	2.94	13	1	64	51	35	61
Haren, Daniel, Pepperdine	10	3	3.08	19	0	108	105	27	77
Graham, Brian, Portland	9	4	3.59	17	0	98	86	32	80
Rust, Evan, Saint Mary's	6	6	3.67	16	0	81	77	33	43
Tucker, Brad, Pepperdine	9	3	4.09	20	0	112	105	48	68
Traber, Billy, LMU	8	6	4.20	20	1	120	135	37	135
Hertel, Jason, Portland	1	5	4.21	17	3	68	90	17	40
Crudale, Mike, Santa Clara	4	7	4.25	17	1	91	95	26	71

TRANSAMERICA CONFERENCE (continued)

Nebel, Jeff, Mercer	10	3	4.28	20	0	107	116	38	104	
Ray, James, Jacksonville	7	1	4.36	20	0	85	87	39	59	
Hepler, Wes, Campbell	5	2	4.57	19	0	89	101	33	59	
Regilio, Nick, Jacksonville	7	2	4.58	13	0	73	77	29	66	
Jackson, Dan, Fla. Atlantic	10	2	4.61	17	0	96	88	55	126	
Lindsey, Michael, Jack. State	5	3	4.75	16	1	53	54	22	45	
Russ, Jason, Troy State	6	6	4.84	21	0	102	115	45	108	
Page, Jason, Mercer	6	3	5.20	30	4	71	76	46	74	

Bonilla, Ben, LMU	7	6	4.27	20	0	99	113	31	73
Morgan-Voyce, Jason, St. M.	6	7	4.38	17	1	123	137	16	59
Jackson, Stosh, Portland	5	3	4.55	14	0	85	99	34	72
Gray, Kevin, San Diego	7	2	4.56	23	1	77	82	33	41
Boyanich, Vince, Santa Clara	2	6	4.57	18	0	89	88	42	53
Amundson, Mike, San Diego	6	5	5.04	19	0	104	119	45	52
Thogersen, Chris, San Fran.	4	4	5.07	11	0	72	86	31	48
Hamilton, Ryan, San Diego	3	6	5.19	18	3	59	69	21	56
Schultz, Mike, LMU	7	6	5.20	19	0	123	138	64	104

WESTERN ATHLETIC CONFERENCE

	Conference		Overall	
*Rice	25	5	59	15
Texas Christian	19	10	32	26
San Jose State	16	11	30	26
Nevada-Las Vegas	16	14	27	34
Hawaii	15	14	37	20
New Mexico	14	15	29	30
Fresno State	14	16	33	30
San Diego State	14	16	27	32
Brigham Young	12	17	26	31
Utah	8	20	22	30
Air Force	5	20	19	32

ALL-CONFERENCE TEAM: C—Mark Silva, Sr., Texas Christian. **1B**—Jamie Aloy, Jr., Hawaii. **2B**—Ryan Pond, Sr., Brigham Young. **3B**—Royce Huffman, Sr., Texas Christian. **SS**—Damon Thames, Sr., Rice. **OF**—Ryan Ludwick, Jr., Nevada-Las Vegas; Charles Williams, Jr., Rice; Anthony Acevedo, Jr., Fresno State. **DH**—Justin Berg, Sr., Rice. **P**—Mario Ramos, Jr., Rice. **RP**—Jesse Kurtz-Nicholl, Sr., Rice.

Player of the Year: Royce Huffman, Texas Christian. **Co-Freshmen of the Year**: Tom Creighton, Fresno State; Junior Ruiz, San Jose State. **Coach of the Year**: Wayne Graham, Rice.

INDIVIDUAL BATTING LEADERS
(Minimum 125 At-Bats)

	AVG	AB	R	H	2B	3B	HR	RBI	SB
Thiessen, Mike, Air Force	.424	191	71	81	15	3	12	50	9
Huffman, Royce, TCU	.422	223	75	94	20	3	15	64	6
Carville, Ryan, Air Force	.407	189	52	77	20	3	9	52	12
Ford, Will, Rice	.398	264	65	105	24	3	12	74	4
Johnson, Gary, BYU	.388	183	55	71	17	1	13	58	8
Gillette, Chris, UNLV	.387	204	53	79	21	2	3	42	15
Acevedo, Anthony, Fresno St.	.383	240	66	92	23	5	6	61	4
Ludwick, Ryan, UNLV	.381	236	70	90	18	4	13	69	19
Thames, Damon, Rice	.377	313	86	118	24	6	11	72	14
Johnerson, Ryan, Utah	.376	210	60	79	16	4	15	44	16
Armstrong, Chris, NM	.371	221	57	82	15	2	7	48	4
Okano, Mark, New Mexico	.371	205	51	76	17	0	4	31	13
Jensen, David, BYU	.368	174	39	64	23	0	6	35	4
Candelaria, Scott, NM	.366	262	58	96	20	3	7	62	5
Robbins, Cory, New Mexico	.366	232	49	85	15	2	17	73	13
Williams, Charles, Rice	.366	317	82	116	22	9	7	50	10
Takamori, Sean, Hawaii	.363	212	58	77	8	2	0	33	34
Aloy, Jamie, Hawaii	.358	179	50	64	17	2	4	39	4
Stolley, Mike, Air Force	.358	137	38	49	11	3	2	16	2
Martines, Scooter, Hawaii	.355	186	29	66	11	2	1	46	1
Campbell, Mike, New Mexico	.354	243	50	86	21	4	5	40	22
Ruiz, Junior, San Jose St.	.354	206	45	73	12	4	2	29	9
Adolph, Chris, UNLV	.352	236	63	83	15	6	2	44	15
Garcia, Nick, Fresno St.	.349	189	36	66	13	3	6	39	1
Hertel, Brian, UNLV	.348	230	48	80	9	4	11	42	8
Sisk, Aaron, New Mexico	.348	256	67	89	22	1	20	76	4
Kaup, Nate, UNLV	.345	174	33	60	10	1	6	36	6
DeMarco, Tony, UNLV	.344	212	37	73	14	1	4	49	0
Delliston, Shane, BYU	.341	223	57	76	18	0	5	43	8
Hillberg, Chad, Air Force	.340	191	39	65	13	2	2	33	17
Pond, Ryan, BYU	.340	209	62	71	13	1	23	65	6
Creighton, Tom, Fresno St.	.335	200	49	67	3	1	0	26	8
Stoner, Matt, UNLV	.335	224	48	75	14	2	3	33	2
Dennis, Dee, New Mexico	.332	205	40	68	14	1	6	37	0
Sarabia, Eliott, UNLV	.332	208	43	69	7	1	1	39	12
Davies, Michael, BYU	.331	136	20	45	10	0	2	25	1
Elzy, Steve, New Mexico	.331	139	33	46	12	0	4	28	3
Wallace, Eric, Utah	.330	182	41	60	17	0	14	33	9
Boomsma, Mike, Air Force	.329	149	39	45	10	3	4	29	5
Gray, Jason, Rice	.327	294	74	96	12	8	20	72	19
Hamilton, Mark, TCU	.327	159	39	52	11	0	7	39	2
Yamaguchi, Lon, NM	.327	254	75	83	12	5	5	54	13

INDIVIDUAL PITCHING LEADERS
(Minimum 50 Innings)

	W	L	ERA	G	SV	IP	H	BB	SO
Baugh, Kenny, Rice	12	2	**2.26**	20	0	112	94	46	103
Ramos, Mario, Rice	13	3	2.51	25	2	154	121	51	**146**
Ho, Randon, Hawaii	6	3	2.57	15	1	63	57	27	55
Atchison, Scott, TCU	10	4	2.58	15	0	101	101	26	115
Kurtz-Nicholl, Jesse, Rice	7	1	2.61	38	**8**	76	68	25	100
LaCorte, Vince, San Jose St.	9	2	2.85	17	2	101	95	26	99
Gwyn, Marc, Rice	7	1	3.22	25	2	81	73	36	74
Murphy, Steve, San Jose St.	5	5	3.67	16	0	69	64	33	43
#Smith, Jimmy, UNLV	0	3	4.03	25	**8**	22	32	5	16
Snider, Rich, Hawaii	6	6	4.24	27	6	81	85	28	48
Bergman, Dusty, Hawaii	4	4	4.35	17	0	68	74	24	47
Harang, Aaron, San Diego St.	8	4	4.47	18	0	109	116	47	101
Smith, Hans, Fresno St.	5	5	4.48	38	1	72	77	16	60
Bradshaw, Chris, TCU	3	4	4.64	15	0	74	75	34	45
Aloy, Jamie, Hawaii	7	6	4.74	15	0	89	101	14	63
Nichols, Jeff, Rice	**15**	4	4.84	25	0	138	165	51	121
Rogelstad, Jeremy, San Jose	6	7	4.85	17	0	106	121	24	89
Scheffels, Bill, UNLV	5	5	4.98	24	0	98	115	36	99
Graham, Tom, Fresno St.	8	6	4.99	20	0	128	149	31	109
Rowe, Casey, Fresno St.	7	9	5.24	17	0	100	102	39	80
Page, Brandon, Utah	6	5	5.57	17	0	84	103	34	59
Samadani, A.J., San Diego St.	7	4	5.96	29	4	74	81	40	80
McCulloch, Andy, UNLV	4	8	5.98	16	0	90	117	27	55

INDEPENDENTS

	Overall	
	W	L
Miami (Fla.)	50	13
Grand Canyon	36	17
Texas-Pan American	30	22
Cal State Northridge	27	29
C.W. Post	15	28
New York Tech	15	32
Pace	14	35
Southern Utah	14	35
Hawaii-Hilo	9	37

INDIVIDUAL BATTING LEADERS
(Minimum 100 At-Bats)

	AVG	AB	R	H	2B	3B	HR	RBI	SB
Woods, Blake, GC	.404	225	55	91	20	0	1	37	0
Kruse, Brian, Southern Utah	.398	196	49	78	12	3	8	43	15
Hellier, Brian, Grand Canyon	.393	229	58	90	21	2	14	60	1
Hill, Bobby, Miami	.391	215	77	84	14	3	10	30	52
Urtnowski, Mike, C.W. Post	.390	159	39	62	11	1	10	58	0
Garza, Steve, UTPA	.381	168	31	64	16	2	1	39	13
Jacobson, Russ, Miami	.380	150	42	57	13	1	14	41	1
Siano, Frank, Pace	.377	122	25	46	10	0	5	28	3
Benson, Tim, C.W. Post	.374	147	29	55	12	0	1	33	0
Mosley, Trevor, Pace	.371	159	42	59	13	1	11	41	0
Rodriguez, Mike, Miami	.371	167	39	62	11	3	1	34	18
Penick, D.J., Southern Utah	.368	190	35	70	15	1	9	58	0
Crespo, Manny, Miami	.364	173	49	63	11	0	12	54	12
Cox, Ryan, C.W. Post	.364	162	41	59	10	1	3	25	5
Curtis, Bill, Grand Canyon	.363	201	49	73	15	1	7	50	5
Critchett, Buddy, GC	.357	140	28	50	9	1	1	23	3
Esquivel, Lale, Miami	.354	229	52	81	16	1	13	58	6
Jaworski, Jason, Pace	.349	195	37	68	11	0	2	40	2
Nettles, Marcus, Miami	.349	109	29	38	3	1	2	20	20
Patrick, Kevin, CS-North.	.349	195	49	68	14	1	7	30	2
Rodriguez, Javier, Miami	.345	139	29	48	3	1	2	22	5
Wigand, Tom, C.W. Post	.340	162	46	55	3	0	11	39	6

INDIVIDUAL PITCHING LEADERS
(Minimum 40 Innings)

	W	L	ERA	G	SV	IP	H	BB	SO
Neu, Michael, Miami	3	1	2.94	46	16	67	36	30	110
Santos, Alex, Miami	13	3	2.95	20	0	122	106	46	144
Gil, David, Miami	12	0	3.19	17	0	93	86	36	103
Curtis, Bill, Grand Canyon	10	2	3.29	13	0	88	102	12	46
DeBiase, Jim, CS Northridge	9	6	3.67	17	0	88	99	35	74
Siff, Ben, Hawaii-Hilo	0	6	3.77	9	0	57	71	12	28
Taber, Justin, Pace	3	4	3.77	11	0	57	59	22	39
Roque, Darryl, Miami	5	1	3.90	13	0	55	47	11	47
Duprey, Hector, C.W. Post	3	6	3.93	14	2	55	65	18	70
Vazquez, Vince, Miami	6	1	4.02	31	2	47	39	28	55
Ortiz, Omar, UTPA	6	5	4.32	15	0	102	87	48	132
Kaholo, Rickard, Hawaii-Hilo	3	4	4.41	11	0	51	55	18	26
Gray, Trevor, CS Northridge	4	2	4.86	18	3	54	62	22	39

SMALLCOLLEGES

Bat controversy rears its head in Division III playoffs

The uncertainty stemming from the NCAA's bat standards controversy spilled onto the field most at the Division III level in 1999.

Two conferences, the New Jersey Athletic Conference (NJAC) and the Wisconsin Intercollegiate Athletics Conference (WIAC), played their regular seasons with wood bats. When their teams reached the postseason, chaos ensued.

Wisconsin-Oshkosh, ranked No. 1 and 31-1 entering the postseason, and Wisconsin-Stevens Point played their regional with wood bats while Minnesota schools St. Thomas and St. Scholastica played with aluminum. Oshkosh fell to St. Thomas twice by one run and failed to qualify for the national tournament.

"I expected teams to use wood bats," said Oshkosh coach Tom Lechnir, whose team had a 1.01 ERA during the regular season. "But when it got to the regional, the topic never came up.

"We were definitely at a competitive disadvantage. It's disheartening, because we had a great chance to win a national championship."

Meanwhile, St. Thomas reached the Division III World Series, where it lost 1-0 in the championship game to North Carolina Wesleyan as Sean Fleming and Buddy Hernandez combined on a six-hitter.

The NJAC, whose members had voted to not participate in postseason play if aluminum bats were used, got luckier. Because all six teams in the Mid-Atlantic regional had used wood during the regular season, four NJAC schools participated in the postseason. William Paterson (N.J.) won the regional, then used aluminum—against the NJAC's wishes—in the World Series, going 2-2 and losing to N.C. Wesleyan in the semifinal.

"The statements are already made, and people aren't listening," Paterson coach Jeff Albies said. "We might face some sanctions, but I've got to cross that bridge later."

DIVISION II

California's Chico State survived a three-run first inning by Kennesaw State (Ga.) and a two-hour, 43-minute rain delay to capture its second Division II title in three years. The Wildcats (50-17) went through the tournament undefeated.

Catcher Casey Glynn led Chico State to an 11-5 victory in the deciding game by breaking a 3-3 tie with a two-run double. Wildcats starter Jason Cly recovered from his rough start to hold Kennesaw State (49-14) to one hit over the next four innings to earn the win. All-American reliever Brian Grover worked the final four innings to pick up his ninth save of the year.

Kennesaw State lost in the final for the second straight year, but along the way senior outfielder Jason Jones set a new Division II hitting-streak record at 39 games.

Saint Rose (N.Y.) senior righthander Nate Kosoc became the fourth pitcher to share the Division II sin-

gle-game strikeout record in an 8-3 win against New Jersey Tech. Kosoc had 21 punchouts.

NAIA

The NAIA World Series was played in Jupiter, Fla., but had a decidedly Idaho flavor. Traditional power Lewis-Clark State knocked off defending champion Albertson 7-2 in the championship game for its 10th World Series crown since 1984. The two teams, meeting for the 10th time in 1999, split two earlier games in the double-elimination tournament.

The Warriors (57-14) gave up just five earned runs in 54 innings over six games to win the national championship.

Mount Vernon Nazarene righthander Andrew Heimbach was selected Baseball America's Small College Player of the Year. An eighth-round pick of the Red Sox, he went 13-2 with a 1.54 ERA and 141 strikeouts in 93 innings.

Andy Heimbach

He threw a perfect game against Malone (Ohio) College on April 27 and set a college career record with 16 shutouts, six in 1999.

JUNIOR COLLEGE

In an all-Texas showdown, Grayson County workhorse Matt Gawer beat San Jacinto 12-7 in the championship game of the Junior College World Series. It was Grayson County's first national championship and came three years after the school reinstituted its baseball program.

Gawer went seven innings in the final, two days after throwing a seven-inning, 14-0 shutout over San Jacinto.

Sacramento City repeated as California Community College champion, scoring three times in the ninth inning to defeat Cypress 4-3. It was the fifth state title for Sac City (42-7).

Seminole State (Okla.) catcher Kade Johnson was selected Baseball America's Junior College Player of the Year. A University of Texas transfer, he broke the national juco record with 38 home runs. The previous record of 31 was set in 1982 by Seminole State's Jamie Doughty, but that mark was broken earlier in

Kade Johnson

1999 by Lamar (Colo.) CC's Dan Wells, who hit 32. Johnson, a second-round pick of the Brewers, hit .434.

Seminole State (58-8) set a national record with 187 homers in 66 games but went 2-2 at the Junior College World Series. Head coach Lloyd Simmons ended the year with 1,549 wins, more than any college coach.

College Baseball

NCAA DIVISION II

WORLD SERIES

Site: Montgomery, Ala.
Participants: Adelphi, N.Y. (31-15); Ashland, Ohio (45-14); Carson-Newman, Tenn. (42-12); Chico State, Calif. (46-17); Kennesaw State, Ga. (46-12); North Alabama (44-10); Rockhurst, Mo. (34-16); West Virginia State (33-9).
Champion: Chico State (5-0).
Runner-Up: Kennesaw State (3-2).
Outstanding Player: John-Eric Hernandez, rhp, Chico State.

ALL-AMERICA TEAM

Pos.	Player, School	Yr.	AVG	HR	RBI
C	Jake Huff, Mesa State (Colo.)	Sr.	.400	17	89
1B	Mike Norfleet, Central Missouri State	Sr.	.435	14	79
2B	Nate Duvall, Mesa State (Colo.)	Sr.	.422	10	55
3B	Mike Simpson, Rockhurst (Mo.)	Sr.	.437	21	87
SS	Josh Willingham, North Alabama	So.	.489	15	89
IF	Jamie Detillion, Ashland (Ohio)	Jr.	.403	23	89
OF	Jason Jones, Kennesaw State (Ga.)	Sr.	.414	25	93
	Dee Haynes, Delta State (Miss.)	So.	.444	26	92
	Josh Rabe, Quincy (Ill.)	So.	.389	10	56
	Mike Moeller, Concordia (N.Y.)	Jr.	.427	19	81
DH	Chance Melvin, West Alabama	Sr.	.435	15	83

		Yr.	W	L	ERA
SP	B.J. Leach, Florida Southern	Sr.	11	2	2.05
	Jeremy McClain, Delta State (Miss.)	Sr.	15	0	2.16
	Tony Pierce, Columbus State (Ga.)	Sr.	12	1	2.07
	Andrew Niederst, Ashland (Ohio)	So.	15	4	4.61
RP	Brian Grover, Chico State (Calif.)	Jr.	4	1	2.56

Player of the Year: B.J. Leach, rhp/2b, Florida Southern (.418-10-55).

NATIONAL LEADERS

BATTING AVERAGE
(Minimum 125 at-bats)

Player, School	AB	H	AVG
Jamie Tucker, Arkansas-Monticello	160	80	.500
Edward Taylor, Albany State (Ga.)	144	71	.493
John Willingham, North Alabama	190	93	.489
Aaron Merhoff, Texas Lutheran	176	86	.489
Brian Arant, Central Oklahoma	133	62	.466
Casey Baker, Morningside (Iowa)	139	64	.460
Mal Higgins, Franklin Pierce (N.H.)	133	61	.459
Marc Thompson, Abilene Christian (Texas)	201	92	.458
Josh Signs, Tusculum (Tenn.)	138	63	.457
Matt Teahan, UC Riverside	180	82	.455
Dee Haynes, Delta State (Miss.)	207	93	.444

Department Leaders: Batting

Dept.	Player, School	G	Total
R	Willie Harris, Kennesaw State (Ga.)	63	86
H	Brian Krot, St. Leo (Fla.)	57	102
TB	Dee Haynes, Delta State (Miss.)	53	197
2B	Jeff Stevens, UC Riverside	50	28
	Chance Melvin, West Alabama	56	28
3B	B.J. Garrison, Florida Southern	57	9
HR	Dee Haynes, Delta State (Miss.)	53	26
RBI	Jason Jones, Kennesaw State (Ga.)	63	93
SB	Rich Devino, Emporia State (Kan.)	41	57

EARNED RUN AVERAGE
(Minimum 50 innings)

Player, School	IP	ER	ERA
Chris McGee, Mansfield (Pa.)	51	5	0.88
Kris Kann, Mansfield (Pa.)	57	8	1.26
Chris Swiatkiewicz, Minn.-Duluth	79	12	1.37
Jeff Tyler, Adelphi (N.Y.)	84	14	1.50
Keith Matlock, Pittsburg State (Kan.)	52	9	1.57
Chris Brown, Bloomsburg (Pa.)	79	14	1.59
Eric Barr, Lock Haven (Pa.)	61	11	1.62
Trevor Bullock, Nebraska-Kearney	66	12	1.64
Bill Bendis, Edinboro (Pa.)	60	11	1.65
Jim Schneider, Dowling (N.Y.)	75	14	1.68

Department Leaders: Pitching

Dept.	Player, School	G	Total
W	Jeremy McClain, Delta State (Miss.)	17	15
	Andrew Niederst, Ashland (Ohio)	28	15
SV	Matt Greenwood, North Alabama	28	12
	John Butler, Carson-Newman (Tenn.)	26	12
SO	Tony Pierce, Columbus State (Ga.)	15	146

NCAA DIVISION III

WORLD SERIES

Site: Salem, Va.
Participants: Aurora, Ill. (38-6); Brandeis, Mass. (33-4); California Lutheran (31-12); Cortland State, N.Y. (35-8); Marietta, Ohio (49-6); North Carolina Wesleyan (37-9); William Paterson, N.J. (29-12); St. Thomas, Minn. (39-5).
Champion: North Carolina Wesleyan (5-0).
Runner-Up: St. Thomas, Minn. (3-2)
Outstanding Player: Barry Blake, ss, North Carolina Wesleyan.

ALL-AMERICA TEAM

Pos.	Player, School	Yr.	AVG	HR	RBI
C	Josh Streit, Marietta (Ohio)	Sr.	.368	13	68
	Casey Kopitzke, Wis.-Oshkosh	Jr.	.366	9	38
1B	Eric Zaleski, Aurora (Ill.)	Sr.	.448	15	67
2B	Keith Heid, Rensselaer (N.Y.)	Sr.	.486	7	38
3B	Dean Muthig, Carthage (Wis.)	Sr.	.405	13	67
SS	Jim Deschaine, Brandeis (Mass.)	Jr.	.448	18	70
OF	Corey Adams, Southern Maine	Sr.	.425	2	32
	Glen Braun, Carthage (Wis.)	Sr.	.458	21	80
	Matt Gelotti, Southwestern (Texas)	Sr.	.455	18	79
	Craig Kerner, Cortland State (N.Y.)	So.	.351	6	43
DH	Ryan Dowdy, Southwestern (Texas)	Jr.	.404	17	84

		Yr.	W	L	ERA
P	David Bradley, Marietta (Ohio)	Sr.	18	2	2.16
	Matt Deegan, Aurora (Ill.)	Sr.	10	1	2.60
	Chris Olean, St. Thomas (Minn.)	Sr.	9	2	0.60
	Jayson Sigley, N.C. Wesleyan	Sr.	9	1	3.01

Player of the Year: Glen Braun, of, Carthage.

NATIONAL LEADERS

BATTING AVERAGE
(Minimum 100 at-bats)

Player, School	AB	H	AVG
Dave DeCew, Bowdoin (Maine)	103	57	.553
Eric Sorensen, John Jay (N.Y.)	106	53	.500
Brad Mercer, Muskingum (Ohio)	142	69	.486
Pat Sweeney, Frostburg State (Md.)	108	52	.481
Bran Slekes, Union (N.Y.)	106	51	.481
Steve Oursler, St. Mary's (Md.)	131	62	.473
Mike Osso, Curry (Mass.)	119	56	.471
Bubba Gentry, Southwestern (Texas)	137	64	.467
Steve Opferman, Bethany (W.Va.)	131	61	.466
Geoff Eriksen, Salem State (Mass.)	142	66	.465
Matt Faulken, St. Thomas (Minn.)	155	72	.465
Gordon Daily, Case Western Reserve (Ohio)	123	57	.463
Adam Olow, Chapman (Calif.)	177	82	.463

Department Leaders: Batting

Dept.	Player, School	G	Total
R	Matt Gelotti, Southwestern (Texas)	51	88
H	Matt Gelotti, Southwestern (Texas)	51	91
TB	Matt Gelotti, Southwestern (Texas)	51	189
2B	Eric Sorensen, John Jay (N.Y.)	31	25
	Jeremy Schlosser, Cal Lutheran	47	25
3B	Matt Gelotti, Southwestern (Texas)	51	12
HR	Glen Braun, Carthage (Wis.)	52	21
RBI	Ryan Dowdy, Southwestern (Texas)	51	84
SB	Mark Schorsch, Mount St. Joseph (Ohio)	43	59

EARNED RUN AVERAGE
(Minimum 40 innings)

Player, School	IP	ER	ERA
Mike Szalkiewicz, Scranton (Pa.)	48	3	0.57
Chris Olean, St. Thomas (Minn.)	89	6	0.60
Craig Glysch, Wisconsin-Oshkosh	71	6	0.76
Matt Wiatrak, Ursinus (Pa.)	75	7	0.84
Kelly Mulroy, Wisconsin-Whitewater	47	5	0.96
Brent Fuchs, Western Maryland	63	7	1.01
Andy Elskamp, Wisconsin-La Crosse	71	8	1.01
Jason Wiertel, Carthage (Wis.)	52	6	1.03
Jacob Chavez, Grinnell (Iowa)	66	8	1.09
Drew Chiesa, Gettysburg (Pa.)	79	10	1.14

Department Leaders: Pitching

Dept.	Player, School	G	Total
W	Dave Bradley, Marietta (Ohio)	22	18
SV	Bubba Gentry, Southwestern (Texas)	24	10
SO	Tom Canale, Cal Lutheran	17	133

NAIA

WORLD SERIES

Site: Jupiter, Fla.
Participants: No. 3 Albertson, Idaho (45-17); No. 5 Belle-vue, Neb. (59-9); No. 6 Birmingham-Southern, Ala. (47-16); No. 9 Culver-Stockton, Mo. (34-17); No. 8 Embry-Riddle, Fla. (44-10); No. 4 Dallas Baptist (46-17); No. 10 Dominican, N.Y. (36-19); No. 7 Indiana Tech (50-20); No. 1 Lewis-Clark State, Idaho (52-13); No. 2 Oklahoma City (56-12).
Champion: Lewis-Clark State (5-1).
Runner-Up: Albertson (5-2).
Outstanding Player: Jason Ellison, of, Lewis-Clark State.

ALL-AMERICA TEAM

Pos.	Player, School	Yr.	AVG	HR	RBI
C	Justin Duarte, Azusa Pacific (Calif.)	Sr.	.358	18	63
	Bryan Grogan, Montreat (N.C.)	Sr.	.436	9	81
1B	John Knott, Azusa Pacific (Calif.)	Sr.	.411	14	68
2B	Joe Bressanelli, Robert Morris (Ill.)	Sr.	.532	12	51
3B	Daniel Sanchez, Williams Baptist (Ark.)	Jr.	.515	14	85
SS	Julio Campos, Missouri Baptist	Jr.	.419	8	40
IF	Enrique Lazu, Campbellsville (Ky.)	Sr.	.491	10	70
OF	Eric Brown, Bellevue (Neb.)	So.	.498	14	82
	Rick Nadeau, Oklahoma City	Sr.	.491	27	110
	Kurt Fillmore, The Master's (Calif.)	Jr.	.394	8	37
	Aaron Merhoff, Texas Lutheran	Sr.	.489	21	85
DH	Dan Swift, Mayville State (N.D.)	Sr.	.416	21	82

		Yr.	W	L	ERA
P	Andy Heimbach, Mt. Vernon Naz. (Ohio) .	Jr.	13	2	1.54
	Jay King, Mobile (Ala.)	Jr.	11	1	2.20
	Jonathon Rouwenhorst, Biola (Calif.) ..	So.	9	2	2.14
	Luke Martin, Embry-Riddle (Fla.)	Jr.	9	2	2.14

Player of the Year: Andy Heimbach, rhp, Mount Vernon Nazarene.

NATIONAL LEADERS

BATTING AVERAGE
(Minimum 125 at-bats)

Player, School	AB	H	AVG
Joe Bressanelli, Robert Morris (Ill.)	123	66	.532
Daniel Sanchez, Williams Baptist (Ark.)	196	101	.515
Eric Brown, Bellevue (Neb.)	227	113	.498
Enrique Lazu, Campbellsville (Ky.)	173	85	.491
Rick Nadeau, Oklahoma City	230	113	.491
Aaron Merhoff, Texas Lutheran	176	86	.489
Randy Ruiz, Bellevue (Neb.)	217	104	.479
Arturo Ramos, St. Thomas (Fla.)	222	106	.477
Nate Barnett, George Fox (Ore.)	152	71	.467
Kevin Coe, Bellevue (Neb.)	240	112	.467
Chris Stanifer, Mt. Vernon Naz. (Ohio)	201	91	.453
Trent Coffee, Lindsey Wilson (Ky.)	169	76	.450
Branden Florence, Albertson (Idaho)	261	117	.448
Travis Bailey, Palm Beach Atlantic. (Fla.)	191	85	.445
Steve Leist, 3b, Lubbock Christian	136	60	.441

Department Leaders: Batting

Dept.	Player, School	G	Total
R	Jeff Pietraszko, Oklahoma City	68	97
H	Branden Florence, Albertson (Idaho)	68	117
2B	Cle Schramm, Bellevue (Neb.)	69	27
3B	Kevin Coe, Bellevue (Neb.)	67	13
HR	Rick Nadeau, Oklahoma City	65	27
RBI	Rick Nadeau, Oklahoma City	65	110
SB	Rob Pregnolato, Palm Beach Atlantic (Fla.)	53	69

EARNED RUN AVERAGE
(Minimum 40 innings)

Player, School	IP	ER	ERA
Andy Heimbach, Mt. Vernon Naz. (Ohio)	93	16	1.54
Dave Byard, Mt. Vernon Naz. (Ohio)	87	16	1.66
Daniel Zunker, Texas Lutheran	64	14	1.98
Jonathon Rouwenhorst, Biola (Calif.)	101	23	2.05
Matt O'Neill, St. Xavier (Ill.)	103	24	2.09
Jason Pannell, Martin Methodist (Tenn.)	71	24	2.09
Luke Martin, Embry-Riddle (Fla.)	106	26	2.14
Jay King, Mobile (Ala.)	118	28	2.20
Nick Priolo, Palm Beach Atlantic (Fla.)	106	26	2.21
Craig Prifogle, Marian (Ind.)	79	20	2.27

Department Leaders: Pitching

Dept.	Player, School	G	Total
W	Tom Franklin, Birmingham-Southern	19	15
SO	Andy Heimbach, Mt. Vernon Naz. (Ohio)	15	141

JUNIOR COLLEGE

WORLD SERIES

Site: Grand Junction, Colo.
Participants: Briarcliffe, N.Y. (31-19); Central Arizona (45-17); Garden City, Kan. (32-24); Grayson County, Texas (50-13); Manatee, Fla. (51-8); Muscatine, Iowa (39-16); San Jacinto, Texas (42-11); Seminole State, Okla. (56-6); Volunteer State, Tenn. (52-11); Wallace State, Ala. (45-15).
Champion: Grayson County (5-0).
Runner-Up: San Jacinto (4-2).
Outstanding Player: Matt Gawer, lhp, Grayson County.

ALL-AMERICA TEAM

C—Kade Johnson, Seminole State (Okla.). **INF**—Nick Green, Georgia Perimeter; Trevor Mote, Yavapai (Ariz.); Terry Tiffee, Pratt (Kan.); Dan Wells, Lamar (Colo.). **OF**—Eric Huber, Alfred State (N.Y.); Lance Williams, McLennan (Texas); Dan Wright, Dixie (Utah). **DH**—Kent Brunen, Jefferson (Mo.). **P**—Mark Carter, Wallace State (Ala.); Billy Keppinger, Lake City (Fla.); Josh Shoulders, Volunteer State (Tenn.).

Player of the Year: Kade Johnson, c, Seminole State (Okla.).

NATIONAL LEADERS

BATTING AVERAGE
(Minimum 75 at-bats)

Player, School	AB	H	AVG
Gerald Crawford, Pitt County (N.C.)	79	41	.519
Oliver Lepine, Briarcliffe (N.Y.)	177	89	.503
Niko Bouzoa, Neosho County (Kan.)	152	74	.487
Luke Johnson, Triton (Ill.)	193	93	.482
Dany Scalabrini, Seminole State (Okla.)	260	122	.469
Pat Gaudreau, Briarcliffe (N.Y.)	171	80	.468
Deke DeCrow, Lamar (Colo.)	92	43	.467
Curtis Murdock, Neosho County (Kan.)	118	54	.458
Garris Gonce, Florida	186	85	.457
Dax O'Daniel, Saint Catharine (Ky.)	158	72	.456

Department Leaders: Batting

Dept.	Player, School	G	Total
HR	Kade Johnson, Seminole State (Okla.)	63	38
RBI	Billy Keppinger, Lake City (Fla.)	58	100
SB	Josh Renick, Manatee (Fla.)	60	72

EARNED RUN AVERAGE
(Minimum 50 innings)

Player, School	IP	ER	ERA
Mark Carter, Wallace State (Ala.)	107	13	1.09
Justin Hampson, Belleville Area (Ill.)	81	13	1.45
Blake Allen, Central Alabama	64	12	1.69
John Rheinecker, Belleville Area (Ill.)	80	17	1.91
Albert Montes, Grayson County (Texas)	84	18	1.93
Kris McWhirter, Volunteer State (Tenn.)	107	23	1.93

Department Leaders: Pitching

Dept.	Player, School	G	Total
W	Mark Carter, Wallace State (Ala.)	16	15
SV	Alex Messier, Briarcliffe (N.Y.)	26	18
SO	Kris McWhirter, Volunteer State (Tenn.)	15	128

NJCAA DIVISION II

WORLD SERIES

Site: Millington, Tenn.
Participants: Baltimore County, Md. (36-17); Carl Albert, Okla. (42-17); Connecticut-Avery Point (33-14); Hinds, Miss. (23-32); Kellogg, Mich. (31-19); Kirkwood, Iowa (50-5); Kishwaukee, Ill. (47-17); Northwest Shoals, Ala. (28-28).
Champion: Kishwaukee (4-0)
Runner-Up: Kellogg (4-2).
Outstanding Player: Matt Salvesen, Kishwaukee.

NJCAA DIVISION III

WORLD SERIES

Site: Batavia, N.Y.
Participants: Columbus State, Ohio (37-16); Gloucester County, N.J. (48-6); Madison Area, Wis. (34-14); Norwalk, Conn. (49-0); Penn State-Beaver (22-6); Richland, Texas (42-10); Schenectady, N.Y. (27-6); Suffolk, N.Y. (31-2).
Champion: Gloucester County (4-0).
Runner-Up: Richland (4-2).
Outstanding Player: Steve Wells, Gloucester County.

HIGH SCHOOL BASEBALL

Lassiter High benefits from powerful youth program, goes wire-to-wire to capture national high school title

BY JOHN ROYSTER

Sitting atop a pyramid of the strongest youth program in the nation, it was inevitable that a high school in Cobb County, Ga., would win the Baseball America/National High School Baseball Coaches Association national championship.

The beneficiary turned out to be Marietta's Lassiter High in 1999.

Lassiter players and those from neighboring schools in the county are veterans of the East Cobb youth program that has won national championships in most every division from Little League to Babe Ruth to AAU over the last two decades. The winning team at the '99 Connie Mack World Series included six players from Lassiter, including tournament MVP Jarrod Schmidt.

Lassiter (35-2) began and ended the 1999 high school season No. 1 in the BA/NHSBCA poll, the first team to accomplish that feat since Sarasota (Fla.) High in 1994. But it was hardly a wire-to-wire performance. The Trojans won their first two games, but then went on a three-game trip to Alabama and came home with two losses, a rainout and a No. 9 ranking.

Coach Mickey McMurtry saw it coming.

"I just thought we were ripe to lose a game," McMurtry said. "We kind of lost our focus, played a little cocky. I think our guys thought we were going to Alabama and teach them the game, which is ridiculous. I wasn't particularly surprised, but I think our kids were."

Jarrod Schmidt

Properly sobered, the Trojans won their last 33 games, their first Georgia 4-A championship and the national title. They reclaimed the No. 1 national ranking immediately after winning the state championship, and held onto it as other states completed play.

Lassiter had twice previously reached the state championship game, in 1995 and 1997, but lost on both occasions.

The Trojans left no doubt about their dominance in their last two games, sweeping Brookwood High of Snellville 10-0 and 6-0 in the state-championship series. The shutouts were pitched by righthanders Schmidt (a one-hitter) and Chad Bendinelli (a two-hitter), next-door neighbors who both signed to play college baseball at Clemson. Schmidt was drafted in the 23rd round by the Florida Marlins but didn't sign.

Schmidt and Bendinelli were two of five Lassiter players who signed with Atlantic Coast Conference schools. Catcher Tyler Parker (.391-13-44), a sixth-round pick of the New York Mets, also didn't sign and

Celebrating a state championship
. . . Turned into a national title for Lassiter High

was attending Georgia Tech. Outfielder Michael DeRosa (.476-19-51) signed with North Carolina, and shortstop Chris Goodman (.287-6-30) signed with North Carolina State.

Other Contenders

It was a good thing for Lassiter that it was so dominant in its state finals. Its closest competitor for No. 1, Bellaire High, was just as dominant in the Texas 5-A state tournament as it tried to overtake the Trojans in the final poll.

Bellaire (38-2) crushed Duncanville High 13-2 in the single-game final, winning in five innings under the Texas mercy rule. Righthander Jon Gonzalez pitched a one-hitter with eight strikeouts. Duncanville was denied in its bid to add the baseball championship to its state titles in football and basketball in the same school year.

The third-ranked team, Westminster Academy of Fort Lauderdale, was a newcomer to the poll with a familiar coach. Rich Hofman was one of the top coaches in the nation at Westminster Christian High in nearby Miami, winning the first BA/NHSBCA national championship in 1992 with shortstop Alex Rodriguez as his star pupil. He didn't expect his new school to join the national elite in his first year, but with eight transfers it went 33-2 and won the Florida 2-A title to go with the No. 3 national ranking.

Westminster Academy earned the nod as the top team in Florida when it won a late-season showdown with No. 6 ranked and 6-A state champion Wellington High, 3-0 in 10 innings.

Of the teams to crack the BA/NHSBCA Top 25, only No. 5 Rose High of Greenville, N.C., went undefeated. The Rampants (26-0) got an outstanding season from 5-foot-10 senior lefthander Ryan Gordon, who went 12-0 with a 0.27 ERA, and spun three no-hitters and three one-hitters. He also slugged 10 home runs, including two in the game that clinched Rose's second state 4-A title in three years. The Rampants also finished fifth nationally in 1997.

Arlington High of Riverside was the top-ranked team in California after winning the California Interscholastic Federation Southern section Division I championship. Ryan Christianson, who hit .519 with seven homers, was the first high school catcher drafted.

Rancho Bernardo High of San Diego, ranked No. 2 nationally in the preseason, overcame an injury-plagued season to win the San Diego CIF Division I sectional championship game and earn a final No. 35 ranking. Righthander Tom Caple, a University of Texas signee, won three of his team's four playoff games and set 17 school batting and pitching records. Star catcher Scott Heard, who was rated the nation's top junior at the start of the season, broke his wrist and returned only for the final two playoff games.

Fairless, Moegle Quit

Hofman's move wasn't the only high-profile coaching change in 1999.

Rodger Fairless, who coached Green Valley High to six straight Nevada championships through 1998, resigned shortly before the season to start a new program at the Junior College of Southern Nevada. He later resigned from that job as well, citing health concerns.

Fairless was a high school coach for 20 seasons, first at Valley High in Las Vegas, where his players included future major leaguers Greg Maddux, Tyler Houston and Doug Mirabelli. His Green Valley alumni included first-round picks Chad Hermansen (Pirates, 1995) and Mike Nannini (Astros, 1998).

Bobby Moegle of Monterey High in Lubbock, Texas, who ranked second nationally in career wins, retired after the season. Moegle won more than 1,100 games and four state championships, and was a state runner-up five times.

The Draft's Impact

High school players had a significant impact on the 1999 draft, reaching uncharted territory in a couple of areas.

Six of the first eight players selected came from high school, including No. 1 overall pick Josh Hamilton, an outfielder from Athens Drive High in Raleigh, N.C.

Of the 1,474 players taken overall, 630 came from

Baseball America's final 1999 Top 50, selected in conjunction with the National High School Baseball Coaches Association.

	SCHOOL, CITY	W-L	Achievement
1.	Lassiter HS, Marietta, Ga.	35-2	Georgia 4-A champion
2.	Bellaire (Texas) HS	38-2	Texas 5-A champion
3.	Westminster Academy, Fort Lauderdale	33-2	Florida 2-A champion
4.	Arlington HS, Riverside, Calif.	29-2	CIF Southern section Div. I champion
5.	Rose HS, Greenville, N.C.	28-0	North Carolina 4-A champion
6.	Wellington (Fla.) HS	33-4	Florida 6-A champion
7.	Chatsworth (Calif.) HS	27-3	Los Angeles city 4-A champion
8.	Catholic Central HS, Redford, Mich.	38-1	Michigan Division I champion
9.	Oakland HS, Murfreesboro, Tenn.	37-2	Tennessee 3-A champion
10.	Moses Lake (Wash.) HS	22-2	
11.	Owasso (Okla.) HS	39-5	Oklahoma 6-A champion
12.	Vestavia Hills (Ala.) HS	30-4	Alabama 6-A champion
13.	Riverdale Baptist HS, Upper Marlboro, Md.	35-4	Maryland private schools champion
14.	Columbus HS, Miami	27-4	
15.	Desert Vista HS, Tempe, Ariz.	34-5	Arizona 5-A champion
16.	Calvary Chapel HS, Santa Ana, Calif.	28-1	CIF Southern section Div. V champion
17.	Durango HS, Las Vegas	35-4	Nevada 4-A champion
18.	Bishop Moore HS, Orlando	31-4	National Classic champion
19.	Barbe HS, Lake Charles, La.	34-3	Louisiana 5-A runner-up
20.	El Dorado HS, Placentia, Calif.	26-5	CIF Southern section Div. III champion
21.	Andrews (Texas) HS	34-3	Texas 4-A champion
22.	Englewood HS, Jacksonville	30-5	Florida 4-A champion
23.	Xaverian HS, Brooklyn	23-5	New York City private school champion
24.	Chaparral HS, Scottsdale, Ariz.	32-2	Arizona 4-A champion
25.	Blue Springs (Mo.) HS	28-2	Missouri 5-A champion
26.	Moody HS, Corpus Christi, Texas	30-3	
27.	Lexington (S.C.) HS	32-3	South Carolina 4-A champion
28.	Mills HS, Little Rock, Ark.	33-4	Arkansas 5-A champion
29.	Jefferson HS, Shenandoah Junction, W.Va.	32-4	West Virginia 3-A champion
30.	Merritt Island (Fla.) HS	31-4	Florida 5-A champion
31.	Providence Catholic HS, New Lenox, Ill.	30-3	Illinois summer champion
32.	Wilson HS, Long Beach	26-5	CIF Southern section Div. I runner-up
33.	Monsignor Pace HS, Miami	29-7	Florida 4-A runner-up
34.	Lakeridge HS, Oswego, Ore.	30-1	Oregon 4-A champion
35.	Rancho Bernardo HS, San Diego	24-6	CIF San Diego section Div. I champion
36.	La Quinta HS, Westminster, Calif.	26-3	
37.	Dunedin (Fla.) HS	28-3	
38.	Steinert HS, Hamilton Township, N.J.	29-3	New Jersey Group IV champion
39.	West Monroe HS, Monroe, La.	31-6	Louisiana 5-A champion
40.	Hattiesburg (Miss.) HS	33-4	Mississippi 5-A runner-up
41.	Alexander HS, Laredo, Texas	28-5	
42.	Servite HS, Anaheim	23-3	
43.	John Adams HS, Ozone Park, N.Y.	44-4	New York City public school champion
44.	Southington (Conn.) HS	19-1	Connecticut LL state champion
45.	Iona Prep, New Rochelle, N.Y.	29-2	New York City private schools runner-up
46.	Elder HS, Cincinnati	27-6	Ohio Division I champion
47.	Andrew HS, Tinley Park, Ill.	37-7	
48.	El Dorado HS, Albuquerque	24-0	New Mexico 4-A champion
49.	Coatesville (Pa.) HS	21-3	
50.	St. Paul's HS, Mobile, Ala.	37-3	Alabama 4-A champion

California does not have a state championship

high schools, 557 from four-year colleges and 280 from junior colleges.

Moses Lake (Wash.) became the first high school team ever to have three players selected in the first two rounds of the same draft. Outfielder B.J. Garbe went fifth overall to the Minnesota Twins. Catcher Ryan Doumit and outfielder Jason Cooper were selected four picks apart in the second round.

Moses Lake finished 10th in the nation with a 22-2 record, despite being ousted from the Washington playoffs by Selah High, a team it had beaten three times previously.

Hamilton was Baseball America's High School Player of the Year, and became a big success in his first professional season in the Tampa Bay Devil Rays organization (see sidebar). But his $3.96 million bonus was exceeded when No. 2 overall pick Josh Beckett signed with the Florida Marlins.

Beckett, a righthander from Spring (Texas) High,

was the most highly regarded high school player in the nation as a junior in 1998. After the '99 draft he held out nearly all summer, finally signing for a bonus of $3.625 million—but for total compensation of $7 million over a four-year major league contract. Hamilton had signed a standard minor league contract.

The $7 million is the largest amount ever given a high school player who signed with the team that drafted him. Beckett began his pro career in instructional league in the fall of 1999.

Two Miami schools shared the distinction of having more players drafted in '99 than any other high school. No. 14 Columbus and No. 33 Monsignor Pace each had four players selected. Two of the Columbus players, righthander Kiki Bengochea and catcher Chris Jaile, went in the third and fourth rounds, respectively.

Highlights

The 1999 season produced its share of outstanding performances:

■ Lefthander Josh Girdley of Jasper (Texas) High struck out 29 batters in 10 innings, but his team lost 2-1 to Lumberton High in 12 innings. Girdley allowed three hits and had two four-strikeout innings. His only non-strikeout outs were a fly to right field, a sacrifice bunt and a 2-3 pickoff. Lumberton scored the winning run on a bases-loaded walk after Girdley left the mound.

Girdley was drafted sixth overall by the Expos, and went 0-2 with a 3.32 ERA in 12 games in the Rookie-level Gulf Coast League.

■ Bill Clayton of Glenwood High in Chatham, Ill., hit three home runs in one inning and pitched a no-hitter in a 27-2 win at Taylorville. The three homers came in the second inning, and tied a national record previously held by Danny Kimura of Iolani High in Honolulu, who did it in 1997.

Clayton, a junior, had eight RBIs in the inning as his team scored 22 runs.

"The wind was blowing about 25 miles an hour, and they've got a short fence in right," said Glenwood coach Pat Moomey. "But all of Billy's were to left, and I've got to think all three were gone without any wind. He hit them good."

■ El Segundo (Calif.) High catcher Alberto Concepcion also tied a national home run record, hitting six straight.

Concepcion homered his last three times up against Banning High and his first three against Burbank. He also had homered earlier in the Banning game, giving him seven in eight at-bats.

The six straight homers tied the record shared by Tim Morgan of Northwest Whitfield in Tunnel Hill, Ga. (1990) and Bob Squires of Waterloo (Ind.) in 1982.

Concepcion was drafted in the second round by the San Diego Padres, but didn't sign. He was attending Southern California.

■ Hattiesburg (Miss.) High, which finished the season ranked 40th in the nation, won a game in which it was no-hit and struck out 16 times. Righthander Mark Broom of West Marion in Foxworth, Miss., lost 1-0 with the run scoring as the result of an error.

"We're just a little old country school here," said Broom's coach Perry Coggins. "I just give him the ball

Player of the Year
Draft's top pick honored

Scouts fell in love with Josh Hamilton in 1999 as he batted .514, hit 13 home runs, won seven games and struck out 95 in 55 innings in a sterling two-way performance for Athens Drive High in Raleigh, N.C. The Tampa Bay Devil Rays liked what they saw and made him the No. 1 pick in the draft.

Baseball America thought he was pretty darned good, too, and named him its 1999 High School Player of the Year.

Hamilton, a lefthanded-hitting center fielder who doubled as the Jaguars ace pitcher, performed admirably under the constant pressure of being the assumed first overall pick all spring.

ROBERT GURGANUS

Josh Hamilton

"I was just trying to work as hard as I could without thinking about everything going on around me," Hamilton said. "I just tried to do my best."

He was pitched around often, walking 26 times in 25 games, but parlayed all the hits and free passes into 17 stolen bases. He also showed a knack for hitting to the opposite field when pitchers stayed away from his power zone.

Three days after being drafted by the Devil Rays Hamilton signed for a $3.96 million bonus, the largest ever by a player signing with the team that drafted him. He became the first No. 1 overall pick to agree to terms so early since Phil Nevin in 1992.

"We got ourselves a real old-fashioned ballplayer," Devil Rays scouting director Dan Jennings said. "Besides all the obvious tools, Josh has all the intangibles you'd want to see in a ballplayer. He has a great natural rhythm and pace to his game."

Hamilton looked every bit the part of a top pick in his first professional summer. He batted .347 with 10 homers, 48 RBIs and 18 stolen bases for Rookie-level Princeton, and earned a late-season promotion to short-season Hudson Valley, where a strong playoff showing helped that team win its first-ever New York-Penn League title. He went 6-for-13 with four RBIs as the Renegades beat Mahoning Valley in three games in the championship series.

The Devil Rays project Hamilton as a right fielder, but he stayed in center for the balance of 1999. The Rays were pleased with his play in the field.

—JOHN ROYSTER

and say, 'See you in two hours.' "

■ Cretin-Derham Hall of St. Paul, Minn., narrowly missed breaking the national record for consecutive wins. The Raiders' streak stood at 66 when they were defeated by Hastings High 11-10 in the opening round

1999 HIGH SCHOOL ALL-AMERICA TEAM

Selected by Baseball America   *Junior

Ryan Christianson

Corey Myers

B.J. Garbe

Bobby Bradley

FIRST TEAM

Pos., Player	School, Hometown	AVG	AB	H	HR	RBI	SB	Drafted (Round)
C Ryan Christianson	Arlington HS, Riverside, Calif.	.519	81	42	7	42	12	Mariners (1)
1B Dom Ambrosini	Connetquot HS, Ronkonkoma, N.Y.	.581	86	50	18	42	14	Expos (6)
INF Neil Jenkins	Dwyer HS, Jupiter, Fla.	.561	82	46	16	45	7	Tigers (3)
INF Corey Myers	Desert Vista HS, Phoenix	.560	125	70	22	77	3	Diamondbacks (1)
INF Jason Repko	Hanford HS, West Richland, Wash.	.581	74	43	18	47	14	Dodgers (1)
OF Rick Asadoorian	Northbridge HS, Whitinsville, Mass.	.500	66	33	7	41	9	Red Sox (1)
OF B.J. Garbe	Moses Lake (Wash.) HS	.500	66	33	6	22	19	Twins (1)
OF Josh Hamilton	Athens Drive HS, Raleigh, N.C.	.514	72	37	13	36	17	Devil Rays (1)
DH Alberto Concepcion	El Segundo (Calif.) HS	.543	92	50	20	67	4	Padres (2)
UT Jarrod Schmidt	Lassiter HS, Marietta, Ga.	.460	100	46	17	52	9	Marlins (23)
		W-L	ERA	IP	H	BB	SO	
P Josh Beckett	Spring (Texas) HS	13-2	0.39	89	31	29	178	Marlins (1)
P Bobby Bradley	Wellington (Fla.) HS	12-1	0.38	92	38	13	156	Pirates (1)
P Josh Girdley	Jasper (Texas) HS	9-2	0.34	82	26	34	178	Expos (1)
P Ryan Gloger	Jesuit HS, Tampa	13-2	0.72	87	39	29	163	Devil Rays (1)
P Dennis Ulacia	Monsignor Pace HS, Miami	13-0	0.52	85	35	27	132	White Sox (8)
UT Jarrod Schmidt	Lassiter HS, Marietta, Ga.	11-1	2.22	63	48	11	73	

SECOND TEAM

Pos., Player	School, Hometown	AVG	AB	H	HR	RBI	SB	Drafted
C Tony Richie*	Bishop Kenny HS, Jacksonville	.580	100	58	9	56	10	Not eligible
1B Brian Stavisky	Port Alleghany (Pa.) HS	.562	73	41	16	54	10	Expos (12)
INF Hank Blalock	Rancho Bernardo HS, San Diego	.515	99	51	12	40	12	Rangers (3)
INF Kevin Howard	Westlake HS, Thousand Oaks, Calif.	.551	78	43	12	38	26	Padres (22)
INF Josh Wilson	Mt. Lebanon HS, Pittsburgh	.612	49	30	7	24	3	Marlins (3)
OF Carl Crawford	Jefferson Davis HS, Houston	.563	64	36	7	28	29	Devil Rays (2)
OF Cody Ross	Carlsbad (N.M.) HS	.525	60	34	12	45	15	Tigers (4)
OF Kyle Smith	Bellaire (Texas) HS	.440	98	44	19	70	27	Not drafted
DH J.R. House	Seabreeze HS, Daytona Beach, Fla.	.592	98	58	15	55	1	Pirates (5)
UT Jeff Baker	Gar-Field HS, Woodbridge, Va.	.544	68	37	12	30	6	Indians (4)
		W-L	ERA	IP	H	BB	SO	
P Brad Baker	Pioneer Valley HS, Leyden, Mass.	9-0	0.96	66	24	22	138	Red Sox (1)
P Josh Cenate	Jefferson HS, Shenandoah Jct., W.Va.	14-1	0.66	96	39	23	198	Orioles (1)
P Brett Myers	Englewood HS, Jacksonville	8-2	0.80	78	25	34	131	Phillies (1)
P Jacob Peavy	St. Paul's HS, Mobile, Ala.	13-0	0.83	90	15	28	151	Padres (15)
P Jason Stumm	Centralia (Wash.) HS	11-0	0.83	68	38	20	105	White Sox (1)
UT Jeff Baker	Gar-Field HS, Woodbridge, Va.	9-0	0.40	70	35	14	111	

PLAYER OF THE YEAR: Josh Hamilton, of-lhp, Athens Drive HS, Raleigh, N.C.

of the state Class AA regional tournament.

They failed to reach the national record of 68, set by Archbishop Molloy of New York from 1963-66.

Cretin-Derham Hall, which fielded a sophomore-dominated club, won twice in the playoff losers' bracket to reach the final, but lost again to Hastings 10-0. The 66-game streak dated to the 1997 season.

■ Desert Vista High of Phoenix broke several records en route to the Arizona 5-A championship and a No. 15 national ranking.

First and foremost was the state record for single-season wins, 34. Shortstop Corey Myers established

seven state offensive records: single-season home runs (22); career home runs (43); single-season runs (70); career runs (144); single-season RBIs (81); career RBIs (182); and single-season hits (70).

The Thunder also broke team records for runs (430), homers (74) and doubles (89). They averaged more than 11 runs per game.

Myers was drafted fourth overall by his hometown Arizona Diamondbacks, and continued his success in pro ball. He batted .274 with five homers for Rookie-level Missoula in the Pioneer League, a circuit dominated by former college players.

AMATEUR BASEBALL

Mission accomplished: U.S qualifies for Olympics

BY JOHN MANUEL

As usual, international baseball supremacy at the 1999 Pan American Games came down to the United States and Cuba. And as usual, Cuba came away with the gold medal, defeating Team USA 5-1 behind righthander Jose Contreras.

But everything else about the baseball competition at the Winnipeg, Manitoba, Games was different. The tournament was the first in which USA Baseball, the sport's governing body in the United States, used professional players to field a team.

Major League Baseball allowed players from its 30 organizations not on 40-man rosters to be eligible for use by national teams. Clubs from the U.S., Canada, Dominican Republic, Mexico and Panama all had minor league players, and even some former major leaguers, like catcher Marcus Jensen, who led Team USA with three homers and nine RBIs.

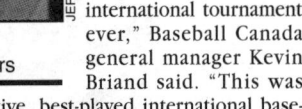

Marcus Jensen
Led U.S. in homers

So while the results and the winners were familiar, the road to the gold-medal game was a very different one from the Pan Am norm. Every game was close in the medal round, and every game was well played and intense.

"This was the greatest international tournament ever," Baseball Canada general manager Kevin Briand said. "This was the most competitive, best-played international baseball tournament of all time."

The tournament's most important games happened the day before the gold-medal matchup, in the semifinals. Cuba and Team USA squeaked to one-run victories against Canada and Mexico, 3-2 and 2-1 respectively. Those wins earned Cuba and the U.S. the two berths in the 2000 Olympics in Sydney, Australia, slotted for the Americas.

"In the big picture, it's mission accomplished," Paul Seiler, USA Baseball's general manager, said after the 10-inning Mexico win that qualified the U.S. for the Olympics. "This team didn't just come here to qualify, it came to win the gold medal. But if you came to me three months ago and guaranteed me a silver medal, I would have taken it."

The result of the gold-medal game seemed almost irrelevant, but it certainly wasn't to Cuba. Contreras, who pitched six innings and threw 83 pitches in Cuba's 3-1 quarterfinal victory against the Dominican Republic, came back on one day of rest to face the Americans with the gold medal on the line. All he did was strike out 13 Team USA batters, giving up just four hits while walking two to get the win.

Veteran Cuban first baseman Orestes Kindelan provided the power, slugging two home runs, enabling Cuba to continue its dominance of international base-

---

2000 OLYMPICS

Eight-team field almost set

With the exception of a series between South Africa and Guam that was scheduled for December 1999 to determine the eighth and final berth, the field for the 2000 Olympics baseball competition, scheduled for Sept. 15-Oct.1 in Sydney, Australia, has been determined.

The field includes defending gold medalist Cuba and the United States, who finished first and second, respectively, at the 1999 Pan American Games in Winnipeg, Manitoba—the qualifying tournament for the Americas.

Korea and Japan qualified from the Asian championships in Seoul, Korea, from Sept. 11-16, while Italy and The Netherlands qualified from the European championships in Italy from July 23-Aug. 3. Australia, as the host country, was granted an automatic bid.

Guam won the Oceanic championship as a host country while South Africa won the All-Africa Games baseball competition, held in Johannesburg, South Africa, from Sept. 9-18.

---

ball. Its national teams have won every Pan Am tournament since 1971, last losing in 1967 in Winnipeg to the United States.

"We knew (Contreras) was on one day's rest, but you just have to tip your cap to him—he threw a great game," Team USA first baseman/DH Jon Zuber (Phillies) said. "We thought he would not have a good fastball because he was on one day's rest, but he had it for about three innings. Then he was locating his split-finger—that's a tough thing to do—and he threw it a couple of different speeds."

Team USA flashed an explosive offense in pool play, ripping the Cubans 10-5 on its way to a 4-1 record. Team USA's only loss came when it blew a three-run lead in the 13th inning to Canada in the opener and lost 7-6.

That began a tournament-long love affair between the host nation and its national team. Team Canada captured the country's attention behind second baseman Stubby Clapp (Cardinals), catcher Andy Stewart (Phillies) and a gritty pitching staff. Stewart led all tournament hitters in home runs and RBIs while batting .462-4-15.

The Canadians beat Team USA and Cuba (8-1) to go undefeated in pool play, only to draw the Cubans again with an Olympic berth on the line. Cuba's veteran third baseman Omar Linares blasted a three-run homer in the third inning, and the pitching of Norge Vera and closer Luis Lazo made the homer hold up in a 3-2 win. Canada beat Mexico for the bronze and finished 6-1, the best record in the tournament, but did not qualify for Sydney.

"I think it's just ridiculous, obviously, that only two teams are going from this tournament," Team USA manager Buddy Bell said. "It's obviously the best baseball in the world." Team Canada manager Ernie Whitt added, "This tournament should send four teams, not two."

Winnipeg, Manitoba
July 24-August 2, 1999

ROUND-ROBIN STANDINGS

POOL A	W	L	RF	RA
Canada	4	0	34	12
United States	3	1	24	15
Cuba	2	2	21	20
Mexico	1	3	13	13
Brazil	0	4	7	39

POOL B	W	L	RF	RA
*Nicaragua	2	1	11	11
Dominican Republic	2	1	20	9
Panama	2	1	18	12
Guatemala	0	3	7	24

*Nicaragua won tiebreaker for top seed.

MEDAL ROUND

QUARTERFINALS: Cuba 3, Dominican Republic 1; Canada 12, Guatemala 2; Mexico 5, Nicaragua 1; United States 5, Panama 2.
SEMIFINALS: Cuba 3, Canada 2; United States 2, Mexico 1 (10 innings).
GOLD MEDAL: Cuba 5, United States 1. **BRONZE MEDAL:** Canada 9, Mexico 2.

INDIVIDUAL BATTING LEADERS
(Minimum 12 At-Bats)

Player, Country	AVG	AB	R	H	2B	3B	HR	RBI	SB
Francisco Matos, DR	.529	17	2	9	0	0	0	4	1
Pablo Ozuna, DR	.500	18	5	9	0	0	0	3	2
Andy Stewart, Canada	.452	31	10	14	3	0	4	15	2
Hector Alvarez, Mexico	.440	25	2	11	0	0	0	5	1
Julio Mosquera, Panama	.438	16	4	7	1	0	0	2	1
Troy Fortin, Canada	.407	27	7	11	1	0	1	4	1
Issac Martinez, Cuba	.391	23	5	9	1	0	1	3	1
Ryan Radmanovich, Can	.391	23	7	9	1	0	2	6	1
Jeremy Ware, Canada	.375	32	6	12	4	0	1	6	3
Adam Kennedy, USA	.367	30	3	11	2	0	0	5	2
Amilcar Estrada, Guat	.357	14	1	5	0	0	1	1	1
Joel Vega, Panama	.357	14	2	5	1	0	1	3	0
Stubby Clapp, Canada	.348	23	6	8	3	0	1	3	1
Lee Delfino, Canada	.348	23	5	8	0	1	0	3	1
Todd Betts, Canada	.345	29	6	10	0	0	1	9	0
Ariel Pestano, Cuba	.333	21	2	7	0	0	0	0	0
Raul Vizcarra, Mexico	.313	16	4	5	1	0	1	3	0
Luis Ulacia, Cuba	.308	26	4	8	0	0	1	1	1
Edgar Lopez, Nic	.308	13	2	4	1	0	0	3	0
Dave Roberts, USA	.308	26	1	8	0	0	0	2	4
Marcus Jensen, USA	.300	20	4	6	1	0	3	9	0
Milton Bradley, USA	.292	24	4	7	2	0	0	0	2
Jason Hardtke, USA	.290	31	4	9	2	0	2	3	1

INDIVIDUAL PITCHING LEADERS
(Minimum 8 Innings)

Player, Country	W	L	ERA	G	SV	IP	H	BB	SO
Steve Green, Canada	1	0	0.00	2	0	10	4	1	5
Tavo Alvarez, Mexico	1	0	0.66	2	0	14	6	4	12
Dario Perez, DR	1	1	0.75	2	0	12	8	1	8
Narciso Elvira, Mexico	1	1	0.82	2	0	11	7	4	5
Jose Contreras, Cuba	3	0	0.98	3	0	18	12	6	22
Luis Lazo, Cuba	0	0	1.13	3	2	8	8	1	13
John Patterson, USA	1	0	1.39	2	0	13	6	0	12
Mark Mulder, USA	1	0	1.42	2	0	13	12	4	7
Jose Ibar, Cuba	1	0	1.74	2	0	10	11	4	10
Norge Vera, Cuba	1	0	2.25	2	0	8	7	1	8
Mike Meyers, Canada	1	1	2.46	2	0	11	7	5	10
Dan Wheeler, USA	1	0	2.70	3	0	10	9	0	11
Jason Gooding, Canada	1	0	2.84	2	0	13	12	4	11
Yan LaChapelle, Canada	2	0	3.27	2	0	11	6	4	8
Len Picota, Panama	0	1	3.60	2	0	10	11	4	8

TEAM USA

BATTING	AVG	AB	R	H	2B	3B	HR	RBI	SB
Charlie Greene, c	.400	5	0	2	1	0	0	0	0
Shawn Gilbert, ss-of	.375	8	1	3	1	0	0	0	1
Adam Kennedy, 2b	.367	30	3	11	2	0	0	5	2
Matthew LeCroy, dh	.333	3	1	1	0	0	0	0	0
Dave Roberts, of	.308	26	1	8	0	0	0	2	4
Marcus Jensen, c-dh	.300	20	4	6	1	0	3	9	0
Milton Bradley, of	.292	24	4	7	2	0	0	0	2
Jason Hardtke, 3b	.290	31	4	9	2	0	2	3	1
Mike Neill, dh-of	.286	7	1	2	1	0	0	1	0
Travis Dawkins, ss	.273	22	2	6	0	0	1	2	2
Craig Paquette, 1b	.227	22	4	5	1	0	2	3	1
Peter Bergeron, of	.217	23	4	5	1	0	0	0	1
Jon Zuber, 1b-dh	.167	18	3	3	1	0	0	2	0
TOTALS	.285	239	32	68	14	0	8	29	14

PITCHING	W	L	ERA	G	SV	IP	H	BB	SO
Ryan Anderson, lhp	1	0	0.00	2	0	7	4	2	9
Bobby Seay, lhp	0	0	0.00	2	1	3	0	1	4
David Holdridge, rhp	0	0	0.00	1	0	1	1	1	0
J.C. Romero, lhp	1	0	0.00	3	0	2	1	3	1
John Patterson, rhp	1	0	1.39	2	0	13	6	0	12
Mark Mulder, lhp	1	0	1.42	2	0	13	12	4	7
Todd Williams, rhp	0	0	1.69	4	1	5	2	2	1
Dan Wheeler, rhp	1	0	2.70	3	0	10	9	0	11
Derek Wallace, rhp	0	0	5.40	3	0	6	3	1	1
Brad Penny, rhp	0	1	6.75	2	0	7	8	3	8
Scott Stewart, lhp	0	0	27.00	1	0	1	2	2	1
TOTALS	5	2	2.49	7	2	65	51	19	55

TEAM CANADA

BATTING	AVG	AB	R	H	2B	3B	HR	RBI	SB
Andy Stewart, c	.452	31	10	14	3	0	4	15	0
Troy Fortin, dh	.407	27	7	11	1	0	1	4	1
Ryan Radmanovich, of	.391	23	7	9	1	0	2	6	0
Jeremy Ware, dh-1b	.375	32	6	12	4	0	1	6	2
Stubby Clapp, 2b	.348	23	6	8	3	0	1	3	1
Lee Delfino, ss	.348	23	5	8	0	1	0	3	0
Todd Betts, 3b	.345	29	6	10	0	0	1	9	0
Matt Logan, 1b	.263	19	2	5	1	0	1	3	0
Aaron Guiel, of	.222	27	5	6	1	0	1	3	1
Colon Dixon, 1b	.222	9	2	2	0	0	1	3	0
Julien Lepine, ss	.000	1	1	0	0	0	0	0	0
Greg Morrison, 1b	.000	6	0	0	0	0	0	0	0
TOTALS	.340	250	57	85	14	1	13	55	5

PITCHING	W	L	ERA	G	SV	IP	H	BB	SO
Steve Green, rhp	1	0	0.00	2	0	10	4	1	5
Clint Lawrence, lhp	0	0	0.00	3	0	3	6	2	2
Jason Green, rhp	1	0	0.00	1	0	1	0	1	1
Dave Ross, lhp	0	0	0.00	1	0	1	1	1	0
Chris Mears, rhp	0	0	0.00	1	0	1	0	0	0
Mark Randall, rhp	0	0	1.42	3	0	6	3	0	0
Mike Meyers, rhp	1	1	2.45	2	0	11	7	5	10
Jason Gooding, lhp	1	0	2.84	2	0	13	12	4	11
Yan LaChapelle, rhp	2	0	3.27	2	0	11	6	4	8
Chad Ricketts, rhp	0	0	7.36	3	1	4	5	1	2
TOTALS	6	1	2.25	7	1	60	41	22	39

GOLD-MEDAL GAME
Cuba 5, USA 1

USA	ab	r	h	rbi	CUBA	ab	r	h	rbi
Roberts lf	3	0	1	0	Ulacia lf	4	0	1	0
Kennedy 2b	3	0	0	0	Martinez rf	3	0	0	0
Hardtke 3b	4	0	0	0	Linares 3b	4	2	0	0
Paquette 1b	3	0	0	0	Kindelan 1b	4	2	3	3
Bradley cf	4	1	1	0	Pierre dh	3	1	2	1
Zuber dh	4	0	0	0	Padilla 2b	4	0	0	0
Jensen c	3	0	1	1	Pestano c	4	0	0	0
Bergeron rf	3	0	1	0	Duenas cf	3	0	1	0
Dawkins ss	2	0	0	0	Videaux cf	0	0	0	0
Neill ph	1	0	0	0	Mesa ss	2	0	1	0
Gilbert ss	0	0	0	0					
Totals	30	1	4	1	Totals	31	5	8	4

USA	000	010	000—1	
Cuba	000	202	01x—5	

E—Dawkins. **DP**—USA 1. **LOB**—USA 5, Cuba 5. **2B**—Bradley, Kindelan, Mesa. **HR**—Kindelan 2, Pierre. **SB**—Roberts, Paquette, Duenas. **CS**—Kennedy, Pierre.

USA	ip	h	r	er	bb	so	CUBA	ip	h	r	er	bb	so
Penny L	4⅓	5	2	2	1	5	Contreras W	8	4	1	1	2	13
Anderson	⅔	1	0	0	0	0	Rodriguez	1	0	0	0	1	3
Wallace	1⅔	1	2	1	0	1							
Romero	⅓	0	1	1	0	0							
Williams	1	1	0	0	1	0							

Romero faced 1 batter in the 8th.
WP—Williams.
A—6,140.

Amateur Baseball

College all-star squad falls short of goal

BY JOHN MANUEL

Never has USA Baseball endured a summer like 1999.

Despite all the challenges the organization endured, it may have had its most successful year since winning its only Olympic gold medal in 1988.

"I think we had some stunning accomplishments," USA Baseball president Dan O'Brien said. "It was a much busier summer than probably USA Baseball has ever had.

"And yet we won gold at the junior world championships. Our youth team (16 and under) won the Police Athletic League tournament. Our junior Olympic (16 and under) tournament expanded to 64 teams. And of course we qualified for the Olympics, which was the most important task of the summer."

For the first time, USA Baseball fielded a team of professionals in international play. Minor leaguers made up the Team USA club that finished second at the Pan American Games in Winnipeg, Manitoba, losing to Cuba in the gold-medal game. The second-place finish qualified the United States for the 2000 Olympics, though.

USA Baseball also fielded a college national team that traveled to Japan and toured the U.S. That club had an erratic season, going 24-15 (winning 15 of its last 18) and finishing seventh at the National Baseball Congress World Series, an event it won handily in 1995.

The summer started haltingly for the collegiate team. Without any formal trials, 41 college players reported to Tucson, USA Baseball's headquarters, in June and were pared down to 24 in two weeks. Retired Arizona coach Jerry Kindall stepped in to run the camp while Team USA coach Mark Johnson coached his Texas A&M club in the College World Series.

Mark Johnson

Soon after Johnson returned, the collegians headed for Japan for the 28th installment of the U.S.-Japan series. A team of Japanese college all-stars defeated the Americans in five consecutive games to shave the Americans' all-time series advantage to 17-11.

"The Japanese were really good," said Johnson, who last coached in the Japan series as a Team USA assistant in 1991. "They were much better than when I'd seen them last."

The U.S. team returned to Tucson from Japan and achieved one of its biggest highlights, an 11-2 win against Korea on July 4 in front of a Hi Corbett Stadium crowd of 7,499.

Team USA finished its season at the 34-team NBC World Series in Wichita. Team USA won the event in 1995 with a team that included current big leaguers such as Troy Glaus, Mark Kotsay, Travis Lee and Randy Wolf.

But the '99 squad was younger and less talented than its '95 predecessor. After winning its first two games by a combined score of 36-1, Team USA lost two close games and finished the tournament with a 3-2 record, tied for seventh place. Team USA's losses came against the Santa Barbara Foresters (California Coastal Collegiate League) and San Diego Stars (Western Semi-Pro Wood Bat League).

"We really had about the youngest team in the tournament," Johnson said. "We played well and I thought we were playing our best at that point of the summer, but we lost a couple of tough ballgames."

Meanwhile, USA Baseball's junior team (18 and under) won

TEAM USA '99

BATTING	AVG	AB	R	H	2B	3B	HR	RBI	SB	College	Class
Xavier Nady, 3b	.414	140	42	58	8	1	17	43	3	California	So.
Keoni DeRenne, ss	.376	125	35	47	11	1	2	18	11	Arizona	So.
Tyrell Godwin, of	.357	129	34	46	10	1	4	22	9	North Carolina	So.
John Gall, 1b-3b	.352	91	19	32	7	2	2	24	2	Stanford	Jr.
Bill Scott, of	.340	141	31	48	8	2	9	32	4	UCLA	So.
Matt Bowser, of	.333	3	0	1	0	0	0	0	0	Central Florida	So.
Manny Crespo, 2b	.320	50	6	16	2	3	2	10	3	Miami	So.
Mike Tonis, c	.310	87	23	27	7	1	8	22	0	California	So.
John Wilson, c	.309	68	14	21	7	1	1	9	0	Kentucky	So.
Taggert Bozied, 1b	.303	132	32	40	10	1	2	23	4	San Francisco	So.
Koyie Hill, 2b	.284	134	23	38	9	6	3	21	2	Wichita State	So.
Daylan Holt, of	.274	113	23	31	6	2	7	29	1	Texas A&M	So.
Jeremy Kurella, ss	.250	8	2	2	1	0	0	1	1	Northwestern	So.
James Jurries, 2b	.250	8	0	2	1	0	0	0	0	Tulane	Fr.
Ryan Howard, 1b	.222	9	3	2	1	0	1	4	0	SW Missouri State	Fr.
Ben Diggins, p-dh	.200	30	9	6	1	2	1	4	0	Arizona	Fr.
Shelley Duncan, of	.154	26	2	4	1	1	1	2	0	Arizona	Fr.
Brian Esposito, c	.000	4	0	0	0	0	0	0	0	Connecticut	So.
Totals	.324	1303	300	422	90	24	60	263	40		

PITCHING	W	L	ERA	G	SV	IP	H	BB	SO	College	Class
Mike Schultz	0	0	0.00	1	0	2	1	2	3	Loyola Marymount	So.
Shane Nance	0	0	1.35	4	0	7	8	4	5	Houston	Jr.
Ben Diggins	2	1	2.05	16	3	22	10	16	17	Arizona	Fr.
Phil Seibel	0	1	2.12	11	1	17	17	3	21	Texas	So.
Len Dinardo	3	1	2.47	11	0	44	34	10	50	Stetson	Fr.
Mark Prior	4	1	2.52	11	0	36	28	10	31	Vanderbilt	Fr.
Brandon Webb	1	0	3.00	1	0	3	5	0	4	Kentucky	So.
Chris Bootcheck	0	0	3.00	1	0	3	3	1	4	Auburn	So.
Aaron Heilman	4	2	3.38	14	2	40	41	12	37	Notre Dame	So.
Josh Karp	4	2	3.72	7	0	36	37	13	35	UCLA	Fr.
Kyle Crowell	2	1	4.03	12	0	29	29	7	33	Houston	So.
Beau Hintz	0	0	4.50	1	0	2	3	0	2	Fresno State	Fr.
Justin Wayne	2	2	4.93	7	0	35	43	11	26	Stanford	So.
Matt Smith	1	1	4.98	8	1	22	26	5	27	Oklahoma State	So.
Jon Brandt	1	2	7.12	9	0	30	38	13	26	UCLA	So.
Jeff Carlsen	0	1	47.25	1	0	1	6	3	1	Washington	So.
Totals	24	15	3.84	39	7	328	329	110	332		

Amateur Baseball

AMERICAS QUALIFYING TOURNAMENT
(World Junior Championship)
Caracas, Venezuela
April 17-24, 1999

ROUND-ROBIN STANDINGS

POOL A	W	L	RF	RA
United States	5	0	62	24
Panama	4	1	63	17
Venezuela	3	2	41	34
Colombia	2	3	40	54
Mexico	1	4	38	43
Costa Rica	0	5	15	81

POOL B	W	L	RF	RA
Cuba	5	0	47	13
Brazil	4	1	61	16
Dominican Republic	3	2	35	25
Guatemala	2	3	45	45
Honduras	1	4	22	60
Argentina	0	5	7	58

GOLD MEDAL—Cuba. **SILVER MEDAL**—Panama. **BRONZE MEDAL**—United States.

FINAL STANDINGS: 1. Cuba; 2. Panama; 3. United States; 4. Venezuela; 5. Dominican Republic; 6. Brazil; 7 (tie). Guatemala, Colombia.

Top five teams qualify for World Junior Championship

TEAM USA

BATTING	AVG	AB	R	H	2B	3B	HR	RBI	SB
Jonah McClanahan, of	.600	5	1	3	0	0	0	1	0
Pat Osborn, ss	.500	30	7	15	0	0	0	11	0
Todd Deininger, p	.500	6	0	3	1	0	0	3	0
Ryan Childs, p	.500	2	0	1	0	0	0	0	0
Travis Wong, 1b	.424	33	8	14	4	0	0	7	0
Drew Meyer, of	.417	36	16	15	5	0	1	9	7
Eric Verbryke, of	.406	32	12	13	1	1	0	4	3
Ryan Garko, of	.400	15	5	6	0	0	0	1	0
Rob Bowen, c	.387	31	6	12	0	0	2	8	1
Dennis Wyrick, 3b	.333	33	7	11	1	3	0	10	2
Dane Artman, 1b-p	.333	9	1	3	1	0	0	2	0
Josh Wilson, 2b	.290	31	14	9	4	1	1	7	0
Mat Thompson, p	.286	7	3	2	1	0	0	2	0
Ryan Schroyer, c	.200	10	4	2	0	0	1	5	0
John Kaye, of	.111	9	3	1	0	0	0	1	0
Totals	.372	298	90	111	18	5	5	72	13

PITCHING	W	L	ERA	G	SV	IP	H	BB	SO
Scott Hindman	1	0	0.00	1	0	2	0	2	2
Josh Wilson	1	0	0.00	1	0	2	0	1	1
Matt Lynch	1	0	2.45	2	0	11	9	3	11
Todd Deininger	1	0	2.57	3	0	14	7	10	8
Ryan Childs	0	1	4.16	3	0	9	10	1	5
Mat Thompson	2	0	4.50	2	0	12	14	3	10
John Thomas	1	0	6.75	3	0	13	22	3	8
Dane Artman	0	0	9.00	1	0	2	1	3	1
Mike Davern	0	0	15.00	3	0	3	7	2	3
Totals	7	1	4.50	8	0	68	70	29	49

WORLD JUNIOR CHAMPIONSHIP
Kaohsiung, Taiwan
August 6-15, 1999

ROUND-ROBIN STANDINGS

POOL A	W	L	POOL B	W	L
Cuba	5	0	Panama	4	1
Taiwan	4	1	United States	4	1
Korea	3	2	Japan	3	2
South Africa	1	3	Australia	2	3
Czech Republic	1	4	Venezuela	1	3
Netherlands	0	4	Guatemala	0	4

GOLD MEDAL—United States. **SILVER MEDAL**—Taiwan. **BRONZE MEDAL**—Cuba.

FINAL STANDINGS: 1. United States; 2. Taiwan; 3. Cuba; 4. Panama.

TEAM USA

BATTING	AVG	AB	R	H	2B	3B	HR	RBI	SB
Drew Jerden, p	1.000	3	3	3	2	0	0	2	0
Joe Torres, p	1.000	1	1	1	0	0	1	2	0
David Espinosa, 3b	.526	19	6	10	3	0	0	3	1
Jeff Baker, ss	.481	27	8	13	4	0	1	12	3
Dave Krynzel, of	.440	25	7	11	6	0	0	7	8
Drew Meyer, 2b	.423	26	10	11	2	0	0	7	7
Eric Verbryke, of-3b	.421	19	7	8	3	0	0	4	3
Scott Heard, c	.412	17	6	7	2	0	2	7	0
Matt Wheatland, p-1b	.400	10	3	4	0	0	1	3	0
Joe Mauer, c	.333	9	2	3	0	0	0	2	0
Travis Wong, 1b	.320	25	5	8	3	0	2	5	0
Carlos Quentin, of	.231	13	5	3	1	0	0	4	3
Brian Hall, of	.143	21	2	3	2	0	0	4	1
Totals	.390	218	65	85	28	0	7	62	26

PITCHING	W	L	ERA	G	SV	IP	H	BB	SO
David Espinosa	0	0	0.00	1	0	1	0	1	1
Danny Core	1	0	1.54	2	0	12	6	5	8
Carmen Pignatiello	1	0	1.64	2	0	11	8	6	7
Joe Torres	2	0	2.16	2	0	8	5	4	10
Ryan Gloger	1	0	2.25	1	0	4	4	0	4
Drew Jerden	1	0	4.50	1	0	6	2	4	8
Sean Rierson	0	0	7.36	3	2	4	4	2	3
Matt Wheatland	0	1	15.43	2	1	2	5	2	2
Todd Deininger	0	0	24.30	2	0	3	8	6	5
Totals	6	1	4.56	7	3	51	42	30	48

close games under adverse conditions in Taiwan on the way to its first gold medal at the World Junior Championships since 1995. After days of torrential rain that forced the cancellation of a number of games in the 12-nation field, the sun finally came out for the title game between host Taiwan and the U.S.

Jeff Baker

In front of 20,000 partisan fans, the U.S. rallied twice from three-run deficits to win 10-9. Shortstop Jeff Baker's two-run single in the eighth inning drove in the winning runs. Baker (Woodbridge, Va.), a fourth-round pick of the Cleveland Indians in the June draft, was named the event's most valuable player. He hit .481 overall.

A day earlier, the U.S. beat two-time defending champion Cuba 3-2 in the semifinals on an eighth-inning solo home run by first baseman Travis Wong (Boise, Idaho).

"Beating Cuba and Taiwan in that environment made it all worthwhile," USA Baseball junior national team director Steve Cohen said. "The only time these young men may ever experience anything like it again is if they play in the seventh game of a World Series on the road. We're in a tie game (8-8 in the eighth inning) in front of 20,000-plus passionate fans, and it was so loud you couldn't even yell to the on-deck batter."

Team USA first ran into logistical nightmares when the Americas qualifying tournament was canceled and rescheduled numerous times. It eventually was played in Caracas, Venezuela, in April 1999 and the U.S. qualified for a berth in the World tournament with a third-place finish.

USA Baseball's defending World champion 16-and-under national team had no forum to compete in on the international stage in 1999, so it participated in the Police Athletic League World Series and won that tournament in convincing fashion, winning eight straight games.

Amateur Baseball

SUMMER PLAYER OF YEAR

X Factor: Bears' Nady powers Team USA

The awards keep piling up for the University of California's Xavier Nady.

In 1998, he was Baseball America's Freshman of the Year, batting .404 with 15 homers and 70 RBIs while splitting time between second base and shortstop for the Bears. As a sophomore, he didn't

Xavier Nady

rest on his laurels, terrorizing pitchers again while moving to third base. Nady batted .374 with 23 homers and 62 RBIs and was a first-team All-American.

After failing to make Team USA's traveling roster for the World Championships in Italy in 1998, Nady became the main cog in a potent Team USA offense in 1999. He led the team in the triple crown categories while batting .414 with 17 homers and 43 RBIs. For that effort, he was named Baseball America's Summer Player of the Year.

"He's kind of a streaky hitter, but when he gets hot he can carry a whole team, and that's what he did with us," said Team USA coach Mark Johnson (Texas A&M). "He really got hot for a while. He can just hit. He's a hitter.

"He really improved for us defensively, and I was more pleased with that than anything else. He worked hard at it after getting off to a slow start."

Nady's home run total tied Travis Lee for the second-best in USA Baseball history, trailing only Tino Martinez, who hit 20 in 1988 when the U.S. won a gold medal in the Olympics. Proving Johnson's point, Nady hit eight homers in a six-game stretch, homering in every game with two multi-homer efforts. Nady also led the team in runs (42) and slugging (.850).

Nady projects as a high first-round pick and could be the first college player selected in the 2000 draft.

SUMMER ALL-AMERICA TEAM

C—Mike Tonis, Team USA (California), 320-8-22. **1B**—Lance Niekro, Orleans/Cape Cod (Florida Southern), .360-13-44. **2B**—Dominic Rich, Brewster/Cape Cod (Auburn), .341-2-28. **3B**—Xavier Nady, Team USA (California), .414-17-43. **SS**—Keoni DeRenne, Team USA (Arizona) .376-2-18. **OF**—Jamie Bubela, Wareham/Cape Cod (Baylor), .370-2-18, 23 SB; Bill Scott, Team USA (UCLA), .340-9-32; Radames Torres, Delaware/Great Lakes (Ohio Dominican), .455-9-42. **DH**—G.R. Schalick, Outer Banks/Coastal Plain (Richmond), .323-11-42; **Util**—Dallas McPherson, Asheboro/Coastal Plain (The Citadel), .349-3-28, 5-2, 2.19.

SP—Taft Cable, Wilson/Coastal Plain (UNC Greensboro), 9-2, 1.83; Rik Currier, Chatham/Cape Cod (Southern California), 7-0, 1.34; John Eric Hernandez, Mat-Su/Alaska (Chico State, Calif.,), 7-1, 0.95; Jim Magrane, Waterloo/Northwoods (Iowa), 9-3, 1.41; Brandon Sloan, El Dorado/Jayhawk (Wichita State), 5-1, 1.15. **RP**—Derrick DePriest, Chatham/Cape Cod (North Carolina), 1-0, 0.00, 15 SV.

GOLDEN SPIKES AWARD

Baylor's Jennings completes trophy haul

For the first time in three years, Pat Burrell wasn't a finalist for the 1999 Golden Spikes Award.

Presented by USA Baseball, the Golden Spikes Award is the top amateur baseball award in the country. Usually, the winner has played for one of USA Baseball's national teams, and 1999 was no exception. But while Baylor righthander/DH Jason Jennings didn't play for Team USA in 1999, his experience with the national team program prepared him well for a big finish to his college career.

Jennings led Baylor to one of its finest seasons ever and its first 50-win campaign by going 13-2, 2.58 while batting .386 with 17 home runs and 68 RBIs. But when the Colorado Rockies drafted him with the 16th overall pick in the 1999 draft, Jennings knew they wanted him for his right arm, not his lefthanded bat.

Jennings, also Baseball America's 1999 College Player of the Year, got his first inkling he would have to focus on pitching while he was a member of Team USA in 1997 and '98. The select team called on Jennings as a reliever in 1997, when he pitched in 11 games (18 innings), but he got just five at-bats.

The next year, Jennings became a starter for Baylor and for Team USA. He made nine appearances (pitching 39 innings) and emerged as one of

Jason Jennings

the nation's top pitchers. But given more of a chance to hit (23 at-bats), Jennings batted just .174-1-5.

"I guess I've always known I was going to pitch mostly when I got drafted," Jennings said. "I have found that out as I've gone along. Hitting is a lot of fun, but I see myself as a pitcher."

Jennings is the third two-way player to win the award, joining Cal State Fullerton's Mark Kotsay (1995) and Wichita State's Darren Dreifort (1993).

Like Dreifort, Jennings has shown power at the plate, but it's his power on the mound that makes the biggest impression.

—JOHN MANUEL

Amateur Baseball

Niekro, Teixeira head thin Cape talent crop

BY JOHN MANUEL

The summer college baseball landscape keeps shifting, with mixed results.

With the NCAA regional field expanded from 48 to 64 teams, a week was added to the college baseball season in 1999. The College World Series ended June 19, 13 days later than in 1998. That meant more players reported late to summer leagues when their teams made the NCAA tournament. Factor in Team USA skimming the top 25 or so players off the top, and the talent pool of eligible college players was considerably thinned out—at least early in the season.

Another factor thinning out talent is the competition among the summer leagues themselves. The Coastal Plain League achieved NCAA certification in 1999, and has joined the Central Illinois, Clark Griffith, Great Lakes, Jayhawk, New England Collegiate, Northwoods and Shenandoah Valley leagues as viable wood-bat alternatives to longtime summer stalwarts such as the Alaska League and Cape Cod League. Both of those leagues suffered a dip in talent from past seasons.

"I attribute that more to college baseball than the Cape, though," said John Schiffner, coach of Cape Cod runner-up Chatham. "The pros are just doing a better job of identifying talent and signing talent."

The best summer talent still plays on the Cape. In 1999, a disproportionate share of talent played in Orleans, which had a prospect-laden infield of corner infielders Lance Niekro (Florida Southern) and Mark Teixeira (Georgia Tech) and shortstop Tim Hummel (Old Dominion)—all of whom may eventually become first-round draft picks. In a Baseball America poll, managers named Teixeira, a freshman, the league's No. 1 prospect. Niekro, the No. 2 prospect and son of former big league pitcher Joe Niekro, led the league in home runs and RBIs and finished second in average.

Lance Niekro

Cotuit also fielded a talented infield that helped lead the Kettleers to the league championship. First baseman Garrett Atkins (UCLA), the playoff MVP, and second baseman Chase Utley (UCLA) powered the offense. Cotuit rallied for a 3-2 win in Game Two of the championship series by scoring two runs in the ninth inning against Chatham reliever Derrick DePriest (North Carolina), who hadn't allowed a run all season while racking up a league-record 15 saves. The Kettleers then won the title with a 7-1 win in the deciding game.

Wareham outfielder Jamie Bubela (Baylor) won the league's batting crown. Gatemen righthander Logan Dale (Missouri) topped big leaguer Jeff Weaver's Cape Cod record with 34 consecutive scoreless innings.

In other summer league news:

■ The Anchorage Bucs and Kenai Peninsula Oilers

Unanimous pick for No. 1
Mark Teixeira impressed Cape managers

claimed the Alaska League's two berths in the National Baseball Congress World Series, while Liberal won the Jayhawk League championship. But the Dallas Phillies upstaged those traditional summer-team powers to claim the NBC title.

The Phillies, who went 38-4 in the regular season in the Dallas Amateur Baseball Association, became the first team from Texas to win the NBC title in 40 years. The team finished third in the 1998 tournament, but got over the hump in 1999 with a potent mix of veteran hitters and hard-throwing college pitchers.

In winning all seven of its games, Dallas relied on players as varied as 33-year-old first baseman Rod Murrell, an ex-pro who hit .393 with a team-best three homers in the tournament, and Marco Cunningham, an outfielder at Texas Tech who hit .393 from the leadoff spot.

Righthander Beau Hale (Texas), who pitched most of the summer in the Cape Cod League and was a late pickup, picked up four saves, an NBC record. He earned his final save in the final game as Dallas rallied from a 4-2 deficit to defeat the Oilers 5-4.

Team USA was the favorite in Wichita, having won the event easily in 1995 in the only other year that it competed. The '99 edition of Team USA, though, was among the NBC's youngest teams and finished 3-2, tied for seventh.

■ The Arlington Senators won their second straight Clark Griffith League title and went on to capture the All-American Amateur Baseball Association championship in Johnstown, Pa., beating Milford, Pa., 17-8 in the final.

Senators outfielder Jared Dufault (Illinois State) set a new league record for hits (61) while batting .409 with six homers and 42 RBIs. He missed a triple crown by one homer.

■ The San Diego Collegiate League ceased operation in January 1999, citing increased costs.

Amateur Baseball

COLLEGE SUMMER LEAGUES

NCAA-CERTIFIED

ATLANTIC COLLEGIATE LEAGUE

WOLFF	W	L	PCT	GB
Quakertown Blazers	26	14	.650	—
New Jersey Colts	22	18	.550	4
Delaware Valley Gulls	21	19	.525	5
Jersey Pilots	21	19	.525	5
KAISER	**W**	**L**	**PCT**	**GB**
Newburgh Generals	28	12	.700	—
Jersey City Colonels	18	22	.450	10
Metro New York Cadets	14	26	.350	14
Nassau Collegians	10	30	.250	18

PLAYOFFS: New Jersey defeated Newburgh 2-0 and Quakertown defeated Jersey City 2-0 in best-of-3 semifinals. New Jersey defeated Quakertown in one-game final.

Most Valuable Player: Jared Musolf, New Jersey (Old Dominion). **Outstanding Pitcher:** Chris Buglovsky, Jersey (College of New Jersey).

INDIVIDUAL BATTING LEADERS
(Minimum 100 Plate Appearances)

	AVG	AB	R	H	2B	3B	HR	RBI	SB
Mullen, Jim, Delaware	.426	115	30	49	12	3	0	25	6
Musolf, Jared, New Jersey	.381	147	30	56	15	5	0	25	14
Weed, B.J., Newburgh	.378	132	34	50	7	4	0	15	24
Eldred, Brad, Jersey City	.367	106	18	39	7	2	4	25	5
Spadt, Eric, Quakertown	.364	143	26	52	15	1	5	34	4
Moccia, Mark, Newburgh	.364	138	40	48	7	4	0	21	30
McCarthy, Bill, New Jersey	.347	101	22	35	5	3	2	13	4
Ellerson, Brian, Jersey City	.342	114	23	39	12	5	1	14	10
Macchio, Paul, Newburgh	.333	132	22	44	6	3	0	24	6
Koslowski, Kasey, Metro	.330	115	15	38	6	0	0	13	3

INDIVIDUAL PITCHING LEADERS
(Minimum 35 Innings)

	W	L	ERA	G	SV	IP	H	BB	SO
Reed, Mike, Quakertown	4	1	0.88	12	2	41	26	23	30
Mazzante, Lou, Delaware	6	0	1.43	8	0	44	25	22	40
Buglovsky, Chris, Jersey	7	1	1.49	10	0	60	39	12	78
Lackett, Chris, New Jersey	3	1	2.25	9	0	48	39	21	30
McGuire, Rich, Metro	4	5	2.44	13	1	67	55	18	36
Fardella, Jason, Metro	2	4	2.78	11	1	46	16	16	18
Myers, Damien, Delaware	5	2	3.03	13	1	50	32	21	30
Pahucki, Dave, Newburgh	8	1	3.08	11	0	61	59	21	41
McKenna, Tim, New Jersey	4	2	3.33	8	0	54	21	16	20

CAPE COD LEAGUE

EAST	W	L	T	PCT	PTS
Chatham A's	30	14	0	.682	60
Orleans Cardinals	28	16	0	.636	56
Yarmouth-Dennis Red Sox	19	23	2	.452	40
Brewster Whitecaps	19	24	1	.442	39
Harwich Mariners	17	27	0	.386	34
WEST	**W**	**L**	**T**	**PCT**	**PTS**
Cotuit Kettleers	26	18	0	.591	52
Wareham Gatemen	24	18	2	.571	50
Bourne Braves	23	20	1	.535	47
Hyannis Mets	18	24	2	.429	38
Falmouth Commodores	12	32	0	.273	24

PLAYOFFS: Chatham defeated Orleans 3-1 and Cotuit defeated Wareham 3-0 in best-of-5 semifinals; Cotuit defeated Chatham 2-1 in best-of-3 final.

ALL-STAR TEAM: C—Curtis Sapp, Hyannis (North Carolina State). **1B**—Garrett Atkins, Cotuit (UCLA). **2B**—Dominic Rich, Brewster (Auburn). **3B**—Lance Niekro, Orleans (Florida Southern). **SS**—Tim Hummel, Orleans (Old Dominion). **OF**—Jaime Bubela, Wareham (Baylor); Rich Thompson, Cotuit (James Madison); David

Cape Cod playoff MVP
Garrett Atkins was the league's top first baseman

DeJesus, Chatham (Rutgers); Shawn Pearson, Cotuit (Old Dominion). **DH**—John Ballon, Bourne (New Orleans). **Util**—Seth Davidson, Chatham (Southern California); Mark Teixeira, Orleans (Georgia Tech). **P**—Rik Currier, Chatham (Southern California); Pat Pinkman, Wareham (Virginia Tech); Greg Montalbano, Orleans (Northeastern); Shawn Weaver, Orleans (Old Dominion). **RP**—Derrick DePriest, Chatham (North Carolina); Kevin Zaug, Harwich (St. John's).

Most Valuable Player: Lance Niekro, Orleans. **Pitchers of the Year:** Pat Pinkman, Wareham; Rik Currier, Chatham.

INDIVIDUAL BATTING LEADERS
(Minimum 119 Plate Appearances)

	AVG	AB	R	H	2B	3B	HR	RBI	SB
Bubela, Jaime, Wareham	.370	165	34	61	7	2	2	18	23
Niekro, Lance, Orleans	.360	172	26	62	9	0	13	44	3
Rich, Dominic, Brewster	.341	132	26	45	12	0	2	28	18
Sapp, Curtis, Hyannis	.327	165	14	54	6	1	3	27	0
Utley, Chase, Cotuit	.322	143	25	46	7	0	5	33	4
Thompson, Rich, Cotuit	.318	176	46	56	6	0	0	14	36
Hartig, Phil, Wareham	.317	161	22	51	7	2	2	32	4
Atkins, Garrett, Cotuit	.312	141	17	44	9	1	1	35	1
Mace, Clark, Wareham	.308	133	17	41	1	0	0	17	12
Pearson, Shawn, Cotuit	.299	127	23	38	6	1	0	23	23
Ballon, John, Bourne	.298	151	21	45	13	0	4	25	3
Hawpe, Brad, Y-D	.293	140	18	41	8	0	8	20	2
Rock, Jamie, Y-D	.292	130	27	38	16	3	4	21	4
DeJesus, David, Chatham	.292	161	25	47	9	2	2	16	11
Teixeira, Mark, Orleans	.289	149	30	43	11	2	7	26	4
Scott, Mike, Hyannis	.288	170	25	49	5	1	2	15	3
Inglett, Joe, Bourne	.287	122	20	35	9	0	3	7	5
Stanley, Steve, Brewster	.286	168	29	48	1	0	0	8	32
Bilezikjian, Charles, Harwich	.286	133	16	38	5	0	2	17	14
Duncan, Jeff, Y-D	.283	145	36	41	8	1	5	27	16
Davidson, Seth, Chatham	.280	164	30	46	5	0	4	16	4
Lambert, Casey, Wareham	.280	150	25	42	7	0	0	19	13
Hooper, Clay, Chatham	.278	133	15	37	8	0	1	15	2
Stockton, Brad, Cotuit	.277	141	22	39	8	0	5	27	4
Hallada, Daryl, Cotuit	.276	123	15	34	4	1	0	11	2
Hummel, Tim, Orleans	.275	149	38	41	11	0	8	28	12
Prince, Bryan, Orleans	.271	133	9	36	2	0	3	18	1

Amateur Baseball

	AVG	AB	R	H	2B	3B	HR	RBI	SB
Jones, Mitch, Y-D	.268	138	25	37	6	1	7	29	2
Cash, Kevin, Falmouth	.262	107	12	28	8	0	2	16	4
Wilfong, Nick, Brewster	.259	112	12	29	3	0	6	18	5
Colson, Jason, Cotuit	.256	125	15	32	8	0	2	19	0
Walter, Scott, Wareham	.252	143	16	36	7	0	3	24	2
Nelson, John, Harwich	.252	147	20	37	5	2	0	18	4
Fagan, Shawn, Hyannis	.252	159	20	40	5	1	1	14	3

INDIVIDUAL PITCHING LEADERS
(Minimum 35 Innings)

	W	L	ERA	G	SV	IP	H	BB	SO
Zaug, Kevin, Harwich	5	2	1.09	23	6	41	29	13	40
Weaver, Shawn, Orleans	1	1	1.11	9	0	65	35	16	54
Ramshaw, James, Cotuit	1	2	1.22	15	2	37	17	19	41
Montalbano, Greg, Orleans	5	1	1.29	9	0	56	26	18	46
Pinkman, Pat, Wareham	7	2	1.34	10	0	74	60	25	71
Currier, Rik, Chatham	7	0	1.34	8	0	47	21	27	44
Treadway, Brion, Wareham	1	1	1.46	21	10	37	19	14	47
Brooks, Conor, Hyannis	5	0	1.49	15	2	42	29	13	38
Leuenberger, Jeff, Chatham	4	2	1.67	8	0	54	40	27	35
Schultz, Mike, Cotuit	5	1	1.81	7	0	45	30	22	34
Sturkie, Scott, Bourne	2	1	2.01	15	2	45	30	9	38
Carlsen, Jeff, Bourne	5	2	2.08	9	1	61	41	11	59
Bonilla, Henry, Cotuit	6	1	2.19	8	0	53	42	17	46
Dale, Logan, Wareham	5	3	2.20	9	0	61	43	18	41
Bouknight, Kip, Chatham	5	2	2.25	9	0	60	44	32	45
Dennis, Jason, Brewster	4	2	2.31	10	0	74	61	18	56
Capuano, Chris, Bourne	2	4	2.35	10	0	61	55	20	60
Berney, Scott, Falmouth	3	1	2.36	15	1	46	36	16	38
Bauer, Peter, Orleans	7	1	2.49	9	0	61	47	28	41
Fontana, Tony, Cotuit	3	3	2.66	7	0	44	41	15	38
D'Amato, Dan, Y-D	3	1	2.72	6	1	36	32	11	34
O'Gara, Dan, Brewster	3	2	2.76	8	0	46	37	19	32
Beal, Andy, Bourne	4	1	2.77	9	1	52	45	19	45
LeClair, Aric, Harwich	2	3	2.80	18	1	45	34	28	44
Stamler, Keith, Orleans	2	3	2.83	18	1	35	31	19	31
Minton, Foye, Hyannis	4	2	2.88	10	1	50	33	15	55
Pember, David, Orleans	2	0	2.93	11	2	46	41	12	36
Stokes, Shaun, Chatham	5	2	2.98	9	0	63	59	21	47

CENTRAL ILLINOIS LEAGUE

EAST	W	L	PCT	GB
Twin City Stars	26	21	.553	—
Danville Dans	24	22	.522	1½
Decatur Blues	13	34	.277	13
WEST	W	L	PCT	GB
Quincy Gems	31	17	.646	—
Bluff City Bombers	29	19	.604	2
Springfield Rifles	19	29	.396	12

PLAYOFF TOURNAMENT: Danville 3-0, Quincy 2-2, Twin City 1-2, Bluff City 1-2, Springfield 0-1, Decatur 0-0.

ALL-STAR TEAM: C—Ben Caffey, Bluff City (Meramec, Mo., CC); Matt Serafini, Twin City (Evansville). **1B**—Ryan Howard, Decatur (Southwest Missouri State); Jayme Sperring, Quincy (Houston). **2B**—Ryan Kyes, Springfield (Ohio); Matt Gardner, Danville (Southwest Missouri State); Chad Opel, Bluff City (Southern Illinois-Edwardsville). **3B**—Mark Gilliam, Twin City (Motlow State, Tenn., CC); Brian Fuess, Bluff City (Southwest Missouri State); Jon Knott, Danville (Mississippi State); Chris Martin, Decatur (Eastern Illinois). **SS**—Brian Brown, Twin City (Bradley); Jesse Smith, Springfield (Bradley). **OF**—Dave Crouthers, Bluff City (SIU-Edwardsville); Travis Dawson, Bluff City (SIU-Edwardsville); Buddy Dubois, Danville (Austin Peay); Jason Beckman, Twin City (Bradley); Darrin Dubois, Danville (Danville Area, Ill., CC). **SP**—John Rheinecker, Danville (Belleville Area, Ill., CC); Mike Weel, Danville (Austin Peay); Brian Forystek, Twin City (Illinois State); Chucky Son, Danville (Louisiana State); Allan Wills, Quincy (Lewis, Ill.); Duncan McAdoo, Quincy (Houston). **RP**—Neal Cotts, Quincy (Illinois State); Jayme Sperring, Quincy (Houston).

Players of the Year: Brian Fuess, Bluff City; Jon Knott, Danville. **Pitcher of the Year:** Chucky Son, Danville.

INDIVIDUAL BATTING LEADERS
(Minimum 106 Plate Appearances)

	AVG	AB	R	H	2B	3B	HR	RBI	SB
Martin, Chris, Decatur	.343	102	16	35	3	0	2	13	6
Fuess, Brian, Bluff City	.343	178	25	61	17	0	6	44	1
Caffey, Ben, Bluff City	.337	166	25	56	10	0	4	47	3
Dubois, Darrin, Danville	.333	111	26	37	8	1	0	23	6
Smith, Jesse, Springfield	.326	193	22	63	13	2	1	24	5
Brown, Brian, Twin City	.323	167	27	54	17	0	3	36	5

	AVG	AB	R	H	2B	3B	HR	RBI	SB
Gardner, Matt, Danville	.323	186	40	60	8	1	2	29	8
Howard, Ryan, Decatur	.319	160	28	51	6	3	11	30	0
Shelton, Tyler, Springfield	.317	126	15	40	3	1	0	9	4
Kyes, Ryan, Springfield	.317	186	27	59	9	0	1	18	6
Gilliam, Mark, Twin City	.317	183	31	58	13	0	1	26	1
Peerman, Michael, Danville	.316	187	28	59	8	0	0	27	3
Sperring, Jayme, Quincy	.310	155	21	48	9	2	7	35	0
Knott, Jon, Danville	.309	191	44	59	16	1	10	43	4
Dawson, Travis, Bluff City	.306	196	54	60	11	2	1	23	30
Crouthers, Dave, Bluff City	.305	187	41	57	4	1	1	27	12
Opel, Chad, Bluff City	.304	171	41	52	13	1	4	27	18
Dubois, Buddy, Danville	.304	191	25	58	11	0	1	25	14
Haines, Andy, Twin City	.302	129	10	39	3	0	1	12	1

INDIVIDUAL PITCHING LEADERS
(Minimum 40 Innings)

	W	L	ERA	G	SV	IP	H	BB	SO
Rheinecker, John, Bluff City	3	2	2.61	7	0	48	41	13	41
Son, Chucky, Danville	7	1	2.70	12	0	73	54	20	45
Weel, Mike, Danville	6	3	2.90	10	0	68	75	18	46
Anderson, Jason, Danville	3	3	2.96	10	0	49	45	10	47
Hoffman, Dave, Danville	3	6	3.02	10	0	60	45	36	38
Andrzejak, Chris, Springfield	4	3	3.11	8	0	64	70	13	39
Fehland, Matt, Twin City	4	5	3.14	11	1	63	56	23	46
Taylor, Kirk, Springfield	3	4	3.22	12	0	50	44	23	26
Forystek, Brian, Twin City	7	2	3.39	10	0	77	78	30	58
McAdoo, Duncan, Quincy	7	1	3.62	10	0	60	69	27	55
Wills, Allan, Quincy	7	1	3.71	11	0	68	60	18	49
Brown, Joel, Decatur	2	6	3.79	13	0	55	48	43	35
Wechsler, Justin, Quincy	4	3	3.86	13	1	61	50	24	59
Feld, Adam, Springfield	4	3	3.88	12	2	72	89	20	62

COASTAL PLAIN LEAGUE

	W	L	PCT	GB
*Wilmington Sharks	33	16	.673	—
+Outer Banks Daredevils	30	18	.625	2½
Edenton Steamers	27	23	.540	6½
Wilson Tobs	25	24	.510	8
Durham Braves	22	26	.458	10½
Thomasville Hi-Toms	21	26	.447	11
Asheboro Copperheads	21	27	.438	11½
Florence Redwolves	15	34	.306	18

*First-half champion +Second-half champion

PLAYOFFS: Wilmington defeated Outer Banks 2-1 in best-of-3 final.

ALL-STAR TEAM: C—Brett Muhlhan, Wilson (UNC Asheville). **1B**—Brandon Blair, Edenton (Mercer). **2B**—Jake Long, Durham (Dayton). **3B**—Kevin Youkilis, Florence (Cincinnati). **SS**—Tim LaVigne, Wilmington (Virginia). **OF**—Kevin Hairr, Edenton (UNC Wilmington); Matt McCay, Thomasville (North Carolina); Max Krance, Wilson (Princeton). **RHP**—Chris Spigner, Edenton (South Carolina). **LHP**—Brian Ross, Outer Banks (Old Dominion). **RP**—Daryll DeSalvo, Outer Banks (Radford).

Most Valuable Player: Dallas McPherson, Asheboro. **Pitcher of the Year:** Taft Cable, Wilson.

INDIVIDUAL BATTING LEADERS
(Minimum 135 Plate Appearances)

	AVG	AB	R	H	2B	3B	HR	RBI	SB
McPherson, Dallas, Ashe.	.349	166	19	58	17	4	3	28	5
Schalick, G.R., Outer Banks	.323	158	31	51	10	0	11	42	1
McCay, Matt, Thomasville	.318	151	28	48	3	0	1	17	6
Martin, Grant, Thomasville	.308	133	14	41	6	0	1	11	2
Walsh, Sean, Thomasville	.306	170	27	52	9	1	2	26	8
Shearin, Jamey, Durham	.306	157	27	48	9	1	4	31	5
LaVigne, Tim, Wilmington	.304	171	26	52	20	1	1	25	13
Knox, Mic, Wilson	.300	150	25	45	15	0	2	18	2
Hairr, Kevin, Edenton	.297	192	30	57	10	0	5	17	13
Sinsabaugh, Jeremy, Dur.	.295	176	29	52	17	1	7	29	9
Oliva, Mike, Thomasville	.294	160	26	47	7	0	1	19	10
Brackley, Carlos, Wilson	.291	141	26	41	8	2	8	30	3
Braun, Scott, Durham	.290	162	28	47	10	3	5	30	9
Troilo, Joe, Wilmington	.288	170	30	49	12	1	3	22	33

INDIVIDUAL PITCHING LEADERS
(Minimum 40 Innings)

	W	L	ERA	G	SV	IP	H	BB	SO
Sigley, Jayson, Wilmington	3	0	1.02	7	0	44	24	15	64
Hernandez, Buddy, Wilmington	9	0	1.19	12	3	45	26	13	70
Spigner, Chris, Edenton	6	1	1.20	12	0	67	35	41	85
Toler, Ted, Outer Banks	4	3	1.36	29	1	53	38	23	43

Batson, Byron, Wilmington	3	2	1.61	20	1	50	39	15	50
Cable, Taft, Wilson	9	2	1.83	14	0	98	72	30	91
Ross, Brian, Outer Banks	6	2	2.07	13	0	83	69	44	68
Clark, Chris, Wilmington	3	4	2.11	11	1	73	56	12	75
McPherson, Dallas, Asheboro	5	2	2.19	12	0	82	65	27	83
Poston, Jamie, Wilmington	7	1	2.30	15	0	70	48	21	75
Helmey, Shaun, Florence	5	5	2.30	11	0	82	63	36	59
Combs, Ryan, Edenton	2	3	2.43	10	0	59	53	18	52
Jansen, Matt, Outer Banks	6	5	2.46	13	0	91	69	13	108

GREAT LAKES LEAGUE

EAST	W	L	PCT	GB
+Northern Ohio	28	10	.737	—
Youngstown Express	22	17	.564	6½
*Columbus All-Americans	19	21	.450	10
Delaware Cows	18	21	.462	10½
Stark County Terriers	15	25	.375	14

WEST	W	L	PCT	GB
*Michigan Monarchs	24	15	.615	—
+Lima Locos	22	18	.550	4
Michigan Panthers	18	21	.462	6
Grand Lake Mariners	17	22	.436	7
Sandusky Bay Stars	13	26	.333	11

*First-half champion +Second-half champion

PLAYOFFS: Northern Ohio defeated Columbus 2-0 and Michigan Monarchs defeated Lima 2-0 in best-of-3 semifinals. Michigan Monarchs defeated Northern Ohio 2-1 in best-of-3 final.

ALL-STAR TEAM: C—Rock Mills, Northern Ohio (Alabama). **1B**—Sean Luellwitz, Stark County (Vanderbilt). **2B**—Chris Burke, Northern Ohio (Tennessee). **3B**—Jeremy Brown, Northern Ohio (Alabama). **SS**—Nate Reeser, Columbus (West Virginia). **OF**—Les Brock, Youngstown (Kent); Radames Torres, Delaware (Ohio Dominican); Ed Weightman, Columbus (West Virginia). **DH**—Brad Bouras, Sandusky (Columbus State). **Util**—Ryan Ellis, Youngstown (Point Park, Pa.). **P**—Josh Axelson, Northern Ohio (Michigan State); Dan Horvath, Michigan Monarchs (Michigan State); Mike Newsted, Michigan Monarchs (Wayne State, Mich.); Nate Tekavec, Lima (Miami, Ohio).

Most Valuable Player: Radames Torres, Delaware. **Pitcher of the Year:** Mike Newsted, Michigan Monarchs.

INDIVIDUAL BATTING LEADERS
(Minimum 100 Plate Appearances)

	AVG	AB	R	H	2B	3B	HR	RBI	SB
Torres, Radames, Delaware	.455	121	30	55	12	1	9	42	1
Burke, Chris, Northern Ohio	.438	130	32	57	10	1	2	21	23
Ellis, Ryan, Youngstown	.408	98	29	40	9	0	0	19	2
Brown, Jeremy, NO	.392	79	26	31	1	0	11	28	1
Haegele, Dan, Delaware	.379	95	17	36	3	0	0	14	2
Mills, Rock, Northern Ohio	.356	90	18	32	4	1	6	25	3
McIlvain, Trent, Delaware	.347	98	16	34	0	0	0	15	3
Bouras, Brad, Sandusky	.346	127	21	44	10	3	6	26	3
Weightman, Ed, Columbus	.342	120	17	41	5	0	4	25	4
Luellwitz, Sean, SC	.341	91	12	31	4	1	4	20	0
Puliafico, Joe, Youngstown	.340	103	16	35	7	1	2	22	1
Broshears, Phil, Lima	.339	127	17	43	6	0	3	14	3
Bogenrife, Jason, Delaware	.333	108	16	36	8	0	3	23	2
Mayor, John, Youngstown	.333	120	20	40	7	1	1	10	13
St. Clair, Blake, Grand Lake	.333	81	10	27	4	1	0	10	3

INDIVIDUAL PITCHING LEADERS
(Minimum 28 Innings)

	W	L	ERA	G	SV	IP	H	BB	SO
Teckavec, Nate, Lima	4	1	1.07	6	0	42	33	11	18
Heath, Bryce, Northern Ohio	6	0	1.30	12	4	28	21	7	19
Kelley, Camden, Monarchs	4	1	1.66	7	0	43	38	21	38
Busbin, Brad, Northern Ohio	2	1	1.91	5	0	28	17	13	23
Wells, Chad, Grand Lake	2	2	1.93	10	2	37	36	10	39
Moenter, Curt, Delaware	3	3	1.99	7	0	45	28	12	33
Menke, Craig, Grand Lake	4	2	2.09	7	1	39	28	13	24
Wilkinson, John, Youngstown	2	3	2.17	15	7	37	40	12	26
Horvath, Dan, Monarchs	6	3	2.20	11	1	57	51	13	38
Harrington, Sean, Panthers	4	3	2.25	11	0	36	32	10	17
Moak, Curtis, Panthers	0	2	2.30	14	0	31	30	14	23
Lammers, Kris, Grand Lake	4	2	2.59	8	0	42	41	11	36
Miller, Brandon, Lima	3	3	2.74	7	0	43	45	11	32
Bolthouse, Adam, Monarchs	4	4	2.78	10	0	55	48	11	47
Newsted, Mike, Monarchs	6	1	2.91	11	0	59	50	9	46

NEW ENGLAND COLLEGIATE LEAGUE

	W	L	PCT	GB
Keene Swamp Bats	27	14	.659	—
Middletown Giants	27	15	.643	½
Rhode Island Reds	25	16	.610	2
Danbury Westerners	23	19	.548	4½
Torrington Twisters	23	19	.548	4½
Rhode Island Gulls	18	24	.429	9½
Central Mass Collegians	13	28	.317	14
Eastern Tides	9	30	.231	17

PLAYOFFS: Danbury defeated Keene 2-1 and Middletown defeated Rhode Island Reds 2-1 in best-of-3 semifinals. Middletown defeated Danbury 3-1 in best-of-5 final.

ALL-STAR TEAM: C—Bob Acabbo, Middletown (Vermont). **1B**—Mike O'Brien, Rhode Island Reds (Rutgers). **2B**—Shaun Larkin, Keene (Cypress, Calif., JC). **3B**—Justin Sherrod, Torrington (Rollins, Fla.). **SS**—Jeff Keppinger, Keene (Georgia). **OF**—Matt Easterday, Danbury (Georgia Southern); Mark Malaska, Danbury (Akron); Jeff Baumtrog, Keene (Tennessee). **DH**—Brian Wolotka, Danbury (Butler). **P**—Josh Novotney, Torrington (Western Kentucky); Chad Coward, Rhode Island Reds (Guilford, N.C.); John Novinsky, Keene (Iona).

Most Valuable Player: Matt Easterday, Danbury. **Pitcher of the Year:** Chad Coward, Rhode Island Reds.

INDIVIDUAL BATTING LEADERS
(Minimum 113 Plate Appearances)

	AVG	AB	R	H	2B	3B	HR	RBI	SB
Morgan, Chris, CM	.396	101	20	40	3	0	5	22	0
Hess, Cy, Eastern	.356	118	20	42	3	3	2	17	10
Houdek, Brian, Torrington	.348	158	27	55	4	0	0	21	14
Souza, Ryan, RI Gulls	.347	118	20	41	11	0	5	28	5
Berigan, Brent, RI Gulls	.343	99	20	34	8	3	2	20	16
Malaska, Mark, Danbury	.317	161	37	51	12	1	6	41	10
Easterday, Matt, Danbury	.312	157	21	49	10	2	1	32	10
Larkin, Shaun, Keene	.310	155	35	48	7	0	10	38	2
Scullin, Jon, RI Gulls	.307	140	30	43	2	1	1	9	16
Hastings, Joe, Keene	.304	125	27	38	6	0	6	27	3
Wissner, Kevin, Middletown	.298	151	26	45	3	2	6	30	6
Baron, Brian, Torrington	.297	138	14	41	7	2	1	32	3
Keppinger, Jeff, Keene	.295	139	30	41	11	0	9	35	7
Merrill, Ronnie, Torrington	.293	174	36	51	8	1	3	23	11
Baumtrog, Jeff, Keene	.293	99	32	29	7	0	3	12	15
Jansen, Andrew, Danbury	.287	150	35	43	11	1	5	33	5

INDIVIDUAL PITCHING LEADERS
(Minimum 34 Innings)

	W	L	ERA	G	SV	IP	H	BB	SO
Huddleston, Mike, Danbury	4	0	0.97	24	3	37	20	16	56
Reeder, Brad, Keene	5	1	1.00	14	4	45	27	23	57
Langone, Stephen, RI Reds	3	1	1.44	6	0	44	24	14	52
Novotney, Josh, Torrington	6	2	1.64	8	0	66	43	19	78
Coward, Chad, RI Reds	6	1	1.73	8	0	62	43	16	48
Novinsky, John, Keene	4	1	2.05	9	0	61	33	25	69
Liriano, Orlando, RI Reds	3	3	2.13	7	0	51	38	22	47
Szuminski, Jason, RI Gulls	5	3	2.45	8	0	59	46	23	42
Gaffney, Chris, RI Gulls	4	3	2.50	11	1	58	48	23	41
Bailin, James, RI Reds	6	1	2.61	8	0	52	40	14	43
Clark, Jeff, Middletown	5	0	2.75	7	0	39	32	11	32
Smith, Cliff, Central Mass	3	3	3.02	10	0	63	53	20	71

NORTHEASTERN LEAGUE

EAST	W	L	PCT	GB
Schenectady Mohawks	27	12	.692	—
Ithaca Lakers	20	20	.500	7½
Cortland Apples	16	23	.410	10
Rome Indians	11	28	.282	14½

WEST	W	L	PCT	GB
Geneva Knights	25	15	.625	—
Newark Raptors	25	15	.625	—
Wellsville Nitros	17	22	.436	7½
Hornell Dodgers	17	23	.425	8

PLAYOFFS: Ithaca defeated Schenectady 2-0 and Newark defeated Geneva 2-1 in best-of-3 semifinals. Newark defeated Ithaca 2-0 in best-of-3 final.

Most Valuable Player: Jeff Haase, Schenectady.

INDIVIDUAL BATTING LEADERS
(Minimum 120 Plate Appearances)

	AVG	AB	R	H	2B	3B	HR	RBI	SB
Haase, Jeff, Schenectady	.389	114	35	56	11	2	8	38	14
O'Brien, Jade, Hornell	.376	133	27	50	17	2	3	43	7
Marcum, Matt, Ithaca	.367	120	17	44	10	0	0	22	6
Shemwell, Foy, Wellsville	.361	119	26	43	2	2	3	18	7
Diaz, Octavio, Schenectady	.346	133	40	46	8	1	2	18	2
Warren, Phil, Newark	.344	128	27	44	12	1	1	25	4
McMains, Derin, Newark	.333	114	27	38	4	3	1	18	10
Navarette, Ray, Geneva	.333	114	24	38	5	1	1	11	10
Klebonis, Dave, Newark	.331	145	18	48	7	4	2	28	5
Ciemniecki, Brian, Hornell	.331	130	42	43	4	2	0	12	30

INDIVIDUAL PITCHING LEADERS
(Minimum 36 Innings)

	W	L	ERA	G	SV	IP	H	BB	SO
McCurdy, Nick, Cortland	6	1	1.65	10	0	60	50	18	34
Erwin, Randy, Newark	5	1	1.94	7	0	46	45	11	39
Fischer, Brian, Schenectady	4	1	2.00	7	0	45	28	16	42
Long, Jerry, Schenectady	5	3	2.37	10	0	46	44	17	34
Emrich, Jeff, Geneva	4	3	2.41	8	0	52	43	19	35
Riley, Chris, Wellsville	1	2	2.55	10	2	35	26	15	23
Barrera, Shawn, Hornell	5	3	2.85	11	0	73	60	31	71
Schulz, Rob, Newark	6	3	2.87	15	2	38	32	13	44
Galbreath, Ben, Wellsville	3	3	3.00	14	0	36	39	12	31
Osgood, John, Ithaca	3	2	3.03	7	1	39	33	18	34

SHENANDOAH VALLEY LEAGUE

	W	L	PCT	GB
Staunton Braves	27	13	.675	—
Harrisonburg Turks	22	18	.550	5
Winchester Royals	21	19	.525	6
New Market Rebels	20	20	.500	7
Waynesboro Generals	19	21	.475	8
Front Royal Cardinals	11	29	.275	16

PLAYOFFS: Winchester defeated Harrisonburg 3-1 and Staunton defeated New Market 3-1 in best-of-5 semifinals. Staunton defeated Winchester 3-0 in best-of-5 final.

Most Valuable Player: Ernesto Durazo, Harrisonburg (Arizona).
Most Outstanding Pitcher: Carl Rowland, Winchester (Arkansas-Little Rock).

INDIVIDUAL BATTING LEADERS
(Minimum 100 Plate Appearances)

	AVG	AB	R	H	2B	3B	HR	RBI	SB
Scott, Luke, Staunton	.366	134	33	49	12	1	6	30	5
Olkowski, Kevin, Wayne.	.359	153	26	55	10	1	4	29	1
Stone, David, Staunton	.348	178	38	62	6	1	0	21	15
Stone, Casey, Winchester	.342	146	27	50	4	0	0	13	12
Shealy, Ryan, Harri.	.339	109	18	37	5	1	3	22	0
Bender, Eric, Staunton	.338	148	37	50	7	0	7	34	4
Goss, Matt, Harrisonburg	.333	126	28	42	5	2	2	16	7
Durazo, Ernesto, Harr.	.330	179	29	59	13	1	4	35	2
Drawdy, Ben, Wayne.	.316	95	15	30	2	1	1	9	7
Olson, Tim, Staunton	.315	184	43	58	13	0	8	49	14
Tyler, John, New Market	.306	111	26	34	3	0	0	5	11
Greenwell, Bill, Front Royal	.301	146	22	44	8	0	4	21	1
Gertz, Jeff, Harrisonburg	.297	118	17	35	14	0	1	20	1
Tracy, Chad, Staunton	.294	119	21	35	4	0	3	26	2
Raffo, John, Front Royal	.290	93	15	27	7	0	5	19	0
Baha, Mark, Harrisonburg	.286	133	22	38	3	0	1	15	6
Brock, Todd, Winchester	.282	181	31	51	12	1	6	33	6
Weishaar, Kasey, New Market	.281	146	27	41	11	1	1	11	8
Turner, Jason, Waynesboro	.279	129	22	36	8	3	3	20	2

INDIVIDUAL PITCHING LEADERS
(Minimum 30 Innings)

	W	L	ERA	G	SV	IP	H	BB	SO
Corcorhan, Roy, Harrisonburg	5	3	1.35	23	5	33	21	23	46
Eagle, Corey, Waynesboro	3	2	1.45	23	8	31	22	14	35
Lynn, Kevin, Staunton	5	0	1.56	7	0	40	30	8	40
Edwards, Brad, Front Royal	4	1	2.39	9	0	60	38	40	75
Rowland, Carl, Winchester	5	2	2.42	11	0	71	70	19	59
Kennedy, Casey, Staunton	7	2	2.57	10	0	74	71	8	73
Hammond, Jamie, Wayne.	4	1	2.71	10	0	66	67	12	65
Goebeler, Dan, Staunton	9	0	2.80	12	0	74	59	23	62
Adinolfi, Tim, New Market	4	2	2.95	12	2	73	66	19	65
Lee, Jon, Waynesboro	2	4	3.20	9	0	59	63	20	38
Pope, Justin, Staunton	5	2	3.26	10	0	61	62	21	47

NON-AFFILIATED LEAGUES

ALASKA LEAGUE

	League				Overall	
	W	L	PCT	GB	W	L
Kenai Peninsula Oilers	17	9	.654	—	35	17
Anchorage Bucs	15	12	.556	2½	24	18
Fairbanks Goldpanners	14	14	.500	4	24	21
Anchorage Glacier Pilots	12	14	.462	5	24	20
Mat-Su Miners	8	17	.320	8½	20	24

ALL-STAR TEAM: C—Eric Frei, Fairbanks (Purdue). **1B**—Jared Pitney, Kenai (Pepperdine). **2B**—Danny Garcia, Kenai (Pepperdine). **3B**—Greg Filson, Mat-Su (George Mason). **SS**—Bryan Anderson, Anchorage Bucs (Southwest Texas State). **OF**—Spencer Oborn, Anchorage Bucs (Cal State Fullerton); Jonah Martin, Fairbanks (Arizona State); Elliot Wheeler, Anchorage Bucs (Santa Clara). **DH**—David Parrish, Anchorage Glacier Pilots (Michigan). **Util**—Kurt Koshelnik, Anchorage Bucs (Lewis-Clark State, Idaho). **P**—Jeff Bowman, Kenai (San Francisco); Jeff Bruksch, Anchorage Bucs (Southern California); David Bush, Fairbanks (Wake Forest); John Eric Hernandez, Mat-Su (Chico State); Steve Madril, Kenai (UC Riverside).

Most Valuable Player: John Eric Hernandez, Kenai.

INDIVIDUAL BATTING LEADERS
(Minimum 100 Plate Appearances)

	AVG	AB	R	H	2B	3B	HR	RBI	SB
Pitney, Jared, Kenai	.361	122	29	44	11	0	4	23	6
Jensen, Dave, Fairbanks	.316	155	24	49	7	1	1	19	7
Garcia, Danny, Kenai	.315	181	50	57	7	6	9	40	19
Oborn, Spencer, Bucs	.314	102	23	32	7	1	2	21	14
Candelaria, Scott, Kenai	.309	191	31	59	10	1	2	27	16
Day, Nick, Bucs	.304	102	21	31	6	1	3	18	3
Clark, Ryan, Kenai	.301	143	21	43	10	0	3	30	4
Downing, Phil, Kenai	.293	116	22	34	6	2	0	10	12
Koshelnik, Kurt, Bucs	.287	115	22	33	9	2	0	13	5
Reece, Eric, Glacier Pilots	.284	95	12	27	4	0	0	12	1
Filson, Greg, Mat-Su	.282	131	21	37	7	0	2	12	7
Jones, Jeff, Kenai	.282	142	27	40	9	0	0	27	3
Peck, Bryan, Glacier Pilots	.282	142	21	40	6	2	2	22	14
Womack, Bobby, Bucs	.282	85	16	29	7	2	0	14	18
Alvarado, Damien, Bucs	.275	80	19	22	2	1	0	15	2
Conrad, Brooks, Fairbanks	.274	164	37	45	7	3	2	21	14
LaBarbera, A.J., Bucs	.272	125	19	34	3	1	0	12	10

INDIVIDUAL PITCHING LEADERS
(Minimum 30 Innings)

	W	L	ERA	G	SV	IP	H	BB	SO
Hernandez, John Eric, Mat-Su	8	1	0.85	10	0	63	40	11	49
Rich, Daniel, Fairbanks	2	2	1.53	7	0	35	30	9	27
Nichols, Jeff, Kenai	4	1	1.74	7	0	41	27	10	38
Reid, Brent, Mat-Su	2	2	1.83	8	0	39	30	13	18
Oglesby, Jason, Glacier Pilots	1	2	1.91	12	5	33	21	18	15
Madril, Steve, Kenai	5	3	2.07	12	0	70	51	18	41
Bruksch, Jeff, Bucs	5	0	2.25	7	0	44	31	13	33
Hamilton, Mark, Bucs	2	1	2.38	7	0	34	25	10	35
Olson, Ryan, Fairbanks	3	1	2.44	13	2	44	35	18	28
Alexander, Nick, Mat-Su	3	2	2.51	21	3	32	26	9	23
Diaz, Paul, Glacier Pilots	1	2	2.65	11	2	37	30	15	20
Bomar, Mike, Glacier Pilots	3	3	2.89	8	0	47	37	11	31
Hintz, Beau, Mat-Su	2	4	2.89	9	0	37	33	18	29
Ralston, Bryce, Glacier Pilots	3	1	2.89	7	0	37	26	10	37
Skaggs, Jon, Kenai	1	2	2.93	8	0	31	16	25	15
Garner, Mike, Kenai	8	2	3.07	12	0	70	56	19	49
Carralejo, George, Bucs	3	1	3.23	7	0	31	18	29	14
Meldahl, Todd, Fairbanks	5	3	3.36	10	0	59	57	18	36

CLARK GRIFFITH COLLEGIATE LEAGUE

	W	L	PCT	GB
*Arlington	31	8	.795	—
Bethesda	23	14	.622	7
Southern Maryland	20	18	.526	10½
Vienna	15	22	.405	15
Reston	5	32	.135	25

*Won both halves of split-season schedule.

Most Valuable Player: Jared Dufault, Arlington (Illinois State).

Amateur Baseball

INDIVIDUAL BATTING LEADERS
(Minimum 85 At-Bats)

	AVG	AB	R	H	2B	3B	HR	RBI	SB
Dufault, Jared, Arlington	.409	149	32	61	9	2	6	42	12
Wood, Taylor, Arlington	.349	149	36	52	10	2	1	18	20
Lunsford, Trey, Arlington	.336	113	23	38	8	0	1	25	5
Crandell, Jeff, So. Maryland	.333	93	12	31	6	1	0	14	4
Floyd, Mike, Arlington	.329	149	23	49	14	3	1	30	17
Easter, Chuck, Bethesda	.321	134	19	43	13	0	0	22	1
Davies, Gregg, Bethesda	.320	122	25	39	7	0	0	14	6
Thomas, Stephen, Bethesda	.316	136	30	43	8	1	1	22	4
McCarty, Justin, Arlington	.312	93	23	29	5	2	0	9	22
Santmyer, Brad, Vienna	.310	100	14	31	8	0	7	23	0

INDIVIDUAL PITCHING LEADERS
(Minimum 30 Innings)

	W	L	ERA	G	SV	IP	H	BB	SO
Wynegar, Adam, Arlington	6	1	1.77	11	0	41	23	20	52
Abraham, Paul, Vienna	2	3	2.17	12	4	37	34	16	39
Rush, Josh, Arlington	4	1	2.60	10	0	45	45	23	28
Little, Jeff, Bethesda	4	1	2.63	7	0	48	28	22	37
Baker, Jason, Arlington	4	2	2.86	10	0	35	36	8	44
Viars, Andy, So. Maryland	2	2	2.90	9	0	50	57	17	40
Dudley, Mark, So. Maryland	4	1	3.08	9	0	38	39	5	18
Wilson, Aaron, Arlington	3	2	3.16	12	1	43	30	18	38
Heagen, Doug, Vienna	4	3	3.17	9	0	54	53	24	47
Sparkman, Kyle, Bethesda	4	1	3.38	8	0	59	48	16	65

NORTHWOODS LEAGUE

SOUTH	W	L	PCT	GB
+Waterloo	44	19	.698	—
*Rochester	40	23	.635	4
Mankato	28	34	.452	15½
Southern Minny	19	41	.463	23½

NORTH	W	L	PCT	GB
*+St. Cloud	43	19	.694	—
Brainerd	35	28	.556	8½
Wisconsin	22	42	.344	22
Grand Forks	19	44	.302	24½

*First-half champion +Second-half champion

PLAYOFFS: Rochester defeated Waterloo 2-0 and St. Cloud defeated Brainerd 2-1 in best-of-3 divisional series. Rochester defeated St. Cloud 2-1 in best-of-3 final.

ALL-STAR TEAM: C—Tony Arnerich, St. Cloud (Santa Rosa, Calif., CC); John Draper, Rochester (Cal State Los Angeles). **1B**—Josh Persell, Wisconsin (Southern California). **2B**—Dan Dement, Waterloo (Alabama-Birmingham). **3B**—Ray Goirigolzarri, Grand Forks (Stetson). **SS**—Mike Rouse, Brainerd (San Jose State). **OF**—Rich Austin, Mankato (Lindenwood, Mo.); Creston Whitaker, Waterloo (Illinois); Jeff Walker, Brainerd (Canada, Calif., JC). **DH**—Tony DeMarco, St. Cloud (Nevada-Las Vegas). **Util**—Chris Basak, St. Cloud (Illinois); Jesse Zimmer, Rochester (Northern Iowa). **RHP**—Steve Hecker, Waterloo (Illinois State); Jim Magrane, Waterloo (Iowa); Jeremy Rogelstad, Brainerd (San Jose State); Brad Steele, St. Cloud (California); Nic Ungs, Rochester (Northern Iowa); David Wells, Wisconsin (Belmont, Tenn.). **LHP**—Britt Carmichael, St. Cloud (Lubbock Christian); William Collazo, Waterloo (Kirkwood, Iowa, CC); Taylor Grant, Grand Forks (Washington); Pete Smart, St. Cloud (Kansas).
Most Valuable Player: Jim Magrane, Waterloo.

INDIVIDUAL BATTING LEADERS
(Minimum 173 Plate Appearances)

	AVG	AB	R	H	2B	3B	HR	RBI	SB
Persell, Josh, Wisconsin	.386	210	41	81	20	0	7	55	3
Rouse, Mike, Brainerd	.381	239	49	91	18	2	1	35	42
Basak, Chris, St. Cloud	.362	243	60	88	16	1	0	30	35
Dement, Dan, Waterloo	.357	199	50	71	21	4	9	50	14
Walker, Jeff, Brainerd	.356	180	39	64	12	0	4	32	4
Huggins, Mike, Mankato	.355	166	35	59	9	0	4	20	10
Whitaker, Creston, Waterloo	.353	150	42	53	7	1	0	16	34
DeMarco, Tony, St. Cloud	.351	194	37	68	14	1	8	50	3

	AVG	AB	R	H	2B	3B	HR	RBI	SB
Austin, Rich, Mankato	.345	145	32	50	8	2	6	33	11
Sark, Dave, Rochester	.333	201	35	67	14	0	5	45	1
Creighton, Tom, Wisconsin	.327	214	40	70	9	0	3	30	30
Christy, Jeff, Wisconsin	.327	196	49	64	16	2	3	32	16
Gates, David, St. Cloud	.325	160	35	52	6	0	8	34	11
Draper, John, Rochester	.325	197	43	64	18	2	4	40	9
Bone, Blake, St. Cloud	.321	196	45	63	22	1	7	42	3

INDIVIDUAL PITCHING LEADERS
(Minimum 51 Innings)

	W	L	ERA	G	SV	IP	H	BB	SO
Magrane, Jim, Waterloo	9	3	1.41	13	1	102	89	28	134
Steele, Brad, St. Cloud	7	1	1.99	10	0	68	65	19	66
Smart, Pete, St. Cloud	10	3	2.33	13	0	81	59	21	66
Grant, Taylor, Grand Forks	4	4	2.43	10	0	63	44	29	61
Collazo, William, Waterloo	9	2	2.50	11	0	86	70	25	82
Walk, Mitch, St. Cloud	5	2	2.63	11	0	51	33	33	55
Pedersen, Mark, Mankato	5	1	2.77	21	2	62	47	29	67
Rogelstad, Jeremy, Brainerd	7	4	2.79	11	0	84	75	14	66
Ungs, Nic, Rochester	8	3	3.12	13	1	69	51	22	68
Baker, Joey, Waterloo	6	3	3.18	14	0	88	89	35	67
Minor, Zach, Brainerd	3	2	3.21	11	0	62	50	36	60
Dickinson, Andy, Waterloo	4	0	3.32	13	2	57	55	17	31
McCasland, Ralph, St. Cloud	3	4	3.36	17	1	67	62	28	40
Lunski, Greg, Grand Forks	3	2	3.48	17	1	52	56	24	50
Floros, Tony, Mankato	3	4	3.53	12	0	74	73	24	45

JAYHAWK LEAGUE

	W	L	PCT	GB
Liberal Bee Jays	27	13	.675	—
Nevada Griffons	24	16	.600	3
El Dorado Broncos	20	17	.541	5½
Hays Larks	20	20	.500	7
Elkhart Dusters	14	25	.359	12½
Topeka Capitals	12	26	.316	14

ALL-STAR TEAM: C—Eli Whiteside, Nevada (Delta State). **1B**—Chris Williamson, Nevada (McNeese State). **2B**—Mickey McKee, Topeka (Tulane). **3B**—Terry Tiffee, Liberal (Louisiana State). **SS**—Kelly Eddlemon, Liberal (Sam Houston State). **OF**—Michael Artman, Nevada (Southern Mississippi); J.R. Warner, Nevada (Missouri); Dee Haynes, Nevada (Delta State). **DH**—Ryan Callaway, El Dorado (Fort Hays State). **Util**—Brian Loeb, Hays (Baylor). **RHP**—R.D. Spiehs, Liberal (Nebraska). **LHP**—Kenny Holubec, Liberal (Northeast Louisiana). **RP**—Chad Durham, Liberal (Texas Christian).

INDIVIDUAL BATTING LEADERS
(Minimum 75 At-Bats)

	AVG	AB	R	H	2B	3B	HR	RBI	SB
Eiquren, Chaz, Liberal	.369	111	22	41	10	1	2	16	2
Tiffee, Terry, Liberal	.361	133	25	48	8	1	4	32	2
Eddlemon, Kelly, Liberal	.351	131	34	46	17	2	5	32	8
Pujols, Albert, Hays	.343	108	22	37	5	1	5	17	10
Johnson, Jeremy, El Dorado	.339	109	15	37	8	1	1	24	3
Warner, J.R., Nevada	.330	112	23	37	5	0	3	12	7
Callaway, Ryan, El Dorado	.324	105	12	34	5	1	1	17	1
Garner, Ty, El Dorado	.319	119	21	38	12	1	1	19	13
Connors, Ryan, Nevada	.310	142	25	44	6	0	2	21	18
McKee, Mickey, Topeka	.310	84	12	26	4	0	0	8	8

INDIVIDUAL PITCHING LEADERS
(Minimum 30 Innings)

	W	L	ERA	G	SV	IP	H	BB	SO
Tarajack, Brian, Hays	2	1	1.78	6	1	30	23	8	18
Holubec, Kenny, Liberal	6	0	2.30	8	0	55	35	21	69
Bullinger, Trey, Elkhart	3	2	2.45	6	0	37	32	16	31
Orr, Ben, El Dorado	2	1	2.45	6	0	37	30	12	28
Glen, Willie, Nevada	3	2	2.47	8	0	44	35	25	30
Gassner, David, Hays	4	5	2.56	11	0	56	38	19	55
Slanina, Jason, Nevada	3	0	2.78	7	0	36	33	12	28
Gregg, Grant, Topeka	2	2	2.84	6	0	38	36	16	34
Williams, Blake, Liberal	6	2	2.96	9	0	46	32	12	36
Thomas, Tom, El Dorado	4	1	3.00	5	0	30	30	11	28

Japan plays its cards right; wins LL Series

Osaka, Japan, saved its best pitcher for the championship game and Kazuki Sumiyama responded with a two-hit, 5-0 shutout over United States champion Phenix City, Ala., at the 1999 Little League World Series (11-12) in Williamsport, Pa.

Sumiyama won two games at the eight-team tournament and had 19 strikeouts while pitching 11 scoreless innings. He also hit .615. Sumiyama was able to pitch in the final because he was lifted after only one inning in Japan's 12-2 semifinal win over Yabucoa, Puerto Rico, when Japan took an early 7-0 lead.

Phenix City was forced to use No. 3 pitcher Zach Martin in the final because its two best pitchers, Colby Rasmus and Bryan Woodall, combined to stop defending champion Toms River, N.J., 3-2 in the other semifinal. Little League rules prohibit a pitcher from working in successive games if he pitches more than one inning in the first.

Japan won its fourth title and first since 1976. Osaka was managed by former Hanshin Tigers outfielder Tsutomu Kameyama.

Minnesota wins Legion

New Brighton, Minn., Post 513 won the 1999 American Legion World Series in Middletown, Conn., by overwhelming two opponents with a floodtide of baserunners on the final day.

It tied a tournament record by leaving 17 runners on base in the semifinals against Gallatin, Tenn., Post 17, but scored nine others in winning 9-6. Hours later, the team from north suburban Minneapolis scored 11 and left 11 in winning the championship 11-5 over Kennewick, Wash., Post 34 to finish the year with a 64-5 record.

"You chip the ice and finally break through. You've got to get guys on base to score," New Brighton manager Jeff Larsen said. "As long as we kept it up . . . then we got some big doubles that brought in some runs."

The big doubles came back-to-back from first baseman Brian Paone and right fielder Peter Wiedewitsch in the eighth inning of the final. They extended New Brighton's 4-3 lead (with nine LOBs) to 8-3.

Wiedewitsch, the tournament MVP, did double duty as a pitcher to beat Chatsworth, Calif., Post 582 in a round-robin game, giving New Brighton four complete games in its five games. At the plate, Wiedewitsch went 11-for-22 with six RBIs.

A Ruthian Feat

San Gabriel Valley, Calif., scored a rare double by winning both the Babe Ruth 16-18 and Babe Ruth 16 World Series on the same day. But the two teams won in quite different fashion.

At Stamford, Conn., the San Gabriel Valley 16-18 team had to overcome an early loss and beat Kent, Wash., twice on the final day, 2-0 and 5-3, to win its seventh title in 11 trips to the tournament.

John Hoyos pitched a two-hitter in the first game for San Gabriel Valley, and Matt Swaydan belted two home runs in the second game to clinch the title and avenge a loss in the 1998 championship game to

Columbia Basin, Wash. By coming through the losers' bracket, San Gabriel had to win eight games.

At Burlington, Iowa, San Gabriel's 16-year-old team stayed in the winners' bracket throughout and won the title in four games, earning a 12-4 victory over Redmond, Wash., in the final.

Shortstop Sergio Santos, a sophomore at Los Altos High, hit a three-run homer in the deciding game to sew up MVP honors.

Elusive Title

East Cobb's highly successful Georgia youth program had won just about every meaningful national title over the last two decades except the Connie Mack World Series (17-18) in Farmington, N.M. The East Cobb Yankees added that tournament to their trophy case in 1999 by beating the Guaynabo (Puerto Rico) Jets 9-4 in the championship game.

"It was the crowning blow," East Cobb manager James Beavers said. "Connie Mack is the best baseball in America because teams are able to stack their rosters. We weren't sure we would be able to compete because all our kids are from the Atlanta area."

Jarrod Schmidt

The Yankees (55-10) won five of six games, outscoring their opponents 64-22. The team featured six players from Lassiter High, the 1999 Baseball America/National High School Baseball Coaches Association national titlist, including series MVP Jarrod Schmidt, who won twice and hit .364 with two homers.

The East Cobb program also won national titles in 1999 at the AAU 15- and 16-year-old World Series, and the U.S. Specialty Sports Association 18-year-old series. It placed second at the AAU 13-year-old series and third at the Colt League (15-16) World Series.

East Cobb's 16-year-old team won the AAU Junior Olympic championship for the fourth straight year, beating Danville, Calif., 2-0 in the final of the 53-team event in Cleveland. That team also went on to win the Super Series, a tournament in Marietta, Ga., featuring the nation's outstanding 16-year-old summer teams.

Team USA Triumphs

With no World Championship tournament on the docket for 16-year-olds in 1999, USA Baseball entered its national team in the Police Athletic League World Series in Jupiter, Fla. Predictably, the U.S. team rolled through the 16-team tournament, winning eight straight games and outscoring opponents 96-11. The all-star team beat Fort Myers, Fla., 17-1 in the final on a two-hitter by Zach Segovia (Forney, Texas).

Outfielder Michael Wilson (Tulsa) led Team USA with three home runs and 10 RBIs while hitting .417. Mark Jecmen (Diamond Bar, Calif.) and Brett Smith (La Habra, Calif.) won two games apiece for the U.S., the reigning 16-year-old world champions.

ALL-AMERICAN AMATEUR BASEBALL ASSOCIATION (AAABA)
HEADQUARTERS: Zanesville, Ohio

Event	Site	Champion	Runner-Up
World Series (21 & u)	Johnstown, Pa.	Arlington (Va.) Senators	Altoona, Pa.

AMATEUR ATHLETIC UNION (AAU)
HEADQUARTERS: Lake Buena Vista, Fla.

9 & under	Orlando	Orlando Blast	San Diego Stars/North
10 & under	Kansas City, Mo.	Florida Sun Devils	Florida Stingers
11 & under	Orlando	Placentia (Calif.) Mustangs	Florida Vipers
12 & under	Burnsville, Minn.	San Diego Stars	Fort Worth Reds
13 & under (90 foot)	Kingsport, Tenn.	Florida Yard Dogs	San Diego Stars
13 & under (80 foot)	Tulsa	Cucamonga (Calif.) Dodgers	East Cobb (Ga.) Mavericks
14 & under	Chickasha, Okla.	Placentia (Calif.) Mustangs	San Diego Stars
15 & under	Millington, Tenn.	East Cobb (Ga.) Astros	Capital City (Calif.) Bombers
Junior Olympics (16 & u)	Cleveland	East Cobb (Ga.) Astros	Danville (Calif.) Norcal
17 & under	Norman, Okla.	Oklahoma Sooners	San Diego Stars
18 & under	Orlando	Kansas City Monarchs	Cucamonga (Calif.) Dodgers

AMERICAN AMATEUR BASEBALL CONGRESS (AABC)
HEADQUARTERS: Marshall, Mich.

Robert Clemente (8 & u)	Wheatridge, Colo.	Puerto Rico	Jefferson County, Colo.
Willie Mays (10 & u)	Olive Branch, Miss.	Vega Baja (P.R.) Mariners	Memphis Tigers
Pee Wee Reese (12 & u)	Toa Baja, P.R.	Dallas Tigers	Puerto Rico Orioles
Sandy Koufax (14 & u)	Jersey City, N.J.	Los Lomas, P.R.	Memphis Tigers
Mickey Mantle (16 & u)	McKinney, Texas	Orange County (Calif.) Dawgs	Dallas Hurricanes
Connie Mack (18 & u)	Farmington, N.M.	East Cobb (Ga.) Yankees	Guaynabo (P.R.) Jets
Stan Musial (open)	Battle Creek, Mich.	Bradenton (Fla.) BB Academy	Battle Creek, Mich.

AMERICAN LEGION BASEBALL
HEADQUARTERS: Indianapolis

World Series (19 & u)	Middletown, Conn.	New Brighton, Minn.	Kennewick, Wash.

BABE RUTH BASEBALL
HEADQUARTERS: Trenton, N.J.

Bambino (11-12)	Mattoon, Ill.	Danbury, Conn.	Honolulu
13-Prep	Tallahassee, Fla.	Tallahassee, Fla.	Jefferson Parish, La.
14	Clifton Park, N.Y.	Peabody, Mass.	Brooklyn
13-15	Abbeville, La.	Sarasota, Fla.	Jefferson Parish, La.
16	Burlington, Iowa	San Gabriel Valley, Calif.	Redmond, Wash.
16-18	Stamford, Conn.	San Gabriel Valley, Calif.	Kent, Wash.

CONTINENTAL AMATEUR BASEBALL ASSOCIATION (CABA)
HEADQUARTERS: Westerville, Ohio

9 & under	Charles City, Iowa	Cincinnati Flames	Honolulu Rainbows
10 & under	Aurelia, Iowa	Woolsey (Ga.) Wizards	Austin Braves
11 & under	Tarkio, Mo.	Marietta (Ga.) Blue Devils	Maryland Orioles
12 & under	Omaha	Miami	Dallas Tigers
13 & under	Broken Arrow, Okla.	Houston Cougars	Encinitas (Calif.) Reds
14 & under	Dublin, Ohio	Denver Gameface	West Covina (Calif.) Dukes
15 & under	Crystal Lake, Ill.	Issaquah (Wash.) Tigers	West Covina (Calif.) Red Sox
16 & under	Arlington, Texas	Duluth (Ga.) Tigers	Dallas Mustangs
High school age	Cleveland	Brooklyn Bergen Beach	Nashville Twitty City Heat
18 & under	Homestead, Fla.	Bayside (N.Y.) Yankees	Duluth (Ga.) Tigers
College	Chicago	Bloomington, Ill., Bobcats	Wheaton, Ill., White Sox
Unlimited	Eau Claire, Wis.	White Bear Lake, Minn.	Chicago Badgers

DIXIE BASEBALL
HEADQUARTERS: Montgomery, Ala.

Dixie Youth (12 & u)	Terrell, Texas	Hilton Head Island, S.C.	Montgomery, Ala.
Dixie 13	Pelham, Ala.	Dothan, Ala.	Lee County, Ga.
Dixie Boys (13-14)	Scottsboro, Ala.	Valdosta, Ga.	Columbus County, N.C.
Dixie Pre-Majors (15-16)	Euless, Texas	Columbia County, Ga.	St. Charles Parish, La.
Dixie Majors (15-18)	Montgomery, Ala.	Prattville, Ala.	Valdosta, Ga.

DIZZY DEAN BASEBALL
HEADQUARTERS: Europa, Miss.

Minor League (9-10)	Oak Grove, Miss.	Alpharetta, Ga.	Oak Grove, Miss.
Freshman (11-12)	Oak Grove, Miss.	North Jackson, Miss.	Laurel, Miss.
Sophomore (13-14)	Panama City Beach, Fla.	Pace, Fla.	Sykesville, Md.
Junior (15-16)	Southaven, Miss.	Panama City, Fla.	Cincinnati
Senior (17-18)	Elkton, Md.	Cincinnati Midland Braves	Hampstead (Md.) Rangers

HAP DUMONT BASEBALL
HEADQUARTERS: Wichita

10 & under	Fordland, Mo.	Dallas Tigers	Shawnee (Okla.) Rangers
11 & under	Russell, Kan.	Tulsa Braves	Alpharetta (Ga.) Cobras

Amateur Baseball

12 & under	Casper, Wyo.	Dallas Mariners	Manhattan (Kan.) Wildcats
13 & under	Omaha	Oklahoma City 89ers	Houston Outlaws
14 & under	Brainerd, Minn.	Wichita Cardinals	Edmond (Wash.) Rays
16 & under	Harrison, Ark.	Lexington (Ky.) Dixie Stars	Wichita Rebels

LITTLE LEAGUE BASEBALL
HEADQUARTERS: Williamsport, Pa.

Little League (11-12)	Williamsport, Pa.	Osaka, Japan	Phenix City, Ala.
Junior League (13-14)	Taylor, Mich.	Arroyo, P.R.	Hermosillo, Mexico
Senior League (15-16)	Kissimmee, Fla.	Kissimmee, Fla.	Maracaibo, Venezuela
Big League (17-18)	Tucson	Clearwater, Fla.	Fraser Valley, B.C.

NATIONAL AMATEUR BASEBALL FEDERATION (NABF)
HEADQUARTERS: Bowie, Md.

Rookie (10 & u)	Cincinnati	Nashville Attack	Joliet, Ill.
Freshman (12 & u)	Sylvania, Ohio	Livonia, Mich.	Columbus, Ohio
Sophomore (14 & u)	Miamisburg, Ohio	Westchester (Ohio) Sluggers	Sweeney (Ohio) Mustangs
Junior (16 & u)	Northville, Mich.	Indiana Bulls	Long Island Tigers
High School (17 & u)	Chillicothe, Ohio	Germantown (Tenn.) Red Devils	Long Island Bulls
Senior (18 & u)	Evansville, Ind.	Hammond, La.	Norwood (Ill.) Blues
College (22 & u)	Baltimore	Salisbury, Md.	Mount Airy, Md.
Major (open)	Louisville	Long Island Storm	Buffalo

POLICE ATHLETIC LEAGUE (PAL)
HEADQUARTERS: North Palm Beach, Fla.

14 & under	Palm Beach County, Fla. Lake Worth (Fla.) Gators	Palm Beach (Fla.) Dream Team
16 & under	Palm Beach County, Fla. Team USA	Fort Myers, Fla.

PONY BASEBALL
HEADQUARTERS: Washington, Pa.

Mustang (9-10)	Irving, Texas	Garden Grove, Calif.	Irving, Texas
Bronco (11-12)	Monterey, Calif.	Tai-Tung, Taiwan	Corona, Calif.
Pony (13-14)	Washington, Pa.	Covina, Calif.	Tai-Tung, Taiwan
Colt (15-16)	Lafayette, Ind.	Lafayette, Ind.	Danville, Calif.
Palomino (17-18)	Greensboro, N.C.	Santa Clara, Calif.	Houston

REVIVING BASEBALL IN INNER CITIES (RBI)
HEADQUARTERS: New York

Junior (13-15)	Orlando	San Juan, P.R.	Houston
Senior (16-18)	Orlando	San Juan, P.R.	Los Angeles

U.S. AMATEUR BASEBALL ASSOCIATION (USABA)
HEADQUARTERS: Edmonds, Wash.

11 & under	Las Vegas	Las Vegas	Caguas, P.R.
12 & under	Las Vegas	Caguas, P.R.	Fresno
14 & under	Seattle	Seattle Indians	Seattle Sonics
15 & under	Victoria, B.C.	Nanaimo, B.C.	Brooklyn, N.Y.
16 & under	South Jordan, Utah	Oakland, Calif.	California Cannons
18 & under	Logan, Utah	Sumner, Wash., Triple Play	Mililan, Hawaii

U.S. AMATEUR BASEBALL FEDERATION (USABF)
HEADQUARTERS: San Diego

12 & under	San Diego	Norcal Rebels	San Diego Stars South
14 & under	San Diego	Encinitas (Calif.) Reds	USABF Stars
16 & under	San Diego	Oceanside (Calif.) Players	Phoenix Yankees
18 & under	San Diego	Colton (Calif.) Knight Hawks	Sylmar (Calif.) Stallions

U.S. JUNIOR OLYMPIC BASEBALL
HEADQUARTERS: Tucson

16 & under	Tucson	Dallas Hurricanes	Texas Horns

U.S. SPECIALTY SPORTS ASSOCIATION (USSSA)
HEADQUARTERS: Liberty, Mo.
MAJOR DIVISION

9 & under	Joplin, Mo.	Texas Heat	Tulsa Lookouts
10 & under	Fort Worth	Woolsey (Ga.) Wizards	Houston Panthers
11 & under	Overland Park, Kan.	Germantown (Tenn.) Giants	Tulsa Braves
12 & under	Hutchinson, Kan.	Fort Worth Reds	Seattle Warriors
13 & under	Tulsa	Florida Yard Dogs	Orange County (Calif.) Juice
14 & under	Houston	Arlington (Texas) Wizards	Houston Cougars
15 & under	Winter Haven, Fla.	Manchester (Ohio) A's	Dallas Longhorns
16 & under	Oklahoma City	Dallas A's	Wichita Cyclones
18 & under	Cocoa, Fla.	East Cobb (Ga.) Stallions	California Valley White Sox

UNIVERSAL BASEBALL GLOBAL CHAMPIONSHIP
HEADQUARTERS: Lancaster, Pa.

18 & under	Millington, Tenn.	United States	Aruba

Amateur Baseball

FIRST-YEAR DRAFT

Despite big bonuses to Hamilton, Beckett, Munson, '99 first-year draft largely free of acrimony

BY DAVID RAWNSLEY

It might very well be that the 1999 first-year player draft is best remembered for ... the players.

There were no loophole free agents and $10 million contracts, no J.D. Drew-style holdouts and few, if any, truly acrimonious negotiations. The commissioner's office attempted no last-minute rule changes and the word arbitrator was never whispered.

In fact, every player from the first round was under contract by the end of August, the first time that had happened since 1990. In 1998, first-round righthanders Jeff Austin (Royals) and Kip Wells (White Sox) held out for more than six months after they were selected.

Happy to start playing
Josh Hamilton signs for $3.96 million

You have to go all the way down to the 12th pick of the second round—the 63rd pick overall—to find a player, outfielder Jason Cooper, now a freshman at Stanford, who didn't sign.

The underlying reason, of course, is the enormous amount of money being spent on top amateur talent. Big league clubs have become almost immune to the size of first-round bonuses, players are overwhelmed and agents are competing harder than ever for players in order to get their slice of the pie.

The average bonus for first-round picks in 1999 was $1,809,767, easily surpassing the 1998 average of $1,637,667. It also topped the record first-round average of $1,794,383 set in 1996, when a draft loophole enabled four players to sign as free agents. Those players received contracts worth a total of $29.275 million.

In 1999, 34 drafted players, including all but one first-rounder, received a signing bonus in excess of $1 million. Seventy-six players in the first 10 rounds received more than $500,000, while 127 prospects in those rounds took home at least $200,000, the major league minimum salary. Even Pirates 39th-round pick Patrick O'Brien signed for $500,000.

The Big Three

Three players dominated speculation for the top pick all spring: righthander Josh Beckett, outfielder Josh Hamilton and catcher Eric Munson.

Hamilton, then 17, shocked scouts in pre-season practice games at Athens Drive High School in Raleigh, N.C., by hitting 95-96 mph from the mound—usually enough by itself to put a high school lefthander in the first round. But Hamilton's athleticism and power potential kept scouts focused on him as an outfielder.

Beckett, 19, came into the spring regarded as one of the most acclaimed high school pitchers in draft history and a candidate to become the first prep righthander ever selected first overall. He did nothing to discourage comparisons to past Texas schoolboy heroes Nolan Ryan, David Clyde and Kerry Wood. He was as dominating as ever on the mound, combining a 94-96 mph fastball with a biting curve to go 13-2 with 178 strikeouts in 89 innings at Spring (Texas) High.

Munson, 21, missed two months of the spring season at the University of Southern California when he was crossed up by lefthander Barry Zito, a fellow first-rounder, and broke his right hand. The injury healed in time for Munson to return for NCAA tournament play before the draft, but he did not vault himself over the two high school players to the top of the draft.

When draft day came, it was obvious that Hamilton was Tampa Bay's choice. The only real question was whether Beckett and Munson's contract demands would drop them out of the top three. Both were known to be seeking long-term big league deals.

That there was a different climate for signing players quickly become obvious when the Devil Rays announced Hamilton's signing hardly 48 hours after selecting the 6-foot-4, 200-pounder. His contract was announced at $3.65 million, though the actual amount that Hamilton will receive before December 21, 2000, will be $3.96 million. The difference between the two

TOP 10 SIGNING BONUSES

Based on the stated bonus in major league contracts and the full compensation to be paid out in standard minor league contracts, here are the 10 largest bonuses of the draft era (as reported to the commissioner's office) that were awarded to players signing with the club that drafted them:

Player, Pos.	Club, Year (Round)	Bonus
1. Josh Hamilton, of	Devil Rays '99 (1)	$3,960,000
2. #Corey Patterson, of	Cubs '98 (1)	3,700,000
3. *Josh Beckett, rhp	Marlins '99 (1)	3,625,000
4. *Eric Munson, c	Tigers '99 (1)	3,500,000
5. #Mark Mulder, lhp	Athletics '98 (1)	3,200,000
6. *Pat Burrell, 3b	Phillies '98 (1)	3,150,000
7. *J.D. Drew, of	Cardinals '98 (1)	3,000,000
8. B.J. Garbe, of	Twins '99 (1)	2,750,000
9. Matt Anderson, rhp	Tigers '97 (1)	2,505,000
10. Rick Ankiel, lhp	Cardinals '97 (2)	2,500,000

* Signed major league contract
# Received contract with provision for deferred interest payments

Amateur Draft

DRAFT '99 TOP 50 PICKS

Signing bonuses do not include scholarships, incentive bonus plans or salaries from a major league contract.
*Highest level of professional baseball attained   #Signed major league contract

Rank. Team. Player. Pos.	School	Hometown	Bonus	B'date	B-T	Ht.	Wt.	AVG	AB	H	HR	RBI	SB	'99 Assignment*
1. Devil Rays. Josh Hamilton, of	Athens Drive HS	Raleigh, N.C	$3,960,000	5-21-81	L-L	6-4	200	.514	72	37	13	36	17	Hudson Valley (A)
3. #Tigers. Eric Munson, c	U. of Southern California	San Diego	3,500,000	10-3-77	L-R	6-3	220	.346	153	53	15	41	5	West Michigan (A)
4. Diamondbacks. Corey Myers, ss	Desert Vista HS	Phoenix	2,000,000	6-5-80	R-R	6-2	205	.560	125	70	22	77	3	Missoula (R)
5. Twins. B.J. Garbe, of	Moses Lake HS	Moses Lake, Wash.	2,750,000	2-3-81	R-R	6-1	195	.500	66	33	6	22	19	Elizabethton (R)
11. Mariners. Ryan Christianson, c	Arlington HS	Riverside, Calif.	2,100,000	4-21-81	R-R	6-2	210	.519	81	42	7	42	12	Everett (A)
17. Red Sox. Rick Asadoorian, of	Northbridge HS	Whitinsville, Mass.	1,725,500	7-23-80	R-R	6-2	180	.500	66	33	7	38	9	Did Not Play
19. Blue Jays. Alex Rios, 3b-of	San Pedro Martin HS	Guaynabo, P.R.	845,000	2-18-81	R-R	6-5	185	No high school team						Medicine Hat (R)
20. Padres. Vince Faison, of	Toombs County HS	Lyons, Ga.	1,415,000	1-22-81	L-R	5-11	185	.531	64	34	6	24	5	Fort Wayne (A)
21. Orioles. Larry Bigbie, of	Ball State U.	Hobart, Ind.	1,200,000	11-4-77	L-R	6-4	187	.419	210	88	17	54	21	Delmarva (A)
23. Orioles. Keith Reed, of	Providence College	Yarmouth Port, Mass.	1,150,000	10-8-78	R-R	6-4	215	.398	274	109	17	79	15	Delmarva (A)
37. Dodgers. Jason Repko, ss	Hanford HS	West Richland, Wash.	660,000	12-27-80	R-R	5-11	175	.581	74	43	18	47	14	Great Falls (R)
42. Astros. Mike Rosamond, of	U. of Mississippi	Madison, Miss.	725,000	4-18-78	R-R	6-5	225	.310	232	72	18	41	6	Michigan (A)
46. Cardinals. Chris Duncan, of	Canyon del Oro HS	Tucson	900,000	5-5-81	L-R	6-5	215	.326	95	31	11	36	5	Johnson City (R)
50. Orioles. Brian Roberts, ss	U. of South Carolina	Chapel Hill, N.C.	650,000	10-9-77	B-R	5-10	170	.353	221	78	12	36	67	Delmarva (A)

Rank. Team. Player. Pos.	School	Hometown	Bonus	B'date	B-T	Ht.	Wt.	W-L	ERA	IP	H	BB	SO	'99 Assignment*
2. #Marlins. Josh Beckett, p	Spring HS	Spring, Texas	$3,625,000	5-15-80	R-R	6-4	200	13-2	0.39	89	31	29	178	Did Not Play
6. Expos. Josh Girdley, p	Jasper HS	Jasper, Texas	1,700,000	8-29-80	L-L	6-4	175	9-2	0.34	82	26	34	178	GCL Expos (R)
7. Royals. Kyle Snyder, p	U. of North Carolina	Sarasota, Fla.	2,100,000	9-9-77	R-R	6-8	215	7-5	3.82	97	85	32	102	Spokane (A)
8. Pirates. Bobby Bradley, p	Wellington HS	Wellington, Fla.	2,250,000	12-15-80	R-R	6-2	170	12-1	0.38	92	38	13	156	GCL Pirates (R)
9. Athletics. Barry Zito, p	U. of Southern California	La Mesa, Calif.	1,590,000	5-13-78	L-L	6-3	200	12-3	3.28	113	93	58	154	Vancouver (AAA)
10. Brewers. Ben Sheets, p	Northeast Louisiana U.	St. Amant, La.	2,450,000	7-18-78	R-R	6-2	195	14-1	3.11	116	100	31	158	Stockton (A)
12. Phillies. Brett Myers, p	Englewood HS	Jacksonville	2,050,000	8-17-80	R-R	6-4	210	8-2	0.80	78	25	34	131	GCL Phillies (R)
13. Orioles. Mike Paradis, p	Clemson U.	Auburn, Mass.	1,700,000	5-3-78	R-R	6-2	205	6-1	4.37	91	94	39	87	Delmarva (A)
14. Reds. Ty Howington, p	Hudson's Bay HS	Vancouver, Wash.	1,750,000	11-4-80	R-L	6-5	220	11-3	2.15	78	57	27	149	Did Not Play
15. White Sox. Jason Stumm, p	Centralia HS	Centralia, Wash.	1,750,000	4-13-81	R-R	6-2	200	11-0	0.83	68	38	20	105	Burlington (A)
16. Rockies. Jason Jennings, p	Baylor U.	Mesquite, Texas	1,675,000	7-17-78	L-R	6-2	235	13-2	2.58	147	102	50	172	Asheville (A)
18. Orioles. Richard Stahl, p	Newton HS	Covington, Ga.	1,795,000	4-11-81	R-L	6-7	185	11-0	2.40	79	38	58	146	Did Not Play
22. White Sox. Matt Ginter, p	Mississippi State U.	Winchester, Ky.	1,275,000	12-24-77	R-R	6-1	215	8-7	4.80	94	81	56	108	Burlington (A)
24. Giants. Kurt Ainsworth, p	Louisiana State U.	Baton Rouge	1,300,000	9-9-78	R-R	6-4	178	13-6	3.45	130	114	48	157	Salem-Keizer (A)
25. Royals. Mike MacDougal, p	Wake Forest U.	Mesa, Ariz.	1,150,000	3-5-77	R-R	6-5	187	13-3	2.62	120	88	65	117	Spokane (A)
26. Cubs. Ben Christensen, p	Wichita State U.	Goddard, Kan.	1,062,500	2-7-78	R-R	6-4	185	9-1	2.40	91	46	17	77	Daytona (A)
27. Yankees. David Walling, p	U. of Arkansas	Lakeside, Calif.	1,075,000	11-12-78	R-R	6-5	195	10-2	3.78	121	104	31	155	Staten Island (A)
28. Padres. Gerik Baxter, p	Edmonds-Woodway HS	Edmonds, Wash.	1,100,000	3-11-80	R-R	6-2	185	6-1	0.73	48	18	14	80	Idaho Falls (R)
29. Padres. Omar Ortiz, p	U. of Texas-Pan Am	Edinburg, Texas	1,050,000	9-11-77	B-R	6-4	180	6-5	4.32	102	87	48	132	Fort Wayne (A)
30. Cardinals. Chance Caple, p	Texas A&M U.	Southlake, Texas	1,200,000	8-9-78	R-R	6-6	215	8-5	4.26	114	107	45	125	New Jersey (A)
31. Diamondbacks. Casey Daigle, p	Sulphur HS	Sulphur, La.	1,300,000	4-4-81	R-R	6-6	208	11-2	1.04	69	45	19	97	Did Not Play
32. Royals. Jay Gehrke, p	Pepperdine U.	Fargo, N.D.	1,025,000	11-1-77	R-R	6-6	225	1-1	0.86	31	19	12	40	Spokane (A)
33. Mariners. Jeff Heaverlo, p	U. of Washington	Ephrata, Wash.	987,500	1-13-78	R-R	6-1	180	10-4	4.72	108	112	45	131	Wisconsin (A)
34. Orioles. Josh Cenate, p	Jefferson HS	Shenandoah Jct., W.Va.	950,000	1-28-81	L-L	6-3	195	14-1	0.66	96	39	23	198	Bluefield (R)
35. White Sox. Brian West, p	West Monroe HS	Monroe, La.	1,000,000	8-4-80	R-R	6-4	240	11-1	2.46	74	42	26	100	Bristol (R)
36. Cardinals. Nick Stocks, p	Florida State U.	Tampa	1,410,000	8-27-78	R-R	6-2	185	13-2	3.25	127	111	41	139	Did Not Play
38. Rangers. Colby Lewis, p	Bakersfield (Calif.) JC	Bakersfield, Calif.	862,500	8-2-79	R-R	6-4	210	4-5	2.80	88	73	34	108	Pulaski (R)
39. Giants. Jerome Williams, p	Waipahu HS	Honolulu	832,500	12-4-81	R-R	6-3	185	8-1	0.12	64	19	9	123	Salem-Keizer (A)
40. Red Sox. Brad Baker, p	Pioneer Valley HS	Leyden, Mass.	844,000	11-6-80	R-R	6-1	175	9-0	0.96	66	24	22	138	GCL Red Sox (R)
41. Padres. Casey Burns, p	U. of Richmond	Pennington, N.J.	750,000	7-24-77	R-R	6-1	185	9-3	3.21	95	72	37	124	Idaho Falls (R)
43. Royals. Jimmy Gobble, p	John Battle HS	Bristol, Va.	725,000	7-19-81	L-L	6-4	175	10-1	0.49	71	23	27	151	GCL Royals (R)
44. Orioles. Scott Rice, p	Royal HS	Simi Valley, Calif.	737,000	9-21-81	L-L	6-6	220	6-1	2.95	55	46	37	72	GCL Orioles (R)
45. White Sox. Rob Purvis, p	Bradley U.	Tipton, Ind.	750,000	8-11-77	R-R	6-2	185	2-8	4.04	78	55	43	81	Burlington (A)
47. Rangers. David Mead, p	Soddy Daisy HS	Chattanooga	600,000	3-21-81	R-R	6-5	185	2-3	3.56	41	30	35	61	GCL Rangers (R)
48. Red Sox. Casey Fossum, p	Texas A&M U.	Waco, Texas	680,000	1-6-78	L-L	6-0	150	12-7	3.64	134	117	52	162	Lowell (A)
49. Padres. Mike Bynum, p	U. of North Carolina	Middleburg, Fla.	650,000	3-20-78	L-L	6-3	200	7-1	3.90	85	85	41	89	Rancho Cuca. (A)

Amateur Draft

numbers is the accrued interest on the lower figure between the signing date and the final payment.

"We got ourselves a real old-fashioned ballplayer," said Tampa Bay scouting director Dan Jennings in describing Hamilton. "Besides all the obvious tools, Josh has all the intangibles you'd want to see in a ballplayer. He has a great natural rhythm and pace to his game."

Hamilton played center field in high school and in his first season of professional baseball but projects as a right fielder. Jennings compared him to Shawn Green, the Toronto Blue Jays outfielder who has combined to hit 77 home runs and steal 55 bases the past two seasons.

The Other Josh

Beckett, selected second by the Florida Marlins, and Munson, picked third by the Detroit Tigers, both held firm on their predraft demands for major league contracts.

Munson agreed to terms with the Tigers quickly on a four-year, $6.75 million deal. Beckett, though, waited out the entire summer before the Marlins finally succumbed to a four-year, $7 million contract.

Beckett and Munson became only the ninth and 10th players in the draft era to sign major league contracts, which allows payments to be spread over several years.

The Marlins were adamantly opposed initially to giving Beckett a major league deal, which will require him to be in the big leagues for good by 2002. Only two major league contracts had ever been given to high school players: Todd Van Poppel by the Athletics in 1990 and Alex Rodriguez by the Mariners in 1993.

Beckett and adviser Michael Moye originally sought a bonus in the $8 million-$10 million range. The Marlins were prepared to pay about half that—about the same amount Hamilton signed for—and focused their early attention instead on Venezuelan shortstop Miguel Cabrera, who signed for $1.8 million. In Cabrera, the club said it already had signed a top-of-the-draft talent in 1999 and believed that would give it leverage in dormant discussions with Beckett.

Josh Beckett

But on Aug. 26, four days before Beckett was scheduled to enroll at Blinn (Texas) Junior College, the Marlins caved in and gave Beckett a $7 million major league deal that included a $3.625 million bonus. He signed too late to begin his career in 1999.

Marlins general manager Dave Dombrowski defended his club's signing of Beckett. "You're talking about a 19-year-old pitcher, not a 17-year-old pitcher," he said. "You're talking about someone with a lot of talent. I think there are a lot of other organizations who, if they were given the same opportunity, would have done that and given (Beckett) a big league contract."

Munson, who received a $3.5 million bonus as part of his package, was assigned to Class A West Michigan to begin his professional career.

"We just want him to be himself," Tigers general manager Randy Smith said. "He's a pretty polished guy right now. He swings the bat very well and we'll

play him every day."

In addition to his bonus, Munson was scheduled to receive payments over four years. He received $250,000 in salary in 1999 an was due $750,000 in 2000, $1 million in 2001 and $1.25 million in 2002.

"History has shown that it's easier for pitchers to move faster than it is for hitters," Smith said. "But I wouldn't bet against him. We expect him to be here quickly."

Because Munson missed much of the 1999 college season because of a broken hand, placing him at Double-A Jacksonville wasn't considered by the Tigers.

"Beginning at West Michigan will present a good challenge for Eric because he hasn't played that much this year," Smith said. "There will be an adjustment period for him."

Surprise Selection

The first and really only major surprise of the first round was Arizona's selection of shortstop Corey Myers from nearby Desert Vista High with the fourth selection. Though Myers rewrote the Arizona high school record book by slamming 21 home runs in

Amateur Draft

1999, questions about his future position and overall athletic ability put him near the top of few, if any, other teams' draft lists.

"Other teams don't know Myers like we do," maintained Diamondbacks scouting director Don Mitchell, who resigned shortly after the draft to become an agent. "We're talking about a player who is a plus hitter, with plus power and tremendous makeup and knowledge of the game. Why take the chance that someone else might pick him?"

Myers was one of several players in the first 10 picks to sign immediately. He agreed to a $2 million signing bonus—well below the $2.7 million bonus that Kansas City paid Jeff Austin in the same slot in 1998.

Lefthander Josh Girdley, selected sixth overall by the Montreal Expos, and righthander Kyle Snyder, picked seventh by the Kansas City Royals, also signed immediately—agreeing to deals that were orchestrated before the draft.

The cash-strapped Expos signed Girdley for $1.7 million. The Jasper (Texas) High lefthander gained national recognition by striking out 29 hitters in a 10 inning no-decision earlier in the spring, but was not considered a true first-round prospect by most teams.

Snyder was a serious candidate to be the first overall pick at the start of the year but he battled tendinitis most of the spring and lost six of his last eight decisions as his velocity dropped. The 6-foot-7 Snyder signed with the Royals for $2.1 million and recovered his velocity during the summer while on strict pitch limits.

Outfielder B.J. Garbe, selected fifth by the Twins, was in on a slice of draft history. When Moses Lake (Wash.) High teammates Ryan Doumit (Pirates) and Jason Cooper (Phillies) were selected in the second round, it marked the first time that a single high school had produced three picks in the first two rounds in the same year. Overall, nine Washington state players were picked in the first two rounds, easily the most bountiful talent harvest in that state's baseball history.

HIGH AND LOW

The highest and lowest bonus paid in each round through the first 10 rounds of the 1999 draft:

Round	Highest Bonus	Lowest Bonus
1	Josh Hamilton, Devil Rays ($3,960,000)	Alexis Rios, Blue Jays ($845,000)
*1	Nick Stocks, Cardinals ($1,410,000)	David Mead, Rangers ($600,000)
2	Carl Crawford, Devil Rays ($1,245,000)	Terry Byron, Marlins ($350,000)
3	Neil Jenkins, Tigers ($900,000)	Sean McGowan, Giants ($127,500)
4	Jeff Randazzo, Twins ($392,000)	Keith Surkont, Athletics ($70,000)
5	Matt McClendon, Braves ($900,000)	Ryan Cox, Giants ($50,000)
6	Charles Frazier, Marlins ($300,000)	J.J. Putz, Mariners ($10,000)
7	Brett Evert, Braves ($169,500)	Rodney Nye, Mets ($20,000)
8	Chris Capuano, Diamondbacks ($145,000)	Ryan Lundquist, Reds ($7,000)
9	Brian Specht, Angels ($600,000)	Mark Ellis, Royals ($1,000)
10	Nathan Cromer, Devil Rays ($140,000)	Brian Wiese, Red Sox ($3,000)

*Supplemental round

NO. 1 DRAFT PICKS, 1965-99

Year Club, Player, Pos.	School	Hometown	High Level (G#)	'99 Team	Bonus
1965 A's. Rick Monday, of	Arizona State U.	Santa Monica, Calif.	Majors (1,996)	Out of Baseball	$104,000
1966 Mets. Steve Chilcott, c	Antelope Valley HS	Lancaster, Calif.	Triple-A (2)	Out of Baseball	75,000
1967 Yankees. Ron Blomberg, 1b	Druid Hills HS	Atlanta	Majors (461)	Out of Baseball	75,000
1968 Mets. Tim Foli, ss	Notre Dame HS	Sherman Oaks	Majors (1,696)	Out of Baseball	75,000
1969 Senators. Jeff Burroughs, of	Wilson HS	Long Beach, Calif.	Majors (1,689)	Out of Baseball	88,000
1970 Padres. Mike Ivie, c	Walker HS	Decatur, Ga.	Majors (857)	Out of Baseball	80,000
1971 White Sox. Danny Goodwin, c	Central HS	Peoria, Ill.	Majors (252)	Out of Baseball	DNS
1972 Padres. Dave Roberts, 3b	U. of Oregon	Corvallis, Ore.	Majors (709)	Out of Baseball	60,000
1973 Rangers. David Clyde, lhp	Westchester, HS	Houston	Majors (84)	Out of Baseball	125,000
1974 Padres. Bill Almon, ss	Brown U.	Warwick, R.I.	Majors (1,236)	Out of Baseball	90,000
1975 Angels. Danny Goodwin, c	Southern U.	Peoria, Ill.	Majors (252)	Out of Baseball	125,000
1976 Astros. Floyd Bannister, lhp	Arizona State U.	Seattle	Majors (431)	Out of Baseball	100,000
1977 White Sox. Harold Baines, of	St. Michaels HS	St. Michaels, Md.	Majors (2,702)	Indians	40,000
1978 Braves. Bob Horner, 3b	Arizona State U.	Glendale, Ariz.	Majors (1,020)	Out of Baseball	175,000
1979 Mariners. Al Chambers, of	Harris HS	Harrisburg, Pa.	Majors (57)	Out of Baseball	60,000
1980 Mets. Darryl Strawberry, of	Crenshaw HS	Los Angeles	Majors (1,583)	Yankees	152,500
1981 Mariners. Mike Moore, rhp	Oral Roberts U.	Eakly, Okla.	Majors (450)	Out of Baseball	100,000
1982 Cubs. Shawon Dunston, ss	Jefferson HS	New York	Majors (1,492)	Mets	100,000
1983 Twins. Tim Belcher, rhp	Mt. Vernon Naz. Coll.	Sparta, Ohio	Majors (353)	Angels	DNS
1984 Mets. Shawn Abner, of	Mechanicsburg HS	Mechanicsburg, Pa.	Majors (392)	Out of Baseball	150,000
1985 Brewers. B.J. Surhoff, c	U. of North Carolina	Rye, N.Y.	Majors (1,716)	Orioles	150,000
1986 Pirates. Jeff King, 3b	U. of Arkansas	Colorado Springs	Majors (1,201)	Royals	160,000
1987 Mariners. Ken Griffey Jr., of	Moeller HS	Cincinnati	Majors (1,535)	Mariners	169,000
1988 Padres. Andy Benes, rhp	U. of Evansville	Evansville, Ind.	Majors (328)	Diamondbacks	235,000
1989 Orioles. Ben McDonald, rhp	Louisiana State U.	Denham Springs, La.	Majors (211)	Injured	*350,000
1990 Braves. Chipper Jones, ss	The Bolles School	Jacksonville	Majors (779)	Braves	275,000
1991 Yankees. Brien Taylor, lhp	East Carteret HS	Beaufort, N.C.	Double-A (27)	Mariners (R)	1,550,000
1992 Astros. Phil Nevin, 3b	Cal State Fullerton	Placentia, Calif.	Majors (381)	Padres	700,000
1993 Mariners. Alex Rodriguez, ss	West. Christian HS	Miami	Majors (642)	Mariners	*1,000,000
1994 Mets. Paul Wilson, rhp	Florida State U.	Orlando	Majors (26)	Mets (AAA)	1,550,000
1995 Angels. Darin Erstad, of	U. of Nebraska	Jamestown, N.D.	Majors (471)	Angels	1,575,000
1996 Pirates. Kris Benson, rhp	Clemson U.	Kennesaw, Ga.	Majors (31)	Pirates	2,000,000
1997 Tigers. Matt Anderson, rhp	Rice U.	Louisville	Majors (79)	Tigers	2,505,000
1998 Phillies. Pat Burrell, 3b	U. of Miami	Boulder Creek, Calif.	Class AAA (10)	Phillies (AAA)	*3,150,000
1999 Devil Rays. Josh Hamilton, of	Athens Drive HS	Raleigh, N.C.	Class A (16)	Devil Rays (A)	3,960,000

*Received major league contract with guaranteed incentives   #No. of games at that level   DNS—Did not sign

Controversial picks

Three picks in the bottom half of the first round were especially notable.

With the No. 19 pick, Toronto chose outfielder Alexis Rios, the first Puerto Rican first-rounder since the Royals picked Juan LeBron, another tall, lanky outfielder, with the 19th selection in 1995. Rios signed immediately after the draft for an $845,000 bonus–the only bonus in the first round less than $1 million.

San Francisco, picking 24th, selected righthander Kurt Ainsworth, who had thrown only eight innings the previous two years after undergoing Tommy John surgery. He was one of more than 10 pitchers in the 1999 draft who had the same surgery. The Giants also signed 11th-rounder Jeff Verplancke, who sat out the entire 1999 season while recovering from Tommy John surgery–yet still signed for $600,000.

The usually conservative and public relations-conscious Chicago Cubs, picking in the No. 26 slot, endured a firestorm of controversy when they cast their lot with Wichita State righthander Ben Christensen, who missed the final six weeks of the college

season after being suspended for hitting and severely injuring Evansville's Anthony Molina before a game.

Christensen claimed he was just trying to brush back Molina, whom he said was trying to time his warmup pitches before the start of a Missouri Valley Conference game. The ball did severe damage to Molina's left eye and Christensen faced potential criminal and civil legal action for the incident.

Most clubs had Christensen as a solid first-round talent and scouting directors contacted by Baseball America said they had not been discouraged from selecting Christensen by their legal departments.

"I am sorry about everything that's happened," Christensen said. "If I could take it back, I definitely would. There's no doubt about it. I will accept any consequences for what happened. Hopefully this will get behind me and him so we can both kind of get on with our lives."

The organization stood firmly behind Christensen.

"Obviously, we're very supportive of Ben," said director of scouting and player development Jim Hendry, who once coached Creighton in the Missouri Valley Conference. "We feel he's a quality young man. We would not have made the decision if we didn't feel he was a quality person off the field."

The Cubs gave Christensen a bonus of $1.0625 million.

Pitcher-Oriented Draft

Pitchers made up 11 of the first 16 picks and 20 of the 30 first-rounders. At one point–from San Francisco's Kurt Ainsworth at No. 24 to St. Louis' Nick Stocks at No. 36–13 straight pitchers heard their name called.

A number of the pitchers were claimed by Baltimore, the Chicago White Sox, Kansas City and San Diego, who combined to make 21 picks before the second round started. The Orioles alone had seven of the first 50 picks and spent $8.1825 million to sign those players.

That the Orioles held so many extra picks highlighted what many perceived to be a flaw in the system for awarding picks as compensation to teams

RELATIVELY SPEAKING

Players drafted in 1999 who are related to current or former big leaguers (unless specified otherwise):

Player, Pos.	Club (Round)	Relative
Syketo Anderson, 2b	Cubs (13)	Brother of Marlon
Marc Bluma, rhp	Blue Jays (13)	Brother of Jaime
Josh Bonifay, ss	Pirates (24)	Nephew of Cam*
Bret Boyer, ss	Expos (7)	Son of Clete
Bill Curtis, of	Angels (45)	Brother of Chad
Chris Duncan, 1b	Cardinals (1)	Son of Dave
Bryan Erstad, of	Reds (42)	Brother of Darin
Willie Eyre, rhp	Twins (24)	Brother of Scott
Brandon Fahey, 3b	Padres (17)	Son of Bill
Carrington Fisk, rhp	Mets (39)	Nephew of Carlton
Scott Hairston, ss	White Sox (18)	Son of Jerry
Drew Hassler, rhp	Orioles (13)	Son of Andy
Jeff Heaverlo, rhp	Mariners (1)	Son of Dave
Joe Kerrigan, ss	Red Sox (45)	Son of Joe
Vince LaCorte, rhp	Angels (5)	Son of Frank
Alex LeFlore, of	Reds (6)	Son of Ron
Dave LaRoche, 1b	Marlins (42)	Son of Dave
David Lemon, of	Cubs (28)	Son of Chet
Ryan Ludwick, of	Athletics (2)	Brother of Eric
Joey Monahan, ss	Twins (36)	Brother of Shane
Rodney Nye, 1b	Mets (7)	Brother of Ryan
Kelvin Pickering, c	Orioles (35)	Brother of Calvin
Jose Pujols, 3b	Cardinals (13)	Son of Luis
Robb Quinlan, 1b	Angels (10)	Brother of Tom
Jordan Remy, 2b	Red Sox (49)	Son of Jerry
Jason Reuss, 1b	Rangers (26)	Son of Jerry
Jon Schuerholz, ss	Braves (37)	Son of John#
Ben Sheets, rhp	Brewers (1)	Cousin of Andy
Justin Sobchuk, rhp	Athletics (10)	Son of Dennis+
Chad Sutter, c	Yankees (23)	Son of Bruce
Garry Templeton, ss	Angels (49)	Son of Garry
Frank Torre, 1b-lhp	Pirates (42)	Son of Frank
Brady Williams, 3b	Red Sox (45)	Son of Jimy

*Pirates GM #Braves GM +Ex-NHL player

Amateur Draft

that lose major league free agents. Because they finished in the bottom half of the American League standings in 1998, the Orioles didn't lose their first-round pick–even after signing free agents Albert Belle, Will Clark, Delino DeShields and Mike Timlin. They lost their picks in the second, third, fourth and fifth rounds.

But by losing free agents Roberto Alomar (Indians), Eric Davis (Cardinals) and Rafael Palmeiro (Rangers) to teams in the upper half of the 1998 standings, the Orioles raked in six extra picks before the second round began.

With their bonanza of multiple picks, the White Sox and Royals decided they would invest heavily in pitching. The White Sox selected pitchers with 14 of their first 15 picks, including their top five, while the Royals drafted pitchers with their top seven picks.

Braves Work Magic

The Atlanta Braves were the final team to make its initial pick, selecting 81st overall. For the Braves, it was the last draft under veteran scouting director Paul Snyder and perhaps one of his best.

Matt McClendon

Despite not having a first-round pick, the Braves spent $3.1 million on their first six picks. They gave $800,000 to second-rounder Matt Butler, $700,000 to third-rounder Pat Manning and $950,000 to fifth-rounder Matt McClendon–the largest bonus ever for that round. McClendon projected as a first-rounder at the start of the year, but a chest injury hampered him over the second half of the season and caused him to slide in the draft.

McClendon was represented by hard-line agent Scott Boras, who didn't have a pick in the first round. Not since 1985 had Boras, the agent for celebrated draft holdout J.D. Drew, not had a player in the first 10 picks.

He eventually struck a $1.3 million deal for Diamondbacks righthander Casey Daigle (31st overall) and $1.41 million for Cardinals righthander Nick Stocks (36th overall)–the two largest bonuses of the compensation round–but he was unable to get second-rounder Bobby Hill to sign with the White Sox. Hill elected not to return to the University of Miami, and in effect renounced his remaining college eligibility.

The Marlins had the greatest success in signing their picks, inking their first 22 and 29 of their first 30–though the contract of 12th-rounder Angel Sanchez was later voided. Only 23rd-round pick Jarrod Schmidt, who decided to attend college at Clemson, went unsigned.

The Rockies signed their first 17 picks, the Blue Jays their first 13, the Giants and Tigers their first 12 and the Expos their first 11.

The Red Sox had the greatest difficulty in signing their premium draft picks. They took a month to sign a single player from the first 10 rounds and never did agree to terms with their selections from the fourth through ninth rounds.

They signed first-round pick Rick Asadoorian just

days before he was scheduled to enroll at the University of Florida. The Whitinsville, Mass., product signed for a club-record $1,725,500–topping the record held by 1998 first-round pick Adam Everett by $500.

One unsigned Red Sox pick, righthander Hank Thoms, snubbed Boston's $3,500 offer as a ninth-round pick to sign with the independent Northern League.

In all, there were 1,474 players drafted, including 256 from California, 186 from Florida, 126 from Texas, 48 from Arizona and 47 each from Oklahoma and Washington.

As usual, there were frenzied negotiations in the days leading up to the draft to sign the top draft-and-follows from the previous year's draft. Two players, A's catcher Gerald Laird (second round, 1998) and Yankees shortstop Ivan Reyes (fourth round), both signed for $1 million bonuses, the first time that a player under control had signed for a seven-figure bonus.

DRAFT '99

CLUB-BY-CLUB SELECTIONS
Boldface indicates player signed; draft order in parentheses

ANAHEIM (17)
1. (Choice to Red Sox as compensation for Type A free agent Mo Vaughn).
2. **John Lackey, rhp, Grayson County (Texas) CC.**
3. **Phil Wilson, rhp, Poway (Calif.) HS.**
4. **Stan Bukowski, rhp, Dunedin (Fla.) HS.**
5. **Vince LaCorte, rhp, San Jose State U.**
6. **Dusty Bergman, lhp, U. of Hawaii.**
7. **Alan Wawrzyniak, rhp, Philadelphia College of Textiles.**
8. **Aaron Franke, rhp, Owens (Ohio) CC.**
9. **Brian Specht, ss/2b, Doherty HS, Colorado Springs.**
10. **Robb Quinlan, 1b, U. of Minnesota.**
11. **Chris Barski, c, New Mexico State U.**
12. **Mike O'Keefe, of, Providence College.**
13. **Alfredo Amezaga, ss, St Petersburg (Fla.) JC.**
14. **Jon Palmieri, 1b, Wake Forest U.**
15. **Sean Brummett, lhp, Indiana State U.**
16. **Brandon Jackson, of, Savannah State (Ga.) U.**
17. **Scott Bikowski, of, Florida Southern College.**
18. Shayne Wright, rhp, Sacramento CC.
19. **Gary Johnson, of, Brigham Young U.**
20. **Brent Haworth, rhp, Rollins (Fla.) College.**
21. **Jeff Wagner, c, U. of Notre Dame.**
22. Pat Osborn, ss, Bakersfield (Calif.) HS.
23. **Alcides Duverge, c, Norwalk (Conn.) CC.**
24. **Ben Grezlovski, rhp, U. of Florida.**
25. **Shayne Ferrier, rhp, Southwest Missouri State U.**
26. **Palmer Ebanks, rhp, Jacksonville U.**
27. **Thomas Gregorio, c, Troy State U.**
28. **Luke Sullivan, lhp, New Mexico State U.**
29. **Brett Schreyer, rhp, Florida Atlantic U.**
30. **Chip Gosewisch, 2b, Arizona State U.**
31. Kevin Tillman, 3b, Arizona State U.
32. **Chris Hills, of, Jackson State U.**
33. **Tim Boeth, 3b/ss, U. of Central Florida.**
34. **Patrick Bowen, rhp, St. Leo (Fla.) College.**
35. **Craig Glysch, rhp, U. of Wisconsin-Oshkosh.**
36. **Pete Orgill, c/1b, U. of Washington.**
37. Jason Farren, rhp, Gulf Coast (Fla.) CC.
38. Jermie Fitzgerald, lhp, Cowley County (Kan.) CC.
39. Robert Ellis, lhp, Mission (Calif.) JC.
40. Ryan Smith, rhp, Chipola (Fla.) JC.
41. **Brandon Martin, of, Riverside (Calif.) CC.**
42. David Wolensky, rhp, Chipola (Fla.) JC.
43. Jeremy Paul, c, Buffalo Grove (Ill.) HS.
44. Moises Feliz, ss, Chipola (Fla.) JC.
45. **Bill Curtis, of, Grand Canyon U.**
46. George Malone, of, Victor Valley HS, Victorville, Calif.
47. Adam Thomas, rhp, St Petersburg (Fla.) CC.
48. Klent Corley, rhp, Greenway HS, Phoenix.
49. **Garry Templeton Jr., ss, North Carolina A&T U.**
50. **Jeff Nebel, rhp, Mercer U.**

ARIZONA (4)
1. **Corey Myers, ss, Desert Vista HS, Phoenix.**
1. **Casey Daigle, rhp, Sulphur (La.) HS** (Supplemental pick—31st—for loss of Type A free agent Devon White).
2. (Choice to Astros as compensation for Type A free agent Randy Johnson).
2. **Jeremy Ward, rhp, Long Beach State U.** (Choice from Dodgers as compensation for White).
3. (Choice to Red Sox as compensation for Type A free agent Greg Swindell).
4. (Choice to Rangers as compensation for Type A free agent Todd Stottlemyre).
5. (Choice to Padres as compensation for Type A free agent Steve Finley).
6. Justin Maureau, lhp, Highlands Ranch (Colo.) HS.
7. **Ryan Owens, ss, Cal State Fullerton.**
8. **Chris Capuano, lhp, Duke U.**
9. **Matt Kata, ss, Vanderbilt U.**
10. Matt Abram, 3b, Chaparral HS, Scottsdale, Ariz.
11. Ben King, lhp/of, Grapevine (Texas) HS.
12. **Doug Devore, of, U. of Indiana.**

13. Jesse Harper, rhp, Brazoswood HS, Clute, Texas.
14. Todd Gelatka, rhp, Trabuco Hills HS, Lake Forest, Calif.
15. **Todd Kasper, c, Yale U.**
16. **Greg Perkin, rhp, Kingwood (Texas) HS.**
17. **Shawn Lagana, ss, Lakewood HS, Cypress, Calif.**
18. **Lyle Overbay, 1b/of, U. of Nevada.**
19. **Jack Santora, ss, UCLA.**
20. **Justin Graham, of, West Virginia State College.**
21. **Tim Stanton, lhp, Florida Southern College.**
22. **Mike Davis, rhp, Lyon County HS, Eddyville, Ky.**
23. **Evan Fahrner, rhp, Bradley U.**
24. **Toby Harris, rhp, U. of Nevada.**
25. **Travis Oglesby, c, Armstrong Atlantic State (Ga.) U.**
26. **Kevin Burns, of, Troy State U.**
27. **Dan Jackson, rhp, St Louis CC-Forest Park.**
28. **Dan Williford, 1b, U. of Mobile.**
29. **Dale Deveraux, rhp, JC of Southern Idaho.**
30. Hans Smith, lhp, Fresno State U.
31. **Joe Kalczynski, c, Michigan State U.**
32. James Kavourias, 1b, Pensacola (Fla.) JC.
33. **Joe Yakopich, ss, St. Thomas of Villanova HS, Amherstburg, Conn.**
34. **Cody Sundbeck, rhp, Dallas Baptist U.**
35. **James Wollscheid, rhp, McMurry (Texas) U.**
36. **Steven Tomshack, c, U. of Maryland.**
37. **Derek Forbes, rhp, South Mountain (Ariz.) CC.**
38. Erick Contreras, ss, Garden City (Kan.) CC.
39. Carlton Wells, lhp, Hillsborough (Fla.) CC.
40. Aaron Sobieraj, rhp, Dunedin (Fla.) HS.
41. **Josh Goldfield, c, Moorpark (Calif.) JC.**
42. **Brian Matzenbacher, rhp, Southern Illinois U-Edwardsville.**
43. **Todd Myers, rhp, Lamar U.**
44. Aaron Pullin, rhp, Midland (Texas) HS.
45. Jered Liebeck, rhp, Mountain Ridge HS, Glendale, Ariz.
46. Scott Buffington, rhp, Lamar (Colo.) CC.
47. **Chris Jorgenson, of, McCoy HS, New Brigden, Alberta.**
48. Keith Schuttler, of, Agua Fria HS, Litchfield Park, Ariz.
49. Chris Churchill, c, Abilene (Texas) HS.
50. Peter Hawley, of, Branford (Conn.) HS.

ATLANTA (30)
1. (Choice to Cardinals as compensation for Type A free agent Brian Jordan).
2. **Matt Butler, rhp, Hattiesburg (Miss.) HS.**
3. **Pat Manning, ss, Mater Dei HS, Anaheim Hills, Calif.**
4. **Alec Zumwalt, of, East Forsyth HS, Kernersville, N.C.**
5. **Matt McClendon, rhp, U. of Florida.**
6. **Andrew Brown, rhp, Trinity Christian Academy, Deltona, Fla.**
7. **Brett Evert, rhp, North Salem HS, Salem, Ore.**
8. Chris Spencer, rhp, Humble (Texas) HS.
9. **Angelo Burrows, of, Killian HS, Miami.**
10. **Bryan Cetani, lhp, Deep Valley Christian HS, Ukiah, Calif.**
11. **Chris Trevino, lhp, Andrews (Texas) HS.**
12. **Ben Kozlowski, lhp, Santa Fe (Fla.) CC.**
13. Shaud Williams, ss, Andrews (Texas) HS.
14. **Garrett Jones, 1b, Andrew HS, Tinley Park, Ill.**
15. David Fiala, rhp, Orange Park (Fla.) HS.
16. **Kevin Green, c, Georgia Perimeter JC.**
17. Efren Lira, rhp, Walnut (Calif.) HS.
18. **Tom Curtiss, lhp, U. of Maryland.**
19. Scott Wade, rhp, Sullivan South HS, Kingsport, Tenn.
20. **Collin Remekie, of, Martin County HS, Stuart, Fla.**
21. **Wes Rasmussen, ss, Moorpark (Calif.) HS.**
22. **Bryce Terveen, c, U. of the Pacific.**
23. **Kyle Colton, rhp, Bishop Moore HS, Longwood, Fla.**
24. **Alva Thompson, c, Southern U.**
25. **Jon Foster, lhp, Lewis-Clark State (Idaho) College.**
26. **Shannin Veronie, rhp, Chico State U.**
27. **Chris Chavez, rhp, Florida State U.**
28. Ryan Hubbard, ss, Huntington Beach (Calif.) HS.
29. Travis Suereth, 1b, Buchholtz HS, Gainesville, Fla.
30. **Jeff Rodriguez, c, Florida International U.**
31. Zachary Parker, lhp, Westwood HS, Austin.
32. **Joseph Francisco, of, Wagner (N.Y.) College.**
33. Thomas Parrott, 3b, Merritt Island (Fla.) HS.
34. **Curt Fiore, 3b, Loyola Marymount U.**
35. Jeremy Barker, lhp, Willows (Calif.) HS.
36. **Shaun Argento, c, New Mexico Highlands U.**
37. John Schuerholz, ss, Lovett School, Atlanta.
38. **Anthony Sclafani, rhp, St. Peters HS, Staten Island, N.Y.**
39. **Ryan Erwin, rhp, Monte Vista HS, Spring Valley, Calif.**
40. Joshua Robinson, rhp, Thompson HS, Alabaster, Ala.
41. Michael Gleason, rhp, Butler County (Kan.) CC.

42. Klint Richardson, rhp, Lyons (N.Y.) HS.
43. Michael Koppin, ss, Stephens County HS, Eastanollee, Ga.
44. Toby Staveland, rhp, Mendocino (Calif.) CC.
45. Grant Abrams, ss, St Petersburg (Fla.) CC.
46. J.C. Barnett, rhp, Fort Meade (Fla.) HS.
47. James Anderson, c, North HS, Riverside, Calif.
48. August Marsala, 3b, Buffalo (Mo.) HS.
49. **Nathan Kent, rhp, U. of Kentucky.**
50. Scott Leitz, lhp, Vanguard HS, Ocala, Fla.

BALTIMORE (13)

1. **Mike Paradis, rhp, Clemson U.**
1. **Richard Stahl, lhp, Newton HS, Covington, Ga.** (Choice from Cardinals as compensation for Type A free agent Eric Davis).
1. **Larry Bigbie, of, Ball State U.** (Choice from Rangers as compensation for Type A free agent Rafael Palmeiro).
1. **Keith Reed, of, Providence College** (Choice from Indians as compensation for Type A free agent Roberto Alomar).
1. **Josh Cenate, lhp, Jefferson HS, Shenandoah Junction, W.Va.** (Supplemental pick—34th—for loss of Alomar).
1. **Scott Rice, lhp, Royal HS, Simi Valley, Calif.** (Supplemental pick—44th—for loss of Davis).
1. **Brian Roberts, ss, U. of South Carolina.** (Supplemental pick—50th—for loss of Palmeiro).
2. (Choice to White Sox as compensation for Type A free agent Albert Belle).
3. (Choice to Mariners as compensation for Type A free agent Mike Timlin).
3. **Jon Kessick, c, Ball State U.** (Choice from Dodgers as compensation for Type B free agent Alan Mills).
4. (Choice to Cardinals as compensation for Type A free agent Delino DeShields).
5. (Choice to Rangers as compensation for Type A free agent Will Clark).
6. **Erik Bedard, lhp, Norwalk (Conn.) CC.**
7. **David Farren, rhp, Texas HS, Texarkana, Texas.**
8. **Matthew Tate, rhp, Holmes County HS, Bonifay, Fla.**
9. **Pete Shier, ss, Hilliard Davidson HS, Columbus, Ohio.**
10. **Octavio Martinez, c, Bakersfield (Calif.) JC.**
11. Kraig Brinkman, rhp, Napa (Calif.) HS.
12. **Brad Rogers, rhp, Wellington SS, Nanaimo, B.C.**
13. Drew Hassler, rhp, Arcadia HS, Phoenix.
14. **Matt Riordan, of, Loyola Marymount U.**
15. Brock Ralph, of, U. of Wyoming.
16. **Shaun Babula, lhp, Philadelphia College of Textiles.**
17. Jason Tourangeau, rhp, South Carroll HS, Mt. Airy, Md.
18. **Kyle Martin, c, Selah (Wash.) HS.**
19. **Nicolas Garcia, ss, Desert View HS, Tucson.**
20. **Steve Salargo, of, East Carolina U.**
21. Shane Waroff, rhp, Fullerton (Calif.) JC.
22. Beau Kemp, rhp, Nathan Hale HS, Tulsa.
23. **Aaron Rakers, rhp, Southern Illinois U-Edwardsville.**
24. **Willie Harris, 2b/ss, Kennesaw State (Ga.) U.**
25. Mitch Jones, 3b, Arizona State U.
26. **Mike Seestedt, c, U of Michigan.**
27. **Rodney Ormond, rhp, North Carolina State U.**
28. Matt Larson, rhp, Corona Del Mar HS, Costa Mesa, Calif.
29. Martin LaRocca, rhp, Archbishop Rummel, Metaire, La.
30. Kyle Yudizky, of, Duncanville (Texas) HS.
31. Kyle Roat, c, Coweta (Okla.) HS.
32. Keven Virtue, rhp, Lucas HS, London, Ontario.
33. **James Phillips, rhp, Maysville HS, Zanesville, Ohio.**
34. Douglas Slaten, lhp, Glendale (Calif.) JC.
35. **Kelvin Pickering, c, King HS, Tampa.**
36. Andrew Corona, 1b, Moorpark (Calif.) CC.
37. Ryan Rocheleau, lhp, Hemet (Calif.) HS.
38. **Charles Dees, of, Chipola (Fla.) JC.**
39. **Gary Cates, 2b, Brandon (Fla.) HS.**
40. Matthew Roy, rhp, Johnstown-Monroe HS, Johnstown, Ohio.
41. Sean White, rhp, Mercer Island (Wash.) HS.
42. Nicholas Vitielliss, rhp, Thomas Stone HS, Waldorf, Md.
43. **Terry Plank, rhp, Methodist (N.C.) College.**
44. **Doug Sowers, 3b, West Virginia State College.**
45. Brad Guglielmelli, 3b, Cuesta (Calif.) JC.
46. Pat Tobin, c, Dun Barton SS, Pickering, Ontario.
47. Judd Richardson, rhp, Country Day HS, Terra Cotta, Ontario.
48. Michael Roga, rhp, Pine Ridge HS, Pickering, Ontario.
49. Mark Perkins, rhp, Claremont SS, Victoria, B.C.
50. Kyle Baumgartner, ss, Olympic HS, Bremerton, Wash.

BOSTON (25)

1. **Rick Asadoorian, of, Northbridge HS, Whitinsville, Mass.** (Choice to Angels as compensation for Type A free agent Mo Vaughn).

1. (Choice to Royals as compensation for Type A free agent Jose Offerman).
1. **Brad Baker, rhp, Pioneer Valley HS, Leyden, Mass.** (Supplemental pick—40th—for loss of Vaughn).
1. **Casey Fossum, lhp, Texas A&M U.** (Supplemental pick—48th—for loss of Type A free agent Greg Swindell).
2. **Mat Thompson, rhp, Timberline HS, Boise, Idaho.**
3. **Richard Rundles, lhp, Jefferson County HS, New Market, Tenn.** (Choice from Diamondbacks as compensation for Swindell).
3. **Antron Seiber, of, Independence (La.) HS.**
4. Rory Shortell, rhp, Madison HS, Portland, Ore.
5. Greg Montalbano, lhp, Northeastern U.
6. Jon Kail, of, Baldwin HS, Pittsburgh.
7. Richard Carroll, 1b, Venice (Fla.) HS.
8. Andrew Heimbach, rhp, Mount Vernon Nazarene (Ohio) College.
9. Hank Thoms, rhp, Mississippi State U.
10. **Brian Wiese, of, Mississippi State U.**
11. **Kregg Jarvais, c, U. of Maine.**
12. **Lew Ford, of, Dallas Baptist U.**
13. **Mike Dwyer, 1b, U. of Richmond.**
14. **B.J. Leach, rhp, Florida Southern College.**
15. Brian Wiley, rhp, The Citadel.
16. Charles Manning, lhp, Polk (Fla.) CC.
17. Trae Duncan, 3b, Mississippi Gulf Coast JC.
18. **Jeff Waldron, c, Boston College.**
19. **Jason Bottenfield, rhp, U. of Texas-Pan American.**
20. **Daniel Generelli, rhp, Quinsigamond (Mass.) CC.**
21. Jason Henderson, rhp, Bishop Hendricken HS, Coventry, R.I.
22. Ellis Debrow, 1b/of, Woodham HS, Pensacola, Fla.
23. Nicolas Puckett, lhp, Timberline HS, Boise, Idaho.
24. Rex Rundgren, ss, Mid Pacific Institute, Honolulu.
25. Tim McCabe, ss, North Catholic HS, Wexford, Pa.
26. Marshall McDougall, 2b, Florida State U.
27. Mark Kiger, 2b, Grossmont (Calif.) JC.
28. **Jonathan Anderson, ss, U. of Illinois.**
29. Bart Hollis, rhp, Lawrence County HS, Moulton, Ala.
30. Charles Frasier, 3b, Santa Rosa (Calif.) JC.
31. Jaime Bubela, of, Baylor U.
32. David Flournoy, of, Deer Valley HS, Antioch, Calif.
33. **Perry Miley, of, William Carey (Miss.) College.**
34. **Dan Giese, rhp, U. of San Diego.**
35. **Ben Marbury, of, Rockford, Ala.**
36. Jon Brandon, of, Panola (Texas) JC.
37. Chris Mabeus, rhp, Eastern Arizona JC.
38. Jesse Cooksey, rhp, Port Neches-Groves HS, Port Arthur, Texas.
39. Matt Ames, 1b, Stanhope Elmore HS, Millbrook, Ala.
40. Anthony Bass, of, Booker T. Washington HS, Tulsa, Okla.
41. Justin Smetana, lhp, Cardinal HS, Huntsburg, Ohio.
42. Brian Rinehart, 2b, Southington (Conn.) HS.
43. Ryan Coffin, rhp, Desert Vista HS, Phoenix.
44. Alan Lindsey, of, Lee-Davis HS, Mechanicsville, Va
45. **Brady Williams, 3b, Pasco-Hernando (Fla.) CC.**
46. **Joe Kerrigan, ss, Temple U.**
47. James Burgess, of, Durango HS, Las Vegas
48. Joseph Kjose, rhp, Cochise County (Ariz.) CC.
49. Jordan Remy, 2b, Weston (Mass.) HS.
50. Brian Buscher, ss, Terry Parker HS, Jacksonville.

CHICAGO-AL (15)

1. **Jason Stumm, rhp, Centralia (Wash.) HS.**
1. **Matt Ginter, rhp, Mississippi State U.** (Choice from Mets as compensation for Type A free agent Robin Ventura).
1. **Brian West, rhp, West Monroe HS, Monroe, La.** (Supplemental pick—35th—for loss of Type A free agent Albert Belle).
1. **Rob Purvis, rhp, Bradley U.** (Supplemental pick—45th—for loss of Type A free agent Robin Ventura).
2. **Danny Wright, rhp, U. of Arkansas** (Choice from Orioles for loss of Belle).
2. Bobby Hill, ss, U. of Miami.
3. **Jon Rauch, rhp, Morehead State U.**
4. Brandon Sloan, rhp, Wichita State U.
5. **Josh Stewart, lhp, U. of Memphis.**
6. David Sanders, lhp, Barton County (Kan.) CC.
7. **Scott Patten, rhp, Tecumseh (Okla.) HS.**
8. **Dennis Ulacia, lhp, Monsignor Pace HS, Opa Locka, Fla.**
9. **Corwin Malone, lhp, Thomasville (Ala.) HS.**
10. **Matt Guerrier, rhp, Kent U.**
11. **Alex Hollifield, rhp, Stranahan HS, Fort Lauderdale, Fla.**
12. **Derek Stanley, of, North Florida JC.**
13. **Casey Rogowski, of, Catholic Central HS, Livonia, Mich.**
14. **Spencer Oborn, of, Cal State Fullerton.**
15. **Julio Reyes, 1b/of, Miami Senior HS.**
16. Ben Birk, of, U. of Minnesota.
17. Ryan Childs, 3b/rhp, Damascus HS, Gaithersburg, Md.
18. Scott Hairston, ss, Canyon del Oro HS, Tucson.

19. Che Done, rhp, Pace HS, Miami.
20. David Brockman, rhp, Glendale (Ariz.) JC.
21. **Daniel Martinez, lhp, Southwestern (Calif.) JC.**
22. **Kris McWhirter, rhp, Volunteer State (Tenn.) CC.**
23. **Joe Curreri, rhp, Long Island U.**
24. **Todd Holt, of, Louisburg (N.C.) JC.**
25. **Rocky Hughes, lhp, Pratt (Kan.) CC.**
26. **Joe Valentine, rhp, Jefferson Davis (Ala.) JC.**
27. Daniel Ortmeier, of/1b, Lewisville HS, Highland Village, Texas.
28. Wally Rosa, c, Brito Private HS, Miami.
29. **Jason Rummel, 2b, Towson State U.**
30. Jonathan Cavin, of, Connors State (Okla.) JC.
31. Juan Gutierrez, of, Coral Park HS, Miami.
32. Michel Valdez, of, Miami-Dade CC.
33. Tony Neal, rhp, Faulkner State (Ala.) JC.
34. Matt Salvesan, 3b, Kishwaukee (Ill.) JC.
35. Greg Sandifer, rhp, Palomar (Calif.) JC.
36. Jeff Bajenaru, rhp, U. of Oklahoma.
37. Michael Eady, of, West Ouachita HS, Eros, La.
38. **Trent Roehler, c, Fort Hays State (Kan.) U.**
39. Paul Beaudreau, c, El Modena HS, Orange, Calif.
40. Jeremy Castillo, of, Southridge HS, Miami.
41. Eric Johnson, rhp, Southridge HS, Miami.
42. John Koonig, rhp, Jefferson (Mo.) JC.
43. Kristopher Gross, rhp, Lees Summit (Mo.) HS.
44. Armando Perez, lhp, Montgomery HS, San Ysidro, Calif.
45. James Hymon, ss, Kishwaukee (Ill.) JC.
46. Dustin Scheffel, rhp, Oak Ridge HS, Cameron Park, Calif.
47. Carlynn Steele, ss, Connors State (Okla.) JC.
48. Mike Cox, c, Riverview HS, Sarasota, Fla.
49. Austin Rappe, of, Virginia Tech.
50. Adam Heiden, rhp, Denison (Iowa) HS.

CHICAGO-NL (26)

1. **Ben Christensen, rhp, Wichita State U.**
2. **Michael Mallory, of, Dinwiddie County HS, Dinwiddie, Va.**
3. **Ryan Gripp, 3b, Creighton U.**
4. **Steve Smyth, lhp, U. of Southern California.**
5. Todd Deininger, rhp, Joliet Township (Ill.) HS.
6. **Ben Shaffar, rhp, U. of Kentucky.**
7. **Mike Dzurilla, 2b, St. Johnís U.**
8. **Dustin Pate, rhp, Daniel HS, Clemson, S.C.**
9. **Chris Curry, c, Mississippi State U.**
10. **Jim Deschaine, ss, Brandeis (Mass.) U.**
11. **Tim Lavery, lhp, U. of Illinois.**
12. **Condor Cash, of, Stephens County School, Toccoa, Ga.**
13. **Syketo Anderson, 2b, Chipola (Fla.) JC.**
14. **Jandin Thornton-Murray, ss, St. Louis HS, Honolulu.**
15. Andrew Earley, rhp, Okaloosa Walton CC.
16. **Tony Gsell, 2b, Old Dominion U.**
17. **Derrick Cohens, of, Lake City (Fla.) CC.**
18. **James Eppeneder, lhp, Diablo Valley (Calif.) CC.**
19. **John Webb, rhp, Manatee (Fla.) CC.**
20. **Brandon Sing, ss/1b, Joliet Township (Ill.) HS.**
21. Ron Ogle, lhp, Long Beach (Calif.) CC.
22. Martin Calderon, ss, El Modena HS, Orange, Calif.
23. **Pete Zoccolillo, 1b/of, Rutgers U.**
24. Kevin Collins, of, Land O'Lakes (Fla.) HS.
25. **Ryan Van Horn, c, U. of Oklahoma.**
26. **Ben Johnstone, of, Yale U.**
27. **Casey Kopitzke, c, U. of Wisconsin-Oshkosh.**
28. David Lemon, of, Eustis HS, Heathrow, Fla.
29. Ryan Jackson, c, McNeil HS, Austin.
30. Raymond Sadler, of, Hill (Texas) JC.
31. Blake Melstrom, c, South Hills HS, West Covina, Calif.
32. Jorge Acevedo, of, Efrain Sanchez Hidalgo HS, Moca, P.R.
33. Greg Hanoian, of, U. of Southern California.
34. Stephen Solwick, rhp, Rio Rancho (N.M.) HS.
35. **Eduardo Marquez, of, Nicholls State U.**
36. Jason MacKintosh, lhp, Cerro Coso (Calif.) CC.
37. **Jeff Ryan, ss, Wichita State U.**
38. Cody Willis, rhp, Deweyville (Texas) HS.
39. Federico Baez, 3b, Jose Alegria HS, Dorado, P.R.
40. Justin Valenti, of, Norwalk (Conn.) CC.
41. Beau Benton, of, Central Florida CC.
42. Donn Bair, lhp/of, Merced (Calif.) HS.
43. Bryan Golden, c, Potomac State (W.Va.) JC.
44. Jeremy Mannin, lhp, Wenatchee (Wash.) HS.
45. Michael Sims, of, Karns HS, Knoxville.
46. **Chris Adams, rhp, McLennan (Texas) CC.**
47. Dale Thayer, rhp, Edison HS, Huntington Beach, Calif.
48. Charles Talanoa, rhp, El Segundo (Calif.) HS.
49. Ryan Johnson, of, Laguna Hills (Calif.) HS.
50. Thomas Syc, rhp, Carl Sandburg HS, Orland Park, Ill.

CINCINNATI (14)

1. **Ty Howington, lhp, Hudson's Bay HS, Vancouver, Wash.**
2. **Ben Broussard, 1b, McNeese State U.**
3. **Brandon Love, rhp, Viola (Ark.) HS.**
4. **Ken Lutz, rhp, Collinsville HS, Caseyville, Ill.**
5. Mike Esposito, rhp, Cimarron-Memorial HS, Las Vegas, Nev.
6. **Alex LeFlore, of, Pinellas Park (Fla.) HS.**
7. **Okorie Barrow, of, Clarke Central HS, Athens, Ga.**
8. **Ryan Lundquist, c, U. of Arkansas.**
9. **Casey Bookout, 1b, U. of Oklahoma.**
10. **Scott Dunn, rhp, U. of Texas.**
11. **Paul Darnell, lhp, Tarleton State (Texas) U.**
12. **Joshua Spoerl, 3b, U. of Texas.**
13. Travis Wong, 1b, Timberline HS, Boise, Idaho.
14. **David Bradley, rhp, Marietta (Ohio) College.**
15. **Rafael Erazo, rhp, Oklahoma Christian U.**
16. **Paco Escamilla, rhp, Lubbock Christian U.**
17. **Kyle Moncrief, 1b, West Monroe HS, Monroe, La.**
18. **Matthew Dehner, ss, Oklahoma City U.**
19. **B.J. Hawes, ss, Augusta (Ga.) Christian School.**
20. **Mark Burnett, 2b, U. of Arkansas.**
21. **Brad Sal mon, rhp, Jefferson Davis (Ala.) CC.**
22. Mike Fawcett, rhp, Central Michigan U.
23. **Matt Nanninga, rhp, Bellevue (Neb.) U.**
24. **Carlos Hines, rhp, Smithfield-Selma HS, Selma, N.C.**
25. **Kevin Schnall, c, Coastal Carolina U.**
26. **Jason Huth, ss, Texas Tech.**
27. **Michael Landkammer, rhp, Mankato State (Minn.) U.**
28. **Thomas Pike, rhp, McMurry (Texas) U.**
29. **Michael Neu, rhp, U of Miami**
30. Jonathan Sheaffer, of, South Mountain (Ariz.) CC.
31. **Corey Ward, of, Odessa (Texas) JC.**
32. Jack Arroyo, 2b, East Union HS, Prundale, Calif.
33. **Jason Howard, c, East Carolina U.**
34. Stace Pape, rhp, U. of Texas-San Antonio.
35. Evan Conley, ss, Manatee HS, Bradenton, Fla.
36. Richard Hill, lhp, Milton (Mass.) HS.
37. **Jerymaine Beasley, rhp, Eastern Washington U.**
38. Blake Bodenmiller, lhp, West Orange HS, Orlando.
39. Josh Andrade, rhp, Sandalwood HS, Jacksonville.
40. Matthew Allen, rhp, Vernon Regional (Texas) JC.
41. Garrett Alwert, lhp, Bethel HS, Puyallup, Wash.
42. Bryan Erstad, of, Jamestown (N.D.) HS.
43. **Nate Rewers, 2b, U. of Richmond.**
44. Marlyn Tisdale, rhp, U. of Tennessee.
45. **Paul Brown, lhp, Citrus (Calif.) JC.**
46. Matt Lynch, lhp, John Carroll HS, Fort Pierce, Fla.
47. **Leon Smith, rhp, Greenbrier HS, Appling, Ga.**
48. Scott Hindman, lhp, Fremd HS, Inverness, Ill.
49. Gerrit Simpson, rhp, Connors State (Okla.) JC.
50. Cory Whitlock, ss, De Soto (Texas) HS.

CLEVELAND (23)

1. (Choice to Orioles as compensation for Type A free agent Roberto Alomar).
2. **Will Hartley, c, Bradford County HS, Stark, Fla.**
3. **Eric Johnson, of, Western Carolina U.**
4. Jeff Baker, ss, Gar-Field HS, Woodbridge, Va.
5. **Curtis Gay, 1b, Oklahoma City U.**
6. **Shane Wallace, lhp, Newman Smith HS, Carrollton, Texas.**
7. Daylon Monette, of, Miller HS, Fontana, Calif.
8. **Devin Rogers, rhp, Nicholls State U.**
9. Stephen Cowie, lhp, Duke U.
10. **Fernando Cabrera, rhp, Discipulus de Cristo HS, Baya-mon, P.R.**
11. Monte Mansfield, rhp, Hesperia (Calif.) HS.
12. **Francis Finnerty, c, Wellington (Fla.) Community HS.**
13. **Adam Barr, lhp, South Williamsport Area HS, Williamsport, Pa.**
14. **Josh Martin, lhp, King Academy, Columbia, S.C.**
15. **Brody Lynn, ss, Kapaun-Mt. Carmel HS, Wichita.**
16. **Anthony Marini, lhp, Kennesaw State U.**
17. **Chris Kelley, rhp, College of William & Mary.**
18. **Kyle Moyer, 1b, Mohawk HS, Tiffin, Ohio.**
19. **Travis Santini, of, Lely HS, Naples, Fla.**
20. Louis Wieben, lhp, St. Mary HS, Secaucus, N.J.
21. Jason Davis, rhp, Cleveland State (Tenn.) CC.
22. Jeffrey Reboin, lhp, Sacramento City CC.
23. Anthony Tomey, rhp, Catholic Central HS, Northville, Mich.
24. **Philip Rosengren, rhp, Northwestern U.**
25. **Chris Lotterhos, 2b, Mississippi State U.**
26. **Kyle Denny, rhp, U. of Oklahoma.**
27. Jordan Olson, lhp, Crescenta Valley HS, La Crescenta, Calif..

28. Matthew Spiess, rhp, Owosso (Mich.) HS.
29. Roberto Vega, c, Adela Brenes Texidor HS, Guayama, P.R.
30. William McKenzie, rhp, Sullivan South HS, Kingsport, Tenn.
31. **Leyson Rivera, rhp, Calderon HS, Carolina, P.R.**
32. Ben Fransico, of, Servite HS, Fullerton, Calif.
33. Scott Thomas, rhp, Watervliet (Mich.) HS.
34. Kerry Hodges, of, New Mexico JC.
35. **Mike Byrd, rhp, Vanderbilt U.**
36. Jerad Doty, of, Rio Vista (Texas) HS.
37. **Teddy Sullivan, rhp, Duke U.**
38. **John Christ, rhp, Johns Hopkins U.**
39. **Byron Ewing, 1b, Howard U.**
40. Neil Dudkowski, lhp, Lassen (Calif.) JC.
41. Roger Ring, lhp, Monte Vista HS, La Mesa, Calif.
42. Anthony Lunetta, ss, Arlington HS, Riverside, Calif.
43. Brad Harrison, of, Mandarin HS, Jacksonville.
44. Michael Bishop, of/c, Kansas State U.
45. Douglas Johnson, rhp, Pelham (N.H.) HS.
46. Jeff Becker, 3b, Duke U.
47. **Samuel Button, lhp, Jacksonville State U.**
48. **Simon Young, lhp, Georgia Tech.**
49. Neal Maybin, of, Brevard (Fla.) CC.
50. John Gall, 1b, Stanford U.

COLORADO (16)

1. **Jason Jennings, rhp, Baylor U.**
2. **Ryan Kibler, rhp, King HS, Tampa.**
3. **Josh Bard, c, Texas Tech.**
4. **Chuck Crowder, lhp, Georgia Tech.**
5. **Chris Testa, of, Palmdale (Calif.) HS.**
6. **Roney Johnson, rhp, Woodcreek HS, Antelope, Calif.**
7. **Carlos Figueroa, ss, Gilberto Concepcion HS, Carolina, P.R.**
8. **Greg Catalanotte, of, U. of Florida.**
9. **Colin Young, lhp, Fordham U.**
10. **Sean Daly, c, Golden West HS, Visalia, Calif.**
11. **Chris Moore, ss, Western Carolina U.**
12. **Craig House, rhp, Memphis State U.**
13. **Rick Cercy, rhp, Morehead State U.**
14. **Eric McQueen, c, Georgia Tech.**
15. **Danny Phillips, 3b/of, Cal State Northridge.**
16. **Cam Esslinger, rhp, Seton Hall U.**
17. **Billy Gasparino, ss, Oklahoma State U.**
18. Brandon Caraway, 2b, U. of Houston.
19. **Dave Mulqueen, 3b, Marquette HS, Milwaukee.**
20. **Aaron Warren, c, Howard U.**
21. **Matt Hoffman, rhp, Oral Roberts U.**
22. Darin Naatjes, of, West Lyon HS, Alvord, Iowa.
23. **Javier Lorenzo, rhp, Miami-Dade CC.**
24. **Deryck Christensen, rhp, Eastside Catholic HS, Issaquah, Wash.**
25. **Ray Aguilar, lhp, Cypress (Calif.) JC.**
26. Bob Brownlie, rhp, Edison (N.J.) HS.
27. Michael Tejada, c, Brigham Young U.
28. Justin Hampson, lhp, Belleville Area (Ill.) CC.
29. Bryce Coppieters, of, Lethbridge (Alberta) CC.
30. Rick Sander, rhp, Riverside (Calif.) CC.
31. Andy Warren, rhp, Sam Houston State U.
32. Casey Kelly, 1b, Westview HS, Portland, Oregon.
33. Darren Clarke, rhp, Plant HS, Tampa.
34. Pat Curran, lhp, Edmonds (Wash.) CC.
35. Don Tolen, rhp, Orange Glen HS, Escondido, Calif.
36. Thomas MacLane, lhp, St. Petersburg (Fla.) CC.
37. Chad Liter, of, Madison (Ind.) Consolidated HS.
38. Jason Kramer, lhp, Marcus HS, Flower Mound, Texas.
39. William Dennis, of, Devine HS, Big Foot, Texas.
40. Nicholas Gor, rhp, Esperanza HS, Yorba Linda, Calif.
41. Eli Lapka, ss, Dodge City (Kan.) CC.
42. Grant Mullen, 1b, St. Christopher's SS, Corunna, Ontario.
43. Cortney Inman, rhp, Parkview HS, Springfield, Mo.
44. Nick Loughmin, rhp, Bishop Verot HS, Cape Coral, Fla.
45. Nick McCurdy, rhp, Jefferson Davis (Ala.) JC.
46. Tobias Bird, of, Mendocino (Calif.) CC.
47. Kendall Jones, c, Broken Arrow (Okla.) HS.
48. Manases Pabon, of, Indian Hills (Iowa) CC.
49. Billy Wheeler, rhp, Crown Point (Ind.) HS.

DETROIT (3)

1. **Eric Munson, c, U. of Southern California.**
2. (Choice to Royals as compensation for Type A free agent Dean Palmer).
3. **Neil Jenkins, 3b, Dwyer HS, Jupiter, Fla.**
4. **Cody Ross, of, Carlsbad (N.M.) HS.**
5. **Dayle Campbell, of, Los Angeles Pierce JC.**
6. **Brant Ust, 3b, U. of Notre Dame.**
7. **Tim Kalita, lhp, U. of Notre Dame.**
8. **Anthony Ware, 3b, Hamilton HS, Los Angeles.**

First college player selected
Tigers picked Southern California's Eric Munson

9. **Casey Rowe, rhp, Fresno State U.**
10. **Jerrod Fuell, rhp, Palo Verde HS, Tucson.**
11. **Erick Burke, lhp, U. of Houston.**
12. **Dan Davis, of, Osceola HS, Kissimmee, Fla.**
13. **Kevin Jackson, 3b, U. of North Florida.**
14. Ross Garland, c, Walters State (Tenn.) CC.
15. **Corey Richardson, of, New Mexico State U.**
16. **Stephen Bess, rhp, Rice U.**
17. Brad Steele, rhp, U. of California.
18. **Randy Leek, lhp, College of William & Mary.**
19. **Casey Williamson, of, Troy State U.**
20. **Dustin Beam, ss, Wright State U.**
21. **Corey McDonald, lhp, U. of North Carolina-Greensboro.**
22. **Aaron Barnett, lhp, Middle Tennessee State U.**
23. **Jeremy Lewis, lhp, Central Cabarrus HS, Concord, N.C.**
24. Nathan Husser, 1b, Middletown HS, Newark, Del.
25. Ed Romprey, ss, Fullerton (Calif.) JC.
26. **Greg Watson, rhp, U. of Tampa.**
27. **Johnny Gordon, of, Warner Southern (Fla.) College.**
28. Ryan Golem, rhp, Dearborn (Mich.) HS.
29. Tim Leveque, rhp, Crespi HS, Northridge, Calif.
30. Joe Urban, of, Santa Ana (Calif.) JC.
31. Randy Thurman, lhp, Ringling (Okla.) HS.
32. Eric Eckenstahler, lhp, Illinois State U.
33. **Jason Frasor, rhp, Southern Illinois U.**
34. **Robert Hlousek, 3b, U. of Missouri-St. Louis.**
35. Dennis Wyrick, ss, Bishop Amat HS, Azusa, Calif.
36. **Jason Siegfried, c, U. of Dayton.**
37. Miles Luuloa, ss, Laney (Calif.) CC.
38. Corey Loomis, ss, Eastwood HS, Pemberville, Ohio.
39. Kaulana Kuhaulua, ss, Los Angeles CC.
40. Francisco Arteaga, rhp, Roosevelt HS, Los Angeles.
41. John-Eric Hernandez, rhp, Chico State (Calif.) U.
42. Peter Pirman, of, Triton (Ill.) JC.
43. Phillip Mixter, rhp, Muskegon (Mich.) HS.
44. **Jayson Drobiak, ss, U. of Connecticut.**

FLORIDA (2)

1. **Josh Beckett, rhp, Spring (Texas) HS.**
2. **Terry Byron, rhp, Indian River (Fla.) JC.**
3. **Josh Wilson, ss, Mt. Lebanon HS, Pittsburgh**
4. **Dominic Woody, c, U. of Washington.**

5. **Nate Robertson, lhp, Wichita State U.**
6. **Charlie Frazier, of, Toms River (N.J.) South HS.**
7. **Jake Laidlaw, ss, Cheyenne HS, Las Vegas.**
8. **Kevin Hooper, 2b, Wichita State U.**
9. **Ben Hickman, rhp, Louisiana Tech.**
10. **Scott Goodman, of, Arizona State U.**
11. **Randy Messenger, rhp, Sparks (Nev.) HS.**
12. **Angel Sanchez, c, Vineland (N.J.) HS.**
13. **Bryan Moore, rhp, U. of Houston.**
14. **Todd Moser, lhp, Florida Atlantic U.**
15. **Barry Schell, of, Palomar (Calif.) JC.**
16. **Jared Wykoff, rhp, Kinder (La.) HS.**
17. **Brad Haynes, rhp, Barren County HS, Glasgow, Ky.**
18. **David Johnston, rhp, Marshalltown (Iowa) HS.**
19. **Kevin Perkins, 2b, UC Riverside.**
20. **Shane Smuin, rhp, Utah Valley State JC.**
21. **Joe Sergent, lhp, Lamar U.**
22. **James Close, of, U. of Nevada-Las Vegas.**
23. **Jarrod Schmidt, 1b/rhp, Lassiter HS, Marietta, Ga.**
24. **Bryan Morse, lhp, Mount Olive (N.C.) College.**
25. **Dennis Anderson, c, U. of Arizona.**
26. **Keith Herbert, ss, Boonsboro HS, Keedysville, Md.**
27. **Thomas Bell, rhp, George Marshall (Va.) HS.**
28. **Matt Ward, lhp, Texas A&M U.**
29. **Matt Postell, 1b, North Carolina State U.**
30. **Brandon Bowe, rhp, Louisiana State U.**
31. Kenny Riley, c, Reed HS, Sparks, Nev.
32. Dustin Griffith, rhp, Dakota Ridge HS, Littleton, Colo.
33. Micheal Flannery, rhp, Gloucester County (N.J.) CC.
34. John Moylan, c, Canada (Calif.) JC.
35. **Enrique Mendieta, of, Norfolk State U.**
36. Kevin Snowden, of, Roosevelt HS, Lanham, Md.
37. Derek Caraway, rhp, Andalusia (Fla.) HS.
38 Robert Glaser, of, San Joaquin Delta (Calif.) JC.
39. Chance Scott, ss, Pleasant Grove (Utah) HS.
40. Matt Krabbe, rhp, Triton (Ill.) JC.
41. Jeff Nichols, rhp, Rice U.
42. David LaRoche, 1b, Fort Scott (Kan.) CC.
43. Darin Phalines, rhp, Gloucester County (N.J.) CC.
44. **Alonso Gomez, 3b, JC of San Mateo (Calif.).**
45. John Anderson, rhp, Pine Bluff (Ark.) HS.
46. Benjamin Vannatter, c, Amelia (Ohio) HS.
47. Jacob Robertson, of, Twin Falls (Idaho) HS.
48. **Quian Davis, of, Buena Regional HS, Minotola, N.J.**
49. John Zamora, rhp, Cabrillo (Calif.) JC.
50. Anthony Aceves, of, Howard HS, Columbia, Md.

HOUSTON (29)

1. (Choice to Padres as compensation for Type A free agent Ken Caminiti).
1. **Michael Rosamond, of, U. of Mississippi** (Supplemental pick—42nd—for loss of Type A free agent Randy Johnson).
2. **Jay Perez, c, Seymour (Conn.) HS** (Choice from Diamondbacks as compensation for Johnson).
2. **Travis Anderson, rhp, U. of Washington.**
3. **Jim Barrett, rhp, Fort Hill HS, Cumberland, Md.**
4. **Jon Topolski, of, Baylor U.**
5. **Mike Gallo, lhp, Long Beach State U.**
6. **Jason Lane, of, U. of Southern California.**
7. **Nick Roberts, rhp, U. of Southern Utah.**
8. **Chris Sampson, ss, Texas Tech U.**
9. **Jonathan Helquist, ss, University Christian HS, Jacksonville.**
10. Greg Dobbs, 3b, Long Beach State U.
11. **Kris Kann, rhp, Mansfield (Pa.) U.**
12. **Royce Huffman, 3b, Texas Christian U.**
13. **Garett Gentry, c, Victor Valley (Calif.) CC.**
14. **Brian Schmitt, 1b, Blinn (Texas) JC.**
15. Bryan Edwards, rhp, Northeast Texas CC.
16. **Daniel Parker, rhp, Diablo Valley (Calif.) JC.**
17. **Ryan Jamison, rhp, U. of Missouri.**
18. **Mike Hill, of/2b, Oral Roberts U.**
19. **Jon Andrianoff, ss, Portville (N.Y.) Central HS.**
20. **Derrick Johnson, lhp, Wallace State (Ala.) CC.**
21. Russ Morgan, rhp, Purdue U.
22. Stephen Ghutzman, c, Spring (Texas) HS.
23. **Jason Maule, 2b, Central Connecticut State U.**
24. **Brian O'Connor, c, Valparaiso U.**
25. **Chris George, rhp, U. of Missouri.**
26. Lance Ericksen, rhp, U. of Utah.
27. Shane Hall, rhp, Sierra Vista HS, Hereford, Az.
28. Marc Gwyn, rhp, Rice U.
29. David Frame, rhp, Westfield HS, Houston.
30. Steven Mortimer, 1b, Richland (Wash.) HS.
31. Javier Andueza, rhp, West Valley (Calif.) JC.

32. Billy Zbacnik, 1b, University HS, San Diego.
33. **Steven Hoover, of, Cal State Stanislaus.**
34. **John Ortiz, lhp, U. of New Mexico.**
35. Justin Toone, rhp, Kingwood (Texas) HS.
36. Jordan Hunt, rhp, Edmonds (Wash.) CC.
37. Abraham Ayala, 3b, Miami Dade CC.
38. Deshain Beasley, of, Kamiakin HS, Kennewick, Wash.
39. **Jeffrey Blitstein, rhp, Chapman (Calif.) College.**
40. Darrick Bingham, rhp, Canada (Calif.) JC.
41. Ray Leyba, lhp, Cowley County (Kan.) CC.

KANSAS CITY (7)

1. **Kyle Snyder, rhp, U. of North Carolina**
1. **Mike MacDougal, rhp, Wake Forest U.** (Choice from Red Sox for loss of Type A free agent Jose Offerman).
1. **Jay Gehrke, rhp, Pepperdine U.** (Supplemental pick—32nd—for loss of Offerman).
1. **Jimmy Gobble, lhp, John Battle HS, Bristol, Va.** (Supplemental pick—43rd—for loss of Type A free agent Dean Palmer).
2. **Brian Sanches, rhp, Lamar U.** (Choice from Tigers as compensation for Palmer).
2. **Wes Obermueller, rhp, U. of Iowa.**
3. Kiki Bengochea, rhp, Columbus HS, Miami.
4. **Mackeel Rodgers, ss, Jackson HS, Miami.**
5. **Ken Harvey, 1b, U. of Nebraska.**
6. **Ryan Baerlocher, rhp, Lewis-Clark State (Idaho) College.**
7. **James McAuley, c, U. of Louisville.**
8. **Eric Nelson, 2b, Baylor U.**
9. **Mark Ellis, ss, U. of Florida.**
10. **Jesse Kurtz-Nicholl, lhp, Rice U.**
11. **Edwin Franco, lhp, Florida International U.**
12. **Tony Cogan, lhp, Stanford U.**
13. **G.J. Raymundo, 3b, Pepperdine U.**
14. **Jarrett Shearin, of, U. of North Carolina.**
15. **Casey Dunn, c, Auburn U.**
16. Sam Smith, rhp, Trinidad State (Colo.) JC.
17. **Brad Stiles, lhp, Lamar (Colo.) HS.**
18. Brandon Medders, rhp, Shelton State (Ala.) CC.
19. **Jermaine Smiley, of, Bellevue (Wash.) CC.**
20. Juan Figueroa, rhp, Juan M. Lazaro HS, Carolina, P.R.
21. Brian Nagore, c, Logan HS, Hayward, Calif.
22. **Chad Santos, 1b, St. Louis HS, Kaneohe, Hawaii.**
23. Pat Magness, 1b, Wichita State U.
24. **Brian Johnson, c, U. of Nebraska.**
25. **Chris Cabaj, rhp, Ball State U.**
26. **Raul Garcia, rhp, Florida International U.**
27. Ben Carter, c, Bowie (Texas) HS.
28. Jason Lockwood, rhp, Torrance (Calif.) HS.
29. Lukas Guidroz, rhp, Enterprise State (Ala.) JC.
30. Richard Frink, c, Mission Bay HS, San Diego.
31. Jason Crear, of, King HS, Houston.
32. Jason Arre, lhp, Toms River South HS, Beachwood, N.J.
33. **Michael Clay, ss/c, Southeastern Oklahoma State U.**
34. William Austin, rhp, Salina (Okla.) HS.
35. Marcus Wyatt, of, Fontana (Calif.) HS.
36. **Julian Gonzalez, of, U. of Virginia.**
37. Bryan Bullington, rhp, Madison (Ind.) Consolidated HS
38. Adam Lingenfelter, rhp, Florida JC.
39. **Abel Garcia, lhp, Laredo (Texas) JC.**
40. Jason Fransz, of, Arlington HS, San Jacinto, Calif.
41. Herman Wright, of, Odem (Texas) HS.
42. Anthony Mercado, rhp, Veve Calzada HS, Fajardo, P.R.
43. **Keronn Walker, c, Bluefield (Va.) College.**
44. Shane Menn, rhp, Calallen HS, Robstown, Texas.
45. **Jacob Baker, 1b, Rice U.**
46. Jason Maloney, rhp, Stranahan HS, Fort Lauderdale.
47. Greg Bauer, rhp, Wichita State U.
48. Lee Peach, rhp, Memorial HS, Newburgh, Ind..
49. Kyle Middleton, rhp, Jefferson Davis (Ala.) JC.
50. Byron Russell, of, Pamlico County HS, Bayboro, N.C.

LOS ANGELES (20)

1. (Choice to Padres as compensation for Type A free agent Kevin Brown).
1. **Jason Repko, ss-of, Hanford HS, West Richland, Wash.** (Supplemental pick—37th—for loss of Type A free agent Scott Radinsky).
2. **Brennan King, ss, Oakland HS, Murfreesboro, Tenn.** (Choice from Cardinals as compensation for Radinsky).
2. (Choice to Diamondbacks as compensation for Type A free agent Devon White).
2. Drew Meyer, ss-of, Bishop England HS, Charleston, S.C. (Supplemental pick—83rd—for loss of Type C free agent Brian Bohanon).
3. (Choice to Orioles as compensation for Type B free agent

Alan Mills)
4. **Joe Thurston, ss, Sacramento CC.**
5. **Phil Devey, lhp, U. of Southwestern Louisiana.**
6. **Shane Victorino, of, St. Anthonyís HS, Wailuku, Hawaii.**
7. **Jose Escalera, of, Carlos Escobar Lopez HS, Loiza, P.R.**
8. **T.J. Nall, rhp, Schaumburg (Ill.) HS.**
9. **Jonathan Berry, rhp, Newberry (S.C.) College.**
10. **Lamont Matthews, of, Oklahoma State U.**
11. **Eric Junge, rhp, Bucknell U.**
12. **Josh Dalton, ss, Louisiana State U.**
13. **Jon Hale, c, Southwest Missouri State U.**
14. **Randy Hadden, rhp, U. of South Carolina.**
15. **Wade Parrish, lhp, Washington State U.**
16. Tymber Lee, rhp, Wichita State U.
17. **Scott Martin, rhp, Central Connecticut State U.**
18. John Rozich, c, Kutztown (Pa.) U.
19. **Harold Eckert, rhp, Florida International U.**
20. Ryan Hamilton, rhp, U. of San Diego.
21. **Chris Snow, of, Desert Vista HS, Phoenix.**
22. Tim Cunningham, lhp, Rocklin (Calif.) HS.
23. Reggie Abercrombie, of, Columbus (Ga.) HS.
24. Shane Nance, lhp, U. of Houston.
25. Clint Chauncey, c, Terry Parker HS, Jacksonville, Fla.
26. Traviss Hodge, 1b, Los Angeles Pierce JC.
27. Lucas Robertson, rhp, Butler County (Kan.) CC.
28. Mike Keirstead, rhp, St Malachy's HS, St. John, N.B.
29. Zachary Cates, 1b, Mesa (Ariz.) CC.
30. Ryan Brnardic, rhp, Sandwich SS, LaSalle, Ontario.
31. Justin Glenn, of, Sheridan HS, Little Rock, Ark.
32. Nolan McManus, rhp, Sierra (Calif.) JC.
33. **Clif Wren, c, Mississippi State U.**
34. Nom Siriveaw, of, Eastern Oklahoma State JC.
35. Kegan O'Toole, c, Jackson HS, Bothell, Wash.
36. Ryan Harris, rhp, Woodstock (N.B.) HS.
37. Miguel Heredia, rhp, Eastern Oklahoma State JC.
38. Chris Hunter, rhp, Mountain View HS, Lindon, Utah.
39. Chris Hanne, lhp, Duluth (Ga.) HS.
40. Michael Pelsnik, rhp, Horizon HS, Phoenix.
41. **Keith Godbolt, of, Hillsborough HS, Tampa, Fla.**
42. Robert Harrand, rhp, Regina, Sask.
43. Kyle Bateman, rhp, Coconino HS, Flagstaff, Ariz.
44. Robby Sumner, 1b, Pace (Fla.) HS.
45. Erik Lohse, rhp, Butte (Calif.) JC.
46. Chris Bell, rhp, Columbus HS, Miami.
47. Joey Black, rhp, Bonneville HS, Ogden, Utah
48. Scott Wilson, c, Ellensburg (Wash.) HS.
49. Jayson Casiano, 1b, Monserrate Leon de Irriza HS, Cabo Rojo, P.R.
50. Jonathan Morel, 1b, Colegio San Agustin HS, Cabo Rojo, P.R.

MILWAUKEE (10)

1. **Ben Sheets, rhp, Northeast Louisiana U.**
2. **Kade Johnson, c, Seminole State (Okla.) JC.**
3. **Ruddy Lugo, rhp, Xaverian HS, Brooklyn, N.Y.**
4. **Travis Horne, lhp, First Coast HS, Jacksonville.**
5. Dustin Lansford, rhp, McLennan CC.
6. **Mark Ernster, 2b, Arizona State U.**
7. **Jeff Robinson, rhp, U. of Southwestern Louisiana.**
8. **David Pember, rhp, Western Carolina U.**
9. **Bryan Tindell, c, Avon Park (Fla.) HS.**
10. **Ben Hendrickson, rhp, Jefferson HS, Bloomington, Minn.**
11. **Will Ford, of, Rice U.**
12. **Frank Wagner, lhp, U. of Minnesota.**
13. **Terry Mayo, of, Eastern Guilford HS, Greensboro, N.C.**
14. **Steven Truitt, of, Texas A&M U.**
15. **Chris McGee, rhp, Mansfield U.**
16. Jason Tibesar, rhp, South Mountain (Ariz.) CC.
17. **Chris Olean, rhp, U. of Saint Thomas (Minn.).**
18. **Steve Scarborough, ss, Texas A&M U.**
19. William Hudson, ss, Fountain Valley (Calif.) HS.
20. Kevin Grater, rhp, U. of Wisconsin-Oshkosh.
21. **Ben Wallace, lhp, Quarbin HS, Hubbardston, Mass.**
22. Chad Clark, rhp, Glendora (Calif.) HS.
23. Chad Sadowski, rhp, U. of Wisconsin-Milwaukee.
24. **Ryan Knox, of, Illinois State U.**
25. **Casey Trout, ss, U. of Maryland.**
26. **Anthony Forelli, 1b, Old Dominion U.**
27. **Brad Ralston, rhp, Texas Tech.**
28. **Jeremy Durkee, lhp, Cuyahoga Falls (Ohio) HS.**
29. **Darrell Gaston, rhp, U. of Mobile.**
30. **Robert Pregnalato, of, Palm Beach Atlantic (Fla.) College.**
31. **Corey Arrieta, lhp, Northeast Louisiana U.**
32. **Justin Gordon, lhp, Massasoit (Mass.) CC.**
33. **Chris Schilling, c, Daniel HS, Central, S.C.**
34. **Jason Kelley, rhp, Bowling Green State U.**

35. **Jeff Kenney, ss, U. of Richmond.**
36. **Jeremy Krismer, rhp, Oklahoma State U.**
37. Devin Butler, 1b, Hillsborough (Fla.) JC.
38. Matt Gieble, lhp, Woodland (Calif.) HS.
39. Sean Sivers, lhp, Kearny HS, San Diego.
40. **Jeff House, rhp, Stetson U.**
41. **Javerro January, ss, Callaway HS, Jackson, Miss.**
42. **Brian Foster, c, Western Alamance HS, Burlington, N.C.**
43. **Chris Simonson, rhp, U. of Wisconsin.**
44. William Vazquez, rhp, Indian Hills (Iowa) CC.
45. Jason France, lhp, Central Arizona JC.
46. Joshua Lake, c, Buena HS, Ventura, Calif.
47. Ryan Warpinski, rhp, Denmark HS, Maribel, Wis.
48. Amos Burgess, of, Lone Peak (Utah) HS.
49. Blair Bourque, of, Taunton (Mass.) HS.

MINNESOTA (5)

1. **B.J. Garbe, of, Moses Lake (Wash.) HS.**
2. **Rob Bowen, c, Homestead HS, Fort Wayne, Ind.**
3. **Justin Morneau, c, New Westminster (B.C.) SS.**
4. **Jeff Randazzo, lhp, Cardinal O'Hara HS, Broomall, Pa.**
5. **Brent Schoening, rhp, Auburn U.**
6. **Brian Wolfe, rhp, Servite HS, Anaheim.**
7. Darren Ciraco, of, Pelham (N.Y.) Memorial HS.
8. **Matt Scanlon, 3b, U. of Minnesota.**
9. Grant Gregg, lhp, McLennan (Texas) CC.
10. Jim Caine, rhp, St. Charles (Ill.) HS.
11. Mike Prochaska, lhp, Leesville Road HS, Raleigh, N.C.
12. Kevin Johnson, rhp, U. of California.
13. Seth Morris, rhp/of, Hamilton (Ohio) HS.
14. Brian Slocum, rhp, Iona Prep School, Eastchester, N.Y.
15. John Wilson, c/of, U. of Kentucky.
16. **Kevin West, of, Mendocino (Fla.) CC.**
17. John Larson, rhp, Eastern Illinois U.
18. **Barry Quickstad, 2b, Waseca (Minn.) HS.**
19. **Paul Poplin, rhp, UNC Charlotte.**
20. Travis Bowyer, rhp, Liberty HS, Bedford, Va.
21. **Chad Wandall, ss, Auburn U.**
22. **Ricky Manning, of, Edison HS, Fresno.**
23. **Willie Eyre, rhp, JC of Eastern Utah.**
24. Daniel Matienzo, c, Columbus HS, Miami.
25. Craig Patterson, c, Cal State Fullerton.
26. **Terry Tiffee, 1b, Pratt (Kan.) CC.**
27. **Jess Turner, rhp, Centralia (Wash.) JC.**
28. **Brad Weis, lhp, Auburn U.**
29. **Sherwin Lockridge, ss, Florida A&M U.**
30. **Matthew Reed, ss, Haines City (Fla.) HS.**
31. Ryan Miller, rhp, U. of Evansville.
32. Jeff Balser, rhp, Venice (Fla.) HS.
33. Billy Keppinger, of, Lake City (Ga.) CC.
34. John Thomman, of, Levelland (Texas) HS.
35. **Jason Richardson, rhp, Polk (Fla.) CC.**
36. Joey Monahan, ss, Wheeler HS, Marietta, Ga.
37. **Digno Torres, of, Lake City (Fla.) CC.**
38. Scott Blackwell, rhp, Lincoln Land (Ill.) CC.
39. William Vaughan, rhp, Mountain Ridge HS, Glendale, Ariz.
40. Richard Smart, lhp, Gulf Coast (Fla.) CC.
41. Michael Stavey, 1b, Eustis (Fla.) HS.
42. **Michael Wrenn, c, St. Leo (Fla.) College.**
43. **Bryan Williamson, of, U. of Washington.**
44. Charles Campbell, rhp, Bay HS, Panama City, Fla.
45. Patrick Neshek, rhp, Park Center HS, Brooklyn Park, Minn.
46. Maurice Powell, rhp, Upland HS, Alta Loma, Calif.
47. Luke Field, rhp, Barton County (Kan.) CC.
48. Casey Rauschenberger, 3b, Oakland HS, Murfreesboro, Tenn.
49. David Slevin, ss, John Carroll HS, Port St. Lucie, Fla.
50. Joseph Ammirato, of, Marina HS, Long Beach.

MONTREAL (6)

1. **Josh Girdley, lhp, Jasper (Texas) HS.**
2. **Brandon Phillips, ss, Redan HS, Stone Mountain, Ga.**
3. **Drew McMillan, c, El Dorado HS, Placentia, Calif.**
4. **Matt Cepicky, of, Southwest Missouri State U.**
5. **Pat Collins, rhp, St. John's U.**
6. **Dom Ambrosini, of, Connetquot HS, Ronkonkoma, N.Y.**
7. **Bret Boyer, ss, Largo (Fla.) HS.**
8. **Luke Lockwood, lhp, Silverado HS, Victorville, Calif.**
9. **Brandon Watson, 2b, Westchester HS, Los Angeles.**
10. **Grant Dorn, rhp, North Carolina State U.**
11. **David Lutz, of, Monte Vista HS, Spring Valley, Calif.**
12. Brian Stavisky, of, Port Allegany (Pa.) HS.
13. **Chris Humrich, rhp, Armstrong Atlantic State (Ga.) U.**
14. **Brian Preston, c, Wichita State U.**
15. **Valentino Pascucci, rhp, U. of Oklahoma.**
16. **Matt Watson, 3b/2b, Xavier U.**

17. Josh Emmerick, c, Rancho Buena Vista HS, Oceanside, Calif.
18. Pat Wyrick, rhp, Atoka (Okla.) HS.
19. Neville Blount, of, Colton (Calif.) HS.
20. Leonard Landeros, lhp, Hanford (Calif.) HS.
21. **Mark Thomas, 1b, Youngstown State U.**
22. **Matt Brown, 3b, Eastern Randolph HS, Randleman, N.C.**
23. Israel Torres, lhp, Cerritos (Calif.) JC.
24. **Eric Charron, rhp, Marie-Anne HS, Montreal.**
25. **Chuck Crumpton, rhp, Arizona State U.**
26. **Lou Melucci, 2b, U. of Pittsburgh.**
27. Manuel Diaz, rhp, John Glenn (Calif.) HS.
28. Mike Natale, rhp, Santa Ana (Calif.) JC.
29. Francisco Chavez, rhp, Socorro HS, El Paso.
30. Alex Groleau, rhp, Edouard Montpetit (Quebec) College.
31. Jason Norderum, lhp, Shasta HS, Redding, Calif.
32. Jason Stevenson, lhp, Foothill HS, Redding, Calif.
33. Victor Rosario, of, Sandalwood HS, Jacksonville, Fla.
34. Eric Langill, c, Des Moines Area CC.
35. **Todd Johannes, c, U. of Florida.**
36. Jerry Alexander, ss, Westchester HS, Hawthorne, Calif.
37. Julio Acosta, c, Perkiomen School, Pennsburg, Pa.
38. Joseph Clark, rhp, JC of Southern Idaho.
39. Travis Edwards, of, Cerritos (Calif.) JC.
40. Wesley Cain, rhp, Marietta (Okla.) HS.
41. Jonnie Mazzeo, rhp, LaSalle SS, Kingston, Ontario.
42. Grant Oltjenbruns, of, Fresno (Calif.) CC.
43. Chris Sieman, c, Blanchard (Okla.) HS.
44. Charles Rohr, rhp, Citrus (Calif.) JC.
45. Chris Richard, of, Norwalk (Conn.) CC.
46. Matt Alexander, c, Trinidad State (Colo.) JC.
47. Matt Romero, of, Utah Valley State JC.
48. **Antonio Garris, 3b/of, Pitt (N.C.) CC.**

NEW YORK-AL (27)

1. **David Walling, rhp, U. of Arkansas.**
2. **Tommy Winrow, of, Bishop Verot HS, Fort Myers, Fla.**
3. **Alex Graman, lhp, Indiana State U.**
4. Robert Corrado, rhp, Oakwood HS, Dayton, Ohio.
5. **Seth Taylor, ss, U. of South Alabama.**
6. **Reggie Laplante, rhp, Ahuntsic College, Montreal.**
7. **Andy Phillips, 3b, U. of Alabama.**
8. **Scott Oliver, rhp, College of Charleston.**
9. **Jeff Leaumont, 1b, Louisiana State U.**
10. **Brad Ticehurst, of, U. of Southern California.**
11. Jeffrey Moye, rhp, Seminole State (Okla.) JC.
12. **Lou Witte, rhp, Xavier U.**
13. **Brian Peeples, lhp, First Coast HS, Jacksonville.**
14. **Todd Mitchell, ss, Illinois State U.**
15. **Casey Baker, ss, Towanda HS, Wysox, Pa.**
16. **Brian Grace, rhp, Louisiana State U.**
17. **Ricky Spears, rhp, Gore (Okla.) HS.**
18. **Dominic Correa, 2b, U. of Southern California.**
19. **John Kremer, rhp, U. of Evansville.**
20. Jesse Floyd, rhp, Nederland (Texas) HS.
21. **Michael Aldridge, c, Eastern Michigan U.**
22. Chris Klosterman, 3b/of, Cypress (Calif.) JC.
23. **Chad Sutter, c, Tulane U.**
24. **Joshua McCloud, rhp, Bowsher HS, Holland, Ohio.**
25. Brian Reed, rhp, Amory (Miss.) HS.
26. Darin Davis, 2b, Palisades (Calif.) HS.
27. John Robert Dimercurio, c, Highlands Ranch (Colo.) HS.
28. Chris Dobbins, rhp, Central Alabama CC.
29. Sean Lichter, rhp, Deer Valley HS, Glendale, Ariz.
30. Sean Henn, lhp, Aledo (Texas) HS.
31. Nathan Thompson, ss, Grayson County (Texas) JC.
32. Ryan Fry, 3b, Nazareth Area HS, Stockertown, Pa.
33. Santiago Narciandi, c, Miami-Dade CC.
34. Chad Bentz, lhp, Douglas HS, Juneau, Alaska.
35. Larry Buckley, rhp, East Central (Mo.) JC.
36. Nathan Bowden, 3b, Northwest Mississippi CC.
37. Michael Hurd, lhp, Arapahoe HS, Littleton, Colo.
38. Michael Brown, of, Centreville HS, Dayton, Ohio.
39. Jacob Pierce, rhp, Navarro (Texas) JC.
40. Jonathan Habrack, lhp, Dallas Senior HS, Shavertown, Pa.
41. Rob Garibaldi, of, Santa Rosa (Calif.) JC.
42. Ben Hedgecock, rhp, Gaither HS, Tampa.
43. **Jason Faigin, rhp, Rowan (N.J.) College.**
44. Jeremiah Porter, rhp, Columbia River HS, Vancouver, Wash.
45. Ruben Mancilla, 3b, Costa Mesa (Calif.) HS.
46. Beau Dannemiller, rhp, Logan (Ill.) JC.
47. John Perry, 1b, Arapahoe HS, Littleton, Colo.
48. David Lower, c, Culver Military Academy, Alexandria, Ind.
49. Henry Caban, rhp, Lehman HS, Bronx.
50. Mark Cooper, 1b, Texas City (Texas) HS.

NEW YORK-NL (22)

1. (Choice to White Sox as compensation for Type A free agent Robin Ventura)
2. **Neal Musser, lhp, Benton Central HS, Otterbein, Ind.**
2. **Jake Joseph, rhp, Cosumnes River (Calif.) JC** (Supplemental pick—84th—for loss of Type C free agent Armando Reynoso).
3. **Jeremy Griffiths, rhp, U. of Toledo.**
4. Angel Pagan, of, Republica De Colombia HS, Rio Piedras, P.R.
5. **Nick James, rhp, Hancock (Calif.) JC.**
6. Tyler Parker, c, Lassiter HS, Marietta, Ga.
7. **Rodney Nye, 3b, U. of Arkansas.**
8. **Forrest Lawson, of, Rogers HS, Puyallup, Wash.**
9. **Wayne Lydon, of, Valley View HS, Jessup, Pa.**
10. **Prentice Redman, of, Bevill State (Ala.) CC.**
11. **Joey Cole, rhp, U. of Texas-Pan American.**
12. **Paul Viole, rhp, Seton Hall U.**
13. **Robert McIntyre, ss, Hillsborough HS, Tampa.**
14. **John Hendricks, lhp, Wake Forest U.**
15. **Steven Elzy, c, U. of New Mexico.**
16. Gene Desalme, lhp, Meramec (Mo.) CC.
17. **Kevin Ciarrachi, c, U. of Northern Iowa.**
18. **Matt Smith, rhp, Southwest Missouri State U.**
19. Jose Pabon, 2b, Potomac HS, Dumfries, Va.
20. Rob Henkel, lhp, UCLA.
21. Adam Manley, of, JC of Southern Idaho.
22. Kyle Woods, of, U. of Washington.
23. Terry Jackson, ss, Westside HS, Augusta, Ga.
24. Dustin Brisson, 1b, U. of Central Florida.
25. **Matt Dyer, c, Manchester (Ind.) College.**
26. **Brad Wright, of, UC Santa Barbara.**
27. **Sam Lopez, ss, Fresno (Calif.) CC.**
28. Steve Bennett, rhp, Gonzaga U.
29. Bryan Loeb, c, Baylor U.
30. Matt Mize, 2b, U. of Texas-Arlington.
31. Orlando Roman, rhp, Indian Hills (Iowa) CC.
32. Brian Williamson, rhp, Cornell U.
33. Lionel Rogers, rhp, Fresno (Calif.) CC.
34. Pat O'Sullivan, of, Austin Peay St U.
35. Jamie Gonzales, rhp, Porterville (Calif.) CC.
36. Aaron Ledbetter, rhp, Cedarville HS, Fort Smith, Ark.
37. **Graeme Brown, rhp, Brown U.**
38. **Michael Jacobs, c, Grossmont (Calif.) JC.**
39. Carrington Fisk, rhp, Keene (N.H.) HS.
40. **Cory Harris, of, Pensacola (Fla.) JC.**
41. Philip Perry, rhp, Walton HS, Marrietta, Ga.
42. Darius Shelby, of, Valley View HS, Moreno Valley, Calif.
43. Ryan Hay, c, St. Paul HS, Niagara Falls, Ontario.
44. Brian Kelly, rhp, Southaven HS, Olive Branch, Miss.
45. Ross Peeples, lhp, Middle Georgia JC.
46. Aaron Gureckis, rhp, Nashua (N.H.) HS.
47. Andre DeCordova, ss, Pace HS, Hialeah, Fla.
48. Vincent White, of, Beaconsfield, Quebec.
49. Eric Bernier, of, Edouard Montpetit (Quebec) College.
50. John Hoyos, lhp, San Gabriel HS, Rosemead, Calif.

OAKLAND (9)

1. **Barry Zito, lhp, U. of Southern California.**
2. **Ryan Ludwick, of, U. of Nevada-Las Vegas.**
3. **Jorge Soto, c-1b, Troy State U.**
4. **Keith Surkont, rhp, Williams (Mass.) College.**
5. **Darin Moore, rhp, U. of the Pacific.**
6. **Mario Ramos, lhp, Rice U.**
7. **Josh Hochgesang, 3b, Stanford U.**
8. **Justin Lehr, rhp/c, U. of Southern California.**
9. **Kirk Asche, of, Jacksonville U.**
10. **Justin Sobchuk, rhp, Sehome HS, Bellingham, Wash.**
11. **Michael Wenner, of, Rider U.**
12. Jay Garthwaite, of, Kent Meridan HS, Kent, Wash.
13. **Jason Pomar, rhp, U. of South Carolina.**
14. **Alvyn Ellis, 1b, Clackamas (Ore.) CC.**
15. Anthony Cicero, c, Cleveland HS, Van Nuys, Calif.
16. Matt Allegra, of, Lake Mary (Fla.) HS.
17. **Bryan Mazur, lhp, U. of North Carolina-Wilmington.**
18. **G.W. Keller, of, U. of Alabama.**
19. **Jason Clements, ss, Oral Roberts U.**
20. **Matt Gage, rhp, Eastern Illinois U.**
21. **Cade Sanchez, rhp, U. of Texas-Arlington.**
22. Edmund Muth, of, Stanford U.
23. **Mike Lockwood, of, Ohio State U.**
24. **Brad Henderson, 2b, U. of Mississippi.**
25. Fernando De Aza, rhp, Colegio Universario, Carolina, P.R.
26. **Jacob Beckman, rhp, Glen Oaks (Mich.) CC.**
27. Donaldo Atencio, rhp, Kirtland Central (N.M.) HS.
28. **Nate Hilton, rhp, Iowa State U.**

29. Andre Marshall, of, Walla Walla (Wash.) CC.
30. Jonathan Edge, of, U. of Tampa.
31. Kris Mancini, of, CC of Rhode Island.
32. **Micah Dunphy, lhp, Sauk Valley (Ill.) CC.**
33. Alex Coleman, of, Poly HS, Long Beach.
34. Geoff Comfort, of, JC of San Mateo (Calif.)
35. Darvin Withers, rhp, Spartanburg (S.C.) Methodist JC.
36. Jerry Knox, rhp, Oakland HS, Murfreesboro, Tenn.
37. **Jorge Ortiz, 3b, Miguel Melendez Munoz HS, Cayey, P.R.**
38. Frank James, lhp, Navarro (Texas) JC.
39. Brandon Bahr, rhp, Gulf Coast HS, Marco Island, Fla.
40. Jared Joaquin, rhp, Lower Columbia (Wash.) CC.
41. James Cole, lhp, Navarro (Texas) JC.
42. Kellyn Shafer, rhp, Lane (Ore.) CC.
43. Zach Gordon, ss, Moorpark (Calif.) JC.
44. Eric Kitchen, 3b, Durango HS, Las Vegas.
45. William Zeier, of, Laney (Calif.) JC.

PHILADELPHIA (12)

1. **Brett Myers, rhp, Englewood HS, Jacksonville.**
2. Jason Cooper, of, Moses Lake (Wash.) HS.
3. **Russ Jacobson, c, U. of Miami.**
4. **Brad Pautz, rhp, U. of Minnesota.**
5. Joe Saunders, lhp, West Springfield HS, Springfield, Va
6. **Daniel Tosca, c, Durant HS, Seffner, Fla.**
7. David Gil, rhp, U. of Miami.
8. **Jesse Thrasher, rhp, Benton HS, St. Joseph, Mo.**
9. **Julio Collazo, ss, Mississippi Delta JC.**
10. **Marlon Byrd, of, Georgia Perimeter JC.**
11. **Allen Legette, rhp, Stratford HS, Goose Creek, S.C.**
12. **Brian Bush, of, U. of Michigan.**
13. **Frank Brooks, lhp, St Peter's College.**
14. Jovanathan Clark, of, Vallejo (Calif.) HS.
15. **Mark Outlaw, lhp, Baylor U.**
16. **Chris Keelin, rhp, Montclair State (N.J.) College.**
17. **Brad Tucker, rhp, Pepperdine U.**
18. **Robert Avila, c, The Masterís (Calif.) College.**
19. Trey Saye, rhp, Newberry (S.C.) HS.
20. **Hector Serrano, c, Juan Ponce de Leon HS, Arecibo, P.R.**
21. **Aaron Merhoff, of, Texas Lutheran University.**
22. **Justin Duarte, 1b, Azusa Pacific (Calif.) U.**
23. **Todd Eagle, c, Albany (Calif.) HS.**
24. **Joe Schley, of, Southern Illinois U.**
25. **Brian Hitchcox, ss, Samford U.**
26. **Justin Fry, rhp, Ohio State U.**
27. **Daniel O'Neill, c, U. of Illinois.**
28. **Tom Batson, 3b, Northwestern State U.**
29. Randon Ho, lhp, U. of Hawaii.
30. **Chad Smith, rhp, Indiana U.**
31. **Wade Van Vark, of, Central (Iowa) College.**
32. **Jay Sitzman, of, Arizona State U.**
33. **Dean Muthig, 3b, Carthage (Wisc.) College.**
34. **Charles Carey, lhp, Cuesta (Calif.) JC.**
35. Chris Herman, ss, Mt. San Antonio (Calif.) CC.
36. Todd Simo, rhp, New Providence (N.J.) HS.
37. **Ryan Brookman, rhp, U. of Wisconsin-Whitewater.**
38. Jon Uhl, rhp, Leto Comprehensive HS, Tampa.
39. Kameron Loe, rhp, Granada Hills HS, Chatsworth, Calif.
40. Lawrence Alexander, of, Chandler (Okla.) HS.
41. **Todd Oetting, c, Jefferson City (Mo.) HS.**
42. **Erick Rivera, c, Luis Munoz Rivera HS, Utuado, P.R.**
43. Nicholas White, rhp, Arapahoe HS, Littleton, Colo.
44. Jordan Pickens, 3b, Atascadero (Calif.) HS.

PITTSBURGH (8)

1. **Bobby Bradley, rhp, Wellington (Fla.) HS.**
2. **Ryan Doumit, c, Moses Lake (Wash.) HS.**
3. **Aron Weston, of, Solon (Ohio) HS.**
4. **Justin Reid, rhp, U. of California-Davis.**
5. **J.R. House, c, Seabreeze HS, Ormond Beach, Fla.**
6. **B.J. Barns, of, Duquesne U.**
7. **Matt Schneider, of, U. of North Florida.**
8. **Jonathan Searles, rhp, Huntington (N.Y.) HS.**
9. **Shane Wright, rhp, Texas Tech.**
10. **Jeremy Sickles, c, Cal State Northridge.**
11. Craig Munroe, 1b, U. of Maryland.
12. **Jay Langston, 3b/of, Georgia State U.**
13. **Josh Hudnall, ss, Ouachita Christian School, Monroe, La.**
14. **Daniel Hudson, of/rhp, Mississippi Gulf Coast JC.**
15. **Joe Burruezo, rhp/of, Jesuit HS, Tampa.**
16. **Justin Martin, 2b, U. of Nevada.**
17. **Cliff Reik, 3b, Cary (N.C.) HS.**
18. **Ryan Dorsey, ss, Riverdale Baptist HS, Upper Marlboro, Md.**
19. Brian Tallet, lhp, Louisiana State U.
20. **Elliott Sarabia, ss, U. of Nevada-Las Vegas.**

21. Derek Ver Helst, lhp, Spearfish (S.D.) HS.
22. Jason Wilson, of/rhp, San Augustine (Texas) HS.
23. **Michael Piercy, of, Kean (N.J.) U.**
24. **Josh Bonifay, ss/2b, U. of North Carolina-Wilmington.**
25. **Aaron Story, lhp, Lawrence County HS, Lawrenceburg, Tenn.**
26. Ja'mar Clanton, ss, Proviso West HS, Bellwood, Ill.
27. Ken Henderson, lhp, New York Tech.
28. Andrew Green, rhp, Ouachita Parish HS, Monroe, La.
29. **Rodney Hancock, lhp, The Citadel.**
30. **Derek Hurley, lhp, Seton Hall U.**
31. **Walter Young, 1b, Purvis (Miss.) HS.**
32. **Jason Biddlestone, rhp, Columbus State (Ohio) CC.**
33. **Michael Sabens, rhp, Berry (Ga.) College.**
34. **Kurt Bultmann, 2b, Clemson U.**
35. **Mo Douglas, 1b, U. of Southwestern Louisiana.**
36. Ryan Fillingim, c/of, Fairhope (Ala.) HS.
37. **Troy Satterfield, lhp, U. of Central Florida.**
38. Ryan Stanek, rhp, New Providence (N.J.) HS.
39. **Patrick O'Brien, rhp, Walsh Jesuit HS, Bath, Ohio.**
40. Seth Hill, lhp/1b, Sandwich (Ill.) HS.
41. **Brian Messer, rhp, U. of New Mexico.**
42. Frank Torre, lhp, Palm Beach Garden, Fla.
43. Daniel Stringer, rhp, Brazoswood HS, Clute, Texas.
44. Michael Oehlberg, lhp, Guilford HS, Rockford, Ill.
45. Raul Nieves, ss, U. of Mobile (Ala.).
46. **Chris Batcheller, c, Washington & Lee (Va.) U.**
47. Bryce Morrison, of, Leander (Texas) HS.
48. Jude Voltz, 1b, U. of Mississippi.
49. **Brian Pollard, of, U. of Florida.**
50. **Landon Jacobsen, rhp, Trinidad State (Colo.) JC.**

ST. LOUIS (18)

1. (Choice to Orioles as compensation for Type A free agent Eric Davis).
1. **Chance Caple, rhp, Texas A&M U.** (Choice from Braves as compensation for Type A free agent Brian Jordan).
1. **Nick Stocks, rhp, Florida State U.** (Supplemental pick—36th—for loss of Jordan).
1. **Chris Duncan, 1b, Canyon del Oro HS, Tucson** (Supplemental pick—46th—for loss of Type A free agent Delino DeShields).
2. (Choice to Dodgers as compensation for Type A free agent Scott Radinsky).
2. **Josh Pearce, rhp, U. of Arizona** (Supplemental pick—82nd—for loss of Type C free agent Tom Lampkin).
3. **B.R. Cook, rhp, Oregon State U.**
4. **Ben Johnson, of, Germantown (Tenn.) HS** (Choice from Orioles as compensation for DeShields).
4. **Jim Journell, rhp, U. of Illinois.**
5. **Charles Williams, of, Rice U.**
6. **Josh Teekel, rhp, Belaire HS, Greenwell Springs, La.**
7. **Covelli Crisp, 2b, Los Angeles Pierce JC.**
8. **Shawn Schumacher, c/3b, Texas A&M U.**
9. **Damon Thames, ss, Rice U.**
10. **Kevin Sprague, lhp, McNeese State U.**
11. Aaron Davidson, 2b, Cuesta (Calif.) CC.
12. **Brent Spooner, c, U. of Central Florida.**
13. **Jose Pujols, 3b, Maple Woods (Mo.) CC.**
14. **Matt Vincent, lhp, Lindsey Wilson (Ky.) College.**
15. **Travis Bailey, 3b, Florida Atlantic U.**
16. **Cheyenne Janke, rhp, Nicholls State U.**
17. **Mike Perkins, rhp, Manatee JC.**
18. **Paul Fahs, rhp, Briar Cliff (N.Y.) JC.**
19. Chris Beck, of, Cal State Fullerton.
20. **Michael Layfield, rhp, Valdosta State (Ga.) U.**
21. **Jeremy Cummings, rhp, West Virginia U.**
22. **Mike Floyd, of, U. of Florida.**
23. **Chris Fiora, rhp, Towson State U.**
24. **Mike Crudale, rhp, Santa Clara U.**
25. **Mark Penberthy, c, The Masters (Calif.) College.**
26. Justin Berg, c, Rice U.
27. **Donavan Graves, rhp, Booneville (Mo.) HS.**
28. **Brandon Peck, lhp, Kansas State U.**
29. **Justin Albertsen, of, El Camino (Calif.) JC.**
30. **Mark Butler, rhp, Bellevue (Neb.) U.**
31. **Matt Parker, rhp, Mercer U.**
32. **Trevor Sansom, rhp, West Virginia State College.**
33. **Bo Hart, ss/2b, Gonzaga U.**
34. Jake Moon, rhp, Cypress (Calif.) JC.
35. **Aaron Dinkel, rhp, JC of Eastern Utah.**
36. Jeff Cruz, lhp, Fullerton (Calif.) CC.
37. **Robert Yates, rhp, U. of Arkansas.**
38. **Chris Buckley, of, North Arkansas CC.**
39. **Monte Lee, of, College of Charleston.**
40. Ron Corona, rhp, Cypress (Calif.) JC.

SAN DIEGO (28)

1. Vince Faison, of, Toombs County HS, Lyons, Ga. (Choice from Dodgers for loss of Type A free agent Kevin Brown).
1. Gerik Baxter, rhp, Edmonds-Woodway HS, Edmonds, Wash.
1. Omar Ortiz, rhp, U. of Texas-Pan American (Choice from Astros as compensation for Type A free agent Ken Caminiti).
1. Casey Burns, rhp, U. of Richmond (Supplemental pick—41st—for loss of Brown).
1. Mike Bynum, lhp, U. of North Carolina (Supplemental pick—49th—for loss of Caminiti).
1. Nick Trzesniak, c, Andrew HS, Tinley Park, Ill. (Supplemental pick—34th—for loss of Type A free agent Steve Finley).
2. Alberto Concepcion, c, El Segundo (Calif.) HS.
3. Josh Vitek, rhp, Fayetteville (Texas) HS.
4. Jason Moore, ss, U. of Texas.
5. Chris Heck, lhp, Clemson U. (Choice from Diamondbacks for loss of Finley).
5. Mike Thompson, rhp, Lamar (Colo.) HS.
6. Blair DeHart, rhp, James Madison U.
7. John Scheschuk, 1b, Texas A&M U.
8. Todd Donovan, of, Siena College.
9. John Puccinelli, ss/3b, Notre Dame HS, Toluca Lake, Calif.
10. Todd Shiyuk, lhp, U. of Alabama-Huntsville.
11. Brian Adams, lhp, Clemson U.
12. Brian Ward, 2b, North Carolina State U.
13. Tony Adler, rhp, Greenhill HS, Dallas.
14. Bobby Scales, 2b, U. of Michigan.
15. Jacob Peavy, rhp, St. Paul's HS, Semmes, Ala.
16. Greg Ienni, of, Cal State Los Angeles.
17. Brandon Fahey, 3b, Duncanville (Texas) HS.
18. Andres Pagan, c, Luis Munoz Marin HS, Yauco, P.R.
19. Richard Huff, c, Mesa State (Colo.) College.
20. Matt Moran, rhp, Cosumnes River (Calif.) JC.
21. Troy Schader, ss, Oregon State U.
22. Kevin Howard, 3b, Westlake HS, Thousand Oaks, Calif.
23. Mike Mueller, rhp, West Bend East HS, West Bend, Wis.
24. Jeremy Alford, 3b, Benton (La.) HS.
25. Anthony Vandemore, of, Truman State (Mo.) U.
26. Shawn Lynn, rhp, Seminole State (Okla.) JC.
27. Chris Adolph, of, U. of Nevada-Las Vegas.
28. Chad Dias, c, Bellevue (Wash.) CC.
29. B.J. Long, of, Evans HS, Martinez, Ga.
30. Jason Hammond, of, West Hills HS, Santee, Calif.
31. Jarrett Roenicke, of, Yuba (Calif.) JC.
32. Jeremy Webster, lhp, Salt Lake (Utah) CC.
33. Shawn Hill, rhp, Bishop Redding HS, Georgetown, Conn.
34. Michael Saunches, 1b, Argenta-Oreana HS, Decautur, Ill.
35. Jeff Rizzo, 3b, Stanford U.
36. Anthony Bianucci, of, Woodson HS, Fairfax, Va.
37. Kevin Okimoto, 1b, Santa Clara U.
38. Marcellus Dawson, of, Wauwatosa East HS, Milwaukee.
39. Chris Wilkins, rhp, The Dalles (Ore.) HS.
40. Jared Vance, rhp, Connorsville (Ind.) HS.

SAN FRANCISCO (24)

1. Kurt Ainsworth, rhp, Louisiana State U.
1. Jerome Williams, rhp, Waipahu HS, Honolulu (Supplemental pick—39th—for loss of Type A free agent Jose Mesa).
2. John Thomas, lhp, Righetti HS, Orcutt, Calif. (Choice from Nariners for loss of Mesa).
2. Jack Taschner, lhp, U. of Wisconsin-Oshkosh.
3. Sean McGowan, 1b, Boston College.
4. Jeremy Cunningham, rhp, Cal Poly San Luis Obispo.
5. Ryan Cox, rhp, Southern Illinois U.-Edwardsville.
6. Ryan Pene, of, Dixie (Utah) JC.
7. Joe Jester, ss, U. of Arkansas.
8. Kevin Vent, rhp, U. of Arkansas.
9. Josh Cook, ss, Yuba (Calif.) CC.
10. Anthony Yacco, rhp, Mahopac (N.Y.) HS.
11. Jeff Verplancke, rhp, Cal State Los Angeles.
12. Ron Merrill, ss, U. of Tampa.
13. Fletcher Lee, rhp, Lewis-Clark State (Idaho) College.
14. Mike Meyer, rhp, U. of Arizona.
15. Hal Featherstone, rhp, North Carolina A&T U.
16. Micah Holst, of, Southwest Missouri State U.
17. Vance Cozier, rhp, St. Bonaventure U.
18. Brian Meagher, lhp, JC of San Mateo (Calif.).
19. Ryan Cheo, lhp, Saddleback (Calif.) CC.
20. Anthony Turco, c, St. Petersburg (Fla.) JC.
21. Ryan Luther, ss, Lewis-Clark State (Idaho) College.
22. Jason Barrow, c, Chemeketa (Ore.) CC.
23. Mike Zirelli, rhp, Cal Poly San Luis Obispo.

24. Bill Murphy, lhp, Arlington HS, Riverside, Calif.
25. Andrew Edwards, rhp, Christ The King HS, Queens, N.Y.
26. Kevin Alexander, ss, Modesto (Calif.) JC.
27. Troy Gustafson, of, Blaine (Minn.) HS.
28. Lars Hansen, c, U. of Hawaii.
29. Troy Ransom, of, South Mountain (Ariz.) CC.
30. Ryan Davis, of, Cosumnes River (Calif.) JC.
31. Scott Daeley, of, Wake Forest U.
32. Tim Gilhooly, c, San Ramon Valley HS, Danville, Calif.
33. Kavonski Chatman, lhp/of, Northeast Texas CC.
34. Scott Shoemaker, rhp, Granite Hills HS, El Cajon, Calif.
35. Robert Lorona, ss, Hayden HS, Winkelman, Ariz.
36. Bryan Lang, of, Scottsdale (Ariz.) CC.
37. Chris Norris, rhp, Central Arizona CC.
38. Drew Endicott, rhp, Carthage (Mo.) HS.
39. Paul Turco, ss, Auburn U.
40. Travis Veracka, lhp, U. of Massachusetts.
41. Winston Woods, of, Broward (Fla.) CC.
42. Jason Hickman, lhp, Ball State U.
43. Brett Cayton, c, Fountain Valley (Calif.) HS.
44. Daniel August, rhp, St Petersburg (Fla.) JC.
45. Chad Ashlock, rhp, U. of Texas-Arlington.
46. Wesley Faust, rhp, Oklahoma Baptist U.
47. Oscar Vargas, ss, Chabot (Calif.) JC
48. Jamie Aloy, 1b, U. of Hawaii.
49. Joshua Sousa, rhp, Modesto (Calif.) JC.
50. Brian Grochol, of, Canada (Calif.) CC.

SEATTLE (11)

1. Ryan Christianson, c, Arlington HS, Riverside, Calif.
1. Jeff Heaverlo, rhp, U. of Washington (Supplemental pick—33rd—for loss of Type A free agent Mike Timlin).
2. (Choice to Giants as compensation for Type A free agent Jose Mesa).
3. Willie Bloomquist, ss, Arizona State U.
3. Sheldon Fulse, ss, George Jenkins HS, Bartow, Fla. (Choice from Orioles as compensation for Timlin).
4. Vaughn Schill, ss, Duke U.
5. Clint Nageotte, rhp, Brooklyn (Ohio) HS.
6. J.J. Putz, rhp, U. of Michigan.
7. Michael Davies, lhp, Westview HS, Beaverton, Ore.
8. Terrmel Sledge, of, Long Beach State U.
9. Steve Kent, lhp, Florida International U.
10. Justin Smith, lhp, U. of Alabama.
11. Hawkeye Wayne, rhp, Columbia U.
12. Larry Brown, of, San Fernando (Calif.) HS.
13. Justin Leone, ss, St. Martin's (Wash.) College.
14. Oscar Ramirez, ss, St Petersburg (Fla.) JC.
15. Tim Burton, rhp, Florida Atlantic U.
16. Sean Parnell, of, U. Wisconsin-Oshkosh.
17. Brian Hertel, 1b, U. of Nevada-Las Vegas.
18. Kris Gundrum, of, Western Michigan U.
19. Brandon Roberson, rhp, Texas Tech U.
20. Kevin Olore, rhp, Marist College.
21. Craig Helmandollar, lhp, Potomac State (W.Va.) College.
22. Jason Edmonds, rhp/3b, De Anza HS, San Pablo, Calif.
23. Zeph Zinsman, 1b, Mission (Calif.) JC.
24. Ryan Simon, rhp, Chamberlain HS, Tampa.
25. Dan Davidson, lhp, Mosley HS, Lynn Haven, Fla.
26. Matthew Walter, rhp, Brandon (Fla.) HS
27. Andrew Rempel, of, W.J. Mouat HS, Abbotsford, B.C.
28. Jonathan Kuelz, rhp, Odessa (Texas) JC.
29. William Gwaltney, rhp, McLennan (Texas) CC.
30. Michael Squibb, lhp, South HS, Hagerstown, Md.
31. Travis Allen, rhp, Quartz Hill HS, Lancaster, Calif.
32. Andrew Wells, rhp, Mounds HS, Bixby, Okla.
33. Chuck Lopez, of, Long Beach State U.
34. Chris Bono, c, Brevard (Fla.) CC.
35. Brian McDevitt, rhp, Waubonsie Valley HS, Naperville, Ill.
36. Eddie Menchaca, rhp, Westwood HS, Mesa, Ariz.
37. Glenn Tucker, rhp, Coral Shores HS, Tavenier, Fla.
38. Richard Harden, rhp, Claremont SS, Victoria, B.C.
39. Kellan Dedge, ss, Suwannee HS, Jasper, Fla.
40. Jeff Thompson, 3b, Torrance HS, Lomita, Calif.
41. Guarionez Rodriguez, 2b, Miami-Dade CC.
42. Tyson Munn, of, Earl Marriott SS, Surrey, B.C.
43. Chris Snyder, c, Spring Woods HS, Houston.
44. Steve Hassett, lhp, Sarasota (Fla.) HS.
45. Jon Nelson, 3b, Dixie (Utah) JC.
46. Ben Ashworth, rhp, Battle Ground Academy, Franklin, Tenn.
47. Jared Cudd, rhp, Sentinel (Okla.) HS.
48. Shawn Bonds, rhp, Lamar (Colo.) CC.
49. Mark Leith, rhp, David Thompson SS, Vancouver, B.C.
50. Nathaniel Doorlag, 1b, Plainwell (Mich.) HS.

TAMPA BAY (1)

1. **Josh Hamilton, of, Athens Drive HS, Raleigh, N.C.**
2. **Carl Crawford, of, Jefferson Davis HS, Houston.**
3. **Doug Waechter, rhp, Northeast HS, St. Petersburg, Fla.**
4. **Alex Santos, rhp, U. of Miami.**
5. **Seth McClung, rhp, Greenbrier East HS, Lewisburg, W.Va.**
6. Eric Henderson, lhp, Santa Fe (Fla.) CC.
7. **Andrew Beinbrink, 3b, Arizona State U.**
8. Ryan Gloger, lhp, Jesuit HS, Tampa.
9. **Dan Ortiz, 1b, Hemet HS, Nuevo, Calif.**
10. **Nathan Cromer, lhp, Lincoln HS, Des Moines.**
11. **Jason Cromer, lhp, Lincoln HS, Des Moines.**
12. **Jorge Maduro, c, Monsignor Pace HS, Miami.**
13. **Jason Pruett, lhp, Brookhaven College.**
14. **Jeff Ridgway, lhp, Port Angeles (Wash.) HS.**
15. **Scott Vandermeer, rhp, McMain HS, New Orleans.**
16. Daniel Lopaze, rhp/ss, Potomac HS, Lakeridge, Va.
17. **Matt Diaz, of, Florida State U.**
18. Ryan Raburn, ss, Durant HS, Dover, Fla.
19. **Oginga Aaron, 2b, Santa Ana (Calif.) JC.**
20. **Chris Crawford, rhp, U. of Georgia.**
21. Mike Fontenot, 2b, Salmen HS, Slidell, La.
22. Cortney Jenkins, rhp, Lamar U.
23. **Travis Minix, rhp, Ball State U.**
24. Mark Carter, lhp, Wallace State (Ala.) CC.
25. **Matt Dailey, lhp, UC Santa Barbara.**
26. Aaron Sheffield, rhp, Pope HS, Marietta, Ga.
27. **Justin Schuda, c, Murietta Valley (Calif.) HS.**
28. Scott Berney, rhp, U. of Connecticut.
29. Michael Hernandez, lhp, Central Union HS, Fresno.
30. Ralph Harrelson, rhp, Modesto (Calif.) JC.
31. Curtis White, lhp, Lindsay (Okla.) HS.
32. Josh Nichols, lhp, Bradford HS, Starke, Fla.
33. Courtney Hill, 2b, Eastern Oklahoma State JC.
34. Phil Klaiber, 3b, Schenectady County (N.Y.) CC.
35. Kevin O'Brien, 1b, Tarpon Springs HS, Dunedin, Fla.
36. Ralph Roberts, of, Lenoir (N.C.) CC.
37. Matt Lederhos, rhp, Westwood (Mass.) HS.
38. Teryn Stanley, ss, Horizon Christian HS, San Diego.
39. Kevin Beavers, lhp, Saddleback (Calif.) CC.
40. Peter Bonifas, rhp, Marquette HS, Bellevue, Iowa.
41. **Glenn Katz, of, U. of Connecticut.**
42. Ben Himes, of, Westlake HS, Austin, Texas.
43. Trevor Tacker, rhp, Carroll HS, Southlake, Texas.
44. Josh Radke, ss, Bozeman HS, Bozeman, Mont.
45. Chad Coder, of, East Lake HS, Redmond, Wash.
46. Robert Ashabraner, rhp, Esperanza HS, Yorba Linda, Calif.
47. Chadd Blasko, rhp, Mishawaka (Ind.) HS.
48. Casey Blalock, rhp, Panola (Texas) JC.
49. Randy Walter, of, Huntley Project HS, Ballantine, Mont.
50. Allen Nevels, rhp, Taloga HS, Putnam, Okla.

TEXAS (21)

1. (Choice to Orioles as compensation for Type A free agent Rafael Palmeiro).
1. **Colby Lewis, rhp, Bakersfield (Calif.) JC** (Supplemental pick—38th—for loss of Type A free agent Todd Stottlemyre).
1. **David Mead, rhp, Soddy Daisy HS, Chattanooga, Tenn.** (Supplemental pick—47th—for loss of Type A free agent Will Clark).
2. **Nick Regilio, rhp, Jacksonville U.**
3. **Hank Blalock, ss, Rancho Bernardo HS, San Diego.**
4. **Kevin Mench, of, U. of Delaware** (Choice from Diamondbacks as compensation for Stottlemyre).
4. **Chris Jaile, c, Columbus HS, Miami.**
5. **Andy Cavazos, rhp, Brazoswood HS, Clute, Texas** (Choice from Orioles as compensation for Clark).
5. **Victor Hillaert, rhp, Shippensburg (Pa.) U.**
6. **Aaron Harang, rhp, San Diego State U.**
7. Luz Portobanco, rhp, Miami Senior HS.
8. **John Rahrer, rhp, Emmett (Idaho) HS.**
9. **Brett Cadiente, of, Arizona State U.**
10. **Jason Bryan, of, New Utrecht HS, Brooklyn.**
11. **Justin Echols, rhp, Greenway HS, Phoenix.**
12. **Mike Scuglik, rhp, Xavier U.**
13. **Jason Jones, of, Kennesaw State U.**
14. **Ernest Villegas, of, Northeast Texas CC.**
15. Dennis Sarfate, rhp, Gilbert HS, Chandler, Ariz.
16. Joel Alvarado, c, Garden City (Kan.) CC.
17. **Orlando Cruz, of, Jose Collazo Colon HS, Juncos, P.R.**
18. Raymond Knight, c, St. Johnis Prep, Jamaica, N.Y.
19. Noah Lowry, lhp, Ventura (Calif.) JC.
20. Kevin Marshall, of, Martin HS, Arlington, Texas.

---

21. Michael Falco, of, Agoura HS, Westlake Village, Calif.
22. Nick Devenney, rhp, Holmes (Miss.) JC.
23. Denny Summerall, of, Armwood HS, Seffner, Fla.
24. Dan Sauer, rhp, Modesto (Calif.) JC.
25. Matt Trepkowski, lhp, Killeen HS, Ft. Hood, Texas.
26. Jason Reuss, 1b, Orange Coast (Calif.) JC.
27. Ryan Mottl, rhp, Clemson U.
28. Justin Sherman, rhp, Durango (Nev.) HS.
29. Erick Monzon, 2b, De Lourdes HS, Carolina, P.R.
30. Dustin Smith, c, Girard (Kan.) HS.
31. Charles Bowman, rhp, Pell City (Ala.) HS.
32. Josue Lopez, 1b, El Toro HS, Trabuco Canyon, Calif.
33. Anthony Piazza, c, Fairview HS, Cody, Wyom.
34. Ignacio Suarez, ss, John Bowne HS, Corona, N.Y.
35. Ed Erickson, 1b, U. of Washington.
36. George Crider, rhp, Phoenix (Ariz.) JC.
37. Jared Hartness, rhp, Jonesboro (Ga.) HS.
38. Richard Gilbert, lhp, JC of Eastern Utah.
39. Chad Williams, lhp, Tucson HS, Arivaca, Ariz.
40. Josh Hollingsworth, 3b, St. Petersburg (Fla.) JC.
41. Andrew Fryson, rhp, Shanks HS, Gretna, Fla.
42. **Adam Poe, of, U. of South Carolina.**
43. Michael Sills, lhp, Leon HS, Tallahassee, Fla.
44. Russel Reeves, lhp, Imperial (Calif.) HS.
45. Brad Hertel, of, Clovis West HS, Fresno.
46. Jason Botts, 1b, Glendale (Calif.) JC.
47. Marty Hayes, rhp, U. of San Diego.
48. Nick Priest, 1b, El Capitan HS, El Cajon, Calif.
49. Nathan Neibauer, of, Overland HS, Aurora, Colo.
50. Clay Chesser, of, Golden West HS, Visalia, Calif.

TORONTO (19)

1. **Alexis Rios, 3b, San Pedro Martir HS, Guaynabo, P.R.**
2. **Michael Snyder, 3b, Ayala HS, Chino Hills, Calif.**
3. **Matt Ford, lhp, Taravella HS, Tamarac, Fla.**
4. **Brian Cardwell, rhp, Sapulpa (Okla.) HS.**
5. **Scott Porter, rhp, Jacksonville U.**
6. **David Hanson, rhp, Richland (Wash.) HS.**
7. **Derrick Nunley, rhp, Englewood HS, Jacksonville.**
8. **Ryan McCullem, lhp, Hickman HS, Columbia, Mo.**
9. **Josh Holliday, c/3b, Oklahoma State U.**
10. **Robert Cosby, ss, Academie Bautista, San Juan, P.R.**
11. **Charles Kegley, rhp, Okaloosa-Walton (Fla.) JC.**
12. **Chris Weekly, ss, New Mexico State U.**
13. **Marc Bluma, rhp, Wichita State U.**
14. Brandon Lyon, rhp, Dixie (Utah) JC.
15. **Tim Newman, rhp, Walla Walla CC.**
16. **Jim Detwiler, lhp, Old Dominion U.**
17. **Reed Johnson, of, Cal State Fullerton.**
18. **Peyton Lewis, rhp, Creighton U.**
19. **Ryan Spille, lhp, Southeast Missouri State U.**
20. **Thom Dreier, rhp, Oklahoma State U.**
21. **Robert Hamann, rhp, Wheaton (Ill.) College.**
22. **Justin Stine, lhp, U. of Missouri.**
23. Andre Monroe, of, Santa Monica HS, Palmdale, Calif.
24. Jeremy Cook, rhp, San Diego State U.
25. Joshua Berry, lhp, Lake Stevens HS, Everett, Wash.
26. **Doug Roper, rhp, Clemson U.**
27. Angel Molina, of, Colegio Cristo Rey, Santa Isabel, P.R.
28. Kirk Gosch, lhp, Coeur D'Alene (Idaho) HS.
29. **Chris Baker, rhp, Oklahoma City U.**
30. Jerome McCoy, ss, Eastern Hills HS, Fort Worth.
31. Charles Tasiaux, rhp, Ahuntsic College, Montreal.
32. **Aaron Fera, of, Georgia College.**
33. Collin Perschon, rhp, Bellevue, Wash.
34. **Lee Southard, rhp, Seminole State (Okla.) JC.**
35. **Matt Bimeal, rhp, Conemaugh Township HS, Davidsville, Pa.**
36. **Douglas Dimma, lhp, Valdosta State (Ga.) U.**
37. Robert Findlay, rhp, Power HS, Etobicoke, Ontario.
38. Mike Tisdale, rhp, St. Peters SS, Peterborough, Ontario.
39. Wilton Reynolds, of, Cosumnes River (Calif.) JC.
40. **Brian Mitchell, 2b, U. of Iowa.**
41. Jeff Flegler, of, Gloucester, N.J.
42. Judson Jones, lhp, Meridian (Miss.) CC.
43. Chad Scarbery, rhp, Clovis HS, Fresno.
44. Jonathan Youngblood, ss, Arkansas HS, Texarkana, Ark.
45. Brendon Stafford, rhp, St. Mathews HS, Gloucester, Ontario.
46. Brooks McNiven, rhp, Kalamalka SS, Vernon, B.C.
47. Garrison Gonce, c, Florida CC.
48. Jonathan Slack, of, Green Valley HS, Henderson, Nev.
49. Phillip Banta, rhp, Bellevue (Wash.) CC.
50. Derek Brehm, lhp, East Central HS, San Antonio.

OBITUARIES/INDEX

OBITUARIES
November 1998-October 1999

Joe Adcock, the Milwaukee Braves' slugging first baseman of the 1950s, died May 3 in Coushatta, La. He was 71. Adcock had several distinctions as a hitter, but is probably best known for breaking up Harvey Haddix' perfect game in the 13th inning in 1959. Adcock also holds a record with 18 total bases in a game. He hit four home runs and a double against the Brooklyn Dodgers in 1954.

Dewey Adkins, a former major league righthander, died Dec. 26, 1998, in Santa Monica, Calif. He was 80. Adkins spent part of the 1942 and '43 seasons with the Washington Senators, and all of the 1949 season with the Cubs. He went 2-4, 5.64 in 38 big league games, and played 13 years in the minors.

Gene Benson, a star Negro Leagues center fielder who used the basket catch before anyone had heard of Willie Mays, died April 5 in Philadelphia. He was 85. Benson played in the high-level Negro leagues from 1936-48, mostly for the Philadelphia Stars.

George Brophy, a longtime front-office executive for the Twins, died of aplastic anemia Nov. 20, 1998, in Edina, Minn. He was 72.

John Brown, a Negro Leagues pitcher from 1944-49, died March 3 in Detroit. He was 81. Brown played for the Cleveland Buckeyes, Chicago American Giants and Houston Eagles, and went 6-2, 3.46 for the Buckeyes' 1945 Negro World Series championship team.

Clay Bryant, a pitching star for the Cubs' 1938 pennant winners, died April 9 in Boca Raton, Fla. He was 87. Bryant, a righthander, went 19-11, 3.10 for the '38 Cubs. His son Clay Jr. pitched in the Yankees organization from 1956-58.

Paul Calvert, a former major league righthander, died Feb. 1 in Sherbrooke, Quebec. He was 81. Calvert went 9-22, 5.31 in seven big league seasons with the Indians, Washington Senators and Tigers. In his season in Washington, he finished in a three-way tie for the American League lead in losses, going 6-17, 5.43.

Paddy Cottrell, a former scout and the coach who led Santa Clara to its only College World Series final in 1962, died July 13 in Santa Clara, Calif. He was 87.

Frank DeMoss, a longtime Cubs scout, died of a heart attack April 25 in Fairmont, W.Va. He was 61. DeMoss spent 40 years in the Cubs organization, the first nine as a jack-of-all-trades minor league player and the rest as a scout. His son David played one season as a Cubs minor league outfielder in 1992.

Ralph DiLullo, a former minor league player and manager and a longtime scout for the Cubs and the Major League Scouting Bureau, died in Paterson, N.J. He was 89. Nicknamed "The Jet," DiLullo was known for having signed Joe Niekro and Bruce Sutter, among others.

Joe DiMaggio, one of the greatest baseball players ever, died March 8 in Hollywood, Fla. He was 84. The Yankee Clipper hit .325 in his 13-year career, with 361 home runs and 1,537 RBIs. A graceful center fielder, he earned MVP honors in 1941, when he hit in a record 56 consecutive games.

Claire Donahoe, the first player ever drafted for the All-American Girls Baseball League, died of a blood clot in a lung Jan. 17 in Bethesda, Md. She was 77.

Jimmy Dudley, the radio voice of the Indians for two decades, died of a stroke Feb. 12 in Tucson. He was 89. After a short stint with the Cubs, Dudley did Indians games from 1948-67. He closed out his career in 1969 by broadcasting the only season of the Seattle Pilots. Dudley was inducted into the broadcasters' wing of the Hall of Fame in 1997.

Jim Dyck, a former major league outfielder/third baseman, died Jan. 11 in Cheney, Wash. He was 76. Dyck batted .246-26-114 in 330 big league games for the St. Louis Browns (1951-53), Indians (1954), Orioles (1955-56) and Reds (1956). He played for 16 seasons in the minors.

Red Flaherty, an American League umpire from 1953-73, died April 1 in Falmouth, Mass. He was 81. Flaherty worked four World Series and three All-Star Games.

Dee Fondy, the Cubs' regular first baseman in the early and middle 1950s, died Aug. 19 in Redlands, Calif. He was 74. Fondy batted .286-69-373 in eight major league seasons with the Cubs, Pirates and Reds. He played six other seasons in the minors in a career that spanned 1946-59.

Greek George, a longtime minor leaguer who also caught Bob Feller's 17-strikeout major league debut in 1936, died Aug. 15 in Metairie, La. He was 86. George never spent a full season in the majors, but he played in the minors from 1932-52 except for 1943 and '49.

George Gill, a former major league righthander, died Feb. 21 in Jackson, Miss. He was 90. Gill went 24-26, 5.05 in three full major league seasons with the Tigers (1937-39) and St. Louis Browns (1939).

Johnny Gorsica, a former Tigers righthander best known for his relief work as a rookie in the 1940 World Series, died Dec. 16, 1998, in Charlottesville, Va. He was 83. Gorsica went 31-39, 4.18 in 204 big league games.

Jack Graham, a legendary minor league slugger from the mid-1930s to the mid-1950s, died Jan. 1 in Long Beach. He was 82. Graham played two full seasons in the majors and batted .231-38-126 in 239 games. Graham's father Peaches Graham was a major league catcher for seven seasons from 1902-12.

Donald Grant, the former Mets chairman who gained infamy for trading Tom Seaver in a salary dispute, died Nov. 28, 1998, in Hobe Sound, Fla. He was 94. Grant was chairman of the board from the team's inception in 1962 until he was forced out after the 1978 season.

Calvin Griffith

Paul Gregory, a former major league righthander and Mississippi State baseball and basketball coach, died of heart failure Sept. 16 in Southaven, Miss. He was 91. After his playing career, Gregory coached the Mississippi State basketball team to a 58-100 record from 1947-55. He became the baseball coach in 1957 and was much more successful, going 328-200 though 1974.

Calvin Griffith, who started with the Washington Senators in 1924 as a 12-year-old batboy and oversaw the team's move to Minnesota as club owner in 1961, died Oct. 16. He was 87. Griffith took over controlling interest in the Senators in 1955 when his uncle Clark Griffith died. He moved the franchise six years later and owned the Minnesota Twins until he sold the team to Carl Pohlad in 1984.

Lee Grissom, an all-star lefthander for the Reds, died Oct. 4 in Corning, Calif. He was 90. Grissom made the National League all-star team in 1935, when he led the league in shutouts with five while going 12-17, 3.26.

Johnny Grodzicki, a former Cardinals righthander who later became a manager, coach and scout, died May 2 in Daytona Beach, Fla. He was 81. Grodzicki went 2-2, 4.43 in 24 big league games in 1941 and 1946-47, all with the Cardinals. After retiring as a player, Grodzicki became a scout, minor league and major league coach.

Howie Haak, a groundbreaking scout for the Pirates, died Feb. 22 in Palm Springs, Calif. He was 87. Haak, who was honored as baseball's first scout of the year in 1984, was a pioneer in scouting Latin America. Among the players he signed were Roberto Clemente, Omar Moreno, Tony Pena and Manny Sanguillen.

Earl Harrist, a former major league righthander, died Sept. 1 in Simsboro, La. He was 79. Harrist went 12-28, 4.34 in five big league seasons with the Reds (1945), White Sox (1947-48, 1953), Washington Senators (1948), St. Louis Browns (1952) and Tigers (1953).

Bob Hartsfield, a Giants special-assignment scout, died

of a kidney condition Jan. 25 in Roswell, Ga. He was 66. Hartsfield was the Giants' scouting coordinator from 1993-97, and had worked as a scout or minor league manager for several organizations since 1963. An infielder, he played in the minors for 11 seasons from 1950-62.

Phil Haugstad, a former major league reliever, died Oct. 21 in Black River Falls, Wis. He was 74. Haugstad, a righthander, went 1-1, 5.59 in 37 major league games with the Brooklyn Dodgers (1947-48, 1951) and the Reds (1952).

Randy Heflin, a righthander who appeared in 25 games for the 1945-46 Red Sox, died Aug. 17 in Fredericksburg, Va. He was 80. Heflin was in the Red Sox starting rotation for much of the 1945 season, going 4-10, 4.06 in 20 games, including 14 starts. His totals for the next year gave him a lifetime record of 4-11, 3.86.

Jim "Catfish" Hunter

Sonny Hirsch, former general manager of the Miami club in the Florida State League and spring training coordinator for the Orioles, died of a heart attack March 26 in Miami Lakes, Fla. He was 65. Hirsch may have been best known in Miami as a broadcaster, especially of University of Miami baseball.

Jerry Hoffberger, owner of the Orioles during their glory years of the 1960s and '70s, died April 9 in Baltimore. He was 80. Hoffberger, whose main business was the National brewery, owned the O's from 1965-79, when he sold them to Edward Bennett Williams for $12 million.

Gene Host, a major league righthander in 1956 and '57, died Aug. 20 in Nashville. He was 65. Host started his only game with the Tigers in '56, then appeared in 11 games for the '57 Kansas City Athletics. He went 0-2, 7.31 lifetime. He made his professional debut with a phenomenal 26-7, 1.81 season with Kinston (Coastal Plain) in 1952.

Jim "Catfish" Hunter, the Hall of Fame righthander for the Athletics and Yankees, died of Lou Gehrig's Disease on Sept. 9 in Hertford, N.C. He was 53. Hunter pitched for the Kansas City and Oakland A's from 1965-74 and the Yankees from 1975-79 and compiled a 224-166, 3.26 record with 42 shutouts.

Henry Kimbro, a star Negro Leagues outfielder, mostly for the Baltimore Elite Giants, died July 11 in Nashville. He was 87. A six-time all-star, Kimbro played for the Elites from 1938-51, except for 1941 when he was traded to the New York Black Yankees for a year. A dangerous leadoff hitter and basestealer and a fine fielder, he was regarded as the top center fielder in the Negro National League during his prime in the mid-'40s.

Tim Layana, a righthander who pitched for the Reds' 1990 World Series champions, was killed in an auto wreck June 26 in Bakersfield, Calif. He was 35. Layana went 5-3, 3.49 in 55 relief appearances for the 1990 Reds, but did not appear in the postseason. He had a lifetime record of 5-5, 4.56 in 78 relief appearances.

Ad Liska, a righthander whose playing career spanned from 1926-49, the last 14 years with Portland of the PCL, died Nov. 30 in Portland, Ore. He was 92. Liska pitched in the majors for five seasons, going 17-18, 3.87 for the Washington Senators (1929-31) and the Phillies (1932-33).

Bill Lohrman, a righthander for five major league teams in the 1930s and '40s, died Sept. 13 in Poughkeepsie, N.Y. He was 86. Lohrman won in double figures three times in a nine-year major league career with the Phillies (1934), New York Giants, Cardinals, Brooklyn Dodgers and Reds.

Doc Marshall, a former New York Giants utility infielder, died Sept. 1 in Lake San Marcos, Calif. He was 93. Marshall reached the majors at the end of his second professional season and batted .258-0-61 from 1929-32.

Verdell Mathis, a star lefthander for the Memphis Red Sox of the Negro American League from 1940-50, died Oct.

30 in Memphis. He was 83. Mathis pitched for poor teams and didn't have impressive won/lost records, but is often regarded as the best Negro Leagues lefthander of the decade. He started and won back-to-back East-West all-star games in 1944 and '45, giving up no runs in either game.

Katsutoshi Miwata, chief scout for the Orix BlueWave of Japan, fell to his death from the 11th floor of an apartment building in Naha, Okinawa. He was 53. Police investigated the death as a suicide, though they wouldn't speculate on motives and said there was no suicide note. Miwata was in negotiations with pitcher Nagisa Arakaki, the team's top pick in the 1998 draft, and Arakaki had said he wouldn't sign.

Wilmer "Vinegar Bend" Mizell, a former major league lefthander and U.S. congressman from North Carolina, died Feb. 21 in Kerrville, Texas. He was 68. Mizell, nicknamed for his hometown of Vinegar Bend, Ala., went 90-88, 3.85 in nine big league seasons with the Cardinals (1952-53, 1956-60), Pirates (1960-62) and Mets (1962). He was a key acquisition for the Pirates during their 1960 pennant drive, going 13-5, 3.12 after coming over from St. Louis.

Pat Mullin, a two-time all-star outfielder for the Tigers, died Aug. 14 in Brownsville, Pa. He was 81. Mullin batted .271-87-385 in 10 big league seasons, all with Detroit from 1940-41 and 1946-53. He made the American League all-star team in '47 and '48, though he missed the 1947 game with an injury. Mullin's best year was '48, when he batted .288-23-80.

Ray Naimoli, the Devil Rays' chief financial officer and the brother of team owner Vince Naimoli, died of cancer March 14 in Phoenix. He was 56. Ray Naimoli began working with his brother in 1991 as a consultant in the bid to secure a Tampa Bay franchise. With the team, he was responsible for the organization's financial structure, information systems management and long-term planning.

Hal Newhouser, the Hall of Fame lefthander for the Tigers, died Nov. 10 in Detroit. He was 77. Newhouser is the only pitcher ever to win back-to-back MVP awards, doing it in 1944 and '45. He won an American League pitching triple crown in '45, going 25-9, 1.81 with 212 strikeouts. Overall, Newhouser went 207-150, 3.06 in 17 big league seasons with the Tigers (1939-53) and Indians (1954-55). He was a seven-time all-star and led the AL in wins four times.

Bill Owens, a shortstop for several Negro League teams from 1923-33, died of complications from diabetes May 5 in Indianapolis. He was 98. Owens was the last surviving player from the 1920s Indianapolis ABCs franchise that was a founding member of the Negro National League, and the last survivor from the Eastern Colored League.

Max Patkin, known as the Clown Prince of Baseball, died Oct. 30 in Paoli, Pa. He was 79. Patkin toured minor league ballparks for more than 50 years, entertaining fans with his antics.

Boots Poffenberger, a former major league righthander, died Sept. 1 in Williamsport, Md. He was 84. Poffenberger went 16-12, 4.75 in 57 big league games with the Tigers (1937-38) and Brooklyn Dodgers (1939). He led the Southern Association in both wins and runs allowed in 1940, going 26-9, 4.58 for Nashville.

Dave Pope, a former major league outfielder, died Aug. 28 in Cleveland. He was 78. Pope batted .265-12-73 in four big league seasons with the Indians and Orioles. He went 0-for-3 with a walk in the 1954 World Series, in which the Indians were swept by the New York Giants.

Harry Postove, a longtime scout for several organizations who signed Hall of Fame shortstop Luis Aparicio and Dodgers infielder Junior Gilliam, died March 1 in Norfolk, Va. He was 86.

Pee Wee Reese, the Hall of Fame Brooklyn Dodgers shortstop, died Aug. 14 in Louisville. He was 81. A nine-time all-star, Reese hit .269-126-885 in 16 major league seasons. He was instrumental in the Dodgers' acceptance of Jackie Robinson as a teammate in 1947.

Johnny Riddle, a former major league catcher who formed a big league battery with his brother, died Dec. 15 in Indianapolis. He was 93. Riddle batted .238-0-11 in 98 big league games spread over seven seasons. He and his brother Elmer, a onetime National League ERA champion and 21-game winner, both played for the '41, '44 and '45 Reds and the '48 Pirates.

Cal Ripken Sr., former Orioles manager and the father of pro players Cal Jr. and Bill Ripken, died of lung cancer March 26 in Baltimore. He was 63. Ripken took over Leesburg (Florida State) late in the 1961 season in just his fifth year as a player, at age 25. He remained in the Orioles organization through 1992, mostly as a minor league manager and a coach for the major league team. Cal Sr.'s brother Bill was a minor league outfielder from 1947-49.

Jay Roberts, a 1981 first-round draft pick of the Braves who never played above Class A, died in a one-car crash Sept. 26 near Bellevue, Wash. He was 35. Roberts never batted higher than .208 in four minor league seasons, and left after 1984 to pursue a football career at the University of Washington.

Ken Robinson, a righthander in the Diamondbacks organization and a former minor leaguer, was killed in an auto accident Feb. 28 in Tucson. He was 29. The vehicle Robinson was riding in was driven by fellow Diamondbacks farmhand John Rosengren. Robinson compiled a 2-2, 3.91 record in 29 major league games from 1995-98.

Leo Schrall, a longtime coach at Bradley University and a former minor league player and manager, died Feb. 3 in Peoria, Ill. He was 91. Schrall was head coach at Bradley from 1949-72, reaching the College World Series twice and winning six Missouri Valley Conference titles.

Walter Sessi, a minor league star whose chances in the major leagues were severely limited by military service in World War II, died April 18 in Mobile, Ala. He was 79. Sessi, an outfielder, spent what would have been his prime years in the service. As it was, he played 20 games in the majors, all for the Cardinals.

Leo "Muscle" Shoals, the No. 10 all-time home run hitter in the minor leagues, died of a heart attack Feb. 23 in Glade Spring, Va. He was 82. Shoals batted .337 with 362 home runs from 1937-55. His Carolina League record of 55 homers set in 1949 still stands.

Dick Sisler, the all-star outfielder whose home run won the 1950 National League pennant for the "Whiz Kids" Phillies, died Nov. 20, 1998, in Nashville. He was 78. Sisler batted .276-55-360 in eight major league seasons with the Cardinals (1946-47, 1952-53), Phillies (1948-51) and Reds (1952). On the final day of the 1950 regular season, his three-run homer in the 10th inning beat the Brooklyn Dodgers and clinched the pennant for the Phillies. Sisler's father was Hall of Fame first baseman George Sisler, who died in 1973. Sisler's brother was ex-American League righthander Dave Sisler.

Cal Ripken Sr.

A. Ray Smith, who owned Louisville (American Association) when it became the first minor league team to draw more than a million fans in a season, died of cancer June 28 in Tulsa. He was 84.

Bernie Snyder, a shortstop who had a brief but successful big league career, died April 15 in Havertown, Pa. He was 85. Snyder had just one .300 season in 10 years in the minors, but went 11-for-32 (.344) in 10 major league games with the 1935 Philadelphia Athletics.

Watson Spoelstra, founder of Baseball Chapel, died of cancer July 20 in St. Petersburg, Fla. He was 89. Spoelstra began the ministry because Sunday day games made it impossible for professional baseball players, coaches and employees to attend regular church services. Spoelstra founded Baseball Chapel after retiring as a sportswriter for The Detroit News in 1973. Today, about 3,000 people attend services each week.

Eddie Stanky, a fiery second baseman who helped three different teams win National League pennants, died of a heart attack June 6 in Fairhope, Ala. He was 83. A four-time all-star, Stanky hit .268-29-364 in an 11-year major league career with the Cubs (1943-44), Brooklyn Dodgers (1944-47), Boston Braves (1948-49), New York Giants (1950-51) and Cardinals (1952-53). Stanky also went 467-435 as a major league manager and 488-193 as a college head coach for 14 seasons at South Alabama from 1969-79 and 1981-83.

Ben Taylor, a longtime minor league first baseman who played briefly for three major league teams, died May 11 in Alma, Okla. He was 74. Taylor played in the minors for 13 seasons from 1944-57, and was a non-playing manager for Johnson City (Appalachian) in '57.

Birdie Tebbetts, who reached the top of the profession as a player, manager and scout, died March 24 in Bradenton, Fla. He was 86. Tebbetts, a catcher, was a four-time all-star in 14 major league seasons with the Tigers, Red Sox and Indians. He batted .270-38-469 lifetime. After his playing career, Tebbetts spent one year managing in the minors and then 11 in the major leagues, where his record was 748-705.

Bob Thurman, whose varied career included a major league debut at age 38, died Oct. 31 in Wichita. He was 81. Thurman was discovered, at first as a pitcher, by the Negro League Homestead Grays while playing for service teams in the Pacific during World War II. He finally debuted in the majors as a Reds outfielder, and batted .246-35-106 for them from 1955-59.

Paul Toth, a former major league righthander, died of a heart attack March 23 in Anaheim. He was 63. Toth went 9-12, 3.80 in three big league seasons with the Cardinals and Cubs.

Jim Turner, whose record of 51 straight years in professional baseball was tied in 1999 by Yankees bench coach Don Zimmer, died Nov. 29, 1998, in Nashville. He was 95. Turner is best known as the pitching coach for the Yankees during their glory years in the 1950s. He retired in 1973 after playing or coaching in 13 World Series.

Harry Walker, who drove home Enos Slaughter from first base with a double to win the 1946 World Series, died of complications from a stroke Aug. 8 in Birmingham. He was 80. Walker, whose nickname "The Hat" came from his habit of adjusting his cap between pitches as a hitter, played in three World Series and was a two-time all-star. Primarily an outfielder, he batted .296-10-214 in 11 major league seasons with the Cardinals.

Johnnie Wittig, a former major league righthander, died Feb. 24 in Nassawadox, Va. He was 84. Wittig went 10-25, 4.89 in five major league seasons. He pitched for the New York Giants in 1938, '39, '41 and '43, then resurfaced for one game with the Red Sox in 1949. He played in the International League for 11 seasons.

William Wrigley, who followed his grandfather and father as owner of the Cubs, died of complications from pneumonia March 8 in Chicago. He was 66. Wrigley's grandfather William Wrigley Jr. founded the family chewing-gum company and bought the Cubs in the early 20th century. Wrigley sold the Cubs to the Chicago Tribune Corp. in 1981.

Whit Wyatt, the popular Brooklyn Dodgers righthander of the 1940s and later a longtime major league pitching coach, died July 16 in Buchanan, Ga. He was 91. His best year was 1941, when he went 22-10, 2.34 for the pennant-winning Dodgers, leading the National League in wins and shutouts.

Early Wynn, the Hall of Fame righthander, died April 4 in Venice, Fla. He was 79. Wynn led the American League in wins twice, in ERA once, in strikeouts twice and in innings pitched three times. He went 23-11 for the 1954 Indians team that won 111 games, and won the 1959 Cy Young Award for another pennant-winning club, going 22-10 with the White Sox. Overall, Wynn went 300-244 in 23 major league seasons with the Washington Senators, Indians and White Sox.

Norm Zauchin, the Red Sox' 1955 rookie star, died of cancer Jan. 31 in Birmingham. He was 69. Zauchin batted .239-29-93 in '55, won the American League Gold Glove at first base and finished second to the Yankees' Elston Howard in rookie-of-the-year balloting. He flamed out after that, and finished his career with .233-50-159 totals in six seasons with the Red Sox and Washington Senators.

Hal Zimmer, a former minor league outfielder/pitcher and the brother of Yankees bench coach Don Zimmer, died July 21 in Fort Myers, Fla. He was 67.

Index

GENERAL INFORMATION

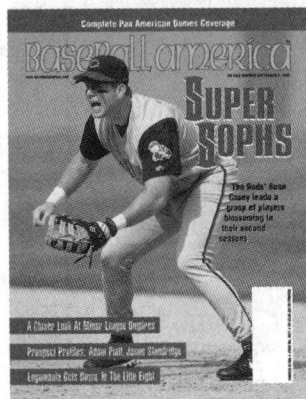